Collins
Italian
Dictionary

Collins
Italian
Dictionary

Second Edition 2005

©HarperCollins Publishers, 2000, 2005

HarperCollins Publishers
Westerhill Road
Bishopbriggs
Glasgow
G64 2QT
Great Britain

ISBN 0–00–712626–3

Collins®, and Bank of English® are registered trademarks of HarperCollins Publishers Limited

www.collins.co.uk

HarperCollins Publishers, Inc.
10 East 53rd Street, New York, NY 10022

ISBN 0–06–078732–5

Library of Congress Cataloging-in-Publication Data has been applied for

www.harpercollins.com

First HarperCollins edition published 2000

HarperCollins books may be purchased for educational, business, or sales promotional use. For information, please write to: Special Markets Department, HarperCollins Publishers Inc., 10 East 53rd Street, New York, NY 10022

A Catalogue record for this book is available from the British Library

This edition typeset by Morton Word Processing Ltd, Scarborough

Printed in Italy by Legoprint S.P.A.

Corpus Acknowledgements

We would like to acknowledge the assistance of the many hundreds of individuals and companies who have kindly given permission for copyright material to be used in the Bank of English. The written sources include many national and regional newspapers in Britain and overseas; magazine and periodical publishers; and book publishers in Britain, the United States and Australia. Extensive spoken data have been provided by radio and television broadcasting companies; research workers at many universities and other institutions; and numerous individual contributors. We are grateful to them all.

INDICE

CONTENTS

Catherine E. Love ● Michela Clari

with/hanno collaborato
Gabriella Bacchelli ● Donatella Boi
Angela Jack ● Daphne Day

editorial staff/segreteria di redazione
Megan Thomson ● Isobel Gordon
Elspeth Anderson ● Anne Convery ● Anne Marie Banks

series editor/collana a cura di
Lorna Sinclair Knight
editorial management/coordinamento redazionale
Vivian Marr

INTRODUZIONE

Se desiderate imparare l'inglese o approfondire le conoscenze già acquisite, se volete leggere o redigere dei testi in inglese, oppure conversare con interlocutori di madrelingua inglese, se siete studenti, turisti, uomini o donne d'affari avete scelto il compagno di viaggio ideale per esprimervi e comunicare in inglese sia a voce che per iscritto. Strumento pratico e moderno, il vostro dizionario dà largo spazio al linguaggio quotidiano in campi quali l'attualità, gli affari, la gestione d'ufficio, l'informatica e il turismo. Come in tutti i nostri dizionari, grande importanza è stata data alla lingua contemporanea e alle espressioni idiomatiche.

COME USARE IL DIZIONARIO

Troverete qui di seguito alcune spiegazioni sul modo in cui le informazioni sono state presentate nel testo. L'obiettivo del dizionario è quello di darvi il maggior numero possibile di informazioni senza tuttavia sacrificare la chiarezza all'interno delle voci.

Le voci

Qui di seguito verranno descritti i vari elementi di cui si compone una voce tipo del vostro dizionario.

La trascrizione fonetica

Come regola generale è stata data la pronuncia di tutte le parole inglesi e quella delle parole italiane che potevano presentare qualche difficoltà per il parlante inglese. Nella parte inglese-italiano, tuttavia, per la pronuncia di nomi composti formati da due parole non unite dal trattino si dovrà cercare la trascrizione di ciascuna di queste parole alla rispettiva posizione alfabetica. La pronuncia si trova tra parentesi quadra, subito dopo il lemma. Come nella maggior parte dei dizionari moderni è stato adottato il sistema noto come "alfabeto fonetico internazionale". Troverete qui di seguito, a pagina xiii e xiv, un elenco completo dei caratteri utilizzati in questo sistema.

La categorie grammaticali

Tutte le parole appartengono ad una categoria grammaticale, cioè possono essere sostantivi, verbi, aggettivi, avverbi, pronomi, articoli, congiunzioni o abbreviazioni. I sostantivi possono essere singolari o plurali, sia in italiano che in inglese, e maschili o femminili in italiano. I verbi possono essere transitivi o intransitivi in entrambe le lingue, ma anche riflessivi o impersonali in italiano. La categoria grammaticale è stata introdotta in *corsivo* subito dopo la pronuncia ed eventuali informazioni di tipo morfologico (plurali irregolari ecc.).

Numerose voci sono state suddivise in varie categorie grammaticali. Per esempio la parola italiana **bene** può essere sia un avverbio che un aggettivo o un sostantivo, e la parola inglese **sneeze** può essere sia un sostantivo (starnuto) che un verbo intransitivo (starnutire). Analogamente il verbo italiano **correre** può essere usato sia come verbo intransitivo ("correre alla stazione") che come transitivo ("correre un rischio"). Per presentare la voce con maggiore chiarezza e permettervi di trovare rapidamente la traduzione che cercate, è stato introdotto il simbolo ♦ per contrassegnare il passaggio da una categoria grammaticale ad un'altra.

Suddivisioni semantiche

La maggior parte delle parole ha più di un significato. Per esempio, la parola **fiocco** può essere sia un'annodatura di un nastro che una falda di neve. Molte parole si traducono in modo diverso a seconda del contesto in cui sono usate: per esempio **scala** si tradurrà in inglese con "staircase" o "stairs" se si tratta di una scala con gradini, con "ladder" se è una scala a pioli. Per permettervi di scegliere la traduzione giusta per ciascuno dei contesti in cui la parola si può trovare, le voci sono state suddivise in categorie di significato. Ciascuna suddivisione è introdotta da un "indicatore d'uso" tra parentesi in *corsivo*. Le voci **fiocco** e **scala** compariranno quindi nel testo nel modo seguente:

fiocco, chi *sm (di nastro)* bow; (*di stoffa, lana*) flock; (*di neve*) flake
scala *sf (a gradini etc)* staircase, stairs *pl*; (*a pioli, di corda*) ladder

Per segnalare la traduzione appropriata sono stati introdotti anche degli indicatori d'ambito d'uso in CORSIVO MAIUSCOLO tra parentesi, spesso in forma abbreviata, come per esempio nel caso della voce **tromba**:

tromba *sf (MUS)* trumpet; (*AUT*) horn

Troverete un elenco completo delle abbreviazioni adottate all'interno del dizionario alle pp x, xi, xii.

Le traduzioni

Per la maggior parte delle parole inglesi ed italiane ci sono traduzioni precise a seconda del significato o del contesto, come risulta dagli esempi riportati fin qui. A volte, tuttavia, le parole non hanno un preciso equivalente nella lingua d'arrivo: in questi casi è stato fornito un equivalente approssimativo, preceduto dal segno ≈, come ad esempio per l'abbreviazione **RAC**, per cui è stato dato l'equivalente italiano "A.C.I.", dato che le due associazioni svolgono nei due paesi funzioni analoghe:

RAC *n abbr (BRIT: = Royal Automobile Club)* ≈ A.C.I. *m (= Automobile Club d' Italia)*

A volte è persino impossibile trovare un equivalente approssimativo. Questo è il caso, per esempio, di piatti tipici di un certo paese, come ad esempio **pandoro**:

pandoro *sm type of sponge cake eaten at Christmas*

In questi casi, al posto della traduzione, che non esiste, comparirà una spiegazione: per maggior chiarezza questa spiegazione o glossa è stata messa in *corsivo*.

Molto spesso la traduzione di una parola può non funzionare all'interno di una data locuzione. Ad esempio alla voce **dare**, verbo spesso tradotto con "to give" in inglese, troviamo varie locuzioni per alcune delle quali la traduzione fornita all'inizio della voce non si può utilizzare: **quanti anni mi dai?** "how old do you think I am?" **danno ancora quel film?** "is that film still showing?", **dare per certo qc** "to consider sth certain", e così via. Ed è proprio in questi casi che potrete verificare l'utilità e la completezza del dizionario, che contiene una ricca gamma di composti, locuzioni e frasi idiomatiche.

Il registro linguistico

In italiano sapete istintivamente scegliere l'espressione corretta da usare a seconda del contesto in cui vi esprimete. Per esempio saprete quando dire **Non me ne importa!** e quando invece potete dire **Chi se ne frega?** Più difficile sarà farlo in inglese, dove avete minore consapevolezza delle sfumature di registro linguistico. Per questo motivo nella parte inglese-italiano le parole ed espressioni inglesi di uso più familiare sono segnalate dall'abbreviazione (*col*), mentre (*col!*) segnala le parole ed espressioni volgari. Nella parte italiano-inglese (*!*) dopo una traduzione segnala che si tratta di una parola od espressione volgare.

Parole chiave

Come vedrete, ad alcune voci è stato riservato un trattamento particolare sia dal punto di vista grafico che da quello linguistico. Si tratta di voci come **essere** o **fare**, o dei loro equivalenti inglesi **be** e **do**, che per la loro importanza e complessità meritano una strutturazione più articolata ed un maggior numero di locuzioni illustrative. Queste voci sono strutturate in diverse categorie di significato contrassegnate da numeri, e le costruzioni sintattiche e locuzioni che illustrano quel particolare significato sono riportate all'interno della relativa categoria.

Informazioni culturali

Le voci che compaiono nel testo delimitate da due linee approfondiscono aspetti della cultura italiana o di quella dei paesi di lingua inglese in argomenti quali la politica, la scuola, i mass media e le festività nazionali.

INTRODUCTION

You may be starting to learn Italian, or you may wish to extend your knowledge of the language. Perhaps you want to read and study Italian books, newspapers and magazines, or perhaps simply have a conversation with Italian speakers. Whatever the reason, whether you're a student, a tourist or want to use Italian for business, this is the ideal book to help you understand and communicate. This modern, user-friendly dictionary gives priority to everyday vocabulary and the language of current affairs, business and tourism. As in all Collins dictionaries, the emphasis is firmly placed on contemporary language and expressions.

HOW TO USE THE DICTIONARY

Below you will find an outline of how information is presented in your dictionary. Our aim is to give you the maximum amount of detail in the clearest and most helpful way.

Entries

A typical entry in your dictionary will be made up of the following elements:

Phonetic transcription

Phonetics appear in square brackets immediately after the headword. They are shown using the International Phonetic Alphabet (IPA), and a complete list of the symbols used in this system can be found on pages xiii and xiv.

Grammatical information

All words belong to one of the following parts of speech: noun, verb, adjective, adverb, pronoun, article, conjunction, preposition, abbreviation. Nouns can be singular or plural and, in Italian, masculine or feminine. Verbs can be transitive, intransitive, reflexive or impersonal. Parts of speech appear in *italics* immediately after the phonetic spelling of the headword.

Often a word can have more than one part of speech. Just as the English word **chemical** can be an adjective or a noun, the Italian word **fondo** can be an adjective ("deep") or a masculine noun ("bottom"). In the same way the verb **to walk** is sometimes transitive, ie it takes an object ("to walk the dog") and sometimes intransitive, ie it doesn't take an object ("to walk to school"). To help you find the meaning you are looking for quickly and for clarity of presentation, the different part of speech categories are separated by a black lozenge ♦.

Meaning divisions

Most words have more than one meaning. Take, for example, **punch** which can be, amongst other things, a blow with the fist or an object used for making holes. Other words are translated differently depending on the context in which they are used. The transitive verb **to roll up**, for example, can be translated by "arrotolare" or "rimboccare" depending on *what* it is you are rolling up. To help you select the most appropriate translation in every context, entries are divided according to meaning. Each different meaning is introduced by an "indicator" in *italics* and in brackets. Thus, the examples given above will be shown as follows:

> **punch** n (*blow*) pugno; (*tool*) punzone m
> **roll up** vt (*carpet, cloth, map*) arrotolare; (*sleeves*) rimboccare

Likewise, some words can have a different meaning when used to talk about a specific subject area or field. For example, **bishop**, which is generally used to mean a high-ranking clergyman, is also the name of a chess piece. To show English speakers which translation to use, we have added "subject field labels" in capitals and in brackets, in this case (*CHESS*):

bishop *n* vescovo; (*CHESS*) alfiere *m*

Field labels are often shortened to save space. You will find a complete list of abbreviations used in the dictionary on pages x, xi, xii.

Translations

Most English words have a direct translation in Italian and vice versa, as shown in the examples given above. Sometimes, however, no exact equivalent exists in the target language. In such cases we have given an approximate equivalent, indicated by the sign ≈. Such is the case of **National Insurance**, the Italian equivalent of which is "Previdenza Sociale". This is not an exact translation since the systems of the two countries in question are quite different:

National Insurance *n* (*BRIT*) ≈ Previdenza Sociale

On occasion it is impossible to find even an approximate equivalent. This may be the case, for example, with the names of types of food:

cottage pie *n piatto a base di carne macinata in sugo e purè di patate*

Here the translation (which doesn't exist) is replaced by an explanation. For increased clarity the explanation, or "gloss", is shown in *italics*.

It is often the case that a word, or a particular meaning of a word, cannot be translated in isolation. The translation of **Dutch**, for example, is "olandese". However, the phrase **to go Dutch** is rendered by "fare alla romana". Even an expression as simple as **washing powder** needs a separate translation since it translates as "detersivo (in polvere)", not "polvere per lavare". This is where your dictionary will prove to be particularly informative and useful since it contains an abundance of compounds, phrases and idiomatic expressions.

Levels of formality and familiarity

In English you instinctively know when to say **I'm broke** *or* **I'm a bit short of cash** and when to say **I don't have any money**. When you are trying to understand someone who is speaking Italian, however, or when you yourself try to speak Italian, it is important to know what is polite and what is less so, and what you can say in a relaxed situation but not in a formal context. To help you with this, on the Italian-English side we have added the label (*fam*) to show that an Italian word or expression is colloquial, while those word or expressions which are vulgar are given an exclamation mark (*fam!*), warning you they can cause serious offence. Note also that on the English-Italian side, translations which are vulgar are followed by an exclamation mark in brackets.

Keywords

Words labelled in the text as *KEYWORDS*, such as **be** and **do** or their Italian equivalents **essere** and **fare**, have been given special treatment because they form the basic elements of the language. This extra help will ensure that you know how to use these complex words with confidence.

Cultural information

Entries which appear separated from the main text by a line above and below them explain aspects of culture in Italy and English-speaking countries. Subject areas covered include politics, education, media and national festivals.

ABBREVIAZIONI

ABBREVIATIONS

abbreviazione	**abbr**	abbreviation
aggettivo	**adj**	adjective
amministrazione	**ADMIN**	administration
avverbio	**adv**	adverb
aeronautica, viaggi aerei	**AER**	flying, air travel
aggettivo	**ag**	adjective
agricoltura	**AGR**	agriculture
amministrazione	**AMM**	administration
anatomia	**ANAT**	anatomy
architettura	**ARCHIT**	architecture
astronomia, astrologia	**ASTR**	astronomy, astrology
l'automobile	**AUT**	the motor car and motoring
verbo ausiliare	**aux vb**	auxiliary verb
avverbio	**av**	adverb
aeronautica, viaggi aerei	**AVIAT**	flying, air travel
biologia	**BIOL**	biology
botanica	**BOT**	botany
inglese della Gran Bretagna	**BRIT**	British English
consonante	**C**	consonant
chimica	**CHIM, CHEM**	chemistry
familiare (! da evitare)	**col(!)**	colloquial usage (! particularly offensive)
commercio, finanza, banca	**COMM**	commerce, finance, banking
informatica	**COMPUT**	computing
congiunzione	**cong**	conjunction
congiunzione	**conj**	conjunction
edilizia	**CONSTR**	building
sostantivo usato come aggettivo, non può essere usato né come attributo, né dopo il sostantivo qualificato	**cpd**	compound element: noun used as adjective and which cannot follow the noun it qualifies
cucina	**CUC, CULIN**	cookery
davanti a	**dav**	before
determinante: articolo, aggettivo dimostrativo o indefinito etc	**det**	determiner: article, demonstrative etc
diritto	**DIR**	law
economia	**ECON**	economics
edilizia	**EDIL**	building
elettricità, elettronica	**ELETTR, ELEC**	electricity, electronics
esclamazione, interiezione	**escl, excl**	exclamation, interjection
specialmente	**esp**	especially
femminile	**f**	feminine
familiare (! da evitare)	**fam(!)**	colloquial usage (! particularly offensive)
ferrovia	**FERR**	railways
figurato	**fig**	figurative use
fisiologia	**FISIOL**	physiology
fotografia	**FOT**	photography
(verbo inglese) la cui particella è inseparabile dal verbo	**fus**	(phrasal verb) where the particle cannot be separated from main verb
nella maggior parte dei sensi; generalmente	**gen**	in most or all senses; generally
geografia, geologia	**GEO**	geography, geology
geometria	**GEOM**	geometry
impersonale	**impers**	impersonal

informatica	**INFORM**	computing
insegnamento, sistema scolastico e universitario	**INS**	schooling, schools and universities
invariabile	**inv**	invariable
irregolare	**irreg**	irregular
grammatica, linguistica	**LING**	grammar, linguistics
maschile	**m**	masculine
matematica	**MAT(H)**	mathematics
termine medico, medicina	**MED**	medical term, medicine
il tempo, meteorologia	**METEOR**	the weather, meteorology
maschile o femminile	**m/f**	either masculine or feminine depending on sex
esercito, linguaggio militare	**MIL**	military matters
musica	**MUS**	music
sostantivo	**n**	noun
nautica	**NAUT**	sailing, navigation
sostantivo che non si usa al plurale	**no pl**	uncountable noun: not used in the plural
numerale (aggettivo, sostantivo)	**num**	numeral adjective or noun
	o.s.	oneself
peggiorativo	**peg, pej**	derogatory, pejorative
fotografia	**PHOT**	photography
fisiologia	**PHYSIOL**	physiology
plurale	**pl**	plural
politica	**POL**	politics
participio passato	**pp**	past participle
preposizione	**prep**	preposition
pronome	**pron**	pronoun
psicologia, psichiatria	**PSIC, PSYCH**	psychology, psychiatry
tempo passato	**pt**	past tense
qualcosa	**qc**	
qualcuno	**qn**	
religione, liturgia	**REL**	religions, church service
sostantivo	**s**	noun
	sb	somebody
insegnamento, sistema scolastico e universitario	**SCOL**	schooling, schools and universities
singolare	**sg**	singular
soggetto (grammaticale)	**sog**	(grammatical) subject
	sth	something
congiuntivo	**sub**	subjunctive
soggetto (grammaticale)	**subj**	(grammatical) subject
termine tecnico, tecnologia	**TECN, TECH**	technical term, technology
telecomunicazioni	**TEL**	telecommunications
tipografia	**TIP**	typography, printing
televisione	**TV**	television
tipografia	**TYP**	typography, printing
inglese degli Stati Uniti	**US**	American English
vocale	**V**	vowel
verbo (ausiliare)	**vb (aus)**	(auxiliary) verb
verbo o gruppo verbale con funzione intransitiva	**vi**	verb or phrasal verb used intransitively
verbo riflessivo	**vr**	reflexive verb
verbo o gruppo verbale con funzione transitiva	**vt**	verb or phrasal verb used transitively
zoologia	**ZOOL**	zoology
marchio registrato	®	registered trademark
introduce un'equivalenza culturale	≈	introduces a cultural equivalent

TRASCRIZIONE FONETICA

<table>
<tr><td colspan="2">**Consonanti**</td><td>**Consonants**</td></tr>
<tr><td colspan="2">NB. **p, b, t, d, k, g** sono seguite da un'aspirazione in inglese.</td><td>NB. **p, b, t, d, k, g** are not aspirated in Italian.</td></tr>
</table>

Italiano		Inglese
_p_adre	p	_p_u_pp_y
_b_am_b_ino	b	_b_a_b_y
_tutt_o	t	_t_en_t_
_d_a_d_o	d	_d_a_dd_y
_c_ane _ch_e	k	_c_or_k_ _k_iss _ch_ord
gola _gh_iro	g	_g_a_g_ _g_uess
_s_ano	s	_s_o ri_c_e _k_i_ss_
_s_vago e_s_ame	z	cou_s_in bu_zz_
_sc_ena	ʃ	_sh_eep _s_ugar
	ʒ	plea_s_ure bei_g_e
pe_c_e lan_c_iare	tʃ	_ch_ur_ch_
giro _gi_oco	dʒ	_j_ud_ge_ _g_eneral
a_f_a _f_aro	f	_f_arm ra_ff_le
_v_ero bra_v_o	v	_v_ery re_v_
	θ	_th_in ma_th_s
	ð	_th_at o_th_er
_l_etto a_l_a	l	_l_itt_le_ ba_ll_
_gl_i	ʎ	
_r_ete ar_c_o	r	_r_at b_r_at
ra_m_o _m_adre	m	_m_u_mm_y co_mb_
_n_o fuma_n_te	n	_n_o ra_n_
_gn_omo	ɲ	
	ŋ	si_ng_ing ba_nk_
	h	_h_at re_h_eat
bu_i_o p_i_acere	j	_y_et
_u_omo g_u_aio	w	_w_all be_w_ail
	x	lo_ch_

Varie		**Miscellaneous**
per l'inglese: la "r" finale viene pronunciata se seguita da una vocale	*	
precede la sillaba accentata	'	precedes the stressed syllable

Come regola generale, in tutte le voci la trascrizione fonetica in parentesi quadra segue il termine cui si riferisce. Tuttavia, dalla parte inglese-italiano del dizionario, per la pronuncia di composti che sono formati da più parole non unite da trattino che appaiono comunque nel dizionario, si veda la trascrizione fonetica di ciascuna di queste parole alla rispettiva posizione alfabetica.

PHONETIC TRANSCRIPTION

Vocali

NB. La messa in equivalenza di certi suoni indica solo una rassomiglianza approssimativa.

Vowels

NB. The pairing of some vowel sounds only indicates approximate equivalence.

Vocali	IPA	Vowels
v_i_no _i_dea	i iː	h_ee_l b_ea_d
	ɪ	h_i_t p_i_ty
st_e_lla _e_d_e_ra	e	
_e_poca ecc_e_tto	ɛ	s_e_t t_e_nt
m_a_mm_a_ _a_more	a æ	_a_pple b_a_t
	ɑː	_a_fter c_a_r c_a_lm
	ʌ	f_u_n c_ou_sin
	ə	ov_er_ _a_bove
	əː	_ur_n f_er_n w_or_k
r_o_sa _o_cchio	ɔ	w_a_sh p_o_t
	ɔː	b_or_n c_or_k
p_o_nte _o_gnun_o_	o	
_u_tile z_u_cca	u	f_u_ll s_oo_t
	uː	b_oo_n l_ew_d

Dittonghi

Diphthongs

IPA	Diphthongs
ɪə	b_eer_ t_ier_
ɛə	t_ear_ f_air_ th_ere_
eɪ	d_a_te pl_ai_ce d_ay_
aɪ	l_i_fe b_uy_ cry
au	_ow_l f_ou_l n_ow_
əu	l_ow_ n_o_
ɔɪ	b_oi_l b_oy_ _oi_ly
uə	p_oor_ t_our_

In general, we give the pronunciation of each entry in square brackets after the word in question. However, on the English-Italian side, where the entry is composed of two or more unhyphenated words, each of which is given elsewhere in this dictionary, you will find the pronunciation of each word in its alphabetical position.

ITALIAN PRONUNCIATION

Vowels

Where the vowel **e** or the vowel **o** appears in a stressed syllable it can be either open [ɛ], [ɔ] or closed [e], [o]. As the open or closed pronunciation of these vowels is subject to regional variation, the distinction is of little importance to the user of this dictionary. Phonetic transcription for headwords containing these vowels will therefore only appear where other pronunciation difficulties are present.

Consonants

c before "e" or "i" is pronounced *tch*.

ch is pronounced like the "k" in "kit".

g before "e" or "i" is pronounced like the "j" in "jet".

gh is pronounced like the "g" in "get".

gl before "e" or "i" is normally pronounced like the "lli" in "million", and in a few cases only like the "gl" in "glove".

gn is pronounced like the "ny" in "canyon".

sc before "e" or "i" is pronounced *sh*.

z is pronounced like the "ts" in "stetson", or like the "d's" in "bird's-eye".

Headwords containing the above consonants and consonantal groups have been given full phonetic transcription in this dictionary.

NB. All double written consonants in Italian are fully sounded: e.g. the *tt* in "tutto" is pronounced as in "ha*t t*rick".

ITALIAN VERBS

1 Gerundio *2* Participio passato *3* Presente *4* Imperfetto *5* Passato remoto *6* Futuro
7 Condizionale *8* Congiuntivo presente *9* Congiuntivo passato *10* Imperativo

accadere *like* **cadere**
accedere *like* **concedere**
accendere *2* acceso *5* accesi, accendesti
accludere *like* **alludere**
accogliere *like* **cogliere**
accondiscendere *like* **scendere**
accorgersi *like* **scorgere**
accorrere *like* **correre**
accrescere *like* **crescere**
addirsi *like* **dire**
addurre *like* **ridurre**
affiggere *2* affisso *5* affissi, affiggesti
affliggere *2* afflitto *5* afflissi, affliggesti
aggiungere *like* **giungere**
alludere *2* alluso *5* allusi, alludesti
ammettere *like* **mettere**
andare *3* vado, vai, va, andiamo, andate,
vanno *6* andrò *etc 8* vada *10* va'!, vada!,
andate!, vadano!
annettere *2* annesso *5* annessi *o* annettei,
annettesti
apparire *2* apparso *3* appaio, appari *o* ap-
parisci, appare *o* apparisce, appaiono *o*
appariscono *5* apparvi *o* apparsi, appa-
risti, apparve *o* apparì *o* apparse, appar-
vero *o* apparirono *o* apparsero *8* appaia *o*
apparisca
appartenere *like* **tenere**
appendere *2* appeso *5* appesi, appendesti
apporre *like* **porre**
apprendere *like* **prendere**
aprire *2* aperto *3* apro *5* aprii *o* apersi,
apristi *8* apra
ardere *2* arso *5* arsi, ardesti
ascendere *like* **scendere**
aspergere *2* asperso *5* aspersi, aspergesti
assalire *like* **salire**
assistere *2* assistito
assolvere *2* assolto *5* assolsi *o* assolvei *o*
assolvetti, assolvesti
assumere *2* assunto *5* assunsi, assumesti
astenersi *like* **tenere**
attendere *like* **tendere**
attingere *like* **tingere**
AVERE *3* ho, hai, ha, abbiamo, avete, hanno *5* ebbi, avesti, ebbe, avemmo, aveste,
ebbero *6* avrò *etc 8* abbia *etc 10* abbi!, abbia!, abbiate!, abbiano!
avvedersi *like* **vedere**
avvenire *like* **venire**
avvincere *like* **vincere**
avvolgere *like* **volgere**
benedire *like* **dire**
bere *1* bevendo *2* bevuto *3* bevo *etc 4* beve-
vo *etc 5* bevvi *o* bevetti, bevesti *6* berrò

etc 8 beva *etc 9* bevessi *etc*
cadere *5* caddi, cadesti *6* cadrò *etc*
chiedere *2* chiesto *5* chiesi, chiedesti
chiudere *2* chiuso *5* chiusi, chiudesti
cingere *2* cinto *5* cinsi, cingesti
cogliere *2* colto *3* colgo, colgono *5* colsi,
cogliesti *8* colga
coincidere *2* coinciso *5* coincisi, coincide-
sti
coinvolgere *like* **volgere**
commettere *like* **mettere**
commuovere *like* **muovere**
comparire *like* **apparire**
compiacere *like* **piacere**
compiangere *like* **piangere**
comporre *like* **porre**
comprendere *like* **prendere**
comprimere *2* compresso *5* compressi,
comprimesti
compromettere *like* **mettere**
concedere *2* concesso *o* conceduto *5* concessi *o* concedei *o* concedetti, concedesti
concludere *like* **alludere**
concorrere *like* **correre**
condurre *like* **ridurre**
confondere *like* **fondere**
congiungere *like* **giungere**
connettere *like* **annettere**
conoscere *2* conosciuto *5* conobbi, cono-
scesti
consistere *like* **assistere**
contendere *like* **tendere**
contenere *like* **tenere**
contorcere *like* **torcere**
contraddire *like* **dire**
contraffare *like* **fare**
contrarre *like* **trarre**
convenire *like* **venire**
convincere *like* **vincere**
coprire *like* **aprire**
correggere *like* **reggere**
correre *2* corso *5* corsi, corresti
corrispondere *like* **rispondere**
corrompere *like* **rompere**
costringere *like* **stringere**
costruire *5* costrussi, costruisti
crescere *2* cresciuto *5* crebbi, crescesti
cuocere *2* cotto *3* cuocio, cociamo, cuocio-
no *5* cossi, cocesti
dare *3* do, dai, dà, diamo, date, danno *5*
diedi *o* detti, desti *6* darò *etc 8* dia *etc 9*
dessi *etc 10* da'!, dai!, date!, diano!
decidere *2* deciso *5* decisi, decidesti
decrescere *like* **crescere**
dedurre *like* **ridurre**

deludere *like* **alludere**
deporre *like* **porre**
deprimere *like* **comprimere**
deridere *like* **ridere**
descrivere *like* **scrivere**
desumere *like* **assumere**
detergere *like* **tergere**
devolvere *2* devoluto
difendere *2* difeso *5* difesi, difendesti
diffondere *like* **fondere**
dipendere *like* **appendere**
dipingere *like* **tingere**
dire *1* dicendo *2* detto *3* dico, dici, dice, diciamo, dite, dicono *4* dicevo *etc 5* dissi, dicesti *6* dirò *etc 8* dica, diciamo, diciate, dicano *9* dicessi *etc 10* di'!, dica!, dite!, dicano!
dirigere *2* diretto *5* diressi, dirigesti
discendere *like* **scendere**
dischiudere *like* **chiudere**
disciogliere *like* **sciogliere**
discorrere *like* **correre**
discutere *2* discusso *5* discussi, discutesti
disfare *like* **fare**
disilludere *like* **alludere**
disperdere *like* **perdere**
dispiacere *like* **piacere**
disporre *like* **porre**
dissolvere *2* dissolto *o* dissoluto *5* dissolsi *o* dissolvetti *o* dissolvei, dissolvesti
dissuadere *like* **persuadere**
distendere *like* **tendere**
distinguere *2* distinto *5* distinsi, distinguesti
distogliere *like* **togliere**
distrarre *like* **trarre**
distruggere *like* **struggere**
divenire *like* **venire**
dividere *2* diviso *5* divisi, dividesti
dolere *3* dolgo, duoli, duole, dolgono *5* dolsi, dolesti *6* dorrò *etc 8* dolga
DORMIRE *1 GERUNDIO* dormendo
　2 PARTICIPIO PASSATO dormito
　3 PRESENTE dormo, dormi, dorme, dormiamo, dormite, dormono
　4 IMPERFETTO dormivo, dormivi, dormiva, dormivamo, dormivate, dormivano
　5 PASSATO REMOTO dormii, dormisti, dormì, dormimmo, dormiste, dormirono
　6 FUTURO dormirò, dormirai, dormirà, dormiremo, dormirete, dormiranno
　7 CONDIZIONALE dormirei, dormiresti, dormirebbe, dormiremmo, dormireste, dormirebbero
　8 CONGIUNTIVO PRESENTE dorma, dorma, dorma, dormiamo, dormiate, dormano
　9 CONGIUNTIVO PASSATO dormissi, dormissi, dormisse, dormissimo, dormiste, dormissero
　10 IMPERATIVO dormi!, dorma!, dormite!, dormano!
dovere *3* devo *o* debbo, devi, deve, dobbiamo, dovete, devono *o* debbono *6* dovrò *etc*

8 debba, dobbiamo, dobbiate, devano *o* debbano
eccellere *2* eccelso *5* eccelsi, eccellesti
eludere *like* **alludere**
emergere *2* emerso *5* emersi, emergesti
emettere *like* **mettere**
erigere *like* **dirigere**
escludere *like* **alludere**
esigere *2* esatto
esistere *2* esistito
espellere *2* espulso *5* espulsi, espellesti
esplodere *2* esploso *5* esplosi, esplodesti
esporre *like* **porre**
esprimere *like* **comprimere**
ESSERE *2* stato *3* sono, sei, è, siamo, siete, sono *4* ero, eri, era, eravamo, eravate, erano *5* fui, fosti, fu, fummo, foste, furono *6* sarò *etc 8* sia *etc 9* fossi, fossi, fosse, fossimo, foste, fossero *10* sii!, sia!, siate!, siano!
estendere *like* **tendere**
estinguere *like* **distinguere**
estrarre *like* **trarre**
evadere *2* evaso *5* evasi, evadesti
evolvere *2* evoluto
fare *1* facendo *2* fatto *3* faccio, fai, fa, facciamo, fate, fanno *4* facevo *etc 5* feci, facesti *6* farò *etc 8* faccia *etc 9* facessi *etc 10* fa'!, faccia!, fate!, facciano!
fingere *like* **cingere**
FINIRE *1 GERUNDIO* finendo
　2 PARTICIPIO PASSATO finito
　3 PRESENTE finisco, finisci, finisce, finiamo, finite, finiscono
　4 IMPERFETTO finivo, finivi, finiva, finivamo, finivate, finivano
　5 PASSATO REMOTO finii, finisti, finì, finimmo, finiste, finirono
　6 FUTURO finirò, finirai, finirà, finiremo, finirete, finiranno
　7 CONDIZIONALE finirei, finiresti, finirebbe, finiremmo, finireste, finirebbero
　8 CONGIUNTIVO PRESENTE finisca, finisca, finisca, finiamo, finiate, finiscano
　9 CONGIUNTIVO PASSATO finissi, finissi, finisse, finissimo, finiste, finissero
　10 IMPERATIVO finisci!, finisca!, finite!, finiscano!
flettere *2* flesso
fondere *2* fuso *5* fusi, fondesti
friggere *2* fritto *5* frissi, friggesti
fungere *2* funto *5* funsi, fungesti
giacere *3* giaccio, giaci, giace, giac(c)iamo, giacete, giacciono *5* giacqui, giacesti *8* giaccia *etc 10* giaci!, giaccia!, giac(c)iamo!, giacete!, giacciano!
giungere *2* giunto *5* giunsi, giungesti
godere *6* godrò *etc*
illudere *like* **alludere**
immergere *like* **emergere**
immettere *like* **mettere**
imporre *like* **porre**
imprimere *like* **comprimere**

incidere *like* **decidere**
includere *like* **alludere**
incorrere *like* **correre**
incutere *like* **discutere**
indulgere 2 indulto 5 indulsi, indulgesti
indurre *like* **ridurre**
inferire[1] 2 inferto 5 infersi, inferisti
inferire[2] 2 inferito 5 inferii, inferisti
infliggere *like* **affliggere**
infrangere 2 infranto 5 infransi, infrangesti
infondere *like* **fondere**
insistere *like* **assistere**
intendere *like* **tendere**
interdire *like* **dire**
interporre *like* **porre**
interrompere *like* **rompere**
intervenire *like* **venire**
intraprendere *like* **prendere**
introdurre *like* **ridurre**
invadere *like* **evadere**
irrompere *like* **rompere**
iscrivere *like* **scrivere**
istruire *like* **costruire**
ledere 2 leso 5 lesi, ledesti
leggere 2 letto 5 lessi, leggesti
maledire *like* **dire**
mantenere *like* **tenere**
mettere 2 messo 5 misi, mettesti
mordere 2 morso 5 morsi, mordesti
morire 2 morto 3 muoio, muori, muore, moriamo, morite, muoiono 6 morirò o morrò *etc* 8 muoia
mungere 2 munto 5 munsi, mungesti
muovere 2 mosso 5 mossi, movesti
nascere 2 nato 5 nacqui, nascesti
nascondere 2 nascosto 5 nascosi, nascondesti
nuocere 2 nuociuto 3 nuoccio, nuoci, nuoce, nociamo o nuociamo, nuocete, nuocciono 4 nuocevo *etc* 5 nocqui, nuocesti 6 nuocerò *etc* 7 nuoccia
occorrere *like* **correre**
offendere *like* **difendere**
offrire 2 offerto 3 offro 5 offersi o offrii, offristi 8 offra
omettere *like* **mettere**
opporre *like* **porre**
opprimere *like* **comprimere**
ottenere *like* **tenere**
parere 2 parso 3 paio, paiamo, paiono 5 parvi o parsi, paresti 6 parrò *etc* 8 paia, paiamo, paiate, paiano
PARLARE 1 *GERUNDIO* parlando
  2 *PARTICIPIO PASSATO* parlato
  3 *PRESENTE* parlo, parli, parla, parliamo, parlate, parlano
  4 *IMPERFETTO* parlavo, parlavi, parlava, parlavamo, parlavate, parlavano
  5 *PASSATO REMOTO* parlai, parlasti, parlò, parlammo, parlaste, parlarono
  6 *FUTURO* parlerò, parlerai, parlerà, parleremo, parlerete, parleranno

  7 *CONDIZIONALE* parlerei, parleresti, parlerebbe, parleremmo, parlereste, parlerebbero
  8 *CONGIUNTIVO PRESENTE* parli, parli, parli, parliamo, parliate, parlino
  9 *CONGIUNTIVO PASSATO* parlassi, parlassi, parlasse, parlassimo, parlaste, parlassero
  10 *IMPERATIVO* parla!, parli!, parlate!, parlino!
percorrere *like* **correre**
percuotere 2 percosso 5 percossi, percotesti
perdere 2 perso o perduto 5 persi o perdei o perdetti, perdesti
permettere *like* **mettere**
persuadere 2 persuaso 5 persuasi, persuadesti
pervenire *like* **venire**
piacere 2 piaciuto 3 piaccio, piacciamo, piacciono 5 piacqui, piacesti 8 piaccia *etc*
piangere 2 pianto 5 piansi, piangesti
piovere 5 piovve
porgere 2 porto 5 porsi, porgesti
porre 1 ponendo 2 posto 3 pongo, poni, pone, poniamo, ponete, pongono 4 ponevo *etc* 5 posi, ponesti 6 porrò *etc* 8 ponga, poniamo, poniate, pongano 9 ponessi *etc*
posporre *like* **porre**
possedere *like* **sedere**
potere 3 posso, puoi, può, possiamo, potete, possono 6 potrò *etc* 8 possa, possiamo, possiate, possano
prediligere 2 prediletto 5 predilessi, prediligesti
predire *like* **dire**
prefiggersi *like* **affiggere**
preludere *like* **alludere**
prendere 2 preso 5 presi, prendesti
preporre *like* **porre**
prescrivere *like* **scrivere**
presiedere *like* **sedere**
presumere *like* **assumere**
pretendere *like* **tendere**
prevalere *like* **valere**
prevedere *like* **vedere**
prevenire *like* **venire**
produrre *like* **ridurre**
proferire *like* **inferire[2]**
profondere *like* **fondere**
promettere *like* **mettere**
promuovere *like* **muovere**
proporre *like* **porre**
prorompere *like* **rompere**
proscrivere *like* **scrivere**
proteggere 2 protetto 5 protessi, proteggesti
provenire *like* **venire**
provvedere *like* **vedere**
pungere 2 punto 5 punsi, pungesti
racchiudere *like* **chiudere**
raccogliere *like* **cogliere**
radere 2 raso 5 rasi, radesti

raggiungere *like* giungere
rapprendere *like* prendere
ravvedersi *like* vedere
recidere *like* decidere
redigere *2* redatto
redimere *2* redento *5* redensi, redimesti
reggere *2* retto *5* ressi, reggesti
rendere *2* reso *5* resi, rendesti
reprimere *like* comprimere
rescindere *like* scindere
respingere *like* spingere
restringere *like* stringere
ricadere *like* cadere
richiedere *like* chiedere
riconoscere *like* conoscere
ricoprire *like* coprire
ricorrere *like* correre
ridere *2* riso *5* risi, ridesti
ridire *like* dire
ridurre *1* riducendo *2* ridotto *3* riduco *etc 4* riducevo *etc 5* ridussi, riducesti *6* ridurrò *etc 8* riduca *etc 9* riducessi *etc*
riempire *1* riempiendo *3* riempio, riempi, riempie, riempiono
rifare *like* fare
riflettere *2* riflettuto *o* riflesso
rifrangere *like* infrangere
rimanere *2* rimasto *3* rimango, rimangono *5* rimasi, rimanesti *6* rimarrò *etc 8* rimanga
rimettere *like* mettere
rimpiangere *like* piangere
rinchiudere *like* chiudere
rincrescere *like* crescere
rinvenire *like* venire
ripercuotere *like* percuotere
riporre *like* porre
riprendere *like* prendere
riprodurre *like* ridurre
riscuotere *like* scuotere
risolvere *like* assolvere
risorgere *like* sorgere
rispondere *2* risposto *5* risposi, rispondesti
ritenere *like* tenere
ritrarre *like* trarre
riuscire *like* uscire
rivedere *like* vedere
rivivere *like* vivere
rivolgere *like* volgere
rodere *2* roso *5* rosi, rodesti
rompere *2* rotto *5* ruppi, rompesti
salire *3* salgo, sali, salgono *8* salga
sapere *3* so, sai, sa, sappiamo, sapete, sanno *5* seppi, sapesti *6* saprò *etc 8* sappia *etc 10* sappi!, sappia!, sappiate!, sappiano!
scadere *like* cadere
scegliere *2* scelto *3* scelgo, scegli, sceglie, scegliamo, scegliete, scelgono *5* scelsi, scegliesti *8* scelga, scegliamo, scegliate, scelgano *10* scegli!, scelga!, scegliamo!, scegliete!, scelgano!
scendere *2* sceso *5* scesi, scendesti

schiudere *like* chiudere
scindere *2* scisso *5* scissi, scindesti
sciogliere *2* sciolto *3* sciolgo, sciolgi, sciogliamo, sciogliete, sciolgono *5* sciolsi, sciogliesti *8* sciolga, sciogliamo, sciogliate, sciolgano *10* sciogli!, sciolga!, sciogliamo!, sciogliete!, sciolgano!
scommettere *like* mettere
scomparire *like* apparire
scomporre *like* porre
sconfiggere *2* sconfitto *5* sconfissi, sconfiggesti
sconvolgere *like* volgere
scoprire *like* aprire
scorgere *2* scorto *5* scorsi, scorgesti
scorrere *like* correre
scrivere *2* scritto *5* scrissi, scrivesti
scuotere *2* scosso *3* scuoto, scuoti, scuote, scotiamo, scotete, scuotono *5* scossi, scotesti *6* scoterò *etc 8* scuota, scotiamo, scotiate, scuotano *10* scuoti!, scuota!, scotiamo!, scotete!, scuotano!
sedere *3* siedo, siedi, siede, siedono *8* sieda
seppellire *2* sepolto
smettere *like* mettere
smuovere *like* muovere
socchiudere *like* chiudere
soccorrere *like* correre
soddisfare *like* fare
soffriggere *like* friggere
soffrire *2* sofferto *5* soffersi *o* soffrii, soffristi
soggiungere *like* giungere
solere *2* solito *3* soglio, suoli, suole, sogliamo, solete, sogliono *8* soglia, sogliamo, sogliate, sogliano
sommergere *like* emergere
sopprimere *like* comprimere
sorgere *2* sorto *3* sorsi, sorgesti
sorprendere *like* prendere
sorreggere *like* reggere
sorridere *like* ridere
sospendere *like* appendere
sospingere *like* spingere
sostenere *like* tenere
sottintendere *like* tendere
spandere *2* spanto
spargere *2* sparso *5* sparsi, spargesti
sparire *5* sparii *o* sparvi, sparisti
spegnere *2* spento *3* spengo, spengono *5* spensi, spegnesti *8* spenga
spendere *2* speso *5* spesi, spendesti
spingere *2* spinto *5* spinsi, spingesti
sporgere *like* porgere
stare *2* stato *3* sto, stai, sta, stiamo, state, stanno *5* stetti, stesti *6* starò *etc 8* stia *etc 9* stessi *etc 10* sta'!, stia!, state!, stiano!
stendere *like* tendere
storcere *like* torcere
stringere *2* stretto *5* strinsi, stringesti
struggere *2* strutto *5* strussi, struggesti
succedere *like* concedere

supporre *like* **porre**
svenire *like* **venire**
svolgere *like* **volgere**
tacere *2* taciuto *3* taccio, tacciono *5* tacqui, tacesti *8* taccia
tendere *2* teso *5* tesi, tendesti *etc*
tenere *3* tengo, tieni, tiene, tengono *5* tenni, tenesti *6* terrò *etc* *8* tenga
tingere *2* tinto *5* tinsi, tingesti
togliere *2* tolto *3* tolgo, togli, toglie, togliamo, togliete, tolgono *5* tolsi, togliesti *8* tolga, togliamo, togliate, tolgano *10* togli!, tolga!, togliamo!, togliete!, tolgano!
torcere *2* torto *5* torsi, torcesti
tradurre *like* **ridurre**
trafiggere *like* **sconfiggere**
transigere *like* **esigere**
trarre *1* traendo *2* tratto *3* traggo, trai, trae, traiamo, traete, traggono *4* traevo *etc* *5* trassi, traesti *6* trarrò *etc* *8* tragga *9* traessi *etc*
trascorrere *like* **correre**
trascrivere *like* **scrivere**
trasmettere *like* **mettere**
trasparire *like* **apparire**
trattenere *like* **tenere**
uccidere *2* ucciso *5* uccisi, uccidesti
udire *3* odo, odi, ode, odono *8* oda
ungere *2* unto *5* unsi, ungesti
uscire *3* esco, esci, esce, escono *8* esca
valere *2* valso *3* valgo, valgono *5* valsi, valesti *6* varrò *etc* *8* valga

vedere *2* visto *o* veduto *5* vidi, vedesti *6* vedrò *etc*
VENDERE *1* GERUNDIO vendendo
  2 PARTICIPIO PASSATO venduto
  3 PRESENTE vendo, vendi, vende, vendiamo, vendete, vendono
  4 IMPERFETTO vendevo, vendevi, vendeva, vendevamo, vendevate, vendevano
  5 PASSATO REMOTO vendei *o* vendetti, vendesti, vendé *o* vendette, vendemmo, vendeste, venderono *o* vendettero
  6 FUTURO venderò, venderai, venderà, venderemo, venderete, venderanno
  7 CONDIZIONALE venderei, venderesti, venderebbe, venderemmo, vendereste, venderebbero
  8 CONGIUNTIVO PRESENTE venda, venda, venda, vendiamo, vendiate, vendano
  9 CONGIUNTIVO PASSATO vendessi, vendessi, vendesse, vendessimo, vendeste, vendessero
  10 IMPERATIVO vendi!, venda!, vendete!, vendano!
venire *2* venuto *3* vengo, vieni, viene, vengono *5* venni, venisti *6* verrò *etc* *8* venga
vincere *2* vinto *5* vinsi, vincesti
vivere *2* vissuto *5* vissi, vivesti
volere *3* voglio, vuoi, vuole, vogliamo, volete, vogliono *5* volli, volesti *6* vorrò *etc* *8* voglia *etc* *10* vogli!, voglia!, vogliate!, vogliano!
volgere *2* volto *5* volsi, volgesti

VERBI INGLESI

present	pt	pp	present	pt	pp
arise	arose	arisen	drive	drove	driven
awake	awoke	awoken	dwell	dwelt	dwelt
be (am, is,	was, were	been	eat	ate	eaten
are;			fall	fell	fallen
being)			feed	fed	fed
bear	bore	born(e)	feel	felt	felt
beat	beat	beaten	fight	fought	fought
become	became	become	find	found	found
befall	befell	befallen	flee	fled	fled
begin	began	begun	fling	flung	flung
behold	beheld	beheld	fly	flew	flown
bend	bent	bent	forbid	forbad(e)	forbidden
beset	beset	beset	forecast	forecast	forecast
bet	bet, betted	bet, betted	forget	forgot	forgotten
bid (at	bid	bid	forgive	forgave	forgiven
auction,			forsake	forsook	forsaken
cards)			freeze	froze	frozen
bid (say)	bade	bidden	get	got	got, (US)
bind	bound	bound			gotten
bite	bit	bitten	give	gave	given
bleed	bled	bled	go (goes)	went	gone
blow	blew	blown	grind	ground	ground
break	broke	broken	grow	grew	grown
breed	bred	bred	hang	hung	hung
bring	brought	brought	hang	hanged	hanged
build	built	built	(execute)		
burn	burnt,	burnt,	have	had	had
	burned	burned	hear	heard	heard
burst	burst	burst	hide	hid	hidden
buy	bought	bought	hit	hit	hit
can	could	(been able)	hold	held	held
cast	cast	cast	hurt	hurt	hurt
catch	caught	caught	keep	kept	kept
choose	chose	chosen	kneel	knelt,	knelt,
cling	clung	clung		kneeled	kneeled
come	came	come	know	knew	known
cost	cost	cost	lay	laid	laid
cost (work	costed	costed	lead	led	led
out price			lean	leant,	leant,
of)				leaned	leaned
creep	crept	crept	leap	leapt,	leapt,
cut	cut	cut		leaped	leaped
deal	dealt	dealt	learn	learnt,	learnt,
dig	dug	dug		learned	learned
do (3rd	did	done	leave	left	left
person:			lend	lent	lent
he/she/it			let	let	let
does)			lie (lying)	lay	lain
draw	drew	drawn	light	lit, lighted	lit, lighted
dream	dreamed,	dreamed,	lose	lost	lost
	dreamt	dreamt	make	made	made
drink	drank	drunk	may	might	—

present	pt	pp	present	pt	pp
mean	meant	meant	speed	sped,	sped,
meet	met	met		speeded	speeded
mistake	mistook	mistaken	spell	spelt,	spelt,
mow	mowed	mown,		spelled	spelled
		mowed	spend	spent	spent
must	(had to)	(had to)	spill	spilt,	spilt,
pay	paid	paid		spilled	spilled
put	put	put	spin	spun	spun
quit	quit,	quit,	spit	spat	spat
	quitted	quitted	spoil	spoiled,	spoiled,
read	read	read		spoilt	spoilt
rid	rid	rid	spread	spread	spread
ride	rode	ridden	spring	sprang	sprung
ring	rang	rung	stand	stood	stood
rise	rose	risen	steal	stole	stolen
run	ran	run	stick	stuck	stuck
saw	sawed	sawed,	sting	stung	stung
		sawn	stink	stank	stunk
say	said	said	stride	strode	stridden
see	saw	seen	strike	struck	struck
seek	sought	sought	strive	strove	striven
sell	sold	sold	swear	swore	sworn
send	sent	sent	sweep	swept	swept
set	set	set	swell	swelled	swollen,
sew	sewed	sewn			swelled
shake	shook	shaken	swim	swam	swum
shear	sheared	shorn,	swing	swung	swung
		sheared	take	took	taken
shed	shed	shed	teach	taught	taught
shine	shone	shone	tear	tore	torn
shoot	shot	shot	tell	told	told
show	showed	shown	think	thought	thought
shrink	shrank	shrunk	throw	threw	thrown
shut	shut	shut	thrust	thrust	thrust
sing	sang	sung	tread	trod	trodden
sink	sank	sunk	wake	woke,	woken,
sit	sat	sat		waked	waked
slay	slew	slain	wear	wore	worn
sleep	slept	slept	weave	wove	woven
slide	slid	slid	weave	weaved	weaved
sling	slung	slung	*(wind)*		
slit	slit	slit	wed	wedded,	wedded,
smell	smelt,	smelt,		wed	wed
	smelled	smelled	weep	wept	wept
sow	sowed	sown,	win	won	won
		sowed	wind	wound	wound
speak	spoke	spoken	wring	wrung	wrung
			write	wrote	written

I NUMERI

NUMBERS

uno(a)	1	one
due	2	two
tre	3	three
quattro	4	four
cinque	5	five
sei	6	six
sette	7	seven
otto	8	eight
nove	9	nine
dieci	10	ten
undici	11	eleven
dodici	12	twelve
tredici	13	thirteen
quattordici	14	fourteen
quindici	15	fifteen
sedici	16	sixteen
diciassette	17	seventeen
diciotto	18	eighteen
diciannove	19	nineteen
venti	20	twenty
ventuno	21	twenty-one
ventidue	22	twenty-two
ventitré	23	twenty-three
ventotto	28	twenty-eight
trenta	30	thirty
quaranta	40	forty
cinquanta	50	fifty
sessanta	60	sixty
settanta	70	seventy
ottanta	80	eighty
novanta	90	ninety
cento	100	a hundred, one hundred
centouno	101	a hundred and one
duecento	200	two hundred
mille	1 000	a thousand, one thousand
milleduecentodue	1 202	one thousand two hundred and two
cinquemila	5 000	five thousand
un milione	1 000 000	a million, one million

I NUMERI

NUMBERS

primo(a), 1°	first, 1st
secondo(a), 2°	second, 2nd
terzo(a), 3°	third, 3rd
quarto(a)	fourth, 4th
quinto(a)	fifth, 5th
sesto(a)	sixth, 6th
settimo(a)	seventh
ottavo(a)	eighth
nono(a)	ninth
decimo(a)	tenth
undicesimo(a)	eleventh
dodicesimo(a)	twelfth
tredicesimo(a)	thirteenth
quattordicesimo(a)	fourteenth
quindicesimo(a)	fifteenth
sedicesimo(a)	sixteenth
diciassettesimo(a)	seventeenth
diciottesimo(a)	eighteenth
diciannovesimo(a)	nineteenth
ventesimo(a)	twentieth
ventunesimo(a)	twenty-first
ventiduesimo(a)	twenty-second
ventitreesimo(a)	twenty-third
ventottesimo(a)	twenty-eighth
trentesimo(a)	thirtieth
centesimo(a)	hundredth
centunesimo(a)	hundred-and-first
millesimo(a)	thousandth
milionesimo(a)	millionth

L'ORA

THE TIME

che ora è?, che ore sono?
è ..., sono ...

what time is it?
it's ...

mezzanotte	midnight
l'una (del mattino)	one o'clock (in the morning) , one (am)
l'una e cinque	five past one
l'una e dieci	ten past one
l'una e un quarto, l'una e quindici	a quarter past one, one fifteen
l'una e venticinque	twenty-five past one, one twenty-five
l'una e mezzo *o* mezza, l'una e trenta	half past one, one thirty
l'una e trentacinque	twenty-five to two, one thirty-five
le due meno venti, l'una e quaranta	twenty to two, one forty
le due meno un quarto, l'una e quarantacinque	a quarter to two, one forty-five
le due meno dieci, l'una e cinquanta	ten to two, one fifty
mezzogiorno	twelve o'clock, midday, noon
le tre, le quindici	three o'clock (in the afternoon), three (pm)
le sette (di sera), le diciannove	seven o'clock (in the evening), seven (pm)

a che ora?

at what time?

a mezzanotte	at midnight
alle sette	at seven o'clock
fra venti minuti	in twenty minutes
venti minuti fa	twenty minutes ago

LA DATA

THE DATE

oggi	today
domani	tomorrow
dopodomani	the day after tomorrow
ieri	yesterday
l'altro ieri	the day before yesterday
il giorno prima	the day before, the previous day
il giorno dopo	the next *or* following day

la mattina	morning
la sera	evening
stamattina	this morning
stasera	this evening
questo pomeriggio	this afternoon
ieri mattina	yesterday morning
ieri sera	yesterday evening
domani mattina	tomorrow morning
domani sera	tomorrow evening
nella notte tra sabato e domenica	during Saturday night, during the night of Saturday to Sunday
viene sabato	he's coming on Saturday
il sabato	on Saturdays
tutti i sabati	every Saturday
sabato scorso, lo scorso sabato	last Saturday
il prossimo sabato	next Saturday
fra due sabati	a week on Saturday
fra tre sabati	a fortnight *or* two weeks on Saturday
da lunedì a sabato	from Monday to Saturday
tutti i giorni	every day
una volta alla settimana	once a week
una volta al mese	once a month
due volte alla settimana	twice a week
una settimana fa	a week ago
quindici giorni fa	a fortnight *or* two weeks ago
l'anno scorso *or* passato	last year
fra due giorni	in two days
fra una settimana	in a week
fra quindici giorni	in a fortnight *or* two weeks
il mese prossimo	next month
l'anno prossimo	next year
che giorno è oggi?	*what day is it?*
il primo/24 ottobre 1996	the 1st/24th of October 1996, October 1st/24th 1996
nel 1996	in 1996
il millenovecentonovantacinque	nineteen ninety-five
44 a.C.	44 BC
14 d.C.	14 AD
nel diciannovesimo secolo, nel XIX secolo, nell'Ottocento	in the nineteenth century
negli anni trenta	in the thirties
c'era una volta ...	once upon a time ...

Italiano-Inglese
Italian-English

_Aa_

A, a [a] _sf o m inv_ (_lettera_) A, a; **A come Ancona** ≈ A for Andrew (_BRIT_), A for Able (_US_); **dalla a alla z** from a to z. **A** _abbr_ (= _altezza_) h; (= _area_) A; (= _autostrada_) ≈ M (_BRIT_).

a (_a + il_ = **al**, _a + lo_ = **allo**, _a + l'_ = **all'**, _a + la_ = **alla**, _a + i_ = **ai**, _a + gli_ = **agli**, _a + le_ = **alle**) _prep_ **1** (_stato in luogo_) at; (: _in_) in; **essere alla stazione** to be at the station; **essere ~ casa/~ scuola/~ Roma** to be at home/at school/in Rome; **è ~ 10 km da qui** it's 10 km from here, it's 10 km away; **restare ~ cena** to stay for dinner
2 (_moto a luogo_) to; **andare ~ casa/~ scuola/alla stazione** to go home/to school/to the station; **andare ~ Roma/al mare** to go to Rome/to the seaside
3 (_tempo_) at; (_epoca, stagione_) in; **alle cinque** at five (o'clock); **~ mezzanotte/Natale** at midnight/Christmas; **al mattino** in the morning; **~ maggio/primavera** in May/spring; **~ cinquant'anni** at fifty (years of age); **~ domani!** see you tomorrow!; **~ lunedì!** see you on Monday!; **~ giorni** within (a few) days
4 (_complemento di termine_) to; **dare qc ~ qn** to give sb sth, give sth to sb; **l'ho chiesto ~ lui** I asked him
5 (_mezzo, modo_) with, by; **~ piedi/cavallo** on foot/horseback; **viaggiare ~ 100 km all'ora** to travel at 100 km an _o_ per hour; **alla televisione/radio** on television/the radio; **fatto ~ mano** made by hand, handmade; **una barca ~ motore** a motorboat; **una stufa ~ gas** a gas heater; **~ uno ~ uno** one by one; **~ fatica** with difficulty; **all'italiana** the Italian way, in the Italian fashion
6 (_rapporto_) a, per; (: _con prezzi_) at; **due volte al giorno/mese** twice a day/month; **prendo 2000 euro al mese** I get 2000 euros a _o_ per month; **pagato ~ ore** paid by the hour; **vendere qc ~ 2 euro il chilo** to sell sth at 2 euros a _o_ per kilo; **cinque ~ zero** (_punteggio_) five nil.

AA _sigla_ = Alto Adige.
AAST _sigla f_ = Azienda Autonoma di Soggiorno e turismo.
AA.VV. _abbr_ = autori vari.
ab. _abbr_ = abitante.
a'bate _sm_ abbot.
abbacchi'ato, a [abbak'kjato] _ag_ downhearted, in low spirits.
abbacin'are [abbatʃi'nare] _vt_ to dazzle.
abbagli'ante [abbaʎ'ʎante] _ag_ dazzling; **~i** _smpl_ (_AUT_): **accendere gli ~i** to put one's headlights on full (_BRIT_) _o_ high (_US_) beam.
abbagli'are [abbaʎ'ʎare] _vt_ to dazzle; (_illudere_) to delude.
ab'baglio [ab'baʎʎo] _sm_ blunder; **prendere un ~** to blunder, make a blunder.
abbai'are _vi_ to bark.
abba'ino _sm_ dormer window; (_soffitta_) attic room.
abbando'nare _vt_ to leave, abandon, desert; (_trascurare_) to neglect; (_rinunciare a_) to abandon, give up; **~rsi** _vr_ to let o.s. go; **~ il campo** (_MIL_) to retreat; **~ la presa** to let go; **~rsi a** (_ricordi, vizio_) to give o.s. up to.
abbando'nato, a _ag_ (_casa_) deserted; (_miniera_) disused; (_trascurato: terreno,_

podere) neglected; (*bambino*) abandoned.

abban'dono *sm* abandoning; neglecting; (*stato*) abandonment; neglect; (*SPORT*) withdrawal; (*fig*) abandon; **in** ~ (*edificio, giardino*) neglected.

abbarbi'carsi *vr*: ~ (**a**) (*anche fig*) to cling (to).

abbassa'mento *sm* lowering; (*di pressione, livello dell'acqua*) fall; (*di prezzi*) reduction; ~ **di temperatura** drop in temperature.

abbas'sare *vt* to lower; (*radio*) to turn down; ~**rsi** *vr* (*chinarsi*) to stoop; (*livello, sole*) to go down; (*fig: umiliarsi*) to demean o.s.; ~ **i fari** (*AUT*) to dip (*BRIT*) *o* dim (*US*) one's lights; ~ **le armi** (*MIL*) to lay down one's arms.

ab'basso *escl*: ~ **il re!** down with the king!

abbas'tanza [abbas'tantsa] *av* (*a sufficienza*) enough; (*alquanto*) quite, rather, fairly; **non è** ~ **furbo** he's not shrewd enough; **un vino** ~ **dolce** quite a sweet wine, a fairly sweet wine; **averne** ~ **di qn/qc** to have had enough of sb/sth.

ab'battere *vt* (*muro, casa, ostacolo*) to knock down; (*albero*) to fell; (: *sog: vento*) to bring down; (*bestie da macello*) to slaughter; (*cane, cavallo*) to destroy, put down; (*selvaggina, aereo*) to shoot down; (*fig: sog: malattia, disgrazia*) to lay low; ~**rsi** *vr* (*avvilirsi*) to lose heart; ~**rsi a terra** *o* **al suolo** to fall to the ground; ~**rsi su** (*sog: maltempo*) to beat down on; (: *disgrazia*) to hit, strike.

abbatti'mento *sm* knocking down; felling; (*di casa*) demolition; (*prostrazione: fisica*) exhaustion; (: *morale*) despondency.

abbat'tuto, a *ag* despondent, depressed.

abba'zia [abbat'tsia] *sf* abbey.

abbece'dario [abbetʃe'darjo] *sm* primer.

abbelli'mento *sm* embellishment.

abbel'lire *vt* to make beautiful; (*ornare*) to embellish.

abbeve'rare *vt* to water; ~**rsi** *vr* to drink.

abbevera'toio *sm* drinking trough.

'abbi, 'abbia, abbi'amo, 'abbiano, abbi'ate *vb vedi* **avere**.

abbiccì [abbit'tʃi] *sm inv* alphabet; (*sillabario*) primer; (*fig*) rudiments *pl*.

abbi'ente *ag* well-to-do, well-off.

abbi'etto, a *ag* = **abietto**.

abbiezi'one [abbjet'tsjone] *sf* = **abiezione**.

abbiglia'mento [abbiʎʎa'mento] *sm* dress *no pl*; (*indumenti*) clothes *pl*; (*industria*) clothing industry.

abbigli'are [abbiʎ'ʎare] *vt* to dress up.

abbina'mento *sm* combination; linking; matching.

abbi'nare *vt*: ~ (**con** *o* **a**) (*gen*) to combine

(with); (*nomi*) to link (with); ~ **qc a qc** (*colori etc*) to match sth with sth.

abbindo'lare *vt* (*fig*) to cheat, trick.

abbocca'mento *sm* (*colloquio*) talks *pl*, meeting; (*TECN: di tubi*) connection.

abboc'care *vt* (*tubi, canali*) to connect, join up ♦ *vi* (*pesce*) to bite; (*tubi*) to join; ~ (**all'amo**) (*fig*) to swallow the bait.

abboc'cato, a *ag* (*vino*) sweetish.

abbona'mento *sm* subscription; (*alle ferrovie etc*) season ticket; **in** ~ for subscribers only; for season ticket holders only; **fare l'**~ (**a**) to take out a subscription (to); to buy a season ticket (for).

abbo'nare *vt* (*cifra*) to deduct; (*fig: perdonare*) to forgive; ~**rsi** *vr*: ~**rsi a un giornale** to take out a subscription to a newspaper; ~**rsi al teatro/alle ferrovie** to take out a season ticket for the theatre/ the train.

abbo'nato, a *sm/f* subscriber; season-ticket holder; **elenco degli** ~**i** telephone directory.

abbon'dante *ag* abundant, plentiful; (*giacca*) roomy.

abbon'danza [abbon'dantsa] *sf* abundance; plenty.

abbon'dare *vi* to abound, be plentiful; ~ **in** *o* **di** to be full of, abound in.

abbor'dabile *ag* (*persona*) approachable; (*prezzo*) reasonable.

abbor'dare *vt* (*nave*) to board; (*persona*) to approach; (*argomento*) to tackle; ~ **una curva** to take a bend.

abbotto'nare *vt* to button up, do up; ~**rsi** *vr* to button (up).

abbotto'nato, a *ag* (*camicia etc*) buttoned (up); (*fig*) reserved.

abbotto'natura *sf* buttons *pl*; **questo cappotto ha l'**~ **da uomo/da donna** this coat buttons on the man's/woman's side.

abboz'zare [abbot'tsare] *vt* to sketch, outline; (*SCULTURA*) to rough-hew; ~ **un sorriso** to give a hint of a smile.

ab'bozzo [ab'bɔttso] *sm* sketch, outline; (*DIR*) draft.

abbracci'are [abbrat'tʃare] *vt* to embrace; (*persona*) to hug, embrace; (*professione*) to take up; (*contenere*) to include; ~**rsi** *vr* to hug *o* embrace (one another).

ab'braccio [ab'brattʃo] *sm* hug, embrace.

abbrevi'are *vt* to shorten; (*parola*) to abbreviate, shorten.

abbreviazi'one [abbrevjat'tsjone] *sf* abbreviation.

abbron'zante [abbron'dzante] *ag* tanning, sun *cpd*.

abbron'zare [abbron'dzare] vt (pelle) to tan; (metalli) to bronze; ~**rsi** vr to tan, get a tan.

abbron'zato, a [abbron'dzato] ag (sun)tanned.

abbronza'tura [abbrondza'tura] sf tan, suntan.

abbrusto'lire vt (pane) to toast; (caffè) to roast.

abbruti'mento sm exhaustion; degradation.

abbru'tire vt (snervare, stancare) to exhaust; (degradare) to degrade; **essere abbrutito dall'alcool** to be ruined by drink.

abbuf'farsi vr (fam): ~ **(di qc)** to stuff o.s. (with sth).

abbuf'fata sf (fam) nosh-up; (fig) binge; **farsi un'**~ to stuff o.s.

abbuo'nare vt = **abbonare**.

abbu'ono sm (COMM) allowance, discount; (SPORT) handicap.

abdi'care vi to abdicate; ~ **a** to give up.

abdicazi'one [abdikat'tsjone] sf abdication.

aberrazi'one [aberrat'tsjone] sf aberration.

abe'taia sf fir wood.

a'bete sm fir (tree); ~ **bianco** silver fir; ~ **rosso** spruce.

abi'etto, a ag despicable, abject.

abiezi'one [abjet'tsjone] sf abjection.

'abile ag (idoneo): ~ **(a qc/a fare qc)** fit (for sth/to do sth); (capace) able; (astuto) clever; (accorto) skilful; ~ **al servizio militare** fit for military service.

abilità sf inv ability; cleverness; skill.

abili'tante ag qualifying; **corsi** ~**i** (INS) ≈ teacher training sg.

abili'tare vt: ~ **qn a qc/a fare qc** to qualify sb for sth/to do sth; **è stato abilitato all'insegnamento** he has qualified as a teacher.

abili'tato, a ag qualified; (TEL) which has an outside line.

abilitazi'one [abilitat'tsjone] sf qualification.

abis'sale ag abysmal; (fig: senza limiti) profound.

abis'sino, a ag, sm/f Abyssinian.

a'bisso sm abyss, gulf.

abitabilità sf: **licenza di** ~ document stating that a property is fit for habitation.

abi'tacolo sm (AER) cockpit; (AUT) inside; (di camion) (driver's) cab.

abi'tante sm/f inhabitant.

abi'tare vt to live in, dwell in ♦ vi: ~ **in campagna/a Roma** to live in the country/in Rome.

abi'tato, a ag inhabited; lived in ♦ sm (anche: **centro** ~) built-up area.

abitazi'one [abitat'tsjone] sf residence; house.

'abito sm dress no pl; (da uomo) suit; (da donna) dress; (abitudine, disposizione, REL) habit; ~**i** smpl (vestiti) clothes; **in** ~ **da cerimonia** in formal dress; **in** ~ **da sera** in evening dress; **"è gradito l'**~ **scuro"** "dress formal"; ~ **mentale** way of thinking.

abitu'ale ag usual, habitual; (cliente) regular.

abitual'mente av usually, normally.

abitu'are vt: ~ **qn a** to get sb used o accustomed to; ~**rsi a** to get used to, accustom o.s. to.

abitudi'nario, a ag of fixed habits ♦ sm/f creature of habit.

abi'tudine sf habit; **aver l'**~ **di fare qc** to be in the habit of doing sth; **d'**~ usually; **per** ~ from o out of habit.

abiu'rare vt to renounce.

abla'tivo sm ablative.

abnegazi'one [abnegat'tsjone] sf (self-) abnegation, self-denial.

ab'norme ag (enorme) extraordinary; (anormale) abnormal.

abo'lire vt to abolish; (DIR) to repeal.

abolizi'one [abolit'tsjone] sf abolition; repeal.

abomi'nevole ag abominable.

abo'rigeno [abo'ridʒeno] sm aborigine.

abor'rire vt to abhor, detest.

abor'tire vi (MED: accidentalmente) to miscarry, have a miscarriage; (: deliberatamente) to have an abortion; (fig) to miscarry, fail.

abor'tista, i, e ag pro-choice, pro-abortion ♦ sm/f pro-choicer.

a'borto sm miscarriage; abortion; (fig) freak; ~ **clandestino** backstreet abortion.

abrasi'one sf abrasion.

abra'sivo, a ag, sm abrasive.

abro'gare vt to repeal, abrogate.

abrogazi'one [abrogat'tsjone] sf repeal.

abruz'zese [abrut'tsese] ag of (o from) the Abruzzi.

A'bruzzo [a'bruttso] sm: **l'**~, **gli** ~**i** the Abruzzi.

ABS [abi'esse] sigla m ABS (= anti-lock braking system).

'abside sf apse.

'Abu 'Dhabi sf Abu Dhabi.

a'bulico, a, ci, che ag lacking in willpower.

abu'sare vi: ~ **di** to abuse, misuse; (approfittare, violare) to take advantage of; ~ **dell'alcool/dei cibi** to drink/eat to excess.

abusi'vismo *sm* (*anche:* ~ **edilizio**) unlawful building, building without planning permission (*BRIT*).

abu'sivo, a *ag* unauthorized, unlawful; (**occupante**) ~ (*di una casa*) squatter.

a'buso *sm* abuse, misuse; excessive use; **fare** ~ **di** (*stupefacenti, medicine*) to abuse.

a.C. *abbr av* (= *avanti Cristo*) BC.

a'cacia, cie [a'katʃa] *sf* acacia.

'acca *sf* letter H; **non capire un'**~ not to understand a thing.

ac'cadde *vb vedi* **accadere**.

acca'demia *sf* (*società*) learned society; (*scuola: d'arte, militare*) academy; ~ **di Belle Arti** art school.

acca'demico, a, ci, che *ag* academic ♦ *sm* academician.

acca'dere *vi* to happen, occur.

acca'duto *sm* event; **raccontare l'**~ to describe what has happened.

accalappia'cani *sm inv* dog-catcher.

accalappi'are *vt* to catch; (*fig*) to trick, dupe.

accal'care *vt*, ~**rsi** *vr* to crowd, throng.

accal'darsi *vr* to grow hot.

accalo'rarsi *vr* (*fig*) to get excited.

accampa'mento *sm* camp.

accam'pare *vt* to encamp; (*fig*) to put forward, advance; ~**rsi** *vr* to camp; ~ **scuse** to make excuses.

accani'mento *sm* fury; (*tenacia*) tenacity, perseverance.

acca'nirsi *vr* (*infierire*) to rage; (*ostinarsi*) to persist.

accanita'mente *av* fiercely; assiduously.

acca'nito, a *ag* (*odio, gelosia*) fierce, bitter; (*lavoratore*) assiduous; (*giocatore*) inveterate; (*tifoso, sostenitore*) keen; **fumatore** ~ chain smoker.

ac'canto *av* near, nearby; ~ **a** *prep* near, beside, close to; **la casa** ~ the house next door.

accanto'nare *vt* (*problema*) to shelve; (*somma*) to set aside.

accaparra'mento *sm* (*COMM*) cornering, buying up.

accapar'rare *vt* (*COMM*) to corner, buy up; (*versare una caparra*) to pay a deposit on; ~**rsi** *vr*: ~**rsi qc** (*fig: simpatia, voti*) to secure sth (for o.s.).

accapigli'arsi [akkapiʎ'ʎarsi] *vr* to come to blows; (*fig*) to quarrel.

accappa'toio *sm* bathrobe.

accappo'nare *vi*: **far** ~ **la pelle a qn** (*fig*) to bring sb out in goosepimples.

accarez'zare [akkaret'tsare] *vt* to caress,

stroke, fondle; (*fig*) to toy with.

accartocci'are [akkartot'tʃare] *vt* (*carta*) to roll up, screw up; ~**rsi** *vr* (*foglie*) to curl up.

acca'sarsi *vr* to set up house; to get married.

accasci'arsi [akkaʃ'ʃarsi] *vr* to collapse; (*fig*) to lose heart.

accatas'tare *vt* to stack, pile.

accatto'naggio [akkatto'naddʒo] *sm* begging.

accat'tone, a *sm/f* beggar.

accaval'lare *vt* (*gambe*) to cross; ~**rsi** *vr* (*sovrapporsi*) to overlap; (*addensarsi*) to gather.

acce'care [attʃe'kare] *vt* to blind ♦ *vi* to go blind.

ac'cedere [at'tʃɛdere] *vi*: ~ **a** to enter; (*richiesta*) to grant, accede to; (*fonte*) to gain access to.

accele'rare [attʃele'rare] *vt* to speed up ♦ *vi* (*AUT*) to accelerate; ~ **il passo** to quicken one's pace.

accele'rato, a [attʃele'rato] *ag* quick, rapid ♦ *sm* (*FERR*) local train, stopping train.

accelera'tore [attʃelera'tore] *sm* (*AUT*) accelerator.

accelerazi'one [attʃelerat'tsjone] *sf* acceleration.

ac'cendere [at'tʃɛndere] *vt* (*fuoco, sigaretta*) to light; (*luce, televisione*) to put o switch o turn on; (*AUT: motore*) to switch on; (*COMM: conto*) to open; (: *debito*) to contract; (: *ipoteca*) to raise; (*fig: suscitare*) to inflame, stir up; ~**rsi** *vr* (*luce*) to come o go on; (*legna*) to catch fire, ignite; (*fig: lotta, conflitto*) to break out.

accen'dino [attʃen'dino], **accendi'sigaro** [attʃendi'sigaro] *sm* (*cigarette*) lighter.

accen'nare [attʃen'nare] *vt* to indicate, point out; (*MUS*) to pick out the notes of; to hum ♦ *vi*: ~ **a** (*fig: alludere a*) to hint at; (: *far atto di*) to make as if; ~ **un saluto** (*con la mano*) to make as if to wave; (*col capo*) to half nod; ~ **un sorriso** to half smile; **accenna a piovere** it looks as if it's going to rain.

ac'cenno [at'tʃenno] *sm* (*cenno*) sign; nod; (*allusione*) hint.

accensi'one [attʃen'sjone] *sf* (*vedi accendere*) lighting; switching on; opening; (*AUT*) ignition.

accen'tare [attʃen'tare] *vt* (*parlando*) to stress; (*scrivendo*) to accent.

accentuazi'one [attʃentuat'tsjone] *sf* accentuation; stressing.

ac'cento [at'tʃɛnto] *sm* accent; (*FONETICA, fig*) stress; (*inflessione*) tone (of voice).

accentra'mento [attʃentra'mento] *sm* centralization.

accen'trare [attʃen'trare] *vt* to centralize.

accentra'tore, 'trice [attʃentra'tore] *ag* (*persona*) unwilling to delegate; **politica ~trice** policy of centralization.

accentu'are [attʃentu'are] *vt* to stress, emphasize; **~rsi** *vr* to become more noticeable.

accerchi'are [attʃer'kjare] *vt* to surround, encircle.

accerta'mento [attʃerta'mento] *sm* check; assessment.

accer'tare [attʃer'tare] *vt* to ascertain; (*verificare*) to check; (*reddito*) to assess; **~rsi** *vr*: **~rsi (di qc/che)** to make sure (of sth/that).

ac'ceso, a [at'tʃeso] *pp di* **accendere ♦** *ag* lit; on; open; (*colore*) bright; **~ di** (*ira, entusiasmo etc*) burning with.

acces'sibile [attʃes'sibile] *ag* (*luogo*) accessible; (*persona*) approachable; (*prezzo*) reasonable; (*idea*): **~ a qn** within the reach of sb.

ac'cesso [at'tʃɛsso] *sm* (*anche INFORM*) access; (*MED*) attack, fit; (*impulso violento*) fit, outburst; **programmi dell'~** (*TV*) educational programmes; **tempo di ~** (*INFORM*) access time; **~ casuale/seriale/ sequenziale** (*INFORM*) random/serial/ sequential access.

accessori'ato, a [attʃesso'rjato] *ag* with accessories.

acces'sorio, a [attʃes'sɔrjo] *ag* secondary, of secondary importance; **~i** *smpl* accessories.

ac'cetta [at'tʃetta] *sf* hatchet.

accet'tabile [attʃet'tabile] *ag* acceptable.

accet'tare [attʃet'tare] *vt* to accept; **~ di fare qc** to agree to do sth.

accettazi'one [attʃettat'tsjone] *sf* acceptance; (*locale di servizio pubblico*) reception; **~ bagagli** (*AER*) check-in (desk); **~ con riserva** qualified acceptance.

ac'cetto, a [at'tʃɛtto] *ag* (*persona*) welcome; **(ben) ~ a tutti** well-liked by everybody.

accezi'one [attʃet'tsjone] *sf* meaning.

acchiap'pare [akkjap'pare] *vt* to catch; (*afferrare*) to seize.

ac'chito [ak'kito] *sm*: **a primo ~** at first sight.

acciac'cato, a [attʃak'kato] *ag* (*persona*) full of aches and pains; (*abito*) crushed.

acci'acco, chi [at'tʃakko] *sm* ailment; **~chi** *smpl* aches and pains.

acciaie'ria [attʃaje'ria] *sf* steelworks *sg*.

acci'aio [at'tʃajo] *sm* steel; **~ inossidabile** stainless steel.

acciden'tale [attʃiden'tale] *ag* accidental.

accidental'mente [attʃidental'mente] *av* (*per caso*) by chance; (*non deliberatamente*) accidentally, by accident.

acciden'tato, a [attʃiden'tato] *ag* (*terreno etc*) uneven.

acci'dente [attʃi'dɛnte] *sm* (*caso imprevisto*) accident; (*disgrazia*) mishap; **~i!** (*fam: per rabbia*) damn (it)!; (: *per meraviglia*) good heavens!; **~i a lui!** damn him!; **non vale un ~** it's not worth a damn; **non capisco un ~** it's as clear as mud to me; **mandare un ~ a qn** to curse sb.

ac'cidia [at'tʃidja] *sf* (*REL*) sloth.

accigli'ato, a [attʃiʎ'ʎato] *ag* frowning.

ac'cingersi [at'tʃindʒersi] *vr*: **~ a fare** to be about to do.

acciotto'lato [attʃotto'lato] *sm* cobbles *pl*.

acciuf'fare [attʃuf'fare] *vt* to seize, catch.

acci'uga, ghe [at'tʃuga] *sf* anchovy; **magro come un'~** as thin as a rake.

accla'mare *vt* (*applaudire*) to applaud; (*eleggere*) to acclaim.

acclamazi'one [akklamat'tsjone] *sf* applause; acclamation.

acclima'tare *vt* to acclimatize; **~rsi** *vr* to become acclimatized.

acclimatazi'one [akklimatat'tsjone] *sf* acclimatization.

ac'cludere *vt* to enclose.

ac'cluso, a *pp di* **accludere ♦** *ag* enclosed.

accocco'larsi *vr* to crouch.

acco'darsi *vr* to follow, tag on (behind).

accogli'ente [akkoʎ'ʎɛnte] *ag* welcoming, friendly.

accogli'enza [akkoʎ'ʎɛntsa] *sf* reception; welcome; **fare una buona ~ a qn** to welcome sb.

ac'cogliere [ak'kɔʎʎere] *vt* (*ricevere*) to receive; (*dare il benvenuto*) to welcome; (*approvare*) to agree to, accept; (*contenere*) to hold, accommodate.

ac'colgo etc *vb vedi* **accogliere**.

accol'lare *vt* (*fig*): **~ qc a qn** to force sth on sb; **~rsi** *vr*: **~rsi qc** to take sth upon o.s., shoulder sth.

accol'lato, a *ag* (*vestito*) high-necked.

ac'colsi etc *vb vedi* **accogliere**.

accoltel'lare *vt* to knife, stab.

ac'colto, a *pp di* **accogliere**.

accoman'dita *sf* (*DIR*) limited partnership.

accomia'tare *vt* to dismiss; **~rsi** *vr*: **~rsi (da)** to take one's leave (of).

accomoda'mento *sm* agreement, settlement.

accomo'dante *ag* accommodating.

accomo'dare *vt* (*aggiustare*) to repair, mend; (*riordinare*) to tidy; (*sistemare: questione, lite*) to settle; ~**rsi** *vr* (*sedersi*) to sit down; (*fig: risolversi: situazione*) to work out; **si accomodi!** (*venga avanti*) come in!; (*si sieda*) take a seat!

accompagna'mento [akkompaɲɲa'mento] *sm* (*MUS*) accompaniment; (*COMM*): **lettera di** ~ accompanying letter.

accompa'gnare [akkompaɲˈɲare] *vt* to accompany, come *o* go with; (*MUS*) to accompany; (*unire*) to couple; ~**rsi** *vr* (*armonizzarsi*) to go well together; ~ **qn a casa** to see sb home; ~ **qn alla porta** to show sb out; ~ **un regalo con un biglietto** to put in *o* send a card with a present; ~ **qn con lo sguardo** to follow sb with one's eyes; ~ **la porta** to close the door gently; ~**rsi a** (*frequentare*) to frequent; (*colori*) to go with, match; (*cibi*) to go with.

accompagna'tore, 'trice [akkompaɲɲa 'tore] *sm/f* companion, escort; (*MUS*) accompanist; (*SPORT*) team manager; ~ **turistico** courier; tour guide.

accomu'nare *vt* to pool, share; (*avvicinare*) to unite.

acconcia'tura [akkontʃa'tura] *sf* hairstyle.

accondiscen'dente [akkondiʃʃen'dɛnte] *ag* affable.

accondi'scendere [akkondiʃˈʃendere] *vi*: ~ **a** to agree *o* consent to.

accondi'sceso, a [akkondiʃˈʃeso] *pp di* **accondiscendere**.

acconsen'tire *vi*: ~ (**a**) to agree *o* consent (to); **chi tace acconsente** silence means consent.

acconten'tare *vt* to satisfy; ~**rsi** *vr*: ~**rsi di** to be satisfied with, content o.s. with; **chi si accontenta gode** there's no point in complaining.

ac'conto *sm* part payment; **pagare una somma in** ~ to pay a sum of money as a deposit; ~ **di dividendo** interim dividend.

accoppia'mento *sm* pairing off; mating; (*ELETTR, INFORM*) coupling.

accoppi'are *vt* to couple, pair off; (*BIOL*) to mate; ~**rsi** *vr* to pair off; to mate.

accoppia'tore *sm* (*TECN*) coupler; ~ **acustico** (*INFORM*) acoustic coupler.

acco'rato, a *ag* heartfelt.

accorci'are [akkor'tʃare] *vt* to shorten; ~**rsi** *vr* to become shorter; (*vestiti: nel lavaggio*) to shrink.

accor'dare *vt* to reconcile; (*colori*) to match; (*MUS*) to tune; (*LING*): ~ **qc con qc** to make sth agree with sth; (*DIR*) to grant; ~**rsi** *vr* to agree, come to an agreement; (*colori*) to match.

ac'cordo *sm* agreement; (*armonia*) harmony; (*MUS*) chord; **essere d'**~ to agree; **andare d'**~ to get on well together; **d'**~! all right!, agreed!; **mettersi d'**~ (**con qn**) to agree *o* come to an agreement with sb; **prendere** ~**i con** to reach an agreement with; ~ **commerciale** trade agreement; **A**~ **generale sulle tariffe ed il commercio** General Agreement on Tariffs and Trade, GATT.

ac'corgersi [ak'kɔrdʒersi] *vr*: ~ **di** to notice; (*fig*) to realize.

accorgi'mento [akkordʒi'mento] *sm* shrewdness *no pl*; (*espediente*) trick, device.

ac'correre *vi* to run up.

ac'corsi *vb vedi* **accorgersi; accorrere**.

ac'corso, a *pp di* **accorrere**.

accor'tezza [akkor'tettsa] *sf* (*avvedutezza*) good sense; (*astuzia*) shrewdness.

ac'corto, a *pp di* **accorgersi** ♦ *ag* shrewd; **stare** ~ to be on one's guard.

accosta'mento *sm* (*di colori etc*) combination.

accos'tare *vt* (*avvicinarsi a*) to approach; (*socchiudere: imposte*) to half-close; (: *porta*) to leave ajar ♦ *vi*: ~ (**a**) (*NAUT*) to come alongside; (*AUT*) to draw up (at); ~**rsi** *vr*: ~**rsi a** to draw near, approach; (*somigliare*) to be like, resemble; (*fede, religione*) to turn to; (*idee politiche*) to come to agree with; ~ **qc a** (*avvicinare*) to bring sth near to, put sth near to; (*colori, stili*) to match sth with; (*appoggiare: scala etc*) to lean sth against.

accovacci'arsi [akkovat'tʃarsi] *vr* to crouch.

accoz'zaglia [akkot'tsaʎʎa] *sf* (*peg: di idee, oggetti*) jumble, hotchpotch; (: *di persone*) odd assortment.

ac'crebbi *etc vb vedi* **accrescere**.

accredi'tare *vt* (*notizia*) to confirm the truth of; (*COMM*) to credit; (*diplomatico*) to accredit; ~**rsi** *vr* (*fig*) to gain credit.

ac'credito *sm* (*COMM: atto*) crediting; (: *effetto*) credit.

ac'crescere [ak'kreʃʃere] *vt* to increase; ~**rsi** *vr* to increase, grow.

accresci'mento [akkreʃʃi'mento] *sm* increase, growth.

accresci'tivo, a [akkreʃʃi'tivo] *ag, sm* (*LING*) augmentative.

accresci'uto, a [akkreʃˈʃuto] *pp di* **accrescere**.

accucci'arsi [akkut'tʃarsi] *vr* (*cane*) to lie down; (*persona*) to crouch down.

accu'dire *vi*: ~ **a** *vt* to attend to; to look after.

acculturazi'one [akkulturat'tsjone] *sf*

(*SOCIOLOGIA*) integration.

accumu'lare *vt* to accumulate; **~rsi** *vr* to accumulate; (*FINANZA*) to accrue.

accumula'tore *sm* (*ELETTR*) accumulator.

accumulazi'one [akkumulat'tsjone] *sf* accumulation.

ac'cumulo *sm* accumulation.

accurata'mente *av* carefully.

accura'tezza [akkura'tettsa] *sf* care; accuracy.

accu'rato, a *ag* (*diligente*) careful; (*preciso*) accurate.

ac'cusa *sf* accusation; (*DIR*) charge; **l'~, la pubblica ~** (*DIR*) the prosecution; **mettere qn sotto ~** to indict sb; **in stato di ~** committed for trial.

accu'sare *vt* (*sentire: dolore*) to feel; **~ qn di qc** to accuse sb of sth; (*DIR*) to charge sb with sth; **~ ricevuta di** (*COMM*) to acknowledge receipt of; **~ la fatica** to show signs of exhaustion; **ha accusato il colpo** (*anche fig*) you could see that he had felt the blow.

accusa'tivo *sm* accusative.

accu'sato, a *smlf* accused.

accusa'tore, 'trice *ag* accusing ♦ *smlf* accuser ♦ *sm* (*DIR*) prosecutor.

a'cerbo, a [a'tʃerbo] *ag* bitter; (*frutta*) sour, unripe; (*persona*) immature.

'acero ['atʃero] *sm* maple.

a'cerrimo, a [a'tʃerrimo] *ag* very fierce.

ace'tato [atʃe'tato] *sm* acetate.

a'ceto [a'tʃeto] *sm* vinegar; **mettere sotto ~** to pickle.

ace'tone [atʃe'tone] *sm* nail varnish remover.

'A.C.I. ['atʃi] *sigla m* (= *Automobile Club d'Italia*) ≈ AA (*BRIT*), AAA (*US*).

acidità [atʃidi'ta] *sf* acidity; sourness; **~ (di stomaco)** heartburn.

'acido, a ['atʃido] *ag* (*sapore*) acid, sour; (*CHIM, colore*) acid ♦ *sm* (*CHIM*) acid.

a'cidulo, a [a'tʃidulo] *ag* slightly sour, slightly acid.

'acino ['atʃino] *sm* berry; **~ d'uva** grape.

'ACLI *sigla fpl* (= *Associazioni Cristiane dei Lavoratori Italiani*) Christian Trade Union Association.

'acme *sf* (*fig*) acme, peak; (*MED*) crisis.

'acne *sf* acne.

ACNUR *sigla m* (= *Alto Commissariato delle Nazioni Unite per i Rifugiati*) UNHCR.

'acqua *sf* water; (*pioggia*) rain; **~e** *sfpl* waters; **fare ~** (*NAUT*) to leak, take in water; **essere con** *o* **avere l'~ alla gola** to be in great difficulty; **tirare ~ al proprio mulino** to feather one's own nest; **navigare in cattive ~e** (*fig*) to be in deep water; **~ in bocca!** mum's the word!; **~ corrente** running water; **~ dolce** fresh water; **~ di mare** sea water; **~ minerale** mineral water; **~ ossigenata** hydrogen peroxide; **~ piovana** rain water; **~ potabile** drinking water; **~ salata** *o* **salmastra** salt water; **~ tonica** tonic water.

acqua'forte, *pl* **acque'forti** *sf* etching.

a'cquaio *sm* sink.

acqua'ragia [akkwa'radʒa] *sf* turpentine.

a'cquario *sm* aquarium; (*dello zodiaco*): **A~** Aquarius; **essere dell'A~** to be Aquarius.

acquartie'rare *vt* (*MIL*) to quarter.

acqua'santa *sf* holy water.

acquas'cooter [akkwas'cuter] *sm inv* Jet Ski ®.

a'cquatico, a, ci, che *ag* aquatic; (*sport, sci*) water *cpd*.

acquat'tarsi *vr* to crouch (down).

acqua'vite *sf* brandy.

acquaz'zone [akkwat'tsone] *sm* cloudburst, heavy shower.

acque'dotto *sm* aqueduct; waterworks *pl*, water system.

'acqueo, a *ag*: **vapore ~** water vapour (*BRIT*) *o* vapor (*US*); **umore ~** aqueous humour (*BRIT*) *o* humor (*US*).

acque'rello *sm* watercolour (*BRIT*), watercolor (*US*).

acque'rugiola [akkwe'rudʒola] *sf* drizzle.

acquie'tare *vt* to appease; (*dolore*) to ease; **~rsi** *vr* to calm down.

acqui'rente *smlf* purchaser, buyer.

acqui'sire *vt* to acquire.

acquisizi'one [akkwizit'tsjone] *sf* acquisition.

acquis'tare *vt* to purchase, buy; (*fig*) to gain ♦ *vi* to improve; **~ in bellezza** to become more beautiful; **ha acquistato in salute** his health has improved.

a'cquisto *sm* purchase; **fare ~i** to go shopping; **ufficio ~i** (*COMM*) purchasing department; **~ rateale** instalment purchase, hire purchase (*BRIT*).

acqui'trino *sm* bog, marsh.

acquo'lina *sf*: **far venire l'~ in bocca a qn** to make sb's mouth water.

a'cquoso, a *ag* watery.

'acre *ag* acrid, pungent; (*fig*) harsh, biting.

a'credine *sf* (*fig*) bitterness.

a'crilico, a, ci, che *ag, sm* acrylic.

a'critico, a, ci, che *ag* uncritical.

a'crobata, i, e *smlf* acrobat.

acro'batico, a, ci, che *ag* (*ginnastica*) acrobatic; (*AER*) aerobatic ♦ *sf* acrobatics *sg*.

acroba'zia [akrobat'tsia] *sf* acrobatic feat;

~**e aeree** aerobatics.

a'**cronimo** *sm* acronym.

a'**cropoli** *sf inv*: **l'A**~ the Acropolis.

acu'**ire** *vt* to sharpen; ~**rsi** *vr* (*gen*) to increase; (*crisi*) to worsen.

a'**culeo** *sm* (*ZOOL*) sting; (*BOT*) prickle.

a'**cume** *sm* acumen, perspicacity.

acumi'**nato, a** *ag* sharp.

a'**custico, a, ci, che** *ag* acoustic ♦ *sf* (*scienza*) acoustics *sg*; (*di una sala*) acoustics *pl*; **apparecchio** ~ hearing aid; **cornetto** ~ ear trumpet.

acu'**tezza** [aku'tettsa] *sf* sharpness; shrillness; acuteness; high pitch; intensity; keenness.

acutiz'**zare** [akutid'dzare] *vt* (*fig*) to intensify; ~**rsi** *vr* (*fig: crisi, malattia*) to become worse, worsen.

a'**cuto, a** *ag* (*appuntito*) sharp, pointed; (*suono, voce*) shrill, piercing; (*MAT, LING, MED*) acute; (*MUS*) high-pitched; (*fig: dolore, desiderio*) intense; (: *perspicace*) acute, keen ♦ *sm* (*MUS*) high note.

ad *prep* (*dav V*) = **a**.

adagi'**are** [ada'dʒare] *vt* to lay *o* set down carefully; ~**rsi** *vr* to lie down, stretch out.

a'**dagio** [a'dadʒo] *av* slowly ♦ *sm* (*MUS*) adagio; (*proverbio*) adage, saying.

ada'**mitico, a, ci, che** *ag*: **in costume** ~ in one's birthday suit.

adat'**tabile** *ag* adaptable.

adattabilità *sf* adaptability.

adatta'**mento** *sm* adaptation; **avere spirito di** ~ to be adaptable.

adat'**tare** *vt* to adapt; (*sistemare*) to fit; ~**rsi** *vr*: ~**rsi (a)** (*ambiente, tempi*) to adapt (to); (*essere adatto*) to be suitable (for); (*accontentarsi*): ~**rsi a qc/a fare qc** to make the best of sth/of doing sth.

adatta'**tore** *sm* (*ELETTR*) adapter, adaptor.

a'**datto, a** *ag*: ~ (**a**) suitable (for), right (for).

addebi'**tare** *vt*: ~ **qc a qn** to debit sb with sth; (*fig: incolpare*) to blame sb for sth.

ad'**debito** *sm* (*COMM*) debit.

addensa'**mento** *sm* thickening; gathering.

adden'**sare** *vt* to thicken; ~**rsi** *vr* to thicken; (*nuvole*) to gather.

adden'**tare** *vt* to bite into.

adden'**trarsi** *vr*: ~ **in** to penetrate, go into.

ad'**dentro** *av* (*fig*): **essere molto** ~ **in qc** to be well-versed in sth.

addestra'**mento** *sm* training; ~ **aziendale** company training.

addes'**trare** *vt*, ~**rsi** *vr* to train; ~**rsi in qc** to practise (*BRIT*) *o* practice (*US*) sth.

ad'**detto, a** *ag*: ~ **a** (*persona*) assigned to; (*oggetto*) intended for ♦ *sm* employee;

(*funzionario*) attaché; ~ **commerciale/ stampa** commercial/press attaché; ~ **al telex** telex operator; **gli** ~**i ai lavori** authorized personnel; (*fig*) those in the know; "**vietato l'ingresso ai non** ~**i ai lavori**" "authorized personnel only".

addì *av* (*AMM*): ~ **3 luglio 1989** on the 3rd of July 1989 (*BRIT*), on July 3rd 1989 (*US*).

addi'**accio** [ad'djattʃo] *sm* (*MIL*) bivouac; **dormire all'**~ to sleep in the open.

addi'**etro** *av* (*indietro*) behind; (*nel passato, prima*) before, ago.

ad'**dio** *sm, escl* goodbye, farewell.

addirit'**tura** *av* (*veramente*) really, absolutely; (*perfino*) even; (*direttamente*) directly, right away.

ad'**dirsi** *vr*: ~ **a** to suit, be suitable for.

'**Addis A'beba** *sf* Addis Ababa.

addi'**tare** *vt* to point out; (*fig*) to expose.

addi'**tivo** *sm* additive.

addizio'**nale** [addittsjo'nale] *ag* additional ♦ *sf* (*anche*: **imposta** ~) surtax.

addizio'**nare** [addittsjo'nare] *vt* (*MAT*) to add (up).

addizi'**one** [addit'tsjone] *sf* addition.

addob'**bare** *vt* to decorate.

ad'**dobbo** *sm* decoration.

addol'**cire** [addol'tʃire] *vt* (*caffè etc*) to sweeten; (*acqua, fig: carattere*) to soften; ~**rsi** *vr* (*fig*) to mellow, soften; ~ **la pillola** (*fig*) to sugar the pill.

addolo'**rare** *vt* to pain, grieve; ~**rsi** *vr*: ~**rsi (per)** to be distressed (by).

addolo'**rato, a** *ag* distressed, upset; **l'A**~**a** (*REL*) Our Lady of Sorrows.

ad'**dome** *sm* abdomen.

addomesti'**care** *vt* to tame.

addomi'**nale** *ag* abdominal; (**muscoli** *mpl*) ~**i** stomach muscles.

addormen'**tare** *vt* to put to sleep; ~**rsi** *vr* to fall asleep, go to sleep.

addormen'**tato, a** *ag* sleeping, asleep; (*fig: tardo*) stupid, dopey.

addos'**sare** *vt* (*appoggiare*): ~ **qc a qc** to lean sth against sth; (*fig*): ~ **la colpa a qn** to lay the blame on sb; ~**rsi** *vr*: ~**rsi qc** (*responsabilità etc*) to shoulder sth.

ad'**dosso** *av* (*sulla persona*) on; ~ **a** *prep* (*sopra*) on; (*molto vicino*) right next to; **mettersi** ~ **il cappotto** to put one's coat on; **andare** (*o* **venire**) ~ **a** (*AUT: altra macchina*) to run into; (: *pedone*) to run over; **non ho soldi** ~ I don't have any money on me; **stare** ~ **a qn** (*fig*) to breathe down sb's neck; **dare** ~ **a qn** (*fig*) to attack sb; **mettere gli occhi** ~ **a qn/qc** to take quite a fancy to sb/sth; **mettere le mani** ~ **a qn** (*picchiare*) to hit sb;

(*catturare*) to seize sb; (*molestare: donna*) to touch sb up.

ad'dotto, a *pp di* **addurre**.

ad'duco *etc vb vedi* **addurre**.

ad'durre *vt* (*DIR*) to produce; (*citare*) to cite.

ad'dussi *etc vb vedi* **addurre**.

adegu'are *vt*: ~ **qc a** to adjust sth to; ~**rsi** *vr* to adapt.

adegua'tezza [adegwa'tettsa] *sf* adequacy; suitability; fairness.

adegu'ato, a *ag* adequate; (*conveniente*) suitable; (*equo*) fair.

a'dempiere *vt* to fulfil (*BRIT*), fulfill (*US*), carry out; (*comando*) to carry out.

adempi'mento *sm* fulfilment (*BRIT*), fulfillment (*US*); carrying out; **nell'**~ **del proprio dovere** in the performance of one's duty.

adem'pire *vt* = **adempiere**.

'Aden: il golfo di ~ *sm* the Gulf of Aden.

ade'noidi *sfpl* adenoids.

a'depto *sm* disciple, follower.

ade'rente *ag* adhesive; (*vestito*) close-fitting ♦ *sm/f* follower.

ade'renza [ade'rɛntsa] *sf* adhesion; ~**e** *sfpl* (*fig*) connections, contacts.

ade'rire *vi* (*stare attaccato*) to adhere, stick; ~ **a** to adhere to, stick to; (*fig: società, partito*) to join; (: *opinione*) to support; (*richiesta*) to agree to.

ades'care *vt* (*attirare*) to lure, entice; (*TECN: pompa*) to prime.

adesi'one *sf* adhesion; (*fig: assenso*) agreement, acceptance; (*appoggio*) support.

ade'sivo, a *ag*, *sm* adhesive.

a'desso *av* (*ora*) now; (*or ora, poco fa*) just now; (*tra poco*) any moment now; **da** ~ **in poi** from now on; **per** ~ for the moment, for now.

adia'cente [adja'tʃɛnte] *ag* adjacent.

adi'bire *vt* (*usare*): ~ **qc a** to turn sth into.

'Adige ['adidʒe] *sm*: **l'**~ the Adige.

'adipe *sm* fat.

adi'poso, a *ag* (*tessuto, zona*) adipose.

adi'rarsi *vr*: ~ (**con** *o* **contro qn per qc**) to get angry (with sb over sth).

adi'rato, a *ag* angry.

a'dire *vt* (*DIR*): ~ **le vie legali** to take legal proceedings; ~ **un'eredità** to take legal possession of an inheritance.

'adito *sm*: **dare** ~ **a** (*sospetti*) to give rise to.

adocchi'are [adok'kjare] *vt* (*scorgere*) to catch sight of; (*occhieggiare*) to eye.

adole'scente [adoleʃ'ʃɛnte] *ag*, *sm/f* adolescent.

adole'scenza [adoleʃ'ʃɛntsa] *sf* adolescence.

adolescenzi'ale [adoleʃʃen'tsjale] *ag* adolescent.

adom'brarsi *vr* (*cavallo*) to shy; (*persona*) to grow suspicious; (: *aversene a male*) to be offended.

adope'rare *vt* to use; ~**rsi** *vr* to strive; ~**rsi per qn/qc** to do one's best for sb/sth.

ado'rabile *ag* adorable.

ado'rare *vt* to adore; (*REL*) to adore, worship.

adorazi'one [adorat'tsjone] *sf* adoration; worship.

ador'nare *vt* to adorn.

a'dorno, a *ag*: ~ (**di**) adorned (with).

adot'tare *vt* to adopt; (*decisione, provvedimenti*) to pass.

adot'tivo, a *ag* (*genitori*) adoptive; (*figlio, patria*) adopted.

adozi'one [adot'tsjone] *sf* adoption; ~ **a distanza** child sponsorship.

adrena'linico, a, ci, che *ag* (*fig: vivace, eccitato*) charged-up.

adri'atico, a, ci, che *ag* Adriatic ♦ *sm*: **l'A**~, **il mare A**~ the Adriatic, the Adriatic Sea.

adu'lare *vt* to flatter.

adula'tore, 'trice *sm/f* flatterer.

adula'torio, a *ag* flattering.

adulazi'one [adulat'tsjone] *sf* flattery.

adulte'rare *vt* to adulterate.

adul'terio *sm* adultery.

a'dultero, a *ag* adulterous ♦ *sm/f* adulterer/adulteress.

a'dulto, a *ag* adult; (*fig*) mature ♦ *sm* adult, grown-up.

adu'nanza [adu'nantsa] *sf* assembly, meeting.

adu'nare *vt*, ~**rsi** *vr* to assemble, gather.

adu'nata *sf* (*MIL*) parade, muster.

a'dunco, a, chi, che *ag* hooked.

aerazi'one [aerat'tsjone] *sf* ventilation; (*TECN*) aeration.

a'ereo, a *ag* air *cpd*; (*radice*) aerial ♦ *sm* aerial; (*aeroplano*) plane; ~ **da caccia** fighter (plane); ~ **di linea** airliner; ~ **a reazione** jet (plane).

ae'robica *sf* aerobics *sg*.

aerodi'namico, a, ci, che *ag* aerodynamic; (*affusolato*) streamlined ♦ *sf* aerodynamics *sg*.

aeromo'dello *sm* model aircraft.

aero'nautica *sf* (*scienza*) aeronautics *sg*; ~ **militare** air force.

aerona'vale *ag* (*forze, manovre*) air and sea *cpd*.

aero'plano *sm* (aero)plane (*BRIT*), (air)plane (*US*).

aero'porto *sm* airport.

aeroportu'ale *ag* airport *cpd*.
aeros'calo *sm* airstrip.
aero'sol *sm inv* aerosol.
aerospazi'ale [aerospat'tsjale] *ag* aerospace.
aeros'tatico, a, ci, che *ag* aerostatic; **pallone** ~ air balloon.
ae'rostato *sm* aerostat.
A.F. *abbr* (= *alta frequenza*) HF; (*AMM*) = **assegni familiari**.
'afa *sf* sultriness.
af'fabile *ag* affable.
affabilità *sf* affability.
affaccen'darsi [affatt ʃen'darsi] *vr*: ~ **intorno a qc** to busy o.s. with sth.
affaccen'dato, a [affatt ʃen'dato] *ag* busy.
affacci'arsi [affat't ʃarsi] *vr*: ~ **(a)** to appear (at); ~ **alla vita** to come into the world.
affa'mato, a *ag* starving; (*fig*): ~ **(di)** eager (for).
affan'nare *vt* to leave breathless; (*fig*) to worry; ~**rsi** *vr*: ~**rsi per qn/qc** to worry about sb/sth.
af'fanno *sm* breathlessness; (*fig*) anxiety, worry.
affannosa'mente *av* with difficulty; anxiously.
affan'noso, a *ag* (*respiro*) difficult; (*fig*) troubled, anxious.
af'fare *sm* (*faccenda*) matter, affair; (*COMM*) piece of business, (business) deal; (*occasione*) bargain; (*DIR*) case; (*fam: cosa*) thing; ~**i** *smpl* (*COMM*) business *sg*; ~ **fatto!** done!, it's a deal!; **sono** ~**i miei** that's my business; **bada agli** ~**i tuoi!** mind your own business!; **uomo d'**~**i** businessman; **ministro degli A**~**i Esteri** Foreign Secretary (*BRIT*), Secretary of State (*US*).
affa'rista, i *sm* profiteer, unscrupulous businessman.
affasci'nante [affaʃʃi'nante] *ag* fascinating.
affasci'nare [affaʃʃi'nare] *vt* to bewitch; (*fig*) to charm, fascinate.
affatica'mento *sm* tiredness.
affati'care *vt* to tire; ~**rsi** *vr* (*durar fatica*) to tire o.s. out.
af'fatto *av* completely; **non** ... ~ not ... at all; **niente** ~ not at all.
affer'mare *vi* (*dire di sì*) to say yes ♦ *vt* (*dichiarare*) to maintain, affirm; ~**rsi** *vr* to assert o.s., make one's name known.
affermativa'mente *av* in the affirmative, affirmatively.
afferma'tivo, a *ag* affirmative.
affer'mato, a *ag* established, well-known.
affermazi'one [affermat'tsjone] *sf* affirmation, assertion; (*successo*) achievement.

affer'rare *vt* to seize, grasp; (*fig: idea*) to grasp; ~**rsi** *vr*: ~**rsi a** to cling to.
Aff. Est. *abbr* = *Affari Esteri*.
affet'tare *vt* (*tagliare a fette*) to slice; (*ostentare*) to affect.
affet'tato, a *ag* sliced; affected ♦ *sm* sliced cold meat.
affetta'trice [affetta'tritʃe] *sf* meat slicer.
affettazi'one [affettat'tsjone] *sf* affectation.
affet'tivo, a *ag* emotional, affective.
af'fetto, a *ag*: **essere** ~ **da** to suffer from ♦ *sm* affection; **gli** ~**i familiari** one's nearest and dearest.
affettuosa'mente *av* affectionately; (*nelle lettere*): **(ti saluto)**, **Maria** love, Maria.
affettuosità *sf inv* affection; ~ *sfpl* (*manifestazioni*) demonstrations of affection.
affettu'oso, a *ag* affectionate.
affezio'narsi [affettsjo'narsi] *vr*: ~ **a** to grow fond of.
affezio'nato, a [affettsjo'nato] *ag*: ~ **a qn/ qc** fond of sb/sth; (*attaccato*) attached to sb/sth.
affezi'one [affet'tsjone] *sf* (*affetto*) affection; (*MED*) ailment, disorder.
affian'care *vt* to place side by side; (*MIL*) to flank; (*fig*) to support; ~ **qc a qc** to place sth next to *o* beside sth; ~**rsi** *vr*: ~**rsi a qn** to stand beside sb.
affiata'mento *sm* understanding.
affia'tato, a *ag*: **essere** ~**i** to work well together *o* get on; **formano una squadra** ~**a** they make a good team.
affibbi'are *vt* to buckle, do up; (*fig: dare*) to give.
affi'dabile *ag* reliable.
affidabilità *sf* reliability.
affida'mento *sm* (*DIR: di bambino*) custody; (*fiducia*): **fare** ~ **su qn** to rely on sb; **non dà nessun** ~ he's not to be trusted.
affi'dare *vt*: ~ **qc** *o* **qn a qn** to entrust sth *o* sb to sb; ~**rsi** *vr*: ~**rsi a** to place one's trust in.
affievo'lirsi *vr* to grow weak.
af'figgere [af'fiddʒere] *vt* to stick up, post up.
affi'lare *vt* to sharpen.
affi'lato, a *ag* (*gen*) sharp; (*volto, naso*) thin.
affili'are *vt* to affiliate; ~**rsi** *vr*: ~**rsi a** to become affiliated to.
affi'nare *vt* to sharpen.
affinché [affin'ke] *cong* in order that, so that.
af'fine *ag* similar.
affinità *sf inv* affinity.

affio'rare *vi* to emerge.

af'fissi *etc vb vedi* **affiggere**.

affissi'one *sf* billposting.

af'fisso, a *pp di* **affiggere** ♦ *sm* bill, poster; (*LING*) affix.

affitta'camere *smf inv* landlord/landlady.

affit'tare *vt* (*dare in affitto*) to let, rent (out); (*prendere in affitto*) to rent.

af'fitto *sm* rent; (*contratto*) lease; **dare in** ~ to rent (out), let; **prendere in** ~ to rent.

affittu'ario *sm* lessee.

af'fliggere [af'fliddʒere] *vt* to torment; ~**rsi** *vr* to grieve.

af'flissi *etc vb vedi* **affliggere**.

af'flitto, a *pp di* **affliggere**.

afflizi'one [afflit'tsjone] *sf* distress, torment.

afflosci'arsi [affloʃ'ʃarsi] *vr* to go limp; (*frutta*) to go soft.

afflu'ente *sm* tributary.

afflu'enza [afflu'ɛntsa] *sf* flow; (*di persone*) crowd.

afflu'ire *vi* to flow; (*fig: merci, persone*) to pour in.

af'flusso *sm* influx.

affo'gare *vt, vi* to drown; ~**rsi** *vr* to drown; (*deliberatamente*) to drown o.s.

affo'gato, a *ag* drowned; (*CUC: uova*) poached.

affolla'mento *sm* crowding; (*folla*) crowd.

affol'lare *vt*, ~**rsi** *vr* to crowd.

affol'lato, a *ag* crowded.

affonda'mento *sm* (*di nave*) sinking.

affon'dare *vt* to sink.

affran'care *vt* to free, liberate; (*AMM*) to redeem; (*lettera*) to stamp; (: *meccanicamente*) to frank (*BRIT*), meter (*US*); ~**rsi** *vr* to free o.s.

affranca'trice [affranka'tritʃe] *sf* franking machine (*BRIT*), postage meter (*US*).

affranca'tura *sf* (*di francobollo*) stamping; franking (*BRIT*), metering (*US*); (*tassa di spedizione*) postage; ~ **a carico del destinatario** postage paid.

af'franto, a *ag* (*esausto*) worn out; (*abbattuto*) overcome.

af'fresco, schi *sm* fresco.

affret'tare *vt* to quicken, speed up; ~**rsi** *vr* to hurry; ~**rsi a fare qc** to hurry *o* hasten to do sth.

affret'tato, a *ag* (*veloce: passo, ritmo*) quick, fast; (*frettoloso: decisione*) hurried, hasty; (: *lavoro*) rushed.

affron'tare *vt* (*pericolo etc*) to face; (*assalire: nemico*) to confront; ~**rsi** *vr* (*reciproco*) to confront each other.

af'fronto *sm* affront, insult; **fare un** ~ **a qn** to insult sb.

affumi'care *vt* to fill with smoke; to blacken with smoke; (*alimenti*) to smoke.

affuso'lato, a *ag* tapering.

af'gano, a *ag, smf* Afghan.

Af'ghanistan [af'ganistan] *sm*: **l'**~ Afghanistan.

af'ghano, a *ag, smf* = **afgano**.

afo'risma, i *sm* aphorism.

a'foso, a *ag* sultry, close.

'Africa *sf*: **l'**~ Africa.

afri'cano, a *ag, smf* African.

afroasi'atico a, ci, che *ag* Afro-Asian.

afrodi'siaco, a, ci, che *ag, sm* aphrodisiac.

AG *sigla* = Agrigento.

a'genda [a'dʒɛnda] *sf* diary; ~ **tascabile/da tavolo** pocket/desk diary.

a'gente [a'dʒɛnte] *sm* agent; ~ **di cambio** stockbroker; ~ **di custodia** prison officer; ~ **marittimo** shipping agent; ~ **di polizia** police officer; ~ **provocatore** agent provocateur; ~ **delle tasse** tax inspector; ~ **di vendita** sales agent; **resistente agli** ~**i atmosferici** weather-resistant.

agen'zia [adʒen'tsia] *sf* agency; (*succursale*) branch; ~ **di collocamento** employment agency; ~ **immobiliare** estate agent's (office) (*BRIT*), real estate office (*US*); **A**~ **Internazionale per l'Energia Atomica (AIEA)** International Atomic Energy Agency (IAEA); ~ **matrimoniale** marriage bureau; ~ **pubblicitaria** advertising agency; ~ **di stampa** press agency; ~ **viaggi** travel agency.

agevo'lare [adʒevo'lare] *vt* to facilitate, make easy.

agevolazi'one [adʒevolat'tsjone] *sf* (*facilitazione economica*) facility; ~ **di pagamento** payment on easy terms; ~**i creditizie** credit facilities; ~**i fiscali** tax concessions.

a'gevole [a'dʒevole] *ag* easy; (*strada*) smooth.

agganci'are [aggan'tʃare] *vt* to hook up; (*FERR*) to couple; ~**rsi** *vr*: ~**rsi a** to hook up to; (*fig: pretesto*) to seize on.

ag'gancio [ag'gantʃo] *sm* (*TECN*) coupling; (*fig: conoscenza*) contact.

ag'geggio [ad'dʒeddʒo] *sm* gadget, contraption.

agget'tivo [addʒet'tivo] *sm* adjective.

agghiacci'ante [aggjat'tʃante] *ag* (*fig*) chilling.

agghiacci'are [aggjat'tʃare] *vt* to freeze; (*fig*) to make one's blood run cold; ~**rsi** *vr* to freeze.

agghin'darsi [aggin'darsi] *vr* to deck o.s. out.

aggiorna'mento [addʒorna'mento] *sm*

updating; revision; postponement; **corso di** ~ refresher course.

aggior'nare [addʒor'nare] *vt* (*opera, manuale*) to bring up-to-date; (: *rivedere*) to revise; (*listino*) to maintain, up-date; (*seduta etc*) to postpone; **~rsi** *vr* to bring (*o keep*) o.s. up-to-date.

aggior'nato, a [addʒor'nato] *ag* up-to-date.

aggio'taggio [addʒo'taddʒo] *sm* (*ECON*) rigging the market.

aggi'rare [addʒi'rare] *vt* to go round; (*fig: ingannare*) to trick; **~rsi** *vr* to wander about; **il prezzo s'aggira sul milione** the price is around the million mark.

aggiudi'care [addʒudi'kare] *vt* to award; (*all'asta*) to knock down; **~rsi qc** to win sth.

aggi'ungere [ad'dʒundʒere] *vt* to add.

aggi'unsi [ad'dʒunsi] *etc vb vedi* **aggiungere**.

aggi'unto, a [ad'dʒunto] *pp di* **aggiungere** ♦ *ag* assistant *cpd* ♦ *sm* assistant ♦ *sf* addition; **sindaco** ~ deputy mayor; **in ~a** … what's more ….

aggius'tare [addʒus'tare] *vt* (*accomodare*) to mend, repair; (*riassettare*) to adjust; (*fig: lite*) to settle; **~rsi** *vr* (*arrangiarsi*) to make do; (*con senso reciproco*) to come to an agreement; **ti aggiusto io!** I'll fix you!

agglome'rato *sm* (*di rocce*) conglomerate; (*di legno*) chipboard; ~ **urbano** built-up area.

aggrap'parsi *vr*: ~ **a** to cling to.

aggrava'mento *sm* worsening.

aggra'vante *ag* (*DIR*) aggravating ♦ *sf* aggravation.

aggra'vare *vt* (*aumentare*) to increase; (*appesantire: anche fig*) to weigh down, make heavy; (*fig: pena*) to make worse; **~rsi** *vr* (*fig*) to worsen, become worse.

ag'gravio *sm*: ~ **di costi** increase in costs.

aggrazi'ato, a [aggrat'tsjato] *ag* graceful.

aggre'dire *vt* to attack, assault.

aggre'gare *vt*: ~ **qn a qc** to admit sb to sth; **~rsi** *vr* to join; **~rsi a** to join, become a member of.

aggre'gato, a *ag* associated ♦ *sm* aggregate; ~ **urbano** built-up area.

aggressi'one *sf* aggression; (*atto*) attack; ~ **a mano armata** armed assault.

aggressività *sf* aggressiveness.

aggres'sivo, a *ag* aggressive.

aggres'sore *sm* aggressor, attacker.

aggrot'tare *vt*: ~ **le sopracciglia** to frown.

aggrovigli'are [aggroviʎ'ʎare] *vt* to tangle; **~rsi** *vr* (*fig*) to become complicated.

agguan'tare *vt* to catch, seize.

aggu'ato *sm* trap; (*imboscata*) ambush; **tendere un** ~ **a qn** to set a trap for sb.

agguer'rito, a *ag* (*sostenitore, nemico*) fierce.

agia'tezza [adʒa'tettsa] *sf* prosperity.

agi'ato, a [a'dʒato] *ag* (*vita*) easy; (*persona*) well-off, well-to-do.

'agile ['adʒile] *ag* agile, nimble.

agilità [adʒili'ta] *sf* agility, nimbleness.

'agio ['adʒo] *sm* ease, comfort; **~i** *smpl* comforts; **mettersi a proprio** ~ to make o.s. at home *o* comfortable; **dare** ~ **a qn di fare qc** to give sb the chance of doing sth.

a'gire [a'dʒire] *vi* to act; (*esercitare un'azione*) to take effect; (*TECN*) to work, function; ~ **contro qn** (*DIR*) to take action against sb.

agi'tare [adʒi'tare] *vt* (*bottiglia*) to shake; (*mano, fazzoletto*) to wave; (*fig: turbare*) to disturb; (: *incitare*) to stir (up); **~rsi** *vr* (*mare*) to be rough; (*malato, dormitore*) to toss and turn; (*bambino*) to fidget; (*emozionarsi*) to get upset; (*POL*) to agitate.

agi'tato, a [adʒi'tato] *ag* rough; restless; fidgety; upset, perturbed.

agita'tore, 'trice [adʒita'tore] *sm/f* (*POL*) agitator.

agitazi'one [adʒitat'tsjone] *sf* agitation; (*POL*) unrest, agitation; **mettere in** ~ **qn** to upset *o* distress sb.

'agli ['aʎʎi] *prep + det vedi* **a**.

'aglio ['aʎʎo] *sm* garlic.

a'gnello [aɲ'ɲɛllo] *sm* lamb.

a'gnostico, a, ci, che [aɲ'ɲɔstiko] *ag*, *sm/f* agnostic.

'ago, *pl* **'aghi** *sm* needle; ~ **da calza** knitting needle.

ago. *abbr* (= *agosto*) Aug.

ago'nia *sf* agony.

ago'nistico, a, ci, che *ag* athletic; (*fig*) competitive.

agoniz'zante [agonid'dzante] *ag* dying.

agoniz'zare [agonid'dzare] *vi* to be dying.

agopun'tura *sf* acupuncture.

agorafo'bia *sf* agoraphobia.

a'gosto *sm* August; *per fraseologia vedi* **luglio**.

a'grario, a *ag* agrarian, agricultural; (*riforma*) land *cpd* ♦ *sm* landowner ♦ *sf* agriculture.

a'gricolo, a *ag* agricultural, farm *cpd*.

agricol'tore *sm* farmer.

agricol'tura *sf* agriculture, farming.

agri'foglio [agri'fɔʎʎo] *sm* holly.

agrimen'sore *sm* land surveyor.

agritu'rismo *sm* farm holidays *pl*.

agritu'ristico, a, ci, che *ag* farm holiday *cpd*.

'agro, a *ag* sour, sharp.

agro'dolce [agro'doltʃe] *ag* bittersweet;

(*salsa*) sweet and sour.

agrono'mia *sf* agronomy.

a'gronomo *sm* agronomist.

a'grume *sm* (*spesso al pl: pianta*) citrus; (*: frutto*) citrus fruit.

agru'meto *sm* citrus grove.

aguz'zare [agut'tsare] *vt* to sharpen; ~ **gli orecchi** to prick up one's ears; ~ **l'ingegno** to use one's wits.

aguz'zino, a [agud'dzino] *sm/f* jailer; (*fig*) tyrant.

a'guzzo, a [a'guttso] *ag* sharp.

'ahi *escl* (*dolore*) ouch!

ahimè *escl* alas!

'ai *prep* + *det vedi* **a.**

'Aia *sf*: **L'**~ The Hague.

'aia *sf* threshing floor.

AIDDA *sigla f* (= *Associazione Imprenditrici Donne Dirigenti d'Azienda*) *association of women entrepreneurs and managers.*

AIDS ['aids] *abbr m o f* AIDS.

AIE *sigla f* (= *Associazione Italiana degli Editori*) *publishers' association.*

AIEA *sigla f vedi* **Agenzia Internazionale per l'Energia Atomica.**

AIED *sigla f* (= *Associazione Italiana Educazione Demografica*) ≈ FPA (= *Family Planning Association*).

AIG *sigla f* (= *Associazione Italiana Alberghi per la Gioventù*) ≈ YHA (*BRIT*).

ai'ola *sf* = **aiuola.**

airbag *sm inv* air bag.

AIRC *abbr f* = *associazione italiana per la ricerca sul cancro.*

ai'rone *sm* heron.

ai'tante *ag* robust.

aiu'ola *sf* flower bed.

aiu'tante *sm/f* assistant ♦ *sm* (*MIL*) adjutant; (*NAUT*) master-at-arms; ~ **di campo** aide-de-camp.

aiu'tare *vt* to help; ~ **qn (a fare)** to help sb (to do).

ai'uto *sm* help, assistance, aid; (*aiutante*) assistant; **venire in** ~ **di qn** to come to sb's aid; ~ **chirurgo** assistant surgeon.

aiz'zare [ait'tsare] *vt* to incite; ~ **i cani contro qn** to set the dogs on sb.

al *prep* + *det vedi* **a.**

a.l. *abbr* = **anno luce.**

'ala, *pl* **'ali** *sf* wing; **fare** ~ to fall back, make way; ~ **destra/sinistra** (*SPORT*) right/left wing.

ala'bastro *sm* alabaster.

'alacre *ag* quick, brisk.

alacrità *sf* promptness, speed.

alam'bicco, chi *sm* still (*CHIM*).

a'lano *sm* Great Dane.

a'lare *ag* wing *cpd*; ~**i** *smpl* firedogs.

A'laska *sf*: **l'**~ Alaska.

a'lato, a *ag* winged.

'alba *sf* dawn; **all'**~ at dawn.

alba'nese *ag*, *sm/f*, *sm* Albanian.

Alba'nia *sf*: **l'**~ Albania.

'albatro *sm* albatross.

albeggi'are [albed'dʒare] *vi*, *vb impers* to dawn.

albe'rato, a *ag* (*viale, piazza*) lined with trees, tree-lined.

albera'tura *sf* (*NAUT*) masts *pl.*

alber'gare *vt* (*dare albergo*) to accommodate ♦ *vi* (*poetico*) to dwell.

alberga'tore, 'trice *sm/f* hotelier, hotel owner.

alberghi'ero, a [alber'gjɛro] *ag* hotel *cpd.*

al'bergo, ghi *sm* hotel; ~ **diurno** *public toilets with washing and shaving facilities etc*; ~ **della gioventù** youth hostel.

'albero *sm* tree; (*NAUT*) mast; (*TECN*) shaft; ~ **a camme** camshaft; ~ **genealogico** family tree; ~ **a gomiti** crankshaft; ~ **maestro** mainmast; ~ **di Natale** Christmas tree; ~ **di trasmissione** transmission shaft.

albi'cocca, che *sf* apricot.

albi'cocco, chi *sm* apricot tree.

al'bino, a *ag*, *sm/f* albino.

'albo *sm* (*registro*) register, roll; (*AMM*) notice board.

'album *sm* album; ~ **da disegno** sketch book.

al'bume *sm* albumen; (*bianco d'uovo*) egg white.

albu'mina *sf* albumin.

'alce ['altʃe] *sm* elk.

al'chimia [al'kimja] *sf* alchemy.

alchi'mista, i [alki'mista] *sm* alchemist.

'alcol *sm inv* = **alcool.**

alcolicità [alkolitʃi'ta] *sf* alcohol(ic) content.

al'colico, a, ci, che *ag* alcoholic ♦ *sm* alcoholic drink.

alco'lismo *sm* alcoholism.

alco'lista, i, e *sm/f* alcoholic.

alcoliz'zato, a [alkolid'dzato] *sm/f* alcoholic.

'alcool *sm inv* alcohol; ~ **denaturato** methylated spirits *pl* (*BRIT*), wood alcohol (*US*); ~ **etilico** ethyl alcohol; ~ **metilico** methyl alcohol.

alco'olico *etc vedi* **alcolico** *etc.*

alco'test *sm inv* Breathalyser ® (*BRIT*), Breathalyzer ® (*US*).

al'cova *sf* alcove.

al'cuno, a *det* (*dav sm*: **alcun** + *C, V*, **alcuno** + *s impura, gn, pn, ps, x, z*; *dav sf*: **alcuna** + *C*, **alcun'** + *V*) (*nessuno*): **non ...** ~ no, not any; ~**i(e)** *det pl, pron pl* some, a few; **non c'è** ~**a fretta** there's no hurry, there isn't any hurry; **senza alcun riguardo** without any consideration.

aldilà *sm inv*: **l'~** the next life, the after-life.

alea'torio, a *ag* (*incerto*) uncertain.

aleggi'are [aled'dʒare] *vi* (*fig: profumo, sospetto*) to be in the air.

Ales'sandria *sf* (*anche*: ~ **d'Egitto**) Alexandria.

a'letta *sf* (*TECN*) fin; tab.

alet'tone *sm* (*AER*) aileron.

Aleu'tine *sfpl*: **le isole** ~ the Aleutian Islands.

alfa'betico, a, ci, che *ag* alphabetical.

alfa'beto *sm* alphabet.

alfanu'merico, a, ci, che *ag* alphanumeric.

alfi'ere *sm* standard-bearer; (*SCACCHI*) bishop.

al'fine *av* finally, in the end.

'alga, ghe *sf* seaweed *no pl*, alga.

'algebra ['aldʒebra] *sf* algebra.

Al'geri [al'dʒeri] *sf* Algiers.

Alge'ria [aldʒe'ria] *sf*: **l'~** Algeria.

alge'rino, a [aldʒe'rino] *ag, sm/f* Algerian.

algo'ritmo *sm* algorithm.

ALI *sigla f* (= *Associazione Librai Italiani*) *booksellers' association*.

ali'ante *sm* (*AER*) glider.

'alibi *sm inv* alibi.

a'lice [a'litʃe] *sf* anchovy.

alie'nare *vt* (*DIR*) to transfer; (*rendere ostile*) to alienate; ~**rsi qn** to alienate sb.

alie'nato, a *ag* alienated; transferred; (*fuor di senno*) insane ♦ *sm* lunatic, insane person.

alienazi'one [aljenat'tsjone] *sf* alienation; transfer; insanity.

ali'eno, a *ag* (*avverso*): ~ (**da**) opposed (to), averse (to) ♦ *sm/f* alien.

alimen'tare *vt* to feed; (*TECN*) to feed, supply; (*fig*) to sustain ♦ *ag* food *cpd*; ~**i** *smpl* foodstuffs; (*anche*: **negozio di** ~**i**) grocer's shop; **regime** ~ diet.

alimenta'tore *sm* (*ELETTR*) feeder.

alimentazi'one [alimentat'tsjone] *sf* feeding; (*cibi*) diet; ~ **di fogli** (*INFORM*) sheet feed.

ali'mento *sm* food; ~**i** *smpl* food *sg*; (*DIR*) alimony.

a'liquota *sf* share; ~ **d'imposta** tax rate; ~ **minima** (*FISCO*) basic rate.

alis'cafo *sm* hydrofoil.

'alito *sm* breath.

all. *abbr* (= *allegato*) enc., encl.

'alla *prep* + *det vedi* **a.**

allaccia'mento [allattʃa'mento] *sm* (*TECN*) connection.

allacci'are [allat'tʃare] *vt* (*scarpe*) to tie, lace (up); (*cintura*) to do up, fasten; (*due località*) to link; (*luce, gas*) to connect; (*amicizia*) to form; ~**rsi** *vr* (*vestito*) to fasten; ~ *o* ~**rsi la cintura** to fasten one's belt.

allaccia'tura [allattʃa'tura] *sf* fastening.

allaga'mento *sm* flooding *no pl*; flood.

alla'gare *vt*, ~**rsi** *vr* to flood.

allampa'nato, a *ag* lanky.

allar'gare *vt* to widen; (*vestito*) to let out; (*aprire*) to open; (*fig: dilatare*) to extend; ~**rsi** *vr* (*gen*) to widen; (*scarpe, pantaloni*) to stretch; (*fig: problema, fenomeno*) to spread.

allar'mare *vt* to alarm; ~**rsi** *vr* to become alarmed.

al'larme *sm* alarm; **mettere qn in** ~ to alarm sb; ~ **aereo** air-raid warning.

allar'mismo *sm* scaremongering.

allar'mista, i, e *sm/f* scaremonger, alarmist.

allat'tare *vt* (*sog: donna*) to (breast-)feed; (: *animale*) to suckle; ~ **artificialmente** to bottle-feed.

'alle *prep* + *det vedi* **a.**

alle'anza [alle'antsa] *sf* alliance; **A**~ **Democratica** (*POL*) *moderate centre-left party*; **A**~ **Nazionale** (*POL*) *party on the far right*.

alle'arsi *vr* to form an alliance.

alle'ato, a *ag* allied ♦ *sm/f* ally.

alleg. *abbr* = **all.**

alle'gare *vt* (*accludere*) to enclose; (*DIR: citare*) to cite, adduce; (*denti*) to set on edge.

alle'gato, a *ag* enclosed ♦ *sm* enclosure; (*di e-mail*) attachment; **in** ~ enclosed; **in** ~ **Vi inviamo …** please find enclosed ….

allegge'rire [alleddʒe'rire] *vt* to lighten, make lighter; (*fig: sofferenza*) to alleviate, lessen; (: *lavoro, tasse*) to reduce.

allego'ria *sf* allegory.

alle'gorico, a, ci, che *ag* allegorical.

alle'gria *sf* gaiety, cheerfulness.

al'legro, a *ag* cheerful, merry; (*un po' brillo*) merry, tipsy; (*vivace: colore*) bright ♦ *sm* (*MUS*) allegro.

allena'mento *sm* training.

alle'nare *vt*, ~**rsi** *vr* to train.

allena'tore *sm* (*SPORT*) trainer, coach.

allen'tare *vt* to slacken; (*disciplina*) to relax; ~**rsi** *vr* to become slack; (*ingranaggio*) to work loose.

aller'gia, 'gie [aller'dʒia] *sf* allergy.

al'lergico, a, ci, che [al'lɛrdʒiko] *ag* allergic.

allesti'mento *sm* preparation, setting up; **in** ~ in preparation.

alles'tire *vt* (*cena*) to prepare; (*esercito, nave*) to equip, fit out; (*spettacolo*) to stage.

allet'tante *ag* attractive, alluring.

allet'tare *vt* to lure, entice.

alleva'mento *sm* breeding, rearing; (*luogo*) stock farm; **pollo d'**~ battery hen.

alle'vare *vt* (*animale*) to breed, rear; (*bambino*) to bring up.

alleva'tore *sm* breeder.

allevi'are *vt* to alleviate.

alli'bire *vi* to turn pale; (*essere turbato*) to be disconcerted.

alli'bito, a *ag* pale; disconcerted.

allibra'tore *sm* bookmaker.

allie'tare *vt* to cheer up, gladden.

alli'evo *sm* pupil; (*apprendista*) apprentice; ~ **ufficiale** cadet.

alliga'tore *sm* alligator.

allinea'mento *sm* alignment.

alline'are *vt* (*persone, cose*) to line up; (*TIP*) to align; (*fig: economia, salari*) to adjust, align; ~**rsi** *vr* to line up; (*fig: a idee*): ~**rsi a** to come into line with.

alline'ato, a *ag* aligned, in line; **paesi non** ~**i** (*POL*) non-aligned countries.

'allo *prep* + *det vedi* **a**.

allo'care *vt* to allocate.

al'locco, a, chi, che *sm* tawny owl ♦ *sm/f* oaf.

allocuzi'one [allokut'tsjone] *sf* address, solemn speech.

al'lodola *sf* (sky)lark.

alloggi'are [allod'dʒare] *vt* to accommodate ♦ *vi* to live.

al'loggio [al'lɔddʒo] *sm* lodging, accommodation (*BRIT*), accommodations (*US*); (*appartamento*) flat (*BRIT*), apartment (*US*).

allontana'mento *sm* removal; dismissal; estrangement.

allonta'nare *vt* to send away, send off; (*impiegato*) to dismiss; (*pericolo*) to avert, remove; (*estraniare*) to alienate; ~**rsi** *vr*: ~**rsi (da)** to go away (from); (*estraniarsi*) to become estranged (from).

al'lora *av* (*in quel momento*) then ♦ *cong* (*in questo caso*) well then; (*dunque*) well then, so; **la gente d'**~ people then *o* in those days; **da** ~ **in poi** from then on; **e** ~**?** (*che fare?*) what now?; (*e con ciò?*) so what?

allor'ché [allor'ke] *cong* (*formale*) when, as soon as.

al'loro *sm* laurel; **riposare** *o* **dormire sugli** ~**i** to rest on one's laurels.

'alluce ['allutʃe] *sm* big toe.

alluci'nante [allutʃi'nante] *ag* (*scena, spettacolo*) awful, terrifying; (*fam: incredibile*) amazing.

alluci'nato, a [allutʃi'nato] *ag* terrified; (*fuori di sé*) bewildered, confused.

allucinazi'one [allutʃinat'tsjone] *sf* hallucination.

al'ludere *vi*: ~ **a** to allude to, hint at.

allu'minio *sm* aluminium (*BRIT*), aluminum (*US*).

allu'naggio [allu'naddʒo] *sm* moon landing.

allu'nare *vi* to land on the moon.

allun'gare *vt* to lengthen; (*distendere*) to prolong, extend; (*diluire*) to water down; ~**rsi** *vr* to lengthen; (*ragazzo*) to stretch, grow taller; (*sdraiarsi*) to lie down, stretch out; ~ **le mani** (*rubare*) to pick pockets; **gli allungò uno schiaffo** he took a swipe at him.

al'lusi *etc vb vedi* **alludere**.

allusi'one *sf* hint, allusion.

al'luso, a *pp di* **alludere**.

alluvi'one *sf* flood.

alma'nacco, chi *sm* almanac.

al'meno *av* at least ♦ *cong*: (**se**) ~ if only; (**se**) ~ **piovesse!** if only it would rain!

a'logeno, a [a'lɔdʒeno] *ag*: **lampada** ~**a** halogen lamp.

a'lone *sm* halo.

al'pestre *ag* (*delle alpi*) alpine; (*montuoso*) mountainous.

'Alpi *sfpl*: **le** ~ the Alps.

alpi'nismo *sm* mountaineering, climbing.

alpi'nista, i, e *sm/f* mountaineer, climber.

al'pino, a *ag* Alpine; mountain *cpd*; ~**i** *smpl* (*MIL*) Italian Alpine troops.

al'quanto *av* rather, a little; ~, **a** *det* a certain amount of, some ♦ *pron* a certain amount, some; ~**i(e)** *det pl, pron pl* several, quite a few.

Al'sazia [al'sattsja] *sf* Alsace.

alt *escl* halt!, stop! ♦ *sm*: **dare l'**~ to call a halt.

alta'lena *sf* (*a funi*) swing; (*in bilico, anche fig*) seesaw.

alta'mente *av* extremely, highly.

al'tare *sm* altar.

alte'rare *vt* to alter, change; (*cibo*) to adulterate; (*registro*) to falsify; (*persona*) to irritate; ~**rsi** *vr* to alter; (*cibo*) to go bad; (*persona*) to lose one's temper.

alterazi'one [alterat'tsjone] *sf* alteration, change; adulteration; falsification; annoyance.

al'terco, chi *sm* altercation, wrangle.

alter'nanza [alter'nantsa] *sf* alternation; (*AGR*) rotation.

alter'nare *vt*, ~**rsi** *vr* to alternate.

alterna'tivo, a *ag* alternative ♦ *sf* alternative; **non abbiamo ~e** we have no alternative.

alter'nato, a *ag* alternate; (*ELETTR*) alternating.

alterna'tore *sm* alternator.

al'terno, a *ag* alternate; **a giorni ~i** on alternate days, every other day; **circolazione a targhe ~e** (*AUT*) *system of restricting vehicle use to odd/even registrations on alternate days.*

al'tero, a *ag* proud.

al'tezza [al'tettsa] *sf* (*di edificio, persona*) height; (*di tessuto*) width, breadth; (*di acqua, pozzo*) depth; (*di suono*) pitch; (*GEO*) latitude; (*titolo*) highness; (*fig: nobiltà*) greatness; **essere all'~ di** to be on a level with; (*fig*) to be up to *o* equal to; **all'~ della farmacia** near the chemist's.

altez'zoso, a [altet'tsoso] *ag* haughty.

al'ticcio, a, ci, ce [al'tittʃo] *ag* tipsy.

altipi'ano *sm* = **altopiano**.

altiso'nante *ag* (*fig*) high-sounding, pompous.

alti'tudine *sf* altitude.

'alto, a *ag* high; (*persona*) tall; (*tessuto*) wide, broad; (*sonno, acque*) deep; (*suono*) high(-pitched); (*GEO*) upper; (: *settentrionale*) northern ♦ *sm* top (part) ♦ *av* high; (*parlare*) aloud, loudly; **il palazzo è ~ 20 metri** the building is 20 metres high; **il tessuto è ~ 70 cm** the material is 70 cm wide; **ad ~a voce** aloud; **a notte ~a** in the dead of night; **in ~** up, upwards; **at the top; mani in ~!** hands up!; **dall'~ in o al basso** up and down; **degli ~i e bassi** (*fig*) ups and downs; **andare a testa ~a** (*fig*) to carry one's head high; **essere in ~ mare** (*fig*) to be far from a solution; **~a fedeltà** high fidelity, hi-fi; **~a moda** haute couture; **l'A~ Medioevo** the Early Middle Ages; **l'~ Po** the upper reaches of the Po.

altoate'sino, a *ag* of (*o* from) the Alto Adige.

alto'forno *sm* blast furnace.

altolo'cato, a *ag* of high rank, highly placed.

altopar'lante *sm* loudspeaker.

altopi'ano, *pl* **alti'piani** *sm* upland plain, plateau.

'Alto 'Volta *sm*: **l'~** Upper Volta.

altret'tanto, a *ag, pron* as much; (*pl*) as many ♦ *av* equally; **tanti auguri! — grazie, ~** all the best! — thank you, the same to you.

'altri *pron inv* (*qualcuno*) somebody; (: *in espressioni negative*) anybody; (*un'altra persona*) another (person).

altri'menti *av* otherwise.

══════════ *PAROLA CHIAVE*

'altro, a *det* **1** (*diverso*) other, different; **questa è un'~a cosa** that's another *o* a different thing; **passami l'~a penna** give me the other pen
2 (*supplementare*) other; **prendi un ~ cioccolatino** have another chocolate; **hai avuto ~e notizie?** have you had any more *o* any other news?; **hai ~ pane?** have you got any more bread?
3 (*nel tempo*): **l'~ giorno** the other day; **l'altr'anno** last year; **l'~ ieri** the day before yesterday; **domani l'~** the day after tomorrow; **quest'~ mese** next month
4: **d'~a parte** on the other hand
♦ *pron* **1** (*persona, cosa diversa o supplementare*): **un ~, un'~a** another (one); **lo farà un ~** someone else will do it; **~i, e** others; **gli ~i** (*la gente*) others, other people; **l'uno e l'~** both (of them); **aiutarsi l'un l'~** to help one another; **prendine un ~** have another (one); **da un giorno all'~** from day to day; (*nel giro di 24 ore*) from one day to the next; (*da un momento all'altro*) any day now
2 (*sostantivato: solo maschile*) something else; (: *in espressioni interrogative*) anything else; **non ho ~ da dire** I have nothing else *o* I don't have anything else to say; **desidera ~?** do you want anything else?; **più che ~** above all; **se non ~** if nothing else, at least; **tra l'~** among other things; **ci mancherebbe ~!** that's all we need!; **non faccio ~ che lavorare** I do nothing but work; **contento? — ~ che!** are you pleased? — I certainly am!; *vedi anche* **senza; noialtri; voialtri; tutto.**

altroché [altro'ke] *escl* certainly!, and how!

al'tronde *av*: **d'~** on the other hand.

al'trove *av* elsewhere, somewhere else.

al'trui *ag inv* other people's ♦ *sm*: **l'~** other people's belongings *pl*.

altru'ismo *sm* altruism.

altru'ista, i, e *ag* altruistic ♦ *sm/f* altruist.

al'tura *sf* (*rialto*) height, high ground; (*alto mare*) open sea; **pesca d'~** deep-sea fishing.

a'lunno, a *sm/f* pupil.

alve'are *sm* hive.

'alveo *sm* riverbed.

alzabandi'era [altsaban'djera] *sm inv* (*MIL*): **l'~** the raising of the flag.

al'zare [al'tsare] *vt* to raise, lift; (*issare*) to hoist; (*costruire*) to build, erect; **~rsi** *vr* to rise; (*dal letto*) to get up; (*crescere*) to grow tall (*o* taller); ~ **le spalle** to shrug one's shoulders; ~ **le carte** to cut the cards; ~ **il gomito** to drink too much; ~ **le mani su qn** to raise one's hand to sb; ~ **i tacchi** to take to one's heels; **~rsi in piedi** to stand up, get to one's feet; **~rsi col piede sbagliato** to get out of bed on the wrong side.

al'zata [al'tsata] *sf* lifting, raising; **un'~ di spalle** a shrug.

A.M. *abbr* = **aeronautica militare**.

a'mabile *ag* lovable; (*vino*) sweet.

'AMAC *sigla f* = **Aeronautica Militare-Aviazione Civile**.

a'maca, che *sf* hammock.

amalga'mare *vt*, **~rsi** *vr* to amalgamate.

a'mante *ag*: ~ **di** (*musica etc*) fond of ♦ *smlf* lover/mistress.

amara'mente *av* bitterly.

ama'ranto *sm* (*BOT*) love-lies-bleeding ♦ *ag inv*: **color** ~ reddish purple.

a'mare *vt* to love; (*amico, musica, sport*) to like.

amareggi'are [amared'dʒare] *vt* to sadden, upset; **~rsi** *vr* to get upset; **~rsi la vita** to make one's life a misery.

amareggi'ato, a [amared'dʒato] *ag* upset, saddened.

ama'rena *sf* sour black cherry.

ama'retto *sm* (*dolce*) macaroon; (*liquore*) bitter liqueur made with almonds.

ama'rezza [ama'rettsa] *sf* bitterness.

a'maro, a *ag* bitter ♦ *sm* bitterness; (*liquore*) bitters *pl*.

ama'rognolo, a [ama'roɲɲolo] *ag* slightly bitter.

a'mato, a *ag* beloved, loved, dear ♦ *smlf* loved one.

ama'tore, 'trice *smlf* (*amante*) lover; (*intenditore: di vini etc*) connoisseur; (*dilettante*) amateur.

a'mazzone [a'maddzone] *sf* (*MITOLOGIA*) Amazon; (*cavallerizza*) horsewoman; (*abito*) riding habit; **cavalcare all'~** to ride sidesaddle; **il Rio delle A~i** the (river) Amazon.

Amaz'zonia [amad'dzonja] *sf* Amazonia.

amaz'zonico, a, ci, che [amad'dzɔniko] *ag* Amazonian; Amazon *cpd*.

ambasce'ria [ambaʃʃe'ria] *sf* embassy.

ambasci'ata [ambaʃ'ʃata] *sf* embassy; (*messaggio*) message.

ambascia'tore, 'trice [ambaʃʃa'tore] *smlf* ambassador/ambassadress.

ambe'due *ag inv*: ~ **i ragazzi** both boys ♦ *pron inv* both.

ambi'destro, a *ag* ambidextrous.

ambien'tale *ag* (*temperatura*) ambient *cpd*; (*problemi, tutela*) environmental.

ambienta'lismo *sm* environmentalism.

ambienta'lista, i, e *ag* environmental ♦ *smlf* environmentalist.

ambien'tare *vt* to acclimatize; (*romanzo, film*) to set; **~rsi** *vr* to get used to one's surroundings.

ambientazi'one [ambjentat'tsjone] *sf* setting.

ambi'ente *sm* environment; (*fig: insieme di persone*) milieu; (*stanza*) room.

ambiguità *sf inv* ambiguity.

am'biguo, a *ag* ambiguous; (*persona*) shady.

am'bire *vt* (*anche: vi*: ~ **a**) to aspire to; **un premio molto ambito** a much sought-after prize.

'ambito *sm* sphere, field.

ambiva'lente *ag* ambivalent; **questo apparecchio è** ~ this is a dual-purpose device.

ambizi'one [ambit'tsjone] *sf* ambition.

ambizi'oso, a [ambit'tsjoso] *ag* ambitious.

'ambo *ag inv* both.

'ambra *sf* amber; ~ **grigia** ambergris.

ambu'lante *ag* travelling, itinerant.

ambu'lanza [ambu'lantsa] *sf* ambulance.

ambulatori'ale *ag* (*MED*) outpatients *cpd*; **operazione** ~ operation as an outpatient; **visita** ~ visit to the doctor's surgery (*BRIT*) *o* office (*US*).

ambula'torio *sm* (*studio medico*) surgery (*BRIT*), doctor's office (*US*).

'AMDI *sigla f* = **Associazione Medici Dentisti Italiani**.

a'meba *sf* amoeba (*BRIT*), ameba (*US*).

amenità *sf inv* pleasantness *no pl*; (*facezia*) pleasantry.

a'meno, a *ag* pleasant; (*strano*) funny, strange; (*spiritoso*) amusing.

A'merica *sf*: **l'~** America; **l'~ latina** Latin America; **l'~ del sud** South America.

america'nata *sf* (*peg*): **le Olimpiadi sono state una vera** ~ the Olympics were a typically vulgar American extravaganza.

america'nismo *sm* Americanism; (*ammirazione*) love of America.

ameri'cano, a *ag*, *smlf* American.

ame'tista *sf* amethyst.

ami'anto *sm* asbestos.

a'mica *sf vedi* **amico**.

ami'chevole [ami'kevole] *ag* friendly.

ami'cizia [ami'tʃittsja] *sf* friendship; **~e** *sfpl* (*amici*) friends; **fare** ~ **con qn** to make friends with sb.

a'mico, a, ci, che *smlf* friend; (*amante*) boyfriend/girlfriend; ~ **del cuore** *o* **intimo**

bosom friend; **~ d'infanzia** childhood friend.

'amido *sm* starch.

ammac'care *vt* (*pentola*) to dent; (*persona*) to bruise; **~rsi** *vr* to bruise.

ammacca'tura *sf* dent; bruise.

ammaes'trare *vt* (*animale*) to train; (*persona*) to teach.

ammai'nare *vt* to lower, haul down.

amma'larsi *vr* to fall ill.

amma'lato, a *ag* ill, sick ♦ *sm/f* sick person; (*paziente*) patient.

ammali'are *vt* (*fig*) to enchant, charm.

ammalia'tore, 'trice *sm/f* enchanter/enchantress.

am'manco, chi *sm* (*ECON*) deficit.

ammanet'tare *vt* to handcuff.

ammani'cato, a, ammanigli'ato, a [ammaniʎ'ʎato] *ag* (*fig*) with friends in high places.

amman'sire *vt* (*animale*) to tame; (*fig*: *persona*) to calm down, placate.

amman'tarsi *vr*: **~ di** (*persona*) to wrap o.s. in; (*fig*: *prato etc*) to be covered in.

amma'raggio [amma'raddʒo] *sm* (*sea*) landing; splashdown.

amma'rare *vi* (*AER*) to make a sea landing; (*astronave*) to splash down.

ammas'sare *vt* (*ammucchiare*) to amass; (*raccogliere*) to gather together; **~rsi** *vr* to pile up; to gather.

am'masso *sm* mass; (*mucchio*) pile, heap; (*ECON*) stockpile.

ammat'tire *vi* to go mad.

ammaz'zare [ammat'tsare] *vt* to kill; **~rsi** *vr* (*uccidersi*) to kill o.s.; (*rimanere ucciso*) to be killed; **~rsi di lavoro** to work o.s. to death.

am'menda *sf* amends *pl*; (*DIR, SPORT*) fine; **fare ~ di qc** to make amends for sth.

am'messo, a *pp di* **ammettere** ♦ *cong*: **~ che** supposing that.

am'mettere *vt* to admit; (*riconoscere: fatto*) to acknowledge, admit; (*permettere*) to allow, accept; (*supporre*) to suppose; **ammettiamo che ...** let us suppose that ....

ammez'zato [ammed'dzato] *sm* (*anche*: **piano ~**) entresol, mezzanine.

ammic'care *vi*: **~ (a)** to wink (at).

amminis'trare *vt* to run, manage; (*REL, DIR*) to administer.

amministra'tivo, a *ag* administrative.

amministra'tore *sm* administrator; (*COMM*) director; **~ aggiunto** associate director; **~ delegato** managing director; **~ fiduciario** trustee; **~ unico** sole director.

amministrazi'one [amministrat'tsjone] *sf* management; administration; **consiglio d'~** board of directors; **l'~ comunale** local government; **~ fiduciaria** trust.

ammi'raglia [ammi'raʎʎa] *sf* flagship.

ammiragli'ato [ammiraʎ'ʎato] *sm* admiralty.

ammi'raglio [ammi'raʎʎo] *sm* admiral.

ammi'rare *vt* to admire.

ammira'tore, 'trice *sm/f* admirer.

ammirazi'one [ammirat'tsjone] *sf* admiration.

am'misi *etc vb vedi* **ammettere**.

ammis'sibile *ag* admissible, acceptable.

ammissi'one *sf* admission; (*approvazione*) acknowledgment.

Amm.ne *abbr* = **amministrazione**.

ammobili'are *vt* to furnish.

ammobili'ato, a *ag* (*camera, appartamento*) furnished.

ammoder'nare *vt* to modernize.

am'modo, a 'modo *av* properly ♦ *ag inv* respectable, nice.

ammogli'are [ammoʎ'ʎare] *vt* to find a wife for; **~rsi** *vr* to marry, take a wife.

am'mollo *sm*: **lasciare in ~** to leave to soak.

ammo'niaca *sf* ammonia.

ammoni'mento *sm* warning; admonishment.

ammo'nire *vt* (*avvertire*) to warn; (*rimproverare*) to admonish; (*DIR*) to caution.

ammonizi'one [ammonit'tsjone] *sf* (*monito: anche SPORT*) warning; (*rimprovero*) reprimand; (*DIR*) caution.

ammon'tare *vi*: **~ a** to amount to ♦ *sm* (total) amount.

ammonticchi'are [ammontik'kjare] *vt* to pile up, heap up.

ammor'bare *vt* (*diffondere malattia*) to infect; (*sog: odore*) to taint, foul.

ammorbi'dente *sm* fabric softener.

ammorbi'dire *vt* to soften.

ammorta'mento *sm* redemption; amortization; **~ fiscale** capital allowance.

ammor'tare *vt* (*FINANZA: debito*) to pay off, redeem; (*: spese d'impianto*) to write off.

ammortiz'zare [ammortid'dzare] *vt* (*FINANZA*) to pay off, redeem; (*: spese d'impianto*) to write off; (*AUT, TECN*) to absorb, deaden.

ammortizza'tore [ammortiddza'tore] *sm* (*AUT, TECN*) shock absorber.

ammucchi'are [ammuk'kjare] *vt*, **~rsi** *vr* to pile up, accumulate.

ammuf'fire *vi* to go mouldy (*BRIT*) o moldy (*US*).

ammutina'mento *sm* mutiny.
ammuti'narsi *vr* to mutiny.
ammuti'nato, a *ag* mutinous ♦ *sm* mutineer.
ammuto'lire *vi* to be struck dumb.
amne'sia *sf* amnesia.
amnis'tia *sf* amnesty.
'amo *sm* (*PESCA*) hook; (*fig*) bait.
amo'rale *ag* amoral.
a'more *sm* love; ~i *smpl* love affairs; **il tuo bambino è un** ~ your baby's a darling; **fare l'**~ *o* **all'**~ to make love; **andare d'**~ **e d'accordo con qn** to get on like a house on fire with sb; **per** ~ **o per forza** by hook or by crook; **amor proprio** self-esteem, pride.
amoreggi'are [amored'dʒare] *vi* to flirt.
amo'revole *ag* loving, affectionate.
a'morfo, a *ag* amorphous; (*fig: persona*) lifeless.
amo'rino *sm* cupid.
amo'roso, a *ag* (*affettuoso*) loving, affectionate; (*d'amore: sguardo*) amorous; (*: poesia, relazione*) love *cpd*.
am'pere [ã'pɛr] *sm inv* amp(ère).
ampi'ezza [am'pjettsa] *sf* width, breadth; spaciousness; (*fig: importanza*) scale, size; ~ **di vedute** broad-mindedness.
'ampio, a *ag* wide, broad; (*spazioso*) spacious; (*abbondante: vestito*) loose; (*: gonna*) full; (*: spiegazione*) ample, full.
am'plesso *sm* (*sessuale*) intercourse.
amplia'mento *sm* (*di strada*) widening; (*di aeroporto*) expansion; (*fig*) broadening.
ampli'are *vt* (*allargare*) to widen; (*fig: discorso*) to enlarge on; ~**rsi** *vr* to grow, increase; ~ **la propria cultura** to broaden one's mind.
amplifi'care *vt* to amplify; (*magnificare*) to extol.
amplifica'tore *sm* (*TECN, MUS*) amplifier.
amplificazi'one [amplifikat'tsjone] *sf* amplification.
am'polla *sf* (*vasetto*) cruet.
ampol'loso, a *ag* bombastic, pompous.
ampu'tare *vt* (*MED*) to amputate.
amputazi'one [amputat'tsjone] *sf* amputation.
'Amsterdam *sf* Amsterdam.
amu'leto *sm* lucky charm.
AN *sigla* = Ancona.
A.N. *sigla f* (*POL*) = **Alleanza Nazionale**.
anabbagli'ante [anabbaʎ'ʎante] *ag* (*AUT*) dipped (*BRIT*), dimmed (*US*); ~**i** *smpl* dipped *o* dimmed headlights.
anaboliz'zante [anabolid'dzante] *sm* anabolic steroid ♦ *ag* (*sostanza*) anabolic.
anacro'nismo *sm* anachronism.

a'nagrafe *sf* (*registro*) register of births, marriages and deaths; (*ufficio*) registry office (*BRIT*), office of vital statistics (*US*).
ana'grafico, a, ci, che *ag* (*AMM*): **dati** ~**ci** personal data; **comune di residenza** ~**a** district where resident.
ana'gramma, i *sm* anagram.
anal'colico, a, ci, che *ag* non-alcoholic ♦ *sm* soft drink; **bevanda** ~**a** soft drink.
a'nale *ag* anal.
analfa'beta, i, e *ag*, *sm/f* illiterate.
analfabe'tismo *sm* illiteracy.
anal'gesico, a, ci, che [anal'dʒɛziko] *ag*, *sm* analgesic.
a'nalisi *sf inv* analysis; (*MED: esame*) test; **in ultima** ~ in conclusion, in the final analysis; ~ **grammaticale** parsing; ~ **del sangue** blood test; ~ **dei sistemi/costi** systems/cost analysis.
ana'lista, i, e *sm/f* analyst; (*PSIC*) (psycho)analyst; ~ **finanziario** financial analyst; ~ **di sistemi** systems analyst.
ana'litico, a, ci, che *ag* analytic(al).
analiz'zare [analid'dzare] *vt* to analyse (*BRIT*), analyze (*US*); (*MED*) to test.
analo'gia, 'gie [analo'dʒia] *sf* analogy.
ana'logico, a, ci, che [analo'lɔdʒiko] *ag* analogical; (*calcolatore, orologio*) analog(ue).
a'nalogo, a, ghi, ghe *ag* analogous.
'ananas *sm inv* pineapple.
anar'chia [anar'kia] *sf* anarchy.
a'narchico, a, ci, che [a'narkiko] *ag* anarchic(al) ♦ *sm/f* anarchist.
anarco-insurreziona'lista [anarko,insurrettsjona'lista] *ag* anarcho-revolutionary.
'A.N.A.S. *sigla f* (= *Azienda Nazionale Autonoma delle Strade*) *national roads department*.
ana'tema, i *sm* anathema.
anato'mia *sf* anatomy.
ana'tomico, a, ci, che *ag* anatomical; (*sedile*) contoured.
'anatra *sf* duck; ~ **selvatica** mallard.
ana'troccolo *sm* duckling.
'ANCA *sigla f* = *Associazione Nazionale Cooperative Agricole*.
'anca, che *sf* (*ANAT*) hip; (*ZOOL*) haunch.
ANCC *sigla f* = *Associazione Nazionale Carabinieri*.
'anche ['anke] *cong* also; (*perfino*) even; **vengo anch'io!** I'm coming too!; ~ **se** even if; ~ **volendo, non finiremmo in tempo** even if we wanted to, we wouldn't finish in time.
ancheggi'are [anked'dʒare] *vi* to wiggle (one's hips).

anchilo'sato, a [ankilo'zato] *ag* stiff.

'ANCI ['antʃi] *sigla f* (= *Associazione Nazionale dei Comuni Italiani*) national confederation of local authorities.

ancone'tano, a *ag* of (*o* from) Ancona.

an'cora *av* still; (*di nuovo*) again; (*di più*) some more; (*persino*): ~ **più forte** even stronger; **non** ~ not yet; ~ **una volta** once more, once again; ~ **un po'** a little more; (*di tempo*) a little longer.

'ancora *sf* anchor; **gettare/levare l'**~ to cast/weigh anchor; ~ **di salvezza** (*fig*) last hope.

anco'raggio [anko'raddʒo] *sm* anchorage.

anco'rare *vt*, ~**rsi** *vr* to anchor.

ANCR *sigla f* (= *Associazione Nazionale Combattenti e Reduci*) servicemen's and ex-servicemen's association.

Andalu'sia *sf*: l'~ Andalusia.

anda'luso, a *ag*, *sm/f* Andalusian.

anda'mento *sm* (*di strada*, *malattia*) course; (*del mercato*) state.

an'dante *ag* (*corrente*) current; (*di poco pregio*) cheap, second-rate ♦ *sm* (*MUS*) andante.

an'dare *sm*: **a lungo** ~ in the long run; **con l'andar del tempo** with the passing of time; **racconta storie a tutto** ~ she's forever talking rubbish ♦ *vi* (*gen*) to go; (*essere adatto*): ~ **a** to suit; (*piacere*): **il suo comportamento non mi va** I don't like the way he behaves; **ti va di** ~ **al cinema?** do you feel like going to the cinema?; ~ **a cavallo** to ride; ~ **in macchina/aereo** to go by car/plane; ~ **a fare qc** to go and do sth; ~ **a pescare/sciare** to go fishing/skiing; **andarsene** to go away; **vado e vengo** I'll be back in a minute; ~ **per i 50** (*età*) to be getting on for 50; ~ **a male** to go bad; ~ **fiero di qc/qn** to be proud of sth/sb; ~ **perduto** to be lost; **come va?** (*lavoro*, *progetto*) how are things?; **come va?** — **bene, grazie!** how are you? — fine, thanks!; **va fatto entro oggi** it's got to be done today; **ne va della nostra vita** our lives are at stake; **se non vado errato** if I'm not mistaken; **le mele vanno molto** apples are selling well; **va da sé** (*è naturale*) it goes without saying; **per questa volta vada** let's say no more about it this time.

an'data *sf* (*viaggio*) outward journey; **biglietto di sola** ~ single (*BRIT*) *o* one-way ticket; **biglietto di** ~ **e ritorno** return (*BRIT*) *o* round-trip (*US*) ticket.

anda'tura *sf* (*modo di andare*) walk, gait; (*SPORT*) pace; (*NAUT*) tack.

an'dazzo [an'dattso] *sm* (*peg*): **prendere un**

brutto ~ to take a turn for the worse.

'Ande *sfpl*: **le** ~ the Andes.

an'dino, a *ag* Andean.

andirivi'eni *sm inv* coming and going.

'andito *sm* corridor, passage.

An'dorra *sf* Andorra.

andrò *etc vb vedi* andare.

an'drone *sm* entrance hall.

a'neddoto *sm* anecdote.

ane'lare *vi*: ~ **a** (*fig*) to long for, yearn for.

a'nelito *sm* (*fig*): ~ **di** longing *o* yearning for.

a'nello *sm* ring; (*di catena*) link.

ane'mia *sf* anaemia (*BRIT*), anemia (*US*).

a'nemico, a, ci, che *ag* anaemic (*BRIT*), anemic (*US*).

a'nemone *sm* anemone.

aneste'sia *sf* anaesthesia (*BRIT*), anesthesia (*US*).

aneste'sista, i, e *sm/f* anaesthetist (*BRIT*), anesthetist (*US*).

anes'tetico, a, ci, che *ag*, *sm* anaesthetic (*BRIT*), anesthetic (*US*).

anestetiz'zare [anestetid'dzare] *vt* to anaesthetize (*BRIT*), anesthetize (*US*).

anfeta'mina *sf* amphetamine.

anfeta'minico, a, ci, che *ag* (*fig*) hyper.

an'fibio, a *ag* amphibious ♦ *sm* amphibian; (*AUT*) amphibious vehicle.

anfite'atro *sm* amphitheatre (*BRIT*), amphitheater (*US*).

anfitri'one *sm* host.

'anfora *sf* amphora.

an'fratto *sm* ravine.

an'gelico, a, ci, che [an'dʒɛliko] *ag* angelic(al).

'angelo ['andʒelo] *sm* angel; ~ **custode** guardian angel; **l'**~ **del focolare** (*fig*) the perfect housewife.

anghe'ria [ange'ria] *sf* vexation.

an'gina [an'dʒina] *sf* tonsillitis; ~ **pectoris** angina.

angli'cano, a *ag* Anglican.

angli'cismo [angli'tʃizmo] *sm* anglicism.

an'glofilo, a *ag* anglophilic ♦ *sm/f* anglophile.

anglo'sassone *ag* Anglo-Saxon.

An'gola *sf*: l'~ Angola.

ango'lano, a *ag*, *sm/f* Angolan.

ango'lare *ag* angular.

angola'tura *sf* angle.

angolazi'one [angolat'tsjone] *sf* (*di angolo*) angulation; (*FOT*, *CINE*, *TV*, *fig*) angle.

'angolo *sm* corner; (*MAT*) angle; ~ **cottura** (*di appartamento etc*) cooking area; **fare** ~ **con** (*strada*) to run into; **dietro l'**~ (*anche fig*) round the corner.

ango'loso, a *ag* (*oggetto*) angular; (*volto*,

corpo) angular, bony.

'**angora** *sf*: **lana d'~** angora.

an'**goscia, sce** [an'gɔʃʃa] *sf* deep anxiety, anguish *no pl*.

angosci'**are** [angoʃ'ʃare] *vt* to cause anguish to; **~rsi** *vr*: **~rsi (per)** (*preoccuparsi*) to become anxious (about); (*provare angoscia*) to get upset (about *o* over).

angosci'**oso, a** [angoʃ'ʃoso] *ag* (*d'angoscia*) anguished; (*che dà angoscia*) distressing, painful.

angu'**illa** *sf* eel.

an'**guria** *sf* watermelon.

an'**gustia** *sf* (*ansia*) anguish, distress; (*povertà*) poverty, want.

angusti'**are** *vt* to distress; **~rsi** *vr*: **~rsi (per)** to worry (about).

an'**gusto, a** *ag* (*stretto*) narrow; (*fig*) mean, petty.

'**anice** ['anitʃe] *sm* (*CUC*) aniseed; (*BOT*) anise; (*liquore*) anisette.

ani'**dride** *sf* (*CHIM*): **~ carbonica/solforosa** carbon/sulphur dioxide.

'**anima** *sf* soul; (*abitante*) ~ **gemella** soul mate; **un'~ in pena** (*anche fig*) a tormented soul; **non c'era ~ viva** there wasn't a living soul; **volere un bene dell'~ a qn** to be extremely fond of sb; **rompere l'~ a qn** to drive sb mad; **il nonno buon'~ ...** Grandfather, God rest his soul ....

ani'**male** *sm*, *ag* animal.

anima'**lesco, a, schi, sche** *ag* (*gesto, atteggiamento*) animal-like.

anima'**lista, i, e** *ag* animal rights *cpd* ♦ *smlf* animal rights activist.

ani'**mare** *vt* to give life to, liven up; (*incoraggiare*) to encourage; **~rsi** *vr* to become animated, come to life.

ani'**mato, a** *ag* animate; (*vivace*) lively, animated; (*: strada*) busy.

anima'**tore, 'trice** *smlf* guiding spirit; (*CINE*) animator; (*di festa*) life and soul.

animazi'**one** [animat'tsjone] *sf* liveliness; (*di strada*) bustle; (*CINE*) animation; **~ teatrale** amateur dramatics.

'**animo** *sm* (*mente*) mind; (*cuore*) heart; (*coraggio*) courage; (*disposizione*) character, disposition; **avere in ~ di fare qc** to intend *o* have a mind to do sth; **farsi ~** to pluck up courage; **fare qc di buon/ mal ~** to do sth willingly/unwillingly; **perdersi d'~** to lose heart.

animosità *sf* animosity.

A'**NITA** *sigla f* = *Associazione Naturista Italiana*.

'**anitra** *sf* = **anatra**.

'**Ankara** *sf* Ankara.

ANM *sigla f* (= *Associazione Nazionale dei Magistrati*) *national association of magistrates*.

ANMI *sigla f* (= *Associazione Nazionale Marinai d'Italia*) *national association of seamen*.

ANMIG *sigla f* (= *Associazione Nazionale fra Mutilati e Invalidi di Guerra*) *national association for disabled ex-servicemen*.

anna'**cquare** *vt* to water down, dilute.

annaffi'**are** *vt* to water.

annaffia'**toio** *sm* watering can.

an'**nali** *smpl* annals.

annas'**pare** *vi* (*nell'acqua*) to flounder; (*fig: nel buio, nell'incertezza*) to grope.

an'**nata** *sf* year; (*importo annuo*) annual amount; **vino di ~** vintage wine.

annebbi'**are** *vt* (*fig*) to cloud; **~rsi** *vr* to become foggy; (*vista*) to become dim.

annega'**mento** *sm* drowning.

anne'**gare** *vt, vi* to drown; **~rsi** *vr* (*accidentalmente*) to drown; (*deliberatamente*) to drown o.s.

anne'**rire** *vt* to blacken ♦ *vi* to become black.

annessi'**one** *sf* (*POL*) annexation.

an'**nesso, a** *pp di* **annettere** ♦ *ag* attached; (*POL*) annexed; **... e tutti gli ~i e connessi** ... and so on and so forth.

an'**nettere** *vt* (*POL*) to annex; (*accludere*) to attach.

annichi'**lire** [anniki'lire] *vt* to annihilate.

anni'**darsi** *vr* to nest.

annienta'**mento** *sm* annihilation, destruction.

annien'**tare** *vt* to annihilate, destroy.

anniver'**sario** *sm* anniversary.

'**anno** *sm* year; **quanti ~i hai? — ho 40 ~i** how old are you? — I'm 40 (years old); **gli ~i 20** the 20s; **porta bene gli ~i** she doesn't look her age; **porta male gli ~i** she looks older than she is; **~ commerciale** business year; **~ giudiziario** legal year; **~ luce** light year; **gli ~i di piombo** *the Seventies in Italy, characterized by terrorist attacks and killings*.

anno'**dare** *vt* to knot, tie; (*fig: rapporto*) to form.

annoi'**are** *vt* to bore; (*seccare*) to annoy; **~rsi** *vr* to be bored; to be annoyed.

an'**noso, a** *ag* (*albero*) old; (*fig: problema etc*) age-old.

anno'**tare** *vt* (*registrare*) to note, note down (*BRIT*); (*commentare*) to annotate.

annotazi'**one** [annotat'tsjone] *sf* note; annotation.

annove'**rare** *vt* to number.

annu'ale *ag* annual.
annual'mente *av* annually, yearly.
annu'ario *sm* yearbook.
annu'ire *vi* to nod; (*acconsentire*) to agree.
annulla'mento *sm* annihilation, destruction; cancellation; annulment; quashing.
annul'lare *vt* to annihilate, destroy; (*contratto, francobollo*) to cancel; (*matrimonio*) to annul; (*sentenza*) to quash; (*risultati*) to declare void.
annunci'are [annun'tʃare] *vt* to announce; (*dar segni rivelatori*) to herald.
annuncia'tore, 'trice [annuntʃa'tore] *sm/f* (*RADIO, TV*) announcer.
Annunciazi'one [annuntʃat'tsjone] *sf* (*REL*): l'~ the Annunciation.
an'nuncio [an'nuntʃo] *sm* announcement; (*fig*) sign; ~ **pubblicitario** advertisement; ~**i economici** classified advertisements, small ads; **piccoli** ~**i** small ads, classified ads; ~**i mortuari** (*colonna*) obituary column.
'annuo, a *ag* annual, yearly.
annu'sare *vt* to sniff, smell; ~ **tabacco** to take snuff.
annuvola'mento *sm* clouding (over).
annuvo'lare *vt* to cloud; ~**rsi** *vr* to become cloudy, cloud over.
'ano *sm* anus.
'anodo *sm* anode.
anoma'lia *sf* anomaly.
a'nomalo, a *ag* anomalous.
anoni'mato *sm* anonymity; **conservare l'~** to remain anonymous.
a'nonimo, a *ag* anonymous ♦ *sm* (*autore*) anonymous writer (*o* painter *etc*); **un tipo** ~ (*peg*) a colourless (*BRIT*) *o* colorless (*US*) character.
anores'sia *sf* anorexia; ~ **nervosa** anorexia nervosa.
ano'ressico, a, ci, che *ag* anorexic.
anor'male *ag* abnormal ♦ *sm/f* subnormal person; (*eufemismo*) homosexual.
anormalità *sf inv* abnormality.
'ANSA *sigla f* (= *Agenzia Nazionale Stampa Associata*) *national press agency.*
'ansa *sf* (*manico*) handle; (*di fiume*) bend.
an'sante *ag* out of breath, panting.
'ANSEA *sigla f* (= *Associazione delle Nazioni del Sud-Est asiatico*) ASEAN.
'ansia *sf* anxiety; **stare in** ~ (**per qn/qc**) to be anxious (about sb/sth).
ansietà *sf* anxiety.
ansi'mare *vi* to pant.
ansi'oso, a *ag* anxious.
'anta *sf* (*di finestra*) shutter; (*di armadio*) door.

antago'nismo *sm* antagonism.
antago'nista, i, e *sm/f* antagonist.
an'tartico, a, ci, che *ag* Antarctic ♦ *sm*: l'A~ the Antarctic.
An'tartide *sf*: l'~ Antarctica.
ante'bellico, a, ci, che *ag* prewar *cpd.*
antece'dente [antetʃe'dɛnte] *ag* preceding, previous.
ante'fatto *sm* previous events *pl*; previous history.
antegu'erra *sm* pre-war period.
ante'nato *sm* ancestor, forefather.
an'tenna *sf* (*RADIO, TV*) aerial; (*ZOOL*) antenna, feeler; **rizzare le** ~**e** (*fig*) to prick up one's ears; ~ **parabolica** (*TV*) satellite dish.
ante'porre *vt*: ~ **qc a qc** to place *o* put sth before sth.
ante'posto, a *pp di* **anteporre.**
ante'prima *sf* preview; ~ **di stampa** (*INFORM*) print preview.
anteri'ore *ag* (*ruota, zampa*) front *cpd*; (*fatti*) previous, preceding.
antesi'gnano [antesiɲ'ɲano] *sm* (*STORIA*) standard-bearer; (*fig*) forerunner.
antiade'rente *ag* non-stick.
antia'ereo, a *ag* anti-aircraft *cpd.*
antial'lergico, a [antial'lɛrdʒiko] *ag, sm* hypoallergenic.
antia'tomico, a, ci, che *ag* anti-nuclear; **rifugio** ~ fallout shelter.
antibi'otico, a, ci, che *ag, sm* antibiotic.
anti'caglia [anti'kaʎʎa] *sf* junk *no pl.*
antical'care *ag* (*prodotto, detersivo*) anti-limescale.
anti'camera *sf* anteroom; **fare** ~ to be kept waiting; **non mi passerebbe neanche per l'~ del cervello** it wouldn't even cross my mind.
anti'carie *ag inv* which fights tooth decay.
antichità [antiki'ta] *sf inv* antiquity; (*oggetto*) antique.
antici'clone [antitʃi'klone] *sm* anticyclone.
antici'pare [antitʃi'pare] *vt* (*consegna, visita*) to bring forward, anticipate; (*somma di denaro*) to pay in advance; (*notizia*) to disclose ♦ *vi* to be ahead of time.
antici'pato, a [antitʃi'pato] *ag* (*prima del previsto*) early; **pagamento** ~ payment in advance.
anticipazi'one [antitʃipat'tsjone] *sf* anticipation; (*di notizia*) advance information; (*somma di denaro*) advance.
an'ticipo [an'titʃipo] *sm* anticipation; (*di denaro*) advance; **in** ~ early, in advance; **con un sensibile** ~ well in advance.
antic'lan *ag inv* (*magistrato, processo*) anti-Mafia.

an'tico, a, chi, che *ag* (*quadro, mobili*) antique; (*dell'antichità*) ancient; **all'~a** old-fashioned.

anticoncezio'nale [antikontʃettsjo'nale] *sm* contraceptive.

anticonfor'mista, i, e *ag, sm/f* nonconformist.

anticonge'lante [antikondʒe'lante] *ag, sm* antifreeze.

anticongiuntu'rale [antikondʒuntu'rale] *ag* (*ECON*): **misure ~i** measures to remedy the economic situation.

anti'corpo *sm* antibody.

anticostituzio'nale [antikostituttsjo'nale] *ag* unconstitutional.

antidepres'sivo, a *ag, sm* antidepressant.

antidiluvi'ano, a *ag* (*fig: antiquato*) ancient.

antidolo'rifico, ci *sm* painkiller.

anti'doping *sm, ag inv* drug testing; **test ~** drugs (*BRIT*) *o* drug (*US*) test.

an'tidoto *sm* antidote.

anti'droga *ag inv* anti-drugs *cpd*.

antie'stetico, a, ci, che *ag* unsightly.

an'tifona *sf* (*MUS, REL*) antiphon; **capire l'~** (*fig*) to take the hint.

anti'forfora *ag inv* anti-dandruff.

anti'furto *sm* anti-theft device.

anti'gelo [anti'dʒɛlo] *ag inv* antifreeze *cpd* ♦ *sm* (*per motore*) antifreeze; (*per cristalli*) de-icer.

an'tigene [an'tidʒene] *sm* antigen.

antigi'enico, a, ci, che [anti'dʒɛniko] *ag* unhygienic.

antiglobalizza'zione [antiglobalizza'tsjone] *ag* anti-globalization *cpd*.

An'tille *sfpl*: **le ~** the West Indies.

an'tilope *sf* antelope.

anti'mafia *ag inv* anti-mafia *cpd*.

antin'cendio [antin'tʃɛndjo] *ag inv* fire *cpd*; **bombola ~** fire extinguisher.

anti'nebbia *sm inv* (*anche*: **faro ~**: *AUT*) fog lamp.

antine'vralgico, a, ci, che [antine'vraldʒiko] *ag* painkilling ♦ *sm* painkiller.

antin'fiammatorio, a *ag, sm* anti-inflammatory.

antio'rario *ag*: **in senso ~** in an anticlockwise (*BRIT*) *o* counterclockwise (*US*) direction, anticlockwise, counterclockwise.

anti'pasto *sm* hors d'œuvre.

antipa'tia *sf* antipathy, dislike.

anti'patico, a, ci, che *ag* unpleasant, disagreeable.

anti'placca *ag inv* (*dentifricio*) anti-plaque.

an'tipodi *smpl*: **essere agli ~** (*fig: di idee* opposte) to be poles apart.

antipro'iettile *ag inv* bulletproof.

antiquari'ato *sm* antique trade; **un pezzo d'~** an antique.

anti'quario *sm* antique dealer.

anti'quato, a *ag* antiquated, old-fashioned.

antirici'claggio [antiritʃi'kladdʒo] *ag* (*attività, operazioni*) anti-laundering.

antiri'flesso *ag inv* (*schermo*) non-glare *cpd*.

anti'ruggine [anti'ruddʒine] *ag* anti-rust *cpd* ♦ *sm inv* rust-preventer.

anti'rughe [anti'ruge] *ag inv* anti-wrinkle.

antise'mita, i, e *ag* anti-semitic.

antisemi'tismo *sm* anti-semitism.

anti'settico, a, ci, che *ag, sm* antiseptic.

antista'minico, a, ci, che *ag, sm* antihistamine.

anti'stante *ag* opposite.

anti'tartaro *ag inv* anti-tartar.

antiterro'rismo *sm* anti-terrorist measures *pl*.

an'titesi *sf* antithesis.

antitraspi'rante *ag* antiperspirant.

anti'vipera *ag inv*: **siero ~** remedy for snake bites.

anti'virus [anti'virus] *sm inv* antivirus software *no pl*.

antolo'gia, 'gie [antolo'dʒia] *sf* anthology.

antono'masia *sf* antonomasia; **per ~** par excellence.

antra'cite [antra'tʃite] *sf* anthracite.

'antro *sm* cavern.

antro'pofago, gi *sm* cannibal.

antropolo'gia [antropolo'dʒia] *sf* anthropology.

antropo'logico, a, ci, che [antropo'lɔdʒiko] *ag* anthropological.

antro'pologo, a, gi, ghe *sm/f* anthropologist.

anu'lare *ag* ring *cpd* ♦ *sm* ring finger.

An'versa *sf* Antwerp.

'anzi ['antsi] *av* (*invece*) on the contrary; (*o meglio*) or rather, or better still.

anzianità [antsjani'ta] *sf* old age; (*AMM*) seniority.

anzi'ano, a [an'tsjano] *ag* old; (*AMM*) senior ♦ *sm/f* old person; senior member.

anziché [antsi'ke] *cong* rather than.

anzi'tempo [antsi'tɛmpo] *av* (*in anticipo*) early.

anzi'tutto [antsi'tutto] *av* first of all.

AO *sigla* = *Aosta*.

a'orta *sf* aorta.

aos'tano, a *ag* of (*o* from) Aosta.

AP *sigla* = *Ascoli Piceno*.

apar'titico, a, ci, che *ag* (*POL*) non-party *cpd*.

apa'tia *sf* apathy, indifference.

a'patico, a, ci, che *ag* apathetic, indifferent.

a.p.c. *abbr* = a pronta cassa.

'ape *sf* bee.

aperi'tivo *sm* apéritif.

aperta'mente *av* openly.

a'perto, a *pp di* aprire ♦ *ag* open ♦ *sm*: all'~ in the open (air); rimanere a bocca ~a (*fig*) to be taken aback.

aper'tura *sf* opening; (*ampiezza*) width, spread; (*POL*) approach; (*FOT*) aperture; ~ alare wing span; ~ mentale open-mindedness; ~ di credito (*COMM*) granting of credit.

API *sigla f* = Associazione Piccole e Medie Industrie.

'apice ['apitʃe] *sm* apex; (*fig*) height.

apicol'tore *sm* beekeeper.

apicol'tura *sf* beekeeping.

ap'nea *sf*: immergersi in ~ to dive without breathing apparatus.

apoca'lisse *sf* apocalypse.

apo'geo [apo'dʒɛo] *sm* (*ASTR*) apogee; (*fig*: *culmine*) zenith.

a'polide *ag* stateless.

apo'litico, a, ci, che *ag* (*neutrale*) nonpolitical; (*indifferente*) apolitical.

apolo'gia, gie [apolo'dʒia] *sf* (*difesa*) apologia; (*esaltazione*) praise; ~ di reato attempt to defend criminal acts.

apoples'sia *sf* (*MED*) apoplexy.

apop'lettico, a, ci, che *ag* apoplectic; colpo ~ apoplectic fit.

a'postolo *sm* apostle.

apostro'fare *vt* (*parola*) to write with an apostrophe; (*persona*) to address.

a'postrofo *sm* apostrophe.

app. *abbr* (= appendice) app.

appaga'mento *sm* satisfaction; fulfilment.

appa'gare *vt* to satisfy; (*desiderio*) to fulfil; ~rsi *vr*: ~rsi di to be satisfied with.

appa'gato, a *ag* satisfied.

appai'are *vt* to couple, pair.

ap'paio *etc vb vedi* apparire.

appallotto'lare *vt* (*carta, foglio*) to screw into a ball; ~rsi *vr* (*gatto*) to roll up into a ball.

appalta'tore *sm* contractor.

ap'palto *sm* (*COMM*) contract; dare/ prendere in ~ un lavoro to let out/ undertake a job on contract.

appan'naggio [appan'naddʒo] *sm* (*compenso*) annuity; (*fig*) privilege, prerogative.

appan'nare *vt* (*vetro*) to mist; (*metallo*) to tarnish; (*vista*) to dim; ~rsi *vr* to mist over; to tarnish; to grow dim.

appa'rato *sm* equipment, machinery; (*ANAT*) apparatus; ~ scenico (*TEAT*) props *pl*.

apparecchi'are [apparek'kjare] *vt* to prepare; (*tavola*) to set ♦ *vi* to set the table.

apparecchia'tura [apparekkja'tura] *sf* equipment; (*macchina*) machine, device.

appa'recchio [appa'rekkjo] *sm* piece of apparatus, device; (*aeroplano*) aircraft *inv*; ~i sanitari bathroom *o* sanitary appliances; ~ televisivo/telefonico television set/telephone.

appa'rente *ag* apparent.

apparente'mente *av* apparently.

appa'renza [appa'rɛntsa] *sf* appearance; in *o* all'~ apparently, to all appearances.

appa'rire *vi* to appear; (*sembrare*) to seem, appear.

appari'scente [appariʃ'ʃɛnte] *ag* (*colore*) garish, gaudy; (*bellezza*) striking.

apparizi'one [apparit'tsjone] *sf* apparition.

ap'parso, a *pp di* apparire.

apparta'mento *sm* flat (*BRIT*), apartment (*US*).

appar'tarsi *vr* to withdraw.

appar'tato, a *ag* (*luogo*) secluded.

apparte'nenza [apparte'nɛntsa] *sf*: ~ (a) (*gen*) belonging (to); (*a un partito, club*) membership (of).

apparte'nere *vi*: ~ a to belong to.

ap'parvi *etc vb vedi* apparire.

appassio'nante *ag* thrilling, exciting.

appassio'nare *vt* to thrill; (*commuovere*) to move; ~rsi *vr*: ~rsi a qc to take a great interest in sth; to be deeply moved by sth.

appassio'nato, a *ag* passionate; (*entusiasta*): ~ (di) keen (on).

appas'sire *vi* to wither.

appel'larsi *vr* (*ricorrere*): ~ a to appeal to; (*DIR*): ~ contro to appeal against.

ap'pello *sm* roll-call; (*implorazione, DIR*) appeal; (*sessione d'esame*) exam session; fare ~ a to appeal to; fare l'~ (*INS*) to call the register *o* roll; (*MIL*) to call the roll.

ap'pena *av* (*a stento*) hardly, scarcely; (*solamente, da poco*) just ♦ *cong* as soon as; (non) ~ furono arrivati ... as soon as they had arrived ...; basta ~ a sfamarli it's scarcely enough to feed them; ho ~ finito I have just finished.

ap'pendere *vt* to hang (up).

appendi'abiti *sm inv* hook, peg; (*mobile*) hall stand (*BRIT*), hall tree (*US*).

appen'dice [appen'ditʃe] *sf* appendix; romanzo d'~ popular serial.

appendi'cite [appendi'tʃite] *sf* appendicitis.

appen'dino *sm* (coat) hook.

Appen'nini *smpl*: gli ~ the Apennines.

appesan'tire *vt* to make heavy; **~rsi** *vr* to grow stout.

ap'peso, a *pp di* **appendere**.

appe'tito *sm* appetite.

appeti'toso, a *ag* appetising; (*fig*) attractive, desirable.

appezza'mento [appettsa'mento] *sm* (*anche*: **~ di terreno**) plot, piece of ground.

appia'nare *vt* to level; (*fig*) to smooth away, iron out; **~rsi** *vr* (*divergenze*) to be ironed out.

appiat'tire *vt* to flatten; **~rsi** *vr* to become flatter; (*farsi piatto*) to flatten o.s.; **~rsi al suolo** to lie flat on the ground.

appic'care *vt*: **~ il fuoco a** to set fire to, set on fire.

appicci'care [appittʃi'kare] *vt* to stick; (*fig*): **~ qc a qn** to palm sth off on sb; **~rsi** *vr* to stick; (*fig: persona*) to cling.

appiccica'ticcio, a, ci, ce [appittʃika'tittʃo] *ag*, **appicci'coso, a** [appittʃi'koso] *ag* sticky; (*fig: persona*): **essere ~** to cling like a leech.

appie'dato, a *ag*: **rimanere ~** to be left without means of transport.

appi'eno *av* fully.

appigli'arsi [appiʎ'ʎarsi] *vr*: **~ a** (*afferrarsi*) to take hold of; (*fig*) to cling to.

ap'piglio [ap'piʎʎo] *sm* hold; (*fig*) pretext.

appiop'pare *vt*: **~ qc a qn** (*nomignolo*) to pin sth on sb; (*compito difficile*) to saddle sb with sth; **gli ha appioppato un pugno sul muso** he punched him in the face.

appiso'larsi *vr* to doze off.

applau'dire *vt*, *vi* to applaud.

ap'plauso *sm* applause *no pl*.

appli'cabile *ag*: **~ (a)** applicable (to).

appli'care *vt* to apply; (*regolamento*) to enforce; **~rsi** *vr* to apply o.s.

appli'cato, a *ag* (*arte, scienze*) applied ♦ *sm* (*AMM*) clerk.

applica'tore *sm* applicator.

applicazi'one [applikat'tsjone] *sf* application; enforcement; **~i tecniche** (*INS*) practical subjects.

appoggi'are [appod'dʒare] *vt* (*mettere contro*): **~ qc a qc** to lean *o* rest sth against sth; (*fig: sostenere*) to support; **~rsi** *vr*: **~rsi a** to lean against; (*fig*) to rely upon.

ap'poggio [ap'pɔddʒo] *sm* support.

appollai'arsi *vr* (*anche fig*) to perch.

ap'pongo, ap'poni *etc vb vedi* **apporre**.

ap'porre *vt* to affix.

appor'tare *vt* to bring.

ap'porto *sm* (*gen*, *FINANZA*) contribution.

ap'posi *etc vb vedi* **apporre**.

apposita'mente *av* (*apposta*) on purpose; (*specialmente*) specially.

ap'posito, a *ag* appropriate.

ap'posta *av* on purpose, deliberately; **neanche a farlo ~**, … by sheer coincidence, ….

appos'tarsi *vr* to lie in wait.

ap'posto, a *pp di* **apporre**.

ap'prendere *vt* (*imparare*) to learn; (*comprendere*) to grasp.

apprendi'mento *sm* learning.

appren'dista, i, e *smlf* apprentice.

apprendi'stato *sm* apprenticeship.

apprensi'one *sf* apprehension.

appren'sivo, a *ag* apprehensive.

ap'preso, a *pp di* **apprendere**.

ap'presso *av* (*accanto, vicino*) close by, near; (*dietro*) behind; (*dopo, più tardi*) after, later ♦ *ag inv* (*dopo*): **il giorno ~** the next day; **~ a** *prep* (*vicino a*) near, close to.

appres'tare *vt* to prepare, get ready; **~rsi** *vr*: **~rsi a fare qc** to prepare *o* get ready to do sth.

ap'pretto *sm* starch.

apprez'zabile [appret'tsabile] *ag* (*notevole*) noteworthy, significant; (*percepibile*) appreciable.

apprezza'mento [apprettsa'mento] *sm* appreciation; (*giudizio*) opinion; (*commento*) comment.

apprez'zare [appret'tsare] *vt* to appreciate.

ap'proccio [ap'prɔttʃo] *sm* approach.

appro'dare *vi* (*NAUT*) to land; (*fig*): **non ~ a nulla** to come to nothing.

ap'prodo *sm* landing; (*luogo*) landing place.

approfit'tare *vi*: **~ di** (*persona, situazione*) to take advantage of; (*occasione, opportunità*) to make the most of, profit by.

approfon'dire *vt* to deepen; (*fig*) to study in depth; **~rsi** *vr* (*gen, fig*) to deepen; (*peggiorare*) to get worse.

appron'tare *vt* to prepare, get ready.

appropri'arsi *vr*: **~ di qc** to appropriate sth, take possession of sth; **~ indebitamente di** to embezzle.

appropri'ato, a *ag* appropriate.

appropriazi'one [approprjat'tsjone] *sf* appropriation; **~ indebita** (*DIR*) embezzlement.

approssi'mare *vt* (*cifra*): **~ per eccesso/per difetto** to round up/down; **~rsi** *vr*: **~rsi a** to approach, draw near.

approssima'tivo, a *ag* approximate, rough; (*impreciso*) inexact, imprecise.

approssimazi'one [approssimat'tsjone] *sf* approximation; **per ~** approximately, roughly.

appro'vare *vt* (*condotta, azione*) to approve of; (*candidato*) to pass; (*progetto di legge*) to approve.

approvazi'one [approvat'tsjone] *sf* approval.

approvvigiona'mento [approvvidʒona'mento] *sm* supplying; stocking up; ~**i** *smpl* (*MIL*) supplies.

approvvigio'nare [approvvidʒo'nare] *vt* to supply; ~**rsi** *vr* to lay in provisions, stock up; ~ **qn di qc** to supply sb with sth.

appunta'mento *sm* appointment; (*amoroso*) date; **darsi** ~ to arrange to meet (one another).

appun'tare *vt* (*rendere aguzzo*) to sharpen; (*fissare*) to pin, fix; (*annotare*) to note down.

appun'tato *sm* (*CARABINIERI*) corporal.

appun'tire *vt* to sharpen.

ap'punto *sm* note; (*rimprovero*) reproach ♦ *av* (*proprio*) exactly, just; **per l'**~!, ~! exactly!

appu'rare *vt* to check, verify.

apr. *abbr* (= *aprile*) Apr.

apribot'tiglie [apribot'tiʎʎe] *sm inv* bottleopener.

a'prile *sm* April; **pesce d'**~! April Fool!; *per fraseologia vedi* **luglio**.

a'prire *vt* to open; (*via, cadavere*) to open up; (*gas, luce, acqua*) to turn on ♦ *vi* to open; ~**rsi** *vr* to open; ~ **le ostilità** (*MIL*) to start up *o* begin hostilities; ~ **una sessione** (*INFORM*) to log on; ~**rsi a qn** to confide in sb, open one's heart to sb; **mi si è aperto lo stomaco** I feel rather peckish; **apriti cielo!** heaven forbid!

apris'catole *sm inv* tin (*BRIT*) *o* can opener.

APT *sigla f* (= *Azienda di Promozione Turistica*) ≈ tourist board.

AQ *sigla* = *L'Aquila*.

aquagym [akwa'dʒim] *sf* aquarobics.

a'quario *sm* = **acquario**.

'aquila *sf* (*ZOOL*) eagle; (*fig*) genius.

aqui'lino, a *ag* aquiline.

aqui'lone *sm* (*giocattolo*) kite; (*vento*) North wind.

AR *sigla* = *Arezzo*.

A/R *abbr* (= *andata e ritorno*) return.

ara'besco *sm* (*decorazione*) arabesque.

A'rabia Sau'dita *sf*: **l'**~ Saudi Arabia.

a'rabico, a, ci, che *ag*: **il Deserto** ~ the Arabian Desert.

a'rabile *ag* arable.

'arabo, a *ag, sm/f* Arab ♦ *sm* (*LING*) Arabic; **parlare** ~ (*fig*) to speak double Dutch (*BRIT*).

a'rachide [a'rakide] *sf* peanut.

ara'gosta *sf* spiny lobster.

a'raldica *sf* heraldry.

a'raldo *sm* herald.

aran'ceto [aran'tʃeto] *sm* orange grove.

a'rancia, ce [a'rantʃa] *sf* orange.

aranci'ata [aran'tʃata] *sf* orangeade.

a'rancio [a'rantʃo] *sm* (*BOT*) orange tree; (*colore*) orange ♦ *ag inv* (*colore*) orange; **fiori di** ~ orange blossom *sg*.

aranci'one [aran'tʃone] *ag inv*: **(color)** ~ bright orange.

a'rare *vt* to plough (*BRIT*), plow (*US*).

ara'tore *sm* ploughman (*BRIT*), plowman (*US*).

a'ratro *sm* plough (*BRIT*), plow (*US*).

ara'tura *sf* ploughing (*BRIT*), plowing (*US*).

a'razzo [a'rattso] *sm* tapestry.

arbi'traggio [arbi'traddʒo] *sm* (*SPORT*) refereeing; umpiring; (*DIR*) arbitration; (*COMM*) arbitrage.

arbi'trare *vt* (*SPORT*) to referee; to umpire; (*DIR*) to arbitrate.

arbi'trario, a *ag* arbitrary.

arbi'trato *sm* arbitration.

ar'bitrio *sm* will; (*abuso, sopruso*) arbitrary act.

'arbitro *sm* arbiter, judge; (*DIR*) arbitrator; (*SPORT*) referee; (: *TENNIS, CRICKET*) umpire.

ar'busto *sm* shrub.

'arca, che *sf* (*sarcofago*) sarcophagus; **l'**~ **di Noè** Noah's ark.

ar'caico, a, ci, che *ag* archaic.

arca'ismo *sm* (*LING*) archaism.

ar'cangelo [ar'kandʒelo] *sm* archangel.

ar'cano, a *ag* arcane, mysterious ♦ *sm* mystery.

ar'cata *sf* (*ARCHIT, ANAT*) arch; (*ordine di archi*) arcade.

archeolo'gia [arkeolo'dʒia] *sf* arch(a)eology.

archeo'logico, a, ci, che [arkeo'lɔdʒiko] *ag* arch(a)eological.

arche'ologo, a, gi, ghe [arke'ɔlogo] *sm/f* arch(a)eologist.

ar'chetipo [ar'kɛtipo] *sm* archetype.

ar'chetto [ar'ketto] *sm* (*MUS*) bow.

architet'tare [arkitet'tare] *vt* (*fig: ideare*) to devise; (: *macchinare*) to plan, concoct.

archi'tetto [arki'tetto] *sm* architect.

architet'tonico, a, ci, che [arkitet'tɔniko] *ag* architectural.

architet'tura [arkitet'tura] *sf* architecture.

archivi'are [arki'vjare] *vt* (*documenti*) to file; (*DIR*) to dismiss.

archiviazi'one [arkivjat'tsjone] *sf* filing; dismissal.

ar'chivio [ar'kivjo] *sm* archives *pl*; (*INFORM*)

file; ~ **principale** (*INFORM*) master file.
archi'vista, i, e [arki'vista] *sm/f* (*AMM*)
archivist; (*in ufficio*) filing clerk.
'ARCI ['artʃi] *sigla f* (= *Associazione Ricreativa
Culturale Italiana*) *cultural society*.
arci'duca, chi [artʃi'duka] *sm* archduke.
arci'ere [ar'tʃɛre] *sm* archer.
ar'cigno, a [ar'tʃiɲɲo] *ag* grim, severe.
arci'pelago, ghi [artʃi'pɛlago] *sm*
archipelago.
arci'vescovo [artʃi'veskovo] *sm*
archbishop.
'arco, chi *sm* (*arma, MUS*) bow; (*ARCHIT*)
arch; (*MAT*) arc; **nell'~ di 3 settimane**
within the space of 3 weeks; ~
costituzionale *political parties involved
in formulating Italy's post-war
constitution.*
arcoba'leno *sm* rainbow.
arcu'ato, a *ag* curved, bent; **dalle gambe**
~e bow-legged.
ar'dente *ag* burning; (*fig*) burning, ardent.
'ardere *vt, vi* to burn; **legna da ~** firewood.
ar'desia *sf* slate.
ardi'mento *sm* daring.
ar'dire *vi* to dare ♦ *sm* daring.
ar'dito, a *ag* brave, daring, bold; (*sfacciato*)
bold.
ar'dore *sm* blazing heat; (*fig*) ardour,
fervour.
'arduo, a *ag* arduous, difficult.
'area *sf* area; (*EDIL*) land, ground; **nell'~ dei**
partiti di sinistra among the parties of the
left; ~ **fabbricabile** building land; ~ **di**
rigore (*SPORT*) penalty area; ~ **di servizio**
(*AUT*) service area.
a'rena *sf* arena; (*per corride*) bullring;
(*sabbia*) sand.
are'naria *sf* sandstone.
are'narsi *vr* to run aground; (*fig: trattative*)
to come to a standstill.
areo'plano *sm* = **aeroplano**.
are'tino, a *ag* of (*o* from) Arezzo.
'argano *sm* winch.
argen'tato, a [ardʒen'tato] *ag* silver-
plated; (*colore*) silver, silvery; (*capelli*)
silver(-grey).
ar'genteo, a [ar'dʒɛnteo] *ag* silver, silvery.
argente'ria [ardʒente'ria] *sf* silverware,
silver.
Argen'tina [ardʒen'tina] *sf*: **l'~** Argentina.
argen'tino, a [ardʒen'tino] *ag, sm/f*
(*dell'Argentina*) Argentinian ♦ *sf* crewneck
sweater.
ar'gento [ar'dʒɛnto] *sm* silver; ~ **vivo**
quicksilver; **avere l'~ (vivo) addosso** (*fig*)
to be fidgety.
ar'gilla [ar'dʒilla] *sf* clay.

argil'loso, a [ardʒil'loso] *ag* (*contenente
argilla*) clayey; (*simile ad argilla*) clay-like.
argi'nare [ardʒi'nare] *vt* (*fiume, acque*) to
embank; (: *con diga*) to dyke up; (*fig:
inflazione, corruzione*) to check; (: *spese*) to
limit.
'argine ['ardʒine] *sm* embankment, bank;
(*diga*) dyke, dike; **far ~ a, porre un ~ a**
(*fig*) to check, hold back.
argomen'tare *vi* to argue.
argo'mento *sm* argument; (*materia, tema*)
subject; **tornare sull'~** to bring the
matter up again.
argu'ire *vt* to deduce.
ar'guto, a *ag* sharp, quick-witted;
(*spiritoso*) witty.
ar'guzia [ar'guttsja] *sf* wit; (*battuta*) witty
remark.
'aria *sf* air; (*espressione, aspetto*) air, look;
(*MUS: melodia*) tune; (: *di opera*) aria; **all'~**
aperta in the open (air); (*spiritoso*) it's
stuffy; **andare all'~** (*piano, progetto*) to
come to nothing; **mandare all'~ qc** to ruin
o upset sth; **darsi delle ~e** to put on airs
and graces; **ha la testa per ~** his head is
in the clouds; **che ~ tira?** (*fig: atmosfera*)
what's the atmosphere like?
aridità *sf* aridity, dryness; (*fig*) lack of
feeling.
'arido, a *ag* arid.
arieggi'are [arjed'dʒare] *vt* (*cambiare aria*)
to air; (*imitare*) to imitate.
ari'ete *sm* ram; (*MIL*) battering ram; (*dello
zodiaco*): **A~** Aries; **essere dell'A~** to be
Aries.
a'ringa, ghe *sf* herring *inv*; ~ **affumicata**
smoked herring, kipper; ~ **marinata**
pickled herring.
ari'oso, a *ag* (*ambiente, stanza*) airy; (*MUS*)
ariose.
'arista *sf* (*CUC*) chine of pork.
aristo'cratico, a, ci, che *ag* aristocratic.
aristocra'zia [aristokrat'tsia] *sf* aristocracy.
arit'metica *sf* arithmetic.
arit'metico, a, ci, che *ag* arithmetical.
arlec'chino [arlek'kino] *sm* harlequin.
'arma, i *sf* weapon, arm; (*parte dell'esercito*)
arm; **alle ~i!** to arms!; **chiamare alle ~i** to
call up (*BRIT*), draft (*US*); **sotto le ~i** in the
army (*o* forces); **combattere ad ~i pari**
(*anche fig*) to fight on equal terms; **essere**
alle prime ~i (*fig*) to be a novice; **passare**
qn per le ~i to execute sb; ~ **a doppio**
taglio (*anche fig*) double-edged weapon; ~
da fuoco firearm; **~i convenzionali/non**
convenzionali conventional/
unconventional weapons; **~i di**
distruzione di massa weapons of mass

destruction.

arma'dietto *sm* (*dei medicinali*) medicine cabinet *o* cupboard; (*in cucina*) (kitchen) cupboard; (*per riporre abiti*) locker.

ar'madio *sm* cupboard; (*per abiti*) wardrobe; ~ **a muro** built-in cupboard.

armamen'tario *sm* equipment, instruments *pl.*

arma'mento *sm* (*MIL*) armament; (: *materiale*) arms *pl*, weapons *pl*; (*NAUT*) fitting out; manning; **la corsa agli** ~**i** the arms race.

ar'mare *vt* to arm; (*arma da fuoco*) to cock; (*NAUT: nave*) to rig, fit out; to man; (*EDIL: volta, galleria*) to prop up, shore up; ~**rsi** *vr* to arm o.s.; (*MIL*) to take up arms.

ar'mato, a *ag:* ~ (**di**) (*anche fig*) armed (with) ♦ *sf* (*MIL*) army; (*NAUT*) fleet; **rapina a mano** ~**a** armed robbery.

arma'tore *sm* shipowner.

arma'tura *sf* (*struttura di sostegno*) framework; (*impalcatura*) scaffolding; (*STORIA*) armour *no pl* (*BRIT*), armor *no pl* (*US*).

armeggi'are [armed'dʒare] *vi* (*affaccendarsi*): ~ (**intorno a qc**) to mess about (with sth).

ar'meno, a *ag, sm/f, sm* Armenian.

arme'ria *sf* (*deposito*) armoury (*BRIT*), armory (*US*); (*collezione*) collection of arms.

armis'tizio [armis'tittsjo] *sm* armistice.

armo'nia *sf* harmony.

ar'monico, a, ci, che *ag* harmonic; (*fig*) harmonious ♦ *sf* (*MUS*) harmonica; ~**a a bocca** mouth organ.

armoni'oso, a *ag* harmonious.

armoniz'zare [armonid'dzare] *vt* to harmonize; (*colori, abiti*) to match ♦ *vi* to be in harmony; to match.

ar'nese *sm* tool, implement; (*oggetto indeterminato*) thing, contraption; **male in** ~ (*malvestito*) badly dressed; (*di salute malferma*) in poor health; (*di condizioni economiche*) down-at-heel.

'arnia *sf* hive.

a'roma, i *sm* aroma; fragrance; ~**i** *smpl* herbs and spices; ~**i naturali/artificiali** natural/artificial flavouring *sg* (*BRIT*) *o* flavoring *sg* (*US*).

aromatera'pia *sf* aromatherapy.

aro'matico, a, ci, che *ag* aromatic; (*cibo*) spicy.

aromatiz'zare [aromatid'dzare] *vt* to season, flavour (*BRIT*), flavor (*US*).

'arpa *sf* (*MUS*) harp.

ar'peggio [ar'peddʒo] *sm* (*MUS*) arpeggio.

ar'pia *sf* (*anche fig*) harpy.

arpi'one *sm* (*gancio*) hook; (*cardine*) hinge; (*PESCA*) harpoon.

arrabat'tarsi *vr* to do all one can, strive.

arrabbi'are *vi* (*cane*) to be affected with rabies; ~**rsi** *vr* (*essere preso dall'ira*) to get angry, fly into a rage.

arrabbi'ato, a *ag* (*cane*) rabid, with rabies; (*persona*) furious, angry.

arrabbia'tura *sf*: **prendersi un'**~ (**per qc**) to become furious (over sth).

arraf'fare *vt* to snatch, seize; (*sottrarre*) to pinch.

arrampi'carsi *vr* to climb (up); ~ **sui vetri** *o* **sugli specchi** (*fig*) to clutch at straws.

arrampi'cata *sf* climb.

arrampica'tore, 'trice *sm/f* (*gen, SPORT*) climber; ~ **sociale** (*fig*) social climber.

arran'care *vi* to limp, hobble; (*fig*) to struggle along.

arrangia'mento [arrandʒa'mento] *sm* (*MUS*) arrangement.

arran'giare [arran'dʒare] *vt* to arrange; ~**rsi** *vr* to manage, do the best one can.

arre'care *vt* to bring; (*causare*) to cause.

arreda'mento *sm* (*studio*) interior design; (*mobili etc*) furnishings *pl.*

arre'dare *vt* to furnish.

arreda'tore, 'trice *sm/f* interior designer.

ar'redo *sm* fittings *pl*, furnishings *pl;* ~ **per uffici** office furnishings.

arrem'baggio [arrem'baddʒo] *sm* (*NAUT*) boarding.

ar'rendersi *vr* to surrender; ~ **all'evidenza (dei fatti)** to face (the) facts.

arren'devole *ag* (*persona*) yielding, compliant.

arrendevo'lezza [arrendevo'lettsa] *sf* compliancy.

ar'reso, a *pp di* **arrendersi**.

arres'tare *vt* (*fermare*) to stop, halt; (*catturare*) to arrest; ~**rsi** *vr* (*fermarsi*) to stop.

arres'tato, a *sm/f* person under arrest.

ar'resto *sm* (*cessazione*) stopping; (*fermata*) stop; (*cattura, MED*) arrest; (*COMM: in produzione*) stoppage; **subire un** ~ to come to a stop *o* standstill; **mettere agli** ~**i** to place under arrest; ~**i domiciliari** (*DIR*) house arrest.

arre'trare *vt, vi* to withdraw.

arre'trato, a *ag* (*lavoro*) behind schedule; (*paese, bambino*) backward; (*numero di giornale*) back *cpd*; ~**i** *smpl* arrears; **gli** ~**i dello stipendio** back pay *sg*.

arricchi'mento [arrikki'mento] *sm* enrichment.

arric'chire [arrik'kire] *vt* to enrich; ~**rsi** *vr* to become rich.

arric'chito, a [arrik'kito] *smf* nouveau riche.

arricci'are [arrit't∫are] *vt* to curl; **~ il naso** to turn up one's nose.

ar'ridere *vi*: **~ a qn** (*fortuna, successo*) to smile on sb.

ar'ringa, ghe *sf* harangue; (*DIR*) address by counsel.

arrischi'are [arris'kjare] *vt* to risk; **~rsi** *vr* to venture, dare.

arrischi'ato, a [arris'kjato] *ag* risky; (*temerario*) reckless, rash.

ar'riso, a *pp di* **arridere**.

arri'vare *vi* to arrive; (*avvicinarsi*) to come; (*accadere*) to happen, occur; **~ a** (*livello, grado etc*) to reach; **lui arriva a Roma alle 7** he gets to *o* arrives at Rome at 7; **~ a fare qc** to manage to do sth, succeed in doing sth; **non ci arrivo** I can't reach it; (*fig: non capisco*) I can't understand it.

arri'vato, a *ag* (*persona: di successo*) successful ♦ *sm/f*: **essere un ~** to have made it; **nuovo ~** newcomer; **ben ~!** welcome!; **non sono l'ultimo ~!** (*fig*) I'm no fool!

arrive'derci [arrive'dert∫i] *escl* goodbye!

arrive'derla *escl* (*forma di cortesia*) goodbye!

arri'vismo *sm* (*ambizione*) ambitiousness; (*sociale*) social climbing.

arri'vista, i, e *sm/f* go-getter.

ar'rivo *sm* arrival; (*SPORT*) finish, finishing line.

arro'gante *ag* arrogant.

arro'ganza [arro'gantsa] *sf* arrogance.

arro'gare *vt*: **~rsi il diritto di fare qc** to assume the right to do sth; **~rsi il merito di qc** to claim credit for sth.

arrossa'mento *sm* reddening.

arros'sare *vt* (*occhi, pelle*) to redden, make red; **~rsi** *vr* to go *o* become red.

arros'sire *vi* (*per vergogna, timidezza*) to blush; (*per gioia*) to flush, blush.

arros'tire *vt* to roast; (*pane*) to toast; (*ai ferri*) to grill.

ar'rosto *sm, ag inv* roast; **~ di manzo** roast beef.

arro'tare *vt* to sharpen; (*investire con un veicolo*) to run over.

arro'tino *sm* knife-grinder.

arroto'lare *vt* to roll up.

arroton'dare *vt* (*forma, oggetto*) to round; (*stipendio*) to add to; (*somma*) to round off.

arrovel'larsi *vr* (*anche*: **~ il cervello**) to rack one's brains.

arroven'tato, a *ag* red-hot.

arruf'fare *vt* to ruffle; (*fili*) to tangle; (*fig:*

questione) to confuse.

arruggi'nire [arrudd3i'nire] *vt* to rust; **~rsi** *vr* to rust; (*fig*) to become rusty.

arruola'mento *sm* (*MIL*) enlistment.

arruo'lare *vt* (*MIL*) to enlist; **~rsi** *vr* to enlist, join up.

arse'nale *sm* (*MIL*) arsenal; (*cantiere navale*) dockyard.

ar'senico *sm* arsenic.

'arsi *vb vedi* **ardere**.

'arso, a *pp di* **ardere** ♦ *ag* (*bruciato*) burnt; (*arido*) dry.

ar'sura *sf* (*calore opprimente*) burning heat; (*siccità*) drought.

art. *abbr* (= *articolo*) art.

'arte *sf* art; (*abilità*) skill; **a regola d'~** (*fig*) perfectly; **senz'~ né parte** penniless and out of a job; **~i figurative** visual arts.

arte'fatto, a *ag* (*stile, modi*) affected; (*cibo*) adulterated.

ar'tefice [ar'tefit∫e] *sm/f* craftsman/woman; (*autore*) author.

ar'teria *sf* artery.

arterioscle'rosi *sf* arteriosclerosis, hardening of the arteries.

arteri'oso, a *ag* arterial.

'artico, a, ci, che *ag* Arctic ♦ *sm*: **l'A~** the Arctic; **il Circolo polare ~** the Arctic Circle; **l'Oceano ~** the Arctic Ocean.

artico'lare *ag* (*ANAT*) of the joints, articular ♦ *vt* to articulate; (*suddividere*) to divide, split up; **~rsi** *vr*: **~rsi in** (*discorso, progetto*) to be divided into.

artico'lato, a *ag* (*linguaggio*) articulate; (*AUT*) articulated.

articolazi'one [artikolat'tsjone] *sf* (*ANAT, TECN*) joint; (*di voce, concetto*) articulation.

ar'ticolo *sm* article; **~ di fondo** (*STAMPA*) leader, leading article; **~i di marca** branded goods; **un bell'~** (*fig*) a real character.

'Artide *sm*: **l'~** the Arctic.

artifici'ale [artifi't∫ale] *ag* artificial.

artifici'ere [artifi't∫εre] *sm* (*MIL*) artificer; (: *per disinnescare bombe*) bomb-disposal expert.

arti'ficio [arti'fit∫o] *sm* (*espediente*) trick, artifice; (*ricerca di effetto*) artificiality.

artifici'oso, a [artifi't∫oso] *ag* cunning; (*non spontaneo*) affected.

artigia'nale [artid3a'nale] *ag* craft *cpd*.

artigia'nato [artid3a'nato] *sm* craftsmanship; craftsmen *pl*.

artigi'ano, a [arti'd3ano] *sm/f* craftsman/woman.

artigli'ere [artiλ'λεre] *sm* artilleryman.

artiglie'ria [artiλλe'ria] *sf* artillery.

ar'tiglio [ar'tiλλo] *sm* claw; (*di rapaci*) talon;

sfoderare gli ~i (*fig*) to show one's claws.
ar'tista, i, e *sm/f* artist; **un lavoro da ~** (*fig*) a professional piece of work.
ar'tistico, a, ci, che *ag* artistic.
'arto *sm* (*ANAT*) limb.
ar'trite *sf* (*MED*) arthritis.
ar'trosi *sf* osteoarthritis.
arzigogo'lato, a [ardzigogo'lato] *ag* tortuous.
ar'zillo, a [ar'dzillo] *ag* lively, sprightly.
a'scella [aʃ'ʃɛlla] *sf* (*ANAT*) armpit.
ascen'dente [aʃʃen'dɛnte] *sm* ancestor; (*fig*) ascendancy; (*ASTR*) ascendant.
a'scendere [aʃ'ʃendere] *vi*: ~ **al trono** to ascend the throne.
ascensi'one [aʃʃen'sjone] *sf* (*ALPINISMO*) ascent; (*REL*): **l'A~** the Ascension; **isola dell'A~** Ascension Island.
ascen'sore [aʃʃen'sore] *sm* lift.
a'scesa [aʃ'ʃesa] *sf* ascent; (*al trono*) accession; (*al potere*) rise.
a'scesi [aʃ'ʃɛzi] *sf* asceticism.
a'sceso, a [aʃ'ʃeso] *pp di* **ascendere**.
a'scesso [aʃ'ʃesso] *sm* (*MED*) abscess.
a'sceta, i [aʃ'ʃeta] *sm* ascetic.
'ascia, *pl* **'asce** ['aʃʃa] *sf* axe.
asciugaca'pelli [aʃʃugaka'pelli] *sm* hair dryer.
asciuga'mano [aʃʃuga'mano] *sm* towel.
asciu'gare [aʃʃu'gare] *vt* to dry; **~rsi** *vr* to dry o.s.; (*diventare asciutto*) to dry.
asciuga'trice [aʃʃuga'tritʃe] *sf* spin-dryer.
asciut'tezza [aʃʃut'tettsa] *sf* dryness; leanness; curtness.
asci'utto, a [aʃ'ʃutto] *ag* dry; (*fig: magro*) lean; (*: burbero*) curt ♦ *sm*: **restare all'~** (*fig*) to be left penniless; **restare a bocca ~a** (*fig*) to be disappointed.
asco'lano, a *ag* of (*o* from) Ascoli.
ascol'tare *vt* to listen to; **~ il consiglio di qn** to listen to *o* heed sb's advice.
ascolta'tore, 'trice *sm/f* listener.
as'colto *sm*: **essere** *o* **stare in ~** to be listening; **dare** *o* **prestare ~ (a)** to pay attention (to); **indice di ~** (*TV, RADIO*) audience rating.
AS. COM. *sigla f* = *Associazione Commercianti*.
as'critto, a *pp di* **ascrivere**.
as'crivere *vt* (*attribuire*): **~ qc a qn** to attribute sth to sb; **~ qc a merito di qn** to give sb credit for sth.
a'settico, a, ci, che *ag* aseptic.
asfal'tare *vt* to asphalt.
as'falto *sm* asphalt.
asfis'sia *sf* asphyxia, asphyxiation.
asfissi'ante *ag* (*gas*) asphyxiating; (*fig: calore, ambiente*) stifling, suffocating;

(*: persona*) tiresome.
asfissi'are *vt* to asphyxiate, suffocate; (*fig: opprimere*) to stifle; (*: infastidire*) to get on sb's nerves ♦ *vi* to suffocate, asphyxiate.
'Asia *sf*: **l'~** Asia.
asi'atico, a, ci, che *ag*, *sm/f* Asiatic, Asian.
a'silo *sm* refuge, sanctuary; **~ (d'infanzia)** nursery(-school); **~ nido** day nursery, crèche (*for children aged 0 to 3*); **~ politico** political asylum.
asim'metrico, a, ci, che *ag* asymmetric(al).
'asino *sm* donkey, ass; **la bellezza dell'~** (*fig: di ragazza*) the beauty of youth; **qui casca l'~**! there's the rub!
ASL [azl] *sigla f* (= *Azienda Sanitaria Locale*) local health centre.
'asma *sf* asthma.
as'matico, a, ci, che *ag*, *sm/f* asthmatic.
asoci'ale [aso'tʃale] *ag* antisocial.
'asola *sf* buttonhole.
as'parago, gi *sm* asparagus *no pl*.
as'pergere [as'pɛrdʒere] *vt*: **~ (di** *o* **con)** to sprinkle (with).
asperità *sf inv* roughness *no pl*; (*fig*) harshness *no pl*.
as'persi *etc vb vedi* **aspergere**.
as'perso, a *pp di* **aspergere**.
aspet'tare *vt* to wait for; (*anche COMM*) to await; (*aspettarsi*) to expect; (*essere in serbo: notizia, evento etc*) to be in store for, lie ahead of ♦ *vi* to wait; **~rsi qc** to expect sth; **~ un bambino** to be expecting (a baby); **questo non me l'aspettavo** I wasn't expecting this; **me l'aspettavo!** I thought as much!
aspetta'tiva *sf* expectation; **inferiore all'~** worse than expected; **essere/mettersi in ~** (*AMM*) to be on/take leave of absence.
as'petto *sm* (*apparenza*) aspect, appearance, look; (*punto di vista*) point of view; **di bell'~** good-looking.
aspi'rante *ag* (*attore etc*) aspiring ♦ *sm/f* candidate, applicant.
aspira'polvere *sm inv* vacuum cleaner.
aspi'rare *vt* (*respirare*) to breathe in, inhale; (*sog: apparecchi*) to suck (up) ♦ *vi*: **~ a** to aspire to.
aspira'tore *sm* extractor fan.
aspirazi'one [aspirat'tsjone] *sf* (*TECN*) suction; (*anelito*) aspiration.
aspi'rina *sf* aspirin.
aspor'tare *vt* (*anche MED*) to remove, take away.
as'prezza [as'prettsa] *sf* sourness, tartness; pungency; harshness; roughness; rugged nature.
'aspro, a *ag* (*sapore*) sour, tart; (*odore*)

acrid, pungent; (*voce, clima, fig*) harsh; (*superficie*) rough; (*paesaggio*) rugged.

Ass. *abbr* = **assicurazione; assicurata; assegno.**

assaggi'are [assad'dʒare] *vt* to taste.

assag'gini [assad'dʒini] *smpl* (*CUC*) *selection of first courses*.

as'saggio [as'saddʒo] *sm* tasting; (*piccola quantità*) taste; (*campione*) sample.

as'sai *av* (*molto*) a lot, much; (: *con ag*) very; (*a sufficienza*) enough ♦ *ag inv* (*quantità*) a lot of, much; (*numero*) a lot of, many; ~ **contento** very pleased.

as'salgo *etc vb vedi* **assalire**.

assa'lire *vt* to attack, assail.

assali'tore, 'trice *sm/f* attacker, assailant.

assal'tare *vt* (*MIL*) to storm; (*banca*) to raid; (*treno, diligenza*) to hold up.

as'salto *sm* attack, assault; **prendere d'~** (*fig: negozio, treno*) to storm; (: *personalità*) to besiege; **d'~** (*editoria, giornalista etc*) aggressive.

assapo'rare *vt* to savour (*BRIT*), savor (*US*).

assassi'nare *vt* to murder; (*POL*) to assassinate; (*fig*) to ruin.

assas'sinio *sm* murder; assassination.

assas'sino, a *ag* murderous ♦ *sm/f* murderer; assassin.

'asse *sm* (*TECN*) axle; (*MAT*) axis ♦ *sf* board; ~ **da stiro** ironing board.

assecon'dare *vt*: ~ **qn (in qc)** to go along with sb (in sth); ~ **i desideri di qn** to go along with sb's wishes; ~ **i capricci di qn** to give in to sb's whims.

assedi'are *vt* to besiege.

as'sedio *sm* siege.

asse'gnare [assep'ɲare] *vt* to assign, allot; (*premio*) to award.

assegna'tario [assepɲa'tarjo] *sm* (*DIR*) assignee; (*COMM*) recipient; **l'~ del premio** the person awarded the prize.

assegnazi'one [assepɲat'tsjone] *sf* (*di casa, somma*) allocation; (*di carica*) assignment; (*di premio, borsa di studio*) awarding.

as'segno [as'sepɲo] *sm* allowance; (*anche*: ~ **bancario**) cheque (*BRIT*), check (*US*); **contro ~** cash on delivery; ~ **circolare** bank draft; ~ **di invalidità** *o* **di malattia** injury *o* sickness benefit; ~ **post-datato** post-dated cheque; ~ **sbarrato** crossed cheque; ~ **non sbarrato** uncrossed cheque; ~ **di studio** study grant; "~ **non trasferibile**" "account payee only"; ~ **di viaggio** travel(l)er's cheque; ~ **a vuoto** dud cheque; ~**i alimentari** alimony *sg*; ~**i familiari** ≈ child benefit *sg*.

assem'blaggio [assem'bladdʒo] *sm* (*INDUSTRIA*) assembly.

assem'blare *vt* to assemble.

assem'blea *sf* assembly; (*raduno, adunanza*) meeting.

assembra'mento *sm* public gathering; **divieto di ~** ban on public meetings.

assen'nato, a *ag* sensible.

as'senso *sm* assent, consent.

assen'tarsi *vr* to go out.

as'sente *ag* absent; (*fig*) faraway, vacant ♦ *sm/f* absentee.

assente'ismo *sm* absenteeism.

assente'ista, i, e *sm/f* (*dal lavoro*) absentee.

assen'tire *vi*: ~ **(a)** to agree (to), assent (to).

as'senza [as'sɛntsa] *sf* absence.

asse'rire *vt* to maintain, assert.

asserragli'arsi [asserraʎ'ʎarsi] *vr*: ~ **(in)** to barricade o.s. (in).

asser'vire *vt* to enslave; (*fig: animo, passioni*) to subdue; ~**rsi** *vr*: ~**rsi (a)** to submit (to).

asserzi'one [asser'tsjone] *sf* assertion.

assesso'rato *sm* councillorship.

asses'sore *sm* councillor.

assesta'mento *sm* (*sistemazione*) arrangement; (*EDIL, GEO*) settlement.

asses'tare *vt* (*mettere in ordine*) to put in order, arrange; ~**rsi** *vr* to settle in; (*GEO*) to settle; ~ **un colpo a qn** to deal sb a blow.

asse'tato, a *ag* thirsty, parched.

as'setto *sm* order, arrangement; (*NAUT, AER*) trim; **in ~ di guerra** on a war footing; ~ **territoriale** country planning.

assicu'rare *vt* (*accertare*) to ensure; (*infondere certezza*) to assure; (*fermare, legare*) to make fast, secure; (*fare un contratto di assicurazione*) to insure; ~**rsi** *vr* (*accertarsi*): ~**rsi (di)** to make sure (of); (*contro il furto etc*): ~**rsi (contro)** to insure o.s. (against).

assicu'rato, a *ag* insured ♦ *sf* (*anche*: **lettera ~a**) registered letter.

assicura'tore, 'trice *ag* insurance *cpd* ♦ *sm/f* insurance agent; **società ~trice** insurance company.

assicurazi'one [assikurat'tsjone] *sf* assurance; insurance; ~ **multi-rischio** comprehensive insurance.

assidera'mento *sm* exposure.

asside'rare *vt* to freeze; ~**rsi** *vr* to freeze; **morire assiderato** to die of exposure.

as'siduo, a *ag* (*costante*) assiduous; (*regolare*) regular.

assi'eme *av* (*insieme*) together ♦ *prep*: ~ **a** (together) with.

assil'lante *ag* (*dubbio, pensiero*) nagging; (*creditore*) pestering.

assil'lare *vt* to pester, torment.
as'sillo *sm* (*fig*) worrying thought.
assimi'lare *vt* to assimilate.
assimilazi'one [assimilat'tsjone] *sf* assimilation.
assi'oma, i *sm* axiom.
assio'matico, a, ci, che *ag* axiomatic.
as'sise *sfpl* (*DIR*) assizes (*BRIT*); **corte** *f* **d'~** court of assizes, ≈ crown court (*BRIT*); *vedi anche* **Corte d'Assise**.
assis'tente *sm/f* assistant; **~ sociale** social worker; **~ universitario** (assistant) lecturer; **~ di volo** (*AER*) steward/ stewardess.
assis'tenza [assis'tɛntsa] *sf* assistance; **~ legale** legal aid; **~ ospedaliera** free hospital treatment; **~ sanitaria** health service; **~ sociale** welfare services *pl*.
assistenzi'ale [assisten'tsjale] *ag* (*ente, organizzazione*) welfare *cpd*; (*opera*) charitable.
assistenzia'lismo [assistentsja'lizmo] *sm* (*peg*) excessive state aid.
as'sistere *vt* (*aiutare*) to assist, help; (*curare*) to treat ♦ *vi*: **~ (a qc)** (*essere presente*) to be present (at sth), attend (sth).
assis'tito, a *pp di* **assistere**.
'asso *sm* ace; **piantare qn in ~** to leave sb in the lurch.
associ'are [asso'tʃare] *vt* to associate; (*rendere partecipe*): **~ qn a** (*affari*) to take sb into partnership in; (*partito*) to make sb a member of; **~rsi** *vr* to enter into partnership; **~rsi a** to become a member of, join; (*dolori, gioie*) to share in; **~ qn alle carceri** to take sb to prison.
associazi'one [assotʃat'tsjone] *sf* association; **~ di categoria** trade association; **~ a o per delinquere** (*DIR*) criminal association; **A~ Europea di Libero Scambio** European Free Trade Association, EFTA; **~ in partecipazione** (*COMM*) joint venture.
asso'dare *vt* (*muro, posizione*) to strengthen; (*fatti, verità*) to ascertain.
asso'dato, a *ag* well-founded.
assogget'tare [assoddʒet'tare] *vt* to subject, subjugate; **~rsi** *vr*: **~rsi a** to submit to.
asso'lato, a *ag* sunny.
assol'dare *vt* to recruit.
as'solsi *etc vb vedi* **assolvere**.
as'solto, a *pp di* **assolvere**.
assoluta'mente *av* absolutely.
asso'luto, a *ag* absolute.
assoluzi'one [assolut'tsjone] *sf* (*DIR*) acquittal; (*REL*) absolution.
as'solvere *vt* (*DIR*) to acquit; (*REL*) to

absolve; (*adempiere*) to carry out, perform.
assomigli'are [assomiʎ'ʎare] *vi*: **~ a** to resemble, look like.
asson'nato, a *ag* sleepy.
asso'pirsi *vr* to doze off.
assor'bente *ag* absorbent ♦ *sm*: **~ igienico** sanitary towel; **~ interno** tampon.
assor'bire *vt* to absorb; (*fig: far proprio*) to assimilate.
assor'dante *ag* (*rumore, musica*) deafening.
assor'dare *vt* to deafen.
assorti'mento *sm* assortment.
assor'tire *vt* (*disporre*) to arrange.
assor'tito, a *ag* assorted; (*colori*) matched, matching.
as'sorto, a *ag* absorbed, engrossed.
assottigli'are [assotti'ʎ'ʎare] *vt* to make thin, thin; (*aguzzare*) to sharpen; (*ridurre*) to reduce; **~rsi** *vr* to grow thin; (*fig: ridursi*) to be reduced.
assue'fare *vt* to accustom; **~rsi** *vr*: **~rsi a** to get used to, accustom o.s. to.
assue'fatto, a *pp di* **assuefare**.
assuefazi'one [assuefat'tsjone] *sf* (*MED*) addiction.
as'sumere *vt* (*impiegato*) to take on, engage; (*responsabilità*) to assume, take upon o.s.; (*contegno, espressione*) to assume, put on; (*droga*) to consume.
as'sunsi *etc vb vedi* **assumere**.
as'sunto, a *pp di* **assumere** ♦ *sm* (*tesi*) proposition.
assunzi'one [assun'tsjone] *sf* (*di impiegati*) employment, engagement; (*REL*): **l'A~** the Assumption.
assurdità *sf inv* absurdity; **dire delle ~** to talk nonsense.
as'surdo, a *ag* absurd.
'asta *sf* pole; (*modo di vendita*) auction.
as'tante *sm* bystander.
astante'ria *sf* casualty department.
as'temio, a *ag* teetotal ♦ *sm/f* teetotaller.
aste'nersi *vr*: **~ (da)** to abstain (from), refrain (from); (*POL*) to abstain (from).
astensi'one *sf* abstention.
astensio'nista, i, e *sm/f* (*POL*) abstentionist.
aste'risco, schi *sm* asterisk.
aste'roide *sm* asteroid.
'astice ['astitʃe] *sm* lobster.
astigi'ano, a [asti'dʒano] *ag* of (*o* from) Asti.
astig'matico, a, ci, che *ag* astigmatic.
asti'nenza [asti'nɛntsa] *sf* abstinence; **essere in crisi di ~** to suffer from withdrawal symptoms.
'astio *sm* rancour, resentment.

asti'oso, a *ag* resentful.

astrat'tismo *sm* (*ARTE*) abstract art.

as'tratto, a *ag* abstract.

astrin'gente [astrin'dʒɛnte] *ag, sm* astringent.

'astro *sm* star.

astrolo'gia [astrolo'dʒia] *sf* astrology.

astro'logico, a, ci, che [astro'lɔdʒiko] *ag* astrological.

as'trologo, a, ghi, ghe *sm/f* astrologer.

astro'nauta, i, e *sm/f* astronaut.

astro'nautica *sf* astronautics *sg*.

astro'nave *sf* space ship.

astrono'mia *sf* astronomy.

astro'nomico, a, ci, che *ag* astronomic(al).

as'tronomo *sm* astronomer.

as'truso, a *ag* (*discorso, ragionamento*) abstruse.

as'tuccio [as'tuttʃo] *sm* case, box, holder.

as'tuto, a *ag* astute, cunning, shrewd.

as'tuzia [as'tuttsja] *sf* astuteness, shrewdness; (*azione*) trick.

AT *sigla* = *Asti*.

a'tavico, a, ci, che *ag* atavistic.

ate'ismo *sm* atheism.

atelier [atə'lje] *sm inv* (*laboratorio*) workshop; (*studio*) studio; (*sartoria*) fashion house.

A'tene *sf* Athens.

ate'neo *sm* university.

ateni'ese *ag, sm/f* Athenian.

'ateo, a *ag, sm/f* atheist.

a'tipico, a, ci, che *ag* atypical.

at'lante *sm* atlas; **i Monti dell'A~** the Atlas Mountains.

at'lantico, a, ci, che *ag* Atlantic ♦ *sm*: **l'A~**, **l'Oceano A~** the Atlantic, the Atlantic Ocean.

at'leta, i, e *sm/f* athlete.

at'letica *sf* athletics *sg*; **~ leggera** track and field events *pl*; **~ pesante** weightlifting and wrestling.

ATM *sigla f* = *Azienda Tranviaria Municipale*.

atmos'fera *sf* atmosphere.

atmos'ferico, a, ci, che *ag* atmospheric.

a'tollo *sm* atoll.

a'tomico, a, ci, che *ag* atomic; (*nucleare*) atomic, atom *cpd*, nuclear.

atomizza'tore [atomiddza'tore] *sm* (*di acqua, lacca*) spray; (*di profumo*) atomizer.

'atomo *sm* atom.

'atono, a *ag* (*FONETICA*) unstressed.

'atrio *sm* entrance hall, lobby.

a'troce [a'trotʃe] *ag* (*che provoca orrore*) dreadful; (*terribile*) atrocious.

atrocità [atrotʃi'ta] *sf inv* atrocity.

atro'fia *sf* atrophy.

attacca'brighe [attakka'brige] *sm/f inv* quarrelsome person.

attacca'mento *sm* (*fig*) attachment, affection.

attacca'panni *sm* hook, peg; (*mobile*) hall stand.

attac'care *vt* (*unire*) to attach; (*cucendo*) to sew on; (*far aderire*) to stick (on); (*appendere*) to hang (up); (*assalire: anche fig*) to attack; (*iniziare*) to begin, start; (*fig: contagiare*) to pass on ♦ *vi* to stick, adhere; **~rsi** *vr* to stick, adhere; (*trasmettersi per contagio*) to be contagious; (*afferrarsi*): **~rsi (a)** to cling (to); (*fig: affezionarsi*): **~rsi (a)** to become attached (to); **~ discorso** to start a conversation; **con me non attacca!** that won't work with me!

attacca'ticcio, a, ci, ce [attakka'tittʃo] *ag* sticky.

attacca'tura *sf* (*di manica*) join; **~ (dei capelli)** hairline.

at'tacco, chi *sm* (*azione offensiva: anche fig*) attack; (*MED*) attack, fit; (*SCI*) binding; (*ELETTR*) socket.

attanagli'are [attanaʎ'ʎare] *vt* (*anche fig*) to grip.

attar'darsi *vr*: **~ a fare qc** (*fermarsi*) to stop to do sth; (*stare più a lungo*) to stay behind to do sth.

attec'chire [attek'kire] *vi* (*pianta*) to take root; (*fig*) to catch on.

atteggia'mento [atteddʒa'mento] *sm* attitude.

atteggi'arsi [atted'dʒarsi] *vr*: **~ a** to pose as.

attem'pato, a *ag* elderly.

atten'dente *sm* (*MIL*) orderly, batman.

at'tendere *vt* to wait for, await ♦ *vi*: **~ a** to attend to.

atten'dibile *ag* (*scusa, storia*) credible; (*fonte, testimone, notizia*) reliable; (*persona*) trustworthy.

atte'nersi *vr*: **~ a** to keep o stick to.

atten'tare *vi*: **~ a** to make an attempt on.

atten'tato *sm* attack; **~ alla vita di qn** attempt on sb's life.

at'tento, a *ag* attentive; (*accurato*) careful, thorough ♦ *escl* be careful!; **stare ~ a qc** to pay attention to sth; **~i!** (*MIL*) attention!; **~i al cane** beware of the dog.

attenu'ante *sf* (*DIR*) extenuating circumstance.

attenu'are *vt* to alleviate, ease; (*diminuire*) to reduce; **~rsi** *vr* to ease, abate.

attenuazi'one [attenuat'tsjone] *sf* alleviation; easing; reduction.

attenzi'one [atten'tsjone] *sf* attention ♦ *escl* watch out!, be careful!; **coprire qn di ~i** to lavish attention on sb.

atter'raggio [atter'raddʒo] *sm* landing; ~ **di fortuna** emergency landing.

atter'rare *vt* to bring down ♦ *vi* to land.

atter'rire *vt* to terrify.

at'tesa *sf vedi* **atteso**.

at'tesi *etc vb vedi* **attendere**.

at'teso, a *pp di* **attendere** ♦ *sf* waiting; (*tempo trascorso aspettando*) wait; **essere in** ~**a di qc** to be waiting for sth; **in** ~**a di una vostra risposta** (*COMM*) awaiting your reply; **restiamo in** ~**a di Vostre ulteriori notizie** (*COMM*) we look forward to hearing (further) from you.

attes'tare *vt*: ~ **qc/che** to testify to sth/(to the fact) that.

attes'tato *sm* certificate.

attestazi'one [attestat'tsjone] *sf* (*certificato*) certificate; (*dichiarazione*) statement.

'attico, ci *sm* attic.

at'tiguo, a *ag* adjacent, adjoining.

attil'lato, a *ag* (*vestito*) close-fitting, tight; (*persona*) dressed up.

'attimo *sm* moment; **in un** ~ in a moment.

atti'nente *ag*: ~ **a** relating to, concerning.

atti'nenza [atti'nentsa] *sf* connection.

at'tingere [at'tindʒere] *vt*: ~ **a** *o* **da** (*acqua*) to draw from; (*denaro, notizie*) to obtain from.

at'tinto, a *pp di* **attingere**.

atti'rare *vt* to attract; ~**rsi delle critiche** to incur criticism.

atti'tudine *sf* (*disposizione*) aptitude; (*atteggiamento*) attitude.

atti'vare *vt* to activate; (*far funzionare*) to set going, start.

atti'vista, i, e *sm/f* activist.

attività *sf inv* activity; (*COMM*) assets *pl*; ~ **liquide** (*COMM*) liquid assets.

at'tivo, a *ag* active; (*COMM*) profit-making ♦ *sm* (*COMM*) assets *pl*; **in** ~ in credit; **chiudere in** ~ to show a profit; **avere qc al proprio** ~ (*fig*) to have sth to one's credit.

attiz'zare [attit'tsare] *vt* (*fuoco*) to poke; (*fig*) to stir up.

attizza'toio [attittsa'tojo] *sm* poker.

'atto, a *ag*: ~ **a** fit for, capable of ♦ *sm* act; (*azione, gesto*) action, act, deed; (*DIR: documento*) deed, document; ~**i** *smpl* (*di congressi etc*) proceedings; **essere in** ~ to be under way; **mettere in** ~ to put into action; **fare** ~ **di fare qc** to make as if to do sth; **all'** ~ **pratico** in practice; **dare** ~ **a qn di qc** to give sb credit for sth; ~ **di nascita/morte** birth/death certificate; ~ **di proprietà** title deed; ~ **pubblico** official document; ~ **di vendita** bill of sale; ~**i osceni (in luogo pubblico)** (*DIR*) indecent exposure; ~**i verbali** transactions.

at'tonito, a *ag* dumbfounded, astonished.

attorcigli'are [attortʃiʎ'ʎare] *vt*, ~**rsi** *vr* to twist.

at'tore, 'trice *sm/f* actor/actress.

attorni'are *vt* (*circondare*) to surround; ~**rsi** *vr*: ~**rsi di** to surround o.s. with.

at'torno *av*, ~ **a** *prep* round, around, about.

attrac'care *vt, vi* (*NAUT*) to dock, berth.

at'tracco, chi *sm* (*NAUT: manovra*) docking, berthing; (*luogo*) berth.

at'trae *etc vb vedi* **attrarre**.

attra'ente *ag* attractive.

at'traggo *etc vb vedi* **attrarre**.

at'trarre *vt* to attract.

at'trassi *etc vb vedi* **attrarre**.

attrat'tiva *sf* attraction, charm.

at'tratto, a *pp di* **attrarre**.

attraversa'mento *sm* crossing; ~ **pedonale** pedestrian crossing.

attraver'sare *vt* to cross; (*città, bosco, fig: periodo*) to go through; (*sog: fiume*) to run through.

attra'verso *prep* through; (*da una parte all'altra*) across.

attrazi'one [attrat'tsjone] *sf* attraction.

attrez'zare [attret'tsare] *vt* to equip; (*NAUT*) to rig.

attrezza'tura [attrettsa'tura] *sf* equipment *no pl*; rigging; ~**e per uffici** office equipment.

at'trezzo [at'trettso] *sm* tool, instrument; (*SPORT*) piece of equipment.

attribu'ire *vt*: ~ **qc a qn** (*assegnare*) to give *o* award sth to sb; (*quadro etc*) to attribute sth to sb.

attri'buto *sm* attribute.

at'trice [at'tritʃe] *sf vedi* **attore**.

at'trito *sm* (*anche fig*) friction.

attu'abile *ag* feasible.

attuabilità *sf* feasibility.

attu'ale *ag* (*presente*) present; (*di attualità*) topical; (*che è in atto*) actual.

attualità *sf inv* topicality; (*avvenimento*) current event; **notizie d'**~ (*TV*) the news *sg*.

attualiz'zare [attualid'dzare] *vt* to update, bring up to date.

attual'mente *av* at the moment.

attu'are *vt* to carry out; ~**rsi** *vr* to be realized.

attuazi'one [attuat'tsjone] *sf* carrying out.

attu'tire *vt* to deaden, reduce; ~**rsi** *vr* to die down.

au'dace [au'datʃe] *ag* audacious, daring; (*provocante*) provocative; (*sfacciato*) impudent.

au'dacia [au'datʃa] *sf* audacity, daring; boldness; provocativeness; impudence.

'audio *sm* (*TV, RADIO, CINE*) sound.

audiocas'setta *sf* (audio) cassette.

audio'leso, a *sm/f* person who is hard of hearing.

audiovi'sivo, a *ag* audiovisual.

audi'torio *sm*, **audi'torium** *sm inv* auditorium.

audizi'one [audit'tsjone] *sf* hearing; (*MUS*) audition.

'auge ['audʒe] *sf* (*della gloria, carriera*) height, peak; **essere in** ~ to be at the top.

augu'rale *ag*: **messaggio** ~ greeting; **biglietto** ~ greetings card.

augu'rare *vt* to wish; **~rsi qc** to hope for sth.

au'gurio *sm* (*presagio*) omen; (*voto di benessere etc*) (good) wish; **essere di buon/cattivo** ~ to be of good omen/be ominous; **fare gli ~i a qn** to give sb one's best wishes; **tanti ~i!** all the best!

'aula *sf* (*scolastica*) classroom; (*universitaria*) lecture theatre; (*di edificio pubblico*) hall; ~ **magna** main hall; ~ **del tribunale** courtroom.

aumen'tare *vt, vi* to increase; ~ **di peso** (*persona*) to put on weight; **la produzione è aumentata del 50%** production has increased by 50%.

au'mento *sm* increase.

'aureo, a *ag* (*di oro*) gold *cpd*; (*fig: colore, periodo*) golden.

au'reola *sf* halo.

au'rora *sf* dawn.

ausili'are *ag, sm, sm/f* auxiliary.

au'silio *sm* aid.

auspi'cabile *ag* desirable.

auspi'care *vt* to call for.

aus'picio [aus'pitʃo] *sm* omen; (*protezione*) patronage; **sotto gli ~i di** under the auspices of; **è di buon** ~ it augurs well.

austerità *sf inv* austerity.

aus'tero, a *ag* austere.

aus'trale *ag* southern.

Aus'tralia *sf*: **l'~** Australia.

australi'ano, a *ag, sm/f* Australian.

'Austria *sf*: **l'~** Austria.

aus'triaco, a, ci, che *ag, sm/f* Austrian.

au'tarchico, a, ci, che [au'tarkiko] *ag* (*sistema*) self-sufficient, autarkic; (*prodotto*) home *cpd*, home-produced.

'aut 'aut *sm inv* ultimatum.

autenti'care *vt* to authenticate.

autenticità [autentitʃi'ta] *sf* authenticity.

au'tentico, a, ci, che *ag* (*quadro, firma*) authentic, genuine; (*fatto*) true, genuine.

au'tista, i *sm* driver; (*personale*) chauffeur.

'auto *sf inv* car; ~ **blu** official car.

autoabbron'zante [autoabbron'dzante] *ag*

self-tanning.

autoade'sivo, a *ag* self-adhesive ♦ *sm* sticker.

autoartico'lato *sm* articulated lorry (*BRIT*), semi (trailer) (*US*).

autobiogra'fia *sf* autobiography.

autobio'grafico, a, ci, che *ag* autobiographic(al).

auto'blinda *sf* armoured (*BRIT*) *o* armored (*US*) car.

auto'bomba *sf inv* car carrying a bomb; **l'~ si trovava a pochi metri** the car bomb was a few metres away.

auto'botte *sf* tanker.

'autobus *sm inv* bus.

autocari'cabile *ag*: **scheda** ~ top-up card.

auto'carro *sm* lorry (*BRIT*), truck.

autocertificazi'one [autotʃertifikat'tsjone] *sf* self-declaration.

autocis'terna [autotʃis'tɛrna] *sf* tanker.

autoco'lonna *sf* convoy.

autocon'trollo *sm* self-control.

autocopia'tivo, a *ag*: **carta** ~a carbonless paper.

autocorri'era *sf* coach, bus.

auto'cratico, a, ci, che *ag* autocratic.

auto'critica, che *sf* self-criticism.

au'toctono, a *ag, sm/f* native.

autodemolizi'one [autodemolit'tsjone] *sf* breaker's yard (*BRIT*).

autodi'datta, i, e *sm/f* autodidact, self-taught person.

autodi'fesa *sf* self-defence.

autoferrotranvi'ario, a *ag* public transport *cpd*.

autogesti'one [autodʒes'tjone] *sf* worker management.

autoges'tito, a [autodʒes'tito] *ag* under worker management.

au'tografo, a *ag, sm* autograph.

auto'grill *sm inv* motorway café (*BRIT*), roadside restaurant (*US*).

autoim'mune *ag* autoimmune.

autolesio'nismo *sm* (fig) self-destruction.

auto'linea *sf* bus route.

au'toma, i *sm* automaton.

auto'matico, a, ci, che *ag* automatic ♦ *sm* (*bottone*) snap fastener; (*fucile*) automatic; **selezione** ~a (*TEL*) direct dialling.

automazi'one [automat'tsjone] *sf*: ~ **delle procedure d'ufficio** office automation.

automedicazi'one [automedikat'tsjone] *sf* (*medicine, farmaci*): **medicinale di** ~ self-medication.

auto'mezzo [auto'mɛddzo] *sm* motor vehicle.

auto'mobile *sf* (motor) car; ~ **da corsa** racing car (*BRIT*), race car (*US*).

automobi'lismo *sm* (*gen*) motoring; (*SPORT*) motor racing.
automobi'lista, i, e *smf* motorist.
automobi'listico, a, ci, che *ag* car *cpd* (*BRIT*), automobile *cpd* (*US*); (*sport*) motor *cpd*.
autono'leggio [autono'leddʒo] *sm* car hire (*BRIT*), car rental.
autono'mia *sf* autonomy; (*di volo*) range.
au'tonomo, a *ag* autonomous; (*sindacato, pensiero*) independent.
auto'parco, chi *sm* (*parcheggio*) car park (*BRIT*), parking lot (*US*); (*insieme di automezzi*) transport fleet.
auto'pompa *sf* fire engine.
autop'sia *sf* post-mortem (examination), autopsy.
auto'radio *sf inv* (*apparecchio*) car radio; (*autoveicolo*) radio car.
au'tore, 'trice *sm/f* author; **l'~ del furto** the person who committed the robbery; **diritti d'~** copyright *sg*; (*compenso*) royalties.
autoregolamentazi'one [autoregolamentat'tsjone] *sf* self-regulation.
auto'revole *ag* authoritative; (*persona*) influential.
autori'messa *sf* garage.
autorità *sf inv* authority.
autori'tratto *sm* self-portrait.
autoriz'zare [autorid'dzare] *vt* to authorize, give permission for.
autorizzazi'one [autoriddzat'tsjone] *sf* authorization; **~ a procedere** (*DIR*) authorization to proceed.
autos'catto *sm* (*FOT*) timer.
autos'contro *sm* dodgem car (*BRIT*), bumper car (*US*).
autoscu'ola *sf* driving school.
autosno'dato *sm* articulated vehicle.
autos'top *sm* hitchhiking.
autostop'pista, i, e *sm/f* hitchhiker.
autos'trada *sf* motorway (*BRIT*), highway (*US*); **~ informatica** information superhighway.
autosuffici'ente [autosuffi't ʃɛnte] *ag* self-sufficient.
autosuffici'enza [autosuffi't ʃɛntsa] *sf* self-sufficiency.
auto'treno *sm* articulated lorry (*BRIT*), semi (trailer) (*US*).
autove'icolo *sm* motor vehicle.
auto'velox ® *sm inv* (police) speed camera.
autovet'tura *sf* (motor) car.
autun'nale *ag* (*di autunno*) autumn *cpd*; (*da autunno*) autumnal.
au'tunno *sm* autumn.
AV *sigla* = Avellino.

aval'lare *vt* (*FINANZA*) to guarantee; (*fig: sostenere*) to back; (: *confermare*) to confirm.
a'vallo *sm* (*FINANZA*) guarantee.
avam'braccio, *pl(f)* **-cia** [avam'brattʃo] *sm* forearm.
avam'posto *sm* (*MIL*) outpost.
A'vana *sf*: **l'~** Havana.
a'vana *sm inv* (*sigaro*) Havana (cigar); (*colore*) Havana brown.
avangu'ardia *sf* vanguard; (*ARTE*) avant-garde.
avansco'perta *sf* (*MIL*) reconnaissance; **andare in ~** to reconnoitre.
a'vanti *av* (*stato in luogo*) in front; (*moto: andare, venire*) forward; (*tempo: prima*) before ♦ *prep* (*luogo*): **~ a** before, in front of; (*tempo*): **~ Cristo** before Christ ♦ *escl* (*entrate*) come (*o* go) in!; (*MIL*) forward!; (*coraggio*) come on! ♦ *sm inv* (*SPORT*) forward; **il giorno ~** the day before; **~ e indietro** backwards and forwards; **andare ~** to go forward; (*continuare*) to go on; (*precedere*) to go (on) ahead; (*orologio*) to be fast; **essere ~ negli studi** to be well advanced in one's studies; **mandare ~ la famiglia** to provide for one's family; **mandare ~ un'azienda** to run a business; **~ il prossimo!** next please!
avan'treno *sm* (*AUT*) front chassis.
avanza'mento [avantsa'mento] *sm* (*gen*) advance; (*fig*) progress; promotion.
avan'zare [avan'tsare] *vt* (*spostare in avanti*) to move forward, advance; (*domanda*) to put forward; (*promuovere*) to promote; (*essere creditore*): **~ qc da qn** to be owed sth by sb ♦ *vi* (*andare avanti*) to move forward, advance; (*fig: progredire*) to make progress; (*essere d'avanzo*) to be left, remain; **basta e avanza** that's more than enough.
avan'zato, a [avan'tsato] *ag* (*teoria, tecnica*) advanced ♦ *sf* (*MIL*) advance; **in età ~a** advanced in years, up in years.
a'vanzo [a'vantso] *sm* (*residuo*) remains *pl*, left-overs *pl*; (*MAT*) remainder; (*COMM*) surplus; (*eccedenza di bilancio*) profit carried forward; **averne d'~ di qc** to have more than enough of sth; **~ di cassa** cash in hand; **~ di galera** (*fig*) jailbird.
ava'ria *sf* (*guasto*) damage; (: *meccanico*) breakdown.
avari'ato, a *ag* (*merce*) damaged; (*cibo*) off.
ava'rizia [ava'rittsja] *sf* avarice; **crepi l'~!** to hang with the expense!
a'varo, a *ag* avaricious, miserly ♦ *sm* miser.
a'vena *sf* oats *pl*.

================= PAROLA CHIAVE

a'vere *sm* (*COMM*) credit; **gli ~i** (*ricchezze*) wealth *sg*, possessions
♦ *vt* **1** (*possedere*) to have; **ha due bambini/una bella casa** she has (got) two children/a lovely house; **ha i capelli lunghi** he has (got) long hair; **non ho da mangiare/bere** I've (got) nothing to eat/drink, I don't have anything to eat/drink
2 (*indossare*) to wear, have on; **aveva una maglietta rossa** he was wearing *o* he had on a red T-shirt; **ha gli occhiali** he wears *o* has glasses
3 (*ricevere*) to get; **hai avuto l'assegno?** did you get *o* have you had the cheque?
4 (*età, dimensione*) to be; **ha 9 anni** he is 9 (years old); **la stanza ha 3 metri di lunghezza** the room is 3 metres in length; *vedi* **fame; paura; sonno** *etc*
5 (*tempo*): **quanti ne abbiamo oggi?** what's the date today?; **ne hai per molto?** will you be long?
6 (*fraseologia*): **avercela con qn** to be angry with sb; **cos'hai?** what's wrong *o* what's the matter (with you)?; **non ha niente a che vedere** *o* **fare con me** it's got nothing to do with me
♦ *vb aus* **1** to have; **aver bevuto/mangiato** to have drunk/eaten; **l'ho già visto** I have seen it already; **l'ho visto ieri** I saw it yesterday; **ci ha creduto?** did he believe it?
2 (+ *da* + *infinito*): **~ da fare qc** to have to do sth; **non ho niente da dire** I have nothing to say; **non hai che da chiederlo** you only have to ask him.

avia'tore, 'trice *sm/f* aviator, pilot.
aviazi'one [avjat'tsjone] *sf* aviation; (*MIL*) air force; **~ civile** civil aviation.
avicol'tura *sf* bird breeding; (*di pollame*) poultry farming.
avidità *sf* eagerness; greed.
'avido, a *ag* eager; (*peg*) greedy.
avi'ere *sm* (*MIL*) airman.
avitami'nosi *sf* vitamin deficiency.
'avo *sm* (*antenato*) ancestor; **i nostri ~i** our ancestors.
avo'cado *sm* avocado.
a'vorio *sm* ivory.
a'vulso, a *ag*: **parole ~e dal contesto** words out of context; **~ dalla società** (*fig*) cut off from society.
Avv. *abbr* = **avvocato.**
avva'lersi *vr*: **~ di** to avail o.s. of.
avvalla'mento *sm* sinking *no pl*; (*effetto*) depression.

avvalo'rare *vt* to confirm.
avvantaggi'are [avvantad'dʒare] *vt* to favour (*BRIT*), favor (*US*); **~rsi** *vr* (*trarre vantaggio*): **~rsi di** to take advantage of; (*prevalere*): **~rsi negli affari/sui concorrenti** to get ahead in business/of one's competitors.
avve'dersi *vr*: **~ di qn/qc** to notice sb/sth.
avve'duto, a *ag* (*accorto*) prudent; (*scaltro*) astute.
avvelena'mento *sm* poisoning.
avvele'nare *vt* to poison.
avve'nente *ag* attractive, charming.
avve'nenza [avve'nɛntsa] *sf* good looks *pl*.
av'vengo *etc vb vedi* **avvenire.**
avveni'mento *sm* event.
avve'nire *vi, vb impers* to happen, occur ♦ *sm* future.
av'venni *etc vb vedi* **avvenire.**
avven'tarsi *vr*: **~ su** *o* **contro qn/qc** to hurl o.s. *o* rush at sb/sth.
avven'tato, a *ag* rash, reckless.
avven'tizio, a [avven'tittsjo] *ag* (*impiegato*) temporary; (*guadagno*) casual.
av'vento *sm* advent, coming; (*REL*): **l'A~** Advent.
avven'tore *sm* customer.
avven'tura *sf* adventure; (*amorosa*) affair; **avere spirito d'~** to be adventurous.
avventu'rarsi *vr* to venture.
avventuri'ero, a *sm/f* adventurer/adventuress.
avventu'roso, a *ag* adventurous.
avve'nuto, a *pp di* **avvenire.**
avve'rarsi *vr* to come true.
av'verbio *sm* adverb.
avverrò *etc vb vedi* **avvenire.**
avver'sare *vt* to oppose.
avver'sario, a *ag* opposing ♦ *sm* opponent, adversary.
avversi'one *sf* aversion.
avversità *sf inv* adversity, misfortune.
av'verso, a *ag* (*contrario*) contrary; (*sfavorevole*) unfavourable (*BRIT*), unfavorable (*US*).
avver'tenza [avver'tɛntsa] *sf* (*ammonimento*) warning; (*cautela*) care; (*premessa*) foreword; **~e** *sfpl* (*istruzioni per l'uso*) instructions.
avverti'mento *sm* warning.
avver'tire *vt* (*avvisare*) to warn; (*rendere consapevole*) to inform, notify; (*percepire*) to feel.
av'vezzo, a [av'vettso] *ag*: **~ a** used to.
avvia'mento *sm* (*atto*) starting; (*effetto*) start; (*AUT*) starting; (: *dispositivo*) starter; (*COMM*) goodwill.
avvi'are *vt* (*mettere sul cammino*) to direct;

(*impresa, trattative*) to begin, start; (*motore*) to start; ~**rsi** *vr* to set off, set out.

avvicenda'mento [avvitʃenda'mento] *sm* alternation; (*AGR*) rotation; **c'è molto** ~ **di personale** there is a high turnover of staff.

avvicen'dare [avvitʃen'dare] *vt*, ~**rsi** *vr* to alternate.

avvicina'mento [avvitʃina'mento] *sm* approach.

avvici'nare [avvitʃi'nare] *vt* to bring near; (*trattare con: persona*) to approach; ~**rsi** *vr*: ~**rsi (a qn/qc)** to approach (sb/sth), draw near (to sb/sth); (*somigliare*) to be similar (to sb/sth), be close (to sb/sth).

avvi'lente *ag* (*umiliante*) humiliating; (*scoraggiante*) discouraging, disheartening.

avvili'mento *sm* humiliation; disgrace; discouragement.

avvi'lire *vt* (*umiliare*) to humiliate; (*degradare*) to disgrace; (*scoraggiare*) to dishearten, discourage; ~**rsi** *vr* (*abbattersi*) to lose heart.

avvilup'pare *vt* (*avvolgere*) to wrap up; (*ingarbugliare*) to entangle.

avvinaz'zato, a [avvinat'tsato] *ag* drunk.

avvin'cente [avvin'tʃɛnte] *ag* (*film, racconto*) enthralling.

av'vincere [av'vintʃere] *vt* to charm, enthral.

avvinghi'are [avvin'gjare] *vt* to clasp; ~**rsi** *vr*: ~**rsi a** to cling to.

av'vinsi *etc vb vedi* **avvincere.**

av'vinto, a *pp di* **avvincere.**

av'vio *sm* start, beginning; **dare l'**~ **a qc** to start sth off; **prendere l'**~ to get going, get under way.

avvi'saglia [avvi'zaʎʎa] *sf* (*sintomo: di temporale etc*) sign; (*di malattia*) manifestation, sign, symptom; (*scaramuccia*) skirmish.

avvi'sare *vt* (*far sapere*) to inform; (*mettere in guardia*) to warn.

avvisa'tore *sm* (*apparecchio d'allarme*) alarm; ~ **acustico** horn; ~ **d'incendio** fire alarm.

av'viso *sm* warning; (*annuncio*) announcement; (*affisso*) notice; (*inserzione pubblicitaria*) advertisement; **a mio** ~ **in** my opinion; **mettere qn sull'**~ to put sb on their guard; **fino a nuovo** ~ until further notice; ~ **di chiamata** (*servizio*) call waiting; (*segnale*) call waiting signal; ~ **di consegna/spedizione** (*COMM*) delivery/ consignment note; ~ **di garanzia** (*DIR*) notification (*of impending investigation and of the right to name a defence laywer*); ~ **di pagamento** (*COMM*) payment advice.

avvista'mento *sm* sighting.

avvis'tare *vt* to sight.

avvi'tare *vt* to screw down (*o* in).

avviz'zire [avvit'tsire] *vi* to wither.

avvo'cato, 'essa *sm/f* (*DIR*) barrister (*BRIT*), lawyer; (*fig*) defender, advocate; ~ **del diavolo: fare l'**~ **del diavolo** to play devil's advocate; ~ **difensore** counsel for the defence; ~ **di parte civile** counsel for the plaintiff.

av'volgere [av'vɔldʒere] *vt* to roll up; (*bobina*) to wind up; (*avviluppare*) to wrap up; ~**rsi** *vr* (*avvilupparsi*) to wrap o.s. up.

avvol'gibile [avvol'dʒibile] *sm* roller blind (*BRIT*), blind.

avvolgi'mento [avvoldʒi'mento] *sm* winding.

av'volsi *etc vb vedi* **avvolgere.**

av'volto, a *pp di* **avvolgere.**

avvol'toio *sm* vulture.

aza'lea [addza'lɛa] *sf* azalea.

Azerbaigi'an [addzɛrbai'dʒan] *sm* Azerbaijan.

azerbaig'iano, a [addzɛrbai'dʒano] *ag* Azerbaijani ♦ *sm/f* (*abitante*) Azerbaijani ♦ *sm* (*LING*) Azerbaijani.

a'zero, a [ad'dzero] *sm/f* Azeri.

azi'enda [ad'dzjɛnda] *sf* business, firm, concern; ~ **agricola** farm; ~ **(autonoma) di soggiorno** tourist board; ~ **a partecipazione statale** *business in which the State has a financial interest*; ~**e pubbliche** public corporations.

azien'dale [addzjen'dale] *ag* company *cpd*; **organizzazione** ~ business administration.

azio'nare [attsjo'nare] *vt* to activate.

azio'nario, a [attsjo'narjo] *ag* share *cpd*; **capitale** ~ share capital; **mercato** ~ stock market.

azi'one [at'tsjone] *sf* action; (*COMM*) share; ~ **sindacale** industrial action; ~**i preferenziali** preference shares (*BRIT*), preferred stock *sg* (*US*).

azio'nista, i, e [attsjo'nista] *sm/f* (*COMM*) shareholder.

a'zoto [ad'dzɔto] *sm* nitrogen.

az'teco, a, ci, che [as'tɛko] *ag*, *sm/f* Aztec.

azzan'nare [attsan'nare] *vt* to sink one's teeth into.

azzar'dare [addzar'dare] *vt* (*soldi, vita*) to risk, hazard; (*domanda, ipotesi*) to hazard, venture; ~**rsi** *vr*: ~**rsi a fare** to dare (to) do.

azzar'dato, a [addzar'dato] *ag* (*impresa*) risky; (*risposta*) rash.

az'zardo [ad'dzardo] *sm* risk; **gioco d'**~ game of chance.

azzec'care [attsek'kare] *vt* (*bersaglio*) to hit, strike; (*risposta, pronostico*) to get right; (*fig: indovinare*) to guess.

azzera'mento [addzera'mento] *sm* (*INFORM*) reset.

azze'rare [addze'rare] *vt* (*MAT, FISICA*) to make equal to zero, reduce to zero; (*TECN: strumento*) to (re)set to zero.

'azzimo, a ['addzimo] *ag* unleavened ♦ *sm* unleavened bread.

azzop'pare [attsop'pare] *vt* to lame, make lame.

Az'zorre [ad'dzorre] *sfpl*: **le** ~ the Azores.

azzuf'farsi [attsuf'farsi] *vr* to come to blows.

az'zurro, a [ad'dzurro] *ag* blue ♦ *sm* (*colore*) blue; **gli** ~**i** (*SPORT*) the Italian national team.

azzur'rognolo, a [addzur'roɲɲolo] *ag* bluish.

B b

B, b [bi] *sf o m inv* (*lettera*) B, b; ~ **come Bologna** ≈ B for Benjamin (*BRIT*), B for Baker (*US*).

BA *sigla* = Bari.

ba'bau *sm inv* ogre, bogey man.

bab'beo *sm* simpleton.

'babbo *sm* (*fam*) dad, daddy; **B**~ **Natale** Father Christmas.

bab'buccia, ce [bab'buttʃa] *sf* slipper; (*per neonati*) bootee.

babbu'ino *sm* baboon.

babilo'nese *ag, smf* Babylonian.

Babi'lonia *sf* Babylonia.

ba'bordo *sm* (*NAUT*) port side.

baby'sitter ['beɪbɪsɪtə*] *smf inv* baby-sitter.

ba'cato, a *ag* worm-eaten, rotten; (*fig: mente*) diseased; (: *persona*) corrupt.

'bacca, che *sf* berry.

baccalà *sm* dried salted cod; (*fig: peg*) dummy.

bac'cano *sm* din, clamour (*BRIT*), clamor (*US*).

bac'cello [bat'tʃɛllo] *sm* pod.

bac'chetta [bak'ketta] *sf* (*verga*) stick, rod; (*di direttore d'orchestra*) baton; (*di tamburo*) drumstick; **comandare a** ~ to rule with a rod of iron; ~ **magica** magic wand.

ba'checa, che [ba'kɛka] *sf* (*mobile*) showcase, display case; (*UNIVERSITÀ, in ufficio*) notice board (*BRIT*), bulletin board (*US*).

bacia'mano [batʃa'mano] *sm*: **fare il** ~ **a qn** to kiss sb's hand.

baci'are [ba'tʃare] *vt* to kiss; ~**rsi** *vr* to kiss (one another).

ba'cillo [ba'tʃillo] *sm* bacillus, germ.

baci'nella [batʃi'nɛlla] *sf* basin.

ba'cino [ba'tʃino] *sm* basin; (*MINERALOGIA*) field, bed; (*ANAT*) pelvis; (*NAUT*) dock; ~ **carbonifero** coalfield; ~ **di carenaggio** dry dock; ~ **petrolifero** oilfield.

'bacio ['batʃo] *sm* kiss.

'baco, chi *sm* worm; ~ **da seta** silkworm.

'bada *sf*: **tenere qn a** ~ (*tener d'occhio*) to keep an eye on sb; (*tenere a distanza*) to hold sb at bay.

ba'dare *vi* (*fare attenzione*) to take care, be careful; ~ **a** (*occuparsi di*) to look after, take care of; (*dar ascolto*) to pay attention to; **è un tipo che non bada a spese** money is no object to him; **bada ai fatti tuoi!** mind your own business!

ba'dia *sf* abbey.

ba'dile *sm* shovel.

'baffi *smpl* moustache *sg*, mustache *sg* (*US*); (*di animale*) whiskers; **leccarsi i** ~ to lick one's lips; **ridere sotto i** ~ to laugh up one's sleeve.

bagagli'aio [bagaʎ'ʎajo] *sm* luggage van (*BRIT*) *o* car (*US*); (*AUT*) boot (*BRIT*), trunk (*US*).

ba'gaglio [ba'gaʎʎo] *sm* luggage *no pl*, baggage *no pl*; **fare/disfare i** ~**i** to pack/unpack; ~ **a mano** hand luggage.

bagat'tella *sf* trifle, trifling matter.

Bag'dad *sf* Baghdad.

baggia'nata [baddʒa'nata] *sf* foolish action; **dire** ~**e** to talk nonsense.

bagli'ore [baʎ'ʎore] *sm* flash, dazzling light; **un** ~ **di speranza** a sudden ray of hope.

ba'gnante [baɲ'ɲante] *smf* bather.

ba'gnare [baɲ'ɲare] *vt* to wet; (*inzuppare*) to soak; (*innaffiare*) to water; (*sog: fiume*) to flow through; (: *mare*) to wash, bathe; (*brindare*) to drink to, toast; ~**rsi** *vr* (*al mare*) to go swimming *o* bathing; (*in vasca*) to have a bath.

ba'gnato, a [baɲ'ɲato] *ag* wet; **era come un pulcino** ~ he looked like a drowned rat.

ba'gnino [baɲ'ɲino] *sm* lifeguard.

'bagno ['baɲɲo] *sm* bath; (*locale*) bathroom; ~**i** *smpl* (*stabilimento*) baths; **fare il** ~ to have a bath; (*nel mare*) to go swimming *o* bathing; **fare il** ~ **a qn** to give sb a bath; **mettere a** ~ to soak.

bagnoma'ria [baɲɲoma'ria] *sm*: **cuocere a**

~ to cook in a double saucepan (*BRIT*) o double boiler (*US*).

bagnoschi'uma [baɲɲoskj'uma] *sm inv* bubble bath.

Ba'hama [ba'ama] *sfpl*: **le** ~ the Bahamas.

Bah'rein [ba'rein] *sm*: **il** ~ Bahrain o Bahrein.

'baia *sf* bay.

baio'netta *sf* bayonet.

'baita *sf* mountain hut.

balaus'trata *sf* balustrade.

balbet'tare *vi* to stutter, stammer; (*bimbo*) to babble ♦ *vt* to stammer out.

bal'buzie [bal'buttsje] *sf* stammer.

balbuzi'ente [balbut'tsjɛnte] *ag* stuttering, stammering.

Bal'cani *smpl*: **i** ~ the Balkans.

bal'canico, a, ci, che *ag* Balkan.

bal'cone *sm* balcony.

baldac'chino [baldak'kino] *sm* canopy; **letto a** ~ four-poster (bed).

bal'danza [bal'dantsa] *sf* self-confidence; boldness.

'baldo, a *ag* bold, daring.

bal'doria *sf*: **fare** ~ to have a riotous time.

Bale'ari *sfpl*: **le isole** ~ the Balearic Islands.

ba'lena *sf* whale.

bale'nare *vb impers*: **balena** there's lightning ♦ *vi* to flash; **mi balenò un'idea** an idea flashed through my mind.

baleni'era *sf* (*per la caccia*) whaler, whaling ship.

ba'leno *sm* flash of lightning; **in un** ~ in a flash.

ba'lera *sf* (*locale*) dance hall; (*pista*) dance floor.

ba'lestra *sf* crossbow.

'balia *sf* wet-nurse; ~ **asciutta** nanny.

ba'lia *sf*: **in** ~ **di** at the mercy of; **essere lasciato in** ~ **di se stesso** to be left to one's own devices.

ba'lilla *sm inv* (*STORIA*) *member of Fascist youth group*.

ba'listico, a, ci, che *ag* ballistic ♦ *sf* ballistics *sg*; **perito** ~ ballistics expert.

'balla *sf* (*di merci*) bale; (*fandonia*) (tall) story.

bal'labile *sm* dance number, dance tune.

bal'lare *vt, vi* to dance.

bal'lata *sf* ballad.

balla'toio *sm* (*terrazzina*) gallery.

balle'rina *sf* dancer; ballet dancer; (*scarpa*) pump; ~ **di rivista** chorus girl.

balle'rino *sm* dancer; ballet dancer.

bal'letto *sm* ballet.

'ballo *sm* dance; (*azione*) dancing *no pl*; ~ **in maschera** o **mascherato** fancy-dress ball;

~ to be involved; (*: cosa*) to be at stake; **tirare in** ~ **qc** to bring sth up, raise sth.

ballot'taggio [ballot'taddʒo] *sm* (*POL*) second ballot.

balne'are *ag* seaside *cpd*; (*stagione*) bathing.

ba'locco, chi *sm* toy.

ba'lordo, a *ag* stupid, senseless.

bal'samico, a, ci, che *ag* (*aria, brezza*) balmy; **pomata** ~**a** balsam.

'balsamo *sm* (*aroma*) balsam; (*lenimento, fig*) balm; (*per capelli*) (hair) conditioner.

'baltico, a, ci, che *ag* Baltic; **il (mar) B**~ the Baltic (Sea).

balu'ardo *sm* bulwark.

'balza ['baltsa] *sf* (*dirupo*) crag; (*di stoffa*) frill.

bal'zano, a [bal'tsano] *ag* (*persona, idea*) queer, odd.

bal'zare [bal'tsare] *vi* to bounce; (*lanciarsi*) to jump, leap; **la verità balza agli occhi** the truth of the matter is obvious.

'balzo ['baltso] *sm* bounce; jump, leap; (*del terreno*) crag; **prendere la palla al** ~ (*fig*) to seize one's opportunity.

bam'bagia [bam'badʒa] *sf* (*ovatta*) cotton wool (*BRIT*), absorbent cotton (*US*); (*cascame*) cotton waste; **tenere qn nella** ~ (*fig*) to mollycoddle sb.

bam'bina *sf vedi* **bambino**.

bambi'naia *sf* nanny, nurse(maid).

bam'bino, a *sm/f* child; **fare il** ~ to behave childishly.

bam'boccio [bam'bɔttʃo] *sm* plump child; (*pupazzo*) rag doll.

'bambola *sf* doll.

bambo'lotto *sm* male doll.

bambù *sm* bamboo.

ba'nale *ag* banal, commonplace.

banalità *sf inv* banality.

ba'nana *sf* banana.

ba'nano *sm* banana tree.

'banca, che *sf* bank; ~ **d'affari** merchant bank; ~ **(di) dati** data bank.

banca'rella *sf* stall.

ban'cario, a *ag* banking, bank *cpd* ♦ *sm* bank clerk.

banca'rotta *sf* bankruptcy; **fare** ~ to go bankrupt.

bancarotti'ere *sm* bankrupt.

ban'chetto [ban'ketto] *sm* banquet.

banchi'ere [ban'kjɛre] *sm* banker.

ban'china [ban'kina] *sf* (*di porto*) quay; (*per pedoni, ciclisti*) path; (*di stazione*) platform; ~ **cedevole** (*AUT*) soft verge (*BRIT*) o shoulder (*US*); ~ **spartitraffico** (*AUT*) central reservation (*BRIT*), median (strip)

(*US*).

ban'chisa [ban'kiza] *sf* pack ice.

'banco, chi *sm* bench; (*di negozio*) counter; (*di mercato*) stall; (*di officina*) (work)bench; (*GEO, banca*) bank; **sotto ~** (*fig*) under the counter; **tenere il ~** (*nei giochi*) to be (the) banker; **tener ~** (*fig*) to monopolize the conversation; **medicinali da ~** over-the-counter medicines; **~ di chiesa** pew; **~ di corallo** coral reef; **~ degli imputati** dock; **~ del Lotto** lottery-ticket office; **~ di prova** (*fig*) testing ground; **~ dei testimoni** witness box (*BRIT*) o stand (*US*).

banco'giro [banko'dʒiro] *sm* credit transfer.

'Bancomat ® *sm inv* automated banking; (*tessera*) cash card.

banco'nota *sf* banknote.

'banda *sf* band; (*di stoffa*) band, stripe; (*lato, parte*) side; (*di calcolatore*) tape; **~ perforata** punch tape.

banderu'ola *sf* (*METEOR*) weathercock, weathervane; **essere una ~** (*fig*) to be fickle.

bandi'era *sf* flag, banner; **battere ~ italiana** (*nave etc*) to fly the Italian flag; **cambiare ~** (*fig*) to change sides; **~ di comodo** flag of convenience.

ban'dire *vt* to proclaim; (*esiliare*) to exile; (*fig*) to dispense with.

ban'dito *sm* outlaw, bandit.

bandi'tore *sm* (*di aste*) auctioneer.

'bando *sm* proclamation; (*esilio*) exile, banishment; **mettere al ~ qn** to exile sb; (*fig*) to freeze sb out; **~ alle ciance!** that's enough talk!

'bandolo *sm* (*di matassa*) end; **trovare il ~ della matassa** (*fig*) to find the key to the problem.

Bang'kok [ban'kɔk] *sf* Bangkok.

Bangla'desh [bangla'dɛʃ] *sm*: **il ~** Bangladesh.

bar *sm inv* bar.

'bara *sf* coffin.

ba'racca, che *sf* shed, hut; (*peg*) hovel; **mandare avanti la ~** to keep things going; **piantare ~ e burattini** to throw everything up.

barac'cato, a *sm/f person living in temporary camp.*

barac'chino [barak'kino] *sm* (*chiosco*) stall; (*apparecchio*) CB radio.

barac'cone *sm* booth, stall; **~i** *smpl* (*luna park*) funfair *sg* (*BRIT*), amusement park; **fenomeno da ~** circus freak.

barac'copoli *sf inv* shanty town.

bara'onda *sf* hubbub, bustle.

ba'rare *vi* to cheat.

'baratro *sm* abyss.

barat'tare *vt*: **~ qc con** to barter sth for, swap sth for.

ba'ratto *sm* barter.

ba'rattolo *sm* (*di latta*) tin; (*di vetro*) jar; (*di coccio*) pot.

'barba *sf* beard; **farsi la ~** to shave; **farla in ~ a qn** (*fig*) to fool sb; **servire qn di ~ e capelli** (*fig*) to teach sb a lesson; **che ~!** what a bore!

barbabi'etola *sf* beetroot (*BRIT*), beet (*US*); **~ da zucchero** sugar beet.

Bar'bados *sfsg* Barbados.

bar'barico, a, ci, che *ag* (*invasione*) barbarian; (*usanze, metodi*) barbaric.

bar'barie *sf* barbarity.

'barbaro, a *ag* barbarous ♦ *sm* barbarian; **i B~i** the Barbarians.

'barbecue ['ba:bikju:] *sm inv* barbecue.

barbi'ere *sm* barber.

barbi'turico, a, ci, che *ag* barbituric ♦ *sm* barbiturate.

bar'bone *sm* (*cane*) poodle; (*vagabondo*) tramp.

bar'buto, a *ag* bearded.

'barca, che *sf* boat; **una ~ di** (*fig*) heaps of, tons of; **mandare avanti la ~** (*fig*) to keep things going; **~ a remi** rowing boat (*BRIT*), rowboat (*US*); **~ a vela** sailing boat (*BRIT*), sailboat (*US*).

barcai'olo *sm* boatman.

barcame'narsi *vr* (*nel lavoro*) to get by; (*a parole*) to beat about the bush.

Barcel'lona [bartʃel'lona] *sf* Barcelona.

barcol'lare *vi* to stagger.

bar'cone *sm* (*per ponti di barche*) pontoon.

ba'rella *sf* (*lettiga*) stretcher.

'Barents: il mar di ~ *sm* the Barents Sea.

ba'rese *ag* of (o from) Bari.

bari'centro [bari'tʃentro] *sm* centre (*BRIT*) o center (*US*) of gravity.

ba'rile *sm* barrel, cask.

ba'rista, i, e *sm/f* barman/barmaid; bar owner.

ba'ritono *sm* baritone.

bar'lume *sm* glimmer, gleam.

'baro *sm* (*CARTE*) cardsharp.

ba'rocco, a, chi, che *ag, sm* baroque.

ba'rometro *sm* barometer.

ba'rone *sm* baron; **i ~i della medicina** (*fig peg*) the top brass in the medical faculty.

baro'nessa *sf* baroness.

'barra *sf* bar; (*NAUT*) helm; (*segno grafico*) stroke.

bar'rare *vt* to bar.

barri'care *vt* to barricade.

barri'cata *sf* barricade; **essere dall'altra parte della ~** (*fig*) to be on the other side of the fence.

barri'era *sf* barrier; (*GEO*) reef; **la Grande B~ Corallina** the Great Barrier Reef.

bar'roccio [bar'rɔttʃo] *sm* cart.

ba'ruffa *sf* scuffle; **fare ~** to squabble.

barzel'letta [bardzel'letta] *sf* joke, funny story.

basa'mento *sm* (*parte inferiore, piedestallo*) base; (*TECN*) bed, base plate.

ba'sare *vt* to base, found; **~rsi** *vr*: **~rsi su** (*sog: fatti, prove*) to be based *o* founded on; (*: persona*) to base one's arguments on.

'basco, a, schi, sche *ag* Basque ♦ *sm/f* Basque ♦ *sm* (*lingua*) Basque; (*copricapo*) beret.

bas'culla *sf* weighing machine, weighbridge.

'base *sf* base; (*fig: fondamento*) basis; (*POL*) rank and file; **di ~** basic; **in ~ a** on the basis of, according to; **in ~ a ciò ...** on that basis ...; **a ~ di caffè** coffee-based; **essere alla ~ di qc** to be at the root of sth; **gettare le ~i per qc** to lay the basis *o* foundations for sth; **avere buone ~i** (*INS*) to have a sound educational background.

'baseball ['beisbɔːl] *sm* baseball.

ba'setta *sf* sideburn.

basi'lare *ag* basic, fundamental.

Basi'lea *sf* Basle.

ba'silica, che *sf* basilica.

ba'silico *sm* basil.

bas'sezza [bas'settsa] *sf* (*d'animo, di sentimenti*) baseness; (*azione*) base action.

bas'sista, i, e *sm/f* bass player.

'basso, a *ag* low; (*di statura*) short; (*meridionale*) southern ♦ *sm* bottom, lower part; (*MUS*) bass; **a occhi ~i** with eyes lowered; **a ~ prezzo** cheap; **scendere da ~** to go downstairs; **cadere in ~** (*fig*) to come down in the world; **la ~a Italia** southern Italy; **il ~ Medioevo** the late Middle Ages.

basso'fondo, *pl* **bassi'fondi** *sm* (*GEO*) shallows *pl*; **i bassifondi** (*della città*) the seediest parts of the town.

bassorili'evo *sm* bas-relief.

bas'sotto, a *ag* squat ♦ *sm* (*cane*) dachshund.

bas'tardo, a *ag* (*animale, pianta*) hybrid, crossbreed; (*persona*) illegitimate, bastard (*peg*) ♦ *sm/f* illegitimate child, bastard (*peg*); (*cane*) mongrel.

bas'tare *vi, vb impers* to be enough, be sufficient; **~ a qn** to be enough for sb; **~ a se stesso** to be self-sufficient; **basta chiedere** *o* **che chieda a un vigile** you have only to *o* need only ask a policeman; **basti dire che ...** suffice it to say that ...; **basta!**

that's enough!, that will do!; **basta così?** (*al bar etc*) will that be all?; **punto e basta!** and that's that!

basti'an *sm*: **~ contrario** awkward customer.

basti'mento *sm* ship, vessel.

basti'one *sm* bastion.

basto'nare *vt* to beat, thrash; **avere l'aria di un cane bastonato** to look crestfallen.

basto'nata *sf* blow (with a stick); **prendere qn a ~e** to give sb a good beating.

baston'cino [baston'tʃino] *sm* (*piccolo bastone*) small stick; (*TECN*) rod; (*SCI*) ski pole; **~i di pesce** (*CUC*) fish fingers (*BRIT*), fish sticks (*US*).

bas'tone *sm* stick; **~i** *smpl* (*CARTE*) suit in *Neapolitan pack of cards*; **~ da passeggio** walking stick; **mettere i ~i fra le ruote a qn** to put a spoke in sb's wheel.

bat'tage [ba'taʒ] *sm inv*: **~ promozionale** *o* **pubblicitario** publicity campaign.

bat'taglia [bat'taʎʎa] *sf* battle.

bat'taglio [bat'taʎʎo] *sm* (*di campana*) clapper; (*di porta*) knocker.

battagli'one [battaʎ'ʎone] *sm* battalion.

bat'tello *sm* boat.

bat'tente *sm* (*imposta: di porta*) wing, flap; (*: di finestra*) shutter; (*per bussare*) knocker; (*di orologio*) hammer; **chiudere i ~i** (*fig*) to shut up shop.

'battere *vt* to beat; (*grano*) to thresh; (*percorrere*) to scour; (*rintoccare: le ore*) to strike ♦ *vi* (*bussare*) to knock; (*urtare*): **~ contro** to hit *o* strike against; (*pioggia, sole*) to beat down; (*cuore*) to beat; (*TENNIS*) to serve; **~rsi** *vr* to fight; **~ le mani** to clap; **~ i piedi** to stamp one's feet; **~ su un argomento** to hammer home an argument; **~ a macchina** to type; **~ il marciapiede** (*peg*) to walk the streets, be on the game; **~ un rigore** (*CALCIO*) to take a penalty; **~ in testa** (*AUT*) to knock; **in un batter d'occhio** in the twinkling of an eye; **senza ~ ciglio** without batting an eyelid; **battersela** to run off.

batte'ria *sf* battery; (*MUS*) drums *pl*; **~ da cucina** pots and pans *pl*.

bat'terio *sm* bacterium; **~i** *smpl* bacteria.

batteriolo'gia [batterjolo'dʒia] *sf* bacteriology.

bat'tesimo *sm* (*sacramento*) baptism; (*rito*) baptism, christening; **tenere qn a ~** to be godfather (*o* godmother) to sb.

battez'zare [batted'dzare] *vt* to baptize; to christen.

battiba'leno *sm*: **in un ~** in a flash.

batti'becco, chi *sm* squabble.

batticu'ore *sm* palpitations *pl*; **avere il ~ to**

be frightened to death.

bat'tigia [bat'tidʒa] *sf* water's edge.

batti'mano *sm* applause.

batti'panni *sm inv* carpet-beater.

battis'tero *sm* baptistry.

battis'trada *sm inv* (*di pneumatico*) tread; (*di gara*) pacemaker.

battitap'peto *sm inv* upright vacuum cleaner.

'battito *sm* beat, throb; ~ **cardiaco** heartbeat; ~ **della pioggia/dell'orologio** beating of the rain/ticking of the clock.

batti'tore *sm* (*CRICKET*) batsman; (*BASEBALL*) batter; (*CACCIA*) beater.

batti'tura *sf* (*anche:* ~ **a macchina**) typing; (*del grano*) threshing.

bat'tuta *sf* blow; (*di macchina da scrivere*) stroke; (*MUS*) bar; beat; (*TEAT*) cue; (*di caccia*) beating; (*POLIZIA*) combing, scouring; (*TENNIS*) service; **fare una** ~ to crack a joke, make a witty remark; **aver la** ~ **pronta** (*fig*) to have a ready answer; **è ancora alle prime** ~**e** it's just started.

ba'tuffolo *sm* wad.

ba'ule *sm* trunk; (*AUT*) boot (*BRIT*), trunk (*US*).

bau'xite [bauk'site] *sf* bauxite.

'bava *sf* (*di animale*) slaver, slobber; (*di lumaca*) slime; (*di vento*) breath.

bava'glino [bavaʎ'ʎino] *sm* bib.

ba'vaglio [ba'vaʎʎo] *sm* gag.

bava'rese *ag, sm/f* Bavarian.

'bavero *sm* collar.

Bavi'era *sf* Bavaria.

ba'zar [bad'dzar] *sm inv* bazaar.

baz'zecola [bad'dzekola] *sf* trifle.

bazzi'care [battsi'kare] *vt* (*persona*) to hang about with; (*posto*) to hang about ♦ *vi*: ~ **in/con** to hang about/hang about with.

BCE *sigla f* (= *Banca centrale europea*) ECB.

be'arsi *vr*: ~ **di qc/a fare qc** to delight in sth/in doing sth; ~ **alla vista di** to enjoy looking at.

beati'tudine *sf* bliss.

be'ato, a *ag* blessed; (*fig*) happy; ~ **te!** lucky you!

bebè *sm inv* baby.

bec'care *vt* to peck; (*fig: raffreddore*) to pick up, catch; ~**rsi** *vr* (*fig*) to squabble.

bec'cata *sf* peck.

beccheggi'are [bekked'dʒare] *vi* to pitch.

beccherò *etc* [bekke'rɔ] *vb vedi* **beccare**.

bec'chime [bek'kime] *sm* birdseed.

bec'chino [bek'kino] *sm* gravedigger.

'becco, chi *sm* beak, bill; (*di caffettiera etc*) spout; lip; **mettere** ~ (*fam*) to butt in; **chiudi il** ~! (*fam*) shut your mouth!; **non**

ho il ~ **di un quattrino** (*fam*) I'm broke.

Be'fana *sf old woman who, according to legend, brings children their presents at the Epiphany*; (*Epifania*) Epiphany; (*donna brutta*): **b**~ hag, witch; *vedi nota nel riquadro.*

BEFANA

*Marking the end of the traditional 12 days of Christmas on 6 January, the **Befana**, or the feast of the Epiphany, is a national holiday in Italy. It is named after the old woman who, legend has it, comes down the chimney the night before, bringing gifts to children who have been good during the year and leaving lumps of coal for those who have not.*

'beffa *sf* practical joke; **farsi** ~ *o* ~**e di qn** to make a fool of sb.

bef'fardo, a *ag* scornful, mocking.

bef'fare *vt* (*anche:* ~**rsi di**) to make a fool of, mock.

'bega, ghe *sf* quarrel.

'begli ['beʎʎi], **'bei** *ag vedi* **bello**.

beige [beʒ] *ag inv* beige.

Bei'rut *sf* Beirut.

bel *ag vedi* **bello**.

be'lare *vi* to bleat.

'belga, gi, ghe *ag, sm/f* Belgian.

'Belgio ['beldʒo] *sm*: **il** ~ Belgium.

Bel'grado *sf* Belgrade.

'bella *sf vedi* **bello**.

bel'lezza [bel'lettsa] *sf* beauty; **chiudere** *o* **finire qc in** ~ to finish sth with a flourish; **che** ~! fantastic!; **ho pagato la** ~ **di 300 euro** I paid 300 euros, no less.

belli'coso, a *ag* warlike.

bellige'rante [bellidʒe'rante] *ag* belligerent.

bellim'busto *sm* dandy.

═══════════════════════ *PAROLA CHIAVE*

'bello, a (*ag: dav sm* **bel** + *C*, **bell'** + *V*, **bello** + *s impura, gn, pn, ps, x, z, pl* **bei** + *C*, **begli** + *s impura etc o V*) *ag* **1** (*oggetto, donna, paesaggio*) beautiful; (*uomo*) handsome; (*tempo*) beautiful, fine, lovely; **farsi** ~ **di qc** to show off about sth; **fare la** ~**a vita** to have an easy life; **le** ~**e arti** fine arts

2 (*quantità*): **una** ~**a cifra** a considerable sum of money; **un bel niente** absolutely nothing

3 (*rafforzativo*): **è una truffa** ~**a e buona!** it's a real fraud!; **oh** ~**a!**, **anche questa è** ~**a!** (*ironico*) that's nice!; **è bell'e finito** it's already finished

♦ *sm/f* (*innamorato*) sweetheart

♦ *sm* **1** (*bellezza*) beauty; (*tempo*) fine

weather
2: **adesso viene il** ~ now comes the best bit;
sul più ~ at the crucial point; **cosa fai di** ~?
are you doing anything interesting?
♦ *sf (anche:* ~**a copia**) fair copy; (*SPORT,
CARTE*) decider
♦ *av*: **fa** ~ the weather is fine, it's fine; **alla
bell'e meglio** somehow or other.

bellu'nese *ag* of (*o* from) Belluno.
'belva *sf* wild animal.
belve'dere *sm inv* panoramic viewpoint.
benché [ben'ke] *cong* although.
'benda *sf* bandage; (*per gli occhi*) blindfold.
ben'dare *vt* to bandage; to blindfold.
bendis'posto, a *ag*: ~ **a qn/qc** well
disposed towards sb/sth.
'bene *av* well; (*completamente, affatto*): **è
ben difficile** it's very difficult ♦ *ag inv*:
gente ~ well-to-do people ♦ *sm* good;
(*COMM*) asset; ~**i** *smpl (averi)* property *sg*,
estate *sg*; **io sto** ~/**poco** ~ I'm well/not
very well; **va** ~ all right; **ben più lungo/
caro** much longer/more expensive; **lo
spero** ~ I certainly hope so; **volere un** ~
dell'anima a qn to love sb very much; **un
uomo per** ~ a respectable man; **fare** ~ to
do the right thing; **fare** ~ **a** (*salute*) to be
good for; **fare del** ~ **a qn** to do sb a good
turn; **di** ~ **in meglio** better and better; ~**i
ambientali** environmental assets; ~**i di
consumo** consumer goods; ~**i di consumo
durevole** consumer durables; ~**i culturali**
cultural heritage; ~**i immateriali**
immaterial *o* intangible assets; ~**i
patrimoniali** fixed assets; ~**i privati**
private property *sg*; ~**i pubblici** public
property *sg*; ~**i reali** tangible assets.
bene'detto, a *pp di* **benedire** ♦ *ag* blessed,
holy.
bene'dire *vt* to bless; to consecrate; **l'ho
mandato a farsi** ~ (*fig*) I told him to go to
hell.
benedizi'one [benedit'tsjone] *sf* blessing.
benedu'cato, a *ag* well-mannered.
benefat'tore, 'trice *sm/f* benefactor/
benefactress.
benefi'cenza [benefi'tʃɛntsa] *sf* charity.
benefici'are [benefi'tʃare] *vi*: ~ **di** to benefit
by, benefit from.
benefici'ario, a [benefi'tʃarjo] *ag, sm/f*
beneficiary.
bene'ficio [bene'fitʃo] *sm* benefit; **con** ~
d'inventario (*fig*) with reservations.
be'nefico, a, ci, che *ag* beneficial;
charitable.
'Benelux *sm*: **il** ~ Benelux, the Benelux
countries.

beneme'renza [beneme'rɛntsa] *sf* merit.
bene'merito, a *ag* meritorious.
bene'placito [bene'platʃito] *sm*
(*approvazione*) approval; (*permesso*)
permission.
be'nessere *sm* well-being.
benes'tante *ag* well-to-do.
benes'tare *sm* consent, approval.
benevo'lenza [benevo'lɛntsa] *sf*
benevolence.
be'nevolo, a *ag* benevolent.
ben'godi *sm* land of plenty.
benia'mino, a *sm/f* favourite (*BRIT*),
favorite (*US*).
be'nigno, a [be'ninɲo] *ag* kind, kindly;
(*critica etc*) favourable (*BRIT*), favorable
(*US*); (*MED*) benign.
benintenzio'nato, a [benintentsjo'nato] *ag*
well-meaning.
benin'teso *av* of course; ~ **che** *cong*
provided that.
benpen'sante *sm/f* conformist.
benser'vito *sm*: **dare il** ~ **a qn** (*sul lavoro*)
to give sb the sack, fire sb; (*fig*) to send sb
packing.
bensì *cong* but (rather).
benve'nuto, a *ag, sm* welcome; **dare il** ~ **a
qn** to welcome sb.
ben'visto, a *ag*: **essere** ~ **(da)** to be well
thought of (by).
benvo'lere *vt*: **farsi** ~ **da tutti** to win
everybody's affection; **prendere a** ~ **qn/
qc** to take a liking to sb/sth.
ben'zina [ben'dzina] *sf* petrol (*BRIT*), gas
(*US*); **fare** ~ to get petrol *o* gas; **rimanere
senza** ~ to run out of petrol *o* gas; ~
verde unleaded petrol, lead-free petrol.
benzi'naio [bendzi'najo] *sm* petrol (*BRIT*) *o*
gas (*US*) pump attendant.
be'one *sm* heavy drinker.
'bere *vt* to drink; (*assorbire*) to soak up;
questa volta non me la dai a ~! I won't be
taken in this time!
berga'masco, a, schi, sche *ag* of (*o* from)
Bergamo.
'Bering ['beriŋ]: **il mar di** ~ *sm* the Bering
Sea.
ber'lina *sf* (*AUT*) saloon (car) (*BRIT*), sedan
(*US*); **mettere alla** ~ (*fig*) to hold up to
ridicule.
Ber'lino *sf* Berlin; ~ **est/ovest** East/West
Berlin.
Ber'muda *sfpl*: **le** ~ Bermuda *sg*.
ber'muda *smpl* (*calzoncini*) Bermuda
shorts.
'Berna *sf* Bern.
ber'noccolo *sm* bump; (*inclinazione*) flair.
ber'retto *sm* cap.

berrò *etc vb vedi* **bere.**

bersagli'are [bersaʎ'ʎare] *vt* to shoot at; (*colpire ripetutamente, fig*) to bombard; **bersagliato dalla sfortuna** dogged by ill fortune.

bersagli'ere [bersaʎ'ʎɛre] *sm member of rifle regiment in Italian army.*

ber'saglio [ber'saʎʎo] *sm* target.

bes'temmia *sf* curse; (*REL*) blasphemy.

bestemmi'are *vi* to curse, swear; to blaspheme ♦ *vt* to curse, swear at; to blaspheme; ~ **come un turco** to swear like a trooper.

'bestia *sf* animal; **lavorare come una** ~ to work like a dog; **andare in** ~ (*fig*) to fly into a rage; **una** ~ **rara** (*fig: persona*) an oddball; ~ **da soma** beast of burden.

besti'ale *ag* bestial, brutish; (*fam*): **fa un caldo** ~ it's terribly hot; **fa un freddo** ~ it's bitterly cold.

besti'ame *sm* livestock; (*bovino*) cattle *pl.*

Bet'lemme *sf* Bethlehem.

betoni'era *sf* cement mixer.

'bettola *sf* (*peg*) dive.

be'tulla *sf* birch.

be'vanda *sf* drink, beverage.

bevi'tore, 'trice *sm/f* drinker.

'bevo *etc vb vedi* **bere.**

be'vuto, a *pp di* **bere** ♦ *sf* drink.

'bevvi *etc vb vedi* **bere.**

BG *sigla* = Bergamo.

BI *sigla f* = Banca d'Italia ♦ *sigla* = Biella.

bi'ada *sf* fodder.

bianche'ria [bjanke'ria] *sf* linen; ~ **intima** underwear; ~ **da donna** ladies' underwear, lingerie.

bi'anco, a, chi, che *ag* white; (*non scritto*) blank ♦ *sm* white; (*intonaco*) whitewash ♦ *sm/f* white, white man/woman; **in** ~ (*foglio, assegno*) blank; **in** ~ **e nero** (*TV, FOT*) black and white; **mangiare in** ~ to follow a bland diet; **pesce in** ~ boiled fish; **andare in** ~ (*non riuscire*) to fail; (*in amore*) to be rejected; **notte** ~**a** *o* **in** ~ sleepless night; **voce** ~**a** (*MUS*) treble (voice); ~ **dell'uovo** egg-white.

bianco'segno [bjanko'seɲɲo] *sm* signature to a blank document.

biancos'pino *sm* hawthorn.

biasci'care [bjaʃʃi'kare] *vt* to mumble.

biasi'mare *vt* to disapprove of, censure.

'bibbia *sf* bible.

bibe'ron *sm inv* feeding bottle.

'bibita *sf* (*soft*) drink.

bibliogra'fia *sf* bibliography.

biblio'teca, che *sf* library; (*mobile*) bookcase.

bibliote'cario, a *sm/f* librarian.

bicame'rale *ag* (*POL*) two-chamber *cpd.*

bicarbo'nato *sm:* ~ **(di sodio)** bicarbonate (of soda).

bicchi'ere [bik'kjɛre] *sm* glass; **è (facile) come bere un bicchier d'acqua** it's as easy as pie.

bici'cletta [bitʃi'kletta] *sf* bicycle; **andare in** ~ to cycle.

bi'cipite [bi'tʃipite] *sm* bicep.

bidè *sm inv* bidet.

bi'dello, a *sm/f* (*INS*) janitor.

bi'det *sm inv* = **bidè.**

bido'nare *vt* (*fam: piantare in asso*) to let down; (: *imbrogliare*) to cheat, swindle.

bido'nata *sf* (*fam*) swindle.

bi'done *sm* drum, can; (*anche:* ~ **dell'immondizia**) (dust)bin; (*fam: truffa*) swindle; **fare un** ~ **a qn** (*fam*) to let sb down; to cheat sb.

bidon'ville [bidɔ̃'vil] *sf inv* shanty town.

bi'eco, a, chi, che *ag* sinister.

Bielo'russia *sf* Belarus.

bielo'russo, a *ag, sm/f* Belarussian.

bien'nale *ag* biennial ♦ *sf:* **la B**~ **di Venezia** the Venice Arts Festival; *vedi nota nel riquadro.*

BIENNALE DI VENEZIA

Dating back to 1895, the **Biennale di Venezia** *is an international festival of the contemporary arts. It takes place every two years in the "Giardini Pubblici". The various countries taking part each put on exhibitions in their own pavilions. There is a section dedicated to the work of young artists, as well as a special exhibition organized around a specific theme for that year.*

---

bi'ennio *sm* period of two years.

bi'erre *sm/f member of the Red Brigades.*

bi'etola *sf* beet.

bifami'liare *ag* (*villa, casetta*) semi-detached.

bifo'cale *ag* bifocal.

bi'folco, a, chi, che *sm/f* (*peg*) bumpkin.

'bifora *sf* (*ARCHIT*) mullioned window.

bifor'carsi *vr* to fork.

biforcazi'one [biforkat'tsjone] *sf* fork.

bifor'cuto, a *ag* (*anche fig*) forked.

biga'mia *sf* bigamy.

'bigamo, a *ag* bigamous ♦ *sm/f* bigamist.

bighello'nare [bigello'nare] *vi* to loaf (about).

bighel'lone, a [bigel'lone] *sm/f* loafer.

bigiotte'ria [bidʒotte'ria] *sf* costume jewellery (*BRIT*) *o* jewelry (*US*); (*negozio*) jeweller's (shop) (*BRIT*) *o* jewelry store (*US*) (*selling only costume jewellery*).

bigli'ardo [biʎˈʎardo] *sm* = **biliardo**.

bigliet'taio, a [biʎʎetˈtajo] *sm/f* (*nei treni*) ticket inspector; (*in autobus etc*) conductor/conductress; (*CINE, TEAT*) box-office attendant.

bigliette'ria [biʎʎetteˈria] *sf* (*di stazione*) ticket office; booking office; (*di teatro*) box office.

bigli'etto [biʎˈʎetto] *sm* (*per viaggi, spettacoli etc*) ticket; (*cartoncino*) card; (*anche:* ~ **di banca**) (bank)note; ~ **d'auguri/da visita** greetings/visiting card; ~ **d'andata e ritorno** return (*BRIT*) *o* round-trip (*US*) ticket; ~ **omaggio** complimentary ticket.

bignè [biɲˈɲɛ] *sm inv* cream puff.

bigo'dino *sm* roller, curler.

bi'gotto, a *ag* over-pious ♦ *sm/f* church fiend.

bi'kini *sm inv* bikini.

bi'lancia, ce [biˈlantʃa] *sf* (*pesa*) scales *pl*; (: *di precisione*) balance; (*dello zodiaco*): **B~** Libra; **essere della B~** to be Libra; ~ **commerciale/dei pagamenti** balance of trade/payments.

bilanci'are [bilanˈtʃare] *vt* (*pesare*) to weigh; (: *fig*) to weigh up; ~ **le uscite e le entrate** (*COMM*) to balance expenditure and revenue.

bi'lancio [biˈlantʃo] *sm* (*COMM*) balance (sheet); (*statale*) budget; **far quadrare il** ~ to balance the books; **chiudere il** ~ **in attivo/passivo** to make a profit/loss; **fare il** ~ **di** (*fig*) to assess; ~ **consolidato** consolidated balance; ~ **consuntivo** (final) balance; ~ **preventivo** budget; ~ **pubblico** national budget; ~ **di verifica** trial balance.

bilate'rale *ag* bilateral.

'bile *sf* bile; (*fig*) rage, anger.

bili'ardo *sm* billiards *sg*; (*tavolo*) billiard table.

'bilico, chi *sm*: **essere in** ~ to be balanced; (*fig*) to be undecided; **tenere qn in** ~ to keep sb in suspense.

bi'lingue *ag* bilingual.

bili'one *sm* (*mille milioni*) thousand million, billion (*US*); (*milione di milioni*) billion (*BRIT*), trillion (*US*).

bilo'cale *sm* two-room flat (*BRIT*) *o* apartment (*US*).

'bimbo, a *sm/f* little boy/girl.

bimen'sile *ag* fortnightly.

bimes'trale *ag* two-monthly, bimonthly.

bi'mestre *sm* two-month period; **ogni** ~ every two months.

bi'nario, a *ag* binary ♦ *sm* (railway) track *o* line; (*piattaforma*) platform; ~ **morto** dead-end track.

bi'nocolo *sm* binoculars *pl*.

bio'chimica [bioˈkimika] *sf* biochemistry.

biodegra'dabile *ag* biodegradable.

biodiversità *sf* biodiversity.

bio'etica *sf* bioethics *sg*.

bio'etico, a, ci, che *ag* bioethical.

bio'fabbrica *sf factory producing biological control agents*.

bio'fisica *sf* biophysics *sg*.

biogra'fia *sf* biography.

bio'grafico, a, ci, che *ag* biographical.

bi'ografo, a *sm/f* biographer.

biolo'gia [biolo'dʒia] *sf* biology.

bio'logico, a, ci, che [bioˈlɔdʒiko] *ag* (*scienze, fenomeni etc*) biological; (*agricoltura, prodotti*) organic.

bi'ologo, a, ghi, ghe *sm/f* biologist.

bi'ondo, a *ag* blond, fair.

bi'onico, a, ci, che *ag* bionic.

biop'sia *sf* biopsy.

bio'ritmo *sm* biorhythm.

bios'fera *sf* biosphere.

biotecnolo'gia [bioteknolo'dʒia] *sf* biotechnology.

bipar'tito, a *ag* (*POL*) two-party *cpd* ♦ *sm* (*POL*) two-party alliance.

'birba *sf* rascal, rogue.

bir'bante *sm* rascal, rogue.

birbo'nata *sf* naughty trick.

bir'bone, a *ag* (*bambino*) naughty ♦ *sm/f* little rascal.

biri'chino, a [biriˈkino] *ag* mischievous ♦ *sm/f* scamp, little rascal.

bi'rillo *sm* skittle (*BRIT*), pin (*US*); ~**i** *smpl* (*gioco*) skittles *sg* (*BRIT*), bowling *no pl* (*US*).

Bir'mania *sf*: **la** ~ Burma.

bir'mano, a *ag, sm/f* Burmese (*inv*).

'biro ® *sf inv* biro ®.

'birra *sf* beer; ~ **scura** stout; **a tutta** ~ (*fig*) at top speed.

birre'ria *sf* (*locale*) ≈ bierkeller; (*fabbrica*) brewery.

bis *escl, sm inv* encore ♦ *ag inv* (*treno, autobus*) relief *cpd* (*BRIT*), additional; (*numero*): **12** ~ 12a.

bi'saccia, ce [biˈzattʃa] *sf* knapsack.

Bi'sanzio [biˈzantsjo] *sf* Byzantium.

bis'betico, a, ci, che *ag* ill-tempered, crabby.

bisbigli'are [bizbiʎˈʎare] *vt, vi* to whisper.

bis'biglio [bizˈbiʎʎo] *sm* whisper; (*notizia*) rumour (*BRIT*), rumor (*US*).

bisbi'glio [bizbiʎˈʎio] *sm* whispering.

bis'boccia, ce [bizˈbɔttʃa] *sf* binge, spree;

fare ~ to have a binge.
'**bisca, sche** *sf* gambling house.
Bis'caglia [bis'kaʎʎa] *sf*: **il golfo di** ~ the Bay of Biscay.
'**bischero** ['biskero] *sm* (*MUS*) peg; (*fam: toscano*) fool, idiot.
'**biscia, sce** ['biʃʃa] *sf* snake; ~ **d'acqua** water snake.
biscot'tato, a *ag* crisp; **fette** ~**e** rusks.
bis'cotto *sm* biscuit.
bisessu'ale *ag, smf* bisexual.
bises'tile *ag*: **anno** ~ leap year.
bisezi'one [biset'tsjone] *sf* dichotomy.
bis'lacco, a, chi, che *ag* odd, weird.
bis'lungo, a, ghi, ghe *ag* oblong.
biso'gnare [bizoɲ'ɲare] *vb impers*: **bisogna che tu parta/lo faccia** you'll have to go/do it; **bisogna parlargli** we'll have to (*o* I'll) have to talk to him ♦ *vi* (*esser utile*) to be necessary.
bi'sogno [bi'zoɲɲo] *sm* need; ~**i** *smpl* (*necessità corporali*): **fare i propri** ~**i** to relieve o.s.; **avere** ~ **di qc/di fare qc** to need sth/to do sth; **al** ~, **in caso di** ~ if need be.
biso'gnoso, a [bizoɲ'ɲoso] *ag* needy, poor; ~ **di** in need of, needing.
bi'sonte *sm* (*ZOOL*) bison.
bis'tecca, che *sf* steak, beefsteak; ~ **al sangue/ai ferri** rare/grilled steak.
bisticci'are [bistit'tʃare] *vi*, ~**rsi** *vr* to quarrel, bicker.
bis'ticcio [bis'tittʃo] *sm* quarrel, squabble; (*gioco di parole*) pun.
bistrat'tare *vt* to maltreat.
'**bisturi** *sm inv* scalpel.
bi'sunto, a *ag* very greasy.
bi'torzolo [bi'tortsolo] *sm* (*sulla testa*) bump; (*sul corpo*) lump.
'**bitter** *sm inv* bitters *pl*.
bi'tume *sm* bitumen.
bivac'care *vi* (*MIL*) to bivouac; (*fig*) to bed down.
bi'vacco, chi *sm* bivouac.
'**bivio** *sm* fork; (*fig*) dilemma.
bizan'tino, a [biddzan'tino] *ag* Byzantine.
'**bizza** ['biddza] *sf* tantrum; **fare le** ~**e** to throw a tantrum.
biz'zarro, a [bid'dzarro] *ag* bizarre, strange.
biz'zeffe [bid'dzɛffe]: **a** ~ *av* in plenty, galore.
BL *sigla* = Belluno.
blan'dire *vt* to soothe; to flatter.
'**blando, a** *ag* mild, gentle.
blas'femo, a *ag* blasphemous ♦ *smf* blasphemer.
bla'sone *sm* coat of arms.

blate'rare *vi* to chatter.
'**blatta** *sf* cockroach.
blin'dare *vt* to armour (*BRIT*), armor (*US*).
blin'data *sf* (*macchina*) armoured car *o* limousine.
blin'dato, a *ag* armoured (*BRIT*), armored (*US*); **camera** ~**a** strongroom; **mezzo** ~ armoured vehicle; **porta** ~**a** a reinforced door; **vita** ~**a** life amid maximum security; **vetro** ~ bulletproof glass.
bloc'care *vt* to block; (*isolare*) to isolate, cut off; (*porto*) to blockade; (*prezzi, beni*) to freeze; (*meccanismo*) to jam; ~**rsi** *vr* (*motore*) to stall; (*freni, porta*) to jam, stick; (*ascensore*) to get stuck, stop; **ha bloccato la macchina** (*AUT*) he jammed on the brakes.
bloccas'terzo [blokkas'tɛrtso] *sm* (*AUT*) steering lock.
blocche'rò *etc* [blokke'rɔ] *vb vedi* **bloccare**.
bloc'chetto [blok'ketto] *sm* notebook; (*di biglietti*) book.
'**blocco, chi** *sm* block; (*MIL*) blockade; (*dei fitti*) restriction; (*quadernetto*) pad; (*fig: unione*) coalition; (*il bloccare*) blocking; isolating, cutting-off; blockading; freezing; jamming; **in** ~ (*nell'insieme*) as a whole; (*COMM*) in bulk; ~ **cardiaco** cardiac arrest.
bloc-'notes [blɔk'nɔt] *sm inv* notebook, notepad.
blu *ag inv, sm inv* dark blue.
bluff [blɛf] *sm inv* bluff.
bluf'fare *vi* (*anche fig*) to bluff.
'**blusa** *sf* (*camiciotto*) smock; (*camicetta*) blouse.
BN *sigla* = Benevento.
BO *sigla* = Bologna.
'**boa** *sm inv* (*ZOOL*) boa constrictor; (*sciarpa*) feather boa ♦ *sf* buoy.
bo'ato *sm* rumble, roar.
bob [bɔb] *sm inv* bobsleigh.
bo'bina *sf* reel, spool; (*di pellicola*) spool; (*di film*) reel; (*ELETTR*) coil.
'**bocca, che** *sf* mouth; **essere di buona** ~ to be a hearty eater; (*fig*) to be easily satisfied; **essere sulla** ~ **di tutti** (*persona, notizia*) to be the talk of the town; **rimanere a** ~ **asciutta** to have nothing to eat; (*fig*) to be disappointed; **in** ~ **al lupo!** good luck!; ~ **di leone** (*BOT*) snapdragon.
boc'caccia, ce [bok'kattʃa] *sf* (*malalingua*) gossip; (*smorfia*): **fare le** ~**ce** to pull faces.
boc'caglio [bok'kaʎʎo] *sm* (*TECN*) nozzle; (*di respiratore*) mouthpiece.
boc'cale *sm* jug; ~ **da birra** tankard.
bocca'scena [bokkaʃ'ʃɛna] *sm inv* proscenium.

boc'cata *sf* mouthful; (*di fumo*) puff; **prendere una ~ d'aria** to go out for a breath of (fresh) air.

boc'cetta [bot'tʃetta] *sf* small bottle.

boccheggi'are [bokked'dʒare] *vi* to gasp.

boc'chino [bok'kino] *sm* (*di sigaretta, sigaro: cannella*) cigarette-holder; cigar-holder; (*di pipa, strumenti musicali*) mouthpiece.

'boccia, ce ['bottʃa] *sf* bottle; (*da vino*) decanter, carafe; (*palla di legno, metallo*) bowl; **gioco delle ~ce** bowls *sg*.

bocci'are [bot'tʃare] *vt* (*proposta, progetto*) to reject; (*INS*) to fail; (*BOCCE*) to hit.

boccia'tura [bottʃa'tura] *sf* failure.

bocci'olo [bot'tʃɔlo] *sm* bud.

'boccolo *sm* curl.

boccon'cino [bokkon'tʃino] *sm* (*pietanza deliziosa*) delicacy.

boc'cone *sm* mouthful, morsel; **mangiare un ~** to have a bite to eat.

boc'coni *av* face downwards.

Bo'emia *sf* Bohemia.

bo'emo, a *ag, sm/f* Bohemian.

bofonchi'are [bofon'kjare] *vi* to grumble.

Bogotá *sf* Bogotá.

'boia *sm inv* executioner; hangman; **fa un freddo ~** (*fam*) it's cold as hell; **mondo ~!**, **~ d'un mondo ladro!** (*fam*) damn!, blast!

boi'ata *sf* botch.

boicot'taggio [boikot'taddʒo] *sm* boycott.

boicot'tare *vt* to boycott.

'bolgia, ge ['bɔldʒa] *sf* (*fig*): **c'era una tale ~ al cinema** the cinema was absolutely mobbed.

'bolide *sm* (*ASTR*) meteor; (*macchina: da corsa*) racing car (*BRIT*), race car (*US*); (*: elaborata*) performance car; **come un ~** like a flash, at top speed; **entrare/uscire come un ~** to charge in/out.

Bo'livia *sf*: **la ~** Bolivia.

bolivi'ano, a *ag, sm/f* Bolivian.

'bolla *sf* bubble; (*MED*) blister; (*COMM*) bill, receipt; **finire in una ~ di sapone** (*fig*) to come to nothing; **~ di accompagnamento** waybill; **~ di consegna** delivery note; **~ papale** papal bull.

bol'lare *vt* to stamp; (*fig*) to brand.

bol'lente *ag* boiling; boiling hot; **calmare i ~i spiriti** to sober up, calm down.

bol'letta *sf* bill; (*ricevuta*) receipt; **essere in ~** to be hard up; **~ di consegna** delivery note; **~ doganale** clearance certificate; **~ di trasporto aereo** air waybill.

bol'lettino *sm* bulletin; (*COMM*) note; **~ meteorologico** weather forecast; **~ di ordinazione** order form; **~ di spedizione** consignment note.

bolli'cina [bolli'tʃina] *sf* bubble; **acqua con**

le ~ fizzy water.

bol'lire *vt, vi* to boil; **qualcosa bolle in pentola** (*fig*) there's something brewing.

bol'lito *sm* (*CUC*) boiled meat.

bolli'tore *sm* (*TECN*) boiler; (*CUC: per acqua*) kettle; (*: per latte*) milk pan.

bolli'tura *sf* boiling.

'bollo *sm* stamp; **imposta di ~** stamp duty; **~ auto** road tax; **~ per patente** driving licence tax; **~ postale** postmark.

bol'lore *sm*: **dare un ~ a qc** to bring sth to the boil (*BRIT*) *o* a boil (*US*); **i ~i della gioventù** youthful enthusiasm *sg*.

Bo'logna [bo'lɔɲɲa] *sf* Bologna.

bolo'gnese [bolɔɲ'ɲese] *ag* Bolognese; **spaghetti alla ~** spaghetti bolognese.

'bomba *sf* bomb; **tornare a ~** (*fig*) to get back to the point; **sei stato una ~!** you were tremendous!; **~ atomica** atom bomb; **~ a mano** hand grenade; **~ ad orologeria** time bomb.

bombarda'mento *sm* bombardment; bombing.

bombar'dare *vt* to bombard; (*da aereo*) to bomb.

bombardi'ere *sm* bomber.

bom'betta *sf* bowler (hat) (*BRIT*), derby (*US*).

'bombola *sf* cylinder; **~ del gas** gas cylinder.

bombo'letta *sf*: **~ f spray** *inv* spray can.

bomboni'era *sf* box of sweets (*as souvenir at weddings, first communions etc*).

bo'naccia, ce [bo'nattʃa] *sf* dead calm.

bonacci'one, a [bonat'tʃone] *ag* good-natured ♦ *sm/f* good-natured sort.

bo'nario, a *ag* good-natured, kind.

bo'nifica, che *sf* reclamation; reclaimed land.

bo'nifico, ci *sm* (*riduzione, abbuono*) discount; (*versamento a terzi*) credit transfer.

Bonn *sf* Bonn.

bontà *sf* goodness; (*cortesia*) kindness; **aver la ~ di fare qc** to be good *o* kind enough to do sth.

'bonus-'malus *sm inv* ≈ no-claims bonus.

bor'bonico, a, ci, che *ag* Bourbon; (*fig*) backward, out of date.

borbot'tare *vi* to mumble; (*stomaco*) to rumble.

borbot'tio, ii *sm* mumbling; rumbling.

'borchia ['borkja] *sf* stud.

borda'tura *sf* (*SARTORIA*) border, trim.

bor'deaux [bor'dɔ] *sm* (*colore*) burgundy, maroon; (*vino*) Bordeaux.

bor'dello *sm* brothel.

'bordo *sm* (*NAUT*) ship's side; (*orlo*) edge;

(*striscia di guarnizione*) border, trim; **a ~ di** (*nave, aereo*) aboard, on board; (*macchina*) in; **sul ~ della strada** at the roadside; **persona d'alto ~** VIP.

bor'dura *sf* border.

bor'gata *sf* hamlet; (*a Roma*) working-class suburb.

bor'ghese [bor'geze] *ag* (*spesso peg*) middle-class; bourgeois; **abito ~** civilian dress; **poliziotto in ~** plainclothes policeman.

borghe'sia [borge'zia] *sf* middle classes *pl*; bourgeoisie.

'borgo, ghi *sm* (*paesino*) village; (*quartiere*) district; (*sobborgo*) suburb.

'boria *sf* self-conceit, arrogance.

bori'oso, a *ag* arrogant.

bor'lotto *sm* kidney bean.

'Borneo *sm*: **il ~** Borneo.

boro'talco *sm* talcum powder.

bor'raccia, ce [bor'rattʃa] *sf* canteen, water-bottle.

'borsa *sf* bag; (*anche: ~ da signora*) handbag; (*ECON*): **la B~** (*valori*) the Stock Exchange; **~ dell'acqua calda** hot-water bottle; **B~ merci** commodity exchange; **~ nera** black market; **~ della spesa** shopping bag; **~ di studio** grant.

borsai'olo *sm* pickpocket.

bor'seggio [bor'seddʒo] *sm* pickpocketing.

borsel'lino *sm* purse.

bor'sello *sm* gent's handbag.

bor'setta *sf* handbag.

bor'sista, i, e *smlf* (*ECON*) speculator; (*INS*) grant-holder.

bos'caglia [bos'kaʎʎa] *sf* woodlands *pl*.

boscai'olo, boscaiu'olo *sm* woodcutter; forester.

bos'chetto [bos'ketto] *sm* copse, grove.

'bosco, schi *sm* wood.

bos'coso, a *ag* wooded.

bos'niaco, a, ci, che *ag, smlf* Bosnian.

'Bosnia-Erze'govina ['bɔsnja erdze'govina] *sf*: **la ~** Bosnia-Herzegovina.

'bossolo *sm* cartridge case.

Bot, bot *sigla m inv vedi* **buono ordinario del Tesoro.**

bo'tanico, a, ci, che *ag* botanical ♦ *sm* botanist ♦ *sf* botany.

'botola *sf* trap door.

Bots'wana [bots'vana] *sm*: **il ~** Botswana.

'botta *sf* blow; (*rumore*) bang; **dare (un sacco di) ~e a qn** to give sb a good thrashing; **~ e risposta** (*fig*) cut and thrust.

'botte *sf* barrel, cask; **essere in una ~ di ferro** (*fig*) to be as safe as houses; **volere la ~ piena e la moglie ubriaca** to want to

have one's cake and eat it.

bot'tega, ghe *sf* shop; (*officina*) workshop; **stare a ~ (da qn)** to serve one's apprenticeship (with sb); **le B~ghe Oscure** *headquarters of the DS, Italian left-wing party*.

botte'gaio, a *smlf* shopkeeper.

botte'ghino [botte'gino] *sm* ticket office; (*del lotto*) public lottery office.

bot'tiglia [bot'tiʎʎa] *sf* bottle.

bottiglie'ria [bottiʎʎe'ria] *sf* wine shop.

bot'tino *sm* (*di guerra*) booty; (*di rapina, furto*) loot; **fare ~ di qc** (*anche fig*) to make off with sth.

'botto *sm* bang; crash; **di ~** suddenly; **d'un ~** (*fam*) in a flash.

bot'tone *sm* button; (*BOT*) bud; **stanza dei ~i** control room; (*fig*) nerve centre; **attaccare (un) ~ a qn** to buttonhole sb.

bo'vino, a *ag* bovine; **~i** *smpl* cattle.

box [bɔks] *sm inv* (*per cavalli*) horsebox; (*per macchina*) lock-up; (*per macchina da corsa*) pit; (*per bambini*) playpen.

boxe [bɔks] *sf* boxing.

'boxer ['bɔkser] *sm inv* (*cane*) boxer ♦ *smpl* (*mutande*): **un paio di ~** a pair of boxer shorts.

'bozza ['bɔttsa] *sf* draft; (*TIP*) proof; **~ di stampa/impaginata** galley/page proof.

boz'zetto [bot'tsetto] *sm* sketch.

'bozzolo ['bɔttsolo] *sm* cocoon.

BR *sigla fpl* = **Brigate Rosse** ♦ *sigla* = Brindisi.

'braca, che *sf* (*gamba di pantalone*) trouser leg; **~che** *sfpl* (*fam*) trousers, pants (*US*); (*mutandoni*) drawers; **calare le ~che** (*fig fam*) to chicken out.

brac'care *vt* to hunt.

brac'cetto [brat'tʃetto] *sm*: **a ~** arm in arm.

braccherò etc [brakke'rɔ] *vb vedi* **braccare.**

bracci'ale [brat'tʃale] *sm* bracelet; (*per nuotare, anche distintivo*) armband.

braccia'letto [brattʃa'letto] *sm* bracelet, bangle.

bracci'ante [brat'tʃante] *sm* (*AGR*) day labourer.

bracci'ata [brat'tʃata] *sf* armful; (*nel nuoto*) stroke.

'braccio ['brattʃo] *sm* (*pl(f)* **braccia:** *ANAT*) arm; (*pl(m)* **bracci:** *di gru, fiume*) arm; (*: di edificio*) wing; **camminare sotto ~** to walk arm in arm; **è il suo ~ destro** he's his right-hand man; **~ di ferro** (*anche fig*) trial of strength; **~ di mare** sound.

bracci'olo [brat'tʃɔlo] *sm* (*appoggio*) arm.

'bracco, chi *sm* hound.

bracconi'ere *sm* poacher.

'brace ['bratʃe] *sf* embers *pl*.

braci'ere [bra'tʃɛre] *sm* brazier.

braci'ola [bra't∫ɔla] *sf (CUC)* chop.
'bradipo *sm (ZOOL)* sloth.
'brado, a *ag*: **allo stato** ~ in the wild *o* natural state.
'brama *sf*: ~ **(di/di fare)** longing (for/to do), yearning (for/to do).
bra'mare *vt*: ~ **(qc/di fare qc)** to long (for sth/to do sth), yearn (for sth/to do sth).
bramo'sia *sf*: ~ **(di)** longing (for), yearning (for).
'branca, che *sf* branch.
'branchia ['brankja] *sf (ZOOL)* gill.
'branco, chi *sm (di cani, lupi)* pack; *(di uccelli, pecore)* flock; *(peg: di persone)* gang, pack.
branco'lare *vi* to grope, feel one's way.
'branda *sf* camp bed.
bran'dello *sm* scrap, shred; **a ~i** in tatters, in rags; **fare a ~i** to tear to shreds.
bran'dina *sf* camp bed (*BRIT*), cot (*US*).
bran'dire *vt* to brandish.
'brano *sm* piece; *(di libro)* passage.
bra'sare *vt* to braise.
bra'sato *sm* braised beef.
Bra'sile *sm*: **il** ~ Brazil.
Bra'silia *sf* Brasilia.
brasili'ano, a *ag, sm/f* Brazilian.
bra'vata *sf (azione spavalda)* act of bravado.
'bravo, a *ag (abile)* clever, capable, skilful; *(buono)* good, honest; *(: bambino)* good; *(coraggioso)* brave; ~! well done!; *(al teatro)* bravo!; **su da** ~! *(fam)* there's a good boy!; **mi sono fatto le mie** ~**e 8 ore di lavoro** I put in a full 8 hours' work.
bra'vura *sf* cleverness, skill.
'breccia, ce ['brett∫a] *sf* breach; **essere sulla** ~ *(fig)* to be going strong; **fare** ~ **nell'animo** *o* **nel cuore di qn** to find the way to sb's heart.
'Brema *sf* Bremen.
bre'saola *sf* kind of dried salted beef.
bresci'ano, a [bre∫'∫ano] *ag* of (*o* from) Brescia.
Bre'tagna [bre'taɲɲa] *sf*: **la** ~ Brittany.
bre'tella *sf (AUT)* link; ~**e** *sfpl* braces.
'bret(t)one *ag, sm/f* Breton.
'breve *ag* brief, short; **in** ~ in short; **per farla** ~ to cut a long story short; **a** ~ *(COMM)* short-term.
brevet'tare *vt* to patent.
bre'vetto *sm* patent; ~ **di pilotaggio** pilot's licence (*BRIT*) *o* license (*US*).
brevità *sf* brevity.
'brezza ['breddza] *sf* breeze.
'bricco, chi *sm* jug; ~ **del caffè** coffeepot.
bricco'nata *sf* mischievous trick.
bric'cone, a *sm/f* rogue, rascal.

'briciola ['brit∫ola] *sf* crumb.
'briciolo ['brit∫olo] *sm (specie fig)* bit.
bridge [bridʒ] *sm* bridge.
'briga, ghe *sf (fastidio)* trouble, bother; **attaccar** ~ to start a quarrel; **pigliarsi la** ~ **di fare qc** to take the trouble to do sth.
brigadi'ere *sm (dei carabinieri etc)* ≈ sergeant.
bri'gante *sm* bandit.
bri'gata *sf (MIL)* brigade; *(gruppo)* group, party; **le B**~**e Rosse** *(POL)* the Red Brigades.
briga'tismo *sm* phenomenon of the Red Brigades.
briga'tista, i, e *sm/f (POL)* member of the Red Brigades.
'briglia ['briʎʎa] *sf* rein; **a** ~ **sciolta** at full gallop; *(fig)* at full speed.
bril'lante *ag* bright; *(anche fig)* brilliant; *(che luccica)* shining ♦ *sm* diamond.
brillan'tina *sf* brilliantine.
bril'lare *vi* to shine; *(mina)* to blow up ♦ *vt (mina)* to set off.
'brillo, a *ag* merry, tipsy.
'brina *sf* hoarfrost.
brin'dare *vi*: ~ **a qn/qc** to drink to *o* toast sb/sth.
'brindisi *sm inv* toast.
'brio *sm* liveliness, go.
bri'oche [bri'ɔʃ] *sf inv* brioche (bun).
bri'oso, a *ag* lively.
'briscola *sf* type of card game; *(seme vincente)* trump(s); *(carta)* trump card.
bri'tannico, a, ci, che *ag* British ♦ *sm/f* Briton; **i B**~**ci** the British *pl*.
'brivido *sm* shiver; *(di ribrezzo)* shudder; *(fig)* thrill; **racconti del** ~ suspense stories.
brizzo'lato, a [brittso'lato] *ag (persona)* going grey; *(barba, capelli)* greying.
'brocca, che *sf* jug.
broc'cato *sm* brocade.
'broccolo *sm* broccoli *no pl*.
bro'daglia [bro'daʎʎa] *sf (peg)* dishwater.
'brodo *sm* broth; *(per cucinare)* stock; ~ **ristretto** consommé; **lasciare (cuocere) qn nel suo** ~ to let sb stew (in his own juice); **tutto fa** ~ every little bit helps.
'broglio ['brɔʎʎo] *sm*: ~ **elettorale** gerrymandering; ~**i** *smpl (DIR)* malpractices.
'bromo *sm (CHIM)* bromine.
bron'chite [bron'kite] *sf (MED)* bronchitis.
'broncio ['bront∫o] *sm* sulky expression; **tenere il** ~ to sulk.
'bronco, chi *sm* bronchial tube.
bronto'lare *vi* to grumble; *(tuono, stomaco)* to rumble.
bronto'lio *sm* grumbling, mumbling.

bronto'lone, a *ag* grumbling ♦ *sm/f* grumbler.

bron'zina [bron'dzina] *sf* (*TECN*) bush.

'bronzo ['brondzo] *sm* bronze; **che faccia di ~!** what a brass neck!

bross. *abbr* = **in brossura**.

bros'sura *sf*: **in ~** (*libro*) limpback.

'browser ['brauzer] *sm inv* (*INFORM*) browser.

bru'care *vt* to browse on, nibble at.

brucherà *etc* [bruke'ra] *vb vedi* **brucare**.

bruciacchi'are [brutʃak'kjare] *vt* to singe, scorch; **~rsi** *vr* to become singed *o* scorched.

brucia'pelo [brutʃa'pelo]: **a ~** *av* point-blank.

bruci'are [bru'tʃare] *vt* to burn; (*scottare*) to scald ♦ *vi* to burn; **~ gli avversari** (*SPORT, fig*) to leave the rest of the field behind; **~ le tappe** *o* **i tempi** (*SPORT, fig*) to shoot ahead; **~rsi la carriera** to put an end to one's career.

brucia'tore [brutʃa'tore] *sm* burner.

brucia'tura [brutʃa'tura] *sf* (*atto*) burning *no pl*; (*segno*) burn; (*scottatura*) scald.

bruci'ore [bru'tʃore] *sm* burning *o* smarting sensation.

'bruco, chi *sm* grub; (*di farfalla*) caterpillar.

'brufolo *sm* pimple, spot.

brughi'era [bru'gjɛra] *sf* heath, moor.

bruli'care *vi* to swarm.

bruli'chio, ii [bruli'kio] *sm* swarming.

'brullo, a *ag* bare, bleak.

'bruma *sf* mist.

'bruno, a *ag* brown, dark; (*persona*) dark(-haired).

brusca'mente *av* (*frenare, fermarsi*) suddenly; (*rispondere, reagire*) sharply.

'brusco, a, schi, sche *ag* (*sapore*) sharp; (*modi, persona*) brusque, abrupt; (*movimento*) abrupt, sudden.

bru'sio *sm* buzz, buzzing.

bru'tale *ag* brutal.

brutalità *sf inv* brutality.

'bruto, a *ag* (*forza*) brute *cpd* ♦ *sm* brute.

'brutta *sf vedi* **brutto**.

brut'tezza [brut'tettsa] *sf* ugliness.

'brutto, a *ag* ugly; (*cattivo*) bad; (*malattia, strada, affare*) nasty, bad ♦ *sm*: **guardare qn di ~** to give sb a nasty look ♦ *sf* rough copy, first draft; **~ tempo** bad weather; **passare un ~ quarto d'ora** to have a nasty time of it; **vedersela ~a** (*per un attimo*) to have a nasty moment; (*per un periodo*) to have a bad time of it.

brut'tura *sf* (*cosa brutta*) ugly thing; (*sudiciume*) filth; (*azione meschina*) mean action.

Bru'xelles [bry'sɛl] *sf* Brussels.

BS *sigla* = Brescia.

BSE [bi'ɛsse'ɛ] *sigla f* BSE (= *bovine spongiform encephalopathy*).

B.T. *abbr* (= *bassa tensione*) LT ♦ *sigla m inv* = **buono del Tesoro**.

btg *abbr* = **battaglione**.

Btp *sigla m* (= *buono del Tesoro poliennale*, *vedi* **buono**.

bub'bone *sm* swelling.

'buca, che *sf* hole; (*avvallamento*) hollow; **~ delle lettere** letterbox.

buca'neve *sm inv* snowdrop.

bu'care *vt* (*forare*) to make a hole (*o* holes) in; (*pungere*) to pierce; (*biglietto*) to punch; **~rsi** *vr* (*con eroina*) to mainline; **~ una gomma** to have a puncture; **avere le mani bucate** (*fig*) to be a spendthrift.

'Bucarest *sf* Bucharest.

bu'cato *sm* (*operazione*) washing; (*panni*) wash, washing.

'buccia, ce ['buttʃa] *sf* skin, peel; (*corteccia*) bark.

bucherel'lare [bukerel'lare] *vt* to riddle with holes.

bucherò *etc* [buke'rɔ] *vb vedi* **bucare**.

'buco, chi *sm* hole; **fare un ~ nell'acqua** to fail, draw a blank; **farsi un ~** (*fam: drogarsi*) to have a fix; **~ nero** (*anche fig*) black hole.

'Budapest *sf* Budapest.

'Budda *sm inv* Buddha.

bud'dismo *sm* Buddhism.

bu'dello *sm* intestine; (*fig: tubo*) tube; (*vicolo*) alley; **~a** *sfpl* bowels, guts.

bu'dino *sm* pudding.

'bue, *pl* **bu'oi** *sm ox*; (*anche:* **carne di ~**) beef; **uovo all'occhio di ~** fried egg.

Bu'enos 'Aires *sf* Buenos Aires.

'bufalo *sm* buffalo.

bu'fera *sf* storm.

buf'fetto *sm* flick.

'buffo, a *ag* funny; (*TEAT*) comic.

buffo'nata *sf* (*azione*) prank, jest; (*parola*) jest.

buf'fone *sm* buffoon.

bugge'rare [buddʒe'rare] *vt* to swindle, cheat.

bu'gia, 'gie [bu'dʒia] *sf* lie; (*candeliere*) candleholder.

bugi'ardo, a [bu'dʒardo] *ag* lying, deceitful ♦ *sm/f* liar.

bugi'gattolo [budʒi'gattolo] *sm* poky little room.

'buio, a *ag* dark ♦ *sm* dark, darkness; **fa ~ pesto** it's pitch-dark.

'bulbo *sm* (*BOT*) bulb; **~ oculare** eyeball.

Bulga'ria *sf*: **la ~** Bulgaria.

'bulgaro, a *ag, sm/f, sm* Bulgarian.

buli'mia *sf* bulimia.

'bullo *sm* (*persona*) tough.

bul'lone *sm* bolt.
bu'oi *smpl di* **bue.**
buona'fede *sf* good faith.
buon'anima *sf* = **buon'anima;** *vedi* **anima.**
buona'notte *escl* good night! ♦ *sf*: **dare la ~**
  a to say good night to.
buona'sera *escl* good evening!
buoncos'tume *sm* public morality; **la**
  (squadra del) ~ *(POLIZIA)* the vice squad.
buondi *escl* hello!
buongi'orno [bwon'dʒorno] *escl* good
  morning *(o* afternoon)!
buon'grado *av*: **di ~** willingly.
buongus'taio, a *sm/f* gourmet.
buon'gusto *sm* good taste.

═══════════════════ *PAROLA CHIAVE*

bu'ono, a *(ag: dav sm* **buon** + *C o V,* **buono**
  + *s impura, gn, pn, ps, x, z; dav sf* **buon'**
  + *V) ag* **1** *(gen)* good; **un buon pranzo/**
  ristorante a good lunch/restaurant; **(stai)**
  ~! behave!; che ~! *(cibo)* this is nice!
  2 *(benevolo)*: **~ (con)** good (to), kind (to)
  3 *(giusto, valido)* right; **al momento ~** at
  the right moment
  4 *(adatto)*: **~ a/da** fit for/to; **essere ~ a**
  nulla to be no good *o* use at anything
  5 *(auguri)*: **buon compleanno!** happy
  birthday!; **buon divertimento!** have a nice
  time!; **~a fortuna!** good luck!; **buon**
  riposo! sleep well!; **buon viaggio!** have a
  good trip!
  6: ad ogni buon conto in any case; **tante**
  ~e cose! all the best!; **di buon cuore**
  (persona) goodhearted; **di buon grado**
  willingly; **le ~e maniere** good manners; **di**
  buon mattino early in the morning; **a**
  buon mercato cheap; **di buon'ora** early;
  mettere una ~a parola to put in a good
  word; **di buon passo** at a good pace; **buon**
  pro ti faccia! much good may it do you!;
  buon senso common sense; **la ~a società**
  the upper classes; **una ~a volta** once and
  for all; **alla ~a** *ag* simple
  ♦ *av* in a simple way, without any fuss; **un**
  tipo alla ~a an easy-going sort
  ♦ *sm/f*: **essere un ~/una ~a** to be a good
  person; **a nulla** good for nothing; **i ~i e i**
  cattivi *(in storia, film)* the goodies and the
  baddies; **accetterà con le ~e o con le**
  cattive one way or another he's going to
  agree to it
  ♦ *sm* **1** *(bontà)* goodness, good
  2 *(COMM)* voucher, coupon; **~ d'acquisto**
  credit note; **~ di cassa** cash voucher; **~ di**
  consegna delivery note; **~ fruttifero**
  interest-bearing bond; **~ ordinario del**
  Tesoro short-term Treasury bond; **~**

postale fruttifero interest-bearing bond
  (issued by Italian Post Office); **~ del Tesoro**
  Treasury bill.

buon'senso *sm* = **buon senso.**
buontem'pone *sm/f* jovial person.
buonu'scita [bwonuʃ'ʃita] *sf (INDUSTRIA)*
  golden handshake; *(di affitti) sum paid for*
  the relinquishing of tenancy rights.
buratti'naio *sm* puppeteer, puppet
  master.
burat'tino *sm* puppet.
'burbero, a *ag* surly, gruff.
'burla *sf* prank, trick.
bur'lare *vt*: **~ qc/qn, ~rsi di qc/qn** to make
  fun of sth/sb.
bu'rocrate *sm* bureaucrat.
buro'cratico, a, ci, che *ag* bureaucratic.
burocra'zia [burokrat'tsia] *sf* bureaucracy.
bur'rasca, sche *sf* storm.
burras'coso, a *ag* stormy.
'burro *sm* butter.
bur'rone *sm* ravine.
bus'care *vt (anche: ~rsi: raffreddore)* to get,
  catch; **buscarle** *(fam)* to get a hiding.
buscherò *etc* [buske'rɔ] *vb vedi* **buscare.**
bus'sare *vi* to knock; **~ a quattrini** *(fig)* to
  ask for money.
'bussola *sf* compass; **perdere la ~** *(fig)* to
  lose one's bearings.
'busta *sf (da lettera)* envelope; *(astuccio)*
  case; **in ~ aperta/chiusa** in an unsealed/
  sealed envelope; **~ paga** pay packet.
busta'rella *sf* bribe, backhander.
bus'tina *sf (piccola busta)* envelope; *(di cibi,*
  farmaci) sachet; *(MIL)* forage cap; **~ di tè**
  tea bag.
'busto *sm* bust; *(indumento)* corset, girdle;
  a mezzo ~ *(fotografia, ritratto)* half-length.
bu'tano *sm* butane.
but'tare *vt* to throw; *(anche: ~ via)* to
  throw away; **~rsi** *vr (saltare)* to jump; **~**
  giù *(scritto)* to scribble down, dash off;
  (cibo) to gulp down; *(edificio)* to pull down,
  demolish; *(pasta, verdura)* to put into
  boiling water; **ho buttato là una frase** I
  mentioned it in passing; **buttiamoci!**
  (saltiamo) let's jump!; *(rischiamo)* let's
  have a go!; **~rsi dalla finestra** to jump out
  of the window.
'buzzo ['buddzo] *sm (fam: pancia)* belly,
  paunch; **di ~ buono** *(con impegno)* with a
  will.

C c

C, c [tʃi] *sf o m inv* (*lettera*) C, c ♦ *abbr* (*GEO*) = **capo**; (= *Celsius, centigrado*) C; (= *conto*) a/c; ~ **come Como** ≈ C for Charlie.

CA *sigla* = Cagliari.

c.a. *abbr* (*ELETTR*) *vedi* **corrente alternata**; (*COMM*) = **corrente anno**.

caba'ret [kaba'rɛ] *sm inv* cabaret.

ca'bina *sf* (*di nave*) cabin; (*da spiaggia*) beach hut; (*di autocarro, treno*) cab; (*di aereo*) cockpit; (*di ascensore*) cage; ~ **di proiezione** (*CINE*) projection booth; ~ **di registrazione** recording booth; ~ **telefonica** callbox, (tele)phone box *o* booth.

cabi'nato *sm* cabin cruiser.

ca'blaggio [ka'bladdʒo] *sm* wiring.

cablo'gramma *sm* cable(gram).

ca'cao *sm* cocoa.

'cacca *sf* (*fam: anche fig*) shit (*!*).

'caccia ['kattʃa] *sf* hunting; (*con fucile*) shooting; (*inseguimento*) chase; (*cacciagione*) game ♦ *sm inv* (*aereo*) fighter; (*nave*) destroyer; **andare a** ~ to go hunting; **andare a** ~ **di guai** to be asking for trouble; ~ **grossa** big-game hunting; ~ **all'uomo** manhunt.

cacciabombardi'ere [kattʃabombar'djɛre] *sm* fighter-bomber.

cacciagi'one [kattʃa'dʒone] *sf* game.

cacci'are [kat'tʃare] *vt* to hunt; (*mandar via*) to chase away; (*ficcare*) to shove, stick ♦ *vi* to hunt; ~**rsi** *vr* (*fam: mettersi*): ~**rsi tra la folla** to plunge into the crowd; **dove s'è cacciata la mia borsa?** where has my bag got to?; ~**rsi nei guai** to get into trouble; ~ **fuori qc** to whip *o* pull sth out; ~ **un urlo** to let out a yell.

caccia'tora [kattʃa'tora] *sf* (*giacca*) hunting jacket; (*CUC*): **pollo** *etc* **alla** ~ chicken *etc* chasseur.

caccia'tore [kattʃa'tore] *sm* hunter; ~ **di frodo** poacher; ~ **di dote** fortune-hunter.

cacciatorpedini'ere [kattʃatorpedi'njɛre] *sm* destroyer.

caccia'vite [kattʃa'vite] *sm inv* screwdriver.

cache'mire [kaʃ'mir] *sm inv* cashmere.

ca'chet [ka'ʃɛ] *sm* (*MED*) capsule; (*: compressa*) tablet; (*compenso*) fee; (*colorante per capelli*) rinse.

'cachi ['kaki] *sm inv* (*albero, frutto*) persimmon; (*colore*) khaki ♦ *ag inv* khaki.

'cacio ['katʃo] *sm* cheese; **essere come il** ~ **sui maccheroni** (*fig*) to turn up at the right moment.

'cactus *sm inv* cactus.

ca'davere *sm* (dead) body, corpse.

cada'verico, a, ci, che *ag* (*fig*) deathly pale.

'caddi *etc vb vedi* **cadere**.

ca'dente *ag* falling; (*casa*) tumbledown; (*persona*) decrepit.

ca'denza [ka'dɛntsa] *sf* cadence; (*andamento ritmico*) rhythm; (*MUS*) cadenza.

ca'dere *vi* to fall; (*denti, capelli*) to fall out; (*tetto*) to fall in; **questa gonna cade bene** this skirt hangs well; **lasciar** ~ (*anche fig*) to drop; ~ **dal sonno** to be falling asleep on one's feet; ~ **ammalato** to fall ill; ~ **dalle nuvole** (*fig*) to be taken aback.

ca'detto *sm* cadet.

cadrò *etc vb vedi* **cadere**.

ca'duto, a *ag* (*morto*) dead ♦ *sm* dead soldier ♦ *sf* fall; **monumento ai** ~**i** war memorial; ~**a di temperatura** drop in temperature; **la** ~**a dei capelli** hair loss; ~**a del sistema** (*INFORM*) system failure.

caffè *sm inv* coffee; (*locale*) café; ~ **corretto** coffee with liqueur; ~ **in grani** coffee beans; ~ **macchiato** coffee with a dash of milk; ~ **macinato** ground coffee.

caffe'ina *sf* caffeine.

caffel'latte *sm inv* white coffee.

caffette'ria *sf* coffee shop.

caffetti'era *sf* coffeepot.

ca'fone *sm* (*contadino*) peasant; (*peg*) boor.

cagio'nare [kadʒo'nare] *vt* to cause, be the cause of.

cagio'nevole [kadʒo'nevole] *ag* delicate, weak.

cagli'are [kaʎ'ʎare] *vi* to curdle.

cagliari'tano, a [kaʎʎari'tano] *ag* of (*o* from) Cagliari.

'cagna ['kaɲɲa] *sf* (*ZOOL, peg*) bitch.

ca'gnara [kaɲ'ɲara] *sf* (*fig*) uproar.

ca'gnesco, a, schi, sche [kaɲ'ɲesko] *ag* (*fig*): **guardare qn in** ~ to scowl at sb.

CAI *sigla m* = Club Alpino Italiano.

'Cairo *sm*: **il** ~ Cairo.

cala'brese *ag, sm/f* Calabrian.

cala'brone *sm* hornet.

Cala'hari [kala'ari]: **il Deserto di** ~ *sm* the Kalahari Desert.

cala'maio *sm* inkpot; inkwell.

cala'maro *sm* squid.

cala'mita *sf* magnet.

calamità _sf inv_ calamity, disaster; ~ **naturale** natural disaster.

ca'lare _vt_ (_far discendere_) to lower; (_MAGLIA_) to decrease ♦ _vi_ (_discendere_) to go (_o_ come) down; (_tramontare_) to set, go down; ~ **di peso** to lose weight.

ca'lata _sf_ (_invasione_) invasion.

'calca _sf_ throng, press.

cal'cagno [kal'kaɲɲo] _sm_ heel.

cal'care _sm_ limestone; (_incrostazione_) (lime)scale ♦ _vt_ (_premere coi piedi_) to tread, press down; (_premere con forza_) to press down; (_mettere in rilievo_) to stress; ~ **la mano** to overdo it, exaggerate; ~ **le scene** (_fig_) to be on the stage; ~ **le orme di qn** (_fig_) to follow in sb's footsteps.

'calce ['kaltʃe] _sm_: **in** ~ at the foot of the page ♦ _sf_ lime; ~ **viva** quicklime.

calces'truzzo [kaltʃes'truttso] _sm_ concrete.

calcherò _etc_ [kalke'rɔ] _vb vedi_ **calcare**.

calci'are [kal'tʃare] _vt_, _vi_ to kick.

calcia'tore [kaltʃa'tore] _sm_ footballer (_BRIT_), (football) player.

cal'cina [kal'tʃina] _sf_ (lime) mortar.

calci'naccio [kaltʃi'nattʃo] _sm_ flake of plaster.

'calcio ['kaltʃo] _sm_ (_pedata_) kick; (_sport_) football, soccer; (_di pistola, fucile_) butt; (_CHIM_) calcium; ~ **d'angolo** (_SPORT_) corner (kick); ~ **di punizione** (_SPORT_) free kick.

'calco, chi _sm_ (_ARTE_) casting, moulding (_BRIT_), molding (_US_); cast, mo(u)ld.

calco'lare _vt_ to calculate, work out, reckon; (_ponderare_) to weigh (up).

calcola'tore, 'trice _ag_ calculating ♦ _sm_ calculator; (_fig_) calculating person ♦ _sf_ (_anche_: **macchina calcolatrice**) calculator; ~ **digitale** digital computer; ~ **elettronico** computer; ~ **da tavolo** desktop computer.

'calcolo _sm_ (_anche MAT_) calculation; (_infinitesimale etc_) calculus; (_MED_) stone; **fare il** ~ **di qc** to work sth out; **fare i propri** ~**i** (_fig_) to weigh the pros and cons; **per** ~ out of self-interest.

cal'daia _sf_ boiler.

caldar'rosta _sf_ roast chestnut.

caldeggi'are [kalded'dʒare] _vt_ to support.

'caldo, a _ag_ warm; (_molto_ ~) hot; (_fig: appassionato_) keen ♦ _sm_ heat; **ho** ~ I'm warm; I'm hot; **fa** ~ it's warm; it's hot; **non mi fa né** ~ **né freddo** I couldn't care less; **a** ~ (_fig_) in the heat of the moment.

caleidos'copio _sm_ kaleidoscope.

calen'dario _sm_ calendar.

ca'lende _sfpl_ calends; **rimandare qc alle** ~ **greche** to put sth off indefinitely.

ca'lesse _sm_ gig.

'calibro _sm_ (_di arma_) calibre, bore; (_TECN_) callipers _pl_; (_fig_) calibre; **di grosso** ~ (_fig_) prominent.

'calice ['kalitʃe] _sm_ goblet; (_REL_) chalice.

Cali'fornia _sf_ California.

californi'ano, a _ag_ Californian.

ca'ligine [ka'lidʒine] _sf_ fog; (_mista con fumo_) smog.

calligra'fia _sf_ (_scrittura_) handwriting; (_arte_) calligraphy.

'callo _sm_ callus; (_ai piedi_) corn; **fare il** ~ **a qc** to get used to sth.

'calma _sf_ calm; **faccia con** ~ take your time.

cal'mante _sm_ sedative, tranquillizer.

cal'mare _vt_ to calm; (_lenire_) to soothe; ~**rsi** _vr_ to grow calm, calm down; (_vento_) to abate; (_dolori_) to ease.

calmi'ere _sm_ controlled price.

'calmo, a _ag_ calm, quiet.

'calo _sm_ (_COMM: di prezzi_) fall; (: _di volume_) shrinkage; (: _di peso_) loss.

ca'lore _sm_ warmth; (_intenso, FISICA_) heat; **essere in** ~ (_ZOOL_) to be on heat.

calo'ria _sf_ calorie.

calo'rifero _sm_ radiator.

calo'roso, a _ag_ warm; **essere** ~ not to feel the cold.

calpes'tare _vt_ to tread on, trample on; "**è vietato** ~ **l'erba**" "keep off the grass".

ca'lunnia _sf_ slander; (_scritta_) libel.

calunni'are _vt_ to slander.

cal'vario _sm_ (_fig_) affliction, cross.

cal'vizie [kal'vittsje] _sf_ baldness.

'calvo, a _ag_ bald.

'calza ['kaltsa] _sf_ (_da donna_) stocking; (_da uomo_) sock; **fare la** ~ to knit; ~**e di nailon** nylons, (nylon) stockings.

calza'maglia [kaltsa'maʎʎa] _sf_ tights _pl_; (_per danza, ginnastica_) leotard.

cal'zare [kal'tsare] _vt_ (_scarpe, guanti: mettersi_) to put on; (: _portare_) to wear ♦ _vi_ to fit; ~ **a pennello** to fit like a glove.

calza'tura [kaltsa'tura] _sf_ footwear.

calzaturi'ficio [kaltsaturi'fitʃo] _sm_ shoe _o_ footwear factory.

cal'zetta [kal'tsetta] _sf_ ankle sock; **una mezza** ~ (_fig_) a nobody.

calzet'tone [kaltset'tone] _sm_ heavy knee-length sock.

cal'zino [kal'tsino] _sm_ sock.

calzo'laio [kaltso'lajo] _sm_ shoemaker; (_che ripara scarpe_) cobbler.

calzole'ria [kaltsole'ria] _sf_ (_negozio_) shoe shop; (_arte_) shoemaking.

calzon'cini [kaltson'tʃini] _smpl_ shorts; ~ **da bagno** (swimming) trunks.

cal'zone [kal'tsone] _sm_ trouser leg; (_CUC_)

savoury turnover made with pizza dough;
~**i** smpl trousers (BRIT), pants (US).
camale'onte sm chameleon.
cambi'ale sf bill (of exchange); (pagherò
cambiario) promissory note; ~ **di comodo**
o **di favore** accommodation bill.
cambia'mento sm change.
cambi'are vt to change; (modificare) to
alter, change; (barattare): ~ **(qc con qn/qc)**
to exchange (sth with sb/for sth)
♦ vi to change, alter; ~**rsi** vr (variare abito)
to change; ~ **casa** to move (house); ~ **idea**
to change one's mind; ~ **treno** to change
trains; ~ **le carte in tavola** (fig) to change
one's tune; ~ **(l')aria in una stanza** to air a
room; **è ora di** ~ **aria** (andarsene) it's time
to move on.
cambiava'lute sm inv exchange office.
'cambio sm change; (modifica) alteration,
change; (scambio, COMM) exchange; (corso
dei cambi) rate (of exchange); (TECN, AUT)
gears pl; **in** ~ **di** in exchange for; **dare il** ~
a qn to take over from sb; **fare il** o **un** ~ to
change (over); ~ **a termine** (COMM)
forward exchange.
'Cambital sigla m = Ufficio Italiano dei
Cambi.
Cam'bogia [kam'bɔdʒa] sf: **la** ~ Cambodia.
cambogi'ano, a [kambo'dʒano] ag, sm/f
Cambodian.
cam'busa sf storeroom.
'camera sf room; (anche: ~ **da letto**)
bedroom; (POL) chamber, house; ~
ardente mortuary chapel; ~ **d'aria** inner
tube; (di pallone) bladder; ~ **blindata**
strongroom; **C~ di Commercio** Chamber
of Commerce; **C~ dei Deputati** Chamber
of Deputies, ≈ House of Commons (BRIT),
≈ House of Representatives (US); vedi nota
nel riquadro; ~ **a gas** gas chamber; ~ **del
lavoro** trades union centre (BRIT), labor
union center (US); ~ **a un letto/a due
letti/matrimoniale** single/twin-bedded/
double room; ~ **oscura** (FOT) dark room;
~ **da pranzo** dining room.

CAMERA DEI DEPUTATI

*The **Camera dei deputati** is the lower house
of the Italian Parliament and is presided over by
the "Presidente della Camera", who is chosen
by the "deputati". Elections to the Chamber are
normally held every five years. Since the
electoral reform of 1993 members have been
voted in via a system which combines a first-
past-the-post element with proportional
representation. See also **Parlamento**.*

---

came'rata, i, e sm/f companion, mate ♦ sf
dormitory.
camera'tismo sm comradeship.
cameri'era sf (domestica) maid; (che serve a
tavola) waitress; (che fa le camere)
chambermaid.
cameri'ere sm (man)servant; (di ristorante)
waiter.
came'rino sm (TEAT) dressing room.
'Camerun sm: **il** ~ Cameroon.
'camice ['kamitʃe] sm (REL) alb; (per medici
etc) white coat.
cami'cetta [kami'tʃetta] sf blouse.
ca'micia, cie [ka'mitʃa] sf (da uomo) shirt;
(da donna) blouse; **nascere con la** ~ (fig) to
be born lucky; **sudare sette** ~**cie** (fig) to
have a hell of a time; ~ **di forza**
straitjacket; ~ **da notte** (da donna)
nightdress; (da uomo) nightshirt; **C~ nera**
(fascista) Blackshirt.
camici'ola [kami'tʃɔla] sf vest.
camici'otto [kami'tʃɔtto] sm casual shirt;
(per operai) smock.
cami'netto sm hearth, fireplace.
ca'mino sm chimney; (focolare) fireplace,
hearth.
'camion sm inv lorry (BRIT), truck
(US).
camion'cino [kamjon'tʃino] sm van.
camio'netta sf jeep.
camio'nista, i sm lorry driver (BRIT), truck
driver (US).
'camma sf cam; **albero a** ~**e**
camshaft.
cam'mello sm (ZOOL) camel; (tessuto)
camel hair.
cam'meo sm cameo.
cammi'nare vi to walk; (funzionare) to
work, go; ~ **a carponi** o **a quattro zampe**
to go on all fours.
cammi'nata sf walk; **fare una** ~ to go for a
walk.
cam'mino sm walk; (sentiero) path;
(itinerario, direzione, tragitto) way; **mettersi
in** ~ to set o start off; **cammin facendo**
the way; **riprendere il** ~ to continue on
one's way.
camo'milla sf camomile; (infuso)
camomile tea.
ca'morra sf Camorra; (fig) racket.
camor'rista, i, e sm/f member of the
Camorra; (fig) racketeer.
ca'moscio [ka'mɔʃʃo] sm chamois.
cam'pagna [kam'paɲɲa] sf country,
countryside; (POL, COMM, MIL) campaign;
in ~ in the country; **andare in** ~ to go to
the country; **fare una** ~ to campaign; ~
promozionale vendite sales campaign.

campa'gnolo, a [kampaɲ'ɲɔlo] *ag* country *cpd* ♦ *sf* (*AUT*) cross-country vehicle.

cam'pale *ag* field *cpd*; (*fig*): **una giornata ~** a hard day.

cam'pana *sf* bell; (*anche:* **~ di vetro**) bell jar; **sordo come una ~** as deaf as a doorpost; **sentire l'altra ~** (*fig*) to hear the other side of the story.

campa'nella *sf* small bell; (*di tenda*) curtain ring.

campa'nello *sm* (*all'uscio, da tavola*) bell.

campa'nile *sm* bell tower, belfry.

campani'lismo *sm* parochialism.

cam'pano, a *ag* of (o from) Campania.

cam'pare *vi* to live; (*tirare avanti*) to get by, manage; **~ alla giornata** to live from day to day.

cam'pato, a *ag*: **~ in aria** unsound, unfounded.

campeggi'are [kamped'dʒare] *vi* to camp; (*risaltare*) to stand out.

campeggia'tore, 'trice [kampeddʒa'tore] *smlf* camper.

cam'peggio [kam'peddʒo] *sm* camping; (*terreno*) camp site; **fare (del) ~** to go camping.

cam'pestre *ag* country *cpd*, rural; **corsa ~** cross-country race.

Campi'doglio [kampi'dɔʎʎo] *sm*: **il ~** the Capitol; *vedi nota nel riquadro*.

CAMPIDOGLIO

The **Campidoglio***, one of the Seven Hills of Rome, is the home of the "Comune di Roma".*

'camping ['kæmpiŋ] *sm inv* camp site.

campiona'mento *sm* sampling.

campio'nario, a *ag*: **fiera ~a** a trade fair ♦ *sm* collection of samples.

campio'nato *sm* championship.

campiona'tura *sf* (*COMM*) production of samples; (*STATISTICA*) sampling.

campi'one, 'essa *smlf* (*SPORT*) champion ♦ *sm* (*COMM*) sample; **~ gratuito** free sample; **prelievi di ~** product samples.

'campo *sm* (*gen*) field; (*MIL*) field; (*: accampamento*) camp; (*spazio delimitato: sportivo etc*) ground; field; (*di quadro*) background; **i ~i** (*campagna*) the countryside; **padrone del ~** (*fig*) victor; **~ da aviazione** airfield; **~ di concentramento** concentration camp; **~ di golf** golf course; **~ lungo** (*CINE, TV, FOT*) long shot; **~ nomadi** travellers' camp; **~ da tennis** tennis court; **~ visivo** field of vision.

campobas'sano, a *ag* of (o from) Campobasso.

campo'santo, *pl* **campi'santi** *sm* cemetery.

camuf'fare *vt* to disguise; **~rsi** *vr*: **~rsi (da)** to disguise o.s. (as); (*per ballo in maschera*) to dress up (as).

CAN *abbr* (= *Costo, Assicurazione e Nolo*) CIF.

Can. *abbr* (*GEO*) = **canale**.

'Canada *sm*: **il ~** Canada.

cana'dese *ag*, *smlf* Canadian ♦ *sf* (*anche:* **tenda ~**) ridge tent.

ca'naglia [ka'naʎʎa] *sf* rabble, mob; (*persona*) scoundrel, rogue.

ca'nale *sm* (*anche fig*) channel; (*artificiale*) canal.

'canapa *sf* hemp; **~ indiana** cannabis.

Ca'narie *sfpl*: **le (isole) ~** the Canary Islands, the Canaries.

cana'rino *sm* canary.

Can'berra *sf* Canberra.

cancel'lare [kantʃel'lare] *vt* (*con la gomma*) to rub out, erase; (*con la penna*) to strike out; (*annullare, disdire*) to cancel.

cancel'lata [kantʃel'lata] *sf* railing(s) (*pl*).

cancelle'ria [kantʃelle'ria] *sf* chancery; (*quanto necessario per scrivere*) stationery.

cancelli'ere [kantʃel'ljɛre] *sm* chancellor; (*di tribunale*) clerk of the court.

can'cello [kan'tʃello] *sm* gate.

cance'rogeno, a [kantʃe'rɔdʒeno] *ag* carcinogenic ♦ *sm* carcinogen.

cance'rologo, a, gi, ghe [kantʃe'rɔlogo] *smlf* cancer specialist.

cance'roso, a [kantʃe'roso] *ag* cancerous ♦ *smlf* cancer patient.

can'crena *sf* gangrene.

'cancro *sm* (*MED*) cancer; (*dello zodiaco*): **C~** Cancer; **essere del C~** to be Cancer.

candeggi'are [kanded'dʒare] *vt* to bleach.

candeg'gina [kanded'dʒina] *sf* bleach.

can'dela *sf* candle; **~ (di accensione)** (*AUT*) spark(ing) plug; **una lampadina da 100 ~e** (*ELETTR*) a 100 watt bulb; **a lume di ~** by candlelight; **tenere la ~** (*fig*) to play gooseberry (*BRIT*), act as chaperone.

cande'labro *sm* candelabra.

candeli'ere *sm* candlestick.

cande'lotto *sm* candle; **~ di dinamite** stick of dynamite; **~ lacrimogeno** tear gas grenade.

candi'dare *vt* to present as candidate; **~rsi** *vr* to present o.s. as candidate.

candi'dato, a *smlf* candidate; (*aspirante a una carica*) applicant.

candida'tura *sf* candidature; application.

'candido, a *ag* white as snow; (*puro*) pure; (*sincero*) sincere, candid.

can'dito, a *ag* candied.

can'dore *sm* brilliant white; purity; sincerity, candour (*BRIT*), candor (*US*).

'cane *sm* dog; (*di pistola, fucile*) cock; **fa un freddo** ~ it's bitterly cold; **non c'era un** ~ there wasn't a soul; **quell'attore è un** ~ he's a rotten actor; ~ **da caccia** hunting dog; ~ **da guardia** guard dog; ~ **lupo** alsatian; ~ **da salotto** lap dog; ~ **da slitta** husky.

ca'nestro *sm* basket; **fare un** ~ (*SPORT*) to shoot a basket.

'canfora *sf* camphor.

cangi'ante [kan'dʒante] *ag* iridescent; **seta** ~ shot silk.

can'guro *sm* kangaroo.

ca'nicola *sf* scorching heat.

ca'nile *sm* kennel; (*di allevamento*) kennels *pl*; ~ **municipale** dog pound.

ca'nino, a *ag*, *sm* canine.

'canna *sf* (*pianta*) reed; (*: indica, da zucchero*) cane; (*bastone*) stick, cane; (*di fucile*) barrel; (*di organo*) pipe; (*DROGA: gergo*) joint; ~ **fumaria** chimney flue; ~ **da pesca** (fishing) rod; ~ **da zucchero** sugar cane.

can'nella *sf* (*CUC*) cinnamon; (*di conduttura, botte*) tap.

cannel'loni *smpl* pasta tubes stuffed with sauce and baked.

can'neto *sm* bed of reeds.

can'nibale *sm* cannibal.

cannocchi'ale [kannok'kjale] *sm* telescope.

canno'nata *sf*: **è una vera** ~! (*fig*) it's (*o* he's *etc*) fantastic!

can'none *sm* (*MIL*) gun; (*: STORIA*) cannon; (*tubo*) pipe, tube; (*piega*) box pleat; (*fig*) ace; **donna** ~ fat woman.

cannoni'ere *sm* (*NAUT*) gunner; (*CALCIO*) goal scorer.

can'nuccia, ce [kan'nuttʃa] *sf* (drinking) straw.

'canone *sm* canon, criterion; (*mensile, annuo*) rent; fee; **legge dell'equo** ~ fair rent act.

ca'nonica, che *sf* presbytery.

ca'nonico, ci *sm* (*REL*) canon.

canoniz'zare [kanonid'dzare] *vt* to canonize.

ca'noro, a *ag* (*uccello*) singing, song *cpd*.

ca'notta *sf* vest.

canot'taggio [kanot'taddʒo] *sm* rowing.

canotti'era *sf* vest (*BRIT*), undershirt (*US*).

ca'notto *sm* small boat, dinghy; canoe.

cano'vaccio [kano'vattʃo] *sm* (*tela*) canvas; (*strofinaccio*) duster; (*trama*) plot.

can'tante *sm/f* singer.

can'tare *vt*, *vi* to sing; ~ **vittoria** to crow;

fare ~ **qn** (*fig*) to make sb talk.

cantas'torie *sm/f inv* storyteller.

cantau'tore, 'trice *sm/f* singer-composer.

canterel'lare *vt*, *vi* to hum, sing to o.s.

canticchi'are [kantik'kjare] *vt*, *vi* to hum, sing to o.s.

canti'ere *sm* (*EDIL*) (building) site; (*anche:* ~ **navale**) shipyard.

canti'lena *sf* (*filastrocca*) lullaby; (*fig*) singsong voice.

can'tina *sf* (*locale*) cellar; (*bottega*) wine shop.

'canto *sm* song; (*arte*) singing; (*REL*) chant; chanting; (*POESIA*) poem, lyric; (*parte di una poesia*) canto; (*parte, lato*): **da un** ~ on the one hand; **d'altro** ~ on the other hand.

canto'nata *sf* (*di edificio*) corner; **prendere una** ~ (*fig*) to blunder.

can'tone *sm* (*in Svizzera*) canton.

cantoni'era *ag*: **(casa)** ~ road inspector's house.

can'tuccio [kan'tuttʃo] *sm* corner, nook.

ca'nuto, a *ag* white, whitehaired.

canzo'nare [kantso'nare] *vt* to tease.

canzona'tura [kantsona'tura] *sf* teasing; (*beffa*) joke.

can'zone [kan'tsone] *sf* song; (*POESIA*) canzone.

canzoni'ere [kantso'njɛre] *sm* (*MUS*) songbook; (*LETTERATURA*) collection of poems.

'caos *sm inv* chaos.

ca'otico, a, ci, che *ag* chaotic.

CAP *sigla m vedi* **codice di avviamento postale**.

cap. *abbr* (= *capitolo*) ch.

ca'pace [ka'patʃe] *ag* able, capable; (*ampio, vasto*) large, capacious; **sei** ~ **di farlo?** can you *o* are you able to do it?; ~ **d'intendere e di volere** (*DIR*) in full possession of one's faculties.

capacità [kapatʃi'ta] *sf inv* ability; (*DIR, di recipiente*) capacity; ~ **produttiva** production capacity.

capaci'tarsi [kapatʃi'tarsi] *vr*: ~ **di** to make out, understand.

ca'panna *sf* hut.

capan'nello *sm* knot (of people).

ca'panno *sm* (*di cacciatori*) hide; (*da spiaggia*) bathing hut.

capan'none *sm* (*AGR*) barn; (*fabbricato industriale*) (factory) shed.

caparbietà *sf* stubbornness.

ca'parbio, a *ag* stubborn.

ca'parra *sf* deposit, down payment.

capa'tina *sf*: **fare una** ~ **da qn/in centro** to pop in on sb/into town.

capeggi'are [kaped'dʒare] *vt* (*rivolta etc*) to

head, lead.
ca'pello *sm* hair; ~**i** *smpl* (*capigliatura*) hair
sg; **averne fin sopra i ~i di qc/qn** to be fed
up to the (back) teeth with sth/sb; **mi ci
hanno tirato per i ~i** (*fig*) they dragged
me into it; **tirato per i ~i** (*spiegazione*)
far-fetched.
capel'lone, a *sm/f* hippie.
capel'luto, a *ag*: **cuoio ~** scalp.
capez'zale [kapet'tsale] *sm* bolster; (*fig*)
bedside.
ca'pezzolo [ka'pettsolo] *sm* nipple.
capi'ente *ag* capacious.
capi'enza [ka'pjɛntsa] *sf* capacity.
capiglia'tura [kapiʎʎa'tura] *sf* hair.
capil'lare *ag* (*fig*) detailed ♦ *sm* (*ANAT*:
anche: **vaso ~**) capillary.
ca'pire *vt* to understand; ~ **al volo** to catch
on straight away; **si capisce!** (*certamente!*)
of course!, certainly!
capi'tale *ag* (*mortale*) capital;
(*fondamentale*) main *cpd*, chief *cpd* ♦ *sf*
(*città*) capital ♦ *sm* (*ECON*) capital; ~
azionario equity capital, share capital; ~
d'esercizio working capital; ~ **fisso**
capital assets, fixed capital; ~ **immobile**
real estate; ~ **liquido** cash assets *pl*; ~
mobile movables *pl*; ~ **di rischio** risk
capital; ~ **sociale** (*di società*) authorized
capital; (*di club*) funds *pl*; ~ **di ventura**
venture capital, risk capital.
capita'lismo *sm* capitalism.
capita'lista, i, e *ag*, *sm/f* capitalist.
capitaliz'zare [kapitalid'dzare] *vt* to
capitalize.
capitalizzazi'one [kapitaliddzat'tsjone] *sf*
capitalization.
capita'nare *vt* to lead; (*CALCIO*) to captain.
capitane'ria *sf*: ~ (**di porto**) port
authorities *pl*.
capi'tano *sm* captain; ~ **di lungo corso**
master mariner; ~ **di ventura** (*STORIA*)
mercenary leader.
capi'tare *vi* (*giungere casualmente*) to
happen to go, find o.s.; (*accadere*) to
happen; (*presentarsi: cosa*) to turn up,
present itself ♦ *vb impers* to happen; ~ **a
proposito/bene/male** to turn up at the
right moment/at a good time/at a bad
time; **mi è capitato un guaio** I've had a
spot of trouble.
capi'tello *sm* (*ARCHIT*) capital.
capito'lare *vi* to capitulate.
capitolazi'one [kapitolat'tsjone] *sf*
capitulation.
ca'pitolo *sm* chapter; ~**i** *smpl* (*COMM*)
items; **non ho voce in ~** (*fig*) I have no say
in the matter.

capi'tombolo *sm* headlong fall, tumble.
'capo *sm* (*ANAT*) head; (*persona*) head,
leader; (: *in ufficio*) head, boss; (: *in tribù*)
chief; (*estremità*: *di tavolo, scale*) head, top;
(: *di filo*) end; (*GEO*) cape; **andare a ~** to
start a new paragraph; "**punto a ~**" "full
stop — new paragraph"; **da ~** over again;
in ~ a (*tempo*) within; **da un ~ all'altro**
from one end to the other; **fra ~ e collo**
(*all'improvviso*) out of the blue; **un
discorso senza né ~ né coda** a senseless *o*
meaningless speech; ~ **d'accusa** (*DIR*)
charge; ~ **di bestiame** head *inv* of cattle;
C~ di Buona Speranza Cape of Good
Hope; ~ **di vestiario** item of clothing.
capo'banda, *pl* capi'banda *sm* (*MUS*)
bandmaster; (*di malviventi, fig*) gang
leader.
ca'poccia [ka'pɔttʃa] *sm inv* (*di lavoranti*)
overseer; (*peg*: *capobanda*) boss.
capo'classe, *pl(m)* capi'classe, *pl(f) inv sm/f*
(*INS*) ≈ form captain (*BRIT*), class
president (*US*).
capocu'oco, chi *sm* head cook.
Capo'danno *sm* New Year.
capofa'miglia, *pl(m)* capifa'miglia, *pl(f)*
inv [kapofa'miʎʎa] *sm/f* head of the family.
capo'fitto: a ~ *av* headfirst, headlong.
capo'giro [kapo'dʒiro] *sm* dizziness *no pl*; **da
~** (*fig*) astonishing, staggering.
capo'gruppo, *pl(m)* capi'gruppo, *pl(f) inv
sm/f* group leader.
capola'voro, i *sm* masterpiece.
capo'linea, *pl* capi'linea *sm* terminus; (*fig*)
end of the line.
capo'lino *sm*: **far ~** to peep out (*o in etc*).
capo'lista, *pl(m)* capi'lista, *pl(f) inv sm/f*
(*POL*) top candidate on electoral list.
capolu'ogo, *pl* ghi *o* capilu'oghi *sm* chief
town, administrative centre (*BRIT*) *o*
center (*US*).
capo'mastro, *pl* i *o* capi'mastri *sm* master
builder.
capo'rale *sm* (*MIL*) lance corporal (*BRIT*),
private first class (*US*).
capore'parto, *pl(m)* capire'parto, *pl(f) inv
sm/f* (*di operai*) foreman; (*di ufficio, negozio*)
head of department.
capo'sala *sf inv* (*MED*) ward sister.
capo'saldo, *pl* capi'saldi *sm* stronghold;
(*fig*: *fondamento*) basis, cornerstone.
capo'squadra, *pl* capi'squadra *sm* (*di
operai*) foreman, ganger; (*MIL*) squad
leader; (*SPORT*) team captain.
capostazi'one, *pl* capistazi'one
[kapostat'tsjone] *sm* station master.
capos'tipite *sm* progenitor; (*fig*) earliest
example.

capo'tavola, pl(m) **capi'tavola,** pl(f) inv sm/f (persona) head of the table; **sedere a** ~ to sit at the head of the table.

ca'pote [ka'pɔt] sf inv (AUT) hood (BRIT), soft top.

capo'treno, pl **capi'treno** o **capo'treni** sm guard.

capouf'ficio, pl(m) **capiuf'ficio,** pl(f) inv [kapouf'fitʃo] sm/f head clerk.

capo'verso sm (di verso, periodo) first line; (TIP) indent; (paragrafo) paragraph; (DIR: comma) section.

capo'volgere [kapo'voldʒere] vt to overturn; (fig) to reverse; ~**rsi** vr to overturn; (barca) to capsize; (fig) to be reversed.

capovolgi'mento [kapovoldʒi'mento] sm (fig) reversal, complete change.

capo'volto, a pp di **capovolgere** ♦ ag upside down; (barca) capsized.

'cappa sf (mantello) cape, cloak; (del camino) hood.

cap'pella sf (REL) chapel.

cappel'lano sm chaplain.

cap'pello sm hat; **Tanto di** ~! (fig) I take my hat off to you!; ~ **a bombetta** bowler (hat), derby (US); ~ **a cilindro** top hat; ~ **di paglia** straw hat.

'cappero sm caper.

cap'pone sm capon.

cappot'tare vi (AUT) to overturn.

cap'potto sm (over)coat.

cappuc'cino [kapput'tʃino] sm (frate) Capuchin monk; (bevanda) cappuccino.

cap'puccio [kap'puttʃo] sm (copricapo) hood; (della biro) cap.

'capra sf (she-)goat.

ca'prese ag from (o of) Capri.

ca'pretto sm kid.

ca'priccio [ka'prittʃo] sm caprice, whim; (bizza) tantrum; **fare i** ~**i** to be very naughty; ~ **della sorte** quirk of fate.

capricci'oso, a [kaprit'tʃoso] ag capricious, whimsical; naughty.

Capri'corno sm Capricorn; **essere del** ~ (dello zodiaco) to be Capricorn.

capri'foglio [kapri'fɔʎʎo] sm honeysuckle.

capri'ola sf somersault.

capri'olo sm roe deer.

'capro sm billy-goat; ~ **espiatorio** (fig) scapegoat.

ca'prone sm billy-goat.

'capsula sf capsule; (di arma, per bottiglie) cap.

cap'tare vt (RADIO, TV) to pick up; (cattivarsi) to gain, win.

CAR sigla m = Centro Addestramento Reclute.

cara'bina sf rifle.

carabini'ere sm member of Italian military police force; vedi nota nel riquadro.

Ca'racas sf Caracas.

ca'raffa sf carafe.

Ca'raibi smpl: **il mar dei** ~ the Caribbean (Sea).

cara'ibico, a, ci, che ag Caribbean.

cara'mella sf sweet.

cara'mello sm caramel.

ca'rato sm (di oro, diamante etc) carat.

ca'rattere sm character; (caratteristica) characteristic, trait; **avere un buon** ~ to be good-natured; **informazione di** ~ **tecnico/confidenziale** information of a technical/confidential nature; **essere in** ~ **con qc** (intonarsi) to be in harmony with sth; ~ **jolly** wild card.

caratte'rino sm difficult nature o character.

caratte'ristico, a, ci, che ag characteristic ♦ sf characteristic, feature; **segni** ~**ci** (su passaporto etc) distinguishing marks.

caratteriz'zare [karatterid'dzare] vt to characterize, distinguish.

carboi'drato sm carbohydrate.

carbo'naio sm (chi fa carbone) charcoal-burner; (commerciante) coalman, coal merchant.

car'bone sm coal; ~ **fossile** (pit) coal; **essere** o **stare sui** ~**i ardenti** to be like a cat on hot bricks.

car'bonio sm (CHIM) carbon.

carboniz'zare [karbonid'dzare] vt (legna) to carbonize; (: parzialmente) to char; **morire carbonizzato** to be burned to death.

carbu'rante sm (motor) fuel.

carbura'tore sm carburettor.

car'cassa sf carcass; (fig: peg: macchina etc) (old) wreck.

carce'rato, a [kartʃe'rato] sm/f prisoner.

'carcere ['kartʃere] sm prison; (pena) imprisonment; ~ **di massima sicurezza** top-security prison.

carceri'ere, a [kartʃe'rjɛre] sm/f (anche fig)

jailer.

carci'ofo [kar'tʃɔfo] *sm* artichoke.

cardel'lino *sm* goldfinch.

car'diaco, a, ci, che *ag* cardiac, heart *cpd*.

cardi'nale *ag, sm* cardinal.

'cardine *sm* hinge.

cardiolo'gia [kardjolo'dʒia] *sf* cardiology.

cardi'ologo, gi *sm* heart specialist, cardiologist.

'cardo *sm* thistle.

ca'rente *ag*: ~ **di** lacking in.

ca'renza [ka'rɛntsa] *sf* lack, scarcity; (*vitaminica*) deficiency.

cares'tia *sf* famine; (*penuria*) scarcity, dearth.

ca'rezza [ka'rettsa] *sf* caress; **dare** *o* **fare una** ~ **a** (*persona*) to caress; (*animale*) to stroke, pat.

carez'zare [karet'tsare] *vt* to caress, stroke, fondle.

carez'zevole [karet'tsevole] *ag* sweet, endearing.

cari'are *vt*, ~**rsi** *vr* (*denti*) to decay.

'carica *sf vedi* **carico**.

caricabatte'rie *sm inv* (*ELETTR*) battery charger.

cari'care *vt* to load; (*aggravare: anche fig*) to weigh down; (*orologio*) to wind up; (*batteria, MIL*) to charge; (*INFORM*) to load; ~**rsi** *vr*: ~**rsi di** to burden *o* load o.s. with; (*fig: di responsabilità, impegni*) to burden o.s. with.

carica'tura *sf* caricature.

'carico, a, chi, che *ag* (*che porta un peso*): ~ **di** loaded *o* laden with; (*fucile*) loaded; (*orologio*) wound up; (*batteria*) charged; (*colore*) deep; (*caffè, tè*) strong ♦ *sm* (*il caricare*) loading; (*ciò che si carica*) load; (*COMM*) shipment; (*fig: peso*) burden, weight ♦ *sf* (*mansione ufficiale*) office, position; (*MIL, TECN, ELETTR*) charge; ~ **di debiti** up to one's ears in debt; **persona a** ~ dependent; **essere a** ~ **di qn** (*spese etc*) to be charged to sb; (*accusa, prova*) to be against sb; **testimone a** ~ witness for the prosecution; **farsi** ~ **di** (*problema, responsabilità*) to take on; **a** ~ **del cliente** at the customer's expense; ~ **di lavoro** (*di ditta, reparto*) workload; ~ **utile** payload; **capacità di** ~ cargo capacity; **entrare/essere in** ~**a** to come into/be in office; **ricoprire** *o* **rivestire una** ~**a** to hold a position; **uscire di** ~**a** to leave office; **dare la** ~**a a** (*orologio*) to wind up; (*fig: persona*) to back up; **tornare alla** ~**a** (*fig*) to insist, persist; **ha una forte** ~**a di simpatia** he's very likeable.

'carie *sf* (*dentaria*) decay.

ca'rino, a *ag* lovely, pretty, nice; (*simpatico*) nice.

ca'risma [ka'rizma] *sm* charisma.

caris'matico, a, ci, che *ag* charismatic.

carità *sf* charity; **per** ~! (*escl di rifiuto*) good heavens, no!

carita'tevole *ag* charitable.

carnagi'one [karna'dʒone] *sf* complexion.

car'nale *ag* (*amore*) carnal; (*fratello*) blood *cpd*.

'carne *sf* flesh; (*bovina, ovina etc*) meat; **in** ~ **e ossa** in the flesh, in person; **essere (bene) in** ~ to be well padded, be plump; **non essere né** ~ **né pesce** (*fig*) to be neither fish nor fowl; ~ **di manzo/maiale/pecora** beef/pork/mutton; ~ **in scatola** tinned *o* canned meat; ~ **tritata** mince (*BRIT*), hamburger meat (*US*), minced (*BRIT*) *o* ground (*US*) meat.

car'nefice [kar'nefitʃe] *sm* executioner; hangman.

carnefi'cina [karnefi'tʃina] *sf* carnage; (*fig*) disaster.

carne'vale *sm* carnival; **C**~ *vedi nota nel riquadro*.

CARNEVALE

Carnevale *is the name given to the period between Epiphany (6 January) and the beginning of Lent, when people throw parties, put on processions with spectacular floats, build bonfires in the "piazze" and dress up in fabulous costumes and masks. Building to a peak just before Lent,* **Carnevale** *culminates in the festivities of "Martedì grasso" (Shrove Tuesday).*

---

car'nivoro, a *ag* carnivorous.

car'noso, a *ag* fleshy; (*pianta, frutto, radice*) pulpy; (*labbra*) full.

'caro, a *ag* (*amato*) dear; (*costoso*) dear, expensive.

ca'rogna [ka'roɲɲa] *sf* carrion; (*fig fam*) swine.

caro'sello *sm* merry-go-round.

ca'rota *sf* carrot.

caro'vana *sf* caravan.

caro'vita *sm* high cost of living.

'carpa *sf* carp.

Car'pazi [kar'patsi] *smpl*: **i** ~ the Carpathian Mountains.

carpente'ria *sf* carpentry.

carpenti'ere *sm* carpenter.

car'pire *vt*: ~ **qc a qn** (*segreto etc*) to get sth out of sb.

car'poni *av* on all fours.

car'rabile *ag* suitable for vehicles; **"passo**

~" "keep clear".

car'raio, a *ag*: **passo** ~ vehicle entrance.

carré *sm* (*acconciatura*) bob.

carreggi'ata [karred'dʒata] *sf* carriageway (*BRIT*), roadway; **rimettersi in** ~ (*fig: recuperare*) to catch up; **tenersi in** ~ (*fig*) to keep to the right path.

carrel'lata *sf* (*CINE, TV: tecnica*) tracking; (: *scena*) running shot; ~ **di successi** medley of hit tunes.

car'rello *sm* trolley; (*AER*) undercarriage; (*CINE*) dolly; (*di macchina da scrivere*) carriage.

car'retta *sf*: **tirare la** ~ (*fig*) to plod along.

car'retto *sm* handcart.

carri'era *sf* career; **fare** ~ to get on; **ufficiale di** ~ (*MIL*) regular officer; **a gran** ~ at full speed.

carri'ola *sf* wheelbarrow.

'carro *sm* cart, wagon; **il Gran/Piccolo C**~ (*ASTR*) the Great/Little Bear; **mettere il** ~ **avanti ai buoi** (*fig*) to put the cart before the horse; ~ **armato** tank; ~ **attrezzi** (*AUT*) breakdown van (*BRIT*), tow truck (*US*); ~ **funebre** hearse; ~ **merci/bestiame** (*FERR*) goods/animal wagon.

car'roccio [kar'rɔtʃo] *sm* (*POL*): **il C**~ symbol of *Lega Nord*.

car'rozza [kar'rɔttsa] *sf* carriage, coach; ~ **letto** (*FERR*) sleeper; ~ **ristorante** (*FERR*) dining car.

carroz'zella [karrot'tsɛlla] *sf* (*per bambini*) pram (*BRIT*), baby carriage (*US*); (*per invalidi*) wheelchair.

carrozze'ria [karrottse'ria] *sf* body, coachwork (*BRIT*); (*officina*) coachbuilder's workshop (*BRIT*), body shop.

carrozzi'ere [karrot'tsjere] *sm* (*AUT: progettista*) car designer; (: *meccanico*) coachbuilder.

carroz'zina [karrot'tsina] *sf* pram (*BRIT*), baby carriage (*US*).

carroz'zone [karrot'tsone] *sm* (*da circo, di zingari*) caravan.

car'rucola *sf* pulley.

'carta *sf* paper; (*al ristorante*) menu; (*GEO*) map; plan; (*documento, da gioco*) card; (*costituzione*) charter; ~**e** *sfpl* (*documenti*) papers, documents; **alla** ~ (*al ristorante*) à la carte; **cambiare le** ~**e in tavola** (*fig*) to shift one's ground; **fare** ~ **e false** (*fig*) to go to great lengths; ~ **assegni** bank card; ~ **assorbente** blotting paper; ~ **bollata** *o* **da bollo** (*AMM*) official stamped paper; ~ **di credito** credit card; ~ **di debito** cash card; ~ **(geografica)** map; ~ **d'identità** identity card; ~ **igienica** toilet paper; ~ **d'imbarco**

(*AER, NAUT*) boarding card, boarding pass; ~ **da lettere** writing paper; ~ **libera** (*AMM*) unstamped paper; ~ **millimetrata** graph paper; ~ **oleata** waxed paper; ~ **da pacchi,** ~ **da imballo** wrapping paper, brown paper; ~ **da parati** wallpaper; ~ **verde** (*AUT*) green card; ~ **vetrata** sandpaper; ~ **da visita** visiting card.

cartacar'bone, *pl* **cartecar'bone** *sf* carbon paper.

car'taccia, ce [kar'tattʃa] *sf* waste paper.

cartamo'dello *sm* (*CUCITO*) paper pattern.

cartamo'neta *sf* paper money.

carta'pecora *sf* parchment.

carta'pesta *sf* papier-mâché.

cartas'traccia [kartas'trattʃa] *sf* waste paper.

car'teggio [kar'teddʒo] *sm* correspondence.

car'tella *sf* (*scheda*) card; (*custodia: di cartone, INFORM*) folder; (: *di uomo d'affari etc*) briefcase; (: *di scolaro*) schoolbag, satchel; ~ **clinica** (*MED*) case sheet.

cartel'lino *sm* (*etichetta*) label; (*su porta*) notice; (*scheda*) card; **timbrare il** ~ (*all'entrata*) to clock in; (*all'uscita*) to clock out; ~ **di presenza** clock card, timecard.

car'tello *sm* sign; (*pubblicitario*) poster; (*stradale*) sign, signpost; (*in dimostrazioni*) placard; (*ECON*) cartel.

cartel'lone *sm* (*pubblicitario*) advertising poster; (*della tombola*) scoring frame; (*TEAT*) playbill; **tenere il** ~ (*spettacolo*) to have a long run.

carti'era *sf* paper mill.

carti'lagine [karti'ladʒine] *sf* cartilage.

car'tina *sf* (*AUT, GEO*) map.

car'toccio [kar'tɔttʃo] *sm* paper bag; **cuocere al** ~ (*CUC*) to bake in tinfoil.

cartogra'fia *sf* cartography.

carto'laio, a *sm/f* stationer.

cartole'ria *sf* stationer's (shop (*BRIT*)).

carto'lina *sf* postcard; ~ **di auguri** greetings card; ~ **precetto** *o* **rosa** (*MIL*) call-up card.

carto'mante *sm/f* fortune-teller (*using cards*).

carton'cino [karton'tʃino] *sm* (*materiale*) thin cardboard; (*biglietto*) card; ~ **della società** compliments slip.

car'tone *sm* cardboard; (*del latte, dell'aranciata*) carton; (*ARTE*) cartoon; ~**i animati** (*CINE*) cartoons.

car'tuccia, ce [kar'tuttʃa] *sf* cartridge; ~ **a salve** blank cartridge; **mezza** ~ (*fig: persona*) good-for-nothing.

'casa *sf* house; (*specialmente la propria* ~) home; (*COMM*) firm, house; **essere a** ~ to be at home; **vado a** ~ **mia/tua** I'm going home/to your house; ~ **di correzione** ≈ community home (*BRIT*), reformatory (*US*); ~ **di cura** nursing home; ~ **editrice** publishing house; **C~ delle Libertà** House of Liberties, *centre-right coalition*; ~ **di riposo** (old people's) home, care home; ~ **dello studente** student hostel; ~ **di tolleranza,** ~ **d'appuntamenti** brothel; ~**e popolari** ≈ council houses (*o* flats) (*BRIT*), ≈ public housing units (*US*).

ca'sacca, che *sf* military coat; (*di fantino*) blouse.

ca'sale *sm* (*gruppo di case*) hamlet; (*casa di campagna*) farmhouse.

casa'lingo, a, ghi, ghe *ag* household, domestic; (*fatto a casa*) home-made; (*semplice*) homely; (*amante della casa*) home-loving ♦ *sf* housewife; ~**ghi** *smpl* (*oggetti*) household articles; **cucina ~a** plain home cooking.

ca'sata *sf* family lineage.

ca'sato *sm* family name.

casca'morto *sm* woman-chaser; **fare il ~** to chase women.

cas'care *vi* to fall; ~ **bene/male** (*fig*) to land lucky/unlucky; ~ **dalle nuvole** (*fig*) to be taken aback; ~ **dal sonno** to be falling asleep on one's feet; **caschi il mondo** no matter what; **non cascherà il mondo se …** it won't be the end of the world if ….

cas'cata *sf* fall; (*d'acqua*) cascade, waterfall.

cascherò *etc* [kaske'rɔ] *vb vedi* **cascare.**

ca'scina [kaʃ'ʃina] *sf* farmstead.

casci'nale [kaʃʃi'nale] *sm* (*casolare*) farmhouse; (*cascina*) farmstead.

'casco, schi *sm* helmet; (*del parrucchiere*) hair-dryer; (*di banane*) bunch; ~ **blu** (*MIL*) blue helmet (*UN soldier*).

caseggi'ato [kased'dʒato] *sm* (*edificio*) large block of flats (*BRIT*) *o* apartment building (*US*); (*gruppo di case*) group of houses.

casei'ficio [kazei'fitʃo] *sm* creamery.

ca'sella *sf* pigeonhole; ~ **postale (C.P.)** post office box (P.O. box).

casel'lario *sm* (*mobile*) filing cabinet; (*raccolta di pratiche*) files *pl*; ~ **giudiziale** court records *pl*; ~ **penale** police files *pl*.

ca'sello *sm* (*di autostrada*) tollgate.

case'reccio, a, ci, ce [kase'rettʃo] *ag* home-made.

ca'serma *sf* barracks *pl*.

caser'tano, a *ag* of (*o* from) Caserta.

ca'sino *sm* (*confusione*) row, racket; (*casa di prostituzione*) brothel.

casinò *sm inv* casino.

ca'sistica *sf* (*MED*) record of cases; **secondo la ~ degli incidenti stradali** according to road accident data.

'caso *sm* chance; (*fatto, vicenda*) event, incident; (*possibilità*) possibility; (*MED, LING*) case; **a ~** at random; **per ~** by chance, by accident; **in ogni ~, in tutti i ~i** in any case, at any rate; **in ~ contrario** otherwise; **al ~** should the opportunity arise; **nel ~ che** in case; ~ **mai** if by chance; **far ~ a qc/qn** to pay attention to sth/sb; **fare** *o* **porre** *o* **mettere il ~ che** to suppose that; **fa proprio al ~ nostro** it's just what we need; **guarda ~ …** strangely enough …; **è il ~ che ce ne andiamo** we'd better go; ~ **limite** borderline case.

caso'lare *sm* cottage.

'Caspio *sm*: **il mar ~** the Caspian Sea.

'caspita *escl* (*di sorpresa*) good heavens!; (*di impazienza*) for goodness' sake!

'cassa *sf* case, crate, box; (*bara*) coffin; (*mobile*) chest; (*involucro: di orologio etc*) case; (*macchina*) cash register; (*luogo di pagamento*) cash desk, checkout (counter); (*fondo*) fund; (*istituto bancario*) bank; **battere ~** (*fig*) to come looking for money; ~ **automatica prelievi** automatic telling machine, cash dispenser; ~ **continua** night safe; **mettere in ~ integrazione** ≈ to lay off; **C~ del Mezzogiorno** *development fund for the South of Italy*; ~ **mutua** *o* **malattia** health insurance scheme; ~ **di risonanza** (*MUS*) soundbox; (*fig*) platform; ~ **di risparmio** savings bank; ~ **rurale e artigiana** credit institution (*serving farmers and craftsmen*); ~ **toracica** (*ANAT*) chest.

cassa'forte, *pl* **casse'forti** *sf* safe.

cassa'panca, *pl* **cassa'panche** *o* **casse'panche** *sf* settle.

casseru'ola, casse'rola *sf* saucepan.

cas'setta *sf* box; (*per registratore*) cassette; (*CINE, TEAT*) box-office takings *pl*; **pane a** *o* **in ~** toasting loaf; **film di ~** (*commerciale*) box-office draw; **far ~** to be a box-office success; ~ **delle lettere** letterbox; ~ **di sicurezza** strongbox.

cas'setto *sm* drawer.

casset'tone *sm* chest of drawers.

cassi'ere, a *sm/f* cashier; (*di banca*) teller.

cassinte'grato, a *sm/f* person who has been laid off.

cas'sone *sm* (*cassa*) large case, large chest.

'casta *sf* caste.

cas'tagna [kas'taɲɲa] *sf* chestnut; **prendere qn in ~** (*fig*) to catch sb in the act.

cas'tagno [kas'taɲɲo] *sm* chestnut (tree).

cas'tano, a *ag* chestnut (brown).

cas'tello *sm* castle; (*TECN*) scaffolding.

casti'gare *vt* to punish.
casti'gato, a *ag* (*casto, modesto*) pure, chaste; (*emendato: prosa, versione*) expurgated, amended.
cas'tigo, ghi *sm* punishment.
castità *sf* chastity.
'casto, a *ag* chaste, pure.
cas'toro *sm* beaver.
cas'trante *ag* frustrating.
cas'trare *vt* to castrate; to geld; to doctor (*BRIT*), fix (*US*); (*fig: iniziativa*) to frustrate.
castrone'ria *sf* (*fam*): **dire ~e** to talk rubbish.
casu'ale *ag* chance *cpd*.
ca'supola *sf* simple little cottage.
catac'lisma, i *sm* (*fig*) catastrophe.
cata'comba *sf* catacomb.
cata'fascio [kata'faʃʃo] *sm*: **andare a ~** to collapse; **mandare a ~** to wreck.
cata'litico, a, ci, che *ag*: **marmitta ~a** (*AUT*) catalytic converter.
cataliz'zare [katalid'dzare] *vt* (*fig*) to act as a catalyst (up)on.
cataliz'zato, a [katalid'dzato] *ag* (*AUT*) with catalytic converter.
catalizza'tore [kataliddza'tore] *sm* (*anche fig*) catalyst; (*AUT*) catalytic converter.
Cata'logna [kata'loɲɲa] *sf*: **la ~** Catalonia.
ca'talogo, ghi *sm* catalogue; **~ dei prezzi** price list.
cata'nese *ag* of (*o* from) Catania.
catanza'rese [katandza'rese] *ag* of (*o* from) Catanzaro.
cata'pecchia [kata'pekkja] *sf* hovel.
cata'pulta *sf* catapult.
catarifran'gente [katarifran'dʒɛnte] *sm* (*AUT*) reflector.
ca'tarro *sm* catarrh.
ca'tarsi *sf inv* catharsis.
ca'tasta *sf* stack, pile.
ca'tasto *sm* land register; land registry office.
ca'tastrofe *sf* catastrophe, disaster.
catas'trofico, a, ci, che *ag* (*evento*) catastrophic; (*persona, previsione*) pessimistic.
cate'chismo [kate'kizmo] *sm* catechism.
catego'ria *sf* category; (*di albergo*) class.
cate'gorico, a, ci, che *ag* categorical.
ca'tena *sf* chain; **reazione a ~** chain reaction; **susseguirsi a ~** to happen in quick succession; **~ alimentare** food chain; **~ di montaggio** assembly line; **~ montuosa** mountain range; **~e da neve** (*AUT*) snow chains.
cate'naccio [kate'nattʃo] *sm* bolt.
cate'nella *sf* (*ornamento*) chain; (*di orologio*) watch chain; (*di porta*) door chain.
cate'ratta *sf* cataract; (*chiusa*) sluice gate.
ca'terva *sf* (*di cose*) loads *pl*, heaps *pl*; (*di persone*) horde.
cate'tere *sm* (*MED*) catheter.
cati'nella *sf*: **piovere a ~e** to pour, rain cats and dogs.
ca'tino *sm* basin.
ca'todico, a, ci, che *ag*: **tubo a raggi ~ci** cathode-ray tube.
ca'torcio [ka'tortʃo] *sm* (*peg*) old wreck.
ca'trame *sm* tar.
'cattedra *sf* teacher's desk; (*di università*) chair; **salire** *o* **montare in ~** (*fig*) to pontificate.
catte'drale *sf* cathedral.
catte'dratico, a, ci, che *ag* (*insegnamento*) university *cpd*; (*ironico*) pedantic ♦ *smf* professor.
catti'veria *sf* (*qualità*) wickedness; (*di bambino*) naughtiness; (*azione*) wicked action; **fare una ~** to do something wicked; to be naughty.
cattività *sf* captivity.
cat'tivo, a *ag* bad; (*malvagio*) bad, wicked; (*turbolento: bambino*) bad, naughty; (*: mare*) rough; (*odore, sapore*) nasty, bad ♦ *smf* bad *o* wicked person; **farsi ~ sangue** to worry, get in a state; **farsi un ~ nome** to earn o.s. a bad reputation; **i ~i** (*nei film*) the baddies (*BRIT*), the bad guys (*US*).
cattocomu'nista, i, e *ag combining Catholic and communist ideas.*
cattoli'cesimo [kattoli'tʃezimo] *sm* Catholicism.
cat'tolico, a, ci, che *ag, smf* (Roman) Catholic.
cat'tura *sf* capture.
cattu'rare *vt* to capture.
cau'casico, a, ci, che *ag, smf* Caucasian.
'Caucaso *sm*: **il ~** the Caucasus.
cauccù [kaut'tʃu] *sm* rubber.
'causa *sf* cause; (*DIR*) lawsuit, case, action; **a ~ di** because of; **per ~ sua** because of him; **fare** *o* **muovere ~ a qn** to take legal action against sb; **parte in ~** litigant.
cau'sale *ag* (*LING*) causal ♦ *sf* cause, reason.
cau'sare *vt* to cause.
'caustico, a, ci, che *ag* caustic.
cau'tela *sf* caution, prudence.
caute'lare *vt* to protect; **~rsi** *vr*: **~rsi (da** *o* **contro)** to take precautions (against).
'cauto, a *ag* cautious, prudent.
cauzio'nare [kauttsjo'nare] *vt* to guarantee.
cauzi'one [kaut'tsjone] *sf* security; (*DIR*) bail; **rilasciare dietro ~** to release on bail.
cav. *abbr* = **cavaliere**.
'cava *sf* quarry.

caval'care *vt* (*cavallo*) to ride; (*muro*) to sit astride; (*sog: ponte*) to span.

caval'cata *sf* ride; (*gruppo di persone*) riding party.

cavalca'via *sm inv* flyover.

cavalci'oni [kaval'tʃoni]: **a ~ di** *prep* astride.

cavali'ere *sm* rider; (*feudale, titolo*) knight; (*soldato*) cavalryman; (*al ballo*) partner.

cavalleg'gero [kavalled'dʒɛro] *sm* (*MIL*) light cavalryman.

cavalle'resco, a, schi, sche *ag* chivalrous.

cavalle'ria *sf* chivalry; (*milizia a cavallo*) cavalry.

cavalle'rizzo, a [kavalle'rittso] *sm/f* riding instructor; circus rider.

caval'letta *sf* grasshopper; (*dannosa*) locust.

caval'letto *sm* (*FOT*) tripod; (*da pittore*) easel.

caval'lina *sf* (*GINNASTICA*) horse; (*gioco*) leap-frog; **correre la ~** (*fig*) to sow one's wild oats.

ca'vallo *sm* horse; (*SCACCHI*) knight; (*AUT: anche:* **~ vapore**) horsepower; (*dei pantaloni*) crotch; **a ~** on horseback; **a ~ di** astride, straddling; **siamo a ~** (*fig*) we've made it; **da ~** (*fig: dose*) drastic; (*: febbre*) raging; **vivere a ~ tra due periodi** to straddle two periods; **~ di battaglia** (*TEAT*) tour de force; (*fig*) hobbyhorse; **~ da corsa** racehorse; **~ a dondolo** rocking horse; **~ da sella** saddle horse; **~ da soma** packhorse.

ca'vare *vt* (*togliere*) to draw out, extract, take out; (*: giacca, scarpe*) to take off; (*: fame, sete, voglia*) to satisfy; **~rsi** *vr*: **~rsi da** (*guai, problemi*) to get out of; **cavarsela** to get away with it; to manage, get on all right; **non ci caverà un bel nulla** you'll get nothing out of it (*o him etc*).

cava'tappi *sm inv* corkscrew.

ca'verna *sf* cave.

caver'noso, a *ag* (*luogo*) cavernous; (*fig: voce*) deep; (*: tosse*) raucous.

ca'vezza [ka'vettsa] *sf* halter.

'cavia *sf* guinea pig.

cavi'ale *sm* caviar.

ca'viglia [ka'viʎʎa] *sf* ankle.

cavil'lare *vi* to quibble.

ca'villo *sm* quibble.

cavil'loso, a *ag* quibbling, hair-splitting.

cavità *sf inv* cavity.

'cavo, a *ag* hollow ♦ *sm* (*ANAT*) cavity; (*grossa corda*) rope, cable; (*ELETTR, TEL*) cable.

cavo'lata *sf* (*fam*) stupid thing.

cavolfi'ore *sm* cauliflower.

'cavolo *sm* cabbage; **non m'importa un ~** (*fam*) I don't give a hoot; **che ~ vuoi?** (*fam*) what the heck do you want?; **~ di Bruxelles** Brussels sprout.

caz'zata [kat'tsata] *sf* (*fam!: stupidaggine*) stupid thing, something stupid.

'cazzo ['kattso] *sm* (*fam!: pene*) prick (*!*); **non gliene importa un ~** (*fig fam!*) he doesn't give a damn about it; **fatti i ~i tuoi** (*fig fam!*) mind your own damn business.

caz'zotto [kat'tsɔtto] *sm* punch; **fare a ~i** to have a punch-up.

cazzu'ola [kat'tswɔla] *sf* trowel.

CB *sigla* = *Campobasso*.

CC *abbr* = *Carabinieri*.

cc *abbr* (= *centimetro cubico*) cc.

C.C. *abbr* = **codice civile**.

c.c. *abbr* (= *conto corrente*) c/a, a/c; (*ELETTR*) *vedi* **corrente continua**.

c/c *abbr* (= *conto corrente*) c/a, a/c.

C.C.D. *sigla m* (*POL* = *Centro Cristiano Democratico*) *party originating from Democrazia Cristiana*.

CCI *sigla f* (= *Camera di Commercio Internazionale*) ICC (= *International Chamber of Commerce*).

CCIAA *abbr* = *Camera di Commercio Industria, Agricoltura e Artigianato*.

CCT *sigla m vedi* **certificato di credito del Tesoro**.

C.D. *abbr* (= *Corpo Diplomatico*) CD ♦ *sm inv* (= *compact disc*) CD.

c.d. *abbr* = *cosiddetto*.

C.d.A. *abbr* = **Consiglio di Amministrazione**.

c.d.d. *abbr* (= *come dovevasi dimostrare*) QED (= *quod erat demonstrandum*).

C.d.M. *abbr* = **Cassa del Mezzogiorno**.

CD-Rom [tʃidi'rɔm] *sigla m inv* (= *Compact Disc Read Only Memory*) CD-Rom.

C.d.U. [tʃidi'u] *sigla m* (= *Cristiano Democratici Uniti*) United Christian Democrats (*Italian centre-right political party*).

CE *sigla* = *Caserta*.

ce [tʃe] *pron, av vedi* **ci**.

C.E. *sigla* = **Consiglio d'Europa**.

cec'chino [tʃek'kino] *sm* sniper; (*POL*) *member of parliament who votes against his own party*.

'cece ['tʃetʃe] *sm* chickpea, garbanzo (*US*).

Ce'cenia [tʃe'tʃenja] *sf* Chechnya.

ce'ceno, a [tʃe'tʃeno] *ag, sm/f* Chechen.

cecità [tʃetʃi'ta] *sf* blindness.

'ceco, a, chi, che ['tʃɛko] *ag, sm/f, sm* Czech; **la Repubblica C~a** the Czech Republic.

Cecoslo'vacchia [tʃekozlo'vakkja] *sf*: **la ~** Czechoslovakia.

cecoslo'vacco, a, chi, che
[tʃekozlo'vakko] ag, sm/f Czechoslovakian.
CED [tʃɛd] sigla m = **centro elaborazione dati**.

'cedere ['tʃɛdere] vt (concedere: posto) to give up; (DIR) to transfer, make over ♦ vi (cadere) to give way, subside; ~ **(a)** to surrender (to), yield (to), give in (to); ~ **il passo (a qn)** to let (sb) pass in front; ~ **il passo a qc** (fig) to give way to sth; ~ **la parola (a qn)** to hand over (to sb).

ce'devole [tʃe'devole] ag (terreno) soft; (fig) yielding.

'cedola ['tʃɛdola] sf (COMM) coupon; voucher.

ce'drata [tʃe'drata] sf citron juice.

'cedro ['tʃɛdro] sm cedar; (albero da frutto, frutto) citron.

'CEE ['tʃee] sigla f vedi **Comunità Economica Europea**.

'ceffo ['tʃɛffo] sm (peg) ugly mug.

cef'fone [tʃef'fone] sm slap, smack.

'ceko, a ['tʃɛko] ag, sm/f, sm = **ceco**.

ce'lare [tʃe'lare] vt to conceal; ~**rsi** vr to hide.

cele'brare [tʃele'brare] vt to celebrate; (cerimonia) to hold; ~ **le lodi di qc/qn** to sing the praises of sth/sb.

celebrazi'one [tʃelebrat'tsjone] sf celebration.

'celebre ['tʃɛlebre] ag famous, celebrated.

celebrità [tʃelebri'ta] sf inv fame; (persona) celebrity.

'celere ['tʃɛlere] ag fast, swift; (corso) crash cpd ♦ sf (POLIZIA) riot police.

ce'leste [tʃe'lɛste] ag celestial; heavenly; (colore) sky-blue.

'celia [tʃɛlja] sf joke; **per** ~ for a joke.

celi'bato [tʃeli'bato] sm celibacy.

'celibe ['tʃɛlibe] ag single, unmarried ♦ sm bachelor.

'cella ['tʃɛlla] sf cell; ~ **di rigore** punishment cell.

cello'phane ® [sɛlo'fan] sm cellophane ®.

'cellula ['tʃɛllula] sf (BIOL, ELETTR, POL) cell.

cellu'lare [tʃellu'lare] ag cellular ♦ sm (furgone) police van; (telefono) cellphone; **segregazione** ~ (DIR) solitary confinement.

cellu'lite [tʃellu'lite] sf cellulitis.

'celta ['tʃɛlta] sm/f Celt.

'celtico, a, ci, che ['tʃɛltiko] ag, sm Celtic.

'cembalo ['tʃembalo] sm (MUS) harpsichord.

cemen'tare [tʃemen'tare] vt (anche fig) to cement.

ce'mento [tʃe'mento] sm cement; ~ **armato** reinforced concrete.

'cena ['tʃena] sf dinner; (leggera) supper.

ce'nacolo [tʃe'nakolo] sm (circolo) coterie, circle; (REL, dipinto) Last Supper.

ce'nare [tʃe'nare] vi to dine, have dinner.

'cencio ['tʃentʃo] sm piece of cloth, rag; (per spolverare) duster; **essere bianco come un** ~ to be as white as a sheet.

'cenere ['tʃenere] sf ash.

Cene'rentola [tʃene'rɛntola] sf (anche fig) Cinderella.

'cenno ['tʃenno] sm (segno) sign, signal; (gesto) gesture; (col capo) nod; (con la mano) wave; (allusione) hint, mention; (breve esposizione) short account; **far** ~ **di si/no** to nod (one's head)/shake one's head; ~ **d'intesa** sign of agreement; ~**i di storia dell'arte** an outline of the history of art.

censi'mento [tʃensi'mento] sm census.

cen'sire [tʃen'sire] vt to take a census of.

'CENSIS ['tʃensis] sigla m (= Centro Studi Investimenti Sociali) independent institute carrying out research on Italy's social and cultural welfare.

cen'sore [tʃen'sore] sm censor.

cen'sura [tʃen'sura] sf censorship; censor's office; (fig) censure.

censu'rare [tʃensu'rare] vt to censor; to censure.

cent. abbr = **centesimo**.

centelli'nare [tʃentelli'nare] vt to sip; (fig) to savour (BRIT), savor (US).

cente'nario, a [tʃente'narjo] ag (che ha cento anni) hundred-year-old; (che ricorre ogni cento anni) centennial, centenary cpd ♦ sm/f centenarian ♦ sm centenary.

cen'tesimo, a [tʃen'tɛzimo] ag, sm hundredth; (di euro, dollaro) cent; **essere senza un** ~ to be penniless.

cen'tigrado, a [tʃen'tigrado] ag centigrade; **20 gradi** ~**i** 20 degrees centigrade.

cen'tilitro [tʃen'tilitro] sm centilitre.

cen'timetro [tʃen'timetro] sm centimetre (BRIT), centimeter (US); (nastro) measuring tape (in centimetres).

centi'naio, pl(f) **-aia** [tʃenti'najo] sm: **un** ~ **(di)** a hundred; about a hundred.

'cento ['tʃento] num a hundred, one hundred; **per** ~ per cent; **al** ~ **per** ~ a hundred per cent; ~ **di questi giorni!** many happy returns (of the day)!

centodi'eci [tʃento'djetʃi] num one hundred and ten; ~ **e lode** (UNIVERSITÀ) ≈ first-class honours.

cento'mila [tʃento'mila] num a o one hundred thousand; **te l'ho detto** ~ **volte** (fig) I've told you a thousand times.

Cen'trafrica [tʃen'trafrika] sm: **il** ~ **the**

Central African Republic.

cen'trale [tʃen'trale] *ag* central ♦ *sf:* ~ **elettrica** electric power station; ~ **del latte** dairy; ~ **di polizia** police headquarters *pl;* ~ **telefonica** (telephone) exchange; **sede** ~ head office.

centrali'nista [tʃentrali'nista] *sm/f* operator.

centra'lino [tʃentra'lino] *sm* (telephone) exchange; (*di albergo etc*) switchboard.

centraliz'zare [tʃentralid'dzare] *vt* to centralize.

cen'trare [tʃen'trare] *vt* to hit the centre (*BRIT*) *o* center (*US*) of; (*TECN*) to centre; ~ **una risposta** to get the right answer; **ha centrato il problema** you've hit the nail on the head.

centra'vanti [tʃentra'vanti] *sm inv* centre forward.

cen'trifuga [tʃen'trifuga] *sf* spin-dryer.

centrifu'gare [tʃentrifu'gare] *vt* (*TECN*) to centrifuge; (*biancheria*) to spin-dry.

'centro ['tʃentro] *sm* centre (*BRIT*), center (*US*); **fare** ~ to hit the bull's eye; (*CALCIO*) to score; (*fig*) to hit the nail on the head; ~ **balneare** seaside resort; ~ **commerciale** shopping centre; (*città*) commercial centre; ~ **di costo** cost centre; ~ **elaborazione dati** data-processing unit; ~ **ospedaliero** hospital complex; ~ **sociale** community centre; ~**i vitali** (*anche fig*) vital organs.

centromedi'ano [tʃentrome'djano] *sm* (*CALCIO*) centre half.

'ceppo ['tʃeppo] *sm* (*di albero*) stump; (*pezzo di legno*) log.

'cera ['tʃera] *sf* wax; (*aspetto*) appearance, look; ~ **per pavimenti** floor polish.

cera'lacca [tʃera'lakka] *sf* sealing wax.

ce'ramica, che [tʃe'ramika] *sf* ceramic; (*ARTE*) ceramics *sg*.

cerbi'atto [tʃer'bjatto] *sm* fawn.

'cerca ['tʃerka] *sf:* **in** *o* **alla** ~ **di** in search of.

cercaper'sone [tʃerkaper'sone] *sm inv* bleeper.

cer'care [tʃer'kare] *vt* to look for, search for ♦ *vi:* ~ **di fare qc** to try to do sth.

cercherò *etc* [tʃerke'rɔ] *vb vedi* **cercare**.

'cerchia ['tʃerkja] *sf* circle.

cerchi'ato, a [tʃer'kjato] *ag:* **occhiali** ~**i d'osso** horn-rimmed spectacles; **avere gli occhi** ~**i** to have dark rings under one's eyes.

'cerchio ['tʃerkjo] *sm* circle; (*giocattolo, di botte*) hoop; **dare un colpo al** ~ **e uno alla botte** (*fig*) to keep two things going at the same time.

cerchi'one [tʃer'kjone] *sm* (wheel)rim.

cere'ale [tʃere'ale] *sm* cereal.

cere'brale [tʃere'brale] *ag* cerebral.

ceri'monia [tʃeri'mɔnja] *sf* ceremony; **senza tante** ~**e** (*senza formalità*) informally; (*bruscamente*) unceremoniously, without so much as a by-your-leave.

cerimoni'ale [tʃerimo'njale] *sm* etiquette; ceremonial.

cerimoni'ere [tʃerimo'njɛre] *sm* master of ceremonies.

cerimoni'oso, a [tʃerimo'njoso] *ag* formal, ceremonious.

ce'rino [tʃe'rino] *sm* wax match.

CERN [tʃern] *sigla m* (= *Comitato Europeo di Ricerche Nucleari*) CERN.

'cernia ['tʃɛrnja] *sf* (*ZOOL*) stone bass.

cerni'era [tʃer'njɛra] *sf* hinge; ~ **lampo** zip (fastener) (*BRIT*), zipper (*US*).

'cernita ['tʃɛrnita] *sf* selection; **fare una** ~ **di** to select.

'cero ['tʃero] *sm* (church) candle.

ce'rone [tʃe'rone] *sm* (*trucco*) greasepaint.

ce'rotto [tʃe'rɔtto] *sm* sticking plaster.

certa'mente [tʃerta'mente] *av* certainly, surely.

cer'tezza [tʃer'tettsa] *sf* certainty.

certifi'care [tʃertifi'kare] *vt* to certify.

certifi'cato [tʃertifi'kato] *sm* certificate; ~ **medico/di nascita** medical/birth certificate; ~ **di credito del Tesoro (CCT)** treasury bill.

certificazi'one [tʃertifikat'tsjone] *sf* certification; ~ **di bilancio** (*COMM*) external audit.

══════════════════ *PAROLA CHIAVE*

'certo, a ['tʃɛrto] *ag* (*sicuro*): ~ **(di/che)** certain *o* sure (of/that)
♦ *det* **1** (*tale*) certain; **un** ~ **signor Smith** a (certain) Mr Smith
2 (*qualche; con valore intensivo*) some; **dopo un** ~ **tempo** after some time; **un fatto di una** ~**a importanza** a matter of some importance; **di una** ~**a età** past one's prime, not so young
♦ *pron:* ~**i, e** *pl* some
♦ *av* (*certamente*) certainly; (*senz'altro*) of course; **di** ~ certainly; **no (di)** ~**!**, ~ **che no!** certainly not!; **sì** ~ yes indeed, certainly.

certo'sino [tʃerto'zino] *sm* Carthusian monk; (*liquore*) chartreuse; **è un lavoro da** ~ it's a pernickety job.

cer'tuni [tʃer'tuni] *pron pl* some (people).

ce'rume [tʃe'rume] *sm* (ear) wax.

'cerva ['tʃerva] *sf* (female) deer, doe.

cer'vello, pl i (*anche:* *pl(f)* **a** *o* **e**) [tʃer'vɛllo] *sm* brain; ~ **elettronico** computer; **avere il** *o* **essere un ~ fino** to be sharp-witted; **è uscito di ~, gli è dato di volta il ~** he's gone off his head.

cervi'cale [tʃervi'kale] *ag* cervical.

'cervo, a ['tʃervo] *sm/f* stag/hind ♦ *sm* deer; ~ **volante** stag beetle.

cesel'lare [tʃezel'lare] *vt* to chisel; (*incidere*) to engrave.

ce'sello [tʃe'zɛllo] *sm* chisel.

ce'soie [tʃe'zoje] *sfpl* shears.

ces'puglio [tʃes'puʎʎo] *sm* bush.

ces'sare [tʃes'sare] *vi, vt* to stop, cease; ~ **di fare qc** to stop doing sth; "**cessato allarme**" "all clear".

ces'sate il fu'oco [tʃes'sate-] *sm* ceasefire.

cessazi'one [tʃessat'tsjone] *sf* cessation; (*interruzione*) suspension.

cessi'one [tʃes'sjone] *sf* transfer.

'cesso ['tʃɛsso] *sm* (*fam: gabinetto*) bog.

'cesta ['tʃesta] *sf* (large) basket.

ces'tello [tʃes'tɛllo] *sm* (*per bottiglie*) crate; (*di lavatrice*) drum.

cesti'nare [tʃesti'nare] *vt* to throw away; (*fig: proposta*) to turn down; (: *romanzo*) to reject.

ces'tino [tʃes'tino] *sm* basket; (*per la carta straccia*) wastepaper basket; ~ **da viaggio** (*FERR*) packed lunch (*o* dinner).

'cesto ['tʃesto] *sm* basket.

ce'sura [tʃe'zura] *sf* caesura.

ce'taceo [tʃe'tatʃeo] *sm* sea mammal.

'ceto ['tʃeto] *sm* (*social*) class.

'cetra ['tʃetra] *sf* (*MUS*) zither; (*fig: di poeta*) lyre.

cetrio'lino [tʃetrio'lino] *sm* gherkin.

cetri'olo [tʃetri'ɔlo] *sm* cucumber.

Cf., Cfr. *abbr* (= *confronta*) cf.

CFC [tʃiɛffe'tʃi] *abbr mpl* (= *clorofluorocarburi*) CFC.

CFS *sigla m* (= *Corpo Forestale dello Stato*) *body responsible for the planting and management of forests.*

cg *abbr* (= *centigrammo*) cg.

C.G.I.L. [tʃidʒi'ɛlle] *sigla f* (= *Confederazione Generale Italiana del Lavoro*) *trades union organization.*

CH *sigla* = *Chieti.*

cha'let [ʃa'lɛ] *sm inv* chalet.

cham'pagne [ʃã'paɲ] *sm inv* champagne.

chance [ʃãs] *sf inv* chance.

charme [ʃarm] *sm* charm.

'charter ['tʃaːtər] *ag inv* (*volo*) charter *cpd*; (*aereo*) chartered ♦ *sm inv* chartered plane.

chat'tare [tʃat'tare] *vi* to chat; (*online*) to chat.

che [ke] *pron* **1** (*relativo: persona: soggetto*) who; (: *oggetto*) whom, that; (: *cosa, animale*) which, that; **il ragazzo ~ è venuto** the boy who came; **l'uomo ~ io vedo** the man (whom) I see; **il libro ~ è sul tavolo** the book which *o* that is on the table; **il libro ~ vedi** the book (which *o* that) you see; **la sera ~ ti ho visto** the evening I saw you

2 (*interrogativo, esclamativo*) what; ~ **(cosa) fai?** what are you doing?; **a ~ (cosa) pensi?** what are you thinking about?; **non sa ~ (cosa) fare** he doesn't know what to do; **sai di ~ si tratta?** do you know what it's about?; ~ **(cosa) succede?** what's happening?; **ma ~ dici!** what are you saying!

3 (*indefinito*): **quell'uomo ha un ~ di losco** there's something suspicious about that man; **un certo non so ~** an indefinable something; **non è un gran ~** it's nothing much

♦ *det* **1** (*interrogativo: tra tanti*) what; (: *tra pochi*) which; ~ **tipo di film preferisci?** what sort of film do you prefer?; ~ **vestito ti vuoi mettere?** what (*o* which) dress do you want to put on?

2 (*esclamativo: seguito da aggettivo*) how; (: *seguito da sostantivo*) what; ~ **buono!** how delicious!; ~ **bel vestito!** what a lovely dress!; ~ **macchina!** what a car!

♦ *cong* **1** (*con proposizioni subordinate*) that; **credo ~ verrà** I think he'll come; **voglio ~ tu studi** I want you to study; **so ~ tu c'eri** I know (that) you were there; **non ~ sia sbagliato, ma**... not that it's wrong, but...

2 (*finale*) so that; **vieni qua, ~ ti veda** come here, so (that) I can see you; **stai attento ~ non cada** mind it doesn't fall

3 (*temporale*): **arrivai ~ eri già partito** you had already left when I arrived; **sono anni ~ non lo vedo** I haven't seen him for years

4 (*in frasi imperative, concessive*): ~ **venga pure!** let him come by all means!; ~ **tu sia benedetto!** may God bless you!; ~ **tu venga o no partiamo lo stesso** we're going whether you come or not

5 (*comparativo: con più, meno*) than; **è più lungo ~ largo** it's longer than it's wide; **più bella ~ mai** more beautiful than ever; *vedi* **anche più; meno; così** *etc.*

'checca, che ['kekka] *sf* (*fam: omosessuale*) fairy.

chef [ʃɛf] *sm inv* chef.

chemiotera'pia [kemjotera'pia] *sf* chemotherapy.

chero'sene [kero'zɛne] *sm* kerosene.

cheru'bino [keru'bino] *sm* cherub.

che'tare [ke'tare] *vt* to hush, silence; ~**rsi** *vr* to quieten down, fall silent.

cheti'chella [keti'kɛlla]: **alla** ~ *av* stealthily, unobtrusively; **andarsene alla** ~ to slip away.

'cheto, a ['keto] *ag* quiet, silent.

═══════════════ *PAROLA CHIAVE*

chi [ki] *pron* **1** (*interrogativo: soggetto*) who; (: *oggetto*) who, whom; ~ **è?** who is it?; **di** ~ **è questo libro?** whose book is this?, whose is this book?; **con** ~ **parli?** who are you talking to?; **a** ~ **pensi?** who are you thinking about?; ~ **di voi?** which of you?; **non so a** ~ **rivolgermi** I don't know who to ask

2 (*relativo*) whoever, anyone who; **dillo a** ~ **vuoi** tell whoever you like; **portate** ~ **volete** bring anyone you like; **so io di** ~ **parlo** I know who I'm talking about; **lo riferirò a** ~ **di dovere** I'll pass it on to the relevant person

3 (*indefinito*): ~ ... ~ ... some ... others ...; ~ **dice una cosa,** ~ **dice un'altra** some say one thing, others say another.

chiacchie'rare [kjakkje'rare] *vi* to chat; (*discorrere futilmente*) to chatter; (*far pettegolezzi*) to gossip.

chiacchie'rata [kjakkje'rata] *sf* chat; **farsi una** ~ to have a chat.

chi'acchiere ['kjakkjere] *sfpl* chatter *no pl*; gossip *no pl*; **fare due** *o* **quattro** ~ to have a chat; **perdersi in** ~ to waste time talking.

chiacchie'rone, a [kjakkje'rone] *ag* talkative, chatty; gossipy ♦ *sm/f* chatterbox; gossip.

chia'mare [kja'mare] *vt* to call; (*rivolgersi a qn*) to call (in), send for; ~**rsi** *vr* (*aver nome*) to be called; **mi chiamo Paolo** my name is Paolo, I'm called Paolo; **mandare a** ~ **qn** to send for sb, call sb in; ~ **alle armi** to call up; ~ **in giudizio** to summon; ~ **qn da parte** to take sb aside.

chia'mata [kja'mata] *sf* (*TEL*) call; (*MIL*) call-up; ~ **interurbana** long-distance call; ~ **con preavviso** person-to-person call; ~ **alle urne** (*POL*) election.

chi'appa ['kjappa] *sf* (*fam: natica*) cheek; ~**e** *sfpl* bottom *sg*.

chi'ara ['kjara] *sf* egg white.

chia'rezza [kja'rettsa] *sf* clearness; clarity.

chiarifi'care [kjarifi'kare] *vt* (*anche fig*) to clarify.

chiarificazi'one [kjarifikat'tsjone] *sf* clarification.

chiari'mento [kjari'mento] *sm* clarification *no pl*, explanation.

chia'rire [kja'rire] *vt* to make clear; (*fig: spiegare*) to clear up, explain; ~**rsi** *vr* to become clear; **si sono chiariti** they've sorted things out.

chi'aro, a ['kjaro] *ag* clear; (*luminoso*) clear, bright; (*colore*) pale, light ♦ *av* (*parlare, vedere*) clearly; **si sta facendo** ~ the day is dawning; **sia** ~**a una cosa** let's get one thing straight; **mettere in** ~ **qc** (*fig*) to clear sth up; **parliamoci** ~ let's be frank; **trasmissione in** ~ (*TV*) uncoded broadcast.

chia'rore [kja'rore] *sm* (*diffuse*) light.

chiaroveg'gente [kjaroved'dʒɛnte] *sm/f* clairvoyant.

chi'asso ['kjasso] *sm* uproar, row; **far** ~ to make a din; (*fig*) to make a fuss; (: *scalpore*) to cause a stir.

chias'soso, a [kjas'soso] *ag* noisy, rowdy; (*vistoso*) showy, gaudy.

'chiatta ['kjatta] *sf* barge.

chi'ave ['kjave] *sf* key ♦ *ag inv* key *cpd*; **chiudere a** ~ to lock; ~ **d'accensione** (*AUT*) ignition key; ~ **a forcella** fork spanner; ~ **inglese** monkey wrench; **in** ~ **politica** in political terms; ~ **di volta** (*anche fig*) keystone; ~**i in mano** (*contratto*) turn-key *cpd*; **prezzo** ~**i in mano** (*di macchina*) on-the-road price.

chiavis'tello [kjavis'tɛllo] *sm* bolt.

chi'azza ['kjattsa] *sf* stain, splash.

chiaz'zare [kjat'tsare] *vt* to stain, splash.

chic [ʃik] *ag inv* chic, elegant.

chicches'sia [kikkes'sia] *pron* anyone, anybody.

'chicco, chi ['kikko] *sm* (*di cereale, riso*) grain; (*di caffè*) bean; ~ **di grandine** hailstone; ~ **d'uva** grape.

chi'edere ['kjɛdere] *vt* (*per sapere*) to ask; (*per avere*) to ask for ♦ *vi*: ~ **di qn** to ask after sb; (*al telefono*) to ask for *o* want sb; ~**rsi** *vr*: ~**rsi (se)** to wonder (whether); ~ **qc a qn** to ask sb sth; to ask sb for sth; ~ **scusa a qn** to apologize to sb; ~ **l'elemosina** to beg; **non chiedo altro** that's all I want.

chieri'chetto [kjeri'ketto] *sm* altar boy.

chi'erico, ci ['kjɛriko] *sm* cleric; altar boy.

chi'esa ['kjɛza] *sf* church.

chi'esi *etc* ['kjɛzi] *vb vedi* **chiedere**.

chi'esto, a ['kjɛsto] *pp di* **chiedere**.

'Chigi ['kidʒi]: **palazzo** ~ *sm* (*POL*) *offices of the Italian Prime Minister*.

'**chiglia** ['kiʎʎa] *sf* keel.

'**chilo** ['kilo] *sm* kilo.

chilo'grammo [kilo'grammo] *sm* kilogram(me).

chilome'traggio [kilome'traddʒo] *sm* (AUT) ≈ mileage.

chilo'metrico, a, ci, che [kilo'mɛtriko] *ag* kilometric; (*fig*) endless.

chi'lometro [ki'lɔmetro] *sm* kilometre (BRIT), kilometer (US).

'**chimico, a, ci, che** ['kimiko] *ag* chemical ♦ *sm/f* chemist ♦ *sf* chemistry.

chi'mono [ki'mɔno] *sm inv* kimono.

'**china** ['kina] *sf* (*pendio*) slope, descent; (BOT) cinchona; (**inchiostro di**) ~ Indian ink; **risalire la** ~ (*fig*) to be on the road to recovery.

chi'nare [ki'nare] *vt* to lower, bend; ~**rsi** *vr* to stoop, bend.

chincaglie'ria [kinkaʎʎe'ria] *sf* fancy-goods shop; ~**e** *sfpl* fancy goods, knick-knacks.

chi'nino [ki'nino] *sm* quinine.

'**chino, a** ['kino] *ag*: **a capo** ~, **a testa** ~**a** head bent *o* bowed.

chi'occia, ce ['kjɔttʃa] *sf* brooding hen.

chi'occio, a, ci, ce ['kjɔttʃo] *ag* (*voce*) clucking.

chi'occiola ['kjɔttʃola] *sf* snail; (*di indirizzo e-mail*) at; **scala a** ~ spiral staircase.

chi'odo ['kjɔdo] *sm* nail; (*fig*) obsession; ~ **scaccia** ~ (*proverbio*) one problem drives away another; **roba da** ~**i!** it's unbelievable!; ~ **di garofano** (CUC) clove.

chi'oma ['kjɔma] *sf* (*capelli*) head of hair; (*di albero*) foliage.

chi'osco, schi ['kjɔsko] *sm* kiosk, stall.

chi'ostro ['kjɔstro] *sm* cloister.

chiro'mante [kiro'mante] *sm/f* palmist; (*indovino*) fortune-teller.

chirur'gia [kirur'dʒia] *sf* surgery.

chi'rurgico, a, ci, che [ki'rurdʒiko] *ag* (*anche fig*) surgical.

chi'rurgo, ghi *o* **gi** [ki'rurgo] *sm* surgeon.

chissà [kis'sa] *av* who knows, I wonder.

chi'tarra [ki'tarra] *sf* guitar.

chitar'rista, i, e [kitar'rista] *sm/f* guitarist, guitar player.

chi'udere ['kjudere] *vt* to close, shut; (*luce, acqua*) to put off, turn off; (*definitivamente: fabbrica*) to close down, shut down; (*strada*) to close; (*recingere*) to enclose; (*porre termine*) to end ♦ *vi* to close, shut; to close down, shut down; to end; ~**rsi** *vr* to shut, close; (*ritirarsi: anche fig*) to shut o.s. away; (*ferita*) to close up;

~ **un occhio su** (*fig*) to turn a blind eye to; **chiudi la bocca!** *o* **il becco!** (*fam*) shut up!

chi'unque [ki'unkwe] *pron* (*relativo*) whoever; (*indefinito*) anyone, anybody; ~ **sia** whoever it is.

'**chiusi** *etc* ['kjusi] *vb vedi* **chiudere**.

chi'uso, a ['kjuso] *pp di* **chiudere** ♦ *ag* (*porta*) shut, closed; (: *a chiave*) locked; (*senza uscita: strada etc*) blocked off; (*rubinetto*) off; (*persona*) uncommunicative; (*ambiente, club*) exclusive ♦ *sm*: **stare al** ~ (*fig*) to be shut up ♦ *sf* (*di corso d'acqua*) sluice, lock; (*recinto*) enclosure; (*di discorso etc*) conclusion, ending; "~" (*negozio etc*) "closed"; "~ **al pubblico**" "no admittance to the public".

chiu'sura [kju'sura] *sf* closing; shutting; closing *o* shutting down; enclosing; putting *o* turning off; ending; (*dispositivo*) catch; fastening; fastener; **orario di** ~ closing time; ~ **lampo** ® zip (fastener) (BRIT), zipper (US).

═══════════════════ *PAROLA CHIAVE*

ci [tʃi] (*dav lo, la, li, le, ne diventa* **ce**) *pron* **1** (*personale: complemento oggetto*) us; (: *a noi: complemento di termine*) (to) us; (: *riflessivo*) ourselves; (: *reciproco*) each other, one another; (*impersonale*): ~ **si veste** we get dressed; ~ **ha visti** he's seen us; **non** ~ **ha dato niente** he gave us nothing; ~ **vestiamo** we get dressed; ~ **amiamo** we love one another *o* each other; ~ **siamo divertiti** we had a good time

2 (*dimostrativo: di ciò, su ciò, in ciò etc*) about (*o* on *o* of) it; **non** ~ **capisco nulla** I can't make head nor tail of it; **non so cosa far**~ I don't know what to do about it; **che** ~ **posso fare?** what can I do about it?; **che c'entro io?** what have I got to do with it?; ~ **puoi giurare** you can bet on it; ~ **puoi contare** you can depend on it; ~ **sei?** (*sei pronto?*) are you ready?; (*hai capito?*) are you with me?

♦ *av* (*qui*) here; (*lì*) there; (*moto attraverso luogo*): ~ **passa sopra un ponte** a bridge passes over it; **non** ~ **passa più nessuno** nobody comes this way any more; **qui** ~ **abito da un anno** I've been living here for a year; **esser**~ *vedi* **essere**.

C.I. *abbr* = **carta d'identità**.

CIA ['tʃia] *sigla f* (= *Central Intelligence Agency*) CIA.

C.ia *abbr* (= *compagnia*) Co.

cia'batta [tʃaˈbatta] *sf* mule, slipper.

ciabat'tino [tʃabatˈtino] *sm* cobbler.

ciac [tʃak] *sm* (*CINE*) clapper board; ~, **si gira!** action!

Ci'ad [tʃad] *sm*: **il ~** Chad.

ci'alda [ˈtʃalda] *sf* (*CUC*) wafer.

cial'trone [tʃalˈtrone] *sm* good-for-nothing.

ciam'bella [tʃamˈbella] *sf* (*CUC*) ring-shaped cake; (*salvagente*) rubber ring.

ci'ancia, ce [ˈtʃantʃa] *sf* gossip *no pl*, tittle-tattle *no pl*.

cianfru'saglie [tʃanfruˈzaʎʎe] *sfpl* bits and pieces.

cia'nuro [tʃaˈnuro] *sm* cyanide.

ci'ao [ˈtʃao] *escl* (*all'arrivo*) hello!; (*alla partenza*) cheerio! (*BRIT*), bye!

ciar'lare [tʃarˈlare] *vi* to chatter; (*peg*) to gossip.

ciarla'tano [tʃarlaˈtano] *sm* charlatan.

cias'cuno, a [tʃasˈkuno] (*dav sm*: **ciascun** +*C, V*, **ciascuno** +*s impura, gn, pn, ps, x, z*; *dav sf*: **ciascuna** +*C*, **ciascun'** +*V*) *det, pron* each.

ci'bare [tʃiˈbare] *vt* to feed; ~**rsi** *vr*: ~**rsi di** to eat.

ci'barie [tʃiˈbarje] *sfpl* foodstuffs.

ciber'netica [tʃiberˈnɛtika] *sf* cybernetics *sg*.

'cibo [ˈtʃibo] *sm* food.

ci'cala [tʃiˈkala] *sf* cicada.

cica'trice [tʃikaˈtritʃe] *sf* scar.

cicatriz'zarsi [tʃikatridˈdzarsi] *vr* to form a scar, heal (up).

'cicca, che [ˈtʃikka] *sf* cigarette end; (*fam*: *sigaretta*) fag; **non vale una ~** (*fig*) it's worthless.

'ciccia [ˈtʃittʃa] *sf* (*fam: carne*) meat; (: *grasso umano*) fat, flesh.

cicci'one, a [tʃitˈtʃone] *smf* (*fam*) fatty.

cice'rone [tʃitʃeˈrone] *sm* guide.

cicla'mino [tʃiklaˈmino] *sm* cyclamen.

ci'clismo [tʃiˈklizmo] *sm* cycling.

ci'clista, i, e [tʃiˈklista] *smf* cyclist.

'ciclo [ˈtʃiklo] *sm* cycle; (*di malattia*) course.

ciclomo'tore [tʃiklomoˈtore] *sm* moped.

ci'clone [tʃiˈklone] *sm* cyclone.

ciclos'tile [tʃiklosˈtile] *sm* cyclostyle (*BRIT*).

ci'cogna [tʃiˈkoɲɲa] *sf* stork.

ci'coria [tʃiˈkɔrja] *sf* chicory.

ci'eco, a, chi, che [ˈtʃɛko] *ag* blind ♦ *smf* blind man/woman; **alla ~a** (*anche fig*) blindly.

ciel'lino, a [tʃielˈlino] *smf* (*POL*) *member of CL movement.*

ci'elo [ˈtʃɛlo] *sm* sky; (*REL*) heaven; **toccare il ~ con un dito** (*fig*) to walk on air; **per amor del ~!** for heavens' sake!

'cifra [ˈtʃifra] *sf* (*numero*) figure, numeral; (*somma di denaro*) sum, figure; (*monogramma*) monogram, initials *pl*; (*codice*) code, cipher.

ci'frare [tʃiˈfrare] *vt* (*messaggio*) to code; (*lenzuola etc*) to embroider with a monogram.

'ciglio [ˈtʃiʎʎo] *sm* (*margine*) edge, verge; (*pl(f)* **ciglia**: *delle palpebre*) (eye)lash; (*sopracciglio*) eyebrow; **non ha battuto ~** (*fig*) he didn't bat an eyelid.

'cigno [ˈtʃiɲɲo] *sm* swan.

cigo'lante [tʃigoˈlante] *ag* squeaking, creaking.

cigo'lare [tʃigoˈlare] *vi* to squeak, creak.

'Cile [ˈtʃile] *sm*: **il ~** Chile.

ci'lecca [tʃiˈlekka] *sf*: **far ~** to fail.

ci'leno, a [tʃiˈlɛno] *ag*, *smf* Chilean.

cili'egia, gie *o* **ge** [tʃiˈljɛdʒa] *sf* cherry.

cili'egina [tʃiljeˈdʒina] *sf* glacé cherry; **la ~ sulla torta** (*fig*) the icing *o* cherry on the cake.

cili'egio [tʃiˈljɛdʒo] *sm* cherry tree.

cilin'drata [tʃilinˈdrata] *sf* (*AUT*) (cubic) capacity; **una macchina di grossa ~** a big-engined car.

ci'lindro [tʃiˈlindro] *sm* cylinder; (*cappello*) top hat.

CIM [tʃim] *sigla m* = *centro d'igiene mentale*.

'cima [ˈtʃima] *sf* (*sommità*) top; (*di monte*) top, summit; (*estremità*) end; (*fig: persona*) genius; **in ~ a** at the top of; **da ~ a fondo** from top to bottom; (*fig*) from beginning to end.

ci'melio [tʃiˈmɛljo] *sm* relic.

cimen'tarsi [tʃimenˈtarsi] *vr*: ~**rsi in** (*atleta, concorrente*) to try one's hand at.

'cimice [ˈtʃimitʃe] *sf* (*ZOOL*) bug; (*puntina*) drawing pin (*BRIT*), thumbtack (*US*).

cimini'era [tʃimiˈnjɛra] *sf* chimney; (*di nave*) funnel.

cimi'tero [tʃimiˈtɛro] *sm* cemetery.

ci'murro [tʃiˈmurro] *sm* (*di cani*) distemper.

'Cina [ˈtʃina] *sf*: **la ~** China.

cin'cin, cin cin [tʃinˈtʃin] *escl* cheers!

cincischi'are [tʃintʃisˈkjare] *vi* to mess about.

'cine [ˈtʃine] *sm inv* (*fam*) cinema.

cine'asta, i, e [tʃineˈasta] *smf* person in the film industry; film-maker.

cinegior'nale [tʃinedʒorˈnale] *sm* newsreel.

'cinema [ˈtʃinema] *sm inv* cinema; ~ **muto** silent films; ~ **d'essai** (*locale*) avant-garde cinema, experimental cinema.

cinemato'grafico, a, ci, che [tʃinematoˈgrafiko] *ag* (*attore, critica*) movie *cpd*, film *cpd*; (*festival*) film *cpd*; **sala ~a** cinema; **successo ~** box-office success.

cinema'tografo [tʃinema'tɔgrafo] *sm* cinema.

cine'presa [tʃine'presa] *sf* cine-camera.

ci'nese [tʃi'nese] *ag, smlf, sm* Chinese *inv*.

cine'teca, che [tʃine'tɛka] *sf* (*collezione*) film collection; (*locale*) film library.

ci'netico, a, ci, che [tʃi'nɛtiko] *ag* kinetic.

'cingere ['tʃindʒere] *vt* (*attorniare*) to surround, encircle; ~ **la vita con una cintura** to put a belt round one's waist; ~ **d'assedio** to besiege, lay siege to.

'cinghia ['tʃingja] *sf* strap; (*cintura, TECN*) belt; **tirare la** ~ (*fig*) to tighten one's belt.

cinghi'ale [tʃin'gjale] *sm* wild boar.

cinguet'tare [tʃingwet'tare] *vi* to twitter.

'cinico, a, ci, che ['tʃiniko] *ag* cynical ♦ *smlf* cynic.

ci'nismo [tʃi'nizmo] *sm* cynicism.

cin'quanta [tʃin'kwanta] *num* fifty.

cinquante'nario [tʃinkwante'narjo] *sm* fiftieth anniversary.

cinquan'tenne [tʃinkwan'tɛnne] *smlf* fifty-year-old man/woman.

cinquan'tesimo, a [tʃinkwan'tɛzimo] *num* fiftieth.

cinquan'tina [tʃinkwan'tina] *sf* (*serie*): **una** ~ (**di**) about fifty; (*età*): **essere sulla** ~ to be about fifty.

'cinque ['tʃinkwe] *num* five; **avere** ~ **anni** to be five (years old); **il** ~ **dicembre 1988** the fifth of December 1988; **alle** ~ (*ora*) at five (o'clock); **siamo in** ~ there are five of us.

cinquecen'tesco, a, schi, sche [tʃinkwetʃen'tesko] *ag* sixteenth-century.

cinque'cento [tʃinkwe'tʃento] *num* five hundred ♦ *sm*: **il C**~ the sixteenth century.

cinque'mila [tʃinkwe'mila] *num* five thousand.

'cinsi *etc* ['tʃinsi] *vb vedi* **cingere**.

'cinta ['tʃinta] *sf* (*anche*: ~ **muraria**) city walls *pl*; **muro di** ~ (*di giardino etc*) surrounding wall.

cin'tare [tʃin'tare] *vt* to enclose.

'cinto, a ['tʃinto] *pp di* **cingere**.

'cintola ['tʃintola] *sf* (*cintura*) belt; (*vita*) waist.

cin'tura [tʃin'tura] *sf* belt; ~ **di salvataggio** lifebelt (*BRIT*), life preserver (*US*); ~ **di sicurezza** (*AUT, AER*) safety *o* seat belt.

cintu'rino [tʃintu'rino] *sm* strap; ~ **dell'orologio** watch strap.

CIO *sigla m* (= *Comitato Internazionale Olimpico*) IOC (= *International Olympic Committee*).

ciò [tʃɔ] *pron* this; that; ~ **che** what; ~ **nonostante** *o* **nondimeno** nevertheless, in spite of that; **con tutto** ~ for all that, in

spite of everything.

ci'occa, che ['tʃɔkka] *sf* (*di capelli*) lock.

ciocco'lata [tʃokko'lata] *sf* chocolate; (*bevanda*) (hot) chocolate; ~ **al latte/ fondente** milk/plain chocolate.

cioccola'tino [tʃokkola'tino] *sm* chocolate.

ciocco'lato [tʃokko'lato] *sm* chocolate.

cio'è [tʃo'ɛ] *av* that is (to say).

ciondo'lare [tʃondo'lare] *vt* (*far dondolare*) to dangle, swing ♦ *vi* to dangle; (*fig*) to loaf (about).

ci'ondolo ['tʃondolo] *sm* pendant; ~ **portafortuna** charm.

ciondo'loni [tʃondo'loni] *av*: **con le braccia/ gambe** ~ with arms/legs dangling.

ciononos'tante [tʃononos'tante] *av* nonetheless, nevertheless.

ci'otola ['tʃɔtola] *sf* bowl.

ci'ottolo ['tʃɔttolo] *sm* pebble; (*di strada*) cobble(stone).

C.I.P. [tʃip] *sigla m* (= *comitato interministeriale prezzi*) *vedi* **comitato**.

Cipe ['tʃipe] *sigla m* (= *comitato interministeriale per la programmazione economica*) *vedi* **comitato**.

'Cipi ['tʃipi] *sigla m* (= *comitato interministeriale per lo sviluppo industriale*) *vedi* **comitato**.

ci'piglio [tʃi'piʎʎo] *sm* frown.

ci'polla [tʃi'polla] *sf* onion; (*di tulipano etc*) bulb.

cipol'lina [tʃipol'lina] *sf* onion; ~**e sottaceto** pickled onions; ~**e sottolio** baby onions in oil.

ci'presso [tʃi'presso] *sm* cypress (tree).

'cipria ['tʃiprja] *sf* (face) powder.

cipri'ota, i, e [tʃipri'ɔta] *ag, smlf* Cypriot.

'Cipro ['tʃipro] *sm* Cyprus.

'circa ['tʃirka] *av* about, roughly ♦ *prep* about, concerning; **a mezzogiorno** ~ about midday.

'circo, chi ['tʃirko] *sm* circus.

circo'lare [tʃirko'lare] *vi* to circulate; (*AUT*) to drive (along), move (along) ♦ *ag* circular ♦ *sf* (*AMM*) circular; (*di autobus*) circle (line); **circola voce che ...** there is a rumour going about that ...; **assegno** ~ banker's draft.

circolazi'one [tʃirkolat'tsjone] *sf* circulation; (*AUT*): **la** ~ (the) traffic; **libretto di** ~ log book, registration book; **tassa di** ~ road tax; ~ **a targhe alterne** *vedi nota nel riquadro*.

CIRCOLAZIONE A TARGHE ALTERNE

Circolazione a targhe alterne *was introduced by some town councils to combat the increase in traffic and pollution in town* *centres. It stipulates that on days with an even date, only cars whose number plate ends in an even number or a zero may be on the road; on days with an odd date, only cars with odd registration numbers may be used. Public holidays are generally, but not always, exempt.*

'circolo ['tʃirkolo] *sm* circle; **entrare in** ~ (*ANAT*) to enter the bloodstream.

circoncisi'one [tʃirkontʃi'zjone] *sf* circumcision.

circon'dare [tʃirkon'dare] *vt* to surround.

circondari'ale [tʃirkonda'rjale] *ag*: **casa di pena** ~ district prison.

circon'dario [tʃirkon'darjo] *sm* (*DIR*) administrative district; (*zona circostante*) neighbourhood (*BRIT*), neighborhood (*US*).

circonfe'renza [tʃirkonfe'rɛntsa] *sf* circumference.

circonvallazi'one [tʃirkonvallat'tsjone] *sf* ring road (*BRIT*), beltway (*US*); (*per evitare una città*) by-pass.

circos'critto, a [tʃirkos'kritto] *pp di* **circoscrivere**.

circos'crivere [tʃirkos'krivere] *vt* to circumscribe; (*fig*) to limit, restrict.

circoscrizi'one [tʃirkoskrit'tsjone] *sf* (*AMM*) district, area; ~ **elettorale** constituency.

circos'petto, a [tʃirkos'pɛtto] *ag* circumspect, cautious.

circos'tante [tʃirkos'tante] *ag* surrounding, neighbouring (*BRIT*), neighboring (*US*).

circos'tanza [tʃirkos'tantsa] *sf* circumstance; (*occasione*) occasion; **parole di** ~ words suited to the occasion.

circu'ire [tʃirku'ire] *vt* (*fig*) to fool, take in.

cir'cuito [tʃir'kuito] *sm* circuit; **andare in** *o* **fare corto** ~ to short-circuit; ~ **integrato** integrated circuit.

ci'rillico, a, ci, che [tʃi'rilliko] *ag* Cyrillic.

cir'rosi [tʃir'rɔzi] *sf*: ~ **epatica** cirrhosis (of the liver).

'C.I.S.A.L. ['tʃizal] *sigla f* (= *Confederazione Italiana Sindacati Autonomi dei Lavoratori*) *trades union organization*.

C.I.S.L. [tʃizl] *sigla f* (= *Confederazione Italiana Sindacati Lavoratori*) *trades union organization*.

'C.I.S.N.A.L. ['tʃiznal] *sigla f* (= *Confederazione Italiana Sindacati Nazionali dei Lavoratori*) *trades union organization*.

'ciste ['tʃiste] *sf* = **cisti**.

cis'terna [tʃis'tɛrna] *sf* tank, cistern.

'cisti ['tʃisti] *sf inv* cyst.

cis'tite [tʃis'tite] *sf* cystitis.

C.I.T. [tʃit] *sigla f* = *Compagnia Italiana Turismo*.

cit. *abbr* (= *citato, citata*) cit.

ci'tare [tʃi'tare] *vt* (*DIR*) to summon; (*autore*) to quote; (*a esempio, modello*) to cite; ~ **qn per danni** to sue sb.

citazi'one [tʃitat'tsjone] *sf* summons *sg*; quotation; (*di persona*) mention.

ci'tofono [tʃi'tɔfono] *sm* entry phone; (*in uffici*) intercom.

cito'logico, a, ci, che [tʃito'lɔdʒiko] *ag*: **esame** ~ test for detection of cancerous cells.

'citrico, a, ci, che ['tʃitriko] *ag* citric.

città [tʃit'ta] *sf inv* town; (*importante*) city; ~ **giardino** garden city; ~ **mercato** shopping centre, mall; ~ **universitaria** university campus; **C**~ **del Capo** Cape Town.

citta'della [tʃitta'dɛlla] *sf* citadel, stronghold.

cittadi'nanza [tʃittadi'nantsa] *sf* citizens *pl*, inhabitants *pl* of a town (*o* city); (*DIR*) citizenship.

citta'dino, a [tʃitta'dino] *ag* town *cpd*; city *cpd* ♦ *sm/f* (*di uno Stato*) citizen; (*abitante di città*) town dweller, city dweller.

ci'uccio ['tʃuttʃo] *sm* (*fam*) comforter, dummy (*BRIT*), pacifier (*US*).

ci'uco, a, chi, che ['tʃuko] *sm/f* ass.

ci'uffo ['tʃuffo] *sm* tuft.

ci'urma ['tʃurma] *sf* (*di nave*) crew.

ci'vetta [tʃi'vetta] *sf* (*ZOOL*) owl; (*fig: donna*) coquette, flirt ♦ *ag inv*: **auto/nave** ~ decoy car/ship; **fare la** ~ **con qn** to flirt with sb.

civet'tare [tʃivet'tare] *vi* to flirt.

civette'ria [tʃivette'ria] *sf* coquetry, coquettishness.

civettu'olo, a [tʃivet'twɔlo] *ag* flirtatious.

'civico, a, ci, che ['tʃiviko] *ag* civic; (*museo*) municipal, town *cpd*; **guardia** ~**a** town policeman; **senso** ~ public spirit.

ci'vile [tʃi'vile] *ag* civil; (*non militare*) civilian; (*nazione*) civilized ♦ *sm* civilian; **stato** ~ marital status; **abiti** ~**i** civvies.

civi'lista, i, e [tʃivi'lista] *sm/f* (*avvocato*) civil lawyer; (*studioso*) expert in civil law.

civiliz'zare [tʃivilid'dzare] *vt* to civilize.

civilizzazi'one [tʃiviliddzat'tsjone] *sf* civilization.

civiltà [tʃivil'ta] *sf* civilization; (*cortesia*) civility.

ci'vismo [tʃi'vizmo] *sm* public spirit.

CL [tʃi'elle] *sigla f* (*POL*: = *Comunione e Liberazione*) *Catholic youth movement* ♦ *sigla* = *Caltanissetta*.

cl *abbr* (= *centilitro*) cl.

'clacson *sm inv* (*AUT*) horn.

cla'more *sm* (*frastuono*) din, uproar, clamour (*BRIT*), clamor (*US*); (*fig*) outcry.

clamo'roso, a *ag* noisy; (*fig*) sensational.

clan *sm inv* clan.

clandestinità *sf* (*di attività*) secret nature; **vivere nella** ~ to live in hiding; (*ricercato politico*) to live underground.

clandes'tino, a *ag* clandestine; (*POL*) underground, clandestine ♦ *sm/f* stowaway; (*anche*: **immigrato** ~) illegal immigrant.

clari'netto *sm* clarinet.

'classe *sf* class; **di** ~ (*fig*) with class; of excellent quality; ~ **turistica** (*AER*) economy class.

classi'cismo [klassi'tʃizmo] *sm* classicism.

'classico, a, ci, che *ag* classical; (*tradizionale: moda*) classic(al) ♦ *sm* classic; classical author; (*anche*: **liceo** ~) *secondary school with emphasis on humanities.*

clas'sifica, che *sf* classification; (*SPORT*) placings *pl*; (*di dischi*) charts *pl*.

classifi'care *vt* to classify; (*candidato, compito*) to grade; ~**rsi** *vr* to be placed.

classifica'tore *sm* filing cabinet.

classificazi'one [klassifikat'tsjone] *sf* classification; grading.

clas'sista, i, e *ag* class-conscious ♦ *sm/f* class-conscious person.

claudi'cante *ag* (*zoppo*) lame; (*fig: prosa*) halting.

'clausola *sf* (*DIR*) clause.

claustro'fobico, a, ci, che *ag* claustrophobic.

clau'sura *sf* (*REL*): **monaca di** ~ nun belonging to an enclosed order; **fare una vita di** ~ (*fig*) to lead a cloistered life.

'clava *sf* club.

clavi'cembalo [klavi'tʃembalo] *sm* harpsichord.

cla'vicola *sf* (*ANAT*) collarbone.

cle'mente *ag* merciful; (*clima*) mild.

cle'menza [kle'mɛntsa] *sf* mercy, clemency; mildness.

clep'tomane *sm/f* kleptomaniac.

cleri'cale *ag* clerical.

'clero *sm* clergy.

cles'sidra *sf* (*a sabbia*) hourglass; (*ad acqua*) water clock.

clic'care *vi* (*INFORM*): ~ **su** to click on.

cliché [kli'ʃe] *sm inv* (*TIP*) plate; (*fig*) cliché.

cli'ente *sm/f* customer, client.

clien'tela *sf* customers *pl*, clientèle.

cliente'lismo *sm*: ~ **politico** political nepotism.

'clima, i *sm* climate.

cli'matico, a, ci, che *ag* climatic; **stazione** ~**a** health resort.

climatizza'tore [klimatiddza'tore] *sm* air

conditioner.

climatizzazi'one [klimatiddzat'tsjone] *sf* air conditioning.

'clinico, a, ci, che *ag* clinical ♦ *sm* (*medico*) clinician ♦ *sf* (*scienza*) clinical medicine; (*casa di cura*) clinic, nursing home; (*settore d'ospedale*) clinic; **quadro** ~ anamnesis; **avere l'occhio** ~ (*fig*) to have an expert eye.

clis'tere *sm* (*MED*) enema; (: *apparecchio*) *device used to give an enema.*

clo'aca, che *sf* sewer.

cloche [klɔʃ] *sf inv* control stick, joystick; **cambio a** ~ (*AUT*) floor-mounted gear lever.

clo'nare *vt* to clone.

clona'zione [clonat'tsjone] *sf* (*BIOL, fig*) cloning.

'cloro *sm* chlorine.

cloro'filla *sf* chlorophyll.

cloro'formio *sm* chloroform.

club *sm inv* club.

cm *abbr* (= *centimetro*) cm.

c.m. *abbr* (= *corrente mese*) inst.

CN *sigla* = *Cuneo*.

c/n *abbr* = *conto nuovo*.

CNEN *sigla m* (= *Comitato Nazionale per l'Energia Nucleare*) ≈ AEA (*BRIT*), AEC (*US*).

CNR *sigla m* (= *Consiglio Nazionale delle Ricerche*) *science research council.*

CNRN *sigla m* = *Comitato Nazionale Ricerche Nucleari.*

CO *sigla* = *Como.*

Co. *abbr* (= *compagnia*) Co.

c/o *abbr* (= *care of*) c/o.

coabi'tare *vi* to live together.

coagu'lare *vt* to coagulate ♦ *vi*, ~**rsi** *vr* to coagulate; (*latte*) to curdle.

coalizi'one [koalit'tsjone] *sf* coalition.

co'atto, a *ag* (*DIR*) compulsory, forced; **condannare al domicilio** ~ to place under house arrest.

'COBAS *sigla mpl* (= *Comitati di base*) *independent trades unions.*

'cobra *sm inv* cobra.

'coca 'cola ® *sf* coca cola ®.

coca'ina *sf* cocaine.

coc'carda *sf* cockade.

cocchi'ere [kok'kjɛre] *sm* coachman.

'cocchio ['kɔkkjo] *sm* (*carrozza*) coach; (*biga*) chariot.

cocci'nella [kottʃi'nɛlla] *sf* ladybird (*BRIT*), ladybug (*US*).

'coccio ['kɔttʃo] *sm* earthenware; (*vaso*) earthenware pot; ~**i** *smpl* fragments (of pottery).

cocciu'taggine [kottʃu'taddʒine] *sf*

stubbornness, pig-headedness.

cocci'uto, a [kot't∫uto] *ag* stubborn, pigheaded.

'**cocco, chi** *sm* (*pianta*) coconut palm; (*frutto*): **noce di** ~ coconut ♦ *smlf* (*fam*) darling; **è il** ~ **della mamma** he's mummy's darling.

cocco'drillo *sm* crocodile.

cocco'lare *vt* to cuddle, fondle.

co'cente [ko't∫ɛnte] *ag* (*anche fig*) burning.

cocerò *etc* [kot∫e'rɔ] *vb vedi* **cuocere**.

co'comero *sm* watermelon.

co'cuzzolo [ko'kuttsolo] *sm* top; (*di capo, cappello*) crown.

cod. *abbr* = **codice**.

'**coda** *sf* tail; (*fila di persone, auto*) queue (*BRIT*), line (*US*); (*di abiti*) train; **con la** ~ **dell'occhio** out of the corner of one's eye; **mettersi in** ~ to queue (up) (*BRIT*), line up (*US*); to join the queue *o* line; ~ **di cavallo** (*acconciatura*) ponytail; **avere la** ~ **di paglia** (*fig*) to have a guilty conscience; ~ **di rospo** (*CUC*) frogfish tail.

codar'dia *sf* cowardice.

co'dardo, a *ag* cowardly ♦ *smlf* coward.

co'desto, a *ag, pron* (*poetico*) this; that.

'**codice** ['kɔdit∫e] *sm* code; (*manoscritto antico*) codex; ~ **di avviamento postale** (**CAP**) postcode (*BRIT*), zip code (*US*); ~ **a barre** bar code; ~ **civile** civil code; ~ **fiscale** tax code; ~ **penale** penal code; ~ **segreto** (*di tessera magnetica*) PIN (number); ~ **della strada** highway code.

co'difica *sf* codification; (*INFORM: di programma*) coding.

codifi'care *vt* (*DIR*) to codify; (*cifrare*) to code.

codificazi'one [kodifikat'tsjone] *sf* coding.

coercizi'one [koert∫it'tsjone] *sf* coercion.

coe'rente *ag* coherent.

coe'renza [koe'rɛntsa] *sf* coherence.

coesi'one *sf* cohesion.

coe'sistere *vi* to coexist.

coe'taneo, a *ag, smlf* contemporary; **essere** ~ **di qn** to be the same age as sb.

cofa'netto *sm* casket; ~ **dei gioielli** jewel case.

'**cofano** *sm* (*AUT*) bonnet (*BRIT*), hood (*US*); (*forziere*) chest.

'**coffa** *sf* (*NAUT*) top.

'**cogli** ['kɔʎʎi] *prep* + *det vedi* **con**.

'**cogliere** ['kɔʎʎere] *vt* (*fiore, frutto*) to pick, gather; (*sorprendere*) to catch, surprise; (*bersaglio*) to hit; (*fig: momento opportuno etc*) to grasp, seize, take; (*: capire*) to grasp; ~ **l'occasione (per fare)** to take the opportunity (to do); ~ **sul fatto** *o* **in flagrante/alla sprovvista** to catch red-

handed/unprepared; ~ **nel segno** (*fig*) to hit the nail on the head.

cogli'one [koʎ'ʎone] *sm* (*fam!: testicolo*): ~**i balls** (*!*); (*: fig: persona sciocca*) jerk; **rompere i** ~**i a qn** to get on sb's tits (*!*).

co'gnac [kɔ'ɲak] *sm inv* cognac.

co'gnato, a [koɲ'ɲato] *smlf* brother-/ sister-in-law.

cognizi'one [koɲɲit'tsjone] *sf* knowledge; **con** ~ **di causa** with full knowledge of the facts.

co'gnome [koɲ'ɲome] *sm* surname.

'**coi** *prep* + *det vedi* **con**.

coi'bente *ag* insulating.

coinci'denza [kointʃi'dɛntsa] *sf* coincidence; (*FERR, AER, di autobus*) connection.

coin'cidere [koin't∫idere] *vi* to coincide.

coin'ciso, a [koin't∫izo] *pp di* **coincidere**.

coinqui'lino *sm* fellow tenant.

cointeres'senza [kointeres'sɛntsa] *sf* (*COMM*): **avere una** ~ **in qc** to own shares in sth; ~ **dei lavoratori** profit-sharing.

coin'volgere [koin'vɔldʒere] *vt*: ~ **in** to involve in.

coinvolgi'mento [koinvoldʒi'mento] *sm* involvement.

coin'volto, a *pp di* **coinvolgere**.

col *prep* + *det vedi* **con**.

Col. *abbr* (= *colonnello*) Col.

colà *av* there.

cola'brodo *sm inv* strainer.

cola'pasta *sm inv* colander.

co'lare *vt* (*liquido*) to strain; (*pasta*) to drain; (*oro fuso*) to pour ♦ *vi* (*sudore*) to drip; (*botte*) to leak; (*cera*) to melt; ~ **a picco** *vt, vi* (*nave*) to sink.

co'lata *sf* (*di lava*) flow; (*FONDERIA*) casting.

colazi'one [kolat'tsjone] *sf* (*anche*: **prima** ~) breakfast; (*anche*: **seconda** ~) lunch; **fare** ~ to have breakfast (*o* lunch); ~ **di lavoro** working lunch.

Coldi'retti *abbr f* (= *Confederazione nazionale coltivatori diretti*) *federation of Italian farmers*.

co'lei *pron vedi* **colui**.

co'lera *sm* (*MED*) cholera.

coleste'rolo *sm* cholesterol.

colf *abbr f* = **collaboratrice familiare**.

'**colgo** *etc vb vedi* **cogliere**.

colibrì *sm* hummingbird.

'**colica** *sf* (*MED*) colic.

co'lino *sm* strainer.

'**colla** *prep* + *det vedi* **con** ♦ *sf* glue; (*di farina*) paste.

collabo'rare *vi* to collaborate; (*con la polizia*) to co-operate; ~ **a** to collaborate on; (*giornale*) to contribute to.

collabora'tore, 'trice *sm/f* collaborator; (*di giornale, rivista*) ~ **esterno** freelance; ~**trice familiare** home help; ~ **di giustizia** = **pentito, a**.

collaborazi'one [kollaborat'tsjone] *sf* collaboration; contribution.

col'lana *sf* necklace; (*collezione*) collection, series.

col'lant [kɔ'lã] *sm inv* tights *pl*.

col'lare *sm* collar.

col'lasso *sm* (*MED*) collapse.

collate'rale *ag* collateral; **effetti** ~**i** side effects.

col'laudo *sm* testing *no pl*; test.

'colle *prep* + *det vedi* **con** ♦ *sm* hill.

col'lega, ghi, ghe *sm/f* colleague.

collega'mento *sm* connection; (*MIL*) liaison; (*RADIO*) link(-up); (*INFORM*) link; **ufficiale di** ~ liaison officer; ~ **ipertestuale** hyperlink.

colle'gare *vt* to connect, join, link; ~**rsi** *vr* (*RADIO, TV*) to link up; ~**rsi con** (*TEL*) to get through to.

collegi'ale [kolle'dʒale] *ag* (*riunione, decisione*) collective; (*INS*) boarding school *cpd* ♦ *sm/f* boarder; (*fig: persona timida e inesperta*) schoolboy/girl.

col'legio [kol'lɛdʒo] *sm* college; (*convitto*) boarding school; ~ **elettorale** (*POL*) constituency.

'collera *sf* anger; **andare in** ~ to get angry.

col'lerico, a, ci, che *ag* quick-tempered, irascible.

col'letta *sf* collection.

collettività *sf* community.

collet'tivo, a *ag* collective; (*interesse*) general, everybody's; (*biglietto, visita etc*) group *cpd* ♦ *sm* (*POL*) (political) group; **società in nome** ~ (*COMM*) partnership.

col'letto *sm* collar; ~**i bianchi** (*fig*) white-collar workers.

collezio'nare [kollettsjo'nare] *vt* to collect.

collezi'one [kollet'tsjone] *sf* collection.

collezio'nista [kollettsjo'nista] *sm/f* collector.

colli'mare *vi* to correspond, coincide.

col'lina *sf* hill.

colli'nare *ag* hill *cpd*.

col'lirio *sm* eyewash.

collisi'one *sf* collision.

'collo *prep* + *det vedi* **con** ♦ *sm* neck; (*di abito*) neck, collar; (*pacco*) parcel; ~ **del piede** instep.

colloca'mento *sm* (*impiego*) employment; (*disposizione*) placing, arrangement; **ufficio di** ~ ≈ Jobcentre (*BRIT*), state (*o* federal) employment agency (*US*); ~ **a riposo** retirement.

collo'care *vt* (*libri, mobili*) to place; (*persona: trovare un lavoro per*) to find a job for, place; (*COMM: merce*) to find a market for; ~ **qn a riposo** to retire sb.

collocazi'one [kollokat'tsjone] *sf* placing; (*di libro*) classification.

colloqui'ale *ag* (*termine etc*) colloquial; (*tono*) informal.

col'loquio *sm* conversation, talk; (*ufficiale, per un lavoro*) interview; (*INS*) preliminary oral exam; **avviare un** ~ **con qn** (*POL etc*) to start talks with sb.

col'loso, a *ag* sticky.

col'lottola *sf* nape *o* scruff of the neck; **afferrare qn per la** ~ to grab sb by the scruff of the neck.

collusi'one *sf* (*DIR*) collusion.

colluttazi'one [kolluttat'tsjone] *sf* scuffle.

col'mare *vt*: ~ **di** (*anche fig*) to fill with; (*dare in abbondanza*) to load *o* overwhelm with; ~ **un divario** (*fig*) to bridge a gap.

'colmo, a *ag*: ~ **(di)** full (of) ♦ *sm* summit, top; (*fig*) height; **al** ~ **della disperazione** in the depths of despair; **è il** ~**!** it's the last straw!; **e per** ~ **di sfortuna** ... and to cap it all ....

co'lomba *sf vedi* **colombo**.

Co'lombia *sf*: **la** ~ Colombia.

colombi'ano, a *ag, sm/f* Colombian.

co'lombo, a *sm/f* dove; pigeon; ~**i** (*fig fam*) lovebirds.

Co'lonia *sf* Cologne.

co'lonia *sf* colony; (*per bambini*) holiday camp; (**acqua di**) ~ (eau de) cologne.

coloni'ale *ag* colonial ♦ *sm/f* colonist, settler.

co'lonico, a, ci, che *ag*: **casa** ~**a** farmhouse.

coloniz'zare [kolonid'dzare] *vt* to colonize.

co'lonna *sf* column; ~ **sonora** (*CINE*) sound track; ~ **vertebrale** spine, spinal column.

colon'nello *sm* colonel.

co'lono *sm* (*coltivatore*) tenant farmer.

colo'rante *sm* colouring (*BRIT*), coloring (*US*).

colo'rare *vt* to colour (*BRIT*), color (*US*); (*disegno*) to colo(u)r in.

co'lore *sm* colour (*BRIT*), color (*US*); (*CARTE*) suit; **a** ~**i** in colo(u)r, colo(u)r *cpd*; **la gente di** ~ colo(u)red people; **diventare di tutti i** ~**i** to turn scarlet; **farne di tutti i** ~**i** to get up to all sorts of mischief; **passarne di tutti i** ~**i** to go through all sorts of problems.

colo'rito, a *ag* coloured (*BRIT*), colored (*US*); (*viso*) rosy, pink; (*linguaggio*) colourful (*BRIT*), colorful (*US*) ♦ *sm* (*tinta*) colour (*BRIT*), color (*US*); (*carnagione*) complexion.

co'loro *pron pl vedi* **colui.**

colos'sale *ag* colossal, enormous.

co'losso *sm* colossus.

'colpa *sf* fault; (*biasimo*) blame;
(*colpevolezza*) guilt; (*azione colpevole*)
offence; (*peccato*) sin; **di chi è la ~?** whose
fault is it?; **è ~ sua** it's his fault; **per ~ di**
through, owing to; **senso di ~** sense of
guilt; **dare la ~ a qn di qc** to blame sb for
sth.

col'pevole *ag* guilty.

colpevoliz'zare [kolpevolid'dzare] *vt*: **~ qn**
to make sb feel guilty.

col'pire *vt* to hit, strike; (*fig*) to strike;
rimanere colpito da qc to be amazed *o*
struck by sth; **è stato colpito da ordine di
cattura** there is a warrant out for his
arrest; **~ nel segno** (*fig*) to hit the nail on
the head, be spot on (*BRIT*).

'colpo *sm* (*urto*) knock; (*fig: affettivo*) blow,
shock; (*: aggressivo*) blow; (*di pistola*) shot;
(*MED*) stroke; (*furto*) raid; **di ~, tutto d'un
~** suddenly; **fare ~** to make a strong
impression; **il motore perde ~i** (*AUT*) the
engine is misfiring; **è morto sul ~** he died
instantly; **mi hai fatto venire un ~!** what a
fright you gave me!; **ti venisse un ~!**
(*fam*) drop dead!; **~ d'aria** chill; **~ in
banca** bank job *o* raid; **~ basso** (*PUGILATO*,
fig) punch below the belt; **~ di fulmine**
love at first sight; **~ di grazia** coup de
grâce; (*fig*) finishing blow; **a ~ d'occhio** at
a glance; **~ di scena** (*TEAT*) coup de
théâtre; (*fig*) dramatic turn of events; **~
di sole** sunstroke; **~i di sole** (*nei capelli*)
highlights; **~ di Stato** coup d'état; **~ di
telefono** phone call; **~ di testa** (sudden)
impulse *o* whim; **~ di vento** gust (of
wind).

col'poso, a *ag*: **omicidio ~** manslaughter.

'colsi *etc vb vedi* **cogliere.**

coltel'lata *sf* stab.

col'tello *sm* knife; **avere il ~ dalla parte del
manico** (*fig*) to have the whip hand; **~ a
serramanico** clasp knife.

colti'vare *vt* to cultivate; (*verdura*) to grow,
cultivate.

coltiva'tore *sm* farmer; **~ diretto** small
independent farmer.

coltivazi'one [koltivat'tsjone] *sf*
cultivation; growing; **~ intensiva**
intensive farming.

'colto, a *pp di* **cogliere** ♦ *ag* (*istruito*)
cultured, educated.

'coltre *sf* blanket.

col'tura *sf* cultivation; **~ alternata** crop
rotation.

co'lui, co'lei, *pl* **co'loro** *pron* the one;
~ che parla the one *o* the man *o* the
person who is speaking; **colei che
amo** the one *o* the woman *o* the person
(whom) I love.

com. *abbr* = **comunale; commissione.**

'coma *sm inv* coma.

comanda'mento *sm* (*REL*) commandment.

coman'dante *sm* (*MIL*) commander,
commandant; (*di reggimento*)
commanding officer; (*NAUT, AER*) captain.

coman'dare *vi* to be in command ♦ *vt* to
command; (*imporre*) to order, command;
~ a qn di fare to order sb to do.

co'mando *sm* (*ingiunzione*) order,
command; (*autorità*) command; (*TECN*)
control; **~ generale** general headquarters
pl; **~ a distanza** remote control.

co'mare *sf* (*madrina*) godmother; (*donna
pettegola*) gossip.

co'masco, a, schi, sche *ag* of (*o* from)
Como.

combaci'are [komba't∫are] *vi* to meet; (*fig:
coincidere*) to coincide, correspond.

combat'tente *ag* fighting ♦ *sm* combatant;
ex-~ ex-serviceman.

com'battere *vt* to fight; (*fig*) to combat,
fight against ♦ *vi* to fight.

combatti'mento *sm* fight; fighting *no pl*; (*di
pugilato*) match; **mettere fuori ~** to knock
out.

combat'tivo, a *ag* pugnacious.

combat'tuto, a *ag* (*incerto: persona*)
uncertain, undecided; (*gara, partita*) hard
fought.

combi'nare *vt* to combine; (*organizzare*) to
arrange; (*fam: fare*) to make, cause ♦ *vi*
(*corrispondere*): **~ (con)** to correspond
(with).

combinazi'one [kombinat'tsjone] *sf*
combination; (*caso fortuito*) coincidence;
per ~ by chance.

com'briccola *sf* (*gruppo*) party; (*banda*)
gang.

combus'tibile *ag* combustible ♦ *sm*
fuel.

combusti'one *sf* combustion.

com'butta *sf* (*peg*) gang; **in ~** in
league.

══════════════════ *PAROLA CHIAVE*

'come *av* **1** (*alla maniera di*) like; **ti comporti
~ lui** you behave like him *o* like he does;
bianco ~ la neve (as) white as snow; **~ se**
as if, as though; **com'è vero Dio!** as God is
my witness!

2 (*in qualità di*) as a; **lavora ~ autista** he
works as a driver

3 (*interrogativo*) how; ~ **ti chiami?** what's your name?; ~ **sta?** how are you?; **com'è il tuo amico?** what is your friend like?; ~? (*prego?*) pardon?, sorry?; ~ **mai?** how come?; ~ **mai non ci hai avvertiti?** how come you didn't warn us?
4 (*esclamativo*): ~ **sei bravo!** how clever you are!; ~ **mi dispiace!** I'm terribly sorry!
♦ *cong* **1** (*in che modo*) how; **mi ha spiegato** ~ **l'ha conosciuto** he told me how he met him; **non so** ~ **sia successo** I don't know how it happened; **attento a** ~ **parli!** watch your mouth!
2 (*correlativo*) as; (*con comparativi di maggioranza*) than; **non è bravo** ~ **pensavo** he isn't as clever as I thought; **è meglio di** ~ **pensassi** it's better than I thought
3 (*quasi se*) as; **è** ~ **se fosse ancora qui** it's as if he was still here; ~ **se niente fosse** as if nothing had happened; ~ **non detto!** let's forget it!
4 (*appena che, quando*) as soon as; ~ **arrivò, iniziò a lavorare** as soon as he arrived, he set to work; *vedi anche* **così**; **oggi**; **ora**.

'**COMECON** *abbr m* (= *Consiglio di Mutua Assistenza Economica*) COMECON.
come'done *sm* blackhead.
co'meta *sf* comet.
'**comico, a, ci, che** *ag* (*TEAT*) comic; (*buffo*) comical ♦ *sm* (*attore*) comedian, comic actor; (*comicità*) comic spirit, comedy.
co'mignolo [ko'miɲɲolo] *sm* chimney top.
cominci'are [komin'tʃare] *vt, vi* to begin, start; ~ **a fare/col fare** to begin to do/by doing; **cominciamo bene!** (*ironico*) we're off to a fine start!
comi'tato *sm* committee; ~ **direttivo** steering committee; ~ **di gestione** works council; ~ **interministeriale prezzi** interdepartmental committee on prices; ~ **interministeriale per la programmazione economica** interdepartmental committee for economic planning; ~ **interministeriale per lo sviluppo industriale** interdepartmental committee for industrial development.
comi'tiva *sf* party, group.
co'mizio [ko'mittsjo] *sm* (*POL*) meeting, assembly; ~ **elettorale** election rally.
'**comma, i** *sm* (*DIR*) subsection.
com'mando *sm inv* commando (squad).
com'media *sf* comedy; (*opera teatrale*) play; (: *che fa ridere*) comedy; (*fig*) playacting *no pl*.

commedi'ante *sm/f* (*peg*) third-rate actor/actress; (: *fig*) sham.
commedi'ografo, a *sm/f* (*autore*) comedy writer.
commemo'rare *vt* to commemorate.
commemorazi'one [kommemorat'tsjone] *sf* commemoration.
commenda'tore *sm official title awarded for services to one's country.*
commen'sale *sm/f* table companion.
commen'tare *vt* to comment on; (*testo*) to annotate; (*RADIO, TV*) to give a commentary on.
commenta'tore, 'trice *sm/f* commentator.
com'mento *sm* comment; (*a un testo, RADIO, TV*) commentary; ~ **musicale** (*CINE*) background music.
commerci'ale [kommer'tʃale] *ag* commercial, trading; (*peg*) commercial.
commercia'lista, i, e [kommertʃa'lista] *sm/f* (*laureato*) graduate in economics and commerce; (*consulente*) business consultant.
commercializ'zare [kommertʃalid'dzare] *vt* to market.
commercializzazi'one [kommertʃaliddzat 'tsjone] *sf* marketing.
commerci'ante [kommer'tʃante] *sm/f* trader, dealer; (*negoziante*) shopkeeper; ~ **all'ingrosso** wholesaler; ~ **in proprio** sole trader.
commerci'are [kommer'tʃare] *vi*: ~ **in** *vt* to deal *o* trade in.
com'mercio [kom'mertʃo] *sm* trade, commerce; **essere in** ~ (*prodotto*) to be on the market *o* on sale; **essere nel** ~ (*persona*) to be in business; ~ **all'ingrosso/al minuto** wholesale/retail trade.
com'messo, a *pp di* **commettere** ♦ *sm/f* shop assistant (*BRIT*), sales clerk (*US*) ♦ *sm* (*impiegato*) clerk ♦ *sf* (*COMM*) order; ~ **viaggiatore** commercial traveller.
commes'tibile *ag* edible; ~**i** *smpl* foodstuffs.
com'mettere *vt* to commit; (*ordinare*) to commission, order.
commi'ato *sm* leave-taking; **prendere** ~ **da qn** to take one's leave of sb.
commi'nare *vt* (*DIR*) to make provision for.
commise'rare *vt* to sympathize with, commiserate with.
commiserazi'one [kommizerat'tsjone] *sf* commiseration.
com'misi *etc vb vedi* **commettere**.
commissaria'mento *sm* temporary receivership.

commissari'are *vt* to put under temporary receivership.

commissari'ato *sm* (*AMM*) commissionership; (*: sede*) commissioner's office; (*: di polizia*) police station.

commis'sario *sm* commissioner; (*di pubblica sicurezza*) ≈ (police) superintendent (*BRIT*), (police) captain (*US*); (*SPORT*) steward; (*membro di commissione*) member of a committee *o* board; **alto** ~ high commissioner; ~ **di bordo** (*NAUT*) purser; ~ **d'esame** member of an examining board; ~ **di gara** race official; ~ **tecnico** (*SPORT*) national coach.

commissio'nare *vt* to order, place an order for.

commissio'nario *sm* (*COMM*) agent, broker.

commissi'one *sf* (*incarico*) errand; (*comitato, percentuale*) commission; (*COMM: ordinazione*) order; ~**i** *sfpl* (*acquisti*) shopping *sg*; ~ **d'esame** examining board; ~ **d'inchiesta** committee of enquiry; ~ **permanente** standing committee; ~**i bancarie** bank charges.

commit'tente *sm/f* (*COMM*) purchaser, customer.

com'mosso, a *pp di* **commuovere**.

commo'vente *ag* moving.

commozi'one [kommot'tsjone] *sf* emotion, deep feeling; ~ **cerebrale** (*MED*) concussion.

commu'overe *vt* to move, affect; ~**rsi** *vr* to be moved.

commu'tare *vt* (*pena*) to commute; (*ELETTR*) to change *o* switch over.

commutazi'one [kommutat'tsjone] *sf* (*DIR, ELETTR*) commutation.

comò *sm inv* chest of drawers.

como'dino *sm* bedside table.

comodità *sf inv* comfort; convenience.

'comodo, a *ag* comfortable; (*facile*) easy; (*conveniente*) convenient; (*utile*) useful, handy ♦ *sm* comfort; convenience; **con** ~ at one's convenience *o* leisure; **fare il proprio** ~ to do as one pleases; **far** ~ to be useful *o* handy; **stia** ~! don't bother to get up!

'compact disc *sm inv* compact disc.

compae'sano, a *sm/f* fellow-countryman/woman; person from the same town.

com'pagine [kom'padʒine] *sf* (*squadra*) team.

compa'gnia [kompaɲ'ɲia] *sf* company; (*gruppo*) gathering; **fare** ~ **a qn** to keep sb company; **essere di** ~ to be sociable.

com'pagno, a [kom'paɲɲo] *sm/f* (*di classe, gioco*) companion; (*POL*) comrade; ~ **di lavoro** workmate; ~ **di scuola** schoolfriend; ~ **di viaggio** fellow traveller.

com'paio *etc vb vedi* **comparire**.

compa'rare *vt* to compare.

compara'tivo, a *ag, sm* comparative.

comparazi'one [komparat'tsjone] *sf* comparison.

com'pare *sm* (*padrino*) godfather; (*complice*) accomplice; (*fam: amico*) old pal, old mate.

compa'rire *vi* to appear; ~ **in giudizio** (*DIR*) to appear before the court.

comparizi'one [komparit'tsjone] *sf* (*DIR*) appearance; **mandato di** ~ summons *sg*.

com'parso, a *pp di* **comparire** ♦ *sf* appearance; (*TEAT*) walk-on; (*CINE*) extra.

comparteci'pare [kompartetʃi'pare] *vi* (*COMM*): ~ **a** to have a share in.

compartecipazi'one [kompartetʃipat 'tsjone] *sf* sharing; (*quota*) share; ~ **agli utili** profit- sharing; **in** ~ jointly.

comparti'mento *sm* compartment; (*AMM*) district.

com'parvi *etc vb vedi* **comparire**.

compas'sato, a *ag* (*persona*) composed; **freddo e** ~ cool and collected.

compassi'one *sf* compassion, pity; **avere** ~ **di qn** to feel sorry for sb, pity sb; **fare** ~ to arouse pity.

compassio'nevole *ag* compassionate.

com'passo *sm* (pair of) compasses *pl*; callipers *pl*.

compa'tibile *ag* (*scusabile*) excusable; (*conciliabile, INFORM*) compatible.

compati'mento *sm* compassion; indulgence; **con aria di** ~ with a condescending air.

compa'tire *vt* (*aver compassione di*) to sympathize with, feel sorry for; (*scusare*) to make allowances for.

compatri'ota, i, e *sm/f* compatriot.

compat'tezza [kompat'tettsa] *sf* (*solidità*) compactness; (*fig: unità*) solidity.

com'patto, a *ag* compact; (*roccia*) solid; (*folla*) dense; (*fig: gruppo, partito*) united, close-knit.

com'pendio *sm* summary; (*libro*) compendium.

compen'sare *vt* (*equilibrare*) to compensate for, make up for; ~**rsi** *vr* (*reciproco*) to balance each other out; ~ **qn di** (*rimunerare*) to pay *o* remunerate sb for; (*risarcire*) to pay compensation to sb for; (*fig: fatiche, dolori*) to reward sb for.

compen'sato *sm* (*anche*: **legno** ~)

plywood.

com'penso *sm* compensation; payment; remuneration; reward; **in** ~ (*d'altra parte*) on the other hand.

'compera *sf* purchase; **fare le** ~**e** to do the shopping.

compe'rare *vt* = **comprare**.

compe'tente *ag* competent; (*mancia*) apt, suitable; (*capace*) qualified; **rivolgersi all'ufficio** ~ to apply to the office concerned.

compe'tenza [kompe'tɛntsa] *sf* competence; (*DIR: autorità*) jurisdiction; (*TECN, COMM*) expertise; ~**e** *sfpl* (*onorari*) fees; **definire le** ~**e** to establish responsibilities.

com'petere *vi* to compete, vie; (*DIR: spettare*): ~ **a** to lie within the competence of.

competitività *sf inv* competitiveness.

competi'tivo, a *ag* competitive.

competi'tore, 'trice *sm/f* competitor.

competizi'one [kompetit'tsjone] *sf* competition; **spirito di** ~ competitive spirit.

compia'cente [kompja'tʃɛnte] *ag* courteous, obliging.

compia'cenza [kompja'tʃɛntsa] *sf* courtesy.

compia'cere [kompja'tʃere] *vi*: ~ **a** to gratify, please ♦ *vt* to please; ~**rsi** *vr* (*provare soddisfazione*): ~**rsi di** *o* **per qc** to be delighted at sth; (*rallegrarsi*): ~**rsi con qn** to congratulate sb; (*degnarsi*): ~**rsi di fare** to be so good as to do.

compiaci'mento [kompjatʃi'mento] *sm* satisfaction.

compiaci'uto, a [kompja'tʃuto] *pp di* **compiacere**.

compi'angere [kom'pjandʒere] *vt* to sympathize with, feel sorry for.

compi'anto, a *pp di* **compiangere** ♦ *ag*: **il** ~ **presidente** the late lamented president ♦ *sm* mourning, grief.

'compiere *vt* (*concludere*) to finish, complete; (*adempiere*) to carry out, fulfil; ~**rsi** *vr* (*avverarsi*) to be fulfilled, come true; ~ **gli anni** to have one's birthday.

compi'lare *vt* to compile; (*modulo*) to complete, fill in (*BRIT*), fill out (*US*).

compila'tore, 'trice *sm/f* compiler.

compilazi'one [kompilat'tsjone] *sf* compilation; completion.

compi'mento *sm* (*termine, conclusione*) completion, fulfilment; **portare a** ~ **qc** to conclude sth, bring sth to a conclusion.

com'pire *vb* = **compiere**.

'compito *sm* (*incarico*) task, duty; (*dovere*) duty; (*INS*) exercise; (*: a casa*) piece of homework; **fare i** ~**i** to do one's homework.

com'pito, a *ag* well-mannered, polite.

compiu'tezza [kompju'tettsa] *sf* (*completezza*) completeness; (*perfezione*) perfection.

compi'uto, a *pp di* **compiere** ♦ *ag*: **a 20 anni** ~**i** at 20 years of age, at age 20; **un fatto** ~ a fait accompli.

comple'anno *sm* birthday.

complemen'tare *ag* complementary; (*INS: materia*) subsidiary.

comple'mento *sm* complement; (*MIL*) reserve (troops); ~ **oggetto** (*LING*) direct object.

comples'sato, a *ag*, *sm/f*: **essere** (**un**) ~ to be full of complexes *o* hang-ups (*fam*).

complessità *sf* complexity.

complessiva'mente *av* (*nell'insieme*) on the whole; (*in tutto*) altogether.

comples'sivo, a *ag* (*globale*) comprehensive, overall; (*totale: cifra*) total; **visione** ~**a** overview.

com'plesso, a *ag* complex ♦ *sm* (*PSIC, EDIL*) complex; (*MUS: corale*) ensemble; (*: orchestrina*) band; (*: di musica pop*) group; **in** *o* **nel** ~ on the whole.

completa'mento *sm* completion.

comple'tare *vt* to complete.

com'pleto, a *ag* complete; (*teatro, autobus*) full ♦ *sm* suit; **al** ~ full; (*tutti presenti*) all present; **essere al** ~ (*teatro*) to be sold out; ~ **da sci** ski suit.

compli'care *vt* to complicate; ~**rsi** *vr* to become complicated.

complicazi'one [komplikat'tsjone] *sf* complication; **salvo** ~**i** unless any difficulties arise.

'complice ['komplitʃe] *sm/f* accomplice.

complicità [komplitʃi'ta] *sf inv* complicity; **un sorriso/uno sguardo di** ~ a knowing smile/look.

complimen'tarsi *vr*: ~ **con** to congratulate.

compli'mento *sm* compliment; ~**i** *smpl* (*cortesia eccessiva*) ceremony *sg*; ~**i!** congratulations!; **senza** ~**i!** don't stand on ceremony!; make yourself at home!; help yourself!

complot'tare *vi* to plot, conspire.

com'plotto *sm* plot, conspiracy.

com'pone *etc vb vedi* **comporre**.

compo'nente *sm/f* member ♦ *sm* component.

com'pongo *etc vb vedi* **comporre**.

compo'nibile *ag* (*mobili, cucina*) fitted.

componi'mento *sm* (*DIR*) settlement; (*INS*) composition; (*poetico, teatrale*) work.

com'porre *vt* (*musica, testo*) to compose; (*mettere in ordine*) to arrange; (*DIR: lite*) to settle; (*TIP*) to set; (*TEL*) to dial; **comporsi** *vr*: **comporsi di** to consist of, be composed of.

comportamen'tale *ag* behavioural (*BRIT*), behavioral (*US*).

comporta'mento *sm* behaviour (*BRIT*), behavior (*US*); (*di prodotto*) performance.

compor'tare *vt* (*implicare*) to involve, entail; (*consentire*) to permit, allow (of); **~rsi** *vr* (*condursi*) to behave.

com'posi *etc vb vedi* **comporre**.

composi'tore, 'trice *sm/f* composer; (*TIP*) compositor, typesetter.

composizi'one [kompozit'tsjone] *sf* composition; (*DIR*) settlement.

com'posta *sf vedi* **composto**.

compos'tezza [kompos'tettsa] *sf* composure; decorum.

com'posto, a *pp di* **comporre** ♦ *ag* (*persona*) composed, self-possessed; (*: decoroso*) dignified; (*formato da più elementi*) compound *cpd* ♦ *sm* compound; (*CUC etc*) mixture ♦ *sf* (*CUC*) stewed fruit *no pl*; (*AGR*) compost.

com'prare *vt* to buy; (*corrompere*) to bribe.

compra'tore, 'trice *sm/f* buyer, purchaser.

compra'vendita *sf* (*COMM*) (contract of) sale; **un atto di ~** a deed of sale.

com'prendere *vt* (*contenere*) to comprise, consist of; (*capire*) to understand.

compren'donio *sm*: **essere duro di ~** to be slow on the uptake.

compren'sibile *ag* understandable.

comprensi'one *sf* understanding.

compren'sivo, a *ag* (*prezzo*): **~ di** inclusive of; (*indulgente*) understanding.

compren'sorio *sm* area, territory; (*AMM*) district.

com'preso, a *pp di* **comprendere** ♦ *ag* (*incluso*) included; **tutto ~** all included, all-in (*BRIT*).

com'pressa *sf vedi* **compresso**.

compressi'one *sf* compression.

com'presso, a *pp di* **comprimere** ♦ *ag* (*vedi comprimere*) pressed; compressed; repressed ♦ *sf* (*MED: garza*) compress; (*: pastiglia*) tablet.

compres'sore *sm* compressor; (*anche*: **rullo ~**) steamroller.

compri'mario, a *sm/f* (*TEAT*) supporting actor/actress.

com'primere *vt* (*premere*) to press; (*FISICA*) to compress; (*fig*) to repress.

compro'messo, a *pp di* **compromettere** ♦ *sm* compromise.

compro'mettere *vt* to compromise; **~rsi** *vr* to compromise o.s.

comproprietà *sf* (*DIR*) joint ownership.

compro'vare *vt* to confirm.

com'punto, a *ag* contrite; **con fare ~** with a solemn air.

compunzi'one [kompun'tsjone] *sf* contrition; solemnity.

compu'tare *vt* to calculate; (*addebitare*): **~ qc a qn** to debit sb with sth.

com'puter [kəm'pju:tər] *sm inv* computer.

computeriz'zato, a [komputerid'dzato] *ag* computerized.

computerizzazi'one [komputeriddzat'tsjone] *sf* computerization.

computiste'ria *sf* accounting, bookkeeping.

'computo *sm* calculation; **fare il ~ di** to count.

comu'nale *ag* municipal, town *cpd*; **consiglio/palazzo ~** town council/hall; **è un impiegato ~** he works for the local council.

Co'mune *sm* (*AMM*) town council; (*sede*) town hall; *vedi nota nel riquadro*.

COMUNE

The **Comune** *is the smallest autonomous political and administrative unit. It keeps records of births, marriages and deaths and has the power to levy taxes and vet proposals for public works and town planning. It is run by a "Giunta comunale", which is elected by the "Consiglio comunale". The* **Comune** *is headed by the "sindaco" (mayor) who since 1993 has been elected directly by the citizens.*

co'mune *ag* common; (*consueto*) common, everyday; (*di livello medio*) average; (*ordinario*) ordinary ♦ *sf* (*di persone*) commune; **fuori del ~** out of the ordinary; **avere in ~** to have in common, share; **mettere in ~** to share; **un nostro ~ amico** a mutual friend of ours; **fare cassa ~** to pool one's money.

comuni'care *vt* (*notizia*) to pass on, convey; (*malattia*) to pass on; (*ansia etc*) to communicate; (*trasmettere: calore etc*) to transmit, communicate; (*REL*) to administer communion to ♦ *vi* to communicate; **~rsi** *vr* (*propagarsi*): **~rsi a** to spread to; (*REL*) to receive communion.

comunica'tivo, a *ag* (*sentimento*) infectious; (*persona*) communicative ♦ *sf* communicativeness.

comuni'cato *sm* communiqué; **~ stampa** press release.

comunicazi'one [komunikat'tsjone] *sf* communication; (*annuncio*) announcement; (*TEL*): ~ **(telefonica)** (telephone) call; **dare la** ~ **a qn** to put sb through; **ottenere la** ~ to get through; **salvo ~i contrarie da parte Vostra** unless we hear from you to the contrary.

comuni'one *sf* communion; ~ **dei beni** (*DIR*: *tra coniugi*) joint ownership of property.

comu'nismo *sm* communism.

comu'nista, i, e *ag, smlf* communist.

comunità *sf inv* community; **C~ Economica Europea (CEE)** European Economic Community (EEC); ~ **terapeutica** *rehabilitation centre run by voluntary organizations for people with drug, alcohol etc dependency.*

comuni'tario, a *ag* community *cpd.*

co'munque *cong* however, no matter how ♦ *av* (*in ogni modo*) in any case; (*tuttavia*) however, nevertheless.

con *prep* (*nei seguenti casi* **con** *può fondersi con l'articolo definito:* con + il = **col**, con + la = **colla**, con + gli = **cogli**, con + i = **coi**, con + le = **colle**) with; **partire col treno** to leave by train; ~ **mio grande stupore** to my great astonishment; ~ **la forza** by force; ~ **questo freddo** in this cold weather; ~ **il 1° di ottobre** as of October 1st; ~ **tutto ciò** in spite of that, for all that; ~ **tutto che era arrabbiato** even though he was angry, in spite of the fact that he was angry; **e** ~ **questo?** so what?

co'nato *sm*: ~ **di vomito** retching.

'conca, che *sf* (*GEO*) valley.

concate'nare *vt* to link up, connect; **~rsi** *vr* to be connected.

'concavo, a *ag* concave.

con'cedere [kon'tʃɛdere] *vt* (*accordare*) to grant; (*ammettere*) to admit, concede; **~rsi qc** to treat o.s. to sth, allow o.s. sth.

concentra'mento [kontʃentra'mento] *sm* concentration.

concen'trare [kontʃen'trare] *vt*, **~rsi** *vr* to concentrate.

concen'trato [kontʃen'trato] *sm* concentrate; ~ **di pomodoro** tomato purée.

concentrazi'one [kontʃentrat'tsjone] *sf* concentration; ~ **orizzontale/verticale** (*ECON*) horizontal/vertical integration.

con'centrico, a, ci, che [kon'tʃɛntriko] *ag* concentric.

conce'pibile [kontʃe'pibile] *ag* conceivable.

concepi'mento [kontʃepi'mento] *sm* conception.

conce'pire [kontʃe'pire] *vt* (*bambino*) to conceive; (*progetto, idea*) to conceive (of);

(*metodo, piano*) to devise; (*situazione*) to imagine, understand.

con'cernere [kon'tʃɛrnere] *vt* to concern; **per quanto mi concerne** as far as I'm concerned.

concer'tare [kontʃer'tare] *vt* (*MUS*) to harmonize; (*ordire*) to devise, plan; **~rsi** *vr* to agree.

concer'tista, i, e [kontʃer'tista] *smlf* (*MUS*) concert performer.

con'certo [kon'tʃɛrto] *sm* (*MUS*) concert; (*: componimento*) concerto.

con'cessi *etc* [kon'tʃɛssi] *vb vedi* **concedere.**

concessio'nario [kontʃessjo'narjo] *sm* (*COMM*) agent, dealer; ~ **esclusivo (di)** sole agent (for).

concessi'one [kontʃes'sjone] *sf* concession.

con'cesso, a [kon'tʃɛsso] *pp di* **concedere.**

con'cetto [kon'tʃɛtto] *sm* (*pensiero, idea*) concept; (*opinione*) opinion; **è un impiegato di** ~ ≈ he's a white-collar worker.

concezi'one [kontʃet'tsjone] *sf* conception; (*idea*) view, idea.

con'chiglia [kon'kiʎʎa] *sf* shell.

'concia ['kontʃa] *sf* (*di pelli*) tanning; (*di tabacco*) curing; (*sostanza*) tannin.

conci'are [kon'tʃare] *vt* (*pelli*) to tan; (*tabacco*) to cure; (*fig: ridurre in cattivo stato*) to beat up; **~rsi** *vr* (*sporcarsi*) to get in a mess; (*vestirsi male*) to dress badly; **ti hanno conciato male o per le feste!** they've really beaten you up!

concili'abile [kontʃi'ljabile] *ag* compatible.

concili'abolo [kontʃi'ljabolo] *sm* secret meeting.

concili'ante [kontʃi'ljante] *ag* conciliatory.

concili'are [kontʃi'ljare] *vt* to reconcile; (*contravvenzione*) to pay on the spot; (*favorire: sonno*) to be conducive to, induce; (*procurare: simpatia*) to gain; **~rsi qc** to gain o win sth (for o.s.); **~rsi qn** to win sb over; **~rsi con** to be reconciled with.

conciliazi'one [kontʃiljat'tsjone] *sf* reconciliation; (*DIR*) settlement; **la C~** (*STORIA*) the Lateran Pact.

con'cilio [kon'tʃiljo] *sm* (*REL*) council.

conci'mare [kontʃi'mare] *vt* to fertilize; (*con letame*) to manure.

con'cime [kon'tʃime] *sm* manure; (*chimico*) fertilizer.

concisi'one [kontʃi'zjone] *sf* concision, conciseness.

con'ciso, a [kon'tʃizo] *ag* concise, succinct.

conci'tato, a [kontʃi'tato] *ag* excited, emotional.

concitta'dino, a [kontʃitta'dino] *smlf* fellow

citizen.

con'clave *sm* conclave.

con'cludere *vt* to conclude; (*portare a compimento*) to conclude, finish, bring to an end; (*operare positivamente*) to achieve ♦ *vi* (*essere convincente*) to be conclusive; ~**rsi** *vr* to come to an end, close.

conclusi'one *sf* conclusion; (*risultato*) result.

conclu'sivo, a *ag* conclusive; (*finale*) final.

con'cluso, a *pp di* **concludere**.

concomi'tanza [konkomi'tantsa] *sf* (*di circostanze, fatti*) combination.

concor'danza [konkor'dantsa] *sf* (*anche LING*) agreement.

concor'dare *vt* (*prezzo*) to agree on; (*LING*) to make agree ♦ *vi* to agree; ~ **una tregua** to agree to a truce.

concor'dato *sm* agreement; (*REL*) concordat.

con'corde *ag* (*d'accordo*) in agreement; (*simultaneo*) simultaneous.

con'cordia *sf* harmony, concord.

concor'rente *ag* competing; (*MAT*) concurrent ♦ *smlf* (*SPORT, COMM*) competitor; (*a un concorso di bellezza*) contestant.

concor'renza [konkor'rɛntsa] *sf* competition; ~ **sleale** unfair competition; **a prezzi di** ~ at competitive prices.

concorrenzi'ale [konkorren'tsjale] *ag* competitive.

con'correre *vi*: ~ **(in)** (*MAT*) to converge *o* meet (in); ~ **(a)** (*competere*) to compete (for); (*: INS: a una cattedra*) to apply (for); (*partecipare: a un'impresa*) to take part (in), contribute (to).

con'corso, a *pp di* **concorrere** ♦ *sm* competition; (*esame*) competitive examination; ~ **di bellezza** beauty contest; ~ **di circostanze** combination of circumstances; ~ **di colpa** (*DIR*) contributory negligence; **un** ~ **ippico** a showjumping event; ~ **in reato** (*DIR*) complicity in a crime; ~ **per titoli** competitive examination for qualified candidates.

con'creto, a *ag* concrete ♦ *sm*: **in** ~ **in** reality.

concu'bina *sf* concubine ♦ *sm*: **sono** ~**i** they are living together.

concussi'one *sf* (*DIR*) extortion.

con'danna *sf* condemnation; sentence; conviction; ~ **a morte** death sentence.

condan'nare *vt* (*disapprovare*) to condemn; (*DIR*): ~ **a** to sentence to; ~ **per** to convict of.

condan'nato, a *smlf* convict.

con'densa *sf* condensation.

conden'sare *vt*, ~**rsi** *vr* to condense.

condensa'tore *sm* capacitor.

condensazi'one [kondensat'tsjone] *sf* condensation.

condi'mento *sm* seasoning; dressing.

con'dire *vt* to season; (*insalata*) to dress.

condiscen'dente [kondiʃʃen'dɛnte] *ag* obliging; compliant.

condiscen'denza [kondiʃʃen'dɛntsa] *sf* (*disponibilità*) obligingness; (*arrendevolezza*) compliance.

condi'scendere [kondiʃ'ʃendere] *vi*: ~ **a** to agree to.

condi'sceso, a [kondiʃ'ʃeso] *pp di* **condiscendere**.

condi'videre *vt* to share.

condi'viso, a *pp di* **condividere**.

condizio'nale [kondittsjo'nale] *ag* conditional ♦ *sm* (*LING*) conditional ♦ *sf* (*DIR*) suspended sentence.

condiziona'mento [kondittsjona'mento] *sm* conditioning; ~ **d'aria** air conditioning.

condizio'nare [kondittsjo'nare] *vt* to condition; **ad aria condizionata** air-conditioned.

condiziona'tore [kondittsjona'tore] *sm* air conditioner.

condizi'one [kondit'tsjone] *sf* condition; ~**i** *sfpl* (*di pagamento etc*) terms, conditions; **a** ~ **che** on condition that, provided that; **a nessuna** ~ on no account; ~**i a convenirsi** terms to be arranged; ~**i di lavoro** working conditions; ~**i di vendita** sales terms.

condogli'anze [kondoʎ'ʎantse] *sfpl* condolences.

condomini'ale *ag*: **riunione** ~ residents' meeting; **spese** ~**i** common charges.

condo'minio *sm* joint ownership; (*edificio*) jointly-owned building.

con'domino *sm* joint owner.

condo'nare *vt* (*DIR*) to remit.

con'dono *sm* remission; ~ **fiscale** *conditional amnesty for people evading tax.*

con'dotta *sf vedi* **condotto**.

con'dotto, a *pp di* **condurre** ♦ *ag*: **medico** ~ local authority doctor (*in country district*) ♦ *sm* (*canale, tubo*) pipe, conduit; (*ANAT*) duct ♦ *sf* (*modo di comportarsi*) conduct, behaviour (*BRIT*), behavior (*US*); (*di un affare etc*) handling; (*di acqua*) piping; (*incarico sanitario*) *country medical practice controlled by a local authority.*

condu'cente [kondu'tʃente] *sm* driver.

con'duco *etc vb vedi* **condurre**.

con'durre *vt* to conduct; (*azienda*) to

manage; (*accompagnare: bambino*) to take; (*automobile*) to drive; (*trasportare: acqua, gas*) to convey, conduct; (*fig*) to lead ♦ *vi* to lead; **condursi** *vr* to behave, conduct o.s.; ~ **a termine** to conclude.

con'**dussi** *etc vb vedi* **condurre.**

condut'**tore,** '**trice** *ag*: ~ **filo** ~ (*fig*) thread; **motivo** ~ leitmotiv ♦ *sm* (*di mezzi pubblici*) driver; (*FISICA*) conductor.

condut'**tura** *sf* (*gen*) pipe; (*di acqua, gas*) main.

conduzi'**one** [kondut'tsjone] *sf* (*di affari, ditta*) management; (*DIR: locazione*) lease; (*FISICA*) conduction.

confabu'**lare** *vi* to confab.

confa'**cente** [konfa'tʃɛnte] *ag*: ~ **a qn/qc** suitable for sb/sth; **clima** ~ **alla salute** healthy climate.

CONFAGRICOL'TURA *abbr f* (= *Confederazione generale dell'Agricoltura Italiana*) *confederation of Italian farmers*.

CON'FAPI *sigla f* = *Confederazione Nazionale della Piccola Industria*.

con'**farsi** *vr*: ~ **a** to suit, agree with.

CONFARTIGIA'NATO [konfartidʒa'nato] *abbr f* = *Confederazione Generale dell'Artigianato Italiano*.

con'**fatto, a** *pp di* **confarsi.**

CONFCOM'MERCIO [konfkom'mertʃo] *abbr f* = *Confederazione Generale del Commercio*.

confederazi'**one** [konfederat'tsjone] *sf* confederation; ~ **imprenditoriale** employers' association.

confe'**renza** [konfe'rɛntsa] *sf* (*discorso*) lecture; (*riunione*) conference; ~ **stampa** press conference.

conferenzi'**ere, a** [konferen'tsjɛre] *sm/f* lecturer.

conferi'**mento** *sm* conferring, awarding.

confe'**rire** *vt*: ~ **qc a qn** to give sth to sb, confer sth on sb ♦ *vi* to confer.

con'**ferma** *sf* confirmation.

confer'**mare** *vt* to confirm.

confes'**sare** *vt*, ~**rsi** *vr* to confess; **andare a** ~**rsi** (*REL*) to go to confession.

confessio'**nale** *ag, sm* confessional.

confessi'**one** *sf* confession; (*setta religiosa*) denomination.

con'**fesso, a** *ag*: **essere reo** ~ to have pleaded guilty.

confes'**sore** *sm* confessor.

con'**fetto** *sm* sugared almond; (*MED*) pill.

confet'**tura** *sf* (*gen*) jam; (*di arance*) marmalade.

confezio'**nare** [konfettsjo'nare] *vt* (*vestito*) to make (up); (*merci, pacchi*) to package.

confezi'**one** [konfet'tsjone] *sf* (*di abiti: da uomo*) tailoring; (: *da donna*) dressmaking; (*imballaggio*) packaging; ~ **regalo** gift pack; ~ **risparmio** economy size; ~ **da viaggio** travel pack; ~**i per signora** ladies' wear *no pl*; ~**i da uomo** menswear *no pl*.

confic'**care** *vt*: ~ **qc in** to hammer o drive sth into; ~**rsi** *vr* to stick.

confi'**dare** *vi*: ~ **in** to confide in, rely on ♦ *vt* to confide; ~**rsi con qn** to confide in sb.

confi'**dente** *sm/f* (*persona amica*) confidant/ confidante; (*informatore*) informer.

confi'**denza** [konfi'dɛntsa] *sf* (*familiarità*) intimacy, familiarity; (*fiducia*) trust, confidence; (*rivelazione*) confidence; **prendersi (troppe)** ~**e** to take liberties; **fare una** ~ **a qn** to confide something to sb.

confidenzi'**ale** [konfiden'tsjale] *ag* familiar, friendly; (*segreto*) confidential; **in via** ~ confidentially.

configu'**rare** *vt* (*INFORM*) to set; ~**rsi** *vr*: ~ **a** to assume the shape o form of.

configurazi'**one** [konfigurat'tsjone] *sf* configuration; (*INFORM*) setting.

confi'**nante** *ag* neighbouring (*BRIT*), neighboring (*US*).

confi'**nare** *vi*: ~ **con** to border on ♦ *vt* (*POL*) to intern; (*fig*) to confine; ~**rsi** *vr* (*isolarsi*): ~**rsi in** to shut o.s. up in.

confi'**nato, a** *ag* interned ♦ *sm/f* internee.

CONFIN'DUSTRIA *sigla f* (= *Confederazione Generale dell'Industria Italiana*) *employers' association*, ≈ CBI (*BRIT*).

con'**fine** *sm* boundary; (*di paese*) border, frontier; **territorio di** ~ border zone.

con'**fino** *sm* internment.

con'**fisca** *sf* confiscation.

confis'**care** *vt* to confiscate.

conflagrazi'**one** [konflagrat'tsjone] *sf* conflagration.

con'**flitto** *sm* conflict; **essere in** ~ **con qc** to clash with sth; **essere in** ~ **con qn** to be at loggerheads with sb.

conflittu'**ale** *ag*: **rapporto** ~ relationship based on conflict.

conflittualità *sf* conflicts *pl*.

conflu'**enza** [konflu'ɛntsa] *sf* (*di fiumi*) confluence; (*di strade*) junction.

conflu'**ire** *vi* (*fiumi*) to flow into each other, meet; (*strade*) to meet.

con'**fondere** *vt* to mix up, confuse; (*imbarazzare*) to embarrass; ~**rsi** *vr* (*mescolarsi*) to mingle; (*turbarsi*) to be confused; (*sbagliare*) to get mixed up; ~ **le idee a qn** to mix sb up, confuse sb.

confor'**mare** *vt* (*adeguare*): ~ **a** to adapt o

conform to; ~**rsi** *vr:* ~**rsi (a)** to conform (to).

con'**forme** *ag:* ~ **a** (*simile*) similar to; (*corrispondente*) in keeping with.

conforme'**mente** *av* accordingly; ~ **a** in accordance with.

confor'**mismo** *sm* conformity.

confor'**mista, i, e** *sm/f* conformist.

conformità *sf* conformity; **in** ~ **a** in conformity with.

confor'**tare** *vt* to comfort, console.

confor'**tevole** *ag* (*consolante*) comforting; (*comodo*) comfortable.

con'**forto** *sm* (*consolazione, sollievo*) comfort, consolation; (*conferma*) support; **a** ~ **di qc** in support of sth; **i** ~**i** (*religiosi*) the last sacraments.

confra'**ternita** *sf* brotherhood.

confron'**tare** *vt* to compare; ~**rsi** *vr* (*scontrarsi*) to have a confrontation.

con'**fronto** *sm* comparison; (*DIR, MIL, POL*) confrontation; **in** *o* **a** ~ **di** in comparison with, compared to; **nei miei** (*o* **tuoi** *etc*) ~**i** towards me (*o* you *etc*).

con'**fusi** *etc vb vedi* **confondere.**

confusi'**one** *sf* confusion; (*imbarazzo*) embarrassment; **far** ~ (*disordine*) to make a mess; (*chiasso*) to make a racket; (*confondere*) to confuse things.

con'**fuso, a** *pp di* **confondere** ♦ *ag* (*vedi confondere*) confused; embarrassed.

confu'**tare** *vt* to refute.

conge'**dare** [kondʒe'dare] *vt* to dismiss; (*MIL*) to demobilize; ~**rsi** *vr* to take one's leave.

con'**gedo** [kon'dʒedo] *sm* (*anche MIL*) leave; **prendere** ~ **da qn** to take one's leave of sb; ~ **assoluto** (*MIL*) discharge.

conge'**gnare** [kondʒeɲ'ɲare] *vt* to construct, put together.

con'**gegno** [kon'dʒeɲɲo] *sm* device, mechanism.

congela'**mento** [kondʒela'mento] *sm* (*gen*) freezing; (*MED*) frostbite; ~ **salariale** wage freeze.

conge'**lare** [kondʒe'lare] *vt*, ~**rsi** *vr* to freeze.

congela'**tore** [kondʒela'tore] *sm* freezer.

con'**genito, a** [kon'dʒenito] *ag* congenital.

con'**gerie** [kon'dʒɛrje] *sf inv* (*di oggetti*) heap; (*di idee*) muddle, jumble.

congestio'**nare** [kondʒestjo'nare] *vt* to congest; **essere congestionato** (*persona, viso*) to be flushed; (*zona: per traffico*) to be congested.

congesti'**one** [kondʒes'tjone] *sf* congestion.

conget'**tura** [kondʒet'tura] *sf* conjecture,

supposition.

con'**giungere** [kon'dʒundʒere] *vt*, ~**rsi** *vr* to join (together).

congiunti'**vite** [kondʒunti'vite] *sf* conjunctivitis.

congiun'**tivo** [kondʒun'tivo] *sm* (*LING*) subjunctive.

congi'**unto, a** [kon'dʒunto] *pp di* **congiungere** ♦ *ag* (*unito*) joined ♦ *sm/f* (*parente*) relative.

congiun'**tura** [kondʒun'tura] *sf* (*giuntura*) junction, join; (*ANAT*) joint; (*circostanza*) juncture; (*ECON*) economic situation.

congiuntu'**rale** [kondʒuntu'rale] *ag* of the economic situation; **crisi** ~ economic crisis.

congiunzi'**one** [kondʒun'tsjone] *sf* (*LING*) conjunction.

congi'**ura** [kon'dʒura] *sf* conspiracy.

congiu'**rare** [kondʒu'rare] *vi* to conspire.

conglome'**rato** *sm* (*GEO*) conglomerate; (*fig*) conglomeration; (*EDIL*) concrete.

'**Congo** *sm*: **il** ~ the Congo.

congo'**lese** *ag, sm/f* Congolese *inv.*

congratu'**larsi** *vr*: ~ **con qn per qc** to congratulate sb on sth.

congratulazi'**oni** [kongratulat'tsjoni] *sfpl* congratulations.

con'**grega, ghe** *sf* band, bunch.

congregazi'**one** [kongregat'tsjone] *sf* congregation.

congres'**sista, i, e** *sm/f* participant at a congress.

con'**gresso** *sm* congress.

'**congruo, a** *ag* (*prezzo, compenso*) adequate, fair; (*ragionamento*) coherent, consistent.

conguagli'**are** [kongwaʎ'ʎare] *vt* to balance; (*stipendio*) to adjust.

congu'**aglio** [kon'gwaʎʎo] *sm* balancing; adjusting; (*somma di denaro*) balance; **fare il** ~ **di** to balance; to adjust.

coni'**are** *vt* to mint, coin; (*fig*) to coin.

coniazi'**one** [konjat'tsjone] *sf* mintage.

'**conico, a, ci, che** *ag* conical.

co'**nifere** *sfpl* conifers.

conigli'**era** [koniʎ'ʎera] *sf* (*gabbia*) rabbit hutch; (*più grande*) rabbit run.

conigli'**etta** [koniʎ'ʎetta] *sf* bunny girl.

conigli'**etto** [koniʎ'ʎetto] *sm* bunny.

co'**niglio** [ko'niʎʎo] *sm* rabbit; **sei un** ~! (*fig*) you're chicken!

coniu'**gale** *ag* (*amore, diritti*) conjugal; (*vita*) married, conjugal.

coniu'**gare** *vt* to combine; (*LING*) to conjugate; ~**rsi** *vr* to get married.

coniu'**gato, a** *ag* (*AMM*) married.

coniugazi'**one** [konjugat'tsjone] *sf* (*LING*)

conjugation.

'**coniuge** ['kɔnjudʒe] *sm/f* spouse.

connatu'rato, a *ag* inborn.

connazio'nale [konnattsjo'nale] *sm/f* fellow-countryman/woman.

connessi'one *sf* connection.

con'nesso, a *pp di* **connettere.**

con'nettere *vt* to connect, join ♦ *vi* (*fig*) to think straight.

connet'tore *sm* (*ELETTR*) connector.

conni'vente *ag* conniving.

conno'tati *smpl* distinguishing marks; **rispondere ai ~i** to fit the description; **cambiare i ~i a qn** (*fam*) to beat sb up.

con'nubio *sm* (*matrimonio*) marriage; (*fig*) union.

'**cono** *sm* cone; ~ **gelato** ice-cream cone.

co'nobbi *etc vb vedi* **conoscere.**

cono'scente [konoʃ'ʃɛnte] *sm/f* acquaintance.

cono'scenza [konoʃ'ʃɛntsa] *sf* (*il sapere*) knowledge *no pl*; (*persona*) acquaintance; (*facoltà sensoriale*) consciousness *no pl*; **essere a ~ di qc** to know sth; **portare qn a ~ di qc** to inform sb of sth; **per vostra ~** for your information; **fare la ~ di qn** to make sb's acquaintance; **perdere ~** to lose consciousness; ~ **tecnica** know-how.

co'noscere [ko'noʃʃere] *vt* to know; **ci siamo conosciuti a Firenze** we (first) met in Florence; ~ **qn di vista** to know sb by sight; **farsi ~** (*fig*) to make a name for o.s.

conosci'tore, 'trice [konoʃʃi'tore] *sm/f* connoisseur.

conosci'uto, a [konoʃ'ʃuto] *pp di* **conoscere** ♦ *ag* well-known.

con'quista *sf* conquest.

conquis'tare *vt* to conquer; (*fig*) to gain, win.

conquista'tore, 'trice *sm/f* (*in guerra*) conqueror ♦ *sm* (*seduttore*) lady-killer.

cons. *abbr* = **consiglio.**

consa'crare *vt* (*REL*) to consecrate; (*: sacerdote*) to ordain; (*dedicare*) to dedicate; (*fig: uso etc*) to sanction; ~**rsi a** to dedicate o.s. to.

consangu'ineo, a *sm/f* blood relation.

consa'pevole *ag*: ~ **di** aware of.

consapevo'lezza [konsapevo'lettsa] *sf* awareness, consciousness.

conscia'mente [konʃa'mente] *av* consciously.

'**conscio, a, sci, sce** ['kɔnʃo] *ag*: ~ **di** aware *o* conscious of.

consecu'tivo, a *ag* consecutive; (*successivo: giorno*) following, next.

con'segna [kon'seɲɲa] *sf* delivery; (*merce consegnata*) consignment; (*custodia*) care,

custody; (*MIL: ordine*) orders *pl*; (*: punizione*) confinement to barracks; **alla ~** on delivery; **dare qc in ~ a qn** to entrust sth to sb; **passare le ~e a qn** to hand over to sb; ~ **a domicilio** home delivery; ~ **in contrassegno, pagamento alla** ~ cash on delivery; ~ **sollecita** prompt delivery.

conse'gnare [konseɲ'ɲare] *vt* to deliver; (*affidare*) to entrust, hand over; (*MIL*) to confine to barracks.

consegna'tario [konseɲɲa'tarjo] *sm* consignee.

consegu'ente *ag* consequent.

conseguente'mente *av* consequently.

consegu'enza [konse'gwɛntsa] *sf* consequence; **per** *o* **di** ~ consequently.

consegui'mento *sm* (*di scopo, risultato etc*) achievement, attainment; **al ~ della laurea** on graduation.

consegu'ire *vt* to achieve ♦ *vi* to follow, result; ~ **la laurea** to graduate, obtain one's degree.

con'senso *sm* approval, consent.

consensu'ale *ag* (*DIR*) by mutual consent.

consen'tire *vi*: ~ **a** to consent *o* agree to ♦ *vt* to allow, permit; **mi si consenta di ringraziare ...** I would like to thank ....

consenzi'ente [konsen'tsjente] *ag* (*gen, DIR*) consenting.

con'serto, a *ag*: **a braccia** ~**e** with one's arms folded.

con'serva *sf* (*CUC*) preserve; ~ **di frutta** jam; ~ **di pomodoro** tomato purée; ~**e alimentari** tinned (*o* canned *o* bottled) foods.

conser'vante *sm* (*per alimenti*) preservative.

conser'vare *vt* (*CUC*) to preserve; (*custodire*) to keep; (*: dalla distruzione etc*) to preserve, conserve; ~**rsi** *vr* to keep.

conserva'tore, 'trice *ag, sm/f* (*POL*) conservative.

conserva'torio *sm* (*di musica*) conservatory.

conservato'rismo *sm* (*POL*) conservatism.

conservazi'one [konservat'tsjone] *sf* preservation; conservation; **istinto di ~** instinct for self-preservation; **a lunga ~** (*latte, panna*) long-life *cpd*.

con'sesso *sm* (*assemblea*) assembly; (*riunione*) meeting.

conside'rabile *ag* worthy of considera-tion.

conside'rare *vt* to consider; (*reputare*) to consider, regard; ~ **molto qn** to think highly of sb.

conside'rato, a *ag* (*prudente*) cautious,

careful; (*stimato*) highly thought of, esteemed.

considerazi'one [konsiderat'tsjone] *sf* (*esame, riflessione*) consideration; (*stima*) regard, esteem; (*pensiero, osservazione*) observation; **prendere in** ~ to take into consideration.

conside'revole *ag* considerable.

consigli'abile [konsiʎ'ʎabile] *ag* advisable.

consigli'are [konsiʎ'ʎare] *vt* (*persona*) to advise; (*metodo, azione*) to recommend, advise, suggest; ~**rsi** *vr*: ~**rsi con qn** to ask sb for advice.

consigli'ere, a [konsiʎ'ʎɛre] *smf* adviser ♦ *sm*: ~ **d'amministrazione** board member; ~ **comunale** town councillor; ~ **delegato** (*COMM*) managing director.

con'siglio [kon'siʎʎo] *sm* (*suggerimento*) advice *no pl*, piece of advice; (*assemblea*) council; ~ **d'amministrazione** board; **C**~ **d'Europa** Council of Europe; ~ **di fabbrica** works council; **il C**~ **dei Ministri** (*POL*) ≈ the Cabinet; **C**~ **di stato** *advisory body to the Italian government on administrative matters and their legal implications*; **C**~ **superiore della magistratura** *state body responsible for judicial appointments and regulations*; *vedi nota nel riquadro.*

CONSIGLI

The **Consiglio dei Ministri**, *the Italian Cabinet, is headed by the "Presidente del Consiglio", the Prime Minister, who is the leader of the Government.*
The **Consiglio superiore della Magistratura**, *the magistrates' governing body, ensures their autonomy and independence as enshrined in the Constitution. Chaired by the "Presidente della Repubblica", it mainly deals with appointments and transfers, and can take disciplinary action as required. Of the 30 magistrates elected to the* **Consiglio** *for a period of four years, 20 are chosen by their fellow magistrates and 10 by Parliament. The "Presidente della Repubblica" and the "Vicepresidente" are ex officio members.*

---

con'simile *ag* similar.

consis'tente *ag* solid; (*fig*) sound, valid.

consis'tenza [konsis'tɛntsa] *sf* (*di impasto*) consistency; (*di stoffa*) texture; **senza** ~ (*sospetti, voci*) ill-founded, groundless; ~ **di cassa/di magazzino** cash/stock in hand; ~ **patrimoniale** financial solidity.

con'sistere *vi*: ~ **in** to consist of.

consis'tito, a *pp di* **consistere.**

'CONSOB *sigla f* (= *Commissione nazionale per le società e la borsa*) *regulatory body for the Italian Stock Exchange.*

consoci'arsi [konso'tʃarsi] *vr* to go into partnership.

consociati'vismo [konsotʃati'vizmo] *sm* (*POL*) pact-building.

consocia'tivo, a [konsotʃa'tivo] *ag* (*POL*: *democrazia*) based on pacts.

consoci'ato, a [konso'tʃato] *ag* associated ♦ *sm/f* associate.

conso'lante *ag* consoling, comforting.

conso'lare *ag* consular ♦ *vt* (*confortare*) to console, comfort; (*rallegrare*) to cheer up; ~**rsi** *vr* to be comforted; to cheer up.

conso'lato *sm* consulate.

consolazi'one [konsolat'tsjone] *sf* consolation, comfort.

'console *sm* consul ♦ *sf* [kɔ̃'sɔl] (*quadro di comando*) console.

consolida'mento *sm* strengthening; consolidation.

consoli'dare *vt* to strengthen, reinforce; (*MIL, terreno*) to consolidate; ~**rsi** *vr* to consolidate.

consolidazi'one [konsolidat'tsjone] *sf* strengthening; consolidation.

consommé [kɔ̃sɔ'me] *sm inv* consommé.

conso'nante *sf* consonant.

conso'nanza [konso'nantsa] *sf* consonance.

'consono, a *ag*: ~ **a** consistent with, consonant with.

con'sorte *sm/f* consort.

con'sorzio [kon'sɔrtsjo] *sm* consortium; ~ **agrario** farmers' cooperative; ~ **di garanzia** (*COMM*) underwriting syndicate.

con'stare *vi*: ~ **di** to consist of ♦ *vb impers*: **mi consta che** it has come to my knowledge that, it appears that; **a quanto mi consta** as far as I know.

consta'tare *vt* to establish, verify; (*notare*) to notice, observe.

constatazi'one [konstatat'tsjone] *sf* observation; ~ **amichevole** (*in incidenti*) *jointly-agreed statement for insurance purposes.*

consu'eto, a *ag* habitual, usual ♦ *sm*: **come di** ~ as usual.

consuetudi'nario, a *ag*: **diritto** ~ (*DIR*) common law.

consue'tudine *sf* habit; (*usanza*) custom.

consu'lente *sm/f* consultant; ~ **aziendale/ tecnico** management/technical consultant.

consu'lenza [konsu'lɛntsa] *sf* consultancy;

~ **medica/legale** medical/legal advice;
ufficio di ~ **fiscale** tax consultancy office;
~ **tecnica** technical consultancy o advice.
consul'tare vt to consult; ~**rsi** vr: ~**rsi con
qn** to seek the advice of sb.
consultazi'one [konsultat'tsjone] sf
consultation; ~**i** sfpl (POL) talks,
consultations; **libro di** ~ reference book.
consul'tivo, a ag consultative.
consul'torio sm: ~ **familiare** o
matrimoniale marriage guidance centre;
~ **pediatrico** children's clinic.
consu'mare vt (logorare: abiti, scarpe) to
wear out; (usare) to consume, use up;
(mangiare, bere) to consume; (DIR) to
consummate; ~**rsi** vr to wear out; to be
used up; (anche fig) to be consumed;
(combustibile) to burn out.
consu'mato, a ag (vestiti, scarpe, tappeto)
worn; (persona: esperto) accomplished.
consuma'tore sm consumer.
consumazi'one [konsumat'tsjone] sf
(bibita) drink; (spuntino) snack; (DIR)
consummation.
consu'mismo sm consumerism.
con'sumo sm consumption; wear; use;
generi o **beni di** ~ consumer goods; **beni
di largo** ~ basic commodities; **imposta sui
~i** tax on consumer goods.
consun'tivo sm (ECON) final balance.
consun'to, a ag worn-out; (viso) wasted.
'**conta** sf (nei giochi): **fare la** ~ to see who is
going to be "it".
con'tabile ag accounts cpd, accounting
♦ smf accountant.
contabilità sf (attività, tecnica) accounting,
accountancy; (insieme dei libri etc) books
pl, accounts pl; (ufficio) ~ accounts
department; ~ **finanziaria** financial
accounting; ~ **di gestione** management
accounting.
contachi'lometri [kontaki'lɔmetri] sm inv
≈ mileometer.
conta'dino, a smlf countryman/woman;
farm worker; (peg) peasant.
contagi'are [konta'dʒare] vt to infect.
con'tagio [kon'tadʒo] sm infection; (per
contatto diretto) contagion; (epidemia)
epidemic.
contagi'oso, a [konta'dʒoso] ag infectious;
contagious.
conta'giri [konta'dʒiri] sm inv (AUT) rev
counter.
conta'gocce [konta'gottʃe] sm inv dropper.
contami'nare vt to contaminate.
contaminazi'one [kontaminat'tsjone] sf
contamination.
con'tante sm cash; **pagare in** ~**i** to pay

cash.
con'tare vt to count; (considerare) to
consider ♦ vi to count, be of importance;
~ **su qn** to count o rely on sb; ~ **di fare qc**
to intend to do sth; **ha i giorni contati, ha
le ore contate** his days are numbered; **la
gente che conta** people who matter.
contas'catti sm inv telephone meter.
conta'tore sm meter.
contat'tare vt to contact.
con'tatto sm contact; **essere in** ~ **con qn** to
be in touch with sb; **fare** ~ (ELETTR: fili) to
touch.
'**conte** sm count.
con'tea sf (STORIA) earldom; (AMM) county.
conteggi'are [konted'dʒare] vt to charge,
put on the bill.
con'teggio [kon'tedd3o] sm calculation.
con'tegno [kon'teɲɲo] sm (comportamento)
behaviour (BRIT), behavior (US);
(atteggiamento) attitude; **darsi un** ~
(ostentare disinvoltura) to act nonchalant;
(ricomporsi) to pull o.s. together.
conte'gnoso, a [konteɲ'ɲoso] ag reserved,
dignified.
contem'plare vt to contemplate, gaze at;
(DIR) to make provision for.
contempla'tivo, a ag contemplative.
contemplazi'one [kontemplat'tsjone] sf
contemplation.
con'tempo sm: **nel** ~ meanwhile, in the
meantime.
contemporanea'mente av
simultaneously; at the same time.
contempo'raneo, a ag, smlf
contemporary.
conten'dente smlf opponent, adversary.
con'tendere vi (competere) to compete;
(litigare) to quarrel ♦ vt: ~ **qc a qn** to
contend with o be in competition with sb
for sth.
conte'nere vt to contain; ~**rsi** vr to contain
o.s.
conteni'tore sm container.
conten'tabile ag: **difficilmente** ~ difficult
to please.
conten'tare vt to please, satisfy; ~**rsi** vr:
~**rsi di** to be satisfied with, content o.s.
with; **si contenta di poco** he is easily
satisfied.
conten'tezza [konten'tettsa] sf
contentment.
conten'tino sm sop.
con'tento, a ag pleased, glad; ~ **di** pleased
with.
conte'nuto ag (ira, entusiasmo) restrained,
suppressed; (forza) contained ♦ sm
contents pl; (argomento) content.

contenzi'oso, a [konten'tsjɔso] *ag* (*DIR*)
contentious ♦ *sm* (*AMM*: *ufficio*) legal
department.
con'teso, a *pp di* **contendere** ♦ *sf* dispute,
argument.
con'tessa *sf* countess.
contes'tare *vt* (*DIR*) to notify; (*fig*) to
dispute; ~ **il sistema** to protest against
the system.
contesta'tore, 'trice *ag* anti-
establishment ♦ *sm/f* protester.
contestazi'one [kontestat'tsjone] *sf* (*DIR*:
disputa) dispute; (: *notifica*) notification;
(*POL*) anti-establishment activity; **in caso
di** ~ if there are any objections.
con'testo *sm* context.
con'tiguo, a *ag*: ~ **(a)** adjacent (to).
continen'tale *ag* continental.
conti'nente *ag* continent ♦ *sm* (*GEO*)
continent; (: *terra ferma*) mainland.
conti'nenza [konti'nɛntsa] *sf* continence.
contin'gente [kontin'dʒɛnte] *ag* contingent
♦ *sm* (*COMM*) quota; (*MIL*) contingent.
contin'genza [kontin'dʒɛntsa] *sf*
circumstance; **(indennità di)** ~ cost-of-
living allowance.
continua'mente *av* (*senza interruzione*)
continuously, nonstop; (*ripetutamente*)
continually.
continu'are *vt* to continue (with), go on
with ♦ *vi* to continue, go on; ~ **a fare qc** to
go on *o* continue doing sth; **continua a
nevicare/a fare freddo** it's still snowing/
cold.
continua'tivo, a *ag* (*occupazione*)
permanent; (*periodo*) consecutive.
continuazi'one [kontinuat'tsjone] *sf*
continuation.
continuità *sf* continuity.
con'tinuo, a *ag* (*numerazione*) continuous;
(*pioggia*) continual, constant; (*ELETTR*:
corrente) direct; **di** ~ continually.
'conto *sm* (*calcolo*) calculation; (*COMM*,
ECON) account; (*di ristorante, albergo*) bill;
(*fig: stima*) consideration, esteem; **avere
un** ~ **in sospeso (con qn)** to have an
outstanding account (with sb); (*fig*) to
have a score to settle (with sb); **fare i ~i
con qn** to settle one's account with sb;
fare ~ **su qn** to count *o* rely on sb; **fare** ~
che (*supporre*) to suppose that; **rendere** ~
a qn di qc to be accountable to sb for sth;
rendersi ~ **di qc/che** to realize sth/that;
tener ~ **di qn/qc** to take sb/sth into
account; **tenere qc da** ~ to take great
care of sth; **ad ogni buon** ~ in any case;
di poco/nessun ~ of little/no importance;
per ~ **di** on behalf of; **per** ~ **mio** as far as

I'm concerned; (*da solo*) on my own; **a** ~**i
fatti, in fin dei** ~**i** all things considered; **mi
hanno detto strane cose sul suo** ~ I've
heard some strange things about him; ~
capitale capital account; ~ **cifrato**
numbered account; ~ **corrente** current
account (*BRIT*), checking account (*US*); ~
corrente postale Post Office account; ~
economico profit and loss account; ~ **in
partecipazione** joint account; ~ **passivo**
account payable; ~ **profitti e perdite**
profit and loss account; ~ **alla rovescia**
countdown; ~ **valutario** foreign currency
account.
con'torcere [kon'tɔrtʃere] *vt* to twist;
(*panni*) to wring (out); ~**rsi** *vr* to twist,
writhe.
contor'nare *vt* to surround; ~**rsi** *vr*: ~**rsi di**
to surround o.s. with.
con'torno *sm* (*linea*) outline, contour;
(*ornamento*) border; (*CUC*) vegetables *pl*;
fare da ~ **a** to surround.
contorsi'one *sf* contortion.
con'torto, a *pp di* **contorcere**.
contrabban'dare *vt* to smuggle.
contrabbandi'ere, a *sm/f* smuggler.
contrab'bando *sm* smuggling,
contraband; **merce di** ~ contraband,
smuggled goods *pl*.
contrab'basso *sm* (*MUS*) (double) bass.
contraccambi'are *vt* (*favore etc*) to return;
vorrei ~ I'd like to show my appreciation.
contraccet'tivo, a [kontratt ʃet'tivo] *ag, sm*
contraceptive.
contrac'colpo *sm* rebound; (*di arma da
fuoco*) recoil; (*fig*) repercussion.
con'trada *sf* street; district; *vedi anche* **Palio**.
contrad'detto, a *pp di* **contraddire**.
contrad'dire *vt* to contradict; ~**rsi** *vr* to
contradict o.s.; (*uso reciproco: persone*) to
contradict each other *o* one another;
(: *testimonianze etc*) to be contradictory.
contraddis'tinguere *vt* (*merce*) to mark;
(*fig: atteggiamento, persona*) to distinguish.
contraddis'tinto, a *pp di*
contraddistinguere.
contraddit'torio, a *ag* contradictory;
(*sentimenti*) conflicting ♦ *sm* (*DIR*) cross-
examination.
contraddizi'one [kontraddit'tsjone] *sf*
contradiction; **cadere in** ~ to contradict
o.s.; **essere in** ~ (*tesi, affermazioni*) to
contradict one another; **spirito di** ~
argumentativeness.
con'trae *etc vb vedi* **contrarre**.
contra'ente *sm* contractor.
contra'erea *sf* (*MIL*) anti-aircraft artillery.
contra'ereo, a *ag* anti-aircraft.

contraf'fare vt (persona) to mimic; (voce) to disguise; (firma) to forge, counterfeit.
contraf'fatto, a pp di **contraffare** ♦ ag counterfeit.
contraffazi'one [kontraffat'tsjone] sf mimicking no pl; disguising no pl; forging no pl; (cosa contraffatta) forgery.
contraf'forte sm (ARCHIT) buttress; (GEO) spur.
con'traggo etc vb vedi **contrarre.**
con'tralto sm (MUS) contralto.
contrap'pello sm (MIL) second roll call.
contrappe'sare vt to counterbalance; (fig: decisione) to weigh up.
contrap'peso sm counterbalance, counterweight.
contrap'porre vt: ~ qc a qc to counter sth with sth; (paragonare) to compare sth with sth; **contrapporsi** vr: **contrapporsi a qc** to contrast with sth, be opposed to sth.
contrap'posto, a pp di **contrapporre.**
contraria'mente av: ~ a contrary to.
contrari'are vt (contrastare) to thwart, oppose; (irritare) to annoy, bother; ~rsi vr to get annoyed.
contrari'ato, a ag annoyed.
contrarietà sf adversity; (fig) aversion.
con'trario, a ag opposite; (sfavorevole) unfavourable (BRIT), unfavorable (US) ♦ sm opposite; **essere ~ a qc** (persona) to be against sth; **al ~** on the contrary; **in caso ~** otherwise; **avere qualcosa in ~** to have some objection; **non ho niente in ~** I have no objection.
con'trarre vt (malattia, debito) to contract; (muscoli) to tense; (abitudine, vizio) to pick up; (accordo, patto) to enter into; **contrarsi** vr to contract; ~ **matrimonio** to marry.
contrasse'gnare [kontrasseɲ'ɲare] vt to mark.
contras'segno [kontras'seɲɲo] sm (distintivo) distinguishing mark; **spedire in ~** (COMM) to send COD.
con'trassi etc vb vedi **contrarre.**
contras'tante ag contrasting.
contras'tare vt (avversare) to oppose; (impedire) to bar; (negare: diritto) to contest, dispute ♦ vi: ~ (essere in disaccordo) to contrast (with); (lottare) to struggle (with).
con'trasto sm contrast; (conflitto) conflict; (litigio) dispute.
contrat'tacco sm counterattack; **passare al ~** (fig) to fight back.
contrat'tare vt, vi to negotiate.
contrat'tempo sm hitch.
con'tratto, a pp di **contrarre** ♦ sm contract; ~ **di acquisto** purchase agreement; ~ **di**

affitto, ~ **di locazione** lease; ~ **collettivo di lavoro** collective agreement; ~ **di lavoro** contract of employment; ~ **a termine** forward contract.
contrattu'ale ag contractual; **forza** ~ (di sindacato) bargaining power.
contravve'nire vi: ~ **a** (legge) to contravene; (obbligo) to fail to meet.
contravven'tore, 'trice sm/f offender.
contravve'nuto, a pp di **contravvenire.**
contravvenzi'one [kontravven'tsjone] sf contravention; (ammenda) fine.
contrazi'one [kontrat'tsjone] sf contraction; (di prezzi etc) reduction.
contribu'ente sm/f taxpayer; ratepayer (BRIT), property tax payer (US).
contribu'ire vi to contribute.
contribu'tivo, a ag contributory.
contri'buto sm contribution; (sovvenzione) subsidy, contribution; (tassa) tax; ~**i previdenziali** ≈ national insurance (BRIT) o welfare (US) contributions; ~**i sindacali** trade union dues.
con'trito, a ag contrite, penitent.
'contro prep against; ~ **di me/lui** against me/him; **pastiglie** ~ **la tosse** throat lozenges; ~ **pagamento** (COMM) on payment; ~ **ogni mia aspettativa** contrary to my expectations; **per** ~ on the other hand.
contro'battere vt (fig: a parole) to answer back; (: confutare) to refute.
controbilanci'are [kontrobilan'tʃare] vt to counterbalance.
controcor'rente av: **andare** ~ (anche fig) to swim against the tide.
controcul'tura sf counterculture.
contro'esodo sm return from holiday.
contro'fax sm inv reply to a fax.
controffen'siva sf counteroffensive.
controfi'gura sf (CINE) double.
controfir'mare vt to countersign.
control'lare vt (accertare) to check; (sorvegliare) to watch, control; (tenere nel proprio potere, fig: dominare) to control; ~**rsi** vr to control o.s.
control'lato, a ag (persona) self-possessed; (reazioni) controlled ♦ sf (COMM: società) associated company.
con'trollo sm check; watch; control; **base di** ~ (AER) ground control; **telefono sotto** ~ tapped telephone; **visita di** ~ (MED) checkup; ~ **doganale** customs inspection; ~ **di gestione** management control; ~ **delle nascite** birth control; ~ **di qualità** quality control.
control'lore sm (FERR, AUTOBUS) (ticket) inspector; ~ **di volo** o **del traffico aereo**

air traffic controller.

contro'luce [kontro'lutʃe] *sf inv* (*FOT*) backlit shot ♦ *av*: **(in)** ~ against the light; (*fotografare*) into the light.

contro'mano *av*: **guidare** ~ to drive on the wrong side of the road; (*in un senso unico*) to drive the wrong way up a one-way street.

contropar'tita *sf* (*fig*: *compenso*): **come** ~ in return.

contropi'ede *sm* (*SPORT*): **azione di** ~ sudden counter-attack; **prendere qn in** ~ (*fig*) to catch sb off his (*o* her) guard.

controprodu'cente [kontroprodu'tʃɛnte] *ag* counterproductive.

con'trordine *sm* counter-order; **salvo** ~ unless I (*o* you *etc*) hear to the contrary.

contro'senso *sm* (*contraddizione*) contradiction in terms; (*assurdità*) nonsense.

controspio'naggio [kontrospio'naddʒo] *sm* counterespionage.

controva'lore *sm* equivalent (value).

contro'vento *av* against the wind; **navigare** ~ (*NAUT*) to sail to windward.

contro'versia *sf* controversy; (*DIR*) dispute; ~ **sindacale** industrial dispute.

contro'verso, a *ag* controversial.

contro'voglia [kontro'vɔʎʎa] *av* unwillingly.

contu'mace [kontu'matʃe] *ag* (*DIR*): **rendersi** ~ to default, fail to appear in court ♦ *smf* (*DIR*) defaulter.

contu'macia [kontu'matʃa] *sf* (*DIR*) default.

contun'dente *ag*: **corpo** ~ blunt instrument.

contur'bante *ag* (*sguardo, bellezza*) disturbing.

contur'bare *vt* to disturb, upset.

contusi'one *sf* (*MED*) bruise.

convale'scente [konvaleʃ'ʃɛnte] *ag, smf* convalescent.

convale'scenza [konvaleʃ'ʃɛntsa] *sf* convalescence.

con'valida *sf* (*DIR*) confirmation; (*di biglietto*) stamping.

convali'dare *vt* (*AMM*) to validate; (*fig*: *sospetto, dubbio*) to confirm.

con'vegno [kon'veɲɲo] *sm* (*incontro*) meeting; (*congresso*) convention, congress; (*luogo*) meeting place.

conve'nevoli *smpl* civilities.

conveni'ente *ag* suitable; (*vantaggioso*) profitable; (: *prezzo*) cheap.

conveni'enza [konve'njɛntsa] *sf* suitability; advantage; cheapness; ~**e** *sfpl* social conventions.

conve'nire *vt* to agree upon ♦ *vi* (*riunirsi*) to

gather, assemble; (*concordare*) to agree; (*tornare utile*) to be worthwhile ♦ *vb impers*: **conviene fare questo** it is advisable to do this; **conviene andarsene** we should go; **ne convengo** I agree; **come convenuto** as agreed; **in data da** ~ on a date to be agreed; **come (si) conviene ad una signorina** as befits a young lady.

conven'ticola *sf* (*cricca*) clique; (*riunione*) secret meeting.

con'vento *sm* (*di frati*) monastery; (*di suore*) convent.

conve'nuto, a *pp di* **convenire** ♦ *sm* (*cosa pattuita*) agreement ♦ *smf* (*DIR*) defendant; **i** ~**i** (*i presenti*) those present.

convenzio'nale [konventsjo'nale] *ag* conventional.

convenzio'nato, a [konventsjo'nato] *ag* (*ospedale, clinica*) providing free health care, ≈ National Health Service *cpd* (*BRIT*).

convenzi'one [konven'tsjone] *sf* (*DIR*) agreement; (*nella società*) convention; **le** ~**i (sociali)** social conventions.

conver'gente [konver'dʒɛnte] *ag* convergent.

conver'genza [konver'dʒɛntsa] *sf* convergence.

con'vergere [kon'vɛrdʒere] *vi* to converge.

con'versa *sf* (*REL*) lay sister.

conver'sare *vi* to have a conversation, converse.

conversazi'one [konversat'tsjone] *sf* conversation; **fare** ~ (*chiacchierare*) to chat, have a chat.

conversi'one *sf* conversion; ~ **ad U** (*AUT*) U-turn.

con'verso, a *pp di* **convergere**; **per** ~ *av* conversely.

conver'tire *vt* (*trasformare*) to change; (*INFORM, POL, REL*) to convert; ~**rsi** *vr*: ~**rsi (a)** to be converted (to).

conver'tito, a *smf* convert.

converti'tore *sm* (*ELETTR*) converter.

con'vesso, a *ag* convex.

convin'cente [konvin'tʃɛnte] *ag* convincing.

con'vincere [kon'vintʃere] *vt* to convince; ~ **qn di qc** to convince sb of sth; (*DIR*) to prove sb guilty of sth; ~ **qn a fare qc** to persuade sb to do sth.

con'vinto, a *pp di* **convincere** ♦ *ag*: **reo** ~ (*DIR*) convicted criminal.

convinzi'one [konvin'tsjone] *sf* conviction, firm belief.

convis'suto, a *pp di* **convivere**.

convi'tato, a *smf* guest.

con'vitto *sm* (*INS*) boarding school.

convi'venza [konvi'vɛntsa] *sf* living together; (*DIR*) cohabitation.
con'vivere *vi* to live together.
convivi'ale *ag* convivial.
convo'care *vt* to call, convene; (*DIR*) to summon.
convocazi'one [konvokat'tsjone] *sf* meeting; summons *sg;* **lettera di** ~ (letter of) notification to appear *o* attend.
convogli'are [konvoʎ'ʎare] *vt* to convey; (*dirigere*) to direct, send.
con'voglio [kon'vɔʎʎo] *sm* (*di veicoli*) convoy; (*FERR*) train; ~ **funebre** funeral procession.
convo'lare *vi:* ~ **a (giuste) nozze** (*scherzoso*) to tie the knot.
convulsi'one *sf* convulsion.
con'vulso, a *ag* (*pianto*) violent, convulsive; (*attività*) feverish.
COOP *abbr f* = **cooperativa.**
coope'rare *vi:* ~ **(a)** to cooperate (in).
coopera'tiva *sf* cooperative.
cooperazi'one [kooperat'tsjone] *sf* cooperation.
coordina'mento *sm* coordination.
coordi'nare *vt* to coordinate.
coordi'nato, a *ag* (*movimenti*) coordinated ♦ *sf* (*LING, GEO, MAT*) coordinate ♦ *smpl:* ~**i** (*MODA*) coordinates.
coordinazi'one [koordinat'tsjone] *sf* coordination.
co'perchio [ko'pɛrkjo] *sm* cover; (*di pentola*) lid.
co'perta *sf* cover; (*di lana*) blanket; (*da viaggio*) rug; (*NAUT*) deck.
coper'tina *sf* (*STAMPA*) cover, jacket.
co'perto, a *pp di* **coprire** ♦ *ag* covered; (*cielo*) overcast ♦ *sm* place setting; (*posto a tavola*) place; (*al ristorante*) cover charge; ~ **di** covered in *o* with.
coper'tone *sm* (*telo impermeabile*) tarpaulin; (*AUT*) rubber tyre.
coper'tura *sf* (*anche ECON, MIL*) cover; (*di edificio*) roofing; **fare un gioco di** ~ (*SPORT*) to play a defensive game; ~ **assicurativa** insurance cover.
'copia *sf* copy; (*FOT*) print; **brutta/bella** ~ rough/final copy; ~ **conforme** (*DIR*) certified copy; ~ **omaggio** presentation copy.
copi'are *vt* to copy.
copia'trice [kopja'tritʃe] *sf* copier, copying machine.
copi'one *sm* (*CINE, TEAT*) script.
'coppa *sf* (*bicchiere*) goblet; (*per frutta, gelato*) dish; (*trofeo*) cup, trophy; ~**e** *sfpl* (*CARTE*) suit in Neapolitan pack of cards; ~ **dell'olio** oil sump (*BRIT*) *o* pan (*US*).

'coppia *sf* (*di persone*) couple; (*di animali, SPORT*) pair.
cop'rente *ag* (*colore, cosmetico*) covering; (*calze*) opaque.
copri'capo *sm* headgear; (*cappello*) hat.
coprifu'oco, chi *sm* curfew.
copri'letto *sm* bedspread.
copripiu'mino *sm inv* duvet cover.
co'prire *vt* to cover; (*occupare: carica, posto*) to hold; ~**rsi** *vr* (*cielo*) to cloud over; (*vestirsi*) to wrap up, cover up; (*ECON*) to cover o.s.; ~**rsi di** (*macchie, muffa*) to become covered in; ~ **qn di baci** to smother sb with kisses; ~ **le spese** to break even; ~**rsi le spalle** (*fig*) to cover o.s.
coque [kɔk] *sf:* **uovo alla** ~ boiled egg.
co'raggio [ko'raddʒo] *sm* courage, bravery; ~**!** (*forza!*) come on!; (*animo!*) cheer up!; **farsi** ~ to pluck up courage; **hai un bel** ~**!** (*sfacciataggine*) you've got a nerve *o* a cheek!
coraggi'oso, a [korad'dʒoso] *ag* courageous, brave.
co'rale *ag* choral; (*approvazione*) unanimous.
co'rallo *sm* coral; **il mar dei C**~**i** the Coral Sea.
co'rano *sm* (*REL*) Koran.
co'razza [ko'rattsa] *sf* armour (*BRIT*), armor (*US*); (*di animali*) carapace, shell; (*MIL*) armo(u)r(-plating).
coraz'zato, a [korat'tsato] *ag* (*MIL*) armoured (*BRIT*), armored (*US*) ♦ *sf* battleship.
corazzi'ere [korat'tsjɛre] *sm* (*STORIA*) cuirassier; (*guardia presidenziale*) carabiniere of the President's guard.
corbelle'ria *sf* stupid remark; ~**e** *sfpl* (*sciocchezze*) nonsense *no pl.*
'corda *sf* cord; (*fune*) rope; (*spago, MUS*) string; **dare** ~ **a qn** (*fig*) to let sb have his (*o* her) way; **tenere sulla** ~ **qn** (*fig*) to keep sb on tenterhooks; **tagliare la** ~ (*fig*) to slip away, sneak off; **essere giù di** ~ to feel down; ~**e vocali** vocal cords.
cor'data *sf* (*ALPINISMO*) roped party; (*fig*) alliance system *in financial and business world.*
cordi'ale *ag* cordial, warm ♦ *sm* (*bevanda*) cordial.
cordialità *sf inv* warmth, cordiality; ~ *sfpl* (*saluti*) best wishes.
cor'doglio [kor'dɔʎʎo] *sm* grief; (*lutto*) mourning.
cor'done *sm* cord, string; (*linea: di polizia*) cordon; ~ **ombelicale** umbilical cord; ~ **sanitario** quarantine line.

Co'rea *sf*: **la ~** Korea; **la ~ del Nord/Sud** North/South Korea.
core'ano, a *ag, sm/f* Korean.
coreogra'fia *sf* choreography.
core'ografo, a *sm/f* choreographer.
cori'aceo, a [ko'rjatʃeo] *ag* (*BOT, ZOOL*) coriaceous; (*fig*) tough.
cori'andolo *sm* (*BOT*) coriander; **~i** *smpl* (*per carnevale etc*) confetti *no pl*.
cori'care *vt* to put to bed; **~rsi** *vr* to go to bed.
coricherò *etc* [korike'rɔ] *vb vedi* **coricare**.
Co'rinto *sf* Corinth.
co'rista, i, e *sm/f* (*REL*) choir member, chorister; (*TEAT*) member of the chorus.
'corna *sfpl vedi* **corno**.
cor'nacchia [kor'nakkja] *sf* crow.
corna'musa *sf* bagpipes *pl*.
'cornea *sf* (*ANAT*) cornea.
'corner *sm inv* (*CALCIO*) corner (kick); **salvarsi in ~** (*fig: in gara, esame etc*) to get through by the skin of one's teeth.
cor'netta *sf* (*MUS*) cornet; (*TEL*) receiver.
cor'netto *sm* (*CUC*) croissant; **~ acustico** ear trumpet.
cor'nice [kor'nitʃe] *sf* frame; (*fig*) background, setting.
cornici'one [korni'tʃone] *sm* (*di edificio*) ledge; (*ARCHIT*) cornice.
'corno *sm* (*ZOOL*: *pl(f)* **~a**, *MUS*) horn; (*fam*): **fare le ~a a qn** to be unfaithful to sb; **dire peste e ~a di qn** to call sb every name under the sun; **un ~!** not on your life!
Corno'vaglia [korno'vaʎʎa] *sf*: **la ~** Cornwall.
cor'nuto, a *ag* (*con corna*) horned; (*fam!: marito*) cuckolded ♦ *sm* (*fam!*) cuckold; (*: insulto*) bastard (*!*).
'coro *sm* chorus; (*REL*) choir.
corol'lario *sm* corollary.
co'rona *sf* crown; (*di fiori*) wreath.
corona'mento *sm* (*di impresa*) completion; (*di carriera*) crowning achievement; **il ~ dei propri sogni** the fulfilment of one's dreams.
coro'nare *vt* to crown.
coro'naria *sf* coronary artery.
'corpo *sm* body; (*cadavere*) (dead) body; (*militare, diplomatico*) corps *inv*; (*di opere*) corpus; **prendere ~** to take shape; **darsi anima e ~ a** to give o.s. heart and soul to; **a ~ a ~** hand-to-hand; **~ d'armata** army corps; **~ di ballo** corps de ballet; **~ dei carabinieri** ≈ police force; **~ celeste** heavenly body; **~ di guardia** (*soldati*) guard; (*locale*) guardroom; **~ insegnante** teaching staff; **~ del reato** material evidence.

corpo'rale *ag* bodily; (*punizione*) corporal.
corpora'tura *sf* build, physique.
corporazi'one [korporat'tsjone] *sf* corporation.
cor'poreo, a *ag* bodily, physical.
cor'poso, a *ag* (*vino*) full-bodied.
corpu'lento, a *ag* stout, corpulent.
corpu'lenza [korpu'lɛntsa] *sf* stoutness, corpulence.
cor'puscolo *sm* corpuscle.
corre'dare *vt*: **~ di** to provide *o* furnish with; **domanda corredata dai seguenti documenti** application accompanied by the following documents.
cor'redo *sm* equipment; (*di sposa*) trousseau.
cor'reggere [kor'rɛddʒere] *vt* to correct; (*compiti*) to correct, mark.
cor'rente *ag* (*fiume*) flowing; (*acqua del rubinetto*) running; (*moneta, prezzo*) current; (*comune*) everyday ♦ *sm*: **essere al ~ (di)** to be well-informed (about) ♦ *sf* (*movimento di liquido*) current, stream; (*spiffero*) draught; (*ELETTR, METEOR*) current; (*fig*) trend, tendency; **mettere al ~ (di)** to inform (of); **la vostra lettera del 5 ~ mese** (*in lettere commerciali*) in your letter of the 5th inst.; **articoli di qualità ~** average-quality products; **~ alternata (c.a.)** alternating current (AC); **~ continua (c.c.)** direct current (DC).
corrente'mente *av* (*comunemente*) commonly; **parlare una lingua ~** to speak a language fluently.
corren'tista, i, e *sm/f* (current (*BRIT*) *o* checking (*US*)) account holder.
cor'reo, a *sm/f* (*DIR*) accomplice.
'correre *vi* to run; (*precipitarsi*) to rush; (*partecipare a una gara*) to race, run; (*fig: diffondersi*) to go round ♦ *vt* (*SPORT: gara*) to compete in; (*rischio*) to run; (*pericolo*) to face; **~ dietro a qn** to run after sb; **corre voce che ...** it is rumoured that ....
corresponsabilità *sf* joint responsibility; (*DIR*) joint liability.
corresponsi'one *sf* payment.
cor'ressi *etc vb vedi* **correggere**.
corret'tezza [korret'tettsa] *sf* (*di comportamento*) correctness; (*SPORT*) fair play.
cor'retto, a *pp di* **correggere** ♦ *ag* (*comportamento*) correct, proper; **caffè ~ al cognac** coffee laced with brandy.
corret'tore, 'trice *sm/f*: **~ di bozze** proofreader ♦ *sm*: (*liquido*) **~ correction** fluid.
correzi'one [korret'tsjone] *sf* correction; marking; **~ di bozze** proofreading.

cor'rida *sf* bullfight.

corri'doio *sm* corridor; **manovre di** ~ (*POL*) lobbying *sg*.

corri'dore *sm* (*SPORT*) runner; (: *su veicolo*) racer.

corri'era *sf* coach (*BRIT*), bus.

corri'ere *sm* (*diplomatico, di guerra*) courier; (*posta*) mail, post; (*spedizioniere*) carrier.

corri'mano *sm* handrail.

corrispet'tivo *sm* amount due; **versare a qn il** ~ **di una prestazione** to pay sb the amount due for his (*o* her) services.

corrispon'dente *ag* corresponding ♦ *sm/f* correspondent.

corrispon'denza [korrispon'dɛntsa] *sf* correspondence; ~ **in arrivo/partenza** incoming/outgoing mail.

corris'pondere *vi* (*equivalere*): ~ **(a)** to correspond (to); (*per lettera*): ~ **con** to correspond with ♦ *vt* (*stipendio*) to pay; (*fig: amore*) to return.

corris'posto, a *pp di* **corrispondere**.

corrobo'rare *vt* to strengthen, fortify; (*fig*) to corroborate, bear out.

cor'rodere *vt*, ~**rsi** *vr* to corrode.

cor'rompere *vt* to corrupt; (*comprare*) to bribe.

corrosi'one *sf* corrosion.

corro'sivo, a *ag* corrosive.

cor'roso, a *pp di* **corrodere**.

corrotta'mente *av* corruptly.

cor'rotto, a *pp di* **corrompere** ♦ *ag* corrupt.

corrucci'arsi [korrut't∫arsi] *vr* to grow angry *o* vexed.

corru'gare *vt* to wrinkle; ~ **la fronte** to knit one's brows.

cor'ruppi *etc vb vedi* **corrompere**.

corrut'tela *sf* corruption, depravity.

corruzi'one [korrut'tsjone] *sf* corruption; bribery; ~ **di minorenne** (*DIR*) corruption of a minor.

'corsa *sf* running *no pl*; (*gara*) race; (*di autobus, taxi*) journey, trip; **fare una** ~ to run, dash; (*SPORT*) to run a race; **andare** *o* **essere di** ~ to be in a hurry; ~ **automobilistica/ciclistica** motor/cycle racing; ~ **campestre** cross-country racing; ~ **ad ostacoli** (*IPPICA*) steeplechase; (*ATLETICA*) hurdles race.

cor'saro, a *ag*: **nave** ~**a** privateer ♦ *sm* privateer.

'corsi *etc vb vedi* **correre**.

cor'sia *sf* (*AUT, SPORT*) lane; (*di ospedale*) ward; ~ **di emergenza** (*AUT*) hard shoulder; ~ **preferenziale** ≈ bus lane; (*fig*)

fast track; ~ **di sorpasso** (*AUT*) overtaking lane.

'Corsica *sf*: **la** ~ Corsica.

cor'sivo *sm* cursive (writing); (*TIP*) italics *pl*.

'corso, a *pp di* **correre** ♦ *ag, sm/f* Corsican ♦ *sm* course; (*strada cittadina*) main street; (*di unità monetaria*) circulation; (*di titoli, valori*) rate, price; **dar libero** ~ **a** to give free expression to; **in** ~ in progress, under way; (*annata*) current; ~ **d'acqua** river; stream; (*artificiale*) waterway; ~ **serale** evening class; **aver** ~ **legale** to be legal tender.

'corte *sf* (*court*)yard; (*DIR, regale*) court; **fare la** ~ **a qn** to court sb; ~ **d'appello** court of appeal; ~ **di cassazione** final court of appeal; **C**~ **dei Conti** *State audit court*; **C**~ **Costituzionale** *special court dealing with constitutional and ministerial matters*; ~ **marziale** court-martial; *vedi nota nel riquadro*.

CORTI

The **Corte d'Appello** *hears appeals against sentences passed by courts in both civil and criminal cases and can modify sentences where necessary. The* **Corte d'Assise** *tries serious crimes such as manslaughter and murder; its judges include both legal professionals and members of the public. Similar in structure, the* **Corte d'Assise d'Appello** *hears appeals imposed by these two courts. The* **Corte di Cassazione** *is the highest judicial authority and ensures that the law is correctly applied by the other courts; it may call for a retrial if required. The politically independent* **Corte Costituzionale** *decides whether laws comply with the principles of the Constitution, and has the power to impeach the "Presidente della Repubblica". The* **Corte dei Conti** *ensures the Government's compliance with the law and the Constitution. Reporting directly to Parliament, it oversees the financial aspects of the state budget.*

---

cor'teccia, ce [kor'tett∫a] *sf* bark.

corteggia'mento [korteddʒa'mento] *sm* courtship.

corteggi'are [korted'dʒare] *vt* to court.

corteggia'tore [korteddʒa'tore] *sm* suitor.

cor'teo *sm* procession; ~ **funebre** funeral cortège.

cor'tese *ag* courteous.

corte'sia *sf* courtesy; **fare una** ~ **a qn** to do sb a favour; **per** ~, **dov'è ...?** excuse me, please, where is ...?

cortigi'ano, a [korti'dʒano] *sm/f* courtier ♦ *sf* courtesan.

cor'tile *sm* (court)yard.

cor'tina *sf* curtain; (*anche fig*) screen.

corti'sone *sm* cortisone.

'corto, a *ag* short ♦ *av*: **tagliare ~** to come straight to the point; **essere a ~ di qc** to be short of sth; **essere a ~ di parole** to be at a loss for words; **la settimana ~a** the 5-day week; **~ circuito** short-circuit.

cortocir'cuito [kortotʃir'kuito] *sm* = **corto circuito.**

cortome'traggio [kortome'traddʒo] *sm* short (feature film).

cor'vino, a *ag* (*capelli*) jet-black.

'corvo *sm* raven.

'cosa *sf* thing; (*faccenda*) affair, matter, business *no pl*; **(che) ~?** what?; **(che) cos'è?** what is it?; **a ~ pensi?** what are you thinking about?; **tante belle ~e!** all the best!; **ormai è ~ fatta!** (*positivo*) it's in the bag!; (*negativo*) it's done now!; **a ~e fatte** when it's all over.

'Cosa 'Nostra *sf* Cosa Nostra.

'cosca, sche *sf* (*di mafiosi*) clan.

'coscia, sce ['kɔʃʃa] *sf* thigh; **~ di pollo** (*CUC*) chicken leg.

cosci'ente [koʃ'ʃɛnte] *ag* conscious; **~ di** conscious *o* aware of.

cosci'enza [koʃ'ʃɛntsa] *sf* conscience; (*consapevolezza*) consciousness; **~ politica** political awareness.

coscienzi'oso, a [koʃʃen'tsjoso] *ag* conscientious.

cosci'otto [koʃ'ʃɔtto] *sm* (*CUC*) leg.

cos'critto *sm* (*MIL*) conscript.

coscrizi'one [koskrit'tsjone] *sf* conscription.

═══════════ *PAROLA CHIAVE*

così *av* **1** (*in questo modo*) like this, (in) this way; (*in tal modo*) so; **le cose stanno ~** this is the way things stand; **non ho detto ~!** I didn't say that!; **come stai? — (e) ~ ~** how are you? — so-so; **e ~ via** and so on; **per ~ dire** so to speak; **~ sia** amen

2 (*tanto*) so; **~ lontano** so far away; **un ragazzo ~ intelligente** such an intelligent boy

♦ *ag inv* (*tale*): **non ho mai visto un film ~** I've never seen such a film

♦ *cong* **1** (*perciò*) so, therefore; **e ~ ho deciso di lasciarlo** so I decided to leave him

2: **~ ... come** as ... as; **non è ~ bravo come te** he's not as good as you; **~ ... che** so ... that.

cosicché [kosik'ke] *cong* so (that).

cosid'detto, a *ag* so-called.

cos'mesi *sf* (*scienza*) cosmetics *sg*; (*prodotti*) cosmetics *pl*; (*trattamento*) beauty treatment.

cos'metico, a, ci, che *ag, sm* cosmetic.

'cosmico, a, ci, che *ag* cosmic.

'cosmo *sm* cosmos.

cosmo'nauta, i, e *sm/f* cosmonaut.

cosmopo'lita, i, e *ag* cosmopolitan.

'coso *sm* (*fam: oggetto*) thing, thingumajig; (: *aggeggio*) contraption; (: *persona*) what's his name, thingumajig.

cos'pargere [kos'pardʒere] *vt*: **~ di** to sprinkle with.

cos'parso, a *pp di* **cospargere.**

cos'petto *sm*: **al ~ di** in front of; in the presence of.

cospicuità *sf* vast quantity.

cos'picuo, a *ag* considerable, large.

cospi'rare *vi* to conspire.

cospira'tore, 'trice *sm/f* conspirator.

cospirazi'one [kospirat'tsjone] *sf* conspiracy.

'cossi *etc vb vedi* **cuocere.**

Cost. *abbr* = **costituzione.**

'costa *sf* (*tra terra e mare*) coast(line); (*litorale*) shore; (*pendio*) slope; (*ANAT*) rib; **navigare sotto ~** to hug the coast; **la C~ Azzurra** the French Riviera; **la C~ d'Avorio** the Ivory Coast; **velluto a ~e** corduroy.

costà *av* there.

cos'tante *ag* constant; (*persona*) steadfast ♦ *sf* constant.

cos'tanza [kos'tantsa] *sf* (*gen*) constancy; (*fermezza*) constancy, steadfastness; **il Lago di C~** Lake Constance.

cos'tare *vi, vt* to cost; **~ caro** to be expensive, cost a lot; **~ un occhio della testa** to cost a fortune; **costi quel che costi** no matter what.

'Costa 'Rica *sf*: **la ~** Costa Rica.

cos'tata *sf* (*CUC: di manzo*) large chop.

cos'tato *sm* (*ANAT*) ribs *pl.*

costeggi'are [kosted'dʒare] *vt* to be close to; to run alongside.

cos'tei *pron vedi* **costui.**

costellazi'one [kostellat'tsjone] *sf* constellation.

coster'nare *vt* to dismay.

coster'nato, a *ag* dismayed.

costernazi'one [kosternat'tsjone] *sf* dismay, consternation.

costi'ero, a *ag* coastal, coast *cpd* ♦ *sf* stretch of coast.

costi'pato, a *ag* (*stitico*) constipated.

costitu'ire *vt* (*comitato, gruppo*) to set up,

form; (*collezione*) to put together, build up; (*sog: elementi, parti: comporre*) to make up, constitute; (*rappresentare*) to constitute; (*DIR*) to appoint; ~**rsi** *vr*: ~**rsi (alla polizia)** to give o.s. up (to the police); ~**rsi parte civile** (*DIR*) *to associate in an action with the public prosecutor for damages*; **il fatto non costituisce reato** this is not a crime.

costitu'tivo, a *ag* constituent, component; **atto** ~ (*DIR: di società*) memorandum of association.

costituzio'nale [kostituttsjo'nale] *ag* constitutional.

costituzi'one [kostitut'tsjone] *sf* setting up; building up; constitution.

'costo *sm* cost; **sotto** ~ for less than cost price; **a ogni** *o* **qualunque** ~, **a tutti i** ~**i** at all costs; ~**i di esercizio** running costs; ~**i fissi** fixed costs; ~**i di gestione** operating costs; ~**i di produzione** production costs.

'costola *sf* (*ANAT*) rib; **ha la polizia alle** ~**e** the police are hard on his heels.

costo'letta *sf* (*CUC*) cutlet.

cos'toro *pron pl vedi* **costui**.

cos'toso, a *ag* expensive, costly.

cos'tretto, a *pp di* **costringere**.

cos'tringere [kos'trindʒere] *vt*: ~ **qn a fare qc** to force sb to do sth.

costrit'tivo, a *ag* coercive.

costrizi'one [kostrit'tsjone] *sf* coercion.

costru'ire *vt* to construct, build.

costrut'tivo, a *ag* (*EDIL*) building *cpd*; (*fig*) constructive.

costruzi'one [kostrut'tsjone] *sf* construction, building; **di** ~ **inglese** British-made.

cos'tui, cos'tei, *pl* **cos'toro** *pron* (*soggetto*) he/she; *pl* they; (*complemento*) him/her; *pl* them; **si può sapere chi è** ~? (*peg*) just who is that fellow?

cos'tume *sm* (*uso*) custom; (*foggia di vestire, indumento*) costume; **il buon** ~ public morality; **donna di facili** ~**i** woman of easy morals; ~ **da bagno** bathing *o* swimming costume (*BRIT*), swimsuit; (*da uomo*) bathing *o* swimming trunks *pl*.

costu'mista, i, e *smf* costume maker, costume designer.

co'tenna *sf* bacon rind.

co'togna [ko'toɲɲa] *sf* quince.

coto'letta *sf* (*di maiale, montone*) chop; (*di vitello, agnello*) cutlet.

coto'nare *vt* (*capelli*) to backcomb.

co'tone *sm* cotton; ~ **idrofilo** cotton wool (*BRIT*), absorbent cotton (*US*).

cotoni'ficio [kotoni'fitʃo] *sm* cotton mill.

'cotta *sf* (*REL*) surplice; (*fam:*

innamoramento) crush.

'cottimo *sm*: **lavorare a** ~ to do piecework.

'cotto, a *pp di* **cuocere** ♦ *ag* cooked; (*fam: innamorato*) head-over-heels in love ♦ *sm* brickwork; ~ **a puntino** cooked to perfection; **dirne di** ~**e e di crude a qn** to call sb every name under the sun; **farne di** ~**e e di crude** to get up to all kinds of mischief; **mattone di** ~ fired brick; **pavimento in** ~ tile floor.

cot'tura *sf* cooking; (*in forno*) baking; (*in umido*) stewing; ~ **a fuoco lento** simmering; **angolo (di)** ~ cooking area.

co'vare *vt* to hatch; (*fig: malattia*) to be sickening for; (*: odio, rancore*) to nurse ♦ *vi* (*fuoco, fig*) to smoulder (*BRIT*), smolder (*US*).

co'vata *sf* (*anche fig*) brood.

'covo *sm* den; ~ **di terroristi** terrorist base.

co'vone *sm* sheaf.

'cozza ['kɔttsa] *sf* mussel.

coz'zare [kot'tsare] *vi*: ~ **contro** to bang into, collide with.

'cozzo ['kɔttso] *sm* collision.

C.P. *abbr* (= *cartolina postale*) pc; (*POSTA*) *vedi* **casella postale**; (*NAUT*) = **capitaneria (di porto)**; (*DIR*) = **codice penale**.

crack *sm inv* (*droga*) crack.

Cra'covia *sf* Cracow.

'crampo *sm* cramp.

'cranio *sm* skull.

cra'tere *sm* crater.

cra'vatta *sf* tie; ~ **a farfalla** bow tie.

cravat'tino *sm* bow tie.

cre'anza [kre'antsa] *sf* manners *pl*; **per buona** ~ out of politeness.

cre'are *vt* to create.

creatività *sf* creativity.

cre'ato *sm* creation.

crea'tore, 'trice *ag* creative ♦ *smf* creator; **un** ~ **di alta moda** fashion designer; **andare al C**~ to go to meet one's maker.

crea'tura *sf* creature; (*bimbo*) baby, infant.

creazi'one [kreat'tsjone] *sf* creation; (*fondazione*) foundation, establishment.

'crebbi *etc vb vedi* **crescere**.

cre'dente *smf* (*REL*) believer.

cre'denza [kre'dentsa] *sf* belief; (*armadio*) sideboard.

credenzi'ali [kreden'tsjali] *sfpl* credentials.

'credere *vt* to believe ♦ *vi*: ~ **in**, ~ **a** to believe in; ~ **qn onesto** to believe sb (to be) honest; ~ **che** to believe *o* think that; ~**rsi furbo** to think one is clever; **lo credo bene!** I can well believe it!; **fai quello che credi** *o* **come credi** do as you please.

cre'dibile *ag* credible, believable.

credibilità *sf* credibility.

credi'tizio, a [kredi'tittsjo] *ag* credit.

'credito *sm (anche COMM)* credit; *(reputazione)* esteem, repute; **comprare a** ~ to buy on credit; ~ **agevolato** easy credit terms; ~ **d'imposta** tax credit.

credi'tore, 'trice *sm/f* creditor.

'credo *sm inv* creed.

'credulo, a *ag* credulous.

credu'lone, a *sm/f* simpleton, sucker *(fam).*

'crema *sf* cream; *(con uova, zucchero etc)* custard; ~ **idratante** moisturizing cream; ~ **pasticciera** confectioner's custard; ~ **solare** sun cream.

cre'mare *vt* to cremate.

crema'torio *sm* crematorium.

cremazi'one [kremat'tsjone] *sf* cremation.

'cremisi *ag inv, sm inv* crimson.

Crem'lino *sm*: il ~ the Kremlin.

cremo'nese *ag* of *(o* from) Cremona.

cre'moso, a *ag* creamy.

'crepa *sf* crack.

cre'paccio [kre'pattʃo] *sm* large crack, fissure; *(di ghiacciaio)* crevasse.

crepacu'ore *sm* broken heart.

crepa'pelle *av*: ridere a ~ to split one's sides laughing.

cre'pare *vi (fam: morire)* to snuff it *(BRIT)*, kick the bucket; ~ **dalle risa** to split one's sides laughing; ~ **dall'invidia** to be green with envy.

crepi'tare *vi (fuoco)* to crackle; *(pioggia)* to patter.

crepi'tio, ii *sm* crackling; pattering.

cre'puscolo *sm* twilight, dusk.

cre'scendo [kreʃ'ʃɛndo] *sm (MUS)* crescendo.

cre'scente [kreʃ'ʃɛnte] *ag (gen)* growing, increasing; *(luna)* waxing.

'crescere ['krɛʃʃere] *vi* to grow ♦ *vt (figli)* to raise.

cre'scione [kreʃ'ʃone] *sm* watercress.

'crescita ['kreʃʃita] *sf* growth.

cresci'uto, a [kreʃ'ʃuto] *pp di* crescere.

'cresima *sf (REL)* confirmation.

cresi'mare *vt* to confirm.

'crespo, a *ag (capelli)* frizzy; *(tessuto)* puckered ♦ *sm* crêpe.

'cresta *sf* crest; *(di polli, uccelli)* crest, comb; **alzare la** ~ *(fig)* to become cocky; **abbassare la** ~ *(fig)* to climb down; **essere sulla** ~ **dell'onda** *(fig)* to be riding high.

'Creta *sf* Crete.

'creta *sf (gesso)* chalk; *(argilla)* clay.

cre'tese *ag, sm/f* Cretan.

creti'nata *sf (fam)*: **dire/fare una** ~ to say/ do a stupid thing.

cre'tino, a *ag* stupid ♦ *sm/f* idiot, fool.

CRI *sigla f* = Croce Rossa Italiana.

cric *sm inv (TECN)* jack.

'cricca, che *sf* clique.

'cricco, chi *sm* = cric.

cri'ceto [kri'tʃeto] *sm* hamster.

crimi'nale *ag, sm/f* criminal.

criminalità *sf* crime; ~ **organizzata** organized crime.

'Criminalpol *abbr* = polizia criminale.

'crimine *sm (DIR)* crime.

criminolo'gia [kriminolo'dʒia] *sf* criminology.

crimi'noso, a *ag* criminal.

cri'nale *sm* ridge.

'crine *sm* horsehair.

crini'era *sf* mane.

'cripta *sf* crypt.

crip'tare *vt (TV: programma)* to encrypt.

crip'tato, a *ag (programma, messaggio)* encrypted.

crisan'temo *sm* chrysanthemum; *vedi anche* **Giorno dei Morti**.

'crisi *sf inv* crisis; *(MED)* attack, fit; **essere in** ~ *(partito, impresa etc)* to be in a state of crisis; ~ **energetica** energy crisis; ~ **di nervi** attack *o* fit of nerves.

cristalle'ria *sf (fabbrica)* crystal glassworks *sg; (oggetti)* crystalware.

cristal'lino, a *ag (MINERALOGIA)* crystalline; *(fig: suono, acque)* crystal clear ♦ *sm (ANAT)* crystalline lens.

cristalliz'zare [kristallid'dzare] *vi,* ~**rsi** *vr* to crystallize; *(fig)* to become fossilized.

cris'tallo *sm* crystal.

cristia'nesimo *sm* Christianity.

cristianità *sf* Christianity; *(i cristiani)* Christendom.

cristi'ano, a *ag, sm/f* Christian; **un povero** ~ *(fig)* a poor soul *o* beggar; **comportarsi da** ~ *(fig)* to behave in a civilized manner.

'cristo *sm*: **C**~ Christ; **(un) povero** ~ (a) poor beggar.

cri'terio *sm* criterion; *(buon senso)* (common) sense.

'critica, che *sf vedi* critico.

criti'care *vt* to criticize.

'critico, a, ci, che *ag* critical ♦ *sm* critic ♦ *sf* criticism; **la** ~**a** *(attività)* criticism; *(persone)* the critics *pl.*

criti'cone, a *sm/f* faultfinder.

crivel'lare *vt*: ~ **(di)** to riddle (with).

cri'vello *sm* riddle.

cro'ato, a *ag, sm/f* Croatian, Croat.

Cro'azia [kro'attsja] *sf*: **la** ~ Croatia.

croc'cante *ag* crisp, crunchy ♦ *sm (CUC)* almond crunch.

'crocchia ['krɔkkja] *sf* chignon, bun.

'crocchio ['krɔkkjo] *sm (di persone)* small

group, cluster.

'**croce** ['krotʃe] *sf* cross; **in** ~ (*di traverso*) crosswise; (*fig*) on tenterhooks; **mettere in** ~ (*anche fig: criticare*) to crucify; (: *tormentare*) to nag to death; **la C**~ **Rossa** the Red Cross; ~ **uncinata** swastika.

croce'**figgere** *etc* [krotʃe'fiddʒere] = **crocifiggere** *etc*.

croceros'**sina** [krotʃeros'sina] *sf* Red Cross nurse.

croce'**via** [krotʃe'via] *sm inv* crossroads *sg*.

croci'**ato, a** [kro'tʃato] *ag* cross-shaped ♦ *sm* (*anche fig*) crusader ♦ *sf* crusade.

cro'**cicchio** [kro'tʃikkjo] *sm* crossroads *sg*.

croci'**era** [kro'tʃɛra] *sf* (*viaggio*) cruise; (*ARCHIT*) transept; **altezza di** ~ (*AER*) cruising height; **velocità di** ~ (*AER, NAUT*) cruising speed.

croci'**figgere** [krotʃi'fiddʒere] *vt* to crucify.

crocifissi'**one** [krotʃifis'sjone] *sf* crucifixion.

croci'**fisso, a** [krotʃi'fisso] *pp di* **crocifiggere** ♦ *sm* crucifix.

crogio'**larsi** [krodʒo'larsi] *vr*: ~ **al sole** to bask in the sun.

crogi'**olo** [kro'dʒɔlo], **crogiu'olo** [kro'dʒwɔlo] *sm* crucible; (*fig*) melting pot.

crol'**lare** *vi* to collapse.

'**crollo** *sm* collapse; (*di prezzi*) slump, sudden fall.

'**croma** *sf* (*MUS*) quaver (*BRIT*), eighth note (*US*).

cro'**mato, a** *ag* chromium-plated.

'**cromo** *sm* chrome, chromium.

cromo'**soma, i** *sm* chromosome.

'**cronaca, che** *sf* chronicle; (*STAMPA*) news *sg*; (: *rubrica*) column; (*TV, RADIO*) commentary; **fatto** *o* **episodio di** ~ news item; ~ **nera** crime news *sg*; crime column.

'**cronico, a, ci, che** *ag* chronic.

cro'**nista, i** *sm* (*STAMPA*) reporter, columnist.

cronis'**toria** *sf* chronicle; (*fig: ironico*) blow-by-blow account.

cro'**nografo** *sm* (*strumento*) chronograph.

cronolo'**gia** [kronolo'dʒia] *sf* chronology.

cronome'**trare** *vt* to time.

cro'**nometro** *sm* chronometer; (*a scatto*) stopwatch.

'**crosta** *sf* crust; (*MED*) scab; (*ZOOL*) shell; (*di ghiaccio*) layer; (*fig peg: quadro*) daub.

cros'**tacei** [kros'tatʃei] *smpl* shellfish.

cros'**tata** *sf* (*CUC*) tart.

cros'**tino** *sm* (*CUC*) croûton; (: *da antipasto*) canapé.

crucci'**are** [krut'tʃare] *vt* to torment, worry; ~**rsi** *vr*: ~**rsi per** to torment o.s. over.

'**cruccio** ['kruttʃo] *sm* worry, torment.

cruci'**ale** [kru'tʃale] *ag* crucial.

cruci'**verba** [krutʃi'vɛrba] *sm inv* crossword (puzzle).

cru'**dele** *ag* cruel.

crudel**tà** *sf* cruelty.

'**crudo, a** *ag* (*non cotto*) raw; (*aspro*) harsh, severe.

cru'**ento, a** *ag* bloody.

cru'**miro** *sm* (*peg*) blackleg (*BRIT*), scab.

'**cruna** *sf* eye (of a needle).

'**crusca** *sf* bran.

crus'**cotto** *sm* (*AUT*) dashboard.

CS *sigla* = Cosenza.

c.s. *abbr* = come sopra.

CSI [tʃi'ɛsse'i] *sigla f* (= *Comunità di Stati Indipendenti*) CIS.

CSM [tʃiɛsse'ɛmme] *sigla m* (= *consiglio superiore della magistratura*) Magistrates' Board of Supervisors.

CT *sigla* = Catania.

c.t. *abbr* = **commissario tecnico**.

'**Cuba** *sf* Cuba.

cu'**bano, a** *ag, sm/f* Cuban.

cu'**betto** *sm* (*small*) cube; ~ **di ghiaccio** ice cube.

'**cubico, a, ci, che** *ag* cubic.

cu'**bista** *sf* podium dancer, *dancer who performs on stage in a club*.

'**cubo, a** *ag* cubic ♦ *sm* cube; **elevare al** ~ (*MAT*) to cube.

cuc'**cagna** [kuk'kaɲɲa] *sf*: **paese della** ~ land of plenty; **albero della** ~ greasy pole (*fig*).

cuc'**cetta** [kut'tʃetta] *sf* (*FERR*) couchette; (*NAUT*) berth.

cucchiai'**ata** [kukkja'jata] *sf* spoonful; tablespoonful.

cucchia'**ino** [kukkja'ino] *sm* teaspoon; coffee spoon.

cucchi'**aio** [kuk'kjajo] *sm* spoon; (*da tavola*) tablespoon; (*cucchiaiata*) spoonful; tablespoonful.

'**cuccia, ce** ['kuttʃa] *sf* dog's bed; **a** ~! down!

cuccio'**lata** [kuttʃo'lata] *sf* litter.

'**cucciolo** ['kuttʃolo] *sm* cub; (*di cane*) puppy.

cu'**cina** [ku'tʃina] *sf* (*locale*) kitchen; (*arte culinaria*) cooking, cookery; (*le vivande*) food, cooking; (*apparecchio*) cooker; **di** ~ (*libro, lezione*) cookery *cpd*; ~ **componibile** fitted kitchen; ~ **economica** kitchen range.

cuci'**nare** [kutʃi'nare] *vt* to cook.

cuci'**nino** [kutʃi'nino] *sm* kitchenette.

cu'**cire** [ku'tʃire] *vt* to sew, stitch; ~ **la bocca a qn** (*fig*) to shut sb up.

cu'cito, a [ku'tʃito] *sm* sewing; (*INS*) sewing, needlework.

cuci'trice [kutʃi'tritʃe] *sf* (*TIP: per libri*) stitching machine; (*per fogli*) stapler.

cuci'tura [kutʃi'tura] *sf* sewing, stitching; (*costura*) seam.

cucù *sm inv,* **cu'culo** *sm* cuckoo.

'cuffia *sf* bonnet, cap; (*da infermiera*) cap; (*da bagno*) (bathing) cap; (*per ascoltare*) headphones *pl,* headset.

cu'gino, a [ku'dʒino] *sm/f* cousin.

================== *PAROLA CHIAVE*

'cui *pron* **1** (*nei complementi indiretti: persona*) whom; (*: oggetto, animale*) which; **la persona/le persone a ~ accennavi** the person/people you were referring to *o* to whom you were referring; **la penna con ~ scrivo** the pen I'm writing with; **il paese da ~ viene** the country he comes from; **i libri di ~ parlavo** the books I was talking about *o* about which I was talking; **parla varie lingue, fra ~ l'inglese** he speaks several languages, including English; **il quartiere in ~ abito** the district where I live; **visto il modo in ~ ti ha trattato** ... considering how he treated you ...; **la ragione per ~** the reason why; **per ~ non so più che fare** that's why I don't know what to do
2 (*inserito tra articolo e sostantivo*) whose; **la donna i ~ figli sono scomparsi** the woman whose children have disappeared; **il signore, dal ~ figlio ho avuto il libro** the man from whose son I got the book.

culi'naria *sf* cookery.

culi'nario, a *ag* culinary.

'culla *sf* cradle.

cul'lare *vt* to rock; (*fig: idea, speranza*) to cherish; **~rsi** *vr* (*gen*) to sway; **~rsi in vane speranze** (*fig*) to cherish fond hopes; **~rsi nel dolce far niente** (*fig*) to sit back and relax.

culmi'nante *ag:* **posizione ~** (*ASTR*) highest point; **punto** *o* **momento ~** (*fig*) climax.

culmi'nare *vi:* **~ in** *o* **con** to culminate in.

'culmine *sm* top, summit.

'culo *sm* (*fam!*) arse (*BRIT!*), ass (*US!*); (*: fig: fortuna*): **aver ~** to have the luck of the devil; **prendere qn per il ~** to take the piss out of sb (*!*).

'culto *sm* (*religione*) religion; (*adorazione*) worship, adoration; (*venerazione: anche fig*) cult.

cul'tura *sf* (*gen*) culture; (*conoscenza*) education, learning; **di ~** (*persona*) cultured; (*istituto*) cultural, of culture; **~ generale** general knowledge; **~ di massa** mass culture.

cultu'rale *ag* cultural.

cultu'rismo *sm* body-building.

cumu'lare *vt* to accumulate, amass.

cumula'tivo, a *ag* cumulative; (*prezzo*) inclusive; (*biglietto*) group *cpd.*

'cumulo *sm* (*mucchio*) pile, heap; (*METEOR*) cumulus; **~ dei redditi** (*FISCO*) combined incomes; **~ delle pene** (*DIR*) consecutive sentences.

'cuneo *sm* wedge.

cu'netta *sf* (*di strada etc*) bump; (*scolo: nelle strade di città*) gutter; (*: di campagna*) ditch.

cu'nicolo *sm* (*galleria*) tunnel; (*di miniera*) pit, shaft; (*di talpa*) hole.

cu'oca *sf vedi* **cuoco.**

cu'ocere ['kwɔtʃere] *vt* (*alimenti*) to cook; (*mattoni etc*) to fire ♦ *vi* to cook; **~ in umido/a vapore/in padella** to stew/steam/fry; **~ al forno** (*pane*) to bake; (*arrosto*) to roast.

cu'oco, a, chi, che *sm/f* cook; (*di ristorante*) chef.

cuoi'ame *sm* leather goods *pl.*

cu'oio *sm* leather; **~ capelluto** scalp; **tirare le ~a** (*fam*) to kick the bucket.

cu'ore *sm* heart; **~i** *smpl* (*CARTE*) hearts; **avere buon ~** to be kind-hearted; **stare a ~ a qn** to be important to sb; **un grazie di ~** heartfelt thanks; **ringraziare di ~** to thank sincerely; **nel profondo del ~** in one's heart of hearts; **avere la morte nel ~** to be sick at heart; **club dei ~i solitari** lonely hearts club.

cupi'digia [kupi'didʒa] *sf* greed, covetousness.

'cupo, a *ag* dark; (*suono*) dull; (*fig*) gloomy, dismal.

'cupola *sf* dome; (*più piccola*) cupola; (*fig*) Mafia high command.

'cura *sf* care; (*MED: trattamento*) (course of) treatment; **aver ~ di** (*occuparsi di*) to look after; **a ~ di** (*libro*) edited by; **fare una ~** to follow a course of treatment; **~ dimagrante** diet.

cu'rabile *ag* curable.

cu'rante *ag:* **medico ~** doctor (in charge of a patient).

cu'rare *vt* (*malato, malattia*) to treat; (*: guarire*) to cure; (*aver cura di*) to take care of; (*testo*) to edit; **~rsi** *vr* to take care of o.s.; (*MED*) to follow a course of treatment; **~rsi di** to pay attention to; (*occuparsi di*) to look after.

cu'rato *sm* parish priest; (*protestante*)

vicar, minister.

cura'tore, 'trice *sm/f* (*DIR*) trustee; (*di antologia etc*) editor; ~ **fallimentare** (official) receiver.

'curdo, a *ag* Kurdish ♦ *sm/f* Kurd.

'curia *sf* (*REL*): **la** ~ **romana** the Roman curia; ~ **notarile** notaries' association *o* guild.

curio'saggine [kurjo'saddʒine] *sf* nosiness.

curio'sare *vi* to look round, wander round; (*tra libri*) to browse; ~ **nei negozi** to look *o* wander round the shops; ~ **nelle faccende altrui** to poke one's nose into other people's affairs.

curiosità *sf inv* curiosity; (*cosa rara*) curio, curiosity.

curi'oso, a *ag* (*che vuol sapere*) curious, inquiring; (*ficcanaso*) curious, inquisitive; (*bizzarro*) strange, curious ♦ *sm/f* busybody, nosy parker; **essere** ~ **di** to be curious about; **una folla di** ~**i** a crowd of onlookers.

cur'riculum *sm inv*: ~ **(vitae)** curriculum vitae.

cur'sore *sm* (*INFORM*) cursor.

'curva *sf* curve; (*stradale*) bend, curve.

cur'vare *vt* to bend ♦ *vi* (*veicolo*) to take a bend; (*strada*) to bend, curve; ~**rsi** *vr* to bend; (*legno*) to warp.

'curvo, a *ag* curved; (*piegato*) bent.

CUS *sigla m* = *Centro Universitario Sportivo*.

cusci'netto [kuʃʃi'netto] *sm* pad; (*TECN*) bearing ♦ *ag inv*: **stato** ~ buffer state; ~ **a sfere** ball bearing.

cu'scino [kuʃ'ʃino] *sm* cushion; (*guanciale*) pillow.

'cuspide *sf* (*ARCHIT*) spire.

cus'tode *sm/f* (*di museo*) keeper, custodian; (*di parco*) warden; (*di casa*) concierge; (*di fabbrica, carcere*) guard.

cus'todia *sf* care; (*DIR*) custody; (*astuccio*) case, holder; **avere qc in** ~ to look after sth; **dare qc in** ~ **a qn** to entrust sth to sb's care; **agente di** ~ prison warder; ~ **delle carceri** prison security; ~ **cautelare** (*DIR*) remand.

custo'dire *vt* (*conservare*) to keep; (*assistere*) to look after, take care of; (*fare la guardia*) to guard.

'cute *sf* (*ANAT*) skin.

cu'ticola *sf* cuticle.

C.V. *abbr* = *cavallo vapore*.

c.v.d. *abbr* (= *come volevasi dimostrare*) QED (= *quod erat demonstrandum*).

c.vo *abbr* = *corsivo*.

cy'clette ® [si'klɛt] *sf inv* exercise bike.

CZ *sigla* = *Catanzaro*.

D d

D, d [di] *sf o m inv* (*lettera*) D, d; **D come Domodossola** ≈ D for David (*BRIT*), D for Dog (*US*).

D *abbr* (= *destra*) R; (*FERR*) = **diretto**.

━━━━━━━━━━━ *PAROLA CHIAVE*

da (*da* + *il* = **dal**, *da* + *lo* = **dallo**, *da* + *l'* = **dall'**, *da* + *la* = **dalla**, *da* + *i* = **dai**, *da* + *gli* = **dagli**, *da* + *le* = **dalle**) *prep* **1** (*agente*) by; **dipinto** ~ **un grande artista** painted by a great artist

2 (*causa*) with; **tremare dalla paura** to tremble with fear

3 (*stato in luogo*) at; **abito** ~ **lui** I'm living at his house *o* with him; **sono dal giornalaio** I'm at the newsagent's; **era** ~ **Francesco** she was at Francesco's (house)

4 (*moto a luogo*) to; (*moto per luogo*) through; **vado** ~ **Pietro/dal giornalaio** I'm going to Pietro's (house)/to the newsagent's; **sono passati dalla finestra** they came in through the window

5 (*provenienza, allontanamento*) from; ~ ... **a** from ... to; **arrivare/partire** ~ **Milano** to arrive/depart from Milan; **scendere dal treno/dalla macchina** to get off the train/out of the car; **viene** ~ **una famiglia povera** he comes from a poor background; **viene dalla Scozia** he comes from Scotland; **ti chiamo** ~ **una cabina** I'm phoning from a call box; **si trova a 5 km** ~ **qui** it's 5 km from here

6 (*tempo: durata*) for; (: *a partire da: nel passato*) since; (: *nel futuro*) from; **vivo qui** ~ **un anno** I've been living here for a year; **è dalle 3 che ti aspetto** I've been waiting for you since 3 (o'clock); ~ **mattina a sera** from morning till night; ~ **oggi in poi** from today onwards; ~ **bambino** as a child, when I (*o he etc*) was a child

7 (*modo, maniera*) like; **comportarsi** ~ **uomo** to behave like a man; **l'ho fatto** ~ **me** I did it (by) myself; **non è** ~ **lui** it's not like him

8 (*descrittivo*): **una macchina** ~ **corsa** a racing car; **è una cosa** ~ **poco** it's nothing special; **una ragazza dai capelli biondi** a

girl with blonde hair; **sordo** ~ **un orecchio**
deaf in one ear; **abbigliamento** ~ **uomo**
menswear; **un vestito** ~ **100 euro** a 100
euro dress; **qualcosa** ~ **bere/mangiare**
something to drink/eat.

dà *vb vedi* **dare**.
dab'bene *ag inv* honest, decent.
'Dacca *sf* Dacca.
dac'capo, da 'capo *av* (*di nuovo*) (once)
again; (*dal principio*) all over again, from
the beginning.
dacché [dak'ke] *cong* since.
'dado *sm* (*da gioco*) dice *o* die (*pl* dice);
(*CUC*) stock cube (*BRIT*), bouillon cube
(*US*); (*TECN*) (screw) nut; ~**i** *smpl* (game of)
dice.
daf'fare, da 'fare *sm* work, toil; **avere un**
gran ~ to be very busy.
'dagli ['daʎʎi], **'dai** *prep* + *det vedi* **da**.
'daino *sm* (fallow) deer *inv*; (*pelle*)
buckskin.
Da'kar *sf* Dakar.
dal *prep* + *det vedi* **da**.
dal *abbr* (= decalitro) dal.
dall', 'dalla, 'dalle, 'dallo *prep* + *det vedi*
da.
dal'tonico, a, ci, che *ag* colour-blind
(*BRIT*), colorblind (*US*).
dam *abbr* (= decametro) dam.
'dama *sf* lady; (*nei balli*) partner; (*gioco*)
draughts *sg* (*BRIT*), checkers *sg* (*US*); **far** ~
(*nel gioco*) to make a crown; ~ **di**
compagnia lady's companion; ~ **di corte**
lady-in-waiting.
Da'masco *sf* Damascus.
dami'gella [dami'dʒɛlla] *sf* (*STORIA*) damsel;
(: *titolo*) mistress; ~ **d'onore** (*di sposa*)
bridesmaid.
damigi'ana [dami'dʒana] *sf* demijohn.
dam'meno *ag inv*: **per non essere** ~ **di qn**
so as not to be outdone by sb.
DAMS *sigla m* (= Disciplina delle Arti, della
Musica, dello Spettacolo) *study of the*
performing arts.
da'naro *sm* = **denaro**.
dana'roso, a *ag* wealthy.
da'nese *ag* Danish ♦ *smf* Dane ♦ *sm* (*LING*)
Danish.
Dani'marca *sf*: **la** ~ Denmark.
dan'nare *vt* (*REL*) to damn; ~**rsi** *vr*: ~**rsi**
(**per**) (*fig: tormentarsi*) to be worried to
death (by); **far** ~ **qn** to drive sb mad; ~**rsi**
l'anima per qc (*affannarsi*) to work o.s. to
death for sth; (*tormentarsi*) to worry o.s.
to death over sth.
dan'nato, a *ag* damned.
dannazi'one [dannat'tsjone] *sf* damnation.

danneggi'are [danned'dʒare] *vt* to damage;
(*rovinare*) to spoil; (*nuocere*) to harm; **la**
parte danneggiata (*DIR*) the injured
party.
'danno *vb vedi* **dare** ♦ *sm* damage; (*a*
persona) harm, injury; ~**i** *smpl* (*DIR*)
damages; **a** ~ **di qn** to sb's detriment;
chiedere/risarcire i ~**i** to sue for/pay
damages.
dan'noso, a *ag*: ~ (**a** *o* **per**) harmful (to),
bad (for).
dan'tesco, a, schi, sche *ag* Dantesque;
l'opera ~**a** Dante's work.
Da'nubio *sm*: **il** ~ the Danube.
'danza ['dantsa] *sf*: **la** ~ dancing; **una** ~ a
dance.
dan'zante [dan'tsante] *ag* dancing; **serata** ~
dance.
dan'zare [dan'tsare] *vt, vi* to dance.
danza'tore, 'trice [dantsa'tore] *smf* dancer.
dapper'tutto *av* everywhere.
dap'poco *ag inv* inept; worthless.
dap'prima *av* at first.
Darda'nelli *smpl*: **i** ~ the Dardanelles.
'dardo *sm* dart.
'dare *sm* (*COMM*) debit ♦ *vt* to give;
(*produrre: frutti, suono*) to produce ♦ *vi*
(*guardare*): ~ **su** to look (out) onto; ~**rsi** *vr*:
~**rsi a** to dedicate o.s. to; **quanti anni mi**
dai? how old do you think I am?; **danno**
ancora quel film? is that film still
showing?; ~ **da mangiare a qn** to give sb
something to eat; ~ **per certo qc** to
consider sth certain; ~ **ad intendere a qn**
che ... to lead sb to believe that ...; ~ **per**
morto qn to give sb up for dead; ~ **qc per**
scontato to take sth for granted; ~**rsi**
ammalato to report sick; ~**rsi alla bella**
vita to have a good time; ~**rsi al bere** to
take to drink; ~**rsi al commercio** to go
into business; ~**rsi da fare per fare qc** to
go to a lot of bother to do sth; ~**rsi per**
vinto to give in; **può** ~**rsi** maybe, perhaps;
si dà il caso che ... it so happens that ...;
darsela a gambe to take to one's heels; **il**
~ **e l'avere** (*ECON*) debits and credits *pl*.
Dar-es-Sa'laam *sf* Dar-es-Salaam.
'darsena *sf* dock.
'data *sf* date; **in** ~ **da destinarsi** on a date
still to be announced; **in** ~ **odierna** as of
today; **amicizia di lunga** *o* **vecchia** ~ long-
standing friendship; ~ **di emissione** date
of issue; ~ **di nascita** date of birth; ~ **di**
scadenza expiry date; ~ **limite d'utilizzo** *o*
di consumo (*COMM*) best-before date.
da'tare *vt* to date ♦ *vi*: ~ **da** to date from.
da'tato, a *ag* dated.
da'tivo *sm* dative.

'dato, a *ag* (*stabilito*) given ♦ *sm* datum; **~i** *smpl* data *pl*; **~ che** given that; **in ~i casi** in certain cases; **è un ~ di fatto** it's a fact.

da'tore, 'trice *sm/f*: **~ di lavoro** employer.

'dattero *sm* date (*BOT*).

dattilogra'fare *vt* to type.

dattilogra'fia *sf* typing.

datti'lografo, a *sm/f* typist.

dattilos'critto *sm* typescript.

da'vanti *av* in front; (*dirimpetto*) opposite ♦ *ag inv* front ♦ *sm* front; **~ a** *prep* in front of; (*dirimpetto a*) facing, opposite; (*in presenza di*) before, in front of.

davan'zale [davan'tsale] *sm* windowsill.

da'vanzo, d'a'vanzo [da'vantso] *av* more than enough.

dav'vero *av* really, indeed; **dico ~** I mean it.

dazi'ario, a [dat'tsjarjo] *ag* excise *cpd*.

'dazio ['dattsjo] *sm* (*somma*) duty; (*luogo*) customs *pl*; **~ d'importazione** import duty.

db *abbr* (= *decibel*) dB.

DC *sigla f* = **Democrazia Cristiana** (*former political party*).

d.C. *av abbr* (= *dopo Cristo*) A.D.

D.D.T. *abbr m* (= *dicloro-difenil-tricloroetano*) D.D.T.

'dea *sf* goddess.

'debbo *etc vb vedi* **dovere**.

debel'lare *vt* to overcome, conquer.

debili'tare *vt* to debilitate.

debita'mente *av* duly, properly.

'debito, a *ag* due, proper ♦ *sm* debt; (*COMM: dare*) debit; **a tempo ~** at the right time; **portare a ~ di qn** to debit sb with; **~ consolidato** consolidated debt; **~ d'imposta** tax liability; **~ pubblico** national debt.

debi'tore, 'trice *sm/f* debtor.

'debole *ag* weak, feeble; (*suono*) faint; (*luce*) dim ♦ *sm* weakness.

debo'lezza [debo'lettsa] *sf* weakness.

debut'tante *sm/f* (*gen*) beginner, novice; (*TEAT*) actor/actress at the beginning of his (*o* her) career.

debut'tare *vi* to make one's début.

de'butto *sm* début.

'decade *sf* period of ten days.

deca'dente *ag* decadent.

deca'denza [deka'dɛntsa] *sf* decline; (*DIR*) loss, forfeiture.

deca'dere *vi* to decline.

deca'duto, a *ag* (*persona*) impoverished; (*norma*) lapsed.

decaffei'nato, a *ag* decaffeinated.

de'calogo *sm* (*fig*) rulebook.

de'cano *sm* (*REL*) dean.

decan'tare *vt* (*virtù, bravura etc*) to praise;

(*persona*) to sing the praises of.

decapi'tare *vt* to decapitate, behead.

decappot'tabile *ag, sf* convertible.

dece'duto, a [detʃe'duto] *ag* deceased.

decele'rare [detʃele'rare] *vt, vi* to decelerate, slow down.

decen'nale [detʃen'nale] *ag* (*che dura 10 anni*) ten-year *cpd*; (*che ricorre ogni 10 anni*) ten-yearly, every ten years ♦ *sm* (*ricorrenza*) tenth anniversary.

de'cenne [de'tʃɛnne] *ag*: **un bambino ~ a** ten-year-old child, a child of ten.

de'cennio [de'tʃɛnnjo] *sm* decade.

de'cente [de'tʃɛnte] *ag* decent, respectable, proper; (*accettabile*) satisfactory, decent.

decentraliz'zare [detʃentralid'dzare] *vt* (*AMM*) to decentralize.

decentra'mento [detʃentra'mento] *sm* decentralization.

decen'trare [detʃen'trare] *vt* to decentralize, move out of the centre.

de'cenza [de'tʃɛntsa] *sf* decency, propriety.

de'cesso [de'tʃɛsso] *sm* death; **atto di ~** death certificate.

de'cidere [de'tʃidere] *vi* to decide, make up one's mind ♦ *vt*: **~ qc** to decide on sth; (*questione, lite*) to settle sth; **~rsi** *vr*: **~rsi (a fare)** to decide (to do), make up one's mind (to do); **~ di fare/che** to decide to do/that; **~ di qc** (*sog: cosa*) to determine sth.

deci'frare [detʃi'frare] *vt* to decode; (*fig*) to decipher, make out.

de'cilitro [de'tʃilitro] *sm* decilitre (*BRIT*), deciliter (*US*).

deci'male [detʃi'male] *ag* decimal.

deci'mare [detʃi'mare] *vt* to decimate.

de'cimetro [de'tʃimetro] *sm* decimetre.

'decimo, a ['dɛtʃimo] *num* tenth.

de'cina [de'tʃina] *sf* ten; (*circa dieci*): **una ~ (di)** about ten.

de'cisi [de'tʃizi] *etc vb vedi* **decidere**.

decisio'nale [detʃizjo'nale] *ag* decision-making *cpd*.

decisi'one [detʃi'zjone] *sf* decision; **prendere una ~** to make a decision; **con ~** decisively, resolutely.

deci'sivo, a [detʃi'zivo] *ag* (*gen*) decisive; (*fattore*) deciding.

de'ciso, a [de'tʃizo] *pp di* **decidere** ♦ *ag* (*persona, carattere*) determined; (*tono*) firm, resolute.

declas'sare *vt* to downgrade; to lower in status; **1ª declassata** (*FERR*) *first-class carriage which may be used by second-class passengers*.

decli'nare *vi* (*pendio*) to slope down; (*fig:*

diminuire) to decline; (*tramontare*) to set, go down ♦ *vt* to decline; ~ **le proprie generalità** (*fig*) to give one's particulars; ~ **ogni responsabilità** to disclaim all responsibility.

declinazi'one [deklinat'tsjone] *sf* (*LING*) declension.

de'clino *sm* decline.

de'clivio *sm* (downward) slope.

decodifi'care *vt* to decode.

decodifica'tore *sm* decoder.

decol'lare *vi* (*AER*) to take off.

décolleté [dekol'te] *ag inv* (*abito*) low-necked, low-cut ♦ *sm* (*di abito*) low neckline; (*di donna*) cleavage.

de'collo *sm* take-off.

decolo'rare *vt* to bleach.

decom'porre *vt*, **decomporsi** *vr* to decompose.

decomposizi'one [dekompozit'tsjone] *sf* decomposition.

decom'posto, a *pp di* **decomporre**.

decompressi'one *sf* decompression.

deconge'lare [dekondʒe'lare] *vt* to defrost.

decongestio'nare [dekondʒestjo'nare] *vt* (*MED, traffico*) to relieve congestion in.

deco'rare *vt* to decorate.

decora'tivo, a *ag* decorative.

decora'tore, 'trice *smlf* (interior) decorator.

decorazi'one [dekorat'tsjone] *sf* decoration.

de'coro *sm* decorum.

deco'roso, a *ag* decorous, dignified.

decor'renza [dekor'rɛntsa] *sf*: **con ~ da** (as) from.

de'correre *vi* to pass, elapse; (*avere effetto*) to run, have effect.

de'corso, a *pp di* **decorrere** ♦ *sm* (*evoluzione: anche MED*) course.

de'crebbi *etc vb vedi* **decrescere**.

de'crepito, a *ag* decrepit.

de'crescere [de'kreʃʃere] *vi* (*diminuire*) to decrease, diminish; (*acque*) to subside, go down; (*prezzi*) to go down.

decresci'uto, a [dekreʃ'ʃuto] *pp di* **decrescere**.

decre'tare *vt* (*norma*) to decree; (*mobilitazione*) to order; ~ **lo stato d'emergenza** to declare a state of emergency; ~ **la nomina di qn** to decide on the appointment of sb.

de'creto *sm* decree; ~ **legge** *decree with the force of law*; ~ **di sfratto** eviction order.

decur'tare *vt* (*debito, somma*) to reduce.

decurtazi'one [dekurtat'tsjone] *sf* reduction.

'dedalo *sm* maze, labyrinth.

'dedica, che *sf* dedication.

dedi'care *vt* to dedicate; ~**rsi** *vr*: ~**rsi a** (*votarsi*) to devote o.s. to.

dedicherò *etc* [dedike'rɔ] *vb vedi* **dedicare**.

'dedito, a *ag*: ~ **a** (*studio etc*) dedicated *o* devoted to; (*vizio*) addicted to.

de'dotto, a *pp di* **dedurre**.

de'duco *etc vb vedi* **dedurre**.

de'durre *vt* (*concludere*) to deduce; (*defalcare*) to deduct.

de'dussi *etc vb vedi* **dedurre**.

deduzi'one [dedut'tsjone] *sf* deduction.

defal'care *vt* to deduct.

defenes'trare *vt* to throw out of the window; (*fig*) to remove from office.

defe'rente *ag* respectful, deferential.

defe'rire *vt* (*DIR*): ~ **a** to refer to.

defezi'one [defet'tsjone] *sf* defection, desertion.

defici'ente [defi'tʃɛnte] *ag* (*mancante*): ~ **di** deficient in; (*insufficiente*) insufficient ♦ *smlf* mental defective; (*peg: cretino*) idiot.

defici'enza [defi'tʃɛntsa] *sf* deficiency; (*carenza*) shortage; (*fig: lacuna*) weakness.

'deficit ['dɛfitʃit] *sm inv* (*ECON*) deficit.

defi'nire *vt* to define; (*risolvere*) to settle; (*questione*) to finalize.

defini'tivo, a *ag* definitive, final ♦ *sf*: **in ~a** (*dopotutto*) when all is said and done; (*dunque*) well then.

defi'nito, a *ag* definite; **ben ~** clear, clear cut.

definizi'one [definit'tsjone] *sf* (*gen*) definition; (*di disputa, vertenza*) settlement; (*di tempi, obiettivi*) establishment.

deflagrazi'one [deflagrat'tsjone] *sf* explosion.

deflazi'one [deflat'tsjone] *sf* (*ECON*) deflation.

deflet'tore *sm* (*AUT*) quarterlight (*BRIT*), deflector (*US*).

deflu'ire *vi*: ~ **da** (*liquido*) to flow away from; (*fig: capitali*) to flow out of.

de'flusso *sm* (*della marea*) ebb.

defor'mare *vt* (*alterare*) to put out of shape; (*corpo*) to deform; (*pensiero, fatto*) to distort; ~**rsi** *vr* to lose its shape.

deformazi'one [deformat'tsjone] *sf* (*MED*) deformation; **questa è ~ professionale!** that's force of habit because of your (*o* his *etc*) job!

de'forme *ag* deformed; disfigured.

deformità *sf inv* deformity.

defrau'dare *vt*: ~ **qn di qc** to defraud sb of sth, cheat sb out of sth.

de'funto, a *ag* late *cpd* ♦ *sm/f* deceased.

degene'rare [dedʒene'rare] *vi* to degenerate.

degenerazi'one [dedʒenerat'tsjone] *sf* degeneration.

de'genere [de'dʒɛnere] *ag* degenerate.

de'gente [de'dʒɛnte] *sm/f* bedridden person; (*ricoverato in ospedale*) in-patient.

de'genza [de'dʒɛntsa] *sf* confinement to bed; ~ ospedaliera period in hospital.

'degli ['deʎʎi] *prep* + *det vedi* di.

deglu'tire *vt* to swallow.

de'gnare [deɲ'ɲare] *vt*: ~ qn della propria presenza to honour sb with one's presence; ~rsi *vr*: ~rsi di fare qc to deign *o* condescend to do sth; non mi ha degnato di uno sguardo he wouldn't even look at me.

'degno, a ['deɲɲo] *ag* dignified; ~ di worthy of; ~ di lode praiseworthy.

degra'dare *vt* (MIL) to demote; (*privare della dignità*) to degrade; ~rsi *vr* to demean o.s.

de'grado *sm*: ~ urbano urban decline.

degus'tare *vt* to sample, taste.

degustazi'one [degustat'tsjone] *sf* sampling, tasting; ~ di vini (*locale*) specialist wine bar; ~ di caffè (*locale*) specialist coffee shop.

'dei *smpl di* dio ♦ *prep* + *det vedi* di.

del *prep* + *det vedi* di.

dela'tore, 'trice *sm/f* police informer.

delazi'one [delat'tsjone] *sf* informing.

'delega, ghe *sf* (*procura*) proxy; per ~ notarile ≈ through a solicitor (BRIT) *o* lawyer.

dele'gare *vt* to delegate.

dele'gato *sm* delegate.

delegazi'one [delegat'tsjone] *sf* delegation.

delegherò *etc* [delege'rɔ] *vb vedi* delegare.

dele'terio, a *ag* deleterious, noxious.

del'fino *sm* (ZOOL) dolphin; (STORIA) dauphin; (*fig*) probable successor.

'Delhi ['dɛli] *sf* Delhi.

de'libera *sf* decision.

delibe'rare *vt* to come to a decision on ♦ *vi* (DIR): ~ (su qc) to rule (on sth).

delica'tezza [delika'tettsa] *sf* delicacy; frailty; thoughtfulness; tactfulness.

deli'cato, a *ag* delicate; (*salute*) delicate, frail; (*fig: gentile*) thoughtful, considerate; (: *che dimostra tatto*) tactful.

delimi'tare *vt* (*anche fig*) to delimit.

deline'are *vt* to outline; ~rsi *vr* to be outlined; (*fig*) to emerge.

delin'quente *sm/f* criminal, delinquent.

delin'quenza [delin'kwɛntsa] *sf* criminality, delinquency; ~ minorile juvenile delinquency.

de'liquio *sm* (MED) swoon; cadere in ~ to swoon.

deli'rante *ag* (MED) delirious; (*fig: folla*) frenzied; (: *discorso, mente*) insane.

deli'rare *vi* to be delirious, rave; (*fig*) to rave.

de'lirio *sm* delirium; (*ragionamento insensato*) raving; (*fig*): andare/mandare in ~ to go/send into a frenzy.

de'litto *sm* crime; ~ d'onore *crime committed to avenge one's honour.*

delittu'oso, a *ag* criminal.

de'lizia [de'littsja] *sf* delight.

delizi'are [delit'tsjare] *vt* to delight; ~rsi *vr*: ~rsi di qc/a fare qc to take delight in sth/ in doing sth.

delizi'oso, a [delit'tsjoso] *ag* delightful; (*cibi*) delicious.

dell', 'della, 'delle, 'dello *prep* + *det vedi* di.

'delta *sm inv* delta.

delta'plano *sm* hang-glider; volo col ~ hang-gliding.

delucidazi'one [delutʃidat'tsjone] *sf* clarification *no pl.*

delu'dente *ag* disappointing.

de'ludere *vt* to disappoint.

delusi'one *sf* disappointment.

de'luso, a *pp di* deludere ♦ *ag* disappointed.

dema'gogico, a, ci, che [dema'gɔdʒiko] *ag* popularity-seeking, demagogic.

dema'gogo, ghi *sm* demagogue.

de'manio *sm* state property.

de'mente *ag* (MED) demented, mentally deranged; (*fig*) crazy, mad.

de'menza [de'mɛntsa] *sf* dementia; madness; ~ senile senile dementia.

demenzi'ale [demen'tsjale] *ag* (*fig*) off-the-wall.

'demmo *vb vedi* dare.

demo'cratico, a, ci, che *ag* democratic.

democra'zia [demokrat'tsia] *sf* democracy; la D~ Cristiana the Christian Democrat Party.

democristi'ano, a *ag*, *sm/f* Christian Democrat.

demogra'fia *sf* demography.

demo'grafico, a, ci, che *ag* demographic; incremento ~ increase in population.

demo'lire *vt* to demolish.

demolizi'one [demolit'tsjone] *sf* demolition.

'demone *sm* demon.

de'monio *sm* demon, devil; il D~ the Devil.

demoniz'zare [demonid'dzare] *vt* to make a monster of.

demonizzazi'one [demoniddzat'tsjone] *sf* demonizing, demonization.

demoraliz'zare [demoralid'dzare] *vt* to demoralize; **~rsi** *vr* to become demoralized.

de'mordere *vi*: **non ~ (da)** to refuse to give up.

demoti'vare *vt*: **~ qn** to take away sb's motivation.

demoti'vato, a *ag* unmotivated, lacking motivation.

de'naro *sm* money; **~i** *smpl* (*CARTE*) *suit in Neapolitan pack of cards*.

denatu'rato, a *ag vedi* **alcool**.

deni'grare *vt* to denigrate, run down.

denomi'nare *vt* to name; **~rsi** *vr* to be named *o* called.

denomina'tore *sm* (*MAT*) denominator.

denominazi'one [denominat'tsjone] *sf* name; denomination; **~ di origine controllata** (**D.O.C.**) *label guaranteeing the quality and origin of a wine*.

deno'tare *vt* to denote, indicate.

densità *sf inv* density; (*di nebbia*) thickness, denseness; **ad alta/bassa ~ di popolazione** densely/sparsely populated.

'denso, a *ag* thick, dense.

den'tale *ag* dental.

den'tario, a *ag* dental.

denta'tura *sf* set of teeth, teeth *pl*; (*TECN: di ruota*) serration.

'dente *sm* tooth; (*di forchetta*) prong; (*GEO: cima*) jagged peak; **al ~** (*CUC: pasta*) *cooked so as to be firm when eaten*; **mettere i ~i** to teethe; **mettere qc sotto i ~i** to have a bite to eat; **avere il ~ avvelenato contro** *o* **con qn** to bear sb a grudge; **~ di leone** (*BOT*) dandelion; **~i del giudizio** wisdom teeth.

'dentice ['dɛntitʃe] *sm* (*ZOOL*) sea bream.

denti'era *sf* (set of) false teeth *pl*.

denti'fricio [denti'fritʃo] *sm* toothpaste.

den'tista, i, e *sm/f* dentist.

'dentro *av* inside; (*in casa*) indoors; (*fig: nell'intimo*) inwardly ♦ *prep*: **~ (a)** in; **piegato in ~** folded over; **qui/là ~** in here/there; **~ di sé** (*pensare, brontolare*) to oneself; **tenere tutto ~** to keep everything bottled up (inside o.s.); **darci ~** (*fig fam*) to slog away, work hard.

denucleariz'zato, a [denuklearid'dzato] *ag* denuclearized, nuclear-free.

denu'dare *vt* (*persona*) to strip; (*parte del corpo*) to bare; **~rsi** *vr* to strip.

de'nuncia, ce *o* **cie** [de'nuntʃa], **de'nunzia** [de'nuntsja] *sf* denunciation; declaration; **fare una ~** *o* **sporgere ~ contro qn** (*DIR*) to report sb to the police; **~ del reddito** (income) tax return.

denunci'are [denun'tʃare], **denunzi'are**

[denun'tsjare] *vt* to denounce; (*dichiarare*) to declare; **~ qn/qc (alla polizia)** to report sb/sth to the police.

denu'trito, a *ag* undernourished.

denutrizi'one [denutrit'tsjone] *sf* malnutrition.

deodo'rante *sm* deodorant.

deontolo'gia [deontolo'dʒia] *sf* (*professionale*) professional code of conduct.

depenalizzazi'one [depenaliddzat'tsjone] *sf* decriminalization.

dépen'dance [depã'dãs] *sf inv* outbuilding.

depe'ribile *ag* perishable; **merce ~** perishables *pl*, perishable goods *pl*.

deperi'mento *sm* (*di persona*) wasting away; (*di merci*) deterioration.

depe'rire *vi* to waste away.

depi'lare *vt* to depilate.

depila'torio, a *ag* hair-removing, depilatory ♦ *sm* hair remover, depilatory.

depilazi'one [depilat'tsjone] *sf* hair removal, depilation.

depis'taggio [depis'taddʒo] *sm* diversion.

depis'tare *vt* to set on the wrong track.

dépli'ant [depli'ã] *sm inv* leaflet; (*opuscolo*) brochure.

deplo'rare *vt* to deplore; to lament.

deplo'revole *ag* deplorable.

de'pone, de'pongo *etc vb vedi* **deporre**.

de'porre *vt* (*depositare*) to put down; (*rimuovere: da una carica*) to remove; (: *re*) to depose; (*DIR*) to testify; **~ le armi** (*MIL*) to lay down arms; **~ le uova** to lay eggs.

depor'tare *vt* to deport.

depor'tato, a *sm/f* deportee.

deportazi'one [deportat'tsjone] *sf* deportation.

de'posi *etc vb vedi* **deporre**.

deposi'tante *sm* (*COMM*) depositor.

deposi'tare *vt* (*gen, GEO, ECON*) to deposit; (*lasciare*) to leave; (*merci*) to store; **~rsi** *vr* (*sabbia, polvere*) to settle.

deposi'tario *sm* (*COMM*) depository.

de'posito *sm* deposit; (*luogo*) warehouse; depot; (: *MIL*) depot; **~ bagagli** left-luggage office; **~ di munizioni** ammunition dump.

deposizi'one [depozit'tsjone] *sf* deposition; (*da una carica*) removal; **rendere una falsa ~** to perjure o.s.

de'posto, a *pp di* **deporre**.

depra'vare *vt* to corrupt, pervert.

depra'vato, a *ag* depraved ♦ *sm/f* degenerate.

depre'care *vt* to deprecate, deplore.

depre'dare *vt* to rob, plunder.

depressi'one *sf* depression; **area** *o* **zona di**

~ (*METEOR*) area of low pressure; (*ECON*) depressed area.

de'presso, a *pp di* **deprimere ♦** *ag* depressed.

deprezza'mento [deprettsa'mento] *sm* depreciation.

deprez'zare [depret'tsare] *vt* (*ECON*) to depreciate.

depri'mente *ag* depressing.

de'primere *vt* to depress.

depu'rare *vt* to purify.

depura'tore *sm*: ~ **d'acqua** water purifier; ~ **di gas** scrubber.

depu'tato, a *sm/f* (*POL*) deputy, ≈ Member of Parliament (*BRIT*), ≈ Congressman/ woman (*US*); *vedi anche* **Camera dei Deputati**.

deputazi'one [deputat'tsjone] *sf* deputation; (*POL*) position of deputy, ≈ parliamentary seat (*BRIT*), ≈ seat in Congress (*US*).

deraglia'mento [deraʎʎa'mento] *sm* derailment.

deragli'are [deraʎ'ʎare] *vi* to be derailed; **far** ~ to derail.

dera'pare *vi* (*veicolo*) to skid; (*SCI*) to sideslip.

derattizzazi'one [derattiddzat'tsjone] *sf* rodent control.

deregolamen'tare *vt* to deregulate.

deregolamentazi'one [deregolamentat'tsjone] *sf* deregulation.

dere'litto, a *ag* derelict.

dere'tano *sm* (*fam*) bottom, buttocks *pl.*

de'ridere *vt* to mock, deride.

de'risi *etc vb vedi* **deridere**.

derisi'one *sf* derision, mockery.

de'riso, a *pp di* **deridere**.

deri'sorio, a *ag* (*gesto, tono*) mocking.

de'riva *sf* (*NAUT, AER*) drift; (*dispositivo*: *AER*) fin; (: *NAUT*) centre-board (*BRIT*), centerboard (*US*); **andare alla** ~ (*anche fig*) to drift.

deri'vare *vi*: ~ **da** to derive from ♦ *vt* to derive; (*corso d'acqua*) to divert.

deri'vato, a *ag* derived ♦ *sm* (*CHIM, LING*) derivative; (*prodotto*) by-product.

derivazi'one [derivat'tsjone] *sf* derivation; diversion.

derma'tite *sf* dermatitis.

dermatolo'gia [dermatolo'dʒia] *sf* dermatology.

derma'tologo, a, gi, ghe *sm/f* dermatologist.

dermoprotet'tivo, a *ag* (*crema, azione*) protecting the skin.

'deroga, ghe *sf* (special) dispensation; **in** ~ **a** as a (special) dispensation to.

dero'gare *vi*: ~ **a** (*DIR*) to repeal in part.

der'rate *sfpl* commodities; ~ **alimentari** foodstuffs.

deru'bare *vt* to rob.

des'critto, a *pp di* **descrivere**.

des'crivere *vt* to describe.

descrizi'one [deskrit'tsjone] *sf* description.

de'serto, a *ag* deserted ♦ *sm* (*GEO*) desert; **isola** ~**a** desert island.

deside'rabile *ag* desirable.

deside'rare *vt* to want, wish for; (*sessualmente*) to desire; ~ **fare/che qn faccia** to want *o* wish to do/sb to do; **desidera fare una passeggiata?** would you like to go for a walk?; **farsi** ~ (*fare il prezioso*) to play hard to get; (*farsi aspettare*) to take one's time; **lascia molto a** ~ it leaves a lot to be desired.

desi'derio *sm* wish; (*più intenso, carnale*) desire.

deside'roso, a *ag*: ~ **di** longing *o* eager for.

desi'gnare [desiɲ'ɲare] *vt* to designate, appoint; (*data*) to fix; **la vittima designata** the intended victim.

designazi'one [desiɲɲat'tsjone] *sf* designation, appointment.

desi'nare *vi* to dine, have dinner ♦ *sm* dinner.

desi'nenza [dezi'nɛntsa] *sf* (*LING*) ending, inflexion.

de'sistere *vi*: ~ **da** to give up, desist from.

desis'tito, a *pp di* **desistere**.

deso'lante *ag* distressing.

deso'lato, a *ag* (*paesaggio*) desolate; (*persona: spiacente*) sorry.

desolazi'one [dezolat'tsjone] *sf* desolation.

'despota, i *sm* despot.

'dessi *etc vb vedi* **dare**.

destabiliz'zare [destabilid'dzare] *vt* to destabilize.

des'tare *vt* to wake (up); (*fig*) to awaken, arouse; ~**rsi** *vr* to wake (up).

'deste *etc vb vedi* **dare**.

desti'nare *vt* to destine; (*assegnare*) to appoint, assign; (*indirizzare*) to address; ~ **qc a qn** to intend to give sth to sb, intend sb to have sth.

destina'tario, a *sm/f* (*di lettera*) addressee; (*di merce*) consignee; (*di mandato*) payee.

destinazi'one [destinat'tsjone] *sf* destination; (*uso*) purpose.

des'tino *sm* destiny, fate.

destitu'ire *vt* to dismiss, remove.

destituzi'one [destitut'tsjone] *sf* dismissal, removal.

'desto, a *ag* (wide) awake.

'destra *sf vedi* **destro**.

destreggi'arsi [destred'dʒarsi] *vr* to manoeuvre (*BRIT*), maneuver (*US*).

des'trezza [des'trettsa] *sf* skill, dexterity.

'destro, a *ag* right, right-hand; (*abile*) skilful (*BRIT*), skillful (*US*), adroit ♦ *sf* (*mano*) right hand; (*parte*) right (side); (*POL*): **la ~a** the right ♦ *sm* (*BOXE*) right; **a ~a** (*essere*) on the right; (*andare*) to the right; **tenere la ~a** to keep to the right.

de'sumere *vt* (*dedurre*) to infer, deduce; (*trarre: informazioni*) to obtain.

de'sunto, a *pp di* **desumere**.

detas'sare *vt* to remove the duty (*o* tax) from.

dete'nere *vt* (*incarico, primato*) to hold; (*proprietà*) to have, possess; (*in prigione*) to detain, hold.

de'tengo, de'tenni *etc vb vedi* **detenere**.

deten'tivo, a *ag*: **mandato ~** imprisonment order; **pena ~a** a prison sentence.

deten'tore, 'trice *sm/f* (*di titolo, primato etc*) holder.

dete'nuto, a *sm/f* prisoner.

detenzi'one [deten'tsjone] *sf* holding; possession; detention.

deter'gente [deter'dʒɛnte] *ag* detergent; (*crema, latte*) cleansing ♦ *sm* detergent.

de'tergere [de'tɛrdʒere] *vt* (*gen*) to clean; (*pelle, viso*) to cleanse; (*sudore*) to wipe (away).

deteriora'mento *sm*: **~ (di)** deterioration (in).

deterio'rare *vt* to damage; **~rsi** *vr* to deteriorate.

deteri'ore *ag* (*merce*) second-rate; (*significato*) pejorative; (*tradizione letteraria*) lesser, minor.

determi'nante *ag* decisive, determining.

determi'nare *vt* to determine.

determina'tivo, a *ag* determining; **articolo ~** (*LING*) definite article.

determi'nato, a *ag* (*gen*) certain; (*particolare*) specific; (*risoluto*) determined, resolute.

determinazi'one [determinat'tsjone] *sf* determination; (*decisione*) decision.

deter'rente *ag, sm* deterrent.

deterrò *etc vb vedi* **detenere**.

deter'sivo *sm* detergent; (*per bucato: in polvere*) washing powder (*BRIT*), soap powder.

de'terso, a *pp di* **detergere**.

detes'tare *vt* to detest, hate.

deti'ene *etc vb vedi* **detenere**.

deto'nare *vi* to detonate.

detona'tore *sm* detonator.

detonazi'one [detonat'tsjone] *sf* (*di*
esplosivo*) detonation, explosion; (*di arma*) bang; (*di motore*) pinking (*BRIT*), knocking.

de'trae, de'traggo *etc vb vedi* **detrarre**.

de'trarre *vt*: **~ (da)** to deduct (from), take away (from).

de'trassi *etc vb vedi* **detrarre**.

de'tratto, a *pp di* **detrarre**.

detrazi'one [detrat'tsjone] *sf* deduction; **~ d'imposta** tax allowance.

detri'mento *sm* detriment, harm; **a ~ di** to the detriment of.

de'trito *sm* (*GEO*) detritus.

detroniz'zare [detronid'dzare] *vt* to dethrone.

'detta *sf*: **a ~ di** according to.

dettagli'ante [dettaʎ'ʎante] *sm/f* (*COMM*) retailer.

dettagli'are [dettaʎ'ʎare] *vt* to detail, give full details of.

dettaglia'mente [dettaʎʎata'mente] *av* in detail.

det'taglio [det'taʎʎo] *sm* detail; (*COMM*): **il ~** retail; **al ~** (*COMM*) retail; separately.

det'tame *sm* dictate, precept.

det'tare *vt* to dictate; **~ legge** (*fig*) to lay down the law.

det'tato *sm* dictation.

detta'tura *sf* dictation.

'detto, a *pp di* **dire** ♦ *ag* (*soprannominato*) called, known as; (*già nominato*) above-mentioned ♦ *sm* saying; **~ fatto** no sooner said than done; **presto ~!** it's easier said than done!

detur'pare *vt* to disfigure; (*moralmente*) to sully.

devas'tante *ag* (*anche fig*) devastating.

devas'tare *vt* to devastate; (*fig*) to ravage.

devastazi'one [devastat'tsjone] *sf* devastation, destruction.

devi'are *vi*: **~ (da)** to turn off (from) ♦ *vt* to divert.

devi'ato, a *ag* (*fig: persona, organizzazione*) corrupt, bent (*col*).

deviazi'one [devjat'tsjone] *sf* (*anche AUT*) diversion; **fare una ~** to make a detour.

'devo *etc vb vedi* **dovere**.

devo'luto, a *pp di* **devolvere**.

devoluzi'one [devolut'tsjone] *sf* (*DIR*) devolution, transfer.

de'volvere *vt* (*DIR*) to transfer, devolve; **~ qc in beneficenza** to give sth to charity.

de'voto, a *ag* (*REL*) devout, pious; (*affezionato*) devoted.

devozi'one [devot'tsjone] *sf* devoutness; (*anche REL*) devotion.

dg *abbr* (= *decigrammo*) dg.

================= *PAROLA CHIAVE*

di (*di* + *il* = **del**, *di* + *lo* = **dello**, *di* + *l'*
= **dell'**, *di* + *la* = **della**, *di* + *i* = **dei**, *di* + *gli*
= **degli**, *di* + *le* = **delle**) *prep* 1 (*possesso,
specificazione*) of; (*composto da, scritto da*)
by; **la macchina ~ Paolo/~ mio fratello**
Paolo's/my brother's car; **un amico ~ mio
fratello** a friend of my brother's, one of
my brother's friends; **la grandezza della
casa** the size of the house; **le foto delle
vacanze** the holiday photos; **la città ~
Firenze** the city of Florence; **il nome ~
Maria** the name Mary; **un quadro ~
Botticelli** a painting by Botticelli
2 (*caratterizzazione, misura*) of; **una casa ~
mattoni** a brick house, a house made of
bricks; **un orologio d'oro** a gold watch; **un
bimbo ~ 3 anni** a child of 3, a 3-year-old
child; **una trota ~ un chilo** a trout
weighing a kilo; **una strada ~ 10 km** a
road 10 km long; **un quadro ~ valore** a
valuable picture
3 (*causa, mezzo, modo*) with; **tremare ~
paura** to tremble with fear; **morire ~
cancro** to die of cancer; **spalmare ~ burro**
to spread with butter
4 (*argomento*) about, of; **discutere ~ sport**
to talk about sport; **parlare ~ politica/
lavoro** to talk about politics/work
5 (*luogo: provenienza*) from; out of; **essere
~ Roma** to be from Rome; **uscire ~ casa**
to come out of o leave the house
6 (*tempo*) in; **d'estate/d'inverno** in (the)
summer/winter; **~ notte** by night, at
night; **~ mattina/sera** in the morning/
evening; **~ lunedì** on Mondays; **~ ora in
ora** by the hour
7 (*partitivo*) of; **alcuni ~ voi/noi** some of
you/us; **il più bravo ~ tutti** the best of all;
il migliore del mondo the best in the
world; **non c'è niente ~ peggio** there's
nothing worse
8 (*paragone*) than; **più veloce ~ me** faster
than me; **guadagna meno ~ me** he earns
less than me
♦ *det* (*una certa quantità di*) some;
(: *negativo*) any; (: *interrogativo*) any, some;
del pane (some) bread; **delle caramelle**
(some) sweets; **degli amici miei** some
friends of mine; **vuoi del vino?** do you
want some *o* any wine?

dì *sm* day; **buon ~!** hallo!; **a ~ =** **addì**.
DIA *sigla f* = *Direzione investigativa antimafia*.
dia'bete *sm* diabetes *sg*.
dia'betico, a, ci, che *ag, sm/f* diabetic.
dia'bolico, a, ci, che *ag* diabolical.

di'acono *sm* (*REL*) deacon.
dia'dema, i *sm* diadem; (*di donna*) tiara.
di'afano, a *ag* (*trasparente*) diaphanous;
(*pelle*) transparent.
dia'framma, i *sm* (*divisione*) screen; (*ANAT,
FOT, contraccettivo*) diaphragm.
di'agnosi [di'aɲɲozi] *sf* diagnosis *sg*.
diagnosti'care [diaɲɲosti'kare] *vt* to
diagnose.
dia'gnostico, a, ci, che [diaɲ'nɔstiko] *ag*
diagnostic; **aiuti ~ci** (*INFORM*) debugging
aids.
diago'nale *ag, sf* diagonal.
dia'gramma, i *sm* diagram; **~ a barre** bar
chart; **~ di flusso** flow chart.
dialet'tale *ag* dialectal; **poesia ~** poetry in
dialect.
dia'letto *sm* dialect.
di'alisi *sf* dialysis.
dialo'gante *ag*: **unità ~** (*INFORM*)
interactive terminal.
dialo'gare *vi*: **~ (con)** to have a dialogue
(with); (*conversare*) to converse (with)
♦ *vt* (*scena*) to write the dialogue for.
di'alogo, ghi *sm* dialogue.
dia'mante *sm* diamond.
di'ametro *sm* diameter.
di'amine *escl*: **che ~ ...?** what on
earth ...?
diaposi'tiva *sf* transparency, slide.
di'aria *sf* daily (expense) allowance.
di'ario *sm* diary; **~ di bordo** (*NAUT*)
log(book); **~ di classe** (*INS*) class register;
~ degli esami (*INS*) exam timetable.
diar'rea *sf* diarrhoea.
dia'triba *sf* diatribe.
diavole'ria *sf* (*azione*) act of mischief;
(*aggeggio*) weird contraption.
di'avolo *sm* devil; **è un buon ~** he's a good
sort; **avere un ~ per capello** to be in a foul
temper; **avere una fame/un freddo del ~**
to be ravenously hungry/frozen stiff;
mandare qn al ~ (*fam*) to tell sb to go to
hell; **fare il ~ a quattro** to kick up a fuss.
di'battere *vt* to debate, discuss; **~rsi** *vr* to
struggle.
dibatti'mento *sm* (*dibattito*) debate,
discussion; (*DIR*) hearing.
di'battito *sm* debate, discussion.
dic. *abbr* (= *dicembre*) Dec.
dicas'tero *sm* ministry.
'dice ['ditʃe] *vb vedi* **dire**.
di'cembre [di'tʃɛmbre] *sm* December; *per
fraseologia vedi* **luglio**.
dice'ria [ditʃe'ria] *sf* rumour (*BRIT*), rumor
(*US*), piece of gossip.
dichia'rare [dikja'rare] *vt* to declare; **~rsi** *vr*
to declare o.s.; (*innamorato*) to declare

one's love; **si dichiara che ...** it is hereby declared that ...; **~rsi vinto** to admit defeat.

dichia'rato, a [dikja'rato] *ag* (*nemico, ateo*) avowed.

dichiarazi'one [dikjarat'tsjone] *sf* declaration; ~ **dei redditi** statement of income; (*modulo*) tax return.

dician'nove [ditʃan'nɔve] *num* nineteen.

dicianno'venne [ditʃanno'vɛnne] *ag, sm/f* nineteen-year-old.

dicias'sette [ditʃas'sɛtte] *num* seventeen.

diciasset'tenne [ditʃasset'tɛnne] *ag, sm/f* seventeen-year-old.

diciot'tenne [ditʃot'tɛnne] *ag, sm/f* eighteen-year-old.

dici'otto [di'tʃɔtto] *num* eighteen ♦ *sm inv* (*INS*) *minimum satisfactory mark awarded in Italian universities*.

dici'tura [ditʃi'tura] *sf* words *pl*, wording.

'**dico** *etc vb vedi* **dire**.

didasca'lia *sf* (*di illustrazione*) caption; (*CINE*) subtitle; (*TEAT*) stage directions *pl*.

di'dattico, a, ci, che *ag* didactic; (*metodo, programma*) teaching; (*libro*) educational ♦ *sf* didactics *sg*; teaching methodology.

di'dentro *av* inside, indoors.

didi'etro *av* behind ♦ *ag inv* (*ruota, giardino*) back, rear *cpd* ♦ *sm* (*di casa*) rear; (*fam: sedere*) backside.

di'eci ['djɛtʃi] *num* ten.

dieci'mila [djɛtʃi'mila] *num* ten thousand.

die'cina [dje'tʃina] *sf* = **decina**.

di'edi *etc vb vedi* **dare**.

di'eresi *sf* dieresis *sg*.

'**diesel** ['di:zəl] *sm inv* diesel engine.

dies'sino, a *ag* (*POL*) of *o* belonging to the Democrats of the Left (*Italian left-wing party*).

di'eta *sf* diet; **essere a** ~ to be on a diet.

die'tetica *sf* dietetics *sg*.

die'tologo, a, gi, ghe *sm/f* dietician.

di'etro *av* behind; (*in fondo*) at the back ♦ *prep* behind; (*tempo: dopo*) after ♦ *sm* (*di foglio, giacca*) back; (*di casa*) back, rear ♦ *ag inv* back *cpd*; **le zampe di** ~ the hind legs; ~ **ricevuta** against receipt; ~ **richiesta** on demand; (*scritta*) on application; **andare** ~ **a** (*anche fig*) to follow; **stare** ~ **a qn** (*sorvegliare*) to keep an eye on sb; (*corteggiare*) to hang around sb; **portarsi** ~ **qn/qc** to bring sb/sth with one, bring sb/sth along; **gli hanno riso/ parlato** ~ they laughed at/talked about him behind his back.

di'etro 'front *escl* about turn! (*BRIT*), about face! (*US*) ♦ *sm* (*MIL*) about-turn, about-face; (*fig*) volte-face, about-turn, about-

face; **fare** ~ (*MIL, fig*) to about-turn, about-face; (*tornare indietro*) to turn round.

di'fatti *cong* in fact, as a matter of fact.

di'fendere *vt* to defend; **~rsi** *vr* (*cavarsela*) to get by; **~rsi da/contro** to defend o.s. from/against; **~rsi dal freddo** to protect o.s. from the cold; **sapersi** ~ to know how to look after o.s.

difen'sivo, a *ag* defensive ♦ *sf*: **stare sulla** ~**a** (*anche fig*) to be on the defensive.

difen'sore, a *sm/f* defender; **avvocato** ~ counsel for the defence (*BRIT*) *o* defense (*US*).

di'fesa *sf vedi* **difeso**.

di'fesi *etc vb vedi* **difendere**.

di'feso, a *pp di* **difendere** ♦ *sf* defence (*BRIT*), defense (*US*); **prendere le** ~**e di qn** to defend sb's part.

difet'tare *vi* to be defective; ~ **di** to be lacking in, lack.

difet'tivo, a *ag* defective.

di'fetto *sm* (*mancanza*): ~ **di** lack of; (*di fabbricazione*) fault, flaw, defect; (*morale*) fault, failing, defect; (*fisico*) defect; **far** ~ to be lacking; **in** ~ at fault; in the wrong.

difet'toso, a *ag* defective, faulty.

diffa'mare *vt* (*a parole*) to slander; (*per iscritto*) to libel.

diffama'torio, a *ag* slanderous; libellous.

diffamazi'one [diffamat'tsjone] *sf* slander; libel.

diffe'rente *ag* different.

diffe'renza [diffe'rɛntsa] *sf* difference; **a** ~ **di** unlike; **non fare** ~ (**tra**) to make no distinction (between).

differenzi'ale [differen'tsjale] *ag, sm* differential; **classi** ~**i** (*INS*) special classes (*for backward children*).

differenzi'are [differen'tsjare] *vt* to differentiate; **~rsi da** to differentiate o.s. from; to differ from.

diffe'rire *vt* to postpone, defer ♦ *vi* to be different.

diffe'rita *sf*: **in** ~ (*trasmettere*) prerecorded.

dif'ficile [dif'fitʃile] *ag* difficult; (*persona*) hard to please, difficult (to please); (*poco probabile*): **è** ~ **che sia libero** it is unlikely that he'll be free ♦ *sm/f*: **fare il(la)** ~ to be difficult, be awkward ♦ *sm* difficult part; difficulty; **essere** ~ **nel mangiare** to be fussy about one's food.

difficil'mente [diffitʃil'mente] *av* (*con difficoltà*) with difficulty; ~ **verrà** he's unlikely to come.

difficoltà *sf inv* difficulty.

difficol'toso, a *ag* (*compito*) difficult, hard; (*persona*) difficult, hard to please;

digestione ~a poor digestion.

dif'fida *sf* (*DIR*) warning, notice.

diffi'dare *vi*: ~ **di** to be suspicious *o* distrustful of ♦ *vt* (*DIR*) to warn; ~ **qn dal fare qc** to warn sb not to do sth, caution sb against doing sth.

diffi'dente *ag* suspicious, distrustful.

diffi'denza [diffi'dɛntsa] *sf* suspicion, distrust.

dif'fondere *vt* (*luce, calore*) to diffuse; (*notizie*) to spread, circulate; ~**rsi** *vr* to spread.

dif'fusi *etc vb vedi* **diffondere.**

diffusi'one *sf* diffusion; spread; (*anche di giornale*) circulation; (*FISICA*) scattering.

dif'fuso, a *pp di* **diffondere** ♦ *ag* (*FISICA*) diffuse; (*notizia, malattia etc*) widespread; **è opinione** ~**a che** ... it's widely held that ....

difi'lato *av* (*direttamente*) straight, directly; (*subito*) straight away.

difte'rite *sf* diphtheria.

'diga, ghe *sf* dam; (*portuale*) breakwater.

dige'rente [didʒe'rɛnte] *ag* (*apparato*) digestive.

dige'rire [didʒe'rire] *vt* to digest.

digesti'one [didʒes'tjone] *sf* digestion.

diges'tivo, a [didʒes'tivo] *ag* digestive ♦ *sm* (*after-dinner*) liqueur.

Digi'one [di'dʒone] *sf* Dijon.

digi'tale [didʒi'tale] *ag* digital; (*delle dita*) finger *cpd*, digital ♦ *sf* (*BOT*) foxglove.

digi'tare [didʒi'tare] *vt* (*dati*) to key (in); (*tasto*) to press.

digiu'nare [didʒu'nare] *vi* to starve o.s.; (*REL*) to fast.

digi'uno, a [di'dʒuno] *ag*: **essere** ~ not to have eaten ♦ *sm* fast; **a** ~ on an empty stomach.

dignità [diɲɲi'ta] *sf inv* dignity.

digni'tario [diɲɲi'tarjo] *sm* dignitary.

digni'toso, a [diɲɲi'toso] *ag* dignified.

'DIGOS *sigla f* (= *Divisione Investigazioni Generali e Operazioni Speciali*) police department dealing with political security.

digressi'one *sf* digression.

digri'gnare [digriɲ'ɲare] *vt*: ~ **i denti** to grind one's teeth.

dila'gare *vi* to flood; (*fig*) to spread.

dilani'are *vt* to tear to pieces.

dilapi'dare *vt* to squander, waste.

dila'tare *vt* to dilate; (*gas*) to cause to expand; (*passaggio, cavità*) to open (up); ~**rsi** *vr* to dilate; (*FISICA*) to expand.

dilatazi'one [dilatat'tsjone] *sf* (*ANAT*) dilation; (*di gas, metallo*) expansion.

dilazio'nare [dilattsjo'nare] *vt* to delay, defer.

dilazi'one [dilat'tsjone] *sf* deferment.

dileggi'are [diled'dʒare] *vt* to mock, deride.

dilegu'are *vi*, ~**rsi** *vr* to vanish, disappear.

di'lemma, i *sm* dilemma.

dilet'tante *sm/f* dilettante; (*anche SPORT*) amateur.

dilet'tare *vt* to give pleasure to, delight; ~**rsi** *vr*: ~**rsi di** to take pleasure in, enjoy.

dilet'tevole *ag* delightful.

di'letto, a *ag* dear, beloved ♦ *sm* pleasure, delight.

dili'gente [dili'dʒɛnte] *ag* (*scrupoloso*) diligent; (*accurato*) careful, accurate.

dili'genza [dili'dʒɛntsa] *sf* diligence; care; (*carrozza*) stagecoach.

dilu'ire *vt* to dilute.

dilun'garsi *vr* (*fig*): ~ **su** to talk at length on *o* about.

diluvi'are *vb impers* to pour (down).

di'luvio *sm* downpour; (*inondazione, fig*) flood; **il** ~ **universale** the Flood.

dima'grante *ag* slimming *cpd*.

dima'grire *vi* to get thinner, lose weight.

dime'nare *vt* to wave, shake; ~**rsi** *vr* to toss and turn; (*fig*) to struggle; ~ **la coda** (*sog: cane*) to wag its tail.

dimensi'one *sf* dimension; (*grandezza*) size; **considerare un discorso nella sua** ~ **politica** to look at a speech in terms of its political significance.

dimenti'canza [dimenti'kantsa] *sf* forgetfulness; (*errore*) oversight, slip; **per** ~ inadvertently.

dimenti'care *vt* to forget; ~**rsi** *vr*: ~**rsi di qc** to forget sth.

dimentica'toio *sm* (*scherzoso*): **cadere/ mettere nel** ~ to sink into/consign to oblivion.

di'mentico, a, chi, che *ag*: ~ **di** (*che non ricorda*) forgetful of; (*incurante*) oblivious of, unmindful of.

di'messo, a *pp di* **dimettere** ♦ *ag* (*voce*) subdued; (*uomo, abito*) modest, humble.

dimesti'chezza [dimesti'kettsa] *sf* familiarity.

di'mettere *vt*: ~ **qn da** to dismiss sb from; (*dall'ospedale*) to discharge sb from; ~**rsi** *vr*: ~**rsi (da)** to resign (from).

dimez'zare [dimed'dzare] *vt* to halve.

diminu'ire *vt* to reduce, diminish; (*prezzi*) to bring down, reduce ♦ *vi* to decrease, diminish; (*rumore*) to die down, die away; (*prezzi*) to fall, go down.

diminu'tivo, a *ag, sm* diminutive.

diminuzi'one [diminut'tsjone] *sf* decreasing, diminishing; **in** ~ on the decrease; ~ **della produttività** fall in productivity.

di'misi *etc vb vedi* **dimettere.**

dimissio'nario, a *ag* outgoing, resigning.

dimissi'oni *sfpl* resignation *sg*; **dare** *o*
presentare le ~ to resign, hand in one's
resignation.

di'mora *sf* residence; **senza fissa** ~ of no
fixed address *o* abode.

dimo'rare *vi* to reside.

dimos'trante *sm/f* (*POL*) demonstrator.

dimos'trare *vt* to demonstrate, show;
(*provare*) to prove, demonstrate; ~**rsi** *vr*:
~**rsi molto abile** to show o.s. *o* prove to be
very clever; **non dimostra la sua età** he
doesn't look his age; **dimostra 30 anni** he
looks about 30 (years old).

dimostra'tivo, a *ag* (*anche* *LING*)
demonstrative.

dimostrazi'one [dimostrat'tsjone] *sf*
demonstration; proof.

di'namico, a, ci, che *ag* dynamic ♦ *sf*
dynamics *sg*.

dina'mismo *sm* dynamism.

dinami'tardo, a *ag*: **attentato** ~ dynamite
attack ♦ *sm/f* dynamiter.

dina'mite *sf* dynamite.

'dinamo *sf inv* dynamo.

di'nanzi [di'nantsi]: ~ **a** *prep* in front of.

dinas'tia *sf* dynasty.

dini'ego, ghi *sm* (*rifiuto*) refusal;
(*negazione*) denial.

dinocco'lato, a *ag* lanky; **camminare** ~ to
walk with a slouch.

dino'sauro *sm* dinosaur.

din'torno *av* round, (round) about; ~**i** *smpl*
outskirts; **nei** ~**i di** in the vicinity *o*
neighbourhood of.

'dio, *pl* **'dei** *sm* god; **D**~ God; **gli dei** the
gods; **si crede un** ~ he thinks he's
wonderful; **D**~ **mio!** my God!; **D**~ **ce la**
mandi buona let's hope for the best; **D**~
ce ne scampi e liberi! God forbid!

di'ocesi [di'ɔtʃezi] *sf inv* diocese.

dios'sina *sf* dioxin.

dipa'nare *vt* (*lana*) to wind into a ball; (*fig*)
to disentangle, sort out.

diparti'mento *sm* department.

dipen'dente *ag* dependent ♦ *sm/f*
employee.

dipen'denza [dipen'dɛntsa] *sf* dependence;
essere alle ~**e di qn** to be employed by sb
o in sb's employ.

di'pendere *vi*: ~ **da** to depend on;
(*finanziariamente*) to be dependent on;
(*derivare*) to come from, be due to.

di'pesi *etc vb vedi* **dipendere.**

di'peso, a *pp di* **dipendere.**

di'pingere [di'pindʒere] *vt* to paint.

di'pinsi *etc vb vedi* **dipingere.**

di'pinto, a *pp di* **dipingere** ♦ *sm* painting.

di'ploma, i *sm* diploma.

diplo'mare *vt* to award a diploma to,
graduate (*US*) ♦ *vi* to obtain a diploma,
graduate (*US*).

diplo'matico, a, ci, che *ag* diplomatic
♦ *sm* diplomat.

diplo'mato, a *ag* qualified ♦ *sm/f* qualified
person, holder of a diploma.

diploma'zia [diplomat'tsia] *sf* diplomacy.

di'porto *sm*: **imbarcazione** *f* **da** ~ pleasure
craft.

dira'dare *vt* to thin (out); (*visite*) to reduce,
make less frequent; ~**rsi** *vr* to disperse;
(*nebbia*) to clear (up).

dira'mare *vt* to issue ♦ *vi*, ~**rsi** *vr* (*strade*) to
branch.

'dire *vt* to say; (*segreto, fatto*) to tell; ~ **qc a**
qn to tell sb sth; ~ **a qn di fare qc** to tell
sb to do sth; ~ **di sì/no** to say yes/no; **si**
dice che ... they say that ...; **mi si dice che**
... I am told that ...; **si direbbe che ...** it
looks (*o* sounds) as though ...; **dica,**
signora? (*in un negozio*) yes, Madam, can I
help you?; **sa quello che dice** he knows
what he's talking about; **lascialo** ~
(*esprimersi*) let him have his say;
(*ignoralo*) just ignore him; **come sarebbe a**
~? what do you mean?; **che ne diresti di**
andarcene? how about leaving?; **chi**
l'avrebbe mai detto! who would have
thought it!; **si dicono esperti** they say
they are experts; **per così** ~ so to speak; **a**
dir poco to say the least; **non c'è che** ~
there's no doubt about it; **non dico di no** I
can't deny it; **il che è tutto** ~ need I say
more?

di'ressi *etc vb vedi* **dirigere.**

di'retta *sf vedi* **diretto.**

diretta'mente *av* (*immediatamente*)
directly, straight; (*personalmente*)
directly; (*senza intermediari*) direct,
straight.

diret'tissima *sf* (*tragitto*) most direct route;
(*DIR*): **processo per** ~ summary
trial.

diret'tissimo *sm* (*FERR*) fast (through)
train.

diret'tivo, a *ag* (*POL, AMM*) executive;
(*COMM*) managerial, executive ♦ *sm*
leadership, leaders *pl* ♦ *sf* directive,
instruction.

di'retto, a *pp di* **dirigere** ♦ *ag* direct ♦ *sm*
(*FERR*) through train ♦ *sf*: **in (linea)** ~**a**
(*RADIO, TV*) live; **il mio** ~ **superiore** my
immediate superior.

diret'tore, 'trice *sm/f* (*di azienda*) director;

manager/ess; (*di scuola elementare*) head (teacher) (*BRIT*), principal (*US*); ~ **amministrativo** company secretary (*BRIT*), corporate executive secretary (*US*); ~ **del carcere** prison governor (*BRIT*) *o* warden (*US*); ~ **di filiale** branch manager; ~ **d'orchestra** conductor; ~ **di produzione** (*CINE*) producer; ~ **sportivo** team manager; ~ **tecnico** (*SPORT*) trainer, coach.

direzi'one [diret'tsjone] *sf* (*senso: anche fig*) direction; (*conduzione: gen*) running; (: *di partito*) leadership; (: *di società*) management; (: *di giornale*) editorship; (*direttori*) management; **in ~ di** in the direction of, towards.

diri'gente [diri'dʒɛnte] *ag* managerial ♦ *smlf* executive; (*POL*) leader; **classe ~** ruling class.

diri'genza [diri'dʒɛntsa] *sf* management; (*POL*) leadership.

dirigenzi'ale [diridʒen'tsjale] *ag* managerial.

di'rigere [di'ridʒere] *vt* to direct; (*impresa*) to run, manage; (*MUS*) to conduct; **~rsi** *vr*: **~rsi verso** *o* **a** to make *o* head for; **~ i propri passi verso** to make one's way towards; **il treno era diretto a Pavia** the train was heading for Pavia.

diri'gibile [diri'dʒibile] *sm* airship.

dirim'petto *av* opposite; **~ a** *prep* opposite, facing.

di'ritto, a *ag* straight; (*onesto*) upright ♦ *av* straight, directly ♦ *sm* right side; (*TENNIS*) forehand; (*MAGLIA*) plain stitch, knit stitch; (*prerogativa*) right; (*leggi, scienza*): **il ~** law; **stare ~** to stand up straight; **aver ~ a qc** to be entitled to sth; **punto ~** plain (stitch); **andare ~** to go straight on; **a buon ~** quite rightly; **~i (d'autore)** royalties; **~ di successione** right of succession.

dirit'tura *sf* (*SPORT*) straight; (*fig*) rectitude.

diroc'cato, a *ag* tumbledown, in ruins.

dirom'pente *ag* (*anche fig*) explosive.

dirotta'mento *sm*: **~ (aereo)** hijack.

dirot'tare *vt* (*nave, aereo*) to change the course of; (*aereo: sotto minaccia*) to hijack; (*traffico*) to divert ♦ *vi* (*nave, aereo*) to change course.

dirotta'tore, 'trice *smlf* hijacker.

di'rotto, a *ag* (*pioggia*) torrential; (*pianto*) unrestrained; **piovere a ~** to pour, rain cats and dogs; **piangere a ~** to cry one's heart out.

di'rupo *sm* crag, precipice.

di'sabile *smlf* disabled person.

disabi'tato, a *ag* uninhabited.

disabitu'arsi *vr*: **~ a** to get out of the habit of.

disac'cordo *sm* disagreement.

disadat'tato, a *ag* (*PSIC*) maladjusted.

disa'dorno, a *ag* plain, unadorned.

disaffezi'one [dizaffet'tsjone] *sf* disaffection.

disa'gevole [disa'dʒevole] *ag* (*scomodo*) uncomfortable; (*difficile*) difficult.

disagi'ato, a [diza'dʒato] *ag* poor, needy; (*vita*) hard.

di'sagio [di'zadʒo] *sm* discomfort; (*disturbo*) inconvenience; (*fig: imbarazzo*) embarrassment; **~i** *smpl* hardship *sg*, poverty *sg*; **essere a ~** to be ill at ease.

di'samina *sf* close examination.

disappro'vare *vt* to disapprove of.

disapprovazi'one [dizapprovat'tsjone] *sf* disapproval.

disap'punto *sm* disappointment.

disarcio'nare [dizartʃo'nare] *vt* to unhorse.

disar'mante *ag* (*fig*) disarming.

disar'mare *vt, vi* to disarm.

di'sarmo *sm* (*MIL*) disarmament.

di'sastro *sm* disaster.

disas'troso, a *ag* disastrous.

disat'tento, a *ag* inattentive.

disattenzi'one [dizatten'tsjone] *sf* carelessness, lack of attention.

disatti'vare *vt* (*bomba*) to de-activate, defuse.

disa'vanzo [diza'vantso] *sm* (*ECON*) deficit.

disavven'tura *sf* misadventure, mishap.

dis'brigo, ghi *sm* (*prompt*) clearing up *o* settlement.

dis'capito *sm*: **a ~ di** to the detriment of.

dis'carica, che *sf* (*di rifiuti*) rubbish tip *o* dump.

discen'dente [diʃʃen'dɛnte] *ag* descending ♦ *smlf* descendant.

di'scendere [diʃ'ʃɛndere] *vt* to go (*o* come) down ♦ *vi* to go (*o* come) down; (*smontare*) to get off; **~ da** (*famiglia*) to be descended from; **~ dalla macchina/dal treno** to get out of the car/out of *o* off the train; **~ da cavallo** to dismount, get off one's horse.

di'scepolo, a [diʃ'ʃepolo] *smlf* disciple.

di'scernere [diʃ'ʃernere] *vt* to discern.

discerni'mento [diʃʃerni'mento] *sm* discernment.

disce'sista [diʃʃe'sista] *smlf* downhill skier.

di'sceso, a [diʃ'ʃeso] *pp di* **discendere** ♦ *sf* descent; (*pendio*) slope; **in ~a** (*strada*) downhill *cpd*, sloping; **~a libera** (*SCI*) downhill race.

dischi'udere [dis'kjudere] *vt* (*aprire*) to open; (*fig: rivelare*) to disclose, reveal.

dischi'usi *etc* [dis'kjusi] *vb vedi* **dischiudere**.
dischi'uso, a [dis'kjuso] *pp di* **dischiudere**.
di'scinto, a [diʃ'ʃinto] *ag* (*anche*: **in abiti ~i**) half-undressed.
disci'ogliere [diʃ'ʃɔʎʎere] *vt*, **~rsi** *vr* to dissolve; (*fondere*) to melt.
disci'plina [diʃʃi'plina] *sf* discipline.
discipli'nare [diʃʃipli'nare] *ag* disciplinary ♦ *vt* to discipline.
'disco, schi *sm* disc, disk; (*SPORT*) discus; (*fonografico*) record; (*INFORM*) disk; **~ magnetico** (*INFORM*) magnetic disk; **~ orario** (*AUT*) parking disc; **~ rigido** (*INFORM*) hard disk; **~ volante** flying saucer.
discogra'fia *sf* (*tecnica*) recording, record-making; (*industria*) record industry.
disco'grafico, a, ci, che *ag* record *cpd*, recording *cpd* ♦ *sm* record producer; **casa ~a** record(ing) company.
'discolo, a *ag* (*bambino*) undisciplined, unruly ♦ *sm/f* rascal.
discol'pare *vt* to clear of blame; **~rsi** *vr* to clear o.s., prove one's innocence; (*giustificarsi*) to excuse o.s.
disco'noscere [disko'noʃʃere] *vt* (*figlio*) to disown; (*meriti*) to ignore, disregard.
disconosci'uto, a [diskonoʃ'ʃuto] *pp di* **disconoscere**.
discon'tinuo, a *ag* (*linea*) broken; (*rendimento, stile*) irregular; (*interesse*) sporadic.
dis'corde *ag* conflicting, clashing.
dis'cordia *sf* discord; (*dissidio*) disagreement, clash.
dis'correre *vi*: **~ (di)** to talk (about).
dis'corso, a *pp di* **discorrere** ♦ *sm* speech; (*conversazione*) conversation, talk.
dis'costo, a *ag* faraway, distant ♦ *av* far away; **~ da** *prep* far from.
disco'teca, che *sf* (*raccolta*) record library; (*luogo di ballo*) disco(theque).
discre'panza [diskre'pantsa] *sf* discrepancy.
dis'creto, a *ag* discreet; (*abbastanza buono*) reasonable, fair.
discrezi'one [diskret'tsjone] *sf* discretion; (*giudizio*) judgment, discernment; **a ~ di** at the discretion of.
discrimi'nante *ag* (*fattore, elemento*) decisive ♦ *sf* (*DIR*) extenuating circumstance.
discrimi'nare *vt* to discrimate.
discriminazi'one [diskriminat'tsjone] *sf* discrimination.
dis'cussi *etc vb vedi* **discutere**.
discussi'one *sf* discussion; (*litigio*) argument; **mettere in ~** to bring into

question; **fuori ~** out of the question.
dis'cusso, a *pp di* **discutere**.
dis'cutere *vt* to discuss, debate; (*contestare*) to question, dispute ♦ *vi* (*conversare*): **~ (di)** to discuss; (*litigare*) to argue.
discu'tibile *ag* questionable.
disde'gnare [dizdeɲ'ɲare] *vt* to scorn.
dis'degno [diz'deɲɲo] *sm* scorn, disdain.
disde'gnoso, a [dizdeɲ'ɲoso] *ag* disdainful, scornful.
dis'detto, a *pp di* **disdire** ♦ *sf* cancellation; (*sfortuna*) bad luck.
disdi'cevole [dizdi'tʃevole] *ag* improper, unseemly.
dis'dire *vt* (*prenotazione*) to cancel; **~ un contratto d'affitto** (*DIR*) to give notice (to quit).
dise'gnare [diseɲ'ɲare] *vt* to draw; (*progettare*) to design; (*fig*) to outline.
disegna'tore, 'trice [diseɲɲa'tore] *sm/f* designer.
di'segno [di'zeɲɲo] *sm* drawing; (*su stoffa etc*) design; (*fig: schema*) outline; **~ industriale** industriale design; **~ di legge** (*DIR*) bill.
diser'bante *sm* weedkiller.
disere'dare *vt* to disinherit.
diser'tare *vt, vi* to desert.
diser'tore *sm* (*MIL*) deserter.
diserzi'one [dizer'tsjone] *sf* (*MIL*) desertion.
disfaci'mento [disfatʃi'mento] *sm* (*di cadavere*) decay; (*fig: di istituzione, impero, società*) decline, decay; **in ~** in decay.
dis'fare *vt* to undo; (*valigie*) to unpack; (*meccanismo*) to take to pieces; (*lavoro, paese*) to destroy; (*neve*) to melt; **~rsi** *vr* to come undone; (*neve*) to melt; **~ il letto** to strip the bed; **~rsi di qn** (*liberarsi*) to get rid of sb.
dis'fatta *sf vedi* **disfatto**.
disfat'tista, i, e *sm/f* defeatist.
dis'fatto, a *pp di* **disfare** ♦ *ag* (*gen*) undone, untied; (*letto*) unmade; (*persona: sfinito*) exhausted, worn-out; (: *addolorato*) grief-stricken ♦ *sf* (*sconfitta*) rout.
disfunzi'one [disfun'tsjone] *sf* (*MED*) dysfunction; **~ cardiaca** heart trouble.
disge'lare [dizdʒe'lare] *vt, vi*, **~rsi** *vr* to thaw.
dis'gelo [diz'dʒɛlo] *sm* thaw.
dis'grazia [diz'grattsja] *sf* (*sventura*) misfortune; (*incidente*) accident, mishap.
disgrazi'ato, a [dizgrat'tsjato] *ag* unfortunate ♦ *sm/f* wretch.
disgre'gare *vt*, **~rsi** *vr* to break up.
disgu'ido *sm* hitch; **~ postale** error in postal delivery.

disgus'tare *vt* to disgust; ~**rsi** *vr*: ~**rsi di** to be disgusted by.

dis'gusto *sm* disgust.

disgus'toso, a *ag* disgusting.

disidra'tare *vt* to dehydrate.

disidra'tato, a *ag* dehydrated.

disil'ludere *vt* to disillusion, disenchant.

disillusi'one *sf* disillusion, disenchantment.

disimpa'rare *vt* to forget.

disimpe'gnare [dizimpeɲ'ɲare] *vt* (*persona: da obblighi*): ~ **da** to release from; (*oggetto dato in pegno*) to redeem, get out of pawn; ~**rsi** *vr*: ~**rsi da** (*obblighi*) to release o.s. from, free o.s. from.

disincagli'are [dizinkaʎ'ʎare] *vt* (*barca*) to refloat; ~**rsi** *vr* to get afloat again.

disincan'tato, a *ag* disenchanted, disillusioned.

disincenti'vare [dizintʃenti'vare] *vt* to discourage.

disinfes'tare *vt* to disinfest.

disinfestazi'one [dizinfestat'tsjone] *sf* disinfestation.

disinfet'tante *ag, sm* disinfectant.

disinfet'tare *vt* to disinfect.

disinfezi'one [dizinfet'tsjone] *sf* disinfection.

disingan'nare *vt* to disillusion.

disin'ganno *sm* disillusion.

disini'bito, a *ag* uninhibited.

disinnes'care *vt* to defuse.

disinnes'tare *vt* (*marcia*) to disengage.

disinqui'nare *vt* to free from pollution.

disinte'grare *vt, vi* to disintegrate.

disinteres'sarsi *vr*: ~ **di** to take no interest in.

disinte'resse *sm* indifference; (*generosità*) unselfishness.

disintossi'care *vt* (*alcolizzato, drogato*) to treat for alcoholism (*o drug addiction*); ~**rsi** *vr* to clear out one's system; (*alcolizzato, drogato*) to be treated for alcoholism (*o drug addiction*).

disintossicazi'one [dizintossikat'tsjone] *sf* treatment for alcoholism (*o drug addiction*).

disin'volto, a *ag* casual, free and easy.

disinvol'tura *sf* casualness, ease.

disles'sia *sf* dyslexia.

disli'vello *sm* difference in height; (*fig*) gap.

dislo'care *vt* to station, position.

dismi'sura *sf* excess; **a** ~ to excess, excessively.

disobbe'dire *etc* = **disubbidire** *etc*.

disoccu'pato, a *ag* unemployed ♦ *sm/f* unemployed person.

disoccupazi'one [dizokkupat'tsjone] *sf* unemployment.

disonestà *sf* dishonesty.

diso'nesto, a *ag* dishonest.

disono'rare *vt* to dishonour (*BRIT*), dishonor (*US*), bring disgrace upon.

diso'nore *sm* dishonour (*BRIT*), dishonor (*US*), disgrace.

di'sopra *av* (*con contatto*) on top; (*senza contatto*) above; (*al piano superiore*) upstairs ♦ *ag inv* (*superiore*) upper ♦ *sm inv* top, upper part; **la gente** ~ the people upstairs; **il piano** ~ the floor above.

disordi'nare *vt* to mess up, disarrange; (*MIL*) to throw into disorder.

disordi'nato, a *ag* untidy; (*privo di misura*) irregular, wild.

di'sordine *sm* (*confusione*) disorder, confusion; (*sregolatezza*) debauchery; ~**i** *smpl* (*POL etc*) disorder *sg*; (*tumulti*) riots.

disor'ganico, a, ci, che *ag* incoherent, disorganized.

disorganiz'zato, a [dizorganid'dzato] *ag* disorganized.

disorienta'mento *sm* (*fig*) confusion, bewilderment.

disorien'tare *vt* to disorientate; ~**rsi** *vr* (*fig*) to get confused, lose one's bearings.

disorien'tato, a *ag* disorientated.

disos'sare *vt* (*CUC*) to bone.

di'sotto *av* below, underneath; (*in fondo*) at the bottom; (*al piano inferiore*) downstairs ♦ *ag inv* (*inferiore*) lower; bottom *cpd* ♦ *sm inv* (*parte inferiore*) lower part; bottom; **la gente** ~ the people downstairs; **il piano** ~ the floor below.

dis'paccio [dis'pattʃo] *sm* dispatch.

dispa'rato, a *ag* disparate.

'dispari *ag inv* odd, uneven.

disparità *sf inv* disparity.

dis'parte : **in** ~ *av* (*da lato*) aside, apart; **tenersi** *o* **starsene in** ~ to keep to o.s., hold aloof.

dis'pendio *sm* (*di denaro, energie*) expenditure; (: *spreco*) waste.

dispendi'oso, a *ag* expensive.

dis'pensa *sf* pantry, larder; (*mobile*) sideboard; (*DIR*) exemption; (*REL*) dispensation; (*fascicolo*) number, issue.

dispen'sare *vt* (*elemosine, favori*) to distribute; (*esonerare*) to exempt.

dispe'rare *vi*: ~ (**di**) to despair (of); ~**rsi** *vr* to despair.

dispe'rato, a *ag* (*persona*) in despair; (*caso, tentativo*) desperate.

disperazi'one [disperat'tsjone] *sf* despair.

dis'perdere *vt* (*disseminare*) to disperse; (*MIL*) to scatter, rout; (*fig: consumare*) to waste, squander; ~**rsi** *vr* to disperse; to scatter.

dispersi'one *sf* dispersion, dispersal; (*FISICA, CHIM*) dispersion.

disper'sivo, a *ag* (*lavoro etc*) disorganized.

dis'perso, a *pp di* **disperdere** ♦ *sm/f* missing person; (*MIL*) missing soldier.

dis'petto *sm* spite *no pl*, spitefulness *no pl*; **fare un** ~ **a qn** to play a (nasty) trick on sb; **a** ~ **di** in spite of; **con suo grande** ~ much to his annoyance.

dispet'toso, a *ag* spiteful.

dispia'cere [dispja't∫ere] *sm* (*rammarico*) regret, sorrow; (*dolore*) grief ♦ *vi*: ~ **a** to displease ♦ *vb impers*: **mi dispiace (che)** I am sorry (that); ~**i** *smpl* (*preoccupazioni*) troubles, worries; **se non le dispiace, me ne vado adesso** if you don't mind, I'll go now.

dispiaci'uto, a [dispja't∫uto] *pp di* **dispiacere** ♦ *ag* sorry.

dis'pone, dis'pongo *etc vb vedi* **disporre**.

dispo'nibile *ag* available; (*persona: solerte, gentile*) helpful.

disponibilità *sf inv* availability; (*solerzia, gentilezza*) helpfulness; **disponibilità** *sfpl* (*economiche*) resources.

dis'porre *vt* (*sistemare*) to arrange; (*preparare*) to prepare; (*DIR*) to order; (*persuadere*): ~ **qn a** to incline *o* dispose sb towards ♦ *vi* (*decidere*) to decide; (*usufruire*): ~ **di** to use, have at one's disposal; (*essere dotato*): ~ **di** to have; **disporsi** *vr* (*ordinarsi*) to place o.s., arrange o.s.; **disporsi a fare** to get ready to do; **disporsi all'attacco** to prepare for an attack; **disporsi in cerchio** to form a circle.

dis'posi *etc vb vedi* **disporre**.

disposi'tivo *sm* (*meccanismo*) device; (*DIR*) pronouncement; ~ **di controllo** *o* **di comando** control device; ~ **di sicurezza** (*gen*) safety device; (*di arma da fuoco*) safety catch.

disposizi'one [dispozit'tsjone] *sf* arrangement, layout; (*stato d'animo*) mood; (*tendenza*) bent, inclination; (*comando*) order; (*DIR*) provision, regulation; **a** ~ **di qn** at sb's disposal; **per** ~ **di legge** by law; ~ **testamentaria** provisions of a will.

dis'posto, a *pp di* **disporre** ♦ *ag* (*incline*): ~ **a fare** disposed *o* prepared to do.

dis'potico, a, ci, che *ag* despotic.

dispo'tismo *sm* despotism.

disprez'zare [dispret'tsare] *vt* to despise.

dis'prezzo [dis'prettso] *sm* contempt; **con** ~ **del pericolo** with a total disregard for the danger involved.

'disputa *sf* dispute, quarrel.

dispu'tare *vt* (*contendere*) to dispute, contest; (*SPORT: partita*) to play; (: *gara*) to take part in ♦ *vi* to quarrel; ~ **di** to discuss; ~**rsi qc** to fight for sth.

disqui'sire *vi* to discourse on.

disquisizi'one [diskwizit'tsjone] *sf* detailed analysis.

dissa'crare *vt* to desecrate.

dissangua'mento *sm* loss of blood.

dissangu'are *vt* (*fig: persona*) to bleed white; (: *patrimonio*) to suck dry; ~**rsi** *vr* (*MED*) to lose blood; (*fig*) to ruin o.s.; **morire dissanguato** to bleed to death.

dissa'pore *sm* slight disagreement.

'disse *vb vedi* **dire**.

disse'care *vt* to dissect.

dissec'care *vt*, ~**rsi** *vr* to dry up.

dissemi'nare *vt* to scatter; (*fig: notizie*) to spread.

dissenna'tezza [dissenna'tettsa] *sf* foolishness.

dis'senso *sm* dissent; (*disapprovazione*) disapproval.

dissente'ria *sf* dysentery.

dissen'tire *vi*: ~ (**da**) to disagree (with).

disseppel'lire *vt* (*esumare: cadavere*) to disinter, exhume; (*dissotterrare: anche fig*) to dig up, unearth; (: *rancori*) to resurrect.

dissertazi'one [dissertat'tsjone] *sf* dissertation.

disser'vizio [disser'vittsjo] *sm* inefficiency.

disses'tare *vt* (*ECON*) to ruin.

disses'tato, a *ag* (*fondo stradale*) uneven; (*economia, finanze*) shaky; "**strada** ~**a**" (*per lavori in corso*) "road up" (*BRIT*), "road out" (*US*).

dis'sesto *sm* (financial) ruin.

disse'tante *ag* refreshing.

disse'tare *vt* to quench the thirst of; ~**rsi** *vr* to quench one's thirst.

dissezi'one [disset'tsjone] *sf* dissection.

'dissi *vb vedi* **dire**.

dissi'dente *ag*, *sm/f* dissident.

dis'sidio *sm* disagreement.

dis'simile *ag* different, dissimilar.

dissimu'lare *vt* (*fingere*) to dissemble; (*nascondere*) to conceal.

dissimula'tore, 'trice *sm/f* dissembler.

dissimulazi'one [dissimulat'tsjone] *sf* dissembling; concealment.

dissi'pare *vt* to dissipate; (*scialacquare*) to squander, waste.

dissipa'tezza [dissipa'tettsa] *sf* dissipation.

dissi'pato, a *ag* dissolute, dissipated.

dissipazi'one [dissipat'tsjone] *sf* squandering.

dissoci'are [disso'tʃare] *vt* to dissociate.
dis'solto, a *pp di* **dissolvere**.
disso'lubile *ag* soluble.
dissolu'tezza [dissolu'tettsa] *sf* dissoluteness.
dissolu'tivo, a *ag* (*forza*) divisive; **processo** ~ (*anche fig*) process of dissolution.
disso'luto, a *pp di* **dissolvere** ♦ *ag* dissolute, licentious.
dissol'venza [dissol'vɛntsa] *sf* (*CINE*) fading.
dis'solvere *vt* to dissolve; (*neve*) to melt; (*fumo*) to disperse; ~**rsi** *vr* to dissolve; to melt; to disperse.
disso'nante *ag* discordant.
disso'nanza [disso'nantsa] *sf* (*fig: di opinioni*) clash.
dissotter'rare *vt* (*cadavere*) to disinter, exhume; (*tesori, rovine*) to dig up, unearth; (*fig: sentimenti, odio*) to bring up again, resurrect.
dissu'adere *vt*: ~ **qn da** to dissuade sb from.
dissuasi'one *sf* dissuasion.
dissu'aso, a *pp di* **dissuadere**.
distacca'mento *sm* (*MIL*) detachment.
distac'care *vt* to detach, separate; (*SPORT*) to leave behind; ~**rsi** *vr* to be detached; (*fig*) to stand out; ~**rsi da** (*fig: allontanarsi*) to grow away from.
dis'tacco, chi *sm* (*separazione*) separation; (*fig: indifferenza*) detachment; (*SPORT*): **vincere con un** ~ **di ...** to win by a distance of ....
dis'tante *av* far away ♦ *ag* distant, far away; **essere** ~ (**da**) to be a long way (from); **è** ~ **da qui?** is it far from here?; **essere** ~ **nel tempo** to be in the distant past.
dis'tanza [dis'tantsa] *sf* distance; **comando a** ~ remote control; **a** ~ **di 2 giorni** 2 days later; **tener qn a** ~ to keep sb at arm's length; **prendere le** ~**e da qc/qn** to dissociate o.s. from sth/sb; **tenere o mantenere le** ~**e** to keep one's distance; ~ **focale** focal length; ~ **di sicurezza** safe distance; (*AUT*) braking distance; ~ **di tiro** range; ~ **di visibilità** visibility.
distanzi'are [distan'tsjare] *vt* to space out, place at intervals; (*SPORT*) to outdistance; (*fig: superare*) to outstrip, surpass.
dis'tare *vi*: **distiamo pochi chilometri da Roma** we are only a few kilometres (away) from Rome; **dista molto da qui?** is it far (away) from here?; **non dista molto** it's not far (away).
dis'tendere *vt* (*coperta*) to spread out; (*gambe*) to stretch (out); (*mettere a*

giacere) to lay; (*rilassare: muscoli, nervi*) to relax; ~**rsi** *vr* (*rilassarsi*) to relax; (*sdraiarsi*) to lie down.
distensi'one *sf* stretching; relaxation; (*POL*) détente.
disten'sivo, a *ag* (*gen*) relaxing, restful; (*farmaco*) tranquillizing; (*POL*) conciliatory.
dis'teso, a *pp di* **distendere** ♦ *ag* (*allungato: persona, gamba*) stretched out; (*rilassato: persona, atmosfera*) relaxed ♦ *sf* expanse, stretch; **avere un volto** ~ to look relaxed.
distil'lare *vt* to distil.
distil'lato *sm* distillate.
distillazi'one [distillat'tsjone] *sf* distillation.
distille'ria *sf* distillery.
dis'tinguere *vt* to distinguish; ~**rsi** *vr* (*essere riconoscibile*) to be distinguished; (*emergere*) to stand out, be conspicuous, distinguish o.s.; **un vino che si distingue per il suo aroma** a wine with a distinctive bouquet.
dis'tinguo *sm inv* distinction.
dis'tinta *sf* (*nota*) note; (*elenco*) list; ~ **di pagamento** receipt; ~ **di versamento** pay-in slip.
distin'tivo, a *ag* distinctive; distinguishing ♦ *sm* badge.
dis'tinto, a *pp di* **distinguere** ♦ *ag* (*dignitoso ed elegante*) distinguished; ~**i saluti** (*in lettera*) yours faithfully.
distinzi'one [distin'tsjone] *sf* distinction; **non faccio** ~**i** (*tra persone*) I don't discriminate; (*tra cose*) it's all one to me; **senza** ~ **di razza/religione ...** no matter what one's race/creed ....
dis'togliere [dis'tɔʎʎere] *vt*: ~ **da** to take away from; (*fig*) to dissuade from.
dis'tolto, a *pp di* **distogliere**.
dis'torcere [dis'tɔrtʃere] *vt* to twist; (*fig*) to twist, distort; ~**rsi** *vr* (*contorcersi*) to twist.
distorsi'one *sf* (*MED*) sprain; (*FISICA, OTTICA*) distortion.
dis'torto, a *pp di* **distorcere**.
dis'trarre *vt* to distract; (*divertire*) to entertain, amuse; **distrarsi** *vr* (*non fare attenzione*) to be distracted, let one's mind wander; (*svagarsi*) to amuse o enjoy o.s.; ~ **lo sguardo** to look away; **non distrarti!** pay attention!
distratta'mente *av* absent-mindedly, without thinking.
dis'tratto, a *pp di* **distrarre** ♦ *ag* absent-minded; (*disattento*) inattentive.
distrazi'one [distrat'tsjone] *sf* absent-mindedness; inattention; (*svago*) distraction, entertainment; **errori di** ~

careless mistakes.

dis'tretto *sm* district.

distribu'ire *vt* to distribute; (*CARTE*) to deal (out); (*consegnare: posta*) to deliver; (*lavoro*) to allocate, assign; (*ripartire*) to share out.

distribu'tore *sm* (*di benzina*) petrol (*BRIT*) *o* gas (*US*) pump; (*AUT, ELETTR*) distributor; (*automatico*) vending machine.

distribuzi'one [distribut'tsjone] *sf* distribution; delivery; allocation, assignment; sharing out.

distri'care *vt* to disentangle, unravel; ~**rsi** *vr* (*tirarsi fuori*): ~**rsi da** to get out of, disentangle o.s. from; (*fig: cavarsela*) to manage, get by.

dis'truggere [dis'truddʒere] *vt* to destroy.

distrut'tivo, a *ag* destructive.

dis'trutto, a *pp di* **distruggere**.

distruzi'one [distrut'tsjone] *sf* destruction.

distur'bare *vt* to disturb, trouble; (*sonno, lezioni*) to disturb, interrupt; ~**rsi** *vr* to put o.s. out; **non si disturbi** please don't bother.

dis'turbo *sm* trouble, bother, inconvenience; (*indisposizione*) (slight) disorder, ailment; ~**i** *smpl* (*RADIO, TV*) static *sg*; ~ **della quiete pubblica** (*DIR*) disturbance of the peace; ~**i di stomaco** stomach trouble *sg*.

disubbidi'ente *ag* disobedient.

disubbidi'enza [dizubbi'djɛntsa] *sf* disobedience; ~ **civile** civil disobedience.

disubbi'dire *vi*: ~ **(a qn)** to disobey (sb).

disuguagli'anza [dizugwaʎ'ʎantsa] *sf* inequality.

disugu'ale *ag* unequal; (*diverso*) different; (*irregolare*) uneven.

disumanità *sf* inhumanity.

disu'mano, a *ag* inhuman; **un grido** ~ a terrible cry.

disuni'one *sf* disunity.

disu'nire *vt* to divide, disunite.

di'suso *sm*: **andare** *o* **cadere in** ~ to fall into disuse.

'dita *sfpl di* **dito**.

di'tale *sm* thimble.

di'tata *sf* (*colpo*) jab (with one's finger); (*segno*) fingermark.

'dito, *pl(f)* **'dita** *sm* finger; (*misura*) finger, finger's breadth; ~ **(del piede)** toe; **mettersi le** ~**a nel naso** to pick one's nose; **mettere il** ~ **sulla piaga** (*fig*) to touch a sore spot; **non ha mosso un** ~ **(per aiutarmi)** he didn't lift a finger (to help me); **ormai è segnato a** ~ everyone knows about him now.

'ditta *sf* firm, business; **macchina della** ~

company car.

dit'tafono *sm* Dictaphone ®.

ditta'tore *sm* dictator.

ditta'tura *sf* dictatorship.

dit'tongo, ghi *sm* diphthong.

di'urno, a *ag* day *cpd*, daytime *cpd*; **ore** ~**e** daytime *sg*; **spettacolo** ~ matinee; **turno** ~ day shift; *vedi anche* **albergo**.

'diva *sf vedi* **divo**.

diva'gare *vi* to digress.

divagazi'one [divagat'tsjone] *sf* digression; ~**i sul tema** variations on a theme.

divam'pare *vi* to flare up, blaze up.

di'vano *sm* sofa; (*senza schienale*) divan; ~ **letto** bed settee, sofa bed.

divari'care *vt* to open wide.

di'vario *sm* difference.

di'vengo *etc vb vedi* **divenire**.

dive'nire *vi* = **diventare**.

di'venni *etc vb vedi* **divenire**.

diven'tare *vi* to become; ~ **famoso/ professore** to become famous/a teacher; ~ **vecchio** to grow old; **c'è da** ~ **matti** it's enough to drive you mad.

dive'nuto, a *pp di* **divenire**.

di'verbio *sm* altercation.

diver'gente [diver'dʒɛnte] *ag* divergent.

diver'genza [diver'dʒɛntsa] *sf* divergence; ~ **d'opinioni** difference of opinion.

di'vergere [di'vɛrdʒere] *vi* to diverge.

diverrò *etc vb vedi* **divenire**.

diversa'mente *av* (*in modo differente*) differently; (*altrimenti*) otherwise; ~ **da quanto stabilito** contrary to what had been decided.

diversifi'care *vt* to diversify, vary; ~**rsi** *vr*: ~**rsi (per)** to differ (in).

diversificazi'one [diversifikat'tsjone] *sf* diversification; difference.

diversi'one *sf* diversion.

diversità *sf inv* difference, diversity; (*varietà*) variety.

diver'sivo, a *ag* diversionary ♦ *sm* diversion, distraction; **fare un'azione** ~**a** to create a diversion.

di'verso, a *ag* (*differente*): ~ **(da)** different (from) ♦ *sm* (*omosessuale*) homosexual; ~**i, e** *det pl* several, various; (*COMM*) sundry ♦ *pron pl* several (people), many (people).

diver'tente *ag* amusing.

diverti'mento *sm* amusement, pleasure; (*passatempo*) pastime, recreation; **buon** ~**!** enjoy yourself!, have a nice time!

diver'tire *vt* to amuse, entertain; ~**rsi** *vr* to amuse *o* enjoy o.s.; **divertiti!** enjoy yourself, have a good time!; ~**rsi alle spalle di qn** to have a laugh at sb's expense.

diver'tito, a *ag* amused.

divi'dendo *sm* dividend.

di'videre *vt* (*anche MAT*) to divide; (*distribuire, ripartire*) to divide (up), split (up); ~**rsi** *vr* (*persone*) to separate, part; (*coppia*) to separate; ~**rsi (in)** (*scindersi*) to divide (into), split up (into); (*ramificarsi*) to fork; **è diviso dalla moglie** he's separated from his wife; **si divide tra casa e lavoro** he divides his time between home and work.

divi'eto *sm* prohibition; "~ **di accesso**" "no entry"; "~ **di caccia**" "no hunting"; "~ **di parcheggio**" "no parking"; "~ **di sosta**" (*AUT*) "no waiting".

divinco'larsi *vr* to wriggle, writhe.

divinità *sf inv* divinity.

di'vino, a *ag* divine.

di'visa *sf* (*MIL etc*) uniform; (*COMM*) foreign currency.

di'visi *etc vb vedi* **dividere**.

divisi'one *sf* division; ~ **in sillabe** syllable division; (*a fine riga*) hyphenation.

di'vismo *sm* (*esibizionismo*) playing to the crowd.

di'viso, a *pp di* **dividere**.

divi'sorio, a *ag* (*siepe, muro esterno*) dividing; (*muro interno*) dividing, partition *cpd* ♦ *sm* (*in una stanza*) partition.

'divo, a *sm/f* star; **come una** ~**a** like a prima donna.

divo'rare *vt* to devour; ~ **qc con gli occhi** to eye sth greedily.

divorzi'are [divor'tsjare] *vi*: ~ (**da qn**) to divorce (sb).

divorzi'ato, a [divor'tsjato] *ag* divorced ♦ *sm/f* divorcee.

di'vorzio [di'vortsjo] *sm* divorce.

divul'gare *vt* to divulge, disclose; (*rendere comprensibile*) to popularize; ~**rsi** *vr* to spread.

divulgazi'one [divulgat'tsjone] *sf* (*vedi vb*) disclosure; popularization; spread.

dizio'nario [dittsjo'narjo] *sm* dictionary.

dizi'one [dit'tsjone] *sf* diction; pronunciation.

Dja'karta [dʒa'karta] *sf* Djakarta.

dl *abbr* (= *decilitro*) dl.

dm *abbr* (= *decimetro*) dm.

DNA [di'ennea] *sigla m* (*BIOL*: = *acido deossiribonucleico*) DNA ♦ *sigla f* = *direzione nazionale antimafia*.

do *sm* (*MUS*) C; (: *solfeggiando la scala*) do(h).

dobbi'amo *vb vedi* **dovere**.

D.O.C. [dɔk] *sigla vedi* **denominazione di origine controllata**.

doc. *abbr* = **documento**.

'doccia, ce ['dottʃa] *sf* (*bagno*) shower; (*condotto*) pipe; **fare la** ~ to have a shower; ~ **fredda** (*fig*) slap in the face.

do'cente [do'tʃɛnte] *ag* teaching ♦ *smlf* teacher; (*di università*) lecturer; **personale non** ~ non-teaching staff.

do'cenza [do'tʃɛntsa] *sf* university teaching *o* lecturing; **ottenere la libera** ~ to become a lecturer.

D.O.C.G. *sigla* (= *denominazione di origine controllata e garantita*) label guaranteeing the quality and origin of a wine.

'docile ['dɔtʃile] *ag* docile.

docilità [dotʃili'ta] *sf* docility.

documen'tare *vt* to document; ~**rsi** *vr*: ~**rsi (su)** to gather information *o* material (about).

documen'tario, a *ag*, *sm* documentary.

documentazi'one [dokumentat'tsjone] *sf* documentation.

docu'mento *sm* document; ~**i** *smpl* (*d'identità etc*) papers.

Dodecan'neso *sm*: **le Isole del** ~ the Dodecanese Islands.

dodi'cenne [dodi'tʃenne] *ag*, *sm/f* twelve-year-old.

dodi'cesimo, a [dodi'tʃezimo] *num* twelfth.

'dodici ['doditʃi] *num* twelve.

do'gana *sf* (*ufficio*) customs *pl*; (*tassa*) (customs) duty; **passare la** ~ to go through customs.

doga'nale *ag* customs *cpd*.

dogani'ere *sm* customs officer.

'doglie ['dɔʎʎe] *sfpl* (*MED*) labour *sg* (*BRIT*), labor *sg* (*US*), labo(u)r pains.

'dogma, i *sm* dogma.

dog'matico, a, ci, che *ag* dogmatic.

'dolce ['doltʃe] *ag* sweet; (*colore*) soft; (*carattere, persona*) gentle, mild; (*fig: mite: clima*) mild; (*non ripido: pendio*) gentle ♦ *sm* (*sapore* ~) sweetness, sweet taste; (*CUC: portata*) sweet, dessert; (: *torta*) cake; **il** ~ **far niente** sweet idleness.

dolcemente *av* (*baciare, trattare*) gently; (*sorridere, cantare*) sweetly; (*parlare*) softly.

dol'cezza [dol'tʃettsa] *sf* sweetness; softness; mildness; gentleness.

dolci'ario, a [dol'tʃarjo] *ag* confectionery *cpd*.

dolci'astro, a [dol'tʃastro] *ag* (*sapore*) sweetish.

dolcifi'cante [doltʃifi'kante] *ag* sweetening ♦ *sm* sweetener.

dolci'umi [dol'tʃumi] *smpl* sweets.

do'lente *ag* sorrowful, sad.

do'lere *vi* to be sore, hurt, ache; ~**rsi** *vr* to complain; (*essere spiacente*): ~**rsi di** to be sorry for; **mi duole la testa** my head aches, I've got a headache.

'dolgo *etc vb vedi* **dolere.**

'dollaro *sm* dollar.

'dolo *sm* (*DIR*) malice; (*frode*) fraud, deceit.

Dolo'miti *sfpl*: **le** ~ the Dolomites.

dolo'rante *ag* aching, sore.

do'lore *sm* (*fisico*) pain; (*morale*) sorrow, grief; **se lo scoprono sono** ~**i!** if they find out there'll be trouble!

dolo'roso, a *ag* painful; sorrowful, sad.

do'loso, a *ag* (*DIR*) malicious; **incendio** ~ arson.

'dolsi *etc vb vedi* **dolere.**

dom. *abbr* (= *domenica*) Sun.

do'manda *sf* (*interrogazione*) question; (*richiesta*) demand; (*: cortese*) request; (*DIR: richiesta scritta*) application; (*ECON*): **la** ~ demand; **fare una** ~ **a qn** to ask sb a question; **fare** ~ **(per un lavoro)** to apply (for a job); **far regolare** ~ **(di qc)** to apply through the proper channels (for sth); **fare** ~ **all'autorità giudiziaria** to apply to the courts; ~ **di divorzio** divorce petition; ~ **di matrimonio** proposal.

doman'dare *vt* (*per avere*) to ask for; (*per sapere*) to ask; (*esigere*) to demand; ~**rsi** *vr* to wonder, ask o.s.; ~ **qc a qn** to ask sb for sth; to ask sb sth.

do'mani *av* tomorrow ♦ *sm* (*l'indomani*) next day, following day; **il** ~ (*il futuro*) the future; (*il giorno successivo*) the next day; **un** ~ some day; ~ **l'altro** the day after tomorrow; ~ **(a) otto** tomorrow week, a week tomorrow; **a** ~**!** see you tomorrow!

do'mare *vt* to tame.

doma'tore, 'trice *sm/f* (*gen*) tamer; ~ **di cavalli** horsebreaker; ~ **di leoni** lion tamer.

domat'tina *av* tomorrow morning.

do'menica, che *sf* Sunday; *per fraseologia vedi* **martedì.**

domeni'cale *ag* Sunday *cpd*.

domeni'cano, a *ag, sm/f* Dominican.

do'mestica, che *sf vedi* **domestico.**

do'mestico, a, ci, che *ag* domestic ♦ *sm/f* servant, domestic; **le pareti** ~**che** one's own four walls; **animale** *m* ~ pet; **una** ~**a a ore** a daily (woman).

domicili'are [domitʃi'ljare] *ag vedi* **arresto.**

domicili'arsi [domitʃi'ljarsi] *vr* to take up residence.

domi'cilio [domi'tʃiljo] *sm* (*DIR*) domicile, place of residence; **visita a** ~ (*MED*) house call; "**recapito a** ~" "deliveries"; **violazione di** ~ (*DIR*) breaking and entering.

domi'nante *ag* (*colore, nota*) dominant;

(*opinione*) prevailing; (*idea*) main *cpd*, chief *cpd*; (*posizione*) dominating *cpd*; (*classe, partito*) ruling *cpd*.

domi'nare *vt* to dominate; (*fig: sentimenti*) to control, master ♦ *vi* to be in the dominant position; ~**rsi** *vr* (*controllarsi*) to control o.s.; ~ **su** (*fig*) to surpass, outclass.

domina'tore, 'trice *ag* ruling *cpd* ♦ *sm/f* ruler.

dominazi'one [dominat'tsjone] *sf* domination.

domini'cano, a *ag*: **la Repubblica D**~**a** the Dominican Republic.

do'minio *sm* dominion; (*fig: campo*) field, domain; ~**i coloniali** colonies; **essere di** ~ **pubblico** (*notizia etc*) to be common knowledge.

don *sm* (*REL*) Father.

do'nare *vt* to give, present; (*per beneficenza etc*) to donate ♦ *vi* (*fig*): ~ **a** to suit, become; ~ **sangue** to give blood.

dona'tore, 'trice *sm/f* donor; ~ **di sangue/ di organi** blood/organ donor.

donazi'one [donat'tsjone] *sf* donation; **atto di** ~ (*DIR*) deed of gift.

'donde *av* (*poetico*) whence.

dondo'lare *vt* (*cullare*) to rock; ~**rsi** *vr* to swing, sway.

'dondolo *sm*: **sedia/cavallo a** ~ rocking chair/horse.

dongio'vanni [dondʒo'vanni] *sm* Don Juan, ladies' man.

'donna *sf* woman; (*titolo*) Donna; (*CARTE*) queen; **figlio di buona** ~**!** (*fam*) son of a bitch!; ~ **di casa** housewife; ~ **a ore** daily (help *o* woman); ~ **delle pulizie** cleaning lady, cleaner; ~ **di servizio** maid; ~ **di vita** *o* **di strada** prostitute, streetwalker.

donnai'olo *sm* ladykiller.

'donnola *sf* weasel.

'dono *sm* gift.

'doping *sm* doping.

'dopo *av* (*tempo*) afterwards; (*: più tardi*) later; (*luogo*) after, next ♦ *prep* after ♦ *cong* (*temporale*): ~ **aver studiato** after having studied ♦ *ag inv*: **il giorno** ~ the following day; ~ **mangiato va a dormire** after having eaten *o* after a meal he goes for a sleep; **un anno** ~ a year later; ~ **di me/lui** after me/him; ~ **che** = **dopoché.**

dopo'barba *sm inv* after-shave.

dopoché [dopo'ke] *cong* after, when.

dopodiché [dopodi'ke] *av* after which.

dopodo'mani *av* the day after tomorrow.

dopogu'erra *sm* postwar years *pl*.

dopola'voro *sm* recreational club.

dopo'pranzo [dopo'prandzo] *av* after lunch

(o dinner).

doposcì [dopoʃ'ʃi] sm inv après-ski outfit.

doposcu'ola sm inv school club offering extra tuition and recreational facilities.

dopo'sole sm inv, ag inv: **(lozione/crema)** ~ aftersun (lotion/cream).

dopo'tutto av after all.

doppi'aggio [dop'pjaddʒo] sm (CINE) dubbing.

doppi'are vt (NAUT) to round; (SPORT) to lap; (CINE) to dub.

doppia'tore, 'trice sm/f dubber.

doppi'etta sf (fucile) double-barrelled (BRIT) o double-barreled (US) shotgun; (sparo) shot from both barrels; (CALCIO) double; (PUGILATO) one-two; (AUT) double-declutch (BRIT), double-clutch (US).

doppi'ezza [dop'pjettsa] sf (fig: di persona) duplicity, double-dealing.

'doppio, a ag double; (fig: falso) double-dealing, deceitful ♦ sm (quantità): **il** ~ **(di)** twice as much (o many), double the amount (o number) of; (SPORT) doubles pl ♦ av double; **battere una lettera in** ~**a copia** to type a letter with a carbon copy; **fare il** ~ **gioco** (fig) to play a double game; **chiudere a** ~**a mandata** to double-lock; ~ **senso** double entendre; **frase a** ~ **senso** sentence with a double meaning; **un utensile a** ~ **uso** a dual-purpose utensil.

doppio'fondo sm (di valigia) false bottom; (NAUT) double hull.

doppi'one sm duplicate (copy).

doppio'petto sm double-breasted jacket.

dop'pista sm/f (TENNIS) doubles player.

do'rare vt to gild; (CUC) to brown; ~ **la pillola** (fig) to sugar the pill.

do'rato, a ag golden; (ricoperto d'oro) gilt, gilded.

dora'tura sf gilding.

dormicchi'are [dormik'kjare] vi to doze.

dormi'ente ag sleeping ♦ sm/f sleeper.

dormigli'one, a [dormiʎ'ʎone] sm/f sleepyhead.

dor'mire vi to sleep; (essere addormentato) to be asleep, be sleeping; **il caffè non mi fa** ~ coffee keeps me awake; ~ **come un ghiro** to sleep like a log; ~ **della grossa** to sleep soundly; ~ **in piedi** (essere stanco) to be asleep on one's feet.

dor'mita sf: **farsi una** ~ to have a good sleep.

dormi'torio sm dormitory; ~ **pubblico** doss house (BRIT) o flophouse (US) (run by local authority).

dormi'veglia [dormi'veʎʎa] sm drowsiness.

dorrò etc vb vedi **dolere**.

dor'sale ag: **spina** ~ backbone, spine.

'dorso sm back; (di montagna) ridge, crest; (di libro) spine; (NUOTO) backstroke; **a** ~ **di cavallo** on horseback.

do'saggio [do'zaddʒo] sm (atto) measuring out; **sbagliare il** ~ to get the proportions wrong.

do'sare vt to measure out; (MED) to dose.

'dose sf quantity, amount; (MED) dose.

dossi'er [do'sje] sm inv dossier, file.

'dosso sm (rilievo) rise; (: di strada) bump; (dorso): **levarsi di** ~ **i vestiti** to take one's clothes off; **levarsi un peso di** ~ (fig) to take a weight off one's mind.

do'tare vt: ~ **di** to provide o supply with; (fig) to endow with.

do'tato, a ag: ~ **di** (attrezzature) equipped with; (bellezza, intelligenza) endowed with; **un uomo** ~ a gifted man.

dotazi'one [dotat'tsjone] sf (insieme di beni) endowment; (di macchine etc) equipment; **dare qc in** ~ **a qn** to issue sb with sth; **i macchinari in** ~ **alla fabbrica** the machinery in use in the factory.

'dote sf (di sposa) dowry; (assegnata a un ente) endowment; (fig) gift, talent.

Dott. abbr (= dottore) Dr.

'dotto, a ag (colto) learned ♦ sm (sapiente) scholar; (ANAT) duct.

dotto'rato sm degree; ~ **di ricerca** doctorate, doctor's degree.

dot'tore, 'essa sm/f doctor.

dot'trina sf doctrine.

Dott.ssa abbr (= dottoressa) Dr.

double-'face [dubl'fas] ag inv reversible.

'dove av where; (in cui) where, in which; (dovunque) wherever ♦ sm: **per ogni** ~ everywhere; **di dov'è?** where are you from?; **da** ~ **abito vedo tutta la città** I can see the whole city from where I live; **per** ~ **si passa?** which way should we go?; **le dò una mano fin** ~ **posso** I'll help you as much as I can.

do'vere sm (obbligo) duty ♦ vt (essere debitore): ~ **qc (a qn)** to owe (sb) sth ♦ vi (seguito dall'infinito: obbligo) to have to; **lui deve farlo** he has to do it, he must do it; **è dovuto partire** he had to leave; **ha dovuto pagare** he had to pay; (: intenzione): **devo partire domani** I'm (due) to leave tomorrow; (: probabilità) **dev'essere tardi** it must be late; **doveva accadere** it was bound to happen; **avere il senso del** ~ to have a sense of duty; **rivolgersi a chi di** ~ to apply to the appropriate authority o person; **a** ~ (bene) properly; (debitamente) as he (o she etc) deserves; **come si deve** (bene) properly; (merita-

tamente) properly, as he (*o* she *etc*) deserves; **una persona come si deve** a respectable person.

dove'roso, a *ag* (right and) proper.

do'vizia [do'vittsja] *sf* abundance.

dovrò *etc vb vedi* **dovere**.

do'vunque *av* (*in qualunque luogo*) wherever; (*dappertutto*) everywhere; ~ **io vada** wherever I go.

dovuta'mente *av* (*debitamente*: redigere, compilare) correctly; (: *rimproverare*) as he (*o* she *etc*) deserves.

do'vuto, a *ag* (*causato*): ~ **a** due to ♦ *sm* due; **nel modo** ~ in the proper way; **ho lavorato più del** ~ I worked more than was necessary.

doz'zina [dod'dzina] *sf* dozen; **una** ~ **di uova** a dozen eggs; **di** *o* **da** ~ (*scrittore, spettacolo*) second-rate.

dozzi'nale [doddzi'nale] *ag* cheap, second-rate.

DP *sigla f* (= *Democrazia Proletaria*) *political party*.

'draga, ghe *sf* dredger.

dra'gare *vt* to dredge.

dragherò *etc* [drage'rɔ] *vb vedi* **dragare**.

'drago, ghi *sm* dragon; (*fig fam*) genius.

'dramma, i *sm* drama; **fare un** ~ **di qc** to make a drama out of sth.

dram'matico, a, ci, che *ag* dramatic.

drammatiz'zare [drammatid'dzare] *vt* to dramatize.

dramma'turgo, ghi *sm* playwright.

drappeggi'are [drapped'dʒare] *vt* to drape.

drap'peggio [drap'peddʒo] *sm* (*tessuto*) drapery; (*di abito*) folds.

drap'pello *sm* (*MIL*) squad; (*gruppo*) band, group.

'drappo *sm* cloth.

'drastico, a, ci, che *ag* drastic.

dre'naggio [dre'naddʒo] *sm* drainage.

dre'nare *vt* to drain.

'Dresda *sf* Dresden.

drib'blare *vi* (*CALCIO*) to dribble ♦ *vt* (*avversario*) to dodge, avoid.

'dritto, a *ag, av* = **diritto** ♦ *sm/f* (*fam: furbo*): **è un** ~ he's a crafty *o* sly one ♦ *sf* (*destra*) right, right hand; (*NAUT*) starboard; **a** ~**a e a manca** (*fig*) on all sides, right, left and centre.

driz'zare [drit'tsare] *vt* (*far tornare diritto*) to straighten; (*volgere: sguardo, occhi*) to turn, direct; (*innalzare: antenna, muro*) to erect; ~**rsi** *vr* to stand up; ~ **le orecchie** to prick up one's ears; ~**rsi in piedi** to rise to one's feet; ~**rsi a sedere** to sit up.

'droga, ghe *sf* (*sostanza aromatica*) spice; (*stupefacente*) drug; ~**ghe pesanti/leggere** hard/soft drugs.

dro'gare *vt* to drug, dope; ~**rsi** *vr* to take drugs.

dro'gato, a *sm/f* drug addict.

droghe'ria [droge'ria] *sf* grocer's (shop) (*BRIT*), grocery (store) (*US*).

drogherò *etc* [droge'rɔ] *vb vedi* **drogare**.

droghi'ere, a [dro'gjɛre] *sm/f* grocer.

drome'dario *sm* dromedary.

DS [di'ɛsse] *smpl* (= *Democratici di Sinistra*) Democrats of the Left (*Italian left-wing party*).

'dubbio, a *ag* (*incerto*) doubtful, dubious; (*ambiguo*) dubious ♦ *sm* (*incertezza*) doubt; **avere il** ~ **che** to be afraid that, suspect that; **essere in** ~ **fra** to hesitate between; **mettere in** ~ **qc** to question sth; **nutrire seri** ~**i su qc** to have grave doubts about sth; **senza** ~ doubtless, no doubt.

dubbi'oso, a *ag* doubtful, dubious.

dubi'tare *vi*: ~ **di** (*onestà*) to doubt; (*risultato*) to be doubtful of; ~ **di qn** to mistrust sb; ~ **di sé** to be unsure of o.s.

Du'blino *sf* Dublin.

'duca, chi *sm* duke.

'duce ['dutʃe] *sm* (*STORIA*) captain; (: *del fascismo*) duce.

du'chessa [du'kessa] *sf* duchess.

'due *num* two; **a** ~ **a** ~ two at a time, two by two; **dire** ~ **parole** to say a few words; **ci metto** ~ **minuti** I'll have it done in a jiffy.

duecen'tesco, a, schi, sche [duetʃen'tesko] *ag* thirteenth-century.

due'cento [due'tʃɛnto] *num* two hundred ♦ *sm*: **il D**~ the thirteenth century.

duel'lare *vi* to fight a duel.

du'ello *sm* duel.

due'mila *num* two thousand ♦ *sm inv*: **il** ~ the year two thousand.

due'pezzi [due'pɛttsi] *sm* (*costume da bagno*) two-piece swimsuit; (*abito femminile*) two-piece suit.

du'etto *sm* duet.

'dulcis in 'fundo ['dultʃisin'fundo] *av* to cap it all.

'duna *sf* dune.

'dunque *cong* (*perciò*) so, therefore; (*riprendendo il discorso*) well (then) ♦ *sm inv*: **venire al** ~ to come to the point.

'duo *sm inv* (*MUS*) duet; (*TEAT, CINE, fig*) duo.

du'ole *etc vb vedi* **dolere**.

du'omo *sm* cathedral.

'duplex *sm inv* (*TEL*) party line.

dupli'cato *sm* duplicate.

'duplice ['duplitʃe] *ag* double, twofold; **in** ~ **copia** in duplicate.

duplicità [duplitʃi'ta] *sf* (*fig*) duplicity.

du'rante *prep* during; **vita natural** ~ for

life.
du'rare *vi* to last; **non può** ~! this can't go on any longer!; ~ **fatica a** to have difficulty in; ~ **in carica** to remain in office.

du'rata *sf* length (of time); duration; **per tutta la** ~ **di** throughout; ~ **media della vita** life expectancy.

dura'turo, a *ag*, **du'revole** *ag* (*ricordo*) lasting; (*materiale*) durable.

du'rezza [du'rettsa] *sf* hardness; stubbornness; harshness; toughness.

'duro, a *ag* (*pietra, lavoro, materasso, problema*) hard; (*persona: ostinato*) stubborn, obstinate; (*: severo*) harsh, hard; (*voce*) harsh; (*carne*) tough ♦ *sm/f* (*persona*) tough one ♦ *av*: **tener** ~ (*resistere*) to stand firm, hold out; **avere la pelle** ~**a** (*fig: persona*) to be tough; **fare il** ~ to act tough; ~ **di comprendonio** slow-witted; ~ **d'orecchi** hard of hearing.

du'rone *sm* hard skin.

'duttile *ag* (*sostanza*) malleable; (*fig: carattere*) docile, biddable; (*: stile*) adaptable.

DVD [divu'di] *sm inv* DVD; (*lettore*) DVD player.

E e

E, e [e] *sf o m inv* (*lettera*) E, e; **E come Empoli** ≈ E for Edward (*BRIT*), E for Easy (*US*).

E *abbr* (= *est*) E; (*AUT*) = *itinerario europeo*.

e, *dav V spesso* **ed** *cong* and; (*avversativo*) but; (*eppure*) and yet; ~ **lui?** what about him?; ~ **compralo!** well buy it then!

è *vb vedi* **essere**.

E.A.D. *sigla f vedi* **elaborazione automatica dei dati**.

ebaniste'ria *sf* cabinet-making; (*negozio*) cabinet-maker's shop.

'ebano *sm* ebony.

eb'bene *cong* well (then).

'ebbi *etc vb vedi* **avere**.

eb'brezza [eb'brettsa] *sf* intoxication.

'ebbro, a *ag* drunk; ~ **di** (*gioia etc*) beside o.s. *o* wild with.

'ebete *ag* stupid, idiotic.

ebe'tismo *sm* stupidity.

ebollizi'one [ebollit'tsjone] *sf* boiling; **punto di** ~ boiling point.

e'braico, a, ci, che *ag* Hebrew, Hebraic ♦ *sm* (*LING*) Hebrew.

e'breo, a *ag* Jewish ♦ *sm/f* Jew/Jewess.

'Ebridi *sfpl*: **le (isole)** ~ the Hebrides.

e'burneo, a *ag* ivory *cpd*.

E/C *abbr* = **estratto conto**.

eca'tombe *sf* (*strage*) slaughter, massacre.

ecc. *abbr av* (= *eccetera*) etc.

ecce'dente [ettʃe'dɛnte] *sm* surplus.

ecce'denza [ettʃe'dɛntsa] *sf* excess, surplus; (*INFORM*) overflow.

ec'cedere [et'tʃɛdere] *vt* to exceed ♦ *vi* to go too far; ~ **nel bere/mangiare** to indulge in drink/food to excess.

eccel'lente [ettʃel'lɛnte] *ag* excellent; (*cadavere, arresto*) of a prominent person.

eccel'lenza [ettʃe'lɛntsa] *sf* excellence; (*titolo*): **Sua E**~ His Excellency.

ec'cellere [et'tʃɛllere] *vi*: ~ **(in)** to excel (at); ~ **su tutti** to surpass everyone.

ec'celso, a [et'tʃɛlso] *pp di* **eccellere** ♦ *ag* (*cima, montagna*) high; (*fig: ingegno*) great, exceptional.

ec'centrico, a, ci, che [et'tʃɛntriko] *ag* eccentric.

ecces'sivo, a [ettʃes'sivo] *ag* excessive.

ec'cesso [et'tʃɛsso] *sm* excess; **all'**~ (*gentile, generoso*) to excess, excessively; **dare in** ~**i** to fly into a rage; ~ **di velocità** (*AUT*) speeding; ~ **di zelo** overzealousness.

ec'cetera [et'tʃɛtera] *av* et cetera, and so on.

ec'cetto [et'tʃɛtto] *prep* except, with the exception of; ~ **che** *cong* except, other than; ~ **che (non)** unless.

eccettu'are [ettʃettu'are] *vt* to except; **eccettuati i presenti** present company excepted.

eccezio'nale [ettʃettsjo'nale] *ag* exceptional; **in via del tutto** ~ in this instance, exceptionally.

eccezi'one [ettʃet'tsjone] *sf* exception; (*DIR*) objection; **a** ~ **di** with the exception of, except for; **d'**~ exceptional; **fare un'**~ **alla regola** to make an exception to the rule.

ec'chimosi [ek'kimozi] *sf inv* bruise.

ec'cidio [et'tʃidjo] *sm* massacre.

ecci'tante [ettʃi'tante] *ag* (*gen*) exciting; (*sostanza*) stimulating ♦ *sm* stimulant.

ecci'tare [ettʃi'tare] *vt* (*curiosità, interesse*) to excite, arouse; (*folla*) to incite; ~**rsi** *vr* to get excited; (*sessualmente*) to become aroused.

eccitazi'one [ettʃitat'tsjone] *sf* excitement.

ecclesi'astico, a, ci, che *ag* ecclesiastical, church *cpd*; clerical ♦ *sm* ecclesiastic.

'ecco *av* (*per dimostrare*): ~ **il treno!** here's *o* here comes the train!; (*dav pronome*): ~**mi!** here I am!; ~**ne uno!** here's one (of them)!; (*dav pp*): ~ **fatto!** there, that's it done!

ec'come *av* rather; **ti piace?** — ~**!** do you like it? — I'll say! *o* and how! *o* rather! (*BRIT*).

ECG *sigla m* = **elettrocardiogramma**.

echeggi'are [eked'dʒare] *vi* to echo.

e'clettico, a, ci, che *ag, sm/f* eclectic.

eclet'tismo *sm* eclecticism.

eclis'sare *vt* to eclipse; (*fig*) to eclipse, overshadow; ~**rsi** *vr* (*persona: scherzoso*) to slip away.

e'clissi *sf* eclipse.

'eco, *pl(m)* **'echi** *sm o f* echo; **suscitò** *o* **ebbe una profonda** ~ it caused quite a stir.

ecogra'fia *sf* (*MED*) ultrasound.

ecolo'gia [ekolo'dʒia] *sf* ecology.

eco'logico, a, ci, che [eko'lɔdʒiko] *ag* ecological.

ecolo'gista, i, e [ekolo'dʒista] *ag* ecological ♦ *sm/f* ecologist, environmentalist.

e'cologo, a, gi, ghe *sm/f* ecologist.

econo'mato *sm* (*INS*) bursar's office.

econo'mia *sf* economy; (*scienza*) economics *sg*; (*risparmio: azione*) saving; **fare** ~ to economize, make economies; **l'**~ **sommersa** the black (*BRIT*) *o* underground (*US*) economy; ~ **di mercato** market economy; ~ **pianificata** planned economy.

eco'nomico, a, ci, che *ag* economic; (*poco costoso*) economical; **edizione** ~**a** economy edition.

econo'mista, i *sm* economist.

economiz'zare [ekonomid'dzare] *vt, vi* to save.

e'conomo, a *ag* thrifty ♦ *sm/f* (*INS*) bursar.

ecosis'tema, i *sm* ecosystem.

'ecstasy ['ekstasi] *sf inv* ecstasy.

'Ecuador *sm*: **l'**~ Ecuador.

ecu'menico, a, ci, che *ag* ecumenical.

ec'zema [ek'dzɛma] *sm* eczema.

ed *cong vedi* **e**.

Ed. *abbr* = **editore**.

ed. *abbr* = **edizione**.

'edera *sf* ivy.

e'dicola *sf* newspaper kiosk *o* stand (*US*).

edico'lante *sm/f* news vendor (*in kiosk*).

edifi'cante *ag* edifying.

edifi'care *vt* to build; (*fig: teoria, azienda*) to establish; (*indurre al bene*) to edify.

edi'ficio [edi'fitʃo] *sm* building; (*fig*) structure.

e'dile *ag* building *cpd*.

edi'lizio, a [edi'littsjo] *ag* building *cpd* ♦ *sf* building, building trade.

Edim'burgo *sf* Edinburgh.

'edito, a *ag* published.

edi'tore, 'trice *ag* publishing *cpd* ♦ *sm/f* publisher; (*curatore*) editor.

edito'ria *sf* publishing.

editori'ale *ag* publishing *cpd* ♦ *sm* (*articolo di fondo*) editorial, leader.

e'ditto *sm* edict.

edizi'one [edit'tsjone] *sf* edition; (*tiratura*) printing; ~ **a tiratura limitata** limited edition.

edo'nismo *sm* hedonism.

e'dotto, a *ag* informed; **rendere qn** ~ **su qc** to inform sb about sth.

edu'canda *sf* boarder.

edu'care *vt* to educate; (*gusto, mente*) to train; ~ **qn a fare** to train sb to do.

educa'tivo, a *ag* educational.

edu'cato, a *ag* polite, well-mannered.

educazi'one [edukat'tsjone] *sf* education; (*familiare*) upbringing; (*comportamento*) (good) manners *pl*; **per** ~ out of politeness; **questa è pura mancanza d'**~**!** this is sheer bad manners!; ~ **fisica** (*INS*) physical training *o* education.

educherò *etc* [eduke'rɔ] *vb vedi* **educare**.

E.E.D. *sigla f vedi* **elaborazione elettronica dei dati**.

EEG *sigla m* = **elettroencefalogramma**.

e'felide *sf* freckle.

effemi'nato, a *ag* effeminate.

effe'rato, a *ag* brutal, savage.

efferve'scente [efferveʃ'ʃɛnte] *ag* effervescent.

effettiva'mente *av* (*in effetti*) in fact; (*a dire il vero*) really, actually.

effet'tivo, a *ag* (*reale*) real, actual; (*impiegato, professore*) permanent; (*MIL*) regular ♦ *sm* (*MIL*) strength; (*di patrimonio etc*) sum total.

ef'fetto *sm* effect; (*COMM: cambiale*) bill; (*fig: impressione*) impression; **far** ~ (*medicina*) to take effect, (start to) work; **cercare l'**~ to seek attention; **in** ~**i** in fact; ~**i attivi** (*COMM*) bills receivable; ~**i passivi** (*COMM*) bills payable; ~**i personali** personal effects, personal belongings; ~ **serra** greenhouse effect; ~**i speciali** (*CINE*) special effects.

effettu'are *vt* to effect, carry out.

effi'cace [effi'katʃe] *ag* effective.

effi'cacia [effi'katʃa] *sf* effectiveness.

effici'ente [effi'tʃɛnte] *ag* efficient.

efficien'tismo [effitʃen'tizmo] *sm* maximum efficiency.

effici'enza [effi'tʃɛntsa] *sf* efficiency.

effigi'are [effi'dʒare] *vt* to represent, portray.

ef'figie [ef'fidʒe] *sf inv* effigy.
ef'fimero, a *ag* ephemeral.
ef'fluvio *sm* (*anche peg, ironico*) scent, perfume.
effusi'one *sf* effusion.
e.g. *abbr* (= *exempli gratia*) e.g.
egemo'nia [edʒemo'nia] *sf* hegemony.
E'geo [e'dʒɛo] *sm*: **l'~, il mare ~** the Aegean (Sea).
'egida ['ɛdʒida] *sf*: **sotto l'~ di** under the aegis of.
E'gitto [e'dʒitto] *sm*: **l'~** Egypt.
egizi'ano, a [edʒit'tsjano] *ag, sm/f* Egyptian.
e'gizio, a [e'dʒittsjo] *ag, sm/f* (ancient) Egyptian.
'egli ['eʎʎi] *pron* he; **~ stesso** he himself.
'ego *sm inv* (*PSIC*) ego.
ego'centrico, a, ci, che [ego'tʃɛntriko] *ag* egocentric(al) ♦ *sm/f* self-centred (*BRIT*) *o* self-centered (*US*) person.
egocen'trismo [egotʃen'trizmo] *sm* egocentricity.
ego'ismo *sm* selfishness, egoism.
ego'ista, i, e *ag* selfish, egoistic ♦ *sm/f* egoist.
ego'istico, a, ci, che *ag* egoistic, selfish.
ego'tismo *sm* egotism.
ego'tista, i, e *ag* egotistic ♦ *sm/f* egotist.
Egr. *abbr* = **Egregio.**
e'gregio, a, gi, gie [e'grɛdʒo] *ag* distinguished; (*nelle lettere*): **E~ Signore** Dear Sir.
eguagli'anza *etc* [egwaʎ'ʎantsa] *vedi* **uguaglianza** *etc*.
eguali'tario, a *ag, sm/f* egalitarian.
E.I. *abbr* = *Esercito Italiano*.
eiaculazi'one [ejakulat'tsjone] *sf* ejaculation; **~ precoce** premature ejaculation.
elabo'rare *vt* (*progetto*) to work out, elaborate; (*dati*) to process; (*digerire*) to digest.
elabora'tore *sm* (*INFORM*): **~ elettronico** computer.
elaborazi'one [elaborat'tsjone] *sf* elaboration; processing; digestion; **~ automatica dei dati (E.A.D.)** (*INFORM*) automatic data processing (A.D.P.); **~ elettronica dei dati (E.E.D.)** (*INFORM*) electronic data processing (E.D.P.); **~ testi** (*INFORM*) text processing.
elar'gire [elar'dʒire] *vt* to hand out.
elargizi'one [elardʒit'tsjone] *sf* donation.
elasticiz'zato, a [elastitʃid'dzato] *ag* (*tessuto*) stretch *cpd*.
e'lastico, a, ci, che *ag* elastic; (*fig: andatura*) springy; (: *decisione, vedute*) flexible ♦ *sm* (*gommino*) rubber band; (*per

il cucito) elastic *no pl*.
ele'fante *sm* elephant.
ele'gante *ag* elegant.
ele'ganza [ele'gantsa] *sf* elegance.
e'leggere [e'lɛddʒere] *vt* to elect.
elemen'tare *ag* elementary; **le (scuole) ~i** *vedi* **scuola elementare; prima ~** first year of primary school, ≈ infants' class (*BRIT*), ≈ 1st grade (*US*).
ele'mento *sm* element; (*parte componente*) element, component, part; **~i** *smpl* (*della scienza etc*) elements, rudiments.
ele'mosina *sf* charity, alms *pl*; **chiedere l'~** to beg.
elemosi'nare *vt* to beg for, ask for ♦ *vi* to beg.
elen'care *vt* to list.
elencherò *etc* [elenke'rɔ] *vb vedi* **elencare.**
e'lenco, chi *sm* list; **~ nominativo** list of names; **~ telefonico** telephone directory.
e'lessi *etc vb vedi* **eleggere.**
elet'tivo, a *ag* (*carica etc*) elected.
e'letto, a *pp di* **eleggere** ♦ *sm/f* (*nominato*) elected member.
eletto'rale *ag* electoral, election *cpd*.
eletto'rato *sm* electorate.
elet'tore, 'trice *sm/f* voter, elector.
elet'trauto *sm inv* workshop for car electrical repairs; (*tecnico*) car electrician.
elettri'cista, i [elettri'tʃista] *sm* electrician.
elettricità [elettritʃi'ta] *sf* electricity.
e'lettrico, a, ci, che *ag* electric(al).
elettrifi'care *vt* to electrify.
elettriz'zante [elettrid'dzante] *ag* (*fig*) electrifying, thrilling.
elettriz'zare [elettrid'dzare] *vt* to electrify; **~rsi** *vr* to become charged with electricity; (*fig: persona*) to be thrilled.
e'lettro... *prefisso* electro....
elettrocardio'gramma, i *sm* electrocardiogram.
e'lettrodo *sm* electrode.
elettrodo'mestico, a, ci, che *ag*: **apparecchi ~ci** domestic (electrical) appliances.
elettroencefalo'gramma, i [elettroentʃefalo'gramma] *sm* electroencephalogram.
elet'trogeno, a [elet'trɔdʒeno] *ag*: **gruppo ~** generator.
elet'trolisi *sf* electrolysis.
elettroma'gnetico, a, ci, che [elettromaɲ'ɲetiko] *ag* electromagnetic.
elettromo'trice [elettromo'tritʃe] *sf* electric tram.
elet'trone *sm* electron.
elet'tronico, a, ci, che *ag* electronic ♦ *sf*

electronics *sg*.
elettro'shock [elettroʃ'ʃɔk] *sm inv*
(electro)shock treatment.
elettro'tecnico, a, ci, che *ag*
electrotechnical ♦ *sm* electrical engineer.
ele'vare *vt* to raise; (*edificio*) to erect;
(*multa*) to impose; ~ **un numero al
quadrato** to square a number.
eleva'tezza [eleva'tettsa] *sf* (*altezza*)
elevation; (*di animo, pensiero*) loftiness.
ele'vato, a *ag* (*gen*) high; (*cime*) high, lofty;
(*fig: stile, sentimenti*) lofty.
elevazi'one [elevat'tsjone] *sf* elevation;
(*l'elevare*) raising.
elezi'one [elet'tsjone] *sf* election; ~**i** *sfpl*
(*POL*) election(s); **patria d'**~ chosen
country.
'elica, che *sf* propeller.
eli'cottero *sm* helicopter.
e'lidere *vt* (*FONETICA*) to elide; ~**rsi** *vr* (*forze*)
to cancel each other out.
elimi'nare *vt* to eliminate.
elimina'toria *sf* eliminating round.
.eliminazi'one [eliminat'tsjone] *sf*
elimination.
'elio *sm* helium.
eli'porto *sm* heliport.
elisabetti'ano, a *ag* Elizabethan.
eli'sir *sm inv* elixir.
e'liso, a *pp di* **elidere**.
elisoc'corso *sm* helicopter ambulance.
eli'tario, a *ag* elitist.
é'lite [e'lit] *sf inv* élite.
'ella *pron* she; (*forma di cortesia*) you; ~
stessa she herself; you yourself.
el'lisse *sf* ellipse.
el'littico, a, ci, che *ag* elliptic(al).
el'metto *sm* helmet.
'elmo *sm* helmet.
elogi'are [elod'dʒare] *vt* to praise.
elogia'tivo, a [elodʒa'tivo] *ag* laudatory.
e'logio [e'lɔdʒo] *sm* (*discorso, scritto*)
eulogy; (*lode*) praise; ~ **funebre** funeral
oration.
elo'quente *ag* eloquent; **questi dati sono**
~**i** these facts speak for themselves.
elo'quenza [elo'kwɛntsa] *sf* eloquence.
e'loquio *sm* speech, language.
elucu'brare *vt* to ponder about *o* over.
elucubrazi'oni [elukubrat'tsjoni] *sfpl* (*anche
ironico*) cogitations, ponderings.
e'ludere *vt* to evade.
e'lusi *etc vb vedi* **eludere**.
elusi'one *sf*: ~ **d'imposta** tax evasion.
elu'sivo, a *ag* evasive.
e'luso, a *pp di* **eludere**.
el'vetico, a, ci, che *ag* Swiss.
emaci'ato, a [ema'tʃato] *ag* emaciated.

e-'mail, e'mail [e'mail] *sf inv, ag inv* email;
indirizzo ~ e-mail address.
ema'nare *vt* to send out, give off; (*fig:
leggi*) to promulgate; (: *decreti*) to issue
♦ *vi*: ~ **da** to come from.
emanazi'one [emanat'tsjone] *sf* (*di raggi,
calore*) emanation; (*di odori*) exhalation;
(*di legge*) promulgation; (*di ordine,
circolare*) issuing.
emanci'pare [emant'ʃi'pare] *vt* to
emancipate; ~**rsi** *vr* (*fig*) to become
liberated *o* emancipated.
emancipazi'one [emantʃipat'tsjone] *sf*
emancipation.
emargi'nare [emardʒi'nare] *vt* (*fig:
socialmente*) to cast out.
emargi'nato, a [emardʒi'nato] *sm/f* outcast.
ematolo'gia [ematolo'dʒia] *sf* haematology
(*BRIT*), hematology (*US*).
ema'toma, i *sm* haematoma (*BRIT*),
hematoma (*US*).
em'blema, i *sm* emblem.
emble'matico, a, ci, che *ag* emblematic;
(*fig: atteggiamento, parole*) symbolic.
embo'lia *sf* embolism.
embrio'nale, i, e *ag* embryonic, embryo
cpd; **allo stadio** ~ at the embryo stage.
embri'one *sm* embryo.
emenda'mento *sm* amendment.
emen'dare *vt* to amend.
emer'gente [emer'dʒɛnte] *ag* emerging.
emer'genza [emer'dʒɛntsa] *sf* emergency;
in caso di ~ in an emergency.
e'mergere [e'mɛrdʒere] *vi* to emerge;
(*sommergibile*) to surface; (*fig:
distinguersi*) to stand out.
e'merito, a *ag* (*insigne*) distinguished; **è un**
~ **cretino!** he's a complete idiot!
e'mersi *etc vb vedi* **emergere**.
e'merso, a *pp di* **emergere** ♦ *ag* (*GEO*): **terre**
~**e** lands above sea level.
e'messo, a *pp di* **emettere**.
e'mettere *vt* (*suono, luce*) to give out, emit;
(*onde radio*) to send out; (*assegno,
francobollo, ordine*) to issue; (*fig: giudizio*)
to express, voice; ~ **la sentenza** (*DIR*) to
pass sentence.
emi'crania *sf* migraine.
emi'grante *ag, sm/f* emigrant.
emi'grare *vi* to emigrate.
emi'grato, a *ag* emigrant ♦ *sm/f* emigrant;
(*STORIA*) émigré.
emigrazi'one [emigrat'tsjone] *sf*
emigration.
emili'ano, a *ag* of (*o* from) Emilia.
emi'nente *ag* eminent, distinguished.
emi'nenza [emi'nɛntsa] *sf* eminence; ~
grigia (*fig*) éminence grise.

emi'rato *sm* emirate; **gli E~i Arabi Uniti** the United Arab Emirates.

e'miro *sm* emir.

emis'fero *sm* hemisphere; ~ **boreale/australe** northern/southern hemisphere.

e'misi *etc vb vedi* **emettere**.

emis'sario *sm* (*GEO*) outlet, effluent; (*inviato*) emissary.

emissi'one *sf* (*vedi emettere*) emission; sending out; issue; (*RADIO*) broadcast.

emit'tente *ag* (*banca*) issuing; (*RADIO*) broadcasting, transmitting ♦ *sf* (*RADIO*) transmitter.

emofi'lia *sf* haemophilia (*BRIT*), hemophilia (*US*).

emofi'liaco, a, ci, che *ag, sm/f* haemophiliac (*BRIT*), hemophiliac (*US*).

emoglo'bina *sf* haemoglobin (*BRIT*), ·hemoglobin (*US*).

emolli'ente *ag* soothing.

emorra'gia, 'gie [emorra'dʒia] *sf* haemorrhage (*BRIT*), hemorrhage (*US*).

emor'roidi *sfpl* haemorrhoids (*BRIT*), hemorrhoids (*US*).

emos'tatico, a, ci, che *ag* haemostatic (*BRIT*), hemostatic (*US*); **laccio ~** tourniquet; **matita ~a** styptic pencil.

emotività *sf* emotionalism.

emo'tivo, a *ag* emotional.

emozio'nante [emottsjo'nante] *ag* exciting, thrilling.

emozio'nare [emottsjo'nare] *vt* (*appassionare*) to thrill, excite; (*commuovere*) to move; (*innervosire*) to upset; ~**rsi** *vr* to be excited; to be moved; to be upset.

emozi'one [emot'tsjone] *sf* emotion; (*agitazione*) excitement.

'empio, a *ag* (*sacrilego*) impious; (*spietato*) cruel, pitiless; (*malvagio*) wicked, evil.

em'pirico, a, ci, che *ag* empirical.

em'porio *sm* general store.

emu'lare *vt* to emulate.

'emulo, a *sm/f* imitator.

emulsi'one *sf* emulsion.

EN *sigla* = *Enna*.

en'ciclica, che [en'tʃiklika] *sf* (*REL*) encyclical.

enciclope'dia [entʃiklope'dia] *sf* encyclop(a)edia.

encomi'abile *ag* commendable, praiseworthy.

encomi'are *vt* to commend, praise.

en'comio *sm* commendation; ~ **solenne** (*MIL*) mention in dispatches.

endove'noso, a *ag* (*MED*) intravenous ♦ *sf* intravenous injection.

E'NEA *sigla f* = *Comitato nazionale per la ricerca e lo sviluppo dell'Energia Nucleare e delle Energie Alternative*.

'E.N.E.L. *sigla m* (= *Ente Nazionale per l'Energia Elettrica*) *national electricity company*.

ener'getico, a, ci, che [ener'dʒetiko] *ag* (*risorse, crisi*) energy *cpd*; (*sostanza, alimento*) energy-giving.

ener'gia, 'gie [ener'dʒia] *sf* (*FISICA*) energy; (*fig*) energy, strength, vigour (*BRIT*), vigor (*US*).

e'nergico, a, ci, che [e'nεrdʒiko] *ag* energetic, vigorous.

'enfasi *sf* emphasis; (*peg*) bombast, pomposity.

en'fatico, a, ci, che *ag* emphatic; pompous.

enfatiz'zare [enfatid'dzare] *vt* to emphasize, stress.

enfi'sema *sm* emphysema.

'ENI *sigla m* = *Ente Nazionale Idrocarburi*.

e'nigma, i *sm* enigma.

enig'matico, a, ci, che *ag* enigmatic.

'ENIT *sigla m* (= *Ente Nazionale Italiano per il Turismo*) *Italian tourist authority*.

en'nesimo, a *ag* (*MAT, fig*) nth; **per l'~a volta** for the umpteenth time.

enolo'gia [enolo'dʒia] *sf* oenology (*BRIT*), enology (*US*).

e'nologo, gi *sm* wine expert.

e'norme *ag* enormous, huge.

enormità *sf inv* enormity, huge size; (*assurdità*) absurdity; **non dire ~!** don't talk nonsense!

eno'teca, che *sf* (*negozio*) wine bar.

'E.N.P.A. *sigla m* (= *Ente Nazionale Protezione Animali*) ≈ RSPCA (*BRIT*), ≈ SPCA (*US*).

'E.N.P.A.S. *sigla m* (= *Ente Nazionale di Previdenza e Assistenza per i Dipendenti Statali*) *welfare organization for State employees*.

'ente *sm* (*istituzione*) body, board, corporation; (*FILOSOFIA*) being; ~ **locale** local authority (*BRIT*), local government (*US*); ~ **pubblico** public body; ~ **di ricerca** research organization.

ente'rite *sf* enteritis.

entità *sf* (*FILOSOFIA*) entity; (*di perdita, danni, investimenti*) extent; (*di popolazione*) size; **di molta/poca ~** (*avvenimento, incidente*) of great/little importance.

en'trambi, e *pron pl* both (of them) ♦ *ag pl*: ~ **i ragazzi** both boys, both of the boys.

en'trante *ag* (*prossimo: mese, anno*) next, coming.

en'trare *vi* to enter, go (*o* come) in; ~ **in** (*luogo*) to enter, go (*o* come) into; (*trovar* *posto, poter stare*) to fit into; (*essere ammesso a: club etc*) to join, become a member of; ~ **in automobile** to get into the car; **far** ~ **qn** (*visitatore etc*) to show sb in; ~ **in società/in commercio con qn** to go into partnership/business with sb; **questo non c'entra** (*fig*) that's got nothing to do with it.

en'trata *sf* entrance, entry; ~**e** *sfpl* (*COMM*) receipts, takings; (*ECON*) income *sg*; "~ **libera**" "admission free"; **con l'~ in vigore dei nuovi provvedimenti** ... once the new measures come into effect ...; ~**e tributarie** tax revenue *sg*.

'entro *prep* (*temporale*) within; ~ **domani** by tomorrow; ~ **e non oltre il 25 aprile** no later than 25th April.

entro'terra *sm inv* hinterland.

entusias'mante *ag* exciting.

entusias'mare *vt* to excite, fill with enthusiasm; ~**rsi** *vr*: ~**rsi (per qc/qn)** to become enthusiastic (about sth/sb).

entusi'asmo *sm* enthusiasm.

entusi'asta, i, e *ag* enthusiastic ♦ *sm/f* enthusiast.

entusi'astico, a, ci, che *ag* enthusiastic.

enucle'are *vt* (*formale: chiarire*) to explain.

enume'rare *vt* to enumerate, list.

enunci'are [enun'tʃare] *vt* (*teoria*) to enunciate, set out.

en'zima, i *sm* enzyme.

e'patico, a, ci, che *ag* hepatic; **cirrosi** ~**a** cirrhosis of the liver.

epa'tite *sf* hepatitis.

'epico, a, ci, che *ag* epic.

epide'mia *sf* epidemic.

epi'dermico, a, ci, che *ag* (*ANAT*) skin *cpd*; (*fig: interesse, impressioni*) superficial.

epi'dermide *sf* skin, epidermis.

Epifa'nia *sf* Epiphany.

e'pigono *sm* imitator.

e'pigrafe *sf* epigraph; (*su libro*) dedication.

epiles'sia *sf* epilepsy.

epi'lettico, a, ci, che *ag*, *sm/f* epileptic.

e'pilogo, ghi *sm* conclusion.

epi'sodico, a, ci, che *ag* (*romanzo, narrazione*) episodic; (*fig: occasionale*) occasional.

epi'sodio *sm* episode; **sceneggiato a** ~**i** serial.

e'pistola *sf* epistle.

episto'lare *ag* epistolary; **essere in rapporto** *o* **relazione** ~ **con qn** to correspond *o* be in correspondence with sb.

e'piteto *sm* epithet.

'epoca, che *sf* (*periodo storico*) age, era; (*tempo*) time; (*GEO*) age; **mobili d'**~ period

furniture; **fare** ~ (*scandalo*) to cause a stir; (*cantante, moda*) to mark a new era.

epo'pea *sf* (*anche fig*) epic.

ep'pure *cong* and yet, nevertheless.

EPT *sigla m* (= *Ente Provinciale per il Turismo*) *district tourist bureau.*

epu'rare *vt* (*POL*) to purge.

equ'anime *ag* (*imparziale*) fair, impartial.

equa'tore *sm* equator.

equazi'one [ekwat'tsjone] *sf* (*MAT*) equation.

e'questre *ag* equestrian.

equi'latero, a *ag* equilateral.

equili'brare *vt* to balance.

equili'brato, a *ag* (*carico, fig: giudizio*) balanced; (*vita*) well-regulated; (*persona*) stable, well-balanced.

equi'librio *sm* balance, equilibrium; **perdere l'**~ to lose one's balance; **stare in** ~ **su** (*persona*) to balance on; (*oggetto*) to be balanced on.

equili'brismo *sm* tightrope walking; (*fig*) juggling.

e'quino, a *ag* horse *cpd*, equine.

equi'nozio [ekwi'nɔttsjo] *sm* equinox.

equipaggia'mento [ekwipaddʒa'mento] *sm* (*operazione: di nave*) equipping, fitting out; (: *di spedizione, esercito*) equipping, kitting out; (*attrezzatura*) equipment.

equipaggi'are [ekwipad'dʒare] *vt* to equip; ~**rsi** *vr* to equip o.s.

equi'paggio [ekwi'paddʒo] *sm* crew.

equipa'rare *vt* to make equal.

é'quipe [e'kip] *sf* (*SPORT, gen*) team.

equità *sf* equity, fairness.

equitazi'one [ekwitat'tsjone] *sf* (horse-) riding.

equiva'lente *ag*, *sm* equivalent.

equiva'lenza [ekwiva'lɛntsa] *sf* equivalence.

equiva'lere *vi*: ~ **a** to be equivalent to; ~**rsi** *vr* (*forze etc*) to counterbalance each other; (*soluzioni*) to amount to the same thing; **equivale a dire che** ... that is the same as saying that ....

equi'valso, a *pp di* **equivalere**.

equivo'care *vi* to misunderstand.

e'quivoco, a, ci, che *ag* equivocal, ambiguous; (*sospetto*) dubious ♦ *sm* misunderstanding; **a scanso di** ~**ci** to avoid any misunderstanding; **giocare sull'**~ to equivocate.

'equo, a *ag* fair, just.

'era *sf* era.

'era *etc vb vedi* **essere**.

erari'ale *ag*: **ufficio** ~ ≈ tax office; **imposte** ~**i** revenue taxes; **spese** ~**i** public expenditure *sg*.

e'rario *sm*: l'~ ≈ the Treasury.

'erba *sf* grass; (*aromatica, medicinale*) herb; in ~ (*fig*) budding; **fare di ogni ~ un fascio** (*fig*) to lump everything (*o* everybody) together.

er'baccia, ce [er'battʃa] *sf* weed.

er'bivoro, a *ag* herbivorous ♦ *sm/f* herbivore.

erbo'rista, i, e *sm/f* herbalist.

erboriste'ria *sf* (*scienza*) study of medicinal herbs; (*negozio*) herbalist's (shop).

er'boso, a *ag* grassy.

e'rede *sm/f* heir; ~ **legittimo** heir-at-law.

eredità *sf* (*DIR*) inheritance; (*BIOL*) heredity; **lasciare qc in ~ a qn** to leave *o* bequeath sth to sb.

eredi'tare *vt* to inherit.

eredi'tario, a *ag* hereditary.

erediti'era *sf* heiress.

ere'mita, i *sm* hermit.

eremi'taggio [eremi'taddʒo] *sm* hermitage.

'eremo *sm* hermitage; (*fig*) retreat.

ere'sia *sf* heresy.

e'ressi *etc vb vedi* **erigere**.

e'retico, a, ci, che *ag* heretical ♦ *sm/f* heretic.

e'retto, a *pp di* **erigere** ♦ *ag* erect, upright.

erezi'one [eret'tsjone] *sf* (*FISIOL*) erection.

ergasto'lano, a *sm/f* prisoner serving a life sentence, lifer (*fam*).

er'gastolo *sm* (*DIR: pena*) life imprisonment; (*: luogo di pena*) prison (*for those serving life sentences*).

ergono'mia *sf* ergonomics *sg*.

ergo'nomico, a, ci, che *ag* ergonomic(al).

'erica *sf* heather.

e'rigere [e'ridʒere] *vt* to erect, raise; (*fig: fondare*) to found.

eri'tema *sm* (*MED*) inflammation, erythema; ~ **solare** sunburn.

Eri'trea *sf* Eritrea.

ermel'lino *sm* ermine.

er'metico, a, ci, che *ag* hermetic.

'ernia *sf* (*MED*) hernia; ~ **del disco** slipped disc.

'ero *vb vedi* **essere**.

e'rodere *vt* to erode.

e'roe *sm* hero.

ero'gare *vt* (*somme*) to distribute; (*gas, servizi*) to supply.

erogazi'one [erogat'tsjone] *sf* distribution; supply.

e'roico, a, ci, che *ag* heroic.

ero'ina *sf* heroine; (*droga*) heroin.

ero'ismo *sm* heroism.

'eros *sm* Eros.

erosi'one *sf* erosion.

e'roso, a *pp di* **erodere**.

e'rotico, a, ci, che *ag* erotic.

ero'tismo *sm* eroticism.

'erpete *sm* herpes *sg*.

'erpice ['erpitʃe] *sm* (*AGR*) harrow.

er'rare *vi* (*vagare*) to wander, roam; (*sbagliare*) to be mistaken.

er'roneo, a *ag* erroneous, wrong.

er'rore *sm* error, mistake; (*morale*) error; **per ~** by mistake; ~ **giudiziario** miscarriage of justice.

'erto, a *ag* (very) steep ♦ *sf* steep slope; **stare all'~a** to be on the alert.

eru'dire *vt* to teach, educate.

eru'dito, a *ag* learned, erudite.

erut'tare *vt* (*sog: vulcano*) to throw out, belch.

eruzi'one [erut'tsjone] *sf* eruption; (*MED*) rash.

es. *abbr* (= *esempio*) e.g.

E.S. *sigla m* (= *elettroshock*) ECT.

E.S.A. ['eza] *sigla m* (= *European Space Agency*) ESA.

esacer'bare [ezatʃer'bare] *vt* to exacerbate.

esage'rare [ezadʒe'rare] *vt* to exaggerate ♦ *vi* to exaggerate; (*eccedere*) to go too far; **senza ~** without exaggeration.

esage'rato, a [ezadʒe'rato] *ag* (*notizia, proporzioni*) exaggerated; (*curiosità, pignoleria*) excessive; (*prezzo*) exorbitant ♦ *sm/f*: **sei il solito ~** you are exaggerating as usual.

esagerazi'one [esadʒerat'tsjone] *sf* exaggeration.

esago'nale *ag* hexagonal.

e'sagono *sm* hexagon.

esa'lare *vt* (*odori*) to give off ♦ *vi*: ~ (**da**) to emanate (from); ~ **l'ultimo respiro** (*fig*) to breathe one's last.

esalazi'one [ezalat'tsjone] *sf* (*emissione*) exhalation; (*odore*) fumes *pl*.

esal'tante *ag* exciting.

esal'tare *vt* to exalt; (*entusiasmare*) to excite, stir; ~**rsi** *vr*: ~**rsi (per qc)** to grow excited (about sth).

esal'tato, a *sm/f* fanatic.

esaltazi'one [ezaltat'tsjone] *sf* (*elogio*) extolling, exalting; (*nervosa*) intense excitement; (*mistica*) exaltation.

e'same *sm* examination; (*INS*) exam, examination; **fare** *o* **dare un ~** to sit *o* take an exam; **fare un ~ di coscienza** to search one's conscience; ~ **di guida** driving test; ~ **del sangue** blood test.

esami'nare *vt* to examine.

e'sangue *ag* bloodless; (*fig: pallido*) pale, wan; (*: privo di vigore*) lifeless.

e'sanime *ag* lifeless.

esaspe'rare *vt* to exasperate; (*situazione*) to exacerbate; ~**rsi** *vr* to become annoyed *o* exasperated.

esasperazi'one [ezasperat'tsjone] *sf* exasperation.

esatta'mente *av* exactly; accurately, precisely.

esat'tezza [ezat'tettsa] *sf* exactitude, accuracy, precision; **per l'**~ to be precise.

e'satto, a *pp di* **esigere** ♦ *ag* (*calcolo, ora*) correct, right, exact; (*preciso*) accurate, precise; (*puntuale*) punctual.

esat'tore *sm* (*di imposte etc*) collector.

esatto'ria *sf*: ~ **comunale** district rates office (*BRIT*) *o* assessor's office (*US*).

esau'dire *vt* to grant, fulfil (*BRIT*), fulfill (*US*).

esauri'ente *ag* exhaustive.

esauri'mento *sm* exhaustion; ~ **nervoso** nervous breakdown; **svendita (fino) ad** ~ **della merce** clearance sale.

esau'rire *vt* (*stancare*) to exhaust, wear out; (*provviste, miniera*) to exhaust; ~**rsi** *vr* to exhaust o.s., wear o.s. out; (*provviste*) to run out.

esau'rito, a *ag* exhausted; (*merci*) sold out; (*libri*) out of print; **essere** ~ (*persona*) to be run down; **registrare il tutto** ~ (*TEAT*) to have a full house.

e'sausto, a *ag* exhausted.

esauto'rare *vt* (*dirigente, funzionario*) to deprive of authority.

esazi'one [ezat'tsjone] *sf* collection (of taxes).

'esca, *pl* **'esche** *sf* bait.

escamo'tage [eskamɔ'taʒ] *sm* subterfuge.

escande'scenza [eskandeʃ'ʃɛntsa] *sf*: **dare in** ~**e** to lose one's temper, fly into a rage.

'esce ['ɛʃʃe] *vb vedi* **uscire.**

eschi'mese [eski'mese] *ag, sm/f, sm* Eskimo.

'esci ['ɛʃʃi] *vb vedi* **uscire.**

escl. *abbr* (= *escluso*) excl.

escla'mare *vi* to exclaim, cry out.

esclama'tivo, a *ag*: **punto** ~ exclamation mark.

esclamazi'one [esklamat'tsjone] *sf* exclamation.

es'cludere *vt* to exclude.

es'clusi *etc vb vedi* **escludere.**

esclusi'one *sf* exclusion; **a** ~ **di, fatta** ~ **per** except (for), apart from; **senza** ~ **(alcuna)** without exception; **procedere per** ~ to follow a process of elimination; **senza** ~ **di colpi** (*fig*) with no holds barred.

esclu'siva *sf vedi* **esclusivo.**

esclusiva'mente *av* exclusively, solely.

esclu'sivo, a *ag* exclusive ♦ *sf* (*DIR, COMM*) exclusive *o* sole rights *pl*.

es'cluso, a *pp di* **escludere** ♦ *ag*: **nessuno** ~ without exception; **IVA** ~**a** excluding VAT, exclusive of VAT.

'esco *vb vedi* **uscire.**

escogi'tare [eskodʒi'tare] *vt* to devise, think up.

'escono *vb vedi* **uscire.**

escoriazi'one [eskorjat'tsjone] *sf* abrasion, graze.

escre'menti *smpl* excrement *sg*, faeces.

es'cudo *sm* (*pl* ~**s**) escudo.

escursi'one *sf* (*gita*) excursion, trip; (: *a piedi*) hike, walk; (*METEOR*): ~ **termica** temperature range.

escursio'nista, i, e *sm/f* (*gitante*) (day) tripper; (: *a piedi*) hiker, walker.

ese'crare *vt* to loathe, abhor.

esecu'tivo, a *ag, sm* executive.

esecu'tore, 'trice *sm/f* (*MUS*) performer; (*DIR*) executor.

esecuzi'one [ezekut'tsjone] *sf* execution, carrying out; (*MUS*) performance; ~ **capitale** execution.

ese'geta, i [eze'dʒɛta] *sm* commentator.

esegu'ire *vt* to carry out, execute; (*MUS*) to perform, execute.

e'sempio *sm* example; **per** ~ for example, for instance; **fare un** ~ to give an example.

esem'plare *ag* exemplary ♦ *sm* example; (*copia*) copy; (*BOT, ZOOL, GEO*) specimen.

esemplifi'care *vt* to exemplify.

esen'tare *vt*: ~ **qn/qc da** to exempt sb/sth from.

esen'tasse *ag inv* tax-free.

e'sente *ag*: ~ **da** (*dispensato da*) exempt from; (*privo di*) free from.

esenzi'one [ezen'tsjone] *sf* exemption.

e'sequie *sfpl* funeral rites; funeral service *sg*.

eser'cente [ezer'tʃɛnte] *sm/f* trader, dealer; shopkeeper.

eserci'tare [ezertʃi'tare] *vt* (*professione*) to practise (*BRIT*), practice (*US*); (*allenare: corpo, mente*) to exercise, train; (*diritto*) to exercise; (*influenza, pressione*) to exert; ~**rsi** *vr* to practise; ~**rsi nella guida** to practise one's driving.

esercitazi'one [ezertʃitat'tsjone] *sf* (*scolastica, militare*) exercise; ~**i di tiro** target practice *sg*.

e'sercito [e'zɛrtʃito] *sm* army.

eser'cizio [ezer'tʃittsjo] *sm* practice; (*compito, movimento*) exercise; (*azienda*) business, concern; (*ECON*): ~ **finanziario** financial year; **in** ~ (*medico etc*) practising (*BRIT*), practicing (*US*); **nell'**~ **delle proprie funzioni** in the execution of one's duties.

esfoli'ante *sm* exfoliator.

esi'bire *vt* to exhibit, display; (*documenti*) to produce, present; ~**rsi** *vr* (*attore*) to perform; (*fig*) to show off.

esibizi'one [ezibit'tsjone] *sf* exhibition; (*di documento*) presentation; (*spettacolo*) show, performance.

esibizio'nista, i, e [ezibittsjo'nista] *sm/f* exhibitionist.

esi'gente [ezi'dʒɛnte] *ag* demanding.

esi'genza [ezi'dʒɛntsa] *sf* demand, requirement.

e'sigere [e'zidʒere] *vt* (*pretendere*) to demand; (*richiedere*) to demand, require; (*imposte*) to collect.

esi'gibile [ezi'dʒibile] *ag* payable.

e'siguo, a *ag* small, slight.

esila'rante *ag* hilarious; **gas** ~ laughing gas.

'**esile** *ag* (*persona*) slender, slim; (*stelo*) thin; (*voce*) faint.

esili'are *vt* to exile.

esili'ato, a *ag* exiled ♦ *sm/f* exile.

e'silio *sm* exile.

e'simere *vt*: ~ **qn/qc da** to exempt sb/sth from; ~**rsi** *vr*: ~**rsi da** to get out of.

esis'tente *ag* existing; (*attuale*) present, current.

esis'tenza [ezis'tɛntsa] *sf* existence.

esistenzia'lismo [ezistentsja'lizmo] *sm* existentialism.

e'sistere *vi* to exist; **esiste più di una versione dell'opera** there is more than one version of the work; **non esiste!** (*fam*) no way!

esis'tito, a *pp di* **esistere**.

esi'tante *ag* hesitant; (*voce*) faltering.

esi'tare *vi* to hesitate.

esitazi'one [ezitat'tsjone] *sf* hesitation.

'**esito** *sm* result, outcome.

'**eskimo** *sm* (*giaccone*) parka.

'**esodo** *sm* exodus.

e'sofago, gi *sm* oesophagus (*BRIT*), esophagus (*US*).

esone'rare *vt*: ~ **qn da** to exempt sb from.

esorbi'tante *ag* exorbitant, excessive.

esor'cismo [ezor'tʃizmo] *sm* exorcism.

esor'cista, i [ezor'tʃista] *sm* exorcist.

esorciz'zare [ezort'ʃid'dzare] *vt* to exorcize.

esordi'ente *sm/f* beginner.

e'sordio *sm* debut.

esor'dire *vi* (*nel teatro*) to make one's debut; (*fig*) to start out, begin (one's career); **esordì dicendo che ...** he began by saying (that) ....

esor'tare *vt*: ~ **qn a fare** to urge sb to do.

esortazi'one [ezortat'tsjone] *sf*

exhortation.

e'soso, a *ag* (*prezzo*) exorbitant; (*persona: avido*) grasping.

eso'terico, a, ci, che *ag* esoteric.

e'sotico, a, ci, che *ag* exotic.

es'pandere *vt* to expand; (*confini*) to extend; (*influenza*) to extend, spread; ~**rsi** *vr* to expand.

espansi'one *sf* expansion.

espansività *sf* expansiveness.

espan'sivo, a *ag* expansive, communicative.

es'panso, a *pp di* **espandere**.

espatri'are *vi* to leave one's country.

es'patrio *sm* expatriation; **permesso di** ~ authorization to leave the country.

espedi'ente *sm* expedient; **vivere di** ~**i** to live by one's wits.

es'pellere *vt* to expel.

esperi'enza [espe'rjɛntsa] *sf* experience; (*SCIENZA: prova*) experiment; **parlare per** ~ to speak from experience.

esperi'mento *sm* experiment; **fare un** ~ to carry out *o* do an experiment.

es'perto, a *ag*, *sm/f* expert.

espi'anto *sm* (*MED*) removal.

espi'are *vt* to atone for.

espiazi'one [espiat'tsjone] *sf*: ~ **(di)** expiation (of), atonement (for).

espi'rare *vt*, *vi* to breathe out.

espleta'mento *sm* (*AMM*) carrying out.

esple'tare *vt* (*AMM*) to carry out.

espli'care *vt* (*attività*) to carry out, perform.

esplica'tivo, a *ag* explanatory.

es'plicito, a [es'plitʃito] *ag* explicit.

es'plodere *vi* (*anche fig*) to explode ♦ *vt* to fire.

esplo'rare *vt* to explore.

esplora'tore, 'trice *sm/f* explorer; (*anche: giovane* ~) (boy) scout/(girl) guide (*BRIT*) *o* scout (*US*) ♦ *sm* (*NAUT*) scout (ship).

esplorazi'one [esplorat'tsjone] *sf* exploration; **mandare qn in** ~ (*MIL*) to send sb to scout ahead.

esplosi'one *sf* (*anche fig*) explosion.

esplo'sivo, a *ag*, *sm* explosive.

es'ploso, a *pp di* **esplodere**.

es'pone *etc vb vedi* **esporre**.

espo'nente *sm/f* (*rappresentante*) representative.

esponenzi'ale [esponen'tsjale] *ag* (*MAT*) exponential.

es'pongo, es'poni *etc vb vedi* **esporre**.

es'porre *vt* (*merci*) to display; (*quadro*) to exhibit, show; (*fatti, idee*) to explain, set out; (*porre in pericolo, FOT*) to expose;

esporsi *vr:* **esporsi a** (*sole, pericolo*) to expose o.s. to; (*critiche*) to lay o.s. open to.

espor'tare *vt* to export.

esporta'tore, 'trice *ag* exporting ♦ *sm* exporter.

esportazi'one [esportat'tsjone] *sf* (*azione*) exportation, export; (*insieme di prodotti*) exports *pl.*

es'pose *etc vb vedi* **esporre.**

espo'simetro *sm* exposure meter.

esposizi'one [espozit'tsjone] *sf* displaying; exhibiting; setting out; (*anche FOT*) exposure; (*mostra*) exhibition; (*narrazione*) explanation, exposition.

es'posto, a *pp di* **esporre** ♦ *ag:* ~ **a nord** facing north, north-facing ♦ *sm* (*AMM*) statement, account; (: *petizione*) petition.

espressi'one *sf* expression.

espres'sivo, a *ag* expressive.

es'presso, a *pp di* **esprimere** ♦ *ag* express ♦ *sm* (*lettera*) express letter; (*anche:* **treno** ~) express train; (*anche:* **caffè** ~) espresso.

es'primere *vt* to express; ~**rsi** *vr* to express o.s.

espropri'are *vt* (*terreni, edifici*) to place a compulsory purchase order on; (*persona*) to dispossess.

espropriazi'one [esproprjat'tsjone] *sf*, **es'proprio** *sm* expropriation; ~ **per pubblica utilità** compulsory purchase.

espu'gnare [espuɲ'ɲare] *vt* to take by force, storm.

es'pulsi *etc vb vedi* **espellere.**

espulsi'one *sf* expulsion.

es'pulso, a *pp di* **espellere.**

'essa *pron f,* **'esse** *pron fpl vedi* **esso.**

es'senza [es'sɛntsa] *sf* essence.

essenzi'ale [essen'tsjale] *ag* essential; (*stile, linea*) simple ♦ *sm:* **l'**~ the main *o* most important thing.

=========== *PAROLA CHIAVE*

'essere *sm* being; ~ **umano** human being
♦ *vb copulativo* **1** (*con attributo, sostantivo*) to be; **sei giovane/simpatico** you are *o* you're young/nice; **è medico** he is *o* he's a doctor

2 (+ *di: appartenere*) to be; **di chi è la penna?** whose pen is it?; **è di Carla** it is *o* it's Carla's, it belongs to Carla

3 (+ *di: provenire*) to be; **è di Venezia** he is *o* he's from Venice

4 (*data, ora*): **è il 15 agosto** it is *o* it's the 15th of August; **è lunedì** it is *o* it's

Monday; **che ora è?, che ore sono?** what time is it?; **è l'una** it is *o* it's one o'clock; **sono le due** it is *o* it's two o'clock

5 (*costare*): **quant'è?** how much is it?; **sono 20 euro** it's 20 euros

♦ *vb aus* **1** (*attivo*): ~ **arrivato/venuto** to have arrived/come; **è già partita** she has already left

2 (*passivo*) to be; ~ **fatto da** to be made by; **è stata uccisa** she has been killed

3 (*riflessivo*): **si sono lavati** they washed, they got washed

4 (+ *da* + *infinito*): **è da farsi subito** it must be done *o* is to be done immediately

♦ *vi* **1** (*esistere, trovarsi*) to be; **sono a casa** I'm at home; ~ **in piedi/seduto** to be standing/sitting

2 (*succedere*): **sarà quel che sarà** what will be will be; **sia quel che sia, io me ne vado** come what may, I'm going now

3: **esserci**: **c'è** there is; **ci sono** there are; **che c'è?** what's the matter?, what is it?; **non c'è niente da fare** there's nothing we can do; **c'è da sperare che ...** one can only hope that ...; **ci sono!** (*sono pronto*) I'm ready; (*ho capito*) I get it!; *vedi anche* **ci**

♦ *vb impers:* **è tardi/Pasqua** it's late/Easter; **è mezzanotte** it's midnight; **è bello/caldo/freddo** it's nice/hot/cold; **è possibile che venga** he may come; **è così** that's the way it is.

'essi *pron mpl vedi* **esso.**

essic'care *vt* (*gen*) to dry; (*legname*) to season; (*cibi*) to desiccate; (*bacino, palude*) to drain; ~**rsi** *vr* (*fiume, pozzo*) to dry up; (*vernice*) to dry (out).

'esso, a *pron* it; (*riferito a persona: soggetto*) he/she; (: *complemento*) him/her; ~**i, e** *pron pl* they; (*complemento*) them.

est *sm* east; **i paesi dell'E**~ the Eastern bloc *sg.*

'estasi *sf* ecstasy.

estasi'are *vt* to send into raptures; ~**rsi** *vr:* ~**rsi (davanti a)** to go into ecstasies (over), go into raptures (over).

es'tate *sf* summer.

es'tatico, a, ci, che *ag* ecstatic.

estempo'raneo, a *ag* (*discorso*) extempore, impromptu; (*brano musicale*) impromptu.

es'tendere *vt* to extend; ~**rsi** *vr* (*diffondersi*) to spread; (*territorio, confini*) to extend.

estensi'one *sf* extension; (*di superficie*) expanse; (*di voce*) range.

estenu'ante *ag* wearing, tiring.

estenu'are *vt* (*stancare*) to wear out, tire

out.

esteri'ore *ag* outward, external.

esteriorità *sf inv* outward appearance.

esterioriz'zare [esterjorid'dzare] *vt* (*gioia etc*) to show.

ester'nare *vt* to express; ~ **un sospetto** to voice a suspicion.

es'terno, a *ag* (*porta, muro*) outer, outside; (*scala*) outside; (*alunno, impressione*) external ♦ *sm* outside, exterior ♦ *sm/f* (*allievo*) day pupil; **"per uso ~"** "for external use only"; **gli ~i sono stati girati a Glasgow** (*CINE*) the location shots were taken in Glasgow.

'estero, a *ag* foreign ♦ *sm*: **all'~** abroad; **Ministero degli E~i, gli E~i** Ministry for Foreign Affairs, ≈ Foreign Office (*BRIT*), ≈ State Department (*US*).

esterofi'lia *sf excessive love of foreign things*.

esterre'fatto, a *ag* (*costernato*) horrified; (*sbalordito*) astounded.

es'tesi *etc vb vedi* **estendere**.

es'teso, a *pp di* **estendere** ♦ *ag* extensive, large; **scrivere per** ~ to write in full.

estetica'mente *av* aesthetically.

es'tetico, a, ci, che *ag* aesthetic ♦ *sf* (*disciplina*) aesthetics *sg*; (*bellezza*) attractiveness; **chirurgia** ~**a** cosmetic surgery; **cura** ~**a** beauty treatment.

este'tista, i, e *sm/f* beautician.

'estimo *sm* valuation; (*disciplina*) surveying.

es'tinguere *vt* to extinguish, put out; (*debito*) to pay off; (*conto*) to close; ~**rsi** *vr* to go out; (*specie*) to become extinct.

es'tinsi *etc vb vedi* **estinguere**.

es'tinto, a *pp di* **estinguere**.

estin'tore *sm* (fire) extinguisher.

estinzi'one [estin'tsjone] *sf* putting out; (*di specie*) extinction; (*di debito*) payment; (*di conto*) closing.

estir'pare *vt* (*pianta*) to uproot, pull up; (*dente*) to extract; (*tumore*) to remove; (*fig: vizio*) to eradicate.

es'tivo, a *ag* summer *cpd*.

'estone *ag, sm/f, sm* Estonian.

Es'tonia *sf*: **l'~** Estonia.

es'torcere [es'tortʃere] *vt*: ~ **qc (a qn)** to extort sth (from sb).

estorsi'one *sf* extortion.

es'torto, a *pp di* **estorcere**.

estra'dare *vt* to extradite.

estradizi'one [estradit'tsjone] *sf* extradition.

es'trae, es'traggo *etc vb vedi* **estrarre**.

es'traneo, a *ag* foreign; (*discorso*) extraneous, unrelated ♦ *sm/f* stranger;

rimanere ~ **a qc** to take no part in sth; **sentirsi** ~ **a** (*famiglia, società*) to feel alienated from; **"ingresso vietato agli ~i"** "no admittance to unauthorized personnel".

estrani'arsi *vr*: ~ (**da**) to cut o.s. off (from).

es'trarre *vt* to extract; (*minerali*) to mine; (*sorteggiare*) to draw; ~ **a sorte** to draw lots.

es'trassi *etc vb vedi* **estrarre**.

es'tratto, a *pp di* **estrarre** ♦ *sm* extract; (*di documento*) abstract; ~ **conto** (bank) statement; ~ **di nascita** birth certificate.

estrazi'one [estrat'tsjone] *sf* extraction; mining; drawing *no pl*; draw.

estrema'mente *av* extremely.

estre'mismo *sm* extremism.

estre'mista, i, e *sm/f* extremist.

estremità *sf inv* extremity, end ♦ *sfpl* (*ANAT*) extremities.

es'tremo, a *ag* extreme; (*ultimo: ora, tentativo*) final, last ♦ *sm* extreme; (*di pazienza, forza*) limit, end; ~**i** *smpl* (*DIR*) essential elements; (*AMM: dati essenziali*) details, particulars; **l'E~ Oriente** the Far East.

estrinse'care *vt* to express, show.

'estro *sm* (*capriccio*) whim, fancy; (*ispirazione creativa*) inspiration.

estro'messo, a *pp di* **estromettere**.

estro'mettere *vt*: ~ (**da**) (*partito, club etc*) to expel (from); (*discussione*) to exclude (from).

estromissi'one *sf* expulsion.

es'troso, a *ag* whimsical, capricious; inspired.

estro'verso, a *ag, sm* extrovert.

estu'ario *sm* estuary.

esube'rante *ag* exuberant; (*COMM*) redundant (*BRIT*).

esube'ranza [ezube'rantsa] *sf* (*di persona*) exuberance; ~ **di personale** (*COMM*) overmanning (*BRIT*), over-staffing (*US*).

e'subero *sm*: ~ **di personale** surplus staff; **in** ~ redundant, due to be laid off.

esu'lare *vi*: ~ **da** (*competenza*) to be beyond; (*compiti*) not to be part of.

'esule *sm/f* exile.

esul'tanza [ezul'tantsa] *sf* exultation.

esul'tare *vi* to exult.

esu'mare *vt* (*salma*) to exhume, disinter; (*fig*) to unearth.

età *sf inv* age; **all'~ di 8 anni** at the age of 8, at 8 years of age; **ha la mia** ~ he (*o* she) is the same age as me *o* as I am; **di mezza** ~ middle-aged; **raggiungere la maggiore** ~ to come of age; **essere in** ~ **minore** to be

under age.
eta'nolo *sm* ethanol.
etc. *abbr* etc.
'etere *sm* ether; **via** ~ on the airwaves.
e'tereo, a *ag* ethereal.
eternità *sf* eternity.
e'terno, a *ag* eternal; (*interminabile: lamenti, attesa*) never-ending; **in** ~ for ever.
etero'geneo, a [etero'dʒɛneo] *ag* heterogeneous.
eterosessu'ale *ag, sm/f* heterosexual.
'etica *sf vedi* **etico.**
eti'chetta [eti'ketta] *sf* label; (*cerimoniale*): **l'**~ etiquette.
'etico, a, ci, che *ag* ethical ♦ *sf* ethics *sg.*
eti'lometro *sm* Breathalyzer ®.
etimolo'gia, 'gie [etimolo'dʒia] *sf* etymology.
etimo'logico, a, ci, che [etimo'lɔdʒiko] *ag* etymological.
e'tiope *ag, sm/f* Ethiopian.
Eti'opia *sf*: **l'**~ Ethiopia.
eti'opico, a, ci, che *ag, sm* (*LING*) Ethiopian.
'Etna *sm*: **l'**~ Etna.
'etnico, a, ci, che *ag* ethnic.
e'trusco, a, schi, sche *ag, sm/f* Etruscan.
'ettaro *sm* hectare (= *10,000 m²*).
'etto *sm abbr* = **ettogrammo.**
etto'grammo *sm* hectogram(me) (= *100 grams*).
et'tolitro *sm* hectolitre (*BRIT*), hectoliter (*US*).
et'tometro *sm* hectometre.
EU *abbr* = **Europa.**
euca'lipto *sm* eucalyptus.
Eucaris'tia *sf*: **l'**~ the Eucharist.
eufe'mismo *sm* euphemism.
eufe'mistico, a, ci, che *ag* euphemistic.
eufo'ria *sf* euphoria.
eu'forico, a, ci, che *ag* euphoric.
Eu'rasia *sf* Eurasia.
eurasi'atico, a, ci, che *ag, sm/f* Eurasian.
Eura'tom *sigla f* (= *Comunità Europea dell'Energia Atomica*) Euratom.
'euro *sm inv* (*divisa*) euro.
euro'corpo *sm* European force.
eurodepu'tato *sm* Euro MP.
eurodi'visa *sf* Eurocurrency.
euro'dollaro *sm* Eurodollar.
Euro'landia *sf* Euroland.
euromer'cato *sm* Euromarket.
euro'missile *sm* Euro-missile.
Eu'ropa *sf*: **l'**~ Europe.
europarlamen'tare *sm/f* Member of the European Parliament, MEP.
euro'peo, a *ag, sm/f* European.
euro'scettico, a, ci, che [euroʃ'ʃɛttiko]

sm/f Euro-sceptic.
euta'nasia *sf* euthanasia.
E.V. *abbr* = *Eccellenza Vostra.*
evacu'are *vt* to evacuate.
evacuazi'one [evakuat'tsjone] *sf* evacuation.
e'vadere *vi* (*fuggire*): ~ **da** to escape from ♦ *vt* (*sbrigare*) to deal with, dispatch; (*tasse*) to evade.
evan'gelico, a, ci, che [evan'dʒɛliko] *ag* evangelical.
evange'lista, i [evandʒe'lista] *sm* evangelist.
evapo'rare *vi* to evaporate.
evaporazi'one [evaporat'tsjone] *sf* evaporation.
e'vasi *etc vb vedi* **evadere.**
evasi'one *sf* (*vedi* **evadere**) escape; dispatch; **dare** ~ **ad un ordine** to carry out *o* execute an order; **letteratura d'**~ escapist literature; ~ **fiscale** tax evasion.
eva'sivo, a *ag* evasive.
e'vaso, a *pp di* **evadere** ♦ *sm* escapee.
eva'sore *sm*: ~ (**fiscale**) tax evader.
eveni'enza [eve'njɛntsa] *sf*: **nell'**~ **che ciò succeda** should that happen; **essere pronto ad ogni** ~ to be ready for anything *o* any eventuality.
e'vento *sm* event.
eventu'ale *ag* possible.
eventualità *sf inv* eventuality, possibility; **nell'**~ **di** in the event of.
eventual'mente *av* if need be, if necessary.
'Everest *sm*: **l'**~, **il Monte** ~ (Mount) Everest.
eversi'one *sf* subversion.
ever'sivo, a *ag* subversive.
evi'dente *ag* evident, obvious.
evidente'mente *av* evidently; (*palesemente*) obviously, evidently.
evi'denza [evi'dɛntsa] *sf* obviousness; **mettere in** ~ to point out, highlight; **tenere in** ~ **qc** to bear sth in mind.
evidenzi'are [eviden'tsjare] *vt* (*sottolineare*) to emphasize, highlight; (*con evidenziatore*) to highlight.
evidenzia'tore [evidentsja'tore] *sm* (*penna*) highlighter.
evi'rare *vt* to castrate.
evi'tabile *ag* avoidable.
evi'tare *vt* to avoid; ~ **di fare** to avoid doing; ~ **qc a qn** to spare sb sth.
'evo *sm* age, epoch.
evo'care *vt* to evoke.
evoca'tivo, a *ag* evocative.
evocherò *etc* [evoke'rɔ] *vb vedi* **evocare.**
evolu'tivo, a *ag* (*gen, BIOL*) evolutionary;

(*MED*) progressive.

evo'luto, a *pp di* **evolversi ♦** *ag* (*popolo,
civiltà*) (highly) developed, advanced;
(*persona: emancipato*) independent;
(: *senza pregiudizi*) broad-minded.

evoluzi'one [evolut'tsjone] *sf* evolution.

e'volversi *vr* to evolve; **con l'~ della
situazione** as the situation develops.

ev'viva *escl* hurrah!; ~ **il re!** long live the
king!, hurrah for the king!

ex *prefisso* ex-, former **♦** *sm/f inv* ex-
boyfriend/girlfriend.

ex 'aequo [ɛg'zɛkwo] *av:* **classificarsi primo
~ to** come joint first, come equal first.

'extra *ag inv, sm inv* extra.

extracomuni'tario, a *ag* non-EEC **♦** *sm/f*
non-EEC national (*often referring to non-
European immigrant*).

extraconiu'gale *ag* extramarital.

extraparlamen'tare *ag*
extraparliamentary.

extrasensori'ale *ag:* **percezione** *f* ~
extrasensory perception.

extrater'restre *ag, sm/f* extraterrestrial.

extraur'bano, a *ag* suburban.

Ff

F, f ['effe] *sf o m inv* (*lettera*) F, f; **F come
Firenze** ≈ F for Frederick (*BRIT*), F for
Fox (*US*).

F *abbr* (= *Fahrenheit*) F.

F. *abbr* (= *fiume*) R.

fa *vb vedi* **fare ♦** *sm inv* (*MUS*) F;
(: *solfeggiando la scala*) fa **♦** *av:* **10 anni** ~
10 years ago.

fabbi'sogno [fabbi'zoɲɲo] *sm* needs *pl*,
requirements *pl*; **il** ~ **nazionale di petrolio**
the country's oil requirements; ~ **del
settore pubblico** public sector borrowing
requirement (*BRIT*), government debt
borrowing (*US*).

'fabbrica *sf* factory.

fabbri'cante *sm* manufacturer, maker.

fabbri'care *vt* to build; (*produrre*) to
manufacture, make; (*fig*) to fabricate,
invent.

fabbri'cato *sm* building.

fabbricazi'one [fabbrikat'tsjone] *sf*
building, fabrication; making,
manufacture, manufacturing.

'fabbro *sm* (black)smith.

fac'cenda [fat'tʃenda] *sf* matter, affair;
(*cosa da fare*) task, chore; **le** ~**e
domestiche** the housework *sg*.

faccendi'ere [fattʃen'djɛre] *sm* wheeler-
dealer, (shady) operator.

fac'cetta [fat'tʃetta] *sf* (*di pietra preziosa*)
facet.

fac'chino [fak'kino] *sm* porter.

'faccia, ce [fat'tʃa] *sf* face; (*di moneta,
medaglia*) side; ~ **a** ~ face to face; **di** ~ **a**
opposite, facing; **avere la** ~ **(tosta) di
dire/fare qc** to have the cheek *o* nerve to
say/do sth; **fare qc alla** ~ **di qn** to do sth to
spite sb; **leggere qc in** ~ **a qn** to see sth
written all over sb's face.

facci'ata [fat'tʃata] *sf* façade; (*di pagina*)
side.

'faccio *etc* ['fattʃo] *vb vedi* **fare.**

fa'cente [fa'tʃente]: ~ **funzione** *sm* (*AMM*)
deputy.

fa'cessi *etc* [fa'tʃessi] *vb vedi* **fare.**

fa'ceto, a [fa'tʃeto] *ag* witty, humorous.

fa'cevo *etc* [fa'tʃevo] *vb vedi* **fare.**

fa'cezia [fa'tʃettsja] *sf* witticism, witty
remark.

fa'chiro [fa'kiro] *sm* fakir.

'facile ['fatʃile] *ag* easy; (*affabile*) easy-
going; (*disposto*): ~ **a** inclined to, prone
to; (*probabile*): **è** ~ **che piova** it's likely to
rain; **donna di** ~**i costumi** woman of easy
virtue, loose woman.

facilità [fatʃili'ta] *sf* easiness; (*disposizione,
dono*) aptitude.

facili'tare [fatʃili'tare] *vt* to make easier.

facilitazi'one [fatʃilitat'tsjone] *sf* (*gen*)
facilities *pl*; ~**i di pagamento** easy terms,
credit facilities.

facil'mente [fatʃil'mente] *av* (*gen*) easily;
(*probabilmente*) probably.

faci'lone, a [fatʃi'lone] *sm/f* (*peg*) happy-go-
lucky person.

facino'roso, a [fatʃino'roso] *ag* violent.

facoltà *sf inv* faculty; (*CHIM*) property;
(*autorità*) power.

facolta'tivo, a *ag* optional; (*fermata
d'autobus*) request *cpd*.

facol'toso, a *ag* wealthy, rich.

fac'simile *sm* facsimile.

'faggio ['faddʒo] *sm* beech.

fagi'ano [fa'dʒano] *sm* pheasant.

fagio'lino [fadʒo'lino] *sm* French (*BRIT*) *o*
string bean.

fagi'olo [fa'dʒɔlo] *sm* bean; **capitare a** ~ to
come at the right time.

fagoci'tare [fagotʃi'tare] *vt* (*fig: industria
etc*) to absorb, swallow up; (*scherzoso:
cibo*) to devour.

fa'gotto *sm* bundle; (*MUS*) bassoon; **far** ~ (*fig*) to pack up and go.

'fai *vb vedi* **fare.**

'faida *sf* feud.

'fai-da-'te *sm inv* DIY, do-it-yourself.

fa'ina *sf* (*ZOOL*) stone marten.

'Fahrenheit ['faːrənheit] *sm* Fahrenheit.

fa'lange [fa'landʒe] *sf* (*ANAT, MIL*) phalanx.

fal'cata *sf* stride.

'falce ['faltʃe] *sf* scythe; ~ **e martello** (*POL*) hammer and sickle.

fal'cetto [fal'tʃetto] *sm* sickle.

falci'are [fal'tʃare] *vt* to cut; (*fig*) to mow down.

falcia'trice [faltʃa'tritʃe] *sf* (*per fieno*) reaping machine; (*per erba*) mowing machine.

'falco, chi *sm* (*anche fig*) hawk.

fal'cone *sm* falcon.

'falda *sf* (*GEO*) layer, stratum; (*di cappello*) brim; (*di cappotto*) tails *pl*; (*di monte*) lower slope; (*di tetto*) pitch; (*di neve*) flake; **abito a** ~**e** tails *pl*.

fale'gname [fale ɲ'ɲame] *sm* joiner.

fa'lena *sf* (*ZOOL*) moth.

'Falkland ['fɔːlklənd] *sfpl*: **le isole** ~ the Falkland Islands.

fal'lace [fal'latʃe] *ag* misleading, deceptive.

'fallico, a, ci, che *ag* phallic.

fallimen'tare *ag* (*COMM*) bankruptcy *cpd*; **bilancio** ~ negative balance, deficit; **diritto** ~ bankruptcy law.

falli'mento *sm* failure; bankruptcy.

fal'lire *vi* (*non riuscire*): ~ **(in)** to fail (in); (*DIR*) to go bankrupt ♦ *vt* (*colpo, bersaglio*) to miss.

fal'lito, a *ag* unsuccessful; bankrupt ♦ *sm/f* bankrupt.

'fallo *sm* error, mistake; (*imperfezione*) defect, flaw; (*SPORT*) foul; fault; (*ANAT*) phallus; **senza** ~ without fail; **cogliere qn in** ~ to catch sb out; **mettere il piede in** ~ to slip.

fal'locrate *sm* male chauvinist.

falò *sm inv* bonfire.

fal'sare *vt* to distort, misrepresent.

falsa'riga, ghe *sf* lined page, ruled page; **sulla** ~ **di ...** (*fig*) along the lines of ....

fal'sario *sm* forger; counterfeiter.

falsifi'care *vt* to forge; (*monete*) to forge, counterfeit.

falsità *sf inv* (*di persona, notizia*) falseness; (*bugia*) falsehood, lie.

'falso, a *ag* false; (*errato*) wrong; (*falsificato*) forged; fake; (: *oro, gioielli*) imitation *cpd* ♦ *sm* forgery; **essere un** ~ **magro** to be heavier than one looks; **giurare il** ~ to commit perjury; ~ **in atto pubblico**

forgery (of a legal document).

'fama *sf* fame; (*reputazione*) reputation, name.

'fame *sf* hunger; **aver** ~ to be hungry; **fare la** ~ (*fig*) to starve, exist at subsistence level.

fa'melico, a, ci, che *ag* ravenous.

famige'rato, a [famidʒe'rato] *ag* notorious, ill-famed.

fa'miglia [fa'miʎʎa] *sf* family.

famili'are *ag* (*della famiglia*) family *cpd*; (*ben noto*) familiar; (*rapporti, atmosfera*) friendly; (*LING*) informal, colloquial ♦ *sm/f* relative, relation; **una vettura** ~ a family car.

familiarità *sf* familiarity; friendliness; informality.

familiariz'zare [familjarid'dzare] *vi*: ~ **con qn** to get to know sb; **abbiamo familiarizzato subito** we got on well together from the start.

fa'moso, a *ag* famous, well-known.

fa'nale *sm* (*AUT*) light, lamp (*BRIT*); (*luce stradale, NAUT*) light; (*di faro*) beacon.

fa'natico, a, ci, che *ag* fanatical; (*del teatro, calcio etc*): ~ **di** *o* **per** mad *o* crazy about ♦ *sm/f* fanatic; (*tifoso*) fan.

fana'tismo *sm* fanaticism.

fanciul'lezza [fantʃul'lettsa] *sf* childhood.

fanci'ullo, a [fan'tʃullo] *sm/f* child.

fan'donia *sf* tall story; ~**e** *sfpl* nonsense *sg*.

fan'fara *sf* brass band; (*musica*) fanfare.

fanfa'rone *sm* braggart.

fan'ghiglia [fan'giʎʎa] *sf* mire, mud.

'fango, ghi *sm* mud; **fare i** ~**ghi** (*MED*) to take a course of mud baths.

fan'goso, a *ag* muddy.

'fanno *vb vedi* **fare.**

fannul'lone, a *sm/f* idler, loafer.

fantasci'enza [fantaʃ'ʃɛntsa] *sf* science fiction.

fanta'sia *sf* fantasy, imagination; (*capriccio*) whim, caprice ♦ *ag inv*: **vestito** ~ patterned dress.

fantasi'oso, a *ag* (*dotato di fantasia*) imaginative; (*bizzarro*) fanciful, strange.

fan'tasma, i *sm* ghost, phantom.

fantasti'care *vi* to daydream.

fantastiche'ria [fantastike'ria] *sf* daydream.

fan'tastico, a, ci, che *ag* fantastic; (*potenza, ingegno*) imaginative.

'fante *sm* infantryman; (*CARTE*) jack, knave (*BRIT*).

fante'ria *sf* infantry.

fan'tino *sm* jockey.

fan'toccio [fan'tɔttʃo] *sm* puppet.

fanto'matico, a, ci, che *ag* (*nave, esercito*)

phantom *cpd*; (*personaggio*) mysterious.

FAO *sigla f* FAO (= *Food and Agriculture Organization*).

fara'butto *sm* crook.

fara'ona *sf* guinea fowl.

fara'one *sm* (*STORIA*) Pharaoh.

fara'onico, a, ci, che *ag* of the Pharaohs; (*fig*) enormous, huge.

far'cire [far'tʃire] *vt* (*carni, peperoni etc*) to stuff; (*torte*) to fill.

fard [far] *sm inv* blusher.

far'dello *sm* bundle; (*fig*) burden.

══════════ *PAROLA CHIAVE*

'**fare** *sm* **1** (*modo di fare*): **con ~ distratto** absent-mindedly; **ha un ~ simpatico** he has a pleasant manner

2: **sul far del giorno/della notte** at daybreak/nightfall

♦ *vt* **1** (*fabbricare, creare*) to make; (*: casa*) to build; (*: assegno*) to make out; **~ una promessa/un film** to make a promise/a film; **~ rumore** to make a noise

2 (*effettuare: lavoro, attività, studi*) to do; (*: sport*) to play; **cosa fa?** (*adesso*) what are you doing?; (*di professione*) what do you do?; **~ psicologia/italiano** to do psychology/Italian; **~ tennis** to play tennis; **~ un viaggio** to go on a trip *o* journey; **~ una passeggiata** to go for a walk; **~ la spesa** to do the shopping

3 (*funzione*) to be; (*TEAT*) to play; **~ il medico** to be a doctor; **~ il malato** (*fingere*) to act the invalid

4 (*suscitare: sentimenti*): **~ paura a qn** to frighten sb; **mi fa rabbia** it makes me angry; (**non**) **fa niente** (*non importa*) it doesn't matter

5 (*ammontare*): **3 più 3 fa 6** 3 and 3 are *o* make 6; **fanno 6 euro** that's 6 euros; **Roma fa oltre 2.000.000 di abitanti** Rome has over 2,000,000 inhabitants; **che ora fai?** what time do you make it?

6 (+ *infinito*): **far ~ qc a qn** (*obbligare*) to make sb do sth; (*permettere*) to let sb do sth; **~ piangere/ridere qn** to make sb cry/laugh; **~ venire qn** to send for sb; **fammi vedere** let me see; **far partire il motore** to start (up) the engine; **far riparare la macchina/costruire una casa** to get *o* have the car repaired/a house built

7: **~rsi**: **~rsi una gonna** to make o.s. a skirt; **~rsi un nome** to make a name for o.s.; **~rsi la permanente** to get a perm; **~rsi notare** to get o.s. noticed; **~rsi tagliare i capelli** to get one's hair cut; **~rsi operare** to have an operation

8 (*fraseologia*): **farcela** to succeed,

manage; **non ce la faccio più** I can't go on; **ce la faremo** we'll make it; **me l'hanno fatta!** I've been done!; **lo facevo più giovane** I thought he was younger; **fare sì/no con la testa** to nod/shake one's head

♦ *vi* **1** (*agire*) to act, do; **fate come volete** do as you like; **~ presto** to be quick; **~ da** to act as; **non c'è niente da ~** it's no use; **saperci ~ con qn/qc** to know how to deal with sb/sth; **ci sa ~** she's very good at it; **faccia pure!** go ahead!

2 (*dire*) to say; "**davvero?" fece** "really?" he said

3: **~ per** (*essere adatto*) to be suitable for; **~ per ~ qc** to be about to do sth; **fece per andarsene** he made as if to leave

4: **~rsi**: **si fa così** you do it like this, this is the way it's done; **non si fa così!** (*rimprovero*) that's no way to behave!; **la festa non si fa** the party is off

5: **~ a gara con qn** to compete with sb; **~ a pugni** to come to blows; **~ in tempo a ~** to be in time to do

♦ *vb impers*: **fa bel tempo** the weather is fine; **fa caldo/freddo** it's hot/cold; **fa notte** it's getting dark

♦ *vr*: **~rsi 1** (*diventare*) to become; **~rsi prete** to become a priest; **~rsi grande/vecchio** to grow tall/old

2 (*spostarsi*): **~rsi avanti/indietro** to move forward/back; **fatti più in là** move along a bit

3 (*fam: drogarsi*) to be a junkie.

fa'retra *sf* quiver.

far'falla *sf* butterfly.

farfugli'are [farfuʎ'ʎare] *vt, vi* to mumble, mutter.

fa'rina *sf* flour; **~ gialla** maize (*BRIT*) *o* corn (*US*) flour; **~ integrale** wholemeal (*BRIT*) *o* whole-wheat (*US*) flour; **questa non è ~ del tuo sacco** (*fig*) this isn't your own idea (*o* work).

fari'nacei [fari'natʃei] *smpl* starches.

fa'ringe [fa'rindʒe] *sf* (*ANAT*) pharynx.

farin'gite [farin'dʒite] *sf* pharyngitis.

fari'noso, a *ag* (*patate*) floury; (*neve, mela*) powdery.

farma'ceutico, a, ci, che [farma'tʃeutiko] *ag* pharmaceutical.

farma'cia, 'cie [farma'tʃia] *sf* pharmacy; (*negozio*) chemist's (shop) (*BRIT*), pharmacy.

farma'cista, i, e [farma'tʃista] *sm/f* chemist (*BRIT*), pharmacist.

'**farmaco, ci** *o* **chi** *sm* drug, medicine.

farneti'care *vi* to rave, be delirious.

'**faro** *sm* (*NAUT*) lighthouse; (*AER*) beacon;

(_AUT_) headlight, headlamp (_BRIT_).

farragi'noso, a [farradʒi'noso] _ag_ (_stile_) muddled, confused.

'farsa _sf_ farce.

far'sesco, a, schi, sche _ag_ farcical.

fasc. _abbr_ = **fascicolo**.

'fascia, sce ['faʃʃa] _sf_ band, strip; (_MED_) bandage; (_di sindaco, ufficiale_) sash; (_parte di territorio_) strip, belt; (_di contribuenti etc_) group, band; **essere in** ~**sce** (_anche fig_) to be in one's infancy; ~ **oraria** time band.

fasci'are [faʃ'ʃare] _vt_ to bind; (_MED_) to bandage; (_bambino_) to put a nappy (_BRIT_) _o_ diaper (_US_) on.

fascia'tura [faʃʃa'tura] _sf_ (_azione_) bandaging; (_fascia_) bandage.

fa'scicolo [faʃ'ʃikolo] _sm_ (_di documenti_) file, dossier; (_di rivista_) issue, number; (_opuscolo_) booklet, pamphlet.

'fascino ['faʃʃino] _sm_ charm, fascination.

'fascio ['faʃʃo] _sm_ bundle, sheaf; (_di fiori_) bunch; (_di luce_) beam; (_POL_): **il F~** the Fascist Party.

fa'scismo [faʃ'ʃizmo] _sm_ fascism.

fa'scista, i, e [faʃ'ʃista] _ag, sm/f_ fascist.

'fase _sf_ phase; (_TECN_) stroke; **in** ~ **di espansione** in a period of expansion; **essere fuori** ~ (_motore_) to be rough (_BRIT_), run roughly; (_fig_) to feel rough (_BRIT_) _o_ rotten.

fas'tidio _sm_ bother, trouble; **dare** ~ **a qn** to bother _o_ annoy sb; **sento** ~ **allo stomaco** my stomach's upset; **avere** ~**i con la polizia** to have trouble _o_ bother with the police.

fastidi'oso, a _ag_ annoying, tiresome; (_schifiltoso_) fastidious.

'fasto _sm_ pomp, splendour (_BRIT_), splendor (_US_).

fas'toso, a _ag_ sumptuous, lavish.

fa'sullo, a _ag_ (_gen_) fake; (_dichiarazione, persona_) false; (_pretesto_) bogus.

'fata _sf_ fairy.

fa'tale _ag_ fatal; (_inevitabile_) inevitable; (_fig_) irresistible.

fata'lismo _sm_ fatalism.

fatalità _sf inv_ inevitability; (_avversità_) misfortune; (_fato_) fate, destiny.

fa'tato, a _ag_ (_spada, chiave_) magic; (_castello_) enchanted.

fa'tica, che _sf_ hard work, toil; (_sforzo_) effort; (_di metalli_) fatigue; **a** ~ with difficulty; **respirare a** ~ to have difficulty (in) breathing; **fare** ~ **a fare qc** to find it difficult to do sth; **animale da** ~ beast of burden.

fati'caccia, ce [fati'kattʃa] _sf_: **fu una** ~ **it was** hard work, it was a hell of a job (_fam_).

fati'care _vi_ to toil; ~ **a fare qc** to have difficulty doing sth.

fati'cata _sf_ hard work.

fa'tichi _etc_ [fa'tiki] _vb vedi_ **faticare**.

fati'coso, a _ag_ (_viaggio, camminata_) tiring, exhausting; (_lavoro_) laborious.

fa'tidico, a, ci, che _ag_ fateful.

'fato _sm_ fate, destiny.

Fatt. _abbr_ (= _fattura_) inv.

fat'taccio [fat'tattʃo] _sm_ foul deed.

fat'tezze [fat'tettse] _sfpl_ features.

fat'tibile _ag_ feasible, possible.

fattis'pecie [fattis'pɛtʃe] _sf_: **nella** _o_ **in** ~ in this case _o_ instance.

'fatto, a _pp di_ **fare** ♦ _ag_: **un uomo** ~ a grown man ♦ _sm_ fact; (_azione_) deed; (_avvenimento_) event, occurrence; (_di romanzo, film_) action, story; ~ **a mano/in casa** hand-/home-made; **è ben** ~**a** she has a nice figure; **cogliere qn sul** ~ to catch sb red-handed; **il** ~ **sta** _o_ **è che** the fact remains _o_ is that; **in** ~ **di** as for, as far as ... is concerned; **fare i** ~**i propri** to mind one's own business; **è uno che sa il** ~ **suo** he knows what he's about; **gli ho detto il** ~ **suo** I told him what I thought of him; **porre qn di fronte al** ~ **compiuto** to present sb with a fait accompli.

fat'tore _sm_ (_AGR_) farm manager; (_MAT_: _elemento costitutivo_) factor.

fatto'ria _sf_ farm; (_casa_) farmhouse.

fatto'rino _sm_ errand boy; (_di ufficio_) office boy; (_d'albergo_) porter.

fattucchi'era [fattuk'kjɛra] _sf_ witch.

fat'tura _sf_ (_COMM_) invoice; (_di abito_) tailoring; (_malia_) spell; **pagamento contro presentazione** ~ payment on invoice.

fattu'rare _vt_ (_COMM_) to invoice; (_prodotto_) to produce; (_vino_) to adulterate.

fattu'rato _sm_ (_COMM_) turnover.

fatturazi'one [fatturat'tsjone] _sf_ billing, invoicing.

'fatuo, a _ag_ vain, fatuous; **fuoco** ~ (_anche fig_) will-o'-the-wisp.

'fauci ['fautʃi] _sfpl_ (_di leone etc_) jaws; (_di vulcano_) mouth _sg_.

'fauna _sf_ fauna.

'fausto, a _ag_ (_formale_) happy; **un** ~ **presagio** a good omen.

fau'tore, 'trice _sm/f_ advocate, supporter.

'fava _sf_ broad bean.

fa'vella _sf_ speech.

fa'villa _sf_ spark.

'favo _sm_ (_di api_) honeycomb.

'favola _sf_ (_fiaba_) fairy tale; (_d'intento morale_) fable; (_fandonia_) yarn; **essere la** ~ **del paese** (_oggetto di critica_) to be the talk of the town; (_zimbello_) to be a

laughing stock.
favo'loso, a *ag* fabulous; (*incredibile*)
incredible.
fa'vore *sm* favour (*BRIT*), favor (*US*); **per ~**
please; **prezzo/trattamento di ~**
preferential price/treatment; **condizioni
di ~** (*COMM*) favo(u)rable terms; **fare un
~ a qn** to do sb a favo(u)r; **col ~ delle
tenebre** under cover of darkness.
favoreggia'mento [favoreddʒa'mento] *sm*
(*DIR*) aiding and abetting.
favo'revole *ag* favourable (*BRIT*),
favorable (*US*).
favo'rire *vt* to favour (*BRIT*), favor (*US*); (*il
commercio, l'industria, le arti*) to promote,
encourage; **vuole ~?** won't you help
yourself?; **favorisca in salotto** please
come into the sitting room; **mi favorisca i
documenti** please may I see your papers?
favori'tismo *sm* favouritism (*BRIT*),
favoritism (*US*).
favo'rito, a *ag, sm/f* favourite (*BRIT*),
favorite (*US*).
fax *sm inv* fax; **mandare qc via ~** to fax sth.
fa'xare *vt* to fax.
fazi'one [fat'tsjone] *sf* faction.
faziosità [fattsjosi'ta] *sf* sectarianism.
fazzo'letto [fattso'letto] *sm* handkerchief;
(*per la testa*) (head)scarf.
F.B.I. *sigla f* (= *Federal Bureau of
Investigation*) FBI.
F.C. *abbr* = **fuoricorso.**
f.co *abbr* = **franco.**
FE *sigla* = *Ferrara.*
febb. *abbr* (= *febbraio*) Feb.
feb'braio *sm* February; *per fraseologia vedi*
luglio.
'febbre *sf* fever; **aver la ~** to have a high
temperature; **~ da fieno** hay fever.
feb'brile *ag* (*anche fig*) feverish.
'feccia, ce ['fettʃa] *sf* dregs *pl.*
'feci ['fɛtʃi] *sfpl* faeces, excrement *sg.*
'feci *etc* ['fɛtʃi] *vb vedi* **fare.**
'fecola *sf* potato flour.
fecon'dare *vt* to fertilize.
fecondazi'one [fekondat'tsjone] *sf*
fertilization; **~ artificiale** artificial
insemination.
fecondità *sf* fertility.
fe'condo, a *ag* fertile.
'Fedcom *sigla m* = *Fondo Europeo di
Cooperazione Monetaria.*
'fede *sf* (*credenza*) belief, faith; (*REL*) faith;
(*fiducia*) faith, trust; (*fedeltà*) loyalty;
(*anello*) wedding ring; (*attestato*)
certificate; **aver ~ in qn** to have faith in
sb; **tener ~ a** (*ideale*) to remain loyal to;
(*giuramento, promessa*) to keep; **in buona/**

cattiva ~ in good/bad faith; **"in ~"** (*DIR*)
"in witness whereof".
fe'dele *ag* (*leale*): **~ (a)** faithful (to);
(*veritiero*) true, accurate ♦ *sm/f* follower;
i ~i (*REL*) the faithful.
fedeltà *sf* faithfulness; (*coniugale*) fidelity;
(*esattezza: di copia, traduzione*) accuracy;
alta ~ (*RADIO*) high fidelity.
'federa *sf* pillowslip, pillowcase.
fede'rale *ag* federal.
federa'lismo *sm* (*POL*) federalism.
federa'lista, i, e *ag, sm/f* (*POL*) federalist.
federazi'one [federat'tsjone] *sf* federation.
Feder'caccia [feder'kattʃa] *abbr f*
(= *Federazione Italiana della Caccia*) hunting
federation.
Feder'calcio [feder'kaltʃo] *abbr m*
(= *Federazione Italiana Gioco Calcio*) Italian
football association.
Federcon'sorzi [federkon'sɔrtsi] *abbr f*
(= *Federazione Italiana dei Consorzi Agrari*)
federation of farmers' cooperatives.
fe'difrago, a, ghi, ghe *ag* faithless,
perfidious.
fe'dina *sf* (*DIR*): **~ (penale)** record; **avere la
~ penale sporca** to have a police record.
'fegato *sm* liver; (*fig*) guts *pl*, nerve;
mangiarsi o rodersi il ~ to be consumed
with rage.
'felce ['feltʃe] *sf* fern.
fe'lice [fe'litʃe] *ag* happy; (*fortunato*) lucky.
felicità [felitʃi'ta] *sf* happiness.
felici'tarsi [felitʃi'tarsi] *vr* (*congratularsi*): **~
con qn per qc** to congratulate sb on sth.
felicitazi'oni [felitʃitat'tsjoni] *sfpl*
congratulations.
fe'lino, a *ag, sm* feline.
'felpa *sf* sweatshirt.
fel'pato, a *ag* (*tessuto*) brushed; (*passo*)
stealthy; **con passo ~** stealthily.
'feltro *sm* felt.
'femmina *sf* (*ZOOL, TECN*) female; (*figlia*)
girl, daughter; (*spesso peg*) woman.
femmi'nile *ag* feminine; (*sesso*) female;
(*lavoro, giornale*) woman's, women's;
(*moda*) women's ♦ *sm* (*LING*) feminine.
femminilità *sf* femininity.
femmi'nismo *sm* feminism.
femmi'nista, i, e *ag, sm/f* feminist.
'femore *sm* thighbone, femur.
'fendere *vt* to cut through.
fendi'nebbia *sm* (*AUT*) fog lamp.
fendi'tura *sf* (*gen*) crack; (*di roccia*) cleft,
crack.
fe'nomeno *sm* phenomenon.
'feretro *sm* coffin.
feri'ale *ag*: **giorno ~** weekday, working
day.

'**ferie** *sfpl* holidays (*BRIT*), vacation *sg* (*US*); **andare in** ~ to go on holiday *o* vacation; **25 giorni di** ~ **pagate** 25 days' holiday *o* vacation with pay.

feri'mento *sm* wounding.

fe'rire *vt* to injure; (*deliberatamente*: *MIL etc*) to wound; (*colpire*) to hurt; ~**rsi** *vr* to hurt o.s., injure o.s.

fe'rito, a *sm/f* wounded *o* injured man/ woman ♦ *sf* injury; wound.

feri'toia *sf* slit.

'**ferma** *sf* (*MIL*) (period of) service; (*CACCIA*): **cane da** ~ pointer.

ferma'carte *sm inv* paperweight.

fermacra'vatta *sm inv* tiepin (*BRIT*), tie tack (*US*).

fer'maglio [fer'maʎʎo] *sm* clasp; (*gioiello*) brooch; (*per documenti*) clip.

ferma'mente *av* firmly.

fer'mare *vt* to stop, halt; (*POLIZIA*) to detain, hold; (*bottone etc*) to fasten, fix ♦ *vi* to stop; ~**rsi** *vr* to stop, halt; ~**rsi a fare qc** to stop to do sth.

fer'mata *sf* stop; ~ **dell'autobus** bus stop.

fermen'tare *vi* to ferment; (*fig*) to be in a ferment.

fermentazi'one [fermentat'tsjone] *sf* fermentation.

fer'mento *sm* (*anche fig*) ferment; (*lievito*) yeast; ~**i lattici** probiotics, probiotic bacteria.

fer'mezza [fer'mettsa] *sf* (*fig*) firmness, steadfastness.

'**fermo, a** *ag* still, motionless; (*veicolo*) stationary; (*orologio*) not working; (*saldo: anche fig*) firm; (*voce, mano*) steady ♦ *escl* stop!; keep still! ♦ *sm* (*chiusura*) catch, lock; (*DIR*): ~ **di polizia** police detention; ~ **restando che** ... it being understood that ....

'**fermo 'posta** *av*, *sm inv* poste restante (*BRIT*), general delivery (*US*).

fe'roce [fe'rotʃe] *ag* (*animale*) wild, fierce, ferocious; (*persona*) cruel, fierce; (*fame, dolore*) raging.

fe'rocia, cie [fe'rotʃa] *sf* ferocity.

Ferr. *abbr* = **ferrovia**.

fer'raglia [fer'raʎʎa] *sf* scrap iron.

ferra'gosto *sm* (*festa*) feast of the Assumption; (*periodo*) August holidays *pl* (*BRIT*) *o* vacation (*US*); *vedi nota nel riquadro*.

FERRAGOSTO

Ferragosto, *15 August, is a national holiday. Marking the feast of the Assumption, its origins are religious but in recent years it has simply become the most important public*

holiday of the summer season. Most people take some extra time off work and head out of town to the holiday resorts. Consequently, most of industry and commerce grind to a standstill.

---

ferra'menta *sfpl* ironmongery *sg* (*BRIT*), hardware *sg*; **negozio di** ~ ironmonger's (*BRIT*), hardware shop *o* store (*US*).

fer'rare *vt* (*cavallo*) to shoe.

fer'rato, a *ag* (*FERR*): **strada** ~**a** railway line (*BRIT*), railroad line (*US*); (*fig*): **essere** ~ **in** (*materia*) to be well up in.

ferra'vecchio [ferra'vɛkkjo] *sm* scrap merchant.

'**ferreo, a** *ag* iron *cpd*.

ferri'era *sf* ironworks *sg o pl*.

'**ferro** *sm* iron; **una bistecca ai** ~**i** a grilled steak; **mettere a** ~ **e fuoco** to put to the sword; **essere ai** ~**i corti** (*fig*) to be at daggers drawn; **tocca** ~! touch wood!; ~ **battuto** wrought iron; ~ **di cavallo** horseshoe; ~ **da stiro** iron; ~**i da calza** knitting needles; **i** ~**i del mestiere** the tools of the trade.

ferrotranvi'ario, a *ag* public transport *cpd*.

Ferrotranvi'eri *abbr f* (= *Federazione Nazionale Lavoratori Autoferrotranvieri e Internavigatori*) *transport workers' union*.

ferro'vecchio [ferro'vɛkkjo] *sm* = **ferravecchio**.

ferro'via *sf* railway (*BRIT*), railroad (*US*).

ferrovi'ario, a *ag* railway *cpd* (*BRIT*), railroad *cpd* (*US*).

ferrovi'ere *sm* railwayman (*BRIT*), railroad man (*US*).

'**fertile** *ag* fertile.

fertilità *sf* fertility.

fertiliz'zante [fertilid'dzante] *sm* fertilizer.

fertiliz'zare [fertilid'dzare] *vt* to fertilize.

fer'vente *ag* fervent, ardent.

'**fervere** *vi*: **fervono i preparativi per** ... they are making feverish preparations for ....

'**fervido, a** *ag* fervent, ardent.

fer'vore *sm* fervour (*BRIT*), fervor (*US*), ardour (*BRIT*), ardor (*US*); (*punto culminante*) height.

'**fesa** *sf* (*CUC*) rump of veal.

fesse'ria *sf* stupidity; **dire** ~**e** to talk nonsense.

'**fesso, a** *pp di* **fendere** ♦ *ag* (*fam: sciocco*) crazy, cracked.

fes'sura *sf* crack, split; (*per gettone, moneta*) slot.

'**festa** *sf* (*religiosa*) feast; (*pubblica*) holiday; (*compleanno*) birthday; (*onomastico*) name day; (*ricevimento*) celebration, party; **far** ~ to have a holiday; (*far baldoria*) to live it up; **far ~ a qn** to give sb a warm welcome; **essere vestito a ~** to be dressed up to the nines; **~ comandata** (*REL*) holiday of obligation; **la ~ della mamma/del papà** Mother's/Father's Day; **la F~ della Repubblica** *vedi nota nel riquadro.*

FESTA DELLA REPUBBLICA

The **Festa della Repubblica***, 2 June, celebrates the founding of the Italian Republic after the fall of the monarchy and the subsequent referendum in 1946. It is marked by military parades and political speeches.*

---

festeggia'menti [festeddʒa'menti] *smpl* celebrations.

festeggi'are [fested'dʒare] *vt* to celebrate; (*persona*) to have a celebration for.

fes'tino *sm* party; (*con balli*) ball.

fes'tivo, a *ag* (*atmosfera*) festive; **giorno ~** holiday.

fes'toso, a *ag* merry, joyful.

fe'tente *ag* (*puzzolente*) fetid; (*comportamento*) disgusting.

fe'ticcio [fe'tittʃo] *sm* fetish.

'feto *sm* foetus (*BRIT*), fetus (*US*).

fe'tore *sm* stench, stink.

'fetta *sf* slice.

fet'tuccia, ce [fet'tuttʃa] *sf* tape, ribbon.

fettuc'cine [fettut'tʃine] *sfpl* (*CUC*) ribbon-shaped pasta.

feu'dale *ag* feudal.

'feudo *sm* (*STORIA*) fief; (*fig*) stronghold.

ff *abbr* (*AMM*) = **facente funzione**; (= *fogli*) pp.

FF.AA *abbr* = **forze armate**.

FG *sigla* = *Foggia*.

FI *sigla* = *Firenze* ♦ *abbr* = **Forza Italia**.

fi'aba *sf* fairy tale.

fia'besco, a, schi, sche *ag* fairy-tale *cpd*.

fi'acca *sf* weariness; (*svogliatezza*) listlessness; **battere la ~** to shirk.

fiac'care *vt* to weaken.

fiaccherò *etc* [fjakke'rɔ] *vb vedi* **fiaccare**.

fi'acco, a, chi, che *ag* (*stanco*) tired, weary; (*svogliato*) listless; (*debole*) weak; (*mercato*) slack.

fi'accola *sf* torch.

fiacco'lata *sf* torchlight procession.

fi'ala *sf* phial.

fi'amma *sf* flame; (*NAUT*) pennant.

fiam'mante *ag* (*colore*) flaming; **nuovo ~** brand new.

fiam'mata *sf* blaze.

fiammeggi'are [fjammed'dʒare] *vi* to blaze.

fiam'mifero *sm* match.

fiam'mingo, a, ghi, ghe *ag* Flemish ♦ *sm/f* Fleming ♦ *sm* (*LING*) Flemish; (*ZOOL*) flamingo; **i F~ghi** the Flemish.

fian'cata *sf* (*di nave etc*) side; (*NAUT*) broadside.

fiancheggi'are [fjanked'dʒare] *vt* to border; (*fig*) to support, back (up); (*MIL*) to flank.

fi'anco, chi *sm* side; (*di persona*) hip; (*MIL*) flank; **di ~** sideways, from the side; **a ~ a ~** side by side; **prestare il proprio ~ alle critiche** to leave o.s. open to criticism; **~ destr/sinistr!** (*MIL*) right/left turn!

Fi'andre *sfpl*: **le ~** Flanders *sg*.

fiaschette'ria [fjaskette'ria] *sf* wine shop.

fi'asco, schi *sm* flask; (*fig*) fiasco; **fare ~** to be a fiasco.

fia'tare *vi* (*fig: parlare*): **senza ~** without saying a word.

fi'ato *sm* breath; (*resistenza*) stamina; **~i** *smpl* (*MUS*) wind instruments; **avere il ~ grosso** to be out of breath; **prendere ~** to catch one's breath; **bere qc tutto d'un ~** to drink sth in one go *o* gulp.

'fibbia *sf* buckle.

'fibra *sf* fibre, fiber (*US*); (*fig*) constitution; **~ ottica** optical fibre; **~ di vetro** fibreglass (*BRIT*), fiberglass (*US*).

ficca'naso, *pl(m)* **~i**, *pl(f) inv sm/f* busybody, nos(e)y parker.

fic'care *vt* to push, thrust, drive; **~rsi** *vr* (*andare a finire*) to get to; **~ il naso negli affari altrui** (*fig*) to poke *o* stick one's nose into other people's business; **~rsi nei pasticci** *o* **nei guai** to get into a fix.

ficcherò *etc* [fikke'rɔ] *vb vedi* **ficcare**.

fiche [fiʃ] *sf inv* (*nei giochi d'azzardo*) chip.

'fico, chi *sm* (*pianta*) fig tree; (*frutto*) fig; **~ d'India** prickly pear; **~ secco** dried fig.

fidanza'mento [fidantsa'mento] *sm* engagement.

fidan'zarsi [fidan'tsarsi] *vr* to get engaged.

fidan'zato, a [fidan'tsato] *sm/f* fiancé/fiancée.

fi'darsi *vr*: **~ di** to trust; **~rsi è bene non ~rsi è meglio** (*proverbio*) better safe than sorry.

fi'dato, a *ag* reliable, trustworthy.

fide'ismo *sm* unquestioning belief.

fide'istico, a, ci, che *ag* (*atteggiamento, posizione*) totally uncritical.

fideius'sore *sm* (*DIR*) guarantor.

'fido, a *ag* faithful, loyal ♦ *sm* (*COMM*) credit.

fi'ducia [fi'dutʃa] *sf* confidence, trust; **incarico di ~** position of trust, responsible position; **persona di ~** reliable person; **è il mio uomo di ~** he is my right-hand man; **porre la questione di ~** (*POL*) to ask for a vote of confidence.

fiduci'oso, a [fidu'tʃoso] *ag* trusting.
fi'ele *sm* (*MED*) bile; (*fig*) bitterness.
fie'nile *sm* hayloft.
fi'eno *sm* hay.
fi'era *sf* fair; (*animale*) wild beast; ~ **di beneficenza** charity bazaar; ~ **campionaria** trade fair.
fie'rezza [fje'rettsa] *sf* pride.
fi'ero, a *ag* proud; (*crudele*) fierce, cruel; (*audace*) bold.
fi'evole *ag* (*luce*) dim; (*suono*) weak.
F.I.F.A. *sigla f* (= *Fédération Internationale de Football Association*) FIFA.
'fifa *sf* (*fam*): **aver** ~ to have the jitters.
fi'fone, a *sm/f* (*fam, scherzoso*) coward.
fig. *abbr* (= *figura*) fig.
FIGC *sigla f* (= *Federazione Italiana Gioco Calcio*) *Italian football association*.
'Figi ['fidʒi] *sfpl*: **le isole** ~ Fiji, the Fiji Islands.
'figlia ['fiʎʎa] *sf* daughter; (*COMM*) counterfoil (*BRIT*), stub.
figli'are [fiʎ'ʎare] *vi* to give birth.
figli'astro, a [fiʎ'ʎastro] *sm/f* stepson/daughter.
'figlio ['fiʎʎo] *sm* son; (*senza distinzione di sesso*) child; ~ **d'arte: essere** ~ **d'arte** to come from a theatrical (*o* musical *etc*) family; ~ **di puttana** (*fam!*) son of a bitch (*!*); ~ **unico** only child.
figli'occio, a, ci, ce [fiʎ'ʎottʃo] *sm/f* godchild, godson/daughter.
figli'ola [fiʎ'ʎola] *sf* daughter; (*fig: ragazza*) girl.
figli'olo [fiʎ'ʎolo] *sm* (*anche fig: ragazzo*) son.
fi'gura *sf* figure; (*forma, aspetto esterno*) form, shape; (*illustrazione*) picture, illustration; **far** ~ to look smart; **fare una brutta** ~ to make a bad impression; **che** ~! how embarrassing!
figu'raccia, ce [figu'rattʃa] *sf*: **fare una** ~ to create a bad impression.
figu'rare *vi* to appear ♦ *vt*: ~**rsi qc** to imagine sth; ~**rsi** *vr*: **figurati!** imagine that!; **ti do noia?** — **ma figurati!** am I disturbing you? — not at all!
figura'tivo, a *ag* figurative.
figu'rina *sf* (*statuetta*) figurine; (*cartoncino*) picture card.
figuri'nista, i, e *sm/f* dress designer.
figu'rino *sm* fashion sketch.
fi'guro *sm*: **un losco** ~ a suspicious character.
figu'rone *sm*: **fare un** ~ (*persona, oggetto*) to look terrific; (*persona: con un discorso etc*) to make an excellent impression.
'fila *sf* row, line; (*coda*) queue; (*serie*) series, string; **di** ~ in succession; **fare la**

~ to queue; **in** ~ **indiana** in single file.
fila'mento *sm* filament.
fi'lanca ® *sf stretch material*.
fi'landa *sf* spinning mill.
fi'lante *ag*: **stella** ~ (*stella cadente*) shooting star; (*striscia di carta*) streamer.
filantro'pia *sf* philanthropy.
filan'tropico, a, ci, che *ag* philanthropic(al).
fi'lantropo *sm* philanthropist.
fi'lare *vt* to spin; (*NAUT*) to pay out ♦ *vi* (*baco, ragno*) to spin; (*formaggio fuso*) to go stringy; (*liquido*) to trickle; (*discorso*) to hang together; (*fam: amoreggiare*) to go steady; (*muoversi a forte velocità*) to go at full speed; (*andarsene lestamente*) to make o.s. scarce ♦ *sm* (*di alberi etc*) row, line; ~ **diritto** (*fig*) to toe the line.
filar'monico, a, ci, che *ag* philharmonic.
filas'trocca, che *sf* nursery rhyme.
filate'lia *sf* philately, stamp collecting.
fi'lato, a *ag* spun ♦ *sm* yarn ♦ *av*: **vai dritto** ~ **a casa** go straight home; **3 giorni** ~**i** 3 days running *o* on end.
fila'tura *sf* spinning; (*luogo*) spinning mill.
fi'letto *sm* (*ornamento*) braid, trimming; (*di vite*) thread; (*di carne*) fillet.
fili'ale *ag* filial ♦ *sf* (*di impresa*) branch.
filibusti'ere *sm* pirate; (*fig*) adventurer.
fili'grana *sf* (*in oreficeria*) filigree; (*su carta*) watermark.
fi'lippica *sf* invective.
Filip'pine *sfpl*: **le** ~ the Philippines.
filip'pino, a *ag, sm/f* Filipino.
film *sm inv* film.
fil'mare *vt* to film.
fil'mato *sm* short film.
fil'mina *sf* film strip.
'filo *sm* (*anche fig*) thread; (*filato*) yarn; (*metallico*) wire; (*di lama, rasoio*) edge; **con un** ~ **di voce** in a whisper; **un** ~ **d'aria** (*fig*) a breath of air; **dare del** ~ **da torcere a qn** to create difficulties for sb, make life difficult for sb; **fare il** ~ **a qn** (*corteggiare*) to be after sb, chase sb; **per** ~ **e per segno** in detail; ~ **d'erba** blade of grass; ~ **interdentale** dental floss; ~ **di perle** string of pearls; ~ **di Scozia** fine cotton yarn; ~ **spinato** barbed wire.
filoameri'cano, a *ag* pro-American.
'filobus *sm inv* trolley bus.
filodiffusi'one *sf* rediffusion.
filodram'matico, a, ci, che *ag*: (**compagnia**) ~**a** amateur dramatic society ♦ *sm/f* amateur actor/actress.
filon'cino [filon'tʃino] *sm* ≈ French stick.
fi'lone *sm* (*di minerali*) seam, vein; (*pane*) ≈ Vienna loaf; (*fig*) trend.

filoso'fia *sf* philosophy.

filo'sofico, a, ci, che *ag* philosophical.

fi'losofo, a *sm/f* philosopher.

filosovi'etico, a, ci, che *ag* pro-Soviet.

filo'via *sf* (*linea*) trolley line; (*bus*) trolley bus.

fil'trare *vt, vi* to filter.

'filtro *sm* filter; (*pozione*) potion; ~ **dell'olio** (*AUT*) oil filter.

'filza ['filtsa] *sf* (*anche fig*) string.

FIN *sigla f* = Federazione Italiana Nuoto.

fin *av, prep* = **fino.**

fi'nale *ag* final ♦ *sm* (*di libro, film*) end, ending; (*MUS*) finale ♦ *sf* (*SPORT*) final.

fina'lista, i, e *sm/f* finalist.

finalità *sf* (*scopo*) aim, purpose.

finaliz'zare [finalid'dzare] *vt*: ~ **a** to direct towards.

final'mente *av* finally, at last.

fi'nanza [fi'nantsa] *sf* finance; ~**e** *sfpl* (*di individuo, Stato*) finances; **(Guardia di)** ~ (*di frontiera*) ≈ Customs and Excise (*BRIT*), ≈ Customs Service (*US*); **(Intendenza di)** ~ ≈ Inland Revenue (*BRIT*), ≈ Internal Revenue Service (*US*); **Ministro delle** ~**e** Minister of Finance, ≈ Chancellor of the Exchequer (*BRIT*), ≈ Secretary of the Treasury (*US*).

finanzia'mento [finantsja'mento] *sm* (*azione*) financing; (*denaro fornito*) funds *pl*.

finanzi'are [finan'tsjare] *vt* to finance, fund.

finanzi'ario, a [finan'tsjarjo] *ag* financial ♦ *sf* (*anche:* **società** ~**a**) investment company; (*anche:* **legge** ~**a**) finance act, ≈ budget (*BRIT*).

finanzia'tore, 'trice *ag*: **ente** ~, **società** ~**trice** backer ♦ *sm/f* backer.

finanzi'ere [finan'tsjɛre] *sm* financier; (*guardia di finanza: doganale*) customs officer; (*: tributaria*) Inland Revenue official (*BRIT*), Internal Revenue official (*US*).

finché [fin'ke] *cong* (*per tutto il tempo che*) as long as; (*fino al momento in cui*) until; ~ **vorrai** as long as you like; **aspetta** ~ **non esca** wait until he goes (*o* comes) out.

'fine *ag* (*lamina, carta*) thin; (*capelli, polvere*) fine; (*vista, udito*) keen, sharp; (*persona*: *raffinata*) refined, distinguished; (*osservazione*) subtle ♦ *sf* end ♦ *sm* aim, purpose; (*esito*) result, outcome; **in** *o* **alla** ~ in the end, finally; **alla fin** ~ at the end of the day, in the end; **che** ~ **ha fatto?** what became of him?; **buona** ~ **e buon principio!** (*augurio*) happy New Year!; **a fin di bene** with the best of intentions; **al** ~ **di fare qc** (in order) to do sth; **condurre**

qc a buon ~ to bring sth to a successful conclusion; **secondo** ~ ulterior motive.

'fine setti'mana *sm* o *f inv* weekend.

fi'nestra *sf* window.

fines'trino *sm* (*di treno, auto*) window.

fi'nezza [fi'nettsa] *sf* thinness; fineness; keenness, sharpness; refinement; subtlety.

'fingere ['findʒere] *vt* to feign; (*supporre*) to imagine, suppose; ~**rsi** *vr*: ~**rsi ubriaco/ pazzo** to pretend to be drunk/crazy; ~ **di fare** to pretend to do.

fini'menti *smpl* (*di cavallo etc*) harness *sg*.

fini'mondo *sm* pandemonium.

fi'nire *vt* to finish ♦ *vi* to finish, end ♦ *sm*: **sul** ~ **della festa** towards the end of the party; ~ **di fare** (*compiere*) to finish doing; (*smettere*) to stop doing; ~ **in galera** to end up *o* finish up in prison; **farla finita** (*con la vita*) to put an end to one's life; **farla finita con qc** to have done with sth; **com'è andata a** ~? what happened in the end?; **finiscila!** stop it!

fini'tura *sf* finish.

finlan'dese *ag* Finnish ♦ *sm/f* Finn ♦ *sm* (*LING*) Finnish.

Fin'landia *sf*: **la** ~ Finland.

'fino, a *ag* (*capelli, seta*) fine; (*oro*) pure; (*fig*: *acuto*) shrewd ♦ *av* (*spesso troncato in* **fin**: *pure, anche*) even ♦ *prep* (*spesso troncato in* **fin**: *tempo*): **fin quando?** till when?; (*: luogo*): **fin qui** as far as here; ~ **a** (*tempo*) until, till; (*luogo*) as far as, (up) to; **fin da domani** from tomorrow onwards; **fin da ieri** since yesterday; **fin dalla nascita** from *o* since birth.

fi'nocchio [fi'nɔkkjo] *sm* fennel; (*fam peg*: *pederasta*) queer.

fi'nora *av* up till now.

'finsi *etc vb vedi* **fingere.**

'finto, a *pp di* **fingere** ♦ *ag* (*capelli, dente*) false; (*fiori*) artificial; (*cuoio, pelle*) imitation *cpd*; (*fig: simulato: pazzia etc*) feigned, sham ♦ *sf* pretence (*BRIT*), pretense (*US*), sham; (*SPORT*) feint; **far** ~**a** (**di fare**) to pretend (to do); **l'ho detto per** ~**a** I was only pretending; (*per scherzo*) I was only kidding.

finzi'one [fin'tsjone] *sf* pretence (*BRIT*), pretense (*US*), sham.

fioc'care *vi* (*neve*) to fall; (*fig: insulti etc*) to fall thick and fast.

fi'occo, chi *sm* (*di nastro*) bow; (*di stoffa, lana*) flock; (*di neve*) flake; (*NAUT*) jib; **coi** ~**chi** (*fig*) first-rate; ~**chi di granoturco** cornflakes.

fi'ocina ['fjɔtʃina] *sf* harpoon.

fi'oco, a, chi, che *ag* faint, dim.

fi'onda *sf* catapult.
fio'raio, a *smf* florist.
fiorda'liso *sm* (*BOT*) cornflower.
fi'ordo *sm* fjord.
fi'ore *sm* flower; **~i** *smpl* (*CARTE*) clubs; **nel ~ degli anni** in one's prime; **a fior d'acqua** on the surface of the water; **a fior di labbra** in a whisper; **aver i nervi a fior di pelle** to be on edge; **fior di latte** cream; **è costato fior di soldi** it cost a pretty penny; **il fior ~ della società** the cream of society; **~ all'occhiello** feather in the cap; **~i di campo** wild flowers.
fio'rente *ag* (*industria, paese*) flourishing; (*salute*) blooming; (*petto*) ample.
fioren'tino, a *ag, smf* Florentine ♦ *sf* (*CUC*) T-bone steak.
fio'retto *sm* (*SCHERMA*) foil.
fio'rino *sm* florin.
fio'rire *vi* (*rosa*) to flower; (*albero*) to blossom; (*fig*) to flourish.
fio'rista, i, e *smf* florist.
fiori'tura *sf* (*di pianta*) flowering, blooming; (*di albero*) blossoming; (*fig: di commercio, arte*) flourishing; (*insieme dei fiori*) flowers *pl*; (*MUS*) fioritura.
fi'otto *sm* (*di lacrime*) flow, flood; (*di sangue*) gush, spurt.
'FIPE *sigla f = Federazione Italiana Pubblici Esercizi.*
Fi'renze [fi'rɛntse] *sf* Florence.
'firma *sf* signature; (*reputazione*) name.
firma'mento *sm* firmament.
fir'mare *vt* to sign.
firma'tario, a *smf* signatory.
fisar'monica, che *sf* accordion.
fis'cale *ag* fiscal, tax *cpd*; (*meticoloso*) punctilious; **medico ~** *doctor employed by Social Security to verify cases of sick leave.*
fisca'lista, i, e *smf* tax consultant.
fiscaliz'zare [fiskalid'dzare] *vt* to exempt from taxes.
fischi'are [fis'kjare] *vi* to whistle ♦ *vt* to whistle; (*attore*) to boo, hiss; **mi fischian le orecchie** my ears are singing; (*fig*) my ears are burning.
fischiet'tare [fiskjet'tare] *vi, vt* to whistle.
fischi'etto [fis'kjetto] *sm* (*strumento*) whistle.
'fischio ['fiskjo] *sm* whistle; **prendere ~i per fiaschi** to get hold of the wrong end of the stick.
'fisco *sm* tax authorities *pl*, ≈ Inland Revenue (*BRIT*), ≈ Internal Revenue Service (*US*).
'fisica *sf vedi* **fisico.**
fisica'mente *av* physically.

'fisico, a, ci, che *ag* physical ♦ *smf* physicist ♦ *sm* physique ♦ *sf* physics *sg.*
'fisima *sf* fixation.
fisiolo'gia [fizjolo'dʒia] *sf* physiology.
fisiono'mia *sf* face, physiognomy.
fisiotera'pia *sf* physiotherapy.
fisiotera'pista *smf* physiotherapist.
fis'saggio [fis'saddʒo] *sm* (*FOT*) fixing.
fis'sante *ag* (*spray, lozione*) holding.
fis'sare *vt* to fix, fasten; (*guardare intensamente*) to stare at; (*data, condizioni*) to fix, establish, set; (*prenotare*) to book; **~rsi** *vr*: **~rsi su** (*sog: sguardo, attenzione*) to focus on; (*fig: idea*) to become obsessed with.
fissazi'one [fissat'tsjone] *sf* (*PSIC*) fixation.
fissi'one *sf* fission.
'fisso, a *ag* fixed; (*stipendio, impiego*) regular ♦ *av*: **guardar ~ qn/qc** to stare at sb/sth; **avere un ragazzo ~** to have a steady boyfriend; **senza ~a dimora** of no fixed abode.
fitoterma'lismo *sm* herbal hydrotherapy.
'fitta *sf vedi* **fitto.**
fit'tavolo *sm* tenant.
fit'tizio, a [fit'tittsjo] *ag* fictitious, imaginary.
'fitto, a *ag* thick, dense; (*pioggia*) heavy ♦ *sm* (*affitto, pigione*) rent ♦ *sf* sharp pain; **una ~a al cuore** (*fig*) a pang of grief; **nel ~ del bosco** in the heart *o* depths of the wood.
fiu'mana *sf* torrent; (*fig*) stream, flood.
fi'ume *sm* river ♦ *ag inv*: **processo ~** long-running trial; **scorrere a ~i** (*acqua, sangue*) to flow in torrents.
fiu'tare *vt* to smell, sniff; (*sog: animale*) to scent; (*fig: inganno*) to get wind of, smell; **~ tabacco** to take snuff; **~ cocaina** to snort cocaine.
fi'uto *sm* (sense of) smell; (*fig*) nose.
'flaccido, a ['flattʃido] *ag* flabby.
fla'cone *sm* bottle.
flagel'lare [fladʒel'lare] *vt* to flog, scourge; (*sog: onde*) to beat against.
fla'gello [fla'dʒello] *sm* scourge.
fla'grante *ag* flagrant; **cogliere qn in ~** to catch sb red-handed.
fla'nella *sf* flannel.
flash [flaʃ] *sm inv* (*FOT*) flash; (*giornalistico*) newsflash.
flau'tista, i *smf* flautist.
'flauto *sm* flute.
'flebile *ag* faint, feeble.
fle'bite *sf* phlebitis.
'flemma *sf* (*calma*) coolness, phlegm; (*MED*) phlegm.
flem'matico, a, ci, che *ag* phlegmatic,

cool.

fles'sibile *ag* pliable; (*fig: che si adatta*) flexible.

flessi'one *sf* (*gen*) bending; (*GINNASTICA: a terra*) sit-up; (: *in piedi*) forward bend; (: *sulle gambe*) knee-bend; (*diminuzione*) slight drop, slight fall; (*LING*) inflection; **fare una ~** to bend; **una ~ economica** a downward trend in the economy.

'**flesso, a** *pp di* **flettere.**

flessu'oso, a *ag* supple, lithe; (*andatura*) flowing, graceful.

'**flettere** *vt* to bend.

'**flipper** ['flipper] *sm inv* pinball machine.

flirt [flɔːt] *sm inv* brief romance, flirtation.

flir'tare *vi* to flirt.

F.lli *abbr* (= *fratelli*) Bros.

'**flora** *sf* flora.

'**florido, a** *ag* flourishing; (*fig*) glowing with health.

'**floscio, a, sci, sce** ['flɔʃʃo] *ag* (*cappello*) floppy, soft; (*muscoli*) flabby.

'**flotta** *sf* fleet.

flot'tante *sm* (*ECON*): **titoli a largo ~** blue chips, stocks on the market.

'**fluido, a** *ag*, *sm* fluid.

flu'ire *vi* to flow.

fluore'scente [fluoreʃˈʃɛnte] *ag* fluorescent.

flu'oro *sm* fluorine.

fluo'ruro *sm* fluoride.

'**flusso** *sm* flow; (*FISICA, MED*) flux; **~ e riflusso** ebb and flow; **~ di cassa** (*COMM*) cash flow.

'**flutti** *smpl* waves.

fluttu'are *vi* to rise and fall; (*ECON*) to fluctuate.

fluvi'ale *ag* river *cpd*, fluvial.

FM *abbr vedi* **modulazione di frequenza.**

FMI *sigla m vedi* **Fondo Monetario Internazionale.**

FO *sigla* = *Forlì.*

fo'bia *sf* phobia.

'**foca, che** *sf* (*ZOOL*) seal.

fo'caccia, ce [foˈkattʃa] *sf kind of pizza*; (*dolce*) bun; **rendere pan per ~** to get one's own back, give tit for tat.

fo'cale *ag* focal.

focaliz'zare [fokalidˈdzare] *vt* (*FOT: immagine*) to get into focus; (*fig: situazione*) to get into perspective; **~ l'attenzione su** to focus one's attention on.

'**foce** ['fotʃe] *sf* (*GEO*) mouth.

fo'chista, i [foˈkista] *sm* (*FERR*) stoker, fireman.

foco'laio *sm* (*MED*) centre (*BRIT*) o center (*US*) of infection; (*fig*) hotbed.

foco'lare *sm* hearth, fireside; (*TECN*) furnace.

fo'coso, a *ag* fiery; (*cavallo*) mettlesome, fiery.

'**fodera** *sf* (*di vestito*) lining; (*di libro, poltrona*) cover.

fode'rare *vt* to line; to cover.

'**fodero** *sm* (*di spada*) scabbard; (*di pugnale*) sheath; (*di pistola*) holster.

'**foga** *sf* enthusiasm, ardour (*BRIT*), ardor (*US*).

'**foggia, ge** ['fɔddʒa] *sf* (*maniera*) style; (*aspetto*) form, shape; (*moda*) fashion, style.

foggi'are [fodˈdʒare] *vt* to shape; to style.

'**foglia** ['fɔʎʎa] *sf* leaf; **ha mangiato la ~** (*fig*) he's caught on; **~ d'argento/d'oro** silver/gold leaf.

fogli'ame [foʎˈʎame] *sm* foliage, leaves *pl*.

fogli'etto [foʎˈʎetto] *sm* (*piccolo foglio*) slip of paper, piece of paper; (*manifestino*) leaflet, handout.

'**foglio** ['fɔʎʎo] *sm* (*di carta*) sheet (of paper); (*di metallo*) sheet; (*documento*) document; (*banconota*) (bank)note; **~ di calcolo** spreadsheet; **~ rosa** (*AUT*) provisional licence; **~ di via** (*DIR*) expulsion order; **~ volante** pamphlet.

'**fogna** ['foɲɲa] *sf* drain, sewer.

fogna'tura [foɲɲaˈtura] *sf* drainage, sewerage.

föhn [føːn] *sm inv* hair-dryer.

fo'lata *sf* gust.

fol'clore *sm* folklore.

folclo'ristico, a, ci, che *ag* folk *cpd*.

folgo'rare *vt* (*sog: fulmine*) to strike down; (: *alta tensione*) to electrocute.

folgorazi'one [folgoratˈtsjone] *sf* electrocution; **ebbe una ~** (*fig: idea*) he had a brainwave.

'**folgore** *sf* thunderbolt.

'**folla** *sf* crowd, throng.

'**folle** *ag* mad, insane; (*TECN*) idle; **in ~** (*AUT*) in neutral.

folleggi'are [folledˈdʒare] *vi* (*divertirsi*) to paint the town red.

fol'letto *sm* elf.

fol'lia *sf* folly, foolishness; foolish act; (*pazzia*) madness, lunacy; **amare qn alla ~** to love sb to distraction; **costare una ~** to cost the earth.

'**folto, a** *ag* thick.

fomen'tare *vt* to stir up, foment.

fon *sm inv* = **föhn.**

fon'dale *sm* (*del mare*) bottom; (*TEAT*) backdrop; **il ~ marino** the sea bed.

fondamen'tale *ag* fundamental, basic.

fondamenta'lista, i, e *ag*, *sm/f* (*REL*) fundamentalist.

fonda'mento *sm* foundation; ~**a** *sfpl* (*EDIL*) foundations.

fon'dare *vt* to found; (*fig: dar base*): ~ **qc su** to base sth on; ~**rsi** *vr* (*teorie*): ~**rsi** (**su**) to be based (on).

fonda'tezza [fonda'tettsa] *sf* (*di ragioni*) soundness; (*di dubbio, sospetto*) basis in fact.

fon'dato, a *ag* (*ragioni*) sound; (*dubbio, sospetto*) well-founded.

fondazi'one [fondat'tsjone] *sf* foundation.

fon'dente *ag*: **cioccolato** ~ plain *o* dark chocolate.

'fondere *vt* (*neve*) to melt; (*metallo*) to fuse, melt; (*fig: colori*) to merge, blend; (: *imprese, gruppi*) to merge ♦ *vi* to melt; ~**rsi** *vr* to melt; (*fig: partiti, correnti*) to unite, merge.

fonde'ria *sf* foundry.

fondi'ario, a *ag* land *cpd*.

fon'dina *sf* (*piatto fondo*) soup plate; (*portapistola*) holster.

'fondo, a *ag* deep ♦ *sm* (*di recipiente, pozzo*) bottom; (*di stanza*) back; (*quantità di liquido che resta, deposito*) dregs *pl*; (*sfondo*) background; (*unità immobiliare*) property, estate; (*somma di denaro*) fund; (*SPORT*) long-distance race; ~**i** *smpl* (*denaro*) funds; **a notte** ~**a** at dead of night; **in** ~ **a** at the bottom of; at the back of; (*strada*) at the end of; **laggiù in** ~ (*lontano*) over there; (*in profondità*) down there; **in** ~ (*fig*) after all, all things considered; **andare fino in** ~ **a** (*fig*) to examine thoroughly; **andare a** ~ (*nave*) to sink; **conoscere a** ~ to know inside out; **dar** ~ **a** (*fig: provvisti, soldi*) to use up; **toccare il** ~ (*fig*) to plumb the depths; **a** ~ **perduto** (*COMM*) without security; ~ **comune di investimento** investment trust; **F~ Monetario Internazionale (FMI)** International Monetary Fund (IMF); ~ **di previdenza** social insurance fund; ~ **di riserva** reserve fund; ~ **urbano** town property; ~**i di caffè** coffee grounds; ~**i d'esercizio** working capital *sg*; ~**i liquidi** ready money *sg*, liquid assets; ~**i di magazzino** old *o* unsold stock *sg*; ~**i neri** slush fund *sg*.

fondo'tinta *sm inv* (*cosmetico*) foundation.

fo'nema *sm* phoneme.

fo'netica *sf* phonetics *sg*.

fo'netico, a, ci, che *ag* phonetic.

fon'tana *sf* fountain.

fonta'nella *sf* drinking fountain.

'fonte *sf* spring, source; (*fig*) source ♦ *sm*: ~ **battesimale** (*REL*) font.

fon'tina *sm full fat hard, sweet cheese.*

'footing ['futiŋ] *sm* jogging.

forag'giare [forad'dʒare] *vt* (*cavalli*) to fodder; (*fig: partito etc*) to bankroll.

fo'raggio [fo'raddʒo] *sm* fodder, forage.

fo'rare *vt* to pierce, make a hole in; (*pallone*) to burst; (*pneumatico*) to puncture; (*biglietto*) to punch; ~**rsi** *vr* (*gen*) to develop a hole; (*AUT, pallone, timpano*) to burst; ~ **una gomma** to burst a tyre (*BRIT*) *o* tire (*US*).

fora'tura *sf* piercing; bursting; puncturing; punching.

'forbici ['fɔrbitʃi] *sfpl* scissors.

forbi'cina [forbi'tʃina] *sf* earwig.

for'bito, a *ag* (*stile, modi*) polished.

'forca, che *sf* (*AGR*) fork, pitchfork; (*patibolo*) gallows *sg*.

for'cella [for'tʃella] *sf* (*TECN*) fork; (*di monte*) pass.

for'chetta [for'ketta] *sf* fork; **essere una buona** ~ to enjoy one's food.

for'cina [for'tʃina] *sf* hairpin.

'forcipe ['fɔrtʃipe] *sm* forceps *pl*.

for'cone *sm* pitchfork.

fo'rense *ag* (*linguaggio*) legal; **avvocato** ~ barrister (*BRIT*), lawyer.

fo'resta *sf* forest; **la F~ Nera** the Black Forest.

fores'tale *ag* forest *cpd*; **guardia** ~ forester.

foreste'ria *sf* (*di convento, palazzo etc*) guest rooms *pl*, guest quarters *pl*.

foresti'ero, a *ag* foreign ♦ *smf* foreigner.

for'fait [fɔr'fɛ] *sm inv*: (**prezzo a**) ~ fixed price, set price; **dichiarare** ~ (*SPORT*) to withdraw; (*fig*) to give up.

forfe'tario, a *ag*: **prezzo** ~ (*da pagare*) fixed *o* set price; (*da ricevere*) lump sum.

'forfora *sf* dandruff.

'forgia, ge ['fɔrdʒa] *sf* forge.

forgi'are [for'dʒare] *vt* to forge.

'forma *sf* form; (*aspetto esteriore*) form, shape; (*DIR: procedura*) procedure; (*per calzature*) last; (*stampo da cucina*) mould (*BRIT*), mold (*US*); ~**e** *sfpl* (*del corpo*) figure, shape; **le** ~**e** (*convenzioni*) appearances; **errori di** ~ stylistic errors; **essere in** ~ to be in good shape; **tenersi in** ~ to keep fit; **in** ~ **ufficiale/privata** officially/privately; **una** ~ **di formaggio** a (whole) cheese.

formag'gino [formad'dʒino] *sm* processed cheese.

for'maggio [for'maddʒo] *sm* cheese.

for'male *ag* formal.

formalità *sf inv* formality.

formaliz'zare [formalid'dzare] *vt* to formalize.

for'mare *vt* to form, shape, make; (*numero*

di telefono) to dial; (*fig: carattere*) to form, mould (*BRIT*), mold (*US*); ~**rsi** *vr* to form, take shape; **il treno si forma a Milano** the train starts from Milan.

for'mato *sm* format, size.

format'tare *vt* (*INFORM*) to format.

formattazi'one [formattat'tsjone] *sf* (*INFORM*) formatting.

formazi'one [format'tsjone] *sf* formation; (*fig: educazione*) training; ~ **professionale** vocational training.

for'mica, che *sf* ant.

formi'caio *sm* anthill.

formico'lare *vi* (*gamba, braccio*) to tingle; (*brulicare: anche fig*): ~ **di** to be swarming with; **mi formicola la gamba** I've got pins and needles in my leg, my leg's tingling.

formico'lio *sm* pins and needles *pl*; swarming.

formi'dabile *ag* powerful, formidable; (*straordinario*) remarkable.

for'moso, a *ag* shapely.

'formula *sf* formula; ~ **di cortesia** (*nelle lettere*) letter ending.

formu'lare *vt* to formulate.

for'nace [for'natʃe] *sf* (*per laterizi etc*) kiln; (*per metalli*) furnace.

for'naio *sm* baker.

for'nello *sm* (*elettrico, a gas*) ring; (*di pipa*) bowl.

for'nire *vt*: ~ **qn di qc**, ~ **qc a qn** to provide *o* supply sb with sth, supply sth to sb; ~**rsi** *vr*: ~**rsi di** (*procurarsi*) to provide o.s. with.

for'nito, a *ag*: **ben** ~ (*negozio*) well-stocked.

forni'tore, 'trice *ag*: **ditta** ~**trice di ...** company supplying ... ♦ *sm/f* supplier.

forni'tura *sf* supply.

'forno *sm* (*di cucina*) oven; (*panetteria*) bakery; (*TECN: per calce etc*) kiln; (: *per metalli*) furnace; **fare i** ~**i** (*MED*) to undergo heat treatment.

'foro *sm* (*buco*) hole; (*STORIA*) forum; (*tribunale*) (law) court.

'forse *av* perhaps, maybe; (*circa*) about; **essere in** ~ to be in doubt.

forsen'nato, a *ag* mad, crazy, insane.

'forte *ag* strong; (*suono*) loud; (*spesa*) considerable, great ♦ *av* strongly; (*velocemente*) fast; (*a voce alta*) loud(ly); (*violentemente*) hard ♦ *sm* (*edificio*) fort; (*specialità*) forte, strong point; **piatto** ~ (*CUC*) main dish; **avere un** ~ **mal di testa/raffreddore** to have a bad headache/cold; **essere** ~ **in qc** to be good at sth; **farsi** ~ **di qc** to make use of sth; **dare man** ~ **a qn** to back sb up, support sb; **usare le maniere**

~**i** to use strong-arm tactics.

for'tezza [for'tettsa] *sf* (*morale*) strength; (*luogo fortificato*) fortress.

fortifi'care *vt* to fortify, strengthen.

for'tuito, a *ag* fortuitous, chance *cpd*.

for'tuna *sf* (*destino*) fortune, luck; (*buona sorte*) success, fortune; (*eredità, averi*) fortune; **per** ~ luckily, fortunately; **di** ~ makeshift, improvised; **atterraggio di** ~ emergency landing.

fortu'nale *sm* storm.

fortunata'mente *av* luckily, fortunately.

fortu'nato, a *ag* lucky, fortunate; (*coronato da successo*) successful.

fortu'noso, a *ag* (*vita*) eventful; (*avvenimento*) unlucky.

fo'runcolo *sm* (*MED*) boil.

forvi'are *vt, vi* = **fuorviare**.

'forza ['fɔrtsa] *sf* strength; (*potere*) power; (*FISICA*) force ♦ *escl* come on!; ~**e** *sfpl* (*fisiche*) strength *sg*; (*MIL*) forces; **per** ~ against one's will; (*naturalmente*) of course; **per** ~ **di cose** by force of circumstances; **a viva** ~ by force; **a** ~ **di** by dint of; **farsi** ~ (*coraggio*) to pluck up one's courage; **bella** ~! (*ironico*) how clever of you (*o* him *etc*)!; ~ **lavoro** work force, manpower; **per causa di** ~ **maggiore** (*DIR*) by reason of an act of God; (*per estensione*) due to circumstances beyond one's control; **la** ~ **pubblica** the police *pl*; ~ **di pace** peacekeeping force; ~ **di vendita** (*COMM*) sales force; ~ **di volontà** willpower; **le** ~**e armate** the armed forces; **F**~ **Italia** (*POL*) *moderate right-wing party*.

for'zare [for'tsare] *vt* to force; (*cassaforte, porta*) to force (open); (*voce*) to strain; ~ **qn a fare** to force sb to do.

for'zato, a [for'tsato] *ag* forced ♦ *sm* (*DIR*) prisoner sentenced to hard labour (*BRIT*) *o* labor (*US*).

forzi'ere [for'tsjɛre] *sm* strongbox; (*di pirati*) treasure chest.

for'zista, i, e [for'tsista] *ag* of Forza Italia ♦ *sm/f* member (*o* supporter) of Forza Italia.

for'zuto, a [for'tsuto] *ag* big and strong.

fos'chia [fos'kia] *sf* mist, haze.

'fosco, a, schi, sche *ag* dark, gloomy; **dipingere qc a tinte** ~**sche** (*fig*) to paint a gloomy picture of sth.

fos'fato *sm* phosphate.

fosfore'scente [fosforeʃ'ʃɛnte] *ag* phosphorescent; (*lancetta dell'orologio etc*) luminous.

'fosforo *sm* phosphorous.

'fossa *sf* pit; (*di cimitero*) grave; ~ **comune**

mass grave.

fos'sato *sm* ditch; (*di fortezza*) moat.

fos'setta *sf* dimple.

'fossi *etc vb vedi* **essere.**

'fossile *ag, sm* fossil (*cpd*).

'fosso *sm* ditch; (*MIL*) trench.

'foste *etc vb vedi* **essere.**

'foto *sf inv* photo; ~ **ricordo** souvenir photo; ~ **tessera** passport(-type) photo.

foto... *prefisso* photo....

foto'camera *sf*: ~ **digitale** digital camera.

fotocomposi'tore *sm* filmsetter.

fotocomposizi'one [fotokompozit'tsjone] *sf* film setting.

foto'copia *sf* photocopy.

fotocopi'are *vt* to photocopy.

fotocopiste'ria *sf* photocopy shop.

foto'genico, a, ci, che [foto'dʒɛniko] *ag* photogenic.

fotogra'fare *vt* to photograph.

fotogra'fia *sf* (*procedimento*) photography; (*immagine*) photograph; **fare una** ~ to take a photograph; **una** ~ **a colori/in bianco e nero** a colour/black and white photograph.

foto'grafico, a, ci, che *ag* photographic; **macchina** ~a camera.

fo'tografo, a *sm/f* photographer.

foto'gramma, i *sm* (*CINE*) frame.

fotomo'dello, a *sm/f* fashion model.

fotomon'taggio [fotomon'taddʒo] *sm* photomontage.

fotore'porter *sm/f inv* newspaper (*o* magazine) photographer.

fotoro'manzo [fotoro'mandzo] *sm* romantic picture story.

foto'sintesi *sf* photosynthesis.

'fottere *vt* (*fam!*: *avere rapporti sessuali*) to fuck (*!*), screw (*!*); (: *rubare*) to pinch, swipe; (: *fregare*): **mi hanno fottuto** they played a dirty trick on me; **vai a farti** ~! fuck off! (*!*).

fot'tuto, a *ag* (*fam!*) bloody, fucking (*!*).

fou'lard [fu'lar] *sm inv* scarf.

FR *sigla* = Frosinone.

fra *prep* = **tra.**

fracas'sare *vt* to shatter, smash; ~**rsi** *vr* to shatter, smash; (*veicolo*) to crash.

fra'casso *sm* smash; crash; (*baccano*) din, racket.

'fradicio, a, ci, ce ['fraditʃo] *ag* (*guasto*) rotten; (*molto bagnato*) soaking (wet); **ubriaco** ~ blind drunk.

'fragile ['fradʒile] *ag* fragile; (*salute*) delicate; (*nervi, vetro*) brittle.

fragilità [fradʒili'ta] *sf* (*vedi ag*) fragility; delicacy; brittleness.

'fragola *sf* strawberry.

fra'gore *sm* (*di cascate, carro armato*) roar; (*di tuono*) rumble.

frago'roso, a *ag* deafening; **ridere in modo** ~ to roar with laughter.

fra'grante *ag* fragrant.

fraintendi'mento *sm* misunderstanding.

frain'tendere *vt* to misunderstand.

frain'teso, a *pp di* **fraintendere.**

fram'mento *sm* fragment.

fram'misto, a *ag*: ~ **a** interspersed with.

'frana *sf* landslide; (*fig*: *persona*): **essere una** ~ to be useless, be a walking disaster area.

fra'nare *vi* to slip, slide down.

franca'mente *av* frankly.

fran'cese [fran'tʃeze] *ag* French ♦ *sm/f* Frenchman/woman ♦ *sm* (*LING*) French; **i F~i** the French.

fran'chezza [fran'kettsa] *sf* frankness, openness.

fran'chigia, gie [fran'kidʒa] *sf* (*AMM*) exemption; (*DIR*) franchise; (*NAUT*) shore leave; ~ **doganale** exemption from customs duty.

'Francia ['frantʃa] *sf*: **la** ~ France.

'franco, a, chi, che *ag* (*COMM*) free; (*sincero*) frank, open, sincere ♦ *sm* (*moneta*) franc; **farla** ~**a** (*fig*) to get off scot-free; ~ **a bordo** free on board; ~ **di dogana** duty-free; ~ **a domicilio** delivered free of charge; ~ **fabbrica** ex factory, ex works; **prezzo** ~ **fabbrica** ex-works price; ~ **magazzino** ex warehouse; ~ **di porto** carriage free; ~ **vagone** free on rail; ~ **tiratore** *sm* sniper; (*POL*) *member of parliament who votes against his own party.*

franco'bollo *sm* (postage) stamp.

franco-cana'dese *ag, sm/f* French Canadian.

Franco'forte *sf* Frankfurt.

fran'gente [fran'dʒɛnte] *sm* (*onda*) breaker; (*scoglio emergente*) reef; (*circostanza*) situation, circumstance.

'frangia, ge ['frandʒa] *sf* fringe.

frangi'flutti [frandʒi'flutti] *sm inv* breakwater.

frangi'vento [frandʒi'vɛnto] *sm* windbreak.

fran'toio *sm* (*AGR*) olive press; (*TECN*) crusher.

frantu'mare *vt*, ~**rsi** *vr* to break into pieces, shatter.

fran'tumi *smpl* pieces, bits; (*schegge*) splinters; **andare in** ~, **mandare in** ~ to shatter, smash to pieces *o* smithereens.

frappé *sm* (*CUC*) milk shake.

fra'sario *sm* (*gergo*) vocabulary, language.

'frasca, sche *sf* (leafy) branch; **saltare di**

palo in ~ to jump from one subject to another.

'**frase** *sf* (*LING*) sentence; (*locuzione, espressione, MUS*) phrase; ~ **fatta** set phrase.

fraseolo'gia [frazeolo'dʒia] *sf* phraseology.

'**frassino** *sm* ash (tree).

frastagli'ato, a [frasta'ʎ'ʎato] *ag* (*costa*) indented, jagged.

frastor'nare *vt* (*intontire*) to daze; (*confondere*) to bewilder, befuddle.

frastor'nato, a *ag* dazed; bewildered.

frastu'ono *sm* hubbub, din.

'**frate** *sm* friar, monk.

fratel'lanza [fratel'lantsa] *sf* brotherhood; (*associazione*) fraternity.

fratel'lastro *sm* stepbrother; (*con genitore in comune*) half brother.

fra'tello *sm* brother; ~**i** *smpl* brothers; (*nel senso di fratelli e sorelle*) brothers and sisters.

fra'terno, a *ag* fraternal, brotherly.

fratri'cida, i, e [fratri'tʃida] *ag* fratricidal ♦ *sm/f* fratricide; **guerra** ~ civil war.

frat'taglie [frat'taʎʎe] *sfpl* (*CUC: gen*) offal *sg*; (: *di pollo*) giblets.

frat'tanto *av* in the meantime, meanwhile.

frat'tempo *sm*: **nel** ~ in the meantime, meanwhile.

frat'tura *sf* fracture; (*fig*) split, break.

frattu'rare *vt* to fracture.

fraudo'lento, a *ag* fraudulent.

fraziona'mento [frattsjona'mento] *sm* division, splitting up.

frazio'nare [frattsjo'nare] *vt* to divide, split up.

frazi'one [frat'tsjone] *sf* fraction; (*borgata*): ~ **di comune** hamlet.

'**freccia, ce** ['frettʃa] *sf* arrow; ~ **di direzione** (*AUT*) indicator.

frec'ciata [fret'tʃata] *sf*: **lanciare una** ~ to make a cutting remark.

fred'dare *vt* to shoot dead.

fred'dezza [fred'dettsa] *sf* coldness.

'**freddo, a** *ag, sm* cold; **fa** ~ it's cold; **aver** ~ to be cold; **soffrire il** ~ to feel the cold; **a** ~ (*fig*) deliberately.

freddo'loso, a *ag* sensitive to the cold.

fred'dura *sf* pun.

'**freezer** ['frizer] *sm inv* fridge-freezer.

fre'gare *vt* to rub; (*fam: truffare*) to take in, cheat; (: *rubare*) to swipe, pinch; **fregarsene** (*fam!*): **chi se ne frega?** who gives a damn (about it)?

fre'gata *sf* rub; (*fam*) swindle; (*NAUT*) frigate.

frega'tura *sf* (*fam: imbroglio*) rip-off; (: *delusione*) let-down.

freghe'rò *etc* [frege'rɔ] *vb vedi* **fregare**.

'**fregio** ['fredʒo] *sm* (*ARCHIT*) frieze; (*ornamento*) decoration.

'**fremere** *vi*: ~ **di** to tremble *o* quiver with; ~ **d'impazienza** to be champing at the bit.

'**fremito** *sm* tremor, quiver.

fre'nare *vt* (*veicolo*) to slow down; (*cavallo*) to rein in; (*lacrime*) to restrain, hold back ♦ *vi* to brake; ~**rsi** *vr* (*fig*) to restrain o.s., control o.s.

fre'nata *sf*: **fare una** ~ to brake.

frene'sia *sf* frenzy.

fre'netico, a, ci, che *ag* frenetic.

'**freno** *sm* brake; (*morso*) bit; **tenere a** ~ (*passioni etc*) to restrain; **tenere a** ~ **la lingua** to hold one's tongue; ~ **a disco** disc brake; ~ **a mano** handbrake.

'**freon** ® *sm inv* (*CHIM*) Freon ®.

frequen'tare *vt* (*scuola, corso*) to attend; (*locale, bar*) to go to, frequent; (*persone*) to see (often).

frequen'tato, a *ag* (*locale*) busy.

fre'quente *ag* frequent; **di** ~ frequently.

fre'quenza [fre'kwentsa] *sf* frequency; (*INS*) attendance.

fre'sare *vt* (*TECN*) to mill.

fres'chezza [fres'kettsa] *sf* freshness.

'**fresco, a, schi, sche** *ag* fresh; (*temperatura*) cool; (*notizia*) recent, fresh ♦ *sm*: **godere il** ~ to enjoy the cool air; ~ **di bucato** straight from the wash, newly washed; **stare** ~ (*fig*) to be in for it; **mettere al** ~ to put in a cool place; (*fig: in prigione*) to put inside *o* in the cooler.

fres'cura *sf* cool.

'**fresia** *sf* freesia.

'**fretta** *sf* hurry, haste; **in** ~ in a hurry; **in** ~ **e furia** in a mad rush; **aver** ~ to be in a hurry; **far** ~ **a qn** to hurry sb.

frettolosa'mente *av* hurriedly, in a rush.

fretto'loso, a *ag* (*persona*) in a hurry; (*lavoro etc*) hurried, rushed.

fri'abile *ag* (*terreno*) friable; (*pasta*) crumbly.

'**friggere** ['friddʒere] *vt* to fry ♦ *vi* (*olio etc*) to sizzle; **vai a farti** ~! (*fam*) get lost!

frigidità [fridʒidi'ta] *sf* frigidity.

'**frigido, a** ['fridʒido] *ag* (*MED*) frigid.

fri'gnare [friɲ'ɲare] *vi* to whine, snivel.

fri'gnone, a [friɲ'ɲone] *sm/f* whiner, sniveller.

'**frigo, ghi** *sm* fridge.

frigo'bar *sm inv* minibar.

frigo'rifero, a *ag* refrigerating ♦ *sm* refrigerator; **cella** ~**a** cold store.

fringu'ello *sm* chaffinch.

'**frissi** *etc vb vedi* **friggere**.

frit'tata *sf* omelet(te); **fare una** ~ (*fig*) to

make a mess of things.

frit'tella *sf* (*CUC*) pancake; (: *ripiena*) fritter.

'fritto, a *pp* di **friggere ♦** *ag* fried **♦** *sm* fried food; **ormai siamo** ~**i!** (*fig fam*) now we've had it!; **è un argomento** ~ **e rifritto** that's old hat; ~ **misto** mixed fry.

frit'tura *sf* (*cibo*) fried food; ~ **di pesce** mixed fried fish.

friu'lano, a *ag* of (*o* from) Friuli.

frivo'lezza [frivo'lettsa] *sf* frivolity.

'frivolo, a *ag* frivolous.

frizi'one [frit'tsjone] *sf* friction; (*di pelle*) rub, rub-down; (*AUT*) clutch.

friz'zante [frid'dzante] *ag* (*anche fig*) sparkling.

'frizzo ['friddzo] *sm* witticism.

fro'dare *vt* to defraud, cheat.

'frode *sf* fraud; ~ **fiscale** tax evasion.

'frodo *sm*: **di** ~ illegal, contraband; **pescatore di** ~, **cacciatore di** ~ poacher.

'frogia, gie ['frɔdʒa] *sf* (*di cavallo etc*) nostril.

'frollo, a *ag* (*carne*) tender; (: *di selvaggina*) high; (*fig: persona*) soft; **pasta** ~**a** short(crust) pastry.

'fronda *sf* (leafy) branch; (*di partito politico*) internal opposition; ~**e** *sfpl* (*di albero*) foliage *sg*.

fron'tale *ag* frontal; (*scontro*) head-on.

'fronte *sf* (*ANAT*) forehead; (*di edificio*) front, façade **♦** *sm* (*MIL, POL, METEOR*) front; **a** ~, **di** ~ facing, opposite; **di** ~ **a** (*posizione*) opposite, facing, in front of; (*a paragone di*) compared with; **far** ~ **a** (*nemico, problema*) to confront; (*responsabilità*) to face up to; (*spese*) to cope with.

fronteggi'are [fronted'dʒare] *vt* (*avversari, difficoltà*) to face, stand up to; (*spese*) to cope with.

frontes'pizio [frontes'pittsjo] *sm* (*ARCHIT*) frontispiece; (*di libro*) title page.

fronti'era *sf* border, frontier.

fron'tone *sm* pediment.

'fronzolo ['frondzolo] *sm* frill.

'frotta *sf* crowd; **in** ~, **a** ~**e** in their hundreds, in droves.

'frottola *sf* fib; **raccontare un sacco di** ~**e** to tell a pack of lies.

fru'gale *ag* frugal.

fru'gare *vi* to rummage **♦** *vt* to search.

frugherò *etc* [fruge'rɔ] *vb vedi* **frugare**.

frui'tore *sm* user.

fruizi'one [fruit'tsjone] *sf* use.

frul'lare *vt* (*CUC*) to whisk **♦** *vi* (*uccelli*) to flutter; **cosa ti frulla in mente?** what is going on in that mind of yours?

frul'lato *sm* (*CUC*) milk shake; (: *con solo*

frutta) fruit drink.

frulla'tore *sm* electric mixer.

frul'lino *sm* whisk.

fru'mento *sm* wheat.

frusci'are [fruʃ'ʃare] *vi* to rustle.

fru'scio [fruʃ'ʃio] *sm* rustle; rustling.

'frusta *sf* whip; (*CUC*) whisk.

frus'tare *vt* to whip.

frus'tata *sf* lash.

frus'tino *sm* riding crop.

frus'trare *vt* to frustrate.

frus'trato, a *ag* frustrated.

frustrazi'one [frustrat'tsjone] *sf* frustration.

'frutta *sf* fruit; (*portata*) dessert; ~ **candita/secca** candied/dried fruit.

frut'tare *vi* (*investimenti, deposito*) to bear dividends, give a return; **il mio deposito in banca (mi) frutta il 10%** my bank deposits bring (me) in 10%; **quella gara gli fruttò la medaglia d'oro** he won the gold medal in that competition.

frut'teto *sm* orchard.

frutticol'tura *sf* fruit growing.

frut'tifero, a *ag* (*albero etc*) fruit-bearing; (*fig: che frutta*) fruitful, profitable; **deposito** ~ interest-bearing deposit.

frutti'vendolo, a *sm/f* greengrocer (*BRIT*), produce dealer (*US*).

'frutto *sm* fruit; (*fig: risultato*) result(s); (*ECON: interesse*) interest; (: *reddito*) income; **è** ~ **della tua immaginazione** it's a figment of your imagination; ~**i di mare** seafood *sg*.

fruttu'oso, a *ag* fruitful, profitable.

FS *abbr* (= *Ferrovie dello Stato*) *Italian railways*.

f.t. *abbr* = **fuori testo**.

f.to *abbr* (= *firmato*) signed.

fu *vb vedi* **essere ♦** *ag inv*: **il** ~ **Paolo Bianchi** the late Paolo Bianchi.

fuci'lare [futʃi'lare] *vt* to shoot.

fuci'lata [futʃi'lata] *sf* rifle shot.

fucilazi'one [futʃilat'tsjone] *sf* execution (by firing squad).

fu'cile [fu'tʃile] *sm* rifle, gun; (*da caccia*) shotgun, gun; ~ **a canne mozze** sawn-off shotgun.

fu'cina [fu'tʃina] *sf* forge.

'fuco, chi *sm* drone.

'fucsia *sf* fuchsia.

'fuga, ghe *sf* escape, flight; (*di gas, liquidi*) leak; (*MUS*) fugue; **mettere qn in** ~ to put sb to flight; ~ **di cervelli** brain drain.

fu'gace [fu'gatʃe] *ag* fleeting, transient.

fu'gare *vt* (*dubbi, incertezze*) to dispel, drive out.

fug'gevole [fud'dʒevole] *ag* fleeting.

fuggi'asco, a, schi, sche [fud'dʒasko] *ag, sm/f* fugitive.

fuggi'fuggi [fuddʒi'fuddʒi] *sm* scramble, stampede.

fug'gire [fud'dʒire] *vi* to flee, run away; (*fig: passar veloce*) to fly ♦ *vt* to avoid.

fuggi'tivo, a [fuddʒi'tivo] *sm/f* fugitive, runaway.

'fui *vb vedi* **essere**.

'fulcro *sm* (*FISICA*) fulcrum; (*fig: di teoria, questione*) central *o* key point.

ful'gore *sm* brilliance, splendour (*BRIT*), splendor (*US*).

fu'liggine [fu'liddʒine] *sf* soot.

fulmi'nare *vt* (*sog: elettricità*) to electrocute; (*con arma da fuoco*) to shoot dead; **~rsi** *vr* (*lampadina*) to go, blow; (*fig: con lo sguardo*): **mi fulminò (con uno sguardo)** he looked daggers at me.

'fulmine *sm* bolt of lightning; **~i** *smpl* lightning *sg*; **~ a ciel sereno** bolt from the blue.

ful'mineo, a *ag* (*fig: scatto*) rapid; (: *minaccioso*) threatening.

'fulvo, a *ag* tawny.

fumai'olo *sm* (*di nave*) funnel; (*di fabbrica*) chimney.

fu'mante *ag* (*piatto etc*) steaming.

fu'mare *vi* to smoke; (*emettere vapore*) to steam ♦ *vt* to smoke.

fu'mario, a *ag*: **canna ~a** flue.

fu'mata *sf* (*segnale*) smoke signal; **farsi una ~** to have a smoke; **~ bianca/nera** (*in Vaticano*) signal that a new pope has/has not been elected.

fuma'tore, 'trice *sm/f* smoker.

fu'metto *sm* comic strip; **giornale** *m* **a ~i** comic.

'fummo *vb vedi* **essere**.

'fumo *sm* smoke; (*vapore*) steam; (*il fumare tabacco*) smoking; **~i** *smpl* (*industriali etc*) fumes; **vendere ~** to deceive, cheat; **è tutto ~ e niente arrosto** it has no substance to it; **i ~i dell'alcool** (*fig*) the after-effects of drink; **~ passivo** passive smoking.

fu'mogeno, a [fu'mɔdʒeno] *ag* (*candelotto*) smoke *cpd* ♦ *sm* smoke bomb; **cortina ~a** smoke screen.

fu'moso, a *ag* smoky; (*fig*) muddled.

fu'nambolo, a *sm/f* tightrope walker.

'fune *sf* rope, cord; (*più grossa*) cable.

'funebre *ag* (*rito*) funeral; (*aspetto*) gloomy, funereal.

fune'rale *sm* funeral.

fu'nesto, a *ag* (*incidente*) fatal; (*errore, decisione*) fatal, disastrous; (*atmosfera*) gloomy, dismal.

'fungere ['fundʒere] *vi*: **~ da** to act as.

'fungo, ghi *sm* fungus; (*commestibile*) mushroom; **~ velenoso** toadstool; **crescere come i ~ghi** (*fig*) to spring up overnight.

funico'lare *sf* funicular railway.

funi'via *sf* cable railway.

'funsi *etc vb vedi* **fungere**.

'funto, a *pp di* **fungere**.

funzio'nare [funtsjo'nare] *vi* to work, function; (*fungere*): **~ da** to act as.

funzio'nario [funtsjo'narjo] *sm* official; **~ statale** civil servant.

funzi'one [fun'tsjone] *sf* function; (*carica*) post, position; (*REL*) service; **in ~** (*meccanismo*) in operation; **in ~ di** (*come*) as; **vive in ~ dei figli** he lives for his children; **far ~ di** to act as; **fare la ~ di qn** (*farne le veci*) to take sb's place.

fu'oco, chi *sm* fire; (*fornello*) ring; (*FOT, FISICA*) focus; **dare ~ a qc** to set fire to sth; **far ~** (*sparare*) to fire; **prendere ~** to catch fire; **~ d'artificio** firework; **~ di paglia** flash in the pan; **~ sacro** *o* **di Sant'Antonio** (*MED fam*) shingles *sg*.

fuorché [fwor'ke] *cong, prep* except.

FU'ORI *sigla m* (= *Fronte Unitario Omosessuale Rivoluzionario Italiano*) *gay liberation movement.*

fu'ori *av* outside; (*all'aperto*) outdoors, outside; (~ *di casa, SPORT*) out; (*esclamativo*) get out! ♦ *prep*: **~ (di)** out of, outside ♦ *sm* outside; **essere in ~** (*sporgere*) to stick out; **lasciar ~ qc/qn** to leave sth/sb out; **far ~** (*fam: soldi*) to spend; (: *cioccolatini*) to eat up; (: *rubare*) to nick; **far ~ qn** (*fam*) to kill sb, do sb in; **essere tagliato ~** (*da un gruppo, ambiente*) to be excluded; **essere ~ di sé** to be beside oneself; **~ luogo** (*inopportuno*) out of place, uncalled for; **~ mano** out of the way, remote; **~ pasto** between meals; **~ pericolo** out of danger; **~ dai piedi!** get out of the way!; **~ servizio** out of order; **~ stagione** out of season; **illustrazione ~ testo** (*STAMPA*) plate; **~ uso** out of use.

fuori'bordo *sm inv* speedboat (with outboard motor); outboard motor.

fuori'busta *sm inv* unofficial payment.

fuori'classe *sm/f inv* (undisputed) champion.

fuori'corso *ag inv* (*moneta*) no longer in circulation; (*INS*): (**studente**) **~** *undergraduate who has not completed a course in due time.*

fuorigi'oco [fwori'dʒɔko] *sm* offside.

fuori'legge [fwori'leddʒe] *sm/f inv* outlaw.

fuoriprog'ramma *sm inv* (*TV, RADIO*)

unscheduled programme; (*fig*) change of plan *o* programme.

fuori'serie *ag inv* (*auto etc*) custom-built ♦ *sf* custom-built car.

fuoris'trada *sm* (*AUT*) cross-country vehicle.

fuoru'scito, a, fuoriu'scito, a [fwor(i)uʃ'ʃito] *sm/f* exile ♦ *sf* (*di gas*) leakage, escape; (*di sangue, linfa*) seepage.

fuorvi'are *vt* to mislead; (*fig*) to lead astray ♦ *vi* to go astray.

furbacchi'one, a [furbak'kjone] *sm/f* cunning old devil.

fur'bizia [fur'bittsja] *sf* (*vedi ag*) cleverness; cunning; **una** ~ a cunning trick.

'furbo, a *ag* clever, smart; (*peg*) cunning ♦ *sm/f*: **fare il** ~ to (try to) be clever *o* smart; **fatti** ~! show a bit of sense!

fu'rente *ag*: ~ (**contro**) furious (with).

fure'ria *sf* (*MIL*) orderly room.

fu'retto *sm* ferret.

fur'fante *sm* rascal, scoundrel.

furgon'cino [furgon'tʃino] *sm* small van.

fur'gone *sm* van.

'furia *sf* (*ira*) fury, rage; (*fig: impeto*) fury, violence; (*fretta*) rush; **a** ~ **di** by dint of; **andare su tutte le** ~**e** to fly into a rage.

furi'bondo, a *ag* furious.

furi'ere *sm* quartermaster.

furi'oso, a *ag* furious; (*mare, vento*) raging.

'furono *vb vedi* **essere**.

fu'rore *sm* fury; (*esaltazione*) frenzy; **far** ~ to be all the rage.

furtiva'mente *av* furtively.

fur'tivo, a *ag* furtive.

'furto *sm* theft; ~ **con scasso** burglary.

'fusa *sfpl*: **fare le** ~ to purr.

fu'scello [fuʃ'ʃello] *sm* twig.

fu'seaux *smpl inv* leggings.

'fusi *etc vb vedi* **fondere**.

fu'sibile *sm* (*ELETTR*) fuse.

fusi'one *sf* (*di metalli*) fusion, melting; (*colata*) casting; (*COMM*) merger; (*fig*) merging.

'fuso, a *pp di* **fondere** ♦ *sm* (*FILATURA*) spindle; **diritto come un** ~ as stiff as a ramrod; ~ **orario** time zone.

fusoli'era *sf* (*AER*) fusillage.

fus'tagno [fus'taɲɲo] *sm* corduroy.

fus'tella *sf* (*su scatola di medicinali*) tear-off tab.

fusti'gare *vt* (*frustare*) to flog; (*fig: costumi*) to censure, denounce.

fus'tino *sm* (*di detersivo*) tub.

'fusto *sm* stem; (*ANAT, di albero*) trunk; (*recipiente*) drum, can; (*fam*) he-man.

'futile *ag* vain, futile.

futilità *sf inv* futility.

futu'rismo *sm* futurism.

G, g [dʒi] *sf o m inv* (*lettera*) G, g; **G come Genova** ≈ G for George.

g *abbr* (= *grammo*) g.

G7 [dʒi'sɛtte] *smpl* G7 (*Group of Seven*).

gabar'dine [gabar'din] *sm* (*tessuto*) gabardine; (*soprabito*) gabardine raincoat.

gab'bare *vt* to take in, dupe; ~**rsi** *vr*: ~**rsi di qn** to make fun of sb.

'gabbia *sf* cage; (*DIR*) dock; (*da imballaggio*) crate; **la** ~ **degli accusati** (*DIR*) the dock; ~ **dell'ascensore** lift (*BRIT*) *o* elevator (*US*) shaft; ~ **toracica** (*ANAT*) rib cage.

gabbi'ano *sm* (sea)gull.

gabi'netto *sm* (*MED etc*) consulting room; (*POL*) ministry; (*di decenza*) toilet, lavatory; (*INS: di fisica etc*) laboratory.

Ga'bon *sm*: **il** ~ Gabon.

ga'elico, a, ci, che *ag, sm* Gaelic.

gaffe [gaf] *sf inv* blunder, boob (*fam*).

gagli'ardo, a [gaʎ'ʎardo] *ag* strong, vigorous.

gai'ezza [ga'jettsa] *sf* gaiety, cheerfulness.

'gaio, a *ag* cheerful.

'gala *sf* (*sfarzo*) pomp; (*festa*) gala.

ga'lante *ag* gallant, courteous; (*avventura, poesia*) amorous.

galante'ria *sf* gallantry.

galantu'omo, pl galantu'omini *sm* gentleman.

Ga'lapagos *sfpl*: **le (isole)** ~ the Galapagos Islands.

ga'lassia *sf* galaxy.

gala'teo *sm* (good) manners *pl*, etiquette.

gale'otto *sm* (*rematore*) galley slave; (*carcerato*) convict.

ga'lera *sf* (*NAUT*) galley; (*prigione*) prison.

'galla *sf*: **a** ~ afloat; **venire a** ~ to surface, come to the surface; (*fig: verità*) to come out.

galleggia'mento [galleddʒa'mento] *sm* floating; **linea di** ~ (*di nave*) waterline.

galleggi'ante [galled'dʒante] *ag* floating ♦ *sm* (*natante*) barge; (*di pescatore, lenza, TECN*) float.

galleggi'are [galled'dʒare] *vi* to float.

galle'ria *sf* (*traforo*) tunnel; (*ARCHIT, d'arte*) gallery; (*TEAT*) circle; (*strada coperta con*

negozi) arcade; ~ **del vento** *o*
aerodinamica *(AER)* wind tunnel.
'**Galles** *sm*: **il** ~ Wales.
gal'lese *ag* Welsh ♦ *sm/f* Welshman/woman
♦ *sm (LING)* Welsh; **i G~i** the Welsh.
gal'letta *sf* cracker; *(NAUT)* ship's biscuit.
gal'letto *sm* young cock, cockerel; *(fig)*
cocky young man; **fare il** ~ to play the
gallant.
'**Gallia** *sf*: **la** ~ Gaul.
gal'lina *sf* hen; **andare a letto con le** ~**e** to
go to bed early.
gal'lismo *sm* machismo.
'**gallo** *sm* cock; **al canto del** ~ at daybreak,
at cockcrow; **fare il** ~ to play the gallant.
gal'lone *sm* piece of braid; *(MIL)* stripe;
(unità di misura) gallon.
galop'pare *vi* to gallop.
galop'pino *sm* errand boy; *(POL)*
canvasser.
ga'loppo *sm* gallop; **al** *o* **di** ~ at a gallop.
galvaniz'zare [galvanid'dzare] *vt* to
galvanize.
'**gamba** *sf* leg; *(asta: di lettera)* stem; **in** ~ *(in buona salute)* well; *(bravo, sveglio)* bright,
smart; **prendere qc sotto** ~ *(fig)* to treat
sth too lightly; **scappare a** ~**e levate** to
take to one's heels; ~**e!** scatter!
gam'bale *sm* legging.
gambe'retto *sm* shrimp.
'**gambero** *sm (di acqua dolce)* crayfish; *(di mare)* prawn.
'**Gambia** *sf*: **la** ~ the Gambia.
gambiz'zare [gambid'dzare] *vt* to kneecap.
'**gambo** *sm* stem; *(di frutta)* stalk.
ga'mella *sf* mess tin.
'**gamma** *sf (MUS)* scale; *(di colori, fig)*
range; ~ **di prodotti** product range.
ga'nascia, sce [ga'naʃʃa] *sf* jaw; ~**sce del**
freno *(AUT)* brake shoes.
'**gancio** ['gantʃo] *sm* hook.
'**Gange** ['gandʒe] *sm*: **il** ~ the Ganges.
'**gangheri** ['gangeri] *smpl*: **uscire dai** ~ *(fig)*
to fly into a temper.
gan'grena *sf* = **cancrena**.
'**gara** *sf* competition; *(SPORT)* competition;
contest; match; *(: corsa)* race; **fare a** ~ to
compete, vie; ~ **d'appalto** *(COMM)* tender.
ga'rage [ga'raʒ] *sm inv* garage.
ga'rante *sm/f* guarantor.
garan'tire *vt* to guarantee; *(debito)* to stand
surety for; *(dare per certo)* to assure.
garan'tismo *sm* protection of civil
liberties.
garan'tista, i, e *ag* concerned with civil
liberties.
garan'zia [garan'tsia] *sf* guarantee; *(pegno)*
security; **in** ~ under guarantee.

gar'bare *vi*: **non mi garba** I don't like it *(o*
him *etc)*.
garba'tezza [garba'tettsa] *sf* courtesy,
politeness.
gar'bato, a *ag* courteous, polite.
'**garbo** *sm (buone maniere)* politeness,
courtesy; *(di vestito etc)* grace, style.
gar'buglio [gar'buʎʎo] *sm* tangle; *(fig)*
muddle, mess.
gareggi'are [gared'dʒare] *vi* to compete.
garga'nella *sf*: **a** ~ from the bottle.
garga'rismo *sm* gargle; **fare i** ~**i** to gargle.
ga'ritta *sf (di caserma)* sentry box.
ga'rofano *sm* carnation; **chiodo di** ~ clove.
gar'retto *sm* hock.
gar'rire *vi* to chirp.
'**garrulo, a** *ag (uccello)* chirping; *(persona: loquace)* garrulous, talkative.
'**garza** ['gardza] *sf (per bende)* gauze.
gar'zone [gar'dzone] *sm (di negozio)* boy.
gas *sm inv* gas; **a tutto** ~ at full speed; **dare**
~ *(AUT)* to accelerate; ~ **lacrimogeno** tear
gas; ~ **naturale** natural gas.
ga'sare *etc* = **gassare** *etc*.
ga'sato, a *sm/f (fam: persona)* freak.
gas'dotto *sm* gas pipeline.
ga'solio *sm* diesel (oil).
ga's(s)are *vt* to aerate, carbonate;
(asfissiare) to gas; ~**rsi** *vr (fam)* to get
excited.
ga's(s)ato, a *ag (bibita)* aerated, fizzy.
gas'soso, a *ag* gaseous; gassy ♦ *sf* fizzy
drink.
'**gastrico, a, ci, che** *ag* gastric.
gast'rite *sf* gastritis.
gastroente'rite *sf* gastroenteritis.
gastrono'mia *sf* gastronomy.
gas'tronomo, a *sm/f* gourmet,
gastronome.
G.A.T.T. *sigla m (= General Agreement on*
Tariffs and Trade) GATT.
'**gatta** *sf* cat, she-cat; **una** ~ **da pelare** *(fam)*
a thankless task; **qui** ~ **ci cova!** I smell a
rat!, there's something fishy going on
here!
gatta'buia *sf (fam scherzoso: prigione)*
clink.
gat'tino *sm* kitten.
'**gatto** *sm* cat, tomcat; ~ **delle nevi** *(AUT,*
SCI) snowcat; ~ **a nove code** cat-o'-nine-
tails; ~ **selvatico** wildcat.
gatto'pardo *sm*: ~ **africano** serval; ~
americano ocelot.
gat'tuccio [gat'tuttʃo] *sm* dogfish.
gau'dente *sm/f* pleasure-seeker.
'**gaudio** *sm* joy, happiness.
ga'vetta *sf (MIL)* mess tin; **venire dalla** ~
(MIL, fig) to rise from the ranks.

'gazza ['gaddza] *sf* magpie.

gaz'zarra [gad'dzarra] *sf* racket, din.

gaz'zella [gad'dzɛlla] *sf* gazelle; (*dei carabinieri*) (high-speed) police car.

gaz'zetta [gad'dzetta] *sf* news sheet; **G~ Ufficiale** *official publication containing details of new laws.*

gaz'zoso, a [gad'dzoso] *ag* = **gassoso.**

Gazz. Uff. *abbr* = **Gazzetta Ufficiale.**

GB *sigla* (= *Gran Bretagna*) GB.

G.C. *abbr* = **genio civile.**

G.d.F. *abbr* = **guardia di finanza.**

GE *sigla* = *Genova.*

gel [dʒɛl] *sm inv* gel.

ge'lare [dʒe'lare] *vt, vi, vb impers* to freeze; **mi ha gelato il sangue** (*fig*) it made my blood run cold.

ge'lata [dʒe'lata] *sf* frost.

gela'taio, a [dʒela'tajo] *sm/f* ice-cream vendor.

gelate'ria [dʒelate'ria] *sf* ice-cream shop.

gela'tina [dʒela'tina] *sf* gelatine; **~ esplosiva** gelignite; **~ di frutta** fruit jelly.

gelati'noso, a [dʒelati'noso] *ag* gelatinous, jelly-like.

ge'lato, a [dʒe'lato] *ag* frozen ♦ *sm* ice cream.

'gelido, a ['dʒɛlido] *ag* icy, ice-cold.

'gelo ['dʒɛlo] *sm* (*temperatura*) intense cold; (*brina*) frost; (*fig*) chill.

ge'lone [dʒe'lone] *sm* chilblain.

gelo'sia [dʒelo'sia] *sf* jealousy.

ge'loso, a [dʒe'loso] *ag* jealous.

'gelso ['dʒɛlso] *sm* mulberry (tree).

gelso'mino [dʒelso'mino] *sm* jasmine.

gemel'laggio [dʒemel'laddʒo] *sm* twinning.

gemel'lare [dʒemel'lare] *ag* twin *cpd* ♦ *vt* (*città*) to twin.

ge'mello, a [dʒe'mɛllo] *ag, sm/f* twin; **~i** *smpl* (*di camicia*) cufflinks; (*dello zodiaco*): **G~i** Gemini *sg*; **essere dei G~i** to be Gemini.

'gemere ['dʒɛmere] *vi* to moan, groan; (*cigolare*) to creak; (*gocciolare*) to drip, ooze.

'gemito ['dʒɛmito] *sm* moan, groan.

'gemma ['dʒɛmma] *sf* (*BOT*) bud; (*pietra preziosa*) gem.

Gen. *abbr* (*MIL*: = *generale*) Gen.

gen. *abbr* (= *generale, generalmente*) gen.

gen'darme [dʒen'darme] *sm* policeman; (*fig*) martinet.

'gene ['dʒɛne] *sm* gene.

genealo'gia, 'gie [dʒenealo'dʒia] *sf* genealogy.

genea'logico, a, ci, che [dʒenea'lɔdʒiko] *ag* genealogical; **albero ~** family tree.

gene'rale [dʒene'rale] *ag, sm* general; **in ~** (*per sommi capi*) in general terms; (*di*

solito) usually, in general; **a ~ richiesta** by popular request.

generalità [dʒenerali'ta] *sfpl* (*dati d'identità*) particulars.

generaliz'zare [dʒeneralid'dzare] *vt, vi* to generalize.

generalizzazi'one [dʒeneraliddzat'tsjone] *sf* generalization.

general'mente [dʒeneral'mente] *av* generally.

gene'rare [dʒene'rare] *vt* (*dar vita*) to give birth to; (*produrre*) to produce; (*causare*) to arouse; (*TECN*) to produce, generate.

genera'tore [dʒenera'tore] *sm* (*TECN*) generator.

generazi'one [dʒenerat'tsjone] *sf* generation.

'genere ['dʒɛnere] *sm* kind, type, sort; (*BIOL*) genus; (*merce*) article, product; (*LING*) gender; (*ARTE, LETTERATURA*) genre; **in ~** generally, as a rule; **cose del o di questo ~** such things; **il ~ umano** mankind; **~i alimentari** foodstuffs; **~i di consumo** consumer goods; **~i di prima necessità** basic essentials.

ge'nerico, a, ci, che [dʒe'nɛriko] *ag* generic; (*vago*) vague, imprecise; **medico ~** general practitioner.

'genero ['dʒɛnero] *sm* son-in-law.

generosità [dʒenerosi'ta] *sf* generosity.

gene'roso, a [dʒene'roso] *ag* generous.

'genesi ['dʒɛnezi] *sf* genesis.

ge'netico, a, ci, che [dʒe'nɛtiko] *ag* genetic ♦ *sf* genetics *sg*.

gen'giva [dʒen'dʒiva] *sf* (*ANAT*) gum.

ge'nia [dʒe'nia] *sf* (*peg*) mob, gang.

geni'ale [dʒe'njale] *ag* (*persona*) of genius; (*idea*) ingenious, brilliant.

'genio ['dʒɛnjo] *sm* genius; (*attitudine, talento*) talent, flair, genius; **andare a ~ a qn** to be to sb's liking, appeal to sb; **~ civile** civil engineers *pl*; **il ~ (militare)** the Engineers.

geni'tale [dʒeni'tale] *ag* genital; **~i** *smpl* genitals.

geni'tore [dʒeni'tore] *sm* parent, father *o* mother; **~i** *smpl* parents.

genn. *abbr* (= *gennaio*) Jan.

gen'naio [dʒen'najo] *sm* January; *per fraseologia vedi* **luglio.**

geno'cidio [dʒeno'tʃidjo] *sm* genocide.

'Genova ['dʒɛnova] *sf* Genoa.

geno'vese [dʒeno'vese] *ag, sm/f* Genoese (*pl inv*).

gen'taglia [dʒen'taʎʎa] *sf* (*peg*) rabble.

'gente ['dʒɛnte] *sf* people *pl*.

gentil'donna [dʒentil'dɔnna] *sf* lady.

gen'tile [dʒen'tile] *ag* (*persona, atto*) kind;

(: *garbato*) courteous, polite; (*nelle lettere*): **G~ Signore** Dear Sir; (: *sulla busta*): **G~ Signor Fernando Villa** Mr Fernando Villa.

genti'lezza [dʒenti'lettsa] *sf* kindness; courtesy, politeness; **per ~** (*per favore*) please.

gentilu'omo, *pl* **gentilu'omini** [dʒenti'lwɔmo] *sm* gentleman.

genuflessi'one [dʒenufles'sjone] *sf* genuflection.

genu'ino, a [dʒenu'ino] *ag* (*prodotto*) natural; (*persona, sentimento*) genuine, sincere.

geogra'fia [dʒeogra'fia] *sf* geography.

geo'grafico, a, ci, che [dʒeo'grafiko] *ag* geographical.

ge'ografo, a [dʒe'ɔgrafo] *sm/f* geographer.

geolo'gia [dʒeolo'dʒia] *sf* geology.

geo'logico, a, ci, che [dʒeo'lɔdʒiko] *ag* geological.

ge'ometra, i, e [dʒe'ɔmetra] *sm/f* (*professionista*) surveyor.

geome'tria [dʒeome'tria] *sf* geometry.

geo'metrico, a, ci, che [dʒeo'mɛtriko] *ag* geometric(al).

geopo'litico, a, ci, che [dʒeopo'litiko] *ag* geopolitical.

Ge'orgia [dʒe'ɔrdʒa] *sf* Georgia.

geor'giano, a [dʒeor'dʒano] *ag, sm/f* Georgian.

ge'ranio [dʒe'ranjo] *sm* geranium.

ge'rarca, chi [dʒe'rarka] *sm* (*STORIA: nel fascismo*) party official.

gerar'chia [dʒerar'kia] *sf* hierarchy.

ge'rarchico, a, ci, che [dʒe'rarkiko] *ag* hierarchical.

ge'rente [dʒe'rɛnte] *sm/f* manager/manageress.

ge'renza [dʒe'rɛntsa] *sf* management.

ger'gale [dʒer'gale] *ag* slang *cpd*.

'gergo, ghi ['dʒɛrgo] *sm* jargon; slang.

geria'tria [dʒerja'tria] *sf* geriatrics *sg*.

geri'atrico, a, ci, che [dʒe'rjatriko] *ag* geriatric.

'gerla ['dʒɛrla] *sf* conical wicker basket.

Ger'mania [dʒer'manja] *sf*: **la ~** Germany; **la ~ occidentale/orientale** West/East Germany.

'germe ['dʒɛrme] *sm* germ; (*fig*) seed.

germinazi'one [dʒerminat'tsjone] *sf* germination.

germogli'are [dʒermoʎ'ʎare] *vi* (*emettere germogli*) to sprout; (*germinare*) to germinate.

ger'moglio [dʒer'moʎʎo] *sm* shoot; (*gemma*) bud.

gero'glifico, ci [dʒero'glifiko] *sm* hieroglyphic.

geron'tologo, a, gi, ghe [dʒeron'tɔlogo] *sm/f* specialist in geriatrics.

ge'rundio [dʒe'rundjo] *sm* gerund.

Gerusa'lemme [dʒeruza'lɛmme] *sf* Jerusalem.

'gesso ['dʒɛsso] *sm* chalk; (*SCULTURA, MED, EDIL*) plaster; (*statua*) plaster figure; (*minerale*) gypsum.

'gesta ['dʒɛsta] *sfpl* (*letterario*) deeds, feats.

ges'tante [dʒes'tante] *sf* expectant mother.

gestazi'one [dʒestat'tsjone] *sf* gestation.

gestico'lare [dʒestiko'lare] *vi* to gesticulate.

gestio'nale [dʒestjo'nale] *ag* administrative, management *cpd*.

gesti'one [dʒes'tjone] *sf* management; **~ di magazzino** stock control; **~ patrimoniale** investment management.

ges'tire [dʒes'tire] *vt* to run, manage.

'gesto ['dʒɛsto] *sm* gesture.

ges'tore [dʒes'tore] *sm* manager.

Gesù [dʒe'zu] *sm* Jesus; **~ bambino** the Christ Child.

gesu'ita, i [dʒezu'ita] *sm* Jesuit.

get'tare [dʒet'tare] *vt* to throw; (*anche*: **~ via**) to throw away *o* out; (*SCULTURA*) to cast; (*EDIL*) to lay; (*acqua*) to spout; (*grido*) to utter; **~rsi** *vr*: **~rsi in** (*impresa*) to throw o.s. into; (*mischia*) to hurl o.s. into; (*sog: fiume*) to flow into; **~ uno sguardo su** to take a quick look at.

get'tata [dʒet'tata] *sf* (*di cemento, gesso, metalli*) cast; (*diga*) jetty.

'gettito ['dʒettito] *sm* revenue.

'getto ['dʒetto] *sm* (*di gas, liquido, AER*) jet; (*BOT*) shoot; **a ~ continuo** uninterruptedly; **di ~** (*fig*) straight off, in one go.

get'tone [dʒet'tone] *sm* token; (*per giochi*) counter; (: *roulette etc*) chip; **~ di presenza** attendance fee; **~ telefonico** telephone token.

gettoni'era [dʒetto'njera] *sf* telephone-token dispenser.

'geyser ['gaizə] *sm inv* geyser.

'Ghana ['gana] *sm*: **il ~** Ghana.

'ghenga, ghe ['gɛnga] *sf* (*fam*) gang, crowd.

ghe'pardo [ge'pardo] *sm* cheetah.

gher'mire [ger'mire] *vt* to grasp, clasp, clutch.

'ghetta ['getta] *sf* (*gambale*) gaiter.

ghettiz'zare [gettid'dzare] *vt* to segregate.

'ghetto ['getto] *sm* ghetto.

ghiacci'aia [gjat'tʃaja] *sf* (*anche fig*) icebox.

ghiacci'aio [gjat'tʃajo] *sm* glacier.

ghiacci'are [gjat'tʃare] *vt* to freeze; (*fig*): **~ qn** to make sb's blood run cold ♦ *vi* to

freeze, ice over.
ghiacci'ato, a [gjat'tʃato] *ag* frozen;
(*bevanda*) ice-cold.
ghi'accio ['gjattʃo] *sm* ice.
ghiacci'olo [gjat'tʃɔlo] *sm* icicle; (*tipo di gelato*) ice lolly (*BRIT*), popsicle (*US*).
ghi'aia ['gjaja] *sf* gravel.
ghi'anda ['gjanda] *sf* (*BOT*) acorn.
ghi'andola ['gjandola] *sf* gland.
ghiando'lare [gjando'lare] *ag* glandular.
ghigliot'tina [giʎʎot'tina] *sf* guillotine.
ghi'gnare [giɲ'ɲare] *vi* to sneer.
'ghigno ['giɲɲo] *sm* (*espressione*) sneer;
(*risata*) mocking laugh.
'ghingheri ['gingeri] *smpl*: **in ~** all dolled up; **mettersi in ~** to put on one's Sunday best.
ghi'otto, a ['gjotto] *ag* greedy; (*cibo*) delicious, appetizing.
ghiot'tone, a [gjot'tone] *sm/f* glutton.
ghiottone'ria [gjottone'ria] *sf* greed, gluttony; (*cibo*) delicacy, titbit (*BRIT*), tidbit (*US*).
ghiri'goro [giri'gɔro] *sm* scribble, squiggle.
ghir'landa [gir'landa] *sf* garland, wreath.
'ghiro ['giro] *sm* dormouse.
'ghisa ['giza] *sf* cast iron.
G.I. *abbr* = **giudice istruttore**.
già [dʒa] *av* already; (*ex, in precedenza*) formerly ♦ *escl* of course!, yes indeed!; **~ che ci sei** ... while you are at it ....
gi'acca, che ['dʒakka] *sf* jacket; **~ a vento** windcheater (*BRIT*), windbreaker (*US*).
giacché [dʒak'ke] *cong* since, as.
giac'chetta [dʒak'ketta] *sf* (light) jacket.
'giaccio *etc* ['dʒattʃo] *vb vedi* **giacere**.
giac'cone [dʒak'kone] *sm* heavy jacket.
gia'cenza [dʒa'tʃɛntsa] *sf*: **merce in ~** goods in stock; **capitale in ~** uninvested capital; **~ e di magazzino** unsold stock.
gia'cere [dʒa'tʃere] *vi* to lie.
giaci'mento [dʒatʃi'mento] *sm* deposit.
gia'cinto [dʒa'tʃinto] *sm* hyacinth.
giaci'uto, a [dʒa'tʃuto] *pp di* **giacere**.
gi'acqui *etc* ['dʒakkwi] *vb vedi* **giacere**.
gi'ada ['dʒada] *sf* jade.
giaggi'olo [dʒad'dʒɔlo] *sm* iris.
giagu'aro [dʒa'gwaro] *sm* jaguar.
gial'lastro, a [dʒal'lastro] *ag* yellowish; (*carnagione*) sallow.
gi'allo ['dʒallo] *ag* yellow; (*carnagione*) sallow ♦ *sm* yellow; (*anche:* **romanzo ~**) detective novel; (*anche:* **film ~**) detective film; **~ dell'uovo** yolk; **il mar G~** the Yellow Sea.
gial'lognolo, a [dʒal'loɲɲolo] *ag* yellowish, dirty yellow.
Gia'maica [dʒa'maika] *sf*: **la ~** Jamaica.

giamai'cano, a [dʒamai'kano] *ag, sm/f* Jamaican.
giam'mai [dʒam'mai] *av* never.
Giap'pone [dʒap'pone] *sm*: **il ~** Japan.
giappo'nese [dʒappo'nese] *ag, sm/f, sm* Japanese *inv*.
gi'ara ['dʒara] *sf* jar.
giardi'naggio [dʒardi'naddʒo] *sm* gardening.
giardi'netta [dʒardi'netta] *sf* estate car (*BRIT*), station wagon (*US*).
giardini'ere, a [dʒardi'njɛre] *sm/f* gardener ♦ *sf* (*misto di sottaceti*) mixed pickles *pl*; (*automobile*) = **giardinetta**.
giar'dino [dʒar'dino] *sm* garden; **~ d'infanzia** nursery school; **~ pubblico** public gardens *pl*, (public) park; **~ zoologico** zoo.
giarretti'era [dʒarret'tjɛra] *sf* garter.
Gi'ava ['dʒava] *sf* Java.
giavel'lotto [dʒavel'lɔtto] *sm* javelin.
gib'boso, a [dʒib'boso] *ag* (*superficie*) bumpy; (*naso*) crooked.
Gibil'terra [dʒibil'tɛrra] *sf* Gibraltar.
gi'gante, 'essa [dʒi'gante] *sm/f* giant ♦ *ag* giant, gigantic; (*COMM*) giant-size.
gigan'tesco, a, schi, sche [dʒigan'tesko] *ag* gigantic.
gigantogra'fia [dʒigantogra'fia] *sf* (*FOT*) blow-up.
'giglio ['dʒiʎʎo] *sm* lily.
gilè [dʒi'lɛ] *sm inv* waistcoat.
gin [dʒin] *sm inv* gin.
gin'cana [dʒin'kana] *sf* gymkhana.
ginecolo'gia [dʒinekolo'dʒia] *sf* gynaecology (*BRIT*), gynecology (*US*).
gine'cologo, a, gi, ghe [dʒine'kɔlogo] *sm/f* gynaecologist (*BRIT*), gynecologist (*US*).
gi'nepro [dʒi'nepro] *sm* juniper.
gi'nestra [dʒi'nɛstra] *sf* (*BOT*) broom.
Gi'nevra [dʒi'nevra] *sf* Geneva; **il Lago di ~** Lake Geneva.
gingil'larsi [dʒindʒil'larsi] *vr* to fritter away one's time; (*giocare*): **~ con** to fiddle with.
gin'gillo [dʒin'dʒillo] *sm* plaything.
gin'nasio [dʒin'nazjo] *sm the 4th and 5th year of secondary school in Italy*.
gin'nasta, i, e [dʒin'nasta] *sm/f* gymnast.
gin'nastica [dʒin'nastika] *sf* gymnastics *sg*; (*esercizio fisico*) keep-fit exercises *pl*; (*INS*) physical education.
'ginnico, a, ci, che ['dʒinniko] *ag* gymnastic.
gi'nocchio [dʒi'nɔkkjo] *pl(m)* **gi'nocchi** *o pl(f)* **gi'nocchia** *sm* knee; **stare in ~** to kneel, be on one's knees; **mettersi in ~** to kneel (down).
ginocchi'oni [dʒinok'kjoni] *av* on one's

knees.

gio'care [dʒo'kare] *vt* to play; (*scommettere*) to stake, wager, bet; (*ingannare*) to take in ♦ *vi* to play; (*a roulette etc*) to gamble; (*fig*) to play a part, be important; (*TECN: meccanismo*) to be loose; ~ **a** (*gioco, sport*) to play; (*cavalli*) to bet on; ~ **d'astuzia** to be crafty; ~**rsi la carriera** to put one's career at risk; ~**rsi tutto** to risk everything; **a che gioco giochiamo?** what are you playing at?

gioca'tore, 'trice [dʒoka'tore] *sm/f* player; gambler.

gio'cattolo [dʒo'kattolo] *sm* toy.

giocherel'lare [dʒokerel'lare] *vi*: ~ **con** to play with.

giocherò *etc* [dʒoke'rɔ] *vb vedi* **giocare**.

gio'chetto [dʒo'ketto] *sm* (*gioco*) game; (*tranello*) trick; (*fig*): **è un** ~ it's child's play.

gi'oco, chi ['dʒɔko] *sm* game; (*divertimento, TECN*) play; (*al casinò*) gambling; (*CARTE*) hand; (*insieme di pezzi etc necessari per un gioco*) set; **per** ~ for fun; **fare il doppio** ~ **con qn** to double-cross sb; **prendersi** ~ **di qn** to pull sb's leg; **stare al** ~ **di qn** to play along with sb; **è in** ~ **la mia reputazione** my reputation is at stake; ~ **d'azzardo** game of chance; ~ **della palla** ball game; ~ **degli scacchi** chess set; **i G**~**chi Olimpici** the Olympic Games.

gioco'forza [dʒoko'fɔrtsa] *sm*: **essere** ~ to be inevitable.

giocoli'ere [dʒoko'ljɛre] *sm* juggler.

gio'coso, a [dʒo'koso] *ag* playful, jesting.

gio'gaia [dʒo'gaja] *sf* (*GEO*) range of mountains.

gi'ogo, ghi ['dʒogo] *sm* yoke.

gi'oia ['dʒɔja] *sf* joy, delight; (*pietra preziosa*) jewel, precious stone.

gioielle'ria [dʒojelle'ria] *sf* jeweller's (*BRIT*) *o* jeweler's (*US*) craft; (*negozio*) jewel(l)er's (shop).

gioielli'ere, a [dʒojel'ljɛre] *sm/f* jeweller (*BRIT*), jeweler (*US*).

gioi'ello [dʒo'jɛllo] *sm* jewel, piece of jewellery (*BRIT*) *o* jewelry (*US*); ~**i** *smpl* (*gioie*) jewel(l)ery *sg*.

gioi'oso, a [dʒo'joso] *ag* joyful.

Gior'dania [dʒor'danja] *sf*: **la** ~ Jordan.

Gior'dano [dʒor'dano] *sm*: **il** ~ the Jordan.

gior'dano, a [dʒor'dano] *ag, sm/f* Jordanian.

giorna'laio, a [dʒorna'lajo] *sm/f* newsagent (*BRIT*), newsdealer (*US*).

gior'nale [dʒor'nale] *sm* (*news*)paper; (*diario*) journal, diary; (*COMM*) journal; ~ **di bordo** (*NAUT*) ship's log; ~ **radio** radio news *sg*.

giorna'letto [dʒorna'letto] *sm* (children's) comic.

giornali'ero, a [dʒorna'ljɛro] *ag* daily.

giorna'lino [dʒorna'lino] *sm* children's comic.

giorna'lismo [dʒorna'lizmo] *sm* journalism.

giorna'lista, i, e [dʒorna'lista] *sm/f* journalist.

giorna'listico, a, ci, che [dʒorna'listiko] *ag* journalistic; **stile** ~ journalese.

giornal'mente [dʒornal'mente] *av* daily.

gior'nata [dʒor'nata] *sf* day; (*paga*) day's wages, day's pay; **durante la** ~ **di ieri** yesterday; **fresco di** ~ (*uovo*) freshly laid; **vivere alla** ~ to live from day to day; ~ **lavorativa** working day.

gi'orno ['dʒorno] *sm* day; (*opposto alla notte*) day, daytime; (*luce del* ~) daylight; **al** ~ per day; **di** ~ by day; ~ **per** ~ day by day; **al** ~ **d'oggi** nowadays; **tutto il santo** ~ all day long; **il G**~ **dei Morti** *vedi nota nel riquadro*.

IL GIORNO DEI MORTI

Il Giorno dei Morti, All Souls' Day, falls on 2 November. At this time of year people visit cemeteries to lay flowers on the graves of their loved ones.

---

gi'ostra ['dʒɔstra] *sf* (*per bimbi*) merry-go-round; (*torneo storico*) joust.

gios'trare [dʒos'trare] *vi* (*STORIA*) to joust, tilt; ~**rsi** *vr* to manage.

giov. *abbr* (= *giovedì*) Thur(s).

giova'mento [dʒova'mento] *sm* benefit, help.

gi'ovane ['dʒovane] *ag* young; (*aspetto*) youthful ♦ *sm/f* youth/girl, young man/woman; **i** ~**i** young people; **è** ~ **del mestiere** he's new to the job.

giova'netto, a [dʒova'netto] *sm/f* young man/woman.

giova'nile [dʒova'nile] *ag* youthful; (*scritti*) early; (*errore*) of youth.

giova'notto [dʒova'nɔtto] *sm* young man.

gio'vare [dʒo'vare] *vi*: ~ **a** (*essere utile*) to be useful to; (*far bene*) to be good for ♦ *vb impers* (*essere bene, utile*) to be useful; ~**rsi** *vr*: ~**rsi di qc** to make use of sth; **a che giova prendersela?** what's the point of getting upset?

Gi'ove ['dʒove] *sm* (*MITOLOGIA*) Jove; (*ASTR*) Jupiter.

giovedì [dʒove'di] *sm inv* Thursday; *per fraseologia vedi* **martedì**.

gio'venca, che [dʒo'vɛnka] *sf* heifer.

gioventù [dʒoven'tu] *sf* (*periodo*) youth; (*i*

giovani) young people *pl*, youth.
giovi'ale [dʒo'vjale] *ag* jovial, jolly.
giovi'nastro [dʒovi'nastro] *sm* young thug.
giovin'cello [dʒovin'tʃɛllo] *sm* young lad.
giovi'nezza [dʒovi'nettsa] *sf* youth.
gip [dʒip] *sigla m inv* (= *giudice per le indagini preliminari*) judge for preliminary enquiries.
gira'dischi [dʒira'diski] *sm inv* record player.
gi'raffa [dʒi'raffa] *sf* giraffe; (*TV, CINE, RADIO*) boom.
gira'mento [dʒira'mento] *sm*: ~ **di testa** fit of dizziness.
gira'mondo [dʒira'mondo] *sm/f inv* globetrotter.
gi'randola [dʒi'randola] *sf* (*fuoco d'artificio*) Catherine wheel; (*giocattolo*) toy windmill; (*banderuola*) weather vane, weathercock.
gi'rante [dʒi'rante] *sm/f* (*di assegno*) endorser.
gi'rare [dʒi'rare] *vt* (*far ruotare*) to turn; (*percorrere, visitare*) to go round; (*CINE*) to shoot; (: *film: come regista*) to make; (*COMM*) to endorse ♦ *vi* to turn; (*più veloce*) to spin; (*andare in giro*) to wander, go around; ~**rsi** *vr* to turn; ~ **attorno a** to go round; to revolve round; **si girava e rigirava nel letto** he tossed and turned in bed; **far** ~ **la testa a qn** to make sb dizzy; (*fig*) to turn sb's head; **gira al largo** keep your distance; **girala come ti pare** (*fig*) look at it whichever way you like; **gira e rigira** … after a lot of driving (*o* walking) about …; (*fig*) whichever way you look at it; **cosa ti gira?** (*fam*) what's got into you?; **mi ha fatto** ~ **le scatole** (*fam*) he drove me crazy.
girar'rosto [dʒirar'rosto] *sm* (*CUC*) spit.
gira'sole [dʒira'sole] *sm* sunflower.
gi'rata [dʒi'rata] *sf* (*passeggiata*) stroll; (*con veicolo*) drive; (*COMM*) endorsement.
gira'tario, a [dʒira'tarjo] *sm/f* endorsee.
gira'volta [dʒira'vɔlta] *sf* twirl, turn; (*curva*) sharp bend; (*fig*) about-turn.
gi'rello [dʒi'rɛllo] *sm* (*di bambino*) Babywalker ® (*BRIT*), go-cart (*US*); (*taglio di carne*) topside (*BRIT*), top round (*US*).
gi'retto [dʒi'retto] *sm* (*passeggiata*) walk, stroll; (: *in macchina*) drive, spin; (: *in bicicletta*) ride.
gi'revole [dʒi'revole] *ag* revolving, turning.
gi'rino [dʒi'rino] *sm* tadpole.
'giro ['dʒiro] *sm* (*circuito, cerchio*) circle; (*di chiave, manovella*) turn; (*viaggio*) tour, excursion; (*passeggiata*) stroll, walk; (*in macchina*) drive; (*in bicicletta*) ride; (*SPORT*:

della pista) lap; (*di denaro*) circulation; (*CARTE*) hand; (*TECN*) revolution; **fare un** ~ to go for a walk (*o* a drive *o* a ride); **fare il** ~ **di** (*parco, città*) to go round; **andare in** ~ (*a piedi*) to go about, walk around; **guardarsi in** ~ to look around; **prendere in** ~ **qn** (*fig*) to take sb for a ride; **a stretto** ~ **di posta** by return of post; **nel** ~ **di un mese** in a month's time; **essere nel** ~ (*fig*) to belong to a circle (of friends); ~ **d'affari** (*viaggio*) business tour; (*COMM*) turnover; ~ **di parole** circumlocution; ~ **di prova** (*AUT*) test drive; ~ **turistico** sightseeing tour; ~ **vita** waist measurement.
giro'collo [dʒiro'kɔllo] *sm*: **a** ~ crewneck *cpd*.
giro'conto [dʒiro'konto] *sm* (*ECON*) credit transfer.
gi'rone [dʒi'rone] *sm* (*SPORT*) series of games; ~ **di andata/ritorno** (*CALCIO*) first/second half of the season.
gironzo'lare [dʒirondzo'lare] *vi* to stroll about.
giro'tondo [dʒiro'tondo] *sm* ring-a-ring-o'roses (*BRIT*), ring-around-the-rosey (*US*); **in** ~ in a circle.
girova'gare [dʒirova'gare] *vi* to wander about.
gi'rovago, a, ghi, ghe [dʒi'rɔvago] *sm/f* (*vagabondo*) tramp; (*venditore*) peddler; **una compagnia di** ~**ghi** (*attori*) a company of strolling actors.
'gita ['dʒita] *sf* excursion, trip; **fare una** ~ to go for a trip, go on an outing.
gi'tano, a [dʒi'tano] *sm/f* gipsy.
gi'tante [dʒi'tante] *sm/f* member of a tour.
giù [dʒu] *av* down; (*dabbasso*) downstairs; **in** ~ downwards, down; **la mia casa è un po' più in** ~ my house is a bit further on; ~ **di lì** (*pressappoco*) thereabouts; **bambini dai 6 anni in** ~ children aged 6 and under; **cadere** ~ **per le scale** to fall down the stairs; ~ **le mani!** hands off!; **essere** ~ (*fig: di salute*) to be run down; (: *di spirito*) to be depressed; **quel tipo non mi va** ~ I can't stand that guy.
gi'ubba ['dʒubba] *sf* jacket.
giub'botto [dʒub'bɔtto] *sm* jerkin; ~ **antiproiettile** bulletproof vest.
giubi'lare [dʒubi'lare] *vi* to rejoice.
gi'ubilo ['dʒubilo] *sm* rejoicing.
giudi'care [dʒudi'kare] *vt* to judge; (*accusato*) to try; (*lite*) to arbitrate in; ~ **qn/qc bello** to consider sb/sth (to be) beautiful.
giudi'cato [dʒudi'kato] *sm* (*DIR*): **passare in** ~ to pass final judgment.

giu'dice ['dʒuditʃe] *sm* judge; ~ **collegiale** member of the court; ~ **conciliatore** justice of the peace; ~ **istruttore** examining (*BRIT*) *o* committing (*US*) magistrate; ~ **popolare** member of a jury.

giudizi'ale [dʒudit'tsjale] *ag* judicial.

giudizi'ario, a [dʒudit'tsjarjo] *ag* legal, judicial.

giu'dizio [dʒu'dittsjo] *sm* judgment; (*opinione*) opinion; (*DIR*) judgment, sentence; (: *processo*) trial; (: *verdetto*) verdict; **aver** ~ to be wise *o* prudent; **essere in attesa di** ~ to be awaiting trial; **citare in** ~ to summons; **l'imputato è stato rinviato a** ~ the accused has been committed for trial.

giudizi'oso, a [dʒudit'tsjoso] *ag* prudent, judicious.

gi'uggiola ['dʒuddʒola] *sf*: **andare in brodo di** ~**e** (*fam*) to be over the moon.

gi'ugno ['dʒuɲɲo] *sm* June; *per fraseologia vedi* **luglio**.

giu'livo, a [dʒu'livo] *ag* merry.

giul'lare [dʒul'lare] *sm* jester.

giu'menta [dʒu'menta] *sf* mare.

gi'unco, chi ['dʒunko] *sm* (*BOT*) rush.

gi'ungere ['dʒundʒere] *vi* to arrive ♦ *vt* (*mani etc*) ~ **a** to arrive at, reach; ~ **nuovo a qn** to come as news to sb; ~ **in porto** to reach harbour; (*fig*) to be brought to a successful outcome.

gi'ungla ['dʒungla] *sf* jungle.

gi'unsi *etc* ['dʒunsi] *vb vedi* **giungere**.

gi'unto, a ['dʒunto] *pp di* **giungere** ♦ *sm* (*TECN*) coupling, joint ♦ *sf* addition; (*organo esecutivo, amministrativo*) council, board; **per** ~**a** into the bargain, in addition; ~**a militare** military junta; *vedi anche* **Comune**; **Provincia**; **Regione**.

giun'tura [dʒun'tura] *sf* joint.

giuo'care [dʒwo'kare] *vt*, *vi* = **giocare**.

giu'oco ['dʒwɔko] *sm* = **gioco**.

giura'mento [dʒura'mento] *sm* oath; ~ **falso** perjury.

giu'rare [dʒu'rare] *vt* to swear ♦ *vi* to swear, take an oath; **gliel'ho giurata** I swore I would get even with him.

giu'rato, a [dʒu'rato] *ag*: **nemico** ~ sworn enemy ♦ *sm/f* juror, juryman/woman.

giu'ria [dʒu'ria] *sf* jury.

giu'ridico, a, ci, che [dʒu'ridiko] *ag* legal.

giurisdizi'one [dʒurizdit'tsjone] *sf* jurisdiction.

giurispru'denza [dʒurispru'dɛntsa] *sf* jurisprudence.

giu'rista, i, e [dʒu'rista] *sm/f* jurist.

giustap'porre [dʒustap'porre] *vt* to juxtapose.

giustapposizi'one [dʒustappozit'tsjone] *sf* juxtaposition.

giustap'posto, a [dʒustap'posto] *pp di* **giustapporre**.

giustifi'care [dʒustifi'kare] *vt* to justify; ~**rsi** *vr*: ~**rsi di** *o* **per qc** to justify *o* excuse o.s. for sth.

giustifica'tivo, a [dʒustifika'tivo] *ag* (*AMM*): **nota** *o* **pezza** ~**a** a receipt.

giustificazi'one [dʒustifikat'tsjone] *sf* justification; (*INS*) (note of) excuse.

gius'tizia [dʒus'tittsja] *sf* justice; **farsi** ~ (**da sé**) (*vendicarsi*) to take the law into one's own hands.

giustizi'are [dʒustit'tsjare] *vt* to execute, put to death.

giustizi'ere [dʒustit'tsjere] *sm* executioner.

gi'usto, a ['dʒusto] *ag* (*equo*) fair, just; (*vero*) true, correct; (*adatto*) right, suitable; (*preciso*) exact, correct ♦ *av* (*esattamente*) exactly, precisely; (*per l'appunto, appena*) just; **arrivare** ~ to arrive just in time; **ho** ~ **bisogno di te** you're just the person I need.

'glabro, a *ag* hairless.

glaci'ale [gla'tʃale] *ag* glacial.

gla'diolo *sm* gladiolus.

'glandola *sf* = **ghiandola**.

'glassa *sf* (*CUC*) icing.

glau'coma *sm* glaucoma.

gli [ʎi] *det mpl* (*dav V, s impura, gn, pn, ps, x, z*) the ♦ *pron* (*a lui*) to him; (*a esso*) to it; (*in coppia con lo, la, li, le, ne: a lui, a lei, a loro etc*): **gliele do** I'm giving them to him (*o* her *o* them); **gliene ho parlato** I spoke to him (*o* her *o* them) about it; *vedi anche* **il**.

glice'mia [glit'ʃe'mia] *sf* glycaemia.

glice'rina [glit'ʃe'rina] *sf* glycerine.

'glicine ['glitʃine] *sm* wistaria.

gli'ela *etc* ['ʎela] *vedi* **gli**.

glo'bale *ag* overall; (*vista*) global.

'globo *sm* globe.

'globulo *sm* (*ANAT*): ~ **rosso/bianco** red/white corpuscle.

'gloria *sf* glory; **farsi** ~ **di qc** to pride o.s. on sth, take pride in sth.

glori'arsi *vr*: ~ **di qc** to pride o.s. on sth, glory *o* take pride in sth.

glorifi'care *vt* to glorify.

glori'oso, a *ag* glorious.

glos'sario *sm* glossary.

glu'cosio *sm* glucose.

'gluteo *sm* gluteus; ~**i** *smpl* buttocks.

GM *abbr* = **genio militare**.

'gnocchi ['ɲɔkki] *smpl* (*CUC*) *small dumplings made of semolina pasta or potato.*

'gnomo [ˈɲɔmo] *sm* gnome.
'gnorri [ˈɲɔrri] *sm/f inv*: **non fare lo** ~! stop acting as if you didn't know anything about it!
GO *sigla* = *Gorizia*.
'goal [ˈgoul] *sm inv* (*SPORT*) goal.
'gobba *sf* (*ANAT*) hump; (*protuberanza*) bump.
'gobbo, a *ag* hunchbacked; (*ricurvo*) round-shouldered ♦ *sm/f* hunchback.
'Gobi *smpl*: **il Deserto dei** ~ the Gobi Desert.
'goccia, ce [ˈgottʃa] *sf* drop; ~ **di rugiada** dewdrop; **somigliarsi come due** ~**ce d'acqua** to be as like as two peas in a pod; **è la** ~ **che fa traboccare il vaso!** it's the last straw!
'goccio [ˈgottʃo] *sm* drop, spot.
goccio'lare [gottʃoˈlare] *vi*, *vt* to drip.
goccio'lio [gottʃoˈlio] *sm* dripping.
go'dere *vi* (*compiacersi*): ~ (**di**) to be delighted (at), rejoice (at); (*trarre vantaggio*): ~ **di** to enjoy, benefit from ♦ *vt* to enjoy; ~**rsi la vita** to enjoy life; **godersela** to have a good time, enjoy o.s.
godi'mento *sm* enjoyment.
godrò *etc vb vedi* **godere**.
gof'faggine [gofˈfaddʒine] *sf* clumsiness.
'goffo, a *ag* clumsy, awkward.
'gogna [ˈgoɲɲa] *sf* pillory.
gol *sm inv* = **goal**.
'gola *sf* (*ANAT*) throat; (*golosità*) gluttony, greed; (*di camino*) flue; (*di monte*) gorge; **fare** ~ (*anche fig*) to tempt; **ricacciare il pianto** *o* **le lacrime in** ~ to swallow one's tears.
go'letta *sf* (*NAUT*) schooner.
golf *sm inv* (*SPORT*) golf; (*maglia*) cardigan.
'golfo *sm* gulf.
goli'ardico, a, ci, che *ag* (*canto, vita*) student *cpd*.
go'loso, a *ag* greedy.
'golpe *sm inv* (*POL*) coup.
gomi'tata *sf*: **dare una** ~ **a qn** to elbow sb; **farsi avanti a (forza** *o* **furia di)** ~**e** to elbow one's way through; **fare a** ~**e per qc** to fight to get sth.
'gomito *sm* elbow; (*di strada etc*) sharp bend.
go'mitolo *sm* ball.
'gomma *sf* rubber; (*colla*) gum; (*per cancellare*) rubber, eraser; (*di veicolo*) tyre (*BRIT*), tire (*US*); ~ **da masticare** chewing gum; ~ **a terra** flat tyre.
gommapi'uma ® *sf* foam rubber.
gom'mino *sm* rubber tip; (*rondella*) rubber washer.
gom'mista, i, e *sm/f* tyre (*BRIT*) *o* tire (*US*)

specialist; (*rivenditore*) tyre *o* tire merchant.
gom'mone *sm* rubber dinghy.
gom'moso, a *ag* rubbery.
'gondola *sf* gondola.
gondoli'ere *sm* gondolier.
gonfa'lone *sm* banner.
gonfi'are *vt* (*pallone*) to blow up, inflate; (*dilatare, ingrossare*) to swell; (*fig: notizia*) to exaggerate; ~**rsi** *vr* to swell; (*fiume*) to rise.
'gonfio, a *ag* swollen; (*stomaco*) bloated; (*palloncino, gomme*) inflated, blown up; (*con pompa*) pumped up; (*vela*) full; **occhi** ~**i di pianto** eyes swollen with tears; ~ **di orgoglio** (*persona*) puffed up (with pride); **avere il portafoglio** ~ to have a bulging wallet.
gonfi'ore *sm* swelling.
gongo'lare *vi* to look pleased with o.s.; ~ **di gioia** to be overjoyed.
'gonna *sf* skirt; ~ **pantalone** culottes *pl*.
'gonzo [ˈgondzo] *sm* simpleton, fool.
gorgheggi'are [gorgedˈdʒare] *vi* to warble; to trill.
gor'gheggio [gorˈgeddʒo] *sm* (*MUS, di uccello*) trill.
'gorgo, ghi *sm* whirlpool.
gorgogli'are [gorgoʎˈʎare] *vi* to gurgle.
gorgo'glio [gorgoʎˈʎio] *sm* gurgling.
go'rilla *sm inv* gorilla; (*guardia del corpo*) bodyguard.
'Gotha *sm inv* (*del cinema, letteratura, industria*) leading lights *pl*.
'gotico, a, ci, che *ag, sm* Gothic.
'gotta *sf* gout.
gover'nante *sm/f* ruler ♦ *sf* (*di bambini*) governess; (*donna di servizio*) housekeeper.
gover'nare *vt* (*stato*) to govern, rule; (*pilotare, guidare*) to steer; (*bestiame*) to tend, look after.
governa'tivo, a *ag* (*politica, decreto*) government *cpd*, governmental; (*stampa*) pro-government.
governa'tore *sm* governor.
go'verno *sm* government; ~ **ombra** shadow cabinet.
'gozzo [ˈgottso] *sm* (*ZOOL*) crop; (*MED*) goitre; (*fig fam*) throat.
gozzovigli'are [gottsoviʎˈʎare] *vi* to make merry, carouse.
GPL [dʒipiˈɛlle] *sigla m* (= *Gas di Petrolio Liquefatto*) LPG (= *Liquefied Petroleum Gas*).
GPS [dʒipiˈɛsse] *sigla m* GPS = (*Global Positioning System*).
gpm *abbr* (= *giri per minuto*) rpm.

GR [dzi'erre] *sigla* = Grosseto ♦ *sigla m*
(= **giornale radio**) radio news.
gracchi'are [grak'kjare] *vi* to caw.
graci'dare [gratʃi'dare] *vi* to croak.
graci'dio, ii [gratʃi'dio] *sm* croaking.
'gracile ['gratʃile] *ag* frail, delicate.
gra'dasso *sm* boaster.
gradata'mente *av* gradually, by degrees.
gradazi'one [gradat'tsjone] *sf* (*sfumatura*)
gradation; ~ **alcolica** alcoholic content.
gra'devole *ag* pleasant, agreeable.
gradi'mento *sm* pleasure, satisfaction;
essere di mio (*o* **tuo** *etc*) ~ to be to my (*o*
your *etc*) liking.
gradi'nata *sf* flight of steps; (*in teatro,
stadio*) tiers *pl*.
gra'dino *sm* step; (*ALPINISMO*) foothold.
gra'dire *vt* (*accettare con piacere*) to accept;
(*desiderare*) to wish, like; **gradisce una
tazza di tè?** would you like a cup of tea?
gra'dito, a *ag* welcome.
'grado *sm* (*MAT, FISICA etc*) degree; (*stadio*)
degree, level; (*MIL, sociale*) rank; **essere in**
~ **di fare** to be in a position to do; **di buon**
~ willingly; **per ~i** by degrees; **un cugino
di primo/secondo** ~ a first/second cousin;
subire il terzo ~ (*anche fig*) to be given the
third degree.
gradu'ale *ag* gradual.
gradu'are *vt* to grade.
gradu'ato, a *ag* (*esercizi*) graded; (*scala,
termometro*) graduated ♦ *sm* (*MIL*) non-
commissioned officer.
gradua'toria *sf* (*di concorso*) list; (*per la
promozione*) order of seniority.
'graffa *sf* (*gancio*) clip; (*segno grafico*)
brace.
graf'fetta *sf* paper clip.
graffi'are *vt* to scratch.
graffia'tura *sf* scratch.
'graffio *sm* scratch.
graf'fiti *smpl* graffiti.
gra'fia *sf* spelling; (*scrittura*) handwriting.
'grafico, a, ci, che *ag* graphic ♦ *sm* graph;
(*persona*) graphic designer ♦ *sf* graphic
arts *pl*; ~ **a torta** pie chart.
gra'migna [gra'miɲɲa] *sf* weed; couch
grass.
gram'matica, che *sf* grammar.
grammati'cale *ag* grammatical.
'grammo *sm* gram(me).
gram'mofono *sm* gramophone.
'gramo, a *ag* (*vita*) wretched.
gran *ag vedi* **grande.**
'grana *sf* (*granello, di minerali, corpi spezzati*)
grain; (*fam: seccatura*) trouble; (: *soldi*)
cash ♦ *sm inv* cheese similar to Parmesan.
gra'naglie [gra'naʎʎe] *sfpl* corn *sg*, seed *sg*.

gra'naio *sm* granary, barn.
gra'nata *sf* (*frutto*) pomegranate; (*pietra
preziosa*) garnet; (*proiettile*) grenade.
granati'ere *sm* (*MIL*) grenadier; (*fig*) fine
figure of a man.
Gran Bre'tagna [granbre'taɲɲa] *sf*: **la** ~
Great Britain.
gran'cassa *sf* (*MUS*) bass drum.
'granchio ['grankjo] *sm* crab; (*fig*) blunder;
prendere un ~ (*fig*) to blunder.
grandango'lare *sm* wide-angle lens *sg*.
gran'dangolo *sm* (*FOT*) wide-angle lens *sg*.
'grande *ag* (*qualche volta* **gran** +*C,* **grand'**
+*V*) (*grosso, largo, vasto*) big, large; (*alto*)
tall; (*lungo*) long; (*in sensi astratti*) great
♦ *sm/f* (*persona adulta*) adult, grown-up; (*chi
ha ingegno e potenza*) great man/woman;
mio fratello più ~ my big *o* older brother;
il gran pubblico the general public; **di
gran classe** (*prodotto*) high-class; **cosa
farai da ~?** what will you be *o* do when
you grow up?; **fare le cose in** ~ to do
things in style; **fare il** ~ (*strafare*) to act
big; **una gran bella donna** a very beautiful
woman; **non è una gran cosa** *o* **un gran
che** it's nothing special; **non ne so gran
che** I don't know very much about it.
grandeggi'are [granded'dʒare] *vi* (*emergere
per grandezza*): ~ **su** to tower over; (*darsi
arie*) to put on airs.
gran'dezza [gran'dettsa] *sf* (*dimensione*)
size; (*fig*) greatness; **in** ~ **naturale** lifesize;
manie di ~ delusions of grandeur.
grandi'nare *vb impers* to hail.
'grandine *sf* hail.
grandi'oso, a *ag* grand, grandiose.
gran'duca, chi *sm* grand duke.
grandu'cato *sm* grand duchy.
grandu'chessa [grandu'kessa] *sf* grand
duchess.
gra'nello *sm* (*di cereali, uva*) seed; (*di frutta*)
pip; (*di sabbia, sale etc*) grain.
gra'nita *sf* kind of water ice.
gra'nito *sm* granite.
'grano *sm* (*in quasi tutti i sensi*) grain;
(*frumento*) wheat; (*di rosario, collana*) bead;
~ **di pepe** peppercorn.
gran'turco *sm* maize.
'granulo *sm* granule; (*MED*) pellet.
'grappa *sf* rough, strong brandy.
'grappolo *sm* bunch, cluster.
'graspo *sm* bunch (of grapes).
gras'setto *sm* (*TIP*) bold (type) (*BRIT*), bold
face.
'grasso, a *ag* fat; (*cibo*) fatty; (*pelle*)
greasy; (*terreno*) rich; (*fig: guadagno,
annata*) plentiful; (: *volgare*) coarse, lewd
♦ *sm* (*di persona, animale*) fat; (*sostanza che*

unge) grease.

gras'soccio, a, ci, ce [gras'sɔttʃo] *ag* plump.

gras'sone, a *sm/f* (*fam: persona*) dumpling.

'grata *sf* grating.

gra'ticcio [gra'tittʃo] *sm* trellis; (*stuoia*) mat.

gra'ticola *sf* grill.

gra'tifica, che *sf* bonus; ~ **natalizia** Christmas bonus.

gratificazi'one [gratifikat'tsjone] *sf* (*soddisfazione*) satisfaction, reward.

grati'nare *vt* (*CUC*) to cook au gratin.

'gratis *av* free, for nothing.

grati'tudine *sf* gratitude.

'grato, a *ag* grateful.

gratta'capo *sm* worry, headache.

grattaci'elo [gratta'tʃɛlo] *sm* skyscraper.

gratta e 'vinci [grattae'vintʃi] *sm* (*lotteria*) lottery; (*biglietto*) scratchcard.

grat'tare *vt* (*pelle*) to scratch; (*raschiare*) to scrape; (*pane, formaggio, carote*) to grate; (*fam: rubare*) to pinch ♦ *vi* (*stridere*) to grate; (*AUT*) to grind; ~**rsi** *vr* to scratch o.s.; ~**rsi la pancia** (*fig*) to twiddle one's thumbs.

grat'tata *sf* scratch; **fare una** ~ (*AUT: fam*) to grind the gears.

grat'tugia, gie [grat'tudʒa] *sf* grater.

grattugi'are [grattu'dʒare] *vt* to grate; **pane** *m* **grattugiato** breadcrumbs *pl*.

gratuità *sf* (*fig*) gratuitousness.

gra'tuito, a *ag* free; (*fig*) gratuitous.

gra'vame *sm* tax; (*fig*) burden, weight.

gra'vare *vt* to burden ♦ *vi*: ~ **su** to weigh on.

'grave *ag* (*danno, pericolo, peccato etc*) grave, serious; (*responsabilità*) heavy, grave; (*contegno*) grave, solemn; (*voce, suono*) deep, low-pitched; (*LING*): **accento** ~ grave accent ♦ *sm* (*FISICA*) (heavy) body; **un malato** ~ a person who is seriously ill.

grave'mente *av* (*ammalato, ferito*) seriously.

gravi'danza [gravi'dantsa] *sf* pregnancy.

'gravido, a *ag* pregnant.

gravità *sf* seriousness; (*anche FISICA*) gravity.

gravi'tare *vi* (*FISICA*): ~ **intorno a** to gravitate round.

gra'voso, a *ag* heavy, onerous.

'grazia ['grattsja] *sf* grace; (*favore*) favour (*BRIT*), favor (*US*); (*DIR*) pardon; **di** ~ (*ironico*) if you please; **troppa** ~! (*ironico*) you're too generous!; **quanta** ~ **di Dio!** what abundance!; **entrare nelle** ~**e di qn** to win sb's favour; **Ministero di G**~ **e**

Giustizia Ministry of Justice, ≈ Lord Chancellor's Office (*BRIT*), ≈ Department of Justice (*US*).

grazi'are [grat'tsjare] *vt* (*DIR*) to pardon.

'grazie ['grattsje] *escl* thank you!; ~ **mille!** *o* **tante!** *o* **infinite!** thank you very much!; ~ **a** thanks to.

grazi'oso, a [grat'tsjoso] *ag* charming, delightful; (*gentile*) gracious.

'Grecia ['grɛtʃa] *sf*: **la** ~ Greece.

'greco, a, ci, che *ag, sm/f, sm* Greek.

gre'gario *sm* (*CICLISMO*) supporting rider.

'gregge, *pl(f)* **i** ['greddʒe] *sm* flock.

'greggio, a, gi, ge ['greddʒo] *ag* raw, unrefined; (*diamante*) rough, uncut; (*tessuto*) unbleached ♦ *sm* (*anche*: **petrolio** ~) crude (oil).

grembi'ule *sm* apron; (*sopravveste*) overall.

'grembo *sm* lap; (*ventre della madre*) womb.

gre'mito, a *ag*: ~ (**di**) packed *o* crowded (with).

'greto *sm* (exposed) gravel bed of a river.

'gretto, a *ag* mean, stingy; (*fig*) narrow-minded.

'greve *ag* heavy.

'grezzo, a ['greddzo] *ag* = **greggio**.

gri'dare *vi* (*per chiamare*) to shout, cry (out); (*strillare*) to scream, yell ♦ *vt* to shout (out), yell (out); ~ **aiuto** to cry *o* shout for help.

'grido, *pl(m)* **i** *o* *pl(f)* **a** *sm* shout, cry; scream, yell; (*di animale*) cry; **di** ~ famous; **all'ultimo** ~ in the latest style.

'grigio, a, gi, gie ['gridʒo] *ag, sm* grey (*BRIT*), gray (*US*).

'griglia ['griʎʎa] *sf* (*per arrostire*) grill; (*ELETTR*) grid; (*inferriata*) grating; **alla** ~ (*CUC*) grilled.

grigli'ata [griʎ'ʎata] *sf* (*CUC*) grill.

gril'letto *sm* trigger.

'grillo *sm* (*ZOOL*) cricket; (*fig*) whim; **ha dei** ~**i per la testa** his head is full of nonsense.

grimal'dello *sm* picklock.

'grinfia *sf*: **cadere nelle** ~**e di qn** (*fig*) to fall into sb's clutches.

'grinta *sf* grim expression; (*SPORT*) fighting spirit; **avere molta** ~ to be very determined.

grintoso, a *ag* forceful.

'grinza ['grintsa] *sf* crease, wrinkle; (*ruga*) wrinkle; **il tuo ragionamento non fa una** ~ your argument is faultless.

grin'zoso, a [grin'tsoso] *ag* wrinkled; creased.

grip'pare *vi* (*TECN*) to seize.

gris'sino *sm* bread-stick.

groenlan'dese *ag* Greenland *cpd* ♦ *sm/f*

Greenlander.

Groen'landia *sf*: la ~ Greenland.

'gronda *sf* eaves *pl*.

gron'daia *sf* gutter.

gron'dante *ag* dripping.

gron'dare *vi* to pour; (*essere bagnato*): ~ **di** to be dripping with ♦ *vt* to drip with.

'groppa *sf* (*di animale*) back, rump; (*fam: dell'uomo*) back, shoulders *pl*.

'groppo *sm* tangle; **avere un ~ alla gola** (*fig*) to have a lump in one's throat.

'grossa *sf* (*unità di misura*) gross.

gros'sezza [gros'settsa] *sf* size; thickness.

gros'sista, i, e *sm/f* (*COMM*) wholesaler.

'grosso, a *ag* big, large; (*di spessore*) thick; (*grossolano: anche fig*) coarse; (*grave, insopportabile*) serious, great; (*tempo, mare*) rough ♦ *sm*: **il ~ di** the bulk of; **un pezzo ~** (*fig*) a VIP, a bigwig; **farla ~a** to do something very stupid; **dirle ~e** to tell tall stories (*BRIT*) o tales (*US*); **questa è ~a!** that's a good one!; **sbagliarsi di ~** to be completely wrong; **dormire della ~a** to sleep like a log.

grossolanità *sf* coarseness.

grosso'lano, a *ag* rough, coarse; (*fig*) coarse, crude; (*: errore*) stupid.

grosso'modo *av* roughly.

'grotta *sf* cave; grotto.

grot'tesco, a, schi, sche *ag* grotesque.

grovi'era *sm o f* gruyère (cheese).

gro'viglio [gro'viʎʎo] *sm* tangle; (*fig*) muddle.

gru *sf inv* crane.

'gruccia, ce ['gruttʃa] *sf* (*per camminare*) crutch; (*per abiti*) coat-hanger.

gru'gnire [gruɲ'ɲire] *vi* to grunt.

gru'gnito [gruɲ'ɲito] *sm* grunt.

'grugno ['gruɲɲo] *sm* snout; (*fam: faccia*) mug.

'grullo, a *ag* silly, stupid.

'grumo *sm* (*di sangue*) clot; (*di farina etc*) lump.

gru'moso, a *ag* lumpy.

'gruppo *sm* group; **~ sanguigno** blood group.

gruvi'era *sm o f* = **groviera**.

'gruzzolo ['gruttsolo] *sm* (*di denaro*) hoard.

GT *abbr* (*AUT: = gran turismo*) GT.

G.U. *abbr* = **Gazzetta Ufficiale**.

guada'gnare [gwadaɲ'ɲare] *vt* (*ottenere*) to gain; (*soldi, stipendio*) to earn; (*vincere*) to win; (*raggiungere*) to reach; **tanto di guadagnato!** so much the better!

gua'dagno [gwa'daɲɲo] *sm* earnings *pl*; (*COMM*) profit; (*vantaggio, utile*) advantage, gain; **~ di capitale** capital gains *pl*; **~ lordo/netto** gross/net earnings

pl.

gu'ado *sm* ford; **passare a ~** to ford.

gu'ai *escl*: ~ **a te** (*o* **lui** *etc*)! woe betide you (*o* him *etc*)!

gua'ina *sf* (*fodero*) sheath; (*indumento per donna*) girdle.

gu'aio *sm* trouble, mishap; (*inconveniente*) trouble, snag.

gua'ire *vi* to whine, yelp.

gua'ito *sm* (*di cane*) yelp, whine; (*il guaire*) yelping, whining.

gu'ancia, ce ['gwantʃa] *sf* cheek.

guanci'ale [gwan'tʃale] *sm* pillow; **dormire fra due ~i** (*fig*) to sleep easy, have no worries.

gu'anto *sm* glove; **trattare qn con i ~i** (*fig*) to handle sb with kid gloves; **gettare/raccogliere il ~** (*fig*) to throw down/take up the gauntlet.

guan'tone *sm* boxing glove.

guarda'boschi [gwarda'bɔski] *sm inv* forester.

guarda'caccia [gwarda'kattʃa] *sm inv* gamekeeper.

guarda'coste *sm inv* coastguard; (*nave*) coastguard patrol vessel.

guarda'linee *sm inv* (*SPORT*) linesman.

guarda'macchine [gwarda'makkine] *sm/f inv* car-park (*BRIT*) o parking lot (*US*) attendant.

guar'dare *vt* (*con lo sguardo: osservare*) to look at; (*film, televisione*) to watch; (*custodire*) to look after, take care of ♦ *vi* to look; (*badare*): ~ **a** to pay attention to; (*luoghi: esser orientato*): ~ **a** to face; **~rsi** *vr* to look at o.s.; ~ **di** to try to; **~rsi da** (*astenersi*) to refrain from; (*stare in guardia*) to beware of; **~rsi dal fare** to take care not to do; **ma guarda un po'!** good heavens!; **e guarda caso** ... as if by coincidence ...; ~ **qn dall'alto in basso** to look down on sb; **non ~ in faccia a nessuno** (*fig*) to have no regard for anybody; ~ **di traverso** to scowl o frown at; ~ **a vista qn** to keep a close watch on sb.

guarda'roba *sm inv* wardrobe; (*locale*) cloakroom.

guardarobi'ere, a *sm/f* cloakroom attendant.

guardasi'gilli [gwardasi'dʒilli] *sm inv* ≈ Lord Chancellor (*BRIT*), ≈ Attorney General (*US*).

gu'ardia *sf* (*individuo, corpo*) guard; (*sorveglianza*) watch; **fare la ~ a qc/qn** to guard sth/sb; **stare in ~** (*fig*) to be on one's guard; **il medico di ~** the doctor on call; **il fiume ha raggiunto il livello di ~**

the river has reached the high-water mark; ~ **carceraria** (prison) warder (*BRIT*) o guard (*US*); ~ **del corpo** bodyguard; ~ **di finanza** (*corpo*) customs *pl*; (*persona*) customs officer; ~ **forestale** forest ranger; ~ **giurata** security guard; ~ **medica** emergency doctor service; ~ **municipale** town policeman; ~ **notturna** night security guard; ~ **di pubblica sicurezza** policeman; *vedi nota nel riquadro.*

GUARDIA DI FINANZA

The **Guardia di Finanza** *is a military body which deals with infringements of the laws governing income tax and monopolies. It reports to the Ministers of Finance, Justice or Agriculture, depending on the function it is performing.*

---

guardia'caccia [gwardja'kattʃa] *sm inv* = **guardacaccia**.

guardi'ano, a *sm/f* (*di carcere*) warder (*BRIT*), guard (*US*); (*di villa etc*) caretaker; (*di museo*) custodian; (*di zoo*) keeper; ~ **notturno** night watchman.

guar'dina *sf* cell.

guar'dingo, a, ghi, ghe *ag* wary, cautious.

guardi'ola *sf* porter's lodge; (*MIL*) look-out tower.

guarigi'one [gwari'dʒone] *sf* recovery.

gua'rire *vt* (*persona, malattia*) to cure; (*ferita*) to heal ♦ *vi* to recover, be cured; to heal (up).

guarnigi'one [gwarni'dʒone] *sf* garrison.

guar'nire *vt* (*ornare: abiti*) to trim; (*CUC*) to garnish.

guarnizi'one [gwarnit'tsjone] *sf* trimming; garnish; (*TECN*) gasket.

guasta'feste *sm/f inv* spoilsport.

guas'tare *vt* to spoil, ruin; (*meccanismo*) to break; ~**rsi** *vr* (*cibo*) to go bad; (*meccanismo*) to break down; (*tempo*) to change for the worse; (*amici*) to quarrel.

gu'asto, a *ag* (*non funzionante*) broken; (: *telefono etc*) out of order; (*andato a male*) bad, rotten; (: *dente*) decayed, bad; (*fig: corrotto*) depraved ♦ *sm* breakdown; (*avaria*) failure; ~ **al motore** engine failure.

Guate'mala *sm*: **il** ~ Guatemala.

guatemal'teco, a, ci, che *ag, sm/f* Guatemalan.

gu'ercio, a, ci, ce ['gwertʃo] *ag* cross-eyed.

gu'erra *sf* war; (*tecnica: atomica, chimica etc*) warfare; **fare la** ~ **(a)** to wage war (against); **la** ~ **fredda** the Cold War; ~ **mondiale** world war; ~ **preventiva**

preventative war; **la prima/seconda** ~ **mondiale** the First/Second World War.

guerrafon'daio *sm* warmonger.

guerreggi'are [gwerred'dʒare] *vi* to wage war.

guerri'ero, a *ag* warlike ♦ *sm* warrior.

guer'riglia [gwer'riʎʎa] *sf* guerrilla warfare.

guerrigli'ero [gwerriʎ'ʎɛro] *sm* guerrilla.

'gufo *sm* owl.

'guglia ['guʎʎa] *sf* (*ARCHIT*) spire; (*di roccia*) needle.

Gui'ana *sf*: **la** ~ **francese** French Guiana.

gu'ida *sf* (*persona*) guide; (*libro*) guide(book); (*comando, direzione*) guidance, direction; (*AUT*) driving; (: *sterzo*) steering; (*tappeto, di tenda, cassetto*) runner; ~ **a destra/sinistra** (*AUT*) right-/left-hand drive; **essere alla** ~ **di** (*governo*) to head; (*spedizione, paese*) to lead; **far da** ~ **a qn** (*mostrare la strada*) to show sb the way; (*in una città*) to show sb (a)round; ~ **telefonica** telephone directory.

gui'dare *vt* to guide; (*condurre a capo*) to lead; (*auto*) to drive; (*aereo, nave*) to pilot; **sa** ~? can you drive?

guida'tore, 'trice *sm/f* (*conducente*) driver.

Gui'nea *sf*: **la Repubblica di** ~ the Republic of Guinea; **la** ~ **Equatoriale** Equatorial Guinea.

guin'zaglio [gwin'tsaʎʎo] *sm* leash, lead.

gu'isa *sf*: **a** ~ **di** like, in the manner of.

guiz'zare [gwit'tsare] *vi* to dart; to flicker; to leap; ~ **via** (*fuggire*) to slip away.

gu'izzo ['gwittso] *sm* (*di animali*) dart; (*di fulmine*) flash.

'guru *sm inv* (*REL, anche fig*) guru.

'guscio ['guʃʃo] *sm* shell.

gus'tare *vt* (*cibi*) to taste; (: *assaporare con piacere*) to enjoy, savour (*BRIT*), savor (*US*); (*fig*) to enjoy, appreciate ♦ *vi*: ~ **a** to please; **non mi gusta affatto** I don't like it at all.

gusta'tivo, a *ag*: **papille** *fpl* ~**e** taste buds.

'gusto *sm* (*senso*) taste; (*sapore*) taste, flavour (*BRIT*), flavor (*US*); (*godimento*) enjoyment; **al** ~ **di fragola** strawberry-flavo(u)red; **di** ~ **barocco** in the baroque style; **mangiare di** ~ to eat heartily; **prenderci** ~: **ci ha preso** ~ he's acquired a taste for it, he's got to like it.

gus'toso, a *ag* tasty; (*fig*) agreeable.

guttu'rale *ag* guttural.

Gu'yana [gu'jana] *sf*: **la** ~ Guyana.

H h   I i

H, h ['akka] *sf o m inv* (*lettera*) H, h ♦ *abbr*
(= *ora*) hr; (= *etto, altezza*) h; **H come hotel**
≈ H for Harry (*BRIT*), H for How (*US*).

ha¹, 'hai [a, ai] *vb vedi* **avere.**

ha² *abbr* (= *ettaro*) ha.

Ha'iti [a'iti] *sf* Haiti.

haiti'ano, a [ai'tjano] *ag, smf* Haitian.

hall [hɔːl] *sf inv* hall, foyer.

'handicap ['handikap] *sm inv* handicap.

handicap'pato, a [andikap'pato] *ag*
handicapped ♦ *smf* handicapped person,
disabled person.

'hanno ['anno] *vb vedi* **avere.**

ha'scisc [aʃ'ʃiʃ] *sm* hashish.

hawai'ano, a [ava'jano] *ag, smf* Hawaiian.

Ha'waii [a'vai] *sfpl:* **le ~** Hawaii *sg.*

'Helsinki ['ɛlsinki] *sf* Helsinki.

'herpes ['ɛrpes] *sm* (*MED*) herpes *sg;* **~**
zoster shingles *sg.*

hg *abbr* (= *ettogrammo*) hg.

'hi-fi ['haifai] *sm inv, ag inv* hi-fi.

Hima'laia [ima'laja] *sm:* **l'~** the Himalayas
pl.

hl *abbr* (= *ettolitro*) hl.

ho [ɔ] *vb vedi* **avere.**

'hobby ['hɔbi] *sm inv* hobby.

'hockey ['hɔki] *sm* hockey; **~ su ghiaccio**
ice hockey.

'holding ['houldiŋ] *sf inv* holding company.

Hon'duras [on'duras] *sm* Honduras.

'Hong Kong ['ɔkɔg] *sf* Hong Kong.

Hono'lulu [ono'lulu] *sf* Honolulu.

'hostess ['houstis] *sf inv* air hostess (*BRIT*) *o*
stewardess.

ho'tel [o'tɛl] *sm inv* hotel.

Hz *abbr* (= *hertz*) Hz.

I, i [i] *sf o m inv* (*lettera*) I, i; **I come Imola** ≈ I
for Isaac (*BRIT*), I for Item (*US*).

i *det mpl* the; *vedi anche* **il.**

IACP *sigla m* (= *Istituto Autonomo per le Case*
Popolari) *public housing association.*

i'ato *sm* hiatus.

i'berico, a, ci, che *ag* Iberian; **la Penisola**
I~a the Iberian Peninsula.

iber'nare *vi* to hibernate ♦ *vt* (*MED*) to
induce hypothermia in.

ibernazi'one [ibernat'tsjone] *sf*
hibernation.

ibid. *abbr* (= *ibidem*) ib(id).

'ibrido, a *ag, sm* hybrid.

IC *abbr* = **intercity.**

'ICE ['itʃe] *sigla m* (= *Istituto nazionale per il*
Commercio Estero) *overseas trade board.*

i'cona *sf* icon.

id *abbr* (= *idem*) do.

Id'dio *sm* God.

i'dea *sf* idea; (*opinione*) opinion, view;
(*ideale*) ideal; **avere le ~e chiare** to know
one's mind; **cambiare ~** to change one's
mind; **dare l'~ di** to seem, look like;
neanche *o* **neppure per ~!** certainly not!,
no way!; **~ fissa** obsession.

ide'ale *ag, sm* ideal.

idea'lismo *sm* idealism.

idea'lista, i, e *smf* idealist.

idea'listico, a, ci, che *ag* idealistic.

idealiz'zare [idealid'dzare] *vt* to idealize.

ide'are *vt* (*immaginare*) to think up,
conceive; (*progettare*) to plan.

idea'tore, 'trice *smf* author.

i'dentico, a, ci, che *ag* identical.

identifi'care *vt* to identify.

identificazi'one [identifikat'tsjone] *sf*
identification.

identità *sf inv* identity.

ideolo'gia, 'gie [ideolo'dʒia] *sf* ideology.

ideo'logico, a, ci, che [ideo'lɔdʒiko] *ag*
ideological.

idil'liaco, a, ci, che *ag* = **idillico.**

i'dillico, a, ci, che *ag* idyllic.

i'dillio *sm* idyll; **tra di loro è nato un ~** they
have fallen in love.

idi'oma, i *sm* idiom, language.

idio'matico, a, ci, che *ag* idiomatic; **frase** *f*

~**a** idiom.
idiosincra'sia *sf* idiosyncrasy.
idi'ota, i, e *ag* idiotic ♦ *smf* idiot.
idio'zia [idjot'tsia] *sf* idiocy; (*atto, discorso*) idiotic thing to do (*o* say).
ido'latra, i, e *ag* idolatrous ♦ *smf* idolater.
idola'trare *vt* to worship; (*fig*) to idolize.
idola'tria *sf* idolatry.
'idolo *sm* idol.
idoneità *sf* suitability; **esame** *m* **di** ~ qualifying examination.
i'doneo, a *ag*: ~ **a** suitable for, fit for; (MIL) fit for; (*qualificato*) qualified for.
i'drante *sm* hydrant.
idra'tante *ag* (*crema*) moisturizing ♦ *sm* moisturizer.
idra'tare *vt* (*pelle*) to moisturize.
idratazi'one [idratat'tsjone] *sf* moisturizing.
i'draulico, a, ci, che *ag* hydraulic ♦ *sm* plumber ♦ *sf* hydraulics *sg*.
'idrico, a, ci, che *ag* water *cpd*.
idrocar'buro *sm* hydrocarbon.
idroe'lettrico, a, ci, che *ag* hydroelectric.
i'drofilo, a *ag*: **cotone** *m* ~ cotton wool (BRIT), absorbent cotton (US).
idrofo'bia *sf* rabies *sg*.
i'drofobo, a *ag* rabid; (*fig*) furious.
i'drogeno [i'drɔdʒeno] *sm* hydrogen.
idroli'pidico, a, ci, che *ag* hydrolipid.
idro'porto *sm* (AER) seaplane base.
idrorepel'lente *ag* water-repellent.
idros'calo *sm* = **idroporto**.
idrovo'lante *sm* seaplane.
i'ella *sf* bad luck.
iel'lato, a *ag* plagued by bad luck.
i'ena *sf* hyena.
ie'ratico, a, ci, che *ag* (REL: *scrittura*) hieratic; (*fig: atteggiamento*) solemn.
i'eri *av*, *sm* yesterday; **il giornale di** ~ yesterday's paper; ~ **l'altro** the day before yesterday; ~ **sera** yesterday evening.
ietta'tore, 'trice *smf* jinx.
igi'ene [i'dʒɛne] *sf* hygiene; **norme d'**~ sanitary regulations; **ufficio d'**~ public health office; ~ **mentale** mental health; ~ **pubblica** public health.
igi'enico, a, ci, che [i'dʒɛniko] *ag* hygienic; (*salubre*) healthy.
igloo [i'glu] *sm inv* igloo; (*tenda*) dome tent.
IGM *sigla m* (= *Ispettorato Generale della Motorizzazione*) *road traffic inspectorate*.
i'gnaro, a [iɲ'ɲaro] *ag*: ~ **di** unaware of, ignorant of.
i'gnifugo, a, ghi, ghe [iɲ'ɲifugo] *ag* flame-resistant, fireproof.
i'gnobile [iɲ'ɲɔbile] *ag* despicable, vile.

igno'minia [iɲɲo'minja] *sf* ignominy.
igno'rante [iɲɲo'rante] *ag* ignorant.
igno'ranza [iɲɲo'rantsa] *sf* ignorance.
igno'rare [iɲɲo'rare] *vt* (*non sapere, conoscere*) to be ignorant *o* unaware of, not to know; (*fingere di non vedere, sentire*) to ignore.
i'gnoto, a [iɲ'ɲɔto] *ag* unknown ♦ *smf*: **figlio di** ~**i** child of unknown parentage; **il Milite I**~ the Unknown Soldier.

=================== *PAROLA CHIAVE*

il (*pl* (*m*) **i**; *diventa* **lo** (*pl* **gli**) *davanti a s impura, gn, pn, ps, x, z; f* **la** (*pl* **le**)) *det m* **1** the; ~ **libro/lo studente/l'acqua** the book/ the student/the water; **gli scolari** the pupils
2 (*astrazione*): ~ **coraggio/l'amore/la giovinezza** courage/love/youth
3 (*tempo*): ~ **mattino/la sera** in the morning/evening; ~ **venerdì** (*abitualmente*) on Fridays; (*quel giorno*) on (the) Friday; **la settimana prossima** next week
4 (*distributivo*) a, an; **2 euro** ~ **chilo/paio** 2 euros a *o* per kilo/pair
5 (*partitivo*) some, any; **hai messo lo zucchero?** have you added sugar?; **hai comprato** ~ **latte?** did you buy (some *o* any) milk?
6 (*possesso*): **aprire gli occhi** to open one's eyes; **rompersi la gamba** to break one's leg; **avere i capelli neri/**~ **naso rosso** to have dark hair/a red nose; **mettiti le scarpe** put your shoes on
7 (*con nomi propri*): ~ **Petrarca** Petrarch; ~ **Presidente Bush** President Bush; **dov'è la Francesca?** where's Francesca?
8 (*con nomi geografici*): ~ **Tevere** the Tiber; **l'Italia** Italy; ~ **Regno Unito** the United Kingdom; **l'Everest** Everest.

'ilare *ag* cheerful.
ilarità *sf* hilarity, mirth.
ill. *abbr* (= *illustrazione; illustrato*) ill.
illangui'dire *vi* to grow weak *o* feeble.
illazi'one [illat'tsjone] *sf* inference, deduction.
il'lecito, a [il'letʃito] *ag* illicit.
ille'gale *ag* illegal.
illegalità *sf* illegality.
illeg'gibile [illed'dʒibile] *ag* illegible.
illegittimità [illeddʒittimi'ta] *sf* illegitimacy.
ille'gittimo, a [ille'dʒittimo] *ag* illegitimate.
il'leso, a *ag* unhurt, unharmed.
illette'rato, a *ag* illiterate.
illiba'tezza [illiba'tettsa] *sf* (*di donna*) virginity.

illi'bato, a *ag*: **donna** ~**a** virgin.
illimi'tato, a *ag* boundless; unlimited.
illivi'dire *vi* (*volto, mani*) to turn livid; (*cielo*) to grow leaden.
ill.mo *abbr* = **illustrissimo.**
il'logico, a, ci, che [il'lɔdʒiko] *ag* illogical.
il'ludere *vt* to deceive, delude; ~**rsi** *vr* to deceive o.s., delude o.s.
illumi'nare *vt* to light up, illuminate; (*fig*) to enlighten; ~**rsi** *vr* to light up; ~ **a giorno** (*con riflettori*) to floodlight.
illumi'nato, a *ag* (*fig: sovrano, spirito*) enlightened.
illuminazi'one [illuminat'tsjone] *sf* lighting; illumination; floodlighting; (*fig*) flash of inspiration.
illumi'nismo *sm* (*STORIA*): **l'l**~ the Enlightenment.
il'lusi *etc vb vedi* **illudere.**
illusi'one *sf* illusion; **farsi delle** ~**i** to delude o.s.
illusio'nismo *sm* conjuring.
illusio'nista, i, e *sm/f* conjurer.
il'luso, a *pp di* **illudere.**
illu'sorio, a *ag* illusory.
illus'trare *vt* to illustrate.
illustra'tivo, a *ag* illustrative.
illustrazi'one [illustrat'tsjone] *sf* illustration.
il'lustre *ag* eminent, renowned.
illus'trissimo, a *ag* (*negli indirizzi*) very revered.
'ILOR *sigla f vedi* **imposta locale sui redditi.**
IM *sigla* = *Imperia.*
imbacuc'care *vt*, ~**rsi** *vr* to wrap up.
imbaldan'zire [imbaldan'tsire] *vt* to give confidence to; ~**rsi** *vr* to grow bold.
imbal'laggio [imbal'laddʒo] *sm* packing *no pl.*
imbal'lare *vt* to pack; (*AUT*) to race; ~**rsi** *vr* (*AUT*) to race.
imbalsa'mare *vt* to embalm.
imbalsa'mato, a *ag* embalmed.
imbambo'lato, a *ag* (*sguardo, espressione*) vacant, blank.
imban'dire *vt*: ~ **un banchetto** to prepare a lavish feast.
imban'dito, a *ag*: **tavola** ~**a** lavishly *o* sumptuously decked table.
imbaraz'zante [imbarat'tsante] *ag* embarrassing, awkward.
imbaraz'zare [imbarat'tsare] *vt* (*mettere a disagio*) to embarrass; (*ostacolare: movimenti*) to hamper; (: *stomaco*) to lie heavily on; ~**rsi** *vr* to become embarrassed.
imbaraz'zato, a [imbarat'tsato] *ag* embarrassed; **avere lo stomaco** ~ to have

an upset stomach.
imba'razzo [imba'rattso] *sm* (*disagio*) embarrassment; (*perplessità*) puzzlement, bewilderment; **essere** *o* **trovarsi in** ~ to be in an awkward situation *o* predicament; **mettere in** ~ to embarrass; ~ **di stomaco** indigestion.
imbarbari'mento *sm* (*di civiltà, costumi*) barbarization.
imbarca'dero *sm* landing stage.
imbar'care *vt* (*passeggeri*) to embark; (*merci*) to load; ~**rsi** *vr*: ~**rsi su** to board; ~**rsi per l'America** to sail for America; ~**rsi in** (*fig: affare*) to embark on.
imbarcazi'one [imbarkat'tsjone] *sf* (small) boat, (small) craft *inv*; ~ **di salvataggio** lifeboat.
im'barco, chi *sm* embarkation; loading; boarding; (*banchina*) landing stage; **carta d'**~ boarding pass (*BRIT*), boarding card.
imbastar'dire *vt* to bastardize, debase; ~**rsi** *vr* to degenerate, become debased.
imbas'tire *vt* (*cucire*) to tack; (*fig: abbozzare*) to sketch, outline.
im'battersi *vr*: ~ **in** (*incontrare*) to bump *o* run into.
imbat'tibile *ag* unbeatable, invincible.
imbavagli'are [imbavaʎ'ʎare] *vt* to gag.
imbec'care *vt* (*uccelli*) to feed; (*fig*) to prompt, put words into sb's mouth.
imbec'cata *sf* (*TEAT*) prompt; **dare l'**~ **a qn** to prompt sb; (*fig*) to give sb their cue.
imbe'cille [imbe'tʃille] *ag* idiotic ♦ *sm/f* idiot; (*MED*) imbecile.
imbecillità [imbetʃilli'ta] *sf inv* (*MED, fig*) imbecility, idiocy; **dire** ~ to talk nonsense.
imbellet'tare *vt* (*viso*) to make up, put make-up on; ~**rsi** *vr* to make o.s. up, put on one's make-up.
imbel'lire *vt* to adorn, embellish ♦ *vi* to grow more beautiful.
im'berbe *ag* beardless; **un giovanotto** ~ a callow youth.
imbestia'lire *vt* to infuriate; ~**rsi** *vr* to become infuriated, fly into a rage.
im'bevere *vt* to soak; ~**rsi** *vr*: ~**rsi di** to soak up, absorb.
imbe'vuto, a *ag*: ~ (**di**) soaked (in).
imbian'care *vt* to whiten; (*muro*) to whitewash ♦ *vi* to become *o* turn white.
imbianca'tura *sf* (*di muro: con bianco di calce*) whitewashing; (: *con altre pitture*) painting.
imbian'chino [imbjan'kino] *sm* (house) painter, painter and decorator.
imbion'dire *vt* (*capelli*) to lighten; (*CUC: cipolla*) to brown; ~**rsi** *vr* (*capelli*) to

lighten, go blonde, go fair; (*messi*) to turn golden, ripen.

imbizzar'rirsi [imbiddzar'rirsi] *vr* (*cavallo*) to become frisky.

imboc'care *vt* (*bambino*) to feed; (*entrare*: *strada*) to enter, turn into ♦ *vi*: ~ **in** (*sog*: *strada*) to lead into; (: *fiume*) to flow into.

imbocca'tura *sf* mouth; (*di strada, porto*) entrance; (*MUS, del morso*) mouthpiece.

im'bocco, chi *sm* entrance.

imboni'tore *sm* (*di spettacolo, circo*) barker.

imborghe'sire [imborge'zire] *vi*, ~**rsi** *vr* to become bourgeois.

imbos'care *vt* to hide; ~**rsi** *vr* (*MIL*) to evade military service.

imbos'cata *sf* ambush.

imbos'cato *sm* draft dodger (*US*).

imboschi'mento [imboski'mento] *sm* afforestation.

imbottigli'are [imbottiʎ'ʎare] *vt* to bottle; (*NAUT*) to blockade; (*MIL*) to hem in; ~**rsi** *vr* to be stuck in a traffic jam.

imbot'tire *vt* to stuff; (*giacca*) to pad; ~**rsi** *vr*: ~**rsi di** (*rimpinzarsi*) to stuff o.s. with.

imbot'tito, a *ag* (*sedia*) upholstered; (*giacca*) padded ♦ *sf* quilt.

imbotti'tura *sf* stuffing; padding.

imbracci'are [imbrat'tʃare] *vt* (*fucile*) to shoulder; (*scudo*) to grasp.

imbra'nato, a *ag* clumsy, awkward ♦ *sm/f* clumsy person.

imbratta'carte *sm/f* (*peg*) scribbler.

imbrat'tare *vt* to dirty, smear, daub; ~**rsi** *vr*: ~**rsi (di)** to dirty o.s. (with).

imbratta'tele *sm/f* (*peg*) dauber.

imbrigli'are [imbriʎ'ʎare] *vt* to bridle.

imbroc'care *vt* (*fig*) to guess correctly.

imbrogli'are [imbroʎ'ʎare] *vt* to mix up; (*fig*: *raggirare*) to deceive, cheat; (: *confondere*) to confuse, mix up; ~**rsi** *vr* to get tangled; (*fig*) to become confused.

im'broglio [im'broʎʎo] *sm* (*groviglio*) tangle; (*situazione confusa*) mess; (*truffa*) swindle, trick.

imbrogli'one, a [imbroʎ'ʎone] *sm/f* cheat, swindler.

imbronci'ato, a [imbron'tʃato] *ag* (*persona*) sulky; (*cielo*) cloudy, threatening.

imbru'nire *vi, vb impers* to grow dark; **all'**~ at dusk.

imbrut'tire *vt* to make ugly ♦ *vi* to become ugly.

imbu'care *vt* to post.

imbur'rare *vt* to butter.

imbuti'forme *ag* funnel-shaped.

im'buto *sm* funnel.

I.M.C.T.C. *sigla* (= *Ispettorato Generale della Motorizzazione Civile e dei Trasporti in*

Concessione) ≈ DVLA.

i'mene *sm* hymen.

imi'tare *vt* to imitate; (*riprodurre*) to copy; (*assomigliare*) to look like.

imita'tore, 'trice *sm/f* (*gen*) imitator; (*TEAT*) impersonator, impressionist.

imitazi'one [imitat'tsjone] *sf* imitation.

immaco'lato, a *ag* spotless; immaculate.

immagazzi'nare [immagaddzi'nare] *vt* to store.

immagi'nabile [immadʒi'nabile] *ag* imaginable.

immagi'nare [immadʒi'nare] *vt* to imagine; (*supporre*) to suppose; (*inventare*) to invent; **s'immagini!** don't mention it!, not at all!

immagi'nario, a [immadʒi'narjo] *ag* imaginary.

immagina'tiva [immadʒina'tiva] *sf* imagination.

immaginazi'one [immadʒinat'tsjone] *sf* imagination; (*cosa immaginata*) fancy.

im'magine [im'madʒine] *sf* image; (*rappresentazione grafica, mentale*) picture.

immagi'noso, a [immadʒi'noso] *ag* (*linguaggio, stile*) fantastic.

immalinco'nire *vt* to sadden, depress; ~**rsi** *vr* to become depressed, become melancholy.

imman'cabile *ag* unfailing.

immancabil'mente *av* without fail, unfailingly.

im'mane *ag* (*smisurato*) huge; (*spaventoso, inumano*) terrible.

imma'nente *ag* (*FILOSOFIA*) inherent, immanent.

immangi'abile [imman'dʒabile] *ag* inedible.

immatrico'lare *vt* to register; ~**rsi** *vr* (*INS*) to matriculate, enrol.

immatricolazi'one [immatrikolat'tsjone] *sf* registration; matriculation, enrolment.

immaturità *sf* immaturity.

imma'turo, a *ag* (*frutto*) unripe; (*persona*) immature; (*prematuro*) premature.

immedesi'marsi *vr*: ~ **in** to identify with.

immediata'mente *av* immediately, at once.

immedia'tezza [immedja'tettsa] *sf* immediacy.

immedi'ato, a *ag* immediate.

immemo'rabile *ag* immemorial; **da tempo** ~ from time immemorial.

im'memore *ag*: ~ **di** forgetful of.

immensità *sf* immensity.

im'menso, a *ag* immense.

im'mergere [im'merdʒere] *vt* to immerse, plunge; ~**rsi** *vr* to plunge; (*sommergibile*) to dive, submerge; (*dedicarsi a*): ~**rsi in** to

immerse o.s. in.
immeri'tato, a *ag* undeserved.
immeri'tevole *ag* undeserving, unworthy.
immersi'one *sf* immersion; (*di sommergibile*) submersion, dive; (*di palombaro*) dive; **linea di ~** (*NAUT*) water line.
im'merso, a *pp di* **immergere**.
im'messo, a *pp di* **immettere**.
im'mettere *vt*: **~ (in)** to introduce (into); **~ dati in un computer** to enter data on a computer.
immi'grante *ag, sm/f* immigrant.
immi'grare *vi* to immigrate.
immi'grato, a *sm/f* immigrant.
immigrazi'one [immigrat'tsjone] *sf* immigration.
immi'nente *ag* imminent.
immi'nenza [immi'nɛntsa] *sf* imminence.
immischi'are [immis'kjare] *vt*: **~ qn in** to involve sb in; **~rsi** *vr*: **~rsi in** to interfere o meddle in.
immiseri'mento *sm* impoverishment.
immise'rire *vt* to impoverish.
immis'sario *sm* (*GEO*) affluent, tributary.
immissi'one *sf* (*gen*) introduction; (*di aria, gas*) intake; **~ di dati** (*INFORM*) data entry.
im'mobile *ag* motionless, still; **(beni) ~i** *smpl* real estate *sg*.
immobili'are *ag* (*DIR*) property *cpd*; **patrimonio ~** real estate; **società ~** property company.
immobi'lismo *sm* inertia.
immobilità *sf* immobility.
immobiliz'zare [immobilid'dzare] *vt* to immobilize; (*ECON*) to lock up.
immobi'lizzo [immobi'liddzo] *sm*: **spese d'~** capital expenditure.
immo'destia *sf* immodesty.
immo'desto, a *ag* immodest.
immo'lare *vt* to sacrifice.
immondez'zaio [immondet'tsajo] *sm* rubbish dump.
immon'dizia [immon'dittsja] *sf* dirt, filth; (*spesso al pl: spazzatura, rifiuti*) rubbish *no pl*, refuse *no pl*.
immo'rale *ag* immoral.
immoralità *sf* immorality.
immorta'lare *vt* to immortalize.
immor'tale *ag* immortal.
immortalità *sf* immortality.
im'mune *ag* (*esente*) exempt; (*MED, DIR*) immune.
immunità *sf* immunity; **~ diplomatica** diplomatic immunity; **~ parlamentare** parliamentary privilege.
immuniz'zare [immunid'dzare] *vt* (*MED*) to immunize.

immunizzazi'one [immuniddzat'tsjone] *sf* immunization.
immunodefi'cienza [immunodefi'tʃɛntsa] *sf*: **~ acquisita** acquired immunodeficiency.
immuno'logico, a, ci, che [immuno'lɔdʒiko] *ag* immunological.
immu'tabile *ag* immutable; unchanging.
impac'care *vt* to pack.
impacchet'tare [impakket'tare] *vt* to pack up.
impacci'are [impat'tʃare] *vt* to hinder, hamper.
impacci'ato, a [impat'tʃato] *ag* awkward, clumsy; (*imbarazzato*) embarrassed.
im'paccio [im'pattʃo] *sm* obstacle; (*imbarazzo*) embarrassment; (*situazione imbarazzante*) awkward situation.
im'pacco, chi *sm* (*MED*) compress.
impadro'nirsi *vr*: **~ di** to seize, take possession of; (*fig: apprendere a fondo*) to master.
impa'gabile *ag* priceless.
impagi'nare [impadʒi'nare] *vt* (*TIP*) to paginate, page (up).
impaginazi'one [impadʒinat'tsjone] *sf* pagination.
impagli'are [impaʎ'ʎare] *vt* to stuff (with straw).
impa'lato, a *ag* (*fig*) stiff as a board.
impalca'tura *sf* scaffolding; (*anche fig*) framework.
impalli'dire *vi* to turn pale; (*fig*) to fade.
impalli'nare *vt* to riddle with shot.
impal'pabile *ag* impalpable.
impa'nare *vt* (*CUC*) to dip (o roll) in breadcrumbs, bread (*US*).
impan'tanarsi *vr* to sink (in the mud); (*fig*) to get bogged down.
impape'rarsi *vr* to stumble over a word.
impappi'narsi *vr* to stammer, falter.
impa'rare *vt* to learn; **così impari!** that'll teach you!
impara'ticcio [impara'tittʃo] *sm* half-baked notions *pl*.
impareggi'abile [impared'dʒabile] *ag* incomparable.
imparen'tarsi *vr*: **~ con** (*famiglia*) to marry into.
'impari *ag inv* (*disuguale*) unequal; (*dispari*) odd.
impar'tire *vt* to bestow, give.
imparzi'ale [impar'tsjale] *ag* impartial, unbiased.
imparzialità [impartsjali'ta] *sf* impartiality.
impas'sibile *ag* impassive.
impas'tare *vt* (*pasta*) to knead; (*colori*) to mix.

impastic'carsi *vr* to pop pills.
im'pasto *sm* (*l'impastare: di pane*) kneading;
(: *di cemento*) mixing; (*pasta*) dough;
(*anche fig*) mixture.
im'patto *sm* impact; ~ **ambientale** impact
on the environment.
impau'rire *vt* to scare, frighten ♦ *vi* (*anche:*
~**rsi**) to become scared *o* frightened.
im'pavido, a *ag* intrepid, fearless.
impazi'ente [impat'tsjɛnte] *ag* impatient.
impazi'enza [impat'tsjɛntsa] *sf* impatience.
impaz'zata [impat'tsata] *sf:* **all'**~
(*precipitosamente*) at breakneck speed;
(*colpire*) wildly.
impaz'zire [impat'tsire] *vi* to go mad; ~ **per
qn/qc** to be crazy about sb/sth.
impec'cabile *ag* impeccable.
impedi'mento *sm* obstacle, hindrance.
impe'dire *vt* (*vietare*): ~ **a qn di fare** to
prevent sb from doing; (*ostruire*) to
obstruct; (*impacciare*) to hamper, hinder.
impe'gnare [impeɲ'ɲare] *vt* (*dare in pegno*)
to pawn; (*onore etc*) to pledge; (*prenotare*)
to book, reserve; (*obbligare*) to oblige;
(*occupare*) to keep busy; (*MIL: nemico*) to
engage; ~**rsi** *vr* (*vincolarsi*): ~**rsi a fare** to
undertake to do; (*mettersi risolutamente*):
~**rsi in qc** to devote o.s. to sth; ~**rsi con qn**
(*accordarsi*) to come to an agreement with
sb.
impegna'tivo, a [impeɲɲa'tivo] *ag* binding;
(*lavoro*) demanding, exacting.
impe'gnato, a [impeɲ'ɲato] *ag* (*occupato*)
busy; (*fig: romanzo, autore*) committed,
engagé.
im'pegno [im'peɲɲo] *sm* (*obbligo*)
obligation; (*promessa*) promise, pledge;
(*zelo*) diligence, zeal; (*compito, d'autore*)
commitment; ~**i di lavoro** business
commitments.
impego'larsi *vr* (*fig*): ~ **in** to get heavily
involved in.
impela'garsi *vr* = **impegolarsi**.
impel'lente *ag* pressing, urgent.
impene'trabile *ag* impenetrable.
impen'narsi *vr* (*cavallo*) to rear up; (*AER*) to
go into a climb; (*fig*) to bridle.
impen'nata *sf* (*di cavallo*) rearing up; (*di
aereo*) climb, nose-up; (*fig: scatto d'ira*)
burst of anger; (: *di prezzi etc*) sudden
increase.
impen'sabile *ag* (*inaccettabile*)
unthinkable; (*difficile da concepire*)
inconceivable.
impen'sato, a *ag* unforeseen, unexpected.
impensie'rire *vt*, ~**rsi** *vr* to worry.
impe'rante *ag* prevailing.
impe'rare *vi* (*anche fig*) to reign, rule.

impera'tivo, a *ag, sm* imperative.
impera'tore, 'trice *sm/f* emperor/empress.
impercet'tibile [impertʃet'tibile] *ag*
imperceptible.
imperdo'nabile *ag* unforgivable,
unpardonable.
imper'fetto, a *ag* imperfect ♦ *sm* (*LING*)
imperfect (tense).
imperfezi'one [imperfet'tsjone] *sf*
imperfection.
imperi'ale *ag* imperial.
imperia'lismo *sm* imperialism.
imperia'lista, i, e *ag* imperialist.
imperi'oso, a *ag* (*persona*) imperious;
(*motivo, esigenza*) urgent, pressing.
imperi'turo, a *ag* everlasting.
impe'rizia [impe'rittsja] *sf* lack of
experience.
imperma'lirsi *vr* to take offence.
imperme'abile *ag* waterproof ♦ *sm*
raincoat.
imperni'are *vt:* ~ **qc su** to hinge sth on;
(*fig: discorso, relazione etc*) to base sth on;
~**rsi** *vr* (*fig*): ~**rsi su** to be based on.
im'pero *sm* empire; (*forza, autorità*) rule,
control.
imperscru'tabile *ag* inscrutable.
imperso'nale *ag* impersonal.
imperso'nare *vt* to personify; (*TEAT*) to
play, act (the part of); ~**rsi** *vr:* ~**rsi in un
ruolo** to get into a part, live a part.
imper'territo, a *ag* unperturbed.
imperti'nente *ag* impertinent.
imperti'nenza [imperti'nɛntsa] *sf*
impertinence.
impertur'babile *ag* imperturbable.
imperver'sare *vi* to rage.
im'pervio, a *ag* (*luogo*) inaccessible;
(*strada*) impassable.
'impeto *sm* (*moto, forza*) force, impetus;
(*assalto*) onslaught; (*fig: impulso*) impulse;
(: *slancio*) transport; **con** ~ (*parlare*)
forcefully, energetically.
impet'tito, a *ag* stiff, erect; **camminare** ~
to strut.
impetu'oso, a *ag* (*vento*) strong, raging;
(*persona*) impetuous.
impian'tare *vt* (*motore*) to install; (*azienda,
discussione*) to establish, start.
impian'tistica *sf* plant design and
installation.
impi'anto *sm* (*installazione*) installation;
(*apparecchiature*) plant; (*sistema*) system;
~ **elettrico** wiring; ~ **sportivo** sports
complex; ~**i di risalita** (*SCI*) ski lifts.
impias'trare, impiastricci'are
[impjastrit't ʃare] *vt* to smear, dirty.
impi'astro *sm* poultice; (*fig fam: persona*)

nuisance.

impiccagi'one [impikka'dʒone] *sf* hanging.

impic'care *vt* to hang; ~**rsi** *vr* to hang o.s.

impicci'are [impit't∫are] *vt* to hinder, hamper; ~**rsi** *vr* to meddle, interfere; **impicciati degli affari tuoi!** mind your own business!

im'piccio [im'pitt∫o] *sm* (*ostacolo*) hindrance; (*seccatura*) trouble, bother; (*affare imbrogliato*) mess; **essere d'**~ to be in the way; **cavare** *o* **togliere qn dagli** ~**i** to get sb out of trouble.

impicci'one, a [impit't∫one] *sm/f* busybody.

impie'gare *vt* (*usare*) to use, employ; (*assumere*) to employ, take on; (*spendere*: *denaro, tempo*) to spend; (*investire*) to invest; ~**rsi** *vr* to get a job, obtain employment; **impiego un quarto d'ora per andare a casa** it takes me *o* I take a quarter of an hour to get home.

impiega'tizio, a [impjega'tittsjo] *ag* clerical, white-collar *cpd*; **lavoro/ceto** ~ clerical *o* white-collar work/workers *pl*.

impie'gato, a *sm/f* employee; ~ **statale** state employee.

impi'ego, ghi *sm* (*uso*) use; (*occupazione*) employment; (*posto di lavoro*) (regular) job, post; (*ECON*) investment; ~ **pubblico** job in the public sector.

impieto'sire *vt* to move to pity; ~**rsi** *vr* to be moved to pity.

impie'toso, a *ag* pitiless, cruel.

impie'trire *vt* (*anche fig*) to petrify.

impigli'are [impiʎ'ʎare] *vt* to catch, entangle; ~**rsi** *vr* to get caught up *o* entangled.

impi'grire *vt* to make lazy ♦ *vi* (*anche*: ~**rsi**) to grow lazy.

impingu'are *vt* (*maiale etc*) to fatten; (*fig*: *tasche, casse dello Stato*) to stuff with money.

impiom'bare *vt* (*pacco*) to seal (with lead); (*dente*) to fill.

impla'cabile *ag* implacable.

implemen'tare *vt* to implement.

impli'care *vt* to imply; (*coinvolgere*) to involve; ~**rsi** *vr*: ~**rsi (in)** to become involved (in).

implicazi'one [implikat'tsjone] *sf* implication.

im'plicito, a [im'plit∫ito] *ag* implicit.

implo'rare *vt* to implore.

implorazi'one [implorat'tsjone] *sf* plea, entreaty.

impolli'nare *vt* to pollinate.

impollinazi'one [impollinat'tsjone] *sf* pollination.

impolve'rare *vt* to cover with dust; ~**rsi** *vr*

to get dusty.

impoma'tare *vt* (*pelle*) to put ointment on; (*capelli*) to pomade; (*baffi*) to wax; ~**rsi** *vr* (*fam*) to get spruced up.

imponde'rabile *ag* imponderable.

im'pone *etc vb vedi* **imporre**.

impo'nente *ag* imposing, impressive.

im'pongo *etc vb vedi* **imporre**.

impo'nibile *ag* taxable ♦ *sm* taxable income.

impopo'lare *ag* unpopular.

impopolarità *sf* unpopularity.

im'porre *vt* to impose; (*costringere*) to force, make; (*far valere*) to impose, enforce; **imporsi** *vr* (*persona*) to assert o.s.; (*cosa*: *rendersi necessario*) to become necessary; (*aver successo*: *moda, attore*) to become popular; ~ **a qn di fare** to force sb to do, make sb do.

impor'tante *ag* important.

impor'tanza [impor'tantsa] *sf* importance; **dare** ~ **a qc** to attach importance to sth; **darsi** ~ to give o.s. airs.

impor'tare *vt* (*introdurre dall'estero*) to import ♦ *vi* to matter, be important ♦ *vb impers* (*essere necessario*) to be necessary; (*interessare*) to matter; **non importa!** it doesn't matter!; **non me ne importa!** I don't care!

importa'tore, 'trice *ag* importing ♦ *sm/f* importer.

importazi'one [importat'tsjone] *sf* importation; (*merci importate*) imports *pl*.

im'porto *sm* (total) amount.

importu'nare *vt* to bother.

impor'tuno, a *ag* irksome, annoying.

im'posi *etc vb vedi* **imporre**.

imposizi'one [impozit'tsjone] *sf* imposition; (*ordine*) order, command; (*onere, imposta*) tax.

imposses'sarsi *vr*: ~ **di** to seize, take possession of.

impos'sibile *ag* impossible; **fare l'**~ to do one's utmost, do all one can.

impossibilità *sf* impossibility; **essere nell'**~ **di fare qc** to be unable to do sth.

impossibili'tato, a *ag*: **essere** ~ **a fare qc** to be unable to do sth.

im'posta *sf* (*di finestra*) shutter; (*tassa*) tax; ~ **indiretta sui consumi** excise duty *o* tax; ~ **locale sui redditi (ILOR)** tax on unearned income; ~ **patrimoniale** property tax; ~ **sul reddito** income tax; ~ **sul reddito delle persone fisiche (IRPEF)** personal income tax; ~ **di successione** capital transfer tax (*BRIT*), inheritance tax (*US*); ~ **sugli utili** tax on profits; ~ **sul valore aggiunto (I.V.A.)** value added tax

(VAT) (*BRIT*), sales tax (*US*).

impos'tare *vt* (*imbucare*) to post; (*servizio, organizzazione*) to set up; (*lavoro*) to organize, plan; (*resoconto, rapporto*) to plan; (*problema*) to set out, formulate; (*TIP: pagina*) to lay out; ~ **la voce** (*MUS*) to pitch one's voice.

impostazi'one [impostat'tsjone] *sf* (*di lettera*) posting (*BRIT*), mailing (*US*); (*di problema, questione*) formulation, statement; (*di lavoro*) organization, planning; (*di attività*) setting up; (*MUS: di voce*) pitch.

im'posto, a *pp di* **imporre**.

impos'tore, a *sm/f* impostor.

impo'tente *ag* weak, powerless; (*anche MED*) impotent.

impo'tenza [impo'tɛntsa] *sf* weakness, powerlessness; impotence.

impove'rire *vt* to impoverish ♦ *vi* (*anche*: ~**rsi**) to become poor.

imprati'cabile *ag* (*strada*) impassable; (*campo da gioco*) unplayable.

imprati'chire [imprati'kire] *vt* to train; ~**rsi** *vr*: ~**rsi in qc** to practise (*BRIT*) *o* practice (*US*) sth.

impre'care *vi* to curse, swear; ~ **contro** to hurl abuse at.

imprecazi'one [imprekat'tsjone] *sf* abuse, curse.

impreci'sato, a [impret'ʃi'zato] *ag* (*non preciso: quantità, numero*) indeterminate.

imprecisi'one [impret'ʃi'zjone] *sf* imprecision; inaccuracy.

impre'ciso, a [impre't'ʃizo] *ag* imprecise, vague; (*calcolo*) inaccurate.

impre'gnare [impreɲ'ɲare] *vt*: ~ **(di)** (*imbevere*) to soak *o* impregnate (with); (*riempire: anche fig*) to fill (with).

imprendi'tore *sm* (*industriale*) entrepreneur; (*appaltatore*) contractor; **piccolo** ~ small businessman.

imprendito'ria *sf* enterprise; (*imprenditori*) entrepreneurs *pl*.

imprenditori'ale *ag* (*ceto, classe*) entrepreneurial.

imprepa'rato, a *ag*: ~ **(a)** (*gen*) unprepared (for); (*lavoratore*) untrained (for); **cogliere qn** ~ to catch sb unawares.

impreparazi'one [impreparat'tsjone] *sf* lack of preparation.

im'presa *sf* (*iniziativa*) enterprise; (*azione*) exploit; (*azienda*) firm, concern; ~ **familiare** family firm; ~ **pubblica** state-owned enterprise.

impre'sario *sm* (*TEAT*) manager, impresario; ~ **di pompe funebri** funeral director.

imprescin'dibile [impreʃʃin'dibile] *ag* not to be ignored.

im'pressi *etc vb vedi* **imprimere**.

impressio'nante *ag* impressive; upsetting.

impressio'nare *vt* to impress; (*turbare*) to upset; (*FOT*) to expose; ~**rsi** *vr* to be easily upset.

impressi'one *sf* impression; (*fig: sensazione*) sensation, feeling; (*stampa*) printing; **fare** ~ (*colpire*) to impress; (*turbare*) to frighten, upset; **fare buona/cattiva** ~ **a** to make a good/bad impression on.

im'presso, a *pp di* **imprimere**.

impres'tare *vt*: ~ **qc a qn** to lend sth to sb.

impreve'dibile *ag* unforeseeable; (*persona*) unpredictable.

imprevi'dente *ag* lacking in foresight.

imprevi'denza [imprevi'dɛntsa] *sf* lack of foresight.

impre'visto, a *ag* unexpected, unforeseen ♦ *sm* unforeseen event; **salvo** ~**i** unless anything unexpected happens.

imprezio'sire [imprettsjo'sire] *vt*: ~ **di** to embellish with.

imprigiona'mento [impridʒona'mento] *sm* imprisonment.

imprigio'nare [impridʒo'nare] *vt* to imprison.

im'primere *vt* (*anche fig*) to impress, stamp; (*comunicare: movimento*) to transmit, give.

impro'babile *ag* improbable, unlikely.

'improbo, a *ag* (*fatica, lavoro*) hard, laborious.

improdut'tivo, a *ag* (*investimento*) unprofitable; (*terreno*) unfruitful; (*fig: sforzo*) fruitless.

im'pronta *sf* imprint, impression, sign; (*di piede, mano*) print; (*fig*) mark, stamp; ~ **digitale** fingerprint; **rilevamento delle** ~**e genetiche** genetic fingerprinting.

impro'perio *sm* insult.

impropo'nibile *ag* which cannot be proposed *o* suggested.

im'proprio, a *ag* improper; **arma** ~**a** offensive weapon.

improro'gabile *ag* (*termine*) that cannot be extended.

improvvisa'mente *av* suddenly; unexpectedly.

improvvi'sare *vt* to improvise; ~**rsi** *vr*: ~**rsi cuoco** to (decide to) act as cook.

improvvi'sata *sf* (pleasant) surprise.

improvvisazi'one [improvvizat'tsjone] *sf* improvisation; **spirito d'** ~ spirit of invention.

improv'viso, a *ag* (*imprevisto*) unexpected; (*subitaneo*) sudden; **all'**~ unexpectedly; suddenly.

impru'dente *ag* foolish, imprudent; (*osservazione*) unwise.

impru'denza [impru'dɛntsa] *sf* foolishness, imprudence; **è stata un'**~ that was a foolish *o* an imprudent thing to do.

impu'dente *ag* impudent.

impu'denza [impu'dɛntsa] *sf* impudence.

impudi'cizia [impudi'tʃittsja] *sf* immodesty.

impu'dico, a, chi, che *ag* immodest.

impu'gnare [impuɲ'ɲare] *vt* to grasp, grip; (*DIR*) to contest.

impugna'tura [impuɲɲa'tura] *sf* grip, grasp; (*manico*) handle; (: *di spada*) hilt.

impulsività *sf* impulsiveness.

impul'sivo, a *ag* impulsive.

im'pulso *sm* impulse; **dare un** ~ **alle vendite** to boost sales.

impune'mente *av* with impunity.

impunità *sf* impunity.

impun'tarsi *vr* to stop dead, refuse to budge; (*fig*) to be obstinate.

impun'tura *sf* stitching.

impurità *sf inv* impurity.

im'puro, a *ag* impure.

impu'tare *vt* (*ascrivere*): ~ **qc a** to attribute sth to; (*DIR: accusare*): ~ **qn di** to charge sb with, accuse sb of.

impu'tato, a *sm/f* (*DIR*) accused, defendant.

imputazi'one [imputat'tsjone] *sf* (*DIR*) charge; (*di spese*) allocation.

imputri'dire *vi* to rot.

=============== *PAROLA CHIAVE*

in (*in* + *il* = **nel**, *in* + *lo* = **nello**, *in* + *l'* = **nell'**, *in* + *la* = **nella**, *in* + *i* = **nei**, *in* + *gli* = **negli**, *in* + *le* = **nelle**) *prep* **1** (*stato in luogo*) in; **vivere** ~ **Italia/città** to live in Italy/ town; **essere** ~ **casa/ufficio** to be at home/the office; **è nel cassetto/**~ **salotto** it's in the drawer/in the sitting room; **se fossi** ~ **te** if I were you

2 (*moto a luogo*) to; (: *dentro*) into; **andare** ~ **Germania/città** to go to Germany/town; **andare** ~ **ufficio** to go to the office; **entrare** ~ **macchina/casa** to get into the car/go into the house

3 (*tempo*) in; **nel 1989** in 1989; ~ **giugno/ estate** in June/summer; **l'ha fatto** ~ **sei mesi** he did it in six months; ~ **gioventù, io ... quando** ~ I was young, I ...

4 (*modo, maniera*) in; ~ **silenzio** in silence; **parlare** ~ **tedesco** to speak (in) German; ~ **abito da sera** in evening

dress; ~ **guerra** at war; ~ **vacanza** on holiday; **Maria Bianchi** ~ **Rossi** Maria Rossi née Bianchi

5 (*mezzo*) by; **viaggiare** ~ **autobus/treno** to travel by bus/train

6 (*materia*) made of; ~ **marmo** made of marble, marble *cpd*; **una collana** ~ **oro** a gold necklace

7 (*misura*) in; **siamo** ~ **quattro** there are four of us; ~ **tutto** in all

8 (*fine*): **dare** ~ **dono** to give as a gift; **spende tutto** ~ **alcool** he spends all his money on drink; ~ **onore di** in honour of.

i'nabile *ag*: ~ **a** incapable of; (*fisicamente, MIL*) unfit for.

inabilità *sf*: ~ **(a)** unfitness (for).

inabis'sare *vt* (*nave*) to sink; ~**rsi** *vr* to go down.

inabi'tabile *ag* uninhabitable.

inabi'tato, a *ag* uninhabited.

inacces'sibile [inattʃes'sibile] *ag* (*luogo*) inaccessible; (*persona*) unapproachable; (*mistero*) unfathomable.

inaccet'tabile [inattʃet'tabile] *ag* unacceptable.

inacer'bire [inatʃer'bire] *vt* to exacerbate; ~**rsi** *vr* (*persona*) to become embittered.

inaci'dire [inatʃi'dire] *vt* (*persona, carattere*) to embitter; ~**rsi** *vr* (*latte*) to go sour; (*fig: persona, carattere*) to become sour, become embittered.

ina'datto, a *ag*: ~ **(a)** unsuitable *o* unfit (for).

inadegu'ato, a *ag* inadequate.

inadempi'ente *ag* defaulting ♦ *sm/f* defaulter.

inadempi'enza [inadem'pjentsa] *sf*: ~ **a un contratto** non-fulfilment of a contract; **dovuto alle** ~**e dei funzionari** due to negligence on the part of the officials.

inadempi'mento *sm* non-fulfilment.

inaffer'rabile *ag* elusive; (*concetto, senso*) difficult to grasp.

'INAIL *sigla m* (= *Istituto Nazionale per l'Assicurazione contro gli Infortuni sul Lavoro*) *state body providing sickness benefit in the event of accidents at work.*

ina'lare *vt* to inhale.

ina'latore *sm* inhaler.

inalazi'one [inalat'tsjone] *sf* inhalation.

inalbe'rare *vt* (*NAUT*) to hoist, raise; ~**rsi** *vr* (*fig*) to flare up, fly off the handle.

inalte'rabile *ag* unchangeable; (*colore*) fast, permanent; (*affetto*) constant.

inalte'rato, a *ag* unchanged.

inami'dare *vt* to starch.

inami'dato, a *ag* starched.

inammis'sibile *ag* inadmissible.

inani'mato, a *ag* inanimate; (*senza vita: corpo*) lifeless.

inappa'gabile *ag* insatiable.

inappel'labile *ag* (*decisione*) final, irrevocable; (*DIR*) final, not open to appeal.

inappe'tenza [inappe'tɛntsa] *sf* (*MED*) lack of appetite.

inappun'tabile *ag* irreproachable, flawless.

inar'care *vt* (*schiena*) to arch; (*sopracciglia*) to raise; **~rsi** *vr* to arch.

inaridi'mento *sm* (*anche fig*) drying up.

inari'dire *vt* to make arid, dry up ♦ *vi* (*anche:* **~rsi**) to dry up, become arid.

inarres'tabile *ag* (*processo*) irreversible; (*emorragia*) that cannot be stemmed; (*corsa del tempo*) relentless.

inascol'tato, a *ag* unheeded, unheard.

inaspettata'mente *av* unexpectedly.

inaspet'tato, a *ag* unexpected.

inas'prire *vt* (*disciplina*) to tighten up, make harsher; (*carattere*) to embitter; (*rapporti*) to make worse; **~rsi** *vr* to become harsher; to become bitter; to become worse.

inattac'cabile *ag* (*anche fig*) unassailable; (*alibi*) cast-iron.

inatten'dibile *ag* unreliable.

inat'teso, a *ag* unexpected.

inat'tivo, a *ag* inactive, idle; (*CHIM*) inactive.

inattu'abile *ag* impracticable.

inau'dito, a *ag* unheard of.

inaugu'rale *ag* inaugural.

inaugu'rare *vt* to inaugurate, open; (*monumento*) to unveil.

inaugurazi'one [inaugurat'tsjone] *sf* inauguration; unveiling.

inavve'duto, a *ag* careless, inadvertent.

inavver'tenza [inavver'tɛntsa] *sf* carelessness, inadvertence.

inavvertita'mente *av* inadvertently, unintentionally.

inavvici'nabile [inavvitʃi'nabile] *ag* unapproachable.

'Inca *ag inv, smf inv* Inca.

incagli'are [inkaʎ'ʎare] *vi* (*NAUT: anche:* **~rsi**) to run aground.

incalco'labile *ag* incalculable.

incal'lito, a *ag* calloused; (*fig*) hardened, inveterate; (: *insensibile*) hard.

incal'zante [inkal'tsante] *ag* urgent, insistent; (*crisi*) imminent.

incal'zare [inkal'tsare] *vt* to follow *o* pursue closely; (*fig*) to press ♦ *vi* (*urgere*) to be pressing; (*essere imminente*) to be imminent.

incame'rare *vt* (*DIR*) to expropriate.

incammi'nare *vt* (*fig: avviare*) to start up; **~rsi** *vr* to set off.

incana'lare *vt* (*anche fig*) to channel; **~rsi** *vr* (*folla*): **~rsi verso** to converge on.

incancre'nire *vi*, **incancre'nirsi** *vi* to become gangrenous.

incande'scente [inkandeʃ'ʃɛnte] *ag* incandescent, white-hot.

incan'tare *vt* to enchant, bewitch; **~rsi** *vr* (*rimanere intontito*) to be spellbound; to be in a daze; (*meccanismo: bloccarsi*) to jam.

incanta'tore, 'trice *ag* enchanting, bewitching ♦ *smf* enchanter/enchantress.

incan'tesimo *sm* spell, charm.

incan'tevole *ag* charming, enchanting.

in'canto *sm* spell, charm, enchantment; (*asta*) auction; **come per ~** as if by magic; **ti sta d'~!** (*vestito etc*) it really suits you!; **mettere all'~** to put up for auction.

incanu'tire *vi* to go white.

inca'pace [inka'patʃe] *ag* incapable.

incapacità [inkapatʃi'ta] *sf* inability; (*DIR*) incapacity; **~ d'intendere e di volere** diminished responsibility.

incapo'nirsi *vr* to be stubborn, be determined.

incap'pare *vi*: **~ in qc/qn** (*anche fig*) to run into sth/sb.

incappucci'are [inkapput'tʃare] *vt* to put a hood on; **~rsi** *vr* (*persona*) to put on a hood.

incapricci'arsi [inkaprit'tʃarsi] *vr*: **~ di** to take a fancy *o* for.

incapsu'lare *vt* (*dente*) to crown.

incarce'rare [inkartʃe'rare] *vt* to imprison.

incari'care *vt*: **~ qn di fare** to give sb the responsibility of doing; **~rsi** *vr*: **~rsi di** to take care *o* charge of.

incari'cato, a *ag*: **~ (di)** in charge (of), responsible (for) ♦ *smf* delegate, representative; **docente ~** (*di università*) lecturer without tenure; **~ d'affari** (*POL*) chargé d'affaires.

in'carico, chi *sm* task, job; (*INS*) temporary post.

incar'nare *vt* to embody; **~rsi** *vr* to be embodied; (*REL*) to become incarnate.

incarnazi'one [inkarnat'tsjone] *sf* incarnation; (*fig*) embodiment.

incarta'mento *sm* dossier, file.

incartapeco'rito, a *ag* (*pelle*) wizened, shrivelled (*BRIT*), shriveled (*US*).

incar'tare *vt* to wrap (in paper).

incasel'lare *vt* (*posta*) to sort; (*fig: nozioni*) to pigeonhole.

incas'sare *vt* (*merce*) to pack (in cases); (*gemma: incastonare*) to set; (*ECON:*

riscuotere) to collect; (*PUGILATO: colpi*) to take, stand up to.

in'casso *sm* cashing, encashment; (*introito*) takings *pl*.

incasto'nare *vt* to set.

incastona'tura *sf* setting.

incas'trare *vt* to fit in, insert; (*fig: intrappolare*) to catch; ~**rsi** *vr* (*combaciare*) to fit together; (*restare bloccato*) to become stuck.

in'castro *sm* slot, groove; (*punto di unione*) joint; **gioco a** ~ interlocking puzzle.

incate'nare *vt* to chain up.

incatra'mare *vt* to tar.

incatti'vire *vt* to make wicked; ~**rsi** *vr* to turn nasty.

in'cauto, a *ag* imprudent, rash.

inca'vare *vt* to hollow out.

inca'vato, a *ag* hollow; (*occhi*) sunken.

in'cavo *sm* hollow; (*solco*) groove.

incavo'larsi *vr* (*fam*) to lose one's temper, get annoyed.

incaz'zarsi [inkat'tsarsi] *vr* (*fam!*) to get steamed up.

in'cedere [in't∫edere] *vi* (*poetico*) to advance solemnly ♦ *sm* solemn gait.

incendi'are [int∫en'djare] *vt* to set fire to; ~**rsi** *vr* to catch fire, burst into flames.

incendi'ario, a [int∫en'djarjo] *ag* incendiary ♦ *sm/f* arsonist.

in'cendio [in't∫endjo] *sm* fire.

incene'rire [int∫ene'rire] *vt* to burn to ashes, incinerate; (*cadavere*) to cremate; ~**rsi** *vr* to be burnt to ashes.

inceneri'tore [int∫eneri'tore] *sm* incinerator.

in'censo [in't∫enso] *sm* incense.

incensu'rato, a [int∫ensu'rato] *ag* (*DIR*): **essere** ~ to have a clean record.

incenti'vare [int∫enti'vare] *vt* (*produzione, vendite*) to boost; (*persona*) to motivate.

incen'tivo [int∫en'tivo] *sm* incentive.

incen'trarsi [int∫en'trarsi] *vr*: ~ **su** (*fig*) to centre (*BRIT*) *o* center (*US*) on.

incep'pare [int∫ep'pare] *vt* to obstruct, hamper; ~**rsi** *vr* to jam.

ince'rata [int∫e'rata] *sf* (*tela*) tarpaulin; (*impermeabile*) oilskins *pl*.

incer'tezza [int∫er'tettsa] *sf* uncertainty.

in'certo, a [in't∫erto] *ag* uncertain; (*irresoluto*) undecided, hesitating ♦ *sm* uncertainty; **gli** ~**i del mestiere** the risks of the job.

incespi'care [int∫espi'kare] *vi*: ~ (**in qc**) to trip (over sth).

inces'sante [int∫es'sante] *ag* incessant.

in'cesto [in't∫esto] *sm* incest.

incestu'oso, a [int∫estu'oso] *ag* incestuous.

in'cetta [in't∫etta] *sf* buying up; **fare** ~ **di qc** to buy up sth.

inchi'esta [in'kjɛsta] *sf* investigation, inquiry.

inchi'nare [inki'nare] *vt* to bow; ~**rsi** *vr* to bend down; (*per riverenza*) to bow; (*: donna*) to curtsy.

in'chino [in'kino] *sm* bow; curtsy.

inchio'dare [inkjo'dare] *vt* to nail (down); ~ **la macchina** (*AUT*) to jam on the brakes.

inchi'ostro [in'kjɔstro] *sm* ink; ~ **simpatico** invisible ink.

inciam'pare [int∫am'pare] *vi* to trip, stumble.

inci'ampo [in't∫ampo] *sm* obstacle; **essere d'**~ **a qn** (*fig*) to be in sb's way.

inciden'tale [int∫iden'tale] *ag* incidental.

incidental'mente [int∫idental'mente] *av* (*per caso*) by chance; (*per inciso*) incidentally, by the way.

inci'dente [int∫i'dente] *sm* accident; (*episodio*) incident; **e con questo l'**~ **è chiuso** and that is the end of the matter; ~ **d'auto** car accident; ~ **diplomatico** diplomatic incident.

inci'denza [int∫i'dentsa] *sf* incidence; **avere una forte** ~ **su qc** to affect sth greatly.

in'cidere [in't∫idere] *vi*: ~ **su** to bear upon, affect ♦ *vt* (*tagliare incavando*) to cut into; (*ARTE*) to engrave; to etch; (*canzone*) to record.

in'cinta [in't∫inta] *ag f* pregnant.

incipi'ente [int∫i'pjɛnte] *ag* incipient.

incipri'are [int∫i'prjare] *vt* to powder.

in'circa [in't∫irka] *av*: **all'**~ more or less, very nearly.

in'cisi *etc* [in't∫izi] *vb vedi* **incidere**.

incisi'one [int∫i'zjone] *sf* cut; (*disegno*) engraving; etching; (*registrazione*) recording; (*MED*) incision.

inci'sivo, a [int∫i'zivo] *ag* incisive; (*ANAT*): (**dente**) ~ incisor.

in'ciso, a [in't∫izo] *pp di* **incidere** ♦ *sm*: **per** ~ incidentally, by the way.

inci'sore [int∫i'zore] *sm* (*ARTE*) engraver.

incita'mento [int∫ita'mento] *sm* incitement.

inci'tare [int∫i'tare] *vt* to incite.

inci'vile [int∫i'vile] *ag* uncivilized; (*villano*) impolite.

incivi'lire [int∫ivi'lire] *vt* to civilize.

inciviltà [int∫ivil'ta] *sf* (*di popolazione*) barbarism; (*fig: di trattamento*) barbarity; (*: maleducazione*) incivility, rudeness.

incl. *abbr* (= *incluso*) encl.

incle'mente *ag* (*giudice, sentenza*) severe, harsh; (*fig: clima*) harsh; (*: tempo*) inclement.

incle'menza [inkle'mentsa] *sf* severity;

harshness; inclemency.
incli'nabile *ag* (*schienale*) reclinable.
incli'nare *vt* to tilt ♦ *vi* (*fig*): ~ **a qc/a fare** to incline towards sth/doing; to tend towards sth/to do; ~**rsi** *vr* (*barca*) to list; (*aereo*) to bank.
incli'nato, a *ag* sloping.
inclinazi'one [inklinat'tsjone] *sf* slope; (*fig*) inclination, tendency.
in'cline *ag*: ~ **a** inclined to.
in'cludere *vt* to include; (*accludere*) to enclose.
inclusi'one *sf* inclusion.
inclu'sivo, a *ag*: ~ **di** inclusive of.
in'cluso, a *pp di* **includere** ♦ *ag* included; enclosed.
incoe'rente *ag* incoherent; (*contraddittorio*) inconsistent.
incoe'renza [inkoe'rɛntsa] *sf* incoherence; inconsistency.
in'cognito, a [in'kɔɲɲito] *ag* unknown ♦ *sm*: **in** ~ incognito ♦ *sf* (*MAT, fig*) unknown quantity.
incol'lare *vt* to glue, gum; (*unire con colla*) to stick together; ~ **gli occhi addosso a qn** (*fig*) to fix one's eyes on sb.
incolla'tura *sf* (*IPPICA*): **vincere/perdere di un'**~ to win/lose by a head.
incolon'nare *vt* to draw up in columns.
inco'lore *ag* colourless (*BRIT*), colorless (*US*).
incol'pare *vt*: ~ **qn di** to charge sb with.
in'colto, a *ag* (*terreno*) uncultivated; (*trascurato: capelli*) neglected; (*persona*) uneducated.
in'columе *ag* safe and sound, unhurt.
incolumità *sf* safety.
incom'bente *ag* (*pericolo*) imminent, impending.
incom'benza [inkom'bɛntsa] *sf* duty, task.
in'combere *vi* (*sovrastare minacciando*): ~ **su** to threaten, hang over.
incominci'are [inkomin'tʃare] *vi*, *vt* to begin, start.
incomo'dare *vt* to trouble, inconvenience; ~**rsi** *vr* to put o.s. out.
in'comodo, a *ag* uncomfortable; (*inopportuno*) inconvenient ♦ *sm* inconvenience, bother.
incompa'rabile *ag* incomparable.
incompa'tibile *ag* incompatible.
incompatibilità *sf* incompatibility; ~ **di carattere** (mutual) incompatibility.
incompe'tente *ag* incompetent.
incompe'tenza [inkompe'tɛntsa] *sf* incompetence.
incompi'uto, a *ag* unfinished, incomplete.
incom'pleto, a *ag* incomplete.

incompren'sibile *ag* incomprehensible.
incomprensi'one *sf* incomprehension.
incom'preso, a *ag* not understood; misunderstood.
inconce'pibile [inkontʃe'pibile] *ag* inconceivable.
inconcili'abile [inkontʃi'ljabile] *ag* irreconcilable.
inconclu'dente *ag* inconclusive; (*persona*) ineffectual.
incondizio'nato, a [inkondittsjo'nato] *ag* unconditional.
inconfes'sabile *ag* (*pensiero, peccato*) unmentionable.
inconfon'dibile *ag* unmistakable.
inconfu'tabile *ag* irrefutable.
incongru'ente *ag* inconsistent.
incongru'enza [inkongru'entsa] *sf* inconsistency.
in'congruo, a *ag* incongruous.
inconsa'pevole *ag*: ~ **di** unaware of, ignorant of.
inconsapevo'lezza [inkonsapevo'lettsa] *sf* ignorance, lack of awareness.
in'conscio, a, sci, sce [in'kɔnʃo] *ag* unconscious ♦ *sm* (*PSIC*): **l'**~ the unconscious.
inconsis'tente *ag* (*patrimonio*) insubstantial; (*dubbio*) unfounded; (*ragionamento, prove*) tenuous, flimsy.
inconsis'tenza [inkonsis'tentsa] *sf* insubstantial nature; lack of foundation; flimsiness.
inconso'labile *ag* inconsolable.
inconsu'eto, a *ag* unusual.
incon'sulto, a *ag* rash.
inconte'nibile *ag* (*rabbia*) uncontrollable; (*entusiasmo*) irrepressible.
inconten'tabile *ag* (*desiderio, avidità*) insatiable; (*persona: capriccioso*) hard to please, very demanding.
incontes'tabile *ag* incontrovertible, indisputable.
incontes'tato, a *ag* undisputed.
inconti'nenza [inkonti'nentsa] *sf* incontinence.
incon'trare *vt* to meet; (*difficoltà*) to meet with; ~**rsi** *vr* to meet.
incon'trario *av*: **all'**~ (*sottosopra*) upside down; (*alla rovescia*) back to front; (*all'indietro*) backwards; (*nel senso contrario*) the other way round.
incontras'tabile *ag* incontrovertible, indisputable.
incontras'tato, a *ag* (*successo, vittoria, verità*) uncontested, undisputed.
in'contro *av*: ~ **a** (*verso*) towards ♦ *sm* meeting; (*SPORT*) match; meeting;

(*fortuito*) encounter; **venire ~ a** (*richieste, esigenze*) to comply with; **~ di calcio** football match (*BRIT*), soccer game (*US*).

incontrol'labile *ag* uncontrollable.

inconveni'ente *sm* drawback, snag.

incoraggia'mento [inkoraddʒa'mento] *sm* encouragement; **premio d'~** consolation prize.

incoraggi'are [inkorad'dʒare] *vt* to encourage.

incor'nare *vt* to gore.

incornici'are [inkorni'tʃare] *vt* to frame.

incoro'nare *vt* to crown.

incoronazi'one [inkoronat'tsjone] *sf* coronation.

incorpo'rare *vt* to incorporate; (*fig: annettere*) to annex.

incorreg'gibile [inkorred'dʒibile] *ag* incorrigible.

in'correre *vi*: **~ in** to meet with, run into.

incorrut'tibile *ag* incorruptible.

in'corso, a *pp di* **incorrere**.

incosci'ente [inkoʃ'ʃɛnte] *ag* (*inconscio*) unconscious; (*irresponsabile*) reckless, thoughtless.

incosci'enza [inkoʃ'ʃɛntsa] *sf* unconsciousness; recklessness, thoughtlessness.

incos'tante *ag* (*studente, impiegato*) inconsistent; (*carattere*) fickle, inconstant; (*rendimento*) sporadic.

incos'tanza [inkos'tantsa] *sf* inconstancy, fickleness.

incostituzio'nale [inkostituttsjo'nale] *ag* unconstitutional.

incre'dibile *ag* incredible, unbelievable.

incredulità *sf* incredulity.

in'credulo, a *ag* incredulous, disbelieving.

incremen'tare *vt* to increase; (*dar sviluppo a*) to promote.

incre'mento *sm* (*sviluppo*) development; (*aumento numerico*) increase, growth.

incresci'oso, a [inkreʃ'ʃoso] *ag* (*spiacevole*) unpleasant; regrettable.

incres'pare *vt* (*capelli*) to curl; (*acque*) to ripple; **~rsi** *vr* (*vedi vt*) to curl; to ripple.

incrimi'nare *vt* (*DIR*) to charge.

incriminazi'one [inkriminat'tsjone] *sf* (*atto d'accusa*) indictment, charge.

incri'nare *vt* to crack; (*fig: rapporti, amicizia*) to cause to deteriorate; **~rsi** *vr* to crack; to deteriorate.

incrina'tura *sf* crack; (*fig*) rift.

incroci'are [inkro'tʃare] *vt* to cross; (*incontrare*) to meet ♦ *vi* (*NAUT, AER*) to cruise; **~rsi** *vr* (*strade*) to cross, intersect; (*persone, veicoli*) to pass each other; **~ le braccia/le gambe** to fold one's arms/cross

one's legs.

incrocia'tore [inkrotʃa'tore] *sm* cruiser.

in'crocio [in'krotʃo] *sm* (*anche FERR*) crossing; (*di strade*) crossroads.

incrol'labile *ag* (*fede*) unshakeable, firm.

incros'tare *vt* to encrust; **~rsi** *vr*: **~rsi di** to become encrusted with.

incrostazi'one [inkrostat'tsjone] *sf* encrustation; (*di calcare*) scale; (*nelle tubature*) fur (*BRIT*), scale.

incru'ento, a *ag* (*battaglia*) without bloodshed, bloodless.

incuba'trice [inkuba'tritʃe] *sf* incubator.

incubazi'one [inkubat'tsjone] *sf* incubation.

'incubo *sm* nightmare.

in'cudine *sf* anvil; **trovarsi o essere tra l'~ e il martello** (*fig*) to be between the devil and the deep blue sea.

incul'care *vt*: **~ qc in** to inculcate sth into, instill sth into.

incune'are *vt* to wedge.

incu'pire *vt* (*rendere scuro*) to darken; (*fig: intristire*) to fill with gloom ♦ *vi* (*vedi vt*) to darken; to become gloomy.

incu'rabile *ag* incurable.

incu'rante *ag*: **~ (di)** heedless (of), careless (of).

in'curia *sf* negligence.

incurio'sire *vt* to make curious; **~rsi** *vr* to become curious.

incursi'one *sf* raid.

incur'vare *vt*, **~rsi** *vr* to bend, curve.

in'cusso, a *pp di* **incutere**.

incusto'dito, a *ag* unguarded, unattended; **passaggio a livello ~** unmanned level crossing.

in'cutere *vt* to arouse; **~ timore/rispetto a qn** to strike fear into sb/command sb's respect.

'indaco *sm* indigo.

indaffa'rato, a *ag* busy.

inda'gare *vt* to investigate.

indaga'tore, 'trice *ag* (*sguardo, domanda*) searching; (*mente*) inquiring.

in'dagine [in'dadʒine] *sf* investigation, inquiry; (*ricerca*) research, study; **~ di mercato** market survey.

indebita'mente *av* (*immeritatamente*) undeservedly; (*erroneamente*) wrongfully.

indebi'tare *vt*: **~ qn** to get sb into debt; **~rsi** *vr* to run o get into debt.

in'debito, a *ag* undeserved; wrongful.

indeboli'mento *sm* weakening; (*debolezza*) weakness.

indebo'lire *vt, vi* (*anche: ~rsi*) to weaken.

inde'cente [inde'tʃɛnte] *ag* indecent.

inde'cenza [inde'tʃɛntsa] *sf* indecency; **è un'~!** (*vergogna*) it's scandalous!, it's a disgrace!

indeci'frabile [indetʃi'frabile] *ag* indecipherable.

indecisi'one [indetʃi'zjone] *sf* indecisiveness; indecision.

inde'ciso, a [inde'tʃizo] *ag* indecisive; (*irresoluto*) undecided.

indeco'roso, a *ag* (*comportamento*) indecorous, unseemly.

inde'fesso, a *ag* untiring, indefatigable.

indefi'nibile *ag* indefinable.

indefi'nito, a *ag* (*anche LING*) indefinite; (*impreciso, non determinato*) undefined.

indefor'mabile *ag* crushproof.

in'degno, a [in'deɲɲo] *ag* (*atto*) shameful; (*persona*) unworthy.

inde'lebile *ag* indelible.

indelica'tezza [indelika'tettsa] *sf* tactlessness.

indeli'cato, a *ag* (*domanda*) indiscreet, tactless.

indemoni'ato, a *ag* possessed (by the devil).

in'denne *ag* unhurt, uninjured.

indennità *sf inv* (*rimborso: di spese*) allowance; (: *di perdita*) compensation, indemnity; ~ **di contingenza** cost-of-living allowance; ~ **di fine rapporto** severance payment (*on retirement, redundancy or when taking up other employment*); ~ **di trasferta** travel expenses *pl*.

indenniz'zare [indennid'dzare] *vt* to compensate.

inden'nizzo [inden'niddzo] *sm* (*somma*) compensation, indemnity.

indero'gabile *ag* binding.

indescri'vibile *ag* indescribable.

indeside'rabile *ag* undesirable.

indeside'rato, a *ag* unwanted.

indetermina'tezza [indetermina'tettsa] *sf* vagueness.

indetermina'tivo, a *ag* (*LING*) indefinite.

indetermi'nato, a *ag* indefinite, indeterminate.

in'detto, a *pp di* **indire**.

'India *sf*: **l'**~ India; **le** ~**e occidentali** the West Indies.

indi'ano, a *ag* Indian ♦ *sm/f* (*d'India*) Indian; (*d'America*) Red Indian; **l'Oceano I**~ the Indian Ocean.

indiavo'lato, a *ag* possessed (by the devil); (*vivace, violento*) wild.

indi'care *vt* (*mostrare*) to show, indicate; (: *col dito*) to point to, point out; (*consigliare*) to suggest, recommend.

indica'tivo, a *ag* indicative ♦ *sm* (*LING*) indicative (mood).

indi'cato, a *ag* (*consigliato*) advisable; (*adatto*): ~ **per** suitable for, appropriate for.

indica'tore, 'trice *ag* indicating ♦ *sm* (*elenco*) guide; directory; (*TECN*) gauge; indicator; **cartello** ~ sign; (*TECN, MAT, nei libri*) index; ~ **azionario** share index; ~ **di velocità** (*AUT*) speedometer; (*AER*) airspeed indicator.

indicazi'one [indikat'tsjone] *sf* indication; (*informazione*) piece of information; ~**i per l'uso** instructions for use.

'indice ['inditʃe] *sm* (*ANAT: dito*) index finger, forefinger; (*lancetta*) needle, pointer; (*fig: indizio*) sign; (*TECN, MAT, nei libri*) index; ~ **azionario** share index; ~ **di gradimento** (*RADIO, TV*) popularity rating; ~ **dei prezzi al consumo** ≈ retail price index.

indicherò *etc* [indike'rɔ] *vb vedi* **indicare**.

indi'cibile [indi't ʃibile] *ag* inexpressible.

indiciz'zare [inditʃid'dzare] *vt*: ~ **al costo della vita** to index-link (*BRIT*), index (*US*).

indiciz'zato, a [inditʃid'dzato] *ag* (*polizza, salario etc*) index-linked (*BRIT*), indexed (*US*).

indicizzazi'one [inditʃiddzat'tsjone] *sf* indexing.

indietreggi'are [indjetred'dʒare] *vi* to draw back, retreat.

indi'etro *av* back; (*guardare*) behind, back; (*andare, cadere: anche*: **all'**~) backwards; **rimanere** ~ to be left behind; **essere** ~ (*col lavoro*) to be behind; (*orologio*) to be slow; **rimandare qc** ~ to send sth back; **non vado né avanti né** ~ (*fig*) I'm not getting anywhere, I'm getting nowhere.

indi'feso, a *ag* (*città, confine*) undefended; (*persona*) defenceless (*BRIT*), defenseless (*US*), helpless.

indiffe'rente *ag* indifferent ♦ *sm*: **fare l'**~ to pretend to be indifferent, be *o* act casual; (*fingere di non vedere o sentire*) to pretend not to notice.

indiffe'renza [indiffe'rɛntsa] *sf* indifference.

in'digeno, a [in'didʒeno] *ag* indigenous, native ♦ *sm/f* native.

indi'gente [indi'dʒɛnte] *ag* poverty-stricken, destitute.

indi'genza [indi'dʒɛntsa] *sf* extreme poverty.

indigesti'one [indidʒes'tjone] *sf* indigestion.

indi'gesto, a [indi'dʒɛsto] *ag* indigestible.

indi'gnare [indiɲ'ɲare] *vt* to fill with indignation; ~**rsi** *vr* to be (*o* get) indignant.

indignazi'one [indiɲɲat'tsjone] *sf* indignation.

indimenti'cabile *ag* unforgettable.

'indio, a *ag, sm/f* (South American) Indian.

indipen'dente *ag* independent.

indipendente'mente *av* independently; ~ **dal fatto che gli piaccia o meno, verrà!** he's coming, whether he likes it or not!

indipen'denza [indipen'dɛntsa] *sf* independence.

in'dire *vt* (*concorso*) to announce; (*elezioni*) to call.

indi'retto, a *ag* indirect.

indiriz'zare [indirit'tsare] *vt* (*dirigere*) to direct; (*mandare*) to send; (*lettera*) to address; ~ **la parola a qn** to address sb.

indiriz'zario [indirit'tsarjo] *sm* mailing list.

indi'rizzo [indi'rittso] *sm* address; (*direzione*) direction; (*avvio*) trend, course; ~ **assoluto** (*INFORM*) absolute address.

indisci'plina [indiʃʃi'plina] *sf* indiscipline.

indiscipli'nato, a [indiʃʃipli'nato] *ag* undisciplined, unruly.

indis'creto, a *ag* indiscreet.

indiscrezi'one [indiskret'tsjone] *sf* indiscretion.

indiscrimi'nato, a *ag* indiscriminate.

indis'cusso, a *ag* unquestioned.

indiscu'tibile *ag* indisputable, unquestionable.

indispen'sabile *ag* indispensable, essential.

indispet'tire *vt* to irritate, annoy ♦ *vi* (*anche*: ~**rsi**) to get irritated *o* annoyed.

indispo'nente *ag* irritating, annoying.

indis'porre *vt* to antagonize.

indisposizi'one [indispozit'tsjone] *sf* (slight) indisposition.

indis'posto, a *pp di* **indisporre** ♦ *ag* indisposed, unwell.

indisso'lubile *ag* indissoluble.

indissolubil'mente *av* indissolubly.

indistinta'mente *av* (*senza distinzioni*) indiscriminately, without exception; (*in modo indefinito: vedere, sentire*) vaguely, faintly.

indis'tinto, a *ag* indistinct.

indistrut'tibile *ag* indestructible.

in'divia *sf* endive.

individu'ale *ag* individual.

individua'lismo *sm* individualism.

individua'lista, i, e *sm/f* individualist.

individualità *sf* individuality.

individual'mente *av* individually.

individu'are *vt* (*dar forma distinta a*) to characterize; (*determinare*) to locate; (*riconoscere*) to single out.

indi'viduo *sm* individual.

indivi'sibile *ag* indivisible; **quei due sono** ~**i** (*fig*) those two are inseparable.

indizi'are [indit'tsjare] *vt*: ~ **qn di qc** to cast suspicion on sb for sth.

indizi'ato, a [indit'tsjato] *ag* suspected ♦ *sm/f* suspect.

in'dizio [in'dittsjo] *sm* (*segno*) sign, indication; (*POLIZIA*) clue; (*DIR*) piece of evidence.

Indo'cina [indo't ʃina] *sf*: **l'**~ Indochina.

'indole *sf* nature, character.

indo'lente *ag* indolent.

indo'lenza [indo'lɛntsa] *sf* indolence.

indolen'zire [indolen'tsire] *vt* (*gambe, braccia etc*) to make stiff, cause to ache; (: *intorpidire*) to numb; ~**rsi** *vr* to become stiff; to go numb.

indolen'zito, a [indolen'tsito] *ag* stiff, aching; (*intorpidito*) numb.

indo'lore *ag* (*anche fig*) painless.

indo'mani *sm*: **l'**~ the next day, the following day.

Indo'nesia [indo'nɛzja] *sf*: **l'**~ Indonesia.

indonesi'ano, a *ag, sm/f, sm* Indonesian.

indo'rare *vt* (*rivestire in oro*) to gild; (*CUC*) to dip in egg yolk; ~ **la pillola** (*fig*) to sugar the pill.

indos'sare *vt* (*mettere indosso*) to put on; (*avere indosso*) to have on.

indossa'tore, 'trice *sm/f* model.

in'dotto, a *pp di* **indurre**.

indottri'nare *vt* to indoctrinate.

indovi'nare *vt* (*scoprire*) to guess; (*immaginare*) to imagine, guess; (*il futuro*) to foretell; **tirare a** ~ to make a shot in the dark.

indovi'nato, a *ag* successful; (*scelta*) inspired.

indovi'nello *sm* riddle.

indo'vino, a *sm/f* fortuneteller.

indù *ag, sm/f* Hindu.

indubbia'mente *av* undoubtedly.

in'dubbio, a *ag* certain, undoubted.

in'duco *etc vb vedi* **indurre**.

indugi'are [indu'dʒare] *vi* to take one's time, delay.

in'dugio [in'dudʒo] *sm* (*ritardo*) delay; **senza** ~ without delay.

indul'gente [indul'dʒɛnte] *ag* indulgent; (*giudice*) lenient.

indul'genza [indul'dʒɛntsa] *sf* indulgence; leniency.

in'dulgere [in'duldʒere] *vi*: ~ **a** (*accondiscendere*) to comply with; (*abbandonarsi*) to indulge in.

in'dulto, a *pp di* **indulgere** ♦ *sm* (*DIR*) pardon.

indu'mento *sm* article of clothing,

garment; ~**i** *smpl* (*vestiti*) clothes; ~**i intimi** underwear *sg*.

induri'mento *sm* hardening.

indu'rire *vt* to harden ♦ *vi* (*anche:* ~**rsi**) to harden, become hard.

in'durre *vt*: ~ **qn a fare qc** to induce *o* persuade sb to do sth; ~ **qn in errore** to mislead sb; ~ **in tentazione** to lead into temptation.

in'dussi *etc vb vedi* **indurre**.

in'dustria *sf* industry; **la piccola/grande** ~ small/big business.

industri'ale *ag* industrial ♦ *sm* industrialist.

industrializ'zare [industrjalid'dzare] *vt* to industrialize.

industrializzazi'one [industrjaliddzat'tsjone] *sf* industrialization.

industri'arsi *vr* to do one's best, try hard.

industri'oso, a *ag* industrious, hardworking.

induzi'one [indut'tsjone] *sf* induction.

inebe'tito, a *ag* dazed, stunned.

inebri'are *vt* (*anche fig*) to intoxicate; ~**rsi** *vr* to become intoxicated.

inecce'pibile [inettʃe'pibile] *ag* unexceptionable.

i'nedia *sf* starvation.

i'nedito, a *ag* unpublished.

inef'fabile *ag* ineffable.

ineffi'cace [ineffi'katʃe] *ag* ineffective.

ineffi'cacia [ineffi'katʃa] *sf* inefficacy, ineffectiveness.

ineffici'ente [ineffi'tʃɛnte] *ag* inefficient.

ineffici'enza [ineffi'tʃɛntsa] *sf* inefficiency.

ineguagli'abile [inegwaʎ'ʎabile] *ag* incomparable, matchless.

ineguagli'anza [inegwaʎ'ʎantsa] *sf* (*sociale*) inequality; (*di superficie, livello*) unevenness.

inegu'ale *ag* unequal; (*irregolare*) uneven.

inelut'tabile *ag* inescapable.

ineluttabilità *sf* inescapability.

inenar'rabile *ag* unutterable.

inequivo'cabile *ag* unequivocal.

ine'rente *ag*: ~ **a** concerning, regarding.

i'nerme *ag* unarmed, defenceless (*BRIT*), defenseless (*US*).

inerpi'carsi *vr*: ~ (**su**) to clamber (up).

i'nerte *ag* inert; (*inattivo*) indolent, sluggish.

i'nerzia [i'nɛrtsja] *sf* inertia; indolence, sluggishness.

inesat'tezza [inezat'tettsa] *sf* inaccuracy.

ine'satto, a *ag* (*impreciso*) inaccurate, inexact; (*erroneo*) incorrect; (*AMM: non riscosso*) uncollected.

inesau'ribile *ag* inexhaustible.

inesis'tente *ag* non-existent.

ineso'rabile *ag* inexorable, relentless.

inesorabil'mente *av* inexorably.

inesperi'enza [inespe'rjɛntsa] *sf* inexperience.

ines'perto, a *ag* inexperienced.

inespli'cabile *ag* inexplicable.

inesplo'rato, a *ag* unexplored.

ines'ploso, a *ag* unexploded.

inespres'sivo, a *ag* (*viso*) expressionless, inexpressive.

ines'presso, a *ag* unexpressed.

inespri'mibile *ag* inexpressible.

inespu'gnabile [inespuɲ'ɲabile] *ag* (*fortezza, torre etc*) impregnable.

ineste'tismo *sm* beauty problem.

inesti'mabile *ag* inestimable; (*valore*) incalculable.

inestir'pabile *ag* ineradicable.

inestri'cabile *ag* (*anche fig*) impenetrable.

inetti'tudine *sf* ineptitude.

i'netto, a *ag* (*incapace*) inept; (*che non ha attitudine*): ~ (**a**) unsuited (to).

ine'vaso, a *ag* (*ordine, corrispondenza*) outstanding.

inevi'tabile *ag* inevitable.

inevitabil'mente *av* inevitably.

i'nezia [i'nɛttsja] *sf* trifle, thing of no importance.

infagot'tare *vt* to bundle up, wrap up; ~**rsi** *vr* to wrap up.

infal'libile *ag* infallible.

infallibilità *sf* infallibility.

infa'mante *ag* (*accusa*) defamatory, slanderous.

infa'mare *vt* to defame.

in'fame *ag* infamous; (*fig: cosa, compito*) awful, dreadful.

in'famia *sf* infamy.

infan'gare *vt* (*sporcare*) to cover with mud; (*nome, reputazione*) to sully; ~**rsi** *vr* to get covered in mud; to be sullied.

infan'tile *ag* child *cpd*; childlike; (*adulto, azione*) childish; **letteratura** ~ children's books *pl*.

in'fanzia [in'fantsja] *sf* childhood; (*bambini*) children *pl*; **prima** ~ babyhood, infancy.

infari'nare *vt* to cover with (*o* sprinkle with *o* dip in) flour; ~ **di zucchero** to sprinkle with sugar.

infarina'tura *sf* (*fig*) smattering.

in'farto *sm* (*MED*): ~ (**cardiaco**) coronary.

infasti'dire *vt* to annoy, irritate; ~**rsi** *vr* to get annoyed *o* irritated.

infati'cabile *ag* tireless, untiring.

in'fatti *cong* as a matter of fact, in fact, actually.

infatu'arsi *vr:* ~ **di** *o* **per** to become infatuated with, fall for.

infatuazi'one [infatuat'tsjone] *sf* infatuation.

in'fausto, a *ag* unpropitious, unfavourable (*BRIT*); unfavorable (*US*).

infecondità *sf* infertility.

infe'condo, a *ag* infertile.

infe'dele *ag* unfaithful.

infedeltà *sf* infidelity.

infe'lice [infe'litʃe] *ag* unhappy; (*sfortunato*) unlucky, unfortunate; (*inopportuno*) inopportune, ill-timed; (*mal riuscito: lavoro*) bad, poor.

infelicità [infelitʃi'ta] *sf* unhappiness.

infel'trire *vi,* ~**rsi** *vr* (*lana*) to become matted.

infe'renza [infe'rɛntsa] *sf* inference.

inferi'ore *ag* lower; (*per intelligenza, qualità*) inferior ♦ *sm/f* inferior; ~ **a** (*numero, quantità*) less *o* smaller than; (*meno buono*) inferior to; ~ **alla media** below average.

inferiorità *sf* inferiority.

infe'rire *vt* (*dedurre*) to infer, deduce.

inferme'ria *sf* infirmary; (*di scuola, nave*) sick bay.

infermi'ere, a *sm/f* nurse.

infermità *sf inv* illness; infirmity; ~ **di mente** mental illness.

in'fermo, a *ag* (*ammalato*) ill; (*debole*) infirm; ~ **di mente** mentally ill.

infer'nale *ag* infernal; (*proposito, complotto*) diabolical; **un tempo** ~ (*fam*) hellish weather.

in'ferno *sm* hell; **soffrire le pene dell'**~ (*fig*) to go through hell.

infero'cire [infero'tʃire] *vt* to make fierce ♦ *vi,* ~**rsi** *vr* to become fierce.

inferri'ata *sf* grating.

infervo'rare *vt* to arouse enthusiasm in; ~**rsi** *vr* to get excited, get carried away.

infes'tare *vt* to infest.

infet'tare *vt* to infect; ~**rsi** *vr* to become infected.

infet'tivo, a *ag* infectious.

in'fetto, a *ag* infected; (*acque*) polluted, contaminated.

infezi'one [infet'tsjone] *sf* infection.

infiac'chire [infjak'kire] *vt* to weaken ♦ *vi* (*anche:* ~**rsi**) to grow weak.

infiam'mabile *ag* inflammable.

infiam'mare *vt* to set alight; (*fig, MED*) to inflame; ~**rsi** *vr* to catch fire; (*MED*) to become inflamed; (*fig*): ~**rsi di** to be fired with.

infiammazi'one [infjammat'tsjone] *sf* (*MED*) inflammation.

infias'care *vt* to bottle.

infici'are [infi'tʃare] *vt* (*DIR: atto, dichiarazione*) to challenge.

in'fido, a *ag* unreliable, treacherous.

infie'rire *vi:* ~ **su** (*fisicamente*) to attack furiously; (*verbalmente*) to rage at; (*epidemia*) to rage over.

in'figgere [in'fiddʒere] *vt:* ~ **qc in** to thrust *o* drive sth into.

infi'lare *vt* (*ago*) to thread; (*mettere: chiave*) to insert; (*: vestito*) to slip *o* put on; (*strada*) to turn into, take; ~**rsi** *vr:* ~**rsi in** to slip into; (*indossare*) to slip on; ~ **un anello al dito** to slip a ring on one's finger; ~ **l'uscio** to slip in; to slip out; ~**rsi la giacca** to put on one's jacket.

infil'trarsi *vr* to penetrate, seep through; (*MIL*) to infiltrate.

infil'trato, a *sm/f* infiltrator.

infiltrazi'one [infiltrat'tsjone] *sf* infiltration.

infil'zare [infil'tsare] *vt* (*infilare*) to string together; (*trafiggere*) to pierce.

'infimo, a *ag* lowest; **un albergo di** ~ **ordine** a third-rate hotel.

in'fine *av* finally; (*insomma*) in short.

infin'gardo, a *ag* lazy ♦ *sm/f* slacker.

infinità *sf* infinity; (*in quantità*): **un'**~ **di** an infinite number of.

infinitesi'male *ag* infinitesimal.

infi'nito, a *ag* infinite; (*LING*) infinitive ♦ *sm* infinity; (*LING*) infinitive; **all'**~ (*senza fine*) endlessly; (*LING*) in the infinitive.

infinocchi'are [infinok'kjare] *vt* (*fam*) to hoodwink.

infiore'scenza [infjoreʃ'ʃɛntsa] *sf* inflorescence.

infir'mare *vt* (*DIR*) to invalidate.

infischi'arsi [infis'kjarsi] *vr:* ~ **di** not to care about.

in'fisso, a *pp di* **infiggere** ♦ *sm* fixture; (*di porta, finestra*) frame.

infit'tire *vt, vi* (*anche:* ~**rsi**) to thicken.

inflazio'nare [inflattsjo'nare] *vt* to inflate.

inflazi'one [inflat'tsjone] *sf* inflation.

inflazio'nistico, a, ci, che [inflattsjo'nistiko] *ag* inflationary.

infles'sibile *ag* inflexible; (*ferreo*) unyielding.

inflessi'one *sf* inflexion.

in'fliggere [in'fliddʒere] *vt* to inflict.

in'flissi *etc vb vedi* **infliggere.**

in'flitto, a *pp di* **infliggere.**

influ'ente *ag* influential.

influ'enza [influ'ɛntsa] *sf* influence; (*MED*) influenza, flu.

influen'zare [influen'tsare] *vt* to influence, have an influence on.

influ'ire *vi:* ~ **su** to influence.

in'flusso *sm* influence.

INFN *sigla m* = *Istituto Nazionale di Fisica Nucleare.*

info'cato, a *ag* = **infuocato**.

info'gnarsi [infoɲ'ɲarsi] *vr (fam)* to get into a mess; ~ **in un mare di debiti** to be up to one's *o* the eyes in debt.

infol'tire *vt, vi* to thicken.

infon'dato, a *ag* unfounded, groundless.

in'fondere *vt:* ~ **qc in qn** to instill sth in sb; ~ **fiducia in qn** to inspire sb with confidence.

infor'care *vt* to fork (up); *(bicicletta, cavallo)* to get on; *(occhiali)* to put on.

infor'male *ag* informal.

infor'mare *vt* to inform, tell; ~**rsi** *vr:* ~**rsi (di o su)** to inquire (about); **tenere informato qn** to keep sb informed.

infor'matico, a, ci, che *ag (settore)* computer *cpd* ♦ *sf* computer science.

informa'tivo, a *ag* informative; **a titolo** ~ for information only.

informatiz'zare [informatid'dzare] *vt* to computerize.

infor'mato, a *ag* informed; **tenersi** ~ **to** keep o.s. (well-)informed.

informa'tore *sm* informer.

informazi'one [informat'tsjone] *sf* piece of information; ~**i** *sfpl* information *sg*; **chiedere un'**~ to ask for (some) information; ~ **di garanzia** *(DIR)* = **avviso di garanzia**.

in'forme *ag* shapeless.

informico'larsi *vr*, **informico'lirsi** *vr*: **mi si è informicolata una gamba** I've got pins and needles in my leg.

infor'nare *vt* to put in the oven.

infor'nata *sf (anche fig)* batch.

infortu'narsi *vr* to injure o.s., have an accident.

infortu'nato, a *ag* injured, hurt ♦ *sm/f* injured person.

infor'tunio *sm* accident; ~ **sul lavoro** industrial accident, accident at work.

infortu'nistica *sf* study of (industrial) accidents.

infos'sarsi *vr (terreno)* to sink; *(guance)* to become hollow.

infos'sato, a *ag* hollow; *(occhi)* deep-set; *(: per malattia)* sunken.

infradici'are [infradi'tʃare] *vt (inzuppare)* to soak, drench; *(marcire)* to rot; ~**rsi** *vr* to get soaked, get drenched; to rot.

infra'dito *sm inv (calzatura)* flip flop *(BRIT)*, thong *(US)*.

in'frangere [in'frandʒere] *vt* to smash; *(fig: legge, patti)* to break; ~**rsi** *vr* to smash, break.

infran'gibile [infran'dʒibile] *ag* unbreakable.

in'franto, a *pp di* **infrangere** ♦ *ag* broken.

infra'rosso, a *ag, sm* infrared.

infrasettima'nale *ag* midweek *cpd*.

infrastrut'tura *sf* infrastructure.

infrazi'one [infrat'tsjone] *sf:* ~ **a** breaking of, violation of.

infredda'tura *sf* slight cold.

infreddo'lito, a *ag* cold, chilled.

infre'quente *ag* infrequent, rare.

infrol'lire *vi*, ~**rsi** *vr (selvaggina)* to become high.

infruttu'oso, a *ag* fruitless.

infuo'cato, a *ag (metallo)* red-hot; *(sabbia)* burning; *(fig: discorso)* heated, passionate.

infu'ori *av* out; **all'**~ outwards; **all'**~ **di** *(eccetto)* except, with the exception of.

infuri'are *vi* to rage; ~**rsi** *vr* to fly into a rage.

infusi'one *sf* infusion.

in'fuso, a *pp di* **infondere** ♦ *ag:* **scienza** ~**a** *(anche ironico)* innate knowledge ♦ *sm* infusion; ~ **di camomilla** camomile tea.

Ing. *abbr* = **ingegnere**.

ingabbi'are *vt* to (put in a) cage.

ingaggi'are [ingad'dʒare] *vt (assumere con compenso)* to take on, hire; *(SPORT)* to sign on; *(MIL)* to engage.

in'gaggio [in'gaddʒo] *sm* hiring; signing on.

ingagliar'dire [ingaʎʎar'dire] *vt* to strengthen, invigorate ♦ *vi (anche:* ~**rsi**) to grow stronger.

ingan'nare *vt* to deceive; *(coniuge)* to be unfaithful to; *(fisco)* to cheat; *(eludere)* to dodge, elude; *(fig: tempo)* to while away ♦ *vi (apparenza)* to be deceptive; ~**rsi** *vr* to be mistaken, be wrong.

inganna'tore, 'trice *ag* deceptive; *(persona)* deceitful.

ingan'nevole *ag* deceptive.

in'ganno *sm* deceit, deception; *(azione)* trick; *(menzogna, frode)* cheat, swindle; *(illusione)* illusion.

ingarbugli'are [ingarbuʎ'ʎare] *vt* to tangle; *(fig)* to confuse, muddle; ~**rsi** *vr* to become confused *o* muddled.

ingarbu'gliato, a [ingarbuʎ'ʎato] *ag* tangled; confused, muddled.

inge'gnarsi [indʒeɲ'ɲarsi] *vr* to do one's best, try hard; ~ **per vivere** to live by one's wits; **basta** ~ **un po'** you just need a bit of ingenuity.

inge'gnere [indʒeɲ'ɲɛre] *sm* engineer; ~ **civile/navale** civil/naval engineer.

ingegne'ria [indʒeɲɲe'ria] *sf* engineering.

in'gegno [in'dʒeɲɲo] *sm (intelligenza)* intelligence, brains *pl*; *(capacità creativa)* ingenuity; (*disposizione*) talent.

ingegnosità [indʒeɲɲosi'ta] *sf* ingenuity.

inge'gnoso, a [indʒeɲ'ɲoso] *ag* ingenious, clever.

ingelo'sire [indʒelo'sire] *vt* to make jealous ♦ *vi* (*anche*: ~rsi) to become jealous.

in'gente [in'dʒɛnte] *ag* huge, enormous.

ingenti'lire [indʒenti'lire] *vt* to refine, civilize; ~rsi *vr* to become more refined, become more civilized.

ingenuità [indʒenui'ta] *sf* ingenuousness.

in'genuo, a [in'dʒɛnuo] *ag* ingenuous, naïve.

inge'renza [indʒe'rɛntsa] *sf* interference.

inge'rire [indʒe'rire] *vt* to ingest.

inges'sare [indʒes'sare] *vt* (*MED*) to put in plaster.

ingessa'tura [indʒessa'tura] *sf* plaster.

Inghil'terra [ingil'tɛrra] *sf*: **l'~** England.

inghiot'tire [ingjot'tire] *vt* to swallow.

in'ghippo [in'gippo] *sm* trick.

ingial'lire [indʒal'lire] *vi* to go yellow.

ingigan'tire [indʒigan'tire] *vt* to enlarge, magnify ♦ *vi* to become gigantic *o* enormous.

inginocchi'arsi [indʒinok'kjarsi] *vr* to kneel (down).

inginocchia'toio [indʒinokkja'tojo] *sm* prie-dieu.

ingioiel'lare [indʒojel'lare] *vt* to bejewel, adorn with jewels.

ingiù [in'dʒu] *av* down, downwards.

ingi'ungere [in'dʒundʒere] *vt*: **~ a qn di fare qc** to enjoin *o* order sb to do sth.

ingi'unto, a [in'dʒunto] *pp di* **ingiungere**.

ingiunzi'one [indʒun'tsjone] *sf* injunction, command; **~ di pagamento** final demand.

ingi'uria [in'dʒurja] *sf* insult; (*fig: danno*) damage.

ingiuri'are [indʒu'rjare] *vt* to insult, abuse.

ingiuri'oso, a [indʒu'rjoso] *ag* insulting, abusive.

ingiusta'mente [indʒusta'mente] *av* unjustly.

ingiustifi'cabile [indʒustifi'kabile] *ag* unjustifiable.

ingiustifi'cato, a [indʒustifi'kato] *ag* unjustified.

ingius'tizia [indʒus'tittsja] *sf* injustice.

ingi'usto, a [in'dʒusto] *ag* unjust, unfair.

in'glese *ag* English ♦ *sm/f* Englishman/ woman ♦ *sm* (*LING*) English; **gli I~i** the English; **andarsene** *o* **filare all'~** to take French leave.

inglori'oso, a [inglo'rjoso] *ag* inglorious.

ingob'bire *vi*, ~rsi *vr* to become stooped.

ingoi'are *vt* to gulp (down); (*fig*) to swallow (up); **ha dovuto ~ il rospo** (*fig*) he had to

accept the situation.

ingol'fare *vt*, ~rsi *vr* (*motore*) to flood.

ingolo'sire *vt*: **~ qn** to make sb's mouth water; (*fig*) to attract sb ♦ *vi* (*anche*: ~rsi): **~ (di)** (*anche fig*) to become greedy (for).

ingom'brante *ag* cumbersome.

ingom'brare *vt* (*strada*) to block; (*stanza*) to clutter up.

in'gombro, a *ag*: **~ di** (*strada*) blocked by; (*stanza*) cluttered up with ♦ *sm* obstacle; **essere d'~** to be in the way; **per ragioni di ~** for reasons of space.

ingor'digia [ingor'didʒa] *sf*: **~ (di)** greed (for); avidity (for).

in'gordo, a *ag*: **~ di** greedy for; (*fig*) greedy *o* avid for ♦ *sm/f* glutton.

ingor'gare *vt* to block; ~rsi *vr* to be blocked up, be choked up.

in'gorgo, ghi *sm* blockage, obstruction; (*anche*: **~ stradale**) traffic jam.

ingoz'zare [ingot'tsare] *vt* (*animali*) to fatten; (*fig: persona*) to stuff; ~rsi *vr*: ~rsi **(di)** to stuff o.s. (with).

ingra'naggio [ingra'naddʒo] *sm* (*TECN*) gear; (*di orologio*) mechanism; **gli ~i della burocrazia** the bureaucratic machinery.

ingra'nare *vi* to mesh, engage ♦ *vt* to engage; **~ la marcia** to get into gear.

ingrandi'mento *sm* enlargement; extension; magnification; growth; expansion.

ingran'dire *vt* (*anche FOT*) to enlarge; (*estendere*) to extend; (*OTTICA, fig*) to magnify ♦ *vi* (*anche*: ~rsi) to become larger *o* bigger; (*aumentare*) to grow, increase; (*espandersi*) to expand.

ingrandi'tore *sm* (*FOT*) enlarger.

ingras'saggio [ingras'saddʒo] *sm* greasing.

ingras'sare *vt* to make fat; (*animali*) to fatten; (*AGR: terreno*) to manure; (*lubrificare*) to grease ♦ *vi* (*anche*: ~rsi) to get fat, put on weight.

ingrati'tudine *sf* ingratitude.

in'grato, a *ag* ungrateful; (*lavoro*) thankless, unrewarding.

ingrazi'are [ingrat'tsjare] *vt*: ~rsi **qn** to ingratiate o.s. with sb.

ingredi'ente *sm* ingredient.

in'gresso *sm* (*porta*) entrance; (*atrio*) hall; (*l'entrare*) entrance, entry; (*facoltà di entrare*) admission; "**~ libero**" "admission free"; **~ principale** main entrance; **~ di servizio** tradesmen's entrance.

ingros'sare *vt* to increase; (*folla, livello*) to swell ♦ *vi* (*anche*: ~rsi) to increase; to swell.

in'grosso *av*: **all'~** (*COMM*) wholesale; (*all'incirca*) roughly, about.

ingru'gnato, a [ingruɲ'ɲato] *ag* grumpy.
inguai'arsi *vr* to get into trouble.
inguai'nare *vt* to sheathe.
ingual'cibile [ingwal'tʃibile] *ag* crease-resistant.
ingua'ribile *ag* incurable.
'inguine *sm* (*ANAT*) groin.
ingurgi'tare [ingurdʒi'tare] *vt* to gulp down.
ini'bire *vt* to forbid, prohibit; (*PSIC*) to inhibit.
ini'bito, a *ag* inhibited ♦ *sm/f* inhibited person.
inibi'torio, a *ag* (*PSIC*) inhibitory, inhibitive; (*provvedimento, misure*) restrictive.
inibizi'one [inibit'tsjone] *sf* prohibition; inhibition.
iniet'tare *vt* to inject; ~**rsi** *vr*: ~**rsi di sangue** (*occhi*) to become bloodshot.
iniet'tore *sm* injector.
iniezi'one [injet'tsjone] *sf* injection.
inimi'care *vt* to alienate, make hostile; ~**rsi** *vr*: ~**rsi con qn** to fall out with sb; **si è inimicato gli amici di un tempo** he has alienated his old friends.
inimi'cizia [inimi'tʃittsja] *sf* animosity.
inimi'tabile *ag* inimitable.
inimmagi'nabile [inimmadʒi'nabile] *ag* unimaginable.
ininfiam'mabile *ag* non-flammable.
inintelli'gibile [inintelli'dʒibile] *ag* unintelligible.
ininterrotta'mente *av* non-stop, continuously.
ininter'rotto, a *ag* (*fila*) unbroken; (*rumore*) uninterrupted.
iniquità *sf inv* iniquity; (*atto*) wicked action.
i'niquo, a *ag* iniquitous.
inizi'ale [init'tsjale] *ag*, *sf* initial.
inizializ'zare [inittsjalid'dzare] *vt* (*INFORM*) to boot.
inizial'mente [inittsjal'mente] *av* initially, at first.
inizi'are [init'tsjare] *vi, vt* to begin, start; ~ **qn a** to initiate sb into; (*pittura etc*) to introduce sb to; ~ **a fare qc** to start doing sth.
inizia'tiva [inittsja'tiva] *sf* initiative; ~ **privata** private enterprise.
inizia'tore, 'trice [inittsja'tore] *sm/f* initiator.
i'nizio [i'nittsjo] *sm* beginning; **all'**~ at the beginning, at the start; **dare** ~ **a qc** to start sth, get sth going; **essere agli** ~**i** (*progetto, lavoro etc*) to be in the initial stages.
innaffi'are *etc* = **annaffiare** *etc*.
innal'zare [innal'tsare] *vt* (*sollevare, alzare*)

to raise; (*rizzare*) to erect; ~**rsi** *vr* to rise.
innamora'mento *sm* falling in love.
innamo'rare *vt* to enchant, charm; ~**rsi** *vr*: ~**rsi (di qn)** to fall in love (with sb).
innamo'rato, a *ag* (*che nutre amore*): ~ **(di)** in love (with); (*appassionato*): ~ **di** very fond of ♦ *sm/f* lover; (*anche scherzoso*) sweetheart.
in'nanzi [in'nantsi] *av* (*stato in luogo*) in front, ahead; (*moto a luogo*) forward, on; (*tempo: prima*) before ♦ *prep* (*prima*) before; ~ **a** in front of; **d'ora** ~ from now on; **farsi** ~ to step forward; ~ **tempo** ahead of time.
innanzi'tutto [innantsi'tutto] *av* above all; (*per prima cosa*) first of all.
in'nato, a *ag* innate.
innatu'rale *ag* unnatural.
inne'gabile *ag* undeniable.
inneggi'are [inned'dʒare] *vi*: ~ **a** to sing hymns to; (*fig*) to sing the praises of.
innervo'sire *vt*: ~ **qn** to get on sb's nerves; ~**rsi** *vr* to get irritated *o* upset.
innes'care *vt* to prime.
in'nesco, schi *sm* primer.
innes'tare *vt* (*BOT, MED*) to graft; (*TECN*) to engage; (*inserire: presa*) to insert.
in'nesto *sm* graft; grafting *no pl*; (*TECN*) clutch; (*ELETTR*) connection.
'inno *sm* hymn; ~ **nazionale** national anthem.
inno'cente [inno'tʃɛnte] *ag* innocent.
inno'cenza [inno'tʃɛntsa] *sf* innocence.
in'nocuo, a *ag* innocuous, harmless.
innomi'nato, a *ag* unnamed.
inno'vare *vt* to change, make innovations in.
innova'tivo, a *ag* innovative.
innovazi'one [innovat'tsjone] *sf* innovation.
innume'revole *ag* innumerable.
inocu'lare *vt* (*MED*) to inoculate.
ino'doro, a *ag* odourless (*BRIT*), odorless (*US*).
inoffen'sivo, a *ag* harmless.
inol'trare *vt* (*AMM*) to pass on, forward; ~**rsi** *vr* (*addentrarsi*) to advance, go forward.
inol'trato, a *ag*: **a notte** ~**a** late at night; **a primavera** ~**a** late in the spring.
i'noltre *av* besides, moreover.
i'noltro *sm* (*AMM*) forwarding.
inon'dare *vt* to flood.
inondazi'one [inondat'tsjone] *sf* flooding *no pl*; flood.
inope'roso, a *ag* inactive, idle.
inopi'nato, a *ag* unexpected.
inoppor'tuno, a *ag* untimely, ill-timed; (*poco adatto*) inappropriate; (*momento*)

inopportune.

inoppu'gnabile [inoppuɲ'ɲabile] *ag* incontrovertible.

inor'ganico, a, ci, che *ag* inorganic.

inorgo'glire [inorgoʎ'ʎire] *vt* to make proud ♦ *vi* (*anche:* ~**rsi**) to become proud; ~**rsi di qc** to pride o.s. on sth.

inorri'dire *vt* to horrify ♦ *vi* to be horrified.

inospi'tale *ag* inhospitable.

inosser'vante *ag*: **essere ~ di** to fail to comply with.

inosser'vato, a *ag* (*non notato*) unobserved; (*non rispettato*) not observed, not kept; **passare ~** to go unobserved, escape notice.

inossi'dabile *ag* stainless.

INPS *sigla m* (= *Istituto Nazionale Previdenza Sociale*) social security service.

inqua'drare *vt* (*foto, immagine*) to frame; (*fig*) to situate, set.

inquadra'tura *sf* (*CINE, FOT: atto*) framing; (: *immagine*) shot; (: *sequenza*) sequence.

inqualifi'cabile *ag* unspeakable.

inquie'tante *ag* disturbing, worrying.

inquie'tare *vt* (*turbare*) to disturb, worry; ~**rsi** *vr* to worry, become anxious; (*impazientirsi*) to get upset.

inqui'eto, a *ag* restless; (*preoccupato*) worried, anxious.

inquie'tudine *sf* anxiety, worry.

inqui'lino, a *sm/f* tenant.

inquina'mento *sm* pollution.

inqui'nare *vt* to pollute.

inqui'rente *ag* (*DIR*): **magistrato ~** examining (*BRIT*) *o* committing (*US*) magistrate; **commissione ~** commission of inquiry.

inqui'sire *vt, vi* to investigate.

inqui'sito, a *ag* (*persona*) under investigation.

inquisi'tore, 'trice *ag* (*sguardo*) inquiring.

inquisizi'one [inkwizit'tsjone] *sf* inquisition.

insabbia'mento *sm* (*fig*) shelving.

insabbi'are *vt* (*fig: pratica*) to shelve; ~**rsi** *vr* (*barca*) to run aground; (*fig: pratica*) to be shelved.

insac'care *vt* (*grano, farina etc*) to bag, put into sacks; (*carne*) to put into sausage skins.

insac'cati *smpl* (*CUC*) sausages.

insa'lata *sf* salad; (*pianta*) lettuce; ~ **mista** mixed salad.

insalati'era *sf* salad bowl.

insa'lubre *ag* unhealthy.

insa'nabile *ag* (*piaga*) which cannot be healed; (*situazione*) irremediable; (*odio*) implacable.

insangui'nare *vt* to stain with blood.

in'sania *sf* insanity.

in'sano, a *ag* (*pazzo, folle*) insane.

insapo'nare *vt* to soap; ~**rsi le mani** to soap one's hands.

insapo'nata *sf*: **dare un'~ a qc** to give sth a (quick) soaping.

insapo'rire *vt* to flavour (*BRIT*), flavor (*US*); (*con spezie*) to season; ~**rsi** *vr* to acquire flavo(u)r.

insa'poro, a *ag* tasteless, insipid.

insa'puta *sf*: **all'~ di qn** without sb knowing.

insazi'abile [insat'tsjabile] *ag* insatiable.

insca'tolare *vt* (*frutta, carne*) to can.

insce'nare [inʃe'nare] *vt* (*TEAT*) to stage, put on; (*fig*) to stage.

inscin'dibile [inʃin'dibile] *ag* (*fattori*) inseparable; (*legame*) indissoluble.

insec'chire [insek'kire] *vt* (*seccare*) to dry up; (: *piante*) to wither ♦ *vi* to dry up, become dry; to wither.

insedia'mento *sm* (*AMM: in carica, ufficio*) installation; (*villaggio, colonia*) settlement.

insedi'are *vt* (*AMM*) to install; ~**rsi** *vr* (*AMM*) to take up office; (*colonia, profughi etc*) to settle; (*MIL*) to take up positions.

in'segna [in'seɲɲa] *sf* sign; (*emblema*) sign, emblem; (*bandiera*) flag, banner; ~**e** *sfpl* (*decorazioni*) insignia *pl*.

insegna'mento [inseɲɲa'mento] *sm* teaching; **trarre ~ da un'esperienza** to learn from an experience, draw a lesson from an experience; **che ti serva da ~** let this be a lesson to you.

inse'gnante [inseɲ'ɲante] *ag* teaching ♦ *sm/f* teacher.

inse'gnare [inseɲ'ɲare] *vt, vi* to teach; ~ **a qn qc** to teach sb sth; ~ **a qn a fare qc** to teach sb (how) to do sth; **come lei ben m'insegna** ... (*ironico*) as you will doubtless be aware ....

insegui'mento *sm* pursuit, chase; **darsi all'~ di qn** to give chase to sb.

insegu'ire *vt* to pursue, chase.

insegui'tore, 'trice *sm/f* pursuer.

insel'lare *vt* to saddle.

inselvati'chire [inselvati'kire] *vt* (*persona*) to make unsociable ♦ *vi* (*anche:* ~**rsi**) to grow wild; (*persona*) to become unsociable.

inseminazi'one [inseminat'tsjone] *sf* insemination.

insena'tura *sf* inlet, creek.

insen'sato, a *ag* senseless, stupid.

insen'sibile *ag* (*anche fig*) insensitive.

insensibilità *sf* insensitivity, insensibility.

insepa'rabile *ag* inseparable.

inse'polto, a *ag* unburied.

inseri'mento *sm* (*gen*) insertion; **problemi di** ~ (*di persona*) adjustment problems.

inse'rire *vt* to insert; (*ELETTR*) to connect; (*allegare*) to enclose; ~**rsi** *vr* (*fig*): ~**rsi in** to become part of; ~ **un annuncio sul giornale** to put *o* place an advertisement in the newspaper.

in'serto *sm* (*pubblicazione*) insert; ~ **filmato** (*film*) clip.

inser'vibile *ag* useless.

inservi'ente *sm/f* attendant.

inserzi'one [inser'tsjone] *sf* insertion; (*avviso*) advertisement; **fare un'**~ **sul giornale** to put an advertisement in the newspaper.

inserzio'nista, i, e [insertsjo'nista] *sm/f* advertiser.

insetti'cida, i [insetti'tʃida] *sm* insecticide.

in'setto *sm* insect.

insicu'rezza [insiku'rettsa] *sf* insecurity.

insi'curo, a *ag* insecure.

in'sidia *sf* snare, trap; (*pericolo*) hidden danger; **tendere un'**~ **a qn** to lay *o* set a trap for sb.

insidi'are *vt* (*MIL*) to harass; ~ **la vita di qn** to make an attempt on sb's life.

insidi'oso, a *ag* insidious.

insi'eme *av* together; (*contemporaneamente*) at the same time ♦ *prep*: ~ **a** *o* **con** together with ♦ *sm* whole; (*MAT, servizio, assortimento*) set; (*MODA*) ensemble, outfit; **tutti** ~ all together; **tutto** ~ all together; (*in una volta*) at one go; **nell'**~ on the whole; **d'**~ (*veduta etc*) overall.

in'signe [in'siɲɲe] *ag* (*persona*) famous, distinguished, eminent; (*città, monumento*) notable.

insignifi'cante [insiɲɲifi'kante] *ag* insignificant.

insi'gnire [insiɲ'ɲire] *vt*: ~ **qn di** to honour (*BRIT*) *o* honor (*US*) sb with, decorate sb with.

insin'cero, a [insin'tʃero] *ag* insincere.

insinda'cabile *ag* unquestionable.

insinu'ante *ag* (*osservazione, sguardo*) insinuating; (*maniere*) ingratiating.

insinu'are *vt* (*introdurre*): ~ **qc in** to slip *o* slide sth into; (*fig*) to insinuate, imply; ~**rsi** *vr*: ~**rsi in** to seep into; (*fig*) to creep into; to worm one's way into.

insinuazi'one [insinuat'tsjone] *sf* (*fig*) insinuation.

in'sipido, a *ag* insipid.

insis'tente *ag* insistent; (*pioggia, dolore*) persistent.

insistente'mente *av* repeatedly.

insis'tenza [insis'tɛntsa] *sf* insistence; persistence.

in'sistere *vi*: ~ **su qc** to insist on sth; ~ **in qc/a fare** (*perseverare*) to persist in sth/in doing.

insis'tito, a *pp di* **insistere**.

'insito, a *ag*: ~ (**in**) inherent (in).

insoddis'fatto, a *ag* dissatisfied.

insoddisfazi'one [insoddisfat'tsjone] *sf* dissatisfaction.

insoffe'rente *ag* intolerant.

insoffe'renza [insoffe'rɛntsa] *sf* impatience.

insolazi'one [insolat'tsjone] *sf* (*MED*) sunstroke.

inso'lente *ag* insolent.

insolen'tire *vi* to grow insolent ♦ *vt* to insult, be rude to.

inso'lenza [inso'lɛntsa] *sf* insolence.

in'solito, a *ag* unusual, out of the ordinary.

inso'lubile *ag* insoluble.

inso'luto, a *ag* (*non risolto*) unsolved; (*non pagato*) unpaid, outstanding.

insol'vente *ag* (*DIR*) insolvent.

insol'venza [insol'vɛntsa] *sf* (*DIR*) insolvency.

insol'vibile *ag* insolvent.

in'somma *av* (*in breve, in conclusione*) in short; (*dunque*) well ♦ *escl* for heaven's sake!

inson'dabile *ag* unfathomable.

in'sonne *ag* sleepless.

in'sonnia *sf* insomnia, sleeplessness.

insonno'lito, a *ag* sleepy, drowsy.

insonorizzazi'one [insonoriddzat'tsjone] *sf* soundproofing.

insoppor'tabile *ag* unbearable.

insoppri'mibile *ag* insuppressible.

insor'genza [insor'dʒɛntsa] *sf* (*di malattia*) onset.

in'sorgere [in'sordʒere] *vi* (*ribellarsi*) to rise up, rebel; (*apparire*) to come up, arise.

insormon'tabile *ag* (*ostacolo*) insurmountable, insuperable.

in'sorsi *etc vb vedi* **insorgere**.

in'sorto, a *pp di* **insorgere** ♦ *sm/f* rebel, insurgent.

insospet'tabile *ag* (*al di sopra di ogni sospetto*) above suspicion; (*inatteso*) unsuspected.

insospet'tire *vt* to make suspicious ♦ *vi* (*anche*: ~**rsi**) to become suspicious.

insoste'nibile *ag* (*posizione, teoria*) untenable; (*dolore, situazione*) intolerable, unbearable; **le spese di manutenzione sono** ~**i** the maintenance costs are excessive.

insostitu'ibile *ag* (*persona*) irreplaceable; (*aiuto, presenza*) invaluable.

insoz'zare [insot'tsare] vt (pavimento) to make dirty; (fig: reputazione, memoria) to tarnish, sully; ~**rsi** vr to get dirty.

inspe'rabile ag: **la guarigione/salvezza era** ~ there was no hope of a cure/of rescue; **abbiamo ottenuto risultati** ~**i** the results we achieved were far better than we had hoped.

inspe'rato, a ag unhoped-for.

inspie'gabile ag inexplicable.

inspi'rare vt to breathe in, inhale.

in'stabile ag (carico, indole) unstable; (tempo) unsettled; (equilibrio) unsteady.

instabilità sf instability; (di tempo) changeability.

instal'lare vt to install; ~**rsi** vr (sistemarsi): ~**rsi in** to settle in.

installazi'one [installat'tsjone] sf installation.

instan'cabile ag untiring, indefatigable.

instau'rare vt to establish.

instaurazi'one [instaurat'tsjone] sf establishment.

instil'lare vt to instil.

instra'dare vt = **istradare**.

insù av up, upwards; **guardare all'**~ to look up o upwards; **naso all'**~ turned-up nose.

insubordinazi'one [insubordinat'tsjone] sf insubordination.

insuc'cesso [insut'tʃɛsso] sm failure, flop.

insudici'are [insudi'tʃare] vt to dirty; ~**rsi** vr to get dirty.

insuffici'ente [insuffi'tʃɛnte] ag insufficient; (compito, allievo) inadequate.

insuffici'enza [insuffi'tʃɛntsa] sf insufficiency; inadequacy; (INS) fail; ~ **di prove** (DIR) lack of evidence.

insu'lare ag insular.

insu'lina sf insulin.

in'sulso, a ag (sciocco) inane, silly; (persona) dull, insipid.

insul'tare vt to insult, affront.

in'sulto sm insult, affront.

insupe'rabile ag (ostacolo, difficoltà) insuperable, insurmountable; (eccellente: qualità, prodotto) unbeatable; (: persona, interpretazione) unequalled.

insuper'bire vt to make proud, make arrogant; ~**rsi** vr to become arrogant.

insurrezi'one [insurret'tsjone] sf revolt, insurrection.

insussis'tente ag non-existent.

intac'care vt (fare tacche) to cut into; (corrodere) to corrode; (fig: cominciare ad usare: risparmi) to break into; (: ledere) to damage.

intagli'are [intaʎ'ʎare] vt to carve.

intaglia'tore, 'trice [intaʎʎa'tore] sm/f engraver.

in'taglio [in'taʎʎo] sm carving.

intan'gibile [intan'dʒibile] ag (bene, patrimonio) untouchable; (fig: diritto) inviolable.

in'tanto av (nel frattempo) meanwhile, in the meantime; (per cominciare) just to begin with; ~ **che** cong while.

intarsi'are vt to inlay.

in'tarsio sm inlaying no pl, marquetry no pl; inlay.

intasa'mento sm (ostruzione) blockage, obstruction; (AUT: ingorgo) traffic jam.

inta'sare vt to choke (up), block (up); (AUT) to obstruct, block; ~**rsi** vr to become choked o blocked.

intas'care vt to pocket.

in'tatto, a ag intact; (puro) unsullied.

intavo'lare vt to start, enter into.

inte'gerrimo, a [inte'dʒɛrrimo] ag honest, upright.

inte'grale ag complete; (pane, farina) wholemeal (BRIT), wholewheat (US); **film in versione** ~ uncut version of a film; **calcolo** ~ (MAT) integral calculus; **edizione** ~ unabridged edition.

inte'grante ag: **parte** f ~ integral part.

inte'grare vt to complete; (MAT) to integrate; ~**rsi** vr (persona) to become integrated.

integra'tivo, a ag (assegno) supplementary; (INS): **esame** ~ assessment test sat when changing schools.

integra'tore sm: ~**i alimentari** nutritional supplements.

integrazi'one [integrat'tsjone] sf integration.

integrità sf integrity.

'integro, a ag (intatto, intero) complete, whole; (retto) upright.

intelaia'tura sf frame; (fig) structure, framework.

intel'letto sm intellect.

intellettu'ale ag, sm/f intellectual.

intellettua'loide (peg) ag pseudo-intellectual ♦ sm/f pseudo-intellectual, would-be intellectual.

intelli'gente [intelli'dʒɛnte] ag intelligent.

intelli'genza [intelli'dʒɛntsa] sf intelligence.

intelli'ghenzia [intelli'gɛntsja] sf intelligentsia.

intelli'gibile [intelli'dʒibile] ag intelligible.

inteme'rato, a ag (persona, vita) blameless, irreproachable; (coscienza) clear; (fama) unblemished.

intempe'rante ag intemperate,

immoderate.

intempe'ranza [intempe'rantsa] *sf* intemperance; **~e** *sfpl* (*eccessi*) excesses.

intem'perie *sfpl* bad weather *sg*.

intempes'tivo, a *ag* untimely.

inten'dente *sm*: **~ di Finanza** inland (*BRIT*) *o* internal (*US*) revenue officer.

inten'denza [inten'dɛntsa] *sf*: **~ di Finanza** inland (*BRIT*) *o* internal (*US*) revenue office.

in'tendere *vt* (*avere intenzione*): **~ fare qc** to intend *o* mean to do sth; (*comprendere*) to understand; (*udire*) to hear; (*significare*) to mean; **~rsi** *vr* (*conoscere*): **~rsi di** to know a lot about, be a connoisseur of; (*accordarsi*) to get on (well); **~rsi con qn su qc** to come to an agreement with sb about sth; **intendersela con qn** (*avere una relazione amorosa*) to have an affair with sb; **mi ha dato a ~ che** ... he led me to believe that ...; **non vuole ~ ragione** he won't listen to reason; **s'intende!** naturally!, of course!; **intendiamoci** let's get it quite clear; **ci siamo intesi?** is that clear?, is that understood?

intendi'mento *sm* (*intelligenza*) understanding; (*proposito*) intention.

intendi'tore, 'trice *sm/f* connoisseur, expert; **a buon intenditor poche parole** (*proverbio*) a word is enough to the wise.

intene'rire *vt* (*fig*) to move (to pity); **~rsi** *vr* (*fig*) to be moved.

intensifi'care *vt*, **~rsi** *vr* to intensify.

intensità *sf* intensity; (*del vento*) force, strength.

inten'sivo, a *ag* intensive.

in'tenso, a *ag* (*luce, profumo*) strong; (*colore*) intense, deep.

inten'tare *vt* (*DIR*): **~ causa contro qn** to start *o* institute proceedings against sb.

inten'tato, a *ag*: **non lasciare nulla d'~** to leave no stone unturned, try everything.

in'tento, a *ag* (*teso, assorto*): **~ (a)** intent (on), absorbed (in) ♦ *sm* aim, purpose; **fare qc con l'~ di** to do sth with the intention of; **riuscire nell'~** to achieve one's aim.

intenzio'nale [intentsjo'nale] *ag* intentional; (*DIR*: *omicidio*) premeditated; **fallo ~** (*SPORT*) deliberate foul.

intenzio'nato, a [intentsjo'nato] *ag*: **essere ~ a fare qc** to intend to do sth, have the intention of doing sth; **ben ~** well-meaning, well-intentioned; **mal ~** ill-intentioned.

intenzi'one [inten'tsjone] *sf* intention; (*DIR*) intent; **avere ~ di fare qc** to intend to do sth, have the intention of doing sth.

intera'gire [intera'dʒire] *vi* to interact.

intera'mente *av* entirely, completely.

interat'tivo, a *ag* interactive.

interazi'one [interat'tsjone] *sf* interaction.

interca'lare *sm* pet phrase, stock phrase ♦ *vt* to insert.

interca'pedine *sf* gap, cavity.

inter'cedere [inter'tʃɛdere] *vi* to intercede.

intercessi'one [intertʃes'sjone] *sf* intercession.

intercetta'mento [intertʃetta'mento] *sm* = **intercettazione**.

intercet'tare [intertʃet'tare] *vt* to intercept.

intercettazi'one [intertʃettat'tsjone] *sf*: **~ telefonica** telephone tapping.

intercity [inter'siti] *sm inv* (*FERR*) ≈ intercity (train).

intercon'nettere *vt* to interconnect.

inter'correre *vi* (*esserci*) to exist; (*passare: tempo*) to elapse.

inter'corso, a *pp di* **intercorrere**.

inter'detto, a *pp di* **interdire** ♦ *ag* forbidden, prohibited; (*sconcertato*) dumbfounded ♦ *sm* (*REL*) interdict; **rimanere ~** to be taken aback.

inter'dire *vt* to forbid, prohibit, ban; (*REL*) to interdict; (*DIR*) to deprive of civil rights.

interdizi'one [interdit'tsjone] *sf* prohibition, ban.

interessa'mento *sm* interest; (*intervento*) intervention, good offices *pl*.

interes'sante *ag* interesting; **essere in stato ~** to be expecting (a baby).

interes'sare *vt* to interest; (*concernere*) to concern, be of interest to; (*far intervenire*): **~ qn a** to draw sb's attention to ♦ *vi*: **~ a** to interest, matter to; **~rsi** *vr* (*mostrare interesse*): **~rsi a** to take an interest in, be interested in; (*occuparsi*): **~rsi di** to take care of; **precipitazioni che interessano le regioni settentrionali** rainfall affecting the north; **si è interessato di farmi avere quei biglietti** he took the trouble to get me those tickets.

interes'sato, a *ag* (*coinvolto*) interested, involved; (*peg*): **essere ~** to act out of pure self-interest ♦ *sm/f* (*coinvolto*) person concerned; **a tutti gli ~i** to all those concerned, to all interested parties.

inte'resse *sm* (*anche COMM*) interest; (*tornaconto*): **fare qc per ~** to do sth out of self-interest; **~ maturato** (*ECON*) accrued interest; **~ privato in atti di ufficio** (*AMM*) abuse of public office.

interes'senza [interes'sɛntsa] *sf* (*ECON*) profit-sharing.

inter'faccia, ce [inter'fattʃa] *sf* (*INFORM*) interface; **~ utente** user interface.

interfacci'are [interfat'tʃare] *vt* (*INFORM*) to interface.

interfe'renza [interfe'rɛntsa] *sf* interference.

interfe'rire *vi* to interfere.

inter'fono *sm* intercom; (*apparecchio*) internal phone.

interiezi'one [interjet'tsjone] *sf* exclamation, interjection.

'interim *sm inv* (*periodo*) interim, interval; **ministro ad** ~ acting *o* interim minister; (*incarico*) temporary appointment.

interi'ora *sfpl* entrails.

interi'ore *ag* inner *cpd*; **parte** *f* ~ inside.

interiorità *sf* inner being.

interioriz'zare [interjorid'dzare] *vt* to internalize.

inter'linea *sf* (*DATTILOGRAFIA*) spacing; (*TIP*) leading; **doppia** ~ double spacing.

interlocu'tore, 'trice *sm/f* speaker.

interlocu'torio, a *ag* interlocutory.

inter'ludio *sm* (*MUS*) interlude.

intermedi'ario, a *ag*, *sm/f* intermediary.

intermediazi'one [intermedjat'tsjone] *sf* mediation.

inter'medio, a *ag* intermediate.

inter'mezzo [inter'mɛddzo] *sm* (*intervallo*) interval; (*breve spettacolo*) intermezzo.

intermi'nabile *ag* interminable, endless.

intermit'tente *ag* intermittent.

intermit'tenza [intermit'tɛntsa] *sf*: **ad** ~ intermittent.

interna'mento *sm* internment; confinement (to a mental hospital).

inter'nare *vt* (*arrestare*) to intern; (*MED*) to confine to a mental hospital.

inter'nato, a *ag* interned; confined (to a mental hospital) ♦ *sm/f* internee; inmate (of a mental hospital) ♦ *sm* (*collegio*) boarding school; (*MED*) period as a houseman (*BRIT*) *o* an intern (*US*).

internazio'nale [internattsjo'nale] *ag* international.

'Internet ['internet] *sf* Internet; **in** ~ on the Internet.

inter'nista, i, e *sm/f* specialist in internal medicine.

in'terno, a *ag* (*di dentro*) internal, interior, inner; (: *mare*) inland; (*nazionale*) domestic; (*allievo*) boarding ♦ *sm* inside, interior; (*di paese*) interior; (*fodera*) lining; (*di appartamento*) flat (*BRIT*) *o* apartment (*US*) (number); (*TEL*) extension ♦ *sm/f* (*INS*) boarder; ~**i** *smpl* (*CINE*) interior shots; **commissione** ~**a** (*INS*) internal examination board; **"per uso** ~**"** (*MED*) "to be taken internally"; **all'**~ inside; **Ministero degli I**~**i** Ministry of the Interior, ≈ Home Office (*BRIT*), ≈ Department of the Interior (*US*); **notizie dall'**~ (*STAMPA*) home news.

in'tero, a *ag* (*integro, intatto*) whole, entire; (*completo, totale*) complete; (*numero*) whole; (*non ridotto: biglietto*) full.

interpel'lanza [interpel'lantsa] *sf*: **presentare un'**~ (*POL*) to ask a (parliamentary) question; ~ **parlamentare** interpellation.

interpel'lare *vt* to consult; (*POL*) to question.

INTER'POL *sigla f* (= *International Criminal Police Organization*) INTERPOL.

inter'porre *vt* (*ostacolo*): ~ **qc a qc** to put sth in the way of sth; (*influenza*) to use; **interporsi** *vr* to intervene; ~ **appello** (*DIR*) to appeal; **interporsi fra** (*mettersi in mezzo*) to come between.

inter'posto, a *pp di* **interporre**.

interpre'tare *vt* (*spiegare, tradurre*) to interpret; (*MUS, TEAT*) to perform; (*personaggio, sonata*) to play; (*canzone*) to sing.

interpretari'ato *sm* interpreting.

interpretazi'one [interpretat'tsjone] *sf* interpretation.

in'terprete *sm/f* interpreter; (*TEAT*) actor/actress, performer; (*MUS*) performer; **farsi** ~ **di** to act as a spokesman for.

interpunzi'one [interpun'tsjone] *sf* punctuation; **segni di** ~ punctuation marks.

inter'rare *vt* (*seme, pianta*) to plant; (*tubature etc*) to lay underground; (*MIL*: *pezzo d'artiglieria*) to dig in; (*riempire di terra*: *canale*) to fill in.

interregio'nale [interredʒo'nale] *sm* train that travels between two or more regions of Italy.

interro'gare *vt* to question; (*INS*) to test.

interroga'tivo, a *ag* (*occhi, sguardo*) questioning, inquiring; (*LING*) interrogative ♦ *sm* question; (*fig*) mystery.

interroga'torio, a *ag* interrogatory, questioning ♦ *sm* (*DIR*) questioning *no pl*.

interrogazi'one [interrogat'tsjone] *sf* questioning *no pl*; (*INS*) oral test; (*POL*): ~ **(parlamentare)** question.

inter'rompere *vt* to interrupt; (*studi, trattative*) to break off, interrupt; ~**rsi** *vr* to break off, stop.

inter'rotto, a *pp di* **interrompere**.

interrut'tore *sm* switch.

interruzi'one [interrut'tsjone] *sf* (*vedi interrompere*) interruption; break; ~ **di gravidanza** termination of pregnancy.

interse'care *vt*, ~**rsi** *vr* to intersect.

inter'stizio [inter'stittsjo] *sm* interstice,

crack.

interur'bano, a *ag* inter-city; (*TEL: chiamata*) trunk *cpd* (*BRIT*), long-distance; (*: telefono*) long-distance ♦ *sf* trunk call (*BRIT*), long-distance call.

inter'vallo *sm* interval; (*spazio*) space, gap; ~ **pubblicitario** (*TV*) commercial break.

interve'nire *vi* (*partecipare*): ~ **a** to take part in; (*intromettersi: anche POL*) to intervene; (*MED: operare*) to operate.

interven'tista, i, e *ag, sm/f* interventionist.

inter'vento *sm* participation; (*intromissione*) intervention; (*MED*) operation; (*breve discorso*) speech; **fare un** ~ **nel corso di** (*dibattito, programma*) to take part in.

interve'nuto, a *pp di* **intervenire** ♦ *sm*: **gli ~i** those present.

inter'vista *sf* interview.

intervis'tare *vt* to interview.

intervista'tore, 'trice *sm/f* interviewer.

in'teso, a *pp di* **intendere** ♦ *ag* agreed ♦ *sf* understanding; (*accordo*) agreement, understanding; **resta** ~ **che** ... it is understood that ...; **non darsi per** ~ **di qc** to take no notice of sth; **uno sguardo d'~a** a knowing look.

in'tessere *vt* to weave together; (*fig: trama, storia*) to weave.

intes'tare *vt* (*lettera*) to address; (*proprietà*): ~ **a** to register in the name of; ~ **un assegno a qn** to make out a cheque to sb.

intesta'tario, a *sm/f* holder.

intestato, a *ag* (*proprietà, casa, conto*) in the name of; (*assegno*) made out to; **carta ~a** headed paper.

intestazi'one [intestat'tsjone] *sf* heading; (*su carta da lettere*) letterhead; (*registrazione*) registration.

intesti'nale *ag* intestinal.

intes'tino, a *ag* (*lotte*) internal, civil ♦ *sm* (*ANAT*) intestine.

intiepi'dire *vt* (*riscaldare*) to warm (up); (*raffreddare*) to cool (down); (*fig: amicizia etc*) to cool; **~rsi** *vr* to warm (up); to cool (down); to cool.

Inti'fada *sf* Intifada.

intima'mente *av* intimately; **sono ~ convinto che** ... I'm firmly *o* deeply convinced that ...; **i due fatti sono ~ connessi** the two events are closely connected.

inti'mare *vt* to order, command; ~ **la resa a qn** (*MIL*) to call upon sb to surrender.

intimazi'one [intimat'tsjone] *sf* order, command.

intimida'torio, a *ag* threatening.

intimidazi'one [intimidat'tsjone] *sf* intimidation.

intimi'dire *vt* to intimidate ♦ *vi* (*anche: ~rsi*) to grow shy.

intimità *sf* intimacy; privacy; (*familiarità*) familiarity.

'intimo, a *ag* intimate; (*affetti, vita*) private; (*fig: profondo*) inmost ♦ *sm* (*persona*) intimate *o* close friend; (*dell'animo*) bottom, depths *pl*; **parti ~e** (*ANAT*) private parts; **rapporti ~i** (*sessuali*) intimate relations.

intimo'rire *vt* to frighten; **~rsi** *vr* to become frightened.

in'tingere [in'tindʒere] *vt* to dip.

in'tingolo *sm* sauce; (*pietanza*) stew.

in'tinto, a *pp di* **intingere**.

intiriz'zire [intirid'dzire] *vt* to numb ♦ *vi* (*anche: ~rsi*) to go numb.

intiriz'zito, a [intirid'dzito] *ag* numb (with cold).

intito'lare *vt* to give a title to; (*dedicare*) to dedicate; **~rsi** *vr* (*libro, film*) to be called.

intolle'rabile *ag* intolerable.

intolle'rante *ag* intolerant.

intolle'ranza [intolle'rantsa] *sf* intolerance.

intona'care *vt* to plaster.

in'tonaco, ci *o* **chi** *sm* plaster.

into'nare *vt* (*canto*) to start to sing; (*armonizzare*) to match; **~rsi** *vr* (*colori*) to go together; **~rsi a** (*carnagione*) to suit; (*abito*) to go with, match.

intonazi'one [intonat'tsjone] *sf* intonation.

inton'tire *vt* to stun, daze ♦ *vi*, **~rsi** *vr* to be stunned *o* dazed.

inton'tito, a *ag* stunned, dazed; ~ **dal sonno** stupid with sleep.

in'toppo *sm* stumbling block, obstacle.

intorbi'dire *vt* (*liquido*) to make turbid; (*mente*) to cloud; ~ **le acque** (*fig*) to muddy the waters.

in'torno *av* around; ~ **a** *prep* (*attorno a*) around; (*riguardo, circa*) about.

intorpi'dire *vt* to numb; (*fig*) to make sluggish ♦ *vi* (*anche: ~rsi*) to grow numb; (*fig*) to become sluggish.

intossi'care *vt* to poison.

intossicazi'one [intossikat'tsjone] *sf* poisoning.

intradu'cibile [intradu'tʃibile] *ag* untranslatable.

intralci'are [intral'tʃare] *vt* to hamper, hold up.

in'tralcio [in'traltʃo] *sm* hitch.

intrallaz'zare [intrallat'tsare] *vi* to intrigue, scheme.

intral'lazzo [intral'lattso] *sm* (*POL*) intrigue, manoeuvre (*BRIT*), maneuver (*US*); (*traffico losco*) racket.

intramon'tabile *ag* timeless.

intramusco'lare *ag* intramuscular.
'Intranet ['intranet] *sf* intranet.
intransi'gente [intransi'dʒɛnte] *ag* intransigent, uncompromising.
intransi'genza [intransi'dʒɛntsa] *sf* intransigence.
intransi'tivo, a *ag, sm* intransitive.
intrappo'lare *vt* to trap; **rimanere intrappolato** to be trapped; **farsi** ~ to get caught.
intrapren'dente *ag* enterprising, go-ahead; (*con le donne*) forward, bold.
intrapren'denza [intrapren'dɛntsa] *sf* audacity, initiative; (*con le donne*) boldness.
intra'prendere *vt* to undertake; (*carriera*) to embark (up)on.
intra'preso, a *pp di* **intraprendere.**
intrat'tabile *ag* intractable.
intratte'nere *vt* (*divertire*) to entertain; (*chiacchierando*) to engage in conversation; (*rapporti*) to have, maintain; ~**rsi** *vr* to linger; ~**rsi su qc** to dwell on sth.
intratteni'mento *sm* entertainment.
intrave'dere *vt* to catch a glimpse of; (*fig*) to foresee.
intrecci'are [intret't∫are] *vt* (*capelli*) to plait, braid; (*intessere: anche fig*) to weave, interweave, intertwine; ~**rsi** *vr* to intertwine, become interwoven; ~ **le mani** to clasp one's hands; ~ **una relazione amorosa** (*fig*) to begin an affair.
in'treccio [in'trett∫o] *sm* (*fig: trama*) plot, story.
in'trepido, a *ag* fearless, intrepid.
intri'care *vt* (*fili*) to tangle; (*fig: faccenda*) to complicate; ~**rsi** *vr* to become tangled; to become complicated.
in'trico, chi *sm* (*anche fig*) tangle.
intri'gante *ag* scheming ♦ *sm/f* schemer, intriguer.
intri'gare *vi* to manoeuvre (*BRIT*), maneuver (*US*), scheme.
in'trigo, ghi *sm* plot, intrigue.
in'trinseco, a, ci, che *ag* intrinsic.
in'triso, a *ag*: ~ (**di**) soaked (in).
intris'tire *vi* (*persona: diventare triste*) to grow sad; (*pianta*) to wilt.
intro'dotto, a *pp di* **introdurre.**
intro'durre *vt* to introduce; (*chiave etc*): ~ **qc in** to insert sth into; (*persona: far entrare*) to show in; **introdursi** *vr* (*moda, tecniche*) to be introduced; **introdursi in** (*persona: penetrare*) to enter; (: *entrare furtivamente*) to steal o slip into.
in'troito *sm* income, revenue.
intro'messo, a *pp di* **intromettersi.**

intro'mettersi *vr* to interfere, meddle; (*interporsi*) to intervene.
intromissi'one *sf* interference, meddling; intervention.
introspezi'one [introspet'tsjone] *sf* introspection.
intro'vabile *ag* (*persona, oggetto*) who (*o* which) cannot be found; (*libro etc*) unobtainable.
intro'verso, a *ag* introverted ♦ *sm/f* introvert.
intrufo'larsi *vr*: ~ (**in**) (*stanza*) to sneak in(to), slip in(to); (*conversazione*) to butt in (on).
in'truglio [in'truʎʎo] *sm* concoction.
intrusi'one *sf* intrusion; interference.
in'truso, a *sm/f* intruder.
intu'ire *vt* to perceive by intuition; (*rendersi conto*) to realize.
in'tuito *sm* intuition; (*perspicacia*) perspicacity.
intuizi'one [intuit'tsjone] *sf* intuition.
inturgi'dire [inturdʒi'dire] *vi*, ~**rsi** *vr* to swell.
inumanità *sf inv* inhumanity.
inu'mano, a *ag* inhuman.
inu'mare *vt* (*seppellire*) to bury, inter.
inumazi'one [inumat'tsjone] *sf* burial, interment.
inumi'dire *vt* to dampen, moisten; ~**rsi** *vr* to become damp *o* wet.
inurba'mento *sm* urbanization.
inusi'tato, a *ag* unusual.
i'nutile *ag* useless; (*superfluo*) pointless, unnecessary; **è stato tutto** ~! it was all in vain!
inutilità *sf* uselessness; pointlessness.
inutiliz'zabile [inutilid'dzabile] *ag* unusable.
inutil'mente *av* (*senza risultato*) fruitlessly; (*senza utilità, scopo*) unnecessarily, needlessly; **l'ho cercato** ~ I looked for him in vain; **ti preoccupi** ~ there's nothing for you to worry about, there's no need for you to worry.
inva'dente *ag* (*fig*) intrusive.
inva'denza [inva'dɛntsa] *sf* intrusiveness.
in'vadere *vt* to invade; (*affollare*) to swarm into, overrun; (*sog: acque*) to flood.
invadi'trice [invadi'trit∫e] *ag f vedi* **invasore.**
inva'ghirsi [inva'girsi] *vr*: ~ **di** to take a fancy to.
invali'cabile *ag* (*montagna*) impassable.
invali'dare *vt* to invalidate.
invalidità *sf* infirmity; disability; (*DIR*) invalidity.
in'valido, a *ag* (*infermo*) infirm; (*al lavoro*) disabled; (*DIR: nullo*) invalid ♦ *sm/f* invalid; disabled person; ~ **di guerra** disabled ex-

serviceman; ~ **del lavoro** industrially
disabled person.

in'valso, a *ag* (*diffuso*) established.

in'vano *av* in vain.

invari'abile *ag* invariable.

invari'ato, a *ag* unchanged.

inva'sare *vt* (*pianta*) to pot.

inva'sato, a *ag* possessed (by the devil)
♦ *sm/f* person possessed by the devil;
urlare come un ~ to shout like a madman.

invasi'one *sf* invasion.

in'vaso, a *pp di* **invadere.**

inva'sore, invadi'trice [invadi'tritʃe] *ag*
invading ♦ *sm* invader.

invecchia'mento [invekkja'mento] *sm*
growing old; ageing; **questo whisky ha un**
~ **di 12 anni** this whisky has been
matured for 12 years.

invecchi'are [invek'kjare] *vi* (*persona*) to
grow old; (*vino, popolazione*) to age;
(*moda*) to become dated ♦ *vt* to age; (*far
apparire più vecchio*) to make look older; **lo
trovo invecchiato** I find he has aged.

in'vece [in'vetʃe] *av* instead; (*al contrario*)
on the contrary; ~ **di** *prep* instead of.

inve'ire *vi*: ~ **contro** to rail against.

invele'nire *vt* to embitter; ~**rsi** *vr* to
become bitter.

inven'duto, a *ag* unsold.

inven'tare *vt* to invent; (*pericoli,
pettegolezzi*) to make up, invent.

inventari'are *vt* to make an inventory of,
inventory.

inven'tario *sm* inventory; (*COMM*)
stocktaking *no pl*.

inven'tivo, a *ag* inventive ♦ *sf*
inventiveness.

inven'tore, 'trice *sm/f* inventor.

invenzi'one [inven'tsjone] *sf* invention;
(*bugia*) lie, story.

invere'condia *sf* shamelessness,
immodesty.

inver'nale *ag* winter *cpd*; (*simile all'inverno*)
wintry.

in'verno *sm* winter; **d'**~ in (the) winter.

invero'simile *ag* unlikely ♦ *sm*: **ha dell'**~
it's hard to believe, it's incredible.

inversi'one *sf* inversion; **"divieto d'**~**"**
(*AUT*) "no U-turns".

in'verso, a *ag* opposite; (*MAT*) inverse ♦ *sm*
contrary, opposite; **in senso** ~ in the
opposite direction; **in ordine** ~ in reverse
order.

inverte'brato, a *ag, sm* invertebrate.

inver'tire *vt* to invert; (*disposizione, posti*)
to change; (*ruoli*) to exchange; ~ **la marcia**
(*AUT*) to do a U-turn; ~ **la rotta** (*NAUT*) to
go about; (*fig*) to do a U-turn.

inver'tito, a *sm/f* homosexual.

investi'gare *vt, vi* to investigate.

investiga'tivo, a *ag*: **squadra** ~**a** detective
squad.

investiga'tore, 'trice *sm/f* investigator,
detective.

investigazi'one [investigat'tsjone] *sf*
investigation, inquiry.

investi'mento *sm* (*ECON*) investment; (*di
veicolo*) crash, collision; (*di pedone*)
knocking down.

inves'tire *vt* (*denaro*) to invest; (*sog:
veicolo: pedone*) to knock down; (*: altro
veicolo*) to crash into; (*apostrofare*) to
assail; (*incaricare*): ~ **qn di** to invest sb
with; ~**rsi** *vr* (*fig*): ~**rsi di una parte** to
enter thoroughly into a role.

investi'tore, 'trice *sm/f* driver responsible
for an accident.

investi'tura *sf* investiture.

invete'rato, a *ag* inveterate.

invet'tiva *sf* invective.

invi'are *vt* to send.

invi'ato, a *sm/f* envoy; (*STAMPA*)
correspondent.

in'vidia *sf* envy; **fare** ~ **a qn** to make sb
envious.

invidi'abile *ag* enviable.

invidi'are *vt*: ~ **qn (per qc)** to envy sb (for
sth); ~ **qc a qn** to envy sb sth; **non aver
nulla da** ~ **a nessuno** to be as good as the
next one.

invidi'oso, a *ag* envious.

invin'cibile [invin'tʃibile] *ag* invincible.

in'vio, 'vii *sm* sending; (*insieme di merci*)
consignment; (*tasto*) Return (key), Enter
(key).

invio'labile *ag* inviolable.

invio'lato, a *ag* (*diritto, segreto*) inviolate;
(*foresta*) virgin *cpd*; (*montagna, vetta*)
unscaled.

invipe'rire *vi*, ~**rsi** *vr* to become furious,
fly into a temper.

invipe'rito, a *ag* furious.

invis'chiare [invis'kjare] *vt* (*fig*): ~ **qn in qc**
to involve sb in sth, mix sb up in sth; ~**rsi**
vr: ~**rsi (con qn/in qc)** to get mixed up *o*
involved (with sb/in sth).

invi'sibile *ag* invisible.

in'viso, a *ag*: ~ **a** unpopular with.

invi'tante *ag* (*proposta, odorino*) inviting;
(*sorriso*) appealing, attractive.

invi'tare *vt* to invite; ~ **qn a fare** to invite
sb to do.

invi'tato, a *sm/f* guest.

in'vito *sm* invitation; **dietro** ~ **del sig. Rossi**
at Mr Rossi's invitation.

invo'care *vt* (*chiedere: aiuto, pace*) to cry

out for; (*appellarsi: la legge, Dio*) to appeal to, invoke.

invogli'are [invoʎ'ʎare] *vt:* ~ **qn a fare to** tempt sb to do, induce sb to do.

involon'tario, a *ag* (*errore*) unintentional; (*gesto*) involuntary.

invol'tino *sm* (*CUC*) roulade.

in'volto *sm* (*pacco*) parcel; (*fagotto*) bundle.

in'volucro *sm* cover, wrapping.

involu'tivo, a *ag:* **subire un processo** ~ **to** regress.

invo'luto, a *ag* involved, intricate.

involuzi'one [involut'tsjone] *sf* (*di stile*) convolutedness; (*regresso*): **subire un'**~ **to** regress.

invulne'rabile *ag* invulnerable.

inzacche'rare [intsakke'rare] *vt* to spatter with mud; ~**rsi** *vr* to get muddy.

inzup'pare [intsup'pare] *vt* to soak; ~**rsi** *vr* to get soaked; **inzuppò i biscotti nel latte** he dipped the biscuits in the milk.

'io *pron* I ♦ *sm inv:* **l'**~ **the** ego, the self; ~ **stesso(a)** I myself; **sono** ~ it's me.

i'odio *sm* iodine.

i'ogurt *sm inv* = **yoghurt.**

i'one *sm* ion.

l'onio *sm:* **lo** ~, **il mar** ~ the Ionian (Sea).

ionizza'tore [joniddza'tore] *sm* ioniser.

'iosa: a ~ *av* in abundance.

'IPAB *sigla fpl* (= *Istituzioni pubbliche di Assistenza e Beneficenza*) *charitable institutions.*

i'perbole *sf* (*LETTERATURA*) hyperbole; (*MAT*) hyperbola.

iper'bolico, a, ci, che *ag* (*LETTERATURA*, *MAT*) hyperbolic(al); (*fig: esagerato*) exaggerated.

ipermer'cato *sm* hypermarket.

ipersen'sibile *ag* (*persona*) hypersensitive; (*FOT: lastra, pellicola*) hypersensitized.

ipertecno'logico, a, ci, che [ipertekno'lɔdʒiko] *ag* hi-tech.

ipertensi'one *sf* high blood pressure, hypertension.

iper'testo *sm* hypertext.

ip'nosi *sf* hypnosis.

ip'notico, a, ci, che *ag* hypnotic.

ipno'tismo *sm* hypnotism.

ipnotiz'zare [ipnotid'dzare] *vt* to hypnotize.

ipoaller'genico, a, ci, che [ipoaller'dʒɛniko] *ag* hypoallergenic.

ipocon'dria *sf* hypochondria.

ipocon'driaco, a, ci, che *ag, sm/f* hypochondriac.

ipocri'sia *sf* hypocrisy.

i'pocrita, i, e *ag* hypocritical ♦ *sm/f* hypocrite.

ipo'sodico, a, ci, che *ag* low sodium *cpd.*

ipo'teca, che *sf* mortgage.

ipote'care *vt* to mortgage.

ipote'nusa *sf* hypotenuse.

i'potesi *sf inv* hypothesis; **facciamo l'**~ **che** ..., **ammettiamo per** ~ **che** ... let's suppose *o* assume that ...; **nella peggiore/migliore delle** ~**i** at worst/best; **nell'**~ **che venga** should he come, if he comes; **se per** ~ **io partissi** ... just supposing I were to leave ....

ipo'tetico, a, ci, che *ag* hypothetical.

ipotiz'zare [ipotid'dzare] *vt:* ~ **che to** form the hypothesis that.

'ippico, a, ci, che *ag* horse *cpd* ♦ *sf* horse-racing.

ippocas'tano *sm* horse chestnut.

ip'podromo *sm* racecourse.

ippo'potamo *sm* hippopotamus.

'ipsilon *sf o m inv* (*lettera*) Y, y; (: *dell'alfabeto greco*) epsilon.

IP'SOA *sigla m* (= *Istituto Post-Universitario per lo Studio dell'Organizzazione Aziendale*) *postgraduate institute of business administration.*

IR *abbr* (*FERR*) = **interregionale.**

IRA *sigla f* (= *Irish Republican Army*) IRA.

'ira *sf* anger, wrath.

ira'cheno, a [ira'kɛno] *ag, sm/f* Iraqi.

l'ran *sm:* **l'**~ Iran.

irani'ano, a *ag, sm/f* Iranian.

l'raq *sm:* **l'**~ Iraq.

iras'cibile [iraʃ'ʃibile] *ag* quick-tempered.

'IRCE ['irtʃe] *sigla m* = *Istituto per le relazioni culturali con l'Estero.*

'IRI *sigla m* (= *Istituto per la Ricostruzione Industriale*) *state-controlled industrial investment office.*

'iride *sf* (*arcobaleno*) rainbow; (*ANAT, BOT*) iris.

'iris *sf inv* iris.

Ir'landa *sf:* **l'**~ Ireland; **l'**~ **del Nord** Northern Ireland, Ulster; **la Repubblica d'**~ Eire, the Republic of Ireland; **il mar d'**~ the Irish Sea.

irlan'dese *ag* Irish ♦ *sm/f* Irishman/woman; **gli l**~**i** the Irish.

iro'nia *sf* irony.

i'ronico, a, ci, che *ag* ironic(al).

ironiz'zare [ironid'dzare] *vt, vi:* ~ **su to** be ironical about.

i'roso, a *ag* (*sguardo, tono*) angry, wrathful; (*persona*) irascible.

'IRPEF *sigla f vedi* **imposta sul reddito delle persone fisiche.**

ir'pino, a *ag* of (*o* from) Irpinia.

irradi'are *vt* to radiate; (*sog: raggi di luce: illuminare*) to shine on ♦ *vi* (*diffondersi:*

anche: ~**rsi**) to radiate.
irradiazi'one [irradjat'tsjone] *sf* radiation.
irraggiun'gibile [irraddʒun'dʒibile] *ag* unreachable; (*fig: meta*) unattainable.
irragio'nevole [irradʒo'nevole] *ag* (*privo di ragione*) irrational; (*fig: persona, pretese, prezzo*) unreasonable.
irrazio'nale [irrattsjo'nale] *ag* irrational.
irre'ale *ag* unreal.
irrealiz'zabile [irrealid'dzabile] *ag* (*sogno, desiderio*) unattainable, unrealizable; (*progetto*) unworkable, impracticable.
irrealtà *sf* unreality.
irrecupe'rabile *ag* (*gen*) irretrievable; (*fig: persona*) irredeemable.
irrecu'sabile *ag* (*offerta*) not to be refused; (*prova*) irrefutable.
irreden'tista, i, e *ag, smf* (*STORIA*) Irredentist.
irrefre'nabile *ag* uncontrollable.
irrefu'tabile *ag* irrefutable.
irrego'lare *ag* irregular; (*terreno*) uneven.
irregolarità *sf inv* irregularity; unevenness *no pl.*
irremo'vibile *ag* (*fig*) unshakeable, unyielding.
irrepa'rabile *ag* irreparable; (*fig*) inevitable.
irrepe'ribile *ag* nowhere to be found.
irrepren'sibile *ag* irreproachable.
irrequi'eto, a *ag* restless.
irresis'tibile *ag* irresistible.
irreso'luto, a *ag* irresolute.
irrespi'rabile *ag* (*aria*) unbreathable; (*fig: opprimente*) stifling, oppressive; (*: malsano*) unhealthy.
irrespon'sabile *ag* irresponsible.
irrestrin'gibile [irrestrin'dʒibile] *ag* unshrinkable, non-shrink (*BRIT*).
irre'tire *vt* to seduce.
irrever'sibile *ag* irreversible.
irrevo'cabile *ag* irrevocable.
irricono'scibile [irrikonoʃ'ʃibile] *ag* unrecognizable.
irridu'cibile [irridu'tʃibile] *ag* irreducible; (*fig*) unshakeable.
irrifles'sivo, a *ag* thoughtless.
irri'gare *vt* (*annaffiare*) to irrigate; (*sog: fiume etc*) to flow through.
irrigazi'one [irrigat'tsjone] *sf* irrigation.
irrigidi'mento [irridʒidi'mento] *sm* stiffening; hardening; tightening.
irrigi'dire [irridʒi'dire] *vt* to stiffen; (*disciplina*) to tighten; ~**rsi** *vr* to stiffen; (*posizione, atteggiamento*) to harden.
irriguar'doso, a *ag* disrespectful.
irrile'vante *ag* (*trascurabile*) insignificant.
irrimedi'abile *ag*: **un errore** ~ a mistake

which cannot be rectified; **non è** ~! we can do something about it!
irrinunci'abile [irrinun'tʃabile] *ag* vital; which cannot be abandoned.
irripe'tibile *ag* unrepeatable.
irri'solto, a *ag* (*problema*) unresolved.
irri'sorio, a *ag* derisory.
irrispet'toso, a *ag* disrespectful.
irri'tabile *ag* irritable.
irri'tante *ag* (*atteggiamento*) irritating, annoying; (*MED*) irritant.
irri'tare *vt* (*mettere di malumore*) to irritate, annoy; (*MED*) to irritate; ~**rsi** *vr* (*stizzirsi*) to become irritated *o* annoyed; (*MED*) to become irritated.
irritazi'one [irritat'tsjone] *sf* irritation; annoyance.
irrive'rente *ag* irreverent.
irrobus'tire *vt* (*persona*) to make stronger, make more robust; (*muscoli*) to strengthen; ~**rsi** *vr* to become stronger.
ir'rompere *vi*: ~ **in** to burst into.
irro'rare *vt* to sprinkle; (*AGR*) to spray.
ir'rotto, a *pp di* **irrompere**.
irru'ente *ag* (*fig*) impetuous, violent.
irru'enza [irru'ɛntsa] *sf* impetuousness; **con** ~ impetuously.
ir'ruppi *etc vb vedi* **irrompere**.
irruvi'dire *vt* to roughen ♦ *vi* (*anche:* ~**rsi**) to become rough.
irruzi'one [irrut'tsjone] *sf*: **fare** ~ **in** to burst into; (*sog: polizia*) to raid.
ir'suto, a *ag* (*petto*) hairy; (*barba*) bristly.
'irto, a *ag* bristly; ~ **di** bristling with. .
ls. *abbr* (= *isola*) I.
ISBN *abbr* (= *International Standard Book Number*) ISBN.
is'crissi *etc vb vedi* **iscrivere**.
is'critto, a *pp di* **iscrivere** ♦ *smf* member; **gli** ~**i alla gara** the competitors; **per** *o* **in** ~ in writing.
is'crivere *vt* to register, enter; (*persona*): ~ **(a)** to register (in), enrol (in); ~**rsi** *vr*: ~**rsi (a)** (*club, partito*) to join; (*università*) to register *o* enrol (at); (*esame, concorso*) to register *o* enter (for).
iscrizi'one [iskrit'tsjone] *sf* (*epigrafe etc*) inscription; (*a scuola, società etc*) enrolment; registration.
'ISEF *sigla m* = *Istituto Superiore di Educazione Fisica.*
ls'lam *sm*: **l'**~ Islam.
is'lamico, a, ci, che *ag* Islamic.
ls'landa *sf*: **l'**~ Iceland.
islan'dese *ag* Icelandic ♦ *smf* Icelander ♦ *sm* (*LING*) Icelandic.
'isola *sf* island; ~ **pedonale** (*AUT*) pedestrian precinct.

isolamento – itinerante

isola'mento *sm* isolation; (*TECN*) insulation; **essere in cella di** ~ to be in solitary confinement; ~ **acustico** soundproofing; ~ **termico** thermal insulation.

iso'lano, a *ag* island *cpd* ♦ *sm/f* islander.

iso'lante *ag* insulating ♦ *sm* insulator.

iso'lare *vt* to isolate; (*TECN*) to insulate; (*: acusticamente*) to soundproof.

iso'lato, a *ag* isolated; insulated ♦ *sm* (*edificio*) block.

isolazio'nismo [izolattsjo'nismo] *sm* isolationism.

i'sotopo *sm* isotope.

ispessi'mento *sm* thickening.

ispes'sire *vt* to thicken; ~**rsi** *vr* to get thicker, thicken.

ispetto'rato *sm* inspectorate.

ispet'tore, 'trice *sm/f* inspector; (*COMM*) supervisor; ~ **di zona** (*COMM*) area supervisor *o* manager; ~ **di reparto** shop walker (*BRIT*), floor walker (*US*).

ispezio'nare [ispettsjo'nare] *vt* to inspect.

ispezi'one [ispet'tsjone] *sf* inspection.

'ispido, a *ag* bristly, shaggy.

ispi'rare *vt* to inspire; ~**rsi** *vr*: ~**rsi a** to draw one's inspiration from; (*conformarsi*) to be based on; **l'idea m'ispira** the idea appeals to me.

ispira'tore, 'trice *ag* inspiring ♦ *sm/f* inspirer; (*di ribellione*) instigator.

ispirazi'one [ispirat'tsjone] *sf* inspiration; **secondo l'~ del momento** according to the mood of the moment.

israeli'ano, a *ag*, *sm/f* Israeli.

israe'lita, i, e *sm/f* Jew/Jewess; (*STORIA*) Israelite.

israe'litico, a, ci, che *ag* Jewish.

is'sare *vt* to hoist; ~ **l'ancora** to weigh anchor.

'Istanbul *sf* Istanbul.

istan'taneo, a *ag* instantaneous ♦ *sf* (*FOT*) snapshot.

is'tante *sm* instant, moment; **all'~, sull'~** instantly, immediately.

is'tanza [is'tantsa] *sf* petition, request; **giudice di prima** ~ (*DIR*) judge of the court of first instance; **giudizio di seconda** ~ judgment on appeal; **in ultima** ~ (*fig*) finally; ~ **di divorzio** petition for divorce.

'ISTAT *sigla m* = *Istituto Centrale di Statistica*.

'ISTEL *sigla f* = *Indagine sull'ascolto delle televisioni in Italia*.

is'terico, a, ci, che *ag* hysterical.

isteri'lire *vt* (*terreno*) to render infertile; (*fig: fantasia*) to dry up; ~**rsi** *vr* to become infertile; to dry up.

iste'rismo *sm* hysteria.

isti'gare *vt* to incite.

istigazi'one [istigat'tsjone] *sf* instigation; ~ **a delinquere** (*DIR*) incitement to crime.

istin'tivo, a *ag* instinctive.

is'tinto *sm* instinct.

istitu'ire *vt* (*fondare*) to institute, found; (*porre: confronto*) to establish; (*intraprendere: inchiesta*) to set up.

isti'tuto *sm* institute; (*di università*) department; (*ente, DIR*) institution; ~ **di bellezza** beauty salon; ~ **di credito** bank, banking institution; ~ **tecnico commerciale** ≈ commercial college; ~ **tecnico industriale statale** ≈ technical college.

istitu'tore, 'trice *sm/f* (*fondatore*) founder; (*precettore*) tutor/governess.

istituzi'one [istitut'tsjone] *sf* institution; ~**i** *sfpl* (*DIR*) institutes; **lotta alle** ~**i** struggle against the Establishment.

'istmo *sm* (*GEO*) isthmus.

isto'gramma, i *sm* histogram.

istra'dare *vt* (*fig: persona*): ~ **(a/verso)** to direct (to/towards).

istri'ano, a *ag*, *sm/f* Istrian.

'istrice ['istrit∫e] *sm* porcupine.

istri'one *sm* (*peg*) ham (actor).

istru'ire *vt* (*insegnare*) to teach; (*ammaestrare*) to train; (*informare*) to instruct, inform; (*DIR*) to prepare.

istru'ito, a *ag* educated.

istrut'tivo, a *ag* instructive.

istrut'tore, 'trice *sm/f* instructor ♦ *ag*: **giudice** ~ examining (*BRIT*) *o* committing (*US*) magistrate.

istrut'toria *sf* (*DIR*) (preliminary) investigation and hearing; **formalizzare un'**~ to proceed to a formal hearing.

istruzi'one [istrut'tsjone] *sf* (*gen*) training; (*INS, cultura*) education; (*direttiva*) instruction; (*DIR*) = **istruttoria**; **Ministero della Pubblica I**~ Ministry of Education; ~**i di spedizione** forwarding instructions; ~**i per l'uso** instructions (for use).

istupi'dire *vt* (*sog: colpo*) to stun, daze; (*: droga, stanchezza*) to stupefy; ~**rsi** *vr* to become stupid.

'ISVE *sigla m* (= *Istituto di Studi per lo Sviluppo Economico*) *institute for research into economic development*.

l'talia *sf*: **l'**~ Italy.

itali'ano, a *ag* Italian ♦ *sm/f* Italian ♦ *sm* (*LING*) Italian; **gli I**~**i** the Italians.

ITC *sigla m* = **istituto tecnico commerciale**.

'iter *sm* passage, course; **l'**~ **burocratico** the bureaucratic process.

itine'rante *ag* wandering, itinerant; **mostra** ~ touring exhibition; **spettacolo** ~

travelling (*BRIT*) *o* traveling (*US*) show,
touring show.

itine'rario *sm* itinerary.

'ITIS *sigla m* = **istituto tecnico industriale statale.**

itte'rizia [itte'rittsja] *sf* (*MED*) jaundice.

'ittico, a, ci, che *ag* fish *cpd*; fishing *cpd*.

IUD *sigla m inv* (= *intra-uterine device*) IUD.

Iugos'lavia *sf* = **Jugoslavia.**

iugos'lavo, a *ag, smlf* = **jugoslavo, a.**

i'uta *sf* jute.

'I.V.A. *sigla f vedi* **imposta sul valore aggiunto.**

'ivi *av* (*formale, poetico*) therein; (*nelle citazioni*) ibid.

Jj

J, j [i'lunga] *sm o f inv* (*lettera*) J, j; **~ come Jersey** ≈ J for Jack (*BRIT*), J for Jig (*US*).

jazz [dʒaz] *sm* jazz.

jaz'zista, i [dʒad'dzista] *sm* jazz player.

jeans [dʒinz] *smpl* jeans.

jeep [dʒip] *sm inv* jeep.

'jersey ['dʒɛrzi] *sm inv* jersey (cloth).

'jockey ['dʒɔki] *sm inv* (*CARTE*) jack; (*fantino*) jockey.

'jogging ['dʒɔgiŋ] *sm* jogging; **fare ~** to go jogging.

'jolly ['dʒɔli] *sm inv* joker.

jr. *abbr* (= *junior*) Jr., jr.

ju'do [dʒu'dɔ] *sm* judo.

Jugos'lavia [jugoz'lavja] *sf*: **la ~** Yugoslavia.

jugos'lavo, a *ag, smlf* Yugoslav(ian).

'juke 'box ['dʒuk'bɔks] *sm inv* jukebox.

Kk

K, k ['kappa] *sf o m inv* (*lettera*) K, k ♦ *abbr* (= *kilo-, chilo-*) k; (*INFORM*) K; **K come Kursaal** ≈ K for King.

Kam'pala *sf* Kampala.

kara'oke [kara'oke] *sm inv* karaoke.

karatè [kara'tɛ] *sm* karate.

'Kashmir ['kaʃmir] *sm*: **il ~** Kashmir.

ka'yak [ka'jak] *sm inv* kayak.

Ka'zakistan [ka'dzakistan] *sm* Kazakhstan.

ka'zako, a [ka'dzako] *ag, smlf* Kazakh.

'Kenia ['kenja] *sm*: **il ~** Kenya.

keni'ano, a, keni'ota, i, e *ag, smlf* Kenyan.

'Kenya ['kenja] *sm*: **il ~** Kenya.

kero'sene [kero'zɛne] *sm* = **cherosene.**

kg *abbr* (= *chilogrammo*) kg.

kib'butz [kib'buts] *sm inv* kibbutz.

Kilimangi'aro [kiliman'dʒaro] *sm*: **il ~** Kilimanjaro.

'killer ['killer] *sm inv* gunman, hired gun.

'kilo *etc* = **chilo** *etc*.

kilt [kilt] *sm inv* kilt.

ki'mono [ki'mɔno] *sm* = **chimono.**

Kir'ghizistan [kir'gidzistan] *sm* Kyrgyzstan.

kir'ghiso, a [kir'gizo] *ag, smlf* Kyrgyz.

kitsch [kitʃ] *sm* kitsch.

'kiwi ['kiwi] *sm inv* kiwi (fruit).

km *abbr* (= *chilometro*) km.

kmq *abbr* (= *chilometro quadrato*) km².

ko'ala [ko'ala] *sm inv* koala (bear).

koso'varo, a *ag, smlf* Kosovan.

'Kosovo *sm* Kosovo.

KR *sigla* = Crotone.

'krapfen ['krapfən] *sm inv* doughnut.

Ku'ala Lum'par *sf* Kuala Lumpur.

Ku'wait [ku'vait] *sm*: **il ~** Kuwait.

kW *abbr* (= *kilowatt, chilowatt*) kW.

kWh *abbr* (= *kilowattora*) kW/h.

L l

L, l ['ɛlle] *sf o m inv* (*lettera*) L, l ♦ *abbr* (= *lira*) L; **L come Livorno** ≈ L for Lucy (*BRIT*), L for Love (*US*).

l *abbr* (= *litro*) l.

l' *det vedi* **la, lo.**

la *det f* (*dav V l'*) the ♦ *pron* (*dav V l'*) (*oggetto: persona*) her; (: *cosa*) it; (: *forma di cortesia*) you ♦ *sm inv* (*MUS*) A; (: *solfeggiando la scala*) la; *vedi anche* **il.**

là *av* there; **di** ~ (*da quel luogo*) from there; (*in quel luogo*) in there; (*dall'altra parte*) over there; **di** ~ **di** beyond; **per di** ~ that way; **più in** ~ further on; (*tempo*) later on; ~ **dentro/sopra/sotto** in/up (*o* on)/under there; ~ **per** ~ (*sul momento*) there and then; **essere in** ~ **con gli anni** to be getting on (in years); **essere più di** ~ **che di qua** to be more dead than alive; **va'** ~! come off it!; **stavolta è andato troppo in** ~ this time he's gone too far; *vedi anche* **quello.**

'labbro *sm* (*pl(f)*: **labbra**: *solo nel senso ANAT*) lip.

'labile *ag* fleeting, ephemeral.

labi'rinto *sm* labyrinth, maze.

labora'torio *sm* (*di ricerca*) laboratory; (*di arti, mestieri*) workshop; ~ **linguistico** language laboratory.

labori'oso, a *ag* (*faticoso*) laborious; (*attivo*) hard-working.

labu'rista, i, e *ag* Labour *cpd* (*BRIT*) ♦ *sm/f* Labour Party member (*BRIT*).

'lacca, che *sf* lacquer; (*per unghie*) nail varnish (*BRIT*), nail polish.

lac'care *vt* (*mobili*) to varnish, lacquer.

'laccio ['lattʃo] *sm* noose; (*legaccio, tirante*) lasso; (*di scarpa*) lace; ~ **emostatico** (*MED*) tourniquet.

lace'rante [latʃe'rante] *ag* (*suono*) piercing, shrill.

lace'rare [latʃe'rare] *vt* to tear to shreds, lacerate; ~**rsi** *vr* to tear.

lacerazi'one [latʃerat'tsjone] *sf* (*anche MED*) tear.

'lacero, a ['latʃero] *ag* (*logoro*) torn, tattered; (*MED*) lacerated; **ferita** ~-**contusa** injury with lacerations and bruising.

la'conico, a, ci, che *ag* laconic, brief.

'lacrima *sf* tear; (*goccia*) drop; **in** ~**e** in tears.

lacri'mare *vi* to water.

lacri'mevole *ag* heartrending, pitiful.

lacri'mogeno, a [lakri'mɔdʒeno] *ag*: **gas** ~ tear gas.

lacri'moso, a *ag* tearful.

la'cuna *sf* (*fig*) gap.

la'custre *ag* lake *cpd*.

lad'dove *cong* whereas.

'ladro *sm* thief; **al** ~! stop thief!

ladro'cinio [ladro'tʃinjo] *sm* theft, robbery.

la'druncolo, a *sm/f* petty thief.

laggiù [lad'dʒu] *av* down there; (*di là*) over there.

'lagna ['laɲɲa] *sf* (*fam: persona, cosa*) drag, bore; **fare la** ~ to whine, moan.

la'gnanza [laɲ'ɲantsa] *sf* complaint.

la'gnarsi [laɲ'ɲarsi] *vr*: ~ (**di**) to complain (about).

'lago, ghi *sm* lake.

'Lagos ['lagos] *sf* Lagos.

'lagrima *etc* = **lacrima** *etc*.

la'guna *sf* lagoon.

lagu'nare *ag* lagoon *cpd*.

'laico, a, ci, che *ag* (*apostolato*) lay; (*vita*) secular; (*scuola*) non-denominational ♦ *sm/f* layman/woman ♦ *sm* lay brother.

'laido, a *ag* filthy, foul; (*fig: osceno*) obscene, filthy.

'lama *sf* blade ♦ *sm inv* (*ZOOL*) llama; (*REL*) lama.

lambic'care *vt* to distil; ~**rsi il cervello** to rack one's brains.

lam'bire *vt* (*fig: sog: fiamme*) to lick; (: *acqua*) to lap.

lam'bretta ® *sf* scooter.

la'mella *sf* (*di metallo etc*) thin sheet, thin strip; (*di fungo*) gill.

lamen'tare *vt* to lament; ~**rsi** *vr* (*emettere lamenti*) to moan, groan; (*rammaricarsi*): ~**rsi (di)** to complain (about).

lamen'tela *sf* complaining *no pl*.

lamen'tevole *ag* (*voce*) complaining, plaintive; (*stato*) lamentable, pitiful.

la'mento *sm* moan, groan; (*per la morte di qn*) lament.

lamen'toso, a *ag* plaintive.

la'metta *sf* razor blade.

lami'era *sf* sheet metal.

'lamina *sf* (*lastra sottile*) thin sheet (*o* layer *o* plate); ~ **d'oro** gold leaf; gold foil.

lami'nare *vt* to laminate.

lami'nato, a *ag* laminated; (*tessuto*) lamé ♦ *sm* laminate.

'lampada *sf* lamp; ~ **a petrolio/a gas** oil/gas lamp; ~ **a spirito** blowlamp (*BRIT*), blowtorch; ~ **a stelo** standard lamp

(*BRIT*), floor lamp; ~ **da tavolo** table lamp.

lampa'dario *sm* chandelier.

lampa'dina *sf* light bulb; ~ **tascabile** pocket torch (*BRIT*), flashlight (*US*).

lam'pante *ag* (*fig: evidente*) crystal clear, evident.

lam'para *sf* fishing lamp; (*barca*) boat for fishing by lamplight (*in Mediterranean*).

lampeggi'are [lamped'dʒare] *vi* (*luce, fari*) to flash ♦ *vb impers:* **lampeggia** there's lightning.

lampeggia'tore [lampeddʒa'tore] *sm* (*AUT*) indicator.

lampi'one *sm* street light *o* lamp (*BRIT*).

'lampo *sm* (*METEOR*) flash of lightning; (*di luce, fig*) flash ♦ *ag inv:* **cerniera** ~ zip (fastener) (*BRIT*), zipper (*US*); **guerra** ~ blitzkrieg; ~**i** *smpl* (*METEOR*) lightning *no pl*; **passare come un** ~ to flash past *o* by.

lam'pone *sm* raspberry.

'lana *sf* wool; ~ **d'acciaio** steel wool; **pura** ~ **vergine** pure new wool; ~ **di vetro** glass wool.

lan'cetta [lan'tʃetta] *sf* (*indice*) pointer, needle; (*di orologio*) hand.

'lancia, ce ['lantʃa] *sf* (*arma*) lance; (: *picca*) spear; (*di pompa antincendio*) nozzle; (*imbarcazione*) launch; **partire** ~ **in resta** (*fig*) to set off ready for battle; **spezzare una** ~ **in favore di qn** (*fig*) to come to sb's defence; ~ **di salvataggio** lifeboat.

lancia'bombe [lantʃa'bombe] *sm inv* (*MIL*) mortar.

lanciafi'amme [lantʃa'fjamme] *sm inv* flamethrower.

lancia'missili [lantʃa'missili] *ag inv* missile-launching ♦ *sm inv* missile launcher.

lancia'razzi [lantʃa'raddzi] *ag inv* rocket-launching ♦ *sm inv* rocket launcher.

lanci'are [lan'tʃare] *vt* to throw, hurl, fling; (*SPORT*) to throw; (*far partire: automobile*) to get up to full speed; (*bombe*) to drop; (*razzo, prodotto, moda*) to launch; (*emettere: grido*) to give out; ~**rsi** *vr:* ~**rsi contro/su** to throw *o* hurl *o* fling o.s. against/on; ~**rsi in** (*fig*) to embark on; ~ **un cavallo** to give a horse his head; ~ **il disco** (*SPORT*) to throw the discus; ~ **il peso** (*SPORT*) to put the shot; ~**rsi all'inseguimento di qn** to set off in pursuit of sb; ~**rsi col paracadute** to parachute.

lanci'ato, a [lan'tʃato] *ag* (*affermato: attore, prodotto*) well-known, famous; (*veicolo*) speeding along, racing along.

lanci'nante [lantʃi'nante] *ag* (*dolore*) shooting, throbbing; (*grido*) piercing.

'lancio ['lantʃo] *sm* throwing *no pl*; throw;

dropping *no pl*; drop; launching *no pl*; launch; ~ **del disco** (*SPORT*) throwing the discus; ~ **del peso** (*SPORT*) putting the shot.

'landa *sf* (*GEO*) moor.

'languido, a *ag* (*fiacco*) languid, weak; (*tenero, malinconico*) languishing.

langu'ire *vi* to languish; (*conversazione*) to flag.

langu'ore *sm* weakness, languor.

lani'ero, a *ag* wool *cpd*, woollen (*BRIT*), woolen (*US*).

lani'ficio [lani'fitʃo] *sm* woollen (*BRIT*) *o* woolen (*US*) mill.

lano'lina *sf* lanolin(e).

la'noso, a *ag* woolly.

lan'terna *sf* lantern; (*faro*) lighthouse.

lanter'nino *sm:* **cercarsele col** ~ to be asking for trouble.

la'nugine [la'nudʒine] *sf* down.

'Laos *sm* Laos.

lapalissi'ano, a *ag* self-evident.

La 'Paz [la'pas] *sf* La Paz.

lapi'dare *vt* to stone.

lapi'dario, a *ag* (*fig*) terse.

'lapide *sf* (*di sepolcro*) tombstone; (*commemorativa*) plaque.

la'pin [la'pɛ̃] *sm inv* coney.

'lapis *sm inv* pencil.

'lappone *ag, sm/f, sm* Lapp.

Lap'ponia *sf:* **la** ~ Lapland.

'lapsus *sm inv* slip.

laptop ['læp tɔp] *sm inv* laptop (computer).

'lardo *sm* bacon fat, lard.

lar'ghezza [lar'gettsa] *sf* width; breadth; looseness; generosity; ~ **di vedute** broad-mindedness.

lar'gire [lar'dʒire] *vt* to give generously.

'largo, a, ghi, ghe *ag* wide, broad; (*maniche*) wide; (*abito: troppo ampio*) loose; (*fig*) generous ♦ *sm* width; breadth; (*mare aperto*): **il** ~ the open sea ♦ *sf:* **stare** *o* **tenersi alla** ~**a (da qn/qc)** to keep one's distance (from sb/sth), keep away (from sb/sth); ~ **due metri** two metres wide; ~ **di spalle** broad-shouldered; **di** ~**ghe vedute** broad-minded; **in** ~**a misura** to a great *o* large extent; **su** ~**a scala** on a large scale; **di manica** ~**a** generous, open-handed; **al** ~ **di Genova** off (the coast of) Genoa; **farsi** ~ **tra la folla** to push one's way through the crowd.

'larice ['laritʃe] *sm* (*BOT*) larch.

la'ringe [la'rindʒe] *sf* larynx.

larin'gite [larin'dʒite] *sf* laryngitis.

laringoi'atra, i, e *sm/f* (*medico*) throat specialist.

'larva *sf* larva; (*fig*) shadow.

la'sagne [la'zaɲɲe] sfpl lasagna sg.

lasciapas'sare [laʃʃapas'sare] sm inv pass, permit.

lasci'are [laʃ'ʃare] vt to leave; (abbandonare) to leave, abandon, give up; (cessare di tenere) to let go of ♦ vb aux: ~ qn fare qc to let sb do sth ♦ vi: ~ di fare (smettere) to stop doing; ~rsi andare/truffare to let o.s. go/be cheated; ~ andare o correre o perdere to let things go their own way; ~ stare qc/qn to leave sth/sb alone; ~ qn erede to make sb one's heir; ~ la presa to lose one's grip; ~ il segno (su qc) to leave a mark (on sth); (fig) to leave one's mark (on sth); ~ (molto) a desiderare to leave much to be desired; ci ha lasciato la vita it cost him his life.

'lascito ['laʃʃito] sm (DIR) legacy.

la'scivia [laʃ'ʃivja] sf lust, lasciviousness.

la'scivo, a [laʃ'ʃivo] ag lascivious.

'laser ['lazer] ag, sm inv: (raggio) ~ laser (beam).

lassa'tivo, a ag, sm laxative.

las'sismo sm laxity.

'lasso sm: ~ di tempo interval.

lassù av up there.

'lastra sf (di pietra) slab; (di metallo, FOT) plate; (di ghiaccio, vetro) sheet; (radiografica) X-ray (plate).

lastri'care vt to pave.

lastri'cato sm paving.

'lastrico, ci o chi sm paving; essere sul ~ (fig) to be penniless; gettare qn sul ~ (fig) to leave sb destitute.

las'trone sm (ALPINISMO) sheer rock face.

la'tente ag latent.

late'rale ag lateral, side cpd; (uscita, ingresso etc) side cpd ♦ sm (CALCIO) half-back.

lateral'mente av sideways.

late'rizio [late'rittsjo] sm (perforated) brick.

latifon'dista, i, e sm/f large agricultural landowner.

lati'fondo sm large estate.

la'tino, a ag, sm Latin.

la'tinoameri'cano, a ag, sm/f Latin-American.

lati'tante ag: essere ~ to be on the run ♦ sm/f fugitive (from justice).

lati'tanza [lati'tantsa] sf: darsi alla ~ to go into hiding.

lati'tudine sf latitude.

'lato, a ag: in senso ~ broadly speaking ♦ sm side; (fig) aspect, point of view; d'altro ~ (d'altra parte) on the other hand.

la'trare vi to bark.

lat'rato sm howling.

la'trina sf public lavatory.

latro'cinio [latro'tʃinjo] sm = ladrocinio.

'latta sf tin (plate); (recipiente) tin, can.

lat'taio, a sm/f (distributore) milkman/woman; (commerciante) dairyman/woman.

lat'tante ag unweaned ♦ sm/f breast-fed baby.

'latte sm milk; fratello di ~ foster brother; avere ancora il ~ alla bocca (fig) to be still wet behind the ears; tutto ~ e miele (fig) all smiles; ~ detergente cleansing milk o lotion; ~ intero full-cream milk; ~ a lunga conservazione UHT milk; ~ magro o scremato skimmed milk; ~ secco o in polvere dried o powdered milk.

'latteo, a ag milky; (dieta, prodotto) milk cpd.

latte'ria sf dairy.

latti'cini [latti'tʃini] smpl dairy o milk products.

lat'tina sf (di birra etc) can.

lat'tuga, ghe sf lettuce.

'laurea sf ≈ degree; ~ breve university degree awarded at the end of a three-year course; avere una ~ in chimica to have a degree in chemistry o a chemistry degree; vedi nota nel riquadro.

LAUREA

The **Laurea** is awarded to students who successfully complete their degree courses. Traditionally, this takes between four and six years; a major element of the final examinations is the presentation and discussion of a dissertation. A shorter, more vocational course of study, taking from two to three years, is also available; at the end of this time students receive a diploma called the **Laurea breve**.

---

laure'ando, a sm/f final-year student.

laure'are vt to confer a degree on; ~rsi vr to graduate.

laure'ato, a ag, sm/f graduate.

'lauro sm laurel.

'lauto, a ag (pranzo, mancia) lavish.

'lava sf lava.

la'vabo sm washbasin.

la'vaggio [la'vaddʒo] sm washing no pl; ~ del cervello brainwashing no pl.

la'vagna [la'vaɲɲa] sf (GEO) slate; (di scuola) blackboard; ~ luminosa overhead projector.

la'vanda sf (anche MED) wash; (BOT) lavender; fare una ~ gastrica a qn to pump sb's stomach.

lavande'ria *sf* (*di ospedale, caserma etc*) laundry; ~ **automatica** launderette; ~ **a secco** dry-cleaner's.

lavan'dino *sm* sink; (*del bagno*) washbasin.

lavapi'atti *sm/f* dishwasher.

la'vare *vt* to wash; **~rsi** *vr* to wash, have a wash; ~ **a secco** to dry-clean; **~rsi le mani/i denti** to wash one's hands/clean one's teeth.

lava'secco *sm o f inv* dry-cleaner's.

lavasto'viglie [lavasto'viʎʎe] *sm o f inv* (*macchina*) dishwasher.

la'vata *sf* wash; (*fig*): **dare una ~ di capo a qn** to give sb a good telling-off.

lava'tivo *sm* (*clistere*) enema; (*buono a nulla*) good-for-nothing, idler.

lava'trice [lava'tritʃe] *sf* washing machine.

lava'tura *sf* washing *no pl*; ~ **di piatti** dishwater.

la'vello *sm* (kitchen) sink.

la'vina *sf* snowslide.

lavo'rare *vi* to work; (*fig: bar, studio etc*) to do good business ♦ *vt* to work; ~ **a** to work on; ~ **a maglia** to knit; ~ **di fantasia** (*suggestionarsi*) to imagine things; (*fantasticare*) to let one's imagination run free; **~rsi qn** (*convincere*) to work on sb.

lavora'tivo, a *ag* working.

lavora'tore, 'trice *sm/f* worker ♦ *ag* working.

lavorazi'one [lavorat'tsjone] *sf* (*gen*) working; (*di legno, pietra*) carving; (*di film*) making; (*di prodotto*) manufacture; (*modo di esecuzione*) workmanship.

lavo'rio *sm* intense activity.

la'voro *sm* work; (*occupazione*) job, work *no pl*; (*opera*) piece of work, job; (*ECON*) labour (*BRIT*), labor (*US*); **Ministero del L~** Department of Employment (*BRIT*), Department of Labor (*US*); (**fare**) **i ~i di casa** (to do) the housework *sg*; **~i forzati** hard labour *sg*; **i ~i del parlamento** the parliamentary session *sg*; **~i pubblici** public works.

lazi'ale [lat'tsjale] *ag* of (*o* from) Lazio.

lazza'retto [laddza'retto] *sm* leper hospital.

lazza'rone [laddza'rone] *sm* scoundrel.

'lazzo ['laddzo] *sm* jest.

LC *sigla* = Lecco.

LE *sigla* = Lecce.

le *det fpl* the ♦ *pron* (*oggetto*) them; (: *a lei, a essa*) (to) her; (: *forma di cortesia*) (to) you; *vedi anche* **il**.

le'ale *ag* loyal; (*sincero*) sincere; (*onesto*) fair.

lea'lista, i, e *sm/f* loyalist.

lealtà *sf* loyalty; sincerity; fairness.

'leasing ['liːzɪŋ] *sm* leasing; lease.

'lebbra *sf* leprosy.

'lecca 'lecca *sm inv* lollipop.

leccapi'edi *sm/f inv* (*peg*) toady, bootlicker.

lec'care *vt* to lick; (*sog: gatto: latte etc*) to lick *o* lap up; (*fig*) to flatter; **~rsi** *vr* (*fig*) to preen o.s.; **~rsi i baffi** to lick one's lips.

lec'cato, a *ag* affected ♦ *sf* lick.

leccherò *etc* [lekke'rɔ] *vb vedi* **leccare**.

'leccio ['lettʃo] *sm* holm oak, ilex.

leccor'nia *sf* titbit, delicacy.

'lecito, a ['lɛtʃito] *ag* permitted, allowed; **se mi è ~** if I may; **mi sia ~ far presente che** … may I point out that ….

'ledere *vt* to damage, injure; ~ **gli interessi di qn** to be prejudicial to sb's interests.

'lega, ghe *sf* (*anche POL*) league; (*di metalli*) alloy; **metallo di bassa ~** base metal; **gente di bassa ~** common *o* vulgar people; **L~ Nord** (*POL*) *federalist party*.

le'gaccio [le'gattʃo] *sm* string, lace.

le'gale *ag* legal ♦ *sm* lawyer; **corso ~ delle monete** official exchange rate; **medicina ~** forensic medicine; **studio ~** lawyer's office.

legalità *sf* legality, lawfulness.

legaliz'zare [legalid'dzare] *vt* to legalize; (*documento*) to authenticate.

legalizzazi'one [legaliddzat'tsjone] *sf* (*vedi vt*) legalization; authentication.

le'game *sm* (*corda, fig: affettivo*) tie, bond; (*nesso logico*) link, connection; ~ **di sangue** *o* **di parentela** family tie.

lega'mento *sm* (*ANAT*) ligament.

le'gare *vt* (*prigioniero, capelli, cane*) to tie (up); (*libro*) to bind; (*CHIM*) to alloy; (*fig: collegare*) to bind, join ♦ *vi* (*far lega*) to unite; (*fig*) to get on well; **è pazzo da ~** (*fam*) he should be locked up.

lega'tario, a *sm/f* (*DIR*) legatee.

le'gato *sm* (*REL*) legate; (*DIR*) legacy, bequest.

legato'ria *sf* (*attività*) bookbinding; (*negozio*) bookbinder's.

lega'tura *sf* (*di libro*) binding; (*MUS*) ligature.

legazi'one [legat'tsjone] *sf* legation.

le'genda [le'dʒɛnda] *sf* (*di carta geografica etc*) = **leggenda**.

'legge ['leddʒe] *sf* law; ~ **procedurale** procedural law.

leg'genda [led'dʒɛnda] *sf* (*narrazione*) legend; (*di carta geografica etc*) key, legend.

leggen'dario, a [leddʒen'darjo] *ag* legendary.

'leggere ['lɛddʒere] *vt, vi* to read; ~ **il pensiero di qn** to read sb's mind *o* thoughts.

legge'rezza [leddʒe'rettsa] *sf* lightness; thoughtlessness; fickleness.

leg'gero, a [led'dʒero] *ag* light; (*agile, snello*) nimble, agile, light; (*tè, caffè*) weak; (*fig: non grave, piccolo*) slight; (: *spensierato*) thoughtless; (: *incostante*) fickle; free and easy; **una ragazza ~a** (*fig*) a flighty girl; **alla ~a** thoughtlessly.

leggi'adro, a [led'dʒadro] *ag* pretty, lovely; (*movimenti*) graceful.

leg'gibile [led'dʒibile] *ag* legible; (*libro*) readable, worth reading.

leg'gio, 'gii [led'dʒio] *sm* lectern; (*MUS*) music stand.

legherò *etc* [lege'rɔ] *vb vedi* **legare**.

le'ghismo [le'gismo] *sm political movement with federalist tendencies.*

le'ghista, i, e [le'gista] (*POL*) *ag* of a "lega" (*especially Lega Nord*) ♦ *smf* member (*o* supporter) of a "lega" (*especially Lega Nord*).

legife'rare [ledʒife'rare] *vi* to legislate.

legio'nario [ledʒo'narjo] *sm* (*romano*) legionary; (*volontario*) legionnaire.

legi'one [le'dʒone] *sf* legion; **~ straniera** foreign legion.

legisla'tivo, a [ledʒizla'tivo] *ag* legislative.

legisla'tore [ledʒizla'tore] *sm* legislator.

legisla'tura [ledʒizla'tura] *sf* legislature.

legislazi'one [ledʒizlat'tsjone] *sf* legislation.

legitti'mare [ledʒitti'mare] *vt* (*figlio*) to legitimize; (*comportamento etc*) to justify.

legittimità [ledʒittimi'ta] *sf* legitimacy.

le'gittimo, a [le'dʒittimo] *ag* legitimate; (*fig: giustificato, lecito*) justified, legitimate; **~a difesa** (*DIR*) self-defence (*BRIT*), self-defense (*US*).

'legna ['leɲɲa] *sf* firewood.

le'gnaia [leɲ'naja] *sf* woodshed.

legnai'olo [leɲɲa'jɔlo] *sm* woodcutter.

le'gname [leɲ'ɲame] *sm* wood, timber.

le'gnata [leɲ'ɲata] *sf* blow with a stick; **dare a qn un sacco di ~e** to give sb a good hiding.

'legno ['leɲɲo] *sm* wood; (*pezzo di ~*) piece of wood; **di ~** wooden; **~ compensato** plywood.

le'gnoso, a [leɲ'ɲoso] *ag* (*di legno*) wooden; (*come il legno*) woody; (*carne*) tough.

le'gume *sm* (*BOT*) pulse; **~i** *smpl* (*fagioli, piselli etc*) pulses.

'lei *pron* (*soggetto*) she; (*oggetto: per dare rilievo, con preposizione*) her; (*forma di cortesia: anche:* **L~**) you ♦ *sf inv:* **la mia ~** my beloved ♦ *sm:* **dare del ~ a qn** to address sb as "lei"; **~ stessa** she herself; you yourself; **è ~** it's her.

'lembo *sm* (*di abito, strada*) edge; (*striscia sottile: di terra*) strip.

'lemma, i *sm* headword.

'lemme 'lemme *av* (very) very slowly.

'lena *sf* (*fig*) energy, stamina; **di buona ~** (*lavorare, camminare*) at a good pace.

Lenin'grado *sf* Leningrad.

le'nire *vt* to soothe.

lenta'mente *av* slowly.

'lente *sf* (*OTTICA*) lens *sg*; **~ d'ingrandimento** magnifying glass; **~i a contatto, ~i corneali** contact lenses; **~i (a contatto) morbide** soft lenses; **~i (a contatto) rigide** hard lenses.

len'tezza [len'tettsa] *sf* slowness.

len'ticchia [len'tikkja] *sf* (*BOT*) lentil.

len'tiggine [len'tiddʒine] *sf* freckle.

'lento, a *ag* slow; (*molle: fune*) slack; (*non stretto: vite, abito*) loose ♦ *sm* (*ballo*) slow dance.

'lenza ['lentsa] *sf* fishing line.

lenzu'olo [len'tswɔlo] *sm* sheet; **~a** *sfpl* pair of sheets; **~ funebre** shroud.

leon'cino [leon't fino] *sm* lion cub.

le'one *sm* lion; (*dello zodiaco*): **L~** Leo; **essere del L~** to be Leo.

leo'pardo *sm* leopard.

lepo'rino, a *ag:* **labbro ~** harelip.

'lepre *sf* hare.

'lercio, a, ci, ce ['lertʃo] *ag* filthy.

lerci'ume [ler't fume] *sm* filth.

'lesbico, a, ci, che *ag, sf* lesbian.

'lesi *etc vb vedi* **ledere**.

lesi'nare *vt* to be stingy with ♦ *vi:* **~ (su)** to skimp (on), be stingy (with).

lesi'one *sf* (*MED*) lesion; (*DIR*) injury, damage; (*EDIL*) crack.

le'sivo, a *ag:* **~ (di)** damaging (to), detrimental (to).

'leso, a *pp di* **ledere** ♦ *ag* (*offeso*) injured; **parte ~a** (*DIR*) injured party; **~a maestà** lese-majesty.

les'sare *vt* (*CUC*) to boil.

'lessi *etc vb vedi* **leggere**.

lessi'cale *ag* lexical.

'lessico, ci *sm* vocabulary; (*dizionario*) lexicon.

lessicogra'fia *sf* lexicography.

lessi'cografo, a *smf* lexicographer.

'lesso, a *ag* boiled ♦ *sm* boiled meat.

'lesto, a *ag* quick; (*agile*) nimble; **~ di mano** (*per rubare*) light-fingered; (*per picchiare*) free with one's fists.

lesto'fante *sm* swindler, con man.

le'tale *ag* lethal, deadly.

leta'maio *sm* dunghill.

le'tame *sm* manure, dung.

le'targo, ghi *sm* lethargy; (*ZOOL*)

hibernation.

le'**tizia** [le'tittsja] *sf* joy, happiness.

'**letta** *sf*: **dare una ~ a qc** to glance *o* look through sth.

'**lettera** *sf* letter; **~e** *sfpl* (*letteratura*) literature *sg*; (*studi umanistici*) arts (subjects); **alla ~** literally; **in ~e** in words, in full; **diventar ~ morta** (*legge*) to become a dead letter; **restar ~ morta** (*consiglio, invito*) to go unheeded; **~ di accompagnamento** accompanying letter; **~ assicurata** registered letter; **~ di cambio** (*COMM*) bill of exchange; **~ di credito** (*COMM*) letter of credit; **~ di intenti** letter of intent; **~ di presentazione** *o* **raccomandazione** letter of introduction; **~ raccomandata** recorded delivery (*BRIT*) *o* certified (*US*) letter; **~ di trasporto aereo** (*COMM*) air waybill.

lette'**rale** *ag* literal.

letteral'**mente** *av* literally.

lette'**rario, a** *ag* literary.

lette'**rato, a** *ag* well-read, scholarly.

lettera'**tura** *sf* literature.

let'**tiga, ghe** *sf* (*portantina*) litter; (*barella*) stretcher.

let'**tino** *sm* cot (*BRIT*), crib (*US*).

'**letto, a** *pp di* **leggere ♦** *sm* bed; **andare a ~** to go to bed; **~ a castello** bunk beds *pl*; **~ a una piazza/a due piazze** *o* **matrimoniale** single/double bed.

'**lettone** *ag, smf* Latvian **♦** *sm* (*LING*) Latvian, Lettish.

Let'**tonia** *sf*: **la ~** Latvia.

lettorato *sm* (*INS*) lectorship, assistantship; (*REL*) lectorate.

let'**tore, 'trice** *smf* reader; (*INS*) (foreign language) assistant (*BRIT*), (foreign) teaching assistant (*US*) **♦** *sm*: **~ ottico** (**di caratteri**) optical character reader; **~ CD** CD player; **~ DVD** DVD player.

let'**tura** *sf* reading.

leuce'**mia** [leut∫e'mia] *sf* leukaemia.

'**leva** *sf* lever; (*MIL*) conscription; **far ~ su qn** to work on sb; **essere di ~** to be due for call-up; **~ del cambio** (*AUT*) gear lever.

le'**vante** *sm* east; (*vento*) East wind; **il L~** the Levant.

le'**vare** *vt* (*occhi, braccio*) to raise; (*sollevare, togliere: tassa, divieto*) to lift; (: *indumenti*) to take off, remove; (*rimuovere*) to take away; (: *dal di sopra*) to take off; (: *dal di dentro*) to take out; **~rsi** *vr* to get up; (*sole*) to rise; **~ le tende** (*fig*) to pack up and leave; **~rsi il pensiero** to put one's mind at rest; **levati di mezzo** *o* **di lì** *o* **di torno!** get out of my way!

le'**vata** *sf* (*di posta*) collection.

leva'**taccia, ce** [leva'tatt∫a] *sf* early rise.

leva'**toio, a** *ag*: **ponte ~** drawbridge.

leva'**trice** [leva'trit∫e] *sf* midwife.

leva'**tura** *sf* intelligence, mental capacity.

levi'**gare** *vt* to smooth; (*con carta vetrata*) to sand.

levi'**gato, a** *ag* (*superficie*) smooth; (*fig: stile*) polished; (: *viso*) flawless.

levi'**tà** *sf* lightness.

levri'**ere** *sm* greyhound.

lezi'**one** [let'tsjone] *sf* lesson; (*all'università, sgridata*) lecture; **fare ~** to teach; to lecture.

lezi'**oso, a** [let'tsjoso] *ag* affected; simpering.

'**lezzo** ['leddzo] *sm* stench, stink.

Ll *sigla* = Livorno.

li *pron pl* (*oggetto*) them.

lì *av* there; **di** *o* **da ~** from there; **per di ~** that way; **di ~ a pochi giorni** a few days later; **~ per ~** there and then; at first; **essere ~ (~) per fare** to be on the point of doing, be about to do; **~ dentro** in there; **~ sotto** under there; **~ sopra** on there; up there; **tutto ~** that's all; *vedi anche* **quello**.

libagi'**one** [liba'dʒone] *sf* libation.

liba'**nese** *ag, smf* Lebanese *inv*.

Li'bano *sm*: **il ~** the Lebanon.

'**libbra** *sf* (*peso*) pound.

li'**beccio** [li'bett∫o] *sm* south-west wind.

li'**bello** *sm* libel.

li'**bellula** *sf* dragonfly.

libe'**rale** *ag, smf* liberal.

liberaliz'**zare** [liberalid'dzare] *vt* to liberalize.

libe'**rare** *vt* (*rendere libero: prigioniero*) to release; (: *popolo*) to free, liberate; (*sgombrare: passaggio*) to clear; (: *stanza*) to vacate; (*produrre: energia*) to release; **~rsi** *vr*: **~rsi di qc/qn** to get rid of sth/sb.

libera'**tore, 'trice** *ag* liberating **♦** *smf* liberator.

liberazi'**one** [liberat'tsjone] *sf* (*di prigioniero*) release; (*di popolo*) liberation; **che ~!** what a relief!; **la L~** *vedi nota nel riquadro*.

LIBERAZIONE

The **Liberazione** is a national holiday which falls on 25 April. It commemorates the liberation of Italy in 1945 from German forces and Mussolini's government and marks the end of the war on Italian soil.

Li'**beria** *sf*: **la ~** Liberia.

liberi'**ano, a** *ag, smf* Liberian.

libe'rismo *sm* (*ECON*) laissez-faire.

'libero, a *ag* free; (*strada*) clear; (*non occupato: posto etc*) vacant, free; (*TEL*) not engaged; ~ **di fare qc** free to do sth; ~ **da** free from; **una donna dai** ~**i costumi** a woman of loose morals; **avere via** ~**a** to have a free hand; **dare via** ~**a a qn** to give sb the go-ahead; **via** ~**a!** all clear!; ~ **arbitrio** free will; ~ **professionista** self-employed professional person; ~ **scambio** free trade; ~**a uscita** (*MIL*) leave.

liberoscam'bismo *sm* (*ECON*) free trade.

libertà *sf inv* freedom; (*tempo disponibile*) free time ♦ *sfpl* (*licenza*) liberties; **essere in** ~ **provvisoria/vigilata** to be released without bail/be on probation; ~ **di riunione** right to hold meetings.

'liberty ['liberti] *ag inv*, *sm* art nouveau.

'Libia *sf:* **la** ~ Libya.

'libico, a, ci, che *ag*, *sm/f* Libyan.

li'bidine *sf* lust.

libidi'noso, a *ag* lustful, libidinous.

li'bido *sf* libido.

li'braio *sm* bookseller.

li'brario, a *ag* book *cpd*.

li'brarsi *vr* to hover.

libre'ria *sf* (*bottega*) bookshop; (*stanza*) library; (*mobile*) bookcase.

li'bretto *sm* booklet; (*taccuino*) notebook; (*MUS*) libretto; ~ **degli assegni** chequebook (*BRIT*), checkbook (*US*); ~ **di circolazione** (*AUT*) logbook; ~ **di deposito** (bank) deposit book; ~ **di risparmio** (savings) bankbook, passbook; ~ **universitario** student's report book.

'libro *sm* book; ~ **bianco** (*POL*) white paper; ~ **di cassa** cash book; ~ **di consultazione** reference book; ~ **mastro** ledger; ~ **paga** payroll; ~ **tascabile** paperback; ~ **di testo** textbook; ~**i contabili** (account) books; ~**i sociali** company records.

li'cantropo *sm* werewolf.

lice'ale [litʃe'ale] *ag* secondary school *cpd* (*BRIT*), high school *cpd* (*US*) ♦ *sm/f* secondary school *o* high school pupil.

li'cenza [li'tʃɛntsa] *sf* (*permesso*) permission, leave; (*di pesca, caccia, circolazione*) permit, licence (*BRIT*), license (*US*); (*MIL*) leave; (*INS*) school-leaving certificate; (*libertà*) liberty; (*sfrenatezza*) licentiousness; **andare in** ~ (*MIL*) to go on leave; **su** ~ **di ...** (*COMM*) under licence from ...; ~ **di esportazione** export licence; ~ **di fabbricazione** manufacturer's licence; ~ **poetica** poetic licence.

licenzia'mento [litʃentsja'mento] *sm* dismissal.

licenzi'are [litʃen'tsjare] *vt* (*impiegato*) to dismiss; (*INS*) to award a certificate to; ~**rsi** *vr* (*impiegato*) to resign, hand in one's notice; (*INS*) to obtain one's school-leaving certificate.

licenziosità [litʃentsjosi'ta] *sf* licentiousness.

licenzi'oso, a [litʃen'tsjoso] *ag* licentious.

li'ceo [li'tʃɛo] *sm* (*INS*) secondary (*BRIT*) *o* high (*US*) school (*for 14 to 19-year-olds*); ~ **classico/scientifico** *secondary or high school specializing in classics/scientific subjects.*

li'chene [li'kɛne] *sm* (*BOT*) lichen.

'lido *sm* beach, shore.

'Liechtenstein ['liktǝnstain] *sm:* **il** ~ Liechtenstein.

li'eto, a *ag* happy, glad; "**molto** ~" (*nelle presentazioni*) "pleased to meet you"; **a** ~ **fine** with a happy ending.

li'eve *ag* light; (*di poco conto*) slight; (*sommesso: voce*) faint, soft.

lievi'tare *vi* (*anche fig*) to rise ♦ *vt* to leaven.

li'evito *sm* yeast; ~ **di birra** brewer's yeast.

'ligio, a, gi, gie ['lidʒo] *ag* faithful, loyal.

li'gnaggio [liɲ'naddʒo] *sm* descent, lineage.

'ligure *ag* Ligurian; **la Riviera L**~ the Italian Riviera.

Li'kud [li'kud] *sm* Likud.

'lilla, lillà *sm inv* lilac.

'Lima *sf* Lima.

'lima *sf* file; ~ **da unghie** nail file.

limacci'oso, a [limat'tʃoso] *ag* muddy.

li'mare *vt* to file (down); (*fig*) to polish.

'limbo *sm* (*REL*) limbo.

li'metta *sf* nail file.

limi'tare *vt* to limit, restrict; (*circoscrivere*) to bound, surround.

limitata'mente *av* to a limited extent; ~ **alle mie possibilità** in so far as I am able.

limi'tato, a *ag* limited, restricted.

limitazi'one [limitat'tsjone] *sf* limitation, restriction.

'limite *sm* limit; (*confine*) border, boundary ♦ *ag inv:* **caso** ~ extreme case; **al** ~ if the worst comes to the worst (*BRIT*), if worst comes to worst (*US*); ~ **di velocità** speed limit.

li'mitrofo, a *ag* neighbouring (*BRIT*), neighboring (*US*).

'limo *sm* mud, slime; (*GEO*) silt.

limo'nata *sf* lemonade (*BRIT*), (lemon) soda (*US*); (*spremuta*) lemon squash (*BRIT*), lemonade (*US*).

li'mone *sm* (*pianta*) lemon tree; (*frutto*) lemon.

limpi'dezza [limpi'dettsa] *sf* clearness; (*di discorso*) clarity.

'**limpido, a** *ag* (*acqua*) limpid, clear; (*cielo*) clear; (*fig*: *discorso*) clear, lucid.

'**lince** ['lintʃe] *sf* lynx.

linci'aggio [lin'tʃaddʒo] *sm* lynching.

linci'are [lin'tʃare] *vt* to lynch.

'**lindo, a** *ag* tidy, spick and span; (*biancheria*) clean.

'**linea** *sf* (*gen*) line; (*di mezzi pubblici di trasporto: itinerario*) route; (: *servizio*) service; (*di prodotto: collezione*) collection; (: *stile*) style; **a grandi ~e** in outline; **mantenere la ~** to look after one's figure; **è caduta la ~** (*TEL*) I (*o* you *etc*) have been cut off; **di ~**: **aereo di ~** airliner; **nave di ~** liner; **volo di ~** scheduled flight; **in ~ diretta da** (*TV, RADIO*) coming to you direct from; **~ aerea** airline; **~ continua** solid line; **~ di partenza/d'arrivo** (*SPORT*) starting/finishing line; **~ punteggiata** dotted line; **~ di tiro** line of fire.

linea'menti *smpl* features; (*fig*) outlines.

line'are *ag* linear; (*fig*) coherent, logical.

line'etta *sf* (*trattino*) dash; (*d'unione*) hyphen.

'**linfa** *sf* (*BOT*) sap; (*ANAT*) lymph; **~ vitale** (*fig*) lifeblood.

lin'gotto *sm* ingot, bar.

'**lingua** *sf* (*ANAT, CUC*) tongue; (*idioma*) language; **mostrare la ~** to stick out one's tongue; **di ~ italiana** Italian-speaking; **~ madre** mother tongue; **una ~ di terra** a spit of land.

lingu'accia [lin'gwattʃa] *sf* (*fig*) spiteful gossip.

linguacci'uto, a [lingwat'tʃuto] *ag* gossipy.

lingu'aggio [lin'gwaddʒo] *sm* language; **~ giuridico** legal language; **~ macchina** (*INFORM*) machine language; **~ di programmazione** (*INFORM*) programming language.

lingu'etta *sf* (*di strumento*) reed; (*di scarpa, TECN*) tongue; (*di busta*) flap.

lingu'ista, i, e *sm/f* linguist.

lingu'istico, a, ci, che *ag* linguistic ♦ *sf* linguistics *sg*.

lini'mento *sm* liniment.

'**lino** *sm* (*pianta*) flax; (*tessuto*) linen.

li'noleum *sm inv* linoleum, lino.

liofiliz'zare [liofilid'dzare] *vt* to freeze-dry.

liofiliz'zati [liofilid'dzati] *smpl* freeze-dried foods.

Li'one *sf* Lyons.

liposuzi'one [liposut'tsjone] *sf* liposuction.

'**LIPU** *sigla f* (= *Lega Italiana Protezione Uccelli*) *society for the protection of birds*.

liqu'ame *sm* liquid sewage.

lique'fare *vt* (*render liquido*) to liquefy;

(*fondere*) to melt; **~rsi** *vr* to liquefy; to melt.

lique'fatto, a *pp di* **liquefare**.

liqui'dare *vt* (*società, beni, persona*: *uccidere*) to liquidate; (*persona*: *sbarazzarsene*) to get rid of; (*conto, problema*) to settle; (*COMM: merce*) to sell off, clear.

liquidazi'one [likwidat'tsjone] *sf* (*di società, persona*) liquidation; (*di conto*) settlement; (*di problema*) settling; (*COMM: di merce*) clearance sale; (*AMM*) severance pay (*on retirement, redundancy, or when taking up other employment*).

liquidità *sf* liquidity.

'**liquido, a** *ag, sm* liquid; **denaro ~** cash, ready money; **~ per freni** brake fluid.

liqui'gas ® *sm inv* Calor gas ® (*BRIT*), butane.

liqui'rizia [likwi'rittsja] *sf* liquorice.

li'quore *sm* liqueur.

liquo'roso, a *ag*: **vino ~** dessert wine.

'**lira** *sf* (*unità monetaria*) lira; (*MUS*) lyre; **~ sterlina** pound sterling.

'**lirico, a, ci, che** *ag* lyric(al); (*MUS*) lyric ♦ *sf* (*poesia*) lyric poetry; (*componimento poetico*) lyric; (*MUS*) opera; **cantante/teatro ~** opera singer/house.

li'rismo *sm* lyricism.

Lis'bona *sf* Lisbon.

'**lisca, sche** *sf* (*di pesce*) fishbone.

lisci'are [liʃ'ʃare] *vt* to smooth; (*fig*) to flatter; **~rsi i capelli** to straighten one's hair.

'**liscio, a, sci, sce** ['liʃʃo] *ag* smooth; (*capelli*) straight; (*mobile*) plain; (*bevanda alcolica*) neat; (*fig*) straightforward, simple ♦ *av*: **andare ~** to go smoothly; **passarla ~a** to get away with it.

'**liso, a** *ag* worn out, threadbare.

'**lista** *sf* (*striscia*) strip; (*elenco*) list; **~ elettorale** electoral roll; **~ delle vivande** menu.

lis'tare *vt*: **~ (di)** to edge (with), border (with).

lis'tato *sm* (*INFORM*) list, listing.

lis'tino *sm* list; **~ di borsa** the Stock Exchange list; **~ dei cambi** (foreign) exchange rate; **~ dei prezzi** price list.

lita'nia *sf* litany.

'**lite** *sf* quarrel, argument; (*DIR*) lawsuit.

liti'gare *vi* to quarrel; (*DIR*) to litigate.

li'tigio [li'tidʒo] *sm* quarrel.

litigi'oso, a [liti'dʒoso] *ag* quarrelsome; (*DIR*) litigious.

litogra'fia *sf* (*sistema*) lithography; (*stampa*) lithograph.

lito'grafico, a, ci, che *ag* lithographic.

lito'rale *ag* coastal, coast *cpd* ♦ *sm* coast.
lito'raneo, a *ag* coastal.
'litro *sm* litre (*BRIT*), liter (*US*).
lit'torio, a *ag* (*STORIA*) lictorial; **fascio** ~ fasces *pl*.
Litu'ania *sf*: **la** ~ Lithuania.
litu'ano, a *ag*, *smf*, *sm* Lithuanian.
litur'gia, 'gie [litur'dʒia] *sf* liturgy.
li'uto *sm* lute.
li'vella *sf* level; ~ **a bolla d'aria** spirit level.
livel'lare *vt* to level, make level; ~**rsi** *vr* to become level; (*fig*) to level out, balance out.
livella'trice [livella'tritʃe] *sf* steamroller.
li'vello *sm* level; (*fig*) level, standard; **ad alto** ~ (*fig*) high-level; **a** ~ **mondiale** world-wide; **a** ~ **di confidenza** confidentially; ~ **di magazzino** stock level; ~ **del mare** sea level; **sul** ~ **del mare** above sea level; ~ **occupazionale** level of employment; ~ **retributivo** salary level.
'livido, a *ag* livid; (*per percosse*) bruised, black and blue; (*cielo*) leaden ♦ *sm* bruise.
li'vore *sm* malice, spite.
Li'vorno *sf* Livorno, Leghorn.
li'vrea *sf* livery.
'lizza ['littsa] *sf* lists *pl*; **essere in** ~ **per** (*fig*) to compete for; **scendere in** ~ (*anche fig*) to enter the lists.
LO *sigla* = *Lodi.*
lo *det m* (*dav s impura, gn, pn, ps, x, z; dav V l'*) the ♦ *pron* (*dav V l'*) (*oggetto: persona*) him; (: *cosa*) it; ~ **sapevo** I knew it; ~ **so** I know; **sii buono, anche se lui non** ~ **è** be good, even if he isn't; *vedi anche* **il**.
lob'bista, i, e *smf* lobbyist.
'lobby *sf inv* lobby.
'lobo *sm* lobe; ~ **dell'orecchio** ear lobe.
lo'cale *ag* local ♦ *sm* room; (*luogo pubblico*) premises *pl*; ~ **notturno** nightclub.
località *sf inv* locality.
localiz'zare [lokalid'dzare] *vt* (*circoscrivere*) to confine, localize; (*accertare*) to locate, place.
lo'canda *sf* inn.
locandi'ere, a *smf* innkeeper.
locan'dina *sf* (*TEAT*) poster.
lo'care *vt* (*casa*) to rent out, let; (*macchina*) to hire out (*BRIT*), rent (out).
loca'tario, a *smf* tenant.
loca'tivo, a *ag* (*DIR*) rentable.
loca'tore, 'trice *smf* landlord/lady.
locazi'one [lokat'tsjone] *sf* (*da parte del locatario*) renting *no pl*; (*da parte del locatore*) renting *no pl*; **(contratto di)** ~ lease; **(canone di)** ~ rent; **dare in** ~ to rent out, let.
locomo'tiva *sf* locomotive.

locomo'tore *sm* electric locomotive.
locomot'rice [lokomo'tritʃe] *sf* = **locomotore**.
locomozi'one [lokomot'tsjone] *sf* locomotion; **mezzi di** ~ vehicles, means of transport.
'loculo *sm* burial recess.
lo'custa *sf* locust.
locuzi'one [lokut'tsjone] *sf* phrase, expression.
lo'dare *vt* to praise.
'lode *sf* praise; (*INS*): **laurearsi con 110 e** ~ ≈ to graduate with first-class honours (*BRIT*), ≈ to graduate summa cum laude (*US*).
'loden *sm inv* (*stoffa*) loden; (*cappotto*) loden overcoat.
lo'devole *ag* praiseworthy.
loga'ritmo *sm* logarithm.
'loggia, ge ['lɔddʒa] *sf* (*ARCHIT*) loggia; (*circolo massonico*) lodge.
loggi'one [lod'dʒone] *sm* (*di teatro*): **il** ~ the Gods *sg*.
logica'mente [lodʒika'mente] *av* naturally, obviously.
logicità [lodʒitʃi'ta] *sf* logicality.
'logico, a, ci, che ['lɔdʒiko] *ag* logical ♦ *sf* logic.
lo'gistica [lo'dʒistika] *sf* logistics *sg*.
'logo *sm inv* logo.
logora'mento *sm* (*di vestiti etc*) wear.
logo'rante *ag* exhausting.
logo'rare *vt* to wear out; (*sciupare*) to waste; ~**rsi** *vr* to wear out; (*fig*) to wear o.s. out.
logo'rio *sm* wear and tear; (*fig*) strain.
'logoro, a *ag* (*stoffa*) worn out, threadbare; (*persona*) worn out.
'Loira *sf*: **la** ~ the Loire.
lom'baggine [lom'baddʒine] *sf* lumbago.
Lombar'dia *sf*: **la** ~ Lombardy.
lom'bardo, a *ag*, *smf* Lombard.
lom'bare *ag* (*ANAT*, *MED*) lumbar.
lom'bata *sf* (*taglio di carne*) loin.
'lombo *sm* (*ANAT*) loin.
lom'brico, chi *sm* earthworm.
londi'nese *ag* London *cpd* ♦ *smf* Londoner.
'Londra *sf* London.
lon'ganime *ag* forbearing.
longevità [londʒevi'ta] *sf* longevity.
lon'gevo, a [lon'dʒevo] *ag* long-lived.
longi'lineo, a [londʒi'lineo] *ag* long-limbed.
longi'tudine [londʒi'tudine] *sf* longitude.
lontana'mente *av* remotely; **non ci pensavo neppure** ~ it didn't even occur to me.
lonta'nanza [lonta'nantsa] *sf* distance; absence.

lon'tano, a *ag* (*distante*) distant, faraway; (*assente*) absent; (*vago: sospetto*) slight, remote; (*tempo: remoto*) far-off, distant; (*parente*) distant, remote ♦ *av* far; **è ~a la casa?** is it far to the house?, is the house far from here?; **è ~ un chilometro** it's a kilometre away *o* a kilometre from here; **più ~** farther; **da** *o* **di ~** from a distance; **~ da** a long way from; **alla ~a** slightly, vaguely.

'lontra *sf* otter.

lo'quace [lo'kwatʃe] *ag* talkative, loquacious; (*fig: gesto etc*) eloquent.

loquacità [lokwatʃi'ta] *sf* talkativeness, loquacity.

'lordo, a *ag* dirty, filthy; (*peso, stipendio*) gross; **~ d'imposta** pre-tax.

Lo'rena *sf* (*GEO*) Lorraine.

'loro *pron pl* (*oggetto, con preposizione*) them; (*complemento di termine*) to them; (*soggetto*) they; (*forma di cortesia: anche:* **L~**) you; to you; **il(la) ~, i(le) ~** *det* their; (*forma di cortesia: anche:* **L~**) your ♦ *pron* theirs; (*forma di cortesia: anche:* **L~**) yours ♦ *sm inv:* **il ~** their (*o* your) money ♦ *sf inv:* **la ~** (*opinione*) their (*o* your) view; **i ~** (*famiglia*) their (*o* your) family; (*amici etc*) their (*o* your) own people; **un ~ amico** a friend of theirs; **è dalla ~** he's on their (*o* your) side; **ne hanno fatto un'altra delle ~** they've (*o* you've) done it again; **~ stessi(e)** they themselves; you yourselves.

lo'sanga, ghe *sf* diamond, lozenge.

Lo'sanna *sf* Lausanne.

'losco, a, schi, sche *ag* (*fig*) shady, suspicious.

'lotta *sf* struggle, fight; (*SPORT*) wrestling; **essere in ~ (con)** to be in conflict (with); **fare la ~ (con)** to wrestle (with); **~ armata** armed struggle; **~ di classe** (*POL*) class struggle; **~ libera** (*SPORT*) all-in wrestling (*BRIT*), freestyle.

lot'tare *vi* to fight, struggle; to wrestle.

lotta'tore, 'trice *sm/f* wrestler.

lotte'ria *sf* lottery; (*di gara ippica*) sweepstake.

lottiz'zare [lottid'dzare] *vt* to divide into plots; (*fig*) to share out.

lottizzazi'one [lottiddzat'tsjone] *sf* division into plots; (*fig*) share-out.

'lotto *sm* (*gioco*) (state) lottery; (*parte*) lot; (*EDIL*) site; **vincere un terno al ~** (*anche fig*) to hit the jackpot.

lozi'one [lot'tsjone] *sf* lotion.

LT *sigla* = *Latina*.

LU *sigla* = *Lucca*.

lubrifi'cante *sm* lubricant.

lubrifi'care *vt* to lubricate.

lu'cano, a *ag* of (*o* from) Lucania.

luc'chetto [luk'ketto] *sm* padlock.

lucci'care [luttʃi'kare] *vi* to sparkle; (*oro*) to glitter; (*stella*) to twinkle; (*occhi*) to glisten.

lucci'chio [luttʃi'kio] *sm* sparkling; glittering; twinkling; glistening.

lucci'cone [luttʃi'kone] *sm:* **avere i ~i agli occhi** to have tears in one's eyes.

'luccio ['luttʃo] *sm* (*ZOOL*) pike.

'lucciola ['luttʃola] *sf* (*ZOOL*) firefly; glow-worm; (*fam, fig: prostituta*) girl (*o* woman) on the game.

'luce ['lutʃe] *sf* light; (*finestra*) window; **alla ~ di** by the light of; **fare qc alla ~ del sole** (*fig*) to do sth in the open; **dare alla ~** (*bambino*) to give birth to; **fare ~ su qc** (*fig*) to shed *o* throw light on sth; **~ del sole/della luna** sun/moonlight.

lu'cente [lu'tʃente] *ag* shining.

lucen'tezza [lutʃen'tettsa] *sf* shine.

lu'cerna [lu'tʃerna] *sf* oil lamp.

lucer'nario [lutʃer'narjo] *sm* skylight.

lu'certola [lu'tʃertola] *sf* lizard.

luci'dare [lutʃi'dare] *vt* to polish; (*ricalcare*) to trace.

lucida'trice [lutʃida'tritʃe] *sf* floor polisher.

lucidità [lutʃidi'ta] *sf* lucidity.

'lucido, a ['lutʃido] *ag* shining, bright; (*lucidato*) polished; (*fig*) lucid ♦ *sm* shine, lustre (*BRIT*), luster (*US*); (*per scarpe etc*) polish; (*disegno*) tracing.

lu'cignolo [lu'tʃiɲɲolo] *sm* wick.

luc'rare *vt* to make money out of.

lucra'tivo, a *ag* lucrative; **a scopo ~** for gain.

'lucro *sm* profit, gain; **a scopo di ~** for gain; **organizzazione senza scopo di ~** non-profit-making (*BRIT*) *o* non-profit (*US*) organization.

lu'croso, a *ag* lucrative, profitable.

luculli'ano, a *ag* (*pasto*) sumptuous.

lu'dibrio *sm* mockery *no pl*; (*oggetto di scherno*) laughing stock.

'lue *sf* syphilis.

'luglio ['luʎʎo] *sm* July; **nel mese di ~** in July, in the month of July; **il primo ~** the first of July; **arrivare il 2 ~** to arrive on the 2nd of July; **all'inizio/alla fine di ~** at the beginning/at the end of July; **durante il mese di ~** during July; **a ~ del prossimo anno** in July of next year; **ogni anno a ~** every July; **che fai a ~?** what are you doing in July?; **ha piovuto molto a ~ quest'anno** July was very wet this year.

'lugubre *ag* gloomy.

'lui *pron* (*soggetto*) he; (*oggetto: per dare*

rilievo, con preposizione) him ♦ *sm inv*: **il mio**
~ my beloved; ~ **stesso** he himself; **è** ~
it's him.

lu'maca, che *sf* slug; (*chiocciola*) snail.

luma'cone *sm* (large) slug; (*fig*) slowcoach
(*BRIT*), slowpoke (*US*).

'lume *sm* light; (*lampada*) lamp; ~ **a olio** oil
lamp; **chiedere** ~**i a qn** (*fig*) to ask sb for
advice; **a** ~ **di naso** (*fig*) by rule of thumb.

lumi'cino [lumi'tʃino] *sm* small *o* faint light;
essere (ridotto) al ~ (*fig*) to be at death's
door.

lumi'era *sf* chandelier.

lumi'nare *sm* luminary.

lumi'naria *sf* (*per feste*) illuminations *pl*.

lumine'scente [lumineʃ'ʃɛnte] *ag*
luminescent.

lu'mino *sm* small light; ~ **da notte** night-
light; ~ **per i morti** candle for the dead.

luminosità *sf* brightness; (*fig: di sorriso,
volto*) radiance.

lumi'noso, a *ag* (*che emette luce*) luminous;
(*cielo, colore, stanza*) bright; (*sorgente*) of
light, light *cpd*; (*fig: sorriso*) bright,
radiant; **insegna** ~**a** neon sign.

lun. *abbr* (= *lunedì*) Mon.

'luna *sf* moon; ~ **nuova/piena** new/full
moon; **avere la** ~ to be in a bad mood; ~
di miele honeymoon.

'luna park *sm inv* amusement park,
funfair.

lu'nare *ag* lunar, moon *cpd*.

lu'nario *sm* almanac; **sbarcare il** ~ to make
ends meet.

lu'natico, a, ci, che *ag* whimsical,
temperamental.

lunedì *sm inv* Monday; *per fraseologia vedi*
martedì.

lun'gaggine [lun'gaddʒine] *sf* slowness; ~**i
della burocrazia** red tape.

lunga'mente *av* (*a lungo*) for a long time;
(*estesamente*) at length.

lun'garno *sm* embankment along the
Arno.

lun'ghezza [lun'gettsa] *sf* length; ~ **d'onda**
(*FISICA*) wavelength.

'lungi ['lundʒi] *av*: ~ **da** *prep* far from.

lungimi'rante [lundʒimi'rante] *ag* far-
sighted.

'lungo, a, ghi, ghe *ag* long; (*lento: persona*)
slow; (*diluito: caffè, brodo*) weak, watery,
thin ♦ *sm* length ♦ *prep* along; ~ **3 metri** 3
metres long; **avere la barba** ~**a** to be
unshaven; **a** ~ for a long time; **a** ~ **andare**
in the long run; **di gran** ~**a** (*molto*) by far;
andare in ~ *o* **per le lunghe** to drag on;
saperla ~**a** to know what's what; **in** ~ **e in
largo** far and wide, all over; ~ **il corso dei**

secoli throughout the centuries;
navigazione di ~ **corso** ocean-going
navigation.

lungofi'ume *sm* embankment.

lungo'lago *sm* road round a lake.

lungo'mare *sm* promenade.

lungome'traggio [lungome'traddʒo] *sm*
(*CINE*) feature film.

lungo'tevere *sm* embankment along the
Tiber.

lu'notto *sm* (*AUT*) rear *o* back window; ~
termico heated rear window.

lu'ogo, ghi *sm* place; (*posto: di incidente
etc*) scene, site; (*punto, passo di libro*)
passage; **in** ~ **di** instead of; **in primo** ~ in
the first place; **aver** ~ to take place; **dar** ~
a to give rise to; ~ **comune**
commonplace; ~ **del delitto** scene of the
crime; ~ **geometrico** locus; ~ **di nascita**
birthplace; (*AMM*) place of birth; ~ **di
pena** prison, penitentiary; ~ **di
provenienza** place of origin.

luogote'nente *sm* (*MIL*) lieutenant.

lupacchi'otto [lupak'kjɔtto] *sm* (*ZOOL*)
(wolf) cub.

lu'para *sf* sawn-off shotgun.

lu'petto *sm* (*ZOOL*) (wolf) cub; (*negli scouts*)
cub scout.

'lupo, a *sm/f* wolf/she-wolf; **cane** ~ alsatian
(dog) (*BRIT*), German shepherd (dog);
tempo da ~**i** filthy weather.

'luppolo *sm* (*BOT*) hop.

'lurido, a *ag* filthy.

luri'dume *sm* filth.

lu'singa, ghe *sf* (*spesso al pl*) flattery *no pl*.

lusin'gare *vt* to flatter.

lusinghi'ero, a [luzin'gjɛro] *ag* flattering,
gratifying.

lus'sare *vt* (*MED*) to dislocate.

lussazi'one [lussat'tsjone] *sf* (*MED*)
dislocation.

lussembur'ghese [lussembur'gese] *ag* of (*o
from*) Luxembourg ♦ *sm/f* native (*o
inhabitant*) of Luxembourg.

Lussem'burgo *sm* (*stato*): **il** ~
Luxembourg ♦ *sf* (*città*) Luxembourg.

'lusso *sm* luxury; **di** ~ luxury *cpd*.

lussu'oso, a *ag* luxurious.

lussureggi'are [lussured'dʒare] *vi* to be
luxuriant.

lus'suria *sf* lust.

lussuri'oso, a *ag* lascivious, lustful.

lus'trare *vt* to polish, shine.

lustras'carpe *sm/f inv* shoeshine.

lus'trino *sm* sequin.

'lustro, a *ag* shiny; (*pelliccia*) glossy ♦ *sm*
shine, gloss; (*fig*) prestige, glory;
(*quinquennio*) five-year period.

lute'rano, a *ag, sm/f*, Lutheran.

'lutto *sm* mourning; **essere in/portare il ~** to be in/wear mourning.

M m

M, m ['ɛmme] *sf o m inv* (*lettera*) M, m; **M come Milano** ≈ M for Mary (*BRIT*), M for Mike (*US*).

m. *abbr* = **mese; metro; miglia; monte.**

ma *cong* but; **~ insomma!** for goodness sake!; **~ no!** of course not!

'macabro, a *ag* gruesome, macabre.

ma'caco, chi *sm* (*ZOOL*) macaque.

macché [mak'ke] *escl* not at all!, certainly not!

macche'roni [makke'roni] *smpl* macaroni *sg*.

'macchia ['makkja] *sf* stain, spot; (*chiazza di diverso colore*) spot; splash, patch; (*tipo di boscaglia*) scrub; **~ d'inchiostro** ink stain; **estendersi a ~ d'olio** (*fig*) to spread rapidly; **darsi/vivere alla ~** (*fig*) to go into/live in hiding.

macchi'are [mak'kjare] *vt* (*sporcare*) to stain, mark; **~rsi** *vr* (*persona*) to get o.s. dirty; (*stoffa*) to stain; **to get stained** *o* marked; **~rsi di un delitto** to be guilty of a crime.

macchi'ato, a [mak'kjato] *ag* (*pelle, pelo*) spotted; **~ di** stained with; **caffè ~** coffee with a dash of milk.

macchi'etta [mak'kjetta] *sf* (*disegno*) sketch, caricature; (*TEAT*) caricature; (*fig: persona*) character.

'macchina ['makkina] *sf* machine; (*motore, locomotiva*) engine; (*automobile*) car; (*fig: meccanismo*) machinery; **andare in ~** (*AUT*) to go by car; (*STAMPA*) to go to press; **salire in ~** to get into the car; **venire in ~** to come by car; **sala ~e** (*NAUT*) engine room; **~ da cucire** sewing machine; **~ fotografica** camera; **~ da presa** cine *o* movie camera; **~ da scrivere** typewriter; **~ utensile** machine tool; **~ a vapore** steam engine.

macchinal'mente [makkinal'mente] *av* mechanically.

macchi'nare [makki'nare] *vt* to plot.

macchi'nario [makki'narjo] *sm* machinery.

macchinazi'one [makkinat'tsjone] *sf* plot, machination.

macchi'netta [makki'netta] *sf* (*fam: caffettiera*) percolator; (*: accendino*) lighter.

macchi'nista, i [makki'nista] *sm* (*di treno*) engine-driver; (*di nave*) engineer; (*TEAT, TV*) stagehand.

macchi'noso, a [makki'noso] *ag* complex, complicated.

ma'cedone [ma'tʃedone] *ag, sm/f* Macedonian.

Mace'donia [matʃe'dɔnja] *sm* Macedonia.

mace'donia [matʃe'dɔnja] *sf* fruit salad.

macel'laio [matʃel'lajo] *sm* butcher.

macel'lare [matʃel'lare] *vt* to slaughter, butcher.

macellazi'one [matʃellat'tsjone] *sf* slaughtering, butchering.

macelle'ria [matʃelle'ria] *sf* butcher's (shop).

ma'cello [ma'tʃello] *sm* (*mattatoio*) slaughterhouse, abattoir (*BRIT*); (*fig*) slaughter, massacre; (*: disastro*) shambles *sg*.

mace'rare [matʃe'rare] *vt* to macerate; (*CUC*) to marinate; **~rsi** *vr* to waste away; (*fig*): **~rsi in** to be consumed with.

macerazi'one [matʃerat'tsjone] *sf* maceration.

ma'cerie [ma'tʃɛrje] *sfpl* rubble *sg*, debris *sg*.

'macero ['matʃero] *sm* (*operazione*) pulping; (*stabilimento*) pulping mill; **carta da ~** paper for pulping.

machia'vellico, a, ci, che [makja'vɛlliko] *ag* (*anche fig*) Machiavellian.

ma'cigno [ma'tʃiɲɲo] *sm* (*masso*) rock, boulder.

maci'lento, a [matʃi'lɛnto] *ag* emaciated.

'macina ['matʃina] *sf* (*pietra*) millstone; (*macchina*) grinder.

macinacaffè [matʃinakaf'fɛ] *sm inv* coffee grinder.

macina'pepe [matʃina'pepe] *sm inv* peppermill.

maci'nare [matʃi'nare] *vt* to grind; (*carne*) to mince (*BRIT*), grind (*US*).

maci'nato [matʃi'nato] *sm* meal, flour; (*carne*) minced (*BRIT*) *o* ground (*US*) meat.

maci'nino [matʃi'nino] *sm* (*per caffè*) coffee grinder; (*per pepe*) peppermill; (*scherzoso: macchina*) old banger (*BRIT*), clunker (*US*).

maciul'lare [matʃul'lare] *vt* (*canapa, lino*) to brake; (*fig: braccio etc*) to crush.

'macro ... *prefisso* macro....

macrobi'otico, a *ag* macrobiotic ♦ *sf* macrobiotics *sg*.

macu'lato, a *ag* (*pelo*) spotted.

Ma'dama: palazzo ~ *sm* (*POL*) *seat of the*

Italian Chamber of Senators.
made in Italy [meɪdɪ'nɪtəlɪ] *sm*: **il** ~ Italian exports *pl* (*especially fashion goods*).
Ma'dera *sf* (*GEO*) Madeira ♦ *sm inv* (*vino*) Madeira.
'madido, a *ag*: ~ **(di)** wet *o* moist (with).
Ma'donna *sf* (*REL*) Our Lady.
mador'nale *ag* enormous, huge.
'madre *sf* mother; (*matrice di bolletta*) counterfoil ♦ *ag inv* mother *cpd*; **ragazza** ~ unmarried mother; **scena** ~ (*TEAT*) principal scene; (*fig*) terrible scene.
madre'lingua *sf* mother tongue, native language.
madre'patria *sf* mother country, native land.
madre'perla *sf* mother-of-pearl.
Ma'drid *sf* Madrid.
madri'gale *sm* madrigal.
madri'leno, a *ag* of (*o* from) Madrid ♦ *sm/f* person from Madrid.
ma'drina *sf* godmother.
maestà *sf inv* majesty; **Sua M**~ **la Regina** Her Majesty the Queen.
maestosità *sf* majesty.
maes'toso, a *ag* majestic.
ma'estra *sf vedi* **maestro**.
maes'trale *sm* north-west wind.
maes'tranze [maes'trantse] *sfpl* workforce *sg*.
maes'tria *sf* mastery, skill.
ma'estro, a *sm/f* (*INS: anche*: ~ **di scuola** *o* **elementare**) primary (*BRIT*) *o* grade school (*US*) teacher; (*esperto*) expert ♦ *sm* (*artigiano, fig: guida*) master; (*MUS*) maestro ♦ *ag* (*principale*) main; (*di grande abilità*) masterly, skilful (*BRIT*), skillful (*US*); **un colpo da** ~ (*fig*) a masterly move; **muro** ~ main wall; **strada** ~**a** main road; ~**a d'asilo** nursery teacher; ~ **di ballo** dancing master; ~ **di cerimonie** master of ceremonies; ~ **d'orchestra** conductor, director (*US*); ~ **di scherma** fencing master; ~ **di sci** ski instructor.
'mafia *sf* Mafia.
mafi'oso *sm* member of the Mafia.
'maga, ghe *sf* sorceress.
ma'gagna [ma'gaɲɲa] *sf* defect, flaw, blemish; (*noia, guaio*) problem.
ma'gari *escl* (*esprime desiderio*): ~ **fosse vero!** if only it were true!; **ti piacerebbe andare in Scozia?** — ~! would you like to go to Scotland? — I certainly would! ♦ *av* (*anche*) even; (*forse*) perhaps.
magazzi'naggio [magaddzi'naddʒo] *sm*: (**spese di**) ~ storage charges *pl*, warehousing charges *pl*.
magazzini'ere [magaddzi'njɛre] *sm* warehouseman.
magaz'zino [magad'dzino] *sm* warehouse; **grande** ~ department store; ~ **doganale** bonded warehouse.
'maggio ['maddʒo] *sm* May; *per fraseologia vedi* **luglio**.
maggio'rana [maddʒo'rana] *sf* (*BOT*) (sweet) marjoram.
maggio'ranza [maddʒo'rantsa] *sf* majority; **nella** ~ **dei casi** in most cases.
maggio'rare [maddʒo'rare] *vt* to increase, raise.
maggiorazi'one [maddʒorat'tsjone] *sf* (*COMM*) rise, increase.
maggior'domo [maddʒor'dɔmo] *sm* butler.
maggi'ore [mad'dʒore] *ag* (*comparativo: più grande*) bigger, larger; taller; greater; (*: più vecchio: sorella, fratello*) older, elder; (*: di grado superiore*) senior; (*: più importante, MIL, MUS*) major; (*superlativo*) biggest, largest; tallest; greatest; oldest, eldest ♦ *sm/f* (*di grado*) superior; (*di età*) elder; (*MIL*) major; (*: AER*) squadron leader; **la maggior parte** the majority; **andare per la** ~ (*cantante, attore etc*) to be very popular, be "in".
maggio'renne [maddʒo'rɛnne] *ag* of age ♦ *sm/f* person who has come of age.
maggiori'tario, a [maddʒori'tarjo] *ag* majority *cpd* ♦ (*POL: anche*: **sistema** ~) first-past-the-post system.
maggior'mente [maddʒor'mente] *av* much more; (*con senso superlativo*) most.
maghre'bino, a *ag, sm/f* Maghrebi.
ma'gia [ma'dʒia] *sf* magic.
'magico, a, ci, che ['madʒiko] *ag* magic; (*fig*) fascinating, charming, magical.
'magio ['madʒo] *sm* (*REL*): **i re Magi** the Magi, the Three Wise Men.
magis'tero [madʒis'tɛro] *sm* teaching; (*fig: maestria*) skill; (*INS*): **Facoltà di M**~ ≈ teachers' training college.
magis'trale [madʒis'trale] *ag* primary (*BRIT*) *o* grade school (*US*) teachers', primary *o* grade school teaching *cpd*; (*abile*) skilful (*BRIT*), skillful (*US*); **istituto** ~ *secondary school for the training of primary teachers*.
magis'trato [madʒis'trato] *sm* magistrate.
magistra'tura [madʒistra'tura] *sf* magistrature; (*magistrati*): **la** ~ the Bench.
'maglia ['maʎʎa] *sf* stitch; (*lavoro ai ferri*) knitting *no pl*; (*tessuto, SPORT*) jersey; (*maglione*) jersey, sweater; (*di catena*) link; (*di rete*) mesh; **avviare/diminuire le** ~**e** to cast on/cast off; **lavorare a** ~, **fare la** ~ to knit; ~ **diritta/rovescia** plain/purl.
magli'aia [maʎ'ʎaja] *sf* knitter.
maglie'ria [maʎʎe'ria] *sf* knitwear;

(*negozio*) knitwear shop; **macchina per** ~ knitting machine.

magli'etta [maʎ'ʎetta] *sf* (*canottiera*) vest; (*tipo camicia*) T-shirt.

magli'ficio [maʎʎi'fitʃo] *sm* knitwear factory.

ma'glina [maʎ'ʎina] *sf* (*tessuto*) jersey.

'maglio ['maʎʎo] *sm* mallet; (*macchina*) power hammer.

magli'one [maʎ'ʎone] *sm* jersey, sweater.

'magma *sm* magma; (*fig*) mass.

ma'gnaccia [maɲ'ɲattʃa] *sm inv* (*peg*) pimp.

magnanimità [maɲɲanimi'ta] *sf* magnanimity.

ma'gnanimo, a [maɲ'ɲanimo] *ag* magnanimous.

ma'gnate [maɲ'ɲate] *sm* tycoon, magnate.

ma'gnesia [maɲ'ɲɛzja] *sf* (*CHIM*) magnesia.

ma'gnesio [maɲ'ɲɛzjo] *sm* (*CHIM*) magnesium; **al** ~ (*lampada, flash*) magnesium *cpd*.

ma'gnete [maɲ'ɲɛte] *sm* magnet.

ma'gnetico, a, ci, che [maɲ'ɲɛtiko] *ag* magnetic.

magne'tismo [maɲɲe'tizmo] *sm* magnetism.

magnetiz'zare [maɲɲetid'dzare] *vt* (*FISICA*) to magnetize; (*fig*) to mesmerize.

magne'tofono [maɲɲe'tɔfono] *sm* tape recorder.

magnifica'mente [maɲɲifika'mente] *av* magnificently, extremely well.

magnifi'cenza [maɲɲifi'tʃɛntsa] *sf* magnificence, splendour (*BRIT*), splendor (*US*).

ma'gnifico, a, ci, che [maɲ'ɲifiko] *ag* magnificent, splendid; (*ospite*) generous.

'magno, a ['maɲɲo] *ag*: **aula** ~**a** main hall.

ma'gnolia [maɲ'ɲɔlja] *sf* magnolia.

'mago, ghi *sm* (*stregone*) magician, wizard; (*illusionista*) magician.

ma'grezza [ma'grettsa] *sf* thinness.

'magro, a *ag* (*very*) thin, skinny; (*carne*) lean; (*formaggio*) low-fat; (*fig: scarso, misero*) meagre (*BRIT*), meager (*US*), poor; (: *meschino: scusa*) poor, lame; **mangiare di** ~ not to eat meat.

'mai *av* (*nessuna volta*) never; (*talvolta*) ever; **non ...** ~ never; ~ **più** never again; **come** ~? why (*o* how) on earth?; **chi/ dove/quando** ~? whoever/wherever/ whenever?

mai'ale *sm* (*ZOOL*) pig; (*carne*) pork.

mai'olica *sf* majolica.

maio'nese *sf* mayonnaise.

Mai'orca *sf* Majorca.

'mais *sm* maize (*BRIT*), corn (*US*).

mai'uscolo, a *ag* (*lettera*) capital ♦ *sf*

capital letter ♦ *sm* capital letters *pl*; (*TIP*) upper case; **scrivere tutto (in)** ~ to write everything in capitals *o* in capital letters.

mal *av, sm vedi* **male.**

'mala *sf* (*gergo*) underworld.

malac'corto, a *ag* rash, careless.

mala'fede *sf* bad faith.

malaf'fare: di ~ *ag* (*gente*) shady, dishonest; **donna di** ~ prostitute.

mala'gevole [mala'dʒevole] *ag* difficult, hard.

mala'grazia [mala'grattsja] *sf*: **con** ~ with bad grace, impolitely.

mala'lingua, *pl* **male'lingue** *sf* gossip (*person*).

mala'mente *av* badly; (*sgarbatamente*) rudely.

malan'dato, a *ag* (*persona: di salute*) in poor health; (: *di condizioni finanziarie*) badly off; (*trascurato*) shabby.

ma'lanimo *sm* ill will, malevolence; **di** ~ unwillingly.

ma'lanno *sm* (*disgrazia*) misfortune; (*malattia*) ailment.

mala'pena *sf*: **a** ~ hardly, scarcely.

ma'laria *sf* malaria.

ma'larico, a, ci, che *ag* malarial.

mala'sorte *sf* bad luck.

mala'ticcio, a [mala'tittʃo] *ag* sickly.

ma'lato, a *ag* ill, sick; (*gamba*) bad; (*pianta*) diseased ♦ *sm/f* sick person; (*in ospedale*) patient; **darsi** ~ (*sul lavoro etc*) to go sick.

malat'tia *sf* (*infettiva etc*) illness, disease; (*cattiva salute*) illness, sickness; (*di pianta*) disease; **mettersi in** ~ to go on sick leave; **fare una** ~ **di qc** (*fig: disperarsi*) to get in a state about sth.

malaugu'rato, a *ag* ill-fated, unlucky.

malau'gurio *sm* bad *o* ill omen; **uccello del** ~ bird of ill omen.

mala'vita *sf* underworld.

malavi'toso, a *sm/f* gangster.

mala'voglia [mala'vɔʎʎa]: **di** ~ *av* unwillingly, reluctantly.

Ma'lawi [ma'lavi] *sm*: **il** ~ Malawi.

Mala'ysia *sf* Malaysia.

malaysi'ano, a *ag, sm/f* Malaysian.

malcapi'tato, a *ag* unlucky, unfortunate ♦ *sm/f* unfortunate person.

mal'concio, a, ci, ce [mal'kontʃo] *ag* in a sorry state.

malcon'tento *sm* discontent.

malcos'tume *sm* immorality.

mal'destro, a *ag* (*inabile*) inexpert, inexperienced; (*goffo*) awkward.

maldi'cente [maldi'tʃɛnte] *ag* slanderous.

maldi'cenza [maldi'tʃɛntsa] *sf* malicious gossip.

maldis'posto, a *ag*: ~ **(verso)** ill-disposed (towards).

Mal'dive *sfpl*: **le** ~ the Maldives.

'male *av* badly ◊ *sm* (*ciò che è ingiusto, disonesto*) evil; (*danno, svantaggio*) harm; (*sventura*) misfortune; (*dolore fisico, morale*) pain, ache; **sentirsi** ~ to feel ill; **aver mal di cuore/fegato** to have a heart/liver complaint; **aver mal di denti/d'orecchie/di testa** to have toothache/earache/a headache; **aver mal di gola** to have a sore throat; **aver** ~ **ai piedi** to have sore feet; **far** ~ (*dolere*) to hurt; **far** ~ **alla salute** to be bad for one's health; **far del** ~ **a qn** to hurt *o* harm sb; **parlar** ~ **di qn** to speak ill of sb; **restare** *o* **rimanere** ~ to be sorry; to be disappointed; to be hurt; **trattar** ~ **qn** to ill-treat sb; **andare a** ~ to go off *o* bad; **come va?** — **non c'è** ~ how are you? — not bad; **di** ~ **in peggio** from bad to worse; **per** ~ **che vada** however badly things go; **non avertene a** ~, **non prendertela a** ~ don't take it to heart; **mal comune mezzo gaudio** (*proverbio*) a trouble shared is a trouble halved; **mal d'auto** carsickness; **mal di mare** seasickness.

male'detto, a *pp di* **maledire** ◊ *ag* cursed, damned; (*fig fam*) damned, blasted.

male'dire *vt* to curse.

maledizi'one [maledit'tsjone] *sf* curse; ~! damn it!

maledu'cato, a *ag* rude, ill-mannered.

maleducazi'one [maledukat'tsjone] *sf* rudeness.

male'fatta *sf* misdeed.

male'ficio [male'fitʃo] *sm* witchcraft.

ma'lefico, a, ci, che *ag* (*aria, cibo*) harmful, bad; (*influsso, azione*) evil.

ma'lese *ag*, *sm/f* Malay(an) ◊ *sm* (*LING*) Malay.

Ma'lesia *sf* Malaya.

ma'lessere *sm* indisposition, slight illness; (*fig*) uneasiness.

malevo'lenza [malevo'lɛntsa] *sf* malevolence.

ma'levolo, a *ag* malevolent.

malfa'mato, a *ag* notorious.

mal'fatto, a *ag* (*persona*) deformed; (*oggetto*) badly made; (*lavoro*) badly done.

malfat'tore, 'trice *sm/f* wrongdoer.

mal'fermo, a *ag* unsteady, shaky; (*salute*) poor, delicate.

malformazi'one [malformat'tsjone] *sf* malformation.

'malga, ghe *sf* Alpine hut.

malgo'verno *sm* maladministration.

mal'grado *prep* in spite of, despite ◊ *cong*

although; **mio** (*o* **tuo** *etc*) ~ against my (*o* your *etc*) will.

ma'lia *sf* spell; (*fig: fascino*) charm.

mali'ardo, a *ag* (*occhi, sorriso*) bewitching ◊ *sf* enchantress.

maligna'mente [maliɲɲa'mente] *av* maliciously.

mali'gnare [maliɲ'ɲare] *vi*: ~ **su** to malign, speak ill of.

malignità [maliɲɲi'ta] *sf inv* (*qualità*) malice, spite; (*osservazione*) spiteful remark; **con** ~ spitefully, maliciously.

ma'ligno, a [ma'liɲɲo] *ag* (*malvagio*) malicious, malignant; (*MED*) malignant.

malinco'nia *sf* melancholy, gloom.

malin'conico, a, ci, che *ag* melancholy.

malincu'ore : a ~ *av* reluctantly, unwillingly.

malinfor'mato, a *ag* misinformed.

malintenzio'nato, a [malintentsjo'nato] *ag* ill-intentioned.

malin'teso, a *ag* misunderstood; (*riguardo, senso del dovere*) mistaken, wrong ◊ *sm* misunderstanding.

ma'lizia [ma'littsja] *sf* (*malignità*) malice; (*furbizia*) cunning; (*espediente*) trick.

malizi'oso, a [malit'tsjoso] *ag* malicious; cunning; (*vivace, birichino*) mischievous.

malle'abile *ag* malleable.

mal'loppo *sm* (*fam: refurtiva*) loot.

malme'nare *vt* to beat up; (*fig*) to ill-treat.

mal'messo, a *ag* shabby.

malnu'trito, a *ag* undernourished.

malnutrizi'one [malnutrit'tsjone] *sf* malnutrition.

'malo, a *ag*: **in** ~ **modo** badly.

ma'locchio [ma'lɔkkjo] *sm* evil eye.

ma'lora *sf* (*fam*): **andare in** ~ to go to the dogs; **va in** ~! go to hell!

ma'lore *sm* (sudden) illness.

malri'dotto, a *ag* (*abiti, scarpe, persona*) in a sorry state; (*casa, macchina*) dilapidated, in a poor state of repair.

mal'sano, a *ag* unhealthy.

malsi'curo, a *ag* unsafe.

'Malta *sf* Malta.

'malta *sf* (*EDIL*) mortar.

mal'tempo *sm* bad weather.

'malto *sm* malt.

mal'tolto *sm* ill-gotten gains *pl*.

maltratta'mento *sm* ill treatment.

maltrat'tare *vt* to ill-treat.

malu'more *sm* bad mood; (*irritabilità*) bad temper; (*discordia*) ill feeling; **di** ~ in a bad mood.

'malva *sf* (*BOT*) mallow ◊ *ag*, *sm inv* mauve.

mal'vagio, a, gi, gie [mal'vadʒo] *ag* wicked, evil.

malvagità [malvadʒi'ta] *sf inv* (*qualità*) wickedness; (*azione*) wicked deed.

malva'sia *sf Italian dessert wine.*

malversazi'one [malversat'tsjone] *sf* (*DIR*) embezzlement.

malves'tito, a *ag* badly dressed, ill-clad.

mal'visto, a *ag:* ~ (**da**) disliked (by), unpopular (with).

malvi'vente *sm* criminal.

malvolenti'eri *av* unwillingly, reluctantly.

malvo'lere *vt:* **farsi** ~ **da qn** to make o.s. unpopular with sb ♦ *sm:* **prendere qn a** ~ to take a dislike to sb.

'mamma *sf* mum(my) (*BRIT*), mom (*US*); ~ **mia!** my goodness!

mam'mario, a *ag* (*ANAT*) mammary.

mam'mella *sf* (*ANAT*) breast; (*di vacca, capra etc*) udder.

mam'mifero *sm* mammal.

mam'mismo *sm* excessive attachment to one's mother.

'mammola *sf* (*BOT*) violet.

'manager ['mænidʒə] *sm inv* manager.

manageri'ale [manadʒe'rjale] *ag* managerial.

ma'nata *sf* (*colpo*) slap; (*quantità*) handful.

'manca *sf* left (hand); **a destra e a** ~ left, right and centre, on all sides.

manca'mento *sm* (*di forze*) (feeling of) faintness, weakness.

man'canza [man'kantsa] *sf* lack; (*carenza*) shortage, scarcity; (*fallo*) fault; (*imperfezione*) failing, shortcoming; **per** ~ **di tempo** through lack of time; **in** ~ **di meglio** for lack of anything better; **sentire la** ~ **di qc/qn** to miss sth/sb.

man'care *vi* (*essere insufficiente*) to be lacking; (*venir meno*) to fail; (*sbagliare*) to be wrong, make a mistake; (*non esserci*) to be missing, not to be there; (*essere lontano*): ~ (**da**) to be away (from) ♦ *vt* to miss; ~ **di** to lack; ~ **a** (*promessa*) to fail to keep; **tu mi manchi** I miss you; **mancò poco che morisse** he very nearly died; **mancano ancora 10 sterline** we're still £10 short; **manca un quarto alle 6** it's a quarter to 6; **non mancherò** I won't forget, I'll make sure I do; **ci mancherebbe altro!** of course I (*o* you *etc*) will!; ~ **da casa** to be away from home; ~ **di rispetto a** *o* **verso qn** to be lacking in respect towards sb, be disrespectful towards sb; ~ **di parola** not to keep one's word, go back on one's word; **sentirsi** ~ to feel faint.

man'cato, a *ag* (*tentativo*) unsuccessful; (*artista*) failed.

manche [mãʃ] *sf inv* (*SPORT*) heat.

mancherò *etc* [manke'rɔ] *vb vedi* **mancare**.

man'chevole [man'kevole] *ag* (*insufficiente*) inadequate, insufficient.

manchevo'lezza [mankevo'lettsa] *sf* (*scorrettezza*) fault, shortcoming.

'mancia, ce ['mantʃa] *sf* tip; ~ **competente** reward.

manci'ata [man'tʃata] *sf* handful.

man'cino, a [man'tʃino] *ag* (*braccio*) left; (*persona*) left-handed; (*fig*) underhand.

'manco *av* (*nemmeno*): ~ **per sogno** *o* **per idea!** not on your life!

man'dante *smf* (*DIR*) principal; (*istigatore*) instigator.

manda'rancio [manda'rantʃo] *sm* clementine.

man'dare *vt* to send; (*far funzionare: macchina*) to drive; (*emettere*) to send out; (: *grido*) to give, utter, let out; ~ **avanti** (*persona*) to send ahead; (*fig: famiglia*) to provide for; (: *ditta*) to look after, run; (: *pratica*) to attend to; ~ **a chiamare qn** to send for sb; ~ **giù** to send down; (*anche fig*) to swallow; ~ **in onda** (*RADIO, TV*) to broadcast; ~ **in rovina** to ruin; ~ **via** to send away; (*licenziare*) to fire.

manda'rino *sm* mandarin (orange); (*cinese*) mandarin.

man'data *sf* (*quantità*) lot, batch; (*di chiave*) turn; **chiudere a doppia** ~ to double-lock.

manda'tario *sm* (*DIR*) representative, agent.

man'dato *sm* (*incarico*) commission; (*DIR: provvedimento*) warrant; (*di deputato etc*) mandate; (*ordine di pagamento*) postal *o* money order; ~ **d'arresto,** ~ **di cattura** warrant for arrest; ~ **di comparizione** summons *sg*; ~ **di perquisizione** search warrant.

man'dibola *sf* mandible, jaw.

mando'lino *sm* mandolin(e).

'mandorla *sf* almond.

mandor'lato *sm* nut brittle.

'mandorlo *sm* almond tree.

'mandria *sf* herd.

mandri'ano *sm* cowherd, herdsman.

man'drino *sm* (*TECN*) mandrel.

maneg'gevole [maned'dʒevole] *ag* easy to handle.

maneggi'are [maned'dʒare] *vt* (*creta, cera*) to mould (*BRIT*), mold (*US*), work, fashion; (*arnesi, utensili*) to handle; (: *adoperare*) to use; (*fig: persone, denaro*) to handle, deal with.

ma'neggio [ma'neddʒo] *sm* moulding (*BRIT*), molding (*US*); handling; use; (*intrigo*) plot, scheme; (*per cavalli*) riding school.

ma'nesco, a, schi, sche *ag* free with one's fists.

ma'nette *sfpl* handcuffs.

manga'nello *sm* club.

manga'nese *sm* manganese.

mange'reccio, a, ci, ce [mandʒe'rettʃo] *ag* edible.

mangi'abile [man'dʒabile] *ag* edible, eatable.

mangia'dischi [mandʒa'diski] *sm inv* record player.

mangia'nastri [mandʒa'nastri] *sm inv* cassette-recorder.

mangi'are [man'dʒare] *vt* to eat; (*intaccare*) to eat into *o* away; (*CARTE, SCACCHI etc*) to take ♦ *vi* to eat ♦ *sm* eating; (*cibo*) food; (*cucina*) cooking; **fare da** ~ to do the cooking; ~**rsi le parole** to mumble; ~**rsi le unghie** to bite one's nails.

mangia'soldi [mandʒa'sɔldi] *ag inv* (*fam*): **macchinetta** ~ one-armed bandit.

mangia'toia [mandʒa'toja] *sf* feeding-trough.

man'gime [man'dʒime] *sm* fodder.

mangiucchi'are [mandʒuk'kjare] *vt* to nibble.

'mango, ghi *sm* mango.

ma'nia *sf* (*PSIC*) mania; (*fig*) obsession, craze; **avere la** ~ **di fare qc** to have a habit of doing sth; ~ **di persecuzione** persecution complex *o* mania.

mania'cale *ag* (*PSIC*) maniacal; (*fanatico*) fanatical.

ma'niaco, a, ci, che *ag* suffering from a mania; ~ (**di**) obsessed (by), crazy (about).

'manica, che *sf* sleeve; (*fig: gruppo*) gang, bunch; (*GEO*): **la M**~, **il Canale della M**~ the (English) Channel; **senza** ~**che** sleeveless; **essere in** ~**che di camicia** to be in one's shirt sleeves; **essere di** ~ **larga/ stretta** to be easy-going/strict; ~ **a vento** (*AER*) wind sock.

manica'retto *sm* titbit (*BRIT*), tidbit (*US*).

mani'chino [mani'kino] *sm* (*di sarto, vetrina*) dummy.

'manico, ci *sm* handle; (*MUS*) neck; ~ **di scopa** broomstick.

mani'comio *sm* mental hospital; (*fig*) madhouse.

mani'cotto *sm* muff; (*TECN*) coupling; sleeve.

mani'cure *sm o f inv* manicure ♦ *sf inv* manicurist.

mani'era *sf* way, manner; (*stile*) style, manner; ~**e** *sfpl* manners; **in** ~ **che** so that; **in** ~ **da** so as to; **alla** ~ **di** in *o* after the style of; **in una** ~ **o nell'altra** one way or another; **in tutte le** ~**e** at all costs; **usare**

buone ~**e con qn** to be polite to sb; **usare le** ~**e forti** to use strong-arm tactics.

manie'rato, a *ag* affected.

mani'ero *sm* manor.

manifat'tura *sf* (*lavorazione*) manufacture; (*stabilimento*) factory.

manifatturi'ero, a *ag* manufacturing.

manifes'tante *sm/f* demonstrator.

manifes'tare *vt* to show, display; (*esprimere*) to express; (*rivelare*) to reveal, disclose ♦ *vi* to demonstrate; ~**rsi** *vr* to show o.s.; ~**rsi amico** to prove o.s. (to be) a friend.

manifestazi'one [manifestat'tsjone] *sf* show, display; expression; (*sintomo*) sign, symptom; (*dimostrazione pubblica*) demonstration; (*cerimonia*) event.

manifes'tino *sm* leaflet.

mani'festo, a *ag* obvious, evident ♦ *sm* poster, bill; (*scritto ideologico*) manifesto.

ma'niglia [ma'niʎʎa] *sf* handle; (*sostegno: negli autobus etc*) strap.

Ma'nila *sf* Manila.

manipo'lare *vt* to manipulate; (*alterare: vino*) to adulterate.

manipolazi'one [manipolat'tsjone] *sf* manipulation; adulteration.

ma'nipolo *sm* (*drappello*) handful.

manis'calco, chi *sm* blacksmith, farrier (*BRIT*).

'manna *sf* (*REL*) manna.

man'naia *sf* (*del boia*) (executioner's) axe *o* ax (*US*); (*per carni*) cleaver.

man'naro, a *ag*: **lupo** ~ werewolf.

'mano, i *sf* hand; (*strato: di vernice etc*) coat; **a** ~ by hand; **cucito a** ~ hand-sewn; **fatto a** ~ handmade; **alla** ~ (*persona*) easy-going; **fuori** ~ out of the way; **di prima** ~ (*notizia*) first-hand; **di seconda** ~ second-hand; **man** ~ little by little, gradually; **man** ~ **che** as; **a piene** ~**i** (*fig*) generously; **avere le** ~**i bucate** to spend money like water; **aver le** ~**i in pasta** to be in the know; **avere qc per le** ~**i** (*progetto, lavoro*) to have sth in hand; **dare una** ~ **a qn** to lend sb a hand; **dare una** ~ **di vernice a qc** to give sth a coat of paint; **darsi** *o* **stringersi la** ~ to shake hands; **forzare la** ~ to go too far; **mettere** ~ **a qc** to have a hand in sth; **mettere le** ~**i avanti** (*fig*) to safeguard o.s.; **restare a** ~**i vuote** to be left empty-handed; **venire alle** ~**i** to come to blows; ~**i in alto!** hands up!; ~**i pulite** *vedi nota nel riquadro*.

MANI PULITE

Mani pulite *("clean hands")* is the term used

to describe the judicial operation of the early 1990s to gather evidence against politicians and industrialists who were implicated in bribery and corruption scandals.

mano'dopera *sf* labour (*BRIT*), labor (*US*).

mano'messo, a *pp di* **manomettere**.

ma'nometro *sm* gauge, manometer.

mano'mettere *vt* (*alterare*) to tamper with; (*aprire indebitamente*) to break open illegally.

manomissi'one *sf* (*di prove etc*) tampering; (*di lettera*) opening.

ma'napola *sf* (*dell'armatura*) gauntlet; (*guanto*) mitt; (*di impugnatura*) hand-grip; (*pomello*) knob.

manos'critto, a *ag* handwritten ♦ *sm* manuscript.

mano'vale *sm* labourer (*BRIT*), laborer (*US*).

mano'vella *sf* handle; (*TECN*) crank.

ma'novra *sf* manoeuvre (*BRIT*), maneuver (*US*); (*FERR*) shunting; **~e di corridoio** palace intrigues.

mano'vrare *vt* (*veicolo*) to manoeuvre (*BRIT*), maneuver (*US*); (*macchina, congegno*) to operate; (*fig: persona*) to manipulate ♦ *vi* to manoeuvre.

manro'vescio [manro'vɛʃʃo] *sm* slap (*with back of hand*).

man'sarda *sf* attic.

mansi'one *sf* task, duty, job.

mansu'eto, a *ag* (*animale*) tame; (*persona*) gentle, docile.

mansue'tudine *sf* tameness; gentleness, docility.

man'tello *sm* cloak; (*fig: di neve etc*) blanket, mantle; (*TECN: involucro*) casing, shell; (*ZOOL*) coat.

mante'nere *vt* to maintain; (*adempiere: promesse*) to keep, abide by; (*provvedere a*) to support, maintain; **~rsi** *vr:* **~rsi calmo/giovane** to stay calm/young; **~ i contatti con qn** to keep in touch with sb.

manteni'mento *sm* maintenance.

mante'nuto, a *sm/f* gigolo/kept woman.

'mantice ['mantitʃe] *sm* bellows *pl*; (*di carrozza, automobile*) hood.

'manto *sm* cloak; **~ stradale** road surface.

'Mantova *sf* Mantua.

manto'vano, a *ag* of (*o from*) Mantua.

manu'ale *ag* manual ♦ *sm* (*testo*) manual, handbook.

manua'listico, a, ci, che *ag* textbook *cpd*.

manual'mente *av* manually, by hand.

ma'nubrio *sm* handle; (*di bicicletta etc*)

handlebars *pl*; (*SPORT*) dumbbell.

manu'fatto *sm* manufactured article; **~i** *smpl* manufactured goods.

manutenzi'one [manuten'tsjone] *sf* maintenance, upkeep; (*d'impianti*) maintenance, servicing.

'manzo ['mandzo] *sm* (*ZOOL*) steer; (*carne*) beef.

Mao'metto *sm* Mohammed.

'mappa *sf* (*GEO*) map.

mappa'mondo *sm* map of the world; (*globo girevole*) globe.

ma'rasma, i *sm* (*fig*) decay, decline.

mara'tona *sf* marathon.

'marca, che *sf* mark; (*bollo*) stamp; (*COMM: di prodotti*) brand; (*contrassegno, scontrino*) ticket, check; **prodotti di (gran) ~** high-class products; **~ da bollo** official stamp.

mar'care *vt* (*munire di contrassegno*) to mark; (*a fuoco*) to brand; (*SPORT: gol*) to score; (*: avversario*) to mark; (*accentuare*) to stress; **~ visita** (*MIL*) to report sick.

mar'cato, a *ag* (*lineamenti, accento etc*) pronounced.

'Marche ['marke] *sfpl:* **le ~** the Marches (*region of central Italy*).

marcherò *etc* [marke'rɔ] *vb vedi* **marcare**.

mar'chese, a [mar'keze] *sm/f* marquis *o* marquess/marchioness.

marchi'ano, a [mar'kjano] *ag* (*errore*) glaring, gross.

marchi'are [mar'kjare] *vt* to brand.

marchigi'ano, a [marki'dʒano] *ag* of (*o* from) the Marches.

'marchio ['markjo] *sm* (*di bestiame, COMM, fig*) brand; **~ depositato** registered trademark; **~ di fabbrica** trademark.

'marcia, ce ['martʃa] *sf* (*anche MUS, MIL*) march; (*funzionamento*) running; (*il camminare*) walking; (*AUT*) gear; **mettere in ~** to start; **mettersi in ~** to get moving; **far ~ indietro** (*AUT*) to reverse; (*fig*) to back-pedal; **~ forzata** forced march; **~ funebre** funeral march.

marciapi'ede [martʃa'pjɛde] *sm* (*di strada*) pavement (*BRIT*), sidewalk (*US*); (*FERR*) platform.

marci'are [mar'tʃare] *vi* to march; (*andare: treno, macchina*) to go; (*funzionare*) to run, work.

'marcio, a, ci, ce ['martʃo] *ag* (*frutta, legno*) rotten, bad; (*MED*) festering; (*fig*) corrupt, rotten ♦ *sm:* **c'è del ~ in questa storia** (*fig*) there's something fishy about this business; **avere torto ~** to be utterly wrong.

mar'cire [mar'tʃire] *vi* (*andare a male*) to go bad, rot; (*suppurare*) to fester; (*fig*) to rot.

marci'ume [mar'tʃume] *sm* (*parte guasta: di cibi etc*) rotten part, bad part; (*di radice, pianta*) rot; (*fig: corruzione*) rottenness, corruption.

'**marco, chi** *sm* (*unità monetaria*) mark.

'**mare** *sm* sea; **di** ~ (*brezza, acqua, uccelli, pesce*) sea *cpd*; **in** ~ at sea; **per** ~ by sea; **sul** ~ (*barca*) on the sea; (*villaggio, località*) by *o* beside the sea; **andare al** ~ (*in vacanza etc*) to go to the seaside; **il mar Caspio** the Caspian Sea; **il mar Morto** the Dead Sea; **il mar Nero** the Black Sea; **il** ~ **del Nord** the North Sea; **il mar Rosso** the Red Sea; **il mar dei Sargassi** the Sargasso Sea; **i** ~**i del Sud** the South Seas.

ma'rea *sf* tide; **alta/bassa** ~ high/low tide.

mareggi'ata [mared'dʒata] *sf* heavy sea.

ma'remma *sf* (*GEO*) maremma, swampy coastal area.

marem'mano, a *ag* (*zona, macchia*) swampy; (*della Maremma*) of (*o* from) the Maremma.

mare'moto *sm* seaquake.

maresci'allo [mareʃ'ʃallo] *sm* (*MIL*) marshal; (: *sottufficiale*) warrant officer.

marez'zato, a [mared'dzato] *ag* (*seta etc*) watered, moiré; (*legno*) veined; (*carta*) marbled.

marga'rina *sf* margarine.

marghe'rita [marge'rita] *sf* (ox-eye) daisy, marguerite; (*di stampante*) daisy wheel.

margheri'tina [margeri'tina] *sf* daisy.

margi'nale [mardʒi'nale] *ag* marginal.

'**margine** ['mardʒine] *sm* margin; (*di bosco, via*) edge, border; **avere un buon** ~ **di tempo/denaro** to have plenty of time/money; ~ **di guadagno** *o* **di utile** profit margin; ~ **di sicurezza** safety margin.

mariju'ana [mæri'waːnə] *sf* marijuana.

ma'rina *sf* navy; (*costa*) coast; (*quadro*) seascape; ~ **mercantile** merchant navy (*BRIT*) *o* marine (*US*); ~ **militare (M.M.)** ≈ Royal Navy (RN) (*BRIT*), Navy (*US*).

mari'naio *sm* sailor.

mari'nare *vt* (*CUC*) to marinate; ~ **la scuola** to play truant.

mari'naro, a *ag* (*tradizione, popolo*) seafaring; (*CUC*) with seafood; **alla** ~**a** (*vestito, cappello*) sailor *cpd*; **borgo** ~ district where fishing folk live.

mari'nata *sf* marinade.

ma'rino, a *ag* sea *cpd*, marine.

mario'netta *sf* puppet.

mari'tare *vt* to marry; ~**rsi** *vr*: ~**rsi a** *o* **con qn** to marry sb, get married to sb.

mari'tato, a *ag* married.

ma'rito *sm* husband; **prendere** ~ to get married; **ragazza (in età) da** ~ girl of marriageable age.

ma'rittimo, a *ag* maritime, sea *cpd*.

mar'maglia [mar'maʎʎa] *sf* mob, riff-raff.

marmel'lata *sf* jam; (*di agrumi*) marmalade.

mar'mitta *sf* (*recipiente*) pot; (*AUT*) silencer; ~ **catalitica** catalytic converter.

'**marmo** *sm* marble.

mar'mocchio [mar'mɔkkjo] *sm* (*fam*) (little) kid.

mar'motta *sf* (*ZOOL*) marmot.

maroc'chino, a [marok'kino] *ag, smf* Moroccan.

Ma'rocco *sm*: **il** ~ Morocco.

ma'roso *sm* breaker.

'**marra** *sf* hoe.

Marra'kesh [marra'keʃ] *sf* Marrakesh.

mar'rone *ag inv* brown ♦ *sm* (*BOT*) chestnut.

mar'sala *sm inv* (*vino*) Marsala (wine).

Mar'siglia [mar'siʎʎa] *sf* Marseilles.

mar'sina *sf* tails *pl*, tail coat.

mar'supio *sm* (*ZOOL*) pouch, marsupium.

mart. *abbr* (= *martedì*) Tue(s).

'**Marte** *sm* (*ASTR, MITOLOGIA*) Mars.

marte'dì *sm inv* Tuesday; **di** *o* **il** ~ on Tuesdays; **oggi è** ~ **3 aprile** (the date) today is Tuesday 3rd April; ~ **stavo male** I wasn't well on Tuesday; **il giornale di** ~ Tuesday's newspaper; ~ **grasso** Shrove Tuesday.

martel'lante *ag* (*fig: dolore*) throbbing.

martel'lare *vt* to hammer ♦ *vi* (*pulsare*) to throb; (: *cuore*) to thump.

martel'letto *sm* (*di pianoforte*) hammer; (*di macchina da scrivere*) typebar; (*di giudice, nelle vendite all'asta*) gavel; (*MED*) percussion hammer.

mar'tello *sm* hammer; (*di uscio*) knocker; **suonare a** ~ (*fig: campane*) to sound the tocsin; ~ **pneumatico** pneumatic drill.

marti'netto *sm* (*TECN*) jack.

martin'gala *sf* (*di giacca*) half-belt; (*di cavallo*) martingale.

'**martire** *smf* martyr.

mar'tirio *sm* martyrdom; (*fig*) agony, torture.

martori'are *vt* to torment, torture.

mar'xismo *sm* Marxism.

mar'xista, i, e *ag, smf* Marxist.

marza'pane [martsa'pane] *sm* marzipan.

marzi'ale [mar'tsjale] *ag* martial.

'**marzo** ['martso] *sm* March; *per fraseologia vedi* **luglio**.

marzo'lino, a [martso'lino] *ag* March *cpd*.

mascalzo'nata [maskaltso'nata] *sf* dirty trick.

mascal'zone [maskal'tsone] *sm* rascal, scoundrel.

mas'cara *sm inv* mascara.

mascar'pone *sm* soft cream cheese often used in desserts.

ma'scella [maʃˈʃɛlla] *sf* (*ANAT*) jaw.

'**maschera** [ˈmaskera] *sf* mask; (*travestimento*) disguise; (: *per un ballo etc*) fancy dress; (*TEAT, CINE*) usher/usherette; (*personaggio del teatro*) stock character; **in** ~ (*mascherato*) masked; **ballo in** ~ fancy-dress ball; **gettare la** ~ (*fig*) to reveal o.s.; ~ **antigas/subacquea** gas/diving mask; ~ **di bellezza** face pack.

masche'rare [maskeˈrare] *vt* to mask; (*travestire*) to disguise; to dress up; (*fig: celare*) to hide, conceal; (*MIL*) to camouflage; ~**rsi** *vr*: ~**rsi da** to disguise o.s. as; to dress up as; (*fig*) to masquerade as.

masche'rina [maskeˈrina] *sf* (*piccola maschera*) mask; (*di animale*) patch; (*di scarpe*) toe-cap; (*AUT*) radiator grill.

mas'chile [masˈkile] *ag* masculine; (*sesso, popolazione*) male; (*abiti*) men's; (*per ragazzi: scuola*) boys'.

'**maschio, a** [ˈmaskjo] *ag* (*BIOL*) male; (*virile*) manly ♦ *sm* (*anche ZOOL, TECN*) male; (*uomo*) man; (*ragazzo*) boy; (*figlio*) son.

masco'lino, a *ag* masculine.

mas'cotte [masˈkɔt] *sf inv* mascot.

maso'chismo [mazoˈkizmo] *sm* masochism.

maso'chista, i, e [mazoˈkista] *ag* masochistic ♦ *sm/f* masochist.

'**massa** *sf* mass; (*di errori etc*): **una** ~ **di** heaps, masses of; (*di gente*) mass, multitude; (*ELETTR*) earth; **in** ~ (*COMM*) in bulk; (*tutti insieme*) en masse; **adunata in** ~ mass meeting; **manifestazione/cultura di** ~ mass demonstration/culture; **produrre in** ~ to mass-produce; **la** ~ (**del popolo**) the masses *pl*.

massa'crante *ag* exhausting, gruelling.

massa'crare *vt* to massacre, slaughter.

mas'sacro *sm* massacre, slaughter; (*fig*) mess, disaster.

massaggi'are [massadˈdʒare] *vt* to massage.

massaggia'tore, 'trice [massaddʒaˈtore] *sm/f* masseur/masseuse.

mas'saggio [masˈsaddʒo] *sm* massage.

mas'saia *sf* housewife.

masse'ria *sf* large farm.

masse'rizie [masseˈrittsje] *sfpl* (household) furnishings.

massicci'ata [massitˈtʃata] *sf* (*di strada, ferrovia*) ballast.

mas'siccio, a, ci, ce [masˈsittʃo] *ag* (*oro, legno*) solid; (*palazzo*) massive;

(*corporatura*) stout ♦ *sm* (*GEO*) massif.

'**massima** *sf vedi* massimo.

massi'male *sm* maximum; (*COMM*) ceiling, limit.

'**massimo, a** *ag, sm* maximum ♦ *sf* (*sentenza, regola*) maxim; (*METEOR*) maximum temperature; **in linea di** ~**a** generally speaking; **arrivare entro il tempo** ~ to arrive within the time limit; **al** ~ at (the) most; **sfruttare qc al** ~ to make full use of sth; **arriverò al** ~ **alle 5** I'll arrive at 5 at the latest; **erano presenti le** ~**e autorità** all the most important dignitaries were there; **il** ~ **della pena** (*DIR*) the maximum penalty.

mas'sivo, a *ag* (*intervento*) en masse; (*emigrazione*) mass; (*emorragia*) massive.

'**masso** *sm* rock, boulder.

mas'sone *sm* freemason.

masso'neria *sf* freemasonry.

mas'sonico, a, ci, che *ag* masonic.

mas'tello *sm* tub.

masteriz'zare [masteridˈdzare] *vt* to burn.

masterizza'tore [masteriddzaˈtore] *sm* CD burner *o* writer.

masti'care *vt* to chew.

'**mastice** [ˈmastitʃe] *sm* mastic; (*per vetri*) putty.

mas'tino *sm* mastiff.

masto'dontico, a, ci, che *ag* gigantic, colossal.

mastur'barsi *vr* to masturbate.

masturbazi'one [masturbatˈtsjone] *sf* masturbation.

ma'tassa *sf* skein.

mate'matico, a, ci, che *ag* mathematical ♦ *sm/f* mathematician ♦ *sf* mathematics *sg*.

materas'sino *sm* mat; ~ **gonfiabile** air bed.

mate'rasso *sm* mattress; ~ **a molle** spring *o* interior-sprung mattress.

ma'teria *sf* (*FISICA*) matter; (*TECN, COMM*) material, matter *no pl*; (*disciplina*) subject; (*argomento*) subject matter, material; **prima di entrare in** ~ ... before discussing the matter in hand ...; **un esperto in** ~ (**di musica etc**) an expert on the subject (of music *etc*); **sono ignorante in** ~ I know nothing about it; ~ **cerebrale** cerebral matter; ~ **grassa** fat; ~ **grigia** (*anche fig*) grey matter; ~**e plastiche** plastics; ~**e prime** raw materials.

materi'ale *ag* material; (*fig: grossolano*) rough, rude ♦ *sm* material; (*insieme di strumenti etc*) equipment *no pl*, materials *pl*; ~ **da costruzione** building materials *pl*.

materia'lista, i, e *ag* materialistic ♦ *sm/f* materialist.

materializ'zarsi [materjalidˈdzarsi] *vr* to

materialize.

material'mente *av* (*fisicamente*) materially; (*economicamente*) financially.

maternità *sf* motherhood, maternity; (*clinica*) maternity hospital; **in (congedo di)** ~ on maternity leave.

ma'terno, a *ag* (*amore, cura etc*) maternal, motherly; (*nonno*) maternal; (*lingua, terra*) mother *cpd*; *vedi anche* **scuola**.

ma'tita *sf* pencil; ~**e colorate** crayons; ~ **per gli occhi** eyeliner (pencil).

ma'trice [ma'tritʃe] *sf* matrix; (*COMM*) counterfoil; (*fig: origine*) background.

ma'tricola *sf* (*registro*) register; (*numero*) registration number; (*nell'università*) freshman, fresher (*BRIT fam*).

ma'trigna [ma'triɲɲa] *sf* stepmother.

matrimoni'ale *ag* matrimonial, marriage *cpd*; **camera/letto** ~ double room/bed.

matri'monio *sm* marriage, matrimony; (*durata*) marriage, married life; (*cerimonia*) wedding.

ma'trona *sf* (*fig*) matronly woman.

matta'toio *sm* abattoir (*BRIT*), slaughterhouse.

mat'tina *sf* morning; **la** *o* **alla** *o* **di** ~ in the morning; **di prima** ~, **la** ~ **presto** early in the morning; **dalla** ~ **alla sera** (*continuamente*) from morning to night; (*improvvisamente: cambiare*) overnight.

matti'nata *sf* morning; (*spettacolo*) matinée, afternoon performance; **in** ~ in the course of the morning; **nella** ~ in the morning; **nella tarda** ~ at the end of the morning; **nella tarda** ~ **di sabato** late on Saturday morning.

mattini'ero, a *ag*: **essere** ~ to be an early riser.

mat'tino *sm* morning; **di buon** ~ early in the morning.

'matto, a *ag* mad, crazy; (*fig: falso*) false, imitation; (: *opaco*) matt, dull ♦ *sm/f* madman/woman; **avere una voglia** ~**a di qc** to be dying for sth; **far diventare** ~ **qn** to drive sb mad *o* crazy; **una gabbia di** ~**i** (*fig*) a madhouse.

mat'tone *sm* brick; (*fig*): **questo libro/ film è un** ~ this book/film is heavy going.

matto'nella *sf* tile.

mattu'tino, a *ag* morning *cpd*.

matu'rare *vi* (*anche*: ~**rsi**) (*frutta, grano*) to ripen; (*ascesso*) to come to a head; (*fig: persona, idea, ECON*) to mature ♦ *vt* to ripen; to (make) mature; ~ **una decisione** to come to a decision.

maturità *sf* maturity; (*di frutta*) ripeness, maturity; (*INS*) school-leaving examination, ≈ GCE A-levels (*BRIT*).

ma'turo, a *ag* mature; (*frutto*) ripe, mature.

ma'tusa *sm/f inv* (*scherzoso*) old fogey.

Mauri'tania *sf*: **la** ~ Mauritania.

Mau'rizio [mau'rittsjo] *sf*: (**l'isola di**) ~ Mauritius.

mauso'leo *sm* mausoleum.

max. *abbr* (= *massimo*) max.

'maxi... *prefisso* maxi....

maxipro'cesso [maksipro'tʃɛsso] *sm vedi nota nel riquadro*.

MAXIPROCESSO

A **maxiprocesso** is a criminal trial which is characterized by a large number of co-defendants. These people are usually members of terrorist or criminal organizations. The trials are often lengthy and many witnesses may be called to give evidence.

---

maxis'chermo [maksis'kermo] *sm* giant screen.

'mazza ['mattsa] *sf* (*bastone*) club; (*martello*) sledge-hammer; (*SPORT: da golf*) club; (: *da baseball, cricket*) bat.

maz'zata [mat'tsata] *sf* (*anche fig*) heavy blow.

maz'zetta [mat'tsetta] *sf* (*di banconote etc*) bundle; (*fig*) rake-off.

'mazzo ['mattso] *sm* (*di fiori, chiavi etc*) bunch; (*di carte da gioco*) pack.

MC *sigla* = Macerata.

m.c.d. *abbr* (= *minimo comune denominatore*) lcd.

m.c.m. *abbr* (= *minimo comune multiplo*) lcm.

ME *sigla* = Messina.

me *pron* me; **sei bravo quanto** ~ you are as clever as I (am) *o* as me.

me'andro *sm* meander.

M.E.C. [mɛk] *abbr m* = **Mercato Comune Europeo**.

'Mecca *sf* (*anche fig*): **La** ~ Mecca.

meccanica'mente *av* mechanically.

mec'canico, a, ci, che *ag* mechanical ♦ *sm* mechanic ♦ *sf* mechanics *sg*; (*attività tecnologica*) mechanical engineering; (*meccanismo*) mechanism; **officina** ~**a** garage.

mecca'nismo *sm* mechanism.

meccaniz'zare [mekkanid'dzare] *vt* to mechanize.

meccanizzazi'one [mekkaniddzat'tsjone] *sf* mechanization.

mece'nate [metʃe'nate] *sm* patron.

mèche [mɛʃ] *sf inv* streak; **farsi le** ~ to have one's hair streaked.

me'daglia [me'daʎʎa] *sf* medal; ~ **d'oro** (*oggetto*) gold medal; (*persona*) gold medallist (*BRIT*) *o* medalist (*US*).

medagli'one [medaʎ'ʎone] *sm* (*ARCHIT*) medallion; (*gioiello*) locket.

me'desimo, a *ag* same; (*in persona*): **io** ~ **I** myself.

'media *sf vedi* medio.

media'mente *av* on average.

medi'ano, a *ag* median; (*valore*) mean ♦ *sm* (*CALCIO*) half-back.

medi'ante *prep* by means of.

medi'are *vt* (*fare da mediatore*) to act as mediator in; (*MAT*) to average.

medi'ato, a *ag* indirect.

media'tore, 'trice *smf* mediator; (*COMM*) middle man, agent; **fare da** ~ **fra** to mediate between.

mediazi'one [medjat'tsjone] *sf* mediation; (*COMM: azione, compenso*) brokerage.

medica'mento *sm* medicine, drug.

medi'care *vt* to treat; (*ferita*) to dress.

medi'cato, a *ag* (*garza, shampoo*) medicated.

medicazi'one [medikat'tsjone] *sf* treatment, medication; dressing; **fare una** ~ **a qn** to dress sb's wounds.

medi'cina [medi'tʃina] *sf* medicine; ~ **legale** forensic medicine.

medici'nale [meditʃi'nale] *ag* medicinal ♦ *sm* drug, medicine.

'medico, a, ci, che *ag* medical ♦ *sm* doctor; ~ **di bordo** ship's doctor; ~ **di famiglia** family doctor; ~ **fiscale** *doctor who examines patients signed off sick for a lengthy period by their private doctor*; ~ **generico** general practitioner, GP.

medie'vale *ag* medieval.

'medio, a *ag* average; (*punto, ceto*) middle; (*altezza, statura*) medium ♦ *sm* (*dito*) middle finger ♦ *sf* average; (*MAT*) mean; (*INS: voto*) end-of-term average; ~**e** *sfpl vedi* **scuola media inferiore; licenza** ~**a** *leaving certificate awarded at the end of 3 years of secondary education*; **in** ~**a** on average; **al di sopra/sotto della** ~**a** above/below average; **viaggiare ad una** ~**a di** ... to travel at an average speed of ...; **il M**~ **Oriente** the Middle East.

medi'ocre *ag* (*gen*) mediocre; (*qualità, stipendio*) poor.

mediocrità *sf* mediocrity; poorness.

medioe'vale *ag* = **medievale**.

Medio'evo *sm* Middle Ages *pl*.

medita'bondo, a *ag* thoughtful.

medi'tare *vt* to ponder over, meditate on; (*progettare*) to plan, think out ♦ *vi* to meditate.

medi'tato, a *ag* (*gen*) meditated; (*parole*) carefully-weighed; (*vendetta*) premeditated; **ben** ~ (*piano*) well worked-out, neat.

meditazi'one [meditat'tsjone] *sf* meditation.

mediter'raneo, a *ag* Mediterranean; **il (mare) M**~ the Mediterranean (Sea).

'medium *sm/f inv* medium.

me'dusa *sf* (*ZOOL*) jellyfish.

me'gafono *sm* megaphone.

mega'lomane *ag, sm/f* megalomaniac.

me'gera [me'dʒɛra] *sf* (*peg: donna*) shrew.

'meglio ['meʎʎo] *av, ag inv* better; (*con senso superlativo*) best ♦ *sm* (*la cosa migliore*): **il** ~ the best (thing); **faresti** ~ **ad andartene** you had better leave; **alla** ~ as best one can; **andar di bene in** ~ to get better and better; **fare del proprio** ~ to do one's best; **per il** ~ for the best; **aver la** ~ **su qn** to get the better of sb.

'mela *sf* apple; ~ **cotogna** quince.

mela'grana *sf* pomegranate.

melan'zana [melan'dzana] *sf* aubergine (*BRIT*), eggplant (*US*).

me'lassa *sf* molasses *sg*, treacle.

me'lenso, a *ag* dull, stupid.

me'lissa *sf* (*BOT*) balm.

mel'lifluo, a *ag* (*peg*) sugary, honeyed.

'melma *sf* mud, mire.

'melo *sm* apple tree.

melo'dia *sf* melody.

me'lodico, a, ci, che *ag* melodic.

melodi'oso, a *ag* melodious.

melo'dramma, i *sm* melodrama.

me'lone *sm* (musk) melon.

'membra *sfpl vedi* **membro**.

mem'brana *sf* membrane.

'membro *sm* member; (*pl(f)* ~**a**: *arto*) limb.

memo'rabile *ag* memorable.

memo'randum *sm inv* memorandum.

'memore *ag*: ~ **di** (*ricordando*) mindful of; (*riconoscente*) grateful for.

me'moria *sf* (*anche INFORM*) memory; ~**e** *sfpl* (*opera autobiografica*) memoirs; **a** ~ (*imparare, sapere*) by heart; **a** ~ **d'uomo** within living memory; ~ **di sola lettura** (*INFORM*) read-only memory; ~ **tampone** (*INFORM*) buffer.

memori'ale *sm* (*raccolta di memorie*) memoirs *pl*; (*DIR*) memorial.

memoriz'zare [memorid'dzare] *vt* (*gen*) to memorize; (*INFORM*) to store.

memorizzazi'one [memoriddzat'tsjone] *sf* memorization; storage.

'mena *sf* scheme.

mena'dito: **a** ~ *av* perfectly, thoroughly;

sapere qc a ~ to have sth at one's fingertips.

mena'gramo *smf inv* jinx, Jonah.

me'nare *vt* to lead; (*picchiare*) to hit, beat; (*dare: colpi*) to deal; ~ **la coda** (*cane*) to wag its tail; ~ **qc per le lunghe** to drag sth out; ~ **il can per l'aia** (*fig*) to beat about (*BRIT*) *o* around (*US*) the bush.

mendi'cante *smf* beggar.

mendi'care *vt* to beg for ♦ *vi* to beg.

menefre'ghismo [menefre'gizmo] *sm* (*fam*) couldn't-care-less attitude.

me'ninge [me'nindʒe] *sf* (*MED*) meninx; **spremersi le** ~**i** to rack one's brains.

menin'gite [menin'dʒite] *sf* meningitis.

me'nisco *sm* (*ANAT, MAT, FISICA*) meniscus.

========== *PAROLA CHIAVE* ==========

'meno *av* **1** (*in minore misura*) less; **dovresti mangiare** ~ you should eat less, you shouldn't eat so much; **è sempre** ~ **facile** it's getting less and less easy; **ne voglio di** ~ I don't want so much

2 (*comparativo*): ~ ... **di** not as ... as, less ... than; **sono** ~ **alto di te** I'm not as tall as you (are), I'm less tall than you (are); ~ ... **che** not as ... as, less ... than; ~ **che mai** less than ever; **è** ~ **intelligente che ricco** he's more rich than intelligent; ~ **fumo più mangio** the less I smoke the more I eat; ~ **di quanto pensassi** less than I thought

3 (*superlativo*) least; **il** ~ **dotato degli studenti** the least gifted of the students; **è quello che compro** ~ **spesso** it's the one I buy least often

4 (*MAT*) minus; **8** ~ **5** 8 minus 5, 8 take away 5; **sono le 8** ~ **un quarto** it's a quarter to 8; ~ **5 gradi** 5 degrees below zero, minus 5 degrees; **mille euro in** ~ a thousand euros less; **ha preso 6** ~ (*a scuola*) he scraped a pass; **cento euro** ~ **le spese** a hundred euros minus *o* less expenses

5 (*fraseologia*): **quanto** ~ **poteva telefonare** he could at least have phoned; **non so se accettare o** ~ I don't know whether to accept or not; **non essere da** ~ **di** not to be outdone by; **fare a** ~ **di qc/qn** to do without sth/sb; **non potevo fare a** ~ **di ridere** I couldn't help laughing; ~ **male!** thank goodness!; ~ **male che sei arrivato** it's a good job that you've come

♦ *ag inv* (*tempo, denaro*) less; (*errori, persone*) fewer; **ha fatto** ~ **errori di tutti** he made fewer mistakes than anyone, he made the fewest mistakes of all

♦ *sm inv* **1**: **il** ~ (*il minimo*) the least; **parlare del più e del** ~ to talk about this and that; **era il** ~ **che ti potesse succedere** it was the least you could have expected

2 (*MAT*) minus

♦ *prep* (*eccetto*) except (for), apart from; **tutti** ~ **lui** everybody apart from *o* except him; **a** ~ **che, a** ~ **di** unless; **a** ~ **che non piova** unless it rains; **non posso, a** ~ **di prendere ferie** I can't, unless I take some leave; *vedi anche* **più**.

═══════════════════════════════

meno'mare *vt* (*danneggiare*) to maim, disable.

meno'mato, a *ag* (*persona*) disabled ♦ *smf* disabled person.

menomazi'one [menomat'tsjone] *sf* disablement.

meno'pausa *sf* menopause.

'mensa *sf* (*locale*) canteen; (: *MIL*) mess; (: *nelle università*) refectory.

men'sile *ag* monthly ♦ *sm* (*periodico*) monthly (magazine); (*stipendio*) monthly salary.

mensil'mente *av* (*ogni mese*) every month; (*una volta al mese*) monthly.

'mensola *sf* bracket; (*ripiano*) shelf; (*ARCHIT*) corbel.

'menta *sf* mint; (*anche*: ~ **piperita**) peppermint; (*bibita*) peppermint cordial; (*caramella*) mint, peppermint.

men'tale *ag* mental.

mentalità *sf inv* mentality.

mental'mente *av* mentally.

'mente *sf* mind; **imparare/sapere qc a** ~ to learn/know sth by heart; **avere in** ~ **qc** to have sth in mind; **avere in** ~ **di fare qc** to intend to do sth; **fare venire in** ~ **qc a qn** to remind sb of sth; **mettersi in** ~ **di fare qc** to make up one's mind to do sth; **passare di** ~ **a qn** to slip sb's mind; **tenere a** ~ **qc** to bear sth in mind; **a** ~ **fredda** objectively; **lasciami fare** ~ **locale** let me think.

mente'catto, a *ag* half-witted ♦ *smf* halfwit, imbecile.

men'tire *vi* to lie.

men'tito, a *ag*: **sotto** ~**e spoglie** under false pretences (*BRIT*) *o* pretenses (*US*).

'mento *sm* chin; **doppio** ~ double chin.

men'tolo *sm* menthol.

'mentre *cong* (*temporale*) while; (*avversativo*) whereas ♦ *sm*: **in quel** ~ at that very moment.

menù *sm inv* (set) menu; ~ **turistico** standard *o* tourists' menu.

menzio'nare [mentsjo'nare] *vt* to mention.

menzi'one [men'tsjone] *sf* mention; **fare** ~ **di** to mention.

men'zogna [men'tsɔɲɲa] *sf* lie.
menzo'gnero, a [mentsoɲ'ɲero] *ag* false,
untrue.
mera'viglia [mera'viʎʎa] *sf* amazement,
wonder; (*persona, cosa*) marvel, wonder; **a**
~ perfectly, wonderfully.
meravigli'are [meraviʎ'ʎare] *vt* to amaze,
astonish; ~**rsi** *vr*: ~**rsi (di)** to marvel (at);
(*stupirsi*) to be amazed (at), be astonished
(at); **mi meraviglio di te!** I'm surprised at
you!; **non c'è da** ~**rsi** it's not surprising.
meravigli'oso, a [meraviʎ'ʎoso] *ag*
wonderful, marvellous (*BRIT*), marvelous
(*US*).
merc. *abbr* (= *mercoledì*) Wed.
mer'cante *sm* merchant; ~ **d'arte** art
dealer; ~ **di cavalli** horse dealer.
mercanteggi'are [merkanted'dʒare] *vt*
(*onore, voto*) to sell ♦ *vi* to bargain, haggle.
mercan'tile *ag* commercial, mercantile;
(*nave, marina*) merchant *cpd* ♦ *sm* (*nave*)
merchantman.
mercan'zia [merkan'tsia] *sf* merchandise,
goods *pl*.
merca'tino *sm* (*rionale*) local street
market; (*ECON*) unofficial stock market.
mer'cato *sm* market; **di** ~ (*economia,
prezzo, ricerche*) market *cpd*; **mettere** *o*
lanciare qc sul ~ to launch sth on the
market; **a buon** ~ *ag, av* cheap; ~ **dei
cambi** exchange market; **M~ Comune
(Europeo)** (European) Common Market;
~ **del lavoro** labour market, job market;
~ **nero** black market; ~ **al rialzo/al
ribasso** (*BORSA*) sellers'/buyers' market.
'merce ['mertʃe] *sf* goods *pl*, merchandise;
~ **deperibile** perishable goods *pl*.
mercé [mer'tʃe] *sf* mercy; **essere alla** ~ **di
qn** to be at sb's mercy.
merce'nario, a [mertʃe'narjo] *ag, sm*
mercenary.
merce'ria [mertʃe'ria] *sf* (*articoli*)
haberdashery (*BRIT*), notions *pl* (*US*); (*bottega*) haberdasher's shop (*BRIT*), notions
store (*US*).
mercoledì *sm inv* Wednesday; ~ **delle
Ceneri** Ash Wednesday; *vedi nota nel
riquadro*; *per fraseologia vedi* **martedì**.

MERCOLEDÌ DELLE CENERI

In the Catholic church, **Mercoledì delle
Ceneri** *signals the beginning of Lent.
Churchgoers are marked on the forehead with
ash from the burning of an olive branch. Ash
Wednesday is traditionally a day of fasting,
abstinence and repentance.*

---

mer'curio *sm* mercury.
'merda *sf* (*fam!*) shit (*!*).
me'renda *sf* afternoon snack.
meren'dina *sf* snack.
meridi'ano, a *ag* (*di mezzogiorno*) midday
cpd, noonday ♦ *sm* meridian ♦ *sf* (*orologio*)
sundial.
meridio'nale *ag* southern ♦ *sm/f*
southerner.
meridi'one *sm* south.
me'ringa, ghe *sf* (*CUC*) meringue.
meri'tare *vt* to deserve, merit ♦ *vb impers*
(*valere la pena*): **merita andare** it is worth
going; **non merita neanche parlarne** it's
not worth talking about; **per quel che
merita** for what it's worth.
meri'tevole *ag* worthy.
'merito *sm* merit; (*valore*) worth; **dare** ~ **a
qn di** to give sb credit for; **finire a pari** ~
to finish joint first (*o* second *etc*); **to tie; in**
~ **a** as regards, with regard to; **entrare
nel** ~ **di una questione** to go into a
matter; **non so niente in** ~ I don't know
anything about it.
meritocra'zia [meritokrat'tsia] *sf*
meritocracy.
meri'torio, a *ag* praiseworthy.
mer'letto *sm* lace.
'merlo *sm* (*ZOOL*) blackbird; (*ARCHIT*)
battlement.
mer'luzzo [mer'luttso] *sm* (*ZOOL*) cod.
'mescere ['meʃʃere] *vt* to pour (out).
meschinità [meskini'ta] *sf* wretchedness;
meagreness; meanness; narrow-
mindedness.
mes'chino, a [mes'kino] *ag* wretched;
(*scarso*) meagre (*BRIT*), meager (*US*);
(*persona: gretta*) mean; (: *limitata*) narrow-
minded, petty; **fare una figura** ~**a** to cut a
poor figure.
'mescita ['meʃʃita] *sf* wine shop.
mesci'uto, a [meʃ'ʃuto] *pp di* **mescere**.
mesco'lanza [mesko'lantsa] *sf* mixture.
mesco'lare *vt* to mix; (*vini, colori*) to blend;
(*mettere in disordine*) to mix up, muddle
up; (*carte*) to shuffle; ~**rsi** *vr* to mix; to
blend; to get mixed up; (*fig*): ~**rsi in** to get
mixed up in, meddle in.
'mese *sm* month; **il** ~ **scorso** last month; **il
corrente** ~ this month.
'messa *sf* (*REL*) mass; (*il mettere*): ~ **a fuoco**
focusing; ~ **in moto** starting; ~ **in piega**
(*acconciatura*) set; ~ **a punto** (*TECN*)
adjustment; (*AUT*) tuning; (*fig*)
clarification; ~ **in scena** = **messinscena**.
messagge'rie [messaddʒe'rie] *sfpl* (*ditta: di
distribuzione*) distributors; (: *di trasporto*)
freight company.

messag'gero [messad'dʒɛro] *sm*
messenger.
messag'gino [messad'dʒino] *sm* (*di
telefonino*) text (message).
mes'saggio [mes'saddʒo] *sm* message.
messag'gistica [messad'dʒistica] *sf*: ~
immediata (*COMPUT*) instant messaging;
programma di ~ **immediata** instant
messenger.
mes'sale *sm* (*REL*) missal.
'messe *sf* harvest.
Mes'sia *sm inv* (*REL*): **il** ~ the Messiah.
messi'cano, a *ag, smlf* Mexican.
'Messico *sm*: **il** ~ Mexico; **Città del** ~
Mexico City.
messin'scena [messin'ʃɛna] *sf* (*TEAT*)
production.
'messo, a *pp di* **mettere** ♦ *sm* messenger.
mestie'rante *smlf* (*peg*) money-grubber;
(: *scrittore*) hack.
mesti'ere *sm* (*professione*) job; (: *manuale*)
trade; (: *artigianale*) craft; (*fig: abilità nel
lavoro*) skill, technique; **di** ~ by *o* to trade;
essere del ~ to know the tricks of the
trade.
mes'tizia [mes'tittsja] *sf* sadness,
melancholy.
'mesto, a *ag* sad, melancholy.
'mestolo *sm* (*CUC*) ladle.
mestru'ale *ag* menstrual.
mestruazi'one [mestruat'tsjone] *sf*
menstruation; **avere le** ~**i** to have one's
period.
'meta *sf* destination; (*fig*) aim, goal.
metà *sf inv* half; (*punto di mezzo*) middle;
dividere qc a *o* **per** ~ to divide sth in half,
halve sth; **fare a** ~ (**di qc con qn**) to go
halves (with sb in sth); **a** ~ **prezzo** at half
price; **a** ~ **settimana** midweek; **a** ~ **strada**
halfway; **verso la** ~ **del mese** halfway
through the month, towards the middle
of the month; **dire le cose a** ~ to leave
some things unsaid; **fare le cose a** ~ to
leave things half-done; **la mia dolce** ~
(*fam scherzoso*) my better half.
metabo'lismo *sm* metabolism.
meta'done *sm* methadone.
meta'fisica *sf* metaphysics *sg*.
me'tafora *sf* metaphor.
meta'forico, a, ci, che *ag* metaphorical.
me'tallico, a, ci, che *ag* (*di metallo*) metal
cpd; (*splendore, rumore etc*) metallic.
metalliz'zato, a [metallid'dzato] *ag*
(*verniciatura*) metallic.
me'tallo *sm* metal; **di** ~ metal *cpd*.
metallur'gia [metallur'dʒia] *sf* metallurgy.
metalmec'canico, a, ci, che *ag*
engineering *cpd* ♦ *sm* engineering worker.

meta'morfosi *sf* metamorphosis.
me'tano *sm* methane.
me'teora *sf* meteor.
meteo'rite *sm* meteorite.
meteorolo'gia [meteorolo'dʒia] *sf*
meteorology.
meteoro'logico, a, ci, che
[meteoro'lɔdʒiko] *ag* meteorological,
weather *cpd*.
meteo'rologo, a, ghi, ghe *smlf*
meteorologist.
me'ticcio, a, ci, ce [me'tittʃo] *smlf* half-
caste, half-breed.
meticolosità *sf* meticulousness.
metico'loso, a *ag* meticulous.
me'todico, a, ci, che *ag* methodical.
'metodo *sm* method; (*manuale*) tutor (*BRIT*),
manual; **far qc con/senza** ~ to do sth
methodically/unmethodically.
me'traggio [me'traddʒo] *sm* (*SARTORIA*)
length; (*CINE*) footage; **film a lungo** ~
feature film; **film a corto** ~ short film.
metra'tura *sf* length.
'metrico, a, ci, che *ag* metric; (*POESIA*)
metrical ♦ *sf* metrics *sg*.
'metro *sm* metre (*BRIT*), meter (*US*);
(*nastro*) tape measure; (*asta*) (metre) rule.
metrò *sm inv* underground (*BRIT*), subway
(*US*).
metro'notte *sm inv* night security guard.
me'tropoli *sf* metropolis.
metropoli'tano, a *ag* metropolitan ♦ *sf*
underground (*BRIT*), subway (*US*); ~**a
leggera** metro (*mainly on the surface*).
'mettere *vt* to put; (*abito*) to put on;
(: *portare*) to wear; (*installare: telefono*) to
put in; (*fig: provocare*): ~ **fame/allegria a
qn** to make sb hungry/happy; (*supporre*):
mettiamo che ... let's suppose *o* say that
...; ~**rsi** *vr* (*persona*) to put o.s.; (*oggetto*) to
go; (*disporsi: faccenda*) to turn out; ~**rsi a
piangere/ridere** to start crying/laughing,
start *o* begin to cry/laugh; ~**rsi a sedere**
to sit down; ~**rsi al lavoro** to set to work;
~**rsi a letto** to get into bed; (*per malattia*)
to take to one's bed; ~**rsi il cappello** to put
on one's hat; ~**rsi sotto** to get down to
things; ~**rsi in società** to set up in
business; **si sono messi insieme** (*coppia*)
they've started going out together (*BRIT*)
o dating (*US*); ~**rci**: ~**rci molta cura/molto
tempo** to take a lot of care/a lot of time;
mettercela tutta to do one's best; **ci ho
messo 3 ore per venire** it's taken me 3
hours to get here; ~ **un annuncio sul
giornale** to place an advertisement in the
paper; ~ **a confronto** to compare; ~ **in
conto** (*somma etc*) to put on account; ~ **in**

luce (*problemi, errori*) to stress, highlight;
~ **a tacere qn/qc** to keep sb/sth quiet; ~
su casa to set up house; ~ **su un negozio**
to start a shop; ~ **su peso** to put on
weight; ~ **via** to put away.

mez'zadro [med'dzadro] *sm* (*AGR*)
sharecropper.

mezza'luna [meddza'luna], *pl* **mezze'lune**
sf half-moon; (*dell'islamismo*) crescent;
(*coltello*) (semicircular) chopping knife.

mezza'nino [meddza'nino] *sm* mezzanine
(floor).

mez'zano, a [med'dzano] *ag* (*medio*)
average, medium; (*figlio*) middle *cpd*
♦ *sm/f* (*intermediario*) go-between; (*ruffiano*)
pimp.

mezza'notte [meddza'nɔtte] *sf* midnight.

'mezzo, a ['mɛddzo] *ag* half; **un ~ litro/**
panino half a litre/roll ♦ *av* half-; ~ **morto**
half-dead ♦ *sm* (*metà*) half; (*parte centrale:*
di strada etc) middle; (*per raggiungere un*
fine) means *sg*; (*veicolo*) vehicle;
(*nell'indicare l'ora*): **le nove e** ~ half past
nine; **mezzogiorno e** ~ half past twelve
♦ *sf*: **la** ~**a** half-past twelve (in the
afternoon); ~**i** *smpl* (*possibilità economiche*)
means; **di** ~**a età** middle-aged; **aver una**
~**a idea di fare qc** to have half a mind to
do sth; **è stato un** ~ **scandalo** it almost
caused a scandal; **un soprabito di** ~**a**
stagione a spring (*o* autumn) coat; **a** ~**a**
voce in an undertone; **una volta e** ~ **più**
grande one and a half times bigger; **di** ~
middle, in the middle; **andarci di** ~ (*patir*
danno) to suffer; **esserci di** ~ (*ostacolo*) to
be in the way; **levarsi** *o* **togliersi di** ~ to
get out of the way; **mettersi di** ~ to
interfere; **togliere di** ~ (*persona, cosa*) to
get rid of; (*fam: uccidere*) to bump off; **non**
c'è una via di ~ there's no middle course;
in ~ **a** in the middle of; **nel bel** ~ **(di)** right
in the middle (of); **per** *o* **a** ~ **di** by means
of; **a** ~ **corriere** by carrier; ~**i di**
comunicazione di massa mass media *pl*;
~**i pubblici** public transport *sg*; ~**i di**
trasporto means of transport.

mezzogi'orno [meddzo'dʒorno] *sm* midday,
noon; (*GEO*) south; **a** ~ at 12 (o'clock) *o*
midday *o* noon; **il** ~ **d'Italia** southern
Italy.

mez'z'ora, mez'zora [med'dzora] *sf* half-
hour, half an hour.

MI *sigla* = *Milano*.

mi *pron* (*dav lo, la, li, le, ne diventa* **me**)
(*oggetto*) me; (*complemento di termine*) (to)
me; (*riflessivo*) myself ♦ *sm* (*MUS*) E;
(*: solfeggiando la scala*) mi; ~ **aiuti?** will
you help me?; **me ne ha parlato** he spoke

to me about it, he told me about it; ~
servo da solo I'll help myself.

'mia *vedi* **mio.**

miago'lare *vi* to miaow, mew.

Mib *sigla m, ag* (= *indice borsa Milano*) Milan
Stock Exchange Index.

'mica *sf* (*CHIM*) mica ♦ *av* (*fam*): **non ...** ~
not ... at all; **non sono** ~ **stanco** I'm not a
bit tired; **non sarà** ~ **partito?** he wouldn't
have left, would he?; ~ **male** not bad.

'miccia, ce ['mittʃa] *sf* fuse.

micidi'ale [mitʃi'djale] *ag* fatal;
(*dannosissimo*) deadly.

'micio, a, ci, cie ['mitʃo] *sm/f* pussy (cat).

microbiolo'gia [mikrobiolo'dʒia] *sf*
microbiology.

'microbo *sm* microbe.

microcir'cuito [mikrotʃir'kuito] *sm*
microcircuit.

micro'fibra *sf* microfibre.

micro'film *sm inv* microfilm.

mi'crofono *sm* microphone.

microinfor'matica *sf* microcomputing.

micro'onda *sf* microwave.

microproces'sore [mikroprotʃes'sore] *sm*
microprocessor.

micros'copico, a, ci, che *ag* microscopic.

micros'copio *sm* microscope.

micro'solco, chi *sm* (*solco*) microgroove;
(*disco: a 33 giri*) long-playing record, LP; (:
a 45 giri) extended-play record, EP.

micros'pia *sf* hidden microphone, bug
(*fam*).

mi'dollo, *pl(f)* ~**a** *sm* (*ANAT*) marrow; ~
spinale spinal cord.

'mie, mi'ei *vedi* **mio.**

mi'ele *sm* honey.

mi'etere *vt* (*AGR*) to reap, harvest; (*fig:*
vite) to take, claim.

mietitrebbia'trice [mjetitrebbja'tritʃe] *sf*
combine harvester.

mieti'trice [mjeti'tritʃe] *sf* (*macchina*)
harvester.

mieti'tura *sf* (*raccolto*) harvest; (*lavoro*)
harvesting; (*tempo*) harvest-time.

'miglia ['miʎʎa] *sfpl di* **miglio.**

migli'aio [miʎ'ʎajo], *pl(f)* ~**a** *sm* thousand;
un ~ **(di)** about a thousand; **a** ~**a** by the
thousand, in thousands.

'miglio ['miʎʎo] *sm* (*BOT*) millet; (*pl(f)* ~**a**:
unità di misura) mile; ~ **marino** *o* **nautico**
nautical mile.

migliora'mento [miʎʎora'mento] *sm*
improvement.

miglio'rare [miʎʎo'rare] *vt, vi* to improve.

migli'ore [miʎ'ʎore] *ag* (*comparativo*)
better; (*superlativo*) best ♦ *sm*: **il** ~ the best
(thing) ♦ *sm/f*: **il(la)** ~ the best (person); **il**

miglior vino di questa regione the best wine in this area; **i ~i auguri** best wishes.

miglio'ria [miʎʎo'ria] *sf* improvement.

'**mignolo** ['miɲɲolo] *sm* (*ANAT*) little finger, pinkie; (: *dito del piede*) little toe.

mi'grare *vi* to migrate.

migrazi'one [migrat'tsjone] *sf* migration.

'**mila** *pl di* **mille.**

mila'nese *ag* Milanese ♦ *smf* person from Milan; **i ~i** the Milanese; **cotoletta alla ~** (*CUC*) Wiener schnitzel; **risotto alla ~** (*CUC*) risotto with saffron.

Mi'lano *sf* Milan.

miliar'dario, a *ag, smf* millionaire.

mili'ardo *sm* thousand million (*BRIT*), billion (*US*).

mili'are *ag*: **pietra ~** milestone.

milio'nario, a *ag, smf* millionaire.

mili'one *sm* million; **un ~ di euro** a million euros.

mili'tante *ag, smf* militant.

mili'tanza [mili'tantsa] *sf* militancy.

mili'tare *vi* (*MIL*) to be a soldier, serve; (*fig: in un partito*) to be a militant ♦ *ag* military ♦ *sm* serviceman; **fare il ~** to do one's military service; **~ di carriera** regular (soldier).

milita'resco, a, schi, sche *ag* (*portamento*) military *cpd*.

'**milite** *sm* soldier.

mi'lizia [mi'littsja] *sf* (*corpo armato*) militia.

milizi'ano [milit'tsjano] *sm* militiaman.

millanta'tore, 'trice *smf* boaster.

millante'ria *sf* (*qualità*) boastfulness.

'**mille** *num* (*pl* **mila**) a *o* one thousand; **diecimila** ten thousand.

mille'foglie [mille'fɔʎʎe] *sm inv* (*CUC*) cream *o* vanilla slice.

mil'lennio *sm* millennium.

millepi'edi *sm inv* centipede.

mil'lesimo, a *ag, sm* thousandth.

milli'grammo *sm* milligram(me).

mil'lilitro *sm* millilitre (*BRIT*), milliliter (*US*).

mil'limetro *sm* millimetre (*BRIT*), millimeter (*US*).

'**milza** ['miltsa] *sf* (*ANAT*) spleen.

mi'metico, a, ci, che *ag* (*arte*) mimetic; **tuta ~a** (*MIL*) camouflage.

mime'tismo *sm* camouflage.

mimetiz'zare [mimetid'dzare] *vt* to camouflage; **~rsi** *vr* to camouflage o.s.

'**mimica** *sf* (*arte*) mime.

'**mimo** *sm* (*attore, componimento*) mime.

mi'mosa *sf* mimosa.

min. *abbr* (= *minuto, minimo*) min.

'**mina** *sf* (*esplosiva*) mine; (*di matita*) lead.

mi'naccia, ce [mi'nattʃa] *sf* threat; **sotto la**

~ di under threat of.

minacci'are [minat'tʃare] *vt* to threaten; **~ qn di morte** to threaten to kill sb; **~ di fare qc** to threaten to do sth; **minaccia di piovere** it looks like rain.

minacci'oso, a [minat'tʃoso] *ag* threatening.

mi'nare *vt* (*MIL*) to mine; (*fig*) to undermine.

mina'tore *sm* miner.

mina'torio, a *ag* threatening.

minchi'one, a [min'kjone] (*fam*) *ag* idiotic ♦ *smf* idiot.

mine'rale *ag, sm* mineral.

mineralo'gia [mineralo'dʒia] *sf* mineralogy.

mine'rario, a *ag* (*delle miniere*) mining; (*dei minerali*) ore *cpd*.

mi'nestra *sf* soup; **~ in brodo** noodle soup; **~ di verdura** vegetable soup.

mines'trone *sm* thick vegetable and pasta soup.

mingher'lino, a [minger'lino] *ag* thin, slender.

'**mini** *ag inv* mini ♦ *sf inv* miniskirt.

minia'tura *sf* miniature.

mini'bar *sm inv* minibar.

minielabora'tore *sm* minicomputer.

mini'era *sf* mine; **~ di carbone** coalmine; (*impresa*) colliery (*BRIT*), coalmine.

mini'gonna *sf* miniskirt.

minima'lista, i, e *ag, smf* minimalist.

minimiz'zare [minimid'dzare] *vt* to minimize.

'**minimo, a** *ag* minimum, least, slightest; (*piccolissimo*) very small, slight; (*il più basso*) lowest, minimum ♦ *sm* minimum; **al ~** at least; **girare al ~** (*AUT*) to idle; **il ~ indispensabile** the bare minimum; **il ~ della pena** the minimum sentence.

minis'tero *sm* (*POL, REL*) ministry; (*governo*) government; (*DIR*): **Pubblico M~** State Prosecutor; **M~ delle Finanze** Ministry of Finance, ≈ Treasury.

mi'nistro *sm* (*POL, REL*) minister; **M~ delle Finanze** Minister of Finance, ≈ Chancellor of the Exchequer (*BRIT*).

mino'ranza [mino'rantsa] *sf* minority; **essere in ~** to be in the minority.

mino'rato, a *ag* handicapped ♦ *smf* physically (*o* mentally) handicapped person.

minorazi'one [minorat'tsjone] *sf* handicap.

Mi'norca *sf* Minorca.

mi'nore *ag* (*comparativo*) less; (: *più piccolo*) smaller; (: *numero*) lower; (: *inferiore*) lower, inferior; (: *meno importante*) minor; (: *più giovane*) younger; (*superlativo*) least; smallest; lowest; least important; youngest ♦ *smf* (*minorenne*) minor, person under age; **in misura** ~ to a lesser extent; **questo è il male** ~ this is the lesser evil.

mino'renne _ag_ under age ♦ _smlf_ minor, person under age.

mino'rile _ag_ juvenile; **carcere** ~ young offenders' institution; **delinquenza** ~ juvenile delinquency.

minori'tario, a _ag_ minority _cpd._

mi'nuscolo, a _ag_ (_scrittura, carattere_) small; (_piccolissimo_) tiny ♦ _sf_ small letter ♦ _sm_ small letters _pl_; (_TIP_) lower case; **scrivere tutto (in)** ~ to write everything in small letters.

mi'nuta _sf_ rough copy, draft.

mi'nuto, a _ag_ tiny, minute; (_pioggia_) fine; (_corporatura_) delicate, fine; (_lavoro_) detailed ♦ _sm_ (_unità di misura_) minute; **al** ~ (_COMM_) retail; **avere i** ~**i contati** to have very little time.

mi'nuzia [mi'nuttsja] _sf_ (_cura_) meticulousness; (_particolare_) detail.

minuziosa'mente [minuttsjosa'mente] _av_ meticulously; in minute detail.

minuzi'oso, a [minut'tsjoso] _ag_ (_persona, descrizione_) meticulous; (_esame_) minute.

'mio, 'mia, mi'ei, 'mie _det_: **il** ~, **la mia** _etc_ my ♦ _pronome_: **il** ~, **la mia** _etc_ mine ♦ _sm_: **ho speso del** ~ I spent my own money ♦ _sf_: **la mia** (_opinione_) my view; **i miei** my family; **un** ~ **amico** a friend of mine; **per amor** ~ for my sake; **è dalla mia** he is on my side; **anch'io ho avuto le mie** (_disavventure_) I've had my problems too; **ne ho fatta una delle mie!** (_sciocchezze_) I've done it again!; **cerco di stare sulle mie** I try to keep myself to myself.

'miope _ag_ short-sighted.

mio'pia _sf_ short-sightedness, myopia; (_fig_) short-sightedness.

'mira _sf_ (_anche fig_) aim; **avere una buona/ cattiva** ~ to be a good/bad shot; **prendere la** ~ to take aim; **prendere di** ~ **qn** (_fig_) to pick on sb.

mi'rabile _ag_ admirable, wonderful.

mi'racolo _sm_ miracle.

miraco'loso, a _ag_ miraculous.

mi'raggio [mi'radd3o] _sm_ mirage.

mi'rare _vi_: ~ **a** to aim at.

mi'riade _sf_ myriad.

mi'rino _sm_ (_TECN_) sight; (_FOT_) viewer, viewfinder.

mir'tillo _sm_ bilberry (_BRIT_), blueberry (_US_), whortleberry.

'mirto _sm_ myrtle.

mi'santropo, a _smlf_ misanthropist.

mi'scela [miʃ'ʃɛla] _sf_ mixture; (_di caffè_) blend.

miscel'lanea [miʃʃel'lanea] _sf_ miscellany.

'mischia ['miskja] _sf_ scuffle; (_RUGBY_) scrum, scrummage.

mischi'are [mis'kjare] _vt_, ~**rsi** _vr_ to mix, blend.

misco'noscere [misko'noʃʃere] _vt_ (_qualità, coraggio etc_) to fail to appreciate.

miscre'dente _ag_ (_REL_) misbelieving; (: _incredulo_) unbelieving ♦ _smlf_ misbeliever; unbeliever.

mis'cuglio [mis'kuʎʎo] _sm_ mixture, hotchpotch, jumble.

'mise _vb vedi_ **mettere**.

mise'rabile _ag_ (_infelice_) miserable, wretched; (_povero_) poverty-stricken; (_di scarso valore_) miserable.

mi'seria _sf_ extreme poverty; (_infelicità_) misery; ~**e** _sfpl_ (_del mondo etc_) misfortunes, troubles; **costare una** ~ to cost next to nothing; **piangere** ~ to plead poverty; **ridursi in** ~ to be reduced to poverty; **porca** ~! (_fam_) (bloody) hell!

miseri'cordia _sf_ mercy, pity.

misericordi'oso, a _ag_ merciful.

'misero, a _ag_ miserable, wretched; (_povero_) poverty-stricken; (_insufficiente_) miserable.

mis'fatto _sm_ misdeed, crime.

'misi _vb vedi_ **mettere**.

mi'sogino [mi'zɔdʒino] _sm_ misogynist.

'missile _sm_ missile; ~ **cruise** _o_ **di crociera** cruise missile; ~ **terra-aria** surface-to-air missile.

missio'nario, a _ag_, _smlf_ missionary.

missi'one _sf_ mission.

misteri'oso, a _ag_ mysterious.

mis'tero _sm_ mystery; **fare** ~ **di qc** to make a mystery out of sth; **quanti** ~**i!** why all the mystery?

'mistico, a, ci, che _ag_ mystic(al) ♦ _sm_ mystic.

mistifi'care _vt_ to fool, bamboozle.

'misto, a _ag_ mixed; (_scuola_) mixed, coeducational ♦ _sm_ mixture; **un tessuto in** ~ **lino** a linen mix.

mis'tura _sf_ mixture.

mi'sura _sf_ measure; (_misurazione, dimensione_) measurement; (_taglia_) size; (_provvedimento_) measure, step; (_moderazione_) moderation; (_MUS_) time; (: _divisione_) bar; (_fig: limite_) bounds _pl_, limit; **in** ~ **di** in accordance with, according to; **nella** ~ **in cui** inasmuch as, insofar as; **in giusta** ~ moderately; **oltre** ~ beyond measure; **su** ~ made to measure; **in ugual** ~ equally, in the same way; **a** ~ **d'uomo** on a human scale; **passare la** ~ to overstep the mark, go too far; **prendere le** ~**e a qn** to take sb's measurements, measure sb; **prendere le ~e di qc** to measure sth; **ho preso le mie ~e** I've taken the necessary steps; **non ha il senso della ~** he doesn't know when to stop; **~ di lunghezza/capacità** measure of length/capacity; **~e di sicurezza/ prevenzione** safety/precautionary measures.

misu'rare *vt* (*ambiente, stoffa*) to measure; (*terreno*) to survey; (*abito*) to try on; (*pesare*) to weigh; (*fig: parole etc*) to weigh up; (: *spese, cibo*) to limit ♦ *vi* to measure; **~rsi** *vr*: **~rsi con qn** to have a confrontation with sb; (*competere*) to compete with sb.

misu'rato, a *ag* (*ponderato*) measured; (*prudente*) cautious; (*moderato*) moderate.

misurazi'one [mizurat'tsjone] *sf* measuring; (*di terreni*) surveying.

'mite *ag* mild; (*prezzo*) moderate, reasonable.

'mitico, a, ci, che *ag* mythical.

miti'gare *vt* to mitigate, lessen; (*lenire*) to soothe, relieve; **~rsi** *vr* (*odio*) to subside; (*tempo*) to become milder.

'mitilo *sm* mussel.

'mito *sm* myth.

mitolo'gia, 'gie [mitolo'dʒia] *sf* mythology.

mito'logico, a, ci, che [mito'lɔdʒiko] *ag* mythological.

'mitra *sf* (*REL*) mitre (*BRIT*), miter (*US*) ♦ *sm inv* (*arma*) sub-machine gun.

mitragli'are [mitraʎ'ʎare] *vt* to machine-gun.

mitraglia'tore, 'trice [mitraʎʎa'tore] *ag*: **fucile** *m* **~** sub-machine gun ♦ *sf* machine gun.

mitteleuro'peo, a *ag* Central European.

mit'tente *smf* sender.

ml *abbr* (= *millilitro*) ml.

MLD *sigla m vedi* **Movimento per la Liberazione della Donna**.

MM *abbr* = Metropolitana Milanese.

mm *abbr* (= *millimetro*) mm.

M.M. *abbr vedi* **marina militare**.

mms ['ɛmme'ɛmme'ɛsse] *sigla m inv* (= *Multimedia Messaging Service*) MMS.

MN *sigla* = Mantova.

M/N, m/n *abbr* (= *motonave*) MV.

MO *sigla* = Modena.

M.O. *abbr* = **Medio Oriente**.

mo' *sm*: **a ~ di** *prep* like; **a ~ di esempio** by way of example.

'mobile *ag* mobile; (*parte di macchina*) moving; (*DIR: bene*) movable, personal ♦ *sm* (*arredamento*) piece of furniture; **~i** *smpl* furniture *sg*.

mo'bilia *sf* furniture.

mobili'are *ag* (*DIR*) personal, movable.

mo'bilio *sm* = mobilia.

mobilità *sf* mobility.

mobili'tare *vt* to mobilize; **~ l'opinione pubblica** to rouse public opinion.

mobilitazi'one [mobilitat'tsjone] *sf* mobilization.

mocas'sino *sm* moccasin.

mocci'oso, a [mot'tʃoso] *smf* (*bambino piccolo*) little kid; (*peg*) snotty-nosed kid.

'moccolo *sm* (*di candela*) candle end; (*fam: bestemmia*) oath; (: *moccio*) snot; **reggere il ~** to play gooseberry (*BRIT*), act as chaperon(e).

'moda *sf* fashion; **alla ~, di ~** fashionable, in fashion.

modalità *sf inv* formality; **seguire attentamente le ~ d'uso** to follow the instructions carefully; **~ giuridiche** legal procedures; **~ di pagamento** method of payment.

mo'della *sf* model.

model'lare *vt* (*creta*) to model, shape; **~rsi** *vr*: **~rsi su** to model o.s. on.

mo'dello *sm* model; (*stampo*) mould (*BRIT*), mold (*US*) ♦ *ag inv* model *cpd*.

'modem *sm inv* modem.

mode'nese *ag* of (*o* from) Modena.

mode'rare *vt* to moderate; **~rsi** *vr* to restrain o.s.; **~ la velocità** to reduce speed; **~ i termini** to weigh one's words.

mode'rato, a *ag* moderate.

modera'tore, 'trice *smf* moderator.

moderazi'one [moderat'tsjone] *sf* moderation.

moderniz'zare [modernid'dzare] *vt* to bring up to date, modernize; **~rsi** *vr* to get up to date.

mo'derno, a *ag* modern.

mo'destia *sf* modesty; **~ a parte ...** in all modesty ..., though I say it myself ....

mo'desto, a *ag* modest.

'modico, a, ci, che *ag* reasonable, moderate.

mo'difica, che *sf* modification; **subire delle ~che** to undergo some modifications.

modifi'cabile *ag* modifiable.

modifi'care *vt* to modify, alter; **~rsi** *vr* to alter, change.

mo'dista *sf* milliner.

'modo *sm* way, manner; (*mezzo*) means, way; (*occasione*) opportunity; (*LING*) mood; (*MUS*) mode; **~i** *smpl* (*maniere*) manners; **a suo ~, a ~ suo** in his own way; **ad** *o* **in ogni ~** anyway; **di** *o* **in ~ che** so that; **in ~ da** so as to; **in tutti i ~i** at all costs; (*comunque sia*) anyway; (*in ogni caso*) in any case; **in un certo qual ~** in a way, in some ways; **in qualche** ~ somehow or other; **oltre** ~ extremely; ~ **di dire** turn of phrase; **per** ~ **di dire** so to speak; **fare a** ~ **proprio** to do as one likes; **fare le cose a** ~ to do things properly; **una persona a** ~ a well-mannered person; **c'è** ~ **e** ~ **di farlo** there's a right way and a wrong way of doing it.

modu'lare *vt* to modulate ♦ *ag* modular.

modulazi'one [modulat'tsjone] *sf* modulation; ~ **di frequenza (FM)** frequency modulation (FM).

'modulo *sm* (*modello*) form; (*ARCHIT, lunare, di comando*) module; ~ **di domanda** application form; ~ **d'iscrizione** enrolment form; ~ **di versamento** deposit slip.

Moga'discio [moga'diʃʃo] *sm* Mogadishu.

'mogano *sm* mahogany.

'mogio, a, gi, gie ['mɔdʒo] *ag* down in the dumps, dejected.

'moglie ['mɔʎʎe] *sf* wife.

mo'hair [mɔ'ɛr] *sm* mohair.

mo'ine *sfpl* cajolery *sg*; (*leziosità*) affectation *sg*; **fare le** ~ **a qn** to cajole sb.

'mola *sf* millstone; (*utensile abrasivo*) grindstone.

mo'lare *vt* to grind ♦ *ag* (*pietra*) mill *cpd* ♦ *sm* (*dente*) molar.

'mole *sf* mass; (*dimensioni*) size; (*edificio grandioso*) massive structure; **una** ~ **di lavoro** masses (*BRIT*) *o* loads of work.

mo'lecola *sf* molecule.

moles'tare *vt* to bother, annoy.

mo'lestia *sf* annoyance, bother; **recar** ~ **a qn** to bother sb; ~**e sessuali** sexual harassment *sg*.

mo'lesto, a *ag* annoying.

moli'sano, a *ag* of (*o from*) Molise.

'molla *sf* spring; ~**e** *sfpl* (*per camino*) tongs; **prendere qn con le** ~**e** to treat sb with kid gloves.

mol'lare *vt* to release, let go; (*NAUT*) to ease; (*fig: ceffone*) to give ♦ *vi* (*cedere*) to give in; ~ **gli ormeggi** (*NAUT*) to cast off; ~ **la presa** to let go.

'molle *ag* soft; (*muscoli*) flabby; (*fig: debole*) weak, feeble.

molleggi'ato, a [molled'dʒato] *ag* (*letto*) sprung; (*auto*) with good suspension.

mol'leggio [mol'leddʒo] *sm* (*per veicoli*) suspension; (*elasticità*) springiness; (*GINNASTICA*) knee-bends *pl*.

mol'letta *sf* (*per capelli*) hairgrip; (*per panni stesi*) clothes peg (*BRIT*) *o* pin (*US*); ~**e** *sfpl* (*per zucchero*) tongs.

mol'lezza [mol'lettsa] *sf* softness; flabbiness; weakness, feebleness; ~**e** *sfpl*:

vivere nelle ~**e** to live in the lap of luxury.

mol'lica, che *sf* crumb, soft part.

mol'liccio, a, ci, ce [mol'littʃo] *ag* (*terreno, impasto*) soggy; (*frutta*) soft; (*floscio: mano*) limp; (: *muscolo*) flabby.

mol'lusco, schi *sm* mollusc.

'molo *sm* jetty, pier.

mol'teplice [mol'teplitʃe] *ag* (*formato di più elementi*) complex; ~**i** *pl* (*svariati: interessi, attività*) numerous, various.

molteplicità [molteplitʃi'ta] *sf* multiplicity.

moltipli'care *vt* to multiply; ~**rsi** *vr* to multiply; (*richieste*) to increase in number.

moltiplicazi'one [moltiplikat'tsjone] *sf* multiplication.

molti'tudine *sf* multitude; **una** ~ **di** a vast number *o* a multitude of.

═══════════════════════ *PAROLA CHIAVE*

'molto, a *det* (*quantità*) a lot of, much; (*numero*) a lot of, many; ~ **pane/carbone** a lot of bread/coal; ~**a gente** a lot of people, many people; ~**i libri** a lot of books, many books; **non ho** ~ **tempo** I haven't got much time; **per** ~ **(tempo)** for a long time; **ci vuole** ~ **(tempo)?** will it take long?; **arriverà fra non** ~ he'll arrive soon; **ne hai per** ~**?** will you be long?

♦ *av* **1** a lot, (very) much; **viaggia** ~ he travels a lot; **non viaggia** ~ he doesn't travel much *o* a lot

2 (*intensivo: con aggettivi, avverbi*) very; (: *con participio passato*) (very) much; ~ **buono** very good; ~ **migliore**, ~ **meglio** much *o* a lot better

♦ *pron* much, a lot; ~**i, e** *pron pl* many, a lot; ~**i pensano che ...** many (people) think that ...; ~**e sono rimaste a casa** a lot of them stayed at home; **c'era gente, ma non** ~**a** there were people there, but not many.

momentanea'mente *av* at the moment, at present.

momen'taneo, a *ag* momentary, fleeting.

mo'mento *sm* moment; **da un** ~ **all'altro** at any moment; (*all'improvviso*) suddenly; **al** ~ **di fare** just as I was (*o* you were *o* he was *etc*) doing; **a** ~**i** (*da un* ~ *all'altro*) any time *o* moment now; (*quasi*) nearly; **per il** ~ for the time being; **dal** ~ **che** ever since; (*dato che*) since; ~ **culminante** climax.

'monaca, che *sf* nun.

'Monaco *sf* Monaco; ~ **(di Baviera)** Munich.

'monaco, ci *sm* monk.

mo'narca, chi *sm* monarch.

monar'chia [monar'kia] *sf* monarchy.

mo'narchico, a, ci, che [mo'narkiko] *ag* (*stato, autorità*) monarchic; (*partito, fede*) monarchist ♦ *sm/f* monarchist.

monas'tero *sm* (*di monaci*) monastery; (*di monache*) convent.

mo'nastico, a, ci, che *ag* monastic.

'monco, a, chi, che *ag* maimed; (*fig*) incomplete; ~ **d'un braccio** one-armed.

mon'cone *sm* stump.

mon'dana *sf* prostitute.

mondanità *sf* (*frivolezza*) worldliness; **le ~** (*piaceri*) the pleasures of the world.

mon'dano, a *ag* (*anche fig*) worldly; (*dell'alta società*) society *cpd*; fashionable.

mon'dare *vt* (*frutta, patate*) to peel; (*piselli*) to shell; (*pulire*) to clean.

mondez'zaio [mondet'tsajo] *sm* rubbish (*BRIT*) *o* garbage (*US*) dump.

mondi'ale *ag* (*campionato, popolazione*) world *cpd*; (*influenza*) world-wide; **di fama ~** world famous.

'mondo *sm* world; (*grande quantità*): **un ~ di** lots of, a host of; **il gran o bel ~** high society; **per niente al ~, per nessuna cosa al ~** not for all the world; **da che ~ è ~** since time *o* the world began; **mandare qn all'altro ~** to kill sb; **mettere/venire al ~** to bring/come into the world; **vivere fuori dal ~** to be out of touch with the real world; **(sono) cose dell'altro ~!** it's incredible!; **com'è piccolo il ~!** it's a small world!

mone'gasco, a, schi, sche *ag, sm/f* Monegasque.

monelle'ria *sf* prank, naughty trick.

mo'nello, a *sm/f* street urchin; (*ragazzo vivace*) scamp, imp.

mo'neta *sf* coin; (*ECON: valuta*) currency; (*denaro spicciolo*) (small) change; **~ estera** foreign currency; **~ legale** legal tender.

mone'tario, a *ag* monetary.

Mon'golia *sf*: **la ~** Mongolia.

mon'golico, a, ci, che *ag* Mongolian.

mongo'lismo *sm* Down's syndrome.

'mongolo, a *ag* Mongolian ♦ *sm/f, sm* Mongol, Mongolian.

mongo'loide *ag, sm/f* (*MED*) mongol.

'monito *sm* warning.

'monitor *sm inv* (*TECN, TV*) monitor.

monito'raggio [monito'raddʒo] *sm* monitoring.

monito'rare *vt* to monitor.

mo'nocolo *sm* (*lente*) monocle, eyeglass.

monoco'lore *ag* (*POL*): **governo ~** one-party government.

monoga'mia *sf* monogamy.

mo'nogamo, a *ag* monogamous ♦ *sm* monogamist.

monogra'fia *sf* monograph.

mono'gramma, i *sm* monogram.

mono'lingue *ag* monolingual.

monolo'cale *sm* ≈ studio flat.

mo'nologo, ghi *sm* monologue.

mono'pattino *sm* scooter.

mono'polio *sm* monopoly; **~ di stato** government monopoly.

monopoliz'zare [monopolid'dzare] *vt* to monopolize.

mono'sillabo, a *ag* monosyllabic ♦ *sm* monosyllable.

monoto'nia *sf* monotony.

mo'notono, a *ag* monotonous.

mono'uso *ag inv* disposable.

monovo'lume *sf inv* people carrier, people mover.

Mons. *abbr* (= *Monsignore*) Mgr.

monsi'gnore [monsiɲ'ɲore] *sm* (*REL: titolo*) Your (*o* His) Grace.

mon'sone *sm* monsoon.

monta'carichi [monta'kariki] *sm inv* hoist, goods lift.

mon'taggio [mon'taddʒo] *sm* (*TECN*) assembly; (*CINE*) editing.

mon'tagna [mon'taɲɲa] *sf* mountain; (*zona montuosa*): **la ~** the mountains *pl*; **andare in ~** to go to the mountains; **aria/strada di ~** mountain air/road; **casa di ~** house in the mountains; **~e russe** roller coaster *sg*.

monta'gnoso, a [montaɲ'ɲoso] *ag* mountainous.

monta'naro, a *ag* mountain *cpd* ♦ *sm/f* mountain dweller.

mon'tano, a *ag* mountain *cpd*.

mon'tante *sm* (*di porta*) jamb; (*di finestra*) upright; (*CALCIO: palo*) post; (*PUGILATO*) upper cut; (*COMM*) total amount.

mon'tare *vt* to go (*o* come) up; (*cavallo*) to ride; (*apparecchiatura*) to set up, assemble; (*CUC*) to whip; (*ZOOL*) to cover; (*incastonare*) to mount, set; (*CINE*) to edit; (*FOT*) to mount ♦ *vi* to go (*o* come) up; (*a cavallo*): **~ bene/male** to ride well/badly; (*aumentare di livello, volume*) to rise; **~rsi** *vr* to become big-headed; **~ qc** to exaggerate sth; **~ qn** *o* **la testa a qn** to turn sb's head; **~rsi la testa** to become big-headed; **~ in bicicletta/macchina/treno** to get on a bicycle/ into a car/on a train; **~ a cavallo** to get on *o* mount a horse; **~ la guardia** (*MIL*) to mount guard.

monta'tura *sf* assembling *no pl*; (*di occhiali*) frames *pl*; (*di gioiello*) mounting, setting; (*fig*): **~ pubblicitaria** publicity stunt.

montavi'vande *sm inv* dumbwaiter.

'**monte** *sm* mountain; **a** ~ upstream; **andare a** ~ (*fig*) to come to nothing; **mandare a** ~ **qc** (*fig*) to upset sth, cause sth to fail; **il M~ Bianco** Mont Blanc; **il M~ Everest** Mount Everest; ~ **di pietà** pawnshop; ~ **premi** prize.

Monteci'torio [montetʃi'tɔrjo] *sm*: **palazzo** ~ (*POL*) *seat of the Italian Chamber of Deputies*.

montene'grino, a *ag, sm/f* Montenegrin.

Monte'negro *sm* Montenegro.

mont'gomery [mɔnt'gʌməri] *sm inv* duffel coat.

mon'tone *sm* (*ZOOL*) ram; (*anche*: **giacca di** ~) sheepskin (jacket); **carne di** ~ mutton.

montuosità *sf* mountainous nature.

montu'oso, a *ag* mountainous.

monu'mento *sm* monument.

mo'quette [mɔ'kɛt] *sf* fitted carpet.

'**mora** *sf* (*del rovo*) blackberry; (*del gelso*) mulberry; (*DIR*) delay; (: *somma*) arrears *pl*.

mo'rale *ag* moral ♦ *sf* (*scienza*) ethics *sg*, moral philosophy; (*complesso di norme*) moral standards *pl*, morality; (*condotta*) morals *pl*; (*insegnamento morale*) moral ♦ *sm* morale; **la** ~ **della favola** the moral of the tale; **essere giù di** ~ to be feeling down; **aver il** ~ **alto/a terra** to be in good/ low spirits.

mora'lista, i, e *ag* moralistic ♦ *sm/f* moralist.

moralità *sf* morality; (*condotta*) morals *pl*.

moraliz'zare [moralid'dzare] *vt* (*costumi, vita pubblica*) to set moral standards for.

moralizzazi'one [moraliddzat'tsjone] *sf* setting of moral standards.

mora'toria *sf* (*DIR*) moratorium.

morbi'dezza [morbi'dettsa] *sf* softness; smoothness; tenderness.

'**morbido, a** *ag* soft; (*pelle*) soft, smooth; (*carne*) tender.

mor'billo *sm* (*MED*) measles *sg*.

'**morbo** *sm* disease.

mor'boso, a *ag* (*fig*) morbid.

'**morchia** ['mɔrkja] *sf* (*residuo grasso*) dregs *pl*; oily deposit.

mor'dente *sm* (*fig*: *di satira, critica*) bite; (: *di persona*) drive.

'**mordere** *vt* to bite; (*addentare*) to bite into; (*corrodere*) to eat into.

mordicchi'are [mordik'kjare] *vt* (*gen*) to chew at.

mo'rente *ag* dying ♦ *sm/f* dying man/ woman.

mor'fina *sf* morphine.

mo'ria *sf* high mortality.

mori'bondo, a *ag* dying, moribund.

morige'rato, a [moridʒe'rato] *ag* of good morals.

mo'rire *vi* to die; (*abitudine, civiltà*) to die out; ~ **di dolore** to die of a broken heart; ~ **di fame** to die of hunger; (*fig*) to be starving; ~ **di freddo** to freeze to death; (*fig*) to be frozen; ~ **d'invidia** to be green with envy; ~ **di noia/paura** to be bored/ scared to death; ~ **dalla voglia di fare qc** to be dying to do sth; **fa un caldo da** ~ it's terribly hot.

mormo'rare *vi* to murmur; (*brontolare*) to grumble; **si mormora che ...** it's rumoured (*BRIT*) *o* rumored (*US*) that ...; **la gente mormora** people are talking.

mormo'rio *sm* murmuring; grumbling.

'**moro, a** *ag* dark(-haired); dark(-complexioned); **i M~i** *smpl* (*STORIA*) the Moors.

mo'roso, a *ag* in arrears ♦ *sm/f* (*fam*: *innamorato*) sweetheart.

'**morsa** *sf* (*TECN*) vice (*BRIT*), vise (*US*); (*fig*: *stretta*) grip.

mor'setto *sm* (*TECN*) clamp; (*ELETTR*) terminal.

morsi'care *vt* to nibble (at), gnaw (at); (*sog*: *insetto*) to bite.

'**morso, a** *pp di* **mordere** ♦ *sm* bite; (*di insetto*) sting; (*parte della briglia*) bit; **dare un** ~ **a qc/qn** to bite sth/sb; **i ~i della fame** pangs of hunger.

morta'della *sf* (*CUC*) mortadella (*type of salted pork meat*).

mor'taio *sm* mortar.

mor'tale *ag, sm* mortal.

mortalità *sf* mortality; (*STATISTICA*) mortality, death rate.

'**morte** *sf* death; **in punto di** ~ at death's door; **ferito a** ~ (*soldato*) mortally wounded; (*in incidente*) fatally injured; **essere annoiato a** ~ to be bored to death *o* to tears; **avercela a** ~ **con qn** to be bitterly resentful of sb; **avere la** ~ **nel cuore** to have a heavy heart.

mortifi'care *vt* to mortify.

'**morto, a** *pp di* **morire** ♦ *ag* dead ♦ *sm/f* dead man/woman; **i** ~**i** the dead; **fare il** ~ (*nell'acqua*) to float on one's back; **un** ~ **di fame** (*fig peg*) a down-and-out; **le campane suonavano a** ~ the funeral bells were tolling; *vedi anche* **Giorno dei Morti**.

mor'torio *sm* (*anche fig*) funeral.

mo'saico, ci *sm* mosaic; **l'ultimo tassello del** ~ (*fig*) the last piece of the puzzle.

'**Mosca** *sf* Moscow.

'**mosca, sche** *sf* fly; **rimanere** *o* **restare con un pugno di** ~**sche** (*fig*) to be left empty-handed; **non si sentiva volare una** ~ (fig) you could have heard a pin drop; ~ **cieca** blind-man's buff.

mos'cato sm muscatel (wine).

mosce'rino [moʃʃe'rino] sm midge, gnat.

mos'chea [mos'kɛa] sf mosque.

mos'chetto [mos'ketto] sm musket.

moschet'tone [mosket'tone] sm (gancio) spring clip; (ALPINISMO) karabiner, snaplink.

moschi'cida, i, e [moski'tʃida] ag fly cpd; **carta** ~ flypaper.

'moscio, a, sci, sce ['moʃʃo] ag (fig) lifeless; **ha la "r"** ~**a** he can't roll his "r"s.

mos'cone sm (ZOOL) bluebottle; (barca) pedalo; (: a remi) kind of pedalo with oars.

mosco'vita, i, e ag, sm/f Muscovite.

'mossa sf movement; (nel gioco) move; **darsi una** ~ (fig) to give o.s. a shake; **prendere le** ~**e da qc** to come about as the result of sth.

'mossi etc vb vedi **muovere**.

'mosso, a pp di **muovere** ♦ ag (mare) rough; (capelli) wavy; (FOT) blurred; (ritmo, prosa) animated.

mos'tarda sf mustard.

'mosto sm must.

'mostra sf exhibition, show; (ostentazione) show; **in** ~ on show; **far** ~ **di** (fingere) to pretend; **far** ~ **di sé** to show off; **mettersi in** ~ to draw attention to o.s.

mos'trare vt to show ♦ vi: ~ **di fare** to pretend to do; ~**rsi** vr to appear; ~ **la lingua** to stick out one's tongue.

'mostro sm monster.

mostru'oso, a ag monstrous.

mo'tel sm inv motel.

moti'vare vt (causare) to cause; (giustificare) to justify, account for.

motivazi'one [motivat'tsjone] sf justification; (PSIC) motivation.

mo'tivo sm (causa) reason, cause; (movente) motive; (letterario) (central) theme; (disegno) motif, design; (MUS) motif; **per quale** ~? why?, for what reason?; **per** ~**i di salute** for health reasons; ~**i personali** personal reasons.

'moto sm (anche FISICA) motion; (movimento, gesto) movement; (esercizio fisico) exercise; (sommossa) rising, revolt; (commozione) feeling, impulse ♦ sf inv (motocicletta) motorbike; **fare del** ~ to take some exercise; **un** ~ **d'impazienza** an impatient gesture; **mettere in** ~ to set in motion; (AUT) to start up; ~ **d'acqua** Jet Ski ®.

moto'carro sm three-wheeler van.

motoci'cletta [mototʃi'kletta] sf motorcycle.

motoci'clismo [mototʃi'klizmo] sm motorcycling, motorcycle racing.

motoci'clista, i, e [mototʃi'klista] sm/f motorcyclist.

moto'nave sf motor vessel.

motopesche'reccio [motopeske'rettʃo] sm motor fishing vessel.

mo'tore, 'trice ag motor; (TECN) driving ♦ sm engine, motor ♦ sf (TECN) engine, motor; **albero** ~ drive shaft; **forza** ~**trice** driving force; **a** ~ motor cpd, power-driven; ~ **a combustione interna/a reazione** internal combustion/jet engine; ~ **di ricerca** (INFORM) search engine.

moto'rino sm moped; ~ **di avviamento** (AUT) starter.

motoriz'zato, a [motorid'dzato] ag (truppe) motorized; (persona) having a car o transport.

motorizzazi'one [motoriddzat'tsjone] sf (ufficio tecnico e organizzativo): **(ufficio della)** ~ road traffic office.

motos'cafo sm motorboat.

motove'detta sf motor patrol vessel.

mo'trice [mo'tritʃe] sf vedi **motore**.

mot'teggio [mot'teddʒo] sm banter.

'motto sm (battuta scherzosa) witty remark; (frase emblematica) motto, maxim.

mountain bike sf inv mountain bike.

'mouse ['maus] sm inv (INFORM) mouse.

mo'vente sm motive.

mo'venza [mo'vɛntsa] sf movement.

movimen'tare vt to liven up.

movimen'tato, a ag (festa, partita) lively; (riunione) animated; (strada, vita) busy; (soggiorno) eventful.

movi'mento sm movement; (fig) activity, hustle and bustle; (MUS) tempo, movement; **essere sempre in** ~ to be always on the go; **fare un po' di** ~ (esercizio fisico) to take some exercise; **c'è molto** ~ **in città** the town is very busy; ~ **di capitali** movement of capital; **M**~ **per la Liberazione della Donna (MLD)** Women's Movement.

movi'ola sf moviola; **rivedere qc alla** ~ to see an action (BRIT) o instant (US) replay of sth.

Mozam'bico [moddzam'biko] sm: **il** ~ Mozambique.

mozi'one [mot'tsjone] sf (POL) motion; ~ **d'ordine** (POL) point of order.

mozzafi'ato [mottsa'fjato] ag inv breathtaking.

moz'zare [mot'tsare] vt to cut off; (coda) to dock; ~ **il fiato** o **il respiro a qn** (fig) to take sb's breath away.

mozza'rella [mottsa'rɛlla] *sf* mozzarella.

mozzi'cone [mottsi'kone] *sm* stub, butt, end; (*anche*: ~ **di sigaretta**) cigarette end.

'mozzo *sm* ['mɔddzo] (*MECCANICA*) hub; ['mottso] (*NAUT*) ship's boy; ~ **di stalla** stable boy.

mq *abbr* (= *metro quadro*) sq.m.

MS *sigla* = *Massa Carrara*.

M.S.I. *sigla m* (= *Movimento Sociale Italiano*) *former right-wing political party.*

Mti *abbr* = *monti*.

'mucca, che *sf* cow; ~ **pazza** BSE; (**morbo della**) ~ **pazza** mad cow disease, BSE; **l'emergenza** ~ **pazza** the mad cow crisis.

'mucchio ['mukkjo] *sm* pile, heap; (*fig*): **un** ~ **di** lots of, heaps of.

mucil'lagine [mutʃil'ladʒine] *sf* (*BOT*) mucilage (*green slime produced by plants growing in water*).

'muco, chi *sm* mucus.

mu'cosa *sf* mucous membrane.

'muesli [mjusli] *sm* muesli.

'muffa *sf* mould (*BRIT*), mold (*US*), mildew; **fare la** ~ to go mouldy (*BRIT*) o moldy (*US*).

mugghi'are [mug'gjare] *vi* (*fig*: *mare, tuono*) to roar; (: *vento*) to howl.

mug'gire [mud'dʒire] *vi* (*vacca*) to low, moo; (*toro*) to bellow; (*fig*) to roar.

mug'gito [mud'dʒito] *sm* moo; bellow; roar.

mu'ghetto [mu'getto] *sm* lily of the valley.

mu'gnaio, a [muɲ'ɲajo] *sm/f* miller.

mugo'lare *vi* (*cane*) to whimper, whine; (*fig*: *persona*) to moan.

mugu'gnare [muguɲ'ɲare] *vi* (*fam*) to mutter, mumble.

mulatti'era *sf* mule track.

mu'latto, a *ag, sm/f* mulatto.

muli'nare *vi* to whirl, spin (round and round).

muli'nello *sm* (*moto vorticoso*) eddy, whirl; (*di canna da pesca*) reel; (*NAUT*) windlass.

mu'lino *sm* mill; ~ **a vento** windmill.

'mulo *sm* mule.

'multa *sf* fine.

mul'tare *vt* to fine.

multico'lore *ag* multicoloured (*BRIT*), multicolored (*US*).

multi'etnico, a, ci, che *ag* multiethnic.

multi'forme *ag* (*paesaggio, attività, interessi*) varied; (*ingegno*) versatile.

multimedi'ale *ag* multimedia *cpd*.

multinazio'nale [multinattsjo'nale] *ag, sf* multinational; **forza** ~ **di pace** multinational peace-keeping force.

'multiplo, a *ag, sm* multiple.

multiu'tenza [multiu'tɛntsa] *sf* (*INFORM*) time sharing.

'mummia *sf* mummy.

'mungere ['mundʒere] *vt* (*anche fig*) to milk.

mungi'tura [mundʒi'tura] *sf* milking.

munici'pale [munitʃi'pale] *ag* (*gen*) municipal; **palazzo** ~ town hall; **autorità** ~**i** local authorities (*BRIT*), local government *sg*.

muni'cipio [muni'tʃipjo] *sm* town council; (*edificio*) town hall; **sposarsi in** ~ ≈ to get married in a registry office (*BRIT*), have a civil marriage.

munifi'cenza [munifi'tʃɛntsa] *sf* munificence.

mu'nifico, a, ci, che *ag* munificent, generous.

mu'nire *vt*: ~ **qc/qn di** to equip sth/sb with; ~ **di firma** (*documento*) to sign.

munizi'oni [munit'tsjoni] *sfpl* (*MIL*) ammunition *sg*.

'munsi *etc vb vedi* **mungere**.

'munto, a *pp di* **mungere**.

mu'oio *etc vb vedi* **morire**.

mu'overe *vt* to move; (*ruota, macchina*) to drive; (*sollevare: questione, obiezione*) to raise, bring up; (: *accusa*) to make, bring forward; ~ **rsi** *vr* to move; ~ **causa a qn** (*DIR*) to take legal action against sb; ~ **a compassione** to move to pity; ~ **guerra a** *o* **contro qn** to wage war against sb; ~ **mari e monti** to move heaven and earth; ~ **al pianto** to move to tears; ~ **i primi passi** to take one's first steps; (*fig*) to be starting out; **muoviti!** hurry up!, get a move on!

'mura *sfpl vedi* **muro**.

mu'raglia [mu'raʎʎa] *sf* (high) wall.

mu'rale *ag* wall *cpd*; mural.

mu'rare *vt* (*persona, porta*) to wall up.

mu'rario, a *ag* building *cpd*; **arte** ~**a** masonry.

mura'tore *sm* (*con pietre*) mason; (*con mattoni*) bricklayer.

mura'tura *sf* (*lavoro murario*) masonry; **casa in** ~ (*di pietra*) stonebuilt house; (*di mattoni*) brick house.

'muro *sm* wall; ~**a** *sfpl* (*cinta cittadina*) walls; **a** ~ wall *cpd*; (*armadio etc*) built-in; **mettere al** ~ (*fucilare*) to shoot *o* execute (by firing squad); ~ **di cinta** surrounding wall; ~ **divisorio** dividing wall; ~ **del suono** sound barrier.

'musa *sf* muse.

'muschio ['muskjo] *sm* (*ZOOL*) musk; (*BOT*) moss.

musco'lare *ag* muscular, muscle *cpd*.

muscola'tura *sf* muscle structure.

'muscolo *sm* (*ANAT*) muscle.

musco'loso, a *ag* muscular.

mu'seo *sm* museum.
museru'ola *sf* muzzle.
'musica *sf* music; ~ **da ballo/camera**
dance/chamber music.
musi'cale *ag* musical.
musicas'setta *sf* (pre-recorded) cassette.
musi'cista, i, e [muzi'tʃista] *sm/f* musician.
musi'comane *sm/f* music lover.
'muso *sm* muzzle; (*di auto, aereo*) nose;
tenere il ~ to sulk.
mu'sone, a *sm/f* sulky person.
'mussola *sf* muslin.
mus(s)ul'mano, a *ag, sm/f* Muslim,
Moslem.
'muta *sf* (*di animali*) moulting (*BRIT*),
molting (*US*); (*di serpenti*) sloughing; (*per
immersioni subacquee*) diving suit; (*gruppo
di cani*) pack.
mu'tabile *ag* changeable.
muta'mento *sm* change.
mu'tande *sfpl* (da uomo) (under)pants.
mutan'dine *sfpl* (*da donna, bambino*) pants
(*BRIT*), briefs; ~ **di plastica** plastic pants.
mu'tare *vt, vi* to change, alter.
mutazi'one [mutat'tsjone] *sf* change,
alteration; (*BIOL*) mutation.
mu'tevole *ag* changeable.
muti'lare *vt* to mutilate, maim; (*fig*) to
mutilate, deface.
muti'lato, a *sm/f* disabled person (*through
loss of limbs*); ~ **di guerra** disabled ex-
serviceman (*BRIT*) *o* war veteran (*US*).
mutilazi'one [mutilat'tsjone] *sf* mutilation.
mu'tismo *sm* (*MED*) mutism;
(*atteggiamento*) (stubborn) silence.
'muto, a *ag* (*MED*) dumb; (*emozione, dolore,
CINE*) silent; (*LING*) silent, mute; (*carta
geografica*) blank; ~ **per lo stupore** *etc*
speechless with amazement *etc*; **ha fatto
scena** ~**a** he didn't utter a word.
'mutua *sf* (*anche:* **cassa** ~) health
insurance scheme; **medico della** ~
≈ National Health Service doctor (*BRIT*).
mutu'are *vt* (*fig*) to borrow.
mutu'ato, a *sm/f* member of a health
insurance scheme.
'mutuo, a *ag* (*reciproco*) mutual ♦ *sm* (*ECON*)
(long-term) loan; ~ **ipotecario** mortgage.

N n

N, n ['ɛnne] *sf o m* (*lettera*) N, n; **N come
Napoli** ≈ N for Nellie (*BRIT*), N for Nan
(*US*).
N *abbr* (= *nord*) N.
n *abbr* (= *numero*) no.
NA *sigla* = *Napoli*.
na'babbo *sm* (*anche fig*) nabob.
'nacchere ['nakkere] *sfpl* castanets.
NAD *sigla m* = **nucleo anti-droga**.
na'dir *sm* (*ASTR*) nadir.
'nafta *sf* naphtha; (*per motori diesel*) diesel
oil.
nafta'lina *sf* (*CHIM*) naphthalene; (*tarmicida*)
mothballs *pl*.
'naia *sf* (*ZOOL*) cobra; (*MIL*) *slang term for
national service*.
na'if [na'if] *ag inv* naïve.
'nailon *sm* = **nylon**.
Nai'robi *sf* Nairobi.
'nanna *sf* (*linguaggio infantile*): **andare a** ~
to go to beddy-byes.
'nano, a *ag, sm/f* dwarf.
napole'tano, a *ag, sm/f* Neapolitan ♦ *sf*
(*macchinetta da caffè*) Neapolitan coffee
pot.
'Napoli *sf* Naples.
'nappa *sf* tassel.
nar'ciso [nar'tʃizo] *sm* narcissus.
'narcos *sm inv* (*colombiano*) Colombian
drug trafficker.
narco'dollari *smpl* drug money *sg*.
nar'cosi *sf* general anaesthesia, narcosis.
nar'cotico, ci *sm* narcotic.
narcotraffi'cante *sm/f* drug trafficker.
narco'traffico *sm* drug trade.
na'rice [na'ritʃe] *sf* nostril.
nar'rare *vt* to tell the story of, recount.
narra'tivo, a *ag* narrative ♦ *sf* (*branca
letteraria*) fiction.
narra'tore, 'trice *sm/f* narrator.
narrazi'one [narrat'tsjone] *sf* narration;
(*racconto*) story, tale.
N.A.S.A. ['naza] *sigla f* (= *National
Aeronautics and Space Administration*)
NASA.
na'sale *ag* nasal.
na'scente [naʃ'ʃɛnte] *ag* (*sole, luna*) rising.
'nascere ['naʃʃere] *vi* (*bambino*) to be born;

(*pianta*) to come *o* spring up; (*fiume*) to rise, have its source; (*sole*) to rise; (*dente*) to come through; (*fig: derivare, conseguire*): ~ **da** to arise from, be born out of; **è nata nel 1952** she was born in 1952; **da cosa nasce cosa** one thing leads to another.

'nascita ['naʃʃita] *sf* birth.

nasci'turo, a [naʃʃi'turo] *sm/f* future child; **come si chiamerà il** ~? what's the baby going to be called?

nas'condere *vt* to hide, conceal; ~**rsi** *vr* to hide.

nascon'diglio [naskon'diʎʎo] *sm* hiding place.

nascon'dino *sm* (*gioco*) hide-and-seek.

nas'cosi *etc vb vedi* **nascondere**.

nas'costo, a *pp di* **nascondere ♦** *ag* hidden; **di** ~ secretly.

na'sello *sm* (*ZOOL*) hake.

'naso *sm* nose.

Nas'sau *sf* Nassau.

'nastro *sm* ribbon; (*magnetico, isolante, SPORT*) tape; ~ **adesivo** adhesive tape; ~ **trasportatore** conveyor belt.

nas'turzio [nas'turtsjo] *sm* nasturtium.

na'tale *ag* of one's birth **♦** *sm* (*REL*): **N**~ Christmas; (*giorno della nascita*) birthday; ~**i** *smpl*: **di illustri/umili** ~**i** of noble/humble birth.

natalità *sf* birth rate.

nata'lizio, a [nata'littsjo] *ag* (*del Natale*) Christmas *cpd*.

na'tante *sm* craft *inv*, boat.

'natica, che *sf* (*ANAT*) buttock.

na'tio, a, 'tii, 'tie *ag* native.

Natività *sf* (*REL*) Nativity.

na'tivo, a *ag, sm/f* native.

'nato, a *pp di* **nascere ♦** *ag*: **un attore** ~ a born actor; ~**a Pieri** née Pieri.

'N.A.T.O. *sigla f* NATO (= *North Atlantic Treaty Organization*).

na'tura *sf* nature; **pagare in** ~ to pay in kind; ~ **morta** still life.

natu'rale *ag* natural **♦** *sm*: **al** ~ (*alimenti*) served plain; (*ritratto*) life-size; (**ma**) **è** ~! (*in risposte*) of course!; **a grandezza** ~ life-size; **acqua** ~ spring water.

natura'lezza [natura'lettsa] *sf* naturalness.

natura'lista, i, e *sm/f* naturalist.

naturaliz'zare [naturalid'dzare] *vt* to naturalize.

natural'mente *av* naturally; (*certamente, sì*) of course.

natu'rismo *sm* naturism, nudism.

natu'rista, i, e *ag, sm/f* naturist, nudist.

naufra'gare *vi* (*nave*) to be wrecked; (*persona*) to be shipwrecked; (*fig*) to fall through.

nau'fragio [nau'fradʒo] *sm* shipwreck; (*fig*) ruin, failure.

'naufrago, ghi *sm* castaway, shipwreck victim.

'nausea *sf* nausea; **avere la** ~ to feel sick (*BRIT*) *o* ill (*US*); **fino alla** ~ ad nauseam.

nausea'bondo, a *ag,* **nause'ante** *ag* nauseating, sickening.

nause'are *vt* to nauseate, make (feel) sick (*BRIT*) *o* ill (*US*).

'nautico, a, ci, che *ag* nautical **♦** *sf* (art of) navigation; **salone** ~ (*mostra*) boat show.

na'vale *ag* naval; **battaglia** ~ naval battle; (*gioco*) battleships *pl*.

na'vata *sf* (*anche:* ~ **centrale**) nave; (*anche:* ~ **laterale**) aisle.

'nave *sf* ship, vessel; ~ **da carico** cargo ship, freighter; ~ **cisterna** tanker; ~ **da guerra** warship; ~ **di linea** liner; ~ **passeggeri** passenger ship; ~ **portaerei** aircraft carrier; ~ **spaziale** spaceship.

na'vetta *sf* shuttle; (*servizio di collegamento*) shuttle (service).

navi'cella [navi'tʃɛlla] *sf* (*di aerostato*) gondola; ~ **spaziale** spaceship.

navi'gabile *ag* navigable.

navi'gante *sm* sailor, seaman.

navi'gare *vi* to sail; ~ **in cattive acque** (*fig*) to be in deep water; ~ **in Internet** to surf the Net.

navi'gato, a *ag* (*fig: esperto*) experienced.

naviga'tore, 'trice *sm/f* (*gen*) navigator; ~ **solitario** single-handed sailor; ~ **satellitare** satellite navigator.

navigazi'one [navigat'tsjone] *sf* navigation; **dopo una settimana di** ~ after a week at sea.

na'viglio [na'viʎʎo] *sm* fleet, ships *pl*; (*canale artificiale*) canal; ~ **da pesca** fishing fleet.

nazio'nale [nattsjo'nale] *ag* national **♦** *sf* (*SPORT*) national team.

naziona'lismo [nattsjona'lizmo] *sm* nationalism.

naziona'lista, i, e [nattsjona'lista] *ag, sm/f* nationalist.

nazionalità [nattsjonali'ta] *sf inv* nationality.

nazionaliz'zare [nattsjonalid'dzare] *vt* to nationalize.

nazionalizzazi'one [nattsjonalid-dzat'tsjone] *sf* nationalization.

nazi'one [nat'tsjone] *sf* nation.

naziskin ['naːtsiskin] *sm inv* Nazi skinhead.

na'zismo [nat'tsizmo] *sm* Nazism.

na'zista, i, e [nat'tsista] *ag, sm/f* Nazi.

NB *abbr* (= *nota bene*) NB.

N.d.A. *abbr* (= *nota dell'autore*) author's

note.

N.d.D. *abbr* = *nota della direzione.*

N.d.E. *abbr* (= *nota dell'editore*) publisher's note.

N.d.R. *abbr* (= *nota della redazione*) editor's note.

'nd'rangheta [nd'rangeta] *sf* Calabrian Mafia.

N.d.T. *abbr* (= *nota del traduttore*) translator's note.

========================= *PAROLA CHIAVE*

ne *pron* **1** (*di lui, lei, loro*) of him/her/them; about him/her/them; ~ **riconosco la voce** I recognize his (*o* her) voice

2 (*di questa, quella cosa*) of it; about it; ~ **voglio ancora** I want some more (of it *o* them); **non parliamone più!** let's not talk about it any more!

3 (*da ciò*) from this; ~ **deduco che l'avete trovato** I gather you've found it; ~ **consegue che** ... it follows therefore that ...

4 (*con valore partitivo*): **hai dei libri? — sì,** ~ **ho** have you any books? — yes, I have (some); **hai del pane? — no, non** ~ **ho** have you any bread? — no, I haven't any; **quanti anni hai? —** ~ **ho 17** how old are you? — I'm 17

♦ *av* (*moto da luogo: da lì*) from there; ~ **vengo ora** I've just come from there.

né *cong*: ~ ... ~ neither ... nor; ~ **l'uno** ~ **l'altro lo vuole** neither of them wants it; ~ **più** ~ **meno** no more no less; **non parla** ~ **l'italiano** ~ **il tedesco** he speaks neither Italian nor German, he doesn't speak either Italian or German; **non piove** ~ **nevica** it isn't raining or snowing.

N.E. *abbr* (= *nordest*) NE.

ne'anche [ne'anke] *av, cong* not even; **non** ... ~ not even; ~ **se volesse potrebbe venire** he couldn't come even if he wanted to; **non l'ho visto — neanch'io** I didn't see him — neither did I *o* I didn't either; ~ **per idea** *o* **sogno!** not on your life!; **non ci penso** ~**!** I wouldn't dream of it!; ~ **a pagarlo lo farebbe** he wouldn't do it even if you paid him.

'nebbia *sf* fog; (*foschia*) mist.

nebbi'oso, a *ag* foggy; misty.

nebulizza'tore [nebuliddza'tore] *sm* atomizer.

nebu'losa *sf* nebula.

nebulosità *sf* haziness.

nebu'loso, a *ag* (*atmosfera, cielo*) hazy; (*fig*) hazy, vague.

néces'saire [nesɛ'sɛr] *sm inv*: ~ **da viaggio** overnight case *o* bag.

necessaria'mente [netʃessarja'mente] *av* necessarily.

neces'sario, a [netʃes'sarjo] *ag* necessary ♦ *sm*: **fare il** ~ to do what is necessary; **lo stretto** ~ the bare essentials *pl.*

necessità [netʃessi'ta] *sf inv* necessity; (*povertà*) need, poverty; **trovarsi nella** ~ **di fare qc** to be forced *o* obliged to do sth, have to do sth.

necessi'tare [netʃessi'tare] *vt* to require ♦ *vi* (*aver bisogno*): ~ **di** to need.

necro'logio [nekro'lɔdʒo] *sm* obituary notice; (*registro*) register of deaths.

ne'fando, a *ag* infamous, wicked.

ne'fasto, a *ag* inauspicious, ill-omened.

ne'gare *vt* to deny; (*rifiutare*) to deny, refuse; ~ **di aver fatto/che** to deny having done/that.

negativa'mente *av* negatively; **rispondere** ~ to give a negative response.

nega'tivo, a *ag, sf, sm* negative.

negazi'one [negat'tsjone] *sf* negation.

negherò *etc* [nege'rɔ] *vb vedi* **negare.**

ne'gletto, a [ne'gletto] *ag* (*trascurato*) neglected.

'negli ['neʎʎi] *prep + det vedi* **in.**

négli'gé [negli'ʒe] *sm inv* negligee.

negli'gente [negli'dʒɛnte] *ag* negligent, careless.

negli'genza [negli'dʒɛntsa] *sf* negligence, carelessness.

negozi'abile [negot'tsjabile] *ag* negotiable.

negozi'ante [negot'tsjante] *sm/f* trader, dealer; (*bottegaio*) shopkeeper (*BRIT*), storekeeper (*US*).

negozi'are [negot'tsjare] *vt* to negotiate ♦ *vi*: ~ **in** to trade *o* deal in.

negozi'ato [negot'tsjato] *sm* negotiation.

negozia'tore, 'trice [negottsja'tore] *sm/f* negotiator.

ne'gozio [ne'gɔttsjo] *sm* (*locale*) shop (*BRIT*), store (*US*); (*affare*) (piece of) business *no pl*; (*DIR*): ~ **giuridico** legal transaction.

negri'ere, a, negri'ero, a *sm* slave trader ♦ *sm/f* (*fig*) slave driver.

'negro, a *ag, sm/f* Negro.

negro'mante *sm/f* necromancer.

negroman'zia [negroman'tsia] *sf* necromancy.

'nei, nel, nell', 'nella, 'nelle, 'nello *prep +det vedi* **in.**

'nembo *sm* (*METEOR*) nimbus.

ne'mico, a, ci, che *ag* hostile; (*MIL*) enemy *cpd* ♦ *sm/f* enemy; **essere** ~ **di** to be strongly averse *o* opposed to.

nem'meno *av, cong* = **neanche**.

'nenia *sf* dirge; (*motivo monotono*) monotonous tune.

'neo *sm* mole; (*fig*) (slight) flaw.

'neo... *prefisso* neo....

neofa'scista, i, e [neofaʃ'ʃista] *sm/f* neofascist.

neolo'gismo [neolo'dʒizmo] *sm* neologism.

'neon *sm* (*CHIM*) neon.

neo'nato, a *ag* newborn ♦ *sm/f* newborn baby.

neozelan'dese [neoddzelan'dese] *ag* New Zealand *cpd* ♦ *sm/f* New Zealander.

Ne'pal *sm*: il ~ Nepal.

nepo'tismo *sm* nepotism.

nep'pure *av, cong* = **neanche**.

ner'bata *sf* (*colpo*) blow; (*sferzata*) whiplash.

'nerbo *sm* lash; (*fig*) strength, backbone.

nerbo'ruto, a *ag* muscular; robust.

ne'retto *sm* (*TIP*) bold type.

'nero, a *ag* black; (*scuro*) dark ♦ *sm* black; **nella miseria più ~a** in utter *o* abject poverty; **essere di umore ~, essere ~** to be in a filthy mood; **mettere qc ~ su bianco** to put sth down in black and white; **vedere tutto ~** to look on the black side (of things).

nero'fumo *sm* lampblack.

nerva'tura *sf* (*ANAT*) nervous system; (*BOT*) veining; (*ARCHIT, TECN*) rib.

'nervo *sm* (*ANAT*) nerve; (*BOT*) vein; **avere i ~i** to be on edge; **dare sui ~i a qn** to get on sb's nerves; **tenere/avere i ~i saldi** to keep/be calm; **che ~i!** damn (it)!

nervo'sismo *sm* (*PSIC*) nervousness; (*irritazione*) irritability.

ner'voso, a *ag* nervous; (*irritabile*) irritable ♦ *sm* (*fam*): **far venire il ~ a qn** to get on sb's nerves; **farsi prendere dal ~** to let o.s. get irritated.

'nespola *sf* (*BOT*) medlar; (*fig*) blow, punch.

'nespolo *sm* medlar tree.

'nesso *sm* connection, link.

=========== *PAROLA CHIAVE*

nes'suno, a (*det: dav sm* **nessun** + *C, V*, **nessuno** + *s impura, gn, pn, ps, x, z; dav sf* **nessuna** + *C*, **nessun'** + *V*) *det* **1** (*non uno*) no, *espressione negativa* + any; **non c'è nessun libro** there isn't any book, there is no book; **nessun altro** no one else, nobody else; **nessun'altra cosa** nothing else; **in nessun luogo** nowhere

2 (*qualche*) any; **hai ~a obiezione?** do you have any objections?

♦ *pron* **1** (*non uno*) no one, nobody,

espressione negativa + any(one); (*: cosa*) none, *espressione negativa* + any; **~ è venuto, non è venuto** ~ nobody came

2 (*qualcuno*) anyone, anybody; **ha telefonato ~?** did anyone phone?

netta'mente *av* clearly.

net'tare *vt* to clean ♦ *sm* ['nɛttare] nectar.

net'tezza [net'tettsa] *sf* cleanness, cleanliness; **~ urbana** cleansing department (*BRIT*), department of sanitation (*US*).

'netto, a *ag* (*pulito*) clean; (*chiaro*) clear, clear-cut; (*deciso*) definite; (*ECON*) net; **tagliare qc di ~** to cut sth clean off; **taglio ~ col passato** (*fig*) clean break with the past.

nettur'bino *sm* dustman (*BRIT*), garbage collector (*US*).

'neuro... *prefisso* neuro....

neurochirur'gia [neurokirur'dʒia] *sf* neurosurgery.

neurolo'gia [neurolo'dʒia] *sf* neurology.

neuro'logico, a, ci, che [neuro'lɔdʒiko] *ag* neurological.

neu'rologo a, gi, ghe *sm/f* neurologist.

neu'rosi *sf inv* = **nevrosi**.

neu'trale *ag* neutral.

neutralità *sf* neutrality.

neutraliz'zare [neutralid'dzare] *vt* to neutralize.

'neutro, a *ag* neutral; (*LING*) neuter ♦ *sm* (*LING*) neuter.

neu'trone *sm* neutron.

ne'vaio *sm* snowfield.

'neve *sf* snow; **montare a ~** (*CUC*) to whip up; **~ carbonica** dry ice.

nevi'care *vb impers* to snow.

nevi'cata *sf* snowfall.

ne'vischio [ne'viskjo] *sm* sleet.

ne'voso, a *ag* snowy; snow-covered.

nevral'gia [nevral'dʒia] *sf* neuralgia.

ne'vralgico, a, ci, che [ne'vraldʒiko] *ag*: **punto ~** (*MED*) nerve centre; (*fig*) crucial point.

nevras'tenico, a, ci, che *ag* (*MED*) neurasthenic; (*fig*) hot-tempered ♦ *sm/f* neurasthenic; hot-tempered person.

ne'vrosi *sf inv* neurosis.

ne'vrotico, a, ci, che *ag, sm/f* (*anche fig*) neurotic.

Nia'gara *sm*: **le cascate del ~** the Niagara Falls.

'nibbio *sm* (*ZOOL*) kite.

Nica'ragua *sm*: **il ~** Nicaragua.

nicaragu'ense *ag, sm/f* Nicaraguan.

'nicchia ['nikkja] *sf* niche; (*naturale*) cavity, hollow; **~ di mercato** (*COMM*) niche market.

nicchi'are [nik'kjare] *vi* to shilly-shally, hesitate.

'nichel ['nikel] *sm* nickel.

nichi'lismo [niki'lizmo] *sm* nihilism.

Nico'sia *sf* Nicosia.

nico'tina *sf* nicotine.

nidi'ata *sf* (*di uccelli, fig*: *di bambini*) brood; (*di altri animali*) litter.

nidifi'care *vi* to nest.

'nido *sm* nest ♦ *ag inv*: **asilo ~** day nursery, crèche (*for children aged 0 to 3*); **a ~ d'ape** (*tessuto etc*) honeycomb *cpd*.

========== *PAROLA CHIAVE*

ni'ente *pron* **1** (*nessuna cosa*) nothing; **~ può fermarlo** nothing can stop him; **~ di ~** absolutely nothing; **grazie! — di ~!** thank you! — not at all!; **nient'altro** nothing else; **nient'altro che** nothing but; **~ affatto** not at all, not in the least; **come se ~ fosse** as if nothing had happened; **cose da ~** trivial matters; **per ~** (*gratis, invano*) for nothing; **non per ~, ma ...** not for any particular reason, but ...; **poco o ~** next to nothing; **un uomo da ~** a man of no consequence

2 (*qualcosa*): **hai bisogno di ~?** do you need anything?

3: **non ... ~** nothing, *espressione negativa +* anything; **non ho visto ~** I saw nothing, I didn't see anything; **non può farci ~** he can't do anything about it; **(non) fa ~** (*non importa*) it doesn't matter; **non ho ~ da dire** I have nothing *o* haven't anything to say

♦ *ag inv*: **~ paura!** never fear!; **e ~ scuse!** and I don't want to hear excuses!

♦ *sm* nothing; **un bel ~** absolutely nothing; **basta un ~ per farla piangere** the slightest thing is enough to make her cry; **finire in ~** to come to nothing

♦ *av* (*in nessuna misura*): **non ... ~** not ... at all; **non è (per) ~ buono** it isn't good at all; **non ci penso per ~** (*non ne ho nessuna intenzione*) I wouldn't think of it; **~ male!** not bad at all!

nientedi'meno, niente'meno *av* actually, even ♦ *escl* really!, I say!

'Niger ['nidʒer] *sm*: **il ~** Niger; (*fiume*) the Niger.

Ni'geria [ni'dʒɛrja] *sf* Nigeria.

nigeri'ano, a [nidʒe'rjano] *ag, sm/f* Nigerian.

'Nilo *sm*: **il ~** the Nile.

'nimbo *sm* halo.

'ninfa *sf* nymph.

nin'fea *sf* water lily.

nin'fomane *sf* nymphomaniac.

ninna'nanna *sf* lullaby.

'ninnolo *sm* (*balocco*) plaything; (*gingillo*) knick-knack.

ni'pote *sm/f* (*di zii*) nephew/niece; (*di nonni*) grandson/daughter, grandchild.

nip'ponico, a, ci, che *ag* Japanese.

niti'dezza [niti'dettsa] *sf* (*gen*) clearness; (*di stile*) clarity; (*FOT, TV*) sharpness.

'nitido, a *ag* clear; (*immagine*) sharp.

ni'trato *sm* nitrate.

'nitrico, a, ci, che *ag* nitric.

ni'trire *vi* to neigh.

ni'trito *sm* (*di cavallo*) neighing *no pl*; neigh; (*CHIM*) nitrite.

nitroglice'rina [nitroglitʃe'rina] *sf* nitroglycerine.

'niveo, a *ag* snow-white.

'Nizza ['nittsa] *sf* Nice.

nn *abbr* (= *numeri*) nos.

NO *sigla* = *Novara*.

no *av* (*risposta*) no; **vieni o ~?** are you coming or not?; **come ~!** of course!, certainly!; **perché ~?** why not?

N.O. *abbr* (= *nordovest*) NW.

nobil'donna *sf* noblewoman.

'nobile *ag* noble ♦ *sm/f* noble, nobleman/woman.

nobili'are *ag* noble.

nobili'tare *vt* (*anche fig*) to ennoble; **~rsi** *vr* (*rendersi insigne*) to distinguish o.s.

nobiltà *sf* nobility; (*di azione etc*) nobleness.

nobilu'omo *sm, pl* **-u'omini** nobleman.

'nocca, che *sf* (*ANAT*) knuckle.

'noccio *etc* ['nɔttʃo] *vb vedi* **nuocere**.

nocci'ola [not'tʃɔla] *sf* hazelnut ♦ *ag inv* (*anche*: **color ~**) hazel, light brown.

noccio'lina [nottʃo'lina] *sf* (*anche*: **~ americana**) peanut.

'nocciolo ['nɔttʃolo] *sm* (*di frutto*) stone; (*fig*) heart, core; [not'tʃɔlo] (*albero*) hazel.

'noce ['notʃe] *sm* (*albero*) walnut tree ♦ *sf* (*frutto*) walnut; **una ~ di burro** (*CUC*) a knob of butter (*BRIT*), a dab of butter (*US*); **~ di cocco** coconut; **~ moscata** nutmeg.

noce'pesca, sche [notʃe'pɛska] *sf* nectarine.

no'cevo *etc* [no'tʃevo] *vb vedi* **nuocere**.

noci'uto [no'tʃuto] *pp di* **nuocere**.

no'civo, a [no'tʃivo] *ag* harmful, noxious.

'nocqui *etc vb vedi* **nuocere**.

'nodo *sm* (*di cravatta, legname, NAUT*) knot; (*AUT, FERR*) junction; (*MED, ASTR, BOT*) node; (*fig: legame*) bond, tie; (: *punto centrale*) heart, crux; **avere un ~ alla gola** to have a lump in one's throat; **tutti i ~i vengono al pettine** (*proverbio*) your sins will find you out.

no'doso, a *ag* (*tronco*) gnarled.

'nodulo *sm* (*ANAT, BOT*) nodule.

no-'global [no'global] *ag inv* anti-globalization *cpd*.

'noi *pron* (*soggetto*) we; (*oggetto: per dare rilievo, con preposizione*) us; ~ stessi(e) we ourselves; (*oggetto*) ourselves; da ~ (*nel nostro paese*) in our country, where we come from; (*a casa nostra*) at our house.

'noia *sf* boredom; (*disturbo, impaccio*) bother *no pl*, trouble *no pl*; avere qn/qc a ~ not to like sb/sth; mi è venuto a ~ I'm tired of it; dare ~ a to annoy; avere delle ~e con qn to have trouble with sb.

noi'altri *pron* we.

noi'oso, a *ag* boring; (*fastidioso*) annoying, troublesome.

noleggi'are [noled'dʒare] *vt* (*prendere a noleggio*) to hire (*BRIT*), rent; (*dare a noleggio*) to hire out (*BRIT*), rent out; (*aereo, nave*) to charter.

noleggia'tore, 'trice [noleddʒa'tore] *sm/f* hirer (*BRIT*), renter; charterer.

no'leggio [no'leddʒo] *sm* hire (*BRIT*), rental; charter.

no'lente *ag*: volente o ~ whether one likes it or not, willy-nilly.

'nolo *sm* hire (*BRIT*), rental; charter; (*per trasporto merci*) freight; prendere/dare a ~ qc to hire/hire out sth (*BRIT*), rent/rent out sth.

'nomade *ag* nomadic ♦ *sm/f* nomad.

noma'dismo *sm* nomadism.

'nome *sm* name; (*LING*) noun; in *o* a ~ di in the name of; di *o* per ~ (*chiamato*) called, named; conoscere qn di ~ to know sb by name; fare il ~ di qn to name sb; faccia pure il mio ~ feel free to mention my name; ~ d'arte stage name; ~ di battesimo Christian name; ~ depositato trade name; ~ di famiglia surname; ~ da ragazza maiden name; ~ da sposata married name.

no'mea *sf* notoriety.

nomencla'tura *sf* nomenclature.

nomenkla'tura *sf* (*di partito, stato*) nomenklatura.

no'mignolo [no'miɲɲolo] *sm* nickname.

'nomina *sf* appointment.

nomi'nale *ag* nominal; (*LING*) noun *cpd*.

nomi'nare *vt* to name; (*eleggere*) to appoint; (*citare*) to mention; non l'ho mai sentito ~ I've never heard of it (*o* him).

nomina'tivo, a *ag* (*intestato: titolo*) registered; (: *libretto*) personal; (*LING*) nominative ♦ *sm* (*nome*) name; (*LING*) nominative; elenco ~ list of names.

non *av* not ♦ *prefisso* non-; grazie — ~ c'è di che thank you — don't mention it; i ~ credenti the unbelievers; *vedi anche* affatto, appena *etc*.

nonché [non'ke] *cong* (*tanto più, tanto meno*) let alone; (*e inoltre*) as well as.

nonconfor'mista, i, e *ag, sm/f* nonconformist.

noncu'rante *ag*: ~ (di) careless (of), indifferent (to); con fare ~ with a nonchalant air.

noncu'ranza [nonku'rantsa] *sf* carelessness, indifference; un'aria di ~ a nonchalant air.

nondi'meno *cong* (*tuttavia*) however; (*nonostante*) nevertheless.

'nonno, a *sm/f* grandfather/mother; (*in senso più familiare*) grandma/grandpa; ~i *smpl* grandparents.

non'nulla *sm inv*: un ~ nothing, a trifle.

'nono, a *num* ninth.

nonos'tante *prep* in spite of, notwithstanding ♦ *cong* although, even though.

non plus 'ultra *sm inv*: il ~ (di) the last word (in).

nontiscordardimé *sm inv* (*BOT*) forget-me-not.

nord *sm* north ♦ *ag inv* north; (*regione*) northern; verso ~ north, northwards; l'America del N~ North America.

nor'dest *sm* north-east.

'nordico, a, ci, che *ag* nordic, northern European.

nor'dista, i, e *ag, sm/f* Yankee.

nor'dovest *sm* north-west.

Norim'berga *sf* Nuremberg.

'norma *sf* (*principio*) norm; (*regola*) regulation, rule; (*consuetudine*) custom, rule; di ~ normally; a ~ di legge according to law, as laid down by law; al di sopra della ~ above average, above the norm; per sua ~ e regola for your information; proporsi una ~ di vita to set o.s. rules to live by; ~e di sicurezza safety regulations; ~e per l'uso instructions for use.

nor'male *ag* normal.

normalità *sf* normality.

normaliz'zare [normalid'dzare] *vt* to normalize, bring back to normal.

normal'mente *av* normally.

Norman'dia *sf*: la ~ Normandy.

nor'manno, a *ag, sm/f* Norman.

norma'tivo, a *ag* normative ♦ *sf* regulations *pl*.

norve'gese [norve'dʒese] *ag, sm/f, sm* Norwegian.

Nor'vegia [nor'vɛdʒa] *sf*: la ~ Norway.

noso'comio *sm* hospital.

nostal'gia [nostal'dʒia] *sf* (*di casa, paese*) homesickness; (*del passato*) nostalgia.

nos'talgico, a, ci, che [nos'taldʒiko] *ag* homesick; nostalgic ♦ *sm/f* (POL) *person who hopes for the return of Fascism.*

nos'trano, a *ag* local; (*pianta, frutta*) home-produced.

'nostro, a *det*: **il(la) ~(a)** *etc* our ♦ *pron*: **il(la) ~(a)** *etc* ours ♦ *sm*: **abbiamo speso del ~** we spent our own money ♦ *sf*: **la ~a** (*opinione*) our view; **i ~i** our family; our own people; **è dei ~i** he's one of us; **è dalla ~a** (*parte*) he's on our side; **anche noi abbiamo avuto le ~e** (*disavventure*) we've had our problems too; **alla ~a!** (*brindisi*) to us!

nos'tromo *sm* boatswain.

'nota *sf* (*segno*) mark; (*comunicazione scritta, MUS*) note; (*fattura*) bill; (*elenco*) list; **prendere ~ di qc** to note sth, make a note of sth, write sth down; (*fig: fare attenzione*) to note sth, take note of sth; **degno di ~** noteworthy, worthy of note; **~e caratteristiche** distinguishing marks *o* features; **~e a piè di pagina** footnotes.

no'tabile *ag* notable; (*persona*) important ♦ *sm* prominent citizen.

no'taio *sm* notary.

no'tare *vt* (*segnare: errori*) to mark; (*registrare*) to note (down), write down; (*rilevare, osservare*) to note, notice; **farsi ~** to get o.s. noticed.

nota'rile *ag*: **atto ~** legal document (*authorized by a notary*); **studio ~** notary's office.

notazi'one [notat'tsjone] *sf* (MUS) notation.

no'tevole *ag* (*talento*) notable, remarkable; (*peso*) considerable.

no'tifica, che *sf* notification.

notifi'care *vt* (DIR): **~ qc a qn** to notify sb of sth, give sb notice of sth.

notificazi'one [notifikat'tsjone] *sf* notification.

no'tizia [no'tittsja] *sf* (piece of) news *sg*; (*informazione*) piece of information; **~e** *sfpl* news *sg*; information *sg*.

notizi'ario [notit'tsjarjo] *sm* (RADIO, TV, STAMPA) news *sg*.

'noto, a *ag* (well-)known.

notorietà *sf* fame; notoriety.

no'torio, a *ag* well-known; (*peg*) notorious.

not'tambulo, a *sm/f* night-bird (*fig*).

not'tata *sf* night.

'notte *sf* night; **di ~** at night; (*durante la ~*) in the night, during the night; **questa ~** (*passata*) last night; (*che viene*) tonight; **nella ~ dei tempi** in the mists of time;

come va? — peggio che andar di ~ how are things? — worse than ever; **~ bianca** sleepless night.

notte'tempo *av* at night; during the night.

'nottola *sf* (ZOOL) noctule.

not'turno, a *ag* nocturnal; (*servizio, guardiano*) night *cpd* ♦ *sf* (SPORT) evening fixture (BRIT) *o* match.

nov. *abbr* (= *novembre*) Nov.

no'vanta *num* ninety.

novan'tenne *ag, sm/f* ninety-year-old.

novan'tesimo, a *num* ninetieth.

novan'tina *sf*: **una ~ (di)** about ninety.

'nove *num* nine.

novecen'tesco, a, schi, sche [novetʃen'tesko] *ag* twentieth-century.

nove'cento [nove'tʃento] *num* nine hundred ♦ *sm*: **il N~** the twentieth century.

no'vella *sf* (LETTERATURA) short story.

novel'lino, a *ag* (*pivello*) green, inexperienced.

novel'lista, i, e *sm/f* short-story writer.

novel'listica *sf* (*arte*) short-story writing; (*insieme di racconti*) short stories *pl*.

no'vello, a *ag* (*piante, patate*) new; (*insalata, verdura*) early; (*sposo*) newly-married.

no'vembre *sm* November; *per fraseologia vedi* **luglio.**

novem'brino, a *ag* November *cpd*.

nove'mila *num* nine thousand.

noven'nale *ag* (*che dura 9 anni*) nine-year *cpd*; (*ogni 9 anni*) nine-yearly.

novi'lunio *sm* (ASTR) new moon.

novità *sf inv* novelty; (*innovazione*) innovation; (*cosa originale, insolita*) something new; (*notizia*) (piece of) news *sg*; **le ~ della moda** the latest fashions.

novizi'ato [novit'tsjato] *sm* (REL) novitiate; (*tirocinio*) apprenticeship.

no'vizio, a [no'vittsjo] *sm/f* (REL) novice; (*tirocinante*) beginner, apprentice.

nozi'one [not'tsjone] *sf* notion, idea; **~i** *sfpl* (*rudimenti*) basic knowledge *sg*, rudiments.

nozio'nismo [nottsjo'nizmo] *sm* superficial knowledge.

nozio'nistico, a, ci, che [nottsjo'nistiko] *ag* superficial.

'nozze ['nɔttse] *sfpl* wedding *sg*, marriage *sg*; **~ d'argento/d'oro** silver/golden wedding *sg*.

ns. *abbr* (COMM) = **nostro.**

NU *sigla* = *Nuoro.*

N.U. *sigla* (= *Nazioni Unite*) UN.

'nube *sf* cloud.

nubi'fragio [nubi'fradʒo] *sm* cloudburst.

'nubile *ag* (*donna*) unmarried, single.

'nuca, che *sf* nape of the neck.

nucle'are *ag* nuclear ♦ *sm*: **il** ~ nuclear energy.

'nucleo *sm* nucleus; (*gruppo*) team, unit, group; (*MIL, POLIZIA*) squad; ~ **antidroga** anti-drugs squad; **il** ~ **familiare** the family unit.

nu'dismo *sm* nudism.

nu'dista, i, e *sm/f* nudist.

nudità *sf inv* nudity, nakedness; (*di paesaggio*) bareness ♦ *sfpl* (*parti nude del corpo*) nakedness *sg*.

'nudo, a *ag* (*persona*) bare, naked, nude; (*membra*) bare, naked; (*montagna*) bare ♦ *sm* (*ARTE*) nude; **a occhio** ~ to the naked eye; **a piedi** ~**i** barefoot; **mettere a** ~ (*cuore, verità*) to lay bare; **gli ha detto** ~ **e crudo che** ... he told him bluntly that ....

'nugolo *sm*: **un** ~ **di** a whole host of.

'nulla *pron, av* = **niente** ♦ *sm*: **il** ~ nothing; **svanire nel** ~ to vanish into thin air; **basta un** ~ **per farlo arrabbiare** he gets annoyed over the slightest thing.

nulla'osta *sm inv* authorization.

nullate'nente *ag*: **essere** ~ to own nothing ♦ *sm/f* person with no property.

nullità *sf inv* nullity; (*persona*) nonentity.

'nullo, a *ag* useless, worthless; (*DIR*) null (and void); (*SPORT*): **incontro** ~ draw.

nume'rale *ag, sm* numeral.

nume'rare *vt* to number.

numera'tore *sm* (*MAT*) numerator; (*macchina*) numbering device.

numerazi'one [numerat'tsjone] *sf* numbering; (*araba, decimale*) notation.

nu'merico, a, ci, che *ag* numerical.

'numero *sm* number; (*romano, arabo*) numeral; (*di spettacolo*) act, turn; **dare i** ~**i** (*farneticare*) not to be all there; **tanto per fare** ~ **invitiamo anche lui** why don't we invite him to make up the numbers?; **ha tutti i** ~**i per riuscire** he's got what it takes to succeed; **che** ~ **tuo fratello!** your brother is a real character!; ~ **civico** house number; ~ **chiuso** (*UNIVERSITÀ*) selective entry system; ~ **doppio** (*di rivista*) issue with supplement; ~ **di scarpe** size of shoe; ~ **verde** (*TEL*) ≈ Freephone ®.

nume'roso, a *ag* numerous, many; (*folla, famiglia*) large.

numis'matica *sf* numismatics *sg*, coin collecting.

'nunzio ['nuntsjo] *sm* (*REL*) nuncio.

nu'occio *etc* ['nwɔttʃo] *vb vedi* **nuocere**.

nu'ocere ['nwɔtʃere] *vi*: ~ **a** to harm, damage; **il tentar non nuoce** (*proverbio*) there's no harm in trying.

nuoci'uto, a [nwo'tʃuto] *pp di* **nuocere**.

nu'ora *sf* daughter-in-law.

nuo'tare *vi* to swim; (*galleggiare: oggetti*) to float; ~ **a rana/sul dorso** to do the breast stroke/backstroke.

nuo'tata *sf* swim.

nuota'tore, 'trice *sm/f* swimmer.

nu'oto *sm* swimming.

nu'ova *sf vedi* **nuovo**.

nuova'mente *av* again.

Nu'ova York *sf* New York.

Nu'ova Ze'landa [-dze'landa] *sf*: **la** ~ New Zealand.

nu'ovo, a *ag* new ♦ *sf* (*notizia*) (piece of) news *sg*; **come** ~ as good as new; **di** ~ again; **fino a** ~ **ordine** until further notice; **il suo volto non mi è** ~ I know his face; **rimettere a** ~ (*cosa, macchina*) to do up like new; **anno** ~, **vita** ~**a!** it's time to turn over a new leaf!; ~ **fiammante** *o* **di zecca** brand-new; **la N**~**a Guinea** New Guinea; **la N**~**a Inghilterra** New England; **la N**~**a Scozia** Nova Scotia.

nu'trice [nu'tritʃe] *sf* wet nurse.

nutri'ente *ag* nutritious, nourishing; (*crema, balsamo*) nourishing.

nutri'mento *sm* food, nourishment.

nu'trire *vt* to feed; (*fig: sentimenti*) to harbour (*BRIT*), harbor (*US*), nurse.

nutri'tivo, a *ag* nutritional; (*alimento*) nutritious.

nu'trito, a *ag* (*numeroso*) large; (*fitto*) heavy; **ben/mal** ~ well/poorly fed.

nutrizi'one [nutrit'tsjone] *sf* nutrition.

'nuvolo, a *ag* cloudy ♦ *sf* cloud.

nuvolosità *sf* cloudiness.

nuvo'loso, a *ag* cloudy.

nuzi'ale [nut'tsjale] *ag* nuptial; wedding *cpd*.

'nylon ['nailən] *sm* nylon.

O o

O, o [ɔ] *sf o m inv* (*lettera*) O, o; ~ **come Otranto** ≈ O for Oliver (*BRIT*), O for Oboe (*US*).

o *cong* (*dav V spesso* **od**) or; ~ ... ~ either ... or; ~ **l'uno** ~ **l'altro** either (of them); ~ **meglio** or rather.

O. *abbr* (= *ovest*) W.

'oasi *sf inv* oasis.

obbedi'ente *etc vedi* **ubbidiente** *etc*.

obbiet'tare *etc vedi* **obiettare** *etc*.

obbli'gare *vt* (*costringere*): ~ qn a fare to force *o* oblige sb to do; (*DIR*) to bind; ~**rsi** *vr*: ~**rsi a fare** to undertake to do; ~**rsi per qn** (*DIR*) to stand surety for sb, act as guarantor for sb.

obbliga'tissimo, a *ag* (*ringraziamento*): ~! much obliged!

obbli'gato, a *ag* (*costretto, grato*) obliged; (*percorso, tappa*) set, fixed; **passaggio** ~ (*fig*) essential requirement.

obbliga'torio, a *ag* compulsory, obligatory.

obbligazi'one [obbligat'tsjone] *sf* obligation; (*COMM*) bond, debenture; ~ **dello Stato** government bond; ~**i convertibili** convertible loan stock, convertible debentures.

obbligazio'nista, i, e [obbligattsjo'nista] *sm/f* bond-holder.

'obbligo, ghi *sm* obligation; (*dovere*) duty; **avere l'**~ **di fare, essere nell'**~ **di fare** to be obliged to do; **essere d'**~ (*discorso, applauso*) to be called for; **avere degli** ~**ghi con** *o* **verso qn** to be under an obligation to sb, be indebted to sb; **le formalità d'**~ the necessary formalities.

obb.mo *abbr* = **obbligatissimo**.

ob'brobrio *sm* disgrace; (*fig*) mess, eyesore.

obe'lisco, schi *sm* obelisk.

obe'rato, a *ag*: ~ **di** (*lavoro*) overloaded *o* overburdened with; (*debiti*) crippled with.

obesità *sf* obesity.

o'beso, a *ag* obese.

obiet'tare *vt*: ~ **che** to object that; ~ **su qc** to object to sth, raise objections concerning sth.

obiettiva'mente *av* objectively.

obiettività *sf* objectivity.

obiet'tivo, a *ag* objective ♦ *sm* (*OTTICA, FOT*) lens *sg*, objective; (*MIL, fig*) objective.

obiet'tore *sm* objector; ~ **di coscienza** conscientious objector.

obiezi'one [objet'tsjone] *sf* objection.

obi'torio *sm* morgue.

o'bliquo, a *ag* oblique; (*inclinato*) slanting; (*fig*) devious, underhand; **sguardo** ~ sidelong glance.

oblite'rare *vt* (*francobollo*) to cancel; (*biglietto*) to stamp.

oblitera'trice [oblitera'tritʃe] *sf* (*anche:* **macchina** ~) cancelling machine; stamping machine.

oblò *sm inv* porthole.

o'blungo, a, ghi, ghe *ag* oblong.

'oboe *sm* oboe.

'obolo *sm* (*elemosina*) (small) offering, mite.

obsole'scenza [obsoleʃ'ʃɛntsa] *sf* (*ECON*) obsolescence.

obso'leto, a *ag* obsolete.

OC *abbr* (= *onde corte*) SW.

'oca, pl 'oche *sf* goose.

o'caggine [o'kaddʒine] *sf* silliness, stupidity.

occasio'nale *ag* (*incontro*) chance; (*cliente, guadagni*) casual, occasional.

occasi'one *sf* (*caso favorevole*) opportunity; (*causa, motivo, circostanza*) occasion; (*COMM*) bargain; **all'**~ should the need arise; **alla prima** ~ at the first opportunity; **d'**~ (*a buon prezzo*) bargain *cpd*; (*usato*) secondhand.

occhi'aia [ok'kjaja] *sf* eye socket; ~**e** *sfpl* (*sotto gli occhi*) shadows (under the eyes).

occhi'ali [ok'kjali] *smpl* glasses, spectacles; ~ **da sole** sunglasses.

occhi'ata [ok'kjata] *sf* look, glance; **dare un'**~ **a** to have a look at.

occhieggi'are [okkjed'dʒare] *vi* (*apparire qua e là*) to peep (out).

occhi'ello [ok'kjɛllo] *sm* buttonhole; (*asola*) eyelet.

'occhio ['ɔkkjo] *sm* eye; ~! careful!, watch out!; **a** ~ **nudo** with the naked eye; **a quattr'**~**i** privately, in private; **avere** ~ to have a good eye; **chiudere un** ~ (**su**) (*fig*) to turn a blind eye (to), shut one's eyes (to); **costare un** ~ **della testa** to cost a fortune; **dare all'**~ *o* **nell'**~ **a qn** to catch sb's eye; **fare l'**~ **a qc** to get used to sth; **tenere d'**~ **qn** to keep an eye on sb; **vedere di buon/mal** ~ **qc** to look favourably/unfavourably on sth.

occhio'lino [okkjo'lino] *sm*: **fare l'**~ **a qn** to wink at sb.

occiden'tale [ottʃiden'tale] *ag* western ♦ *sm/f* Westerner.

occi'dente [ottʃi'dɛnte] *sm* west; (*POL*): **l'O**~ the West; **a** ~ in the west.

oc'cipite [ot'tʃipite] *sm* back of the head, occiput (*ANAT*).

oc'cludere *vt* to block.

occlusi'one *sf* blockage, obstruction.

oc'cluso, a *pp di* **occludere**.

occor'rente *ag* necessary ♦ *sm* all that is necessary.

occor'renza [okkor'rɛntsa] *sf* necessity, need; **all'**~ in case of need.

oc'correre *vi* to be needed, be required ♦ *vb impers*: **occorre farlo** it must be done; **occorre che tu parta** you must leave, you'll have to leave; **mi occorrono i soldi** I need the money.

oc'corso, a *pp di* **occorrere**.

occulta'mento *sm* concealment.

occul'tare *vt* to hide, conceal.

oc'culto, a *ag* hidden, concealed; (*scienze, forze*) occult.

occu'pante *sm/f* (*di casa*) occupier, occupant; ~ **abusivo** squatter.

occu'pare *vt* to occupy; (*manodopera*) to employ; (*ingombrare*) to occupy, take up; ~**rsi** *vr* to occupy o.s., keep o.s. busy; (*impiegarsi*) to get a job; ~**rsi di** (*interessarsi*) to take an interest in; (*prendersi cura di*) to look after, take care of.

occu'pato, a *ag* (*MIL, POL*) occupied; (*persona: affaccendato*) busy; (*posto, sedia*) taken; (*toilette, TEL*) engaged.

occupazio'nale [okkupattsjo'nale] *ag* employment *cpd*, of employment.

occupazi'one [okkupat'tsjone] *sf* occupation; (*impiego, lavoro*) job; (*ECON*) employment.

Oce'ania [ot∫e'anja] *sf*: **l'**~ Oceania.

o'ceano [o't∫eano] *sm* ocean.

'ocra *sf* ochre.

'OCSE *sigla f* (= *Organizzazione per la Cooperazione e lo Sviluppo Economico*) OECD (= *Organization for Economic Cooperation and Development*).

ocu'lare *ag* ocular, eye *cpd*; **testimone** ~ eye witness.

ocula'tezza [okula'tettsa] *sf* caution; shrewdness.

ocu'lato, a *ag* (*attento*) cautious, prudent; (*accorto*) shrewd.

ocu'lista, i, e *sm/f* eye specialist, oculist.

od *cong vedi* **o**.

'ode *sf* ode.

'ode *etc vb vedi* **udire**.

odi'are *vt* to hate, detest.

odi'erno, a *ag* today's, of today; (*attuale*) present; **in data** ~**a** (*formale*) today.

'odio *sm* hatred; **avere in** ~ **qc/qn** to hate *o* detest sth/sb.

odi'oso, a *ag* hateful, odious; **rendersi** ~ (**a**) to make o.s. unpopular (with).

'odo *etc vb vedi* **udire**.

odontoi'atra, i, e *sm/f* dentist, dental surgeon.

odontoia'tria *sf* dentistry.

odo'rare *vt* (*annusare*) to smell; (*profumare*) to perfume, scent ♦ *vi*: ~ (**di**) to smell (of).

odo'rato *sm* sense of smell.

o'dore *sm* smell; **gli** ~**i** *smpl* (*CUC*) (aromatic) herbs; **sentire** ~ **di qc** to smell sth; **morire in** ~ **di santità** (*REL*) to die in the odour (*BRIT*) *o* odor (*US*) of sanctity.

odo'roso, a *ag* sweet-smelling.

of'fendere *vt* to offend; (*violare*) to break, violate; (*insultare*) to insult; (*ferire*) to hurt;

~**rsi** *vr* (*con senso reciproco*) to insult one another; (*risentirsi*): ~**rsi (di)** to take offence (at), be offended (by).

offen'sivo, a *ag, sf* offensive.

offen'sore *sm* offender; (*MIL*) aggressor.

offe'rente *sm* (*in aste*): **al migliore** ~ to the highest bidder.

of'ferto, a *pp di* **offrire** ♦ *sf* offer; (*donazione, anche REL*) offering; (*in gara d'appalto*) tender; (*in aste*) bid; (*ECON*) supply; **fare un'**~**a** to make an offer; (*per appalto*) to tender; (*ad un'asta*) to bid; ~**a pubblica d'acquisto (OPA)** takeover bid; ~**a pubblica di vendita (OPV)** public offer for sale; ~**a reale** tender; **"**~**e d'impiego"** (*STAMPA*) "situations vacant" (*BRIT*), "help wanted" (*US*).

of'feso, a *pp di* **offendere** ♦ *ag* offended; (*fisicamente*) hurt, injured ♦ *sm/f* offended party ♦ *sf* insult, affront; (*MIL*) attack; (*DIR*) offence (*BRIT*), offense (*US*); **essere** ~ **con qn** to be annoyed with sb; **parte** ~**a** (*DIR*) plaintiff.

offi'ciare [offi't∫are] *vi* (*REL*) to officiate.

offi'cina [offi't∫ina] *sf* workshop.

of'frire *vt* to offer; ~**rsi** *vr* (*proporsi*) to offer (o.s.), volunteer; (*occasione*) to present itself; (*esporsi*): ~**rsi a** to expose o.s. to; **ti offro da bere** I'll buy you a drink; **"offresi posto di segretaria"** "secretarial vacancy", "vacancy for secretary"; **"segretaria offresi"** "secretary seeks post".

offus'care *vt* to obscure, darken; (*fig: intelletto*) to dim, cloud; (: *fama*) to obscure, overshadow; ~**rsi** *vr* to grow dark; to cloud, grow dim; to be obscured.

of'talmico, a, ci, che *ag* ophthalmic.

oggettività [oddʒettivi'ta] *sf* objectivity.

ogget'tivo, a [oddʒet'tivo] *ag* objective.

og'getto [od'dʒetto] *sm* object; (*materia, argomento*) subject (matter); (*in lettere commerciali*): ~ ... re ...; **essere** ~ **di** (*critiche, controversia*) to be the subject of; (*odio, pietà etc*) to be the object of; **essere** ~ **di scherno** to be a laughing stock; **in** ~ **a quanto detto** (*in lettere*) as regards the matter mentioned above; ~**i preziosi** valuables, articles of value; ~**i smarriti** lost property *sg* (*BRIT*), lost and found *sg* (*US*).

'oggi ['oddʒi] *av, sm* today; ~ **stesso** today, this very day; ~ **come** ~ at present, as things stand; **dall'** ~ **al domani** from one day to the next; **a tutt'**~ up till now, till today; **le spese a tutt'**~ **sono** ... expenses to date are ...; ~ **a otto** a week today.

oggigi'orno [oddʒi'dʒorno] *av* nowadays.

o'giva [o'dʒiva] *sf* ogive, pointed arch.

OGM [ɔdʒi'ɛmme] *sigla mpl* (= *organismi geneticamente modificati*) GMO (= *genetically modified organisms*).

'ogni ['oɲɲi] *det* every, each; (*tutti*) all; (*con valore distributivo*) every; ~ **uomo è mortale** all men are mortal; **viene** ~ **due giorni** he comes every two days; ~ **cosa** everything; **ad** ~ **costo** at all costs, at any price; **in** ~ **luogo** everywhere; ~ **tanto** every so often; ~ **volta che** every time that.

Ognis'santi [oɲɲis'santi] *sm* All Saints' Day.

o'gnuno [oɲ'ɲuno] *pron* everyone, everybody.

'ohi *escl* oh!; (*esprimente dolore*) ow!

ohimè *escl* oh dear!

'OIL *sigla f* (= *Organizzazione Internazionale del Lavoro*) ILO.

OL *abbr* (= *onde lunghe*) LW.

O'landa *sf*: **l'**~ Holland.

olan'dese *ag* Dutch ♦ *sm* (*LING*) Dutch ♦ *sm/f* Dutchman/woman; **gli O**~**i** the Dutch.

ole'andro *sm* oleander.

ole'ato, a *ag*: **carta** ~**a** greaseproof paper (*BRIT*), wax paper (*US*).

oleo'dotto *sm* oil pipeline.

ole'oso, a *ag* oily; (*che contiene olio*) oil *cpd*.

o'lezzo [o'leddzo] *sm* fragrance.

ol'fatto *sm* sense of smell.

oli'are *vt* to oil.

olia'tore *sm* oil can, oiler.

oli'era *sf* oil cruet.

oligar'chia [oligar'kia] *sf* oligarchy.

olim'piadi *sfpl* Olympic Games.

o'limpico, a, ci, che *ag* Olympic.

'olio *sm* oil; (*PITTURA*): **un (quadro a)** ~ an oil painting; **sott'**~ (*CUC*) in oil; ~ **di fegato di merluzzo** cod liver oil; ~ **d'oliva** olive oil; ~ **santo** holy oil; ~ **di semi** vegetable oil; ~ **solare** suntan oil.

o'liva *sf* olive.

oli'vastro, a *ag* olive(-coloured) (*BRIT*), olive(-colored) (*US*); (*carnagione*) sallow.

oli'veto *sm* olive grove.

o'livo *sm* olive tree.

'olmo *sm* elm.

olo'causto *sm* holocaust.

OLP *sigla f* (= *Organizzazione per la Liberazione della Palestina*) PLO.

oltraggi'are [oltrad'dʒare] *vt* to offend, insult.

ol'traggio [ol'traddʒo] *sm* offence (*BRIT*), offense (*US*), insult; (*DIR*): ~ **al pudore** indecent behaviour (*BRIT*) o behavior (*US*); ~ **alla corte** contempt of court.

oltraggi'oso, a [oltrad'dʒoso] *ag* offensive.

ol'tralpe *av* beyond the Alps.

ol'tranza [ol'trantsa] *sf*: **a** ~ to the last, to the bitter end; **sciopero ad** ~ all-out strike.

oltran'zismo [oltran'tsizmo] *sm* (*POL*) extremism.

oltran'zista, i, e [oltran'tsista] *sm/f* (*POL*) extremist.

'oltre *av* (*più in là*) further; (*di più: aspettare*) longer, more ♦ *prep* (*di là da*) beyond, over, on the other side of; (*più di*) more than, over; (*in aggiunta a*) besides; (*eccetto*): ~ **a** except, apart from; ~ **a tutto** on top of all that.

oltrecor'tina *av* behind the Iron Curtain; **paesi d'**~ Iron Curtain countries.

oltre'manica *av* across the Channel.

oltre'mare *av* overseas.

oltre'modo *av* extremely, greatly.

oltreo'ceano [oltreo't ʃano] *av* overseas ♦ *sm*: **paesi d'**~ overseas countries.

oltrepas'sare *vt* to go beyond, exceed.

oltre'tomba *sm inv*: **l'**~ the hereafter.

OM *abbr* (= *onde medie*) MW; (*MIL*) = *ospedale militare*.

o'maggio [o'maddʒo] *sm* (*dono*) gift; (*segno di rispetto*) homage, tribute; ~**i** *smpl* (*complimenti*) respects; **in** ~ (*copia, biglietto*) complimentary; **rendere** ~ **a** to pay homage *o* tribute to; **presentare i propri** ~**i a qn** (*formale*) to pay one's respects to sb.

'Oman *sm*: **l'**~ Oman.

ombeli'cale *ag* umbilical.

ombe'lico, chi *sm* navel.

'ombra *sf* (*zona non assolata, fantasma*) shade; (*sagoma scura*) shadow ♦ *ag inv*: **bandiera** ~ flag of convenience; **governo** ~ (*POL*) shadow cabinet; **sedere all'**~ to sit in the shade; **nell'**~ (*tramare, agire*) secretly; **restare nell'**~ (*fig: persona*) to remain in obscurity; **senza** ~ **di dubbio** without the shadow of a doubt.

ombreggi'are [ombred'dʒare] *vt* to shade.

om'brello *sm* umbrella; ~ **da sole** parasol, sunshade.

ombrel'lone *sm* beach umbrella.

om'bretto *sm* eyeshadow.

om'broso, a *ag* shady, shaded; (*cavallo*) nervous, skittish; (*persona*) touchy, easily offended.

ome'lette [ɔmə'lɛt] *sf inv* omelet(te).

ome'lia *sf* (*REL*) homily, sermon.

ome'opata *sm/f* hom(o)eopath.

omeopa'tia *sf* hom(o)eopathy.

omeo'patico, a, ci, che *ag* hom(o)eopathic ♦ *sm* hom(o)eopath.

omertà *sf* conspiracy of silence.

o'messo, a *pp di* **omettere.**

o'mettere *vt* to omit, leave out; ~ **di fare** to omit *o* fail to do.

omi'cida, i, e [omi'tʃida] *ag* homicidal, murderous ♦ *sm/f* murderer/murderess.

omi'cidio [omi'tʃidjo] *sm* murder; ~ **colposo** (*DIR*) culpable homicide; ~ **premeditato** (*DIR*) murder.

o'misi *etc vb vedi* **omettere.**

omissi'one *sf* omission; **reato d'**~ criminal negligence; ~ **di atti d'ufficio** negligence (*by a public employee*); ~ **di denuncia** failure to report a crime; ~ **di soccorso** (*DIR*) failure to stop and give assistance.

omogeneiz'zato [omodʒeneid'dzato] *sm* baby food.

omo'geneo, a [omo'dʒɛneo] *ag* homogeneous.

omolo'gare *vt* (*DIR*) to approve, recognize; (*ratificare*) to ratify.

omologazi'one [omologat'tsjone] *sf* approval; ratification.

o'mologo, a, ghi, ghe *ag* homologous, corresponding ♦ *sm/f* opposite number.

o'monimo, a *sm/f* namesake ♦ *sm* (*LING*) homonym.

omosessu'ale *ag, sm/f* homosexual.

O.M.S. *sigla f vedi* **Organizzazione Mondiale della Sanità.**

On. *abbr* (*POL*) = **onorevole.**

'oncia, ce ['ontʃa] *sf* ounce.

'onda *sf* wave; **mettere** *o* **mandare in** ~ (*RADIO, TV*) to broadcast; **andare in** ~ (*RADIO, TV*) to go on the air; ~**e corte/ medie/lunghe** short/medium/long wave *sg*; **l'**~ **verde** (*AUT*) synchronized traffic lights *pl*.

on'data *sf* wave, billow; (*fig*) wave, surge; **a** ~**e** in waves; ~ **di caldo** heatwave; ~ **di freddo** cold spell *o* snap.

'onde *cong* (*affinché: con il congiuntivo*) so that, in order that; (*: con l'infinito*) so as to, in order to.

ondeggi'are [onded'dʒare] *vi* (*acqua*) to ripple; (*muoversi sulle onde: barca*) to rock, roll; (*fig: muoversi come le onde, barcollare*) to sway; (*: essere incerto*) to waver.

on'doso, a *ag* (*moto*) of the waves.

ondu'lato, a *ag* (*capelli*) wavy; (*terreno*) undulating; **cartone** ~ corrugated paper; **lamiera** ~**a** sheet of corrugated iron.

ondula'torio, a *ag* undulating; (*FISICA*) undulatory, wave *cpd*.

ondulazi'one [ondulat'tsjone] *sf* undulation; (*acconciatura*) wave.

one'rato, a *ag*: ~ **di** burdened with, loaded with.

'onere *sm* burden; ~ **finanziario** financial

charge; ~**i fiscali** taxes.

one'roso, a *ag* (*fig*) heavy, onerous.

onestà *sf* honesty.

onesta'mente *av* honestly; fairly; virtuously; (*in verità*) honestly, frankly.

o'nesto, a *ag* (*probo, retto*) honest; (*giusto*) fair; (*casto*) chaste, virtuous.

'onice ['ɔnitʃe] *sf* onyx.

o'nirico, a, ci, che *ag* dreamlike, dream *cpd*.

onnipo'tente *ag* omnipotent.

onnipre'sente *ag* omnipresent; (*scherzoso*) ubiquitous.

onnisci'ente [onniʃ'ʃɛnte] *ag* omniscient.

onniveg'gente [onnived'dʒɛnte] *ag* all-seeing.

ono'mastico, ci *sm* name day.

onomato'pea *sf* onomatopoeia.

onomato'peico, a, ci, che *ag* onomatopoeic.

ono'ranze [ono'rantse] *sfpl* honours (*BRIT*), honors (*US*).

ono'rare *vt* to honour (*BRIT*), honor (*US*); (*far onore a*) to do credit to; ~**rsi** *vr*: ~**rsi di qc/di fare** to feel hono(u)red by sth/to do.

ono'rario, a *ag* honorary ♦ *sm* fee.

onora'tissimo, a *ag* (*in presentazioni*): ~! delighted to meet you!

ono'rato, a *ag* (*reputazione, famiglia, carriera*) distinguished; **essere** ~ **di fare qc** to have the honour to do sth *o* of doing sth; ~ **di conoscerla!** (it is) a pleasure to meet you!

o'nore *sm* honour (*BRIT*), honor (*US*); **in** ~ **di** in hono(u)r of; **fare gli** ~**i di casa** to play host (*o* hostess); **fare** ~ **a** to hono(u)r; (*pranzo*) to do justice to; (*famiglia*) to be a credit to; **farsi** ~ to distinguish o.s.; **posto d'**~ place of hono(u)r; **a onor del vero ...** to tell the truth ....

ono'revole *ag* honourable (*BRIT*), honorable (*US*) ♦ *sm/f* (*POL*) ≈ Member of Parliament (*BRIT*), ≈ Congressman/ woman (*US*).

onorifi'cenza [onorifi'tʃɛntsa] *sf* honour (*BRIT*), honor (*US*); decoration.

ono'rifico, a, ci, che *ag* honorary.

'onta *sf* shame, disgrace; **ad** ~ **di** despite, notwithstanding.

on'tano *sm* alder.

'O.N.U. *sigla f* (= *Organizzazione delle Nazioni Unite*) UN, UNO.

'OPA *sigla f vedi* **offerta pubblica d'acquisto.**

o'paco, a, chi, che *ag* (*vetro*) opaque; (*metallo*) dull, matt.

o'pale *sm o f* opal.

'O.P.E.C. *sigla f* (= *Organization of Petroleum Exporting Countries*) OPEC.

'opera *sf* (*gen*) work; (*azione rilevante*) action, deed, work; (*MUS*) work; opus; (: *melodramma*) opera; (: *teatro*) opera house; (*ente*) institution, organization; **per ~ sua** thanks to him; **fare ~ di persuasione presso qn** to try to convince sb; **mettersi/essere all'~** to get down to/be at work; **~ d'arte** work of art; **~ buffa** comic opera; **~ lirica** (grand) opera; **~ pia** religious charity; **~e pubbliche (OO.PP.)** public works; **~e di restauro/di scavo** restoration/excavation work *sg*.

ope'raio, a *ag* working-class; workers'; (*ZOOL: ape, formica*) worker *cpd* ♦ *sm/f* worker; **classe ~a** working class; **~ di fabbrica** factory worker; **~ a giornata** day labourer (*BRIT*) *o* laborer (*US*); **~ specializzato** *o* **qualificato** skilled worker; **~ non specializzato** semi-skilled worker.

ope'rare *vt* to carry out, make; (*MED*) to operate on ♦ *vi* to operate, work; (*rimedio*) to act, work; (*MED*) to operate; **~rsi** *vr* to occur, take place; (*MED*) to have an operation; **~rsi d'appendicite** to have one's appendix out; **~ qn d'urgenza** to perform an emergency operation on sb.

opera'tivo, a *ag* operative, operating; **piano ~** (*MIL*) plan of operations.

ope'rato *sm* (*comportamento*) actions *pl*.

opera'tore, 'trice *sm/f* operator; (*TV, CINE*) cameraman; **aperto solo agli ~i** (*COMM*) open to the trade only; **~ di borsa** dealer on the stock exchange; **~ ecologico** refuse collector; **~ economico** agent, broker; **~ del suono** sound recordist; **~ turistico** tour operator.

opera'torio, a *ag* (*MED*) operating.

operazi'one [operat'tsjone] *sf* operation.

ope'retta *sf* (*MUS*) operetta, light opera.

operosità *sf* industry.

ope'roso, a *ag* industrious, hard-working.

opi'ficio [opi'fitʃo] *sm* factory, works *pl*.

opi'nabile *ag* (*discutibile*) debatable, questionable; **è ~** it is a matter of opinion.

opini'one *sf* opinion; **avere il coraggio delle proprie ~i** to have the courage of one's convictions; **l'~ pubblica** public opinion.

opinio'nista, i, e *sm/f* (political) columnist.

op là *escl* (*per far saltare*) hup!; (*a bimbo che è caduto*) upsy-daisy!

'oppio *sm* opium.

oppi'omane *sm/f* opium addict.

oppo'nente *ag* opposing ♦ *sm/f* opponent.

op'pongo *etc vb vedi* **opporre**.

op'porre *vt* to oppose; **opporsi** *vr*: **opporsi (a qc)** to oppose (sth); to object (to sth); **~ resistenza/un rifiuto** to offer resistance/to refuse.

opportu'nista, i, e *sm/f* opportunist.

opportunità *sf inv* opportunity; (*convenienza*) opportuneness, timeliness.

oppor'tuno, a *ag* timely, opportune; (*giusto*) right, appropriate; **a tempo ~** at the right *o* the appropriate time.

op'posi *etc vb vedi* **opporre**.

opposi'tore, 'trice *sm/f* opposer, opponent.

opposizi'one [oppozit'tsjone] *sf* opposition; (*DIR*) objection; **essere in netta ~** (*idee, opinioni*) to clash, be in complete opposition; **fare ~ a qn/qc** to oppose sb/sth.

op'posto, a *pp di* **opporre** ♦ *ag* opposite; (*opinioni*) conflicting ♦ *sm* opposite, contrary; **all'~** on the contrary.

oppressi'one *sf* oppression.

oppres'sivo, a *ag* oppressive.

op'presso, a *pp di* **opprimere**.

oppres'sore *sm* oppressor.

oppri'mente *ag* (*caldo, noia*) oppressive; (*persona*) tiresome; (: *deprimente*) depressing.

op'primere *vt* (*premere, gravare*) to weigh down; (*estenuare: sog: caldo*) to suffocate, oppress; (*tiranneggiare: popolo*) to oppress.

oppu'gnare [oppuɲˈɲare] *vt* (*fig*) to refute.

op'pure *cong* or (else).

op'tare *vi*: **~ per** (*scegliere*) to opt for, decide upon; (*BORSA*) to take (out) an option on.

'optimum *sm inv* optimum.

opu'lento, a *ag* (*ricco*) rich, wealthy, affluent; (: *arredamento etc*) opulent.

opu'lenza [opu'lɛntsa] *sf* (*vedi ag*) richness, wealth, affluence; opulence.

o'puscolo *sm* booklet, pamphlet.

OPV *sigla f vedi* **offerta pubblica di vendita**.

opzio'nale [optsjo'nale] *ag* optional.

opzi'one [op'tsjone] *sf* option.

OR *sigla* = Oristano.

'ora *sf* (*60 minuti*) hour; (*momento*) time ♦ *av* (*adesso*) now; (*poco fa*): **è uscito proprio ~** he's just gone out; (*tra poco*) presently, in a minute; (*correlativo*): **~ ... ~** now ... now; **che ~ è?, che ~e sono?** what time is it?; **domani a quest'~** this time tomorrow; **non veder l'~ di fare** to long to do, look forward to doing; **fare le ~e piccole** to stay up till the early hours (of the morning) *o* the small hours; **è ~ di partire** it's time to go; **di buon' ~** early; **alla buon'~!** at last!; **~ legale** *o* **estiva** summer time (*BRIT*), daylight saving time (*US*); **~ locale** local time; **~ di pranzo** lunchtime; **~ di punta** (*AUT*) rush hour; **d'~ in avanti** *o* **poi** from now on; **or**

~ just now, a moment ago; ~ **come** ~ right now, at present; **10 anni or sono** 10 years ago.

o'racolo *sm* oracle.

'orafo *sm* goldsmith.

o'rale *ag, sm* oral.

oral'mente *av* orally.

ora'mai *av* = **ormai**.

o'rario, a *ag* hourly; (*fuso, segnale*) time *cpd*; (*velocità*) per hour ♦ *sm* timetable, schedule; (*di visite etc*) hours *pl*, time(s *pl*); ~ **di apertura/chiusura** opening/closing time; ~ **di apertura degli sportelli** bank opening hours; ~ **elastico** *o* **flessibile** (*INDUSTRIA*) flexitime; ~ **ferroviario** railway timetable; ~ **di lavoro/d'ufficio** working/office hours.

o'rata *sf* sea bream.

ora'tore, 'trice *sm/f* speaker; orator.

ora'torio, a *ag* oratorical ♦ *sm* (*REL*) oratory; (*MUS*) oratorio ♦ *sf* (*arte*) oratory.

orazi'one [orat'tsjone] *sf* (*REL*) prayer; (*discorso*) speech, oration.

or'bene *cong* so, well (then).

'orbita *sf* (*ASTR, FISICA*) orbit; (*ANAT*) (eye-) socket.

orbi'tare *vi* to orbit.

'orbo, a *ag* blind.

'Orcadi *sfpl*: **le (isole)** ~ the Orkney Islands, the Orkneys.

or'chestra [or'kɛstra] *sf* orchestra.

orches'trale [orkes'trale] *ag* orchestral ♦ *sm/f* orchestra player.

orches'trare [orkes'trare] *vt* to orchestrate; (*fig*) to stage-manage.

orchi'dea [orki'dɛa] *sf* orchid.

'orcio ['ortʃo] *sm* jar.

'orco, chi *sm* ogre.

'orda *sf* horde.

or'digno [or'diɲɲo] *sm*: ~ **esplosivo** explosive device.

ordi'nale *ag, sm* ordinal.

ordina'mento *sm* order, arrangement; (*regolamento*) regulations *pl*, rules *pl*; ~ **scolastico/giuridico** education/legal system.

ordi'nanza [ordi'nantsa] *sf* (*DIR, MIL*) order; (*AMM: decreto*) decree; (*persona: MIL*) orderly, batman; **d'**~ (*MIL*) regulation *cpd*; **ufficiale d'**~ orderly; ~ **municipale** by(e)-law.

ordi'nare *vt* (*mettere in ordine*) to arrange, organize; (*COMM*) to order; (*prescrivere: medicina*) to prescribe; (*comandare*): ~ **a qn di fare qc** to order *o* command sb to do sth; (*REL*) to ordain.

ordi'nario, a *ag* (*comune*) ordinary; (*grossolano*) coarse, common ♦ *sm*

ordinary; (*di università*) full professor.

ordina'tivo, a *ag* regulating, governing ♦ *sm* (*COMM*) order.

ordi'nato, a *ag* tidy, orderly.

ordinazi'one [ordinat'tsjone] *sf* (*COMM*) order; (*REL*) ordination; **fare un'**~ **di qc** to put in an order for sth, order sth; **eseguire qc su** ~ to make sth to order.

'ordine *sm* order; (*carattere*): **d'**~ **pratico** of a practical nature; **all'**~ (*COMM: assegno*) to order; **di prim'**~ first-class; **fino a nuovo** ~ until further notice; **essere in** ~ (*documenti*) to be in order; (*persona, stanza*) to be tidy; **mettere in** ~ to put in order, tidy (up); **richiamare all'**~ to call to order; **le forze dell'**~ the forces of law and order; ~ **d'acquisto** purchase order; **l'**~ **degli avvocati** ≈ the Bar; ~ **del giorno** (*di seduta*) agenda; (*MIL*) order of the day; **l'**~ **dei medici** ≈ the Medical Association; ~ **di pagamento** standing order (*BRIT*), automatic payment (*US*); **l'**~ **pubblico** law and order; ~**i (sacri)** (*REL*) holy orders.

or'dire *vt* (*fig*) to plot, scheme.

or'dito *sm* (*di tessuto*) warp.

orecchi'abile [orek'kjabile] *ag* (*canzone*) catchy.

orec'chino [orek'kino] *sm* earring.

o'recchio [o'rekkjo], *pl*(*f*) **o'recchie** *sm* (*ANAT*) ear; **avere** ~ to have a good ear (for music); **venire all'**~ **di qn** to come to sb's attention; **fare** ~**e da mercante (a)** to turn a deaf ear (to).

orecchi'oni [orek'kjoni] *smpl* (*MED*) mumps *sg*.

o'refice [o'refitʃe] *sm* goldsmith; jeweller (*BRIT*), jeweler (*US*).

orefice'ria [orefitʃe'ria] *sf* (*arte*) goldsmith's art; (*negozio*) jeweller's (shop) (*BRIT*), jewelry store (*US*).

'orfano, a *ag* orphan(ed) ♦ *sm/f* orphan; ~ **di padre/madre** fatherless/motherless.

orfano'trofio *sm* orphanage.

orga'netto *sm* barrel organ; (*fam: armonica a bocca*) mouth organ; (: *fisarmonica*) accordion.

or'ganico, a, ci, che *ag* organic ♦ *sm* personnel, staff.

organi'gramma, i *sm* organization chart; (*INFORM*) computer flow chart.

orga'nismo *sm* (*BIOL*) organism; (*ANAT, AMM*) body, organism.

orga'nista, i, e *sm/f* organist.

organiz'zare [organid'dzare] *vt* to organize; ~**rsi** *vr* to get organized.

organizza'tivo, a [organiddza'tivo] *ag* organizational.

organizza'tore, 'trice [organiddza'tore] *ag*

organizing ♦ *smf* organizer.

organizzazi'one [organiddzat'tsjone] *sf*
(*azione*) organizing, arranging; (*risultato*)
organization; **O~ Mondiale della Sanità
(O.M.S.)** World Health Organization
(WHO).

'organo *sm* organ; (*di congegno*) part;
(*portavoce*) spokesman/woman,
mouthpiece; **~i di trasmissione** (*TECN*)
transmission (unit) *sg*.

or'gasmo *sm* (*FISIOL*) orgasm; (*fig*)
agitation, anxiety.

'orgia, ge ['ɔrdʒa] *sf* orgy.

or'goglio [or'ɡoʎʎo] *sm* pride.

orgogli'oso, a [orɡoʎ'ʎoso] *ag* proud.

orien'tabile *ag* adjustable.

orien'tale *ag* (*paese, regione*) eastern;
(*tappeti, lingua, civiltà*) oriental.

orienta'mento *sm* positioning;
orientation; direction; **senso di ~** sense of
direction; **perdere l'~** to lose one's
bearings; **~ professionale** careers
guidance.

orien'tare *vt* (*situare*) to position; (*carta,
bussola*) to orientate; (*fig*) to direct; **~rsi** *vr*
to find one's bearings; (*fig: tendere*) to
tend, lean; (: *indirizzarsi*): **~rsi verso** to
take up, go in for.

orienta'tivo, a *ag* indicative, for guidance;
a scopo ~ for guidance.

ori'ente *sm* east; **l'O~** the East, the Orient;
il Medio/l'Estremo O~ the Middle/Far
East; **a ~** in the east.

ori'ficio [ori'fitʃo], **ori'fizio** [ori'fittsjo] *sm*
(*apertura*) opening; (: *di tubo*) mouth;
(*ANAT*) orifice.

o'rigano *sm* oregano.

origi'nale [oridʒi'nale] *ag* original; (*bizzarro*)
eccentric ♦ *sm* original.

originalità [oridʒinali'ta] *sf* originality;
eccentricity.

origi'nare [oridʒi'nare] *vt* to bring about,
produce ♦ *vi*: **~ da** to arise *o* spring from.

origi'nario, a [oridʒi'narjo] *ag* original;
essere ~ di to be a native of; (*animale,
pianta*) to be indigenous to, be native to.

o'rigine [o'ridʒine] *sf* origin; **all'~**
originally; **d'~ inglese** of English origin;
avere ~ da to originate from; **dare ~ a** to
give rise to.

origli'are [oriʎ'ʎare] *vi*: **~ (a)** to eavesdrop
(on).

o'rina *sf* urine.

ori'nale *sm* chamberpot.

ori'nare *vi* to urinate ♦ *vt* to pass.

orina'toio *sm* (public) urinal.

ori'undo, a *ag*: **essere ~ di Milano** *etc* to be
of Milanese *etc* extraction *o* origin

♦ *smf* person of foreign extraction *o* origin.

orizzon'tale [oriddzon'tale] *ag* horizontal.

oriz'zonte [orid'dzonte] *sm* horizon.

ORL *sigla f* (*MED*: = *otorinolaringoiatria*) ENT.

or'lare *vt* to hem.

orla'tura *sf* (*azione*) hemming *no pl*; (*orlo*)
hem.

'orlo *sm* edge, border; (*di recipiente*) rim,
brim; (*di vestito etc*) hem; **pieno fino all'~**
full to the brim, brimful; **sull'~ della
pazzia/della rovina** on the brink *o* verge
of madness/ruin; **~ a giorno** hemstitch.

'orma *sf* (*di persona*) footprint; (*di animale*)
track; (*impronta, traccia*) mark, trace;
seguire *o* calcare le ~e di qn to follow in
sb's footsteps.

or'mai *av* by now, by this time; (*adesso*)
now; (*quasi*) almost, nearly.

ormeggi'are [ormed'dʒare] *vt*, **~rsi** *vr*
(*NAUT*) to moor.

or'meggio [or'meddʒo] *sm* (*atto*) mooring *no
pl*; (*luogo*) moorings *pl*; **posto d'~** berth.

ormo'nale *ag* hormonal; (*disfunzione, cura*)
hormone *cpd*; **terapia ~** hormone therapy.

or'mone *sm* hormone.

ornamen'tale *ag* ornamental, decorative.

orna'mento *sm* ornament, decoration.

or'nare *vt* to adorn, decorate; **~rsi** *vr*: **~rsi
(di)** to deck o.s. (out) (with).

or'nato, a *ag* ornate.

ornitolo'gia [ornitolo'dʒia] *sf* ornithology.

orni'tologo, a, gi, ghe *smf* ornithologist.

'oro *sm* gold; **d'~, in ~** gold *cpd*; **d'~** (*colore,
occasione*) golden; (*persona*) marvellous
(*BRIT*), marvelous (*US*); **un affare d'~** a
real bargain; **prendere qc per ~ colato** to
take sth as gospel (truth); **~ nero** black
gold; **~ zecchino** pure gold.

orologe'ria [orolodʒe'ria] *sf* watchmaking
no pl; watchmaker's (shop); clockmaker's
(shop); **bomba a ~** time bomb.

orologi'aio [orolo'dʒajo] *sm* watchmaker;
clockmaker.

oro'logio [oro'lɔdʒo] *sm* clock; (*da tasca, da
polso*) watch; **~ biologico** biological
clock; **~ da polso** wristwatch; **~ al quarzo**
quartz watch; **~ a sveglia** alarm clock.

o'roscopo *sm* horoscope.

or'rendo, a *ag* (*spaventoso*) horrible,
awful; (*bruttissimo*) hideous.

or'ribile *ag* horrible.

'orrido, a *ag* fearful, horrid.

orripi'lante *ag* hair-raising, horrifying.

or'rore *sm* horror; **avere in ~ qn/qc** to
loathe *o* detest sb/sth; **mi fanno ~** I loathe
o detest them.

orsacchi'otto [orsak'kjɔtto] *sm* teddy bear.

'orso *sm* bear; **~ bruno/bianco** brown/polar

bear.

orsù *escl* come now!

or'taggio [or'taddʒo] *sm* vegetable.

or'tensia *sf* hydrangea.

or'tica, che *sf* (stinging) nettle.

orti'caria *sf* nettle rash.

orticol'tura *sf* horticulture.

'orto *sm* vegetable garden, kitchen garden; (*AGR*) market garden (*BRIT*), truck farm (*US*); ~ **botanico** botanical garden(s *pl*).

orto'dosso, a *ag* orthodox.

ortofrut'ticolo, a *ag* fruit and vegetable *cpd*.

ortogo'nale *ag* perpendicular.

ortogra'fia *sf* spelling.

orto'lano, a *smlf* (*venditore*) greengrocer (*BRIT*), produce dealer (*US*).

ortope'dia *sf* orthopaedics *sg* (*BRIT*), orthopedics *sg* (*US*).

orto'pedico, a, ci, che *ag* orthopaedic (*BRIT*), orthopedic (*US*) ♦ *sm* orthopaedic specialist (*BRIT*), orthopedist (*US*).

orzai'olo [ordza'jɔlo], **orzaiu'olo** [ordza'jwɔlo] *sm* (*MED*) stye.

or'zata [or'dzata] *sf* barley water.

'orzo ['ɔrdzo] *sm* barley.

'OSA *sigla f* (= *Organizzazione degli Stati Americani*) OAS (= *Organization of American States*).

o'sare *vt, vi* to dare; ~ **fare** to dare (to) do; **come osi?** how dare you?

oscenità [oʃʃeni'ta] *sf inv* obscenity.

o'sceno, a [oʃ'ʃɛno] *ag* obscene; (*ripugnante*) ghastly.

oscil'lare [oʃʃil'lare] *vi* (*pendolo*) to swing; (*dondolare: al vento etc*) to rock; (*variare*) to fluctuate; (*TECN*) to oscillate; (*fig*): ~ **fra** to waver between.

oscillazi'one [oʃʃillat'tsjone] *sf* oscillation; (*di prezzi, temperatura*) fluctuation.

oscura'mento *sm* darkening; obscuring; (*in tempo di guerra*) blackout.

oscu'rare *vt* to darken, obscure; (*fig*) to obscure; ~**rsi** *vr* (*cielo*) to darken, cloud over; (*persona*): **si oscurò in volto** his face clouded over.

oscurità *sf* (*vedi ag*) darkness; obscurity; gloominess.

os'curo, a *ag* dark; (*fig: incomprensibile*) obscure; (: *umile: vita, natali*) humble, obscure; (: *triste: pensiero*) gloomy, sombre ♦ *sm*: **all'**~ in the dark; **tenere qn all'**~ **di qc** to keep sb in the dark about sth.

'Oslo *sf* Oslo.

ospe'dale *sm* hospital.

ospedali'ero, a *ag* hospital *cpd*.

ospi'tale *ag* hospitable.

ospitalità *sf* hospitality.

ospi'tare *vt* to give hospitality to; (*sog: albergo*) to accommodate.

'ospite *smlf* (*persona che ospita*) host/hostess; (*persona ospitata*) guest.

os'pizio [os'pittsjo] *sm* (*per vecchi etc*) home.

'ossa *sfpl vedi* **osso**.

os'sario *sm* (*MIL*) war memorial (*with burial place*).

ossa'tura *sf* (*ANAT*) skeletal structure, frame; (*TECN, fig*) framework.

'osseo, a *ag* bony; (*tessuto etc*) bone *cpd*.

osse'quente *ag*: ~ **alla legge** law-abiding.

os'sequio *sm* deference, respect; ~**i** *smpl* (*saluto*) respects, regards; **porgere i propri** ~**i a qn** (*formale*) to pay one's respects to sb; ~**i alla signora!** (give my) regards to your wife!

ossequi'oso, a *ag* obsequious.

osser'vanza [osser'vantsa] *sf* observance.

osser'vare *vt* to observe, watch; (*esaminare*) to examine; (*notare, rilevare*) to notice, observe; (*DIR: la legge*) to observe, respect; (*mantenere: silenzio*) to keep, observe; **far** ~ **qc a qn** to point sth out to sb.

osserva'tore, 'trice *ag* observant, perceptive ♦ *smlf* observer.

osserva'torio *sm* (*ASTR*) observatory; (*MIL*) observation post.

osservazi'one [osservat'tsjone] *sf* observation; (*di legge etc*) observance; (*considerazione critica*) observation, remark; (*rimprovero*) reproof; **in** ~ under observation; **fare un'**~ to make a remark; to raise an objection; **fare un'**~ **a qn** to criticize sb.

ossessio'nare *vt* to obsess, haunt; (*tormentare*) to torment, harass.

ossessi'one *sf* obsession; (*seccatura*) nuisance.

osses'sivo, a *ag* obsessive, haunting; troublesome.

os'sesso, a *ag* (*spiritato*) possessed.

os'sia *cong* that is, to be precise.

ossi'buchi [ossi'buki] *smpl di* **ossobuco**.

ossi'dare *vt*, ~**rsi** *vr* to oxidize.

ossidazi'one [ossidat'tsjone] *sf* oxidization, oxidation.

'ossido *sm* oxide; ~ **di carbonio** carbon monoxide.

ossige'nare [ossidʒe'nare] *vt* to oxygenate; (*decolorare*) to bleach; **acqua ossigenata** hydrogen peroxide.

os'sigeno [os'sidʒeno] *sm* oxygen.

'osso *sm* (*pl(f)* **ossa** *nel senso ANAT*) bone; **d'**~ (*bottone etc*) of bone, bone *cpd*; **avere**

le ~**a rotte** to be dead *o* dog tired;
bagnato fino all'~ soaked to the skin;
essere ridotto all'~ (*fig: magro*) to be just
skin and bone; (: *senza soldi*) to be in dire
straits; **rompersi l'**~ **del collo** to break
one's neck; **rimetterci l'**~ **del collo** (*fig*) to
ruin o.s., lose everything; **un** ~ **duro**
(*persona, impresa*) a tough number; ~ **di
seppia** cuttlebone.

osso'buco, *pl* **ossi'buchi** *sm* (*CUC*)
marrowbone; (: *piatto*) *stew made with
knuckle of veal in tomato sauce.*

os'suto, a *ag* bony.

ostaco'lare *vt* to block, obstruct.

os'tacolo *sm* obstacle; (*EQUITAZIONE*)
hurdle, jump; **essere di** ~ **a qn/qc** (*fig*) to
stand in the way of sb/sth.

os'taggio [os'taddʒo] *sm* hostage.

'oste, os'tessa *sm/f* innkeeper.

osteggi'are [osted'dʒare] *vt* to oppose, be
opposed to.

os'tello *sm* hostel; ~ **della gioventù** youth
hostel.

osten'sorio *sm* (*REL*) monstrance.

osten'tare *vt* to make a show of, flaunt.

ostentazi'one [ostentat'tsjone] *sf*
ostentation, show.

oste'ria *sf* inn.

os'tessa *sf vedi* **oste.**

os'tetrico, a, ci, che *ag* obstetric ♦ *sm*
obstetrician ♦ *sf* midwife.

'ostia *sf* (*REL*) host; (*per medicinali*) wafer.

'ostico, a, ci, che *ag* difficult, tough.

os'tile *ag* hostile.

ostilità *sf* hostility ♦ *sfpl* (*MIL*) hostilities.

osti'narsi *vr* to insist, dig one's heels in; ~
a fare to persist (obstinately) in doing.

osti'nato, a *ag* (*caparbio*) obstinate;
(*tenace*) persistent, determined.

ostinazi'one [ostinat'tsjone] *sf* obstinacy;
persistence.

ostra'cismo [ostra'tʃizmo] *sm* ostracism.

'ostrica, che *sf* oyster.

ostru'ire *vt* to obstruct, block.

ostruzi'one [ostrut'tsjone] *sf* obstruction,
blockage.

ostruzio'nismo [ostruttsjo'nizmo] *sm* (*POL*)
obstructionism; (*SPORT*) obstruction; **fare
dell'**~ **a** (*progetto, legge*) to obstruct; ~
sindacale work-to-rule (*BRIT*), slowdown
(*US*).

o'tite *sf* ear infection.

oto'rino(laringoi'atra), i, e *sm/f* ear, nose
and throat specialist.

'otre *sm* (*recipiente*) goatskin.

ott. *abbr* (= *ottobre*) Oct.

ottago'nale *ag* octagonal.

ot'tagono *sm* octagon.

ot'tano *sm* octane; **numero di** ~**i** octane
rating.

ot'tanta *num* eighty.

ottan'tenne *ag* eighty-year-old ♦ *sm/f*
octogenarian.

ottan'tesimo, a *num* eightieth.

ottan'tina *sf*: **una** ~ (**di**) about eighty.

ot'tavo, a *num* eighth ♦ *sf* octave.

ottempe'ranza [ottempe'rantsa] *sf*: **in** ~ **a**
(*AMM*) in accordance with, in compliance
with.

ottempe'rare *vi*: ~ **a** to comply with, obey.

ottene'brare *vt* to darken; (*fig*) to cloud.

otte'nere *vt* to obtain, get; (*risultato*) to
achieve, obtain.

'ottico, a, ci, che *ag* (*della vista: nervo*)
optic; (*dell'ottica*) optical ♦ *sm* optician
♦ *sf* (*scienza*) optics *sg*; (*FOT: lenti, prismi
etc*) optics *pl*.

otti'male *ag* optimal, optimum.

ottima'mente *av* excellently, very well.

otti'mismo *sm* optimism.

otti'mista, i, e *sm/f* optimist.

ottimiz'zare [ottimid'dzare] *vt* to optimize.

ottimizzazi'one [ottimiddzat'tsjone] *sf*
optimization.

'ottimo, a *ag* excellent, very good.

'otto *num* eight.

ot'tobre *sm* October; *per fraseologia vedi*
luglio.

otto'brino, a *ag* October *cpd*.

ottocen'tesco, a, schi, sche
[ottotʃen'tesko] *ag* nineteenth-century.

otto'cento [otto'tʃento] *num* eight hundred
♦ *sm*: **l'O**~ the nineteenth century.

otto'mila *num* eight thousand.

ot'tone *sm* brass; **gli** ~**i** (*MUS*) the brass.

ottuage'nario, a [ottuadʒe'narjo] *ag, sm/f*
octogenarian.

ot'tundere *vt* (*fig*) to dull.

ottu'rare *vt* to close (up); (*dente*) to fill.

ottura'tore *sm* (*FOT*) shutter; (*nelle armi*)
breechblock.

otturazi'one [otturat'tsjone] *sf* closing
(up); (*dentaria*) filling.

ottusità *sf* (*vedi ag*) obtuseness; dullness.

ot'tuso, a *pp di* **ottundere** ♦ *ag* (*MAT, fig*)
obtuse; (*suono*) dull.

o'vaia *sf*, **o'vaio** *sm* (*ANAT*) ovary.

o'vale *ag, sm* oval.

o'varico, a *ag* ovarian.

o'vatta *sf* cotton wool; (*per imbottire*)
padding, wadding.

ovat'tare *vt* (*imbottire*) to pad; (*fig:
smorzare*) to muffle.

ovazi'one [ovat'tsjone] *sf* ovation.

'ovest *sm* west; **a** ~ (**di**) west (of); **verso** ~
westward(s).

o'**vile** *sm* pen, enclosure; **tornare all'**~ (*fig*) to return to the fold.

o'**vino, a** *ag* sheep *cpd*, ovine.

'**O.V.N.I.** *sigla m* (= *oggetto volante non identificato*) UFO.

ovulazi'one [ovulat'tsjone] *sf* ovulation.

'**ovulo** *sm* (*FISIOL*) ovum.

o'**vunque** *av* = **dovunque**.

ov'**vero** *cong* (*ossia*) that is, to be precise; (*oppure*) or (else).

ovvi'are *vi*: ~ **a** to obviate.

'**ovvio, a** *ag* obvious.

ozi'are [ot'tsjare] *vi* to laze around.

'**ozio** ['ɔttsjo] *sm* idleness; (*tempo libero*) leisure; **ore d'**~ leisure time; **stare in** ~ to be idle.

ozi'oso, a [ot'tsjoso] *ag* idle.

o'**zono** [od'dzɔno] *sm* ozone; **lo strato d'**~ the ozone layer.

ozonos'fera [oddzonos'fɛra] *sf* ozone layer.

P p

P, p [pi] *sf o m inv* (*lettera*) P, p; **P come Padova** ≈ P for Peter.

P *abbr* (= *peso*) wt; (= *parcheggio*) P.

p. *abbr* (= *pagina*) p.

P2 *abbr f*: **la (loggia)** ~ the P2 masonic lodge.

PA *sigla* = Palermo.

P.A. *abbr* = **pubblica amministrazione**.

pa'**care** *vt* to calm; ~**rsi** *vr* (*tempesta*, *disordini*) to subside.

paca'tezza [paka'tettsa] *sf* quietness, calmness.

pa'**cato, a** *ag* quiet, calm.

'**pacca, che** *sf* slap.

pac'**chetto** [pak'ketto] *sm* packet; ~ **applicativo** (*INFORM*) applications package; ~ **azionario** (*FINANZA*) shareholding; ~ **software** (*INFORM*) software package; ~ **turistico** package holiday (*BRIT*) *o* tour.

pacchi'ano, a [pak'kjano] *ag* (*colori*) garish; (*abiti, arredamento*) vulgar, garish.

'**pacco, chi** *sm* parcel; (*involto*) bundle; ~ **postale** parcel.

paccot'tiglia [pakkot'tiʎʎa] *sf* trash, junk.

'**pace** ['patʃe] *sf* peace; **darsi** ~ to resign o.s.; **fare (la)** ~ **con qn** to make it up with sb.

pachis'tano, a [pakis'tano] *ag, smf* Pakistani.

pacifi'care [patʃifi'kare] *vt* (*riconciliare*) to reconcile, make peace between; (*mettere in pace*) to pacify.

pacificazi'one [patʃifikat'tsjone] *sf* (*vedi vt*) reconciliation; pacification.

pa'**cifico, a, ci, che** [pa'tʃifiko] *ag* (*persona*) peaceable; (*vita*) peaceful; (*fig: indiscusso*) indisputable; (: *ovvio*) obvious, clear ♦ *sm*: **il P**~, **l'Oceano P**~ the Pacific (Ocean).

paci'fismo [patʃi'fizmo] *sm* pacifism.

paci'fista, i, e [patʃi'fista] *smf* pacifist.

pa'**dano, a** *ag* of the Po; **la pianura** ~**a** the Lombardy plain.

pa'**della** *sf* frying pan; (*per infermi*) bedpan.

padigli'one [padiʎ'ʎone] *sm* pavilion.

'**Padova** *sf* Padua.

pado'vano, a *ag* of (*o* from) Padua.

'**padre** *sm* father; ~**i** *smpl* (*antenati*) forefathers.

Padre'terno *sm*: **il** ~ God the Father.

pa'**drino** *sm* godfather.

padro'nale *ag* (*scala, entrata*) main, principal; **casa** ~ country house.

padro'nanza [padro'nantsa] *sf* command, mastery.

padro'nato *sm*: **il** ~ the ruling class.

pa'**drone, a** *smf* master/mistress; (*proprietario*) owner; (*datore di lavoro*) employer; **essere** ~ **di sé** to be in control of o.s.; ~**/a di casa** master/mistress of the house; (*per gli inquilini*) landlord/lady.

padroneggi'are [padroned'dʒare] *vt* (*fig: sentimenti*) to master, control; (: *materia*) to master, know thoroughly; ~**rsi** *vr* to control o.s.

pae'saggio [pae'zaddʒo] *sm* landscape.

paesag'gista, i, e [paezad'dʒista] *smf* (*pittore*) landscape painter.

pae'sano, a *ag* country *cpd* ♦ *smf* villager; countryman/woman.

pa'ese *sm* (*nazione*) country, nation; (*terra*) country, land; (*villaggio*) village; ~ **di provenienza** country of origin; **i P**~**i Bassi** the Netherlands.

paf'futo, a *ag* chubby, plump.

'**paga, ghe** *sf* pay, wages *pl*; **giorno di** ~ pay day.

pa'gabile *ag* payable; ~ **alla consegna/a vista** payable on delivery/on demand.

pa'gaia *sf* paddle.

paga'mento *sm* payment; ~ **anticipato** payment in advance; ~ **alla consegna** payment on delivery; ~ **all'ordine** cash with order; **la TV a** ~ pay TV.

pa'gano, a *ag, smf* pagan.

pa'gare *vt* to pay; (*acquisto, fig: colpa*) to

pay for; (*contraccambiare*) to repay, pay back ♦ *vi* to pay; **quanto l'ha pagato?** how much did you pay for it?; ~ **con carta di credito** to pay by credit card; ~ **in contanti** to pay cash; ~ **di persona** (*fig*) to suffer the consequences; **l'ho pagata cara** (*fig*) I paid dearly for it.

pa'gella [pa'dʒɛlla] *sf* (*INS*) school report (*BRIT*), report card (*US*).

'paggio ['paddʒo] *sm* page(boy).

paghe'rò [page'rɔ] *vb vedi* **pagare** ♦ *sm inv* IOU; ~ **cambiario** promissory note.

'pagina ['padʒina] *sf* page; **P~e bianche** phone book, telephone directory; **P~e Gialle** ® Yellow Pages ®.

'paglia ['paʎʎa] *sf* straw; **avere la coda di** ~ (*fig*) to have a guilty conscience; **fuoco di** ~ (*fig*) flash in the pan.

pagliac'cetto [paʎʎat'tʃetto] *sm* (*per bambini*) rompers *pl*.

pagliac'ciata [paʎʎat'tʃata] *sf* farce.

pagli'accio [paʎ'ʎattʃo] *sm* clown.

pagli'aio [paʎ'ʎajo] *sm* haystack.

paglie'riccio [paʎʎe'rittʃo] *sm* straw mattress.

paglie'rino, a [paʎʎe'rino] *ag*: **giallo** ~ pale yellow.

pagli'etta [paʎ'ʎetta] *sf* (*cappello per uomo*) (straw) boater; (*per tegami etc*) steel wool.

pagli'uzza [paʎ'ʎuttsa] *sf* (*blade of*) straw; (*d'oro etc*) tiny particle, speck.

pa'gnotta [paɲ'ɲɔtta] *sf* round loaf.

'pago, a, ghi, ghe *ag*: ~ **(di)** satisfied (with).

pa'goda *sf* pagoda.

pail'lette [pa'jɛt] *sf inv* sequin.

'paio, pl(f) 'paia *sm* pair; **un** ~ **di occhiali** a pair of glasses; **un** ~ **di** (*alcuni*) a couple of; **è un altro** ~ **di maniche** (*fig*) that's another kettle of fish.

'paio *etc vb vedi* **parere**.

pai'olo, paiu'olo *sm* (copper) pot.

'Pakistan *sm*: **il** ~ Pakistan.

pakis'tano, a *ag, sm/f* = **pachistano**.

pal. *abbr* = **palude**.

'pala *sf* shovel; (*di remo, ventilatore, elica*) blade; (*di ruota*) paddle.

palan'drana *sf* (*scherzoso: abito lungo e largo*) tent.

pa'lata *sf* shovelful; **fare soldi a** ~**e** to make a mint.

pala'tale *ag* (*ANAT, LING*) palatal.

pa'lato *sm* palate.

pa'lazzo [pa'lattso] *sm* (*reggia*) palace; (*edificio*) building; ~ **di giustizia** courthouse; ~ **dello sport** sports stadium; *vedi nota nel riquadro*.

---

pal'chetto [pal'ketto] *sm* shelf.

'palco, chi *sm* (*TEAT*) box; (*tavolato*) platform, stand; (*ripiano*) layer.

palco'scenico, ci [palkoʃ'ʃɛniko] *sm* (*TEAT*) stage.

palermi'tano, a *ag* of (*o from*) Palermo ♦ *sm/f* person from Palermo.

Pa'lermo *sf* Palermo.

pale'sare *vt* to reveal, disclose; ~**rsi** *vr* to reveal *o* show o.s.

pa'lese *ag* clear, evident.

Pales'tina *sf*: **la** ~ Palestine.

palesti'nese *ag, sm/f* Palestinian.

pa'lestra *sf* gymnasium; (*esercizio atletico*) exercise, training; (*fig*) training ground, school.

paletot [pal'to] *sm inv* overcoat.

pa'letta *sf* spade; (*per il focolare*) shovel; (*del capostazione*) signalling disc.

pa'letto *sm* stake, peg; (*spranga*) bolt.

palin'sesto *sm* (*STORIA*) palimpsest; (*TV, RADIO*) programme (*BRIT*) *o* program (*US*) schedule.

'palio *sm* (*gara*): **il P**~ *horserace run at Siena*; **mettere qc in** ~ to offer sth as a prize; *vedi nota nel riquadro*.

---

palis'sandro *sm* rosewood.
paliz'zata [palit'tsata] *sf* palisade.
'palla *sf* ball; (*pallottola*) bullet; **prendere la ~ al balzo** (*fig*) to seize one's opportunity.
pallaca'nestro *sf* basketball.
pallanu'oto *sf* water polo.
palla'volo *sf* volleyball.
palleggi'are [palled'dʒare] *vi* (*CALCIO*) to practise (*BRIT*) *o* practice (*US*) with the ball; (*TENNIS*) to knock up.
pallia'tivo *sm* palliative; (*fig*) stopgap measure.
'pallido, a *ag* pale.
pal'lina *sf* (*bilia*) marble.
pal'lino *sm* (*BILIARDO*) cue ball; (*BOCCE*) jack; (*proiettile*) pellet; (*pois*) dot; **bianco a ~i blu** white with blue dots; **avere il ~ di** (*fig*) to be crazy about.
pallon'cino [pallon'tʃino] *sm* balloon; (*lampioncino*) Chinese lantern.
pal'lone *sm* (*palla*) ball; (*CALCIO*) football; (*aerostato*) balloon; **gioco del ~** ball game.
pal'lore *sm* pallor, paleness.
pal'lottola *sf* pellet; (*proiettile*) bullet.
'palma *sf* (*ANAT*) = **palmo**; (*BOT*) palm; **~ da datteri** date palm.
pal'mato, a *ag* (*ZOOL: piede*) webbed; (*BOT*) palmate.
pal'mipede *ag* web-footed.
pal'mizio [pal'mittsjo] *sm* (*palma*) palm tree; (*ramo*) palm.
'palmo *sm* (*ANAT*) palm; **essere alto un ~** (*fig*) to be tiny; **restare con un ~ di naso** (*fig*) to be badly disappointed.
'palo *sm* (*legno appuntito*) stake; (*sostegno*) pole; **fare da** *o* **il ~** (*fig*) to act as look-out; **saltare di ~ in frasca** (*fig*) to jump from one topic to another.
palom'baro *sm* diver.
pa'lombo *sm* (*pesce*) dogfish.
pal'pare *vt* to feel, finger.
'palpebra *sf* eyelid.
palpi'tare *vi* (*cuore, polso*) to beat; (: *più forte*) to pound, throb; (*fremere*) to quiver.
palpitazi'one [palpitat'tsjone] *sf* palpitation.
'palpito *sm* (*del cuore*) beat; (*fig: d'amore etc*) throb.
paltò *sm inv* overcoat.
pa'lude *sf* marsh, swamp.
palu'doso, a *ag* marshy, swampy.
pa'lustre *ag* marsh *cpd*, swamp *cpd*.
'pampino *sm* vine leaf.
pana'cea [pana'tʃɛa] *sf* panacea.
'Panama *sf* Panama; **il canale di ~** the Panama Canal.
pana'mense *ag, sm/f* Panamanian.

'panca, che *sf* bench.
pancarrè *sm* sliced bread.
pan'cetta [pan'tʃetta] *sf* (*CUC*) bacon.
pan'chetto [pan'ketto] *sm* stool; footstool.
pan'china [pan'kina] *sf* garden seat; (*di giardino pubblico*) (park) bench.
'pancia, ce ['pantʃa] *sf* belly, stomach; **mettere** *o* **fare ~** to be getting a paunch; **avere mal di ~** to have stomach ache *o* a sore stomach.
panci'era [pan'tʃɛra] *sf* corset.
panci'olle [pan'tʃɔlle] *av*: **stare in ~** to lounge about (*BRIT*) *o* around.
panci'otto [pan'tʃɔtto] *sm* waistcoat.
panci'uto, a [pan'tʃuto] *ag* (*persona*) potbellied; (*vaso, bottiglia*) rounded.
'pancreas *sm inv* pancreas.
'panda *sm inv* panda.
pande'monio *sm* pandemonium.
pan'doro *sm* type of sponge cake eaten at Christmas.
'pane *sm* bread; (*pagnotta*) loaf (of bread); (*forma*): **un ~ di burro/cera** *etc* a pat of butter/bar of wax *etc*; **guadagnarsi il ~** to earn one's living; **dire ~ al ~, vino al vino** (*fig*) to call a spade a spade; **rendere pan per focaccia** (*fig*) to give tit for tat; **~ casereccio** homemade bread; **~ a cassetta** sliced bread; **~ integrale** wholemeal bread; **~ di segale** rye bread; **pan di Spagna** sponge cake; **~ tostato** toast.
pane'girico [pane'dʒiriko] *sm* (*fig*) panegyric.
panet'teria *sf* (*forno*) bakery; (*negozio*) baker's (shop), bakery.
panetti'ere, a *sm/f* baker.
panet'tone *sm* a kind of spiced brioche with sultanas, eaten at Christmas.
'panfilo *sm* yacht.
pan'forte *sm* Sienese nougat-type delicacy.
pangrat'tato *sm* breadcrumbs *pl*.
'panico, a, ci, che *ag, sm* panic; **essere in preda al ~** to be panic-stricken; **lasciarsi prendere dal ~** to panic.
pani'ere *sm* basket.
panifica'tore, trice *sm/f* bread-maker, baker.
pani'ficio [pani'fitʃo] *sm* (*forno*) bakery; (*negozio*) baker's (shop), bakery.
pa'nino *sm* roll; **~ imbottito** filled roll; sandwich.
panino'teca, che *sf* sandwich bar.
'panna *sf* (*CUC*) cream; (*AUT*) = **panne**; **~ di cucina** cooking cream; **~ montata** whipped cream.
'panne [pan] *sf inv* (*AUT*) breakdown; **essere in ~** to have broken down.

pan'nello *sm* panel; ~ **di controllo** control panel; ~ **solare** solar panel.

'panno *sm* cloth; ~**i** *smpl* (*abiti*) clothes; **mettiti nei miei** ~**i** (*fig*) put yourself in my shoes.

pan'nocchia [pan'nɔkkja] *sf* (*di mais etc*) ear.

panno'lino *sm* (*per bambini*) nappy (*BRIT*), diaper (*US*).

pano'rama, i *sm* panorama.

pano'ramico, a, ci, che *ag* panoramic; **strada** ~**a** scenic route.

pantacol'lant *smpl* leggings.

panta'loni *smpl* trousers (*BRIT*), pants (*US*), pair *sg* of trousers *o* pants.

pan'tano *sm* bog.

pan'tera *sf* panther.

'pantheon ['panteon] *sm inv* pantheon.

pan'tofola *sf* slipper.

panto'mimo *sf* pantomime.

pan'zana [pan'tsana] *sf* fib, tall story.

pao'nazzo, a [pao'nattso] *ag* purple.

'papa, i *sm* pope.

papà *sm inv* dad(dy); **figlio di** ~ spoilt young man.

pa'pale *ag* papal.

pa'pato *sm* papacy.

pa'pavero *sm* poppy.

'papero, a *sm/f* (*ZOOL*) gosling ♦ *sf* (*fig*) slip of the tongue, blunder.

papi'llon [papi'jɔ̃] *sm inv* bow tie.

pa'piro *sm* papyrus.

'pappa *sf* baby cereal.

pappa'gallo *sm* parrot; (*fig: uomo*) Romeo.

pappa'gorgia, ge [pappa'gɔrdʒa] *sf* double chin.

pappar'della *sf* (*fig*) rigmarole.

pap'pare *vt* (*fam: anche:* ~**rsi**) to gobble up.

par. *abbr* (= *paragrafo*) par.

'para *sf*: **suole di** ~ crepe soles.

parà *abbr m inv* (= *paracadutista*) para.

pa'rabola *sf* (*MAT*) parabola; (*REL*) parable.

para'bolico, a, ci, che *ag* (*MAT*) parabolic; *vedi anche* **antenna**.

para'brezza [para'breddza] *sm inv* (*AUT*) windscreen (*BRIT*), windshield (*US*).

paracadu'tare *vt*, ~**rsi** *vr* to parachute.

paraca'dute *sm inv* parachute.

paracadu'tismo *sm* parachuting.

paracadu'tista, i, e *sm/f* parachutist; (*MIL*) paratrooper.

para'carro *sm* kerbstone (*BRIT*), curbstone (*US*).

paradi'siaco, a, ci, che *ag* heavenly.

para'diso *sm* paradise; ~ **fiscale** tax haven.

parados'sale *ag* paradoxical.

para'dosso *sm* paradox.

para'fango, ghi *sm* mudguard.

paraf'fina *sf* paraffin, paraffin wax.

parafra'sare *vt* to paraphrase.

pa'rafrasi *sf inv* paraphrase.

para'fulmine *sm* lightning conductor.

pa'raggi [pa'raddʒi] *smpl*: **nei** ~ in the vicinity, in the neighbourhood (*BRIT*) *o* neighborhood (*US*).

parago'nare *vt*: ~ **con/a** to compare with/ to.

para'gone *sm* comparison; (*esempio analogo*) analogy, parallel; **reggere al** ~ to stand comparison.

pa'ragrafo *sm* paragraph.

paraguai'ano, a *ag, sm/f* Paraguayan.

Paragu'ay [para'gwai] *sm*: **il** ~ Paraguay.

pa'ralisi *sf inv* paralysis.

para'litico, a, ci, che *ag, sm/f* paralytic.

paraliz'zare [paralid'dzare] *vt* to paralyze.

parallela'mente *av* in parallel.

paralle'pipedo *sm* parallelepiped.

paralle'lismo *sm* (*MAT*) parallelism; (*fig: corrispondenza*) similarities *pl*.

paral'lelo, a *ag* parallel ♦ *sm* (*GEO*) parallel; (*comparazione*): **fare un** ~ **tra** to draw a parallel between ♦ *sf* parallel (line); ~**e** *sfpl* (*attrezzo ginnico*) parallel bars.

para'lume *sm* lampshade.

para'medico, a, ci, che *ag* paramedical.

para'menti *smpl* (*REL*) vestments.

pa'rametro *sm* parameter.

paramili'tare *ag* paramilitary.

pa'ranco, chi *sm* hoist.

para'noia *sf* paranoia; **andare/mandare in** ~ (*fam*) to freak/be freaked out.

para'noico, a, ci, che *ag, sm/f* paranoid; (*fam: angosciato*) freaked (out).

paranor'male *ag* paranormal.

para'occhi [para'ɔkki] *smpl* blinkers (*BRIT*), blinders (*US*).

para'petto *sm* parapet.

para'piglia [para'piʎʎa] *sm* commotion.

parapsicolo'gia [parapsikolo'dʒia] *sf* parapsychology.

pa'rare *vt* (*addobbare*) to adorn, deck; (*proteggere*) to shield, protect; (*scansare: colpo*) to parry; (*CALCIO*) to save ♦ *vi*: **dove vuole andare a** ~**?** what are you driving at?; ~**rsi** *vr* (*presentarsi*) to appear, present o.s.

parasco'lastico, a, ci, che *ag* (*attività*) extracurricular.

para'sole *sm inv* parasol, sunshade.

paras'sita, i *sm* parasite.

parassi'tario, a *ag* parasitic.

parasta'tale *ag* state-controlled.

paras'tato *sm employees in the state-controlled sector.*

pa'rata *sf* (*SPORT*) save; (*MIL*) review,

parade.

pa'rati *smpl* hangings *pl*; **carta da** ~ wallpaper.

para'tia *sf* (*di nave*) bulkhead.

para'urti *sm inv* (*AUT*) bumper.

para'vento *sm* folding screen; **fare da** ~ **a qn** (*fig*) to shield sb.

par'cella [par'tʃɛlla] *sf* fee.

parcheggi'are [parked'dʒare] *vt* to park.

parcheggia'tore, trice [parkeddʒa'tore] *sm/f* parking attendant.

par'cheggio [par'keddʒo] *sm* parking *no pl*; (*luogo*) car park (*BRIT*), parking lot (*US*); (*singolo posto*) parking space.

par'chimetro [par'kimetro] *sm* parking meter.

'parco, chi *sm* park; (*spazio per deposito*) depot; (*complesso di veicoli*) fleet.

'parco, a, chi, che *ag*: ~ (**in**) (*sobrio*) moderate (in); (*avaro*) sparing (with).

par'cometro *sm* (*AUTO*) (Pay and Display) ticket machine.

pa'recchio, a [pa'rekkjo] *det* quite a lot of; (*tempo*) quite a lot of, a long ♦ *pron* quite a lot, quite a bit; (*tempo*) quite a while, a long time ♦ *av* (*con ag*) quite, rather; (*con vb*) quite a lot, quite a bit; ~**i(e)** *det pl* quite a lot of, several ♦ *pron pl* quite a lot, several.

pareggi'are [pared'dʒare] *vt* to make equal; (*terreno*) to level, make level; (*bilancio, conti*) to balance ♦ *vi* (*SPORT*) to draw.

pa'reggio [pa'reddʒo] *sm* (*ECON*) balance; (*SPORT*) draw.

paren'tado *sm* relatives *pl*, relations *pl*.

pa'rente *sm/f* relative, relation.

paren'tela *sf* (*vincolo di sangue, fig*) relationship; (*insieme dei parenti*) relations *pl*, relatives *pl*.

pa'rentesi *sf* (*segno grafico*) bracket, parenthesis; (*frase incisa*) parenthesis; (*digressione*) parenthesis, digression; **tra** ~ in brackets; (*fig*) incidentally.

pa'rere *sm* (*opinione*) opinion; (*consiglio*) advice, opinion; **a mio** ~ in my opinion ♦ *vi* to seem, appear ♦ *vb impers*: **pare che** it seems *o* appears that, they say that; **mi pare che** it seems to me that; **mi pare di si/no** I think so/don't think so; **fai come ti pare** do as you like; **che ti pare del mio libro?** what do you think of my book?

pa'rete *sf* wall.

'pari *ag inv* (*uguale*) equal, same; (*in giochi*) equal; drawn, tied; (*MAT*) even ♦ *sm inv* (*POL: di Gran Bretagna*) peer ♦ *sm/f inv* peer, equal; **copiato** ~ ~ copied word for word; **siamo** ~ (*fig*) we are quits *o* even; **alla** ~ on the same level; (*BORSA*) at par; **ragazza**

alla ~ au pair (girl); **mettersi alla** ~ **con** to place o.s. on the same level as; **mettersi in** ~ **con** to catch up with; **andare di** ~ **passo con qn** to keep pace with sb.

parifi'care *vt* (*scuola*) to recognize officially.

parifi'cato, a *ag*: **scuola** ~**a** *officially recognized private school*.

Pa'rigi [pa'ridʒi] *sf* Paris.

pari'gino, a [pari'dʒino] *ag, sm/f* Parisian.

pa'riglia [pa'riʎʎa] *sf* pair; **rendere la** ~ to give tit for tat.

parità *sf* parity, equality; (*SPORT*) draw, tie.

pari'tetico, a, ci, che *ag*: **commissione** ~**a** joint committee; **rapporto** ~ equal relationship.

parlamen'tare *ag* parliamentary ♦ *sm/f* ≈ Member of Parliament (*BRIT*), ≈ Congressman/woman (*US*) ♦ *vi* to negotiate, parley.

parla'mento *sm* parliament; *vedi nota nel riquadro*.

---

parlan'tina *sf* (*fam*) talkativeness; **avere una buona** ~ to have the gift of the gab.

par'lare *vi* to speak, talk; (*confidare cose segrete*) to talk ♦ *vt* to speak; ~ (**a qn**) **di** to speak *o* talk (to sb) about; ~ **chiaro** to speak one's mind; ~ **male di** to speak ill of; ~ **del più e del meno** to talk of this and that; **ne ho sentito** ~ I have heard it mentioned; **non parliamone più** let's just forget about it; **i dati parlano** (*fig*) the facts speak for themselves.

par'lata *sf* (*dialetto*) dialect.

parla'tore, 'trice *sm/f* speaker.

parla'torio *sm* (*di carcere etc*) visiting room; (*REL*) parlour (*BRIT*), parlor (*US*).

parlot'tare *vi* to mutter.

parmigi'ano, a [parmi'dʒano] *ag* Parma *cpd*, of (*o* from) Parma ♦ *sm* (*grana*) Parmesan (cheese); **alla** ~**a** (*CUC*) with Parmesan cheese.

paro'dia *sf* parody.

pa'rola *sf* word; (*facoltà*) speech; ~**e** *sfpl* (*chiacchiere*) talk *sg*; **chiedere la** ~ to ask permission to speak; **dare la** ~ **a qn** to call on sb to speak; **dare la propria** ~ **a qn** to give sb one's word; **mantenere la** ~ to keep one's word; **mettere una buona ~ per qn** to put in a good word for sb; **passare dalle ~e ai fatti** to get down to business; **prendere la** ~ to take the floor; **rimanere senza** ~e to be speechless; **rimangiarsi la** ~ to go back on one's word; **non ho ~e per ringraziarla** I don't know how to thank you; **rivolgere la** ~ **a qn** to speak to sb; **non è detta l'ultima** ~ that's not the end of the matter; **è una persona di** ~ he is a man of his word; **in ~e povere** in plain English; ~ **d'onore** word of honour; ~ **d'ordine** (MIL) password; ~**e incrociate** crossword (puzzle) sg.

paro'laccia, ce [paro'lattʃa] sf bad word, swearword.

paros'sismo sm paroxysm.

par'quet [par'kɛ] sm parquet (flooring).

parrò etc vb vedi **parere**.

par'rocchia [par'rɔkkja] sf parish; (chiesa) parish church.

parrocchi'ano, a [parrok'kjano] sm/f parishioner.

'parroco, ci sm parish priest.

par'rucca, che sf wig.

parrucchi'ere, a [parruk'kjɛre] sm/f hairdresser ♦ sm barber.

parruc'cone sm (peg) old fogey.

parsi'monia sf frugality, thrift.

parsimoni'oso, a ag frugal, thrifty.

'parso, a pp di **parere**.

'parte sf part; (lato) side; (quota spettante a ciascuno) share; (direzione) direction; (POL) party; faction; (DIR) party; **a** ~ ag separate ♦ av separately; **scherzi a** ~ joking aside; **a** ~ **ciò** apart from that; **inviare a** ~ (campioni etc) to send under separate cover; **da** ~ (in disparte) to one side, aside; **mettere/prendere da** ~ to put/take aside; **d'altra** ~ on the other hand; **da** ~ **di** (per conto di) on behalf of; **da** ~ **mia** as far as I'm concerned, as for me; **da** ~ **di madre** on his (o her etc) mother's side; **essere dalla** ~ **della ragione** to be in the right; **da** ~ **a** ~ right through; **da qualche** ~ somewhere; **da nessuna** ~ nowhere; **da questa** ~ (in questa direzione) this way; **da ogni** ~ on all sides, everywhere; (moto da luogo) from all sides; **fare** ~ **di qc** to belong to sth; **prendere** ~ **a qc** to take part in sth; **prendere le ~i di qn** to take sb's side; **mettere qn a** ~ **di qc** to inform sb of sth; **costituirsi** ~ **civile contro qn** (DIR) to associate in an action with the public prosecutor against sb; **la** ~ **lesa** (DIR) the injured party; **le ~i in causa** the parties

concerned; ~**i sociali** representatives of workers and employers.

parteci'pante [partetʃi'pante] sm/f: ~ **(a)** (a riunione, dibattito) participant (in); (a gara sportiva) competitor (in); (a concorso) entrant (to).

parteci'pare [partetʃi'pare] vi: ~ **a** to take part in, participate in; (utili etc) to share in; (spese etc) to contribute to; (dolore, successo di qn) to share (in) ♦ vt: ~ **le nozze (a)** to announce one's wedding (to).

partecipazi'one [partetʃipat'tsjone] sf participation; sharing; (ECON) interest; ~ **a banda armata** (DIR) belonging to an armed gang; ~ **di maggioranza/minoranza** controlling/minority interest; ~ **agli utili** profit-sharing; ~**i di nozze** wedding announcement card; **ministro delle P~i statali** minister responsible for companies in which the state has a financial interest.

par'tecipe [par'tetʃipe] ag participating; **essere** ~ **di** to take part in, participate in; (gioia, dolore) to share (in); (consapevole) to be aware of.

parteggi'are [parted'dʒare] vi: ~ **per** to side with, be on the side of.

par'tenza [par'tɛntsa] sf departure; (SPORT) start; **essere in** ~ to be about to leave, be leaving; **passeggeri in** ~ **per** passengers travelling (BRIT) o traveling (US) to; **siamo tornati al punto di** ~ (fig) we are back where we started; **falsa** ~ (anche fig) false start.

parti'cella [parti'tʃɛlla] sf particle.

parti'cipio [parti'tʃipjo] sm participle.

partico'lare ag (specifico) particular; (proprio) personal, private; (speciale) special, particular; (caratteristico) distinctive; (fuori dal comune) peculiar ♦ sm detail, particular; **in** ~ in particular, particularly; **entrare nei ~i** to go into details.

particolareggi'ato, a [partikolared'dʒato] ag (extremely) detailed.

particolarità sf inv (carattere eccezionale) peculiarity; (dettaglio) particularity, detail; (caratteristica) characteristic, feature.

partigi'ano, a [parti'dʒano] ag partisan ♦ sm (fautore) supporter, champion; (MIL) partisan.

par'tire vi to go, leave; (allontanarsi) to go (o drive etc) away o off; (petardo, colpo) to go off; (fig: avere inizio, SPORT) to start; **sono partita da Roma alle 7** I left Rome at 7; **il volo parte da Ciampino** the flight leaves from Ciampino; **a** ~ **da** from; **la**

seconda a ~ **da destra** the second from the right; ~ **in quarta** to drive off at top speed; (*fig*) to be very enthusiastic.

par'tita *sf* (*COMM*) lot, consignment; (*ECON: registrazione*) entry, item; (*CARTE, SPORT: gioco*) game; (: *competizione*) match, game; ~ **di caccia** hunting party; ~ **IVA** VAT account; ~ **semplice/doppia** (*COMM*) single-/double-entry book-keeping.

par'tito *sm* (*POL*) party; (*decisione*) decision, resolution; (*persona da maritare*) match; **per** ~ **preso** on principle; **mettere la testa a** ~ to settle down.

partitocra'zia [partitokrat'tsia] *sf* hijacking of institutions by the party system.

parti'tura *sf* (*MUS*) score.

'**parto** *sm* (*MED*) labour (*BRIT*), labor (*US*); **sala** ~ labo(u)r room; **morire di** ~ to die in childbirth.

partori'ente *sf* woman in labour (*BRIT*) o labor (*US*).

parto'rire *vt* to give birth to; (*fig*) to produce.

par'venza [par'vɛntsa] *sf* semblance.

'**parvi** *etc vb vedi* **parere**.

parzi'ale [par'tsjale] *ag* (*limitato*) partial; (*non obiettivo*) biased, partial.

parzialità [partsjali'ta] *sf*: ~ (**a favore di**) partiality (for), bias (towards); ~ (**contro**) bias (against).

'**pascere** ['paʃʃere] *vi* to graze ♦ *vt* (*brucare*) to graze on; (*far pascolare*) to graze, pasture.

pasci'uto, a [paʃ'ʃuto] *pp di* **pascere** ♦ *ag*: **ben** ~ plump.

pasco'lare *vt, vi* to graze.

'**pascolo** *sm* pasture.

'**Pasqua** *sf* Easter; **isola di** ~ Easter Island.

pas'quale *ag* Easter *cpd*.

pasqu'etta *sf* Easter Monday.

pas'sabile *ag* fairly good, passable.

pas'saggio [pas'saddʒo] *sm* passing *no pl*, passage; (*traversata*) crossing *no pl*, passage; (*luogo, prezzo della traversata, brano di libro etc*) passage; (*su veicolo altrui*) lift (*BRIT*), ride; (*SPORT*) pass; **di** ~ (*persona*) passing through; ~ **pedonale/a livello** pedestrian/level (*BRIT*) o grade (*US*) crossing; ~ **di proprietà** transfer of ownership.

passamane'ria *sf* braid, trimming.

passamon'tagna [passamon'taɲɲa] *sm inv* balaclava.

pas'sante *sm/f* passer-by ♦ *sm* loop.

passa'porto *sm* passport.

pas'sare *vi* (*andare*) to go; (*veicolo, pedone*) to pass (by), go by; (*fare una breve sosta: postino etc*) to come, call; (: *amico: per fare*

una visita) to call o drop in; (*sole, aria, luce*) to get through; (*trascorrere: giorni, tempo*) to pass, go by; (*fig: proposta di legge*) to be passed; (: *dolore*) to pass, go away; (*CARTE*) to pass ♦ *vt* (*attraversare*) to cross; (*trasmettere: messaggio*): ~ **qc a qn** to pass sth on to sb; (*dare*): ~ **qc a qn** to pass sth to sb, give sb sth; (*trascorrere: tempo*) to spend; (*superare: esame*) to pass; (*triturare: verdura*) to strain; (*approvare*) to pass, approve; (*oltrepassare, sorpassare: anche fig*) to go beyond, pass; (*fig: subire*) to go through; ~ **da ... a** to pass from ... to; ~ **di padre in figlio** to be handed down o to pass from father to son; ~ **per** (*anche fig*) to go through; ~ **per stupido/un genio** to be taken for a fool/a genius; ~ **sopra** (*anche fig*) to pass over; ~ **attraverso** (*anche fig*) to go through; ~ **ad altro** to change the subject; (*in una riunione*) to discuss the next item; ~ **in banca/ufficio** to call (in) at the bank/office; ~ **alla storia** to pass into history; ~ **a un esame** to go up (to the next class) after an exam; ~ **di moda** to go out of fashion; ~ **a prendere qc/qn** to call and pick sth/sb up; **le passo il Signor X** (*al telefono*) here is Mr X, I'm putting you through to Mr X; **farsi** ~ **per** to pass o.s. off as, pretend to be; **lasciar** ~ **qn/qc** to let sb/sth through; **col** ~ **degli anni** (*riferito al presente*) as time goes by; (*riferito al passato*) as time passed o went by; **il peggio è passato** the worst is over; **30 anni e passa** well over 30 years ago; ~ **una mano di vernice su qc** to give sth a coat of paint; **passarsela: come te la passi?** how are you getting on o along?

pas'sata *sf*: **dare una** ~ **di vernice a qc** to give sth a coat of paint; **dare una** ~ **al giornale** to have a look at the paper, skim through the paper.

passa'tempo *sm* pastime, hobby.

pas'sato, a *ag* (*scorso*) last; (*finito: gloria, generazioni*) past; (*usanze*) out of date; (*sfiorito*) faded ♦ *sm* past; (*LING*) past (tense); **l'anno** ~ last year; **nel corso degli anni** ~**i** over the past years; **nei tempi** ~**i** in the past; **sono le 8** ~**e** it's past o after 8 o'clock; **è acqua** ~**a** (*fig*) it's over and done with; ~ **prossimo** (*LING*) present perfect; ~ **remoto** (*LING*) past historic; ~ **di verdura** (*CUC*) vegetable purée.

passa'tutto *sm inv*, **passaver'dura** *sm inv* vegetable mill.

passeg'gero, a [passed'dʒero] *ag* passing ♦ *sm/f* passenger.

passeggi'are [passed'dʒare] *vi* to go for a walk; (*in veicolo*) to go for a drive.

passeggi'ata [passed'dʒata] *sf* walk; drive; (*luogo*) promenade; **fare una ~** to go for a walk (*o* drive).

passeg'gino [passed'dʒino] *sm* pushchair (*BRIT*), stroller (*US*).

pas'seggio [pas'seddʒo] *sm* walk, stroll; (*luogo*) promenade; **andare a ~** to go for a walk *o* a stroll.

passe'rella *sf* footbridge; (*di nave, aereo*) gangway; (*pedana*) catwalk.

'passero *sm* sparrow.

pas'sibile *ag*: **~ di** liable to.

passio'nale *ag* (*temperamento*) passionate; **delitto ~** crime of passion.

passi'one *sf* passion.

passività *sf* (*qualità*) passivity, passiveness; (*COMM*) liability.

pas'sivo, a *ag* passive ♦ *sm* (*LING*) passive; (*ECON*) debit; (: *complesso dei debiti*) liabilities *pl*.

'passo *sm* step; (*andatura*) pace; (*rumore*) (foot)step; (*orma*) footprint; (*passaggio, fig: brano*) passage; (*valico*) pass; **a ~ d'uomo** at walking pace; (*AUT*) dead slow; **~ (a) ~** step by step; **fare due** *o* **quattro ~i** to go for a walk *o* a stroll; **andare al ~ coi tempi** to keep up with the times; **di questo ~** (*fig*) at this rate; **fare i primi ~i** (*anche fig*) to take one's first steps; **fare il gran ~** (*fig*) to take the plunge; **fare un ~ falso** (*fig*) to make the wrong move; **tornare sui propri ~i** to retrace one's steps; "**~ carraio**" "vehicle entrance — keep clear".

'pasta *sf* (*CUC*) dough; (: *impasto per dolce*) pastry; (: *anche*: **~ alimentare**) pasta; (*massa molle di materia*) paste; (*fig: indole*) nature; **~e** *sfpl* (*pasticcini*) pastries; **~ in brodo** noodle soup; **~ sfoglia** puff pastry *o* paste (*US*).

pastasci'utta [pastaʃ'ʃutta] *sf* pasta.

pasteggi'are [pasted'dʒare] *vi*: **~ a vino/champagne** to have wine/champagne with one's meal.

pas'tella *sf* batter.

pas'tello *sm* pastel.

pas'tetta *sf* (*CUC*) = **pastella**.

pas'ticca, che *sf* = **pastiglia**.

pasticce'ria [pastittʃe'ria] *sf* (*pasticcini*) pastries *pl*, cakes *pl*; (*negozio*) cake shop; (*arte*) confectionery.

pasticci'are [pastit'tʃare] *vt* to mess up, make a mess of ♦ *vi* to make a mess.

pasticci'ere, a [pastit'tʃere] *sm/f* pastrycook; confectioner.

pastic'cino [pastit'tʃino] *sm* petit four.

pas'ticcio [pas'tittʃo] *sm* (*CUC*) pie; (*lavoro disordinato, imbroglio*) mess; **trovarsi nei**

~i to get into trouble.

pasti'ficio [pasti'fitʃo] *sm* pasta factory.

pas'tiglia [pas'tiʎʎa] *sf* pastille, lozenge.

pas'tina *sf* small pasta shapes used in soup.

pasti'naca, che *sf* parsnip.

'pasto *sm* meal; **vino da ~** table wine.

pas'toia *sf* (*fig*): **~ burocratica** red tape.

pas'tone *sm* (*per animali*) mash; (*peg*) overcooked stodge.

pasto'rale *ag* pastoral.

pas'tore *sm* shepherd; (*REL*) pastor, minister; (*anche*: **cane ~**) sheepdog; **~ scozzese** (*ZOOL*) collie; **~ tedesco** (*ZOOL*) Alsatian (dog) (*BRIT*), German shepherd (dog).

pasto'rizia [pasto'rittsja] *sf* sheep-rearing, sheep farming.

pastoriz'zare [pastorid'dzare] *vt* to pasteurize.

pas'toso, a *ag* doughy; pasty; (*fig: voce, colore*) mellow, soft.

pas'trano *sm* greatcoat.

pa'tacca, che *sf* (*distintivo*) medal, decoration; (*fig: macchia*) grease spot, grease mark; (: *articolo scadente*) bit of rubbish.

pa'tata *sf* potato; **~e fritte** chips (*BRIT*), French fries.

pata'tine *sfpl* (potato) crisps (*BRIT*) *o* chips (*US*).

pata'trac *sm* (*crollo: anche fig*) crash.

pâté [pa'te] *sm inv* pâté; **~ di fegato d'oca** pâté de foie gras.

pa'tella *sf* (*ZOOL*) limpet.

pa'tema, i *sm* anxiety, worry.

paten'tato, a *ag* (*munito di patente*) licensed, certified; (*fig scherzoso: qualificato*) utter, thorough.

pa'tente *sf* licence (*BRIT*), license (*US*); (*anche*: **~ di guida**) driving licence (*BRIT*), driver's license (*US*); **~ a punti** *driving licence with penalty points*.

paten'tino *sm* temporary licence (*BRIT*) *o* license (*US*).

paterna'lismo *sm* paternalism.

paterna'lista *sm* paternalist.

paterna'listico, a, ci, che *ag* paternalistic.

paternità *sf* paternity, fatherhood.

pa'terno, a *ag* (*affetto, consigli*) fatherly; (*casa, autorità*) paternal.

pa'tetico, a, ci, che *ag* pathetic; (*commovente*) moving, touching.

'pathos ['patos] *sm* pathos.

pa'tibolo *sm* gallows *sg*, scaffold.

pati'mento *sm* suffering.

'patina *sf* (*su rame etc*) patina; (*sulla lingua*)

fur, coating.

pa'tire *vt*, *vi* to suffer.

pa'tito, a *sm/f* enthusiast, fan, lover.

patolo'gia [patolo'dʒia] *sf* pathology.

pato'logico, a, ci, che [pato'lɔdʒiko] *ag* pathological.

pa'tologo, a, gi, ghe *sm/f* pathologist.

'patria *sf* homeland; **amor di ~** patriotism.

patri'arca, chi *sm* patriarch.

pa'trigno [pa'triɲɲo] *sm* stepfather.

patrimoni'ale *ag* (*rendita*) from property ♦ *sf* (*anche*: **imposta ~**) property tax.

patri'monio *sm* estate, property; (*fig*) heritage; **mi è costato un ~** (*fig*) it cost me a fortune, I paid a fortune for it; **~ spirituale/culturale** spiritual/cultural heritage; **~ ereditario** (*fig*) hereditary characteristics *pl*; **~ pubblico** public property.

'patrio, a, ii, ie *ag* (*di patria*) native *cpd*, of one's country; (*DIR*): **~a potestà** parental authority; **amor ~** love of one's country.

patri'ota, i, e *sm/f* patriot.

patri'ottico, a, ci, che *ag* patriotic.

patriot'tismo *sm* patriotism.

patroci'nare [patrotʃi'nare] *vt* (*DIR*: *difendere*) to defend; (*sostenere*) to sponsor, support.

patro'cinio [patro'tʃinjo] *sm* defence (*BRIT*), defense (*US*); support, sponsorship.

patro'nato *sm* patronage; (*istituzione benefica*) charitable institution *o* society.

pa'trono *sm* (*REL*) patron saint; (*socio di patronato*) patron; (*DIR*) counsel.

'patta *sf* flap; (*dei pantaloni*) fly.

patteggia'mento [patteddʒa'mento] *sm* (*DIR*) plea bargaining.

patteggi'are [patted'dʒare] *vt*, *vi* to negotiate.

patti'naggio [patti'naddʒo] *sm* skating.

patti'nare *vi* to skate; **~ sul ghiaccio** to ice-skate.

pattina'tore, 'trice *sm/f* skater.

'pattino *sm* skate; (*di slitta*) runner; (*AER*) skid; (*TECN*) sliding block; **~i (da ghiaccio)** (ice) skates; **~i in linea** rollerblades; **~i a rotelle** roller skates.

pat'tino *sm* (*barca*) kind of pedalo with oars.

pat'tista, i, e *ag* (*POL*) of Patto per l'Italia ♦ *sm/f* (*POL*) member (*o* supporter) of Patto per l'Italia.

'patto *sm* (*accordo*) pact, agreement; (*condizione*) term, condition; **a ~ che** on condition that; **a nessun ~** under no circumstances; **venire** *o* **scendere a ~i (con)** to come to an agreement (with); **P~ per l'Italia** (*POL*) *centrist party*.

pat'tuglia [pat'tuʎʎa] *sf* (*MIL*) patrol.

pattugli'are [pattuʎ'ʎare] *vt* to patrol.

pattu'ire *vt* to reach an agreement on.

pattumi'era *sf* (dust)bin (*BRIT*), ashcan (*US*).

pa'ura *sf* fear; **aver ~ di/di fare/che** to be frightened *o* afraid of/of doing/that; **far ~ a** to frighten; **per ~ di/che** for fear of/that; **ho ~ di sì/no** I am afraid so/not.

pau'roso, a *ag* (*che fa paura*) frightening; (*che ha paura*) fearful, timorous.

'pausa *sf* (*sosta*) break; (*nel parlare, MUS*) pause.

paven'tato, a *ag* much-feared.

pa'vese *ag* of (*o* from) Pavia.

'pavido, a *ag* (*letterario*) fearful.

pavimen'tare *vt* (*stanza*) to floor; (*strada*) to pave.

pavimentazi'one [pavimentat'tsjone] *sf* flooring, paving.

pavi'mento *sm* floor.

pa'vone *sm* peacock.

pavoneggi'arsi [pavoned'dʒarsi] *vr* to strut about, show off.

pazien'tare [pattsjen'tare] *vi* to be patient.

pazi'ente [pat'tsjɛnte] *ag*, *sm/f* patient.

pazi'enza [pat'tsjɛntsa] *sf* patience; **perdere la ~** to lose (one's) patience.

pazza'mente [pattsa'mente] *av* madly; **essere ~ innamorato** to be madly in love.

paz'zesco, a, schi, sche [pat'tsesko] *ag* mad, crazy.

paz'zia [pat'tsia] *sf* (*MED*) madness, insanity; (*di azione, decisione*) madness, folly; **è stata una ~!** it was sheer madness!

'pazzo, a ['pattso] *ag* (*MED*) mad, insane; (*strano*) wild, mad ♦ *sm/f* madman/woman; **~ di** (*gioia, amore etc*) mad *o* crazy with; **~ per qc/qn** mad *o* crazy about sth/sb; **essere ~ da legare** to be raving mad *o* a raving lunatic.

PC *sigla = Piacenza* ♦ [pi'tʃi] *sigla m inv* (= *personal computer*) PC.

p.c. *abbr* = *per condoglianze; per conoscenza*.

p.c.c. *abbr* (= *per copia conforme*) cc.

P.C.I. *sigla m* (= *Partito Comunista Italiano*) *former political party*.

PCUS *sigla m* = *Partito Comunista dell'Unione Sovietica*.

PD *sigla = Padova*.

P.D. *abbr = partita doppia*.

PE *sigla = Pescara*.

'pecca, che *sf* defect, flaw, fault.

peccami'noso, a *ag* sinful.

pec'care *vi* to sin; (*fig*) to err.

pec'cato *sm* sin; **è un ~ che** it's a pity that; **che ~!** what a shame *o* pity!; **un ~ di**

gioventù (*fig*) a youthful error *o* indiscretion.

pecca'tore, **'trice** *sm/f* sinner.

pecche'rò *etc* [pekke'rɔ] *vb vedi* **peccare**.

'pece ['petʃe] *sf* pitch.

pechi'nese [peki'nese] *ag, sm/f* Pekin(g)ese (*inv*) ♦ *sm* (*anche:* **cane** ~) Pekin(g)ese *inv*, Peke.

Pe'chino [pe'kino] *sf* Beijing, Peking.

'pecora *sf* sheep; ~ **nera** (*fig*) black sheep.

peco'raio *sm* shepherd.

peco'rella *sf* lamb; **la** ~ **smarrita** the lost sheep; **cielo a** ~**e** (*fig: nuvole*) mackerel sky.

peco'rino *sm* sheep's milk cheese.

pecu'lato *sm* (*DIR*) embezzlement.

peculi'are *ag*: ~ **di** peculiar to.

peculiarità *sf* peculiarity.

pecuni'ario, a *ag* financial, money *cpd*.

pe'daggio [pe'daddʒo] *sm* toll.

pedago'gia [pedago'dʒia] *sf* pedagogy, educational methods *pl*.

peda'gogico, a, ci, che [peda'gɔdʒiko] *ag* pedagogic(al).

peda'gogo, a, ghi, ghe *sm/f* pedagogue.

peda'lare *vi* to pedal; (*andare in bicicletta*) to cycle.

pe'dale *sm* pedal.

pe'dana *sf* footboard; (*SPORT: nel salto*) springboard; (: *nella scherma*) piste.

pe'dante *ag* pedantic ♦ *sm/f* pedant.

pedante'ria *sf* pedantry.

pe'data *sf* (*impronta*) footprint; (*colpo*) kick; **prendere a** ~**e qn/qc** to kick sb/sth.

pede'rasta, i *sm* pederast.

pe'destre *ag* prosaic, pedestrian.

pedi'atra, i, e *sm/f* paediatrician (*BRIT*), pediatrician (*US*).

pedia'tria *sf* paediatrics *sg* (*BRIT*), pediatrics *sg* (*US*).

pedi'atrico, a, ci, che *ag* pediatric.

pedi'cure *sm/f inv* chiropodist (*BRIT*), podiatrist (*US*).

pedigree *sm inv* pedigree.

pedi'luvio *sm* footbath.

pe'dina *sf* (*della dama*) draughtsman (*BRIT*), draftsman (*US*); (*fig*) pawn.

pedi'nare *vt* to shadow, tail.

pe'dofilo, a *ag, sm/f* paedophile.

pedo'nale *ag* pedestrian.

pe'done, a *sm/f* pedestrian ♦ *sm* (*SCACCHI*) pawn.

peeling ['piling] *sm inv* (*COSMESI*) facial scrub.

'peggio ['pɛddʒo] *av, ag inv* worse ♦ *sm o f*: **il** *o* **la** ~ the worst; **cambiare in** ~ to get *o* become worse; **alla** ~ at worst, if the worst comes to the worst; **tirare avanti**

alla meno ~ to get along as best one can; **avere la** ~ to come off worse, get the worst of it.

peggiora'mento [peddʒora'mento] *sm* worsening.

peggio'rare [peddʒo'rare] *vt* to make worse, worsen ♦ *vi* to grow worse, worsen.

peggiora'tivo, a [peddʒora'tivo] *ag* pejorative.

peggi'ore [ped'dʒore] *ag* (*comparativo*) worse; (*superlativo*) worst ♦ *sm/f*: **il(la)** ~ the worst (person); **nel** ~ **dei casi** if the worst comes to the worst.

'pegno ['peɲɲo] *sm* (*DIR*) security, pledge; (*nei giochi di società*) forfeit; (*fig*) pledge, token; **dare in** ~ **qc** to pawn sth; **in** ~ **d'amicizia** as a token of friendship; **banco dei** ~**i** pawnshop.

pelapa'tate *sm inv* potato peeler.

pe'lare *vt* (*spennare*) to pluck; (*spellare*) to skin; (*sbucciare*) to peel; (*fig*) to make pay through the nose; ~**rsi** *vr* to go bald.

pe'lato, a *ag* (*sbucciato*) peeled; (*calvo*) bald; (*pomodori*) ~**i** peeled tomatoes.

pel'lame *sm* skins *pl*, hides *pl*.

'pelle *sf* skin; (*di animale*) skin, hide; (*cuoio*) leather; **essere** ~ **ed ossa** to be skin and bone; **avere la** ~ **d'oca** to have goose pimples *o* goose flesh; **avere i nervi a fior di** ~ to be edgy; **non stare più nella** ~ **dalla gioia** to be beside o.s. with delight; **lasciarci la** ~ to lose one's life; **amici per la** ~ firm *o* close friends.

pellegri'naggio [pellegri'naddʒo] *sm* pilgrimage.

pelle'grino, a *sm/f* pilgrim.

pelle'rossa, pelli'rossa, *pl* **pelli'rosse** *sm/f* Red Indian.

pellette'ria *sf* (*articoli*) leather goods *pl*; (*negozio*) leather goods shop.

pelli'cano *sm* pelican.

pellicce'ria [pellittʃe'ria] *sf* (*negozio*) furrier's (shop); (*quantità di pellicce*) furs *pl*.

pel'liccia, ce [pel'littʃa] *sf* (*mantello di animale*) coat, fur; (*indumento*) fur coat; ~ **ecologica** fake fur.

pellicci'aio [pellit'tʃajo] *sm* furrier.

pel'licola *sf* (*membrana sottile*) film, layer; (*FOT, CINE*) film.

pelli'rossa *sm/f* = **pellerossa**.

'pelo *sm* hair; (*pelame*) coat, hair; (*pelliccia*) fur; (*di tappeto*) pile; (*di liquido*) surface; **per un** ~: **per un** ~ **non ho perduto il treno** I very nearly missed the train; **c'è mancato un** ~ **che affogasse** he narrowly escaped drowning; **cercare il** ~ **nell'uovo**

(*fig*) to pick holes, split hairs; **non aver ~i sulla lingua** (*fig*) to speak one's mind.

pe'loso, a *ag* hairy.

'peltro *sm* pewter.

pe'luche [pə'lyʃ] *sm* plush; **giocattoli di ~** soft toys.

pe'luria *sf* down.

'pelvi *sf inv* pelvis.

'pelvico, a, ci, che *ag* pelvic.

'pena *sf* (*DIR*) sentence; (*punizione*) punishment; (*sofferenza*) sadness *no pl*, sorrow; (*fatica*) trouble *no pl*, effort; (*difficoltà*) difficulty; **far ~** to be pitiful; **mi fai ~** I feel sorry for you; **essere** *o* **stare in ~ (per qc/qn)** to worry *o* be anxious (about sth/sb); **prendersi** *o* **darsi la ~ di fare** to go to the trouble of doing; **vale la ~ farlo** it's worth doing, it's worth it; **non ne vale la ~** it's not worth the effort, it's not worth it; **~ di morte** death sentence; **~ pecuniaria** fine.

pe'nale *ag* penal ♦ *sf* (*anche:* **clausola ~**) penalty clause; **causa ~** criminal trial; **diritto ~** criminal law; **pagare la ~** to pay the penalty.

pena'lista, i, e *sm/f* (*avvocato*) criminal lawyer.

penalità *sf inv* penalty.

penaliz'zare [penalid'dzare] *vt* (*SPORT*) to penalize.

penalizzazi'one [penaliddzat'tsjone] *sf* (*SPORT*) penalty.

pe'nare *vi* (*patire*) to suffer; (*faticare*) to struggle.

pen'dente *ag* hanging; leaning ♦ *sm* (*ciondolo*) pendant; (*orecchino*) drop earring.

pen'denza [pen'dɛntsa] *sf* slope, slant; (*grado d'inclinazione*) gradient; (*ECON*) outstanding account.

'pendere *vi* (*essere appeso*): **~ da** to hang from; (*essere inclinato*) to lean; (*fig: incombere*): **~ su** to hang over.

pen'dice [pen'ditʃe] *sf* (*di monte*) slope.

pen'dio, ii *sm* slope, slant; (*luogo in pendenza*) slope.

'pendola *sf* pendulum clock.

pendo'lare *ag* pendulum *cpd*, pendular ♦ *sm/f* commuter.

pendola'rismo *sm* commuting.

pendo'lino *sm* (*FERR*) high-speed tilting train.

'pendolo *sm* (*peso*) pendulum; (*anche:* **orologio a ~**) pendulum clock.

'pene *sm* penis.

pene'trante *ag* piercing, penetrating.

pene'trare *vi* to come *o* get in ♦ *vt* to penetrate; **~ in** to enter; (*sog: proiettile*) to

penetrate; (: *acqua, aria*) to go *o* come into.

penetrazi'one [penetrat'tsjone] *sf* penetration.

penicil'lina [penitʃil'lina] *sf* penicillin.

peninsu'lare *ag* peninsular; **l'Italia ~** mainland Italy.

pe'nisola *sf* peninsula.

peni'tente *sm/f* penitent.

peni'tenza [peni'tɛntsa] *sf* penitence; (*punizione*) penance.

penitenzi'ario [peniten'tsjarjo] *sm* prison.

'penna *sf* (*di uccello*) feather; (*per scrivere*) pen; **~e** *sfpl* (*CUC*) quills (*type of pasta*); **~ a feltro/stilografica/a sfera** felt-tip/fountain/ballpoint pen.

pen'nacchio [pen'nakkjo] *sm* (*ornamento*) plume.

penna'rello *sm* felt(-tip) pen.

pennel'lare *vi* to paint.

pennel'lata *sf* brushstroke.

pen'nello *sm* brush; (*per dipingere*) (paint)brush; **a ~** (*perfettamente*) to perfection, perfectly; **~ per la barba** shaving brush.

Pen'nini *smpl*: **i ~** the Pennines.

pen'nino *sm* nib.

pen'none *sm* (*NAUT*) yard; (*stendardo*) banner, standard.

pen'nuto *sm* bird.

pe'nombra *sf* half-light, dim light.

pe'noso, a *ag* painful, distressing; (*faticoso*) tiring, laborious.

pen'sare *vi* to think ♦ *vt* to think; (*inventare, escogitare*) to think out; **~ a** to think of; (*amico, vacanze*) to think of *o* about; (*problema*) to think about; **~ di fare qc** to think of doing sth; **~ bene/male di qn** to think well/badly of sb, have a good/bad opinion of sb; **penso di sì** I think so; **penso di no** I don't think so; **a pensarci bene ...** on second thoughts (*BRIT*) *o* thought (*US*) **...**; **non voglio nemmeno pensarci** I don't even want to think about it; **ci penso io** I'll see to *o* take care of it.

pen'sata *sf* (*trovata*) idea, thought.

pensa'tore, 'trice *sm/f* thinker.

pense'rino *sm* (*dono*) little gift; (*pensiero*): **ci farò un ~** I'll think about it.

pensi'ero *sm* thought; (*modo di pensare, dottrina*) thinking *no pl*; (*preoccupazione*) worry, care, trouble; **darsi ~ per qc** to worry about sth; **stare in ~ per qn** to be worried about sb; **un ~ gentile** (*anche fig: dono etc*) a kind thought.

pensie'roso, a *ag* thoughtful.

'pensile *ag* hanging.

pensi'lina *sf* (*in stazione*) platform roof.

pensiona'mento *sm* retirement; **~**

anticipato early retirement.
pensio'nante *sm/f* (*presso una famiglia*)
lodger; (*di albergo*) guest.
pensio'nato, a *sm/f* pensioner ♦ *sm* (*istituto*)
hostel.
pensi'one *sf* (*al prestatore di lavoro*)
pension; (*vitto e alloggio*) board and
lodging; (*albergo*) boarding house; **andare
in** ~ to retire; **mezza** ~ half board; ~
completa full board; ~ **d'invalidità**
disablement pension; ~ **di anzianità** old-
age pension.
pensio'nistico, a, ci, che *ag* pension *cpd*.
pen'soso, a *ag* thoughtful, pensive, lost in
thought.
pen'tagono *sm* pentagon; **il P**~ the
Pentagon.
pentag'ramma, i *sm* (*MUS*) staff, stave.
pentapar'tito *sm* (*POL*) five-party coalition
government.
'pentathlon ['pɛntatlon] *sm* (*SPORT*)
pentathlon.
Pente'coste *sf* Pentecost, Whit Sunday
(*BRIT*).
penti'mento *sm* repentance, contrition.
pen'tirsi *vr*: ~ **di** to repent of;
(*rammaricarsi*) to regret, be sorry for.
penti'tismo *sm confessions from terrorists
and members of organized crime rackets;
vedi nota nel riquadro.*

PENTITISMO

*The practice of **pentitismo** first emerged in
Italy during the 1970s, a period marked by
major terrorist activity. Once arrested, some
members of terrorist groups would collaborate
with the authorities by providing information in
return for a reduced sentence, or indeed for
their own reasons. In recent years it has
become common practice for members of
Mafia organizations to become "pentiti", and
special legislation has had to be introduced to
provide for the sentencing and personal
protection of these informants.*

---

pen'tito, a *sm/f* ≈ supergrass (*BRIT*),
*terrorist/criminal who turns police
informer.*
'pentola *sf* pot; ~ **a pressione** pressure
cooker.
pe'nultimo, a *ag* last but one (*BRIT*), next
to last, penultimate.
pe'nuria *sf* shortage.
penzo'lare [pendzo'lare] *vi* to dangle, hang
loosely.
penzo'loni [pendzo'loni] *av* dangling,
hanging down; **stare** ~ to dangle, hang

down.
pe'pato, a *ag* (*condito con pepe*) peppery,
hot; (*fig: pungente*) sharp.
'pepe *sm* pepper; ~ **macinato/in grani/nero**
ground/whole/black pepper.
pepero'nata *sf stewed peppers, tomatoes
and onions.*
peperon'cino [peperon'tʃino] *sm* chilli
pepper.
pepe'rone *sm*: ~ **(rosso)** red pepper,
capsicum; ~ **(verde)** green pepper,
capsicum; **rosso come un** ~ as red as a
beetroot (*BRIT*), fire-engine red (*US*); ~**i
ripieni** stuffed peppers.
pe'pita *sf* nugget.

═══════════ *PAROLA CHIAVE*

per *prep* **1** (*moto attraverso luogo*) through; **i
ladri sono passati** ~ **la finestra** the thieves
got in (*o* out) through the window; **l'ho
cercato** ~ **tutta la casa** I've searched the
whole house *o* all over the house for it
2 (*moto a luogo*) for, to; **partire** ~ **la
Germania/il mare** to leave for Germany/
the sea; **il treno** ~ **Roma** the Rome train,
the train for *o* to Rome; **proseguire** ~
Londra to go on to London
3 (*stato in luogo*): **seduto/sdraiato** ~ **terra**
sitting/lying on the ground
4 (*tempo*) for; ~ **anni/tanto tempo** for
years/a long time; ~ **tutta l'estate**
throughout the summer, all summer
long; **lo rividi** ~ **Natale** I saw him again at
Christmas; **lo faccio** ~ **lunedì** I'll do it for
Monday
5 (*mezzo, maniera*) by; ~ **lettera/ferrovia/
via aerea** by letter/rail/airmail; **prendere
qn** ~ **un braccio** to take sb by the arm
6 (*causa, scopo*) for; **assente** ~ **malattia**
absent because of *o* through *o* owing to
illness; **ottimo** ~ **il mal di gola** excellent
for sore throats; ~ **abitudine** out of habit,
from habit
7 (*limitazione*) for; **è troppo difficile** ~ **lui**
it's too difficult for him; ~ **quel che mi
riguarda** as far as I'm concerned; ~ **poco
che sia** however little it may be; ~ **questa
volta ti perdono** I'll forgive you this time
8 (*prezzo, misura*) for; (*distributivo*) a, per;
venduto ~ **3 milioni** sold for 3 million; **la
strada continua** ~ **3 km** the street goes on
for 3 km; **15 euro** ~ **persona** 15 euros a *o*
per person; **una** ~ **volta** one at a time;
uno ~ **uno** one by one; **due** ~ **parte** two
either side; **5** ~ **cento** 5 per cent; **3** ~ **4 fa
12** 3 times 4 equals 12; **dividere/moltipli-
care 12** ~ **4** to divide/multiply 12 by 4
9 (*in qualità di*) as; (*al posto di*) for; **avere**

qn ~ **professore** to have sb as a teacher; **ti ho preso ~ Mario** I mistook you for Mario; **dare ~ morto qn** to give sb up for dead; **lo prenderanno ~ pazzo** they'll think he's crazy

10 (*seguito da vb: finale*): ~ **fare qc** (so as) to do sth, in order to do sth; (: *causale*): ~ **aver fatto qc** for having done sth; **studia ~ passare l'esame** he's studying in order to *o* (so as) to pass his exam; **l'hanno punito ~ aver rubato i soldi** he was punished for having stolen the money; **è abbastanza grande ~ andarci da solo** he's big enough to go on his own.

'**pera** *sf* pear.
pe'raltro *av* moreover, what's more.
per'bacco *escl* by Jove!
per'bene *ag inv* respectable, decent ♦ *av* (*con cura*) properly, well.
perbe'nismo *sm* (so-called) respectability.
percentu'ale [pertʃentu'ale] *sf* percentage; (*commissione*) commission.
perce'pire [pertʃe'pire] *vt* (*sentire*) to perceive; (*ricevere*) to receive.
percet'tibile [pertʃet'tibile] *ag* perceptible.
percezi'one [pertʃet'tsjone] *sf* perception.

═══════ *PAROLA CHIAVE*

perché [per'ke] *av* why; ~ **no?** why not?; ~ **non vuoi andarci?** why don't you want to go?; **spiegami ~ l'hai fatto** tell me why you did it
♦ *cong* **1** (*causale*) because; **non posso uscire ~ ho da fare** I can't go out because *o* as I've a lot to do
2 (*finale*) in order that, so that; **te lo do ~ tu lo legga** I'm giving it to you so (that) you can read it
3 (*consecutivo*): **è troppo forte ~ si possa batterlo** he's too strong to be beaten
♦ *sm inv* reason; **il ~ di** the reason for; **non c'è un vero ~** there's no real reason for it.

perciò [per'tʃɔ] *cong* so, for this (*o* that) reason.
per'correre *vt* (*luogo*) to go all over; (: *paese*) to travel up and down, go all over; (*distanza*) to cover.
percor'ribile *ag* (*strada*) which can be followed.
per'corso, a *pp di* **percorrere** ♦ *sm* (*tragitto*) journey; (*tratto*) route.
per'cosso, a *pp di* **percuotere** ♦ *sf* blow.
percu'otere *vt* to hit, strike.
percussi'one *sf* percussion; **strumenti a ~** (*MUS*) percussion instruments.
per'dente *ag* losing ♦ *sm/f* loser.

'**perdere** *vt* to lose; (*lasciarsi sfuggire*) to miss; (*sprecare: tempo, denaro*) to waste; (*mandare in rovina: persona*) to ruin ♦ *vi* to lose; (*serbatoio etc*) to leak; ~**rsi** *vr* (*smarrirsi*) to get lost; (*svanire*) to disappear, vanish; **saper ~** to be a good loser; **lascia ~!** forget it!, never mind!; **non ho niente da ~** (*fig*) I've got nothing to lose; **è un'occasione da non ~** it's a marvellous opportunity; (*affare*) it's a great bargain; **è fatica persa** it's a waste of effort; ~ **al gioco** to lose money gambling; ~ **di vista qn** (*anche fig*) to lose sight of sb; ~**rsi di vista** to lose sight of each other; (*fig*) to lose touch; ~**rsi alla vista** to disappear from sight; ~**rsi in chiacchiere** to waste time talking.
perdifi'ato : a ~ *av* (*correre*) at breathtaking speed; (*gridare*) at the top of one's voice.
perdigi'orno [perdi'dʒorno] *sm/f inv* idler, waster.
'**perdita** *sf* loss; (*spreco*) waste; (*fuoriuscita*) leak; **siamo in ~** (*COMM*) we are running at a loss; **a ~ d'occhio** as far as the eye can see.
perdi'tempo *sm/f inv* waster, idler.
perdizi'one [perdit'tsjone] *sf* (*REL*) perdition, damnation; **luogo di ~** place of ill repute.
perdo'nare *vt* to pardon, forgive; (*scusare*) to excuse, pardon; **per farsi ~** in order to be forgiven; **perdona la domanda ...** if you don't mind my asking ...; **vogliate ~ il (mio) ritardo** my apologies for being late; **un male che non perdona** an incurable disease.
per'dono *sm* forgiveness; (*DIR*) pardon; **chiedere ~ a qn (per)** to ask for sb's forgiveness (for); (*scusarsi*) to apologize to sb (for).
perdu'rare *vi* to go on, last; (*perseverare*) to persist.
perduta'mente *av* desperately, passionately.
per'duto, a *pp di* **perdere** ♦ *ag* (*gen*) lost; **sentirsi** *o* **vedersi ~** (*fig*) to realize the hopelessness of one's position; **una donna ~a** (*fig*) a fallen woman.
peregri'nare *vi* to wander, roam.
pe'renne *ag* eternal, perpetual, perennial; (*BOT*) perennial.
peren'torio, a *ag* peremptory; (*definitivo*) final.
perfetta'mente *av* perfectly; **sai ~ che ...** you know perfectly well that ....
per'fetto, a *ag* perfect ♦ *sm* (*LING*) perfect (tense).

perfeziona'mento [perfettsjona'mento] *sm*:
~ **(di)** improvement (in), perfection (of);
corso di ~ proficiency course.
perfezio'nare [perfettsjo'nare] *vt* to
improve, perfect; **~rsi** *vr* to improve.
perfezi'one [perfet'tsjone] *sf* perfection.
perfezio'nismo [perfettsjo'nizmo] *sm*
perfectionism.
perfezio'nista, i, e [perfettsjo'nista] *smf*
perfectionist.
per'fidia *sf* perfidy.
'perfido, a *ag* perfidious, treacherous.
per'fino *av* even.
perfo'rare *vt* to pierce; (*MED*) to perforate;
(*banda, schede*) to punch; (*trivellare*) to
drill.
perfora'tore, 'trice *sm/f* punch-card
operator ♦ *sm* (*utensile*) punch; (*INFORM*):
~ **di schede** card punch ♦ *sf* (*TECN*) boring
o drilling machine; (*INFORM*) card punch.
perforazi'one [perforat'tsjone] *sf* piercing;
perforation; punching; drilling.
perga'mena *sf* parchment.
'pergola *sf* pergola.
pergo'lato *sm* pergola.
perico'lante *ag* precarious.
pe'ricolo *sm* danger; **essere fuori** ~ to be
out of danger; (*MED*) to be off the danger
list; **mettere in** ~ to endanger, put in
danger.
perico'loso, a *ag* dangerous.
perife'ria *sf* (*anche fig*) periphery; (*di città*)
outskirts *pl*.
peri'ferico, a, ci, che *ag* (*ANAT, INFORM*)
peripheral; (*zona*) outlying.
pe'rifrasi *sf inv* circumlocution.
pe'rimetro *sm* perimeter.
peri'odico, a, ci, che *ag* periodic(al);
(*MAT*) recurring ♦ *sm* periodical.
pe'riodo *sm* period; ~ **contabile**
accounting period; ~ **di prova** trial
period.
peripe'zie [peripet'tsie] *sfpl* ups and downs,
vicissitudes.
'periplo *sm* circumnavigation.
pe'rire *vi* to perish, die.
peris'copio *sm* periscope.
pe'rito, a *ag* expert, skilled ♦ *sm/f* expert;
(*agronomo, navale*) surveyor; **un** ~
chimico a qualified chemist.
perito'nite *sf* peritonitis.
pe'rizia [pe'rittsja] *sf* (*abilità*) ability;
(*giudizio tecnico*) expert opinion; expert's
report; ~ **psichiatrica** psychiatrist's
report.
peri'zoma, i [peri'dʒoma] *sm* G-string.
'perla *sf* pearl.
per'lina *sf* bead.

perli'nato *sm* matchboarding.
perlo'meno *av* (*almeno*) at least.
perlopiù *av* (*quasi sempre*) in most cases,
usually.
perlus'trare *vt* to patrol.
perlustrazi'one [perlustrat'tsjone] *sf* patrol,
reconnaissance; **andare in** ~ to go on
patrol.
perma'loso, a *ag* touchy.
perma'nente *ag* permanent ♦ *sf*
permanent wave, perm.
perma'nenza [perma'nɛntsa] *sf*
permanence; (*soggiorno*) stay; **buona** ~!
enjoy your stay!
perma'nere *vi* to remain.
per'mango, per'masi *etc vb vedi*
permanere.
perme'abile *ag* permeable.
perme'are *vt* to permeate.
per'messo, a *pp di* **permettere** ♦ *sm*
(*autorizzazione*) permission, leave; (*dato a
militare, impiegato*) leave; (*licenza*) licence
(*BRIT*), license (*US*), permit; (*MIL: foglio*)
pass; ~**?, è** ~**?** (*posso entrare?*) may I
come in?; (*posso passare?*) excuse me; ~
di lavoro/pesca work/fishing permit.
per'mettere *vt* to allow, permit; ~ **a qn**
qc/di fare qc to allow sb sth/to do sth; **~rsi**
vr: **~rsi qc/di fare qc** (*concedersi*) to allow
o.s. sth/to do sth; (*avere la possibilità*) to
afford sth/to do sth; **permettete che mi**
presenti let me introduce myself, may I
introduce myself?; **mi sia permesso di**
sottolineare che ... may I take the liberty
of pointing out that ….
per'misi *etc vb vedi* **permettere**.
permis'sivo, a *ag* permissive.
'permuta *sf* (*DIR*) transfer; (*COMM*) trade-
in; **accettare qc in** ~ to take sth as a
trade-in; **valore di** ~ (*di macchina etc*)
trade-in value.
permu'tare *vt* to exchange; (*MAT*) to
permute.
per'nacchia [per'nakkja] *sf* (*fam*): **fare una**
~ to blow a raspberry.
per'nice [per'nitʃe] *sf* partridge.
'perno *sm* pivot.
pernotta'mento *sm* overnight stay.
pernot'tare *vi* to spend the night, stay
overnight.
'pero *sm* pear tree.
però *cong* (*ma*) but; (*tuttavia*) however,
nevertheless.
pero'rare *vt* (*DIR, fig*): ~ **la causa di qn** to
plead sb's case.
perpendico'lare *ag, sf* perpendicular.
perpen'dicolo *sm*: **a** ~ perpendicularly.
perpe'trare *vt* to perpetrate.

perpetu'are *vt* to perpetuate.

per'petuo, a *ag* perpetual.

perplessità *sf inv* perplexity.

per'plesso, a *ag* perplexed, puzzled.

perqui'sire *vt* to search.

perquisizi'one [perkwizit'tsjone] *sf* (police) search; **mandato di** ~ search warrant.

'perse *etc vb vedi* **perdere**.

persecu'tore *sm* persecutor.

persecuzi'one [persekut'tsjone] *sf* persecution.

persegu'ibile *ag* (*DIR*): **essere** ~ **per legge** to be liable to prosecution.

persegu'ire *vt* to pursue; (*DIR*) to prosecute.

persegui'tare *vt* to persecute.

perseve'rante *ag* persevering.

perseve'ranza [perseve'rantsa] *sf* perseverance.

perseve'rare *vi* to persevere.

'persi *etc vb vedi* **perdere**.

'Persia *sf*: **la** ~ Persia.

persi'ano, a *ag*, *sm/f* Persian ♦ *sf* shutter; ~**a avvolgibile** roller blind.

'persico, a, ci, che *ag*: **il golfo P**~ the Persian Gulf; **pesce** ~ perch.

per'sino *av* = **perfino**.

persis'tente *ag* persistent.

persis'tenza [persis'tentsa] *sf* persistence.

per'sistere *vi* to persist; ~ **a fare** to persist in doing.

persis'tito, a *pp di* **persistere**.

'perso, a *pp di* **perdere** ♦ *ag* (*smarrito: anche fig*) lost; (*sprecato*) wasted; **fare qc a tempo** ~ to do sth in one's spare time; ~ **per** ~ I've (*o* we've *etc*) got nothing further to lose.

per'sona *sf* person; (*qualcuno*): **una** ~ someone, somebody, *espressione interrogativa* + anyone *o* anybody; ~**e** *sfpl* people *pl*; **non c'è** ~ **che** ... there's nobody who ..., there isn't anybody who ...; **in** ~, **di** ~ in person; **per interposta** ~ through an intermediary *o* a third party; ~ **giuridica** (*DIR*) legal person.

perso'naggio [perso'naddʒo] *sm* (*persona ragguardevole*) personality, figure; (*tipo*) character, individual; (*LETTERATURA*) character.

perso'nale *ag* personal ♦ *sm* staff, personnel; (*figura fisica*) build ♦ *sf* (*mostra*) one-man (*o* one-woman) exhibition.

personalità *sf inv* personality.

personaliz'zare [personalid'dzare] *vt* (*arredamento, stile*) to personalize; (*adattare*) to customize.

personaliz'zato, a [personalid'dzato] *ag* personalized.

personal'mente *av* personally.

personifi'care *vt* to personify; (*simboleggiare*) to embody.

personificazi'one [personifikat'tsjone] *sf* (*vedi vb*) personification; embodiment.

perspi'cace [perspi'katʃe] *ag* shrewd, discerning.

perspi'cacia [perspi'katʃa] *sf* perspicacity, shrewdness.

persu'adere *vt*: ~ **qn** (**di qc/a fare**) to persuade sb (of sth/to do).

persuasi'one *sf* persuasion.

persua'sivo, a *ag* persuasive.

persu'aso, a *pp di* **persuadere**.

per'tanto *cong* (*quindi*) so, therefore.

'pertica, che *sf* pole.

perti'nace [perti'natʃe] *ag* determined; persistent.

perti'nente *ag*: ~ (**a**) relevant (to), pertinent (to).

perti'nenza [perti'nentsa] *sf* (*attinenza*) pertinence, relevance; (*competenza*): **essere di** ~ **di qn** to be sb's business.

per'tosse *sf* whooping cough.

per'tugio [per'tudʒo] *sm* hole, opening.

pertur'bare *vt* to disrupt; (*persona*) to disturb, perturb.

perturbazi'one [perturbat'tsjone] *sf* disruption; disturbance.

Perù *sm*: **il** ~ Peru.

peru'gino, a [peru'dʒino] *ag* of (*o* from) Perugia.

peruvi'ano, a *ag*, *sm/f* Peruvian.

per'vadere *vt* to pervade.

per'vaso, a *pp di* **pervadere**.

perve'nire *vi*: ~ **a** to reach, arrive at, come to; (*venire in possesso*): **gli pervenne una fortuna** he inherited a fortune; **far** ~ **qc a** to have sth sent to.

perve'nuto, a *pp di* **pervenire**.

perversi'one *sf* perversion.

perversità *sf* perversity.

per'verso, a *ag* perverted.

perver'tire *vt* to pervert.

perver'tito, a *sm/f* pervert.

pervi'cace [pervi'katʃe] *ag* stubborn, obstinate.

pervi'cacia [pervi'katʃa] *sf* stubbornness, obstinacy.

per'vinca, che *sf* periwinkle ♦ *sm inv* (*colore*) periwinkle (blue).

p.es. *abbr* (= *per esempio*) e.g.

'pesa *sf* weighing *no pl*; weighbridge.

pe'sante *ag* heavy; (*fig: noioso*) dull, boring.

pesan'tezza [pesan'tettsa] *sf* (*anche fig*) heaviness; **avere** ~ **di stomaco** to feel bloated.

pesaper'sone *ag inv:* (**bilancia**) ~ (weighing) scales *pl*; (*automatica*) weighing machine.

pe'sare *vt* to weigh ♦ *vi* (*avere un peso*) to weigh; (*essere pesante*) to be heavy; (*fig*) to carry weight; ~ **su** (*fig*) to lie heavy on; to influence; to hang over; **mi pesa sgridarlo** I find it hard to scold him; **tutta la responsabilità pesa su di lui** all the responsibility rests on his shoulders; **è una situazione che mi pesa** it's a difficult situation for me; **il suo parere pesa molto** his opinion counts for a lot; ~ **le parole** to weigh one's words.

'pesca *sf* (*pl* **pesche:** *frutto*) peach; (*il pescare*) fishing; **andare a** ~ to go fishing; ~ **di beneficenza** (*lotteria*) lucky dip; ~ **con la lenza** angling; ~ **subacquea** underwater fishing.

pes'caggio [pes'kaddʒo] *sm* (*NAUT*) draught (*BRIT*), draft (*US*).

pes'care *vt* (*pesce*) to fish for; to catch; (*qc nell'acqua*) to fish out; (*fig: trovare*) to get hold of, find.

pesca'tore *sm* fisherman; (*con lenza*) angler.

'pesce ['peʃʃe] *sm* fish *gen inv*; **P~i** (*dello zodiaco*) Pisces; **essere dei P~i** to be Pisces; **non saper che ~i prendere** (*fig*) not to know which way to turn; ~ **d'aprile!** April Fool! *vedi nota nel riquadro*; ~ **martello** hammerhead; ~ **rosso** goldfish; ~ **spada** swordfish.

IL PESCE D'APRILE

Il pesce d'aprile *is a sort of April Fool's joke, played on 1 April. Originally it took its name from a paper fish which was secretly attached to a person's back but nowadays all sorts of practical jokes are popular.*

---

pesce'cane [peʃʃe'kane] *sm* shark.

pesche'reccio [peske'rettʃo] *sm* fishing boat.

pesche'ria [peske'ria] *sf* fishmonger's (shop) (*BRIT*), fish store (*US*).

pescherò *etc* [peske'rɔ] *vb vedi* **pescare.**

peschi'era [pes'kjɛra] *sf* fishpond.

pesci'vendolo, a [peʃʃi'vendolo] *smf* fishmonger (*BRIT*), fish merchant (*US*).

'pesco, schi *sm* peach tree.

pes'coso, a *ag* teeming with fish.

pe'seta *sf* peseta.

'peso *sm* weight; (*SPORT*) shot; **dar ~ a qc** to attach importance to sth; **essere di ~ a qn** (*fig*) to be a burden to sb; **rubare sul ~** to give short weight; **lo portarono via di ~**

they carried him away bodily; **avere due ~i e due misure** (*fig*) to have double standards; ~ **lordo/netto** gross/net weight; ~ **piuma/mosca/gallo/medio/massimo** (*PUGILATO*) feather/fly/bantam/middle/heavyweight.

pessi'mismo *sm* pessimism.

pessi'mista, i, e *ag* pessimistic ♦ *smf* pessimist.

'pessimo, a *ag* very bad, awful; **di ~a qualità** of very poor quality.

pes'tare *vt* to tread on, trample on; (*sale, pepe*) to grind; (*uva, aglio*) to crush; (*fig: picchiare*): ~ **qn** to beat sb up; ~ **i piedi** to stamp one's feet; ~ **i piedi a qn** (*anche fig*) to tread on sb's toes.

'peste *sf* plague; (*persona*) nuisance, pest.

pes'tello *sm* pestle.

pesti'cida, i [pesti't ʃida] *sm* pesticide.

pes'tifero, a *ag* (*anche fig*) pestilential, pestiferous; (*odore*) noxious.

pesti'lenza [pesti'lɛntsa] *sf* pestilence; (*fetore*) stench.

'pesto, a *ag:* **c'è buio ~** it's pitch dark ♦ *sm* (*CUC*) sauce made with basil, garlic, cheese and oil; **occhio ~** black eye.

'petalo *sm* (*BOT*) petal.

pe'tardo *sm* firecracker, banger (*BRIT*).

petizi'one [petit'tsjone] *sf* petition; **fare una ~ a** to petition.

'peto *sm* (*fam!*) fart (*!*).

petro'dollaro *sm* petrodollar.

petrol'chimica [petrol'kimika] *sf* petrochemical industry.

petroli'era *sf* (*nave*) oil tanker.

petroli'ere *sm* (*industriale*) oilman; (*tecnico*) worker in the oil industry.

petroli'ero, a *ag* oil *cpd*.

petro'lifero, a *ag* oil *cpd*.

pe'trolio *sm* oil, petroleum; (*per lampada, fornello*) paraffin (*BRIT*), kerosene (*US*); **lume a** ~ oil *o* paraffin *o* kerosene lamp; ~ **grezzo** crude oil.

pettego'lare *vi* to gossip.

pettego'lezzo [pettego'leddzo] *sm* gossip *no pl*; **fare ~i** to gossip.

pet'tegolo, a *ag* gossipy ♦ *smf* gossip.

petti'nare *vt* to comb (the hair of); ~**rsi** *vr* to comb one's hair.

pettina'tura *sf* (*acconciatura*) hairstyle.

'pettine *sm* comb; (*ZOOL*) scallop.

petti'rosso *sm* robin.

'petto *sm* chest; (*seno*) breast, bust; (*CUC: di carne bovina*) brisket; (: *di pollo etc*) breast; **prendere qn/qc di ~** to face up to sb/sth; **a doppio ~** (*abito*) double-breasted.

petto'rina *sf* (*di grembiule*) bib.

petto'ruto, a _ag_ broad-chested; full-breasted.

petu'lante _ag_ insolent.

pe'tunia _sf_ petunia.

'pezza ['pɛttsa] _sf_ piece of cloth; (_toppa_) patch; (_cencio_) rag, cloth; (_AMM_): ~ **d'appoggio** _o_ **giustificativa** voucher; **trattare qn come una ~ da piedi** to treat sb like a doormat.

pez'zato, a [pet'tsato] _ag_ piebald.

pez'zente [pet'tsɛnte] _sm/f_ beggar.

'pezzo ['pɛttso] _sm_ (_gen_) piece; (_brandello, frammento_) piece, bit; (_di macchina, arnese etc_) part; (_STAMPA_) article; (_di tempo_): **aspettare un ~** to wait quite a while _o_ some time; **andare a ~i** to break into pieces; **essere a ~i** (_oggetto_) to be in pieces _o_ bits; (_fig: persona_) to be shattered; **un bel ~ d'uomo** a fine figure of a man; **abito a due ~i** two-piece suit; **essere tutto d'un ~** (_fig_) to be a man (_o_ woman) of integrity; **~ di cronaca** (_STAMPA_) report; **~ grosso** (_fig_) bigwig; **~ di ricambio** spare part.

PG _sigla_ = _Perugia_.

P.G. _abbr_ = **procuratore generale**.

pH [pi'akka] _sm inv_ (_CHIM_) pH.

PI _sigla_ = _Pisa_.

P.I. _abbr_ = **Pubblica Istruzione**.

pi'accio _etc_ ['pjattʃo] _vb vedi_ **piacere**.

pia'cente [pja'tʃɛnte] _ag_ attractive, pleasant.

pia'cere [pja'tʃere] _vi_ to please; ♦ _sm_ pleasure; (_favore_) favour (_BRIT_), favor (_US_); **una ragazza che piace** (_piacevole_) a likeable girl; (_attraente_) an attractive girl; **~ a: mi piace** I like it; **quei ragazzi non mi piacciono** I don't like those boys; **gli piacerebbe andare al cinema** he would like to go to the cinema; **il suo discorso è piaciuto molto** his speech was well received; **"~!"** (_nelle presentazioni_) "pleased to meet you!"; **con ~** certainly, with pleasure; **per ~** please; **fare un ~ a qn** to do sb a favour; **mi fa ~ per lui** I am pleased for him; **mi farebbe ~ rivederlo** I would like to see him again.

pia'cevole [pja'tʃevole] _ag_ pleasant, agreeable.

piaci'mento [pjatʃi'mento] _sm_: **a ~** (_a volontà_) as much as one likes, at will; **lo farà a suo ~** he'll do it when it suits him.

piaci'uto, a [pja'tʃuto] _pp di_ **piacere**.

pi'acqui _etc vb vedi_ **piacere**.

pi'aga, ghe _sf_ (_lesione_) sore; (_ferita: anche fig_) wound; (_fig: flagello_) scourge, curse; (: _persona_) pest, nuisance.

piagnis'teo [pjaɲɲis'tɛo] _sm_ whining, whimpering.

piagnuco'lare [pjaɲɲuko'lare] _vi_ to whimper.

piagnuco'lio, ii [pjaɲɲuko'lio] _sm_ whimpering.

piagnuco'loso, a [pjaɲɲuko'loso] _ag_ whiny, whimpering, moaning.

pi'alla _sf_ (_arnese_) plane.

pial'lare _vt_ to plane.

pialla'trice [pjalla'tritʃe] _sf_ planing machine.

pi'ana _sf_ stretch of level ground; (_più esteso_) plain.

pianeggi'ante [pjaned'dʒante] _ag_ flat, level.

piane'rottolo _sm_ landing.

pia'neta _sm_ (_ASTR_) planet.

pi'angere ['pjandʒere] _vi_ to cry, weep; (_occhi_) to water ♦ _vt_ to cry, weep; (_lamentare_) to bewail, lament; **~ la morte di qn** to mourn sb's death.

pianifi'care _vt_ to plan.

pianificazi'one [pjanifikat'tsjone] _sf_ (_ECON_) planning; **~ aziendale** corporate planning.

pia'nista, i, e _sm/f_ pianist.

pi'ano, a _ag_ (_piatto_) flat, level; (_MAT_) plane; (_facile_) straightforward, simple; (_chiaro_) clear, plain ♦ _av_ (_adagio_) slowly; (_a bassa voce_) softly; (_con cautela_) carefully ♦ _sm_ (_MAT_) plane; (_GEO_) plain; (_livello_) level, plane; (_di edificio_) floor; (_programma_) plan; (_MUS_) piano; **pian ~** very slowly; (_poco a poco_) little by little; **una casa di 3 ~i** a 3-storey (_BRIT_) _o_ 3-storied (_US_) house; **al ~ di sopra/di sotto** on the floor above/below; **all'ultimo ~** on the top floor; **al ~ terra** on the ground floor; **in primo/secondo ~** (_FOT, CINE etc_) in the foreground/background; **fare un primo ~** (_FOT, CINE_) to take a close-up; **di primo ~** (_fig_) prominent, high-ranking; **un fattore di secondo ~** a secondary _o_ minor factor; **passare in secondo ~** to become less important; **mettere tutto sullo stesso ~** to lump everything together, give equal importance to everything; **tutto secondo i ~i** all according to plan; **~ di lavoro** (_superficie_) worktop; (_programma_) work plan; **~ regolatore** (_URBANISTICA_) town-planning scheme; **~ stradale** road surface.

piano'forte _sm_ piano, pianoforte.

piano'terra _sm inv_ = **piano terra**.

pi'ansi _etc vb vedi_ **piangere**.

pi'anta _sf_ (_BOT_) plant; (_ANAT: anche_: **~ del piede**) sole (of the foot); (_grafico_) plan; (_cartina topografica_) map; **ufficio a ~ aperta** open-plan office; **in ~ stabile** on the permanent staff; ~ **stradale** street map, street plan.

piantagi'one [pjanta'dʒone] *sf* plantation.

pianta'grane *sm/f inv* troublemaker.

pian'tare *vt* to plant; (*conficcare*) to drive *o* hammer in; (*tenda*) to put up, pitch; (*fig: lasciare*) to leave, desert; ~**rsi** *vr*: ~**rsi davanti a qn** to plant o.s. in front of sb; ~ **qn in asso** to leave sb in the lurch; ~ **grane** (*fig*) to cause trouble; **piantala!** (*fam*) cut it out!

pian'tato, a *ag*: **ben** ~ (*persona*) well-built.

pianta'tore *sm* planter.

pianter'reno *sm* ground floor.

pi'anto, a *pp di* **piangere** ♦ *sm* tears *pl*, crying.

pianto'nare *vt* to guard, watch over.

pian'tone *sm* (*vigilante*) sentry, guard; (*soldato*) orderly; (*AUT*) steering column.

pia'nura *sf* plain.

pi'astra *sf* plate; (*di pietra*) slab; (*di fornello*) hotplate; **panino alla** ~ ≈ toasted sandwich; ~ **di registrazione** tape deck.

pias'trella *sf* tile.

piastrel'lare *vt* to tile.

pias'trina *sf* (*ANAT*) platelet; (*MIL*) identity disc (*BRIT*) *o* tag (*US*).

piatta'forma *sf* (*anche fig*) platform; ~ **continentale** (*GEO*) continental shelf; ~ **girevole** (*TECN*) turntable; ~ **di lancio** (*MIL*) launching pad *o* platform; ~ **rivendicativa** *document prepared by the unions in an industry, setting out their claims.*

piat'tello *sm* clay pigeon; **tiro al** ~ clay-pigeon shooting (*BRIT*), trapshooting.

piat'tino *sm* (*di tazza*) saucer.

pi'atto, a *ag* flat; (*fig: scialbo*) dull ♦ *sm* (*recipiente, vivanda*) dish; (*portata*) course; (*parte piana*) flat (part); ~**i** *smpl* (*MUS*) cymbals; **un** ~ **di minestra** a plate of soup; ~ **fondo** soup dish; ~ **forte** main course; ~ **del giorno** dish of the day, plat du jour; ~ **dei giradischi** turntable; ~**i già pronti** (*CUC*) ready-cooked dishes.

pi'azza ['pjattsa] *sf* square; (*COMM*) market; (*letto, lenzuolo*): **a una** ~ single; **a due** ~**e** double; **far** ~ **pulita** to make a clean sweep; **mettere in** ~ (*fig: rendere pubblico*) to make public; **scendere in** ~ (*fig*) to take to the streets, demonstrate; ~ **d'armi** (*MIL*) parade ground.

piazza'forte [pjattsa'forte], *pl* **piazze'forti** *sf* (*MIL*) stronghold.

piaz'zale [pjat'tsale] *sm* (large) square.

piazza'mento [pjattsa'mento] *sm* (*SPORT*) place, placing.

piaz'zare [pjat'tsare] *vt* to place; (*COMM*) to market, sell; ~**rsi** *vr* (*SPORT*) to be placed;

~**rsi bene** to finish with the leaders *o* in a good position.

piaz'zista, i [pjat'tsista] *sm* (*COMM*) commercial traveller.

piaz'zola [pjat'tsɔla] *sf* (*AUT*) lay-by (*BRIT*), (roadside) stopping place; (*di tenda*) pitch.

'picca, che *sf* pike; ~**che** *sfpl* (*CARTE*) spades; **rispondere** ~**che a qn** (*fig*) to give sb a flat refusal.

pic'cante *ag* hot, pungent; (*fig*) racy.

pic'carsi *vr*: ~ **di fare** to pride o.s. on one's ability to do; ~ **per qc** to take offence (*BRIT*) *o* offense (*US*) at sth.

picchet'taggio [pikket'taddʒo] *sm* picketing.

picchet'tare [pikket'tare] *vt* to picket.

pic'chetto [pik'ketto] *sm* (*MIL, di scioperanti*) picket.

picchi'are [pik'kjare] *vt* (*persona: colpire*) to hit, strike; (: *prendere a botte*) to beat (up); (*battere*) to beat; (*sbattere*) to bang ♦ *vi* (*bussare*) to knock; (: *con forza*) to bang; (*colpire*) to hit, strike; (*sole*) to beat down.

picchi'ata [pik'kjata] *sf* knock; bang; blow; (*percosse*) beating, thrashing; (*AER*) dive; **scendere in** ~ to (nose-)dive.

picchiet'tare [pikkjet'tare] *vt* (*punteggiare*) to spot, dot; (*colpire*) to tap.

'picchio ['pikkjo] *sm* woodpecker.

pic'cino, a [pit'tʃino] *ag* tiny, very small.

picci'olo [pit'tʃɔlo] *sm* (*BOT*) stalk.

piccio'naia [pittʃo'naja] *sf* pigeon-loft; (*TEAT*): **la** ~ the gods *sg* (*BRIT*), the gallery.

picci'one [pit'tʃone] *sm* pigeon; **pigliare due** ~**i con una fava** (*fig*) to kill two birds with one stone.

'picco, chi *sm* peak; **a** ~ vertically; **colare a** ~ (*NAUT, fig*) to sink.

picco'lezza [pikko'lettsa] *sf* (*dimensione*) smallness; (*fig: grettezza*) meanness, pettiness; (: *inezia*) trifle.

'piccolo, a *ag* small; (*oggetto, mano, di età: bambino*) small, little (*dav sostantivo*); (*di breve durata: viaggio*) short; (*fig*) mean, petty ♦ *sm/f* child, little one ♦ *sm*: **nel mio** ~ in my own small way; ~**i** *smpl* (*di animale*) young *pl*; **in** ~ in miniature; **la** ~**a borghesia** the lower middle classes; (*peg*) the petty bourgeoisie.

pic'cone *sm* pick(-axe).

pic'cozza [pik'kɔttsa] *sf* ice-axe.

pic'nic *sm inv* picnic; **fare un** ~ to have a picnic.

pidies'sino, a *ag* (*POL*) of P.D.S. ♦ *sm/f* member (*o* supporter) of P.D.S.

pi'docchio [pi'dɔkkjo] *sm* louse.

pidocchi'oso, a [pidok'kjoso] *ag* (*infestato*)

lousy; (fig: taccagno) mean, stingy, tight.
pidu'ista, i, e ag P2 cpd (masonic lodge) ♦ sm
member of the P2 masonic lodge.
piè sm inv: **a ogni ~ sospinto** (fig) at every
step; **saltare a ~ pari** (omettere) to skip; **a
~ di pagina** at the foot of the page; **note a
~ di pagina** footnotes.
pi'ede sm foot; (di mobile) leg; **in ~i**
standing; **a ~i** on foot; **a ~i nudi** barefoot;
su due ~i (fig) at once; **mettere qc in ~i**
(azienda etc) to set sth up; **prendere ~** (fig)
to gain ground, catch on; **puntare i ~i** (fig)
to dig one's heels in; **sentirsi mancare la
terra sotto i ~i** to feel lost; **non sta in ~i**
(persona) he can't stand; (fig: scusa etc) it
doesn't hold water; **tenere in ~i** (persona)
to keep on his (o her) feet; (fig: ditta etc) to
keep going; **a ~ libero** (DIR) on bail; **sul ~
di guerra** (MIL) ready for action; **~ di
porco** crowbar.
piedipi'atti sm inv (peg: poliziotto) cop.
piedis'tallo, piedes'tallo sm pedestal.
pi'ega, ghe sf (piegatura, GEO) fold; (di
gonna) pleat; (di pantaloni) crease; (grinza)
wrinkle, crease; **prendere una brutta o
cattiva ~** (fig: persona) to get into bad
ways; (: situazione) to take a turn for the
worse; **non fa una ~** (fig: ragionamento)
it's faultless; **non ha fatto una ~** (fig:
persona) he didn't bat an eye(lid) (BRIT) o
an eye(lash) (US).
piega'mento sm folding; bending; **~ sulle
gambe** (GINNASTICA) kneebend.
pie'gare vt to fold; (braccia, gambe, testa) to
bend ♦ vi to bend; **~rsi** vr to bend; (fig):
~rsi (a) to yield (to), submit (to).
piega'tura sf folding no pl; bending no pl;
fold; bend.
pieghe'rò etc [pjege'rɔ] vb vedi **piegare**.
pieghet'tare [pjeget'tare] vt to pleat.
pie'ghevole [pje'gevole] ag pliable,
flexible; (porta) folding; (fig) yielding.
Pie'monte sm: **il ~** Piedmont.
piemon'tese ag, smf Piedmontese.
pi'ena sf vedi **pieno**.
pie'nezza [pje'nettsa] sf fullness.
pi'eno, a ag full; (muro, mattone) solid ♦ sm
(colmo) height, peak; (carico) full load ♦ sf
(di fiume) flood, spate; (gran folla) crowd,
throng; **~ di** full of; **a ~e mani**
abundantly; **a tempo ~** full-time; **a ~i voti**
(eleggere) unanimously; **laurearsi a ~i voti**
to graduate with full marks; **in ~ giorno**
in broad daylight; **in ~ inverno** in the
depths of winter; **in ~a notte** in the
middle of the night; **in ~a stagione** at the
height of the season; **in ~** (completamente:
sbagliare) completely; (colpire, centrare)

bang o right in the middle; **avere ~i
poteri** to have full powers; **nel ~ possesso
delle sue facoltà** in full possession of his
faculties; **fare il ~ (di benzina)** to fill up
(with petrol).
pie'none sm: **c'era il ~ al cinema/al teatro**
the cinema/the theatre was packed.
'piercing ['pirsing] sm: **farsi il ~
all'ombelico** to have one's navel pierced.
pietà sf pity; (REL) piety; **senza ~** (agire)
ruthlessly; (persona) pitiless, ruthless;
avere ~ di (compassione) to pity, feel
sorry for; (misericordia) to have pity o
mercy on; **far ~** to arouse pity; (peg) to be
terrible.
pie'tanza [pje'tantsa] sf dish, course.
pie'toso, a ag (compassionevole) pitying,
compassionate; (che desta pietà) pitiful.
pi'etra sf stone; **mettiamoci una ~ sopra**
(fig) let bygones be bygones; **~ preziosa**
precious stone, gem; **~ dello scandalo**
(fig) cause of scandal.
pie'traia sf (terreno) stony ground.
pietrifi'care vt to petrify; (fig) to transfix,
paralyze.
piet'rina sf (per accendino) flint.
pie'trisco, schi sm crushed stone, road
metal.
pi'eve sf parish church.
'piffero sm (MUS) pipe.
pigi'ama [pi'dʒama] sm pyjamas pl.
'pigia 'pigia ['pidʒa'pidʒa] sm crowd, press.
pigi'are [pi'dʒare] vt to press.
pigia'trice [pidʒa'tritʃe] sf (macchina) wine
press.
pigi'one [pi'dʒone] sf rent.
pigli'are [piʎ'ʎare] vt to take, grab;
(afferrare) to catch.
'piglio ['piʎʎo] sm look, expression.
pig'mento sm pigment.
pig'meo, a smf pygmy.
'pigna ['piɲɲa] sf pine cone.
pignole'ria [piɲɲole'ria] sf fastidiousness,
fussiness.
pi'gnolo, a [piɲ'ɲolo] ag pernickety.
pigno'rare [piɲɲo'rare] vt (DIR) to distrain.
pigo'lare vi to cheep, chirp.
pigo'lio sm cheeping, chirping.
pigra'mente av lazily.
pi'grizia [pi'grittsja] sf laziness.
'pigro, a ag lazy; (fig: ottuso) slow, dull.
PIL sigla m vedi **prodotto interno lordo**.
'pila sf (catasta, di ponte) pile; (ELETTR)
battery; (fam: torcia) torch (BRIT),
flashlight; **a ~, a ~e** battery-operated.
pi'lastro sm pillar.
'pile ['pail] sm inv fleece.
'pillola sf pill; **prendere la ~** (contraccettivo)

to be on the pill; ~ **del giorno dopo** morning-after pill.

pi'lone sm (di ponte) pier; (di linea elettrica) pylon.

pi'lota, i, e sm/f pilot; (AUT) driver ♦ ag inv pilot cpd; ~ **automatico** automatic pilot.

pilo'taggio [pilo'taddʒo] sm: **cabina di** ~ flight deck.

pilo'tare vt to pilot; to drive.

piluc'care vt to nibble at.

pi'mento sm pimento, allspice.

pim'pante ag lively, full of beans.

pinaco'teca, che sf art gallery.

pi'neta sf pinewood.

ping-'pong [pɪŋ'pɔŋ] sm table tennis.

'pingue ag fat, corpulent.

pingu'edine sf corpulence.

pingu'ino sm (ZOOL) penguin.

'pinna sf fin; (di pinguino, spatola di gomma) flipper.

pin'nacolo sm pinnacle.

'pino sm pine (tree).

pi'nolo sm pine kernel.

'pinta sf pint.

'pinza ['pintsa] sf pliers pl; (MED) forceps pl; (ZOOL) pincer.

pinzette [pin'tsette] sfpl tweezers.

'pio, a, 'pii, 'pie ag pious; (opere, istituzione) charitable, charity cpd.

piogge'rella [pjoddʒe'rɛlla] sf drizzle.

pi'oggia, ge ['pjoddʒa] sf rain; (fig: di regali, fiori) shower; (di insulti) hail; **sotto la** ~ in the rain; ~ **acida** acid rain.

pi'olo sm peg; (di scala) rung.

piom'bare vi to fall heavily; (gettarsi con impeto): ~ **su** to fall upon, assail ♦ vt (dente) to fill.

piomba'tura sf (di dente) filling.

piom'bino sm (sigillo) (lead) seal; (del filo a piombo) plummet; (PESCA) sinker.

pi'ombo sm (CHIM) lead; (sigillo) (lead) seal; (proiettile) (lead) shot; **a** ~ (cadere) straight down; (muro etc) plumb; **andare con i piedi di** ~ (fig) to tread carefully; **senza** ~ (benzina) unleaded, lead-free; **anni di** ~ (fig) era of terrorist outrages.

pioni'ere, a sm/f pioneer.

pi'oppo sm poplar.

pio'vano, a ag: **acqua** ~a rainwater.

pi'overe vb impers to rain ♦ vi (fig: scendere dall'alto) to rain down; (: affluire in gran numero): ~ **in** to pour into; **non ci piove sopra** (fig) there's no doubt about it.

pioviggi'nare [pjoviddʒi'nare] vb impers to drizzle.

piovosità sf rainfall.

pio'voso, a ag rainy.

pi'ovra sf octopus.

pi'ovve etc vb vedi **piovere**.

'pipa sf pipe.

pipì sf (fam): **fare** ~ to have a wee (wee).

pipis'trello sm (ZOOL) bat.

pi'ramide sf pyramid.

pi'ranha sm inv piranha.

pi'rata, i sm pirate; ~ **informatico** hacker; ~ **della strada** hit-and-run driver.

Pire'nei smpl: **i** ~ the Pyrenees.

pi'retro sm pyrethrum.

'pirico, a, ci, che ag: **polvere** ~a gunpowder.

pi'rite sf pyrite.

piro'etta sf pirouette.

pi'rofilo, a ag heat-resistant ♦ sf heat-resistant glass; (tegame) heat-resistant dish.

pi'roga, ghe sf dug-out canoe.

pi'romane sm/f arsonist.

pi'roscafo sm steamer, steamship.

'Pisa sf Pisa.

pi'sano, a ag Pisan.

pisci'are [piʃ'ʃare] vi (fam!) to piss (!), pee (!).

pi'scina [piʃ'ʃina] sf (swimming) pool.

pi'sello sm pea.

piso'lino sm nap; **fare un** ~ to have a nap.

'pista sf (traccia) track, trail; (di stadio) track; (di pattinaggio) rink; (da sci) run; (AER) runway; (di circo) ring; ~ **da ballo** dance floor; ~ **ciclabile** cycle lane; ~ **di lancio** launch(ing) pad; ~ **di rullaggio** (AER) taxiway; ~ **di volo** (AER) runway.

pis'tacchio [pis'takkjo] sm pistachio (tree); pistachio (nut).

pis'tillo sm (BOT) pistil.

pis'tola sf pistol, gun; ~ **a spruzzo** spray gun; ~ **a tamburo** revolver.

pis'tone sm piston.

pi'tocco, chi sm skinflint, miser.

pi'tone sm python.

'pittima sf (fig) bore.

pit'tore, 'trice sm/f painter.

pitto'resco, a, schi, sche ag picturesque.

pit'torico, a, ci, che ag of painting, pictorial.

pit'tura sf painting; ~ **fresca** wet paint.

pittu'rare vt to paint.

══════ PAROLA CHIAVE

più av 1 (in maggiore quantità) more; ~ **del solito** more than usual; **in** ~, **di** ~ more; **ne voglio di** ~ I want some more; **ci sono 3 persone in** o **di** ~ there are 3 more o extra people; **costa di** ~ it's more expensive; **una volta di** ~ once more; ~ **o meno** more or less; **né** ~ **né meno** no more, no less; **per di** ~ (inoltre) what's more, moreover; **è sempre ~ difficile** it is getting more and more difficult; **chi ~ chi meno hanno tutti contribuito** everybody made a contribution of some sort; **~ dormo e ~ dormirei** the more I sleep the more I want to sleep

2 (*comparativo*) more; (*se monosillabo, spesso*): + ...**er**; **~ ... di/che** more ... than; **~ intelligente di lui** more intelligent than him; **~ furbo di te** smarter than you; **~ tardi di** ... later than ...; **lavoro ~ di te/di Paola** I work harder than you/than Paola; **è ~ fortunato che bravo** he is lucky rather than skilled; **~ di quanto pensassi** more than I thought; **~ che altro** mainly; **~ che mai** more than ever

3 (*superlativo*) most; (*se monosillabico, spesso*): + ...**est**; **il ~ grande/intelligente** the biggest/most intelligent; **è quello che compro ~ spesso** that's the one I buy most often; **al ~ presto** as soon as possible; **al ~ tardi** at the latest

4 (*negazione*): **non ... ~** no more, no longer; **non ho ~ soldi** I've got no more money, I don't have any more money; **non lavoro ~** I'm no longer working, I don't work any more; **non ce n'è ~** there isn't any left; **non c'è ~ nessuno** there's no one left; **non c'è ~ niente da fare** there's nothing more to be done; **a ~ non posso** (*gridare*) at the top of one's voice; (*correre*) as fast as one can

5 (*MAT*) plus; **4 ~ 5 fa 9** 4 plus 5 equals 9; **~ 5 gradi** 5 degrees above freezing, plus 5; **6 ~** (*a scuola*) just above a pass

♦ *prep* plus; **500.000 ~ le spese** 500,000 plus expenses; **siamo in quattro ~ il nonno** there are four of us, plus grandpa ♦ *ag inv* **1: ~ ... (di)** more ... (than); **~ denaro/tempo** more money/time; **~ persone di quante ci aspettassimo** more people than we expected

2 (*numerosi, diversi*) several; **l'aspettai per ~ giorni** I waited for it for several days ♦ *sm* **1** (*la maggior parte*): **il ~ è fatto** most of it is done; **il ~ delle volte** more often than not, generally; **parlare del ~ e del meno** to talk about this and that

2 (*MAT*) plus (sign)

3: i ~ the majority.

piuccheper'fetto [pjukkeper'fɛtto] *sm* (*LING*) pluperfect, past perfect.

pi'uma *sf* feather; **~e** *sfpl* down *sg*; (*piumaggio*) plumage *sg*, feathers.

piu'maggio [pju'maddʒo] *sm* plumage, feathers *pl*.

piu'mino *sm* (eider)down; (*per letto*) eiderdown; (: *tipo danese*) duvet, continental quilt; (*giacca*) quilted jacket (*with goose-feather padding*); (*per cipria*) powder puff; (*per spolverare*) feather duster.

piut'tosto *av* rather; **~ che** (*anziché*) rather than.

'piva *sf*: **con le ~e nel sacco** (*fig*) empty-handed.

pi'vello, a *sm/f* greenhorn.

'pizza ['pittsa] *sf* (*CUC*) pizza; (*CINE*) reel.

pizze'ria [pittse'ria] *sf place where pizzas are made, sold or eaten.*

pizzi'cagnolo, a [pittsi'kaɲɲolo] *sm/f* specialist grocer.

pizzi'care [pittsi'kare] *vt* (*stringere*) to nip, pinch; (*pungere*) to sting; to bite; (*MUS*) to pluck ♦ *vi* (*prudere*) to itch, be itchy; (*cibo*) to be hot *o* spicy.

pizziche'ria [pittsike'ria] *sf* delicatessen (shop).

'pizzico, chi ['pittsiko] *sm* (*pizzicotto*) pinch, nip; (*piccola quantità*) pinch, dash; (*d'insetto*) sting; bite.

pizzi'cotto [pittsi'kɔtto] *sm* pinch, nip.

'pizzo ['pittso] *sm* (*merletto*) lace; (*barbetta*) goatee beard; (*tangente*) protection money.

pla'care *vt* to placate, soothe; **~rsi** *vr* to calm down.

'placca, che *sf* plate; (*con iscrizione*) plaque; (*anche*: **~ dentaria**) (dental) plaque.

plac'care *vt* to plate; **placcato in oro/ argento** gold-/silver-plated.

pla'centa [pla't ʃɛnta] *sf* placenta.

placidità [platʃidi'ta] *sf* calm, peacefulness.

'placido, a ['platʃido] *ag* placid, calm.

plafoni'era *sf* ceiling light.

plagi'are [pla'dʒare] *vt* (*copiare*) to plagiarize; (*DIR: influenzare*) to coerce.

'plagio ['pladʒo] *sm* plagiarism; (*DIR*) duress.

plaid [plɛd] *sm inv* (travelling) rug (*BRIT*), lap robe (*US*).

pla'nare *vi* (*AER*) to glide.

'plancia, ce ['plantʃa] *sf* (*NAUT*) bridge; (*AUT: cruscotto*) dashboard.

'plancton *sm inv* plankton.

plane'tario, a *ag* planetary ♦ *sm* (*locale*) planetarium.

planis'fero *sm* planisphere.

plan'tare *sm* arch support.

'plasma *sm* plasma.

plas'mare *vt* to mould (*BRIT*), mold (*US*), shape.

'plastico, a, ci, che *ag* plastic ♦ *sm* (*rappresentazione*) relief model;

(*esplosivo*): **bomba al** ~ plastic bomb ♦ *sf*
(*arte*) plastic arts *pl*; (*MED*) plastic
surgery; (*sostanza*) plastic; **in materiale** ~
plastic.
plasti'lina ® *sf* plasticine ®.
'platano *sm* plane tree.
pla'tea *sf* (*TEAT*) stalls *pl* (*BRIT*), orchestra
(*US*).
plate'ale *ag* (*gesto, atteggiamento*)
theatrical.
plateal'mente *av* theatrically.
'platino *sm* platinum.
pla'tonico, a, ci, che *ag* platonic.
plau'dire *vi*: ~ **a** to applaud.
plau'sibile *ag* plausible.
'plauso *sm* (*fig*) approval.
'playback ['plei bæk] *sm*: **cantare in** ~ to
mime.
'playboy ['pleibɔi] *sm inv* playboy.
'playmaker ['pleimeikə*] *sm/f inv* (*SPORT*)
playmaker.
'play-off ['pleiɔf] *sm inv* (*SPORT*) play-off.
ple'baglia [ple'baʎʎa] *sf* (*peg*) rabble, mob.
'plebe *sf* common people.
ple'beo, a *ag* plebeian; (*volgare*) coarse,
common.
plebi'scito [plebiʃ'ʃito] *sm* plebiscite.
ple'nario, a *ag* plenary.
pleni'lunio *sm* full moon.
plenipotenzi'ario, a [plenipoten'tsjarjo] *ag*
plenipotentiary.
'plenum *sm inv* plenum.
'plettro *sm* plectrum.
'pleura *sf* (*ANAT*) pleura.
pleu'rite *sf* pleurisy.
P.L.I. *sigla m* (= *Partito Liberale Italiano*)
former political party.
'plico, chi *sm* (*pacco*) parcel; **in** ~ **a parte**
(*COMM*) under separate cover.
plissé [pli'se] *ag inv* plissé *cpd* ♦ *sm inv* (*anche*:
tessuto ~) plissé.
plisset'tato, a *ag* plissé *cpd*.
plo'tone *sm* (*MIL*) platoon; ~ **d'esecuzione**
firing squad.
'plumbeo, a *ag* leaden.
plu'rale *ag, sm* plural.
plura'lismo *sm* pluralism.
pluralità *sf* plurality; (*maggioranza*)
majority.
plusva'lenza [pluzva'lɛntsa] *sf* capital gain.
plusva'lore *sm* (*ECON*) surplus.
plu'tonio *sm* plutonium.
pluvi'ale *ag* rain *cpd*.
pluvi'ometro *sm* rain gauge.
P.M. *abbr* (*POL*) = **Pubblico Ministero**;
(= *Polizia Militare*) MP (= *Military Police*).
pm *abbr* = **peso molecolare**.
PN *sigla* = **Pordenone**.

pneu'matico, a, ci, che *ag* inflatable;
(*TECN*) pneumatic ♦ *sm* (*AUT*) tyre (*BRIT*),
tire (*US*).
PNL *sigla m vedi* **prodotto nazionale lordo**.
PO *sigla* = **Prato**.
Po *sm*: **il** ~ the Po.
po' *av, sm vedi* **poco**.
P.O. *abbr* = **posta ordinaria**.
po'chezza [po'kettsa] *sf* insufficiency,
shortage; (*fig: meschinità*) meanness,
smallness.

=========================== *PAROLA CHIAVE*

'poco, a, chi, che *ag* (*quantità*) little, not
much; (*numero*) few, not many; ~ **pane/
denaro/spazio** little *o* not much bread/
money/space; **con** ~**a spesa** without
spending much; **a** ~ **prezzo** at a low price,
cheap; ~ **(tempo) fa** a short time ago;
~**che persone/idee** few *o* not many
people/ideas; **è un tipo di** ~**che parole** he's
a man of few words
♦ *av* **1** (*in piccola quantità*) little, not much;
(*numero limitato*) few, not many;
guadagna ~ he doesn't earn much, he
earns little
2 (*con ag, av*) (a) little, not very; **è** ~ **più
vecchia di lui** she's a little *o* slightly older
than him; **è** ~ **socievole** he's not very
sociable; **sta** ~ **bene** he isn't very well
3 (*tempo*): ~ **dopo/prima** shortly
afterwards/before; **il film dura** ~ the film
doesn't last very long; **ci vediamo molto**
~ we don't see each other very often, we
hardly ever see each other
4: **un po'** a little, a bit; **è un po' corto** it's a
little *o* a bit short; **arriverà fra un po'** he'll
arrive shortly *o* in a little while
5: **a dir** ~ to say the least; **a** ~ **a** ~ little by
little; **per** ~ **non cadevo** I nearly fell; **è
una cosa da** ~ it's nothing, it's of no
importance; **una persona da** ~ **a**
worthless person
♦ *pron* (a) little; ~**chi**, ~**che** *pron pl* (*persone*)
few (people); (*cose*) few; **ci vediamo tra** ~
see you soon; ~**chi lo sanno** not many
people know it; **ci vuole tempo ed io ne ho**
~ it takes time, and I haven't got much to
spare
♦ *sm* **1** little; **vive del** ~ **che ha** he lives on
the little he has
2: **un po'** a little; **un po' di zucchero** a
little sugar; **un bel po' di denaro** quite a
lot of money; **un po' per ciascuno** a bit
each.

po'dere *sm* (*AGR*) farm.
pode'roso, a *ag* powerful.

podestà *sm inv* (*nel fascismo*) podestà, mayor.

'podio *sm* dais, platform; (*MUS*) podium.

po'dismo *sm* (*SPORT: marcia*) walking; (: *corsa*) running.

po'dista, i, e *sm/f* walker; runner.

po'ema, i *sm* poem.

poe'sia *sf* (*arte*) poetry; (*componimento*) poem.

po'eta, 'essa *sm/f* poet/poetess.

poe'tare *vi* to write poetry.

po'etico, a, ci, che *ag* poetic(al).

poggi'are [pod'dʒare] *vt* to lean, rest; (*posare*) to lay, place.

poggia'testa [poddʒa'tɛsta] *sm inv* (*AUT*) headrest.

'poggio ['poddʒo] *sm* hillock, knoll.

poggi'olo [pod'dʒɔlo] *sm* balcony.

'poi *av* then; (*alla fine*) finally, at last ♦ *sm*: **pensare al** ~ to think of the future; **e** ~ (*inoltre*) and besides; **questa** ~ (**è bella**) (*ironico*) that's a good one!; **d'ora in** ~ from now on; **da domani in** ~ from tomorrow onwards.

poi'ana *sf* buzzard.

poiché [poi'ke] *cong* since, as.

pois [pwa] *sm inv* spot, (polka) dot; **a** ~ spotted, polka-dot *cpd*.

'poker *sm* poker.

po'lacco, a, chi, che *ag* Polish ♦ *sm/f* Pole.

po'lare *ag* polar.

polariz'zare [polarid'dzare] *vt* (*anche fig*) to polarize.

'polca, che *sf* polka.

po'lemico, a, ci, che *ag* polemic(al), controversial ♦ *sf* controversy; **fare** ~**che** to be contentious.

polemiz'zare [polemid'dzare] *vi*: ~ (**su qc**) to argue (about sth).

po'lenta *sf* (*CUC*) sort of thick porridge made with maize flour.

polen'tone, a *sm/f* slowcoach (*BRIT*), slowpoke (*US*).

pole'sano, a *ag* of (*o* from) Polesine (*area between the Po and the Adige*).

POL'FER *abbr f* = Polizia Ferroviaria.

'poli... *prefisso* poly....

poliambula'torio *sm* (*MED*) health clinic.

poli'clinico, ci *sm* general hospital.

poli'edro *sm* polyhedron.

poli'estere *sm* polyester.

poliga'mia *sf* polygamy.

po'ligono *sm* polygon; ~ **di tiro** rifle range.

Poli'nesia *sf*: **la** ~ Polynesia.

polinesi'ano, a *ag, sm/f* Polynesian.

'polio(mie'lite) *sf* polio(myelitis).

'polipo *sm* polyp.

polisti'rolo *sm* polystyrene.

poli'tecnico, ci *sm* postgraduate technical college.

po'litica, che *sf vedi* **politico**.

politi'cante *sm/f* (*peg*) petty politician.

politiciz'zare [polititʃid'dzare] *vt* to politicize.

po'litico, a, ci, che *ag* political ♦ *sm/f* politician ♦ *sf* politics *sg*; (*linea di condotta*) policy; **elezioni** ~**che** parliamentary (*BRIT*) *o* congressional (*US*) election(s); **uomo** ~ politician; **darsi alla** ~**a** to go into politics; **fare** ~**a** (*militante*) to be a political activist; (*come professione*) to be in politics; **la** ~**a del governo** the government's policies; ~**a aziendale** company policy; ~**a estera** foreign policy; ~**a dei prezzi** prices policy; ~**a dei redditi** incomes policy.

poliva'lente *ag* multi-purpose.

poli'zia [polit'tsia] *sf* police; ~ **giudiziaria** ≈ Criminal Investigation Department (CID) (*BRIT*), Federal Bureau of Investigation (FBI) (*US*); ~ **sanitaria/ tributaria** health/tax inspectorate; ~ **stradale** traffic police; ~ **di stato** *vedi nota nel riquadro*.

POLIZIA DI STATO

The remit of the **polizia di stato** *is to maintain public order, to uphold the law, and to prevent and investigate crime. This is a civilian branch of the police force; male and female officers perform similar duties. The* **polizia di stato** *reports to the Minister of the Interior.*

---

polizi'esco, a, schi, sche [polit'tsjesko] *ag* police *cpd*; (*film, romanzo*) detective *cpd*.

polizi'otto [polit'tsjɔtto] *sm* policeman; **cane** ~ police dog; **donna** ~ policewoman; ~ **di quartiere** local police officer.

'polizza ['pɔlittsa] *sf* (*COMM*) bill; ~ **di assicurazione** insurance policy; ~ **di carico** bill of lading.

pol'laio *sm* henhouse.

pollai'olo, a *sm/f* poulterer (*BRIT*), poultryman.

pol'lame *sm* poultry.

pol'lastra *sf* pullet; (*fig: ragazza*) chick.

pol'lastro *sm* (*ZOOL*) cockerel.

'pollice ['pɔllitʃe] *sm* thumb; (*unità di misura*) inch.

'polline *sm* pollen.

'pollo *sm* chicken; **far ridere i** ~**i** (*situazione, persona*) to be utterly ridiculous.

polmo'nare *ag* lung *cpd*, pulmonary.

pol'mone *sm* lung.

polmo'nite *sf* pneumonia; ~ **atipica** SARS.

'Polo *sm* (POL) centre-right coalition.

'polo *sm* (GEO, FISICA) pole; (gioco) polo ♦ *sf inv* (maglia) polo shirt; **il P~ sud/nord** the South/North Pole.

Po'lonia *sf:* **la** ~ Poland.

'polpa *sf* flesh, pulp; (carne) lean meat.

pol'paccio [pol'pattʃo] *sm* (ANAT) calf.

polpas'trello *sm* fingertip.

pol'petta *sf* (CUC) meatball.

polpet'tone *sm* (CUC) meatloaf.

'polpo *sm* octopus.

pol'poso, a *ag* fleshy.

pol'sino *sm* cuff.

'polso *sm* (ANAT) wrist; (pulsazione) pulse; (fig: forza) drive, vigour (BRIT), vigor (US); **avere** ~ (fig) to be strong; **un uomo di** ~ a man of nerve.

pol'tiglia [pol'tiʎʎa] *sf* (composto) mash, mush; (di fango e neve) slush.

pol'trire *vi* to laze about.

pol'trona *sf* armchair; (TEAT: posto) seat in the front stalls (BRIT) o the orchestra (US).

poltron'cina [poltron'tʃina] *sf* (TEAT) seat in the back stalls (BRIT) o the orchestra (US).

pol'trone *ag* lazy, slothful.

'polvere *sf* dust; (anche: ~ **da sparo**) (gun)powder; (sostanza ridotta minutissima) powder, dust; **caffè in** ~ instant coffee; **latte in** ~ dried o powdered milk; **sapone in** ~ soap powder; ~ **d'oro** gold dust; ~ **pirica** o **da sparo** gunpowder; ~**i sottili** particulates.

polveri'era *sf* powder magazine.

polve'rina *sf* (gen, MED) powder; (gergo: cocaina) snow.

polveriz'zare [polverid'dzare] *vt* to pulverize; (nebulizzare) to atomize; (fig) to crush, pulverize; (: record) to smash.

polve'rone *sm* thick cloud of dust.

polve'roso, a *ag* dusty.

po'mata *sf* ointment, cream.

po'mello *sm* knob.

pomeridi'ano, a *ag* afternoon cpd; **nelle ore** ~**e** in the afternoon.

pome'riggio [pome'riddʒo] *sm* afternoon; **nel primo/tardo** ~ in the early/late afternoon.

'pomice ['pomitʃe] *sf* pumice.

pomici'are [pomi'tʃare] *vi* (fam: sbaciucchiarsi) to neck.

'pomo *sm* (mela) apple; (ornamentale) knob; (di sella) pommel; ~ **d'Adamo** (ANAT) Adam's apple.

pomo'doro *sm* tomato.

'pompa *sf* pump; (sfarzo) pomp (and ceremony); ~ **antincendio** fire hose; ~ **di**

benzina petrol (BRIT) o gas (US) pump; (distributore) filling o gas (US) station; (impresa di) ~**e funebri** funeral parlour sg (BRIT), undertaker's sg, mortician's (US).

pom'pare *vt* to pump; (trarre) to pump out; (gonfiare d'aria) to pump up.

pompei'ano, a *ag of* (o from) Pompei.

pom'pelmo *sm* grapefruit.

pompi'ere *sm* fireman.

pom'pon [pom'pɔn] *sm inv* pompom, pompon.

pom'poso, a *ag* pompous.

ponde'rare *vt* to ponder over, consider carefully.

ponde'roso, a *ag* (anche fig) weighty.

po'nente *sm* west.

'pongo, 'poni *etc vb vedi* **porre**.

'ponte *sm* bridge; (di nave) deck; (: anche: ~ **di comando**) bridge; (impalcatura) scaffold; **vivere sotto i** ~**i** to be a tramp; **fare il** ~ (fig) to take the extra day off (between 2 public holidays); **governo** ~ interim government; ~ **aereo** airlift; ~ **di barche** (MIL) pontoon bridge; ~ **di coperta** (NAUT) upper deck; ~ **levatoio** drawbridge; ~ **radio** radio link; ~ **sospeso** suspension bridge.

pon'tefice [pon'tefitʃe] *sm* (REL) pontiff.

ponti'cello [ponti'tʃello] *sm* (di occhiali, MUS) bridge.

pontifi'care *vi* (anche fig) to pontificate.

pontifi'cato *sm* pontificate.

ponti'ficio, a, ci, cie [ponti'fitʃo] *ag* papal; **Stato P~** Papal State.

pon'tile *sm* jetty.

'pony ['pɔni] *sm inv* pony.

pool [puːl] *sm inv* (consorzio) consortium; (organismo internazionale) pool; (di esperti, ricercatori) team; (antimafia, antidroga) working party.

pop [pɔp] *ag inv* pop cpd.

'popcorn ['pɔpkɔːn] *sm inv* popcorn.

'popeline ['pɔpelin] *sm* poplin.

popò *sm inv* (sedere) botty.

popo'lano, a *ag* popular, of the people ♦ *sm/f* man/woman of the people.

popo'lare *ag* popular; (quartiere, clientela) working-class; (POL) of P.P.I. ♦ *sm/f* (POL) member (o supporter) of P.P.I. ♦ *vt* (rendere abitato) to populate; ~**rsi** *vr* to fill with people, get crowded; **manifestazione** ~ mass demonstration; **repubblica** ~ people's republic.

popolarità *sf* popularity.

popolazi'one [popolat'tsjone] *sf* population.

'popolo *sm* people.

popo'loso, a *ag* densely populated.

po'**pone** *sm* melon.

'**poppa** *sf* (*di nave*) stern; (*fam: mammella*) breast; **a** ~ aft, astern.

pop'**pante** *sm/f* unweaned infant; (*fig: inesperto*) whippersnapper.

pop'**pare** *vt* to suck.

pop'**pata** *sf* (*allattamento*) feed.

poppa'**toio** *sm* (feeding) bottle.

popu'**lista, i, e** *ag* populist.

por'**caio** *sm* (*anche fig*) pigsty.

por'**cata** *sf* (*libro, film etc*) load of rubbish; **fare una** ~ **a qn** to play a dirty trick on sb.

porcel'**lana** [portʃel'lana] *sf* porcelain, china; (*oggetto*) piece of porcelain.

porcel'**lino, a** [portʃel'lino] *sm/f* piglet; ~ **d'India** guinea pig.

porche'**ria** [porke'ria] *sf* filth, muck; (*fig: oscenità*) obscenity; (: *azione disonesta*) dirty trick; (: *cosa mal fatta*) rubbish.

por'**chetta** [por'ketta] *sf* roast sucking pig.

por'**cile** [por'tʃile] *sm* pigsty.

por'**cino, a** [por'tʃino] *ag* of pigs, pork *cpd* ♦ *sm* (*fungo*) *type of edible mushroom*.

'**porco, ci** *sm* pig; (*carne*) pork.

porcos'**pino** *sm* porcupine.

'**porfido** *sm* porphyry.

'**porgere** ['pɔrdʒere] *vt* to hand, give; (*tendere*) to hold out.

'**porno** *ag inv* porn, porno.

pornogra'**fia** *sf* pornography.

porno'**grafico, a, ci, che** *ag* pornographic.

'**poro** *sm* pore.

po'**roso, a** *ag* porous.

'**porpora** *sf* purple.

'**porre** *vt* (*mettere*) to put; (*collocare*) to place; (*posare*) to lay (down), put (down); (*fig: supporre*): **poniamo (il caso) che ...** let's suppose that ...; **porsi** *vr* (*mettersi*): **porsi a sedere/in cammino** to sit down/ set off; ~ **le basi di** (*fig*) to lay the foundations of, establish; ~ **una domanda a qn** to ask sb a question, put a question to sb; ~ **la propria fiducia in qn** to place one's trust in sb; ~ **fine o termine a qc** to put an end *o* a stop to sth; **posto che ...** supposing that ..., on the assumption that ...; **porsi in salvo** to save o.s.

'**porro** *sm* (*BOT*) leek; (*MED*) wart.

'**porsi** *etc vb vedi* **porgere**.

'**porta** *sf* door; (*SPORT*) goal; (*INFORM*) port; ~**e** *sfpl* (*di città*) gates; **mettere qn alla** ~ to throw sb out; **sbattere** *o* **chiudere la** ~ **in faccia a qn** (*anche fig*) to slam the door in sb's face; **trovare tutte le** ~**e chiuse** (*fig*) to find the way barred; **a** ~**e chiuse** (*DIR*) in camera; **l'inverno è alle** ~**e** (*fig*) winter is upon us; **vendita** ~ **a** ~ door-to-door

selling; ~ **di servizio** tradesmen's entrance; ~ **di sicurezza** emergency exit; ~ **stagna** watertight door.

portaba'**gagli** [portaba'gaʎʎi] *sm inv* (*facchino*) porter; (*AUT, FERR*) luggage rack.

portabandi'**era** *sm inv* standard bearer.

porta'**borse** *sm inv* (*peg*) lackey.

portabot'**tiglie** [portabot'tiʎʎe] *sm inv* bottle rack.

porta-**CD** [portatʃi'di] *sm inv* CD rack; (*astuccio*) CD holder.

porta'**cenere** [porta'tʃenere] *sm inv* ashtray.

portachi'**avi** [porta'kjavi] *sm inv* keyring.

porta'**cipria** [porta'tʃiprja] *sm inv* powder compact.

porta'**erei** *sf inv* (*nave*) aircraft carrier ♦ *sm inv* (*aereo*) aircraft transporter.

portafi'**nestra**, *pl* **portefi'nestre** *sf* French window.

porta'**foglio** [porta'fɔʎʎo] *sm* (*busta*) wallet; (*cartella*) briefcase; (*POL, BORSA*) portfolio; ~ **titoli** investment portfolio.

portagi'**oie** [porta'dʒɔje] *sm inv*, portagioi'**elli** [portadʒo'jelli] *sm inv* jewellery (*BRIT*) *o* jewelry (*US*) box.

por'**tale** *sm* portal.

porta'**lettere** *sm/f inv* postman/woman (*BRIT*), mailman/woman (*US*).

porta'**mento** *sm* carriage, bearing.

portamo'**nete** *sm inv* purse.

por'**tante** *ag* (*muro etc*) supporting, load-bearing.

portan'**tina** *sf* sedan chair; (*per ammalati*) stretcher.

portaog'**getti** [portaod'dʒetti] *ag inv*: **vano** ~ (*in macchina*) glove compartment.

portaom'**brelli** *sm inv* umbrella stand.

porta'**pacchi** [porta'pakki] *sm inv* (*di moto, bicicletta*) luggage rack.

por'**tare** *vt* (*sostenere, sorreggere: peso, bambino, pacco*) to carry; (*indossare: abito, occhiali*) to wear; (: *capelli lunghi*) to have; (*avere: nome, titolo*) to have, bear; (*recare*): ~ **qc a qn** to take (*o* bring) sth to sb; (*fig: sentimenti*) to bear; ~**rsi** *vr* (*recarsi*) to go; ~ **avanti** (*discorso, idea*) to pursue; ~ **via** to take away; (*rubare*) to take; ~ **i bambini a spasso** to take the children for a walk; ~ **fortuna** to bring good luck; ~ **qc alla bocca** to lift *o* put sth to one's lips; **porta bene i suoi anni** he's wearing well; **dove porta questa strada?** where does this road lead?, where does this road take you?; **il documento porta la tua firma** the document has *o* bears your signature; **non gli porto rancore** I don't bear him a grudge; **la polizia si è portata sul luogo**

del disastro the police went to the scene of the disaster.
portarit'ratti sm inv photo(graph) frame.
portari'viste sm inv magazine rack.
portasa'pone sm inv soap dish.
portasiga'rette sm inv cigarette case.
portas'pilli sm inv pincushion.
por'tata sf (vivanda) course; (AUT) carrying (o loading) capacity; (di arma) range; (volume d'acqua) (rate of) flow; (fig: limite) scope, capability; (: importanza) impact, import; **alla** ~ **di tutti** (conoscenza) within everybody's capabilities; (prezzo) within everybody's means; **a/fuori** ~ **(di)** within/out of reach (of); **a** ~ **di mano** within (arm's) reach; **di grande** ~ of great importance.
por'tatile ag portable.
por'tato, a ag (incline): ~ **a** inclined o apt to.
porta'tore, 'trice sm/f (anche COMM) bearer; (MED) carrier; **pagabile al** ~ payable to the bearer; ~ **di handicap** disabled person.
portatovagli'olo [portatovaʎ'ʎɔlo] sm napkin ring.
portau'ovo sm inv eggcup.
porta'voce [porta'votʃe] sm/f inv spokesman/woman.
por'tello sm (di portone) door; (NAUT) hatch.
portel'lone sm (NAUT, AER) hold door.
por'tento sm wonder, marvel.
porten'toso, a ag wonderful, marvellous (BRIT), marvelous (US).
porti'cato sm portico.
'portico, ci sm portico; (riparo) lean-to.
porti'era sf (AUT) door.
porti'ere sm (portinaio) concierge, caretaker; (di hotel) porter; (nel calcio) goalkeeper.
porti'naio, a sm/f concierge, caretaker.
portine'ria sf caretaker's lodge.
'porto, a pp di porgere ♦ sm (NAUT) harbour (BRIT), harbor (US), port; (spesa di trasporto) carriage ♦ sm inv port (wine); **andare** o **giungere in** ~ (fig) to come to a successful conclusion; **condurre qc in** ~ to bring sth to a successful conclusion; ~ **d'armi** gun licence (BRIT) o license (US); ~ **fluviale** river port; ~ **franco** free port; ~ **marittimo** seaport; ~ **militare** naval base; ~ **pagato** carriage paid, post free o paid; ~ **di scalo** port of call.
Porto'gallo sm: **il** ~ Portugal.
porto'ghese [porto'gese] ag, sm/f, sm Portuguese inv.
por'tone sm main entrance, main door.

portori'cano, a ag, sm/f Puerto Rican.
Porto'rico sf Puerto Rico.
portu'ale ag harbour cpd (BRIT), harbor cpd (US), port cpd ♦ sm dock worker.
porzi'one [por'tsjone] sf portion, share; (di cibo) portion, helping.
'posa sf (FOT) exposure; (atteggiamento, di modello) pose; (riposo): **lavorare senza** ~ to work without a break; **mettersi in** ~ to pose; **teatro di** ~ photographic studio.
posa'cenere [posa'tʃenere] sm inv ashtray.
po'sare vt to put (down), lay (down) ♦ vi (ponte, edificio, teoria): ~ **su** to rest on; (FOT, atteggiarsi) to pose; ~**rsi** vr (ape, aereo) to land; (uccello) to alight; (sguardo) to settle.
po'sata sf piece of cutlery; ~**e** sfpl cutlery sg.
posa'tezza [posa'tettsa] sf (di persona) composure; (di discorso) balanced nature.
po'sato, a ag steady; (discorso) balanced.
pos'critto sm postscript.
'posi etc vb vedi **porre**.
positiva'mente av positively; (rispondere) in the affirmative, affirmatively.
posi'tivo, a ag positive.
posizi'one [pozit'tsjone] sf position; **farsi una** ~ to make one's way in the world; **prendere** ~ (fig) to take a stand; **luci di** ~ (AUT) sidelights.
posolo'gia, 'gie [pozolo'dʒia] sf dosage, directions pl for use.
pos'porre vt to place after; (differire) to postpone, defer.
pos'posto, a pp di **posporre**.
posse'dere vt to own, possess; (qualità, virtù) to have, possess; (conoscere a fondo: lingua etc) to have a thorough knowledge of; (sog: ira etc) to possess.
possedi'mento sm possession.
pos'sente ag strong, powerful.
posses'sivo, a ag possessive.
pos'sesso sm possession; **essere in** ~ **di qc** to be in possession of sth; **prendere** ~ **di qc** to take possession of sth; **entrare in** ~ **dell'eredità** to come into one's inheritance.
posses'sore sm owner.
pos'sibile ag possible ♦ sm: **fare tutto il** ~ to do everything possible; **nei limiti del** ~ as far as possible; **al più tardi** ~ as late as possible; **vieni prima** ~ come as soon as possible.
possibi'lista, i, e ag: **essere** ~ to keep an open mind.
possibilità sf inv possibility ♦ sfpl (mezzi) means; **aver la** ~ **di fare** to be in a position to do; to have the opportunity to do; **nei**

limiti delle nostre ~ in so far as we can.
possibil'mente *av* if possible.
possi'dente *sm/f* landowner.
possi'edo *etc vb vedi* **possedere**.
'**posso** *etc vb vedi* **potere**.
post... *prefisso* post....
'**posta** *sf* (*servizio*) post, postal service;
(*corrispondenza*) post, mail; (*ufficio postale*)
post office; (*nei giochi d'azzardo*) stake;
(*CACCIA*) hide (*BRIT*), blind (*US*); ~**e** *sfpl*
(*amministrazione*) post office; **fare la** ~ **a**
qn (*fig*) to lie in wait for sb; **la** ~ **in gioco è**
troppo alta (*fig*) there's too much at stake;
a bella ~ (*apposta*) on purpose; **piccola** ~
(*su giornale*) letters to the editor, letters
page; ~ **aerea** airmail; ~ **elettronica**
electronic mail; ~ **ordinaria**
≈ second-class mail; ~ **prioritaria** first
class (post); **P**~**e e Telecomunicazioni**
(**PP.TT.**) *postal and telecommunications*
service; **ministro delle P**~**e e**
Telecomunicazioni Postmaster General.
posta'giro [posta'dʒiro] *sm* post office
cheque (*BRIT*) *o* check (*US*), postal giro
(*BRIT*).
pos'tale *ag* postal, post office *cpd* ♦ *sm*
(*treno*) mail train; (*nave*) mail boat;
(*furgone*) mail van; **timbro** ~ postmark.
postazi'one [postat'tsjone] *sf* (*MIL*)
emplacement.
post'bellico, a, ci, che *ag* postwar.
postda'tare *vt* to postdate.
posteggi'are [posted'dʒare] *vt*, *vi* to park.
posteggia'tore, 'trice [posteddʒa'tore] *sm/f*
car-park attendant (*BRIT*), parking-lot
attendant (*US*).
pos'teggio [pos'teddʒo] *sm* car park (*BRIT*),
parking lot (*US*); (*di taxi*) rank (*BRIT*),
stand (*US*).
postelegra'fonico, a, ci, che *ag* postal
and telecommunications *cpd*.
'**poster** *sm inv* poster.
'**posteri** *smpl* posterity *sg*; **i nostri** ~ our
descendants.
posteri'ore *ag* (*dietro*) back; (*dopo*) later
♦ *sm* (*fam: sedere*) behind.
posteri'ori: a ~ *ag inv* after the event (*dopo*
sostantivo) ♦ *av* looking back.
posterità *sf* posterity.
pos'ticcio, a, ci, ce [pos'tittʃo] *ag* false
♦ *sm* hairpiece.
postici'pare [postitʃi'pare] *vt* to defer,
postpone.
pos'tilla *sf* marginal note.
pos'tino *sm* postman (*BRIT*), mailman (*US*).
'**posto, a** *pp di* **porre** ♦ *sm* (*sito, posizione*)
place; (*impiego*) job; (*spazio libero*) room,
space; (*di parcheggio*) space; (*sedile: al*

teatro, in treno etc) seat; (*MIL*) post; **a** ~ (*in*
ordine) in place, tidy; (*fig*) settled;
(: *persona*) reliable; **mettere a** ~
(*riordinare*) to tidy (up), put in order;
(*faccende: sistemare*) to straighten out;
prender ~ to take a seat; **al** ~ **di** in place
of; **sul** ~ on the spot; ~ **di blocco**
roadblock; ~ **di lavoro** job; ~ **di polizia**
police station; ~ **telefonico pubblico**
(**P.T.P.**) public telephone; ~ **di**
villeggiatura holiday (*BRIT*) *o* tourist spot;
~**i in piedi** (*TEAT*, *in autobus*) standing
room.
postopera'torio, a *ag* (*MED*)
postoperative.
pos'tribolo *sm* brothel.
post'scriptum *sm inv* postscript.
'**postumo, a** *ag* posthumous; (*tardivo*)
belated; ~**i** *smpl* (*conseguenze*) after-
effects, consequences.
po'tabile *ag* drinkable; **acqua** ~ drinking
water.
po'tare *vt* to prune.
po'tassio *sm* potassium.
pota'tura *sf* pruning.
po'tente *ag* (*nazione*) strong, powerful;
(*veleno, farmaco*) potent, strong.
poten'tino, a *ag* of (*o from*) Potenza.
Po'tenza [po'tɛntsa] *sf* Potenza.
po'tenza [po'tɛntsa] *sf* power; (*forza*)
strength; **all'ennesima** ~ to the nth
degree; **le Grandi P**~**e** the Great Powers;
~ **militare** military might *o* strength.
potenzi'ale [poten'tsjale] *ag, sm* potential.
potenzia'mento [potentsja'mento] *sm*
development.
potenzi'are [poten'tsjare] *vt* to develop.

PAROLA CHIAVE

po'tere *sm* power; **al** ~ (*partito etc*) in
power; ~ **d'acquisto** purchasing power; ~
esecutivo executive power; ~ **giudiziario**
legal power; ~ **legislativo** legislative
power
♦ *vb aus* **1** (*essere in grado di*) can, be able
to; **non ha potuto ripararlo** he couldn't *o*
he wasn't able to repair it; **non è potuto**
venire he couldn't *o* he wasn't able to
come; **spiacente di non poter aiutare**
sorry not to be able to help
2 (*avere il permesso*) can, may, be allowed
to; **posso entrare?** can *o* may I come in?;
posso chiederti dove sei stato? where,
may I ask, have you been?
3 (*eventualità*) may, might, could;
potrebbe essere vero it might *o* could be
true; **può aver avuto un incidente** he may
o might *o* could have had an accident;

può darsi perhaps; **può darsi** o **può essere che non venga** he may o might not come **4** (*augurio*): **potessi almeno parlargli!** if only I could speak to him! **5** (*suggerimento*): **potresti almeno scusarti!** you could at least apologize! ♦ *vt* can, be able to; **può molto per noi** he can do a lot for us; **non ne posso più** (*per stanchezza*) I'm exhausted; (*per rabbia*) I can't take any more.

potestà *sf* (*potere*) power; (*DIR*) authority.
potrò *etc vb vedi* **potere**.
pove'raccio, a, ci, ce [pove'rattʃo] *smf* poor devil.
'povero, a *ag* poor; (*disadorno*) plain, bare ♦ *smf* poor man/woman; **i ~i** the poor; **~ di** lacking in, having little; **minerale ~ di ferro** ore with a low iron content; **paese ~ di risorse** country short of o lacking in resources.
povertà *sf* poverty.
pozi'one [pot'tsjone] *sf* potion.
'pozza ['pottsa] *sf* pool.
poz'zanghera [pot'tsangera] *sf* puddle.
'pozzo ['pottso] *sm* well; (*cava: di carbone*) pit; (*di miniera*) shaft; **~ nero** cesspit; **~ petrolifero** oil well.
pp. *abbr* (= *pagine*) pp.
p.p. *abbr* (= *per procura*) pp.
P.P.I. *sigla m* (*POL*) (= *Partito Popolare Italiano*) *party originating from D.C.*
PP.TT. *abbr* = **Poste e Telecomunicazioni**; *vedi* **posta**.
PR *sigla* = *Parma* ♦ *sigla m* (*POL*) = *Partito Radicale*.
P.R. *abbr* = **piano regolatore; procuratore della Repubblica**.
'Praga *sf* Prague.
prag'matico, a, ci, che *ag* pragmatic.
pram'matica *sf* custom; **essere di ~** to be customary.
pranotera'pia *sf* pranotherapy.
pran'zare [pran'dzare] *vi* to dine, have dinner; to lunch, have lunch.
'pranzo ['prandzo] *sm* dinner; (*a mezzogiorno*) lunch.
'prassi *sf* usual procedure.
'pratica, che *sf* practice; (*esperienza*) experience; (*conoscenza*) knowledge, familiarity; (*tirocinio*) training, practice; (*AMM: affare*) matter, case; (*: incartamento*) file, dossier; **in ~** (*praticamente*) in practice; **mettere in ~** to put into practice; **fare le ~che per** (*AMM*) to do the paperwork for; **~ restrittiva** restrictive practice; **~che illecite** dishonest practices.

prati'cabile *ag* (*progetto*) practicable, feasible; (*luogo*) passable, practicable.
pratica'mente *av* (*in modo pratico*) in a practical way, practically; (*quasi*) practically, almost.
prati'cante *smf* apprentice, trainee; (*REL*) (regular) churchgoer.
prati'care *vt* to practise (*BRIT*), practice (*US*); (*SPORT: tennis etc*) to play; (: *nuoto, scherma etc*) to go in for; (*eseguire: apertura, buco*) to make; **~ uno sconto** to give a discount.
praticità [pratitʃi'ta] *sf* practicality, practicalness; **per ~** for practicality's sake.
'pratico, a, ci, che *ag* practical; **~ di** (*esperto*) experienced o skilled in; (*familiare*) familiar with; **all'atto ~** in practice; **è ~ del mestiere** he knows his trade; **mi è più ~ venire di pomeriggio** it's more convenient for me to come in the afternoon.
'prato *sm* meadow; (*di giardino*) lawn.
preal'larme *sm* warning (signal).
Pre'alpi *sfpl* **~** (the) Pre-Alps.
preal'pino, a *ag* of the Pre-Alps.
pre'ambolo *sm* preamble; **senza tanti ~i** without beating about (*BRIT*) o around (*US*) the bush.
preannunci'are [preannun'tʃare], **preannunzi'are** [preannun'tsjare] *vt* to give advance notice of.
preavvi'sare *vt* to give advance notice of.
preav'viso *sm* notice; **telefonata con ~** personal o person to person call.
pre'bellico, a, ci, che *ag* prewar *cpd*.
precari'ato *sm* temporary employment.
precarietà *sf* precariousness.
pre'cario, a *ag* precarious; (*INS*) temporary, without tenure.
precauzio'nale [prekauttsjo'nale] *ag* precautionary.
precauzi'one [prekaut'tsjone] *sf* caution, care; (*misura*) precaution; **prendere ~i** to take precautions.
prece'dente [pretʃe'dɛnte] *ag* previous ♦ *sm* precedent; **il discorso/film ~** the previous o preceding speech/film; **senza ~i** unprecedented; **~i penali** (*DIR*) criminal record *sg*.
precedente'mente [pretʃedente'mente] *av* previously.
prece'denza [pretʃe'dɛntsa] *sf* priority, precedence; (*AUT*) right of way; **dare ~ assoluta a qc** to give sth top priority.
pre'cedere [pre'tʃɛdere] *vt* to precede, go (*o come*) before.
precet'tare [pretʃet'tare] *vt* (*lavoratori*) to

order back to work (*via an injunction*).

precettazi'one [pretʃettat'tsjone] *sf* (*di lavoratori*) order to resume work.

pre'cetto [pre'tʃɛtto] *sm* precept; (*MIL*) call-up notice.

precet'tore [pretʃet'tore] *sm* (private) tutor.

precipi'tare [pretʃipi'tare] *vi* (*cadere*) to fall headlong; (*fig: situazione*) to get out of control ♦ *vt* (*gettare dall'alto in basso*) to hurl, fling; (*fig: affrettare*) to rush; ~**rsi** *vr* (*gettarsi*) to hurl *o* fling o.s.; (*affrettarsi*) to rush.

precipi'tato, a [pretʃipi'tato] *ag* hasty ♦ *sm* (*CHIM*) precipitate.

precipitazi'one [pretʃipitat'tsjone] *sf* (*METEOR*) precipitation; (*fig*) haste.

precipi'toso, a [pretʃipi'toso] *ag* (*caduta, fuga*) headlong; (*fig: avventato*) rash, reckless; (: *affrettato*) hasty, rushed.

preci'pizio [pretʃi'pittsjo] *sm* precipice; **a** ~ (*fig: correre*) headlong.

pre'cipuo, a [pre'tʃipuo] *ag* principal, main.

precisa'mente [pretʃiza'mente] *av* (*gen*) precisely; (*con esattezza*) exactly.

preci'sare [pretʃi'zare] *vt* to state, specify; (*spiegare*) to explain (in detail); **vi preciseremo la data in seguito** we'll let you know the exact date later; **tengo a ~ che ...** I must point out that ....

precisazi'one [pretʃizat'tsjone] *sf* clarification.

precisi'one [pretʃi'zjone] *sf* precision; accuracy; **strumenti di** ~ precision instruments.

pre'ciso, a [pre'tʃizo] *ag* (*esatto*) precise; (*accurato*) accurate, precise; (*deciso: idea*) precise, definite; (*uguale*): **2 vestiti** ~**i** 2 dresses exactly the same; **sono le 9** ~**e** it's exactly 9 o'clock.

pre'cludere *vt* to block, obstruct.

pre'cluso, a *pp di* **precludere**.

pre'coce [pre'kɔtʃe] *ag* early; (*bambino*) precocious; (*vecchiaia*) premature.

precocità [prekotʃi'ta] *sf* (*di morte*) untimeliness; (*di bambino*) precociousness.

precon'cetto, a [prekon'tʃɛtto] *ag* preconceived ♦ *sm* preconceived idea, prejudice.

pre'correre *vt* to anticipate; ~ **i tempi** to be ahead of one's time.

precorri'tore, 'trice *sm/f* precursor, forerunner.

pre'corso, a *pp di* **precorrere**.

precur'sore *sm* forerunner, precursor.

'preda *sf* (*bottino*) booty; (*animale, fig*) prey; **essere** ~ **di** to fall prey to; **essere in** ~ **a** to be prey to.

pre'dare *vt* to plunder.

preda'tore *sm* predator.

predeces'sore, a [predetʃes'sore] *sm/f* predecessor.

pre'della *sf* platform, dais; altar-step.

predesti'nare *vt* to predestine.

predestinazi'one [predestinat'tsjone] *sf* predestination.

pre'detto, a *pp di* **predire** ♦ *ag* aforesaid, aforementioned.

'predica, che *sf* sermon; (*fig*) lecture, talking-to.

predi'care *vt, vi* to preach.

predica'tivo, a *ag* predicative.

predi'cato *sm* (*LING*) predicate.

predi'letto, a *pp di* **prediligere** ♦ *ag, sm/f* favourite (*BRIT*), favorite (*US*).

predilezi'one [predilet'tsjone] *sf* fondness, partiality; **avere una** ~ **per qc/qn** to be partial to sth/fond of sb.

predi'ligere [predi'lidʒere] *vt* to prefer, have a preference for.

pre'dire *vt* to foretell, predict.

predis'porre *vt* to get ready, prepare; ~ **qn a qc** to predispose sb to sth.

predisposizi'one [predispozit'tsjone] *sf* (*MED*) predisposition; (*attitudine*) bent, aptitude; **avere** ~ **alla musica** to have a bent for music.

predis'posto, a *pp di* **predisporre**.

predizi'one [predit'tsjone] *sf* prediction.

predomi'nante *ag* predominant.

predomi'nare *vi* (*prevalere*) to predominate; (*eccellere*) to excel.

predo'minio *sm* predominance; supremacy.

preesis'tente *ag* pre-existent.

pree'sistere *vi* to pre-exist.

preesis'tito, a *pp di* **preesistere**.

prefabbri'cato, a *ag* (*EDIL*) prefabricated.

prefazi'one [prefat'tsjone] *sf* preface, foreword.

prefe'renza [prefe'rɛntsa] *sf* preference; **a** ~ **di** rather than; **di** ~ preferably, by preference; **non ho** ~**e** I have no preferences either way, I don't mind.

preferenzi'ale [preferen'tsjale] *ag* preferential; **corsia** ~ (*AUT*) bus and taxi lane.

prefe'ribile *ag*: ~ (**a**) preferable (to), better (than); **sarebbe** ~ **andarsene** it would be better to go.

preferibil'mente *av* preferably.

prefe'rire *vt* to prefer, like better; ~ **il caffè al tè** to prefer coffee to tea, like coffee better than tea.

pre'fetto *sm* prefect.

prefet'tura *sf* prefecture.
pre'figgersi [pre'fidd3ersi] *vr*: ~ **uno scopo** to set o.s. a goal.
prefigu'rare *vt* (*simboleggiare*) to foreshadow; (*prevedere*) to foresee.
pre'fisso, a *pp di* **prefiggersi** ♦ *sm* (*LING*) prefix; (*TEL*) dialling (*BRIT*) *o* dial (*US*) code.
Preg. *abbr* = **pregiatissimo**.
pre'gare *vi* to pray ♦ *vt* (*REL*) to pray to; (*implorare*) to beg; (*chiedere*): ~ **qn di fare** to ask sb to do; **farsi** ~ to need coaxing *o* persuading.
pre'gevole [pre'd3evole] *ag* valuable.
pregherò *etc* [prege'rɔ] *vb vedi* **pregare**.
preghi'era [pre'gjɛra] *sf* (*REL*) prayer; (*domanda*) request.
pregi'arsi [pre'd3arsi] *vr*: **mi pregio di farle sapere che ...** I am pleased to inform you that ....
pregia'tissimo, a [pred3a'tissimo] *ag* (*in lettere*): ~ **Signor G. Agnelli** G. Agnelli Esquire.
pregi'ato, a [pre'd3ato] *ag* (*opera*) valuable; (*tessuto*) fine; (*valuta*) strong; **vino** ~ vintage wine.
'pregio ['prɛd3o] *sm* (*stima*) esteem, regard; (*qualità*) (good) quality, merit; (*valore*) value, worth; **il** ~ **di questo sistema è ...** the merit of this system is ...; **oggetto di** ~ valuable object.
pregiudi'care [pred3udi'kare] *vt* to prejudice, harm, be detrimental to.
pregiudi'cato, a [pred3udi'kato] *sm/f* (*DIR*) previous offender.
pregiu'dizio [pred3u'dittsjo] *sm* (*idea errata*) prejudice; (*danno*) harm *no pl*.
preg'nante [preɲ'ɲante] *ag* (*fig*) pregnant, meaningful.
'pregno, a ['preɲɲo] *ag* (*saturo*): ~ **di** full of, saturated with.
'prego *escl* (*a chi ringrazia*) don't mention it!; (*invitando qn ad accomodarsi*) please sit down!; (*invitando qn ad andare prima*) after you!
pregus'tare *vt* to look forward to.
preis'toria *sf* prehistory.
preis'torico, a, ci, che *ag* prehistoric.
pre'lato *sm* prelate.
prela'vaggio [prela'vadd3o] *sm* pre-wash.
prelazi'one [prelat'tsjone] *sf* (*DIR*) pre-emption; **avere il diritto di** ~ **su qc** to have the first option on sth.
preleva'mento *sm* (*BANCA*) withdrawal; (*di merce*) picking up, collection.
prele'vare *vt* (*denaro*) to withdraw; (*campione*) to take; (*merce*) to pick up, collect; (*sog: polizia*) to take, capture.

preli'evo *sm* (*BANCA*) withdrawal; (*MED*): **fare un** ~ **(di)** to take a sample (of).
prelimi'nare *ag* preliminary; ~**i** *smpl* preliminary talks; preliminaries.
pre'ludere *vi*: ~ **a** (*preannunciare: crisi, guerra, temporale*) to herald, be a sign of; (*introdurre: dibattito etc*) to introduce, be a prelude to.
pre'ludio *sm* prelude.
pre'luso, a *pp di* **preludere**.
pre-ma'man [prema'mã] *sm inv* maternity dress.
prematrimoni'ale *ag* premarital.
prema'turo, a *ag* premature.
premedi'tare *vt* to premeditate, plan.
premeditazi'one [premeditat'tsjone] *sf* (*DIR*) premeditation; **con** ~ *ag* premeditated ♦ *av* with intent.
'premere *vt* to press ♦ *vi*: ~ **su** to press down on; (*fig*) to put pressure on; ~ **a** (*fig: importare*) to matter to; ~ **il grilletto** to pull the trigger.
pre'messo, a *pp di* **premettere** ♦ *sf* introductory statement, introduction; **mancano le** ~**e per una buona riuscita** we lack the basis for a successful outcome.
pre'mettere *vt* to put before; (*dire prima*) to start by saying, state first; **premetto che ...** I must say first of all that ...; **premesso che ...** given that ...; **ciò premesso ...** that having been said ....
premi'are *vt* to give a prize to; (*fig: merito, onestà*) to reward.
premiazi'one [premjat'tsjone] *sf* prize giving.
'premier ['prɛmjer] *sm inv* premier.
premi'nente *ag* pre-eminent.
'premio *sm* prize; (*ricompensa*) reward; (*COMM*) premium; (*AMM: indennità*) bonus; **in** ~ **per** as a prize (*o* reward) for; ~ **d'ingaggio** (*SPORT*) signing-on fee; ~ **di produzione** productivity bonus.
pre'misi *etc vb vedi* **premettere**.
premoni'tore, 'trice *ag* premonitory.
premonizi'one [premonit'tsjone] *sf* premonition.
premu'nirsi *vr*: ~ **di** to provide o.s. with; ~ **contro** to protect o.s. from, guard o.s. against.
pre'mura *sf* (*fretta*) haste, hurry; (*riguardo*) attention, care; **aver** ~ to be in a hurry; **far** ~ **a qn** to hurry sb; **usare ogni** ~ **nei riguardi di qn, circondare qn di** ~**e** to be very attentive to sb.
premu'roso, a *ag* thoughtful, considerate.
prena'tale *ag* antenatal.
'prendere *vt* to take; (*andare a prendere*) to get, fetch; (*ottenere*) to get; (*guadagnare*)

to get, earn; (*catturare: ladro, pesce*) to catch; (*collaboratore, dipendente*) to take on; (*passeggero*) to pick up; (*chiedere: somma, prezzo*) to charge, ask; (*trattare: persona*) to handle ♦ *vi* (*colla, cemento*) to set; (*pianta*) to take; (*fuoco: nel camino*) to catch; (*voltare*): ~ **a destra** to turn (to the) right; ~**rsi** *vr* (*azzuffarsi*): ~**rsi a pugni** to come to blows; **prende qualcosa?** (*da bere, da mangiare*) would you like something to eat (*o* drink)?; **prendo un caffè** I'll have a coffee; ~ **a fare qc** to start doing sth; ~ **qn/qc per** (*scambiare*) to take sb/sth for; ~ **l'abitudine di** to get into the habit of; ~ **fuoco** to catch fire; ~ **le generalità di qn** to take down sb's particulars; ~ **nota di** to take note of; ~ **parte a** to take part in; ~**rsi cura di qn/qc** to look after sb/sth; ~**rsi un impegno** to take on a commitment; **prendersela** (*adirarsi*) to get annoyed; (*preoccuparsi*) to get upset, worry.
prendi'sole *sm inv* sundress.
preno'tare *vt* to book, reserve.
prenotazi'one [prenotat'tsjone] *sf* booking, reservation.
'prensile *ag* prehensile.
preoccu'pante *ag* worrying.
preoccu'pare *vt* to worry; ~**rsi** *vr*: ~**rsi di qn/qc** to worry about sb/sth; ~**rsi per qn** to be anxious for sb.
preoccupazi'one [preokkupat'tsjone] *sf* worry, anxiety.
preordi'nato, a *ag* preordained.
prepa'rare *vt* to prepare; (*esame, concorso*) to prepare for; ~**rsi** *vr* (*vestirsi*) to get ready; ~**rsi a qc/a fare** to get ready *o* prepare (o.s.) for sth/to do; ~ **da mangiare** to prepare a meal.
prepara'tivi *smpl* preparations.
prepa'rato, a *ag* (*gen*) prepared; (*pronto*) ready ♦ *sm* (*prodotto*) preparation.
prepara'torio, a *ag* preparatory.
preparazi'one [preparat'tsjone] *sf* preparation; **non ha la necessaria ~ per svolgere questo lavoro** he lacks the qualifications necessary for the job.
prepensiona'mento *sm* early retirement.
preponde'rante *ag* predominant.
pre'porre *vt* to place before; (*fig*) to prefer.
preposizi'one [prepozit'tsjone] *sf* (*LING*) preposition.
pre'posto, a *pp di* **preporre**.
prepo'tente *ag* (*persona*) domineering, arrogant; (*bisogno, desiderio*) overwhelming, pressing ♦ *sm/f* bully.
prepo'tenza [prepo'tɛntsa] *sf* arrogance;

(*comportamento*) arrogant behaviour (*BRIT*) *o* behavior (*US*).
pre'puzio [pre'puttsjo] *sm* (*ANAT*) foreskin.
preroga'tiva *sf* prerogative.
'presa *sf* taking *no pl*; catching *no pl*; (*di città*) capture; (*indurimento: di cemento*) setting; (*appiglio, SPORT*) hold; (*di acqua, gas*) (supply) point; (*ELETTR*): ~ **(di corrente)** socket; (: *al muro*) point; (*piccola quantità: di sale etc*) pinch; (*CARTE*) trick; **far ~** (*colla*) to set; **ha fatto ~ sul pubblico** (*fig*) it caught the public's imagination; **a ~ rapida** (*cemento*) quick-setting; **di forte ~** (*fig*) with wide appeal; **essere alle ~e con qc** (*fig*) to be struggling with sth; **macchina da ~** (*CINE*) cine camera (*BRIT*), movie camera (*US*); ~ **d'aria** air inlet; ~ **diretta** (*AUT*) direct drive; ~ **in giro** leg-pull (*BRIT*), joke; ~ **di posizione** stand.
pre'sagio [pre'zadʒo] *sm* omen.
presa'gire [preza'dʒire] *vt* to foresee.
presa'lario *sm* (*INS*) grant.
'presbite *ag* long-sighted.
presbiteri'ano, a *ag, sm/f* Presbyterian.
presbi'terio *sm* presbytery.
pre'scindere [preʃ'ʃindere] *vi*: ~ **da** to leave out of consideration; **a ~ da** apart from.
pre'scisso, a [preʃ'ʃisso] *pp di* **prescindere**.
presco'lastico, a, ci, che *ag* pre-school *cpd*.
pres'critto, a *pp di* **prescrivere**.
pres'crivere *vt* to prescribe.
prescrizi'one [preskrit'tsjone] *sf* (*MED, DIR*) prescription; (*norma*) rule, regulation; **cadere in ~** (*DIR*) to become statute-barred.
'prese *etc vb vedi* **prendere**.
presen'tare *vt* to present; (*far conoscere*): ~ **qn (a)** to introduce sb (to); (*AMM: inoltrare*) to submit; ~**rsi** *vr* (*recarsi, farsi vedere*) to present o.s., appear; (*farsi conoscere*) to introduce o.s.; (*occasione*) to arise; ~ **qc in un'esposizione** to show *o* display sth at an exhibition; ~ **qn in società** to introduce sb into society; ~**rsi come candidato** (*POL*) to stand (*BRIT*) *o* run (*US*) as a candidate; ~**rsi bene/male** to have a good/poor appearance; **la situazione si presenta difficile** things aren't looking too good, things look a bit tricky.
presentazi'one [prezentat'tsjone] *sf* presentation; introduction.
pre'sente *ag* present; (*questo*) this ♦ *sm* present ♦ *sf* (*lettera*): **con la ~ vi comunico … ** this is to inform you that … ♦ *sm/f* person present; **i ~i** those present; **aver ~ qc/qn** to remember sth/sb; **essere ~ a una**

riunione to be present at o attend a meeting; **tener** ~ **qn/qc** to keep sb/sth in mind; **esclusi i** ~**i** present company excepted.

presenti'mento sm premonition.

pre'senza [pre'zentsa] sf presence; (aspetto esteriore) appearance; **in** ~ **di** in (the) presence of; **di bella** ~ of good appearance; ~ **di spirito** presence of mind.

presenzi'are [prezen'tsjare] vi: ~ **a** to be present at, attend.

pre'sepio, pre'sepe sm crib.

preser'vare vt to protect.

preserva'tivo sm sheath, condom.

'presi etc vb vedi **prendere**.

'preside smlf (INS) head (teacher) (BRIT), principal (US); (di facoltà universitaria) dean.

presi'dente sm (POL) president; (di assemblea, COMM) chairman; **il P**~ **della Camera** (POL) ≈ the Speaker; **P**~ **del Consiglio (dei Ministri)** ≈ Prime Minister; **P**~ **della Repubblica** President of the Republic; vedi nota nel riquadro.

PRESIDENTE

The **Presidente del Consiglio**, the Italian Prime Minister, is the leader of the Government. He or she submits nominations for ministerial posts to the "Presidente della Repubblica", who then appoints them if approved. The **Presidente del Consiglio** is appointed by the "Presidente della Repubblica", in consultation with the leaders of the parliamentary parties, former heads of state, the "Presidente della Camera" and the "Presidente del Senato". The **Presidente della Repubblica** is the head of state. He or she must be an Italian citizen of at least 50 years of age, and is elected by Parliament and by three delegates from each of the Italian regions. He has the power to suspend the implementation of legislation and to dissolve one or both chambers of Parliament, and he presides over the magistrates' governing body (the "Consiglio Superiore della Magistratura").

---

presiden'tessa sf president; (moglie) president's wife; (di assemblea, COMM) chairwoman.

presi'denza [presi'dentsa] sf presidency; office of president; chairmanship; **assumere la** ~ to become president; to take the chair; **essere alla** ~ to be president (o chairman); **candidato alla** ~ presidential candidate; candidate for the

chairmanship.

presidenzi'ale [presiden'tsjale] ag presidential.

presidi'are vt to garrison.

pre'sidio sm garrison.

presi'edere vt to preside over ♦ vi: ~ **a** to direct, be in charge of.

'preso, a pp di **prendere**.

'pressa sf (TECN) press.

pres'sante ag (bisogno, richiesta) urgent, pressing.

pressap'poco av about, roughly, approximately.

pres'sare vt (anche fig) to press; ~ **qn con richieste** to pursue sb with demands.

pressi'one sf pressure; **far** ~ **su qn** to put pressure on sb; **subire forti** ~**i** to be under strong pressure; ~ **sanguigna** blood pressure.

'presso av (vicino) nearby, close at hand ♦ prep (vicino a) near; (accanto a) beside, next to; (in casa di): ~ **qn** at sb's home; (nelle lettere) care of (abbr c/o); (alle dipendenza di): **lavora** ~ **di noi** he works for o with us ♦ smpl: **nei** ~**i di** near, in the vicinity of; **ha avuto grande successo** ~ **i giovani** it has been a hit with young people.

pressoché [presso'ke] av nearly, almost.

pressuriz'zare [pressurid'dzare] vt to pressurize.

prestabi'lire vt to arrange beforehand, arrange in advance.

presta'nome smlf inv (peg) figurehead.

pres'tante ag good-looking.

pres'tanza [pres'tantsa] sf (robust) good looks pl.

pres'tare vt: ~ **(qc a qn)** to lend (sb sth o sth to sb); ~**rsi** vr (offrirsi): ~**rsi a fare** to offer to do; (essere adatto): ~**rsi a** to lend itself to, be suitable for; ~ **aiuto** to lend a hand; ~ **ascolto** o **orecchio** to listen; ~ **attenzione** to pay attention; ~ **fede a qc/ qn** to give credence to sth/sb; ~ **giuramento** to take an oath; **la frase si presta a molteplici interpretazioni** the phrase lends itself to numerous interpretations.

prestazi'one [prestat'tsjone] sf (TECN, SPORT) performance; ~**i** sfpl (di persona: servizi) services.

prestigia'tore, 'trice [prestidʒa'tore] smlf conjurer.

pres'tigio [pres'tidʒo] sm (potere) prestige; (illusione): **gioco di** ~ conjuring trick.

prestigi'oso, a [presti'dʒoso] ag prestigious.

'**prestito** *sm* lending *no pl*; loan; **dar in** ~ to lend; **prendere in** ~ to borrow; ~ **bancario** bank loan; ~ **pubblico** public borrowing.

'**presto** *av* (*tra poco*) soon; (*in fretta*) quickly; (*di buon'ora*) early; **a** ~ see you soon; ~ **o tardi** sooner or later; **fare** ~ **a fare qc** to hurry up and do sth; (*non costare fatica*) to have no trouble doing sth; **si fa** ~ **a criticare** it's easy to criticize; **è ancora** ~ **per decidere** it's still too early *o* too soon to decide.

pre'**sumere** *vt* to presume, assume.

presu'**mibile** *ag* (*dati, risultati*) likely.

pre'**sunsi** *etc vb vedi* **presumere**.

pre'**sunto, a** *pp di* **presumere** ♦ *ag*: **il** ~ **colpevole** the alleged culprit.

presuntu'**oso, a** *ag* presumptuous.

presunzi'**one** [prezun'tsjone] *sf* presumption.

presup'**porre** *vt* to suppose; to presuppose.

presup'**posto, a** *pp di* **presupporre** ♦ *sm* (*premessa*) supposition, premise; **partendo dal** ~ **che** ... assuming that ...; **mancano i** ~**i necessari** the necessary conditions are lacking.

'**prete** *sm* priest.

preten'**dente** *sm/f* pretender ♦ *sm* (*corteggiatore*) suitor.

pre'**tendere** *vt* (*esigere*) to demand, require; (*sostenere*): ~ **che** to claim that; **pretende di aver sempre ragione** he thinks he's always right.

pretenzi'**oso, a** [preten'tsjoso] *ag* pretentious.

preterintenzio'**nale** [preterintentsjo'nale] *ag* (*DIR*): **omicidio** ~ manslaughter.

pre'**teso, a** *pp di* **pretendere** ♦ *sf* (*esigenza*) claim, demand; (*presunzione, sfarzo*) pretentiousness; **avanzare una** ~**a** to put forward a claim *o* demand; **senza** ~**e** *ag* unpretentious ♦ *av* unpretentiously.

pre'**testo** *sm* pretext, excuse; **con il** ~ **di** on the pretext of.

pretestu'**oso, a** *ag* (*data, motivo*) used as an excuse.

pre'**tore** *sm* magistrate.

pre'**tura** *sf* (*DIR: sede*) magistrate's court (*BRIT*), circuit *o* superior court (*US*); (*: magistratura*) magistracy.

preva'**lente** *ag* prevailing.

prevalente'**mente** *av* mainly, for the most part.

preva'**lenza** [preva'lɛntsa] *sf* predominance.

preva'**lere** *vi* to prevail.

pre'**valso, a** *pp di* **prevalere**.

prevari'**care** *vi* (*abusare del potere*) to abuse one's power.

prevaricazi'**one** [prevarikat'tsjone] *sf* (*abuso di potere*) abuse of power.

preve'**dere** *vt* (*indovinare*) to foresee; (*presagire*) to foretell; (*considerare*) to make provision for; **nulla lasciava** ~ **che** ... there was nothing to suggest *o* make one think that ...; **come previsto** as expected; **spese previste** anticipated expenditure; **previsto per martedì** scheduled for Tuesday.

prev'**edibile** *ag* predictable; **non era assolutamente** ~ **che** ... no one could have foreseen that ....

prevedibil'**mente** *av* as one would expect.

preve'**nire** *vt* (*anticipare: obiezione*) to forestall; (: *domanda*) to anticipate; (*evitare*) to avoid, prevent; (*avvertire*): ~ **qn (di)** to warn sb (of); to inform sb (of).

preventi'**vare** *vt* (*COMM*) to estimate.

preven'**tivo, a** *ag* preventive ♦ *sm* (*COMM*) estimate; **fare un** ~ to give an estimate; **bilancio** ~ budget; **carcere** ~ custody (*pending trial*).

preve'**nuto, a** *ag* (*mal disposto*): ~ **(contro qc/qn)** prejudiced (against sth/sb).

prevenzi'**one** [preven'tsjone] *sf* prevention; (*preconcetto*) prejudice.

previ'**dente** *ag* showing foresight; prudent.

previ'**denza** [previ'dɛntsa] *sf* foresight; **istituto di** ~ provident institution; ~ **sociale** social security (*BRIT*), welfare (*US*).

pre'**vidi** *etc vb vedi* **prevedere**.

'**previo, a** *ag* (*COMM*): ~ **avviso** upon notice; ~ **pagamento** upon payment.

previsi'**one** *sf* forecast, prediction; ~**i meteorologiche** *o* **del tempo** weather forecast *sg*.

pre'**visto, a** *pp di* **prevedere** ♦ *sm*: **più/meno del** ~ more/less than expected; **prima del** ~ earlier than expected.

prezi'**oso, a** [pret'tsjoso] *ag* precious; (*aiuto, consiglio*) invaluable ♦ *sm* jewel; valuable.

prez'**zemolo** [pret'tsɛmolo] *sm* parsley.

'**prezzo** ['prɛttso] *sm* price; **a** ~ **di costo** at cost, at cost price (*BRIT*); **tirare sul** ~ to bargain, haggle; **il** ~ **pattuito è 1000 di euro** the agreed price is 1000 euros; ~ **d'acquisto/di vendita** buying/selling price; ~ **di fabbrica** factory price; ~ **di mercato** market price; ~ **scontato** reduced price; ~ **unitario** unit price.

P.R.I. *sigla m* (= *Partito Repubblicano Italiano*) *former political party*.

prigi'one [pri'dʒone] *sf* prison.

prigio'nia [pridʒo'nia] *sf* imprisonment.

prigioni'ero, a [pridʒo'njɛro] *ag* captive ♦ *sm/f* prisoner.

'prima *sf vedi* **primo** ♦ *av* before; (*in anticipo*) in advance, beforehand; (*per l'addietro*) at one time, formerly; (*più presto*) sooner, earlier; (*in primo luogo*) first ♦ *cong*: ~ **di fare/che parta** before doing/he leaves; ~ **di** *prep* before; ~ **o poi** sooner or later; **due giorni** ~ two days before *o* earlier; ~ **d'ora** before now.

pri'mario, a *ag* primary; (*principale*) chief, leading, primary ♦ *sm/f* (*medico*) head physician, chief physician.

pri'mate *sm* (*REL, ZOOL*) primate.

prima'tista, i, e *sm/f* (*SPORT*) record holder.

pri'mato *sm* supremacy; (*SPORT*) record.

prima'vera *sf* spring.

primave'rile *ag* spring *cpd*.

primeggi'are [primed'dʒare] *vi* to excel, be one of the best.

primi'tivo, a *ag* (*gen*) primitive; (*significato*) original.

pri'mizie [pri'mittsje] *sfpl* early produce *sg*.

'primo, a *ag* first; (*fig*) initial; basic; prime ♦ *sm/f* first (one) ♦ *sm* (*CUC*) first course; (*in date*): **il** ~ **luglio** the first of July ♦ *sf* (*TEAT*) first night; (*CINE*) première; (*AUT*) first (gear); **le** ~**e ore del mattino** the early hours of the morning; **di** ~**a mattina** early in the morning; **in** ~**a pagina** (*STAMPA*) on the front page; **ai** ~**i freddi** at the first sign of cold weather; **ai** ~**i di maggio** at the beginning of May; **i** ~**i del Novecento** the early twentieth century; **viaggiare in** ~**a** to travel first-class; **per** ~**a cosa** firstly; **in** ~ **luogo** first of all, in the first place; **di prim'ordine** *o* ~**a qualità** first-class, first-rate; **in un** ~ **tempo** *o* **momento** at first; ~**a donna** leading lady; (*di opera lirica*) prima donna.

primo'genito, a [primo'dʒɛnito] *ag, sm/f* firstborn.

pri'mordi *smpl* beginnings.

primordi'ale *ag* primordial.

'primula *sf* primrose.

princi'pale [printʃi'pale] *ag* main, principal ♦ *sm* manager, boss; **sede** ~ head office.

principal'mente [printʃipal'mente] *av* mainly, principally.

princi'pato [printʃi'pato] *sm* principality.

'principe ['printʃipe] *sm* prince; ~ **ereditario** crown prince.

princi'pesco, a, schi, sche [printʃi'pesko] *ag* (*anche fig*) princely.

princi'pessa [printʃi'pessa] *sf* princess.

principi'ante [printʃi'pjante] *sm/f* beginner.

principi'are [printʃi'pjare] *vt, vi* to start, begin.

prin'cipio [prin'tʃipjo] *sm* (*inizio*) beginning, start; (*origine*) origin, cause; (*concetto, norma*) principle; **al** *o* **in** ~ at first; **fin dal** ~ right from the start; **per** ~ on principle; **una questione di** ~ a matter of principle; **una persona di sani** ~**i morali** a person of sound moral principles; ~ **attivo** active ingredient.

pri'ore *sm* (*REL*) prior.

pri'ori: a ~ *ag inv* prior; a priori ♦ *av* at first glance; initially; a priori.

priorità *sf* priority; **avere la** ~ (**su**) to have priority (over).

priori'tario, a *ag* (*scelta*) first; (*interesse*) overriding; **posta** ~ first class (post).

'prisma, i *sm* prism.

pri'vare *vt*: ~ **qn di** to deprive sb of; ~**rsi** *vr*: ~**rsi di** to go *o* do without.

priva'tiva *sf* (*ECON*) monopoly.

privatiz'zare [privatid'dzare] *vt* to privatize.

privatizzazi'one [privatiddzat'tsjone] *sf* privatization.

pri'vato, a *ag* private ♦ *sm/f* (*anche*: ~ **cittadino**) private citizen; **in** ~ in private; **diritto** ~ (*DIR*) civil law; **ritirarsi a vita** ~**a** to withdraw from public life; "**non vendiamo a** ~**i**" "wholesale only".

privazi'one [privat'tsjone] *sf* privation, hardship.

privilegi'are [privile'dʒare] *vt* to favour (*BRIT*), favor (*US*).

privilegi'ato, a [privile'dʒato] *ag* (*individuo, classe*) privileged; (*trattamento, COMM: credito*) preferential; **azioni** ~**e** preference shares (*BRIT*), preferred stock (*US*).

privi'legio [privi'lɛdʒo] *sm* privilege; **avere il** ~ **di fare** to have the privilege of doing, be privileged to do.

'privo, a *ag*: ~ **di** without, lacking.

pro *prep* for, on behalf of ♦ *sm inv* (*utilità*) advantage, benefit; **a che** ~? what's the use?; **il** ~ **e il contro** the pros and cons.

pro'babile *ag* probable, likely.

probabilità *sf inv* probability; **con molta** ~ very probably, in all probability.

probabil'mente *av* probably.

pro'bante *ag* convincing.

pro'blema, i *sm* problem.

proble'matico, a, ci, che *ag* problematic; (*incerto*) doubtful ♦ *sf* problems *pl*.

pro'boscide [pro'bɔʃʃide] *sf* (*di elefante*) trunk.

procacci'are [prokat'tʃare] *vt* to get, obtain.

procaccia'tore [prokattʃa'tore] *sm*: ~

d'affari sales executive.

pro'cace [pro'katʃe] *ag* (*donna, aspetto*) provocative.

pro'cedere [pro'tʃɛdere] *vi* to proceed; (*comportarsi*) to behave; (*iniziare*): ~ **a** to start; ~ **contro** (*DIR*) to start legal proceedings against; ~ **oltre** to go on ahead; **prima di** ~ **oltre** before going any further; **gli affari procedono bene** business is going well; **bisogna** ~ **con cautela** we have to proceed cautiously; **non luogo a** ~ (*DIR*) nonsuit.

procedi'mento [protʃedi'mento] *sm* (*modo di condurre*) procedure; (*di avvenimenti*) course; (*TECN*) process; ~ **penale** (*DIR*) criminal proceedings *pl*.

proce'dura [protʃe'dura] *sf* (*DIR*) procedure.

proces'sare [protʃes'sare] *vt* (*DIR*) to try.

processi'one [protʃes'sjone] *sf* procession.

pro'cesso [pro'tʃɛsso] *sm* (*DIR*) trial; proceedings *pl*; (*metodo*) process; **essere sotto** ~ to be on trial; **mettere sotto** ~ (*anche fig*) to put on trial; ~ **di fabbricazione** manufacturing process; ~ **di pace** peace process.

processu'ale [protʃessu'ale] *ag* (*DIR*): **atti** ~**i** records of a trial; **spese** ~**i** legal costs.

Proc. Gen. *abbr* = **procuratore generale**.

pro'cinto [pro'tʃinto] *sm*: **in** ~ **di fare** about to do, on the point of doing.

pro'clama, i *sm* proclamation.

procla'mare *vt* to proclaim.

proclamazi'one [proklamat'tsjone] *sf* proclamation, declaration.

procrasti'nare *vt* (*data*) to postpone; (*pagamento*) to defer.

procre'are *vt* to procreate.

pro'cura *sf* (*DIR*) proxy, power of attorney; (*ufficio*) attorney's office; **per** ~ by proxy; **la P**~ **della Repubblica** the Public Prosecutor's Office.

procu'rare *vt*: ~ **qc a qn** (*fornire*) to get *o* obtain sth for sb; (*causare: noie etc*) to bring *o* give sb sth.

procura'tore, 'trice *smlf* (*DIR*) ≈ solicitor; (*: chi ha la procura*) holder of power of attorney; ~ **generale** (*in corte d'appello*) public prosecutor; (*in corte di cassazione*) Attorney General; ~ **legale** ≈ solicitor (*BRIT*), lawyer; ~ **della Repubblica** (*in corte d'assise, tribunale*) public prosecutor.

prodi'gare *vt* to be lavish with; ~**rsi** *vr*: ~**rsi per qn** to do all one can for sb.

pro'digio [pro'didʒo] *sm* marvel, wonder; (*persona*) prodigy.

prodigi'oso, a [prodi'dʒoso] *ag* prodigious; phenomenal.

'prodigo, a, ghi, ghe *ag* lavish, extravagant.

pro'dotto, a *pp di* **produrre** ♦ *sm* product; ~ **di base** primary product; ~ **finale** end product; ~ **interno lordo (PIL)** gross domestic product (GDP); ~ **nazionale lordo (PNL)** gross national product (GNP); ~**i agricoli** farm produce *sg*; ~**i di bellezza** cosmetics; ~**i chimici** chemicals.

pro'duco *etc vb vedi* **produrre**.

pro'durre *vt* to produce.

pro'dussi *etc vb vedi* **produrre**.

produttività *sf* productivity.

produt'tivo, a *ag* productive.

produt'tore, 'trice *ag* producing *cpd* ♦ *smlf* producer; **paese** ~ **di petrolio** oil-producing country.

produzi'one [produt'tsjone] *sf* production; (*rendimento*) output; ~ **in serie** mass production.

pro'emio *sm* introduction, preface.

Prof. *abbr* (= *professore*) Prof.

profa'nare *vt* to desecrate.

pro'fano, a *ag* (*mondano*) secular, profane; (*sacrilego*) profane.

profe'rire *vt* to utter.

profes'sare *vt* to profess; (*medicina etc*) to practise (*BRIT*), practice (*US*).

professio'nale *ag* professional; **scuola** ~ training college.

professi'one *sf* profession; **di** ~ professional, by profession; **libera** ~ profession.

professio'nista, i, e *smlf* professional.

profes'sore, 'essa *smlf* (*INS*) teacher; (*: di università*) lecturer; (*: titolare di cattedra*) professor; ~ **d'orchestra** member of an orchestra.

pro'feta, i *sm* prophet.

pro'fetico, a, ci, che *ag* prophetic.

profetiz'zare [profetid'dzare] *vt* to prophesy.

profe'zia [profet'tsia] *sf* prophecy.

pro'ficuo, a *ag* useful, profitable.

profi'lare *vt* to outline; (*ornare: vestito*) to edge; ~**rsi** *vr* to stand out, be silhouetted; to loom up.

profi'lassi *sf* (*MED*) preventive treatment, prophylaxis.

profi'lattico, a, ci, che *ag* prophylactic ♦ *sm* (*anticoncezionale*) sheath, condom.

pro'filo *sm* profile; (*breve descrizione*) sketch, outline; **di** ~ in profile.

profit'tare *vi*: ~ **di** (*trarre profitto*) to profit by; (*approfittare*) to take advantage of.

pro'fitto *sm* advantage, profit, benefit; (*fig: progresso*) progress; (*COMM*) profit; **ricavare un** ~ **da** to make a profit from *o* out of; **vendere con** ~ to sell at a profit;

profondere – promozione

conto ~**i e perdite** profit and loss account.
pro'fondere *vt* (*lodi*) to lavish; (*denaro*) to squander; ~**rsi** *vr*: ~**rsi in** to be profuse in.
profondità *sf inv* depth.
pro'fondo, a *ag* deep; (*rancore, meditazione*) profound ♦ *sm* depth(s *pl*), bottom; ~ **8 metri** 8 metres deep.
pro'forma *ag* routine *cpd* ♦ *sm inv* formality ♦ *av*: **fare qc** ~ to do sth as a formality.
'profugo, a, ghi, ghe *sm/f* refugee.
profu'mare *vt* to perfume ♦ *vi* to be fragrant; ~**rsi** *vr* to put on perfume *o* scent.
profumata'mente *av*: **pagare qc** ~ to pay through the nose for sth.
profu'mato, a *ag* (*fiore, aria*) fragrant; (*fazzoletto, saponetta*) scented; (*pelle*) sweet-smelling; (*persona*) with perfume on.
profume'ria *sf* perfumery; (*negozio*) perfume shop.
pro'fumo *sm* (*prodotto*) perfume, scent; (*fragranza*) scent, fragrance.
profusi'one *sf* profusion; **a** ~ in plenty.
pro'fuso, a *pp di* **profondere**.
progeni'tore, 'trice [prodʒeni'tore] *sm/f* ancestor.
proget'tare [prodʒet'tare] *vt* to plan; (*TECN: edificio*) to plan, design; ~ **di fare qc** to plan to do sth.
progettazi'one [prodʒettat'tsjone] *sf* planning; **in corso di** ~ at the planning stage.
proget'tista, i, e [prodʒet'tista] *sm/f* designer.
pro'getto [pro'dʒetto] *sm* plan; (*idea*) plan, project; **avere in** ~ **di fare qc** to be planning to do sth; ~ **di legge** (*POL*) bill.
'prognosi ['proɲɲozi] *sf* (*MED*) prognosis; **essere in** ~ **riservata** to be on the danger list.
pro'gramma, i *sm* programme (*BRIT*), program (*US*); (*TV, RADIO*) program(me)s *pl*; (*INS*) syllabus, curriculum; (*INFORM*) program; **avere in** ~ **di fare qc** to be planning to do sth; ~ **applicativo** (*INFORM*) application program.
program'mare *vt* (*TV, RADIO*) to put on; (*INFORM*) to program; (*ECON*) to plan.
programma'tore, 'trice *sm/f* (*INFORM*) computer programmer (*BRIT*) *o* programer (*US*).
programmazi'one [programmat'tsjone] *sf* programming (*BRIT*), programing (*US*); planning.
progre'dire *vi* to progress, make progress.
progressi'one *sf* progression.
progres'sista, i, e *ag, sm/f* progressive.

progressiva'mente *av* progressively.
progres'sivo, a *ag* progressive.
pro'gresso *sm* progress *no pl*; **fare** ~**i** to make progress.
proi'bire *vt* to forbid, prohibit; ~ **a qn di fare qc** (*vietare*) to forbid sb to do sth; (*impedire*) to prevent sb from doing sth.
proi'bitivo, a *ag* prohibitive.
proi'bito, a *ag* forbidden; **"è** ~ **l'accesso"** "no admittance"; **"è** ~ **fumare"** "no smoking".
proibizi'one [proibit'tsjone] *sf* prohibition.
proibizio'nismo [proibittsjo'nizmo] *sm* prohibition.
proiet'tare *vt* (*gen, GEOM, CINE*) to project; (: *presentare*) to show, screen; (*luce, ombra*) to throw, cast, project.
proi'ettile *sm* projectile, bullet (*o* shell *etc*).
proiet'tore *sm* (*CINE*) projector; (*AUT*) headlamp; (*MIL*) searchlight.
proiezi'one [projet'tsjone] *sf* (*CINE*) projection; showing.
'prole *sf* children *pl*, offspring.
proletari'ato *sm* proletariat.
prole'tario, a *ag, sm/f* proletarian.
prolife'rare *vi* (*fig*) to proliferate.
pro'lifico, a, ci, che *ag* prolific.
pro'lisso, a *ag* verbose.
'prologo, ghi *sm* prologue.
pro'lunga, ghe *sf* (*di cavo elettrico etc*) extension.
prolunga'mento *sm* (*gen*) extension; (*di strada*) continuation.
prolun'gare *vt* (*discorso, attesa*) to prolong; (*linea, termine*) to extend.
prome'moria *sm inv* memorandum.
pro'messa *sf* promise; **fare/mantenere una** ~ to make/keep a promise.
pro'messo, a *pp di* **promettere**.
promet'tente *ag* promising.
pro'mettere *vt* to promise ♦ *vi* to be *o* look promising; ~ **a qn di fare** to promise sb that one will do.
promi'nente *ag* prominent.
promi'nenza [promi'nɛntsa] *sf* prominence.
promiscuità *sf* promiscuousness.
pro'miscuo, a *ag*: **matrimonio** ~ mixed marriage; **nome** ~ (*LING*) common-gender noun.
pro'misi *etc vb vedi* **promettere**.
promon'torio *sm* promontory, headland.
pro'mosso, a *pp di* **promuovere**.
promo'tore, 'trice *sm/f* promoter, organizer.
promozio'nale [promottsjo'nale] *ag* promotional; **"vendita** ~**"** "special offer".
promozi'one [promot'tsjone] *sf* promotion;

~ **delle vendite** sales promotion.
promul'gare *vt* to promulgate.
promulgazi'one [promulgat'tsjone] *sf* promulgation.
promu'overe *vt* to promote.
proni'pote *smf* (*di nonni*) great-grandchild, great-grandson/granddaughter; (*di zii*) great-nephew/niece; ~**i** *smpl* (*discendenti*) descendants.
pro'nome *sm* (*LING*) pronoun.
pronomi'nale *ag* pronominal.
pronosti'care *vt* to foretell, predict.
pro'nostico, ci *sm* forecast.
pron'tezza [pron'tettsa] *sf* readiness; quickness, promptness; ~ **di riflessi** quick reflexes; ~ **di spirito/mente** readiness of wit/mind.
'pronto, a *ag* ready; (*rapido*) fast, quick, prompt; ~! (*TEL*) hello!; **essere** ~ **a fare qc** to be ready to do sth; ~ **all'ira** quick-tempered; **a** ~**a cassa** (*COMM*) cash (*BRIT*) *o* collect (*US*) on delivery; ~**a consegna** (*COMM*) prompt delivery; ~ **soccorso** (*trattamento*) first aid; (*reparto*) A&E (*BRIT*) ER (*US*).
prontu'ario *sm* manual, handbook.
pro'nuncia [pro'nuntʃa] *sf* pronunciation.
pronunci'are [pronun'tʃare] *vt* (*parola*, *sentenza*) to pronounce; (*dire*) to utter; (*discorso*) to deliver; ~**rsi** *vr* to declare one's opinion; ~**rsi a favore di/contro** to pronounce o.s. in favour of/against; **non mi pronuncio** I'm not prepared to comment.
pronunci'ato, a [pronun'tʃato] *ag* (*spiccato*) pronounced, marked; (*sporgente*) prominent.
pro'nunzia *etc* [pro'nuntsja] = **pronuncia** *etc.*
propa'ganda *sf* propaganda.
propagan'dare *vt* (*idea*) to propagandize; (*prodotto, invenzione*) to push, plug (*fam*).
propa'gare *vt* (*FISICA, BIOL*) to propagate; (*notizia, idea, malattia*) to spread; ~**rsi** *vr* to propagate; to spread.
propagaz'ione [propagat'tsjone] *sf* (*vedi vb*) propagation; spreading.
prope'deutico, a, ci, che *ag* (*corso*, *trattato*) introductory.
pro'pendere *vi*: ~ **per** to favour (*BRIT*), favor (*US*), lean towards.
propensi'one *sf* inclination, propensity; **avere** ~ **a credere che** ... to be inclined to think that ....
pro'penso, a *pp di* **propendere** ♦ *ag*: **essere** ~ **a qc** to be in favour (*BRIT*) *o* favor (*US*) of sth; **essere** ~ **a fare qc** to be inclined to do sth.

propi'nare *vt* to administer.
pro'pizio, a [pro'pittsjo] *ag* favourable (*BRIT*), favorable (*US*).
pro'porre *vt* (*suggerire*): ~ **qc (a qn)** to suggest sth (to sb); (*candidato*) to put forward; (*legge, brindisi*) to propose; ~ **di fare** to suggest *o* propose doing; **proporsi di fare** to propose *o* intend to do; **proporsi una meta** to set o.s. a goal.
proporzio'nale [proportsjo'nale] *ag* proportional; (**sistema**) ~ (*POL*) proportional representation system.
proporzio'nato, a [proportsjo'nato] *ag*: ~ **a** proportionate to, proportional to; **ben** ~ well-proportioned.
proporzi'one [propor'tsjone] *sf* proportion; **in** ~ **a** in proportion to.
pro'posito *sm* (*intenzione*) intention, aim; (*argomento*) subject, matter; **a** ~ **di** regarding, with regard to; **a questo** ~ on this subject; **di** ~ (*apposta*) deliberately, on purpose; **a** ~ by the way; **capitare a** ~ (*cosa, persona*) to turn up at the right time.
proposizi'one [propozit'tsjone] *sf* (*LING*) clause; (: *periodo*) sentence.
pro'posto, a *pp di* **proporre** ♦ *sf* proposal; (*suggerimento*) suggestion; **fare una** ~**a** to put forward a proposal; to make a suggestion; ~**a di legge** (*POL*) bill.
propria'mente *av* (*correttamente*) properly, correctly; (*in modo specifico*) specifically; ~ **detto** in the strict sense of the word.
proprietà *sf inv* (*ciò che si possiede*) property *gen no pl*, estate; (*caratteristica*) property; (*correttezza*) correctness; **essere di** ~ **di qn** to belong to sb; ~ **edilizia** (developed) property; ~ **privata** private property.
proprie'tario, a *smf* owner; (*di albergo etc*) proprietor, owner; (*per l'inquilino*) landlord/lady; ~ **terriero** landowner.
'proprio, a *ag* (*possessivo*) own; (: *impersonale*) one's; (*esatto*) exact, correct, proper; (*senso, significato*) literal; (*LING: nome*) proper; (*particolare*): ~ **di** characteristic of, peculiar to ♦ *av* (*precisamente*) just, exactly; (*davvero*) really; (*affatto*): **non** ... ~ not ... at all ♦ *sm* (*COMM*): **mettersi in** ~ to set up on one's own; **l'ha visto con i (suoi)** ~**i occhi** he saw it with his own eyes.
propu'gnare [propuɲ'ɲare] *vt* to support.
propulsi'one *sf* propulsion; **a** ~ **atomica** atomic-powered.
propul'sore *sm* (*TECN*) propeller.
'prora *sf* (*NAUT*) bow(s *pl*), prow.
'proroga, ghe *sf* extension; postponement.

proro'gare *vt* to extend; (*differire*) to postpone, defer.

pro'rompere *vi* to burst out.

pro'rotto, a *pp di* **prorompere.**

pro'ruppi *etc vb vedi* **prorompere.**

'prosa *sf* prose; (*TEAT*): **la stagione della ~** the theatre season; **attore di ~** theatre actor; **compagnia di ~** theatrical company.

pro'saico, a, ci, che *ag* (*fig*) prosaic, mundane.

pro'sciogliere [proʃ'ʃɔʎʎere] *vt* to release; (*DIR*) to acquit.

prosciogli'mento [proʃʃoʎʎi'mento] *sm* acquittal.

prosci'olto, a [proʃ'ʃɔlto] *pp di* **prosciogliere.**

prosciu'gare [proʃʃu'gare] *vt* (*terreni*) to drain, reclaim; **~rsi** *vr* to dry up.

prosci'utto [proʃ'ʃutto] *sm* ham.

pros'critto, a *pp di* **proscrivere** ♦ *sm/f* exile; outlaw.

pros'crivere *vt* to exile, banish.

proscrizi'one [proskrit'tsjone] *sf* (*esilio*) banishment, exile.

prosecuzi'one [prosekut'tsjone] *sf* continuation.

prosegui'mento *sm* continuation; **buon ~!** all the best!

prosegu'ire *vt* to carry on with, continue ♦ *vi* to carry on, go on.

pro'selito *sm* (*REL, POL*) convert.

prospe'rare *vi* to thrive.

prosperità *sf* prosperity.

'prospero, a *ag* (*fiorente*) flourishing, thriving, prosperous.

prospe'roso, a *ag* (*robusto*) hale and hearty; (: *ragazza*) buxom.

prospet'tare *vt* (*esporre*) to point out, show; (*ipotesi*) to advance; (*affare*) to outline; **~rsi** *vr* to look, appear.

prospet'tiva *sf* (*ARTE*) perspective; (*veduta*) view; (*fig: previsione, possibilità*) prospect.

pros'petto *sm* (*DISEGNO*) elevation; (*veduta*) view, prospect; (*facciata*) façade, front; (*tabella*) table; (*sommario*) summary.

prospici'ente [prospi'tʃɛnte] *ag:* **~ qc** facing *o* overlooking sth.

prossima'mente *av* soon.

prossimità *sf* nearness, proximity; **in ~ di** near (to), close to; **in ~ delle feste natalizie** as Christmas approaches.

'prossimo, a *ag* (*vicino*): **~ a** near (to), close to; (*che viene subito dopo*) next; (*parente*) close ♦ *sm* neighbour (*BRIT*), neighbor (*US*), fellow man; **nei ~i giorni**

in the next few days; **in un ~ futuro** in the near future; **~ venturo (pv)** (*AMM*): **venerdì ~ venturo** next Friday.

'prostata *sf* prostate (gland).

prostitu'irsi *vr* to prostitute o.s.

prosti'tuta *sf* prostitute.

prostituzi'one [prostitut'tsjone] *sf* prostitution.

pros'trare *vt* (*fig*) to exhaust, wear out; **~rsi** *vr* (*fig*) to humble o.s.; **prostrato dal dolore** overcome *o* prostrate with grief.

prostrazi'one [prostrat'tsjone] *sf* prostration.

protago'nista, i, e *sm/f* protagonist.

pro'teggere [pro'tɛddʒere] *vt* to protect.

proteggi'slip [protɛddʒi'slip] *sm inv* panty liner.

pro'teico, a, ci, che *ag* protein *cpd*; **altamente ~** high in protein.

prote'ina *sf* protein.

pro'tendere *vt* to stretch out.

'protesi *sf inv* (*MED*) prosthesis.

pro'teso, a *pp di* **protendere.**

pro'testa *sf* protest.

protes'tante *ag, sm/f* Protestant.

protes'tare *vt, vi* to protest; **~rsi** *vr:* **~rsi innocente** to protest one's innocence.

pro'testo *sm* (*DIR*) protest; **mandare una cambiale in ~** to dishonour (*BRIT*) *o* dishonor (*US*) a bill.

protet'tivo, a *ag* protective.

pro'tetto, a *pp di* **proteggere.**

protetto'rato *sm* protectorate.

protet'tore, 'trice *sm/f* protector; (*sostenitore*) patron ♦ *ag* (*REL*): **santo ~** patron saint; **società ~trice dei consumatori** consumer protection society.

protezi'one [protet'tsjone] *sf* protection; (*patrocinio*) patronage; **misure di ~** protective measures; **~ civile** civil defence (*BRIT*) *o* defense (*US*).

protezio'nismo [protettsjo'nizmo] *sm* protectionism.

protocol'lare *vt* to register ♦ *ag* formal; of protocol.

proto'collo *sm* protocol; (*registro*) register of documents ♦ *ag inv:* **foglio ~** foolscap; **numero di ~** reference number.

pro'tone *sm* proton.

pro'totipo *sm* prototype.

pro'trarre *vt* (*prolungare*) to prolong; **protrarsi** *vr* to go on, continue.

pro'tratto, a *pp di* **protrarre.**

protube'ranza [protube'rantsa] *sf* protuberance, bulge.

Prov. *abbr* (= *provincia*) Prov.

'prova *sf* (*esperimento, cimento*) test,

trial; (*tentativo*) attempt, try; (*MAT, testimonianza etc*) proof *no pl*; (*DIR*) evidence *no pl*, proof *no pl*; (*INS*) exam, test; (*TEAT*) rehearsal; (*di abito*) fitting; **a ~ di** (*in testimonianza di*) as proof of; **a ~ di fuoco** fireproof; **assumere in ~** (*per lavoro*) to employ on a trial basis; **essere in ~** (*persona: per lavoro*) to be on trial; **mettere alla ~** to put to the test; **giro di ~** test *o* trial run; **fino a ~ contraria** until (it's) proved otherwise; **~ a carico/a discarico** (*DIR*) evidence for the prosecution/for the defence; **~ documentale** (*DIR*) documentary evidence; **~ generale** (*TEAT*) dress rehearsal.

pro'vare *vt* (*sperimentare*) to test; (*tentare*) to try, attempt; (*assaggiare*) to try, taste; (*sperimentare in sé*) to experience; (*sentire*) to feel; (*cimentare*) to put to the test; (*dimostrare*) to prove; (*abito*) to try on; **~rsi** *vr*: **~rsi (a fare)** to try *o* attempt (to do); **~ a fare** to try *o* attempt to do.

proveni'enza [prove'njɛntsa] *sf* origin, source.

prove'nire *vi*: **~ da** to come from.

pro'venti *smpl* revenue *sg*.

prove'nuto, a *pp di* **provenire**.

Pro'venza [pro'ventsa] *sf*: **la ~** Provence.

proven'zale [proven'tsale] *ag* Provençal.

pro'verbio *sm* proverb.

pro'vetta *sf* test tube; **bambino in ~** test-tube baby.

pro'vetto, a *ag* skilled, experienced.

pro'vider [pro'vaider] *sm inv* (*INFORM*) service provider.

pro'vincia, ce *o* **cie** [pro'vintʃa] *sf* province; *vedi nota nel riquadro*.

PROVINCIA

A **Provincia** *is the autonomous political and administrative unit which is on a level between a "Comune" and a "Regione"; there are 103 in the whole of Italy. The* **Provincia** *is responsible for public health and sanitation, for the maintenance of major roads and public buildings such as schools, and for agriculture and fisheries. Situated in the "capoluogo", or chief town, each* **Provincia** *is run by a "Giunta provinciale", which is elected by the "Consiglio provinciale"; both of these bodies are presided over by a "Presidente".*

---

provinci'ale [provin'tʃale] *ag* provincial; (**strada**) **~** main road (*BRIT*), highway (*US*).

pro'vino *sm* (*CINE*) screen test; (*campione*) specimen.

provo'cante *ag* (*attraente*) provocative.

provo'care *vt* (*causare*) to cause, bring about; (*eccitare: riso, pietà*) to arouse; (*irritare, sfidare*) to provoke.

provoca'tore, 'trice *sm/f* agitator ♦ *ag*: **agente ~** agent provocateur.

provoca'torio, a *ag* provocative.

provocazi'one [provokat'tsjone] *sf* provocation.

provve'dere *vi* (*disporre*): **~ (a)** to provide (for); (*prendere un provvedimento*) to take steps, act ♦ *vt*: **~ qc a qn** to supply sth to sb; **~rsi** *vr*: **~rsi di** to provide o.s. with.

provvedi'mento *sm* measure; (*di previdenza*) precaution; **~ disciplinare** disciplinary measure.

provvedito'rato *sm* (*AMM*): **~ agli studi** divisional education offices *pl*.

provvedi'tore *sm* (*AMM*): **~ agli studi** divisional director of education.

provvi'denza [provvi'dɛntsa] *sf*: **la ~** providence.

provvidenzi'ale [provviden'tsjale] *ag* providential.

provvigi'one [provvi'dʒone] *sf* (*COMM*) commission; **lavoro/stipendio a ~** job/salary on a commission basis.

provvi'sorio, a *ag* temporary; (*governo*) temporary, provisional.

prov'vista *sf* (*riserva*) supply, stock; **fare ~ di** to stock up with.

prov'visto, a *pp di* **provvedere** ♦ *sf* provision, supply.

pro'zia [prot'tsia] *sf* great-aunt.

pro'zio, zii [prot'tsio] *sm* great-uncle.

'prua *sf* (*NAUT*) = **prora**.

pru'dente *ag* cautious, prudent; (*assennato*) sensible, wise.

pru'denza [pru'dɛntsa] *sf* prudence, caution; wisdom; **per ~** as a precaution, to be on the safe side.

'prudere *vi* to itch, be itchy.

'prugna ['pruɲɲa] *sf* plum; **~ secca** prune.

prurigi'noso, a [pruridʒi'noso] *ag* itchy.

pru'rito *sm* itchiness *no pl*; itch.

PS *sigla* = Pesaro.

P.S. *abbr* (= *postscriptum*) P.S.; (*COMM*) = **partita semplice** ♦ *sigla f vedi* **Pubblica Sicurezza**.

P.S.D.I. *sigla m* (= *Partito Socialista Democratico Italiano*) *former political party*.

pseu'donimo *sm* pseudonym.

PSI *sigla m* (*POL*) = Partito Socialista Italiano.

psica'nalisi *sf* psychoanalysis.

psicana'lista, i, e *sm/f* psychoanalyst.

psicanaliz'zare [psikanalid'dzare] *vt* to psychoanalyse.

'psiche ['psike] *sf* psyche.

psiche'delico, a, ci, che [psike'dɛliko] *ag* psychedelic.

psichi'atra, i, e [psi'kjatra] *sm/f* psychiatrist.

psichia'tria [psikja'tria] *sf* psychiatry.

psichi'atrico, a, ci, che [psi'kjatriko] *ag* (*caso*) psychiatric; (*reparto, ospedale*) psychiatric, mental.

'psichico, a, ci, che ['psikiko] *ag* psychological.

psico'farmaco, ci *sm* (*MED*) drug used in treatment of mental conditions.

psicolo'gia [psikolo'dʒia] *sf* psychology.

psico'logico, a, ci, che [psiko'lɔdʒiko] *ag* psychological.

psi'cologo, a, gi, ghe *sm/f* psychologist.

psico'patico, a, ci, che *ag* psychopathic ♦ *sm/f* psychopath.

psi'cosi *sf inv* (*MED*) psychosis; (*fig*) obsessive fear.

psicoso'matico, a, ci, che *ag* psychosomatic.

PT *sigla* = Pistoia.

Pt. *abbr* (*GEO*: = punta) Pt.

P.T. *abbr* (= Posta e Telegrafi) ≈ PO (= Post Office); (*FISCO*) = polizia tributaria.

P.ta *abbr* = porta.

pubbli'care *vt* to publish.

pubblicazi'one [pubblikat'tsjone] *sf* publication; ~ **periodica** periodical; ~**i (matrimoniali)** *sfpl* (marriage) banns.

pubbli'cista, i, e [pubbli'tʃista] *sm/f* (*STAMPA*) freelance journalist.

pubblicità [pubblitʃi'ta] *sf* (*diffusione*) publicity; (*attività*) advertising; (*annunci nei giornali*) advertisements *pl*; **fare** ~ **a qc** to advertise sth.

pubblici'tario, a [pubblitʃi'tarjo] *ag* advertising *cpd*; (*trovata, film*) publicity *cpd* ♦ *sm* advertising agent; **annuncio** *o* **avviso** ~ advertisement.

'pubblico, a, ci, che *ag* public; (*statale: scuola etc*) state *cpd* ♦ *sm* public; (*spettatori*) audience; **in** ~ in public; **la** ~**a amministrazione** public administration; **un** ~ **esercizio** a catering (*o* hotel *o* entertainment) business; ~ **funzionario** civil servant; **Ministero della P~a Istruzione** ≈ Department of Education and Science (*BRIT*), ≈ Department of Health, Education and Welfare (*US*); **P~ Ministero** Public Prosecutor's Office; **la P~a Sicurezza (P.S.)** the police.

'pube *sm* (*ANAT*) pubis.

pubertà *sf* puberty.

'pudico, a, ci, che *ag* modest.

pu'dore *sm* modesty.

puericul'tura *sf* infant care.

pue'rile *ag* childish.

pu'erpera *sf* woman who has just given birth.

pugi'lato [pudʒi'lato] *sm* boxing.

'pugile ['pudʒile] *sm* boxer.

pugli'ese [puʎ'ʎese] *ag* of (*o* from) Puglia.

pugna'lare [puɲɲa'lare] *vt* to stab.

pu'gnale [puɲ'ɲale] *sm* dagger.

'pugno ['puɲɲo] *sm* fist; (*colpo*) punch; (*quantità*) fistful; **avere qn in** ~ to have sb in the palm of one's hand; **tenere la situazione in** ~ to have control of the situation; **scrivere qc di proprio** ~ to write sth in one's own hand.

'pulce ['pultʃe] *sf* flea.

pul'cino [pul'tʃino] *sm* chick.

pu'ledro, a *sm/f* colt/filly.

pu'leggia, ge [pu'leddʒa] *sf* pulley.

pu'lire *vt* to clean; (*lucidare*) to polish; **far** ~ **qc** to have sth cleaned; ~ **a secco** to dry-clean.

pu'lito, a *ag* (*anche fig*) clean; (*ordinato*) neat, tidy ♦ *sf* quick clean; **avere la coscienza** ~**a** to have a clear conscience.

puli'tura *sf* cleaning; ~ **a secco** dry-cleaning.

puli'zia [pulit'tsia] *sf* (*atto*) cleaning; (*condizione*) cleanness; **fare le** ~**e** to do the cleaning, do the housework; ~ **etnica** ethnic cleansing.

'pullman *sm inv* coach (*BRIT*), bus.

pul'lover *sm inv* pullover, jumper.

pullu'lare *vi* to swarm, teem.

pul'mino *sm* minibus.

'pulpito *sm* pulpit.

pul'sante *sm* (push-)button.

pul'sare *vi* to pulsate, beat.

pulsazi'one [pulsat'tsjone] *sf* beat.

pul'viscolo *sm* fine dust.

'puma *sm inv* puma.

pun'gente [pun'dʒɛnte] *ag* prickly; stinging; (*anche fig*) biting.

'pungere ['pundʒere] *vt* to prick; (*sog: insetto, ortica*) to sting; (: *freddo*) to bite; ~ **qn sul vivo** (*fig*) to cut sb to the quick.

pungigli'one [pundʒiʎ'ʎone] *sm* sting.

pungo'lare *vt* to goad.

pu'nire *vt* to punish.

puni'tivo, a *ag* punitive.

punizi'one [punit'tsjone] *sf* punishment; (*SPORT*) penalty.

'punsi *etc vb vedi* **pungere**.

'punta *sf* point; (*parte terminale*) tip, end; (*di monte*) peak; (*di costa*) promontory; (*minima parte*) touch, trace; **in** ~ **di piedi** on tiptoe; **ore di** ~ peak hours; **uomo di** ~ (*SPORT, POL*) front-rank *o* leading man; **doppie** ~**e** split ends.

pun'tare _vt (piedi a terra, gomiti sul tavolo)_ to plant; _(dirigere: pistola)_ to point; _(scommettere)_: ~ **su** to bet on ♦ _vi (mirare)_: ~ **a** to aim at; _(avviarsi)_: ~ **su** to head _o_ make for; _(fig: contare)_: ~ **su** to count _o_ rely on.

puntas'pilli _sm inv_ = **portaspilli**.

pun'tata _sf (gita)_ short trip; _(scommessa)_ bet; _(parte di opera)_ instalment _(BRIT)_, installment _(US)_; **farò una ~ a Parigi** I'll pay a flying visit to Paris; **romanzo a ~e** serial.

punteggi'are [punted'dʒare] _vt_ to punctuate.

punteggia'tura [punteddʒa'tura] _sf_ punctuation.

pun'teggio [pun'teddʒo] _sm_ score.

puntel'lare _vt_ to support.

pun'tello _sm_ prop, support.

punteru'olo _sm (TECN)_ punch; _(: per stoffa)_ bodkin.

pun'tiglio [pun'tiʎʎo] _sm_ obstinacy, stubbornness.

puntigli'oso, a [puntiʎ'ʎoso] _ag_ punctilious.

pun'tina _sf_: ~ **da disegno** drawing pin _(BRIT)_, thumb tack _(US)_; ~**e** _sfpl (AUT)_ points.

pun'tino _sm_ dot; **fare qc a ~** to do sth properly; **arrivare a ~** to arrive just at the right moment; **cotto a ~** cooked to perfection; **mettere i ~i sulle "i"** _(fig)_ to dot the i's and cross the t's.

'punto, a _pp di_ **pungere** ♦ _sm (segno, macchiolina)_ dot; _(LING)_ full stop; _(MAT, momento, di punteggio, fig: argomento)_ point; _(di indirizzo e-mail)_ dot; _(posto)_ spot; _(a scuola)_ mark; _(nel cucire, nella maglia, MED)_ stitch ♦ _av_: **non … ~** not … at all; **due ~i** _sm inv (LING)_ colon; **ad un certo ~** at a certain point; **fino ad un certo ~** _(fig)_ to a certain extent; **sul ~ di fare** (just) about to do; **fare il ~** _(NAUT)_ to take a bearing; **fare il ~ della situazione** _(analisi)_ to take stock of the situation; _(riassunto)_ to sum up the situation; **alle 6 in ~** at 6 o'clock sharp _o_ on the dot; **essere a buon ~** to have reached a satisfactory stage; **mettere a ~** to adjust; _(motore)_ to tune; _(cannocchiale)_ to focus; _(fig)_ to settle; **venire al ~** to come to the point; **vestito di tutto ~** all dressed up; **di ~ in bianco** point-blank; ~ **d'arrivo** arrival point; ~ **cardinale** point of the compass, cardinal point; ~ **debole** weak point; ~ **esclamativo/interrogativo** exclamation/ question mark; ~ **d'incontro** meeting place, meeting point; ~ **morto** standstill;

~ **nero** _(comedone)_ blackhead; ~ **nevralgico** _(anche fig)_ nerve centre _(BRIT)_ _o_ center _(US)_; ~ **di partenza** _(anche fig)_ starting point; ~ **di riferimento** landmark; _(fig)_ point of reference; ~ **di vendita** retail outlet; ~ **e virgola** semicolon; ~ **di vista** _(fig)_ point of view; ~**i di sospensione** suspension points.

puntu'ale _ag_ punctual.

puntualità _sf_ punctuality.

puntualiz'zare [puntualid'dzare] _vt_ to make clear.

puntual'mente _av (gen)_ on time; _(ironico: al solito)_ as usual.

pun'tura _sf (di ago)_ prick; _(di insetto)_ sting, bite; _(MED)_ puncture; _(: iniezione)_ injection; _(dolore)_ sharp pain.

punzecchi'are [puntsek'kjare] _vt_ to prick; _(fig)_ to tease.

punzo'nare [puntso'nare] _vt (TECN)_ to stamp.

pun'zone [pun'tsone] _sm (per metalli)_ stamp, die.

può, pu'oi _vb vedi_ **potere**.

'pupa _sf_ doll.

pu'pazzo [pu'pattso] _sm_ puppet.

pu'pillo, a _sm/f (DIR)_ ward; _(prediletto)_ favourite _(BRIT)_, favorite _(US)_, pet ♦ _sf (ANAT)_ pupil.

purché [pur'ke] _cong_ provided that, on condition that.

'pure _cong (tuttavia)_ and yet, nevertheless; _(anche se)_ even if ♦ _av (anche)_ too, also; **pur di** _(al fine di)_ just to; **faccia ~!** go ahead!, please do!

purè _sm_, **pu'rea** _sf (CUC)_ purée; _(: di patate)_ mashed potatoes.

pu'rezza [pu'rettsa] _sf_ purity.

'purga, ghe _sf_ purging _no pl_; purge.

pur'gante _sm (MED)_ purgative, purge.

pur'gare _vt (MED, POL)_ to purge; _(pulire)_ to clean.

purga'torio _sm_ purgatory.

purifi'care _vt_ to purify; _(metallo)_ to refine.

purificazi'one [purifikat'tsjone] _sf_ purification; refinement.

puri'tano, a _ag, sm/f_ puritan.

'puro, a _ag_ pure; _(acqua)_ clear, limpid; _(vino)_ undiluted; **di razza ~a** thoroughbred; **per ~ caso** by sheer chance, purely by chance.

puro'sangue _sm/f inv_ thoroughbred.

pur'troppo _av_ unfortunately.

pus _sm_ pus.

pusil'lanime _ag_ cowardly.

'pustola _sf_ pimple.

puta'caso _av_ just supposing, suppose.

puti'ferio _sm_ rumpus, row.

putre'fare *vi* to putrefy, rot.
putre'fatto, a *pp di* **putrefare.**
putrefazi'one [putrefat'tsjone] *sf* putrefaction.
'putrido, a *ag* putrid, rotten.
put'tana *sf* (*fam!*) whore (*!*).
'putto *sm* cupid.
'puzza ['puttsa] *sf* = **puzzo.**
puz'zare [put'tsare] *vi* to stink; **la faccenda puzza (d'imbroglio)** the whole business stinks.
'puzzo ['puttso] *sm* stink, foul smell.
'puzzola ['puttsola] *sf* polecat.
puzzo'lente [puttso'lɛnte] *ag* stinking.
PV *sigla* = Pavia.
pv *abbr vedi* **prossimo venturo.**
P.V.C. [pivi't ʃi] *sigla m* (= *polyvinyl chloride*) PVC.
PZ *sigla* = Potenza.
p. zza *abbr* = **piazza.**

Q q

Q, q [ku] *sf o m inv* (*lettera*) Q, q; **Q come Quarto** ≈ Q for Queen.
q *abbr* (= *quintale*) q.
Qa'tar [ka'tar] *sm*: **il ~** Qatar.
q.b. *abbr* (= *quanto basta*) as needed; **zucchero ~** sugar to taste.
Q.G. *abbr* = **quartier generale.**
Q.I. *abbr vedi* **quoziente d'intelligenza.**
qua *av* here; **in ~** (*verso questa parte*) this way; **~ dentro/sotto** *etc* in/under here *etc*; **da un anno in ~** for a year now; **da quando in ~?** since when?; **per di ~** (*passare*) this way; **al di ~ di** (*fiume, strada*) on this side of; *vedi* **questo.**
'quacchero, a ['kwakkero] *sm/f* Quaker.
qua'derno *sm* notebook; (*per scuola*) exercise book.
qua'drangolo *sm* quadrangle.
qua'drante *sm* quadrant; (*di orologio*) face.
qua'drare *vi* (*bilancio*) to balance, tally; (*fig: corrispondere*): **~ (con)** to correspond (with) ♦ *vt* (*MAT*) to square; **far ~ il bilancio** to balance the books; **non mi quadra** I don't like it.
qua'drato, a *ag* square; (*fig: equilibrato*) level-headed, sensible; (: *peg*) square ♦ *sm* (*MAT*) square; (*PUGILATO*) ring; **5 al ~** 5 squared.
quadret'tato, a *ag* (*foglio*) squared; (*tessuto*) checked.
qua'dretto *sm*: **a ~i** (*tessuto*) checked; (*foglio*) squared.
quadrien'nale *ag* (*che dura 4 anni*) four-year *cpd*; (*che avviene ogni 4 anni*) four-yearly.
quadri'foglio [kwadri'fɔʎʎo] *sm* four-leaf clover.
quadri'mestre *sm* (*periodo*) four-month period; (*INS*) term.
'quadro *sm* (*pittura*) painting, picture; (*quadrato*) square; (*tabella*) table, chart; (*TECN*) board, panel; (*TEAT*) scene; (*fig: scena, spettacolo*) sight; (: *descrizione*) outline, description; **~i** *smpl* (*POL*) party organizers; (*COMM*) managerial staff; (*MIL*) cadres; (*CARTE*) diamonds; **a ~i** (*disegno*) checked; **fare un ~ della situazione** to outline the situation; **~ clinico** (*MED*) case history; **~ di comando** control panel; **~i intermedi** middle management *sg.*
qua'drupede *sm* quadruped.
quadrupli'care *vt* to quadruple.
'quadruplo, a *ag, sm* quadruple.
quaggiù [kwad'dʒu] *av* down here.
'quaglia ['kwaʎʎa] *sf* quail.

════════════ *PAROLA CHIAVE*

'qualche ['kwalke] *det* **1** some, a few; (*in interrogative*) any; **ho comprato ~ libro** I've bought some *o* a few books; **~ volta** sometimes; **hai ~ sigaretta?** have you any cigarettes?
2 (*uno*): **c'è ~ medico?** is there a doctor?; **in ~ modo** somehow
3 (*un certo, parecchio*) some; **un personaggio di ~ rilievo** a figure of some importance
4: **~ cosa** = **qualcosa.**

qualche'duno [kwalke'duno] *pron* = **qualcuno.**
qual'cosa *pron* something; (*in espressioni interrogative*) anything; **qualcos'altro** something else; anything else; **~ di nuovo** something new; anything new; **~ da mangiare** something to eat; anything to eat; **c'è ~ che non va?** is there something *o* anything wrong?
qual'cuno *pron* (*persona*) someone, somebody; (: *in espressioni interrogative*) anyone, anybody; (*alcuni*) some; **~ è favorevole a noi** some are on our side; **qualcun altro** someone *o* somebody else; anyone *o* anybody else.

═══════════════ *PAROLA CHIAVE*

'quale (*spesso troncato in* **qual**) *det* **1**
(*interrogativo*) what; (: *scegliendo tra due o
più cose o persone*) which; ~ **uomo/
denaro?** what man/money?; which man/
money?; ~**i sono i tuoi programmi?** what
are your plans?; ~ **stanza preferisci?**
which room do you prefer?
2 (*relativo: come*): **il risultato fu** ~ **ci si
aspettava** the result was as expected
3 (*in elenchi*) such as, like; **piante** ~**i
l'edera** plants such as o like ivy
4 (*esclamativo*) what; ~ **disgrazia!** what
bad luck!
5: **in un certo qual modo** in a way, in
some ways; **per la qual cosa** for which
reason
♦ *pron* **1** (*interrogativo*) which; ~ **dei due
scegli?** which of the two do you want?
2 (*relativo*) ~ (*persona: soggetto*)
who; (: *oggetto, con preposizione*) whom;
(*cosa*) which; (*possessivo*) whose; **suo
padre, il** ~ **è avvocato,** ... his father, who
is a lawyer, ...; **a tutti coloro i** ~**i fossero
interessati** ... to whom it may concern ...;
il signore con il ~ **parlavo** the gentleman
to whom I was speaking; **l'albergo al** ~ **ci
siamo fermati** the hotel where we stayed
o which we stayed at; **la signora della** ~
ammiriamo la bellezza the lady whose
beauty we admire
♦ *av* (*in qualità di, come*) as; ~ **sindaco di
questa città** as mayor of this town.

qua'lifica, che *sf* qualification; (*titolo*) title.
qualifi'care *vt* to qualify; (*definire*): ~ **qn/
qc come** to describe sb/sth as; ~**rsi** *vr*
(*anche SPORT*) to qualify; ~**rsi a un
concorso** to pass a competitive exam.
qualifica'tivo, a *ag* qualifying.
qualifi'cato, a *ag* (*dotato di qualifica*)
qualified; (*esperto, abile*) skilled; **non mi
ritengo** ~ **per questo lavoro** I don't think
I'm qualified for this job; **è un medico
molto** ~ he is a very distinguished
doctor.
qualificazi'one [kwalifikat'tsjone] *sf*
qualification; **gara di** ~ (*SPORT*) qualifying
event.
qualità *sf inv* quality; **di ottima** o **prima** ~
top quality; **in** ~ **di** in one's capacity as; **in
** ~ **di amica** as a friend; **articoli di ogni** ~
all sorts of goods; **controllo (di)** ~ quality
control; **prodotto di** ~ quality product.
qualita'tivo, a *ag* qualitative.
qua'lora *cong* in case, if.
qual'siasi, qua'lunque *det inv* any; (*quale*

che sia) whatever; (*discriminativo*)
whichever; (*posposto: mediocre*) poor,
indifferent; ordinary; **mettiti un vestito** ~
put on any old dress; ~ **cosa** anything; ~
cosa accada whatever happens; **a** ~ **costo**
at any cost, whatever the cost; **l'uomo** ~
the man in the street; ~ **persona** anyone,
anybody.
qualunqu'ista, i, e *sm/f* person *indifferent
to politics*.
'quando *cong, av* when; ~ **sarò ricco** when
I'm rich; **da** ~ (*dacché*) since;
(*interrogativo*): **da** ~ **sei qui?** how long
have you been here?; **di** ~ **in** ~ from time
to time; **quand'anche** even if.
quantifi'care *vt* to quantify.
quantità *sf inv* quantity; (*gran numero*): **una
** ~ **di** a great deal of; a lot of; **in grande** ~
in large quantities.
quantita'tivo, a *ag* quantitative ♦ *sm*
(*COMM: di merce*) amount, quantity.

═══════════════ *PAROLA CHIAVE*

'quanto, a *det* **1** (*interrogativo: quantità*) how
much; (: *numero*) how many; ~ **pane/
denaro?** how much bread/money?; ~**i
libri/ragazzi?** how many books/boys?; ~
tempo? how long?; ~**i anni hai?** how old
are you?
2 (*esclamativo*): ~**e storie!** what a lot of
nonsense!; ~ **tempo sprecato!** what a
waste of time!
3 (*relativo: quantità*) as much ... as;
(: *numero*) as many ... as; **ho** ~ **denaro mi
occorre** I have as much money as I need;
prendi ~**i libri vuoi** take as many books as
you like
♦ *pron* **1** (*interrogativo: quantità*) how much;
(: *numero*) how many; (: *tempo*) how long;
~ **mi dai?** how much will you give me?;
~**i me ne hai portati?** how many did you
bring me?; ~ **starai via?** how long will you
be away (for)?; **da** ~ **sei qui?** how long
have you been here?; ~**i ne abbiamo
oggi?** what's the date today?
2 (*relativo: quantità*) as much as;
(: *numero*) as many as; **farò** ~ **posso** I'll do
as much as I can; **a** ~ **dice lui** according
to him; **in risposta a** ~ **esposto nella sua
lettera** ... in answer to the points raised
in your letter; **possono venire
** ~**i sono stati invitati** all those who have
been invited can come
♦ *av* **1** (*interrogativo: con ag, av*) how; (: *con
vb*) how much; ~ **stanco ti sembrava?** how
tired did he seem to you?; ~ **corre la tua
moto?** how fast can your motorbike go?;
~ **costa?** how much does it cost?;

quant'è? how much is it?
2 (*esclamativo: con ag, av*) how; (: *con vb*)
how much; ~ **sono felice!** how happy I
am!; **sapessi ~ abbiamo camminato!** if
you knew how far we've walked!;
studierò ~ posso I'll study as much as *o*
all I can; ~ **prima** as soon as possible; ~
più ... tanto meno the more ... the less; ~
più ... tanto più the more ... the more
3: **in ~** (*in qualità di*) as; (*perché, per il fatto
che*) as, since; **in ~ legale della signora** as
the lady's lawyer; **non è possibile in ~
non possiamo permettercelo** it isn't
possible, since we can't afford it; **(in)** ~ **a**
(*per ciò che riguarda*) as for, as regards;
(in) ~ **a lui** as far as he's concerned
4: **per ~** (*nonostante, anche se*) however;
per ~ si sforzi, non ce la farà try as he
may, he won't manage it; **per ~ sia brava,
fa degli errori** however good she may be,
she makes mistakes; **per ~ io sappia** as
far as I know.

quan'tunque *cong* although, though.
qua'ranta *num* forty.
quaran'tena *sf* quarantine.
quaran'tenne *ag, sm/f* forty-year-old.
quaran'tennio *sm* (period of) forty
years.
quaran'tesimo, a *num* fortieth.
quaran'tina *sf*: **una ~ (di)** about forty.
quaran'totto *sm inv* forty-eight; **fare un ~**
(*fam*) to raise hell.
Qua'resima *sf*: **la ~** Lent.
'quarta *sf vedi* quarto.
quar'tetto *sm* quartet(te).
quarti'ere *sm* district, area; (*MIL*) quarters
pl; ~ **generale (Q.G.)** headquarters *pl*
(HQ); ~ **residenziale** residential area *o*
district; **i ~i alti** the smart districts.
'quarto, a *ag* fourth ♦ *sm* fourth; (*quarta
parte*) quarter ♦ *sf* (*AUT*) fourth (gear);
(*INS: elementare*) *fourth year of primary
school*; (: *superiore*) *seventh year of
secondary school*; **un ~ di vino** a quarter-
litre (*BRIT*) *o* quarter-liter (*US*) bottle of
wine; **le 6 e un ~** a quarter past (*BRIT*) *o*
after (*US*) 6; ~ **d'ora** quarter of an hour;
tre ~i d'ora three quarters of an hour; **le
otto e tre ~i, le nove meno un ~** (a)
quarter to (*BRIT*) *o* of (*US*) nine; **passare
un brutto ~ d'ora** (*fig*) to have a bad *o*
nasty time of it; **~i di finale** (*SPORT*)
quarter finals.
'quarzo ['kwartso] *sm* quartz.
'quasi *av* almost, nearly ♦ *cong* (*anche*:
~ **che**) as if; (*non*) ... ~ **mai** hardly ever;
~ ~ **me ne andrei** I've half a mind to

leave.
quassù *av* up here.
'quatto, a *ag* crouched, squatting;
(*silenzioso*) silent; ~ ~ very quietly;
stealthily.
quattordi'cenne [kwattordi'tʃɛnne] *ag, sm/f*
fourteen-year-old.
quat'tordici [kwat'torditʃi] *num* fourteen.
quat'trini *smpl* money *sg*, cash *sg*.
'quattro *num* four; **in ~ e quattr'otto** in less
than no time; **dirne ~ a qn** to give sb a
piece of one's mind; **fare il diavolo a ~** to
kick up a rumpus; **fare ~ chiacchiere** to
have a chat; **farsi in ~ per qn** to go out of
one's way for sb, put o.s. out for sb.
quat'trocchi [kwat'trɔkki] *sm inv* (*fig fam*:
persona con occhiali) four-eyes; **a ~** *av* (*tra
2 persone*) face to face; (*privatamente*) in
private.
quattrocen'tesco, a, schi, sche
[kwattrotʃen'tesko] *ag* fifteenth-
century.
quattro'cento [kwattro'tʃɛnto] *num*
four hundred ♦ *sm*: **il Q~** the fifteenth
century.
quattro'mila *num* four thousand.

──────── *PAROLA CHIAVE*

'quello, a (*dav sm* **quel** + C, **quell'** + V,
quello + *s impura, gn, pn, ps, x, z; pl* **quei** +
C, **quegli** + V *o s impura, gn, pn, ps, x, z; dav
sf* **quella** + C, **quell'** + V; *pl* **quelle**) *det* that;
those *pl*; ~**a casa** that house; **quegli
uomini** those men; **voglio** ~**a camicia (lì** *o*
là) I want that shirt; ~ **è mio fratello**
that's my brother
♦ *pron* **1** (*dimostrativo*) that (one); those
(ones) *pl*; (*ciò*) that; **conosci** ~**a?** do you
know her?; **prendo ~ bianco** I'll take the
white one; **chi è** ~**?** who's that?;
prendiamo ~ (lì *o* **là)** let's take that one
(there); **in quel di Milano** in the Milan
area *o* region
2 (*relativo*): ~**(a) che** (*persona*) the one
(who); (*cosa*) the one (which), the one
(that); ~**i(e) che** (*persone*) those who;
(*cose*) those which; **è lui ~ che non voleva
venire** he's the one who didn't want to
come; **ho fatto ~ che potevo** I did what I
could; **è** ~**a che ti ho prestato** that's the
one I lent you; **è proprio ~ che gli ho
detto** that's exactly what I told him; **da ~
che ho sentito** from what I've heard.

'quercia, ce ['kwɛrtʃa] *sf* oak (tree); (*legno*)
oak; **la Q**~(*POL*) *symbol of P.D.S.*
que'rela *sf* (*DIR*) (legal) action.
quere'lare *vt* to bring an action against.

que'sito *sm* question, query; problem.
'questi *pron* (*poetico*) this person.
questio'nario *sm* questionnaire.
questi'one *sf* problem, question;
(*controversia*) issue; (*litigio*) quarrel; **in ~**
in question; **il caso in ~** the matter at
hand; **la persona in ~** the person
involved; **non voglio essere chiamato in ~**
I don't want to be dragged into the
argument; **fuor di ~** out of the question; **è
~ di tempo** it's a matter *o* question of
time.

═══════════ *PAROLA CHIAVE*

'questo, a *det* **1** (*dimostrativo*) this; these *pl*;
~ libro (qui *o* **qua)** this book; **io prendo ~
cappotto, tu quello** I'll take this coat, you
take that one; **quest'oggi** today; **~a sera**
this evening
2 (*enfatico*): **non fatemi più prendere di
~e paure** don't frighten me like that
again
♦ *pron* (*dimostrativo*) this (one); these
(ones) *pl*; (*ciò*) this; **prendo ~ (qui** *o* **qua)**
I'll take this one; **preferisci ~i o quelli?** do
you prefer these (ones) or those (ones)?;
~ intendevo io this is what I meant; **~
non dovevi dirlo** you shouldn't have said
that; **e con ~?** so what?; **e con ~ se n'è
andato** and with that he left; **con tutto ~**
in spite of this, despite all this; **~ è
quanto** that's all.

ques'tore *sm* public official in charge of
the police in the provincial capital,
reporting to the prefetto; ≈ chief
constable (*BRIT*), ≈ police commissioner
(*US*).
'questua *sf* collection (of alms).
ques'tura *sf* police headquarters *pl*.
questu'rino *sm* (*fam: poliziotto*) cop.
qui *av* here; **da** *o* **di ~** from here; **di ~ in
avanti** from now on; **di ~ a poco/una
settimana** in a little while/a week's time;
~ dentro/sopra/vicino in/up/near here;
vedi **questo**.
quie'tanza [kwje'tantsa] *sf* receipt.
qui'ete *sf* quiet, quietness; calmness;
stillness; peace; **turbare la ~ pubblica**
(*DIR*) to disturb the peace.
qui'eto, a *ag* quiet; (*notte*) calm, still;
(*mare*) calm; **l'ho fatto per il ~ vivere** I did
it for a quiet life.
'quindi *av* then ♦ *cong* therefore, so.
quindi'cenne [kwindi'tʃɛnne] *ag, sm/f*
fifteen-year-old.
'quindici ['kwinditʃi] *num* fifteen; **~ giorni** a
fortnight (*BRIT*), two weeks.

quindi'cina [kwindi'tʃina] *sf* (*serie*): **una ~
(di)** about fifteen; **fra una ~ di giorni** in a
fortnight (*BRIT*) *o* two weeks.
quindici'nale [kwinditʃi'nale] *ag* fortnightly
(*BRIT*), semimonthly (*US*) ♦ *sm* (*rivista*)
fortnightly magazine (*BRIT*), semimonthly
(*US*).
quinquen'nale *ag* (*che dura 5 anni*) five-
year *cpd*; (*che avviene ogni 5 anni*) five-
yearly.
quin'quennio *sm* period of five years.
quinta *sf vedi* **quinto**.
quin'tale *sm* quintal (*100 kg*).
quin'tetto *sm* quintet(te).
'quinto, a *num* fifth ♦ *sf* (*AUT*) fifth (gear);
(*INS: elementare*) *fifth year of primary
school; (: superiore*) *final year of
secondary school; (TEAT*) wing; **un ~ della
popolazione** a fifth of the population; **tre
~i** three fifths; **in ~a pagina** on the fifth
page, on page five.
qui pro quo *sm inv* misunderstanding.
Quiri'nale *sm vedi nota nel riquadro*.

┌──────────────────────────────────┐
│ **QUIRINALE** │
│ │
│ *The* **Quirinale** *takes its name from one of the
Seven Hills of Rome on which it stands. It is the
official residence of the "Presidente della
Repubblica".* │
└──────────────────────────────────┘

'Quito *sf* Quito.
quiz [kwidz] *sm inv* (*domanda*) question;
(*anche: gioco a ~*) quiz game.
'quorum *sm* quorum.
'quota *sf* (*parte*) quota, share; (*AER*) height,
altitude; (*IPPICA*) odds *pl*; **prendere/
perdere ~** (*AER*) to gain/lose height *o*
altitude; **~ imponibile** taxable income; **~
d'iscrizione** (*INS*) enrolment fee; (*ad una
gara*) entry fee; (*ad un club*) membership
fee; **~ di mercato** market share.
quo'tare *vt* (*BORSA*) to quote; (*valutare:
anche fig*) to value; **è un pittore molto
quotato** he is rated highly as a painter.
quotazi'one [kwotat'tsjone] *sf* quotation.
quotidiana'mente *av* daily, every day.
quotidi'ano, a *ag* daily; (*banale*) everyday
♦ *sm* (*giornale*) daily (paper).
quozi'ente [kwot'tsjɛnte] *sm* (*MAT*)
quotient; **~ di crescita zero** zero growth
rate; **~ d'intelligenza (Q.I.)** intelligence
quotient (IQ).

R r

R, r ['ɛrre] *sf o m* (*lettera*) R, r; **R come Roma** ≈ R for Robert (*BRIT*), R for Roger (*US*).
R *abbr* (*POSTA*) = **raccomandata;** (*FERR*) = **rapido.**
RA *sigla* = *Ravenna*.
ra'barbaro *sm* rhubarb.
Ra'bat *sf* Rabat.
rabberci'are [rabber'tʃare] *vt* (*anche fig*) to patch up.
'rabbia *sf* (*ira*) anger, rage; (*accanimento, furia*) fury; (*MED: idrofobia*) rabies *sg*.
rab'bino *sm* rabbi.
rabbi'oso, a *ag* angry, furious; (*facile all'ira*) quick-tempered; (*forze, acqua etc*) furious, raging; (*MED*) rabid, mad.
rabbo'nire *vt*, **~rsi** *vr* to calm down.
rabbrivi'dire *vi* to shudder, shiver.
rabbui'arsi *vr* to grow dark.
rabdo'mante *sm* water diviner.
racc. *abbr* (*POSTA*) = **raccomandata.**
raccapez'zarsi [rakkapet'tsarsi] *vr*: **non ~** to be at a loss.
raccapricci'ante [rakkaprit'tʃante] *ag* horrifying.
racca'priccio [rakka'prittʃo] *sm* horror.
raccatta'palle *sm inv* (*SPORT*) ballboy.
raccat'tare *vt* to pick up.
rac'chetta [rak'ketta] *sf* (*per tennis*) racket; (*per ping-pong*) bat; **~ da neve** snowshoe; **~ da sci** ski stick.
'racchio, a ['rakkjo] *ag* (*fam*) ugly.
racchi'udere [rak'kjudere] *vt* to contain.
racchi'uso, a [rak'kjuso] *pp di* **racchiudere.**
rac'cogliere [rak'kɔʎʎere] *vt* to collect; (*raccattare*) to pick up; (*frutti, fiori*) to pick, pluck; (*AGR*) to harvest; (*approvazione, voti*) to win; (*profughi*) to take in; (*vele*) to furl; (*capelli*) to put up; **~rsi** *vr* to gather; (*fig*) to gather one's thoughts; to meditate; **non ha raccolto** (*allusione*) he didn't take the hint; (*frecciata*) he took no notice of it; **~ i frutti del proprio lavoro** (*fig*) to reap the benefits of one's work; **~ le idee** (*fig*) to gather one's thoughts.
raccogli'mento [rakkoʎʎi'mento] *sm* meditation.
raccogli'tore [rakkoʎʎi'tore] *sm* (*cartella*) folder, binder; **~ a fogli mobili** loose-leaf binder.
rac'colto, a *pp di* **raccogliere** ♦ *ag* (*persona: pensoso*) thoughtful; (*luogo: appartato*) secluded, quiet ♦ *sm* (*AGR*) crop, harvest ♦ *sf* collecting *no pl*; collection; (*AGR*) harvesting *no pl*, gathering *no pl*; harvest, crop; **fare la ~a di qc** to collect sth; **chiamare a ~a** to gather together; **~a differenziata** (*dei rifiuti*) separate collection of different kinds of household waste.
raccoman'dabile *ag* (highly) commendable; **è un tipo poco ~** he is not to be trusted.
raccoman'dare *vt* to recommend; (*affidare*) to entrust; **~rsi** *vr*: **~rsi a qn** to commend o.s. to sb; **~ a qn di fare qc** to recommend that sb does sth; **~ a qn di non fare qc** to tell o warn sb not to do sth; **~ qn a qn/alle cure di qn** to entrust sb to sb/to sb's care; **mi raccomando!** don't forget!
raccoman'dato, a *ag* (*lettera, pacco*) recorded-delivery (*BRIT*), certified (*US*); (*candidato*) recommended ♦ *sm/f*: **essere un(a) ~(a) di ferro** to have friends in high places ♦ *sf* (*anche:* **lettera ~a**) recorded-delivery letter; **~a con ricevuta di ritorno** (**Rrr**) recorded-delivery letter with advice of receipt.
raccomandazi'one [rakkomandat'tsjone] *sf* recommendation; **lettera di ~** letter of introduction.
raccomo'dare *vt* (*riparare*) to repair, mend.
raccon'tare *vt*: **~ (a qn)** (*dire*) to tell (sb); (*narrare*) to relate (to sb), tell (sb) about; **a me non la racconti** don't try and kid me; **cosa mi racconti di nuovo?** what's new?
rac'conto *sm* telling *no pl*, relating *no pl*; (*fatto raccontato*) story, tale; (*genere letterario*) short story; **~i per bambini** children's stories.
raccorci'are [rakkor'tʃare] *vt* to shorten.
raccor'dare *vt* to link up, join.
rac'cordo *sm* (*TECN: giunzione*) connection, joint; (*AUT: di autostrada*) slip road (*BRIT*), entrance (*o exit*) ramp (*US*); **~ anulare** (*AUT*) ring road (*BRIT*), beltway (*US*).
ra'chitico, a, ci, che [ra'kitiko] *ag* suffering from rickets; (*fig*) scraggy, scrawny.
rachi'tismo [raki'tizmo] *sm* (*MED*) rickets *sg*.
racimo'lare [ratʃimo'lare] *vt* (*fig*) to scrape together, glean.
'rada *sf* (natural) harbour (*BRIT*) *o* harbor (*US*).
'radar *sm inv* radar.

raddol'cire [raddol'tʃire] vt (*persona, carattere*) to soften; ~rsi vr (*tempo*) to grow milder; (*persona*) to soften, mellow.
raddoppia'mento sm doubling.
raddoppi'are vt, vi to double.
rad'doppio sm (*gen*) doubling; (*BILIARDO*) double; (*EQUITAZIONE*) gallop.
raddriz'zare [raddrit'tsare] vt to straighten; (*fig: correggere*) to put straight, correct.
'radere vt (*barba*) to shave off; (*mento*) to shave; (*fig: rasentare*) to graze; to skim; ~rsi vr to shave (o.s.); ~ **al suolo** to raze to the ground.
radi'ale ag radial.
radi'ante ag (*calore, energia*) radiant.
radi'are vt to strike off.
radia'tore sm radiator.
radiazi'one [radjat'tsjone] sf (*FISICA*) radiation; (*cancellazione*) striking off.
'radica sf (*BOT*): ~ **di noce** walnut (wood).
radi'cale ag radical ♦ sm (*LING*) root; (*MAT, POL*) radical.
radi'cato, a ag (*pregiudizio, credenza*) deep-seated, deeply-rooted.
ra'dicchio [ra'dikkjo] sm *variety of chicory.*
ra'dice [ra'ditʃe] sf root; **segno di** ~ (*MAT*) radical sign; **colpire alla** ~ (*fig*) to strike at the root; **mettere** ~i (*idee, odio etc*) to take root; (*persona*) to put down roots; ~ **quadrata** (*MAT*) square root.
'radio sf inv radio ♦ sm (*CHIM*) radium; **trasmettere per** ~ to broadcast; **stazione/ ponte** ~ radio station/link; ~ **ricevente/ trasmittente** receiver/transmitter.
radioabbo'nato, a sm/f radio subscriber.
radioama'tore, 'trice sm/f amateur radio operator, ham (*fam*).
radioascolta'tore, 'trice sm/f (radio) listener.
radioattività sf radioactivity.
radioat'tivo, a ag radioactive.
radiocoman'dare vt to operate by remote control.
radiocoman'dato, a ag remote-controlled.
radioco'mando sm remote control.
radiocomunicazi'one [radjokomunikat'tsjone] sf radio message.
radio'cronaca, che sf radio commentary.
radiocro'nista, i, e sm/f radio commentator.
radiodiffusi'one sf (radio) broadcasting.
radio'fonico, a, ci, che ag radio cpd.
radiogra'fare vt to X-ray.
radiogra'fia sf radiography; (*foto*) X-ray photograph.
radio'lina sf portable radio, transistor (radio).

radiolo'gia [radjolo'dʒia] sf radiology.
radi'ologo, a, gi, ghe sm/f radiologist.
radiorice'vente [radjoritʃe'vɛnte] sf (anche: **apparecchio** ~) receiver.
radi'oso, a ag radiant.
radiostazi'one [radjostat'tsjone] sf radio station.
radios'veglia [radjoz'veʎʎa] sf radio alarm.
radio'taxi sm inv radio taxi.
radio'tecnico, a, ci, che ag radio engineering cpd ♦ sm radio engineer.
radiotelegra'fista, i, e sm/f radiotelegrapher.
radiotera'pia sf radiotherapy.
radiotrasmit'tente ag (radio) broadcasting cpd ♦ sf (radio) broadcasting station.
'rado, a ag (*capelli*) sparse, thin; (*visite*) infrequent; **di** ~ rarely; **non di** ~ not uncommonly.
radu'nare vt, ~rsi vr to gather, assemble.
radu'nata sf (*MIL*) muster.
ra'duno sm gathering, meeting.
ra'dura sf clearing.
'rafano sm horseradish.
raffazzo'nare [raffattso'nare] vt to patch up.
raf'fermo, a ag stale.
'raffica, che sf (*METEOR*) gust (of wind); ~ **di colpi** (*di fucile*) burst of gunfire.
raffigu'rare vt to represent.
raffigurazi'one [raffigurat'tsjone] sf representation, depiction.
raffi'nare vt to refine.
raffina'tezza [raffina'tettsa] sf refinement.
raffi'nato, a ag refined.
raffinazi'one [raffinat'tsjone] sf (*di sostanza*) refining; ~ **del petrolio** oil refining.
raffine'ria sf refinery.
raffor'zare [raffor'tsare] vt to reinforce.
rafforza'tivo, a [raffortsa'tivo] ag (*LING*) intensifying ♦ sm (*LING*) intensifier.
raffredda'mento sm cooling.
raffred'dare vt to cool; (*fig*) to dampen, have a cooling effect on; ~rsi vr to grow cool o cold; (*prendere un raffreddore*) to catch a cold; (*fig*) to cool (off).
raffred'dato, a ag (*MED*): **essere** ~ to have a cold.
raffred'dore sm (*MED*) cold.
raffron'tare vt to compare.
raf'fronto sm comparison.
'rafia sf (*fibra*) raffia.
raga'nella sf (*ZOOL*) tree frog.
ra'gazzo, a [ra'gattso] sm/f boy/girl; (*fam: fidanzato*) boyfriend/girlfriend; **nome da** ~a maiden name; ~a **madre** unmarried

mother; ~**a squillo** call girl.
ragge'lare [raddʒe'lare] *vt, vi,* ~**rsi** *vr* to freeze.
raggi'ante [rad'dʒante] *ag* radiant, shining; ~ **di gioia** beaming *o* radiant with joy.
raggi'era [rad'dʒɛra] *sf* (*di ruota*) spokes *pl*; **a** ~ with a sunburst pattern.
'**raggio** ['raddʒo] *sm* (*di sole etc*) ray; (*MAT, distanza*) radius; (*di ruota etc*) spoke; **nel** ~ **di 20 km** within a radius of 20 km *o* a 20-km radius; **a largo** ~ (*esplorazione, incursione*) wide-ranging; ~ **d'azione** range; ~ **laser** laser beam; ~**i X** X-rays.
raggi'rare [raddʒi'rare] *vt* to take in, trick.
rag'giro [rad'dʒiro] *sm* trick.
raggi'ungere [rad'dʒundʒere] *vt* to reach; (*persona: riprendere*) to catch up (with); (*bersaglio*) to hit; (*fig: meta*) to achieve; ~ **il proprio scopo** to reach one's goal, achieve one's aim; ~ **un accordo** to come to *o* reach an agreement.
raggi'unto, a [rad'dʒunto] *pp di* **raggiungere**.
raggomito'larsi *vr* to curl up.
raggranel'lare *vt* to scrape together.
raggrin'zare [raggrin'tsare] *vt, vi* (*anche:* ~**rsi**) to wrinkle.
raggrin'zire [raggrin'tsire] *vt* = **raggrinzare**.
raggru'mare *vt,* ~**rsi** *vr* (*sangue, latte*) to clot.
raggruppa'mento *sm* (*azione*) grouping; (*gruppo*) group; (: *MIL*) unit.
raggrup'pare *vt* to group (together).
ragguagli'are [raggwaʎ'ʎare] *vt* (*paragonare*) to compare; (*informare*) to inform.
raggu'aglio [rag'gwaʎʎo] *sm* comparison; (*informazione, relazione*) piece of information.
ragguar'devole *ag* (*degno di riguardo*) distinguished, notable; (*notevole: somma*) considerable.
'**ragia** ['radʒa] *sf:* **acqua** ~ turpentine.
ragiona'mento [radʒona'mento] *sm* reasoning *no pl*; argument.
ragio'nare [radʒo'nare] *vi* (*usare la ragione*) to reason; (*discorrere*): ~ (**di**) to argue (about); **cerca di** ~ be reasonable.
ragi'one [ra'dʒone] *sf* reason; (*dimostrazione, prova*) argument, reason; (*diritto*) right; **aver** ~ to be right; **aver** ~ **di qn** to get the better of sb; **dare** ~ **a qn** (*sog: persona*) to side with sb; (: *fatto*) to prove sb right; **farsi una** ~ **di qc** to accept sth, come to terms with sth; **in** ~ **di** at the rate of; **a** *o* **con** ~ rightly, justly; **perdere la** ~ to become insane; (*fig*) to take leave of one's senses; **a ragion veduta** after due

consideration; **per** ~**i di famiglia** for family reasons; ~ **di scambio** terms of trade; ~ **sociale** (*COMM*) corporate name; **ragion di stato** reason of State.
ragione'ria [radʒone'ria] *sf* accountancy; (*ufficio*) accounts department.
ragio'nevole [radʒo'nevole] *ag* reasonable.
ragioni'ere, a [radʒo'njɛre] *sm/f* accountant.
ragli'are [raʎ'ʎare] *vi* to bray.
ragna'tela [raɲɲa'tela] *sf* cobweb, spider's web.
'**ragno** ['raɲɲo] *sm* spider; **non cavare un** ~ **dal buco** (*fig*) to draw a blank.
ragù *sm inv* (*CUC*) meat sauce (*for pasta*).
RAI-TV [raiti'vu] *sigla f* (= *Radio televisione italiana*) Italian Broadcasting Company.
rallegra'menti *smpl* congratulations.
ralle'grare *vt* to cheer up; ~**rsi** *vr* to cheer up; (*provare allegrezza*) to rejoice; ~**rsi con qn** to congratulate sb.
rallenta'mento *sm* slowing down; slackening.
rallen'tare *vt, vi* to slow down; ~ **il passo** to slacken one's pace.
rallenta'tore *sm* (*CINE*) slow-motion camera; **al** ~ (*anche fig*) in slow motion.
raman'zina [raman'dzina] *sf* lecture, telling-off.
ra'mare *vt* (*superficie*) to copper, coat with copper; (*AGR: vite*) to spray with copper sulphate.
ra'marro *sm* green lizard.
ra'mato, a *ag* (*oggetto: rivestito di rame*) copper-coated, coppered; (*capelli, barba*) coppery, copper-coloured (*BRIT*), copper-colored (*US*).
'**rame** *sm* (*CHIM*) copper; **di** ~ copper *cpd*; **incisione su** ~ copperplate.
ramifi'care *vi* (*BOT*) to put out branches; ~**rsi** *vr* (*diramarsi*) to branch out; (*MED: tumore, vene*) to ramify; ~**rsi in** (*biforcarsi*) to branch into.
ramificazi'one [ramifikat'tsjone] *sf* ramification.
ra'mingo, a, ghi, ghe *ag* (*poetico*): **andare** ~ to go wandering, wander.
ra'mino *sm* (*CARTE*) rummy.
rammari'carsi *vr:* ~ (**di**) (*rincrescersi*) to be sorry (about), regret; (*lamentarsi*) to complain (about).
ram'marico, chi *sm* regret.
rammen'dare *vt* to mend; (*calza*) to darn.
ram'mendo *sm* mending *no pl*; darning *no pl*; mend; darn.
rammen'tare *vt* to remember, recall; ~**rsi** *vr:* ~**rsi (di qc)** to remember (sth); ~ **qc a qn** to remind sb of sth.

rammol'lire *vt* to soften ♦ *vi* (*anche:* ~**rsi**) to go soft.

rammol'lito, a *ag* weak ♦ *sm/f* weakling.

'ramo *sm* branch; (*di commercio*) field; **non è il mio** ~ it's not my field *o* line.

ramo'scello [ramoʃˈʃɛllo] *sm* twig.

'rampa *sf* flight (of stairs); ~ **di lancio** launching pad.

rampi'cante *ag* (*BOT*) climbing.

ram'pino *sm* (*gancio*) hook; (*NAUT*) grapnel.

ram'pollo *sm* (*di acqua*) spring; (*BOT*: *germoglio*) shoot; (*fig*: *discendente*) descendant.

ram'pone *sm* harpoon; (*ALPINISMO*) crampon.

'rana *sf* frog; ~ **pescatrice** angler fish.

'rancido, a [ˈrantʃido] *ag* rancid.

'rancio [ˈrantʃo] *sm* (*MIL*) mess; **ora del** ~ mess time.

ran'core *sm* rancour (*BRIT*), rancor (*US*), resentment; **portare** ~ **a qn, provare** ~ **per** *o* **verso qn** to bear sb a grudge.

ran'dagio, a, gi, gie *o* **ge** [ranˈdadʒo] *ag* (*gatto, cane*) stray.

ran'dello *sm* club, cudgel.

'rango, ghi *sm* (*grado*) rank; (*condizione sociale*) station, social standing; **persone di** ~ **inferiore** people of lower standing; **uscire dai** ~**ghi** (*fig*) to step out of line.

Ran'gun *sf* Rangoon.

rannicchi'arsi [rannikˈkjarsi] *vr* to crouch, huddle.

rannuvo'larsi *vr* to cloud over, become overcast.

ra'nocchio [raˈnɔkkjo] *sm* (edible) frog.

ranto'lare *vi* to wheeze.

ranto'lio *sm* (*il respirare affannoso*) wheezing; (: *di agonizzante*) death rattle.

'rantolo *sm* wheeze; death rattle.

ra'nuncolo *sm* (*BOT*) buttercup.

'rapa *sf* (*BOT*) turnip.

ra'pace [raˈpatʃe] *ag* (*animale*) predatory; (*fig*) rapacious, grasping ♦ *sm* bird of prey.

ra'pare *vt* (*capelli*) to crop, cut very short.

'rapida *sf vedi* **rapido**.

rapida'mente *av* quickly, rapidly.

rapidità *sf* speed.

'rapido, a *ag* fast; (*esame, occhiata*) quick, rapid ♦ *sm* (*FERR*) express (train) ♦ *sf* (*di fiume*) rapid.

rapi'mento *sm* kidnapping; (*fig*) rapture.

ra'pina *sf* robbery; ~ **in banca** bank robbery; ~ **a mano armata** armed robbery.

rapi'nare *vt* to rob.

rapina'tore, 'trice *sm/f* robber.

ra'pire *vt* (*cose*) to steal; (*persone*) to kidnap; (*fig*) to enrapture, delight.

ra'pito, a *ag* (*persona*) kidnapped; (*fig*: *in estasi*): **ascoltare** ~ **qn** to be captivated by sb's words ♦ *sm/f* kidnapped person.

rapi'tore, 'trice *sm/f* kidnapper.

rappacifi'care [rappatʃifiˈkare] *vt* (*riconciliare*) to reconcile; ~**rsi** *vr* (*uso reciproco*) to be reconciled, make it up (*fam*).

rappacificazi'one [rappatʃifikatˈtsjone] *sf* reconciliation.

rappez'zare [rappetˈtsare] *vt* to patch.

rappor'tare *vt* (*confrontare*) to compare; (*riprodurre*) to reproduce.

rap'porto *sm* (*resoconto*) report; (*legame*) relationship; (*MAT, TECN*) ratio; ~**i** *smpl* (*fra persone, paesi*) relations; **in** ~ **a quanto è successo** with regard to *o* in relation to what happened; **fare** ~ **a qn su qc** to report sth to sb; **andare a** ~ **da qn** to report to sb; **chiamare qn a** ~ (*MIL*) to summon sb; **essere in buoni/cattivi** ~**i con qn** to be on good/bad terms with sb; ~ **d'affari,** ~ **di lavoro** business relations; ~ **di compressione** (*TECN*) pressure ratio; ~ **coniugale** marital relationship; ~ **di trasmissione** (*TECN*) gear; ~**i sessuali** sexual intercourse *sg*.

rap'prendersi *vr* to coagulate, clot; (*latte*) to curdle.

rappre'saglia [rappreˈsaʎʎa] *sf* reprisal, retaliation.

rappresen'tante *sm/f* representative; ~ **di commercio** sales representative, sales rep (*fam*); ~ **sindacale** union delegate *o* representative.

rappresen'tanza [rapprezenˈtantsa] *sf* delegation, deputation; (*COMM*: *ufficio, sede*) agency; **in** ~ **di qn** on behalf of sb; **spese di** ~ entertainment expenses; **macchina di** ~ official car; **avere la** ~ **di** to be the agent for; ~ **esclusiva** sole agency; **avere la** ~ **esclusiva** to be sole agent.

rappresen'tare *vt* to represent; (*TEAT*) to perform; **farsi** ~ **dal proprio legale** to be represented by one's lawyer.

rappresenta'tivo, a *ag* representative ♦ *sf* (*di partito, sindacale*) representative group; (*SPORT*: *squadra*) representative (team).

rappresentazi'one [rapprezentatˈtsjone] *sf* representation; performing *no pl*; (*spettacolo*) performance; **prima** ~ **assoluta** world première.

rap'preso, a *pp di* **rapprendere**.

rapso'dia *sf* rhapsody.

'raptus *sm inv*: ~ **di follia** fit of madness.
rara'mente *av* seldom, rarely.
rare'fare *vt*, **~rsi** *vr* to rarefy.
rare'fatto, a *pp di* **rarefare** ♦ *ag* rarefied.
rarefazi'one [rarefat'tsjone] *sf* rarefaction.
rarità *sf inv* rarity.
'raro, a *ag* rare.
ra'sare *vt* (*barba etc*) to shave off; (*siepi, erba*) to trim, cut; **~rsi** *vr* to shave (o.s.).
ra'sato, a *ag* (*erba*) trimmed, cut; (*tessuto*) smooth; **avere la barba ~a** to be clean-shaven.
rasa'tura *sf* shave.
raschia'mento [raskja'mento] *sm* (*MED*) curettage; ~ **uterino** D and C.
raschi'are [ras'kjare] *vt* to scrape; (*macchia, fango*) to scrape off ♦ *vi* to clear one's throat.
rasen'tare *vt* (*andar rasente*) to keep close to; (*sfiorare*) to skim along (*o* over); (*fig*) to border on.
ra'sente *prep*: ~ **(a)** close to, very near.
'raso, a *pp di* **radere** ♦ *ag* (*barba*) shaved; (*capelli*) cropped; (*con misure di capacità*) level; (*pieno: bicchiere*) full to the brim ♦ *sm* (*tessuto*) satin; ~ **terra** close to the ground; **volare ~ terra** to hedgehop; **un cucchiaio ~ a** a level spoonful.
ra'soio *sm* razor; ~ **elettrico** electric shaver *o* razor.
ras'pare *vt* (*levigare*) to rasp; (*grattare*) to scratch.
'raspo *sm* (*di uva*) grape stalk.
ras'segna [ras'seɲɲa] *sf* (*MIL*) inspection, review; (*esame*) inspection; (*resoconto*) review, survey; (*pubblicazione letteraria etc*) review; (*mostra*) exhibition, show; **passare in ~** (*MIL, fig*) to review.
rasse'gnare [rasseɲ'ɲare] *vt*: ~ **le dimissioni** to resign, hand in one's resignation; **~rsi** *vr* (*accettare*): **~rsi (a qc/a fare)** to resign o.s. (to sth/to doing).
rassegnazi'one [rasseɲɲat'tsjone] *sf* resignation.
rasse're'nare *vt* (*persona*) to cheer up; **~rsi** *vr* (*tempo*) to clear up.
rasset'tare *vt* to tidy, put in order; (*aggiustare*) to repair, mend.
rassicu'rante *ag* reassuring.
rassicu'rare *vt* to reassure; **~rsi** *vr* to take heart, recover one's confidence.
rassicurazi'one [rassikurat'tsjone] *sf* reassurance.
rasso'dare *vt* to harden, stiffen; (*fig*) to strengthen, consolidate.
rassomigli'anza [rassomiʎ'ʎantsa] *sf* resemblance.
rassomigli'are [rassomiʎ'ʎare] *vi*: ~ **a** to resemble, look like.

rastrella'mento *sm* (*MIL, di polizia*) (thorough) search.
rastrel'lare *vt* to rake; (*fig: perlustrare*) to comb.
rastrelli'era *sf* rack; (*per piatti*) dish rack.
ras'trello *sm* rake.
'rata *sf* (*quota*) instalment, installment (*US*); **pagare a ~e** to pay by instal(l)ments *o* on hire purchase (*BRIT*); **comprare/vendere a ~e** to buy/sell on hire purchase (*BRIT*) *o* on the installment plan (*US*).
rate'ale *ag*: **pagamento ~** payment by instal(l)ments; **vendita ~** hire purchase (*BRIT*), installment plan (*US*).
rate'are, rateiz'zare [rateid'dzare] *vt* to divide into instal(l)ments.
rateazi'one [rateat'tsjone] *sf* division into instal(l)ments.
'rateo *sm* (*COMM*) accrual.
ra'tifica, che *sf* ratification.
ratifi'care *vt* (*DIR*) to ratify.
'ratto *sm* (*DIR*) abduction; (*ZOOL*) rat.
rattop'pare *vt* to patch.
rat'toppo *sm* patching *no pl*; patch.
rattrap'pire *vt* to make stiff; **~rsi** *vr* to be stiff.
rattris'tare *vt* to sadden; **~rsi** *vr* to become sad.
rau'cedine [rau'tʃedine] *sf* hoarseness.
'rauco, a, chi, che *ag* hoarse.
rava'nello *sm* radish.
raven'nate *ag* of (*o* from) Ravenna.
ravi'oli *smpl* ravioli *sg*.
ravve'dersi *vr* to mend one's ways.
ravvi'are *vt* (*capelli*) to tidy; **~rsi i capelli** to tidy one's hair.
ravvicina'mento [ravvitʃina'mento] *sm* (*tra persone*) reconciliation; (*POL: tra paesi etc*) rapprochement.
ravvici'nare [ravvitʃi'nare] *vt* (*avvicinare*): ~ **qc a** to bring sth nearer to; (*oggetti*) to bring closer together; (*fig: persone*) to reconcile, bring together; **~rsi** *vr* to be reconciled.
ravvi'sare *vt* to recognize.
ravvi'vare *vt* to revive; (*fig*) to brighten up, enliven; **~rsi** *vr* to revive; to brighten up.
Rawal'pindi [raval'pindi] *sf* Rawalpindi.
razio'cinio [rattsjo'tʃinjo] *sm* reasoning *no pl*; reason; (*buon senso*) common sense.
razio'nale [rattsjo'nale] *ag* rational.
razionalità [rattsjonali'ta] *sf* rationality; (*buon senso*) common sense.
razionaliz'zare [rattsjonalid'dzare] *vt* (*metodo, lavoro, programma*) to rationalize; (*problema, situazione*) to approach rationally.

raziona'mento [rattsjona'mento] *sm* rationing.

razio'nare [rattsjo'nare] *vt* to ration.

razi'one [rat'tsjone] *sf* ration; (*porzione*) portion, share.

'razza ['rattsa] *sf* race; (*ZOOL*) breed; (*discendenza, stirpe*) stock, race; (*sorta*) sort, kind.

raz'zia [rat'tsia] *sf* raid, foray.

razzi'ale [rat'tsjale] *ag* racial.

raz'zismo [rat'tsizmo] *sm* racism, racialism.

raz'zista, i, e [rat'tsista] *ag, smf* racist, racialist.

'razzo ['raddzo] *sm* rocket; ~ **di segnalazione** flare; ~ **vettore** vector rocket.

razzo'lare [rattso'lare] *vi* (*galline*) to scratch about.

RC *sigla = Reggio Calabria.*

RDT *sigla f vedi* **Repubblica Democratica Tedesca.**

RE *sigla = Reggio Emilia.*

re *sm inv* (*sovrano*) king; (*MUS*) D; (*: solfeggiando la scala*) re.

rea'gente [rea'dʒɛnte] *sm* reagent.

rea'gire [rea'dʒire] *vi* to react.

re'ale *ag* real; (*di, da re*) royal ♦ *sm*: **il** ~ reality; **i R~i** the Royal family.

rea'lismo *sm* realism.

rea'lista, i, e *smf* realist; (*POL*) royalist.

rea'listico, a, ci, che *ag* realistic.

realiz'zare [realid'dzare] *vt* (*progetto etc*) to realize, carry out; (*sogno, desiderio*) to realize, fulfil; (*scopo*) to achieve; (*COMM: titoli etc*) to realize; (*CALCIO etc*) to score; ~**rsi** *vr* to be realized.

realizzazi'one [realiddzat'tsjone] *sf* realization; fulfilment; achievement; ~ **scenica** stage production.

rea'lizzo [rea'liddzo] *sm* (*conversione in denaro*) conversion into cash; (*vendita forzata*) clearance sale.

real'mente *av* really, actually.

realtà *sf inv* reality; **in** ~ (*in effetti*) in fact; (*a dire il vero*) really.

re'ame *sm* kingdom, realm; (*fig*) realm.

re'ato *sm* offence (*BRIT*), offense (*US*).

reat'tore *sm* (*FISICA*) reactor; (*AER: aereo*) jet; (*: motore*) jet engine.

reazio'nario, a [reattsjo'narjo] *ag, smf* (*POL*) reactionary.

reazi'one [reat'tsjone] *sf* reaction; **motore/ aereo a** ~ jet engine/plane; **forze della** ~ reactionary forces; ~ **a catena** (*anche fig*) chain reaction.

'rebbio *sm* prong.

'rebus *sm inv* rebus; (*fig*) puzzle; enigma.

recapi'tare *vt* to deliver.

re'capito *sm* (*indirizzo*) address; (*consegna*) delivery; **ha un** ~ **telefonico?** do you have a telephone number where you can be reached?; ~ **a domicilio** home delivery (service).

re'care *vt* (*portare*) to bring; (*avere su di sé*) to carry, bear; (*cagionare*) to cause, bring; ~**rsi** *vr* to go; ~ **danno a qn** to harm sb, cause harm to sb.

re'cedere [re'tʃedere] *vi* to withdraw.

recensi'one [retʃen'sjone] *sf* review.

recen'sire [retʃen'sire] *vt* to review.

recen'sore, a [retʃen'sore] *smf* reviewer.

re'cente [re'tʃɛnte] *ag* recent; **di** ~ recently; **più** ~ latest, most recent.

recente'mente [retʃente'mente] *av* recently.

rece'pire [retʃe'pire] *vt* to understand, take in.

recessi'one [retʃes'sjone] *sf* (*ECON*) recession.

re'cesso [re'tʃɛsso] *sm* (*azione*) recession, receding; (*DIR*) withdrawal; (*luogo*) recess.

recherò *etc* [reke'rɔ] *vb vedi* **recare.**

re'cidere [re'tʃidere] *vt* to cut off, chop off.

reci'divo, a [retʃi'divo] *smf* (*DIR*) second (*o* habitual) offender, recidivist ♦ *sf* recidivism.

recin'tare [retʃin'tare] *vt* to enclose, fence off.

re'cinto [re'tʃinto] *sm* enclosure; (*ciò che recinge*) fence; surrounding wall.

recinzi'one [retʃin'tsjone] *sf* (*azione*) enclosure, fencing-off; (*recinto: di legno*) fence; (*: di mattoni*) wall; (*: reticolato*) wire fencing; (*: a sbarre*) railings *pl*.

recipi'ente [retʃi'pjɛnte] *sm* container.

re'ciproco, a, ci, che [re'tʃiproko] *ag* reciprocal.

re'ciso, a [re'tʃizo] *pp di* **recidere.**

'recita ['rɛtʃita] *sf* performance.

'recital ['rɛtʃital] *sm inv* recital.

reci'tare [retʃi'tare] *vt* (*poesia, lezione*) to recite; (*dramma*) to perform; (*ruolo*) to play *o* act (the part of).

recitazi'one [retʃitat'tsjone] *sf* recitation; (*di attore*) acting; **scuola di** ~ drama school.

recla'mare *vi* to complain ♦ *vt* (*richiedere*) to demand.

ré'clame [re'klam] *sf inv* advertising *no pl*; advertisement, advert (*BRIT*), ad (*fam*).

reclamiz'zare [reklamid'dzare] *vt* to advertise.

re'clamo *sm* complaint; **sporgere** ~ **a** to complain to, make a complaint to.

recli'nabile *ag* (*sedile*) reclining.
recli'nare *vt* (*capo*) to bow, lower; (*sedile*) to tilt.
reclusi'one *sf* (*DIR*) imprisonment.
re'cluso, a *sm/f* prisoner.
'recluta *sf* recruit.
recluta'mento *sm* recruitment.
reclu'tare *vt* to recruit.
re'condito, a *ag* secluded; (*fig*) secret, hidden.
'record *ag inv* record *cpd* ♦ *sm inv* record; **in tempo ~, a tempo di ~** in record time; **detenere il ~ di** to hold the record for; **~ mondiale** world record.
recrimi'nare *vi*: **~ (su qc)** to complain (about sth).
recriminazi'one [rekriminat'tsjone] *sf* recrimination.
recrude'scenza [rekrudeʃ'ʃɛntsa] *sf* fresh outbreak.
recupe'rare *etc* = **ricuperare** *etc*.
re'dassi *etc vb vedi* **redigere**.
re'datto, a *pp di* **redigere**.
redat'tore, 'trice *sm/f* (*STAMPA*) editor; (: *di articolo*) writer; (*di dizionario etc*) compiler; **~ capo** chief editor.
redazi'one [redat'tsjone] *sf* editing; writing; (*sede*) editorial office(s); (*personale*) editorial staff; (*versione*) version.
reddi'tizio, a [reddi'tittsjo] *ag* profitable.
'reddito *sm* income; (*dello Stato*) revenue; (*di un capitale*) yield; **~ complessivo** gross income; **~ disponibile** disposable income; **~ fisso** fixed income; **~ imponibile/non imponibile** taxable/non-taxable income; **~ da lavoro** earned income; **~ nazionale** national income; **~ pubblico** public revenue.
re'densi *etc vb vedi* **redimere**.
re'dento, a *pp di* **redimere**.
reden'tore *sm*: **il R~** the Redeemer.
redenzi'one [reden'tsjone] *sf* redemption.
re'digere [re'didʒere] *vt* to write; (*contratto*) to draw up.
re'dimere *vt* to deliver; (*REL*) to redeem.
'redini *sfpl* reins.
redi'vivo, a *ag* returned to life, reborn.
'reduce ['redutʃe] *ag* (*gen*): **~ da** returning from, back from ♦ *sm/f* survivor; (*veterano*) veteran; **essere ~ da** (*esame*, *colloquio*) to have been through; (*malattia*) to be just over.
'refe *sm* thread.
refe'rendum *sm inv* referendum.
refe'renza [refe'rɛntsa] *sf* reference.
re'ferto *sm* medical report.
refezi'one [refet'tsjone] *sf* (*INS*) school meal.

refrat'tario, a *ag* refractory; (*fig*): **essere ~ alla matematica** to have no aptitude for mathematics.
refrige'rare [refridʒe'rare] *vt* to refrigerate; (*rinfrescare*) to cool, refresh.
refrigerazi'one [refridʒerat'tsjone] *sf* refrigeration; (*TECN*) cooling; **~ ad acqua** (*AUT*) water-cooling.
refri'gerio [refri'dʒɛrjo] *sm*: **trovare ~** to find somewhere cool.
refur'tiva *sf* stolen goods *pl*.
Reg. *abbr* (= *reggimento*) Regt; (*AMM*) = *regolamento*.
rega'lare *vt* to give (as a present).
re'gale *ag* regal.
re'galo *sm* gift, present ♦ *ag inv*: **confezione ~** gift pack; **fare un ~ a qn** to give sb a present; **"articoli da ~"** "gifts".
re'gata *sf* regatta.
reg'gente [red'dʒɛnte] *ag* (*proposizione*) main; (*sovrano*) reigning ♦ *sm/f* regent; **principe ~** prince regent.
reg'genza [red'dʒɛntsa] *sf* regency.
'reggere ['reddʒere] *vt* (*tenere*) to hold; (*sostenere*) to support, bear, hold up; (*portare*) to carry, bear; (*resistere*) to withstand; (*dirigere: impresa*) to manage, run; (*governare*) to rule, govern; (*LING*) to take, be followed by ♦ *vi* (*resistere*): **~ a** to stand up to, hold out against; (*sopportare*): **~ a** to stand; (*durare*) to last; (*fig: teoria etc*) to hold water; **~rsi** *vr* (*stare ritto*) to stand; (*fig: dominarsi*) to control o.s.; **~rsi sulle gambe** *o* **in piedi** to stand up.
'reggia, ge ['rɛddʒa] *sf* royal palace.
reggi'calze [reddʒi'kaltse] *sm inv* suspender belt.
reggi'mento [reddʒi'mento] *sm* (*MIL*) regiment.
reggi'petto [reddʒi'pɛtto] *sm*, **reggi'seno** [reddʒi'seno] *sm* bra.
re'gia, 'gie [re'dʒia] *sf* (*TV, CINE etc*) direction.
re'gime [re'dʒime] *sm* (*POL*) regime; (*DIR*: *aureo, patrimoniale etc*) system; (*MED*) diet; (*TECN*) (engine) speed; **~ di giri** (*di motore*) revs *pl* per minute; **~ vegetariano** vegetarian diet.
re'gina [re'dʒina] *sf* queen.
'regio, a, gi, gie ['rɛdʒo] *ag* royal.
regio'nale [redʒo'nale] *ag* regional.
regi'one [re'dʒone] *sf* (*gen*) region; (*territorio*) region, area; *vedi nota nel riquadro*.

REGIONE

The **Regione** *is the biggest administrative unit in Italy. Each of the 20* **Regioni** *consists of a* *variable number of "Province", which in turn are subdivided into "Comuni". Each of the regions has a "capoluogo", its chief province (for example, Florence is the chief province of the region of Tuscany). Five regions have special status and wider powers: Val d'Aosta, Friuli-Venezia Giulia, Trentino-Alto Adige, Sicily and Sardinia. A **Regione** is run by the "Giunta regionale", which is elected by the "Consiglio regionale"; both are presided over by a "Presidente". The "Giunta" has legislative powers within the region over the police, public health, schools, town planning and agriculture.*

re'gista, i, e [reˈdʒista] *sm/f* (*TV, CINE etc*) director.

regis'trare [redʒisˈtrare] *vt* (*AMM*) to register; (*COMM*) to enter; (*notare*) to report, note; (*canzone, conversazione, sog: strumento di misura*) to record; (*mettere a punto*) to adjust, regulate; ~ **i bagagli** (*AER*) to check in one's luggage; ~ **i freni** (*TECN*) to adjust the brakes.

registra'tore [redʒistraˈtore] *sm* (*strumento*) recorder, register; (*magnetofono*) tape recorder; ~ **di cassa** cash register; ~ **a cassette** cassette recorder; ~ **di volo** (*AER*) flight recorder, black box (*fam*).

registrazi'one [redʒistratˈtsjone] *sf* registration; entry; reporting; recording; adjustment; ~ **bagagli** (*AER*) check-in.

re'gistro [reˈdʒistro] *sm* (*libro, MUS, TECN, LING*) register; (*DIR*) registry; (*COMM*): ~ **(di cassa)** ledger; **ufficio del** ~ registrar's office; ~ **di bordo** logbook; **~i contabili** (account) books.

re'gnante [reɲˈɲante] *ag* reigning, ruling ♦ *sm/f* ruler.

re'gnare [reɲˈɲare] *vi* to reign, rule; (*fig*) to reign.

'regno [ˈreɲɲo] *sm* kingdom; (*periodo*) reign; (*fig*) realm; **il** ~ **animale/vegetale** the animal/vegetable kingdom; **il R~ Unito** the United Kingdom.

'regola *sf* rule; **a** ~ **d'arte** duly; perfectly; **essere in** ~ (*dipendente*) to be a registered employee; (*fig: essere pulito*) to be clean; **fare le cose in** ~ to do things properly; **avere le carte in** ~ (*gen*) to have one's papers in order; (*fig: essere adatto*) to be the right person; **per tua (norma e)** ~ for your information; **un'eccezione alla** ~ an exception to the rule.

rego'labile *ag* adjustable.

regolamen'tare *ag* (*distanza, velocità*) regulation *cpd*, proper; (*disposizione*) statutory ♦ *vt* (*gen*) to control; **entro il tempo** ~ within the time allowed, within the prescribed time.

regola'mento *sm* (*complesso di norme*) regulations *pl*; (*di debito*) settlement; ~ **di conti** (*fig*) settling of scores.

rego'lare *ag* regular; (*velocità*) steady; (*superficie*) even; (*passo*) steady, even; (*in regola: documento*) in order ♦ *vt* to regulate, control; (*apparecchio*) to adjust, regulate; (*questione, conto, debito*) to settle; ~**rsi** *vr* (*moderarsi*): ~**rsi nel bere/nello spendere** to control one's drinking/spending; (*comportarsi*) to behave, act; **presentare** ~ **domanda** to apply through the proper channels; ~ **i conti** (*fig*) to settle old scores.

regolarità *sf inv* regularity; steadiness; evenness; (*nel pagare*) punctuality.

regolariz'zare [regolaridˈdzare] *vt* (*posizione*) to regularize; (*debito*) to settle.

rego'lata *sf*: **darsi una** ~ to pull o.s. together.

regola'tezza [regolaˈtettsa] *sf* (*ordine*) orderliness; (*moderazione*) moderation.

rego'lato, a *ag* (*ordinato*) orderly; (*moderato*) moderate.

regola'tore *sm* (*TECN*) regulator; ~ **di frequenza/di volume** frequency/volume control.

'regolo *sm* ruler; ~ **calcolatore** slide rule.

regre'dire *vi* to regress.

regressi'one *sf* regression.

re'gresso *sm* (*fig: declino*) decline.

rei'etto, a *sm/f* outcast.

reincarnazi'one [reinkarnatˈtsjone] *sf* reincarnation.

reinte'grare *vt* (*produzione*) to restore; (*energie*) to recover; (*dipendente*) to reinstate.

reintegrazi'one [reintegratˈtsjone] *sf* (*di produzione*) restoration; (*di dipendente*) reinstatement.

relativa'mente *av* relatively.

relatività *sf* relativity.

rela'tivo, a *ag* relative; (*attinente*) relevant; (*rispettivo*) respective; ~ **a** (*che concerne*) relating to, concerning; (*proporzionato*) in proportion to.

rela'tore, 'trice *sm/f* (*gen*) spokesman/woman; (*INS: di tesi*) supervisor.

re'lax [reˈlaks] *sm* relaxation.

relazi'one [relatˈtsjone] *sf* (*fra cose,*

persone) relation(ship); (resoconto) report, account; ~i sfpl (conoscenze) connections; **essere in** ~ to be connected; **mettere in** ~ (fatti, elementi) to make the connection between; **in** ~ **a quanto detto prima** with regard to what has already been said; **essere in buone** ~i **con qn** to be on good terms with sb; **fare una** ~ to make a report, give an account; ~i **pubbliche (RP)** public relations (PR).

rele'gare vt to banish; (fig) to relegate.

religi'one [reli'dʒone] sf religion.

religi'oso, a [reli'dʒoso] ag religious ♦ sm/f monk/nun.

re'liquia sf relic.

re'litto sm wreck; (fig) down-and-out.

re'mainder [ri'meində*] sm inv (libro) remainder.

're'make ['ri:'meik] sm inv (CINE) remake.

re'mare vi to row.

remini'scenze [reminiʃˈʃɛntse] sfpl reminiscences.

remissi'one sf remission; (deferenza) submissiveness, compliance; ~ **del debito** remission of debt; ~ **di querela** (DIR) withdrawal of an action.

remissività sf submissiveness.

remis'sivo, a ag submissive, compliant.

're'mo sm oar.

're'mora sf (poetico: indugio) hesitation.

re'moto, a ag remote.

remune'rare etc = rimunerare etc.

're'na sf sand.

re'nale ag kidney cpd.

're'ndere vt (ridare) to return, give back; (: saluto etc) to return; (produrre) to yield, bring in; (esprimere, tradurre) to render; (far diventare): ~ **qc possibile** to make sth possible ♦ vi (fruttare: ditta) to be profitable; (: investimento, campo) to yield, be productive; ~ **grazie a qn** to thank sb; ~ **omaggio a qn** to honour sb; ~ **un servizio a qn** to do sb a service; ~ **una testimonianza** to give evidence; ~ **la visita** to pay a return visit; **non so se rendo l'idea** I don't know whether I'm making myself clear; ~**rsi utile** to make o.s. useful; ~**rsi conto di qc** to realize sth.

rendi'conto sm (rapporto) report, account; (AMM, COMM) statement of account.

rendi'mento sm (reddito) yield; (di manodopera, TECN) efficiency; (capacità di produrre) output; (di studenti) performance.

're'ndita sf (di individuo) private o unearned income; (COMM) revenue; ~ **annua** annuity; ~ **vitalizia** life annuity.

're'ne sm kidney.

're'ni sfpl back sg.

reni'tente ag reluctant, unwilling; ~ **ai consigli di qn** unwilling to follow sb's advice; **essere** ~ **alla leva** (MIL) to fail to report for military service.

're'nna sf reindeer inv.

'Reno sm: **il** ~ the Rhine.

're'o, a sm/f (DIR) offender.

re'parto sm department, section; (MIL) detachment; ~ **acquisti** purchasing office.

repel'lente ag repulsive; (CHIM: insettifugo): **liquido** ~ (liquid) repellent.

repen'taglio [repen'taʎʎo] sm: **mettere a** ~ to jeopardize, risk.

repen'tino, a ag sudden, unexpected.

repe'ribile ag available.

repe'rire vt to find, trace.

re'perto sm (ARCHEOLOGIA) find; (MED) report; (anche: ~ **giudiziario**) exhibit.

reper'torio sm (TEAT) repertory; (elenco) index, (alphabetical) list.

'replica, che sf repetition; reply, answer; (obiezione) objection; (TEAT, CINE) repeat performance; (copia) replica.

repli'care vt (ripetere) to repeat; (rispondere) to answer, reply.

repor'tage [rəpɔr'taʒ] sm inv (STAMPA) report.

repressi'one sf repression.

repres'sivo, a ag repressive.

re'presso, a pp di reprimere.

re'primere vt to suppress, repress.

re'pubblica, che sf republic; **la R**~ **Democratica Tedesca (RDT)** the German Democratic Republic (GDR); **la R**~ **Federale Tedesca (RFT)** the Federal Republic of Germany (FRG); **la Prima/la Seconda R**~ terms used to refer to Italy before and after the political changes resulting from the 1994 elections; vedi anche **Festa della Repubblica**; **Seconda Repubblica**.

repubbli'cano, a ag, sm/f republican.

repu'tare vt to consider, judge.

reputazi'one [reputat'tsjone] sf reputation; **farsi una cattiva** ~ to get o.s. a bad name.

're'quie sf rest; **dare** ~ **a qn** to give sb some peace; **senza** ~ unceasingly.

're'quiem sm inv (preghiera) requiem, prayer for the dead; (fig: ufficio funebre) requiem.

requi'sire vt to requisition.

requi'sito sm requirement; **avere i** ~**i necessari per un lavoro** to have the necessary qualifications for a job.

requisi'toria *sf* (*DIR*) closing speech (for the prosecution).

requisizi'one [rekwizit'tsjone] *sf* requisition.

'resa *sf* (*l'arrendersi*) surrender; (*restituzione, rendimento*) return; ~ **dei conti** rendering of accounts; (*fig*) day of reckoning.

re'scindere [reʃ'ʃindere] *vt* (*DIR*) to rescind, annul.

re'scisso, a [reʃ'ʃisso] *pp di* **rescindere**.

reset'tare *vt* (*INFORM*) to reset.

'resi *etc vb vedi* **rendere**.

resi'dente *ag* resident.

resi'denza [resi'dɛntsa] *sf* residence.

residenzi'ale [residen'tsjale] *ag* residential.

re'siduo, a *ag* residual, remaining ♦ *sm* remainder; (*CHIM*) residue; ~**i industriali** industrial waste *sg*.

'resina *sf* resin.

resis'tente *ag* (*che resiste*): ~ **a** resistant to; (*forte*) strong; (*duraturo*) long-lasting, durable; ~ **all'acqua** waterproof; ~ **al caldo** heat-resistant; ~ **al fuoco** fireproof; ~ **al gelo** frost-resistant.

resis'tenza [resis'tɛntsa] *sf* (*gen, ELETTR*) resistance; (*di persona: fisica*) stamina, endurance; (*: mentale*) endurance, resistance; **opporre** ~ (**a**) to offer *o* put up resistance (to); (*decisione, scelta*) to show opposition (to); **la R**~ *vedi nota nel riquadro*.

RESISTENZA

The Italian **Resistenza** *fought against both the Nazis and the Fascists during the Second World War. It was particularly active after the fall of the Fascist Government on 25 July 1943, throughout the German occupation and during the period of Mussolini's Republic of Salò in northern Italy. Resistance members spanned the whole political spectrum and played a vital role in the Liberation and the formation of the new democratic government.*

---

re'sistere *vi* to resist; ~ **a** to resist; (*dolore, sog: pianta*) to withstand; (*non patir danno*) to be resistant to.

resis'tito, a *pp di* **resistere**.

'reso, a *pp di* **rendere**.

reso'conto *sm* report, account.

respin'gente [respin'dʒɛnte] *sm* (*FERR*) buffer.

res'pingere [res'pindʒere] *vt* to drive back, repel; (*rifiutare: pacco, lettera*) to return; (*: invito*) to refuse; (*: proposta*) to reject, turn down; (*INS: bocciare*) to fail.

res'pinto, a *pp di* **respingere**.

respi'rare *vi* to breathe; (*fig*) to get one's breath; to breathe again ♦ *vt* to breathe (in), inhale.

respira'tore *sm* respirator.

respira'torio, a *ag* respiratory.

respirazi'one [respirat'tsjone] *sf* breathing; ~ **artificiale** artificial respiration; ~ **bocca a bocca** mouth-to-mouth resuscitation, kiss of life (*fam*).

res'piro *sm* breathing *no pl*; (*singolo atto*) breath; (*fig*) respite, rest; **mandare un** ~ **di sollievo** to give a sigh of relief; **trattenere il** ~ to hold one's breath; **lavorare senza** ~ to work non-stop; **di ampio** ~ (*opera, lavoro*) far-reaching.

respon'sabile *ag* responsible ♦ *smf* person responsible; (*capo*) person in charge; ~ **di** responsible for; (*DIR*) liable for.

responsabilità *sf inv* responsibility; (*legale*) liability; **assumere la** ~ **di** to take on the responsibility for; **affidare a qn la** ~ **di qc** to make sb responsible for sth; ~ **patrimoniale** debt liability; ~ **penale** criminal liability.

responsabiliz'zare [responsabilid'dzare] *vt*: ~ **qn** to make sb feel responsible.

res'ponso *sm* answer; (*DIR*) verdict.

'ressa *sf* crowd, throng.

'ressi *etc vb vedi* **reggere**.

res'tare *vi* (*rimanere*) to remain, stay; (*diventare*): ~ **orfano/cieco** to become *o* be left an orphan/become blind; (*trovarsi*): ~ **sorpreso** to be surprised; (*avanzare*) to be left, remain; ~ **d'accordo** to agree; **non resta più niente** there's nothing left; **restano pochi giorni** there are only a few days left; **che resti tra di noi** this is just between ourselves; ~ **in buoni rapporti** to remain on good terms; ~ **senza parole** to be left speechless.

restau'rare *vt* to restore.

restaura'tore, 'trice *sm/f* restorer.

restaurazi'one [restaurat'tsjone] *sf* (*POL*) restoration.

res'tauro *sm* (*di edifici etc*) restoration; **in** ~ under repair; **sotto** ~ (*dipinto*) being restored; **chiuso per** ~**i** closed for repairs.

res'tio, a, 'tii, 'tie *ag* restive; (*persona*): ~ **a** reluctant to.

restitu'ire *vt* to return, give back; (*energie, forze*) to restore.

restituzi'one [restitut'tsjone] *sf* return; (*di soldi*) repayment.

'resto *sm* remainder, rest; (*denaro*) change; (*MAT*) remainder; ~**i** *smpl* leftovers; (*di città*) remains; **del** ~ moreover, besides; ~**i mortali** (mortal) remains.

res'tringere [res'trindʒere] *vt* to reduce; (*vestito*) to take in; (*stoffa*) to shrink; (*fig*) to restrict, limit; **~rsi** *vr* (*strada*) to narrow; (*stoffa*) to shrink.

restrit'tivo, a *ag* restrictive.

restrizi'one [restrit'tsjone] *sf* restriction.

resurrezi'one [resurret'tsjone] *sf* = **risurrezione.**

resusci'tare [resuʃʃi'tare] *vt, vi* = **risuscitare.**

re'tata *sf* (*PESCA*) haul, catch; **fare una ~ di** (*fig*: *persone*) to round up.

'rete *sf* net; (*di recinzione*) wire netting; (*AUT, FERR, di spionaggio etc*) network; (*fig*) trap, snare; **segnare una ~** (*CALCIO*) to score a goal; **~ ferroviaria/stradale/di distribuzione** railway/road/distribution network; **~ del letto** (sprung) bed base; **~ da pesca** fishing net; **~ (televisiva)** (*sistema*) network; (*canale*) channel; **la R~** the Web; **calze a ~** fishnet tights *o* stockings.

reti'cente [reti'tʃɛnte] *ag* reticent.

reti'cenza [reti'tʃɛntsa] *sf* reticence.

retico'lato *sm* grid; (*rete metallica*) wire netting; (*di filo spinato*) barbed wire fence.

'retina *sf* (*ANAT*) retina.

re'torico, a, ci, che *ag* rhetorical ♦ *sf* rhetoric.

retribu'ire *vt* to pay; (*premiare*) to reward; **un lavoro mal retribuito** a poorly-paid job.

retribu'tivo, a *ag* pay *cpd.*

retribuzi'one [retribut'tsjone] *sf* payment; reward.

re'trivo, a *ag* (*fig*) reactionary.

'retro *sm inv* back ♦ *av* (*dietro*): **vedi ~** see over(leaf).

retroattività *sf* retroactivity.

retroat'tivo, a *ag* (*DIR*: *legge*) retroactive; (*AMM*: *salario*) backdated.

retrobot'tega, ghe *sf* back shop.

retro'cedere [retro'tʃɛdere] *vi* to withdraw ♦ *vt* (*CALCIO*) to relegate; (*MIL*) to degrade; (*AMM*) to demote.

retrocessi'one [retrotʃes'sjone] *sf* (*di impiegato*) demotion.

retro'cesso, a [retro'tʃɛsso] *pp di* **retrocedere.**

retroda'tare *vt* (*AMM*) to backdate.

re'trogrado, a *ag* (*fig*) reactionary, backward-looking.

retrogu'ardia *sf* (*anche fig*) rearguard.

retro'marcia [retro'martʃa] *sf* (*AUT*) reverse; (: *dispositivo*) reverse gear.

retro'scena [retroʃ'ʃɛna] *sf inv* (*TEAT*) backstage ♦ *sm inv* (*fig*) behind-the-scenes activity.

retrospet'tivo, a *ag* retrospective ♦ *sf* (*ARTE*) retrospective (exhibition).

retros'tante *ag*: **~ (a)** at the back (of).

retro'terra *sm* hinterland.

retro'via *sf* (*MIL*) zone behind the front; **mandare nelle ~e** to send to the rear.

retrovi'sore *sm* (*AUT*) (rear-view) mirror.

'retta *sf* (*MAT*) straight line; (*di convitto*) charge for bed and board; (*fig*: *ascolto*): **dar ~ a** to listen to, pay attention to.

rettango'lare *ag* rectangular.

ret'tangolo, a *ag* right-angled ♦ *sm* rectangle.

ret'tifica, che *sf* rectification, correction.

rettifi'care *vt* (*curva*) to straighten; (*fig*) to rectify, correct.

'rettile *sm* reptile.

retti'lineo, a *ag* rectilinear.

retti'tudine *sf* rectitude, uprightness.

'retto, a *pp di* **reggere** ♦ *ag* straight; (*MAT*): **angolo ~** right angle; (*onesto*) honest, upright; (*giusto, esatto*) correct, proper, right.

ret'tore *sm* (*REL*) rector; (*di università*) ≈ chancellor.

reuma'tismo *sm* rheumatism.

Rev. *abbr* (= *Reverendo*) Rev(d).

reve'rendo, a *ag*: **il ~ padre Belli** the Reverend Father Belli.

reve'rente *ag* = **riverente.**

reve'renza [reve'rɛntsa] *sf* = **riverenza.**

rever'sibile *ag* reversible.

revisio'nare *vt* (*conti*) to audit; (*TECN*) to overhaul, service; (*DIR*: *processo*) to review; (*componimento*) to revise.

revisi'one *sf* auditing *no pl*; audit; servicing *no pl*; overhaul; review; revision; **~ di bilancio** audit; **~ di bozze** proofreading; **~ contabile interna** internal audit.

revi'sore *sm*: **~ di conti/bozze** auditor/proofreader.

'revoca *sf* revocation.

revo'care *vt* to revoke.

re'volver *sm inv* revolver.

revolve'rata *sf* revolver shot.

'Reykjavik ['reikjavik] *sf* Reykjavik.

RFT *sigla f vedi* **Repubblica Federale Tedesca.**

ri'abbia *etc vb vedi* **riavere.**

riabili'tare *vt* to rehabilitate; (*fig*) to restore to favour (*BRIT*) *o* favor (*US*).

riabilitazi'one [riabilitat'tsjone] *sf* rehabilitation.

riac'cendere [riat'tʃɛndere] *vt* (*sigaretta, fuoco, gas*) to light again; (*luce, radio, TV*) to switch on again; (*fig*: *sentimenti, interesse*) to rekindle, revive; **~rsi** *vr* (*fuoco*) to catch again; (*luce, radio, TV*) to come back on again; (*fig*: *sentimenti*) to revive, be rekindled.

riac'ceso, a [riat't∫eso] *pp di* **riaccendere.**

riacqui'stare *vt* (*gen*) to buy again; (*ciò che si era venduto*) to buy back; (*fig: buonumore, sangue freddo, libertà*) to regain; ~ **la salute** to recover (one's health); ~ **le forze** to regain one's strength.

Ri'ad *sf* Riyadh.

riaddormen'tare *vt* to put to sleep again; ~**rsi** *vr* to fall asleep again.

riallac'ciare [riallat't∫are] *vt* (*cintura, cavo etc*) to refasten, tie up *o* fasten again; (*fig: rapporti, amicizia*) to resume, renew; ~**rsi** *vr*: ~**rsi a** (*fig: a discorso, tema*) to resume, take up again.

rial'zare [rial'tsare] *vt* to raise, lift; (*alzare di più*) to heighten, raise; (*aumentare: prezzi*) to increase, raise ♦ *vi* (*prezzi*) to rise, increase.

rial'zato, a [rial'tsato] *ag*: **piano** ~ mezzanine, entresol.

rial'zista, i [rial'tsista] *sm* (*BORSA*) bull.

ri'alzo [ri'altso] *sm* (*di prezzi*) increase, rise; (*sporgenza*) rise; **giocare al** ~ (*BORSA*) to bull.

rian'dare *vi*: ~ **(in)**, ~ **(a)** to go back (to), return (to).

riani'mare *vt* (*MED*) to resuscitate; (*fig: rallegrare*) to cheer up; (: *dar coraggio*) to give heart to; ~**rsi** *vr* to recover consciousness; to cheer up; to take heart.

rianimazi'one [rianimat'tsjone] *sf* (*MED*) resuscitation; **centro di** ~ intensive care unit.

ria'perto, a *pp di* **riaprire.**

riaper'tura *sf* reopening.

riappa'rire *vi* to reappear.

riap'parso, a *pp di* **riapparire.**

riap'pendere *vt* to rehang; (*TEL*) to hang up.

ria'prire *vt*, ~**rsi** *vr* to reopen, open again.

ri'armo *sm* (*MIL*) rearmament.

ri'arso, a *ag* (*terreno*) arid; (*gola*) parched; (*labbra*) dry.

riasset'tare *vt* (*vedi sm*) to rearrange; to reorganize.

rias'setto *sm* (*di stanza etc*) rearrangement; (*ordinamento*) reorganization.

rias'sumere *vt* (*riprendere*) to resume; (*impiegare di nuovo*) to re-employ; (*sintetizzare*) to summarize.

rias'sunto, a *pp di* **riassumere** ♦ *sm* summary.

riattac'care *vt* (*attaccare di nuovo*): ~ **(a)** (*manifesto, francobollo*) to stick back (on); (*bottone*) to sew back (on); (*quadro, chiavi*) to hang back up (on); ~ **(il telefono** *o* **il**

ricevitore) to hang up (the receiver).

riatti'vare *vt* to reactivate.

ria'vere *vt* to have again; (*avere indietro*) to get back; (*riacquistare*) to recover; ~**rsi** *vr* to recover; (*da svenimento, stordimento*) to come round.

riba'dire *vt* (*fig*) to confirm.

ri'balta *sf* (*sportello*) flap; (*TEAT: proscenio*) front of the stage; (: *apparecchio d'illuminazione*) footlights *pl*; (*fig*) limelight; **tornare alla** ~ (*personaggio*) to make a comeback; (*problema*) to come up again.

ribal'tabile *ag* (*sedile*) tip-up.

ribal'tare *vt*, *vi* (*anche*: ~**rsi**) to turn over, tip over.

ribas'sare *vt* to lower, bring down ♦ *vi* to come down, fall.

ribas'sista, i *sm* (*BORSA*) bear.

ri'basso *sm* reduction, fall; **essere in** ~ (*azioni, prezzi*) to be down; (*fig: popolarità*) to be on the decline; **giocare al** ~ (*BORSA*) to bear.

ri'battere *vt* (*battere di nuovo*) to beat again; (*con macchina da scrivere*) to type again; (*palla*) to return; (*confutare*) to refute; ~ **che** to retort that.

ribattez'zare [ribatted'dzare] *vt* to rename.

ribel'larsi *vr*: ~ **(a)** to rebel (against).

ri'belle *ag* (*soldati*) rebel; (*ragazzo*) rebellious ♦ *smf* rebel.

ribelli'one *sf* rebellion.

'ribes *sm inv* currant; ~ **nero** blackcurrant; ~ **rosso** redcurrant.

ribol'lire *vi* (*fermentare*) to ferment; (*fare bolle*) to bubble, boil; (*fig*) to seethe.

ri'brezzo [ri'breddzo] *sm* disgust, loathing; **far** ~ **a** to disgust.

ribut'tante *ag* disgusting, revolting.

ricacci'are [rikat't∫are] *vt* (*respingere*) to drive back; ~ **qn fuori** to throw sb out.

rica'dere *vi* to fall again; (*scendere a terra, fig: nel peccato etc*) to fall back; (*vestiti, capelli etc*) to hang (down); (*riversarsi: fatiche, colpe*): ~ **su** to fall on.

rica'duta *sf* (*MED*) relapse.

rical'care *vt* (*disegni*) to trace; (*fig*) to follow faithfully.

ricalci'trare [rikalt∫i'trare] *vi* (*cavalli, asini, muli*) to kick.

rica'mare *vt* to embroider.

ricambi'are *vt* to change again; (*contraccambiare*) to return.

ri'cambio *sm* exchange, return; (*FISIOL*) metabolism; ~**i** *smpl*, **pezzi di** ~ spare parts; ~ **della manodopera** labour turnover.

ri'camo *sm* embroidery; **senza** ~**i** (*fig*)

without frills.

ricapito'lare *vt* to recapitulate, sum up.

ricapitolazi'one [rikapitolat'tsjone] *sf* recapitulation, summary.

ricari'care *vt* (*arma, macchina fotografica*) to reload; (*penna*) to refill; (*orologio, giocattolo*) to rewind; (*ELETTR*) to recharge.

ricat'tare *vt* to blackmail.

ricatta'tore, 'trice *sm/f* blackmailer.

ri'catto *sm* blackmail; **fare un ~ a qn** to blackmail sb; **subire un ~** to be blackmailed.

rica'vare *vt* (*estrarre*) to draw out, extract; (*ottenere*) to obtain, gain.

rica'vato *sm* (*di vendite*) proceeds *pl*.

ri'cavo *sm* proceeds *pl*; (*CONTABILITÀ*) revenue.

ric'chezza [rik'kettsa] *sf* wealth; (*fig*) richness; **~e** *sfpl* (*beni*) wealth *sg*, riches; **~e naturali** natural resources.

'riccio, a, ci, ce ['rittʃo] *ag* curly ♦ *sm* (*ZOOL*) hedgehog; (*: anche*: **~ di mare**) sea urchin.

'ricciolo ['rittʃolo] *sm* curl.

ricci'uto, a [rit'tʃuto] *ag* curly.

'ricco, a, chi, che *ag* rich; (*persona, paese*) rich, wealthy ♦ *sm/f* rich man/woman; **i ~chi** the rich; **~ di** (*idee, illustrazioni etc*) full of; (*risorse, fauna etc*) rich in.

ri'cerca, che [ri'tʃerka] *sf* search; (*indagine*) investigation, inquiry; (*studio*): **la ~** research; **una ~** piece of research; **mettersi alla ~ di** to go in search of, look *o* search *o* hunt for; **essere alla ~ di** to be searching for, be looking for; **~ di mercato** market research; **~ operativa** operational research.

ricer'care [ritʃer'kare] *vt* (*motivi, cause*) to look for, try to determine; (*successo, piacere*) to pursue; (*onore, gloria*) to seek.

ricerca'tezza [ritʃerka'tettsa] *sf* (*raffinatezza*) refinement; (*: peg*) affectation.

ricer'cato, a [ritʃer'kato] *ag* (*apprezzato*) much sought-after; (*affettato*) studied, affected ♦ *sm/f* (*POLIZIA*) wanted man/woman.

ricerca'tore, 'trice [ritʃerka'tore] *sm/f* (*INS*) researcher.

ricetrasmit'tente [ritʃetrazmit'tɛnte] *sf* two-way radio, transceiver.

ri'cetta [ri'tʃetta] *sf* (*MED*) prescription; (*CUC*) recipe; (*fig: antidoto*): **~ contro** remedy for.

ricet'tacolo [ritʃet'takolo] *sm* (*peg: luogo malfamato*) den.

ricet'tario [ritʃet'tarjo] *sm* (*MED*)

prescription pad; (*CULIN*) recipe book.

ricetta'tore, 'trice [ritʃetta'tore] *sm/f* (*DIR*) receiver (of stolen goods).

ricettazi'one [ritʃettat'tsjone] *sf* (*DIR*) receiving (stolen goods).

ricet'tivo, a [ritʃet'tivo] *ag* receptive.

rice'vente [ritʃe'vɛnte] *ag* (*RADIO, TV*) receiving ♦ *sm/f* (*COMM*) receiver.

ri'cevere [ri'tʃevere] *vt* to receive; (*stipendio, lettera*) to get, receive; (*accogliere: ospite*) to welcome; (*vedere: cliente, rappresentante etc*) to see; "**confermiamo di aver ricevuto tale merce**" (*COMM*) "we acknowledge receipt of these goods".

ricevi'mento [ritʃevi'mento] *sm* receiving *no pl*; (*trattenimento*) reception; **al ~ della merce** on receipt of the goods.

ricevi'tore [ritʃevi'tore] *sm* (*TECN*) receiver; **~ delle imposte** tax collector.

ricevito'ria [ritʃevito'ria] *sf* (*FISCO*): **~ (delle imposte)** Inland Revenue (*BRIT*) *o* Internal Revenue (*US*) Office; **~ del lotto** lottery office.

rice'vuta [ritʃe'vuta] *sf* receipt; **accusare ~ di qc** (*COMM*) to acknowledge receipt of sth; **~ fiscale** official receipt (for tax purposes); **~ di ritorno** (*POSTA*) advice of receipt; **~ di versamento** receipt of payment.

ricezi'one [ritʃet'tsjone] *sf* (*RADIO, TV*) reception.

richia'mare [rikja'mare] *vt* (*chiamare indietro, ritelefonare*) to call back; (*ambasciatore, truppe*) to recall; (*rimproverare*) to reprimand; (*attirare*) to attract, draw; **~rsi** *vr*: **~rsi a** (*riferirsi a*) to refer to; **~ qn all'ordine** to call sb to order; **desidero ~ la vostra attenzione su** … I would like to draw your attention to ….

richi'amo [ri'kjamo] *sm* call; recall; reprimand; attraction.

richie'dente [rikje'dɛnte] *sm/f* applicant.

richi'edere [ri'kjɛdere] *vt* to ask again for; (*chiedere indietro*): **~ qc** to ask for sth back; (*chiedere: per sapere*) to ask; (*: per avere*) to ask for; (*AMM: documenti*) to apply for; (*esigere*) to need, require; **essere molto richiesto** to be in great demand.

richi'esto, a [ri'kjɛsto] *pp di* **richiedere** ♦ *sf* (*domanda*) request; (*AMM*) application, request; (*esigenza*) demand, request; **a ~a** on request.

rici'claggio [ritʃi'kladdʒo] *sm* (*fig*) laundering; **~ di materiale** recycling; **~ di denaro sporco** money laundering.

rici'clare [ritʃi'klare] vt (*vetro, carta, bottiglie*) to recycle; (*fig: personale*) to retrain.

'ricino ['ritʃino] sm: **olio di** ~ castor oil.

ricogni'tore [rikoɲɲi'tore] sm (*AER*) reconnaissance aircraft.

ricognizi'one [rikoɲɲit'tsjone] sf (*MIL*) reconnaissance; (*DIR*) recognition, acknowledgement.

ricolle'gare vt (*collegare nuovamente: gen*) to join again, link again; (*connettere: fatti*): ~ **(a, con)** to connect (with); ~**rsi** vr: ~**rsi a** (*sog: fatti: connettersi*) to be connected to; (*: persona: riferirsi*) to refer to.

ri'colmo, a ag: ~ **(di)** (*bicchiere*) full to the brim (with); (*stanza*) full (of).

ricominci'are [rikomin'tʃare] vt, vi to start again, begin again; ~ **a fare qc** to begin doing o to do sth again, start doing o to do sth again.

ricom'pensa sf reward.

ricompen'sare vt to reward.

ricom'porsi vr to compose o.s., regain one's composure.

ricom'posto, a pp di **ricomporsi**.

riconcili'are [rikontʃi'ljare] vt to reconcile; ~**rsi** vr to be reconciled.

riconciliazi'one [rikontʃiliat'tsjone] sf reconciliation.

ricon'dotto, a pp di **ricondurre**.

ricon'durre vt to bring (o take) back.

ricon'ferma sf reconfirmation.

riconfer'mare vt to reconfirm.

ricono'scente [rikonoʃ'ʃente] ag grateful.

ricono'scenza [rikonoʃ'ʃentsa] sf gratitude.

rico'noscere [riko'noʃʃere] vt to recognize; (*DIR: figlio, debito*) to acknowledge; (*ammettere: errore*) to admit, acknowledge; ~ **qn colpevole** to find sb guilty.

riconosci'mento [rikonoʃʃi'mento] sm recognition; acknowledgement; (*identificazione*) identification; **come** ~ **dei servizi resi** in recognition of services rendered; **documento di** ~ means of identification; **segno di** ~ distinguishing mark.

riconosci'uto, a [rikonoʃ'ʃuto] pp di **riconoscere**.

riconquis'tare vt (*MIL*) to reconquer; (*libertà, stima*) to win back.

rico'perto, a pp di **ricoprire**.

ricopi'are vt to copy.

rico'prire vt to re-cover; (*coprire*) to cover; (*occupare: carica*) to hold.

ricor'dare vt to remember, recall; (*richiamare alla memoria*): ~ **qc a qn** to remind sb of sth; ~**rsi** vr: ~**rsi (di)** to remember; ~**rsi di qc/di aver fatto** to remember sth/having done.

ri'cordo sm memory; (*regalo*) keepsake, souvenir; (*di viaggio*) souvenir; ~**i** smpl (*memorie*) memoirs.

ricor'rente ag recurrent, recurring.

ricor'renza [rikor'rɛntsa] sf recurrence; (*festività*) anniversary.

ri'correre vi (*ripetersi*) to recur; ~ **a** (*rivolgersi*) to turn to; (*: DIR*) to appeal to; (*servirsi di*) to have recourse to; ~ **in appello** to lodge an appeal.

ri'corso, a pp di **ricorrere** ♦ sm recurrence; (*DIR*) appeal; **far** ~ **a** = **ricorrere a**.

ricostitu'ente ag (*MED*): **cura** ~ tonic treatment ♦ sm (*MED*) tonic.

ricostitu'ire vt (*società*) to build up again; (*governo, partito*) to re-form; ~**rsi** vr (*gruppo etc*) to re-form.

ricostru'ire vt (*casa*) to rebuild; (*fatti*) to reconstruct.

ricostruzi'one [rikostrut'tsjone] sf rebuilding no pl; reconstruction.

ri'cotta sf soft white unsalted cheese made from sheep's milk.

ricove'rare vt to give shelter to; ~ **qn in ospedale** to admit sb to hospital.

ricove'rato, a sm/f patient.

ri'covero sm shelter, refuge; (*MIL*) shelter; (*MED*) admission (to hospital); ~ **antiaereo** air-raid shelter.

ricre'are vt to recreate; (*rinvigorire*) to restore; (*fig: distrarre*) to amuse.

ricrea'tivo, a ag recreational.

ricreazi'one [rikreat'tsjone] sf recreation, entertainment; (*INS*) break.

ri'credersi vr to change one's mind.

ricupe'rare vt (*rientrare in possesso di*) to recover, get back; (*tempo perduto*) to make up for; (*NAUT*) to salvage; (*: naufraghi*) to rescue; (*delinquente*) to rehabilitate; ~ **lo svantaggio** (*SPORT*) to close the gap.

ri'cupero sm (*gen*) recovery; (*di relitto etc*) salvaging; **capacità di** ~ resilience.

ricu'sare vt to refuse.

ridacchi'are [ridak'kjare] vi to snigger.

ri'dare vt to return, give back.

'ridda sf (*di ammiratori etc*) swarm; (*di pensieri*) jumble.

ri'dente ag (*occhi, volto*) smiling; (*paesaggio*) delightful.

'ridere vi to laugh; (*deridere, beffare*): ~ **di** to laugh at, make fun of; **non c'è niente da** ~, **c'è poco da** ~ it's not a laughing matter.

rides'tare vt (*fig: ricordi, passioni*) to reawaken.

ri'detto, a pp di **ridire**.

ridico'laggine [ridiko'laddʒine] sf (*di

situazione) absurdity; (*cosa detta o fatta*) nonsense *no pl*.

ridicoliz'zare [ridikolid'dzare] *vt* to ridicule.

ri'dicolo, a *ag* ridiculous, absurd ♦ *sm*: **cadere nel** ~ to become ridiculous; **rendersi** ~ to make a fool of o.s.

ridimensiona'mento *sm* reorganization; (*di fatto storico*) reappraisal.

ridimensio'nare *vt* to reorganize; (*fig*) to see in the right perspective.

ri'dire *vt* to repeat; (*criticare*) to find fault with; to object to; **trova sempre qualcosa da** ~ he always manages to find fault.

ridon'dante *ag* redundant.

ri'dosso *sm*: **a** ~ **di** (*dietro*) behind; (*contro*) against.

ri'dotto, a *pp di* **ridurre**.

ri'duco *etc vb vedi* **ridurre**.

ri'durre *vt* (*anche* CHIM, MAT) to reduce; (*prezzo, spese*) to cut, reduce; (*accorciare*: *opera letteraria*) to abridge; (: RADIO, TV) to adapt; **ridursi** *vr* (*diminuirsi*) to be reduced, shrink; **ridursi a** to be reduced to; **ridursi a pelle e ossa** to be reduced to skin and bone.

ri'dussi *etc vb vedi* **ridurre**.

ridut'tore *sm* (TECN, CHIM, ELETTR) reducer.

riduzi'one [ridut'tsjone] *sf* reduction; abridgement; adaptation.

ri'ebbi *etc vb vedi* **riavere**.

riecheg'giare [rieked'dʒare] *vi* to re-echo.

riedu'care *vt* (*persona, arto*) to re-educate; (*malato*) to rehabilitate.

rieducazi'one [riedukat'tsjone] *sf* re-education; rehabilitation; **centro di** ~ rehabilitation centre.

rie'leggere [rie'lɛddʒere] *vt* to re-elect.

rie'letto, a *pp di* **rieleggere**.

riempi'mento *sm* filling (up).

riem'pire *vt* to fill (up); (*modulo*) to fill in *o* out; ~**rsi** *vr* to fill (up); (*mangiare troppo*) to stuff o.s.; ~ **qc di** to fill sth (up) with.

riempi'tivo, a *ag* filling ♦ *sm* (*anche fig*) filler.

rien'tranza [rien'trantsa] *sf* recess; indentation.

rien'trare *vi* (*entrare di nuovo*) to go (*o* come) back in; (*tornare*) to return; (*fare una rientranza*) to go in, curve inwards; to be indented; (*riguardare*): ~ **in** to be included among, form part of; ~ (**a casa**) to get back home; **non rientriamo nelle spese** we are not within our budget.

ri'entro *sm* (*ritorno*) return; (*di astronave*) re-entry; **è iniziato il grande** ~ (*estivo*) people are coming back from their (summer) holidays.

riepilo'gare *vt* to summarize ♦ *vi* to

recapitulate.

rie'pilogo, ghi *sm* recapitulation; **fare un** ~ **di qc** to summarize sth.

rie'same *sm* re-examination.

riesami'nare *vt* to re-examine.

ri'esco *etc vb vedi* **riuscire**.

ri'essere *vi*: **ci risiamo!** (*fam*) we're back to this again!

rievo'care *vt* (*passato*) to recall; (*commemorare*: *figura, meriti*) to commemorate.

rievocazi'one [rievokat'tsjone] *sf* (*vedi vt*) recalling; commemoration.

rifaci'mento [rifatʃi'mento] *sm* (*di film*) remake; (*di opera letteraria*) rehashing.

ri'fare *vt* to do again; (*ricostruire*) to make again; (*nodo*) to tie again, do up again; (*imitare*) to imitate, copy; ~**rsi** *vr* (*risarcirsi*): ~**rsi di** to make up for; (*vendicarsi*): ~**rsi di qc su qn** to get one's own back on sb for sth; (*riferirsi*): ~**rsi a** (*periodo, fenomeno storico*) to go back to; ~ **il letto** to make the bed; ~**rsi una vita** to make a new life for o.s.

ri'fatto, a *pp di* **rifare**.

riferi'mento *sm* reference; **in** *o* **con** ~ **a** with reference to; **far** ~ **a** to refer to.

rife'rire *vt* (*riportare*) to report; (*ascrivere*): ~ **qc a** to attribute sth to ♦ *vi* to do a report; ~**rsi** *vr*: ~**rsi a** to refer to; **riferirò** I'll pass on the message.

rifi'lare *vt* (*tagliare a filo*) to trim; (*fam*: *affibbiare*): ~ **qc a qn** to palm sth off on sb.

rifi'nire *vt* to finish off, put the finishing touches to.

rifini'tura *sf* finishing touch; ~**e** *sfpl* (*di mobile, auto*) finish *sg*.

rifiu'tare *vt* to refuse; ~ **di fare** to refuse to do.

rifi'uto *sm* refusal; ~**i** *smpl* (*spazzatura*) rubbish *sg*, refuse *sg*; ~**i solidi urbani** solid urban waste *sg*.

riflessi'one *sf* (FISICA) reflection; (*il pensare*) thought, reflection; (*osservazione*) remark.

rifles'sivo, a *ag* (*persona*) thoughtful, reflective; (LING) reflexive.

ri'flesso, a *pp di* **riflettere** ♦ *sm* (*di luce, su specchio*) reflection; (FISIOL) reflex; (*su capelli*) light; (*fig*) effect; **di** *o* **per** ~ indirectly; **avere i** ~**i pronti** to have quick reflexes.

riflessolo'gia [riflessolo'dʒia] *sf*: ~ **(plantare)** reflexology.

ri'flettere *vt* to reflect ♦ *vi* to think; ~**rsi** *vr* to be reflected; (*ripercuotersi*): ~**rsi su** to have repercussions on; ~ **su** to think over.

riflet'tore *sm* reflector; (*proiettore*) floodlight; (: *MIL*) searchlight.

ri'flusso *sm* flowing back; (*della marea*) ebb; **un'epoca di** ~ an era of nostalgia.

rifocil'larsi [rifotʃil'larsi] *vr* (*poetico*) to take refreshment.

rifondazi'one [rifondat'tsjone] *sf* (*POL*): **R~ Comunista** *hard left party, originating from former P.C.I.*

ri'fondere *vt* (*rimborsare*) to refund, repay; ~ **le spese a qn** to refund sb's expenses; ~ **i danni a qn** to compensate sb for damages.

ri'forma *sf* reform; (*MIL*) declaration of unfitness for service; discharge (*on health grounds*); **la R~** (*REL*) the Reformation.

rifor'mare *vt* to re-form; (*cambiare, innovare*) to reform; (*MIL: recluta*) to declare unfit for service; (: *soldato*) to invalid out, discharge.

riforma'tore, 'trice *ag* reforming ♦ *sm/f* reformer.

riforma'torio *sm* (*DIR*) community home (*BRIT*), reformatory (*US*).

rifor'mista, i, e *ag, sm/f* reformist.

riforni'mento *sm* supplying, providing; restocking; (*di carburante*) refuelling; ~**i** *smpl* supplies, provisions; **fare** ~ **di** (*viveri*) to stock up with; (*benzina*) to fill up with; **posto di** ~ filling *o* gas (*US*) station.

rifor'nire *vt* (*provvedere*): ~ **di** to supply *o* provide with; (*fornire di nuovo: casa etc*) to restock.

ri'frangere [ri'frandʒere] *vt* to refract.

ri'fratto, a *pp di* **rifrangere**.

rifrazi'one [rifrat'tsjone] *sf* refraction.

rifug'gire [rifud'dʒire] *vi* to escape again; (*fig*): ~ **da** to shun.

rifugi'arsi [rifu'dʒarsi] *vr* to take refuge.

rifugi'ato, a [rifu'dʒato] *sm/f* refugee.

ri'fugio [ri'fudʒo] *sm* refuge, shelter; (*in montagna*) shelter; ~ **antiaereo** air-raid shelter.

ri'fuso, a *pp di* **rifondere**.

'riga, ghe *sf* line; (*striscia*) stripe; (*di persone, cose*) line, row; (*regolo*) ruler; (*scriminatura*) parting; **mettersi in** ~ to line up; **a** ~**ghe** (*foglio*) lined; (*vestito*) striped; **buttare giù due** ~**ghe** (*note*) to jot down a few notes; **mandami due** ~**ghe appena arrivi** drop me a line as soon as you arrive.

ri'gagnolo [ri'gaɲɲolo] *sm* rivulet.

ri'gare *vt* (*foglio*) to rule ♦ *vi*: ~ **diritto** (*fig*) to toe the line.

riga'toni *smpl* (*CUC*) *short, ridged pasta shapes.*

rigatti'ere *sm* junk dealer.

riga'tura *sf* (*di pagina, quaderno*) lining, ruling; (*di fucile*) rifling.

rigene'rare [ridʒene'rare] *vt* (*gen, TECN*) to regenerate; (*forze*) to restore; (*gomma*) to retread; ~**rsi** *vr* (*gen*) to regenerate; (*ramo, tumore*) to regenerate, grow again; **gomma rigenerata** retread.

rigenerazi'one [ridʒenerat'tsjone] *sf* regeneration.

riget'tare [ridʒet'tare] *vt* (*gettare indietro*) to throw back; (*fig: respingere*) to reject; (*vomitare*) to bring *o* throw up.

ri'getto [ri'dʒetto] *sm* (*anche MED*) rejection.

ri'ghello [ri'gello] *sm* ruler.

righerò etc [rige'rɔ] *vb vedi* **rigare**.

rigi'dezza [ridʒi'dettsa], **rigidità** [ridʒidi'ta] *sf* rigidity; stiffness; severity, rigours *pl* (*BRIT*), rigors *pl* (*US*); strictness.

'rigido, a [ˈridʒido] *ag* rigid, stiff; (*membra etc: indurite*) stiff; (*METEOR*) harsh, severe; (*fig*) strict.

rigi'rare [ridʒi'rare] *vt* to turn; ~**rsi** *vr* to turn round; (*nel letto*) to turn over; ~ **qc tra le mani** to turn sth over in one's hands; ~ **il discorso** to change the subject.

'rigo, ghi *sm* line; (*MUS*) staff, stave.

rigogli'oso, a [rigoʎ'ʎoso] *ag* (*pianta*) luxuriant; (*fig: commercio, sviluppo*) thriving.

rigonfia'mento *sm* (*ANAT*) swelling; (*su legno, intonaco etc*) bulge.

ri'gonfio, a *ag* swollen; (*grembiule, sporta*): ~ **di** bulging with.

ri'gore *sm* (*METEOR*) harshness, rigours *pl* (*BRIT*), rigors *pl* (*US*); (*fig*) severity, strictness; (*anche: calcio di* ~) penalty; **di** ~ compulsory; **"è di** ~ **l'abito da sera"** "evening dress"; **area di** ~ (*CALCIO*) penalty box (*BRIT*); **a rigor di termini** strictly speaking.

rigorosità *sf* strictness; rigour (*BRIT*), rigor (*US*).

rigo'roso, a *ag* (*severo: persona, ordine*) strict; (*preciso*) rigorous.

rigover'nare *vt* to wash (up).

riguar'dare *vt* to look at again; (*considerare*) to regard, consider; (*concernere*) to regard, concern; ~**rsi** *vr* (*aver cura di sé*) to look after o.s.; **per quel che mi riguarda** as far as I'm concerned; **sono affari che non ti riguardano** it's none of your business.

rigu'ardo *sm* (*attenzione*) care; (*considerazione*) regard, respect; ~ **a** concerning, with regard to; **per** ~ **a** out of respect for; **ospite/persona di** ~ very important guest/person; **non aver ~i nell'agire/nel parlare** to act/speak freely.

riguar'doso, a *ag* (*rispettoso*) respectful; (*premuroso*) considerate, thoughtful.

rigurgi'tare [rigurdʒi'tare] *vi* (*liquido*): ~ **da** to gush out from; (*recipiente: traboccare*): ~ **di** to overflow with.

ri'gurgito [ri'gurdʒito] *sm* (*MED*) regurgitation; (*fig: ritorno, risveglio*) revival.

rilanci'are [rilan'tʃare] *vt* (*lanciare di nuovo: gen*) to throw again; (: *moda*) to bring back; (: *prodotto*) to re-launch; ~ **un'offerta** (*asta*) to make a higher bid.

ri'lancio [ri'lantʃo] *sm* (*CARTE, di offerta*) raising.

rilasci'are [rilaʃ'ʃare] *vt* (*rimettere in libertà*) to release; (*AMM: documenti*) to issue; (*intervista*) to give; ~ **delle dichiarazioni** to make a statement.

ri'lascio [ri'laʃʃo] *sm* release; issue.

rilassa'mento *sm* (*gen, MED*) relaxation.

rilas'sare *vt* to relax; ~**rsi** *vr* to relax; (*fig: disciplina*) to become slack.

rilassa'tezza [rilassa'tettsa] *sf* (*fig: di costumi, disciplina*) laxity.

rilas'sato, a *ag* (*persona, muscoli*) relaxed; (*disciplina, costumi*) lax.

rile'gare *vt* (*libro*) to bind.

rilega'tura *sf* binding.

ri'leggere [ri'lɛddʒere] *vt* to reread, read again; (*rivedere*) to read over.

ri'lento: a ~ *av* slowly.

ri'letto, a *pp di* **rileggere**.

rilet'tura *sf* (*vedi vt*) rereading; reading over.

rileva'mento *sm* (*topografico, statistico*) survey; (*NAUT*) bearing.

rile'vante *ag* considerable; important.

rile'vanza [rile'vantsa] *sf* importance.

rile'vare *vt* (*ricavare*) to find; (*notare*) to notice; (*mettere in evidenza*) to point out; (*venire a conoscere: notizia*) to learn; (*raccogliere: dati*) to gather, collect; (*TOPOGRAFIA*) to survey; (*MIL*) to relieve; (*COMM*) to take over.

rilevazi'one [rilevat'tsjone] *sf* survey.

rili'evo *sm* (*ARTE, GEO*) relief; (*fig: rilevanza*) importance; (*osservazione*) point, remark; (*TOPOGRAFIA*) survey; **dar** ~ **a** *o* **mettere in** ~ **qc** (*fig*) to bring sth out, highlight sth; **di poco/nessun** ~ (*fig*) of little/no importance; **un personaggio di** ~ an important person.

rilut'tante *ag* reluctant.

rilut'tanza [rilut'tantsa] *sf* reluctance.

'rima *sf* rhyme; (*verso*) verse; **far** ~ **con** to rhyme with; **rispondere a qn per le ~e** to

give sb tit for tat.

riman'dare *vt* to send again; (*restituire, rinviare*) to send back, return; (*differire*): ~ **qc (a)** to postpone sth *o* put sth off (till); (*fare riferimento*): ~ **qn a** to refer sb to; **essere rimandato** (*INS*) to have to resit one's exams.

ri'mando *sm* (*rinvio*) return; (*dilazione*) postponement; (*riferimento*) cross-reference.

rimaneggi'are [rimaned'dʒare] *vt* (*testo*) to reshape, recast; (*POL*) to reshuffle.

rima'nente *ag* remaining ♦ *sm* rest, remainder; **i ~i** (*persone*) the rest of them, the others.

rima'nenza [rima'nɛntsa] *sf* rest, remainder; ~**e** *sfpl* (*COMM*) unsold stock *sg*.

rima'nere *vi* (*restare*) to remain, stay; (*avanzare*) to be left, remain; (*restare stupito*) to be amazed; (*restare, mancare*): **rimangono poche settimane a Pasqua** there are only a few weeks left till Easter; (*diventare*): ~ **vedovo** to be left a widower; (*trovarsi*): ~ **confuso/sorpreso** to be confused/surprised; **rimane da vedere se** it remains to be seen whether.

rimangi'are [riman'dʒare] *vt* to eat again; ~**rsi la parola/una promessa** (*fig*) to go back on one's word/one's promise.

ri'mango *etc vb vedi* **rimanere**.

ri'mare *vt, vi* to rhyme.

rimargi'nare [rimardʒi'nare] *vt, vi* (*anche*: ~**rsi**) to heal.

ri'masto, a *pp di* **rimanere**.

rima'sugli [rima'suʎʎi] *smpl* leftovers.

rimbal'zare [rimbal'tsare] *vi* to bounce back, rebound; (*proiettile*) to ricochet.

rim'balzo [rim'baltso] *sm* rebound; ricochet.

rimbam'bire *vi* to be in one's dotage; (*rincretinire*) to grow foolish.

rimbam'bito, a *ag* senile, gaga (*fam*); **un vecchio** ~ a doddering old man.

rimbec'care *vt* (*persona*) to answer back; (*offesa*) to return.

rimbecil'lire [rimbetʃil'lire] *vi*, ~**rsi** *vr* to become stupid.

rimboc'care *vt* (*orlo*) to turn up; (*coperta*) to tuck in; (*maniche, pantaloni*) to turn *o* roll up.

rimbom'bare *vi* to resound; (*artiglieria*) to boom; (*tuono*) to rumble.

rim'bombo *sm* (*vedi vi*) boom; rumble.

rimbor'sare *vt* to pay back, repay; ~ **qc a qn** to reimburse sb for sth.

rim'borso *sm* repayment; (*di spese, biglietto*) refund; ~ **d'imposta** tax rebate.

rimboschi'mento [rimboski'mento] *sm* reafforestation.

rimbos'chire [rimbos'kire] *vt* to reafforest.

rimbrot'tare *vt* to reproach.

rim'brotto *sm* reproach.

rimedi'are *vi:* ~ a to remedy ♦ *vt* (*fam: procurarsi*) to get *o* scrape together; ~ **da vivere** to scrape a living.

ri'medio *sm* (*medicina*) medicine; (*cura, fig*) remedy, cure; **porre** ~ **a qc** to remedy sth; **non c'è** ~ there's no way out, there's nothing to be done about it.

rimesco'lare *vt* to mix well, stir well; (*carte*) to shuffle; **sentirsi** ~ **il sangue** (*per rabbia*) to feel one's blood boil.

ri'messa *sf* (*locale: per veicoli*) garage; (: *per aerei*) hangar; (*COMM: di merce*) consignment; (: *di denaro*) remittance; (*TENNIS*) return; (*CALCIO: anche:* ~ **in gioco**) throw-in.

ri'messo, a *pp di* **rimettere**.

rimes'tare *vt* (*mescolare*) to mix well, stir well; (*fig: passato*) to drag up again.

ri'mettere *vt* (*mettere di nuovo*) to put back; (*indossare di nuovo*): ~ **qc** to put sth back on, put sth on again; (*restituire*) to return, give back; (*affidare*) to entrust; (: *decisione*) to refer; (*condonare*) to remit; (*COMM: merci*) to deliver; (: *denaro*) to remit; (*vomitare*) to bring up; (*perdere: anche:* **rimetterci**) to lose; ~**rsi** *vr:* ~**rsi a** (*affidarsi*) to trust; ~ **a nuovo** (*casa etc*) to do up (*BRIT*) *o* over (*US*); **rimetterci di tasca propria** to be out of pocket; ~**rsi al bello** (*tempo*) to clear up; ~**rsi in cammino** to set off again; ~**rsi al lavoro** to start working again; ~**rsi in salute** to get better, recover one's health.

rimi'nese *ag* of (*o* from) Rimini.

ri'misi *etc vb vedi* **rimettere**.

'rimmel ® *sm inv* mascara.

rimoderna'mento *sm* modernization.

rimoder'nare *vt* to modernize.

ri'monta *sf* (*SPORT, gen*) recovery.

rimon'tare *vt* (*meccanismo*) to reassemble; (*tenda*) to put up again ♦ *vi* (*salire di nuovo*): ~ **in** (*macchina, treno*) to get back into; (*SPORT*) to close the gap.

rimorchi'are [rimor'kjare] *vt* to tow; (*fig: ragazza*) to pick up.

rimorchia'tore [rimorkja'tore] *sm* (*NAUT*) tug(boat).

ri'morchio [ri'mɔrkjo] *sm* tow; (*veicolo*) trailer; **andare a** ~ to be towed; **prendere a** ~ to tow; **cavo da** ~ towrope; **autocarro con** ~ articulated lorry (*BRIT*), semi(trailer) (*US*).

ri'morso *sm* remorse; **avere il** ~ **di aver fatto qc** to deeply regret having done sth.

ri'mosso, a *pp di* **rimuovere**.

rimos'tranza [rimos'trantsa] *sf* protest, complaint; **fare le proprie** ~ **e a qn** to remonstrate with sb.

rimozi'one [rimot'tsjone] *sf* removal; (*da un impiego*) dismissal; (*PSIC*) repression; "~ **forzata**" "illegally parked vehicles will be removed at owner's expense".

rimpas'tare *vt* (*POL: ministero*) to reshuffle.

rim'pasto *sm* (*POL*) reshuffle; ~ **ministeriale** cabinet reshuffle.

rimpatri'are *vi* to return home ♦ *vt* to repatriate.

rim'patrio *sm* repatriation.

rimpi'angere [rim'pjandʒere] *vt* to regret; (*persona*) to miss; ~ **di (non) aver fatto qc** to regret (not) having done sth.

rimpi'anto, a *pp di* **rimpiangere** ♦ *sm* regret.

rimpiat'tino *sm* hide-and-seek.

rimpiaz'zare [rimpjat'tsare] *vt* to replace.

rimpiccio'lire [rimpittʃo'lire] *vt* to make smaller ♦ *vi* (*anche:* ~**rsi**) to become smaller.

rimpin'zare [rimpin'tsare] *vt:* ~ **di** to cram *o* stuff with.

rimprove'rare *vt* to rebuke, reprimand.

rim'provero *sm* rebuke, reprimand; **di** ~ (*tono, occhiata*) reproachful; (*parole*) of reproach.

rimugi'nare [rimudʒi'nare] *vt* (*fig*) to turn over in one's mind.

rimune'rare *vt* (*retribuire*) to remunerate; (*ricompensare: sacrificio etc*) to reward; **un lavoro ben rimunerato** a well-paid job.

rimunera'tivo, a *ag* (*lavoro, attività*) remunerative, profitable.

rimunerazi'one [rimunerat'tsjone] *sf* remuneration; (*premio*) reward.

rimu'overe *vt* to remove; (*destituire*) to dismiss; (*fig: distogliere*) to dissuade.

rinascimen'tale [rinaʃʃimen'tale] *ag* Renaissance *cpd*, of the Renaissance.

Rinasci'mento [rinaʃʃi'mento] *sm:* **il** ~ the Renaissance.

ri'nascita [ri'naʃʃita] *sf* rebirth, revival.

rincal'zare [rinkal'tsare] *vt* (*palo, albero*) to support, prop up; (*lenzuola*) to tuck in.

rin'calzo [rin'kaltso] *sm* support, prop; (*rinforzo*) reinforcement; (*SPORT*) reserve (player); ~**i** *smpl* (*MIL*) reserves.

rinca'rare *vt* to increase the price of ♦ *vi* to go up, become more expensive; ~ **la dose** (*fig*) to pile it on.

rin'caro *sm:* ~ **(di)** (*prezzi, costo della vita*) increase (in); (*prodotto*) increase in the price (of).

rinca'sare *vi* to go home.
rinchi'udere [rin'kjudere] *vt* to shut (*o* lock) up; ~**rsi** *vr*: ~**rsi in** to shut o.s. up in; ~**rsi in se stesso** to withdraw into o.s.
rinchi'uso, a [rin'kjuso] *pp di* **rinchiudere**.
rincitrul'lirsi [rintʃitrul'lirsi] *vr* to grow foolish.
rin'correre *vt* to chase, run after.
rin'corso, a *pp di* **rincorrere ♦** *sf* short run.
rin'crescere [rin'kreʃʃere] *vb impers*: **mi rincresce che/di non poter fare** I'm sorry that/I can't do, I regret that/being unable to do.
rincresci'mento [rinkreʃʃi'mento] *sm* regret.
rincresci'uto, a [rinkreʃ'ʃuto] *pp di* **rincrescere**.
rincu'lare *vi* to draw back; (*arma*) to recoil.
rinfacci'are [rinfat'tʃare] *vt* (*fig*): ~ **qc a qn** to throw sth in sb's face.
rinfoco'lare *vt* (*fig: odio, passioni*) to rekindle; (: *risentimento, rabbia*) to stir up.
rinfor'zare [rinfor'tsare] *vt* to reinforce, strengthen ♦ *vi* (*anche:* ~**rsi**) to grow stronger.
rin'forzo [rin'fɔrtso] *sm*: **mettere un** ~ **a** to strengthen; ~**i** *smpl* (*MIL*) reinforcements; **di** ~ (*asse, sbarra*) strengthening; (*esercito*) supporting; (*personale*) extra, additional.
rinfran'care *vt* to encourage, reassure.
rinfres'cante *ag* (*bibita*) refreshing.
rinfres'care *vt* (*atmosfera, temperatura*) to cool (down); (*abito, pareti*) to freshen up ♦ *vi* (*tempo*) to grow cooler; ~**rsi** *vr* (*ristorarsi*) to refresh o.s.; (*lavarsi*) to freshen up; ~ **la memoria a qn** to refresh sb's memory.
rin'fresco, schi *sm* (*festa*) party; ~**schi** *smpl* (*cibi e bevande*) refreshments.
rin'fusa *sf*: **alla** ~ in confusion, higgledy-piggledy.
ringhi'are [rin'gjare] *vi* to growl, snarl.
ringhi'era [rin'gjɛra] *sf* railing; (*delle scale*) banister(s *pl*).
'ringhio ['ringjo] *sm* growl, snarl.
ringhi'oso, a [rin'gjoso] *ag* growling, snarling.
ringiova'nire [rindʒova'nire] *vt* (*sog: vestito, acconciatura etc*): ~ **qn** to make sb look younger; (: *vacanze etc*) to rejuvenate ♦ *vi* (*anche:* ~**rsi**) to become (*o* look) younger.
ringrazia'mento [ringrattsja'mento] *sm* thanks *pl*; **lettera/biglietto di** ~ thank you letter/card.
ringrazi'are [ringrat'tsjare] *vt* to thank; ~ **qn di qc** to thank sb for sth; ~ **qn per aver fatto qc** to thank sb for doing sth.

rinne'gare *vt* (*fede*) to renounce; (*figlio*) to disown, repudiate.
rinne'gato, a *sm/f* renegade.
rinnova'mento *sm* renewal; (*economico*) revival.
rinno'vare *vt* to renew; (*ripetere*) to repeat, renew; ~**rsi** *vr* (*fenomeno*) to be repeated, recur.
rin'novo *sm* (*di contratto*) renewal; "**chiuso per** ~ (**dei**) **locali**" (*negozio*) "closed for alterations".
rinoce'ronte [rinotʃe'ronte] *sm* rhinoceros.
rino'mato, a *ag* renowned, celebrated.
rinsal'dare *vt* to strengthen.
rinsa'vire *vi* to come to one's senses.
rinsec'chito, a [rinsek'kito] *ag* (*vecchio, albero*) thin, gaunt.
rinta'narsi *vr* (*animale*) to go into its den; (*persona: nascondersi*) to hide.
rintoc'care *vi* (*campana*) to toll; (*orologio*) to strike.
rin'tocco, chi *sm* toll.
rintracci'are [rintrat'tʃare] *vt* to track down; (*persona scomparsa, documento*) to trace.
rintro'nare *vi* to boom, roar ♦ *vt* (*assordare*) to deafen; (*stordire*) to stun.
rintuz'zare [rintut'tsare] *vt* (*fig: sentimento*) to check, repress; (: *accusa*) to refute.
ri'nuncia [ri'nuntʃa] *sf* renunciation; ~ **a** (*carica*) resignation from; (*eredità*) relinquishment of; ~ **agli atti del giudizio** (*DIR*) abandonment of a claim.
rinunci'are [rinun'tʃare] *vi*: ~ **a** to give up, renounce; ~ **a fare qc** to give up doing sth.
rinuncia'tario, a [rinuntʃa'tarjo] *ag* defeatist.
ri'nunzia *etc* [ri'nuntsja] = **rinuncia** *etc*.
rinveni'mento *sm* (*ritrovamento*) recovery; (*scoperta*) discovery; (*METALLURGIA*) tempering.
rinve'nire *vt* to find, recover; (*scoprire*) to discover, find out ♦ *vi* (*riprendere i sensi*) to come round; (*riprendere l'aspetto naturale*) to revive.
rinve'nuto, a *pp di* **rinvenire**.
rinver'dire *vi* (*bosco, ramo*) to become green again.
rinvi'are *vt* (*rimandare indietro*) to send back, return; (*differire*): ~ **qc (a)** to postpone sth *o* put sth off (till); (: *seduta*) to adjourn sth (till); (*fare un rimando*): ~ **qn a** to refer sb to; ~ **a giudizio** (*DIR*) to commit for trial.
rinvigo'rire *vt* to strengthen.
rin'vio, 'vii *sm* (*rimando*) return; (*differimento*) postponement; (: *di seduta*)

adjournment; (*in un testo*) cross-reference; ~ **a giudizio** (*DIR*) indictment.

riò *etc vb vedi* **riavere**.

'Rio de Ja'neiro ['riodedʒa'neiro] *sf* Rio de Janeiro.

rio'nale *ag* (*mercato, cinema*) local, district *cpd*.

ri'one *sm* district, quarter.

riordina'mento *sm* (*di ente, azienda*) reorganization.

riordi'nare *vt* (*rimettere in ordine*) to tidy; (*riorganizzare*) to reorganize.

riorganiz'zare [riorganid'dzare] *vt* to reorganize.

riorganizzazi'one [riorganiddzat'tsjone] *sf* reorganization.

ripa'gare *vt* to repay.

ripa'rare *vt* (*proteggere*) to protect, defend; (*correggere: male, torto*) to make up for; (: *errore*) to put right; (*aggiustare*) to repair ♦ *vi* (*mettere rimedio*): ~ **a** to make up for; ~**rsi** *vr* (*rifugiarsi*) to take refuge *o* shelter.

ripa'rato, a *ag* (*posto*) sheltered.

riparazi'one [riparat'tsjone] *sf* (*di un torto*) reparation; (*di guasto, scarpe*) repairing *no pl*; repair; (*risarcimento*) compensation; (*INS*): **esame di** ~ resit (*BRIT*), test retake (*US*).

ri'paro *sm* (*protezione*) shelter, protection; (*rimedio*) remedy; **al** ~ **da** (*sole, vento*) sheltered from; **mettersi al** ~ to take shelter; **correre ai** ~**i** (*fig*) to take remedial action.

ripar'tire *vt* (*dividere*) to divide up; (*distribuire*) to share out, distribute ♦ *vi* to leave again; (*motore*) to start again.

ripartizi'one [ripartit'tsjone] *sf* division; sharing out, distribution; (*AMM: dipartimento*) department.

ripas'sare *vi* to come (*o* go) back ♦ *vt* (*scritto, lezione*) to go over (again).

ri'passo *sm* (*di lezione*) revision (*BRIT*), review (*US*).

ripensa'mento *sm* second thoughts *pl* (*BRIT*), change of mind; **avere un** ~ to have second thoughts, change one's mind.

ripen'sare *vi* to think; (*cambiare idea*) to change one's mind; (*tornare col pensiero*): ~ **a** to recall; **a ripensarci** ... on thinking it over ....

riper'correre *vt* (*itinerario*) to travel over again; (*strada*) to go along again; (*fig: ricordi, passato*) to go back over.

riper'corso, a *pp di* **ripercorrere**.

riper'cosso, a *pp di* **ripercuotersi**.

ripercu'otersi *vr*: ~ **su** (*fig*) to have repercussions on.

ripercussi'one *sf* (*fig*): **avere una** ~ *o* **delle** ~**i su** to have repercussions on.

ripes'care *vt* (*pesce*) to catch again; (*persona, cosa*) to fish out; (*fig: ritrovare*) to dig out.

ripe'tente *smf* student repeating the year, repeater (*US*).

ri'petere *vt* to repeat; (*ripassare*) to go over.

ripeti'tore *sm* (*RADIO, TV*) relay.

ripetizi'one [ripetit'tsjone] *sf* repetition; (*di lezione*) revision; ~**i** *sfpl* (*INS*) private tutoring *o* coaching *sg*; **fucile a** ~ repeating rifle.

ripetuta'mente *av* repeatedly, again and again.

ripi'ano *sm* (*GEO*) terrace; (*di mobile*) shelf.

ri'picca *sf*: **per** ~ out of spite.

'ripido, a *ag* steep.

ripiega'mento *sm* (*MIL*) retreat.

ripie'gare *vt* to refold; (*piegare più volte*) to fold (up) ♦ *vi* (*MIL*) to retreat, fall back; (*fig: accontentarsi*): ~ **su** to make do with; ~**rsi** *vr* to bend.

ripi'ego, ghi *sm* expedient; **una soluzione di** ~ a makeshift solution.

ripi'eno, a *ag* full; (*CUC*) stuffed; (: *panino*) filled ♦ *sm* (*CUC*) stuffing.

ri'pone, ri'pongo *etc vb vedi* **riporre**.

ri'porre *vt* (*porre al suo posto*) to put back, replace; (*mettere via*) to put away; (*fiducia, speranza*): ~ **qc in qn** to place *o* put sth in sb.

ripor'tare *vt* (*portare indietro*) to bring (*o* take) back; (*riferire*) to report; (*citare*) to quote; (*ricevere*) to receive, get; (*vittoria*) to gain; (*successo*) to have; (*MAT*) to carry; (*COMM*) to carry forward; ~**rsi** *vr*: ~**rsi a** (*anche fig*) to go back to; (*riferirsi a*) to refer to; ~ **danni** to suffer damage; **ha riportato gravi ferite** he was seriously injured.

ri'porto *sm* amount carried over; amount carried forward.

ripo'sante *ag* (*gen*) restful; (*musica, colore*) soothing.

ripo'sare *vt* (*bicchiere, valigia*) to put down; (*dare sollievo*) to rest ♦ *vi* to rest; ~**rsi** *vr* to rest; **qui riposa** ... (*su tomba*) here lies ....

ripo'sato, a *ag* (*viso, aspetto*) rested; (*mente*) fresh.

ri'posi *etc vb vedi* **riporre**.

ri'poso *sm* rest; (*MIL*): ~! at ease!; **a** ~ (*in pensione*) retired; **giorno di** ~ day off; "**oggi** ~" (*CINE, TEAT*) "no performance today"; (*ristorante*) "closed today".

ripos'tiglio [ripos'tiʎʎo] *sm* lumber room

(*BRIT*), storage room (*US*).

ri'posto, a *pp di* **riporre** ♦ *ag* (*fig: senso, significato*) hidden.

ri'prendere *vt* (*prigioniero, fortezza*) to recapture; (*prendere indietro*) to take back; (*ricominciare: lavoro*) to resume; (*andare a prendere*) to fetch, come back for; (*assumere di nuovo: impiegati*) to take on again, re-employ; (*rimproverare*) to tell off; (*restringere: abito*) to take in; (*CINE*) to shoot; ~**rsi** *vr* to recover; (*correggersi*) to correct o.s.; ~ **a fare qc** to start doing sth again; ~ **il cammino** to set off again; ~ **i sensi** to recover consciousness; ~ **sonno** to go back to sleep.

ripresen'tare *vt* (*certificato*) to submit again; (*domanda*) to put forward again; (*persona*) to introduce again; ~**rsi** *vr* (*ritornare: persona*) to come back; (: *occasione*) to arise again; ~**rsi a** (*esame*) to sit (*BRIT*) o take (*US*) again; (*concorso*) to enter again; ~**rsi come candidato** (*POL*) to stand (*BRIT*) o run (*US*) again (as a candidate).

ri'preso, a *pp di* **riprendere** ♦ *sf* recapture; resumption; (*economica, da malattia, emozione*) recovery; (*AUT*) acceleration *no pl*; (*TEAT, CINE*) rerun; (*CINE: presa*) shooting *no pl*; shot; (*SPORT*) second half; (: *PUGILATO*) round; **a più ~e** on several occasions, several times.

ripristi'nare *vt* to restore.

ri'pristino *sm* (*gen*) restoration; (*di tradizioni*) revival.

ripro'dotto, a *pp di* **riprodurre.**

ripro'durre *vt* to reproduce; **riprodursi** *vr* (*BIOL*) to reproduce; (*riformarsi*) to form again.

riprodut'tivo, a *ag* reproductive.

riprodut'tore, 'trice *ag* (*organo*) reproductive ♦ *sm*: ~ **acustico** pick-up; ~ **a cassetta** cassette player.

riproduzi'one [riprodut'tsjone] *sf* reproduction; ~ **vietata** all rights reserved.

ripro'messo, a *pp di* **ripromettersi.**

ripro'mettersi *vt* (*aspettarsi*): ~ **qc da** to expect sth from; (*intendere*): ~ **di fare qc** to intend to do sth.

ripro'porre *vt*: **riproporsi di fare qc** to intend to do sth.

ripro'posto, a *pp di* **riproporre.**

ri'prova *sf* confirmation; **a ~ di** as confirmation of.

ripro'vare *vt* (*provare di nuovo: gen*) to try again; (: *vestito*) to try on again; (: *sensazione*) to experience again ♦ *vi* (*tentare*): ~ **(a fare qc)** to try (to do sth)

again; **riproverò più tardi** I'll try again later.

ripro'vevole *ag* reprehensible.

ripudi'are *vt* to repudiate, disown.

ri'pudio *sm* repudiation, disowning.

ripu'gnante [ripuɲ'ɲante] *ag* disgusting, repulsive.

ripu'gnanza [ripuɲ'ɲantsa] *sf* repugnance, disgust.

ripu'gnare [ripuɲ'ɲare] *vi*: ~ **a qn** to repel o disgust sb.

ripu'lire *vt* to clean up; (*sog: ladri*) to clean out; (*perfezionare*) to polish, refine.

ripulsi'one *sf* (*FISICA, fig*) repulsion.

ri'quadro *sm* square; (*ARCHIT*) panel.

ri'sacca, che *sf* backwash.

ri'saia *sf* paddy field.

risa'lire *vi* (*ritornare in su*) to go back up; ~ **a** (*ritornare con la mente*) to go back to; (*datare da*) to date back to, go back to.

risa'lita *sf*: **mezzi di ~** (*SCI*) ski lifts.

risal'tare *vi* (*fig: distinguersi*) to stand out; (*ARCHIT*) to project, jut out.

ri'salto *sm* prominence; (*sporgenza*) projection; **mettere** o **porre in ~ qc** to make sth stand out.

risana'mento *sm* (*economico*) improvement; (*bonifica*) reclamation; ~ **del bilancio** reorganization of the budget; ~ **edilizio** building improvement.

risa'nare *vt* (*guarire*) to heal, cure; (*palude*) to reclaim; (*economia*) to improve; (*bilancio*) to reorganize.

risa'pere *vt*: ~ **qc** to come to know of sth.

risa'puto, a *ag*: **è ~ che** ... everyone knows that ..., it's common knowledge that ....

risarci'mento [risartʃi'mento] *sm*: ~ **(di)** compensation (for); **aver diritto al ~ dei danni** to be entitled to damages.

risar'cire [risar'tʃire] *vt* (*cose*) to pay compensation for; (*persona*): ~ **qn di qc** to compensate sb for sth; ~ **i danni a qn** to pay sb damages.

ri'sata *sf* laugh.

riscalda'mento *sm* heating; ~ **centrale** central heating.

riscal'dare *vt* (*scaldare*) to heat; (: *mani, persona*) to warm; (*minestra*) to reheat; ~**rsi** *vr* to warm up.

ris'caldo *sm* (*fam*) (slight) inflammation.

riscat'tare *vt* (*prigioniero*) to ransom, pay a ransom for; (*DIR*) to redeem; ~**rsi** *vr* (*da disonore*) to redeem o.s.

ris'catto *sm* ransom; redemption.

rischia'rare [riskja'rare] *vt* (*illuminare*) to light up; (*colore*) to make lighter; ~**rsi** *vr* (*tempo*) to clear up; (*cielo*) to clear; (*fig: volto*) to brighten up; ~**rsi la voce** to clear one's throat.

rischi'are [ris'kjare] vt to risk ♦ vi: ~ **di fare qc** to risk o run the risk of doing sth.

'rischio ['riskjo] sm risk; **a** ~ (zona, situazione) at risk, vulnerable; **a proprio** ~ **e pericolo** at one's own risk; **correre il** ~ **di fare qc** to run the risk of doing sth; ~ **del mestiere** occupational hazard.

rischi'oso, a [ris'kjoso] ag risky, dangerous.

risciac'quare [riʃʃak'kware] vt to rinse.

risci'acquo [riʃ'ʃakkwo] sm rinse.

riscon'trare vt (confrontare: due cose) to compare; (esaminare) to check, verify; (rilevare) to find.

ris'contro sm comparison; check, verification; (AMM: lettera di risposta) reply; **mettere a** ~ to compare; **in attesa di un vostro cortese** ~ we look forward to your reply.

risco'perto, a pp di **riscoprire**.

risco'prire vt to rediscover.

riscossi'one sf collection.

ris'cosso, a pp di **riscuotere** ♦ sf (riconquista) recovery, reconquest.

riscu'otere vt (ritirare una somma dovuta) to collect; (: stipendio) to draw, collect; (fig: successo etc) to win, earn; ~**rsi** vr: ~**rsi (da)** to shake o.s. (out of), rouse o.s. (from); ~ **un assegno** to cash a cheque.

'rise etc vb vedi **ridere**.

risenti'mento sm resentment.

risen'tire vt to hear again; (provare) to feel ♦ vi: ~ **di** to feel (o show) the effects of; ~**rsi** vr: ~**rsi di** o **per** to take offence (BRIT) o offense (US) at, resent.

risen'tito, a ag resentful.

ri'serbo sm reserve.

ri'serva sf reserve; (di caccia, pesca) preserve; (restrizione, di indigeni) reservation; (CALCIO) substitute; **fare** ~ **di** (cibo) to get in a supply of; **tenere di** ~ to keep in reserve; **con le dovute** ~**e** with certain reservations; **ha accettato con la** ~ **di potersi ritirare** he accepted with the proviso that he could pull out.

riser'vare vt (tenere in serbo) to keep, put aside; (prenotare) to book, reserve; ~**rsi** vr: ~**rsi di fare qc** to intend to do sth; ~**rsi il diritto di fare qc** to reserve the right to do sth.

riserva'tezza [riserva'tettsa] sf reserve.

riser'vato, a ag (prenotato, fig: persona) reserved; (confidenziale) confidential.

'risi etc vb vedi **ridere**.

ri'sibile ag laughable.

risi'cato, a ag (vittoria etc) very narrow.

risi'edere vi: ~ **a** o **in** to reside in.

'risma sf (di carta) ream; (fig) kind, sort.

'riso, a pp di **ridere** ♦ sm (pianta) rice; (pl(f) ~**a**: il ridere): **un** ~ a laugh; **il** ~ laughter; **uno scoppio di** ~**a** a burst of laughter.

riso'lino sm snigger.

risolle'vare vt (sollevare di nuovo: testa) to raise again, lift up again; (fig: questione) to raise again, bring up again; (: morale) to raise; ~**rsi** vr (da terra) to rise again; (fig: da malattia) to recover; ~ **le sorti di qc** to improve the chances of sth.

ri'solsi etc vb vedi **risolvere**.

ri'solto, a pp di **risolvere**.

risolu'tezza [risolu'tettsa] sf determination.

risolu'tivo, a ag (determinante) decisive; (che risolve): **arrivare ad una formula** ~**a** to come up with a formula to resolve a situation.

riso'luto, a ag determined, resolute.

risoluzi'one [risolut'tsjone] sf solving no pl; (MAT) solution; (decisione, di immagine) resolution.

ri'solvere vt (difficoltà, controversia) to resolve; (problema) to solve; (decidere): ~ **di fare** to resolve to do; ~**rsi** vr (decidersi): ~**rsi a fare** to make up one's mind to do; (andare a finire): ~**rsi in** to end up, turn out; ~**rsi in nulla** to come to nothing.

risol'vibile ag solvable.

riso'nanza [riso'nantsa] sf resonance; **aver vasta** ~ (fig: fatto etc) to be known far and wide; ~ **magnetica** magnetic resonance.

riso'nare vt, vi = **risuonare**.

ri'sorgere [ri'sordʒere] vi to rise again.

risorgimen'tale [risordʒimen'tale] ag of the Risorgimento.

risorgi'mento [risordʒi'mento] sm revival; **il R~** (STORIA) the Risorgimento; vedi nota nel riquadro.

RISORGIMENTO

The **Risorgimento**, the period stretching from the early nineteenth century to 1861 and the proclamation of the Kingdom of Italy, saw considerable upheaval and change. Political and personal freedom took on new importance as the events of the French Revolution unfolded. The **Risorgimento** paved the way for the unification of Italy in 1871.

ri'sorsa sf expedient, resort; ~**e** sfpl (naturali, finanziarie etc) resources; **persona piena di** ~**e** resourceful person.

ri'sorsi etc vb vedi **risorgere**.

ri'sorto, a pp di **risorgere**.

ri'sotto sm (CUC) risotto.

risparmi'are *vt* to save; (*non uccidere*) to spare ♦ *vi* to save; ~ **qc a qn** to spare sb sth; ~ **fatica/fiato** to save one's energy/ breath; **risparmiati il disturbo** *o* **la fatica** (*anche ironico*) save yourself the trouble.

risparmia'tore, 'trice *sm/f* saver.

ris'parmio *sm* saving *no pl*; (*denaro*) savings *pl*.

rispecchi'are [rispek'kjare] *vt* to reflect; ~**rsi** *vr* to be reflected.

rispe'dire *vt* to send back; ~ **qc a qn** to send sth back to sb.

rispet'tabile *ag* respectable; (*considerevole: somma*) sizeable, considerable.

rispet'tare *vt* to respect; (*legge*) to obey, comply with, abide by; (*promessa*) to keep; **farsi** ~ to command respect; ~ **le distanze** to keep one's distance; ~ **i tempi** to keep to schedule; **ogni medico che si rispetti** every self-respecting doctor.

rispettiva'mente *av* respectively.

rispet'tivo, a *ag* respective.

ris'petto *sm* respect; ~**i** *smpl* (*saluti*) respects, regards; ~ **a** (*in paragone a*) compared to; (*in relazione a*) as regards, as for; ~ **(di** *o* **per)** (*norme, leggi*) observance (of), compliance (with); **portare** ~ **a qn/qc** to have *o* feel respect for sb/sth; **mancare di** ~ **a qn** to be disrespectful to sb; **con** ~ **parlando** with respect, if you will excuse my saying so; **(porga) i miei** ~**i alla signora** (give) my regards to your wife.

rispet'toso, a *ag* respectful.

risplen'dente *ag* (*giornata, sole*) bright, shining; (*occhi*) sparkling.

ris'plendere *vi* to shine.

rispon'dente *ag*: ~ **a** in keeping *o* conformity with.

rispon'denza [rispon'dɛntsa] *sf* correspondence.

ris'pondere *vi* to answer, reply; (*freni*) to respond; ~ **a** (*domanda*) to answer, reply to; (*persona*) to answer; (*invito*) to reply to; (*provocazione, sog: veicolo, apparecchio*) to respond to; (*corrispondere a*) to correspond to; (: *speranze, bisogno*) to answer; ~ **a qn di qc** (*essere responsabile*) to be answerable to sb for sth.

rispo'sarsi *vr* to get married again, remarry.

ris'posto, a *pp di* **rispondere** ♦ *sf* answer, reply; **in** ~**a a** in reply to; **dare una** ~**a** to give an answer; **diamo** ~**a alla vostra lettera del** ... in reply to your letter of ....

'rissa *sf* brawl.

ris'soso, a *ag* quarrelsome.

rist. *abbr* = **ristampa**.

ristabi'lire *vt* to re-establish, restore; (*persona: sog: riposo etc*) to restore to health; ~**rsi** *vr* to recover.

rista'gnare [ristaɲ'ɲare] *vi* (*acqua*) to become stagnant; (*sangue*) to cease flowing; (*fig: industria*) to stagnate.

ris'tagno [ris'taɲɲo] *sm* stagnation; **c'è un** ~ **delle vendite** business is slack.

ris'tampa *sf* reprinting *no pl*; reprint.

ristam'pare *vt* to reprint.

risto'rante *sm* restaurant.

risto'rare *vt* (*persona, forze*) to revive, refresh; ~**rsi** *vr* (*rifocillarsi*) to have something to eat and drink; (*riposarsi*) to rest, have a rest.

ristora'tore, 'trice *ag* refreshing, reviving ♦ *sm* (*gestore di ristorante*) restaurateur.

ris'toro *sm* (*bevanda, cibo*) refreshment; **posto di** ~ (*FERR*) buffet, snack bar; **servizio di** ~ (*FERR*) refreshments *pl*.

ristret'tezza [ristret'tettsa] *sf* (*strettezza*) narrowness; (*fig: scarsezza*) scarcity, lack; (: *meschinità*) meanness; ~**e** *sfpl* (*povertà*) poverty *sg*.

ris'tretto, a *pp di* **restringere** ♦ *ag* (*racchiuso*) enclosed, hemmed in; (*angusto*) narrow; (*limitato*): ~ **(a)** restricted *o* limited (to); (*CUC: brodo*) thick; (: *caffè*) extra strong.

ristruttu'rare *vt* (*azienda*) to reorganize; (*edificio*) to restore; (*appartamento*) to alter; (*sog: crema, balsamo*) to repair.

ristrutturazi'one [ristrutturat'tsjone] *sf* reorganization; restoration; alteration.

risucchi'are [risuk'kjare] *vt* to suck in.

ri'succhio [ri'sukkjo] *sm* (*di acqua*) undertow, pull; (*di aria*) suction.

risul'tare *vi* (*dimostrarsi*) to prove (to be), turn out (to be); (*riuscire*): ~ **vincitore** to emerge as the winner; ~ **da** (*provenire*) to result from, be the result of; **mi risulta che** ... I understand that ..., as far as I know ...; **(ne) risulta che** ... it follows that ...; **non mi risulta** not as far as I know.

risul'tato *sm* result.

risuo'nare *vi* (*rimbombare*) to resound.

risurrezi'one [risurret'tsjone] *sf* (*REL*) resurrection.

risusci'tare [risuʃʃi'tare] *vt* to resuscitate, restore to life; (*fig*) to revive, bring back ♦ *vi* to rise (from the dead).

risvegli'are [rizveʎ'ʎare] *vt* (*gen*) to wake up, waken; (*fig: interesse*) to stir up, arouse; (: *curiosità*) to arouse; (*fig: dall'inerzia etc*): ~ **qn (da)** to rouse sb (from); ~**rsi** *vr* to wake up, awaken; (*fig: interesse, curiosità*) to be aroused.

ris'veglio [riz've\\o] *sm* waking up; (*fig*) revival.

ris'volto *sm* (*di giacca*) lapel; (*di pantaloni*) turn-up (*BRIT*), cuff (*US*); (*di manica*) cuff; (*di tasca*) flap; (*di libro*) inside flap; (*fig*) implication.

ritagli'are [rita\'\are] *vt* (*tagliar via*) to cut out.

ri'taglio [ri'ta\\o] *sm* (*di giornale*) cutting, clipping; (*di stoffa etc*) scrap; **nei ~i di tempo** in one's spare time.

ritar'dare *vi* (*persona, treno*) to be late; (*orologio*) to be slow ♦ *vt* (*rallentare*) to slow down; (*impedire*) to delay, hold up; (*differire*) to postpone, delay; **~ il pagamento** to defer payment.

ritarda'tario, a *sm/f* latecomer.

ritar'dato, a *ag* (*PSIC*) retarded.

ri'tardo *sm* delay; (*di persona aspettata*) lateness *no pl*; (*fig: mentale*) backwardness; **in ~** late.

ri'tegno [ri'teɲɲo] *sm* restraint.

ritem'prare *vt* (*forze, spirito*) to restore.

rite'nere *vt* (*trattenere*) to hold back; (: *somma*) to deduct; (*giudicare*) to consider, believe.

ri'tengo, ri'tenni *etc vb vedi* **ritenere**.

riten'tare *vt* to try again, make another attempt at.

rite'nuta *sf* (*sul salario*) deduction; **~ d'acconto** advance deduction of tax; **~ alla fonte** (*FISCO*) taxation at source.

riterrò, riti'ene *etc vb vedi* **ritenere**.

riti'rare *vt* to withdraw; (*POL: richiamare*) to recall; (*andare a prendere: pacco etc*) to collect, pick up; **~rsi** *vr* to withdraw; (*da un'attività*) to retire; (*stoffa*) to shrink; (*marea*) to recede; **gli hanno ritirato la patente** they disqualified him from driving (*BRIT*), they took away his licence (*BRIT*) *o* license (*US*); **~rsi a vita privata** to withdraw from public life.

riti'rata *sf* (*MIL*) retreat; (*latrina*) lavatory.

riti'rato, a *ag* secluded; **fare vita ~a** to live in seclusion.

ri'tiro *sm* (*di truppe, candidati, soldi*) withdrawal; (*di pacchi*) collection; (*di passaporto*) confiscation; (*da attività*) retirement; (*luogo appartato*) retreat.

rit'mato, a *ag* rhythmic(al).

'ritmico, a, ci, che *ag* rhythmic(al).

'ritmo *sm* rhythm; (*fig*) rate; (: *della vita*) pace, tempo; **al ~ di** at a speed *o* rate of; **ballare al ~ di valzer** to waltz.

'rito *sm* rite; **di ~** usual, customary.

ritoc'care *vt* (*disegno, fotografia*) to touch up; (*testo*) to alter.

ri'tocco, chi *sm* touching up *no pl*; alteration.

ri'torcere [ri'tɔrtʃere] *vt* (*filato*) to twist; (*fig: accusa, insulto*) to throw back; **~rsi** *vr* (*tornare a danno di*): **~rsi contro** to turn against.

ritor'nare *vi* to return, go (*o* come) back; (*ripresentarsi*) to recur; (*ridiventare*): **~ ricco** to become rich again ♦ *vt* (*restituire*) to return, give back.

ritor'nello *sm* refrain.

ri'torno *sm* return; **durante il (viaggio di) ~** on the return trip, on the way back; **al ~** (*tornando*) on the way back; **essere di ~** to be back; **far ~** to return; **avere un ~ di fiamma** (*AUT*) to backfire; (*fig: persona*) to be back in love again.

ritorsi'one *sf* (*rappresaglia*) retaliation.

ri'torto, a *pp di* **ritorcere** ♦ *ag* (*cotone, corda*) twisted.

ri'trarre *vt* (*trarre indietro, via*) to withdraw; (*distogliere: sguardo*) to turn away; (*rappresentare*) to portray, depict; (*ricavare*) to get, obtain; **ritrarsi** *vr* to move back.

ritrat'tare *vt* (*disdire*) to retract, take back; (*trattare nuovamente*) to deal with again.

ritrattazi'one [ritrattat'tsjone] *sf* withdrawal.

ritrat'tista, i, e *sm/f* portrait painter.

ri'tratto, a *pp di* **ritrarre** ♦ *sm* portrait.

ritro'sia *sf* (*riluttanza*) reluctance, unwillingness; (*timidezza*) shyness.

ri'troso, a *ag* (*restio*): **~ (a)** reluctant (to); (*schivo*) shy; **andare a ~** to go backwards.

ritrova'mento *sm* (*di cadavere, oggetto smarrito etc*) finding; (*oggetto ritrovato*) find.

ritro'vare *vt* to find; (*salute*) to regain; (*persona*) to find; to meet again; **~rsi** *vr* (*essere, capitare*) to find o.s.; (*raccapezzarsi*) to find one's way; (*con senso reciproco*) to meet (again).

ritro'vato *sm* discovery.

ri'trovo *sm* meeting place; **~ notturno** night club.

'ritto, a *ag* (*in piedi*) standing, on one's feet; (*levato in alto*) erect, raised; (: *capelli*) standing on end; (*posto verticalmente*) upright.

ritu'ale *ag, sm* ritual.

riuni'one *sf* (*adunanza*) meeting; (*riconciliazione*) reunion; **essere in ~** to be at a meeting.

riu'nire *vt* (*ricongiungere*) to join (together); (*riconciliare*) to reunite, bring together (again); **~rsi** *vr* (*adunarsi*) to meet; (*tornare a stare insieme*) to be reunited; **siamo qui riuniti per festeggiare il vostro**

anniversario we are gathered here to celebrate your anniversary.

riu'scire [riuʃ'ʃire] vi (uscire di nuovo) to go out again, go back out; (aver esito: fatti, azioni) to go, turn out; (aver successo) to succeed, be successful; (essere, apparire) to be, prove; (raggiungere il fine) to manage, succeed; ~ **a fare qc** to manage o be able to do sth; **questo mi riesce nuovo** this is new to me.

riu'scita [riuʃ'ʃita] sf (esito) result, outcome; (buon esito) success.

riutiliz'zare [riutilid'dzare] vt to use again, re-use.

'riva sf (di fiume) bank; (di lago, mare) shore; **in ~ al mare** on the (sea) shore.

ri'vale ag rival cpd ♦ sm/f rival; **non avere ~i** (anche fig) to be unrivalled.

rivaleggi'are [rivaled'dʒare] vi to compete, vie.

rivalità sf rivalry.

ri'valsa sf (rivincita) revenge; (risarcimento) compensation; **prendersi una ~ su qn** to take revenge on sb.

rivalu'tare vt (ECON) to revalue.

rivalutazi'one [rivalutat'tsjone] sf (ECON) revaluation; (fig) re-evaluation.

rivan'gare vt (ricordi etc) to dig up (again).

rive'dere vt to see again; (ripassare) to revise; (verificare) to check.

rivedrò etc vb vedi **rivedere**.

rive'lare vt to reveal; (divulgare) to reveal, disclose; (dare indizio) to reveal, show; ~**rsi** vr (manifestarsi) to be revealed; ~**rsi onesto** etc to prove to be honest etc.

rivela'tore, 'trice ag revealing ♦ sm (TECN) detector; (FOT) developer.

rivelazi'one [rivelat'tsjone] sf revelation.

ri'vendere vt (vendere: di nuovo) to resell, sell again; (: al dettaglio) to retail, sell retail.

rivendi'care vt to claim, demand.

rivendicazi'one [rivendikat'tsjone] sf claim; ~**i salariali** wage claims.

ri'vendita sf (bottega) retailer's (shop); ~ **di tabacchi** tobacconist's (shop).

rivendi'tore, 'trice sm/f retailer; ~ **autorizzato** authorized dealer.

riverbe'rare vt to reflect.

ri'verbero sm (di luce, calore) reflection; (di suono) reverberation.

rive'rente ag reverent, respectful.

rive'renza [rive'rɛntsa] sf reverence; (inchino) bow; curtsey.

rive'rire vt (rispettare) to revere; (salutare) to pay one's respects to.

river'sare vt (anche fig) to pour; ~**rsi** vr (fig: persone) to pour out.

rivesti'mento sm covering; coating.

rives'tire vt to dress again; (ricoprire) to cover; (: con vernice) to coat; (fig: carica) to hold; ~**rsi** vr to get dressed again; to change (one's clothes); ~ **di piastrelle** to tile.

ri'vidi etc vb vedi **rivedere**.

rivi'era sf coast; **la ~ italiana** the Italian Riviera.

ri'vincita [ri'vintʃita] sf (SPORT) return match; (fig) revenge; **prendersi la ~ (su qn)** to take o get one's revenge (on sb).

rivis'suto, a pp di **rivivere**.

ri'vista sf review; (periodico) magazine, review; (TEAT) revue; variety show.

ri'visto, a pp di **rivedere**.

rivitaliz'zante [rivitalid'dzante] ag revitalizing.

rivitaliz'zare [rivitalid'dzare] vt to revitalize.

ri'vivere vi (riacquistare forza) to come alive again; (tornare in uso) to be revived ♦ vt to relive.

'rivo sm stream.

ri'volgere [ri'vɔldʒere] vt (attenzione, sguardo) to turn, direct; (parole) to address; ~**rsi** vr to turn round; (fig: dirigersi per informazioni): ~**rsi a** to go and see, go and speak to; ~ **un'accusa/una critica a qn** to accuse/criticize sb; ~**rsi all'ufficio competente** to apply to the office concerned.

rivolgi'mento [rivoldʒi'mento] sm upheaval.

ri'volsi etc vb vedi **rivolgere**.

ri'volta sf revolt, rebellion.

rivol'tante ag revolting, disgusting.

rivol'tare vt to turn over; (con l'interno all'esterno) to turn inside out; (disgustare: stomaco) to upset, turn; (: fig) to revolt, disgust; ~**rsi** vr (ribellarsi): ~**rsi (a)** to rebel (against).

rivol'tella sf revolver.

ri'volto, a pp di **rivolgere**.

rivol'toso, a ag rebellious ♦ sm/f rebel.

rivoluzio'nare [rivoluttsjo'nare] vt to revolutionize.

rivoluzio'nario, a [rivoluttsjo'narjo] ag, sm/f revolutionary.

rivoluzi'one [rivolut'tsjone] sf revolution.

riz'zare [rit'tsare] vt to raise, erect; ~**rsi** vr to stand up; (capelli) to stand on end; ~**rsi in piedi** to stand up, get to one's feet.

RN sigla = Rimini.

RNA sigla m RNA (= ribonucleic acid).

RO sigla = Rovigo.

'roba sf stuff, things pl; (possessi, beni) belongings pl, things pl, possessions pl; ~

da mangiare things to eat, food; ~ **da matti!** it's sheer madness *o* lunacy!

robi'vecchi [robi'vɛkki] *sm/f inv* junk dealer.

'robot *sm inv* robot.

ro'botica *sf* robotics *sg*.

robus'tezza [robus'tettsa] *sf* (*di persona, pianta*) robustness, sturdiness; (*di edificio, ponte*) soundness.

ro'busto, a *ag* robust, sturdy; (*solido: catena*) strong; (: *edificio, ponte*) sound, solid; (*vino*) full-bodied.

'rocca, che *sf* fortress.

rocca'forte *sf* stronghold.

roc'chetto [rok'ketto] *sm* reel, spool.

'roccia, ce ['rottʃa] *sf* rock; **fare ~** (*SPORT*) to go rock climbing.

roccia'tore, 'trice [rottʃa'tore] *sm/f* rock climber.

rocci'oso, a [rot'tʃoso] *ag* rocky; **le Montagne R~e** the Rocky Mountains.

'roco, a, chi, che *ag* hoarse.

ro'daggio [ro'daddʒo] *sm* running (*BRIT*) *o* breaking (*US*) in; **in ~** running *o* breaking in; **periodo di ~** (*fig*) period of adjustment.

'Rodano *sm*: **il ~** the Rhone.

ro'dare *vt* (*AUT, TECN*) to run (*BRIT*) *o* break (*US*) in.

ro'deo *sm* rodeo.

'rodere *vt* to gnaw (at); (*distruggere poco a poco*) to eat into.

'Rodi *sf* Rhodes.

rodi'tore *sm* (*ZOOL*) rodent.

rodo'dendro *sm* rhododendron.

'rogito ['rɔdʒito] *sm* (*DIR*) (notary's) deed.

'rogna ['rɔɲɲa] *sf* (*MED*) scabies *sg*; (*di animale*) mange; (*fig*) bother, nuisance.

ro'gnone [roɲ'ɲone] *sm* (*CUC*) kidney.

ro'gnoso, a [roɲ'ɲoso] *ag* (*persona*) scabby; (*animale*) mangy; (*fig*) troublesome.

'rogo, ghi *sm* (*per cadaveri*) (funeral) pyre; (*supplizio*): **il ~** the stake.

rol'lare *vi* (*NAUT, AER*) to roll.

rol'lino *sm* = **rullino**.

rol'lio *sm* roll(ing).

'Roma *sf* Rome.

roma'gnolo, a [romaɲ'ɲɔlo] *ag* of (*o* from) Romagna.

roma'nesco, a, schi, sche *ag* Roman ♦ *sm* Roman dialect.

Roma'nia *sf*: **la ~** Romania.

ro'manico, a, ci, che *ag* Romanesque.

ro'mano, a *ag, sm/f* Roman; **fare alla ~a** to go Dutch.

romantiche'ria [romantike'ria] *sf* sentimentality.

romanti'cismo [romanti'tʃizmo] *sm* romanticism.

ro'mantico, a, ci, che *ag* romantic.

ro'manza [ro'mandza] *sf* (*MUS, LETTERATURA*) romance.

roman'zare [roman'dzare] *vt* to romanticize.

roman'zesco, a, schi, sche [roman'dzesko] *ag* (*stile, personaggi*) fictional; (*fig*) storybook *cpd*.

romanzi'ere [roman'dzjɛre] *sm* novelist.

ro'manzo, a [ro'mandzo] *ag* (*LING*) romance *cpd* ♦ *sm* (*medievale*) romance; (*moderno*) novel; ~ **d'amore** love story; ~ **d'appendice** serial (story); ~ **cavalleresco** tale of chivalry; ~ **poliziesco**, ~ **giallo** detective story; ~ **rosa** romantic novel.

rom'bare *vi* to rumble, thunder, roar.

'rombo *sm* rumble, thunder, roar; (*MAT*) rhombus; (*ZOOL*) turbot.

ro'meno, a *ag, sm/f, sm* = **rumeno**.

'rompere *vt* to break; (*conversazione, fidanzamento*) to break off ♦ *vi* to break; ~**rsi** *vr* to break; **mi rompe le scatole** (*fam*) he (*o* she) is a pain in the neck; ~**rsi un braccio** to break an arm.

rompi'capo *sm* worry, headache; (*indovinello*) puzzle; (*in enigmistica*) brain-teaser.

rompi'collo *sm* daredevil.

rompighi'accio [rompi'gjattʃo] *sm* (*NAUT*) icebreaker.

rompis'catole *sm/f inv* (*fam*) pest, pain in the neck.

'ronda *sf* (*MIL*) rounds *pl*, patrol.

ron'della *sf* (*TECN*) washer.

'rondine *sf* (*ZOOL*) swallow.

ron'done *sm* (*ZOOL*) swift.

ron'fare *vi* (*russare*) to snore.

ron'zare [ron'dzare] *vi* to buzz, hum.

ron'zino [ron'dzino] *sm* (*peg: cavallo*) nag.

ron'zio, ii [ron'dzio] *sm* buzzing, humming; ~ **auricolare** (*MED*) tinnitus *sg*.

'rosa *sf* rose; (*fig: gruppo*): ~ **dei candidati** list of candidates ♦ *ag inv, sm* pink.

ro'saio *sm* (*pianta*) rosebush, rose tree; (*giardino*) rose garden.

ro'sario *sm* (*REL*) rosary.

ro'sato, a *ag* pink, rosy ♦ *sm* (*vino*) rosé (wine).

ro'seo, a *ag* (*anche fig*) rosy.

ro'seto *sm* rose garden.

ro'setta *sf* (*diamante*) rose-cut diamond; (*rondella*) washer.

'rosi *vb vedi* **rodere**.

rosicchi'are [rosik'kjare] *vt* to gnaw (at); (*mangiucchiare*) to nibble (at).

rosma'rino *sm* rosemary.

'roso, a *pp di* **rodere**.

roso'lare *vt* (*CUC*) to brown.

roso'lia *sf* (*MED*) German measles *sg*, rubella.

'rospo *sm* (*ZOOL*) toad; **mandar giù** *o* **ingoiare un** *o* **il** ~ (*fig*) to swallow a bitter pill; **sputa il** ~! out with it!

ros'setto *sm* (*per labbra*) lipstick; (*per guance*) rouge.

ros'siccio, a, ci, ce [ros'sittʃo] *ag* reddish.

'rosso, a *ag, sm, sm/f* red; **diventare** ~ (**per la vergogna**) to blush *o* go red (with *o* for shame); **il mar R**~ the Red Sea; ~ **d'uovo** egg yolk.

ros'sore *sm* flush, blush.

rosticce'ria [rostittʃe'ria] *sf shop selling roast meat and other cooked food.*

'rostro *sm* rostrum; (*becco*) beak.

ro'tabile *ag* (*percorribile*): **strada** ~ roadway; (*FERR*): **materiale** ~ rolling stock.

ro'taia *sf* rut, track; (*FERR*) rail.

ro'tare *vt, vi* to rotate.

rota'tivo, a *ag* rotating, rotation *cpd*.

rotazi'one [rotat'tsjone] *sf* rotation.

rote'are *vt, vi* to whirl; ~ **gli occhi** to roll one's eyes.

ro'tella *sf* small wheel; (*di mobile*) castor.

roto'calco, chi *sm* (*TIP*) rotogravure; (*rivista*) illustrated magazine.

roto'lare *vt, vi* to roll; ~**rsi** *vr* to roll (about).

roto'lio *sm* rolling.

'rotolo *sm* (*di carta, stoffa*) roll; (*di corda*) coil; **andare a** ~**i** (*fig*) to go to rack and ruin; **mandare a** ~**i** (*fig*) to ruin.

ro'tondo, a *ag* round ♦ *sf* rotunda.

ro'tore *sm* rotor.

'rotta *sf* (*AER, NAUT*) course, route; (*MIL*) rout; **a** ~ **di collo** at breakneck speed; **essere in** ~ **con qn** to be on bad terms with sb; **fare** ~ **su** *o* **per** *o* **verso** to head for *o* towards; **cambiare** ~ (*anche fig*) to change course; **in** ~ **di collisione** on a collision course; **ufficiale di** ~ navigator, navigating officer.

rotta'mare *vt to scrap old vehicles in return for incentives.*

rottama'zione [rottamat'tsjone] *sf the scrapping of old vehicles in return for incentives.*

rot'tame *sm* fragment, scrap, broken bit; ~**i** *smpl* (*di nave, aereo etc*) wreckage *sg*; ~**i di ferro** scrap iron *sg*.

'rotto, a *pp di* **rompere** ♦ *ag* broken; (*calzoni*) torn, split; (*persona: pratico, resistente*): ~ **a** accustomed *o* inured to ♦ *sm*: **per il** ~ **della cuffia** by the skin of one's teeth; ~**i** *smpl*: **20 euro e** ~**i** 20-odd euros.

rot'tura *sf* (*azione*) breaking *no pl*; (*di rapporti*) breaking off; (*MED*) fracture,

break.

rou'lotte [ru'lɔt] *sf inv* caravan.

ro'vente *ag* red-hot.

'rovere *sm* oak.

ro'vescia [ro'vɛʃʃa] *sf*: **alla** ~ upside-down; inside-out; **oggi mi va tutto alla** ~ everything is going wrong (for me) today.

rovesci'are [roveʃ'ʃare] *vt* (*versare in giù*) to pour; (*: accidentalmente*) to spill; (*capovolgere*) to turn upside down; (*gettare a terra*) to knock down; (*: fig: governo*) to overthrow; (*piegare all'indietro: testa*) to throw back; ~**rsi** *vr* (*sedia, macchina*) to overturn; (*barca*) to capsize; (*liquido*) to spill; (*fig: situazione*) to be reversed.

ro'vescio, sci [ro'vɛʃʃo] *sm* other side, wrong side; (*della mano*) back; (*di moneta*) reverse; (*pioggia*) sudden downpour; (*fig*) setback; (*MAGLIA: anche: punto* ~) purl (stitch); (*TENNIS*) backhand (stroke); **a** ~ (*sottosopra*) upside-down; (*con l'esterno all'interno*) inside-out; **capire qc a** ~ to misunderstand sth; ~ **di fortuna** setback.

ro'vina *sf* ruin; ~**e** *sfpl* ruins; **andare in** ~ (*andare a pezzi*) to collapse; (*fig*) to go to rack and ruin; **mandare qc/qn in** ~ to ruin sth/sb.

rovi'nare *vi* to collapse, fall down ♦ *vt* (*far cadere giù: casa*) to demolish; (*danneggiare, fig*) to ruin.

rovi'nato, a *ag* ruined, damaged; (*fig: persona*) ruined.

rovi'noso, a *ag* ruinous.

rovis'tare *vt* (*casa*) to ransack; (*tasche*) to rummage in (*o* through).

'rovo *sm* (*BOT*) blackberry *o* bramble bush.

roz'zezza [rod'dzettsa] *sf* roughness, coarseness.

'rozzo, a ['roddzo] *ag* rough, coarse.

RP *sigla fpl vedi* **relazioni pubbliche.**

R.R. *abbr* (*POSTA*) = **ricevuta di ritorno.**

Rrr *abbr* (*POSTA*) = **raccomandata con ricevuta di ritorno.**

RSVP *abbr* (= *répondez s'il vous plaît*) RSVP.

'ruba *sf*: **andare a** ~ to sell like hot cakes.

rubacu'ori *sm inv* ladykiller.

ru'bare *vt* to steal; ~ **qc a qn** to steal sth from sb.

rubi'condo, a *ag* ruddy.

rubi'netto *sm* tap, faucet (*US*).

ru'bino *sm* ruby.

ru'bizzo, a [ru'bittso] *ag* lively, sprightly.

'rublo *sm* rouble.

ru'brica, che *sf* (*di giornale: colonna*) column; (*: pagina*) page; (*quadernetto*) index book; (*: per indirizzi*) address book.

'rude *ag* tough, rough.

'**rudere** *sm* (*rovina*) ruins *pl*.
rudimen'tale *ag* rudimentary, basic.
rudi'menti *smpl* rudiments; basic principles.
ruffi'ano *sm* pimp.
'**ruga, ghe** *sf* wrinkle.
'**ruggine** ['ruddʒine] *sf* rust.
rug'gire [rud'dʒire] *vi* to roar.
rug'gito [rud'dʒito] *sm* roar.
rugi'ada [ru'dʒada] *sf* dew.
ru'goso, a *ag* wrinkled; (*scabro: superficie etc*) rough.
rul'lare *vi* (*tamburo, nave*) to roll; (*aereo*) to taxi.
rul'lino *sm* (*FOT*) roll of film, spool.
rul'lio, ii *sm* (*di tamburi*) roll.
'**rullo** *sm* (*di tamburi*) roll; (*arnese cilindrico, TIP*) roller; ~ **compressore** steam roller; ~ **di pellicola** roll of film.
rum *sm* rum.
ru'meno, a *ag, sm/f, sm* Romanian.
rumi'nante *sm* (*ZOOL*) ruminant.
rumi'nare *vt* (*ZOOL*) to ruminate; (*fig*) to ruminate on *o* over, chew over.
ru'more *sm*: **un** ~ a noise, a sound; **il** ~ noise; **fare** ~ to make a noise; **un** ~ **di passi** the sound of footsteps; **la notizia ha fatto molto** ~ (*fig*) the news aroused great interest.
rumoreggi'are [rumored'dʒare] *vi* (*tuono etc*) to rumble; (*fig: folla*) to clamour (*BRIT*), clamor (*US*).
rumo'roso, a *ag* noisy.
ru'olo *sm* (*TEAT, fig*) role, part; (*elenco*) roll, register, list; **di** ~ permanent, on the permanent staff; **professore di** ~ (*INS*) ≈ lecturer with tenure; **fuori** ~ (*personale, insegnante*) temporary.
ru'ota *sf* wheel; **a** ~ (*forma*) circular; ~ **anteriore/posteriore** front/back wheel; **andare a** ~ **libera** to freewheel; **parlare a** ~ **libera** (*fig*) to speak freely; ~ **di scorta** spare wheel.
ruo'tare *vt, vi* = rotare.
'**rupe** *sf* cliff, rock.
ru'pestre *ag* rocky.
ru'pia *sf* rupee.
'**ruppi** *etc vb vedi* rompere.
ru'rale *ag* rural, country *cpd*.
ru'scello [ruʃ'ʃɛllo] *sm* stream.
'**ruspa** *sf* excavator.
rus'pante *ag* (*pollo*) free-range.
rus'sare *vi* to snore.
'**Russia** *sf*: **la** ~ Russia.
'**russo, a** *ag, sm/f, sm* Russian.
'**rustico, a, ci, che** *ag* country *cpd*, rural; (*arredamento*) rustic; (*fig*) rough, unrefined ♦ *sm* (*fabbricato: per attrezzi*)

shed; (*per abitazione*) farm labourer's (*BRIT*) *o* farmhand's cottage.
'**ruta** *sf* (*BOT*) rue.
rut'tare *vi* to belch.
'**rutto** *sm* belch.
'**ruvido, a** *ag* rough, coarse.
ruzzo'lare [ruttso'lare] *vi* to tumble down.
ruzzo'lone [ruttso'lone] *sm* tumble, fall.
ruzzo'loni [ruttso'loni] *av*: **cadere** ~ to tumble down; **fare le scale** ~ to tumble down the stairs.

Ss

S, s ['ɛsse] *sf o m* (*lettera*) S, s; **S come Savona** ≈ S for Sugar.
s *abbr* (= *secondo*) sec.
S. *abbr* (= *sud*) S; (= *santo*) St.
SA *sigla* = *Salerno* ♦ *abbr vedi* **società anonima**.
sa *vb vedi* **sapere**.
sab. *abbr* (= *sabato*) Sat.
'**sabato** *sm* Saturday; *per fraseologia vedi* **martedì**.
'**sabbia** *sf* sand; ~**e mobili** quicksand(s *pl*).
sabbia'tura *sf* (*MED*) sand bath; (*TECN*) sand-blasting; **fare le** ~**e** to take sand baths.
sabbi'oso, a *ag* sandy.
sabo'taggio [sabo'taddʒo] *sm* sabotage.
sabo'tare *vt* to sabotage.
sabota'tore, 'trice *sm/f* saboteur.
'**sacca, che** *sf* bag; (*bisaccia*) haversack; (*insenatura*) inlet; ~ **d'aria** air pocket; ~ **da viaggio** travelling bag.
sacca'rina *sf* saccharin(e).
sac'cente [sat't ʃɛnte] *sm/f* know-all (*BRIT*), know-it-all (*US*).
saccheggi'are [sakked'dʒare] *vt* to sack, plunder.
sac'cheggio [sak'keddʒo] *sm* sack(ing).
sac'chetto [sak'ketto] *sm* (small) bag; (small) sack; ~ **di carta/di plastica** paper/plastic bag.
'**sacco, chi** *sm* bag; (*per carbone etc*) sack; (*ANAT, BIOL*) sac; (*tela*) sacking; (*saccheggio*) sack(ing); (*fig: grande quantità*): **un** ~ **di** lots of, heaps of; **cogliere** *o* **prendere qn con le mani nel** ~ to catch sb red-handed; **vuotare il** ~ to confess, spill the beans; **mettere qn nel** ~

to cheat sb; **colazione** f **al** ~ packed lunch; ~ **a pelo** sleeping bag; ~ **per i rifiuti** bin bag (BRIT), garbage bag (US).

sacer'dote [satʃer'dɔte] sm priest.

sacer'dozio [satʃer'dɔttsjo] sm priesthood.

'Sacra Co'rona U'nita sf the mafia in Puglia.

sacra'mento sm sacrament.

sa'crario sm memorial chapel.

sacres'tano sm = sagrestano.

sacres'tia sf = sagrestia.

sacrifi'care vt to sacrifice; ~**rsi** vr to sacrifice o.s.; (privarsi di qc) to make sacrifices.

sacrifi'cato, a ag sacrificed; (non valorizzato) wasted; **una vita** ~**a** a life of sacrifice.

sacri'ficio [sakri'fitʃo] sm sacrifice.

sacri'legio [sacri'lɛdʒo] sm sacrilege.

sa'crilego, a, ghi, ghe ag (REL) sacrilegious.

'sacro, a ag sacred.

sacro'santo, a ag sacrosanct.

'sadico, a, ci, che ag sadistic ♦ sm/f sadist.

sa'dismo sm sadism.

sadomaso'chismo [sadomazo'kismo] sm sadomasochism.

sa'etta sf arrow; (fulmine: anche fig) thunderbolt.

sa'fari sm inv safari.

sa'gace [sa'gatʃe] ag shrewd, sagacious.

sa'gacia [sa'gatʃa] sf sagacity, shrewdness.

sag'gezza [sad'dʒettsa] sf wisdom.

saggi'are [sad'dʒare] vt (metalli) to assay; (fig) to test.

'saggio, a, gi, ge ['saddʒo] ag wise ♦ sm (persona) sage; (operazione sperimentale) test; (: dell'oro) assay; (fig: prova) proof; (campione indicativo) sample; (scritto: letterario) essay; (: INS) written test; **dare** ~ **di** to give proof of; **in** ~ as a sample.

sag'gistica [sad'dʒistika] sf ≈ non-fiction.

Sagit'tario [sadʒit'tarjo] sm Sagittarius; **essere del** ~ to be Sagittarius.

'sagoma sf (profilo) outline, profile; (forma) form, shape; (TECN) template; (bersaglio) target; (fig: persona) character.

'sagra sf festival.

sa'grato sm churchyard.

sagres'tano sm sacristan; sexton.

sagres'tia sf sacristy; (culto protestante) vestry.

Sa'hara [sa'ara] sm: **il (Deserto del)** ~ the Sahara (Desert).

sahari'ana [saa'rjana] sf bush jacket.

'sai vb vedi **sapere**.

'saio sm (REL) habit.

'sala sf hall; (stanza) room; (CINE: di proiezione) screen; ~ **d'aspetto** waiting room; ~ **da ballo** ballroom; ~ (**dei**) **comandi** control room; ~ **per concerti** concert hall; ~ **per conferenze** (INS) lecture hall; (in aziende) conference room; ~ **corse** betting shop; ~ **giochi** amusement arcade; ~ **macchine** (NAUT) engine room; ~ **operatoria** (MED) operating theatre (BRIT) o room (US); ~ **da pranzo** dining room; ~ **per ricevimenti** banqueting hall; ~ **delle udienze** (DIR) courtroom.

sa'lace [sa'latʃe] ag (spinto, piccante) salacious, saucy; (mordace) cutting, biting.

sala'mandra sf salamander.

sa'lame sm salami no pl, salami sausage.

sala'moia sf (CUC) brine.

sa'lare vt to salt.

salari'ale ag wage cpd, pay cpd; **aumento** ~ wage o pay increase (BRIT) o raise (US).

salari'ato, a sm/f wage-earner.

sa'lario sm pay, wages pl; ~ **base** basic wage; ~ **minimo garantito** guaranteed minimum wage.

salas'sare vt (MED) to bleed.

sa'lasso sm (MED) bleeding, bloodletting; (fig: forte spesa) drain.

sala'tino sm cracker, salted biscuit.

sa'lato, a ag (sapore) salty; (CUC) salted, salt cpd; (fig: discorso etc) biting, sharp; (: prezzi) steep, stiff.

sal'dare vt (congiungere) to join, bind; (parti metalliche) to solder; (: con saldatura autogena) to weld; (conto) to settle, pay.

salda'tore sm (operaio) solderer; welder; (utensile) soldering iron.

salda'trice [salda'tritʃe] sf (macchina) welder, welding machine; ~ **ad arco** arc welder.

salda'tura sf soldering; welding; (punto saldato) soldered joint; weld; ~ **autogena** welding; ~ **dolce** soft soldering.

sal'dezza [sal'dettsa] sf firmness, strength.

'saldo, a ag (resistente, forte) strong, firm; (fermo) firm, steady, stable; (fig) firm, steadfast ♦ sm (svendita) sale; (di conto) settlement; (ECON) balance; **pagare a** ~ to pay in full; ~ **attivo** credit; ~ **passivo** deficit; ~ **da riportare** balance carried forward.

'sale sm salt; (fig) wit; ~**i** smpl (MED: da annusare) smelling salts; **sotto** ~ salted; **restare di** ~ (fig) to be dumbfounded; **ha poco** ~ **in zucca** he doesn't have much sense; ~ **da cucina,** ~ **grosso** cooking salt; ~ **da tavola,** ~ **fino** table salt; ~**i da bagno** bath salts; ~**i minerali** mineral salts; ~**i e**

tabacchi tobacconist's (shop).
sal'gemma [sal'dʒɛmma] *sm* rock salt.
'salgo etc *vb vedi* **salire.**
'salice ['salitʃe] *sm* willow; ~ **piangente**
weeping willow.
sali'ente *ag (fig)* salient, main.
sali'era *sf* salt cellar.
sa'lino, a *ag* saline ♦ *sf* saltworks *sg.*
sa'lire *vi* to go (*o* come) up; (*aereo etc*) to
climb, go up; (*passeggero*) to get on;
(*sentiero, prezzi, livello*) to go up, rise ♦ *vt*
(*scale, gradini*) to go (*o* come) up; ~ **su** to
climb (up); ~ **sul treno/sull'autobus** to
board the train/the bus; ~ **in macchina** to
get into the car; ~ **a cavallo** to mount; ~
al potere to rise to power; ~ **al trono** to
ascend the throne; ~ **alle stelle** (*prezzi*) to
rocket.
sali'scendi [saliʃ'ʃendi] *sm inv* latch.
sa'lita *sf* climb, ascent; (*erta*) hill, slope; **in**
~ *ag, av* uphill.
sa'liva *sf* saliva.
'salma *sf* corpse.
sal'mastro, a *ag (acqua)* salt *cpd*; (*sapore*)
salty ♦ *sm* (*sapore*) salty taste; (*odore*)
salty smell.
salmì *sm (CUC)* salmi; **lepre in** ~ salmi of
hare.
'salmo *sm* psalm.
sal'mone *sm* salmon.
salmo'nella *sf* salmonella.
Salo'mone: le isole ~ *sfpl* the Solomon
Islands.
sa'lone *sm (stanza)* sitting room, lounge; (*in*
albergo) lounge; (*di ricevimento*) reception
room; (*su nave*) lounge, saloon; (*mostra*)
show, exhibition; (*negozio: di parrucchiere*)
hairdresser's (salon); ~ **dell'automobile**
motor show; ~ **di bellezza** beauty salon.
salo'pette [salɔ'pɛt] *sf inv* dungarees *pl.*
salotti'ero, a *ag* mundane.
sa'lotto *sm* lounge, sitting room; (*mobilio*)
lounge suite.
sal'pare *vi (NAUT)* to set sail; (*anche:* ~
l'ancora) to weigh anchor.
'salsa *sf (CUC)* sauce; **in tutte le** ~**e** *(fig)* in
all kinds of ways; ~ **di pomodoro** tomato
sauce.
sal'sedine *sf (del mare, vento)* saltiness;
(*incrostazione*) (dried) salt.
sal'siccia, ce [sal'sittʃa] *sf* pork sausage.
salsi'era *sf* sauceboat *(BRIT)*, gravy boat.
'salso *sm* saltiness.
sal'tare *vi* to jump, leap; (*esplodere*) to
blow up, explode; (*: valvola*) to blow; (*venir*
via) to pop off; (*non aver luogo: corso etc*)
to be cancelled ♦ *vt* to jump (over), leap
(over); (*fig: pranzo, capitolo*) to skip, miss

(out); (*CUC*) to sauté; **far** ~ to blow up;
(*serratura: forzare*) to break; **far** ~ **il banco**
(*GIOCO*) to break the bank; **farsi** ~ **le**
cervella to blow one's brains out; **ma che**
ti salta in mente? what are you thinking
of?; ~ **da un argomento all'altro** to jump
from one subject to another; ~ **addosso a**
qn (*aggredire*) to attack sb; ~ **fuori** to
jump out, leap out; (*venire trovato*) to turn
up; ~ **fuori con** (*frase, commento*) to come
out with; ~ **giù da qc** to jump off sth,
jump down from sth.
saltel'lare *vi* to skip; to hop.
sal'tello *sm* hop, little jump.
saltim'banco, chi *sm* acrobat.
'salto *sm* jump; (*SPORT*) jumping;
(*dislivello*) drop; **fare un** ~ to jump, leap;
fare un ~ **da qn** to pop over to sb's
(place); ~ **in alto/lungo** high/long jump; ~
con l'asta pole vaulting; ~ **mortale**
somersault; **un** ~ **di qualità**
(*miglioramento*) significant improvement.
saltu'ario, a *ag* occasional, irregular.
sa'lubre *ag* healthy, salubrious.
sa'lume *sm (CUC)* cured pork; ~**i** *smpl*
(*insaccati*) cured pork meats.
salume'ria *sf* delicatessen.
salumi'ere, a *sm/f* ≈ delicatessen owner.
salumi'ficio [salumi'fitʃo] *sm* cured pork
meat factory.
salu'tare *ag* healthy; *(fig)* salutary,
beneficial ♦ *vt* (*per dire buon giorno, fig*) to
greet; (*per dire addio*) to say goodbye to;
(*MIL*) to salute; **mi saluti sua moglie** my
regards to your wife.
sa'lute *sf* health; ~! (*a chi starnutisce*) bless
you!; (*nei brindisi*) cheers!; **bere alla** ~ **di**
qn to drink (to) sb's health; **la** ~ **pubblica**
public welfare; **godere di buona** ~ to be
healthy, enjoy good health.
sa'luto *sm (gesto)* wave; (*parola*) greeting;
(*MIL*) salute; **gli ha tolto il** ~ he no longer
says hello to him; **cari** ~**i, tanti** ~**i** best
regards; **vogliate gradire i nostri più**
distinti ~**i** yours faithfully; **i miei** ~**i alla**
sua signora my regards to your wife.
'salva *sf* salvo.
salvacon'dotto *sm (MIL)* safe-conduct.
salvada'naio *sm* moneybox, piggy bank.
salvado'regno, a [salvado'reɲɲo] *ag, sm/f*
Salvadorean.
salva'gente [salva'dʒɛnte] *sm (NAUT)*
lifebuoy; (*pl inv: stradale*) traffic island; ~
a ciambella lifebelt; ~ **a giubbotto**
lifejacket *(BRIT)*, life preserver *(US)*.
salvaguar'dare *vt* to safeguard.
salvagu'ardia *sf* safeguard; **a** ~ **di** for the
safeguard of.

sal'vare *vt* to save; (*trarre da un pericolo*) to rescue; (*proteggere*) to protect; **~rsi** *vr* to save o.s.; to escape; **~ la vita a qn** to save sb's life; **~ le apparenze** to keep up appearances; **si salvi chi può!** every man for himself!

salvas'chermo [salvas'kermo] *sm* (*INFORM*) screen saver.

salva'slip ® *sm inv* pantyliner.

salva'taggio [salva'taddʒo] *sm* rescue.

salva'tore, **'trice** *sm/f* saviour (*BRIT*), savior (*US*).

salvazi'one [salvat'tsjone] *sf* (*REL*) salvation.

'salve *escl* (*fam*) hi!

sal'vezza [sal'vettsa] *sf* salvation; (*sicurezza*) safety.

'salvia *sf* (*BOT*) sage.

salvi'etta *sf* napkin, serviette.

'salvo, a *ag* safe, unhurt, unharmed; (*fuori pericolo*) safe, out of danger ♦ *sm*: **in ~** safe ♦ *prep* (*eccetto*) except; **~ che** *cong* (*a meno che*) unless; (*eccetto che*) except (that); **mettere qc in ~** to put sth in a safe place; **mettersi in ~** to reach safety; **portare qn in ~** to lead sb to safety; **~ contrordini** barring instructions to the contrary; **~ errori e omissioni** errors and omissions excepted; **~ imprevisti** barring accidents.

sam'buca *sf* (*liquore*) sambuca (*type of anisette*).

sam'buco *sm* elder (tree).

sa'nare *vt* to heal, cure; (*economia*) to put right.

sana'toria *sf* (*DIR*) act of indemnity.

sana'torio *sm* sanatorium (*BRIT*), sanitarium (*US*).

san'cire [san'tʃire] *vt* to sanction.

'sandalo *sm* (*BOT*) sandalwood; (*calzatura*) sandal.

sang'ria [san'gria] *sf* (*bibita*) sangria.

'sangue *sm* blood; **farsi cattivo ~** to fret, get worked up; **all'ultimo ~** (*duello, lotta*) to the death; **non corre buon ~ tra di loro** there's bad blood between them; **buon ~ non mente!** blood will out!; **~ freddo** (*fig*) sang-froid, calm; **a ~ freddo** in cold blood.

sangu'igno, a [san'gwiɲɲo] *ag* blood *cpd*; (*colore*) blood-red.

sangui'nante *ag* bleeding.

sangui'nare *vi* to bleed.

sangui'nario, a *ag* bloodthirsty.

sangui'noso, a *ag* bloody.

sangui'suga, ghe *sf* leech.

sani'tà *sf* health; (*salubrità*) healthiness; **Ministero della S~** Department of Health;

~ mentale sanity; **~ pubblica** public health.

sani'tario, a *ag* health *cpd*; (*condizioni*) sanitary ♦ *sm* (*AMM*) doctor; **Ufficiale S~** Health Officer; (**impianti**) **~i** *smpl* bathroom *o* sanitary fittings.

San Ma'rino *sf*: **la Repubblica di ~** the Republic of San Marino.

'sanno *vb vedi* **sapere**.

'sano, a *ag* healthy; (*denti, costituzione*) healthy, sound; (*integro*) whole, unbroken; (*fig: politica, consigli*) sound; **~ di mente** sane; **di ~a pianta** completely, entirely; **~ e salvo** safe and sound.

Santi'ago *sf*: **~ (del Cile)** Santiago (de Chile).

santifi'care *vt* to sanctify; (*feste*) to observe.

san'tino *sm* holy picture.

san'tissimo, a *ag*: **il S~ Sacramento** the Holy Sacrament; **il Padre S~** (*papa*) the Holy Father.

santi'tà *sf* sanctity; holiness; **Sua/Vostra ~** (*titolo di papa*) His/Your Holiness.

'santo, a *ag* holy; (*fig*) saintly; (*seguito da nome proprio: dav sm* **san** + *C*, **sant'** + *V*, **santo** + *s impura, gn, pn, ps, x, z; dav sf* **santa** + *C*, **sant'** + *V*) saint ♦ *sm/f* saint; **parole ~e!** very true!; **tutto il ~ giorno** the whole blessed day, all day long; **non c'è ~ che tenga!** that's no excuse!; **la S~a Sede** the Holy See.

san'tone *sm* holy man.

santu'ario *sm* sanctuary.

sanzio'nare [santsjo'nare] *vt* to sanction.

sanzi'one [san'tsjone] *sf* sanction; (*penale, civile*) sanction, penalty; **~i economiche** economic sanctions.

sa'pere *vt* to know; (*essere capace di*): **so nuotare** I know how to swim, I can swim ♦ *vi*: **~ di** (*aver sapore*) to taste of; (*aver odore*) to smell of ♦ *sm* knowledge; **far ~ qc a qn** to inform sb about sth, let sb know sth; **venire a ~ qc (da qn)** to find out *o* hear about sth (from sb); **non ne vuole più ~ di lei** he doesn't want to have anything more to do with her; **mi sa che non sia vero** I don't think that's true.

sapi'ente *ag* (*dotto*) learned; (*che rivela abilità*) masterly ♦ *sm/f* scholar.

sapien'tone, a *sm/f* (*peg*) know-all (*BRIT*), know-it-all (*US*).

sapi'enza [sa'pjɛntsa] *sf* wisdom.

sa'pone *sm* soap; **~ da barba** shaving soap; **~ da bucato** washing soap; **~ liquido** liquid soap; **~ in scaglie** soapflakes *pl*.

sapo'netta *sf* cake *o* bar *o* tablet of soap.

sa'pore *sm* taste, flavour (*BRIT*), flavor (*US*).

sapo'rito, a _ag_ tasty; (_fig: arguto_) witty; (_: piccante_) racy.

sappi'amo _vb vedi_ **sapere.**

saprò _etc vb vedi_ **sapere.**

sapu'tello, a _sm/f_ know-all (_BRIT_), know-it-all (_US_).

sarà _etc vb vedi_ **essere.**

sara'banda _sf_ (_fig_) uproar.

saraci'nesca, sche [saratʃi'neska] _sf_ (_serranda_) rolling shutter.

sar'casmo _sm_ sarcasm _no pl_; sarcastic remark.

sar'castico, a, ci, che _ag_ sarcastic.

sarchi'are [sar'kjare] _vt_ (_AGR_) to hoe.

sar'cofago, gi _o_ **ghi** _sm_ sarcophagus.

Sar'degna [sar'deɲɲa] _sf_: **la ~** Sardinia.

sar'dina _sf_ sardine.

'sardo, a _ag, sm/f_ Sardinian.

sar'donico, a, ci, che _ag_ sardonic.

sa'rei _etc vb vedi_ **essere.**

SARS _sf_ SARS (= _severe acute respiratory syndrome_).

'sarta _sf vedi_ **sarto.**

'sartia _sf_ (_NAUT_) stay.

'sarto, a _sm/f_ tailor/dressmaker; **~ d'alta moda** couturier.

sarto'ria _sf_ tailor's (shop); dressmaker's (shop); (_casa di moda_) fashion house; (_arte_) couture.

sassai'ola _sf_ hail of stones.

sas'sata _sf_ blow with a stone; **tirare una ~ contro** _o_ **a qc/qn** to throw a stone at sth/sb.

'sasso _sm_ stone; (_ciottolo_) pebble; (_masso_) rock; **restare** _o_ **rimanere di ~** to be dumbfounded.

sassofo'nista, i, e _sm/f_ saxophonist.

sas'sofono _sm_ saxophone.

sas'sone _ag, sm/f, sm_ Saxon.

sas'soso, a _ag_ stony; pebbly.

'Satana _sm_ Satan.

sa'tanico, a, ci, che _ag_ satanic, fiendish.

sa'tellite _sm, ag_ satellite.

'satira _sf_ satire.

satireggi'are [satired'dʒare] _vt_ to satirize ♦ _vi_ (_fare della satira_) to be satirical; (_scrivere satire_) to write satires.

sa'tirico, a, ci, che _ag_ satiric(al).

sa'tollo, a _ag_ full, replete.

satu'rare _vt_ to saturate.

saturazi'one [saturat'tsjone] _sf_ saturation.

'saturo, a _ag_ saturated; (_fig_): **~ di** full of; **~ d'acqua** (_terreno_) waterlogged.

'SAUB _sigla f_ (= _Struttura Amministrativa Unificata di Base_) _state welfare system._

'sauna _sf_ sauna; **fare la ~** to have _o_ take a sauna.

sa'vana _sf_ savannah.

'savio, a _ag_ wise, sensible ♦ _sm_ wise man.

Sa'voia _sf_: **la ~** Savoy.

savoi'ardo, a _ag_ of Savoy, Savoyard ♦ _sm_ (_biscotto_) sponge finger.

sazi'are [sat'tsjare] _vt_ to satisfy, satiate; **~rsi** _vr_ (_riempirsi di cibo_): **~rsi (di)** to eat one's fill (of); (_fig_): **~rsi di** to grow tired _o_ weary of.

sazietà [sattsje'ta] _sf_ satiety, satiation.

'sazio, a ['sattsjo] _ag_: **~ (di)** sated (with), full (of); (_fig: stufo_) fed up (with), sick (of).

sbada'taggine [zbada'taddʒine] _sf_ (_sventatezza_) carelessness; (_azione_) oversight.

sba'dato, a _ag_ careless, inattentive.

sbadigli'are [zbadiʎ'ʎare] _vi_ to yawn.

sba'diglio [zba'diʎʎo] _sm_ yawn; **fare uno ~** to yawn.

'sbafo _sm_: **a ~** at somebody else's expense.

sbagli'are [zbaʎ'ʎare] _vt_ to make a mistake in, get wrong ♦ _vi_ (_fare errori_) to make a mistake (_o_ mistakes), be mistaken; (_ingannarsi_) to be wrong; (_operare in modo non giusto_) to err; **~rsi** _vr_ to make a mistake, be mistaken, be wrong; **~ la mira/strada** to miss one's aim/take the wrong road; **scusi, ho sbagliato numero** (_TEL_) sorry, I've got the wrong number; **non c'è da ~rsi** there can be no mistake.

sbagli'ato, a [zbaʎ'ʎato] _ag_ (_gen_) wrong; (_compito_) full of mistakes; (_conclusione_) erroneous.

'sbaglio ['zbaʎʎo] _sm_ mistake, error; (_morale_) error; **fare uno ~** to make a mistake.

sbales'trato, a _ag_ (_persona: scombussolato_) unsettled.

sbal'lare _vt_ (_merce_) to unpack ♦ _vi_ (_nel fare un conto_) to overestimate; (_DROGA: gergo_) to get high.

sbal'lato, a _ag_ (_calcolo_) wrong; (_fam: ragionamento, persona_) screwy.

'sballo _sm_ (_DROGA: gergo_) trip.

sballot'tare _vt_ to toss (about).

sbalor'dire _vt_ to stun, amaze ♦ _vi_ to be stunned, be amazed.

sbalordi'tivo, a _ag_ amazing; (_prezzo_) incredible, absurd.

sbal'zare [zbal'tsare] _vt_ to throw, hurl; (_fig: da una carica_) to remove, dismiss ♦ _vi_ (_balzare_) to bounce; (_saltare_) to leap, bound.

'sbalzo ['zbaltso] _sm_ (_spostamento improvviso_) jolt, jerk; **a ~i** jerkily; (_fig_) in fits and starts; **uno ~ di temperatura** a sudden change in temperature.

sban'care _vt_ (_nei giochi_) to break the bank

at (o of); (*fig*) to ruin, bankrupt.

sbanda'mento *sm* (*NAUT*) list; (*AUT*) skid; (*fig*: *di persona*) confusion; **ha avuto un periodo di ~** he went off the rails for a bit.

sban'dare *vi* (*NAUT*) to list; (*AUT*) to skid; **~rsi** *vr* (*folla*) to disperse; (*truppe*) to scatter; (*fig*: *famiglia*) to break up.

sban'data *sf* (*AUT*) skid; (*NAUT*) list; **prendere una ~ per qn** (*fig*) to fall for sb.

sban'dato, a *sm/f* mixed-up person.

sbandie'rare *vt* (*bandiera*) to wave; (*fig*) to parade, show off.

'sbando *sm*: **essere allo ~** to drift.

sbarac'care *vt* (*libri, piatti etc*) to clear (up).

sbaragli'are [zbaraʎ'ʎare] *vt* (*MIL*) to rout; (*in gare sportive etc*) to beat, defeat.

sba'raglio [zba'raʎʎo] *sm*: **gettarsi allo ~** (*soldato*) to throw o.s. into the fray; (*fig*) to risk everything.

sbaraz'zarsi [zbarat'tsarsi] *vr*: **~ di** to get rid of, rid o.s. of.

sbaraz'zino, a [zbarat'tsino] *ag* impish, cheeky.

sbar'bare *vt*, **~rsi** *vr* to shave.

sbarba'tello *sm* novice, greenhorn.

sbar'care *vt* (*passeggeri*) to disembark; (*merci*) to unload ♦ *vi* to disembark.

'sbarco *sm* disembarkation; unloading; (*MIL*) landing.

'sbarra *sf* bar; (*di passaggio a livello*) barrier; (*DIR*): **mettere/presentarsi alla ~** to bring/appear before the court.

sbarra'mento *sm* (*stradale*) barrier; (*diga*) dam, barrage; (*MIL*) barrage; (*POL*) cut-off point (*level of support below which a political party is excluded from representation in Parliament*).

sbar'rare *vt* (*bloccare*) to block, bar; (*cancellare*: *assegno*) to cross (*BRIT*); **~ il passo** to bar the way; **~ gli occhi** to open one's eyes wide.

sbar'rato, a *ag* (*porta*) barred; (*passaggio*) blocked, barred; (*strada*) blocked, obstructed; (*occhi*) staring; (*assegno*) crossed (*BRIT*).

'sbattere *vt* (*porta*) to bang; (*tappeti, ali, CUC*) to beat; (*urtare*) to knock, hit ♦ *vi* (*porta, finestra*) to bang; (*agitarsi*: *ali, vele etc*) to flap; **~ qn fuori/in galera** to throw sb out/into prison; **me ne sbatto!** (*fam*) I don't give a damn!

sbat'tuto, a *ag* (*viso, aria*) dejected, worn out; (*uovo*) beaten.

sba'vare *vi* to dribble; (*colore*) to smear, smudge.

sbava'tura *sf* (*di persone*) dribbling; (*di lumache*) slime; (*di rossetto, vernice*) smear.

sbelli'carsi *vr*: **~ dalle risa** to split one's sides laughing.

'sberla *sf* slap.

sber'leffo *sm*: **fare uno ~ a qn** to make a face at sb.

sbia'dire *vi* (*anche*: **~rsi**), *vt* to fade.

sbia'dito, a *ag* faded; (*fig*) colourless (*BRIT*), colorless (*US*), dull.

sbian'care *vt* to whiten; (*tessuto*) to bleach ♦ *vi* (*impallidire*) to grow pale o white.

sbi'eco, a, chi, che *ag* (*storto*) askew; **di ~**: **guardare qn di ~** (*fig*) to look askance at sb; **tagliare una stoffa di ~** to cut material on the bias.

sbigot'tire *vt* to dismay, stun ♦ *vi* (*anche*: **~rsi**) to be dismayed.

sbilanci'are [zbilan'tʃare] *vt* to throw off balance; **~rsi** *vr* (*perdere l'equilibrio*) to overbalance, lose one's balance; (*fig*: *compromettersi*) to compromise o.s.

sbi'lenco, a, chi, che *ag* (*persona*) crooked, misshapen; (*fig*: *idea, ragionamento*) twisted.

sbirci'are [zbir'tʃare] *vt* to cast sidelong glances at, eye.

sbirci'ata [zbir'tʃata] *sf*: **dare una ~ a qc** to glance at sth, have a look at sth.

'sbirro *sm* (*peg*) cop.

sbizzar'rirsi [zbiddzar'rirsi] *vr* to indulge one's whims.

sbloc'care *vt* to unblock, free; (*freno*) to release; (*prezzi, affitti*) to free from controls; **~rsi** *vr* (*gen*) to become unblocked; (*passaggio, strada*) to clear, become unblocked; **la situazione si è sbloccata** things are moving again.

'sblocco, chi *sm* (*vedi vt*) unblocking, freeing; release.

sboc'care *vi*: **~ in** (*fiume*) to flow into; (*strada*) to lead into; (*persona*) to come (out) into; (*fig*: *concludersi*) to end (up) in.

sboc'cato, a *ag* (*persona*) foul-mouthed; (*linguaggio*) foul.

sbocci'are [zbot'tʃare] *vi* (*fiore*) to bloom, open (out).

'sbocco, chi *sm* (*di fiume*) mouth; (*di strada*) end; (*di tubazione, COMM*) outlet; (*uscita*: *anche fig*) way out; **una strada senza ~** a dead end; **siamo in una situazione senza ~chi** there's no way out of this for us.

sbocconcel'lare [zbokkontʃel'lare] *vt*: **~ (qc)** to nibble (at sth).

sbollen'tare *vt* (*CUC*) to parboil.

sbol'lire *vi* (*fig*) to cool down, calm down.

'sbornia *sf* (*fam*): **prendersi una ~** to get plastered.

sbor'sare *vt* (*denaro*) to pay out.

sbot'tare *vi:* ~ **in una risata/per la collera** to burst out laughing/explode with anger.

sbotto'nare *vt* to unbutton, undo.

sbra'cato, a *ag* slovenly.

sbracci'arsi [zbrat'tʃarsi] *vr* to wave (one's arms about).

sbracci'ato, a [zbrat'tʃato] *ag* (*camicia*) sleeveless; (*persona*) bare-armed.

sbrai'tare *vi* to yell, bawl.

sbra'nare *vt* to tear to pieces.

sbricio'lare [zbritʃo'lare] *vt,* ~**rsi** *vr* to crumble.

sbri'gare *vt* to deal with, get through; (*cliente*) to attend to, deal with; ~**rsi** *vr* to hurry (up).

sbriga'tivo, a *ag* (*persona, modo*) quick, expeditious; (*giudizio*) hasty.

sbrina'mento *sm* defrosting.

sbri'nare *vt* to defrost.

sbrindel'lato, a *ag* tattered, in tatters.

sbrodo'lare *vt* to stain, dirty.

sbron'zarsi [zbron'tsarsi] *vr* (*fam*) to get sozzled.

'sbronzo, a ['zbrontso] (*fam*) *ag* sozzled
♦ *sf*: **prendersi una** ~**a** to get sozzled.

sbruf'fone, a *sm/f* boaster, braggart.

sbu'care *vi* (*apparire*) to pop out (*o* up).

sbucci'are [zbut'tʃare] *vt* (*arancia, patata*) to peel; (*piselli*) to shell; ~**rsi un ginocchio** to graze one's knee.

sbucherò *etc* [zbuke'rɔ] *vb vedi* **sbucare.**

sbudel'larsi *vr:* ~ **dalle risa** to split one's sides laughing.

sbuf'fare *vi* (*persona, cavallo*) to snort; (: *ansimare*) to puff, pant; (*treno*) to puff.

'sbuffo *sm* (*di aria, fumo, vapore*) puff; **maniche a** ~ puff(ed) sleeves.

sc. *abbr* (*TEAT*: = *scena*) sc.

'scabbia *sf* (*MED*) scabies *sg.*

'scabro, a *ag* rough, harsh; (*fig*) concise, terse.

sca'broso, a *ag* (*fig: difficile*) difficult, thorny; (: *imbarazzante*) embarrassing; (: *sconcio*) indecent.

scacchi'era [skak'kjɛra] *sf* chessboard.

scacchiere [skak'kjɛre] *sm* (*MIL*) sector; **S~** (*in Gran Bretagna*) Exchequer.

scaccia'cani [skattʃa'kani] *sm o f inv* pistol with blanks.

scacciapensi'eri [skattʃapen'sjɛri] *sm inv* (*MUS*) jew's-harp.

scacci'are [skat'tʃare] *vt* to chase away *o* out, drive away *o* out; ~ **qn di casa** to turn sb out of the house.

'scacco, chi *sm* (*pezzo del gioco*) chessman; (*quadretto di scacchiera*) square; (*fig*) setback, reverse; ~**chi** *smpl* (*gioco*) chess *sg*; **a** ~**chi** (*tessuto*) check(ed); **subire uno** ~ (*fig: sconfitta*) to suffer a setback.

scacco'matto *sm* checkmate; **dare** ~ **a qn** (*anche fig*) to checkmate sb.

'scaddi *etc vb vedi* **scadere.**

sca'dente *ag* shoddy, of poor quality.

sca'denza [ska'dɛntsa] *sf* (*di cambiale, contratto*) maturity; (*di passaporto*) expiry date; **a breve/lunga** ~ short-/long-term; **data di** ~ expiry date; ~ **a termine** fixed deadline.

sca'dere *vi* (*contratto etc*) to expire; (*debito*) to fall due; (*valore, forze, peso*) to decline, go down.

sca'fandro *sm* (*di palombaro*) diving suit; (*di astronauta*) spacesuit.

scaffala'tura *sf* shelving, shelves *pl.*

scaf'fale *sm* shelf; (*mobile*) set of shelves.

sca'fista *sm* (*di immigrati*) people smuggler (*by boat*).

'scafo *sm* (*NAUT, AER*) hull.

scagio'nare [skadʒo'nare] *vt* to exonerate, free from blame.

'scaglia ['skaʎʎa] *sf* (*ZOOL*) scale; (*scheggia*) chip, flake.

scagli'are [skaʎ'ʎare] *vt* (*lanciare: anche fig*) to hurl, fling; ~**rsi** *vr:* ~**rsi su** *o* **contro** to hurl *o* fling o.s. at; (*fig*) to rail at.

scagliona'mento [skaʎʎona'mento] *sm* (*MIL*) arrangement in echelons.

scaglio'nare [skaʎʎo'nare] *vt* (*pagamenti*) to space out, spread out; (*MIL*) to echelon.

scagli'one [skaʎ'ʎone] *sm* (*MIL*) echelon; (*GEO*) terrace; **a** ~**i** in groups.

sca'gnozzo [skaɲ'ɲɔttso] *sm* (*peg*) lackey.

'Scala *sf*: **la** ~ *vedi nota nel riquadro.*

LA SCALA

Milan's **la Scala** *first opened its doors in 1778 with a performance of Salieri's opera, "L'Europa riconosciuta". Built on the site of the church of Santa Maria della Scala, the theatre suffered serious damage in the bombing campaigns of 1943 but reopened in 1946 with a concert conducted by Toscanini. Enjoying world-wide renown for its opera,* **la Scala** *also has a famous school of classical dance.*

'scala *sf* (*a gradini etc*) staircase, stairs *pl*; (*a pioli, di corda*) ladder; (*MUS, GEO, di colori, valori, fig*) scale; ~**e** *sfpl* (*scalinata*) stairs; **su larga** *o* **vasta** ~ on a large scale; **su piccola** ~, **su** ~ **ridotta** on a small scale; **su** ~ **nazionale/mondiale** on a national/worldwide scale; **in** ~ **di 1 a 100.000** on a scale of 1 cm to 1 km; **riproduzione in** ~

reproduction to scale; ~ **a chiocciola** spiral staircase; ~ **a libretto** stepladder; ~ **di misure** system of weights and measures; ~ **mobile** escalator; (*ECON*) sliding scale; ~ **mobile (dei salari)** index-linked pay scale; ~ **di sicurezza** (*antincendio*) fire escape.

sca'lare *vt* (*ALPINISMO, muro*) to climb, scale; (*debito*) to scale down, reduce.

sca'lata *sf* scaling *no pl*, climbing *no pl*; (*arrampicata, fig*) climb; **dare la** ~ **a** (*fig*) to make a bid for.

scala'tore, 'trice *sm/f* climber.

scalca'gnato, a [skalkaɲ'ɲato] *ag* (*logoro*) worn; (*persona*) shabby.

scalci'are [skal'tʃare] *vi* to kick.

scalci'nato, a [skaltʃi'nato] *ag* (*fig peg*) shabby.

scalda'bagno [skalda'baɲɲo] *sm* water heater.

scal'dare *vt* to heat; ~**rsi** *vr* to warm up, heat up; (*al fuoco, al sole*) to warm o.s.; (*fig*) to get excited; ~ **la sedia** (*fig*) to twiddle one's thumbs.

scaldavi'vande *sm inv* dish warmer.

scal'dino *sm* (*per mani*) hand-warmer; (*per piedi*) foot-warmer; (*per letto*) bedwarmer.

scal'fire *vt* to scratch.

scalfit'tura *sf* scratch.

scali'nata *sf* staircase.

sca'lino *sm* (*anche fig*) step; (*di scala a pioli*) rung.

scal'mana *sf* (hot) flush.

scalma'narsi *vr* (*affaticarsi*) to rush about, rush around; (*agitarsi, darsi da fare*) to get all hot and bothered; (*arrabbiarsi*) to get excited, get steamed up.

scalma'nato, a *sm/f* hothead.

'scalo *sm* (*NAUT*) slipway; (*: porto d'approdo*) port of call; (*AER*) stopover; **fare** ~ **(a)** (*NAUT*) to call (at), put in (at); (*AER*) to land (at), make a stop (at); **volo senza** ~ non-stop flight; ~ **merci** (*FERR*) goods (*BRIT*) *o* freight yard.

sca'logna [ska'loɲɲa] *sf* (*fam*) bad luck.

scalo'gnato, a [skaloɲ'ɲato] *ag* (*fam*) unlucky.

scalop'pina *sf* (*CUC*) escalope.

scal'pello *sm* chisel.

scalpi'tare *vi* (*cavallo*) to paw the ground; (*persona*) to stamp one's feet.

scal'pore *sm* noise, row; **far** ~ (*notizia*) to cause a sensation *o* a stir.

'scaltro, a *ag* cunning, shrewd.

scal'zare [skal'tsare] *vt* (*albero*) to bare the roots of; (*muro, fig: autorità*) to undermine.

'scalzo, a ['skaltso] *ag* barefoot.

scambi'are *vt* to exchange; (*confondere*): ~

qn/qc per to take *o* mistake sb/sth for; **mi hanno scambiato il cappello** they've given me the wrong hat.

scambi'evole *ag* mutual, reciprocal.

'scambio *sm* exchange; (*COMM*) trade; (*FERR*) points *pl*; **fare (uno)** ~ to make a swap; **libero** ~ free trade; ~**i con l'estero** foreign trade.

scamosci'ato, a [skamoʃ'ʃato] *ag* suede.

scampa'gnata [skampaɲ'ɲata] *sf* trip to the country.

scampa'nare *vi* to peal.

scam'pare *vt* (*salvare*) to rescue, save; (*evitare: morte, prigione*) to escape ♦ *vi*: ~ **(a qc)** to survive (sth), escape (sth); **scamparla bella** to have a narrow escape.

'scampo *sm* (*salvezza*) escape; (*ZOOL*) prawn; **cercare** ~ **nella fuga** to seek safety in flight; **non c'è (via di)** ~ there's no way out.

'scampolo *sm* remnant.

scanala'tura *sf* (*incavo*) channel, groove.

scandagli'are [skandaʎ'ʎare] *vt* (*NAUT*) to sound; (*fig*) to sound out; to probe.

scanda'listico, a, ci, che *ag* (*settimanale etc*) sensational.

scandaliz'zare [skandalid'dzare] *vt* to shock, scandalize; ~**rsi** *vr* to be shocked.

'scandalo *sm* scandal; **dare** ~ to cause a scandal.

scanda'loso, a *ag* scandalous, shocking.

Scandi'navia *sf*: **la** ~ Scandinavia.

scandi'navo, a *ag, sm/f* Scandinavian.

scan'dire *vt* (*versi*) to scan; (*parole*) to articulate, pronounce distinctly; ~ **il tempo** (*MUS*) to beat time.

scan'nare *vt* (*animale*) to butcher, slaughter; (*persona*) to cut *o* slit the throat of.

'scanner ['skanner] *sm inv* scanner.

scanneriz'zare [skannerid'dzare] *vt* to scan.

'scanno *sm* seat, bench.

scansafa'tiche [skansafa'tike] *sm/f inv* idler, loafer.

scan'sare *vt* (*rimuovere*) to move (aside), shift; (*schivare: schiaffo*) to dodge; (*sfuggire*) to avoid; ~**rsi** *vr* to move aside.

scan'sia *sf* shelves *pl*; (*per libri*) bookcase.

'scanso *sm*: **a** ~ **di** in order to avoid, as a precaution against; **a** ~ **di equivoci** to avoid (any) misunderstanding.

scanti'nato *sm* basement.

scanto'nare *vi* to turn the corner; (*svignarsela*) to sneak off.

scanzo'nato, a [skantso'nato] *ag* easy-going.

scapacci'one [skapat'tʃone] *sm* clout, slap.

scapes'trato, a *ag* dissolute.

'**scapito** *sm* (*perdita*) loss; (*danno*) damage, detriment; **a ~ di** to the detriment of.
'**scapola** *sf* shoulder blade.
'**scapolo** *sm* bachelor.
scappa'mento *sm* (*AUT*) exhaust.
scap'pare *vi* (*fuggire*) to escape; (*andare via in fretta*) to rush off; **~ di prigione** to escape from prison; **~ di mano** (*oggetto*) to slip out of one's hands; **~ di mente a qn** to slip sb's mind; **lasciarsi ~** (*occasione, affare*) to miss, let go by; (*dettaglio*) to overlook; (*parola*) to let slip; (*prigioniero*) to let escape; **mi scappò detto** I let it slip.
scap'pata *sf* quick visit *o* call.
scappa'tella *sf* escapade.
scappa'toia *sf* way out.
scara'beo *sm* beetle.
scarabocchi'are [skarabok'kjare] *vt* to scribble, scrawl.
scara'bocchio [skara'bɔkkjo] *sm* scribble, scrawl.
scara'faggio [skara'faddʒo] *sm* cockroach.
scaraman'zia [skaraman'tsia] *sf*: **per ~** for luck.
scara'muccia, ce [skara'muttʃa] *sf* skirmish.
scaraven'tare *vt* to fling, hurl.
scarce'rare [skartʃe'rare] *vt* to release (from prison).
scarcerazi'one [skartʃerat'tsjone] *sf* release (from prison).
scardi'nare *vt* to take off its hinges.
'**scarica, che** *sf* (*di più armi*) volley of shots; (*di sassi, pugni*) hail, shower; (*ELETTR*) discharge; **~ di mitra** burst of machine-gun fire.
scari'care *vt* (*merci, camion etc*) to unload; (*passeggeri*) to set down; (*da Internet*) to download; (*arma*) to unload; (: *sparare, ELETTR*) to discharge; (*sog: corso d'acqua*) to empty, pour; (*fig: liberare da un peso*) to unburden, relieve; **~rsi** *vr* (*orologio*) to run *o* wind down; (*batteria, accumulatore*) to go flat (*BRIT*) *o* dead; (*fig: rilassarsi*) to unwind; (: *sfogarsi*) to let off steam; **~ le proprie responsabilità su qn** to off-load one's responsibilities onto sb; **~ la colpa addosso a qn** to blame sb; **il fulmine si scaricò su un albero** the lightning struck a tree.
scarica'tore *sm* loader; (*di porto*) docker.
'**scarico, a, chi, che** *ag* unloaded; (*orologio*) run down; (*batteria, accumulatore*) dead, flat (*BRIT*) ♦ *sm* (*di merci, materiali*) unloading; (*di immondizie*) dumping, tipping (*BRIT*); (: *luogo*) rubbish dump; (*TECN: deflusso*) draining; (: *dispositivo*) drain; (*AUT*) exhaust; **~ del**

lavandino waste outlet.
scarlat'tina *sf* scarlet fever.
scar'latto, a *ag* scarlet.
'**scarno, a** *ag* thin, bony.
'**scarpa** *sf* shoe; **fare le ~e a qn** (*fig*) to double-cross sb; **~e da ginnastica** gym shoes; **~e coi tacchi (alti)** high-heeled shoes; **~e col tacco basso** low-heeled shoes; **~e senza tacco** flat shoes; **~e da tennis** tennis shoes.
scar'pata *sf* escarpment.
scarpi'era *sf* shoe rack.
scar'pone *sm* boot; **~i da montagna** climbing boots; **~i da sci** ski-boots.
scarroz'zare [skarrot'tsare] *vt* to drive around.
scarseggi'are [skarsed'dʒare] *vi* to be scarce; **~ di** to be short of, lack.
scar'sezza [skar'settsa] *sf* scarcity, lack.
'**scarso, a** *ag* (*insufficiente*) insufficient, meagre (*BRIT*), meager (*US*); (*povero: annata*) poor, lean; (*INS: voto*) poor; **~ di** lacking in; **3 chili ~i** just under 3 kilos.
scartabel'lare *vt* to skim through, glance through.
scarta'faccio [skarta'fattʃo] *sm* notebook.
scarta'mento *sm* (*FERR*) gauge; **~ normale/ridotto** standard/narrow gauge.
scar'tare *vt* (*pacco*) to unwrap; (*idea*) to reject; (*MIL*) to declare unfit for military service; (*carte da gioco*) to discard; (*CALCIO*) to dodge (past) ♦ *vi* to swerve.
'**scarto** *sm* (*cosa scartata, anche COMM*) reject; (*di veicolo*) swerve; (*differenza*) gap, difference; **~ salariale** wage differential.
scar'toffie *sfpl* (*peg*) papers *pl*.
scas'sare *vt* (*fam: rompere*) to wreck.
scassi'nare *vt* to break, force.
'**scasso** *sm vedi* **furto**.
scate'nare *vt* (*fig*) to incite, stir up; **~rsi** *vr* (*temporale*) to break; (*rivolta*) to break out; (*persona: infuriarsi*) to rage.
scate'nato, a *ag* wild.
'**scatola** *sf* box; (*di latta*) tin (*BRIT*), can; **cibi in ~** tinned (*BRIT*) *o* canned foods; **una ~ di cioccolatini** a box of chocolates; **comprare qc a ~ chiusa** to buy sth sight unseen; **~ cranica** cranium.
scato'lone *sm* box.
scat'tante *ag* quick off the mark; (*agile*) agile.
scat'tare *vt* (*fotografia*) to take ♦ *vi* (*congegno, molla etc*) to be released; (*balzare*) to spring up; (*SPORT*) to put on a spurt; (*fig: per l'ira*) to fly into a rage; (*legge, provvedimento*) to come into effect; **~ in piedi** to spring to one's feet; **far ~ to**

release.

'scatto *sm* (*dispositivo*) release; (: *di arma da fuoco*) trigger mechanism; (*rumore*) click; (*balzo*) jump, start; (*SPORT*) spurt; (*fig: di ira etc*) fit; (: *di stipendio*) increment; **di ~** suddenly; **serratura a ~** spring lock.

scatu'rire *vi* to gush, spring.

scaval'care *vt* (*ostacolo*) to pass (*o* climb) over; (*fig*) to get ahead of, overtake.

sca'vare *vt* (*terreno*) to dig; (*legno*) to hollow out; (*pozzo, galleria*) to bore; (*città sepolta etc*) to excavate.

scava'trice [skava'tritʃe] *sf* (*macchina*) excavator.

scavezza'collo [skavettsa'kɔllo] *sm* daredevil.

'scavo *sm* excavating *no pl*; excavation.

scazzot'tare [skattsot'tare] *vt* (*fam*) to beat up, give a thrashing to.

'scegliere ['ʃeʎʎere] *vt* (*gen*) to choose; (*candidato, prodotto*) to choose, select; **~ di fare** to choose to do.

sce'icco, chi [ʃe'ikko] *sm* sheik.

'scelgo *etc* ['ʃelgo] *vb vedi* **scegliere**.

scelle'rato, a [ʃelle'rato] *ag* wicked, evil.

scel'lino [ʃel'lino] *sm* shilling.

'scelto, a ['ʃelto] *pp di* **scegliere ♦** *ag* (*gruppo*) carefully selected; (*frutta, verdura*) choice, top quality; (*MIL: specializzato*) crack *cpd*, highly skilled ♦ *sf* choice; (*selezione*) selection, choice; **frutta o formaggi a ~a** a choice of fruit or cheese; **fare una ~a** to make a choice, choose; **non avere ~a** to have no choice *o* option; **di prima ~a** top grade *o* quality.

sce'mare [ʃe'mare] *vt, vi* to diminish.

sce'menza [ʃe'mentsa] *sf* stupidity *no pl*; stupid thing (to do *o* say).

'scemo, a ['ʃemo] *ag* stupid, silly.

'scempio ['ʃempjo] *sm* slaughter, massacre; (*fig*) ruin; **far ~ di** (*fig*) to play havoc with, ruin.

'scena ['ʃɛna] *sf* (*gen*) scene; (*palcoscenico*) stage; **le ~e** (*fig: teatro*) the stage; **andare in ~** to be staged *o* put on *o* performed; **mettere in ~** to stage; **uscire di ~** to leave the stage; (*fig*) to leave the scene; **fare una ~** (*fig*) to make a scene; **ha fatto ~ muta** (*fig*) he didn't open his mouth.

sce'nario [ʃe'narjo] *sm* scenery; (*di film*) scenario.

sce'nata [ʃe'nata] *sf* row, scene.

'scendere ['ʃendere] *vi* to go (*o* come) down; (*strada, sole*) to go down; (*notte*) to fall; (*passeggero: fermarsi*) to get out, alight; (*fig: temperatura, prezzi*) to fall, drop ♦ *vt* (*scale, pendio*) to go (*o* come) down; **~ dalle scale** to go (*o* come) down the stairs;

~ dal treno to get off *o* out of the train; **~ dalla macchina** to get out of the car; **~ da cavallo** to dismount, get off one's horse; **~ ad un albergo** to put up *o* stay at a hotel.

sceneggi'ato [ʃenedʒ'dʒato] *sm* television drama.

sceneggia'tore, 'trice [ʃenedʒa'tore] *sm/f* script-writer.

sceneggia'tura [ʃenedʒa'tura] *sf* (*TEAT*) scenario; (*CINE*) screenplay, scenario.

'scenico, a, ci, che ['ʃeniko] *ag* stage *cpd*.

scenogra'fia [ʃenogra'fia] *sf* (*TEAT*) stage design; (*CINE*) set design; (*elementi scenici*) scenery.

sce'nografo, a [ʃe'nɔgrafo] *sm/f* set designer.

sce'riffo [ʃe'riffo] *sm* sheriff.

scervel'larsi [ʃervel'larsi] *vr*: **~ (su qc)** to rack one's brains (over sth).

scervel'lato, a [ʃervel'lato] *ag* featherbrained.

'sceso, a ['ʃeso] *pp di* **scendere**.

scetti'cismo [ʃetti'tʃizmo] *sm* scepticism (*BRIT*), skepticism (*US*).

'scettico, a, ci, che ['ʃettiko] *ag* sceptical (*BRIT*), skeptical (*US*).

'scettro ['ʃettro] *sm* sceptre (*BRIT*), scepter (*US*).

'scheda ['skɛda] *sf* (index) card; (*TV, RADIO*) (brief) report; **~ audio** (*INFORM*) sound card; **~ bianca/nulla** (*POL*) unmarked/spoiled ballot paper; **~ a circuito stampato** printed-circuit board; **~ elettorale** ballot paper; **~ madre** (*INFORM*) motherboard; **~ perforata** punch card; **~ ricaricabile** (*TEL*) top-up card; **~ telefonica** phone card; **~ video** (*INFORM*) video card.

sche'dare [ske'dare] *vt* (*dati*) to file; (*libri*) to catalogue; (*registrare: anche POLIZIA*) to put on one's files.

sche'dario [ske'darjo] *sm* file; (*mobile*) filing cabinet.

sche'dato, a [ske'dato] *ag* with a (police) record ♦ *sm/f* person with a (police) record.

sche'dina [ske'dina] *sf* ≈ pools coupon (*BRIT*).

'scheggia, ge ['skeddʒa] *sf* splinter, sliver; **~ impazzita** (*fig*) maverick.

sche'letrico, a, ci, che [ske'lɛtriko] *ag* (*anche ANAT*) skeletal; (*fig: essenziale*) skeleton *cpd*.

'scheletro ['skɛletro] *sm* skeleton; **avere uno ~ nell'armadio** (*fig*) to have a skeleton in the cupboard.

'schema, i ['skɛma] *sm* (*diagramma*) diagram, sketch; (*progetto, abbozzo*)

outline, plan; **ribellarsi agli** ~**i** to rebel
against traditional values; **secondo gli** ~**i**
tradizionali in accordance with
traditional values.

sche'matico, a, ci, che [ske'matiko] *ag*
schematic.

schematiz'zare [skematid'dzare] *vt* to
schematize.

'scherma ['skerma] *sf* fencing.

scher'maglia [sker'maʎʎa] *sf* (*fig*) skirmish.

scher'mirsi [sker'mirsi] *vr* to defend o.s.

'schermo ['skermo] *sm* shield, screen;
(*CINE, TV*) screen.

schermogra'fia [skermogra'fia] *sf* X-rays
pl.

scher'nire [sker'nire] *vt* to mock, sneer at.

'scherno ['skerno] *sm* mockery, derision;
farsi ~ **di** to sneer at; **essere oggetto di** ~
to be a laughing stock.

scher'zare [sker'tsare] *vi* to joke.

'scherzo ['skertso] *sm* joke; (*tiro*) trick;
(*MUS*) scherzo; **è uno** ~**!** (*una cosa facile*)
it's child's play!, it's easy!; **per** ~ for a
joke *o* a laugh; **fare un brutto** ~ **a qn** to
play a nasty trick on sb; ~**i a parte**
seriously, joking apart.

scher'zoso, a [sker'tsoso] *ag* (*tono, gesto*)
playful; (*osservazione*) facetious; **è un tipo**
~ he likes a joke.

schiaccia'noci [skjattʃa'notʃi] *sm inv*
nutcracker.

schiacci'ante [skjat'tʃante] *ag*
overwhelming.

schiacci'are [skjat'tʃare] *vt* (*dito*) to crush;
(*noci*) to crack; ~ **un pisolino** to have a
nap.

schiaffeggi'are [skjaffed'dʒare] *vt* to slap.

schi'affo ['skjaffo] *sm* slap; **prendere qn a**
~**i** to slap sb's face; **uno** ~ **morale** a slap
in the face, a rebuff.

schiamaz'zare [skjamat'tsare] *vi* to
squawk, cackle.

schia'mazzo [skja'mattso] *sm* (*fig: chiasso*)
din, racket.

schian'tare [skjan'tare] *vt* to break, tear
apart; ~**rsi** *vr* to break (up), shatter; ~**rsi**
al suolo (*aereo*) to crash (to the ground).

schi'anto ['skjanto] *sm* (*rumore*) crash;
tearing sound; **è uno** ~**!** (*fam*) it's (*o* he's *o*
she's) terrific!; **di** ~ all of a sudden.

schia'rire [skja'rire] *vt* to lighten, make
lighter ♦ *vi* (*anche:* ~**rsi**) to grow lighter;
(*tornar sereno*) to clear, brighten up; ~**rsi**
la voce to clear one's throat.

schia'rita [skja'rita] *sf* (*METEOR*) bright
spell; (*fig*) improvement, turn for the
better.

schiat'tare [skjat'tare] *vi* to burst; ~

d'invidia to be green with envy; ~ **di**
rabbia to be beside o.s. with rage.

schiavitù [skjavi'tu] *sf* slavery.

schiaviz'zare [skjavid'dzare] *vt* to enslave.

schi'avo, a ['skjavo] *sm/f* slave.

schi'ena ['skjɛna] *sf* (*ANAT*) back.

schie'nale [skje'nale] *sm* (*di sedia*) back.

schi'era ['skjɛra] *sf* (*MIL*) rank; (*gruppo*)
group, band; **villette a** ~ ≈ terraced
houses.

schiera'mento [skjera'mento] *sm* (*MIL,
SPORT*) formation; (*fig*) alliance.

schie'rare [skje'rare] *vt* (*esercito*) to line up,
draw up, marshal; ~**rsi** *vr* to line up; (*fig*):
~**rsi con** *o* **dalla parte di/contro qn** to side
with/oppose sb.

schi'etto, a ['skjetto] *ag* (*puro*) pure; (*fig*)
frank, straightforward.

schi'fare [ski'fare] *vt* to disgust.

schi'fezza [ski'fettsa] *sf*: **essere una** ~ (*cibo,
bibita etc*) to be disgusting; (*film, libro*) to
be dreadful.

schifil'toso, a [skifil'toso] *ag* fussy,
difficult.

'schifo ['skifo] *sm* disgust; **fare** ~ (*essere
fatto male, dare pessimi risultati*) to be
awful; **mi fa** ~ it makes me sick, it's
disgusting; **quel libro è uno** ~ that book's
rotten.

schi'foso, a [ski'foso] *ag* disgusting,
revolting; (*molto scadente*) rotten, lousy.

schioc'care [skjok'kare] *vt* (*frusta*) to crack;
(*dita*) to snap; (*lingua*) to click; ~ **le labbra**
to smack one's lips.

schioppet'tata [skjoppet'tata] *sf* gunshot.

schi'oppo ['skjɔppo] *sm* rifle, gun.

schi'udere ['skjudere] *vt*, ~**rsi** *vr* to open.

schi'uma ['skjuma] *sf* foam; (*di sapone*)
lather; (*di latte*) froth.

schiu'mare [skju'mare] *vt* to skim ♦ *vi* to
foam.

schi'uso, a ['skjuso] *pp di* **schiudere**.

schi'vare [ski'vare] *vt* to dodge, avoid.

'schivo, a ['skivo] *ag* (*ritroso*) stand-offish,
reserved; (*timido*) shy.

schizofre'nia [skiddzofre'nia] *sf*
schizophrenia.

schizo'frenico, a, ci, che [skiddzo'frɛniko]
ag schizophrenic.

schiz'zare [skit'tsare] *vt* (*spruzzare*) to
spurt, squirt; (*sporcare*) to splash, spatter;
(*fig: abbozzare*) to sketch ♦ *vi* to spurt,
squirt; (*saltar fuori*) to dart up (*o* off *etc*);
~ **via** (*animale, persona*) to dart away;
(*macchina, moto*) to accelerate away.

schizzi'noso, a [skittsi'noso] *ag* fussy,
finicky.

'schizzo ['skittso] *sm* (*di liquido*) spurt;

splash, spatter; (*abbozzo*) sketch.

sci [ʃi] *sm inv* (*attrezzo*) ski; (*attività*) skiing; **~ di fondo** cross-country skiing, ski touring (*US*); **~ nautico** water-skiing.

'scia, *pl* **'scie** ['ʃia] *sf* (*di imbarcazione*) wake; (*di profumo*) trail.

scià [ʃa] *sm inv* shah.

sci'abola ['ʃabola] *sf* sabre (*BRIT*), saber (*US*).

scia'callo [ʃa'kallo] *sm* jackal; (*fig peg: profittatore*) shark, profiteer; (: *ladro*) looter.

sciac'quare [ʃak'kware] *vt* to rinse.

scia'gura [ʃa'gura] *sf* disaster, calamity.

sciagu'rato, a [ʃagu'rato] *ag* unfortunate; (*malvagio*) wicked.

scialac'quare [ʃalak'kware] *vt* to squander.

scia'lare [ʃa'lare] *vi* to throw one's money around.

sci'albo, a ['ʃalbo] *ag* pale, dull; (*fig*) dull, colourless (*BRIT*), colorless (*US*).

sci'alle ['ʃalle] *sm* shawl.

sci'alo ['ʃalo] *sm* squandering, waste.

scia'luppa [ʃa'luppa] *sf* (*NAUT*) sloop; (*anche*: **~ di salvataggio**) lifeboat.

scia'mare [ʃa'mare] *vi* to swarm.

sci'ame ['ʃame] *sm* swarm.

scian'cato, a [ʃan'kato] *ag* lame; (*mobile*) rickety.

sci'are [ʃi'are] *vi* to ski; **andare a ~** to go skiing.

sci'arpa ['ʃarpa] *sf* scarf; (*fascia*) sash.

scia'tore, 'trice [ʃia'tore] *sm/f* skier.

sciat'tezza [ʃat'tettsa] *sf* slovenliness.

sci'atto, a ['ʃatto] *ag* (*persona: nell'aspetto*) slovenly, unkempt; (: *nel lavoro*) sloppy, careless.

'scibile ['ʃibile] *sm* knowledge.

scien'tifico, a, ci, che [ʃen'tifiko] *ag* scientific; **la (polizia) ~a** the forensic department.

sci'enza ['ʃɛntsa] *sf* science; (*sapere*) knowledge; **~e** *sfpl* (*INS*) science *sg*; **~e naturali** natural sciences; **~e politiche** political science *sg*.

scienzi'ato, a [ʃen'tsjato] *sm/f* scientist.

'Scilly ['ʃilli]: **le isole ~** *sfpl* the Scilly Isles.

'scimmia ['ʃimmja] *sf* monkey.

scimmiot'tare [ʃimmjot'tare] *vt* to ape, mimic.

scimpanzé [ʃimpan'tse] *sm inv* chimpanzee.

scimu'nito, a [ʃimu'nito] *ag* silly, idiotic.

'scindere ['ʃindere] *vt*, **~rsi** *vr* to split (up).

scin'tilla [ʃin'tilla] *sf* spark.

scintil'lare [ʃintil'lare] *vi* to spark; (*acqua, occhi*) to sparkle.

scintil'lio [ʃintil'lio] *sm* sparkling.

scioc'care [ʃok'kare] *vt* to shock.

scioc'chezza [ʃok'kettsa] *sf* stupidity *no pl*; stupid *o* foolish thing; **dire ~e** to talk nonsense.

sci'occo, a, chi, che ['ʃɔkko] *ag* stupid, foolish.

sci'ogliere ['ʃɔʎʎere] *vt* (*nodo*) to untie; (*capelli*) to loosen; (*persona, animale*) to untie, release; (*fig: persona*): **~ da** to release from; (*neve*) to melt; (*nell'acqua: zucchero etc*) to dissolve; (*fig: mistero*) to solve; (*porre fine a: contratto*) to cancel; (: *società, matrimonio*) to dissolve; (: *riunione*) to bring to an end; **~rsi** *vr* to loosen, come untied; to melt; to dissolve; (*assemblea, corteo, duo*) to break up; **~ i muscoli** to limber up; **~ il ghiaccio** (*fig*) to break the ice; **~ le vele** (*NAUT*) to set sail; **~rsi dai legami** (*fig*) to free o.s. from all ties.

sci'olgo *etc* ['ʃɔlgo] *vb vedi* **sciogliere**.

sciol'tezza [ʃol'tettsa] *sf* agility; suppleness; ease.

sci'olto, a ['ʃɔlto] *pp di* **sciogliere** ♦ *ag* loose; (*agile*) agile, nimble; (*disinvolto*) free and easy; **essere ~ nei movimenti** to be supple; **versi ~i** (*POESIA*) blank verse.

sciope'rante [ʃope'rante] *sm/f* striker.

sciope'rare [ʃope'rare] *vi* to strike, go on strike.

sci'opero ['ʃɔpero] *sm* strike; **fare ~** to strike; **entrare in ~** to go on *o* come out on strike; **~ bianco** work-to-rule (*BRIT*), slowdown (*US*); **~ della fame** hunger strike; **~ selvaggio** wildcat strike; **~ a singhiozzo** on-off strike; **~ di solidarietà** sympathy strike.

sciori'nare [ʃori'nare] *vt* (*ostentare*) to show off, display.

scio'via [ʃio'via] *sf* ski lift.

sciovi'nismo [ʃovi'nizmo] *sm* chauvinism.

sciovi'nista, i, e [ʃovi'nista] *sm/f* chauvinist.

sci'pito, a [ʃi'pito] *ag* insipid.

scip'pare [ʃip'pare] *vt*: **~ qn** to snatch sb's bag.

scippa'tore [ʃippa'tore] *sm* bag-snatcher.

'scippo ['ʃippo] *sm* bag-snatching.

sci'rocco [ʃi'rɔkko] *sm* sirocco.

sci'roppo [ʃi'rɔppo] *sm* syrup; **~ per la tosse** cough syrup, cough mixture.

'scisma, i ['ʃizma] *sm* (*REL*) schism.

scissi'one [ʃis'sjone] *sf* (*anche fig*) split, division; (*FISICA*) fission.

'scisso, a ['ʃisso] *pp di* **scindere**.

sciu'pare [ʃu'pare] *vt* (*abito, libro, appetito*) to spoil, ruin; (*tempo, denaro*) to waste; **~rsi** *vr* to get spoilt *o* ruined; (*rovinarsi la salute*) to ruin one's health.

scivo'lare [ʃivo'lare] vi to slide o glide along; (involontariamente) to slip, slide.
'scivolo ['ʃivolo] sm slide; (TECN) chute.
scivo'loso, a [ʃivo'loso] ag slippery.
scle'rosi sf sclerosis.
scoc'care vt (freccia) to shoot ♦ vi (guizzare) to shoot up; (battere: ora) to strike.
scoccherò etc [skokke'rɔ] vb vedi scoccare.
scocci'are [skot'tʃare] vt to bother, annoy; ~rsi vr to be bothered o annoyed.
scoccia'tore, 'trice [skottʃa'tore] sm/f nuisance, pest (fam).
scoccia'tura [skottʃa'tura] sf nuisance, bore.
sco'della sf bowl.
scodinzo'lare [skodintso'lare] vi to wag its tail.
scogli'era [skoʎ'ʎɛra] sf reef; (rupe) cliff.
'scoglio ['skɔʎʎo] sm (al mare) rock; (fig: ostacolo) difficulty, stumbling block.
scogli'oso, a [skoʎ'ʎoso] ag rocky.
scoi'attolo sm squirrel.
scola'pasta sm inv colander.
sco'lare ag: età ~ school age ♦ vt to drain ♦ vi to drip.
scola'resca sf schoolchildren pl, pupils pl.
sco'laro, a sm/f pupil, schoolboy/girl.
sco'lastico, a, ci, che ag (gen) scholastic; (libro, anno, divisa) school cpd.
scol'lare vt (staccare) to unstick; ~rsi vr to come unstuck.
scol'lato, a ag (vestito) low-cut, low-necked; (donna) wearing a low-cut dress (o blouse etc).
scolla'tura sf neckline.
'scolo sm drainage; (sbocco) drain; (acqua) waste water; canale di ~ drain; tubo di ~ drainpipe.
scolo'rire vt to fade; to discolour (BRIT), discolor (US) ♦ vi (anche: ~rsi) to fade; to become discolo(u)red; (impallidire) to turn pale.
scol'pire vt to carve, sculpt.
scombi'nare vt to mess up, upset.
scombi'nato, a ag confused, muddled.
scombusso'lare vt to upset.
scom'messo, a pp di scommettere ♦ sf bet, wager; fare una ~a to bet.
scom'mettere vt, vi to bet.
scomo'dare vt to trouble, bother, disturb; (fig: nome famoso) to involve, drag in; ~rsi vr to put o.s. out; ~rsi a fare to go to the bother o trouble of doing.
scomodità sf inv (di sedia, letto etc) discomfort; (di orario, sistemazione etc) inconvenience.
'scomodo, a ag uncomfortable; (sistemazione, posto) awkward,

inconvenient.
scompagi'nare [skompadʒi'nare] vt to upset, throw into disorder.
scompag'nato, a [skompaɲ'ɲato] ag (calzini, guanti) odd.
scompa'rire vi (sparire) to disappear, vanish; (fig) to be insignificant.
scom'parso, a pp di scomparire ♦ sf disappearance; (fig: morte) passing away, death.
scomparti'mento sm (FERR) compartment; (sezione) division.
scom'parto sm compartment, division.
scom'penso sm imbalance, lack of balance.
scompigli'are [skompiʎ'ʎare] vt (cassetto, capelli) to mess up, disarrange; (fig: piani) to upset.
scom'piglio [skom'piʎʎo] sm mess, confusion.
scom'porre vt (parola, numero) to break up; (CHIM) to decompose; scomporsi vr (CHIM) to decompose; (fig) to get upset, lose one's composure; senza scomporsi unperturbed.
scom'posto, a pp di scomporre ♦ ag (gesto) unseemly; (capelli) ruffled, dishevelled.
sco'munica, che sf excommunication.
scomuni'care vt to excommunicate.
sconcer'tante [skontʃer'tante] ag disconcerting.
sconcer'tare [skontʃer'tare] vt to disconcert, bewilder.
'sconcio, a, ci, ce ['skontʃo] ag (osceno) indecent, obscene ♦ sm (cosa riprovevole, mal fatta) disgrace.
sconclusio'nato, a ag incoherent, illogical.
sconfes'sare vt to renounce, disavow; to repudiate.
scon'figgere [skon'fiddʒere] vt to defeat, overcome.
sconfi'nare vi to cross the border; (in proprietà privata) to trespass; (fig): ~ da to stray o digress from.
sconfi'nato, a ag boundless, unlimited.
scon'fitto, a pp di sconfiggere ♦ sf defeat.
sconfor'tante, a ag discouraging, disheartening.
sconfor'tare vt to discourage, dishearten; ~rsi vr to become discouraged, become disheartened, lose heart.
scon'forto sm despondency.
sconge'lare [skondʒe'lare] vt to defrost.
scongiu'rare [skondʒu'rare] vt (implorare) to beseech, implore; (eludere: pericolo) to ward off, avert.
scongi'uro [skon'dʒuro] sm (esorcismo)

exorcism; **fare gli** ~**i** to touch wood (*BRIT*), knock on wood (*US*).

scon'nesso, a *ag* (*fig: discorso*) incoherent, rambling.

sconosci'uto, a [skonoʃ'ʃuto] *ag* unknown; new, strange ♦ *sm/f* stranger, unknown person.

sconquas'sare *vt* to shatter, smash.

scon'quasso *sm* (*danno*) damage; (*fig*) confusion.

sconside'rato, a *ag* thoughtless, rash.

sconsigli'are [skonsiʎ'ʎare] *vt*: ~ **qc a qn** to advise sb against sth; ~ **qn dal fare qc** to advise sb not to do *o* against doing sth.

sconso'lato, a *ag* disconsolate.

scon'tare *vt* (*COMM: detrarre*) to deduct; (: *debito*) to pay off; (: *cambiale*) to discount; (*pena*) to serve; (*colpa, errori*) to pay for, suffer for.

scon'tato, a *ag* (*previsto*) foreseen, taken for granted; (*prezzo, merce*) discounted, at a discount; **dare per** ~ **che** to take it for granted that.

sconten'tare *vt* to displease, dissatisfy.

sconten'tezza [skonten'tettsa] *sf* displeasure, dissatisfaction.

scon'tento, a *ag*: ~ **(di)** discontented *o* dissatisfied (with) ♦ *sm* discontent, dissatisfaction.

'sconto *sm* discount; **fare** *o* **concedere uno** ~ to give a discount; **uno** ~ **del 10%** a 10% discount.

scon'trarsi *vr* (*treni etc*) to crash, collide; (*venire ad uno scontro, fig*) to clash; ~ **con** to crash into, collide with.

scon'trino *sm* ticket.

'scontro *sm* (*MIL, fig*) clash; (*di veicoli*) crash, collision; ~ **a fuoco** shoot-out.

scon'troso, a *ag* sullen, surly; (*permaloso*) touchy.

sconveni'ente *ag* unseemly, improper.

sconvol'gente [skonvol'dʒɛnte] *ag* (*notizia, brutta esperienza*) upsetting, disturbing; (*bellezza*) amazing; (*passione*) overwhelming.

scon'volgere [skon'vɔldʒere] *vt* to throw into confusion, upset; (*turbare*) to shake, disturb, upset.

scon'volto, a *pp di* **sconvolgere** ♦ *ag* (*persona*) distraught, very upset.

'scopa *sf* broom; (*CARTE*) Italian card game.

sco'pare *vt* to sweep; (*fam!*) to bonk (*!*).

sco'pata *sf* (*fam!*) bonk (*!*).

scoperchi'are [skoper'kjare] *vt* (*pentola, vaso*) to take the lid off, uncover; (*casa*) to take the roof off.

sco'perto, a *pp di* **scoprire** ♦ *ag* uncovered; (*capo*) uncovered, bare; (*macchina*) open; (*MIL*) exposed, without cover; (*conto*) overdrawn ♦ *sf* discovery ♦ *sm*: **allo** ~ (*dormire etc*) out in the open; **assegno** ~ uncovered cheque; **avere un conto** ~ to be overdrawn.

'scopo *sm* aim, purpose; **a che** ~**?** what for?; **adatto allo** ~ fit for its purpose; **allo** ~ **di fare qc** in order to do sth; **a** ~ **di lucro** for gain *o* money; **senza** ~ (*fare, cercare*) pointlessly.

scoppi'are *vi* (*spaccarsi*) to burst; (*esplodere*) to explode; (*fig*) to break out; ~ **in pianto** *o* **a piangere** to burst out crying; ~ **dalle risa** *o* **dal ridere** to split one's sides laughing; ~ **dal caldo** to be boiling; ~ **di salute** to be the picture of health.

scoppiet'tare *vi* to crackle.

'scoppio *sm* explosion; (*di tuono, arma etc*) crash, bang; (*di pneumatico*) bang; (*fig: di guerra*) outbreak; **a** ~ **ritardato** delayed-action; **reazione a** ~ **ritardato** delayed *o* slow reaction; **uno** ~ **di risa** a burst of laughter; **uno** ~ **di collera** an explosion of anger.

sco'prire *vt* to discover; (*liberare da ciò che copre*) to uncover; (: *monumento*) to unveil; ~**rsi** *vr* to put on lighter clothes; (*fig*) to give o.s. away.

scopri'tore, 'trice *sm/f* discoverer.

scoraggi'are [skorad'dʒare] *vt* to discourage; ~**rsi** *vr* to become discouraged, lose heart.

scor'butico, a, ci, che *ag* (*fig*) cantankerous.

scorcia'toia [skortʃa'toja] *sf* short cut.

'scorcio ['skortʃo] *sm* (*ARTE*) foreshortening; (*di secolo, periodo*) end, close; ~ **panoramico** vista.

scor'dare *vt* to forget; ~**rsi** *vr*: ~**rsi di qc/di fare** to forget sth/to do.

sco'reggia [sko'reddʒa] (*fam!*) *sf* fart (*!*).

scoreggi'are [skored'dʒare] (*fam!*) *vi* to fart (*!*).

'scorgere ['skɔrdʒere] *vt* to make out, distinguish, see.

sco'ria *sf* (*di metalli*) slag; (*vulcanica*) scoria; ~**e radioattive** (*FISICA*) radioactive waste *sg*.

'scorno *sm* ignominy, disgrace.

scorpacci'ata [skorpat'tʃata] *sf*: **fare una** ~ **(di)** to stuff o.s. (with), eat one's fill (of).

scorpi'one *sm* scorpion; (*dello zodiaco*): **S**~ Scorpio; **essere dello S**~ to be Scorpio.

'scorporo *sm* (*POL*) *transfer of votes aimed at increasing the chances of representation for minority parties.*

scorraz'zare [skorrat'tsare] *vi* to run about.
'scorrere *vt* (*giornale, lettera*) to run *o* skim through ♦ *vi* (*liquido, fiume*) to run, flow; (*fune*) to run; (*cassetto, porta*) to slide easily; (*tempo*) to pass (by).
scorre'ria *sf* raid, incursion.
scorret'tezza [skorret'tettsa] *sf* incorrectness; lack of politeness, rudeness; unfairness; **commettere una ~** (*essere sleale*) to be unfair.
scor'retto, a *ag* (*sbagliato*) incorrect; (*sgarbato*) impolite; (*sconveniente*) improper; (*sleale*) unfair; (*gioco*) foul.
scor'revole *ag* (*porta*) sliding; (*fig: stile*) fluent, flowing.
scorri'banda *sf* (*MIL*) raid; (*escursione*) trip, excursion.
'scorsi *etc vb vedi* **scorgere**.
'scorso, a *pp di* **scorrere** ♦ *ag* last ♦ *sf* quick look, glance; **lo ~ mese** last month.
scor'soio, a *ag*: **nodo ~** noose.
'scorta *sf* (*di personalità, convoglio*) escort; (*provvista*) supply, stock; **sotto la ~ di due agenti** escorted by two policemen; **fare ~ di** to stock up with, get in a supply of; **di ~** (*materiali*) spare; **ruota di ~** spare wheel.
scor'tare *vt* to escort.
scor'tese *ag* discourteous, rude.
scorte'sia *sf* discourtesy, rudeness; (*azione*) discourtesy.
scorti'care *vt* to skin.
'scorto, a *pp di* **scorgere**.
'scorza ['skɔrdza] *sf* (*di albero*) bark; (*di agrumi*) peel, skin.
sco'sceso, a [skoʃ'ʃeso] *ag* steep.
'scosso, a *pp di* **scuotere** ♦ *ag* (*turbato*) shaken, upset ♦ *sf* jerk, jolt, shake; (*ELETTR, fig*) shock; **prendere la ~ a** to get an electric shock; **~a di terremoto** earth tremor.
scos'sone *sm*: **dare uno ~ a qn** to give sb a shake; **procedere a ~i** to jolt *o* jerk along.
scos'tante *ag* (*fig*) off-putting (*BRIT*), unpleasant.
scos'tare *vt* to move (away), shift; **~rsi** to move away.
scostu'mato, a *ag* immoral, dissolute.
scotch [skɔtʃ] *sm inv* (*whisky*) Scotch; ® (*nastro adesivo*) Scotch tape ®, Sellotape ®.
scot'tante *ag* (*fig: urgente*) pressing; (: *delicato*) delicate.
scot'tare *vt* (*ustionare*) to burn; (: *con liquido bollente*) to scald ♦ *vi* to burn; (*caffè*) to be too hot.
scotta'tura *sf* burn; scald.
'scotto, a *ag* overcooked ♦ *sm* (*fig*): **pagare lo ~ (di)** to pay the penalty (for).
sco'vare *vt* to drive out, flush out; (*fig*) to

discover.
'Scozia ['skɔttsja] *sf*: **la ~** Scotland.
scoz'zese [skot'tsese] *ag* Scottish ♦ *sm/f* Scot.
screan'zato, a [skrean'tsato] *ag* ill-mannered ♦ *sm/f* boor.
scredi'tare *vt* to discredit.
scre'mare *vt* to skim.
scre'mato, a *ag* skimmed; **parzialmente ~** semi-skimmed.
screpo'lare *vi*, **~rsi** *vr* to crack.
screpola'tura *sf* cracking *no pl*; crack.
screzi'ato, a [skret'tsjato] *ag* streaked.
'screzio ['skrɛttsjo] *sm* disagreement.
scribac'chino [skribak'kino] *sm* (*peg: impiegato*) penpusher; (: *scrittore*) hack.
scricchio'lare [skrikkjo'lare] *vi* to creak, squeak.
scricchio'lio [skrikkjo'lio] *sm* creaking.
'scricciolo ['skrittʃolo] *sm* wren.
'scrigno ['skriɲɲo] *sm* casket.
scrimina'tura *sf* parting.
'scrissi *etc vb vedi* **scrivere**.
'scritto, a *pp di* **scrivere** ♦ *ag* written ♦ *sm* writing; (*lettera*) letter, note ♦ *sf* inscription; **~i** *smpl* (*letterari etc*) work(s), writings; **per** *o* **in ~** in writing.
scrit'toio *sm* writing desk.
scrit'tore, 'trice *sm/f* writer.
scrit'tura *sf* writing; (*COMM*) entry; (*contratto*) contract; (*REL*): **la Sacra S~** the Scriptures *pl*; **~e** *sfpl* (*COMM*) accounts, books.
scrittu'rare *vt* (*TEAT, CINE*) to sign up, engage; (*COMM*) to enter.
scriva'nia *sf* desk.
scri'vano *sm* (*amanuense*) scribe; (*impiegato*) clerk.
scri'vente *sm/f* writer.
'scrivere *vt* to write; **come si scrive?** how is it spelt?, how do you write it?; **~ qc a qn** to write sth to sb; **~ qc a macchina** to type sth; **~ a penna/matita** to write in pen/pencil; **~ qc maiuscolo/minuscolo** to write sth in capital/small letters.
scroc'care *vt* (*fam*) to scrounge, cadge.
scroc'cone, a *sm/f* scrounger.
'scrofa *sf* (*ZOOL*) sow.
scrol'lare *vt* to shake; **~rsi** *vr* (*anche fig*) to give o.s. a shake; **~ le spalle/il capo** to shrug one's shoulders/shake one's head; **~rsi qc di dosso** (*ache fig*) to shake sth off.
scrol'lata *sf* shake; **~ di spalle** shrug (of one's shoulders).
scrosci'ante [skroʃ'ʃante] *ag* (*pioggia*) pouring; (*fig: applausi*) thunderous.
scrosci'are [skroʃ'ʃare] *vi* (*pioggia*) to pour down, pelt down; (*torrente, fig: applausi*) to

thunder, roar.

'**scroscio** ['skrɔʃʃo] *sm* pelting; thunder, roar; (*di applausi*) burst.

scros'tare *vt* (*intonaco*) to scrape off, strip; ~**rsi** *vr* to peel off, flake off.

'**scrupolo** *sm* scruple; (*meticolosità*) care, conscientiousness; **essere senza** ~**i** to be unscrupulous.

scrupo'loso, a *ag* scrupulous; conscientious.

scru'tare *vt* to scrutinize; (*intenzioni, causa*) to examine, scrutinize.

scruta'tore, trice *sm/f* (*POL*) scrutineer.

scruti'nare *vt* (*voti*) to count.

scru'tinio *sm* (*votazione*) ballot; (*insieme delle operazioni*) poll; (*INS*) (*meeting for*) assignment of marks at end of a term or year.

scu'cire [sku'tʃire] *vt* (*orlo etc*) to unpick, undo; ~**rsi** *vr* to come unstitched.

scude'ria *sf* stable.

scu'detto *sm* (*SPORT*) (championship) shield; (*distintivo*) badge.

scu'discio [sku'diʃʃo] *sm* (riding) crop, (riding) whip.

'**scudo** *sm* shield; **farsi** ~ **di** *o* **con qc** to shield o.s. with sth; ~ **aereo/missilistico** air/missile defence (*BRIT*) *o* defense (*US*); ~ **termico** heat shield.

sculacci'are [skulat'tʃare] *vt* to spank.

sculacci'one [skulat'tʃone] *sm* spanking.

scul'tore, 'trice *sm/f* sculptor.

scul'tura *sf* sculpture.

scu'ola *sf* school; ~ **elementare** *o* **primaria** primary (*BRIT*) *o* grade (*US*) school (*for children from 6 to 11 years of age*); ~ **guida** driving school; ~ **materna** *o* **dell'infanzia** nursery school (*for children aged 3 to 6*); ~ **first 3 years of secondary school, for children from 11 to 14 years of age*); ~ **secondaria di secondo grado** secondary school (*for children aged 14 to 18*) ~ **dell' obbligo** compulsory education; ~ **privata/pubblica** private/state school; ~**e serali** evening classes, night school *sg*; ~ **tecnica** technical college; *vedi nota nel riquadro.*

SCUOLA

Italian children first go to school at the age of three. They remain at the "scuola materna" until they are six, when they move on to the "scuola primaria" for another five years. After this come three years of "scuola secondaria di primo grado". Students who wish to continue their schooling attend "scuola secondaria di secondo grado", choosing between several types of institution which specialize in different subject areas.

---

scu'otere *vt* to shake; ~**rsi** *vr* to jump, be startled; (*fig: muoversi*) to rouse o.s., stir o.s.; (: *turbarsi*) to be shaken.

'**scure** *sf* axe, ax (*US*).

scu'rire *vt* to darken, make darker.

'**scuro, a** *ag* dark; (*fig: espressione*) grim ♦ *sm* darkness; dark colour (*BRIT*) *o* color (*US*); (*imposta*) (window) shutter; **verde/ rosso** *etc* ~ dark green/red *etc.*

scur'rile *ag* scurrilous.

'**scusa** *sf* excuse; ~**e** *sfpl* apology *sg*, apologies; **chiedere** ~ **a qn (per)** to apologize to sb (for); **chiedo** ~ I'm sorry; (*disturbando etc*) excuse me; **vi prego di accettare le mie** ~**e** please accept my apologies.

scu'sare *vt* to excuse; ~**rsi** *vr:* ~**rsi (di)** to apologize (for); (**mi) scusi** I'm sorry; (*per richiamare l'attenzione*) excuse me.

S.C.V. *sigla = Stato della Città del Vaticano.*

sdebi'tarsi *vt:* ~**rsi (con qn di** *o* **per qc)** (*anche fig*) to repay (sb for sth).

sde'gnare [zdeɲ'ɲare] *vt* to scorn, despise; ~**rsi** *vr* (*adirarsi*) to get angry.

sde'gnato, a [zdeɲ'ɲato] *ag* indignant, angry.

'**sdegno** ['zdeɲɲo] *sm* scorn, disdain.

sdegnosa'mente [zdeɲɲosa'mente] *av* scornfully, disdainfully.

sde'gnoso, a [zdeɲ'ɲoso] *ag* scornful, disdainful.

sdilin'quirsi *vr* (*illanguidirsi*) to become sentimental.

sdoga'nare *vt* (*COMM*) to clear through customs.

sdolci'nato, a [zdoltʃi'nato] *ag* mawkish, oversentimental.

sdoppia'mento *sm* (*CHIM: di composto*) splitting; (*PSIC*): ~ **della personalità** split personality.

sdoppi'are *vt* (*dividere*) to divide *o* split in two.

sdrai'arsi *vr* to stretch out, lie down.

'**sdraio** *sm:* **sedia a** ~ deck chair.

sdrammatiz'zare [zdrammatid'dzare] *vt* to play down, minimize.

sdruccio'lare [zdruttʃo'lare] *vi* to slip, slide.

sdruccio'levole [zdruttʃo'levole] *ag* slippery.

sdru'cito, a [zdru'tʃito] *ag* (*strappato*) torn; (*logoro*) threadbare.

═══════════ *PAROLA CHIAVE*

se *pron vedi* **si**
♦ *cong* **1** (*condizionale, ipotetica*) if; ~ **nevica non vengo** I won't come if it

S.E. – sede

snows; ~ **fossi in te** if I were you; **sarei rimasto** ~ **me l'avessero chiesto** I would have stayed if they'd asked me; **non puoi fare altro** ~ **non telefonare** all you can do is phone; ~ **mai** if, if ever; **siamo noi** ~ **mai che le siamo grati** it is we who should be grateful to you; ~ **no** (*altrimenti*) or (else), otherwise; ~ **non** (*anzi*) if not; (*tranne*) except; ~ **non altro** if nothing else, at least; ~ **solo** *o* **solamente** if only

2 (*in frasi dubitative, interrogative indirette*) if, whether; **non so** ~ **scrivere o telefonare** I don't know whether *o* if I should write or phone.

S.E. *abbr* (= *sud-est*) SE; (= *Sua Eccellenza*) HE.

sé *pron* (*gen*) oneself; (*esso, essa, lui, lei, loro*) itself; himself; herself; themselves; ~ **stesso(a)** *pron* oneself; itself; himself; herself; ~ **stessi(e)** *pron pl* themselves; **di per** ~ **non è un problema** it's no problem in itself; **parlare tra** ~ **e** ~ to talk to oneself; **va da** ~ **che** ... it goes without saying that ..., it's obvious that ..., it stands to reason that ...; **è un caso a** ~ *o* **a** ~ **stante** it's a special case; **un uomo che s'è fatto da** ~ a self-made man.

S.E.A.T.O. *sigla f* (= *Southeast Asia Treaty Organization*) SEATO.

seb'bene *cong* although, though.

'sebo *sm* sebum.

sec. *abbr* (= *secolo*) c.

'SECAM *sigla m* (= *séquentiel couleur à mémoire*) SECAM.

'secca *sf vedi* **secco**.

secca'mente *av* (*rispondere, rifiutare*) sharply, curtly.

sec'care *vt* to dry; (*prosciugare*) to dry up; (*fig: importunare*) to annoy, bother ♦ *vi* to dry; to dry up; ~**rsi** *vr* to dry; to dry up; (*fig*) to grow annoyed; **si è seccato molto** he was very annoyed.

sec'cato, a *ag* (*fig: infastidito*) bothered, annoyed; (: *stufo*) fed up.

secca'tore, 'trice *sm/f* nuisance, bother.

secca'tura *sf* (*fig*) bother *no pl*, trouble *no pl*.

seccherò *etc* [sekke'rɔ] *vb vedi* **seccare**.

'secchia ['sekkja] *sf* bucket, pail.

secchi'ello [sek'kjɛllo] *sm* (*per bambini*) bucket, pail.

'secchio ['sekkjo] *sm* bucket, pail; ~ **della spazzatura** *o* **delle immondizie** dustbin

(*BRIT*), garbage can (*US*).

'secco, a, chi, che *ag* dry; (*fichi, pesce*) dried; (*foglie, ramo*) withered; (*magro: persona*) thin, skinny; (*fig: risposta, modo di fare*) curt, abrupt; (: *colpo*) clean, sharp ♦ *sm* (*siccità*) drought ♦ *sf* (*del mare*) shallows *pl*; **restarci** ~ (*fig: morire sul colpo*) to drop dead; **avere la gola** ~**a** to feel dry, be parched; **lavare a** ~ to dry-clean; **tirare a** ~ (*barca*) to beach.

secen'tesco, a, schi, sche [setʃen'tesko] *ag* = **seicentesco**.

se'cernere [se'tʃɛrnere] *vt* to secrete.

seco'lare *ag* age-old, centuries-old; (*laico, mondano*) secular.

'secolo *sm* century; (*epoca*) age.

se'conda *sf vedi* **secondo**; **S~ Repubblica** *vedi nota nel riquadro*.

SECONDA REPUBBLICA

Seconda Repubblica *is the term used, especially by the Italian media, to refer to the Government and the country in general since the 1994 elections. This is when the old party system collapsed, following the "Tangentopoli" scandals. New political parties were set up and the electoral system was reformed, a first-past-the-post element being introduced side by side with proportional representation.*

---

secondaria'mente *av* secondly.

secon'dario, a *ag* secondary; **scuola/ istruzione** ~**a** secondary school/ education.

secon'dino *sm* prison officer, warder (*BRIT*).

se'condo, a *ag* second ♦ *sm* second; (*di pranzo*) main course ♦ *sf* (*AUT*) second (gear); (*FERR*) second class ♦ *prep* according to; (*nel modo prescritto*) in accordance with; ~ **me** in my opinion, to my mind; ~ **la legge/ quanto si era deciso** in accordance with the law/the decision taken; **di** ~**a classe** second-class; **di** ~**a mano** second-hand; **viaggiare in** ~**a** to travel second-class; **comandante** *m* **in** ~**a** second-in-command; **a** ~**a di** *prep* according to; in accordance with.

'sedano *sm* celery.

se'dare *vt* (*dolore*) to soothe; (*rivolta*) to put down, suppress.

seda'tivo, a *ag, sm* sedative.

'sede *sf* (*luogo di residenza*) (place of) residence; (*di ditta: principale*) head office; (: *secondaria*) branch (office); (*di* *organizzazione*) headquarters pl; (*di governo, parlamento*) seat; (*REL*) see; **in ~ di** (*in occasione di*) during; **in altra ~** on another occasion; **in ~ legislativa** in legislative sitting; **prendere ~** to take up residence; **~ centrale** head office; **~ sociale** registered office.

seden'tario, a *ag* sedentary.

se'dere *vi* to sit, be seated; **~rsi** *vr* to sit down ♦ *sm* (*deretano*) bottom; **posto a ~** seat.

'sedia *sf* chair; **~ elettrica** electric chair; **~ a rotelle** wheelchair.

sedi'cenne [sedi't∫εnne] *ag, smf* sixteen-year-old.

sedi'cente [sedi't∫εnte] *ag* self-styled.

sedi'cesimo, a [sedi't∫εzimo] *num* sixteenth.

'sedici ['sedit∫i] *num* sixteen.

se'dile *sm* seat; (*panchina*) bench.

sedimen'tare *vi* to leave a sediment.

sedi'mento *sm* sediment.

sedizi'one [sedit'tsjone] *sf* revolt, rebellion.

sedizi'oso, a [sedit'tsjoso] *ag* seditious.

se'dotto, a *pp di* **sedurre.**

sedu'cente [sedu't∫εnte] *ag* seductive; (*proposta*) very attractive.

se'durre *vt* to seduce.

se'duta *sf* session, sitting; (*riunione*) meeting; **essere in ~** to be in session, be sitting; **~ stante** (*fig*) immediately; **~ spiritica** seance.

sedut'tore, 'trice *smf* seducer/seductress.

seduzi'one [sedut'tsjone] *sf* seduction; (*fascino*) charm, appeal.

SEeO *abbr* (= *salvo errori e omissioni*) E & OE.

'sega, ghe *sf* saw; **~ circolare** circular saw; **~ a mano** handsaw.

'segale *sf* rye.

se'gare *vt* to saw; (*recidere*) to saw off.

sega'tura *sf* (*residuo*) sawdust.

'seggio ['sεddʒo] *sm* seat; **~ elettorale** polling station.

'seggiola ['sεddʒola] *sf* chair.

seggio'lino [sεddʒo'lino] *sm* seat; (*per bambini*) child's chair; **~ di sicurezza** (*AUT*) child safety seat.

seggio'lone [sεddʒo'lone] *sm* (*per bambini*) highchair.

seggio'via [sεddʒo'via] *sf* chairlift.

seghe'ria [sege'ria] *sf* sawmill.

seghe'rò *etc* [sege'rɔ] *vb vedi* **segare.**

seghet'tato, a [seget'tato] *ag* serrated.

se'ghetto [se'getto] *sm* hacksaw.

seg'mento *sm* segment.

segna'lare [seɲɲa'lare] *vt* (*essere segno di*) to indicate, be a sign of; (*avvertire*) to signal; (*menzionare*) to indicate; (: *fatto, risultato, aumento*) to report; (: *errore, dettaglio*) to point out; (*AUT*) to signal, indicate; **~rsi** *vr* (*distinguersi*) to distinguish o.s.; **~ qn a qn** (*per lavoro etc*) to bring sb to sb's attention.

segnalazi'one [seɲɲalat'tsjone] *sf* (*azione*) signalling; (*segnale*) signal; (*annuncio*) report; (*raccomandazione*) recommendation.

se'gnale [seɲ'ɲale] *sm* signal; (*cartello*): **~ stradale** road sign; **~ acustico** acoustic o sound signal; (*di segreteria telefonica*) tone; **~ d'allarme** alarm; (*FERR*) communication cord; **~ di linea libera** (*TEL*) dialling (*BRIT*) o dial (*US*) tone; **~ luminoso** light signal; **~ di occupato** (*TEL*) engaged tone (*BRIT*), busy signal (*US*); **~ orario** (*RADIO*) time signal.

segna'letica [seɲɲa'lεtika] *sf* signalling, signposting; **~ stradale** road signs pl.

segna'libro [seɲɲa'libro] *sm* (*anche INFORM*) bookmark.

segna'punti [seɲɲa'punti] *smf inv* scorer, scorekeeper.

se'gnare [seɲ'ɲare] *vt* to mark; (*prendere nota*) to note; (*indicare*) to indicate, mark; (*SPORT: goal*) to score; **~rsi** *vr* (*REL*) to make the sign of the cross, cross o.s.

'segno ['seɲɲo] *sm* sign; (*impronta, contrassegno*) mark; (*bersaglio*) target; **fare ~ di sì/no** to nod (one's head)/shake one's head; **fare ~ a qn di fermarsi** to motion (to) sb to stop; **cogliere** o **colpire nel ~** (*fig*) to hit the mark; **in** o **come ~ d'amicizia** as a mark o token of friendship; **"~i particolari"** (*su documento etc*) "distinguishing marks".

segre'gare *vt* to segregate, isolate.

segregazi'one [segregat'tsjone] *sf* segregation.

se'greta *sf vedi* **segreto.**

segre'tario, a *smf* secretary; **~ comunale** town clerk; **~ del partito** party leader; **S~ di Stato** Secretary of State.

segrete'ria *sf* (*di ditta, scuola*) (secretary's) office; (*d'organizzazione internazionale*) secretariat; (*POL etc: carica*) office of Secretary; **~ telefonica** answering service.

segre'tezza [segre'tettsa] *sf* secrecy; **notizie della massima ~** confidential information; **in tutta ~** in secret; (*confidenzialmente*) in confidence. ♦

se'greto, a *ag* secret ♦ *sm* secret ♦ *sf*

dungeon; **in** ~ in secret, secretly; **il** ~ **professionale** professional secrecy; **un** ~ **professionale** a professional secret.

segu'ace [se'gwatʃe] *sm/f* follower, disciple.

segu'ente *ag* following, next; **nel modo** ~ as follows, in the following way.

se'gugio [se'gudʒo] *sm* hound, hunting dog; (*fig*) private eye, sleuth.

segu'ire *vt* to follow; (*frequentare: corso*) to attend ♦ *vi* to follow; (*continuare: testo*) to continue; ~ **i consigli di qn** to follow o to take sb's advice; ~ **gli avvenimenti di attualità** to follow o keep up with current events; **come segue** as follows; **"segue"** "to be continued".

segui'tare *vt* to continue, carry on with ♦ *vi* to continue, carry on.

'seguito *sm* (*scorta*) suite, retinue; (*discepoli*) followers *pl*; (*serie*) sequence, series *sg*; (*continuazione*) continuation; (*conseguenza*) result; **di** ~ at a stretch, on end; **in** ~ later on; **in** ~ **a, a** ~ **di** following; (*a causa di*) as a result of, owing to; **essere al** ~ **di qn** to be among sb's suite, be one of sb's retinue; **non aver** ~ (*conseguenze*) to have no repercussions; **facciamo** ~ **alla lettera del** ... further to o in answer to your letter of ....

'sei *vb vedi* **essere** ♦ *num* six.

Sei'celle [sei'tʃɛlle] *sfpl*: **le** ~ the Seychelles.

seicen'tesco, a, schi, sche [seitʃen'tesko] *ag* seventeenth-century.

sei'cento [sei'tʃento] *num* six hundred ♦ *sm*: **il S**~ the seventeenth century.

sei'mila *num* six thousand.

'selce ['seltʃe] *sf* flint, flintstone.

selci'ato [sel'tʃato] *sm* cobbled surface.

selet'tivo, a *ag* selective.

selet'tore *sm* (*TECN*) selector.

selezio'nare [selettsjo'nare] *vt* to select.

selezi'one [selet'tsjone] *sf* selection; **fare una** ~ to make a selection o choice.

'sella *sf* saddle.

sel'lare *vt* to saddle.

sel'lino *sm* saddle.

seltz *sm inv* soda (water).

'selva *sf* (*bosco*) wood; (*foresta*) forest.

selvag'gina [selvad'dʒina] *sf* (*animali*) game.

sel'vaggio, a, gi, ge [sel'vaddʒo] *ag* wild; (*tribù*) savage, uncivilized; (*fig: brutale*) savage, brutal; (: *incontrollato: fenomeno, aumento etc*) uncontrolled ♦ *sm/f* savage; **inflazione** ~**a** runaway inflation.

sel'vatico, a, ci, che *ag* wild.

S.Em. *abbr* (= *Sua Eminenza*) HE.

se'maforo *sm* (*AUT*) traffic lights *pl*.

se'mantico, a *ag* semantic ♦ *sf* semantics *sg*.

sembi'anza [sem'bjantsa] *sf* (*poetico: aspetto*) appearance; ~**e** *sfpl* (*lineamenti*) features; (*fig: falsa apparenza*) semblance *sg*.

sem'brare *vi* to seem ♦ *vb impers*: **sembra che** it seems that; **mi sembra che** it seems to me that; (*penso che*) I think (that); ~ **di essere** to seem to be; **non mi sembra vero!** I can't believe it!

'seme *sm* seed; (*sperma*) semen; (*CARTE*) suit.

se'mente *sf* seed.

semes'trale *ag* (*che dura 6 mesi*) six-month *cpd*; (*che avviene ogni 6 mesi*) six-monthly.

se'mestre *sm* half-year, six-month period.

'semi ... *prefisso* semi ....

semi'cerchio [semi'tʃerkjo] *sm* semicircle.

semicondut'tore *sm* semiconductor.

semidetenzi'one [semideten'tsjone] *sf custodial sentence whereby individual must spend a minimum of 10 hours per day in prison.*

semifi'nale *sf* semifinal.

semi'freddo, a *ag* (*CUC*) chilled ♦ *sm* ice-cream cake.

semilibertà *sf custodial sentence which allows prisoner to study or work outside prison for part of the day.*

'semina *sf* (*AGR*) sowing.

semi'nare *vt* to sow.

semi'nario *sm* seminar; (*REL*) seminary.

semi'nato *sm*: **uscire dal** ~ (*fig*) to wander off the point.

seminter'rato *sm* basement; (*appartamento*) basement flat (*BRIT*) o apartment (*US*).

semi'ologo, a, gi, ghe *sm/f* semiologist.

semi'otica *sf* semiotics *sg*.

se'mitico, a, ci, che *ag* semitic.

semivu'oto, a *ag* half-empty.

sem'mai = **se mai**.

'semola *sf* bran; ~ **di grano duro** durum wheat.

semo'lato *ag*: **zucchero** ~ caster sugar.

semo'lino *sm* semolina.

'semplice ['semplitʃe] *ag* simple; (*di un solo elemento*) single; **è una** ~ **formalità** it's a mere formality.

semplice'mente [semplitʃe'mente] *av* simply.

sempli'cistico, a, ci, che [sempli'tʃistiko] *ag* simplistic.

semplicità [semplitʃi'ta] *sf* simplicity.

semplifi'care *vt* to simplify.
semplificazi'one [semplifikat'tsjone] *sf* simplification; **fare una ~ di** to simplify.
'sempre *av* always; (*ancora*) still; **posso ~ tentare** I can always *o* still try; **da ~** always; **per ~** forever; **una volta per ~** once and for all; **~ che** *cong* as long as, provided (that); **~ più** more and more; **~ meno** less and less; **va ~ meglio** things are getting better and better; **è ~ più giovane** she gets younger and younger; **è ~ meglio che niente** it's better than nothing; **è (pur) ~ tuo fratello** he is still your brother (however); **c'è ~ la possibilità che ...** there's still a chance that ..., there's always the possibility that ....
sempre'verde *ag, sm o f* (*BOT*) evergreen.
Sen. *abbr* (= *senatore*) Sen.
'senape *sf* (*CUC*) mustard.
se'nato *sm* senate; **il S~** *vedi nota nel riquadro*.

SENATO

The **Senato** *is the upper house of the Italian Parliament, with similar functions to the "Camera dei deputati". Candidates must be at least 40 years of age and electors must be 25 or over. Elections are held every five years. Former heads of state become senators for life, as do five distinguished members of the public who are chosen by the head of state for their scientific, social, artistic or literary achievements. The Chamber is presided over by the "Presidente del Senato", who is elected by the senators.*

---

sena'tore, 'trice *sm/f* senator.
'Senegal *sm*: **il ~** Senegal.
senega'lese *ag, sm/f* Senegalese *inv*.
se'nese *ag* of (*o* from) Siena.
se'nile *ag* senile.
'Senna *sf*: **la ~** the Seine.
'senno *sm* judgment, (common) sense; **col ~ di poi** with hindsight.
sennò *av* = **se no**.
'seno *sm* (*ANAT*: *petto, mammella*) breast; (: *grembo, fig*) womb; (: *cavità*) sinus; (*GEO*) inlet, creek; (*MAT*) sine; **in ~ al partito** within the party.
sen'sale *sm* (*COMM*) agent.
sensa'tezza [sensa'tettsa] *sf* good sense, good judgment.
sen'sato, a *ag* sensible.
sensazio'nale [sensattsjo'nale] *ag* sensational.
sensazi'one [sensat'tsjone] *sf* feeling,

sensation; **fare ~** to cause a sensation, create a stir; **avere la ~ che** to have a feeling that.
sen'sibile *ag* sensitive; (*ai sensi*) perceptible; (*rilevante, notevole*) appreciable, noticeable; **~ a** sensitive to.
sensibilità *sf* sensitivity.
sensibiliz'zare [sensibilid'dzare] *vt* (*fig*) to make aware, awaken.
'senso *sm* (*FISIOL, istinto*) sense; (*impressione, sensazione*) feeling, sensation; (*significato*) meaning, sense; (*direzione*) direction; **~i** *smpl* (*coscienza*) consciousness *sg*; (*sensualità*) senses; **perdere/riprendere i ~i** to lose/regain consciousness; **avere ~ pratico** to be practical; **avere un sesto ~** to have a sixth sense; **fare ~ a** (*ripugnare*) to disgust, repel; **ciò non ha ~** that doesn't make sense; **senza o privo di ~** meaningless; **nel ~ che** in the sense that; **nel vero ~ della parola** in the true sense of the word; **nel ~ della lunghezza** lengthwise, lengthways; **nel ~ della larghezza** widthwise; **ho dato disposizioni in quel ~** I've given instructions to that end *o* effect; **~ comune** common sense; **~ del dovere** sense of duty; **in ~ opposto** in the opposite direction; **in ~ orario/antiorario** clockwise/anticlockwise; **~ dell'umorismo** sense of humour; **a ~ unico** one-way.
sensu'ale *ag* sensual; sensuous.
sensualità *sf* sensuality; sensuousness.
sen'tenza [sen'tεntsa] *sf* (*DIR*) sentence; (*massima*) maxim.
sentenzi'are [senten'tsjare] *vi* (*DIR*) to pass judgment.
senti'ero *sm* path.
sentimen'tale *ag* sentimental; (*vita, avventura*) love *cpd*.
senti'mento *sm* feeling.
senti'nella *sf* sentry.
sen'tire *vt* (*percepire al tatto, fig*) to feel; (*udire*) to hear; (*ascoltare*) to listen to; (*odore*) to smell; (*avvertire con il gusto, assaggiare*) to taste ♦ *vi*: **~ di** (*avere sapore*) to taste of; (*avere odore*) to smell of; **~rsi** *vr* (*uso reciproco*) to be in touch; **~rsi bene/male** to feel well/unwell *o* ill; **~rsi di fare qc** (*essere disposto*) to feel like doing sth; **~ la mancanza di qn** to miss sb; **ho sentito dire che ...** I have heard that ...; **a ~ lui ...** to hear him talk ...; **fatti ~** keep in touch; **intendo ~ il mio legale** I'm going to consult my lawyer.
sentita'mente *av* sincerely; **ringraziare ~** to thank sincerely.

sen'tito, a *ag* (*sincero*) sincere, warm; **per** ~ **dire** by hearsay.

sen'tore *sm* rumour (*BRIT*), rumor (*US*), talk; **aver** ~ **di qc** to hear about sth.

'senza ['sɛntsa] *prep, cong* without; ~ **dir nulla** without saying a word; ~ **dire che** ... not to mention the fact that ...; ~ **contare che** ... without considering that ...; **fare** ~ **qc** to do without sth; ~ **di me** without me; ~ **che io lo sapessi** without my knowing; ~ **amici** friendless; **senz'altro** of course, certainly; ~ **dubbio** no doubt; ~ **scrupoli** unscrupulous; **i** ~ **lavoro** the jobless, the unemployed.

senza'tetto [sentsa'tetto] *sm/f inv* homeless person; **i** ~ the homeless.

sepa'rare *vt* to separate; (*dividere*) to divide; (*tenere distinto*) to distinguish; **~rsi** *vr* (*coniugi*) to separate, part; (*amici*) to part; **~rsi da** (*coniuge*) to separate *o* part from; (*amico, socio*) to part company with; (*oggetto*) to part with.

separata'mente *av* separately.

sepa'rato, a *ag* (*letti, conto etc*) separate; (*coniugi*) separated.

separazi'one [separat'tsjone] *sf* separation; ~ **dei beni** division of property.

séparé [sepa're] *sm inv* screen.

se'polcro *sm* sepulchre (*BRIT*), sepulcher (*US*).

se'polto, a *pp di* **seppellire**.

sepol'tura *sf* burial; **dare** ~ **a qn** to bury sb.

seppel'lire *vt* to bury.

'seppi *etc vb vedi* **sapere**.

'seppia *sf* cuttlefish ♦ *ag inv* sepia.

sep'pure *cong* even if.

se'quela *sf* (*di avvenimenti*) series, sequence; (*di offese, ingiurie*) string.

se'quenza [se'kwentsa] *sf* sequence.

sequenzi'ale [sekwen'tsjale] *ag* sequential.

seques'trare *vt* (*DIR*) to impound; (*rapire*) to kidnap; (*costringere in un luogo*) to keep, confine.

se'questro *sm* (*DIR*) impoundment; ~ **di persona** kidnapping.

se'quoia *sf* sequoia.

'sera *sf* evening; **di** ~ in the evening; **domani** ~ tomorrow evening, tomorrow night; **questa** ~ this evening, tonight.

se'rale *ag* evening *cpd*; **scuola** ~ evening classes *pl*, night school.

se'rata *sf* evening; (*ricevimento*) party.

ser'bare *vt* to keep; (*mettere da parte*) to put aside; ~ **rancore/odio verso qn** to bear sb a grudge/hate sb.

serba'toio *sm* tank; (*cisterna*) cistern.

'serbo *ag* Serbian ♦ *sm/f* Serbian, Serb ♦ *sm*

(*LING*) Serbian; (*il serbare*): **mettere/tenere** *o* **avere in** ~ **qc** to put/keep sth aside.

serbocro'ato, a *ag, sm* Serbo-Croat.

serena'mente *av* serenely, calmly.

sere'nata *sf* (*MUS*) serenade.

serenità *sf* serenity.

se'reno, a *ag* (*tempo, cielo*) clear; (*fig*) serene, calm ♦ *sm* (*tempo*) good weather; **un fulmine a ciel** ~ (*fig*) a bolt from the blue.

serg. *abbr* (= *sergente*) Sgt.

ser'gente [ser'dʒɛnte] *sm* (*MIL*) sergeant.

seri'ale *ag* (*INFORM*) serial.

seria'mente *av* (*con serietà, in modo grave*) seriously; **lavorare** ~ to take one's job seriously.

'serie *sf inv* (*successione*) series *inv*; (*gruppo, collezione: di chiavi etc*) set; (*SPORT*) division; league; (*COMM*): **modello di** ~/ **fuori** ~ standard/custom-built model; **in** ~ in quick succession; (*COMM*) mass *cpd*; **tutta una** ~ **di problemi** a whole string *o* series of problems.

serietà *sf* seriousness; reliability.

'serio, a *ag* serious; (*impiegato*) responsible, reliable; (*ditta, cliente*) reliable, dependable; **sul** ~ (*davvero*) really, truly; (*seriamente*) seriously, in earnest; **dico sul** ~ I'm serious; **faccio sul** ~ I mean it; **prendere qc/qn sul** ~ to take sth/sb seriously.

seri'oso, a *ag* (*persona, modi*): **un po'** ~ a bit too serious.

ser'mone *sm* sermon.

'serpe *sf* snake; (*fig peg*) viper.

serpeggi'are [serped'dʒare] *vi* to wind; (*fig*) to spread.

ser'pente *sm* snake; ~ **a sonagli** rattlesnake.

'serra *sf* greenhouse; hothouse; (*GEO*) sierra.

serra'manico *sm*: **coltello a** ~ jack-knife.

ser'randa *sf* roller shutter.

ser'rare *vt* to close, shut; (*a chiave*) to lock; (*stringere*) to tighten; (*premere: nemico*) to close in on; ~ **i pugni/i denti** to clench one's fists/teeth; ~ **le file** to close ranks.

ser'rata *sf* (*INDUSTRIA*) lockout.

ser'rato, a *ag* (*veloce*): **a ritmo** ~ quickly, fast.

serra'tura *sf* lock.

'serva *sf vedi* **servo**.

'server ['server] *sm inv* (*INFORM*) server.

ser'vigio [ser'vidʒo] *sm* favour (*BRIT*), favor (*US*), service.

ser'vire *vt* to serve; (*clienti: al ristorante*) to wait on; (*: al negozio*) to serve, attend to; (*fig: giovare*) to aid, help; (*CARTE*) to deal

♦ *vi* (*TENNIS*) to serve; (*essere utile*): ~ **a qn** to be of use to sb; ~ **a qc/a fare** (*utensile etc*) to be used for sth/for doing; ~ **(a qn) da** to serve as (for sb); ~**rsi** *vr* (*usare*): ~**rsi di** to use; (*prendere: cibo*): ~**rsi (di)** to help o.s. (to); (*essere cliente abituale*): ~**rsi da** to be a regular customer at, go to; **non mi serve più** I don't need it any more; **non serve che lei vada** you don't need to go.

servitù *sf* servitude; slavery; (*personale di servizio*) servants *pl*, domestic staff.

servizi'evole [servit'tsjevole] *ag* obliging, willing to help.

ser'vizio [ser'vittsjo] *sm* service; (*al ristorante: sul conto*) service (charge); (*STAMPA, TV, RADIO*) report; (*da tè, caffè etc*) set, service; ~**i** *smpl* (*di casa*) kitchen and bathroom; (*ECON*) services; **essere di** ~ to be on duty; **fuori** ~ (*telefono etc*) out of order; ~ **compreso/escluso** service included/not included; **entrata di** ~ service *o* tradesman's (*BRIT*) entrance; **casa con doppi** ~**i** house with two bathrooms; ~ **assistenza clienti** after-sales service; ~ **civile** ≈ community service; ~ **in diretta** (*TV, RADIO*) live coverage; ~ **fotografico** (*STAMPA*) photo feature; ~ **militare** military service; ~ **d'ordine** (*POLIZIA*) police patrol; (*di manifestanti*) team of stewards (*responsible for crowd control*); ~**i segreti** secret service *sg*; ~**i di sicurezza** security forces.

'servo, a *sm/f* servant.

servo'freno *sm* (*AUT*) servo brake.

servos'terzo [servos'tɛrtso] *sm* (*AUT*) power steering.

'sesamo *sm* (*BOT*) sesame.

ses'santa *num* sixty.

sessan'tenne *ag, sm/f* sixty-year-old.

sessan'tesimo, a *num* sixtieth.

sessan'tina *sf*: **una** ~ **(di)** about sixty.

sessantot'tino, a *sm/f* a person who took part in the events of 1968.

sessan'totto *sm vedi nota nel riquadro*.

sessi'one *sf* session.

'sesso *sm* sex; **il** ~ **debole/forte** the weaker/stronger sex.

sessu'ale *ag* sexual, sex *cpd*.

sessualità *sf* sexuality.

sessu'ologo, a, gi, ghe *sm/f* sexologist, sex specialist.

ses'tante *sm* sextant.

'sesto, a *num* sixth ♦ *sm*: **rimettere in** ~ (*aggiustare*) to put back in order; (*fig: persona*) to put back on his (*o* her) feet; **rimettersi in** ~ (*riprendersi*) to recover, get well; (*riassettarsi*) to tidy o.s. up.

'seta *sf* silk.

setacci'are [setat'tʃare] *vt* (*farina etc*) to sift, sieve; (*fig: zona*) to search, comb.

se'taccio [se'tattʃo] *sm* sieve; **passare al** ~ (*fig*) to search, comb.

'sete *sf* thirst; **avere** ~ to be thirsty; ~ **di potere** thirst for power.

seti'ficio [seti'fitʃo] *sm* silk factory.

'setola *sf* bristle.

sett. *abbr* (= *settembre*) Sept.

'setta *sf* sect.

set'tanta *num* seventy.

settan'tenne *ag, sm/f* seventy-year-old.

settan'tesimo, a *num* seventieth.

settan'tina *sf*: **una** ~ **(di)** about seventy.

'sette *num* seven.

settecen'tesco, a, schi, sche [settetʃen'tesko] *ag* eighteenth-century.

sette'cento [sette'tʃɛnto] *num* seven hundred ♦ *sm*: **il S**~ the eighteenth century.

set'tembre *sm* September; *per fraseologia vedi* **luglio**.

sette'mila *num* seven thousand.

settentrio'nale *ag* northern ♦ *sm/f* northerner.

settentri'one *sm* north.

'settico, a, ci, che *ag* (*MED*) septic.

setti'mana *sf* week; **la** ~ **scorsa/prossima** last/next week; **a metà** ~ in the middle of the week; ~ **bianca** winter-sports holiday.

settima'nale *ag, sm* weekly.

'settimo, a *num* seventh.

set'tore *sm* sector; ~ **privato/pubblico** private/public sector; ~ **terziario** service industries *pl*.

Se'ul *sf* Seoul.

severità *sf* severity.

se'vero, a *ag* severe.

sevizi'are [sevit'tsjare] *vt* to torture.

se'vizie [se'vittsje] *sfpl* torture *sg*.

'sexy ['seksi] *ag inv* sexy.

sez. *abbr* = **sezione**.

sezio'nare [settsjo'nare] *vt* to divide into sections; (*MED*) to dissect.

sezi'one [set'tsjone] *sf* section; (*MED*) dissection.

sfaccen'dato, a [sfattʃen'dato] *ag* idle.

sfaccetta'tura [sfattʃetta'tura] *sf* (*azione*) faceting; (*parte sfaccettata, fig*) facet.

sfacchi'nare [sfakki'nare] *vi* (*fam*) to toil, drudge.

sfacchi'nata [sfakki'nata] *sf* (*fam*) chore, drudgery *no pl*.

sfaccia'taggine [sfattʃa'taddʒine] *sf* insolence, cheek.

sfacci'ato, a [sfat't ʃato] *ag* (*maleducato*) cheeky, impudent; (*vistoso*) gaudy.

sfa'celo [sfa't ʃɛlo] *sm* (*fig*) ruin, collapse.

sfal'darsi *vr* to flake (off).

sfal'sare *vt* to offset.

sfa'mare *vt* (*nutrire*) to feed; (*soddisfare la fame*): ~ **qn** to satisfy sb's hunger; ~**rsi** *vr* to satisfy one's hunger, fill o.s. up.

sfarfal'lio *sm* (*CINE, TV*) flickering.

'sfarzo ['sfartso] *sm* pomp, splendour (*BRIT*), splendor (*US*).

sfar'zoso, a [sfar'tsoso] *ag* splendid, magnificent.

sfasa'mento *sm* (*ELETTR*) phase displacement; (*fig*) confusion, bewilderment.

sfa'sato, a *ag* (*ELETTR, motore*) out of phase; (*fig: persona*) confused, bewildered.

sfasci'are [sfaʃ'ʃare] *vt* (*ferita*) to unbandage; (*distruggere: porta*) to smash, shatter; ~**rsi** *vr* (*rompersi*) to smash, shatter.

sfa'tare *vt* (*leggenda*) to explode.

sfati'cato, a *sm/f* idler, loafer.

'sfatto, a *ag* (*letto*) unmade; (*orlo etc*) undone; (*gelato, neve*) melted; (*frutta*) overripe; (*riso, pasta etc*) overdone, overcooked; (*fam: persona, corpo*) flabby.

sfavil'lare *vi* to spark, send out sparks; (*risplendere*) to sparkle.

sfa'vore *sm* disfavour (*BRIT*), disfavor (*US*), disapproval.

sfavo'revole *ag* unfavourable (*BRIT*), unfavorable (*US*).

sfega'tato, a *ag* fanatical.

'sfera *sf* sphere.

'sferico, a, ci, che *ag* spherical.

sfer'rare *vt* (*fig: colpo*) to land, deal; (: *attacco*) to launch.

sfer'zante [sfer'tsante] *ag* (*critiche, parole*) stinging.

sfer'zare [sfer'tsare] *vt* to whip; (*fig*) to lash out at.

sfian'care *vt* to wear out, exhaust; ~**rsi** *vr*

to exhaust o.s., wear o.s. out.

sfia'tare *vi* to allow air (*o gas etc*) to escape.

sfiata'toio *sm* blowhole; (*TECN*) vent.

sfi'brante *ag* exhausting, energy-sapping.

sfi'brare *vt* (*indebolire*) to exhaust, enervate.

sfi'brato, a *ag* exhausted, worn out.

'sfida *sf* challenge.

sfi'dante *ag* challenging ◊ *sm/f* challenger.

sfi'dare *vt* to challenge; (*fig*) to defy, brave; ~ **qn a fare qc** to challenge sb to do sth; ~ **un pericolo** to brave a danger; **sfido che** ... I dare say (that) ....

sfi'ducia [sfi'dutʃa] *sf* distrust, mistrust; **avere** ~ **in qn/qc** to distrust sb/sth.

sfiduci'ato, a [sfidu'tʃato] *ag* lacking confidence.

sfi'gato, a (*fam*) *ag*: **essere** ~ (*sfortunato*) to be unlucky ◊ *sm/f* (*fallito, sfortunato*) loser; (*fuori moda*) dork.

sfigu'rare *vt* (*persona*) to disfigure; (*quadro, statua*) to deface ◊ *vi* (*far cattiva figura*) to make a bad impression.

sfilacci'are [sfilat'tʃare] *vt, vi*, ~**rsi** *vr* to fray.

sfi'lare *vt* (*ago*) to unthread; (*abito, scarpe*) to slip off ◊ *vi* (*truppe*) to march past, parade; (*manifestanti*) to march; ~**rsi** *vr* (*perle etc*) to come unstrung; (*orlo, tessuto*) to fray; (*calza*) to run, ladder.

sfi'lata *sf* (*MIL*) parade; (*di manifestanti*) march; ~ **di moda** fashion show.

'sfilza ['sfiltsa] *sf* (*di case*) row; (*di errori*) series *inv*.

'sfinge ['sfindʒe] *sf* sphinx.

sfini'mento *sm* exhaustion.

sfi'nito, a *ag* exhausted.

sfio'rare *vt* to brush (against); (*argomento*) to touch upon; ~ **la velocità di 150 km/h** to touch 150 km/h.

sfio'rire *vi* to wither, fade.

'sfitto, a *ag* vacant, empty.

sfo'cato, a *ag* (*FOT*) out of focus.

sfoci'are [sfo'tʃare] *vi*: ~ **in** to flow into; (*fig: malcontento*) to develop into.

sfode'rato, a *ag* (*vestito*) unlined.

sfo'gare *vt* to vent, pour out; ~**rsi** *vr* (*sfogare la propria rabbia*) to give vent to one's anger; (*confidarsi*): ~**rsi (con)** to pour out one's feelings (to); **non sfogarti su di me!** don't take your bad temper out on me!

sfoggi'are [sfod'dʒare] *vt, vi* to show off.

'sfoggio ['sfɔddʒo] *sm* show, display; **fare** ~ **di** to show off, display.

sfoghe'rò etc [sfoge'rɔ] *vb vedi* **sfogare**.

'sfoglia ['sfɔʎʎa] *sf* sheet of pasta dough;

pasta ~ (*CUC*) puff pastry.

sfogli'are [sfoʎ'ʎare] *vt* (*libro*) to leaf through.

'**sfogo, ghi** *sm* outlet; (*eruzione cutanea*) rash; (*fig*) outburst; **dare ~ a** (*fig*) to give vent to.

sfolgo'rante *ag* (*luce*) blazing; (*fig: vittoria*) brilliant.

sfolgo'rare *vi* to blaze.

sfolla'gente [sfolla'dʒɛnte] *sm inv* truncheon (*BRIT*), billy (*US*).

sfol'lare *vt* to empty, clear ♦ *vi* to disperse; ~ **da** (*città*) to evacuate.

sfol'lato, a *ag* evacuated ♦ *sm/f* evacuee.

sfol'tire *vt*, ~**rsi** *vr* to thin (out).

sfon'dare *vt* (*porta*) to break down; (*scarpe*) to wear a hole in; (*cesto, scatola*) to burst, knock the bottom out of; (*MIL*) to break through ♦ *vi* (*riuscire*) to make a name for o.s.

sfon'dato, a *ag* (*scarpe*) worn out; (*scatola*) burst; (*sedia*) broken, damaged; **essere ricco ~** to be rolling in it.

'**sfondo** *sm* background.

sfo'rare *vi* to overrun.

sfor'mare *vt* to put out of shape, knock out of shape; ~**rsi** *vr* to lose shape, get out of shape.

sfor'mato, a *ag* (*che ha perso forma*) shapeless ♦ *sm* (*CUC*) type of soufflé.

sfor'nare *vt* (*pane*) to take out of the oven; (*fig*) to churn out.

sfor'nito, a *ag*: ~ **di** lacking in, without; (*negozio*) out of.

sfor'tuna *sf* misfortune, ill luck *no pl*; **avere ~** to be unlucky; **che ~!** how unfortunate!

sfortu'nato, a *ag* unlucky; (*impresa, film*) unsuccessful.

sfor'zare [sfor'tsare] *vt* to force; (*voce, occhi*) to strain; ~**rsi** *vr*: ~**rsi di** *o* **a** *o* **per fare** to try hard to do.

'**sforzo** ['sfɔrtso] *sm* effort; (*tensione eccessiva, TECN*) strain; **fare uno ~** to make an effort; **essere sotto ~** (*motore, macchina, fig: persona*) to be under stress.

'**sfottere** *vt* (*fam*) to tease.

sfracel'lare [sfratʃel'lare] *vt*, ~**rsi** *vr* to smash.

sfrat'tare *vt* to evict.

'**sfratto** *sm* eviction; **dare lo ~ a qn** to give sb notice to quit.

sfrecci'are [sfret'tʃare] *vi* to shoot *o* flash past.

sfre'gare *vt* (*strofinare*) to rub; (*graffiare*) to scratch; ~**rsi le mani** to rub one's hands; ~ **un fiammifero** to strike a match.

sfregi'are [sfre'dʒare] *vt* to slash, gash; (*persona*) to disfigure; (*quadro*) to deface.

'**sfregio** ['sfredʒo] *sm* gash; scar; (*fig*) insult.

sfre'nato, a *ag* (*fig*) unrestrained, unbridled.

sfron'dare *vt* (*albero*) to prune, thin out; (*fig: discorso, scritto*) to prune (down).

sfronta'tezza [sfronta'tettsa] *sf* impudence, cheek.

sfron'tato, a *ag* impudent, cheeky.

sfrutta'mento *sm* exploitation.

sfrut'tare *vt* (*terreno*) to overwork, exhaust; (*miniera*) to exploit, work; (*fig: operai, occasione, potere*) to exploit.

sfrutta'tore, 'trice *sm/f* exploiter.

sfug'gente [sfud'dʒɛnte] *ag* (*fig: sguardo*) elusive; (*mento*) receding.

sfug'gire [sfud'dʒire] *vi* to escape; ~ **a** (*custode*) to escape (from); (*morte*) to escape; ~ **a qn** (*dettaglio, nome*) to escape sb; ~ **di mano a qn** to slip out of sb's hand (*o* hands); **lasciarsi ~ un'occasione** to let an opportunity go by; ~ **al controllo** (*macchina*) to go out of control; (*situazione*) to be no longer under control.

sfug'gita [sfud'dʒita] *sf*: **di ~** (*rapidamente, in fretta*) in passing.

sfu'mare *vt* (*colori, contorni*) to soften, shade off ♦ *vi* to shade (off), fade; (*fig: svanire*) to vanish, disappear; (: *speranze*) to come to nothing.

sfuma'tura *sf* shading off *no pl*; (*tonalità*) shade, tone; (*fig*) touch, hint.

sfuo'cato, a *ag* = **sfocato**.

sfuri'ata *sf* (*scatto di collera*) fit of anger; (*rimprovero*) sharp rebuke.

'**sfuso, a** *ag* (*caramelle etc*) loose, unpacked; (*vino*) unbottled; (*birra*) draught (*BRIT*), draft (*US*).

sg. *abbr* = **seguente**.

sga'bello *sm* stool.

sgabuz'zino [zgabud'dzino] *sm* lumber room.

sgambet'tare *vi* to kick one's legs about.

sgam'betto *sm*: **far lo ~ a qn** to trip sb up; (*fig*) to oust sb.

sganasci'arsi [zganaʃ'ʃarsi] *vr*: ~ **dalle risa** to roar with laughter.

sganci'are [zgan'tʃare] *vt* to unhook; (*chiusura*) to unfasten, undo; (*FERR*) to uncouple; (*bombe: da aereo*) to release, drop; (*fig: fam: soldi*) to fork out; ~**rsi** *vr* to come unhooked; to come unfastened, come undone; to uncouple; (*fig*): ~**rsi (da)** to get away (from).

sganghe'rato, a [zgange'rato] *ag* (*porta*) off its hinges; (*auto*) ramshackle; (*riso*) wild, boisterous.

sgar'bato, a *ag* rude, impolite.

'sgarbo *sm*: **fare uno ~ a qn** to be rude to sb.

sgargi'ante [zgar'dʒante] *ag* gaudy, showy.

sgar'rare *vi* (*persona*) to step out of line; (*orologio*: *essere avanti*) to gain; (: *essere indietro*) to lose.

'sgarro *sm* inaccuracy.

sgattaio'lare *vi* to sneak away *o* off.

sge'lare [zdʒe'lare] *vi*, *vt* to thaw.

'sghembo, a ['zgembo] *ag* (*obliquo*) slanting; (*storto*) crooked.

sghignaz'zare [zgiɲɲat'tsare] *vi* to laugh scornfully.

sghignaz'zata [zgiɲɲat'tsata] *sf* scornful laugh.

sgob'bare *vi* (*fam: scolaro*) to swot; (: *operaio*) to slog.

sgoccio'lare [zgottʃo'lare] *vt* (*vuotare*) to drain (to the last drop) ♦ *vi* (*acqua*) to drip; (*recipiente*) to drain.

'sgoccioli ['zgottʃoli] *smpl*: **essere agli ~** (*lavoro, provviste etc*) to be nearly finished; (*periodo*) to be nearly over; **siamo agli ~** we've nearly finished, the end is in sight.

sgo'larsi *vr* to talk (*o* shout *o* sing) o.s. hoarse.

sgomb(e)'rare *vt* to clear; (*andarsene da: stanza*) to vacate; (*evacuare*) to evacuate.

'sgombero *sm vedi* **sgombro**.

'sgombro, a *ag*: **~ (di)** clear (of), free (from) ♦ *sm* (*ZOOL*) mackerel; (*anche*: **sgombero**) clearing; vacating; evacuation; (: *trasloco*) removal.

sgomen'tare *vt* to dismay; **~rsi** *vr* to be dismayed.

sgo'mento, a *ag* dismayed ♦ *sm* dismay, consternation.

sgomi'nare *vt* (*nemico*) to rout; (*avversario*) to defeat; (*fig: epidemia*) to overcome.

sgonfi'are *vt* to let down, deflate; **~rsi** *vr* to go down.

'sgonfio, a *ag* (*pneumatico, pallone*) flat.

'sgorbio *sm* blot; scribble.

sgor'gare *vi* to gush (out).

sgoz'zare [zgot'tsare] *vt* to cut the throat of.

sgra'devole *ag* unpleasant, disagreeable.

sgra'dito, a *ag* unpleasant, unwelcome.

sgraffi'gnare [zgraffiɲ'ɲare] *vt* (*fam*) to pinch, swipe.

sgrammati'cato, a *ag* ungrammatical.

sgra'nare *vt* (*piselli*) to shell; **~ gli occhi** to open one's eyes wide.

sgran'chirsi [zgran'kirsi] *vr* to stretch; **~ le gambe** to stretch one's legs.

sgranocchi'are [zgranok'kjare] *vt* to munch.

sgras'sare *vt* to remove the grease from.

'sgravio *sm*: **~ fiscale** *o* **contributivo** tax relief.

sgrazi'ato, a [zgrat'tsjato] *ag* clumsy, ungainly.

sgreto'lare *vt* to cause to crumble; **~rsi** *vr* to crumble.

sgri'dare *vt* to scold.

sgri'data *sf* scolding.

sguai'ato, a *ag* coarse, vulgar.

sguai'nare *vt* to draw, unsheathe.

sgual'cire [zgwal'tʃire] *vt* to crumple (up), crease.

sgual'drina *sf* (*peg*) slut.

sgu'ardo *sm* (*occhiata*) look, glance; (*espressione*) look (in one's eye); **dare uno ~ a qc** to glance at sth, cast a glance *o* an eye over sth; **alzare** *o* **sollevare lo ~** to raise one's eyes, look up; **cercare qc/qn con lo ~** to look (a)round for sth/sb.

'sguattero, a *sm/f* scullery boy/maid.

sguaz'zare [zgwat'tsare] *vi* (*nell'acqua*) to splash about; (*nella melma*) to wallow; **~ nell'oro** to be rolling in money.

sguinzagli'are [zgwintsaʎ'ʎare] *vt* to let off the leash; (*fig: persona*): **~ qn dietro a qn** to set sb on sb.

sgusci'are [zguʃ'ʃare] *vt* to shell ♦ *vi* (*sfuggire di mano*) to slip; **~ via** to slip *o* slink away.

'shaker ['ʃeikə*] *sm inv* (*cocktail*) shaker.

'shampoo ['ʃampo] *sm inv* shampoo.

'shiatzu ['tʃiatsu] *sm, ag inv* shiatsu.

shoc'care [ʃok'kare] *vt* = **shockare**.

shock [ʃɔk] *sm inv* shock.

shoc'kare [ʃok'kare] *vt* to shock.

SI *sigla* = *Siena*.

═══════════════════════ **PAROLA CHIAVE**

si (*dav* **lo, la, li, le, ne** *diventa* **se**) *pron* **1** (*riflessivo: maschile*) himself; (: *femminile*) herself; (: *neutro*) itself; (: *impersonale*) oneself; (: *pl*) themselves; **lavarsi** to wash (oneself); **~ è tagliato** he has cut himself; **~ credono importanti** they think a lot of themselves

2 (*con complemento oggetto*): **lavarsi le mani** to wash one's hands; **sporcarsi i pantaloni** to get one's trousers dirty; **~ sta lavando i capelli** he (*o* she) is washing his (*o* her) hair

3 (*reciproco*) one another, each other; **si amano** they love one another *o* each other

4 (*passivo*): **~ ripara facilmente** it is easily repaired; **affittasi camera** room to let

5 (*impersonale*): **~ dice che ...** they *o* people say that ...; **~ vede che è vecchio** one *o* you can see that it's old; **non ~ fa**

credito we do not give credit; **ci ~ sbaglia facilmente** it's easy to make a mistake **6** (*noi*) we; **tra poco ~ parte** we're leaving soon.

sì *av* yes ♦ *sm*: **non mi aspettavo un ~** I didn't expect him (*o* her *etc*) to say yes; **per me è ~** I should think so, I expect so; **saranno stati ~ e no in 20** there must have been about 20 of them; **uno ~ e uno no** every other one; **un giorno ~ e uno no** every other day; **dire di ~** to say yes; **spero/penso di ~** I hope/think so; **fece di ~ col capo** he nodded (his head); **e ~ che ... and to think that ....**

'**sia** *cong*: **~ ... ~** (*o* ... *o*): **~ che lavori, ~ che non lavori** whether he works or not; (*tanto ... quanto*): **verranno ~ Luigi ~ suo fratello** both Luigi and his brother will be coming.

'**sia** *etc vb vedi* **essere**.

SIAE *sigla f* = *Società Italiana Autori ed Editori*.

Si'am *sm*: **il ~** Siam.

sia'mese *ag, sm/f* siamese *inv*.

si'amo *vb vedi* **essere**.

Si'beria *sf*: **la ~** Siberia.

siberi'ano, a *ag, sm/f* Siberian.

sibi'lare *vi* to hiss; (*fischiare*) to whistle.

'**sibilo** *sm* hiss; whistle.

si'cario *sm* hired killer.

sicché [sik'ke] *cong* (*perciò*) so (that), therefore; (*e quindi*) (and) so.

siccità [sittʃi'ta] *sf* drought.

sic'come *cong* since, as.

Si'cilia [si'tʃilja] *sf*: **la ~** Sicily.

sicili'ano, a [sitʃi'ljano] *ag, sm/f* Sicilian.

sico'moro *sm* sycamore.

'**siculo, a** *ag, sm/f* Sicilian.

si'cura *sf* (*di arma, spilla*) safety catch; (*di portiera*) safety lock.

sicura'mente *av* certainly.

sicu'rezza [siku'rettsa] *sf* safety; security; confidence; certainty; **di ~** safety *cpd*; **la ~ stradale** road safety; **avere la ~ di qc** to be sure *o* certain of sth; **lo so con ~** I am quite certain; **ha risposto con molta ~** he answered very confidently.

si'curo, a *ag* safe; (*ben difeso*) secure; (*fiducioso*) confident; (*certo*) sure, certain; (*notizia, amico*) reliable; (*esperto*) skilled ♦ *av* (*anche*: **di ~**) certainly ♦ *sm*: **andare sul ~** to play safe; **essere/mettere al ~** to be safe/put in a safe place; **~ di sé** self-confident, sure of o.s.; **sentirsi ~** to feel safe *o* secure; **essere ~ di/che** to be sure of/that; **da fonte ~a** from reliable sources.

siderur'gia [siderur'dʒia] *sf* iron and steel industry.

side'rurgico, a, ci, che [side'rurdʒiko] *ag* iron and steel *cpd*.

'**sidro** *sm* cider.

si'edo *etc vb vedi* **sedere**.

si'epe *sf* hedge.

si'ero *sm* (*MED*) serum; **~ antivipera** snake bite serum; **~ del latte** whey.

sieronegatività *sf inv* HIV-negative status.

sieronega'tivo, a *ag* HIV-negative ♦ *sm/f* HIV-negative person.

sieropositività *sf inv* HIV-positive status.

sieroposi'tivo, a *ag* HIV-positive ♦ *sm/f* HIV-positive person.

si'erra *sf* (*GEO*) sierra.

Si'erra Le'one *sf*: **la ~** Sierra Leone.

si'esta *sf* siesta, (afternoon) nap.

si'ete *vb vedi* **essere**.

si'filide *sf* syphilis.

si'fone *sm* siphon.

Sig. *abbr* (= *signore*) Mr.

siga'retta *sf* cigarette.

'**sigaro** *sm* cigar.

Sigg. *abbr* (= *signori*) Messrs.

sigil'lare [sidʒil'lare] *vt* to seal.

si'gillo [si'dʒillo] *sm* seal.

'**sigla** *sf* (*iniziali*) initials *pl*; (*abbreviazione*) acronym, abbreviation; **~ automobilistica** *abbreviation of province on vehicle number plate*; **~ musicale** signature tune.

si'glare *vt* to initial.

Sig.na *abbr* (= *signorina*) Miss.

signifi'care [siɲɲifi'kare] *vt* to mean; **cosa significa?** what does this mean?

significa'tivo, a [siɲɲifika'tivo] *ag* significant.

signifi'cato [siɲɲifi'kato] *sm* meaning.

si'gnora [siɲ'ɲora] *sf* lady; **la ~ X** Mrs ['mɪsɪz] X; **buon giorno S~/Signore/Signorina** good morning; (*deferente*) good morning Madam/Sir/Madam; (*quando si conosce il nome*) good morning Mrs/Mr/Miss X; **Gentile S~/Signore/Signorina** (*in una lettera*) Dear Madam/Sir/Madam; **Gentile** (*o* **Cara**) **S~ Rossi** Dear Mrs Rossi; **Gentile S~ Anna Rossi** (*sulle buste*) Mrs Anna Rossi; **il signor Rossi e ~** Mr Rossi and his wife; **~e e signori** ladies and gentlemen; **le presento la mia ~** may I introduce my wife?

si'gnore [siɲ'ɲore] *sm* gentleman; (*padrone*) lord, master; (*REL*): **il S~** the Lord; **il signor X** Mr ['mɪstə*] X; **signor Presidente** Mr Chairman; **Gentile** (*o* **Caro**) **Signor Rossi** (*in lettere*) Dear Mr Rossi; **Gentile Signor Paolo Rossi** (*sulle buste*) Mr Paolo Rossi; **i ~i Bianchi** (*coniugi*) Mr and Mrs

Bianchi; *vedi anche* **signora.**

signo'ria [siɲɲo'ria] *sf* (*STORIA*) seignory, signoria; **S~ Vostra (S.V.)** (*AMM*) you.

signo'rile [siɲɲo'rile] *ag* refined.

signorilità [siɲɲorili'ta] *sf* (*raffinatezza*) refinement; (*eleganza*) elegance.

signo'rina [siɲɲo'rina] *sf* young lady; **la ~ X** Miss X; **Gentile** (*o* **Cara**) **S~ Rossi** (*in lettere*) Dear Miss Rossi; **Gentile S~ Anna Rossi** (*sulle buste*) Miss Anna Rossi; *vedi anche* **signora.**

signo'rino [siɲɲo'rino] *sm* young master.

Sig.ra *abbr* (= *signora*) Mrs.

silenzia'tore [silentsja'tore] *sm* silencer.

si'lenzio [si'lentsjo] *sm* silence; **fare ~** to be quiet, stop talking; **far passare qc sotto ~** to keep quiet about sth, hush sth up.

silenzi'oso, a [silen'tsjoso] *ag* silent, quiet.

'silice ['silitʃe] *sf* silica.

si'licio [si'litʃo] *sm* silicon; **piastrina di ~** silicon chip.

sili'cone *sm* silicone.

'sillaba *sf* syllable.

silu'rare *vt* to torpedo; (*fig: privare del comando*) to oust.

si'luro *sm* torpedo.

simbi'osi *sf* (*BIOL*, *fig*) symbiosis.

simboleggi'are [simboled'dʒare] *vt* to symbolize.

sim'bolico, a, ci, che *ag* symbolic(al).

simbo'lismo *sm* symbolism.

'simbolo *sm* symbol.

simi'lare *ag* similar.

'simile *ag* (*analogo*) similar; (*di questo tipo*): **un uomo ~** such a man, a man like this ♦ *sm* (*persona*) fellow man; **libri ~i** such books; **~ a** similar to; **non ho mai visto niente di ~** I've never seen anything like that; **è insegnante o qualcosa di ~** he's a teacher or something like that; **vendono vasi e ~i** they sell vases and things like that; **i suoi ~i** one's fellow men; one's peers.

simili'tudine *sf* (*LING*) simile.

simme'tria *sf* symmetry.

sim'metrico, a, ci, che *ag* symmetric(al).

simpa'tia *sf* (*qualità*) pleasantness; (*inclinazione*) liking; **avere ~ per qn** to like sb, have a liking for sb; **con ~** (*su lettera etc*) with much affection.

sim'patico, a, ci, che *ag* (*persona*) nice, pleasant, likeable; (*casa, albergo etc*) nice, pleasant.

simpatiz'zante [simpatid'dzante] *sm/f* sympathizer.

simpatiz'zare [simpatid'dzare] *vi:* **~ con** to take a liking to.

sim'posio *sm* symposium.

simu'lacro *sm* (*monumento*, *statua*) image; (*fig*) semblance.

simu'lare *vt* to sham, simulate; (*TECN*) to simulate.

simulazi'one [simulat'tsjone] *sf* shamming; simulation.

simul'taneo, a *ag* simultaneous.

sin. *abbr* (= *sinistra*) L.

sina'goga, ghe *sf* synagogue.

sincera'mente [sintʃera'mente] *av* (*gen*) sincerely; (*francamente*) honestly, sincerely.

since'rarsi [sintʃe'rarsi] *vr:* **~ (di qc)** to make sure (of sth).

sincerità [sintʃeri'ta] *sf* sincerity.

sin'cero, a [sin'tʃero] *ag* (*genuino*) sincere; (*onesto*) genuine.

'sincope *sf* syncopation; (*MED*) blackout.

sincro'nia *sf* (*di movimento*) synchronism.

sin'cronico, a, ci, che *ag* synchronic.

sincroniz'zare [sinkronid'dzare] *vt* to synchronize.

sinda'cale *ag* (trade-)union *cpd*.

sindaca'lista, i, e *sm/f* trade unionist.

sinda'care *vt* (*controllare*) to inspect; (*fig: criticare*) to criticize.

sinda'cato *sm* (*di lavoratori*) (trade) union; **~ dei datori di lavoro** employers' association.

'sindaco, ci *sm* mayor.

'sindrome *sf* (*MED*) syndrome.

siner'gia, gie [siner'dʒia] *sf* (*anche fig*) synergy.

sinfo'nia *sf* (*MUS*) symphony.

sin'fonico, a, ci, che *ag* symphonic; (*orchestra*) symphony *cpd*.

singa'lese *ag*, *sm/f*, *sm* Sin(g)halese *inv*.

Singa'pore *sf* Singapore.

singhioz'zare [singjot'tsare] *vi* to sob; to hiccup.

singhi'ozzo [sin'gjottso] *sm* (*di pianto*) sob; (*MED*) hiccup; **avere il ~** to have the hiccups; **a ~** (*fig*) by fits and starts.

singo'lare *ag* (*insolito*) remarkable, singular; (*LING*) singular ♦ *sm* (*LING*) singular; (*TENNIS*): **~ maschile/femminile** men's/women's singles.

singolar'mente *av* (*separatamente*) individually, one at a time; (*in modo strano*) strangely, peculiarly, oddly.

'singolo, a *ag* single, individual ♦ *sm* (*persona*) individual; (*TENNIS*) = **singolare**; **ogni ~ individuo** each individual; **camera ~a** a single room.

sinis'trato, a *ag* damaged ♦ *sm/f* disaster victim; **zona ~a** a disaster area.

si'nistro, a *ag* left, left-hand; (*fig*) sinister ♦ *sm* (*incidente*) accident ♦ *sf* (*POL*) left (wing); **a ~a** on the left; (*direzione*) to the left; **a ~a di** to the left of; **di ~a** left-wing; **tenere la ~a** to keep to the left; **guida a ~a** left-hand drive.

'**sino** *prep* = **fino**.

si'**nonimo, a** *ag* synonymous ♦ *sm* synonym; **~ di** synonymous with.

sin'**tassi** *sf* syntax.

sin'**tattico, a, ci, che** *ag* syntactic.

'**sintesi** *sf* synthesis; (*riassunto*) summary, résumé; **in ~** in brief, in short.

sin'**tetico, a, ci, che** *ag* synthetic; (*conciso*) brief, concise.

sintetiz'**zare** [sintetid'dzare] *vt* to synthesize; (*riassumere*) to summarize.

sintetizza'**tore** [sintetiddza'tore] *sm* (*MUS*) synthesizer; **~ di voce** voice synthesizer.

sinto'**matico, a, ci, che** *ag* symptomatic.

'**sintomo** *sm* symptom.

sinto'**nia** *sf* (*RADIO*) tuning; **essere in ~ con qn** (*fig*) to be on the same wavelength as sb.

sintoniz'**zare** [sintonid'dzare] *vt* to tune (in); **~rsi** *vr*: **~rsi su** to tune in to.

sintonizza'**tore** [sintoniddza'tore] *sm* tuner.

sinu'**oso, a** *ag* (*strada*) winding.

sinu'**site** *sf* sinusitis.

SIP *sigla f* (= *Società Italiana per l'esercizio telefonico*) *former name of Italian telephone company.*

si'**pario** *sm* (*TEAT*) curtain.

si'**rena** *sf* (*apparecchio*) siren; (*nella mitologia, fig*) siren, mermaid; **~ d'allarme** (*per incendio*) fire alarm; (*per furto*) burglar alarm.

'**Siria** *sf*: **la ~** Syria.

siri'**ano, a** *ag, sm/f* Syrian.

si'**ringa, ghe** *sf* syringe.

'**sisma, i** *sm* earthquake.

'**SISMI** *sigla m* (= *Servizio per l'Informazione e la Sicurezza Militari*) *military security service.*

'**sismico, a, ci, che** *ag* seismic; (*zona*) earthquake *cpd*.

sis'**mografo** *sm* seismograph.

sissi'**gnore** [sissiɲ'ɲore] *av* (*a un superiore*) yes, sir; (*enfatico*) yes indeed, of course.

sis'**tema, i** *sm* system; (*metodo*) method, way; **trovare il ~ per fare qc** to find a way to do sth; **~ decimale/metrico** decimal/metric system; **~ operativo** (*INFORM*) operating system; **~ solare** solar system; **~ di vita** way of life.

siste'**mare** *vt* (*mettere a posto*) to tidy, put in order; (*risolvere: questione*) to sort out, settle; (*procurare un lavoro a*) to find a job for; (*dare un alloggio a*) to settle, find accommodation (*BRIT*) *o* accommodations

(*US*) for; **~rsi** *vr* (*problema*) to be settled; (*persona: trovare alloggio*) to find accommodation(s); (: *trovarsi un lavoro*) to get fixed up with a job; **ti sistemo io!** I'll soon sort you out!; **~ qn in un albergo** to fix sb up with a hotel.

sistematica'**mente** *av* systematically.

siste'**matico, a, ci, che** *ag* systematic.

sistemazi'**one** [sistemat'tsjone] *sf* arrangement, order; settlement; employment; accommodation (*BRIT*), accommodations (*US*).

'**sito, a** *ag* (*AMM*) situated ♦ *sm* (*letterario*) place; **~ Internet** website.

situ'**are** *vt* to site, situate.

situ'**ato, a** *ag*: **~ a/su** situated at/on.

situazi'**one** [situat'tsjone] *sf* situation; **vista la sua ~ familiare** given your family situation *o* circumstances; **nella sua ~** in your position *o* situation; **mi trovo in una ~ critica** I'm in a very difficult position.

'**skai** ® *sm* Leatherette ®.

ski-lift [ski'lift] *sm inv* ski lift.

ski pass [ski'pɑːs] *sm inv* ski pass.

slacci'**are** [zlat'tʃare] *vt* to undo, unfasten.

slanci'**arsi** [zlan'tʃarsi] *vr* to dash, fling o.s.

slanci'**ato, a** [zlan'tʃato] *ag* slender.

'**slancio** ['zlantʃo] *sm* dash, leap; (*fig*) surge; **in uno ~ d'affetto** in a burst *o* rush of affection; **di ~** impetuously.

sla'**vato, a** *ag* faded, washed out; (*fig: viso, occhi*) pale, colourless (*BRIT*), colorless (*US*).

sla'**vina** *sf* snowslide.

'**slavo, a** *ag* Slav(onic), Slavic.

sle'**ale** *ag* disloyal; (*concorrenza etc*) unfair.

sleal'**tà** *sf* disloyalty; unfairness.

sle'**gare** *vt* to untie.

slip *sm inv* (*mutandine*) briefs *pl*; (*da bagno: per uomo*) (swimming) trunks *pl*; (: *per donna*) bikini bottoms *pl*.

'**slitta** *sf* sledge; (*trainata*) sleigh.

slitta'**mento** *sm* slipping; skidding; postponement; **~ salariale** wage drift.

slit'**tare** *vi* to slip, slide; (*AUT*) to skid; (*incontro, conferenza*) to be put off, be postponed.

s.l.m. *abbr* (= *sul livello del mare*) a.s.l.

slo'**gare** *vt* (*MED*) to dislocate; (: *caviglia, polso*) to sprain.

sloga'**tura** *sf* dislocation; sprain.

sloggi'**are** [zlod'dʒare] *vt* (*inquilino*) to turn out; (*nemico*) to drive out, dislodge ♦ *vi* to move out.

Slo'vacchia [zlo'vakkja] *sf* Slovakia.

slo'**vacco, a, ci, che** *ag, sm/f* Slovak, Slovakian; **la Repubblica S~a** the Slovak Republic.

Slo'venia *sf* Slovenia.

slo'veno, a *ag, sm/f* Slovene, Slovenian ♦ *sm* (*LING*) Slovene.

S.M. *abbr* (*MIL*) = **Stato Maggiore**; (= *Sua Maestà*) HM.

smac'cato, a *ag* (*fig*) excessive.

smacchi'are [zmak'kjare] *vt* to remove stains from.

smacchia'tore [zmakkja'tore] *sm* stain remover.

'smacco, chi *sm* humiliating defeat.

smagli'ante [zmaʎ'ʎante] *ag* brilliant, dazzling.

smagli'are [zmaʎ'ʎare] *vt, ~***rsi** *vr* (*calza*) to ladder.

smaglia'tura [zmaʎʎa'tura] *sf* (*su maglia, calza*) ladder (*BRIT*), run; (*MED: sulla pelle*) stretch mark.

sma'grire *vt* to make thin ♦ *vi* to get *o* grow thin, lose weight.

sma'grito, a *ag*: **essere ~** to have lost a lot of weight.

smalizi'ato, a [smalit'tsjato] *ag* shrewd, cunning.

smal'tare *vt* to enamel; (*ceramica*) to glaze; (*unghie*) to varnish.

smalti'mento *sm* (*di rifiuti*) disposal.

smal'tire *vt* (*merce*) to sell off; (*rifiuti*) to dispose of; (*cibo*) to digest; (*peso*) to lose; (*rabbia*) to get over; **~ la sbornia** to sober up.

'smalto *sm* (*anche di denti*) enamel; (*per ceramica*) glaze; **~ per unghie** nail varnish.

smance'rie [zmantʃe'rie] *sfpl* mawkishness *sg*.

'smania *sf* agitation, restlessness; (*fig*): **~ di** thirst for, craving for; **avere la ~ addosso** to have the fidgets; **avere la ~ di fare** to long *o* yearn to do.

smani'are *vi* (*agitarsi*) to be restless *o* agitated; (*fig*): **~ di fare** to long *o* yearn to do.

smantella'mento *sm* dismantling.

smantel'lare *vt* to dismantle.

smar'carsi *vr* (*SPORT*) to get free of marking.

smargi'asso [zmar'dʒasso] *sm* show-off.

smarri'mento *sm* loss; (*fig*) bewilderment; dismay.

smar'rire *vt* to lose; (*non riuscire a trovare*) to mislay; **~rsi** *vr* (*perdersi*) to lose one's way, get lost; (*: oggetto*) to go astray.

smar'rito, a *ag* (*oggetto*) lost; (*fig: confuso: persona*) bewildered, nonplussed; (*: sguardo*) bewildered; **ufficio oggetti ~i** lost property office (*BRIT*), lost and found (*US*).

smasche'rare [zmaske'rare] *vt* to unmask.

SME *abbr* = **Stato Maggiore Esercito** ♦ *sigla m* (= *Sistema Monetario Europeo*) EMS (= *European Monetary System*).

smem'brare *vt* (*gruppo, partito etc*) to split; **~rsi** *vr* to split up.

smemo'rato, a *ag* forgetful.

smen'tire *vt* (*negare*) to deny; (*testimonianza*) to refute; (*reputazione*) to give the lie to; **~rsi** *vr* to be inconsistent.

smen'tita *sf* denial; refutation.

sme'raldo *sm, ag inv* emerald.

smerci'are [zmer'tʃare] *vt* (*COMM*) to sell; (*: svendere*) to sell off.

'smercio ['zmɛrtʃo] *sm* sale; **avere poco/ molto ~** to have poor/good sales.

smerigli'ato, a [zmeriʎ'ʎato] *ag*: **carta ~a** emery paper; **vetro ~** frosted glass.

sme'riglio [zme'riʎʎo] *sm* emery.

'smesso, a *pp di* **smettere** ♦ *ag*: **abiti** *mpl* **~i** cast-offs.

'smettere *vt* to stop; (*vestiti*) to stop wearing ♦ *vi* to stop, cease; **~ di fare** to stop doing.

smidol'lato, a *ag* spineless ♦ *sm/f* spineless person.

smilitarizzazi'one [zmilitariddzat'tsjone] *sf* demilitarization.

'smilzo, a ['zmiltso] *ag* thin, lean.

sminu'ire *vt* to diminish, lessen; (*fig*) to belittle; **~ l'importanza di qc** to play sth down.

sminuz'zare [zminut'tsare] *vt* to break into small pieces; to crumble.

'smisi *etc vb vedi* **smettere**.

smista'mento *sm* (*di posta*) sorting; (*FERR*) shunting.

smis'tare *vt* (*pacchi etc*) to sort; (*FERR*) to shunt.

smisu'rato, a *ag* boundless, immeasurable; (*grandissimo*) immense, enormous.

smitiz'zare [zmitid'dzare] *vt* to debunk.

smobili'tare *vt* to demobilize.

smobilitazi'one [zmobilitat'tsjone] *sf* demobilization.

smobi'lizzo [zmobi'liddzo] *sm* (*COMM*) disinvestment.

smo'dato, a *ag* excessive, unrestrained.

smode'rato, a *ag* immoderate.

smog [zmɔg] *sm inv* smog.

'smoking ['smoukiŋ] *sm inv* dinner jacket (*BRIT*), tuxedo (*US*).

smon'tare *vt* (*mobile, macchina etc*) to take to pieces, dismantle; (*fig: scoraggiare*) to dishearten ♦ *vi* (*scendere: da cavallo*) to dismount; (*: da treno*) to get off; (*terminare il lavoro*) to stop (work); **~rsi** *vr* to lose heart; to lose one's enthusiasm.

'**smorfia** *sf* grimace; (*atteggiamento lezioso*) simpering; **fare** ~**e** to make faces; to simper.

smorfi'oso, a *ag* simpering.

'**smorto, a** *ag* (*viso*) pale, wan; (*colore*) dull.

smor'zare [zmor'tsare] *vt* (*suoni*) to deaden; (*colori*) to tone down; (*luce*) to dim; (*sete*) to quench; (*entusiasmo*) to dampen; ~**rsi** *vr* (*suono, luce*) to fade; (*entusiasmo*) to dampen.

'**smosso, a** *pp di* **smuovere**.

smotta'mento *sm* landslide.

sms *sm inv* text (message).

'**smunto, a** *ag* haggard, pinched.

smu'overe *vt* to move, shift; (*fig: commuovere*) to move; (: *dall'inerzia*) to rouse, stir; ~**rsi** *vr* to move, shift.

smus'sare *vt* (*angolo*) to round off, smooth; (*lama etc*) to blunt; ~**rsi** *vr* to become blunt.

s.n. *abbr* = *senza numero*.

snatu'rato, a *ag* inhuman, heartless.

snazionaliz'zare [znattsjonalid'dzare] *vt* to denationalize.

snelli'mento *sm* (*di traffico*) speeding up; (*di procedura*) streamlining.

snel'lire *vt* (*persona*) to make slim; (*traffico*) to speed up; (*procedura*) to streamline; ~**rsi** *vr* (*persona*) to (get) slim; (*traffico*) to speed up.

'**snello, a** *ag* (*agile*) agile; (*svelto*) slender, slim.

sner'vante *ag* (*attesa, lavoro*) exasperating.

sner'vare *vt* to enervate, wear out; ~**rsi** *vr* to become enervated.

sni'dare *vt* to drive out, flush out.

snob'bare *vt* to snub.

sno'bismo *sm* snobbery.

snoccio'lare [znottʃo'lare] *vt* (*frutta*) to stone; (*fig: orazioni*) to rattle off; (: *verità*) to blab; (: *fam: soldi*) to shell out.

sno'dabile *ag* (*lampada*) adjustable; (*tubo, braccio*) hinged; **rasoio con testina** ~ swivel-head razor.

sno'dare *vt* to untie, undo; (*rendere agile, mobile*) to loosen; ~**rsi** *vr* to come loose; (*articolarsi*) to bend; (*strada, fiume*) to wind.

SO *sigla* = *Sondrio*.

so *vb vedi* **sapere**.

S.O. *abbr* (= *sudovest*) SW.

so'ave *ag* (*voce, maniera*) gentle; (*volto*) delicate, sweet; (*musica*) soft, sweet; (*profumo*) delicate.

soavità *sf* gentleness; delicacy; sweetness; softness.

sobbal'zare [sobbal'tsare] *vi* to jolt, jerk; (*trasalire*) to jump, start.

sob'balzo [sob'baltso] *sm* jerk, jolt; jump, start.

sobbar'carsi *vr*: ~ **a** to take on, undertake.

sob'borgo, ghi *sm* suburb.

sobil'lare *vt* to stir up, incite.

'**sobrio, a** *ag* sober.

Soc. *abbr* (= *società*) Soc.

socchi'udere [sok'kjudere] *vt* (*porta*) to leave ajar; (*occhi*) to half-close.

socchi'uso, a [sok'kjuso] *pp di* **socchiudere** ♦ *ag* (*porta, finestra*) ajar; (*occhi*) half-closed.

soc'combere *vi* to succumb, give way.

soc'correre *vt* to help, assist.

soccorri'tore, 'trice *smf* rescuer.

soc'corso, a *pp di* **soccorrere** ♦ *sm* help, aid, assistance; ~**i** *smpl* relief *sg*, aid *sg*; **prestare** ~ **a qn** to help *o* assist sb; **venire in** ~ **di qn** to help sb, come to sb's aid; **operazioni di** ~ rescue operations; ~ **stradale** breakdown service.

socialdemo'cratico, a, ci, che [sotʃaldemo'kratiko] *sm/f* Social Democrat.

soci'ale [so'tʃale] *ag* social; (*di associazione*) club *cpd*, association *cpd*.

socia'lismo [sotʃa'lizmo] *sm* socialism.

socia'lista, i, e [sotʃa'lista] *ag, sm/f* socialist.

socializ'zare [sotʃalid'dzare] *vi* to socialize.

società [sotʃe'ta] *sf inv* society; (*sportiva*) club; (*COMM*) company; **in** ~ **con qn** in partnership with sb; **mettersi in** ~ **con qn** to go into business with sb; **l'alta** ~ high society; ~ **anonima (SA)** ≈ limited (*BRIT*) *o* incorporated (*US*) company; ~ **per azioni (S.p.A.)** joint-stock company; ~ **di comodo** shell company; ~ **fiduciaria** trust company; ~ **di mutuo soccorso** friendly society (*BRIT*), benefit society (*US*); ~ **a responsabilità limitata (S.r.l.)** *type of limited liability company*.

soci'evole [so'tʃevole] *ag* sociable.

socievo'lezza [sotʃevo'lettsa] *sf* sociableness.

'**socio** ['sɔtʃo] *sm* (*DIR, COMM*) partner; (*membro di associazione*) member.

sociolo'gia [sotʃolo'dʒia] *sf* sociology.

soci'ologo, a, gi, ghe [so'tʃɔlogo] *sm/f* sociologist.

'**soda** *sf* (*CHIM*) soda; (*acqua gassata*) soda (water).

soda'lizio [soda'littsjo] *sm* association, society.

soddisfa'cente [soddisfa'tʃɛnte] *ag* satisfactory.

soddis'fare *vt, vi*: ~ **a** to satisfy; (*impegno*) to fulfil; (*debito*) to pay off; (*richiesta*) to meet, comply with; (*offesa*) to make amends for.

soddis'fatto, a *pp di* **soddisfare** ♦ *ag*
satisfied, pleased; **essere ~ di** to be
satisfied *o* pleased with.

soddisfazi'one [soddisfat'tsjone] *sf*
satisfaction.

'sodio *sm* (*CHIM*) sodium.

'sodo, a firm, hard ♦ *sm*: **venire al ~** to
come to the point ♦ *av* (*picchiare, lavorare*)
hard; **dormire ~** to sleep soundly.

sofà *sm inv* sofa.

soffe'renza [soffe'rɛntsa] *sf* suffering;
(*COMM*): **in ~** unpaid.

sof'ferto, a *pp di* **soffrire** ♦ *ag* (*vittoria*)
hard-fought; (*distacco, decisione*) painful.

soffi'are *vt* to blow; (*notizia, segreto*) to
whisper ♦ *vi* to blow; (*sbuffare*) to puff
(and blow); **~rsi il naso** to blow one's
nose; **~ qc/qn a qn** (*fig*) to pinch *o* steal
sth/sb from sb; **~ via qc** to blow sth away.

soffi'ata *sf* (*fam*) tip-off; **fare una ~ alla
polizia** to tip off the police.

'soffice ['sɔffitʃe] *ag* soft.

soffi'etto *sm* (*MUS, per fuoco*) bellows *pl*;
porta a ~ folding door.

'soffio *sm* (*di vento*) breath; (*di fumo*) puff;
(*MED*) murmur.

soffi'one *sm* (*BOT*) dandelion.

sof'fitta *sf* attic.

sof'fitto *sm* ceiling.

soffo'cante *ag* suffocating, stifling.

soffo'care *vi* (*anche*: **~rsi**) to suffocate,
choke ♦ *vt* to suffocate, choke; (*fig*) to
stifle, suppress.

soffocazi'one [soffokat'tsjone] *sf*
suffocation.

sof'friggere [sof'friddʒere] *vt* to fry lightly.

sof'frire *vt* to suffer, endure; (*sopportare*)
to bear, stand ♦ *vi* to suffer; to be in pain;
~ (di) qc (*MED*) to suffer from sth.

sof'fritto, a *pp di* **soffriggere** ♦ *sm* (*CUC*)
fried mixture of herbs, bacon and onions.

sof'fuso, a *ag* (*di luce*) suffused.

So'fia *sf* (*GEO*) Sofia.

sofisti'care *vt* (*vino, cibo*) to adulterate.

sofisti'cato, a *ag* sophisticated; (*vino*)
adulterated.

sofisticazi'one [sofistikat'tsjone] *sf*
adulteration.

'software ['sɔftwɛə] *sm*: **~ applicativo**
applications package.

sogget'tivo, a [soddʒet'tivo] *ag* subjective.

sog'getto, a [sod'dʒɛtto] *ag*: **~ a**
(*sottomesso*) subject to; (*esposto: a
variazioni, danni etc*) subject *o* liable to
♦ *sm* subject; **~ a tassa** taxable; **recitare
a ~** (*TEAT*) to improvise.

soggezi'one [soddʒet'tsjone] *sf* subjection;
(*timidezza*) awe; **avere ~ di qn** to be ill at
ease in sb's presence.

sogghi'gnare [soggiɲ'ɲare] *vi* to sneer.

sog'ghigno [sog'giɲɲo] *sm* sneer.

soggia'cere [soddʒa'tʃere] *vi*: **~ a** to be
subjected to.

soggio'gare [soddʒo'gare] *vt* to subdue,
subjugate.

soggior'nare [soddʒor'nare] *vi* to stay.

soggi'orno [sod'dʒorno] *sm* (*invernale,
marino*) stay; (*stanza*) living room.

soggi'ungere [sod'dʒundʒere] *vt* to add.

soggi'unto, a [sod'dʒunto] *pp di*
soggiungere.

'soglia ['sɔʎʎa] *sf* doorstep; (*anche fig*)
threshold.

'sogliola ['sɔʎʎola] *sf* (*ZOOL*) sole.

so'gnante [soɲ'ɲante] *ag* dreamy.

so'gnare [soɲ'ɲare] *vt, vi* to dream; **~ a
occhi aperti** to daydream.

sogna'tore, 'trice [soɲɲa'tore] *sm/f*
dreamer.

'sogno ['soɲɲo] *sm* dream.

'soia *sf* (*BOT*) soya.

sol *sm* (*MUS*) G; (*: solfeggiando la scala*)
so(h).

so'laio *sm* (*soffitta*) attic.

sola'mente *av* only, just.

so'lare *ag* solar, sun *cpd*.

sol'care *vt* (*terreno, fig: mari*) to plough
(*BRIT*), plow (*US*).

'solco, chi *sm* (*scavo, fig: ruga*) furrow;
(*incavo*) rut, track; (*di disco*) groove; (*scia*)
wake.

sol'dato *sm* soldier; **~ di leva** conscript; **~
semplice** private.

'soldo *sm* (*fig*): **non avere un ~** to be
penniless; **non vale un ~** it's not worth a
penny; **~i** *smpl* (*denaro*) money *sg*.

'sole *sm* sun; (*luce*) sun(light); (*tempo
assolato*) sun(shine); **prendere il ~** to
sunbathe; **il S~ che ride** (*POL*) *symbol of
the Italian Green party*.

soleggi'ato, a [soled'dʒato] *ag* sunny.

so'lenne *ag* solemn.

solennità *sf* solemnity; (*festività*) holiday,
feast day.

so'lere *vt*: **~ fare qc** to be in the habit of
doing sth ♦ *vb impers*: **come suole accadere**
as is usually the case, as usually
happens; **come si suol dire** as they say.

so'lerte *ag* diligent.

so'lerzia [so'lɛrtsja] *sf* diligence.

so'letta *sf* (*per scarpe*) insole.

sol'fato *sm* sulphate (*BRIT*), sulfate (*US*).

sol'forico, a, ci, che *ag* sulphuric (*BRIT*),
sulfuric (*US*); **acido ~** sulphuric *o*
sulfuric acid.

sol'furo *sm* sulphur (*BRIT*), sulfur (*US*).

soli'dale _ag_ in agreement; **essere ~ con qn** (_essere d'accordo_) to be in agreement with sb; (_appoggiare_) to be behind sb.

solidarietà _sf_ solidarity.

solidifi'care _vt, vi_ (_anche:_ ~**rsi**) to solidify.

solidità _sf_ solidity.

'solido, a _ag_ solid; (_forte, robusto_) sturdy, solid; (_fig: ditta_) sound, solid ♦ _sm_ (_MAT_) solid.

soli'loquio _sm_ soliloquy.

so'lista, i, e _ag_ solo ♦ _sm/f_ soloist.

solita'mente _av_ usually, as a rule.

soli'tario, a _ag_ (_senza compagnia_) solitary, lonely; (_solo, isolato_) solitary, lone; (_deserto_) lonely ♦ _sm_ (_gioiello, gioco_) solitaire.

'solito, a _ag_ usual; **essere ~ fare** to be in the habit of doing; **di ~** usually; **più tardi del ~** later than usual; **come al ~** as usual; **siamo alle ~e!** (_fam_) here we go again!

soli'tudine _sf_ solitude.

sollaz'zare [sollat'tsare] _vt_ to entertain; ~**rsi** _vr_ to amuse o.s.

sol'lazzo [sol'lattso] _sm_ amusement.

solleci'tare [solletʃi'tare] _vt_ (_lavoro_) to speed up; (_persona_) to urge on; (_chiedere con insistenza_) to press for, request urgently; (_stimolare_): ~ **qn a fare** to urge sb to do; (_TECN_) to stress.

sollecitazi'one [solletʃitat'tsjone] _sf_ entreaty, request; (_fig_) incentive; (_TECN_) stress; **lettera di ~** (_COMM_) reminder.

sol'lecito, a [sol'letʃito] _ag_ prompt, quick ♦ _sm_ (_COMM_) reminder; ~ **di pagamento** payment reminder.

solleci'tudine [solletʃi'tudine] _sf_ promptness, speed.

solleti'care _vt_ to tickle.

sol'letico _sm_ tickling; **soffrire il ~** to be ticklish.

solleva'mento _sm_ raising; lifting; (_ribellione_) revolt; ~ **pesi** (_sport_) weight-lifting.

solle'vare _vt_ to lift, raise; (_fig: persona: alleggerire_): ~ (**da**) to relieve (of); (_: dar conforto_) to comfort, relieve; (_: questione_) to raise; (_: far insorgere_) to stir (to revolt); ~**rsi** _vr_ to rise; (_fig: riprendersi_) to recover; (_: ribellarsi_) to rise up; ~**rsi da terra** (_persona_) to get up from the ground; (_aereo_) to take off; **sentirsi sollevato** to feel relieved.

solli'evo _sm_ relief; (_conforto_) comfort; **con mio grande ~** to my great relief.

'solo, a _ag_ alone; (_in senso spirituale: isolato_) lonely; (_unico_): **un ~ libro** only one book, a single book; (_con ag numerale_): **veniamo**

noi tre ~i just _o_ only the three of us are coming ♦ _av_ (_soltanto_) only, just; ~ **che** _cong_ but; **è il ~ proprietario** he's the sole proprietor; **l'incontrò due ~e volte** he only met him twice; **non ~ ... ma anche** not only ... but also; **fare qc da ~** to do sth (all) by oneself; **vive (da) ~** he lives on his own; **possiamo vederci da ~i?** can I see you in private?

sol'stizio [sol'stittsjo] _sm_ solstice.

sol'tanto _av_ only.

so'lubile _ag_ (_sostanza_) soluble; **caffè ~** instant coffee.

soluzi'one [solut'tsjone] _sf_ solution; **senza ~ di continuità** uninterruptedly.

sol'vente _ag, sm_ solvent; ~ **per unghie** nail polish remover; ~ **per vernici** paint remover.

sol'venza [sol'vɛntsa] _sf_ (_COMM_) solvency.

'soma _sf_ load, burden; **bestia da ~** beast of burden.

So'malia _sf_: **la ~** Somalia.

'somalo, a _ag, sm/f, sm_ Somali.

so'maro _sm_ ass, donkey.

so'matico, a, ci, che _ag_ somatic.

somigli'anza [somiʎ'ʎantsa] _sf_ resemblance.

somigli'are [somiʎ'ʎare] _vi_: ~ **a** to be like, resemble; (_nell'aspetto fisico_) to look like; ~**rsi** _vr_ to be (_o_ look) alike.

'somma _sf_ (_MAT_) sum; (_di denaro_) sum (of money); (_complesso di varie cose_) whole amount, sum total; **tirare le ~e** (_fig_) to sum up; **tirate le ~e** (_fig_) all things considered.

som'mare _vt_ to add up; (_aggiungere_) to add; **tutto sommato** all things considered.

som'mario, a _ag_ (_racconto, indagine_) brief; (_giustizia_) summary ♦ _sm_ summary.

som'mergere [som'mɛrdʒere] _vt_ to submerge.

sommer'gibile [sommer'dʒibile] _sm_ submarine.

som'merso, a _pp di_ **sommergere**.

som'messo, a _ag_ (_voce_) soft, subdued.

somminis'trare _vt_ to give, administer.

sommità _sf inv_ summit, top; (_fig_) height.

'sommo, a _ag_ highest; (_rispetto_) highest, greatest; (_poeta, artista_) great, outstanding ♦ _sm_ (_fig_) height; **per ~i capi** in short, in brief.

som'mossa _sf_ uprising.

sommozza'tore [sommottsa'tore] _sm_ (deep-sea) diver; (_MIL_) frogman.

so'naglio [so'naʎʎo] _sm_ (_di mucche etc_) bell; (_per bambini_) rattle.

so'nante _ag_: **denaro** _o_ **moneta ~** (ready)

cash.
so'nare *etc* = **suonare** *etc*.
'sonda *sf* (*MED, METEOR, AER*) probe;
(*MINERALOGIA*) drill ♦ *ag inv*: **pallone** *m* ~
weather balloon.
son'daggio [son'daddʒo] *sm* sounding;
probe; boring, drilling; (*indagine*) survey;
~ **d'opinioni** opinion poll.
son'dare *vt* (*NAUT*) to sound; (*atmosfera,
piaga*) to probe; (*MINERALOGIA*) to bore,
drill; (*fig: opinione etc*) to survey, poll.
so'netto *sm* sonnet.
son'nambulo, a *sm/f* sleepwalker.
sonnecchi'are [sonnek'kjare] *vi* to doze,
nod.
sonnel'lino *sm* nap.
son'nifero *sm* sleeping drug (*o* pill).
'sonno *sm* sleep; **aver** ~ to be sleepy;
prendere ~ to fall asleep.
sonno'lento, a *ag* sleepy, drowsy;
(*movimenti*) sluggish.
sonno'lenza [sonno'lɛntsa] *sf* sleepiness,
drowsiness.
'sono *vb vedi* **essere**.
sonoriz'zare [sonorid'dzare] *vt* (*LING*) to
voice; (*CINE*) to add a sound-track to.
so'noro, a *ag* (*ambiente*) resonant; (*voce*)
sonorous, ringing; (*onde, film*) sound *cpd*
♦ *sm*: **il** ~ (*CINE*) the talkies *pl*.
sontu'oso, a *ag* sumptuous.
so'pire *vt* (*fig: dolore, tensione*) to soothe.
so'pore *sm* drowsiness.
sopo'rifero, a *ag* soporific.
soppe'rire *vi*: ~ **a** to provide for; ~ **alla
mancanza di qc** to make up for the lack of
sth.
soppe'sare *vt* to weigh in one's hand(s),
feel the weight of; (*fig*) to weigh up.
soppian'tare *vt* to supplant.
soppi'atto *av*: **di** ~ secretly; furtively.
soppor'tabile *ag* tolerable, bearable.
soppor'tare *vt* (*reggere*) to support; (*subire:
perdita, spese*) to bear, sustain; (*soffrire:
dolore*) to bear, endure; (*sog: cosa: freddo*)
to withstand; (: *persona: freddo, vino*) to
take; (*tollerare*) to put up with, tolerate.
sopportazi'one [sopportat'tsjone] *sf*
patience; **avere spirito di** ~, **avere
capacità di** ~ to be long-suffering.
soppressi'one *sf* abolition; withdrawal;
suppression; deletion; elimination,
liquidation.
sop'presso, a *pp di* **sopprimere**.
sop'primere *vt* (*carica, privilegi etc*) to
abolish, do away with; (*servizio*) to
withdraw; (*pubblicazione*) to suppress;
(*parola, frase*) to delete; (*uccidere*) to
eliminate, liquidate.

'sopra *prep* (*gen*) on; (*al di sopra di, più in
alto di*) above; over; (*riguardo a*) on, about
♦ *av* on top; (*attaccato, scritto*) on it; (*al di
sopra*) above; (*al piano superiore*) upstairs;
donne ~ **i 30 anni** women over 30 (years
of age); **100 metri** ~ **il livello del mare** 100
metres above sea level; **5 gradi** ~ **lo zero**
5 degrees above zero; **abito di** ~ I live
upstairs; **essere al di** ~ **di ogni sospetto** to
be above suspicion; **per i motivi** ~
illustrati for the above-mentioned
reasons, for the reasons shown above;
dormirci ~ (*fig*) to sleep on it; **passar** ~ **a
qc** (*anche fig*) to pass over sth.
so'prabito *sm* overcoat.
sopraccen'nato, a [soprattʃen'nato] *ag*
above-mentioned.
soprac'ciglio [soprat'tʃiʎʎo], *pl*(*f*)
soprac'ciglia *sm* eyebrow.
sopracco'perta *sf* (*di letto*) bedspread; (*di
libro*) jacket.
soprad'detto, a *ag* aforesaid.
sopraf'fare *vt* to overcome, overwhelm.
sopraf'fatto, a *pp di* **sopraffare**.
sopraffazi'one [sopraffat'tsjone] *sf*
overwhelming, overpowering.
sopraf'fino, a *ag* (*pranzo, vino*) excellent;
(*fig*) masterly.
sopraggi'ungere [soprad'dʒundʒere] *vi*
(*giungere all'improvviso*) to arrive
(unexpectedly); (*accadere*) to occur
(unexpectedly).
sopraggi'unto, a [soprad'dʒunto] *pp di*
sopraggiungere.
soprallu'ogo, ghi *sm* (*di esperti*)
inspection; (*di polizia*) on-the-spot
investigation.
sopram'mobile *sm* ornament.
soprannatu'rale *ag* supernatural.
sopran'nome *sm* nickname.
soprannomi'nare *vt* to nickname.
sopran'numero *av*: **in** ~ in excess.
so'prano, a *sm/f* (*persona*) soprano ♦ *sm*
(*voce*) soprano.
soprappensi'ero *av* lost in thought.
soprappiù *sm* surplus, extra; **in** ~ extra,
surplus; (*per giunta*) besides, in addition.
sopras'salto *sm*: **di** ~ with a start, with a
jump.
soprasse'dere *vi*: ~ **a** to delay, put off.
soprat'tassa *sf* surtax.
soprat'tutto *av* (*anzitutto*) above all;
(*specialmente*) especially.
sopravvalu'tare *vt* (*persona, capacità*) to
overestimate.
sopravve'nire *vi* to arrive, appear; (*fatto*)
to occur.
soprav'vento *sm*: **avere/prendere il** ~ **su**

qn to have/get the upper hand over sb.
sopravvis'suto, a *pp di* **sopravvivere ♦** *sm/f*
survivor.
sopravvi'venza [sopravvi'vɛntsa] *sf*
survival.
soprav'vivere *vi* to survive; (*continuare a
vivere*): ~ **(in)** to live on (in); ~ **a** (*incidente
etc*) to survive; (*persona*) to outlive.
soprele'vata *sf* (*di strada, ferrovia*) elevated
section.
soprinten'dente *sm/f* supervisor; (*statale*:
di belle arti etc) keeper.
soprinten'denza [soprinten'dɛntsa] *sf*
supervision; (*ente*): ~ **alle Belle Arti**
*government department responsible for
monuments and artistic treasures.*
soprin'tendere *vi*: ~ **a** to superintend,
supervise.
soprin'teso, a *pp di* **soprintendere.**
so'pruso *sm* abuse of power; **subire un** ~
to be abused.
soq'quadro *sm*: **mettere a** ~ to turn
upside-down.
sor'betto *sm* sorbet, water ice (*BRIT*).
sor'bire *vt* to sip; (*fig*) to put up with.
'sorcio ['sortʃo] *sm* mouse.
'sordido, a *ag* sordid; (*fig*: *gretto*) stingy.
sor'dina *sf*: **in** ~ softly; (*fig*) on the sly.
sordità *sf* deafness.
'sordo, a *ag* deaf; (*rumore*) muffled;
(*dolore*) dull; (*lotta*) silent, hidden; (*odio,
rancore*) veiled ♦ *sm/f* deaf person.
sordo'muto, a *ag* deaf-and-dumb ♦ *sm/f*
deaf-mute.
so'rella *sf* sister.
sorel'lastra *sf* stepsister; (*con genitore in
comune*) half sister.
sor'gente [sor'dʒɛnte] *sf* (*acqua che sgorga*)
spring; (*di fiume, FISICA, fig*) source; **acqua
di** ~ spring water; ~ **di calore** source of
heat; ~ **termale** thermal spring.
'sorgere ['sordʒere] *vi* to rise; (*scaturire*) to
spring, rise; (*fig: difficoltà*) to arise ♦ *sm*: **al**
~ **del sole** at sunrise.
sori'ano, a *ag, sm/f* tabby.
sormon'tare *vt* (*fig*) to overcome,
surmount.
sorni'one, a *ag* sly.
sorpas'sare *vt* (*AUT*) to overtake; (*fig*) to
surpass; (: *eccedere*) to exceed, go
beyond; ~ **in altezza** to be higher than;
(*persona*) to be taller than.
sorpas'sato, a *ag* (*metodo, moda*)
outmoded, old-fashioned; (*macchina*)
obsolete.
sor'passo *sm* (*AUT*) overtaking.
sorpren'dente *ag* surprising; (*eccezionale,
inaspettato*) astonishing, amazing.

sor'prendere *vt* (*cogliere: in flagrante etc*) to
catch; (*stupire*) to surprise; ~**rsi** *vr*: ~**rsi
(di)** to be surprised (at).
sor'preso, a *pp di* **sorprendere ♦** *sf* surprise;
fare una ~**a a qn** to give sb a surprise;
prendere qn di ~**a** to take sb by surprise
o unawares.
sor'reggere [sor'rɛddʒere] *vt* to support,
hold up; (*fig*) to sustain.
sor'retto, a *pp di* **sorreggere.**
sor'ridere *vi* to smile.
sor'riso, a *pp di* **sorridere ♦** *sm* smile.
sor'sata *sf* gulp; **bere a** ~**e** to gulp.
sorseggi'are [sorsed'dʒare] *vt* to sip.
'sorsi *etc vb vedi* **sorgere.**
'sorso *sm* sip; **d'un** ~, **in un** ~ **solo** at one
gulp.
'sorta *sf* sort, kind; **di** ~ whatever, of any
kind at all; **ogni** ~ **di** all sorts of; **di ogni** ~
of every kind.
'sorte *sf* (*fato*) fate, destiny; (*evento fortuito*)
chance; **tirare a** ~ to draw lots; **tentare la**
~ to try one's luck.
sorteggi'are [sorted'dʒare] *vt* to draw for.
sor'teggio [sor'tedd ʒo] *sm* draw.
sorti'legio [sorti'ledʒo] *sm* witchcraft *no pl*;
(*incantesimo*) spell; **fare un** ~ **a qn** to cast
a spell on sb.
sor'tire *vt* (*ottenere*) to produce.
sor'tita *sf* (*MIL*) sortie.
'sorto, a *pp di* **sorgere.**
sorvegli'ante [sorveʎ'ʎante] *sm/f* (*di carcere*)
guard, warder (*BRIT*); (*di fabbrica etc*)
supervisor.
sorvegli'anza [sorveʎ'ʎantsa] *sf* watch;
supervision; (*POLIZIA, MIL*) surveillance.
sorvegli'are [sorveʎ'ʎare] *vt* (*bambino,
bagagli, prigioniero*) to watch, keep an eye
on; (*malato*) to watch over; (*territorio, casa*)
to watch *o* keep watch over; (*lavori*) to
supervise.
sorvo'lare *vt* (*territorio*) to fly over ♦ *vi*: ~
su (*fig*) to skim over.
S.O.S. *sigla m* mayday, SOS.
'sosia *sm inv* double.
sos'pendere *vt* (*appendere*) to hang (up);
(*interrompere, privare di una carica*) to
suspend; (*rimandare*) to defer; ~ **un
quadro al muro/un lampadario al soffitto**
to hang a picture on the wall/a chandelier
from the ceiling; ~ **qn dal suo incarico** to
suspend sb from office.
sospensi'one *sf* (*anche CHIM, AUT*)
suspension; deferment; ~ **condizionale
della pena** (*DIR*) suspended sentence.
sos'peso, a *pp di* **sospendere ♦** *ag* (*appeso*):
~ **a** hanging on (*o* from); (*treno, autobus*)
cancelled; **in** ~ in abeyance; (*conto*)

outstanding; **tenere in** ~ (*fig*) to keep in suspense; **col fiato** ~ with bated breath.

sospet'tare *vt* to suspect ♦ *vi*: ~ **di** to suspect; (*diffidare*) to be suspicious of.

sos'petto, a *ag* suspicious ♦ *sm* suspicion; **destare** ~**i** to arouse suspicion.

sospet'toso, a *ag* suspicious.

sos'pingere [sos'pindʒere] *vt* to drive, push.

sos'pinto, a *pp di* **sospingere**.

sospi'rare *vi* to sigh ♦ *vt* to long for, yearn for.

sos'piro *sm* sigh; ~ **di sollievo** sigh of relief.

'sosta *sf* (*fermata*) stop, halt; (*pausa*) pause, break; **senza** ~ non-stop, without a break.

sostanti'vato, a *ag* (*LING*): **aggettivo** ~ adjective used as a noun.

sostan'tivo *sm* noun, substantive.

sos'tanza [sos'tantsa] *sf* substance; ~**e** *sfpl* (*ricchezze*) wealth *sg*, possessions; **in** ~ in short, to sum up; **la** ~ **del discorso** the essence of the speech.

sostanzi'ale [sostan'tsjale] *ag* substantial.

sostanzi'oso, a [sostan'tsjoso] *ag* (*cibo*) nourishing, substantial.

sos'tare *vi* (*fermarsi*) to stop (for a while), stay; (*fare una pausa*) to take a break.

sos'tegno [sos'teɲɲo] *sm* support; **a** ~ **di** in support of; **muro di** ~ supporting wall.

soste'nere *vt* to support; (*prendere su di sé*) to take on, bear; (*resistere*) to withstand, stand up to; (*affermare*): ~ **che** to maintain that; ~**rsi** *vr* to hold o.s. up, support o.s.; (*fig*) to keep up one's strength; ~ **qn** (*moralmente*) to be a support to sb; (*difendere*) to stand up for sb, take sb's part; ~ **gli esami** to sit exams; ~ **il confronto** to bear *o* stand comparison.

soste'nibile *ag* (*tesi*) tenable; (*spese*) bearable; (*sviluppo*) sustainable.

sosteni'tore, 'trice *sm/f* supporter.

sostenta'mento *sm* maintenance, support; **mezzi di** ~ means of support.

soste'nuto, a *ag* (*stile*) elevated; (*velocità, ritmo*) sustained; (*prezzo*) high ♦ *sm/f*: **fare il(la)** ~**(a)** to be standoffish, keep one's distance.

sostitu'ire *vt* (*mettere al posto di*): ~ **qn/qc a** to substitute sb/sth for; (*prendere il posto di*) to replace, take the place of.

sostitu'tivo, a *ag* (*AMM*: *documento, certificato*) equivalent.

sosti'tuto, a *sm/f* substitute; ~ **procuratore della Repubblica** (*DIR*) deputy public prosecutor.

sostituzi'one [sostitut'tsjone] *sf* substitution; **in** ~ **di** as a substitute for, in

place of.

sotta'ceti [sotta't ʃeti] *smpl* pickles.

sot'tana *sf* (*sottoveste*) underskirt; (*gonna*) skirt; (*REL*) soutane, cassock.

sot'tecchi [sot'tekki] *av*: **guardare di** ~ to steal a glance at.

sotter'fugio [sotter'fudʒo] *sm* subterfuge.

sotter'raneo, a *ag* underground ♦ *sm* cellar.

sotter'rare *vt* to bury.

sottigli'ezza [sottiʎ'ʎettsa] *sf* thinness; slimness; (*fig*: *acutezza*) subtlety; shrewdness; ~**e** *sfpl* (*pedanteria*) quibbles.

sot'tile *ag* thin; (*figura, caviglia*) thin, slim, slender; (*fine*: *polvere, capelli*) fine; (*fig*: *leggero*) light; (: *vista*) sharp, keen; (: *olfatto*) fine, discriminating; (: *mente*) subtle; shrewd ♦ *sm*: **non andare per il** ~ not to mince matters.

sottiliz'zare [sottilid'dzare] *vi* to split hairs.

sottin'tendere *vt* (*intendere qc non espresso*) to understand; (*implicare*) to imply; **lasciare** ~ **che** to let it be understood that.

sottin'teso, a *pp di* **sottintendere** ♦ *sm* allusion; **parlare senza** ~**i** to speak plainly.

'sotto *prep* (*gen*) under; (*più in basso di*) below ♦ *av* underneath, beneath; below; (*al piano inferiore*): **(al piano) di** ~ downstairs; ~ **il monte** at the foot of the mountain; ~ **la pioggia/il sole** in the rain/sun(shine); **tutti quelli** ~ **i 18 anni** all those under 18 (years of age) (*BRIT*) *o* under age 18 (*US*); ~ **il livello del mare** below sea level; ~ **il chilo** under *o* less than a kilo; **ha 5 impiegati** ~ **di sé** he has 5 clerks under him; **siamo** ~ **Natale/Pasqua** it's nearly Christmas/Easter; ~ **un certo punto di vista** in a sense; ~ **forma di** in the form of; ~ **falso nome** under a false name; ~ **terra** underground; ~ **voce** in a low voice; **chiuso** ~ **vuoto** vacuum packed.

sotto'banco *av* (*di nascosto*: *vendere, comprare*) under the counter; (*agire*) in an underhand way.

sottobicchi'ere [sottobik'kjɛre] *sm* mat, coaster.

sotto'bosco, schi *sm* undergrowth *no pl*.

sotto'braccio [sotto'brattʃo] *av* by the arm; **prendere qn** ~ to take sb by the arm; **camminare** ~ **a qn** to walk arm in arm with sb.

sottochi'ave [sotto'kjave] *av* under lock and key.

sottoco'perta *av* (*NAUT*) below deck.

sotto'costo *av* below cost (price).

sottocu'taneo, a *ag* subcutaneous.
sottoes'posto, a *ag* (*fotografia, pellicola*) underexposed.
sotto'fondo *sm* background; ~ **musicale** background music.
sotto'gamba *av*: **prendere qc** ~ not to take sth seriously.
sotto'gonna *sf* underskirt.
sottogo'verno *sm* political patronage.
sotto'gruppo *sm* subgroup; (*di partito*) faction.
sottoline'are *vt* to underline; (*fig*) to emphasize, stress.
sot't'olio *av, ag inv* in oil.
sotto'mano *av* (*a portata di mano*) within reach, to hand; (*di nascosto*) secretly.
sottoma'rino, a *ag* (*flora*) submarine; (*cavo, navigazione*) underwater ♦ *sm* (*NAUT*) submarine.
sotto'messo, a *pp di* **sottomettere** ♦ *ag* submissive.
sotto'mettere *vt* to subdue, subjugate; ~**rsi** *vr* to submit.
sottomissi'one *sf* submission.
sottopas'saggio [sottopas'saddʒo] *sm* (*AUT*) underpass; (*pedonale*) subway, underpass.
sotto'porre *vt* (*costringere*) to subject; (*fig: presentare*) to submit; **sottoporsi** *vr* to submit; **sottoporsi a** (*subire*) to undergo.
sotto'posto, a *pp di* **sottoporre**.
sottopro'dotto *sm* by-product.
sottoproduzi'one [sottoprodut'tsjone] *sf* underproduction.
sottoproletari'ato *sm*: **il** ~ the underprivileged class.
sot'tordine *av*: **passare in** ~ to become of minor importance.
sottos'cala *sm inv* (*ripostiglio*) cupboard (*BRIT*) o closet (*US*) under the stairs; (*stanza*) room under the stairs.
sottos'critto, a *pp di* **sottoscrivere** ♦ *sm/f*: **io** ~, **il** ~ the undersigned.
sottos'crivere *vt* to sign ♦ *vi*: ~ **a** to subscribe to.
sottoscrizi'one [sottoskrit'tsjone] *sf* signing; subscription.
sottosegre'tario *sm*: **S**~ **di Stato** undersecretary of state (*BRIT*), assistant secretary of state (*US*).
sotto'sopra *av* upside-down.
sottos'tante *ag* (*piani*) lower; **nella valle** ~ in the valley below.
sottos'tare *vi*: ~ **a** (*assoggettarsi a*) to submit to; (*: richieste*) to give in to; (*subire: prova*) to undergo.
sottosu'olo *sm* subsoil.
sottosvilup'pato, a *ag* underdeveloped.

sottosvi'luppo *sm* underdevelopment.
sottote'nente *sm* (*MIL*) second lieutenant.
sotto'terra *av* underground.
sotto'tetto *sm* attic.
sotto'titolo *sm* subtitle.
sottovalu'tare *vt* (*persona, prova*) to underestimate, underrate.
sotto'vento *av* (*NAUT*) leeward(s) ♦ *ag inv* (*lato*) leeward, lee.
sotto'veste *sf* underskirt.
sotto'voce [sotto'votʃe] *av* in a low voice.
sottovu'oto *av*: **confezionare** ~ to vacuum-pack ♦ *ag*: **confezione** *f* ~ vacuum pack.
sot'trarre *vt* (*MAT*) to subtract, take away; **sottrarsi** *vr*: **sottrarsi a** (*sfuggire*) to escape; (*evitare*) to avoid; ~ **qn/qc a** (*togliere*) to remove sb/sth from; (*salvare*) to save o rescue sb/sth from; ~ **qc a qn** (*rubare*) to steal sth from sb; **sottratte le spese** once expenses have been deducted.
sot'tratto, a *pp di* **sottrarre**.
sottrazi'one [sottrat'tsjone] *sf* (*MAT*) subtraction; (*furto*) removal.
sottuffici'ale [sottuffi'tʃale] *sm* (*MIL*) non-commissioned officer; (*NAUT*) petty officer.
soufflé [su'fle] *sm inv* (*CUC*) soufflé.
souve'nir [suv(ə)'nir] *sm inv* souvenir.
so'vente *av* often.
soverchi'are [sover'kjare] *vt* to overpower, overwhelm.
soverchie'ria [soverkje'ria] *sf* (*prepotenza*) abuse (of power).
sovi'etico, a, ci, che *ag* Soviet ♦ *sm/f* Soviet citizen.
sovrabbon'dante *ag* overabundant.
sovrabbon'danza [sovrabbon'dantsa] *sf* overabundance; **in** ~ in excess.
sovraccari'care *vt* to overload.
sovrac'carico, a, chi, che *ag*: ~ **(di)** overloaded (with) ♦ *sm* excess load; ~ **di lavoro** extra work.
sovraesposizi'one [sovraespozit'tsjone] *sf* (*FOT*) overexposure.
sovraffol'lato, a *ag* overcrowded.
sovraimmagazzi'nare [sovraimmagaddzi-'nare] *vt* to overstock.
sovranità *sf* sovereignty; (*fig: superiorità*) supremacy.
sovrannatu'rale *ag* = **soprannaturale**.
so'vrano, a *ag* sovereign; (*fig: sommo*) supreme ♦ *sm/f* sovereign, monarch.
sovrappopolazi'one [sovrappopolat'tsjone] *sf* overpopulation.
sovrap'porre *vt* to place on top of, put on top of; (*FOT, GEOM*) to superimpose; **sovrapporsi** *vr* (*fig: aggiungersi*) to be

added; (*FOT*) to be superimposed.

sovrapposizi'one [sovrapposit'tsjone] *sf* superimposition.

sovrap'posto, a *pp di* **sovrapporre.**

sovrapproduzi'one [sovrapprodut'tsjone] *sf* overproduction.

sovras'tante *ag* overhanging; (*fig*) imminent.

sovras'tare *vi:* ~ **a** *vt* (*vallata, fiume*) to overhang; (*fig*) to hang over, threaten.

sovrastrut'tura *sf* superstructure.

sovrecci'tare [sovrettʃi'tare] *vt* to overexcite.

sovrimpressi'one *sf* (*FOT, CINE*) double exposure; **immagini in** ~ superimposed images.

sovrinten'dente *etc* = **soprintendente** *etc.*

sovru'mano, a *ag* superhuman.

sovve'nire *vi* (*venire in mente*): ~ **a** to occur to.

sovvenzio'nare [sovventsjo'nare] *vt* to subsidize.

sovvenzi'one [sovven'tsjone] *sf* subsidy, grant.

sovver'sivo, a *ag* subversive.

sovverti'mento *sm* subversion, undermining.

sovver'tire *vt* (*POL: ordine, stato*) to subvert, undermine.

'sozzo, a ['sottso] *ag* filthy, dirty.

SP *sigla* = La Spezia.

S.P. *abbr* = **strada provinciale**; *vedi* **provinciale.**

S.p.A. *abbr vedi* **società per azioni.**

spac'care *vt* to split, break; (*legna*) to chop; (*fig*) to divide; ~**rsi** *vr* to split, break.

spacca'tura *sf* split.

spaccherò [spakke'rɔ] *etc vb vedi* **spaccare.**

spacci'are [spat'tʃare] *vt* (*vendere*) to sell (off); (*mettere in circolazione*) to circulate; (*droga*) to peddle, push; ~**rsi** *vr:* ~**rsi per** (*farsi credere*) to pass o.s. off as, pretend to be.

spacci'ato, a [spat'tʃato] *ag* (*fam: malato, fuggiasco*): **essere** ~ to be done for.

spaccia'tore, 'trice [spattʃa'tore] *sm/f* (*di droga*) pusher; (*di denaro falso*) dealer.

'spaccio ['spattʃo] *sm* (*di merce rubata, droga*): ~ **(di)** trafficking (in); (*di denaro falso*): ~ **(di)** passing (of); (*vendita*) sale; (*bottega*) shop.

'spacco, chi *sm* (*fenditura*) split, crack; (*strappo*) tear; (*di gonna*) slit.

spac'cone *sm/f* boaster, braggart.

'spada *sf* sword.

spadroneggi'are [spadroned'dʒare] *vi* to swagger.

spae'sato, a *ag* disorientated, lost.

spaghet'tata [spaget'tata] *sf* spaghetti meal.

spa'ghetti [spa'getti] *smpl* (*CUC*) spaghetti *sg.*

'Spagna ['spaɲɲa] *sf:* **la** ~ Spain.

spa'gnolo, a [spaɲ'ɲɔlo] *ag* Spanish ♦ *sm/f* Spaniard ♦ *sm* (*LING*) Spanish; **gli S~i** the Spanish.

'spago, ghi *sm* string, twine; **dare** ~ **a qn** (*fig*) to let sb have his (*o* her) way.

spai'ato, a *ag* (*calza, guanto*) odd.

spalan'care *vt,* ~**rsi** *vr* to open wide.

spa'lare *vt* to shovel.

'spalla *sf* shoulder; (*fig: TEAT*) stooge; ~**e** *sfpl* (*dorso*) back; **di** ~**e** from behind; **seduto alle mie** ~**e** sitting behind me; **prendere/colpire qn alle** ~**e** to take/hit sb from behind; **mettere qn con le** ~**e al muro** (*fig*) to put sb with his (*o* her) back to the wall; **vivere alle** ~**e di qn** (*fig*) to live off sb.

spal'lata *sf* (*urto*) shove *o* push with the shoulder; **dare una** ~ **a qc** to give sth a push *o* shove with one's shoulder.

spalleggi'are [spalled'dʒare] *vt* to back up, support.

spal'letta *sf* (*parapetto*) parapet.

spalli'era *sf* (*di sedia etc*) back; (*di letto: di capo*) head(board); (: *da piedi*) foot(board); (*GINNASTICA*) wall bars *pl.*

spal'lina *sf* (*MIL*) epaulette; (*di sottoveste, maglietta*) strap; **senza** ~**e** strapless.

spal'mare *vt* to spread.

'spalti *smpl* (*di stadio*) terraces (*BRIT*), ≈ bleachers (*US*).

'spandere *vt* to spread; (*versare*) to pour (out); ~**rsi** *vr* to spread; ~ **lacrime** to shed tears.

'spanto, a *pp di* **spandere.**

spa'rare *vt* to fire ♦ *vi* (*far fuoco*) to fire; (*tirare*) to shoot; ~ **a qn/qc** to shoot sb/sth, fire at sb/sth.

spa'rato *sm* (*di camicia*) dicky.

spara'tore *sm* gunman.

spara'toria *sf* exchange of shots.

sparecchi'are [sparek'kjare] *vt:* ~ **(la tavola)** to clear the table.

spa'reggio [spa'reddʒo] *sm* (*SPORT*) play-off.

'spargere ['spardʒere] *vt* (*sparpagliare*) to scatter; (*versare: vino*) to spill; (: *lacrime, sangue*) to shed; (*diffondere*) to spread; (*emanare*) to give off (*o* out); ~**rsi** *vr* (*voce, notizia*) to spread; (*persone*) to scatter; **si è sparsa una voce sul suo conto** there is a rumour going round about him.

spargi'mento [spardʒi'mento] *sm*

scattering; spilling; shedding; ~ **di sangue** bloodshed.

spa'rire vi to disappear, vanish; ~ **dalla circolazione** (fig fam) to lie low, keep a low profile.

sparizi'one [sparit'tsjone] sf disappearance.

spar'lare vi: ~ **di** to run down, speak ill of.

'sparo sm shot.

sparpagli'are [sparpaʎ'ʎare] vt, ~**rsi** vr to scatter.

'sparso, a pp di **spargere** ♦ ag scattered; (sciolto) loose; **in ordine** ~ (MIL) in open order.

sparti'acque sm (GEO) watershed.

sparti'neve sm inv snowplough (BRIT), snowplow (US).

spar'tire vt (eredità, bottino) to share out; (avversari) to separate.

spar'tito sm (MUS) score.

sparti'traffico sm inv (AUT) central reservation (BRIT), median (strip) (US).

spartizi'one [spartit'tsjone] sf division.

spa'ruto, a ag (viso etc) haggard.

sparvi'ero sm (ZOOL) sparrowhawk.

spasi'mante sm suitor.

spasi'mare vi to be in agony; ~ **di fare** (fig) to yearn to do; ~ **per qn** to be madly in love with sb.

'spasimo sm pang.

'spasmo sm (MED) spasm.

spas'modico, a, ci, che ag (angoscioso) agonizing; (MED) spasmodic.

spas'sarsela vi to enjoy o.s., have a good time.

spassio'nato, a ag dispassionate, impartial.

'spasso sm (divertimento) amusement, enjoyment; **andare a** ~ to go out for a walk; **essere a** ~ (fig) to be out of work; **mandare qn a** ~ (fig) to give sb the sack.

spas'soso, a ag amusing, entertaining.

'spastico, a, ci, che ag, sm/f spastic.

'spatola sf spatula.

spau'racchio [spau'rakkjo] sm scarecrow.

spau'rire vt to frighten, terrify.

spavalde'ria sf boldness, arrogance.

spa'valdo, a ag arrogant, bold.

spaventa'passeri sm inv scarecrow.

spaven'tare vt to frighten, scare; ~**rsi** vr to become frightened, become scared.

spa'vento sm fear, fright; **far** ~ **a qn** to give sb a fright.

spaven'toso, a ag frightening, terrible; (fig fam) tremendous, fantastic.

spazi'ale [spat'tsjale] ag (volo, nave, tuta) space cpd; (ARCHIT, GEOM) spatial.

spazia'tura [spattsja'tura] sf (TIP) spacing.

spazien'tire [spattsjen'tire] vi (anche: ~**rsi**) to lose one's patience.

'spazio ['spattsjo] sm space; (posto) room, space; **fare** ~ **per qc/qn** to make room for sth/sb; **nello** ~ **di un'ora** within an hour, in the space of an hour; **dare** ~ **a** (fig) to make room for; ~ **aereo** airspace.

spazi'oso, a [spat'tsjoso] ag spacious.

spazzaca'mino [spattsaka'mino] sm chimney sweep.

spazza'neve [spattsa'neve] sm inv (spartineve, SCI) snowplough (BRIT), snowplow (US).

spaz'zare [spat'tsare] vt to sweep; (foglie etc) to sweep up; (cacciare) to sweep away.

spazza'tura [spattsa'tura] sf sweepings pl; (immondizia) rubbish.

spaz'zino [spat'tsino] sm street sweeper.

'spazzola ['spattsola] sf brush; **capelli a** ~ crew cut sg; ~ **per abiti** clothesbrush; ~ **da capelli** hairbrush.

spazzo'lare [spattso'lare] vt to brush.

spazzo'lino [spattso'lino] sm (small) brush; ~ **da denti** toothbrush.

specchi'arsi [spek'kjarsi] vr to look at o.s. in a mirror; (riflettersi) to be mirrored, be reflected.

specchi'era [spek'kjɛra] sf large mirror; (mobile) dressing table.

specchi'etto [spek'kjetto] sm (tabella) table, chart; ~ **da borsetta** pocket mirror; ~ **retrovisore** (AUT) rear-view mirror.

'specchio ['spɛkkjo] sm mirror; (tabella) table, chart; **uno** ~ **d'acqua** a sheet of water.

speci'ale [spe't∫ale] ag special; **in special modo** especially; **inviato** ~ (RADIO, TV, STAMPA) special correspondent; **offerta** ~ special offer; **poteri/leggi** ~**i** (POL) emergency powers/legislation.

specia'lista, i, e [spet∫a'lista] sm/f specialist.

specia'listico, a, ci, che [spet∫a'listiko] ag (conoscenza, preparazione) specialized.

specialità [spet∫ali'ta] sf inv speciality; (branca di studio) special field, speciality.

specializ'zare [spet∫alid'dzare] vt (industria) to make more specialized; ~**rsi** vr: ~**rsi (in)** to specialize (in).

specializ'zato, a [spet∫alid'dzato] ag (manodopera) skilled; **operaio non** ~ semiskilled worker; **essere** ~ **in** to be a specialist in.

specializzazi'one [spet∫aliddzat'tsjone] sf specialization; **prendere la** ~ **in** to specialize in.

special'mente [spet∫al'mente] av especially, particularly.

'specie ['spɛtʃe] *sf inv* (*BIOL, BOT, ZOOL*) species *inv*; (*tipo*) kind, sort ♦ *av* especially, particularly; **una ~ di** a kind of; **fare ~ a qn** to surprise sb; **la ~ umana** mankind.

spe'cifica, che [spe'tʃifika] *sf* specification.

specifi'care [spetʃifi'kare] *vt* to specify, state.

specificata'mente [spetʃifikata'mente] *av* in detail.

spe'cifico, a, ci, che [spe'tʃifiko] *ag* specific.

speck [ʃpɛk] *sm inv* *kind of smoked ham*.

specu'lare *vi*: **~ su** (*COMM*) to speculate in; (*sfruttare*) to exploit; (*meditare*) to speculate on.

specula'tore, 'trice *sm/f* (*COMM*) speculator.

speculazi'one [spekulat'tsjone] *sf* speculation.

spe'dire *vt* to send; (*COMM*) to dispatch, forward; **~ per posta** to post (*BRIT*), mail (*US*); **~ per mare** to ship.

spedita'mente *av* quickly; **camminare ~** to walk at a brisk pace.

spe'dito, a *ag* (*gen*) quick; **con passo ~** at a brisk pace.

spedizi'one [spedit'tsjone] *sf* sending; (*collo*) consignment; (*scientifica etc*) expedition; (*COMM*) forwarding; shipping; **fare una ~** to send a consignment; **agenzia di ~** forwarding agency; **spese di ~** postal charges; (*COMM*) forwarding charges.

spedizioni'ere [spedittsjo'njɛre] *sm* forwarding agent, shipping agent.

'spegnere ['speɲɲere] *vt* (*fuoco, sigaretta*) to put out, extinguish; (*apparecchio elettrico*) to turn *o* switch off; (*gas*) to turn off; (*fig: suoni, passioni*) to stifle; (*debito*) to extinguish; **~rsi** *vr* to go out; to go off; (*morire*) to pass away.

speleolo'gia [speleolo'dʒia] *sf* (*studio*) speleology; (*pratica*) potholing (*BRIT*), speleology.

spele'ologo, a, gi, ghe *sm/f* speleologist; potholer.

spel'lare *vt* (*scuoiare*) to skin; (*scorticare*) to graze; **~rsi** *vr* to peel.

spendacci'one, a [spendat'tʃone] *sm/f* spendthrift.

'spendere *vt* to spend; **~ una buona parola per qn** (*fig*) to put in a good word for sb.

'spengo *etc vb vedi* **spegnere** ♦

spen'nare *vt* to pluck.

'spensi *etc vb vedi* **spegnere**.

spensiera'tezza [spensjera'tettsa] *sf* carefreeness, lightheartedness.

spensie'rato, a *ag* carefree.

'spento, a *pp di* **spegnere** ♦ *ag* (*suono*) muffled; (*colore*) dull; (*sigaretta*) out; (*civiltà, vulcano*) extinct.

spe'ranza [spe'rantsa] *sf* hope; **nella ~ di rivederti** hoping to see *o* in the hope of seeing you again; **pieno di ~** hopeful; **senza ~** (*situazione*) hopeless; (*amare*) without hope.

speran'zoso, a [speran'tsoso] *ag* hopeful.

spe'rare *vt* to hope for ♦ *vi*: **~ in** to trust in; **~ che/di fare** to hope that/to do; **lo spero, spero di sì** I hope so; **tutto fa ~ per il meglio** everything leads one to hope for the best.

sper'duto, a *ag* (*isolato*) out-of-the-way; (*persona: smarrita, a disagio*) lost.

spergi'uro, a [sper'dʒuro] *sm/f* perjurer ♦ *sm* perjury.

sperico'lato, a *ag* fearless, daring; (*guidatore*) reckless.

sperimen'tale *ag* experimental; **fare qc in via ~** to try sth out.

sperimen'tare *vt* to experiment with, test; (*fig*) to test, put to the test.

sperimentazi'one [sperimentat'tsjone] *sf* experimentation.

'sperma, i *sm* (*BIOL*) sperm.

spermato'zoo, i [spermatod'dzɔo] *sm* spermatozoon.

spe'rone *sm* spur.

sperpe'rare *vt* to squander.

'sperpero *sm* (*di denaro*) squandering, waste; (*di cibo, materiali*) waste.

'spesa *sf* (*soldi spesi*) expense; (*costo*) cost; (*acquisto*) purchase; (*fam: acquisto del cibo quotidiano*) shopping; **~e** *sfpl* expenses; (*COMM*) costs; charges; **ridurre le ~e** (*gen*) to cut down; (*COMM*) to reduce expenditure; **fare la ~** to do the shopping; **fare le ~e di qc** (*fig*) to pay the price for sth; **a ~e di** (*a carico di*) at the expense of; **con la modica ~ di 200 euro** for the modest sum *o* outlay of 200 euros; **~ pubblica** public expenditure; **~e accessorie** incidental expenses; **~e generali** overheads; **~e di gestione** operating expenses; **~ d'impianto** initial outlay; **~e legali** legal costs; **~e di manutenzione, ~e di mantenimento** maintenance costs; **~e postali** postage *sg*; **~e di sbarco e sdoganamento** landing charges; **~e di trasporto** handling charge; **~e di viaggio** travelling (*BRIT*) *o* traveling (*US*) expenses.

spe'sare *vt*: **viaggio tutto spesato** all-expenses-paid trip.

'speso, a *pp di* **spendere**.

'**spesso, a** *ag* (*fitto*) thick; (*frequente*) frequent ♦ *av* often; ~**e volte** frequently, often.

spes'sore *sm* thickness; **ha uno ~ di 20 cm** it is 20 cm thick.

Spett. *abbr vedi* **spettabile.**

spet'tabile *ag* (*abbr:* **Spett.**: *in lettere*): ~ **ditta X** Messrs X and Co; **avvertiamo la ~ clientela** … we inform our customers ….

spettaco'lare *ag* spectacular.

spet'tacolo *sm* (*rappresentazione*) performance, show; (*vista, scena*) sight; **dare ~ di sé** to make an exhibition *o* a spectacle of o.s.

spettaco'loso, a *ag* spectacular.

spet'tanza [spet'tantsa] *sf* (*competenza*) concern; **non è di mia ~** it's no concern of mine.

spet'tare *vi*: ~ **a** (*decisione*) to be up to; (*stipendio*) to be due to; **spetta a lei decidere** it's up to you to decide.

spetta'tore, 'trice *sm/f* (*CINE, TEAT*) member of the audience; (*di avvenimento*) onlooker, witness.

spettego'lare *vi* to gossip.

spetti'nare *vt*: ~ **qn** to ruffle sb's hair; ~**rsi** *vr* to get one's hair in a mess.

spet'trale *ag* spectral, ghostly.

'**spettro** *sm* (*fantasma*) spectre (*BRIT*), specter (*US*); (*FISICA*) spectrum.

'**spezie** ['spɛttsje] *sfpl* (*CUC*) spices.

spez'zare [spet'tsare] *vt* (*rompere*) to break; (*fig: interrompere*) to break up; ~**rsi** *vr* to break.

spezza'tino [spettsa'tino] *sm* (*CUC*) stew.

spez'zato, a [spet'tsato] *ag* (*unghia, ramo, braccio*) broken ♦ *sm* (*abito maschile*) coordinated jacket and trousers (*BRIT*) *o* pants (*US*); **fare orario ~** to work a split shift.

spezzet'tare [spettset'tare] *vt* to break up (*o* chop) into small pieces.

spez'zino, a [spet'tsino] *ag* of (*o* from) La Spezia.

spez'zone [spet'tsone] *sm* (*CINE*) clip.

'**spia** *sf* spy; (*confidente della polizia*) informer; (*ELETTR*) indicating light; warning light; (*fessura*) peephole; (*fig: sintomo*) sign, indication; ~ **dell'olio** (*AUT*) oil warning light.

spiacci'care [spjattʃi'kare] *vt* to squash, crush.

spia'cente [spja'tʃɛnte] *ag* sorry; **essere ~ di qc/di fare qc** to be sorry about sth/for doing sth; **siamo ~i di dovervi annunciare che** … we regret to announce that ….

spia'cevole [spja'tʃevole] *ag* unpleasant, disagreeable.

spi'aggia, ge ['spjaddʒa] *sf* beach.

spia'nare *vt* (*terreno*) to level, make level; (*edificio*) to raze to the ground; (*pasta*) to roll out; (*rendere liscio*) to smooth (out).

spi'ano *sm*: **a tutto ~** (*lavorare*) non-stop, without a break; (*spendere*) lavishly.

spian'tato, a *ag* penniless, ruined.

spi'are *vt* to spy on; (*occasione etc*) to watch *o* wait for.

spi'ata *sf* tip-off.

spiattel'lare *vt* (*fam: verità, segreto*) to blurt out.

spi'azzo ['spjattso] *sm* open space; (*radura*) clearing.

spic'care *vt* (*assegno, mandato di cattura*) to issue ♦ *vi* (*risaltare*) to stand out; ~ **il volo** to fly off; (*fig*) to spread one's wings; ~ **un balzo** to jump, leap.

spic'cato, a *ag* (*marcato*) marked, strong; (*notevole*) remarkable.

spiccherò *etc* [spikke'rɔ] *vb vedi* **spiccare.**

'**spicchio** ['spikkjo] *sm* (*di agrumi*) segment; (*di aglio*) clove; (*parte*) piece, slice.

spicci'are [spit'tʃare] *vt* (*faccenda, impegno*) to finish off; ~**rsi** *vr* (*fare in fretta*) to hurry up, get a move on.

'**spiccio, a, ci, ce** ['spittʃo] *ag* (*modi, mezzi*) quick; **andare per le ~ce** to be quick off the mark, waste no time.

spiccio'lata [spittʃo'lata] *av*: **alla ~** in dribs and drabs, a few at a time.

'**spicciolo, a** ['spittʃolo] *ag*: **moneta ~a, ~i** *smpl* (small) change.

'**spicco, chi** *sm*: **fare ~** to stand out; **di ~** outstanding, prominent; (*tema*) main, principal.

spie'dino *sm* (*utensile*) skewer; (*cibo*) kebab.

spi'edo *sm* (*CUC*) spit; **pollo allo ~** spit-roasted chicken.

spiega'mento *sm* (*MIL*): ~ **di forze** deployment of forces.

spie'gare *vt* (*far capire*) to explain; (*tovaglia*) to unfold; (*vele*) to unfurl; ~**rsi** *vr* to explain o.s., make o.s. clear; ~ **qc a qn** to explain sth to sb; **il problema si spiega** one can understand the problem; **non mi spiego come** … I can't understand how ….

spiegazi'one [spjegat'tsjone] *sf* explanation; **avere una ~ con qn** to have it out with sb.

spiegaz'zare [spjegat'tsare] *vt* to crease, crumple.

spiegherò *etc* [spjege'rɔ] *vb vedi* **spiegare.**

spie'tato, a *ag* ruthless, pitiless.

spiffe'rare *vt* (*fam*) to blurt out, blab.

'**spiffero** *sm* draught (*BRIT*), draft (*US*).

'**spiga, ghe** *sf* (*BOT*) ear.
spigli'ato, a [spiʎ'ʎato] *ag* self-possessed, self-confident.
spigo'lare *vt* (*anche fig*) to glean.
'**spigolo** *sm* corner; (*GEOM*) edge.
spigo'loso, a *ag* (*mobile*) angular; (*persona, carattere*) difficult.
'**spilla** *sf* brooch; (*da cravatta, cappello*) pin.
spil'lare *vt* (*vino, fig*) to tap; ~ **denaro/ notizie a qn** to tap sb for money/ information.
'**spillo** *sm* pin; (*spilla*) brooch; **tacco a** ~ stiletto heel (*BRIT*), spike heel (*US*); ~ **di sicurezza** *o* **da balia** safety pin; ~ **di sicurezza** (*MIL*) (safety) pin.
spilorce'ria [spilortʃe'ria] *sf* meanness, stinginess.
spi'lorcio, a, ci, ce [spi'lortʃo] *ag* mean, stingy.
spilun'gone *sm/f* beanpole.
'**spina** *sf* (*BOT*) thorn; (*ZOOL*) spine, prickle; (*di pesce*) bone; (*ELETTR*) plug; (*di botte*) bunghole; **birra alla** ~ draught beer; **stare sulle** ~**e** (*fig*) to be on tenterhooks; ~ **dorsale** (*ANAT*) backbone.
spi'nacio [spi'natʃo] *sm* spinach *no pl*; (*CUC*): ~**i** spinach *sg*.
spi'nale *ag* (*ANAT*) spinal.
spi'nato, a *ag* (*fornito di spine*): **filo** ~ barbed wire; (*tessuto*) herringbone *cpd*.
spi'nello *sm* (*DROGA: gergo*) joint.
'**spingere** ['spindʒere] *vt* to push; (*condurre: anche fig*) to drive; (*stimolare*): ~ **qn a fare** to urge *o* press sb to do; ~**rsi** *vr* (*inoltrarsi*) to push on, carry on; ~**rsi troppo lontano** (*anche fig*) to go too far.
'**spino** *sm* (*BOT*) thorn bush.
spi'noso, a *ag* thorny, prickly.
'**spinsi** *etc vb vedi* **spingere**.
spinte'rogeno [spinte'rɔdʒeno] *sm* (*AUT*) coil ignition.
'**spinto, a** *pp di* **spingere** ♦ *sf* (*urto*) push; (*FISICA*) thrust; (*fig: stimolo*) incentive, spur; (: *appoggio*) string-pulling *no pl*; **dare una** ~**a a qn** (*fig*) to pull strings for sb.
spinto'nare *vt* to shove, push.
spin'tone *sm* push, shove.
spio'naggio [spio'naddʒo] *sm* espionage, spying.
spion'cino [spion'tʃino] *sm* peephole.
spi'one, a *sm/f* (*spia*) informer; (*ragazzino, collega*) telltale, sneak.
spio'nistico, a, ci, che *ag* (*organizzazione*) spy *cpd*; **rete** ~**a** spy ring.
spi'overe *vi* (*scorrere*) to flow down; (*ricadere*) to hang down, fall.
'**spira** *sf* coil.
spi'raglio [spi'raʎʎo] *sm* (*fessura*) chink,

narrow opening; (*raggio di luce, fig*) glimmer, gleam.
spi'rale *sf* spiral; (*contraccettivo*) coil; **a** ~ spiral(-shaped); ~ **inflazionistica** inflationary spiral.
spi'rare *vi* (*vento*) to blow; (*morire*) to expire, pass away.
spiri'tato, a *ag* possessed; (*fig: persona, espressione*) wild.
spiri'tismo *sm* spiritualism.
'**spirito** *sm* (*REL, CHIM, disposizione d'animo, di legge etc, fantasma*) spirit; (*pensieri, intelletto*) mind; (*arguzia*) wit; (*umorismo*) humour, wit; **in buone condizioni di** ~ in the right frame of mind; **è una persona di** ~ he has a sense of humour (*BRIT*) *o* humor (*US*); **battuta di** ~ joke; ~ **di classe** class consciousness; **non ha** ~ **di parte** he never takes sides; **lo S**~ **Santo** the Holy Spirit *o* Ghost.
spirito'saggine [spirito'saddʒine] *sf* witticism; (*peg*) wisecrack.
spiri'toso, a *ag* witty.
spiritu'ale *ag* spiritual.
splen'dente *ag* (*giornata*) bright, sunny; (*occhi*) shining; (*pavimento*) shining, gleaming.
'**splendere** *vi* to shine.
'**splendido, a** *ag* splendid; (*splendente*) shining; (*sfarzoso*) magnificent, splendid.
splen'dore *sm* splendour (*BRIT*), splendor (*US*); (*luce intensa*) brilliance, brightness.
spodes'tare *vt* to deprive of power; (*sovrano*) to depose.
'**spoglia** ['spɔʎʎa] *sf vedi* **spoglio**.
spogli'are [spoʎ'ʎare] *vt* (*svestire*) to undress; (*privare, fig: depredare*): ~ **qn di qc** to deprive sb of sth; (*togliere ornamenti: anche fig*): ~ **qn/qc di** to strip sb/sth of; ~**rsi** *vr* to undress, strip; ~**rsi di** (*ricchezze etc*) to deprive o.s. of, give up; (*pregiudizi*) to rid o.s. of.
spoglia'rello [spoʎʎa'rɛllo] *sm* striptease.
spoglia'toio [spoʎʎa'tojo] *sm* dressing room; (*di scuola etc*) cloakroom; (*SPORT*) changing room.
'**spoglio, a** ['spɔʎʎo] *ag* (*pianta, terreno*) bare; (*privo*): ~ **di** stripped of; lacking in, without ♦ *sm* (*di voti*) counting ♦ *sf* (*ZOOL*) skin, hide; (: *di rettile*) slough; ~**e** *sfpl* (*salma*) remains; (*preda*) spoils, booty *sg*.
'**spola** *sf* shuttle; (*bobina*) spool; **fare la** ~ (**fra**) to go to and fro *o* shuttle (between).
spo'letta *sf* (*CUCITO: bobina*) spool; (*di bomba*) fuse.
spol'pare *vt* to strip the flesh off.
spolve'rare *vt* (*anche CUC*) to dust; (*con spazzola*) to brush; (*con battipanni*) to beat;

(*fig: mangiare*) to polish off ♦ *vi* to dust.
spolve'rino *sm* (*soprabito*) dust coat.
'sponda *sf* (*di fiume*) bank; (*di mare, lago*)
shore; (*bordo*) edge.
sponsoriz'zare [sponsorid'dzare] *vt* to
sponsor.
sponsorizzazi'one [sponsoriddzat'tsjone]
sf sponsorship.
spontanea'mente *av* (*comportarsi*)
naturally; (*agire*) spontaneously; (*reagire*)
instinctively, spontaneously.
spon'taneo, a *ag* spontaneous; (*persona*)
unaffected, natural; **di sua ~a volontà** of
his own free will.
spopo'lare *vt* to depopulate ♦ *vi* (*attirare
folla*) to draw the crowds; **~rsi** *vr* to
become depopulated.
spo'radico, a, ci, che *ag* sporadic.
sporcacci'one, a [sporkat'tʃone] *sm/f* (*peg*)
pig, filthy person.
spor'care *vt* to dirty, make dirty; (*fig*) to
sully, soil; **~rsi** *vr* to get dirty.
spor'cizia [spor'tʃittsja] *sf* (*stato*) dirtiness;
(*sudiciume*) dirt, filth; (*fig: cosa oscena*)
obscenity.
'sporco, a, chi, che *ag* dirty, filthy; **avere
la coscienza ~a** to have a guilty
conscience.
spor'genza [spor'dʒɛntsa] *sf* projection.
'sporgere ['spɔrdʒere] *vt* to put out, stretch
out ♦ *vi* (*venire in fuori*) to stick out; **~rsi** *vr*
to lean out; **~ querela contro qn** (*DIR*) to
take legal action against sb.
'sporsi *etc vb vedi* **sporgere.**
sport *sm inv* sport.
'sporta *sf* shopping bag.
spor'tello *sm* (*di treno, auto etc*) door; (*di
banca, ufficio*) window, counter; **~
automatico** (*BANCA*) cash dispenser,
automated telling machine.
spor'tivo, a *ag* (*gara, giornale*) sports *cpd*;
(*persona*) sporty; (*abito*) casual; (*spirito,
atteggiamento*) sportsman/ ♦ *sm/f* sportsman/
woman; **campo ~** playing field; **giacca ~a**
sports (*BRIT*) *o* sport (*US*) jacket.
'sporto, a *pp di* **sporgere.**
'sposa *sf* bride; (*moglie*) wife; **abito** *o*
vestito da ~ wedding dress.
sposa'lizio [spoza'littsjo] *sm* wedding.
spo'sare *vt* to marry; (*fig: idea, fede*) to
espouse; **~rsi** *vr* to get married, marry;
~rsi con qn to marry sb, get married to
sb.
spo'sato, a *ag* married.
'sposo *sm* (*bride*)groom; (*marito*) husband;
gli ~i the newlyweds.
spos'sante *ag* exhausting.
spossa'tezza [spossa'tettsa] *sf* exhaustion.

spos'sato, a *ag* exhausted, weary.
sposta'mento *sm* movement, change of
position.
spos'tare *vt* to move, shift; (*cambiare:
orario*) to change; **~rsi** *vr* to move; **hanno
spostato la partenza di qualche giorno**
they postponed *o* put off their departure
by a few days.
spot [spɔt] *sm inv* (*faretto*) spotlight, spot;
(*TV*) advert, commercial, ad.
'spranga, ghe *sf* (*sbarra*) bar; (*catenaccio*)
bolt.
spran'gare *vt* to bar; to bolt.
spray ['sprai] *sm inv* (*dispositivo, sostanza*)
spray ♦ *ag inv* (*bombola, confezione*) spray
cpd.
'sprazzo ['sprattso] *sm* (*di sole etc*) flash;
(*fig: di gioia etc*) burst.
spre'care *vt* to waste; **~rsi** *vr* (*persona*) to
waste one's energy.
'spreco, chi *sm* waste.
spre'gevole [spre'dʒevole] *ag* contemptible,
despicable.
'spregio ['spredʒo] *sm* scorn, disdain.
spregiudi'cato, a [spredʒudi'kato] *ag*
unprejudiced, unbiased; (*peg*)
unscrupulous.
'spremere *vt* to squeeze; **~rsi le meningi**
(*fig*) to rack one's brains.
spre'muta *sf* fresh fruit juice; **~ d'arancia**
fresh orange juice.
sprez'zante [spret'tsante] *ag* scornful,
contemptuous.
'sprezzo ['sprɛttso] *sm* contempt, scorn,
disdain.
sprigio'nare [spridʒo'nare] *vt* to give off,
emit; **~rsi** *vr* to emanate; (*uscire con
impeto*) to burst out.
spriz'zare [sprit'tsare] *vt, vi* to spurt; **~
gioia/salute** to be bursting with joy/
health.
sprofon'dare *vi* to sink; (*casa*) to collapse;
(*suolo*) to give way, subside; **~rsi** *vr*: **~rsi
in** (*poltrona*) to sink into; (*fig*) to become
immersed *o* absorbed in.
sproloqui'are *vi* to ramble on.
spro'loquio *sm* rambling speech.
spro'nare *vt* to spur (on).
'sprone *sm* (*sperone, fig*) spur.
sproporzio'nato, a [sproportsjo'nato] *ag*
disproportionate, out of all proportion.
sproporzi'one [spropor'tsjone] *sf*
disproportion.
sproposi'tato, a *ag* (*lettera, discorso*) full
of mistakes; (*fig: costo*) excessive,
enormous.
spro'posito *sm* blunder; **a ~** at the wrong
time; (*rispondere, parlare*) irrelevantly.

sprovve'duto, a *ag* inexperienced, naïve.

sprov'visto, a *ag* (*mancante*): ~ **di** lacking in, without; **ne siamo** ~**i** (*negozio*) we are out of it (*o* them); **alla** ~**a** unawares.

spruz'zare [sprut'tsare] *vt* (*a nebulizzazione*) to spray; (*aspergere*) to sprinkle; (*inzaccherare*) to splash.

spruzza'tore [spruttsa'tore] *sm* (*per profumi*) spray, atomizer; (*per biancheria*) sprinkler, spray.

'spruzzo ['spruttso] *sm* spray; splash; **verniciatura a** ~ spray painting.

spudora'tezza [spudora'tettsa] *sf* shamelessness.

spudo'rato, a *ag* shameless.

'spugna ['spuɲɲa] *sf* (*ZOOL*) sponge; (*tessuto*) towelling.

spu'gnoso, a [spuɲ'ɲoso] *ag* spongy.

spulci'are [spul'tʃare] *vt* (*animali*) to rid of fleas; (*fig: testo, compito*) to examine thoroughly.

'spuma *sf* (*schiuma*) foam; (*bibita*) fizzy drink.

spu'mante *sm* sparkling wine.

spumeggi'ante [spumed'dʒante] *ag* (*vino, fig*) sparkling; (*birra, mare*) foaming.

spu'mone *sm* (*CUC*) mousse.

spun'tare *sm*: **allo** ~ **del sole** at sunrise; **allo** ~ **del giorno** at daybreak ♦ *vt* (*coltello*) to break the point of; (*capelli*) to trim; (*elenco*) to tick off (*BRIT*), check off (*US*) ♦ *vi* (*uscire: germogli*) to sprout; (: *capelli*) to begin to grow; (: *denti*) to come through; (*apparire*) to appear (suddenly); ~**rsi** *vr* to become blunt, lose its point; **spuntarla** (*fig*) to make it, win through.

spun'tino *sm* snack.

'spunto *sm* (*TEAT, MUS*) cue; (*fig*) starting point; **dare lo** ~ **a** to give rise to; **prendere** ~ **da qc** to take sth as one's starting point.

spur'gare *vt* (*fogna*) to clean, clear; ~**rsi** *vr* (*MED*) to expectorate.

spu'tare *vt* to spit out; (*fig*) to belch (out) ♦ *vi* to spit.

'sputo *sm* spittle *no pl*, spit *no pl*.

sputta'nare *vt* (*fam*) to bad-mouth.

'squadra *sf* (*strumento*) (set) square; (*gruppo*) team, squad; (*di operai*) gang, squad; (*MIL*) squad; (: *AER, NAUT*) squadron; (*SPORT*) team; **lavoro a** ~**e** teamwork; ~ **mobile/del buon costume** (*POLIZIA*) flying/vice squad.

squa'drare *vt* to square, make square; (*osservare*) to look at closely.

squa'driglia [skwa'driʎʎa] *sf* (*AER*) flight; (*NAUT*) squadron.

squa'drone *sm* squadron.

squagli'arsi [skwaʎ'ʎarsi] *vr* to melt; (*fig*) to sneak off.

squa'lifica, che *sf* disqualification.

squalifi'care *vt* to disqualify.

'squallido, a *ag* wretched, bleak.

squal'lore *sm* wretchedness, bleakness.

'squalo *sm* shark.

'squama *sf* scale.

squa'mare *vt* to scale; ~**rsi** *vr* to flake *o* peel (off).

squarcia'gola [skwartʃa'gola]: **a** ~ *av* at the top of one's voice.

squarci'are [skwar'tʃare] *vt* (*muro, corpo*) to rip open; (*tessuto*) to rip; (*fig: tenebre, silenzio*) to split; (: *nuvole*) to pierce.

'squarcio ['skwartʃo] *sm* (*ferita*) gash; (*in lenzuolo, abito*) rip; (*in un muro*) breach; (*in una nave*) hole; (*brano*) passage, excerpt; **uno** ~ **di sole** a burst of sunlight.

squar'tare *vt* to quarter, cut up; (*cadavere*) to dismember.

squattri'nato, a *ag* penniless ♦ *sm/f* pauper.

squili'brare *vt* to unbalance.

squili'brato, a *ag* (*PSIC*) unbalanced ♦ *sm/f* deranged person.

squi'librio *sm* (*differenza, sbilancio*) imbalance; (*PSIC*) derangement.

squil'lante *ag* (*suono*) shrill, sharp; (*voce*) shrill.

squil'lare *vi* (*campanello, telefono*) to ring (out); (*tromba*) to blare.

'squillo *sm* ring, ringing *no pl*; blare ♦ *sf inv* (*anche: ragazza* ~) call girl.

squi'sito, a *ag* exquisite; (*cibo*) delicious; (*persona*) delightful.

squit'tire *vi* (*uccello*) to squawk; (*topo*) to squeak.

SR *sigla* = Siracusa.

sradi'care *vt* to uproot; (*fig*) to eradicate.

sragio'nare [zradʒo'nare] *vi* to talk nonsense, rave.

sregola'tezza [zregola'tettsa] *sf* (*nel mangiare, bere*) lack of moderation; (*di vita*) dissoluteness, dissipation.

srego'lato, a *ag* (*senza ordine: vita*) disorderly; (*smodato*) immoderate; (*dissoluto*) dissolute.

Sri 'Lanka [sri'lanka] *sm*: **lo** ~ Sri Lanka.

S.r.l. *abbr vedi* **società a responsabilità limitata**.

sroto'lare *vt*, ~**rsi** *vr* to unroll.

SS *sigla* = Sassari.

S.S. *abbr* (*REL*) = Sua Santità; Santa Sede; santi, santissimo; (*AUT*) = **strada statale**; *vedi* **statale**.

S.S.N. *abbr* (= Servizio Sanitario Nazionale) ≈

NHS.

sta *etc vb vedi* **stare**.

'**stabbio** *sm* (*recinto*) pen, fold; (*di maiali*) pigsty; (*letame*) manure.

'**stabile** *ag* stable, steady; (*tempo: non variabile*) settled; (*TEAT: compagnia*) resident ♦ *sm* (*edificio*) building; **teatro** ~ civic theatre.

stabili'mento *sm* (*edificio*) establishment; (*fabbrica*) plant, factory; ~ **balneare** bathing establishment; ~ **tessile** textile mill.

stabi'lire *vt* to establish; (*fissare: prezzi, data*) to fix; (*decidere*) to decide; ~**rsi** *vr* (*prendere dimora*) to settle; **resta stabilito che** ... it is agreed that ....

stabilità *sf* stability.

stabiliz'zare [stabilid'dzare] *vt* to stabilize.

stabilizza'tore [stabiliddza'tore] *sm* stabilizer; (*fig*) stabilizing force.

stabilizzazi'one [stabiliddzat'tsjone] *sf* stabilization.

stacano'vista, i, e *sm/f* (*ironico*) eager beaver.

stac'care *vt* (*levare*) to detach, remove; (*separare: anche fig*) to separate, divide; (*strappare*) to tear off (*o* out); (*scandire: parole*) to pronounce clearly; (*SPORT*) to leave behind; ~**rsi** *vr* (*bottone etc*) to come off; (*scostarsi*): ~**rsi** (**da**) to move away (from); (*fig: separarsi*): ~**rsi da** to leave; **non** ~ **gli occhi da qn** not to take one's eyes off sb; ~ **la televisione/il telefono** to disconnect the television/the phone; ~ **un assegno** to write a cheque.

staccio'nata [stattʃo'nata] *sf* (*gen*) fence; (*IPPICA*) hurdle.

'**stacco, chi** *sm* (*intervallo*) gap; (: *tra due scene*) break; (*differenza*) difference; (*SPORT: nel salto*) takeoff.

sta'dera *sf* lever scales *pl*.

'**stadio** *sm* (*SPORT*) stadium; (*periodo, fase*) phase, stage.

'**staffa** *sf* (*di sella, TECN*) stirrup; **perdere le** ~**e** (*fig*) to fly off the handle.

staf'fetta *sf* (*messo*) dispatch rider; (*SPORT*) relay race.

stagflazi'one [stagflat'tsjone] *sf* (*ECON*) stagflation.

stagio'nale [stadʒo'nale] *ag* seasonal ♦ *sm/f* seasonal worker.

stagio'nare [stadʒo'nare] *vt* (*legno*) to season; (*formaggi, vino*) to mature.

stagio'nato, a [stadʒo'nato] *ag* (*vedi vb*) seasoned; matured; (*scherzoso: attempato*) getting on in years.

stagi'one [sta'dʒone] *sf* season; **alta/bassa** ~ high/low season.

stagli'arsi [staʎ'ʎarsi] *vr* to stand out, be silhouetted.

sta'gnante [staɲ'ɲante] *ag* stagnant.

sta'gnare [staɲ'ɲare] *vt* (*vaso, tegame*) to tin-plate; (*barca, botte*) to make watertight; (*sangue*) to stop ♦ *vi* to stagnate.

sta'gnino [staɲ'ɲino] *sm* tinsmith.

'**stagno, a** ['staɲɲo] *ag* (*a tenuta d'acqua*) watertight; (*a tenuta d'aria*) airtight ♦ *sm* (*acquitrino*) pond; (*CHIM*) tin.

sta'gnola [staɲ'ɲɔla] *sf* tinfoil.

stalag'mite *sf* stalagmite.

stalat'tite *sf* stalactite.

stali'nismo *sm* (*POL*) Stalinism.

'**stalla** *sf* (*per bovini*) cowshed; (*per cavalli*) stable.

stalli'ere *sm* groom, stableboy.

'**stallo** *sm* stall, seat; (*SCACCHI*) stalemate; (*AER*) stall; **situazione di** ~ (*fig*) stalemate.

stal'lone *sm* stallion.

sta'mani, stamat'tina *av* this morning.

stam'becco, chi *sm* ibex.

stam'berga, ghe *sf* hovel.

'**stampa** *sf* (*TIP, FOT: tecnica*) printing; (*impressione, copia fotografica*) print; (*insieme di quotidiani, giornalisti etc*): **la** ~ the press; **andare in** ~ to go to press; **mandare in** ~ to pass for press; **errore di** ~ printing error; **prova di** ~ print sample; **libertà di** ~ freedom of the press; "~**e**" "printed matter".

stam'pante *sf* (*INFORM*) printer; ~ **seriale/termica** serial/thermal printer.

stam'pare *vt* to print; (*pubblicare*) to publish; (*coniare*) to strike, coin; (*imprimere: anche fig*) to impress.

stampa'tello *sm* block letters *pl*.

stam'pato, a *ag* printed ♦ *sm* (*opuscolo*) leaflet; (*modulo*) form; ~**i** *smpl* printed matter *sg*.

stam'pella *sf* crutch.

stampigli'are [stampiʎ'ʎare] *vt* to stamp.

stampiglia'tura [stampiʎʎa'tura] *sf* (*atto*) stamping; (*marchio*) stamp.

'**stampo** *sm* mould; (*fig: indole*) type, kind, sort.

sta'nare *vt* to drive out.

stan'care *vt* to tire, make tired; (*annoiare*) to bore; (*infastidire*) to annoy; ~**rsi** *vr* to get tired, tire o.s. out; ~**rsi** (**di**) (*stufarsi*) to grow weary (of), grow tired (of).

stan'chezza [stan'kettsa] *sf* tiredness, fatigue.

'**stanco, a, chi, che** *ag* tired; ~ **di** tired of, fed up with.

stand [stand] *sm inv* (*in fiera*) stand.

'**standard** ['standərd] *sm inv* (*livello*)

standard.

standardiz'zare [standardid'dzare] *vt* to standardize.

stan'dista, i, e *sm/f* (*in una fiera etc*) person responsible for a stand.

'stanga, ghe *sm* bar; (*di carro*) shaft.

stan'gare *vt* (*fig: cliente*) to overcharge; (: *studente*) to fail.

stan'gata *sf* (*colpo: anche fig*) blow; (*cattivo risultato*) poor result; (*CALCIO*) shot.

stan'ghetta [stan'getta] *sf* (*di occhiali*) leg; (*MUS, di scrittura*) bar.

'stanno *vb vedi* **stare**.

sta'notte *av* tonight; (*notte passata*) last night.

'stante *prep* owing to, because of; **a sé** ~ (*appartamento, casa*) independent, separate.

stan'tio, a, 'tii, 'tie *ag* stale; (*burro*) rancid; (*fig*) old.

stan'tuffo *sm* piston.

'stanza ['stantsa] *sf* room; (*POESIA*) stanza; **essere di** ~ **a** (*MIL*) to be stationed in; ~ **da bagno** bathroom; ~ **da letto** bedroom.

stanzia'mento [stantsja'mento] *sm* allocation.

stanzi'are [stan'tsjare] *vt* to allocate.

stan'zino [stan'tsino] *sm* (*ripostiglio*) storeroom; (*spogliatoio*) changing room (*BRIT*), locker room (*US*).

stap'pare *vt* to uncork; (*tappo a corona*) to uncap.

star [star] *sf* (*attore, attrice etc*) star.

'stare *vi* (*restare in un luogo*) to stay, remain; (*abitare*) to stay, live; (*essere situato*) to be, be situated; (*anche*: ~ **in piedi**) to stand; (*essere, trovarsi*) to be; (*dipendere*): **se stesse in me** if it were up to me, if it depended on me; (*seguito da gerundio*): **sta studiando** he's studying; ~ **per fare qc** to be about to do sth; **starci** (*esserci spazio*): **nel baule non ci sta più niente** there's no more room in the boot; (*accettare*): **ci stai?** is that okay with you?; ~ **a** (*attenersi a*) to follow, stick to; (*seguito dall'infinito*): ~ **a sentire** to listen; **staremo a vedere** let's wait and see; **stiamo a discutere** we're talking; (*toccare a*): **sta a te giocare** it's your turn to play; **sta a te decidere** it's up to you to decide; ~ **a qn** (*abiti etc*) to fit sb; **queste scarpe mi stanno strette** these shoes are tight for me; **il rosso ti sta bene** red suits you; **come sta?** how are you?; **io sto bene/male** I'm very well/not very well; ~ **fermo** to keep *o* stay still; ~ **seduto** to sit, be sitting; ~ **zitto** to keep quiet; **stando così le cose** given the situation; **stando a ciò**

che dice lui according to him *o* to his version.

starnaz'zare [starnat'tsare] *vi* to squawk.

starnu'tire *vi* to sneeze.

star'nuto *sm* sneeze.

sta'sera *av* this evening, tonight.

'stasi *sf* (*MED, fig*) stasis.

sta'tale *ag* state *cpd*, government *cpd* ♦ *sm/f* state employee; (*nell'amministrazione*) ≈ civil servant; **bilancio** ~ national budget; **strada** ~ ≈ trunk (*BRIT*) *o* main road.

stataliz'zare [statalid'dzare] *vt* to nationalize, put under state control.

'statico, a, ci, che *ag* (*ELETTR, fig*) static.

sta'tista, i *sm* statesman.

sta'tistico, a, ci, che *ag* statistical ♦ *sf* statistic; (*scienza*) statistics *sg*; **fare una** ~**a** to carry out a statistical examination.

'stato, a *pp di* **essere, stare** ♦ *sm* (*condizione*) state, condition; (*POL*) state; (*DIR*) status; **essere in** ~ **d'accusa** (*DIR*) to be committed for trial; **essere in** ~ **d'arresto** (*DIR*) to be under arrest; **essere in** ~ **interessante** to be pregnant; ~ **d'assedio/ d'emergenza** state of siege/emergency; ~ **civile** (*AMM*) marital status; ~ **di famiglia** (*AMM*) *certificate giving details of a household and its dependents*; ~ **maggiore** (*MIL*) general staff; ~ **patrimoniale** (*COMM*) statement of assets and liabilities; **gli S**~**i Uniti (d'America)** the United States (of America).

'statua *sf* statue.

statuni'tense *ag* United States *cpd*, of the United States.

sta'tura *sf* (*ANAT*) height; (*fig*) stature; **essere alto/basso di** ~ to be tall/short *o* small.

sta'tuto *sm* (*DIR*) statute; **regione a** ~ **speciale** *Italian region with political autonomy in certain matters*; ~ **della società** (*COMM*) articles *pl* of association.

sta'volta *av* this time.

staziona'mento [stattsjona'mento] *sm* (*AUT*) parking; (: *sosta*) waiting; **freno di** ~ handbrake.

stazio'nare [stattsjo'nare] *vi* (*veicoli*) to be parked.

stazio'nario, a [stattsjo'narjo] *ag* stationary; (*fig*) unchanged.

stazi'one [stat'tsjone] *sf* station; (*balneare, invernale etc*) resort; ~ **degli autobus** bus station; ~ **balneare** seaside resort; ~ **climatica** health resort; ~ **ferroviaria** railway (*BRIT*) *o* railroad (*US*) station; ~ **invernale** winter sports resort; ~ **di lavoro** work station; ~ **di polizia** police station (*in small town*); ~ **di servizio**

service *o* petrol (*BRIT*) *o* filling station; ~
termale spa.

'**stazza** ['stattsa] *sf* tonnage.

st. civ. *abbr* = **stato civile**.

'**stecca, che** *sf* stick; (*di ombrello*) rib; (*di
sigarette*) carton; (*MED*) splint; (*stonatura*):
fare una ~ to sing (*o* play) a wrong note.

stec'cato *sm* fence.

stec'chito, a [stek'kito] *ag* dried up;
(*persona*) skinny; **lasciar** ~ **qn** (*fig*) to
leave sb flabbergasted; **morto** ~ stone
dead.

'**stella** *sf* star; ~ **alpina** (*BOT*) edelweiss; ~
cadente *o* **filante** shooting star; ~ **di mare**
(*ZOOL*) starfish; ~ **di Natale** (*BOT*)
poinsettia.

stel'lato, a *ag* (*cielo, notte*) starry.

'**stelo** *sm* stem; (*asta*) rod; **lampada a** ~
standard lamp (*BRIT*), floor lamp.

'**stemma, i** *sm* coat of arms.

'**stemmo** *vb vedi* **stare**.

stempe'rare *vt* (*calce, colore*) to dissolve.

stempi'ato, a *ag* with a receding hairline.

stempia'tura *sf* receding hairline.

sten'dardo *sm* standard.

'**stendere** *vt* (*braccia, gambe*) to stretch
(out); (*tovaglia*) to spread (out); (*bucato*) to
hang out; (*mettere a giacere*) to lay (down);
(*spalmare: colore*) to spread; (*mettere per
iscritto*) to draw up; ~**rsi** *vr* (*coricarsi*) to
stretch out, lie down; (*estendersi*) to
extend, stretch.

stendibianche'ria [stendibjanke'ria] *sm inv*
clotheshorse.

stendi'toio *sm* (*locale*) drying room;
(*stendibiancheria*) clotheshorse.

stenodattilogra'fia *sf* shorthand typing
(*BRIT*), stenography (*US*).

stenodatti'lografo, a *smf* shorthand
typist (*BRIT*), stenographer (*US*).

stenogra'fare *vt* to take down in
shorthand.

stenogra'fia *sf* shorthand.

ste'nografo, a *smf* stenographer.

sten'tare *vi*: ~ **a fare** to find it hard to do,
have difficulty doing.

sten'tato, a *ag* (*compito, stile*) laboured
(*BRIT*), labored (*US*); (*sorriso*) forced.

'**stento** *sm* (*fatica*) difficulty; ~**i** *smpl*
(*privazioni*) hardship *sg*, privation *sg*; **a** ~ *av*
with difficulty, barely.

'**steppa** *sf* steppe.

'**sterco** *sm* dung.

stereofo'nia *sf* stereophony.

'**stereo('fonico, a, ci, che)** *ag*
stereo(phonic).

stereoti'pato, a *ag* stereotyped.

stere'otipo *sm* stereotype; **pensare per** ~**i**
to think in clichés.

'**sterile** *ag* sterile; (*terra*) barren; (*fig*) futile,
fruitless.

sterilità *sf* sterility.

steriliz'zare [sterilid'dzare] *vt* to sterilize.

sterilizzazi'one [steriliddzat'tsjone] *sf*
sterilization.

ster'lina *sf* pound (sterling).

stermi'nare *vt* to exterminate, wipe out.

stermi'nato, a *ag* immense, endless.

ster'minio *sm* extermination, destruction;
campo di ~ death camp.

'**sterno** *sm* (*ANAT*) breastbone.

ster'paglia [ster'paλλa] *sf* brushwood.

'**sterpo** *sm* dry twig.

ster'rare *vt* to excavate.

ster'zare [ster'tsare] *vt, vi* (*AUT*) to steer.

'**sterzo** ['stertso] *sm* steering; (*volante*)
steering wheel.

'**steso, a** *pp di* **stendere**.

'**stessi** *etc vb vedi* **stare**.

'**stesso, a** *ag* same; (*rafforzativo: in persona,
proprio*): **il re** ~ the king himself *o* in
person ♦ *pron*: **lo(la)** ~**(a)** the same (one);
quello ~ **giorno** that very day; **i suoi** ~**i**
avversari lo ammirano even his enemies
admire him; **fa lo** ~ it doesn't matter;
parto lo ~ I'm going all the same; **per me**
è lo ~ it's all the same to me, it doesn't
matter to me; *vedi* **io, tu** *etc*.

ste'sura *sf* (*azione*) drafting *no pl*, drawing
up *no pl*; (*documento*) draft.

stetos'copio *sm* stethoscope.

'**stetti** *etc vb vedi* **stare**.

'**stia** *sf* hutch.

'**stia** *etc vb vedi* **stare**.

'**stigma, i** *sm* stigma.

'**stigmate** *sfpl* (*REL*) stigmata.

sti'lare *vt* to draw up, draft.

'**stile** *sm* style; (*classe*) style, class; (*SPORT*):
~ **libero** freestyle; **mobili in** ~ period
furniture; **in grande** ~ in great style; **è**
proprio nel suo ~ (*fig*) it's just like him.

sti'lismo *sm* concern for style.

sti'lista, i, e *smf* designer.

sti'listico, a, ci, che *ag* stylistic.

stiliz'zato, a [stilid'dzato] *ag* stylized.

stil'lare *vi* (*trasudare*) to ooze; (*gocciolare*) to
drip.

stilli'cidio [stilli't fidjo] *sm* (*fig*) continual
pestering (*o* moaning *etc*).

stilo'grafica, che *sf* (*anche*: **penna** ~)
fountain pen.

Stim. *abbr* = **stimata**.

'**stima** *sf* esteem; valuation; assessment,
estimate; **avere** ~ **di qn** to have respect
for sb; **godere della** ~ **di qn** to enjoy sb's
respect; **fare la** ~ **di qc** to estimate the

value of sth.

sti'mare *vt* (*persona*) to esteem, hold in high regard; (*terreno, casa etc*) to value; (*stabilire in misura approssimativa*) to estimate, assess; (*ritenere*): ~ **che** to consider that; ~**rsi fortunato** to consider o.s. (to be) lucky.

Stim.ma *abbr* = **stimatissima**.

stimo'lante *ag* stimulating ♦ *sm* (*MED*) stimulant.

stimo'lare *vt* to stimulate; (*incitare*): ~ **qn (a fare)** to spur sb on (to do).

stimolazi'one [stimolat'tsjone] *sf* stimulation.

'stimolo *sm* (*anche fig*) stimulus.

'stinco, chi *sm* shin; shinbone.

'stingere ['stindʒere] *vt, vi* (*anche*: ~**rsi**) to fade.

'stinto, a *pp di* **stingere**.

sti'pare *vt* to cram, pack; ~**rsi** *vr* (*accalcarsi*) to crowd, throng.

stipendi'are *vt* (*pagare*) to pay (a salary to).

stipendi'ato, a *ag* salaried ♦ *sm/f* salaried worker.

sti'pendio *sm* salary.

'stipite *sm* (*di porta, finestra*) jamb.

stipu'lare *vt* (*redigere*) to draw up.

stipulazi'one [stipulat'tsjone] *sf* (*di contratto: stesura*) drafting; (: *firma*) signing.

stiracchi'are [stirak'kjare] *vt* (*fig: significato di una parola*) to stretch, force; ~**rsi** *vr* (*persona*) to stretch.

stira'mento *sm* (*MED*) sprain.

sti'rare *vt* (*abito*) to iron; (*distendere*) to stretch; (*strappare: muscolo*) to strain; ~**rsi** *vr* (*fam*) to stretch (o.s.).

stira'tura *sf* ironing.

'stirpe *sf* birth, stock; descendants *pl*.

stiti'chezza [stiti'kettsa] *sf* constipation.

'stitico, a, ci, che *ag* constipated.

'stiva *sf* (*di nave*) hold.

sti'vale *sm* boot.

stiva'letto *sm* ankle boot.

sti'vare *vt* to stow, load.

'stizza ['stittsa] *sf* anger, vexation.

stiz'zire [stit'tsire] *vt* to irritate ♦ *vi*, ~**rsi** *vr* to become irritated, become vexed.

stiz'zoso, a [stit'tsoso] *ag* (*persona*) quick-tempered, irascible; (*risposta*) angry.

stocca'fisso *sm* stockfish, dried cod.

Stoc'carda *sf* Stuttgart.

stoc'cata *sf* (*colpo*) stab, thrust; (*fig*) gibe, cutting remark.

Stoc'colma *sf* Stockholm.

stock [stɔk] *sm inv* (*COMM*) stock.

'stoffa *sf* material, fabric; (*fig*): **aver la ~ di**

to have the makings of; **avere della ~** to have what it takes.

stoi'cismo [stoi'tʃizmo] *sm* stoicism.

'stoico, a, ci, che *ag* stoic(al).

sto'ino *sm* doormat.

'stola *sf* stole.

stol'tezza [stol'tettsa] *sf* stupidity; (*azione*) foolish action.

'stolto, a *ag* stupid, foolish.

'stomaco, chi *sm* stomach; **dare di ~ to** vomit, be sick.

sto'nare *vt* to sing (*o* play) out of tune ♦ *vi* to be out of tune, sing (*o* play) out of tune; (*fig*) to be out of place, jar; (: *colori*) to clash.

sto'nato, a *ag* (*persona*) off-key; (*strumento*) off-key, out of tune.

stona'tura *sf* (*suono*) false note.

stop *sm inv* (*TELEGRAFIA*) stop; (*AUT: cartello*) stop sign; (: *fanalino d'arresto*) brake-light (*BRIT*), stoplight.

'stoppa *sf* tow.

'stoppia *sf* (*AGR*) stubble.

stop'pino *sm* (*di candela*) wick; (*miccia*) fuse.

'storcere ['stɔrtʃere] *vt* to twist; ~**rsi** *vr* to writhe, twist; ~ **il naso** (*fig*) to turn up one's nose; ~**rsi la caviglia** to twist one's ankle.

stordi'mento *sm* (*gen*) dizziness; (*da droga*) stupefaction.

stor'dire *vt* (*intontire*) to stun, daze; ~**rsi** *vr*: ~**rsi col bere** to dull one's senses with drink.

stor'dito, a *ag* stunned; (*sventato*) scatterbrained, heedless.

'storia *sf* (*scienza, avvenimenti*) history; (*racconto, bugia*) story; (*faccenda, questione*) business *no pl*; (*pretesto*) excuse, pretext; ~**e** *sfpl* (*smancerie*) fuss *sg*; **passare alla ~** to go down in history; **non ha fatto ~e** he didn't make a fuss.

storicità [storitʃi'ta] *sf* historical authenticity.

'storico, a, ci, che *ag* historic(al) ♦ *sm/f* historian.

storiogra'fia *sf* historiography.

stori'one *sm* (*ZOOL*) sturgeon.

stor'mire *vi* to rustle.

'stormo *sm* (*di uccelli*) flock.

stor'nare *vt* (*COMM*) to transfer.

stor'nello *sm* kind of folk song.

'storno *sm* starling.

storpi'are *vt* to cripple, maim; (*fig: parole*) to mangle; (: *significato*) to twist.

storpia'tura *sf* (*fig: di parola*) twisting, distortion.

'storpio, a *ag* crippled, maimed.

'storsi etc vb vedi storcere.

'storto, a pp di storcere ♦ ag (chiodo) twisted, bent; (gamba, quadro) crooked; (fig: ragionamento) false, wrong ♦ sf (distorsione) sprain, twist; (recipiente) retort ♦ av: guardare ~ qn (fig) to look askance at sb; andar ~ to go wrong.

sto'viglie [sto'viλλe] sfpl dishes pl, crockery.

str. abbr (GEO) = stretto.

'strabico, a, ci, che ag squint-eyed; (occhi) squint.

strabili'ante ag astonishing, amazing.

strabili'are vi to astonish, amaze.

stra'bismo sm squinting.

strabuz'zare [strabud'dzare] vt: ~ gli occhi to open one's eyes wide.

stra'carico, a, chi, che ag overloaded.

strac'chino [strak'kino] sm type of soft cheese.

stracci'are [strat'tʃare] vt to tear.

'straccio, a, ci, ce ['strattʃo] ag: carta ~a waste paper ♦ sm rag; (per pulire) cloth, duster.

stracci'one, a [strat'tʃone] sm/f ragamuffin.

stracci'vendolo [strattʃi'vendolo] sm ragman.

'stracco, a, chi, che ag: ~ (morto) exhausted, dead tired.

stra'cotto, a ag overcooked ♦ sm (CUC) beef stew.

'strada sf road; (di città) street; (cammino, via, fig) way; ~ facendo on the way; tre ore di ~ (a piedi)/(in macchina) three hours' walk/drive; essere sulla buona ~ (nella vita) to be on the right road o path; (con indagine etc) to be on the right track; essere fuori ~ (fig) to be on the wrong track; fare ~ a qn to show sb the way; fare o farsi ~ (fig: persona) to get on in life; portare qn sulla cattiva ~ to lead sb astray; donna di ~ (fig peg) streetwalker; ragazzo di ~ (fig peg) street urchin; ~ ferrata railway (BRIT), railroad (US); ~ principale main road; ~ senza uscita dead end, cul-de-sac.

stra'dale ag road cpd; (polizia, regolamento) traffic cpd.

stra'dario sm street guide.

stra'dino sm road worker.

strafalci'one [strafal'tʃone] sm blunder, howler.

stra'fare vi to overdo it.

stra'fatto, a pp di strafare.

stra'foro : di ~ av (di nascosto) on the sly.

strafot'tente ag: è ~ he doesn't give a damn, he couldn't care less.

strafot'tenza [strafot'tɛntsa] sf arrogance.

'strage ['stradʒe] sf massacre, slaughter.

stra'grande ag: la ~ maggioranza the overwhelming majority.

stralci'are [stral'tʃare] vt to remove.

'stralcio ['straltʃo] sm (COMM): vendere in ~ to sell off (at bargain prices) ♦ ag inv: legge ~ abridged version of an act.

stralu'nato, a ag (occhi) rolling; (persona) beside o.s., very upset.

stramaz'zare [stramat'tsare] vi to fall heavily.

strambe'ria sf eccentricity.

'strambo, a ag strange, queer.

strampa'lato, a ag odd, eccentric.

strana'mente av oddly, strangely; e lui, ~, ha accettato and, surprisingly, he agreed.

stra'nezza [stra'nettsa] sf strangeness.

strango'lare vt to strangle; ~rsi vr to choke.

strani'ero, a ag foreign ♦ sm/f foreigner.

stra'nito, a ag dazed.

'strano, a ag strange, odd.

straordi'nario, a ag extraordinary; (treno etc) special ♦ sm (lavoro) overtime.

strapaz'zare [strapat'tsare] vt to ill-treat; ~rsi vr to tire o.s. out, overdo things.

strapaz'zato, a [strapat'tsato] ag: uova ~e scrambled eggs.

stra'pazzo [stra'pattso] sm strain, fatigue; da ~ (fig) third-rate.

strapi'eno, a ag full to overflowing.

strapi'ombo sm overhanging rock; a ~ overhanging.

strapo'tere sm excessive power.

strappa'lacrime ag inv (fam): romanzo (o film etc) ~ tear-jerker.

strap'pare vt (gen) to tear, rip; (pagina etc) to tear off, tear out; (sradicare) to pull up; (togliere): ~ qc a qn to snatch sth from sb; (fig) to wrest sth from sb; ~rsi vr (lacerarsi) to rip, tear; (rompersi) to break; ~rsi un muscolo to tear a muscle.

strap'pato, a ag torn, ripped.

'strappo sm (strattone) pull, tug; (lacerazione) tear, rip; (fig fam: passaggio) lift (BRIT), ride (US); fare uno ~ alla regola to make an exception to the rule; ~ muscolare torn muscle.

strapun'tino sm jump o foldaway seat.

strari'pare vi to overflow.

Stras'burgo sf Strasbourg.

strasci'care [straʃʃi'kare] vt to trail; (piedi) to drag; ~ le parole to drawl.

'strascico, chi ['straʃʃiko] sm (di abito) train; (conseguenza) after-effect.

strata'gemma, i [strata'dʒɛmma] sm stratagem.

stra'tega, ghi sm strategist.

strate'gia, 'gie [strate'dʒia] *sf* strategy.
stra'tegico, a, ci, che [stra'tɛdʒiko] *ag* strategic.
'strato *sm* layer; (*rivestimento*) coat, coating; (*GEO, fig*) stratum; (*METEOR*) stratus.
stratos'fera *sf* stratosphere.
strat'tone *sm* tug, jerk; **dare uno ~ a qc** to tug *o* jerk sth, give sth a tug *o* jerk.
stravac'cato, a *ag* sprawling.
strava'gante *ag* odd, eccentric.
strava'ganza [strava'gantsa] *sf* eccentricity.
stra'vecchio, a [stra'vɛkkjo] *ag* very old.
strave'dere *vi*: **~ per qn** to dote on sb.
stra'visto, a *pp di* **stravedere**.
stra'vizio [stra'vittsjo] *sm* excess.
stra'volgere [stra'vɔldʒere] *vt* (*volto*) to contort; (*fig: animo*) to trouble deeply; (: *verità*) to twist, distort.
stra'volto, a *pp di* **stravolgere ♦** *ag* (*persona: per stanchezza etc*) in a terrible state; (: *per sofferenza*) distraught.
strazi'ante [strat'tsjante] *ag* (*scena*) harrowing; (*urlo*) bloodcurdling; (*dolore*) excruciating.
strazi'are [strat'tsjare] *vt* to torture, torment.
'strazio ['strattsjo] *sm* torture; (*fig: cosa fatta male*): **essere uno ~** to be appalling; **fare ~ di** (*corpo, vittima*) to mutilate.
'strega, ghe *sf* witch.
stre'gare *vt* to bewitch.
stre'gone *sm* (*mago*) wizard; (*di tribù*) witch doctor.
stregone'ria *sf* (*pratica*) witchcraft; **fare una ~** to cast a spell.
'stregua *sf*: **alla ~ di** by the same standard as.
stre'mare *vt* to exhaust.
'stremo *sm*: **essere allo ~** to be at the end of one's tether.
'strenna *sf*: **~ natalizia** (*regalo*) Christmas present; (*libro*) book *published for the Christmas market.*
'strenuo, a *ag* brave, courageous.
strepi'tare *vi* to yell and shout.
'strepito *sm* (*di voci, folla*) clamour (*BRIT*), clamor (*US*); (*di catene*) clanking, rattling.
strepi'toso, a *ag* clamorous, deafening; (*fig: successo*) resounding.
stres'sante *ag* stressful.
stres'sare *vt* to put under stress.
stres'sato, a *ag* under stress.
'stretta *sf vedi* **stretto**.
stretta'mente *av* tightly; (*rigorosamente*) strictly.
stret'tezza [stret'tettsa] *sf* narrowness; **~e**

sfpl (*povertà*) poverty *sg*, straitened circumstances.
'stretto, a *pp di* **stringere ♦** *ag* (*corridoio, limiti*) narrow; (*gonna, scarpe, nodo, curva*) tight; (*intimo: parente, amico*) close; (*rigoroso: osservanza*) strict; (*preciso: significato*) precise, exact **♦** *sm* (*braccio di mare*) strait **♦** *sf* (*di mano*) grasp; (*finanziaria*) squeeze; (*fig: dolore, turbamento*) pang; **a denti ~i** with clenched teeth; **lo ~ necessario** the bare minimum; **una ~a di mano** a handshake; **una ~a al cuore** a sudden sadness; **essere alle ~e** to have one's back to the wall.
stret'toia *sf* bottleneck; (*fig*) tricky situation.
stri'ato, a *ag* streaked.
stria'tura *sf* (*atto*) streaking; (*effetto*) streaks *pl*.
stric'nina *sf* strychnine.
'strida *sfpl* screaming *sg*.
stri'dente *ag* strident.
'stridere *vi* (*porta*) to squeak; (*animale*) to screech, shriek; (*colori*) to clash.
'strido, *pl(f)* **strida** *sm* screech, shriek.
stri'dore *sm* screeching, shrieking.
'stridulo, a *ag* shrill.
'striglia ['striʎʎa] *sf* currycomb.
strigli'are [striʎ'ʎare] *vt* (*cavallo*) to curry.
strigli'ata [striʎ'ʎata] *sf* (*di cavallo*) currying; (*fig*): **dare una ~ a qn** to give sb a scolding.
stril'lare *vt, vi* to scream, shriek.
'strillo *sm* scream, shriek.
stril'lone *sm* newspaper seller.
strimin'zito, a [strimin'tsito] *ag* (*misero*) shabby; (*molto magro*) skinny.
strimpel'lare *vt* (*MUS*) to strum.
'stringa, ghe *sf* lace; (*INFORM*) string.
strin'gare *vt* (*fig: discorso*) to condense.
strin'gato, a *ag* (*fig*) concise.
'stringere ['strindʒere] *vt* (*avvicinare due cose*) to press (together), squeeze (together); (*tenere stretto*) to hold tight, clasp, clutch; (*pugno, mascella, denti*) to clench; (*labbra*) to compress; (*avvitare*) to tighten; (*abito*) to take in; (*sog: scarpe*) to pinch, be tight for; (*fig: concludere: patto*) to make; (: *accelerare: passo*) to quicken **♦** *vi* (*incalzare*) to be pressing; **~rsi** *vr* (*accostarsi*): **~rsi a** to press o.s. up against; **~ la mano a qn** to shake sb's hand; **~ gli occhi** to screw up one's eyes; **~ amicizia con qn** to make friends with sb; **stringi stringi** in conclusion; **il tempo stringe** time is short.
'strinsi *etc vb vedi* **stringere**.
'striscia, sce ['striʃʃa] *sf* (*di carta, tessuto*

etc) strip; (*riga*) stripe; ~**sce (pedonali)** zebra crossing *sg*; **a** ~**sce** striped.

strisci'ante [striʃ'ʃante] *ag* (*fig peg*) unctuous; (*ECON: inflazione*) creeping.

strisci'are [striʃ'ʃare] *vt* (*piedi*) to drag; (*muro, macchina*) to graze ♦ *vi* to crawl, creep.

'striscio ['striʃʃo] *sm* graze; (*MED*) smear; **colpire di** ~ to graze.

strisci'one [striʃ'ʃone] *sm* banner.

strito'lare *vt* to grind.

striz'zare [strit'tsare] *vt* (*arancia*) to squeeze; (*panni*) to wring (out); ~ **l'occhio** to wink.

striz'zata [strit'tsata] *sf*: **dare una** ~ **a qc** to give sth a wring; **una** ~ **d'occhio** a wink.

'strofa *sf*, **'strofe** *sf inv* strophe.

strofi'naccio [strofi'nattʃo] *sm* duster, cloth; (*per piatti*) dishcloth; (*per pavimenti*) floorcloth.

strofi'nare *vt* to rub.

stron'care *vt* to break off; (*fig: ribellione*) to suppress, put down; (*: film, libro*) to tear to pieces.

'stronzo ['strontso] *sm* (*sterco*) turd; (*fig fam!: persona*) shit (*!*).

stropicci'are [stropit'tʃare] *vt* to rub.

stroz'zare [strot'tsare] *vt* (*soffocare*) to choke, strangle; ~**rsi** *vr* to choke.

strozza'tura [strottsa'tura] *sf* (*restringimento*) narrowing; (*di strada etc*) bottleneck.

stroz'zino, a [strot'tsino] *sm/f* (*usuraio*) usurer; (*fig*) shark.

struc'care *vt* to remove make-up from; ~**rsi** *vr* to remove one's make-up.

'struggere ['struddʒere] *vt* (*fig*) to consume; ~**rsi** *vr* (*fig*): ~**rsi di** to be consumed with.

struggi'mento [struddʒi'mento] *sm* (*desiderio*) yearning.

strumen'tale *ag* (*MUS*) instrumental.

strumentaliz'zare [strumentalid'dzare] *vt* to exploit, use to one's own ends.

strumentalizzazi'one [strumentaliddzat'tsjone] *sf* exploitation.

strumentazi'one [strumentat'tsjone] *sf* (*MUS*) orchestration; (*TECN*) instrumentation.

stru'mento *sm* (*arnese, fig*) instrument, tool; (*MUS*) instrument; ~ **a corda** *o* **ad arco/a fiato** string(ed)/wind instrument.

'strussi *etc vb vedi* **struggere**.

'strutto *sm* lard.

strut'tura *sf* structure.

struttu'rare *vt* to structure.

'struzzo ['struttso] *sm* ostrich; **fare lo** ~, **fare la politica dello** ~ to bury one's head in the sand.

stuc'care *vt* (*muro*) to plaster; (*vetro*) to putty; (*decorare con stucchi*) to stucco.

stucca'tore, 'trice *sm/f* plasterer; (*artista*) stucco worker.

stuc'chevole [stuk'kevole] *ag* nauseating; (*fig*) tedious, boring.

'stucco, chi *sm* plaster; (*da vetri*) putty; (*ornamentale*) stucco; **rimanere di** ~ (*fig*) to be dumbfounded.

stu'dente, 'essa *sm/f* student; (*scolaro*) pupil, schoolboy/girl.

studen'tesco, a, schi, sche *ag* student *cpd*.

studi'are *vt* to study; ~**rsi** *vr* (*sforzarsi*): ~**rsi di fare** to try *o* endeavour (*BRIT*) *o* endeavor (*US*) to do.

studi'ato, a *ag* (*modi, sorriso*) affected.

'studio *sm* studying; (*ricerca, saggio, stanza*) study; (*di professionista*) office; (*di artista, CINE, TV, RADIO*) studio; (*di medico*) surgery (*BRIT*), office (*US*); ~**i** *smpl* (*INS*) studies; **alla fine degli** ~**i** at the end of one's course (of studies); **secondo recenti** ~**i, appare che ...** recent research indicates that ...; **la proposta è allo** ~ the proposal is under consideration; ~ **legale** lawyer's office.

studi'oso, a *ag* studious, hardworking ♦ *sm/f* scholar.

'stufa *sf* stove; ~ **elettrica** electric fire *o* heater; ~ **a legna/carbone** wood-burning/ coal stove.

stu'fare *vt* (*CUC*) to stew; (*fig fam*) to bore.

stu'fato *sm* (*CUC*) stew.

'stufo, a *ag* (*fam*): **essere** ~ **di** to be fed up with, be sick and tired of.

stu'oia *sf* mat.

stu'olo *sm* crowd, host.

stupefa'cente [stupefa'tʃente] *ag* stunning, astounding ♦ *sm* drug, narcotic.

stupe'fare *vt* to stun, astound.

stupe'fatto, a *pp di* **stupefare**.

stupefazi'one [stupefat'tsjone] *sf* astonishment.

stu'pendo, a *ag* marvellous, wonderful.

stupi'daggine [stupi'daddʒine] *sf* stupid thing (to do *o* say).

stupidità *sf* stupidity.

'stupido, a *ag* stupid.

stu'pire *vt* to amaze, stun ♦ *vi* (*anche*: ~**rsi**): ~ **(di)** to be amazed (at), be stunned (by); **non c'è da** ~**rsi** that's not surprising.

stu'pore *sm* amazement, astonishment.

stu'prare *vt* to rape.

stupra'tore *sm* rapist.

'stupro *sm* rape.

stu'rare *vt* (*lavandino*) to clear.

stuzzica'denti [stuttsika'dɛnti] *sm*

toothpick.

stuzzi'cante [stuttsi'kante] *ag* (*gen*) stimulating; (*appetitoso*) appetizing.

stuzzi'care [stuttsi'kare] *vt* (*ferita etc*) to poke (at), prod (at); (*fig*) to tease; (: *appetito*) to whet; (: *curiosità*) to stimulate; ~ **i denti** to pick one's teeth.

===================== *PAROLA CHIAVE*

su (*su* + *il* = **sul**, *su* + *lo* = **sullo**, *su* + *l'* = **sull'**, *su* + *la* = **sulla**, *su* + *i* = **sui**, *su* + *gli* = **sugli**, *su* + *le* = **sulle**) *prep* **1** (*gen*) on; (*moto*) on(to); (*in cima a*) on (top of); **mettilo sul tavolo** put it on the table; **salire sul treno** to get on the train; **un paesino sul mare** a village by the sea; **è sulla destra** it's on the right; **cento metri sul livello del mare** a hundred metres above sea level; **fecero rotta ~ Palermo** they set out for Palermo; **sul vestito portava un golf rosso** she was wearing a red sweater over her dress

2 (*argomento*) about, on; **un libro ~ Cesare** a book on *o* about Caesar

3 (*circa*) about; **costerà sui 3 milioni** it will cost about 3 million; **una ragazza sui 17 anni** a girl of about 17 (years of age)

4: ~ **misura** made to measure; ~ **ordinazione** to order; ~ **richiesta** on request; **3 casi ~ dieci** 3 cases out of 10

♦ *av* **1** (*in alto, verso l'alto*) up; **vieni ~** come on up; **guarda ~** look up; **andare ~ e giù** to go up and down; ~ **le mani!** hands up!; **in ~** (*verso l'alto*) up(wards); (*in poi*) onwards; **vieni ~ da me?** are you going to come up?; **dai 20 anni in ~** from the age of 20 onwards

2 (*addosso*) on; **cos'hai ~?** what have you got on?

♦ *escl* come on!; ~ **avanti, muoviti!** come on, hurry up!; ~ **coraggio!** come on, cheer up!

'**sua** *vedi* **suo**.

sua'dente *ag* persuasive.

sub *sm/f inv* skin-diver.

su'bacqueo, a *ag* underwater ♦ *sm* skin-diver.

subaffit'tare *vt* to sublet.

subaf'fitto *sm* (*contratto*) sublet.

subal'terno, a *ag, sm* subordinate; (*MIL*) subaltern.

subappal'tare *vt* to subcontract.

subap'palto *sm* subcontract.

sub'buglio [sub'buʎʎo] *sm* confusion, turmoil; **essere/mettere in ~** to be in/ throw into a turmoil.

sub'conscio, a [sub'kɔnʃo],

subcosci'ente [subkoʃ'ʃɛnte] *ag, sm* subconscious.

'**subdolo, a** *ag* underhand, sneaky.

suben'trare *vi*: ~ **a qn in qc** to take over sth from sb; **sono subentrati altri problemi** other problems arose.

su'bire *vt* to suffer, endure.

subis'sare *vt* (*fig*): ~ **di** to overwhelm with, load with.

subi'taneo, a *ag* sudden.

'**subito** *av* immediately, at once, straight away.

subli'mare *vt* (*PSIC*) to sublimate; (*CHIM*) to sublime.

su'blime *ag* sublime.

sublo'care *vt* to sublease.

sublocazi'one [sublokat'tsjone] *sf* sublease.

subnor'male *ag* subnormal ♦ *sm/f* mentally handicapped person.

subodo'rare *vt* (*insidia etc*) to smell, suspect.

subordi'nare *vt* to subordinate.

subordi'nato, a *ag* subordinate; (*dipendente*): ~ **a** dependent on, subject to.

subordinazi'one [subordinat'tsjone] *sf* subordination.

su'bordine *sm*: **in ~** secondarily.

subur'bano, a *ag* suburban.

succe'daneo [suttʃe'daneo] *sm* substitute.

suc'cedere [sut'tʃɛdere] *vi* (*prendere il posto di qn*): ~ **a** to succeed; (*venire dopo*): ~ **a** to follow; (*accadere*) to happen; ~**rsi** *vr* to follow each other; ~ **al trono** to succeed to the throne; **sono cose che succedono** these things happen.

successi'one [suttʃes'sjone] *sf* succession; **tassa di ~** death duty (*BRIT*), inheritance tax (*US*).

successiva'mente [suttʃessiva'mente] *av* subsequently.

succes'sivo, a [suttʃes'sivo] *ag* successive; **il giorno ~** the following day; **in un momento ~** subsequently.

suc'cesso, a [sut'tʃɛsso] *pp di* **succedere** ♦ *sm* (*esito*) outcome; (*buona riuscita*) success; **di ~** (*libro, personaggio*) successful; **avere ~** (*persona*) to be successful; (*idea*) to be well received.

succes'sore [suttʃes'sore] *sm* successor.

succhi'are [suk'kjare] *vt* to suck (up).

succhi'otto [suk'kjɔtto] *sm* dummy (*BRIT*), pacifier (*US*), comforter (*US*).

suc'cinto, a [sut'tʃinto] *ag* (*discorso*) succinct; (*abito*) brief.

'**succo, chi** *sm* juice; (*fig*) essence, gist; ~ **di frutta/pomodoro** fruit/tomato juice.

suc'coso, a *ag* juicy; (*fig*) pithy.

'**succube** *sm/f* victim; **essere ~ di qn** to be dominated by sb.

succur'sale *sf* branch (office).

sud *sm* south ♦ *ag inv* south; (*regione*) southern; **verso ~** south, southwards; **l'Italia del S~** Southern Italy; **l'America del S~** South America.

Su'dafrica *sm*: **il ~** South Africa.

sudafri'cano, a *ag, sm/f* South African.

Suda'merica *sm*: **il ~** South America.

sudameri'cano, a *ag, sm/f* South American.

Su'dan *sm*: **il ~** (the) Sudan.

suda'nese *ag, sm/f* Sudanese *inv*.

su'dare *vi* to perspire, sweat; **~ freddo** to come out in a cold sweat.

su'dato, a *ag* (*persona, mani*) sweaty; (*fig: denaro*) hard-earned ♦ *sf* (*anche fig*) sweat; **una vittoria ~a** a hard-won victory; **ho fatto una bella ~a per finirlo in tempo** it was a real sweat to get it finished in time.

sud'detto, a *ag* above-mentioned.

suddi'tanza [suddi'tantsa] *sf* subjection; (*cittadinanza*) citizenship.

sud'dito, a *sm/f* subject.

suddi'videre *vt* to subdivide.

suddivisi'one *sf* subdivision.

suddi'viso, a *pp di* **suddividere**.

su'dest *sm* south-east; **vento di ~** south-easterly wind; **il ~ asiatico** South-East Asia.

sudice'ria [suditʃe'ria] *sf* (*qualità*) filthiness, dirtiness; (*cosa sporca*) dirty thing.

'**sudicio, a, ci, ce** ['suditʃo] *ag* dirty, filthy.

sudici'ume [sudi'tʃume] *sm* dirt, filth.

su'dore *sm* perspiration, sweat.

su'dovest *sm* south-west; **vento di ~** south-westerly wind.

'**sue** *vedi* **suo**.

'**Suez** ['suez] *sm*: **il Canale di ~** the Suez Canal.

suffici'ente [suffi'tʃɛnte] *ag* enough, sufficient; (*borioso*) self-important; (*INS*) satisfactory.

sufficiente'mente [suffitʃente'mente] *av* sufficiently, enough; (*guadagnare, darsi da fare*) enough.

suffici'enza [suffi'tʃɛntsa] *sf* (*INS*) pass mark; **con un'aria di ~** (*fig*) with a condescending air; **a ~** enough; **ne ho avuto a ~!** I've had enough of this!

suf'fisso *sm* (*LING*) suffix.

suffra'gare *vt* to support.

suf'fragio [suf'fradʒo] *sm* (*voto*) vote; **~ universale** universal suffrage.

suggel'lare [suddʒel'lare] *vt* (*fig*) to seal.

suggeri'mento [suddʒeri'mento] *sm* suggestion; (*consiglio*) piece of advice, advice *no pl*; **dietro suo ~** on his advice.

sugge'rire [suddʒe'rire] *vt* (*risposta*) to tell; (*consigliare*) to advise; (*proporre*) to suggest; (*TEAT*) to prompt; **~ a qn di fare qc** to suggest to sb that he (*o she*) do sth.

suggeri'tore, 'trice [suddʒeri'tore] *sm/f* (*TEAT*) prompter.

suggestio'nare [suddʒestjo'nare] *vt* to influence.

suggesti'one [suddʒes'tjone] *sf* (*PSIC*) suggestion; (*istigazione*) instigation.

sugges'tivo, a [suddʒes'tivo] *ag* (*paesaggio*) evocative; (*teoria*) interesting, attractive.

'**sughero** ['sugero] *sm* cork.

'**sugli** ['suʎʎi] *prep +det vedi* **su**.

'**sugo, ghi** *sm* (*succo*) juice; (*di carne*) gravy; (*condimento*) sauce; (*fig*) gist, essence.

su'goso, a *ag* (*frutto*) juicy; (*fig: articolo etc*) pithy.

'**sui** *prep +det vedi* **su**.

sui'cida, i, e [sui'tʃida] *ag* suicidal ♦ *sm/f* suicide.

suici'darsi [suitʃi'darsi] *vr* to commit suicide.

sui'cidio [sui'tʃidjo] *sm* suicide.

su'ino, a *ag*: **carne ~a** pork ♦ *sm* pig; **~i** *smpl* swine *pl*.

sul, sull', 'sulla, 'sulle, 'sullo *prep + det vedi* **su**.

sulfa'midico, a, ci, che *ag, sm* (*MED*) sulphonamide.

sulta'nina *sf*: (**uva**) **~** sultana.

sul'tano, a *sm/f* sultan/sultana.

Su'matra *sf* Sumatra.

'**summit** ['summit] *sm inv* summit.

S.U.N.I.A. *sigla m* (= *sindacato unitario nazionale inquilini e assegnatari*) *national association of tenants.*

sunnomi'nato, a *ag* aforesaid *cpd*.

'**sunto** *sm* summary.

'**suo, 'sua, 'sue, su'oi** *det*: **il ~, la sua** *etc* (*di lui*) his; (*di lei*) her; (*di esso*) its; (*con valore indefinito*) one's, his/her; (*forma di cortesia: anche*: **S~**) your ♦ *pron*: **il ~, la sua** *etc* his; hers; yours ♦ *sm*: **ha speso del ~** he (*o she etc*) spent his (*o her etc*) own money ♦ *sf*: **la ~a** (*opinione*) his (*o her etc*) view; **i suoi** (*parenti*) his (*o her etc*) family; **un ~ amico** a friend of his (*o hers etc*); **è dalla ~a** he's on his (*o her etc*) side; **anche lui ha avuto le ~e** (*disavventure*) he's had his problems too; **sta sulle ~e** he keeps himself to himself.

su'ocero, a ['swɔtʃero] *sm/f* father/mother-in-law; **i ~i** *smpl* father- and mother-in-law.

su'oi *vedi* **suo**.

su'ola *sf* (*di scarpa*) sole.

su'olo *sm* (*terreno*) ground; (*terra*) soil.

suo'nare *vt* (*MUS*) to play; (*campana*) to ring; (*ore*) to strike; (*clacson, allarme*) to sound ♦ *vi* to play; (*telefono, campana*) to ring; (*ore*) to strike; (*clacson, fig: parole*) to sound.

suo'nato, a *ag* (*compiuto*): **ha cinquant'anni** ~**i** he is well over fifty.

suona'tore, 'trice *sm/f* player; ~ **ambulante** street musician.

suone'ria *sf* alarm.

su'ono *sm* sound.

su'ora *sf* (*REL*) nun; **Suor Maria** Sister Maria.

'super *ag inv*: (*benzina*) ~ ≈ four-star (petrol) (*BRIT*), premium (*US*).

supera'mento *sm* (*di ostacolo*) overcoming; (*di montagna*) crossing.

supe'rare *vt* (*oltrepassare: limite*) to exceed, surpass; (*attraversare: fiume*) to cross; (*sorpassare: veicolo*) to overtake; (*fig: essere più bravo di*) to surpass, outdo; (: *difficoltà*) to overcome; (: *esame*) to get through; ~ **qn in altezza/peso** to be taller/heavier than sb; **ha superato la cinquantina** he's over fifty (years of age); ~ **i limiti di velocità** to exceed the speed limit; **stavolta ha superato se stesso** this time he has surpassed himself.

supe'rato, a *ag* outmoded.

supe'rattico, ci *sm* penthouse.

su'perbia *sf* pride.

su'perbo, a *ag* proud; (*fig*) magnificent, superb.

supercondut'tore *sm* superconductor.

superena'lotto *sm* Italian national lottery.

superfici'ale [superfi't∫ale] *ag* superficial.

superficialità [superfit∫ali'ta] *sf* superficiality.

super'ficie, ci [super'fit∫e] *sf* surface; **tornare in** ~ (*a galla*) to return to the surface; (*problemi*) to resurface; ~ **alare** (*AER*) wing area; ~ **velica** (*NAUT*) sail area.

su'perfluo, a *ag* superfluous.

superi'ora *sf* (*REL: anche*: **madre** ~) mother superior.

superi'ore *ag* (*piano, arto, classi*) upper; (*più elevato: temperatura, livello*): ~ (**a**) higher (than); (*migliore*): ~ (**a**) superior (to) ♦ *sf pl*: **le** ~**i** (*INS*) *vedi* **scuola media superiore**; **il corso** ~ **di un fiume** the upper reaches of a river; **scuola media** ~ ≈ senior comprehensive school (*BRIT*); ≈ senior high (school) (*US*).

superiorità *sf* superiority.

superla'tivo, a *ag, sm* superlative.

superla'voro *sm* overwork.

super'market [super'market] *sm inv* = **supermercato**.

supermer'cato *sm* supermarket.

super'nova *sf* supernova.

superpo'tenza [superpo'tentsa] *sf* (*POL*) superpower.

super'sonico, a, ci, che *ag* supersonic.

su'perstite *ag* surviving ♦ *sm/f* survivor.

superstizi'one [superstit'tsjone] *sf* superstition.

superstizi'oso, a [superstit'tsjoso] *ag* superstitious.

super'strada *sf* ≈ expressway.

supervisi'one *sf* supervision.

supervi'sore *sm* supervisor.

su'pino, a *ag* supine; **accettazione** ~**a** (*fig*) blind acceptance.

suppel'lettile *sf* furnishings *pl*.

suppergiù [supper'dʒu] *av* more or less, roughly.

suppl. *abbr* (= *supplemento*) supp(l).

supplemen'tare *ag* extra; (*treno*) relief *cpd*; (*entrate*) additional.

supple'mento *sm* supplement.

sup'plente *ag* temporary; (*insegnante*) supply *cpd* (*BRIT*), substitute *cpd* (*US*) ♦ *sm/f* temporary member of staff; supply (*o* substitute) teacher.

supp'lenza [sup'plentsa] *sf*: **fare** ~ to do supply (*BRIT*) *o* substitute (*US*) teaching.

supple'tivo, a *ag* (*gen*) supplementary; (*sessione d'esami*) extra.

'supplica, che *sf* (*preghiera*) plea; (*domanda scritta*) petition, request.

suppli'care *vt* to implore, beseech.

suppli'chevole [suppli'kevole] *ag* imploring.

sup'plire *vi*: ~ **a** to make up for.

sup'plizio [sup'plittsjo] *sm* torture.

sup'pongo, sup'poni *etc vb vedi* **supporre**.

sup'porre *vt* to suppose; **supponiamo che** ... let's *o* just suppose that ....

sup'porto *sm* (*sostegno*) support.

supposizi'one [suppozit'tsjone] *sf* supposition.

sup'posta *sf* (*MED*) suppository.

sup'posto, a *pp di* **supporre**.

suppu'rare *vi* to suppurate.

suprema'zia [supremat'tsia] *sf* supremacy.

su'premo, a *ag* supreme; **S**~**a Corte (di Cassazione)** Supreme Court.

surclas'sare *vt* to outclass.

surge'lare [surdʒe'lare] *vt* to (deep-)freeze.

surge'lato, a [surdʒe'lato] *ag* (deep-)frozen ♦ *smpl*: **i** ~**i** frozen food *sg*.

surme'nage [syrmə'naʒ] *sm* (*fisico*) overwork; (*mentale*) mental strain; (*SPORT*) overtraining.

sur'plus *sm inv* (*ECON*) surplus; ~ **di manodopera** overmanning.
surre'ale *ag* surrealistic.
surriscalda'mento *sm* (*gen, TECN*) overheating.
surriscal'dare *vt* to overheat.
surro'gato *sm* substitute.
suscet'tibile [suʃʃet'tibile] *ag* (*sensibile*) touchy, sensitive; (*soggetto*): ~ **di miglioramento** that can be improved, open to improvement.
suscettibilità [suʃʃettibili'ta] *sf* touchiness; **urtare la** ~ **di qn** to hurt sb's feelings.
susci'tare [suʃʃi'tare] *vt* to provoke, arouse.
su'sina *sf* plum.
su'sino *sm* plum (tree).
sussegu'ire *vt* to follow; **~rsi** *vr* to follow one another.
sussidi'ario, a *ag* subsidiary; (*treno*) relief *cpd*; (*fermata*) extra.
sus'sidio *sm* subsidy; (*aiuto*) aid; **~i didattici/audiovisivi** teaching/audiovisual aids; ~ **di disoccupazione** unemployment benefit (*BRIT*) *o* benefits (*US*); ~ **per malattia** sickness benefit.
sussi'ego *sm* haughtiness; **con aria di** ~ haughtily.
sussis'tenza [sussis'tɛntsa] *sf* subsistence.
sus'sistere *vi* to exist; (*essere fondato*) to be valid *o* sound.
sussul'tare *vi* to shudder.
sus'sulto *sm* start.
sussur'rare *vt, vi* to whisper, murmur; **si sussurra che** ... it's rumoured (*BRIT*) *o* rumored (*US*) that ....
sus'surro *sm* whisper, murmur.
su'tura *sf* (*MED*) suture.
sutu'rare *vt* to stitch up, suture.
suv'via *escl* come on!
SV *sigla* = Savona.
S.V. *abbr vedi* **Signoria Vostra**.
sva'gare *vt* (*divertire*) to amuse; (*distrarre*): ~ **qn** to take sb's mind off things; **~rsi** *vr* to amuse o.s.; to take one's mind off things.
sva'gato, a *ag* (*persona*) absent-minded; (*scolaro*) inattentive.
'svago, ghi *sm* (*riposo*) relaxation; (*ricreazione*) amusement; (*passatempo*) pastime.
svaligi'are [zvali'dʒare] *vt* to rob, burgle (*BRIT*), burglarize (*US*).
svaligia'tore, 'trice [zvalidʒa'tore] *sm/f* (*di banca*) robber; (*di casa*) burglar.
svalu'tare *vt* (*ECON*) to devalue; (*fig*) to belittle; **~rsi** *vr* (*ECON*) to be devalued.
svalutazi'one [zvalutat'tsjone] *sf* devaluation.

svam'pito, a *ag* absent-minded ♦ *sm/f* absent-minded person.
sva'nire *vi* to disappear, vanish.
sva'nito, a *ag* (*fig: persona*) absent-minded.
svantaggi'ato, a [zvantad'dʒato] *ag* at a disadvantage.
svan'taggio [zvan'taddʒo] *sm* disadvantage; (*inconveniente*) drawback, disadvantage; **tornerà a suo** ~ it will work against you.
svantaggi'oso, a [zvantad'dʒoso] *ag* disadvantageous; **è un'offerta ~a per me** it's not in my interest to accept this offer; **è un prezzo** ~ it is not an attractive price.
svapo'rare *vi* to evaporate.
svapo'rato, a *ag* (*bibita*) flat.
svari'ato, a *ag* (*vario, diverso*) varied; (*numeroso*) various.
'svastica, che *sf* swastika.
sve'dese *ag* Swedish ♦ *sm/f* Swede ♦ *sm* (*LING*) Swedish.
'sveglia ['zveʎʎa] *sf* waking up; (*orologio*) alarm (clock); **suonare la** ~ (*MIL*) to sound the reveille; ~ **telefonica** alarm call.
svegli'are [zveʎ'ʎare] *vt* to wake up; (*fig*) to awaken, arouse; **~rsi** *vr* to wake up; (*fig*) to be revived, reawaken.
'sveglio, a ['zveʎʎo] *ag* awake; (*fig*) alert, quick-witted.
sve'lare *vt* to reveal.
svel'tezza [zvel'tettsa] *sf* (*gen*) speed; (*mentale*) quick-wittedness.
svel'tire *vt* (*gen*) to speed up; (*procedura*) to streamline.
'svelto, a *ag* (*passo*) quick; (*mente*) quick, alert; (*linea*) slim, slender; **alla ~a** quickly.
'svendere *vt* to sell off, clear.
'svendita *sf* (*COMM*) (clearance) sale.
sve'nevole *ag* mawkish.
'svengo *etc vb vedi* **svenire**.
sveni'mento *sm* fainting fit, faint.
sve'nire *vi* to faint.
sven'tare *vt* to foil, thwart.
sventa'tezza [zventa'tettsa] *sf* (*distrazione*) absent-mindedness; (*mancanza di prudenza*) rashness.
sven'tato, a *ag* (*distratto*) scatterbrained; (*imprudente*) rash.
'sventola *sf* (*colpo*) slap; **orecchie a** ~ sticking-out ears.
svento'lare *vt, vi* to wave, flutter.
sven'trare *vt* to disembowel.
sven'tura *sf* misfortune.
sventu'rato, a *ag* unlucky, unfortunate.
sve'nuto, a *pp di* **svenire**.
svergo'gnare [zvergoɲ'ɲare] *vt* to shame.

svergo'gnato, a [zvergoɲ'ɲato] *ag* shameless ♦ *sm/f* shameless person.

sver'nare *vi* to spend the winter.

sverrò *etc vb vedi* **svenire**.

sves'tire *vt* to undress; ~**rsi** *vr* to get undressed.

'Svezia ['zvɛttsja] *sf*: **la** ~ Sweden.

svez'zare [zvet'tsare] *vt* to wean.

svi'are *vt* to divert; (*fig*) to lead astray; ~**rsi** *vr* to go astray.

svico'lare *vi* to slip down an alley; (*fig*) to sneak off.

svi'gnarsela [zviɲ'ɲarsela] *vr* to slip away, sneak off.

svili'mento *sm* debasement.

svi'lire *vt* to debase.

svilup'pare *vt*, ~**rsi** *vr* to develop.

svi'luppo *sm* development; (*di industria*) expansion; **in via di** ~ in the process of development; **paesi in via di** ~ developing countries.

svinco'lare *vt* to free, release; (*merce*) to clear.

'svincolo *sm* (*COMM*) clearance; (*stradale*) motorway (*BRIT*) *o* expressway (*US*) intersection.

svisce'rare [zviʃʃe'rare] *vt* (*fig: argomento*) to examine in depth.

svisce'rato, a [zviʃʃe'rato] *ag* (*amore, odio*) passionate.

'svista *sf* oversight.

svi'tare *vt* to unscrew.

'Svizzera ['zvittsera] *sf*: **la** ~ Switzerland.

'svizzero, a ['zvittsero] *ag, sm/f* Swiss.

svoglia'tezza [zvoʎʎa'tettsa] *sf* listlessness; indolence.

svogli'ato, a [zvoʎ'ʎato] *ag* listless; (*pigro*) lazy, indolent.

svolaz'zare [zvolat'tsare] *vi* to flutter.

'svolgere ['zvɔldʒere] *vt* to unwind; (*srotolare*) to unroll; (*fig: argomento*) to develop; (: *piano, programma*) to carry out; ~**rsi** *vr* to unwind; to unroll; (*fig: aver luogo*) to take place; (: *procedere*) to go on; **tutto si è svolto secondo i piani** everything went according to plan.

svolgi'mento [zvoldʒi'mento] *sm* development; carrying out; (*andamento*) course.

'svolsi *etc vb vedi* **svolgere**.

'svolta *sf* (*atto*) turning *no pl*; (*curva*) turn, bend; (*fig*) turning-point; **essere ad una** ~ **nella propria vita** to be at a crossroads in one's life.

svol'tare *vi* to turn.

'svolto, a *pp di* **svolgere**.

svuo'tare *vt* to empty (out).

'Swaziland ['swadziland] *sm*: **lo** ~ Swaziland.

T t

T, t [ti] *sf o m inv* (*lettera*) T, t; **T come Taranto** ≈ T for Tommy.

T *abbr* = **tabaccheria**.

t *abbr* = **tara; tonnellata**.

TA *sigla* = *Taranto*.

tabac'caio, a *sm/f* tobacconist.

tabacche'ria [tabakke'ria] *sf* tobacconist's (shop).

tabacchi'era [tabak'kjɛra] *sf* snuffbox.

ta'bacco, chi *sm* tobacco.

ta'bella *sf* (*tavola*) table; (*elenco*) list; ~ **di marcia** schedule; ~ **dei prezzi** price list.

tabel'lone *sm* (*per pubblicità*) billboard; (*per informazioni*) notice board (*BRIT*), bulletin board (*US*); (: *in stazione*) timetable board.

taber'nacolo *sm* tabernacle.

tabù *ag, sm inv* taboo.

'tabula 'rasa *sf* tabula rasa; **fare** ~ (*fig*) to make a clean sweep.

tabu'lare *vt* to tabulate.

tabu'lato *sm* (*INFORM*) printout.

tabula'tore *sm* tabulator.

TAC *sigla f* (*MED*: = *Tomografia Assiale Computerizzata*) CAT.

'tacca, che *sf* notch, nick; **di mezza** ~ (*fig*) mediocre.

taccagne'ria [takkaɲɲe'ria] *sf* meanness, stinginess.

tac'cagno, a [tak'kaɲɲo] *ag* mean, stingy.

tac'cheggio [tak'keddʒo] *sm* shoplifting.

tac'chino [tak'kino] *sm* turkey.

'taccia, ce ['tattʃa] *sf* bad reputation.

tacci'are [tat'tʃare] *vt*: ~ **qn di** (*vigliaccheria etc*) to accuse sb of.

'taccio *etc* ['tattʃo] *vb vedi* **tacere**.

'tacco, chi *sm* heel.

taccu'ino *sm* notebook.

ta'cere [ta'tʃere] *vi* to be silent *o* quiet; (*smettere di parlare*) to fall silent ♦ *vt* to keep to oneself, say nothing about; **far** ~ **qn** to make sb be quiet; (*fig*) to silence sb; **mettere a** ~ **qc** to hush sth up.

tachicar'dia [takikar'dia] *sf* (*MED*) tachycardia.

ta'chimetro [ta'kimetro] *sm* speedometer.

'tacito, a ['tatʃito] *ag* silent; (*sottinteso*) tacit, unspoken.

taci'turno, a [tatʃi'turno] *ag* taciturn.

taci'uto, a [ta't∫uto] *pp di* **tacere**.
'tacqui *etc vb vedi* **tacere**.
ta'fano *sm* horsefly.
taffe'ruglio [taffe'ruʎʎo] *sm* brawl, scuffle.
taffettà *sm* taffeta.
'taglia ['taʎʎa] *sf* (*statura*) height; (*misura*) size; (*riscatto*) ransom; (*ricompensa*) reward; **~e forti** (*ABBIGLIAMENTO*) outsize.
taglia'boschi [taʎʎa'bɔski] *sm inv* woodcutter.
taglia'carte [taʎʎa'karte] *sm inv* paperknife.
taglia'legna [taʎʎa'leɲɲa] *sm inv* woodcutter.
tagli'ando [taʎ'ʎando] *sm* coupon.
tagli'are [taʎ'ʎare] *vt* to cut; (*recidere, interrompere*) to cut off; (*intersecare*) to cut across, intersect; (*carne*) to carve; (*vini*) to blend ♦ *vi* to cut; (*prendere una scorciatoia*) to take a short-cut; **~ la strada a qn** to cut across in front of sb; **~ corto** (*fig*) to cut short.
taglia'telle [taʎʎa'tɛlle] *sfpl* tagliatelle *pl*.
tagli'ato, a [taʎ'ʎato] *ag*: **essere ~ per qc** (*fig*) to be cut out for sth.
taglia'unghie [taʎʎa'ungje] *sm inv* nail clippers *pl*.
tagli'ente [taʎ'ʎɛnte] *ag* sharp.
tagli'ere [taʎ'ʎɛre] *sm* chopping board; (*per il pane*) bread board.
'taglio ['taʎʎo] *sm* (*anche fig*) cut; (*azione*) cutting *no pl*; (*di carne*) piece; (*di stoffa*) length; (*di vini*) blending; **di ~** on edge, edgeways; **banconote di piccolo/grosso ~** notes of small/large denomination; **un bel ~ di capelli** a nice haircut *o* hairstyle; **pizza al ~** pizza by the slice.
tagli'one [taʎ'ʎone] *sm*: **la legge del ~** the concept of an eye for an eye and a tooth for a tooth.
tagliuz'zare [taʎʎut'tsare] *vt* to cut into small pieces.
Ta'hiti [ta'iti] *sf* Tahiti.
tailan'dese *ag, sm/f, sm* Thai.
Tai'landia *sf*: **la ~** Thailand.
tai'lleur [ta'jœr] *sm inv* lady's suit.
'talco *sm* talcum powder.

============= *PAROLA CHIAVE* =============

'tale *det* **1** (*simile, così grande*) such; **un(a) ~ ... such (a) ...;** **non accetto ~i discorsi** I won't allow such talk; **è di una ~ arroganza** he is so arrogant; **fa una ~ confusione!** he makes such a mess!
2 (*persona o cosa indeterminata*) such-and-such; **il giorno ~ all'ora ~** on such-and-such a day at such-and-such a time; **la tal persona** that person; **ha telefonato una ~ Giovanna** somebody called

Giovanna phoned
3 (*nelle similitudini*): **~ ... ~** like ... like; **~ padre ~ figlio** like father, like son; **hai il vestito ~ quale il mio** your dress is just *o* exactly like mine
♦ *pron* (*indefinito: persona*): **un(a) ~** someone; **quel (o quella) ~** that person, that man (*o* woman); **il tal dei ~i** what's-his-name.

tale'bano *sm* Taliban.
ta'lento *sm* talent.
talis'mano *sm* talisman.
talk-'show [tɔlk'∫o] *sm inv* talk *o* chat show.
tallo'nare *vt* to pursue; **~ il pallone** (*CALCIO, RUGBY*) to heel the ball.
tallon'cino [tallon't∫ino] *sm* counterfoil (*BRIT*), stub; **~ del prezzo** (*di medicinali*) tear-off tag.
tal'lone *sm* heel.
tal'mente *av* so.
ta'lora *av* = **talvolta**.
'talpa *sf* (*anche fig*) mole.
tal'volta *av* sometimes, at times.
tambu'rello *sm* tambourine.
tambu'rino *sm* drummer boy.
tam'buro *sm* drum; **freni a ~** drum brakes; **a ~ battente** (*fig*) immediately, at once.
Ta'migi [ta'midʒi] *sm*: **il ~** the Thames.
tampona'mento *sm* (*AUT*) collision; **~ a catena** pile-up.
tampo'nare *vt* (*otturare*) to plug; (*urtare: macchina*) to crash *o* ram into.
tam'pone *sm* (*MED*) wad, pad; (*per timbri*) ink-pad; (*respingente*) buffer; **~ assorbente** tampon.
'tamtam *sm inv* (*fig*) grapevine.
'tana *sf* lair, den; (*fig*) den, hideout.
'tanfo *sm* stench.
tan'gente [tan'dʒɛnte] *ag* (*MAT*): **~ a** tangential to ♦ *sf* tangent; (*quota*) share; (*denaro estorto*) rake-off (*fam*), cut.
tangen'topoli [tandʒen'topoli] *sf* (*POL, MEDIA*) Bribesville; *vedi nota nel riquadro*.

TANGENTOPOLI

Tangentopoli *refers to the corruption scandal of the early 1990s which involved a large number of politicians from all parties, including government ministers, as well as leading industrialists and business people. Subsequent investigations unearthed a complex series of illegal payments and bribes involving both public and private money. The scandal began in Milan, which came to be known as* **Tangentopoli**, *or "Bribesville".*

tangenzi'ale [tandʒen'tsjale] _sf_ (_strada_) bypass.

'Tangeri ['tandʒeri] _sf_ Tangiers.

tan'gibile [tan'dʒibile] _ag_ tangible.

tangibil'mente [tandʒibil'mente] _av_ tangibly.

'tango, ghi _sm_ tango.

'tanica, che _sf_ jerry can.

tan'nino _sm_ tannin.

tan'tino: un ~ _av_ (un po'); a little, a bit; (_alquanto_) rather.

══════════ _PAROLA CHIAVE_

'tanto, a _det_ **1** (_molto: quantità_) a lot of, much; (: _numero_) a lot of, many; ~ **pane/ latte** a lot of bread/milk; ~ **tempo** a lot of time, a long time; ~**i auguri!** all the best!; ~**e grazie** many thanks; ~ **persone** a lot of people, many people; ~**e volte** many times, often; **ogni** ~**i chilometri** every so many kilometres

2: (_così_ ~: _quantità_) so much, such a lot of; (: _numero_) so many, such a lot of; ~**a fatica per niente!** a lot of trouble for nothing!; **ha** ~ **coraggio che** ... he's got so much courage that ..., he's so brave that ...; **ho aspettato per** ~ **tempo** I waited so long _o_ for such a long time

3: ~ ... **quanto** (_quantità_) as much ... as; (_numero_) as many ... as; **ho** ~**a pazienza quanta ne hai tu** I have as much patience as you have _o_ as you; **ha** ~**i amici quanti nemici** he has as many friends as he has enemies

♦ _pron_ **1** (_molto_) much, a lot; (_così_ ~) so much, such a lot; ~**i, e** many, a lot; so many, such a lot; **credevo ce ne fosse** ~ I thought there was (such) a lot, I thought there was plenty; **una persona come** ~**e a** person just like any other; **è passato** ~ (_tempo_) it's been so long; **è** ~ **che aspetto** I've been waiting for a long time; ~ **di guadagnato!** so much the better!

2: ~ **quanto** (_denaro_) as much as; (_cioccolatini_) as many as; **ne ho** ~ **quanto basta** I have as much as I need; **due volte** ~ twice as much

3 (_indeterminato_) so much; ~ **per l'affitto,** ~ **per il gas** so much for the rent, so much for the gas; **costa un** ~ **al metro** it costs so much per metre; **di** ~ **in** ~, **ogni** ~ every so often; ~ **vale che** ... I (_o_ we _etc_) may as well ...; ~ **meglio!** so much the better!; ~ **peggio per lui!** so much the worse for him!; **se** ~ **mi dà** ~ if that's how things are; **guardare qc con** ~ **d'occhi** to gaze wide-eyed at sth

♦ _av_ **1** (_molto_) very; **vengo** ~ **volentieri** I'd be very glad to come; **non ci vuole** ~ **a capirlo** it doesn't take much to understand it

2 (_così_ ~: _con ag, av_) so; (: _con vb_) so much, such a lot; **è** ~ **bella!** she's so beautiful!; **non urlare** ~ **(forte)** don't shout so much; **sto** ~ **meglio adesso** I'm so much better now; **era** ~ **bella da non credere** she was incredibly beautiful; ~ ... **che** so ... (that); ~ ... **da** so ... as

3: ~ ... **quanto** as ... as; **conosco** ~ **Carlo quanto suo padre** I know both Carlo and his father; **non è poi** ~ **complicato quanto sembra** it's not as difficult as it seems; **è** ~ **bella quanto buona** she is as good as she is beautiful; ~ **più insisti,** ~ **più non mollerà** the more you insist, the more stubborn he'll be; **quanto più** ... ~ **meno** the more ... the less; **quanto più lo conosco** ~ **meno mi piace** the better I know him the less I like him

4 (_solamente_) just; ~ **per cambiare/ scherzare** just for a change/a joke; **una volta** ~ for once

5 (_a lungo_) (for) long

♦ _cong_ after all; **non insistere,** ~ **è inutile** don't keep on, it's no use; **lascia stare,** ~ **è troppo tardi** forget it, it's too late.

──────────

Tanza'nia [tandza'nia] _sf_: **la** ~ Tanzania.

tapi'oca _sf_ tapioca.

ta'piro _sm_ (_ZOOL_) tapir.

'tappa _sf_ (_luogo di sosta, fermata_) stop, halt; (_parte di un percorso_) stage, leg; (_SPORT_) lap; **a** ~**e** in stages; **bruciare le** ~**e** (_fig_) to be a whizz kid.

tappa'buchi [tappa'buki] _sm inv_ stopgap; **fare da** ~ to act as a stopgap.

tap'pare _vt_ to plug, stop up; (_bottiglia_) to cork; ~**rsi il naso** to hold one's nose; ~**rsi le orecchie** to turn a deaf ear; ~**rsi gli occhi** to turn a blind eye.

tappa'rella _sf_ rolling shutter.

tappe'tino _sm_ (_per auto_) car mat; ~ **antiscivolo** (_da bagno_) non-slip mat.

tap'peto _sm_ carpet; (_anche:_ **tappetino**) rug; (_di tavolo_) cloth; (_SPORT_) andare al ~ to go down for the count; **mettere sul** ~ (_fig_) to bring up for discussion.

tappez'zare [tappet'tsare] _vt_ (_con carta_) to paper; (_rivestire_): ~ **qc (di)** to cover sth (with).

tappezze'ria [tappettse'ria] _sf_ (_arredamento_) soft furnishings _pl_; (_carta da parati_) wall covering; (_di automobile_) upholstery; **far da** ~ (_fig_) to be a wallflower.

tappezzi'ere [tappet'tsjere] _sm_ upholsterer.

'**tappo** *sm* stopper; (*in sughero*) cork; ~ **a corona** bottle top; ~ **a vite** screw top.

TAR *sigla m* = *Tribunale Amministrativo Regionale*.

'**tara** *sf* (*peso*) tare; (*MED*) hereditary defect; (*difetto*) flaw.

taran'tella *sf* tarantella.

ta'rantola *sf* tarantula.

ta'rare *vt* (*COMM*) to tare; (*TECN*) to calibrate.

ta'rato, a *ag* (*COMM*) tared; (*MED*) with a hereditary defect.

tara'tura *sf* (*COMM*) taring; (*TECN*) calibration.

tarchi'ato, a [tar'kjato] *ag* stocky, thickset.

tar'dare *vi* to be late ♦ *vt* to delay; ~ **a fare** to delay doing.

'**tardi** *av* late; **più** ~ later (on); **al più** ~ at the latest; **sul** ~ (*verso sera*) late in the day; **far** ~ to be late; (*restare alzato*) to stay up late.

tar'divo, a *ag* (*primavera*) late; (*rimedio*) belated, tardy; (*fig: bambino*) retarded.

'**tardo, a** *ag* (*lento, fig: ottuso*) slow; (*tempo: avanzato*) late.

tar'dona *sf* (*peg*): **essere una** ~ to be mutton dressed as lamb.

'**targa, ghe** *sf* plate; (*AUT*) number (*BRIT*) *o* license (*US*) plate; *vedi anche* **circolazione**.

tar'gare *vt* (*AUT*) to register.

targ'hetta [tar'getta] *sf* (*con nome: su porta*) nameplate; (: *su bagaglio*) name tag.

ta'riffa *sf* (*gen*) rate, tariff; (*di trasporti*) fare; (*elenco*) price list; tariff; **la** ~ **in vigore** the going rate; ~ **normale/ridotta** standard/reduced rate; (*su mezzi di trasporto*) full/concessionary fare; ~ **salariale** wage rate; ~ **unica** flat rate; ~**e doganali** customs rates *o* tariff; ~**e postali/telefoniche** postal/telephone charges.

tarif'fario, ii *ag*: **aumento** ~ increase in charges *o* rates ♦ *sm* tariff, table of charges.

'**tarlo** *sm* woodworm.

'**tarma** *sf* moth.

tarmi'cida, i [tarmi't∫ida] *ag, sm* moth-killer.

ta'rocco, chi *sm* tarot card; ~**chi** *smpl* (*gioco*) tarot *sg*.

tar'pare *vt* (*fig*): ~ **le ali a qn** to clip sb's wings.

tartagli'are [tartaʎ'ʎare] *vi* to stutter, stammer.

'**tartaro, a** *ag, sm* (*in tutti i sensi*) tartar.

tarta'ruga, ghe *sf* tortoise; (*di mare*) turtle; (*materiale*) tortoiseshell.

tartas'sare *vt* (*fam*): ~ **qn** to give sb the works; ~ **qn a un esame** to give sb a grilling at an exam.

tar'tina *sf* canapé.

tar'tufo *sm* (*BOT*) truffle.

'**tasca, sche** *sf* pocket; **da** ~ pocket *cpd*; **fare i conti in** ~ **a qn** (*fig*) to meddle in sb's affairs.

tas'cabile *ag* (*libro*) pocket *cpd*.

tasca'pane *sm* haversack.

tas'chino [tas'kino] *sm* breast pocket.

Tas'mania *sf*: **la** ~ Tasmania.

'**tassa** *sf* (*imposta*) tax; (*doganale*) duty; (*per iscrizione: a scuola etc*) fee; ~ **di circolazione/di soggiorno** road/tourist tax.

tas'sametro *sm* taximeter.

tas'sare *vt* to tax; to levy a duty on.

tassa'tivo, a *ag* peremptory.

tassazi'one [tassat'tsjone] *sf* taxation; **soggetto a** ~ taxable.

tas'sello *sm* (*di legno, pietra*) plug; (*assaggio*) wedge.

tassì *sm inv* = **taxi**.

tas'sista, i, e *sm/f* taxi driver.

'**tasso** *sm* (*di natalità, d'interesse etc*) rate; (*BOT*) yew; (*ZOOL*) badger; ~ **di cambio/ d'interesse** rate of exchange/interest; ~ **di crescita** growth rate.

tas'tare *vt* to feel; ~ **il terreno** (*fig*) to see how the land lies.

tasti'era *sf* keyboard.

tastie'rino *sm*: ~ **numerico** numeric keypad.

'**tasto** *sm* key; (*tatto*) touch, feel; **toccare un** ~ **delicato** (*fig*) to touch on a delicate subject; **toccare il** ~ **giusto** (*fig*) to strike the right note; ~ **funzione** (*INFORM*) function key; ~ **delle maiuscole** (*su macchina da scrivere etc*) shift key.

tas'toni *av*: **procedere (a)** ~ to grope one's way forward.

'**tata** *sf* (*linguaggio infantile*) nanny.

'**tattico, a, ci, che** *ag* tactical ♦ *sf* tactics *pl*.

'**tatto** *sm* (*senso*) touch; (*fig*) tact; **duro al** ~ hard to the touch; **aver** ~ to be tactful, have tact.

tatu'aggio [tatu'addʒo] *sm* tattooing; (*disegno*) tattoo.

tatu'are *vt* to tattoo.

tauma'turgico, a, ci, che [tauma'turdʒiko] *ag* (*fig*) miraculous.

ta'verna *sf* (*osteria*) tavern.

'**tavola** *sf* table; (*asse*) plank, board; (*lastra*) tablet; (*quadro*) panel (painting); (*illustrazione*) plate; ~ **calda** snack bar; ~ **pieghevole** folding table.

tavo'lata *sf* company at table.

tavo'lato *sm* boarding; (*pavimento*) wooden

floor.

tavo'letta *sf* tablet, bar; **a** ~ (*AUT*) flat out.

tavo'lino *sm* small table; (*scrivania*) desk; ~ **da tè/gioco** coffee/card table; **mettersi a** ~ to get down to work; **decidere qc a** ~ (*fig*) to decide sth on a theoretical level.

'tavolo *sm* table; ~ **da disegno** drawing board; ~ **da lavoro** desk; (*TECN*) workbench; ~ **operatorio** (*MED*) operating table.

tavo'lozza [tavo'lɔttsa] *sf* (*ARTE*) palette.

'taxi *sm inv* taxi.

'tazza ['tattsa] *sf* cup; ~ **da caffè/tè** coffee/tea cup; **una** ~ **di caffè/tè** a cup of coffee/tea.

taz'zina [tat'tsina] *sf* coffee cup.

TBC *abbr f* (= *tubercolosi*) TB.

TCI *sigla m* = *Touring Club Italiano*.

TE *sigla* = *Teramo*.

te *pron* (*soggetto: in forme comparative, oggetto*) you.

tè *sm inv* tea; (*trattenimento*) tea party.

tea'trale *ag* theatrical.

te'atro *sm* theatre; ~ **comico** comedy; ~ **di posa** film studio.

'tecnico, a, ci, che *ag* technical ♦ *sm/f* technician ♦ *sf* technique; (*tecnologia*) technology.

tecnolo'gia [teknolo'dʒia] *sf* technology; **alta** ~ high technology, hi-tech.

tecno'logico, a, ci, che [tekno'lɔdʒiko] *ag* technological.

te'desco, a, schi, sche *ag*, *sm/f*, *sm* German; ~ **orientale/occidentale** East/West German.

tedi'are *vt* (*infastidire*) to bother, annoy; (*annoiare*) to bore.

'tedio *sm* tedium, boredom.

tedi'oso, a *ag* tedious, boring.

te'game *sm* (*CUC*) pan; **al** ~ fried.

'teglia ['teʎʎa] *sf* (*CUC: per dolci*) (baking) tin (*BRIT*), cake pan (*US*); (*: per arrosti*) (roasting) tin.

'tegola *sf* tile.

Teh'ran *sf* Tehran.

tei'era *sf* teapot.

te'ina *sf* (*CHIM*) theine.

tel. *abbr* (= *telefono*) tel.

'tela *sf* (*tessuto*) cloth; (*per vele, quadri*) canvas; (*dipinto*) canvas, painting; **di** ~ (*calzoni*) (heavy) cotton *cpd*; (*scarpe, borsa*) canvas *cpd*; ~ **cerata** oilcloth; ~ **di ragno** spider's web.

te'laio *sm* (*apparecchio*) loom; (*struttura*) frame.

Tel A'viv *sf* Tel Aviv.

tele... *prefisso* tele....

teleabbo'nato *sm* television licence

holder.

tele'camera *sf* television camera.

telecoman'dare *vt* to operate by remote control.

teleco'mando *sm* remote control; (*dispositivo*) remote-control device.

telecomunicazi'oni [telekomunikat'tsjoni] *sfpl* telecommunications.

teleconfe'renza *sf* teleconferencing.

tele'cronaca, che *sf* television report.

telecro'nista, i, e *sm/f* (television) commentator.

tele'ferica, che *sf* cableway.

tele'film *sm inv* television film.

telefo'nare *vi* to telephone, ring; (*fare una chiamata*) to make a phone call ♦ *vt* to telephone; ~ **a qn** to telephone sb, phone *o* ring *o* call sb (up).

telefo'nata *sf* (*telephone*) call; ~ **urbana/interurbana** local/long-distance call; ~ **a carico del destinatario** reverse-charge (*BRIT*) *o* collect (*US*) call; ~ **con preavviso** person-to-person call.

telefonica'mente *av* by (tele)phone.

tele'fonico, a, ci, che *ag* (tele)phone *cpd*.

telefo'nino *sm* (*cellulare*) mobile phone.

telefo'nista, i, e *sm/f* telephonist; (*d'impresa*) switchboard operator.

te'lefono *sm* telephone; **essere al** ~ to be on the (tele)phone; ~ **a gettoni** ≈ pay phone; ~ **azzurro** ≈ Childline; ~ **interno** internal phone; ~ **pubblico** public phone, call box (*BRIT*); ~ **rosa** ≈ rape crisis.

telegior'nale [teledʒor'nale] *sm* television news (programme).

telegra'fare *vt*, *vi* to telegraph, cable.

tele'grafico, a, ci, che *ag* telegraph *cpd*, telegraphic.

telegra'fista, i, e *sm/f* telegraphist.

te'legrafo *sm* telegraph; (*ufficio*) telegraph office.

tele'gramma, i *sm* telegram.

telela'voro *sm* teleworking.

tele'matica *sf* data transmission; telematics *sg*.

teleno'vela *sf* soap opera.

teleobiet'tivo *sm* telephoto lens *sg*.

telepa'tia *sf* telepathy.

tele'quiz [tele'kwits] *sm inv* (*TV*) game show.

teles'chermo [teles'kɛrmo] *sm* television screen.

teles'copio *sm* telescope.

telescri'vente *sf* teleprinter (*BRIT*), teletypewriter (*US*).

teleselet'tivo, a *ag*: **prefisso** ~ dialling code (*BRIT*), dial code (*US*).

teleselezi'one [teleselet'tsjone] *sf* direct dialling.

telespetta'tore, **'trice** *sm/f* (television) viewer.
tele'text *sm inv* teletext.
tele'vendita *sf* teleshopping.
tele'video *sm* videotext service.
televisi'one *sf* television; ~ **digitale** digital TV; *vedi nota nel riquadro.*

TELEVISIONE

Three state-owned channels, RAI 1, 2 and 3, and a large number of private companies broadcast television programmes in Italy. Some of the latter function at purely local level, while others are regional; some form part of a network, while others remain independent. As a public corporation, RAI reports to the Post and Telecommunications Ministry. Both RAI and the private-sector channels compete for advertising revenues.

---

televi'sore *sm* television set.
'telex *sm inv* telex.
'telo *sm* length of cloth.
te'lone *sm* (*per merci etc*) tarpaulin; (*sipario*) drop curtain.
'tema, i *sm* theme; (*INS*) essay.
te'matica *sf* basic themes *pl.*
teme'rario, a *ag* rash, reckless.
te'mere *vt* to fear, be afraid of; (*essere sensibile a: freddo, calore*) to be sensitive to ♦ *vi* to be afraid; (*essere preoccupato*): ~ **per** to worry about, fear for; ~ **di/che** to be afraid of/that.
'tempera *sf* (*pittura*) tempera; (*dipinto*) painting in tempera.
temperama'tite *sm inv* pencil sharpener.
tempera'mento *sm* temperament.
tempe'rante *ag* moderate.
tempe'rare *vt* (*aguzzare*) to sharpen; (*fig*) to moderate, control, temper.
tempe'rato, a *ag* moderate, temperate; (*clima*) temperate.
tempera'tura *sf* temperature; ~ **ambiente** room temperature.
tempe'rino *sm* penknife.
tem'pesta *sf* storm; ~ **di sabbia/neve** sand/snowstorm.
tempes'tare *vt* (*percuotere*): ~ **qn di colpi** to rain blows on sb; (*bombardare*): ~ **qn di domande** to bombard sb with questions; (*ornare*) to stud.
tempes'tivo, a *ag* timely.
tempes'toso, a *ag* stormy.
'tempia *sf* (*ANAT*) temple.
'tempio *sm* (*edificio*) temple.
tem'pismo *sm* sense of timing.

tem'pistiche [tem'pistike] *sfpl* (*COMM*) time and motion.
'tempo *sm* (*METEOR*) weather; (*cronologico*) time; (*epoca*) time, times *pl*; (*di film, gioco: parte*) part; (*MUS*) time; (: *battuta*) beat; (*LING*) tense; **un** ~ once; **da** ~ for a long time now; ~ **fa** some time ago; **poco** ~ **dopo** not long after; **a** ~ **e luogo** at the right time and place; **ogni cosa a suo** ~ we'll (*o* you'll *etc*) deal with it in due course; **al** ~ **stesso** *o* **a un** ~ at the same time; **per** ~ early; **per qualche** ~ for a while; **trovare il** ~ **di fare qc** to find the time to do sth; **aver fatto il proprio** ~ to have had its (*o* his *etc*) day; **primo/ secondo** ~ (*TEAT*) first/second part; (*SPORT*) first/second half; **rispettare i** ~**i** to keep to the timetable; **stringere i** ~**i** to speed things up; **con i** ~**i che corrono** these days; **in questi ultimi** ~**i** of late; **ai miei** ~**i** in my day; ~ **di cottura** cooking time; **in** ~ **utile** in due time *o* course; ~**i di esecuzione** (*COMM*) time scale *sg*; ~**i di lavorazione** (*COMM*) throughput time *sg*; ~**i morti** (*COMM*) downtime *sg*, idle time *sg.*
tempo'rale *ag* temporal ♦ *sm* (*METEOR*) (thunder)storm.
tempora'lesco, a, schi, sche *ag* stormy.
tempo'raneo, a *ag* temporary.
temporeggi'are [tempored'dʒare] *vi* to play for time, temporize.
'tempra *sf* (*TECN: atto*) tempering, hardening; (: *effetto*) temper; (*fig: costituzione fisica*) constitution; (: *intellettuale*) temperament.
tem'prare *vt* to temper.
te'nace [te'natʃe] *ag* strong, tough; (*fig*) tenacious.
te'nacia [te'natʃa] *sf* tenacity.
te'naglie [te'naʎʎe] *sfpl* pincers *pl.*
'tenda *sf* (*riparo*) awning; (*di finestra*) curtain; (*per campeggio etc*) tent.
ten'daggio [ten'daddʒo] *sm* curtaining, curtains *pl*, drapes *pl* (*US*).
ten'denza [ten'dɛntsa] *sf* tendency; (*orientamento*) trend; **avere** ~ **a** *o* **per qc** to have a bent for sth; ~ **al rialzo/ribasso** (*BORSA*) upward/downward trend.
tendenziosità [tendentsjosi'ta] *sf* tendentiousness.
tendenzi'oso, a [tenden'tsjoso] *ag* tendentious, bias(s)ed.
'tendere *vt* (*allungare al massimo*) to stretch, draw tight; (*porgere: mano*) to hold out; (*fig: trappola*) to lay, set ♦ *vi*: ~ **a qc/a fare** to tend towards sth/to do; **tutti i nostri sforzi sono tesi a ...** all our efforts

are geared towards ...; ~ **l'orecchio** to
prick up one's ears; **il tempo tende al
caldo** the weather is getting hot; **un blu
che tende al verde** a greenish blue.

ten'dina *sf* curtain.

'tendine *sm* tendon, sinew.

ten'done *sm* (*da circo*) big top.

ten'dopoli *sf inv* (large) camp.

'tenebre *sfpl* darkness *sg*.

tene'broso, a *ag* dark, gloomy.

te'nente *sm* lieutenant.

te'nere *vt* to hold; (*conservare, mantenere*)
to keep; (*ritenere, considerare*) to consider;
(*spazio: occupare*) to take up, occupy;
(*seguire: strada*) to keep to; (*dare: lezione,
conferenza*) to give ♦ *vi* to hold; (*colori*) to
be fast; (*dare importanza*): ~ **a** to care
about; ~ **a fare** to want to do, be keen
to do; ~**rsi** *vr* (*stare in una determinata
posizione*) to stand; (*stimarsi*) to
consider o.s.; (*aggrapparsi*): ~**rsi a** to hold
on to; (*attenersi*): ~**rsi a** to stick to; ~ **in
gran conto** *o* **considerazione qn** to have a
high regard for sb, think highly of sb; ~
conto di qc to take sth into consideration;
~ **presente qc** to bear sth in mind; **non ci
sono scuse che tengano** I'll take no
excuses; ~**rsi per la mano** (*uso reciproco*)
to hold hands; ~**rsi in piedi** to stay on
one's feet.

tene'rezza [tene'rettsa] *sf* tenderness.

'tenero, a *ag* tender; (*pietra, cera, colore*)
soft; (*fig*) tender, loving ♦ *sm*: **tra quei due
c'è del** ~ there's a romance budding
between those two.

'tengo *etc vb vedi* **tenere**.

'tenia *sf* tapeworm.

'tenni *etc vb vedi* **tenere**.

'tennis *sm* tennis; ~ **da tavolo** table tennis.

ten'nista, i, e *sm/f* tennis player.

te'nore *sm* (*tono*) tone; (*MUS*) tenor; ~ **di
vita** way of life; (*livello*) standard of
living.

tensi'one *sf* tension; **ad alta** ~ (*ELETTR*)
high-voltage *cpd*, high-tension *cpd*.

tentaco'lare *ag* tentacular; (*fig: città*)
magnet-like.

ten'tacolo *sm* tentacle.

ten'tare *vt* (*indurre*) to tempt; (*provare*): ~
qc/di fare to attempt *o* try sth/to do; ~ **la
sorte** to try one's luck.

tenta'tivo *sm* attempt.

tentazi'one [tentat'tsjone] *sf* temptation;
aver la ~ **di fare** to be tempted to do.

tentenna'mento *sm* (*fig*) hesitation,
wavering; **dopo molti** ~**i** after much
hesitation.

tenten'nare *vi* to shake, be unsteady; (*fig*)

to hesitate, waver ♦ *vt*: ~ **il capo** to shake
one's head.

ten'toni *av*: **andare a** ~ (*anche fig*) to grope
one's way.

'tenue *ag* (*sottile*) fine; (*colore*) soft; (*fig*)
slender, slight.

te'nuta *sf* (*capacità*) capacity; (*divisa*)
uniform; (*abito*) dress; (*AGR*) estate; **a** ~
d'aria airtight; ~ **di strada** roadholding
power; **in** ~ **da lavoro** in one's working
clothes; **in** ~ **da sci** in a skiing outfit.

teolo'gia [teolo'dʒia] *sf* theology.

teo'logico, a, ci, che [teo'lɔdʒiko] *ag*
theological.

te'ologo, gi *sm* theologian.

teo'rema, i *sm* theorem.

teo'ria *sf* theory; **in** ~ in theory,
theoretically.

te'orico, a, ci, che *ag* theoretic(al) ♦ *sm*
theorist, theoretician; **a livello** ~, **in linea**
~**a** theoretically.

teoriz'zare [teorid'dzare] *vt* to theorize.

'tepido, a *ag* = **tiepido**.

te'pore *sm* warmth.

'teppa *sf* mob, hooligans *pl*.

tep'paglia [tep'paʎʎa] *sf* hooligans *pl*.

tep'pismo *sm* hooliganism.

tep'pista, i *sm* hooligan.

tera'peutico, a, ci, che *ag* therapeutic.

tera'pia *sf* therapy; ~ **di gruppo** group
therapy.

tera'pista, i, e *sm/f* therapist.

tergicris'tallo [terdʒikris'tallo] *sm*
windscreen (*BRIT*) *o* windshield (*US*)
wiper.

tergiver'sare [terdʒiver'sare] *vi* to shilly-
shally.

'tergo *sm*: **a** ~ behind; **vedi a** ~ please turn
over.

'terital ® *sm inv* Terylene ®.

ter'male *ag* thermal.

'terme *sfpl* thermal baths.

'termico, a, ci, che *ag* thermal; **centrale**
~**a** thermal power station.

termi'nale *ag* (*fase, parte*) final; (*MED*)
terminal ♦ *sm* terminal; **tratto** ~ (*di fiume*)
lower reaches *pl*.

termi'nare *vt* to end; (*lavoro*) to finish ♦ *vi*
to end.

terminazi'one [terminat'tsjone] *sf* (*fine*)
end; (*LING*) ending; ~**i nervose** (*ANAT*)
nerve endings.

'termine *sm* term; (*fine, estremità*) end; (*di
territorio*) boundary, limit; **fissare un** ~ to
set a deadline; **portare a** ~ **qc** to bring sth
to a conclusion; **contratto a** ~ (*COMM*)
forward contract; **a breve/lungo** ~ short-
/long-term; **ai** ~**i di legge** by law; **in altri**

~i in other words; **parlare senza mezzi** ~i to talk frankly, not to mince one's words.

terminolo'gia [terminolo'dʒia] *sf* terminology.

'**termite** *sf* termite.

termoco'perta *sf* electric blanket.

ter'mometro *sm* thermometer.

termonucle'are *ag* thermonuclear.

'**termos** *sm inv* = **thermos**.

termosi'fone *sm* radiator; **(riscaldamento a)** ~ central heating.

ter'mostato *sm* thermostat.

'**terna** *sf* set of three; (*lista di tre nomi*) list of three candidates.

'**terno** *sm* (*al lotto etc*) (set of) three winning numbers; **vincere un** ~ **al lotto** (*fig*) to hit the jackpot.

'**terra** *sf* (*gen, ELETTR*) earth; (*sostanza*) soil, earth; (*opposto al mare*) land *no pl*; (*regione, paese*) land; (*argilla*) clay; ~**e** *sfpl* (*possedimento*) lands, land *sg*; **a o per** ~ (*stato*) on the ground (*o floor*); (*moto*) to the ground, down; **mettere a** ~ (*ELETTR*) to earth; **essere a** ~ (*fig: depresso*) to be at rock bottom; **via** ~ (*viaggiare*) by land, overland; **strada in** ~ **battuta** dirt track; ~ **di nessuno** no man's land; **la T**~ **Santa** the Holy Land; ~ **di Siena** sienna; ~ ~ (*fig: persona, argomento*) prosaic, pedestrian.

'**terra-'aria** *ag inv* (*MIL*) ground-to-air.

terra'cotta *sf* terracotta; **vasellame di** ~ earthenware.

terra'ferma *sf* dry land, terra firma; (*continente*) mainland.

ter'raglia [ter'raʎʎa] *sf* pottery; ~**e** *pl* (*oggetti*) crockery *sg*, earthenware *sg*.

Terra'nova *sf*: **la** ~ Newfoundland.

terrapi'eno *sm* embankment, bank.

'**terra-'terra** *ag inv* (*MIL*) surface-to-surface.

ter'razza [ter'rattsa] *sf*, **ter'razzo** [ter'rattso] *sm* terrace.

terremo'tato, a *ag* (*zona*) devastated by an earthquake ♦ *sm/f* earthquake victim.

terre'moto *sm* earthquake.

ter'reno, a *ag* (*vita, beni*) earthly ♦ *sm* (*suolo, fig*) ground; (*COMM*) land *no pl*, plot (of land); site; (*SPORT, MIL*) field; **perdere** ~ (*anche fig*) to lose ground; **un** ~ **montuoso** a mountainous terrain; ~ **alluvionale** (*GEO*) alluvial soil.

'**terreo, a** *ag* (*viso, colorito*) wan.

ter'restre *ag* (*superficie*) of the earth, earth's; (*di terra: battaglia, animale*) land *cpd*; (*REL*) earthly, worldly.

ter'ribile *ag* terrible, dreadful.

ter'riccio [ter'rittʃo] *sm* soil.

terri'ero, a *ag*: **proprietà** ~**a** landed

property; **proprietario** ~ landowner.

terrifi'cante *ag* terrifying.

ter'rina *sf* (*zuppiera*) tureen.

territori'ale *ag* territorial.

terri'torio *sm* territory.

ter'rone, a *sm/f derogatory term used by Northern Italians to describe Southern Italians.*

ter'rore *sm* terror; **avere il** ~ **di qc** to be terrified of sth.

terro'rismo *sm* terrorism.

terro'rista, i, e *sm/f* terrorist.

terroriz'zare [terrorid'dzare] *vt* to terrorize.

'**terso, a** *ag* clear.

ter'zetto [ter'tsetto] *sm* (*MUS*) trio, terzetto; (*di persone*) trio.

terzi'ario, a [ter'tsjarjo] *ag* (*GEO, ECON*) tertiary.

ter'zino [ter'tsino] *sm* (*CALCIO*) fullback, back.

'**terzo, a** ['tɛrtso] *ag* third ♦ *sm* (*frazione*) third; (*DIR*) third party ♦ *sf* (*gen*) third; (*AUT*) third (gear); (*di trasporti*) third class; (*SCOL: elementare*) third year at primary school; (: *media*) third year at secondary school; (: *superiore*) sixth year at secondary school; ~**i** *smpl* (*altri*) others, other people; **agire per conto di** ~**i** to act on behalf of a third party; **assicurazione contro** ~**i** third-party insurance (*BRIT*), liability insurance (*US*); **la** ~**a età** old age; **il** ~ **mondo** the Third World; **di terz'ordine** third rate; **la** ~**a pagina** (*STAMPA*) the Arts page.

'**tesa** *sf* brim; **a larghe** ~**e** wide-brimmed.

'**teschio** ['tɛskjo] *sm* skull.

'**tesi** *sf inv* thesis; ~ **di laurea** degree thesis.

'**tesi** *etc vb vedi* **tendere**.

'**teso, a** *pp di* **tendere** ♦ *ag* (*tirato*) taut, tight; (*fig*) tense.

tesore'ria *sf* treasury.

tesori'ere *sm* treasurer.

te'soro *sm* treasure; **il Ministero del T**~ the Treasury; **far** ~ **dei consigli di qn** to take sb's advice to heart.

'**tessera** *sf* (*documento*) card; (*di abbonato*) season ticket; (*di giornalista*) pass; **ha la** ~ **del partito** he's a party member.

tesse'rare *vt* (*iscrivere*) to give a membership card to.

tesse'rato, a *sm/f* (*di società sportiva etc*) (fully paid-up) member; (*POL*) (card-carrying) member.

'**tessere** *vt* to weave; ~ **le lodi di qn** (*fig*) to sing sb's praises.

'**tessile** *ag, sm* textile.

tessi'tore, 'trice *sm/f* weaver.

tessi'tura *sf* weaving.

tes'suto *sm* fabric, material; (*BIOL*) tissue; (*fig*) web.

'testa *sf* head; (*di cose: estremità, parte anteriore*) head, front; **5.000 euro a** ~ 5,000 euros apiece *o* a head *o* per person; **a** ~ **alta** with one's head held high; **a** ~ **bassa** (*correre*) headlong; (*con aria dimessa*) with head bowed; **di** ~ *ag* (*vettura etc*) front; **dare alla** ~ to go to one's head; **fare di** ~ **propria** to go one's own way; **in** ~ (*SPORT*) in the lead; **essere in** ~ **alla classifica** (*corridore*) to be number one; (*squadra*) to be at the top of the league table; (*disco*) to be top of the charts, be number one; **essere alla** ~ **di qc** (*società*) to be the head of; (*esercito*) to be at the head of; **tenere** ~ **a qn** (*nemico etc*) to stand up to sb; **una** ~ **d'aglio** a bulb of garlic; ~ **o croce?** heads or tails?; **avere la** ~ **dura** to be stubborn; ~ **di serie** (*TENNIS*) seed, seeded player.

'testa-'coda *sm inv* (*AUT*) spin.

testamen'tario, a *ag* (*DIR*) testamentary; **le sue disposizioni** ~**e** the provisions of his will.

testa'mento *sm* (*atto*) will, testament; **l'Antico/il Nuovo T**~ (*REL*) the Old/New Testament.

testar'daggine [testar'daddʒine] *sf* stubbornness, obstinacy.

tes'tardo, a *ag* stubborn, pig-headed.

tes'tare *vt* to test.

tes'tata *sf* (*parte anteriore*) head; (*intestazione*) heading; **missile a** ~ **nucleare** missile with a nuclear warhead.

'teste *sm/f* witness.

tes'ticolo *sm* testicle.

testi'era *sf* (*del letto*) headboard; (*di cavallo*) headpiece.

testi'mone *sm/f* (*DIR*) witness; **fare da** ~ **alle nozze di qn** to be a witness at sb's wedding; ~ **oculare** eye witness.

testimoni'anza [testimo'njantsa] *sf* (*atto*) deposition; (*effetto*) evidence; (*fig: prova*) proof; **accusare qn di falsa** ~ to accuse sb of perjury; **rilasciare una** ~ to give evidence.

testimoni'are *vt* to testify; (*fig*) to bear witness to, testify to ♦ *vi* to give evidence, testify; ~ **il vero** to tell the truth; ~ **il falso** to perjure o.s.

tes'tina *sf* (*di giradischi, registratore*) head.

'testo *sm* text; **fare** ~ (*opera, autore*) to be authoritative; (*fig: dichiarazione*) to carry weight.

testoste'rone *sm* testosterone.

testu'ale *ag* textual; **le sue parole** ~**i** his (*o* her) actual words.

tes'tuggine [tes'tuddʒine] *sf* tortoise; (*di mare*) turtle.

'tetano *sm* (*MED*) tetanus.

'tetro, a *ag* gloomy.

'tetta *sf* (*fam*) boob, tit.

tetta'rella *sf* teat.

'tetto *sm* roof; **abbandonare il** ~ **coniugale** to desert one's family; ~ **a cupola** dome.

tet'toia *sf* roofing; canopy.

'Tevere *sm*: **il** ~ the Tiber.

TG [tid'dʒi] *abbr m* (= *telegiornale*) TV news *sg*.

'thermos ® ['tɛrmos] *sm inv* vacuum *o* Thermos ® flask.

'thriller ['θrilə], **'thrilling** ['θriliŋ] *sm inv* thriller.

ti *pron* (*dav lo, la, li, le, ne diventa* **te**) (*oggetto*) you; (*complemento di termine*) (to) you; (*riflessivo*) yourself; ~ **aiuto?** can I give you a hand?; **te lo ha dato?** did he give it to you?; ~ **sei lavato?** have you washed?

ti'ara *sf* (*REL*) tiara.

'Tibet *sm*: **il** ~ Tibet.

tibe'tano, a *ag, sm/f* Tibetan.

'tibia *sf* tibia, shinbone.

tic *sm inv* tic, (nervous) twitch; (*fig*) mannerism.

ticchet'tio [tikket'tio] *sm* (*di macchina da scrivere*) clatter; (*di orologio*) ticking; (*della pioggia*) patter.

'ticchio ['tikkjo] *sm* (*ghiribizzo*) whim; (*tic*) tic, (nervous) twitch.

'ticket *sm inv* (*MED*) prescription charge (*BRIT*).

ti'ene *etc vb vedi* **tenere**.

ti'epido, a *ag* lukewarm, tepid.

ti'fare *vi*: ~ **per** to be a fan of; (*parteggiare*) to side with.

'tifo *sm* (*MED*) typhus; (*fig*): **fare il** ~ **per** to be a fan of.

tifoi'dea *sf* typhoid.

ti'fone *sm* typhoon.

ti'foso, a *sm/f* (*SPORT etc*) fan.

tight ['tait] *sm inv* morning suit.

tigì [tid'dʒi] *sm inv* TV news.

'tiglio ['tiʎʎo] *sm* lime (tree), linden (tree).

'tigna ['tiɲɲa] *sf* (*MED*) ringworm.

ti'grato, a *ag* striped.

'tigre *sf* tiger.

tilt *sm*: **andare in** ~ (*fig*) to go haywire.

tim'ballo *sm* (*strumento*) kettledrum; (*CUC*) timbale.

tim'brare *vt* to stamp; (*annullare: francobolli*) to postmark; ~ **il cartellino** to clock in.

'timbro *sm* stamp; (*MUS*) timbre, tone.

timi'dezza [timi'dettsa] *sf* shyness, timidity.

'timido, a *ag* shy, timid.

'**timo** *sm* thyme.

ti'**mone** *sm* (*NAUT*) rudder.

timoni'**ere** *sm* helmsman.

timo'**rato, a** *ag* conscientious; ~ **di Dio** God-fearing.

ti'**more** *sm* (*paura*) fear; (*rispetto*) awe; **avere ~ di qc/qn** (*paura*) to be afraid of sth/sb.

timo'**roso, a** *ag* timid, timorous.

'**timpano** *sm* (*ANAT*) eardrum; (*MUS*): ~**i** kettledrums, timpani.

'**tinca, che** *sf* (*ZOOL*) tench.

ti'**nello** *sm* small dining room.

'**tingere** ['tindʒere] *vt* to dye.

'**tino** *sm* vat.

ti'**nozza** [ti'nɔttsa] *sf* tub.

'**tinsi** *etc vb vedi* **tingere.**

'**tinta** *sf* (*materia colorante*) dye; (*colore*) colour (*BRIT*), color (*US*), shade.

tinta'**rella** *sf* (*fam*) (sun)tan.

tintin'**nare** *vi* to tinkle.

tintin'**nio** *sm* tinkling.

'**tinto, a** *pp di* **tingere.**

tinto'**ria** *sf* (*officina*) dyeworks *sg*; (*lavasecco*) dry cleaner's (shop).

tin'**tura** *sf* (*operazione*) dyeing; (*colorante*) dye; ~ **di iodio** tincture of iodine.

'**tipico, a, ci, che** *ag* typical.

'**tipo** *sm* type; (*genere*) kind, type; (*fam*) chap, fellow; **vestiti di tutti i** ~**i** all kinds of clothes; **sul ~ di questo** of this sort; **sei un bel ~!** you're a fine one!

tipogra'**fia** *sf* typography.

tipo'**grafico, a, ci, che** *ag* typographic(al).

ti'**pografo** *sm* typographer.

tip '**tap** [tip'tap] *sm* (*ballo*) tap dancing.

T.I.R. *sigla m* (= *Transports Internationaux Routiers*) *International Heavy Goods Vehicle.*

'**tira e 'molla** *sm inv* tug-of-war.

ti'**raggio** [ti'raddʒo] *sm* (*di camino etc*) draught (*BRIT*), draft (*US*).

Ti'**rana** *sf* Tirana.

tiranneggi'**are** [tiranned'dʒare] *vt* to tyrannize.

tiran'**nia** *sf* tyranny.

ti'**ranno, a** *ag* tyrannical ♦ *sm* tyrant.

ti'**rante** *sm* (*NAUT*, *di tenda etc*) guy; (*EDIL*) brace.

tirapi'**edi** *sm/f inv* hanger-on.

tira'**pugni** [tira'puɲɲi] *sm inv* knuckle-duster.

ti'**rare** *vt* (*gen*) to pull; (*estrarre*): ~ **qc da** to take *o* pull sth out of; to get sth out of; to extract sth from; (*chiudere: tenda etc*) to draw, pull; (*tracciare, disegnare*) to draw, trace; (*lanciare: sasso, palla*) to throw; (*stampare*) to print; (*pistola, freccia*) to fire

♦ *vi* (*pipa, camino*) to draw; (*vento*) to blow; (*abito*) to be tight; (*fare fuoco*) to fire; (*fare del tiro, CALCIO*) to shoot; ~ **qn da parte** to take *o* draw sb aside; ~ **un sospiro (di sollievo)** to heave a sigh (of relief); ~ **a indovinare** to take a guess; ~ **sul prezzo** to bargain; ~ **avanti** *vi* to struggle on ♦ *vt* (*famiglia*) to provide for; (*ditta*) to look after; ~ **fuori** to take out, pull out; ~ **giù** to pull down; ~ **su** to pull up; (*capelli*) to put up; (*fig: bambino*) to bring up; ~**rsi indietro** to move back; (*fig*) to back out; ~**rsi su** to pull o.s. up; (*fig*) to cheer o.s. up.

ti'**rato, a** *ag* (*teso*) taut; (*fig: teso, stanco*) drawn.

tira'**tore** *sm* gunman; **un buon ~** a good shot; ~ **scelto** marksman.

tira'**tura** *sf* (*azione*) printing; (*di libro*) (print) run; (*di giornale*) circulation.

tirchie'**ria** [tirkje'ria] *sf* meanness, stinginess.

'**tirchio, a** ['tirkjo] *ag* mean, stingy.

tiri'**tera** *sf* drivel, hot air.

'**tiro** *sm* shooting *no pl*, firing *no pl*; (*colpo, sparo*) shot; (*di palla: lancio*) throwing *no pl*; throw; (*fig*) trick; **essere a ~** to be in range; **giocare un brutto ~** *o* **un ~ mancino a qn** to play a dirty trick on s.b.; **cavallo da ~** draught (*BRIT*) *o* draft (*US*) horse; ~ **a segno** target shooting; (*luogo*) shooting range.

tiroci'**nante** [tirotʃi'nante] *ag*, *sm/f* apprentice (*cpd*); trainee (*cpd*).

tiro'**cinio** [tiro'tʃinjo] *sm* apprenticeship; (*professionale*) training.

ti'**roide** *sf* thyroid (gland).

tiro'**lese** *ag*, *sm/f* Tyrolean, Tyrolese *inv*.

Ti'**rolo** *sm*: **il ~** the Tyrol.

tir'**renico, a, ci, che** *ag* Tyrrhenian.

Tir'**reno** *sm*: **il (mar) ~** the Tyrrhenian Sea.

ti'**sana** *sf* herb tea.

'**tisi** *sf* (*MED*) consumption.

'**tisico, a, ci, che** *ag* (*MED*) consumptive; (*fig: gracile*) frail ♦ *sm/f* consumptive (person).

ti'**tanico, a, ci, che** *ag* gigantic, enormous.

ti'**tano** *sm* (*MITOLOGIA, fig*) titan.

tito'**lare** *ag* appointed; (*sovrano*) titular ♦ *sm/f* incumbent; (*proprietario*) owner; (*CALCIO*) regular player.

tito'**lato, a** *ag* (*persona*) titled.

'**titolo** *sm* title; (*di giornale*) headline; (*diploma*) qualification; (*COMM*) security; (*: azione*) share; **a che ~?** for what reason?; **a ~ di amicizia** out of friendship; **a ~ di cronaca** for your information; **a ~ di premio** as a prize; ~ **di credito** share; ~

obbligazionario bond; ~ **al portatore** bearer bond; ~ **di proprietà** title deed; ~**i di stato** government securities; ~**i di testa** (*CINE*) credits.

titu'bante *ag* hesitant, irresolute.

tivù *sf inv* (*fam*) telly (*BRIT*), TV.

'tizio, a ['tittsjo] *smf* fellow, chap.

tiz'zone [tit'tsone] *sm* brand.

T.M.G. *abbr* (= *tempo medio di Greenwich*) GMT.

TN *sigla* = *Trento*.

TNT *sigla m* (= *trinitrotoluolo*) TNT.

TO *sigla* = *Torino*.

toast [toust] *sm inv* toasted sandwich.

toc'cante *ag* touching.

toc'care *vt* to touch; (*tastare*) to feel; (*fig: riguardare*) to concern; (: *commuovere*) to touch, move; (: *pungere*) to hurt, wound; (: *far cenno a: argomento*) to touch on, mention ♦ *vi*: ~ **a** (*accadere*) to happen to; (*spettare*) to be up to; **tocca a te difenderci** it's up to you to defend us; **a chi tocca?** whose turn is it?; **mi toccò pagare** I had to pay; ~ **il fondo** (*in acqua*) to touch the bottom; (*fig*) to touch rock bottom; ~ **con mano** (*fig*) to find out for o.s.; ~ **qn sul vivo** to cut sb to the quick.

tocca'sana *sm inv* cure-all, panacea.

toccherò *etc* [tokke'rɔ] *vb vedi* **toccare**.

'tocco, chi *sm* touch; (*ARTE*) stroke, touch.

toe'letta *sf* = **toilette**.

'toga, ghe *sf* toga; (*di magistrato, professore*) gown.

'togliere ['tɔʎʎere] *vt* (*rimuovere*) to take away (*o* off), remove; (*riprendere, non concedere più*) to take away, remove; (*MAT*) to take away, subtract; (*liberare*) to free; ~ **qc a qn** to take sth (away) from sb; **ciò non toglie che** ... nevertheless ..., be that as it may ...; ~**rsi il cappello** to take off one's hat.

'Togo *sm*: **il** ~ Togo.

toilette [twa'lɛt] *sf inv* (*gabinetto*) toilet; (*cosmesi*) make-up; (*abbigliamento*) gown, dress; (*mobile*) dressing table; **fare** ~ to get made up, make o.s. beautiful.

'Tokyo *sf* Tokyo.

to'letta *sf* = **toilette**.

'tolgo *etc vb vedi* **togliere**.

tolle'rante *ag* tolerant.

tolle'ranza [tolle'rantsa] *sf* tolerance; **casa di** ~ brothel.

tolle'rare *vt* to tolerate; **non tollero repliche** I won't stand for objections; **non sono tollerati i ritardi** lateness will not be tolerated.

To'losa *sf* Toulouse.

'tolsi *etc vb vedi* **togliere**.

'tolto, a *pp di* **togliere**.

to'maia *sf* (*di scarpa*) upper.

'tomba *sf* tomb.

tom'bale *ag*: **pietra** ~ tombstone, gravestone.

tom'bino *sm* manhole cover.

'tombola *sf* (*gioco*) tombola; (*ruzzolone*) tumble.

'tomo *sm* volume.

tomogra'fia *sf* (*MED*) tomography; ~ **assiale computerizzata** computerized axial tomography.

to'nare *vi* = **tuonare**.

'tondo, a *ag* round.

'tonfo *sm* splash; (*rumore sordo*) thud; (*caduta*): **fare un** ~ to take a tumble.

'tonico, a, ci, che *ag* tonic ♦ *sm* tonic; (*cosmetico*) toner.

tonifi'cante *ag* invigorating, bracing.

tonifi'care *vt* (*muscoli, pelle*) to tone up; (*irrobustire*) to invigorate, brace.

ton'nara *sf* tuna-fishing nets *pl*.

ton'nato, a *ag* (*CUC*): **salsa** ~**a** tuna fish sauce; **vitello** ~ veal with tuna fish sauce.

tonnel'laggio [tonnel'laddʒo] *sm* (*NAUT*) tonnage.

tonnel'lata *sf* ton.

'tonno *sm* tuna (fish).

'tono *sm* (*gen, MUS*) tone; (*di colore*) shade, tone; **rispondere a** ~ (*a proposito*) to answer to the point; (*nello stesso modo*) to answer in kind; (*per le rime*) to answer back.

ton'silla *sf* tonsil.

tonsil'lite *sf* tonsillitis.

ton'sura *sf* tonsure.

'tonto, a *ag* dull, stupid ♦ *smf* blockhead, dunce; **fare il finto** ~ to play dumb.

top [tɔp] *sm inv* (*vertice, camicetta*) top.

to'paia *sf* (*di topo*) mousehole; (*di ratto*) rat's nest; (*fig: casa etc*) hovel, dump.

to'pazio [to'pattsjo] *sm* topaz.

topi'cida, i [topi'tʃida] *sm* rat poison.

'topless ['tɔplis] *sm inv* topless bathing costume.

'topo *sm* mouse; ~ **d'albergo** (*fig*) hotel thief; ~ **di biblioteca** (*fig*) bookworm.

topogra'fia *sf* topography.

topog'rafico, a, ci, che *ag* topographic, topographical.

to'ponimo *sm* place name.

'toppa *sf* (*serratura*) keyhole; (*pezza*) patch.

to'race [to'ratʃe] *sm* chest.

'torba *sf* peat.

'torbido, a *ag* (*liquido*) cloudy; (: *fiume*) muddy; (*fig*) dark; troubled ♦ *sm*: **pescare nel** ~ (*fig*) to fish in troubled waters.

'torcere ['tɔrtʃere] *vt* to twist; (*biancheria*) to wring (out); ~**rsi** *vr* to twist, writhe; **dare del filo da** ~ **a qn** to make life *o* things difficult for sb.

torchi'are [tor'kjare] *vt* to press.

'torchio ['tɔrkjo] *sm* press; **mettere qn sotto il** ~ (*fig fam: interrogare*) to grill sb; ~ **tipografico** printing press.

'torcia, ce ['tɔrtʃa] *sf* torch; ~ **elettrica** torch (*BRIT*), flashlight (*US*).

torci'collo [tortʃi'kɔllo] *sm* stiff neck.

'tordo *sm* thrush.

to'rero *sm* bullfighter, toreador.

tori'nese *ag* of (*o* from) Turin ♦ *smf* person from Turin.

To'rino *sf* Turin.

tor'menta *sf* snowstorm.

tormen'tare *vt* to torment; ~**rsi** *vr* to fret, worry o.s.

tor'mento *sm* torment.

torna'conto *sm* advantage, benefit.

tor'nado *sm* tornado.

tor'nante *sm* hairpin bend (*BRIT*) *o* curve (*US*).

tor'nare *vi* to return, go (*o* come) back; (*ridiventare: anche fig*) to become (again); (*riuscire giusto, esatto: conto*) to work out; (*risultare*) to turn out (to be), prove (to be); ~ **al punto di partenza** to start again; ~ **a casa** to go (*o* come) home; **i conti tornano** the accounts balance; ~ **utile** to prove *o* turn out (to be) useful.

torna'sole *sm inv* litmus.

tor'neo *sm* tournament.

'tornio *sm* lathe.

tor'nire *vt* (*TECN*) to turn (on a lathe); (*fig*) to shape, polish.

tor'nito, a *ag* (*gambe, caviglie*) well-shaped.

'toro *sm* bull; (*dello zodiaco*): **T**~ Taurus; **essere del T**~ to be Taurus.

tor'pedine *sf* torpedo.

torpedini'era *sf* torpedo boat.

tor'pore *sm* torpor.

'torre *sf* tower; (*SCACCHI*) rook, castle; ~ **di controllo** (*AER*) control tower.

torrefazi'one [torrefat'tsjone] *sf* roasting.

torreggi'are [torred'dʒare] *vi*: ~ **(su)** to tower (over).

tor'rente *sm* torrent.

torren'tizio, a [torren'tittsjo] *ag* torrential.

torrenzi'ale [torren'tsjale] *ag* torrential.

tor'retta *sf* turret.

'torrido, a *ag* torrid.

torri'one *sm* keep.

tor'rone *sm* nougat.

'torsi *etc vb vedi* **torcere**.

torsi'one *sf* twisting; (*TECN*) torsion.

'torso *sm* torso, trunk; (*ARTE*) torso; **a** ~ **nudo** bare-chested.

'torsolo *sm* (*di cavolo etc*) stump; (*di frutta*) core.

'torta *sf* cake.

tortel'lini *smpl* (*CUC*) tortellini.

torti'era *sf* cake tin (*BRIT*), cake pan (*US*).

'torto, a *pp di* **torcere** ♦ *ag* (*ritorto*) twisted; (*storto*) twisted, crooked ♦ *sm* (*ingiustizia*) wrong; (*colpa*) fault; **a** ~ wrongly; **a** ~ **o a ragione** rightly or wrongly; **aver** ~ to be wrong; **fare un** ~ **a qn** to wrong sb; **essere/passare dalla parte del** ~ to be/put o.s. in the wrong; **lui non ha tutti i** ~**i** there's something in what he says.

'tortora *sf* turtle dove.

tortu'oso, a *ag* (*strada*) twisting; (*fig*) tortuous.

tor'tura *sf* torture.

tortu'rare *vt* to torture.

'torvo, a *ag* menacing, grim.

tosa'erba *sm o f inv* (lawn)mower.

to'sare *vt* (*pecora*) to shear; (*cane*) to clip; (*siepe*) to clip, trim.

tosa'tura *sf* (*di pecore*) shearing; (*di cani*) clipping; (*di siepi*) trimming, clipping.

Tos'cana *sf*: **la** ~ Tuscany.

tos'cano, a *ag, smf* Tuscan ♦ *sm* (*anche*: **sigaro** ~) strong Italian cigar.

'tosse *sf* cough.

tossicità [tossitʃi'ta] *sf* toxicity.

'tossico, a, ci, che *ag* toxic.

tossicodipen'dente *smf* drug addict.

tossicodipen'denza [tossikodipen'dɛntsa] *sf* drug addiction.

tossi'comane *smf* drug addict.

tossicoma'nia *sf* drug addiction.

tos'sina *sf* toxin.

tos'sire *vi* to cough.

tosta'pane *sm inv* toaster.

tos'tare *vt* to toast; (*caffè*) to roast.

tosta'tura *sf* (*di pane*) toasting; (*di caffè*) roasting.

'tosto, a *ag*: **faccia** ~**a** cheek ♦ *av* at once, immediately; ~ **che** as soon as.

to'tale *ag, sm* total.

totalità *sf*: **la** ~ **di** all of, the total amount (*o* number) of; the whole + *sg*.

totali'tario, a *ag* totalitarian; (*totale*) complete, total; **adesione** ~**a** complete support.

totalita'rismo *sm* (*POL*) totalitarianism.

totaliz'zare [totalid'dzare] *vt* to total; (*SPORT: punti*) to score.

totalizza'tore [totaliddza'tore] *sm* (*TECN*) totalizator; (*IPPICA*) totalizator, tote (*fam*).

to'tip *sm gambling pool betting on horse racing*.

toto'calcio [toto'kaltʃo] *sm gambling pool*

betting on football results, ≈ (football) pools *pl* (*BRIT*).

tou'pet [tu'pɛ] *sm inv* toupee.

tour [tur] *sm inv* (*giro*) tour; (*CICLISMO*) tour de France.

tour de 'force ['tur də 'fɔrs] *sm inv* (*SPORT: anche fig*) tour de force.

tour'née [tur'ne] *sf* tour; **essere in** ~ to be on tour.

to'vaglia [to'vaʎʎa] *sf* tablecloth.

tovagli'olo [tovaʎ'ʎɔlo] *sm* napkin.

'tozzo, a ['tɔttso] *ag* squat ♦ *sm*: ~ **di pane** crust of bread.

TP *sigla* = Trapani.

TR *sigla* = Terni.

Tr *abbr* (*COMM*) = **tratta**.

tra *prep* (*di due persone, cose*) between; (*di più persone, cose*) among(st); (*tempo: entro*) within, in; **prendere qn** ~ **le braccia** to take sb in one's arms; **litigano** ~ **(di) loro** they're fighting amongst themselves; ~ **5 giorni** in 5 days' time; ~ **breve** *o* **poco** soon; ~ **sé e sé** (*parlare etc*) to oneself; **sia detto** ~ **noi** ... between you and me ...; ~ **una cosa e l'altra** what with one thing and another.

trabal'lante *ag* shaky.

trabal'lare *vi* to stagger, totter.

tra'biccolo *sm* (*peg: auto*) old banger (*BRIT*), jalopy.

trabocc'care *vi* to overflow.

traboc'chetto [trabok'ketto] *sm* (*fig*) trap ♦ *ag inv* trap *cpd*; **domanda** ~ trick question.

traca'gnotto, a [trakaɲ'ɲɔtto] *ag* dumpy ♦ *sm/f* dumpy person.

tracan'nare *vt* to gulp down.

'traccia, ce ['trattʃa] *sf* (*segno, striscia*) trail, track; (*orma*) tracks *pl*; (*residuo, testimonianza*) trace, sign; (*abbozzo*) outline; **essere sulle** ~**ce di qn** to be on sb's trail.

tracci'are [trat'tʃare] *vt* to trace, mark (out); (*disegnare*) to draw; (*fig: abbozzare*) to outline; ~ **un quadro della situazione** to outline the situation.

tracci'ato [trat'tʃato] *sm* (*grafico*) layout, plan; ~ **di gara** (*SPORT*) race route.

tra'chea [tra'kɛa] *sf* windpipe, trachea.

tra'colla *sf* shoulder strap; **portare qc a** ~ to carry sth over one's shoulder; **borsa a** ~ shoulder bag.

tra'collo *sm* (*fig*) collapse, ruin; ~ **finanziario** crash; **avere un** ~ (*MED*) to have a setback; (*COMM*) to collapse.

traco'tante *ag* overbearing, arrogant.

traco'tanza [trako'tantsa] *sf* arrogance.

trad. *abbr* = **traduzione**.

tradi'mento *sm* betrayal; (*DIR, MIL*) treason; **a** ~ by surprise; **alto** ~ high treason.

tra'dire *vt* to betray; (*coniuge*) to be unfaithful to; (*doveri: mancare*) to fail in; (*rivelare*) to give away, reveal; **ha tradito le attese di tutti** he let everyone down.

tradi'tore, 'trice *sm/f* traitor.

tradizio'nale [tradittsjo'nale] *ag* traditional.

tradizi'one [tradit'tsjone] *sf* tradition.

tra'dotto, a *pp di* **tradurre** ♦ *sf* (*MIL*) troop train.

tra'durre *vt* to translate; (*spiegare*) to render, convey; (*DIR*): ~ **qn in carcere/ tribunale** to take sb to prison/court; ~ **in cifre** to put into figures; ~ **in atto** (*fig*) to put into effect.

tradut'tore, 'trice *sm/f* translator.

traduzi'one [tradut'tsjone] *sf* translation; (*DIR*) transfer.

'trae *vb vedi* **trarre**.

tra'ente *sm/f* (*ECON*) drawer.

trafe'lato, a *ag* out of breath.

traffi'cante *sm/f* dealer; (*peg*) trafficker.

traffi'care *vi* (*commerciare*): ~ **(in)** to trade (in), deal (in); (*affaccendarsi*) to busy o.s. ♦ *vt* (*peg*) to traffic in.

traffi'cato, a *ag* (*strada, zona*) busy.

'traffico, ci *sm* traffic; (*commercio*) trade, traffic; ~ **aereo/ferroviario** air/rail traffic; ~ **di droga** drug trafficking; ~ **stradale** traffic.

tra'figgere [tra'fiddʒere] *vt* to run through, stab; (*fig*) to pierce.

tra'fila *sf* procedure.

trafi'letto *sm* (*di giornale*) short article.

tra'fitto, a *pp di* **trafiggere**.

trafo'rare *vt* to bore, drill.

tra'foro *sm* (*azione*) boring, drilling; (*galleria*) tunnel.

trafu'gare *vt* to purloin.

tra'gedia [tra'dʒɛdja] *sf* tragedy.

'traggo *etc vb vedi* **trarre**.

traghet'tare [traget'tare] *vt* to ferry.

tra'ghetto [tra'getto] *sm* crossing; (*barca*) ferry(boat).

tragicità [tradʒitʃi'ta] *sf* tragedy.

'tragico, a, ci, che ['tradʒiko] *ag* tragic ♦ *sm* (*autore*) tragedian; **prendere tutto sul** ~ (*fig*) to take everything far too seriously.

tragi'comico, a, ci, che [tradʒi'kɔmiko] *ag* tragicomic.

tra'gitto [tra'dʒitto] *sm* (*passaggio*) crossing; (*viaggio*) journey.

tragu'ardo *sm* (*SPORT*) finishing line; (*fig*) goal, aim.

'trai *etc vb vedi* **trarre**.

traiet'toria *sf* trajectory.
trai'nante *ag* (*cavo, fune*) towing; (*fig: persona, settore*) driving.
trai'nare *vt* to drag, haul; (*rimorchiare*) to tow.
'training ['trɛinin(g)] *sm inv* training.
'traino *sm* (*carro*) wagon; (*slitta*) sledge; (*carico*) load.
tralasci'are [tralaʃ'ʃare] *vt* (*studi*) to neglect; (*dettagli*) to leave out, omit.
'tralcio ['traltʃo] *sm* (*BOT*) shoot.
tra'liccio [tra'littʃo] *sm* (*tela*) ticking; (*struttura*) trellis; (*ELETTR*) pylon.
tram *sm inv* tram (*BRIT*), streetcar (*US*).
'trama *sf* (*filo*) weft, woof; (*fig: argomento, maneggio*) plot.
traman'dare *vt* to pass on, hand down.
tra'mare *vt* (*fig*) to scheme, plot.
tram'busto *sm* turmoil.
trames'tio *sm* bustle.
tramez'zino [tramed'dzino] *sm* sandwich.
tra'mezzo [tra'mɛddzo] *sm* partition.
'tramite *prep* through ♦ *sm* means *pl*; **agire/fare da** ~ to act as/be a go-between.
tramon'tana *sf* (*METEOR*) north wind.
tramon'tare *vi* to set, go down.
tra'monto *sm* setting; (*del sole*) sunset.
tramor'tire *vi* to faint ♦ *vt* to stun.
trampo'lino *sm* (*per tuffi*) springboard, diving board; (*per lo sci*) ski-jump.
'trampolo *sm* stilt.
tramu'tare *vt*: ~ **in** to change into.
trance [traːns] *sf inv* (*di medium*) trance; **cadere in** ~ to fall into a trance.
'trancia, ce ['trantʃa] *sf* slice; (*cesoia*) shearing machine.
tranci'are [tran'tʃare] *vt* (*TECN*) to shear.
'trancio ['trantʃo] *sm* slice.
tra'nello *sm* trap; **tendere un** ~ **a qn** to set a trap for sb.
trangugi'are [trangu'dʒare] *vt* to gulp down.
'tranne *prep* except (for), but (for); ~ **che** *cong* unless; **tutti i giorni** ~ **il venerdì** every day except *o* with the exception of Friday.
tranquil'lante *sm* (*MED*) tranquillizer.
tranquillità *sf* calm, stillness; quietness; peace of mind.
tranquilliz'zare [trankwillid'dzare] *vt* to reassure.
tran'quillo, a *ag* calm, quiet; (*bambino, scolaro*) quiet; (*sereno*) with one's mind at rest; **sta'** ~ don't worry.
transat'lantico, a, ci, che *ag* transatlantic ♦ *sm* transatlantic liner; (*POL*) *corridor used as a meeting place by members of the lower chamber of the Italian*

Parliament; vedi nota nel riquadro.

TRANSATLANTICO

The **transatlantico** *is a room in the Palazzo di Montecitorio which is used by "deputati" between parliamentary sessions for relaxation and conversation. It is also used for media interviews and press conferences.*

---

tran'satto, a *pp di* transigere.
transazi'one [transat'tsjone] *sf* (*DIR*) settlement; (*COMM*) transaction, deal.
tran'senna *sf* barrier.
tran'setto *sm* transept.
trans'genico, a, ci, che [trans'dʒɛniko] *ag* genetically modified.
transiberi'ano, a *ag* trans-Siberian.
tran'sigere [tran'sidʒere] *vi* (*DIR*) to reach a settlement; (*venire a patti*) to compromise, come to an agreement.
tran'sistor *sm inv*, **transis'tore** *sm* transistor.
transi'tabile *ag* passable.
transi'tare *vi* to pass.
transi'tivo, a *ag* transitive.
'transito *sm* transit; **di** ~ (*merci*) in transit; (*stazione*) transit *cpd*; **"divieto di** ~**"** "no entry"; **"**~ **interrotto"** "road closed".
transi'torio, a *ag* transitory, transient; (*provvisorio*) provisional.
transizi'one [transit'tsjone] *sf* transition.
tran 'tran *sm* routine; **il solito** ~ the same old routine.
tran'via *sf* tramway (*BRIT*), streetcar line (*US*).
tranvi'ario, a *ag* tram *cpd* (*BRIT*), streetcar *cpd* (*US*); **linea** ~**a** tramline, streetcar line.
tranvi'ere *sm* (*conducente*) tram driver (*BRIT*), streetcar driver (*US*); (*bigliettaio*) tram *o* streetcar conductor.
trapa'nare *vt* (*TECN*) to drill.
'trapano *sm* (*utensile*) drill; (: *MED*) trepan.
trapas'sare *vt* to pierce.
trapas'sato *sm* (*LING*) past perfect.
tra'passo *sm* passage; ~ **di proprietà** (*di case*) conveyancing; (*di auto etc*) legal transfer.
trape'lare *vi* to leak, drip; (*fig*) to leak out.
tra'pezio [tra'pɛttsjo] *sm* (*MAT*) trapezium; (*attrezzo ginnico*) trapeze.
trape'zista, i, e [trapet'tsista] *sm/f* trapeze artist.
trapian'tare *vt* to transplant.
trapi'anto *sm* transplanting; (*MED*) transplant.
'trappola *sf* trap.
tra'punta *sf* quilt.

'**trarre** *vt* to draw, pull; (*prendere, tirare fuori*) to take (out), draw; (*derivare*) to obtain; ~ **beneficio** *o* **profitto da qc** to benefit from sth; ~ **le conclusioni** to draw one's own conclusions; ~ **esempio da qn** to follow sb's example; ~ **guadagno** to make a profit; ~ **qn d'impaccio** to get sb out of an awkward situation; ~ **origine da qc** to have its origins *o* originate in sth; ~ **in salvo** to rescue.

trasa'lire *vi* to start, jump.

trasan'dato, a *ag* shabby.

trasbor'dare *vt* to transfer; (*NAUT*) to tran(s)ship ♦ *vi* (*NAUT*) to change ship; (*AER*) to change plane; (*FERR*) to change (trains).

trascenden'tale [traʃʃenden'tale] *ag* transcendental.

tra'scendere [traʃ'ʃendere] *vt* (*FILOSOFIA, REL*) to transcend; (*fig: superare*) to surpass, go beyond.

tra'sceso, a [traʃ'ʃeso] *pp di* **trascendere**.

trasci'nare [traʃʃi'nare] *vt* to drag; ~**rsi** *vr* to drag o.s. along; (*fig*) to drag on.

tras'correre *vt* (*tempo*) to spend, pass ♦ *vi* to pass.

tras'corso, a *pp di* **trascorrere** ♦ *ag* past ♦ *sm* mistake.

tras'critto, a *pp di* **trascrivere**.

tras'crivere *vt* to transcribe.

trascrizi'one [traskrit'tsjone] *sf* transcription.

trascu'rare *vt* to neglect; (*non considerare*) to disregard.

trascura'tezza [traskura'tettsa] *sf* carelessness, negligence.

trascu'rato, a *ag* (*casa*) neglected; (*persona*) careless, negligent.

traseco'lato, a *ag* astounded, amazed.

trasferi'mento *sm* transfer; (*trasloco*) removal, move.

trasfe'rire *vt* to transfer; ~**rsi** *vr* to move.

tras'ferta *sf* transfer; (*indennità*) travelling expenses *pl*; (*SPORT*) away game.

trasfigu'rare *vt* to transfigure.

trasfor'mare *vt* to transform, change.

trasforma'tore *sm* transformer.

trasformazi'one [trasformat'tsjone] *sf* transformation.

trasfusi'one *sf* (*MED*) transfusion.

trasgre'dire *vt* to break, infringe; (*ordini*) to disobey.

trasgressi'one *sf* breaking, infringement; disobeying.

trasgres'sivo, a *ag* (*personaggio, atteggiamento*) rule-breaking.

trasgres'sore, trasgredi'trice [trazgredi'tritʃe] *sm/f* (*DIR*) transgressor.

tras'lato, a *ag* metaphorical, figurative.

traslo'care *vt* to move, transfer; ~**rsi** *vr* to move.

tras'loco, chi *sm* removal.

tras'messo, a *pp di* **trasmettere**.

tras'mettere *vt* (*passare*): ~ **qc a qn** to pass sth on to sb; (*mandare*) to send; (*TECN, TEL, MED*) to transmit; (*TV, RADIO*) to broadcast.

trasmetti'tore *sm* transmitter.

trasmissi'one *sf* (*gen, FISICA, TECN*) transmission; (*passaggio*) transmission, passing on; (*TV, RADIO*) broadcast.

trasmit'tente *sf* transmitting *o* broadcasting station.

traso'gnato, a [trasoɲ'ɲato] *ag* dreamy.

traspa'rente *ag* transparent.

traspa'renza [traspa'rentsa] *sf* transparency; **guardare qc in** ~ to look at sth against the light.

traspa'rire *vi* to show (through).

tras'parso, a *pp di* **trasparire**.

traspi'rare *vi* to perspire; (*fig*) to come to light, leak out.

traspirazi'one [traspirat'tsjone] *sf* perspiration.

tras'porre *vt* to transpose.

traspor'tare *vt* to carry, move; (*merce*) to transport, convey; **lasciarsi** ~ (**da qc**) (*fig*) to let o.s. be carried away (by sth).

tras'porto *sm* transport; (*fig*) rapture, passion; **con** ~ passionately; **compagnia di** ~ carriers *pl*; (*per strada*) hauliers *pl* (*BRIT*), haulers *pl* (*US*); **mezzi di** ~ means of transport; **nave/aereo da** ~ transport ship/aircraft *inv*; ~ (**funebre**) funeral procession; ~ **marittimo/aereo** sea/air transport; ~ **stradale** (road) haulage; **i** ~**i pubblici** public transport.

tras'posto, a *pp di* **trasporre**.

'**trassi** *etc vb vedi* **trarre**.

trastul'lare *vt* to amuse; ~**rsi** *vr* to amuse o.s.

tras'tullo *sm* game.

trasu'dare *vi* (*filtrare*) to ooze; (*sudare*) to sweat ♦ *vt* to ooze with.

trasver'sale *ag* (*taglio, sbarra*) cross(-); (*retta*) transverse; **via** ~ side street.

trasvo'lare *vt* to fly over.

'**tratta** *sf* (*ECON*) draft; (*di persone*): **la** ~ **delle bianche** the white slave trade; ~ **documentaria** documentary bill of exchange.

tratta'mento *sm* treatment; (*servizio*) service; **ricevere un buon** ~ (*cliente*) to get good service; ~ **di bellezza** beauty treatment; ~ **di fine rapporto** (*COMM*) severance pay.

trat'tare vt (gen) to treat; (commerciare) to deal in; (svolgere: argomento) to discuss, deal with; (negoziare) to negotiate ♦ vi: ~ **di** to deal with; ~ **con** (persona) to deal with; **si tratta di** ... it's about ...; **si tratterebbe solo di poche ore** it would just be a matter of a few hours.

tratta'tiva sf negotiation; ~**e** sfpl (tra governi, stati) talks; **essere in** ~ **con** to be in negotiation with.

trat'tato sm (testo) treatise; (accordo) treaty; ~ **commerciale** trade agreement; ~ **di pace** peace treaty.

trattazi'one [trattat'tsjone] sf treatment.

tratteggi'are [tratted'dʒare] vt (disegnare: a tratti) to sketch, outline; (: col tratteggio) to hatch.

trat'teggio [trat'teddʒo] sm hatching.

tratte'nere vt (far rimanere: persona) to detain; (tenere, frenare, reprimere) to hold back, keep back; (astenersi dal consegnare) to hold, keep; (detrarre: somma) to deduct; ~**rsi** vr (astenersi) to restrain o.s., stop o.s.; (soffermarsi) to stay, remain; **sono stato trattenuto in ufficio** I was delayed at the office.

tratteni'mento sm entertainment; (festa) party.

tratte'nuta sf deduction.

trat'tino sm dash; (in parole composte) hyphen.

'**tratto, a** pp di **trarre** ♦ sm (di penna, matita) stroke; (parte) part, piece; (di strada) stretch; (di mare, cielo) expanse; (di tempo) period (of time); ~**i** smpl (caratteristiche) features; (modo di fare) ways, manners; **a un** ~, **d'un** ~ suddenly.

trat'tore sm tractor.

tratto'ria sf (small) restaurant.

'**trauma, i** sm trauma; ~ **cranico** concussion.

trau'matico, a, ci, che ag traumatic.

traumatiz'zare [traumatid'dzare] vt (MED) to traumatize; (fig: impressionare) to shock.

tra'vaglio [tra'vaʎʎo] sm (angoscia) pain, suffering; (MED) pains pl; ~ **di parto** labour pains.

trava'sare vt to pour; (vino) to decant.

tra'vaso sm pouring; decanting.

trava'tura sf beams pl.

'**trave** sf beam.

tra'veggole sfpl: **avere le** ~ to be seeing things.

tra'versa sf (trave) crosspiece; (via) sidestreet; (FERR) sleeper (BRIT),

(railroad) tie (US); (CALCIO) crossbar.

traver'sare vt to cross.

traver'sata sf crossing; (AER) flight, trip.

traver'sie sfpl mishaps, misfortunes.

traver'sina sf (FERR) sleeper (BRIT), (railroad) tie (US).

tra'verso, a ag oblique; **di** ~ ag askew ♦ av sideways; **andare di** ~ (cibo) to go down the wrong way; **messo di** ~ sideways on; **guardare di** ~ to look askance at; **via** ~**a** side road; **ottenere qc per vie** ~**e** (fig) to obtain sth in an underhand way.

travesti'mento sm disguise.

traves'tire vt to disguise; ~**rsi** vr to disguise o.s.

traves'tito sm transvestite.

travi'are vt (fig) to lead astray.

travi'sare vt (fig) to distort, misrepresent.

travol'gente [travol'dʒɛnte] ag overwhelming.

tra'volgere [tra'vɔldʒere] vt to sweep away, carry away; (fig) to overwhelm.

tra'volto, a pp di **travolgere**.

trazi'one [trat'tsjone] sf traction; ~ **anteriore/posteriore** (AUT) front-wheel/rear-wheel drive.

tre num three.

tre'alberi sm inv (NAUT) three-master.

'**trebbia** sf (AGR: operazione) threshing; (: stagione) threshing season.

trebbi'are vt to thresh.

trebbia'trice [trebbja'tritʃe] sf threshing machine.

trebbia'tura sf threshing.

'**treccia, ce** ['trettʃa] sf plait, braid; **lavorato a** ~**ce** (pullover etc) cable-knit.

trecen'tesco, a, schi, sche [tretʃen'tesko] ag fourteenth-century.

tre'cento [tre'tʃɛnto] num three hundred ♦ sm: **il T**~ the fourteenth century.

tredi'cenne [tredi'tʃɛnne] ag, smf thirteen-year-old.

tredi'cesimo, a [tredi'tʃɛzimo] num thirteenth ♦ sf Christmas bonus of a month's pay.

'**tredici** ['treditʃi] num thirteen ♦ sm inv: **fare** ~ (TOTOCALCIO) to win the pools (BRIT).

'**tregua** sf truce; (fig) respite; **senza** ~ non-stop, without stopping, uninterruptedly.

tre'mante ag trembling, shaking.

tre'mare vi to tremble, shake; ~ **di** (freddo etc) to shiver o tremble with; (paura, rabbia) to shake o tremble with.

trema'rella sf shivers pl.

tremen'tina sf turpentine.

tre'mila num three thousand.

'**tremito** sm trembling no pl; shaking no pl; shivering no pl.

tremo'lare *vi* to tremble; (*luce*) to flicker; (*foglie*) to quiver.

tremo'lio *sm* (*vedi vi*) tremble; flicker; quiver.

tre'more *sm* tremor.

'treno *sm* train; (*AUT*): ~ **di gomme** set of tyres; ~ **locale/diretto/espresso** local/fast/express train; ~ **merci** goods (*BRIT*) *o* freight train; ~ **rapido** express (train) (*for which supplement must be paid*); ~ **straordinario** special train; ~ **viaggiatori** passenger train; *vedi nota nel riquadro.*

TRENI

There are several different types of train in Italy. "Regionali" and "interregionali" are local trains which stop at every small town and village; the former operate within regional boundaries, while the latter may cross them. "Diretti" are ordinary trains for which passengers do not pay a supplement; the main difference from "espressi" is that the latter are long-distance and mainly run at night. "Intercity" and "eurocity" are faster and entail a supplement. "Rapidi" only contain first-class seats, and the high-speed "pendolino", which offers both first- and second-class travel, runs between the major cities.

'trenta *num* thirty ♦ *sm inv* (*INS*): ~ **e lode** full marks plus distinction *o* cum laude.

tren'tenne *ag, sm/f* thirty-year-old.

tren'tennio *sm* period of thirty years.

tren'tesimo, a *num* thirtieth.

tren'tina *sf:* **una** ~ **(di)** thirty or so, about thirty.

tren'tino, a *ag* of (*o* from) Trento.

trepi'dante *ag* anxious.

trepi'dare *vi* to be anxious; ~ **per qn** to be anxious about sb.

'trepido, a *ag* anxious.

treppi'ede *sm* tripod; (*CUC*) trivet.

tre'quarti *sm inv* three-quarter-length coat.

'tresca, sche *sf* (*fig*) intrigue; (*: relazione amorosa*) affair.

'trespolo *sm* trestle.

trevigi'ano, a [trevi'dʒano] *ag* of (*o* from) Treviso.

triango'lare *ag* triangular.

tri'angolo *sm* triangle.

tribo'lare *vi* (*patire*) to suffer; (*fare fatica*) to have a lot of trouble.

tribolazi'one [tribolat'tsjone] *sf* suffering, tribulation.

tri'bordo *sm* (*NAUT*) starboard.

tribù *sf inv* tribe.

tri'buna *sf* (*podio*) platform; (*in aule etc*) gallery; (*di stadio*) stand; ~ **della stampa/riservata al pubblico** press/public gallery.

tribu'nale *sm* court; **presentarsi** *o* **comparire in** ~ to appear in court; ~ **militare** military tribunal; ~ **supremo** supreme court.

tribu'tare *vt* to bestow; ~ **gli onori dovuti a qn** to pay tribute to sb.

tribu'tario, a *ag* (*imposta*) fiscal, tax *cpd*; (*GEO*): **essere** ~ **di** to be a tributary of.

tri'buto *sm* tax; (*fig*) tribute.

tri'checo, chi [tri'kɛko] *sm* (*ZOOL*) walrus.

tri'ciclo [tri'tʃiklo] *sm* tricycle.

trico'lore *ag* three-coloured (*BRIT*), three-coloured (*US*) ♦ *sm* tricolo(u)r; (*bandiera italiana*) Italian flag.

tri'dente *sm* trident.

trien'nale *ag* (*che dura 3 anni*) three-year *cpd*; (*che avviene ogni 3 anni*) three-yearly.

tri'ennio *sm* period of three years.

tries'tino, a *ag* of (*o* from) Trieste.

tri'fase *ag* (*ELETTR*) three-phase.

tri'foglio [tri'fɔʎʎo] *sm* clover.

trifo'lato, a *ag* (*CUC*) cooked in oil, garlic and parsley.

'triglia ['triʎʎa] *sf* red mullet.

trigonome'tria *sf* trigonometry.

tril'lare *vi* (*MUS*) to trill.

'trillo *sm* trill.

tri'mestre *sm* period of three months; (*INS*) term, quarter (*US*); (*COMM*) quarter.

trimo'tore *sm* (*AER*) three-engined plane.

'trina *sf* lace.

trin'cea [trin'tʃea] *sf* trench.

trince'rare [trintʃe'rare] *vt* to entrench.

trinci'are [trin'tʃare] *vt* to cut up.

'Trinidad *sm:* ~ **e Tobago** Trinidad and Tobago.

Trinità *sf* (*REL*) Trinity.

'trio, *pl* **'trii** *sm* trio.

trion'fale *ag* triumphal, triumphant.

trion'fante *ag* triumphant.

trion'fare *vi* to triumph, win; ~ **su** to triumph over, overcome.

tri'onfo *sm* triumph.

tripli'care *vt* to triple.

'triplice ['triplitʃe] *ag* triple; **in** ~ **copia** in triplicate.

'triplo, a *ag* triple, treble ♦ *sm:* **il** ~ **(di)** three times as much (as); **la spesa è** ~**a** it costs three times as much.

'tripode *sm* tripod.

'Tripoli *sf* Tripoli.

'trippa *sf* (*CUC*) tripe.

tri'pudio *sm* triumph, jubilation; (*fig: di colori*) galaxy.

tris *sm inv* (*CARTE*): ~ **d'assi/di re** *etc* three aces/kings *etc*.

'**triste** *ag* sad; (*luogo*) dreary, gloomy.
tris'tezza [tris'tettsa] *sf* sadness;
gloominess.
'**tristo, a** *ag* (*cattivo*) wicked, evil;
(*meschino*) sorry, poor.
trita'carne *sm inv* mincer, grinder (*US*).
trita'ghiaccio [trita'gjattʃo] *sm inv* ice
crusher.
tri'tare *vt* to mince, grind (*US*).
trita'tutto *sm inv* mincer, grinder (*US*).
'**trito, a** *ag* (*tritato*) minced, ground (*US*); ~
e ritrito (*idee*, *argomenti*, *frasi*) trite,
hackneyed.
tri'tolo *sm* trinitrotoluene.
tri'tone *sm* (*ZOOL*) newt.
'**trittico, ci** *sm* (*ARTE*) triptych.
tritu'rare *vt* to grind.
tri'vella *sf* drill.
trivel'lare *vt* to drill.
trivellazi'one [trivellat'tsjone] *sf* drilling;
torre di ~ derrick.
trivi'ale *ag* vulgar, low.
trivialità *sf inv* (*volgarità*) coarseness,
crudeness; (: *osservazione*) coarse *o* crude
remark.
tro'feo *sm* trophy.
'**trogolo** *sm* (*per maiali*) trough.
'**troia** *sf* (*ZOOL*) sow; (*fig peg*) whore.
'**tromba** *sf* (*MUS*) trumpet; (*AUT*) horn; ~
d'aria whirlwind; ~ **delle scale** stairwell.
trombet'tista, i, e *sm/f* trumpeter,
trumpet (player).
trom'bone *sm* trombone.
trom'bosi *sf* thrombosis.
tron'care *vt* to cut off; (*spezzare*) to break
off.
'**tronco, a, chi, che** *ag* cut off; broken off;
(*LING*) truncated ♦ *sm* (*BOT*, *ANAT*) trunk;
(*fig: tratto*) section; (: *pezzo: di lancia*)
stump; **licenziare qn in** ~ (*fig*) to fire sb on
the spot.
troneggi'are [troned'dʒare] *vi:* ~ **(su)** to
tower (over).
'**tronfio, a** *ag* conceited.
'**trono** *sm* throne.
tropi'cale *ag* tropical.
'**tropico, ci** *sm* tropic; ~ **del Cancro/**
Capricorno Tropic of Cancer/Capricorn; **i**
~**ci** the tropics.

============ *PAROLA CHIAVE* ============

'**troppo, a** *det* (*in eccesso: quantità*) too
much; (: *numero*) too many; **ho messo** ~
zucchero I put too much sugar in; **c'era**
~**a gente** there were too many people
♦ *pron* (*in eccesso: quantità*) too much; (:
numero) too many; **ne hai messo** ~
you've put in too much; **meglio** ~**i che**

pochi better too many than too few
♦ *av* (*eccessivamente: con ag, av*) too; (: *con*
vb) too much; ~ **amaro/tardi** too bitter/
late; **lavora** ~ he works too much; ~
buono da parte tua! (*anche ironico*) you're
too kind!; **di** ~ too much; too many;
qualche tazza di ~ a few cups too many; **5**
euro di ~ 5 euros too much; **essere di** ~ to
be in the way.

'**trota** *sf* trout.
trot'tare *vi* to trot.
trotterel'lare *vi* to trot along; (*bambino*) to
toddle.
'**trotto** *sm* trot.
'**trottola** *sf* spinning top.
tro'vare *vt* to find; (*giudicare*): **trovo che** I
find *o* think that; ~**rsi** *vr* (*reciproco*:
incontrarsi) to meet; (*essere, stare*) to be;
(*arrivare, capitare*) to find o.s.; **andare a** ~
qn to go and see sb; ~ **qn colpevole** to find
sb guilty; **trovo giusto/sbagliato che ...** I
think/don't think it's right that ...; ~**rsi**
bene/male (*in un luogo, con qn*) to get on
well/badly; ~**rsi d'accordo con qn** to be in
agreement with sb.
tro'vata *sf* good idea; ~ **pubblicitaria**
advertising gimmick.
trova'tello, a *sm/f* foundling.
truc'care *vt* (*falsare*) to fake; (*attore etc*) to
make up; (*travestire*) to disguise; (*SPORT*)
to fix; (*AUT*) to soup up; ~**rsi** *vr* to make up
(one's face).
trucca'tore, 'trice *sm/f* (*CINE, TEAT*) make-
up artist.
'**trucco, chi** *sm* trick; (*cosmesi*) make-up; **i**
~**chi del mestiere** the tricks of the trade.
'**truce** ['trutʃe] *ag* fierce.
truci'dare [trutʃi'dare] *vt* to slaughter.
tru'ciolo ['trutʃolo] *sm* shaving.
'**truffa** *sf* fraud, swindle.
truf'fare *vt* to swindle, cheat.
truffa'tore, 'trice *sm/f* swindler, cheat.
'**truppa** *sf* troop.
TS *sigla* = **Trieste**.
tu *pron* you; ~ **stesso(a)** you yourself; **dare**
del ~ **a qn** to address sb as "tu"; **trovarsi**
a ~ **per** ~ **con qn** to find o.s. face to face
with sb.
'**tua** *vedi* **tuo**.
'**tuba** *sf* (*MUS*) tuba; (*cappello*) top hat.
tu'bare *vi* to coo.
tuba'tura *sf*, **tubazi'one** [tubat'tsjone] *sf*
piping *no pl*, pipes *pl*.
tuberco'losi *sf* tuberculosis.
'**tubero** *sm* (*BOT*) tuber.
tu'betto *sm* tube.
tu'bino *sm* (*cappello*) bowler (*BRIT*), derby

(*US*); (*abito da donna*) sheath dress.

'**tubo** *sm* tube; (*per conduttore*) pipe; ~ **digerente** (*ANAT*) alimentary canal, digestive tract; ~ **di scappamento** (*AUT*) exhaust pipe.

tubo'lare *ag* tubular ♦ *sm* tubeless tyre (*BRIT*) *o* tire (*US*).

'**tue** *vedi* **tuo**.

tuf'fare *vt* to plunge; (*intingere*) to dip; ~**rsi** *vr* to plunge, dive.

tuffa'tore, 'trice *smlf* (*SPORT*) diver.

'**tuffo** *sm* dive; (*breve bagno*) dip.

tu'gurio *sm* hovel.

tuli'pano *sm* tulip.

'**tulle** *sm* (*tessuto*) tulle.

tume'fare *vt* to cause to swell; ~**rsi** *vr* to swell.

'**tumido, a** *ag* swollen.

tu'more *sm* (*MED*) tumour (*BRIT*), tumor (*US*).

tumulazi'one [tumulat'tsjone] *sf* burial.

tu'multo *sm* uproar, commotion; (*sommossa*) riot; (*fig*) turmoil.

tumultu'oso, a *ag* rowdy, unruly; (*fig*) turbulent, stormy.

tungs'teno *sm* tungsten.

'**tunica, che** *sf* tunic.

'**Tunisi** *sf* Tunis.

Tuni'sia *sf*: **la** ~ Tunisia.

tuni'sino, a *ag, smlf* Tunisian.

'**tunnel** *sm inv* tunnel.

'**tuo, 'tua, tu'oi, 'tue** *det*: **il** ~, **la tua** *etc* your ♦ *pron*: **il** ~, **la tua** *etc* yours ♦ *sm*: **hai speso del** ~? did you spend your own money? ♦ *sf*: **la** ~**a** (*opinione*) your view; **i tuoi** (*genitori, famiglia*) your family; **una** ~**a amica** a friend of yours; **è dalla** ~**a** he is on your side; **alla** ~**a!** (*brindisi*) your health!; **ne hai fatta una delle** ~**e!** (*sciocchezze*) you've done it again!

tuo'nare *vi* to thunder; **tuona** it is thundering, there's some thunder.

tu'ono *sm* thunder.

tu'orlo *sm* yolk.

tu'racciolo [tu'rattʃolo] *sm* cap, top; (*di sughero*) cork.

tu'rare *vt* to stop, plug; (*con sughero*) to cork; ~**rsi il naso** to hold one's nose.

'**turba** *sf* (*folla*) crowd, throng; (: *peg*) mob; ~**e** *sfpl* disorder(s); **soffrire di** ~**e psichiche** to suffer from a mental disorder.

turba'mento *sm* disturbance; (*di animo*) anxiety, agitation.

tur'bante *sm* turban.

tur'bare *vt* to disturb, trouble; ~ **la quiete pubblica** (*DIR*) to disturb the peace.

tur'bato, a *ag* upset; (*preoccupato, ansioso*) anxious.

tur'bina *sf* turbine.

turbi'nare *vi* to whirl.

'**turbine** *sm* whirlwind; ~ **di neve** swirl of snow; ~ **di polvere/sabbia** dust/ sandstorm.

turbi'noso, a *ag* (*vento, danza etc*) whirling.

turbo'lento, a *ag* turbulent; (*ragazzo*) boisterous, unruly.

turbo'lenza [turbo'lentsa] *sf* turbulence.

turboreat'tore *sm* turbojet engine.

tur'chese [tur'kese] *ag, sm, sf* turquoise.

Tur'chia [tur'kia] *sf*: **la** ~ Turkey.

tur'chino, a [tur'kino] *ag* deep blue.

'**turco, a, chi, che** *ag* Turkish ♦ *smlf* Turk/ Turkish woman ♦ *sm* (*LING*) Turkish; **parlare** ~ (*fig*) to talk double Dutch.

'**turgido, a** ['turdʒido] *ag* swollen.

tu'rismo *sm* tourism.

tu'rista, i, e *smlf* tourist.

tu'ristico, a, ci, che *ag* tourist *cpd*.

tur'nista, i, e *smlf* shift worker.

'**turno** *sm* turn; (*di lavoro*) shift; **di** ~ (*soldato, medico, custode*) on duty; **a** ~ (*rispondere*) in turn; (*lavorare*) in shifts; **fare a** ~ **a fare qc** to take turns to do sth; **è il suo** ~ it's your (*o his etc*) turn.

'**turpe** *ag* filthy, vile.

turpi'loquio *sm* obscene language.

'**tuta** *sf* overalls *pl*; (*SPORT*) tracksuit; ~ **mimetica** (*MIL*) camouflage clothing; ~ **spaziale** spacesuit; ~ **subacquea** wetsuit.

tu'tela *sf* (*DIR: di minore*) guardianship; (: *protezione*) protection; (*difesa*) defence (*BRIT*), defense (*US*); ~ **dell'ambiente** environmental protection; ~ **del consumatore** consumer protection.

tute'lare *vt* to protect, defend ♦ *ag* (*DIR*): **giudice** ~ *judge with responsibility for guardianship cases*.

tu'tore, 'trice *smlf* (*DIR*) guardian.

tutta'via *cong* nevertheless, yet.

=========================== *PAROLA CHIAVE*

'**tutto, a** *det* **1** (*intero*) all; ~ **il latte** all the milk; ~**a la notte** all night, the whole night; ~ **il libro** the whole book; ~**a una bottiglia** a whole bottle; **in** ~ **il mondo** all over the world

2 (*pl, collettivo*) all; every; ~**i i libri** all the books; ~**e le notti** every night; ~**i i venerdì** every Friday; ~**i gli uomini** all the men; (*collettivo*) all men; ~**e le volte che** every time (that); ~**i e due** both *o* each of us (*o them o you*); ~**i e cinque** all five of us (*o them o you*)

3 (*completamente*): **era** ~**a sporca** she was all dirty; **tremava** ~ he was trembling all over; **è** ~**a sua madre** she's just *o* exactly

like her mother
4: a tutt'oggi so far, up till now; **a ~a velocità** at full *o* top speed
♦ *pron* **1** (*ogni cosa*) everything, all; (*qualsiasi cosa*) anything; **ha mangiato ~** he's eaten everything; **dimmi ~** tell me all about it; **~ compreso** all included, all-in (*BRIT*); **~ considerato** all things considered; **con ~ che** (*malgrado*) although; **del ~** completely; **100 euro in ~** 100 euros in all; **in ~ eravamo 50** there were 50 of us in all; **in ~ e per ~** completely; **il che è ~ dire** and that's saying a lot
2: ~**i, e** (*ognuno*) all, everybody; **vengono** ~**i** they are all coming, everybody's coming; ~**i sanno che** everybody knows that; ~**i quanti** all and sundry
♦ *av* (*completamente*) entirely, quite; **è ~ il contrario** it's quite the opposite; **tutt'al più: saranno stati tutt'al più una cinquantina** there were about fifty of them at (the very) most; **tutt'al più possiamo prendere un treno** if the worst comes to the worst we can take a train; **tutt'altro** on the contrary; **è tutt'altro che felice** he's anything but happy; **tutt'intorno** all around; **tutt'a un tratto** suddenly
♦ *sm*: **il ~** the whole lot, all of it; **il ~ si è svolto senza incidenti** it all went off without incident; **il ~ le costerà due milioni** the whole thing will cost you two million.

tutto'fare *ag inv*: **domestica ~** general maid; **ragazzo ~** office boy ♦ *sm/f inv* handyman/woman.
tut'tora *av* still.
tutù *sm inv* tutu, ballet skirt.
TV [ti'vu] *sf inv* (= *televisione*) TV ♦ *sigla* = Treviso.

U u

U, u [u] *sf o m inv* (*lettera*) U, u; **U come Udine** ≈ U for Uncle; **inversione ad U** U-turn.
ub'bia *sf* (*letterario*) irrational fear.
ubbidi'ente *ag* obedient.
ubbidi'enza [ubbi'djɛntsa] *sf* obedience.
ubbi'dire *vi* to obey; **~ a** to obey; (*sog:

veicolo, macchina) to respond to.
ubicazi'one [ubikat'tsjone] *sf* site, location.
ubiquità *sf*: **non ho il dono dell'~** I can't be everywhere at once.
ubria'care *vt*: **~ qn** to get sb drunk; (*sog: alcool*) to make sb drunk; (*fig*) to make sb's head spin *o* reel; **~rsi** *vr* to get drunk; **~rsi di** (*fig*) to become intoxicated with.
ubria'chezza [ubria'kettsa] *sf* drunkenness.
ubri'aco, a, chi, che *ag, sm/f* drunk.
ubria'cone *sm* drunkard.
uccellagi'one [uttʃella'dʒone] *sf* bird catching.
uccelli'era [uttʃel'ljɛra] *sf* aviary.
uccel'lino [uttʃel'lino] *sm* baby bird, chick.
uc'cello [ut'tʃɛllo] *sm* bird.
uc'cidere [ut'tʃidere] *vt* to kill; **~rsi** *vr* (*suicidarsi*) to kill o.s.; (*perdere la vita*) to be killed.
uccisi'one [uttʃi'zjone] *sf* killing.
uc'ciso, a [ut'tʃizo] *pp di* **uccidere**.
ucci'sore [uttʃi'zore] *sm* killer.
U'craina *sf* Ukraine.
u'craino, a *ag, sm/f* Ukrainian.
UD *sigla* = *Udine*.
U.D.C. *sigla f* (*POL*: = *Unione di Centro*) *centre party*.
u'dente *sm/f*: **i non udenti** the hard of hearing.
udi'enza [u'djɛntsa] *sf* audience; (*DIR*) hearing; **dare ~ (a)** to grant an audience (to); **~ a porte chiuse** hearing in camera.
u'dire *vt* to hear.
udi'tivo, a *ag* auditory.
u'dito *sm* (sense of) hearing.
udi'tore, 'trice *sm/f* listener; (*INS*) unregistered student (*attending lectures*).
udi'torio *sm* (*persone*) audience.
UE *sigla f* (= *Unione Europea*) EU.
UEFA *sigla f* UEFA (= *Union of European Football Associations*).
UEM *sigla f* (*Unione economica e monetaria*) EMU.
'uffa *escl* tut!
uffici'ale [uffi'tʃale] *ag* official ♦ *sm* (*AMM*) official, officer; (*MIL*) officer; **pubblico ~** public official; **~ giudiziario** clerk of the court; **~ di marina** naval officer; **~ sanitario** health inspector; **~ di stato civile** registrar.
ufficializ'zare [uffitʃalid'dzare] *vt* to make official.
uf'ficio [uf'fitʃo] *sm* (*gen*) office; (*dovere*) duty; (*mansione*) task, function, job; (*agenzia*) agency, bureau; (*REL*) service; **d'~** *ag* office *cpd*; official ♦ *av* officially; **provvedere d'~** to act officially; **convocare d'~** (*DIR*) to summons;

difensore o **avvocato d'~** (*DIR*) court-appointed counsel for the defence; ~ **brevetti** patent office; ~ **di collocamento** employment office; ~ **informazioni** information bureau; ~ **oggetti smarriti** lost property office (*BRIT*), lost and found (*US*); ~ **postale** post office; ~ **vendite/del personale** sales/personnel department.

uffici'oso, a [uffi'tʃoso] *ag* unofficial.

'UFO *sm inv* (= *unidentified flying object*) UFO.

'ufo: a ~ *av* free, for nothing.

U'ganda *sf*: **l'~** Uganda.

'uggia ['uddʒa] *sf* (*noia*) boredom; (*fastidio*) bore; **avere/prendere qn in ~** to dislike/take a dislike to sb.

uggi'oso, a [ud'dʒoso] *ag* tiresome; (*tempo*) dull.

'ugola *sf* uvula.

uguagli'anza [ugwaʎ'ʎantsa] *sf* equality.

uguagli'are [ugwaʎ'ʎare] *vt* to make equal; (*essere uguale*) to equal, be equal to; (*livellare*) to level; ~**rsi** *vr*: ~**rsi a** o **con qn** (*paragonarsi*) to compare o.s. to sb.

ugu'ale *ag* equal; (*identico*) identical, the same; (*uniforme*) level, even ♦ *av*: **costano ~** they cost the same; **sono bravi ~** they're equally good.

ugual'mente *av* equally; (*lo stesso*) all the same.

U.I. *abbr* = *uso interno*.

UIL *sigla f* (= *Unione Italiana del Lavoro*) trade union federation.

'ulcera ['ultʃera] *sf* ulcer.

ulcerazi'one [ultʃerat'tsjone] *sf* ulceration.

u'liva *etc* = *oliva etc*.

U'livo *sm* (*POL*) *centre-left coalition*.

ulteri'ore *ag* further.

ultima'mente *av* lately, of late.

ulti'mare *vt* to finish, complete.

ulti'matum *sm inv* ultimatum.

ulti'missime *sfpl* latest news *sg*.

'ultimo, a *ag* (*finale*) last; (*estremo*) farthest, utmost; (*recente: notizia, moda*) latest; (*fig: sommo, fondamentale*) ultimate ♦ *sm/f* last (one); **fino all'~** to the last, until the end; **da ~, in ~** in the end; **per ~** (*entrare, arrivare*) last; **abitare all'~ piano** to live on the top floor; **in ~a pagina** (*di giornale*) on the back page; **negli ~i tempi** recently; **all'~ momento** at the last minute; **... la vostra lettera del 7 aprile ~ scorso ...** your letter of April 7th last; **in ~a analisi** in the final o last analysis; **in ~ luogo** finally.

ultrà *sm/f* ultra.

ultrasi'nistra *sf* (*POL*) extreme left.

ultrasu'ono *sm* ultrasound.

ultravio'letto, a *ag* ultraviolet.

ulu'lare *vi* to howl.

ulu'lato *sm* howling *no pl*; howl.

umana'mente *av* (*con umanità*) humanely; (*nei limiti delle capacità umane*) humanly.

uma'nesimo *sm* humanism.

umanità *sf* humanity.

umani'tario, a *ag* humanitarian.

umaniz'zare [umanid'dzare] *vt* to humanize.

u'mano, a *ag* human; (*comprensivo*) humane.

umbi'lico *sm* = ombelico.

'umbro, a *ag* of (o from) Umbria.

umet'tare *vt* to dampen, moisten.

umi'diccio, a, ci, ce [umi'dittʃo] *ag* (*terreno*) damp; (*mano*) moist, clammy.

umidifi'care *vt* to humidify.

umidifica'tore *sm* humidifier.

umidità *sf* dampness; moistness; humidity.

'umido, a *ag* damp; (*mano, occhi*) moist; (*clima*) humid ♦ *sm* dampness, damp; **carne in ~** stew.

'umile *ag* humble.

umili'ante *ag* humiliating.

umili'are *vt* to humiliate; ~**rsi** *vr* to humble o.s.

umiliazi'one [umiljat'tsjone] *sf* humiliation.

umiltà *sf* humility, humbleness.

u'more *sm* (*disposizione d'animo*) mood; (*carattere*) temper; **di buon/cattivo ~** in a good/bad mood.

umo'rismo *sm* humour (*BRIT*), humor (*US*); **avere il senso dell'~** to have a sense of humo(u)r.

umo'rista, i, e *sm/f* humorist.

umo'ristico, a, ci, che *ag* humorous, funny.

un, un', una *vedi* uno.

u'nanime *ag* unanimous.

unanimità *sf* unanimity; **all'~** unanimously.

'una 'tantum *ag* one-off *cpd* ♦ *sf* (*imposta*) one-off tax.

unci'nato, a [untʃi'nato] *ag* (*amo*) barbed; (*ferro*) hooked; **croce ~a** swastika.

un'cino [un'tʃino] *sm* hook.

undi'cenne [undi'tʃɛnne] *ag*, *sm/f* eleven-year-old.

undi'cesimo, a [undi'tʃɛzimo] eleventh.

'undici ['unditʃi] *num* eleven.

U'NESCO *sigla f* (= *United Nations Educational, Scientific and Cultural Organization*) UNESCO.

'ungere ['undʒere] *vt* to grease, oil; (*REL*) to anoint; (*fig*) to flatter, butter up; ~**rsi** *vr* (*sporcarsi*) to get covered in grease; ~**rsi con la crema** to put on cream.

unghe'rese [unge'rese] *ag, sm/f, sm* Hungarian.

Unghe'ria [unge'ria] *sf:* **l'~** Hungary.

'unghia ['ungja] *sf* (*ANAT*) nail; (*di animale*) claw; (*di rapace*) talon; (*di cavallo*) hoof; **pagare sull'~** (*fig*) to pay on the nail

unghi'ata [un'gjata] *sf* (*graffio*) scratch.

ungu'ento *sm* ointment.

unica'mente *av* only.

'UNICEF ['unitʃɛf] *sigla m* (= *United Nations International Children's Emergency Fund*) UNICEF.

'unico, a, ci, che *ag* (*solo*) only; (*ineguagliabile*) unique; (*singolo: binario*) single; **è figlio ~** he's an only child; **atto ~** (*TEAT*) one-act play; **agente ~** (*COMM*) sole agent.

uni'corno *sm* unicorn.

unifi'care *vt* to unite, unify; (*sistemi*) to standardize.

unificazi'one [unifikat'tsjone] *sf* unification; standardization.

unifor'mare *vt* (*terreno, superficie*) to level; **~rsi** *vr:* **~rsi a** to conform to; **~ qc a** to adjust o relate sth to.

uni'forme *ag* uniform; (*superficie*) even ♦ *sf* (*divisa*) uniform; **alta ~** dress uniform.

uniformità *sf* uniformity; evenness.

unilate'rale *ag* one-sided; (*DIR, POL*) unilateral.

uninomi'nale *ag* (*POL: collegio, sistema*) single-candidate *cpd*.

uni'one *sf* union; (*fig: concordia*) unity, harmony; **U~ economica e monetaria** economic and monetary union; **U~ Europea** European Union; **l'U~ Sovietica** the Soviet Union.

u'nire *vt* to unite; (*congiungere*) to join, connect; (*: ingredienti, colori*) to combine; (*in matrimonio*) to unite, join together; **~rsi** *vr* to unite; (*in matrimonio*) to be joined together; **~ qc a** to unite sth with; to join o connect sth with; to combine sth with; **~rsi a** (*gruppo, società*) to join.

u'nisono *sm:* **all'~** in unison.

unità *sf inv* (*unione, concordia*) unity; (*MAT, MIL, COMM, di misura*) unit; **~ centrale (di elaborazione)** (*INFORM*) central processing unit; **~ disco** (*INFORM*) disk drive; **~ monetaria** monetary unit.

uni'tario, a *ag* unitary; **prezzo ~** price per unit.

u'nito, a *ag* (*paese*) united; (*amici, famiglia*) close; **in tinta ~a** plain, self-coloured (*BRIT*), self-colored (*US*).

univer'sale *ag* universal; general.

universalità *sf* universality.

universal'mente *av* universally.

università *sf inv* university.

universi'tario, a *ag* university *cpd* ♦ *sm/f* (*studente*) university student; (*insegnante*) academic, university lecturer.

uni'verso *sm* universe.

u'nivoco, a, ci, che *ag* unambiguous.

═══════════════════ *PAROLA CHIAVE*

'uno, a (*dav sm* **un** + *C, V,* **uno** + *s impura, gn, pn, ps, x, z; dav sf* **un'** + *V,* **una** + *C*) *det*
1 a; (*dav vocale*) an; **un bambino** a child; **~a strada** a street; **~ zingaro** a gypsy
2 (*intensivo*): **ho avuto ~a paura!** I got such a fright!

♦ *pron* **1** one; **ce n'è ~ qui** there's one here; **prendine ~** take one (of them); **l'~ o l'altro** either (of them); **l'~ e l'altro** both (of them); **aiutarsi l'un l'altro** to help one another; **sono entrati l'~ dopo l'altro** they came in one after the other; **a ~ a ~** one by one; **metà per ~** half each
2 (*un tale*) someone, somebody; **ho incontrato ~ che ti conosce** I met somebody who knows you
3 (*con valore impersonale*) one, you; **se ~ vuole** if one wants, if you want; **cosa fa ~ in quella situazione?** what does one do in that situation?

♦ *num* one; **~a mela e due pere** one apple and two pears; **~ più ~ fa due** one plus one equals two, one and one are two
♦ *sf:* **è l'~a** it's one (o'clock).

'unsi *etc vb vedi* **ungere**.

'unto, a *pp di* **ungere** ♦ *ag* greasy, oily ♦ *sm* grease.

untu'oso, a *ag* greasy, oily.

unzi'one [un'tsjone] *sf:* **l'Estrema U~** (*REL*) Extreme Unction.

u'omo, *pl* **u'omini** *sm* man; **da ~** (*abito, scarpe*) men's, for men; **a memoria d'~** since the world began; **a passo d'~** at walking pace; **~ d'affari** businessman; **~ d'azione** man of action; **~ di fiducia** right-hand man; **~ di mondo** man of the world; **~ di paglia** stooge; **l'~ della strada** the man in the street.

u'opo *sm:* **all'~** if necessary.

u'ovo, *pl(f)* **u'ova** *sm* egg; **cercare il pelo nell'~** (*fig*) to split hairs; **~ affogato** *o* **in camicia** poached egg; **~ bazzotto/sodo** soft-/hard-boiled egg; **~ alla coque** boiled egg; **~ di Pasqua** Easter egg; **~ al tegame** *o* **all'occhio di bue** fried egg; **uova strapazzate** scrambled eggs.

ura'gano *sm* hurricane.

U'rali *smpl:* **gli ~, i Monti ~** the Urals, the Ural Mountains.

u'ranio *sm* uranium; ~ **impoverito** depleted uranium.

urba'nista, i, e *sm/f* town planner.

urba'nistica *sf* town planning.

urbanità *sf* urbanity.

ur'bano, a *ag* urban, city *cpd*, town *cpd*; (*TEL: chiamata*) local; (*fig*) urbane.

ur'gente [ur'dʒɛnte] *ag* urgent.

ur'genza [ur'dʒɛntsa] *sf* urgency; **in caso d'~** in (case of) an emergency; **d'~** *ag* emergency ♦ *av* urgently, as a matter of urgency; **non c'è ~** there's no hurry; **questo lavoro va fatto con ~** this work is urgent.

'urgere ['urdʒere] *vi* to be needed urgently.

u'rina *etc* = **orina** *etc*.

ur'lare *vi* (*persona*) to scream, yell; (*animale, vento*) to howl ♦ *vt* to scream, yell.

'urlo, *pl(m)* **'urli**, *pl(f)* **'urla** *sm* scream, yell; howl.

'urna *sf* urn; (*elettorale*) ballot box; **andare alle ~e** to go to the polls.

urrà *escl* hurrah!

U.R.S.S. *sigla f* (= *Unione delle Repubbliche Socialiste Sovietiche*): **l'~** the USSR.

ur'tare *vt* to bump into, knock against; (*fig: irritare*) to annoy ♦ *vi*: ~ **contro** *o* **in** to bump into, knock against; (*fig: imbattersi*) to come up against; **~rsi** *vr* (*reciproco: scontrarsi*) to collide; (*: fig*) to clash; (*irritarsi*) to get annoyed.

'urto *sm* (*colpo*) knock, bump; (*scontro*) crash, collision; (*fig*) clash; **terapia d'~** (*MED*) shock treatment.

uruguai'ano, a *ag, sm/f* Uruguayan.

Urugu'ay *sm*: **l'~** Uruguay.

u.s. *abbr* = **ultimo scorso**.

'USA *smpl*: **gli ~** the USA.

u'sanza [u'zantsa] *sf* custom; (*moda*) fashion.

u'sare *vt* to use, employ ♦ *vi* (*essere di moda*) to be fashionable; (*servirsi*): ~ **di** to use; (*: diritto*) to exercise; (*essere solito*): ~ **fare** to be in the habit of doing, be accustomed to doing ♦ *vb impers*: **qui usa così** it's the custom round here; ~ **la massima cura nel fare qc** to exercise great care when doing sth.

u'sato, a *ag* used; (*consumato*) worn; (*di seconda mano*) used, second-hand ♦ *sm* second-hand goods *pl*.

u'scente [uʃ'ʃɛnte] *ag* (*AMM*) outgoing.

usci'ere [uʃ'ʃɛre] *sm* usher.

'uscio ['uʃʃo] *sm* door.

u'scire [uʃ'ʃire] *vi* (*gen*) to come out; (*partire, andare a passeggio, a uno spettacolo etc*) to go out; (*essere sorteggiato: numero*) to come up; ~ **da** (*gen*) to leave; (*posto*) to go (*o* come) out of, leave; (*solco, vasca etc*) to come out of; (*muro*) to stick out of; (*competenza etc*) to be outside; (*infanzia, adolescenza*) to leave behind; (*famiglia nobile etc*) to come from; ~ **da** *o* **di casa** to go out; (*fig*) to leave home; ~ **in automobile** to go out in the car, go for a drive; ~ **di strada** (*AUT*) to go off *o* leave the road.

u'scita [uʃ'ʃita] *sf* (*passaggio, varco*) exit, way out; (*per divertimento*) outing; (*ECON: somma*) expenditure; (*fig: battuta*) witty remark; **"vietata l'~"** "no exit"; ~ **di sicurezza** emergency exit.

usi'gnolo [uziɲ'ɲɔlo] *sm* nightingale.

'uso *sm* (*utilizzazione*) use; (*esercizio*) practice (*BRIT*), practise (*US*); (*abitudine*) custom; **fare ~ di qc** to use sth; **con l'~** with practice; **a ~ di** for (the use of); **d'~** (*corrente*) in use; **fuori ~** out of use; **essere in ~** to be in common *o* current use.

ustio'nare *vt* to burn; **~rsi** *vr* to burn o.s.

usti'one *sf* burn.

usu'ale *ag* common, everyday.

usufru'ire *vi*: ~ **di** (*giovarsi di*) to take advantage of, make use of.

usu'frutto *sm* (*DIR*) usufruct.

u'sura *sf* usury; (*logoramento*) wear (and tear).

usu'raio *sm* usurer.

usur'pare *vt* to usurp.

usurpa'tore, 'trice *sm/f* usurper.

uten'sile *sm* tool, implement ♦ *ag*: **macchina ~** machine tool; **~i da cucina** kitchen utensils.

utensile'ria *sf* (*utensili*) tools *pl*; (*reparto*) tool room.

u'tente *sm/f* user; (*di gas etc*) consumer; (*del telefono*) subscriber; ~ **finale** end user.

'utero *sm* uterus, womb; ~ **in affitto** host womb.

'utile *ag* useful ♦ *sm* (*vantaggio*) advantage, benefit; (*ECON: profitto*) profit; **rendersi ~** to be helpful; **in tempo ~ per** in time for; **unire l'~ al dilettevole** to combine business with pleasure; **partecipare agli ~i** (*ECON*) to share in the profits.

utilità *sf* usefulness *no pl*; use; (*vantaggio*) benefit; **essere di grande ~** to be very useful.

utili'tario, a *ag* utilitarian ♦ *sf* (*AUT*) economy car.

utiliz'zare [utilid'dzare] *vt* to use, make use of, utilize.

utilizzazi'one [utiliddzat'tsjone] *sf*

utilization, use.

uti'lizzo [uti'liddzo] *sm* (*AMM*) utilization; (*BANCA: di credito*) availment.

util'mente *av* usefully, profitably.

uto'pia *sf* utopia; **è pura ~** that's sheer utopianism.

uto'pistico, a, ci, che *ag* utopian.

UVA *abbr* = *ultravioletto prossimo*.

'uva *sf* grapes *pl*; **~ passa** raisins *pl*; **~ spina** gooseberry.

UVB *abbr* = (*ultravioletto lontano*) UVB.

V v

V, v [vi, vu] *sf o m inv* (*lettera*) V, v; **V come Venezia** ≈ V for Victor.

V *abbr* (= *volt*) V.

v. *abbr* (= *vedi, verso, versetto*) v.

VA *sigla* = *Varese*.

va, va' *vb vedi* **andare**.

va'cante *ag* vacant.

va'canza [va'kantsa] *sf* (*l'essere vacante*) vacancy; (*riposo, ferie*) holiday(s *pl*) (*BRIT*), vacation (*US*); (*giorno di permesso*) day off, holiday; **~e** *sfpl* (*periodo di ferie*) holidays, vacation *sg*; **essere/andare in ~** to be/go on holiday *o* vacation; **far ~** to have a holiday; **~e estive** summer holiday(s) *o* vacation.

'vacca, che *sf* cow.

vacci'nare [vattʃi'nare] *vt* to vaccinate; **farsi ~** to have a vaccination, get vaccinated.

vaccinazi'one [vattʃinat'tsjone] *sf* vaccination.

vac'cino [vat'tʃino] *sm* (*MED*) vaccine.

vacil'lante [vatʃil'lante] *ag* (*edificio, vecchio*) shaky, unsteady; (*fiamma*) flickering; (*salute, memoria*) shaky, failing.

vacil'lare [vatʃil'lare] *vi* to sway; (*fiamma*) to flicker; (*fig: memoria, coraggio*) to be failing, falter.

'vacuo, a *ag* (*fig*) empty, vacuous ♦ *sm* vacuum.

'vado *etc vb vedi* **andare**.

vagabon'daggio [vagabon'daddʒo] *sm* wandering, roaming; (*DIR*) vagrancy.

vagabon'dare *vi* to roam, wander.

vaga'bondo, a *sm/f* tramp, vagrant; (*fannullone*) idler, loafer.

va'gare *vi* to wander.

vagheggi'are [vaged'dʒare] *vt* to long for, dream of.

vagherò *etc* [vage'rɔ] *vb vedi* **vagare**.

va'ghezza [va'gettsa] *sf* vagueness.

va'gina [va'dʒina] *sf* vagina.

va'gire [va'dʒire] *vi* to whimper.

va'gito [va'dʒito] *sm* cry, wailing.

'vaglia ['vaʎʎa] *sm inv* money order; **~ cambiario** promissory note; **~ postale** postal order.

vagli'are [vaʎ'ʎare] *vt* to sift; (*fig*) to weigh up.

'vaglio ['vaʎʎo] *sm* sieve; **passare al ~** (*fig*) to examine closely.

'vago, a, ghi, ghe *ag* vague.

va'gone *sm* (*FERR: per passeggeri*) carriage (*BRIT*), car (*US*); (*: per merci*) truck, wagon; **~ letto** sleeper, sleeping car; **~ ristorante** dining *o* restaurant car.

'vai *vb vedi* **andare**.

vai'olo *sm* smallpox.

val. *abbr* = **valuta**.

va'langa, ghe *sf* avalanche.

va'lente *ag* able, talented.

va'lenza [va'lɛntsa] *sf* (*fig: significato*) content; (*CHIM*) valency.

va'lere *vi* (*avere forza, potenza*) to have influence; (*essere valido*) to be valid; (*avere vigore, autorità*) to hold, apply; (*essere capace: poeta, studente*) to be good, be able ♦ *vt* (*prezzo, sforzo*) to be worth; (*corrispondere*) to correspond to; (*procurare*): **~ qc a qn** to earn sb sth; **~rsi** *vr*: **~rsi di** to make use of, take advantage of; **far ~** (*autorità etc*) to assert; **far ~ le proprie ragioni** to make o.s. heard; **farsi ~** to make o.s. appreciated *o* respected; **vale a dire** that is to say; **~ la pena** to be worth the effort *o* worth it; **l'uno vale l'altro** the one is as good as the other, they amount to the same thing; **non vale niente** it's worthless; **~rsi dei consigli di qn** to act upon sb's advice.

valeri'ana *sf* (*BOT, MED*) valerian.

va'levole *ag* valid.

'valgo *etc vb vedi* **valere**.

vali'care *vt* to cross.

'valico, chi *sm* (*passo*) pass.

validità *sf* validity.

'valido, a *ag* valid; (*rimedio*) effective; (*persona*) worthwhile; **essere di ~ aiuto a qn** to be a great help to sb.

valige'ria [validʒe'ria] *sf* (*assortimento*) leather goods *pl*; (*fabbrica*) leather goods factory; (*negozio*) leather goods shop.

vali'getta [vali'dʒetta] *sf*: **~ ventiquattrore** overnight bag *o* case.

va'ligia, gie *o* **ge** [va'lidʒa] *sf* (suit)case;

fare le ~**gie** to pack (up); ~ **diplomatica** diplomatic bag.

val'lata *sf* valley.

'**valle** *sf* valley; **a** ~ (*di fiume*) downstream; **scendere a** ~ to go downhill.

val'letto *sm* valet.

valligi'ano, a [valli'dʒano] *sm/f* inhabitant of a valley.

va'lore *sm* (*gen, COMM*) value; (*merito*) merit, worth; (*coraggio*) valour (*BRIT*), valor (*US*), courage; (*FINANZA: titolo*) security; ~**i** *smpl* (*oggetti preziosi*) valuables; **crescere/diminuire di** ~ to go up/down in value, gain/lose in value; **è di gran** ~ it's worth a lot, it's very valuable; **privo di** ~ worthless; ~ **contabile** book value; ~ **effettivo** real value; ~ **nominale** *o* **facciale** nominal value; ~ **di realizzo** break-up value; ~ **di riscatto** surrender value; ~**i bollati** (revenue) stamps.

valoriz'zare [valorid'dzare] *vt* (*terreno*) to develop; (*fig*) to make the most of.

valo'roso, a *ag* courageous.

'**valso, a** *pp di* **valere**.

va'luta *sf* currency, money; (*BANCA*): ~ **15 gennaio** interest to run from January 15th; ~ **estera** foreign currency.

valu'tare *vt* (*casa, gioiello, fig*) to value; (*stabilire: peso, entrate, fig*) to estimate.

valu'tario, a *ag* (*FINANZA: norme*) currency *cpd*.

valutazi'one [valutat'tsjone] *sf* valuation; estimate.

'**valva** *sf* (*ZOOL, BOT*) valve.

'**valvola** *sf* (*TECN, ANAT*) valve; (*ELETTR*) fuse; ~ **a farfalla del carburatore** (*AUT*) throttle; ~ **di sicurezza** safety valve.

'**valzer** ['valtser] *sm inv* waltz.

vam'pata *sf* (*di fiamma*) blaze; (*di calore*) blast; (: *al viso*) flush.

vam'piro *sm* vampire.

vana'gloria *sf* boastfulness.

van'dalico, a, ci, che *ag* vandal *cpd*; **atto** ~ act of vandalism.

vanda'lismo *sm* vandalism.

'**vandalo** *sm* vandal.

vaneggia'mento [vaneddʒa'mento] *sm* raving, delirium.

vaneggi'are [vaned'dʒare] *vi* to rave.

va'nesio, a *ag* vain, conceited.

'**vanga, ghe** *sf* spade.

van'gare *vt* to dig.

van'gelo [van'dʒɛlo] *sm* gospel.

vanifi'care *vt* to nullify.

va'niglia [va'niʎʎa] *sf* vanilla.

vanigli'ato, a [vaniʎ'ʎato] *ag*: **zucchero** ~ (*CUC*) vanilla sugar.

vanità *sf* vanity; (*di promessa*) emptiness;

(*di sforzo*) futility.

vani'toso, a *ag* vain, conceited.

'**vanno** *vb vedi* **andare**.

'**vano, a** *ag* vain ♦ *sm* (*spazio*) space; (*apertura*) opening; (*stanza*) room; **il** ~ **della porta** the doorway; **il** ~ **portabagagli** (*AUT*) the boot (*BRIT*), the trunk (*US*).

van'taggio [van'taddʒo] *sm* advantage; **trarre** ~ **da qc** to benefit from sth; **essere/portarsi in** ~ (*SPORT*) to be in/take the lead.

vantaggi'oso, a [vantad'dʒoso] *ag* advantageous, favourable (*BRIT*), favorable (*US*).

van'tare *vt* to praise, speak highly of; ~**rsi** *vr*: ~**rsi (di/di aver fatto)** to boast *o* brag (about/about having done).

vante'ria *sf* boasting.

'**vanto** *sm* boasting; (*merito*) virtue, merit; (*gloria*) pride.

'**vanvera** *sf*: **a** ~ haphazardly; **parlare a** ~ to talk nonsense.

va'pore *sm* vapour (*BRIT*), vapor (*US*); (*anche:* ~ **acqueo**) steam; (*nave*) steamer; **a** ~ (*turbina etc*) steam *cpd*; **al** ~ (*CUC*) steamed.

vapo'retto *sm* steamer.

vapori'era *sf* (*FERR*) steam engine.

vaporiz'zare [vaporid'dzare] *vt* to vaporize.

vaporizza'tore [vaporiddza'tore] *sm* spray.

vaporizzazi'one [vaporiddzat'tsjone] *sf* vaporization.

vapo'roso, a *ag* (*tessuto*) filmy; (*capelli*) soft and full.

va'rare *vt* (*NAUT, fig*) to launch; (*DIR*) to pass.

var'care *vt* to cross.

'**varco, chi** *sm* passage; **aprirsi un** ~ **tra la folla** to push one's way through the crowd.

vare'china [vare'kina] *sf* bleach.

vari'abile *ag* variable; (*tempo, umore*) changeable, variable ♦ *sf* (*MAT*) variable.

vari'ante *sf* (*gen*) variation, change; (*di piano*) modification; (*LING*) variant; (*SPORT*) alternative route.

vari'are *vt, vi* to vary; ~ **di opinione** to change one's mind.

variazi'one [varjat'tsjone] *sf* variation, change; (*MUS*) variation; **una** ~ **di programma** a change of plan.

va'rice [va'ritʃe] *sf* varicose vein.

vari'cella [vari'tʃɛlla] *sf* chickenpox.

vari'coso, a *ag* varicose.

varie'gato, a *ag* variegated.

varietà *sf inv* variety ♦ *sm inv* variety show.

'**vario, a** *ag* varied; (*parecchi: col sostantivo al pl*) various; (*mutevole: umore*)

changeable; ~**e** *sfpl*: ~**e ed eventuali**
(*nell'ordine del giorno*) any other business.
vario'pinto, a *ag* multicoloured (*BRIT*),
multicolored (*US*).
'**varo** *sm* (*NAUT*, *fig*) launch; (*di leggi*)
passing.
varrò *etc vb vedi* **valere**.
Var'savia *sf* Warsaw.
va'saio *sm* potter.
'**vasca, sche** *sf* basin; (*anche*: ~ **da bagno**)
bathtub, bath.
va'scello [vaʃ'ʃɛllo] *sm* (*NAUT*) vessel, ship.
vas'chetta [vas'ketta] *sf* (*per gelato*) tub;
(*per sviluppare fotografie*) dish.
vase'lina *sf* vaseline.
vasel'lame *sm* (*stoviglie*) crockery; (: *di
porcellana*) china; ~ **d'oro/d'argento** gold/
silver plate.
'**vaso** *sm* (*recipiente*) pot; (: *barattolo*) jar;
(: *decorativo*) vase; (*ANAT*) vessel; ~ **da
fiori** vase; (*per piante*) flowerpot.
vas'sallo *sm* vassal.
vas'soio *sm* tray.
vastità *sf* vastness.
'**vasto, a** *ag* vast, immense; **di** ~**e
proporzioni** (*incendio*) huge; (*fenomeno,
rivolta*) widespread; **su** ~**a scala** on a vast
o huge scale.
Vati'cano *sm*: **il** ~ the Vatican; **la Città del**
~ the Vatican City.
VB *sigla* = *Vibo Valenza*.
VC *sigla* = *Vercelli*.
VE *sigla* = *Venezia* ♦ *abbr* = *Vostra Eccellenza*.
ve *pron*, *av vedi* **vi**.
vecchi'aia [vek'kjaja] *sf* old age.
'**vecchio, a** ['vɛkkjo] *ag* old ♦ *smlf* old man/
woman; **i** ~**i** the old; **è un mio** ~ **amico**
he's an old friend of mine; **è un uomo**
~ **stile** *o* **stampo** he's an old-fashioned
man; **è** ~ **del mestiere** he's an old hand at
the job.
'**vece** ['vetʃe] *sf*: **in** ~ **di** in the place of, for;
fare la ~**i di qn** to take sb's place; **firma
del padre o di chi ne fa le** ~**i** signature of
the father or guardian.
ve'dere *vt, vi* to see; ~**rsi** *vr* to meet, see one
another; ~ **di fare qc** to see (to it) that sth
is done, make sure that sth is done; **avere
a che** ~ **con** to have to do with; **far** ~ **qc a
qn** to show sb sth; **farsi** ~ to show o.s.;
(*farsi vivo*) to show one's face; **farsi** ~ **da
un medico** to go and see a doctor; **modo
di** ~ outlook, view of things; **vedi pagina 8**
(*rimando*) see page 8; **è da** ~ **se ...** it
remains to be seen whether ...; **non vedo
la ragione di farlo** I can't see any reason
to do it; **si era visto costretto a ...** he
found himself forced to ...; **non (ci) si**

vede (*è buio etc*) you can't see a thing; **ci
vediamo domani!** see you tomorrow!; **non
lo posso** ~ (*fig*) I can't stand him.
ve'detta *sf* (*sentinella, posto*) look-out;
(*NAUT*) patrol boat.
ve'dette [və'dɛt] *sf inv* (*attrice*) star.
'**vedovo, a** *smlf* widower/widow; **rimaner** ~
to be widowed.
vedrò *etc vb vedi* **vedere**.
ve'duta *sf* view; **di larghe** *o* **ampie** ~**e**
broad-minded; **di** ~**e limitate** narrow-
minded.
vee'mente *ag* (*discorso, azione*) vehement;
(*assalto*) vigorous; (*passione*)
overwhelming.
vee'menza [vee'mɛntsa] *sf* vehemence; **con**
~ vehemently.
vege'tale [vedʒe'tale] *ag, sm* vegetable.
vege'tare [vedʒe'tare] *vi* (*fig*) to vegetate.
vegetari'ano, a [vedʒeta'rjano] *ag, smlf*
vegetarian.
vegeta'tivo, a *ag* vegetative.
vegetazi'one [vedʒetat'tsjone] *sf*
vegetation.
'**vegeto, a** ['vɛdʒeto] *ag* (*pianta*) thriving;
(*persona*) strong, vigorous.
veg'gente [ved'dʒɛnte] *smlf* (*indovino*)
clairvoyant.
'**veglia** ['veʎʎa] *sf* (*sorveglianza*) watch;
(*trattenimento*) evening gathering; **tra la** ~
e il sonno half awake; **fare la** ~ **a un
malato** to watch over a sick person; ~
funebre wake.
vegli'ardo, a [veʎ'ʎardo] *smlf* venerable old
man/woman.
vegli'are [veʎ'ʎare] *vi* to stay *o* sit up; (*stare
vigile*) to watch; to keep watch ♦ *vt*
(*malato, morto*) to watch over, sit up with.
vegli'one [veʎ'ʎone] *sm* ball, dance.
ve'icolo *sm* vehicle; ~ **spaziale** spacecraft
inv.
'**vela** *sf* (*NAUT*: *tela*) sail; (*sport*) sailing;
tutto va a gonfie ~**e** (*fig*) everything is
going perfectly.
ve'lare *vt* to veil; ~**rsi** *vr* (*occhi, luna*) to mist
over; (*voce*) to become husky; ~**rsi il viso**
to cover one's face (with a veil).
ve'lato, a *ag* veiled.
vela'tura *sf* (*NAUT*) sails *pl*.
veleggi'are [veled'dʒare] *vi* to sail; (*AER*) to
glide.
ve'leno *sm* poison.
vele'noso, a *ag* poisonous.
ve'letta *sf* (*di cappello*) veil.
veli'ero *sm* sailing ship.
ve'lina *sf* (*anche*: **carta** ~: *per imballare*)
tissue paper; (: *per copie*) flimsy paper;
(*copia*) carbon copy.

ve'lista, i, e *sm/f* yachtsman/woman.
ve'livolo *sm* aircraft.
velleità *sf inv* vain ambition, vain desire.
vellei'tario, a *ag* unrealistic.
'vello *sm* fleece.
vellu'tato, a *ag* (*stoffa, pesca, colore*) velvety; (*voce*) mellow.
vel'luto *sm* velvet; ~ **a coste** cord.
'velo *sm* veil; (*tessuto*) voile.
ve'loce [ve'lotʃe] *ag* fast, quick ♦ *av* fast, quickly.
velo'cista, i, e [velo'tʃista] *sm/f* (*SPORT*) sprinter.
velocità [velotʃi'ta] *sf* speed; **a forte** ~ at high speed; ~ **di crociera** cruising speed.
ve'lodromo *sm* velodrome.
ven. *abbr* (= *venerdì*) Fri.
'vena *sf* (*gen*) vein; (*filone*) vein, seam; (*fig: ispirazione*) inspiration; (: *umore*) mood; **essere in** ~ **di qc** to be in the mood for sth.
ve'nale *ag* (*prezzo, valore*) market *cpd*; (*fig*) venal; mercenary.
venalità *sf* venality.
ve'nato, a *ag* (*marmo*) veined, streaked; (*legno*) grained.
vena'torio, a *ag* hunting; **la stagione** ~a the hunting season.
vena'tura *sf* (*di marmo*) vein, streak; (*di legno*) grain.
ven'demmia *sf* (*raccolta*) grape harvest; (*quantità d'uva*) grape crop, grapes *pl*; (*vino ottenuto*) vintage.
vendemmi'are *vt* to harvest ♦ *vi* to harvest the grapes.
'vendere *vt* to sell; ~ **all'ingrosso/al dettaglio** *o* **minuto** to sell wholesale/ retail; ~ **all'asta** to auction, sell by auction; "**vendesi**" "for sale".
ven'detta *sf* revenge.
vendi'care *vt* to avenge; ~**rsi** *vr*: ~**rsi (di)** to avenge o.s. (for); (*per rancore*) to take one's revenge (for); ~**rsi su qn** to revenge o.s. on sb.
vendica'tivo, a *ag* vindictive.
'vendita *sf* sale; **la** ~ (*attività*) selling; (*smercio*) sales *pl*; **in** ~ on sale; **mettere in** ~ to put on sale; **in** ~ **presso** on sale at; **contratto di** ~ sales agreement; **reparto** ~**e** sales department; ~ **all'asta** sale by auction; ~ **al dettaglio** *o* **minuto** retail; ~ **all'ingrosso** wholesale.
vendi'tore, 'trice *sm/f* seller, vendor; (*gestore di negozio*) trader, dealer.
ven'duto, a *ag* (*merce*) sold; (*fig: corrotto*) corrupt.
ve'nefico, a, ci, che *ag* poisonous.
vene'rabile *ag*, **vene'rando, a** *ag*

venerable.
vene'rare *vt* to venerate.
venerazi'one [venerat'tsjone] *sf* veneration.
venerdì *sm inv* Friday; **V~ Santo** Good Friday; *per fraseologia vedi* **martedì**.
'Venere *sm, sf* Venus.
ve'nereo, a *ag* venereal.
'veneto, a *ag* of (*o* from) the Veneto.
'veneto-giuli'ano, a ['vɛnetodʒu'ljano] *ag* of (*o* from) Venezia-Giulia.
Ve'nezia [ve'nɛttsja] *sf* Venice.
venezi'ano, a [venet'tsjano] *ag*, *sm/f* Venetian.
Venezu'ela [venettsu'ela] *sm*: **il** ~ Venezuela.
venezue'lano, a [venettsue'lano] *ag*, *sm/f* Venezuelan.
'vengo *etc vb vedi* **venire**.
veni'ale *ag* venial.
ve'nire *vi* to come; (*riuscire: dolce, fotografia*) to turn out; (*come ausiliare: essere*): **viene ammirato da tutti** he is admired by everyone; ~ **da** to come from; **quanto viene?** how much does it cost?; **far** ~ (*mandare a chiamare*) to send for; (*medico*) to call, send for; ~ **a capo di qc** to unravel sth, sort sth out; ~ **al dunque** *o* **nocciolo** *o* **fatto** to come to the point; ~ **fuori** to come out; ~ **giù** to come down; ~ **meno** (*svenire*) to faint; ~ **meno a qc** not to fulfil sth; ~ **su** to come up; ~ **via** to come away; ~ **a sapere qc** to learn sth; ~ **a trovare qn** to come and see sb; **negli anni a** ~ in the years to come, in future; **è venuto il momento di ...** the time has come to ....
'venni *etc vb vedi* **venire**.
ven'taglio [ven'taʎʎo] *sm* fan.
ven'tata *sf* gust (of wind).
venten'nale *ag* (*che dura 20 anni*) twenty-year *cpd*; (*che ricorre ogni 20 anni*) which takes place every twenty years.
ven'tenne *ag*, *sm/f* twenty-year-old.
ven'tennio *sm* period of twenty years; **il** ~ **fascista** the Fascist period.
ven'tesimo, a *num* twentieth.
'venti *num* twenty.
venti'lare *vt* (*stanza*) to air, ventilate; (*fig: idea, proposta*) to air.
venti'lato, a *ag* (*camera, zona*) airy; **poco** ~ airless.
ventila'tore *sm* fan; (*su parete, finestra*) ventilator, fan.
ventilazi'one [ventilat'tsjone] *sf* ventilation.
ven'tina *sf*: **una** ~ **(di)** around twenty, twenty or so.

ventiquat'tr'ore *sfpl* (*periodo*) twenty-four hours ♦ *sf inv* (*SPORT*) twenty-four-hour race; (*valigetta*) overnight case.

venti'sette *num* twenty-seven; **il** ~ (*giorno di paga*) (monthly) pay day.

ventitré *num* twenty-three ♦ *sfpl*: **portava il cappello sulle** ~ he wore his hat at a jaunty angle.

'**vento** *sm* wind; **c'è** ~ it's windy; **un colpo di** ~ a gust of wind; **contro** ~ against the wind; ~ **contrario** (*NAUT*) headwind.

'**ventola** *sf* (*AUT, TECN*) fan.

ven'tosa *sf* (*ZOOL*) sucker; (*di gomma*) suction pad.

ven'toso, a *ag* windy.

ven'totto *num* twenty-eight.

'**ventre** *sm* stomach.

ven'triloquo *sm* ventriloquist.

ven'tuno *num* twenty-one.

ven'tura *sf*: **andare alla** ~ to trust to luck; **soldato di** ~ mercenary.

ven'turo, a *ag* next, coming.

ve'nuto, a *pp di* venire ♦ *sm/f*: **il(la) primo(a)** ~**(a)** the first person who comes along ♦ *sf* coming, arrival.

ver. *abbr* = **versamento**.

'**vera** *sf* wedding ring.

ve'race [ve'ratʃe] *ag* (*testimone*) truthful; (*testimonianza*) accurate; (*cibi*) real, genuine.

vera'mente *av* really.

ve'randa *sf* veranda(h).

ver'bale *ag* verbal ♦ *sm* (*di riunione*) minutes *pl*; **accordo** ~ verbal agreement; **mettere a** ~ to place in the minutes *o* on record.

'**verbo** *sm* (*LING*) verb; (*parola*) word; (*REL*): **il V**~ the Word.

ver'boso, a *ag* verbose, wordy.

ver'dastro, a *ag* greenish.

'**verde** *ag, sm* green; ~ **bottiglia/oliva** *ag inv* bottle/olive green; **benzina** ~ lead-free *o* unleaded petrol; **i V**~**i** (*POL*) the Greens; **essere al** ~ (*fig*) to be broke.

verdeggi'ante [verded'dʒante] *ag* green, verdant.

verde'rame *sm* verdigris.

ver'detto *sm* verdict.

ver'dura *sf* vegetables *pl*.

vere'condia *sf* modesty.

vere'condo, a *ag* modest.

'**verga, ghe** *sf* rod.

ver'gato, a *ag* (*foglio*) ruled.

vergi'nale [verdʒi'nale] *ag* virginal.

'**vergine** ['verdʒine] *sf* virgin; (*dello zodiaco*): **V**~ Virgo ♦ *ag* virgin; (*ragazza*): **essere** ~ to be a virgin; **essere della V**~ (*dello zodiaco*) to be Virgo; **pura lana** ~ pure

new wool; **olio** ~ **d'oliva** unrefined olive oil.

verginità [verdʒini'ta] *sf* virginity.

ver'gogna [ver'goɲɲa] *sf* shame; (*timidezza*) shyness, embarrassment.

vergo'gnarsi [vergoɲ'ɲarsi] *vr*: ~ (**di**) to be *o* feel ashamed (of); to be shy (about), be embarrassed (about).

vergo'gnoso, a [vergoɲ'ɲoso] *ag* ashamed; (*timido*) shy, embarrassed; (*causa di vergogna: azione*) shameful.

veridicità [veriditʃi'ta] *sf* truthfulness.

ve'ridico, a, ci, che *ag* truthful.

ve'rifica, che *sf* checking *no pl*; check; **fare una** ~ **di** (*freni, testimonianza, firma*) to check; ~ **contabile** (*FINANZA*) audit.

verifi'care *vt* (*controllare*) to check; (*confermare*) to confirm, bear out; (*FINANZA*) to audit.

verità *sf inv* truth; **a dire la** ~, **per la** ~ truth to tell, actually.

veriti'ero, a *ag* (*che dice la verità*) truthful; (*conforme a verità*) true.

'**verme** *sm* worm.

vermi'celli [vermi'tʃelli] *smpl* vermicelli *sg*.

ver'miglio [ver'miʎʎo] *sm* vermilion, scarlet.

'**vermut** *sm inv* vermouth.

ver'nacolo *sm* vernacular.

ver'nice [ver'nitʃe] *sf* (*colorazione*) paint; (*trasparente*) varnish; (*pelle*) patent leather; "~ **fresca**" "wet paint".

vernici'are [verni'tʃare] *vt* to paint; to varnish.

vernicia'tura [vernitʃa'tura] *sf* painting; varnishing.

'**vero, a** *ag* (*veridico: fatti, testimonianza*) true; (*autentico*) real ♦ *sm* (*verità*) truth; (*realtà*) (real) life; **un** ~ **e proprio delinquente** a real criminal, an out and out criminal; **tant'è** ~ **che** ... so much so that ...; **a onor del** ~, **a dire il** ~ to tell the truth.

Ve'rona *sf* Verona.

vero'nese *ag* of (*o* from) Verona.

vero'simile *ag* likely, probable.

verrò *etc vb vedi* **venire**.

ver'ruca, che *sf* wart.

versa'mento *sm* (*pagamento*) payment; (*deposito di denaro*) deposit.

ver'sante *sm* slopes *pl*, side.

ver'sare *vt* (*fare uscire: vino, farina*) to pour (out); (*spargere: lacrime, sangue*) to shed; (*rovesciare*) to spill; (*ECON*) to pay; (: *depositare*) to deposit, pay in ♦ *vi*: ~ **in gravi difficoltà** to find o.s. with serious problems; ~**rsi** *vr* (*rovesciarsi*) to spill; (*fiume, folla*): ~**rsi (in)** to pour (into).

versa'tile *ag* versatile.
versatilità *sf* versatility.
ver'sato, a *ag:* ~ **in** to be (well-)versed in.
ver'setto *sm* (*REL*) verse.
versi'one *sf* version; (*traduzione*)
 translation.
'verso *sm* (*di poesia*) verse, line; (*di animale,
 uccello, venditore ambulante*) cry;
 (*direzione*) direction; (*modo*) way; (*di foglio
 di carta*) verso; (*di moneta*) reverse; ~**i** *smpl*
 (*poesia*) verse *sg*; **per un** ~ **o per l'altro** one
 way or another; **prendere qn/qc per il** ~
 giusto to approach sb/sth the right way;
 rifare il ~ **a qn** (*imitare*) to mimic sb; **non
 c'è** ~ **di persuaderlo** there's no way of
 persuading him, he can't be persuaded ♦
 prep (*in direzione di*) toward(s); (*nei pressi
 di*) near, around (about); (*in senso
 temporale*) about, around; (*nei confronti di*)
 for; ~ **di me** towards me; ~ **l'alto**
 upwards; ~ **il basso** downwards; ~ **sera**
 towards evening.
'vertebra *sf* vertebra.
verte'brale *ag* vertebral; **colonna** ~ spinal
 column, spine.
verte'brato, a *ag, sm* vertebrate.
ver'tenza [ver'tɛntsa] *sf* (*lite*) lawsuit, case;
 (*sindacale*) dispute.
'vertere *vi:* ~ **su** to deal with, be about.
verti'cale *ag, sf* vertical.
'vertice ['vɛrtitʃe] *sm* summit, top; (*MAT*)
 vertex; **conferenza al** ~ (*POL*) summit
 conference.
ver'tigine [ver'tidʒine] *sf* dizziness *no pl*;
 dizzy spell; (*MED*) vertigo; **avere le** ~**i** to
 feel dizzy.
vertigi'noso, a [vertidʒi'noso] *ag* (*altezza*)
 dizzy; (*fig*) breathtakingly high (*o deep
 etc*).
'verza ['vɛrdza] *sf* Savoy cabbage.
ve'scica, che [veʃ'ʃika] *sf* (*ANAT*) bladder;
 (*MED*) blister.
vesco'vile *ag* episcopal.
'vescovo *sm* bishop.
'vespa *sf* wasp; (®: *veicolo*) (motor)
 scooter.
ves'paio *sm* wasps' nest; **suscitare un** ~
 (*fig*) to stir up a hornets' nest.
vespasi'ano *sm* urinal.
'vespro *sm* (*REL*) vespers *pl*.
ves'sare *vt* to oppress.
vessazi'one [vessat'tsjone] *sf* oppression.
ves'sillo *sm* standard; (*bandiera*) flag.
ves'taglia [ves'taʎʎa] *sf* dressing gown,
 robe (*US*).
'veste *sf* garment; (*rivestimento*) covering;
 (*qualità, facoltà*) capacity; ~**i** *sfpl* clothes,
 clothing *sg*; **in** ~ **ufficiale** (*fig*) in an official

capacity; **in** ~ **di** in the guise of, as; ~ **da
 camera** dressing gown, robe (*US*); ~
 editoriale layout.
vesti'ario *sm* wardrobe, clothes *pl*; **capo di**
 ~ article of clothing, garment.
ves'tibolo *sm* (*entrance*) hall.
ves'tigia [ves'tidʒa] *sfpl* (*tracce*) vestiges,
 traces; (*rovine*) ruins, remains.
ves'tire *vt* (*bambino, malato*) to dress;
 (*avere indosso*) to have on, wear; ~**rsi** *vr* to
 dress, get dressed; ~**rsi da** (*negozio, sarto*)
 to buy *o* get one's clothes at.
ves'tito, a *ag* dressed ♦ *sm* garment; (*da
 donna*) dress; (*da uomo*) suit; ~**i** *smpl*
 (*indumenti*) clothes; ~ **di bianco** dressed
 in white.
Ve'suvio *sm:* **il** ~ Vesuvius.
vete'rano, a *ag, sm/f* veteran.
veteri'nario, a *ag* veterinary ♦ *sm*
 veterinary surgeon (*BRIT*), veterinarian
 (*US*), vet ♦ *sf* veterinary medicine.
'veto *sm inv* veto; **porre il** ~ **a qc** to veto sth.
ve'traio *sm* glassmaker; (*per finestre*)
 glazier.
ve'trato, a *ag* (*porta, finestra*) glazed; (*che
 contiene vetro*) glass *cpd* ♦ *sf* glass door (*o*
 window); (*di chiesa*) stained glass
 window; **carta** ~**a** sandpaper.
vetre'ria *sf* (*stabilimento*) glassworks *sg*;
 (*oggetti di vetro*) glassware.
ve'trina *sf* (*di negozio*) (shop) window;
 (*armadio*) display cabinet.
vetri'nista, i, e *sm/f* window dresser.
ve'trino *sm* slide.
vetri'olo *sm* vitriol.
'vetro *sm* glass; (*per finestra, porta*) pane (of
 glass); ~ **blindato** bulletproof glass; ~
 infrangibile shatterproof glass; ~ **di
 sicurezza** safety glass; **i** ~**i di Murano**
 Murano glassware *sg*.
ve'troso, a *ag* vitreous.
'vetta *sf* peak, summit, top.
vet'tore *sm* (*MAT, FISICA*) vector; (*chi
 trasporta*) carrier.
vetto'vaglie [vetto'vaʎʎe] *sfpl* supplies.
vet'tura *sf* (*carrozza*) carriage; (*FERR*)
 carriage (*BRIT*), car (*US*); (*auto*) car (*BRIT*),
 automobile (*US*); ~ **di piazza** hackney carriage.
vettu'rino *sm* coach driver, coachman.
vezzeggi'are [vettsed'dʒare] *vt* to fondle,
 caress.
vezzeggia'tivo [vettseddʒa'tivo] *sm* (*LING*)
 term of endearment.
'vezzo ['vettso] *sm* habit; ~**i** *smpl*
 (*smancerie*) affected ways; (*leggiadria*)
 charms.
vez'zoso, a [vet'tsoso] *ag* (*grazioso*)

charming, pretty; (*lezioso*) affected.

V.F. *abbr* = **vigili del fuoco.**

V.G. *abbr* = *Vostra Grazia.*

VI *sigla* = *Vicenza.*

vi (*dav lo, la, li, le, ne diventa* **ve**) *pron* (*oggetto*) you; (*complemento di termine*) (to) you; (*riflessivo*) yourselves; (*reciproco*) each other ♦ *av* (*lì*) there; (*qui*) here; (*per questo/quel luogo*) through here/there; ~ **è/sono** there is/are.

'via *sf* (*gen*) way; (*strada*) street; (*sentiero, pista*) path, track; (*AMM*: *procedimento*) channels *pl* ♦ *prep* (*passando per*) via, by way of ♦ *av* away ♦ *escl* go away!; (*suvvia*) come on!; (*SPORT*) go! ♦ *sm* (*SPORT*) starting signal; **per** ~ **di** (*a causa di*) because of, on account of; **in** *o* **per** ~ **on** the way; **in** ~ **di guarigione** (*fig*) on the road to recovery; **per** ~ **aerea** by air; (*lettere*) by airmail; ~ **satellite** by satellite; **andare/essere** ~ to go/be away; ~ ~ (*pian piano*) gradually; ~ ~ **che** (*a mano a mano*) as; **e** ~ **dicendo, e** ~ **di questo passo** and so on (and so forth); **dare il** ~ (*SPORT*) to give the starting signal; **dare il** ~ **a un progetto** to give the green light to a project; **hanno dato il** ~ **ai lavori** they've begun *o* started work; **in** ~ **amichevole** in a friendly manner; **comporre una disputa in** ~ **amichevole** (*DIR*) to settle a dispute out of court; **in** ~ **eccezionale** as an exception; **in** ~ **privata** *o* **confidenziale** (*dire etc*) in confidence; **in** ~ **provvisoria** provisionally; **V**~ **lattea** (*ASTR*) Milky Way; ~ **di mezzo** middle course; **non c'è** ~ **di scampo** *o* **d'uscita** there's no way out; ~**e di comunicazione** communication routes.

viabilità *sf* (*di strada*) practicability; (*rete stradale*) roads *pl*, road network.

via'dotto *sm* viaduct.

viaggi'are [viad'dʒare] *vi* to travel; **le merci viaggiano via mare** the goods go *o* are sent by sea.

viaggia'tore, 'trice [viaddʒa'tore] *ag* travelling (*BRIT*), traveling (*US*) ♦ *sm* traveller (*BRIT*), traveler (*US*); (*passeggero*) passenger.

vi'aggio [vi'addʒo] *sm* travel(ling); (*tragitto*) journey, trip; **buon** ~! have a good trip!; ~ **d'affari** business trip; ~ **di nozze** honeymoon; ~ **organizzato** package tour *o* holiday.

vi'ale *sm* avenue.

vian'dante *sm/f* vagrant.

vi'atico, ci *sm* (*REL*) viaticum; (*fig*) encouragement.

via'vai *sm* coming and going, bustle.

vi'brare *vi* to vibrate; (*agitarsi*): ~ (**di**) to quiver (with).

vibra'tore *sm* vibrator.

vibrazi'one [vibrat'tsjone] *sf* vibration.

vi'cario *sm* (*apostolico etc*) vicar.

'vice ['vitʃe] *sm/f* deputy ♦ *prefisso* vice.

vice'console [vitʃe'kɔnsole] *sm* vice-consul.

vicediret'tore, 'trice [vitʃediret'tore] *sm/f* assistant manager/manageress; (*di giornale etc*) deputy editor.

vi'cenda [vi'tʃɛnda] *sf* event; ~**e** *sfpl* (*sorte*) fortunes; **a** ~ in turn; **con alterne** ~**e** with mixed fortunes.

vicen'devole [vitʃen'devole] *ag* mutual, reciprocal.

vicen'tino, a [vitʃen'tino] *ag* of (*o* from) Vicenza.

vicepresi'dente [vitʃepresi'dɛnte] *sm* vice-president, vice-chairman.

vice'versa [vitʃe'vɛrsa] *av* vice versa; **da Roma a Pisa e** ~ from Rome to Pisa and back.

vi'chingo, a, ghi, ghe [vi'kingo] *ag*, *sm/f* Viking.

vici'nanza [vitʃi'nantsa] *sf* nearness, closeness; ~**e** *sfpl* (*paraggi*) neighbourhood (*BRIT*), neighborhood (*US*), vicinity.

vici'nato [vitʃi'nato] *sm* neighbourhood (*BRIT*), neighborhood (*US*); (*vicini*) neighbo(u)rs *pl*.

vi'cino, a [vi'tʃino] *ag* (*gen*) near; (*nello spazio*) near, nearby; (*accanto*) next; (*nel tempo*) near, close at hand ♦ *sm/f* neighbour (*BRIT*), neighbor (*US*) ♦ *av* near, close; **da** ~ (*guardare*) close up; (*esaminare, seguire*) closely; (*conoscere*) well, intimately; ~ **a** *prep* near (to), close to; (*accanto a*) beside; **mi sono stati molto** ~**i** (*fig*) they were very supportive towards me; ~ **di casa** neighbo(u)r.

vicissi'tudini [vitʃissi'tudini] *sfpl* trials and tribulations.

'vicolo *sm* alley; ~ **cieco** blind alley.

'video *sm inv* (*TV*: *schermo*) screen.

video'camera *sf* camcorder.

videocas'setta *sf* videocassette.

videodipen'dente *sm/f* telly addict ♦ *ag*: **un pigrone** ~ a couch potato.

videofo'nino *sm* video mobile.

videogi'oco, chi [video'dʒɔko] *sm* video game.

videono'leggio [videono'leddʒo] *sm* video rental.

videoregistra'tore [videoredʒistra'tore] *sm* (*apparecchio*) video (recorder).

video'teca, che *sf* video shop.

videote'lefono *sm* videophone.

videotermi'nale *sm* visual display unit.

'**vidi** *etc vb vedi* **vedere**.
vidi'mare *vt* (*AMM*) to authenticate.
vidimazi'one [vidimat'tsjone] *sf* (*AMM*) authentication.
Vi'enna *sf* Vienna.
vien'nese *ag, sm/f* Viennese *inv*.
vie'tare *vt* to forbid; (*AMM*) to prohibit; (*libro*) to ban; ~ **a qn di fare** to forbid sb to do; to prohibit sb from doing.
vie'tato, a *ag* (*vedi vb*) forbidden; prohibited; banned; "~ **fumare/ l'ingresso**" "no smoking/admittance"; ~ **ai minori di 14/18 anni** prohibited to children under 14/18; "**senso ~**" (*AUT*) "no entry"; "**sosta ~a**" (*AUT*) "no parking".
Viet'nam *sm*: **il** ~ Vietnam.
vietna'mita, i, e *ag, sm/f, sm* Vietnamese *inv*.
vi'gente [vi'dʒɛnte] *ag* in force.
'**vigere** ['vidʒere] *vi* (*difettivo: si usa solo alla terza persona*) to be in force; **in casa mia vige l'abitudine di ...** at home we are in the habit of ....
vigi'lante [vidʒi'lante] *ag* vigilant, watchful.
vigi'lanza [vidʒi'lantsa] *sf* vigilance; (*sorveglianza: di operai, alunni*) supervision; (: *di sospetti, criminali*) surveillance.
vigi'lare [vidʒi'lare] *vt* to watch over, keep an eye on; ~ **che** to make sure that, see to it that.
vigi'lato, a [vidʒi'lato] *sm/f* (*DIR*) person under police surveillance.
vigila'trice [vidʒila'tritʃe] *sf*: ~ **d'infanzia** nursery-school teacher; ~ **scolastica** school health officer.
'**vigile** ['vidʒile] *ag* watchful ♦ *sm* (*anche*: ~ **urbano**) policeman (*in towns*); ~ **del fuoco** fireman; *vedi nota nel riquadro*.

vigi'lessa [vidʒi'lessa] *sf* (*traffic*) policewoman.
vi'gilia [vi'dʒilja] *sf* (*giorno antecedente*) eve; **la ~ di Natale** Christmas Eve.
vigliacche'ria [viʎʎakke'ria] *sf* cowardice.
vigli'acco, a, chi, che [viʎ'ʎakko] *ag* cowardly ♦ *sm/f* coward.
'**vigna** ['viɲɲa] *sf*, **vi'gneto** [viɲ'ɲeto] *sm* vineyard.
vi'gnetta [viɲ'ɲetta] *sf* cartoon.
vi'gore *sm* vigour (*BRIT*), vigor (*US*); (*DIR*):

essere/entrare in ~ to be in/come into force; **non è più in** ~ it is no longer in force, it no longer applies.
vigo'roso, a *ag* vigorous.
'**vile** *ag* (*spregevole*) low, mean, base; (*codardo*) cowardly.
vili'pendere *vt* to despise, scorn.
vili'pendio *sm* contempt, scorn.
vili'peso, a *pp di* **vilipendere**.
'**villa** *sf* villa.
vil'laggio [vil'laddʒo] *sm* village; ~ **turistico** holiday village.
villa'nia *sf* rudeness, lack of manners; **fare** (*o* **dire**) **una** ~ **a qn** to be rude to sb.
vil'lano, a *ag* rude, ill-mannered ♦ *sm/f* boor.
villeggi'ante [villed'dʒante] *sm/f* holidaymaker (*BRIT*), vacationer (*US*).
villeggi'are [villed'dʒare] *vi* to holiday, spend one's holidays, vacation (*US*).
villeggia'tura [villeddʒa'tura] *sf* holiday(s *pl*) (*BRIT*), vacation (*US*); **luogo di** ~ (holiday) resort.
vil'letta *sf*, **vil'lino** *sm* small house (with a garden), cottage.
vil'loso, a *ag* hairy.
viltà *sf* cowardice *no pl*; (*gesto*) cowardly act.
Vimi'nale *sm vedi nota nel riquadro*.

'**vimine** *sm* wicker; **mobili di ~i** wicker furniture *sg*.
vi'naio *sm* wine merchant.
'**vincere** ['vintʃere] *vt* (*in guerra, al gioco, a una gara*) to defeat, beat; (*premio, guerra, partita*) to win; (*fig*) to overcome, conquer ♦ *vi* to win; ~ **qn in** (*abilità, bellezza*) to surpass sb in.
'**vincita** ['vintʃita] *sf* win; (*denaro vinto*) winnings *pl*.
vinci'tore, 'trice [vintʃi'tore] *sm/f* winner; (*MIL*) victor.
vinco'lante *ag* binding.
vinco'lare *vt* to bind; (*COMM: denaro*) to tie up.
vinco'lato, a *ag*: **deposito** ~ (*COMM*) fixed deposit.
'**vincolo** *sm* (*fig*) bond, tie; (*DIR*) obligation.
vi'nicolo, a *ag* wine *cpd*; **regione ~a** wine-producing area.
vinificazi'one [vinifikat'tsjone] *sf* wine-

making.

'**vino** *sm* wine; ~ **bianco/rosso** white/red wine.

'**vinsi** *etc vb vedi* **vincere**.

'**vinto, a** *pp di* vincere ♦ *ag*: **darla** ~**a a qn** to let sb have his (*o* her) way; **darsi per** ~ to give up, give in.

vi'**ola** *sf* (*BOT*) violet; (*MUS*) viola ♦ *ag, sm inv* (*colore*) purple.

vio'**lare** *vt* (*chiesa*) to desecrate, violate; (*giuramento, legge*) to violate.

violazi'**one** [violat'tsjone] *sf* desecration; violation; ~ **di domicilio** (*DIR*) breaking and entering.

violen'**tare** *vt* to use violence on; (*donna*) to rape.

vio'**lento, a** *ag* violent.

vio'**lenza** [vio'lɛntsa] *sf* violence; ~ **carnale** rape.

vio'**letto, a** *ag, sm* (*colore*) violet ♦ *sf* (*BOT*) violet.

violi'**nista, i, e** *smf* violinist.

vio'**lino** *sm* violin.

violoncel'**lista, i, e** [violontʃel'lista] *smf* cellist, cello player.

violon'**cello** [violon'tʃɛllo] *sm* cello.

vi'**ottolo** *sm* path, track.

VIP *smf inv* (= *Very Important Person*) VIP.

'**vipera** *sf* viper, adder.

vi'**raggio** [vi'raddʒo] *sm* (*NAUT, AER*) turn; (*FOT*) toning.

vi'**rale** *ag* viral.

vi'**rare** *vi* (*NAUT*) to come about; (*AER*) to turn; (*FOT*) to tone; ~ **di bordo** to change course.

vi'**rata** *sf* coming about; turning; change of course.

'**virgola** *sf* (*LING*) comma; (*MAT*) point.

virgo'**lette** *sfpl* inverted commas, quotation marks.

vi'**rile** *ag* (*proprio dell'uomo*) masculine; (*non puerile, da uomo*) manly, virile.

virilità *sf* masculinity; manliness; (*sessuale*) virility.

virtù *sf inv* virtue; **in** *o* **per** ~ **di** by virtue of, by.

virtu'**ale** *ag* virtual.

virtu'**oso, a** *ag* virtuous ♦ *smf* (*MUS etc*) virtuoso.

viru'**lento, a** *ag* virulent.

'**virus** *sm inv* virus.

visa'**gista, i, e** [viza'dʒista] *smf* beautician.

visce'**rale** [viʃʃe'rale] *ag* (*MED*) visceral; (*fig*) profound, deep-rooted.

'**viscere** ['viʃʃere] *sm* (*ANAT*) internal organ ♦ *sfpl* (*di animale*) entrails *pl*; (*fig*) depths *pl*, bowels *pl*.

'**vischio** ['viskjo] *sm* (*BOT*) mistletoe; (*pania*) birdlime.

vischi'**oso, a** [vis'kjoso] *ag* sticky.

visci'**dità** [viʃʃidi'ta] *sf* sliminess.

'**viscido, a** ['viʃʃido] *ag* slimy.

vis'**conte, 'essa** *smf* viscount/viscountess.

visco'**sità** *sf* viscosity.

vis'**coso, a** *ag* viscous.

vi'**sibile** *ag* visible.

visi'**bilio** *sm*: **andare in** ~ to go into raptures.

visibilità *sf* visibility.

visi'**era** *sf* (*di elmo*) visor; (*di berretto*) peak.

visio'**nare** *vt* (*gen*) to look at, examine; (*CINE*) to screen.

visio'**nario, a** *ag, smf* visionary.

visi'**one** *sf* vision; **prendere** ~ **di qc** to examine sth, look sth over; **prima/seconda** ~ (*CINE*) first/second showing.

'**visita** *sf* visit; (*MED*) visit, call; (: *esame*) examination; **far** ~ **a qn, andare in** ~ **da qn** to visit sb, pay sb a visit; **in** ~ **ufficiale in Italia** on an official visit to Italy; **orario di** ~**e** (*ospedale*) visiting hours; ~ **di controllo** (*MED*) checkup; ~ **a domicilio** house call; ~ **guidata** guided tour; ~ **sanitaria** sanitary inspection.

visi'**tare** *vt* to visit; (*MED*) to visit, call on; (: *esaminare*) to examine.

visita'**tore, 'trice** *smf* visitor.

vi'**sivo, a** *ag* visual.

'**viso** *sm* face; **fare buon** ~ **a cattivo gioco** to make the best of things.

vi'**sone** *sm* mink.

vi'**sore** *sm* (*FOT*) viewer.

'**vispo, a** *ag* quick, lively.

'**vissi** *etc vb vedi* **vivere**.

vis'**suto, a** *pp di* vivere ♦ *ag* (*aria, modo di fare*) experienced.

'**vista** *sf* (*facoltà*) (eye)sight; (*fatto di vedere*): **la** ~ **di** the sight of; (*veduta*) view; **con** ~ **sul lago** with a view over the lake; **sparare a** ~ to shoot on sight; **pagabile a** ~ payable on demand; **in** ~ in sight; **avere in** ~ **qc** to have sth in view; **mettersi in** ~ to draw attention to o.s.; (*peg*) to show off; **perdere qn di** ~ to lose sight of sb; (*fig*) to lose touch with sb; **far** ~ **di fare** to pretend to do; **a** ~ **d'occhio** as far as the eye can see; (*fig*) before one's very eyes.

vis'**tare** *vt* to approve; (*AMM: passaporto*) to visa.

'**visto, a** *pp di* vedere ♦ *sm* visa; ~ **che** *cong* seeing (that); ~ **d'ingresso/di transito** entry/transit visa; ~ **permanente/di soggiorno** permanent/tourist visa.

vis'**toso, a** *ag* gaudy, garish; (*ingente*) considerable.

visu'**ale** *ag* visual.

visualiz'zare [vizualid'dzare] *vt* to visualize.
visualizza'tore [vizualiddza'tore] *sm*
(*INFORM*) visual display unit, VDU.
visualizzazi'one [vizualiddzat'tsjone] *sf*
(*INFORM*) display.
'vita *sf* life; (*ANAT*) waist; **essere in** ~ to be
alive; **pieno di** ~ full of life; **a** ~ for life;
membro a ~ life member.
vi'tale *ag* vital.
vitalità *sf* vitality.
vita'lizio, a [vita'littsjo] *ag* life *cpd* ♦ *sm* life
annuity.
vita'mina *sf* vitamin.
'vite *sf* (*BOT*) vine; (*TECN*) screw; **giro di** ~
(*anche fig*) turn of the screw.
vi'tello *sm* (*ZOOL*) calf; (*carne*) veal; (*pelle*)
calfskin.
vi'ticcio [vi'tittʃo] *sm* (*BOT*) tendril.
viticol'tore *sm* wine grower.
viticol'tura *sf* wine growing.
'vitreo, a *ag* vitreous; (*occhio, sguardo*)
glassy.
'vittima *sf* victim.
vitti'mismo *sm* self-pity.
'vitto *sm* food; (*in un albergo etc*) board; ~ **e
alloggio** board and lodging.
vit'toria *sf* victory.
vittori'ano, a *ag* Victorian.
vittori'oso, a *ag* victorious.
vitupe'rare *vt* to rail at *o* against.
vi'uzza [vi'uttsa] *sf* (*in città*) alley.
'viva *escl*: ~ **il re!** long live the king!
vivacchi'are [vivak'kjare] *vi* to scrape a
living.
vi'vace [vi'vatʃe] *ag* (*vivo, animato*) lively;
(*: mente*) lively, sharp; (*colore*) bright.
vivacità [vivatʃi'ta] *sf* liveliness;
brightness.
vivaciz'zare [vivatʃid'dzare] *vt* to liven up.
vi'vaio *sm* (*di pesci*) hatchery; (*AGR*)
nursery.
viva'mente *av* (*commuoversi*) deeply,
profoundly; (*ringraziare etc*) sincerely,
warmly.
vi'vanda *sf* food; (*piatto*) dish.
viva'voce [viva'votʃe] *sm inv* (*dispositivo*)
loudspeaker ♦ *ag inv*: **telefono** ~
speakerphone; **mettere in** ~ to switch on
the loudspeaker.
vi'vente *ag* living, alive; **i** ~**i** the living.
'vivere *vi* to live ♦ *vt* to live; (*passare: brutto
momento*) to live through, go through;
(*sentire: gioie, pene di qn*) to share ♦ ~ **la
vita** life; (*anche*: **modo di** ~) way of life; ~**i** *smpl*
food *sg*, provisions; ~ **di** to live on.
vi'veur [vi'vœr] *sm inv* pleasure-seeker.
'vivido, a *ag* (*colore*) vivid, bright.
vivifi'care *vt* to enliven, give life to; (*piante
etc*) to revive.
vivisezi'one [viviset'tsjone] *sf* vivisection.
'vivo, a *ag* (*vivente*) alive, living; (*fig*)
lively; (*: colore*) bright, brilliant ♦ *sm*:
entrare nel ~ **di una questione** to get to
the heart of a matter; **i** ~**i** the living;
esperimenti su animali ~**i** experiments on
live *o* living animals; ~ **e vegeto** hale and
hearty; **farsi** ~ (*fig*) to show one's face; to
keep in touch; **con** ~ **rammarico** with
deep regret; **congratulazioni vivissime**
heartiest congratulations; **con i più** ~**i**
ringraziamenti with deepest *o* warmest
thanks; **ritrarre dal** ~ to paint from life;
pungere qn nel ~ (*fig*) to cut sb to the
quick.
vivrò *etc vb vedi* **vivere**.
vizi'are [vit'tsjare] *vt* (*bambino*) to spoil;
(*corrompere moralmente*) to corrupt; (*DIR*)
to invalidate.
vizi'ato, a [vit'tsjato] *ag* spoilt; (*aria, acqua*)
polluted; (*DIR*) invalid, invalidated.
'vizio ['vittsjo] *sm* (*morale*) vice; (*cattiva
abitudine*) bad habit; (*imperfezione*) flaw,
defect; (*errore*) fault, mistake; ~ **di forma**
legal flaw *o* irregularity; ~ **procedurale**
procedural error.
vizi'oso, a [vit'tsjoso] *ag* depraved;
(*inesatto*) incorrect; **circolo** ~ vicious
circle.
V.le *abbr* = **viale**.
vocabo'lario *sm* (*dizionario*) dictionary;
(*lessico*) vocabulary.
vo'cabolo *sm* word.
vo'cale *ag* vocal ♦ *sf* vowel.
vocazi'one [vokat'tsjone] *sf* vocation; (*fig*)
natural bent.
'voce ['votʃe] *sf* voice; (*diceria*) rumour
(*BRIT*), rumor (*US*); (*di un elenco, in
bilancio*) item; (*di dizionario*) entry; **parlare
a alta/bassa** ~ to speak in a loud/low *o*
soft voice; **fare la** ~ **grossa** to raise one's
voice; **dar** ~ **a qc** to voice sth, give voice
to sth; **a gran** ~ in a loud voice, loudly; **te
lo dico a** ~ I'll tell you when I see you; **a
una** ~ unanimously; **aver** ~ **in capitolo**
(*fig*) to have a say in the matter; ~**i di
corridoio** rumours.
voci'are [vo'tʃare] *vi* to shout, yell.
vocife'rante [votʃife'rante] *ag* noisy.
vo'cio [vo'tʃio] *sm* shouting.
'vodka *sf inv* vodka.
'voga *sf* (*NAUT*) rowing; (*usanza*): **essere in**
~ to be in fashion *o* in vogue.
vo'gare *vi* to row.
voga'tore, 'trice *sm/f* oarsman/woman
♦ *sm* rowing machine.
vogherò *etc* [voge'rɔ] *vb vedi* **vogare**.

'**voglia** ['vɔʎʎa] *sf* desire, wish; (*macchia*) birthmark; **aver ~ di qc/di fare** to feel like sth/like doing; (*più forte*) to want sth/to do; **di buona ~** willingly.

'**voglio** *etc* ['vɔʎʎo] *vb vedi* **volere**.

vogli'oso, a [voʎ'ʎoso] *ag* (*sguardo etc*) longing; (*più forte*) full of desire.

'**voi** *pron* you; **~ stessi(e)** you yourselves.

voi'altri *pron* you.

vol. *abbr* (= *volume*) vol.

vo'lano *sm* (SPORT) shuttlecock; (TECN) flywheel.

vo'lant [vɔ'lã] *sm inv* frill.

vo'lante *ag* flying ♦ *sm* (steering) wheel ♦ *sf* (POLIZIA: *anche*: **squadra ~**) flying squad.

volanti'naggio [volanti'naddʒo] *sm* leafleting.

volanti'nare *vt* (*distribuire volantini*) to leaflet, hand out leaflets.

volan'tino *sm* leaflet.

vo'lare *vi* (*uccello, aereo, fig*) to fly; (*cappello*) to blow away *o* off, fly away *o* off; **~ via** to fly away *o* off.

vo'lata *sf* flight; (*d'uccelli*) flock, flight; (*corsa*) rush; (SPORT) final sprint; **passare di ~ da qn** to drop in on sb briefly.

vo'latile *ag* (CHIM) volatile ♦ *sm* (ZOOL) bird.

volatiliz'zarsi [volatilid'dzarsi] *vr* (CHIM) to volatilize; (*fig*) to vanish, disappear.

vo'lente *ag*: **verrai ~ o nolente** you'll come whether you like it or not.

volente'roso, a *ag* willing, keen.

volenti'eri *av* willingly; "**~**" "with pleasure", "I'd be glad to".

vo'lere *sm* will, wish(es); **contro il ~ di** against the wishes of; **per ~ di qn** in obedience to sb's will *o* wishes
♦ *vt* **1** (*esigere, desiderare*) to want; **~ fare qc** to want to do sth; **~ che qn faccia qc** to want sb to do sth; **vorrei andarmene** I'd like to go; **vorrei che se ne andasse** I'd like him to go; **vorrei quello lì!** I'd like that one; **volevo parlartene** I meant to talk to you about it; **come vuoi** as you like; **la vogliono al telefono** there's a call for you; **che tu lo voglia o no** whether you like it or not; **vuoi un caffè?** would you like a coffee?; **senza ~** (*inavvertitamente*) without meaning to, unintentionally; **te la sei voluta** you asked for it; **la tradizione vuole che ...** custom requires that ...; **la leggenda vuole che ...** legend has it that ...

2 (*consentire*): **vogliate attendere, per piacere** please wait; **vogliamo andare?** shall we go?; **vuole essere così gentile da ...?** would you be so kind as to ...?; **non ha voluto ricevermi** he wouldn't see me

3: **volerci** (*essere necessario: materiale, attenzione*) to be needed; (: *tempo*) to take; **quanta farina ci vuole per questa torta?** how much flour do you need for this cake?; **ci vuole un'ora per arrivare a Venezia** it takes an hour to get to Venice; **è quel che ci vuole** it's just what is needed

4: **voler bene a qn** (*amore*) to love sb; (*affetto*) to be fond of sb, like sb very much; **voler male a qn** to dislike sb; **volerne a qn** to bear sb a grudge; **voler dire** to mean; **voglio dire ...** I mean ...; **volevo ben dire!** I thought as much!

vol'gare *ag* vulgar.

volgarità *sf* vulgarity.

volgariz'zare [volgarid'dzare] *vt* to popularize.

volgar'mente *av* (*in modo volgare*) vulgarly, coarsely; (*del popolo*) commonly, popularly.

'**volgere** ['vɔldʒere] *vt* to turn ♦ *vi* to turn; (*tendere*): **~ a**: **il tempo volge al brutto/al bello** the weather is breaking/is setting fair; **un rosso che volge al viola** a red verging on purple; **~rsi** *vr* to turn; **~ al peggio** to take a turn for the worse; **~ al termine** to draw to an end.

'**volgo** *sm* common people.

voli'era *sf* aviary.

voli'tivo, a *ag* strong-willed.

'**volli** *etc vb vedi* **volere**.

'**volo** *sm* flight; **ci sono due ore di ~ da Londra a Milano** it's a two-hour flight between London and Milan; **al ~**: **colpire qc al ~** to hit sth as it flies past; **prendere al ~** (*autobus, treno*) to catch at the last possible moment; (*palla*) to catch as it flies past; (*occasione*) to seize; **capire al ~** to understand straight away; **veduta a ~ d'uccello** bird's-eye view; **~ di linea** scheduled flight.

volontà *sf inv* will; **a ~** (*mangiare, bere*) as much as one likes; **buona/cattiva ~** goodwill/lack of goodwill; **le sue ultime ~** (*testamento*) his last will and testament *sg*.

volontaria'mente *av* voluntarily.

volontari'ato *sm* (MIL) voluntary service; (*lavoro*) voluntary work.

volon'tario, a *ag* voluntary ♦ *sm* (MIL) volunteer.

'**volpe** *sf* fox.

vol'pino, a *ag* (*pelo, coda*) fox's; (*aspetto, astuzia*) fox-like ♦ *sm* (*cane*) Pomeranian.

vol'pone, a *sm/f* (*fig*) old fox.

'**volsi** *etc vb vedi* **volgere**.

volt *sm inv* (*ELETTR*) volt.

'volta *sf* (*momento, circostanza*) time; (*turno, giro*) turn; (*curva*) turn, bend; (*ARCHIT*) vault; (*direzione*): **partire alla ~ di** to set off for; **a mia** (*o* **tua** *etc*) **~** in turn; **una ~** once; **una ~ sola** only once; **c'era una ~** once upon a time there was; **le cose di una ~** the things of the past; **due ~e** twice; **tre ~e** three times; **una cosa per ~** one thing at a time; **una ~ o l'altra** one of these days; **una ~ per tutte** once and for all; **una ~ tanto** just for once; **lo facciamo un'altra ~** we'll do it another time *o* some other time; **a ~e** at times, sometimes; **di ~ in ~** from time to time; **una ~ che** (*temporale*) once; (*causale*) since; **3 ~e 4** times 4; **ti ha dato di ~ il cervello?** have you gone out of your mind?

volta'faccia [volta'fattʃa] *sm inv* (*fig*) volte-face.

vol'taggio [vol'taddʒo] *sm* (*ELETTR*) voltage.

vol'tare *vt* to turn; (*girare: moneta*) to turn over; (*rigirare*) to turn round ♦ *vi* to turn; **~rsi** *vr* to turn; to turn over; to turn round.

voltas'tomaco *sm* nausea; (*fig*) disgust.

volteggi'are [volted'dʒare] *vi* (*volare*) to circle; (*in equitazione*) to do trick riding; (*in ginnastica*) to vault.

'volto, a *pp di* **volgere** ♦ *ag* (*inteso a*): **il mio discorso è ~ a spiegare ...** in my speech I intend to explain ... ♦ *sm* face.

vo'lubile *ag* changeable, fickle.

vo'lume *sm* volume.

volumi'noso, a *ag* voluminous, bulky.

vo'luta *sf* (*gen*) spiral; (*ARCHIT*) volute.

voluttà *sf* sensual pleasure *o* delight.

voluttu'oso, a *ag* voluptuous.

vomi'tare *vt, vi* to vomit.

'vomito *sm* vomit; **ho il ~** I feel sick.

'vongola *sf* clam.

vo'race [vo'ratʃe] *ag* voracious, greedy.

voracità [voratʃi'ta] *sf* voracity, voraciousness.

vo'ragine [vo'radʒine] *sf* abyss, chasm.

vorrò *etc vb vedi* **volere**.

'vortice ['vortitʃe] *sm* whirl, vortex; (*fig*) whirl.

vorti'coso, a *ag* whirling.

'vostro, a *det*: **il(la) ~(a)** *etc* your ♦ *pron*: **il(la) ~(a)** *etc* yours ♦ *sm*: **avete speso del ~?** did you spend your own money? ♦ *sf*: **la ~a** (*opinione*) your view; **i ~i** (*famiglia*) your family; **un ~ amico** a friend of yours; **è dei ~i, è dalla ~a** he's on your side; **l'ultima ~a** (*COMM: lettera*) your most recent letter; **alla ~a!** (*brindisi*) here's to you!, your health!

vo'tante *sm/f* voter.

vo'tare *vi* to vote ♦ *vt* (*sottoporre a votazione*) to take a vote on; (*approvare*) to vote for; (*REL*): **~ qc a** to dedicate sth to; **~rsi** *vr* to devote o.s. to.

votazi'one [votat'tsjone] *sf* vote, voting; **~i** *sfpl* (*POL*) votes; (*INS*) marks.

'voto *sm* (*POL*) vote; (*INS*) mark (*BRIT*), grade (*US*); (*REL*) vow; (*: offerta*) votive offering; **aver ~i belli/brutti** (*INS*) to get good/bad marks *o* grades; **prendere i ~i** to take one's vows; **~ di fiducia** vote of confidence.

V.P. *abbr* (= *vicepresidente*) VP.

VR *sigla* = **Verona**.

v.r. *abbr* (= *vedi retro*) PTO.

vs. *abbr* (= *vostro*) yr.

v.s. *abbr* = *vedi sopra*.

VT *sigla* = **Viterbo**.

V.U. *abbr* = **vigile urbano**.

vul'canico, a, ci, che *ag* volcanic.

vulcanizzazi'one [vulkaniddzat'tsjone] *sf* vulcanization.

vul'cano *sm* volcano.

vulne'rabile *ag* vulnerable.

vulnerabilità *sf* vulnerability.

vu'oi, vu'ole *vb vedi* **volere**.

vuo'tare *vt*, **~rsi** *vr* to empty.

vu'oto, a *ag* empty; (*fig: privo*): **~ di** (*senso etc*) devoid of ♦ *sm* empty space, gap; (*spazio in bianco*) blank; (*FISICA*) vacuum; (*fig: mancanza*) gap, void; **a mani ~e** empty-handed; **assegno a ~** dud cheque (*BRIT*), bad check (*US*); **~ d'aria** air pocket; **"~ a perdere"** "no deposit"; **"~ a rendere"** "returnable bottle".

W w

W, w ['dɔppjovu] *sf o m inv* (*lettera*) W, w; **W come Washington** ≈ W for William.

W *abbr* = **viva, evviva**.

'wafer ['vafer] *sm inv* (*CUC, ELETTR*) wafer.

wagon-'lit [vagɔ̃'li] *sm inv* (*FERR*) sleeping car.

'walkman ® ['wɔːkmən] *sm inv* Walkman ®.

'water 'closet ['wɔːtə'klɔzɪt] *sm inv* toilet, lavatory.

watt [vat] *sm inv* (*ELETTR*) watt.

wat'tora [vat'tora] *sm inv* (*ELETTR*) watt-hour.

WC *sm inv* WC.
web [ueb] *sm*: **il** ~ **the Web**; **cercare nel** ~ **to**
  search the Web ◆ *ag inv*: **pagina** ~
  webpage.
'weekend ['wiːkɛnd] *sm inv* weekend.
'western ['wɛstərn] *ag* (*CINE*) cowboy *cpd*
  ◆ *sm inv* western, cowboy film; ~
  all'italiana spaghetti western.
'whisky ['wiski] *sm inv* whisky.
'windsurf ['windsəːf] *sm inv* (*tavola*)
  windsurfer, sailboard; (*sport*)
  windsurfing.
'würstel ['vyrstəl] *sm inv* frankfurter.

X x

X, x [iks] *sf o m inv* (*lettera*) X, x; **X come**
  Xeres ≈ X for Xmas.
xenofo'bia [ksenofo'bia] *sf* xenophobia.
xe'nofobo, a [kse'nɔfobo] *ag* xenophobic
  ◆ *sm/f* xenophobe.
'xeres ['ksɛres] *sm inv* (*vino*) sherry.
xero'copia [ksero'kɔpja] *sf* xerox ®,
  photocopy.
xerocopi'are [kseroko'pjare] *vt* to
  photocopy.
xi'lofono [ksi'lɔfono] *sm* xylophone.

Y y

Y, y ['ipsilon] *sf o m inv* (*lettera*) Y, y; **Y come**
  Yacht ≈ Y for Yellow (*BRIT*), Y for Yoke
  (*US*).
yacht [jɔt] *sm inv* yacht.
'yankee ['jæŋki] *sm/f inv* Yank, Yankee.
Y.C.I. *abbr* = Yacht Club d'Italia.
'Yemen ['jemen] *sm*: **lo** ~ Yemen.
yen [jen] *sm inv* (*moneta*) yen.
'yiddish ['jidiʃ] *ag inv, sm inv* Yiddish.
'yoga ['jɔga] *ag inv, sm* yoga (*cpd*).
yogurt ['jɔgurt] *sm inv* yog(h)urt.

Z z

Z, z ['dzɛta] *sf o m inv* (*lettera*) Z, z; **Z come**
  Zara ≈ Z for Zebra.
zabai'one [dzaba'jone] *sm dessert made of*
  egg yolks, sugar and marsala.
zaf'fata [tsaf'fata] *sf* (*tanfo*) stench.
zaffe'rano [dzaffe'rano] *sm* saffron.
zaf'firo [dzaf'firo] *sm* sapphire.
'zagara ['dzagara] *sf* orange blossom.
'zaino ['dzaino] *sm* rucksack.
Za'ire [dza'ire] *sm*: **lo** ~ Zaire.
'Zambia ['dzambja] *sm*: **lo** ~ Zambia.
'zampa ['tsampa] *sf* (*di animale: gamba*) leg;
  (*: piede*) paw; **a quattro** ~**e** on all fours;
  ~**e di gallina** (*calligrafia*) scrawl; (*rughe*)
  crow's feet.
zam'pata [tsam'pata] *sf* (*di cane, gatto*) blow
  with a paw.
zampet'tare [tsampet'tare] *vi* to scamper.
zampil'lare [tsampil'lare] *vi* to gush, spurt.
zam'pillo [tsam'pillo] *sm* gush, spurt.
zam'pino [tsam'pino] *sm* paw; **qui c'è sotto**
  il suo ~ (*fig*) he's had a hand in this.
zam'pogna [tsam'poɲɲa] *sf instrument*
  similar to bagpipes.
'zanna ['tsanna] *sf* (*di elefante*) tusk; (*di*
  carnivori) fang.
zan'zara [dzan'dzara] *sf* mosquito.
zanzari'era [dzandza'rjɛra] *sf* mosquito net.
'zappa ['tsappa] *sf* hoe.
zap'pare [tsap'pare] *vt* to hoe.
zappa'tura [tsappa'tura] *sf* (*AGR*) hoeing.
'zapping ['tsapiŋ] *sm* (*TV*) channel-hopping.
zar, za'rina [tsar, tsa'rina] *sm/f* tsar/tsarina.
'zattera ['dzattera] *sf* raft.
za'vorra [dza'vorra] *sf* ballast.
'zazzera ['tsattsera] *sf* shock of hair.
'zebra ['dzɛbra] *sf* zebra; ~**e** *sfpl* (*AUT*) zebra
  crossing *sg* (*BRIT*), crosswalk *sg* (*US*).
ze'brato, a [dze'brato] *ag* with black and
  white stripes; **strisce** ~**e, attraversamento**
  ~ (*AUT*) zebra crossing (*BRIT*), crosswalk
  (*US*).
'zecca, che ['tsekka] *sf* (*ZOOL*) tick; (*officina*
  di monete) mint.
zec'chino [tsek'kino] *sm* gold coin; **oro** ~
  pure gold.
ze'lante [dze'lante] *ag* zealous.
'zelo ['dzɛlo] *sm* zeal.

'zenit ['dzɛnit] *sm* zenith.

'zenzero ['dzendzero] *sm* ginger.

'zeppa ['tseppa] *sf* wedge.

'zeppo, a ['tseppo] *ag*: ~ **di** crammed *o* packed with.

zer'bino [dzer'bino] *sm* doormat.

'zero ['dzero] *sm* zero, nought; **vincere per tre a** ~ (*SPORT*) to win three-nil.

'zeta ['dzeta] *sm o f* zed, (the letter) z.

'zia ['tsia] *sf* aunt.

zibel'lino [dzibel'lino] *sm* sable.

zi'gano, a [tsi'gano] *ag, sm/f* gypsy.

'zigomo ['dzigomo] *sm* cheekbone.

zigri'nare [dzigri'nare] *vt* (*gen*) to knurl; (*pellame*) to grain; (*monete*) to mill.

zig'zag [dzig'dzag] *sm inv* zigzag; **andare a** ~ to zigzag.

Zim'babwe [tsim'babwe] *sm*: **lo** ~ Zimbabwe.

zim'bello [dzim'bɛllo] *sm* (*oggetto di burle*) laughing-stock.

'zinco ['dzinko] *sm* zinc.

zinga'resco, a, schi, sche [dzinga'resko] *ag* gypsy *cpd*.

'zingaro, a ['dzingaro] *sm/f* gipsy.

'zio ['tsio], *pl* **'zii** *sm* uncle; **zii** *smpl* (*zio e zia*) uncle and aunt.

zip'pare [dzip'pare] *vt* (*INFORM*) to zip.

zi'tella [dzi'tɛlla] *sf* spinster; (*peg*) old maid.

zit'tire [tsit'tire] *vt* to silence, hush *o* shut up ♦ *vi* to hiss.

'zitto, a ['tsitto] *ag* quiet, silent; **sta'** ~! be quiet!

ziz'zania [dzid'dzanja] *sf* (*BOT*) darnel; (*fig*) discord; **gettare** *o* **seminare** ~ to sow discord.

'zoccolo ['tsɔkkolo] *sm* (*calzatura*) clog; (*di cavallo etc*) hoof; (*ARCHIT*) plinth; (*di parete*) skirting (board); (*di armadio*) base.

zodia'cale [dzodia'kale] *ag* zodiac *cpd*; **segno** ~ sign of the zodiac.

zo'diaco [dzo'diako] *sm* zodiac.

zolfa'nello [tsolfa'nɛllo] *sm* (*sulphur*) match.

'zolfo ['tsolfo] *sm* sulphur (*BRIT*), sulfur (*US*).

'zolla ['dzolla] *sf* clod (of earth).

zol'letta [dzol'letta] *sf* sugar lump.

'zona ['dzɔna] *sf* zone, area; ~ **di depressione** (*METEOR*) trough of low pressure; ~ **erogena** erogenous zone; ~ **pedonale** pedestrian precinct; ~ **verde** (*di abitato*) green area.

'zonzo ['dzondzo]: **a** ~ *av*: **andare a** ~ to wander about, stroll about.

'zoo ['dzɔo] *sm inv* zoo.

zoolo'gia [dzoolo'dʒia] *sf* zoology.

zoo'logico, a, ci, che [dzoo'lɔdʒiko] *ag* zoological.

zo'ologo, a, gi, ghe [dzo'ɔlogo] *sm/f* zoologist.

zoosa'fari [dzoosa'fari] *sm inv* safari park.

zoo'tecnico, a, ci, che [dzoo'tɛkniko] *ag* zootechnical; **il patrimonio** ~ **di un paese** a country's livestock resources.

zoppi'care [tsoppi'kare] *vi* to limp; (*fig: mobile*) to be shaky, rickety.

'zoppo, a ['tsɔppo] *ag* lame; (*fig: mobile*) shaky, rickety.

zoti'cone [dzoti'kone] *sm* lout.

ZTL [dzetati'ɛlle] *sigla f* (= *Zona a Traffico Limitato*) controlled traffic zone.

zu'ava [dzu'ava] *sf*: **pantaloni** *mpl* **alla** ~ knickerbockers.

'zucca, che ['tsukka] *sf* (*BOT*) marrow (*BRIT*), vegetable marrow (*US*); pumpkin; (*scherzoso*) head.

zucche'rare [tsukke'rare] *vt* to put sugar in.

zucche'rato, a [tsukke'rato] *ag* sweet, sweetened.

zuccheri'era [tsukke'rjera] *sf* sugar bowl.

zuccheri'ficio [tsukkeri'fitʃo] *sm* sugar refinery.

zucche'rino, a [tsukke'rino] *ag* sugary, sweet.

'zucchero ['tsukkero] *sm* sugar; ~ **di canna** cane sugar; ~ **caramellato** caramel; ~ **filato** candy floss, cotton candy (*US*); ~ **a velo** icing sugar (*BRIT*), confectioner's sugar (*US*).

zucche'roso, a [tsukke'roso] *ag* sugary.

zuc'china [tsuk'kina] *sf*, **zuc'chino** [tsuk'kino] *sm* courgette (*BRIT*), zucchini (*US*).

zuc'cotto [tsuk'kɔtto] *sm* ice-cream sponge.

'zuffa ['tsuffa] *sf* brawl.

zufo'lare [tsufo'lare] *vt, vi* to whistle.

'zufolo ['tsufolo] *sm* (*MUS*) flageolet.

'zuppa ['tsuppa] *sf* soup; (*fig*) mixture, muddle; ~ **inglese** (*CUC*) *dessert made with sponge cake, custard and chocolate*, ≈ trifle (*BRIT*).

zuppi'era [tsup'pjɛra] *sf* soup tureen.

'zuppo, a ['tsuppo] *ag*: ~ **(di)** drenched (with), soaked (with).

Zu'rigo [dzu'rigo] *sf* Zurich.

English-Italian
Inglese-Italiano

A a

A, a [eɪ] n (letter) A, a for m inv; (SCOL: mark)
≈ 10 (ottimo); (MUS): **A** la m; **A for Andrew**,
(US) **A for Able** ≈ A come Ancona;
from A to Z dall'A alla Z; **A road** n (BRIT
AUT) ≈ strada statale; **A shares** npl (BRIT
STOCK EXCHANGE) azioni fpl senza diritto
di voto; **A to Z** ® n stradario.

===================== KEYWORD

a [ə] (before vowel or silent h: **an**) indef art **1**
un (uno +s impure, gn, pn, ps, x, z), f una
(un' +vowel); ~ **book** un libro; ~ **mirror**
uno specchio; **an apple** una mela; **she's** ~
doctor è medico
2 (instead of the number "one") un(o), f
una; ~ **year ago** un anno fa; ~ **hundred/
thousand pounds** cento/mille sterline
3 (in expressing ratios, prices etc) a, per; **3**
~ **day/week** 3 al giorno/alla settimana; **10
km an hour** 10 km all'ora; **£5** ~ **person** 5
sterline a persona or per persona.

AA n abbr (BRIT: = Automobile Association)
≈ A.C.I. m (= Automobile Club d'Italia);
(US: = Associate in Art) titolo di studio;
(= Alcoholics Anonymous) A.A. f
(= Anonima Alcolisti); (MIL) = **anti-aircraft**.
AAA n abbr (= American Automobile
Association) ≈ A.C.I. m (= Automobile
Club d'Italia); (BRIT) = Amateur Athletics
Association.
AB abbr (BRIT) see **able-bodied seaman**;
(Canada) = Alberta.
aback [ə'bæk] adv: **to be taken** ~ essere
sbalordito(a).
abacus, pl **abaci** ['æbəkəs, -saɪ] n
pallottoliere m, abaco.
abandon [ə'bændən] vt abbandonare ♦ n

abbandono; **to** ~ **ship** abbandonare la
nave.
abandoned [ə'bændənd] adj (child, house
etc) abbandonato(a); (unrestrained:
manner) disinvolto(a).
abase [ə'beɪs] vt: **to** ~ **o.s. (so far as to do)**
umiliarsi or abbassarsi (al punto di fare).
abashed [ə'bæʃt] adj imbarazzato(a).
abate [ə'beɪt] vi calmarsi.
abatement [ə'beɪtmənt] n (of pollution,
noise) soppressione f, eliminazione f;
noise ~ **society** associazione f per la lotta
contro i rumori.
abattoir ['æbətwɑː*] n (BRIT) mattatoio.
abbey ['æbɪ] n abbazia, badia.
abbot ['æbət] n abate m.
abbreviate [ə'briːvɪeɪt] vt abbreviare.
abbreviation [əbriːvɪ'eɪʃən] n
abbreviazione f.
ABC n abbr (= American Broadcasting
Company) rete televisiva americana.
abdicate ['æbdɪkeɪt] vt abdicare a ♦ vi
abdicare.
abdication [æbdɪ'keɪʃən] n abdicazione f.
abdomen ['æbdəmən] n addome m.
abdominal [æb'dɔmɪnl] adj addominale.
abduct [æb'dʌkt] vt rapire.
abduction [æb'dʌkʃən] n rapimento.
Aberdonian [æbə'dəunɪən] adj di Aberdeen
♦ n abitante m/f di Aberdeen; originario/a
di Aberdeen.
aberration [æbə'reɪʃən] n aberrazione f.
abet [ə'bɛt] vt see **aid**.
abeyance [ə'beɪəns] n: **in** ~ in sospeso.
abhor [əb'hɔː*] vt aborrire.
abhorrent [əb'hɔrənt] adj odioso(a).
abide [ə'baɪd] vt sopportare.
▶**abide by** vt fus conformarsi a.

abiding [ə'baɪdɪŋ] *adj* (*memory etc*) persistente, duraturo(a).

ability [ə'bɪlɪtɪ] *n* abilità *f inv*; **to the best of my ~** con il massimo impegno.

abject ['æbdʒɛkt] *adj* (*poverty*) abietto(a); (*apology*) umiliante; (*coward*) indegno(a), vile.

ablaze [ə'bleɪz] *adj* in fiamme; **~ with light** risplendente di luce.

able ['eɪbl] *adj* capace; **to be ~ to do sth** essere capace di fare qc, poter fare qc.

able-bodied ['eɪbl'bɔdɪd] *adj* robusto(a).

able-bodied seaman (AB) *n* (*BRIT*) marinaio scelto.

ably ['eɪblɪ] *adv* abilmente.

ABM *n abbr* (= *anti-ballistic missile*) ABM *m*.

abnormal [æb'nɔːməl] *adj* anormale.

abnormality [æbnɔː'mælɪtɪ] *n* (*condition*) anormalità; (*instance*) anomalia.

aboard [ə'bɔːd] *adv* a bordo ♦ *prep* a bordo di; **~ the train** in *or* sul treno.

abode [ə'bəud] *n* (*old*) dimora; (*LAW*) domicilio, dimora; **of no fixed ~** senza fissa dimora.

abolish [ə'bɔlɪʃ] *vt* abolire.

abolition [æbəu'lɪʃən] *n* abolizione *f*.

abominable [ə'bɔmɪnəbl] *adj* abominevole.

aborigine [æbə'rɪdʒɪnɪ] *n* aborigeno/a.

abort [ə'bɔːt] *vt* (*MED, fig*) abortire; (*COMPUT*) interrompere l'esecuzione di.

abortion [ə'bɔːʃən] *n* aborto; **to have an ~** avere un aborto, abortire.

abortionist [ə'bɔːʃənɪst] *n* abortista *m/f*.

abortive [ə'bɔːtɪv] *adj* abortivo(a).

abound [ə'baund] *vi* abbondare; **to ~ in** abbondare di.

━━━━━━━━━━━━━━━ *KEYWORD*

about [ə'baut] *adv* **1** (*approximately*) circa, quasi; **~ a hundred/thousand** un centinaio/migliaio, circa cento/mille; **it takes ~ 10 hours** ci vogliono circa 10 ore; **at ~ 2 o'clock** verso le 2; **I've just ~ finished** ho quasi finito; **it's ~ here** è qui intorno, è qui vicino
2 (*referring to place*) qua e là, in giro; **to leave things lying ~** lasciare delle cose in giro; **to run ~** correre qua e là; **to walk ~** camminare; **is Paul ~?** (*BRIT*) hai visto Paul in giro?; **it's the other way ~** (*BRIT*) è il contrario
3: **to be ~ to do sth** stare per fare qc; **I'm not ~ to do all that for nothing** non ho intenzione di fare tutto questo per niente
♦ *prep* **1** (*relating to*) su, di; **a book ~ London** un libro su Londra; **what is it ~?** di che si tratta?; (*book, film etc*) di cosa tratta?; **we talked ~ it** ne abbiamo

parlato; **do something ~ it!** fai qualcosa!; **what or how ~ doing this?** che ne dici di fare questo?
2 (*referring to place*): **to walk ~ the town** camminare per la città; **her clothes were scattered ~ the room** i suoi vestiti erano sparsi *or* in giro per tutta la stanza.

about-face [ə'baut'feɪs] *n*, **about-turn** [ə'baut'təːn] *n* (*MIL*) dietro front *m inv*.

above [ə'bʌv] *adv, prep* sopra; **mentioned ~** suddetto; **costing ~ £10** più caro di 10 sterline; **he's not ~ a bit of blackmail** non rifuggirebbe dal ricatto; **~ all** soprattutto.

aboveboard [ə'bʌv'bɔːd] *adj* aperto(a); onesto(a).

abrasion [ə'breɪʒən] *n* abrasione *f*.

abrasive [ə'breɪzɪv] *adj* abrasivo(a).

abreast [ə'brɛst] *adv* di fianco; **3 ~** per 3 di fronte; **to keep ~ of** tenersi aggiornato su.

abridge [ə'brɪdʒ] *vt* ridurre.

abroad [ə'brɔːd] *adv* all'estero; **there is a rumour ~ that ...** (*fig*) si sente dire in giro che ..., circola la voce che ....

abrupt [ə'brʌpt] *adj* (*steep*) erto(a); (*sudden*) improvviso(a); (*gruff, blunt*) brusco(a).

abscess ['æbsɪs] *n* ascesso.

abscond [əb'skɔnd] *vi* scappare.

absence ['æbsəns] *n* assenza; **in the ~ of** (*person*) in assenza di; (*thing*) in mancanza di.

absent ['æbsənt] *adj* assente; **to be ~ without leave (AWOL)** (*MIL etc*) essere assente ingiustificato.

absentee [æbsən'tiː] *n* assente *m/f*.

absenteeism [æbsən'tiːɪzəm] *n* assenteismo.

absent-minded ['æbsənt'maɪndɪd] *adj* distratto(a).

absent-mindedness ['æbsənt'maɪndɪdnɪs] *n* distrazione *f*.

absolute ['æbsəluːt] *adj* assoluto(a).

absolutely [æbsə'luːtlɪ] *adv* assolutamente.

absolve [əb'zɔlv] *vt*: **to ~ sb (from)** (*sin etc*) assolvere qn (da); **to ~ sb from** (*oath*) sciogliere qn da.

absorb [əb'sɔːb] *vt* assorbire; **to be ~ed in a book** essere immerso(a) in un libro.

absorbent [əb'sɔːbənt] *adj* assorbente.

absorbent cotton *n* (*US*) cotone *m* idrofilo.

absorbing [əb'sɔːbɪŋ] *adj* avvincente, molto interessante.

absorption [əb'sɔːpʃən] *n* assorbimento.

abstain [əb'steɪn] *vi*: **to ~ (from)** astenersi (da).

abstemious [əb'stiːmɪəs] *adj* astemio(a).

abstention [əb'stɛnʃən] *n* astensione *f*.

abstinence ['æbstɪnəns] n astinenza.

abstract ['æbstrækt] adj astratto(a) ♦ n (summary) riassunto ♦ vt [æb'strækt] estrarre.

absurd [əb'sɔːd] adj assurdo(a).

absurdity [əb'sɔːdɪtɪ] n assurdità f inv.

ABTA ['æbtə] n abbr = Association of British Travel Agents.

Abu Dhabi ['æbuː'dɑːbɪ] n Abu Dhabi f.

abundance [ə'bʌndəns] n abbondanza.

abundant [ə'bʌndənt] adj abbondante.

abuse n [ə'bjuːs] abuso; (insults) ingiurie fpl ♦ vt [ə'bjuːz] abusare di; **open to** ~ che si presta ad abusi.

abusive [ə'bjuːsɪv] adj ingiurioso(a).

abysmal [ə'bɪzməl] adj spaventoso(a).

abyss [ə'bɪs] n abisso.

AC n abbr (US) = athletic club.

a/c abbr (BANKING etc: = account, current account) c.

academic [ækə'dɛmɪk] adj accademico(a); (pej: issue) puramente formale ♦ n universitario/a.

academic year n anno accademico.

academy [ə'kædəmɪ] n (learned body) accademia; (school) scuola privata; **military/naval** ~ scuola militare/navale; ~ **of music** conservatorio.

ACAS ['eɪkæs] n abbr (BRIT: = Advisory Conciliation and Arbitration Service) comitato governativo per il miglioramento della contrattazione collettiva.

accede [æk'siːd] vi: **to** ~ **to** (request) accedere a; (throne) ascendere a.

accelerate [æk'sɛləreɪt] vt, vi accelerare.

acceleration [æksɛlə'reɪʃən] n accelerazione f.

accelerator [æk'sɛləreɪtə*] n acceleratore m.

accent ['æksɛnt] n accento.

accentuate [æk'sɛntjueɪt] vt (syllable) accentuare; (need, difference etc) accentuare, mettere in risalto or in evidenza.

accept [ək'sɛpt] vt accettare.

acceptable [ək'sɛptəbl] adj accettabile.

acceptance [ək'sɛptəns] n accettazione f; **to meet with general** ~ incontrare il favore or il consenso generale.

access ['æksɛs] n accesso ♦ vt (COMPUT) accedere a; **to have** ~ **to** avere accesso a; **the burglars gained** ~ **through a window** i ladri sono riusciti a penetrare da or attraverso una finestra.

accessible [æk'sɛsəbl] adj accessibile.

accession [æk'sɛʃən] n (addition) aggiunta; (to library) accessione f, acquisto; (of king)

ascesa or salita al trono.

accessory [æk'sɛsərɪ] n accessorio; **toilet accessories** npl (BRIT) articoli mpl da toilette.

access road n strada d'accesso; (to motorway) raccordo di entrata.

access time n (COMPUT) tempo di accesso.

accident ['æksɪdənt] n incidente m; (chance) caso; **to meet with** or **to have an** ~ avere un incidente; **~s at work** infortuni mpl sul lavoro; **by** ~ per caso.

accidental [æksɪ'dɛntl] adj accidentale.

accidentally [æksɪ'dɛntəlɪ] adv per caso.

accident insurance n assicurazione f contro gli infortuni.

accident-prone ['æksɪdənt'prəun] adj: **he's very** ~ è un vero passaguai.

acclaim [ə'kleɪm] vt acclamare ♦ n acclamazione f.

acclamation [æklə'meɪʃən] n (approval) acclamazione f; (applause) applauso.

acclimatize [ə'klaɪmətaɪz], (US) **acclimate** [ə'klaɪmeɪt] vt: **to become** ~**d** acclimatarsi.

accolade ['ækəleɪd] n encomio.

accommodate [ə'kɔmədeɪt] vt alloggiare; (oblige, help) favorire; **this car** ~**s 4 people comfortably** quest'auto può trasportare comodamente 4 persone.

accommodating [ə'kɔmədeɪtɪŋ] adj compiacente.

accommodation, (US) **accommodations** [əkɔmə'deɪʃən(z)] n(pl) alloggio; **seating** ~ (BRIT) posti a sedere; **"~ to let"** (BRIT) "camere in affitto"; **have you any** ~? avete posto?

accompaniment [ə'kʌmpənɪmənt] n accompagnamento.

accompanist [ə'kʌmpənɪst] n (MUS) accompagnatore/trice.

accompany [ə'kʌmpənɪ] vt accompagnare.

accomplice [ə'kʌmplɪs] n complice m/f.

accomplish [ə'kʌmplɪʃ] vt compiere; (achieve) ottenere.

accomplished [ə'kʌmplɪʃt] adj (person) esperto(a).

accomplishment [ə'kʌmplɪʃmənt] n compimento; (thing achieved) risultato; ~**s** npl (skills) doti fpl.

accord [ə'kɔːd] n accordo ♦ vt accordare; **of his own** ~ di propria iniziativa; **with one** ~ all'unanimità, di comune accordo.

accordance [ə'kɔːdəns] n: **in** ~ **with** in conformità con.

according [ə'kɔːdɪŋ]: ~ **to** prep secondo; **it went** ~ **to plan** è andata secondo il previsto.

accordingly [ə'kɔːdɪŋlɪ] adv in conformità.

accordion [ə'kɔːdɪən] n fisarmonica.

accost [ə'kɔst] _vt_ avvicinare.

account [ə'kaunt] _n_ (_COMM_) conto; (_report_) descrizione _f_; ~**s** _npl_ (_COMM_) conti; "_~ payee only_" (_BRIT_) "assegno non trasferibile"; **to keep an ~ of** tenere nota di; **to bring sb to ~ for sth/for having done sth** chiedere a qn di render conto di qc/per aver fatto qc; **by all ~s** a quanto si dice; **of little ~** di poca importanza; **on ~** in acconto; **to buy sth on ~** comprare qc a credito; **on no ~** per nessun motivo; **on ~ of** a causa di; **to take into ~**, **take ~ of** tener conto di.

▶**account for** _vt fus_ (_explain_) spiegare; giustificare; **all the children were ~ed for** nessun bambino mancava all'appello.

accountability [ə'kauntə'bɪlɪtɪ] _n_ responsabilità.

accountable [ə'kauntəbl] _adj_ responsabile; **to be held ~ for sth** dover rispondere di qc.

accountancy [ə'kauntənsɪ] _n_ ragioneria.

accountant [ə'kauntənt] _n_ ragioniere/a.

accounting [ə'kauntɪŋ] _n_ contabilità.

accounting period _n_ esercizio finanziario, periodo contabile.

account number _n_ numero di conto.

account payable _n_ conto passivo.

account receivable _n_ conto da esigere.

accredited [ə'krɛdɪtɪd] _adj_ accreditato(a).

accretion [ə'kriːʃən] _n_ accrescimento.

accrue [ə'kruː] _vi_ (_mount up_) aumentare; **to ~ to** derivare a; **~d charges** ratei _mpl_ passivi; **~d interest** interesse _m_ maturato.

accumulate [ə'kjuːmjuleɪt] _vt_ accumulare ♦ _vi_ accumularsi.

accumulation [əkjuːmju'leɪʃən] _n_ accumulazione _f_.

accuracy ['ækjurəsɪ] _n_ precisione _f_.

accurate ['ækjurɪt] _adj_ preciso(a).

accurately ['ækjurɪtlɪ] _adv_ precisamente.

accusation [ækju'zeɪʃən] _n_ accusa.

accusative [ə'kjuːzətɪv] _n_ (_LING_) accusativo.

accuse [ə'kjuːz] _vt_ accusare.

accused [ə'kjuːzd] _n_ accusato/a.

accuser [ə'kjuːzə*] _n_ accusatore/trice.

accustom [ə'kʌstəm] _vt_ abituare; **to ~ o.s. to sth** abituarsi a qc.

accustomed [ə'kʌstəmd] _adj_ (_usual_) abituale; **~ to** abituato(a) a.

AC/DC _abbr_ (= _alternating current/direct current_) c.a./c.c.

ACE [eɪs] _n abbr_ = _American Council on Education_.

ace [eɪs] _n_ asso; **within an ~ of** (_BRIT_) a un pelo da.

acerbic [ə'səːbɪk] _adj_ (_also fig_) acido(a).

acetate ['æsɪteɪt] _n_ acetato.

ache [eɪk] _n_ male _m_, dolore _m_ ♦ _vi_ (_be sore_) far male, dolere; (_yearn_): **to ~ to do sth** morire dalla voglia di fare qc; **I've got stomach ~** _or_ (_US_) **a stomach ~** ho mal di stomaco; **my head ~s** mi fa male la testa; **I'm aching all over** mi duole dappertutto.

achieve [ə'tʃiːv] _vt_ (_aim_) raggiungere; (_victory_, _success_) ottenere; (_task_) compiere.

achievement [ə'tʃiːvmənt] _n_ compimento; successo.

Achilles heel [ə'kɪliːz-] _n_ tallone _m_ d'Achille.

acid ['æsɪd] _adj_ acido(a) ♦ _n_ acido.

acidity [ə'sɪdɪtɪ] _n_ acidità.

acid rain _n_ pioggia acida.

acid test _n_ (_fig_) prova del fuoco.

acknowledge [ək'nɔlɪdʒ] _vt_ riconoscere; (_letter: also_: ~ **receipt of**) accusare ricevuta di.

acknowledgement [ək'nɔlɪdʒmənt] _n_ riconoscimento; (_of letter_) conferma; ~**s** (_in book_) ringraziamenti _mpl_.

ACLU _n abbr_ (= _American Civil Liberties Union_) _unione americana per le libertà civili_.

acme ['ækmɪ] _n_ culmine _m_, acme _m_.

acne ['æknɪ] _n_ acne _f_.

acorn ['eɪkɔːn] _n_ ghianda.

acoustic [ə'kuːstɪk] _adj_ acustico(a); _see also_ **acoustics**.

acoustic coupler [-'kʌplə*] _n_ (_COMPUT_) accoppiatore _m_ acustico.

acoustics [ə'kuːstɪks] _n_, _npl_ acustica.

acquaint [ə'kweɪnt] _vt_: **to ~ sb with sth** far sapere qc a qn; **to be ~ed with** (_person_) conoscere.

acquaintance [ə'kweɪntəns] _n_ conoscenza; (_person_) conoscente _m/f_; **to make sb's ~** fare la conoscenza di qn.

acquiesce [ækwɪ'ɛs] _vi_ (_agree_): **to ~ (in)** acconsentire (a).

acquire [ə'kwaɪə*] _vt_ acquistare.

acquired [ə'kwaɪəd] _adj_ acquisito(a); **it's an ~ taste** è una cosa che si impara ad apprezzare.

acquisition [ækwɪ'zɪʃən] _n_ acquisto.

acquisitive [ə'kwɪzɪtɪv] _adj_ a cui piace accumulare le cose.

acquit [ə'kwɪt] _vt_ assolvere; **to ~ o.s. well** comportarsi bene.

acquittal [ə'kwɪtl] _n_ assoluzione _f_.

acre ['eɪkə*] _n_ acro (= _4047 m²_).

acreage ['eɪkərɪdʒ] _n_ superficie _f_ in acri.

acrid ['ækrɪd] _adj_ (_smell_) acre, pungente; (_fig_) pungente.

acrimonious [ækrɪ'məʊnɪəs] *adj* astioso(a).

acrobat ['ækrəbæt] *n* acrobata *m/f*.

acrobatic [ækrə'bætɪk] *adj* acrobatico(a).

acrobatics [ækrə'bætɪks] *n* acrobatica ♦ *npl* acrobazie *fpl*.

Acropolis [ə'krɒpəlɪs] *n*: **the ~** l'Acropoli *f*.

across [ə'krɒs] *prep* (*on the other side*) dall'altra parte di; (*crosswise*) attraverso ♦ *adv* dall'altra parte; in larghezza; **to walk ~ (the road)** attraversare (la strada); **to take sb ~ the road** far attraversare la strada a qn; **~ from** di fronte a; **the lake is 12 km ~** il lago ha una larghezza di 12 km *or* è largo 12 km; **to get sth ~ to sb** (*fig*) far capire qc a qn.

acrylic [ə'krɪlɪk] *adj* acrilico(a) ♦ *n* acrilico.

ACT ® *n abbr* (= *American College Test*) *esame di ammissione a college.*

act [ækt] *n* atto; (*in music-hall etc*) numero; (*LAW*) decreto ♦ *vi* agire; (*THEAT*) recitare; (*pretend*) fingere ♦ *vt* (*part*) recitare; **to catch sb in the ~** cogliere qn in flagrante *or* sul fatto; **it's only an ~** è tutta scena, è solo una messinscena; **~ of God** (*LAW*) calamità *f inv* naturale; **to ~ Hamlet** (*BRIT*) recitare la parte di Amleto; **to ~ the fool** (*BRIT*) fare lo stupido; **to ~ as** agire da; **it ~s as a deterrent** serve da deterrente; **~ing in my capacity as chairman, I …** in qualità di presidente, io ….

▶**act on** *vt*: **to ~ on sth** agire in base a qc.

▶**act out** *vt* (*event*) ricostruire; (*fantasies*) dare forma concreta a.

acting ['æktɪŋ] *adj* che fa le funzioni di ♦ *n* (*of actor*) recitazione *f*; (*activity*): **to do some ~** fare del teatro (*or* del cinema); **he is the ~ manager** fa le veci del direttore.

action ['ækʃən] *n* azione *f*; (*MIL*) combattimento; (*LAW*) processo; **to take ~** agire; **to put a plan into ~** realizzare un piano; **out of ~** fuori combattimento; (*machine etc*) fuori servizio; **killed in ~** (*MIL*) ucciso in combattimento; **to bring an ~ against sb** (*LAW*) intentare causa contro qn.

action replay *n* (*BRIT TV*) replay *m inv*.

activate ['æktɪveɪt] *vt* (*mechanism*) fare funzionare; (*CHEM, PHYSICS*) rendere attivo(a).

active ['æktɪv] *adj* attivo(a); **to play an ~ part in** partecipare attivamente a.

active duty (AD) *n* (*US MIL*) = **active service**.

actively ['æktɪvlɪ] *adv* attivamente.

active partner *n* (*COMM*) socio effettivo.

active service *n* (*BRIT MIL*): **to be on ~** prestar servizio in zona di operazioni.

activist ['æktɪvɪst] *n* attivista *m/f*.

activity [æk'tɪvɪtɪ] *n* attività *f inv*.

activity holiday *n* vacanza attiva (*in bici, a cavallo, in barca a vela ecc.*).

actor ['æktə*] *n* attore *m*.

actress ['æktrɪs] *n* attrice *f*.

actual ['æktjuəl] *adj* reale, vero(a).

actually ['æktjuəlɪ] *adv* veramente; (*even*) addirittura.

actuary ['æktjuərɪ] *n* attuario/a.

actuate ['æktjueɪt] *vt* attivare.

acuity [ə'kjuːɪtɪ] *n* acutezza.

acumen ['ækjumən] *n* acume *m*; **business ~** fiuto negli affari.

acupuncture ['ækjupʌŋktʃə*] *n* agopuntura.

AD *adv abbr* (= *Anno Domini*) d. C. ♦ *n abbr* (*US MIL*) *see* **active duty**.

ad [æd] *n abbr* = **advertisement**.

adamant ['ædəmənt] *adj* irremovibile.

Adam's apple ['ædəmz-] *n* pomo di Adamo.

adapt [ə'dæpt] *vt* adattare ♦ *vi*: **to ~ (to)** adattarsi (a).

adaptability [ədæptə'bɪlɪtɪ] *n* adattabilità.

adaptable [ə'dæptəbl] *adj* (*device*) adattabile; (*person*) che sa adattarsi.

adaptation [ædæp'teɪʃən] *n* adattamento.

adapter, adaptor [ə'dæptə*] *n* (*ELEC*) adattatore *m*.

ADC *n abbr* (*MIL*) = **aide-de-camp**; (*US*: = *Aid to Dependent Children*) *sussidio per figli a carico.*

add [æd] *vt* aggiungere; (*figures*) addizionare ♦ *vi*: **to ~ to** (*increase*) aumentare.

▶**add on** *vt* aggiungere.

▶**add up** *vt* (*figures*) addizionare ♦ *vi* (*fig*): **it doesn't ~ up** non ha senso; **it doesn't ~ up to much** non è un granché.

adder ['ædə*] *n* vipera.

addict ['ædɪkt] *n* tossicomane *m/f*; (*fig*) fanatico/a; **heroin ~** eroinomane *m/f*; **drug ~** tossicodipendente *m/f*, tossicomane *m/f*.

addicted [ə'dɪktɪd] *adj*: **to be ~ to** (*drink etc*) essere dedito(a) a; (*fig: football etc*) essere tifoso(a) di.

addiction [ə'dɪkʃən] *n* (*MED*) tossicomania.

adding machine ['ædɪŋ-] *n* addizionatrice *f*.

addition [ə'dɪʃən] *n* addizione *f*; **in ~** inoltre; **in ~ to** oltre.

additional [ə'dɪʃənl] *adj* supplementare.

additive ['ædɪtɪv] *n* additivo.

address [ə'drɛs] *n* (*gen, COMPUT*) indirizzo; (*talk*) discorso ♦ *vt* indirizzare; (*speak to*) fare un discorso a; **form of ~** (*gen*) formula di cortesia; (*in letters*) formula d'indirizzo *or* di intestazione; **to ~ o.s. to sth** indirizzare le proprie energie verso qc; **absolute/relative** ~ (*COMPUT*) indirizzo assoluto/relativo.

address book *n* rubrica.

addressee [ædrɛ'siː] *n* destinatario/a.

Aden ['eɪdən] *n*: **the Gulf of** ~ il golfo di Aden.

adenoids ['ædɪnɔɪdz] *npl* adenoidi *fpl*.

adept ['ædɛpt] *adj*: ~ **at** esperto(a) in.

adequate ['ædɪkwɪt] *adj* (*description, reward*) adeguato(a); (*amount*) sufficiente; **to feel** ~ **to a task** sentirsi all'altezza di un compito.

adequately ['ædɪkwɪtlɪ] *adv* adeguatamente; sufficientemente.

adhere [əd'hɪə*] *vi*: **to** ~ **to** aderire a; (*fig: rule, decision*) seguire.

adhesion [əd'hiːʒən] *n* adesione *f*.

adhesive [əd'hiːzɪv] *adj* adesivo(a) ♦ *n* adesivo; ~ **tape** (*BRIT: for parcels etc*) nastro adesivo; (*US: MED*) cerotto adesivo.

ad hoc [æd'hɔk] *adj* (*decision*) ad hoc *inv*; (*committee*) apposito(a).

ad infinitum ['ædɪnfɪ'naɪtəm] *adv* all'infinito.

adjacent [ə'dʒeɪsənt] *adj* adiacente; ~ **to** accanto a.

adjective ['ædʒɛktɪv] *n* aggettivo.

adjoin [ə'dʒɔɪn] *vt* essere contiguo(a) *or* attiguo(a) a.

adjoining [ə'dʒɔɪnɪŋ] *adj* accanto *inv*, adiacente ♦ *prep* accanto a.

adjourn [ə'dʒəːn] *vt* rimandare, aggiornare; (*US: end*) sospendere ♦ *vi* sospendere la seduta; (*PARLIAMENT*) sospendere i lavori; (*go*) spostarsi; **to** ~ **a meeting till the following week** aggiornare *or* rinviare un incontro alla settimana seguente; **they** ~**ed to the pub** (*col*) si sono trasferiti al pub.

adjournment [ə'dʒəːnmənt] *n* rinvio, aggiornamento; sospensione *f*.

Adjt *abbr* (*MIL*) = **adjutant**.

adjudicate [ə'dʒuːdɪkeɪt] *vt* (*contest*) giudicare; (*claim*) decidere su.

adjudication [ədʒuːdɪ'keɪʃən] *n* decisione *f*.

adjust [ə'dʒʌst] *vt* aggiustare; (*COMM*) rettificare ♦ *vi*: **to** ~ (**to**) adattarsi (a).

adjustable [ə'dʒʌstəbl] *adj* regolabile.

adjuster [ə'dʒʌstə*] *n see* **loss adjuster**.

adjustment [ə'dʒʌstmənt] *n* adattamento; (*of prices, wages*) aggiustamento.

adjutant ['ædʒətənt] *n* aiutante *m*.

ad-lib [æd'lɪb] *vt, vi* improvvisare ♦ *n* improvvisazione *f* ♦ *adv*: **ad lib** a piacere, a volontà.

adman ['ædmæn] *n* (*col*) pubblicitario/a.

admin [æd'mɪn] *n abbr* (*col*)

= **administration**.

administer [əd'mɪnɪstə*] *vt* amministrare; (*justice*) somministrare.

administration [ədmɪnɪs'treɪʃən] *n* amministrazione *f*; **the A**~ (*US*) il Governo.

administrative [əd'mɪnɪstrətɪv] *adj* amministrativo(a).

administrator [əd'mɪnɪstreɪtə*] *n* amministratore/trice.

admirable ['ædmərəbl] *adj* ammirevole.

admiral ['ædmərəl] *n* ammiraglio.

Admiralty ['ædmərəltɪ] *n* (*BRIT: also:* ~ **Board**) Ministero della Marina.

admiration [ædmə'reɪʃən] *n* ammirazione *f*.

admirer [əd'maɪərə*] *n* ammiratore/trice.

admiring [əd'maɪərɪŋ] *adj* (*glance etc*) di ammirazione.

admissible [əd'mɪsəbl] *adj* ammissibile.

admission [əd'mɪʃən] *n* ammissione *f*; (*to exhibition, night club etc*) ingresso; (*confession*) confessione *f*; **by his own** ~ per sua ammissione; "**~ free**", "**free ~**" "ingresso gratuito".

admit [əd'mɪt] *vt* ammettere; far entrare; (*agree*) riconoscere; "**children not** ~**ted**" "vietato l'ingresso ai bambini"; **this ticket** ~**s two** questo biglietto è valido per due persone; **I must** ~ **that** ... devo ammettere *or* confessare che ....

►**admit of** *vt fus* lasciare adito a.

►**admit to** *vt fus* riconoscere.

admittance [əd'mɪtəns] *n* ingresso; "**no** ~" "vietato l'ingresso".

admittedly [əd'mɪtɪdlɪ] *adv* bisogna pur riconoscere (che).

admonish [əd'mɔnɪʃ] *vt* ammonire.

ad nauseam [æd'nɔːzɪæm] *adv* fino alla nausea, a non finire.

ado [ə'duː] *n*: **without (any) more** ~ senza più indugi.

adolescence [ædəu'lɛsns] *n* adolescenza.

adolescent [ædəu'lɛsnt] *adj, n* adolescente (*m/f*).

adopt [ə'dɔpt] *vt* adottare.

adopted [ə'dɔptɪd] *adj* adottivo(a).

adoption [ə'dɔpʃən] *n* adozione *f*.

adore [ə'dɔː*] *vt* adorare.

adoring [ə'dɔːrɪŋ] *adj* adorante; **his** ~ **wife** sua moglie che lo adora.

adoringly [ə'dɔːrɪŋlɪ] *adv* con adorazione.

adorn [ə'dɔːn] *vt* ornare.

adornment [ə'dɔːnmənt] *n* ornamento.

ADP *n abbr see* **automatic data processing**.

adrenalin [ə'drɛnəlɪn] *n* adrenalina; **it gets the** ~ **going** ti dà una carica.

Adriatic (Sea) [eɪdrɪ'ætɪk-] *n* Adriatico.

adrift [ə'drɪft] *adv* alla deriva; **to come** ~

(*boat*) andare alla deriva; (*wire, rope etc*) essersi staccato(a) *or* sciolto(a).

adroit [ə'drɔɪt] *adj* abile, destro(a).

ADT *abbr* (*US:* = *Atlantic Daylight Time*) ora legale di New York.

adult ['ædʌlt] *n* adulto/a.

adult education *n* scuola per adulti.

adulterate [ə'dʌltəreɪt] *vt* adulterare.

adulterer [ə'dʌltərə*] *n* adultero.

adulteress [ə'dʌltərɪs] *n* adultera.

adultery [ə'dʌltərɪ] *n* adulterio.

adulthood ['ædʌlthud] *n* età adulta.

advance [əd'vɑːns] *n* avanzamento; (*money*) anticipo ♦ *vt* avanzare; (*date, money*) anticipare ♦ *vi* avanzare; **in** ~ in anticipo; **to make** ~**s to sb** (*gen*) fare degli approcci a qn; (*amorously*) fare delle avances a qn.

advanced [əd'vɑːnst] *adj* avanzato(a); (*SCOL: studies*) superiore; ~ **in years** avanti negli anni.

advancement [əd'vɑːnsmənt] *n* avanzamento.

advance notice *n* preavviso.

advantage [əd'vɑːntɪdʒ] *n* (*also TENNIS*) vantaggio; **to take** ~ **of** approfittarsi di; **it's to our** ~ è nel nostro interesse, torna a nostro vantaggio.

advantageous [ædvən'teɪdʒəs] *adj* vantaggioso(a).

advent ['ædvənt] *n* avvento; **A**~ (*REL*) Avvento.

Advent calendar *n* calendario dell'Avvento.

adventure [əd'vɛntʃə*] *n* avventura.

adventure playground *n* area attrezzata di giochi per bambini con funi, strutture in legno etc.

adventurous [əd'vɛntʃərəs] *adj* avventuroso(a).

adverb ['ædvəːb] *n* avverbio.

adversary ['ædvəsərɪ] *n* avversario/a.

adverse ['ædvəːs] *adj* avverso(a); **in** ~ **circumstances** nelle avversità; ~ **to** contrario(a) a.

adversity [əd'vəːsɪtɪ] *n* avversità.

advert ['ædvəːt] *n abbr* (*BRIT*) = **advertisement.**

advertise ['ædvətaɪz] *vi* (*vt*) fare pubblicità *or* réclame (a); fare un'inserzione (per vendere); **to** ~ **for** (*staff*) cercare tramite annuncio.

advertisement [əd'vəːtɪsmənt] *n* (*COMM*) réclame *f inv*, pubblicità *f inv*; (*in classified ads*) inserzione *f*.

advertiser ['ædvətaɪzə*] *n* azienda che reclamizza un prodotto; (*in newspaper*) inserzionista *m/f*.

advertising ['ædvətaɪzɪŋ] *n* pubblicità.

advertising agency *n* agenzia pubblicitaria *or* di pubblicità.

advertising campaign *n* campagna pubblicitaria.

advice [əd'vaɪs] *n* consigli *mpl*; (*notification*) avviso; **piece of** ~ consiglio; **to ask (sb) for** ~ chiedere il consiglio (di qn), chiedere un consiglio (a qn); **legal** ~ consulenza legale.

advice note *n* (*BRIT*) avviso di spedizione.

advisable [əd'vaɪzəbl] *adj* consigliabile.

advise [əd'vaɪz] *vt* consigliare; **to** ~ **sb of sth** informare qn di qc; **to** ~ **sb against sth/against doing sth** sconsigliare qc a qn/a qn di fare qc; **you will be well/ill** ~**d to go** fareste bene/male ad andare.

advisedly [əd'vaɪzɪdlɪ] *adv* (*deliberately*) deliberatamente.

adviser [əd'vaɪzə*] *n* consigliere/a; (*in business*) consulente *m/f*, consigliere/a.

advisory [əd'vaɪzərɪ] *adj* consultivo(a); **in an** ~ **capacity** in veste di consulente.

advocate *n* ['ædvəkɪt] (*upholder*) sostenitore/trice ♦ *vt* ['ædvəkeɪt] propugnare; **to be an** ~ **of** essere a favore di.

advt. *abbr* = **advertisement.**

AEA *n abbr* (*BRIT:* = *Atomic Energy Authority*) ente di controllo sulla ricerca e lo sviluppo dell'energia atomica.

AEC *n abbr* (*US:* = *Atomic Energy Commission*) ente di controllo sulla ricerca e lo sviluppo dell'energia atomica.

Aegean (Sea) [iː'dʒiːən-] *n* (mare *m*) Egeo.

aegis ['iːdʒɪs] *n*: **under the** ~ **of** sotto gli auspici di.

aeon ['iːən] *n* eternità *f inv*.

aerial ['ɛərɪəl] *n* antenna ♦ *adj* aereo(a).

aerobatics ['ɛərəu'bætɪks] *npl* acrobazia aerea *sg*; (*stunts*) acrobazie *fpl* aeree.

aerobics [ɛə'rəubɪks] *n* aerobica.

aerodrome ['ɛərədrəum] *n* (*BRIT*) aerodromo.

aerodynamic ['ɛərəudaɪ'næmɪk] *adj* aerodinamico(a).

aeronautics [ɛərə'nɔːtɪks] *n* aeronautica.

aeroplane ['ɛərəpleɪn] *n* aeroplano.

aerosol ['ɛərəsɔl] *n* aerosol *m inv*.

aerospace industry ['ɛərəuspeɪs-] *n* industria aerospaziale.

aesthetic [ɪs'θɛtɪk] *adj* estetico(a).

afar [ə'fɑː*] *adv* lontano; **from** ~ da lontano.

AFB *n abbr* (*US*) = *Air Force Base.*

AFDC *n abbr* (*US*) = *Aid to Families with Dependent Children.*

affable ['æfəbl] *adj* affabile.

affair [ə'fɛə*] n affare m; (also: **love** ~) relazione f amorosa; ~**s** (business) affari; **the Watergate** ~ il caso Watergate.

affect [ə'fɛkt] vt toccare; (feign) fingere.

affectation [æfɛk'teɪʃən] n affettazione f.

affected [ə'fɛktɪd] adj affettato(a).

affection [ə'fɛkʃən] n affetto m.

affectionate [ə'fɛkʃənɪt] adj affettuoso(a).

affectionately [ə'fɛkʃənɪtlɪ] adv affettuosamente.

affidavit [æfɪ'deɪvɪt] n (LAW) affidavit m inv.

affiliated [ə'fɪlɪeɪtɪd] adj affiliato(a); ~ **company** filiale f.

affinity [ə'fɪnɪtɪ] n affinità f inv.

affirm [ə'fɜːm] vt affermare, asserire.

affirmation [æfə'meɪʃən] n affermazione f.

affirmative [ə'fɜːmətɪv] adj affermativo(a) ♦ n: **in the** ~ affermativamente.

affix [ə'fɪks] vt apporre; attaccare.

afflict [ə'flɪkt] vt affliggere.

affliction [ə'flɪkʃən] n afflizione f.

affluence ['æfluəns] n ricchezza.

affluent ['æfluənt] adj ricco(a); **the** ~ **society** la società del benessere.

afford [ə'fɔːd] vt permettersi; (provide) fornire; **I can't** ~ **the time** non ho veramente il tempo; **can we** ~ **a car?** possiamo permetterci un'automobile?

affordable [ə'fɔːdəbl] adj (che ha un prezzo) abbordabile.

affray [ə'freɪ] n (BRIT LAW) rissa.

affront [ə'frʌnt] n affronto.

affronted [ə'frʌntɪd] adj insultato(a).

Afghan ['æfgæn] adj, n afgano(a).

Afghanistan [æf'gænɪstɑːn] n Afganistan m.

afield [ə'fiːld] adv: **far** ~ lontano.

AFL-CIO n abbr (= American Federation of Labor and Congress of Industrial Organizations) confederazione sindacale.

afloat [ə'fləut] adj, adv a galla.

afoot [ə'fut] adv: **there is something** ~ si sta preparando qualcosa.

aforementioned [ə'fɔːmɛnʃənd] adj suddetto(a).

aforesaid [ə'fɔːsɛd] adj suddetto(a).

afraid [ə'freɪd] adj impaurito(a); **to be** ~ **of** aver paura di; **to be** ~ **of doing** or **to do** aver paura di fare; **I am** ~ **that I'll be late** mi dispiace, ma farò tardi; **I'm** ~ **so!** ho paura di sì!, temo proprio di sì!; **I'm** ~ **not** no, mi dispiace, purtroppo no.

afresh [ə'frɛʃ] adv di nuovo.

Africa ['æfrɪkə] n Africa.

African ['æfrɪkən] adj, n africano(a).

Afrikaans [æfrɪ'kɑːns] n afrikaans m.

Afrikaner [æfrɪ'kɑːnə*] n africander m inv.

Afro-American ['æfrəuə'mɛrɪkən] adj afroamericano(a).

Afro-Caribbean ['æfrəkæri'biːən] adj afrocaraibico(a).

AFT n abbr (= American Federation of Teachers) sindacato degli insegnanti.

aft [ɑːft] adv a poppa, verso poppa.

after ['ɑːftə*] prep, adv dopo; ~ **dinner** dopo cena; **the day** ~ **tomorrow** dopodomani; **what/who are you** ~? che/chi cerca?; **the police are** ~ **him** è ricercato dalla polizia; ~ **you!** dopo di lei!; ~ **all** dopo tutto.

afterbirth ['ɑːftəbəːθ] n placenta.

aftercare ['ɑːftəkɛə*] n (BRIT MED) assistenza medica post-degenza.

after-effects ['ɑːftərɪfɛkts] npl conseguenze fpl; (of illness) postumi mpl.

afterlife ['ɑːftəlaɪf] n vita dell'al di là.

aftermath ['ɑːftəmæθ] n conseguenze fpl; **in the** ~ **of** nel periodo dopo.

afternoon ['ɑːftə'nuːn] n pomeriggio; **good** ~! buon giorno!

afters ['ɑːftəz] n (BRIT col: dessert) dessert m inv.

after-sales service [ɑːftə'seɪlz-] n servizio assistenza clienti.

after-shave (lotion) ['ɑːftəʃeɪv-] n dopobarba m inv.

aftershock ['ɑːftəʃɔk] n scossa di assestamento.

aftersun ['ɑːftəsʌn] adj: ~ **(lotion/cream)** (lozione f/crema) doposole m inv.

aftertaste ['ɑːftəteɪst] n retrogusto.

afterthought ['ɑːftəθɔːt] n: **as an** ~ come aggiunta.

afterwards ['ɑːftəwədz] adv dopo.

again [ə'gɛn] adv di nuovo; **to begin/see** ~ ricominciare/rivedere; **he opened it** ~ l'ha aperto di nuovo, l'ha riaperto; **not** ... ~ **non** ... più; ~ **and** ~ ripetutamente; **now and** ~ di tanto in tanto, a volte.

against [ə'gɛnst] prep contro; ~ **a blue background** su uno sfondo azzurro; **leaning** ~ **the desk** appoggiato alla scrivania; **(as)** ~ (BRIT) in confronto a.

age [eɪdʒ] n età f inv ♦ vt, vi invecchiare; **what** ~ **is he?** quanti anni ha?; **he is 20 years of** ~ ha 20 anni; **under** ~ minorenne; **to come of** ~ diventare maggiorenne; **it's been** ~**s since** ... sono secoli che ....

aged ['eɪdʒd] adj: ~ **10** di 10 anni; **the** ~ ['eɪdʒɪd] npl (elderly) gli anziani.

age group n generazione f; **the 40 to 50** ~ le persone fra i 40 e i 50 anni.

ageing ['eɪdʒɪŋ] adj che diventa vecchio(a); **an** ~ **filmstar** una diva stagionata.

ageless ['eɪdʒlɪs] adj senza età.

age limit n limite m d'età.

agency ['eɪdʒənsɪ] *n* agenzia; **through** *or* **by the** ~ **of** grazie a.

agenda [ə'dʒɛndə] *n* ordine *m* del giorno; **on the** ~ all'ordine del giorno.

agent ['eɪdʒənt] *n* agente *m*.

aggravate ['ægrəveɪt] *vt* aggravare, peggiorare; (*annoy*) esasperare.

aggravation [ægrə'veɪʃən] *n* peggioramento; esasperazione *f*.

aggregate ['ægrɪgeɪt] *n* aggregato; **on** ~ (*SPORT*) con punteggio complessivo.

aggression [ə'grɛʃən] *n* aggressione *f*.

aggressive [ə'grɛsɪv] *adj* aggressivo(a).

aggressiveness [ə'grɛsɪvnɪs] *n* aggressività.

aggressor [ə'grɛsə*] *n* aggressore *m*.

aggrieved [ə'griːvd] *adj* addolorato(a).

aggro ['ægrəu] *n* (*col: behaviour*) aggressività *f inv*; (: *hassle*) rottura.

aghast [ə'gɑːst] *adj* sbigottito(a).

agile ['ædʒaɪl] *adj* agile.

agility [ə'dʒɪlɪtɪ] *n* agilità *f inv*.

agitate ['ædʒɪteɪt] *vt* turbare; agitare ♦ *vi*: **to** ~ **for** agitarsi per.

agitator ['ædʒɪteɪtə*] *n* agitatore/trice.

AGM *n abbr see* **annual general meeting**.

agnostic [æg'nɔstɪk] *adj*, *n* agnostico(a).

ago [ə'gəu] *adv*: **2 days** ~ 2 giorni fa; **not long** ~ poco tempo fa; **as long** ~ **as 1960** già nel 1960; **how long** ~? quanto tempo fa?

agog [ə'gɔg] *adj*: **(all)** ~ **(for)** ansioso(a) (di), impaziente (di).

agonize ['ægənaɪz] *vi*: **to** ~ **(over)** angosciarsi (per).

agonizing ['ægənaɪzɪŋ] *adj* straziante.

agony ['ægənɪ] *n* agonia; **I was in** ~ avevo dei dolori atroci.

agony aunt *n* (*BRIT col*) chi tiene la rubrica della posta del cuore.

agony column *n* posta del cuore.

agree [ə'griː] *vt* (*price*) pattuire ♦ *vi*: **to** ~ **(with)** essere d'accordo (con); (*LING*) concordare (con); **to** ~ **to sth/to do sth** accettare qc/di fare qc; **to** ~ **that** (*admit*) ammettere che; **to** ~ **on sth** accordarsi su qc; **it was** ~**d that** ... è stato deciso (di comune accordo) che ...; **garlic doesn't** ~ **with me** l'aglio non mi va.

agreeable [ə'griːəbl] *adj* gradevole; (*willing*) disposto(a); **are you** ~ **to this?** è d'accordo con questo?

agreed [ə'griːd] *adj* (*time*, *place*) stabilito(a); **to be** ~ essere d'accordo.

agreement [ə'griːmənt] *n* accordo; **in** ~ d'accordo; **by mutual** ~ di comune accordo.

agricultural [ægrɪ'kʌltʃərəl] *adj* agricolo(a).

agriculture ['ægrɪkʌltʃə*] *n* agricoltura.

aground [ə'graund] *adv*: **to run** ~ arenarsi.

ahead [ə'hɛd] *adv* avanti; davanti; ~ **of** davanti a; (*fig: schedule etc*) in anticipo su; ~ **of time** in anticipo; **go** ~! avanti!; **go right** *or* **straight** ~ tiri diritto; **they were (right)** ~ **of us** erano (proprio) davanti a noi.

AI *n abbr* = **Amnesty International**; (*COMPUT*) *see* **artificial intelligence**.

AID *n abbr* = **artificial insemination by donor**; (*US*: = **Agency for International Development**) A.I.D. *f*.

aid [eɪd] *n* aiuto ♦ *vt* aiutare; **with the** ~ **of** con l'aiuto di; **in** ~ **of** a favore di; **to** ~ **and abet** (*LAW*) essere complice di.

aide [eɪd] *n* (*person*) aiutante *m*.

aide-de-camp (ADC) ['eɪddə'kɔŋ] *n* (*MIL*) aiutante *m* di campo.

AIDS [eɪdz] *n abbr* (= **acquired immune** *or* **immuno-deficiency syndrome**) A.I.D.S. *f*.

AIH *n abbr* = **artificial insemination by husband**.

ailing ['eɪlɪŋ] *adj* sofferente; (*fig: economy*, *industry etc*) in difficoltà.

ailment ['eɪlmənt] *n* indisposizione *f*.

aim [eɪm] *vt*: **to** ~ **sth at** (*gun*) mirare qc a, puntare qc a; (*camera*, *remark*) rivolgere qc a; (*missile*) lanciare qc contro; (*blow etc*) tirare qc a ♦ *vi* (*also*: **to take** ~) prendere la mira ♦ *n* mira; **to** ~ **at** mirare; **to** ~ **to do** aver l'intenzione di fare.

aimless ['eɪmlɪs] *adj*, **aimlessly** ['eɪmlɪslɪ] *adv* senza scopo.

ain't [eɪnt] (*col*) = **am not**; **aren't**; **isn't**.

air [ɛə*] *n* aria ♦ *vt* (*room*, *bed*) arieggiare; (*clothes*) far prendere aria a; (*idea*, *grievance*) esprimere pubblicamente, manifestare; (*views*) far conoscere ♦ *cpd* (*currents*) d'aria; (*attack*) aereo(a); **by** ~ (*travel*) in aereo; **to be on the** ~ (*RADIO*, *TV*: *station*) trasmettere; (: *programme*) essere in onda.

air bag *n* airbag *m inv*.

air base *n* base *f* aerea.

airbed ['ɛəbɛd] *n* (*BRIT*) materassino.

airborne ['ɛəbɔːn] *adj* (*plane*) in volo; (*troops*) aerotrasportato(a); **as soon as the plane was** ~ appena l'aereo ebbe decollato.

air cargo *n* carico trasportato per via aerea.

air-conditioned ['ɛəkən'dɪʃənd] *adj* con *or* ad aria condizionata.

air conditioning *n* condizionamento d'aria.

air-cooled ['ɛəkuːld] *adj* raffreddato(a) ad

aria.

aircraft ['ɛəkrɑːft] *n* (*pl inv*) apparecchio.

aircraft carrier *n* portaerei *f inv*.

air cushion *n* cuscino gonfiabile; (*TECH*) cuscino d'aria.

airfield ['ɛəfiːld] *n* campo d'aviazione.

Air Force *n* aviazione *f* militare.

air freight *n* spedizione *f* di merci per via aerea; (*goods*) carico spedito per via aerea.

airgun ['ɛəgʌn] *n* fucile *m* ad aria compressa.

air hostess *n* hostess *f inv*.

airily ['ɛərɪlɪ] *adv* con disinvoltura.

airing ['ɛərɪŋ] *n*: **to give an ~ to** (*linen*) far prendere aria a; (*room*) arieggiare; (*fig: ideas etc*) ventilare.

air letter *n* (*BRIT*) aerogramma *m*.

airlift ['ɛəlɪft] *n* ponte *m* aereo.

airline ['ɛəlaɪn] *n* linea aerea.

airliner ['ɛəlaɪnə*] *n* aereo di linea.

airlock ['ɛəlɔk] *n* cassa d'aria.

air mail *n* posta aerea; **by ~** per via *or* posta aerea.

air mattress *n* materasso gonfiabile.

airplane ['ɛəpleɪn] *n* (*US*) aeroplano.

air pocket *n* vuoto d'aria.

airport ['ɛəpɔːt] *n* aeroporto.

air rage *n* comportamento aggressivo dei passeggeri di un aereo.

air raid *n* incursione *f* aerea.

air rifle *n* fucile *m* ad aria compressa.

airsick ['ɛəsɪk] *adj*: **to be ~** soffrire di mal d'aereo.

airspace ['ɛəspeɪs] *n* spazio aereo.

airspeed ['ɛəspiːd] *n* velocità *f inv* di crociera (*AER*).

airstrip ['ɛəstrɪp] *n* pista d'atterraggio.

air terminal *n* air-terminal *m inv*.

airtight ['ɛətaɪt] *adj* ermetico(a).

air time *n* (*RADIO*) spazio radiofonico; (*TV*) spazio televisivo.

air traffic control *n* controllo del traffico aereo.

air traffic controller *n* controllore *m* del traffico aereo.

airway ['ɛəweɪ] *n* (*AVIAT*) rotte *fpl* aeree; (*ANAT*) vie *fpl* respiratorie.

airy ['ɛərɪ] *adj* arioso(a); (*manners*) noncurante.

aisle [aɪl] *n* (*of church*) navata laterale; navata centrale; (*of plane*) corridoio.

aisle seat *n* (*on plane*) posto sul corridoio.

ajar [ə'dʒɑː*] *adj* socchiuso(a).

AK *abbr* (*US*) = Alaska.

aka *abbr* (= *also known as*) alias.

akin [ə'kɪn] *prep* simile a.

AL *abbr* (*US*) = Alabama.

Ala. *abbr* (*US*) = Alabama.

à la carte [ɑːlɑː'kɑːt] *adv* alla carta.

alacrity [ə'lækrɪtɪ] *n*: **with ~** con prontezza.

alarm [ə'lɑːm] *n* allarme *m* ♦ *vt* allarmare.

alarm clock *n* sveglia.

alarmed [ə'lɑːmd] *adj* (*person*) allarmato(a); (*house, car etc*) dotato(a) di allarme.

alarming [ə'lɑːmɪŋ] *adj* allarmante, preoccupante.

alarmingly [ə'lɑːmɪŋlɪ] *adv* in modo allarmante; **~ close** pericolosamente vicino.

alarmist [ə'lɑːmɪst] *n* allarmista *m/f*.

alas [ə'læs] *excl* ohimè!, ahimè!

Alas. *abbr* (*US*) = Alaska.

Alaska [ə'læskə] *n* Alasca.

Albania [æl'beɪnɪə] *n* Albania.

Albanian [æl'beɪnɪən] *adj* albanese ♦ *n* albanese *m/f*; (*LING*) albanese *m*.

albatross ['ælbətrɔs] *n* albatros *m inv*.

albeit [ɔːl'biːɪt] *conj* sebbene + *sub*, benché + *sub*.

album ['ælbəm] *n* album *m inv*; (*L.P.*) 33 giri *m inv*, L.P. *m inv*.

albumen ['ælbjumɪn] *n* albume *m*.

alchemy ['ælkɪmɪ] *n* alchimia.

alcohol ['ælkəhɔl] *n* alcool *m*.

alcohol-free ['ælkəhɔl'friː] *adj* analcolico(a).

alcoholic [ælkə'hɔlɪk] *adj* alcolico(a) ♦ *n* alcolizzato/a.

alcoholism ['ælkəhɔlɪzəm] *n* alcolismo.

alcove ['ælkəuv] *n* alcova.

alderman ['ɔːldəmən] *n* consigliere *m* comunale.

ale [eɪl] *n* birra.

alert [ə'lɜːt] *adj* vivo(a); (*watchful*) vigile ♦ *n* allarme *m* ♦ *vt*: **to ~ sb (to sth)** avvisare qn (di qc), avvertire qn (di qc); **to ~ sb to the dangers of sth** mettere qn in guardia contro qc; **on the ~** all'erta.

Aleutian Islands [ə'luːʃən-] *npl* isole *fpl* Aleutine.

A level *n* (*BRIT*) diploma di studi superiori.

Alexandria [ælɪg'zændrɪə] *n* Alessandria (d'Egitto).

alfresco [æl'freskəu] *adj*, *adv* all'aperto.

algebra ['ældʒɪbrə] *n* algebra.

Algeria [æl'dʒɪərɪə] *n* Algeria.

Algerian [æl'dʒɪərɪən] *adj*, *n* algerino(a).

Algiers [æl'dʒɪəz] *n* Algeri *f*.

algorithm ['ælgərɪðəm] *n* algoritmo.

alias ['eɪlɪəs] *adv* alias ♦ *n* pseudonimo, falso nome *m*.

alibi ['ælɪbaɪ] *n* alibi *m inv*.

alien ['eɪlɪən] *n* straniero/a ♦ *adj*: **~ (to)** estraneo(a) (a).

alienate ['eɪlɪəneɪt] *vt* alienare.

alienation [eɪlɪə'neɪʃən] *n* alienazione *f*.

alight [ə'laɪt] adj acceso(a) ♦ vi scendere;
(bird) posarsi.
align [ə'laɪn] vt allineare.
alignment [ə'laɪnmənt] n allineamento; **out
of ~ (with)** non allineato (con).
alike [ə'laɪk] adj simile ♦ adv allo stesso
modo; **to look ~** assomigliarsi; **winter
and summer ~** sia d'estate che d'inverno.
alimony ['ælɪmənɪ] n (payment) alimenti
mpl.
alive [ə'laɪv] adj vivo(a); (active) attivo(a); **~
with** pieno(a) di; **~ to** conscio(a) di.
alkali ['ælkəlaɪ] n alcali m inv.

================== *KEYWORD* ==================

all [ɔːl] adj tutto(a); **~ day** tutto il giorno; **~
night** tutta la notte; **~ men** tutti gli
uomini; **~ five girls** tutt'e cinque le
ragazze; **~ five came** sono venuti tutti e
cinque; **~ the books** tutti i libri; **~ the
food** tutto il cibo; **~ the time** tutto il
tempo; (always) sempre; **~ his life** tutta la
vita; **for ~ their efforts** nonostante tutti i
loro sforzi
♦ pron **1** tutto(a); **is that ~?** non c'è altro?;
(in shop) basta così?; **~ of them** tutti(e); **~
of it** tutto(a); **I ate it ~, I ate ~ of it** l'ho
mangiato tutto; **~ of us went** tutti noi
siamo andati; **~ of the boys went** tutti i
ragazzi sono andati
2 (in phrases): **above ~** soprattutto; **after
~** dopotutto; **at ~:** **not at ~** (in answer to
question) niente affatto; (in answer to
thanks) prego!, di niente!, s'immagini!;
I'm not at ~ tired non sono affatto stanco;
anything at ~ will do andrà bene
qualsiasi cosa; **~ in ~** tutto sommato
♦ adv: **~ alone** tutto(a) solo(a); **to be/feel ~
in** (BRIT col) essere/sentirsi sfinito(a) or
distrutto(a); **~ out** adv: **to go ~ out**
mettercela tutta; **it's not as hard as ~
that** non è poi così difficile; **~ the more/
the better** tanto più/meglio; **~ but** quasi;
the score is two ~ il punteggio è di due a
due or due pari.

allay [ə'leɪ] vt (fears) dissipare.
all clear n (MIL) cessato allarme m inv; (fig)
okay m.
allegation [ælɪ'geɪʃən] n asserzione f.
allege [ə'lɛdʒ] vt asserire; **he is ~d to have
said** ... avrebbe detto che ....
alleged [ə'lɛdʒd] adj presunto(a).
allegedly [ə'lɛdʒɪdlɪ] adv secondo quanto si
asserisce.
allegiance [ə'liːdʒəns] n fedeltà.
allegory ['ælɪgərɪ] n allegoria.
all-embracing ['ɔːlɪm'breɪsɪŋ] adj

universale.
allergic [ə'lɔːdʒɪk] adj: **~ to** allergico(a) a.
allergy ['ælədʒɪ] n allergia.
alleviate [ə'liːvɪeɪt] vt alleviare.
alley ['ælɪ] n vicolo; (in garden) vialetto.
alleyway ['ælɪweɪ] n vicolo.
alliance [ə'laɪəns] n alleanza.
allied ['ælaɪd] adj alleato(a).
alligator ['ælɪgeɪtə*] n alligatore m.
all-important ['ɔːlɪm'pɔːtənt] adj
importantissimo(a).
all-in ['ɔːlɪn] adj (BRIT: also adv: charge) tutto
compreso.
all-in wrestling n (BRIT) lotta americana.
alliteration [əlɪtə'reɪʃən] n allitterazione f.
all-night ['ɔːl'naɪt] adj aperto(a) (or che
dura) tutta la notte.
allocate ['æləkeɪt] vt (share out) distribuire;
(duties, sum, time): **to ~ sth to** assegnare
qc a; **to ~ sth for** stanziare qc per.
allocation [æləu'keɪʃən] n: **~ (of money)**
stanziamento.
allot [ə'lɔt] vt (share out) spartire; **to ~ sth
to** (time) dare qc a; (duties) assegnare qc
a; **in the ~ted time** nel tempo fissato or
prestabilito.
allotment [ə'lɔtmənt] n (share) spartizione
f; (garden) lotto di terra.
all-out ['ɔːlaut] adj (effort etc) totale ♦ adv: **to
go all out for** mettercela tutta per.
allow [ə'lau] vt (practice, behaviour)
permettere; (sum to spend etc) accordare;
(sum, time estimated) dare; (concede): **to ~
that** ammettere che; **to ~ sb to do**
permettere a qn di fare; **he is ~ed to (do
it)** lo può fare; **smoking is not ~ed** è
vietato fumare, non è permesso fumare;
we must ~ 3 days for the journey
dobbiamo calcolare 3 giorni per il
viaggio.
▶**allow for** vt fus tener conto di.
allowance [ə'lauəns] n (money received)
assegno; (for travelling, accommodation)
indennità f inv; (TAX) detrazione f di
imposta; **to make ~(s) for** tener conto di;
(person) scusare.
alloy ['ælɔɪ] n lega.
all right adv (feel, work) bene; (as answer)
va bene.
all-round ['ɔːl'raund] adj completo(a).
all-rounder [ɔːl'raundə*] n (BRIT): **to be a
good ~** essere bravo(a) in tutto.
allspice ['ɔːlspaɪs] n pepe m della Giamaica.
all-time ['ɔːl'taɪm] adj (record) assoluto(a).
allude [ə'luːd] vi: **to ~ to** alludere a.
alluring [ə'ljuərɪŋ] adj seducente.
allusion [ə'luːʒən] n allusione f.
alluvium [ə'luːvɪəm] n materiale m

alluvionale.

ally *n* ['ælaɪ] alleato ♦ *vt* [ə'laɪ]: **to ~ o.s. with** allearsi con.

almighty [ɔːl'maɪtɪ] *adj* onnipotente.

almond ['ɑːmənd] *n* mandorla.

almost ['ɔːlməust] *adv* quasi; **he ~ fell** per poco non è caduto.

alms [ɑːmz] *n* elemosina.

aloft [ə'lɔft] *adv* in alto; (*NAUT*) sull'alberatura.

alone [ə'ləun] *adj*, *adv* solo(a); **to leave sb ~** lasciare qn in pace; **to leave sth ~** lasciare stare qc; **let ~ ...** figuriamoci poi ..., tanto meno ....

along [ə'lɔŋ] *prep* lungo ♦ *adv*: **is he coming ~?** viene con noi?; **he was limping ~** veniva zoppicando; **~ with** insieme con.

alongside [ə'lɔŋ'saɪd] *prep* accanto a; lungo ♦ *adv* accanto; (*NAUT*) sottobordo; **we brought our boat ~** (*of a pier/shore etc*) abbiamo accostato la barca (al molo/alla riva *etc*).

aloof [ə'luːf] *adj* distaccato(a) ♦ *adv* a distanza, in disparte; **to stand ~** tenersi a distanza *or* in disparte.

aloofness [ə'luːfnɪs] *n* distacco, riserbo.

aloud [ə'laud] *adv* ad alta voce.

alphabet ['ælfəbɛt] *n* alfabeto.

alphabetical [ælfə'bɛtɪkəl] *adj* alfabetico(a); **in ~ order** in ordine alfabetico.

alphanumeric [ælfənjuː'mɛrɪk] *adj* alfanumerico(a).

alpine ['ælpaɪn] *adj* alpino(a); **~ hut** rifugio alpino; **~ pasture** pascolo alpestre; **~ skiing** sci alpino.

Alps [ælps] *npl*: **the ~** le Alpi.

already [ɔːl'rɛdɪ] *adv* già.

alright ['ɔːl'raɪt] *adv* (*BRIT*) = **all right**.

Alsatian [æl'seɪʃən] *n* (*BRIT*: *dog*) pastore *m* tedesco, (cane *m*) lupo.

also ['ɔːlsəu] *adv* anche.

Alta. *abbr* (*Canada*) = Alberta.

altar ['ɔltə*] *n* altare *m*.

alter ['ɔltə*] *vt*, *vi* alterare.

alteration [ɔltə'reɪʃən] *n* modificazione *f*, alterazione *f*; **~s** (*SEWING*, *ARCHIT*) modifiche *fpl*; **timetable subject to ~** orario soggetto a variazioni.

altercation [ɔːltə'keɪʃən] *n* alterco, litigio.

alternate *adj* [ɔl'tɜːnɪt] alterno(a) ♦ *vi* ['ɔltɜːneɪt] alternare; **on ~ days** ogni due giorni.

alternately [ɔl'tɜːnɪtlɪ] *adv* alternatamente.

alternating current ['ɔltəneɪtɪŋ-] *n* corrente *f* alternata.

alternative [ɔl'tɜːnətɪv] *adj* (*solutions*) alternativo(a); (*solution*) altro(a) ♦ *n*

(*choice*) alternativa; (*other possibility*) altra possibilità.

alternatively [ɔl'tɜːnətɪvlɪ] *adv* altrimenti, come alternativa.

alternative medicine *n* medicina alternativa.

alternator ['ɔltɜːneɪtə*] *n* (*AUT*) alternatore *m*.

although [ɔːl'ðəu] *conj* benché + *sub*, sebbene + *sub*.

altitude ['æltɪtjuːd] *n* altitudine *f*.

alto ['æltəu] *n* contralto.

altogether [ɔːltə'gɛðə*] *adv* del tutto, completamente; (*on the whole*) tutto considerato; (*in all*) in tutto; **how much is that ~?** quant'è in tutto?

altruism ['æltruːzəm] *n* altruismo.

altruistic [æltruː'ɪstɪk] *adj* altruistico(a).

aluminium [ælju'mɪnɪəm], (*US*) **aluminum** [ə'luːmɪnəm] *n* alluminio.

always ['ɔːlweɪz] *adv* sempre.

Alzheimer's ['æltshaɪməz] *n* (*also*: **~ disease**) morbo di Alzheimer.

AM *abbr* (= *amplitude modulation*) AM ♦ *n abbr* (= *Assembly Member*) deputato gallese.

am [æm] *vb see* **be**.

a.m. *adv abbr* (= *ante meridiem*) della mattina.

AMA *n abbr* = *American Medical Association*.

amalgam [ə'mælgəm] *n* amalgama *m*.

amalgamate [ə'mælgəmeɪt] *vt* amalgamare ♦ *vi* amalgamarsi.

amalgamation [əmælgə'meɪʃən] *n* amalgamazione *f*; (*COMM*) fusione *f*.

amass [ə'mæs] *vt* ammassare.

amateur ['æmətə*] *n* dilettante *m/f* ♦ *adj* (*SPORT*) dilettante; **~ dramatics** *n* filodrammatica.

amateurish ['æmətərɪʃ] *adj* (*pej*) da dilettante.

amaze [ə'meɪz] *vt* stupire; **to be ~d (at)** essere sbalordito(a) (da).

amazement [ə'meɪzmənt] *n* stupore *m*.

amazing [ə'meɪzɪŋ] *adj* sorprendente, sbalorditivo(a); (*bargain, offer*) sensazionale.

amazingly [ə'meɪzɪŋlɪ] *adv* incredibilmente, sbalorditivamente.

Amazon ['æməzən] *n* (*MYTHOLOGY*) Amazzone *f*; (*river*): **the ~** il Rio delle Amazzoni ♦ *cpd* (*basin, jungle*) amazzonico(a).

Amazonian [æmə'zəunɪən] *adj* amazzonico(a).

ambassador [æm'bæsədə*] *n* ambasciatore/trice.

amber ['æmbə*] *n* ambra; **at ~** (*BRIT AUT*) giallo.

ambidextrous [æmbɪ'dɛkstrəs] *adj* ambidestro(a).
ambience ['æmbɪəns] *n* ambiente *m*.
ambiguity [æmbɪ'gjuɪtɪ] *n* ambiguità *f inv*.
ambiguous [æm'bɪgjuəs] *adj* ambiguo(a).
ambition [æm'bɪʃən] *n* ambizione *f*; **to achieve one's** ~ realizzare le proprie aspirazioni *or* ambizioni.
ambitious [æm'bɪʃəs] *adj* ambizioso(a).
ambivalent [æm'bɪvələnt] *adj* ambivalente.
amble ['æmbl] *vi* (*gen*: **to** ~ **along**) camminare tranquillamente.
ambulance ['æmbjuləns] *n* ambulanza.
ambush ['æmbuʃ] *n* imboscata ♦ *vt* fare un'imboscata a.
ameba [ə'mi:bə] *n* (*US*) = **amoeba**.
ameliorate [ə'mi:lɪəreɪt] *vt* migliorare.
amen ['ɑ:'mɛn] *excl* così sia, amen.
amenable [ə'mi:nəbl] *adj*: ~ **to** (*advice etc*) ben disposto(a) a.
amend [ə'mɛnd] *vt* (*law*) emendare; (*text*) correggere ♦ *vi* emendarsi; **to make** ~**s** fare ammenda.
amendment [ə'mɛndmənt] *n* emendamento; correzione *f*.
amenities [ə'mi:nɪtɪz] *npl* attrezzature *fpl* ricreative e culturali.
amenity [ə'mi:nɪtɪ] *n* amenità *f inv*.
America [ə'mɛrɪkə] *n* America.
American [ə'mɛrɪkən] *adj, n* americano(a).
americanize [ə'mɛrɪkənaɪz] *vt* americanizzare.
amethyst ['æmɪθɪst] *n* ametista.
Amex ['æmɛks] *n abbr* = **American Stock Exchange**.
amiable ['eɪmɪəbl] *adj* amabile, gentile.
amicable ['æmɪkəbl] *adj* amichevole.
amicably ['æmɪkəblɪ] *adv*: **to part** ~ lasciarsi senza rancori.
amid(st) [ə'mɪd(st)] *prep* fra, tra, in mezzo a.
amiss [ə'mɪs] *adj, adv*: **there's something** ~ c'è qualcosa che non va bene; **don't take it** ~ non avertene a male.
ammo ['æməu] *n abbr* (*col*) = **ammunition**.
ammonia [ə'məunɪə] *n* ammoniaca.
ammunition [æmju'nɪʃən] *n* munizioni *fpl*; (*fig*) arma.
ammunition dump *n* deposito di munizioni.
amnesia [æm'ni:zɪə] *n* amnesia.
amnesty ['æmnɪstɪ] *n* amnistia; **to grant an** ~ **to** concedere l'amnistia a, amnistiare.
Amnesty International *n* Amnesty International *f*.
amoeba, (*US*) **ameba** [ə'mi:bə] *n* ameba.
amok [ə'mɔk] *adv*: **to run** ~ diventare pazzo(a) furioso(a).

among(st) [ə'mʌŋ(st)] *prep* fra, tra, in mezzo a.
amoral [eɪ'mɔrəl] *adj* amorale.
amorous ['æmərəs] *adj* amoroso(a).
amorphous [ə'mɔːfəs] *adj* amorfo(a).
amortization [əmɔːtaɪ'zeɪʃən] *n* (*COMM*) ammortamento.
amount [ə'maunt] *n* (*sum of money*) somma; (*of bill etc*) importo; (*quantity*) quantità *f inv* ♦ *vi*: **to** ~ **to** (*total*) ammontare a; (*be same as*) essere come; **this** ~**s to a refusal** questo equivale a un rifiuto.
amp(ère) ['æmp(ɛə*)] *n* ampere *m inv*; **a 13** ~ **plug** una spina con fusibile da 13 ampere.
ampersand ['æmpəsænd] *n* e *f* commerciale.
amphetamine [æm'fɛtəmi:n] *n* anfetamina.
amphibian [æm'fɪbɪən] *n* anfibio.
amphibious [æm'fɪbɪəs] *adj* anfibio(a).
amphitheatre, (*US*) **amphitheater** ['æmfɪθɪətə*] *n* anfiteatro.
ample ['æmpl] *adj* ampio(a); spazioso(a); (*enough*): **this is** ~ questo è più che sufficiente; **to have** ~ **time/room** avere assai tempo/posto.
amplifier ['æmplɪfaɪə*] *n* amplificatore *m*.
amplify ['æmplɪfaɪ] *vt* amplificare.
amply ['æmplɪ] *adv* ampiamente.
ampoule, (*US*) **ampule** ['æmpu:l] *n* (*MED*) fiala.
amputate ['æmpjuteɪt] *vt* amputare.
amputee [æmpju'ti:] *n* mutilato/a, chi ha subito un'amputazione.
Amsterdam [æmstə'dæm] *n* Amsterdam *f*.
amt *abbr* = **amount**.
amuck [ə'mʌk] *adv* = **amok**.
amuse [ə'mju:z] *vt* divertire; **to** ~ **o.s. with sth/by doing sth** divertirsi con qc/a fare qc; **to be** ~**d at** essere divertito da; **he was not** ~**d** non l'ha trovato divertente.
amusement [ə'mju:zmənt] *n* divertimento; **much to my** ~ con mio grande spasso.
amusement arcade *n* sala giochi (*solo con macchinette a gettoni*).
amusement park *n* luna park *m inv*.
amusing [ə'mju:zɪŋ] *adj* divertente.
an [æn, ən, n] *indef art see* **a**.
ANA *n abbr* = **American Newspaper Association; American Nurses Association**.
anachronism [ə'nækrənɪzəm] *n* anacronismo.
anaemia [ə'ni:mɪə] *n* anemia.
anaemic [ə'ni:mɪk] *adj* anemico(a).
anaesthetic [ænɪs'θɛtɪk] *adj* anestetico(a) ♦ *n* anestetico; **local/general** ~ anestesia locale/totale; **under the** ~ sotto anestesia.
anaesthetist [æ'ni:sθɪtɪst] *n* anestesista *m/f*.

anagram ['ænəgræm] *n* anagramma *m.*

anal ['eɪnl] *adj* anale.

analgesic [ænæl'dʒiːsɪk] *adj* analgesico(a) ♦ *n* analgesico.

analogous [ə'næləgəs] *adj:* ~ **to** *or* **with** analogo(a) a.

analog(ue) ['ænəlɔg] *adj* (*watch, computer*) analogico(a).

analogy [ə'nælədʒɪ] *n* analogia; **to draw an** ~ **between** fare un'analogia tra.

analyse ['ænəlaɪz] *vt* (*BRIT*) analizzare.

analysis, *pl* **analyses** [ə'næləsɪs, -siːz] *n* analisi *f inv*; **in the last** ~ in ultima analisi.

analyst ['ænəlɪst] *n* (*political* ~ *etc*) analista *m/f*; (*US*) (psic)analista *m/f.*

analytic(al) [ænə'lɪtɪk(l)] *adj* analitico(a).

analyze ['ænəlaɪz] *vt* (*US*) = **analyse.**

anarchic [æ'nɑːkɪk] *adj* anarchico(a).

anarchist ['ænəkɪst] *adj, n* anarchico(a).

anarchy ['ænəkɪ] *n* anarchia.

anathema [ə'næθɪmə] *n*: **it is** ~ **to him** non ne vuol neanche sentir parlare.

anatomical [ænə'tɒmɪkl] *adj* anatomico(a).

anatomy [ə'nætəmɪ] *n* anatomia.

ANC *n abbr* = *African National Congress.*

ancestor ['ænsɪstə*] *n* antenato/a.

ancestral [æn'sɛstrəl] *adj* avito(a).

ancestry ['ænsɪstrɪ] *n* antenati *mpl*; ascendenza.

anchor ['æŋkə*] *n* ancora ♦ *vi* (*also:* **to drop** ~) gettare l'ancora ♦ *vt* ancorare; **to weigh** ~ salpare *or* levare l'ancora.

anchorage ['æŋkərɪdʒ] *n* ancoraggio.

anchor man *n* (*TV, RADIO*) anchorman *m inv.*

anchor woman *n* (*TV, RADIO*) anchorwoman *f inv.*

anchovy ['æntʃəvɪ] *n* acciuga.

ancient ['eɪnʃənt] *adj* antico(a); (*fig*) anziano(a); ~ **monument** monumento storico.

ancillary [æn'sɪlərɪ] *adj* ausiliario(a).

and [ænd] *conj* e (*often ed before vowel*); ~ **so on** e così via; **try** ~ **do it** prova a farlo; **come** ~ **sit here** vieni a sedere qui; **better** ~ **better** sempre meglio; **more** ~ **more** sempre di più.

Andes ['ændiːz] *npl*: **the** ~ le Ande.

Andorra [æn'dɔːrə] *n* Andorra.

anecdote ['ænɪkdəʊt] *n* aneddoto.

anemia [ə'niːmɪə] *etc* = **anaemia** *etc.*

anemone [ə'nɛmənɪ] *n* (*BOT*) anemone *m*; (*sea* ~) anemone *m* di mare, attinia.

anesthetic [ænɪs'θɛtɪk] *etc* = **anaesthetic** *etc.*

anew [ə'njuː] *adv* di nuovo.

angel ['eɪndʒəl] *n* angelo.

angel dust *n sedativo usato a scopo*

allucinogeno.

anger ['æŋgə*] *n* rabbia ♦ *vt* arrabbiare.

angina [æn'dʒaɪnə] *n* angina pectoris.

angle ['æŋgl] *n* angolo ♦ *vi*: **to** ~ **for** (*fig*) cercare di avere; **from their** ~ dal loro punto di vista.

angler ['æŋglə*] *n* pescatore *m* con la lenza.

Anglican ['æŋglɪkən] *adj, n* anglicano(a).

anglicize ['æŋglɪsaɪz] *vt* anglicizzare.

angling ['æŋglɪŋ] *n* pesca con la lenza.

Anglo- ['æŋgləʊ] *prefix* anglo...; ~**Italian** *adj, n* italobritannico(a).

Anglo-Saxon ['æŋgləʊ'sæksən] *adj, n* anglosassone (*m/f*).

Angola [æŋ'gəʊlə] *n* Angola.

Angolan [æŋ'gəʊlən] *adj, n* angolano(a).

angrily ['æŋgrɪlɪ] *adv* con rabbia.

angry ['æŋgrɪ] *adj* arrabbiato(a), furioso(a); **to be** ~ **with sb/at sth** essere in collera con qn/per qc; **to get** ~ arrabbiarsi; **to make sb** ~ fare arrabbiare qn.

anguish ['æŋgwɪʃ] *n* angoscia.

anguished ['æŋgwɪʃt] *adj* angosciato(a), pieno(a) d'angoscia.

angular ['æŋgjʊlə*] *adj* angolare.

animal ['ænɪməl] *adj, n* animale (*m*).

animal rights *npl* diritti *mpl* degli animali.

animate *vt* ['ænɪmeɪt] animare ♦ *adj* ['ænɪmɪt] animato(a).

animated ['ænɪmeɪtɪd] *adj* animato(a).

animation [ænɪ'meɪʃən] *n* animazione *f.*

animosity [ænɪ'mɒsɪtɪ] *n* animosità.

aniseed ['ænɪsiːd] *n* semi *mpl* di anice.

Ankara ['æŋkərə] *n* Ankara.

ankle ['æŋkl] *n* caviglia.

ankle socks *npl* calzini *mpl.*

annex *n* ['ænɛks] (*also: BRIT:* annexe) edificio annesso ♦ *vt* [ə'nɛks] annettere.

annexation [ænɛk'seɪʃən] *n* annessione *f.*

annihilate [ə'naɪəleɪt] *vt* annientare.

annihilation [ənaɪə'leɪʃən] *n* annientamento.

anniversary [ænɪ'vɜːsərɪ] *n* anniversario.

anniversary dinner *n* cena commemorativa.

annotate ['ænəuteɪt] *vt* annotare.

announce [ə'naʊns] *vt* annunciare; **he** ~**d that he wasn't going** ha dichiarato che non (ci) sarebbe andato.

announcement [ə'naʊnsmənt] *n* annuncio; (*letter, card*) partecipazione *f*; **I'd like to make an** ~ ho una comunicazione da fare.

announcer [ə'naʊnsə*] *n* (*RADIO, TV*: *between programmes*) annunciatore/trice; (: *in a programme*) presentatore/trice.

annoy [ə'nɔɪ] *vt* dare fastidio a; **to be** ~**ed (at sth/with sb)** essere seccato *or* irritato

(per qc/con qn); **don't get** ~**ed!** non
irritarti!

annoyance [ə'nɔɪəns] n fastidio; (*cause of*
~) noia.

annoying [ə'nɔɪɪŋ] adj irritante,
seccante.

annual ['ænjuəl] adj annuale ♦ n (*BOT*)
pianta annua; (*book*) annuario.

annual general meeting (AGM) n (*BRIT*)
assemblea generale.

annually ['ænjuəlɪ] adv annualmente.

annual report n relazione f annuale.

annuity [ə'njuːɪtɪ] n annualità f inv; **life** ~
vitalizio.

annul [ə'nʌl] vt annullare; (*law*) rescindere.

annulment [ə'nʌlmənt] n annullamento;
rescissione f.

annum ['ænəm] n see **per annum**.

Annunciation [ənʌnsɪ'eɪʃən] n
Annunciazione f.

anode ['ænəud] n anodo.

anoint [ə'nɔɪnt] vt ungere.

anomalous [ə'nɔmələs] adj anomalo(a).

anomaly [ə'nɔməlɪ] n anomalia.

anon. [ə'nɔn] abbr = **anonymous**.

anonymity [ænə'nɪmɪtɪ] n anonimato.

anonymous [ə'nɔnɪməs] adj anonimo(a); **to
remain** ~ mantenere l'anonimato.

anorak ['ænəræk] n giacca a vento.

anorexia [ænə'rɛksɪə] n (*also:* ~ **nervosa**)
anoressia.

anorexic [ænə'rɛksɪk] adj, n anoressico(a).

another [ə'nʌðə*] adj: ~ **book** (*one more*)
un altro libro, ancora un libro; (*a
different one*) un altro libro ♦ pron un
altro(un'altra), ancora uno(a); ~ **drink?**
ancora qualcosa da bere?; **in** ~ **5 years**
fra altri 5 anni; *see also* **one**.

ANSI n abbr (= *American National Standards
Institute*) Istituto americano di
standardizzazione.

answer ['ɑːnsə*] n risposta; soluzione f ♦ vi
rispondere ♦ vt (*reply to*) rispondere a;
(*problem*) risolvere; (*prayer*) esaudire; **in**
~ **to your letter** in risposta alla sua
lettera; **to** ~ **the phone** rispondere (al
telefono); **to** ~ **the bell** rispondere al
campanello; **to** ~ **the door** aprire la
porta.

▶**answer back** vi ribattere.

▶**answer for** vt fus essere responsabile di.

▶**answer to** vt fus (*description*)
corrispondere a.

answerable ['ɑːnsərəbl] adj: ~ (**to sb/for
sth**) responsabile (verso qn/di qc); **I am** ~
to no one non devo rispondere a
nessuno.

answering machine ['ɑːnsərɪŋ-] n

segreteria (telefonica) automatica.

ant [ænt] n formica.

antagonism [æn'tægənɪzəm] n
antagonismo.

antagonist [æn'tægənɪst] n antagonista m/f.

antagonistic [æntægə'nɪstɪk] adj
antagonistico(a).

antagonize [æn'tægənaɪz] vt provocare
l'ostilità di.

Antarctic [ænt'ɑːktɪk] n: **the** ~ l'Antartide f
♦ adj antartico(a).

Antarctica [ænt'ɑːktɪkə] n Antartide f.

Antarctic Circle n Circolo polare
antartico.

Antarctic Ocean n Oceano antartico.

ante ['æntɪ] n (*CARDS, fig*): **to up the** ~
alzare la posta in palio.

ante... ['æntɪ] prefix anti..., ante..., pre....

anteater ['æntiːtə*] n formichiere m.

antecedent [æntɪ'siːdənt] n antecedente m,
precedente m.

antechamber ['æntɪtʃeɪmbə*] n
anticamera.

antelope ['æntɪləup] n antilope f.

antenatal ['æntɪ'neɪtl] adj prenatale.

antenatal clinic n assistenza medica
preparto.

antenna, pl **antennae** [æn'tɛnə, -niː] n
antenna.

anthem ['ænθəm] n antifona; **national** ~
inno nazionale.

ant-hill ['ænthɪl] n formicaio.

anthology [æn'θɔlədʒɪ] n antologia.

anthropologist [ænθrə'pɔlədʒɪst] n
antropologo/a.

anthropology [ænθrə'pɔlədʒɪ] n
antropologia.

anti- ['æntɪ] prefix anti....

anti-aircraft ['æntɪ'eəkrɑːft] adj
antiaereo(a).

anti-aircraft defence n difesa antiaerea.

antiballistic ['æntɪbə'lɪstɪk] adj
antibalistico(a).

antibiotic ['æntɪbaɪ'ɔtɪk] adj antibiotico(a)
♦ n antibiotico.

antibody ['æntɪbɔdɪ] n anticorpo.

anticipate [æn'tɪsɪpeɪt] vt prevedere;
pregustare; (*wishes, request*) prevenire;
as ~**d** come previsto; **this is worse than I**
~**d** è peggio di quel che immaginavo or
pensavo.

anticipation [æntɪsɪ'peɪʃən] n anticipazione
f; (*expectation*) aspettative fpl; **thanking
you in** ~ vi ringrazio in anticipo.

anticlimax ['æntɪ'klaɪmæks] n: **it was an** ~
fu una completa delusione.

anticlockwise ['æntɪ'klɔkwaɪz] adj in senso
antiorario.

antics ['æntɪks] *npl* buffonerie *fpl.*

anticyclone ['æntɪ'saɪkləun] *n* anticiclone *m.*

antidote ['æntɪdəut] *n* antidoto.

antifreeze ['æntɪfriːz] *n* anticongelante *m.*

anti-globalization ['æntɪɡləubəlaɪ'zeɪʃən] *adj* antiglobalizzazione *inv.*

antihistamine [æntɪ'hɪstəmɪn] *n* antistaminico.

Antilles [æn'tɪliːz] *npl:* **the ~** le Antille.

antipathy [æn'tɪpəθɪ] *n* antipatia.

antiperspirant ['æntɪ'pə:spərənt] *adj* antitraspirante.

Antipodean [æntɪpə'diːən] *adj* degli Antipodi.

Antipodes [æn'tɪpədiːz] *npl:* **the ~** gli Antipodi.

antiquarian [æntɪ'kwɛərɪən] *adj:* ~ **bookshop** libreria antiquaria ♦ *n* antiquario/a.

antiquated ['æntɪkweɪtɪd] *adj* antiquato(a).

antique [æn'tiːk] *n* antichità *f inv* ♦ *adj* antico(a).

antique dealer *n* antiquario/a.

antique shop *n* negozio d'antichità.

antiquity [æn'tɪkwɪtɪ] *n* antichità *f inv.*

anti-semitic ['æntɪsɪ'mɪtɪk] *adj* antisemitico(a), antisemita.

anti-semitism ['æntɪ'sɛmɪtɪzəm] *n* antisemitismo.

antiseptic [æntɪ'sɛptɪk] *adj* antisettico(a) ♦ *n* antisettico.

antisocial ['æntɪ'səuʃəl] *adj* asociale; (*against society*) antisociale.

antitank [æntɪ'tæŋk] *adj* anticarro *inv.*

antithesis, *pl* **antitheses** [æn'tɪθɪsɪs, -siːz] *n* antitesi *f inv;* (*contrast*) carattere *m* antitetico.

anti-trust [æntɪ'trʌst] *adj* (*COMM*): ~ **legislation** legislazione *f* antitrust *inv.*

antlers ['æntləz] *npl* palchi *mpl.*

Antwerp ['æntwə:p] *n* Anversa.

anus ['eɪnəs] *n* ano.

anvil ['ænvɪl] *n* incudine *f.*

anxiety [æŋ'zaɪətɪ] *n* ansia; (*keenness*): ~ **to do** smania di fare.

anxious ['æŋkʃəs] *adj* ansioso(a), inquieto(a); (*keen*): ~ **to do/that** impaziente di fare/che + *sub;* **I'm very ~ about you** sono molto preoccupato *or* in pensiero per te.

anxiously ['æŋkʃəslɪ] *adv* ansiosamente, con ansia.

============ *KEYWORD*

any ['ɛnɪ] *adj* **1** (*in questions etc*): **have you ~ butter?** hai del burro?, hai un po' di burro?; **have you ~ children?** hai

bambini?; **if there are ~ tickets left** se ci sono ancora (dei) biglietti, se c'è ancora qualche biglietto

2 (*with negative*): **I haven't ~ money/ books** non ho soldi/libri; **without ~ difficulty** senza nessuna *or* alcuna difficoltà

3 (*no matter which*) qualsiasi, qualunque; **choose ~ book you like** scegli un libro qualsiasi

4 (*in phrases*): **in ~ case** in ogni caso; ~ **day now** da un giorno all'altro; **at ~ moment** in qualsiasi momento, da un momento all'altro; **at ~ rate** ad ogni modo

♦ *pron* **1** (*in questions, with negative*): **have you got ~?** ne hai?; **can ~ of you sing?** qualcuno di voi sa cantare?; **I haven't ~ (of them)** non ne ho

2 (*no matter which one(s)*): **take ~ of those books (you like)** prendi uno qualsiasi di quei libri

♦ *adv* **1** (*in questions etc*): **do you want ~ more soup/sandwiches?** vuoi ancora un po' di minestra/degli altri panini?; **are you feeling ~ better?** ti senti meglio?

2 (*with negative*): **I can't hear him ~ more** non lo sento più; **don't wait ~ longer** non aspettare più.

anybody ['ɛnɪbɔdɪ] *pron* qualsiasi persona; (*in interrogative sentences*) qualcuno; (*in negative sentences*): **I don't see ~** non vedo nessuno.

anyhow ['ɛnɪhau] *adv* in qualsiasi modo; (*haphazard*) come capita; **I shall go ~** ci andrò lo stesso *or* comunque.

anyone ['ɛnɪwʌn] *pron* = **anybody**.

anyplace ['ɛnɪpleɪs] *pron* (*US col*) = **anywhere**.

anything ['ɛnɪθɪŋ] *pron* qualsiasi cosa; (*in interrogative sentences*) qualcosa; (*in negative sentences*) non ... niente, non ... nulla; ~ **else?** (*in shop*) basta (così)?; **it can cost ~ between £15 and £20** può costare qualcosa come 15 o 20 sterline.

anytime ['ɛnɪtaɪm] *adv* in qualunque momento; quando vuole.

anyway ['ɛnɪweɪ] *adv* in *or* ad ogni modo.

anywhere ['ɛnɪwɛə*] *adv* da qualsiasi parte; (*in interrogative sentences*) da qualche parte; **I don't see him ~** non lo vedo da nessuna parte; ~ **in the world** dovunque nel mondo.

Anzac ['ænzæk] *n abbr* (= *Australia-New Zealand Army Corps*) A.N.Z.A.C. *m.*

Anzac Day *n see boxed note.*

ANZAC DAY

*L'**Anzac Day** è una festa nazionale australiana e neozelandese che cade il 25 aprile e commemora il famoso sbarco delle forze armate congiunte dei due paesi a Gallipoli nel 1915, durante la prima guerra mondiale.*

apart [ə'pɑːt] *adv* (*to one side*) a parte; (*separately*) separatamente; **with one's legs** ~ con le gambe divaricate; **10 miles/a long way** ~ a 10 miglia di distanza/molto lontani l'uno dall'altro; **they are living** ~ sono separati; ~ **from** *prep* a parte, eccetto.

apartheid [ə'pɑːteɪt] *n* apartheid *f*.

apartment [ə'pɑːtmənt] *n* (*US*) appartamento; ~**s** *npl* appartamento ammobiliato.

apartment building *n* (*US*) stabile *m*, caseggiato.

apathetic [æpə'θεtɪk] *adj* apatico(a).

apathy ['æpəθɪ] *n* apatia.

APB *n abbr* (*US*: = *all points bulletin*: *police expression*) espressione della polizia che significa "*trovate e arrestate il sospetto*".

ape [eɪp] *n* scimmia ♦ *vt* scimmiottare.

Apennines ['æpənaɪnz] *npl*: **the** ~ gli Apennini.

aperitif [ə'pεrɪtiːf] *n* aperitivo.

aperture ['æpətʃjuə*] *n* apertura.

APEX ['eɪpεks] *n abbr* (*AVIAT*: = *advance purchase excursion*) APEX *m inv*.

apex ['eɪpεks] *n* apice *m*.

aphrodisiac [æfrəu'dɪzɪæk] *adj* afrodisiaco(a) ♦ *n* afrodisiaco.

apiece [ə'piːs] *adv* ciascuno(a).

aplomb [ə'plɔm] *n* disinvoltura.

APO *n abbr* (*US*: = *Army Post Office*) ufficio postale dell'esercito.

apocalypse [ə'pɔkəlɪps] *n* apocalisse *f*.

apolitical [eɪpə'lɪtɪkl] *adj* apolitico(a).

apologetic [əpɔlə'dʒεtɪk] *adj* (*tone*, *letter*) di scusa; **to be very** ~ **about** scusarsi moltissimo di.

apologetically [əpɔlə'dʒεtɪkəlɪ] *adv* per scusarsi.

apologize [ə'pɔlədʒaɪz] *vi*: **to** ~ **(for sth to sb)** scusarsi (di qc a qn), chiedere scusa (a qn per qc).

apology [ə'pɔlədʒɪ] *n* scuse *fpl*; **please accept my apologies** la prego di accettare le mie scuse.

apoplexy ['æpəplεksɪ] *n* apoplessia.

apostle [ə'pɔsl] *n* apostolo.

apostrophe [ə'pɔstrəfɪ] *n* (*sign*) apostrofo.

appal [ə'pɔːl] *vt* atterrire; sgomentare.

Appalachian Mountains [æpə'leɪʃən-] *npl*: **the** ~ i Monti Appalachi.

appalling [ə'pɔːlɪŋ] *adj* spaventoso(a); **she's an** ~ **cook** è un disastro come cuoca.

apparatus [æpə'reɪtəs] *n* apparato.

apparel [ə'pærl] *n* (*US*) abbigliamento, confezioni *fpl*.

apparent [ə'pærənt] *adj* evidente.

apparently [ə'pærəntlɪ] *adv* evidentemente, a quanto pare.

apparition [æpə'rɪʃən] *n* apparizione *f*.

appeal [ə'piːl] *vi* (*LAW*) appellarsi alla legge ♦ *n* (*LAW*) appello; (*request*) richiesta; (*charm*) attrattiva; **to** ~ **for** chiedere (con insistenza); **to** ~ **to** (*subj*: *person*) appellarsi a; (: *thing*) piacere a; **to** ~ **to sb for mercy** chiedere pietà a qn; **it doesn't** ~ **to me** mi dice poco; **right of** ~ diritto d'appello.

appealing [ə'piːlɪŋ] *adj* (*moving*) commovente; (*attractive*) attraente.

appear [ə'pɪə*] *vi* apparire; (*LAW*) comparire; (*publication*) essere pubblicato(a); (*seem*) sembrare; **it would** ~ **that** sembra che; **to** ~ **in Hamlet** recitare nell'Amleto; **to** ~ **on TV** presentarsi in televisione.

appearance [ə'pɪərəns] *n* apparizione *f*; (*look*, *aspect*) aspetto; **to put in** *or* **make an** ~ fare atto di presenza; **by order of** ~ (*THEAT*) in ordine di apparizione; **to keep up** ~**s** salvare le apparenze; **to all** ~**s** a giudicar dalle apparenze.

appease [ə'piːz] *vt* calmare, appagare.

appeasement [ə'piːzmənt] *n* (*POL*) appeasement *m inv*.

append [ə'pεnd] *vt* (*COMPUT*) aggiungere in coda.

appendage [ə'pεndɪdʒ] *n* aggiunta.

appendicitis [əpεndɪ'saɪtɪs] *n* appendicite *f*.

appendix, *pl* **appendices** [ə'pεndɪks, -siːz] *n* appendice *f*; **to have one's** ~ **out** operarsi *or* farsi operare di appendicite.

appetite ['æpɪtaɪt] *n* appetito; **that walk has given me an** ~ la passeggiata mi ha messo appetito.

appetizer ['æpɪtaɪzə*] *n* (*food*) stuzzichino; (*drink*) aperitivo.

appetizing ['æpɪtaɪzɪŋ] *adj* appetitoso(a).

applaud [ə'plɔːd] *vt*, *vi* applaudire.

applause [ə'plɔːz] *n* applauso.

apple ['æpl] *n* mela; (*also*: ~ **tree**) melo; **the** ~ **of one's eye** la pupilla dei propri occhi.

apple turnover *n* sfogliatella alle mele.

appliance [ə'plaɪəns] *n* apparecchio; **electrical** ~**s** elettrodomestici *mpl*.

applicable [ə'plɪkəbl] *adj* applicabile; **to be**

~ **to** essere valido per; **the law is** ~ **from January** la legge entrerà in vigore in gennaio.
applicant ['æplɪkənt] *n* candidato/a; (*ADMIN: for benefit etc*) chi ha fatto domanda *or* richiesta.
application [æplɪ'keɪʃən] *n* applicazione *f*; (*for a job, a grant etc*) domanda; **on** ~ su richiesta.
application form *n* modulo di domanda.
application program *n* (*COMPUT*) programma applicativo.
applications package *n* (*COMPUT*) software *m inv* applicativo.
applied [ə'plaɪd] *adj* applicato(a); ~ **arts** arti *fpl* applicate.
apply [ə'plaɪ] *vt*: **to** ~ **(to)** (*paint, ointment*) dare (a); (*theory, technique*) applicare (a) ♦ *vi*: **to** ~ **to** (*ask*) rivolgersi a; (*be suitable for, relevant to*) riguardare, riferirsi a; **to** ~ **(for)** (*permit, grant, job*) fare domanda (per); **to** ~ **the brakes** frenare; **to** ~ **o.s. to** dedicarsi a.
appoint [ə'pɔɪnt] *vt* nominare.
appointee [əpɔɪn'tiː] *n* incaricato/a.
appointment [ə'pɔɪntmənt] *n* nomina; (*arrangement to meet*) appuntamento; **by** ~ su *or* per appuntamento; **to make an** ~ **with sb** prendere un appuntamento con qn; (*PRESS*): **"~s (vacant)"** "offerte *fpl* di impiego".
apportion [ə'pɔːʃən] *vt* attribuire.
appraisal [ə'preɪzl] *n* valutazione *f*.
appraise [ə'preɪz] *vt* (*value*) valutare, fare una stima di; (*situation etc*) fare il bilancio di.
appreciable [ə'priːʃəbl] *adj* apprezzabile.
appreciably [ə'priːʃəblɪ] *adv* notevolmente, sensibilmente.
appreciate [ə'priːʃɪeɪt] *vt* (*like*) apprezzare; (*be grateful for*) essere riconoscente di; (*be aware of*) rendersi conto di ♦ *vi* (*COMM*) aumentare; **I ~d your help** ti sono grato per l'aiuto.
appreciation [əpriːʃɪ'eɪʃən] *n* apprezzamento; (*FINANCE*) aumento del valore.
appreciative [ə'priːʃɪətɪv] *adj* (*person*) sensibile; (*comment*) elogiativo(a).
apprehend [æprɪ'hɛnd] *vt* (*arrest*) arrestare; (*understand*) comprendere.
apprehension [æprɪ'hɛnʃən] *n* (*fear*) inquietudine *f*.
apprehensive [æprɪ'hɛnsɪv] *adj* apprensivo(a).
apprentice [ə'prɛntɪs] *n* apprendista *m/f* ♦ *vt*: **to be ~d to** lavorare come apprendista presso.

apprenticeship [ə'prɛntɪsʃɪp] *n* apprendistato; **to serve one's** ~ fare il proprio apprendistato *or* tirocinio.
appro. ['æprəu] *abbr* (*BRIT COMM: col*) = **approval**.
approach [ə'prəutʃ] *vi* avvicinarsi ♦ *vt* (*come near*) avvicinarsi a; (*ask, apply to*) rivolgersi a; (*subject, passer-by*) avvicinare ♦ *n* approccio; accesso; (*problem*) modo di affrontare; **to** ~ **sb about sth** rivolgersi a qn per qc.
approachable [ə'prəutʃəbl] *adj* accessibile.
approach road *n* strada d'accesso.
approbation [æprə'beɪʃən] *n* approvazione *f*, benestare *m*.
appropriate *vt* [ə'prəuprɪeɪt] (*take*) appropriarsi di ♦ *adj* [ə'prəuprɪɪt] appropriato(a); adatto(a); **it would not be** ~ **for me to comment** non sta a me fare dei commenti.
appropriately [ə'prəuprɪɪtlɪ] *adv* in modo appropriato.
appropriation [əprəuprɪ'eɪʃən] *n* stanziamento.
approval [ə'pruːvəl] *n* approvazione *f*; **on** ~ (*COMM*) in prova, in esame; **to meet with sb's** ~ soddisfare qn, essere di gradimento di qn.
approve [ə'pruːv] *vt*, *vi* approvare.
▶**approve of** *vt fus* approvare.
approved school *n* (*BRIT: old*) riformatorio.
approvingly [ə'pruːvɪŋlɪ] *adv* in approvazione.
approx. *abbr* = **approximately**.
approximate *adj* [ə'prɔksɪmɪt] approssimativo(a) ♦ *vt* [ə'prɔksɪmeɪt] essere un'approssimazione di, avvicinarsi a.
approximately [ə'prɔksɪmətlɪ] *adv* circa.
approximation [ə'prɔksɪ'meɪʃən] *n* approssimazione *f*.
APR *n abbr* (= *annual percentage rate*) tasso di percentuale annuo.
Apr. *abbr* (= *April*) apr.
apricot ['eɪprɪkɔt] *n* albicocca.
April ['eɪprəl] *n* aprile *m*; ~ **fool!** pesce d'aprile!; *for phrases see also* **July**.
April Fools' Day *see boxed note*.

APRIL FOOLS' DAY

April Fools' Day *è il primo aprile, il giorno degli scherzi e delle burle. Il nome deriva dal fatto che, se una persona cade nella trappola che gli è stata tesa, fa la figura del* **fool**, *cioè dello sciocco. Di recente gli scherzi stanno diventando sempre più elaborati, e persino i*

giornalisti a volte inventano vicende incredibili
per burlarsi dei lettori.

apron ['eɪprən] *n* grembiule *m*; (*AVIAT*) area
di stazionamento.

apse [æps] *n* (*ARCHIT*) abside *f*.

APT *n abbr* (*BRIT*: = *advanced passenger train*)
treno ad altissima velocità.

apt [æpt] *adj* (*suitable*) adatto(a); (*able*)
capace; (*likely*): **to be ~ to do** avere
tendenza a fare.

Apt. *abbr* = **apartment**.

aptitude ['æptɪtjuːd] *n* abilità *f inv*.

aptitude test *n* test *m inv* attitudinale.

aptly ['æptlɪ] *adv* appropriatamente, in
modo adatto.

aqualung ['ækwəlʌŋ] *n* autorespiratore *m*.

aquarium [ə'kwɛərɪəm] *n* acquario.

Aquarius [ə'kwɛərɪəs] *n* Acquario; **to be ~**
essere dell'Acquario.

aquatic [ə'kwætɪk] *adj* acquatico(a).

aqueduct ['ækwɪdʌkt] *n* acquedotto.

AR *abbr* (*US*) = *Arkansas*.

ARA *n abbr* (*BRIT*) = *Associate of the Royal
Academy*.

Arab ['ærəb] *adj, n* arabo(a).

Arabia [ə'reɪbɪə] *n* Arabia.

Arabian [ə'reɪbɪən] *adj* arabo(a).

Arabian Desert *n* Deserto arabico.

Arabian Sea *n* mare *m* Arabico.

Arabic ['ærəbɪk] *adj* arabico(a) ♦ *n* arabo.

Arabic numerals *npl* numeri arabi *mpl*,
numerazione *f* araba.

arable ['ærəbl] *adj* arabile.

ARAM *n abbr* (*BRIT*) = *Associate of the Royal
Academy of Music*.

arbitrary ['ɑːbɪtrərɪ] *adj* arbitrario(a).

arbitrate ['ɑːbɪtreɪt] *vi* arbitrare.

arbitration [ɑːbɪ'treɪʃən] *n* (*LAW*) arbitrato;
(*INDUSTRY*) arbitraggio.

arbitrator ['ɑːbɪtreɪtə*] *n* arbitro.

ARC *n abbr* (= *American Red Cross*) C.R.I. *f*
(= *Croce Rossa Italiana*).

arc [ɑːk] *n* arco.

arcade [ɑː'keɪd] *n* portico; (*passage with
shops*) galleria.

arch [ɑːtʃ] *n* arco; (*of foot*) arco plantare
♦ *vt* inarcare ♦ *prefix*: ~(-) grande (*before
n*); per eccellenza.

archaeological [ɑːkɪə'lɔdʒɪkəl] *adj*
archeologico(a).

archaeologist [ɑːkɪ'ɔlədʒɪst] *n*
archeologo/a.

archaeology [ɑːkɪ'ɔlədʒɪ] *n* archeologia.

archaic [ɑː'keɪɪk] *adj* arcaico(a).

archangel ['ɑːkeɪndʒəl] *n* arcangelo.

archbishop [ɑːtʃ'bɪʃəp] *n* arcivescovo.

arched [ɑːtʃt] *adj* arcuato(a), ad arco.

arch-enemy ['ɑːtʃ'ɛnɪmɪ] *n* arcinemico/a.

archeology [ɑːkɪ'ɔlədʒɪ] *etc* = **archaeology**
etc.

archer ['ɑːtʃə*] *n* arciere *m*.

archery ['ɑːtʃərɪ] *n* tiro all'arco.

archetypal ['ɑːkɪtaɪpəl] *adj* tipico(a).

archipelago [ɑːkɪ'pelɪgəu] *n* arcipelago.

architect ['ɑːkɪtɛkt] *n* architetto.

architectural [ɑːkɪ'tɛktʃərəl] *adj*
architettonico(a).

architecture ['ɑːkɪtɛktʃə*] *n* architettura.

archive file *n* (*COMPUT*) file *m inv* di
archivio.

archives ['ɑːkaɪvz] *npl* archivi *mpl*.

archivist ['ɑːkɪvɪst] *n* archivista *m/f*.

archway ['ɑːtʃweɪ] *n* arco.

ARCM *n abbr* (*BRIT*) = *Associate of the Royal
College of Music*.

Arctic ['ɑːktɪk] *adj* artico(a) ♦ *n*: **the ~**
l'Artico.

Arctic Circle *n* Circolo polare artico.

Arctic Ocean *n* Oceano artico.

ARD *n abbr* (*US MED*) = *acute respiratory
disease*.

ardent ['ɑːdənt] *adj* ardente.

ardour, (*US*) **ardor** ['ɑːdə*] *n* ardore *m*.

arduous ['ɑːdjuəs] *adj* arduo(a).

are [ɑː*] *vb see* **be**.

area ['ɛərɪə] *n* (*GEOM*) area; (*zone*) zona;
(: *smaller*) settore *m*; **dining ~** zona
pranzo; **the London ~** la zona di Londra.

area code *n* (*US TEL*) prefisso.

arena [ə'riːnə] *n* arena.

aren't [ɑːnt] = **are not**.

Argentina [ɑːdʒən'tiːnə] *n* Argentina.

Argentinian [ɑːdʒən'tɪnɪən] *adj, n*
argentino(a).

arguable ['ɑːgjuəbl] *adj* discutibile; **it is ~
whether … ** è una cosa discutibile se … +
sub.

arguably ['ɑːgjuəblɪ] *adv*: **it is ~ …** si può
sostenere che sia ….

argue ['ɑːgjuː] *vi* (*quarrel*) litigare; (*reason*)
ragionare ♦ *vt* (*debate: case, matter*)
dibattere; **to ~ that** sostenere che; **to ~
about sth (with sb)** litigare per *or* a
proposito di qc (con qn).

argument ['ɑːgjumənt] *n* (*reasons*)
argomento; (*quarrel*) lite *f*; (*debate*)
discussione *f*; **~ for/against** argomento a
or in favore di/contro.

argumentative [ɑːgju'mɛntətɪv] *adj*
litigioso(a).

aria ['ɑːrɪə] *n* aria.

ARIBA *n abbr* (*BRIT*) = *Associate of the Royal
Institute of British Architects*.

arid ['ærɪd] *adj* arido(a).

aridity [ə'rɪdɪtɪ] *n* aridità.

Aries ['ɛərɪz] n Ariete m; **to be** ~ essere dell'Ariete.

arise, pt **arose**, pp **arisen** [ə'raɪz, ə'rəuz, ə'rɪzn] vi alzarsi; (opportunity, problem) presentarsi; **to** ~ **from** risultare da; **should the need** ~ dovesse presentarsi la necessità, in caso di necessità.

aristocracy [ærɪs'tɔkrəsɪ] n aristocrazia.

aristocrat ['ærɪstəkræt] n aristocratico/a.

aristocratic [ærɪstə'krætɪk] adj aristocratico(a).

arithmetic [ə'rɪθmətɪk] n aritmetica.

arithmetical [ærɪθ'mɛtɪkəl] adj aritmetico(a).

Ariz. abbr (US) = Arizona.

ark [ɑːk] n: **Noah's A**~ l'arca di Noè.

Ark. abbr (US) = Arkansas.

arm [ɑːm] n braccio; (MIL: branch) arma ♦ vt armare; ~ **in** ~ a braccetto; see also **arms**.

armaments ['ɑːməmənts] npl (weapons) armamenti mpl.

armband ['ɑːmbænd] n bracciale m.

armchair ['ɑːmtʃɛə*] n poltrona.

armed [ɑːmd] adj armato(a).

armed forces npl forze fpl armate.

armed robbery n rapina a mano armata.

Armenia [ɑː'miːnɪə] n Armenia.

Armenian [ɑː'miːnɪən] adj armeno(a) ♦ n armeno/a; (LING) armeno.

armful ['ɑːmful] n bracciata.

armistice ['ɑːmɪstɪs] n armistizio.

armour, (US) **armor** ['ɑːmə*] n armatura; (also: ~-**plating**) corazza, blindatura; (MIL: tanks) mezzi mpl blindati.

armo(u)red car n autoblinda f inv.

armo(u)ry ['ɑːmərɪ] n arsenale m.

armpit ['ɑːmpɪt] n ascella.

armrest ['ɑːmrɛst] n bracciolo.

arms [ɑːmz] npl (weapons) armi fpl; (HERALDRY) stemma m.

arms control n controllo degli armamenti.

arms race n corsa agli armamenti.

army ['ɑːmɪ] n esercito.

aroma [ə'rəumə] n aroma.

aromatherapy [ərəumə'θɛrəpɪ] n aromaterapia.

aromatic [ærə'mætɪk] adj aromatico(a).

arose [ə'rəuz] pt of **arise**.

around [ə'raund] adv attorno, intorno ♦ prep intorno a; (fig: about): ~ **£5/3 o'clock** circa 5 sterline/le 3; **is he** ~**?** è in giro?

arousal [ə'rauzəl] n (sexual etc) eccitazione f; (awakening) risveglio.

arouse [ə'rauz] vt (sleeper) svegliare; (curiosity, passions) suscitare.

arrange [ə'reɪndʒ] vt sistemare; (programme) preparare ♦ vi: **we have** ~**d for a taxi to pick you up** la faremo venire

a prendere da un taxi; **it was** ~**d that ...** è stato deciso or stabilito che ...; **to** ~ **to do sth** mettersi d'accordo per fare qc.

arrangement [ə'reɪndʒmənt] n sistemazione f; (plans etc): ~**s** progetti mpl, piani mpl; **by** ~ su richiesta; **to come to an** ~ **(with sb)** venire ad un accordo (con qn), mettersi d'accordo or accordarsi (con qn); **I'll make** ~**s for you to be met** darò disposizioni or istruzioni perché ci sia qualcuno ad incontrarla.

arrant ['ærənt] adj: ~ **nonsense** colossali sciocchezze fpl.

array [ə'reɪ] n fila; (COMPUT) array m inv, insiemi mpl.

arrears [ə'rɪəz] npl arretrati mpl; **to be in** ~ **with one's rent** essere in arretrato con l'affitto.

arrest [ə'rɛst] vt arrestare; (sb's attention) attirare ♦ n arresto; **under** ~ in arresto.

arresting [ə'rɛstɪŋ] adj (fig) che colpisce.

arrival [ə'raɪvəl] n arrivo; (person) arrivato/a; **new** ~ nuovo venuto.

arrive [ə'raɪv] vi arrivare.

▶**arrive at** vt fus arrivare a.

arrogance ['ærəgəns] n arroganza.

arrogant ['ærəgənt] adj arrogante.

arrow ['ærəu] n freccia.

arse [ɑːs] n (BRIT col!) culo(!).

arsenal ['ɑːsɪnl] n arsenale m.

arsenic ['ɑːsnɪk] n arsenico.

arson ['ɑːsn] n incendio doloso.

art [ɑːt] n arte f; (craft) mestiere m; **work of** ~ opera d'arte; see also **arts**.

artefact, (US) **artifact** ['ɑːtɪfækt] n manufatto.

arterial [ɑː'tɪərɪəl] adj (ANAT) arterioso(a); (road etc) di grande comunicazione; ~ **roads** le (grandi or principali) arterie.

artery ['ɑːtərɪ] n arteria.

artful ['ɑːtful] adj furbo(a).

art gallery n galleria d'arte.

arthritis [ɑː'θraɪtɪs] n artrite f.

artichoke ['ɑːtɪtʃəuk] n carciofo; **Jerusalem** ~ topinambur m inv.

article ['ɑːtɪkl] n articolo; ~**s** npl (BRIT LAW: training) contratto di tirocinio; ~**s of clothing** indumenti mpl.

articles of association npl (COMM) statuto sociale.

articulate adj [ɑː'tɪkjulɪt] (person) che si esprime forbitamente; (speech) articolato(a) ♦ vi [ɑː'tɪkjuleɪt] articolare.

articulated lorry n (BRIT) autotreno.

artifact ['ɑːtɪfækt] n (US) = **artefact**.

artifice ['ɑːtɪfɪs] n (cunning) abilità, destrezza; (trick) artificio.

artificial [ɑːtɪ'fɪʃəl] adj artificiale.

artificial insemination [-ɪnsɛmɪ'neɪʃən] *n* fecondazione *f* artificiale.

artificial intelligence (AI) *n* intelligenza artificiale (IA).

artificial respiration *n* respirazione *f* artificiale.

artillery [ɑː'tɪlərɪ] *n* artiglieria.

artisan ['ɑːtɪzæn] *n* artigiano/a.

artist ['ɑːtɪst] *n* artista *m/f*.

artistic [ɑː'tɪstɪk] *adj* artistico(a).

artistry ['ɑːtɪstrɪ] *n* arte *f*.

artless ['ɑːtlɪs] *adj* semplice, ingenuo(a).

arts [ɑːts] *npl* (*SCOL*) lettere *fpl*.

art school *n* scuola d'arte.

artwork ['ɑːtwɔːk] *n* materiale *m* illustrativo.

ARV *n abbr* (= *American Revised Version*) *traduzione della Bibbia*.

AS *n abbr* (*US SCOL*: = *Associate in Science*) *titolo di studio*.

═══════════════ *KEYWORD*

as [æz] *conj* **1** (*referring to time*) mentre; ~ **the years went by** col passare degli anni; **he came in** ~ **I was leaving** arrivò mentre stavo uscendo; ~ **from tomorrow** da domani

2 (*in comparisons*): ~ **big** ~ grande come; **twice** ~ **big** ~ due volte più grande di; ~ **much/many** ~ tanto quanto/tanti quanti; ~ **soon** ~ **possible** prima possibile

3 (*since, because*) dal momento che, siccome

4 (*referring to manner, way*) come; **big** ~ **it is** grande com'è; **much** ~ **I like them**, … per quanto mi siano simpatici, …; **do** ~ **you wish** fa' come vuoi; ~ **she said** come ha detto lei

5 (*concerning*): ~ **for** *or* **to that** per quanto riguarda *or* quanto a quello

6: ~ **if** *or* **though** come se; **he looked** ~ **if he was ill** sembrava stare male; *see also* **long; such; well**

♦ *prep*: **he works** ~ **a driver** fa l'autista; ~ **chairman of the company, he** … come presidente della compagnia, lui …; **he gave me it** ~ **a present** me lo ha regalato.

ASA *n abbr* (= *American Standards Association*) *associazione per la normalizzazione*; (*BRIT*: = *Advertising Standards Association*) ≈ Istituto di Autodisciplina Pubblicitaria.

a.s.a.p. *abbr* (= *as soon as possible*) prima possibile.

asbestos [æz'bɛstəs] *n* asbesto, amianto.

ascend [ə'sɛnd] *vt* salire.

ascendancy [ə'sɛndənsɪ] *n* ascendente *m*.

ascendant [ə'sɛndənt] *n*: **to be in the** ~ essere in auge.

ascension [ə'sɛnʃən] *n*: **the A**~ (*REL*) l'Ascensione *f*.

Ascension Island *n* isola dell'Ascensione.

ascent [ə'sɛnt] *n* salita.

ascertain [æsə'teɪn] *vt* accertare.

ascetic [ə'sɛtɪk] *adj* ascetico(a).

asceticism [ə'sɛtɪsɪzəm] *n* ascetismo.

ASCII ['æskiː] *n abbr* (= *American Standard Code for Information Interchange*) ASCII *m*.

ascribe [ə'skraɪb] *vt*: **to** ~ **sth to** attribuire qc a.

ASCU *n abbr* (*US*) = *Association of State Colleges and Universities*.

ASE *n abbr* = *American Stock Exchange*.

ASH [æʃ] *n abbr* (*BRIT*: = *Action on Smoking and Health*) *iniziativa contro il fumo*.

ash [æʃ] *n* (*dust*) cenere *f*; ~ (**tree**) frassino.

ashamed [ə'ʃeɪmd] *adj* vergognoso(a); **to be** ~ **of** vergognarsi di; **to be** ~ (**of o.s.**) **for having done** vergognarsi di aver fatto.

ashen ['æʃən] *adj* (*pale*) livido(a).

ashore [ə'ʃɔː*] *adv* a terra; **to go** ~ sbarcare.

ashtray ['æʃtreɪ] *n* portacenere *m*.

Ash Wednesday *n* Mercoledì *m inv* delle Ceneri.

Asia Minor *n* Asia minore.

Asian ['eɪʃən] *adj*, *n* asiatico(a).

Asiatic [eɪsɪ'ætɪk] *adj* asiatico(a).

aside [ə'saɪd] *adv* da parte ♦ *n* a parte *m*; **to take sb** ~ prendere qn da parte; ~ **from** (*as well as*) oltre a; (*except for*) a parte.

ask [ɑːsk] *vt* (*request*) chiedere; (*question*) domandare; (*invite*) invitare; **to** ~ **about sth** informarsi su *or* di qc; **to** ~ **sb sth/sb to do sth** chiedere qc a qn/a qn di fare qc; **to** ~ **sb about sth** chiedere a qn di qc; **to** ~ (**sb**) **a question** fare una domanda (a qn); **to** ~ **sb the time** chiedere l'ora a qn; **to** ~ **sb out to dinner** invitare qn a mangiare fuori; **you should** ~ **at the information desk** dovreste rivolgersi all'ufficio informazioni.

▶**ask after** *vt fus* chiedere di.

▶**ask for** *vt fus* chiedere; **it's just** ~**ing for trouble** *or* **for it** è proprio (come) andarsele a cercare.

askance [ə'skɑːns] *adv*: **to look** ~ **at sb** guardare qn di traverso.

askew [ə'skjuː] *adv* di traverso, storto.

asking price ['ɑːskɪŋ-] *n* prezzo di partenza.

asleep [ə'sliːp] *adj* addormentato(a); **to be** ~ dormire; **to fall** ~ addormentarsi.

ASLEF ['æzlɛf] *n abbr* (*BRIT*: = *Associated*

Society of Locomotive Engineers and Firemen) sindacato dei conducenti dei treni e dei macchinisti.
asp [æsp] *n* cobra *m inv* egiziano.
asparagus [əs'pærəgəs] *n* asparagi *mpl.*
asparagus tips *npl* punte *fpl* d'asparagi.
ASPCA *n abbr* (= *American Society for the Prevention of Cruelty to Animals*) ≈ E.N.P.A. *m* (*Ente Nazionale per la Protezione degli Animali*).
aspect ['æspɛkt] *n* aspetto.
aspersions [əs'pə:ʃənz] *npl*: **to cast ~ on** diffamare.
asphalt ['æsfælt] *n* asfalto.
asphyxiate [æs'fıksıeıt] *vt* asfissiare.
asphyxiation [æsfıksı'eıʃən] *n* asfissia.
aspiration [æspə'reıʃən] *n* aspirazione *f.*
aspire [əs'paıə*] *vi*: **to ~ to** aspirare a.
aspirin ['æsprın] *n* aspirina.
aspiring [əs'paıərıŋ] *adj* aspirante.
ass [æs] *n* asino; (*US col!*) culo(*!*).
assail [ə'seıl] *vt* assalire.
assailant [ə'seılənt] *n* assalitore *m.*
assassin [ə'sæsın] *n* assassino.
assassinate [ə'sæsıneıt] *vt* assassinare.
assassination [əsæsı'neıʃən] *n* assassinio.
assault [ə'sɔ:lt] *n* (*MIL*) assalto; (*gen: attack*) aggressione *f*; (*LAW*): **~ (and battery)** minacce e vie di fatto *fpl* ♦ *vt* assaltare; aggredire; (*sexually*) violentare.
assemble [ə'sɛmbl] *vt* riunire; (*TECH*) montare ♦ *vi* riunirsi.
assembly [ə'sɛmblı] *n* (*meeting*) assemblea; (*construction*) montaggio.
assembly language *n* (*COMPUT*) linguaggio assemblativo.
assembly line *n* catena di montaggio.
assent [ə'sɛnt] *n* assenso, consenso ♦ *vi* assentire; **to ~ (to sth)** approvare (qc).
assert [ə'sə:t] *vt* asserire; (*insist on*) far valere; **to ~ o.s.** farsi valere.
assertion [ə'sə:ʃən] *n* asserzione *f.*
assertive [ə'sə:tıv] *adj* che sa imporsi.
assess [ə'sɛs] *vt* valutare.
assessment [ə'sɛsmənt] *n* valutazione *f*; (*judgment*): **~ (of)** giudizio (su).
assessor [ə'sɛsə*] *n* perito; funzionario del fisco.
asset ['æsɛt] *n* vantaggio; (*person*) elemento prezioso; **~s** *npl* (*COMM*) beni *mpl*; disponibilità *fpl*; attivo.
asset-stripping ['æsɛt'strıpıŋ] *n* (*COMM*) acquisto di una società in fallimento con lo scopo di rivenderne le attività.
assiduous [ə'sıdjuəs] *adj* assiduo(a).
assign [ə'saın] *vt*: **to ~ (to)** (*task*) assegnare (a); (*resources*) riservare (a); (*cause, meaning*) attribuire (a); **to ~ a date to sth**

fissare la data di qc.
assignment [ə'saınmənt] *n* compito.
assimilate [ə'sımıleıt] *vt* assimilare.
assimilation [əsımı'leıʃən] *n* assimilazione *f.*
assist [ə'sıst] *vt* assistere, aiutare.
assistance [ə'sıstəns] *n* assistenza, aiuto.
assistant [ə'sıstənt] *n* assistente *m/f*; (*BRIT: also*: **shop ~**) commesso/a.
assistant manager *n* vicedirettore *m.*
assizes [ə'saızız] *npl* assise *fpl.*
associate [ə'səuʃııt] *adj* associato(a); (*member*) aggiunto(a) ♦ *n* collega *m/f*; (*in business*) socio/a ♦ *vb* [ə'səuʃıeıt] *vt* associare ♦ *vi*: **to ~ with sb** frequentare qn.
associated company [ə'səusı'eıtıd-] *n* società collegata.
associate director *n* amministratore *m* aggiunto.
association [əsəusı'eıʃən] *n* associazione *f*; **in ~ with** in collaborazione con.
association football *n* (*BRIT*) (gioco del) calcio.
assorted [ə'sɔ:tıd] *adj* assortito(a); **in ~ sizes** in diverse taglie.
assortment [ə'sɔ:tmənt] *n* assortimento.
Asst. *abbr* = **assistant.**
assuage [ə'sweıdʒ] *vt* alleviare.
assume [ə'sju:m] *vt* supporre; (*responsibilities etc*) assumere; (*attitude, name*) prendere.
assumed name *n* nome *m* falso.
assumption [ə'sʌmpʃən] *n* supposizione *f*, ipotesi *f inv*; **on the ~ that ...** partendo dal presupposto che ....
assurance [ə'ʃuərəns] *n* assicurazione *f*; (*self-confidence*) fiducia in se stesso; **I can give you no ~s** non posso assicurarle *or* garantirle niente.
assure [ə'ʃuə*] *vt* assicurare.
assured [ə'ʃuəd] *adj* (*confident*) sicuro(a); (*certain: promotion etc*) assicurato(a).
AST *abbr* (*US*: = *Atlantic Standard Time*) ora invernale di New York.
asterisk ['æstərısk] *n* asterisco.
astern [ə'stə:n] *adv* a poppa.
asteroid ['æstərɔıd] *n* asteroide *m.*
asthma ['æsmə] *n* asma.
asthmatic [æs'mætık] *adj, n* asmatico(a).
astigmatism [ə'stıgmətızəm] *n* astigmatismo.
astir [ə'stə:*] *adv* in piedi; (*excited*) in fermento.
astonish [ə'stɔnıʃ] *vt* stupire.
astonishing [ə'stɔnıʃıŋ] *adj* sorprendente, stupefacente; **I find it ~ that ...** mi stupisce che ....

astonishingly [əˈstɔnɪʃɪŋlɪ] *adv*
straordinariamente, incredibilmente.
astonishment [əˈstɔnɪʃmənt] *n* stupore *m*;
to my ~ con mia gran meraviglia, con
mio grande stupore.
astound [əˈstaund] *vt* sbalordire.
astray [əˈstreɪ] *adv*: **to go ~** smarrirsi; (*fig*)
traviarsi; **to go ~ in one's calculations**
sbagliare i calcoli.
astride [əˈstraɪd] *adv* a cavalcioni ♦ *prep* a
cavalcioni di.
astringent [əsˈtrɪndʒənt] *adj*, *n* astringente
(*m*).
astrologer [əsˈtrɔlədʒə*] *n* astrologo/a.
astrology [əsˈtrɔlədʒɪ] *n* astrologia.
astronaut [ˈæstrənɔːt] *n* astronauta *m/f*.
astronomer [əsˈtrɔnəmə*] *n* astronomo/a.
astronomical [æstrəˈnɔmɪkl] *adj*
astronomico(a).
astronomy [əsˈtrɔnəmɪ] *n* astronomia.
astrophysics [ˈæstrəuˈfɪzɪks] *n* astrofisica.
astute [əsˈtjuːt] *adj* astuto(a).
asunder [əˈsʌndə*] *adv*: **to tear ~** strappare.
ASV *n abbr* (= *American Standard Version*)
traduzione della Bibbia.
asylum [əˈsaɪləm] *n* asilo; (*lunatic ~*)
manicomio; **to seek political ~** chiedere
asilo politico.
asymmetric(al) [eɪsɪˈmɛtrɪk(əl)] *adj*
asimmetrico(a).

──────────── *KEYWORD*

at [æt] *prep* **1** (*referring to position, direction*)
a; **~ the top** in cima; **~ the desk** al banco,
alla scrivania; **~ home/school** a casa/
scuola; **~ Paolo's** da Paolo; **~ the baker's**
dal panettiere; **to look ~ sth** guardare qc;
to throw sth ~ sb lanciare qc a qn
2 (*referring to time*) a; **~ 4 o'clock** alle 4; **~
night** di notte; **~ Christmas** a Natale; **~
times** a volte
3 (*referring to rates, speed etc*) a; **~ £1 a
kilo** a 1 sterlina al chilo; **two ~ a time**
due alla volta, due per volta; **~ 50 km/h** a
50 km/h; **~ full speed** a tutta velocità
4 (*referring to manner*): **~ a stroke** d'un
solo colpo; **~ peace** in pace
5 (*referring to activity*): **to be ~ work**
essere al lavoro; **to play ~ cowboys**
giocare ai cowboy; **to be good ~ sth/
doing sth** essere bravo in qc/a fare qc
6 (*referring to cause*): **shocked/surprised/
annoyed ~ sth** colpito da/sorpreso da/
arrabbiato per qc; **I went ~ his
suggestion** ci sono andato dietro suo
consiglio.

ate [eɪt] *pt of* **eat**.

atheism [ˈeɪθɪɪzəm] *n* ateismo.
atheist [ˈeɪθɪɪst] *n* ateo/a.
Athenian [əˈθiːnɪən] *adj*, *n* ateniese (*m/f*).
Athens [ˈæθɪnz] *n* Atene *f*.
athlete [ˈæθliːt] *n* atleta *m/f*.
athletic [æθˈlɛtɪk] *adj* atletico(a).
athletics [æθˈlɛtɪks] *n* atletica.
Atlantic [ətˈlæntɪk] *adj* atlantico(a) ♦ *n*: **the
~ (Ocean)** l'Atlantico, l'Oceano Atlantico.
atlas [ˈætləs] *n* atlante *m*.
Atlas Mountains *npl*: **the ~** i Monti
dell'Atlante.
A.T.M. *abbr* (= *automated teller machine*)
cassa automatica prelievi, sportello
automatico.
atmosphere [ˈætməsfɪə*] *n* atmosfera; (*air*)
aria.
atmospheric [ætməsˈfɛrɪk] *adj*
atmosferico(a).
atmospherics [ætməsˈfɛrɪks] *npl* (*RADIO*)
scariche *fpl*.
atoll [ˈætɔl] *n* atollo.
atom [ˈætəm] *n* atomo.
atomic [əˈtɔmɪk] *adj* atomico(a).
atom(ic) bomb *n* bomba atomica.
atomizer [ˈætəmaɪzə*] *n* atomizzatore *m*.
atone [əˈtəun] *vi*: **to ~ for** espiare.
atonement [əˈtəunmənt] *n* espiazione *f*.
ATP *n abbr* = *Association of Tennis
Professionals*.
atrocious [əˈtrəuʃəs] *adj* atroce,
pessimo(a).
atrocity [əˈtrɔsɪtɪ] *n* atrocità *f inv*.
atrophy [ˈætrəfɪ] *n* atrofia ♦ *vi* atrofizzarsi.
attach [əˈtætʃ] *vt* attaccare; (*document,
letter*) allegare; (*MIL: troops*) assegnare; **to
be ~ed to sb/sth** (*to like*) essere
affezionato(a) a qn/qc; **the ~ed letter** la
lettera acclusa *or* allegata.
attaché [əˈtæʃeɪ] *n* addetto.
attaché case *n* valigetta per documenti.
attachment [əˈtætʃmənt] *n* (*tool*)
accessorio; (*love*): **~ (to)** affetto (per);
(*COMPUT*) allegato.
attack [əˈtæk] *vt* attaccare; (*task etc*)
iniziare; (*problem*) affrontare ♦ *n* attacco;
(*also: heart ~*) infarto.
attacker [əˈtækə*] *n* aggressore *m*,
assalitore/trice.
attain [əˈteɪn] *vt* (*also: to ~ to*) arrivare a,
raggiungere.
attainments [əˈteɪnmənts] *npl* cognizioni
fpl.
attempt [əˈtɛmpt] *n* tentativo ♦ *vt* tentare;
~ed murder (*LAW*) tentato omicidio; **to
make an ~ on sb's life** attentare alla vita
di qn; **he made no ~ to help** non ha
(neanche) tentato *or* cercato di aiutare.

attend [ə'tɛnd] _vt_ frequentare; (_meeting, talk_) andare a; (_patient_) assistere.

►**attend to** _vt fus_ (_needs, affairs etc_) prendersi cura di; (_customer_) occuparsi di.

attendance [ə'tɛndəns] _n_ (_being present_) presenza; (_people present_) gente _f_ presente.

attendant [ə'tɛndənt] _n_ custode _m/f_; persona di servizio ♦ _adj_ concomitante.

attention [ə'tɛnʃən] _n_ attenzione _f_; ~**s** premure _fpl_, attenzioni _fpl_; ~! (_MIL_) attenti!; **at** ~ (_MIL_) sull'attenti; **for the** ~ **of** (_ADMIN_) per l'attenzione di; **it has come to my** ~ **that** ... sono venuto a conoscenza (del fatto) che ....

attentive [ə'tɛntɪv] _adj_ attento(a); (_kind_) premuroso(a).

attentively [ə'tɛntɪvlɪ] _adv_ attentamente.

attenuate [ə'tɛnjueɪt] _vt_ attenuare ♦ _vi_ attenuarsi.

attest [ə'tɛst] _vi_: **to** ~ **to** attestare.

attic ['ætɪk] _n_ soffitta.

attire [ə'taɪə*] _n_ abbigliamento.

attitude ['ætɪtjuːd] _n_ (_behaviour_) atteggiamento; (_posture_) posa; (_view_): ~ (**to**) punto di vista (nei confronti di).

attorney [ə'tɜːnɪ] _n_ (_US: lawyer_) avvocato; (_having proxy_) mandatario; **power of** ~ procura.

Attorney General _n_ (_BRIT_) Procuratore _m_ Generale; (_US_) Ministro della Giustizia.

attract [ə'trækt] _vt_ attirare.

attraction [ə'trækʃən] _n_ (_gen pl: pleasant things_) attrattiva; (_PHYSICS, fig: towards sth_) attrazione _f_.

attractive [ə'træktɪv] _adj_ attraente; (_idea, offer, price_) allettante, interessante.

attribute _n_ ['ætrɪbjuːt] attributo ♦ _vt_ [ə'trɪbjuːt]: **to** ~ **sth to** attribuire qc a.

attrition [ə'trɪʃən] _n_: **war of** ~ guerra di logoramento.

Atty. Gen. _abbr_ = **Attorney General**.

atypical [eɪ'tɪpɪkl] _adj_ atipico(a).

AU _n abbr_ (= _African Union_) Unione Africana.

aubergine ['əubəʒiːn] _n_ melanzana.

auburn ['ɔːbən] _adj_ tizianesco(a).

auction ['ɔːkʃən] _n_ (_also:_ **sale by** ~) asta ♦ _vt_ (_also:_ **to sell by** ~) vendere all'asta; (_also:_ **to put up for** ~) mettere all'asta.

auctioneer [ɔːkʃə'nɪə*] _n_ banditore _m_.

auction room _n_ sala dell'asta.

audacious [ɔː'deɪʃəs] _adj_ (_bold_) audace; (_impudent_) sfrontato(a).

audacity [ɔː'dæsɪtɪ] _n_ audacia.

audible ['ɔːdɪbl] _adj_ udibile.

audience ['ɔːdɪəns] _n_ (_people_) pubblico; spettatori _mpl_; ascoltatori _mpl_; (_interview_) udienza.

audio-typist ['ɔːdɪəu'taɪpɪst] _n_ dattilografo/a che trascrive da nastro.

audiovisual [ɔːdɪəu'vɪzjuəl] _adj_ audiovisivo(a); ~ **aids** sussidi _mpl_ audiovisivi.

audit ['ɔːdɪt] _n_ revisione _f_, verifica ♦ _vt_ rivedere, verificare.

audition [ɔː'dɪʃən] _n_ (_THEAT_) audizione _f_; (_CINE_) provino ♦ _vi_ fare un'audizione (_or_ un provino).

auditor ['ɔːdɪtə*] _n_ revisore _m_.

auditorium [ɔːdɪ'tɔːrɪəm] _n_ sala, auditorio.

Aug. _abbr_ (= _August_) ago., ag.

augment [ɔːg'mɛnt] _vt_, _vi_ aumentare.

augur ['ɔːgə*] _vt_ (_be a sign of_) predire ♦ _vi_: **it** ~**s well** promette bene.

August ['ɔːgəst] _n_ agosto; _for phrases see also_ **July.**

august [ɔː'gʌst] _adj_ augusto(a).

aunt [ɑːnt] _n_ zia.

auntie, aunty ['ɑːntɪ] _n_ zietta.

au pair ['əu'pɛə*] _n_ (_also:_ ~ **girl**) (ragazza _f_) alla pari _inv_.

aura ['ɔːrə] _n_ aura.

auspices ['ɔːspɪsɪz] _npl_: **under the** ~ **of** sotto gli auspici di.

auspicious [ɔːs'pɪʃəs] _adj_ propizio(a).

austere [ɔs'tɪə*] _adj_ austero(a).

austerity [ɔs'tɛrɪtɪ] _n_ austerità _f inv_.

Australasia [ɔstrə'leɪzɪə] _n_ Australasia.

Australia [ɔs'treɪlɪə] _n_ Australia.

Australian [ɔs'treɪlɪən] _adj_, _n_ australiano(a).

Austria ['ɔstrɪə] _n_ Austria.

Austrian ['ɔstrɪən] _adj_, _n_ austriaco(a).

AUT _n abbr_ (_BRIT_: = _Association of University Teachers_) associazione dei docenti universitari.

authentic [ɔː'θɛntɪk] _adj_ autentico(a).

authenticate [ɔː'θɛntɪkeɪt] _vt_ autenticare.

authenticity [ɔːθɛn'tɪsɪtɪ] _n_ autenticità.

author ['ɔːθə*] _n_ autore/trice.

authoritarian [ɔːθɔrɪ'tɛərɪən] _adj_ autoritario(a).

authoritative [ɔː'θɔrɪtətɪv] _adj_ (_account etc_) autorevole; (_manner_) autoritario(a).

authority [ɔː'θɔrɪtɪ] _n_ autorità _f inv_; (_permission_) autorizzazione _f_; **the authorities** _npl_ le autorità; **to have** ~ **to do sth** avere l'autorizzazione a fare _or_ il diritto di fare qc.

authorization [ɔːθəraɪ'zeɪʃən] _n_ autorizzazione _f_.

authorize ['ɔːθəraɪz] _vt_ autorizzare.

authorized capital _n_ capitale _m_ nominale.

authorship ['ɔːθəʃɪp] _n_ paternità (_letteraria etc_).

autistic [ɔː'tɪstɪk] _adj_ autistico(a).

auto ['ɔːtəu] n (US) auto f inv.
autobiography [ɔːtəbaɪ'ɔgrəfɪ] n autobiografia.
autocratic [ɔːtə'krætɪk] adj autocratico(a).
Autocue ® ['ɔːtəukjuː] n (BRIT) gobbo (TV).
autograph ['ɔːtəgrɑːf] n autografo ♦ vt firmare.
autoimmune [ɔːtəuɪ'mjuːn] adj autoimmune.
automat ['ɔːtəmæt] n (US) tavola calda fornita esclusivamente di distributori automatici.
automated ['ɔːtəmeɪtɪd] adj automatizzato(a).
automatic [ɔːtə'mætɪk] adj automatico(a) ♦ n (gun) arma automatica; (car) automobile f con cambio automatico; (washing machine) lavatrice f automatica.
automatically [ɔːtə'mætɪklɪ] adv automaticamente.
automatic data processing (ADP) n elaborazione f automatica dei dati (EAD).
automation [ɔːtə'meɪʃən] n automazione f.
automaton, pl automata [ɔː'tɔmətən, -tə] n automa m.
automobile ['ɔːtəməbiːl] n (US) automobile f.
autonomous [ɔː'tɔnəməs] adj autonomo(a).
autopsy ['ɔːtɔpsɪ] n autopsia.
autumn ['ɔːtəm] n autunno.
auxiliary [ɔːg'zɪlɪərɪ] adj ausiliario(a) ♦ n ausiliare m/f.
AV n abbr (= Authorized Version) traduzione inglese della Bibbia ♦ abbr = **audiovisual**.
Av. abbr = **avenue**.
avail [ə'veɪl] vt: to ~ o.s. of servirsi di; approfittarsi di ♦ n: to no ~ inutilmente.
availability [əveɪlə'bɪlɪtɪ] n disponibilità.
available [ə'veɪləbl] adj disponibile; **every ~ means** tutti i mezzi disponibili; **to make sth ~ to sb** mettere qc a disposizione di qn; **is the manager ~?** è libero il direttore?
avalanche ['ævəlɑːnʃ] n valanga.
avant-garde ['ævɑ̃ŋ'gɑːd] adj d'avanguardia.
avarice ['ævərɪs] n avarizia.
avaricious [ævə'rɪʃəs] adj avaro(a).
avdp. abbr (= avoirdupois) sistema ponderale anglosassone basato su libbra, oncia e multipli.
Ave. abbr = **avenue**.
avenge [ə'vɛndʒ] vt vendicare.
avenue ['ævənjuː] n viale m.
average ['ævərɪdʒ] n media ♦ adj medio(a) ♦ vt (also: ~ out at) aggirarsi in media su, essere in media di; **on ~** in media; **above/below (the) ~** sopra/sotto la media.

averse [ə'vɜːs] adj: **to be ~ to sth/doing** essere contrario(a) a qc/a fare; **I wouldn't be ~ to a drink** non avrei nulla in contrario a bere qualcosa.
aversion [ə'vɜːʃən] n avversione f.
avert [ə'vɜːt] vt evitare, prevenire; (one's eyes) distogliere.
avian flu ['eɪvɪən-] n influenza aviaria.
aviary ['eɪvɪərɪ] n voliera, uccelliera.
aviation [eɪvɪ'eɪʃən] n aviazione f.
avid ['ævɪd] adj avido(a).
avidly ['ævɪdlɪ] adv avidamente.
avocado [ævə'kɑːdəu] n (also: BRIT: ~ pear) avocado m inv.
avoid [ə'vɔɪd] vt evitare.
avoidable [ə'vɔɪdəbl] adj evitabile.
avoidance [ə'vɔɪdəns] n l'evitare m.
avowed [ə'vaud] adj dichiarato(a).
AVP n abbr (US) = assistant vice-president.
AWACS ['eɪwæks] n abbr (= airborne warning and control system) sistema di allarme e controllo in volo.
await [ə'weɪt] vt aspettare; **~ing attention** (COMM: letter) in attesa di risposta; (: order) in attesa di essere evaso; **long ~ed** tanto atteso(a).
awake [ə'weɪk] adj sveglio(a) ♦ vb (pt awoke [ə'wəuk], pp awoken [ə'wəukən] or awaked) vt svegliare ♦ vi svegliarsi; ~ **to** consapevole di.
awakening [ə'weɪknɪŋ] n risveglio.
award [ə'wɔːd] n premio; (LAW) decreto ♦ vt assegnare; (LAW: damages) decretare.
aware [ə'wɛə*] adj: ~ **of** (conscious) conscio(a) di; (informed) informato(a) di; **to become ~ of** accorgersi di; **politically/socially ~** politicamente/socialmente preparato; **I am fully ~ that ...** mi rendo perfettamente conto che ....
awareness [ə'wɛənɪs] n consapevolezza; coscienza; **to develop people's ~ (of)** sensibilizzare la gente (a).
awash [ə'wɔʃ] adj: ~ **(with)** inondato(a) (da).
away [ə'weɪ] adj, adv via; lontano(a); **two kilometres ~** a due chilometri di distanza; **two hours ~ by car** a due ore di distanza in macchina; **the holiday was two weeks ~** mancavano due settimane alle vacanze; ~ **from** lontano da; **he's ~ for a week** è andato via per una settimana; **he's ~ in Milan** è (andato) a Milano; **to take ~** vt portare via; **he was working/pedalling** etc ~ la particella indica la continuità e l'energia dell'azione: lavorava/pedalava etc più che poteva; **to fade/wither** etc ~ la particella rinforza l'idea della

diminuzione.

away game n (_SPORT_) partita fuori casa.

awe [ɔ:] n timore m.

awe-inspiring ['ɔ:ɪnspaɪərɪŋ], **awesome** ['ɔ:səm] adj imponente.

awestruck ['ɔ:strʌk] adj sgomento(a).

awful ['ɔ:fəl] adj terribile; **an ~ lot of** (_people, cars, dogs_) un numero incredibile di; (_jam, flowers_) una quantità incredibile di.

awfully ['ɔ:flɪ] adv (_very_) terribilmente.

awhile [ə'waɪl] adv (per) un po'.

awkward ['ɔ:kwəd] adj (_clumsy_) goffo(a); (_inconvenient_) scomodo(a); (_embarrassing_) imbarazzante; (_difficult_) delicato(a), difficile.

awkwardness ['ɔ:kwədnɪs] n goffaggine f; scomodità; imbarazzo; delicatezza, difficoltà.

awl ['ɔ:l] n punteruolo.

awning ['ɔ:nɪŋ] n (_of tent_) veranda; (_of shop, hotel etc_) tenda.

awoke [ə'wəuk] pt of **awake**.

awoken [ə'wəukən] pp of **awake**.

AWOL ['eɪwɔl] abbr (_MIL etc_) see **absent without leave**.

awry [ə'raɪ] adv di traverso ♦ adj storto(a); **to go ~** andare a monte.

axe, (_US_) **ax** [æks] n scure f ♦ vt (_project etc_) abolire; (_jobs_) sopprimere; **to have an ~ to grind** (_fig_) fare i propri interessi _or_ il proprio tornaconto.

axiom ['æksɪəm] n assioma m.

axiomatic [æksɪəu'mætɪk] adj assiomatico(a).

axis, pl **axes** ['æksɪs, -si:z] n asse m.

axle ['æksl] n (_also:_ **~-tree**) asse m.

ay(e) [aɪ] excl (_yes_) sì.

AYH n abbr = _American Youth Hostels._

AZ abbr (_US_) = _Arizona._

azalea [ə'zeɪlɪə] n azalea.

Azerbaijan [æzəbaɪ'dʒɑ:n] n Azerbaigian m.

Azerbaijani [æzəbaɪ'dʒɑ:nɪ], **Azeri** [ə'zɛərɪ] adj, n azerbaigiano(a), azero(a).

Azores [ə'zɔ:z] npl: **the ~** le Azzorre.

AZT n abbr (= _azidothymidine_) AZT m.

Aztec ['æztɛk] adj, n azteco(a).

azure ['eɪʒə*] adj azzurro(a).

B b

B, b [bi:] n (_letter_) B, b f or m inv; (_SCOL: mark_) ≈ 8 (_buono_); (_MUS_): **B** si m; **B for Benjamin**, (_US_) **B for Baker** ≈ B come Bologna; **B road** n (_BRIT AUT_) ≈ strada secondaria.

b. abbr = **born.**

BA n abbr = _British Academy_; (_SCOL_) see **Bachelor of Arts.**

babble ['bæbl] vi cianciare; mormorare ♦ n ciance fpl; mormorio.

babe [beɪb] n (_col_): **she's a real ~** è uno schianto di ragazza.

baboon [bə'bu:n] n babbuino.

baby ['beɪbɪ] n bambino/a.

baby carriage n (_US_) carrozzina.

babyhood ['beɪbɪhud] n prima infanzia.

babyish ['beɪbɪɪʃ] adj infantile.

baby-minder ['beɪbɪ'maɪndə*] n (_BRIT_) bambinaia (_che tiene i bambini mentre la madre lavora_).

baby-sit ['beɪbɪsɪt] vi fare il (_or_ la) babysitter.

baby-sitter ['beɪbɪsɪtə*] n baby-sitter m/f inv.

bachelor ['bætʃələ*] n scapolo; **B~ of Arts/Science (BA/BSc)** ≈ laureato/a in lettere/scienze; **B~ of Arts/Science degree (BA/BSc)** n ≈ laurea in lettere/scienze; see boxed note.

BACHELOR'S DEGREE

Il **Bachelor's Degree** è il riconoscimento che viene conferito a chi ha completato un corso di laurea di tre o quattro anni all'università. I Bachelor's degree più importanti sono il "BA" (_Bachelor of Arts_), il "BSc" (_Bachelor of Science_), il "BEd" (_Bachelor of Education_), e il "LLB" (_Bachelor of Laws_); vedi anche **Master's degree, doctorate.**

---

bachelor party n (_US_) festa di addio al celibato.

back [bæk] n (_of person, horse_) dorso, schiena; (_of hand_) dorso; (_of house, car_) didietro; (_of train_) coda; (_of chair_) schienale m; (_of page_) rovescio; (_FOOTBALL_) difensore m; **~ to front**

all'incontrario; **to break the ~ of a job**
(BRIT) fare il grosso or il peggio di un
lavoro; **to have one's ~ to the wall** (fig)
essere or trovarsi con le spalle al muro
♦ vt (financially) finanziare; (candidate: also:
~ up) appoggiare; (horse: at races)
puntare su; (car) guidare a marcia
indietro ♦ vi indietreggiare; (car etc) fare
marcia indietro ♦ adj (in compounds)
posteriore, di dietro; arretrato(a); ~
seats/wheels (AUT) sedili mpl/ruote fpl
posteriori; ~ **payments/rent** arretrati
mpl; ~ **garden/room** giardino/stanza sul
retro (della casa); **to take a ~ seat** (fig)
restare in secondo piano ♦ adv (not
forward) indietro; (returned): **he's ~ è**
tornato; **when will you be ~?** quando
torni?; **he ran ~** tornò indietro di corsa;
(restitution): **throw the ball ~** ritira la
palla; **can I have it ~?** posso riaverlo?;
(again): **he called ~** ha richiamato.
▶**back down** vi (fig) fare marcia indietro.
▶**back on to** vt fus: **the house ~s on to the
golf course** il retro della casa dà sul
campo da golf.
▶**back out** vi (of promise) tirarsi indietro.
▶**back up** vt (support) appoggiare,
sostenere; (COMPUT) fare una copia di
riserva di.
backache ['bækeɪk] n mal m di schiena.
back benches npl posti in Parlamento
occupati dai backbencher; see boxed note.

backbencher ['bæk'bɛntʃə*] n (BRIT)
parlamentare che non ha incarichi né al
governo né all'opposizione.
backbiting ['bækbaɪtɪŋ] n maldicenza.
backbone ['bækbəʊn] n spina dorsale; **the
~ of the organization** l'anima
dell'organizzazione.
backchat ['bæktʃæt] n (BRIT col)
impertinenza.
backcloth ['bækklɔθ] n (BRIT) scena di
sfondo.
backcomb ['bækkəʊm] vt (BRIT) cotonare.
backdate [bæk'deɪt] vt (letter) retrodatare;
~**d pay rise** aumento retroattivo.
backdrop ['bækdrɔp] n = **backcloth**.

backer ['bækə*] n sostenitore/trice; (COMM)
fautore m.
backfire ['bæk'faɪə*] vi (AUT) dar ritorni di
fiamma; (plans) fallire.
backgammon ['bækgæmən] n tavola reale.
background ['bækgraʊnd] n sfondo; (of
events, COMPUT) background m inv; (basic
knowledge) base f; (experience) esperienza
♦ cpd (noise, music) di fondo; ~ **reading**
letture fpl sull'argomento; **family ~**
ambiente m familiare.
backhand ['bækhænd] n (TENNIS: also: ~
stroke) rovescio.
backhanded [bæk'hændɪd] adj (fig)
ambiguo(a).
backhander ['bækhændə*] n (BRIT: bribe)
bustarella.
backing [bækɪŋ] n (COMM) finanziamento;
(MUS) accompagnamento; (fig) appoggio.
backlash ['bæklæʃ] n contraccolpo,
ripercussione f.
backlog ['bæklɔg] n: ~ **of work** lavoro
arretrato.
back number n (of magazine etc) numero
arretrato.
backpack ['bækpæk] n zaino.
backpacker ['bækpækə*] n chi viaggia con
zaino e sacco a pelo.
back pay n arretrato di paga.
backpedal ['bækpɛdl] vi pedalare
all'indietro; (fig) far marcia indietro.
backseat driver ['bæksiːt-] n passeggero
che dà consigli non richiesti al guidatore.
backside [bæk'saɪd] n (col) sedere m.
backslash ['bækslæʃ] n backslash m inv,
barra obliqua inversa.
backslide ['bækslaɪd] vi ricadere.
backspace ['bækspeɪs] vi (in typing) battere
il tasto di ritorno.
backstage [bæk'steɪdʒ] adv nel retroscena.
back street n vicolo.
backstroke ['bækstrəʊk] n nuoto sul dorso.
backtrack ['bæktræk] vi = **backpedal**.
backup ['bækʌp] adj (train, plane)
supplementare; (COMPUT) di riserva ♦ n
(support) appoggio, sostegno; (COMPUT:
also: ~ **file**) file m inv di riserva.
backward ['bækwəd] adj (movement)
indietro inv; (person) tardivo(a); (country)
arretrato(a); ~ **and forward movement**
movimento avanti e indietro.
backwards ['bækwədz] adv indietro; (fall,
walk) all'indietro; **to know sth ~ or** (US) ~
and forwards (col) sapere qc a menadito.
backwater ['bækwɔːtə*] n (fig) posto
morto.
back yard n cortile m sul retro.
bacon ['beɪkən] n pancetta.

bacteria [bæk'tɪərɪə] *npl* batteri *mpl.*
bacteriology [bæktɪərɪ'ɔlədʒɪ] *n* batteriologia.
bad [bæd] *adj* cattivo(a); (*child*) cattivello(a); (*meat, food*) andato(a) a male; **his** ~ **leg** la sua gamba malata; **to go** ~ (*meat, food*) andare a male; **to have a** ~ **time of it** passarsela male; **I feel** ~ **about it** (*guilty*) mi sento un po' in colpa; ~ **debt** credito difficile da recuperare; ~ **faith** malafede *f.*
baddie, baddy ['bædɪ] *n* (*col: CINE etc*) cattivo/a.
bade [bæd] *pt of* **bid.**
badge [bædʒ] *n* insegna; (*of policeman*) stemma *m*; (*stick-on*) adesivo.
badger ['bædʒə*] *n* tasso ♦ *vt* tormentare.
badly ['bædlɪ] *adv* (*work, dress etc*) male; **things are going** ~ le cose vanno male; ~ **wounded** gravemente ferito; **he needs it** ~ ne ha gran bisogno; ~ **off** *adj* povero(a).
bad-mannered [bæd'mænəd] *adj* maleducato(a), sgarbato(a).
badminton ['bædmɪntən] *n* badminton *m.*
bad-tempered [bæd'tɛmpəd] *adj* irritabile; (*in bad mood*) di malumore.
baffle ['bæfl] *vt* (*puzzle*) confondere.
baffling ['bæflɪŋ] *adj* sconcertante.
bag [bæg] *n* sacco; (*handbag etc*) borsa; (*of hunter*) carniere *m*; bottino ♦ *vt* (*col: take*) mettersi in tasca; prendersi; ~**s of** (*col: lots of*) un sacco di; **to pack one's** ~**s** fare le valigie; ~**s under the eyes** borse sotto gli occhi.
bagful ['bægful] *n* sacco (pieno).
baggage ['bægɪdʒ] *n* bagagli *mpl.*
baggage allowance *n* peso bagaglio consentito.
baggage car *n* (*US*) bagagliaio.
baggage claim *n* ritiro bagagli.
baggy ['bægɪ] *adj* largo(a), sformato(a).
Baghdad [bæg'dæd] *n* Bagdad *f.*
bag lady *n* (*col*) stracciona, barbona.
bagpipes ['bægpaɪps] *npl* cornamusa.
bag-snatcher ['bægsnætʃə*] *n* (*BRIT*) scippatore/trice.
Bahamas [bə'hɑːməz] *npl*: **the** ~ le isole Bahama.
Bahrain [bɑː'reɪn] *n* Bahrein *m.*
bail [beɪl] *n* cauzione *f* ♦ *vt* (*prisoner: gen: to grant* ~ **to**) concedere la libertà provvisoria su cauzione a; (*NAUT: also:* ~ **out**) *see* **bale out; to be released on** ~ essere rilasciato(a) su cauzione.
▶**bail out** *vt* (*prisoner*) ottenere la libertà provvisoria su cauzione di; (*fig*) tirare fuori dai guai ♦ *vi see* **bale out.**
bailiff ['beɪlɪf] *n* usciere *m*; fattore *m.*

bait [beɪt] *n* esca ♦ *vt* (*hook*) innescare; (*trap*) munire di esca; (*fig*) tormentare.
bake [beɪk] *vt* cuocere al forno ♦ *vi* cuocersi al forno.
baked beans *npl* fagioli *mpl* all'uccelletto.
baked potato *n* patata (con la buccia) cotta al forno.
baker ['beɪkə*] *n* fornaio/a, panettiere/a.
bakery ['beɪkərɪ] *n* panetteria.
baking ['beɪkɪŋ] *n* cottura (al forno).
baking powder *n* lievito in polvere.
baking tin *n* stampo, tortiera.
baking tray *n* teglia.
balaclava [bælə'klɑːvə] *n* (*also:* ~ **helmet**) passamontagna *m inv.*
balance ['bæləns] *n* equilibrio; (*COMM: sum*) bilancio; (*scales*) bilancia ♦ *vt* tenere in equilibrio; (*pros and cons*) soppesare; (*budget*) far quadrare; (*account*) pareggiare; (*compensate*) contrappesare; ~ **of trade/payments** bilancia commerciale/ dei pagamenti; ~ **brought forward** saldo riportato; ~ **carried forward** saldo da riportare; **to** ~ **the books** fare il bilancio.
balanced ['bælənst] *adj* (*personality, diet*) equilibrato(a).
balance sheet *n* bilancio.
balcony ['bælkənɪ] *n* balcone *m.*
bald [bɔːld] *adj* calvo(a).
baldness ['bɔːldnɪs] *n* calvizie *f.*
bale [beɪl] *n* balla.
▶**bale out** *vt* (*NAUT: water*) vuotare; (*: boat*) aggottare ♦ *vi* (*of a plane*) gettarsi col paracadute.
Balearic [bælɪ'ærɪk] *adj*: **the** ~ **Islands** le (isole) Baleari.
baleful ['beɪlful] *adj* funesto(a).
balk [bɔːlk] *vi*: **to** ~ (**at**) tirarsi indietro (davanti a); (*horse*) recalcitrare (davanti a).
Balkan ['bɔːlkən] *adj* balcanico(a) ♦ *n*: **the** ~**s** i Balcani.
ball [bɔːl] *n* palla; (*football*) pallone *m*; (*for golf*) pallina; (*dance*) ballo; **to play** ~ (**with sb**) giocare a palla (con qn); (*fig*) stare al gioco (di qn); **to be on the** ~ (*fig: competent*) essere in gamba; (*: alert*) stare all'erta; **to start the** ~ **rolling** (*fig*) fare la prima mossa; **the** ~ **is in your court** (*fig*) a lei la prossima mossa; *see also* **balls.**
ballad ['bæləd] *n* ballata.
ballast ['bæləst] *n* zavorra.
ball bearing *n* cuscinetto a sfere.
ball cock *n* galleggiante *m.*
ballerina [bælə'riːnə] *n* ballerina.
ballet ['bæleɪ] *n* balletto.
ballet dancer *n* ballerino/a.
ballistic [bə'lɪstɪk] *adj* balistico(a).
ballistics [bə'lɪstɪks] *n* balistica.

balloon [bə'luːn] n pallone m; (in comic strip) fumetto ♦ vi gonfiarsi.
balloonist [bə'luːnɪst] n aeronauta m/f.
ballot ['bælət] n scrutinio.
ballot box n urna (per le schede).
ballot paper n scheda.
ballpark ['bɔːlpɑːk] n (US) stadio di baseball.
ballpark figure n (col) cifra approssimativa.
ball-point pen ['bɔːlpɔɪnt-] n penna a sfera.
ballroom ['bɔːlrum] n sala da ballo.
balls [bɔːlz] npl (col!) coglioni mpl (!).
balm [bɑːm] n balsamo.
balmy ['bɑːmɪ] adj (breeze, air) balsamico(a); (BRIT col) = **barmy**.
BALPA ['bælpə] n abbr (= British Airline Pilots' Association) sindacato dei piloti.
balsam ['bɔːlsəm] n balsamo.
balsa (wood) ['bɔːlsə-] n (legno di) balsa.
Baltic ['bɔːltɪk] adj, n: **the ~ (Sea)** il (mar) Baltico.
balustrade [bæləs'treɪd] n balaustrata.
bamboo [bæm'buː] n bambù m.
bamboozle [bæm'buːzl] vt (col) infinocchiare.
ban [bæn] n interdizione f ♦ vt interdire; **he was ~ned from driving** (BRIT) gli hanno ritirato la patente.
banal [bə'nɑːl] adj banale.
banana [bə'nɑːnə] n banana.
band [bænd] n banda; (at a dance) orchestra; (MIL) fanfara.
▶**band together** vi collegarsi.
bandage ['bændɪdʒ] n benda.
Band-Aid ® ['bændeɪd] n (US) cerotto.
bandit ['bændɪt] n bandito.
bandstand ['bændstænd] n palco dell'orchestra.
bandwagon ['bændwægən] n: **to jump on the ~** (fig) seguire la corrente.
bandy ['bændɪ] vt (jokes, insults) scambiare.
▶**bandy about** vt far circolare.
bandy-legged ['bændɪ'lɛgɪd] adj dalle gambe storte.
bane [beɪn] n: **it** (or **he** etc) **is the ~ of my life** è la mia rovina.
bang [bæŋ] n botta; (of door) lo sbattere; (blow) colpo ♦ vt battere (violentemente); (door) sbattere ♦ vi scoppiare; sbattere; **to ~ at the door** picchiare alla porta; **to ~ into sth** sbattere contro qc ♦ adv: **to be ~ on time** (BRIT col) spaccare il secondo; see also **bangs**.
banger ['bæŋə*] n (BRIT: car: also: **old ~**) macinino; (BRIT col: sausage) salsiccia; (firework) mortaretto.
Bangkok ['bæŋkɔk] n Bangkok f.

Bangladesh [bɑːŋglə'dɛʃ] n Bangladesh m.
bangle ['bæŋgl] n braccialetto.
bangs [bæŋz] npl (US: fringe) frangia, frangetta.
banish ['bænɪʃ] vt bandire.
banister(s) ['bænɪstə(z)] n(pl) ringhiera.
banjo, ~es or **~s** ['bændʒəu] n banjo m inv.
bank [bæŋk] n (for money) banca, banco; (of river, lake) riva, sponda; (of earth) banco.
▶**bank on** vt fus contare su.
bank account n conto in banca.
bank balance n saldo; **a healthy ~** un solido conto in banca.
bank card n = **banker's card**.
bank charges npl (BRIT) spese fpl bancarie.
bank draft n assegno circolare or bancario.
banker ['bæŋkə*] n banchiere m; **~'s card** (BRIT) carta f assegni inv; **~'s order** (BRIT) ordine m di banca.
bank giro n bancogiro.
bank holiday n (BRIT) giorno di festa; see boxed note.

BANK HOLIDAY

Una **bank holiday**, in Gran Bretagna, è una giornata in cui le banche e molti negozi sono chiusi. Generalmente le **bank holidays** cadono di lunedì e molti ne approfittano per fare una breve vacanza fuori città. Di conseguenza, durante questi fine settimana lunghi ("bank holiday weekends") si verifica un notevole aumento del traffico sulle strade, negli aeroporti e nelle stazioni e molte località turistiche registrano il tutto esaurito.

---

banking ['bæŋkɪŋ] n attività bancaria; professione f di banchiere.
banking hours npl orario di sportello.
bank loan n prestito bancario.
bank manager n direttore m di banca.
banknote ['bæŋknəut] n banconota.
bank rate n tasso bancario.
bankrupt ['bæŋkrʌpt] adj, n fallito(a); **to go ~** fallire.
bankruptcy ['bæŋkrʌptsɪ] n fallimento.
bank statement n estratto conto.
banned substance ['bænd-] n sostanza al bando (nello sport).
banner ['bænə*] n striscione m.
bannister(s) ['bænɪstə(z)] n(pl) = **banister(s)**.
banns [bænz] npl pubblicazioni fpl di matrimonio.
banquet ['bæŋkwɪt] n banchetto.
bantam-weight ['bæntəmweɪt] n peso gallo.
banter ['bæntə*] n scherzi mpl bonari.

baptism ['bæptɪzəm] *n* battesimo.
Baptist ['bæptɪst] *adj, n* battista (*m/f*).
baptize [bæp'taɪz] *vt* battezzare.
bar [bɑ:*] *n* barra; (*of window etc*) sbarra; (*of chocolate*) tavoletta; (*fig*) ostacolo; restrizione *f*; (*pub*) bar *m inv*; (*counter: in pub*) banco; (*MUS*) battuta ♦ *vt* (*road, window*) sbarrare; (*person*) escludere; (*activity*) interdire; ~ **of soap** saponetta; **the B~** (*LAW*) l'Ordine *m* degli avvocati; **behind ~s** (*prisoner*) dietro le sbarre; ~ **none** senza eccezione.
Barbados [bɑ:'beɪdɔs] *n* Barbados *fsg*.
barbaric [bɑ:'bærɪk], **barbarous** ['bɑ:bərəs] *adj* barbaro(a); barbarico(a).
barbecue ['bɑ:bɪkju:] *n* barbecue *m inv*.
barbed wire ['bɑ:bd-] *n* filo spinato.
barber ['bɑ:bə*] *n* barbiere *m*.
barbiturate [bɑ:'bɪtjurɪt] *n* barbiturico.
Barcelona [bɑ:sɪ'ləunə] *n* Barcellona.
bar chart *n* diagramma *m* di frequenza.
bar code *n* codice *m* a barre.
bare [bɛə*] *adj* nudo(a) ♦ *vt* scoprire, denudare; (*teeth*) mostrare; **the ~ essentials** lo stretto necessario.
bareback ['bɛəbæk] *adv* senza sella.
barefaced ['bɛəfeɪst] *adj* sfacciato(a).
barefoot ['bɛəfut] *adj, adv* scalzo(a).
bareheaded [bɛə'hɛdɪd] *adj, adv* a capo scoperto.
barely ['bɛəlɪ] *adv* appena.
Barents Sea ['bærənts-] *n*: **the ~** il mar di Barents.
bargain ['bɑ:gɪn] *n* (*transaction*) contratto; (*good buy*) affare *m* ♦ *vi* (*haggle*) tirare sul prezzo; (*trade*) contrattare; **into the ~** per giunta.
▶**bargain for** *vt fus* (*col*): **to ~ for sth** aspettarsi qc; **he got more than he ~ed for** gli è andata peggio di quel che si aspettasse.
bargaining ['bɑ:gənɪŋ] *n* contrattazione *f*.
bargaining position *n*: **to be in a weak/ strong ~** non avere/avere potere contrattuale.
barge [bɑ:dʒ] *n* chiatta.
▶**barge in** *vi* (*walk in*) piombare dentro; (*interrupt talk*) intromettersi a sproposito.
▶**barge into** *vt fus* urtare contro.
baritone ['bærɪtəun] *n* baritono.
barium meal ['bɛərɪəm-] *n* (pasto di) bario.
bark [bɑ:k] *n* (*of tree*) corteccia; (*of dog*) abbaio ♦ *vi* abbaiare.
barley ['bɑ:lɪ] *n* orzo.
barley sugar *n* zucchero d'orzo.
barmaid ['bɑ:meɪd] *n* cameriera al banco.
barman ['bɑ:mən] *n* barista *m*.
barmy ['bɑ:mɪ] *adj* (*BRIT col*) tocco(a).

barn [bɑ:n] *n* granaio; (*for animals*) stalla.
barnacle ['bɑ:nəkl] *n* cirripede *m*.
barn owl *n* barbagianni *m inv*.
barometer [bə'rɔmɪtə*] *n* barometro.
baron ['bærən] *n* barone *m*; (*fig*) magnate *m*; **the oil ~s** i magnati del petrolio; **the press ~s** i baroni della stampa.
baroness ['bærənɪs] *n* baronessa.
baronet ['bærənɪt] *n* baronetto.
barrack ['bærək] *vt* (*BRIT*): **to ~ sb** subissare qn di grida e fischi.
barracks ['bærəks] *npl* caserma.
barrage ['bærɑ:ʒ] *n* (*MIL*) sbarramento; **a ~ of questions** una raffica di *or* un fuoco di fila di domande.
barrel ['bærəl] *n* barile *m*; (*of gun*) canna.
barrel organ *n* organetto a cilindro.
barren ['bærən] *adj* sterile; (*soil*) arido(a).
barricade [bærɪ'keɪd] *n* barricata ♦ *vt* barricare.
barrier ['bærɪə*] *n* barriera; (*BRIT: also*: **crash ~**) guardrail *m inv*.
barrier cream *n* (*BRIT*) crema protettiva.
barring ['bɑ:rɪŋ] *prep* salvo.
barrister ['bærɪstə*] *n* (*BRIT*) avvocato; *see boxed note*.

BARRISTER

Il **barrister** *è un membro della più prestigiosa delle due branche della professione legale (l'altra è quella dei "solicitors"); la sua funzione è quella di rappresentare i propri clienti in tutte le corti ("magistrates' court", "crown court" e "Court of Appeal"), generalmente seguendo le istruzioni del caso preparate dai "solicitors".*

---

barrow ['bærəu] *n* (*cart*) carriola.
barstool ['bɑ:stu:l] *n* sgabello.
Bart. *abbr* (*BRIT*) = **baronet**.
bartender ['bɑ:tɛndə*] *n* (*US*) barista *m*.
barter ['bɑ:tə*] *n* baratto ♦ *vt*: **to ~ sth for** barattare qc con.
base [beɪs] *n* base *f* ♦ *adj* vile ♦ *vt*: **to ~ sth on** basare qc su; **to ~ at** (*troops*) mettere di stanza a; **coffee-~d** a base di caffè; **a Paris-~d firm** una ditta con sede centrale a Parigi; **I'm ~d in London** sono di base *or* ho base a Londra.
baseball ['beɪsbɔ:l] *n* baseball *m*.
baseboard ['beɪsbɔ:d] *n* (*US*) zoccolo, battiscopa *m inv*.
base camp *n* campo *m* base *inv*.
Basel [bɑ:l] *n* = **Basle**.
baseline ['beɪslaɪn] *n* (*TENNIS*) linea di fondo.
basement ['beɪsmənt] *n* seminterrato; (*of shop*) sotterraneo.

base rate n tasso di base.

bases ['beɪsiːz] npl of **basis**; ['beɪsɪz] npl of **base**.

bash [bæʃ] vt (col) picchiare ♦ n: **I'll have a ~ (at it)** (BRIT col) ci proverò; **~ed in** adj sfondato(a).

▶**bash up** vt (col: car) sfasciare; (: BRIT: person) riempire di or prendere a botte.

bashful ['bæʃful] adj timido(a).

bashing ['bæʃɪŋ] n: **Paki-/queer-~** atti mpl di violenza contro i pachistani/gli omosessuali.

BASIC ['beɪsɪk] n (COMPUT) BASIC m.

basic ['beɪsɪk] adj (principles, precautions, rules) elementare; (salary) base inv (after n).

basically ['beɪsɪklɪ] adv fondamentalmente, sostanzialmente.

basic rate n (of tax) aliquota minima.

basil ['bæzl] n basilico.

basin ['beɪsn] n (vessel, also GEO) bacino; (also: **wash~**) lavabo; (BRIT: for food) terrina.

basis, pl **bases** ['beɪsɪs, -siːz] n base f; **on the ~ of what you've said** in base alle sue asserzioni.

bask [bɑːsk] vi: **to ~ in the sun** crogiolarsi al sole.

basket ['bɑːskɪt] n cesta; (smaller) cestino; (with handle) paniere m.

basketball ['bɑːskɪtbɔːl] n pallacanestro f.

basketball player n cestista m/f.

Basle [bɑːl] n Basilea.

basmati rice [bəz'mætɪ-] n riso basmati.

Basque [bæsk] adj, n basco(a).

bass [beɪs] n (MUS) basso.

bass clef n chiave f di basso.

bassoon [bə'suːn] n fagotto.

bastard ['bɑːstəd] n bastardo/a; (col!) stronzo (!).

baste [beɪst] vt (CULIN) ungere con grasso; (SEWING) imbastire.

bastion ['bæstɪən] n bastione m; (fig) baluardo.

bat [bæt] n pipistrello; (for baseball etc) mazza; (BRIT: for table tennis) racchetta; **off one's own ~** di propria iniziativa ♦ vt: **he didn't ~ an eyelid** non batté ciglio.

batch [bætʃ] n (of bread) infornata; (of papers) cumulo; (of applicants, letters) gruppo; (of work) sezione f; (of goods) partita, lotto.

batch processing n (COMPUT) elaborazione f a blocchi.

bated ['beɪtɪd] adj: **with ~ breath** col fiato sospeso.

bath [bɑːθ, pl bɑːðz] n bagno; (bathtub) vasca da bagno ♦ vt far fare il bagno a; **to**

have a ~ fare un bagno; see also **baths**.

bathchair ['bɑːθtʃɛə*] n (BRIT) poltrona a rotelle.

bathe [beɪð] vi fare il bagno ♦ vt bagnare; (wound etc) lavare.

bather ['beɪðə*] n bagnante m/f.

bathing ['beɪðɪŋ] n bagni mpl.

bathing cap n cuffia da bagno.

bathing costume, (US) **bathing suit** n costume m da bagno.

bathmat ['bɑːθmæt] n tappetino da bagno.

bathrobe ['bɑːθrəub] n accappatoio.

bathroom ['bɑːθrum] n stanza da bagno.

baths [bɑːðz] npl bagni mpl pubblici.

bath towel n asciugamano da bagno.

bathtub ['bɑːθtʌb] n (vasca da) bagno.

batman ['bætmən] n (BRIT MIL) attendente m.

baton ['bætən] n bastone m; (MUS) bacchetta.

battalion [bə'tælɪən] n battaglione m.

batten ['bætən] n (CARPENTRY) assicella, correntino; (for flooring) tavola per pavimenti; (NAUT) serretta; (: on sail) stecca.

▶**batten down** vt (NAUT): **to ~ down the hatches** chiudere i boccaporti.

batter ['bætə*] vt battere ♦ n pastetta.

battered ['bætəd] adj (hat) sformato(a); (pan) ammaccato(a); **~ wife/baby** consorte f/bambino(a) maltrattato(a).

battering ram ['bætərɪŋ-] n ariete m.

battery ['bætərɪ] n batteria; (of torch) pila.

battery charger n caricabatterie m inv.

battle ['bætl] n battaglia ♦ vi battagliare, lottare; **to fight a losing ~** (fig) battersi per una causa persa; **that's half the ~** (col) è già una mezza vittoria.

battle dress n uniforme f da combattimento.

battlefield ['bætlfiːld] n campo di battaglia.

battlements ['bætlmənts] npl bastioni mpl.

battleship ['bætlʃɪp] n nave f da guerra.

batty ['bætɪ] adj (col: person) svitato(a), strambo(a); (: behaviour, idea) strampalato(a).

bauble ['bɔːbl] n ninnolo.

baud [bɔːd] n (COMPUT) baud m inv.

baulk [bɔːlk] vi = **balk**.

bauxite ['bɔːksaɪt] n bauxite f.

Bavaria [bə'vɛərɪə] n Bavaria.

Bavarian [bə'vɛərɪən] adj, n bavarese (m/f).

bawdy ['bɔːdɪ] adj piccante.

bawl [bɔːl] vi urlare.

bay [beɪ] n (of sea) baia; (BRIT: for parking) piazzola di sosta; (loading) piazzale m di (sosta e) carico; **to hold sb at ~** tenere qn a bada.

bay leaf *n* foglia d'alloro.
bayonet ['beɪənɪt] *n* baionetta.
bay tree *n* alloro.
bay window *n* bovindo.
bazaar [bə'zɑː*] *n* bazar *m inv*; vendita di beneficenza.
bazooka [bə'zuːkə] *n* bazooka *m inv*.
BB *n abbr* (*BRIT*: = Boys' Brigade) *organizzazione giovanile a fine educativo*.
B & B *n abbr see* **bed and breakfast**.
BBB *n abbr* (*US*: = Better Business Bureau) *organismo per la difesa dei consumatori*.
BBC *n abbr* = British Broadcasting Corporation; *see boxed note*.

BBC

La **BBC** è l'azienda statale che fornisce il servizio radiofonico e televisivo in Gran Bretagna. Pur dovendo rispondere al Parlamento del proprio operato, la BBC non è soggetta al controllo dello stato per scelte e programmi, anche perché si autofinanzia con il ricavato dei canoni d'abbonamento. La BBC fornisce anche un servizio di informazione internazionale, il "BBC World Service", trasmesso in tutto il mondo.

BBE *n abbr* (*US*: = Benevolent and Protective Order of Elks) *organizzazione filantropica*.
BC *adv abbr* (= before Christ) a.C. ♦ *abbr* (*Canada*) = British Columbia.
BCG *n abbr* (= Bacillus Calmette-Guérin) *vaccino antitubercolare*.
BD *n abbr* (= Bachelor of Divinity) *titolo di studio*.
B/D *abbr* = bank draft.
BDS *n abbr* (= Bachelor of Dental Surgery) *titolo di studio*.

===================== *KEYWORD*

be [biː] (*pt* was, were, *pp* been) *aux vb* **1** (*with present participle: forming continuous tenses*): **what are you doing?** che fai?, che stai facendo?; **they're coming tomorrow** vengono domani; **I've been waiting for her for hours** sono ore che l'aspetto **2** (*with pp: forming passives*) essere; **to ~ killed** essere *or* venire ucciso(a); **the box had been opened** la scatola era stata aperta; **the thief was nowhere to ~ seen** il ladro non si trovava da nessuna parte **3** (*in tag questions*): **it was fun, wasn't it?** è stato divertente, no?; **he's good-looking, isn't he?** è un bell'uomo, vero?; **she's back, is she?** così è tornata, eh? **4** (+*to* + *infinitive*): **the house is to ~ sold**

abbiamo (*or* hanno *etc*) intenzione di vendere casa; **you're to ~ congratulated for all your work** dovremo farvi i complimenti per tutto il vostro lavoro; **am I to understand that …?** devo dedurre che …?; **he's not to open it** non deve aprirlo; **he was to have come yesterday** sarebbe dovuto venire ieri
♦ *vb* +*complement* **1** (*gen*) essere; **I'm English** sono inglese; **I'm tired** sono stanco(a); **I'm hot/cold** ho caldo/freddo; **he's a doctor** è medico; **2 and 2 are 4** 2 più 2 fa 4; **~ careful!** sta attento!; **~ good** sii buono; **if I were you …** se fossi in te … **2** (*of health*) stare; **how are you?** come sta?; **he's very ill** sta molto male **3** (*of age*): **how old are you?** quanti anni hai?; **I'm sixteen (years old)** ho sedici anni **4** (*cost*) costare; **how much was the meal?** quant'era *or* quanto costava il pranzo?; **that'll ~ £5, please** (sono) 5 sterline, per favore
♦ *vi* **1** (*exist, occur etc*) essere, esistere; **the best singer that ever was** il migliore cantante mai esistito *or* di tutti tempi; **~ that as it may** comunque sia, sia come sia; **so ~ it** sia pure, e sia **2** (*referring to place*) essere, trovarsi; **I won't ~ here tomorrow** non ci sarò domani; **Edinburgh is in Scotland** Edimburgo si trova in Scozia **3** (*referring to movement*): **where have you been?** dove sei stato?; **I've been to China** sono stato in Cina
♦ *impers vb* **1** (*referring to time, distance*) essere; **it's 5 o'clock** sono le 5; **it's the 28th of April** è il 28 aprile; **it's 10 km to the village** di qui al paese sono 10 km **2** (*referring to the weather*) fare; **it's too hot/cold** fa troppo caldo/freddo; **it's windy** c'è vento **3** (*emphatic*): **it's me** sono io; **it's only me** sono solo io; **it was Maria who paid the bill** è stata Maria che ha pagato il conto.

B/E *abbr* = bill of exchange.
beach [biːtʃ] *n* spiaggia ♦ *vt* tirare in secco.
beach buggy *n* dune buggy *f inv*.
beachcomber ['biːtʃkəumə*] *n* vagabondo (che s'aggira sulla spiaggia).
beachwear ['biːtʃwɛə*] *n* articoli *mpl* da spiaggia.
beacon ['biːkən] *n* (*lighthouse*) faro; (*marker*) segnale *m*; (*radio ~*) radiofaro.
bead [biːd] *n* perlina; (*of dew, sweat*) goccia; **~s** (*necklace*) collana.
beady ['biːdɪ] *adj*: **~ eyes** occhi *mpl* piccoli e

penetranti.

beagle ['biːgl] n cane m da lepre.

beak [biːk] n becco.

beaker ['biːkə*] n coppa.

beam [biːm] n trave f; (of light) raggio; (RADIO) fascio (d'onde) ♦ vi brillare; (smile): **to** ~ **at sb** rivolgere un radioso sorriso a qn; **to drive on full** or **main** ~ or (US) **high** ~ guidare con gli abbaglianti accesi.

beaming ['biːmɪŋ] adj (sun, smile) raggiante.

bean [biːn] n fagiolo; (of coffee) chicco.

beanpole ['biːnpəul] n (col) spilungone/a.

beansprouts ['biːnsprauts] npl germogli mpl di soia.

bear [bɛə*] n orso; (STOCK EXCHANGE) ribassista m/f ♦ vb (pt **bore**, pp **borne** [bɔː*, bɔːn]) vt (gen) portare; (produce: fruit) produrre, dare; (: traces, signs) mostrare; (COMM: interest) fruttare; (endure) sopportare ♦ vi: **to** ~ **right/left** piegare a destra/sinistra; **to** ~ **the responsibility of** assumersi la responsabilità di; **to** ~ **comparison with** reggere al paragone con; **I can't** ~ **him** non lo posso soffrire or sopportare; **to bring pressure to** ~ **on sb** fare pressione su qn.

▶**bear out** vt (theory, suspicion) confermare, convalidare.

▶**bear up** vi farsi coraggio; **he bore up well under the strain** ha sopportato bene lo stress.

▶**bear with** vt fus (sb's moods, temper) sopportare (con pazienza); ~ **with me a minute** solo un attimo, prego.

bearable ['bɛərəbl] adj sopportabile.

beard [bɪəd] n barba.

bearded ['bɪədɪd] adj barbuto(a).

bearer ['bɛərə*] n portatore m; (of passport) titolare m/f.

bearing ['bɛərɪŋ] n portamento; (connection) rapporto; **(ball)** ~**s** npl cuscinetti mpl a sfere; **to take a** ~ fare un rilevamento; **to find one's** ~**s** orientarsi.

beast [biːst] n bestia.

beastly ['biːstlɪ] adj meschino(a); (weather) da cani.

beat [biːt] n colpo; (of heart) battito; (MUS) tempo; battuta; (of policeman) giro ♦ vt (pt **beat**, pp **beaten**) battere; **off the** ~**en track** fuori mano; **to** ~ **about the bush** menare il cane per l'aia; **to** ~ **time** battere il tempo; **that** ~**s everything!** (col) questo è il colmo!

▶**beat down** vt (door) abbattere, buttare giù; (price) far abbassare; (seller) far scendere ♦ vi (rain) scrosciare; (sun)

picchiare.

▶**beat off** vt respingere.

▶**beat up** vt (col: person) picchiare.

beater ['biːtə*] n (for eggs, cream) frullino.

beating ['biːtɪŋ] n botte fpl; (defeat) batosta; **to take a** ~ prendere una (bella) batosta.

beat-up [biːt'ʌp] adj (col) scassato(a).

beautician [bjuː'tɪʃən] n estetista m/f.

beautiful ['bjuːtɪful] adj bello(a).

beautify ['bjuːtɪfaɪ] vt abbellire.

beauty ['bjuːtɪ] n bellezza; (concept) bello; **the** ~ **of it is that ...** il bello è che ....

beauty contest n concorso di bellezza.

beauty queen n miss f inv, reginetta di bellezza.

beauty salon n istituto di bellezza.

beauty sleep n: **to get one's** ~ farsi un sonno ristoratore.

beauty spot n neo; (BRIT: TOURISM) luogo pittoresco.

beaver ['biːvə*] n castoro.

becalmed [bɪ'kɑːmd] adj in bonaccia.

became [bɪ'keɪm] pt of **become**.

because [bɪ'kɔz] conj perché; ~ **of** prep a causa di.

beck [bɛk] n: **to be at sb's** ~ **and call** essere a completa disposizione di qn.

beckon ['bɛkən] vt (also: ~ **to**) chiamare con un cenno.

become [bɪ'kʌm] vt (irreg: like **come**) diventare; **to** ~ **fat/thin** ingrassarsi/dimagrire; **to** ~ **angry** arrabbiarsi; **it became known that ...** si è venuto a sapere che ...; **what has** ~ **of him?** che gli è successo?

becoming [bɪ'kʌmɪŋ] adj (behaviour) che si conviene; (clothes) grazioso(a).

BEd n abbr (= Bachelor of Education) laurea con abilitazione all'insegnamento.

bed [bɛd] n letto; (of flowers) aiuola; (of coal, clay) strato; (of sea, lake) fondo; **to go to** ~ andare a letto.

▶**bed down** vi sistemarsi (per dormire).

bed and breakfast (B & B) n (terms) camera con colazione; (place) ≈ pensione f familiare; see boxed note.

BED AND BREAKFAST

I **bed and breakfasts**, anche **B & Bs**, sono piccole pensioni a conduzione familiare, in case private o fattorie, dove si affittano camere e viene servita al mattino la tradizionale colazione all'inglese. Queste pensioni offrono un servizio di camera con prima colazione, appunto "bed and breakfast", a prezzi più contenuti rispetto agli alberghi.

bedbug ['bɛdbʌg] *n* cimice *f*.
bedclothes ['bɛdkləuðz] *npl* coperte e lenzuola *fpl*.
bedcover ['bɛdkʌvə*] *n* copriletto.
bedding ['bɛdɪŋ] *n* coperte e lenzuola *fpl*.
bedevil [bɪ'dɛvl] *vt* (*person*) tormentare; (*plans*) ostacolare continuamente.
bedfellow ['bɛdfɛləu] *n*: **they are strange ~s** (*fig*) fanno una coppia ben strana.
bedlam ['bɛdləm] *n* baraonda.
bedpan ['bɛdpæn] *n* padella.
bedpost ['bɛdpəust] *n* colonnina del letto.
bedraggled [bɪ'drægld] *adj* sbrindellato(a); (*wet*) fradicio(a).
bedridden ['bɛdrɪdən] *adj* costretto(a) a letto.
bedrock ['bɛdrɔk] *n* (*GEO*) basamento; (*fig*) fatti *mpl* di base.
bedroom ['bɛdrum] *n* camera da letto.
Beds *abbr* (*BRIT*) = *Bedfordshire.*
bed settee *n* divano *m* letto *inv*.
bedside ['bɛdsaɪd] *n*: **at sb's ~** al capezzale di qn.
bedside lamp *n* lampada da comodino.
bedsit(ter) ['bɛdsɪt(ə*)] *n* (*BRIT*) monolocale *m*.
bedspread ['bɛdsprɛd] *n* copriletto.
bedtime ['bɛdtaɪm] *n*: **it's ~** è ora di andare a letto.
bee [biː] *n* ape *f*; **to have a ~ in one's bonnet (about sth)** avere la fissazione (di qc).
beech [biːtʃ] *n* faggio.
beef [biːf] *n* manzo.
▶**beef up** *vt* (*col*) rinforzare.
beefburger ['biːfbəːgə*] *n* hamburger *m inv*.
beefeater ['biːfiːtə*] *n* guardia della Torre di Londra.
beehive ['biːhaɪv] *n* alveare *m*.
bee-keeping ['biːkiːpɪŋ] *n* apicoltura.
beeline ['biːlaɪn] *n*: **to make a ~ for** buttarsi a capo fitto verso.
been [biːn] *pp of* **be**.
beep [biːp] *n* (*of horn*) colpo di clacson; (*of phone etc*) segnale *m* (acustico), bip *m inv* ♦ *vi* suonare.
beeper ['biːpə*] *n* (*of doctor etc*) cercapersone *m inv*.
beer [bɪə*] *n* birra.
beer belly *n* (*col*) stomaco da bevitore.
beer can *n* lattina di birra.
beetle ['biːtl] *n* scarafaggio; coleottero.
beetroot ['biːtruːt] *n* (*BRIT*) barbabietola.
befall [bɪ'fɔːl] *vi(vt)* (*irreg: like* **fall**) accadere (a).
befit [bɪ'fɪt] *vt* addirsi a.
before [bɪ'fɔː*] *prep* (*in time*) prima di; (*in*

space) davanti a ♦ *conj* prima che + *sub*; prima di ♦ *adv* prima; ~ **going** prima di andare; ~ **she goes** prima che vada; **the week** ~ la settimana prima; **I've seen it** ~ l'ho già visto; **I've never seen it** ~ è la prima volta che lo vedo.
beforehand [bɪ'fɔːhænd] *adv* in anticipo.
befriend [bɪ'frɛnd] *vt* assistere; mostrarsi amico a.
befuddled [bɪ'fʌdld] *adj* confuso(a).
beg [bɛg] *vi* chiedere l'elemosina ♦ *vt* chiedere in elemosina; (*favour*) chiedere; (*entreat*) pregare; **I ~ your pardon** (*apologising*) mi scusi; (*not hearing*) scusi?; **this ~s the question of ...** questo presuppone che sia già risolto il problema di ....
began [bɪ'gæn] *pt of* **begin**.
beggar ['bɛgə*] *n* (*also*: ~**man**, ~**woman**) mendicante *m/f*.
begin, *pt* **began**, *pp* **begun** [bɪ'gɪn, bɪ'gæn, bɪ'gʌn] *vt*, *vi* cominciare; **to ~ doing** *or* **to do sth** incominciare *or* iniziare a fare qc; **I can't ~ to thank you** non so proprio come ringraziarla; **to ~ with, I'd like to know ...** tanto per cominciare vorrei sapere ...; ~**ning from Monday** a partire da lunedì.
beginner [bɪ'gɪnə*] *n* principiante *m/f*.
beginning [bɪ'gɪnɪŋ] *n* inizio, principio; **right from the ~** fin dall'inizio.
begrudge [bɪ'grʌdʒ] *vt*: **to ~ sb sth** dare qc a qn a malincuore; invidiare qn per qc.
beguile [bɪ'gaɪl] *vt* (*enchant*) incantare.
beguiling [bɪ'gaɪlɪŋ] *adj* (*charming*) allettante; (*deluding*) ingannevole.
begun [bɪ'gʌn] *pp of* **begin**.
behalf [bɪ'hɑːf] *n*: **on ~ of**, (*US*) **in ~ of** per conto di; a nome di.
behave [bɪ'heɪv] *vi* comportarsi; (*well*: *also*: ~ **o.s.**) comportarsi bene.
behaviour, (*US*) **behavior** [bɪ'heɪvjə*] *n* comportamento, condotta.
behead [bɪ'hɛd] *vt* decapitare.
beheld [bɪ'hɛld] *pt*, *pp of* **behold**.
behind [bɪ'haɪnd] *prep* dietro; (*followed by pronoun*) dietro di; (*time*) in ritardo con ♦ *adv* dietro; in ritardo ♦ *n* didietro; **we're ~ them in technology** siamo più indietro *or* più arretrati di loro nella tecnica; ~ **the scenes** dietro le quinte; **to be ~ (schedule) with sth** essere indietro con qc; (*payments*) essere in arretrato con qc; **to leave sth ~** dimenticare di prendere qc.
behold [bɪ'həuld] *vt* (*irreg: like* **hold**) vedere, scorgere.

beige [beɪʒ] *adj* beige *inv*.
Beijing [beɪ'dʒɪŋ] *n* Pechino *f*.
being ['biːɪŋ] *n* essere *m*; **to come into** ~ cominciare ad esistere.
Beirut [beɪ'ruːt] *n* Beirut *f*.
Belarus ['bɛlærus] *n* Bielorussia.
Belarussian [bɛlə'rʌʃən] *adj* bielorusso(a) ♦ *n* bielorusso/a; (*LING*) bielorusso.
belated [bɪ'leɪtɪd] *adj* tardo(a).
belch [bɛltʃ] *vi* ruttare ♦ *vt* (*gen*: ~ **out**: *smoke etc*) eruttare.
beleaguered [bɪ'liːgəd] *adj* (*city*) assediato(a); (*army*) accerchiato(a); (*fig*) assillato(a).
Belfast ['bɛlfɑːst] *n* Belfast *f*.
belfry ['bɛlfrɪ] *n* campanile *m*.
Belgian ['bɛldʒən] *adj, n* belga (*m/f*).
Belgium ['bɛldʒəm] *n* Belgio.
Belgrade [bɛl'greɪd] *n* Belgrado *f*.
belie [bɪ'laɪ] *vt* smentire; (*give false impression of*) nascondere.
belief [bɪ'liːf] *n* (*opinion*) opinione *f*, convinzione *f*; (*trust, faith*) fede *f*; (*acceptance as true*) credenza; **in the** ~ **that** nella convinzione che; **it's beyond** ~ è incredibile.
believe [bɪ'liːv] *vt, vi* credere; **to** ~ **in** (*God*) credere in; (*ghosts*) credere a; (*method*) avere fiducia in; **I don't** ~ **in corporal punishment** sono contrario alle punizioni corporali; **he is** ~**d to be abroad** si pensa (che) sia all'estero.
believer [bɪ'liːvə*] *n* (*REL*) credente *m/f*; (*in idea, activity*): **to be a** ~ **in** credere in.
belittle [bɪ'lɪtl] *vt* sminuire.
Belize [bɛ'liːz] *n* Belize *m*.
bell [bɛl] *n* campana; (*small, on door, electric*) campanello; **that rings a** ~ (*fig*) mi ricorda qualcosa.
bell-bottoms ['bɛlbɔtəmz] *npl* calzoni *mpl* a zampa d'elefante.
bellboy ['bɛlbɔɪ], (*US*) **bellhop** ['bɛlhɔp] *n* ragazzo d'albergo, fattorino d'albergo.
belligerent [bɪ'lɪdʒərənt] *adj* (*at war*) belligerante; (*fig*) bellicoso(a).
bellow ['bɛləu] *vi* muggire; (*cry*) urlare (a squarciagola) ♦ *vt* (*orders*) urlare (a squarciagola).
bellows ['bɛləuz] *npl* soffietto.
bell push *n* (*BRIT*) pulsante *m* del campanello.
belly ['bɛlɪ] *n* pancia.
bellyache ['bɛlɪeɪk] *n* mal *m* di pancia ♦ *vi* (*col*) mugugnare.
bellybutton ['bɛlɪbʌtn] *n* ombelico.
bellyful ['bɛlɪful] *n* (*col*): **to have had a** ~ **of** (*fig*) averne piene le tasche (di).
belong [bɪ'lɔŋ] *vi*: **to** ~ **to** appartenere a;

(*club etc*) essere socio di; **this book** ~**s here** questo libro va qui.
belongings [bɪ'lɔŋɪŋz] *npl* cose *fpl*, roba; **personal** ~ effetti *mpl* personali.
Belorussia [bɛləu'rʌʃə] *n* Bielorussia.
Belorussian [bɛləu'rʌʃən] *adj, n* = **Belarussian**.
beloved [bɪ'lʌvɪd] *adj* adorato(a).
below [bɪ'ləu] *prep* sotto, al di sotto di ♦ *adv* sotto, di sotto; giù; **see** ~ vedi sotto *or* oltre; **temperatures** ~ **normal** temperature al di sotto del normale.
belt [bɛlt] *n* cintura; (*TECH*) cinghia ♦ *vt* (*thrash*) picchiare ♦ *vi* (*BRIT col*) filarsela; **industrial** ~ zona industriale.
▶**belt out** *vt* (*song*) cantare a squarciagola.
▶**belt up** *vi* (*BRIT col*) chiudere la boccaccia.
beltway ['bɛltweɪ] *n* (*US AUT*) circonvallazione *f*; (: *motorway*) autostrada.
bemoan [bɪ'məun] *vt* lamentare.
bemused [bɪ'mjuːzd] *adj* perplesso(a), stupito(a).
bench [bɛntʃ] *n* panca; (*in workshop*) banco; **the B~** (*LAW*) la Corte.
bench mark *n* banco di prova.
bend [bɛnd] *vb* (*pt, pp* **bent** [bɛnt]) *vt* curvare; (*leg, arm*) piegare ♦ *vi* curvarsi; piegarsi ♦ *n* (*BRIT: in road*) curva; (*in pipe, river*) gomito.
▶**bend down** *vi* chinarsi.
▶**bend over** *vi* piegarsi.
bends [bɛndz] *npl* (*MED*) embolia.
beneath [bɪ'niːθ] *prep* sotto, al di sotto di; (*unworthy of*) indegno(a) di ♦ *adv* sotto, di sotto.
benefactor ['bɛnɪfæktə*] *n* benefattore *m*.
benefactress ['bɛnɪfæktrɪs] *n* benefattrice *f*.
beneficial [bɛnɪ'fɪʃəl] *adj* che fa bene; vantaggioso(a); ~ **to** che giova a.
beneficiary [bɛnɪ'fɪʃərɪ] *n* (*LAW*) beneficiario/a.
benefit ['bɛnɪfɪt] *n* beneficio, vantaggio; (*allowance of money*) indennità *f inv* ♦ *vt* far bene a ♦ *vi*: **he'll** ~ **from it** ne trarrà beneficio *or* profitto.
benefit performance *n* spettacolo di beneficenza.
Benelux ['bɛnɪlʌks] *n* Benelux *m*.
benevolent [bɪ'nɛvələnt] *adj* benevolo(a).
BEng *n abbr* (= *Bachelor of Engineering*) laurea in ingegneria.
benign [bɪ'naɪn] *adj* benevolo(a); (*MED*) benigno(a).
bent [bɛnt] *pt, pp of* **bend** ♦ *n* inclinazione *f* ♦ *adj* (*wire, pipe*) piegato(a), storto(a); (*col: dishonest*) losco(a); **to be** ~ **on** essere

deciso(a) a.

bequeath [bɪ'kwiːð] *vt* lasciare in eredità.

bequest [bɪ'kwɛst] *n* lascito.

bereaved [bɪ'riːvd] *adj* in lutto ♦ *npl*: **the ~ i** familiari in lutto.

bereavement [bɪ'riːvmənt] *n* lutto.

beret ['bɛreɪ] *n* berretto.

Bering Sea ['bɛrɪŋ-] *n*: **the ~ il mar di** Bering.

berk [bəːk] *n* (*BRIT col!*) coglione/a (*!*).

Berks *abbr* (*BRIT*) = Berkshire.

Berlin [bəː'lɪn] *n* Berlino *f*; **East/West ~** Berlino est/ovest.

berm [bəːm] *n* (*US AUT*) corsia d'emergenza.

Bermuda [bəː'mjuːdə] *n* le Bermude.

Bermuda shorts *npl* bermuda *mpl*.

Bern [bəːn] *n* Berna *f*.

berry ['bɛrɪ] *n* bacca.

berserk [bə'səːk] *adj*: **to go ~** montare su tutte le furie.

berth [bəːθ] *n* (*bed*) cuccetta; (*for ship*) ormeggio ♦ *vi* (*in harbour*) entrare in porto; (*at anchor*) gettare l'ancora; **to give sb a wide ~** (*fig*) tenersi alla larga da qn.

beseech, *pt, pp* **besought** [bɪ'siːtʃ, bɪ'sɔːt] *vt* implorare.

beset, *pt, pp* **beset** [bɪ'sɛt] *vt* assalire ♦ *adj*: **a policy ~ with dangers** una politica irta *or* piena di pericoli.

besetting [bɪ'sɛtɪŋ] *adj*: **his ~ sin** il suo più grande difetto.

beside [bɪ'saɪd] *prep* accanto a; (*compared with*) rispetto a, in confronto a; **to be ~ o.s. (with anger)** essere fuori di sé; **that's ~ the point** non c'entra.

besides [bɪ'saɪdz] *adv* inoltre, per di più ♦ *prep* oltre a; (*except*) a parte.

besiege [bɪ'siːdʒ] *vt* (*town*) assediare; (*fig*) tempestare.

besotted [bɪ'sɔtɪd] *adj* (*BRIT*): **~ with** infatuato(a) di.

besought [bɪ'sɔːt] *pt, pp of* **beseech**.

bespectacled [bɪ'spɛktɪkld] *adj* occhialuto(a).

bespoke [bɪ'spəuk] *adj* (*BRIT*: *garment*) su misura; **~ tailor** sarto.

best [bɛst] *adj* migliore ♦ *adv* meglio; **the ~ thing to do is …** la cosa migliore da fare *or* farsi è …; **the ~ part of** (*quantity*) la maggior parte di; **at ~** tutt'al più; **to make the ~ of sth** cavare il meglio possibile da qc; **to do one's ~** fare del proprio meglio; **to the ~ of my knowledge** per quel che ne so; **to the ~ of my ability** al massimo delle mie capacità; **he's not exactly patient at the ~ of times**

non è mai molto paziente.

best-before date *n* (*COMM*) data limite d'utilizzo *or* di consumo.

best man *n* testimone *m* dello sposo.

bestow [bɪ'stəu] *vt*: **to ~ sth on sb** conferire qc a qn.

bestseller ['bɛst'sɛlə*] *n* bestseller *m inv*.

bet [bɛt] *n* scommessa ♦ *vt, vi* (*pt, pp* **bet** *or* **betted**) scommettere; **it's a safe ~** (*fig*) è molto probabile.

Bethlehem ['bɛθlɪhɛm] *n* Betlemme *f*.

betray [bɪ'treɪ] *vt* tradire.

betrayal [bɪ'treɪəl] *n* tradimento.

better ['bɛtə*] *adj* migliore ♦ *adv* meglio ♦ *vt* migliorare ♦ *n*: **to get the ~ of** avere la meglio su; **you had ~ do it** è meglio che lo faccia; **he thought ~ of it** cambiò idea; **to get ~** migliorare; **a change for the ~** un cambiamento in meglio; **that's ~!** così va meglio!; **I had ~ go** dovrei andare; **~ off** *adj* più ricco(a); (*fig*): **you'd be ~ off this way** starebbe meglio così.

betting ['bɛtɪŋ] *n* scommesse *fpl*.

betting shop *n* (*BRIT*) ufficio dell'allibratore.

between [bɪ'twiːn] *prep* tra ♦ *adv* in mezzo, nel mezzo; **the road ~ here and London** la strada da qui a Londra; **we only had £5 ~ us** fra tutti e due avevamo solo 5 sterline.

bevel ['bɛvl] *n* (*also*: **~(led) edge**) profilo smussato.

beverage ['bɛvərɪdʒ] *n* bevanda.

bevy ['bɛvɪ] *n*: **a ~ of** una banda di.

bewail [bɪ'weɪl] *vt* lamentare.

beware [bɪ'wɛə*] *vt, vi*: **to ~ (of)** stare attento(a) (a).

bewildered [bɪ'wɪldəd] *adj* sconcertato(a), confuso(a).

bewildering [bɪ'wɪldərɪŋ] *adj* sconcertante, sbalorditivo(a).

bewitching [bɪ'wɪtʃɪŋ] *adj* affascinante.

beyond [bɪ'jɔnd] *prep* (*in space*) al di là di; (*exceeding*) al di sopra di ♦ *adv* di là; **~ doubt** senza dubbio; **~ repair** irreparabile.

b/f *abbr see* **brought forward**.

bhp *n abbr* (*AUT*: = brake horsepower) c.v. (= *cavallo vapore*).

bi... [baɪ] *prefix* bi....

biannual [baɪ'ænjuəl] *adj* semestrale.

bias ['baɪəs] *n* (*prejudice*) pregiudizio; (*preference*) preferenza.

bias(s)ed ['baɪəst] *adj* parziale; **to be ~ against** essere prevenuto(a) contro.

biathlon [baɪ'æθlən] *n* biathlon *m*.

bib [bɪb] *n* bavaglino.

Bible ['baɪbl] *n* Bibbia.

bibliography [bɪblɪ'ɔgrəfɪ] n bibliografia.
bicarbonate of soda [baɪ'kɑːbənɪt-] n bicarbonato (di sodio).
bicentenary [baɪsɛn'tiːnərɪ], **bicentennial** [baɪsɛn'tɛnɪəl] n bicentenario.
biceps ['baɪsɛps] n bicipite m.
bicker ['bɪkə*] vi bisticciare.
bicycle ['baɪsɪkl] n bicicletta.
bicycle path n, **bicycle track** n sentiero ciclabile.
bicycle pump n pompa della bicicletta.
bid [bɪd] n offerta; (attempt) tentativo ♦ vb (pt **bade** [bæd] or **bid**, pp **bidden** ['bɪdn] or **bid**) vi fare un'offerta ♦ vt fare un'offerta di; **to ~ sb good day** dire buon giorno a qn.
bidder ['bɪdə*] n: **the highest ~** il maggior offerente.
bidding ['bɪdɪŋ] n offerte fpl.
bide [baɪd] vt: **to ~ one's time** aspettare il momento giusto.
bidet ['biːdeɪ] n bidè m inv.
bidirectional ['baɪdɪ'rɛkʃənl] adj bidirezionale.
biennial [baɪ'ɛnɪəl] adj biennale ♦ n (pianta) biennale f.
bier [bɪə*] n bara.
bifocals [baɪ'fəuklz] npl occhiali mpl bifocali.
big [bɪg] adj grande; grosso(a); **my ~ brother** mio fratello maggiore; **to do things in a ~ way** fare le cose in grande.
bigamy ['bɪgəmɪ] n bigamia.
big dipper [-'dɪpə*] n montagne fpl russe, otto m inv volante.
big end n (AUT) testa di biella.
biggish ['bɪgɪʃ] adj (see big) piuttosto grande; piuttosto grosso(a); **a ~ rent** un affitto piuttosto alto.
bigheaded ['bɪg'hɛdɪd] adj presuntuoso(a).
big-hearted ['bɪg'hɑːtɪd] adj generoso(a).
bigot ['bɪgət] n persona gretta.
bigoted ['bɪgətɪd] adj gretto(a).
bigotry ['bɪgətrɪ] n grettezza.
big toe n alluce m.
big top n tendone m del circo.
big wheel n (at fair) ruota (panoramica).
bigwig ['bɪgwɪg] n (col) pezzo grosso.
bike [baɪk] n bici f inv.
bike lane n pista ciclabile.
bikini [bɪ'kiːnɪ] n bikini m inv.
bilateral [baɪ'lætərl] adj bilaterale.
bile [baɪl] n bile f.
bilingual [baɪ'lɪŋgwəl] adj bilingue.
bilious ['bɪlɪəs] adj biliare; (fig) bilioso(a).
bill [bɪl] n (in hotel, restaurant) conto; (COMM) fattura; (for gas, electricity) bolletta, conto; (POL) atto; (US: banknote) banconota; (notice) avviso; (THEAT): **on the ~** in cartellone; (of bird) becco ♦ vt mandare il conto a; **may I have the ~ please?** posso avere il conto per piacere?; **"stick** or **post no ~s"** "divieto di affissione"; **to fit** or **fill the ~** (fig) fare al caso; **~ of exchange** cambiale f, tratta; **~ of lading** polizza di carico; **~ of sale** atto di vendita.
billboard ['bɪlbɔːd] n tabellone m.
billet ['bɪlɪt] n alloggio ♦ vt (troops etc) alloggiare.
billfold ['bɪlfəuld] n (US) portafoglio.
billiards ['bɪljədz] n biliardo.
billion ['bɪljən] n (BRIT) bilione m; (US) miliardo.
billow ['bɪləu] n (of smoke) nuvola; (of sail) rigonfiamento ♦ vi (smoke) alzarsi in volute; (sail) gonfiarsi.
bills payable (B/P, b.p.) npl effetti mpl passivi.
bills receivable (B/R, b.r.) npl effetti mpl attivi.
billy goat ['bɪlɪgəut] n caprone m, becco.
bimbo ['bɪmbəu] n (col) pollastrella, svampitella.
bin [bɪn] n bidone m; (BRIT: also: **dust~**) pattumiera; (: also: **litter ~**) cestino.
binary ['baɪnərɪ] adj binario(a).
bind, pt, pp **bound** [baɪnd, baund] vt legare; (oblige) obbligare.
▶**bind over** vt (LAW) dare la condizionale a.
▶**bind up** vt (wound) fasciare, bendare; **to be bound up in** (work, research etc) essere completamente assorbito da; **to be bound up with** (person) dedicarsi completamente a.
binder ['baɪndə*] n (file) classificatore m.
binding ['baɪndɪŋ] n (of book) legatura ♦ adj (contract) vincolante.
binge [bɪndʒ] n (col): **to go on a ~** fare baldoria.
bingo ['bɪŋgəu] n gioco simile alla tombola.
bin liner n sacchetto per l'immondizia.
binoculars [bɪ'nɔkjuləz] npl binocolo.
biochemistry [baɪəu'kɛmɪstrɪ] n biochimica.
biodegradable ['baɪəudɪ'greɪdəbl] adj biodegradabile.
biodiversity ['baɪəudaɪ'vəːsɪtɪ] n biodiversità f inv.
biofuel ['baɪəufjuəl] n carburante m biologico.
biographer [baɪ'ɔgrəfə*] n biografo/a.
biographic(al) [baɪə'græfɪk(l)] adj biografico(a).
biography [baɪ'ɔgrəfɪ] n biografia.
biological [baɪə'lɔdʒɪkl] adj biologico(a).
biological clock n orologio biologico.

biologist [baɪ'ɔlədʒɪst] *n* biologo/a.
biology [baɪ'ɔlədʒɪ] *n* biologia.
biophysics [baɪəu'fɪzɪks] *n* biofisica.
biopic ['baɪəupɪk] *n* film *m inv* biografia *inv*.
biosphere ['baɪəusfɪə*] *n* biosfera.
biopsy ['baɪɔpsɪ] *n* biopsia.
biotechnology [baɪəutɛk'nɔlədʒɪ] *n*
  biotecnologia.
bioterrorism [baɪəu'tɛrərɪzəm] *n*
  bioterrorismo.
birch [bə:tʃ] *n* betulla.
bird [bə:d] *n* uccello; (*BRIT col: girl*)
  bambola.
bird flu *n* influenza aviaria.
bird of prey *n* (uccello) rapace *m*.
bird's-eye view ['bə:dzaɪ-] *n* vista
  panoramica.
bird watcher *n* ornitologo/a dilettante.
Biro ® ['baɪrəu] *n* biro ® *f inv*.
birth [bə:θ] *n* nascita; **to give ~ to** dare alla
  luce; (*fig*) dare inizio a.
birth certificate *n* certificato di nascita.
birth control *n* controllo delle nascite;
  contraccezione *f*.
birthday ['bə:θdeɪ] *n* compleanno.
birthmark ['bə:θmɑ:k] *n* voglia.
birthplace ['bə:θpleɪs] *n* luogo di nascita.
birth rate *n* indice *m* di natalità.
Biscay ['bɪskeɪ] *n*: **the Bay of** ~ il golfo di
  Biscaglia.
biscuit ['bɪskɪt] *n* (*BRIT*) biscotto; (*US*)
  panino al latte.
bisect [baɪ'sɛkt] *vt* tagliare in due (parti);
  (*MATH*) bisecare.
bisexual ['baɪ'sɛksjuəl] *adj, n* bissessual (*m/f*).
bishop ['bɪʃəp] *n* vescovo; (*CHESS*) alfiere *m*.
bistro ['bi:strəu] *n* bistrò *m inv*.
bit [bɪt] *pt of* **bite** ♦ *n* pezzo; (*of tool*) punta;
  (*of horse*) morso; (*COMPUT*) bit *m inv*; (*US:
  coin*) ottavo di dollaro; **a ~ of** un po' di; **a
  ~ mad/dangerous** un po' matto/
  pericoloso; **~ by** ~ a poco a poco; **to do
  one's** ~ fare la propria parte; **to come to
  ~s** (*break*) andare a pezzi; **bring all your
  ~s and pieces** porta tutte le tue cose.
bitch [bɪtʃ] *n* (*dog*) cagna; (*col!*) puttana (*!*).
bite [baɪt] *vt, vi* (*pt* **bit** [bɪt], *pp* **bitten** ['bɪtn])
  mordere ♦ *n* morso; (*insect* ~) puntura;
  (*mouthful*) boccone *m*; **let's have a** ~ (**to
  eat**) mangiamo un boccone; **to** ~ **one's
  nails** mangiarsi le unghie.
biting ['baɪtɪŋ] *adj* pungente.
bit part *n* (*THEAT*) particina.
bitten ['bɪtn] *pp of* **bite.**
bitter ['bɪtə*] *adj* amaro(a); (*wind, criticism*)
  pungente; (*icy: weather*) gelido(a) ♦ *n*
  (*BRIT: beer*) birra amara; **to the** ~ **end** a
  oltranza.

bitterly ['bɪtəlɪ] *adv* (*disappoint, complain,
  weep*) amaramente; (*oppose, criticise*)
  aspramente; (*jealous*) profondamente; **it's
  ~ cold** fa un freddo gelido.
bitterness ['bɪtənɪs] *n* amarezza; gusto
  amaro.
bittersweet ['bɪtəswi:t] *adj* agrodolce.
bitty ['bɪtɪ] *adj* (*BRIT col*) frammentario(a).
bitumen ['bɪtjumɪn] *n* bitume *m*.
bivouac ['bɪvuæk] *n* bivacco.
bizarre [bɪ'zɑ:*] *adj* bizzarro(a).
bk *abbr* = **bank; book.**
BL *n abbr* (= *Bachelor of Law(s), Bachelor of
  Letters*) titolo di studio; (*US:* = *Bachelor of
  Literature*) titolo di studio.
B/L *abbr* = **bill of lading.**
blab [blæb] *vi* parlare troppo ♦ *vt* (*also:* ~
  out) spifferare.
black [blæk] *adj* nero(a) ♦ *n* nero; (*person*):
  B~ negro/a ♦ *vt* (*BRIT INDUSTRY*)
  boicottare; ~ **coffee** caffè *m inv* nero; **to
  give sb a** ~ **eye** fare un occhio nero a qn;
  in the ~ (*in credit*) in attivo; **there it is in** ~
  and white (*fig*) eccolo nero su bianco; ~
  and blue *adj* tutto(a) pesto(a).
► **black out** *vi* (*faint*) svenire.
black belt *n* (*SPORT*) cintura nera; (*US:
  area*): **the** ~ zona abitata principalmente
  da negri.
blackberry ['blækbərɪ] *n* mora.
blackbird ['blækbə:d] *n* merlo.
blackboard ['blækbɔ:d] *n* lavagna.
black box *n* (*AVIAT*) scatola nera.
Black Country *n* (*BRIT*): **the** ~ zona
  carbonifera del centro dell'Inghilterra.
blackcurrant [blæk'kʌrənt] *n* ribes *m inv*.
black economy *n* (*BRIT*) economia
  sommersa.
blacken ['blækn] *vt* annerire.
Black Forest *n*: **the** ~ la Foresta Nera.
blackhead ['blækhɛd] *n* punto nero,
  comedone *m*.
black hole *n* (*ASTRON*) buco nero.
black ice *n* strato trasparente di ghiaccio.
blackjack ['blækdʒæk] *n* (*CARDS*) ventuno;
  (*US: truncheon*) manganello.
blackleg ['blæklɛg] *n* (*BRIT*) crumiro.
blacklist ['blæklɪst] *n* lista nera ♦ *vt* mettere
  sulla lista nera.
blackmail ['blækmeɪl] *n* ricatto ♦ *vt* ricattare.
blackmailer ['blækmeɪlə*] *n* ricattatore/
  trice.
black market *n* mercato nero.
blackout ['blækaut] *n* oscuramento;
  (*fainting*) svenimento; (*TV*) interruzione *f*
  delle trasmissioni.
black pepper *n* pepe *m* nero.
Black Sea *n*: **the** ~ il mar Nero.

black sheep n pecora nera.
blacksmith ['blæksmɪθ] n fabbro ferraio.
black spot n (AUT) luogo famigerato per gli incidenti.
bladder ['blædə*] n vescica.
blade [bleɪd] n lama; (of oar) pala; ~ **of grass** filo d'erba.
blame [bleɪm] n colpa ♦ vt: **to ~ sb/sth for sth** dare la colpa di qc a qn/qc; **who's to ~?** chi è colpevole?; **I'm not to ~** non è colpa mia.
blameless ['bleɪmlɪs] adj irreprensibile.
blanch [blɑːntʃ] vi (person) sbiancare in viso ♦ vt (CULIN) scottare.
bland [blænd] adj mite; (taste) blando(a).
blank [blæŋk] adj bianco(a); (look) distratto(a) ♦ n spazio vuoto; (cartridge) cartuccia a salve; **to draw a ~** (fig) non aver nessun risultato.
blank cheque, (US) **blank check** n assegno in bianco; **to give sb a ~ to do** (fig) dare carta bianca a qn per fare.
blanket ['blæŋkɪt] n coperta ♦ adj (statement, agreement) globale.
blanket cover n: **to give ~** (subj: insurance policy) coprire tutti i rischi.
blare [blɛə*] vi strombettare; (radio) suonare a tutto volume.
blasé ['blɑːzeɪ] adj blasé inv.
blasphemous ['blæsfɪməs] adj blasfemo(a).
blasphemy ['blæsfɪmɪ] n bestemmia.
blast [blɑːst] n (of wind) raffica; (of air, steam) getto; (bomb ~) esplosione f ♦ vt far saltare ♦ excl (BRIT col) mannaggia!; **(at) full ~** a tutta forza.
▶**blast off** vi (SPACE) essere lanciato(a).
blast-off ['blɑːstɔf] n (SPACE) lancio.
blatant ['bleɪtənt] adj flagrante.
blatantly ['bleɪtəntlɪ] adv: **it's ~ obvious** è lampante.
blaze [bleɪz] n (fire) incendio; (glow: of fire, sun etc) bagliore m; (fig) vampata ♦ vi (fire) ardere, fiammeggiare; (fig) infiammarsi ♦ vt: **to ~ a trail** (fig) tracciare una via nuova; **in a ~ of publicity** circondato da grande pubblicità.
blazer ['bleɪzə*] n blazer m inv.
bleach [bliːtʃ] n (also: **household ~**) varechina ♦ vt (material) candeggiare.
bleached ['bliːtʃt] adj (hair) decolorato(a).
bleachers ['bliːtʃəz] npl (US) posti mpl di gradinata.
bleak [bliːk] adj (prospect, future) tetro(a); (landscape) desolato(a); (weather) gelido(a); (smile) pallido(a).
bleary-eyed ['blɪərɪ'aɪd] adj dagli occhi offuscati.
bleat [bliːt] vi belare.

bleed, pt, pp **bled** [bliːd, blɛd] vt dissanguare; (brakes, radiator) spurgare ♦ vi sanguinare; **my nose is ~ing** mi viene fuori sangue dal naso.
bleep [bliːp] n breve segnale m acustico, bip m inv ♦ vi suonare ♦ vt (doctor) chiamare con il cercapersone.
bleeper ['bliːpə*] n (of doctor etc) cercapersone m inv.
blemish ['blɛmɪʃ] n macchia.
blend [blɛnd] n miscela ♦ vt mescolare ♦ vi (colours etc) armonizzare.
blender ['blɛndə*] n (CULIN) frullatore m.
bless, pt, pp **blessed** or **blest** [blɛs, blɛst] vt benedire; **~ you!** (sneezing) salute!; **to be ~ed with** godere di.
blessed ['blɛsɪd] adj (REL: holy) benedetto(a); (happy) beato(a); **every ~ day** tutti i santi giorni.
blessing ['blɛsɪŋ] n benedizione f; fortuna; **to count one's ~s** ringraziare Iddio, ritenersi fortunato; **it was a ~ in disguise** in fondo è stato un bene.
blest [blɛst] pt, pp of **bless**.
blew [bluː] pt of **blow**.
blight [blaɪt] n (of plants) golpe f ♦ vt (hopes etc) deludere; (life) rovinare.
blimey ['blaɪmɪ] excl (BRIT col) accidenti!
blind [blaɪnd] adj cieco(a) ♦ n (for window) avvolgibile m; (Venetian ~) veneziana ♦ vt accecare; **to turn a ~ eye (on or to)** chiudere un occhio (su).
blind alley n vicolo cieco.
blind corner n (BRIT) svolta cieca.
blind date n appuntamento combinato (tra due persone che non si conoscono).
blinders ['blaɪndəz] npl (US) = **blinkers**.
blindfold ['blaɪndfəʊld] n benda ♦ adj, adv bendato(a) ♦ vt bendare gli occhi a.
blinding ['blaɪndɪŋ] adj (flash, light) accecante; (pain) atroce.
blindly ['blaɪndlɪ] adv ciecamente.
blindness ['blaɪndnɪs] n cecità.
blind spot n (AUT etc) punto cieco; (fig) punto debole.
blink [blɪŋk] vi battere gli occhi; (light) lampeggiare ♦ n: **to be on the ~** (col) essere scassato(a).
blinkers ['blɪŋkəz] npl (BRIT) paraocchi mpl.
blinking ['blɪŋkɪŋ] adj (BRIT col): **this ~ ...** questo(a) maledetto(a) ....
blip [blɪp] n (on radar etc) segnale m intermittente; (on graph) piccola variazione f; (fig) momentanea battuta d'arresto.
bliss [blɪs] n estasi f.
blissful ['blɪsfəl] adj (event, day) stupendo(a), meraviglioso(a); (smile)

beato(a); **in ~ ignorance** nella (più) beata ignoranza.

blissfully ['blɪsfəlɪ] *adj* (*sigh, smile*) beatamente; **~ happy** magnificamente felice.

blister ['blɪstə*] *n* (*on skin*) vescica; (*on paintwork*) bolla ♦ *vi* (*paint*) coprirsi di bolle.

blithe [blaɪð] *adj* gioioso(a), allegro(a).

blithely ['blaɪðlɪ] *adv* allegramente.

blithering ['blɪðərɪŋ] *adj* (*col*): **this ~ idiot** questa razza d'idiota.

BLit(t) *n abbr* (= *Bachelor of Literature*) titolo di studio.

blitz [blɪts] *n* blitz *m*; **to have a ~ on sth** (*fig*) prendere d'assalto qc.

blizzard ['blɪzəd] *n* bufera di neve.

bloated ['bləʊtɪd] *adj* gonfio(a).

blob [blɔb] *n* (*drop*) goccia; (*stain, spot*) macchia.

bloc [blɔk] *n* (*POL*) blocco.

block [blɔk] *n* (*gen, COMPUT*) blocco; (*in pipes*) ingombro; (*toy*) cubo; (*of buildings*) isolato ♦ *vt* (*gen, COMPUT*) bloccare; **~ of flats** caseggiato; **3 ~s from here** a 3 isolati di distanza da qui; **mental ~** blocco mentale.

►**block up** *vt* bloccare; (*pipe*) ingorgare, intasare.

blockade [blɔ'keɪd] *n* blocco ♦ *vt* assediare.

blockage ['blɔkɪdʒ] *n* ostacolo.

block and tackle *n* (*TECH*) paranco.

block booking *n* prenotazione *f* in blocco.

blockbuster ['blɔkbʌstə*] *n* libro *or* film *etc* sensazionale.

block capitals *npl* stampatello.

blockhead ['blɔkhɛd] *n* testa di legno.

block letters *npl* stampatello.

block release *n* (*BRIT*) periodo pagato concesso al tirocinante per effettuare studi superiori.

block vote *n* (*BRIT*) voto per delega.

bloke [bləʊk] *n* (*BRIT col*) tizio.

blond [blɔnd] *n* (*man*) biondo ♦ *adj* biondo(a).

blonde [blɔnd] *n* (*woman*) bionda ♦ *adj* biondo(a).

blood [blʌd] *n* sangue *m*; **new ~** (*fig*) nuova linfa.

blood bank *n* banca del sangue.

blood count *n* conteggio di globuli rossi e bianchi.

bloodcurdling ['blʌdkəːdlɪŋ] *adj* raccapricciante, da far gelare il sangue.

blood donor *n* donatore/trice di sangue.

blood group *n* gruppo sanguigno.

bloodhound ['blʌdhaʊnd] *n* segugio.

bloodless ['blʌdlɪs] *adj* (*pale*) smorto(a), esangue; (*coup*) senza spargimento di sangue.

bloodletting ['blʌdlɛtɪŋ] *n* (*MED*) salasso; (*fig*) spargimento di sangue.

blood poisoning *n* setticemia.

blood pressure *n* pressione *f* sanguigna; **to have high/low ~** avere la pressione alta/bassa.

bloodshed ['blʌdʃɛd] *n* spargimento di sangue.

bloodshot ['blʌdʃɔt] *adj*: **~ eyes** occhi iniettati di sangue.

bloodstained ['blʌdsteɪnd] *adj* macchiato(a) di sangue.

bloodstream ['blʌdstriːm] *n* flusso del sangue.

blood test *n* analisi *f inv* del sangue.

bloodthirsty ['blʌdθəːstɪ] *adj* assetato(a) di sangue.

blood transfusion *n* trasfusione *f* di sangue.

blood type *n* gruppo sanguigno.

blood vessel *n* vaso sanguigno.

bloody ['blʌdɪ] *adj* sanguinoso(a); (*BRIT col!*): **this ~ ...** questo maledetto ...; **a ~ awful day** (*col!*) una giornata di merda (*!*); **~ good** (*col!*) maledettamente buono.

bloody-minded ['blʌdɪ'maɪndɪd] *adj* (*BRIT col*) indisponente.

bloom [bluːm] *n* fiore *m* ♦ *vi* essere in fiore.

blooming ['bluːmɪŋ] *adj* (*col*): **this ~ ...** questo(a) dannato(a) ....

blossom ['blɔsəm] *n* fiore *m*; (*with pl sense*) fiori *mpl* ♦ *vi* essere in fiore; **to ~ into** (*fig*) diventare.

blot [blɔt] *n* macchia ♦ *vt* macchiare; **to be a ~ on the landscape** rovinare il paesaggio; **to ~ one's copy book** (*fig*) farla grossa.

►**blot out** *vt* (*memories*) cancellare; (*view*) nascondere; (*nation, city*) annientare.

blotchy ['blɔtʃɪ] *adj* (*complexion*) coperto(a) di macchie.

blotter ['blɔtə*] *n* tampone *m* (di carta assorbente).

blotting paper ['blɔtɪŋ-] *n* carta assorbente.

blotto ['blɔtəʊ] *adj* (*col*) sbronzo(a).

blouse [blaʊz] *n* camicetta.

blow [bləʊ] *n* colpo ♦ *vb* (*pt* **blew,** *pp* **blown** [bluː, bləʊn]) *vi* soffiare ♦ *vt* (*fuse*) far saltare; **to come to ~s** venire alle mani; **to ~ one's nose** soffiarsi il naso; **to ~ a whistle** fischiare.

►**blow away** *vi* volare via ♦ *vt* portare via.

►**blow down** *vt* abbattere.

►**blow off** *vt* far volare via; **to ~ off course** far uscire di rotta.

►**blow out** *vi* scoppiare.

▶**blow over** *vi* calmarsi.

▶**blow up** *vi* saltare in aria ♦ *vt* far saltare in aria; (*tyre*) gonfiare; (*PHOT*) ingrandire.

blow-dry ['bləudraɪ] *n* (*hairstyle*) messa in piega a föhn ♦ *vt* asciugare con il föhn.

blowlamp ['bləulæmp] *n* (*BRIT*) lampada a benzina per saldare.

blown [bləun] *pp of* **blow**.

blowout ['bləuaut] *n* (*of tyre*) scoppio; (*col*: *big meal*) abbuffata.

blowtorch ['bləutɔ:tʃ] *n* lampada a benzina per saldare.

blowzy ['blauzɪ] *adj* trasandato(a).

BLS *n abbr* (*US*) = *Bureau of Labor Statistics*.

blubber ['blʌbə*] *n* grasso di balena ♦ *vi* (*pej*) piangere forte.

bludgeon ['blʌdʒən] *vt* prendere a randellate.

blue [blu:] *adj* azzurro(a), celeste; (*darker*) blu *inv*; ~ **film/joke** film/barzelletta pornografico(a); (**only**) **once in a ~ moon** a ogni morte di papa; **out of the ~** (*fig*) all'improvviso; *see also* **blues**.

blue baby *n* neonato cianotico.

bluebell ['blu:bɛl] *n* giacinto di bosco.

bluebottle ['blu:bɔtl] *n* moscone *m*.

blue cheese *n* formaggio tipo gorgonzola.

blue-chip ['blu:tʃɪp] *adj*: ~ **investment** investimento sicuro.

blue-collar worker ['blu:kɔlə*-] *n* operaio/a.

blue jeans *npl* blue-jeans *mpl*.

blueprint ['blu:prɪnt] *n* cianografia; (*fig*): ~ (**for**) formula (di).

blues [blu:z] *npl*: **the** ~ (*MUS*) il blues; **to have the** ~ (*col*: *feeling*) essere a terra.

bluff [blʌf] *vi* bluffare ♦ *n* bluff *m inv*; (*promontory*) promontorio scosceso ♦ *adj* (*person*) brusco(a); **to call sb's** ~ mettere alla prova il bluff di qn.

blunder ['blʌndə*] *n* abbaglio ♦ *vi* prendere un abbaglio; **to** ~ **into sb/sth** andare a sbattere contro qn/qc.

blunt [blʌnt] *adj* (*edge*) smussato(a); (*point*) spuntato(a); (*knife*) che non taglia; (*person*) brusco(a) ♦ *vt* smussare; spuntare; **this pencil is** ~ questa matita non ha più la punta; ~ **instrument** (*LAW*) corpo contundente.

bluntly ['blʌntlɪ] *adv* (*speak*) senza mezzi termini.

bluntness ['blʌntnɪs] *n* (*of person*) brutale franchezza.

blur [blə:*] *n* cosa offuscata ♦ *vt* offuscare.

blurb [blə:b] *n* trafiletto pubblicitario.

blurred [blə:d] *adj* (*photo*) mosso(a); (*TV*) sfuocato(a).

blurt out [blə:t-] *vt* lasciarsi sfuggire.

blush [blʌʃ] *vi* arrossire ♦ *n* rossore *m*.

blusher ['blʌʃə*] *n* fard *m inv*.

bluster ['blʌstə*] *n* spacconate *fpl*; (*threats*) vuote minacce *fpl* ♦ *vi* fare lo spaccone; minacciare a vuoto.

blustering ['blʌstərɪŋ] *adj* (*tone etc*) da spaccone.

blustery ['blʌstərɪ] *adj* (*weather*) burrascoso(a).

Blvd *abbr* = **boulevard**.

BM *n abbr* = *British Museum*; (*SCOL*: = *Bachelor of Medicine*) titolo di studio.

BMA *n abbr* = *British Medical Association*.

BMJ *n abbr* = *British Medical Journal*.

BMus *n abbr* (= *Bachelor of Music*) titolo di studio.

BMX *n abbr* (= *bicycle motocross*) BMX *f inv*; ~ **bike** mountain bike *f inv* per cross.

bn *abbr* = **billion**.

BO *n abbr* (*col*: = *body odour*) odori *mpl* sgradevoli (del corpo); = **box office**.

boar [bɔ:*] *n* cinghiale *m*.

board [bɔ:d] *n* tavola; (*on wall*) tabellone *m*; (*for chess etc*) scacchiera; (*committee*) consiglio, comitato; (*in firm*) consiglio d'amministrazione; (*NAUT, AVIAT*): **on** ~ a bordo ♦ *vt* (*ship*) salire a bordo di; (*train*) salire su; **full** ~ (*BRIT*) pensione *f* completa; **half** ~ (*BRIT*) mezza pensione; ~ **and lodging** vitto e alloggio; **above** ~ (*fig*) regolare; **across the** ~ (*fig*) *adv* per tutte le categorie ♦ *adj* generale; **to go by the** ~ venir messo(a) da parte.

▶**board up** *vt* (*door*) chiudere con assi.

boarder ['bɔ:də*] *n* pensionante *m/f*; (*SCOL*) convittore/trice.

board game *n* gioco da tavolo.

boarding card ['bɔ:dɪŋ-] *n* (*AVIAT, NAUT*) carta d'imbarco.

boarding house *n* pensione *f*.

boarding party *n* squadra di ispezione (*del carico di una nave*).

boarding pass *n* (*BRIT*) = **boarding card**.

boarding school *n* collegio.

board meeting *n* riunione *f* di consiglio.

board room *n* sala del consiglio.

boardwalk ['bɔ:dwɔ:k] *n* (*US*) passeggiata a mare.

boast [bəust] *vi*: **to** ~ (**about** *or* **of**) vantarsi (di) ♦ *vt* vantare ♦ *n* vanteria; vanto.

boastful ['bəustful] *adj* vanaglorioso(a).

boastfulness ['bəustfulnɪs] *n* vanagloria.

boat [bəut] *n* nave *f*; (*small*) barca; **to go by** ~ andare in barca *or* in nave; **we're all in the same** ~ (*fig*) siamo tutti nella stessa barca.

boater ['bəutə*] *n* (*hat*) paglietta.

boating ['bəutɪŋ] *n* canottaggio.

boat people n boat people mpl.
boatswain ['bəusn] n nostromo.
bob [bɔb] vi (boat, cork on water: also: ~ **up and down**) andare su e giù ♦ n (BRIT col) = shilling.
▶**bob up** vi saltare fuori.
bobbin ['bɔbɪn] n bobina; (of sewing machine) rocchetto.
bobby ['bɔbɪ] n (BRIT col) ≈ poliziotto.
bobsleigh ['bɔbsleɪ] n bob m inv.
bode [bəud] vi: **to ~ well/ill (for)** essere di buon/cattivo auspicio (per).
bodice ['bɔdɪs] n corsetto.
bodily ['bɔdɪlɪ] adj (comfort, needs) materiale; (pain) fisico(a) ♦ adv (carry) in braccio; (lift) di peso.
body ['bɔdɪ] n corpo; (of car) carrozzeria; (of plane) fusoliera; (organization) associazione f, organizzazione f; (quantity) quantità f inv; (of speech, document) parte f principale; (also: ~ **stocking**) body m inv; **in a ~** in massa; **ruling ~** direttivo; **a wine with ~** un vino corposo.
body blow n (fig) duro colpo.
body-building ['bɔdɪ'bɪldɪŋ] n culturismo.
bodyguard ['bɔdɪɡɑːd] n guardia del corpo.
body language n linguaggio del corpo.
body repairs npl (AUT) lavori mpl di carrozzeria.
body search n perquisizione f personale; **to submit to** or **undergo a ~** essere sottoposto(a) a perquisizione personale.
bodywork ['bɔdɪwɔːk] n carrozzeria.
boffin ['bɔfɪn] n scienziato.
bog [bɔg] n palude f ♦ vt: **to get ~ged down** (fig) impantanarsi.
bogey ['bəuɡɪ] n (worry) spauracchio; (also: ~ **man**) babau m inv.
boggle ['bɔgl] vi: **the mind ~s** è incredibile.
Bogotá [bəuɡə'tɑː] n Bogotà f.
bogus ['bəuɡəs] adj falso(a); finto(a).
Bohemia [bəu'hiːmɪə] n Boemia.
Bohemian [bəu'hiːmɪən] adj, n boemo(a).
boil [bɔɪl] vt, vi bollire ♦ n (MED) foruncolo; **to come to the** or (US) **a ~** raggiungere l'ebollizione; **to bring to the** or (US) **a ~** portare a ebollizione; ~**ed egg** uovo alla coque; ~**ed potatoes** patate fpl bollite or lesse.
▶**boil down** vi (fig): **to ~ down to** ridursi a.
▶**boil over** vi traboccare (bollendo).
boiler ['bɔɪlə*] n caldaia.
boiler suit n (BRIT) tuta.
boiling ['bɔɪlɪŋ] adj bollente; **I'm ~ (hot)** (col) sto morendo di caldo.
boiling point n punto di ebollizione.

boil-in-the-bag [bɔɪlɪnðə'bæg] adj (rice etc) da bollire nel sacchetto.
boisterous ['bɔɪstərəs] adj chiassoso(a).
bold [bəuld] adj audace; (child) impudente; (outline) chiaro(a); (colour) deciso(a).
boldness ['bəuldnɪs] n audacia; impudenza.
bold type n (TYP) neretto, grassetto.
Bolivia [bə'lɪvɪə] n Bolivia.
Bolivian [bə'lɪvɪən] adj, n boliviano(a).
bollard ['bɔləd] n (NAUT) bitta; (BRIT AUT) colonnina luminosa.
bolshy ['bɔlʃɪ] adj (BRIT col) piantagrane, ribelle; **to be in a ~ mood** essere in vena di piantar grane.
bolster ['bəulstə*] n capezzale m.
▶**bolster up** vt sostenere.
bolt [bəult] n chiavistello; (with nut) bullone m ♦ adv: ~ **upright** diritto(a) come un fuso ♦ vt serrare; (food) mangiare in fretta ♦ vi scappare via; **a ~ from the blue** (fig) un fulmine a ciel sereno.
bomb [bɔm] n bomba ♦ vt bombardare.
bombard [bɔm'bɑːd] vt bombardare.
bombardment [bɔm'bɑːdmənt] n bombardamento.
bombastic [bɔm'bæstɪk] adj ampolloso(a).
bomb disposal n: ~ **expert** artificiere m; ~ **unit** corpo degli artificieri.
bomber ['bɔmə*] n bombardiere m; (terrorist) dinamitardo/a.
bombing ['bɔmɪŋ] n bombardamento.
bomb scare n stato di allarme (per sospetta presenza di una bomba).
bombshell ['bɔmʃel] n (fig) notizia bomba.
bomb site n luogo bombardato.
bona fide ['bəunə'faɪdɪ] adj sincero(a); (offer) onesto(a).
bonanza [bə'nænzə] n cuccagna.
bond [bɔnd] n legame m; (binding promise, FINANCE) obbligazione f; **in ~** (of goods) in attesa di sdoganamento.
bondage ['bɔndɪdʒ] n schiavitù f.
bonded warehouse ['bɔndɪd-] n magazzino doganale.
bone [bəun] n osso; (of fish) spina, lisca ♦ vt disossare; togliere le spine a.
bone china n porcellana fine.
bone-dry ['bəun'draɪ] adj asciuttissimo(a).
bone idle adj: **to be ~** essere un(a) fannullone(a).
bone marrow n midollo osseo.
boner ['bəunə*] n (US) gaffe f inv.
bonfire ['bɔnfaɪə*] n falò m inv.
bonk [bɔŋk] vt, vi (hum, col) scopare (!).
bonkers ['bɔŋkəz] adj (BRIT col) suonato(a).
Bonn [bɔn] n Bonn f.
bonnet ['bɔnɪt] n cuffia; (BRIT: of car) cofano.

bonny ['bɒnɪ] adj (esp Scottish) bello(a), carino(a).

bonus ['bəunəs] n premio; (on wages) gratifica.

bony ['bəunɪ] adj (thin: person) ossuto(a), angoloso(a); (arm, face, MED: tissue) osseo(a); (meat) pieno(a) di ossi; (fish) pieno(a) di spine.

boo [bu:] excl ba! ♦ vt fischiare ♦ n fischio.

boob [bu:b] n (col: breast) tetta; (: BRIT: mistake) gaffe f inv.

booby prize ['bu:bɪ-] n premio per il peggior contendente.

booby trap ['bu:bɪ-] n trabocchetto; (bomb) congegno che esplode al contatto.

booby-trapped ['bu:bɪtræpt] adj: **a ~ car** una macchina con dell'esplosivo a bordo.

book [buk] n libro; (of stamps etc) blocchetto ♦ vt (ticket, seat, room) prenotare; (driver) multare; (football player) ammonire; **~s** npl (COMM) conti mpl; **to keep the ~s** (COMM) tenere la contabilità; **by the ~** secondo le regole; **to throw the ~ at sb** incriminare qn seriamente or con tutte le aggravanti.

►**book in** vi (BRIT: at hotel) prendere una camera.

►**book up** vt riservare, prenotare; **the hotel is ~ed up** l'albergo è al completo; **all seats are ~ed up** è tutto esaurito.

bookable ['bukəbl] adj: **seats are ~** si possono prenotare i posti.

bookcase ['bukkeɪs] n scaffale m.

book ends npl reggilibri mpl.

booking ['bukɪŋ] n (BRIT) prenotazione f.

booking office n (BRIT) biglietteria.

book-keeping ['buk'ki:pɪŋ] n contabilità.

booklet ['buklɪt] n opuscolo, libretto.

bookmaker ['bukmeɪkə*] n allibratore m.

bookmark ['bukmɑːk] n (also COMPUT) segnalibro ♦ vt (COMPUT) mettere un segnalibro a; (Internet Explorer) aggiungere a "Preferiti".

bookseller ['bukselə*] n libraio.

bookshelf ['bukʃelf] n mensola (per libri); **bookshelves** npl (bookcase) libreria.

bookshop ['bukʃɔp] n libreria.

bookstall ['bukstɔːl] n bancarella di libri.

bookstore ['bukstɔː*] n = **bookshop**.

book token n buono m libri inv.

book value n valore m contabile.

bookworm ['bukwɜːm] n (fig) topo di biblioteca.

boom [bu:m] n (noise) rimbombo; (busy period) boom m inv ♦ vi rimbombare; andare a gonfie vele.

boomerang ['bu:məræŋ] n boomerang m inv ♦ vi (fig) avere effetto contrario; **to ~ on** sb (fig) ritorcersi contro qn.

boom town n città f inv in rapidissima espansione.

boon [bu:n] n vantaggio.

boorish ['buərɪʃ] adj maleducato(a).

boost [bu:st] n spinta ♦ vt spingere; (increase: sales, production) incentivare; **to give a ~ to** (morale) tirar su; **it gave a ~ to his confidence** è stata per lui un'iniezione di fiducia.

booster ['bu:stə*] n (ELEC) amplificatore m; (TV) amplificatore m di segnale; (also: ~ rocket) razzo vettore; (MED) richiamo.

booster seat n (AUT: for children) seggiolino di sicurezza.

boot [bu:t] n stivale m; (ankle ~) stivaletto; (for hiking) scarpone m da montagna; (for football etc) scarpa; (BRIT: of car) portabagagli m inv ♦ vt (COMPUT) inizializzare; **to ~** (in addition) per giunta, in più; **to give sb the ~** (col) mettere qn alla porta.

booth [bu:ð] n (at fair) baraccone m; (of cinema, telephone etc) cabina; (also: **voting ~**) cabina (elettorale).

bootleg ['bu:tleg] adj di contrabbando; **~ record** registrazione f pirata inv.

booty ['bu:tɪ] n bottino.

booze [bu:z] (col) n alcool m ♦ vi trincare.

boozer ['bu:zə*] n (col: person) beone m; (BRIT col: pub) osteria.

border ['bɔːdə*] n orlo; margine m; (of a country) frontiera; **the B~** la frontiera tra l'Inghilterra e la Scozia; **the B~s** la zona di confine tra l'Inghilterra e la Scozia.

►**border on** vt fus confinare con.

borderline ['bɔːdəlaɪn] n (fig) linea di demarcazione ♦ adj: **~ case** caso limite.

bore [bɔː*] pt of **bear** ♦ vt (hole) perforare; (person) annoiare ♦ n (person) seccatore/trice; (of gun) calibro; **he's ~d to tears** or **~d to death** or **~d stiff** è annoiato a morte, si annoia da morire.

boredom ['bɔːdəm] n noia.

boring ['bɔːrɪŋ] adj noioso(a).

born [bɔːn] adj: **to be ~** nascere; **I was ~ in 1960** sono nato nel 1960; **~ blind** cieco dalla nascita; **a ~ comedian** un comico nato.

born-again [bɔːnə'gen] adj: **~ Christian** convertito(a) alla chiesa evangelica.

borne [bɔːn] pp of **bear**.

Borneo ['bɔːnɪəu] n Borneo.

borough ['bʌrə] n comune m.

borrow ['bɒrəu] vt: **to ~ sth (from sb)** prendere in prestito qc (da qn); **may I ~ your car?** può prestarmi la macchina?

borrower ['bɒrəuə*] n (gen) chi prende a

prestito; (*ECON*) mutuatario/a.
borrowing ['bɔrəuɪŋ] *n* prestito.
borstal ['bɔːstl] *n* (*BRIT*) riformatorio.
Bosnia ['bɔznɪə] *n* Bosnia.
Bosnia-Herzegovina
['bɔznɪəhɜːrzə'gəuviːnə] *n* (*also*: **Bosnia-Hercegovina**) Bosnia-Erzegovina.
Bosnian ['bɔznɪən] *adj, n* bosniaco(a).
bosom ['buzəm] *n* petto; (*fig*) seno.
bosom friend *n* amico/a del cuore.
boss [bɔs] *n* capo ♦ *vt* (*also*: ~ **about** *or* **around**) comandare a bacchetta; **stop ~ing everyone about!** smettila di dare ordini a tutti!
bossy ['bɔsɪ] *adj* prepotente.
bosun ['bəusn] *n* nostromo.
botanical [bə'tænɪkl] *adj* botanico(a).
botanist ['bɔtənɪst] *n* botanico/a.
botany ['bɔtənɪ] *n* botanica.
botch [bɔtʃ] *vt* fare un pasticcio di.
both [bəuθ] *adj* entrambi(e), tutt'e due ♦ *pron*: ~ (**of them**) entrambi(e) ♦ *adv*: **they sell ~ meat and poultry** vendono insieme la carne ed il pollame; ~ **of us went, we** ~ **went** ci siamo andati tutt'e due.
bother ['bɔðə*] *vt* (*worry*) preoccupare; (*annoy*) infastidire ♦ *vi* (*gen*: ~ **o.s.**) preoccuparsi ♦ *n*: **it is a ~ to have to do** è una seccatura dover fare ♦ *excl* uffa!, accidenti!; **to ~ doing sth** darsi la pena di fare qc; **I'm sorry to ~ you** mi dispiace disturbarla; **please don't ~** non si scomodi; **it's no ~** non c'è problema.
Botswana [bɔt'swɑːnə] *n* Botswana *m*.
bottle ['bɔtl] *n* bottiglia; (*of perfume, shampoo etc*) flacone *m*; (*baby's*) biberon *m inv* ♦ *vt* imbottigliare; ~ **of wine/milk** bottiglia di vino/latte; **wine/milk ~** bottiglia da vino/del latte.
▶**bottle up** *vt* contenere.
bottle bank *n* contenitore *m* per la raccolta del vetro.
bottle-fed ['bɔtlfɛd] *adj* allattato(a) artificialmente.
bottleneck ['bɔtlnɛk] *n* ingorgo.
bottle-opener ['bɔtləupnə*] *n* apribottiglie *m inv*.
bottom ['bɔtəm] *n* fondo; (*of mountain, tree, hill*) piedi *mpl*; (*buttocks*) sedere *m* ♦ *adj* più basso(a); ultimo(a); **at the ~ of** in fondo a; **to get to the ~ of sth** (*fig*) andare al fondo di *or* in fondo a qc.
bottomless ['bɔtəmlɪs] *adj* senza fondo.
bottom line *n*: **the ~ is ...** in ultima analisi ....
botulism ['bɔtjulɪzəm] *n* botulismo.
bough [bau] *n* ramo.
bought [bɔːt] *pt, pp of* **buy.**

boulder ['bəuldə*] *n* masso (tondeggiante).
boulevard ['buːlvɑːd] *n* viale *m*.
bounce [bauns] *vi* (*ball*) rimbalzare; (*cheque*) essere restituito(a) ♦ *vt* far rimbalzare ♦ *n* (*rebound*) rimbalzo; **to ~ in** entrare di slancio *or* con foga; **he's got plenty of ~** (*fig*) è molto esuberante.
bouncer ['baunsə*] *n* buttafuori *m inv*.
bouncy castle ® ['baunsɪ-] *n grande castello gonfiabile per giocare.*
bound [baund] *pt, pp of* **bind** ♦ *n* (*gen pl*) limite *m*; (*leap*) salto ♦ *vt* (*leap*) saltare; (*limit*) delimitare ♦ *adj*: **to be ~ to do sth** (*obliged*) essere costretto(a) a fare qc; **he's ~ to fail** (*likely*) è certo di fallire; ~ **for** diretto(a) a; **out of ~s** il cui accesso è vietato.
boundary ['baundrɪ] *n* confine *m*.
boundless ['baundlɪs] *adj* illimitato(a).
bountiful ['bauntɪful] *adj* (*person*) munifico(a); (*God*) misericordioso(a); (*supply*) abbondante.
bounty ['bauntɪ] *n* (*generosity*) liberalità, munificenza; (*reward*) taglia.
bounty hunter *n* cacciatore *m* di taglie.
bouquet ['bukeɪ] *n* bouquet *m inv*.
bourbon ['buəbən] *n* (*US: also*: ~ **whiskey**) bourbon *m inv*.
bourgeois ['buəʒwɑː] *adj, n* borghese (*m/f*).
bout [baut] *n* periodo; (*of malaria etc*) attacco; (*BOXING etc*) incontro.
boutique [buː'tiːk] *n* boutique *f inv*.
bow¹ *n* [bəu] nodo; (*weapon*) arco; (*MUS*) archetto; (*NAUT: also*: ~**s**) prua.
bow² [bau] *n* (*with body*) inchino ♦ *vi* inchinarsi; (*yield*): **to ~ to** *or* **before** sottomettersi a; **to ~ to the inevitable** rassegnarsi all'inevitabile.
bowels [bauəlz] *npl* intestini *mpl*; (*fig*) viscere *fpl*.
bowl [bəul] *n* (*for eating*) scodella; (*for washing*) bacino; (*ball*) boccia; (*of pipe*) fornello; (*US: stadium*) stadio ♦ *vi* (*CRICKET*) servire (la palla); *see also* **bowls.**
▶**bowl over** *vt* (*fig*) sconcertare.
bow-legged ['bəu'lɛgɪd] *adj* dalle gambe storte.
bowler ['bəulə*] *n* giocatore *m* di bocce; (*CRICKET*) giocatore che serve la palla; (*BRIT: also*: ~ **hat**) bombetta.
bowling ['bəulɪŋ] *n* (*game*) gioco delle bocce; bowling *m*.
bowling alley *n* pista da bowling.
bowling green *n* campo di bocce.
bowls [bəulz] *n* gioco delle bocce.
bow tie *n* cravatta a farfalla.
box [bɔks] *n* scatola; (*also*: **cardboard ~**) (scatola di) cartone *m*; (*crate; also for*

money) cassetta; (*THEAT*) palco; (*BRIT AUT*) area d'incrocio ♦ *vi* mettere in (una) scatola; (*SPORT*) combattere contro.

boxer ['bɔksə*] *n* (*person*) pugile *m*; (*dog*) boxer *m inv*.

boxing ['bɔksɪŋ] *n* (*SPORT*) pugilato.

Boxing Day *n* (*BRIT*) ≈ Santo Stefano; *see boxed note*.

BOXING DAY

Il **Boxing Day** *è il primo giorno infrasettimanale dopo Natale e cade generalmente il 26 di dicembre. Prende il nome dall'usanza di donare pacchi regalo natalizi, un tempo chiamati "Christmas boxes", a fornitori e dipendenti, ed è un giorno di festa.*

---

boxing gloves *npl* guantoni *mpl* da pugile.

boxing ring *n* ring *m inv*.

box number *n* (*for advertisements*) casella.

box office *n* biglietteria.

box room *n* ripostiglio.

boy [bɔɪ] *n* ragazzo; (*small*) bambino; (*son*) figlio; (*servant*) servo.

boy band *n gruppo pop di soli ragazzi maschi creato per far presa su un pubblico giovane.*

boycott ['bɔɪkɔt] *n* boicottaggio ♦ *vt* boicottare.

boyfriend ['bɔɪfrɛnd] *n* ragazzo.

boyish ['bɔɪɪʃ] *adj* di *or* da ragazzo.

bp *abbr* = **bishop**.

bra [brɑː] *n* reggipetto, reggiseno.

brace [breɪs] *n* sostegno; (*on teeth*) apparecchio correttore; (*tool*) trapano; (*TYP: also:* ~ **bracket**) graffa ♦ *vt* rinforzare, sostenere; **to** ~ **o.s.** (*fig*) farsi coraggio; *see also* **braces**.

bracelet ['breɪslɪt] *n* braccialetto.

braces ['breɪsɪz] *npl* (*BRIT*) bretelle *fpl*.

bracing ['breɪsɪŋ] *adj* invigorante.

bracken ['brækən] *n* felce *f*.

bracket ['brækɪt] *n* (*TECH*) mensola; (*group*) gruppo; (*TYP*) parentesi *f inv* ♦ *vt* mettere fra parentesi; (*fig: also:* ~ **together**) mettere insieme; **in** ~**s** tra parentesi; **round/square** ~**s** parentesi tonde/quadre; **income** ~ fascia di reddito.

brag [bræg] *vi* vantarsi.

braid [breɪd] *n* (*trimming*) passamano; (*of hair*) treccia.

Braille [breɪl] *n* braille *m*.

brain [breɪn] *n* cervello; ~**s** *npl* cervella *fpl*; **he's got** ~**s** è intelligente.

brainchild ['breɪntʃaɪld] *n* creatura, creazione *f*.

braindead ['breɪndɛd] *adj* (*MED*) che ha subito inizio cerebrale.

brainless ['breɪnlɪs] *adj* deficiente, stupido(a).

brainstorm ['breɪnstɔːm] *n* (*fig*) attacco di pazzia; (*US*) = **brainwave**.

brainwash ['breɪnwɔʃ] *vt* fare un lavaggio di cervello a.

brainwave ['breɪnweɪv] *n* lampo di genio.

brainy ['breɪnɪ] *adj* intelligente.

braise [breɪz] *vt* brasare.

brake [breɪk] *n* (*on vehicle*) freno ♦ *vt, vi* frenare.

brake light *n* (fanalino dello) stop *m inv*.

brake pedal *n* pedale *m* del freno.

bramble ['bræmbl] *n* rovo; (*fruit*) mora.

bran [bræn] *n* crusca.

branch [brɑːntʃ] *n* ramo; (*COMM*) succursale *f*, filiale *f* ♦ *vi* diramarsi.

▶**branch out** *vi*: **to** ~ **out into** intraprendere una nuova attività nel ramo di.

branch line *n* (*RAIL*) linea secondaria.

branch manager *n* direttore *m* di filiale.

brand [brænd] *n* marca ♦ *vt* (*cattle*) marcare (a ferro rovente); (*fig: pej*): **to** ~ **sb a communist** *etc* definire qn come comunista *etc*.

brandish ['brændɪʃ] *vt* brandire.

brand name *n* marca.

brand-new ['brænd'njuː] *adj* nuovo(a) di zecca.

brandy ['brændɪ] *n* brandy *m inv*.

brash [bræʃ] *adj* sfacciato(a).

brass [brɑːs] *n* ottone *m*; **the** ~ (*MUS*) gli ottoni.

brass band *n* fanfara.

brassière ['bræsɪə*] *n* reggipetto, reggiseno.

brass tacks *npl*: **to get down to** ~ (*col*) venire al sodo.

brat [bræt] *n* (*pej*) marmocchio, monello/a.

bravado [brə'vɑːdəʊ] *n* spavalderia.

brave [breɪv] *adj* coraggioso(a) ♦ *n* guerriero *m* pellerossa *inv* ♦ *vt* affrontare.

bravery ['breɪvərɪ] *n* coraggio.

bravo [brɑː'vəʊ] *excl* bravo!, bene!

brawl [brɔːl] *n* rissa ♦ *vi* azzuffarsi.

brawn [brɔːn] *n* muscolo; (*meat*) carne *f* di testa di maiale.

brawny ['brɔːnɪ] *adj* muscoloso(a).

bray [breɪ] *n* raglio ♦ *vi* ragliare.

brazen ['breɪzn] *adj* svergognato(a) ♦ *vt*: **to** ~ **it out** fare lo sfacciato.

brazier ['breɪzɪə*] *n* braciere *m*.

Brazil [brə'zɪl] *n* Brasile *m*.

Brazilian [brə'zɪljən] *adj, n* brasiliano(a).

Brazil nut *n* noce *f* del Brasile.

breach [briːtʃ] vt aprire una breccia in ♦ n (gap) breccia, varco; (estrangement) rottura; (of duty) abuso; (breaking): ~ **of contract** rottura di contratto; ~ **of the peace** violazione f dell'ordine pubblico; ~ **of trust** abuso di fiducia.

bread [brɛd] n pane m; (col: money) grana; **to earn one's daily** ~ guadagnarsi il pane; **to know which side one's** ~ **is buttered on** saper fare i propri interessi; ~ **and butter** n pane e burro; (fig) mezzi mpl di sussistenza.

breadbin ['brɛdbɪn] n (BRIT) cassetta f portapane inv.

breadboard ['brɛdbɔːd] n tagliere m (per il pane); (COMPUT) pannello per esperimenti.

breadbox ['brɛdbɔks] n (US) cassetta f portapane inv.

breadcrumbs ['brɛdkrʌmz] npl briciole fpl; (CULIN) pangrattato.

breadline ['brɛdlaɪn] n: **to be on the** ~ avere appena denaro per vivere.

breadth [brɛtθ] n larghezza.

breadwinner ['brɛdwɪnə*] n chi guadagna il pane per tutta la famiglia.

break [breɪk] vb (pt **broke** [brəuk], pp **broken** ['brəukən]) vt rompere; (law) violare; (promise) mancare a ♦ vi rompersi; (weather) cambiare ♦ n (gap) breccia; (fracture) rottura; (rest, also SCOL) intervallo; (: short) pausa; (chance) possibilità f inv; (holiday) vacanza; **to** ~ **one's leg** etc rompersi la gamba etc; **to** ~ **a record** battere un primato; **to** ~ **the news to sb** comunicare per primo la notizia a qn; **to** ~ **with sb** (fig) rompere con qn; **to** ~ **even** vi coprire le spese; **to** ~ **free** or **loose** vi liberarsi; **without a** ~ senza una pausa; **to have** or **take a** ~ (few minutes) fare una pausa; (holiday) prendere un po' di riposo; **a lucky** ~ un colpo di fortuna.

▶**break down** vt (figures, data) analizzare; (door etc) buttare giù, abbattere; (resistance) stroncare ♦ vi crollare; (MED) avere un esaurimento (nervoso); (AUT) guastarsi.

▶**break in** vt (horse etc) domare ♦ vi (burglar) fare irruzione.

▶**break into** vt fus (house) fare irruzione in.

▶**break off** vi (speaker) interrompersi; (branch) troncarsi ♦ vt (talks, engagement) rompere.

▶**break open** vt (door etc) sfondare.

▶**break out** vi evadere; **to** ~ **out in spots** coprirsi di macchie.

▶**break through** vi: **the sun broke through** il sole ha fatto capolino tra le nuvole ♦ vt (defences, barrier) sfondare, penetrare in; (crowd) aprirsi un varco in or tra, aprirsi un passaggio in or tra.

▶**break up** vi (partnership) sciogliersi; (friends) separarsi ♦ vt fare in pezzi, spaccare; (fight etc) interrompere, far cessare; (marriage) finire.

breakable ['breɪkəbl] adj fragile; ~**s** npl oggetti mpl fragili.

breakage ['breɪkɪdʒ] n rottura; **to pay for** ~**s** pagare i danni.

breakaway ['breɪkəweɪ] adj (group etc) scissionista, dissidente.

break-dancing ['breɪkdɑːnsɪŋ] n breakdance f.

breakdown ['breɪkdaun] n (AUT) guasto; (in communications) interruzione f; (MED: also: **nervous** ~) esaurimento nervoso; (of payments etc) resoconto.

breakdown service n (BRIT) servizio riparazioni.

breakdown van n carro m attrezzi inv.

breaker ['breɪkə*] n frangente m.

breakeven ['breɪk'iːvn] cpd: ~ **chart** diagramma m del punto di rottura or pareggio; ~ **point** punto di rottura or pareggio.

breakfast ['brɛkfəst] n colazione f.

breakfast cereal n fiocchi mpl d'avena or di mais etc.

break-in ['breɪkɪn] n irruzione f.

breaking point ['breɪkɪŋ-] n punto di rottura.

breakthrough ['breɪkθruː] n (MIL) breccia; (fig) passo avanti.

break-up ['breɪkʌp] n (of partnership, marriage) rottura.

break-up value n (COMM) valore m di realizzo.

breakwater ['breɪkwɔːtə*] n frangiflutti m inv.

breast [brɛst] n (of woman) seno; (chest) petto.

breast-feed ['brɛstfiːd] vt, vi (irreg: like **feed**) allattare (al seno).

breast pocket n taschino.

breast-stroke ['brɛststrəuk] n nuoto a rana.

breath [brɛθ] n fiato; **out of** ~ senza fiato; **to go out for a** ~ **of air** andare a prendere una boccata d'aria.

Breathalyser ® ['brɛθəlaɪzə*] n alcoltest m inv.

breathe [briːð] vt, vi respirare; **I won't** ~ **a word about it** non fiaterò.

▶**breathe in** vi inspirare ♦ vt respirare.

▶**breathe out** vt, vi espirare.

breather ['bri:ðə*] n attimo di respiro.
breathing ['bri:ðɪŋ] n respiro, respirazione f.
breathing space n (fig) attimo di respiro.
breathless ['brɛθlɪs] adj senza fiato; (with excitement) con il fiato sospeso.
breath-taking ['brɛθteɪkɪŋ] adj sbalorditivo(a).
breath test n ≈ prova del palloncino.
-bred [brɛd] suffix: **to be well/ill~** essere ben educato(a)/maleducato(a).
breed [bri:d] vb (pt, pp **bred** [brɛd]) vt allevare; (fig: hate, suspicion) generare, provocare ♦ vi riprodursi ♦ n razza, varietà f inv.
breeder ['bri:də*] n (PHYSICS: also: ~ **reactor**) reattore m autofertilizzante.
breeding ['bri:dɪŋ] n riproduzione f; allevamento.
breeze [bri:z] n brezza.
breeze block n (BRIT) mattone composto di scorie di coke.
breezy ['bri:zɪ] adj arioso(a); allegro(a).
Breton ['brɛtən] adj, n brettone (m/f).
brevity ['brɛvɪtɪ] n brevità.
brew [bru:] vt (tea) fare un infuso di; (beer) fare; (plot) tramare ♦ vi (tea) essere in infusione; (beer) essere in fermentazione; (fig) bollire in pentola.
brewer ['bru:ə*] n birraio.
brewery ['bru:ərɪ] n fabbrica di birra.
briar ['braɪə*] n (thorny bush) rovo; (wild rose) rosa selvatica.
bribe [braɪb] n bustarella ♦ vt comprare; **to ~ sb to do sth** pagare qn sottobanco perché faccia qc.
bribery ['braɪbərɪ] n corruzione f.
bric-a-brac ['brɪkəbræk] n bric-a-brac m.
brick [brɪk] n mattone m.
bricklayer ['brɪkleɪə*] n muratore m.
brickwork ['brɪkwə:k] n muratura in mattoni.
brickworks ['brɪkwə:ks] n fabbrica di mattoni.
bridal ['braɪdl] adj nuziale; ~ **party** corteo nuziale.
bride [braɪd] n sposa.
bridegroom ['braɪdgru:m] n sposo.
bridesmaid ['braɪdzmeɪd] n damigella d'onore.
bridge [brɪdʒ] n ponte m; (NAUT) ponte di comando; (of nose) dorso; (CARDS, DENTISTRY) bridge m inv ♦ vt (river) fare un ponte sopra; (gap) colmare.
bridging loan ['brɪdʒɪŋ-] n (BRIT) anticipazione f sul mutuo.
bridle ['braɪdl] n briglia ♦ vt tenere a freno; (horse) mettere la briglia a ♦ vi (in anger etc) adombrarsi, adontarsi.
bridle path n sentiero (per cavalli).
brief [bri:f] adj breve ♦ n (LAW) comparsa ♦ vt (MIL etc) dare istruzioni a; **in ~** ... in breve ..., a farla breve ...; **to ~ sb (about sth)** mettere qn al corrente (di qc); see also **briefs**.
briefcase ['bri:fkeɪs] n cartella.
briefing ['bri:fɪŋ] n istruzioni fpl.
briefly ['bri:flɪ] adv (speak, visit) brevemente; (glimpse) di sfuggita.
briefness ['bri:fnɪs] n brevità.
briefs [bri:fs] npl mutande fpl.
Brig. abbr = **brigadier**.
brigade [brɪ'geɪd] n (MIL) brigata.
brigadier [brɪgə'dɪə*] n generale m di brigata.
bright [braɪt] adj luminoso(a); (person) sveglio(a); (colour) vivace; **to look on the ~ side** vedere il lato positivo delle cose.
brighten ['braɪtn] (also: ~ **up**) vt (room) rendere luminoso(a); rallegrare ♦ vi schiarirsi; (person) rallegrarsi.
brightly ['braɪtlɪ] adv (shine) vivamente, intensamente; (smile) radiosamente; (talk) con animazione.
brill [brɪl] excl (BRIT col) stupendo!, fantastico!
brilliance ['brɪljəns] n splendore m; (fig: of person) genialità, talento.
brilliant ['brɪljənt] adj brillante; (sunshine) sfolgorante.
brim [brɪm] n orlo.
brimful ['brɪm'ful] adj pieno(a) or colmo(a) fino all'orlo; (fig) pieno(a).
brine [braɪn] n acqua salmastra; (CULIN) salamoia.
bring, pt, pp **brought** [brɪŋ, brɔ:t] vt portare; **to ~ sth to an end** mettere fine a qc; **I can't ~ myself to sack him** non so risolvermi a licenziarlo.
▶**bring about** vt causare.
▶**bring back** vt riportare.
▶**bring down** vt (lower) far scendere; (shoot down) abbattere; (government) far cadere.
▶**bring forward** vt portare avanti; (in time) anticipare; (BOOK-KEEPING) riportare.
▶**bring in** vt (person) fare entrare; (object) portare; (POL: bill) presentare; (: legislation) introdurre; (LAW: verdict) emettere; (produce: income) rendere.
▶**bring off** vt (task, plan) portare a compimento; (deal) concludere.
▶**bring out** vt (meaning) mettere in evidenza; (new product) lanciare; (book) pubblicare, fare uscire.
▶**bring round** or **to** vt (unconscious person)

far rinvenire.

▶**bring up** *vt* allevare; (*question*) introdurre.

brink [brɪŋk] *n* orlo; **on the ~ of doing sth** sul punto di fare qc; **she was on the ~ of tears** era lì lì per piangere.

brisk [brɪsk] *adj* (*person, tone*) spiccio(a), sbrigativo(a); (: *abrupt*) brusco(a); (*wind*) fresco(a); (*trade etc*) vivace, attivo(a); **to go for a ~ walk** fare una camminata di buon passo; **business is ~** gli affari vanno bene.

bristle ['brɪsl] *n* setola ♦ *vi* rizzarsi; **bristling with** irto(a) di.

bristly ['brɪslɪ] *adj* (*chin*) ispido(a); (*beard, hair*) irsuto(a), setoloso(a).

Brit [brɪt] *n abbr* (*col*: = *British person*) britannico/a.

Britain ['brɪtən] *n* Gran Bretagna.

British ['brɪtɪʃ] *adj* britannico(a); **the ~** *npl* i Britannici; **the ~ Isles** *npl* le Isole Britanniche.

British Summer Time *n* ora legale (*in Gran Bretagna*).

Briton ['brɪtən] *n* britannico/a.

Brittany ['brɪtənɪ] *n* Bretagna.

brittle ['brɪtl] *adj* fragile.

Br(o) *abbr* (*REL*) = **brother**.

broach [brəʊtʃ] *vt* (*subject*) affrontare.

broad [brɔːd] *adj* largo(a); (*distinction*) generale; (*accent*) spiccato(a) ♦ *n* (*US col*) bellona; **~ hint** allusione *f* esplicita; **in ~ daylight** in pieno giorno; **the ~ outlines** le grandi linee.

broadband ['brɔːdbænd] *adj* (*COMPUT*) a banda larga ♦ *n* banda larga.

broad bean *n* fava.

broadcast ['brɔːdkɑːst] *n* trasmissione *f* ♦ *vb* (*pt, pp* **broadcast**) *vt* trasmettere per radio (*or* per televisione) ♦ *vi* fare una trasmissione.

broadcaster ['brɔːdkɑːstə*] *n* annunciatore/trice radiotelevisivo(a) (*or* radiofonico(a)).

broadcasting ['brɔːdkɑːstɪŋ] *n* radiodiffusione *f*; televisione *f*.

broaden ['brɔːdn] *vt* allargare ♦ *vi* allargarsi.

broadly ['brɔːdlɪ] *adv* (*fig*) in generale.

broad-minded ['brɔːd'maɪndɪd] *adj* di mente aperta.

broadsheet ['brɔːdʃiːt] *n* (*BRIT*) giornale *m* (*si contrappone al tabloid che è di formato più piccolo*).

broccoli ['brɔkəlɪ] *n* (*BOT*) broccolo; (*CULIN*) broccoli *mpl*.

brochure ['brəʊʃjʊə*] *n* dépliant *m inv*.

brogue [brəʊg] *n* (*shoe*) scarpa rozza in cuoio; (*accent*) accento irlandese.

broil [brɔɪl] *vt* cuocere a fuoco vivo.

broke [brəʊk] *pt of* **break** ♦ *adj* (*col*) squattrinato(a); **to go ~** fare fallimento.

broken ['brəʊkən] *pp of* **break** ♦ *adj* (*gen*) rotto(a); (*stick, promise, vow*) spezzato(a); (*marriage*) fallito(a); **he comes from a ~ home** i suoi sono divisi; **in ~ French/English** in un francese/inglese stentato.

broken-down ['brəʊkən'daʊn] *adj* (*car*) in panne, rotto(a); (*machine*) guasto(a), fuori uso; (*house*) abbandonato(a), in rovina.

broken-hearted ['brəʊkən'hɑːtɪd] *adj*: **to be ~** avere il cuore spezzato.

broker ['brəʊkə*] *n* agente *m*.

brokerage ['brəʊkərɪdʒ] *n* (*COMM*) commissione *f* di intermediazione.

brolly ['brɔlɪ] *n* (*BRIT col*) ombrello.

bronchitis [brɔŋ'kaɪtɪs] *n* bronchite *f*.

bronze [brɔnz] *n* bronzo.

bronzed [brɔnzd] *adj* abbronzato(a).

brooch [brəʊtʃ] *n* spilla.

brood [bruːd] *n* covata ♦ *vi* (*hen*) covare; (*person*) rimuginare.

broody ['bruːdɪ] *adj* (*fig*) cupo(a) e taciturno(a).

brook [brʊk] *n* ruscello.

broom [brʊm] *n* scopa.

broomstick ['brʊmstɪk] *n* manico di scopa.

Bros. *abbr* (*COMM*: = *brothers*) F.lli (= *Fratelli*).

broth [brɔθ] *n* brodo.

brothel ['brɔθl] *n* bordello.

brother ['brʌðə*] *n* fratello.

brotherhood ['brʌðəhʊd] *n* fratellanza; confraternità *f inv*.

brother-in-law ['brʌðərɪnlɔː] *n* cognato.

brotherly ['brʌðəlɪ] *adj* fraterno(a).

brought [brɔːt] *pt, pp of* **bring**.

brought forward (**b/f**) *adj* (*COMM*) riportato(a).

brow [braʊ] *n* fronte *f*; (*rare, gen*: **eye~**) sopracciglio; (*of hill*) cima.

browbeat ['braʊbiːt] *vt* intimidire.

brown [braʊn] *adj* bruno(a), marrone; (*hair*) castano(a) ♦ *n* (*colour*) color *m* bruno *or* marrone ♦ *vt* (*CULIN*) rosolare; **to go ~** (*person*) abbronzarsi; (*leaves*) ingiallire.

brown bread *n* pane *m* integrale, pane nero.

brownie ['braʊnɪ] *n* giovane esploratrice *f*.

brown paper *n* carta da pacchi *or* da imballaggio.

brown rice *n* riso greggio.

brown sugar *n* zucchero greggio.

browse [braʊz] *vi* (*animal*) brucare; (*in bookshop etc*) curiosare; (*COMPUT*) navigare (in Internet) ♦ *vt*: **to ~ the Web** navigare in Internet ♦ *n*: **to have a ~ (around)** dare un'occhiata (in giro); **to ~ through a book** sfogliare un libro.

browser ['brauzə*] *n* (*COMPUT*) browser *sm inv*.

bruise [bru:z] *n* ammaccatura; (*on person*) livido ♦ *vt* ammaccare; (*leg etc*) farsi un livido a; (*fig: feelings*) urtare ♦ *vi* (*fruit*) ammaccarsi.

Brum [brʌm] *n abbr*, **Brummagem** ['brʌmədʒəm] *n* (*col*) = Birmingham.

Brummie ['brʌmɪ] *n* (*col*) abitante *m/f* di Birmingham; originario/a di Birmingham.

brunch [brʌntʃ] *n ricca colazione consumata in tarda mattinata.*

brunette [bru:'nɛt] *n* bruna.

brunt [brʌnt] *n*: **the ~ of** (*attack, criticism etc*) il peso maggiore di.

brush [brʌʃ] *n* spazzola; (*quarrel*) schermaglia ♦ *vt* spazzolare; (*gen*: ~ **past**, ~ **against**) sfiorare; **to have a ~ with sb** (*verbally*) avere uno scontro con qn; (*physically*) venire a diverbio *or* alle mani con qn; **to have a ~ with the police** avere delle noie con la polizia.

▶**brush aside** *vt* scostare.

▶**brush up** *vt* (*knowledge*) rinfrescare.

brushed [brʌʃt] *adj* (*TECH: steel, chrome etc*) sabbiato(a); (*nylon, denim etc*) pettinato(a).

brush-off ['brʌʃɔf] *n*: **to give sb the ~** dare il ben servito a qn.

brushwood ['brʌʃwud] *n* macchia.

brusque [bru:sk] *adj* (*person, manner*) brusco(a); (*tone*) secco(a).

Brussels ['brʌslz] *n* Bruxelles *f*.

Brussels sprout *n* cavolo di Bruxelles.

brutal ['bru:tl] *adj* brutale.

brutality [bru:'tælɪtɪ] *n* brutalità.

brutalize ['bru:təlaɪz] *vt* (*harden*) abbrutire; (*ill-treat*) brutalizzare.

brute [bru:t] *n* bestia; **by ~ force** con la forza, a viva forza.

brutish ['bru:tɪʃ] *adj* da bruto.

BS *n abbr* (*US*: = Bachelor of Science*) titolo di studio.*

bs *abbr* = **bill of sale**.

BSA *n abbr* (*US*) = Boy Scouts of America.

BSc *n abbr see* **Bachelor of Science**.

BSE *n abbr* (= bovine spongiform encephalopathy*) encefalite *f* bovina spongiforme.*

BSI *n abbr* (= British Standards Institution*) associazione per la normalizzazione.*

BST *abbr* (= British Summer Time*) ora legale.*

Bt. *abbr* (*BRIT*) = baronet.

btu *n abbr* (= British thermal unit*) Btu *m* (= 1054.2 joules).*

bubble ['bʌbl] *n* bolla ♦ *vi* ribollire; (*sparkle, fig*) essere effervescente.

bubble bath *n* bagno *m* schiuma *inv*.

bubblejet printer ['bʌbldʒɛt-] *n* stampante *f* a getto d'inchiostro.

bubbly ['bʌblɪ] *adj* (*also fig*) frizzante ♦ *n* (*col*) (*champagne*) spumante *m*.

Bucharest [bu:kə'rɛst] *n* Bucarest *f*.

buck [bʌk] *n* maschio (*di camoscio, caprone, coniglio etc*); (*US col*) dollaro ♦ *vi* sgroppare; **to pass the ~ (to sb)** scaricare (su di qn) la propria responsabilità.

▶**buck up** *vi* (*cheer up*) rianimarsi ♦ *vt*: **to ~ one's ideas up** mettere la testa a partito.

bucket ['bʌkɪt] *n* secchio ♦ *vi* (*BRIT col*): **the rain is ~ing (down)** piove a catinelle.

Buckingham Palace ['bʌkɪŋəm-] *n see boxed note.*

buckle ['bʌkl] *n* fibbia ♦ *vt* affibbiare; (*warp*) deformare.

▶**buckle down** *vi* mettersi sotto.

Bucks [bʌks] *abbr* (*BRIT*) = Buckinghamshire.

bud [bʌd] *n* gemma; (*of flower*) boccio ♦ *vi* germogliare; (*flower*) sbocciare.

Budapest [bju:də'pɛst] *n* Budapest *f*.

Buddha ['budə] *n* Budda *m*.

Buddhism ['budɪzəm] *n* buddismo.

Buddhist ['budɪst] *adj*, *n* buddista (*m/f*).

budding ['bʌdɪŋ] *adj* (*flower*) in boccio; (*poet etc*) in erba.

buddy ['bʌdɪ] *n* (*US*) compagno.

budge [bʌdʒ] *vt* scostare ♦ *vi* spostarsi.

budgerigar ['bʌdʒərɪgɑ:*] *n* pappagallino.

budget ['bʌdʒɪt] *n* bilancio preventivo ♦ *vi*: **to ~ for sth** fare il bilancio per qc; **I'm on a tight ~** devo contare la lira; **she works out her ~ every month** fa il preventivo delle spese ogni mese.

budgie ['bʌdʒɪ] *n* = **budgerigar**.

Buenos Aires ['bweɪnɔs'aɪrɪz] *n* Buenos Aires *f*.

buff [bʌf] *adj* color camoscio *inv* ♦ *n* (*enthusiast*) appassionato/a.

buffalo, *pl* ~ *or* ~**es** ['bʌfələu] *n* bufalo; (*US*) bisonte *m*.
buffer ['bʌfə*] *n* respingente *m*; (*COMPUT*) memoria tampone, buffer *m inv*.
buffer state *n* stato cuscinetto.
buffer zone *n* zona *f* cuscinetto *inv*.
buffet *n* ['bufeɪ] (*food, BRIT: bar*) buffet *m inv* ♦ *vt* ['bʌfɪt] schiaffeggiare; scuotere; urtare.
buffet car *n* (*BRIT RAIL*) ≈ servizio ristoro.
buffet lunch *n* pranzo in piedi.
buffoon [bə'fuːn] *n* buffone *m*.
bug [bʌg] *n* (*insect*) cimice *f*; (: *gen*) insetto; (*fig: germ*) virus *m inv*; (*spy device*) microfono spia; (*COMPUT*) bug *m inv*, errore *m* nel programma ♦ *vt* mettere sotto controllo; (*room*) installare microfoni spia in; (*annoy*) scocciare; **I've got the travel** ~ (*fig*) mi è presa la mania dei viaggi.
bugbear ['bʌgbɛə*] *n* spauracchio.
bugger ['bʌgə*] (*col!*) *n* bastardo (*!*) ♦ *vb*: ~ **off!** vaffanculo! (*!*); ~ **(it)!** merda! (*!*).
bugle ['bjuːgl] *n* tromba.
build [bɪld] *n* (*of person*) corporatura ♦ *vt* (*pt, pp* **built** [bɪlt]) costruire.
▶**build on** *vt fus* (*fig*) prendere il via da.
▶**build up** *vt* (*establish: business*) costruire; (: *reputation*) fare, consolidare; (*increase: production*) allargare, incrementare; **don't** ~ **your hopes up too soon** non sperarci troppo.
builder ['bɪldə*] *n* costruttore *m*.
building ['bɪldɪŋ] *n* costruzione *f*; edificio; (*also:* ~ **trade**) edilizia.
building contractor *n* costruttore *m*, imprenditore *m* (edile).
building industry *n* industria edilizia.
building site *n* cantiere *m* di costruzione.
building society *n* *società immobiliare e finanziaria*; *see boxed note*.

building trade *n* = **building industry**.
build-up ['bɪldʌp] *n* (*of gas etc*) accumulo; (*publicity*): **to give sb/sth a good** ~ fare buona pubblicità a qn/qc.
built [bɪlt] *pt, pp of* **build**; **well-**~ robusto(a).
built-in ['bɪlt'ɪn] *adj* (*cupboard*) a muro; (*device*) incorporato(a).

built-up area ['bɪltʌp-] *n* abitato.
bulb [bʌlb] *n* (*BOT*) bulbo; (*ELEC*) lampadina.
Bulgaria [bʌl'gɛərɪə] *n* Bulgaria.
Bulgarian [bʌl'gɛərɪən] *adj* bulgaro(a) ♦ *n* bulgaro/a; (*LING*) bulgaro.
bulge [bʌldʒ] *n* rigonfiamento; (*in birth rate, sales*) punta ♦ *vi* essere protuberante *or* rigonfio(a); **to be bulging with** essere pieno(a) *or* zeppo(a) di.
bulimia [bə'lɪmɪə] *n* bulimia.
bulk [bʌlk] *n* massa, volume *m*; **the** ~ **of** il grosso di; (**to buy) in** ~ (comprare) in grande quantità.
bulk buying *n* acquisto di merce in grande quantità.
bulk carrier *n* grossa nave *f* da carico.
bulkhead ['bʌlkhɛd] *n* paratia.
bulky ['bʌlkɪ] *adj* grosso(a); voluminoso(a).
bull [bul] *n* toro; (*STOCK EXCHANGE*) rialzista *m/f*; (*REL*) bolla (papale).
bulldog ['buldɔg] *n* bulldog *m inv*.
bulldoze ['buldəuz] *vt* aprire *or* spianare col bulldozer; **I was** ~**d into doing it** (*fig col*) mi ci hanno costretto con la prepotenza.
bulldozer ['buldəuzə*] *n* bulldozer *m inv*.
bullet ['bulɪt] *n* pallottola.
bulletin ['bulɪtɪn] *n* bollettino.
bulletin board *n* (*COMPUT*) bulletin board *m inv*.
bullet point *n* punto; ~**s** elenco *sg* puntato.
bullet-proof ['bulɪtpruːf] *adj* a prova di proiettile; ~ **vest** giubbotto antiproiettile.
bullfight ['bulfaɪt] *n* corrida.
bullfighter ['bulfaɪtə*] *n* torero.
bullfighting ['bulfaɪtɪŋ] *n* tauromachia.
bullion ['buljən] *n* oro in lingotti.
bullock ['bulək] *n* giovenco.
bullring ['bulrɪŋ] *n* arena (per corride).
bull's-eye ['bulzaɪ] *n* centro del bersaglio.
bullshit ['bulʃɪt] (*col!*) *excl, n* stronzate *fpl* (*!*) ♦ *vi* raccontare stronzate (*!*) ♦ *vt* raccontare stronzate a (*!*).
bully ['bulɪ] *n* prepotente *m* ♦ *vt* angariare; (*frighten*) intimidire.
bullying ['bulɪŋ] *n* prepotenze *fpl*.
bum [bʌm] *n* (*col: backside*) culo; (*tramp*) vagabondo/a; (*US: idler*) fannullone/a.
▶**bum around** *vi* (*col*) fare il vagabondo.
bumblebee ['bʌmblbiː] *n* (*ZOOL*) bombo.
bumf [bʌmf] *n* (*col: forms etc*) scartoffie *fpl*.
bump [bʌmp] *n* (*blow*) colpo; (*jolt*) scossa; (*noise*) botto; (*on road etc*) protuberanza; (*on head*) bernoccolo ♦ *vt* battere; (*car*) urtare, sbattere.
▶**bump along** *vi* procedere sobbalzando.
▶**bump into** *vt fus* scontrarsi con; (*col*:

meet) imbattersi in, incontrare per caso.

bumper ['bʌmpə*] n (*BRIT*) paraurti m inv
♦ adj: ~ **harvest** raccolto eccezionale.

bumper cars npl (*US*) autoscontri mpl.

bumph [bʌmf] n = **bumf.**

bumptious ['bʌmpʃəs] adj presuntuoso(a).

bumpy ['bʌmpɪ] adj (*road*) dissestato(a);
(*journey, flight*) movimentato(a).

bun [bʌn] n focaccia; (*of hair*) crocchia.

bunch [bʌntʃ] n (*of flowers, keys*) mazzo; (*of bananas*) ciuffo; (*of people*) gruppo; ~ **of grapes** grappolo d'uva.

bundle ['bʌndl] n fascio ♦ vt (*also*: ~ **up**)
legare in un fascio; (*put*): **to ~ sth/sb into**
spingere qc/qn in.

▶**bundle off** vt (*person*) mandare via in
gran fretta.

▶**bundle out** vt far uscire (senza tante
cerimonie).

bun fight n (*BRIT*: *col*) tè m inv (*ricevimento*).

bung [bʌŋ] n tappo ♦ vt (*BRIT*: *throw*: *also*: ~
into) buttare; (*also*: ~ **up**: *pipe, hole*)
tappare, otturare; **my nose is ~ed up**
(*col*) ho il naso otturato.

bungalow ['bʌŋgələu] n bungalow m inv.

bungee jumping ['bʌndʒiː'dʒʌmpɪŋ] n salto
nel vuoto da ponti, grattacieli etc con un
cavo fissato alla caviglia.

bungle ['bʌŋgl] vt abborracciare.

bunion ['bʌnjən] n callo (al piede).

bunk [bʌŋk] n cuccetta.

▶**bunk off** vi (*BRIT col*): **to ~ off school**
marinare la scuola; **I'll ~ off at 3 this
afternoon** oggi me la filo dal lavoro alle 3.

bunk beds npl letti mpl a castello.

bunker ['bʌŋkə*] n (*coal store*) ripostiglio
per il carbone; (*MIL, GOLF*) bunker m inv.

bunny ['bʌnɪ] n (*also*: ~ **rabbit**) coniglietto.

bunny hill n (*US SKI*) pista per principianti.

bunting ['bʌntɪŋ] n pavesi mpl, bandierine
fpl.

buoy [bɔɪ] n boa.

▶**buoy up** vt tenere a galla; (*fig*) sostenere.

buoyancy ['bɔɪənsɪ] n (*of ship*)
galleggiabilità.

buoyant ['bɔɪənt] adj galleggiante; (*fig*)
vivace; (*COMM*: *market*) sostenuto(a);
(*prices, currency*) stabile.

burden ['bəːdn] n carico, fardello ♦ vt
caricare; (*oppress*) opprimere; **to be a ~
to sb** essere di peso a qn.

bureau, pl ~**x** ['bjuərəu, -z] n (*BRIT*: *writing
desk*) scrivania; (*US*: *chest of drawers*)
cassettone m; (*office*) ufficio, agenzia.

bureaucracy [bjuə'rɔkrəsɪ] n burocrazia.

bureaucrat ['bjuərəkræt] n burocrate m/f.

bureaucratic [bjuərə'krætɪk] adj
burocratico(a).

burgeon ['bəːdʒən] vi svilupparsi
rapidamente.

burger ['bəːgə*] n hamburger m inv.

burglar ['bəːglə*] n scassinatore m.

burglar alarm n antifurto m inv.

burglarize ['bəːgləraɪz] vt (*US*) svaligiare.

burglary ['bəːglərɪ] n furto con scasso.

burgle ['bəːgl] vt svaligiare.

burial ['berɪəl] n sepoltura.

burial ground n cimitero.

burly ['bəːlɪ] adj robusto(a).

Burma ['bəːmə] n Birmania; *see* **Myanmar.**

Burmese [bəː'miːz] adj birmano(a) ♦ n (*pl
inv*) birmano/a; (*LING*) birmano.

burn [bəːn] vt, vi (*pt, pp* **burned** *or* **burnt**
[bəːnt]) bruciare ♦ n bruciatura,
scottatura; (*MED*) ustione f; **I've ~t
myself!** mi sono bruciato!; **the cigarette
~t a hole in her dress** si è fatta un buco
nel vestito con la sigaretta.

▶**burn down** vt distruggere col fuoco.

▶**burn out** vt (*subj*: *writer etc*): **to ~ o.s. out**
esaurirsi.

burner ['bəːnə*] n fornello.

burning ['bəːnɪŋ] adj (*building, forest*) in
fiamme; (*issue, question*) scottante.

burnish ['bəːnɪʃ] vt brunire.

Burns Night n *see boxed note.*

BURNS NIGHT

Burns Night è la festa celebrata il 25
gennaio per commemorare il poeta scozzese
Robert Burns (1759-1796). Gli scozzesi
festeggiano questa data con una cena a base di
"haggis" e whisky, spesso al suono di una
cornamusa; durante la cena vengono recitate le
poesie di Robert Burns e vengono letti discorsi
alla sua memoria.

---

burnt [bəːnt] pt, pp of **burn.**

burp [bəːp] (*col*) n rutto ♦ vi ruttare.

burrow ['bʌrəu] n tana ♦ vt scavare.

bursar ['bəːsə*] n economo/a; (*BRIT*: *student*)
borsista m/f.

bursary ['bəːsərɪ] n (*BRIT*) borsa di studio.

burst [bəːst] vb (*pt, pp* **burst**) vt far
scoppiare *or* esplodere ♦ vi esplodere;
(*tyre*) scoppiare ♦ n scoppio; (*also*: ~ **pipe**)
rottura nel tubo, perdita; ~ **of energy/
laughter** scoppio d'energia/di risa; **a ~ of
applause** uno scroscio d'applausi; **a ~ of
speed** uno scatto (di velocità); ~ **blood
vessel** rottura di un vaso sanguigno; **the
river has ~ its banks** il fiume ha rotto gli
argini *or* ha straripato; **to ~ into flames/
tears** scoppiare in fiamme/lacrime; **to be
~ing with** essere pronto a scoppiare di;

to ~ out laughing scoppiare a ridere; **to ~ open** *vi* aprirsi improvvisamente; (*door*) spalancarsi.

▶**burst into** *vt fus* (*room etc*) irrompere in.

▶**burst out of** *vt fus* precipitarsi fuori da.

bury ['bɛrɪ] *vt* seppellire; **to ~ one's face in one's hands** nascondere la faccia tra le mani; **to ~ one's head in the sand** (*fig*) fare (la politica dello) struzzo; **to ~ the hatchet** (*fig*) seppellire l'ascia di guerra.

bus, ~es [bʌs, 'bʌsɪz] *n* autobus *m inv*.

bus boy *n* (*US*) aiuto *inv* cameriere/a.

bush [buʃ] *n* cespuglio; (*scrub land*) macchia.

bushed [buʃt] *adj* (*col*) distrutto(a).

bushel ['buʃl] *n* staio.

bushfire ['buʃfaɪə*] *n* grande incendio in aperta campagna.

bushy ['buʃɪ] *adj* (*plant, tail, beard*) folto(a); (*eyebrows*) irsuto(a).

busily ['bɪzɪlɪ] *adv* con impegno, alacremente.

business ['bɪznɪs] *n* (*matter*) affare *m*; (*trading*) affari *mpl*; (*firm*) azienda; (*job, duty*) lavoro; **to be away on ~** essere andato via per affari; **I'm here on ~** sono qui per affari; **to do ~ with sb** fare affari con qn; **he's in the insurance ~** lavora nel campo delle assicurazioni; **it's none of my ~** questo non mi riguarda; **he means ~** non scherza.

business address *n* indirizzo di lavoro *or* d'ufficio.

business card *n* biglietto da visita della ditta.

businesslike ['bɪznɪslaɪk] *adj* serio(a); efficiente.

businessman ['bɪznɪsmən] *n* uomo d'affari.

business trip *n* viaggio d'affari.

businesswoman ['bɪznɪswumən] *n* donna d'affari.

busker ['bʌskə*] *n* (*BRIT*) suonatore/trice ambulante.

bus lane *n* (*BRIT*) corsia riservata agli autobus.

bus shelter *n* pensilina (*alla fermata dell'autobus*).

bus station *n* stazione *f* delle autolinee, autostazione *f*.

bus stop *n* fermata d'autobus.

bust [bʌst] *n* (*ART*) busto; (*bosom*) seno ♦ *adj* (*broken*) rotto(a) ♦ *vt* (*col: POLICE: arrest*) pizzicare, beccare; **to go ~** fallire.

bustle ['bʌsl] *n* movimento, attività ♦ *vi* darsi da fare.

bustling ['bʌslɪŋ] *adj* (*person*) indaffarato(a); (*town*) animato(a).

bust-up ['bʌstʌp] *n* (*BRIT col*) lite *f*.

busty ['bʌstɪ] *adj* (*col*) tettone(a).

busy ['bɪzɪ] *adj* occupato(a); (*shop, street*) molto frequentato(a) ♦ *vt*: **to ~ o.s.** darsi da fare; **he's a ~ man** (*normally*) è un uomo molto occupato; (*temporarily*) ha molto da fare, è molto occupato.

busybody ['bɪzɪbɔdɪ] *n* ficcanaso *m/f inv*.

busy signal *n* (*US*) segnale *m* di occupato.

═══════════════════ *KEYWORD*

but [bʌt] *conj* ma; **I'd love to come, ~ I'm busy** vorrei tanto venire, ma ho da fare ♦ *prep* (*apart from, except*) eccetto, tranne, meno; **nothing ~** nient'altro che; **he was nothing ~ trouble** non dava altro che guai; **no-one ~ him** solo lui; **no-one ~ him can do it** nessuno può farlo tranne lui; **the last ~ one** (*BRIT*) il(la) penultimo(a); **~ for you/your help** se non fosse per te/ per il tuo aiuto; **anything ~ that** tutto ma non questo; **anything ~ finished** tutt'altro che finito
♦ *adv* (*just, only*) solo, soltanto; **she's ~ a child** è solo una bambina; **had I ~ known** se solo avessi saputo; **I can ~ try** tentar non nuoce; **all ~ finished** quasi finito.

butane ['bjuːteɪn] *n* (*also: ~ gas*) butano.

butch [butʃ] *adj* (*woman: pej*) mascolino(a); (*man*) macho *inv*.

butcher ['butʃə*] *n* macellaio ♦ *vt* macellare; **~'s (shop)** macelleria.

butler ['bʌtlə*] *n* maggiordomo.

butt [bʌt] *n* (*cask*) grossa botte *f*; (*thick end*) estremità *f inv* più grossa; (*of gun*) calcio; (*of cigarette*) mozzicone *m*; (*BRIT fig: target*) oggetto ♦ *vt* cozzare.

▶**butt in** *vi* (*interrupt*) interrompere.

butter ['bʌtə*] *n* burro ♦ *vt* imburrare.

buttercup ['bʌtəkʌp] *n* ranuncolo.

butter dish *n* burriera.

butterfingers ['bʌtəfɪŋgəz] *n* (*col*) mani *fpl* di ricotta.

butterfly ['bʌtəflaɪ] *n* farfalla; (*SWIMMING: also: ~ stroke*) (nuoto a) farfalla.

buttocks ['bʌtəks] *npl* natiche *fpl*.

button ['bʌtn] *n* bottone *m* ♦ *vt* (*also: ~ up*) abbottonare ♦ *vi* abbottonarsi.

buttonhole ['bʌtnhəul] *n* asola, occhiello ♦ *vt* (*person*) attaccar bottone a.

buttress ['bʌtrɪs] *n* contrafforte *m*.

buxom ['bʌksəm] *adj* formoso(a).

buy [baɪ] *vt* (*pt, pp* **bought** [bɔːt]) comprare, acquistare ♦ *n*: **a good/bad ~** un buon/ cattivo acquisto *or* affare; **to ~ sb sth/ sth from sb** comprare qc per qn/qc da qn; **to ~ sb a drink** offrire da bere a qn.

▶**buy back** *vt* riprendersi, prendersi

indietro.
►**buy in** vt (BRIT: goods) far provvista di.
►**buy into** vt fus (BRIT COMM) acquistare delle azioni di.
►**buy off** vt (col: bribe) comprare.
►**buy out** vt (business) rilevare.
►**buy up** vt accaparrare.
buyer ['baɪə*] n compratore/trice; ~'**s market** mercato favorevole ai compratori.
buy-out ['baɪaut] n (COMM) acquisto di una società da parte dei suoi dipendenti.
buzz [bʌz] n ronzio; (col: phone call) colpo di telefono ♦ vi ronzare ♦ vt (call on intercom) chiamare al citofono; (: with buzzer) chiamare col cicalino; (AVIAT: plane, building) passare rasente; **my head is** ~**ing** mi gira la testa.
►**buzz off** vi (BRIT col) filare, levarsi di torno.
buzzard ['bʌzəd] n poiana.
buzzer ['bʌzə*] n cicalino.
buzz word n (col) termine m in voga.

========================= KEYWORD

by [baɪ] prep **1** (referring to cause, agent) da; **killed** ~ **lightning** ucciso da un fulmine; **surrounded** ~ **a fence** circondato da uno steccato; **a painting** ~ **Picasso** un quadro di Picasso
2 (referring to method, manner, means): ~ **bus/car/train** in autobus/macchina/treno, con l'autobus/la macchina/il treno; **to pay** ~ **cheque** pagare con (un) assegno; ~ **moonlight** al chiaro di luna; ~ **saving hard, he** ... risparmiando molto, lui ...
3 (via, through) per; **we came** ~ **Dover** siamo venuti via Dover
4 (close to, past) accanto a; **the house** ~ **the river** la casa sul fiume; **a holiday** ~ **the sea** una vacanza al mare; **she sat** ~ **his bed** si sedette accanto al suo letto; **she rushed** ~ **me** mi è passata accanto correndo; **I go** ~ **the post office every day** passo davanti all'ufficio postale ogni giorno
5 (not later than) per, entro; ~ **4 o'clock** per or entro le 4; ~ **this time tomorrow** domani a quest'ora; ~ **the time I got here it was too late** quando sono arrivato era ormai troppo tardi
6 (during): ~ **day/night** di giorno/notte
7 (amount) a; ~ **the kilo** a chili; **paid** ~ **the hour** pagato all'ora; **to increase** ~ **the hour** aumentare di ora in ora; **one** ~ **one** uno per uno; **little** ~ **little** a poco a poco
8 (MATH, measure): **to divide/multiply** ~ **3** dividere/moltiplicare per 3; **a room 3**

metres ~ **4** una stanza di 3 metri per 4; **it's broader** ~ **a metre** è un metro più largo, è più largo di un metro
9 (according to) per; **to play** ~ **the rules** attenersi alle regole; **it's all right** ~ **me** per me va bene
10: **(all)** ~ **oneself** (tutto(a)) solo(a); **he did it (all)** ~ **himself** lo ha fatto (tutto) da solo
11: ~ **the way** a proposito; **this wasn't my idea** ~ **the way** tra l'altro l'idea non è stata mia
♦ adv **1** see **go**; **pass** etc
2: ~ **and** ~ (in past) poco dopo; (in future) fra breve; ~ **and large** nel complesso.

bye(-bye) ['baɪ('baɪ)] excl ciao!, arrivederci!
by(e)-law ['baɪlɔ:] n legge f locale.
by-election ['baɪɪlɛkʃən] n (BRIT) elezione f straordinaria; see boxed note.

┌─────────────────────────────────────┐
│ **BY-ELECTION**
│
│ Una **by-election** in Gran Bretagna e in alcuni
│ paesi del Commonwealth è un'elezione che si
│ tiene per coprire un posto in Parlamento resosi
│ vacante, a governo ancora in carica. È
│ importante in quanto serve a misurare il
│ consenso degli elettori in vista delle successive
│ elezioni politiche.
└─────────────────────────────────────┘

Byelorussia [bjɛləu'rʌʃə] n Bielorussia, Belorussia.
Byelorussian [bjɛləu'rʌʃən] adj, n = **Belarussian**.
bygone ['baɪgɔn] adj passato(a) ♦ n: **let** ~**s be** ~**s** mettiamoci una pietra sopra.
bypass ['baɪpɑːs] n circonvallazione f; (MED) by-pass m inv ♦ vt fare una deviazione intorno a.
by-product ['baɪprɔdʌkt] n sottoprodotto; (fig) conseguenza secondaria.
byre ['baɪə*] n (BRIT) stalla.
bystander ['baɪstændə*] n spettatore/trice.
byte [baɪt] n (COMPUT) byte m inv.
byway ['baɪweɪ] n strada secondaria.
byword ['baɪwəːd] n: **to be a** ~ **for** essere sinonimo di.
by-your-leave ['baɪjɔː'liːv] n: **without so much as a** ~ senza nemmeno chiedere il permesso.

Cc

C, c [si:] n (*letter*) C, c f or m inv; (*SCOL: mark*)
≈ 6 (*sufficiente*); (*MUS*): **C** do; ~ **for Charlie**
≈ C come Como.

C abbr (= *Celsius, centigrade*) C.

c. abbr (= *century*) sec.; (= *circa*) c; (*US etc*)
= **cent(s).**

CA abbr = **Central America**; (*US*) = *California*
♦ n abbr (*BRIT*) see **chartered accountant.**

ca. abbr (= *circa*) ca.

c/a abbr = **capital account; credit account;
current account.**

CAA n abbr (*BRIT*: = *Civil Aviation Authority,
US*: = *Civil Aeronautics Authority*)
*organismo di controllo e di sviluppo
dell'aviazione civile.*

CAB n abbr (*BRIT*: = *Citizens' Advice Bureau*)
*organizzazione per la tutela del
consumatore.*

cab [kæb] n taxi m inv; (*of train, truck*) cabina;
(*horsedrawn*) carrozza.

cabaret ['kæbəreɪ] n cabaret m inv.

cabbage ['kæbɪdʒ] n cavolo.

cabbie, cabby ['kæbɪ] n (*col*), **cab driver** n
tassista m/f.

cabin ['kæbɪn] n capanna; (*on ship*) cabina.

cabin cruiser n cabinato.

cabinet ['kæbɪnɪt] n (*POL*) consiglio dei
ministri; (*furniture*) armadietto; (*also:*
display ~) vetrinetta; **cocktail** ~ mobile m
bar *inv.*

cabinet-maker ['kæbɪnɪt'meɪkə*] n
stipettaio.

cabinet minister n ministro (*membro del
Consiglio*).

cable ['keɪbl] n cavo; fune f; (*TEL*)
cablogramma m ♦ vt telegrafare.

cable-car ['keɪblkɑ:*] n funivia.

cablegram ['keɪblgræm] n cablogramma m.

cable railway n funicolare f.

cable television n televisione f via cavo.

cache [kæʃ] n nascondiglio; **a** ~ **of food** *etc*
un deposito segreto di viveri *etc.*

cackle ['kækl] vi schiamazzare.

cactus, pl **cacti** ['kæktəs, -taɪ] n cactus m inv.

CAD n abbr (= *computer-aided design*)
progettazione f con l'ausilio
dell'elaboratore.

caddie ['kædɪ] n caddie m inv.

cadet [kə'dɛt] n (*MIL*) cadetto; **police** ~
allievo poliziotto.

cadge [kædʒ] vt (*col*) scroccare; **to** ~ **a
meal (off sb)** scroccare un pranzo (a qn).

cadre ['kædrɪ] n quadro.

Caesarean, (*US*) **Cesarean** [si:'zɛərɪən] adj:
~ **(section)** (taglio) cesareo.

CAF abbr (*BRIT*: = *cost and freight*) Caf m.

café ['kæfeɪ] n caffè m inv.

cafeteria [kæfɪ'tɪərɪə] n self-service m inv.

caffein(e) ['kæfi:n] n caffeina.

cage [keɪdʒ] n gabbia ♦ vt mettere in
gabbia.

cagey ['keɪdʒɪ] adj (*col*) chiuso(a);
guardingo(a).

cagoule [kə'gu:l] n K-way ® m inv.

cahoots [kə'hu:ts] n: **to be in** ~ **(with sb)**
essere in combutta (con qn).

CAI n abbr (= *computer-aided instruction*)
istruzione f assistita dall'elaboratore.

Cairo ['kaɪərəu] n il Cairo.

cajole [kə'dʒəul] vt allettare.

cake [keɪk] n torta; ~ **of soap** saponetta; **it's
a piece of** ~ (*col*) è una cosa da nulla; **he
wants to have his** ~ **and eat it (too)** (*fig*)
vuole la botte piena e la moglie ubriaca.

caked [keɪkt] adj: ~ **with** incrostato(a) di.

cake shop n pasticceria.

Cal. abbr (*US*) = *California.*

calamitous [kə'læmɪtəs] adj disastroso(a).

calamity [kə'læmɪtɪ] n calamità f inv.

calcium ['kælsɪəm] n calcio.

calculate ['kælkjuleɪt] vt calcolare;
(*estimate: chances, effect*) valutare.

▶**calculate on** vt fus: **to** ~ **on sth/on doing
sth** contare su qc/di fare qc.

calculated ['kælkjuleɪtɪd] adj calcolato(a),
intenzionale; **a** ~ **risk** un rischio
calcolato.

calculating ['kælkjuleɪtɪŋ] adj
calcolatore(trice).

calculation [kælkju'leɪʃən] n calcolo.

calculator ['kælkjuleɪtə*] n calcolatrice f.

calculus ['kælkjuləs] n calcolo; **integral/
differential** ~ calcolo integrale/
differenziale.

calendar ['kæləndə*] n calendario.

calendar year n anno civile.

calf, pl **calves** [kɑ:f, kɑ:vz] n (*of cow*)
vitello; (*of other animals*) piccolo; (*also:*
~**skin**) (pelle f di) vitello; (*ANAT*)
polpaccio.

caliber, (*US*) = **calibre.**

calibrate ['kælɪbreɪt] vt (*gun etc*) calibrare;
(*scale of measuring instrument*) tarare.

calibre, (*US*) **caliber** ['kælɪbə*] n calibro.

calico ['kælɪkəu] n tela grezza, cotone m
grezzo; (*US*) cotonina stampata.

Calif. *abbr* (*US*) = *California*.
California [kælɪ'fɔːnɪə] *n* California.
calipers ['kælɪpəz] *npl* (*US*) = **callipers**.
call [kɔːl] *vt* (*gen, also TEL*) chiamare;
(*announce: flight*) annunciare; (*meeting, strike*) indire, proclamare ♦ *vi* chiamare;
(*visit: also:* ~ **in,** ~ **round**) passare ♦ *n* (*shout*)
grido, urlo; visita; (*summons: for flight etc*)
chiamata; (*fig: lure*) richiamo; (*also:*
telephone ~) telefonata; **to be on** ~ essere
a disposizione; **to make a** ~ telefonare,
fare una telefonata; **please give me a** ~ **at 7**
per piacere mi chiami alle 7; **to pay a** ~ **on**
sb fare (una) visita a qn; **there's not much** ~
for these items non c'è molta richiesta
di questi articoli; **she's** ~**ed Jane** si
chiama Jane; **who is** ~**ing?** (*TEL*) chi
parla?; **London** ~**ing** (*RADIO*) qui Londra.
►**call at** *vt fus* (*subj: ship*) fare scalo a; (:
train) fermarsi a.
►**call back** *vi* (*return*) ritornare; (*TEL*)
ritelefonare, richiamare ♦ *vt* (*TEL*)
ritelefonare a, richiamare.
►**call for** *vt fus* (*demand: action etc*)
richiedere; (*collect: person*) passare a
prendere; (: *goods*) ritirare.
►**call in** *vt* (*doctor, expert, police*) chiamare,
far venire.
►**call off** *vt* (*meeting, race*) disdire; (*deal*)
cancellare; (*dog*) richiamare; **the strike**
was ~**ed off** lo sciopero è stato revocato.
►**call on** *vt fus* (*visit*) passare da; (*request*):
to ~ **on sb to do** chiedere a qn di fare.
►**call out** *vi* urlare ♦ *vt* (*doctor, police,*
troops) chiamare.
►**call up** *vt* (*MIL*) richiamare.
Callanetics ® [kælə'nɛtɪks] *nsg* tipo di
ginnastica basata sulla ripetizione di
piccoli movimenti.
callbox ['kɔːlbɔks] *n* (*BRIT*) cabina
telefonica.
call centre *n* centre informazioni
telefoniche.
caller ['kɔːlə*] *n* persona che chiama;
visitatore/trice; **hold the line,** ~! (*TEL*)
rimanga in linea, signore (*or* signora)!
call girl *n* ragazza *f* squillo *inv*.
call-in ['kɔːlɪn] *n* (*US*) = **phone-in**.
calling ['kɔːlɪŋ] *n* vocazione *f*.
calling card *n* (*US*) biglietto da visita.
callipers, (*US*) **calipers** ['kælɪpəz] *npl* (*MED*)
gambale *m*; (*MATH*) calibro.
callous ['kæləs] *adj* indurito(a), insensibile.
callow ['kæləu] *adj* immaturo(a).
calm [kɑːm] *adj* calmo(a) ♦ *n* calma ♦ *vt*
calmare.
►**calm down** *vi* calmarsi ♦ *vt* calmare.
calmly ['kɑːmlɪ] *adv* con calma.

calmness ['kɑːmnɪs] *n* calma.
Calor gas ® ['kælə*-] *n* (*BRIT*) butano.
calorie ['kælərɪ] *n* caloria; **low-~ product**
prodotto a basso contenuto di calorie.
calve [kɑːv] *vi* figliare.
calves [kɑːvz] *npl of* **calf**.
CAM *n abbr* (= *computer-aided*
manufacturing) fabbricazione *f* con
l'ausilio dell'elaboratore.
camber ['kæmbə*] *n* (*of road*) bombatura.
Cambodia [kæm'bəudjə] *n* Cambogia.
Cambodian [kæm'bəudɪən] *adj, n*
cambogiano(a).
Cambs *abbr* (*BRIT*) = *Cambridgeshire*.
camcorder ['kæmkɔːdə*] *n* videocamera.
came [keɪm] *pt of* **come**.
camel ['kæməl] *n* cammello.
cameo ['kæmɪəu] *n* cammeo.
camera ['kæmərə] *n* macchina fotografica;
(*CINE, TV*) telecamera; (*also:* **cine~, movie**
~) cinepresa; **in** ~ a porte chiuse.
cameraman ['kæmərəmæn] *n* cameraman
m inv.
camera phone *n* telefonino con
fotocamera integrata.
Cameroon, Cameroun ['kæməruːn] *n*
Camerun *m*.
camouflage ['kæməflɑːʒ] *n* camuffamento;
(*MIL*) mimetizzazione *f* ♦ *vt* camuffare;
mimetizzare.
camp [kæmp] *n* campeggio; (*MIL*) campo ♦
vi campeggiare; accamparsi; **to go** ~**ing**
andare in campeggio.
campaign [kæm'peɪn] *n* (*MIL, POL etc*)
campagna ♦ *vi*: **to** ~ **(for/against)** (*also fig*)
fare una campagna (per/contro).
campaigner [kæm'peɪnə*] *n*: ~ **for** fautore/
trice di; ~ **against** oppositore/trice di.
campbed ['kæmp'bɛd] *n* (*BRIT*) brandina.
camper ['kæmpə*] *n* campeggiatore/trice.
camping ['kæmpɪŋ] *n* campeggio.
camp(ing) site *n* campeggio.
campus ['kæmpəs] *n* campus *m inv*.
camshaft ['kæmʃɑːft] *n* albero a camme.
can [kæn] *aux vb see next headword* ♦ *n* (*of milk*)
scatola; (*of oil*) bidone *m*; (*of water*) tanica;
(*tin*) scatola ♦ *vt* mettere in scatola; **a** ~ **of**
beer una lattina di birra; **to carry the** ~
(*BRIT col*) prendere la colpa.

━━━━━━━━━━━━━━━━━━━━━━━ *KEYWORD*

can [kæn] (*negative* **cannot, can't**; *conditional*
and pt **could**) *aux vb* **1** (*be able to*) potere; **I**
~**'t go any further** non posso andare
oltre; **you** ~ **do it if you try** sei in grado di
farlo — basta provarci; **I'll help you all I**
~ ti aiuterò come potrò; **I** ~**'t see you** non
ti vedo; ~ **you hear me?** mi senti?, riesci

a sentirmi?

2 (*know how to*) sapere, essere capace di; **I ~ swim** so nuotare; **~ you speak French?** parla francese?

3 (*may*) potere; **could I have a word with you?** posso parlarle un momento?

4 (*expressing disbelief, puzzlement etc*): **it ~'t be true!** non può essere vero!; **what CAN he want?** cosa può mai volere?

5 (*expressing possibility, suggestion etc*): **he could be in the library** può darsi che sia in biblioteca; **they could have forgotten** potrebbero essersene dimenticati; **she could have been delayed** può aver avuto un contrattempo.

Canada ['kænədə] *n* Canada *m.*
Canadian [kə'neɪdɪən] *adj, n* canadese (*m/f*).
canal [kə'næl] *n* canale *m.*
canary [kə'neərɪ] *n* canarino.
Canary Islands, Canaries [kə'neərɪz] *npl*: **the ~** le (isole) Canarie.
Canberra ['kænbərə] *n* Camberra.
cancel ['kænsəl] *vt* annullare; (*train*) sopprimere; (*cross out*) cancellare.
▶**cancel out** *vt* (*MATH*) semplificare; (*fig*) annullare; **they ~ each other out** (*also fig*) si annullano a vicenda.
cancellation [kænsə'leɪʃən] *n* annullamento; soppressione *f*; cancellazione *f*; (*TOURISM*) prenotazione *f* annullata.
cancer ['kænsə*] *n* cancro; **C~** (*sign*) Cancro; **to be C~** essere del Cancro.
cancerous ['kænsərəs] *adj* canceroso(a).
cancer patient *n* malato/a di cancro.
cancer research *n* ricerca sul cancro.
C and F *abbr* (*BRIT*: = *cost and freight*) Caf *m.*
candid ['kændɪd] *adj* onesto(a).
candidacy ['kændɪdəsɪ] *n* candidatura.
candidate ['kændɪdeɪt] *n* candidato/a.
candidature ['kændɪdətʃə*] *n* (*BRIT*) = **candidacy.**
candied ['kændɪd] *adj* candito(a); **~ apple** (*US*) mela caramellata.
candle ['kændl] *n* candela.
candlelight ['kændl'laɪt] *n*: **by ~** a lume di candela.
candlestick ['kændlstɪk] *n* (*also*: **candle holder**) bugia; (*bigger, ornate*) candeliere *m.*
candour, (*US*) **candor** ['kændə*] *n* sincerità.
candy ['kændɪ] *n* zucchero candito; (*US*) caramella; caramelle *fpl.*
candy-floss ['kændɪflɔs] *n* (*BRIT*) zucchero filato.
candy store *n* (*US*) ≈ pasticceria.

cane [keɪn] *n* canna; (*for baskets, chairs etc*) bambù *m*; (*SCOL*) verga; (*for walking*) bastone *m* (da passeggio) ♦ *vt* (*BRIT SCOL*) punire a colpi di verga.
canine ['keɪnaɪn] *adj* canino(a).
canister ['kænɪstə*] *n* scatola metallica.
cannabis ['kænəbɪs] *n* canapa indiana.
canned ['kænd] *adj* (*food*) in scatola; (*col: recorded: music*) registrato(a); (*BRIT col: drunk*) sbronzo(a); (*US col: worker*) licenziato(a).
cannibal ['kænɪbəl] *n* cannibale *m/f.*
cannibalism ['kænɪbəlɪzəm] *n* cannibalismo.
cannon, *pl* **~** *or* **~s** ['kænən] *n* (*gun*) cannone *m.*
cannonball ['kænənbɔːl] *n* palla di cannone.
cannon fodder *n* carne *f* da macello.
cannot ['kænɔt] = **can not.**
canny ['kænɪ] *adj* furbo(a).
canoe [kə'nuː] *n* canoa; (*SPORT*) canotto.
canoeing [kə'nuːɪŋ] *n* (*sport*) canottaggio.
canoeist [kə'nuːɪst] *n* canottiere *m.*
canon ['kænən] *n* (*clergyman*) canonico; (*standard*) canone *m.*
canonize ['kænənaɪz] *vt* canonizzare.
can opener [-'əupnə*] *n* apriscatole *m inv.*
canopy ['kænəpɪ] *n* baldacchino.
cant [kænt] *n* gergo ♦ *vt* inclinare ♦ *vi* inclinarsi.
can't [kænt] = **can not.**
Cantab. *abbr* (*BRIT*: = *cantabrigiensis*) *of Cambridge.*
cantankerous [kæn'tæŋkərəs] *adj* stizzoso(a).
canteen [kæn'tiːn] *n* mensa; (*BRIT*: *of cutlery*) portaposate *m inv.*
canter ['kæntə*] *n* piccolo galoppo ♦ *vi* andare al piccolo galoppo.
cantilever ['kæntɪliːvə*] *n* trave *f* a sbalzo.
canvas ['kænvəs] *n* tela; **under ~** (*camping*) sotto la tenda; (*NAUT*) sotto la vela.
canvass ['kænvəs] *vt* (*COMM: district*) fare un'indagine di mercato in; (: *citizens, opinions*) fare un sondaggio di; (*POL: district*) fare un giro elettorale di; (: *person*) fare propaganda elettorale a.
canvasser ['kænvəsə*] *n* (*COMM*) agente *m* viaggiatore, piazzista *m*; (*POL*) propagandista *m/f* (elettorale).
canvassing ['kænvəsɪŋ] *n* sollecitazione *f.*
canyon ['kænjən] *n* canyon *m inv.*
CAP *n abbr* (= *Common Agricultural Policy*) PAC *f.*
cap [kæp] *n* (*also FOOTBALL*) berretto; (*of pen*) coperchio; (*of bottle*) tappo; (*for swimming*) cuffia; (*BRIT: contraceptive: also*: **Dutch ~**) diaframma *m* ♦ *vt* tappare;

(*outdo*) superare; ~**ped with** ricoperto(a) di; **and to ~ it all, he ...** (*BRIT*) e per completare l'opera, lui ....

capability [keɪpə'bɪlɪtɪ] *n* capacità *f inv*, abilità *f inv*.

capable ['keɪpəbl] *adj* capace; ~ **of** capace di; suscettibile di.

capacious [kə'peɪʃəs] *adj* capace.

capacity [kə'pæsɪtɪ] *n* capacità *f inv*; (*of lift etc*) capienza; **in his ~ as** nella sua qualità di; **to work at full ~** lavorare al massimo delle proprie capacità; **filled to ~** pieno zeppo; **in an advisory ~** a titolo consultativo.

cape [keɪp] *n* (*garment*) cappa; (*GEO*) capo.

Cape of Good Hope *n* Capo di Buona Speranza.

caper ['keɪpə*] *n* (*CULIN: also:* ~**s**) cappero; (*leap*) saltello; (*escapade*) birichinata.

Cape Town *n* Città del Capo.

capita ['kæpɪtə] *see* **per capita**.

capital ['kæpɪtl] *n* (*also:* ~ **city**) capitale *f*; (*money*) capitale *m*; (*also:* ~ **letter**) (lettera) maiuscola.

capital account *n* conto capitale.

capital allowance *n* ammortamento fiscale.

capital assets *npl* capitale *m* fisso.

capital expenditure *n* spese *fpl* in capitale.

capital gains tax *n* imposta sulla plusvalenza.

capital goods *n* beni *mpl* d'investimento, beni *mpl* capitali.

capital-intensive ['kæpɪtlɪn'tɛnsɪv] *adj* ad alta intensità di capitale.

capitalism ['kæpɪtəlɪzəm] *n* capitalismo.

capitalist ['kæpɪtəlɪst] *adj, n* capitalista (*m/f*).

capitalize ['kæpɪtəlaɪz] *vt* (*provide with capital*) capitalizzare.

►**capitalize on** *vt fus* (*fig*) trarre vantaggio da.

capital punishment *n* pena capitale.

capital transfer tax *n* (*BRIT*) imposta sui trasferimenti di capitali.

Capitol ['kæpɪtl] *n*: **the ~** il Campidoglio; *see boxed note*.

CAPITOL

Il **Capitol** *è l'edificio che ospita le riunioni del Congresso degli Stati Uniti. È situato sull'omonimo colle, "Capitol Hill", a Washington DC. In molti stati americani il termine Capitol viene usato per indicare l'edificio dove si riuniscono i rappresentanti dello stato.*

---

capitulate [kə'pɪtjuleɪt] *vi* capitolare.

capitulation [kəpɪtju'leɪʃən] *n* capitolazione *f*.

capricious [kə'prɪʃəs] *adj* capriccioso(a).

Capricorn ['kæprɪkɔːn] *n* Capricorno; **to be ~** essere del Capricorno.

caps [kæps] *abbr* = **capital letters**.

capsize [kæp'saɪz] *vt* capovolgere ♦ *vi* capovolgersi.

capstan ['kæpstən] *n* argano.

capsule ['kæpsjuːl] *n* capsula.

Capt. *abbr* (= *captain*) Cap.

captain ['kæptɪn] *n* capitano ♦ *vt* capitanare.

caption ['kæpʃən] *n* leggenda.

captivate ['kæptɪveɪt] *vt* avvincere.

captive ['kæptɪv] *adj, n* prigioniero(a).

captivity [kæp'tɪvɪtɪ] *n* prigionia; **in ~** (*animal*) in cattività.

captor ['kæptə*] *n* (*lawful*) chi ha catturato; (*unlawful*) rapitore *m*.

capture ['kæptʃə*] *vt* catturare, prendere; (*attention*) attirare ♦ *n* cattura; (*data ~*) registrazione *f or* rilevazione *f* di dati.

car [kaː*] *n* macchina, automobile *f*; (*US RAIL*) carrozza; **by ~** in macchina.

carafe [kə'ræf] *n* caraffa.

carafe wine *n* (*in restaurant*) ≈ vino sfuso.

caramel ['kærəməl] *n* caramello.

carat ['kærət] *n* carato; **18 ~ gold** oro a 18 carati.

caravan ['kærəvæn] *n* roulotte *f inv*.

caravan site *n* (*BRIT*) campeggio per roulotte.

caraway ['kærəweɪ] *n*: ~ **seed** seme *m* di cumino.

carbohydrates [kaːbəu'haɪdreɪts] *npl* (*foods*) carboidrati *mpl*.

car bomb *n* ordigno esplosivo collocato in una macchina; **a ~ went off yesterday** ieri è esplosa un'autobomba.

carbon ['kaːbən] *n* carbonio.

carbonated ['kaːbəneɪtəd] *adj* (*drink*) gassato(a).

carbon copy *n* copia *f* carbone *inv*.

carbon dioxide [-daɪ'ɔksaɪd] *n* diossido di carbonio.

carbon paper *n* carta carbone.

carbon ribbon *n* nastro carbonato.

car boot sale *n* mercatino dell'usato dove la merce viene esposta nel bagagliaio delle macchine.

carburettor, (*US*) **carburetor** [kaːbju'rɛtə*] *n* carburatore *m*.

carcass ['kaːkəs] *n* carcassa.

carcinogenic [kaːsɪnə'dʒɛnɪk] *adj*

cancerogeno(a).

card [kɑːd] *n* carta; (*thin cardboard*) cartoncino; (*visiting ~ etc*) biglietto; (*membership ~*) tessera; (*Christmas ~ etc*) cartolina; **to play ~s** giocare a carte.

cardamom ['kɑːdəməm] *n* cardamomo.

cardboard ['kɑːdbɔːd] *n* cartone *m*.

cardboard box *n* (scatola di) cartone *m*.

cardboard city *n luogo dove dormono in scatole di cartone emarginati senzatetto.*

card-carrying member ['kɑːd'kærɪɪŋ-] *n* tesserato/a.

card game *n* gioco di carte.

cardiac ['kɑːdɪæk] *adj* cardiaco(a).

cardigan ['kɑːdɪɡən] *n* cardigan *m inv*.

cardinal ['kɑːdɪnl] *adj*, *n* cardinale (*m*).

card index *n* schedario.

cardphone ['kɑːdfəʊn] *n* telefono a scheda (magnetica).

cardsharp ['kɑːdʃɑːp] *n* baro.

card vote *n* (*BRIT*) voto (palese) per delega.

CARE [keə*] *n abbr* = *Cooperative for American Relief Everywhere.*

care [keə*] *n* cura, attenzione *f*; (*worry*) preoccupazione *f* ♦ *vi*: **to ~ about** interessarsi di; **would you ~ to/for ...?** le piacerebbe ...?; **I wouldn't ~ to do it** non lo vorrei fare; **in sb's ~** alle cure di qn; **to take ~** fare attenzione; **to take ~ of** curarsi di; (*details, arrangements*) occuparsi di; **I don't ~** non me ne importa; **I couldn't ~ less** non me ne importa un bel niente; **~ of (c/o)** (*on letter*) presso; "**with ~**" "fragile"; **the child has been taken into ~** il bambino è stato preso in custodia.

▶**care for** *vt fus* aver cura di; (*like*) voler bene a.

careen [kə'riːn] *vi* (*ship*) sbandare ♦ *vt* carenare.

career [kə'rɪə*] *n* carriera; (*occupation*) professione *f* ♦ *vi* (*also*: **~ along**) andare di (gran) carriera.

career girl *n* donna dedita alla carriera.

careers officer *n* consulente *m/f* d'orientamento professionale.

carefree ['keəfriː] *adj* sgombro(a) di preoccupazioni.

careful ['keəful] *adj* attento(a); (*cautious*) cauto(a); (**be**) **~!** attenzione!; **he's very ~ with his money** bada molto alle spese.

carefully ['keəfəlɪ] *adv* con cura; cautamente.

careless ['keəlɪs] *adj* negligente; (*remark*) privo(a) di tatto.

carelessly ['keəlɪslɪ] *adv* negligentemente; senza tatto; (*without thinking*)

distrattamente.

carelessness ['keəlɪsnɪs] *n* negligenza; mancanza di tatto.

carer ['keərə*] *n chi si occupa di un familiare anziano o invalido.*

caress [kə'rɛs] *n* carezza ♦ *vt* accarezzare.

caretaker ['keəteɪkə*] *n* custode *m*.

caretaker government *n* (*BRIT*) governo *m* ponte *inv*.

car-ferry ['kɑːfɛrɪ] *n* traghetto.

cargo, ~es ['kɑːɡəʊ] *n* carico.

cargo boat *n* cargo.

cargo plane *n* aereo di linea da carico.

car hire *n* (*BRIT*) autonoleggio.

Caribbean [kærɪ'biːən] *adj* caraibico(a); **the ~** (**Sea**) il Mar dei Caraibi.

caricature ['kærɪkətjʊə*] *n* caricatura.

caring ['keərɪŋ] *adj* (*person*) premuroso(a); (*society, organization*) umanitario(a).

carnage ['kɑːnɪdʒ] *n* carneficina.

carnal ['kɑːnl] *adj* carnale.

carnation [kɑː'neɪʃən] *n* garofano.

carnival ['kɑːnɪvəl] *n* (*public celebration*) carnevale *m*; (*US: funfair*) luna park *m inv*.

carnivorous [kɑː'nɪvərəs] *adj* carnivoro(a).

carol ['kærəl] *n*: (**Christmas**) **~** canto di Natale.

carouse [kə'rauz] *vi* far baldoria.

carousel [kærə'sɛl] *n* (*US*) giostra.

carp [kɑːp] *n* (*fish*) carpa.

▶**carp at** *vt fus* trovare a ridire su.

car park *n* parcheggio.

carpenter ['kɑːpɪntə*] *n* carpentiere *m*.

carpentry ['kɑːpɪntrɪ] *n* carpenteria.

carpet ['kɑːpɪt] *n* tappeto; (*BRIT: fitted ~*) moquette *f inv* ♦ *vt* coprire con tappeto.

carpet bombing *n* bombardamento a tappeto.

carpet slippers *npl* pantofole *fpl*.

carpet sweeper *n* scopatappeti *m inv*.

car phone *n* telefonino per auto.

car rental *n* (*US*) autonoleggio.

carriage ['kærɪdʒ] *n* vettura; (*of goods*) trasporto; (*of typewriter*) carrello; (*bearing*) portamento; **~ forward** porto assegnato; **~ free** franco di porto; **~ paid** porto pagato.

carriage return *n* (*on typewriter etc*) leva (*or* tasto) del ritorno a capo.

carriageway ['kærɪdʒweɪ] *n* (*BRIT: part of road*) carreggiata.

carrier ['kærɪə*] *n* (*of disease*) portatore/trice; (*COMM*) impresa di trasporti; (*NAUT*) portaerei *f inv*.

carrier bag *n* (*BRIT*) sacchetto.

carrier pigeon *n* colombo viaggiatore.

carrion ['kærɪən] *n* carogna.

carrot ['kærət] *n* carota.

carry ['kærɪ] vt (subj: person) portare; (: vehicle) trasportare; (a motion, bill) far passare; (involve: responsibilities etc) comportare; (COMM: goods) tenere; (: interest) avere; (MATH: figure) riportare ♦ vi (sound) farsi sentire; **this loan carries 10% interest** questo prestito è sulla base di un interesse del 10%; **to be carried away** (fig) farsi trascinare.

▶**carry forward** vt (MATH, COMM) riportare.

▶**carry on** vi: **to ~ on with sth/doing** continuare qc/a fare ♦ vt mandare avanti.

▶**carry out** vt (orders) eseguire; (investigation) svolgere; (accomplish etc: plan) realizzare; (perform, implement: idea, threat) mettere in pratica.

carrycot ['kærɪkɔt] n (BRIT) culla portabile.

carry-on [kærɪ'ɔn] n (col: fuss) casino, confusione f; (: annoying behaviour): **I've had enough of your ~!** mi hai proprio scocciato!

cart [kɑːt] n carro ♦ vt (col) trascinare, scarrozzare.

carte blanche ['kɑːt'blɔnʃ] n: **to give sb ~** dare carta bianca a qn.

cartel [kɑː'tɛl] n (COMM) cartello.

cartilage ['kɑːtɪlɪdʒ] n cartilagine f.

cartographer [kɑː'tɔɡrəfə*] n cartografo/a.

cartography [kɑː'tɔɡrəfɪ] n cartografia.

carton ['kɑːtən] n (box) scatola di cartone; (of yogurt) cartone m; (of cigarettes) stecca.

cartoon [kɑː'tuːn] n (in newspaper etc) vignetta; (CINE, TV) cartone m animato; (ART) cartone.

cartoonist [kɑː'tuːnɪst] n vignettista m/f; cartonista m/f.

cartridge ['kɑːtrɪdʒ] n (for gun, pen) cartuccia; (for camera) caricatore m; (music tape) cassetta; (of record player) testina.

cartwheel ['kɑːtwiːl] n: **to turn a ~** (SPORT etc) fare la ruota.

carve [kɑːv] vt (meat) trinciare; (wood, stone) intagliare.

▶**carve up** vt (meat) tagliare; (fig: country) suddividere.

carving ['kɑːvɪŋ] n (in wood etc) scultura.

carving knife n trinciante m.

car wash n lavaggio auto.

Casablanca [kæsə'blæŋkə] n Casablanca.

cascade [kæs'keɪd] n cascata ♦ vi scendere a cascata.

case [keɪs] n caso; (LAW) causa, processo; (box) scatola; (also: **suit~**) valigia; (TYP): **lower/upper ~** (carattere m) minuscolo/maiuscolo; **to have a good ~** avere

pretese legittime; **there's a strong ~ for reform** ci sono validi argomenti a favore della riforma; **in ~ of** in caso di; **in ~ he** caso mai lui; **just in ~** in caso di bisogno.

case history n (MED) cartella clinica.

case-sensitive ['keɪs'sensɪtɪv] adj (COMPUT) sensibile alle maiuscole o minuscole.

case study n studio di un caso.

cash [kæʃ] n (coins, notes) soldi mpl, denaro; (col: money) quattrini mpl ♦ vt incassare; **to pay (in) ~** pagare in contanti; **to be short of ~** essere a corto di soldi; **~ with order/on delivery (COD)** (COMM) pagamento all'ordinazione/alla consegna.

▶**cash in** vt (insurance policy etc) riscuotere, riconvertire.

▶**cash in on** vt fus: **to ~ in on sth** sfruttare qc.

cash account n conto m cassa inv.

cash-and-carry ['kæʃənd'kærɪ] n cash and carry m inv.

cashbook ['kæʃbuk] n giornale m di cassa.

cash box n cassetta per il denaro spicciolo.

cash card n carta per prelievi automatici.

cash desk n (BRIT) cassa.

cash discount n sconto per contanti.

cash dispenser n sportello automatico.

cashew [kæ'ʃuː] n (also: ~ **nut**) anacardio.

cash flow n cash-flow m inv, liquidità f inv.

cashier [kæ'ʃɪə*] n cassiere/a ♦ vt (esp MIL) destituire.

cashmere ['kæʃmɪə*] n cachemire m.

cash payment n pagamento in contanti.

cash price n prezzo per contanti.

cash register n registratore m di cassa.

cash sale n vendita per contanti.

casing ['keɪsɪŋ] n rivestimento.

casino [kə'siːnəu] n casinò m inv.

cask [kɑːsk] n botte f.

casket ['kɑːskɪt] n cofanetto; (US: coffin) bara.

Caspian Sea ['kæspɪən-] n: **the ~** il mar Caspio.

casserole ['kæsərəul] n casseruola; (food): **chicken ~** pollo in casseruola.

cassette [kæ'sɛt] n cassetta.

cassette deck n piastra di registrazione.

cassette player n riproduttore m a cassette.

cassette recorder n registratore m a cassette.

cast [kɑːst] vt (pt, pp **cast**) (throw) gettare; (shed) perdere; spogliarsi di; (metal) gettare, fondere ♦ n (THEAT) complesso di attori; (mould) forma; (also: **plaster ~**) ingessatura; (THEAT): **to ~ sb as Hamlet** scegliere qn per la parte di Amleto; **to ~**

one's vote votare, dare il voto.

▶**cast aside** vt (*reject*) mettere da parte.

▶**cast off** vi (*NAUT*) salpare; (*KNITTING*) diminuire, calare ♦ vt (*NAUT*) disormeggiare; (*KNITTING*) diminuire, calare.

▶**cast on** vt (*KNITTING*) avviare ♦ vi avviare (le maglie).

castanets [kæstə'nɛts] npl castagnette fpl.

castaway ['kɑːstəwəɪ] n naufrago/a.

caste [kɑːst] n casta.

caster sugar ['kɑːstə-] n zucchero semolato.

casting vote ['kɑːstɪŋ-] n (*BRIT*) voto decisivo.

cast iron n ghisa ♦ adj: **cast-iron** (*fig: will, alibi*) di ferro, d'acciaio.

castle ['kɑːsl] n castello; (*fortified*) rocca.

castor ['kɑːstə*] n (*wheel*) rotella.

castor oil n olio di ricino.

castrate [kæs'treɪt] vt castrare.

casual ['kæʒjul] adj (*by chance*) casuale, fortuito(a); (*irregular: work etc*) avventizio(a); (*unconcerned*) noncurante, indifferente; ~ **wear** casual m.

casual labour n manodopera avventizia.

casually ['kæʒjulɪ] adv con disinvoltura; (*by chance*) casualmente.

casualty ['kæʒjultɪ] n ferito/a; (*dead*) morto/a, vittima; **heavy casualties** npl grosse perdite fpl.

casualty ward n (*BRIT*) pronto soccorso.

cat [kæt] n gatto.

catacombs ['kætəkuːmz] npl catacombe fpl.

catalogue, (*US*) **catalog** ['kætələg] n catalogo ♦ vt catalogare.

catalyst ['kætəlɪst] n catalizzatore m.

catalytic converter [kætə'lɪtɪkkən'vɔːtə*] n marmitta catalitica, catalizzatore m.

catapult ['kætəpʌlt] n catapulta; fionda.

cataract ['kætərækt] n (*also MED*) cateratta.

catarrh [kə'tɑː*] n catarro.

catastrophe [kə'tæstrəfɪ] n catastrofe f.

catastrophic [kætə'strɔfɪk] adj catastrofico(a).

catcall ['kætkɔːl] n (*at meeting etc*) fischio.

catch [kætʃ] vb (pt, pp **caught** [kɔːt]) vt (*train, thief, cold*) acchiappare; (*ball*) afferrare; (*person: by surprise*) sorprendere; (*understand*) comprendere; (*get entangled*) impigliare ♦ vi (*fire*) prendere ♦ n (*fish etc caught*) retata, presa; (*trick*) inganno; (*TECH*) gancio; **to ~ sb's attention** or **eye** attirare l'attenzione di qn; **to ~ fire** prendere fuoco; **to ~ sight of** scorgere.

▶**catch on** vi (*become popular*) affermarsi, far presa; (*understand*): **to ~ on (to sth)** capire (qc).

▶**catch out** vt (*BRIT fig: with trick question*) cogliere in fallo.

▶**catch up** vi mettersi in pari ♦ vt (*also:* ~ **up with**) raggiungere.

catching ['kætʃɪŋ] adj (*MED*) contagioso(a).

catchment area ['kætʃmənt-] n (*BRIT SCOL*) circoscrizione f scolare; (*GEO*) bacino pluviale.

catch phrase n slogan m inv; frase f fatta.

catch-22 ['kætʃtwɛntɪ'tuː] n: **it's a ~ situation** non c'è via d'uscita.

catchy ['kætʃɪ] adj orecchiabile.

catechism ['kætɪkɪzəm] n catechismo.

categoric(al) [kætɪ'gɔrɪk(l)] adj categorico(a).

categorize ['kætɪgəraɪz] vt categorizzare.

category ['kætɪgərɪ] n categoria.

cater ['keɪtə*] vi (*gen:* ~ **for**) provvedere da mangiare (per).

▶**cater for** vt fus (*BRIT: needs*) provvedere a; (*: consumers*) incontrare i gusti di.

caterer ['keɪtərə*] n fornitore m.

catering ['keɪtərɪŋ] n approvvigionamento.

catering trade n settore m ristoranti.

caterpillar ['kætəpɪlə*] n (*ZOOL*) bruco ♦ cpd (*vehicle*) cingolato(a); ~ **track** cingolo.

cat flap n gattaiola.

cathedral [kə'θiːdrəl] n cattedrale f, duomo.

cathode ['kæθəud] n catodo.

cathode ray tube n tubo a raggi catodici.

catholic ['kæθəlɪk] adj universale; aperto(a); eclettico(a); **C~** adj, n (*REL*) cattolico(a).

CAT scanner [kæt-] n (*MED:* = *computerized axial tomography scanner*) (rilevatore m per la) TAC f inv.

cat's-eye ['kæts'aɪ] n (*BRIT AUT*) catarifrangente m.

catsup ['kætsəp] n (*US*) ketchup m inv.

cattle ['kætl] npl bestiame m, bestie fpl.

catty ['kætɪ] adj maligno(a), dispettoso(a).

catwalk ['kætwɔːk] n passerella.

Caucasian [kɔː'keɪzɪən] adj, n caucasico(a).

caucus ['kɔːkəs] n (*US POL*) (riunione f del) comitato elettorale; (*BRIT POL: group*) comitato di dirigenti; *see boxed note.*

CAUCUS

Caucus è il termine usato, specialmente negli Stati Uniti, per indicare una riunione informale dei rappresentanti di spicco di un partito politico che precede una riunione ufficiale. Con uso estensivo, la parola indica il nucleo direttivo di un partito politico.

---

caught [kɔːt] pt, pp of **catch**.

cauliflower ['kɔlɪflauə*] n cavolfiore m.

cause [kɔːz] *n* causa ♦ *vt* causare; **there is no** ~ **for concern** non c'è ragione di preoccuparsi; **to** ~ **sb to do sth** far fare qc a qn; **to** ~ **sth to be done** far fare qc.

causeway ['kɔːzweɪ] *n* strada rialzata.

caustic ['kɔːstɪk] *adj* caustico(a).

caution ['kɔːʃən] *n* prudenza; (*warning*) avvertimento ♦ *vt* ammonire.

cautious ['kɔːʃəs] *adj* cauto(a), prudente.

cautiously ['kɔːʃəslɪ] *adv* prudentemente.

cautiousness ['kɔːʃəsnɪs] *n* cautela.

cavalier [kævə'lɪə*] *n* (*knight*) cavaliere *m* ♦ *adj* (*pej: offhand*) brusco(a).

cavalry ['kævəlrɪ] *n* cavalleria.

cave [keɪv] *n* caverna, grotta ♦ *vi*: **to go caving** fare speleologia.

▶**cave in** *vi* (*roof etc*) crollare.

caveman ['keɪvmæn] *n* uomo delle caverne.

cavern ['kævən] *n* caverna.

caviar(e) ['kævɪɑː*] *n* caviale *m*.

cavity ['kævɪtɪ] *n* cavità *f inv*.

cavity wall insulation *n* isolamento per pareti a intercapedine.

cavort [kə'vɔːt] *vi* far capriole.

cayenne (pepper) [keɪ'ɛn-] *n* pepe *m* di Caienna.

CB *n abbr* (*BRIT:* = *Companion (of the Order) of the Bath*) titolo; (= *Citizens' Band (Radio)*) C.B. *m*; ~ **radio (set)** baracchino.

CBC *n abbr* = *Canadian Broadcasting Corporation*.

CBE *n abbr* (*BRIT:* = *Companion (of the Order) of the British Empire*) titolo.

CBI *n abbr* (= *Confederation of British Industry*) ≈ CONFINDUSTRIA (= *Confederazione Generale dell'Industria Italiana*).

CBS *n abbr* (*US*) = *Columbia Broadcasting System*.

CC *abbr* (*BRIT*) = *county council*.

cc *abbr* (= *cubic centimetre*) cc; (*on letter etc*) = **carbon copy**.

CCA *n abbr* (*US:* = *Circuit Court of Appeals*) corte *f* d'appello itinerante.

CCTV *n abbr* = **closed-circuit television**.

CCU *n abbr* (*US:* = *coronary care unit*) unità coronarica.

CD *n abbr* (= *compact disk*) compact disc *m inv*; ~ **player** lettore *m* CD; (*MIL*) = *Civil Defence (Corps)* (*BRIT*), *Civil Defense (US)* ♦ *abbr* (*BRIT:* = *Corps Diplomatique*) C.D.

CD burner *n* masterizzatore *m*.

CDC *n abbr* (*US*) = *center for disease control*.

CD-I ® *n* CD-I *m inv*, compact disc *m inv* interattivo.

Cdr. *abbr* (= *commander*) Com.

CD-ROM ['siː'diː'rɔm] *n abbr* (= *compact disc*

read-only memory) CD-ROM *m inv*.

CDT *abbr* (*US:* = *Central Daylight Time*) ora legale del centro; (*BRIT SCOL:* = *Craft, Design and Technology*) educazione tecnica.

CDW *n abbr see* **collision damage waiver**.

CD writer *n* masterizzatore *m*.

cease [siːs] *vt*, *vi* cessare.

ceasefire ['siːsfaɪə*] *n* cessate il fuoco *m inv*.

ceaseless ['siːslɪs] *adj* incessante.

CED *n abbr* (*US*) = *Committee for Economic Development*.

cedar ['siːdə*] *n* cedro.

cede [siːd] *vt* cedere.

CEEB *n abbr* (*US:* = *College Entrance Examination Board*) commissione *f* per l'esame di ammissione al college.

ceilidh ['keɪlɪ] *n festa con musiche e danze popolari scozzesi o irlandesi*.

ceiling ['siːlɪŋ] *n* soffitto; (*fig: upper limit*) tetto, limite *m* massimo.

celebrate ['sɛlɪbreɪt] *vt*, *vi* celebrare.

celebrated ['sɛlɪbreɪtɪd] *adj* celebre.

celebration [sɛlɪ'breɪʃən] *n* celebrazione *f*.

celebrity [sɪ'lɛbrɪtɪ] *n* celebrità *f inv*.

celeriac [sə'lɛrɪæk] *n* sedano *m* rapa *inv*.

celery ['sɛlərɪ] *n* sedano.

celestial [sɪ'lɛstɪəl] *adj* celeste.

celibacy ['sɛlɪbəsɪ] *n* celibato.

cell [sɛl] *n* cella; (*BIOL*) cellula; (*ELEC*) elemento (di batteria).

cellar ['sɛlə*] *n* sottosuolo, cantina.

cellist ['tʃɛlɪst] *n* violoncellista *m/f*.

cello ['tʃɛləu] *n* violoncello.

cellophane ® ['sɛləfeɪn] *n* cellophane ® *m*.

cellphone ['sɛlfəun] *n* cellulare *m*.

cellular ['sɛljulə*] *adj* cellulare.

celluloid ['sɛljulɔɪd] *n* celluloide *f*.

cellulose ['sɛljuləus] *n* cellulosa.

Celsius ['sɛlsɪəs] *adj* Celsius *inv*.

Celt [kɛlt, sɛlt] *n* celta *m/f*.

Celtic ['kɛltɪk, 'sɛltɪk] *adj* celtico(a) ♦ *n* (*LING*) celtico.

cement [sə'mɛnt] *n* cemento ♦ *vt* cementare.

cement mixer *n* betoniera.

cemetery ['sɛmɪtrɪ] *n* cimitero.

cenotaph ['sɛnətɑːf] *n* cenotafio.

censor ['sɛnsə*] *n* censore *m* ♦ *vt* censurare.

censorship ['sɛnsəʃɪp] *n* censura.

censure ['sɛnʃə*] *vt* censurare.

census ['sɛnsəs] *n* censimento.

cent [sɛnt] *n* (*of dollar, euro*) centesimo; *see also* **per cent**.

centenary [sɛn'tiːnərɪ], **centennial** [sɛn'tɛnɪəl] *n* centenario.

center ['sɛntə*] *n*, *vt* (*US*) = **centre**.

centigrade ['sɛntɪgreɪd] *adj* centigrado(a).

centilitre, (*US*) **centiliter** ['sɛntɪliːtə*] *n* centilitro.

centimetre, (*US*) **centimeter** ['sɛntɪmiːtə*] *n* centimetro.

centipede ['sɛntɪpiːd] *n* centopiedi *m inv.*

central ['sɛntrəl] *adj* centrale.

Central African Republic *n* Repubblica centrafricana.

Central America *n* America centrale.

central heating *n* riscaldamento centrale.

centralize ['sɛntrəlaɪz] *vt* accentrare.

central processing unit (CPU) *n* (*COMPUT*) unità *f inv* centrale di elaborazione.

central reservation *n* (*BRIT AUT*) banchina *f* spartitraffico *inv.*

centre, (*US*) **center** ['sɛntə*] *n* centro ♦ *vt* (*concentrate*): **to ~ (on)** concentrare (su).

centrefold, (*US*) **centerfold** ['sɛntəfəʊld] *n* (*PRESS*) poster *m* (all'interno di rivista).

centre-forward ['sɛntə'fɔːwəd] *n* (*SPORT*) centroavanti *m inv.*

centre-half ['sɛntə'hɑːf] *n* (*SPORT*) centromediano.

centrepiece, (*US*) **centerpiece** ['sɛntəpiːs] *n* centrotavola *m*; (*fig*) punto centrale.

centre spread *n* (*BRIT*) pubblicità a doppia pagina.

centre-stage [sɛntə'steɪdʒ] *n*: **to take ~** porsi al centro dell'attenzione.

centrifugal [sɛn'trɪfjugəl] *adj* centrifugo(a).

centrifuge ['sɛntrɪfjuːʒ] *n* centrifuga.

century ['sɛntjʊrɪ] *n* secolo; **in the twentieth ~** nel ventesimo secolo.

CEO *n abbr see* **chief executive officer.**

ceramic [sɪ'ræmɪk] *adj* ceramico(a).

cereal ['siːrɪəl] *n* cereale *m.*

cerebral ['sɛrɪbrəl] *adj* cerebrale.

ceremonial [sɛrɪ'məʊnɪəl] *n* cerimoniale *m*; (*rite*) rito.

ceremony ['sɛrɪmənɪ] *n* cerimonia; **to stand on ~** fare complimenti.

cert [səːt] *n* (*BRIT col*): **it's a dead ~** non c'è alcun dubbio.

certain ['səːtən] *adj* certo(a); **to make ~ of** assicurarsi di; **for ~** per certo, di sicuro.

certainly ['səːtənlɪ] *adv* certamente, certo.

certainty ['səːtəntɪ] *n* certezza.

certificate [sə'tɪfɪkɪt] *n* certificato; diploma *m.*

certified letter ['səːtɪfaɪd-] *n* (*US*) lettera raccomandata.

certified public accountant (CPA) ['səːtɪfaɪd-] *n* (*US*) ≈ commercialista *m/f.*

certify ['səːtɪfaɪ] *vt* certificare ♦ *vi*: **to ~ to** attestare a.

cervical ['səːvɪkl] *adj*: **~ cancer** cancro della

cervice, tumore *m* al collo dell'utero; **~ smear** Pap-test *m inv.*

cervix ['səːvɪks] *n* cervice *f.*

Cesarean [siː'zɛərɪən] *adj, n* (*US*) = **Caesarean.**

cessation [sə'seɪʃən] *n* cessazione *f*; arresto.

cesspit ['sɛspɪt] *n* pozzo nero.

CET *abbr* (= *Central European Time*) *fuso orario.*

Ceylon [sɪ'lɔn] *n* Ceylon *f.*

cf. *abbr* (= *compare*) cfr.

c/f *abbr* (*COMM*) = *carried forward.*

CFC *n abbr* (= *chlorofluorocarbon*) CFC *m inv.*

CG *n abbr* (*US*) = **coastguard.**

cg *abbr* (= *centigram*) cg.

CH *n abbr* (*BRIT*: = *Companion of Honour*) *titolo.*

ch. *abbr* (= *chapter*) cap.

Chad [tʃæd] *n* Chad *m.*

chafe [tʃeɪf] *vt* fregare, irritare ♦ *vi* (*fig*): **to ~ against** scontrarsi con.

chaffinch ['tʃæfɪntʃ] *n* fringuello.

chagrin ['ʃægrɪn] *n* disappunto, dispiacere *m.*

chain [tʃeɪn] *n* catena ♦ *vt* (*also*: ~ **up**) incatenare.

chain reaction *n* reazione *f* a catena.

chain-smoke ['tʃeɪnsməʊk] *vi* fumare una sigaretta dopo l'altra.

chain store *n* negozio a catena.

chair [tʃɛə*] *n* sedia; (*armchair*) poltrona; (*of university*) cattedra ♦ *vt* (*meeting*) presiedere; **the ~** (*US: electric ~*) la sedia elettrica.

chairlift ['tʃɛəlɪft] *n* seggiovia.

chairman ['tʃɛəmən] *n* presidente *m.*

chairperson ['tʃɛəpəːsn] *n* presidente/essa.

chairwoman ['tʃɛəwumən] *n* presidentessa.

chalet ['ʃæleɪ] *n* chalet *m inv.*

chalice ['tʃælɪs] *n* calice *m.*

chalk [tʃɔːk] *n* gesso.

▶**chalk up** *vt* scrivere col gesso; (*fig: success*) ottenere; (*: victory*) riportare.

challenge ['tʃælɪndʒ] *n* sfida ♦ *vt* sfidare; (*statement, right*) mettere in dubbio; **to ~ sb to a fight/game** sfidare qn a battersi/ ad una partita; **to ~ sb to do** sfidare qn a fare.

challenger ['tʃælɪndʒə*] *n* (*SPORT*) sfidante *m/f.*

challenging ['tʃælɪndʒɪŋ] *adj* sfidante; (*remark, look*) provocatorio(a).

chamber ['tʃeɪmbə*] *n* camera; **~ of commerce** camera di commercio.

chambermaid ['tʃeɪmbəmeɪd] *n* cameriera.

chamber music *n* musica da camera.

chamberpot ['tʃeɪmbəpɔt] *n* vaso da notte.
chameleon [kə'miːlɪən] *n* camaleonte *m*.
chamois ['ʃæmwɑː] *n* camoscio.
chamois leather ['ʃæmɪ-] *n* pelle *f* di camoscio.
champagne [ʃæm'peɪn] *n* champagne *m inv*.
champers ['ʃæmpəz] *nsg* (*col*) sciampagna.
champion ['tʃæmpɪən] *n* campione/essa; (*of cause*) difensore *m* ♦ *vt* difendere.
championship ['tʃæmpɪənʃɪp] *n* campionato.
chance [tʃɑːns] *n* caso; (*opportunity*) occasione *f*; (*likelihood*) possibilità *f inv* ♦ *vt*: **to ~ it** rischiare, provarci ♦ *adj* fortuito(a); **there is little ~ of his coming** è molto improbabile che venga; **to take a ~** rischiare; **by ~** per caso; **it's the ~ of a lifetime** è un'occasione unica; **the ~s are that ...** probabilmente ..., è probabile che ... + *sub*; **to ~ to do sth** (*formal: happen*) fare per caso qc.
►**chance (up)on** *vt fus* (*person*) incontrare per caso, imbattersi in; (*thing*) trovare per caso.
chancel ['tʃɑːnsəl] *n* coro.
chancellor ['tʃɑːnsələ*] *n* cancelliere *m*; (*of university*) rettore *m* (onorario); **C~ of the Exchequer** (*BRIT*) Cancelliere *m* dello Scacchiere.
chandelier [ʃændə'lɪə*] *n* lampadario.
change [tʃeɪndʒ] *vt* cambiare; (*transform*): **to ~ sb into** trasformare qn in ♦ *vi* cambiarsi; (*be transformed*): **to ~ into** trasformarsi in ♦ *n* cambiamento; (*money*) resto; **to ~ one's mind** cambiare idea; **to ~ gear** (*AUT*) cambiare (marcia); **she ~d into an old skirt** si è cambiata e ha messo una vecchia gonna; **a ~ of clothes** un cambio (di vestiti); **for a ~** tanto per cambiare; **small ~** spiccioli *mpl*, moneta; **keep the ~** tenga il resto; **can you give me ~ for £1?** mi può cambiare una sterlina?
changeable ['tʃeɪndʒəbl] *adj* (*weather*) variabile; (*person*) mutevole.
change machine *n* distributore *m* automatico di monete.
changeover ['tʃeɪndʒəʊvə*] *n* cambiamento, passaggio.
changing ['tʃeɪndʒɪŋ] *adj* che cambia; (*colours*) cangiante.
changing room *n* (*BRIT: in shop*) camerino; (: *SPORT*) spogliatoio.
channel ['tʃænl] *n* canale *m*; (*of river, sea*) alveo ♦ *vt* canalizzare; (*fig: interest, energies*): **to ~ into** concentrare su, indirizzare verso; **through the usual ~s** per le solite vie; **the (English) C~** la Manica; **green/red ~** (*CUSTOMS*) uscita "niente da dichiarare"/"merci da dichiarare".
channel-hopping ['tʃænl,hɔpɪŋ] *n* (*TV*) zapping *m*.
Channel Islands *npl*: **the ~** le Isole Normanne.
Channel Tunnel *n*: **the ~** il tunnel della Manica.
chant [tʃɑːnt] *n* canto; salmodia; (*of crowd*) slogan *m inv* ♦ *vt* cantare; salmodiare; **the demonstrators ~ed their disapproval** i dimostranti lanciavano slogan di protesta.
chaos ['keɪɔs] *n* caos *m*.
chaos theory *n* teoria del caos.
chaotic [keɪ'ɔtɪk] *adj* caotico(a).
chap [tʃæp] *n* (*BRIT col: man*) tipo ♦ *vt* (*skin*) screpolare; **old ~** vecchio mio.
chapel ['tʃæpl] *n* cappella.
chaperone ['ʃæpərəʊn] *n* accompagnatore/trice ♦ *vt* accompagnare.
chaplain ['tʃæplɪn] *n* cappellano.
chapped [tʃæpt] *adj* (*skin, lips*) screpolato(a).
chapter ['tʃæptə*] *n* capitolo.
char [tʃɑː*] *vt* (*burn*) carbonizzare ♦ *vi* (*BRIT: cleaner*) lavorare come domestica (a ore) ♦ *n* (*BRIT*) = **charlady**.
character ['kærɪktə*] *n* (*gen, COMPUT*) carattere *m*; (*in novel, film*) personaggio; (*eccentric*) originale *m*; **a person of good ~** una persona a modo.
character code *n* (*COMPUT*) codice *m* di carattere.
characteristic ['kærɪktə'rɪstɪk] *adj* caratteristico(a) ♦ *n* caratteristica; **~ of** tipico(a) di.
characterize ['kærɪktəraɪz] *vt* caratterizzare; (*describe*): **to ~ (as)** descrivere (come).
charade [ʃə'rɑːd] *n* sciarada.
charcoal ['tʃɑːkəʊl] *n* carbone *m* di legna.
charge [tʃɑːdʒ] *n* accusa; (*cost*) prezzo; (*of gun, battery, MIL: attack*) carica ♦ *vt* (*gun, battery, MIL: enemy*) caricare; (*customer*) fare pagare a; (*sum*) fare pagare; (*LAW*): **to ~ sb (with)** accusare qn (di) ♦ *vi* (*gen with: up, along etc*) lanciarsi; **~s** *npl*: **bank ~s** commissioni *fpl* bancarie; **labour ~s** costi *mpl* del lavoro; **to ~ in/out** precipitarsi dentro/fuori; **to ~ up/down** lanciarsi su/giù per; **is there a ~?** c'è da pagare?; **there's no ~** non c'è niente da pagare; **extra ~** supplemento; **to take ~ of** incaricarsi di; **to be in ~ of** essere responsabile per; **to have ~ of sb** aver cura di qn; **how much do you ~ for this**

repair? quanto chiede per la riparazione?; **to ~ an expense (up) to sb** addebitare una spesa a qn; **~ it to my account** lo metta *or* addebiti sul mio conto.

charge account *n* conto.

charge card *n* carta di credito commerciale.

chargé d'affaires ['ʃɑːʒeɪdæ'fɛə*] *n* incaricato d'affari.

chargehand ['tʃɑːdʒhænd] *n* (*BRIT*) caposquadra *m/f*.

charger ['tʃɑːdʒə*] *n* (*also*: **battery ~**) caricabatterie *m inv*; (*old*: *warhorse*) destriero.

chariot ['tʃærɪət] *n* carro.

charitable ['tʃærɪtəbl] *adj* caritatevole.

charity ['tʃærɪtɪ] *n* carità; (*organization*) opera pia.

charlady ['tʃɑːleɪdɪ] *n* (*BRIT*) domestica a ore.

charlatan ['ʃɑːlətən] *n* ciarlatano.

charm [tʃɑːm] *n* fascino; (*on bracelet*) ciondolo ♦ *vt* affascinare, incantare.

charm bracelet *n* braccialetto con ciondoli.

charming ['tʃɑːmɪŋ] *adj* affascinante.

chart [tʃɑːt] *n* tabella; grafico; (*map*) carta nautica; (*weather ~*) carta del tempo ♦ *vt* fare una carta nautica di; (*sales, progress*) tracciare il grafico di; **to be in the ~s** (*record, pop group*) essere in classifica.

charter ['tʃɑːtə*] *vt* (*plane*) noleggiare ♦ *n* (*document*) carta; **on ~** a nolo.

chartered accountant (CA) ['tʃɑːtəd-] *n* (*BRIT*) ragioniere/a professionista.

charter flight *n* volo *m* charter *inv*.

charwoman ['tʃɑːwumən] *n* = **charlady**.

chase [tʃeɪs] *vt* inseguire; (*also*: **~ away**) cacciare ♦ *n* caccia.

▶**chase down** *vt* (*US*) = **chase up**.

▶**chase up** *vt* (*BRIT*: *person*) scovare; (*: information*) scoprire, raccogliere.

chasm ['kæzəm] *n* abisso.

chassis ['ʃæsɪ] *n* telaio.

chastened ['tʃeɪsnd] *adj* abbattuto(a), provato(a).

chastening ['tʃeɪsnɪŋ] *adj* che fa riflettere.

chastise [tʃæs'taɪz] *vt* punire, castigare.

chastity ['tʃæstɪtɪ] *n* castità.

chat [tʃæt] *vi* (*also*: **have a ~**) chiacchierare ♦ *n* chiacchierata.

▶**chat up** *vt* (*BRIT col*: *girl*) abbordare.

chatline ['tʃætlaɪn] *n* chat line *f inv*.

chat room *n* chat line *f inv*.

chat show *n* (*BRIT*) talk show *m inv*, conversazione *f* televisiva.

chattel ['tʃætl] *n see* **goods**.

chatter ['tʃætə*] *vi* (*person*) ciarlare ♦ *n*

ciarle *fpl*; **her teeth were ~ing** batteva i denti.

chatterbox ['tʃætəbɔks] *n* chiacchierone/a.

chattering classes ['tʃætərɪŋ-] *npl*: **the ~** (*col, pej*) ≈ gli intellettuali da salotto.

chatty ['tʃætɪ] *adj* (*style*) familiare; (*person*) chiacchierino(a).

chauffeur ['ʃəufə*] *n* autista *m*.

chauvinism ['ʃəuvɪnɪzəm] *n* (*also*: **male ~**) maschilismo; (*nationalism*) sciovinismo.

chauvinist ['ʃəuvɪnɪst] *n* (*also*: **male ~**) maschilista *m*; (*nationalist*) sciovinista *m/f*.

chauvinistic [ʃəuvɪ'nɪstɪk] *adj* sciovinistico(a).

ChE *abbr* = *chemical engineer*.

cheap [tʃiːp] *adj* a buon mercato; (*reduced*: *fare, ticket*) ridotto(a); (*joke*) grossolano(a); (*poor quality*) di cattiva qualità ♦ *adv* a buon mercato; **~er** meno caro; **~ day return** biglietto giornaliero ridotto di andata e ritorno; **~ money** denaro a basso tasso di interesse.

cheapen ['tʃiːpn] *vt* ribassare; (*fig*) avvilire.

cheaply ['tʃiːplɪ] *adv* a buon prezzo, a buon mercato.

cheat [tʃiːt] *vi* imbrogliare; (*at school*) copiare ♦ *vt* ingannare; (*rob*) defraudare ♦ *n* imbroglione *m*; copione *m*; (*trick*) inganno; **he's been ~ing on his wife** ha tradito sua moglie.

cheating ['tʃiːtɪŋ] *n* imbrogliare *m*; copiare *m*.

check [tʃɛk] *vt* verificare; (*passport, ticket*) controllare; (*halt*) fermare; (*restrain*) contenere ♦ *vi* (*official etc*) informarsi ♦ *n* verifica; controllo; (*curb*) freno; (*bill*) conto; (*pattern*: *gen pl*) quadretti *mpl*; (*US*) = **cheque** ♦ *adj* (*also*: **~ed**: *pattern, cloth*) a scacchi, a quadretti; **to ~ with sb** chiedere a qn; **to keep a ~ on sb/sth** controllare qn/qc.

▶**check in** *vi* (*in hotel*) registrare; (*at airport*) presentarsi all'accettazione ♦ *vt* (*luggage*) depositare.

▶**check off** *vt* segnare.

▶**check out** *vi* (*from hotel*) saldare il conto ♦ *vt* (*luggage*) ritirare; (*investigate*: *story*) controllare, verificare; (*: person*) prendere informazioni su.

▶**check up** *vi*: **to ~ up (on sth)** investigare (qc); **to ~ up on sb** informarsi sul conto di qn.

checkbook ['tʃɛkbuk] *n* (*US*) = **chequebook**.

checkered ['tʃɛkəd] *adj* (*US*) = **chequered**.

checkers ['tʃɛkəz] *n* (*US*) dama.

check guarantee card *n* (*US*) carta *f*

assegni *inv*.

check-in ['tʃɛkɪn] *n* (*also*: ~ **desk**: *at airport*) check-in *m inv*, accettazione *f* (bagagli *inv*).

checking account ['tʃɛkɪŋ-] *n* (*US*) conto corrente.

checklist ['tʃɛklɪst] *n* lista di controllo.

checkmate ['tʃɛkmeɪt] *n* scaccomatto.

checkout ['tʃɛkaut] *n* (*in supermarket*) cassa.

checkpoint ['tʃɛkpɔɪnt] *n* posto di blocco.

checkroom ['tʃɛkrum] *n* (*US*) deposito *m* bagagli *inv*.

checkup ['tʃɛkʌp] *n* (*MED*) controllo medico.

cheek [tʃiːk] *n* guancia; (*impudence*) faccia tosta.

cheekbone ['tʃiːkbəun] *n* zigomo.

cheeky ['tʃiːkɪ] *adj* sfacciato(a).

cheep [tʃiːp] *n* (*of bird*) pigolio ♦ *vi* pigolare.

cheer [tʃɪə*] *vt* applaudire; (*gladden*) rallegrare ♦ *vi* applaudire ♦ *n* (*gen pl*) applausi *mpl*; evviva *mpl*; ~s! salute!

►**cheer on** *vt* (*person etc*) incitare.

►**cheer up** *vi* rallegrarsi, farsi animo ♦ *vt* rallegrare.

cheerful ['tʃɪəful] *adj* allegro(a).

cheerfulness ['tʃɪəfulnɪs] *n* allegria.

cheerio ['tʃɪərɪ'əu] *excl* (*BRIT*) ciao!

cheerleader ['tʃɪəliːdə*] *n* cheerleader *f inv*.

cheerless ['tʃɪəlɪs] *adj* triste.

cheese [tʃiːz] *n* formaggio.

cheeseboard ['tʃiːzbɔːd] *n* piatto del (*or* per il) formaggio.

cheeseburger ['tʃiːzbəːgə*] *n* cheeseburger *m inv*.

cheesecake ['tʃiːzkeɪk] *n* specie di torta di ricotta, a volte con frutta.

cheetah ['tʃiːtə] *n* ghepardo.

chef [ʃɛf] *n* capocuoco.

chemical ['kɛmɪkl] *adj* chimico(a) ♦ *n* prodotto chimico.

chemical engineering *n* ingegneria chimica.

chemist ['kɛmɪst] *n* (*BRIT*: *pharmacist*) farmacista *m/f*; (*scientist*) chimico/a; ~'s **shop** *n* (*BRIT*) farmacia.

chemistry ['kɛmɪstrɪ] *n* chimica.

chemo ['kiːməu] *n* chemio *f inv*.

chemotherapy [kiːməu'θɛrəpɪ] *n* chemioterapia.

cheque, (*US*) **check** [tʃɛk] *n* assegno; **to pay by** ~ pagare per assegno *or* con un assegno.

chequebook, (*US*) **checkbook** ['tʃɛkbuk] *n* libretto degli assegni.

cheque card *n* (*BRIT*) carta *f* assegni *inv*.

chequered, (*US*) **checkered** ['tʃɛkəd] *adj* (*fig*) movimentato(a).

cherish ['tʃɛrɪʃ] *vt* aver caro; (*hope etc*) nutrire.

cheroot [ʃə'ruːt] *n* sigaro spuntato.

cherry ['tʃɛrɪ] *n* ciliegia.

Ches *abbr* (*BRIT*) = Cheshire.

chess [tʃɛs] *n* scacchi *mpl*.

chessboard ['tʃɛsbɔːd] *n* scacchiera.

chessman ['tʃɛsmæn] *n* pezzo degli scacchi.

chessplayer ['tʃɛspleɪə*] *n* scacchista *m/f*.

chest [tʃɛst] *n* petto; (*box*) cassa; **to get sth off one's** ~ (*col*) sputare il rospo; ~ **of drawers** cassettone *m*.

chest measurement *n* giro *m* torace *inv*.

chestnut ['tʃɛsnʌt] *n* castagna; (*also*: ~ *tree*) castagno ♦ *adj* castano(a).

chesty ['tʃɛstɪ] *adj*: ~ **cough** tosse *f* bronchiale.

chew [tʃuː] *vt* masticare.

chewing gum ['tʃuːɪŋ-] *n* chewing gum *m*.

chic [ʃiːk] *adj* elegante.

chick [tʃɪk] *n* pulcino; (*US col*) pollastrella.

chicken ['tʃɪkɪn] *n* pollo; (*col*: *coward*) coniglio.

►**chicken out** *vi* (*col*) avere fifa; **to** ~ **out of sth** tirarsi indietro da qc per fifa *or* paura.

chicken feed *n* (*fig*) miseria.

chickenpox ['tʃɪkɪnpɔks] *n* varicella.

chick flick *n* (*col*) filmetto rosa.

chickpea ['tʃɪkpiː] *n* cece *m*.

chicory ['tʃɪkərɪ] *n* cicoria.

chide [tʃaɪd] *vt* rimproverare.

chief [tʃiːf] *n* capo ♦ *adj* principale; **C~ of Staff** (*MIL*) Capo di Stato Maggiore.

chief constable *n* (*BRIT*) ≈ questore *m*.

chief executive, (*US*) **chief executive officer (CEO)** *n* direttore *m* generale.

chiefly ['tʃiːflɪ] *adv* per lo più, soprattutto.

chiffon ['ʃɪfən] *n* chiffon *m inv*.

chilblain ['tʃɪlbleɪn] *n* gelone *m*.

child, *pl* ~ren [tʃaɪld, 'tʃɪldrən] *n* bambino/a.

child abuse *n* molestie *fpl* a minori.

child abuser [-ə'bjuːzə*] *n* molestatore/trice di bambini.

child benefit *n* (*BRIT*) ≈ assegni *mpl* familiari.

childbirth ['tʃaɪldbəːθ] *n* parto.

childhood ['tʃaɪldhud] *n* infanzia.

childish ['tʃaɪldɪʃ] *adj* puerile.

childless ['tʃaɪldlɪs] *adj* senza figli.

childlike ['tʃaɪldlaɪk] *adj* fanciullesco(a).

child minder *n* (*BRIT*) bambinaia.

child prodigy *n* bambino *m* prodigio *inv*.

children ['tʃɪldrən] *npl of* child.

children's home *n* istituto per l'infanzia.

Chile ['tʃɪlɪ] *n* Cile *m*.

Chilean ['tʃɪlɪən] *adj, n* cileno(a).
chill [tʃɪl] *n* freddo; (*MED*) infreddatura ♦ *adj* freddo(a), gelido(a) ♦ *vt* raffreddare; (*CULIN*) mettere in fresco; **"serve ~ed"** "servire fresco".
▶**chill out** *vi* (*esp US*: *col*) darsi una calmata.
chilli, (US) chili ['tʃɪlɪ] *n* peperoncino.
chilling ['tʃɪlɪŋ] *adj* agghiacciante; (*wind*) gelido(a).
chilly ['tʃɪlɪ] *adj* freddo(a), fresco(a); (*sensitive to cold*) freddoloso(a); **to feel ~** sentirsi infreddolito(a).
chime [tʃaɪm] *n* carillon *m inv* ♦ *vi* suonare, scampanare.
chimney ['tʃɪmnɪ] *n* camino.
chimney sweep *n* spazzacamino.
chimpanzee [tʃɪmpæn'zi:] *n* scimpanzé *m inv*.
chin [tʃɪn] *n* mento.
China ['tʃaɪnə] *n* Cina.
china ['tʃaɪnə] *n* porcellana.
Chinese [tʃaɪ'ni:z] *adj* cinese ♦ *n* (*pl inv*) cinese *m/f*; (*LING*) cinese *m*.
chink [tʃɪŋk] *n* (*opening*) fessura; (*noise*) tintinnio.
chip [tʃɪp] *n* (*gen pl: CULIN*) patatina fritta; (: *US*: *also*: **potato ~**) patatina; (*of wood, glass, stone*) scheggia; (*in gambling*) fiche *f inv*; (*COMPUT*: **micro~**) chip *m inv* ♦ *vt* (*cup, plate*) scheggiare; **when the ~s are down** (*fig*) al momento critico.
▶**chip in** *vi* (*col*: *contribute*) contribuire; (: *interrupt*) intromettersi.
chipboard ['tʃɪpbɔ:d] *n* agglomerato.
chipmunk ['tʃɪpmʌŋk] *n* tamia *m* striato.
chippings ['tʃɪpɪŋz] *npl*: **loose ~** brecciame *m*.
chip shop *n* (*BRIT*) *see boxed note.*

> **CHIP SHOP**
>
> *I* **chip shops**, *anche chiamati "fish-and-chip shops", sono friggitorie che vendono principalmente filetti di pesce impanati e patatine fritte che un tempo venivano serviti ai clienti avvolti in carta di giornale.*

chiropodist [kɪ'rɔpədɪst] *n* (*BRIT*) pedicure *m/f inv*.
chiropody [kɪ'rɔpədɪ] *n* (*BRIT*) mestiere *m* di callista.
chirp [tʃə:p] *n* cinguettio; (*of crickets*) cri cri *m* ♦ *vi* cinguettare.
chirpy ['tʃə:pɪ] *adj* (*col*) frizzante.
chisel ['tʃɪzl] *n* cesello.
chit [tʃɪt] *n* biglietto.
chitchat ['tʃɪttʃæt] *n* (*col*) chiacchiere *fpl*.

chivalrous ['ʃɪvəlrəs] *adj* cavalleresco(a).
chivalry ['ʃɪvəlrɪ] *n* cavalleria; cortesia.
chives [tʃaɪvz] *npl* erba cipollina.
chloride ['klɔ:raɪd] *n* cloruro.
chlorinate ['klɔrɪneɪt] *vt* clorare.
chlorine ['klɔ:ri:n] *n* cloro.
chock-a-block ['tʃɔkə'blɔk], **chockfull** ['tʃɔk'ful] *adj* pieno(a) zeppo(a).
chocolate ['tʃɔklɪt] *n* (*substance*) cioccolato, cioccolata; (*drink*) cioccolata; (*a sweet*) cioccolatino.
choice [tʃɔɪs] *n* scelta ♦ *adj* scelto(a); **a wide ~** un'ampia scelta; **I did it by** *or* **from ~** l'ho fatto di mia volontà *or* per mia scelta.
choir ['kwaɪə*] *n* coro.
choirboy ['kwaɪəbɔɪ] *n* corista *m* fanciullo.
choke [tʃəuk] *vi* soffocare ♦ *vt* soffocare; (*block*) ingombrare ♦ *n* (*AUT*) valvola dell'aria.
cholera ['kɔlərə] *n* colera *m*.
cholesterol [kə'lɛstərəl] *n* colesterolo.
choose, *pt* chose, *pp* chosen [tʃu:z, tʃəuz, 'tʃəuzn] *vt* scegliere; **to ~ to do** decidere di fare; preferire fare; **to ~ between** scegliere tra; **to ~ from** scegliere da *or* tra.
choosy ['tʃu:zɪ] *adj*: **(to be) ~** (fare lo(la)) schizzinoso(a).
chop [tʃɔp] *vt* (*wood*) spaccare; (*CULIN*: *also*: **~ up**) tritare ♦ *n* colpo netto; (*CULIN*) costoletta; **to get the ~** (*BRIT col*: *project*) essere bocciato(a); (: *person: be sacked*) essere licenziato(a); *see also* **chops**.
▶**chop down** *vt* (*tree*) abbattere.
choppy ['tʃɔpɪ] *adj* (*sea*) mosso(a).
chops [tʃɔps] *npl* (*jaws*) mascelle *fpl*.
chopsticks ['tʃɔpstɪks] *npl* bastoncini *mpl* cinesi.
choral ['kɔːrəl] *adj* corale.
chord [kɔːd] *n* (*MUS*) accordo.
chore [tʃɔː*] *n* faccenda; **household ~s** faccende *fpl* domestiche.
choreographer [kɔrɪ'ɔɡrəfə*] *n* coreografo/a.
choreography [kɔrɪ'ɔɡrəfɪ] *n* coreografia.
chorister ['kɔrɪstə*] *n* corista *m/f*.
chortle ['tʃɔːtl] *vi* ridacchiare.
chorus ['kɔːrəs] *n* coro; (*repeated part of song, also fig*) ritornello.
chose [tʃəuz] *pt of* **choose**.
chosen ['tʃəuzn] *pp of* **choose**.
chowder ['tʃaudə*] *n* zuppa di pesce.
Christ [kraɪst] *n* Cristo.
christen ['krɪsn] *vt* battezzare.
christening ['krɪsnɪŋ] *n* battesimo.
Christian ['krɪstɪən] *adj, n* cristiano(a).
Christianity [krɪstɪ'ænɪtɪ] *n* cristianesimo.

Christian name *n* nome *m* di battesimo.
Christmas ['krɪsməs] *n* Natale *m*; **happy** *or* **merry** ~! Buon Natale!
Christmas card *n* cartolina di Natale.
Christmas Day *n* il giorno di Natale.
Christmas Eve *n* la vigilia di Natale.
Christmas Island *n* isola di Christmas.
Christmas tree *n* albero di Natale.
chrome [krəum] *n* = **chromium**.
chromium ['krəumɪəm] *n* cromo; (*also:* ~ **plating**) cromatura.
chromosome ['krəuməsəum] *n* cromosoma *m*.
chronic ['krɒnɪk] *adj* cronico(a); (*fig: liar, smoker*) incallito(a).
chronicle ['krɒnɪkl] *n* cronaca.
chronological [krɒnə'lɒdʒɪkl] *adj* cronologico(a).
chrysanthemum [krɪ'sænθəməm] *n* crisantemo.
chubby ['tʃʌbɪ] *adj* paffuto(a).
chuck [tʃʌk] *vt* buttare, gettare; **to** ~ (**up** *or* **in**) (*BRIT: job, person*) piantare.
▶**chuck out** *vt* buttar fuori.
chuckle ['tʃʌkl] *vi* ridere sommessamente.
chuffed [tʃʌft] *adj* (*col*): **to be** ~ **about sth** essere arcicontento(a) di qc.
chug [tʃʌg] *vi* (*also:* ~ **along**: *train*) muoversi sbuffando.
chum [tʃʌm] *n* compagno/a.
chump [tʃʌmp] *n* (*col*) idiota *m/f*.
chunk [tʃʌŋk] *n* pezzo; (*of bread*) tocco.
chunky [tʃʌŋkɪ] *adj* (*furniture etc*) basso(a) e largo(a); (*person*) ben piantato(a); (*knitwear*) di lana grossa.
Chunnel ['tʃʌnəl] *n* = **Channel Tunnel**.
church [tʃəːtʃ] *n* chiesa; **the C**~ **of England** la Chiesa anglicana.
churchyard ['tʃəːtʃjɑːd] *n* sagrato.
churlish ['tʃəːlɪʃ] *adj* rozzo(a), sgarbato(a).
churn [tʃəːn] *n* (*for butter*) zangola; (*also:* **milk** ~) bidone *m*.
▶**churn out** *vt* sfornare.
chute [ʃuːt] *n* cascata; (*also:* **rubbish** ~) canale *m* di scarico; (*BRIT: children's slide*) scivolo.
chutney ['tʃʌtnɪ] *n* salsa piccante (di frutta, zucchero e spezie).
CIA *n abbr* (*US:* = *Central Intelligence Agency*) C.I.A. *f*.
CID *n abbr* (*BRIT*) *see* **Criminal Investigation Department**.
cider ['saɪdə*] *n* sidro.
CIF *abbr* (= *cost, insurance, and freight*) C.I.F. *m*.
cigar [sɪ'gɑː*] *n* sigaro.
cigarette [sɪgə'rɛt] *n* sigaretta.
cigarette case *n* portasigarette *m inv*.

cigarette end *n* mozzicone *m*.
cigarette holder *n* bocchino.
C-in-C *abbr see* **commander-in-chief**.
cinch [sɪntʃ] *n* (*col*): **it's a** ~ è presto fatto; (*sure thing*) è una cosa sicura.
cinder ['sɪndə*] *n* cenere *f*.
Cinderella [sɪndə'rɛlə] *n* Cenerentola.
cine-camera ['sɪnɪ'kæmərə] *n* (*BRIT*) cinepresa.
cine-film ['sɪnɪfɪlm] *n* (*BRIT*) pellicola.
cinema ['sɪnəmə] *n* cinema *m inv*.
cine-projector ['sɪnɪprə'dʒɛktə*] *n* (*BRIT*) proiettore *m*.
cinnamon ['sɪnəmən] *n* cannella.
cipher ['saɪfə*] *n* cifra; (*fig: faceless employee etc*) persona di nessun conto; **in** ~ in codice.
circa ['səːkə] *prep* circa.
circle ['səːkl] *n* cerchio; (*of friends etc*) circolo; (*in cinema*) galleria ♦ *vi* girare in circolo ♦ *vt* (*surround*) circondare; (*move round*) girare intorno a.
circuit ['səːkɪt] *n* circuito.
circuit board *n* (*COMPUT*) tavola dei circuiti.
circuitous [səː'kjuɪtəs] *adj* indiretto(a).
circular ['səːkjulə*] *adj* circolare ♦ *n* (*letter*) circolare *f*; (*as advertisement*) volantino pubblicitario.
circulate ['səːkjuleɪt] *vi* circolare; (*person: socially*) girare e andare un po' da tutti ♦ *vt* far circolare.
circulating capital ['səːkjuleɪtɪŋ-] *n* (*COMM*) capitale *m* d'esercizio.
circulation [səːkju'leɪʃən] *n* circolazione *f*; (*of newspaper*) tiratura.
circumcise ['səːkəmsaɪz] *vt* circoncidere.
circumference [sə'kʌmfərəns] *n* circonferenza.
circumflex ['səːkəmflɛks] *n* (*also:* ~ **accent**) accento circonflesso.
circumscribe ['səːkəmskraɪb] *vt* circoscrivere; (*fig: limit*) limitare.
circumspect ['səːkəmspɛkt] *adj* circospetto(a).
circumstances ['səːkəmstənsɪz] *npl* circostanze *fpl*; (*financial condition*) condizioni *fpl* finanziarie; **in the** ~**s** date le circostanze; **under no** ~**s** per nessun motivo.
circumstantial ['səːkəm'stænʃəl] *adj* (*report, statement*) circostanziato(a), dettagliato(a); ~ **evidence** prova indiretta.
circumvent [səːkəm'vɛnt] *vt* (*rule etc*) aggirare.
circus ['səːkəs] *n* circo; (*also:* **C**~: *in place names*) piazza (di forma circolare).

cirrhosis [sɪ'rəʊsɪs] *n* (*also*: ~ **of the liver**) cirrosi *f inv* (epatica).
CIS *n abbr* (= *Commonwealth of Independent States*) CSI *f*.
cissy ['sɪsɪ] *n* = **sissy**.
cistern ['sɪstən] *n* cisterna; (*in toilet*) serbatoio d'acqua.
citation [saɪ'teɪʃən] *n* citazione *f*.
cite [saɪt] *vt* citare.
citizen ['sɪtɪzn] *n* (*POL*) cittadino/a; (*resident*): **the ~s of this town** gli abitanti di questa città.
Citizens' Advice Bureau *n* (*BRIT*) *organizzazione di volontari che offre gratuitamente assistenza legale e finanziaria*.
citizenship ['sɪtɪznʃɪp] *n* cittadinanza.
citric ['sɪtrɪk] *adj*: ~ **acid** acido citrico.
citrus fruit ['sɪtrəs-] *n* agrume *m*.
city ['sɪtɪ] *n* città *f inv*; **the C~** la Città di Londra (*centro commerciale*).
city centre *n* centro della città.
City Hall *n* (*US*) ≈ Comune *m*.
City Technology College *n* (*BRIT*) istituto tecnico superiore (*finanziato dall'industria*).
civic ['sɪvɪk] *adj* civico(a).
civic centre *n* (*BRIT*) centro civico.
civil ['sɪvɪl] *adj* civile; (*polite*) educato(a), gentile.
civil disobedience *n* disubbidienza civile.
civil engineer *n* ingegnere *m* civile.
civil engineering *n* ingegneria civile.
civilian [sɪ'vɪlɪən] *adj, n* borghese (*m/f*).
civilization [sɪvɪlaɪ'zeɪʃən] *n* civiltà *f inv*.
civilized ['sɪvɪlaɪzd] *adj* civilizzato(a); (*fig*) cortese.
civil law *n* codice *m* civile; (*study*) diritto civile.
civil liberties *npl* libertà *fpl* civili.
civil rights *npl* diritti *mpl* civili.
civil servant *n* impiegato/a statale.
Civil Service *n* amministrazione *f* statale.
civil war *n* guerra civile.
civvies ['sɪvɪz] *npl* (*col*): **in** ~ in borghese.
CJD *n abbr* (= *Creutzfeldt-Jakob disease*) malattia di Creutzfeldt-Jakob.
cl *abbr* (= *centilitre*) cl.
clad [klæd] *adj*: ~ (**in**) vestito(a) (di).
claim [kleɪm] *vt* (*rights etc*) rivendicare; (*damages*) richiedere; (*assert*) sostenere, pretendere ♦ *vi* (*for insurance*) fare una domanda d'indennizzo ♦ *n* rivendicazione *f*; pretesa; (*right*) diritto; **to** ~ **that/to be** sostenere che/di essere; (**insurance**) ~ domanda d'indennizzo; **to put in a** ~ **for sth** fare una richiesta di qc.
claimant ['kleɪmənt] *n* (*ADMIN, LAW*)

richiedente *m/f*.
claim form *n* (*gen*) modulo di richiesta; (*for expenses*) modulo di rimborso spese.
clairvoyant [klɛə'vɔɪənt] *n* chiaroveggente *m/f*.
clam [klæm] *n* vongola.
▶**clam up** *vi* (*col*) azzittirsi.
clamber ['klæmbə*] *vi* arrampicarsi.
clammy ['klæmɪ] *adj* (*weather*) caldo(a) umido(a); (*hands*) viscido(a).
clamour, (*US*) **clamor** ['klæmə*] *n* (*noise*) clamore *m*; (*protest*) protesta ♦ *vi*: **to** ~ **for sth** chiedere a gran voce qc.
clamp [klæmp] *n* pinza; morsa ♦ *vt* ammorsare.
▶**clamp down** *vt fus* (*fig*): **to** ~ **down (on)** dare un giro di vite (a).
clampdown ['klæmpdaun] *n* stretta, giro di vite; **a** ~ **on sth/sb** un giro di vite a qc/ qn.
clan [klæn] *n* clan *m inv*.
clandestine [klæn'dɛstɪn] *adj* clandestino(a).
clang [klæŋ] *n* fragore *m*, suono metallico.
clanger ['klæŋə*] *n*: **to drop a** ~ (*BRIT col*) fare una gaffe.
clansman ['klænzmən] *n* membro di un clan.
clap [klæp] *vi* applaudire ♦ *vt*: **to** ~ **one's hands** battere le mani ♦ *n*: **a** ~ **of thunder** un tuono.
clapping ['klæpɪŋ] *n* applausi *mpl*.
claptrap ['klæptræp] *n* (*col*) stupidaggini *fpl*.
claret ['klærət] *n* vino di Bordeaux.
clarification [klærɪfɪ'keɪʃən] *n* (*fig*) chiarificazione *f*, chiarimento.
clarify ['klærɪfaɪ] *vt* chiarificare, chiarire.
clarinet [klærɪ'nɛt] *n* clarinetto.
clarity ['klærɪtɪ] *n* chiarezza.
clash [klæʃ] *n* frastuono; (*fig*) scontro ♦ *vi* (*MIL, fig: have an argument*) scontrarsi; (*colours*) stridere; (*dates, events*) coincidere.
clasp [klɑːsp] *n* fermaglio, fibbia ♦ *vt* stringere.
class [klɑːs] *n* classe *f*; (*group, category*) tipo, categoria ♦ *vt* classificare.
class-conscious ['klɑːskɔnʃəs] *adj* che ha coscienza di classe.
class consciousness *n* coscienza di classe.
classic ['klæsɪk] *adj* classico(a) ♦ *n* classico.
classical ['klæsɪkəl] *adj* classico(a).
classics ['klæsɪks] *npl* (*SCOL*) studi *mpl* umanistici.
classification [klæsɪfɪ'keɪʃən] *n* classificazione *f*.
classified ['klæsɪfaɪd] *adj* (*information*)

segreto(a), riservato(a); ~ **ads** annunci economici.

classify ['klæsifai] vt classificare.

classless society ['klɑːslɪs-] n società f inv senza distinzioni di classe.

classmate ['klɑːsmeit] n compagno/a di classe.

classroom ['klɑːsrum] n aula.

classroom assistant n assistente m/f in classe dell'insegnante.

clatter ['klætə*] n acciottolio; scalpitio ♦ vi acciottolare; scalpitare.

clause [klɔːz] n clausola; (LING) proposizione f.

claustrophobia [klɔːstrə'fəubiə] n claustrofobia.

claustrophobic [klɔːstrə'fəubik] adj claustrofobico(a).

claw [klɔː] n tenaglia; (of bird of prey) artiglio; (of lobster) pinza ♦ vt graffiare; afferrare.

clay [klei] n argilla.

clean [kliːn] adj pulito(a); (clear, smooth) netto(a) ♦ vt pulire ♦ adv: he ~ **forgot** si è completamente dimenticato; **to come ~** (col: admit guilt) confessare; **to have a ~ driving licence** or (US) **record** non aver mai preso contravvenzioni; **to ~ one's teeth** (BRIT) lavarsi i denti.

▶**clean off** vt togliere.

▶**clean out** vt ripulire.

▶**clean up** vi far pulizia ♦ vt (also fig) ripulire; (fig: make profit): **to ~ up on** fare una barca di soldi con.

clean-cut ['kliːn'kʌt] adj (man) curato(a); (situation etc) ben definito(a).

cleaner ['kliːnə*] n (person) uomo/donna delle pulizie; (also: **dry ~**) tintore/a; (product) smacchiatore m.

cleaning ['kliːnɪŋ] n pulizia.

cleaning lady n donna delle pulizie.

cleanliness ['klɛnlɪnɪs] n pulizia.

cleanly ['kliːnlɪ] adv in modo netto.

cleanse [klɛnz] vt pulire; purificare.

cleanser ['klɛnzə*] n detergente m; (cosmetic) latte m detergente.

clean-shaven ['kliːn'ʃeivn] adj sbarbato(a).

cleansing department ['klɛnzɪŋ-] n (BRIT) nettezza urbana.

clean sweep n: **to make a ~ (of)** fare piazza pulita (di).

clean-up ['kliːnʌp] n pulizia.

clear [kliə*] adj chiaro(a); (road, way) libero(a); (profit, majority) netto(a) ♦ vt sgombrare; liberare; (site, woodland) spianare; (COMM: goods) liquidare; (LAW: suspect) discolpare; (obstacle) superare; (cheque) fare la compensazione di ♦ vi

(weather) rasserenarsi; (fog) andarsene ♦ adv: ~ **of** distante da ♦ n: **to be in the ~** (out of debt) essere in attivo; (out of suspicion) essere a posto; (out of danger) essere fuori pericolo; **to ~ the table** sparecchiare (la tavola); **to ~ one's throat** schiarirsi la gola; **to ~ a profit** avere un profitto netto; **to make o.s. ~** spiegarsi bene; **to make it ~ to sb that ...** far capire a qn che ...; **I have a ~ day tomorrow** (BRIT) non ho impegni domani; **to keep ~ of sb/sth** tenersi lontano da qn/qc, stare alla larga da qn/qc.

▶**clear off** vi (col: leave) svignarsela.

▶**clear up** vi schiarirsi ♦ vt mettere in ordine; (mystery) risolvere.

clearance ['kliərəns] n (removal) sgombro; (free space) spazio; (permission) autorizzazione f, permesso.

clearance sale n vendita di liquidazione.

clear-cut ['kliə'kʌt] adj ben delineato(a), distinto(a).

clearing ['kliərɪŋ] n radura; (BRIT BANKING) clearing m.

clearing bank n (BRIT) banca che fa uso della camera di compensazione.

clearing house n (COMM) camera di compensazione.

clearly ['kliəlɪ] adv chiaramente.

clearway ['kliəwei] n (BRIT) strada con divieto di sosta.

cleavage ['kliːvidʒ] n (of woman) scollatura.

cleaver ['kliːvə*] n mannaia.

clef [klɛf] n (MUS) chiave f.

cleft [klɛft] n (in rock) crepa, fenditura.

clemency ['klɛmənsɪ] n clemenza.

clement ['klɛmənt] adj (weather) mite, clemente.

clench [klɛntʃ] vt stringere.

clergy ['klɜːdʒɪ] n clero.

clergyman ['klɜːdʒɪmən] n ecclesiastico.

clerical ['klɛrikl] adj d'impiegato; (REL) clericale.

clerk [klɑːk, (US) klɜːrk] n impiegato/a; (US: salesman/woman) commesso/a; **C~ of the Court** (LAW) cancelliere m.

clever ['klɛvə*] adj (mentally) intelligente; (deft, skilful) abile; (device, arrangement) ingegnoso(a).

cleverly ['klɛvəlɪ] adv abilmente.

clew [kluː] n (US) = **clue**.

cliché ['kliːʃei] n cliché m inv.

click [klik] vi scattare ♦ vt: **to ~ one's tongue** schioccare la lingua; **to ~ one's heels** battere i tacchi.

clickable ['klikəbl] adj cliccabile.

client ['klaiənt] n cliente m/f.

clientele [kliː̃ãːn'tɛl] *n* clientela.
cliff [klɪf] *n* scogliera scoscesa, rupe *f*.
cliffhanger ['klɪfhæŋə*] *n* (*TV, fig*) episodio (*or* situazione *etc*) ricco(a) di suspense.
climactic [klaɪ'mæktɪk] *adj* culminante.
climate ['klaɪmɪt] *n* clima *m*.
climax ['klaɪmæks] *n* culmine *m*; (*of play etc*) momento più emozionante; (*sexual ~*) orgasmo.
climb [klaɪm] *vi* salire; (*clamber*) arrampicarsi; (*plane*) prendere quota ♦ *vt* salire; (*CLIMBING*) scalare ♦ *n* salita; arrampicata; scalata; **to ~ over a wall** scavalcare un muro.
▶**climb down** *vi* scendere; (*BRIT fig*) far marcia indietro.
climbdown ['klaɪmdaun] *n* (*BRIT*) ritirata.
climber ['klaɪmə*] *n* (*also*: **rock ~**) rocciatore/trice; alpinista *m/f*.
climbing ['klaɪmɪŋ] *n* (*also*: **rock ~**) alpinismo.
clinch [klɪntʃ] *vt* (*deal*) concludere.
clincher ['klɪntʃə*] *n* (*col*): **that was the ~** quello è stato il fattore decisivo.
cling, *pt, pp* **clung** [klɪŋ, klʌŋ] *vi*: **to ~ (to)** tenersi stretto(a) (a); (*of clothes*) aderire strettamente (a).
clingfilm ['klɪŋfɪlm] *n* pellicola trasparente (*per alimenti*).
clinic ['klɪnɪk] *n* clinica; (*session*) seduta; serie *f* di sedute.
clinical ['klɪnɪkəl] *adj* clinico(a); (*fig*) freddo(a), distaccato(a).
clink [klɪŋk] *vi* tintinnare.
clip [klɪp] *n* (*for hair*) forcina; (*also*: **paper ~**) graffetta; (*BRIT: also*: **bulldog ~**) fermafogli *m inv*; (*holding hose etc*) anello d'attacco ♦ *vt* (*also*: **~ together**: *papers*) attaccare insieme; (*hair, nails*) tagliare; (*hedge*) tosare.
clippers ['klɪpəz] *npl* macchinetta per capelli; (*also*: **nail ~**) forbicine *fpl* per le unghie.
clipping ['klɪpɪŋ] *n* (*from newspaper*) ritaglio.
clique [kliːk] *n* cricca.
cloak [kləuk] *n* mantello ♦ *vt* avvolgere.
cloakroom ['kləukrum] *n* (*for coats etc*) guardaroba *m inv*; (*BRIT: W.C.*) gabinetti *mpl*.
clock [klɔk] *n* orologio; (*of taxi*) tassametro; **around the ~** ventiquattr'ore su ventiquattro; **to sleep round the ~** *or* **the ~ round** dormire un giorno intero; **to work against the ~** lavorare in gara col tempo; **30,000 on the ~** (*BRIT AUT*) 30.000 sul contachilometri.
▶**clock in, clock on** *vi* (*BRIT*) timbrare il cartellino (all'entrata).
▶**clock off, clock out** *vi* (*BRIT*) timbrare il cartellino (all'uscita).
▶**clock up** *vt* (*miles, hours etc*) fare.
clockwise ['klɔkwaɪz] *adv* in senso orario.
clockwork ['klɔkwəːk] *n* movimento *or* meccanismo a orologeria ♦ *adj* (*toy, train*) a molla.
clog [klɔg] *n* zoccolo ♦ *vt* intasare ♦ *vi* intasarsi, bloccarsi.
cloister ['klɔɪstə*] *n* chiostro.
clone [kləun] *n* clone *m* ♦ *vt* clonare.
close *adj, adv and derivatives* [kləus] *adj* vicino(a); (*writing, texture*) fitto(a); (*watch*) stretto(a); (*examination*) attento(a); (*weather*) afoso(a) ♦ *adv* vicino, dappresso; **~ to** *prep* vicino a; **~ by, ~ at hand** qui (*or* lì) vicino; **how ~ is Edinburgh to Glasgow?** quanto dista Edimburgo da Glasgow?; **a ~ friend** un amico intimo; **to have a ~ shave** (*fig*) scamparla bella; **at ~ quarters** da vicino
♦ *vb, n and derivatives* [kləuz] *vt* chiudere; (*bargain, deal*) concludere ♦ *vi* (*shop etc*) chiudere; (*lid, door etc*) chiudersi; (*end*) finire ♦ *n* (*end*) fine *f*; **to bring sth to a ~** terminare qc.
▶**close down** *vt* chiudere (definitivamente) ♦ *vi* cessare (definitivamente).
▶**close in** *vi* (*hunters*) stringersi attorno; (*evening, night, fog*) calare; **to ~ in on sb** accerchiare qn; **the days are closing in** le giornate si accorciano.
▶**close off** *vt* (*area*) chiudere.
closed [kləuzd] *adj* chiuso(a).
closed-circuit ['kləuzd'səːkɪt] *adj*: **~ television** televisione *f* a circuito chiuso.
closed shop *n* azienda o fabbrica che impiega solo aderenti ai sindacati.
close-knit ['kləus'nɪt] *adj* (*family, community*) molto unito(a).
closely ['kləuslɪ] *adv* (*examine, watch*) da vicino; **we are ~ related** siamo parenti stretti; **a ~ guarded secret** un assoluto segreto.
close season ['kləuz-] *n* (*FOOTBALL*) periodo di vacanza del campionato; (*HUNTING*) stagione *f* di chiusura (*di caccia, pesca etc*).
closet ['klɔzɪt] *n* (*cupboard*) armadio.
close-up ['kləusʌp] *n* primo piano.
closing ['kləuzɪŋ] *adj* (*stages, remarks*) conclusivo(a), finale; **~ price** (*STOCK EXCHANGE*) prezzo di chiusura.
closing time *n* orario di chiusura.
closure ['kləuʒə*] *n* chiusura.
clot [klɔt] *n* (*also*: **blood ~**) coagulo; (*col*:

idiot) scemo/a ♦ *vi* coagularsi.
cloth [klɔθ] *n* (*material*) tessuto, stoffa;
(*BRIT: also*: **tea**~) strofinaccio; (*also*:
table~) tovaglia.
clothe [kləuð] *vt* vestire.
clothes [kləuðz] *npl* abiti *mpl*, vestiti *mpl*; **to
put one's** ~ **on** vestirsi; **to take one's** ~
off togliersi i vestiti, svestirsi.
clothes brush *n* spazzola per abiti.
clothes line *n* corda (per stendere il
bucato).
clothes peg, (*US*) **clothes pin** *n* molletta.
clothing [ˈkləuðɪŋ] *n* = **clothes.**
clotted cream [ˈklɔtɪd-] *n* (*BRIT*) panna
rappresa.
cloud [klaud] *n* nuvola; (*of dust, smoke, gas*)
nube *f* ♦ *vt* (*liquid*) intorbidire; **to** ~ **the
issue** distogliere dal problema; **every** ~
has a silver lining (*proverb*) non tutto il
male vien per nuocere.
▶**cloud over** *vi* rannuvolarsi; (*fig*)
offuscarsi.
cloudburst [ˈklaudbə:st] *n* acquazzone *m*.
cloud-cuckoo-land [ˈklaudˈkukuːˈlænd] *n*
(*BRIT*) mondo dei sogni.
cloudy [ˈklaudɪ] *adj* nuvoloso(a); (*liquid*)
torbido(a).
clout [klaut] *n* (*blow*) colpo; (*fig*) influenza
♦ *vt* dare un colpo a.
clove [kləuv] *n* chiodo di garofano; ~ **of
garlic** spicchio d'aglio.
clover [ˈkləuvə*] *n* trifoglio.
cloverleaf [ˈkləuvəliːf] *n* foglia di trifoglio;
(*AUT*) raccordo (a quadrifoglio).
clown [klaun] *n* pagliaccio ♦ *vi* (*also*: ~
about, ~ **around**) fare il pagliaccio.
cloying [ˈklɔɪɪŋ] *adj* (*taste, smell*)
nauseabondo(a).
club [klʌb] *n* (*society*) club *m inv*, circolo;
(*weapon, GOLF*) mazza ♦ *vt* bastonare ♦ *vi*:
to ~ **together** associarsi; ~**s** *npl* (*CARDS*)
fiori *mpl*.
club car *n* (*US RAIL*) carrozza *or* vagone *m*
ristorante.
club class *n* (*AVIAT*) classe *f* club.
clubhouse [ˈklʌbhaus] *n* sede *f* del circolo.
club soda *n* (*US*) = **soda.**
cluck [klʌk] *vi* chiocciare.
clue [kluː] *n* indizio; (*in crosswords*)
definizione *f*; **I haven't a** ~ non ho la
minima idea.
clued up, (*US*) **clued in** [kluːd-] *adj* (*col*)
(ben) informato(a).
clump [klʌmp] *n*: ~ **of trees** folto d'alberi.
clumsy [ˈklʌmzɪ] *adj* (*person*) goffo(a),
maldestro(a); (*object*) malfatto(a), mal
costruito(a).
clung [klʌŋ] *pt, pp of* **cling.**

cluster [ˈklʌstə*] *n* gruppo ♦ *vi*
raggrupparsi.
clutch [klʌtʃ] *n* (*grip, grasp*) presa, stretta;
(*AUT*) frizione *f* ♦ *vt* afferrare, stringere
forte; **to** ~ **at** aggrapparsi a.
clutter [ˈklʌtə*] *vt* (*also*: ~ **up**) ingombrare
♦ *n* confusione *f*, disordine *m*.
cm *abbr* (= *centimetre*) cm.
CNAA *n abbr* (*BRIT*: = *Council for National
Academic Awards*) *organizzazione che
conferisce premi accademici.*
CND *n abbr* (*BRIT*) = *Campaign for Nuclear
Disarmament.*
CO *n abbr* (= *commanding officer*) Com.;
(*BRIT*) = *Commonwealth Office* ♦ *abbr* (*US*)
= *Colorado.*
Co. *abbr* = **county;** (= *company*) C., C.ia.
c/o *abbr* (= *care of*) c/o.
coach [kəutʃ] *n* (*bus*) pullman *m inv*; (*horse-
drawn, of train*) carrozza; (*SPORT*)
allenatore/trice ♦ *vt* allenare.
coach trip *n* viaggio in pullman.
coagulate [kəuˈægjuleɪt] *vt* coagulare ♦ *vi*
coagularsi.
coal [kəul] *n* carbone *m*.
coalface [ˈkəulfeɪs] *n* fronte *f*.
coalfield [ˈkəulfiːld] *n* bacino carbonifero.
coalition [kəuəˈlɪʃən] *n* coalizione *f*.
coalman [ˈkəulmən] *n* negoziante *m* di
carbone.
coalmine [ˈkəulmaɪn] *n* miniera di carbone.
coalminer [ˈkəulmaɪnə*] *n* minatore *m*.
coalmining [ˈkəulmaɪnɪŋ] *n* estrazione *f* del
carbone.
coarse [kɔːs] *adj* (*salt, sand etc*) grosso(a);
(*cloth, person*) rozzo(a); (*vulgar: character,
laugh*) volgare.
coast [kəust] *n* costa ♦ *vi* (*with cycle etc*)
scendere a ruota libera.
coastal [ˈkəustəl] *adj* costiero(a).
coaster [ˈkəustə*] *n* (*NAUT*) nave *f* da
cabotaggio; (*for glass*) sottobicchiere *m*.
coastguard [ˈkəustgaːd] *n* guardia
costiera.
coastline [ˈkəustlaɪn] *n* linea costiera.
coat [kəut] *n* cappotto; (*of animal*) pelo; (*of
paint*) mano *f* ♦ *vt* coprire; ~ **of arms** *n*
stemma *m*.
coat hanger *n* attaccapanni *m inv*.
coating [ˈkəutɪŋ] *n* rivestimento.
co-author [ˈkəuˈɔːθə*] *n* coautore/trice.
coax [kəuks] *vt* indurre (con moine).
cob [kɔb] *n see* **corn.**
cobbler [ˈkɔblə*] *n* calzolaio.
cobbles [ˈkɔblz], **cobblestones**
[ˈkɔblstəunz] *npl* ciottoli *mpl*.
COBOL [ˈkəubɔl] *n* COBOL *m*.
cobra [ˈkəubrə] *n* cobra *m inv*.

cobweb ['kɔbwɛb] n ragnatela.

cocaine [kə'keɪn] n cocaina.

cock [kɔk] n (rooster) gallo; (male bird) maschio ♦ vt (gun) armare; **to ~ one's ears** (fig) drizzare le orecchie.

cock-a-hoop [kɔkə'huːp] adj euforico(a).

cockerel ['kɔkərəl] n galletto.

cock-eyed ['kɔkaɪd] adj (fig) storto(a); strampalato(a).

cockle ['kɔkl] n cardio.

cockney ['kɔknɪ] n cockney m/f inv (abitante dei quartieri popolari dell'East End di Londra).

cockpit ['kɔkpɪt] n abitacolo.

cockroach ['kɔkrəutʃ] n blatta.

cocktail ['kɔkteɪl] n cocktail m inv; **prawn ~, (US) shrimp ~** cocktail m inv di gamberetti.

cocktail cabinet n mobile m bar inv.

cocktail party n cocktail m inv.

cocktail shaker n shaker m inv.

cocky ['kɔkɪ] adj spavaldo(a), arrogante.

cocoa ['kəukəu] n cacao.

coconut ['kəukənʌt] n noce f di cocco.

cocoon [kə'kuːn] n bozzolo.

COD abbr see **cash on delivery,** (US) see **collect on delivery.**

cod [kɔd] n merluzzo.

code [kəud] n codice m; **~ of behaviour** regole fpl di condotta; **~ of practice** codice professionale.

codeine ['kəudiːn] n codeina.

codger ['kɔdʒəʳ] n (BRIT col): **an old ~** un simpatico nonnetto.

codicil ['kɔdɪsɪl] n codicillo.

codify ['kəudɪfaɪ] vt codificare.

cod-liver oil ['kɔdlɪvəʳ-] n olio di fegato di merluzzo.

co-driver ['kəu'draɪvəʳ] n (in race) copilota m; (of lorry) secondo autista m.

co-ed ['kəu'ɛd] adj abbr = **coeducational** ♦ n abbr (US: female student) studentessa presso un'università mista; (BRIT: school) scuola mista.

coeducational ['kəuɛdju'keɪʃənl] adj misto(a).

coerce [kəu'əːs] vt costringere.

coercion [kəu'əːʃən] n coercizione f.

coexistence ['kəuɪg'zɪstəns] n coesistenza.

C. of C. n abbr = **chamber of commerce.**

C of E abbr = **Church of England.**

coffee ['kɔfɪ] n caffè m inv; **white ~,** (US) **~ with cream** caffellatte m.

coffee bar n (BRIT) caffè m inv.

coffee bean n grano or chicco di caffè.

coffee break n pausa per il caffè.

coffeecake ['kɔfɪkeɪk] n (US) panino dolce all'uva.

coffee cup n tazzina da caffè.

coffeepot ['kɔfɪpɔt] n caffettiera.

coffee table n tavolino da tè.

coffin ['kɔfɪn] n bara.

C of I abbr = Church of Ireland.

C of S abbr = Church of Scotland.

cog [kɔg] n dente m.

cogent ['kəudʒənt] adj convincente.

cognac ['kɔnjæk] n cognac m inv.

cogwheel ['kɔgwiːl] n ruota dentata.

cohabit [kəu'hæbɪt] vi (formal): **to ~ (with sb)** coabitare (con qn).

coherent [kəu'hɪərənt] adj coerente.

cohesion [kəu'hiːʒən] n coesione f.

cohesive [kəu'hiːsɪv] adj (fig) unificante, coesivo(a).

COI n abbr (BRIT) = Central Office of Information.

coil [kɔɪl] n rotolo; (one loop) anello; (AUT, ELEC) bobina; (contraceptive) spirale f; (of smoke) filo ♦ vt avvolgere.

coin [kɔɪn] n moneta ♦ vt (word) coniare.

coinage ['kɔɪnɪdʒ] n sistema m monetario.

coin-box ['kɔɪnbɔks] n (BRIT) cabina telefonica.

coincide [kəuɪn'saɪd] vi coincidere.

coincidence [kəu'ɪnsɪdəns] n combinazione f.

coin-operated ['kɔɪn'ɔpəreɪtɪd] adj (machine) (che funziona) a monete.

Coke ® [kəuk] n (Coca-Cola) coca f inv.

coke [kəuk] n coke m.

Col. abbr = **colonel**; (US) = Colorado.

COLA n abbr (US: = cost-of-living adjustment) ≈ scala mobile.

colander ['kɔləndəʳ] n colino.

cold [kəuld] adj freddo(a) ♦ n freddo; (MED) raffreddore m; **it's ~** fa freddo; **to be ~** aver freddo; **to catch ~** prendere freddo; **to catch a ~** prendere un raffreddore; **in ~ blood** a sangue freddo; **to have ~ feet** avere i piedi freddi; (fig) aver la fifa; **to give sb the ~ shoulder** ignorare qn.

cold-blooded [kəuld'blʌdɪd] adj (ZOOL) a sangue freddo.

cold call n chiamata pubblicitaria non richiesta.

cold cream n crema emolliente.

coldly ['kəuldlɪ] adv freddamente.

cold sore n erpete m.

cold sweat n: **to be in a ~ (about sth)** sudare freddo (per qc).

cold turkey n (col): **to go ~** avere la scimmia (drogato).

Cold War n: **the ~** la guerra fredda.

coleslaw ['kəulslɔː] n insalata di cavolo bianco.

colic ['kɔlɪk] n colica.

colicky ['kɒlɪkɪ] *adj* che soffre di coliche.
collaborate [kə'læbəreɪt] *vi* collaborare.
collaboration [kəlæbə'reɪʃən] *n*
  collaborazione *f*.
collaborator [kə'læbəreɪtə*] *n*
  collaboratore/trice.
collage [kɒ'lɑːʒ] *n* (*ART*) collage *m inv*.
collagen ['kɒlədʒən] *n* collageno.
collapse [kə'læps] *vi* (*gen*) crollare;
  (*government*) cadere; (*MED*) avere un
  collasso; (*plans*) fallire ♦ *n* crollo; caduta;
  collasso; fallimento.
collapsible [kə'læpsəbl] *adj* pieghevole.
collar ['kɒlə*] *n* (*of coat, shirt*) colletto; (*for
  dog*) collare *m*; (*TECH*) anello, fascetta ♦ *vt*
  (*col: person, object*) beccare.
collarbone ['kɒləbəun] *n* clavicola.
collate [kɒ'leɪt] *vt* collazionare.
collateral [kɒ'lætərəl] *n* garanzia.
collation [kɒ'leɪʃən] *n* collazione *f*.
colleague ['kɒliːg] *n* collega *m/f*.
collect [kə'lɛkt] *vt* (*gen*) raccogliere; (*as a
  hobby*) fare collezione di; (*BRIT: call for*)
  prendere; (*money owed, pension*)
  riscuotere; (*donations, subscriptions*) fare
  una colletta di ♦ *vi* (*people*) adunarsi,
  riunirsi; (*rubbish etc*) ammucchiarsi ♦ *adv*
  (*US TEL*): **to call** ~ fare una chiamata a
  carico del destinatario; **to** ~ **one's
  thoughts** raccogliere le idee; ~ **on
  delivery (COD)** (*US COMM*) pagamento alla
  consegna.
collected [kə'lɛktɪd] *adj*: ~ **works** opere *fpl*
  raccolte.
collection [kə'lɛkʃən] *n* collezione *f*;
  raccolta; (*for money*) colletta; (*POST*)
  levata.
collective [kə'lɛktɪv] *adj* collettivo(a) ♦ *n*
  collettivo.
collective bargaining *n* trattative *fpl*
  (sindacali) collettive.
collector [kə'lɛktə*] *n* collezionista *m/f*; (*of
  taxes*) esattore *m*; ~**'s item** *or* **piece** pezzo
  da collezionista.
college ['kɒlɪdʒ] *n* (*BRIT, US SCOL*) college *m
  inv*; (*of technology, agriculture etc*) istituto
  superiore; (*body*) collegio; ~ **of education**
  ≈ facoltà *f inv* di Magistero.
collide [kə'laɪd] *vi*: **to** ~ (**with**) scontrarsi
  (con).
collie ['kɒlɪ] *n* (*dog*) collie *m inv*.
colliery ['kɒlɪərɪ] *n* (*BRIT*) miniera di
  carbone.
collision [kə'lɪʒən] *n* collisione *f*, scontro; **to
  be on a** ~ **course** (*also fig*) essere in rotta
  di collisione.
collision damage waiver (CDW) *n*
  (*INSURANCE*) copertura per i danni alla
  vettura.

colloquial [kə'ləukwɪəl] *adj* familiare.
collusion [kə'luːʒən] *n* collusione *f*; **in** ~
  with in accordo segreto con.
Colo. *abbr* (*US*) = Colorado.
Cologne [kə'ləun] *n* Colonia.
cologne [kə'ləun] *n* (*also*: **eau de** ~) acqua
  di colonia.
Colombia [kə'lɒmbɪə] *n* Colombia.
Colombian [kə'lɒmbɪən] *adj, n*
  colombiano(a).
colon ['kəulən] *n* (*sign*) due punti *mpl*; (*MED*)
  colon *m inv*.
colonel ['kəːnl] *n* colonnello.
colonial [kə'ləunɪəl] *adj* coloniale.
colonize ['kɒlənaɪz] *vt* colonizzare.
colony ['kɒlənɪ] *n* colonia.
color *etc* ['kʌlə*] (*US*) = **colour** *etc*.
Colorado beetle [kɒlə'rɑːdəu-] *n* dorifora.
colossal [kə'lɒsl] *adj* colossale.
colour, (*US*) **color** ['kʌlə*] *n* colore *m* ♦ *vt*
  colorare; (*tint, dye*) tingere; (*fig: affect*)
  influenzare ♦ *vi* arrossire ♦ *cpd* (*film,
  photograph, television*) a colori; ~**s** *npl* (*of
  party, club*) emblemi *mpl*.
colo(u)r bar *n* discriminazione *f* razziale
  (*in locali etc*).
colo(u)r-blind ['kʌləblaɪnd] *adj*
  daltonico(a).
colo(u)red ['kʌləd] *adj* colorato(a); (*photo*)
  a colori ♦ *n*: ~**s** gente *f* di colore.
colo(u)r film *n* (*for camera*) pellicola a
  colori.
colo(u)rful ['kʌləful] *adj* pieno(a) di colore,
  a vivaci colori; (*personality*) colorato(a).
colo(u)ring ['kʌlərɪŋ] *n* colorazione *f*;
  (*complexion*) colorito.
colo(u)r scheme *n* combinazione *f* di colori.
colour supplement *n* (*BRIT PRESS*)
  supplemento a colori.
colo(u)r television *n* televisione *f* a colori.
colt [kəult] *n* puledro.
column ['kɒləm] *n* colonna; (*fashion* ~,
  sports ~ *etc*) rubrica; **the editorial** ~
  l'articolo di fondo.
columnist ['kɒləmnɪst] *n* articolista *m/f*.
coma ['kəumə] *n* coma *m inv*.
comb [kəum] *n* pettine *m* ♦ *vt* (*hair*)
  pettinare; (*area*) battere a tappeto.
combat ['kɒmbæt] *n* combattimento ♦ *vt*
  combattere, lottare contro.
combination [kɒmbɪ'neɪʃən] *n*
  combinazione *f*.
combination lock *n* serratura a
  combinazione.
combine *vb* [kəm'baɪn] *vt* combinare; (*one
  quality with another*): **to** ~ **sth with sth**
  unire qc a qc ♦ *vi* unirsi; (*CHEM*)

combinarsi ♦ *n* ['kɔmbaɪn] lega; (*ECON*) associazione *f*; **a ~d effort** uno sforzo collettivo.
combine (harvester) *n* mietitrebbia.
combo ['kɔmbəʊ] *n* (*JAZZ etc*) gruppo.
combustible [kəm'bʌstɪbl] *adj* combustibile.
combustion [kəm'bʌstʃən] *n* combustione *f*.
come, *pt* **came,** *pp* **come** [kʌm, keɪm] *vi* venire; (*arrive*) venire, arrivare; **~ with me** vieni con me; **we've just ~ from Paris** siamo appena arrivati da Parigi; **nothing came of it** non è saltato fuori niente; **to ~ into sight** *or* **view** apparire; **to ~ to** (*decision etc*) raggiungere; **to ~ undone/ loose** slacciarsi/allentarsi; **coming!** vengo!; **if it ~s to it** nella peggiore delle ipotesi.
▶**come about** *vi* succedere.
▶**come across** *vt fus* trovare per caso; **to ~ across well/badly** fare una buona/cattiva impressione.
▶**come along** *vi* (*pupil, work*) fare progressi; **~ along!** avanti!, andiamo!, forza!
▶**come apart** *vi* andare in pezzi; (*become detached*) staccarsi.
▶**come away** *vi* venire via; (*become detached*) staccarsi.
▶**come back** *vi* ritornare; (*reply: col*): **can I ~ back to you on that one?** possiamo riparlarne più tardi?
▶**come by** *vt fus* (*acquire*) ottenere; procurarsi.
▶**come down** *vi* scendere; (*prices*) calare; (*buildings*) essere demolito(a).
▶**come forward** *vi* farsi avanti; presentarsi.
▶**come from** *vt fus* venire da; provenire da.
▶**come in** *vi* entrare.
▶**come in for** *vt fus* (*criticism etc*) ricevere.
▶**come into** *vt fus* (*money*) ereditare.
▶**come off** *vi* (*button*) staccarsi; (*stain*) andar via; (*attempt*) riuscire.
▶**come on** *vi* (*lights, electricity*) accendersi; (*pupil, undertaking*) fare progressi; **~ on!** avanti!, andiamo!, forza!
▶**come out** *vi* uscire; (*strike*) entrare in sciopero.
▶**come over** *vt fus*: **I don't know what's ~ over him!** non so cosa gli sia successo!
▶**come round** *vi* (*after faint, operation*) riprendere conoscenza, rinvenire.
▶**come through** *vi* (*survive*) sopravvivere, farcela; **the call came through** ci hanno passato la telefonata.

▶**come to** *vi* rinvenire ♦ *vt* (*add up to: amount*): **how much does it ~ to?** quanto costa?, quanto viene?
▶**come under** *vt fus* (*heading*) trovarsi sotto; (*influence*) cadere sotto, subire.
▶**come up** *vi* venire su.
▶**come up against** *vt fus* (*resistance, difficulties*) urtare contro.
▶**come up to** *vt fus* arrivare (fino) a; **the film didn't ~ up to our expectations** il film ci ha delusi.
▶**come up with** *vt fus*: **he came up with an idea** venne fuori con un'idea.
▶**come upon** *vt fus* trovare per caso.
comeback ['kʌmbæk] *n* (*THEAT etc*) ritorno; (*reaction*) reazione *f*; (*response*) risultato, risposta.
comedian [kə'miːdɪən] *n* comico.
comedienne [kəmiːdɪ'ɛn] *n* attrice *f* comica.
comedown ['kʌmdaʊn] *n* rovescio.
comedy ['kɔmɪdɪ] *n* commedia.
comet ['kɔmɪt] *n* cometa.
comeuppance [kʌm'ʌpəns] *n*: **to get one's ~** ricevere ciò che si merita.
comfort ['kʌmfət] *n* comodità *f inv*, benessere *m*; (*solace*) consolazione *f*, conforto ♦ *vt* consolare, confortare; *see also* **comforts**.
comfortable ['kʌmfətəbl] *adj* comodo(a); (*income, majority*) più che sufficiente; **I don't feel very ~ about it** non mi sento molto tranquillo.
comfortably ['kʌmfətəblɪ] *adv* (*sit*) comodamente; (*live*) bene.
comforter ['kʌmfətə*] *n* (*US*) trapunta.
comforts ['kʌmfəts] *npl* comforts *mpl*, comodità *fpl*.
comfort station *n* (*US*) gabinetti *mpl*.
comic ['kɔmɪk] *adj* comico(a) ♦ *n* comico; (*magazine*) giornaletto.
comical ['kɔmɪkl] *adj* divertente, buffo(a).
comic strip *n* fumetto.
coming ['kʌmɪŋ] *n* arrivo ♦ *adj* (*next*) prossimo(a); (*future*) futuro(a); **in the ~ weeks** nelle prossime settimane.
coming(s) and going(s) *n(pl)* andirivieni *m inv*.
Comintern ['kɔmɪntəːn] *n* KOMINTERN *m*.
comma ['kɔmə] *n* virgola.
command [kə'mɑːnd] *n* ordine *m*, comando; (*MIL: authority*) comando; (*mastery*) padronanza; (*COMPUT*) command *m inv*, comando ♦ *vt* comandare; **to ~ sb to do** ordinare a qn di fare; **to have/take ~ of** avere/prendere il comando di; **to have at one's ~** (*money, resources etc*) avere a propria disposizione.

command economy n = **planned economy**.

commandeer [kɔmən'dɪə*] vt requisire.

commander [kə'mɑːndə*] n capo; (MIL) comandante m.

commander-in-chief (C-in-C) [kə'mɑːndər-ɪn'tʃiːf] n (MIL) comandante m in capo.

commanding [kə'mɑːndɪŋ] adj (appearance) imponente; (voice, tone) autorevole; (lead, position) dominante.

commanding officer n comandante m.

commandment [kə'mɑːndmənt] n (REL) comandamento.

command module n (SPACE) modulo di comando.

commando [kə'mɑːndəu] n commando m inv; membro di un commando.

commemorate [kə'mɛməreɪt] vt commemorare.

commemoration [kəmɛmə'reɪʃən] n commemorazione f.

commemorative [kə'mɛmərətɪv] adj commemorativo(a).

commence [kə'mɛns] vt, vi cominciare.

commend [kə'mɛnd] vt lodare; raccomandare.

commendable [kə'mɛndəbl] adj lodevole.

commendation [kɔmɛn'deɪʃən] n lode f; raccomandazione f; (for bravery etc) encomio.

commensurate [kə'mɛnʃərɪt] adj: ~ **with** proporzionato(a) a.

comment ['kɔmɛnt] n commento ♦ vi: to ~ **(on)** fare commenti (su); to ~ **that** osservare che; "no ~" "niente da dire".

commentary ['kɔməntərɪ] n commentario; (SPORT) radiocronaca; telecronaca.

commentator ['kɔmənteɪtə*] n commentatore/trice; (SPORT) radiocronista m/f; telecronista m/f.

commerce ['kɔmɔːs] n commercio.

commercial [kə'mɔːʃəl] adj commerciale ♦ n (TV: also: ~ **break**) pubblicità f inv.

commercial bank n banca commerciale.

commercial college n ≈ istituto commerciale.

commercialism [kə'mɔːʃəlɪzəm] n affarismo.

commercial television n televisione f commerciale.

commercial traveller n commesso viaggiatore.

commercial vehicle n veicolo commerciale.

commiserate [kə'mɪzəreɪt] vi: to ~ **with** condolersi con.

commission [kə'mɪʃən] n commissione f;

(for salesman) commissione, provvigione f ♦ vt (MIL) nominare (al comando); (work of art) commissionare; I get 10% ~ ricevo il 10% sulle vendite; out of ~ (NAUT) in disarmo; (machine) fuori uso; to ~ **sb to do sth** incaricare qn di fare qc; to ~ **sth from sb** (painting etc) commissionare qc a qn; ~ **of inquiry** (BRIT) commissione f d'inchiesta.

commissionaire [kəmɪʃə'nɛə*] n (BRIT: at shop, cinema etc) portiere m in livrea.

commissioner [kə'mɪʃənə*] n commissionario; (POLICE) questore m.

commit [kə'mɪt] vt (act) commettere; (to sb's care) affidare; to ~ **o.s.** (to do) impegnarsi (a fare); to ~ **suicide** suicidarsi; to ~ **sb for trial** rinviare qn a giudizio.

commitment [kə'mɪtmənt] n impegno.

committed [kə'mɪtɪd] adj (writer) impegnato(a); (Christian) convinto(a).

committee [kə'mɪtɪ] n comitato; to be on a ~ far parte di un comitato or di una commissione.

committee meeting n riunione f di comitato or di commissione.

commodity [kə'mɔdɪtɪ] n prodotto, articolo; (food) derrata.

commodity exchange n borsa f merci inv.

common ['kɔmən] adj comune; (pej) volgare; (usual) normale ♦ n terreno comune; in ~ in comune; in ~ **use** di uso comune; it's ~ **knowledge** that è di dominio pubblico che; to the ~ **good** nell'interesse generale, per il bene comune; see also **Commons**.

common cold n: the ~ il raffreddore.

common denominator n denominatore m comune.

commoner ['kɔmənə*] n cittadino/a (non nobile).

common ground n (fig) terreno comune.

common land n terreno di uso pubblico.

common law n diritto consuetudinario.

common-law ['kɔmənlɔː] adj: ~ **wife** convivente f more uxorio.

commonly ['kɔmənlɪ] adv comunemente, usualmente.

Common Market n Mercato Comune.

commonplace ['kɔmənpleɪs] adj banale, ordinario(a).

commonroom ['kɔmənrum] n sala di riunione; (SCOL) sala dei professori.

Commons ['kɔmənz] npl (BRIT POL): the **(House of)** ~ la Camera dei Comuni.

common sense n buon senso.

Commonwealth ['kɔmənwɛlθ] *n:* **the ~** il Commonwealth; *see boxed note.*

COMMONWEALTH

Il **Commonwealth** *è un'associazione di stati sovrani indipendenti e di alcuni territori annessi che facevano parte dell'antico Impero Britannico. Ancora oggi molti stati del Commonwealth riconoscono simbolicamente il sovrano britannico come capo di stato, e i loro rappresentanti si riuniscono per discutere questioni di comune interesse.*

---

commotion [kə'məuʃən] *n* confusione *f*, tumulto.
communal ['kɔmjuːnl] *adj* (*life*) comunale; (*for common use*) pubblico(a).
commune *n* ['kɔmjuːn] (*group*) comune *f* ♦ *vi* [kə'mjuːn]: **to ~ with** mettersi in comunione con.
communicate [kə'mjuːnɪkeɪt] *vt* comunicare, trasmettere ♦ *vi:* **to ~ (with)** comunicare (con).
communication [kəmjuːnɪ'keɪʃən] *n* comunicazione *f*.
communication cord *n* (*BRIT*) segnale *m* d'allarme.
communications network *n* rete *f* delle comunicazioni.
communications satellite *n* satellite *m* per telecomunicazioni.
communicative [kə'mjuːnɪkətɪv] *adj* (*gen*) loquace.
communion [kə'mjuːnɪən] *n* (*also:* **Holy C~**) comunione *f*.
communiqué [kə'mjuːnɪkeɪ] *n* comunicato.
communism ['kɔmjunɪzəm] *n* comunismo.
communist ['kɔmjunɪst] *adj, n* comunista (*m/f*).
community [kə'mjuːnɪtɪ] *n* comunità *f inv.*
community centre *n* circolo ricreativo.
community chest *n* (*US*) fondo di beneficenza.
community health centre *n* centro socio-sanitario.
community home *n* (*BRIT*) riformatorio.
community service *n* (*BRIT*) ≈ lavoro sostitutivo.
community spirit *n* spirito civico.
commutation ticket [kɔmjuˈteɪʃən-] *n* (*US*) biglietto di abbonamento.
commute [kə'mjuːt] *vi* fare il pendolare ♦ *vt* (*LAW*) commutare.
commuter [kə'mjuːtə*] *n* pendolare *m/f.*
compact *adj* [kəm'pækt] compatto(a) ♦ *n* ['kɔmpækt] (*also:* **powder ~**) portacipria *m inv.*

compact disc *n* compact disc *m inv;* **~ player** lettore *m* CD *inv.*
companion [kəm'pænjən] *n* compagno/a.
companionship [kəm'pænjənʃɪp] *n* compagnia.
companionway [kəm'pænjənweɪ] *n* (*NAUT*) scala.
company ['kʌmpənɪ] *n* (*also COMM, MIL, THEAT*) compagnia; **he's good ~** è di buona compagnia; **we have ~** abbiamo ospiti; **to keep sb ~** tenere compagnia a qn; **to part ~ with** separarsi da; **Smith and C~** Smith e soci.
company car *n* macchina (di proprietà) della ditta.
company director *n* amministratore *m*, consigliere *m* di amministrazione.
company secretary *n* (*BRIT COMM*) segretario/a generale.
comparable ['kɔmpərəbl] *adj* comparabile.
comparative [kəm'pærətɪv] *adj* (*freedom, cost*) relativo(a); (*adjective, adverb etc*) comparativo(a); (*literature*) comparato(a).
comparatively [kəm'pærətɪvlɪ] *adv* relativamente.
compare [kəm'pɛə*] *vt:* **to ~ sth/sb with/to** confrontare qc/qn con/a ♦ *vi:* **to ~ (with)** reggere il confronto (con); **~d with** *or* **to** a paragone di, rispetto a; **how do the prices ~?** che differenza di prezzo c'è?
comparison [kəm'pærɪsn] *n* confronto; **in ~ (with)** a confronto (di).
compartment [kəm'pɑːtmənt] *n* compartimento; (*RAIL*) scompartimento.
compass ['kʌmpəs] *n* bussola; (**a pair of**) **~es** (*MATH*) compasso; **within the ~ of** entro i limiti di.
compassion [kəm'pæʃən] *n* compassione *f*.
compassionate [kəm'pæʃənɪt] *adj* compassionevole; **on ~ grounds** per motivi personali.
compassionate leave *n* congedo straordinario (*per gravi motivi di famiglia*).
compatibility [kəmpætɪ'bɪlɪtɪ] *n* compatibilità.
compatible [kəm'pætɪbl] *adj* compatibile.
compel [kəm'pɛl] *vt* costringere, obbligare.
compelling [kəm'pɛlɪŋ] *adj* (*fig: argument*) irresistibile.
compendium [kəm'pɛndɪəm] *n* compendio.
compensate ['kɔmpənseɪt] *vt* risarcire ♦ *vi:* **to ~ for** compensare.
compensation [kɔmpən'seɪʃən] *n* compensazione *f*; (*money*) risarcimento.
compère ['kɔmpɛə*] *n* presentatore/trice.
compete [kəm'piːt] *vi* (*take part*) concorrere; (*vie*): **to ~ (with)** fare concorrenza (a).

competence ['kɔmpɪtəns] *n* competenza.

competent ['kɔmpɪtənt] *adj* competente.

competing [kəm'piːtɪŋ] *adj* (*theories, ideas*) opposto(a); (*companies*) in concorrenza; **three ~ explanations (of)** tre spiegazioni contrastanti tra di loro (di).

competition [kɔmpɪ'tɪʃən] *n* gara, concorso; (*SPORT*) gara; (*ECON*) concorrenza; **in ~ with** in concorrenza con.

competitive [kəm'pɛtɪtɪv] *adj* (*sports*) agonistico(a); (*person*) che ha spirito di competizione; (*ECON*) concorrenziale.

competitive examination *n* concorso.

competitor [kəm'pɛtɪtə*] *n* concorrente *m/f*.

compile [kəm'paɪl] *vt* compilare.

complacency [kəm'pleɪsnsɪ] *n* compiacenza di sé.

complacent [kəm'pleɪsnt] *adj* compiaciuto(a) di sé.

complain [kəm'pleɪn] *vi*: **to ~ (about)** lagnarsi (di); (*in shop etc*) reclamare (per).

▶**complain of** *vt fus* (*MED*) accusare.

complaint [kəm'pleɪnt] *n* lamento; reclamo; (*MED*) malattia.

complement *n* ['kɔmplɪmənt] complemento; (*especially of ship's crew etc*) effettivo ♦ *vt* ['kɔmplɪmɛnt] (*enhance*) accompagnarsi bene a.

complementary [kɔmplɪ'mɛntərɪ] *adj* complementare.

complete [kəm'pliːt] *adj* completo(a) ♦ *vt* completare; (*a form*) riempire; **it's a ~ disaster** è un vero disastro.

completely [kəm'pliːtlɪ] *adv* completamente.

completion [kəm'pliːʃən] *n* completamento; **to be nearing ~** essere in fase di completamento; **on ~ of contract** alla firma del contratto.

complex ['kɔmplɛks] *adj* complesso(a) ♦ *n* (*PSYCH, buildings etc*) complesso.

complexion [kəm'plɛkʃən] *n* (*of face*) carnagione *f*; (*of event etc*) aspetto.

complexity [kəm'plɛksɪtɪ] *n* complessità *f inv*.

compliance [kəm'plaɪəns] *n* acquiescenza; **in ~ with** (*orders, wishes etc*) in conformità con.

compliant [kəm'plaɪənt] *adj* acquiescente, arrendevole.

complicate ['kɔmplɪkeɪt] *vt* complicare.

complicated ['kɔmplɪkeɪtɪd] *adj* complicato(a).

complication [kɔmplɪ'keɪʃən] *n* complicazione *f*.

compliment *n* ['kɔmplɪmənt] complimento

♦ *vt* ['kɔmplɪmɛnt] fare un complimento a; **~s** *npl* complimenti *mpl*; rispetti *mpl*; **to pay sb a ~** fare un complimento a qn; **to ~ sb (on sth/on doing sth)** congratularsi *or* complimentarsi con qn (per qc/per aver fatto qc).

complimentary [kɔmplɪ'mɛntərɪ] *adj* complimentoso(a), elogiativo(a); (*free*) in omaggio.

complimentary ticket *n* biglietto d'omaggio.

compliments slip *n* cartoncino della società.

comply [kəm'plaɪ] *vi*: **to ~ with** assentire a; conformarsi a.

component [kəm'pəunənt] *adj*, *n* componente (*m*).

compose [kəm'pəuz] *vt* comporre; **to ~ o.s.** ricomporsi; **~d of** composto(a) di.

composed [kəm'pəuzd] *adj* calmo(a).

composer [kəm'pəuzə*] *n* (*MUS*) compositore/trice.

composite ['kɔmpəzɪt] *adj* composito(a); (*MATH*) composto(a).

composition [kɔmpə'zɪʃən] *n* composizione *f*.

compost ['kɔmpɔst] *n* composta, concime *m*.

composure [kəm'pəuʒə*] *n* calma.

compound ['kɔmpaund] *n* (*CHEM, LING*) composto; (*enclosure*) recinto ♦ *adj* composto(a) ♦ *vt* (*fig: problem, difficulty*) peggiorare.

compound fracture *n* frattura esposta.

compound interest *n* interesse *m* composto.

comprehend [kɔmprɪ'hɛnd] *vt* comprendere, capire.

comprehension [kɔmprɪ'hɛnʃən] *n* comprensione *f*.

comprehensive [kɔmprɪ'hɛnsɪv] *adj* comprensivo(a).

comprehensive insurance policy *n* polizza multi-rischio *inv*.

comprehensive (school) *n* (*BRIT*) scuola *secondaria aperta a tutti*.

compress *vt* [kəm'prɛs] comprimere ♦ *n* ['kɔmprɛs] (*MED*) compressa.

compression [kəm'prɛʃən] *n* compressione *f*.

comprise [kəm'praɪz] *vt* (*also*: **be ~d of**) comprendere.

compromise ['kɔmprəmaɪz] *n* compromesso ♦ *vt* compromettere ♦ *vi* venire a un compromesso ♦ *cpd* (*decision, solution*) di compromesso.

compulsion [kəm'pʌlʃən] *n* costrizione *f*; **under ~** sotto pressioni.

compulsive [kəm'pʌlsɪv] *adj* (*PSYCH*) incontrollabile; **he's a ~ smoker** non riesce a controllarsi nel fumare.

compulsory [kəm'pʌlsərɪ] *adj* obbligatorio(a).

compulsory purchase *n* espropriazione *f*.

compunction [kəm'pʌŋkʃən] *n* scrupolo; **to have no ~ about doing sth** non farsi scrupoli a fare qc.

computer [kəm'pju:tə*] *n* computer *m inv*, elaboratore *m* elettronico.

computer game *n* computer game *m inv*.

computerization [kəmpju:tərɑɪ'zeɪʃən] *n* computerizzazione *f*.

computerize [kəm'pju:tərɑɪz] *vt* computerizzare.

computer language *n* linguaggio *m* macchina *inv*.

computer literate *adj*: **to be ~** essere in grado di usare il computer.

computer peripheral *n* unità periferica.

computer program *n* programma *m* di computer.

computer programmer *n* programmatore/trice.

computer programming *n* programmazione *f* di computer.

computer science *n* informatica.

computer scientist *n* informatico/a.

computing [kəm'pju:tɪŋ] *n* informatica.

comrade ['kɔmrɪd] *n* compagno/a.

comradeship ['kɔmrɪdʃɪp] *n* cameratismo.

Comsat ® ['kɔmsæt] *n abbr* = **communications satellite.**

con [kɔn] *vt* (*col*) truffare ♦ *n* truffa; **to ~ sb into doing sth** indurre qn a fare qc con raggiri.

concave ['kɔn'keɪv] *adj* concavo(a).

conceal [kən'si:l] *vt* nascondere.

concede [kən'si:d] *vt* concedere ♦ *vi* fare una concessione.

conceit [kən'si:t] *n* presunzione *f*, vanità.

conceited [kən'si:tɪd] *adj* presuntuoso(a), vanitoso(a).

conceivable [kən'si:vəbl] *adj* concepibile; **it is ~ that ...** può anche darsi che ....

conceivably [kən'si:vəblɪ] *adv*: **he may ~ be right** può anche darsi che abbia ragione.

conceive [kən'si:v] *vt* concepire ♦ *vi* concepire un bambino; **to ~ of sth/of doing sth** immaginare qc/di fare qc.

concentrate ['kɔnsəntreɪt] *vi* concentrarsi ♦ *vt* concentrare.

concentration [kɔnsən'treɪʃən] *n* concentrazione *f*.

concentration camp *n* campo di concentramento.

concentric [kɔn'sɛntrɪk] *adj* concentrico(a).

concept ['kɔnsɛpt] *n* concetto.

conception [kən'sɛpʃən] *n* concezione *f*; (*idea*) idea, concetto.

concern [kən'sə:n] *n* affare *m*; (*COMM*) azienda, ditta; (*anxiety*) preoccupazione *f* ♦ *vt* riguardare; **to be ~ed** (*about*) preoccuparsi (di); **to be ~ed with** occuparsi di; **as far as I am ~ed** per quanto mi riguarda; **"to whom it may ~"** "a tutti gli interessati"; **the department ~ed** (*under discussion*) l'ufficio in questione; (*relevant*) l'ufficio competente.

concerning [kən'sə:nɪŋ] *prep* riguardo a, circa.

concert ['kɔnsət] *n* concerto; **in ~** di concerto.

concerted [kən'sə:tɪd] *adj* concertato(a).

concert hall *n* sala da concerti.

concertina [kɔnsə'ti:nə] *n* piccola fisarmonica ♦ *vi* ridursi come una fisarmonica.

concerto [kən'tʃɔ:təʊ] *n* concerto.

concession [kən'sɛʃən] *n* concessione *f*.

concessionaire [kənsɛʃə'nɛə*] *n* concessionario.

concessionary [kən'sɛʃənərɪ] *adj* (*ticket, fare*) a prezzo ridotto.

conciliation [kənsɪlɪ'eɪʃən] *n* conciliazione *f*.

conciliatory [kən'sɪlɪətrɪ] *adj* conciliativo(a).

concise [kən'saɪs] *adj* conciso(a).

conclave ['kɔnkleɪv] *n* riunione *f* segreta; (*REL*) conclave *m*.

conclude [kən'klu:d] *vt* concludere ♦ *vi* (*speaker*) concludere; (*events*): **to ~ (with)** concludersi (con).

concluding [kən'klu:dɪŋ] *adj* (*remarks etc*) conclusivo(a), finale.

conclusion [kən'klu:ʒən] *n* conclusione *f*; **come to the ~ that ...** concludere che ..., arrivare alla conclusione che ....

conclusive [kən'klu:sɪv] *adj* conclusivo(a).

concoct [kən'kɔkt] *vt* inventare.

concoction [kən'kɔkʃən] *n* (*food, drink*) miscuglio.

concord ['kɔnkɔːd] *n* (*harmony*) armonia, concordia; (*treaty*) accordo.

concourse ['kɔŋkɔːs] *n* (*hall*) atrio.

concrete ['kɔŋkriːt] *n* calcestruzzo ♦ *adj* concreto(a); (*CONSTR*) di calcestruzzo.

concrete mixer *n* betoniera.

concur [kən'kɔː*] *vi* concordare.

concurrently [kən'kʌrntlɪ] *adv* simultaneamente.

concussion [kən'kʌʃən] *n* (*MED*) commozione *f* cerebrale.

condemn [kən'dɛm] *vt* condannare.

condemnation [kɔndɛm'neɪʃən] *n*

condanna.

condensation [kɔndɛn'seɪʃən] *n* condensazione *f*.

condense [kən'dɛns] *vi* condensarsi ♦ *vt* condensare.

condensed milk *n* latte *m* condensato.

condescend [kɔndɪ'sɛnd] *vi* condiscendere; **to ~ to do sth** degnarsi di fare qc.

condescending [kɔndɪ'sɛndɪŋ] *adj* condiscendente.

condition [kən'dɪʃən] *n* condizione *f*; (*disease*) malattia ♦ *vt* condizionare, regolare; **in good/poor ~** in buone/cattive condizioni; **to have a heart ~** soffrire di (mal di) cuore; **weather ~s** condizioni meteorologiche; **on ~ that a** condizione che + *sub*, a condizione di.

conditional [kən'dɪʃənl] *adj* condizionale; **to be ~ upon** dipendere da.

conditioner [kən'dɪʃənə*] *n* (*for hair*) balsamo.

condo ['kɔndəu] *n abbr* (*US col*) = **condominium**.

condolences [kən'dəulənsɪz] *npl* condoglianze *fpl*.

condom ['kɔndəm] *n* preservativo.

condominium [kɔndə'mɪnɪəm] *n* (*US*) condominio.

condone [kən'dəun] *vt* condonare.

conducive [kən'djuːsɪv] *adj*: **~ to** favorevole a.

conduct *n* ['kɔndʌkt] condotta ♦ *vt* [kən'dʌkt] condurre; (*manage*) dirigere; amministrare; (*MUS*) dirigere; **to ~ o.s.** comportarsi.

conductor [kən'dʌktə*] *n* (*of orchestra*) direttore *m* d'orchestra; (*on bus*) bigliettaio; (*US RAIL*) controllore *m*; (*ELEC*) conduttore *m*.

conductress [kən'dʌktrɪs] *n* (*on bus*) bigliettaia.

conduit ['kɔndɪt] *n* condotto; tubo.

cone [kəun] *n* cono; (*BOT*) pigna.

confectioner [kən'fɛkʃənə*] *n*: **~'s (shop)** ≈ pasticceria.

confectionery [kən'fɛkʃənərɪ] *n* dolciumi *mpl*.

confederate [kən'fɛdərɪt] *adj* confederato(a) ♦ *n* (*pej*) complice *m/f*; (*US HISTORY*) confederato.

confederation [kənfɛdə'reɪʃən] *n* confederazione *f*.

confer [kən'fəː*] *vt*: **to ~ sth on** conferire qc a ♦ *vi* conferire; **to ~ (with sb about sth)** consultarsi (con qn su qc).

conference ['kɔnfərns] *n* congresso; **to be in ~** essere in riunione.

conference room *n* sala *f* conferenze *inv*.

confess [kən'fɛs] *vt* confessare, ammettere ♦ *vi* confessarsi.

confession [kən'fɛʃən] *n* confessione *f*.

confessional [kən'fɛʃənl] *n* confessionale *m*.

confessor [kən'fɛsə*] *n* confessore *m*.

confetti [kən'fɛtɪ] *n* coriandoli *mpl*.

confide [kən'faɪd] *vi*: **to ~ in** confidarsi con.

confidence ['kɔnfɪdns] *n* confidenza; (*trust*) fiducia; (*also:* **self-~**) sicurezza di sé; **to tell sb sth in strict ~** dire qc a qn in via strettamente confidenziale; **to have (every) ~ that ...** essere assolutamente certo(a) che ...; **motion of no ~** mozione *f* di sfiducia.

confidence trick *n* truffa.

confident ['kɔnfɪdənt] *adj* sicuro(a); (*also:* **self-~**) sicuro(a) di sé.

confidential [kɔnfɪ'dɛnʃəl] *adj* riservato(a); (*secretary*) particolare.

confidentiality ['kɔnfɪdɛnʃɪ'ælɪtɪ] *n* riservatezza, carattere *m* confidenziale.

configuration [kən'fɪgju'reɪʃən] *n* (*COMPUT*) configurazione *f*.

confine [kən'faɪn] *vt* limitare; (*shut up*) rinchiudere; **to ~ o.s. to doing sth** limitarsi a fare qc; *see also* **confines**.

confined [kən'faɪnd] *adj* (*space*) ristretto(a).

confinement [kən'faɪnmənt] *n* prigionia; (*MIL*) consegna; (*MED*) parto.

confines ['kɔnfaɪnz] *npl* confini *mpl*.

confirm [kən'fəːm] *vt* confermare; (*REL*) cresimare.

confirmation [kɔnfə'meɪʃən] *n* conferma; cresima.

confirmed [kən'fəːmd] *adj* inveterato(a).

confiscate ['kɔnfɪskeɪt] *vt* confiscare.

confiscation [kɔnfɪs'keɪʃən] *n* confisca.

conflagration [kɔnflə'greɪʃən] *n* conflagrazione *f*.

conflict *n* ['kɔnflɪkt] conflitto ♦ *vi* [kən'flɪkt] essere in conflitto.

conflicting [kən'flɪktɪŋ] *adj* contrastante; (*reports, evidence, opinions*) contraddittorio(a).

conform [kən'fɔːm] *vi*: **to ~ (to)** conformarsi (a).

conformist [kən'fɔːmɪst] *n* conformista *m/f*.

confound [kən'faund] *vt* confondere; (*amaze*) sconcertare.

confounded [kən'faundɪd] *adj* maledetto(a).

confront [kən'frʌnt] *vt* confrontare; (*enemy, danger*) affrontare.

confrontation [kɔnfrən'teɪʃən] *n* scontro.

confrontational [kɔnfrən'teɪʃənəl] *adj* polemico(a), aggressivo(a).

confuse [kən'fjuːz] *vt* imbrogliare; (*one*

thing with another) confondere.
confused [kən'fjuːzd] *adj* confuso(a); **to get** ~ confondersi.
confusing [kən'fjuːzɪŋ] *adj* che fa confondere.
confusion [kən'fjuːʒən] *n* confusione *f*.
congeal [kən'dʒiːl] *vi* (*blood*) congelarsi.
congenial [kən'dʒiːnɪəl] *adj* (*person*) simpatico(a); (*place, work, company*) piacevole.
congenital [kən'dʒɛnɪtl] *adj* congenito(a).
conger eel ['kɔŋgər-] *n* grongo.
congested [kən'dʒɛstɪd] *adj* congestionato(a); (*telephone lines*) sovraccarico(a).
congestion [kən'dʒɛstʃən] *n* congestione *f*.
congestion charge *n pedaggio da pagare per poter circolare in automobile nel centro di alcune città, introdotto per la prima volta a Londra nel 2002.*
conglomerate [kən'glɔmərɪt] *n* (*COMM*) conglomerato.
conglomeration [kənglɔmə'reɪʃən] *n* conglomerazione *f*.
Congo ['kɔŋgəu] *n* Congo.
congratulate [kən'grætjuleɪt] *vt*: **to** ~ **sb** (**on**) congratularsi con qn (per *or* di).
congratulations [kəngrætju'leɪʃənz] *npl*: ~ (**on**) congratulazioni *fpl* (per) ♦ *excl* congratulazioni!, rallegramenti!
congregate ['kɔŋgrɪgeɪt] *vi* congregarsi, riunirsi.
congregation [kɔŋgrɪ'geɪʃən] *n* congregazione *f*.
congress ['kɔŋgrɛs] *n* congresso; (*US POL*): **C**~ il Congresso; *see boxed note.*

CONGRESS

Il **Congress** *è l'assemblea statunitense che si riunisce a Washington D.C. nel "Capitol" per elaborare e discutere le leggi federali. È costituita dalla "House of Representatives" (435 membri, eletti nei vari stati in base al numero degli abitanti) e dal "Senate" (100 senatori, due per ogni stato). Sia i membri della "House of Representatives" che quelli del "Senate" sono eletti direttamente dal popolo.*

---

congressman ['kɔŋgrɛsmən] *n* (*US*) membro del Congresso.
congresswoman ['kɔŋgrɛswumən] *n* (*US*) (*donna*) membro del Congresso.
conical ['kɔnɪkl] *adj* conico(a).
conifer ['kɔnɪfə*] *n* conifero.
coniferous [kə'nɪfərəs] *adj* di conifere.
conjecture [kən'dʒɛktʃə*] *n* congettura ♦ *vt, vi* congetturare.

conjoined twin [kən'dʒɔɪnd-] *n* fratello (*or* sorella) siamese.
conjugal ['kɔndʒugl] *adj* coniugale.
conjugate ['kɔndʒugeɪt] *vt* coniugare.
conjugation [kɔndʒə'geɪʃən] *n* coniugazione *f*.
conjunction [kən'dʒʌŋkʃən] *n* congiunzione *f*; **in** ~ **with** in accordo con, insieme con.
conjunctivitis [kəndʒʌŋktɪ'vaɪtɪs] *n* congiuntivite *f*.
conjure ['kʌndʒə*] *vi* fare giochi di prestigio.
▶**conjure up** *vt* (*ghost, spirit*) evocare; (*memories*) rievocare.
conjurer ['kʌndʒərə*] *n* prestigiatore/trice, prestidigitatore/trice.
conjuring trick ['kʌndʒərɪŋ-] *n* gioco di prestigio.
conker ['kɔŋkə*] *n* (*BRIT col*) castagna (d'ippocastano).
conk out [kɔŋk-] *vi* (*col*) andare in panne.
conman ['kɔnmæn] *n* truffatore *m*.
Conn. *abbr* (*US*) = Connecticut.
connect [kə'nɛkt] *vt* connettere, collegare; (*ELEC*) collegare; (*fig*) associare ♦ *vi* (*train*): **to** ~ **with** essere in coincidenza con; **to be** ~**ed with** aver rapporti con; essere imparentato(a) con; **I am trying to** ~ **you** (*TEL*) sto cercando di darle la linea.
connection [kə'nɛkʃən] *n* relazione *f*, rapporto; (*ELEC*) connessione *f*; (*TEL*) collegamento; (*train etc*) coincidenza; **in** ~ **with** con riferimento a, a proposito di; **what is the** ~ **between them?** in che modo sono legati?; **business** ~**s** rapporti d'affari; **to miss/get one's** ~ (*train etc*) perdere/prendere la coincidenza.
connexion [kə'nɛkʃən] *n* (*BRIT*) = connection.
conning tower ['kɔnɪŋ-] *n* torretta di comando.
connive [kə'naɪv] *vi*: **to** ~ **at** essere connivente in.
connoisseur [kɔnɪ'səː*] *n* conoscitore/ trice.
connotation [kɔnə'teɪʃən] *n* connotazione *f*.
connubial [kə'njuːbɪəl] *adj* coniugale.
conquer ['kɔŋkə*] *vt* conquistare; (*feelings*) vincere.
conqueror ['kɔŋkərə*] *n* conquistatore *m*.
conquest ['kɔŋkwɛst] *n* conquista.
cons [kɔnz] *npl see* **pro**; **convenience**.
conscience ['kɔnʃəns] *n* coscienza; **in all** ~ onestamente, in coscienza.
conscientious [kɔnʃɪ'ɛnʃəs] *adj* coscienzioso(a).
conscientious objector *n* obiettore *m* di coscienza.

conscious ['kɔnʃəs] *adj* consapevole; (*MED*) conscio(a); (*deliberate*: *insult, error*) intenzionale, voluto(a); **to become ~ of sth/that** rendersi conto di qc/che.

consciousness ['kɔnʃəsnɪs] *n* consapevolezza; (*MED*) coscienza; **to lose/regain ~** perdere/riprendere coscienza.

conscript ['kɔnskrɪpt] *n* coscritto.

conscription [kən'skrɪpʃən] *n* coscrizione *f*.

consecrate ['kɔnsɪkreɪt] *vt* consacrare.

consecutive [kən'sɛkjutɪv] *adj* consecutivo(a); **on 3 ~ occasions** 3 volte di fila.

consensus [kən'sɛnsəs] *n* consenso; **the ~ of opinion** l'opinione *f* unanime *or* comune.

consent [kən'sɛnt] *n* consenso ♦ *vi*: **to ~ (to)** acconsentire (a); **age of ~età** legale (per avere rapporti sessuali); **by common ~** di comune accordo.

consenting adults [kən'sɛntɪŋ-] *npl* adulti *mpl* consenzienti.

consequence ['kɔnsɪkwəns] *n* conseguenza, risultato; importanza; **in ~** di conseguenza.

consequently ['kɔnsɪkwəntlɪ] *adv* di conseguenza, dunque.

conservation [kɔnsə'veɪʃən] *n* conservazione *f*; (*also*: **nature ~**) tutela dell'ambiente; **energy ~** risparmio energetico.

conservationist [kɔnsə'veɪʃənɪst] *n* fautore/trice della tutela dell'ambiente.

conservative [kən'sə:vətɪv] *adj* conservatore(trice); (*cautious*) cauto(a); **C~** *adj*, *n* (*BRIT POL*) conservatore(trice); **the C~ Party** il partito conservatore.

conservatory [kən'sə:vətrɪ] *n* (*greenhouse*) serra.

conserve [kən'sə:v] *vt* conservare ♦ *n* conserva.

consider [kən'sɪdə*] *vt* considerare; (*take into account*) tener conto di; **to ~ doing sth** considerare la possibilità di fare qc; **all things ~ed** tutto sommato *or* considerato; **~ yourself lucky** puoi dirti fortunato.

considerable [kən'sɪdərəbl] *adj* considerevole, notevole.

considerably [kən'sɪdərəblɪ] *adv* notevolmente, decisamente.

considerate [kən'sɪdərɪt] *adj* premuroso(a).

consideration [kənsɪdə'reɪʃən] *n* considerazione *f*; (*reward*) rimunerazione *f*; **out of ~ for** per riguardo a; **under ~ in** esame; **my first ~ is my family** il mio primo pensiero è per la mia famiglia.

considered [kən'sɪdəd] *adj*: **it is my ~ opinion that** ... dopo lunga riflessione il mio parere è che ....

considering [kən'sɪdərɪŋ] *prep* in considerazione di; **~ (that)** se si considera (che).

consign [kən'saɪn] *vt* consegnare; (*send*: *goods*) spedire.

consignee [kɔnsaɪ'ni:] *n* consegnatario/a, destinatario/a.

consignment [kən'saɪnmənt] *n* consegna; spedizione *f*.

consignment note *n* (*COMM*) nota di spedizione.

consist [kən'sɪst] *vi*: **to ~ of** constare di, essere composto(a) di.

consistency [kən'sɪstənsɪ] *n* consistenza; (*fig*) coerenza.

consistent [kən'sɪstənt] *adj* coerente; (*constant*) costante; **~ with** compatibile con.

consolation [kɔnsə'leɪʃən] *n* consolazione *f*.

console *vt* [kən'səul] consolare ♦ *n* ['kɔnsəul] quadro di comando.

consolidate [kən'sɔlɪdeɪt] *vt* consolidare.

consols ['kɔnsɔlz] *npl* (*STOCK EXCHANGE*) titoli *mpl* del debito consolidato.

consommé [kən'sɔmeɪ] *n* consommé *m inv*, brodo ristretto.

consonant ['kɔnsənənt] *n* consonante *f*.

consort ['kɔnsɔ:t] *n* consorte *m/f*; **prince ~** principe *m* consorte ♦ *vi* (*often pej*): **to ~ with sb** frequentare qn.

consortium [kən'sɔ:tɪəm] *n* consorzio.

conspicuous [kən'spɪkjuəs] *adj* cospicuo(a); **to make o.s. ~** farsi notare.

conspiracy [kən'spɪrəsɪ] *n* congiura, cospirazione *f*.

conspiratorial [kənspɪrə'tɔ:rɪəl] *adj* cospiratorio(a).

conspire [kən'spaɪə*] *vi* congiurare, cospirare.

constable ['kʌnstəbl] *n* (*BRIT*: *also*: **police ~**) ≈ poliziotto, agente *m* di polizia.

constabulary [kən'stæbjulərɪ] *n* forze *fpl* dell'ordine.

constant ['kɔnstənt] *adj* costante; continuo(a).

constantly ['kɔnstəntlɪ] *adv* costantemente; continuamente.

constellation [kɔnstə'leɪʃən] *n* costellazione *f*.

consternation [kɔnstə'neɪʃən] *n* costernazione *f*.

constipated ['kɔnstɪpeɪtɪd] *adj* stitico(a).

constipation [kɔnstɪ'peɪʃən] *n* stitichezza.

constituency [kən'stɪtjuənsɪ] *n* collegio elettorale; (*people*) elettori *mpl* (del collegio); *see boxed note.*

CONSTITUENCY

Con il termine **constituency** *viene indicato sia un collegio elettorale che i suoi elettori. In Gran Bretagna ogni collegio elegge un rappresentante che in seguito incontra regolarmente i propri elettori in riunioni chiamate "surgeries" per discutere questioni di interesse locale.*

---

constituency party *n* sezione *f* locale (del partito).
constituent [kən'stɪtjuənt] *n* elettore/trice; (*part*) elemento componente.
constitute ['kɔnstɪtjuːt] *vt* costituire.
constitution [kɔnstɪ'tjuːʃən] *n* costituzione *f*.
constitutional [kɔnstɪ'tjuːʃənl] *adj* costituzionale.
constitutional monarchy *n* monarchia costituzionale.
constrain [kən'streɪn] *vt* costringere.
constrained [kən'streɪnd] *adj* costretto(a).
constraint [kən'streɪnt] *n* (*restraint*) limitazione *f*, costrizione *f*; (*embarrassment*) imbarazzo, soggezione *f*.
constrict [kən'strɪkt] *vt* comprimere; opprimere.
construct [kən'strʌkt] *vt* costruire.
construction [kən'strʌkʃən] *n* costruzione *f*; (*fig: interpretation*) interpretazione *f*; **under** ~ in costruzione.
construction industry *n* edilizia, industria edile.
constructive [kən'strʌktɪv] *adj* costruttivo(a).
construe [kən'struː] *vt* interpretare.
consul ['kɔnsl] *n* console *m*.
consulate ['kɔnsjulɪt] *n* consolato.
consult [kən'sʌlt] *vt*: **to** ~ **sb (about sth)** consultare qn (su *or* riguardo a qc).
consultancy [kən'sʌltənsɪ] *n* consulenza.
consultancy fee *n* onorario di consulenza.
consultant [kən'sʌltənt] *n* (*MED*) consulente *m* medico; (*other specialist*) consulente ♦ *cpd*: ~ **engineer** *n* ingegnere *m* consulente; ~ **paediatrician** *n* specialista *m/f* in pediatria; **legal/management** ~ consulente legale/gestionale.
consultation [kɔnsəl'teɪʃən] *n* consultazione *f*; (*MED, LAW*) consulto; **in** ~ **with** consultandosi con.
consultative [kən'sʌltətɪv] *adj* di consulenza.
consulting room [kən'sʌltɪŋ-] *n* (*BRIT*) ambulatorio.

consume [kən'sjuːm] *vt* consumare.
consumer [kən'sjuːmə*] *n* consumatore/trice; (*of electricity, gas etc*) utente *m/f*.
consumer credit *n* credito al consumatore.
consumer durables *npl* prodotti *mpl* di consumo durevole.
consumer goods *npl* beni *mpl* di consumo.
consumerism [kən'sjuːmərɪzəm] *n* (*consumer protection*) tutela del consumatore; (*ECON*) consumismo.
consumer society *n* società dei consumi.
consumer watchdog *n* comitato di difesa dei consumatori.
consummate ['kɔnsʌmeɪt] *vt* consumare.
consumption [kən'sʌmpʃən] *n* consumo; (*MED*) consunzione *f*; **not fit for human** ~ non commestibile.
cont. *abbr* (= *continued*) segue.
contact ['kɔntækt] *n* contatto; (*person*) conoscenza ♦ *vt* mettersi in contatto con; **to be in** ~ **with sb/sth** essere in contatto con qn/qc; **business** ~**s** contatti *mpl* d'affari.
contact lenses *npl* lenti *fpl* a contatto.
contagious [kən'teɪdʒəs] *adj* contagioso(a).
contain [kən'teɪn] *vt* contenere; **to** ~ **o.s.** contenersi.
container [kən'teɪnə*] *n* recipiente *m*; (*for shipping etc*) container *m*.
containerize [kən'teɪnəraɪz] *vt* mettere in container.
container ship *n* nave *f* container *inv*.
contaminate [kən'tæmɪneɪt] *vt* contaminare.
contamination [kəntæmɪ'neɪʃən] *n* contaminazione *f*.
cont'd *abbr* (= *continued*) segue.
contemplate ['kɔntəmpleɪt] *vt* contemplare; (*consider*) pensare a (*or* di).
contemplation [kɔntəm'pleɪʃən] *n* contemplazione *f*.
contemporary [kən'tɛmpərərɪ] *adj* contemporaneo(a); (*design*) moderno(a) ♦ *n* contemporaneo/a; (*of the same age*) coetaneo/a.
contempt [kən'tɛmpt] *n* disprezzo; ~ **of court** (*LAW*) oltraggio alla Corte.
contemptible [kən'tɛmptəbl] *adj* spregevole, vergognoso(a).
contemptuous [kən'tɛmptjuəs] *adj* sdegnoso(a).
contend [kən'tɛnd] *vt*: **to** ~ **that** sostenere che ♦ *vi*: **to** ~ **with** lottare contro; **he has a lot to** ~ **with** ha un sacco di guai.
contender [kən'tɛndə*] *n* contendente *m/f*; concorrente *m/f*.
content [kən'tɛnt] *adj* contento(a),

contented – contravention

soddisfatto(a) ♦ *vt* contentare, soddisfare
♦ *n* ['kɔntɛnt] contenuto; ~**s** *npl* contenuto;
(*of barrel etc*: *capacity*) capacità *f inv*; **(table
of)** ~**s** indice *m*; **to be** ~ **with** essere
contento di; **to** ~ **o.s. with sth/with doing
sth** accontentarsi di qc/di fare qc.
contented [kən'tɛntɪd] *adj* contento(a),
soddisfatto(a).
contentedly [kən'tɛntɪdlɪ] *adv* con
soddisfazione.
contention [kən'tɛnʃən] *n* contesa;
(*assertion*) tesi *f inv*; **bone of** ~pomo della
discordia.
contentious [kən'tɛnʃəs] *adj* polemico(a).
contentment [kən'tɛntmənt] *n*
contentezza.
contest *n* ['kɔntɛst] lotta; (*competition*)
gara, concorso ♦ *vt* [kən'tɛst] contestare;
(*LAW*) impugnare; (*compete for*)
contendere.
contestant [kən'tɛstənt] *n* concorrente *m/f*;
(*in fight*) avversario/a.
context ['kɔntɛkst] *n* contesto; **in/out of** ~
nel/fuori dal contesto.
continent ['kɔntɪnənt] *n* continente *m*; **the
C**~ (*BRIT*) l'Europa continentale; **on the
C**~ in Europa.
continental [kɔntɪ'nɛntl] *adj* continentale
♦ *n* (*BRIT*) abitante *m/f* dell'Europa
continentale.
continental breakfast *n* colazione *f*
all'europea.
continental quilt *n* (*BRIT*) piumino.
contingency [kən'tɪndʒənsɪ] *n* eventualità *f
inv*.
contingency plan *n* misura d'emergenza.
contingent [kən'tɪndʒənt] *n* contingenza
♦ *adj*: **to be** ~ **upon** dipendere da.
continual [kən'tɪnjuəl] *adj* continuo(a).
continually [kən'tɪnjuəlɪ] *adv* di continuo.
continuation [kəntɪnju'eɪʃən] *n*
continuazione *f*; (*after interruption*)
ripresa; (*of story*) seguito.
continue [kən'tɪnjuː] *vi* continuare ♦ *vt*
continuare; (*start again*) riprendere; **to be**
~**d** (*story*) continua; ~**d on page 10** segue
or continua a pagina 10.
continuing education [kən'tɪnjuɪŋ-] *n*
corsi *mpl* per adulti.
continuity [kɔntɪ'njuːɪtɪ] *n* continuità;
(*CINE*) (*ordine m della*) sceneggiatura.
continuity girl *n* (*CINE*) segretaria di
edizione.
continuous [kən'tɪnjuəs] *adj* continuo(a),
ininterrotto(a); ~ **performance** (*CINE*)
spettacolo continuato; ~ **stationery**
(*COMPUT*) carta a moduli continui.
continuously [kən'tɪnjuəslɪ] *adv* (*repeatedly*)

continuamente; (*uninterruptedly*)
ininterrottamente.
contort [kən'tɔːt] *vt* contorcere.
contortion [kən'tɔːʃən] *n* contorcimento;
(*of acrobat*) contorsione *f*.
contortionist [kən'tɔːʃənɪst] *n*
contorsionista *m/f*.
contour ['kɔntuə*] *n* contorno, profilo;
(*also*: ~ **line**) curva di livello.
contraband ['kɔntrəbænd] *n* contrabbando
♦ *adj* di contrabbando.
contraception [kɔntrə'sɛpʃən] *n*
contraccezione *f*.
contraceptive [kɔntrə'sɛptɪv] *adj*
contraccettivo(a) ♦ *n* contraccettivo.
contract *n* ['kɔntrækt] contratto ♦ *cpd*
['kɔntrækt] (*price, date*) del contratto;
(*work*) a contratto ♦ *vi* [kən'trækt] (*COMM*):
to ~ **to do sth** fare un contratto per fare
qc; (*become smaller*) contrarre; **to be
under** ~ **to do sth** aver stipulato un
contratto per fare qc; ~ **of employment**
contratto di lavoro.
▶**contract in** *vi* impegnarsi (con un
contratto); (*BRIT ADMIN*) scegliere di
pagare i contributi per una pensione.
▶**contract out** *vi*: **to** ~ **out (of)** ritirarsi
(da); (*BRIT ADMIN*) (*scegliere di*) non
pagare i contributi per una pensione.
contraction [kən'trækʃən] *n* contrazione *f*.
contractor [kən'træktə*] *n* imprenditore *m*.
contractual [kən'træktjuəl] *adj*
contrattuale.
contradict [kɔntrə'dɪkt] *vt* contraddire.
contradiction [kɔntrə'dɪkʃən] *n*
contraddizione *f*; **to be in** ~ **with**
discordare con.
contradictory [kɔntrə'dɪktərɪ] *adj*
contraddittorio(a).
contralto [kən'træltəu] *n* contralto.
contraption [kən'træpʃən] *n* (*pej*) aggeggio.
contrary ['kɔntrərɪ] *adj* contrario(a);
(*unfavourable*) avverso(a), contrario(a);
[kən'trɛərɪ] (*perverse*) bisbetico(a) ♦ *n*
contrario; **on the** ~ al contrario; **unless
you hear to the** ~ a meno che non si
disdica; ~ **to what we thought** a
differenza di *or* contrariamente a quanto
pensavamo.
contrast *n* ['kɔntrɑːst] contrasto ♦ *vt*
[kən'trɑːst] mettere in contrasto; **in** ~ **to**
or **with** a differenza di, contrariamente
a.
contrasting [kən'trɑːstɪŋ] *adj* contrastante,
di contrasto.
contravene [kɔntrə'viːn] *vt* contravvenire.
contravention [kɔntrə'vɛnʃən] *n*: ~ **(of)**
contravvenzione *f* (a), infrazione *f* (di).

contribute [kən'trɪbjuːt] *vi* contribuire ♦ *vt*:
to ~ £10/an article to dare 10 sterline/un
articolo a; **to ~ to** contribuire a;
(*newspaper*) scrivere per; (*discussion*)
partecipare a.

contribution [kɔntrɪ'bjuːʃən] *n*
contribuzione *f*.

contributor [kən'trɪbjutə*] *n* (*to newspaper*)
collaboratore/trice.

contributory [kən'trɪbjutərɪ] *adj* (*cause*) che
contribuisce; **it was a ~ factor in ...**
quello ha contribuito a ....

contributory pension scheme *n* (*BRIT*)
*sistema di pensionamento finanziato
congiuntamente dai contributi del
lavoratore e del datore di lavoro.*

contrite ['kɔntraɪt] *adj* contrito(a).

contrivance [kən'traɪvəns] *n* congegno;
espediente *m*.

contrive [kən'traɪv] *vt* inventare;
escogitare ♦ *vi*: **to ~ to do** fare in modo di
fare.

control [kən'trəul] *vt* dominare; (*firm,
operation etc*) dirigere; (*check*)
controllare; (*disease, fire*) arginare,
limitare ♦ *n* controllo; **~s** *npl* comandi *mpl*;
to take ~ of assumere il controllo di; **to
be in ~ of** aver autorità su; essere
responsabile di; controllare; **to ~ o.s.**
controllarsi; **everything is under ~** tutto è
sotto controllo; **the car went out of ~** la
macchina non rispondeva ai comandi;
circumstances beyond our ~ circostanze
fpl che non dipendono da noi.

control key *n* (*COMPUT*) tasto di controllo.

controlled substance [kən'trəuld-] *n*
sostanza stupefacente.

controller [kən'trəulə*] *n* controllore *m*.

controlling interest [kən'trəulɪŋ-] *n*
(*COMM*) maggioranza delle azioni.

control panel *n* (*on aircraft, ship, TV etc*)
quadro dei comandi.

control point *n* punto di controllo.

control room *n* (*NAUT, MIL*) sala di
comando; (*RADIO, TV*) sala di regia.

control tower *n* (*AVIAT*) torre *f* di
controllo.

control unit *n* (*COMPUT*) unità *f inv* di
controllo.

controversial [kɔntrə'vəːʃl] *adj*
controverso(a), polemico(a).

controversy ['kɔntrəvəːsɪ] *n* controversia,
polemica.

conurbation [kɔnəː'beɪʃən] *n* conurbazione
f.

convalesce [kɔnvə'lɛs] *vi* rimettersi in
salute.

convalescence [kɔnvə'lɛsns] *n*
convalescenza.

convalescent [kɔnvə'lɛsnt] *adj, n*
convalescente (*m/f*).

convector [kən'vɛktə*] *n* convettore *m*.

convene [kən'viːn] *vt* convocare; (*meeting*)
organizzare ♦ *vi* convenire, adunarsi.

convenience [kən'viːnɪəns] *n* comodità *f inv*;
at your ~ a suo comodo; **at your earliest
~** (*COMM*) appena possibile; **all modern
~s**, (*BRIT*) **all mod cons** tutte le comodità
moderne.

convenience foods *npl* cibi *mpl* precotti.

convenient [kən'viːnɪənt] *adj* conveniente,
comodo(a); **if it is ~ to you** se per lei va
bene, se non la incomoda.

conveniently [kən'viːnɪəntlɪ] *adv* (*happen*) a
proposito; (*situated*) in un posto comodo.

convent ['kɔnvənt] *n* convento.

convention [kən'vɛnʃən] *n* convenzione *f*;
(*meeting*) convegno.

conventional [kən'vɛnʃənl] *adj*
convenzionale.

convent school *n* scuola retta da suore.

converge [kən'vəːdʒ] *vi* convergere.

conversant [kən'vəːsnt] *adj*: **to be ~ with**
essere al corrente di; essere pratico(a)
di.

conversation [kɔnvə'seɪʃən] *n*
conversazione *f*.

conversational [kɔnvə'seɪʃənl] *adj* non
formale; (*COMPUT*) conversazionale; **~
Italian** l'italiano parlato.

conversationalist [kɔnvə'seɪʃnəlɪst] *n*
conversatore/trice.

converse *n* ['kɔnvəːs] contrario, opposto
♦ *vi* [kən'vəːs]: **to ~ (with sb about sth)**
conversare (con qn su qc).

conversely [kɔn'vəːslɪ] *adv* al contrario

conversion [kən'vəːʃən] *n* conversione *f*;
(*BRIT: of house*) trasformazione *f*,
rimodernamento.

conversion table *n* tavola di equivalenze.

convert *vt* [kən'vəːt] (*REL, COMM*)
convertire; (*alter*) trasformare ♦ *n*
['kɔnvəːt] convertito/a.

convertible [kən'vəːtəbl] *n* macchina
decappottabile.

convex ['kɔnvɛks] *adj* convesso(a).

convey [kən'veɪ] *vt* trasportare; (*thanks*)
comunicare; (*idea*) dare.

conveyance [kən'veɪəns] *n* (*of goods*)
trasporto; (*vehicle*) mezzo di trasporto.

conveyancing [kən'veɪənsɪŋ] *n* (*LAW*)
redazione *f* di transazioni di proprietà.

conveyor belt *n* nastro trasportatore.

convict *vt* [kən'vɪkt] dichiarare colpevole
♦ *n* ['kɔnvɪkt] carcerato/a.

conviction [kən'vɪkʃən] *n* condanna; (*belief*)

convinzione f.

convince [kən'vɪns] vt: **to ~ sb (of sth/that)** convincere qn (di qc/che).

convincing [kən'vɪnsɪŋ] adj convincente.

convincingly [kən'vɪnsɪŋlɪ] adv in modo convincente.

convivial [kən'vɪvɪəl] adj allegro(a).

convoluted ['kɔnvəluːtɪd] adj (shape) attorcigliato(a), avvolto(a); (argument) involuto(a).

convoy ['kɔnvɔɪ] n convoglio.

convulse [kən'vʌls] vt sconvolgere; **to be ~d with laughter** contorcersi dalle risa.

convulsion [kən'vʌlʃən] n convulsione f.

coo [kuː] vi tubare.

cook [kuk] vt cucinare, cuocere; (meal) preparare ♦ vi cuocere; (person) cucinare ♦ n cuoco/a.

►**cook up** vt (col: excuse, story) improvvisare, inventare.

cookbook ['kukbuk] n = **cookery book**.

cooker ['kukə*] n fornello, cucina.

cookery book n (BRIT) libro di cucina.

cookie ['kukɪ] n (US) biscotto; (COMPUT) cookie m inv.

cooking ['kukɪŋ] n cucina ♦ cpd (apples, chocolate) da cuocere; (utensils, salt, foil) da cucina.

cookout ['kukaut] n (US) pranzo (cucinato) all'aperto.

cool [kuːl] adj fresco(a); (not afraid) calmo(a); (unfriendly) freddo(a); (impertinent) sfacciato(a) ♦ vt raffreddare, rinfrescare ♦ vi raffreddarsi, rinfrescarsi; **it's ~** (weather) fa fresco; **to keep sth ~** or **in a ~ place** tenere qc in fresco.

►**cool down** vi raffreddarsi; (fig: person, situation) calmarsi.

coolant ['kuːlənt] n (liquido) refrigerante m.

cool box, (US) **cooler** ['kuːlə*] n borsa termica.

cooling ['kuːlɪŋ] adj (breeze) fresco(a).

cooling tower n torre f di raffreddamento.

coolly ['kuːlɪ] adv (calmly) con calma, tranquillamente; (audaciously) come se niente fosse; (unenthusiastically) freddamente.

coolness ['kuːlnɪs] n freschezza; sangue m freddo, calma.

coop [kuːp] n stia ♦ vt: **to ~ up** (fig) rinchiudere.

co-op ['kəuɔp] n abbr (= cooperative (society)) coop f.

cooperate [kəu'ɔpəreɪt] vi cooperare, collaborare.

cooperation [kəuɔpə'reɪʃən] n cooperazione f, collaborazione f.

cooperative [kəu'ɔpərətɪv] adj cooperativo(a) ♦ n cooperativa.

coopt [kəu'ɔpt] vt: **to ~ sb into sth** cooptare qn per qc.

coordinate vt [kəu'ɔːdɪneɪt] coordinare ♦ n [kəu'ɔːdɪnət] (MATH) coordinata; **~s** npl (clothes) coordinati mpl.

coordination [kəuɔːdɪ'neɪʃən] n coordinazione f.

coot [kuːt] n folaga.

co-ownership [kəu'əunəʃɪp] n comproprietà.

cop [kɔp] n (col) sbirro.

cope [kəup] vi farcela; **to ~ with** (problems) far fronte a.

Copenhagen [kəupən'heɪgən] n Copenhagen f.

copier ['kɔpɪə*] n (also: **photo~**) (foto)copiatrice f.

co-pilot ['kəupaɪlət] n secondo pilota m.

copious ['kəupɪəs] adj copioso(a), abbondante.

copper ['kɔpə*] n rame m; (col: policeman) sbirro; **~s** npl spiccioli mpl.

coppice ['kɔpɪs], **copse** [kɔps] n bosco ceduo.

copulate ['kɔpjuleɪt] vi accoppiarsi.

copy ['kɔpɪ] n copia; (book etc) esemplare m; (material: for printing) materiale m, testo ♦ vt (gen, COMPUT) copiare; (imitate) imitare; **rough/fair ~** brutta/bella (copia); **to make good ~** (fig) fare notizia.

►**copy out** vt ricopiare, trascrivere.

copycat ['kɔpɪkæt] n (pej) copione m.

copyright ['kɔpɪraɪt] n diritto d'autore; **~ reserved** tutti i diritti riservati.

copy typist n dattilografo/a.

copywriter ['kɔpɪraɪtə*] n redattore m pubblicitario.

coral ['kɔrəl] n corallo.

coral reef n barriera corallina.

Coral Sea n: **the ~** il mar dei Coralli.

cord [kɔːd] n corda; (ELEC) filo; (fabric) velluto a coste; **~s** npl (trousers) calzoni mpl (di velluto) a coste.

cordial ['kɔːdɪəl] adj, n cordiale (m).

cordless ['kɔːdlɪs] adj senza cavo.

cordon ['kɔːdn] n cordone m.

►**cordon off** vt fare cordone intorno a.

corduroy ['kɔːdərɔɪ] n fustagno.

CORE [kɔː*] n abbr (US) = Congress of Racial Equality.

core [kɔː*] n (of fruit) torsolo; (TECH) centro; (of earth, nuclear reactor) nucleo; (of problem etc) cuore m, nocciolo ♦ vt estrarre il torsolo da; **rotten to the ~**

marcio fino al midollo.
Corfu [kɔːˈfuː] n Corfù f.
coriander [kɔrɪˈændə*] n coriandolo.
cork [kɔːk] n sughero; (of bottle) tappo.
corkage [ˈkɔːkɪdʒ] n somma da pagare se il cliente porta il proprio vino.
corked [kɔːkt], (US) **corky** [ˈkɔːkɪ] adj (wine) che sa di tappo.
corkscrew [ˈkɔːkskruː] n cavatappi m inv.
cormorant [ˈkɔːmərnt] n cormorano.
corn [kɔːn] n (BRIT: wheat) grano; (US: maize) granturco; (on foot) callo; ~ **on the cob** (CULIN) pannocchia cotta.
cornea [ˈkɔːnɪə] n cornea.
corned beef [ˈkɔːnd-] n carne f di manzo in scatola.
corner [ˈkɔːnə*] n angolo; (AUT) curva; (FOOTBALL: also: ~ **kick**) corner m inv, calcio d'angolo ♦ vt intrappolare; mettere con le spalle al muro; (COMM: market) accaparrare ♦ vi prendere una curva; **to cut ~s** (fig) prendere una scorciatoia.
corner flag n (FOOTBALL) bandierina d'angolo.
corner kick n (FOOTBALL) calcio d'angolo.
cornerstone [ˈkɔːnəstəun] n pietra angolare.
cornet [ˈkɔːnɪt] n (MUS) cornetta; (BRIT: of ice-cream) cono.
cornflakes [ˈkɔːnfleɪks] npl fiocchi mpl di granturco.
cornflour [ˈkɔːnflauə*] n (BRIT) ≈ fecola di patate.
cornice [ˈkɔːnɪs] n cornicione m; cornice f.
Cornish [ˈkɔːnɪʃ] adj della Cornovaglia.
corn oil n olio di mais.
cornstarch [ˈkɔːnstɑːtʃ] n (US) = **cornflour**.
cornucopia [kɔːnjuˈkəupɪə] n grande abbondanza.
Cornwall [ˈkɔːnwəl] n Cornovaglia.
corny [ˈkɔːnɪ] adj (col) trito(a).
corollary [kəˈrɔlərɪ] n corollario.
coronary [ˈkɔrənərɪ] n: ~ **(thrombosis)** trombosi f coronaria.
coronation [kɔrəˈneɪʃən] n incoronazione f.
coroner [ˈkɔrənə*] n magistrato incaricato di indagare la causa di morte in circostanze sospette.
coronet [ˈkɔrənɪt] n diadema m.
Corp. abbr = **corporation**.
corporal [ˈkɔːpərl] n caporalmaggiore m ♦ adj: ~ **punishment** pena corporale.
corporate [ˈkɔːpərɪt] adj comune; (COMM) costituito(a) (in corporazione).
corporate hospitality n omaggi mpl ai clienti (come biglietti per spettacoli, cene etc).
corporate identity, corporate image n

(of organization) immagine f di marca.
corporation [kɔːpəˈreɪʃən] n (of town) consiglio comunale; (COMM) ente m.
corporation tax n ≈ imposta societaria.
corps [kɔː*], pl **corps** [kɔːz] n corpo; **press ~** ufficio m stampa inv.
corpse [kɔːps] n cadavere m.
corpuscle [ˈkɔːpʌsl] n corpuscolo.
corral [kəˈrɑːl] n recinto.
correct [kəˈrɛkt] adj (accurate) corretto(a), esatto(a); (proper) corretto(a) ♦ vt correggere; **you are ~** ha ragione.
correction [kəˈrɛkʃən] n correzione f.
correlate [ˈkɔrɪleɪt] vt mettere in correlazione ♦ vi: **to ~ with** essere in rapporto con.
correlation [kɔrɪˈleɪʃən] n correlazione f.
correspond [kɔrɪsˈpɔnd] vi corrispondere.
correspondence [kɔrɪsˈpɔndəns] n corrispondenza.
correspondence course n corso per corrispondenza.
correspondent [kɔrɪsˈpɔndənt] n corrispondente m/f.
corridor [ˈkɔrɪdɔː*] n corridoio.
corroborate [kəˈrɔbəreɪt] vt corroborare, confermare.
corrode [kəˈrəud] vt corrodere ♦ vi corrodersi.
corrosion [kəˈrəuʒən] n corrosione f.
corrosive [kəˈrəuzɪv] adj corrosivo(a).
corrugated [ˈkɔrəgeɪtɪd] adj increspato(a); ondulato(a).
corrugated iron n lamiera di ferro ondulata.
corrupt [kəˈrʌpt] adj corrotto(a) ♦ vt corrompere; ~ **practices** (dishonesty, bribery) pratiche fpl illecite.
corruption [kəˈrʌpʃən] n corruzione f.
corset [ˈkɔːsɪt] n busto.
Corsica [ˈkɔːsɪkə] n Corsica.
Corsican [ˈkɔːsɪkən] adj, n corso(a).
cortège [kɔːˈteɪʒ] n corteo.
cortisone [ˈkɔːtɪzəun] n cortisone m.
coruscating [ˈkɔrəskeɪtɪŋ] adj scintillante.
cosh [kɔʃ] n (BRIT) randello (corto).
cosignatory [kəuˈsɪgnətərɪ] n cofirmatario/a.
cosiness [ˈkəuzɪnɪs] n intimità.
cos lettuce [ˈkɔs-] n lattuga romana.
cosmetic [kɔzˈmɛtɪk] n cosmetico ♦ adj (preparation) cosmetico(a); (surgery) estetico(a); (fig: reforms) ornamentale.
cosmic [ˈkɔzmɪk] adj cosmico(a).
cosmonaut [ˈkɔzmənɔːt] n cosmonauta m/f.
cosmopolitan [kɔzməˈpɔlɪtn] adj cosmopolita.
cosmos [ˈkɔzmɔs] n cosmo.

cosset ['kɔsɪt] vt vezzeggiare.

cost [kɔst] n costo ♦ vb (pt, pp **cost**) vi costare ♦ vt stabilire il prezzo di; ~**s** npl (LAW) spese fpl; **it** ~**s £5/too much** costa 5 sterline/troppo; **it** ~ **him his life/job** gli costò la vita/il suo lavoro; **how much does it** ~? quanto costa?, quanto viene?; **what will it** ~ **to have it repaired?** quanto costerà farlo riparare?; ~ **of living** costo della vita; **at all** ~**s** a ogni costo.

cost accountant n analizzatore m dei costi.

co-star ['kəustɑː*] n attore/trice della stessa importanza del protagonista.

Costa Rica ['kɔstə'riːkə] n Costa Rica.

cost centre n centro di costo.

cost control n controllo dei costi.

cost-effective ['kɔstɪ'fɛktɪv] adj (gen) conveniente, economico(a); (COMM) redditizio(a), conveniente.

cost-effectiveness ['kɔstɪ'fɛktɪvnɪs] n convenienza.

costing ['kɔstɪŋ] n (determinazione f dei) costi mpl.

costly ['kɔstlɪ] adj costoso(a), caro(a).

cost-of-living ['kɔstəv'lɪvɪŋ] adj: ~ **allowance** indennità f inv di contingenza; ~ **index** indice m della scala mobile.

cost price n (BRIT) prezzo all'ingrosso.

costume ['kɔstjuːm] n costume m; (lady's suit) tailleur m inv; (BRIT: also: **swimming** ~) costume da bagno.

costume jewellery n bigiotteria.

cosy, (US) **cozy** ['kəuzɪ] adj intimo(a); (room, atmosphere) accogliente.

cot [kɔt] n (BRIT: child's) lettino; (US: folding bed) brandina.

cot death n improvvisa e inspiegabile morte nel sonno di un neonato.

Cotswolds ['kɔtswəuldz] npl: **the** ~ zona collinare del Gloucestershire.

cottage ['kɔtɪdʒ] n cottage m inv.

cottage cheese n fiocchi mpl di latte magro.

cottage industry n industria artigianale basata sul lavoro a cottimo.

cottage pie n piatto a base di carne macinata in sugo e purè di patate.

cotton ['kɔtn] n cotone m; ~ **dress** etc vestito etc di cotone.

▶**cotton on** vi (col): **to** ~ **on (to sth)** afferrare (qc).

cotton wool n (BRIT) cotone m idrofilo.

couch [kautʃ] n sofà m inv; (in doctor's surgery) lettino ♦ vt esprimere.

couchette [kuː'ʃɛt] n cuccetta.

couch potato n (col) pigrone/a teledipendente.

cough [kɔf] vi tossire ♦ n tosse f.

cough drop n pasticca per la tosse.

cough mixture, cough syrup n sciroppo per la tosse.

could [kud] pt of **can**.

couldn't ['kudnt] = **could not**.

council ['kaunsl] n consiglio; **city** or **town** ~ consiglio comunale; **C~ of Europe** Consiglio d'Europa.

council estate n (BRIT) quartiere m di case popolari.

council house n (BRIT) casa popolare.

council housing n alloggi mpl popolari.

councillor ['kaunsələ*] n consigliere/a.

council tax n (BRIT) tassa comunale sulla proprietà.

counsel ['kaunsl] n avvocato; consultazione f ♦ vt: **to** ~ **sth/sb to do sth** consigliare qc/a qn di fare qc; ~ **for the defence/the prosecution** avvocato difensore/di parte civile.

counsellor, (US) **counselor** ['kaunslə*] n consigliere/a; (US: lawyer) avvocato/essa.

count [kaunt] vt, vi contare ♦ n conto; (nobleman) conte m; **to** ~ **(up) to 10** contare fino a 10; **to** ~ **the cost of** calcolare il costo di; **not** ~**ing the children** senza contare i bambini; **10** ~**ing him** 10 compreso lui; ~ **yourself lucky** considerati fortunato; **it** ~**s for very little** non conta molto, non ha molta importanza; **to keep** ~ **of sth** tenere il conto di qc.

▶**count on** vt fus contare su; **to** ~ **on doing sth** contare di fare qc.

▶**count up** vt addizionare.

countdown ['kauntdaun] n conto alla rovescia.

countenance ['kauntɪnəns] n volto, aspetto ♦ vt approvare.

counter ['kauntə*] n banco; (position: in post office, bank) sportello; (in game) gettone m; (TECH) contatore m ♦ vt opporsi a; (blow) parare ♦ adv: ~ **to** contro; in opposizione a; **to buy under the** ~ (fig) comperare sottobanco; **to** ~ **sth with sth/by doing sth** rispondere a qc con qc/facendo qc.

counteract [kauntər'ækt] vt agire in opposizione a; (poison etc) annullare gli effetti di.

counterattack ['kauntərətæk] n contrattacco ♦ vi contrattaccare.

counterbalance ['kauntəbæləns] vt contrappesare.

counter-clockwise ['kauntə'klɔkwaɪz] adv in senso antiorario.

counter-espionage [kauntər'espɪənɑːʒ] n

controspionaggio.

counterfeit ['kauntəfɪt] n contraffazione f, falso ♦ vt contraffare, falsificare ♦ adj falso(a).

counterfoil ['kauntəfɔɪl] n matrice f.

counterintelligence ['kauntərɪn'tɛlɪdʒəns] n = **counter-espionage.**

countermand ['kauntəmɑːnd] vt annullare.

countermeasure ['kauntəmɛʒə*] n contromisura.

counteroffensive ['kauntərə'fɛnsɪv] n controffensiva.

counterpane ['kauntəpeɪn] n copriletto m inv.

counterpart ['kauntəpɑːt] n (of document etc) copia; (of person) corrispondente m/f.

counterproductive ['kauntəprə'dʌktɪv] adj controproducente.

countersign ['kauntəsaɪn] vt controfirmare.

countersink ['kauntəsɪŋk] vt (hole) svasare.

countess ['kauntɪs] n contessa.

countless ['kauntlɪs] adj innumerevole.

countrified ['kʌntrɪfaɪd] adj rustico(a)

country ['kʌntrɪ] n paese m; (native land) patria; (as opposed to town) campagna; (region) regione f; **in the ~** in campagna; **mountainous ~** territorio montagnoso.

country and western (music) n musica country e western, country m.

country dancing n (BRIT) danza popolare.

country house n villa in campagna.

countryman ['kʌntrɪmən] n (national) compatriota m; (rural) contadino.

countryside ['kʌntrɪsaɪd] n campagna.

country-wide ['kʌntrɪ'waɪd] adj diffuso(a) in tutto il paese ♦ adv in tutto il paese.

county ['kauntɪ] n contea.

county council n (BRIT) consiglio di contea.

county town n (BRIT) capoluogo.

coup, ~s [kuː, -z] n (also: ~ **d'état**) colpo di Stato; (triumph) bel colpo.

coupé [kuː'peɪ] n coupé m inv.

couple ['kʌpl] n coppia ♦ vt (carriages) agganciare; (TECH) accoppiare; (ideas, names) associare; **a ~ of** un paio di.

couplet ['kʌplɪt] n distico.

coupling ['kʌplɪŋ] n (RAIL) agganciamento.

coupon ['kuːpɔn] n (voucher) buono; (COMM) coupon m inv.

courage ['kʌrɪdʒ] n coraggio.

courageous [kə'reɪdʒəs] adj coraggioso(a).

courgette [kuə'ʒɛt] n (BRIT) zucchina.

courier ['kurɪə*] n corriere m; (for tourists) guida.

course [kɔːs] n corso; (of ship) rotta; (for golf) campo; (part of meal) piatto; **first ~** primo piatto; **of ~** adv senz'altro,

naturalmente; **(no) of ~ not!** certo che no!, no di certo!; **in the ~ of the next few days** nel corso dei prossimi giorni; **in due ~** a tempo debito; **~ (of action)** modo d'agire; **the best ~ would be to ...** la cosa migliore sarebbe ...; **we have no other ~ but to ...** non possiamo far altro che ...; **~ of lectures** corso di lezioni; **a ~ of treatment** (MED) una cura.

court [kɔːt] n corte f; (TENNIS) campo ♦ vt (woman) fare la corte a; (fig: favour, popularity) cercare di conquistare; (: death, disaster) sfiorare, rasentare; **out of ~** (LAW: settle) in via amichevole; **to take to ~** citare in tribunale; **C~ of Appeal** corte d'appello.

courteous ['kɔːtɪəs] adj cortese.

courtesan [kɔːtɪ'zæn] n cortigiana.

courtesy ['kɔːtəsɪ] n cortesia; **by ~ of** per gentile concessione di.

courtesy bus n navetta gratuita (di hotel, aeroporto).

courtesy car n vettura sostitutiva.

courtesy light n (AUT) luce f interna.

court-house ['kɔːthaus] n (US) palazzo di giustizia.

courtier ['kɔːtɪə*] n cortigiano/a.

courtmartial, pl **courtsmartial** ['kɔːt'mɑːʃəl] n corte f marziale.

courtroom ['kɔːtrum] n tribunale m.

court shoe n scarpa f décolleté inv.

courtyard ['kɔːtjɑːd] n cortile m.

cousin ['kʌzn] n cugino/a.

cove [kəuv] n piccola baia.

covenant ['kʌvənənt] n accordo ♦ vt: **to ~ to do sth** impegnarsi (per iscritto) a fare qc.

Coventry ['kɔvəntrɪ] n: **to send sb to ~** (fig) dare l'ostracismo a qn.

cover ['kʌvə*] vt (gen) coprire; (distance) coprire, percorrere; (PRESS: report on) fare un servizio su ♦ n (of pan) coperchio; (over furniture) fodera; (of book) copertina; (shelter) riparo; (COMM, INSURANCE) copertura; **to take ~** mettersi al coperto; **under ~** al riparo; **under ~ of darkness** protetto dall'oscurità; **under separate ~** (COMM) a parte, in plico separato; **£10 will ~ everything** 10 sterline saranno sufficienti.

►**cover up** vt (child, object): **to ~ up (with)** coprire (di); (fig: hide: truth, facts) nascondere ♦ vi: **to ~ up for sb** (fig) coprire qn.

coverage ['kʌvərɪdʒ] n (PRESS, TV, RADIO): **to give full ~ to** fare un ampio servizio su.

coveralls ['kʌvərɔːlz] npl (US) tuta.

cover charge n coperto.
covering ['kʌvərɪŋ] n copertura.
covering letter, (US) **cover letter** n lettera d'accompagnamento.
cover note n (INSURANCE) polizza (di assicurazione) provvisoria.
cover price n prezzo di copertina.
covert ['kʌvət] adj nascosto(a); (glance) di sottecchi, furtivo(a).
cover-up ['kʌvərʌp] n occultamento (di informazioni).
covet ['kʌvɪt] vt bramare.
cow [kau] n vacca ♦ cpd femmina ♦ vt intimidire; ~ **elephant** n elefantessa.
cowardice ['kauədɪs] n vigliaccheria.
cowardly ['kauədlɪ] adj vigliacco(a).
cowboy ['kaubɔɪ] n cow-boy m inv.
cower ['kauə*] vi acquattarsi.
cowshed ['kauʃɛd] n stalla.
cowslip ['kauslɪp] n (BOT) primula (odorata).
coxswain ['kɔksn] n (abbr: cox) timoniere m.
coy [kɔɪ] adj falsamente timido(a).
coyote [kɔɪ'əutɪ] n coyote m inv.
cozy ['kəuzɪ] adj (US) = **cosy**.
CP n abbr (= Communist Party) P.C. m.
cp. abbr (= compare) cfr.
CPA n abbr (US) see **certified public accountant**.
CPI n abbr (US: = Consumer Price Index) indice dei prezzi al consumo.
Cpl. abbr = **corporal**.
CP/M n abbr (= Control Program for Microcomputers) CP/M m.
c.p.s. abbr (= characters per second) c.p.s.
CPSA n abbr (BRIT: = Civil and Public Services Association) sindacato dei servizi pubblici.
CPU n abbr see **central processing unit**.
cr. abbr = **credit; creditor**.
crab [kræb] n granchio.
crab apple n mela selvatica.
crack [kræk] n (split, slit) fessura, crepa; incrinatura; (noise) schiocco; (: of gun) scoppio; (joke) battuta; (col: attempt): **to have a ~ at sth** tentare qc; (DRUGS) crack m inv ♦ vt spaccare; incrinare; (whip) schioccare; (nut) schiacciare; (case, mystery: solve) risolvere; (code) decifrare ♦ cpd (athlete) di prim'ordine; **to ~ jokes** (col) dire battute, scherzare; **to get ~ing** (col) darsi una mossa.
►**crack down on** vt fus prendere serie misure contro, porre freno a.
►**crack up** vi crollare.
crackdown ['krækdaun] n repressione f.
cracked [krækt] adj (col) matto(a).

cracker ['krækə*] n cracker m inv; (firework) petardo; (Christmas ~) mortaretto natalizio (con sorpresa); **a ~ of a ...** (BRIT col) un(a) ... formidabile; **he's ~s** (BRIT col) è tocco.
crackle ['krækl] vi crepitare.
crackling ['kræklɪŋ] n crepitio; (on radio, telephone) disturbo; (of pork) cotenna croccante (del maiale).
crackpot ['krækpɔt] n (col) imbecille m/f con idee assurde, assurdo/a.
cradle ['kreɪdl] n culla ♦ vt (child) tenere fra le braccia; (object) reggere tra le braccia.
craft [krɑ:ft] n mestiere m; (cunning) astuzia; (boat) naviglio.
craftsman ['krɑ:ftsmən] n artigiano.
craftsmanship ['krɑ:ftsmənʃɪp] n abilità.
crafty ['krɑ:ftɪ] adj furbo(a), astuto(a).
crag [kræg] n roccia.
cram [kræm] vt (fill): **to ~ sth with** riempire qc di; (put): **to ~ sth into** stipare qc in.
cramming ['kræmɪŋ] n (fig: pej) sgobbare m.
cramp [kræmp] n crampo ♦ vt soffocare, impedire.
cramped [kræmpt] adj ristretto(a).
crampon ['kræmpən] n (CLIMBING) rampone m.
cranberry ['krænbərɪ] n mirtillo.
crane [kreɪn] n gru f inv ♦ vt, vi: **to ~ forward, to ~ one's neck** allungare il collo.
cranium, pl **crania** ['kreɪnɪəm, 'kreɪnɪə] n cranio.
crank [kræŋk] n manovella; (person) persona stramba.
crankshaft ['kræŋkʃɑ:ft] n albero a gomiti.
cranky ['kræŋkɪ] adj eccentrico(a); (bad-tempered): **to be ~** avere i nervi.
cranny ['krænɪ] n see **nook**.
crap [kræp] n (col!) fesserie fpl; **to have a ~** cacare (!).
crappy ['kræpɪ] adj (col) di merda (!).
crash [kræʃ] n fragore m; (of car) incidente m; (of plane) caduta; (of business) fallimento; (STOCK EXCHANGE) crollo ♦ vt fracassare ♦ vi (plane) fracassarsi; (car) avere un incidente; (two cars) scontrarsi; (fig) fallire, andare in rovina; **to ~ into** scontrarsi con; **he ~ed the car into a wall** andò a sbattere contro un muro con la macchina.
crash barrier n (BRIT AUT) guardrail m inv.
crash course n corso intensivo.
crash helmet n casco.
crash landing n atterraggio di fortuna.
crass [kræs] adj crasso(a).
crate [kreɪt] n gabbia.
crater ['kreɪtə*] n cratere m.

cravat(e) [krə'væt] n fazzoletto da collo.
crave [kreɪv] vi: **to ~ for** desiderare ardentemente.
craving ['kreɪvɪŋ] n: **~ (for)** (for food, cigarettes etc) (gran) voglia (di).
crawl [krɔːl] vi strisciare carponi; (child) andare a gattoni; (vehicle) avanzare lentamente ♦ n (SWIMMING) crawl m; **to ~ to sb** (col: suck up) arruffianarsi qn.
crawler lane ['krɔːlə*-] n (BRIT AUT) corsia riservata al traffico lento.
crayfish ['kreɪfɪʃ] n (pl inv) gambero (d'acqua dolce).
crayon ['kreɪən] n matita colorata.
craze [kreɪz] n mania.
crazed [kreɪzd] adj (look, person) folle, pazzo(a); (pottery, glaze) incrinato(a).
crazy ['kreɪzɪ] adj matto(a); **to go ~** uscir di senno, impazzire; **to be ~ about sb** (col: keen) essere pazzo di qn; **to be ~ about sth** andare matto per qc.
crazy paving n (BRIT) lastricato a mosaico irregolare.
creak [kriːk] vi cigolare, scricchiolare.
cream [kriːm] n crema; (fresh) panna ♦ adj (colour) color crema inv; **whipped ~** panna montata.
▶**cream off** vt (best talents, part of profits) portarsi via.
cream cake n torta alla panna.
cream cheese n formaggio fresco.
creamery ['kriːmərɪ] n (shop) latteria; (factory) caseificio.
creamy ['kriːmɪ] adj cremoso(a).
crease [kriːs] n grinza; (deliberate) piega ♦ vt sgualcire ♦ vi sgualcirsi.
crease-resistant ['kriːsrɪzɪstənt] adj ingualcibile.
create [kriː'eɪt] vt creare; (fuss, noise) fare.
creation [kriː'eɪʃən] n creazione f.
creative [kriː'eɪtɪv] adj creativo(a).
creativity [kriːeɪ'tɪvɪtɪ] n creatività.
creator [kriː'eɪtə*] n creatore/trice.
creature ['kriːtʃə*] n creatura.
crèche, creche [krɛʃ] n asilo infantile.
credence ['kriːdns] n credenza, fede f.
credentials [krɪ'denʃlz] npl (papers) credenziali fpl; (letters of reference) referenze fpl.
credibility [kredɪ'bɪlɪtɪ] n credibilità.
credible ['kredɪbl] adj credibile; (witness, source) attendibile.
credit ['kredɪt] n credito; onore m; (SCOL: esp US) certificato del compimento di una parte del corso universitario ♦ vt (COMM) accreditare; (believe: also: **give ~ to**) credere, prestar fede a; **to ~ £5 to sb** accreditare 5 sterline a qn; **to ~ sb with**

sth (fig) attribuire qc a qn; **on ~ a** credito; **to one's ~ a** proprio onore; **to take the ~ for** farsi il merito di; **to be in ~** (person) essere creditore(trice); (bank account) essere coperto(a); **he's a ~ to his family** fa onore alla sua famiglia; see also **credits**.
creditable ['kredɪtəbl] adj che fa onore, degno(a) di lode.
credit account n conto di credito.
credit agency n (BRIT) agenzia di analisi di credito.
credit balance n saldo attivo.
credit bureau n (US) agenzia di analisi di credito.
credit card n carta di credito.
credit control n controllo dei crediti.
credit facilities npl agevolazioni fpl creditizie.
credit limit n limite m di credito.
credit note n (BRIT) nota di credito.
creditor ['kredɪtə*] n creditore/trice.
credits ['kredɪts] npl (CINE) titoli mpl.
credit transfer n bancogiro, postagiro.
creditworthy ['kredɪt'wəːðɪ] adj autorizzabile al credito.
credulity [krɪ'djuːlɪtɪ] n credulità.
creed [kriːd] n credo; dottrina.
creek [kriːk] n insenatura; (US) piccolo fiume m.
creel ['kriːl] n cestino per il pesce; (also: **lobster ~**) nassa.
creep [kriːp] vi (pt, pp **crept** [krept]) avanzare furtivamente (or pian piano); (plant) arrampicarsi ♦ n (col): **he's a ~ è** un tipo viscido; **it gives me the ~s** (col) mi fa venire la pelle d'oca; **to ~ up on sb** avvicinarsi quatto quatto a qn; (fig: old age etc) cogliere qn alla sprovvista.
creeper ['kriːpə*] n pianta rampicante.
creepers ['kriːpəz] npl (US: rompers) tutina.
creepy ['kriːpɪ] adj (frightening) che fa accapponare la pelle.
creepy-crawly ['kriːpɪ'krɔːlɪ] n (col) bestiolina, insetto.
cremate [krɪ'meɪt] vt cremare.
cremation [krɪ'meɪʃən] n cremazione f.
crematorium, pl **crematoria** [kremə'tɔːrɪəm, -'tɔːrɪə] n forno crematorio.
creosote ['krɪəsəut] n creosoto.
crêpe [kreɪp] n crespo.
crêpe bandage n (BRIT) fascia elastica.
crêpe paper n carta crespa.
crêpe sole n suola di para.
crept [krept] pt, pp of **creep**.
crescendo [krɪ'ʃendəu] n crescendo.
crescent ['kresnt] n (shape) mezzaluna;

(*street*) strada semicircolare.

cress [krɛs] *n* crescione *m*.

crest [krɛst] *n* cresta; (*of helmet*) pennacchiera; (*of coat of arms*) cimiero.

crestfallen ['krɛstfɔːlən] *adj* mortificato(a).

Crete ['kriːt] *n* Creta.

crevasse [krɪ'væs] *n* crepaccio.

crevice ['krɛvɪs] *n* fessura, crepa.

crew [kruː] *n* equipaggio; (*CINE*) troupe *f inv*; (*gang*) banda, compagnia.

crew-cut ['kruːkʌt] *n*: **to have a ~** avere i capelli a spazzola.

crew-neck ['kruːnɛk] *n* girocollo.

crib [krɪb] *n* culla; (*REL*) presepio ♦ *vt* (*col*) copiare.

cribbage ['krɪbɪdʒ] *n* tipo di gioco di carte.

crick [krɪk] *n* crampo; **~ in the neck** torcicollo.

cricket ['krɪkɪt] *n* (*insect*) grillo; (*game*) cricket *m*.

cricketer ['krɪkɪtə*] *n* giocatore *m* di cricket.

crime [kraɪm] *n* (*in general*) criminalità; (*instance*) crimine *m*, delitto.

crime wave *n* ondata di criminalità.

criminal ['krɪmɪnl] *adj*, *n* criminale (*m/f*); **C~ Investigation Department (CID)** ≈ polizia giudiziaria.

crimp [krɪmp] *vt* arricciare.

crimson ['krɪmzn] *adj* color cremisi *inv*.

cringe [krɪndʒ] *vi* acquattarsi; (*fig*) essere servile.

crinkle ['krɪŋkl] *vt* arricciare, increspare.

cripple ['krɪpl] *n* zoppo/a ♦ *vt* azzoppare; (*ship, plane*) avariare; (*production, exports*) rovinare; **~d with arthritis** sciancato(a) per l'artrite.

crippling ['krɪplɪŋ] *adj* (*taxes, debts*) esorbitante; (*disease*) molto debilitante.

crisis, pl crises ['kraɪsɪs, -siːz] *n* crisi *f inv*.

crisp [krɪsp] *adj* croccante; (*fig*) frizzante; vivace; deciso(a).

crisps [krɪsps] *npl* (*BRIT*) patatine *fpl* fritte.

criss-cross ['krɪskrɔs] *adj* incrociato(a) ♦ *vt* incrociarsi.

criterion, pl criteria [kraɪ'tɪərɪən, -'tɪərɪə] *n* criterio.

critic ['krɪtɪk] *n* critico/a.

critical ['krɪtɪkl] *adj* critico(a); **to be ~ of sb/sth** criticare qn/qc, essere critico verso qn/qc.

critically ['krɪtɪklɪ] *adv* criticamente; **~ ill** gravemente malato.

criticism ['krɪtɪsɪzəm] *n* critica.

criticize ['krɪtɪsaɪz] *vt* criticare.

critique [krɪ'tiːk] *n* critica, saggio critico.

croak [krəuk] *vi* gracchiare.

Croat ['krəuæt] *adj*, *n* = **Croatian**.

Croatia [krəu'eɪʃɪə] *n* Croazia.

Croatian [krəu'eɪʃɪən] *adj* croato(a) ♦ *n* croato/a; (*LING*) croato.

crochet ['krəuʃeɪ] *n* lavoro all'uncinetto.

crock [krɔk] *n* coccio; (*col: person: also*: **old ~**) rottame *m*; (*: car etc*) caffettiera, rottame *m*.

crockery ['krɔkərɪ] *n* vasellame *m*; (*plates, cups etc*) stoviglie *fpl*.

crocodile ['krɔkədaɪl] *n* coccodrillo.

crocus ['krəukəs] *n* croco.

croft [krɔft] *n* (*BRIT*) piccolo podere *m*.

crofter ['krɔftə*] *n* (*BRIT*) affittuario di un piccolo podere.

crone [krəun] *n* strega.

crony ['krəunɪ] *n* (*col*) amicone/a.

crook [kruk] *n* truffatore *m*; (*of shepherd*) bastone *m*.

crooked ['krukɪd] *adj* curvo(a), storto(a); (*person, action*) disonesto(a).

crop [krɔp] *n* raccolto; (*produce*) coltivazione *f*; (*of bird*) gozzo, ingluvie *f* ♦ *vt* (*cut: hair*) tagliare, rapare; (*subj: animals: grass*) brucare.

▶**crop up** *vi* presentarsi.

cropper ['krɔpə*] *n*: **to come a ~** (*col*) fare fiasco.

crop spraying *n* spruzzatura di antiparassitari.

croquet ['krəukeɪ] *n* croquet *m*.

croquette [krə'kɛt] *n* crocchetta.

cross [krɔs] *n* croce *f*; (*BIOL*) incrocio ♦ *vt* (*street etc*) attraversare; (*arms, legs, BIOL*) incrociare; (*cheque*) sbarrare; (*thwart: person, plan*) contrastare, ostacolare ♦ *vi*: **the boat ~es from ... to ...** la barca fa la traversata da ... a ... ♦ *adj* di cattivo umore; **to ~ o.s.** fare il segno della croce, segnarsi; **we have a ~ed line** (*BRIT: on telephone*) c'è un'interferenza; **they've got their lines ~ed** (*fig*) si sono fraintesi; **to be/get ~ with sb (about sth)** essere arrabbiato(a)/arrabbiarsi con qn (per qc).

▶**cross out** *vt* cancellare.

▶**cross over** *vi* attraversare.

crossbar ['krɔsbɑː*] *n* traversa.

crossbow ['krɔsbəu] *n* balestra.

crossbreed ['krɔsbriːd] *n* incrocio.

cross-Channel ferry ['krɔs'tʃænl-] *n* traghetto che attraversa la Manica.

cross-check ['krɔstʃɛk] *n* controprova ♦ *vi* fare una controprova.

crosscountry (race) [krɔs'kʌntrɪ-] *n* cross-country *m inv*.

cross-dressing [krɔs'drɛsɪŋ] *n* travestitismo.

cross-examination ['krɔsɪgzæmɪ'neɪʃən] *n*

(*LAW*) controinterrogatorio.
cross-examine ['krɔsɪg'zæmɪn] *vt* (*LAW*)
sottoporre a controinterrogatorio.
cross-eyed ['krɔsaɪd] *adj* strabico(a).
crossfire ['krɔsfaɪə*] *n* fuoco incrociato.
crossing ['krɔsɪŋ] *n* incrocio; (*sea-passage*)
traversata; (*also*: **pedestrian** ~) passaggio
pedonale.
crossing point *n* valico di frontiera.
cross-purposes ['krɔs'pɜ:pəsɪz] *npl*: **to be
at** ~ **with sb** (*misunderstand*) fraintendere
qn; **to talk at** ~ fraintendersi.
cross-question [krɔs'kwɛstʃən] *vt* (*LAW*) =
cross-examine; (*fig*) sottoporre ad un
interrogatorio.
cross-reference ['krɔs'rɛfərəns] *n* rinvio,
rimando.
crossroads ['krɔsrəudz] *n* incrocio.
cross section *n* (*BIOL*) sezione *f*
trasversale; (*in population*) settore *m*
rappresentativo.
crosswalk ['krɔswɔ:k] *n* (*US*) strisce *fpl*
pedonali, passaggio pedonale.
crosswind ['krɔswɪnd] *n* vento di traverso.
crosswise ['krɔswaɪz] *adv* di traverso.
crossword ['krɔswɜ:d] *n* cruciverba *m inv*.
crotch [krɔtʃ] *n* (*ANAT*) inforcatura; (*of
garment*) pattina.
crotchet ['krɔtʃɪt] *n* (*MUS*) semiminima.
crotchety ['krɔtʃɪtɪ] *adj* (*person*)
burbero(a).
crouch [krautʃ] *vi* acquattarsi;
rannicchiarsi.
croup [kru:p] *n* (*MED*) crup *m*.
crouton ['kru:tɔn] *n* crostino.
crow [krəu] *n* (*bird*) cornacchia; (*of cock*)
canto del gallo ♦ *vi* (*cock*) cantare; (*fig*)
vantarsi; cantar vittoria.
crowbar ['krəubɑ:*] *n* piede *m* di porco.
crowd [kraud] *n* folla ♦ *vt* affollare, stipare
♦ *vi* affollarsi; **~s of people** un sacco di
gente.
crowded ['kraudɪd] *adj* affollato(a); ~ **with**
stipato(a) di.
crowd scene *n* (*CINE, THEAT*) scena di
massa.
crown [kraun] *n* corona; (*of head*) calotta
cranica; (*of hat*) cocuzzolo; (*of hill*) cima
♦ *vt* incoronare; (*tooth*) incapsulare; **and
to** ~ **it all ...** (*fig*) e per giunta ..., e come
se non bastasse ...; *see boxed note*.

---

crowning ['kraunɪŋ] *adj* (*achievement, glory*)
supremo(a).
crown jewels *npl* gioielli *mpl* della Corona.
crown prince *n* principe *m* ereditario.
crow's-feet ['krəuzfi:t] *npl* zampe *fpl* di
gallina.
crow's-nest ['krəuznɛst] *n* (*on sailing-ship*)
coffa.
crucial ['kru:ʃl] *adj* cruciale, decisivo(a); ~
to essenziale per.
crucifix ['kru:sɪfɪks] *n* crocifisso.
crucifixion [kru:sɪ'fɪkʃən] *n* crocifissione *f*.
crucify ['kru:sɪfaɪ] *vt* crocifiggere, mettere
in croce; (*fig*) distruggere, fare a pezzi.
crude [kru:d] *adj* (*materials*) greggio(a); non
raffinato(a); (*fig*: *basic*) crudo(a),
primitivo(a); (: *vulgar*) rozzo(a),
grossolano(a).
crude (oil) *n* (petrolio) greggio.
cruel ['kruəl] *adj* crudele.
cruelty ['kruəltɪ] *n* crudeltà *f inv*.
cruet ['kru:ɪt] *n* ampolla.
cruise [kru:z] *n* crociera ♦ *vi* andare a
velocità di crociera; (*taxi*) circolare.
cruise missile *n* missile *m* cruise *inv*.
cruiser ['kru:zə*] *n* incrociatore *m*.
cruising speed ['kru:zɪŋ-] *n* velocità *f inv* di
crociera.
crumb [krʌm] *n* briciola.
crumble ['krʌmbl] *vt* sbriciolare ♦ *vi*
sbriciolarsi; (*plaster etc*) sgretolarsi;
(*land, earth*) franare; (*building, fig*)
crollare.
crumbly ['krʌmblɪ] *adj* friabile.
crummy ['krʌmɪ] *adj* (*col*: *cheap*) di infima
categoria; (: *depressed*) giù inv.
crumpet ['krʌmpɪt] *n* specie di frittella.
crumple ['krʌmpl] *vt* raggrinzare,
spiegazzare.
crunch [krʌntʃ] *vt* sgranocchiare;
(*underfoot*) scricchiolare ♦ *n* (*fig*) punto *or*
momento cruciale.
crunchy ['krʌntʃɪ] *adj* croccante.
crusade [kru:'seɪd] *n* crociata ♦ *vi* (*fig*): **to** ~
for/against fare una crociata per/contro.
crusader [kru:'seɪdə*] *n* crociato; (*fig*): ~
(for) sostenitore/trice (di).
crush [krʌʃ] *n* folla; (*love*): **to have a** ~ **on
sb** avere una cotta per qn; (*drink*): **lemon**
~ spremuta di limone ♦ *vt* schiacciare;
(*crumple*) sgualcire; (*grind, break up*: garlic,

ice) tritare; (: *grapes*) pigiare.
crushing ['krʌʃɪŋ] *adj* schiacciante.
crust [krʌst] *n* crosta.
crustacean [krʌs'teɪʃən] *n* crostaceo.
crusty ['krʌstɪ] *adj* (*bread*) croccante; (*person*) brontolone(a).
crutch [krʌtʃ] *n* (*MED*) gruccia; (*support*) sostegno; (*also*: **crotch**) pattina.
crux [krʌks] *n* nodo.
cry [kraɪ] *vi* piangere; (*shout*: *also*: ~ **out**) urlare ♦ *n* urlo, grido; (*of animal*) verso; **to ~ for help** gridare aiuto; **what are you ~ing about?** perché piangi?; **she had a good ~** si è fatta un bel pianto; **it's a far ~ from** ... (*fig*) è tutt'un'altra cosa da ....
▶**cry off** *vi* ritirarsi.
crying ['kraɪɪŋ] *adj* (*fig*) palese; urgente.
crypt [krɪpt] *n* cripta.
cryptic ['krɪptɪk] *adj* ermetico(a).
crystal ['krɪstl] *n* cristallo.
crystal-clear ['krɪstl'klɪə*] *adj* cristallino(a); (*fig*) chiaro(a) (come il sole).
crystallize ['krɪstəlaɪz] *vi* cristallizzarsi ♦ *vt* (*fig*) concretizzarsi, concretare; ~**d fruits** (*BRIT*) frutta candita.
CSA *n abbr* (*US*) = *Confederate States of America*; (*BRIT*: = *Child Support Agency*) *istituto a difesa dei figli di coppie separate, che si adopera affinché venga rispettato l'obbligo del mantenimento.*
CSC *n abbr* (= *Civil Service Commission*) *commissione per il reclutamento dei funzionari statali.*
CS gas *n* (*BRIT*) *tipo di gas lacrimogeno.*
CST *abbr* (*US*: = *central standard time*) *fuso orario.*
CT *abbr* (*US*) = *Connecticut.*
ct *abbr* = *cent, court.*
CTC *n abbr* (*BRIT*: = *city technology college*) *istituto tecnico superiore.*
cu. *abbr* = **cubic**.
cub [kʌb] *n* cucciolo; (*also*: ~ **scout**) lupetto.
Cuba ['kju:bə] *n* Cuba.
Cuban ['kju:bən] *adj*, *n* cubano(a).
cubbyhole ['kʌbɪhəʊl] *n* angolino.
cube [kju:b] *n* cubo ♦ *vt* (*MATH*) elevare al cubo.
cube root *n* radice *f* cubica.
cubic ['kju:bɪk] *adj* cubico(a); ~ **metre** *etc* metro *etc* cubo; ~ **capacity** (*AUT*) cilindrata.
cubicle ['kju:bɪkl] *n* scompartimento separato; cabina.
cuckoo ['kuku:] *n* cucù *m inv*.
cuckoo clock *n* orologio a cucù.
cucumber ['kju:kʌmbə*] *n* cetriolo.

cud [kʌd] *n*: **to chew the** ~ ruminare.
cuddle ['kʌdl] *vt* abbracciare, coccolare ♦ *vi* abbracciarsi.
cuddly ['kʌdlɪ] *adj* da coccolare.
cudgel ['kʌdʒl] *n* randello ♦ *vt*: **to** ~ **one's brains** scervellarsi, spremere le meningi.
cue [kju:] *n* stecca; (*THEAT etc*) segnale *m*.
cuff [kʌf] *n* (*of shirt, coat etc*) polsino; (*US*: on *trousers*) = **turnup**; (*blow*) schiaffo ♦ *vt* dare uno schiaffo a; **off the** ~ *adv* improvvisando.
cufflink ['kʌflɪŋk] *n* gemello.
cu. ft. *abbr* = *cubic feet.*
cu. in. *abbr* = *cubic inches.*
cuisine [kwɪ'zi:n] *n* cucina.
cul-de-sac ['kʌldəsæk] *n* vicolo cieco.
culinary ['kʌlɪnərɪ] *adj* culinario(a).
cull [kʌl] *vt* (*kill selectively*: *animals*) selezionare e abbattere.
culminate ['kʌlmɪneɪt] *vi*: **to** ~ **in** culminare con.
culmination [kʌlmɪ'neɪʃən] *n* culmine *m*.
culottes [kju:'lɔts] *npl* gonna *f* pantalone *inv*.
culpable ['kʌlpəbl] *adj* colpevole.
culprit ['kʌlprɪt] *n* colpevole *m/f*.
cult [kʌlt] *n* culto.
cult figure *n* idolo.
cultivate ['kʌltɪveɪt] *vt* (*also fig*) coltivare.
cultivation [kʌltɪ'veɪʃən] *n* coltivazione *f*.
cultural ['kʌltʃərəl] *adj* culturale.
culture ['kʌltʃə*] *n* (*also fig*) cultura.
cultured ['kʌltʃəd] *adj* colto(a).
cumbersome ['kʌmbəsəm] *adj* ingombrante.
cumin ['kʌmɪn] *n* (*spice*) cumino.
cumulative ['kju:mjulətɪv] *adj* cumulativo(a).
cunning ['kʌnɪŋ] *n* astuzia, furberia ♦ *adj* astuto(a), furbo(a); (*clever*: *device*, *idea*) ingegnoso(a).
cunt [kʌnt] (*col!*) *n* figa (!); (*insult*) stronzo/a (!).
cup [kʌp] *n* tazza; (*prize*) coppa; **a** ~ **of tea** una tazza di tè.
cupboard ['kʌbəd] *n* armadio.
cup final *n* (*BRIT FOOTBALL*) finale *f* di coppa.
Cupid ['kju:pɪd] *n* Cupido; (*figurine*): **c**~ cupido.
cupidity [kju:'pɪdɪtɪ] *n* cupidigia.
cupola ['kju:pələ] *n* cupola.
cuppa ['kʌpə] *n* (*BRIT col*) tazza di tè.
cup-tie ['kʌptaɪ] *n* (*BRIT FOOTBALL*) partita di coppa.
curable ['kjuərəbl] *adj* curabile.
curate ['kjuərɪt] *n* cappellano.
curator [kjuə'reɪtə*] *n* direttore *m* (*di museo*

etc).

curb [kəːb] *vt* tenere a freno; (*expenditure*) limitare ♦ *n* freno; (*US*) = **kerb**.

curd cheese [kəːd-] *n* cagliata.

curdle ['kəːdl] *vi* cagliare.

curds [kəːdz] *npl* latte *m* cagliato.

cure [kjuə*] *vt* guarire; (*CULIN*) trattare; affumicare; essiccare ♦ *n* rimedio; **to be ~d of sth** essere guarito(a) da qc.

cure-all ['kjuərɔːl] *n* (*also fig*) panacea, toccasana *m inv*.

curfew ['kəːfjuː] *n* coprifuoco.

curio ['kjuərɪəu] *n* curiosità *f inv*.

curiosity [kjuərɪ'ɔsɪtɪ] *n* curiosità.

curious ['kjuərɪəs] *adj* curioso(a); **I'm ~ about him** m'incuriosisce.

curiously ['kjuərɪəslɪ] *adv* con curiosità; (*strangely*) stranamente; **~ enough,** ... per quanto possa sembrare strano, ...

curl [kəːl] *n* riccio; (*of smoke etc*) anello ♦ *vt* ondulare; (*tightly*) arricciare ♦ *vi* arricciarsi.

▶**curl up** *vi* avvolgersi a spirale; rannicchiarsi.

curler ['kəːlə*] *n* bigodino; (*SPORT*) giocatore/trice di curling.

curlew ['kəːluː] *n* chiurlo.

curling ['kəːlɪŋ] *n* (*SPORT*) curling *m*.

curling tongs, (*US*) **curling irons** *npl* (*for hair*) arricciacapelli *m inv*.

curly ['kəːlɪ] *adj* ricciuto(a).

currant ['kʌrnt] *n* uva passa.

currency ['kʌrnsɪ] *n* moneta; **foreign ~** divisa estera; **to gain ~** (*fig*) acquistare larga diffusione.

current ['kʌrnt] *adj* corrente; (*tendency, price, event*) attuale ♦ *n* corrente *f*; **in ~ use** in uso corrente, d'uso comune; **the ~ issue of a magazine** l'ultimo numero di una rivista; **direct/alternating ~** (*ELEC*) corrente continua/alternata.

current account *n* (*BRIT*) conto corrente.

current affairs *npl* attualità *fpl*.

current assets (*COMM*) attivo realizzabile e disponibile.

current liabilities *npl* (*COMM*) passività *fpl* correnti.

currently ['kʌrntlɪ] *adv* attualmente.

curriculum, *pl* **~s** *or* **curricula** [kə'rɪkjuləm, -lə] *n* curriculum *m inv*.

curriculum vitae (CV) [-'viːtaɪ] *n* curriculum vitae *m inv*.

curry ['kʌrɪ] *n* curry *m inv* ♦ *vt*: **to ~ favour with** cercare di attirarsi i favori di; **chicken ~** pollo al curry.

curry powder *n* curry *m*.

curse [kəːs] *vt* maledire ♦ *vi* bestemmiare ♦ *n* maledizione *f*; bestemmia.

cursor ['kəːsə*] *n* (*COMPUT*) cursore *m*.

cursory ['kəːsərɪ] *adj* superficiale.

curt [kəːt] *adj* secco(a).

curtail [kəː'teɪl] *vt* (*visit etc*) accorciare; (*expenses etc*) ridurre, decurtare.

curtain ['kəːtn] *n* tenda; (*THEAT*) sipario; **to draw the ~s** (*together*) chiudere *or* tirare le tende; (*apart*) aprire le tende.

curtain call *n* (*THEAT*) chinata alla ribalta.

curts(e)y ['kəːtsɪ] *n* inchino, riverenza ♦ *vi* fare un inchino *or* una riverenza.

curvature ['kəːvətʃə*] *n* curvatura.

curve [kəːv] *n* curva ♦ *vt* curvare ♦ *vi* curvarsi; (*road*) fare una curva.

curved [kəːvd] *adj* curvo(a).

cushion ['kuʃən] *n* cuscino ♦ *vt* (*shock*) fare da cuscinetto a.

cushy ['kuʃɪ] *adj* (*col*): **a ~ job** un lavoro di tutto riposo; **to have a ~ time** spassarsela.

custard ['kʌstəd] *n* (*for pouring*) crema.

custard powder *n* (*BRIT*) crema pasticcera in polvere.

custodial sentence [kʌs'təudɪəl-] *n* condanna a pena detentiva.

custodian [kʌs'təudɪən] *n* custode *m/f*; (*of museum etc*) soprintendente *m/f*.

custody ['kʌstədɪ] *n* (*of child*) custodia; (*for offenders*) arresto; **to take sb into ~** mettere qn in detenzione preventiva; **in the ~ of** alla custodia di.

custom ['kʌstəm] *n* costume *m*, usanza; (*LAW*) consuetudine *f*; (*COMM*) clientela; *see also* **customs**.

customary ['kʌstəmərɪ] *adj* consueto(a); **it is ~ to do** è consuetudine fare.

custom-built ['kʌstəm'bɪlt] *adj see* **custom-made**.

customer ['kʌstəmə*] *n* cliente *m/f*; **he's an awkward ~** (*col*) è un tipo incontentabile.

customer profile *n* profilo del cliente.

customized ['kʌstəmaɪzd] *adj* personalizzato(a); (*car*) fuoriserie *inv*.

custom-made ['kʌstəm'meɪd] *adj* (*clothes*) fatto(a) su misura; (*other goods: also:* **custom-built**) fatto(a) su ordinazione.

customs ['kʌstəmz] *npl* dogana; **to go through (the) ~** passare la dogana.

Customs and Excise *n* (*BRIT*) Ufficio Dazi e Dogana.

customs officer *n* doganiere *m*.

cut [kʌt] *vb* (*pt, pp* **cut**) *vt* tagliare; (*shape, make*) intagliare; (*reduce*) ridurre; (*col: avoid: class, lecture, appointment*) saltare ♦ *vi* tagliare; (*intersect*) tagliarsi ♦ *n* taglio; (*in salary etc*) riduzione *f*; **cold ~s** *npl* (*US*) affettati *mpl*; **power ~** mancanza di corrente elettrica; **to ~ one's finger** tagliarsi un dito; **to get one's hair ~** farsi tagliare i capelli; **to ~ a tooth** mettere un dente; **to ~ sb/sth short** interrompere qn/qc; **to ~ sb dead** ignorare qn completamente.

► **cut back** vt (plants) tagliare; (production, expenditure) ridurre.

► **cut down** vt (tree) abbattere; (consumption, expenses) ridurre; **to ~ sb down to size*** (fig) sgonfiare or ridimensionare qn.

► **cut down on** vt fus ridurre.

► **cut in** vi (interrupt conversation): **to ~ in (on)** intromettersi (in); (AUT) tagliare la strada (a).

► **cut off** vt tagliare; (fig) isolare; **we've been ~ off** (TEL) è caduta la linea.

► **cut out** vt tagliare; (picture) ritagliare.

► **cut up** vt (gen) tagliare; (chop: food) sminuzzare.

cut-and-dried ['kʌtən'draɪd] adj (also: **cut-and-dry**) assodato(a).

cutback ['kʌtbæk] n riduzione f.

cute [kjuːt] adj grazioso(a); (clever) astuto(a).

cut glass n cristallo.

cuticle ['kjuːtɪkl] n (on nail) pellicina, cuticola.

cutlery ['kʌtlərɪ] n posate fpl.

cutlet ['kʌtlɪt] n costoletta.

cutoff ['kʌtɔf] n (also: ~ point) limite m.

cutoff switch n interruttore m.

cutout ['kʌtaut] n (switch) interruttore m; (paper, cardboard figure) ritaglio.

cut-price ['kʌt'praɪs], (US) **cut-rate** ['kʌt'reɪt] adj a prezzo ridotto.

cutthroat ['kʌtθrəut] n assassino ♦ adj: ~ **competition** concorrenza spietata.

cutting ['kʌtɪŋ] adj tagliente; (fig) pungente ♦ n (BRIT: PRESS) ritaglio (di giornale); (: RAIL) trincea; (CINE) montaggio.

cutting edge n (of knife) taglio, filo; **on** or **at the ~ of sth** all'avanguardia di qc.

cut-up ['kʌtʌp] adj stravolto(a).

CV n abbr see **curriculum vitae**.

C & W n abbr = **country and western (music)**.

cwt. abbr = **hundredweight**.

cyanide ['saɪənaɪd] n cianuro.

cybercafé ['saɪbə,kæfeɪ] n cybercaffè m inv

cybernetics [saɪbə'nɛtɪks] n cibernetica.

cyberterrorism [saɪbə'tɛrərɪzəm] n ciberterrorismo.

cyclamen ['sɪkləmən] n ciclamino.

cycle ['saɪkl] n ciclo; (bicycle) bicicletta ♦ vi andare in bicicletta.

cycle path n percorso ciclabile.

cycle race n gara or corsa ciclistica.

cycle rack n portabiciclette m inv.

cycle track n percorso ciclabile; (in velodrome) pista.

cycling ['saɪklɪŋ] n ciclismo; **to go on a ~ holiday** (BRIT) fare una vacanza in bicicletta.

cyclist ['saɪklɪst] n ciclista m/f.

cyclone ['saɪkləun] n ciclone m.

cygnet ['sɪgnɪt] n cigno giovane.

cylinder ['sɪlɪndə*] n cilindro.

cylinder capacity n cilindrata.

cylinder head n testata.

cylinder head gasket n guarnizione f della testata del cilindro.

cymbals ['sɪmblz] npl cembali mpl.

cynic ['sɪnɪk] n cinico/a.

cynical ['sɪnɪkl] adj cinico(a).

cynicism ['sɪnɪsɪzəm] n cinismo.

cypress ['saɪprɪs] n cipresso.

Cypriot ['sɪprɪət] adj, n cipriota (m/f).

Cyprus ['saɪprəs] n Cipro.

cyst [sɪst] n cisti f inv.

cystitis [sɪ'staɪtɪs] n cistite f.

CZ n abbr (US: = Canal Zone) zona del Canale di Panama.

Czech [tʃɛk] adj ceco(a) ♦ n ceco/a; (LING) ceco; **the ~ Republic** la Repubblica Ceca.

Czechoslovak [tʃɛkə'sləuvæk] adj, n = **Czechoslovakian**.

Czechoslovakia [tʃɛkəslə'vækɪə] n Cecoslovacchia.

Czechoslovakian [tʃɛkəslə'vækɪən] adj, n cecoslovacco(a).

D d

D, d [diː] n (letter) D, d f or m inv; (MUS): **D** re m; **D for David**, (US) **D for Dog** ≈ D come Domodossola.

D abbr (US POL) = **Democrat(ic)**.

d abbr (BRIT: old) = **penny**.

d. abbr = **died**.

DA n abbr (US) see **district attorney**.

dab [dæb] vt (eyes, wound) tamponare; (paint, cream) applicare (con leggeri colpetti); **a ~ of paint** un colpetto di vernice.

dabble ['dæbl] vi: **to ~ in** occuparsi (da dilettante) di.

Dacca ['dækə] n Dacca f.

dachshund ['dækshund] n bassotto.

dad, daddy [dæd, 'dædɪ] n babbo, papà m inv.

daddy-long-legs [dædɪ'lɒŋlɛgz] n tipula, zanzarone m.

daffodil ['dæfədɪl] n trombone m, giunchiglia.

daft [dɑːft] adj sciocco(a); **to be ~ about sb** perdere la testa per qn; **to be ~ about sth** andare pazzo per qc.

dagger ['dægə*] n pugnale m.

dahlia ['deɪljə] n dalia.

daily ['deɪlɪ] adj quotidiano(a), giornaliero(a) ♦ n quotidiano; (BRIT: servant) donna di servizio ♦ adv tutti i giorni; **twice ~** due volte al giorno.

dainty ['deɪntɪ] adj delicato(a), grazioso(a).

dairy ['dɛərɪ] n (shop) latteria; (on farm) caseificio ♦ cpd caseario(a).

dairy cow n mucca da latte.

dairy farm n caseificio.

dairy produce n latticini mpl.

dais ['deɪɪs] n pedana, palco.

daisy ['deɪzɪ] n margherita.

daisy wheel n (on printer) margherita.

daisy-wheel printer ['deɪzɪwiːl-] n stampante f a margherita.

Dakar ['dækə*] n Dakar f.

dale [deɪl] n valle f.

dally ['dælɪ] vi trastullarsi.

dalmatian [dæl'meɪʃən] n (dog) dalmata m.

dam [dæm] n diga; (reservoir) bacino artificiale ♦ vt sbarrare; costruire dighe su.

damage ['dæmɪdʒ] n danno, danni mpl; (fig) danno ♦ vt danneggiare; (fig) recar danno a; **~ to property** danni materiali.

damages ['dæmɪdʒɪz] npl (LAW) danni mpl; **to pay £5000 in ~** pagare 5000 sterline di indennizzo.

damaging ['dæmɪdʒɪŋ] adj: **~ (to)** nocivo(a) (a).

Damascus [də'mɑːskəs] n Damasco f.

dame [deɪm] n (title, US col) donna; (THEAT) vecchia signora (ruolo comico di donna recitato da un uomo).

damn [dæm] vt condannare; (curse) maledire ♦ n (col): **I don't give a ~** non me ne importa un fico ♦ adj (col): **this ~ ...** questo maledetto ...; **~ (it)!** accidenti!

damnable ['dæmnəbl] adj (col: behaviour) vergognoso(a); (: weather) schifoso(a).

damnation [dæm'neɪʃən] n (REL) dannazione f ♦ excl (col) dannazione!, diavolo!

damning ['dæmɪŋ] adj (evidence) schiacciante.

damp [dæmp] adj umido(a) ♦ n umidità, umido ♦ vt (also: ~en) (cloth, rag) inumidire, bagnare; (enthusiasm etc) spegnere.

dampcourse ['dæmpkɔːs] n strato m isolante antiumido inv.

damper ['dæmpə*] n (MUS) sordina; (of fire) valvola di tiraggio; **to put a ~ on sth** (fig: atmosphere) gelare; (: enthusiasm) far sbollire.

dampness ['dæmpnɪs] n umidità, umido.

damson ['dæmzən] n susina damaschina.

dance [dɑːns] n danza, ballo; (ball) ballo ♦ vi ballare; **to ~ about** saltellare.

dance hall n dancing m inv, sala da ballo.

dancer ['dɑːnsə*] n danzatore/trice; (professional) ballerino/a.

dancing ['dɑːnsɪŋ] n danza, ballo.

D and C n abbr (MED: = dilation and curettage) raschiamento.

dandelion ['dændɪlaɪən] n dente m di leone.

dandruff ['dændrəf] n forfora.

dandy ['dændɪ] n dandy m inv, elegantone m ♦ adj (US col) fantastico(a).

Dane [deɪn] n danese m/f.

danger ['deɪndʒə*] n pericolo; **there is a ~ of fire** c'è pericolo di incendio; **in ~** in pericolo; **out of ~** fuori pericolo; **he was in ~ of falling** rischiava di cadere.

danger list n (MED): **on the ~ list** in prognosi riservata.

dangerous ['deɪndʒrəs] adj pericoloso(a).

dangerously ['deɪndʒrəslɪ] adv: **~ ill** in pericolo di vita.

danger zone n area di pericolo.

dangle ['dæŋgl] vt dondolare; (fig) far balenare ♦ vi pendolare.

Danish ['deɪnɪʃ] adj danese ♦ n (LING) danese m.

Danish pastry n dolce m di pasta sfoglia.

dank [dæŋk] adj freddo(a) e umido(a).

Danube ['dænjuːb] n: **the ~** il Danubio.

dapper ['dæpə*] adj lindo(a).

Dardanelles [dɑːdə'nɛlz] npl Dardanelli mpl.

dare [dɛə*] vt: **to ~ sb to do** sfidare qn a fare ♦ vi: **to ~ (to) do sth** osare fare qc; **I ~n't tell him** (BRIT) non oso dirglielo; **I ~ say he'll turn up** immagino che spunterà.

daredevil ['dɛədɛvl] n scavezzacollo m/f.

Dar-es-Salaam ['dɑːrɛssə'lɑːm] n Dar-es-Salaam f.

daring ['dɛərɪŋ] adj audace, ardito(a).

dark [dɑːk] adj (night, room) buio(a), scuro(a); (colour, complexion) scuro(a); (fig) cupo(a), tetro(a), nero(a) ♦ n: **in the ~** al buio; **it is/is getting ~** è/si sta facendo buio; **in the ~ about** (fig) all'oscuro di; **after ~** a notte fatta; **~**

chocolate cioccolata amara.

darken ['dɑːkən] vt (room) oscurare; (photo, painting) far scuro(a) ♦ vi oscurarsi; imbrunirsi.

dark glasses npl occhiali mpl scuri.

dark horse n (fig) incognita.

darkly ['dɑːklɪ] adv (gloomily) cupamente, con aria cupa; (in a sinister way) minacciosamente.

darkness ['dɑːknɪs] n oscurità, buio.

darkroom ['dɑːkruːm] n camera oscura.

darling ['dɑːlɪŋ] adj caro(a) ♦ n tesoro.

darn [dɑːn] vt rammendare.

dart [dɑːt] n freccetta ♦ vi: to ~ towards (also: make a ~ towards) precipitarsi verso; to ~ along passare come un razzo; to ~ away guizzare via; see also **darts**.

dartboard ['dɑːtbɔːd] n bersaglio (per freccette).

darts [dɑːts] n tiro al bersaglio (con freccette).

dash [dæʃ] n (sign) lineetta; (small quantity: of liquid) goccio, goccino; (: of soda) spruzzo ♦ vt (missile) gettare; (hopes) infrangere ♦ vi: to ~ towards (also: make a ~ towards) precipitarsi verso.

▶**dash away** vi scappare via.

dashboard ['dæʃbɔːd] n cruscotto.

dashing ['dæʃɪŋ] adj ardito(a).

dastardly ['dæstədlɪ] adj vile.

DAT n abbr (= digital audio tape) cassetta f digitale audio inv.

data ['deɪtə] npl dati mpl.

database ['deɪtəbeɪs] n database m, base f di dati.

data capture n registrazione f or rilevazione f di dati.

data processing n elaborazione f (elettronica) dei dati.

data transmission n trasmissione f di dati.

date [deɪt] n data; (appointment) appuntamento; (fruit) dattero ♦ vt datare; (col: girl etc) uscire con; what's the ~ today? quanti ne abbiamo oggi?; ~ of birth data di nascita; closing ~ scadenza, termine m; to ~ adv fino a oggi; out of ~ scaduto(a); (old-fashioned) passato(a) di moda; up to ~ moderno(a); aggiornato(a); to bring up to ~ (correspondence, information) aggiornare; (method) modernizzare; (person) aggiornare, mettere al corrente; ~d the 13th datato il 13; thank you for your letter ~d 5th July or (US) July 5th la ringrazio per la sua lettera in data 5 luglio.

dated ['deɪtɪd] adj passato(a) di moda.

dateline ['deɪtlaɪn] n linea del

cambiamento di data.

date rape n stupro perpetrato da persona conosciuta.

date stamp n timbro datario.

daub [dɔːb] vt imbrattare.

daughter ['dɔːtə*] n figlia.

daughter-in-law ['dɔːtərɪnlɔː] n nuora.

daunt [dɔːnt] vt intimidire.

daunting ['dɔːntɪŋ] adj non invidiabile.

dauntless ['dɔːntlɪs] adj intrepido(a).

dawdle ['dɔːdl] vi bighellonare; to ~ over one's work gingillarsi con il lavoro.

dawn [dɔːn] n alba ♦ vi (day) spuntare; (fig) venire in mente; at ~ all'alba; from ~ to dusk dall'alba al tramonto; it ~ed on him that ... gli è venuto in mente che ....

dawn chorus n (BRIT) coro mattutino degli uccelli.

day [deɪ] n giorno; (as duration) giornata; (period of time, age) tempo, epoca; the ~ before il giorno avanti or prima; the ~ after, the following ~ il giorno dopo, il giorno seguente; the ~ before yesterday l'altroieri; the ~ after tomorrow dopodomani; (on) that ~ quel giorno; (on) the ~ that ... il giorno che or in cui ...; to work an 8-hour ~ avere una giornata lavorativa di 8 ore; by ~ di giorno; ~ by ~ giorno per giorno; paid by the ~ pagato(a) a giornata; these ~s, in the present ~ di questi tempi, oggigiorno.

daybook ['deɪbuk] n (BRIT) brogliaccio.

day boy n (SCOL) alunno esterno.

daybreak ['deɪbreɪk] n spuntar m del giorno.

day care centre n scuola materna.

daydream ['deɪdriːm] n sogno a occhi aperti ♦ vi sognare a occhi aperti.

day girl n (SCOL) alunna esterna.

daylight ['deɪlaɪt] n luce f del giorno.

daylight robbery n: it's ~! (BRIT col) è un vero furto!

Daylight Saving Time n (US) ora legale.

day release n: to be on ~ avere un giorno di congedo alla settimana per formazione professionale.

day return (ticket) n (BRIT) biglietto giornaliero di andata e ritorno.

day shift n turno di giorno.

daytime ['deɪtaɪm] n giorno.

day-to-day ['deɪtə'deɪ] adj (routine) quotidiano(a); (expenses) giornaliero(a); on a ~ basis a giornata.

day trader n (STOCK EXCHANGE) day dealer m/f inv, operatore che compra e vende titoli nel corso della stessa giornata.

day trip n gita (di un giorno).

day tripper n gitante m/f.

daze [deɪz] *vt* (*subj: drug*) inebetire; (: *blow*) stordire ♦ *n:* **in a ~** inebetito(a); stordito(a).

dazzle ['dæzl] *vt* abbagliare.

dazzling ['dæzlɪŋ] *adj* (*light*) abbagliante; (*colour*) violento(a); (*smile*) smagliante.

dB *abbr* (= *decibel*) db.

DC *abbr* (*ELEC:* = *direct current*) c.c.; (*US*) = *District of Columbia*.

DCC ® *n abbr* = *digital compact cassette*.

DD *n abbr* (= *Doctor of Divinity*) titolo di studio.

dd. *abbr* (*COMM*) = *delivered*.

DD *abbr* = **direct debit**.

D-day ['di:deɪ] *n* giorno dello sbarco alleato in Normandia.

DDS *n abbr* (*US:* = *Doctor of Dental Science*; *Doctor of Dental Surgery*) titoli di studio.

DDT *n abbr* (= *dichlorodiphenyl trichloroethane*) D.D.T. *m*.

DE *abbr* (*US*) = *Delaware*.

deacon ['di:kən] *n* diacono.

dead [dɛd] *adj* morto(a); (*numb*) intirizzito(a) ♦ *adv* assolutamente, perfettamente; **the ~** *npl* i morti; **he was shot ~** fu colpito a morte; **~ on time** in perfetto orario; **~ tired** stanco(a) morto(a); **to stop ~** fermarsi in tronco; **the line has gone ~** (*TEL*) è caduta la linea.

dead beat *adj* (*col*) stanco(a) morto(a).

deaden ['dɛdn] *vt* (*blow, sound*) ammortire; (*make numb*) intirizzire.

dead end *n* vicolo cieco.

dead-end ['dɛdɛnd] *adj:* **a ~ job** un lavoro senza sbocchi.

dead heat *n* (*SPORT*): **to finish in a ~** finire alla pari.

dead-letter office [dɛd'lɛtə-] *n* ufficio della posta in giacenza.

deadline ['dɛdlaɪn] *n* scadenza; **to work to a ~** avere una scadenza.

deadlock ['dɛdlɔk] *n* punto morto.

dead loss *n* (*col*): **to be a ~** (*person, thing*) non valere niente.

deadly ['dɛdlɪ] *adj* mortale; (*weapon, poison*) micidiale ♦ *adv:* **~ dull** di una noia micidiale.

deadpan ['dɛdpæn] *adj* a faccia impassibile.

Dead Sea *n:* **the ~** il mar Morto.

deaf [dɛf] *adj* sordo(a); **to turn a ~ ear to sth** fare orecchi da mercante a qc.

deaf-aid ['dɛfeɪd] *n* apparecchio per la sordità.

deaf-and-dumb ['dɛfən'dʌm] *adj* (*person*) sordomuto(a); (*alphabet*) dei sordomuti.

deafen ['dɛfn] *vt* assordare.

deafening ['dɛfnɪŋ] *adj* fragoroso(a), assordante.

deaf-mute ['dɛfmjuːt] *n* sordomuto/a.

deafness ['dɛfnɪs] *n* sordità.

deal [diːl] *n* accordo; (*business ~*) affare *m* ♦ *vt* (*pt, pp* **dealt** [dɛlt]) (*blow, cards*) dare; **to strike a ~ with sb** fare un affare con qn; **it's a ~!** (*col*) affare fatto!; **he got a bad/fair ~ from them** l'hanno trattato male/bene; **a good ~ of, a great ~ of** molto(a).

▶**deal in** *vt fus* (*COMM*) occuparsi di.

▶**deal with** *vt fus* (*COMM*) fare affari con, trattare con; (*handle*) occuparsi di; (*be about: book etc*) trattare di.

dealer ['diːlə*] *n* commerciante *m/f*.

dealership ['diːləʃɪp] *n* rivenditore *m*.

dealings ['diːlɪŋz] *npl* rapporti *mpl*; (*in goods, shares*) transazioni *fpl*.

dealt [dɛlt] *pt, pp of* **deal**.

dean [diːn] *n* (*REL*) decano; (*SCOL*) preside *m* di facoltà (*or* di collegio).

dear [dɪə*] *adj* caro(a) ♦ *n:* **my ~** caro mio/cara mia; **~ me!** Dio mio!; **D~ Sir/Madam** (*in letter*) Egregio Signore/Egregia Signora; **D~ Mr/Mrs X** Gentile Signor/Signora X.

dearly ['dɪəlɪ] *adv* (*love*) moltissimo; (*pay*) a caro prezzo.

dear money *n* (*COMM*) denaro ad alto interesse.

dearth [dɜːθ] *n* scarsità, carestia.

death [dɛθ] *n* morte *f*; (*ADMIN*) decesso.

deathbed ['dɛθbɛd] *n* letto di morte.

death certificate *n* atto di decesso.

death duty *n* (*BRIT*) imposta *or* tassa di successione.

deathly ['dɛθlɪ] *adj* di morte ♦ *adv* come un cadavere.

death penalty *n* pena di morte.

death rate *n* indice *m* di mortalità.

death row [-rəu] *n* (*US*): **to be on ~** essere nel braccio della morte.

death sentence *n* condanna a morte.

death squad *n* squadra della morte.

deathtrap ['dɛθtræp] *n* trappola mortale.

deb [dɛb] *n abbr* (*col*) = **debutante**.

debacle [deɪ'bɑːkl] *n* (*defeat*) disfatta; (*collapse*) sfacelo.

debar [dɪ'bɑː*] *vt:* **to ~ sb from a club** *etc* escludere qn da un club *etc*; **to ~ sb from doing** vietare a qn di fare.

debase [dɪ'beɪs] *vt* (*currency*) adulterare; (*person*) degradare.

debatable [dɪ'beɪtəbl] *adj* discutibile; **it is ~ whether ...** è in dubbio se ....

debate [dɪ'beɪt] *n* dibattito ♦ *vt* dibattere, discutere ♦ *vi* (*consider*): **to ~ whether** riflettere se.

debauchery [dɪ'bɔːtʃərɪ] *n* dissolutezza.
debenture [dɪ'bɛntʃə*] *n* (*COMM*)
obbligazione *f.*
debilitate [dɪ'bɪlɪteɪt] *vt* debilitare.
debit ['dɛbɪt] *n* debito ♦ *vt*: **to ~ a sum to sb**
or **to sb's account** addebitare una somma
a qn.
debit balance *n* saldo debitore.
debit note *n* nota di addebito.
debonair [dɛbə'nɛə*] *adj* gioviale e
disinvolto(a).
debrief [diː'briːf] *vt* chiamare a rapporto (a
operazione ultimata).
debriefing [diː'briːfɪŋ] *n* rapporto.
debris ['dɛbriː] *n* detriti *mpl.*
debt [dɛt] *n* debito; **to be in ~** essere
indebitato(a); **~s of £5000** debiti per 5000
sterline; **bad ~** debito insoluto.
debt collector *n* agente *m* di recupero
crediti.
debtor ['dɛtə*] *n* debitore/trice.
debug [diː'bʌg] *vt* (*COMPUT*) localizzare e
rimuovere errori in.
debunk [diː'bʌŋk] *vt* (*col: theory*)
demistificare; (: *claim*) smentire;
(: *person, institution*) screditare.
debut ['deɪbjuː] *n* debutto.
debutante ['dɛbjutɑːnt] *n* debuttante *f.*
Dec. *abbr* (= *December*) dic.
decade ['dɛkeɪd] *n* decennio.
decadence ['dɛkədəns] *n* decadenza.
decadent ['dɛkədənt] *adj* decadente.
de-caff ['diːkæf] *n* (*col*) decaffeinato.
decaffeinated [dɪ'kæfɪneɪtɪd] *adj*
decaffeinato(a).
decamp [dɪ'kæmp] *vi* (*col*) filarsela, levare
le tende.
decant [dɪ'kænt] *vt* (*wine*) travasare.
decanter [dɪ'kæntə*] *n* caraffa.
decarbonize [diː'kɑːbənaɪz] *vt* (*AUT*)
decarburare.
decathlon [dɪ'kæθlən] *n* decathlon *m.*
decay [dɪ'keɪ] *n* decadimento;
imputridimento; (*fig*) rovina; (*also*: **tooth**
~) carie *f* ♦ *vi* (*rot*) imputridire; (*fig*)
andare in rovina.
decease [dɪ'siːs] *n* decesso.
deceased [dɪ'siːst] *n*: **the ~** il(la)
defunto(a).
deceit [dɪ'siːt] *n* inganno.
deceitful [dɪ'siːtful] *adj* ingannevole,
perfido(a).
deceive [dɪ'siːv] *vt* ingannare; **to ~ o.s.**
illudersi, ingannarsi.
decelerate [diː'sɛləreɪt] *vt, vi* rallentare.
December [dɪ'sɛmbə*] *n* dicembre *m*; *for
phrases see also* **July.**
decency ['diːsənsɪ] *n* decenza.

decent ['diːsənt] *adj* decente; **they were**
very ~ about it si sono comportati da
signori riguardo a ciò.
decently ['diːsəntlɪ] *adv* (*respectably*)
decentemente, convenientemente;
(*kindly*) gentilmente.
decentralization [diːsɛntrəlaɪ'zeɪʃən] *n*
decentramento.
decentralize [diː'sɛntrəlaɪz] *vt* decentrare.
deception [dɪ'sɛpʃən] *n* inganno.
deceptive [dɪ'sɛptɪv] *adj* ingannevole.
decibel ['dɛsɪbɛl] *n* decibel *m inv.*
decide [dɪ'saɪd] *vt* (*person*) far prendere
una decisione a; (*question, argument*)
risolvere, decidere ♦ *vi* decidere,
decidersi; **to ~ to do/that** decidere di
fare/che; **to ~ on** decidere per; **to ~**
against doing sth decidere di non fare
qc.
decided [dɪ'saɪdɪd] *adj* (*resolute*) deciso(a);
(*clear, definite*) netto(a), chiaro(a).
decidedly [dɪ'saɪdɪdlɪ] *adv* indubbiamente;
decisamente.
deciding [dɪ'saɪdɪŋ] *adj* decisivo(a).
deciduous [dɪ'sɪdjuəs] *adj* deciduo(a).
decimal ['dɛsɪməl] *adj, n* decimale (*m*); **to 3**
~ places al terzo decimale.
decimalize ['dɛsɪməlaɪz] *vt* (*BRIT*)
convertire al sistema metrico decimale.
decimal point *n* ≈ virgola.
decimate ['dɛsɪmeɪt] *vt* decimare.
decipher [dɪ'saɪfə*] *vt* decifrare.
decision [dɪ'sɪʒən] *n* decisione *f*; **to make a**
~ prendere una decisione.
decisive [dɪ'saɪsɪv] *adj* (*victory, factor*)
decisivo(a); (*influence*) determinante;
(*manner, person*) risoluto(a), deciso(a);
(*reply*) deciso(a), categorico(a).
deck [dɛk] *n* (*NAUT*) ponte *m*; (*of cards*)
mazzo; (*of bus*): **top ~** imperiale *m*; **to go**
up on ~ salire in coperta; **below ~** sotto
coperta; **cassette ~** piastra (di
registrazione); **record ~** piatto
(giradischi).
deckchair ['dɛktʃɛə*] *n* sedia a sdraio.
deck hand *n* marinaio.
declaration [dɛklə'reɪʃən] *n* dichiarazione *f.*
declare [dɪ'klɛə*] *vt* dichiarare.
declassify [diː'klæsɪfaɪ] *vt* rendere
accessibile al pubblico.
decline [dɪ'klaɪn] *n* (*decay*) declino;
(*lessening*) ribasso ♦ *vt* declinare; rifiutare
♦ *vi* declinare; diminuire; **~ in living**
standards abbassamento del tenore di
vita; **to ~ to do sth** rifiutar(si) di fare qc.
declutch [diː'klʌtʃ] *vi* (*BRIT*) premere la
frizione.
decode [diː'kəud] *vt* decifrare.

decoder [di:'kəʊdə*] n (*COMPUT, TV*) decodificatore m.

decompose [di:kəm'pəʊz] vi decomporre.

decomposition [di:kɔmpə'zɪʃən] n decomposizione f.

decompression [di:kəm'prɛʃən] n decompressione f.

decompression chamber n camera di decompressione.

decongestant [di:kən'dʒɛstənt] n decongestionante m.

decontaminate [di:kən'tæmɪneɪt] vt decontaminare.

decontrol [di:kən'trəʊl] vt (*trade*) liberalizzare; (*prices*) togliere il controllo governativo a.

decor ['deɪkɔ:*] n decorazione f.

decorate ['dɛkəreɪt] vt (*adorn, give a medal to*) decorare; (*paint and paper*) pitturare e tappezzare.

decoration [dɛkə'reɪʃən] n decorazione f.

decorative ['dɛkərətɪv] adj decorativo(a).

decorator ['dɛkəreɪtə*] n decoratore/trice.

decorum [dɪ'kɔ:rəm] n decoro.

decoy ['di:kɔɪ] n zimbello; **they used him as a ~ for the enemy** l'hanno usato come esca per il nemico.

decrease n ['di:kri:s] diminuzione f ♦ vt, vi [di:'kri:s] diminuire; **to be on the ~** essere in diminuzione.

decreasing [di:'kri:sɪŋ] adj sempre meno inv.

decree [dɪ'kri:] n decreto ♦ vt: **to ~ (that)** decretare (che + sub); **~ absolute** sentenza di divorzio definitiva; **~ nisi** [-'naɪsaɪ] sentenza provvisoria di divorzio.

decrepit [dɪ'krɛpɪt] adj decrepito(a); (*building*) cadente.

decry [dɪ'kraɪ] vt condannare, deplorare.

dedicate ['dɛdɪkeɪt] vt consacrare; (*book etc*) dedicare.

dedicated ['dɛdɪkeɪtɪd] adj coscienzioso(a); (*COMPUT*) specializzato(a), dedicato(a).

dedication [dɛdɪ'keɪʃən] n (*devotion*) dedizione f; (*in book*) dedica.

deduce [dɪ'dju:s] vt dedurre.

deduct [dɪ'dʌkt] vt: **to ~ sth (from)** dedurre qc (da); (*from wage etc*) trattenere qc (da).

deduction [dɪ'dʌkʃən] n (*deducting*) deduzione f; (*from wage etc*) trattenuta; (*deducing*) deduzione f, conclusione f.

deed [di:d] n azione f, atto; (*LAW*) atto; **~ of covenant** atto di donazione.

deem [di:m] vt (*formal*) giudicare, ritenere; **to ~ it wise to do** ritenere prudente fare.

deep [di:p] adj profondo(a) ♦ adv: **~ in snow** affondato(a) nella neve; **spectators stood**

20 ~ c'erano 20 file di spettatori; **knee-~ in water** in acqua fino alle ginocchia; **4 metres ~** profondo(a) 4 metri; **he took a ~ breath** fece un respiro profondo.

deepen ['di:pn] vt (*hole*) approfondire ♦ vi approfondirsi; (*darkness*) farsi più intenso(a).

deep-freeze [di:p'fri:z] n congelatore m ♦ vt congelare.

deep-fry ['di:p'fraɪ] vt friggere in olio abbondante.

deeply ['di:plɪ] adv profondamente; **to regret sth ~** rammaricarsi sinceramente di qc.

deep-rooted ['di:p'ru:tɪd] adj (*prejudice*) profondamente radicato(a); (*affection*) profondo(a); (*habit*) inveterato(a).

deep-sea diver ['di:p'si:-] n palombaro.

deep-sea diving n immersione f in alto mare.

deep-sea fishing n pesca d'alto mare.

deep-seated ['di:p'si:tɪd] adj (*beliefs*) radicato(a).

deep-set ['di:psɛt] adj (*eyes*) infossato(a).

deep-vein thrombosis (DVT) n trombosi f inv venosa profonda.

deer [dɪə*] n (*pl inv*): **the ~** i cervidi (*ZOOL*); **(red) ~** cervo; **(fallow) ~** daino; **(roe) ~** capriolo.

deerskin ['dɪəskɪn] n pelle f di daino.

deerstalker ['dɪəstɔ:kə*] n berretto da cacciatore.

deface [dɪ'feɪs] vt imbrattare.

defamation [dɛfə'meɪʃən] n diffamazione f.

defamatory [dɪ'fæmətərɪ] adj diffamatorio(a).

default [dɪ'fɔ:lt] vi (*LAW*) essere contumace; (*gen*) essere inadempiente ♦ n (*COMPUT: also:* **~ value**) default m inv; **by ~** (*LAW*) in contumacia; (*SPORT*) per abbandono; **to ~ on a debt** non onorare un debito.

defaulter [dɪ'fɔ:ltə*] n (*on debt*) inadempiente m/f.

default option n (*COMPUT*) opzione f di default.

defeat [dɪ'fi:t] n sconfitta ♦ vt (*team, opponents*) sconfiggere; (*fig: plans, efforts*) frustrare.

defeatism [dɪ'fi:tɪzəm] n disfattismo.

defeatist [dɪ'fi:tɪst] adj, n disfattista (*m/f*).

defecate ['dɛfəkeɪt] vi defecare.

defect n ['di:fɛkt] difetto ♦ vi [dɪ'fɛkt]: **to ~ to the enemy/the West** passare al nemico/all'Ovest; **physical ~** difetto fisico; **mental ~** anomalia mentale.

defective [dɪ'fɛktɪv] adj difettoso(a).

defector [dɪ'fɛktə*] n rifugiato(a)

politico(a).

defence, (US) **defense** [dɪ'fɛns] n difesa; **in** ~ **of** in difesa di; **the Ministry of D~,** (US) **the Department of Defense** il Ministero della Difesa; **witness for the** ~ teste m/f a difesa.

defenceless [dɪ'fɛnslɪs] adj senza difesa.

defend [dɪ'fɛnd] vt difendere; (decision, action) giustificare; (opinion) sostenere.

defendant [dɪ'fɛndənt] n imputato/a.

defender [dɪ'fɛndə*] n difensore/a.

defending champion n (SPORT) campione/essa in carica.

defending counsel n (LAW) avvocato difensore.

defense [dɪ'fɛns] n (US) = **defence.**

defensive [dɪ'fɛnsɪv] adj difensivo(a) ♦ n difensiva; **on the** ~ sulla difensiva.

defer [dɪ'fəː*] vt (postpone) differire, rinviare ♦ vi (submit): **to** ~ **to sb/sth** rimettersi a qn/qc.

deference ['dɛfərəns] n deferenza; riguardo; **out of** or **in** ~ **to** per riguardo a.

defiance [dɪ'faɪəns] n sfida; **in** ~ **of** a dispetto di.

defiant [dɪ'faɪənt] adj (attitude) di sfida; (person) ribelle.

defiantly [dɪ'faɪəntlɪ] adv con aria di sfida.

deficiency [dɪ'fɪʃənsɪ] n deficienza; carenza; (COMM) ammanco.

deficiency disease n malattia da carenza.

deficient [dɪ'fɪʃənt] adj deficiente; insufficiente; **to be** ~ **in** mancare di.

deficit ['dɛfɪsɪt] n disavanzo.

defile vb [dɪ'faɪl] vt contaminare ♦ vi sfilare ♦ n ['diːfaɪl] gola, stretta.

define [dɪ'faɪn] vt (gen, COMPUT) definire.

definite ['dɛfɪnɪt] adj (fixed) definito(a), preciso(a); (clear, obvious) ben definito(a), esatto(a); (LING) determinativo(a); **he was** ~ **about it** ne era sicuro.

definitely ['dɛfɪnɪtlɪ] adv indubbiamente.

definition [dɛfɪ'nɪʃən] n definizione f.

definitive [dɪ'fɪnɪtɪv] adj definitivo(a).

deflate [diː'fleɪt] vt sgonfiare; (ECON) deflazionare; (pompous person) fare abbassare la cresta a.

deflation [diː'fleɪʃən] n (ECON) deflazione f.

deflationary [diː'fleɪʃənrɪ] adj (ECON) deflazionistico(a).

deflect [dɪ'flɛkt] vt deflettere, deviare.

defog ['diː'fɔg] vt (US AUT) sbrinare.

defogger ['diː'fɔgə*] n (US AUT) sbrinatore m.

deform [dɪ'fɔːm] vt deformare.

deformed [dɪ'fɔːmd] adj deforme.

deformity [dɪ'fɔːmɪtɪ] n deformità f inv.

Defra n abbr (BRIT): = Department for

Environment, Food and Rural Affairs.

defraud [dɪ'frɔːd] vt: **to** ~ **(of)** defraudare (di).

defray [dɪ'freɪ] vt: **to** ~ **sb's expenses** sostenere le spese di qn.

defrost [diː'frɔst] vt (fridge) disgelare; (frozen food) scongelare.

deft [dɛft] adj svelto(a), destro(a).

defunct [dɪ'fʌŋkt] adj defunto(a).

defuse [diː'fjuːz] vt disinnescare; (fig) distendere.

defy [dɪ'faɪ] vt sfidare; (efforts etc) resistere a; (refuse to obey: person) rifiutare di obbedire a.

degenerate vi [dɪ'dʒɛnəreɪt] degenerare ♦ adj [dɪ'dʒɛnərɪt] degenere.

degradation [dɛgrə'deɪʃən] n degradazione f.

degrade [dɪ'greɪd] vt degradare.

degrading [dɪ'greɪdɪŋ] adj degradante.

degree [dɪ'griː] n grado; (SCOL) laurea (universitaria); **10** ~**s below freezing** 10 gradi sotto zero; **a (first)** ~ **in maths** una laurea in matematica; **a considerable** ~ **of risk** una grossa percentuale di rischio; **by** ~**s** (gradually) gradualmente, a poco a poco; **to some** ~, **to a certain** ~ fino a un certo punto, in certa misura.

dehydrated [diːhaɪ'dreɪtɪd] adj disidratato(a); (milk, eggs) in polvere.

dehydration [diːhaɪ'dreɪʃən] n disidratazione f.

de-ice [diː'aɪs] vt (windscreen) disgelare.

de-icer ['diː'aɪsə*] n sbrinatore m.

deign [deɪn] vi: **to** ~ **to do** degnarsi di fare.

deity ['diːɪtɪ] n divinità f inv; dio/dea.

déjà vu [deɪʒɑː'vuː] n déjà vu m inv.

dejected [dɪ'dʒɛktɪd] adj abbattuto(a), avvilito(a).

dejection [dɪ'dʒɛkʃən] n abbattimento, avvilimento.

Del. abbr (US) = Delaware.

delay [dɪ'leɪ] vt (journey, operation) ritardare, rinviare; (travellers, trains) ritardare; (payment) differire ♦ n ritardo; **without** ~ senza ritardo.

delayed-action [dɪ'leɪd'ækʃən] adj a azione ritardata.

delectable [dɪ'lɛktəbl] adj delizioso(a).

delegate n ['dɛlɪgɪt] delegato/a ♦ vt ['dɛlɪgeɪt] delegare; **to** ~ **sth to sb/sb to do sth** delegare qc a qn/qn a fare qc.

delegation [dɛlɪ'geɪʃən] n delegazione f; (of work etc) delega.

delete [dɪ'liːt] vt (gen, COMPUT) cancellare.

Delhi ['dɛlɪ] n Delhi f.

deli ['dɛlɪ] n = **delicatessen.**

deliberate adj [dɪ'lɪbərɪt] (intentional)

intenzionale; (*slow*) misurato(a) ♦ *vi*
[dɪ'lɪbəreɪt] deliberare, riflettere.
deliberately [dɪ'lɪbərɪtlɪ] *adv* (*on purpose*)
deliberatamente.
deliberation [dɪlɪbə'reɪʃən] *n* (*consideration*)
riflessione *f*; (*discussion*) discussione *f*,
deliberazione *f*.
delicacy ['dɛlɪkəsɪ] *n* delicatezza.
delicate ['dɛlɪkɪt] *adj* delicato(a).
delicately ['dɛlɪkɪtlɪ] *adv* (*gen*)
delicatamente; (*act, express*) con
delicatezza.
delicatessen [dɛlɪkə'tɛsn] *n* ≈ salumeria.
delicious [dɪ'lɪʃəs] *adj* delizioso(a),
squisito(a).
delight [dɪ'laɪt] *n* delizia, gran piacere *m*
♦ *vt* dilettare; **it is a ~ to the eyes** è un
piacere guardarlo; **to take ~ in** divertirsi
a; **to be the ~ of** essere la gioia di.
delighted [dɪ'laɪtɪd] *adj*: **~ (at or with sth)**
contentissimo(a) (di qc), felice (di qc); **to
be ~ to do sth/that** essere felice di fare
qc/che + *sub*; **I'd be ~** con grande piacere.
delightful [dɪ'laɪtful] *adj* (*person, place,
meal*) delizioso(a); (*smile, manner*)
incantevole.
delimit [di:'lɪmɪt] *vt* delimitare.
delineate [dɪ'lɪnɪeɪt] *vt* delineare.
delinquency [dɪ'lɪŋkwənsɪ] *n* delinquenza.
delinquent [dɪ'lɪŋkwənt] *adj, n* delinquente
(*m/f*).
delirious [dɪ'lɪrɪəs] *adj* (*MED, fig*) delirante,
in delirio; **to be ~** delirare; (*fig*)
farneticare.
delirium [dɪ'lɪrɪəm] *n* delirio.
deliver [dɪ'lɪvə*] *vt* (*mail*) distribuire;
(*goods*) consegnare; (*speech*)
pronunciare; (*free*) liberare; (*MED*) far
partorire; **to ~ a message** fare
un'ambasciata; **to ~ the goods** (*fig*)
partorire.
deliverance [dɪ'lɪvrəns] *n* liberazione *f*.
delivery [dɪ'lɪvərɪ] *n* distribuzione *f*,
consegna; (*of speaker*) dizione *f*; (*MED*)
parto; **to take ~ of** prendere in consegna.
delivery note *n* bolla di consegna.
delivery van, (*US*) **delivery truck** *n*
furgoncino (per le consegne).
delta ['dɛltə] *n* delta *m*.
delude [dɪ'lu:d] *vt* deludere, illudere.
deluge ['dɛlju:dʒ] *n* diluvio ♦ *vt* (*fig*): **to ~
(with)** subissare (di), inondare (di).
delusion [dɪ'lu:ʒən] *n* illusione *f*.
de luxe [də'lʌks] *adj* di lusso.
delve [dɛlv] *vi*: **to ~ into** frugare in;
(*subject*) far ricerche in.
Dem. *abbr* (*US POL*) = **Democrat(ic)**.
demagogue ['dɛməgɔg] *n* demagogo.

demand [dɪ'mɑ:nd] *vt* richiedere ♦ *n*
richiesta; (*ECON*) domanda; **to ~ sth (from
or of sb)** pretendere qc (da qn), esigere
qc (da qn); **in ~** ricercato(a), richiesto(a);
on ~ a richiesta.
demand draft *n* (*COMM*) tratta a vista.
demanding [dɪ'mɑ:ndɪŋ] *adj* (*boss*)
esigente; (*work*) impegnativo(a).
demarcation [di:mɑ:'keɪʃən] *n*
demarcazione *f*.
demarcation dispute *n* (*INDUSTRY*)
controversia settoriale (*or* di categoria).
demean [dɪ'mi:n] *vt*: **to ~ o.s.** umiliarsi.
demeanour, (*US*) **demeanor** [dɪ'mi:nə*] *n*
comportamento; contegno.
demented [dɪ'mɛntɪd] *adj* demente,
impazzito(a).
demilitarized zone [di:'mɪlɪtəraɪzd-] *n* zona
smilitarizzata.
demise [dɪ'maɪz] *n* decesso.
demist [di:'mɪst] *vt* (*BRIT AUT*) sbrinare.
demister [di:'mɪstə*] *n* (*BRIT AUT*)
sbrinatore *m*.
demo ['dɛmɔu] *n abbr* (*col*) =
demonstration.
demobilize [di:'məubɪlaɪz] *vt* smobilitare.
democracy [dɪ'mɔkrəsɪ] *n* democrazia.
democrat ['dɛməkræt] *n* democratico/a.
democratic [dɛmə'krætɪk] *adj*
democratico(a); **the D~ Party** (*US*) il
partito democratico.
demography [dɪ'mɔgrəfɪ] *n* demografia.
demolish [dɪ'mɔlɪʃ] *vt* demolire.
demolition [dɛmə'lɪʃən] *n* demolizione *f*.
demon ['di:mən] *n* (*also fig*) demonio ♦ *cpd*:
a ~ squash player un mago dello squash;
a ~ driver un guidatore folle.
demonstrate ['dɛmənstreɪt] *vt* dimostrare,
provare ♦ *vi*: **to ~ (for/against)**
dimostrare (per/contro), manifestare
(per/contro).
demonstration [dɛmən'streɪʃən] *n*
dimostrazione *f*; (*POL*) manifestazione *f*,
dimostrazione; **to hold a ~** (*POL*) tenere
una manifestazione, fare una
dimostrazione.
demonstrative [dɪ'mɔnstrətɪv] *adj*
dimostrativo(a).
demonstrator ['dɛmənstreɪtə*] *n* (*POL*)
dimostrante *m/f*; (*COMM: sales person*)
dimostratore/trice; (: *car, computer etc*)
modello per dimostrazione.
demoralize [dɪ'mɔrəlaɪz] *vt* demoralizzare.
demote [dɪ'məut] *vt* far retrocedere.
demotion [dɪ'məuʃən] *n* retrocessione *f*,
degradazione *f*.
demur [dɪ'mə:*] *vi* (*formal*): **to ~ (at)**
sollevare obiezioni (a *or* su) ♦ *n*: **without**

~ senza obiezioni.

demure [dɪ'mjuə*] *adj* contegnoso(a).

demurrage [dɪ'mʌrɪdʒ] *n* diritti *mpl* di immagazzinaggio; spese *fpl* di controstallia.

den [dɛn] *n* tana, covo.

denationalization ['di:næʃnəlaɪ'zeɪʃən] *n* denazionalizzazione *f*.

denationalize [di:'næʃnəlaɪz] *vt* snazionalizzare.

denial [dɪ'naɪəl] *n* diniego; rifiuto.

denier ['dɛnɪə*] *n* denaro (*di filati, calze*).

denigrate ['dɛnɪgreɪt] *vt* denigrare.

denim ['dɛnɪm] *n* tessuto di cotone ritorto; *see also* **denims**.

denim jacket *n* giubbotto di jeans.

denims ['dɛnɪmz] *npl* blue jeans *mpl*.

denizen ['dɛnɪzən] *n* (*inhabitant*) abitante *m/f*; (*foreigner*) straniero(a) naturalizzato(a).

Denmark ['dɛnmɑːk] *n* Danimarca.

denomination [dɪnɔmɪ'neɪʃən] *n* (*money*) valore *m*; (*REL*) confessione *f*.

denominator [dɪ'nɔmɪneɪtə*] *n* denominatore *m*.

denote [dɪ'nəut] *vt* denotare.

denounce [dɪ'nauns] *vt* denunciare.

dense [dɛns] *adj* fitto(a); (*stupid*) ottuso(a), duro(a).

densely ['dɛnslɪ] *adv*: ~ **wooded** fittamente boscoso(a); ~ **populated** densamente popolato(a).

density ['dɛnsɪtɪ] *n* densità *f inv*; **single/double** ~ **disk** (*COMPUT*) disco a singola/doppia densità di registrazione.

dent [dɛnt] *n* ammaccatura ♦ *vt* (*also*: **make a** ~ **in**) ammaccare; (*fig*) intaccare.

dental ['dɛntl] *adj* dentale.

dental floss [-flɔs] *n* filo interdentale.

dental surgeon *n* medico/a dentista.

dentist ['dɛntɪst] *n* dentista *m/f*; ~**'s surgery** (*BRIT*) gabinetto dentistico.

dentistry ['dɛntɪstrɪ] *n* odontoiatria.

denture(s) ['dɛntʃə(z)] *n*(*pl*) dentiera.

denunciation [dɪnʌnsɪ'eɪʃən] *n* denuncia.

deny [dɪ'naɪ] *vt* negare; (*refuse*) rifiutare; **he denies having said it** nega di averlo detto.

deodorant [di:'əudərənt] *n* deodorante *m*.

depart [dɪ'pɑːt] *vi* partire; **to** ~ **from** (*leave*) allontanarsi da, partire da; (*fig*) deviare da.

departed [dɪ'pɑːtɪd] *adj* estinto(a) ♦ *n*: **the** ~ il caro estinto/la cara estinta.

department [dɪ'pɑːtmənt] *n* (*COMM*) reparto; (*SCOL*) sezione *f*, dipartimento; (*POL*) ministero; **that's not my** ~ (*also fig*) questo non è di mia competenza; **D~ of State** (*US*) Dipartimento di Stato.

departmental [di:pɑːt'mɛntl] *adj* (*dispute*) settoriale; (*meeting*) di sezione; ~ **manager** caporeparto *m/f*.

department store *n* grande magazzino.

departure [dɪ'pɑːtʃə*] *n* partenza; (*fig*): ~ **from** deviazione *f* da; **a new** ~ una novità.

departure lounge *n* sala d'attesa.

depend [dɪ'pɛnd] *vi*: **to** ~ (**up)on** dipendere da; (*rely on*) contare su; (*be dependent on*) dipendere (economicamente) da, essere a carico di; **it** ~**s** dipende; ~**ing on the result** ... a seconda del risultato ....

dependable [dɪ'pɛndəbl] *adj* fidato(a); (*car etc*) affidabile.

dependant [dɪ'pɛndənt] *n* persona a carico.

dependence [dɪ'pɛndəns] *n* dipendenza.

dependent [dɪ'pɛndənt] *adj*: **to be** ~ (**on**) (*gen*) dipendere (da); (*child, relative*) essere a carico (di) ♦ *n* = **dependant**.

depict [dɪ'pɪkt] *vt* (*in picture*) dipingere; (*in words*) descrivere.

depilatory [dɪ'pɪlətərɪ] *n* (*also*: ~ **cream**) crema depilatoria.

depleted [dɪ'pliːtɪd] *adj* diminuito(a).

deplorable [dɪ'plɔːrəbl] *adj* deplorevole, lamentevole.

deplore [dɪ'plɔː*] *vt* deplorare.

deploy [dɪ'plɔɪ] *vt* dispiegare.

depopulate [di:'pɔpjuleɪt] *vt* spopolare.

depopulation ['di:pɔpju'leɪʃən] *n* spopolamento.

deport [dɪ'pɔːt] *vt* deportare; espellere.

deportation [di:pɔː'teɪʃən] *n* deportazione *f*.

deportation order *n* foglio di via obbligatorio.

deportee [di:pɔː'tiː] *n* deportato/a.

deportment [dɪ'pɔːtmənt] *n* portamento.

depose [dɪ'pəuz] *vt* deporre.

deposit [dɪ'pɔzɪt] *n* (*COMM, GEO*) deposito; (*of ore, oil*) giacimento; (*CHEM*) sedimento; (*part payment*) acconto; (*for hired goods etc*) cauzione *f* ♦ *vt* depositare; dare in acconto; (*luggage etc*) mettere or lasciare in deposito; **to put down a** ~ **of £50** versare una caparra di 50 sterline.

deposit account *n* conto vincolato.

depositor [dɪ'pɔzɪtə*] *n* depositante *m/f*.

depository [dɪ'pɔzɪtərɪ] *n* (*person*) depositario/a; (*place*) deposito.

depot ['dɛpəu] *n* deposito.

depraved [dɪ'preɪvd] *adj* depravato(a).

depravity [dɪ'prævɪtɪ] *n* depravazione *f*.

deprecate ['dɛprɪkeɪt] *vt* deprecare.

deprecating ['dɛprɪkeɪtɪŋ] *adj* (*disapproving*) di biasimo; (*apologetic*): **a** ~ **smile** un sorriso di scusa.

depreciate [dɪ'priːʃɪeɪt] *vt* svalutare ♦ *vi*

svalutarsi.

depreciation [dɪpriːʃɪ'eɪʃən] *n* svalutazione *f*.

depress [dɪ'prɛs] *vt* deprimere; (*press down*) premere.

depressant [dɪ'prɛsnt] *n* (*MED*) sedativo.

depressed [dɪ'prɛst] *adj* (*person*) depresso(a), abbattuto(a); (*area*) depresso(a); (*COMM: market, trade*) stagnante, in ribasso; **to get ~** deprimersi.

depressing [dɪ'prɛsɪŋ] *adj* deprimente.

depression [dɪ'prɛʃən] *n* depressione *f*.

deprivation [dɛprɪ'veɪʃən] *n* privazione *f*; (*state*) indigenza; (*PSYCH*) carenza affettiva.

deprive [dɪ'praɪv] *vt*: **to ~ sb of** privare qn di.

deprived [dɪ'praɪvd] *adj* disgraziato(a).

dept. *abbr* = **department**.

depth [dɛpθ] *n* profondità *f inv*; **at a ~ of 3 metres** a una profondità di 3 metri, a 3 metri di profondità; **in the ~s of** nel profondo di; nel cuore di; **in the ~s of winter** in pieno inverno; **to study sth in ~** studiare qc in profondità; **to be out of one's ~** (*BRIT: swimmer*) essere dove non si tocca; (*fig*) non sentirsi all'altezza della situazione.

depth charge *n* carica di profondità.

deputation [dɛpjuˈteɪʃən] *n* deputazione *f*, delegazione *f*.

deputize ['dɛpjutaɪz] *vi*: **to ~ for** svolgere le funzioni di.

deputy ['dɛpjutɪ] *n* (*replacement*) supplente *m/f*; (*second in command*) vice *m/f* ♦ *cpd*: **~ chairman** vicepresidente *m*; **~ head** (*SCOL*) vicepreside *m/f*; **~ leader** (*BRIT POL*) sottosegretario.

derail [dɪ'reɪl] *vt* far deragliare; **to be ~ed** deragliare.

derailment [dɪ'reɪlmənt] *n* deragliamento.

deranged [dɪ'reɪndʒd] *adj*: **to be (mentally) ~** essere pazzo(a).

derby ['dɜːbɪ] *n* (*US*) bombetta.

deregulate [diː'rɛgjuleɪt] *vt* eliminare la regolamentazione di.

deregulation ['diːrɛgjuˈleɪʃən] *n* eliminazione *f* della regolamentazione.

derelict ['dɛrɪlɪkt] *adj* abbandonato(a).

deride [dɪ'raɪd] *vt* deridere.

derision [dɪ'rɪʒən] *n* derisione *f*.

derisive [dɪ'raɪsɪv] *adj* di derisione.

derisory [dɪ'raɪsərɪ] *adj* (*sum*) irrisorio(a).

derivation [dɛrɪ'veɪʃən] *n* derivazione *f*.

derivative [dɪ'rɪvətɪv] *n* derivato ♦ *adj* derivato(a).

derive [dɪ'raɪv] *vt*: **to ~ sth from** derivare

qc da; **trarre qc da** ♦ *vi*: **to ~ from** derivare da.

dermatitis [dəːmə'taɪtɪs] *n* dermatite *f*.

dermatology [dəːmə'tɔlədʒɪ] *n* dermatologia.

derogatory [dɪ'rɔgətərɪ] *adj* denigratorio(a).

derrick ['dɛrɪk] *n* gru *f inv*; (*for oil*) derrick *m inv*.

derv [dəːv] *n* (*BRIT*) gasolio.

desalination [diːsælɪ'neɪʃən] *n* desalinizzazione *f*, dissalazione *f*.

descend [dɪ'sɛnd] *vt*, *vi* discendere, scendere; **to ~ from** discendere da; **in ~ing order of importance** in ordine decrescente d'importanza.

▶**descend on** *vt fus* (*subj: enemy, angry person*) assalire, piombare su; (: *misfortune*) arrivare addosso a; (: *fig: gloom, silence*) scendere su; **visitors ~ed (up)on us** ci sono arrivate visite tra capo e collo.

descendant [dɪ'sɛndənt] *n* discendente *m/f*.

descent [dɪ'sɛnt] *n* discesa; (*origin*) discendenza, famiglia.

describe [dɪs'kraɪb] *vt* descrivere.

description [dɪs'krɪpʃən] *n* descrizione *f*; (*sort*) genere *m*, specie *f*; **of every ~** di ogni genere e specie.

descriptive [dɪs'krɪptɪv] *adj* descrittivo(a).

desecrate ['dɛsɪkreɪt] *vt* profanare.

desert *n* ['dɛzət] deserto ♦ *vb* [dɪ'zəːt] *vt* lasciare, abbandonare ♦ *vi* (*MIL*) disertare; *see also* **deserts**.

deserter [dɪ'zəːtə*] *n* disertore *m*.

desertion [dɪ'zəːʃən] *n* diserzione *f*.

desert island *n* isola deserta.

deserts [dɪ'zəːts] *npl*: **to get one's just ~** avere ciò che si merita.

deserve [dɪ'zəːv] *vt* meritare.

deservedly [dɪ'zəːvɪdlɪ] *adv* meritatamente, giustamente.

deserving [dɪ'zəːvɪŋ] *adj* (*person*) meritevole, degno(a); (*cause*) meritorio(a).

desiccated ['dɛsɪkeɪtɪd] *adj* essiccato(a).

design [dɪ'zaɪn] *n* (*sketch*) disegno; (: *of dress, car*) modello; (*layout, shape*) linea; (*pattern*) fantasia; (*COMM*) disegno tecnico; (*intention*) intenzione *f* ♦ *vt* disegnare; progettare; **to have ~s on** aver mire su; **well-~ed** ben concepito(a); **industrial ~** disegno industriale.

designate *vt* ['dɛzɪgneɪt] designare ♦ *adj* ['dɛzɪgnɪt] designato(a).

designation [dɛzɪg'neɪʃən] *n* designazione *f*.

designer [dɪ'zaɪnə*] *n* (*TECH*) disegnatore/

trice, progettista *m/f*; (*of furniture*) designer *m/f inv*; (*fashion ~*) disegnatore/trice di moda; (*of theatre sets*) scenografo/a.

designer baby *n* bambino progettato geneticamente prima della nascita.

desirability [dɪzaɪərə'bɪlɪtɪ] *n* desiderabilità; vantaggio.

desirable [dɪ'zaɪərəbl] *adj* desiderabile; **it is ~ that** è opportuno che + *sub*.

desire [dɪ'zaɪə*] *n* desiderio, voglia ♦ *vt* desiderare, volere; **to ~ sth/to do sth/that** desiderare qc/di fare qc/che + *sub*.

desirous [dɪ'zaɪərəs] *adj*: **~ of** desideroso(a) di.

desk [dɛsk] *n* (*in office*) scrivania; (*for pupil*) banco; (*BRIT: in shop, restaurant*) cassa; (*in hotel*) ricevimento; (*at airport*) accettazione *f*.

desk job *n* lavoro d'ufficio.

desktop computer ['dɛsktɔp-] *n* personal *m inv*, personal computer *m inv*.

desktop publishing *n* desktop publishing *m*.

desolate ['dɛsəlɪt] *adj* desolato(a).

desolation [dɛsə'leɪʃən] *n* desolazione *f*.

despair [dɪs'pɛə*] *n* disperazione *f* ♦ *vi*: **to ~ of** disperare di; **in ~** disperato(a).

despatch [dɪs'pætʃ] *n, vt* = **dispatch**.

desperate ['dɛspərɪt] *adj* disperato(a); (*measures*) estremo(a); (*fugitive*) capace di tutto; **we are getting ~** siamo sull'orlo della disperazione.

desperately ['dɛspərɪtlɪ] *adv* disperatamente; (*very*) terribilmente, estremamente; **~ ill** in pericolo di vita.

desperation [dɛspə'reɪʃən] *n* disperazione *f*; **in ~** per disperazione.

despicable [dɪs'pɪkəbl] *adj* disprezzabile.

despise [dɪs'paɪz] *vt* disprezzare, sdegnare.

despite [dɪs'paɪt] *prep* malgrado, a dispetto di, nonostante.

despondent [dɪs'pɔndənt] *adj* abbattuto(a), scoraggiato(a).

despot ['dɛspɔt] *n* despota *m*.

dessert [dɪ'zəːt] *n* dolce *m*; frutta.

dessertspoon [dɪ'zəːtspuːn] *n* cucchiaio da dolci.

destabilize [diː'steɪbɪlaɪz] *vt* privare di stabilità; (*fig*) destabilizzare.

destination [dɛstɪ'neɪʃən] *n* destinazione *f*.

destine ['dɛstɪn] *vt* destinare.

destined ['dɛstɪnd] *adj*: **to be ~ to do sth** essere destinato(a) a fare qc; **~ for London** diretto a Londra, con destinazione Londra.

destiny ['dɛstɪnɪ] *n* destino.

destitute ['dɛstɪtjuːt] *adj* indigente,

bisognoso(a); **~ of** privo(a) di.

destroy [dɪs'trɔɪ] *vt* distruggere.

destroyer [dɪs'trɔɪə*] *n* (*NAUT*) cacciatorpediniere *m*.

destruction [dɪs'trʌkʃən] *n* distruzione *f*.

destructive [dɪs'trʌktɪv] *adj* distruttivo(a).

desultory ['dɛsəltərɪ] *adj* (*reading*) disordinato(a); (*conversation*) sconnesso(a); (*contact*) saltuario(a), irregolare.

detach [dɪ'tætʃ] *vt* staccare, distaccare.

detachable [dɪ'tætʃəbl] *adj* staccabile.

detached [dɪ'tætʃt] *adj* (*attitude*) distante.

detached house *n* villa.

detachment [dɪ'tætʃmənt] *n* (*MIL*) distaccamento; (*fig*) distacco.

detail ['diːteɪl] *n* particolare *m*, dettaglio; (*MIL*) piccolo distaccamento ♦ *vt* dettagliare, particolareggiare; (*MIL*): **to ~ sb (for)** assegnare qn (a); **in ~** nei particolari; **to go into ~(s)** scendere nei particolari.

detailed ['diːteɪld] *adj* particolareggiato(a).

detain [dɪ'teɪn] *vt* trattenere; (*in captivity*) detenere.

detainee [diːteɪ'niː] *n* detenuto/a.

detect [dɪ'tɛkt] *vt* scoprire, scorgere; (*MED, POLICE, RADAR etc*) individuare.

detection [dɪ'tɛkʃən] *n* scoperta; individuazione *f*; **crime ~** indagini *fpl* criminali; **to escape ~** (*criminal*) eludere le ricerche; (*mistake*) passare inosservato(a).

detective [dɪ'tɛktɪv] *n* investigatore/trice; **private ~** investigatore *m* privato.

detective story *n* giallo.

detector [dɪ'tɛktə*] *n* rivelatore *m*.

détente [deɪ'tɑːnt] *n* distensione *f*.

detention [dɪ'tɛnʃən] *n* detenzione *f*; (*SCOL*) permanenza forzata per punizione.

deter [dɪ'təː*] *vt* dissuadere.

detergent [dɪ'təːdʒənt] *n* detersivo.

deteriorate [dɪ'tɪərɪəreɪt] *vi* deteriorarsi.

deterioration [dɪtɪərɪə'reɪʃən] *n* deterioramento.

determination [dɪtəːmɪ'neɪʃən] *n* determinazione *f*.

determine [dɪ'təːmɪn] *vt* determinare; **to ~ to do sth** decidere di fare qc.

determined [dɪ'təːmɪnd] *adj* (*person*) risoluto(a), deciso(a); **to be ~ to do sth** essere determinato *or* deciso a fare qc; **a ~ effort** uno sforzo di volontà.

deterrence [dɪ'tɛrəns] *n* deterrenza.

deterrent [dɪ'tɛrənt] *n* deterrente *m*; **to act as a ~** fungere da deterrente.

detest [dɪ'tɛst] *vt* detestare.

detestable [dɪ'tɛstəbl] *adj* detestabile,

abominevole.

detonate ['dɛtəneɪt] *vi* detonare ♦ *vt* far detonare.

detonator ['dɛtəneɪtə*] *n* detonatore *m*.

detour ['diːtuə*] *n* deviazione *f*.

detract [dɪ'trækt] *vt*: **to ~ from** detrarre da.

detractor [dɪ'træktə*] *n* detrattore/trice.

detriment ['dɛtrɪmənt] *n*: **to the ~ of** a detrimento di; **without ~ to** senza danno a.

detrimental [dɛtrɪ'mɛntl] *adj*: **~ to** dannoso(a) a, nocivo(a) a.

deuce [djuːs] *n* (*TENNIS*) quaranta pari *m inv*.

devaluation [diːvæljuː'eɪʃən] *n* svalutazione *f*.

devalue ['diːvæljuː] *vt* svalutare.

devastate ['dɛvəsteɪt] *vt* devastare; **he was ~d by the news** la notizia fu per lui un colpo terribile.

devastating ['dɛvəsteɪtɪŋ] *adj* devastatore(trice).

devastation [dɛvə'steɪʃən] *n* devastazione *f*.

develop [dɪ'vɛləp] *vt* sviluppare; (*habit*) prendere (gradualmente) ♦ *vi* svilupparsi; (*facts, symptoms: appear*) manifestarsi, rivelarsi; **to ~ a taste for sth** imparare a gustare qc; **to ~ into** diventare.

developer [dɪ'vɛləpə*] *n* (*PHOT*) sviluppatore *m*; **property ~** costruttore *m* (edile).

developing country [dɪ'vɛləpɪŋ-] *n* paese *m* in via di sviluppo.

development [dɪ'vɛləpmənt] *n* sviluppo.

development area *n* area di sviluppo industriale.

deviant ['diːvɪənt] *adj* deviante.

deviate ['diːvɪeɪt] *vi*: **to ~ (from)** deviare (da).

deviation [diːvɪ'eɪʃən] *n* deviazione *f*.

device [dɪ'vaɪs] *n* (*apparatus*) congegno; (*explosive ~*) ordigno esplosivo.

devil ['dɛvl] *n* diavolo; demonio.

devilish ['dɛvlɪʃ] *adj* diabolico(a).

devil-may-care ['dɛvlmeɪ'kɛə*] *adj* impudente.

devil's advocate *n*: **to play ~** fare l'avvocato del diavolo.

devious ['diːvɪəs] *adj* (*means*) indiretto(a), tortuoso(a); (*person*) subdolo(a).

devise [dɪ'vaɪz] *vt* escogitare, concepire.

devoid [dɪ'vɔɪd] *adj*: **~ of** privo(a) di.

devolution [diːvə'luːʃən] *n* (*POL*) decentramento.

devolve [dɪ'vɔlv] *vi*: **to ~ (up)on** ricadere su.

devote [dɪ'vəut] *vt*: **to ~ sth to** dedicare qc a.

devoted [dɪ'vəutɪd] *adj* devoto(a); **to be ~ to** essere molto attaccato(a) a.

devotee [dɛvəu'tiː] *n* (*REL*) adepto/a; (*MUS, SPORT*) appassionato/a.

devotion [dɪ'vəuʃən] *n* devozione *f*, attaccamento; (*REL*) atto di devozione, preghiera.

devour [dɪ'vauə*] *vt* divorare.

devout [dɪ'vaut] *adj* pio(a), devoto(a).

dew [djuː] *n* rugiada.

dexterity [dɛks'tɛrɪtɪ] *n* destrezza.

dext(e)rous ['dɛkstrəs] *adj* (*skilful*) destro(a), abile; (*movement*) agile.

DfEE *n abbr* (*BRIT*: = Department for Education and Employment) Ministero della pubblica instruzione e dell'occupazione.

dg *abbr* (= *decigram*) dg.

diabetes [daɪə'biːtiːz] *n* diabete *m*.

diabetic [daɪə'bɛtɪk] *adj* diabetico(a); (*chocolate, jam*) per diabetici ♦ *n* diabetico/a.

diabolical [daɪə'bɔlɪkl] *adj* diabolico(a); (*col: dreadful*) infernale, atroce.

diaeresis [daɪ'ɛrɪsɪs] *n* dieresi *f inv*.

diagnose [daɪəg'nəuz] *vt* diagnosticare.

diagnosis, *pl* **diagnoses** [daɪəg'nəusɪs, -siːz] *n* diagnosi *f inv*.

diagonal [daɪ'ægənl] *adj*, *n* diagonale (*f*).

diagram ['daɪəgræm] *n* diagramma *m*.

dial ['daɪəl] *n* quadrante *m*; (*on telephone*) disco combinatore ♦ *vt* (*number*) fare; **to ~ a wrong number** sbagliare numero; **can I ~ London direct?** si può chiamare Londra in teleselezione?

dial. *abbr* = **dialect.**

dialect ['daɪəlɛkt] *n* dialetto.

dialling code ['daɪəlɪŋ-], (*US*) **area code** *n* prefisso.

dialling tone ['daɪəlɪŋ-], (*US*) **dial tone** *n* segnale *m* di linea libera.

dialogue ['daɪəlɔg] *n* dialogo.

dialysis [daɪ'ælɪsɪs] *n* dialisi *f*.

diameter [daɪ'æmɪtə*] *n* diametro.

diametrically [daɪə'mɛtrɪklɪ] *adv*: **~ opposed (to)** diametralmente opposto(a) (a).

diamond ['daɪəmənd] *n* diamante *m*; (*shape*) rombo; **~s** *npl* (*CARDS*) quadri *mpl*.

diamond ring *n* anello di brillanti; (*with one diamond*) anello con brillante.

diaper ['daɪəpə*] *n* (*US*) pannolino.

diaphragm ['daɪəfræm] *n* diaframma *m*.

diarrhoea, (*US*) **diarrhea** [daɪə'riːə] *n* diarrea.

diary ['daɪərɪ] *n* (*daily account*) diario; (*book*) agenda; **to keep a ~** tenere un diario.

diatribe ['daɪətraɪb] n diatriba.

dice [daɪs] n (pl inv) dado ♦ vt (CULIN) tagliare a dadini.

dicey ['daɪsɪ] adj (col): **it's a bit ~** è un po' un rischio.

dichotomy [daɪ'kɔtəmɪ] n dicotomia.

dickhead ['dɪkhɛd] n (BRIT col!) testa m di cazzo(!).

Dictaphone ® ['dɪktəfəun] n dittafono.

dictate vt [dɪk'teɪt] dettare ♦ vi: **to ~ to** (person) dare ordini a, dettar legge a ♦ n ['dɪkteɪt] dettame m; **I won't be ~d to** non ricevo ordini.

dictation [dɪk'teɪʃən] n dettato; (to secretary etc) dettatura; **at ~ speed** a velocità di dettatura.

dictator [dɪk'teɪtə*] n dittatore m.

dictatorship [dɪk'teɪtəʃɪp] n dittatura.

diction ['dɪkʃən] n dizione f.

dictionary ['dɪkʃənrɪ] n dizionario.

did [dɪd] pt of **do**.

didactic [daɪ'dæktɪk] adj didattico(a).

didn't = **did not**.

die [daɪ] n (pl: **dies**) conio; matrice f; stampo ♦ vi morire; **to be dying** star morendo; **to be dying for sth/to do sth** morire dalla voglia di qc/di fare qc; **to ~ (of or from)** morire (di).

▶**die away** vi spegnersi a poco a poco.

▶**die down** vi abbassarsi.

▶**die out** vi estinguersi.

diehard ['daɪhɑːd] n reazionario/a.

diesel ['diːzl] n diesel m.

diesel engine n motore m diesel inv.

diesel fuel, diesel oil n gasolio (per motori diesel).

diet ['daɪət] n alimentazione f; (restricted food) dieta ♦ vi (also: **be on a ~**) stare a dieta; **to live on a ~ of** nutrirsi di.

dietician [daɪə'tɪʃən] n dietologo/a.

differ ['dɪfə*] vi: **to ~ from sth** differire da qc; essere diverso(a) da qc; **to ~ from sb over sth** essere in disaccordo con qn su qc.

difference ['dɪfrəns] n differenza; (quarrel) screzio; **it makes no ~ to me** per me è lo stesso; **to settle one's ~s** risolvere la situazione.

different ['dɪfrənt] adj diverso(a).

differential [dɪfə'rɛnʃəl] n (AUT, wages) differenziale m.

differentiate [dɪfə'rɛnʃɪeɪt] vi differenziarsi; **to ~ between** discriminare fra, fare differenza fra.

differently ['dɪfrəntlɪ] adv diversamente.

difficult ['dɪfɪkəlt] adj difficile; **~ to understand** difficile da capire.

difficulty ['dɪfɪkəltɪ] n difficoltà f inv; **to**

have difficulties with (police, landlord etc) avere noie con; **to be in ~** essere or trovarsi in difficoltà.

diffidence ['dɪfɪdəns] n mancanza di sicurezza.

diffident ['dɪfɪdənt] adj sfiduciato(a).

diffuse adj [dɪ'fjuːs] diffuso(a) ♦ vt [dɪ'fjuːz] diffondere, emanare.

dig [dɪg] vb (pt, pp **dug** [dʌg]) vt (hole) scavare; (garden) vangare ♦ vi scavare ♦ n (prod) gomitata; (fig) frecciata; (ARCHAEOLOGY) scavo, scavi mpl; **to ~ into** (snow, soil) scavare; **to ~ into one's pockets for sth** frugarsi le tasche cercando qc; **to ~ one's nails into** conficcare le unghie in; see also **digs**.

▶**dig in** vi (col: eat) attaccare a mangiare; (also: **~ o.s. in**: MIL) trincerarsi; (: fig) insediarsi, installarsi ♦ vt (compost) interrare; (knife, claw) affondare; **to ~ in one's heels** (fig) impuntarsi.

▶**dig out** vt (survivors, car from snow) tirar fuori (scavando), estrarre (scavando).

▶**dig up** vt scavare; (tree etc) sradicare.

digest [daɪ'dʒɛst] vt digerire.

digestible [dɪ'dʒɛstəbl] adj digeribile.

digestion [dɪ'dʒɛstʃən] n digestione f.

digestive [dɪ'dʒɛstɪv] adj digestivo(a); **~ system** apparato digerente.

digit ['dɪdʒɪt] n cifra; (finger) dito.

digital ['dɪdʒɪtəl] adj digitale.

digital camera n fotocamera digitale.

digital compact cassette n piastra digitale per CD.

digital radio n radio digitale.

digital TV n televisione f digitale.

dignified ['dɪgnɪfaɪd] adj dignitoso(a).

dignitary ['dɪgnɪtərɪ] n dignitario.

dignity ['dɪgnɪtɪ] n dignità f.

digress [daɪ'grɛs] vi: **to ~ from** divagare da.

digression [daɪ'grɛʃən] n digressione f.

digs [dɪgz] npl (BRIT col) camera ammobiliata.

dilapidated [dɪ'læpɪdeɪtɪd] adj cadente.

dilate [daɪ'leɪt] vt dilatare ♦ vi dilatarsi.

dilatory ['dɪlətərɪ] adj dilatorio(a).

dilemma [daɪ'lɛmə] n dilemma m; **to be in a ~** essere di fronte a un dilemma.

diligent ['dɪlɪdʒənt] adj diligente.

dill [dɪl] n aneto.

dilly-dally ['dɪlɪdælɪ] vi gingillarsi.

dilute [daɪ'luːt] vt diluire; (with water) annacquare ♦ adj diluito(a).

dim [dɪm] adj (light, eyesight) debole; (memory, outline) vago(a); (stupid) ottuso(a) ♦ vt (light: also: US AUT) abbassare; **to take a ~ view of sth** non vedere di buon occhio qc.

dime [daɪm] *n* (*US*) = 10 cents.
dimension [dɪ'mɛnʃən] *n* dimensione *f*.
-dimensional [dɪ'mɛnʃənl] *adj suffix*: **two**~ bi-dimensionale.
diminish [dɪ'mɪnɪʃ] *vt*, *vi* diminuire.
diminished [dɪ'mɪnɪʃt] *adj*: ~ **responsibility** (*LAW*) incapacità d'intendere e di volere.
diminutive [dɪ'mɪnjutɪv] *adj* minuscolo(a) ♦ *n* (*LING*) diminutivo.
dimly ['dɪmlɪ] *adv* debolmente; indistintamente.
dimmer ['dɪmə*] *n* (*also*: ~ **switch**) dimmer *m inv*, interruttore *m* a reostato; ~**s** (*US AUT*) anabbaglianti *mpl*; (: *parking lights*) luci *fpl* di posizione.
dimple ['dɪmpl] *n* fossetta.
dim-witted ['dɪm'wɪtɪd] *adj* (*col*) sciocco(a).
din [dɪn] *n* chiasso, fracasso ♦ *vt*: **to** ~ **sth into sb** (*col*) ficcare qc in testa a qn.
dine [daɪn] *vi* pranzare.
diner ['daɪnə*] *n* (*person*: *in restaurant*) cliente *m*; (*RAIL*) carrozza *or* vagone *m* ristorante; (*US*: *eating place*) tavola calda.
dinghy ['dɪŋgɪ] *n* battello pneumatico; (*also*: **sailing** ~) dinghy *m inv*.
dingy ['dɪndʒɪ] *adj* grigio(a).
dining area ['daɪnɪŋ-] *n* zona pranzo *inv*.
dining car *n* vagone *m* ristorante.
dining room *n* sala da pranzo.
dinner ['dɪnə*] *n* pranzo; (*evening meal*) cena; (*public*) banchetto; ~'**s ready!** a tavola!
dinner jacket *n* smoking *m inv*.
dinner party *n* cena.
dinner service *n* servizio da tavola.
dinner time *n* ora di pranzo (*or* cena).
dinosaur ['daɪnəsɔ:*] *n* dinosauro.
dint [dɪnt] *n*: **by** ~ **of (doing) sth** a forza di (fare) qc.
diocese ['daɪəsɪs] *n* diocesi *f inv*.
dioxide [daɪ'ɔksaɪd] *n* biossido.
dip [dɪp] *n* (*slope*) discesa; (*in sea*) bagno ♦ *vt* immergere, bagnare; (*BRIT AUT*: *lights*) abbassare ♦ *vi* (*road*) essere in pendenza; (*bird*, *plane*) abbassarsi.
Dip. *abbr* (*BRIT*) = **diploma**.
diphtheria [dɪf'θɪərɪə] *n* difterite *f*.
diphthong ['dɪfθɔŋ] *n* dittongo.
diploma [dɪ'pləumə] *n* diploma *m*.
diplomacy [dɪ'pləuməsɪ] *n* diplomazia.
diplomat ['dɪpləmæt] *n* diplomatico.
diplomatic [dɪplə'mætɪk] *adj* diplomatico(a); **to break off** ~ **relations** rompere le relazioni diplomatiche.
diplomatic corps *n* corpo diplomatico.
diplomatic immunity *n* immunità *f inv* diplomatica.
dipstick ['dɪpstɪk] *n* (*AUT*) indicatore *m* di livello dell'olio.
dipswitch ['dɪpswɪtʃ] *n* (*BRIT AUT*) levetta dei fari.
dire [daɪə*] *adj* terribile; estremo(a).
direct [daɪ'rɛkt] *adj* diretto(a); (*manner*, *person*) franco(a), esplicito(a) ♦ *vt* dirigere; **to** ~ **sb to do sth** dare direttive a qn di fare qc; **can you** ~ **me to ...?** mi può indicare la strada per ...?
direct cost *n* (*COMM*) costo diretto.
direct current *n* (*ELEC*) corrente *f* continua.
direct debit *n* (*BANKING*) addebito effettuato per ordine di un cliente di banca.
direct dialling *n* (*TEL*) ≈ teleselezione *f*.
direct hit *n* (*MIL*) colpo diretto.
direction [dɪ'rɛkʃən] *n* direzione *f*; (*of play*, *film*, *programme*) regia; ~**s** *npl* (*advice*) chiarimenti *mpl*; (*instructions*: *to a place*) indicazioni *fpl*; ~**s for use** istruzioni *fpl*; **to ask for** ~**s** chiedere la strada; **sense of** ~ senso dell'orientamento; **in the** ~ **of** in direzione di.
directive [dɪ'rɛktɪv] *n* direttiva, ordine *m*; **a government** ~ una disposizione governativa.
direct labour *n* manodopera diretta.
directly [dɪ'rɛktlɪ] *adv* (*in straight line*) direttamente; (*at once*) subito.
direct mail *n* pubblicità diretta.
direct mailshot *n* (*BRIT*) materiale *m* pubblicitario ad approccio diretto.
directness [daɪ'rɛktnɪs] *n* (*of person*, *speech*) franchezza.
director [dɪ'rɛktə*] *n* direttore/trice; amministratore/trice; (*THEAT*, *CINE*, *TV*) regista *m/f*; **D**~ **of Public Prosecutions (DPP)** (*BRIT*) ≈ Procuratore *m* della Repubblica.
directory [dɪ'rɛktərɪ] *n* elenco; (*street* ~) stradario; (*trade* ~) repertorio del commercio; (*COMPUT*) directory *m inv*.
directory enquiries, (*US*) **directory assistance** *n* (*TEL*) servizio informazioni, informazioni *fpl* elenco abbonati.
dirt [dɜːt] *n* sporcizia; immondizia; **to treat sb like** ~ trattare qn come uno straccio.
dirt-cheap ['dɜːt'tʃiːp] *adj* da due soldi.
dirt road *n* strada non asfaltata.
dirty ['dɜːtɪ] *adj* sporco(a) ♦ *vt* sporcare; ~ **bomb** bomba convenzionale contenente materiale radioattivo; ~ **story** storia oscena; ~ **trick** brutto scherzo.
disability [dɪsə'bɪlɪtɪ] *n* invalidità *f inv*; (*LAW*) incapacità *f inv*.
disability allowance *n* pensione *f* d'invalidità.

disable [dɪs'eɪbl] vt (subj: illness, accident) rendere invalido(a); (tank, gun) mettere fuori uso.

disabled [dɪs'eɪbld] adj invalido(a); (maimed) mutilato(a); (through illness, old age) inabile.

disadvantage [dɪsəd'vɑːntɪdʒ] n svantaggio.

disadvantaged [dɪsəd'vɑːntɪdʒd] adj (person) svantaggiato(a).

disadvantageous [dɪsædvɑːn'teɪdʒəs] adj svantaggioso(a).

disaffected [dɪsə'fɛktɪd] adj: ~ (to or towards) scontento(a) di, insoddisfatto(a) di.

disaffection [dɪsə'fɛkʃən] n malcontento, insoddisfazione f.

disagree [dɪsə'griː] vi (differ) discordare; (be against, think otherwise): to ~ (with) essere in disaccordo (con), dissentire (da); I ~ with you non sono d'accordo con lei; **garlic ~s with me** l'aglio non mi va.

disagreeable [dɪsə'griːəbl] adj sgradevole; (person) antipatico(a).

disagreement [dɪsə'griːmənt] n disaccordo; (quarrel) dissapore m; **to have a ~ with sb** litigare con qn.

disallow ['dɪsə'lau] vt respingere; (BRIT FOOTBALL: goal) annullare.

disappear [dɪsə'pɪə*] vi scomparire.

disappearance [dɪsə'pɪərəns] n scomparsa.

disappoint [dɪsə'pɔɪnt] vt deludere.

disappointed [dɪsə'pɔɪntɪd] adj deluso(a).

disappointing [dɪsə'pɔɪntɪŋ] adj deludente.

disappointment [dɪsə'pɔɪntmənt] n delusione f.

disapproval [dɪsə'pruːvəl] n disapprovazione f.

disapprove [dɪsə'pruːv] vi: **to ~ of** disapprovare.

disapproving [dɪsə'pruːvɪŋ] adj di disapprovazione.

disarm [dɪs'ɑːm] vt disarmare.

disarmament [dɪs'ɑːməmənt] n disarmo.

disarming [dɪs'ɑːmɪŋ] adj (smile) disarmante.

disarray [dɪsə'reɪ] n: **in ~** (troops) in rotta; (thoughts) confuso(a); (clothes) in disordine; **to throw into ~** buttare all'aria.

disaster [dɪ'zɑːstə*] n disastro.

disaster area n zona disastrata.

disastrous [dɪ'zɑːstrəs] adj disastroso(a).

disband [dɪs'bænd] vt sbandare; (MIL) congedare ♦ vi sciogliersi.

disbelief ['dɪsbə'liːf] n incredulità; **in ~** incredulo(a).

disbelieve ['dɪsbə'liːv] vt (person, story) non credere a, mettere in dubbio; **I don't ~ you** vorrei poterle credere.

disc [dɪsk] n disco.

disc. abbr (COMM) = **discount**.

discard [dɪs'kɑːd] vt (old things) scartare; (fig) abbandonare.

disc brake n freno a disco.

discern [dɪ'səːn] vt discernere, distinguere.

discernible [dɪ'səːnəbl] adj percepibile.

discerning [dɪ'səːnɪŋ] adj perspicace.

discharge vt [dɪs'tʃɑːdʒ] (duties) compiere; (settle: debt) pagare, estinguere; (ELEC, waste etc) scaricare; (MED) emettere; (patient) dimettere; (employee) licenziare; (soldier) congedare; (defendant) liberare ♦ n ['dɪstʃɑːdʒ] (ELEC) scarica; (MED, of gas, chemicals) emissione f; (vaginal ~) perdite fpl (bianche); (dismissal) licenziamento; congedo; liberazione f; **to ~ one's gun** fare fuoco.

discharged bankrupt [dɪs'tʃɑːdʒd-] n fallito cui il tribunale ha concesso la riabilitazione.

disciple [dɪ'saɪpl] n discepolo.

disciplinary ['dɪsɪplɪnərɪ] adj disciplinare; **to take ~ action against sb** prendere un provvedimento disciplinare contro qn.

discipline ['dɪsɪplɪn] n disciplina ♦ vt disciplinare; (punish) punire; **to ~ o.s. to do sth** imporsi di fare qc.

disc jockey (DJ) n disc jockey m inv.

disclaim [dɪs'kleɪm] vt negare, smentire.

disclaimer [dɪs'kleɪmə*] n smentita; **to issue a ~** pubblicare una smentita.

disclose [dɪs'kləuz] vt rivelare, svelare.

disclosure [dɪs'kləuʒə*] n rivelazione f.

disco ['dɪskəu] n abbr = **discothèque**.

discolour, (US) **discolor** [dɪs'kʌlə*] vt scolorire; (sth white) ingiallire ♦ vi sbiadire, scolorirsi; (sth white) ingiallire.

discolo(u)ration [dɪskʌlə'reɪʃən] n scolorimento.

discolo(u)red [dɪs'kʌləd] adj scolorito(a); ingiallito(a).

discomfort [dɪs'kʌmfət] n disagio; (lack of comfort) scomodità f inv.

disconcert [dɪskən'səːt] vt sconcertare.

disconnect [dɪskə'nɛkt] vt sconnettere, staccare; (ELEC, RADIO) staccare; (gas, water) chiudere.

disconnected [dɪskə'nɛktɪd] adj (speech, thought) sconnesso(a).

disconsolate [dɪs'kɔnsəlɪt] adj sconsolato(a).

discontent [dɪskən'tɛnt] n scontentezza.

discontented [dɪskən'tɛntɪd] adj scontento(a).

discontinue [dɪskən'tɪnjuː] vt smettere,

cessare; "~**d**" (*COMM*) "sospeso".

discord ['dɪskɔːd] *n* disaccordo; (*MUS*) dissonanza.

discordant [dɪs'kɔːdənt] *adj* discordante; dissonante.

discothèque ['dɪskəutɛk] *n* discoteca.

discount *n* ['dɪskaunt] sconto ♦ *vt* [dɪs'kaunt] scontare; (*report etc*) non badare a; **at a ~** con uno sconto; **to give sb a ~ on sth** fare uno sconto a qn su qc; **~ for cash** sconto *m* cassa *inv*.

discount house *n* (*FINANCE*) casa di sconto, discount house *f inv*; (*COMM: also*: **discount store**) discount *m inv*.

discount rate *n* tasso di sconto.

discourage [dɪs'kʌrɪdʒ] *vt* scoraggiare; (*dissuade, deter*) tentare di dissuadere.

discouragement [dɪs'kʌrɪdʒmənt] *n* (*dissuasion*) disapprovazione *f*; (*depression*) scoraggiamento; **to act as a ~ to** ostacolare.

discouraging [dɪs'kʌrɪdʒɪŋ] *adj* scoraggiante.

discourteous [dɪs'kɔːtɪəs] *adj* scortese.

discover [dɪs'kʌvə*] *vt* scoprire.

discovery [dɪs'kʌvərɪ] *n* scoperta.

discredit [dɪs'krɛdɪt] *vt* screditare; mettere in dubbio ♦ *n* discredito.

discreet [dɪ'skriːt] *adj* discreto(a).

discreetly [dɪ'skriːtlɪ] *adv* con discrezione.

discrepancy [dɪ'skrɛpənsɪ] *n* discrepanza.

discretion [dɪ'skrɛʃən] *n* discrezione *f*; **use your own ~** giudichi lei.

discretionary [dɪs'krɛʃənərɪ] *adj* (*powers*) discrezionale.

discriminate [dɪ'skrɪmɪneɪt] *vi*: **to ~ between** distinguere tra; **to ~ against** discriminare contro.

discriminating [dɪs'krɪmɪneɪtɪŋ] *adj* (*ear, taste*) fine, giudizioso(a); (*person*) esigente; (*tax, duty*) discriminante.

discrimination [dɪskrɪmɪ'neɪʃən] *n* discriminazione *f*; (*judgement*) discernimento; **racial/sexual ~** discriminazione razziale/sessuale.

discus ['dɪskəs] *n* disco.

discuss [dɪ'skʌs] *vt* discutere; (*debate*) dibattere.

discussion [dɪ'skʌʃən] *n* discussione *f*; **under ~** in discussione.

disdain [dɪs'deɪn] *n* disdegno.

disease [dɪ'ziːz] *n* malattia.

diseased [dɪ'ziːzd] *adj* malato(a).

disembark [dɪsɪm'baːk] *vt, vi* sbarcare.

disembarkation [dɪsɛmbaː'keɪʃən] *n* sbarco.

disembodied [dɪsɪm'bɔdɪd] *adj* disincarnato(a).

disembowel [dɪsɪm'bauəl] *vt* sbudellare, sventrare.

disenchanted [dɪsɪn'tʃaːntɪd] *adj* disincantato(a); **~ (with)** deluso(a) (da).

disenfranchise [dɪsɪn'fræntʃaɪz] *vt* privare del diritto di voto; (*COMM*) revocare una condizione di privilegio commerciale a.

disengage [dɪsɪn'geɪdʒ] *vt* disimpegnare; (*TECH*) distaccare; (*AUT*) disinnestare.

disentangle [dɪsɪn'tæŋgl] *vt* sbrogliare.

disfavour, (US) disfavor [dɪs'feɪvə*] *n* sfavore *m*; disgrazia.

disfigure [dɪs'fɪgə*] *vt* sfigurare.

disgorge [dɪs'gɔːdʒ] *vt* (*subj: river*) riversare.

disgrace [dɪs'greɪs] *n* vergogna; (*disfavour*) disgrazia ♦ *vt* disonorare, far cadere in disgrazia.

disgraceful [dɪs'greɪsful] *adj* scandaloso(a), vergognoso(a).

disgruntled [dɪs'grʌntld] *adj* scontento(a), di cattivo umore.

disguise [dɪs'gaɪz] *n* travestimento ♦ *vt* travestire; (*voice*) contraffare; (*feelings etc*) mascherare; **to ~ o.s. as** travestirsi da; **in ~** travestito(a); **there's no disguising the fact that** ... non si può nascondere (il fatto) che ....

disgust [dɪs'gʌst] *n* disgusto, nausea ♦ *vt* disgustare, far schifo a.

disgusting [dɪs'gʌstɪŋ] *adj* disgustoso(a).

dish [dɪʃ] *n* piatto; **to do** *or* **wash the ~es** fare i piatti.

▶**dish out** *vt* (*food*) servire; (*advice*) elargire; (*money*) tirare fuori; (*exam papers*) distribuire.

▶**dish up** *vt* (*food*) servire; (*facts, statistics*) presentare.

dishcloth ['dɪʃklɔθ] *n* strofinaccio dei piatti.

dishearten [dɪs'haːtn] *vt* scoraggiare.

dishevelled, (US) disheveled [dɪ'ʃɛvəld] *adj* arruffato(a); scapigliato(a).

dishonest [dɪs'ɔnɪst] *adj* disonesto(a).

dishonesty [dɪs'ɔnɪstɪ] *n* disonestà.

dishonour, (US) dishonor [dɪs'ɔnə*] *n* disonore *m*.

dishono(u)rable [dɪs'ɔnərəbl] *adj* disonorevole.

dish soap *n* (*US*) detersivo liquido (per stoviglie).

dishtowel ['dɪʃtauəl] *n* strofinaccio dei piatti.

dishwasher ['dɪʃwɔʃə*] *n* lavastoviglie *f inv*; (*person*) sguattero/a.

dishy ['dɪʃɪ] *adj* (*BRIT col*) figo(a).

disillusion [dɪsɪ'luːʒən] *vt* disilludere, disingannare ♦ *n* disillusione *f*; **to become**

~**ed (with)** perdere le illusioni (su).
disillusionment [dısı'luːʒənmənt] *n*
disillusione *f*.
disincentive [dısın'sɛntıv] *n*: **to act as a ~
(to)** agire da freno (su); **to be a ~ to**
scoraggiare.
disinclined [dısın'klaınd] *adj*: **to be ~ to do
sth** essere poco propenso(a) a fare qc.
disinfect [dısın'fɛkt] *vt* disinfettare.
disinfectant [dısın'fɛktənt] *n* disinfettante
m.
disinflation [dısın'fleıʃən] *n* disinflazione *f*.
disinformation [dısınfə'meıʃən] *n*
disinformazione *f*.
disinherit [dısın'hɛrıt] *vt* diseredare.
disintegrate [dıs'ıntıgreıt] *vi* disintegrarsi.
disinterested [dıs'ıntrəstıd] *adj*
disinteressato(a).
disjointed [dıs'dʒɔıntıd] *adj* sconnesso(a).
disk [dısk] *n* (*COMPUT*) disco; **single-/
double-sided** ~ disco *m* monofaccia *inv*/a
doppia faccia.
disk drive *n* disk drive *m inv*, unità *f inv* a
dischi magnetici.
disk operating system (DOS) *n* sistema
m operativo a disco.
diskette [dıs'kɛt] *n* (*COMPUT*) dischetto.
dislike [dıs'laık] *n* antipatia, avversione *f*
♦ *vt*: **he ~s it** non gli piace; **I ~ the idea**
l'idea non mi va; **to take a ~ to sb/sth**
prendere in antipatia qn/qc.
dislocate ['dısləkeıt] *vt* (*MED*) slogare; (*fig*)
disorganizzare; **he ~d his shoulder** si è
lussato una spalla.
dislodge [dıs'lɔdʒ] *vt* rimuovere, staccare;
(*enemy*) sloggiare.
disloyal [dıs'lɔıəl] *adj* sleale.
dismal ['dızml] *adj* triste, cupo(a).
dismantle [dıs'mæntl] *vt* smantellare,
smontare; (*fort, warship*) disarmare.
dismast [dıs'mɑːst] *vt* disalberare.
dismay [dıs'meı] *n* costernazione *f* ♦ *vt*
sgomentare; **much to my ~** con mio gran
stupore.
dismiss [dıs'mıs] *vt* congedare; (*employee*)
licenziare; (*idea*) scacciare; (*LAW*)
respingere ♦ *vi* (*MIL*) rompere i ranghi.
dismissal [dıs'mısəl] *n* congedo;
licenziamento.
dismount [dıs'maunt] *vi* scendere ♦ *vt*
(*rider*) disarcionare.
disobedience [dısə'biːdıəns] *n*
disubbidienza.
disobedient [dısə'biːdıənt] *adj*
disubbidiente.
disobey [dısə'beı] *vt* disubbidire; (*rule*)
trasgredire.
disorder [dıs'ɔːdə*] *n* disordine *m*; (*rioting*)

tumulto; (*MED*) disturbo; **civil** ~ disordini
mpl interni.
disorderly [dıs'ɔːdəlı] *adj* disordinato(a);
tumultuoso(a).
disorderly conduct *n* (*LAW*)
comportamento atto a turbare l'ordine
pubblico.
disorganize [dıs'ɔːgənaız] *vt*
disorganizzare.
disorganized [dıs'ɔːgənaızd] *adj* (*person,
life*) disorganizzato(a); (*system, meeting*)
male organizzato(a).
disorientated [dıs'ɔːrıenteıtıd] *adj*
disorientato(a).
disown [dıs'əun] *vt* ripudiare.
disparaging [dıs'pærıdʒıŋ] *adj*
spregiativo(a), sprezzante; **to be ~ about
sb/sth** denigrare qn/qc.
disparate ['dıspərıt] *adj* disparato(a).
disparity [dıs'pærıtı] *n* disparità *f inv*.
dispassionate [dıs'pæʃənət] *adj* calmo(a),
freddo(a); imparziale.
dispatch [dıs'pætʃ] *vt* spedire, inviare;
(*deal with: business*) sbrigare ♦ *n*
spedizione *f*, invio; (*MIL, PRESS*) dispaccio.
dispatch department *n* reparto
spedizioni.
dispatch rider *n* (*MIL*) corriere *m*,
portaordini *m inv*.
dispel [dıs'pɛl] *vt* dissipare, scacciare.
dispensary [dıs'pɛnsərı] *n* farmacia; (*in
chemist's*) dispensario.
dispense [dıs'pɛns] *vt* distribuire,
amministrare; (*medicine*) preparare e
dare; **to ~ sb from** dispensare qn da.
►**dispense with** *vt fus* fare a meno di;
(*make unnecessary*) rendere superfluo(a).
dispenser [dıs'pɛnsə*] *n* (*container*)
distributore *m*.
dispensing chemist *n* (*BRIT*) farmacista
m/f.
dispersal [dıs'pəːsl] *n* dispersione *f*.
disperse [dıs'pəːs] *vt* disperdere;
(*knowledge*) disseminare ♦ *vi* disperdersi.
dispirited [dıs'pırıtıd] *adj* scoraggiato(a),
abbattuto(a).
displace [dıs'pleıs] *vt* spostare.
displaced person *n* (*POL*) profugo/a.
displacement [dıs'pleısmənt] *n*
spostamento.
display [dıs'pleı] *n* mostra; esposizione *f*;
(*of feeling etc*) manifestazione *f*; (*military
~*) parata (militare); (*computer ~*) display
m inv; (*pej*) ostentazione *f* ♦ *vt* mostrare;
(*goods*) esporre; (*results*) affiggere;
(*departure times*) indicare; **on ~** (*gen*) in
mostra; (*goods*) in vetrina.
display advertising *n* pubblicità

tabellare.

displease [dɪs'pliːz] *vt* dispiacere a, scontentare; **~d with** scontento(a) di.

displeasure [dɪs'plɛʒə*] *n* dispiacere *m*.

disposable [dɪs'pəuzəbl] *adj* (*pack etc*) a perdere; (*income*) disponibile; **~ nappy** (*BRIT*) pannolino di carta.

disposal [dɪs'pəuzl] *n* (*of rubbish*) evacuazione *f*; distruzione *f*; (*of property etc: by selling*) vendita *f*; (: *by giving away*) cessione *f*; **at one's ~** alla sua disposizione; **to put sth at sb's ~** mettere qc a disposizione di qn.

dispose [dɪs'pəuz] *vt* disporre.
▶**dispose of** *vt fus* (*time, money*) disporre di; (*COMM: sell*) vendere; (*unwanted goods*) sbarazzarsi di; (*problem*) eliminare.

disposed [dɪs'pəuzd] *adj*: **~ to do** disposto(a) a fare.

disposition [dɪspə'zɪʃən] *n* disposizione *f*; (*temperament*) carattere *m*.

dispossess ['dɪspə'zɛs] *vt*: **to ~ sb (of)** spossessare qn (di).

disproportion [dɪsprə'pɔːʃən] *n* sproporzione *f*.

disproportionate [dɪsprə'pɔːʃənət] *adj* sproporzionato(a).

disprove [dɪs'pruːv] *vt* confutare.

dispute [dɪs'pjuːt] *n* disputa; (*also*: **industrial ~**) controversia (sindacale) ♦ *vt* contestare; (*matter*) discutere; (*victory*) disputare; **to be in** *or* **under ~** (*matter*) essere in discussione; (*territory*) essere oggetto di contesa.

disqualification [dɪskwɔlɪfɪ'keɪʃən] *n* squalifica; **~ (from driving)** (*BRIT*) ritiro della patente.

disqualify [dɪs'kwɔlɪfaɪ] *vt* (*SPORT*) squalificare; **to ~ sb from sth/from doing** rendere qn incapace a qc/a fare; squalificare qn da qc/da fare; **to ~ sb from driving** (*BRIT*) ritirare la patente a qn.

disquiet [dɪs'kwaɪət] *n* inquietudine *f*.

disquieting [dɪs'kwaɪətɪŋ] *adj* inquietante, allarmante.

disregard [dɪsrɪ'gɑːd] *vt* non far caso a, non badare a ♦ *n* (*indifference*): **~ (for)** (*feelings*) insensibilità (a, indifferenza (verso); (*danger*) noncuranza (di); (*money*) disprezzo (di).

disrepair [dɪsrɪ'pɛə*] *n* cattivo stato; **to fall into ~** (*building*) andare in rovina; (*street*) deteriorarsi.

disreputable [dɪs'rɛpjutəbl] *adj* (*person*) di cattiva fama; (*area*) malfamato(a), poco raccomandabile.

disrepute ['dɪsrɪ'pjuːt] *n* disonore *m*,

vergogna; **to bring into ~** rovinare la reputazione di.

disrespectful [dɪsrɪ'spɛktful] *adj* che manca di rispetto.

disrupt [dɪs'rʌpt] *vt* (*meeting, lesson*) disturbare, interrompere; (*public transport*) creare scompiglio in; (*plans*) scombussolare.

disruption [dɪs'rʌpʃən] *n* disordine *m*; interruzione *f*.

disruptive [dɪs'rʌptɪv] *adj* (*influence*) negativo(a), deleterio(a); (*strike action*) paralizzante.

dissatisfaction [dɪssætɪs'fækʃən] *n* scontentezza, insoddisfazione *f*.

dissatisfied [dɪs'sætɪsfaɪd] *adj*: **~ (with)** scontento(a) *or* insoddisfatto(a) (di).

dissect [dɪ'sɛkt] *vt* sezionare; (*fig*) sviscerare.

disseminate [dɪ'sɛmɪneɪt] *vt* disseminare.

dissent [dɪ'sɛnt] *n* dissenso.

dissenter [dɪ'sɛntə*] *n* (*REL, POL etc*) dissidente *m/f*.

dissertation [dɪsə'teɪʃən] *n* (*SCOL*) tesi *f inv*, dissertazione *f*.

disservice [dɪs'səːvɪs] *n*: **to do sb a ~** fare un cattivo servizio a qn.

dissident ['dɪsɪdnt] *adj* dissidente; (*speech, voice*) di dissenso ♦ *n* dissidente *m/f*.

dissimilar [dɪ'sɪmɪlə*] *adj*: **~ (to)** dissimile *or* diverso(a) (da).

dissipate ['dɪsɪpeɪt] *vt* dissipare.

dissipated ['dɪsɪpeɪtɪd] *adj* dissipato(a).

dissociate [dɪ'səuʃɪeɪt] *vt* dissociare; **to ~ o.s. from** dichiarare di non avere niente a che fare con.

dissolute ['dɪsəluːt] *adj* dissoluto(a), licenzioso(a).

dissolve [dɪ'zɔlv] *vt* dissolvere, sciogliere; (*COMM, POL, marriage*) sciogliere ♦ *vi* dissolversi, sciogliersi; (*fig*) svanire.

dissuade [dɪ'sweɪd] *vt*: **to ~ sb (from)** dissuadere qn (da).

distaff side ['dɪstɑːf-] *n* ramo *femminile di una famiglia*.

distance ['dɪstns] *n* distanza; **in the ~** in lontananza; **what's the ~ to London?** quanto dista Londra?; **it's within walking ~** ci si arriva a piedi; **at a ~ of 2 metres** a 2 metri di distanza.

distant ['dɪstnt] *adj* lontano(a), distante; (*manner*) riservato(a), freddo(a).

distaste [dɪs'teɪst] *n* ripugnanza.

distasteful [dɪs'teɪstful] *adj* ripugnante, sgradevole.

Dist. Atty. *abbr* (*US*) = **district attorney**.

distemper [dɪs'tɛmpə*] *n* (*paint*) tempera; (*of dogs*) cimurro.

distend [dɪs'tɛnd] *vt* dilatare ♦ *vi* dilatarsi.
distended [dɪs'tɛndɪd] *adj* (*stomach*) dilatato(a).
distil, (*US*) **distill** [dɪs'tɪl] *vt* distillare.
distillery [dɪs'tɪlərɪ] *n* distilleria.
distinct [dɪs'tɪŋkt] *adj* distinto(a); (*preference, progress*) definito(a); **as ~ from** a differenza di.
distinction [dɪs'tɪŋkʃən] *n* distinzione *f*; (*in exam*) lode *f*; **to draw a ~ between** fare distinzione tra; **a writer of ~** uno scrittore di notevoli qualità.
distinctive [dɪs'tɪŋktɪv] *adj* distintivo(a).
distinctly [dɪs'tɪŋktlɪ] *adv* distintamente; (*remember*) chiaramente; (*unhappy, better*) decisamente.
distinguish [dɪs'tɪŋgwɪʃ] *vt* distinguere; discernere ♦ *vi*: **to ~ (between)** distinguere (tra); **to ~ o.s.** distinguersi.
distinguished [dɪs'tɪŋgwɪʃt] *adj* (*eminent*) eminente; (*career*) brillante; (*refined*) distinto(a), signorile.
distinguishing [dɪs'tɪŋgwɪʃɪŋ] *adj* (*feature*) distinto(a), caratteristico(a).
distort [dɪs'tɔːt] *vt* (*also fig*) distorcere; (*account*) falsare; (*TECH*) deformare.
distortion [dɪs'tɔːʃən] *n* (*gen*) distorsione *f*; (*of truth etc*) alterazione *f*; (*of facts*) travisamento; (*TECH*) deformazione *f*.
distract [dɪs'trækt] *vt* distrarre.
distracted [dɪs'træktɪd] *adj* distratto(a).
distraction [dɪs'trækʃən] *n* distrazione *f*; **to drive sb to ~** spingere qn alla pazzia.
distraught [dɪs'trɔːt] *adj* stravolto(a).
distress [dɪs'trɛs] *n* angoscia; (*pain*) dolore *m* ♦ *vt* affliggere; **in ~** (*ship etc*) in pericolo, in difficoltà; **~ed area** (*BRIT*) zona sinistrata.
distressing [dɪs'trɛsɪŋ] *adj* doloroso(a), penoso(a).
distress signal *n* segnale *m* di pericolo.
distribute [dɪs'trɪbjuːt] *vt* distribuire.
distribution [dɪstrɪ'bjuːʃən] *n* distribuzione *f*.
distribution cost *n* costo di distribuzione.
distributor [dɪs'trɪbjutə*] *n* distributore *m*; (*COMM*) concessionario.
district ['dɪstrɪkt] *n* (*of country*) regione *f*; (*of town*) quartiere *m*; (*ADMIN*) distretto.
district attorney (DA) *n* (*US*) ≈ sostituto procuratore *m* della Repubblica.
district council *n organo di amministrazione locale*; *see boxed note.*

DISTRICT COUNCIL

*In Inghilterra e in Galles, il **district council** è l'organo responsabile dell'amministrazione dei*

paesi più piccoli e dei distretti di campagna. È finanziato tramite una tassa locale e riceve un contributo da parte del governo. I **district councils** *vengono eletti a livello locale ogni quattro anni. L'organo amministrativo nelle città è invece il "city council".*

---

district nurse *n* (*BRIT*) infermiera di quartiere.
distrust [dɪs'trʌst] *n* diffidenza, sfiducia ♦ *vt* non aver fiducia in.
distrustful [dɪs'trʌstful] *adj* diffidente.
disturb [dɪs'tɜːb] *vt* disturbare; (*inconvenience*) scomodare; **sorry to ~ you** scusi se la disturbo.
disturbance [dɪs'tɜːbəns] *n* disturbo; (*political etc*) tumulto; (*by drunks etc*) disordini *mpl*; **~ of the peace** disturbo della quiete pubblica; **to cause a ~** provocare disordini.
disturbed [dɪs'tɜːbd] *adj* turbato(a); **to be emotionally ~** avere problemi emotivi; **to be mentally ~** essere malato(a) di mente.
disturbing [dɪs'tɜːbɪŋ] *adj* sconvolgente.
disuse [dɪs'juːs] *n*: **to fall into ~** cadere in disuso.
disused [dɪs'juːzd] *adj* abbandonato(a).
ditch [dɪtʃ] *n* fossa ♦ *vt* (*col*) piantare in asso.
dither ['dɪðə*] *vi* vacillare.
ditto ['dɪtəu] *adv* idem.
divan [dɪ'væn] *n* divano.
divan bed *n* divano letto *inv*.
dive [daɪv] *n* tuffo; (*of submarine*) immersione *f*; (*AVIAT*) picchiata; (*pej*) buco ♦ *vi* tuffarsi.
diver ['daɪvə*] *n* tuffatore/trice; (*deep-sea ~*) palombaro.
diverge [daɪ'vɜːdʒ] *vi* divergere.
divergent [daɪ'vɜːdʒənt] *adj* divergente.
diverse [daɪ'vɜːs] *adj* vario(a).
diversification [daɪvɜːsɪfɪ'keɪʃən] *n* diversificazione *f*.
diversify [daɪ'vɜːsɪfaɪ] *vt* diversificare.
diversion [daɪ'vɜːʃən] *n* (*BRIT AUT*) deviazione *f*; (*distraction*) divertimento.
diversionary tactics [daɪ'vɜːʃənrɪ-] *npl* tattica *fsg* diversiva.
diversity [daɪ'vɜːsɪtɪ] *n* diversità *f inv*, varietà *f inv*.
divert [daɪ'vɜːt] *vt* (*traffic, river*) deviare; (*train, plane*) dirottare; (*amuse*) divertire.
divest [daɪ'vɛst] *vt*: **to ~ sb of** spogliare qn di.
divide [dɪ'vaɪd] *vt* dividere; (*separate*) separare ♦ *vi* dividersi; **to ~ (between or**

among) dividere (tra), ripartire (tra); **40
~d by 5** 40 diviso 5.

▶**divide out** *vt*: **to ~ out (between** *or*
among) (*sweets etc*) distribuire (tra);
(*tasks*) distribuire *or* ripartire (tra).

divided [dɪ'vaɪdɪd] *adj* (*country*) diviso(a);
(*opinions*) discordi.

divided highway *n* (*US*) strada a doppia
carreggiata.

divided skirt *n* gonna *f* pantalone *inv.*

dividend ['dɪvɪdɛnd] *n* dividendo.

dividend cover *n* rapporto dividendo
profitti.

dividers [dɪ'vaɪdəz] *npl* compasso a punte
fisse.

divine [dɪ'vaɪn] *adj* divino(a) ♦ *vt* (*future*)
divinare, predire; (*truth*) indovinare;
(*water, metal*) individuare tramite
radioestesia.

diving ['daɪvɪŋ] *n* tuffo.

diving board *n* trampolino.

diving suit *n* scafandro.

divinity [dɪ'vɪnɪtɪ] *n* divinità *f inv*;
teologia.

division [dɪ'vɪʒən] *n* divisione *f*;
separazione *f*; (*BRIT FOOTBALL*) serie *f inv*;
~ of labour divisione *f* del lavoro.

divisive [dɪ'vaɪsɪv] *adj* che è causa di
discordia.

divorce [dɪ'vɔːs] *n* divorzio ♦ *vt* divorziare
da.

divorced [dɪ'vɔːst] *adj* divorziato(a).

divorcee [dɪvɔː'siː] *n* divorziato/a.

divot ['dɪvət] *n* (*GOLF*) zolla di terra
(*sollevata accidentalmente*).

divulge [daɪ'vʌldʒ] *vt* divulgare,
rivelare.

D.I.Y. *adj, n abbr* (*BRIT*) *see* **do-it-yourself.**

dizziness ['dɪzɪnɪs] *n* vertigini *fpl.*

dizzy ['dɪzɪ] *adj* (*height*) vertiginoso(a); **to
make sb ~** far girare la testa a qn; **to feel
~** avere il capogiro; **I feel ~** mi gira la
testa, ho il capogiro.

DJ *n abbr see* **disc jockey.**

dj *n abbr* = **dinner jacket.**

Djakarta [dʒə'kɑːtə] *n* Giakarta.

DJIA *n abbr* (*US STOCK EXCHANGE*: = *Dow-
Jones Industrial Average*) indice *m* Dow-
Jones.

dl *abbr* (= *decilitre*) dl.

DLit(t) *n abbr* = *Doctor of Literature*; *Doctor of
Letters.*

dm *abbr* (= *decimetre*) dm.

DMus *n abbr* = *Doctor of Music.*

DMZ *n abbr* (= *demilitarized zone*) zona
smilitarizzata.

DNA *n abbr* (= *deoxyribonucleic acid*) DNA
m; **~ test** test *m inv* del DNA.

do [duː] (*pt* **did**, *pp* **done**) *n* (*col: party etc*)
festa; **it was rather a grand ~** è stato un
ricevimento piuttosto importante
♦ *vb* **1** (*in negative constructions*) *non
tradotto*; **I don't understand** non capisco
2 (*to form questions*) *non tradotto*; **didn't
you know?** non lo sapevi?; **why didn't you
come?** perché non sei venuto?
3 (*for emphasis, in polite expressions*): **she
does seem rather late** sembra essere
piuttosto in ritardo; **I DO wish I could …**
magari potessi …; **but I DO like it!** sì che
mi piace!; **~ sit down** si accomodi la
prego, prego si sieda; **~ take care!** mi
raccomando, stai attento!
4 (*used to avoid repeating vb*): **she swims
better than I ~** lei nuota meglio di me; **~
you agree? — yes, I ~/no, I don't** sei
d'accordo? — sì/no; **she lives in Glasgow
— so ~ I** lei vive a Glasgow — anch'io; **he
asked me to help him and I did** mi ha
chiesto di aiutarlo ed io l'ho fatto; **they
come here often — ~ they?** vengono qui
spesso — ah sì?, davvero?
5 (*in question tags*): **you like him, don't
you?** ti piace, vero?; **I don't know him, ~
I?** non lo conosco, vero?
♦ *vt* (*gen, carry out, perform etc*) fare; **what
are you ~ing tonight?** che fai stasera?;
what can I ~ for you? (*in shop*) desidera?;
I'll ~ all I can farò tutto il possibile; **to ~
the cooking** cucinare; **to ~ the washing-
up** fare i piatti; **to ~ one's teeth** lavarsi i
denti; **to ~ one's hair/nails** farsi i capelli/
le unghie; **the car was ~ing 100** la
macchina faceva i 100 all'ora; **how ~ you
like your steak done?** come preferisce la
bistecca?; **well done** ben cotto(a)
♦ *vi* **1** (*act, behave*) fare; **~ as I ~** faccia
come me, faccia come faccio io; **what did
he ~ with the cat?** che ne ha fatto del
gatto?
2 (*get on, fare*) andare; **he's ~ing well/
badly at school** va bene/male a scuola;
how ~ you ~? piacere!
3 (*suit*) andare bene; **this room will ~**
questa stanza va bene
4 (*be sufficient*) bastare; **will £10 ~?**
basteranno 10 sterline?; **that'll ~** basta
così; **that'll ~!** (*in annoyance*) ora basta!;
to make ~ (with) arrangiarsi (con)

▶**do away with** *vt fus* (*kill*) far fuori;
(*abolish*) abolire

▶**do for** *vt fus* (*BRIT col: clean for*) fare i
servizi per

▶**do out of** *vt fus*: **to ~ sb out of sth**

fregare qc a qn
▶**do up** *vt* (*laces*) allacciare; (*dress, buttons*) abbottonare; (*renovate: room, house*) rimettere a nuovo, rifare; **to ~ o.s. up** farsi bello(a)
▶**do with** *vt fus* (*need*) aver bisogno di; **I could ~ with some help/a drink** un aiuto/un bicchierino non guasterebbe; **it could ~ with a wash** una lavata non gli farebbe male; (*be connected*): **what has it got to ~ with you?** e tu che c'entri?; **I won't have anything to ~ with it** non voglio avere niente a che farci; **it has to ~ with money** si tratta di soldi
▶**do without** *vi* fare senza ♦ *vt fus* fare a meno di.

do. *abbr* = **ditto.**
DOA *abbr* (= *dead on arrival*) morto(a) durante il trasporto.
d.o.b. *abbr* = **date of birth.**
doc [dɔk] *n* (*col*) dottore/essa.
docile ['dəusaɪl] *adj* docile.
dock [dɔk] *n* bacino; (*wharf*) molo; (*LAW*) banco degli imputati ♦ *vi* entrare in bacino ♦ *vt* (*pay etc*) decurtare.
dock dues *npl* diritti *mpl* di banchina.
docker ['dɔkə*] *n* scaricatore *m*.
docket ['dɔkɪt] *n* (*on parcel etc*) etichetta, cartellino.
dockyard ['dɔkjɑːd] *n* cantiere *m* navale.
doctor ['dɔktə*] *n* medico, dottore/essa; (*PhD etc*) dottore/essa ♦ *vt* (*interfere with: food, drink*) adulterare; (: *text, document*) alterare, manipolare; **~'s office** (*US*) gabinetto medico, ambulatorio; **D~ of Philosophy (PhD)** dottorato di ricerca; (*person*) titolare *m/f* di un dottorato di ricerca.
doctorate ['dɔktərɪt] *n* dottorato di ricerca; *see boxed note.*

DOCTORATE

Il **doctorate** è il riconoscimento accademico più prestigioso in tutti i campi del sapere e viene conferito in seguito alla presentazione di una tesi originale di fronte ad una commissione di esperti. Generalmente tale tesi è un compendio del lavoro svolto durante più anni di studi; vedi anche **Bachelor's degree**, **Master's degree**.

---

doctrine ['dɔktrɪn] *n* dottrina.
docudrama [dɔkju'drɑːmə] *n* (*TV*) ricostruzione *f* filmata.
document *n* ['dɔkjumənt] documento ♦ *vt* ['dɔkjumɛnt] documentare.

documentary [dɔkju'mɛntərɪ] *adj* documentario(a); (*evidence*) documentato(a) ♦ *n* documentario.
documentation [dɔkjumən'teɪʃən] *n* documentazione *f*.
DOD *n abbr* (*US*) = **Department of Defense**; *see* **defence**.
doddering ['dɔdərɪŋ] *adj* traballante.
doddery ['dɔdərɪ] *adj* malfermo(a).
doddle ['dɔdl] *n*: **it's a ~** (*col*) è un gioco da ragazzi.
dodge [dɔdʒ] *n* trucco; schivata ♦ *vt* schivare, eludere ♦ *vi* scansarsi; (*SPORT*) fare una schivata; **to ~ out of the way** scansarsi; **to ~ through the traffic** destreggiarsi nel traffico.
dodgems ['dɔdʒəmz] *npl* (*BRIT*) autoscontri *mpl*.
dodgy ['dɔdʒɪ] *adj* (*col: uncertain*) rischioso(a); (*untrustworthy*) sospetto(a).
DOE *n abbr* (*US*) = **Department of Energy**; *see* **energy**.
doe [dəu] *n* (*deer*) femmina di daino; (*rabbit*) coniglia.
does [dʌz] *see* **do.**
doesn't ['dʌznt] = **does not.**
dog [dɔg] *n* cane *m* ♦ *vt* (*follow closely*) pedinare; (*fig: memory etc*) perseguitare; **to go to the ~s** (*person*) ridursi male, lasciarsi andare; (*nation etc*) andare in malora.
dog biscuits *npl* biscotti *mpl* per cani.
dog collar *n* collare *m* di cane; (*fig*) collarino.
dog-eared ['dɔgɪəd] *adj* (*book*) con orecchie.
dog food *n* cibo per cani.
dogged ['dɔgɪd] *adj* ostinato(a), tenace.
doggie, doggy ['dɔgɪ] *n* (*col*) cane *m*, cagnolino.
doggy bag *n* sacchetto per gli avanzi (*da portare a casa*).
dogma ['dɔgmə] *n* dogma *m*.
dogmatic [dɔg'mætɪk] *adj* dogmatico(a).
do-gooder [duː'gudə*] *n* (*col pej*): **to be a ~** fare il filantropo.
dogsbody ['dɔgzbɔdɪ] *n* (*BRIT*) factotum *m inv*.
doily ['dɔɪlɪ] *n* centrino di carta sottopiatto.
doing ['duːɪŋ] *n*: **this is your ~** è opera tua, sei stato tu; **~s** *npl* attività *fpl*.
do-it-yourself (DIY) ['duːɪtjɔː'sɛlf] *n* il far da sé.
doldrums ['dɔldrəmz] *npl* (*fig*): **to be in the ~** essere giù; (*business*) attraversare un momento difficile.
dole [dəul] *n* (*BRIT*) sussidio di disoccupazione; **to be on the ~** vivere del

sussidio.

▶**dole out** *vt* distribuire.

doleful ['dəulful] *adj* triste, doloroso(a).

doll [dɔl] *n* bambola.

▶**doll up** *vt*: **to ~ o.s. up** farsi bello(a).

dollar ['dɔlə*] *n* dollaro.

dollop ['dɔləp] *n* (*of food*) cucchiaiata.

dolly ['dɔlɪ] *n* bambola.

dolphin ['dɔlfɪn] *n* delfino.

domain [də'meɪn] *n* dominio; (*fig*) campo, sfera.

dome [dəum] *n* cupola.

domestic [də'mestɪk] *adj* (*duty, happiness, animal*) domestico(a); (*policy, affairs, flights*) nazionale; (*news*) dall'interno.

domesticated [də'mestɪkeɪtɪd] *adj* addomesticato(a); (*person*) casalingo(a).

domesticity [dəumes'tɪsɪtɪ] *n* vita di famiglia.

domestic servant *n* domestico/a.

domicile ['dɔmɪsaɪl] *n* domicilio.

dominant ['dɔmɪnənt] *adj* dominante.

dominate ['dɔmɪneɪt] *vt* dominare.

domination [dɔmɪ'neɪʃən] *n* dominazione *f*.

domineering [dɔmɪ'nɪərɪŋ] *adj* dispotico(a), autoritario(a).

Dominican Republic [də'mɪnɪkən-] *n* Repubblica Dominicana.

dominion [də'mɪnɪən] *n* dominio; sovranità; (*BRIT POL*) dominion *m inv*.

domino, ~**es** ['dɔmɪnəu] *n* domino; ~**es** *n* (*game*) gioco del domino.

don [dɔn] *n* (*BRIT*) docente *m/f* universitario(a) ♦ *vt* indossare.

donate [də'neɪt] *vt* donare.

donation [də'neɪʃən] *n* donazione *f*.

done [dʌn] *pp of* **do**.

donkey ['dɔŋkɪ] *n* asino.

donkey-work ['dɔŋkɪwəːk] *n* (*BRIT col*) lavoro ingrato.

donor ['dəunə*] *n* donatore/trice.

donor card *n* tessera di donatore di organi.

don't [dəunt] *vb* = **do not**.

donut ['dəunʌt] *n* (*US*) = **doughnut**.

doodle ['duːdl] *n* scarabocchio ♦ *vi* scarabocchiare.

doom [duːm] *n* destino; rovina ♦ *vt*: **to be ~ed** (**to failure**) essere predestinato(a) (a fallire).

doomsday ['duːmzdeɪ] *n* il giorno del Giudizio.

door [dɔː*] *n* porta; (*of vehicle*) sportello, portiera; **from ~ to ~** di porta in porta.

doorbell ['dɔːbel] *n* campanello.

door handle *n* maniglia.

doorman ['dɔːmæn] *n* (*in hotel*) portiere *m* in livrea; (*in block of flats*) portinaio.

doormat ['dɔːmæt] *n* stuoia della porta.

doorstep ['dɔːstep] *n* gradino della porta.

door-to-door ['dɔːtə'dɔː*] *adj*: ~ **selling** vendita porta a porta.

doorway ['dɔːweɪ] *n* porta; **in the ~** nel vano della porta.

dope [dəup] *n* (*col: drugs*) roba; (*: information*) dati *mpl* ♦ *vt* (*horse etc*) drogare.

dopey ['dəupɪ] *adj* (*col*) inebetito(a).

dormant ['dɔːmənt] *adj* inattivo(a); (*fig*) latente.

dormer ['dɔːmə*] *n* (*also*: ~ **window**) abbaino.

dormice ['dɔːmaɪs] *npl of* **dormouse**.

dormitory ['dɔːmɪtrɪ] *n* dormitorio; (*US: hall of residence*) casa dello studente.

dormouse, *pl* **dormice** ['dɔːmaus, -maɪs] *n* ghiro.

DOS [dɔs] *n abbr see* **disk operating system**.

dosage ['dəusɪdʒ] *n* (*on medicine bottle*) posologia.

dose [dəus] *n* dose *f*; (*BRIT: bout*) attacco ♦ *vt*: **to ~ sb with sth** somministrare qc a qn; **a ~ of flu** una bella influenza.

dosser ['dɔsə*] *n* (*BRIT col*) barbone/a.

doss house ['dɔs-] *n* (*BRIT*) asilo notturno.

dossier ['dɔsɪeɪ] *n* dossier *m inv*.

DOT *n abbr* (*US*) = **Department of Transportation;** *see* **transportation.**

dot [dɔt] *n* punto; macchiolina ♦ *vt*: ~**ted with** punteggiato(a) di; **on the ~** in punto.

dot command *n* (*COMPUT*) dot command *m inv*.

dote [dəut]: **to ~ on** *vt fus* essere infatuato(a) di.

dot-matrix printer [dɔt'meɪtrɪks-] *n* stampante *f* a matrice a punti.

dotted line ['dɔtɪd-] *n* linea punteggiata; **to sign on the ~** firmare (nell'apposito spazio); (*fig*) accettare.

dotty ['dɔtɪ] *adj* (*col*) strambo(a).

double ['dʌbl] *adj* doppio(a) ♦ *adv* (*fold*) in due, doppio; (*twice*): **to cost ~** (**sth**) costare il doppio (di qc) ♦ *n* sosia *m inv*; (*CINE*) controfigura ♦ *vt* raddoppiare; (*fold*) piegare doppio *or* in due ♦ *vi* raddoppiarsi; **spelt with a ~ "l"** scritto con due elle *or* con doppia elle; ~ **five two six (5526)** (*BRIT TEL*) cinque cinque due sei; **on the ~,** (*BRIT*) **at the ~** a passo di corsa; **to ~ as** (*have two uses etc*) funzionare *or* servire anche da; *see also* **doubles.**

▶**double back** *vi* (*person*) tornare sui propri passi.

▶**double up** *vi* (*bend over*) piegarsi in due; (*share room*) dividere la stanza.

double bass *n* contrabbasso.
double bed *n* letto matrimoniale.
double-breasted ['dʌbl'brɛstɪd] *adj* a doppio petto.
double-check ['dʌbl'tʃɛk] *vt, vi* ricontrollare.
double-clutch ['dʌbl'klʌtʃ] *vi* (*US*) fare la doppietta.
double cream *n* (*BRIT*) doppia panna.
doublecross ['dʌbl'krɔs] *vt* fare il doppio gioco con.
doubledecker ['dʌbl'dɛkə*] *n* autobus *m inv* a due piani.
double declutch *vi* (*BRIT*) fare la doppietta.
double exposure *n* (*PHOT*) sovrimpressione *f*.
double glazing *n* (*BRIT*) doppi vetri *mpl*.
double-page ['dʌblpeɪdʒ] *adj*: ~ spread pubblicità a doppia pagina.
double parking *n* parcheggio in doppia fila.
double room *n* camera per due.
doubles ['dʌblz] *n* (*TENNIS*) doppio.
double time *n* tariffa doppia per lavoro straordinario.
double whammy [-'wæmɪ] *n* doppia mazzata (*fig*).
doubly ['dʌblɪ] *adv* doppiamente.
doubt [daut] *n* dubbio ♦ *vt* dubitare di; **to ~ that** dubitare che + *sub*; **without (a) ~** senza dubbio; **beyond ~** fuor di dubbio; **I ~ it very much** ho i miei dubbi, nutro seri dubbi in proposito.
doubtful ['dautful] *adj* dubbioso(a), incerto(a); (*person*) equivoco(a); **to be ~ about sth** avere dei dubbi su qc, non essere convinto di qc; **I'm a bit ~** non ne sono sicuro.
doubtless ['dautlɪs] *adv* indubbiamente.
dough [dəu] *n* pasta, impasto; (*col: money*) grana.
doughnut, (*US*) **donut** ['dəunʌt] *n* bombolone *m*.
dour [duə*] *adj* arcigno(a).
douse [daus] *vt* (*with water*) infradiciare; (*flames*) spegnere.
dove [dʌv] *n* colombo/a.
Dover ['dəuvə*] *n* Dover *f*.
dovetail ['dʌvteɪl] *n*: ~ joint incastro a coda di rondine ♦ *vi* (*fig*) combaciare.
dowager ['dauədʒə*] *n* vedova titolata.
dowdy ['daudɪ] *adj* trasandato(a); malvestito(a).
Dow-Jones average ['dau'dʒəunz-] *n* (*US*) indice *m* Dow-Jones.
down [daun] *n* (*fluff*) piumino; (*hill*) collina, colle *m* ♦ *adv* giù, di sotto ♦ *prep* giù per

♦ *vt* (*col: drink*) scolarsi; ~ **there** laggiù, là in fondo; ~ **here** quaggiù; **I'll be ~ in a minute** scendo tra un minuto; **the price of meat is ~** il prezzo della carne è sceso; **I've got it ~ in my diary** ce l'ho sulla mia agenda; **to pay £2 ~** dare 2 sterline in acconto *or* di anticipo; **I've been ~ with flu** sono stato a letto con l'influenza; **England is two goals ~** l'Inghilterra sta perdendo per due goal; **to ~ tools** (*BRIT*) incrociare le braccia; ~ **with X!** abbasso X!
down-and-out ['daunəndaut] *n* (*tramp*) barbone *m*.
down-at-heel ['daunət'hi:l] *adj* scalcagnato(a); (*fig*) trasandato(a).
downbeat ['daunbi:t] *n* (*MUS*) tempo in battere ♦ *adj* (*col*) volutamente distaccato(a).
downcast ['daunka:st] *adj* abbattuto(a).
downer ['daunə*] *n* (*col: drug*) farmaco depressivo; **to be on a ~** (*depressed*) essere giù.
downfall ['daunfɔ:l] *n* caduta; rovina.
downgrade ['daungreɪd] *vt* (*job, hotel*) declassare; (*employee*) degradare.
downhearted [daun'ha:tɪd] *adj* scoraggiato(a).
downhill ['daun'hɪl] *adv* verso il basso ♦ *n* (*SKI: also*: ~ race) discesa libera; **to go ~** andare in discesa; (*business*) andare a rotoli.
Downing Street ['daunɪŋ-] *n*: **10 ~** *residenza del primo ministro inglese*; *see boxed note*.

download ['daunləud] *vt* (*COMPUT*) trasferire (*per esempio da un grosso calcolatore ad un microcalcolatore*).
down-market ['daun'ma:kɪt] *adj* rivolto(a) ad una fascia di mercato inferiore.
down payment *n* acconto.
downplay ['daunpleɪ] *vt* (*US*) minimizzare.
downpour ['daunpɔ:*] *n* scroscio di pioggia.
downright ['daunraɪt] *adj* franco(a); (*refusal*) assoluto(a).

downsize ['daun'saɪz] *vt* (*workforce*) ridurre.

Down's syndrome *n* sindrome *f* di Down.

downstairs ['daun'stɛəz] *adv* di sotto; al piano inferiore; **to come** ~, **go** ~ scendere giù.

downstream ['daun'striːm] *adv* a valle.

downtime ['dauntaɪm] *n* (*COMM*) tempi *mpl* morti.

down-to-earth ['dauntu'əːθ] *adj* pratico(a).

downtown ['daun'taun] *adv* in città ♦ *adj* (*US*): ~ **Chicago** il centro di Chicago.

downtrodden ['dauntrɔdn] *adj* oppresso(a).

down under *adv* agli antipodi.

downward ['daunwəd] *adj* in giù, in discesa; **a** ~ **trend** una diminuzione progressiva.

downward(s) ['daunwəd(z)] *adv* in giù, in discesa.

dowry ['dauri] *n* dote *f*.

doz. *abbr* = **dozen.**

doze [dəuz] *vi* sonnecchiare.

▶ **doze off** *vi* appisolarsi.

dozen ['dʌzn] *n* dozzina; **a** ~ **books** una dozzina di libri; **80p a** ~ 80 pence la dozzina; ~**s of times** centinaia *or* migliaia di volte.

DPh, DPhil *n abbr* (= *Doctor of Philosophy*) ≈ dottorato di ricerca.

DPP *n abbr* (*BRIT*) *see* **Director of Public Prosecutions.**

DPT *n abbr* (*MED*: = *diphtheria, pertussis, tetanus*) *vaccino*.

Dr, Dr. *abbr* (= *doctor*) Dr, Dott./Dott.ssa.

dr *abbr* (*COMM*) = **debtor.**

Dr. *abbr* (*in street names*) = **drive.**

drab [dræb] *adj* tetro(a), grigio(a).

draft [drɑːft] *n* abbozzo; (*COMM*) tratta; (*US MIL*) contingente *m*; (: *call-up*) leva *f* ♦ *vt* abbozzare; (*document, report*) stendere (in versione preliminare); *see also* **draught.**

drag [dræg] *vt* trascinare; (*river*) dragare ♦ *vi* trascinarsi ♦ *n* (*AVIAT, NAUT*) resistenza (aerodinamica); (*col: person*) noioso/a; (: *task*) noia; (*women's clothing*): **in** ~ travestito (da donna).

▶ **drag away** *vt*: **to** ~ **away (from)** tirare via (da).

▶ **drag on** *vi* tirar avanti lentamente.

dragnet ['drægnɛt] *n* giacchio; (*fig*) rastrellamento.

dragon ['drægən] *n* drago.

dragonfly ['drægənflaɪ] *n* libellula.

dragoon [drə'guːn] *n* (*cavalryman*) dragone *m* ♦ *vt*: **to** ~ **sb into doing sth** (*BRIT*) costringere qn a fare qc.

drain [dreɪn] *n* canale *m* di scolo; (*for sewage*) fogna; (*on resources*) salasso ♦ *vt*

(*land, marshes*) prosciugare; (*vegetables*) scolare; (*reservoir etc*) vuotare ♦ *vi* (*water*) defluire; **to feel** ~**ed** sentirsi svuotato(a), sentirsi sfinito(a).

drainage ['dreɪnɪdʒ] *n* prosciugamento; fognatura.

draining board ['dreɪnɪŋ-], **drainboard** (*US*) ['dreɪnbɔːd] *n* piano del lavello.

drainpipe ['dreɪnpaɪp] *n* tubo di scarico.

drake [dreɪk] *n* maschio dell'anatra.

dram [dræm] *n* bicchierino (di whisky *etc*).

drama ['drɑːmə] *n* (*art*) dramma *m*, teatro; (*play*) commedia; (*event*) dramma.

dramatic [drə'mætɪk] *adj* drammatico(a).

dramatically [drə'mætɪklɪ] *adv* in modo spettacolare.

dramatist ['dræmətɪst] *n* drammaturgo/a.

dramatize ['dræmətaɪz] *vt* (*events etc*) drammatizzare; (*adapt: novel: for TV*) ridurre *or* adattare per la televisione; (: *for cinema*) ridurre *or* adattare per lo schermo.

drank [dræŋk] *pt of* **drink.**

drape [dreɪp] *vt* drappeggiare; *see also* **drapes.**

draper ['dreɪpə*] *n* (*BRIT*) negoziante *m/f* di stoffe.

drapes [dreɪps] *npl* (*US*) tende *fpl*.

drastic ['dræstɪk] *adj* drastico(a).

drastically ['dræstɪklɪ] *adv* drasticamente.

draught, (*US*) **draft** [drɑːft] *n* corrente *f* d'aria; (*NAUT*) pescaggio; **on** ~ (*beer*) alla spina; *see also* **draughts.**

draught beer *n* birra alla spina.

draughtboard ['drɑːftbɔːd] *n* scacchiera.

draughts [drɑːfts] *n* (*BRIT*) (gioco della) dama.

draughtsman, (*US*) **draftsman** ['drɑːftsmən] *n* disegnatore *m*.

draughtsmanship, (*US*) **draftsmanship** ['drɑːftsmənʃɪp] *n* disegno tecnico; (*skill*) arte *f* del disegno.

draw [drɔː] *vb* (*pt* **drew,** *pp* **drawn** [druː, drɔːn]) *vt* tirare; (*attract*) attirare; (*picture*) disegnare; (*line, circle*) tracciare; (*money*) ritirare; (*formulate: conclusion*) trarre, ricavare; (: *comparison, distinction*): **to** ~ **(between)** fare (tra) ♦ *vi* (*SPORT*) pareggiare ♦ *n* (*SPORT*) pareggio; (*in lottery*) estrazione *f*; (*attraction*) attrazione *f*; **to** ~ **to a close** avvicinarsi alla conclusione; **to** ~ **near** *vi* avvicinarsi.

▶ **draw back** *vi*: **to** ~ **back (from)** indietreggiare (di fronte a), tirarsi indietro (di fronte a).

▶ **draw in** *vi* (*BRIT: car*) accostarsi; (: *train*) entrare in stazione.

▶ **draw on** *vt* (*resources*) attingere a;

(*imagination, person*) far ricorso a.

▶**draw out** *vi* (*lengthen*) allungarsi ♦ *vt* (*money*) ritirare.

▶**draw up** *vi* (*stop*) arrestarsi, fermarsi ♦ *vt* (*document*) compilare; (*plans*) formulare.

drawback ['drɔːbæk] *n* svantaggio, inconveniente *m*.

drawbridge ['drɔːbrɪdʒ] *n* ponte *m* levatoio.

drawee [drɔː'iː] *n* trattario.

drawer [drɔː*] *n* cassetto; ['drɔːə*] (*of cheque*) riscuotitore/trice.

drawing ['drɔːɪŋ] *n* disegno.

drawing board *n* tavola da disegno.

drawing pin *n* (*BRIT*) puntina da disegno.

drawing room *n* salotto.

drawl [drɔːl] *n* pronuncia strascicata.

drawn [drɔːn] *pp of* **draw** ♦ *adj* (*haggard: with tiredness*) tirato(a); (: *with pain*) contratto(a) (dal dolore).

drawstring ['drɔːstrɪŋ] *n* laccio (*per stringere maglie, sacche etc*).

dread [drɛd] *n* terrore *m* ♦ *vt* tremare all'idea di.

dreadful ['drɛdful] *adj* terribile; **I feel ~!** (*ill*) mi sento uno straccio!; (*ashamed*) vorrei scomparire (dalla vergogna)!

dream [driːm] *n* sogno ♦ *vt, vi* (*pt, pp* **dreamed** *or* **dreamt** [drɛmt]) sognare; **to have a ~ about sb/sth** fare un sogno su qn/qc; **sweet ~s!** sogni d'oro!

▶**dream up** *vt* (*reason, excuse*) inventare; (*plan, idea*) escogitare.

dreamer ['driːmə*] *n* sognatore/trice.

dreamt [drɛmt] *pt, pp of* **dream**.

dreamy ['driːmɪ] *adj* (*look, voice*) sognante; (*person*) distratto(a), sognatore(trice).

dreary ['drɪərɪ] *adj* tetro(a); monotono(a).

dredge [drɛdʒ] *vt* dragare.

▶**dredge up** *vt* tirare alla superficie; (*fig: unpleasant facts*) rivangare.

dredger ['drɛdʒə*] *n* draga; (*BRIT: also:* **sugar ~**) spargizucchero *m inv*.

dregs [drɛgz] *npl* feccia.

drench [drɛntʃ] *vt* inzuppare; **~ed to the skin** bagnato(a) fino all'osso, bagnato(a) fradicio(a).

dress [drɛs] *n* vestito; (*clothing*) abbigliamento ♦ *vt* vestire; (*wound*) fasciare; (*food*) condire; preparare; (*shop window*) allestire ♦ *vi* vestirsi; **to ~ o.s., to get ~ed** vestirsi; **she ~es very well** veste molto bene.

▶**dress up** *vi* vestirsi a festa; (*in fancy dress*) vestirsi in costume.

dress circle *n* prima galleria.

dress designer *n* disegnatore/trice di moda.

dresser ['drɛsə*] *n* (*THEAT*) assistente *m/f* del camerino; (*also:* **window ~**) vetrinista *m/f*; (*furniture*) credenza.

dressing ['drɛsɪŋ] *n* (*MED*) benda; (*CULIN*) condimento.

dressing gown *n* (*BRIT*) vestaglia.

dressing room *n* (*THEAT*) camerino; (*SPORT*) spogliatoio.

dressing table *n* toilette *f inv*.

dressmaker ['drɛsmeɪkə*] *n* sarta.

dressmaking ['drɛsmeɪkɪŋ] *n* sartoria; confezioni *fpl* per donna.

dress rehearsal *n* prova generale.

dress shirt *n* camicia da sera.

dressy ['drɛsɪ] *adj* (*col*) elegante.

drew [druː] *pt of* **draw**.

dribble ['drɪbl] *vi* gocciolare; (*baby*) sbavare; (*FOOTBALL*) dribblare ♦ *vt* dribblare.

dried [draɪd] *adj* (*fruit, beans*) secco(a); (*eggs, milk*) in polvere.

drier ['draɪə*] *n* = **dryer**.

drift [drɪft] *n* (*of current etc*) direzione *f*; forza; (*of sand, snow*) cumulo; (*general meaning*) senso ♦ *vi* (*boat*) essere trasportato(a) dalla corrente; (*sand, snow*) ammucchiarsi; **to catch sb's ~** capire dove qn vuole arrivare; **to let things ~** lasciare che le cose vadano come vogliono; **to ~ apart** (*friends*) perdersi di vista; (*lovers*) allontanarsi l'uno dall'altro.

drifter ['drɪftə*] *n* persona che fa una vita da zingaro.

driftwood ['drɪftwud] *n* resti *mpl* della mareggiata.

drill [drɪl] *n* trapano; (*MIL*) esercitazione *f* ♦ *vt* trapanare; (*soldiers*) esercitare, addestrare; (*pupils: in grammar*) fare esercitare ♦ *vi* (*for oil*) fare trivellazioni.

drilling ['drɪlɪŋ] *n* (*for oil*) trivellazione *f*.

drilling rig *n* (*on land*) torre *f* di perforazione; (*at sea*) piattaforma (per trivellazioni subacquee).

drily ['draɪlɪ] *adv* = **dryly**.

drink [drɪŋk] *n* bevanda, bibita ♦ *vt, vi* (*pt* **drank**, *pp* **drunk** [dræŋk, drʌŋk]) bere; **to have a ~** bere qualcosa; **a ~ of water** un bicchier d'acqua; **would you like something to ~?** vuole qualcosa da bere?; **we had ~s before lunch** abbiamo preso l'aperitivo.

▶**drink in** *vt* (*subj: person: fresh air*) aspirare; (: *story*) ascoltare avidamente; (: *sight*) ammirare, bersi con gli occhi.

drinkable ['drɪŋkəbl] *adj* (*not poisonous*) potabile; (*palatable*) bevibile.

drink-driving ['drɪŋk'draɪvɪŋ] *n* guida in

stato di ebbrezza.

drinker ['drɪŋkə*] *n* bevitore/trice.

drinking ['drɪŋkɪŋ] *n* (*drunkenness*) il bere, alcoolismo.

drinking fountain *n* fontanella.

drinking water *n* acqua potabile.

drip [drɪp] *n* goccia; (~*ping*) sgocciolio; (*MED*) fleboclisi *f inv*; (*col: spineless person*) lavativo ♦ *vi* gocciolare; (*washing*) sgocciolare; (*wall*) trasudare.

drip-dry ['drɪp'draɪ] *adj* (*shirt*) che non si stira.

drip-feed ['drɪpfiːd] *vt* alimentare mediante fleboclisi.

dripping ['drɪpɪŋ] *n* (*CULIN*) grasso d'arrosto ♦ *adj*: ~ **wet** fradicio(a).

drive [draɪv] *n* passeggiata *or* giro in macchina; (*also:* ~**way**) viale *m* d'accesso; (*energy*) energia; (*PSYCH*) impulso; bisogno; (*push*) sforzo eccezionale; campagna; (*SPORT*) drive *m inv*; (*TECH*) trasmissione *f*; (*COMPUT: also:* **disk** ~) disk drive *m inv*, unità *f inv* a dischi magnetici ♦ *vb* (*pt* **drove**, *pp* **driven** [drəuv, 'drɪvn]) *vt* (*vehicle*) guidare; (*nail*) piantare; (*push*) cacciare, spingere; (*TECH: motor*) azionare; far funzionare ♦ *vi* (*AUT: at controls*) guidare; (*: travel*) andare in macchina; **to go for a** ~ andare a fare un giro in macchina; **it's 3 hours'** ~ **from London** è a 3 ore di macchina da Londra; **left-/right-hand** ~ (*AUT*) guida a sinistra/destra; **front-/rear-wheel** ~ (*AUT*) trazione *f* anteriore/posteriore; **to** ~ **sb to (do) sth** spingere qn a (fare) qc; **he** ~**s a taxi** fa il tassista; **to** ~ **at 50 km an hour** guidare *or* andare a 50 km all'ora.

►**drive at** *vt fus* (*fig: intend, mean*) mirare a, voler dire.

►**drive on** *vi* proseguire, andare (più) avanti ♦ *vt* (*incite, encourage*) sospingere, spingere.

drive-by ['draɪvbaɪ] *n* (*also:* ~ **shooting**) sparatoria dalla macchina; **he was killed in a** ~ **shooting** lo hanno ammazzato sparandogli da una macchina in corsa.

drive-in ['draɪvɪn] *adj, n* (*esp US*) drive-in (*m inv*).

drive-in window *n* (*US*) sportello di drive-in.

drivel ['drɪvl] *n* (*col: nonsense*) ciance *fpl*.

driven ['drɪvn] *pp of* **drive**.

driver ['draɪvə*] *n* conducente *m/f*; (*of taxi*) tassista *m*; (*of bus*) autista *m*; (*COMPUT*) driver *m inv*.

driver's license *n* (*US*) patente *f* di guida.

driveway ['draɪvweɪ] *n* viale *m* d'accesso.

driving ['draɪvɪŋ] *adj*: ~ **rain** pioggia

sferzante ♦ *n* guida.

driving force *n* forza trainante.

driving instructor *n* istruttore/trice di scuola guida.

driving lesson *n* lezione *f* di guida.

driving licence *n* (*BRIT*) patente *f* di guida.

driving school *n* scuola *f* guida *inv*.

driving test *n* esame *m* di guida.

drizzle ['drɪzl] *n* pioggerella ♦ *vi* piovigginare.

droll [drəul] *adj* buffo(a).

dromedary ['drɔmədərɪ] *n* dromedario.

drone [drəun] *n* ronzio; (*male bee*) fuco ♦ *vi* (*bee, aircraft, engine*) ronzare; (*also:* ~ **on:** *person*) continuare a parlare (in modo monotono); (*: voice*) continuare a ronzare.

drool [druːl] *vi* sbavare; **to** ~ **over sb/sth** (*fig*) andare in estasi per qn/qc.

droop [druːp] *vi* abbassarsi; languire.

drop [drɔp] *n* goccia; (*fall: in price*) calo, ribasso; (*: in salary*) riduzione *f*, taglio; (*also:* **parachute** ~) lancio; (*steep incline*) salto ♦ *vt* lasciar cadere; (*voice, eyes, price*) abbassare; (*set down from car*) far scendere ♦ *vi* cascare; (*decrease: wind, temperature, price, voice*) calare; (*numbers, attendance*) diminuire; ~**s** *npl* (*MED*) gocce *fpl*; **cough** ~**s** pastiglie *fpl* per la tosse; **a** ~ **of 10%** un calo del 10%; **to** ~ **sb a line** mandare due righe a qn; **to** ~ **anchor** gettare l'ancora.

►**drop in** *vi* (*col: visit*): **to** ~ **in (on)** fare un salto (da), passare (da).

►**drop off** *vi* (*sleep*) addormentarsi ♦ *vt*: **to** ~ **sb off** far scendere qn.

►**drop out** *vi* (*withdraw*) ritirarsi; (*student etc*) smettere di studiare.

droplet ['drɔplɪt] *n* gocciolina.

dropout ['drɔpaut] *n* (*from society/university*) chi ha abbandonato (la società/gli studi).

dropper ['drɔpə*] *n* (*MED*) contagocce *m inv*.

droppings ['drɔpɪŋz] *npl* sterco.

dross [drɔs] *n* scoria; scarto.

drought [draut] *n* siccità *f inv*.

drove [drəuv] *pt of* **drive** ♦ *n*: ~**s of people** una moltitudine di persone.

drown [draun] *vt* affogare; (*also:* ~ **out:** *sound*) coprire ♦ *vi* affogare.

drowse [drauz] *vi* sonnecchiare.

drowsy ['drauzɪ] *adj* sonnolento(a), assonnato(a).

drudge [drʌdʒ] *n* (*person*) uomo/donna di fatica; (*job*) faticaccia.

drudgery ['drʌdʒərɪ] *n* fatica improba; **housework is sheer** ~ le faccende domestiche sono alienanti.

drug [drʌg] *n* farmaco; (*narcotic*) droga ♦ *vt* drogare; **he's on** ~**s** si droga; (*MED*) segue una cura.

drug abuser [-ə'bjuːzə*] *n* chi fa uso di droghe.

drug addict *n* tossicomane *m/f*.

druggist ['drʌgɪst] *n* (*US*) farmacista *m/f*.

drug peddler *n* spacciatore/trice di droga.

drugstore ['drʌgstɔː*] *n* (*US*) negozio di generi vari e di articoli di farmacia con un bar.

drum [drʌm] *n* tamburo; (*for oil, petrol*) fusto ♦ *vt*: **to ~ one's fingers on the table** tamburellare con le dita sulla tavola; **~s** *npl* (*MUS*) batteria.

►**drum up** *vt* (*enthusiasm, support*) conquistarsi.

drummer ['drʌmə*] *n* batterista *m/f*.

drum roll *n* rullio di tamburi.

drumstick ['drʌmstɪk] *n* (*MUS*) bacchetta; (*chicken leg*) coscia di pollo.

drunk [drʌŋk] *pp of* **drink** ♦ *adj* ubriaco(a); ebbro(a) ♦ *n* ubriacone/a; **to get ~** ubriacarsi, prendere una sbornia.

drunkard ['drʌŋkəd] *n* ubriacone/a.

drunken ['drʌŋkən] *adj* ubriaco(a); da ubriaco; **~ driving** guida in stato di ebbrezza.

drunkenness ['drʌŋkənnɪs] *n* ubriachezza; ebbrezza.

dry [draɪ] *adj* secco(a); (*day, clothes, fig: humour*) asciutto(a); (*uninteresting: lecture, subject*) poco avvincente ♦ *vt* seccare; (*clothes, hair, hands*) asciugare ♦ *vi* asciugarsi; **on ~ land** sulla terraferma; **to ~ one's hands/hair/eyes** asciugarsi le mani/i capelli/gli occhi.

►**dry up** *vi* seccarsi; (*source of supply*) esaurirsi; (*fig: imagination etc*) inaridirsi; (*fall silent: speaker*) azzittirsi.

dry-clean [draɪ'kliːn] *vt* pulire *or* lavare a secco.

dry-cleaner's [draɪ'kliːnəz] *n* lavasecco *m inv*.

dry-cleaning [draɪ'kliːnɪŋ] *n* pulitura a secco.

dry dock *n* (*NAUT*) bacino di carenaggio.

dryer ['draɪə*] *n* (*for hair*) föhn *m inv*, asciugacapelli *m inv*; (*for clothes*) asciugabiancheria *m inv*.

dry goods *npl* (*COMM*) tessuti *mpl* e mercerie *fpl*.

dry goods store *n* (*US*) negozio di stoffe.

dry ice *n* ghiaccio secco.

dryly ['draɪlɪ] *adv* con fare asciutto.

dryness ['draɪnɪs] *n* secchezza; (*of ground*) aridità.

dry rot *n* fungo del legno.

dry run *n* (*fig*) prova.

dry ski slope *n* pista artificiale.

DSc *n abbr* (= *Doctor of Science*) titolo di studio.

DSS *n abbr* (*BRIT*) = **Department of Social Security**; *see* **social security**.

DST *abbr* = **Daylight Saving Time**.

DTI *n abbr* (*BRIT*) = **Department of Trade and Industry**; *see* **trade**.

DTP *n abbr* = **desktop publishing**; (*MED*: = *diphtheria, tetanus, pertussis*) *vaccino*.

DT's *n abbr* (*col*) = **delirium tremens**.

dual ['djuəl] *adj* doppio(a).

dual carriageway *n* (*BRIT*) strada a doppia carreggiata.

dual-control ['djuəlkən'trəul] *adj* con doppi comandi.

dual nationality *n* doppia nazionalità.

dual-purpose ['djuəl'pəːpəs] *adj* a doppio uso.

dubbed [dʌbd] *adj* (*CINE*) doppiato(a); (*nicknamed*) soprannominato(a).

dubious ['djuːbɪəs] *adj* dubbio(a); (*character, manner*) ambiguo(a), equivoco(a); **I'm very ~ about it** ho i miei dubbi in proposito.

Dublin ['dʌblɪn] *n* Dublino *f*.

Dubliner ['dʌblɪnə*] *n* dublinese *m/f*.

duchess ['dʌtʃɪs] *n* duchessa.

duck [dʌk] *n* anatra ♦ *vi* abbassare la testa ♦ *vt* spingere sotto (acqua).

duckling ['dʌklɪŋ] *n* anatroccolo.

duct [dʌkt] *n* condotto; (*ANAT*) canale *m*.

dud [dʌd] *n* (*shell*) proiettile *m* che fa cilecca; (*object, tool*): **it's a ~** è inutile, non funziona ♦ *adj* (*BRIT: cheque*) a vuoto; (*note, coin*) falso(a).

due [djuː] *adj* dovuto(a); (*expected*) atteso(a); (*fitting*) giusto(a) ♦ *n* dovuto ♦ *adv*: **~ north** diritto verso nord; **~s** *npl* (*for club, union*) quota; (*in harbour*) diritti *mpl* di porto; **in ~ course** a tempo debito; finalmente; **~ to** dovuto a; a causa di; **the rent's ~ on the 30th** l'affitto scade il 30; **the train is ~ at 8** il treno è atteso per le 8; **she is ~ back tomorrow** dovrebbe essere di ritorno domani; **I am ~ 6 days' leave** mi spettano 6 giorni di ferie.

due date *n* data di scadenza.

duel ['djuəl] *n* duello.

duet [djuː'ɛt] *n* duetto.

duff [dʌf] *adj* (*BRIT col*) barboso(a).

duffelbag, duffle bag ['dʌflbæg] *n* sacca da viaggio di tela.

duffelcoat, duffle coat ['dʌflkəut] *n* montgomery *m inv*.

duffer ['dʌfə*] *n* (*col*) schiappa.

dug [dʌg] *pt, pp of* **dig**.

dugout ['dʌgaut] *n* (*FOOTBALL*) panchina.

duke [djuːk] *n* duca *m*.

dull [dʌl] *adj* (*boring*) noioso(a); (*slow-witted*) ottuso(a); (*sound, pain*) sordo(a); (*weather, day*) fosco(a), scuro(a); (*blade*) smussato(a) ♦ *vt* (*pain, grief*) attutire; (*mind, senses*) intorpidire.

duly ['dju:lɪ] *adv* (*on time*) a tempo debito; (*as expected*) debitamente.

dumb [dʌm] *adj* muto(a); (*stupid*) stupido(a); **to be struck** ~ (*fig*) ammutolire, restare senza parole.

dumbbell ['dʌmbɛl] *n* (*SPORT*) manubrio, peso.

dumbfounded [dʌm'faundɪd] *adj* stupito(a), stordito(a).

dummy ['dʌmɪ] *n* (*tailor's model*) manichino; (*SPORT*) finto; (*BRIT: for baby*) tettarella ♦ *adj* falso(a), finto(a).

dummy run *n* giro di prova.

dump [dʌmp] *n* mucchio di rifiuti; (*place*) luogo di scarico; (*MIL*) deposito; (*COMPUT*) scaricamento, dump *m inv* ♦ *vt* (*put down*) scaricare; mettere giù; (*get rid of*) buttar via; (*COMM: goods*) svendere; (*COMPUT*) scaricare; **to be (down) in the** ~**s** (*col*) essere giù di corda.

dumping ['dʌmpɪŋ] *n* (*ECON*) dumping *m*; (*of rubbish*): **"no** ~**"** "vietato lo scarico".

dumpling ['dʌmplɪŋ] *n* specie di gnocco.

dumpy ['dʌmpɪ] *adj* tracagnotto(a).

dunce [dʌns] *n* asino.

dune [dju:n] *n* duna.

dung [dʌŋ] *n* concime *m*.

dungarees [dʌŋgə'ri:z] *npl* tuta.

dungeon ['dʌndʒən] *n* prigione *f* sotterranea.

dunk [dʌŋk] *vt* inzuppare.

duo ['dju:əu] *n* (*gen, MUS*) duo *m inv*.

duodenal [dju:əu'di:nl] *adj* (*ulcer*) duodenale.

duodenum [dju:əu'di:nəm] *n* duodeno.

dupe [dju:p] *vt* gabbare, ingannare.

duplex ['dju:plɛks] *n* (*US: also:* ~ **apartment**) appartamento su due piani.

duplicate *n* ['dju:plɪkət] doppio; (*copy of letter etc*) duplicato ♦ *vt* ['dju:plɪkeɪt] raddoppiare; (*on machine*) ciclostilare ♦ *adj* (*copy*) conforme, esattamente uguale; **in** ~ in duplice copia; ~ **key** duplicato (della chiave).

duplicating machine ['dju:plɪkeɪtɪŋ-], **duplicator** ['dju:plɪkeɪtə*] *n* duplicatore *m*.

duplicity [dju:'plɪsɪtɪ] *n* doppiezza, duplicità.

Dur. *abbr* (*BRIT*) = *Durham*.

durability [djuərə'bɪlɪtɪ] *n* durevolezza; resistenza.

durable ['djuərəbl] *adj* durevole; (*clothes, metal*) resistente.

duration [djuə'reɪʃən] *n* durata.

duress [djuə'rɛs] *n*: **under** ~ sotto costrizione.

Durex ® ['djuərɛks] *n* (*BRIT*) preservativo.

during ['djuərɪŋ] *prep* durante, nel corso di.

dusk [dʌsk] *n* crepuscolo.

dusky ['dʌskɪ] *adj* scuro(a).

dust [dʌst] *n* polvere *f* ♦ *vt* (*furniture*) spolverare; (*cake etc*): **to** ~ **with** cospargere con.

▶**dust off** *vt* rispolverare.

dustbin ['dʌstbɪn] *n* (*BRIT*) pattumiera.

duster ['dʌstə*] *n* straccio per la polvere.

dust jacket *n* sopraccoperta.

dustman ['dʌstmən] *n* (*BRIT*) netturbino.

dustpan ['dʌstpæn] *n* pattumiera.

dusty ['dʌstɪ] *adj* polveroso(a).

Dutch [dʌtʃ] *adj* olandese ♦ *n* (*LING*) olandese *m* ♦ *adv*: **to go** ~ *or* **d**~ fare alla romana; **the** ~ gli Olandesi.

Dutch auction *n* asta all'olandese.

Dutchman ['dʌtʃmən], **Dutchwoman** ['dʌtʃwumən] *n* olandese *m/f*.

dutiable ['dju:tɪəbl] *adj* soggetto(a) a dazio.

dutiful ['dju:tɪful] *adj* (*child*) rispettoso(a); (*husband*) premuroso(a); (*employee*) coscienzioso(a).

duty ['dju:tɪ] *n* dovere *m*; (*tax*) dazio, tassa; **duties** *npl* mansioni *fpl*; **on** ~ di servizio; (*MED: in hospital*) di guardia; **off** ~ libero(a), fuori servizio; **to make it one's** ~ **to do sth** assumersi l'obbligo di fare qc; **to pay** ~ **on sth** pagare il dazio su qc.

duty-free ['dju:tɪ'fri:] *adj* esente da dazio; ~ **shop** duty free *m inv*.

duty officer *n* (*MIL etc*) ufficiale *m* di servizio.

duvet ['du:veɪ] *n* piumino, piumone *m*.

DV *abbr* (= *Deo volente*) D.V.

DVD *n abbr* (= *digital versatile or video disc*) DVD *m inv*.

DVD player *n* lettore *m* DVD.

DVLA *n abbr* (*BRIT*: = *Driver and Vehicle Licensing Agency*) ≈ I.M.C.T.C. *m* (= *Ispettorato Generale della Motorizzazione Civile e dei Trasporti in Concessione*).

DVM *n abbr* (*US*: = *Doctor of Veterinary Medicine*) titolo di studio.

DVT *n abbr* = *deep-vein thrombosis*.

dwarf [dwɔ:f] *n* nano/a ♦ *vt* far apparire piccolo.

dwell, *pt*, *pp* **dwelt** [dwɛl, dwɛlt] *vi* dimorare.

▶**dwell on** *vt fus* indugiare su.

dweller ['dwɛlə*] *n* abitante *m/f*; **city** ~ cittadino/a.

dwelling ['dwɛlɪŋ] *n* dimora.

dwelt [dwɛlt] *pt*, *pp of* **dwell**.

dwindle ['dwɪndl] *vi* diminuire, decrescere.

dwindling ['dwɪndlɪŋ] *adj* (*strength, interest*) che si affievolisce; (*resources, supplies*) in diminuzione.

dye [daɪ] *n* colore *m*; (*chemical*) colorante *m*, tintura ♦ *vt* tingere; **hair** ~ tinta per capelli.

dyestuffs ['daɪstʌfs] *npl* coloranti *mpl*.

dying ['daɪɪŋ] *adj* morente, moribondo(a).

dyke [daɪk] *n* diga; (*channel*) canale *m* di scolo; (*causeway*) sentiero rialzato.

dynamic [daɪ'næmɪk] *adj* dinamico(a).

dynamics [daɪ'næmɪks] *n or npl* dinamica.

dynamite ['daɪnəmaɪt] *n* dinamite *f* ♦ *vt* far saltare con la dinamite.

dynamo ['daɪnəməu] *n* dinamo *f inv*.

dynasty ['dɪnəstɪ] *n* dinastia.

dysentery ['dɪsntrɪ] *n* dissenteria.

dyslexia [dɪs'lɛksɪə] *n* dislessia.

dyslexic [dɪs'lɛksɪk] *adj*, *n* dislessico(a).

dyspepsia [dɪs'pɛpsɪə] *n* dispepsia.

dystrophy ['dɪstrəfɪ] *n* distrofia; **muscular** ~ distrofia muscolare.

E e

E, e [iː] *n* (*letter*) E, e *f or m inv*; (*MUS*): **E** mi *m*; **E for Edward,** (*US*) **E for Easy** ≈ E come Empoli.

E *abbr* (= *east*) E ♦ *n abbr* (= *Ecstasy*) ecstasy *f inv*.

e- ['iː] *prefix* e-.

E111 *n abbr* (*also*: **form** ~) E111 (*modulo UE per rimborso spese mediche*).

ea. *abbr* = **each**.

each [iːtʃ] *adj* ogni, ciascuno(a) ♦ *pron* ciascuno(a), ognuno(a); ~ **one** ognuno(a); ~ **other** si (*or* ci *etc*); **they hate** ~ **other** si odiano (l'un l'altro); **you are jealous of** ~ **other** siete gelosi l'uno dell'altro; ~ **day** ogni giorno; **they have 2 books** ~ hanno 2 libri ciascuno; **they cost £5** ~ costano 5 sterline l'uno; ~ **of us** ciascuno *or* ognuno di noi.

eager ['iːɡə*] *adj* impaziente; desideroso(a); ardente; (*keen: pupil*) appassionato(a), attento(a); **to be** ~ **to do sth** non veder l'ora di fare qc; essere desideroso di fare qc; **to be** ~ **for** essere desideroso di, aver gran voglia di.

eagle ['iːɡl] *n* aquila.

E & OE *abbr* (= *errors and omissions excepted*) S.E.O.

ear [ɪə*] *n* orecchio; (*of corn*) pannocchia; **up to the** ~**s in debt** nei debiti fino al collo.

earache ['ɪəreɪk] *n* mal *m* d'orecchi.

eardrum ['ɪədrʌm] *n* timpano.

earful ['ɪəful] *n*: **to give sb an** ~ fare una ramanzina a qn.

earl [əːl] *n* conte *m*.

earlier ['əːlɪə*] *adj* (*date etc*) anteriore; (*edition etc*) precedente, anteriore ♦ *adv* prima; **I can't come any** ~ non posso venire prima.

early ['əːlɪ] *adv* presto, di buon'ora; (*ahead of time*) in anticipo ♦ *adj* precoce; anticipato(a); che si fa vedere di buon'ora; (*man*) primitivo(a); (*Christians, settlers*) primo(a); ~ **in the morning/ afternoon** nelle prime ore del mattino/del pomeriggio; **you're** ~! sei in anticipo!; **have an** ~ **night/start** vada a letto/parta presto; **in the** ~ *or* ~ **in the spring/19th century** all'inizio della primavera/ dell'Ottocento; **she's in her** ~ **forties** ha appena passato la quarantina; **at your earliest convenience** (*COMM*) non appena possibile.

early retirement *n* ritiro anticipato.

early warning system *n* sistema *m* del preallarme.

earmark ['ɪəmaːk] *vt*: **to** ~ **sth for** destinare qc a.

earn [əːn] *vt* guadagnare; (*rest, reward*) meritare; (*COMM: yield*) maturare; **to** ~ **one's living** guadagnarsi da vivere; **this** ~**ed him much praise, he** ~**ed much praise for this** si è attirato grandi lodi per questo.

earned income *n* reddito da lavoro.

earnest ['əːnɪst] *adj* serio(a) ♦ *n* (*also*: ~ **money**) caparra; **in** ~ *adv* sul serio.

earnings ['əːnɪŋz] *npl* guadagni *mpl*; (*of company etc*) proventi *mpl*; (*salary*) stipendio.

ear, nose and throat specialist *n* otorinolaringoiatra *m/f*.

earphones ['ɪəfəunz] *npl* cuffia.

earplugs ['ɪəplʌɡz] *npl* tappi *mpl* per le orecchie.

earring ['ɪərɪŋ] *n* orecchino.

earshot ['ɪəʃɔt] *n*: **out of/within** ~ fuori portata/a portata d'orecchio.

earth [əːθ] *n* (*gen, also BRIT ELEC*) terra; (*of fox etc*) tana ♦ *vt* (*BRIT ELEC*) mettere a terra.

earthenware ['əːθənwɛə*] *n* terracotta;

stoviglie *fpl* di terracotta ♦ *adj* di terracotta.

earthly ['ɔːθlɪ] *adj* terreno(a); ~ **paradise** paradiso terrestre; **there is no ~ reason to think** ... non vi è ragione di pensare....

earthquake ['ɔːθkweɪk] *n* terremoto.

earth-shattering ['ɔːθʃætərɪŋ] *adj* stupefacente.

earth tremor *n* scossa sismica.

earthworks ['ɔːθwɔːks] *npl* lavori *mpl* di sterro.

earthworm ['ɔːθwɔːm] *n* lombrico.

earthy ['ɔːθɪ] *adj* (*fig*) grossolano(a).

earwax ['ɪəwæks] *n* cerume *m*.

earwig ['ɪəwɪg] *n* forbicina.

ease [iːz] *n* agio, comodo ♦ *vt* (*soothe*) calmare; (*loosen*) allentare ♦ *vi* (*situation*) allentarsi, distendersi; **life of** ~ vita comoda; **with** ~ senza difficoltà; **at** ~ a proprio agio; (*MIL*) a riposo; **to feel at** ~/ **ill at** ~ sentirsi a proprio agio/a disagio; **to** ~ **sth out/in** tirare fuori/infilare qc con delicatezza; facilitare l'uscita/ l'entrata di qc.

▶**ease off, ease up** *vi* diminuire; (*slow down*) rallentarsi; (*fig*) rilassarsi.

easel ['iːzl] *n* cavalletto.

easily ['iːzɪlɪ] *adv* facilmente.

easiness ['iːzɪnɪs] *n* facilità, semplicità; (*of manners*) disinvoltura.

east [iːst] *n* est *m* ♦ *adj* dell'est ♦ *adv* a oriente; **the E~** l'Oriente *m*; (*POL*) i Paesi dell'Est.

Easter ['iːstə*] *n* Pasqua ♦ *adj* (*holidays*) pasquale, di Pasqua.

Easter egg *n* uovo di Pasqua.

Easter Island *n* isola di Pasqua.

easterly ['iːstəlɪ] *adj* dall'est, d'oriente.

Easter Monday *n* Pasquetta.

eastern ['iːstən] *adj* orientale, d'oriente; **E~ Europe** l'Europa orientale; **the E~ bloc** (*POL*) i Paesi dell'Est.

Easter Sunday *n* domenica di Pasqua.

East Germany *n* Germania dell'Est.

eastward(s) ['iːstwəd(z)] *adv* verso est, verso levante.

easy ['iːzɪ] *adj* facile; (*manner*) disinvolto(a); (*carefree: life*) agiato(a), tranquillo(a) ♦ *adv*: **to take it** *or* **things** ~ prendersela con calma; **I'm** ~ (*col*) non ho problemi; **easier said than done** tra il dire e il fare c'è di mezzo il mare; **payment on** ~ **terms** (*COMM*) facilitazioni *fpl* di pagamento.

easy chair *n* poltrona.

easy-going ['iːzɪ'gəʊɪŋ] *adj* accomodante.

eat, *pt* **ate**, *pp* **eaten** [iːt, eɪt, 'iːtn] *vt* mangiare.

▶**eat away** *vt* (*subj: sea*) erodere; (: *acid*) corrodere.

▶**eat away at, eat into** *vt fus* rodere.

▶**eat out** *vi* mangiare fuori.

▶**eat up** *vt* (*meal etc*) finire di mangiare; **it** ~**s up electricity** consuma un sacco di corrente.

eatable ['iːtəbl] *adj* mangiabile; (*safe to eat*) commestibile.

eaten ['iːtn] *pp of* **eat**.

eau de Cologne ['əʊdəkə'ləʊn] *n* acqua di colonia.

eaves [iːvz] *npl* gronda.

eavesdrop ['iːvzdrɒp] *vi*: **to** ~ **(on a conversation)** origliare (una conversazione).

ebb [ɛb] *n* riflusso ♦ *vi* rifluire; (*fig: also*: ~ **away**) declinare; ~ **and flow** flusso e riflusso; **to be at a low** ~ (*fig: person, spirits*) avere il morale a terra; (: *business*) andar male.

ebony ['ɛbənɪ] *n* ebano.

ebullient [ɪ'bʌlɪənt] *adj* esuberante.

ECB *n abbr* (= *European Central Bank*) BCE *f*

eccentric [ɪk'sɛntrɪk] *adj*, *n* eccentrico(a).

ecclesiastic [ɪkliːzɪ'æstɪk] *n* ecclesiastico.

ecclesiastic(al) [ɪkliːzɪ'æstɪk(əl)] *adj* ecclesiastico(a).

ECG *n abbr see* **electrocardiogram**.

echo, ~**es** ['ɛkəʊ] *n* eco *m or f* ♦ *vt* ripetere; fare eco a ♦ *vi* echeggiare; dare un eco.

éclair ['eɪkleə*] *n* ≈ bignè *m inv*.

eclipse [ɪ'klɪps] *n* eclissi *f inv* ♦ *vt* eclissare.

eco... ['iːkəʊ] *prefix* eco....

eco-friendly [iːkəʊ'frɛndlɪ] *adj* ecologico(a).

ecological [iːkə'lɒdʒɪkəl] *adj* ecologico(a).

ecologist [ɪ'kɒlədʒɪst] *n* ecologo/a.

ecology [ɪ'kɒlədʒɪ] *n* ecologia.

e-commerce ['iːkɒmɜːs] *n* commercio elettronico, e-commerce *m inv*.

economic [iːkə'nɒmɪk] *adj* economico(a); (*profitable: price*) vantaggioso(a); (*business*) che rende.

economical [iːkə'nɒmɪkəl] *adj* economico(a); (*person*) economo(a).

economically [iːkə'nɒmɪklɪ] *adv* con economia; (*regarding economics*) dal punto di vista economico.

economics [iːkə'nɒmɪks] *n* economia ♦ *npl* aspetto *or* lato economico.

economist [ɪ'kɒnəmɪst] *n* economista *m/f*.

economize [ɪ'kɒnəmaɪz] *vi* risparmiare, fare economia.

economy [ɪ'kɒnəmɪ] *n* economia; **economies of scale** (*COMM*) economie *fpl* di scala.

economy class *n* (*AVIAT etc*) classe *f* turistica.

economy size n confezione f economica.
ecosystem ['iːkəʊsɪstəm] n ecosistema m.
eco-tourism [iːkəʊ'tʊərɪzəm] n ecoturismo.
ECSC n abbr (= European Coal & Steel Community) C.E.C.A. f (= Comunità Europea del Carbone e dell'Acciaio).
ecstasy ['ɛkstəsɪ] n estasi f inv; **to go into ecstasies over** andare in estasi davanti a; **E~** (drug) ecstasy f inv.
ecstatic [ɛks'tætɪk] adj estatico(a), in estasi.
ECT n abbr see **electroconvulsive therapy**.
ECU, ecu ['eɪkjuː] n abbr (= European Currency Unit) ECU f inv, ecu f inv.
Ecuador ['ɛkwədɔː*] n Ecuador m.
ecumenical [iːkjuː'mɛnɪkl] adj ecumenico(a).
eczema ['ɛksɪmə] n eczema m.
eddy ['ɛdɪ] n mulinello.
edge [ɛdʒ] n margine m; (of table, plate, cup) orlo; (of knife etc) taglio ♦ vt bordare ♦ vi: **to ~ away from** sgattaiolare da; **to ~ past** passar rasente; **to ~ forward** avanzare a poco a poco; **on ~** (fig) = **edgy**; **to have the ~ on** essere in vantaggio su.
edgeways ['ɛdʒweɪz] adv di fianco; **he couldn't get a word in ~** non riuscì a dire una parola.
edging ['ɛdʒɪŋ] n bordo.
edgy ['ɛdʒɪ] adj nervoso(a).
edible ['ɛdɪbl] adj commestibile; (meal) mangiabile.
edict ['iːdɪkt] n editto.
edifice ['ɛdɪfɪs] n edificio.
edifying ['ɛdɪfaɪɪŋ] adj edificante.
Edinburgh ['ɛdɪnbərə] n Edimburgo f.
edit ['ɛdɪt] vt curare; (newspaper, magazine) dirigere; (COMPUT) correggere e modificare, editare.
edition [ɪ'dɪʃən] n edizione f.
editor ['ɛdɪtə*] n (in newspaper) redattore/trice; redattore/trice capo; (of sb's work) curatore/trice; (film ~) responsabile m/f del montaggio.
editorial [ɛdɪ'tɔːrɪəl] adj redazionale, editoriale ♦ n editoriale m; **the ~ staff** la redazione.
EDP n abbr see **electronic data processing**.
EDT abbr (US: = Eastern Daylight Time) ora legale di New York.
educate ['ɛdjukeɪt] vt istruire; educare.
educated guess ['ɛdjukeɪtɪd-] n ipotesi f ben fondata.
education [ɛdju'keɪʃən] n (teaching) insegnamento; istruzione f; (knowledge, culture) cultura; (SCOL: subject etc) pedagogia; **primary** or (US) **elementary/secondary ~** scuola primaria/secondaria.

educational [ɛdju'keɪʃənl] adj pedagogico(a); scolastico(a); istruttivo(a); **~ technology** tecnologie fpl applicate alla didattica.
Edwardian [ɛd'wɔːdɪən] adj edoardiano(a).
EE abbr = **electrical engineer**.
EEG n abbr see **electroencephalogram**.
eel [iːl] n anguilla.
EENT n abbr (US MED) = eye, ear, nose and throat.
EEOC n abbr (US) = **Equal Employment Opportunity Commission**.
eerie ['ɪərɪ] adj che fa accapponare la pelle.
EET abbr (= Eastern European Time) fuso orario.
effect [ɪ'fɛkt] n effetto ♦ vt effettuare; **to take ~** (law) entrare in vigore; (drug) fare effetto; **to have an ~ on sb/sth** avere or produrre un effetto su qn/qc; **to put into ~** (plan) attuare; **in ~** effettivamente; **his letter is to the ~ that …** il contenuto della sua lettera è che …; see also **effects**.
effective [ɪ'fɛktɪv] adj efficace; (striking: display, outfit) che fa colpo; **~ date** data d'entrata in vigore; **to become ~** (law) entrare in vigore.
effectively [ɪ'fɛktɪvlɪ] adv (efficiently) efficacemente; (strikingly) ad effetto; (in reality) di fatto; (in effect) in effetti.
effectiveness [ɪ'fɛktɪvnɪs] n efficacia.
effects [ɪ'fɛkts] npl (THEAT) effetti mpl scenici; (property) effetti mpl.
effeminate [ɪ'fɛmɪnɪt] adj effeminato(a).
effervescent [ɛfə'vɛsnt] adj effervescente.
efficacy ['ɛfɪkəsɪ] n efficacia.
efficiency [ɪ'fɪʃənsɪ] n efficienza; rendimento effettivo.
efficiency apartment n (US) miniappartamento.
efficient [ɪ'fɪʃənt] adj efficiente; (remedy, product, system) efficace; (machine, car) che ha un buon rendimento.
efficiently [ɪ'fɪʃəntlɪ] adv efficientemente; efficacemente.
effigy ['ɛfɪdʒɪ] n effigie f.
effluent ['ɛfluənt] n effluente m.
effort ['ɛfət] n sforzo; **to make an ~ to do sth** sforzarsi di fare qc.
effortless ['ɛfətlɪs] adj senza sforzo, facile.
effrontery [ɪ'frʌntərɪ] n sfrontatezza.
effusive [ɪ'fjuːsɪv] adj (person) espansivo(a); (welcome, letter) caloroso(a); (thanks, apologies) interminabile.
EFL n abbr (SCOL) = English as a foreign language.
EFTA ['ɛftə] n abbr (= European Free Trade Association) E.F.T.A. f.

e.g. adv abbr (= exempli gratia: for example) p.es.

egalitarian [ɪgælɪ'tɛərɪən] adj egualitario(a).

egg [ɛg] n uovo.

▶**egg on** vt incitare.

eggcup ['ɛgkʌp] n portauovo m inv.

eggplant ['ɛgplɑ:nt] n (esp US) melanzana.

eggshell ['ɛgʃɛl] n guscio d'uovo ♦ adj (colour) guscio d'uovo inv.

egg-timer ['ɛgtaɪmə*] n clessidra (per misurare il tempo di cottura delle uova).

egg white n albume m, bianco d'uovo.

egg yolk n tuorlo, rosso (d'uovo).

ego ['i:gəu] n ego m inv.

egoism ['ɛgəuɪzəm] n egoismo.

egoist ['ɛgəuɪst] n egoista m/f.

egotism ['ɛgəutɪzəm] n egotismo.

egotist ['ɛgəutɪst] n egotista m/f.

ego trip n: **to be on an ~** gasarsi.

Egypt ['i:dʒɪpt] n Egitto.

Egyptian [ɪ'dʒɪpʃən] adj, n egiziano(a).

eiderdown ['aɪdədaun] n piumino.

eight [eɪt] num otto.

eighteen ['eɪ'ti:n] num diciotto.

eighth [eɪtθ] num ottavo(a).

eighty [eɪtɪ] num ottanta.

Eire ['ɛərə] n Repubblica d'Irlanda.

EIS n abbr (= Educational Institute of Scotland) principale sindacato degli insegnanti in Scozia.

either ['aɪðə*] adj l'uno(a) o l'altro(a); (both, each) ciascuno(a); **on ~ side** su ciascun lato ♦ pron: **~ (of them)** (o) l'uno(a) o l'altro(a); **I don't like ~** non mi piace né l'uno né l'altro ♦ adv neanche; **no, I don't ~** no, neanch'io ♦ conj: **~ good or bad** o buono o cattivo; **I haven't seen ~ one or the other** non ho visto né l'uno né l'altro.

ejaculation [ɪdʒækju'leɪʃən] n (PHYSIOL) eiaculazione f.

eject [ɪ'dʒɛkt] vt espellere; lanciare ♦ vi (pilot) catapultarsi.

ejector seat [ɪ'dʒɛktə-] n sedile m eiettabile.

eke [i:k]: **to ~ out** vt far durare; aumentare.

EKG n abbr (US) = **electrocardiogram**.

el [ɛl] n abbr (US col) see **elevated railroad**.

elaborate adj [ɪ'læbərɪt] elaborato(a), minuzioso(a) ♦ vb [ɪ'læbəreɪt] vt elaborare ♦ vi entrare in dettagli.

elapse [ɪ'læps] vi trascorrere, passare.

elastic [ɪ'læstɪk] adj elastico(a) ♦ n elastico.

elastic band n (BRIT) elastico.

elasticity [ɪlæs'tɪsɪtɪ] n elasticità.

elated [ɪ'leɪtɪd] adj pieno(a) di gioia.

elation [ɪ'leɪʃən] n gioia.

elbow ['ɛlbəu] n gomito ♦ vt: **to ~ one's way through the crowd** farsi largo tra la folla a gomitate.

elbow grease n: **to use a bit of ~** usare un po' di olio di gomiti.

elbowroom ['ɛlbəurum] n spazio.

elder ['ɛldə*] adj maggiore, più vecchio(a) ♦ n (tree) sambuco; **one's ~s** i più anziani.

elderly ['ɛldəlɪ] adj anziano(a) ♦ npl: **the ~** gli anziani.

elder statesman n anziano uomo politico in pensione, ma ancora influente; (of company) anziano/a consigliere/a.

eldest ['ɛldɪst] adj, n: **the ~ (child)** il(la) maggiore (dei bambini).

elect [ɪ'lɛkt] vt eleggere; (choose): **to ~ to do** decidere di fare ♦ adj: **the president ~** il presidente designato.

election [ɪ'lɛkʃən] n elezione f; **to hold an ~** indire un'elezione.

election campaign n campagna elettorale.

electioneering [ɪlɛkʃə'nɪərɪŋ] n propaganda elettorale.

elector [ɪ'lɛktə*] n elettore/trice.

electoral [ɪ'lɛktərəl] adj elettorale.

electoral college n collegio elettorale.

electoral roll n (BRIT) registro elettorale.

electoral system n sistema m elettorale.

electorate [ɪ'lɛktərɪt] n elettorato.

electric [ɪ'lɛktrɪk] adj elettrico(a).

electrical [ɪ'lɛktrɪkəl] adj elettrico(a).

electrical engineer n ingegnere m elettrotecnico.

electrical failure n guasto all'impianto elettrico.

electric blanket n coperta elettrica.

electric chair n sedia elettrica.

electric cooker n cucina elettrica.

electric current n corrente f elettrica.

electric fire n (BRIT) stufa elettrica.

electrician [ɪlɛk'trɪʃən] n elettricista m.

electricity [ɪlɛk'trɪsɪtɪ] n elettricità; **to switch on/off the ~** attaccare/staccare la corrente.

electricity board n (BRIT) ente m regionale per l'energia elettrica.

electric light n luce f elettrica.

electric shock n scossa (elettrica).

electrify [ɪ'lɛktrɪfaɪ] vt (RAIL) elettrificare; (audience) elettrizzare.

electro... [ɪ'lɛktrəu] prefix elettro....

electrocardiogram (ECG) [ɪ'lɛktrə-'kɑ:dɪəgræm] n elettrocardiogramma m.

electro-convulsive therapy (ECT) [ɪ'lɛktrəkən'vʌlsɪv-] n elettroshockterapia.

electrocute [ɪ'lɛktrəkju:t] vt fulminare.

electrode [ɪ'lɛktrəud] n elettrodo.

electroencephalogram (EEG)
[ɪˈlɛktrəuenˈsefələɡræm] n (MED)
elettroencefalogramma m (EEG).
electrolysis [ɪlɛkˈtrɔlɪsɪs] n elettrolisi f.
electromagnetic [ɪˈlɛktrəumæɡˈnɛtɪk] n
elettromagnetico(a).
electron [ɪˈlɛktrɔn] n elettrone m.
electronic [ɪlɛkˈtrɔnɪk] adj elettronico(a);
see also **electronics**.
electronic data processing (EDP) n
elaborazione f elettronica di dati.
electronic mail n posta elettronica.
electronics [ɪlɛkˈtrɔnɪks] n elettronica.
electron microscope n microscopio
elettronico.
electroplated [ɪˈlɛktrəuˈpleɪtɪd] adj
galvanizzato(a).
electrotherapy [ɪˈlɛktrəuˈθɛrəpɪ] n
elettroterapia.
elegance [ˈɛliɡəns] n eleganza.
elegant [ˈɛliɡənt] adj elegante.
element [ˈɛlɪmənt] n elemento; (of heater,
kettle etc) resistenza.
elementary [ɛlɪˈmɛntərɪ] adj elementare.
elementary school n (US) see boxed note.

ELEMENTARY SCHOOL

Negli Stati Uniti e in Canada i bambini
frequentano la **elementary school** per
almeno sei anni, a volte anche per otto. Negli
Stati Uniti si chiama anche "grade school" o
"grammar school".

---

elephant [ˈɛlɪfənt] n elefante/essa.
elevate [ˈɛlɪveɪt] vt elevare.
elevated railroad (el) n (US) (ferrovia)
soprelevata.
elevation [ɛlɪˈveɪʃən] n elevazione f;
(height) altitudine f.
elevator [ˈɛlɪveɪtə*] n elevatore m; (US: lift)
ascensore m.
eleven [ɪˈlɛvn] num undici.
elevenses [ɪˈlɛvnzɪz] npl (BRIT) caffè m a
metà mattina.
eleventh [ɪˈlɛvnθ] adj undicesimo(a); **at the
~ hour** (fig) all'ultimo minuto.
elf, pl **elves** [ɛlf, ɛlvz] n elfo.
elicit [ɪˈlɪsɪt] vt: **to ~ (from)** trarre (da),
cavare fuori (da); **to ~ sth (from sb)**
strappare qc (a qn).
eligible [ˈɛlɪdʒəbl] adj eleggibile; (for
membership) che ha i requisiti; **to be ~
for a pension** essere pensionabile.
eliminate [ɪˈlɪmɪneɪt] vt eliminare.
elimination [ɪlɪmɪˈneɪʃən] n eliminazione f;
by process of ~ per eliminazione.
élite [eɪˈliːt] n élite f inv.

elitist [eɪˈliːtɪst] adj (pej) elitario(a).
elixir [ɪˈlɪksə*] n elisir m inv.
Elizabethan [ɪlɪzəˈbiːθən] n
elisabettiano(a).
ellipse [ɪˈlɪps] n ellisse f.
elliptical [ɪˈlɪptɪkl] adj ellittico(a).
elm [ɛlm] n olmo.
elocution [ɛləˈkjuːʃən] n elocuzione f.
elongated [ˈiːlɔŋɡeɪtɪd] adj allungato(a).
elope [ɪˈləup] vi (lovers) scappare.
eloquence [ˈɛləkwəns] n eloquenza.
eloquent [ˈɛləkwənt] adj eloquente.
else [ɛls] adv altro; **something ~**
qualcos'altro; **somewhere ~** altrove;
everywhere ~ in qualsiasi altro luogo;
where ~? in quale altro luogo?; **little ~**
poco altro; **everyone ~** tutti gli altri;
nothing ~ nient'altro; **or ~** (otherwise)
altrimenti; **is there anything ~ I can do?**
posso fare qualcos'altro?
elsewhere [ɛlsˈwɛə*] adv altrove.
ELT n abbr (SCOL) = English Language
Teaching.
elucidate [ɪˈluːsɪdeɪt] vt delucidare.
elude [ɪˈluːd] vt eludere.
elusive [ɪˈluːsɪv] adj elusivo(a); (answer)
evasivo(a); **he is very ~** è proprio
inafferrabile or irraggiungibile.
elves [ɛlvz] npl of **elf**.
emaciated [ɪˈmeɪsɪeɪtɪd] adj emaciato(a).
E-mail, e-mail [ˈiːmeɪl] n abbr (= electronic
mail) posta elettronica ♦ vt: **to ~ sb**
comunicare con qn mediante posta
elettronica; **~ address** indirizzo di posta
elettronica; **~ account** account m inv di
posta elettronica.
emanate [ˈɛməneɪt] vi: **to ~ from** emanare
da.
emancipate [ɪˈmænsɪpeɪt] vt emancipare.
emancipation [ɪmænsɪˈpeɪʃən] n
emancipazione f.
emasculate [ɪˈmæskjuleɪt] vt (fig) rendere
impotente.
embalm [ɪmˈbɑːm] vt imbalsamare.
embankment [ɪmˈbæŋkmənt] n (of road,
railway) massicciata; (riverside) argine m;
(dyke) diga.
embargo [ɪmˈbɑːɡəu] n (pl ~es: COMM,
NAUT) embargo ♦ vt mettere l'embargo
su; **to put an ~ on sth** mettere l'embargo
su qc.
embark [ɪmˈbɑːk] vi: **to ~ (on)** imbarcarsi
(su) ♦ vt imbarcare; **to ~ on** (fig)
imbarcarsi in; (journey) intraprendere.
embarkation [ɛmbɑːˈkeɪʃən] n imbarco.
embarkation card n carta d'imbarco.
embarrass [ɪmˈbærəs] vt imbarazzare; **to
be ~ed** essere imbarazzato(a).

embarrassing [ɪm'bærəsɪŋ] *adj* imbarazzante.
embarrassment [ɪm'bærəsmənt] *n* imbarazzo.
embassy ['ɛmbəsɪ] *n* ambasciata; **the Italian E~** l'ambasciata d'Italia.
embed [ɪm'bɛd] *vt* conficcare; incastrare.
embellish [ɪm'bɛlɪʃ] *vt* abbellire; **to ~ (with)** (*fig: story, truth*) infiorare (con).
embers ['ɛmbəz] *npl* braci *fpl*.
embezzle [ɪm'bɛzl] *vt* appropriarsi indebitamente di.
embezzlement [ɪm'bɛzlmənt] *n* appropriazione *f* indebita.
embezzler [ɪm'bɛzlə*] *n* malversatore/ trice.
embitter [ɪm'bɪtə*] *vt* amareggiare; inasprire.
emblem ['ɛmbləm] *n* emblema *m*.
embodiment [ɪm'bɒdɪmənt] *n* personificazione *f*, incarnazione *f*.
embody [ɪm'bɒdɪ] *vt* (*features*) racchiudere, comprendere; (*ideas*) dar forma concreta a, esprimere.
embolden [ɪm'bəuldn] *vt* incitare.
embolism ['ɛmbəlɪzəm] *n* embolia.
embossed [ɪm'bɒst] *adj* in rilievo; goffrato(a); **~ with ... con** in rilievo ....
embrace [ɪm'breɪs] *vt* abbracciare; (*include*) comprendere ♦ *vi* abbracciarsi ♦ *n* abbraccio.
embroider [ɪm'brɔɪdə*] *vt* ricamare; (*fig: story*) abbellire.
embroidery [ɪm'brɔɪdərɪ] *n* ricamo.
embroil [ɪm'brɔɪl] *vt:* **to become ~ed (in sth)** restare invischiato(a) (in qc).
embryo ['ɛmbrɪəu] *n* (*also fig*) embrione *m*.
emcee [ɛm'siː] *n abbr* = **master of ceremonies**.
emend [ɪ'mɛnd] *vt* (*text*) correggere, emendare.
emerald ['ɛmərəld] *n* smeraldo.
emerge [ɪ'məːdʒ] *vi* apparire, sorgere; **it ~s that** (*BRIT*) risulta che.
emergence [ɪ'məːdʒəns] *n* apparizione *f*; (*of nation*) nascita.
emergency [ɪ'məːdʒənsɪ] *n* emergenza; **in an ~** in caso di emergenza; **to declare a state of ~** dichiarare lo stato di emergenza.
emergency exit *n* uscita di sicurezza.
emergency landing *n* atterraggio forzato.
emergency lane *n* (*US AUT*) corsia d'emergenza.
emergency road service *n* (*US*) servizio riparazioni.

emergency service *n* servizio di pronto intervento.
emergency stop *n* (*BRIT AUT*) frenata improvvisa.
emergent [ɪ'məːdʒənt] *adj:* **~ nation** paese *m* in via di sviluppo.
emery board ['ɛmərɪ-] *n* limetta di carta smerigliata.
emery paper *n* carta smerigliata.
emetic [ɪ'mɛtɪk] *n* emetico.
emigrant ['ɛmɪgrənt] *n* emigrante *m/f*.
emigrate ['ɛmɪgreɪt] *vi* emigrare.
emigration [ɛmɪ'greɪʃən] *n* emigrazione *f*.
émigré ['ɛmɪgreɪ] *n* emigrato/a.
eminence ['ɛmɪnəns] *n* eminenza.
eminent ['ɛmɪnənt] *adj* eminente.
eminently ['ɛmɪnəntlɪ] *adv* assolutamente, perfettamente.
emirate [ɛ'mɪərɪt] *n* emirato.
emission [ɪ'mɪʃən] *n* (*of gas, radiation*) emissione *f*.
emit [ɪ'mɪt] *vt* emettere.
emolument [ɪ'mɒljumənt] *n* (*often pl: formal*) emolumento.
emotion [ɪ'məuʃən] *n* emozione *f*; (*love, jealousy etc*) sentimento.
emotional [ɪ'məuʃənl] *adj* (*person*) emotivo(a); (*scene*) commovente; (*tone, speech*) carico(a) d'emozione.
emotionally [ɪ'məuʃnəlɪ] *adv* (*behave, be involved*) sentimentalmente; (*speak*) con emozione; **~ disturbed** con turbe emotive.
emotive [ɪ'məutɪv] *adj* emotivo(a); **~ power** capacità di commuovere.
empathy ['ɛmpəθɪ] *n* immedesimazione *f*; **to feel ~ with sb** immedesimarsi nei sentimenti di qn.
emperor ['ɛmpərə*] *n* imperatore *m*.
emphasis, *pl* -ases ['ɛmfəsɪs, -siːz] *n* enfasi *f inv*; importanza; **to lay** *or* **place ~ on sth** (*fig*) mettere in risalto *or* in evidenza qc; **the ~ is on sport** si dà molta importanza allo sport.
emphasize ['ɛmfəsaɪz] *vt* (*word, point*) sottolineare; (*feature*) mettere in evidenza.
emphatic [ɪm'fætɪk] *adj* (*strong*) vigoroso(a); (*unambiguous, clear*) netto(a), categorico(a).
emphatically [ɪm'fætɪkəlɪ] *adv* vigorosamente; nettamente.
emphysema [ɛmfɪ'siːmə] *n* (*MED*) enfisema *m*.
empire ['ɛmpaɪə*] *n* impero.
empirical [ɛm'pɪrɪkl] *adj* empirico(a).
employ [ɪm'plɔɪ] *vt* (*make use of: thing, method, person*) impiegare, servirsi di;

(*give job to*) dare lavoro a, impiegare; **he's ~ed in a bank** lavora in banca.

employee [implɔɪˈiː] *n* impiegato/a.

employer [imˈplɔɪə*] *n* principale *m/f*, datore *m* di lavoro.

employment [imˈplɔɪmənt] *n* impiego; **to find ~** trovare impiego *or* lavoro; **without ~** disoccupato(a); **place of ~** posto di lavoro.

employment agency *n* agenzia di collocamento.

employment exchange *n* (*BRIT*) ufficio *m* collocamento *inv*.

empower [imˈpauə*] *vt*: **to ~ sb to do** concedere autorità a qn di fare.

empress [ˈɛmpris] *n* imperatrice *f*.

emptiness [ˈɛmptinis] *n* vuoto.

empty [ˈɛmpti] *adj* vuoto(a); (*street, area*) deserto(a); (*threat, promise*) vano(a) ♦ *n* (*bottle*) vuoto ♦ *vt* vuotare ♦ *vi* vuotarsi; (*liquid*) scaricarsi; **on an ~ stomach** a stomaco vuoto.

empty-handed [ɛmptiˈhændid] *adj* a mani vuote.

empty-headed [ɛmptiˈhɛdid] *adj* sciocco(a).

EMS *n abbr* (= *European Monetary System*) S.M.E. *m*.

EMT *n abbr* (*US*) = *emergency medical technician*.

EMU *n abbr* (= *European Monetary Union*) Unità *f* monetaria europea; (= *economic and monetary union*) UEM *f*.

emulate [ˈɛmjuleit] *vt* emulare.

emulsion [iˈmʌlʃən] *n* emulsione *f*; (*also*: **~ paint**) colore *m* a tempera.

enable [iˈneibl] *vt*: **to ~ sb to do** permettere a qn di fare.

enact [inˈækt] *vt* (*law*) emanare; (*play, scene*) rappresentare.

enamel [iˈnæməl] *n* smalto.

enamel paint *n* vernice *f* a smalto.

enamoured [iˈnæməd] *adj*: **~ of** innamorato(a) di.

encampment [inˈkæmpmənt] *n* accampamento.

encased [inˈkeist] *adj*: **~ in** racchiuso(a) in; rivestito(a) di.

enchant [inˈtʃɑːnt] *vt* incantare; (*subj: magic spell*) catturare.

enchanting [inˈtʃɑːntiŋ] *adj* incantevole, affascinante.

encircle [inˈsəːkl] *vt* accerchiare.

enc(l). *abbr* (*on letters etc*: = *enclosed, enclosure*) all., alleg.

enclose [inˈkləuz] *vt* (*land*) circondare, recingere; (*letter etc*): **to ~ (with)** allegare (con); **please find ~d** trovi qui accluso.

enclosure [inˈkləuʒə*] *n* recinto; (*COMM*) allegato.

encoder [inˈkəudə*] *n* (*COMPUT*) codificatore *m*.

encompass [inˈkʌmpəs] *vt* comprendere.

encore [ɔŋˈkɔː*] *excl, n* bis (*m inv*).

encounter [inˈkauntə*] *n* incontro ♦ *vt* incontrare.

encourage [inˈkʌridʒ] *vt* incoraggiare; (*industry, growth etc*) favorire; **to ~ sb to do sth** incoraggiare qn a fare qc.

encouragement [inˈkʌridʒmənt] *n* incoraggiamento.

encouraging [inˈkʌridʒiŋ] *adj* incoraggiante.

encroach [inˈkrəutʃ] *vi*: **to ~ (up)on** (*rights*) usurpare; (*time*) abusare di; (*land*) oltrepassare i limiti di.

encrusted [inˈkrʌstid] *adj*: **~ with** incrostato(a) di.

encumbered [inˈkʌmbəd] *adj*: **to be ~ (with)** essere carico(a) di.

encyclop(a)edia [ɛnsaikləuˈpiːdiə] *n* enciclopedia.

end [ɛnd] *n* fine *f*; (*aim*) fine *m*; (*of table*) bordo estremo; (*of line, rope etc*) estremità *f inv*; (*of pointed object*) punta; (*of town*) parte *f* ♦ *vt* finire; (*also*: **bring to an ~, put an ~ to**) mettere fine a ♦ *vi* finire; **from ~ to ~** da un'estremità all'altra; **to come to an ~** arrivare alla fine, finire; **to be at an ~** essere finito(a); **in the ~** alla fine; **at the ~ of the street** in fondo alla strada; **at the ~ of the day** (*BRIT fig*) in fin dei conti; **on ~** (*object*) ritto(a); **to stand on ~** (*hair*) rizzarsi; **for 5 hours on ~** per 5 ore di fila; **for hours on ~** per ore e ore; **to this ~, with this ~ in view** a questo fine; **to ~ (with)** concludere (con).

▶**end up** *vi*: **to ~ up in** finire in.

endanger [inˈdeindʒə*] *vt* mettere in pericolo; **an ~ed species** una specie in via di estinzione.

endear [inˈdiə*] *vt*: **to ~ o.s. to sb** accattivarsi le simpatie di qn.

endearing [inˈdiəriŋ] *adj* accattivante.

endearment [inˈdiəmənt] *n*: **to whisper ~s** sussurrare tenerezze; **term of ~** vezzeggiativo, parola affettuosa.

endeavour, (*US*) **endeavor** [inˈdɛvə*] *n* sforzo, tentativo ♦ *vi*: **to ~ to do** cercare *or* sforzarsi di fare.

endemic [ɛnˈdɛmik] *adj* endemico(a).

ending [ˈɛndiŋ] *n* fine *f*, conclusione *f*; (*LING*) desinenza.

endive [ˈɛndaiv] *n* (*curly*) indivia (riccia); (*smooth, flat*) indivia belga.

endless ['ɛndlɪs] *adj* senza fine; (*patience, resources*) infinito(a); (*possibilities*) illimitato(a).

endorse [ɪn'dɔːs] *vt* (*cheque*) girare; (*approve*) approvare, appoggiare.

endorsee [ɪndɔː'siː] *n* giratario/a.

endorsement [ɪn'dɔːsmənt] *n* (*approval*) approvazione *f*; (*signature*) firma; (*BRIT: on driving licence*) *contravvenzione registrata sulla patente.*

endorser [ɪn'dɔːsə*] *n* girante *m/f*.

endow [ɪn'dau] *vt* (*prize*) istituire; (*hospital*) fondare; (*provide with money*) devolvere denaro a; (*equip*): **to ~ with** fornire di, dotare di.

endowment [ɪn'daumənt] *n* istituzione *f*; fondazione *f*; (*amount*) donazione *f*.

endowment mortgage *n mutuo che viene ripagato sotto forma di un'assicurazione a vita.*

endowment policy *n* polizza-vita mista.

end product *n* (*INDUSTRY*) prodotto finito; (*fig*) risultato.

end result *n* risultato finale.

endurable [ɪn'djuərəbl] *adj* sopportabile.

endurance [ɪn'djuərəns] *n* resistenza; pazienza.

endurance test *n* prova di resistenza.

endure [ɪn'djuə*] *vt* sopportare, resistere a ♦ *vi* durare.

enduring [ɪn'djuərɪŋ] *adj* duraturo(a).

end user *n* (*COMPUT*) consumatore(trice) effettivo(a).

enema ['ɛnɪmə] *n* (*MED*) clistere *m*.

enemy ['ɛnəmɪ] *adj, n* nemico(a); **to make an ~ of sb** inimicarsi qn.

energetic [ɛnə'dʒɛtɪk] *adj* energico(a); attivo(a).

energy ['ɛnədʒɪ] *n* energia; **Department of E~** Ministero dell'Energia.

energy crisis *n* crisi *f* energetica.

energy-saving ['ɛnədʒɪ'seɪvɪŋ] *adj* (*policy*) del risparmio energetico; (*device*) che risparmia energia.

enervating ['ɛnəːveɪtɪŋ] *adj* debilitante.

enforce [ɪn'fɔːs] *vt* (*LAW*) applicare, far osservare.

enforced [ɪn'fɔːst] *adj* forzato(a).

enfranchise [ɪn'fræntʃaɪz] *vt* (*give vote to*) concedere il diritto di voto a; (*set free*) affrancare.

engage [ɪn'geɪdʒ] *vt* (*hire*) assumere; (*lawyer*) incaricare; (*attention, interest*) assorbire; (*MIL*) attaccare; (*TECH*): **to ~ gear/the clutch** innestare la marcia/la frizione ♦ *vi* (*TECH*) ingranare; **to ~ in** impegnarsi in; **he is ~d in research/a survey** si occupa di ricerca/di

un'inchiesta; **to ~ sb in conversation** attaccare conversazione con qn.

engaged [ɪn'geɪdʒd] *adj* (*BRIT: busy, in use*) occupato(a); (*betrothed*) fidanzato(a); **to get ~** fidanzarsi.

engaged tone *n* (*BRIT TEL*) segnale *m* di occupato.

engagement [ɪn'geɪdʒmənt] *n* impegno, obbligo; appuntamento; (*to marry*) fidanzamento; (*MIL*) combattimento; **I have a previous ~** ho già un impegno.

engagement ring *n* anello di fidanzamento.

engaging [ɪn'geɪdʒɪŋ] *adj* attraente.

engender [ɪn'dʒɛndə*] *vt* produrre, causare.

engine ['ɛndʒɪn] *n* (*AUT*) motore *m*; (*RAIL*) locomotiva.

engine driver *n* (*BRIT: of train*) macchinista *m*.

engineer [ɛndʒɪ'nɪə*] *n* ingegnere *m*; (*BRIT: for domestic appliances*) tecnico; (*US RAIL*) macchinista *m*; **civil/mechanical ~** ingegnere civile/meccanico.

engineering [ɛndʒɪ'nɪərɪŋ] *n* ingegneria ♦ *cpd* (*works, factory, worker etc*) metalmeccanico(a).

engine failure *n* guasto al motore.

engine trouble *n* panne *f*.

England ['ɪŋglənd] *n* Inghilterra.

English ['ɪŋglɪʃ] *adj* inglese ♦ *n* (*LING*) inglese *m*; **the ~** *npl* gli Inglesi; **to be an ~ speaker** essere anglofono(a).

English Channel *n*: **the ~** il Canale della Manica.

Englishman ['ɪŋglɪʃmən], **Englishwoman** ['ɪŋglɪʃwumən] *n* inglese *m/f*.

English-speaking ['ɪŋglɪʃspiːkɪŋ] *adj* di lingua inglese.

engrave [ɪn'greɪv] *vt* incidere.

engraving [ɪn'greɪvɪŋ] *n* incisione *f*.

engrossed [ɪn'grəust] *adj*: **~ in** assorbito(a) da, preso(a) da.

engulf [ɪn'gʌlf] *vt* inghiottire.

enhance [ɪn'hɑːns] *vt* accrescere; (*position, reputation*) migliorare.

enigma [ɪ'nɪgmə] *n* enigma *m*.

enigmatic [ɛnɪg'mætɪk] *adj* enigmatico(a).

enjoy [ɪn'dʒɔɪ] *vt* godere; (*have: success, fortune*) avere; (*have benefit of: health*) godere (di); **I ~ dancing** mi piace ballare; **to ~ o.s.** godersela, divertirsi.

enjoyable [ɪn'dʒɔɪəbl] *adj* piacevole.

enjoyment [ɪn'dʒɔɪmənt] *n* piacere *m*, godimento.

enlarge [ɪn'lɑːdʒ] *vt* ingrandire ♦ *vi*: **to ~ on** (*subject*) dilungarsi su.

enlarged [ɪn'lɑːdʒd] *adj* (*edition*)

ampliato(a); (MED: organ, gland)
ingrossato(a).

enlargement [ɪnˈlɑːdʒmənt] n (PHOT)
ingrandimento.

enlighten [ɪnˈlaɪtn] vt illuminare; dare
chiarimenti a.

enlightened [ɪnˈlaɪtnd] adj illuminato(a).

enlightening [ɪnˈlaɪtnɪŋ] adj istruttivo(a).

enlightenment [ɪnˈlaɪtnmənt] n progresso
culturale; chiarimenti mpl; (HISTORY): **the
E~** l'Illuminismo.

enlist [ɪnˈlɪst] vt arruolare; (support)
procurare ♦ vi arruolarsi; **~ed man** (US
MIL) soldato semplice.

enliven [ɪnˈlaɪvn] vt (people) rallegrare;
(events) ravvivare.

enmity [ˈɛnmɪtɪ] n inimicizia.

ennoble [ɪˈnəubl] vt nobilitare; (with title)
conferire un titolo nobiliare a.

enormity [ɪˈnɔːmɪtɪ] n enormità f inv.

enormous [ɪˈnɔːməs] adj enorme.

enormously [ɪˈnɔːməslɪ] adv enormemente.

enough [ɪˈnʌf] adj, n: **~ time/books** assai
tempo/libri; **have you got ~?** ne ha
abbastanza or a sufficienza? ♦ adv: **big ~**
abbastanza grande; **he has not worked ~**
non ha lavorato abbastanza; **~! basta!;**
it's hot ~ (as it is)! fa abbastanza caldo
così!; **will £5 be ~?** bastano 5 sterline?;
that's ~ basta; **I've had ~!** non ne posso
più!; **he was kind ~ to lend me the money**
è stato così gentile da prestarmi i soldi;
... which, funnily ~ ... che, strano a dirsi.

enquire [ɪnˈkwaɪə*] vt, vi = **inquire.**

enrage [ɪnˈreɪdʒ] vt fare arrabbiare.

enrich [ɪnˈrɪtʃ] vt arricchire.

enrol, (US) **enroll** [ɪnˈrəul] vt iscrivere; (at
university) immatricolare ♦ vi iscriversi.

enrol(l)ment [ɪnˈrəulmənt] n iscrizione f.

en route [ɔnˈruːt] adv: **~ for/from/to** in
viaggio per/da/a.

ensconced [ɪnˈskɔnst] adj: **~ in** ben
sistemato(a) in.

ensemble [ɑ̃ːnˈsɑ̃ːmbl] n (MUS) ensemble m
inv.

enshrine [ɪnˈʃraɪn] vt conservare come una
reliquia.

ensign n (NAUT) [ˈɛnsən] bandiera; (MIL)
[ˈɛnsaɪn] portabandiera m inv.

enslave [ɪnˈsleɪv] vt fare schiavo.

ensue [ɪnˈsjuː] vi seguire, risultare.

ensure [ɪnˈʃuə*] vt assicurare; garantire; **to
~ that** assicurarsi che.

ENT n abbr (MED: = ear, nose, and throat)
O.R.L.

entail [ɪnˈteɪl] vt comportare.

entangle [ɪnˈtæŋgl] vt (thread etc)
impigliare; **to become ~d in sth** (fig)

rimanere impegolato in qc.

enter [ˈɛntə*] vt (gen) entrare in; (club)
associarsi a; (profession) intraprendere;
(army) arruolarsi in; (competition)
partecipare a; (sb for a competition)
iscrivere; (write down) registrare;
(COMPUT: data) introdurre, inserire ♦ vi
entrare.

►**enter for** vt fus iscriversi a.

►**enter into** vt fus (explanation) cominciare
a dare; (debate) partecipare a;
(agreement) concludere; (negotiations)
prendere parte a.

►**enter (up)on** vt fus cominciare.

enteritis [ɛntəˈraɪtɪs] n enterite f.

enterprise [ˈɛntəpraɪz] n (undertaking,
company) impresa; (spirit) iniziativa.

enterprising [ˈɛntəpraɪzɪŋ] adj
intraprendente.

entertain [ɛntəˈteɪn] vt divertire; (invite)
ricevere; (idea, plan) nutrire.

entertainer [ɛntəˈteɪnə*] n comico/a.

entertaining [ɛntəˈteɪnɪŋ] adj divertente
♦ n: **to do a lot of ~** avere molti ospiti.

entertainment [ɛntəˈteɪnmənt] n
(amusement) divertimento; (show)
spettacolo.

entertainment allowance n spese fpl di
rappresentanza.

enthral [ɪnˈθrɔːl] vt affascinare, avvincere.

enthralled [ɪnˈθrɔːld] adj affascinato(a).

enthralling [ɪnˈθrɔːlɪŋ] adj avvincente.

enthuse [ɪnˈθuːz] vi: **to ~ (about or over)**
entusiasmarsi (per).

enthusiasm [ɪnˈθuːzɪæzəm] n entusiasmo.

enthusiast [ɪnˈθuːzɪæst] n entusiasta m/f; **a
jazz etc ~** un appassionato di jazz etc.

enthusiastic [ɪnθuːzɪˈæstɪk] adj entusiasta,
entusiastico(a); **to be ~ about sth/sb**
essere appassionato di qc/entusiasta di
qn.

entice [ɪnˈtaɪs] vt allettare, sedurre.

enticing [ɪnˈtaɪsɪŋ] adj allettante.

entire [ɪnˈtaɪə*] adj intero(a).

entirely [ɪnˈtaɪəlɪ] adv completamente,
interamente.

entirety [ɪnˈtaɪərətɪ] n: **in its ~** nel suo
complesso.

entitle [ɪnˈtaɪtl] vt (give right): **to ~ sb to
sth/to do** dare diritto a qn a qc/a fare.

entitled [ɪnˈtaɪtld] adj (book) che si intitola;
to be ~ to sth/to do sth avere diritto a
qc/a fare qc.

entity [ˈɛntɪtɪ] n entità f inv.

entrails [ˈɛntreɪlz] npl interiora fpl.

entrance n [ˈɛntrns] entrata, ingresso; (of
person) entrata ♦ vt [ɪnˈtrɑːns] incantare,
rapire; **to gain ~ to** (university etc) essere

ammesso a.
entrance examination *n (to school)*
esame *m* di ammissione.
entrance fee *n* tassa d'iscrizione; *(to museum etc)* prezzo d'ingresso.
entrance ramp *n (US AUT)* rampa di accesso.
entrancing [ɪn'trɑːnsɪŋ] *adj* incantevole.
entrant ['ɛntrnt] *n* partecipante *m/f*; concorrente *m/f*; *(BRIT: in exam)* candidato/a.
entreat [ɛn'triːt] *vt* supplicare.
entreaty [ɪn'triːtɪ] *n* supplica, preghiera.
entrée ['ɔntreɪ] *n (CULIN)* prima portata.
entrenched [ɛn'trɛntʃt] *adj* radicato(a).
entrepreneur ['ɔntrəprə'nəː*] *n* imprenditore *m*.
entrepreneurial ['ɔntrəprə'nəːrɪəl] *adj* imprenditoriale.
entrust [ɪn'trʌst] *vt*: to ~ sth to affidare qc a.
entry ['ɛntrɪ] *n* entrata; *(way in)* entrata, ingresso; *(in dictionary)* voce *f*; *(in diary, ship's log)* annotazione *f*; *(in account book, ledger, list)* registrazione *f*; **"no ~"** "vietato l'ingresso"; *(AUT)* "divieto di accesso"; **single/double ~ book-keeping** partita semplice/doppia.
entry form *n* modulo d'iscrizione.
entry phone *n (BRIT)* citofono.
entwine [ɪn'twaɪn] *vt* intrecciare.
E number *n sigla di additivo alimentare*.
enumerate [ɪ'njuːməreɪt] *vt* enumerare.
enunciate [ɪ'nʌnsɪeɪt] *vt* enunciare; pronunciare.
envelop [ɪn'vɛləp] *vt* avvolgere, avviluppare.
envelope ['ɛnvələup] *n* busta.
enviable ['ɛnvɪəbl] *adj* invidiabile.
envious ['ɛnvɪəs] *adj* invidioso(a).
environment [ɪn'vaɪərənmənt] *n* ambiente *m*; **Department of the E~** *(BRIT)* ≈ Ministero dell'Ambiente.
environmental [ɪnvaɪərən'mɛntl] *adj* ecologico(a); ambientale; ~ **studies** *(in school etc)* ecologia.
environmentalist [ɪn'vaɪərən'mɛntəlɪst] *n* studioso/a della protezione dell'ambiente.
environmentally [ɪnvaɪərən'mɛntəlɪ] *adv*: ~ **sound/friendly** che rispetta l'ambiente.
Environmental Protection Agency (EPA) *n (US)* ≈ Ministero dell'Ambiente.
envisage [ɪn'vɪzɪdʒ] *vt* immaginare; prevedere.
envision [ɪn'vɪʒən] *vt* concepire, prevedere.
envoy ['ɛnvɔɪ] *n* inviato/a.

envy ['ɛnvɪ] *n* invidia ♦ *vt* invidiare; **to ~ sb sth** invidiare qn per qc.
enzyme ['ɛnzaɪm] *n* enzima *m*.
EPA *n abbr (US) see* **Environmental Protection Agency**.
ephemeral [ɪ'fɛmərəl] *adj* effimero(a).
epic ['ɛpɪk] *n* poema *m* epico ♦ *adj* epico(a).
epicentre, (US) epicenter ['ɛpɪsɛntə*] *n* epicentro.
epidemic [ɛpɪ'dɛmɪk] *n* epidemia.
epilepsy ['ɛpɪlɛpsɪ] *n* epilessia.
epileptic [ɛpɪ'lɛptɪk] *adj, n* epilettico(a).
epilogue ['ɛpɪlɔg] *n* epilogo.
Epiphany [ɪ'pɪfənɪ] *n* Epifania.
episcopal [ɪ'pɪskəpəl] *adj* episcopale.
episode ['ɛpɪsəud] *n* episodio.
epistle [ɪ'pɪsl] *n* epistola.
epitaph ['ɛpɪtɑːf] *n* epitaffio.
epithet ['ɛpɪθɛt] *n* epiteto.
epitome [ɪ'pɪtəmɪ] *n* epitome *f*; quintessenza.
epitomize [ɪ'pɪtəmaɪz] *vt (fig)* incarnare.
epoch ['iːpɔk] *n* epoca.
epoch-making ['iːpɔkmeɪkɪŋ] *adj* che fa epoca.
eponymous [ɪ'pɔnɪməs] *adj* dello stesso nome.
equable ['ɛkwəbl] *adj* uniforme; *(climate)* costante; *(character)* equilibrato(a).
equal ['iːkwl] *adj, n* uguale *(m/f)* ♦ *vt* uguagliare; ~ **to** *(task)* all'altezza di.
equality [iː'kwɔlɪtɪ] *n* uguaglianza.
equalize ['iːkwəlaɪz] *vt, vi* pareggiare.
equalizer ['iːkwəlaɪzə*] *n* punto del pareggio.
equally ['iːkwəlɪ] *adv* ugualmente; **they are** ~ **clever** sono intelligenti allo stesso modo.
Equal Opportunities Commission, (US) Equal Employment Opportunity Commission *n commissione contro discriminazioni sessuali o razziali nel mondo del lavoro*.
equal(s) sign *n* segno d'uguaglianza.
equanimity [ɛkwə'nɪmɪtɪ] *n* serenità.
equate [ɪ'kweɪt] *vt*: **to ~ sth with** considerare qc uguale a; *(compare)* paragonare qc con; **to ~ A to B** mettere in equazione A e B.
equation [ɪ'kweɪʃən] *n (MATH)* equazione *f*.
equator [ɪ'kweɪtə*] *n* equatore *m*.
Equatorial Guinea [ɛkwə'tɔːrɪəl-] *n* Guinea Equatoriale.
equestrian [ɪ'kwɛstrɪən] *adj* equestre ♦ *n* cavaliere/amazzone.
equilibrium [iːkwɪ'lɪbrɪəm] *n* equilibrio.
equinox ['iːkwɪnɔks] *n* equinozio.
equip [ɪ'kwɪp] *vt* equipaggiare, attrezzare;

to ~ sb/sth with fornire qn/qc di; **~ped with** (*machinery etc*) dotato(a) di; **he is well ~ped for the job** ha i requisiti necessari per quel lavoro.

equipment [ɪ'kwɪpmənt] *n* attrezzatura; (*electrical etc*) apparecchiatura.

equitable ['ɛkwɪtəbl] *adj* equo(a), giusto(a).

equities ['ɛkwɪtɪz] *npl* (*BRIT COMM*) azioni *fpl* ordinarie.

equity ['ɛkwɪtɪ] *n* equità.

equity capital *n* capitale *m* azionario.

equivalent [ɪ'kwɪvələnt] *adj, n* equivalente (*m*); **to be ~ to** equivalere a.

equivocal [ɪ'kwɪvəkl] *adj* equivoco(a); (*open to suspicion*) dubbio(a).

equivocate [ɪ'kwɪvəkeɪt] *vi* esprimersi in modo equivoco.

equivocation [ɪkwɪvə'keɪʃən] *n* parole *fpl* equivoche.

ER *abbr* (*BRIT*) = *Elizabeth Regina*.

ERA *n abbr* (*US POL*) = *Equal Rights Amendment*.

era ['ɪərə] *n* era, età *f inv*.

eradicate [ɪ'rædɪkeɪt] *vt* sradicare.

erase [ɪ'reɪz] *vt* cancellare.

eraser [ɪ'reɪzə*] *n* gomma.

erect [ɪ'rɛkt] *adj* eretto(a) ♦ *vt* costruire; (*monument, tent*) alzare.

erection [ɪ'rɛkʃən] *n* (*also PHYSIOL*) erezione *f*; (*of building*) costruzione *f*; (*of machinery*) montaggio.

ergonomics [ə:gə'nɔmɪks] *n* ergonomia.

ERISA *n abbr* (*US*: = *Employee Retirement Income Security Act*) *legge relativa al pensionamento statale*.

Eritrea [ɛrɪ'treɪə] *n* Eritrea.

ERM *n abbr* (= *Exchange Rate Mechanism*) meccanismo dei tassi di cambio.

ermine ['ə:mɪn] *n* ermellino.

ERNIE ['ə:nɪ] *n abbr* (*BRIT*: = *Electronic Random Number Indicator Equipment*) *sistema che seleziona i numeri vincenti di buoni del Tesoro*.

erode [ɪ'rəud] *vt* erodere; (*metal*) corrodere.

erogenous zone [ɪ'rɔdʒənəs-] *n* zona erogena.

erosion [ɪ'rəuʒən] *n* erosione *f*.

erotic [ɪ'rɔtɪk] *adj* erotico(a).

eroticism [ɪ'rɔtɪsɪzəm] *n* erotismo.

err [ə:*] *vi* errare; (*REL*) peccare.

errand ['ɛrənd] *n* commissione *f*; **to run ~s** fare commissioni; **~ of mercy** atto di carità.

errand boy *n* fattorino.

erratic [ɪ'rætɪk] *adj* imprevedibile; (*person, mood*) incostante.

erroneous [ɪ'rəunɪəs] *adj* erroneo(a).

error ['ɛrə*] *n* errore *m*; **typing/spelling ~** errore di battitura/di ortografia; **in ~** per errore; **~s and omissions excepted** salvo errori ed omissioni.

error message *n* (*COMPUT*) messaggio di errore.

erstwhile ['ə:stwaɪl] *adv* allora, un tempo ♦ *adj* di allora.

erudite ['ɛrjudaɪt] *adj* erudito(a).

erupt [ɪ'rʌpt] *vi* erompere; (*volcano*) mettersi (*or* essere) in eruzione.

eruption [ɪ'rʌpʃən] *n* eruzione *f*; (*of anger, violence*) esplosione *f*.

ESA *n abbr* (= *European Space Agency*) ESA *f*.

escalate ['ɛskəleɪt] *vi* intensificarsi; (*costs*) salire.

escalation [ɛskə'leɪʃən] *n* escalation *f*; (*of prices*) aumento.

escalation clause *n* clausola di revisione.

escalator ['ɛskəleɪtə*] *n* scala mobile.

escapade [ɛskə'peɪd] *n* scappatella; avventura.

escape [ɪ'skeɪp] *n* evasione *f*; fuga; (*of gas etc*) fuga, fuoriuscita ♦ *vi* fuggire; (*from jail*) evadere, scappare; (*fig*) sfuggire; (*leak*) uscire ♦ *vt* sfuggire a; **to ~ from sb** sfuggire a qn; **to ~ to** (*another place*) fuggire in; (*freedom, safety*) fuggire verso; **to ~ notice** passare inosservato(a).

escape artist *n* mago della fuga.

escape clause *n* clausola scappatoia.

escapee [ɪskeɪ'pi:] *n* evaso/a.

escape hatch *n* (*in submarine, space rocket*) portello di sicurezza.

escape key *n* (*COMPUT*) tasto di escape, tasto per cambio di codice.

escape route *n* percorso della fuga.

escapism [ɪs'keɪpɪzəm] *n* evasione *f* (dalla realtà).

escapist [ɪs'keɪpɪst] *adj* d'evasione ♦ *n* persona che cerca di evadere dalla realtà.

escapologist [ɛskə'pɔlədʒɪst] *n* (*BRIT*) = **escape artist**.

escarpment [ɪs'kɑ:pmənt] *n* scarpata.

eschew [ɪs'tʃu:] *vt* evitare.

escort *n* ['ɛskɔ:t] scorta; (*to dance etc*): **her ~** il suo cavaliere; **his ~** la sua dama ♦ *vt* [ɪ'skɔ:t] scortare; accompagnare.

escort agency *n* agenzia di hostess.

Eskimo ['ɛskɪməu] *adj* eschimese ♦ *n* eschimese *m/f*; (*LING*) eschimese *m*.

ESL *n abbr* (*SCOL*) = *English as a Second Language*.

esophagus [i:'sɔfəgəs] *n* (*US*) = **oesophagus**.

esoteric [ɛsəu'tɛrɪk] *adj* esoterico(a).

ESP *n abbr see* **extrasensory perception**; (*SCOL*) = *English for Specific* (*or Special*) *Purposes*.

esp. *abbr* (= *especially*) spec.

especially [ɪ'spɛʃlɪ] *adv* specialmente; (*above all*) soprattutto; (*specifically*) espressamente; (*particularly*) particolarmente.

espionage ['ɛspɪənɑːʒ] *n* spionaggio.

esplanade [ɛsplə'neɪd] *n* lungomare *m*.

espouse [ɪ'spauz] *vt* abbracciare.

Esquire [ɪ'skwaɪə*] *n* (*BRIT: abbr* **Esq.**): J. Brown, ~ Signor J. Brown.

essay ['ɛseɪ] *n* (*SCOL*) composizione *f*; (*LITERATURE*) saggio.

essence ['ɛsns] *n* essenza; **in** ~ in sostanza; **speed is of the** ~ la velocità è di estrema importanza.

essential [ɪ'sɛnʃəl] *adj* essenziale; (*basic*) fondamentale ♦ *n* elemento essenziale; **it is** ~ **that** è essenziale che + *sub*.

essentially [ɪ'sɛnʃəlɪ] *adv* essenzialmente.

EST *abbr* (*US*: = *Eastern Standard Time*) *fuso orario*.

est. *abbr* = *established*; *estimate(d)*.

establish [ɪ'stæblɪʃ] *vt* stabilire; (*business*) mettere su; (*one's power etc*) confermare; (*prove: fact, identity, sb's innocence*) dimostrare.

establishment [ɪs'tæblɪʃmənt] *n* stabilimento; (*business*) azienda; **the E~** la classe dirigente; l'establishment *m*; **a teaching** ~ un istituto d'istruzione.

estate [ɪ'steɪt] *n* proprietà *f inv*; (*LAW*) beni *mpl*, patrimonio; (*BRIT: also:* **housing** ~) complesso edilizio.

estate agency *n* (*BRIT*) agenzia immobiliare.

estate agent *n* (*BRIT*) agente *m* immobiliare.

estate car *n* (*BRIT*) giardiniera.

esteem [ɪ'stiːm] *n* stima ♦ *vt* considerare; stimare; **I hold him in high** ~ gode di tutta la mia stima.

esthetic [ɪs'θɛtɪk] *adj* (*US*) = **aesthetic**.

estimate *n* ['ɛstɪmət] stima; (*COMM*) preventivo ♦ *vb* ['ɛstɪmeɪt] *vt* stimare, valutare ♦ *vi* (*BRIT COMM*): **to** ~ **for** fare il preventivo per; **to give sb an** ~ **of** fare a qn una valutazione approssimativa (*or* un preventivo) di; **at a rough** ~ approssimativamente.

estimation [ɛstɪ'meɪʃən] *n* stima; opinione *f*; **in my** ~ a mio giudizio, a mio avviso.

Estonia [ɛ'stəunɪə] *n* Estonia.

Estonian [ɛ'stəunɪən] *adj* estone *inv* ♦ *n* estone *m/f*; (*LING*) estone *m*.

estranged [ɪ'streɪndʒd] *adj* separato(a).

estrangement [ɪs'treɪndʒmənt] *n* alienazione *f*.

estrogen ['iːstrəudʒən] *n* (*US*) = **oestrogen**.

estuary ['ɛstjuərɪ] *n* estuario.

ET *abbr* (= *Eastern Time*) *fuso orario*

ETA *n abbr* (= *estimated time of arrival*) ora di arrivo prevista.

e-tailer ['iːteɪlə*] *n* venditore/trice *m* in Internet.

e-tailing ['iːteɪlɪŋ] *n* commercio in Internet.

et al. *abbr* (= *et alii: and others*) ed altri.

etc. *abbr* (= *et cetera*) ecc., etc.

etch [ɛtʃ] *vt* incidere all'acquaforte.

etching ['ɛtʃɪŋ] *n* acquaforte *f*.

ETD *n abbr* (= *estimated time of departure*) ora di partenza prevista.

eternal [ɪ'təːnl] *adj* eterno(a).

eternity [ɪ'təːnɪtɪ] *n* eternità.

ether ['iːθə*] *n* etere *m*.

ethereal [ɪ'θɪərɪəl] *adj* etereo(a).

ethical ['ɛθɪkl] *adj* etico(a), morale.

ethics ['ɛθɪks] *n* etica ♦ *npl* morale *f*.

Ethiopia [iːθɪ'əupɪə] *n* Etiopia.

Ethiopian [iːθɪ'əupɪən] *adj, n* etiope (*m/f*).

ethnic ['ɛθnɪk] *adj* etnico(a).

ethnic cleansing [-'klɛnzɪŋ] *n* pulizia etnica.

ethnic minority *n* minoranza etnica.

ethnology [ɛθ'nɔlədʒɪ] *n* etnologia.

ethos ['iːθɔs] *n* (*of culture, group*) norma di vita.

e-ticket ['iːtɪkɪt] *n* e-ticket *m inv*; biglietto elettronico.

etiquette ['ɛtɪkɛt] *n* etichetta.

ETV *n abbr* (*US*) = *Educational Television*.

etymology [ɛtɪ'mɔlədʒɪ] *n* etimologia.

EU *n abbr* (= *European Union*) UE *f*.

eucalyptus [juːkə'lɪptəs] *n* eucalipto.

eulogy ['juːlədʒɪ] *n* elogio.

euphemism ['juːfəmɪzəm] *n* eufemismo.

euphemistic [juːfə'mɪstɪk] *adj* eufemistico(a).

euphoria [juː'fɔːrɪə] *n* euforia.

Eurasia [juə'reɪʃə] *n* Eurasia.

Eurasian [juə'reɪʃən] *adj, n* eurasiano(a).

Euratom [juə'rætəm] *n abbr* (= *European Atomic Energy Community*) EURATOM *f*.

euro ['juərəu] *n* (*currency*) euro *m inv*.

Euro- ['juərəu] *prefix* euro-.

Eurocheque ['juərəutʃɛk] *n* eurochèque *m inv*.

Eurocrat ['juərəukræt] *n* eurocrate *m/f*.

Eurodollar ['juərəudɔlə*] *n* eurodollaro.

Euroland ['juərəu,lænd] *n* Eurolandia.

Europe ['juərəp] *n* Europa.

European [juərə'piːən] *adj, n* europeo(a).

European Court of Justice *n* Corte *f* di

Giustizia della Comunità Europea.
Europol ['jʊərəʊpɒl] n Europol f.
Euro-sceptic ['jʊərəʊskɛptɪk] n
euroscettico/a.
Eurozone ['jʊərəʊzəʊn] n zona euro.
euthanasia [ju:θə'neɪzɪə] n eutanasia.
evacuate [ɪ'vækjʊeɪt] vt evacuare.
evacuation [ɪvækju'eɪʃən] n evacuazione f.
evacuee [ɪvækju'i:] n sfollato/a.
evade [ɪ'veɪd] vt eludere; (duties etc)
sottrarsi a.
evaluate [ɪ'væljʊeɪt] vt valutare.
evangelist [ɪ'vændʒəlɪst] n evangelista m.
evangelize [ɪ'vændʒəlaɪz] vt evangelizzare.
evaporate [ɪ'væpəreɪt] vi evaporare ♦ vt far
evaporare.
evaporated milk n latte m concentrato.
evaporation [ɪvæpə'reɪʃən] n evaporazione
f.
evasion [ɪ'veɪʒən] n evasione f.
evasive [ɪ'veɪsɪv] adj evasivo(a).
eve [i:v] n: **on the ~ of** alla vigilia di.
even ['i:vn] adj regolare; (number) pari inv
♦ adv anche, perfino; ~ **if**, ~ **though** anche
se; ~ **more** ancora di più; **he loves her** ~
more la ama anche di più; ~ **faster**
ancora più veloce; ~ **so** ciò nonostante;
not ~ ... nemmeno ...; **to break** ~ finire in
pari or alla pari; **to get** ~ **with sb** dare la
pari a qn.
▶**even out** vi pareggiare.
even-handed ['i:vn'hændɪd] adj imparziale,
equo(a).
evening ['i:vnɪŋ] n sera; (as duration, event)
serata; **in the** ~ la sera; **this** ~ stasera,
questa sera; **tomorrow/yesterday** ~
domani/ieri sera.
evening class n corso serale.
evening dress n (woman's) abito da sera;
in ~ (man) in abito scuro; (woman) in
abito lungo.
evenly ['i:vənlɪ] adv (distribute, space,
spread) uniformemente; (divide) in parti
uguali.
evensong ['i:vnsɒŋ] n ≈ vespro.
event [ɪ'vɛnt] n avvenimento; (SPORT)
gara; **in the** ~ **of** in caso di; **at all** ~s
(BRIT) in any ~ in ogni caso; **in the** ~ in
realtà, di fatto; **in the course of** ~s nel
corso degli eventi.
eventful [ɪ'vɛntful] adj denso(a) di eventi.
eventing [ɪ'vɛntɪŋ] n (HORSERIDING)
concorso ippico.
eventual [ɪ'vɛntʃʊəl] adj finale.
eventuality [ɪvɛntʃu'ælɪtɪ] n possibilità f
inv, eventualità f inv.
eventually [ɪ'vɛntʃʊəlɪ] adv finalmente.
ever ['ɛvə*] adv mai; (at all times) sempre;

for ~ per sempre; **the best** ~ il migliore
che ci sia mai stato; **hardly** ~ non ... quasi
mai; **did you** ~ **meet him?** l'ha mai
incontrato?; **have you** ~ **been there?** c'è
mai stato?; ~ **so pretty** così bello(a);
thank you ~ **so much** grazie mille; **yours**
~ (BRIT: in letters) sempre tuo; ~ **since** adv
da allora ♦ conj sin da quando.
Everest ['ɛvərɪst] n (also: **Mount** ~) Everest
m.
evergreen ['ɛvəgri:n] n sempreverde m.
everlasting [ɛvə'lɑ:stɪŋ] adj eterno(a).
every ['ɛvrɪ] adj ogni; ~ **day** tutti i giorni,
ogni giorno; ~ **other/third day** ogni due/
tre giorni; ~ **other car** una macchina su
due; ~ **now and then** ogni tanto, di
quando in quando; **I have** ~ **confidence in
him** ho piena fiducia in lui.
everybody ['ɛvrɪbɒdɪ] pron ognuno, tutti pl;
~ **else** tutti gli altri; ~ **knows about it** lo
sanno tutti.
everyday ['ɛvrɪdeɪ] adj quotidiano(a); di
ogni giorno; (use, occurrence, experience)
comune; (expression) di uso corrente.
everyone ['ɛvrɪwʌn] = **everybody**.
everything ['ɛvrɪθɪŋ] pron tutto, ogni cosa;
~ **is ready** è tutto pronto; **he did** ~
possible ha fatto tutto il possibile.
everywhere ['ɛvrɪwɛə*] adv in ogni luogo,
dappertutto; (wherever) ovunque; ~ **you
go you meet** ... ovunque si vada si trova
....
evict [ɪ'vɪkt] vt sfrattare.
eviction [ɪ'vɪkʃən] n sfratto.
eviction notice n avviso di sfratto.
evidence ['ɛvɪdəns] n (proof) prova; (of
witness) testimonianza; (sign): **to show** ~
of dare segni di; **to give** ~ deporre; **in** ~
(obvious) in evidenza; in vista.
evident ['ɛvɪdənt] adj evidente.
evidently ['ɛvɪdəntlɪ] adv evidentemente.
evil ['i:vl] adj cattivo(a), maligno(a) ♦ n
male m.
evince [ɪ'vɪns] vt manifestare.
evocative [ɪ'vɒkətɪv] adj evocativo(a).
evoke [ɪ'vəʊk] vt evocare; (admiration)
suscitare.
evolution [i:və'lu:ʃən] n evoluzione f.
evolve [ɪ'vɒlv] vt elaborare ♦ vi svilupparsi,
evolversi.
ewe [ju:] n pecora.
ex- [ɛks] prefix ex; (out of): **the price** ~ **works**
il prezzo franco fabbrica.
exacerbate [ɪk'sæsəbeɪt] vt (pain)
aggravare; (fig: relations, situation)
esacerbare, esasperare.
exact [ɪg'zækt] adj esatto(a) ♦ vt: **to** ~ **sth**
(**from**) estorcere qc (da); esigere qc (da).

exacting [ɪg'zæktɪŋ] *adj* esigente; (*work*) faticoso(a).

exactitude [ɪg'zæktɪtjuːd] *n* esattezza, precisione *f*.

exactly [ɪg'zæktlɪ] *adv* esattamente; ~! esatto!

exaggerate [ɪg'zædʒəreɪt] *vt, vi* esagerare.

exaggeration [ɪgzædʒə'reɪʃən] *n* esagerazione *f*.

exalt [ɪg'zɔːlt] *vt* esaltare; elevare.

exalted [ɪg'zɔːltɪd] *adj* (*rank, person*) elevato(a); (*elated*) esaltato(a).

exam [ɪg'zæm] *n abbr* (*SCOL*) = **examination**.

examination [ɪgzæmɪ'neɪʃən] *n* (*SCOL*) esame *m*; (*MED*) controllo; **to take** *or* (*BRIT*) **sit an** ~ sostenere *or* dare un esame; **the matter is under** ~ la questione è all'esame.

examine [ɪg'zæmɪn] *vt* esaminare; (*SCOL: orally, LAW: person*) interrogare; (*inspect: machine, premises*) ispezionare; (*luggage, passport*) controllare; (*MED*) visitare.

examiner [ɪg'zæmɪnə*] *n* esaminatore/trice.

example [ɪg'zɑːmpl] *n* esempio; **for** ~ ad *or* per esempio; **to set a good/bad** ~ dare il buon/cattivo esempio.

exasperate [ɪg'zɑːspəreɪt] *vt* esasperare; ~d **by** (*or* **at** *or* **with**) esasperato da.

exasperating [ɪg'zɑːspəreɪtɪŋ] *adj* esasperante.

exasperation [ɪgzɑːspə'reɪʃən] *n* esasperazione *f*.

excavate ['ɛkskəveɪt] *vt* scavare.

excavation [ɛkskə'veɪʃən] *n* escavazione *f*.

excavator ['ɛkskəveɪtə*] *n* scavatore *m*, scavatrice *f*.

exceed [ɪk'siːd] *vt* superare; (*one's powers, time limit*) oltrepassare.

exceedingly [ɪk'siːdɪŋlɪ] *adv* eccessivamente.

excel [ɪk'sɛl] *vi* eccellere ♦ *vt* sorpassare; **to** ~ **o.s.** (*BRIT*) superare se stesso.

excellence ['ɛksələns] *n* eccellenza.

Excellency ['ɛksələnsɪ] *n*: **His** ~ Sua Eccellenza.

excellent ['ɛksələnt] *adj* eccellente.

except [ɪk'sɛpt] *prep* (*also*: ~ **for**, ~**ing**) salvo, all'infuori di, eccetto ♦ *vt* escludere; ~ **if/when** salvo se/quando; ~ **that** salvo che.

exception [ɪk'sɛpʃən] *n* eccezione *f*; **to take** ~ **to** trovare a ridire su; **with the** ~ **of** ad eccezione di.

exceptional [ɪk'sɛpʃnl] *adj* eccezionale.

excerpt ['ɛksəːpt] *n* estratto.

excess [ɪk'sɛs] *n* eccesso; **in** ~ **of** al di sopra di.

excess baggage *n* bagaglio in eccedenza.

excess fare *n* supplemento.

excessive [ɪk'sɛsɪv] *adj* eccessivo(a).

excess supply *n* eccesso di offerta.

exchange [ɪks'tʃeɪndʒ] *n* scambio; (*also:* **telephone** ~) centralino ♦ *vt*: **to** ~ (**for**) scambiare (con); **in** ~ **for** in cambio di; **foreign** ~ (*COMM*) cambio.

exchange control *n* controllo sui cambi.

exchange market *n* mercato dei cambi.

exchange rate *n* tasso di cambio.

Exchequer [ɪks'tʃɛkə*] *n*: **the** ~ (*BRIT*) lo Scacchiere, ≈ il ministero delle Finanze.

excisable [ɪk'saɪzəbl] *adj* soggetto(a) a dazio.

excise *n* ['ɛksaɪz] imposta, dazio ♦ *vt* [ɛk'saɪz] recidere.

excise duties *npl* dazi *mpl*.

excitable [ɪk'saɪtəbl] *adj* eccitabile.

excite [ɪk'saɪt] *vt* eccitare; **to get** ~d eccitarsi.

excitement [ɪk'saɪtmənt] *n* eccitazione *f*, agitazione *f*.

exciting [ɪk'saɪtɪŋ] *adj* avventuroso(a); (*film, book*) appassionante.

excl. *abbr* (= *excluding, exclusive (of)*) escl.

exclaim [ɪk'skleɪm] *vi* esclamare.

exclamation [ɛksklə'meɪʃən] *n* esclamazione *f*.

exclamation mark *n* punto esclamativo.

exclude [ɪk'skluːd] *vt* escludere.

excluding [ɪk'skluːdɪŋ] *prep*: ~ **VAT** IVA esclusa.

exclusion [ɪk'skluːʒən] *n* esclusione *f*; **to the** ~ **of** escludendo.

exclusion clause *n* clausola di esclusione.

exclusion zone *n* area interdetta.

exclusive [ɪk'skluːsɪv] *adj* esclusivo(a); (*club*) selettivo(a); (*district*) snob *inv* ♦ *adv* (*COMM*) non compreso; ~ **of VAT** IVA esclusa; ~ **of postage** spese postali escluse; ~ **of service** servizio escluso; **from 1st to 15th March** ~ dal 1° al 15 marzo esclusi; ~ **rights** *npl* (*COMM*) diritti *mpl* esclusivi.

exclusively [ɪk'skluːsɪvlɪ] *adv* esclusivamente.

excommunicate [ɛkskə'mjuːnɪkeɪt] *vt* scomunicare.

excrement ['ɛkskrəmənt] *n* escremento.

excruciating [ɪk'skruːʃɪeɪtɪŋ] *adj* straziante, atroce.

excursion [ɪk'skəːʃən] *n* escursione *f*, gita.

excursion ticket *n* biglietto a tariffa escursionistica.

excusable [ɪk'skjuːzəbl] *adj* scusabile.

excuse *n* [ɪk'skjuːs] scusa ♦ *vt* [ɪk'skjuːz] scusare; (*justify*) giustificare; **to make** ~s

for sb trovare giustificazioni per qn; **to ~ sb from** (*activity*) dispensare qn da; **~ me!** mi scusi!; **now if you will ~ me, ...** ora, mi scusi ma ...; **to ~ o.s. (for (doing) sth)** giustificarsi (per (aver fatto) qc).

ex-directory ['ɛksdɪ'rɛktərɪ] *adj* (*BRIT*): **~ (phone) number** numero non compreso nell'elenco telefonico.

execrable ['ɛksɪkrəbl] *adj* (*gen*) pessimo(a); (*manners*) esecrabile.

execute ['ɛksɪkjuːt] *vt* (*prisoner*) giustiziare; (*plan etc*) eseguire.

execution [ɛksɪ'kjuːʃən] *n* esecuzione *f*.

executioner [ɛksɪ'kjuːʃnə*] *n* boia *m inv*.

executive [ɪg'zɛkjutɪv] *n* (*COMM*) dirigente *m*; (*POL*) esecutivo ♦ *adj* esecutivo(a); (*secretary*) di direzione; (*offices, suite*) della direzione; (*car, plane*) dirigenziale; (*position, job, duties*) direttivo(a).

executive director *n* amministratore/ trice.

executor [ɪg'zɛkjutə*] *n* esecutore(trice) testamentario(a).

exemplary [ɪg'zɛmplərɪ] *adj* esemplare.

exemplify [ɪg'zɛmplɪfaɪ] *vt* esemplificare.

exempt [ɪg'zɛmpt] *adj*: **~ (from)** (*person: from tax*) esentato(a) (da); (: *from military service etc*) esonerato(a) (da); (*goods*) esente (da) ♦ *vt*: **to ~ sb from** esentare qn da.

exemption [ɪg'zɛmpʃən] *n* esenzione *f*.

exercise ['ɛksəsaɪz] *n* esercizio ♦ *vt* esercitare; (*dog*) portar fuori ♦ *vi* (*also*: **take ~**) fare del movimento *or* moto.

exercise bike *n* cyclette ® *f inv*.

exercise book *n* quaderno.

exert [ɪg'zəːt] *vt* esercitare; (*strength, force*) impiegare; **to ~ o.s.** sforzarsi.

exertion [ɪg'zəːʃən] *n* sforzo.

ex gratia ['ɛks'greɪʃə] *adj*: **~ payment** gratifica.

exhale [ɛks'heɪl] *vt, vi* espirare.

exhaust [ɪg'zɔːst] *n* (*also*: **~ fumes**) scappamento; (*also*: **~ pipe**) tubo di scappamento ♦ *vt* esaurire; **to ~ o.s.** sfiancarsi.

exhausted [ɪg'zɔːstɪd] *adj* esaurito(a).

exhausting [ɪg'zɔːstɪŋ] *adj* estenuante.

exhaustion [ɪg'zɔːstʃən] *n* esaurimento; **nervous ~** sovraffaticamento mentale.

exhaustive [ɪg'zɔːstɪv] *adj* esauriente.

exhibit [ɪg'zɪbɪt] *n* (*ART*) oggetto esposto; (*LAW*) documento *or* oggetto esibito ♦ *vt* esporre; (*courage, skill*) dimostrare.

exhibition [ɛksɪ'bɪʃən] *n* mostra, esposizione *f*; (*of rudeness etc*) spettacolo; **to make an ~ of o.s.** dare spettacolo di sé.

exhibitionist [ɛksɪ'bɪʃənɪst] *n* esibizionista *m/f*.

exhibitor [ɪg'zɪbɪtə*] *n* espositore/trice.

exhilarating [ɪg'zɪləreɪtɪŋ] *adj* esilarante; stimolante.

exhilaration [ɪgzɪlə'reɪʃən] *n* esaltazione *f*, ebbrezza.

exhort [ɪg'zɔːt] *vt* esortare.

exile ['ɛksaɪl] *n* esilio; (*person*) esiliato/a ♦ *vt* esiliare; **in ~** in esilio.

exist [ɪg'zɪst] *vi* esistere.

existence [ɪg'zɪstəns] *n* esistenza; **to be in ~** esistere.

existentialism [ɛgzɪs'tɛnʃəlɪzəm] *n* esistenzialismo.

existing [ɪg'zɪstɪŋ] *adj* (*laws, regime*) attuale.

exit ['ɛksɪt] *n* uscita ♦ *vi* (*COMPUT, THEAT*) uscire.

exit poll *n* exit poll *m inv*, sondaggio all'uscita dei seggi.

exit ramp *n* (*US AUT*) rampa di uscita.

exit visa *n* visto d'uscita.

exodus ['ɛksədəs] *n* esodo.

ex officio ['ɛksə'fɪʃɪəu] *adj, adv* d'ufficio.

exonerate [ɪg'zɔnəreɪt] *vt*: **to ~ from** discolpare da.

exorbitant [ɪg'zɔːbɪtənt] *adj* (*price*) esorbitante; (*demands*) spropositato(a).

exorcize ['ɛksɔːsaɪz] *vt* esorcizzare.

exotic [ɪg'zɔtɪk] *adj* esotico(a).

expand [ɪk'spænd] *vt* (*chest, economy etc*) sviluppare; (*market, operations*) espandere; (*influence*) estendere; (*horizons*) allargare ♦ *vi* svilupparsi; (*also gas*) espandersi; (*metal*) dilatarsi; **to ~ on** (*notes, story etc*) ampliare.

expanse [ɪk'spæns] *n* distesa, estensione *f*.

expansion [ɪk'spænʃən] *n* (*gen*) espansione *f*; (*of town, economy*) sviluppo; (*of metal*) dilatazione *f*.

expansionism [ɪk'spænʃənɪzəm] *n* espansionismo.

expansionist [ɪk'spænʃənɪst] *adj* espansionistico(a).

expatriate *n* [ɛks'pætrɪət] espatriato/a ♦ *vt* [ɛks'pætrɪeɪt] espatriare.

expect [ɪk'spɛkt] *vt* (*anticipate*) prevedere, aspettarsi, prevedere *or* aspettarsi che + *sub*; (*count on*) contare su; (*hope for*) sperare; (*require*) richiedere, esigere; (*suppose*) supporre; (*await, also baby*) aspettare ♦ *vi*: **to be ~ing** essere in stato interessante; **to ~ sb to do** aspettarsi che qn faccia; **to ~ to do sth** pensare *or* contare di fare qc; **as ~ed** come previsto; **I ~ so** credo di sì.

expectancy [ɪk'spɛktənsɪ] *n* attesa; **life ~**

probabilità _fpl_ di vita.
expectant [ɪk'spɛktənt] _adj_ pieno(a) di
aspettative.
expectantly [ɪk'spɛktəntlɪ] _adv_ (_look, listen_)
con un'aria d'attesa.
expectant mother _n_ gestante _f._
expectation [ɛkspɛk'teɪʃən] _n_ aspettativa;
speranza; **in** ~ **of** in previsione di;
against _or_ **contrary to all** ~(**s**) contro
ogni aspettativa; **to come** _or_ **live up
to sb's** ~**s** rispondere alle attese
di qn.
expedience, expediency [ɪk'spiːdɪəns,
ɪk'spiːdɪənsɪ] _n_ convenienza; **for the sake
of** ~ per una questione di comodità.
expedient [ɪk'spiːdɪənt] _adj_ conveniente;
vantaggioso(a) ♦ _n_ espediente _m._
expedite ['ɛkspədaɪt] _vt_ sbrigare;
facilitare.
expedition [ɛkspə'dɪʃən] _n_ spedizione _f._
expeditionary force [ɛkspə'dɪʃənərɪ-] _n_
corpo di spedizione.
expeditious [ɛkspə'dɪʃəs] _adj_ sollecito(a),
rapido(a).
expel [ɪk'spɛl] _vt_ espellere.
expend [ɪk'spɛnd] _vt_ spendere; (_use up_)
consumare.
expendable [ɪk'spɛndəbl] _adj_ sacrificabile.
expenditure [ɪk'spɛndɪtʃə*] _n_ spesa; (_of
time, effort_) dispendio.
expense [ɪk'spɛns] _n_ spesa; (_high cost_)
costo; ~**s** _npl_ (_COMM_) spese _fpl_, indennità
fpl; **to go to the** ~ **of** sobbarcarsi la spesa
di; **at great** ~ con grande impiego di
mezzi; **at the** ~ **of** a spese di.
expense account _n_ conto _m_ spese _inv._
expensive [ɪk'spɛnsɪv] _adj_ caro(a),
costoso(a); **she has** ~ **tastes** le piacciono
le cose costose.
experience [ɪk'spɪərɪəns] _n_ esperienza ♦ _vt_
(_pleasure_) provare; (_hardship_) soffrire; **to
learn by** ~ imparare per esperienza.
experienced [ɪk'spɪərɪənst] _adj_ che ha
esperienza.
experiment _n_ [ɪk'spɛrɪmənt] esperimento,
esperienza ♦ _vi_ [ɪk'spɛrɪmɛnt] fare
esperimenti; **to perform** _or_ **carry out an** ~
fare un esperimento; **as an** ~ a titolo di
esperimento; **to** ~ **with a new vaccine**
sperimentare un nuovo vaccino.
experimental [ɪkspɛrɪ'mɛntl] _adj_
sperimentale; **at the** ~ **stage** in via di
sperimentazione.
expert ['ɛkspəːt] _adj, n_ esperto(a); ~
witness (_LAW_) esperto/a; ~ **in** _or_ **at doing
sth** esperto nel fare qc; **an** ~ **on sth** un
esperto di qc.
expertise [ɛkspəː'tiːz] _n_ competenza.

expire [ɪk'spaɪə*] _vi_ (_period of time, licence_)
scadere.
expiry [ɪk'spaɪərɪ] _n_ scadenza.
explain [ɪk'spleɪn] _vt_ spiegare.
▶**explain away** _vt_ dar ragione di.
explanation [ɛksplə'neɪʃən] _n_ spiegazione _f_;
to find an ~ **for sth** trovare la
spiegazione di qc.
explanatory [ɪk'splænətrɪ] _adj_
esplicativo(a).
expletive [ɪk'spliːtɪv] _n_ imprecazione _f._
explicit [ɪk'splɪsɪt] _adj_ esplicito(a); (_definite_)
netto(a).
explode [ɪk'spləʊd] _vi_ esplodere ♦ _vt_ (_fig:
theory_) demolire; **to** ~ **a myth**
distruggere un mito.
exploit _n_ ['ɛksplɔɪt] impresa ♦ _vt_ [ɪk'splɔɪt]
sfruttare.
exploitation [ɛksplɔɪ'teɪʃən] _n_
sfruttamento.
exploration [ɛksplə'reɪʃən] _n_ esplorazione _f._
exploratory [ɪk'splɔrətrɪ] _adj_ (_fig: talks_)
esplorativo(a); ~ **operation** (_MED_)
intervento d'esplorazione.
explore [ɪk'splɔː*] _vt_ esplorare;
(_possibilities_) esaminare.
explorer [ɪk'splɔːrə*] _n_ esploratore/trice.
explosion [ɪk'spləʊʒən] _n_ esplosione _f._
explosive [ɪk'spləʊsɪv] _adj_ esplosivo(a) ♦ _n_
esplosivo.
exponent [ɪk'spəʊnənt] _n_ esponente _m/f._
export _vt_ [ɛk'spɔːt] esportare ♦ _n_ ['ɛkspɔːt]
esportazione _f_; articolo di esportazione
♦ _cpd_ d'esportazione.
exportation [ɛkspɔː'teɪʃən] _n_ esportazione
_f._
exporter [ɪk'spɔːtə*] _n_ esportatore _m._
export licence _n_ licenza d'esportazione.
expose [ɪk'spəʊz] _vt_ esporre; (_unmask_)
smascherare; **to** ~ **o.s.** (_LAW_) oltraggiare
il pudore.
exposed [ɪk'spəʊzd] _adj_ (_land, house_)
esposto(a); (_ELEC: wire_) scoperto(a); (_pipe,
beam_) a vista.
exposition [ɛkspə'zɪʃən] _n_ esposizione _f._
exposure [ɪk'spəʊʒə*] _n_ esposizione _f_;
(_PHOT_) posa; (_MED_) assideramento; **to die
of** ~ morire assiderato(a).
exposure meter _n_ esposimetro.
expound [ɪk'spaʊnd] _vt_ esporre; (_theory,
text_) spiegare.
express [ɪk'sprɛs] _adj_ (_definite_) chiaro(a),
espresso(a); (_BRIT: letter etc_) espresso _inv_
♦ _n_ (_train_) espresso ♦ _adv_: **to send sth** ~
spedire qc per espresso ♦ _vt_ esprimere;
to ~ **o.s.** esprimersi.
expression [ɪk'sprɛʃən] _n_ espressione _f._
expressionism [ɪk'sprɛʃənɪzəm] _n_

espressionismo.
expressive [ɪk'sprɛsɪv] *adj* espressivo(a).
expressly [ɪk'sprɛslɪ] *adv* espressamente.
expressway [ɪk'sprɛsweɪ] *n* (*US*)
autostrada che attraversa la città.
expropriate [ɛks'prəuprɪeɪt] *vt* espropriare.
expulsion [ɪk'spʌlʃən] *n* espulsione *f*.
exquisite [ɛk'skwɪzɪt] *adj* squisito(a).
ex-serviceman ['ɛks'sə:vɪsmən] *n* ex
combattente *m*.
ext. *abbr* (*TEL*: = *extension*) int. (= *interno*).
extemporize [ɪk'stɛmpəraɪz] *vi*
improvvisare.
extend [ɪk'stɛnd] *vt* (*visit*) protrarre; (*road*,
deadline) prolungare; (*building*) ampliare;
(*offer*) offrire, porgere; (*COMM*: *credit*)
accordare ♦ *vi* (*land*) estendersi.
extension [ɪk'stɛnʃən] *n* (*of road, term*)
prolungamento; (*of contract, deadline*)
proroga; (*building*) annesso; (*to wire, table*)
prolunga; (*telephone*) interno; (: *in private
house*) apparecchio supplementare; ~
3718 (*TEL*) interno 3718.
extension cable *n* (*ELEC*) prolunga.
extensive [ɪk'stɛnsɪv] *adj* esteso(a),
ampio(a); (*damage*) su larga scala;
(*alterations*) notevole; (*inquiries*)
esauriente; (*use*) grande.
extensively [ɪk'stɛnsɪvlɪ] *adv* (*altered,
damaged etc*) radicalmente; **he's travelled**
~ ha viaggiato molto.
extent [ɪk'stɛnt] *n* estensione *f*; (*of
knowledge, activities, power*) portata;
(*degree*: *of damage, loss*) proporzioni *fpl*; **to
some** ~ fino a un certo punto; **to a
certain/large** ~ in certa/larga misura; **to
what** ~? fino a che punto?; **to such an** ~
that ... a tal punto che ....
extenuating [ɪk'stɛnjueɪtɪŋ] *adj*: ~
circumstances attenuanti *fpl*.
exterior [ɛk'stɪərɪə*] *adj* esteriore,
esterno(a) ♦ *n* esteriore *m*, esterno;
aspetto (esteriore).
exterminate [ɪk'stə:mɪneɪt] *vt* sterminare.
extermination [ɪkstə:mɪ'neɪʃən] *n*
sterminio.
external [ɛk'stə:nl] *adj* esterno(a), esteriore
♦ *n*: **the** ~**s** le apparenze; **for** ~ **use only**
(*MED*) solo per uso esterno; ~ **affairs** (*POL*)
affari *mpl* esteri.
externally [ɛk'stə:nəlɪ] *adv* esternamente.
extinct [ɪk'stɪŋkt] *adj* estinto(a).
extinction [ɪk'stɪŋkʃən] *n* estinzione *f*.
extinguish [ɪk'stɪŋgwɪʃ] *vt* estinguere.
extinguisher [ɪk'stɪŋgwɪʃə*] *n* estintore *m*.
extol, ** (*US*) **extoll [ɪk'stəul] *vt* (*merits,
virtues*) magnificare; (*person*) celebrare.
extort [ɪk'stɔ:t] *vt*: **to** ~ **sth** (**from**)

estorcere qc (da).
extortion [ɪk'stɔ:ʃən] *n* estorsione *f*.
extortionate [ɪk'stɔ:ʃənɪt] *adj* esorbitante.
extra ['ɛkstrə] *adj* extra *inv*, supplementare
♦ *adv* (*in addition*) di più ♦ *n* supplemento;
(*THEAT*) comparso; **wine will cost** ~ il
vino è extra; ~ **large sizes** taglie *fpl* forti.
extra... ['ɛkstrə] *prefix* extra....
extract *vt* [ɪk'strækt] estrarre; (*money,
promise*) strappare ♦ *n* ['ɛkstrækt]
estratto; (*passage*) brano.
extraction [ɪk'strækʃən] *n* estrazione *f*;
(*descent*) origine *f*.
extractor fan [ɪk'stræktə*-] *n* aspiratore *m*.
extracurricular [ɛkstrəkə'rɪkjulə*] *adj*
(*SCOL*) parascolastico(a).
extradite ['ɛkstrədaɪt] *vt* estradare.
extradition [ɛkstrə'dɪʃən] *n* estradizione *f*.
extramarital [ɛkstrə'mærɪtl] *adj*
extraconiugale.
extramural [ɛkstrə'mjuərl] *adj* fuori
dell'università.
extraneous [ɛk'streɪnɪəs] *adj*: ~ **to**
estraneo(a) a.
extraordinary [ɪk'strɔ:dnrɪ] *adj*
straordinario(a); **the** ~ **thing is that** ... la
cosa strana è che ....
extraordinary general meeting *n*
assemblea straordinaria.
extrapolation [ɪkstræpə'leɪʃən] *n*
estrapolazione *f*.
extrasensory perception (ESP)
[ɛkstrə'sɛnsərɪ-] *n* percezione *f*
extrasensoriale.
extra time *n* (*FOOTBALL*) tempo
supplementare.
extravagance [ɪk'strævəgəns] *n* (*excessive
spending*) sperpero; (*thing bought*)
stravaganza.
extravagant [ɪk'strævəgənt] *adj*
stravagante; (*in spending*: *person*)
prodigo(a); (: *tastes*) dispendioso(a).
extreme [ɪk'stri:m] *adj* estremo(a) ♦ *n*
estremo; ~**s of temperature** eccessivi
sbalzi *mpl* di temperatura; **the** ~ **left/right**
(*POL*) l'estrema sinistra/destra.
extremely [ɪk'stri:mlɪ] *adv* estremamente.
extremist [ɪk'stri:mɪst] *adj, n* estremista
(*m/f*).
extremity [ɪk'strɛmɪtɪ] *n* estremità *f inv*.
extricate ['ɛkstrɪkeɪt] *vt*: **to** ~ **sth** (**from**)
districare qc (da).
extrovert ['ɛkstrəvɔ:t] *n* estroverso/a.
exuberance [ɪg'zu:bərəns] *n* esuberanza.
exuberant [ɪg'zju:bərənt] *adj* esuberante.
exude [ɪg'zju:d] *vt* trasudare; (*fig*)
emanare.
exult [ɪg'zʌlt] *vi* esultare, gioire.

exultant [ɪg'zʌltənt] *adj* (*person, smile*) esultante; (*shout, expression*) di giubilo.

exultation [ɛgzʌl'teɪʃən] *n* giubilo; **in ~** per la gioia.

eye [aɪ] *n* occhio; (*of needle*) cruna ♦ *vt* osservare; **to keep an ~ on** tenere d'occhio; **in the public ~** esposto(a) al pubblico; **as far as the ~ can see** a perdita d'occhio; **with an ~ to doing sth** (*BRIT*) con l'idea di far qc; **to have an ~ for sth** avere occhio per qc; **there's more to this than meets the ~** non è così semplice come sembra.

eyeball ['aɪbɔːl] *n* globo dell'occhio.

eyebath ['aɪbɑːθ] *n* occhino.

eyebrow ['aɪbrau] *n* sopracciglio.

eyebrow pencil *n* matita per le sopracciglia.

eye-catching ['aɪkætʃɪŋ] *adj* che colpisce l'occhio.

eye cup *n* (*US*) = **eyebath**.

eyedrops ['aɪdrɔps] *npl* gocce *fpl* oculari, collirio.

eyeful ['aɪful] *n*: **to get an ~ (of sth)** (*col*) avere l'occasione di dare una bella sbirciata (a qc).

eyeglass ['aɪglɑːs] *n* monocolo.

eyelash ['aɪlæʃ] *n* ciglio.

eyelet ['aɪlɪt] *n* occhiello.

eye-level ['aɪlɛvl] *adj* all'altezza degli occhi.

eyelid ['aɪlɪd] *n* palpebra.

eyeliner ['aɪlaɪnə*] *n* eye-liner *m inv*.

eye-opener ['aɪəupnə*] *n* rivelazione *f*.

eyeshadow ['aɪʃædəu] *n* ombretto.

eyesight ['aɪsaɪt] *n* vista.

eyesore ['aɪsɔː*] *n* pugno nell'occhio.

eyestrain ['aɪstreɪn] *n*: **to get ~** stancarsi gli occhi.

eye-tooth, *pl* **-teeth** ['aɪtuːθ, -tiːθ] *n* canino superiore; **to give one's eye-teeth for sth/to do sth** (*fig*) dare non so che cosa per qc/per fare qc.

eyewash ['aɪwɔʃ] *n* collirio; (*fig*) sciocchezze *fpl*.

eye witness *n* testimone *m/f* oculare.

eyrie ['ɪərɪ] *n* nido (d'aquila).

Ff

F, f [ɛf] *n* (*letter*) F, f *f or m inv*; (*MUS*): F fa *m*; **F for Frederick**, (*US*) **F for Fox** ≈ F come Firenze.

F. *abbr* (= *Fahrenheit*) F.

FA *n abbr* (*BRIT*) = *Football Association*.

FAA *n abbr* (*US*) = *Federal Aviation Administration*.

fable ['feɪbl] *n* favola.

fabric ['fæbrɪk] *n* stoffa, tessuto; (*ARCHIT*) struttura.

fabricate ['fæbrɪkeɪt] *vt* fabbricare.

fabrication [fæbrɪ'keɪʃən] *n* fabbricazione *f*.

fabric ribbon *n* (*for typewriter*) dattilonastro di tessuto.

fabulous ['fæbjuləs] *adj* favoloso(a); (*col: super*) favoloso(a), fantastico(a).

façade [fə'sɑːd] *n* facciata; (*fig*) apparenza.

face [feɪs] *n* faccia, viso, volto; (*expression*) faccia; (*grimace*) smorfia; (*of clock*) quadrante *m*; (*of building*) facciata; (*side, surface*) faccia; (*of mountain, cliff*) parete *f* ♦ *vt* fronteggiare; (*fig*) affrontare; **~ down** (*person*) bocconi; (*object*) a faccia in giù; **to lose/save ~** perdere/salvare la faccia; **to pull a ~** fare una smorfia; **in the ~ of** (*difficulties etc*) di fronte a; **on the ~ of it** a prima vista; **to ~ the fact that …** riconoscere *or* ammettere che ….

▸**face up to** *vt fus* affrontare, far fronte a.

face cloth *n* (*BRIT*) guanto di spugna.

face cream *n* crema per il viso.

faceless ['feɪslɪs] *adj* anonimo(a).

face lift *n* lifting *m inv*; (*of façade etc*) ripulita.

face powder *n* cipria.

face-saving ['feɪs'seɪvɪŋ] *adj* che salva la faccia.

facet ['fæsɪt] *n* faccetta, sfaccettatura; (*fig*) sfaccettatura.

facetious [fə'siːʃəs] *adj* faceto(a).

face-to-face ['feɪstə'feɪs] *adv* faccia a faccia.

face value ['feɪs'væljuː] *n* (*of coin*) valore *m* facciale *or* nominale; **to take sth at ~** (*fig*) giudicare qc dalle apparenze.

facia ['feɪʃɪə] *n* = **fascia**.

facial ['feɪʃəl] *adj* facciale ♦ *n* trattamento del viso.

facile ['fæsaɪl] *adj* facile; superficiale.

facilitate [fə'sɪlɪteɪt] *vt* facilitare.

facility [fə'sɪlɪtɪ] *n* facilità; **facilities** *npl* attrezzature *fpl*; **credit facilities** facilitazioni *fpl* di credito.

facing ['feɪsɪŋ] *n* (*of wall etc*) rivestimento; (*SEWING*) paramontura.

facsimile [fæk'sɪmɪlɪ] *n* facsimile *m inv.*

facsimile machine *n* telecopiatrice *f*.

fact [fækt] *n* fatto; **in** ~ infatti; **to know for a** ~ **that** ... sapere per certo che ...; **the** ~ **(of the matter) is that** ... la verità è che ...; **the** ~**s of life** (*sex*) i fatti riguardanti la vita sessuale; (*fig*) le realtà della vita.

fact-finding ['fæktfaɪndɪŋ] *adj*: **a** ~ **tour/ mission** un viaggio/una missione d'inchiesta.

faction ['fækʃən] *n* fazione *f*.

factional ['fækʃənl] *adj*: ~ **fighting** scontri *mpl* tra fazioni.

factor ['fæktə*] *n* fattore *m*; (*COMM*: *company*) *organizzazione specializzata nell'incasso di crediti per conto terzi*; (*: agent*) agente *m* depositario ♦ *vi* incassare crediti per conto terzi; **human** ~ elemento umano; **safety** ~ coefficiente *m* di sicurezza.

factory ['fæktərɪ] *n* fabbrica, stabilimento.

factory farming *n* (*BRIT*) allevamento su scala industriale.

factory floor *n*: **the** ~ (*workers*) gli operai; (*area*) il reparto produzione; **on the** ~ nel reparto produzione.

factory ship *n* nave *f* fattoria *inv.*

factual ['fæktjuəl] *adj* che si attiene ai fatti.

faculty ['fækəltɪ] *n* facoltà *f inv*; (*US*: *teaching staff*) corpo insegnante.

fad [fæd] *n* mania; capriccio.

fade [feɪd] *vi* sbiadire, sbiadirsi; (*light, sound, hope*) attenuarsi, affievolirsi; (*flower*) appassire.

▶**fade in** *vt* (*picture*) aprire in dissolvenza; (*sound*) aumentare gradualmente d'intensità.

▶**fade out** *vt* (*picture*) chiudere in dissolvenza; (*sound*) diminuire gradualmente d'intensità.

faeces, (*US*) **feces** ['fiːsiːz] *npl* feci *fpl*.

fag [fæg] *n* (*BRIT col*: *cigarette*) cicca; (*: chore*) sfacchinata; (*US col*: *homosexual*) frocio.

fag end *n* (*BRIT col*) mozzicone *m*.

fagged out ['fægd-] *adj* (*BRIT col*) stanco(a) morto(a).

fail [feɪl] *vt* (*exam*) non superare; (*candidate*) bocciare; (*subj*: *courage, memory*) mancare a ♦ *vi* fallire; (*student*) essere respinto(a); (*supplies*) mancare; (*eyesight, health, light*: *also*: **be** ~**ing**) venire a mancare; (*brakes*) non funzionare; **to** ~ **to do sth** (*neglect*) mancare di fare qc; (*be unable*) non riuscire a fare qc; **without** ~ senza fallo; certamente.

failing ['feɪlɪŋ] *n* difetto ♦ *prep* in mancanza di; ~ **that** se questo non è possibile.

failsafe ['feɪlseɪf] *adj* (*device etc*) di sicurezza.

failure ['feɪljə*] *n* fallimento; (*person*) fallito/a; (*mechanical etc*) guasto; (*in exam*) insuccesso, bocciatura; (*of crops*) perdita; **his** ~ **to come** il fatto che non sia venuto; **it was a complete** ~ è stato un vero fiasco.

faint [feɪnt] *adj* debole; (*recollection*) vago(a); (*mark*) indistinto(a); (*smell, breeze, trace*) leggero(a) ♦ *vi* svenire; **to feel** ~ sentirsi svenire.

faintest ['feɪntɪst] *adj*: **I haven't the** ~ **idea** non ho la più pallida idea.

faint-hearted [feɪnt'hɑːtɪd] *adj* pusillanime.

faintly ['feɪntlɪ] *adv* debolmente; vagamente.

faintness ['feɪntnɪs] *n* debolezza.

fair [fɛə*] *adj* (*person, decision*) giusto(a), equo(a); (*hair etc*) biondo(a); (*skin, complexion*) bianco(a); (*weather*) bello(a), clemente; (*good enough*) assai buono(a); (*sizeable*) bello(a) ♦ *adv*: **to play** ~ giocare correttamente ♦ *n* fiera; (*BRIT*: *funfair*) luna park *m inv*; (*also*: **trade** ~) fiera campionaria; **it's not** ~! non è giusto!; **a** ~ **amount of** un bel po' di.

fair copy *n* bella copia.

fair game *n*: **to be** ~ (*person*) essere bersaglio legittimo.

fairground ['fɛəgraʊnd] *n* luna park *m inv.*

fair-haired [fɛə'hɛəd] *adj* (*person*) biondo(a).

fairly ['fɛəlɪ] *adv* equamente; (*quite*) abbastanza.

fairness ['fɛənɪs] *n* equità, giustizia; **in all** ~ per essere giusti, a dire il vero.

fair play *n* correttezza.

fair trade *n* commercio equo e solidale.

fairy ['fɛərɪ] *n* fata.

fairy godmother *n* fata buona.

fairy lights *npl* (*BRIT*) lanternine *fpl* colorate.

fairy tale *n* fiaba.

faith [feɪθ] *n* fede *f*; (*trust*) fiducia; (*sect*) religione *f*, fede *f*; **to have** ~ **in sb/sth** avere fiducia in qn/qc.

faithful ['feɪθful] *adj* fedele.

faithfully ['feɪθfəlɪ] *adv* fedelmente; **yours** ~ (*BRIT*: *in letters*) distinti saluti.

faith healer *n* guaritore/trice.

fake [feɪk] *n* imitazione *f*; (*picture*) falso; (*person*) impostore/a ♦ *adj* falso(a) ♦ *vt* (*accounts*) falsificare; (*illness*) fingere; (*painting*) contraffare; **his illness is a** ~ **fa** finta di essere malato.

falcon ['fɔːlkən] *n* falco, falcone *m*.

Falkland Islands ['fɔːlklənd-] *npl*: **the** ~ **le** isole Falkland.

fall [fɔːl] *n* caduta; (*decrease*) diminuzione *f*, calo; (*in temperature*) abbassamento; (*in price*) ribasso; (*US: autumn*) autunno ♦ *vi* (*pt* **fell**, *pp* **fallen** [fɛl, 'fɔːlən) cadere; (*temperature, price*) abbassare; **a** ~ **of earth** uno smottamento; **a** ~ **of snow** (*BRIT*) una nevicata; **to** ~ **in love (with sb/sth)** innamorarsi (di qn/qc); **to** ~ **short of** (*sb's expectations*) non corrispondere a; **to** ~ **flat** *vi* (*on one's face*) cadere bocconi; (*joke*) fare cilecca; (*plan*) fallire; *see also* **falls.**

▶**fall apart** *vi* cadere a pezzi.

▶**fall back** *vi* indietreggiare; (*MIL*) ritirarsi.

▶**fall back on** *vt fus* ripiegare su; **to have sth to** ~ **back on** avere qc di riserva.

▶**fall behind** *vi* rimanere indietro; (*fig: with payments*) essere in arretrato.

▶**fall down** *vi* (*person*) cadere; (*building, hopes*) crollare.

▶**fall for** *vt fus* (*person*) prendere una cotta per; **to** ~ **for a trick** (*or* **a story** *etc*) cascarci.

▶**fall in** *vi* crollare; (*MIL*) mettersi in riga.

▶**fall in with** *vt fus* (*sb's plans etc*) trovarsi d'accordo con.

▶**fall off** *vi* cadere; (*diminish*) diminuire, abbassarsi.

▶**fall out** *vi* (*friends etc*) litigare.

▶**fall over** *vi* cadere.

▶**fall through** *vi* (*plan, project*) fallire.

fallacy ['fæləsɪ] *n* errore *m*.

fallback ['fɔːlbæk] *adj*: ~ **position** posizione *f* di ripiego.

fallen ['fɔːlən] *pp of* **fall.**

fallible ['fælɪbl] *adj* fallibile.

falling ['fɔːlɪŋ] *adj*: ~ **market** (*COMM*) mercato in ribasso.

falling-off ['fɔːlɪŋ'ɔf] *n* calo.

fallopian tube [fə'ləupɪən-] *n* (*ANAT*) tuba di Falloppio.

fallout ['fɔːlaut] *n* fall-out *m*.

fallout shelter *n* rifugio antiatomico.

fallow ['fæləu] *adj* incolto(a); a maggese.

falls [fɔːlz] *npl* (*waterfall*) cascate *fpl*.

false [fɔːls] *adj* falso(a); **under** ~ **pretences** con l'inganno.

false alarm *n* falso allarme *m*.

falsehood ['fɔːlshud] *n* menzogna.

falsely ['fɔːlslɪ] *adv* (*accuse*) a torto.

false teeth *npl* (*BRIT*) denti *mpl* finti.

falsify ['fɔːlsɪfaɪ] *vt* falsificare; (*figures*) alterare.

falter ['fɔːltə*] *vi* esitare, vacillare.

fame [feɪm] *n* fama, celebrità.

familiar [fə'mɪlɪə*] *adj* familiare; (*common*) comune; (*close*) intimo(a); **to be** ~ **with** (*subject*) conoscere; **to make o.s.** ~ **with** familiarizzarsi con; **to be on** ~ **terms with** essere in confidenza con.

familiarity [fəmɪlɪ'ærɪtɪ] *n* familiarità; intimità.

familiarize [fə'mɪlɪəraɪz] *vt*: **to** ~ **sb with sth** far conoscere qc a qn.

family ['fæmɪlɪ] *n* famiglia.

family allowance *n* (*BRIT*) assegni *mpl* familiari.

family business *n* impresa familiare.

family credit *n* (*BRIT*) ≈ assegni *mpl* familiari.

family doctor *n* medico di famiglia.

family life *n* vita familiare.

family man *n* padre *m* di famiglia.

family planning clinic *n* consultorio familiare.

family tree *n* albergo genealogico.

famine ['fæmɪn] *n* carestia.

famished ['fæmɪʃt] *adj* affamato(a); **I'm** ~! (*col*) ho una fame da lupo!

famous ['feɪməs] *adj* famoso(a).

famously ['feɪməslɪ] *adv* (*get on*) a meraviglia.

fan [fæn] *n* (*folding*) ventaglio; (*machine*) ventilatore *m*; (*person*) ammiratore/trice; (*SPORT*) tifoso/a ♦ *vt* far vento a; (*fire, quarrel*) alimentare.

▶**fan out** *vi* spargersi (a ventaglio).

fanatic [fə'nætɪk] *n* fanatico/a.

fanatical [fə'nætɪkl] *adj* fanatico(a).

fan belt *n* cinghia del ventilatore.

fancied ['fænsɪd] *adj* immaginario(a).

fanciful ['fænsɪful] *adj* fantasioso(a); (*object*) di fantasia.

fan club *n* fan club *m inv*.

fancy ['fænsɪ] *n* immaginazione *f*, fantasia; (*whim*) capriccio ♦ *cpd* (di) fantasia *inv* ♦ *vt* (*feel like, want*) aver voglia di; (*imagine*) immaginare, credere; **to take a** ~ **to** incapricciarsi di; **it took** *or* **caught my** ~ mi è piaciuto; **when the** ~ **takes him** quando ne ha voglia; **to** ~ **that** immaginare che; **he fancies her** gli piace.

fancy dress *n* costume *m* (per maschera).

fancy-dress ball *n* ballo in maschera.

fancy goods *npl* articoli *mpl* di ogni genere.

fanfare ['fænfɛə*] *n* fanfara.

fanfold paper ['fænfəuld-] *n* carta a moduli

continui.

fang [fæŋ] n zanna; (of snake) dente m.

fan heater n (BRIT) stufa ad aria calda.

fanlight ['fænlaɪt] n lunetta.

fanny ['fænɪ] n (BRIT col!) figa(!); (US col) culo(!).

fantasize ['fæntəsaɪz] vi fantasticare, sognare.

fantastic [fæn'tæstɪk] adj fantastico(a).

fantasy ['fæntəsɪ] n fantasia, immaginazione f; fantasticheria; chimera.

fanzine ['fænziːn] n rivista specialistica (per appassionati).

FAO n abbr (= Food and Agriculture Organization) FAO f.

FAQ abbr (= free alongside quay) franco lungo banchina; (COMPUT: = frequently asked question(s)) FAQ.

far [fɑː*] adj: **the ~ side/end** l'altra parte/ l'altro capo; **the ~ left/right** (POL) l'estrema sinistra/destra ♦ adv lontano; **is it ~ to London?** è lontana Londra?; **it's not ~ (from here)** non è lontano (da qui); **~ away, ~ off** lontano, distante; **~ better** assai migliore; **~ from** lontano da; **by ~** di gran lunga; **as ~ back as the 13th century** già nel duecento; **go as ~ as the farm** vada fino alla fattoria; **as ~ as I know** per quel che so; **as ~ as possible** nei limiti del possibile; **how ~ have you got with your work?** dov'è arrivato con il suo lavoro?

faraway ['fɑːrəweɪ] adj lontano(a); (voice, look) assente.

farce [fɑːs] n farsa.

farcical ['fɑːsɪkəl] adj farsesco(a).

fare [fɛə*] n (on trains, buses) tariffa; (in taxi) prezzo della corsa; (food) vitto, cibo ♦ vi passarsela.

Far East n: **the ~** l'Estremo Oriente m.

farewell [fɛə'wɛl] excl, n addio ♦ cpd (party etc) d'addio.

far-fetched ['fɑː'fɛtʃt] adj (explanation) stiracchiato(a), forzato(a); (idea, scheme, story) inverosimile.

farm [fɑːm] n fattoria, podere m ♦ vt coltivare.

▶**farm out** vt (work) dare in consegna.

farmer ['fɑːmə*] n coltivatore/trice; agricoltore/trice.

farmhand ['fɑːmhænd] n bracciante m agricolo.

farmhouse ['fɑːmhaus] n fattoria.

farming ['fɑːmɪŋ] n agricoltura; **intensive ~** coltura intensiva; **sheep ~** allevamento di pecore.

farm labourer n = **farmhand**.

farmland ['fɑːmlænd] n terreno da coltivare.

farm produce n prodotti mpl agricoli.

farm worker n = **farmhand**.

farmyard ['fɑːmjɑːd] n aia.

Faroe Islands ['fɛərəu-], **Faroes** ['fɛərəuz] npl: **the ~** le isole Faeroer.

far-reaching ['fɑː'riːtʃɪŋ] adj di vasta portata.

far-sighted ['fɑː'saɪtɪd] adj presbite; (fig) lungimirante.

fart [fɑːt] (col!) n scoreggia(!) ♦ vi scoreggiare (!).

farther ['fɑːðə*] adv più lontano ♦ adj più lontano(a).

farthest ['fɑːðɪst] superlative of **far**.

FAS abbr (BRIT: = free alongside ship) franco banchina nave.

fascia ['feɪʃɪə] n (AUT) cruscotto; (of mobile phone) mascherina.

fascinate ['fæsɪneɪt] vt affascinare.

fascinating ['fæsɪneɪtɪŋ] adj affascinante.

fascination [fæsɪ'neɪʃən] n fascino.

fascism ['fæʃɪzəm] n fascismo.

fascist ['fæʃɪst] adj, n fascista (m/f).

fashion ['fæʃən] n moda; (manner) maniera, modo ♦ vt foggiare, formare; **in ~** alla moda; **out of ~** passato(a) di moda; **after a ~** (finish, manage etc) così così; **in the Greek ~** alla greca.

fashionable ['fæʃənəbl] adj alla moda, di moda; (writer) di grido.

fashion designer n disegnatore/trice di moda.

fashion show n sfilata di moda.

fast [fɑːst] adj rapido(a), svelto(a), veloce; (clock): **to be ~** andare avanti; (dye, colour) solido(a) ♦ adv rapidamente; (stuck, held) saldamente ♦ n digiuno ♦ vi digiunare; **~ asleep** profondamente addormentato; **as ~ as I can** più in fretta possibile; **my watch is 5 minutes ~** il mio orologio va avanti di 5 minuti; **to make a boat ~** (BRIT) ormeggiare una barca.

fasten ['fɑːsn] vt chiudere, fissare; (coat) abbottonare, allacciare ♦ vi chiudersi, fissarsi; abbottonarsi, allacciarsi.

▶**fasten (up)on** vt fus (idea) cogliere al volo.

fastener ['fɑːsnə*], **fastening** ['fɑːsnɪŋ] n fermaglio, chiusura; (BRIT: zip ~) chiusura lampo.

fast food n fast food m inv.

fastidious [fæs'tɪdɪəs] adj esigente, difficile.

fast lane n (AUT) ≈ corsia di sorpasso.

fat [fæt] adj grasso(a) ♦ n grasso; **to live off the ~ of the land** vivere nel lusso, avere

ogni ben di Dio.

fatal ['feɪtl] adj fatale; mortale; disastroso(a).

fatalism ['feɪtəlɪzəm] n fatalismo.

fatality [fə'tælɪtɪ] n (road death etc) morto/a, vittima.

fatally ['feɪtəlɪ] adv a morte.

fate [feɪt] n destino; (of person) sorte f; **to meet one's** ~ trovare la morte.

fated ['feɪtɪd] adj (governed by fate) destinato(a); (person, project etc) destinato(a) a finire male.

fateful ['feɪtful] adj fatidico(a).

fat-free ['fæt'friː] adj senza grassi.

father ['fɑːðə*] n padre m.

Father Christmas n Babbo Natale.

fatherhood ['fɑːðəhuːd] n paternità.

father-in-law ['fɑːðərɪnlɔː] n suocero.

fatherland ['fɑːðəlænd] n patria.

fatherly ['fɑːðəlɪ] adj paterno(a).

fathom ['fæðəm] n braccio (= 1828 mm) ♦ vt (mystery) penetrare, sondare.

fatigue [fə'tiːg] n stanchezza; (MIL) corvé f; **metal** ~ fatica del metallo.

fatness ['fætnɪs] n grassezza.

fatten ['fætn] vt, vi ingrassare; **chocolate is** ~**ing** la cioccolata fa ingrassare.

fatty ['fætɪ] adj (food) grasso(a) ♦ n (col) ciccione/a.

fatuous ['fætjuəs] adj fatuo(a).

faucet ['fɔːsɪt] n (US) rubinetto.

fault [fɔːlt] n colpa; (TENNIS) fallo; (defect) difetto; (GEO) faglia ♦ vt criticare; **it's my** ~ è colpa mia; **to find** ~ **with** trovare da ridire su; **at** ~ in fallo; **generous to a** ~ eccessivamente generoso.

faultless ['fɔːltlɪs] adj perfetto(a); senza difetto; impeccabile.

faulty ['fɔːltɪ] adj difettoso(a).

fauna ['fɔːnə] n fauna.

faux pas [fəu'pɑː] n gaffe f inv.

favour, (US) **favor** ['feɪvə*] n favore m ♦ vt (proposition) favorire, essere favorevole a; (pupil etc) favorire; (team, horse) dare per vincente; **to do sb a** ~ fare un favore or una cortesia a qn; **in** ~ **of** in favore di; **to be in** ~ **of sth/of doing sth** essere favorevole a qc/a fare qc; **to find** ~ **with sb** (subj: person) entrare nelle buone grazie di qn; (: suggestion) avere l'approvazione di qn.

favo(u)rable ['feɪvərəbl] adj favorevole.

favo(u)rably ['feɪvərəblɪ] adv favorevolmente.

favo(u)rite ['feɪvrɪt] adj, n favorito(a).

favo(u)ritism ['feɪvrɪtɪzəm] n favoritismo.

fawn [fɔːn] n daino ♦ adj (also: ~-**coloured**) marrone chiaro inv ♦ vi: **to** ~ (**up)on**
adulare servilmente.

fax [fæks] n (document, machine) facsimile m inv ♦ vt teletrasmettere, spedire in facsimile.

FBI n abbr (US: = Federal Bureau of Investigation) FBI f.

FCC n abbr (US) = Federal Communications Commission.

FCO n abbr (BRIT: = Foreign and Commonwealth Office) ≈ Ufficio affari esteri.

FD n abbr (US) = **fire department**.

FDA n abbr (US) = Food and Drug Administration.

FE n abbr = **further education**.

fear [fɪə*] n paura, timore m ♦ vt aver paura di, temere ♦ vi: **to** ~ **for** temere per, essere in ansia per; ~ **of heights** vertigini fpl; **for** ~ **of** per paura di; **to** ~ **that** avere paura di (or che + sub), temere di (or che + sub).

fearful ['fɪəful] adj pauroso(a); (sight, noise) terribile, spaventoso(a); (frightened): **to be** ~ **of** temere.

fearfully ['fɪəfəlɪ] adv (timidly) timorosamente; (col: very) terribilmente, spaventosamente.

fearless ['fɪəlɪs] adj intrepido(a), senza paura.

fearsome ['fɪəsəm] adj (opponent) formidabile, terribile; (sight) terrificante.

feasibility [fiːzə'bɪlɪtɪ] n praticabilità.

feasibility study n studio delle possibilità di realizzazione.

feasible ['fiːzəbl] adj fattibile, realizzabile.

feast [fiːst] n festa, banchetto; (REL: also: ~ **day**) festa ♦ vi banchettare; **to** ~ **on** godersi, gustare.

feat [fiːt] n impresa, fatto insigne.

feather ['fɛðə*] n penna ♦ cpd (mattress, bed, pillow) di piume ♦ vt: **to** ~ **one's nest** (fig) arricchirsi.

feather-weight ['fɛðəweɪt] n peso m piuma inv.

feature ['fiːtʃə*] n caratteristica; (article) articolo ♦ vt (subj: film) avere come protagonista ♦ vi figurare; ~**s** npl (of face) fisionomia; **a (special)** ~ **on sth/sb** un servizio speciale su qc/qn; **it** ~**d prominently in** ... ha avuto un posto di prima importanza in ....

feature film n film m inv principale.

featureless ['fiːtʃəlɪs] adj anonimo(a), senza caratteri distinti.

Feb. [fɛb] abbr (= February) feb.

February ['fɛbruərɪ] n febbraio; for phrases see also **July**.

feces ['fiːsiːz] npl (US) = **faeces**.

feckless ['fɛklɪs] *adj* irresponsabile, incosciente.

Fed [fɛd] *abbr* (*US*) = **federal; federation.**

fed [fɛd] *pt, pp of* **feed; to be** ~ **up** essere stufo(a).

Fed. [fɛd] *n abbr* (*US col*) = **Federal Reserve Board.**

federal ['fɛdərəl] *adj* federale.

Federal Republic of Germany (FRG) *n* Repubblica Federale Tedesca (RFT).

Federal Reserve Board (Fed.) *n* (*US*) *organo di controllo del sistema bancario statunitense.*

Federal Trade Commission (FTC) *n* (*US*) *organismo di protezione contro le pratiche commerciali abusive.*

federation [fɛdə'reɪʃən] *n* federazione *f.*

fee [fiː] *n* pagamento *m*; (*of doctor, lawyer*) onorario; (*for examination*) tassa d'esame; **school** ~**s** tasse *fpl* scolastiche; **entrance** ~, **membership** ~ quota d'iscrizione; **for a small** ~ per una somma modesta.

feeble ['fiːbl] *adj* debole.

feeble-minded [fiːbl'maɪndɪd] *adj* deficiente.

feed [fiːd] *n* (*of baby*) pappa ♦ *vt* (*pt, pp* **fed** [fɛd]) nutrire; (*horse etc*) dare da mangiare a; (*fire, machine*) alimentare ♦ *vi* (*baby, animal*) mangiare; **to** ~ **material into sth** introdurre materiale in qc; **to** ~ **data/information into sth** inserire dati/ informazioni in qc.

▶**feed back** *vt* (*results*) riferire.

▶**feed on** *vt fus* nutrirsi di.

feedback ['fiːdbæk] *n* feed-back *m*; (*from person*) reazioni *fpl.*

feeder ['fiːdə*] *n* (*bib*) bavaglino.

feeding bottle ['fiːdɪŋ-] *n* (*BRIT*) biberon *m inv.*

feel [fiːl] *n* sensazione *f*; (*sense of touch*) tatto; (*of substance*) consistenza ♦ *vt* (*pt, pp* **felt** [fɛlt]) toccare; palpare; tastare; (*cold, pain, anger*) sentire; (*grief*) provare; (*think, believe*): **to** ~ (**that**) pensare che; **I** ~ **that you ought to do it** penso che dovreste farlo; **to** ~ **hungry/cold** aver fame/ freddo; **to** ~ **lonely/better** sentirsi solo/ meglio; **I don't** ~ **well** non mi sento bene; **to** ~ **sorry for** dispiacersi per; **it** ~**s soft** è morbido al tatto; **it** ~**s colder out here** sembra più freddo qui fuori; **it** ~**s like velvet** sembra velluto (al tatto); **to** ~ **like** (*want*) aver voglia di; **to** ~ **about** *or* **around for** cercare a tastoni; **to** ~ **about** *or* **around in one's pocket for** frugarsi in tasca per cercare; **I'm still** ~**ing my way** (*fig*) sto ancora tastando il terreno; **to get the** ~ **of sth** (*fig*) abituarsi a qc.

feeler ['fiːlə*] *n* (*of insect*) antenna; **to put out** ~**s** (*fig*) fare un sondaggio.

feelgood ['fiːlgud] *adj* (*film, song*) allegro(a) e a lieto fine.

feeling ['fiːlɪŋ] *n* sensazione *f*; sentimento; (*impression*) senso, impressione *f*; **to hurt sb's** ~**s** offendere qn; **what are your** ~**s about the matter?** che cosa ne pensa?; **my** ~ **is that** ... ho l'impressione che ...; **I got the** ~ **that** ... ho avuto l'impressione che ...; ~**s ran high about it** la cosa aveva provocato grande eccitazione.

fee-paying school ['fiːpeɪɪŋ-] *n* scuola privata.

feet [fiːt] *npl of* **foot.**

feign [feɪn] *vt* fingere, simulare.

felicitous [fɪ'lɪsɪtəs] *adj* felice.

fell [fɛl] *pt of* **fall** ♦ *vt* (*tree*) abbattere; (*person*) atterrare ♦ *adj*: **with one** ~ **blow** con un colpo terribile; **at one** ~ **swoop** in un colpo solo ♦ *n* (*BRIT*: *mountain*) monte *m*; (: *moorland*): **the** ~**s** la brughiera.

fellow ['fɛləu] *n* individuo, tipo; (*comrade*) compagno; (*of learned society*) membro; (*of university*) ≈ docente *m/f* ♦ *cpd*: **their** ~ **prisoners/students** i loro compagni di prigione/studio.

fellow citizen *n* concittadino/a.

fellow countryman *n* compatriota *m.*

fellow feeling *n* simpatia.

fellow men *npl* simili *mpl.*

fellowship ['fɛləuʃɪp] *n* associazione *f*; compagnia; (*SCOL*) specie di borsa di studio universitaria.

fellow traveller *n* compagno/a di viaggio; (*POL*) simpatizzante *m/f.*

fell-walking ['fɛlwɔːkɪŋ] *n* (*BRIT*) passeggiate *fpl* in montagna.

felon ['fɛlən] *n* (*LAW*) criminale *m/f.*

felony ['fɛlənɪ] *n* (*LAW*) reato, crimine *m.*

felt [fɛlt] *pt, pp of* **feel** ♦ *n* feltro.

felt-tip pen ['fɛlttɪp-] *n* pennarello.

female ['fiːmeɪl] *n* (*ZOOL*) femmina; (*pej*: *woman*) donna, femmina ♦ *adj* femminile; (*BIOL, ELEC*) femmina *inv*; **male and** ~ **students** studenti e studentesse.

female impersonator *n* (*THEAT*) *attore comico che fa parti da donna.*

feminine ['fɛmɪnɪn] *adj, n* femminile (*m*).

femininity [fɛmɪ'nɪnɪtɪ] *n* femminilità.

feminism ['fɛmɪnɪzəm] *n* femminismo.

feminist ['fɛmɪnɪst] *n* femminista *m/f.*

fen [fɛn] *n* (*BRIT*): **the F**~**s** la regione delle Fen.

fence [fɛns] *n* recinto; (*SPORT*) ostacolo; (*col*: *person*) ricettatore/trice ♦ *vt* (*also*: ~ **in**) recingere ♦ *vi* schermire; **to sit on the** ~ (*fig*) rimanere neutrale.

fencing ['fɛnsɪŋ] *n* (*SPORT*) scherma.
fend [fɛnd] *vi*: **to ~ for o.s.** arrangiarsi.
▶**fend off** *vt* (*attack, attacker*) respingere,
difendersi da; (*blow*) parare; (*awkward
question*) eludere.
fender ['fɛndə*] *n* parafuoco; (*US*)
parafango; paraurti *m inv*.
fennel ['fɛnl] *n* finocchio.
ferment *vi* [fə'mɛnt] fermentare ♦ *n*
['fə:mɛnt] agitazione *f*, eccitazione *f*.
fermentation [fə:mɛn'teɪʃən] *n*
fermentazione *f*.
fern [fə:n] *n* felce *f*.
ferocious [fə'rəʊʃəs] *adj* feroce.
ferocity [fə'rɔsɪtɪ] *n* ferocità.
ferret ['fɛrɪt] *n* furetto.
▶**ferret about, ferret around** *vi* frugare.
▶**ferret out** *vt* (*person*) scovare, scoprire;
(*secret, truth*) scoprire.
ferry ['fɛrɪ] *n* (*small*) traghetto; (*large: also:*
~**boat**) nave *f* traghetto *inv* ♦ *vt*
traghettare; **to ~ sth/sb across** *or* **over**
traghettare qc/qn da una parte all'altra.
ferryman ['fɛrɪmən] *n* traghettatore *m*.
fertile ['fə:taɪl] *adj* fertile; (*BIOL*)
fecondo(a); ~ **period** periodo di
fecondità.
fertility [fə'tɪlɪtɪ] *n* fertilità; fecondità.
fertility drug *n* farmaco fecondativo.
fertilize ['fə:tɪlaɪz] *vt* fertilizzare;
fecondare.
fertilizer ['fə:tɪlaɪzə*] *n* fertilizzante *m*.
fervent ['fə:vənt] *adj* ardente, fervente.
fervour, (*US*) **fervor** ['fə:və*] *n* fervore *m*,
ardore *m*.
fester ['fɛstə*] *vi* suppurare.
festival ['fɛstɪvəl] *n* (*REL*) festa; (*ART, MUS*)
festival *m inv*.
festive ['fɛstɪv] *adj* di festa; **the ~ season**
(*BRIT: Christmas*) il periodo delle feste.
festivities [fɛs'tɪvɪtɪz] *npl* festeggiamenti
mpl.
festoon [fɛ'stu:n] *vt*: **to ~ with** ornare di;
decorare con.
fetch [fɛtʃ] *vt* andare a prendere; (*sell for*)
essere venduto(a) per; **how much did it
~?** a *or* per quanto lo ha venduto?
▶**fetch up** *vi* (*BRIT*) andare a finire.
fetching ['fɛtʃɪŋ] *adj* attraente.
fête [feɪt] *n* festa.
fetid ['fɛtɪd] *adj* fetido(a).
fetish ['fɛtɪʃ] *n* feticcio.
fetter ['fɛtə*] *vt* (*person*) incatenare; (*horse*)
legare, (*fig*) ostacolare.
fetters ['fɛtəz] *npl* catene *fpl*.
fettle ['fɛtl] *n* (*BRIT*): **in fine ~** in gran
forma.
fetus ['fi:təs] *n* (*US*) = **foetus**.

feud [fju:d] *n* contesa, lotta ♦ *vi* essere in
lotta; **a family ~** una lite in famiglia.
feudal ['fju:dl] *adj* feudale.
feudalism ['fju:dəlɪzəm] *n* feudalesimo.
fever ['fi:və*] *n* febbre *f*; **he has a ~** ha la
febbre.
feverish ['fi:vərɪʃ] *adj* (*also fig*) febbrile;
(*person*) febbricitante.
few [fju:] *adj* pochi(e) ♦ *pron* alcuni(e); ~
succeed pochi ci riescono; **they were ~**
erano pochi; **a ~ ...** qualche ...; **I know a
~** ne conosco alcuni; **a good ~, quite a ~**
parecchi; **in the next ~ days** nei prossimi
giorni; **in the past ~ days** negli ultimi
giorni, in questi ultimi giorni; **every ~
days/months** ogni due o tre giorni/mesi;
a ~ more days qualche altro giorno.
fewer ['fju:ə*] *adj* meno *inv*; meno
numerosi(e) ♦ *pron* meno; **they are ~ now**
adesso ce ne sono di meno.
fewest ['fju:ɪst] *adj* il minor numero di.
FFA *n abbr* = *Future Farmers of America*.
FH *abbr* (*BRIT*) = **fire hydrant**.
FHA *n abbr* (*US*) = *Federal Housing
Administration*.
fiancé [fɪ'ɑ:ŋseɪ] *n* fidanzato.
fiancée [fɪ'ɑ:ŋseɪ] *n* fidanzata.
fiasco [fɪ'æskəʊ] *n* fiasco.
fib [fɪb] *n* piccola bugia.
fibre, (*US*) **fiber** ['faɪbə*] *n* fibra.
fibreboard, (*US*) **fiberboard** ['faɪbəbɔ:d] *n*
pannello di fibre.
fibre-glass, (*US*) **fiber-glass** ['faɪbəglɑ:s] *n*
fibra di vetro.
fibrositis [faɪbrə'saɪtɪs] *n* cellulite *f*.
FICA *n abbr* (*US*) = *Federal Insurance
Contributions Act*.
fickle ['fɪkl] *adj* incostante, capriccioso(a).
fiction ['fɪkʃən] *n* narrativa; (*sth made up*)
finzione *f*.
fictional ['fɪkʃənl] *adj* immaginario(a).
fictionalize ['fɪkʃənəlaɪz] *vt* romanzare.
fictitious [fɪk'tɪʃəs] *adj* fittizio(a).
fiddle ['fɪdl] *n* (*MUS*) violino; (*cheating*)
imbroglio; truffa ♦ *vt* (*BRIT: accounts*)
falsificare, falsare; **tax ~** frode *f* fiscale;
to work a ~ fare un imbroglio.
▶**fiddle with** *vt fus* gingillarsi con.
fiddler ['fɪdlə*] *n* violinista *m/f*.
fiddly ['fɪdlɪ] *adj* (*task*) da certosino; (*object*)
complesso(a).
fidelity [fɪ'dɛlɪtɪ] *n* fedeltà; (*accuracy*)
esattezza.
fidget ['fɪdʒɪt] *vi* agitarsi.
fidgety ['fɪdʒɪtɪ] *adj* agitato(a).
fiduciary [fɪ'du:ʃɪərɪ] *n* fiduciario.
field [fi:ld] *n* (*gen, COMPUT*) campo; **to lead
the ~** (*SPORT, COMM*) essere in testa,

essere al primo posto; **to have a ~ day** (*fig*) divertirsi, spassarsela.

field glasses *npl* binocolo (da campagna).

field hospital *n* ospedale *m* da campo.

field marshal (FM) *n* feldmaresciallo.

fieldwork ['fiːldwəːk] *n* ricerche *fpl* esterne; (*ARCHEOLOGY, GEO*) lavoro sul campo.

fiend [fiːnd] *n* demonio.

fiendish ['fiːndɪʃ] *adj* demoniaco(a).

fierce [fɪəs] *adj* (*look, fighting*) fiero(a); (*wind*) furioso(a); (*attack*) feroce; (*enemy*) acerrimo(a).

fiery ['faɪərɪ] *adj* ardente; infocato(a).

FIFA ['fiːfə] *n abbr* (= *Fédération Internationale de Football Association*) F.I.F.A. *f*.

fifteen [fɪf'tiːn] *num* quindici.

fifth [fɪfθ] *num* quinto(a).

fiftieth ['fɪftɪɪθ] *num* cinquantesimo(a).

fifty ['fɪftɪ] *num* cinquanta.

fifty-fifty ['fɪftɪ'fɪftɪ] *adj, adv*: **to go ~ with sb** fare a metà con qn; **we have a ~ chance of success** abbiamo una probabilità su due di successo.

fig [fɪg] *n* fico.

fight [faɪt] *n* zuffa, rissa; (*MIL*) battaglia, combattimento; (*against cancer etc*) lotta ♦ *vb* (*pt, pp* **fought** [fɔːt]) *vt* combattere; (*cancer, alcoholism*) lottare contro, combattere; (*LAW: case*) difendere ♦ *vi* battersi, combattere; (*quarrel*): **to ~ (with sb)** litigare (con qn); (*fig*): **to ~ (for/against)** lottare (per/contro).

▶**fight back** *vi* difendersi; (*SPORT, after illness*) riprendersi ♦ *vt* (*tears*) ricacciare.

▶**fight down** *vt* (*anger, anxiety*) vincere; (*urge*) reprimere.

▶**fight off** *vt* (*attack, attacker*) respingere; (*disease, sleep, urge*) lottare contro.

▶**fight out** *vt*: **to ~ it out** risolvere la questione a pugni.

fighter ['faɪtə*] *n* combattente *m*; (*plane*) aeroplano da caccia.

fighter-bomber ['faɪtəbɔmə*] *n* cacciabombardiere *m*.

fighter pilot *n* pilota *m* di caccia.

fighting ['faɪtɪŋ] *n* combattimento; (*in streets*) scontri *mpl*.

figment ['fɪgmənt] *n*: **a ~ of the imagination** un parto della fantasia.

figurative ['fɪgjurətɪv] *adj* figurato(a).

figure ['fɪgə*] *n* (*DRAWING, GEOM, person*) figura; (*number, cipher*) cifra; (*body, outline*) forma ♦ *vi* (*appear*) figurare; (*US: make sense*) spiegarsi; essere logico(a) ♦ *vt* (*US: think, calculate*) pensare, immaginare; **public ~** personaggio pubblico; **~ of speech** figura retorica.

▶**figure on** *vt fus* (*US*) contare su.

▶**figure out** *vt* riuscire a capire; calcolare.

figurehead ['fɪgəhɛd] *n* (*NAUT*) polena; (*pej*) prestanome *m/f inv*.

figure skating *n* pattinaggio artistico.

Fiji (Islands) ['fiːdʒiː-] *n(pl)* le (isole) Figi.

filament ['fɪləmənt] *n* filamento.

filch [fɪltʃ] *vt* (*col: steal*) grattare.

file [faɪl] *n* (*tool*) lima; (*for nails*) limetta; (*dossier*) incartamento; (*in cabinet*) scheda; (*folder*) cartellina; (*for loose leaf*) raccoglitore *m*; (*row*) fila; (*COMPUT*) archivio, file *m inv* ♦ *vt* (*nails, wood*) limare; (*papers*) archiviare; (*LAW: claim*) presentare ♦ *vi*: **to ~ in/out** entrare/uscire in fila; **to ~ past** marciare in fila davanti a; **to ~ a suit against sb** intentare causa contro qn.

file name *n* (*COMPUT*) nome *m* del file.

filibuster ['fɪlɪbʌstə*] (*esp US POL*) *n* (*also*: **~er**) ostruzionista *m/f* ♦ *vi* fare ostruzionismo.

filing ['faɪlɪŋ] *n* archiviare *m*; see also **filings**.

filing cabinet *n* casellario.

filing clerk *n* archivista *m/f*.

filings ['faɪlɪŋz] *npl* limatura.

Filipino [fɪlɪ'piːnəu] *n* filippino/a; (*LING*) tagal *m*.

fill [fɪl] *vt* riempire; (*tooth*) otturare; (*job*) coprire; (*supply: order, requirements, need*) soddisfare ♦ *n*: **to eat one's ~** mangiare a sazietà; **we've already ~ed that vacancy** abbiamo già assunto qualcuno per quel posto.

▶**fill in** *vt* (*hole*) riempire; (*form*) compilare; (*details, report*) completare ♦ *vi*: **to ~ in for sb** sostituire qn; **to ~ sb in on sth** (*col*) mettere qn al corrente di qc.

▶**fill out** *vt* (*form, receipt*) riempire.

▶**fill up** *vt* riempire ♦ *vi* (*AUT*) fare il pieno; **~ it up, please** (*AUT*) mi faccia il pieno, per piacere.

fillet ['fɪlɪt] *n* filetto.

fillet steak *n* bistecca di filetto.

filling ['fɪlɪŋ] *n* (*CULIN*) impasto, ripieno; (*for tooth*) otturazione *f*.

filling station *n* stazione *f* di rifornimento.

fillip ['fɪlɪp] *n* incentivo, stimolo.

filly ['fɪlɪ] *n* puledra.

film [fɪlm] *n* (*CINE*) film *m inv*; (*PHOT*) pellicola; (*thin layer*) velo ♦ *vt* (*scene*) filmare.

film script *n* copione *m*.

film star *n* divo/a dello schermo.

filmstrip ['fɪlmstrɪp] *n* filmina.

film studio *n* studio cinematografico.

Filofax ® ['faɪləufæks] *n* agenda ad anelli.

filter ['fɪltə*] *n* filtro ♦ *vt* filtrare.

▶**filter in, filter through** *vi* (*news*) trapelare.

filter coffee *n* caffè *m* da passare al filtro.

filter lane *n* (*BRIT AUT*) corsia di svincolo.

filter tip *n* filtro.

filth [fɪlθ] *n* sporcizia; (*fig*) oscenità.

filthy ['fɪlθɪ] *adj* lordo(a), sozzo(a); (*language*) osceno(a).

fin [fɪn] *n* (*of fish*) pinna.

final ['faɪnl] *adj* finale, ultimo(a); definitivo(a) ♦ *n* (*SPORT*) finale *f*; ~**s** *npl* (*SCOL*) esami *mpl* finali; ~ **demand** ingiunzione *f* di pagamento.

finale [fɪ'nɑːlɪ] *n* finale *m*.

finalist ['faɪnəlɪst] *n* (*SPORT*) finalista *m/f*.

finality [faɪ'nælɪtɪ] *n* irrevocabilità; **with an air of** ~ con risolutezza.

finalize ['faɪnəlaɪz] *vt* mettere a punto.

finally ['faɪnəlɪ] *adv* (*lastly*) alla fine; (*eventually*) finalmente; (*once and for all*) definitivamente.

finance [faɪ'næns] *n* finanza; (*funds*) fondi *mpl*, capitale *m* ♦ *vt* finanziare; ~**s** *npl* finanze *fpl*.

financial [faɪ'nænʃəl] *adj* finanziario(a); ~ **statement** estratto conto finanziario.

financial adviser *n* consulente *m/f* finanziario(a).

financially [faɪ'nænʃəlɪ] *adv* finanziariamente.

financial year *n* anno finanziario, esercizio finanziario.

financier [faɪ'nænsɪə*] *n* finanziatore *m*.

find [faɪnd] *vt* (*pt, pp* **found** [faund]) trovare; (*lost object*) ritrovare ♦ *n* trovata, scoperta; **to** ~ **(some) difficulty in doing sth** trovare delle difficoltà nel fare qc; **to** ~ **sb guilty** (*LAW*) giudicare qn colpevole.

▶**find out** *vt* informarsi di; (*truth, secret*) scoprire; (*person*) cogliere in fallo ♦ *vi*: **to** ~ **out about** informarsi su; (*by chance*) venire a sapere.

findings ['faɪndɪŋz] *npl* (*LAW*) sentenza, conclusioni *fpl*; (*of report*) conclusioni.

fine [faɪn] *adj* bello(a); ottimo(a); (*thin, subtle*) fine ♦ *adv* (*well*) molto bene; (*small*) finemente ♦ *n* (*LAW*) multa ♦ *vt* (*LAW*) multare; **he's** ~ sta bene; **the weather is** ~ il tempo è bello; **you're doing** ~ te la cavi benissimo; **to cut it** ~ (*of time, money*) farcela per un pelo.

fine arts *npl* belle arti *fpl*.

finely ['faɪnlɪ] *adv* (*splendidly*) in modo stupendo; (*chop*) finemente; (*adjust*) con precisione.

fine print *n*: **the** ~ i caratteri minuti.

finery ['faɪnərɪ] *n* abiti *mpl* eleganti.

finesse [fɪ'nɛs] *n* finezza.

fine-tooth comb ['faɪntuːθ-] *n*: **to go through sth with a** ~ (*fig*) passare qc al setaccio.

finger ['fɪŋgə*] *n* dito ♦ *vt* toccare, tastare.

fingernail ['fɪŋgəneɪl] *n* unghia.

fingerprint ['fɪŋgəprɪnt] *n* impronta digitale ♦ *vt* (*person*) prendere le impronte digitali di.

fingerstall ['fɪŋgəstɔːl] *n* ditale *m*.

fingertip ['fɪŋgətɪp] *n* punta del dito; **to have sth at one's** ~**s** (*fig*) avere qc sulla punta delle dita.

finicky ['fɪnɪkɪ] *adj* esigente, pignolo(a); minuzioso(a).

finish ['fɪnɪʃ] *n* fine *f*; (*SPORT: place*) traguardo; (*polish etc*) finitura ♦ *vt* finire; (*use up*) esaurire ♦ *vi* finire; (*session*) terminare; **to** ~ **doing sth** finire di fare qc; **to** ~ **first/second** (*SPORT*) arrivare primo/secondo; **she's** ~**ed with him** ha chiuso con lui.

▶**finish off** *vt* compiere; (*kill*) uccidere.

▶**finish up** *vi, vt* finire.

finished ['fɪnɪʃt] *adj* (*product*) finito(a); (*performance*) perfetto(a); (*col: tired*) sfinito(a).

finishing line ['fɪnɪʃɪŋ-] *n* linea d'arrivo.

finishing school *n* scuola privata di perfezionamento (*per signorine*).

finishing touches *npl* ultimi ritocchi *mpl*.

finite ['faɪnaɪt] *adj* limitato(a); (*verb*) finito(a).

Finland ['fɪnlənd] *n* Finlandia.

Finn [fɪn] *n* finlandese *m/f*.

Finnish ['fɪnɪʃ] *adj* finlandese ♦ *n* (*LING*) finlandese *m*.

fiord [fjɔːd] *n* fiordo.

fir [fəː*] *n* abete *m*.

fire [faɪə*] *n* fuoco; incendio ♦ *vt* (*discharge*): **to** ~ **a gun** scaricare un fucile; (*fig*) infiammare; (*dismiss*) licenziare ♦ *vi* sparare, far fuoco; **on** ~ in fiamme; **insured against** ~ assicurato contro gli incendi; **electric/gas** ~ stufa elettrica/a gas; **to set** ~ **to sth, set sth on** ~ dar fuoco a qc, incendiare qc; **to be/come under** ~ (**from**) essere/finire sotto il fuoco *or* il tiro (di).

fire alarm *n* allarme *m* d'incendio.

firearm ['faɪərɑːm] *n* arma da fuoco.

fire brigade *n* (*BRIT*) (corpo dei) pompieri *mpl*.

fire chief *n* (*US*) = **fire master**.

fire department *n* (*US*) = **fire brigade**.

fire door *n* porta *f* rompifuoco *inv*.

fire drill *n* esercitazione *f* antincendio.

fire engine *n* autopompa.

fire escape *n* scala di sicurezza.

fire extinguisher n estintore m.

fireguard ['faɪəgɑːd] n (BRIT) parafuoco.

fire hazard n: **that's a** ~ comporta rischi in caso d'incendio.

fire hydrant n idrante m.

fire insurance n assicurazione f contro gli incendi.

fireman ['faɪəmən] n pompiere m.

fire master n (BRIT) comandante m dei vigili del fuoco.

fireplace ['faɪəpleɪs] n focolare m.

fireplug ['faɪəplʌg] n (US) = **fire hydrant**.

fire practice n = **fire drill**.

fireproof ['faɪəpruːf] adj resistente al fuoco.

fire regulations npl norme fpl antincendio.

fire screen n parafuoco.

fireside ['faɪəsaɪd] n angolo del focolare.

fire station n caserma dei pompieri.

firewood ['faɪəwud] n legna.

firework ['faɪəwəːk] n fuoco d'artificio.

firing ['faɪərɪŋ] n (MIL) spari mpl, tiro.

firing line n linea del fuoco; **to be in the** ~ (fig) essere sotto tiro.

firing squad n plotone m d'esecuzione.

firm [fəːm] adj fermo(a); (offer, decision) definitivo(a) ♦ n ditta, azienda; **to be a** ~ **believer in sth** credere fermamente in qc.

firmly ['fəːmlɪ] adv fermamente.

firmness ['fəːmnɪs] n fermezza.

first [fəːst] adj primo(a) ♦ adv (before others) il primo, la prima; (before other things) per primo; (for the first time) per la prima volta; (when listing reasons etc) per prima cosa ♦ n (person: in race) primo/a; (BRIT SCOL) laurea con lode; (AUT) prima; **at** ~ dapprima, all'inizio; ~ **of all** prima di tutto; **in the** ~ **instance** prima di tutto, in primo luogo; **I'll do it** ~ **thing tomorrow** lo farò per prima cosa domani; **from the (very)** ~ fin dall'inizio, fin dal primo momento; **the** ~ **of January** il primo (di) gennaio.

first aid n pronto soccorso.

first-aid kit ['fəːst'eɪd-] n cassetta pronto soccorso.

first-class ['fəːst'klɑːs] adj di prima classe.

first-class mail n ≈ espresso.

first-hand ['fəːst'hænd] adj di prima mano; diretto(a).

first lady n (US) moglie f del presidente.

firstly ['fəːstlɪ] adv in primo luogo.

first name n nome m di battesimo.

first night n (THEAT) prima.

first-rate ['fəːst'reɪt] adj di prima qualità, ottimo(a).

first-time buyer ['fəːsttaɪm-] n acquirente m/f di prima casa.

First World War n: **the** ~ la prima guerra mondiale.

fir tree n abete m.

fiscal ['fɪskəl] adj fiscale; ~ **year** anno fiscale.

fish [fɪʃ] n (pl inv) pesce m ♦ vt, vi pescare; **to** ~ **a river** pescare in un fiume; **to go** ~**ing** andare a pesca.

▶**fish out** vt (from water) ripescare; (from box etc) tirare fuori.

fish-and-chip shop [fɪʃən'tʃɪp-] n ≈ friggitoria; see **chip shop**.

fishbone ['fɪʃbəun] n lisca, spina.

fisherman ['fɪʃəmən] n pescatore m.

fishery ['fɪʃərɪ] n zona da pesca.

fish factory n (BRIT) fabbrica per la lavorazione del pesce.

fish farm n vivaio.

fish fingers npl (BRIT) bastoncini mpl di pesce (surgelati).

fish hook n amo.

fishing boat ['fɪʃɪŋ-] n barca da pesca.

fishing industry n industria della pesca.

fishing line n lenza.

fishing net n rete f da pesca.

fishing rod n canna da pesca.

fishing tackle n attrezzatura da pesca.

fish market n mercato del pesce.

fishmonger ['fɪʃmʌŋgə*] n pescivendolo; ~**'s (shop)** pescheria.

fish slice n (BRIT) posata per servire il pesce.

fish sticks npl (US) = **fish fingers**.

fishy ['fɪʃɪ] adj (fig) sospetto(a).

fission ['fɪʃən] n fissione f; **atomic/nuclear** ~ fissione atomica/nucleare.

fissure ['fɪʃə*] n fessura.

fist [fɪst] n pugno.

fistfight ['fɪstfaɪt] n scazzottata.

fit [fɪt] adj (MED, SPORT) in forma; (proper) adatto(a), appropriato(a); conveniente ♦ vt (subj: clothes) stare bene a; (match: facts etc) concordare con; (: description) corrispondere a; (adjust) aggiustare; (put in, attach) mettere; installare; (equip) fornire, equipaggiare ♦ vi (clothes) stare bene; (parts) andare bene, adattarsi; (in space, gap) entrare ♦ n (MED) attacco; ~ **to** in grado di; ~ **for** adatto(a) a; degno(a) di; **to keep** ~ tenersi in forma; ~ **for work** (after illness) in grado di riprendere il lavoro; **do as you think** or **see** ~ faccia come meglio crede; **this dress is a tight/ good** ~ questo vestito è stretto/sta bene; ~ **of anger/enthusiasm** accesso d'ira/ d'entusiasmo; **to have a** ~ (MED) avere un attacco di convulsioni; (col) andare su tutte le furie; **by** ~**s and starts** a sbalzi.

▶**fit in** vi accordarsi; adattarsi ♦ vt (object)

far entrare; (*fig: appointment, visitor*) trovare il tempo per; **to ~ in with sb's plans** adattarsi ai progetti di qn.

▶**fit out** *vt* (*BRIT: also:* ~ **up**) equipaggiare.

fitful ['fɪtful] *adj* saltuario(a).

fitment ['fɪtmənt] *n* componibile *m*.

fitness ['fɪtnɪs] *n* (*MED*) forma fisica; (*of remark*) appropriatezza.

fitted ['fɪtɪd] *adj*: ~ **carpet** moquette *f inv*; ~ **cupboards** armadi *mpl* a muro; ~ **kitchen** (*BRIT*) cucina componibile.

fitter ['fɪtə*] *n* aggiustatore *m or* montatore *m* meccanico; (*DRESSMAKING*) sarto/a.

fitting ['fɪtɪŋ] *adj* appropriato(a) ♦ *n* (*of dress*) prova; (*of piece of equipment*) montaggio, aggiustaggio; *see also* **fittings**.

fitting room *n* (*in shop*) camerino.

fittings ['fɪtɪŋz] *npl* impianti *mpl*.

five [faɪv] *num* cinque.

five-day week ['faɪvdeɪ-] *n* settimana di 5 giorni (lavorativi).

fiver ['faɪvə*] *n* (*col: BRIT*) biglietto da cinque sterline; (: *US*) biglietto da cinque dollari.

fix [fɪks] *vt* fissare; (*mend*) riparare; (*make ready: meal, drink*) preparare ♦ *n*: **to be in a** ~ essere nei guai; **the fight was a** ~ (*col*) l'incontro è stato truccato.

▶**fix up** *vt* (*arrange: date, meeting*) fissare, stabilire; **to** ~ **sb up with sth** procurare qc a qn.

fixation [fɪk'seɪʃən] *n* (*PSYCH, fig*) fissazione *f*, ossessione *f*.

fixed [fɪkst] *adj* (*prices etc*) fisso(a); **there's a** ~ **charge** c'è una quota fissa; **how are you** ~ **for money?** (*col*) a soldi come stai?

fixed assets *npl* beni *mpl* patrimoniali.

fixed penalty (fine) *n* contravvenzione *f* a importo fisso.

fixture ['fɪkstʃə*] *n* impianto (fisso); (*SPORT*) incontro (del calendario sportivo).

fizz [fɪz] *vi* frizzare.

fizzle ['fɪzl] *vi* frizzare; (*also:* ~ **out**: *enthusiasm, interest*) smorzarsi, svanire; (: *plan*) fallire.

fizzy ['fɪzɪ] *adj* frizzante; gassato(a).

fjord [fjɔːd] *n* = **fiord**.

FL, Fla. *abbr* (*US*) = *Florida*.

flabbergasted ['flæbəgɑːstɪd] *adj* sbalordito(a).

flabby ['flæbɪ] *adj* flaccido(a).

flag [flæg] *n* bandiera; (*also:* ~**stone**) pietra da lastricare ♦ *vi* stancarsi; affievolirsi; ~ **of convenience** bandiera di convenienza.

▶**flag down** *vt* fare segno (di fermarsi) a.

flagon ['flægən] *n* bottiglione *m*.

flagpole ['flægpəul] *n* albero.

flagrant ['fleɪgrənt] *adj* flagrante.

flag stop *n* (*US: for bus*) fermata facoltativa, fermata a richiesta.

flair [flɛə*] *n* (*for business etc*) fiuto; (*for languages etc*) facilità.

flak [flæk] *n* (*MIL*) fuoco d'artiglieria; (*col: criticism*) critiche *fpl*.

flake [fleɪk] *n* (*of rust, paint*) scaglia; (*of snow, soap powder*) fiocco ♦ *vi* (*also:* ~ **off**) sfaldarsi.

flaky ['fleɪkɪ] *adj* (*paintwork*) scrostato(a); (*skin*) squamoso(a); ~ **pastry** (*CULIN*) pasta sfoglia.

flamboyant [flæm'bɔɪənt] *adj* sgargiante.

flame [fleɪm] *n* fiamma; **old** ~ (*col*) vecchia fiamma.

flamingo [flə'mɪŋgəu] *n* fenicottero, fiammingo.

flammable ['flæməbl] *adj* infiammabile.

flan [flæn] *n* (*BRIT*) flan *m inv*.

Flanders ['flɑːndəz] *n* Fiandre *fpl*.

flange [flændʒ] *n* flangia; (*on wheel*) suola.

flank [flæŋk] *n* fianco.

flannel ['flænl] *n* (*BRIT: also:* **face** ~) guanto di spugna; (*fabric*) flanella; ~**s** *npl* pantaloni *mpl* di flanella.

flannelette [flænə'let] *n* flanella di cotone.

flap [flæp] *n* (*of pocket*) patta; (*of envelope*) lembo; (*AVIAT*) flap *m inv* ♦ *vt* (*wings*) battere ♦ *vi* (*sail, flag*) sbattere; (*col: also:* **be in a** ~) essere in agitazione.

flapjack ['flæpdʒæk] *n* (*US: pancake*) frittella; (*BRIT: biscuit*) biscotto di avena.

flare [flɛə*] *n* razzo; (*in skirt etc*) svasatura.

▶**flare up** *vi* andare in fiamme; (*fig: person*) infiammarsi di rabbia; (: *revolt*) scoppiare.

flared ['flɛəd] *adj* (*trousers*) svasato(a).

flash [flæʃ] *n* vampata; (*also:* **news** ~) notizia *f* lampo *inv*; (*PHOT*) flash *m inv*; (*US: torch*) torcia elettrica, lampadina tascabile ♦ *vt* accendere e spegnere; (*send: message*) trasmettere; (*flaunt*) ostentare ♦ *vi* brillare; (*light on ambulance, eyes etc*) lampeggiare; **in a** ~ in un lampo; ~ **of inspiration** lampo di genio; **to** ~ **one's headlights** lampeggiare; **he** ~**ed by** *or* **past** ci passò davanti come un lampo.

flashback ['flæʃbæk] *n* flashback *m inv*.

flashbulb ['flæʃbʌlb] *n* cubo *m* flash *inv*.

flash card *n* (*SCOL*) scheda didattica.

flashcube ['flæʃkjuːb] *n* flash *m inv*.

flasher ['flæʃə*] *n* (*AUT*) lampeggiatore *m*.

flashlight ['flæʃlaɪt] *n* (*torch*) lampadina tascabile.

flashpoint ['flæʃpɔɪnt] *n* punto di infiammabilità; (*fig*) livello critico.

flashy ['flæʃɪ] *adj* (*pej*) vistoso(a).

flask [flɑːsk] n fiasco; (*CHEM*) beuta; (*also*: **vacuum** ~) thermos ® m inv.

flat [flæt] adj piatto(a); (*tyre*) sgonfio(a), a terra; (*battery*) scarico(a); (*denial*) netto(a); (*MUS*) bemolle inv; (: *voice*) stonato(a); (: *instrument*) scordato(a) ♦ n (*BRIT*: *rooms*) appartamento; (*MUS*) bemolle m; (*AUT*) pneumatico sgonfio ♦ adv: (**to work**) ~ **out** (lavorare) a più non posso; ~ **rate of pay** tariffa unica di pagamento.

flat-footed ['flæt'futɪd] adj: **to be** ~ avere i piedi piatti.

flatly ['flætlɪ] adv categoricamente, nettamente.

flatmate ['flætmeɪt] n (*BRIT*): **he's my** ~ divide l'appartamento con me.

flatness ['flætnɪs] n (*of land*) assenza di rilievi.

flat-pack ['flætpæk] adj: ~ **furniture** mobili mpl in kit ♦ n: **flat pack** kit m inv.

flat-screen ['flætskriːn] adj a schermo piatto.

flatten ['flætn] vt (*also*: ~ **out**) appiattire; (*house*, *city*) abbattere, radere al suolo.

flatter ['flætə*] vt lusingare; (*show to advantage*) donare a.

flatterer ['flætərə*] n adulatore/trice.

flattering ['flætərɪŋ] adj lusinghiero(a); (*clothes etc*) che dona, che abbellisce.

flattery ['flætərɪ] n adulazione f.

flatulence ['flætjuləns] n flatulenza.

flaunt [flɔːnt] vt fare mostra di.

flavour, (*US*) **flavor** ['fleɪvə*] n gusto, sapore m ♦ vt insaporire, aggiungere sapore a; **vanilla-~ed** al gusto di vaniglia.

flavo(u)ring ['fleɪvərɪŋ] n essenza (artificiale).

flaw [flɔː] n difetto.

flawless ['flɔːlɪs] adj senza difetti.

flax [flæks] n lino.

flaxen ['flæksən] adj biondo(a).

flea [fliː] n pulce f.

flea market n mercato delle pulci.

fleck [flɛk] n (*of mud*, *paint*, *colour*) macchiolina; (*of dust*) granello ♦ vt (*with blood*, *mud etc*) macchiettare; **brown ~ed with white** marrone screziato di bianco.

fled [flɛd] pt, pp of **flee**.

fledg(e)ling ['flɛdʒlɪŋ] n uccellino.

flee, pt, pp **fled** [fliː, flɛd] vt fuggire da ♦ vi fuggire, scappare.

fleece [fliːs] n vello; (*garment*) pile sm inv ♦ vt (*col*) pelare.

fleecy ['fliːsɪ] adj (*blanket*) soffice; (*cloud*) come ovatta.

fleet [fliːt] n flotta; (*of lorries etc*) convoglio; (*of cars*) parco.

fleeting ['fliːtɪŋ] adj fugace; (*visit*) volante.

Flemish ['flɛmɪʃ] adj fiammingo(a) ♦ n (*LING*) fiammingo; **the** ~ npl i Fiamminghi.

flesh [flɛʃ] n carne f; (*of fruit*) polpa.

flesh wound n ferita superficiale.

flew [fluː] pt of **fly**.

flex [flɛks] n filo (flessibile) ♦ vt flettere; (*muscles*) contrarre.

flexibility [flɛksɪˈbɪlɪtɪ] n flessibilità.

flexible ['flɛksəbl] adj flessibile.

flexitime ['flɛksɪtaɪm] n orario flessibile.

flick [flɪk] n colpetto; *see also* **flicks**.

▶**flick through** vt fus sfogliare.

flicker ['flɪkə*] vi tremolare ♦ n tremolio; **a ~ of light** un breve bagliore.

flick knife n (*BRIT*) coltello a serramanico.

flicks npl: **the** ~ (*col*) il cine.

flier ['flaɪə*] n aviatore m.

flight [flaɪt] n volo; (*escape*) fuga; (*also*: ~ **of steps**) scalinata; **to take** ~ darsi alla fuga; **to put to** ~ mettere in fuga.

flight attendant n (*US*) steward m, hostess f inv.

flight crew n equipaggio.

flight deck n (*AVIAT*) cabina di controllo; (*NAUT*) ponte m di comando.

flight path n (*of aircraft*) rotta di volo; (*of rocket*, *projectile*) traiettoria.

flight recorder n registratore m di volo.

flimsy ['flɪmzɪ] adj (*fabric*) inconsistente; (*excuse*) meschino(a).

flinch [flɪntʃ] vi ritirarsi; **to** ~ **from** tirarsi indietro di fronte a.

fling, pt, pp **flung** [flɪŋ, flʌŋ] vt lanciare, gettare ♦ n (*love affair*) avventura.

flint [flɪnt] n selce f; (*in lighter*) pietrina.

flip [flɪp] n colpetto ♦ vt dare un colpetto a; (*US*: *pancake*) far saltare (in aria) ♦ vi: **to ~ for sth** (*US*) fare a testa e croce per qc.

▶**flip through** vt fus (*book*, *records*) dare una scorsa a.

flippant ['flɪpənt] adj senza rispetto, irriverente.

flipper ['flɪpə*] n pinna.

flip side n (*of record*) retro.

flirt [fləːt] vi flirtare ♦ n civetta.

flirtation [fləːˈteɪʃən] n flirt m inv.

flit [flɪt] vi svolazzare.

float [fləut] n galleggiante m; (*in procession*) carro; (*sum of money*) somma ♦ vi galleggiare; (*bather*) fare il morto; (*COMM*: *currency*) fluttuare ♦ vt far galleggiare; (*loan*, *business*) lanciare; **to ~ an idea** ventilare un'idea.

floating ['fləutɪŋ] adj a galla; ~ **vote** voto oscillante; ~ **voter** elettore m indeciso.

flock [flɔk] n gregge m; (*of people*) folla; (*of birds*) stormo.

floe [fləu] *n* (*also*: **ice** ~) banchisa.

flog [flɒg] *vt* flagellare.

flood [flʌd] *n* alluvione *f*; (*of words, tears etc*) diluvio ♦ *vt* inondare, allagare; (*AUT*: *carburettor*) ingolfare; **in** ~ in pieno; **to** ~ **the market** (*COMM*) inondare il mercato.

flooding ['flʌdɪŋ] *n* inondazione *f*.

floodlight ['flʌdlaɪt] *n* riflettore *m* ♦ *vt* illuminare a giorno.

floodlit ['flʌdlɪt] *pt*, *pp of* **floodlight** ♦ *adj* illuminato(a) a giorno.

flood tide *n* alta marea, marea crescente.

floodwater ['flʌdwɔːtə*] *n* acque *fpl* (*di inondazione*).

floor [flɔː*] *n* pavimento; (*storey*) piano; (*of sea*, *valley*) fondo; (*fig*: *at meeting*): **the** ~ il pubblico ♦ *vt* pavimentare; (*knock down*) atterrare; (*baffle*) confondere; (*silence*) far tacere; **on the** ~ sul pavimento, per terra; **ground** ~, (*US*) **first** ~ pianterreno; **first** ~, (*US*) **second** ~ primo piano; **top** ~ ultimo piano; **to have the** ~ (*speaker*) prendere la parola.

floorboard ['flɔːbɔːd] *n* tavellone *m* di legno.

flooring ['flɔːrɪŋ] *n* (*floor*) pavimento; (*material*) materiale *m* per pavimentazioni.

floor lamp *n* (*US*) lampada a stelo.

floor show *n* spettacolo di varietà.

floorwalker ['flɔːwɔːkə*] *n* (*esp US*) ispettore *m* di reparto.

flop [flɒp] *n* fiasco ♦ *vi* (*fail*) far fiasco.

floppy ['flɒpɪ] *adj* floscio(a), molle ♦ *n* (*COMPUT*) = **floppy disk**; ~ **hat** cappello floscio.

floppy disk *n* floppy disk *m inv*.

flora ['flɔːrə] *n* flora.

floral ['flɔːrl] *adj* floreale.

Florence ['flɒrəns] *n* Firenze *f*.

Florentine ['flɒrəntaɪn] *adj* fiorentino(a).

florid ['flɒrɪd] *adj* (*complexion*) florido(a); (*style*) fiorito(a).

florist ['flɒrɪst] *n* fioraio/a; **at the** ~'**s (shop)** dal fioraio.

flotation [fləu'teɪʃən] *n* (*COMM*) lancio.

flounce [flauns] *n* balzo.

▶**flounce out** *vi* uscire stizzito(a).

flounder ['flaundə*] *vi* annaspare ♦ *n* (*ZOOL*) passera di mare.

flour ['flauə*] *n* farina.

flourish ['flʌrɪʃ] *vi* fiorire ♦ *vt* brandire ♦ *n* abbellimento; svolazzo; (*of trumpets*) fanfara.

flourishing ['flʌrɪʃɪŋ] *adj* prosperoso(a), fiorente.

flout [flaut] *vt* (*order*) contravvenire a; (*convention*) sfidare.

flow [fləu] *n* flusso; circolazione *f*; (*of river*, *also ELEC*) corrente *f* ♦ *vi* fluire; (*traffic*, *blood in veins*) circolare; (*hair*) scendere.

flow chart *n* schema *m* di flusso.

flow diagram *n* organigramma *m*.

flower ['flauə*] *n* fiore *m* ♦ *vi* fiorire; **in** ~ in fiore.

flower bed *n* aiuola.

flowerpot ['flauəpɔt] *n* vaso da fiori.

flowery ['flauərɪ] *adj* fiorito(a).

flown [fləun] *pp of* **fly**.

flu [fluː] *n* influenza.

fluctuate ['flʌktjueɪt] *vi* fluttuare, oscillare.

fluctuation [flʌktju'eɪʃən] *n* fluttuazione *f*, oscillazione *f*.

flue [fluː] *n* canna fumaria.

fluency ['fluːənsɪ] *n* facilità, scioltezza; **his** ~ **in English** la sua scioltezza nel parlare l'inglese.

fluent ['fluːənt] *adj* (*speech*) facile, sciolto(a); **he's a** ~ **speaker/reader** si esprime/legge senza difficoltà; **he speaks** ~ **Italian, he's** ~ **in Italian** parla l'italiano correntemente.

fluently ['fluːəntlɪ] *adv* con facilità; correntemente.

fluff [flʌf] *n* lanugine *f*.

fluffy ['flʌfɪ] *adj* lanuginoso(a); (*toy*) di peluche.

fluid ['fluːɪd] *adj* fluido(a) ♦ *n* fluido; (*in diet*) liquido.

fluid ounce *n* (*BRIT*) = 0.028 l; 0.05 pints.

fluke [fluːk] *n* (*col*) colpo di fortuna.

flummox ['flʌməks] *vt* rendere perplesso(a).

flung [flʌŋ] *pt*, *pp of* **fling**.

flunky ['flʌŋkɪ] *n* tirapiedi *m/f inv*.

fluorescent [fluə'rɛsnt] *adj* fluorescente.

fluoride ['fluəraɪd] *n* fluoruro.

fluorine ['fluəriːn] *n* fluoro.

flurry ['flʌrɪ] *n* (*of snow*) tempesta; **a** ~ **of activity/excitement** una febbre di attività/un'improvvisa agitazione.

flush [flʌʃ] *n* rossore *m*; (*fig*) ebbrezza ♦ *vt* ripulire con un getto d'acqua; (*also*: ~ **out**: *birds*) far alzare in volo; (: *animals*, *fig*: *criminal*) stanare ♦ *vi* arrossire ♦ *adj*: ~ **with** a livello di, pari a; ~ **against** aderente a; **hot** ~**es** (*MED*) vampate *fpl* di calore; **to** ~ **the toilet** tirare l'acqua.

flushed [flʌʃt] *adj* tutto(a) rosso(a).

fluster ['flʌstə*] *n* agitazione *f*.

flustered ['flʌstəd] *adj* sconvolto(a).

flute [fluːt] *n* flauto.

flutter ['flʌtə*] *n* agitazione *f*; (*of wings*) frullio ♦ *vi* (*bird*) battere le ali.

flux [flʌks] *n*: **in a state of** ~ in continuo mutamento.

fly [flaɪ] n (insect) mosca; (on trousers: also: **flies**) bracchetta ♦ vb (pt **flew**, pp **flown** [fluː, fləʊn]) vt pilotare; (passengers, cargo) trasportare (in aereo); (distances) percorrere ♦ vi volare; (passengers) andare in aereo; (escape) fuggire; (flag) sventolare; **to ~ open** spalancarsi all'improvviso; **to ~ off the handle** perdere le staffe, uscire dai gangheri.

►**fly away** vi volar via.

►**fly in** vi (plane) arrivare; (person) arrivare in aereo.

►**fly off** vi volare via.

►**fly out** vi (plane) partire; (person) partire in aereo.

fly-fishing ['flaɪfɪʃɪŋ] n pesca con la mosca.

flying ['flaɪɪŋ] n (activity) aviazione f; (action) volo ♦ adj: **~ visit** visita volante; **with ~ colours** con risultati brillanti; **he doesn't like ~** non gli piace viaggiare in aereo.

flying buttress n arco rampante.

flying picket n picchetto (proveniente da fabbriche non direttamente coinvolte nello sciopero).

flying saucer n disco volante.

flying squad n (POLICE) (squadra) volante f.

flying start n: **to get off to a ~ start** partire come un razzo.

flyleaf ['flaɪliːf] n risguardo.

flyover ['flaɪəʊvə*] n (BRIT: bridge) cavalcavia m inv.

flypast ['flaɪpɑːst] n esibizione f della pattuglia aerea.

flysheet ['flaɪʃiːt] n (for tent) sopratetto.

flyweight ['flaɪweɪt] n (SPORT) peso m mosca inv.

flywheel ['flaɪwiːl] n volano.

FM abbr see **frequency modulation**; (BRIT MIL) see **Field Marshal**.

FMB n abbr (US) = Federal Maritime Board.

FMCS n abbr (US: = Federal Mediation and Conciliation Service) organismo di conciliazione in caso di conflitti sul lavoro.

FO n abbr (BRIT) see **Foreign Office**.

foal [fəʊl] n puledro.

foam [fəʊm] n schiuma ♦ vi schiumare.

foam rubber n gommapiuma ®.

FOB abbr (= free on board) franco a bordo.

fob [fɔb] vt: **to ~ sb off with** appioppare qn con; sbarazzarsi di qn con ♦ n (also: **watch ~**: chain) catena per orologio; (: band of cloth) nastro per orologio.

foc abbr (BRIT) = **free of charge**.

focal ['fəʊkəl] adj focale.

focal point n punto focale.

focus ['fəʊkəs] n (pl ~es) fuoco; (of interest) centro ♦ vt (field glasses etc) mettere a fuoco; (light rays) far convergere ♦ vi: **to ~ on** (with camera) mettere a fuoco; (person) fissare lo sguardo su; **in ~** a fuoco; **out of ~** sfocato(a).

focus group n (POL) gruppo di discussione, focus group m inv.

fodder ['fɔdə*] n foraggio.

FOE n abbr (= Friends of the Earth) Amici mpl della Terra; (US: = Fraternal Order of Eagles) organizzazione filantropica.

foe [fəʊ] n nemico.

foetus, (US) **fetus** ['fiːtəs] n feto.

fog [fɔg] n nebbia.

fogbound ['fɔgbaʊnd] adj fermo(a) a causa della nebbia.

foggy ['fɔgɪ] adj nebbioso(a); **it's ~** c'è nebbia.

fog lamp, (US) **fog light** n (AUT) faro m antinebbia inv.

foible ['fɔɪbl] n debolezza, punto debole.

foil [fɔɪl] vt confondere, frustrare ♦ n lamina di metallo; (also: **kitchen ~**) foglio di alluminio; (FENCING) fioretto; **to act as a ~ to** (fig) far risaltare.

foist [fɔɪst] vt: **to ~ sth on sb** rifilare qc a qn.

fold [fəʊld] n (bend, crease) piega; (AGR) ovile m; (fig) gregge m ♦ vt piegare; **to ~ one's arms** incrociare le braccia.

►**fold up** vi (map etc) piegarsi; (business) crollare ♦ vt (map etc) piegare, ripiegare.

folder ['fəʊldə*] n (for papers) cartella; cartellina; (binder) raccoglitore m.

folding ['fəʊldɪŋ] adj (chair, bed) pieghevole.

foliage ['fəʊliɪdʒ] n fogliame m.

folk [fəʊk] npl gente f ♦ cpd popolare; **~s** npl famiglia.

folklore ['fəʊklɔː*] n folclore m.

folk music n musica folk inv.

folk singer n cantante m/f folk inv.

folksong ['fəʊksɔŋ] n canto popolare.

follow ['fɔləʊ] vt seguire ♦ vi seguire; (result) conseguire, risultare; **to ~ sb's advice** seguire il consiglio di qn; **I don't quite ~ you** non ti capisco or seguo affatto; **to ~ in sb's footsteps** seguire le orme di qn; **it ~s that** ... ne consegue che ...; **he ~ed suit** lui ha fatto lo stesso.

►**follow on** vi (continue): **to ~ on from** seguire.

►**follow out** vt (implement: idea, plan) eseguire, portare a termine.

►**follow through** vt = **follow out**.

►**follow up** vt (victory) sfruttare; (letter, offer) fare seguito a; (case) seguire.

follower ['fɔləʊə*] n seguace m/f,

discepolo/a.

following ['fɔləʊɪŋ] *adj* seguente, successivo(a) ♦ *n* seguito, discepoli *mpl*.

follow-up ['fɔləʊʌp] *n* seguito.

folly ['fɔlɪ] *n* pazzia, follia.

fond [fɔnd] *adj* (*memory, look*) tenero(a), affettuoso(a); **to be ~ of** volere bene a; **she's ~ of swimming** le piace nuotare.

fondle ['fɔndl] *vt* accarezzare.

fondly ['fɔndlɪ] *adv* (*lovingly*) affettuosamente; (*naïvely*): **he ~ believed that … ** ha avuto l'ingenuità di credere che ….

fondness ['fɔndnɪs] *n* affetto; **~ (for sth)** predilezione *f* (per qc).

font [fɔnt] *n* (*REL*) fonte *m* (battesimale); (*TYP*) stile *m* di carattere.

food [fuːd] *n* cibo.

food chain *n* catena alimentare.

food mixer *n* frullatore *m*.

food poisoning *n* intossicazione *f* alimentare.

food processor *n* tritatutto *m inv* elettrico.

food stamp *n* (*US*) *buono alimentare dato agli indigenti*.

foodstuffs ['fuːdstʌfs] *npl* generi *fpl* alimentari.

fool [fuːl] *n* sciocco/a; (*HISTORY: of king*) buffone *m*; (*CULIN*) frullato ♦ *vt* ingannare ♦ *vi* (*gen*: **~ around**) fare lo sciocco; **to make a ~ of sb** prendere in giro qn; **to make a ~ of o.s.** coprirsi di ridicolo; **you can't ~ me** non mi inganna.

▶**fool about, fool around** *vi* (*waste time*) perdere tempo.

foolhardy ['fuːlhɑːdɪ] *adj* avventato(a).

foolish ['fuːlɪʃ] *adj* scemo(a), stupido(a); imprudente.

foolishly ['fuːlɪʃlɪ] *adv* stupidamente.

foolishness ['fuːlɪʃnɪs] *n* stupidità.

foolproof ['fuːlpruːf] *adj* (*plan etc*) sicurissimo(a).

foolscap ['fuːlskæp] *n* carta protocollo.

foot [fʊt] *n* (*pl* **feet** [fiːt]) piede *m*; (*measure*) piede (= *304 mm*; *12 inches*); (*of animal*) zampa; (*of page, stairs etc*) fondo ♦ *vt* (*bill*) pagare; **on ~** a piedi; **to put one's ~ down** (*AUT*) schiacciare l'acceleratore; (*say no*) imporsi; **to find one's feet** ambientarsi.

footage ['fʊtɪdʒ] *n* (*CINE: length*) ≈ metraggio; (: *material*) sequenza.

foot and mouth (disease) *n* afta epizootica.

football ['fʊtbɔːl] *n* pallone *m*; (*sport: BRIT*) calcio; (: *US*) football *m* americano.

footballer ['fʊtbɔːlə*] *n* (*BRIT*) = **football player**.

football ground *n* campo di calcio.

football match *n* (*BRIT*) partita di calcio.

football player *n* (*BRIT*) calciatore *m*; (*US*) giocatore *m* di football americano.

footbrake ['fʊtbreɪk] *n* freno a pedale.

footbridge ['fʊtbrɪdʒ] *n* passerella.

foothills ['fʊthɪlz] *npl* contrafforti *fpl*.

foothold ['fʊthəʊld] *n* punto d'appoggio.

footing ['fʊtɪŋ] *n* (*fig*) posizione *f*; **to lose one's ~** mettere un piede in fallo; **on an equal ~** in condizioni di parità.

footlights ['fʊtlaɪts] *npl* luci *fpl* della ribalta.

footman ['fʊtmən] *n* lacchè *m inv*.

footnote ['fʊtnəʊt] *n* nota (a piè di pagina).

footpath ['fʊtpɑːθ] *n* sentiero; (*in street*) marciapiede *m*.

footprint ['fʊtprɪnt] *n* orma, impronta.

footrest ['fʊtrɛst] *n* poggiapiedi *m inv*.

footsie ['fʊtsɪ] *n* (*col*): **to play ~ with sb** fare piedino a qn.

Footsie (index) ['fʊtsɪ-] *n* (*col*) = *Financial Times Stock Exchange 100 Index*.

footsore ['fʊtsɔː*] *adj*: **to be ~** avere mal di piedi.

footstep ['fʊtstɛp] *n* passo.

footwear ['fʊtwɛə*] *n* calzatura.

FOR *abbr* (= *free on rail*) franco vagone.

═══════════════════════ *KEYWORD*

for [fɔː*] *prep* **1** (*indicating destination, intention, purpose*) per; **the train ~ London** il treno per Londra; **he went ~ the paper** è andato a prendere il giornale; **it's time ~ lunch** è ora di pranzo; **what's it ~?** a che serve?; **what ~?** (*why*) perché?

2 (*on behalf of, representing*) per; **to work ~ sb/sth** lavorare per qn/qc; **I'll ask him ~ you** glielo chiederò a nome tuo; **G ~ George** G come George

3 (*because of*) per, a causa di; **~ this reason** per questo motivo

4 (*with regard to*) per; **it's cold ~ July** è freddo per luglio; **~ everyone who voted yes, 50 voted no** per ogni voto a favore ce n'erano 50 contro

5 (*in exchange for*) per; **I sold it ~ £5** l'ho venduto per 5 sterline

6 (*in favour of*) per, a favore di; **are you ~ or against us?** sei con noi o contro di noi?; **I'm all ~ it** sono completamente a favore

7 (*referring to distance, time*) per; **there are roadworks ~ 5 km** ci sono lavori in corso per 5 km; **he was away ~ 2 years** è stato via per 2 anni; **she will be away ~ a month** starà via un mese; **it hasn't rained ~ 3 weeks** non piove da 3 settimane; **can**

you do it ~ **tomorrow?** può farlo per domani?
8 (*with infinitive clauses*): **it is not ~ me to decide** non sta a me decidere; **it would be best ~ you to leave** sarebbe meglio che lei se ne andasse; **there is still time ~ you to do it** ha ancora tempo per farlo; **~ this to be possible** ... perché ciò sia possibile ...
9 (*in spite of*) nonostante; **~ all his complaints, he's very fond of her** nonostante tutte le sue lamentele, le vuole molto bene
♦ *conj* (*since, as: rather formal*) dal momento che, poiché.

forage ['fɔrɪdʒ] *vi* foraggiare.
forage cap *n* bustina.
foray ['fɔreɪ] *n* incursione *f*.
forbad(e) [fə'bæd] *pt of* **forbid**.
forbearing [fɔ:'bɛərɪŋ] *adj* paziente, tollerante.
forbid, *pt* **forbad(e)**, *pp* **forbidden** [fə'bɪd, -'bæd, -'bɪdn] *vt* vietare, interdire; **to ~ sb to do sth** proibire a qn di fare qc.
forbidding [fə'bɪdɪŋ] *adj* arcigno(a), d'aspetto minaccioso.
force [fɔ:s] *n* forza ♦ *vt* forzare; (*obtain by ~: smile, confession*) strappare; **the F~s** *npl* (*BRIT*) le forze armate; **in ~** (*in large numbers*) in gran numero; (*law*) in vigore; **to come into ~** entrare in vigore; **a ~ 5 wind** un vento forza 5; **to join ~s** unire le forze; **the sales ~** (*COMM*) l'effettivo dei rappresentanti; **to ~ sb to do sth** costringere qn a fare qc.
▶**force back** *vt* (*crowd, enemy*) respingere; (*tears*) ingoiare.
▶**force down** *vt* (*food*) sforzarsi di mangiare.
forced [fɔ:st] *adj* forzato(a).
force-feed ['fɔ:sfi:d] *vt* sottoporre ad alimentazione forzata.
forceful ['fɔ:sful] *adj* forte, vigoroso(a).
forcemeat ['fɔ:smi:t] *n* (*BRIT CULIN*) ripieno.
forceps ['fɔ:sɪps] *npl* forcipe *m*.
forcibly ['fɔ:səblɪ] *adv* con la forza; (*vigorously*) vigorosamente.
ford [fɔ:d] *n* guado ♦ *vt* guadare.
fore [fɔ:*] *n*: **to the ~** in prima linea; **to come to the ~** mettersi in evidenza.
forearm ['fɔ:rɑ:m] *n* avambraccio.
forebear ['fɔ:bɛə*] *n* antenato.
foreboding [fɔ:'bəudɪŋ] *n* presagio di male.
forecast ['fɔ:kɑ:st] *n* previsione *f*; (*weather ~*) previsioni *fpl* del tempo ♦ *vt* (*irreg: like* **cast**) prevedere.
foreclose [fɔ:'kləuz] *vt* (*LAW: also: ~ on*)

sequestrare l'immobile ipotecato di.
foreclosure [fɔ:'kləuʒə*] *n* sequestro di immobile ipotecato.
forecourt ['fɔ:kɔ:t] *n* (*of garage*) corte *f* esterna.
forefathers ['fɔ:fɑ:ðəz] *npl* antenati *mpl*, avi *mpl*.
forefinger ['fɔ:fɪŋɡə*] *n* (dito) indice *m*.
forefront ['fɔ:frʌnt] *n*: **in the ~ of** all'avanguardia di.
forego [fɔ:'ɡəu] *vt* = **forgo**.
foregoing ['fɔ:ɡəuɪŋ] *adj* precedente.
foregone ['fɔ:ɡɔn] *pp of* **forego** ♦ *adj*: **it's a ~ conclusion** è una conclusione scontata.
foreground ['fɔ:ɡraund] *n* primo piano ♦ *cpd* (*COMPUT*) foreground *inv*, di primo piano.
forehand ['fɔ:hænd] *n* (*TENNIS*) diritto.
forehead ['fɔrɪd] *n* fronte *f*.
foreign ['fɔrən] *adj* straniero(a); (*trade*) estero(a).
foreign body *n* corpo estraneo.
foreign currency *n* valuta estera.
foreigner ['fɔrənə*] *n* straniero/a.
foreign exchange *n* cambio di valuta; (*currency*) valuta estera.
foreign exchange market *n* mercato delle valute.
foreign exchange rate *n* cambio.
foreign investment *n* investimento all'estero.
foreign minister *n* ministro degli Affari esteri.
Foreign Office (FO) *n* (*BRIT*) Ministero degli Esteri.
foreign secretary *n* (*BRIT*) ministro degli Affari esteri.
foreleg ['fɔ:lɛɡ] *n* zampa anteriore.
foreman ['fɔ:mən] *n* caposquadra *m*; (*LAW: of jury*) portavoce *m* della giuria.
foremost ['fɔ:məust] *adj* principale; più in vista ♦ *adv*: **first and ~** innanzitutto.
forename ['fɔ:neɪm] *n* nome *m* di battesimo.
forensic [fə'rɛnsɪk] *adj*: **~ medicine** medicina legale; **~ expert** esperto della (polizia) scientifica.
foreplay ['fɔ:pleɪ] *n* preliminari *mpl*.
forerunner ['fɔ:rʌnə*] *n* precursore *m*.
foresee, *pt* **foresaw**, *pp* **foreseen** [fɔ:'si:, -'sɔ:, -'si:n] *vt* prevedere.
foreseeable [fɔ:'si:əbl] *adj* prevedibile.
foreseen [fɔ:'si:n] *pp of* **foresee**.
foreshadow [fɔ:'ʃædəu] *vt* presagire, far prevedere.
foreshorten [fɔ:'ʃɔ:tn] *vt* (*figure, scene*) rappresentare in scorcio.
foresight ['fɔ:saɪt] *n* previdenza.

foreskin ['fɔːskɪn] *n* (*ANAT*) prepuzio.
forest ['fɔrɪst] *n* foresta.
forestall [fɔː'stɔːl] *vt* prevenire.
forestry ['fɔrɪstrɪ] *n* silvicoltura.
foretaste ['fɔːteɪst] *n* pregustazione *f*.
foretell, *pt*, *pp* **foretold** [fɔː'tɛl, -'təʊld] *vt* predire.
forethought ['fɔːθɔːt] *n* previdenza.
foretold [fɔː'təʊld] *pt*, *pp of* **foretell**.
forever [fə'rɛvə*] *adv* per sempre; (*fig*) sempre, di continuo.
forewarn [fɔː'wɔːn] *vt* avvisare in precedenza.
forewent [fɔː'wɛnt] *pt of* **forego**.
foreword ['fɔːwəːd] *n* prefazione *f*.
forfeit ['fɔːfɪt] *n* ammenda, pena ♦ *vt* perdere; (*one's happiness, health*) giocarsi.
forgave [fə'geɪv] *pt of* **forgive**.
forge [fɔːdʒ] *n* fucina ♦ *vt* falsificare; (*signature*) contraffare, falsificare; (*wrought iron*) fucinare, foggiare.
►**forge ahead** *vi* tirare avanti.
forger ['fɔːdʒə*] *n* contraffattore *m*.
forgery ['fɔːdʒərɪ] *n* falso; (*activity*) contraffazione *f*.
forget, *pt* **forgot**, *pp* **forgotten** [fə'gɛt, -'gɔt, -'gɔtn] *vt*, *vi* dimenticare.
forgetful [fə'gɛtful] *adj* di corta memoria; ~ **of** dimentico(a) di.
forgetfulness [fə'gɛtfulnɪs] *n* smemoratezza; (*oblivion*) oblio.
forget-me-not [fə'gɛtmɪnɔt] *n* nontiscordardimé *m inv*.
forgive, *pt* **forgave**, *pp* **forgiven** [fə'gɪv, -'geɪv, -'gɪvn] *vt* perdonare; **to** ~ **sb for** sth/for doing sth perdonare qc a qn/a qn di aver fatto qc.
forgiveness [fə'gɪvnɪs] *n* perdono.
forgiving [fə'gɪvɪŋ] *adj* indulgente.
forgo, *pt* **forwent**, *pp* **forgone** [fɔː'gəʊ, -'wɛnt, -'gɔn] *vt* rinunciare a.
forgot [fə'gɔt] *pt of* **forget**.
forgotten [fə'gɔtn] *pp of* **forget**.
fork [fɔːk] *n* (*for eating*) forchetta; (*for gardening*) forca; (*of roads*) bivio; (*of railways*) inforcazione *f* ♦ *vi* (*road*) biforcarsi.
►**fork out** (*col: pay*) *vt* sborsare ♦ *vi* pagare.
forked [fɔːkt] *adj* (*lightning*) a zigzag.
fork-lift truck ['fɔːklɪft-] *n* carrello elevatore.
forlorn [fə'lɔːn] *adj* (*person*) sconsolato(a); (*deserted: cottage*) abbandonato(a); (*desperate: attempt*) disperato(a).
form [fɔːm] *n* forma; (*SCOL*) classe *f*; (*questionnaire*) modulo ♦ *vt* formare; (*circle, queue etc*) fare; **in the** ~ **of** a forma di, sotto forma di; **to be in good** ~

(*SPORT, fig*) essere in forma; **in top** ~ in gran forma; **to** ~ **part of sth** far parte di qc.
formal ['fɔːməl] *adj* (*offer, receipt*) vero(a) e proprio(a); (*person*) cerimonioso(a); (*occasion, dinner*) formale, ufficiale; (*ART, PHILOSOPHY*) formale; ~ **dress** abito da cerimonia; (*evening dress*) abito da sera.
formality [fɔː'mælɪtɪ] *n* formalità *f inv*.
formalize ['fɔːməlaɪz] *vt* rendere ufficiale.
formally ['fɔːməlɪ] *adv* ufficialmente; formalmente; cerimoniosamente; **to be** ~ **invited** ricevere un invito ufficiale.
format ['fɔːmæt] *n* formato ♦ *vt* (*COMPUT*) formattare.
formation [fɔː'meɪʃən] *n* formazione *f*.
formative ['fɔːmətɪv] *adj*: ~ **years** anni *mpl* formativi.
former ['fɔːmə*] *adj* vecchio(a) (*before n*), ex *inv* (*before n*); **the** ~ **president** l'ex presidente; **the** ~ ... **the latter** quello ... questo; **the** ~ **Yugoslavia/Soviet Union** l'ex Jugoslavia/Unione Sovietica.
formerly ['fɔːməlɪ] *adv* in passato.
form feed *n* (*on printer*) alimentazione *f* modulo.
formidable ['fɔːmɪdəbl] *adj* formidabile.
formula ['fɔːmjulə] *n* formula; **F~ One** (*AUT*) formula uno.
formulate ['fɔːmjuleɪt] *vt* formulare.
fornicate ['fɔːnɪkeɪt] *vi* fornicare.
forsake, *pt* **forsook**, *pp* **forsaken** [fə'seɪk, -'suk, -'seɪkən] *vt* abbandonare.
fort [fɔːt] *n* forte *m*; **to hold the** ~ (*fig*) prendere le redini (della situazione).
forte ['fɔːtɪ] *n* forte *m*.
forth [fɔːθ] *adv* in avanti; **to go back and** ~ andare avanti e indietro; **and so** ~ e così via.
forthcoming [fɔːθ'kʌmɪŋ] *adj* prossimo(a); (*character*) aperto(a), comunicativo(a).
forthright ['fɔːθraɪt] *adj* franco(a), schietto(a).
forthwith [fɔːθ'wɪθ] *adv* immediatamente, subito.
fortieth ['fɔːtɪɪθ] *num* quarantesimo(a).
fortification [fɔːtɪfɪ'keɪʃən] *n* fortificazione *f*.
fortified wine *n* vino ad alta gradazione alcolica.
fortify ['fɔːtɪfaɪ] *vt* fortificare.
fortitude ['fɔːtɪtjuːd] *n* forza d'animo.
fortnight ['fɔːtnaɪt] *n* (*BRIT*) quindici giorni *mpl*, due settimane *fpl*; **it's a** ~ **since ...** sono due settimane da quando ....
fortnightly ['fɔːtnaɪtlɪ] *adj* bimensile ♦ *adv* ogni quindici giorni.
FORTRAN ['fɔːtræn] *n* FORTRAN *m*.

fortress ['fɔːtrɪs] n fortezza, rocca.

fortuitous [fɔː'tjuːɪtəs] adj fortuito(a).

fortunate ['fɔːtʃənɪt] adj fortunato(a); **he is ~ to have ...** ha la fortuna di avere ...; **it is ~ that** è una fortuna che + sub.

fortunately ['fɔːtʃənɪtlɪ] adv fortunatamente.

fortune ['fɔːtʃən] n fortuna; **to make a ~** farsi una fortuna.

fortuneteller ['fɔːtʃəntɛlə*] n indovino/a.

forty ['fɔːtɪ] num quaranta.

forum ['fɔːrəm] n foro; (fig) luogo di pubblica discussione.

forward ['fɔːwəd] adj (movement, position) in avanti; (not shy) sfacciato(a); (COMM: delivery, sales, exchange) a termine ♦ n (SPORT) avanti m inv ♦ vt (letter) inoltrare; (parcel, goods) spedire; (fig) promuovere, appoggiare; **to move ~** avanzare; **"please ~"** "si prega di inoltrare"; **~ planning** programmazione f in anticipo.

forward(s) ['fɔːwəd(z)] adv avanti.

forwent [fɔː'wɛnt] pt of **forgo**.

fossil ['fɔsl] adj, n fossile (m); **~ fuel** combustibile m fossile.

foster ['fɔstə*] vt incoraggiare, nutrire; (child) avere in affidamento.

foster brother n fratellastro.

foster child n bambino(a) preso(a) in affidamento.

foster mother n madre f affidataria.

fought [fɔːt] pt, pp of **fight**.

foul [faul] adj (smell, food) cattivo(a); (weather) brutto(a), orribile; (language) osceno(a); (deed) infame ♦ n (FOOTBALL) fallo ♦ vt sporcare; (football player) commettere un fallo su; (entangle: anchor, propeller) impigliarsi in.

foul play n (SPORT) gioco scorretto; **~ is not suspected** si è scartata l'ipotesi del delitto (or dell'attentato etc).

found [faund] pt, pp of **find** ♦ vt (establish) fondare.

foundation [faun'deɪʃən] n (act) fondazione f; (base) base f; (also: **~ cream**) fondo tinta; **~s** npl (of building) fondamenta fpl; **to lay the ~s** gettare le fondamenta.

foundation stone n prima pietra.

founder ['faundə*] n fondatore/trice ♦ vi affondare.

founding ['faundɪŋ] adj: **~ fathers** (US) padri mpl fondatori; **~ member** socio fondatore.

foundry ['faundrɪ] n fonderia.

fount [faunt] n fonte f; (TYP) stile m di carattere.

fountain ['fauntɪn] n fontana.

fountain pen n penna stilografica.

four [fɔː*] num quattro; **on all ~s** a carponi.

four-letter word ['fɔːlɛtə-] n parolaccia.

four-poster ['fɔː'pəustə*] n (also: **~ bed**) letto a quattro colonne.

foursome ['fɔːsəm] n partita a quattro; uscita in quattro.

fourteen ['fɔː'tiːn] num quattordici.

fourth [fɔːθ] num quarto(a) ♦ n (AUT: also: **~ gear**) quarta.

four-wheel drive ['fɔːwiːl-] n (AUT): **with ~** con quattro ruote motrici.

fowl [faul] n pollame m; volatile m.

fox [fɔks] n volpe f ♦ vt confondere.

fox fur n volpe f, pelliccia di volpe.

foxglove ['fɔksglʌv] n (BOT) digitale f.

fox-hunting ['fɔkshʌntɪŋ] n caccia alla volpe.

foyer ['fɔɪeɪ] n atrio; (THEAT) ridotto.

FPA n abbr (BRIT: = Family Planning Association) ≈ A.I.E.D. f (= Associazione Italiana Educazione Demografica).

Fr. abbr (REL) = **father; friar**.

fr. abbr (= franc) fr.

fracas ['frækɑː] n rissa, lite f.

fraction ['frækʃən] n frazione f.

fractionally ['frækʃnəlɪ] adv un tantino, minimamente.

fractious ['frækʃəs] adj irritabile.

fracture ['fræktʃə*] n frattura ♦ vt fratturare.

fragile ['frædʒaɪl] adj fragile.

fragment ['frægmənt] n frammento.

fragmentary ['frægməntərɪ] adj frammentario(a).

fragrance ['freɪɡrəns] n fragranza, profumo.

fragrant ['freɪɡrənt] adj fragrante, profumato(a).

frail [freɪl] adj debole, delicato(a).

frame [freɪm] n (of building) armatura; (of human, animal) ossatura, corpo; (of picture) cornice f; (of door, window) telaio; (of spectacles: also: **~s**) montatura ♦ vt (picture) incorniciare; **to ~ sb** (col) incastrare qn; **~ of mind** stato d'animo.

framework ['freɪmwɔːk] n struttura.

France [frɑːns] n Francia.

franchise ['fræntʃaɪz] n (POL) diritto di voto; (COMM) concessione f.

franchisee [fræntʃaɪ'ziː] n concessionaria.

franchiser ['fræntʃaɪzə*] n concedente m.

frank [fræŋk] adj franco(a), aperto(a) ♦ vt (letter) affrancare.

Frankfurt ['fræŋkfɔːt] n Francoforte f.

frankfurter ['fræŋkfɔːtə*] n würstel m inv.

franking machine ['fræŋkɪŋ-] n macchina affrancatrice.

frankly ['fræŋklɪ] adv francamente,

sinceramente.

frankness ['fræŋknɪs] *n* franchezza.

frantic ['fræntɪk] *adj* (*activity, pace*) frenetico(a); (*desperate: need, desire*) pazzo(a), sfrenato(a); (*: search*) affannoso(a); (*person*) fuori di sé.

frantically ['fræntɪklɪ] *adv* freneticamente; affannosamente.

fraternal [frə'təːnl] *adj* fraterno(a).

fraternity [frə'təːnɪtɪ] *n* (*club*) associazione *f*; (*spirit*) fratellanza.

fraternize ['frætənaɪz] *vi* fraternizzare.

fraud [frɔːd] *n* truffa; (*LAW*) frode *f*; (*person*) impostore/a.

fraudulent ['frɔːdjulənt] *adj* fraudolento(a).

fraught [frɔːt] *adj* (*tense*) teso(a); ~ **with** pieno(a) di, intriso(a) da.

fray [freɪ] *n* baruffa ♦ *vt* logorare ♦ *vi* logorarsi; **to return to the** ~ tornare nella mischia; **tempers were getting** ~**ed** cominciavano ad innervosirsi; **her nerves were** ~**ed** aveva i nervi a pezzi.

FRB *n abbr* (*US*) = **Federal Reserve Board**.

FRCM *n abbr* (*BRIT*) = *Fellow of the Royal College of Music*.

FRCO *n abbr* (*BRIT*) = *Fellow of the Royal College of Organists*.

FRCP *n abbr* (*BRIT*) = *Fellow of the Royal College of Physicians*.

FRCS *n abbr* (*BRIT*) = *Fellow of the Royal College of Surgeons*.

freak [friːk] *n* fenomeno, mostro; (*col: enthusiast*) fanatico/a ♦ *adj* (*storm, conditions*) anormale; (*victory*) inatteso(a).

▶**freak out** *vi* (*col*) andare fuori di testa.

freakish ['friːkɪʃ] *adj* (*result, appearance*) strano(a), bizzarro(a); (*weather*) anormale.

freckle ['frɛkl] *n* lentiggine *f*.

free [friː] *adj* libero(a); (*gratis*) gratuito(a); (*liberal*) generoso(a) ♦ *vt* (*prisoner, jammed person*) liberare; (*jammed object*) districare; ~ (**of charge**) gratuitamente; **admission** ~ entrata libera; **to give sb a** ~ **hand** dare carta bianca a qn; ~ **and easy** rilassato.

freebie ['friːbɪ] *n* (*col*): **it's a** ~ è in omaggio.

freedom ['friːdəm] *n* libertà.

freedom fighter *n* combattente *m/f* per la libertà.

free enterprise *n* liberalismo economico.

Freefone ® ['friːfəun] *n* (*BRIT*) ≈ numero verde.

free-for-all ['friːfərɔːl] *n* parapiglia *m* generale.

free gift *n* regalo, omaggio.

freehold ['friːhəuld] *n* proprietà assoluta.

free kick *n* (*SPORT*) calcio libero.

freelance ['friːlɑːns] *adj* indipendente; ~ **work** collaborazione *f* esterna.

freeloader ['friːləudə*] *n* (*pej*) scroccone/a.

freely ['friːlɪ] *adv* liberamente; (*liberally*) liberalmente.

free-market economy [friː'mɑːkɪt-] *n* economia di libero mercato.

freemason ['friːmeɪsn] *n* massone *m*.

freemasonry ['friːmeɪsnrɪ] *n* massoneria.

freepost ['friːpəust] *n* affrancatura a carica del destinatario.

free-range ['friː'reɪndʒ] *adj* (*eggs*) di gallina ruspante.

free sample *n* campione *m* gratuito.

free speech *n* libertà di parola.

freestyle ['friːstaɪl] *n* (*in swimming*) stile *m* libero.

free trade *n* libero scambio.

freeway ['friːweɪ] *n* (*US*) superstrada.

freewheel [friː'wiːl] *vi* andare a ruota libera.

freewheeling [friː'wiːlɪŋ] *adj* a ruota libera.

free will *n* libero arbitrio; **of one's own** ~ di spontanea volontà.

freeze [friːz] *vb* (*pt* **froze**, *pp* **frozen** [frəuz, 'frəuzn]) *vi* gelare ♦ *vt* gelare; (*food*) congelare; (*prices, salaries*) bloccare ♦ *n* gelo; blocco.

▶**freeze over** *vi* (*lake, river*) ghiacciarsi; (*windows, windscreen*) coprirsi di ghiaccio.

▶**freeze up** *vi* gelarsi.

freeze-dried ['friːzdraɪd] *adj* liofilizzato(a).

freezer ['friːzə*] *n* congelatore *m*.

freezing ['friːzɪŋ] *adj*: **I'm** ~ mi sto congelando ♦ *n* (*also*: ~ **point**) punto di congelamento; **3 degrees below** ~ 3 gradi sotto zero.

freight [freɪt] *n* (*goods*) merce *f*, merci *fpl*; (*money charged*) spese *fpl* di trasporto; ~ **forward** spese a carico del destinatario; ~ **inward** spese di trasporto sulla merce in entrata.

freight car *n* (*US*) carro *m* merci *inv*.

freighter ['freɪtə*] *n* (*NAUT*) nave *f* da carico.

freight forwarder [-'fɔːwədə*] *n* spedizioniere *m*.

freight train *n* (*US*) treno *m* merci *inv*.

French [frɛntʃ] *adj* francese ♦ *n* (*LING*) francese *m*; **the** ~ *npl* i Francesi.

French bean *n* fagiolino.

French Canadian *adj, n* franco-canadese (*m/f*).

French dressing *n* (*CULIN*) condimento per insalata.

French fried potatoes, (*US*) **French fries**

npl patate *fpl* fritte.

French Guiana [-gaɪ'ænə] *n* Guiana francese.

French loaf *n* ≈ filoncino.

Frenchman ['frɛntʃmən] *n* francese *m*.

French Riviera *n*: **the** ~ la Costa Azzurra.

French stick *n* baguette *f inv*.

French window *n* portafinestra.

Frenchwoman ['frɛntʃwumən] *n* francese *f*.

frenetic [frə'nɛtɪk] *adj* frenetico(a).

frenzy ['frɛnzɪ] *n* frenesia.

frequency ['friːkwənsɪ] *n* frequenza.

frequency modulation (FM) *n* modulazione *f* di frequenza (F.M.).

frequent *adj* ['friːkwənt] frequente ♦ *vt* [frɪ'kwɛnt] frequentare.

frequently ['friːkwəntlɪ] *adv* frequentemente, spesso.

fresco ['frɛskəu] *n* affresco.

fresh [frɛʃ] *adj* fresco(a); (*new*) nuovo(a); (*cheeky*) sfacciato(a); **to make a ~ start** cominciare da capo.

freshen ['frɛʃən] *vi* (*wind, air*) rinfrescare.

▶**freshen up** *vi* rinfrescarsi.

freshener ['frɛʃnə*] *n*: **skin** ~ tonico rinfrescante; **air** ~ deodorante *m* per ambienti.

fresher ['frɛʃə*] *n* (*BRIT SCOL: col*) = **freshman**.

freshly ['frɛʃlɪ] *adv* di recente, di fresco.

freshman ['frɛʃmən] *n* (*SCOL*) matricola.

freshness ['frɛʃnɪs] *n* freschezza.

freshwater ['frɛʃwɔːtə*] *adj* (*fish*) d'acqua dolce.

fret [frɛt] *vi* agitarsi, affliggersi.

fretful ['frɛtful] *adj* (*child*) irritabile.

Freudian ['frɔɪdɪən] *adj* freudiano(a); ~ **slip** lapsus *m inv* freudiano.

FRG *n abbr see* **Federal Republic of Germany**.

Fri. *abbr* (= *Friday*) ven.

friar ['fraɪə*] *n* frate *m*.

friction ['frɪkʃən] *n* frizione *f*, attrito.

friction feed *n* (*on printer*) trascinamento ad attrito.

Friday ['fraɪdɪ] *n* venerdì *m inv*; *for phrases see also* **Tuesday**.

fridge [frɪdʒ] *n* (*BRIT*) frigo, frigorifero.

fridge-freezer ['frɪdʒ'friːzə*] *n* freezer *m inv*.

fried [fraɪd] *pt, pp of* **fry** ♦ *adj* fritto(a); ~ **egg** uovo fritto.

friend [frɛnd] *n* amico/a; **to make ~s with** fare amicizia con.

friendliness ['frɛndlɪnɪs] *n* amichevolezza.

friendly ['frɛndlɪ] *adj* amichevole ♦ *n* (*also:* ~ **match**) partita amichevole; **to be ~ with** essere amico di; **to be ~ to** essere cordiale con.

friendly fire *n* fuoco amico.

friendship ['frɛndʃɪp] *n* amicizia.

frieze [friːz] *n* fregio.

frigate ['frɪgɪt] *n* (*NAUT: modern*) fregata.

fright [fraɪt] *n* paura, spavento; **to take ~** spaventarsi; **she looks a ~!** guarda com'è conciata!

frighten ['fraɪtn] *vt* spaventare, far paura a.

▶**frighten away, frighten off** *vt* (*birds, children etc*) scacciare (facendogli paura).

frightened ['fraɪtnd] *adj*: **to be ~ (of)** avere paura (di).

frightening ['fraɪtnɪŋ] *adj* spaventoso(a), pauroso(a).

frightful ['fraɪtful] *adj* orribile.

frightfully ['fraɪtfulɪ] *adv* terribilmente; **I'm ~ sorry** mi dispiace moltissimo.

frigid ['frɪdʒɪd] *adj* (*woman*) frigido(a).

frigidity [frɪ'dʒɪdɪtɪ] *n* frigidità.

frill [frɪl] *n* balza; **without ~s** (*fig*) senza fronzoli.

frilly ['frɪlɪ] *adj* (*clothes, lampshade*) pieno(a) di fronzoli.

fringe [frɪndʒ] *n* frangia; (*edge: of forest etc*) margine *m*; (*fig*): **on the ~** al margine.

fringe benefits *npl* vantaggi *mpl*.

fringe theatre *n* teatro d'avanguardia.

Frisbee ® ['frɪzbɪ] *n* frisbee ® *m inv*.

frisk [frɪsk] *vt* perquisire.

frisky ['frɪskɪ] *adj* vivace, vispo(a).

fritter ['frɪtə*] *n* frittella.

▶**fritter away** *vt* sprecare.

frivolity [frɪ'vɔlɪtɪ] *n* frivolezza.

frivolous ['frɪvələs] *adj* frivolo(a).

frizzy ['frɪzɪ] *adj* crespo(a).

fro [frəu] *adv*: **to and ~** avanti e indietro.

frock [frɔk] *n* vestito.

frog [frɔg] *n* rana; **to have a ~ in one's throat** avere la voce rauca.

frogman ['frɔgmən] *n* uomo *m* rana *inv*.

frogmarch ['frɔgmɑːtʃ] *vt* (*BRIT*): **to ~ sb in/out** portar qn dentro/fuori con la forza.

frolic ['frɔlɪk] *vi* sgambettare.

═══════════════════════════════ *KEYWORD*

from [frɔm] *prep* **1** (*indicating starting place, origin etc*) da; **where do you come ~?**, **where are you ~?** da dove viene?, di dov'è?; **where has he come ~?** da dove arriva?; ~ **London to Glasgow** da Londra a Glasgow; **a letter ~ my sister** una lettera da mia sorella; **tell him ~ me that** … gli dica da parte mia che …

2 (*indicating time*) da; ~ **one o'clock to** *or* **until** *or* **till two** dall'una alle due; (**as**) ~ **Friday** a partire da venerdì; ~ **January**

(on) da gennaio, a partire da gennaio
3 (*indicating distance*) da; **the hotel is 1 km
~ the beach** l'albergo è a 1 km dalla
spiaggia
4 (*indicating price, number etc*) da; **~ a
pound** da una sterlina in su; **prices range
~ £10 to £50** i prezzi vanno dalle 10 alle
50 sterline
5 (*indicating difference*) da; **he can't tell
red ~ green** non sa distinguere il rosso
dal verde
6 (*because of, on the basis of*): **~ what he
says** da quanto dice lui; **weak ~ hunger**
debole per la fame.

frond [frɔnd] *n* fronda.
front [frʌnt] *n* (*of house, dress*) davanti *m
inv*; (*of train*) testa; (*of book*) copertina;
(*promenade: also:* **sea ~**) lungomare *m*;
(*MIL, POL, METEOR*) fronte *m*; (*fig:
appearances*) fronte *f* ♦ *adj* primo(a);
anteriore, davanti *inv* ♦ *vi*: **to ~ onto sth**
dare su qc, guardare verso qc; **in ~ (of)**
davanti (a).
frontage ['frʌntɪdʒ] *n* facciata.
frontal ['frʌntl] *adj* frontale.
front bench *n posti in Parlamento occupati dai frontbencher; see boxed note.*

frontbencher ['frʌnt'bentʃə*] *n* (*BRIT*)
*parlamentare con carica al governo o
all'opposizione.*
front desk *n* (*US: in hotel*) reception *f inv*; (*:
at doctor's*) accettazione *f*.
front door *n* porta d'entrata; (*of car*)
sportello anteriore.
frontier ['frʌntɪə*] *n* frontiera.
frontispiece ['frʌntɪspiːs] *n* frontespizio.
front page *n* prima pagina.
front room *n* (*BRIT*) salotto.
front runner *n* (*fig*) favorito/a.
front-wheel drive ['frʌntwiːl-] *n*
trasmissione *f* anteriore.
frost [frɔst] *n* gelo; (*also:* **hoar~**) brina.
frostbite ['frɔstbaɪt] *n* congelamento.
frosted ['frɔstɪd] *adj* (*glass*) smerigliato(a);
(*US: cake*) glassato(a).

frosting ['frɔstɪŋ] *n* (*US: on cake*) glassa.
frosty ['frɔstɪ] *adj* (*window*) coperto(a) di
ghiaccio; (*welcome*) gelido(a).
froth ['frɔθ] *n* spuma; schiuma.
frown [fraun] *n* cipiglio ♦ *vi* accigliarsi.
▶**frown on** *vt fus* (*fig*) disapprovare.
froze [frəuz] *pt of* **freeze**.
frozen ['frəuzn] *pp of* **freeze** ♦ *adj* (*food*)
congelato(a); (*COMM: assets*) bloccato(a).
FRS *n abbr* (*BRIT*) = *Fellow of the Royal
Society*; (*US:* = *Federal Reserve System*)
sistema bancario degli Stati Uniti.
frugal ['fruːgəl] *adj* frugale; (*person*)
economo(a).
fruit [fruːt] *n* (*pl inv*) frutto; (*collectively*)
frutta.
fruiterer ['fruːtərə*] *n* fruttivendolo; **at the
~'s (shop)** dal fruttivendolo.
fruit fly *n* mosca della frutta.
fruitful ['fruːtful] *adj* fruttuoso(a); (*plant*)
fruttifero(a); (*soil*) fertile.
fruition [fruː'ɪʃən] *n*: **to come to ~**
realizzarsi.
fruit juice *n* succo di frutta.
fruitless ['fruːtlɪs] *adj* (*fig*) vano(a), inutile.
fruit machine *n* (*BRIT*) macchina *f*
mangiasoldi *inv*.
fruit salad *n* macedonia.
frump [frʌmp] *n*: **to feel a ~** sentirsi
infagottato(a).
frustrate [frʌs'treɪt] *vt* frustrare.
frustrated [frʌs'treɪtɪd] *adj* frustrato(a).
frustrating [frʌs'treɪtɪŋ] *adj* (*job*)
frustrante; (*day*) disastroso(a).
frustration [frʌs'treɪʃən] *n* frustrazione *f*.
fry, *pt, pp* **fried** [fraɪ, -d] *vt* friggere ♦ *npl*: **the
small ~** i pesci piccoli.
frying pan ['fraɪɪŋ-] *n* padella.
FT *n abbr* (*BRIT*: = *Financial Times*) *giornale
finanziario;* **the ~ index** l'indice FT.
ft. *abbr* = **foot, feet**.
FTC *n abbr* (*US*) *see* **Federal Trade
Commission**.
FT-SE 100 Index *n abbr* = *Financial Times
Stock Exchange 100 Index.*
fuchsia ['fjuːʃə] *n* fucsia.
fuck [fʌk] *vt, vi* (*col!*) fottere (*!*); **~ off!**
vaffanculo! (*!*).
fuddled ['fʌdld] *adj* (*muddled*) confuso(a);
(*col: tipsy*) brillo(a).
fuddy-duddy ['fʌdɪdʌdɪ] *n* (*pej*) parruccone
m.
fudge [fʌdʒ] *n* (*CULIN*) *specie di caramella
a base di latte, burro e zucchero* ♦ *vt*
(*issue, problem*) evitare.
fuel [fjuəl] *n* (*for heating*) combustibile *m*;
(*for propelling*) carburante *m* ♦ *vt* (*furnace
etc*) alimentare; (*aircraft, ship etc*)

rifornire di carburante.
fuel oil *n* nafta.
fuel pump *n* (*AUT*) pompa del carburante.
fuel tank *n* deposito *m* nafta *inv*; (*on vehicle*) serbatoio (della benzina).
fug [fʌg] *n* (*BRIT*) aria viziata.
fugitive ['fjuːdʒɪtɪv] *n* fuggitivo/a, profugo/a; (*from prison*) evaso/a.
fulfil, (*US*) **fulfill** [ful'fɪl] *vt* (*function*) compiere; (*order*) eseguire; (*wish, desire*) soddisfare, appagare.
fulfilled [ful'fɪld] *adj* (*person*) realizzato(a), soddisfatto(a).
fulfil(l)ment [ful'fɪlmənt] *n* (*of wishes*) soddisfazione *f*, appagamento.
full [ful] *adj* pieno(a); (*details, skirt*) ampio(a); (*price*) intero(a) ♦ *adv*: **to know ~ well that** sapere benissimo che; **~ (up)** (*hotel etc*) al completo; **I'm ~ (up)** sono pieno; **a ~ two hours** due ore intere; **at ~ speed** a tutta velocità; **in ~** per intero; **to pay in ~** pagare tutto; **~ name** nome *m* e cognome *m*; **~ employment** piena occupazione; **~ fare** tariffa completa.
fullback ['fulbæk] *n* (*RUGBY, FOOTBALL*) terzino.
full-blooded ['ful'blʌdɪd] *adj* (*vigorous: attack*) energico(a); (*virile: male*) virile.
full-cream ['ful'kriːm] *adj*: **~ milk** (*BRIT*) latte *m* intero.
full-grown ['ful'grəun] *adj* maturo(a).
full-length ['ful'lɛŋθ] *adj* (*portrait*) in piedi; (*film*) a lungometraggio.
full moon *n* luna piena.
full-scale ['fulskeɪl] *adj* (*plan, model*) in grandezza naturale; (*search, retreat*) su vasta scala.
full-sized ['ful'saɪzd] *adj* (*portrait etc*) a grandezza naturale.
full stop *n* punto.
full-time ['ful'taɪm] *adj, adv* (*work*) a tempo pieno ♦ *n* (*SPORT*) fine *f* partita.
fully ['fulɪ] *adv* interamente, pienamente, completamente; (*at least*): **~ as big** almeno così grosso.
fully-fledged ['fulɪ'flɛdʒd] *adj* (*bird*) adulto(a); (*fig: teacher, member etc*) a tutti gli effetti.
fulsome ['fulsəm] *adj* (*pej: praise*) esagerato(a), eccessivo(a); (*: manner*) insincero.
fumble ['fʌmbl] *vi* brancolare, andare a tentoni ♦ *vt* (*ball*) lasciarsi sfuggire.
►**fumble with** *vt fus* trafficare.
fume [fjuːm] *vi* essere furioso(a); **~s** *npl* esalazioni *fpl*, vapori *mpl*.
fumigate ['fjuːmɪgeɪt] *vt* suffumicare.
fun [fʌn] *n* divertimento, spasso; **to have ~**

divertirsi; **for ~** per scherzo; **it's not much ~** non è molto divertente; **to make ~ of** prendersi gioco di.
function ['fʌŋkʃən] *n* funzione *f*; cerimonia, ricevimento ♦ *vi* funzionare; **to ~ as** fungere da, funzionare da.
functional ['fʌŋkʃənl] *adj* funzionale.
function key *n* (*COMPUT*) tasto di funzioni.
fund [fʌnd] *n* fondo, cassa; (*source*) fondo; (*store*) riserva; **~s** *npl* (*money*) fondi *mpl*.
fundamental [fʌndə'mɛntl] *adj* fondamentale; **~s** *npl* basi *fpl*.
fundamentalism [fʌndə'mɛntəlɪzəm] *n* fondamentalismo.
fundamentalist [fʌndə'mɛntəlɪst] *n* fondamentalista *m/f*.
fundamentally [fʌndə'mɛntəlɪ] *adv* essenzialmente, fondamentalmente.
funding ['fʌndɪŋ] *n* finanziamento.
fund-raising ['fʌndreɪzɪŋ] *n* raccolta di fondi.
funeral ['fjuːnərəl] *n* funerale *m*.
funeral director *n* impresario di pompe funebri.
funeral parlour *n* impresa di pompe funebri.
funeral service *n* ufficio funebre.
funereal [fjuː'nɪərɪəl] *adj* funereo(a), lugubre.
fun fair *n* luna park *m inv*.
fungus, *pl* **fungi** ['fʌŋgəs, -gaɪ] *n* fungo; (*mould*) muffa.
funicular [fjuː'nɪkjulə*] *adj* (*also: ~ railway*) funicolare *f*.
funky ['fʌŋkɪ] *adj* (*music*) funky *inv*; (*col: excellent*) figo(a).
funnel ['fʌnl] *n* imbuto; (*of ship*) ciminiera.
funnily ['fʌnɪlɪ] *adv* in modo divertente; (*oddly*) stranamente.
funny ['fʌnɪ] *adj* divertente, buffo(a); (*strange*) strano(a), bizzarro(a).
funny bone *n* osso cubitale.
fun run *n* marcia non competitiva.
fur [fəː*] *n* pelo; pelliccia; pelle *f*; (*BRIT: in kettle etc*) deposito calcare.
fur coat *n* pelliccia.
furious ['fjuərɪəs] *adj* furioso(a); (*effort*) accanito(a); (*argument*) violento(a).
furiously ['fjuərɪəslɪ] *adv* furiosamente; accanitamente.
furl [fəːl] *vt* (*sail*) piegare.
furlong ['fəːlɔŋ] *n* = 201.17 m (*termine ippico*).
furlough ['fəːləu] *n* (*US*) congedo, permesso.
furnace ['fəːnɪs] *n* fornace *f*.
furnish ['fəːnɪʃ] *vt* ammobiliare; (*supply*) fornire; **~ed flat** *or* (*US*) **apartment**

appartamento ammobiliato.

furnishings ['fɜːnɪʃɪŋz] *npl* mobili *mpl*, mobilia.

furniture ['fɜːnɪtʃə*] *n* mobili *mpl*; **piece of** ~ mobile *m*.

furore [fjuə'rɔːrɪ] *n* (*protests*) scalpore *m*; (*enthusiasm*) entusiasmo.

furrier ['fʌrɪə*] *n* pellicciaio/a.

furrow ['fʌrəu] *n* solco ♦ *vt* (*forehead*) segnare di rughe.

furry ['fɜːrɪ] *adj* (*animal*) peloso(a); (*toy*) di peluche.

further ['fɜːðə*] *adj* supplementare, altro(a); nuovo(a); più lontano(a) ♦ *adv* più lontano; (*more*) di più; (*moreover*) inoltre ♦ *vt* favorire, promuovere; **until** ~ **notice** fino a nuovo avviso; **how much** ~ **is it?** quanto manca *or* dista?; ~ **to your letter of** ... (*COMM*) con riferimento alla vostra lettera del ...; **to** ~ **one's interests** fare i propri interessi.

further education *n* ≈ corsi *mpl* di formazione.

furthermore [fɜːðə'mɔː*] *adv* inoltre, per di più.

furthermost ['fɜːðəməust] *adj* più lontano(a).

furthest ['fɜːðɪst] *superlative of* **far**.

furtive ['fɜːtɪv] *adj* furtivo(a).

fury ['fjuərɪ] *n* furore *m*.

fuse, (*US*) **fuze** [fjuːz] *n* fusibile *m*; (*for bomb etc*) miccia, spoletta ♦ *vt* fondere; (*ELEC*): **to** ~ **the lights** far saltare i fusibili ♦ *vi* fondersi; **a** ~ **has blown** è saltato un fusibile.

fuse box *n* cassetta dei fusibili.

fuselage ['fjuːzəlɑːʒ] *n* fusoliera.

fuse wire *n* filo (di fusibile).

fusillade [fjuːzɪ'leɪd] *n* scarica di fucileria; (*fig*) fuoco di fila, serie *f inv* incalzante.

fusion ['fjuːʒən] *n* fusione *f*.

fuss [fʌs] *n* chiasso, trambusto, confusione *f*; (*complaining*) storie *fpl* ♦ *vt* (*person*) infastidire, scocciare ♦ *vi* agitarsi; **to make a** ~ fare delle storie; **to make a** ~ **of sb** coprire qn di attenzioni.

►**fuss over** *vt fus* (*person*) circondare di premure.

fusspot ['fʌspɔt] *n* (*col*): **he's such a** ~ fa sempre tante storie.

fussy ['fʌsɪ] *adj* (*person*) puntiglioso(a), esigente; che fa le storie; (*dress*) carico(a) di fronzoli; (*style*) elaborato(a); **I'm not** ~ (*col*) per me è lo stesso.

fusty ['fʌstɪ] *adj* (*pej: archaic*) stantio(a); (: *smell*) che sa di stantio.

futile ['fjuːtaɪl] *adj* futile.

futility [fjuː'tɪlɪtɪ] *n* futilità.

futon ['fuːtɔn] *n* futon *m inv*, letto giapponese.

future ['fjuːtʃə*] *adj* futuro(a) ♦ *n* futuro, avvenire *m*; (*LING*) futuro; **in** ~ in futuro; **in the near** ~ in un prossimo futuro; **in the immediate** ~ nell'immediato futuro.

futures ['fjuːtʃəz] *npl* (*COMM*) operazioni *fpl* a termine.

futuristic [fjuːtʃə'rɪstɪk] *adj* futuristico(a).

fuze [fjuːz] *n, vt, vi* (*US*) = **fuse**.

fuzzy ['fʌzɪ] *adj* (*PHOT*) indistinto(a), sfocato(a); (*hair*) crespo(a).

fwd. *abbr* = **forward**.

fwy *abbr* (*US*) = **freeway**.

FY *abbr* = **fiscal year**.

FYI *abbr* = **for your information**.

Gg

G, g [dʒiː] *n* (*letter*) G, g *f or m inv*; (*MUS*): **G** sol *m*; **G for George** ≈ G come Genova.

G *n abbr* (*BRIT SCOL: mark*: = *good*) ≈ buono; (*US CINE*: = *general audience*) per tutti.

g *abbr* (= *gram*; *gravity*) g.

G7 *n abbr* (*POL*: = *Group of Seven*) G7 *mpl*.

GA *abbr* (*US POST*) = **Georgia**.

gab [gæb] *n* (*col*): **to have the gift of the** ~ avere parlantina.

gabble ['gæbl] *vi* borbottare; farfugliare.

gaberdine [gæbə'diːn] *n* gabardine *m inv*.

gable ['geɪbl] *n* frontone *m*.

Gabon [gə'bɔn] *n* Gabon *m*.

gad about [gæd-] *vi* (*col*) svolazzare (qua e là).

gadget ['gædʒɪt] *n* aggeggio.

Gaelic ['geɪlɪk] *adj* gaelico(a) ♦ *n* (*language*) gaelico.

gaffe [gæf] *n* gaffe *f inv*.

gaffer ['gæfə*] *n* (*BRIT col*) capo.

gag [gæg] *n* bavaglio; (*joke*) facezia, scherzo ♦ *vt* (*prisoner etc*) imbavagliare ♦ *vi* (*choke*) soffocare.

gaga ['gɑːgɑː] *adj*: **to go** ~ rimbambirsi.

gage [geɪdʒ] *n, vt* (*US*) = **gauge**.

gaiety ['geɪtɪ] *n* gaiezza.

gaily ['geɪlɪ] *adv* allegramente.

gain [geɪn] *n* guadagno, profitto ♦ *vt* guadagnare ♦ *vi* (*watch*) andare avanti; **to** ~ **in/by** aumentare di/con; **to** ~ **3lbs (in weight)** aumentare di 3 libbre; **to** ~ **ground** guadagnare terreno.

▶**gain (up)on** vt fus accorciare le distanze da, riprendere.

gainful ['geɪnful] adj profittevole, lucrativo(a).

gainfully ['geɪnfəlɪ] adv: to be ~ **employed** avere un lavoro retribuito.

gainsay [geɪn'seɪ] vt irreg (like **say**) contraddire; negare.

gait [geɪt] n andatura.

gal. abbr = **gallon.**

gala ['gɑ:lə] n gala; swimming ~ manifestazione f di nuoto.

Galapagos Islands [gə'læpəgəs-] npl: the ~ le isole Galapagos.

galaxy ['gæləksɪ] n galassia.

gale [geɪl] n vento forte; burrasca; ~ **force 10** vento forza 10.

gall [gɔ:l] n (ANAT) bile f; (fig: impudence) fegato, faccia ♦ vt urtare (i nervi a).

gall. abbr = **gallon.**

gallant ['gælənt] adj valoroso(a); (towards ladies) galante, cortese.

gallantry ['gæləntrɪ] n valore m militare; galanteria, cortesia.

gall bladder ['gɔ:l-] n cistifellea.

galleon ['gælɪən] n galeone m.

gallery ['gælərɪ] n galleria; loggia; (for spectators) tribuna; (in theatre) loggione m, balconata; (also: **art** ~: state-owned) museo; (: private) galleria.

galley ['gælɪ] n (ship's kitchen) cambusa; (ship) galea; (also: ~ **proof**) bozza in colonna.

Gallic ['gælɪk] adj gallico(a); (French) francese.

galling ['gɔ:lɪŋ] adj irritante.

gallon ['gælən] n gallone m (BRIT: = 4.543 l; 8 pints; US = 3.785 l).

gallop ['gæləp] n galoppo ♦ vi galoppare; ~**ing inflation** inflazione f galoppante.

gallows ['gæləuz] n forca.

gallstone ['gɔ:lstəun] n calcolo biliare.

Gallup Poll ['gæləp-] n sondaggio a campione.

galore [gə'lɔ:*] adv a iosa, a profusione.

galvanize ['gælvənaɪz] vt galvanizzare; to ~ **sb into action** (fig) galvanizzare qn, spronare qn all'azione.

Gambia ['gæmbɪə] n Gambia m.

gambit ['gæmbɪt] n (fig): (opening) ~ prima mossa.

gamble ['gæmbl] n azzardo, rischio calcolato ♦ vt, vi giocare; to ~ **on** (fig) giocare su; to ~ **on the Stock Exchange** giocare in Borsa.

gambler ['gæmblə*] n giocatore/trice d'azzardo.

gambling ['gæmblɪŋ] n gioco d'azzardo.

gambol ['gæmbəl] vi saltellare.

game [geɪm] n gioco; (event) partita; (HUNTING) selvaggina ♦ adj coraggioso(a); (ready): to be ~ **(for sth/to do)** essere pronto(a) (a qc/a fare); ~**s** npl (SCOL) attività fpl sportive; **big** ~ selvaggina grossa.

game bird n uccello selvatico.

gamekeeper ['geɪmki:pə*] n guardacaccia m inv.

gamely ['geɪmlɪ] adv coraggiosamente.

game reserve n riserva di caccia.

games console n console f inv dei videogame.

gameshow ['geɪmʃəu] n gioco a premi.

gamesmanship ['geɪmzmənʃɪp] n abilità.

gaming ['geɪmɪŋ] n gioco d'azzardo.

gammon ['gæmən] n (bacon) quarto di maiale; (ham) prosciutto affumicato.

gamut ['gæmət] n gamma.

gang [gæŋ] n banda, squadra ♦ vi: to ~ **up on sb** far combutta contro qn.

Ganges ['gændʒi:z] n: the ~ il Gange.

gangland ['gæŋlænd] adj della malavita; ~ **killer** sicario.

gangling ['gæŋglɪŋ] adj allampanato(a).

gangly ['gæŋglɪ] adj = **gangling.**

gangplank ['gæŋplæŋk] n passerella.

gangrene ['gæŋgri:n] n cancrena.

gangster ['gæŋstə*] n gangster m inv.

gangway ['gæŋweɪ] n passerella; (BRIT: of bus) passaggio.

gantry ['gæntrɪ] n (for crane, railway signal) cavalletto; (for rocket) torre f di lancio.

GAO n abbr (US: = General Accounting Office) ≈ Corte f dei Conti.

gaol [dʒeɪl] n, vt (BRIT) = **jail.**

gap [gæp] n buco; (in time) intervallo; (fig) lacuna; vuoto.

gape [geɪp] vi restare a bocca aperta.

gaping ['geɪpɪŋ] adj (hole) squarciato(a).

gap year n anno di pausa preso prima di iniziare l'università, per lavorare o viaggiare.

garage ['gærɑ:ʒ] n garage m inv.

garb [gɑ:b] n abiti mpl, veste f.

garbage ['gɑ:bɪdʒ] n immondizie fpl, rifiuti mpl; (fig: film, book) porcheria, robaccia; (: nonsense) fesserie fpl.

garbage can n (US) bidone m della spazzatura.

garbage collector n (US) spazzino/a.

garbage disposal unit n tritarifiuti m inv.

garbage truck n (US) camion m inv della spazzatura.

garbled ['gɑ:bld] adj deformato(a); ingarbugliato(a).

garden ['gɑ:dn] n giardino ♦ vi lavorare nel

giardino; **~s** *npl* (*public*) giardini pubblici; (*private*) parco.
garden centre *n* vivaio.
garden city *n* (*BRIT*) città *f inv* giardino *inv*.
gardener ['gɑ:dnə*] *n* giardiniere/a.
gardening ['gɑ:dnɪŋ] *n* giardinaggio.
gargle ['gɑ:gl] *vi* fare gargarismi ♦ *n* gargarismo.
gargoyle ['gɑ:gɔɪl] *n* gargouille *f inv*.
garish ['gɛərɪʃ] *adj* vistoso(a).
garland ['gɑ:lənd] *n* ghirlanda; corona.
garlic ['gɑ:lɪk] *n* aglio.
garment ['gɑ:mənt] *n* indumento.
garner ['gɑ:nə*] *vt* ammucchiare, raccogliere.
garnish ['gɑ:nɪʃ] *vt* guarnire.
garret ['gærɪt] *n* soffitta.
garrison ['gærɪsn] *n* guarnigione *f* ♦ *vt* guarnire.
garrulous ['gærjuləs] *adj* ciarliero(a), loquace.
garter ['gɑ:tə*] *n* giarrettiera; (*US: suspender*) gancio (di reggicalze).
garter belt *n* (*US*) reggicalze *m inv*.
gas [gæs] *n* gas *m inv*; (*used as anaesthetic*) etere *m*; (*US: gasoline*) benzina ♦ *vt* asfissiare con il gas; (*MIL*) gasare.
gas cooker *n* (*BRIT*) cucina a gas.
gas cylinder *n* bombola del gas.
gaseous ['gæsɪəs] *adj* gassoso(a).
gas fire *n* (*BRIT*) radiatore *m* a gas.
gas-fired ['gæsfaɪəd] *adj* (alimentato(a)) a gas.
gash [gæʃ] *n* sfregio ♦ *vt* sfregiare.
gasket ['gæskɪt] *n* (*AUT*) guarnizione *f*.
gas mask *n* maschera *f* antigas *inv*.
gas meter *n* contatore *m* del gas.
gasoline ['gæsəli:n] *n* (*US*) benzina.
gasp [gɑ:sp] *vi* ansare, boccheggiare; (*in surprise*) restare senza fiato.
▶ **gasp out** *vt* dire affannosamente.
gas ring *n* fornello a gas.
gas station *n* (*US*) distributore *m* di benzina.
gas stove *n* cucina a gas.
gassy ['gæsɪ] *adj* gassoso(a).
gas tank *n* (*US AUT*) serbatoio (di benzina).
gas tap *n* (*on cooker*) manopola del gas; (*on pipe*) rubinetto del gas.
gastric ['gæstrɪk] *adj* gastrico(a).
gastric ulcer *n* ulcera gastrica.
gastroenteritis ['gæstrəuentə'raɪtɪs] *n* gastroenterite *f*.
gastronomy [gæs'trɒnəmɪ] *n* gastronomia.
gasworks ['gæswə:ks] *n or npl* impianto di produzione del gas.
gate [geɪt] *n* cancello; (*of castle, town*) porta; (*at airport*) uscita; (*at level crossing*)
barriera.
gâteau, *pl* **~x** ['gætəu, -z] *n* torta.
gatecrash ['geɪtkræʃ] *vt* partecipare senza invito a.
gatecrasher ['geɪtkræʃə*] *n* intruso(a), ospite *m/f* non invitato(a).
gatehouse ['geɪthaus] *n* casetta del custode (*all'entrata di un parco*).
gateway ['geɪtweɪ] *n* porta.
gather ['gæðə*] *vt* (*flowers, fruit*) cogliere; (*pick up*) raccogliere; (*assemble*) radunare; raccogliere; (*understand*) capire ♦ *vi* (*assemble*) radunarsi; (*dust*) accumularsi; (*clouds*) addensarsi; **to ~ speed** acquistare velocità; **to ~ (from/that)** comprendere (da/che), dedurre (da/che); **as far as I can ~** da quel che ho potuto capire.
gathering ['gæðərɪŋ] *n* adunanza.
GATT [gæt] *n abbr* (= *General Agreement on Tariffs and Trade*) G.A.T.T. *m*.
gauche [gəuʃ] *adj* goffo(a), maldestro(a).
gaudy ['gɔ:dɪ] *adj* vistoso(a).
gauge [geɪdʒ] *n* (*standard measure*) calibro; (*RAIL*) scartamento; (*instrument*) indicatore *m* ♦ *vt* misurare; (*fig: sb's capabilities, character*) valutare, stimare; **to ~ the right moment** calcolare il momento giusto; **petrol ~**, (*US*) **gas ~** indicatore *m* or spia della benzina.
gaunt [gɔ:nt] *adj* scarno(a); (*grim, desolate*) desolato(a).
gauntlet ['gɔ:ntlɪt] *n* (*fig*): **to run the ~ through an angry crowd** passare sotto il fuoco di una folla ostile; **to throw down the ~** gettare il guanto.
gauze [gɔ:z] *n* garza.
gave [geɪv] *pt of* **give**.
gawky ['gɔ:kɪ] *adj* goffo(a), sgraziato(a).
gawp [gɔ:p] *vi*: **to ~ at** guardare a bocca aperta.
gay [geɪ] *adj* (*person*) gaio(a), allegro(a); (*colour*) vivace, vivo(a); (*col*) omosessuale.
gaze [geɪz] *n* sguardo fisso ♦ *vi*: **to ~ at** guardare fisso.
gazelle [gə'zɛl] *n* gazzella.
gazette [gə'zɛt] *n* (*newspaper*) gazzetta; (*official publication*) gazzetta ufficiale.
gazetteer [gæzə'tɪə*] *n* (*book*) dizionario dei nomi geografici; (*section of book*) indice *m* dei nomi geografici.
gazump [gə'zʌmp] *vt* (*BRIT*): **to ~ sb** *nella compravendita di immobili, venire meno all'impegno preso con un acquirente accettando un'offerta migliore fatta da altri.*
GB *abbr* (= *Great Britain*) GB.

GBH *n abbr* (*BRIT LAW: col*) *see* **grievous bodily harm**.

GC *n abbr* (*BRIT*: = *George Cross*) *decorazione al valore*.

GCE *n abbr* (*BRIT*: = *General Certificate of Education*) ≈ diploma *m* di maturità.

GCHQ *n abbr* (*BRIT*: = *General Communications Headquarters*) *centro per l'intercettazione delle telecomunicazioni straniere*.

GCSE *n abbr* (*BRIT*: = *General Certificate of Secondary Education*) *diploma di istruzione secondaria conseguito a 16 anni in Inghilterra e Galles*.

Gdns. *abbr* = *gardens*.

GDP *n abbr* = **gross domestic product**.

GDR *n abbr* (*HIST*) *see* **German Democratic Republic**.

gear [gɪə*] *n* attrezzi *mpl*, equipaggiamento; (*belongings*) roba; (*TECH*) ingranaggio; (*AUT*) marcia ♦ *vt* (*fig*: *adapt*) adattare; **top** *or* (*US*) **high/low/bottom** ~ quarta (*or* quinta)/ seconda/ prima; **in** ~ in marcia; **out of** ~ in folle; **our service is** ~**ed to meet the needs of the disabled** la nostra organizzazione risponde espressamente alle esigenze degli handicappati.

▶**gear up** *vi*: **to** ~ **up (to do)** prepararsi (a fare).

gear box *n* scatola del cambio.

gear lever, (*US*) **gear shift** *n* leva del cambio.

GED *n abbr* (*US SCOL*) = *general educational development*.

geese [giːs] *npl of* **goose**.

geezer ['giːzə*] *n* (*BRIT col*) tizio.

Geiger counter ['gaɪgə-] *n* geiger *m inv*.

gel [dʒɛl] *n* gel *m inv*.

gelatin(e) ['dʒɛlətiːn] *n* gelatina.

gelignite ['dʒɛlɪgnaɪt] *n* nitroglicerina.

gem [dʒɛm] *n* gemma.

Gemini ['dʒɛmɪnaɪ] *n* Gemelli *mpl*; **to be** ~ essere dei Gemelli.

gen [dʒɛn] *n* (*BRIT col*): **to give sb the** ~ **on sth** mettere qn al corrente di qc.

Gen. *abbr* (*MIL*: = *General*) Gen.

gen. *abbr* (= *general, generally*) gen.

gender ['dʒɛndə*] *n* genere *m*.

gene [dʒiːn] *n* (*BIOL*) gene *m*.

genealogy [dʒiːnɪ'ælədʒɪ] *n* genealogia.

general ['dʒɛnərl] *n* generale *m* ♦ *adj* generale; **in** ~ in genere; **the** ~ **public** il grande pubblico.

general anaesthetic *n* anestesia totale.

general delivery *n* (*US*) fermo posta *m*.

general election *n* elezioni *fpl* generali.

generalization ['dʒɛnrəlaɪ'zeɪʃən] *n* generalizzazione *f*.

generalize ['dʒɛnrəlaɪz] *vi* generalizzare.

generally ['dʒɛnrəlɪ] *adv* generalmente.

general manager *n* direttore *m* generale.

general practitioner (GP) *n* medico generico; **who's your GP?** qual è il suo medico di fiducia?

general strike *n* sciopero generale.

generate ['dʒɛnəreɪt] *vt* generare.

generation [dʒɛnə'reɪʃən] *n* generazione *f*; (*of electricity etc*) produzione *f*.

generator ['dʒɛnəreɪtə*] *n* generatore *m*.

generic [dʒɪ'nɛrɪk] *adj* generico(a).

generosity [dʒɛnə'rɔsɪtɪ] *n* generosità.

generous ['dʒɛnərəs] *adj* generoso(a); (*copious*) abbondante.

genesis ['dʒɛnɪsɪs] *n* genesi *f*.

genetic [dʒɪ'nɛtɪk] *adj* genetico(a); ~ **engineering** ingegneria genetica.

genetically modified [dʒɪ'nɛtɪklɪ 'mɔdɪfaɪd] *adj* geneticamente modificato(a), transgenico(a); ~ **organism** organismo geneticamente modificato.

genetic fingerprinting [-fɪŋgəprɪntɪŋ] *n* rilevamento delle impronte genetiche.

genetics [dʒɪ'nɛtɪks] *n* genetica.

Geneva [dʒɪ'niːvə] *n* Ginevra; **Lake** ~ il lago di Ginevra.

genial ['dʒiːnɪəl] *adj* geniale, cordiale.

genitals ['dʒɛnɪtlz] *npl* genitali *mpl*.

genitive ['dʒɛnɪtɪv] *n* genitivo.

genius ['dʒiːnɪəs] *n* genio.

Genoa ['dʒɛnəuə] *n* Genova.

genocide ['dʒɛnəusaɪd] *n* genocidio.

Genoese [dʒɛnəu'iːz] *adj, n* (*pl inv*) genovese (*m/f*).

gent [dʒɛnt] *n abbr* (*BRIT col*) = **gentleman**.

genteel [dʒɛn'tiːl] *adj* raffinato(a), distinto(a).

gentle ['dʒɛntl] *adj* delicato(a); (*person*) dolce.

gentleman ['dʒɛntlmən] *n* signore *m*; (*well-bred man*) gentiluomo; ~'**s agreement** impegno sulla parola.

gentlemanly ['dʒɛntlmənlɪ] *adj* da gentiluomo.

gentleness ['dʒɛntlnɪs] *n* delicatezza; dolcezza.

gently ['dʒɛntlɪ] *adv* delicatamente.

gentry ['dʒɛntrɪ] *n* nobiltà minore.

gents [dʒɛnts] *n* W.C. *m* (per signori).

genuine ['dʒɛnjuɪn] *adj* autentico(a); sincero(a).

genuinely ['dʒɛnjuɪnlɪ] *adv* genuinamente.

geographer [dʒɪ'ɔgrəfə*] *n* geografo/a.

geographic(al) [dʒɪə'græfɪk(l)] *adj* geografico(a).

geography [dʒɪ'ɔgrəfɪ] *n* geografia.

geological [dʒɪə'lɔdʒɪkl] *adj* geologico(a).

geologist [dʒɪ'ɔlədʒɪst] *n* geologo/a.

geology [dʒɪ'ɔlədʒɪ] *n* geologia.

geometric(al) [dʒɪə'metrɪk(l)] *adj* geometrico(a).

geometry [dʒɪ'ɔmətrɪ] *n* geometria.

Geordie ['dʒɔːdɪ] *n* (*col*) abitante *m/f* del Tyneside; originario/a del Tyneside.

Georgia ['dʒɔːdʒə] *n* Georgia.

Georgian ['dʒɔːdʒən] *adj* georgiano(a) ♦ *n* georgiano/a; (*LING*) georgiano.

geranium [dʒɪ'reɪnɪəm] *n* geranio.

geriatric [dʒerɪ'ætrɪk] *adj* geriatrico(a).

germ [dʒəːm] *n* (*MED*) microbo; (*BIOL, fig*) germe *m*.

German ['dʒəːmən] *adj* tedesco(a) ♦ *n* tedesco/a; (*LING*) tedesco.

German Democratic Republic (GDR) *n* Repubblica Democratica Tedesca (R.D.T.).

germane [dʒə'meɪn] *adj* (*formal*): **to be ~ to** **sth** essere attinente a qc.

German measles *n* rosolia.

Germany ['dʒəːmənɪ] *n* Germania.

germination [dʒə:mɪ'neɪʃən] *n* germinazione *f*.

germ warfare *n* guerra batteriologica.

gerrymandering ['dʒerɪmændərɪŋ] *n* manipolazione *f* dei distretti elettorali.

gestation [dʒes'teɪʃən] *n* gestazione *f*.

gesticulate [dʒes'tɪkjuleɪt] *vi* gesticolare.

gesture ['dʒestjə*] *n* gesto; **as a ~ of** **friendship** in segno d'amicizia.

===================== *KEYWORD*

get [ɡet] (*pt, pp* **got**, (*US*) *pp* **gotten**) *vi* **1** (*become, be*) diventare, farsi; **to ~ drunk** ubriacarsi; **to ~ killed** venire *or* rimanere ucciso(a); **it's ~ting late** si sta facendo tardi; **to ~ old** invecchiare; **to ~ paid** venire pagato(a); **to ~ ready** prepararsi; **to ~ shaved** farsi la barba; **to ~ tired** stancarsi; **to ~ washed** lavarsi

2 (*go*): **to ~ to/from** andare a/da; **to ~** **home** arrivare *or* tornare a casa; **how did** **you ~ here?** come sei venuto?; **he got** **across the bridge** ha attraversato il ponte; **he got under the fence** è passato sotto il recinto

3 (*begin*) mettersi a, cominciare a; **to ~** **to know sb** incominciare a conoscere qn; **let's ~ going** *or* **started** muoviamoci

4 (*modal aux vb*): **you've got to do it** devi

farlo

♦ *vt* **1**: **to ~ sth done** (*do*) fare qc; (*have* *done*) far fare qc; **to ~ sth/sb ready** preparare qc/qn; **to ~ one's hair cut** tagliarsi *or* farsi tagliare i capelli; **to ~** **sb to do sth** far fare qc a qn

2 (*obtain: money, permission, results*) ottenere; (*find: job, flat*) trovare; (*fetch: person, doctor*) chiamare; (*: object*) prendere; **to ~ sth for sb** prendere *or* procurare qc a qn; **~ me Mr Jones,** **please** (*TEL*) mi passi il signor Jones, per favore; **can I ~ you a drink?** le posso offrire da bere?

3 (*receive: present, letter, prize*) ricevere; (*acquire: reputation*) farsi; **how much did** **you ~ for the painting?** quanto le hanno dato per il quadro?

4 (*catch*) prendere; (*hit: target etc*) colpire; **to ~ sb by the arm/throat** afferrare qn per un braccio/alla gola; **~ him!** prendetelo!; **he really ~s me** (*fig: annoy*) mi dà proprio sui nervi

5 (*take, move*) portare; **to ~ sth to sb** far avere qc a qn; **do you think we'll ~ it** **through the door?** pensi che riusciremo a farlo passare per la porta?

6 (*catch, take: plane, bus etc*) prendere; **he** **got the last bus** ha preso l'ultimo autobus; **she got the morning flight to** **Milan** ha preso il volo per Milano del mattino

7 (*understand*) afferrare; (*hear*) sentire; **I've got it!** ci sono arrivato!, ci sono!; **I'm** **sorry, I didn't ~ your name** scusi, non ho capito (*or* sentito) come si chiama

8 (*have, possess*): **to have got** avere; **how** **many have you got?** quanti ne ha?

▶**get about** *vi* muoversi; (*news*) diffondersi

▶**get across** *vt*: **to ~ across (to)** (*message,* *meaning*) comunicare (a) ♦ *vi*: **to ~ across** **to** (*subj: speaker*) comunicare con

▶**get along** *vi* (*agree*) andare d'accordo; (*depart*) andarsene; (*manage*) = **get by**

▶**get at** *vt fus* (*attack*) prendersela con; (*reach*) raggiungere, arrivare a; **what are** **you ~ting at?** dove vuoi arrivare?

▶**get away** *vi* partire, andarsene; (*escape*) scappare

▶**get away with** *vt fus*: **he'll never ~ away** **with it!** non riuscirà a farla franca!

▶**get back** *vi* (*return*) ritornare, tornare ♦ *vt* riottenere, riavere; **to ~ back to** (*start* *again*) ritornare a; (*contact again*) rimettersi in contatto con

▶**get back at** *vt fus* (*col*): **to ~ back at sb** **(for sth)** rendere pan per focaccia a qn

(per qc)

▶**get by** *vi* (*pass*) passare; (*manage*) farcela; **I can ~ by in Dutch** mi arrangio in olandese

▶**get down** *vi*, *vt fus* scendere ♦ *vt* far scendere; (*depress*) buttare giù

▶**get down to** *vt fus* (*work*) mettersi a (fare); **to ~ down to business** venire al dunque

▶**get in** *vi* entrare; (*train*) arrivare; (*arrive home*) ritornare, tornare ♦ *vt* (*bring in: harvest*) raccogliere; (: *coal, shopping, supplies*) fare provvista di; (*insert*) far entrare, infilare

▶**get into** *vt fus* entrare in; **to ~ into a rage** incavolarsi; **to ~ into bed** mettersi a letto

▶**get off** *vi* (*from train etc*) scendere; (*depart: person, car*) andare via; (*escape*) cavarsela ♦ *vt* (*remove: clothes, stain*) levare; (*send off*) spedire; (*have as leave: days, time*): **we got 2 days off** abbiamo avuto 2 giorni liberi ♦ *vt fus* (*train, bus*) scendere da; **to ~ off to a good start** (*fig*) cominciare bene

▶**get on** *vi*: **how did you ~ on?** com'è andata?; **he got on quite well** ha fatto bene, (gli) è andata bene; **to ~ on (with sb)** andare d'accordo (con qn); **how are you ~ting on?** come va la vita? ♦ *vt fus* montare in; (*horse*) montare su

▶**get on to** *vt fus* (*BRIT col: contact: on phone etc*) contattare, rintracciare; (: *deal with*) occuparsi di

▶**get out** *vi* uscire; (*of vehicle*) scendere ♦ *vt* tirar fuori, far uscire; **to ~ out (of)** (*money from bank etc*) ritirare (da)

▶**get out of** *vt fus* uscire da; (*duty etc*) evitare; **what will you ~ out of it?** cosa ci guadagni?

▶**get over** *vt fus* (*illness*) riaversi da; (*communicate: idea etc*) comunicare, passare; **let's ~ it over (with)** togliamoci il pensiero

▶**get round** *vt fus* aggirare; (*fig: person*) rigirare ♦ *vi*: **to ~ round to doing sth** trovare il tempo di fare qc

▶**get through** *vi* (*TEL*) avere la linea ♦ *vt fus* (*finish: work*) sbrigare; (: *book*) finire

▶**get through to** *vt fus* (*TEL*) parlare a

▶**get together** *vi* riunirsi ♦ *vt* raccogliere; (*people*) adunare

▶**get up** *vi* (*rise*) alzarsi ♦ *vt fus* salire su per

▶**get up to** *vt fus* (*reach*) raggiungere; (*prank etc*) fare.

getaway ['gɛtəweɪ] *n* fuga.
getaway car *n* macchina per la fuga.

get-together ['gɛttəgɛðə*] *n* (piccola) riunione *f*; (*party*) festicciola.
get-up ['gɛtʌp] *n* (*col: outfit*) tenuta.
get-well card [gɛt'wɛl-] *n* cartolina di auguri di pronta guarigione.
geyser ['giːzə*] *n* scaldabagno; (*GEO*) geyser *m inv*. ·
Ghana ['gɑːnə] *n* Ghana *m*.
Ghanaian [gɑː'neɪən] *adj*, *n* ganaense (*m/f*).
ghastly ['gɑːstlɪ] *adj* orribile, orrendo(a).
gherkin ['gəːkɪn] *n* cetriolino.
ghetto ['gɛtəu] *n* ghetto.
ghetto blaster [-'blɑːstə*] *n* maxistereo portatile.
ghost [gəust] *n* fantasma *m*, spettro ♦ *vt* (*book*) fare lo scrittore ombra per.
ghostly ['gəustlɪ] *adj* spettrale.
ghostwriter ['gəustraɪtə*] *n* scrittore/trice ombra *inv*.
ghoul [guːl] *n* vampiro che si nutre di cadaveri.
ghoulish ['guːlɪʃ] *adj* (*tastes etc*) macabro(a).
GHQ *n abbr* (*MIL*: = *general headquarters*) ≈ comando di Stato maggiore.
GI *n abbr* (*US col*: = *government issue*) G.I. *m*, soldato americano.
giant ['dʒaɪənt] *n* gigante/essa ♦ *adj* gigante, enorme; **~ (size) packet** confezione *f* gigante.
giant killer *n* (*SPORT*) *piccola squadra che riesce a batterne una importante.*
gibber ['dʒɪbə*] *vi* (*monkey*) squittire confusamente; (*idiot*) farfugliare.
gibberish ['dʒɪbərɪʃ] *n* parole *fpl* senza senso.
gibe [dʒaɪb] *n* frecciata ♦ *vi*: **to ~ at** lanciare frecciate a.
giblets ['dʒɪblɪts] *npl* frattaglie *fpl*.
Gibraltar [dʒɪ'brɔːltə*] *n* Gibilterra.
giddiness ['gɪdɪnɪs] *n* vertigine *f*.
giddy ['gɪdɪ] *adj* (*dizzy*): **to be ~** aver le vertigini; (*height*) vertiginoso(a); **I feel ~** mi gira la testa.
gift [gɪft] *n* regalo; (*donation, ability*) dono; (*COMM: also: free ~*) omaggio; **to have a ~ for sth** (*talent*) avere il dono di qc.
gifted ['gɪftɪd] *adj* dotato(a).
gift token, gift voucher *n* buono (acquisto).
gig [gɪg] *n* (*col: of musician*) serata.
gigabyte [gɪːgəbaɪt] *n* gigabyte *m inv*.
gigantic [dʒaɪ'gæntɪk] *adj* gigantesco(a).
giggle ['gɪgl] *vi* ridere scioccamente ♦ *n* risolino (sciocco).
GIGO ['gaɪgəu] *abbr* (*COMPUT: col*: = *garbage in, garbage out*) qualità di input = qualità di output.

gild [gɪld] *vt* dorare.

gill [dʒɪl] *n* (*measure*) = 0.25 pints (*BRIT* = 0.148 *l*; *US* = 0.118 *l*).

gills [gɪlz] *npl* (*of fish*) branchie *fpl*.

gilt [gɪlt] *n* doratura ♦ *adj* dorato(a).

gilt-edged ['gɪltedʒd] *adj* (*stocks, securities*) della massima sicurezza.

gimlet ['gɪmlɪt] *n* succhiello.

gimmick ['gɪmɪk] *n* trucco; **sales** ~ trovata commerciale.

gin [dʒɪn] *n* (*liquor*) gin *m inv*.

ginger ['dʒɪndʒə*] *n* zenzero.

▶**ginger up** *vt* scuotere; animare.

ginger ale, ginger beer *n* bibita gassosa allo zenzero.

gingerbread ['dʒɪndʒəbred] *n* pan *m* di zenzero.

ginger group *n* (*BRIT*) gruppo di pressione.

ginger-haired ['dʒɪndʒə'heəd] *adj* rossiccio(a).

gingerly ['dʒɪndʒəlɪ] *adv* cautamente.

gingham ['gɪŋəm] *n* percalle *m* a righe (*or* quadretti).

ginseng ['dʒɪnsɛŋ] *n* ginseng *m*.

gipsy ['dʒɪpsɪ] *n* zingaro/a ♦ *adj* degli zingari.

giraffe [dʒɪ'rɑːf] *n* giraffa.

girder ['gɜːdə*] *n* trave *f*.

girdle ['gɜːdl] *n* (*corset*) guaina.

girl [gɜːl] *n* ragazza; (*young unmarried woman*) signorina; (*daughter*) figlia, figliola; **a little** ~ una bambina.

girl band *n* gruppo pop di sole ragazze creato per far presa su un pubblico giovane.

girlfriend ['gɜːlfrend] *n* (*of girl*) amica; (*of boy*) ragazza.

girlish ['gɜːlɪʃ] *adj* da ragazza.

Girl Scout *n* (*US*) Giovane Esploratrice *f*.

Giro ['dʒaɪrəu] *n*: **the National** ~ (*BRIT*) ≈ la *or* il Bancoposta.

giro ['dʒaɪrəu] *n* (*bank* ~) versamento bancario; (*post office* ~) postagiro.

girth [gɜːθ] *n* circonferenza; (*of horse*) cinghia.

gist [dʒɪst] *n* succo.

give [gɪv] *n* (*of fabric*) elasticità ♦ *vb* (*pt* **gave**, *pp* **given** [geɪv, 'gɪvn]) *vt* dare ♦ *vi* cedere; **to** ~ **sb sth**, ~ **sth to sb** dare qc a qn; **to** ~ **a cry/sigh** emettere un grido/sospiro; **how much did you** ~ **for it?** quanto (l')hai pagato?; **12 o'clock**, ~ **or take a few minutes** mezzogiorno, minuto più minuto meno; **to** ~ **way** *vi* cedere; (*BRIT AUT*) dare la precedenza.

▶**give away** *vt* dare via; (*give free*) fare dono di; (*betray*) tradire; (*disclose*)

rivelare; (*bride*) condurre all'altare.

▶**give back** *vt* rendere.

▶**give in** *vi* cedere ♦ *vt* consegnare.

▶**give off** *vt* emettere.

▶**give out** *vt* distribuire; annunciare ♦ *vi* (*be exhausted: supplies*) esaurirsi, venir meno; (*fail: engine*) fermarsi; (: *strength*) mancare.

▶**give up** *vi* rinunciare ♦ *vt* rinunciare a; **to** ~ **up smoking** smettere di fumare; **to** ~ **o.s. up** arrendersi.

give-and-take [gɪvən'teɪk] *n* (*col*) elasticità (da ambo le parti), concessioni *fpl* reciproche.

giveaway ['gɪvəweɪ] *n* (*col*): **her expression was a** ~ le si leggeva tutto in volto; **the exam was a** ~! l'esame è stato uno scherzo! ♦ *cpd*: ~ **prices** prezzi stracciati.

given ['gɪvn] *pp of* **give** ♦ *adj* (*fixed: time, amount*) dato(a), determinato(a) ♦ *conj*: ~ (**that**) ... dato che ...; ~ **the circumstances** ... date le circostanze ....

glacial ['gleɪsɪəl] *adj* glaciale.

glacier ['glæsɪə*] *n* ghiacciaio.

glad [glæd] *adj* lieto(a), contento(a); **to be** ~ **about sth/that** essere contento *or* lieto di qc/che + *sub*; **I was** ~ **of his help** gli sono stato grato del suo aiuto.

gladden ['glædn] *vt* rallegrare, allietare.

glade [gleɪd] *n* radura.

gladioli [glædɪ'əulaɪ] *npl* gladioli *mpl*.

gladly ['glædlɪ] *adv* volentieri.

glamorous ['glæmərəs] *adj* (*gen*) favoloso(a); (*person*) affascinante, seducente; (*occasion*) brillante, elegante.

glamour ['glæmə*] *n* fascino.

glance [glɑːns] *n* occhiata, sguardo ♦ *vi*: **to** ~ **at** dare un'occhiata a.

▶**glance off** *vt fus* (*bullet*) rimbalzare su.

glancing ['glɑːnsɪŋ] *adj* (*blow*) che colpisce di striscio.

gland [glænd] *n* ghiandola.

glandular ['glændjulə*] *adj*: ~ **fever** (*BRIT*) mononucleosi *f*.

glare [gleə*] *n* riverbero, luce *f* abbagliante; (*look*) sguardo furioso ♦ *vi* abbagliare; **to** ~ **at** guardare male.

glaring ['gleərɪŋ] *adj* (*mistake*) madornale.

glasnost ['glæznɔst] *n* glasnost *f*.

glass [glɑːs] *n* (*substance*) vetro; (*tumbler*) bicchiere *m*; (*also*: **looking** ~) specchio; *see also* **glasses**.

glass-blowing ['glɑːsbləuɪŋ] *n* soffiatura del vetro.

glass ceiling *n* (*fig*) barriera invisibile.

glasses ['glɑːsɪz] *npl* (*spectacles*) occhiali *mpl*.

glass fibre *n* fibra di vetro.

glasshouse ['glɑːshaus] n serra.
glassware ['glɑːswɛə*] n vetrame m.
glassy ['glɑːsɪ] adj (eyes) vitreo(a).
Glaswegian [glæs'wiːdʒən] adj di Glasgow ♦ n abitante m/f di Glasgow; originario/a di Glasgow.
glaze [gleɪz] vt (door) fornire di vetri; (pottery) smaltare; (CULIN) glassare ♦ n smalto; glassa.
glazed ['gleɪzd] adj (eye) vitreo(a); (tiles, pottery) smaltato(a).
glazier ['gleɪzɪə*] n vetraio.
gleam [gliːm] n barlume m; raggio ♦ vi luccicare; **a ~ of hope** un barlume di speranza.
gleaming ['gliːmɪŋ] adj lucente.
glean [gliːn] vt (information) racimolare.
glee [gliː] n allegrezza, gioia.
gleeful ['gliːful] adj allegro(a), gioioso(a).
glen [glɛn] n valletta.
glib [glɪb] adj dalla parola facile; facile.
glide [glaɪd] vi scivolare; (AVIAT, birds) planare ♦ n scivolata; planata.
glider ['glaɪdə*] n (AVIAT) aliante m.
gliding ['glaɪdɪŋ] n (AVIAT) volo a vela.
glimmer ['glɪmə*] vi luccicare ♦ n barlume m.
glimpse [glɪmps] n impressione f fugace ♦ vt vedere di sfuggita; **to catch a ~ of** vedere di sfuggita.
glint [glɪnt] n luccichio ♦ vi luccicare.
glisten ['glɪsn] vi luccicare.
glitter ['glɪtə*] vi scintillare ♦ n scintillio.
glitz [glɪts] n (col) chiasso, chiassosità.
gloat [gləut] vi: **to ~ (over)** gongolare di piacere (per).
global ['gləubl] adj globale; (world-wide) mondiale.
global warming n riscaldamento dell'atmosfera terrestre.
globe [gləub] n globo, sfera.
globetrotter ['gləubtrɔtə*] n giramondo m/f inv.
globule ['glɔbjuːl] n (ANAT) globulo; (of water etc) gocciolina.
gloom [gluːm] n oscurità, buio; (sadness) tristezza, malinconia.
gloomy ['gluːmɪ] adj fosco(a), triste; **to feel ~** sentirsi giù or depresso.
glorification [glɔːrɪfɪ'keɪʃən] n glorificazione f.
glorify ['glɔːrɪfaɪ] vt glorificare; celebrare, esaltare.
glorious ['glɔːrɪəs] adj glorioso(a); magnifico(a).
glory ['glɔːrɪ] n gloria; splendore m ♦ vi: **to ~ in** gloriarsi di or in.
glory hole n (col) ripostiglio.

Glos abbr (BRIT) = Gloucestershire.
gloss [glɔs] n (shine) lucentezza; (also: ~ paint) vernice f a olio.
▶**gloss over** vt fus scivolare su.
glossary ['glɔsərɪ] n glossario.
glossy ['glɔsɪ] adj lucente ♦ n (also: ~ magazine) rivista di lusso.
glove [glʌv] n guanto.
glove compartment n (AUT) vano portaoggetti.
glow [gləu] vi ardere; (face) essere luminoso(a) ♦ n bagliore m; (of face) colorito acceso.
glower ['glauə*] vi: **to ~ (at sb)** guardare (qn) in cagnesco.
glowing ['gləuɪŋ] adj (fire) ardente; (complexion) luminoso(a); (fig: report, description etc) entusiasta.
glow-worm ['gləuwəːm] n lucciola.
glucose ['gluːkəus] n glucosio.
glue [gluː] n colla ♦ vt incollare.
glue-sniffing ['gluːsnɪfɪŋ] n sniffare m (colla).
glum [glʌm] adj abbattuto(a).
glut [glʌt] n eccesso ♦ vt saziare; (market) saturare.
glutinous ['gluːtɪnəs] adj colloso(a), appiccicoso(a).
glutton ['glʌtn] n ghiottone/a; **a ~ for work** un(a) patito(a) del lavoro.
gluttonous ['glʌtənəs] adj ghiotto(a), goloso(a).
gluttony ['glʌtənɪ] n ghiottoneria; (sin) gola.
glycerin(e) ['glɪsəriːn] n glicerina.
GM adj abbr = **genetically modified**.
gm abbr = **gram**.
GMAT n abbr (US: = Graduate Management Admissions Test) esame di ammissione all'ultimo biennio di scuola superiore.
GM-free [dʒiːɛm'friː] adj privo(a) di OGM.
GMO n abbr (= genetically modified organism) OGM m inv.
GMT abbr (= Greenwich Mean Time) T.M.G.
gnarled [nɑːld] adj nodoso(a).
gnash [næʃ] vt: **to ~ one's teeth** digrignare i denti.
gnat [næt] n moscerino.
gnaw [nɔː] vt rodere.
gnome [nəum] n gnomo.
GNP n abbr = **gross national product**.
go [gəu] vb (pt **went**, pp **gone** [wɛnt, gɔn]) vi andare; (depart) partire, andarsene; (work) funzionare; (break etc) cedere; (be sold): **to ~ for £10** essere venduto per 10 sterline; (fit, suit): **to ~ with** andare bene con; (become): **to ~ pale** diventare pallido(a); **to ~ mouldy** ammuffire ♦ n (pl

~es): **to have a** ~ **(at)** provare; **to be on the** ~ essere in moto; **whose** ~ **is it?** a chi tocca?; **to** ~ **by car/on foot** andare in macchina/a piedi; **he's** ~**ing to do** sta per fare; **to** ~ **for a walk** andare a fare una passeggiata; **to** ~ **dancing/shopping** andare a ballare/fare la spesa; **to** ~ **looking for sb/sth** andare in cerca di qn/qc; **to** ~ **to sleep** addormentarsi; **to** ~ **and see sb, to** ~ **to see sb** andare a trovare qn; **how is it** ~**ing?** come va (la vita)?; **how did it** ~? com'è andato?; **to** ~ **round the back/by the shop** passare da dietro/davanti al negozio; **my voice has gone** m'è andata via la voce; **the cake is all gone** il dolce è finito tutto; **I'll take whatever is** ~**ing** (*BRIT*) prendo quello che c'è; ... **to** ~ (*US: food*) ... da portar via; **the money will** ~ **towards our holiday** questi soldi li mettiamo per la vacanza.

▶**go about** *vi* (*also:* ~ **around**) aggirarsi; (: *rumour*) correre, circolare ♦ *vt fus:* **how do I** ~ **about this?** qual è la prassi per questo?; **to** ~ **about one's business** occuparsi delle proprie faccende.

▶**go after** *vt fus* (*pursue*) correr dietro a, rincorrere; (*job, record etc*) mirare a.

▶**go against** *vt fus* (*be unfavourable to*) essere contro; (*be contrary to*) andare contro.

▶**go ahead** *vi* andare avanti; ~ **ahead!** faccia pure!

▶**go along** *vi* andare, avanzare ♦ *vt fus* percorrere; **to** ~ **along with** (*accompany*) andare con, accompagnare; (*agree with:* *idea*) sottoscrivere, appoggiare.

▶**go away** *vi* partire, andarsene.

▶**go back** *vi* tornare, ritornare; (*go again*) andare di nuovo.

▶**go back on** *vt fus* (*promise*) non mantenere.

▶**go by** *vi* (*years, time*) scorrere ♦ *vt fus* attenersi a, seguire (alla lettera); prestar fede a.

▶**go down** *vi* scendere; (*ship*) affondare; (*sun*) tramontare ♦ *vt fus* scendere; **that should** ~ **down well with him** dovrebbe incontrare la sua approvazione.

▶**go for** *vt fus* (*fetch*) andare a prendere; (*like*) andar matto(a) per; (*attack*) attaccare; saltare addosso a.

▶**go in** *vi* entrare.

▶**go in for** *vt fus* (*competition*) iscriversi a; (*be interested in*) interessarsi di.

▶**go into** *vt fus* entrare in; (*investigate*) indagare, esaminare; (*embark on*) lanciarsi in.

▶**go off** *vi* partire, andar via; (*food*) guastarsi; (*explode*) esplodere, scoppiare; (*lights etc*) spegnersi; (*event*) passare ♦ *vt fus:* **I've gone off chocolate** la cioccolata non mi piace più; **the gun went off** il fucile si scaricò; **the party went off well** la festa è andata *or* è riuscita bene; **to** ~ **off to sleep** addormentarsi.

▶**go on** *vi* continuare; (*happen*) succedere; (*lights*) accendersi ♦ *vt fus* (*be guided by:* *evidence etc*) basarsi su, fondarsi su; **to** ~ **on doing** continuare a fare; **what's** ~**ing on here?** che succede *or* che sta succedendo qui?

▶**go on at** *vt fus* (*nag*) assillare.

▶**go on with** *vt fus* continuare, proseguire.

▶**go out** *vi* uscire; (*fire, light*) spegnersi; (*ebb: tide*) calare; **to** ~ **out with sb** uscire con qn.

▶**go over** *vi* (*ship*) ribaltarsi ♦ *vt fus* (*check*) esaminare; **to** ~ **over sth in one's mind** pensare bene a qc.

▶**go round** *vi* (*circulate: news, rumour*) circolare; (*revolve*) girare; (*visit*): **to** ~ **round (to sb's)** passare (da qn); (*make a detour*): **to** ~ **round (by)** passare (per); (*suffice*) bastare (per tutti).

▶**go through** *vt fus* (*town etc*) attraversare; (*search through*) frugare in; (*examine: list, book*) leggere da capo a fondo; (*perform*) fare.

▶**go through with** *vt fus* (*plan, crime*) mettere in atto, eseguire; **I couldn't** ~ **through with it** non sono riuscito ad andare fino in fondo.

▶**go under** *vi* (*sink: ship*) affondare, colare a picco; (: *person*) andare sotto; (*fig: business, firm*) fallire.

▶**go up** *vi* salire ♦ *vt fus* salire su per; **to** ~ **up in flames** andare in fiamme.

▶**go without** *vt fus* fare a meno di.

goad [gəud] *vt* spronare.

go-ahead ['gəuəhɛd] *adj* intraprendente ♦ *n:* **to give sb/sth the** ~ dare l'okay a qn/qc.

goal [gəul] *n* (*SPORT*) gol *m*, rete *f*; (: *place*) porta; (*fig: aim*) fine *m*, scopo.

goal difference *n* differenza *f* reti *inv*.

goalie ['gəulɪ] *n* (*col*) portiere *m*.

goalkeeper ['gəulki:pə*] *n* portiere *m*.

goalpost ['gəulpəust] *n* palo (della porta).

goat [gəut] *n* capra.

gobble ['gɔbl] *vt* (*also:* ~ **down**, ~ **up**) ingoiare.

go-between ['gəubɪtwi:n] *n* intermediario/a.

Gobi Desert ['gəubɪ-] *n:* **the** ~ il Deserto dei Gobi.

goblet ['gɔblɪt] *n* calice *m*, coppa.

goblin ['gɔblɪn] n folletto.
go-cart ['gəukɑːt] n go-kart m inv ♦ cpd: ~
racing n kartismo.
god [gɔd] n dio; **G**~ Dio.
god-awful [gɔd'ɔːfəl] adj (col) di merda (!).
godchild ['gɔdtʃaɪld] n figlioccio/a.
goddamn(ed) ['gɔddæm(d)] (esp US: col)
excl: **goddamn!** porca miseria! ♦ adj
fottuto(a) (!), maledetto(a) ♦ adv
maledettamente.
goddaughter ['gɔddɔːtə*] n figlioccia.
goddess ['gɔdɪs] n dea.
godfather ['gɔdfɑːðə*] n padrino.
god-fearing ['gɔdfɪərɪŋ] adj timorato(a) di
Dio.
god-forsaken ['gɔdfəseɪkən] adj
desolato(a), sperduto(a).
godmother ['gɔdmʌðə*] n madrina.
godparents ['gɔdpɛərənts] npl: **the** ~ il
padrino e la madrina.
godsend ['gɔdsɛnd] n dono del cielo.
godson ['gɔdsʌn] n figlioccio.
goes [gəuz] vb see **go**.
gofer ['gəufə*] n (col) tuttofare m/f,
tirapiedi m/f inv.
go-getter ['gəugɛtə*] n arrivista m/f.
goggle ['gɔgl] vi: **to** ~ **(at)** stare con gli
occhi incollati or appiccicati (a or
addosso a).
goggles ['gɔglz] npl occhiali mpl (di
protezione).
going ['gəuɪŋ] n (conditions) andare m, stato
del terreno ♦ adj: **the** ~ **rate** la tariffa in
vigore; **a** ~ **concern** un'azienda avviata; **it
was slow** ~ si andava a rilento.
going-over [gəuɪŋ'əuvə*] n (col)
controllata; (violent attack) pestaggio.
goings-on ['gəuɪŋz'ɔn] npl (col) fatti mpl
strani, cose fpl strane.
go-kart ['gəukɑːt] n = **go-cart**.
gold [gəuld] n oro ♦ adj d'oro; (reserves)
aureo(a).
golden ['gəuldən] adj (made of gold) d'oro;
(gold in colour) dorato(a).
golden age n età d'oro.
golden handshake n (BRIT) gratifica di
fine servizio.
golden rule n regola principale.
goldfish ['gəuldfɪʃ] n pesce m dorato or
rosso.
gold leaf n lamina d'oro.
gold medal n (SPORT) medaglia d'oro.
goldmine ['gəuldmaɪn] n miniera d'oro.
gold-plated ['gəuld'pleɪtɪd] adj placcato(a)
oro inv.
goldsmith ['gəuldsmɪθ] n orefice m, orafo.
gold standard n tallone m aureo.
golf [gɔlf] n golf m.

golf ball n pallina da golf.
golf club n circolo di golf; (stick) bastone m
or mazza da golf.
golf course n campo di golf.
golfer ['gɔlfə*] n giocatore/trice di golf.
golfing ['gɔlfɪŋ] n il giocare a golf.
gondola ['gɔndələ] n gondola.
gondolier [gɔndə'lɪə*] n gondoliere m.
gone [gɔn] pp of **go**.
goner ['gɔnə*] n (col): **I thought you were a**
~ pensavo che ormai fossi spacciato.
gong [gɔŋ] n gong m inv.
good [gud] adj buono(a); (kind) buono(a),
gentile; (child) bravo(a) ♦ n bene m; ~!
bene!, ottimo!; **to be** ~ **at** essere bravo(a)
in; **it's** ~ **for you** fa bene; **it's a** ~ **thing
you were there** meno male che c'era; **she
is** ~ **with children/her hands** ci sa fare
coi bambini/è abile nei lavori manuali; **to
feel** ~ sentirsi bene; **it's** ~ **to see you** che
piacere vederla; **he's up to no** ~ ne sta
combinando qualcuna; **it's no** ~
complaining brontolare non serve a
niente; **for the common** ~ nell'interesse
generale, per il bene comune; **for** ~ (for
ever) per sempre, definitivamente; **would
you be** ~ **enough to ...?** avrebbe la
gentilezza di ...?; **that's very** ~ **of you** è
molto gentile da parte sua; **is this any** ~
(will it do?) va bene questo?; (what's it
like?) com'è?; **a** ~ **deal (of)** molto(a), una
buona quantità (di); **a** ~ **many** molti(e);
~ **morning!** buon giorno!; ~ **afternoon/
evening!** buona sera!; ~ **night!** buona
notte!; see also **goods**.
goodbye [gud'baɪ] excl arrivederci!; **to say**
~ **to** (person) salutare.
good faith n buona fede.
good-for-nothing ['gudfənʌθɪŋ] n buono/a
a nulla, vagabondo/a.
Good Friday n Venerdì Santo.
good-humoured [gud'hjuːməd] adj (person)
di buon umore; (remark, joke)
bonario(a).
good-looking [gud'lukɪŋ] adj bello(a).
good-natured [gud'neɪtʃəd] adj (person)
affabile; (discussion) amichevole,
cordiale.
goodness ['gudnɪs] n (of person) bontà; **for**
~ **sake!** per amor di Dio!; ~ **gracious!**
santo cielo!, mamma mia!
goods [gudz] npl (COMM etc) merci fpl,
articoli mpl; ~ **and chattels** beni mpl e
effetti mpl.
goods train n (BRIT) treno m merci inv.
goodwill [gud'wɪl] n amicizia,
benevolenza; (COMM) avviamento.
goody-goody ['gudɪgudɪ] n (pej)

santarellino/a.

gooey ['guːɪ] *adj* (*BRIT col*: *sticky*) appiccicoso(a); (*cake, dessert*) troppo zuccherato(a).

goose, *pl* **geese** [guːs, giːs] *n* oca.

gooseberry ['guzbərɪ] *n* uva spina; **to play** ~ (*BRIT*) tenere la candela.

gooseflesh ['guːsfleʃ] *n*, **goosepimples** ['guːspɪmplz] *npl* pelle *f* d'oca.

goose step *n* (*MIL*) passo dell'oca.

GOP *n abbr* (*US POL*: *col*: = *Grand Old Party*) partito repubblicano.

gopher ['gəʊfə*] *n* = **gofer**.

gore [gɔ:*] *vt* incornare ♦ *n* sangue *m* (coagulato).

gorge [gɔːdʒ] *n* gola ♦ *vt*: **to** ~ **o.s. (on)** ingozzarsi (di).

gorgeous ['gɔːdʒəs] *adj* magnifico(a).

gorilla [gə'rɪlə] *n* gorilla *m inv*.

gormless ['gɔːmlɪs] *adj* (*BRIT col*) tonto(a); (: *stronger*) deficiente.

gorse [gɔːs] *n* ginestrone *m*.

gory ['gɔːrɪ] *adj* sanguinoso(a).

go-slow ['gəʊ'sləʊ] *n* (*BRIT*) rallentamento dei lavori (*per agitazione sindacale*).

gospel ['gɔspl] *n* vangelo.

gossamer ['gɔsəmə*] *n* (*cobweb*) fili *mpl* della Madonna *or* di ragnatela; (*light fabric*) stoffa sottilissima.

gossip ['gɔsɪp] *n* chiacchiere *fpl*; pettegolezzi *mpl*; (*person*) pettegolo/a ♦ *vi* chiacchierare; (*maliciously*) pettegolare; **a piece of** ~ un pettegolezzo.

gossip column *n* cronaca mondana.

got [gɔt] *pt, pp of* **get**.

Gothic ['gɔθɪk] *adj* gotico(a).

gotten ['gɔtn] (*US*) *pp of* **get**.

gouge [gaudʒ] *vt* (*also*: ~ **out**: *hole etc*) scavare; (: *initials*) scolpire; (: *sb's eyes*) cavare.

gourd [guəd] *n* zucca.

gourmet ['guəmeɪ] *n* buongustaio/a.

gout [gaut] *n* gotta.

govern ['gʌvən] *vt* governare; (*LING*) reggere.

governess ['gʌvənɪs] *n* governante *f*.

governing ['gʌvənɪŋ] *adj* (*POL*) al potere, al governo; ~ **body** consiglio di amministrazione.

government ['gʌvnmənt] *n* governo; (*BRIT*: *ministers*) ministero ♦ *cpd* statale; **local** ~ amministrazione *f* locale.

governmental [gʌvn'mentl] *adj* governativo(a).

government housing *n* (*US*) alloggi *mpl* popolari.

government stock *n* titoli *mpl* di stato.

governor ['gʌvənə*] *n* (*of state, bank*) governatore *m*; (*of school, hospital*) amministratore *m*; (*BRIT*: *of prison*) direttore/trice.

Govt *abbr* = **government**.

gown [gaun] *n* vestito lungo; (*of teacher, judge*) toga.

GP *n abbr* (*MED*) *see* **general practitioner**.

GPMU *n abbr* (*BRIT*) = Graphical, Paper and Media Union.

GPO *n abbr* (*BRIT*: *old*) = General Post Office; (*US* = *Government Printing Office*) ≈ Poligrafici dello Stato.

gr. *abbr* (*COMM*) = **gross**.

grab [græb] *vt* afferrare, arraffare; (*property, power*) impadronirsi di ♦ *vi*: **to** ~ **at** tentare disperatamente di afferrare.

grace [greɪs] *n* grazia; (*graciousness*) garbo, cortesia ♦ *vt* onorare; **5 days'** ~ dilazione *f* di 5 giorni; **to say** ~ dire il benedicite; **with a good/bad** ~ volentieri/ malvolentieri; **his sense of humour is his saving** ~ il suo senso dell'umorismo è quello che lo salva.

graceful ['greɪsful] *adj* elegante, aggraziato(a).

gracious ['greɪʃəs] *adj* grazioso(a); misericordioso(a) ♦ *excl*: (**good**) ~! madonna (mia)!

gradation [grə'deɪʃən] *n* gradazione *f*.

grade [greɪd] *n* (*COMM*) qualità *f inv*; classe *f*; categoria; (*in hierarchy*) grado; (*US SCOL*) voto; classe; (*gradient*) pendenza, gradiente *m* ♦ *vt* classificare; ordinare; graduare; **to make the** ~ (*fig*) farcela.

grade crossing *n* (*US*) passaggio a livello.

grade school *n* (*US*) scuola elementare *or* primaria.

gradient ['greɪdɪənt] *n* pendenza, gradiente *m*.

gradual ['grædjuəl] *adj* graduale.

gradually ['grædjuəlɪ] *adv* man mano, a poco a poco.

graduate *n* ['grædjuɪt] laureato/a; (*US SCOL*) diplomato/a, licenziato/a ♦ *vi* ['grædjueɪt] laurearsi.

graduated pension ['grædjueɪtɪd-] *n* pensione calcolata sugli ultimi stipendi.

graduation [grædju'eɪʃən] *n* cerimonia del conferimento della laurea; (*US SCOL*) consegna dei diplomi.

graffiti [grə'fiːtɪ] *npl* graffiti *mpl*.

graft [grɑːft] *n* (*AGR, MED*) innesto ♦ *vt* innestare; **hard** ~ (*col*) duro lavoro.

grain [greɪn] *n* (*no pl*: *cereals*) cereali *mpl*; (*US*: *corn*) grano; (*of sand*) granello; (*of wood*) venatura; **it goes against the** ~ (*fig*) va contro la mia (*or* la sua *etc*)

natura.
gram [græm] *n* grammo.
grammar ['græmə*] *n* grammatica.
grammar school *n* (*BRIT*) ≈ liceo; (*US*) ≈ scuola elementare.
grammatical [grə'mætɪkl] *adj* grammaticale.
gramme [græm] *n* = **gram**.
gramophone ['græməfəun] *n* (*BRIT*) grammofono.
granary ['grænərɪ] *n* granaio.
grand [grænd] *adj* grande, magnifico(a); grandioso(a) ♦ *n* (*col: thousand*) mille dollari *mpl* (*or* sterline *fpl*).
grandchild, *pl* **-children** ['græntʃaɪld, -tʃɪldrən] *n* nipote *m*.
granddad ['grændæd] *n* (*col*) nonno.
granddaughter ['grændɔːtə*] *n* nipote *f*.
grandeur ['grændjə*] *n* (*of style, house*) splendore *m*; (*of occasion, scenery etc*) grandiosità, maestà.
grandfather ['grændfɑːðə*] *n* nonno.
grandiose ['grændɪəus] *adj* grandioso(a); (*pej*) pomposo(a).
grand jury *n* (*US*) giuria (*formata da 12 a 23 membri*).
grandma ['grænmɑː] *n* (*col*) nonna.
grandmother ['grænmʌðə*] *n* nonna.
grandpa ['grænpɑː] *n* (*col*) = **granddad**.
grandparent ['grænpɛərənt] *n* nonno/a.
grand piano *n* pianoforte *m* a coda.
Grand Prix ['grɑ̃:'priː] *n* (*AUT*) Gran Premio, Grand Prix *m inv*.
grandson ['grænsʌn] *n* nipote *m*.
grandstand ['grændstænd] *n* (*SPORT*) tribuna.
grand total *n* somma complessiva.
granite ['grænɪt] *n* granito.
granny ['grænɪ] *n* (*col*) nonna.
grant [grɑːnt] *vt* accordare; (*a request*) accogliere; (*admit*) ammettere, concedere ♦ *n* (*SCOL*) borsa; (*ADMIN*) sussidio, sovvenzione *f*; **to take sth for ~ed** dare qc per scontato.
granulated ['grænjuleɪtɪd] *adj*: **~ sugar** zucchero cristallizzato.
granule ['grænjuːl] *n* granello.
grape [greɪp] *n* chicco d'uva, acino; **a bunch of ~s** un grappolo d'uva.
grapefruit ['greɪpfruːt] *n* pompelmo.
grapevine ['greɪpvaɪn] *n* vite *f*; **I heard it on the ~** (*fig*) me l'ha detto l'uccellino.
graph [grɑːf] *n* grafico.
graphic ['græfɪk] *adj* grafico(a); (*vivid*) vivido(a); *see also* **graphics**.
graphic designer *n* grafico/a.
graphic equalizer *n* equalizzatore *m* grafico.

graphics ['græfɪks] *n* (*art, process*) grafica; (*pl: drawings*) illustrazioni *fpl*.
graphite ['græfaɪt] *n* grafite *f*.
graph paper *n* carta millimetrata.
grapple ['græpl] *vi*: **to ~ with** essere alle prese con.
grappling iron ['græplɪŋ-] *n* (*NAUT*) grappino.
grasp [grɑːsp] *vt* afferrare ♦ *n* (*grip*) presa; (*fig*) potere *m*; comprensione *f*; **to have sth within one's ~** avere qc a portata di mano; **to have a good ~ of** (*subject*) avere una buona padronanza di.
▶**grasp at** *vt fus* (*rope etc*) afferrarsi a, aggrapparsi a; (*fig: opportunity*) non farsi sfuggire, approfittare di.
grasping ['grɑːspɪŋ] *adj* avido(a).
grass [grɑːs] *n* erba; (*pasture*) pascolo, prato; (*BRIT col: informer*) informatore/ trice; (*ex-terrorist*) pentito/a.
grasshopper ['grɑːshɔpə*] *n* cavalletta.
grassland ['grɑːslænd] *n* prateria.
grass roots *npl* (*fig*) base *f*.
grass snake *n* natrice *f*.
grassy ['grɑːsɪ] *adj* erboso(a).
grate [greɪt] *n* graticola (del focolare) ♦ *vi* cigolare, stridere ♦ *vt* (*CULIN*) grattugiare.
grateful ['greɪtful] *adj* grato(a), riconoscente.
gratefully ['greɪtfulɪ] *adv* con gratitudine.
grater ['greɪtə*] *n* grattugia.
gratification [grætɪfɪ'keɪʃən] *n* soddisfazione *f*.
gratify ['grætɪfaɪ] *vt* appagare; (*whim*) soddisfare.
gratifying ['grætɪfaɪŋ] *adj* gradito(a); soddisfacente.
grating ['greɪtɪŋ] *n* (*iron bars*) grata ♦ *adj* (*noise*) stridente, stridulo(a).
gratitude ['grætɪtjuːd] *n* gratitudine *f*.
gratuitous [grə'tjuːɪtəs] *adj* gratuito(a).
gratuity [grə'tjuːɪtɪ] *n* mancia.
grave [greɪv] *n* tomba ♦ *adj* grave, serio(a).
gravedigger ['greɪvdɪgə*] *n* becchino.
gravel ['grævl] *n* ghiaia.
gravely ['greɪvlɪ] *adv* gravemente, solennemente; **~ ill** in pericolo di vita.
gravestone ['greɪvstəun] *n* pietra tombale.
graveyard ['greɪvjɑːd] *n* cimitero.
gravitate ['grævɪteɪt] *vi* gravitare.
gravity ['grævɪtɪ] *n* (*all senses*) gravità.
gravy ['greɪvɪ] *n* intingolo della carne; salsa.
gravy boat *n* salsiera.
gravy train *n*: **the ~** (*col*) l'albero della cuccagna.
gray [greɪ] *adj* (*US*) = **grey**.

graze [greɪz] *vi* pascolare, pascere ♦ *vt*
(*touch lightly*) sfiorare; (*scrape*) escoriare
♦ *n* (*MED*) escoriazione *f*.

grazing ['greɪzɪŋ] *n* pascolo.

grease [griːs] *n* (*fat*) grasso; (*lubricant*)
lubrificante *m* ♦ *vt* ingrassare; lubrificare;
to ~ the skids (*US: fig*) spianare la strada.

grease gun *n* ingrassatore *m*.

greasepaint ['griːspeɪnt] *n* cerone *m*.

greaseproof paper ['griːspruːf-] *n* (*BRIT*)
carta oleata.

greasy ['griːsɪ] *adj* grasso(a); untuoso(a);
(*BRIT: road, surface*) scivoloso(a); (*hands,
clothes*) unto(a).

great [greɪt] *adj* grande; (*pain, heat*) forte,
intenso(a); (*col*) magnifico(a),
meraviglioso(a); **they're ~ friends** sono
grandi amici; **the ~ thing is that ...** il
bello è che ...; **it was ~!** è stato
fantastico!; **we had a ~ time** ci siamo
divertiti un mondo.

Great Barrier Reef *n*: **the ~** la Grande
Barriera Corallina.

Great Britain *n* Gran Bretagna.

great-grandchild, *pl* **-children**
[greɪt'grænt∫aɪld, -t∫ɪldrən] *n* pronipote *m/f*.

great-grandfather [greɪt'grændfɑːðə*] *n*
bisnonno.

great-grandmother [greɪt'grænmʌðə*] *n*
bisnonna.

Great Lakes *npl*: **the ~** i Grandi Laghi.

greatly ['greɪtlɪ] *adv* molto.

greatness ['greɪtnɪs] *n* grandezza.

Grecian ['griː∫ən] *adj* greco(a).

Greece [griːs] *n* Grecia.

greed [griːd] *n* (*also*: **~iness**) avarizia; (*for
food*) golosità, ghiottoneria.

greedily ['griːdɪlɪ] *adv* avidamente;
golosamente.

greedy ['griːdɪ] *adj* avido(a); goloso(a),
ghiotto(a).

Greek [griːk] *adj* greco(a) ♦ *n* greco/a; (*LING*)
greco; **ancient/modern ~** greco antico/
moderno.

green [griːn] *adj* (*also POL*) verde;
(*inexperienced*) inesperto(a), ingenuo(a)
♦ *n* verde *m*; (*stretch of grass*) prato; (*also:
village ~*) ≈ piazza del paese; **~s** *npl*
(*vegetables*) verdura; (*of golf course*)
green *m inv*; **to have ~ fingers** *or* (*US*) **a ~
thumb** (*fig*) avere il pollice verde; **the G~
Party** (*BRIT POL*) i Verdi.

green belt *n* (*round town*) cintura di verde.

green card *n* (*AUT*) carta verde.

greenery ['griːnərɪ] *n* verde *m*.

greenfly ['griːnflaɪ] *n* afide *f*.

greengage ['griːngeɪdʒ] *n* susina Regina
Claudia.

greengrocer ['griːnɡrəʊsə*] *n* (*BRIT*)
fruttivendolo/a, erbivendolo/a.

greenhouse ['griːnhaʊs] *n* serra.

greenhouse effect *n*: **the ~** l'effetto
serra.

greenhouse gas *n* gas *m inv* responsabile
dell'effetto serra.

greenish ['griːnɪ∫] *adj* verdastro(a).

Greenland ['griːnlənd] *n* Groenlandia.

Greenlander ['griːnləndə*] *n* groenlandese
m/f.

green light *n*: **to give sb the ~** dare via
libera a qn.

green pepper *n* peperone *m* verde.

greet [griːt] *vt* salutare.

greeting ['griːtɪŋ] *n* saluto; **Christmas/
birthday ~s** auguri *mpl* di Natale/di
compleanno; **Season's ~s** Buone Feste.

greeting(s) card *n* cartolina d'auguri.

gregarious [ɡrə'ɡɛərɪəs] *adj* gregario(a);
socievole.

grenade [ɡrə'neɪd] *n* (*also*: **hand ~**)
granata.

grew [ɡruː] *pt of* **grow**.

grey [ɡreɪ] *adj* grigio(a); **to go ~** diventar
grigio.

greyhound ['ɡreɪhaʊnd] *n* levriere *m*.

grid [ɡrɪd] *n* grata; (*ELEC*) rete *f*; (*US AUT*)
area d'incrocio.

griddle ['ɡrɪdl] *n* piastra.

gridiron ['ɡrɪdaɪən] *n* graticola.

gridlock ['ɡrɪdlɒk] *n* (*traffic jam*) paralisi *f inv*
del traffico.

grief [ɡriːf] *n* dolore *m*; **to come to ~** (*plan*)
naufragare; (*person*) finire male.

grievance ['ɡriːvəns] *n* doglianza, lagnanza;
(*cause for complaint*) motivo di
risentimento.

grieve [ɡriːv] *vi* addolorarsi, soffrire ♦ *vt*
addolorare; **to ~ for sb** compiangere qn;
(*dead person*) piangere qn.

grievous bodily harm (GBH) ['ɡriːvəs-] *n*
(*LAW*) aggressione *f*.

grill [ɡrɪl] *n* (*on cooker*) griglia ♦ *vt* (*BRIT*)
cuocere ai ferri; (*question*) interrogare
senza sosta; **~ed meat** carne *f* ai ferri *or*
alla griglia.

grille [ɡrɪl] *n* grata; (*AUT*) griglia.

grill(room) ['ɡrɪl(rum)] *n* rosticceria.

grim [ɡrɪm] *adj* sinistro(a); brutto(a).

grimace [ɡrɪ'meɪs] *n* smorfia ♦ *vi* fare
smorfie.

grime [ɡraɪm] *n* sudiciume *m*.

grimy ['ɡraɪmɪ] *adj* sudicio(a).

grin [ɡrɪn] *n* sorriso smagliante ♦ *vi*: **to ~
(at)** sorridere (a), fare un gran sorriso
(a).

grind [ɡraɪnd] *vb* (*pt, pp* **ground** [ɡraʊnd]) *vt*

macinare; (*US: meat*) tritare, macinare; (*make sharp*) arrotare; (*polish: gem, lens*) molare ♦ *vi* (*car gears*) grattare ♦ *n* (*work*) sgobbata; **to ~ one's teeth** digrignare i denti; **to ~ to a halt** (*vehicle*) arrestarsi con uno stridio di freni; (*fig: talks, scheme*) insabbiarsi; (: *work, production*) cessare del tutto; **the daily ~** (*col*) il trantran quotidiano.

grinder ['graɪndə*] *n* (*machine: for coffee*) macinino.

grindstone ['graɪndstəun] *n*: **to keep one's nose to the ~** darci sotto.

grip [grɪp] *n* presa; (*holdall*) borsa da viaggio ♦ *vt* afferrare; **to come to ~s with** affrontare; cercare di risolvere; **to ~ the road** (*tyres*) far presa sulla strada; (*car*) tenere bene la strada; **to lose one's ~** perdere *or* allentare la presa; (*fig*) perdere la grinta.

gripe [graɪp] *n* (*MED*) colica; (*col: complaint*) lagna ♦ *vi* (*col*) brontolare.

gripping ['grɪpɪŋ] *adj* avvincente.

grisly ['grɪzlɪ] *adj* macabro(a), orrido(a).

grist [grɪst] *n* (*fig*): **it's (all) ~ to the mill** tutto aiuta.

gristle ['grɪsl] *n* cartilagine *f*.

grit [grɪt] *n* ghiaia; (*courage*) fegato ♦ *vt* (*road*) coprire di sabbia; **to ~ one's teeth** stringere i denti; **I've got a piece of ~ in my eye** ho un bruscolino nell'occhio.

grits [grɪts] *npl* (*US*) macinato grosso (di avena *etc*).

grizzle ['grɪzl] *vi* (*BRIT*) piagnucolare.

grizzly ['grɪzlɪ] *n* (*also: ~ bear*) orso grigio, grizzly *m inv*.

groan [grəun] *n* gemito ♦ *vi* gemere.

grocer ['grəusə*] *n* negoziante *m* di generi alimentari; **~'s (shop)** negozio di alimentari.

groceries ['grəusərɪz] *npl* provviste *fpl*.

grocery ['grəusərɪ] *n* (*shop*) (negozio di) alimentari.

grog [grɔg] *n* grog *m inv*.

groggy ['grɔgɪ] *adj* barcollante.

groin [grɔɪn] *n* inguine *m*.

groom [gruːm] *n* palafreniere *m*; (*also: bride~*) sposo ♦ *vt* (*horse*) strigliare; (*fig*): **to ~ sb for** avviare qn a.

groove [gruːv] *n* scanalatura, solco.

grope [grəup] *vi* andare a tentoni; **to ~ for sth** cercare qc a tastoni.

gross [grəus] *adj* grossolano(a); (*COMM*) lordo(a) ♦ *n* (*pl inv*) (*twelve dozen*) grossa ♦ *vt* (*COMM*) incassare, avere un incasso lordo di.

gross domestic product (GDP) *n* prodotto interno lordo (P.I.L.).

grossly ['grəuslɪ] *adv* (*greatly*) molto.

gross national product (GNP) *n* prodotto nazionale lordo (P.N.L.).

grotesque [grəu'tɛsk] *adj* grottesco(a).

grotto ['grɔtəu] *n* grotta.

grotty ['grɔtɪ] *adj* (*BRIT col*) squallido(a).

grouch [grautʃ] (*col*) *vi* brontolare ♦ *n* (*person*) brontolone/a.

ground [graund] *pt, pp of* **grind** ♦ *adj* (*coffee etc*) macinato(a) ♦ *n* suolo, terra; (*land*) terreno; (*SPORT*) campo; (*reason: gen pl*) ragione *f*; (*US: also: ~ wire*) (presa a) terra ♦ *vt* (*plane*) tenere a terra; (*US ELEC*) mettere la presa a terra a ♦ *vi* (*ship*) arenarsi; **~s** *npl* (*of coffee etc*) fondi *mpl*; (*gardens etc*) terreno, giardini *mpl*; **on/to the ~** per/a terra; **below ~** sottoterra; **common ~** terreno comune; **to gain/lose ~** guadagnare/perdere terreno; **he covered a lot of ~ in his lecture** ha toccato molti argomenti nel corso della conferenza.

ground cloth *n* (*US*) = **groundsheet**.

ground control *n* (*AVIAT, SPACE*) base *f* di controllo.

ground floor *n* pianterreno.

grounding ['graundɪŋ] *n* (*in education*) basi *fpl*.

groundless ['graundlɪs] *adj* infondato(a).

groundnut ['graundnʌt] *n* arachide *f*.

ground rent *n* (*BRIT*) canone *m* di affitto di un terreno.

ground rules *npl* regole *fpl* fondamentali.

groundsheet ['graundʃiːt] *n* (*BRIT*) telone *m* impermeabile.

groundsman ['graundzmən], (*US*) **groundskeeper** ['graundzkiːpə*] *n* (*SPORT*) custode *m* (di campo sportivo).

ground staff *n* personale *m* di terra.

groundswell ['graundswɛl] *n* maremoto; (*fig*) movimento.

ground-to-air ['graundtu'ɛə*] *adj* terra-aria *inv*.

ground-to-ground ['grauntə'graund] *adj*: **~ missile** missile *m* terra-terra.

groundwork ['graundwəːk] *n* preparazione *f*.

group [gruːp] *n* gruppo; (*MUS: pop ~*) complesso, gruppo ♦ *vt* raggruppare ♦ *vi* raggrupparsi.

groupie ['gruːpɪ] *n* groupie *m/f inv*, fan *m/f inv* scatenato(a).

group therapy *n* terapia di gruppo.

grouse [graus] *n* (*pl inv*) (*bird*) tetraone *m* ♦ *vi* (*complain*) brontolare.

grove [grəuv] *n* boschetto.

grovel ['grɔvl] *vi* (*fig*): **to ~ (before)** strisciare (di fronte a).

grow, pt **grew,** pp **grown** [grəu, gru:, grəun] vi crescere; (increase) aumentare; (become): **to ~ rich/weak** arricchirsi/indebolirsi ♦ vt coltivare, far crescere; **to ~ tired of waiting** stancarsi di aspettare.

▶**grow apart** vi (fig) estraniarsi.

▶**grow away from** vt fus (fig) allontanarsi da, staccarsi da.

▶**grow on** vt fus: **that painting is ~ing on me** quel quadro più lo guardo più mi piace.

▶**grow out of** vt fus (clothes) diventare troppo grande per indossare; (habit) perdere (col tempo); **he'll ~ out of it** gli passerà.

▶**grow up** vi farsi grande, crescere.

grower ['grəuə*] n coltivatore/trice.

growing ['grəuiŋ] adj (fear, amount) crescente; **~ pains** (also fig) problemi mpl di crescita.

growl [graul] vi ringhiare.

grown [grəun] pp of **grow** ♦ adj adulto(a), maturo(a).

grown-up [grəun'ʌp] n adulto/a, grande m/f.

growth [grəuθ] n crescita, sviluppo; (what has grown) crescita, (MED) escrescenza, tumore m.

growth rate n tasso di crescita.

grub [grʌb] n larva; (col: food) roba (da mangiare).

grubby ['grʌbɪ] adj sporco(a).

grudge [grʌdʒ] n rancore m ♦ vt: **to ~ sb sth** dare qc a qn di malavoglia; invidiare qc a qn; **to bear sb a ~ (for)** serbar rancore a qn (per).

grudgingly ['grʌdʒiŋlɪ] adv di malavoglia, di malincuore.

gruelling, (US) **grueling** ['gruəliŋ] adj estenuante.

gruesome ['gru:səm] adj orribile.

gruff [grʌf] adj rozzo(a).

grumble ['grʌmbl] vi brontolare, lagnarsi.

grumpy ['grʌmpɪ] adj stizzito(a).

grunge [grʌndʒ] n (MUS) grunge m inv; (style) moda f grunge inv.

grunt [grʌnt] vi grugnire ♦ n grugnito.

G-string ['dʒi:striŋ] n (garment) tanga m inv.

GT abbr (AUT: = gran turismo) GT.

GU abbr (US POST) = Guam.

guarantee [gærən'ti:] n garanzia ♦ vt garantire; **he can't ~ (that) he'll come** non può garantire che verrà.

guarantor [gærən'tɔ:*] n garante m/f.

guard [gɑ:d] n guardia; (protection) riparo, protezione f; (BOXING) difesa; (one man) guardia, sentinella; (BRIT RAIL) capotreno; (safety device: on machine) schermo protettivo; (also: **fire ~**) parafuoco ♦ vt

fare la guardia a; **to ~ (against or from)** proteggere (da), salvaguardare (da); **to be on one's ~** (fig) stare in guardia.

▶**guard against** vi: **to ~ against doing sth** guardarsi dal fare qc.

guard dog n cane m da guardia.

guarded ['gɑ:dɪd] adj (fig) cauto(a), guardingo(a).

guardian ['gɑ:dɪən] n custode m; (of minor) tutore/trice.

guard's van n (BRIT RAIL) vagone m di servizio.

Guatemala [gwɑ:tə'mɑ:lə] n Guatemala m.

Guernsey ['gə:nzɪ] n Guernesey f.

guerrilla [gə'rɪlə] n guerrigliero.

guerrilla warfare n guerriglia.

guess [gɛs] vi indovinare ♦ vt indovinare; (US) credere, pensare ♦ n congettura; **to take** or **have a ~** cercare di indovinare; **my ~ is that ...** suppongo che ...; **to keep sb ~ing** tenere qn in sospeso or sulla corda; **I ~ you're right** mi sa che hai ragione.

guesstimate ['gɛstɪmɪt] n (col) stima approssimativa.

guesswork ['gɛswə:k] n: **I got the answer by ~** ho azzeccato la risposta.

guest [gɛst] n ospite m/f; (in hotel) cliente m/f; **be my ~** (col) fai come (se fossi) a casa tua.

guest-house ['gɛsthaus] n pensione f.

guest room n camera degli ospiti.

guff [gʌf] n (col) stupidaggini fpl, assurdità fpl.

guffaw [gʌ'fɔ:] n risata sonora ♦ vi scoppiare di una risata sonora.

guidance ['gaɪdəns] n guida, direzione f; **marriage/vocational ~** consulenza matrimoniale/per l'avviamento professionale.

guide [gaɪd] n (person, book etc) guida; (also: **girl ~**) giovane esploratrice f ♦ vt guidare; **to be ~d by sb/sth** farsi or lasciarsi guidare da qn/qc.

guidebook ['gaɪdbuk] n guida.

guided missile n missile m telecomandato.

guide dog n (BRIT) cane m guida inv.

guidelines ['gaɪdlaɪnz] npl (fig) indicazioni fpl, linee fpl direttive.

guild [gɪld] n arte f, corporazione f; associazione f.

guildhall ['gɪldhɔ:l] n (BRIT) palazzo municipale.

guile [gaɪl] n astuzia.

guileless ['gaɪllɪs] adj candido(a).

guillotine ['gɪləti:n] n ghigliottina.

guilt [gɪlt] n colpevolezza.

guilty ['gɪltɪ] *adj* colpevole; **to feel ~ (about)** sentirsi in colpa (per); **to plead ~/not ~** dichiararsi colpevole/innocente.

Guinea ['gɪnɪ] *n*: **Republic of ~** Repubblica di Guinea.

guinea ['gɪnɪ] *n* (*BRIT*) ghinea (= *21 shillings: valuta ora fuori uso*).

guinea pig *n* cavia.

guise [gaɪz] *n* maschera.

guitar [gɪ'tɑː*] *n* chitarra.

guitarist [gɪ'tɑːrɪst] *n* chitarrista *m/f*.

gulch [gʌltʃ] *n* (*US*) burrone *m*.

gulf [gʌlf] *n* golfo; (*abyss*) abisso; **the (Persian) G~** il Golfo Persico.

Gulf States *npl*: **the ~** i paesi del Golfo Persico.

Gulf Stream *n*: **the ~** la corrente del Golfo.

gull [gʌl] *n* gabbiano.

gullet ['gʌlɪt] *n* gola.

gullibility [gʌlɪ'bɪlɪtɪ] *n* semplicioneria.

gullible ['gʌlɪbl] *adj* credulo(a).

gully ['gʌlɪ] *n* burrone *m*; gola; canale *m*.

gulp [gʌlp] *vi* deglutire; (*from emotion*) avere il nodo in gola ♦ *vt* (*also:* ~ **down**) tracannare, inghiottire ♦ *n* (*of liquid*) sorso; (*of food*) boccone *m*; **in** *or* **at one** ~ in un sorso, d'un fiato.

gum [gʌm] *n* (*ANAT*) gengiva; (*glue*) colla; (*sweet*) gelatina di frutta; (*also:* **chewing-**~) chewing-gum *m* ♦ *vt* incollare.

▶**gum up** *vt*: **to ~ up the works** (*col*) mettere il bastone tra le ruote.

gumboil ['gʌmbɔɪl] *n* ascesso (dentario).

gumboots ['gʌmbuːts] *npl* (*BRIT*) stivali *mpl* di gomma.

gumption ['gʌmpʃən] *n* buon senso, senso pratico.

gun [gʌn] *n* fucile *m*; (*small*) pistola, rivoltella; (*rifle*) carabina; (*shotgun*) fucile da caccia; (*cannon*) cannone *m* ♦ *vt* (*also:* ~ **down**) abbattere a colpi di pistola *or* fucile; **to stick to one's ~s** (*fig*) tener duro.

gunboat ['gʌnbəut] *n* cannoniera.

gun dog *n* cane *m* da caccia.

gunfire ['gʌnfaɪə*] *n* spari *mpl*.

gung-ho ['gʌŋ'həu] *adj* (*col*) stupidamente entusiasta.

gunk [gʌŋk] *n* porcherie *fpl*.

gunman ['gʌnmən] *n* bandito armato.

gunner ['gʌnə*] *n* artigliere *m*.

gunpoint ['gʌnpɔɪnt] *n*: **at ~** sotto minaccia di fucile.

gunpowder ['gʌnpaudə*] *n* polvere *f* da sparo.

gunrunning ['gʌnrʌnɪŋ] *n* contrabbando d'armi.

gunshot ['gʌnʃɔt] *n* sparo; **within ~** a portata di fucile.

gunsmith ['gʌnsmɪθ] *n* armaiolo.

gurgle ['gəːgl] *n* gorgoglio ♦ *vi* gorgogliare.

guru ['guruː] *n* guru *m inv*.

gush [gʌʃ] *n* fiotto, getto ♦ *vi* sgorgare; (*fig*) abbandonarsi a effusioni.

gushing ['gʌʃɪŋ] *adj* che fa smancerie.

gusset ['gʌsɪt] *n* gherone *m*; (*in tights, pants*) rinforzo.

gust [gʌst] *n* (*of wind*) raffica.

gusto ['gʌstəu] *n* entusiasmo.

gusty ['gʌstɪ] *adj* (*wind*) a raffiche; (*day*) tempestoso(a).

gut [gʌt] *n* intestino, budello; (*MUS etc*) minugia; **~s** *npl* (*col: innards*) budella *fpl*; (: *of animals*) interiora *fpl*; (*courage*) fegato ♦ *vt* (*poultry, fish*) levare le interiora a, sventrare; (*building*) svuotare; (: *subj: fire*) divorare l'interno di; **to hate sb's ~s** odiare qn a morte.

gut reaction *n* reazione *f* istintiva.

gutsy ['gʌtsɪ] *adj* (*col: style*) che ha mordente; (*plucky*) coraggioso(a).

gutted ['gʌtɪd] *adv* (*col: upset*) scioccato(a).

gutter ['gʌtə*] *n* (*of roof*) grondaia; (*in street*) cunetta.

gutter press *n*: **the ~** la stampa scandalistica.

guttural ['gʌtərl] *adj* gutturale.

guy [gaɪ] *n* (*also:* ~**rope**) cavo *or* corda di fissaggio; (*col: man*) tipo, elemento; (*figure*) effigie di Guy Fawkes.

Guyana [gaɪ'ænə] *n* Guyana *f*.

Guy Fawkes Night [-'fɔːks-] *n* (*BRIT*) see *boxed note*.

GUY FAWKES NIGHT

La sera del 5 novembre, in occasione della **Guy Fawkes Night**, *altrimenti chiamata* **Bonfire Night**, *viene commemorato con falò e fuochi d'artificio il fallimento della Congiura delle Polveri contro Giacomo I nel 1605. La festa prende il nome dal principale congiurato della cospirazione, Guy Fawkes, la cui effigie viene bruciata durante i festeggiamenti.*

---

guzzle ['gʌzl] *vi* gozzovigliare ♦ *vt* trangugiare.

gym [dʒɪm] *n* (*also:* **gymnasium**) palestra; (*also:* **gymnastics**) ginnastica.

gymkhana [dʒɪm'kɑːnə] *n* gimkana.

gymnasium [dʒɪm'neɪzɪəm] *n* palestra.

gymnast ['dʒɪmnæst] *n* ginnasta *m/f*.

gymnastics [dʒɪm'næstɪks] *n, npl* ginnastica.

gym shoes *npl* scarpe *fpl* da ginnastica.

gym slip n (*BRIT*) grembiule m da scuola (*per ragazze*).

gynaecologist, (*US*) **gynecologist** [gaɪnɪ'kɔlədʒɪst] n ginecologo/a.

gynaecology, (*US*) **gynecology** [gaɪnə'kɔlədʒɪ] n ginecologia.

gypsy ['dʒɪpsɪ] n = **gipsy.**

gyrate [dʒaɪ'reɪt] vi girare.

gyroscope ['dʒaɪərəskəup] n giroscopio.

H h

H, h [eɪtʃ] n (*letter*) H, h f or m inv; **H for Harry,** (*US*) **H for How** ≈ H come Hotel.

habeas corpus ['heɪbɪəs'kɔːpəs] n (*LAW*) habeas corpus m inv.

haberdashery ['hæbədæʃərɪ] n merceria.

habit ['hæbɪt] n abitudine f; (*costume*) abito; (*REL*) tonaca; **to get out of/into the ~ of doing sth** perdere/prendere l'abitudine di fare qc.

habitable ['hæbɪtəbl] adj abitabile.

habitat ['hæbɪtæt] n habitat m inv.

habitation [hæbɪ'teɪʃən] n abitazione f.

habitual [hə'bɪtjuəl] adj abituale; (*drinker, liar*) inveterato(a).

habitually [hə'bɪtjuəlɪ] adv abitualmente, di solito.

hack [hæk] vt tagliare, fare a pezzi ♦ n (*cut*) taglio; (*blow*) colpo; (*old horse*) ronzino; (*pej: writer*) negro.

hacker ['hækə*] n (*COMPUT*) pirata m informatico.

hackles ['hæklz] npl: **to make sb's ~ rise** (*fig*) rendere qn furioso.

hackney cab ['hæknɪ-] n carrozza a nolo.

hackneyed ['hæknɪd] adj comune, trito(a).

hacksaw ['hæksɔː] n seghetto (per metallo).

had [hæd] pt, pp of **have.**

haddock ['hædək] n eglefino.

hadn't ['hædnt] = **had not.**

haematology, (*US*) **hematology** [hiːmə'tɔlədʒɪ] n ematologia.

haemoglobin, (*US*) **hemoglobin** [hiːməu'gləubɪn] n emoglobina.

haemophilia, (*US*) **hemophilia** [hiːməu'fɪlɪə] n emofilia.

haemorrhage, (*US*) **hemorrhage** ['hemərɪdʒ] n emorragia.

haemorrhoids, (*US*) **hemorrhoids** ['hemərɔɪdz] npl emorroidi fpl.

hag [hæg] n (*ugly*) befana; (*nasty*) megera; (*witch*) strega.

haggard ['hægəd] adj smunto(a).

haggis ['hægɪs] n (*Scottish*) insaccato a base di frattaglie di pecora e avena.

haggle ['hægl] vi: **to ~ (over)** contrattare (su); (*argue*) discutere (su).

haggling ['hæglɪŋ] n contrattazioni fpl.

Hague [heɪg] n: **The ~** L'Aia.

hail [heɪl] n grandine f ♦ vt (*call*) chiamare; (*greet*) salutare ♦ vi grandinare; **to ~ (as)** acclamare (come); **he ~s from Scotland** viene dalla Scozia.

hailstone ['heɪlstəun] n chicco di grandine.

hailstorm ['heɪlstɔːm] n grandinata.

hair [hɛə*] n capelli mpl; (*single hair: on head*) capello; (: *on body*) pelo; **to do one's ~** pettinarsi.

hairbrush ['hɛəbrʌʃ] n spazzola per capelli.

haircut ['hɛəkʌt] n taglio di capelli; **I need a ~** devo tagliarmi i capelli.

hairdo ['hɛəduː] n acconciatura.

hairdresser ['hɛədrɛsə*] n parrucchiere/a.

hair-dryer ['hɛədraɪə*] n asciugacapelli m inv.

-haired [hɛəd] suffix: **fair/long~** dai capelli biondi/lunghi.

hairgrip ['hɛəgrɪp] n forcina.

hairline ['hɛəlaɪn] n attaccatura dei capelli.

hairline fracture n incrinatura.

hair oil n brillantina.

hairpiece ['hɛəpiːs] n toupet m inv.

hairpin ['hɛəpɪn] n forcina.

hairpin bend, (*US*) **hairpin curve** n tornante m.

hair-raising ['hɛəreɪzɪŋ] adj orripilante.

hair remover n crema depilatoria.

hair spray n lacca per capelli.

hairstyle ['hɛəstaɪl] n pettinatura, acconciatura.

hairy ['hɛərɪ] adj irsuto(a); peloso(a); (*col: frightening*) spaventoso(a).

Haiti ['heɪtɪ] n Haiti f.

hake, pl **~** or **~s** [heɪk] n nasello.

halal [hɑː'lɑːl] n: **~ meat** carne macellata secondo la legge mussulmana.

halcyon ['hælsɪən] adj sereno(a).

hale [heɪl] adj: **~ and hearty** che scoppia di salute.

half [hɑːf] n (pl **halves** [hɑːvz]) mezzo, metà f inv; (*SPORT: of match*) tempo; (: *of ground*) metà campo ♦ adj mezzo(a) ♦ adv a mezzo, a metà; **~ an hour** mezz'ora; **~ a dozen** mezza dozzina; **~ a pound** mezza libbra; **two and a ~** due e mezzo; **a week and a ~** una settimana e mezza; **~ (of it)** la metà; **~ (of)** la metà di; **~ the amount of** la metà di; **to cut sth in** ~ tagliare qc in due; ~ **empty/closed** mezzo vuoto/chiuso, semivuoto/semichiuso; ~ **past 3** le 3 e mezza; **to go halves (with sb)** fare a metà (con qn).

half-back ['hɑːfbæk] n (SPORT) mediano.

half-baked [hɑːf'beɪkt] adj (fig col: idea, scheme) mal combinato(a), che non sta in piedi.

half-breed ['hɑːfbriːd] n = **half-caste**.

half-brother ['hɑːfbrʌðə*] n fratellastro.

half-caste ['hɑːfkɑːst] n meticcio/a.

half-hearted [hɑːf'hɑːtɪd] adj tiepido(a).

half-hour [hɑːf'auə*] n mezz'ora.

half-mast ['hɑːf'mɑːst] n: **at** ~ (flag) a mezz'asta.

halfpenny ['heɪpnɪ] n mezzo penny m inv.

half-price ['hɑːf'praɪs] adj a metà prezzo ♦ adv (also: **at** ~) a metà prezzo.

half term n (BRIT SCOL) vacanza a or di metà trimestre.

half-time [hɑːf'taɪm] n (SPORT) intervallo.

halfway [hɑːf'weɪ] adv a metà strada; **to meet sb** ~ (fig) arrivare a un compromesso con qn.

halfway house n (hostel) ostello dove possono alloggiare temporaneamente ex detenuti; (fig) via di mezzo.

half-wit ['hɑːfwɪt] n (col) idiota m/f.

half-yearly [hɑːf'jɪəlɪ] adv semestralmente, ogni sei mesi ♦ adj semestrale.

halibut ['hælɪbət] n (pl inv) ippoglosso.

halitosis [hælɪ'təusɪs] n alitosi f.

hall [hɔːl] n sala, salone m; (entrance way) entrata; (corridor) corridoio; (mansion) grande villa, maniero; ~ **of residence** n (BRIT) casa dello studente.

hallmark ['hɔːlmɑːk] n marchio di garanzia; (fig) caratteristica.

hallo [hə'ləu] excl = **hello**.

Halloween ['hæləu'iːn] n vigilia d'Ognissanti; see boxed note.

hallucination [həluːsɪ'neɪʃən] n allucinazione f.

hallucinogenic [həluːsɪnəu'dʒenɪk] adj allucinogeno(a).

hallway ['hɔːlweɪ] n ingresso; corridoio.

halo ['heɪləu] n (of saint etc) aureola; (of sun)

alone m.

halt [hɔːlt] n fermata ♦ vt fermare ♦ vi fermarsi; **to call a** ~ **(to sth)** (fig) mettere or porre fine (a qc).

halter ['hɔːltə*] n (for horse) cavezza.

halterneck ['hɔːltənɛk] adj allacciato(a) dietro il collo.

halve [hɑːv] vt (apple etc) dividere a metà; (expense) ridurre di metà.

halves [hɑːvz] npl of **half**.

ham [hæm] n prosciutto; (col: also: **radio** ~) radioamatore/trice; (also: ~ **actor**) attore/trice senza talento.

Hamburg ['hæmbəːg] n Amburgo f.

hamburger ['hæmbəːgə*] n hamburger m inv.

ham-fisted ['hæm'fɪstɪd], (US) **ham-handed** ['hæm'hændɪd] adj maldestro(a).

hamlet ['hæmlɪt] n paesetto.

hammer ['hæmə*] n martello ♦ vt martellare; (fig) sconfiggere duramente ♦ vi (at door) picchiare; **to** ~ **a point home to sb** cacciare un'idea in testa a qn.

►**hammer out** vt (metal) spianare (a martellate); (fig: solution, agreement) mettere a punto.

hammock ['hæmək] n amaca.

hamper ['hæmpə*] vt impedire ♦ n cesta.

hamster ['hæmstə*] n criceto.

hamstring ['hæmstrɪŋ] n (ANAT) tendine m del ginocchio.

hand [hænd] n mano f; (of clock) lancetta; (handwriting) scrittura; (at cards) mano; (: game) partita; (worker) operaio/a; (measurement: of horse) ≈ dieci centimetri ♦ vt dare, passare; **to give sb a** ~ dare una mano a qn; **at** ~ a portata di mano; **in** ~ a disposizione; (work) in corso; **we have the matter in** ~ ci stiamo occupando della cosa; **we have the situation in** ~ abbiamo la situazione sotto controllo; **to be on** ~ (person) essere disponibile; (emergency services) essere pronto(a) a intervenire; **to** ~ (information etc) a portata di mano; **to force sb's** ~ forzare la mano a qn; **to have a free** ~ avere carta bianca; **to have in one's** ~ (also fig) avere in mano or in pugno; **on the one** ~ ..., **on the other** ~ da un lato ..., dall'altro.

►**hand down** vt passare giù; (tradition, heirloom) tramandare; (US: sentence, verdict) emettere.

►**hand in** vt consegnare.

►**hand out** vt (leaflets) distribuire; (advice) elargire.

►**hand over** vt passare; cedere.

►**hand round** vt (BRIT: information, papers)

far passare; (*distribute: chocolates etc*) far
girare; (*subj: hostess*) offrire.
handbag ['hændbæg] *n* borsetta.
hand baggage *n* bagaglio a mano.
handball ['hændbɔːl] *n* pallamano *f*.
handbasin ['hændbeɪsn] *n* lavandino.
handbook ['hændbuk] *n* manuale *m*.
handbrake ['hændbreɪk] *n* freno a mano.
hand cream *n* crema per le mani.
handcuffs ['hændkʌfs] *npl* manette *fpl*.
handful ['hændful] *n* manciata, pugno.
hand-held ['hænd'held] *adj* portatile.
handicap ['hændɪkæp] *n* handicap *m inv* ♦ *vt*
handicappare; **to be mentally ~ped**
essere un handicappato mentale; **to be**
physically ~ped essere handicappato.
handicraft ['hændɪkrɑːft] *n* lavoro
d'artigiano.
handiwork ['hændɪwəːk] *n* lavorazione *f* a
mano; **this looks like his ~** (*pej*) qui c'è il
suo zampino.
handkerchief ['hæŋkətʃɪf] *n* fazzoletto.
handle ['hændl] *n* (*of door etc*) maniglia; (*of*
cup etc) ansa; (*of knife etc*) impugnatura;
(*of saucepan*) manico; (*for winding*)
manovella ♦ *vt* toccare, maneggiare;
manovrare; (*deal with*) occuparsi di;
(*treat: people*) trattare; "*~* **with care**"
"fragile".
handlebar(s) ['hændlbɑː(z)] *n(pl)* manubrio.
handling ['hændlɪŋ] *n* (*AUT*)
maneggevolezza; (*of issue*) modo di
affrontare.
handling charges *npl* commissione *f* per
la prestazione; (*for goods*) spese *fpl* di
trasporto; (*BANKING*) spese *fpl* bancarie.
hand-luggage ['hændlʌgɪdʒ] *n* bagagli *mpl*
a mano.
handmade [hænd'meɪd] *adj* fatto(a) a
mano; (*biscuits etc*) fatto(a) in casa.
handout ['hændaut] *n* (*leaflet*) volantino;
(*press ~*) comunicato stampa.
hand-picked [hænd'pɪkt] *adj* (*produce*)
scelto(a), selezionato(a); (*staff etc*)
scelto(a).
handrail ['hændreɪl] *n* (*on staircase etc*)
corrimano.
handset ['hændset] *n* (*TEL*) ricevitore *m*.
hands-free ['hændzfriː] *adj* (*telephone*) con
auricolare; (*microphone*) vivavoce.
handshake ['hændʃeɪk] *n* stretta di mano;
(*COMPUT*) colloquio.
handsome ['hænsəm] *adj* bello(a); (*reward*)
generoso(a); (*profit, fortune*)
considerevole.
hands-on ['hændz'ɔn] *adj:* **~ experience**
esperienza diretta *or* pratica.
handstand ['hændstænd] *n:* **to do a ~** fare

la verticale.
hand-to-mouth ['hændtə'mauθ] *adj*
(*existence*) precario(a).
handwriting ['hændraɪtɪŋ] *n* scrittura.
handwritten ['hændrɪtn] *adj* scritto(a) a
mano, manoscritto(a).
handy ['hændɪ] *adj* (*person*) bravo(a); (*close*
at hand) a portata di mano; (*convenient*)
comodo(a), utile; **to come in ~** servire.
handyman ['hændɪmæn] *n* tuttofare *m inv*;
tools for the ~ arnesi per il fatelo-da-voi.
hang, *pt, pp* **hung** [hæŋ, hʌŋ] *vt* appendere;
(*criminal: pt, pp* **hanged**) impiccare ♦ *vi*
pendere; (*hair*) scendere; (*drapery*)
cadere; **to get the ~ of** (*doing*) **sth** (*col*)
cominiciare a capire (come si fa) qc.
►**hang about** *vi* bighellonare, ciondolare.
►**hang back** *vi* (*hesitate*): **to ~ back (from**
doing) essere riluttante (a fare).
►**hang on** *vi* (*wait*) aspettare ♦ *vt fus*
(*depend on: decision etc*) dipendere da; **to**
~ on to (*keep hold of*) aggrapparsi a,
attaccarsi a; (*keep*) tenere.
►**hang out** *vt* (*washing*) stendere (fuori);
(*col: live*) stare ♦ *vi* penzolare, pendere.
►**hang together** *vi* (*argument etc*) stare in
piedi.
►**hang up** *vi* (*TEL*) riattaccare ♦ *vt*
appendere; **to ~ up on sb** (*TEL*) metter
giù il ricevitore a qn.
hangar ['hæŋə*] *n* hangar *m inv*.
hangdog ['hæŋdɔg] *adj* (*guilty: look,*
expression) da cane bastonato.
hanger ['hæŋə*] *n* gruccia.
hanger-on [hæŋər'ɔn] *n* parassita *m*.
hang-glider ['hæŋglaɪdə*] *n* deltaplano.
hang-gliding ['hæŋglaɪdɪŋ] *n* volo col
deltaplano.
hanging ['hæŋɪŋ] *n* (*execution*)
impiccagione *f*.
hangman ['hæŋmən] *n* boia *m*, carnefice *m*.
hangover ['hæŋəuvə*] *n* (*after drinking*)
postumi *mpl* di sbornia.
hang-up ['hæŋʌp] *n* complesso.
hank [hæŋk] *n* matassa.
hanker ['hæŋkə*] *vi:* **to ~ after** bramare.
hankering ['hæŋkərɪŋ] *n:* **to have a ~ for**
sth/to do sth avere una gran voglia di
qc/di fare qc.
hankie, hanky ['hæŋkɪ] *n abbr =*
handkerchief.
Hants *abbr* (*BRIT*) = Hampshire.
haphazard [hæp'hæzəd] *adj* a casaccio, alla
carlona.
hapless ['hæplɪs] *adj* disgraziato(a);
(*unfortunate*) sventurato(a).
happen ['hæpən] *vi* accadere, succedere;

she ~ed to be free per caso era libera; **if anything ~ed to him** se dovesse succedergli qualcosa; **as it ~s** guarda caso; **what's ~ing?** cosa succede?, cosa sta succedendo?
▶**happen (up)on** *vt fus* capitare su.
happening ['hæpnɪŋ] *n* avvenimento.
happily ['hæpɪlɪ] *adv* felicemente; fortunatamente.
happiness ['hæpɪnɪs] *n* felicità, contentezza.
happy ['hæpɪ] *adj* felice, contento(a); ~ **with** (*arrangements etc*) soddisfatto(a) di; **yes, I'd be ~ to** (certo,) con piacere, (ben) volentieri; ~ **birthday!** buon compleanno!; ~ **Christmas/New Year!** buon Natale/anno!
happy-go-lucky ['hæpɪɡəʊ'lʌkɪ] *adj* spensierato(a).
happy hour *n orario in cui i pub hanno prezzi ridotti.*
harangue [hə'ræŋ] *vt* arringare.
harass ['hærəs] *vt* molestare.
harassed ['hærəst] *adj* assillato(a).
harassment ['hærəsmənt] *n* molestia.
harbour, (*US*) **harbor** ['hɑːbə*] *n* porto ♦ *vt* dare rifugio a; (*retain: grudge etc*) covare, nutrire.
harbo(u)r dues *npl* diritti *mpl* portuali.
harbo(u)r master *n* capitano di porto.
hard [hɑːd] *adj* duro(a) ♦ *adv* (*work*) sodo; (*think, try*) bene; **to look ~ at** guardare fissamente; esaminare attentamente; **to drink ~** bere forte; ~ **luck!** peccato!; **no ~ feelings!** senza rancore!; **to be ~ of hearing** essere duro(a) d'orecchio; **to be ~ on sb** essere severo con qn; **to be ~ done by** essere trattato(a) ingiustamente; **I find it ~ to believe that** ... stento *or* faccio fatica a credere che ... + *sub.*
hard-and-fast ['hɑːdən'fɑːst] *adj* ferreo(a).
hardback ['hɑːdbæk] *n* libro rilegato.
hardboard ['hɑːdbɔːd] *n* legno precompresso.
hard-boiled egg ['hɑːd'bɔɪld-] *n* uovo sodo.
hard cash *n* denaro in contanti.
hard copy *n* (*COMPUT*) hard copy *f inv*, terminale *m* di stampa.
hard-core ['hɑːd'kɔː*] *adj* (*pornography*) hardcore *inv*; (*supporters*) irriducibile.
hard court *n* (*TENNIS*) campo in terra battuta.
hard disk *n* (*COMPUT*) hard disk *m inv*, disco rigido.
harden ['hɑːdn] *vt* indurire; (*steel*) temprare; (*fig: determination*) rafforzare ♦ *vi* (*substance*) indurirsi.

hardened ['hɑːdnd] *adj* (*criminal*) incallito(a); **to be ~ to sth** essere (diventato) insensibile a qc.
hard graft *n:* **by sheer ~** lavorando da matti.
hard-headed ['hɑːd'hɛdɪd] *adj* pratico(a).
hard-hearted ['hɑːd'hɑːtɪd] *adj* che non si lascia commuovere, dal cuore duro.
hard-hitting ['hɑːd'hɪtɪŋ] *adj* molto duro(a); **a ~ documentary** un documentario *m* verità *inv.*
hard labour *n* lavori forzati *mpl.*
hardliner [hɑːd'laɪnə*] *n* fautore/trice della linea dura.
hard-luck story [hɑːd'lʌk-] *n* storia lacrimosa (*con un fine ben preciso*).
hardly ['hɑːdlɪ] *adv* (*scarcely*) appena, a mala pena; **it's ~ the case** non è proprio il caso; ~ **anyone/anywhere** quasi nessuno/da nessuna parte; **I can ~ believe it** stento a crederci.
hardness ['hɑːdnɪs] *n* durezza.
hard-nosed ['hɑːd'nəʊzd] *adj* (*people*) con i piedi per terra.
hard-pressed ['hɑːd'prɛst] *adj* in difficoltà.
hard sell *n* (*COMM*) intensa campagna promozionale.
hardship ['hɑːdʃɪp] *n* avversità *f inv*; privazioni *fpl.*
hard shoulder *n* (*BRIT AUT*) corsia d'emergenza.
hard-up [hɑːd'ʌp] *adj* (*col*) al verde.
hardware ['hɑːdwɛə*] *n* ferramenta *fpl*; (*COMPUT*) hardware *m.*
hardware shop *n* (negozio di) ferramenta *fpl.*
hard-wearing [hɑːd'wɛərɪŋ] *adj* resistente, robusto(a).
hard-won ['hɑːd'wʌn] *adj* sudato(a).
hard-working ['hɑːd'wəːkɪŋ] *adj* lavoratore(trice).
hardy ['hɑːdɪ] *adj* robusto(a); (*plant*) resistente al gelo.
hare [hɛə*] *n* lepre *f.*
hare-brained ['hɛəbreɪnd] *adj* folle; scervellato(a).
harelip ['hɛəlɪp] *n* (*MED*) labbro leporino.
harem [hɑː'riːm] *n* harem *m inv.*
hark back [hɑːk-] *vi:* **to ~ back to** (*former days*) rievocare; (*earlier occasion*) ritornare a *or* su.
harm [hɑːm] *n* male *m*; (*wrong*) danno ♦ *vt* (*person*) fare male a; (*thing*) danneggiare; **to mean no ~** non avere l'intenzione d'offendere; **out of ~'s way** al sicuro; **there's no ~ in trying** tentar non nuoce.
harmful ['hɑːmful] *adj* dannoso(a).
harmless ['hɑːmlɪs] *adj* innocuo(a);

inoffensivo(a).

harmonic [hɑːˈmɔnɪk] *adj* armonico(a).

harmonica [hɑːˈmɔnɪkə] *n* armonica.

harmonics [hɑːˈmɔnɪks] *npl* armonia.

harmonious [hɑːˈməunɪəs] *adj* armonioso(a).

harmonium [hɑːˈməunɪəm] *n* armonium *m inv.*

harmonize [ˈhɑːmənaɪz] *vt, vi* armonizzare.

harmony [ˈhɑːmənɪ] *n* armonia.

harness [ˈhɑːnɪs] *n* bardatura, finimenti *mpl* ♦ *vt (horse)* bardare; *(resources)* sfruttare.

harp [hɑːp] *n* arpa ♦ *vi:* **to ~ on about** insistere tediosamente su.

harpist [ˈhɑːpɪst] *n* arpista *m/f.*

harpoon [hɑːˈpuːn] *n* arpione *m.*

harpsichord [ˈhɑːpsɪkɔːd] *n* clavicembalo.

harrow [ˈhærəu] *n (AGR)* erpice *m.*

harrowing [ˈhærəuɪŋ] *adj* straziante.

harry [ˈhærɪ] *vt (MIL)* saccheggiare; *(person)* assillare.

harsh [hɑːʃ] *adj (hard)* duro(a); *(severe)* severo(a); *(unpleasant: sound)* rauco(a); *(: colour)* chiassoso(a); violento(a).

harshly [ˈhɑːʃlɪ] *adv* duramente; severamente.

harshness [ˈhɑːʃnɪs] *n* durezza; severità.

harvest [ˈhɑːvɪst] *n* raccolto; *(of grapes)* vendemmia ♦ *vt* fare il raccolto di, raccogliere; vendemmiare ♦ *vi* fare il raccolto; vendemmiare.

harvester [ˈhɑːvɪstə*] *n (machine)* mietitrice *f*; *(also:* **combine ~**) mietitrebbia; *(person)* mietitore/trice.

has [hæz] *see* **have**.

has-been [ˈhæzbiːn] *n (col: person):* **he's/ she's a ~** ha fatto il suo tempo.

hash [hæʃ] *n (CULIN)* specie di spezzatino *fatto con carne già cotta*; *(fig: mess)* pasticcio ♦ *n abbr (col)* = **hashish**.

hashish [ˈhæʃɪʃ] *n* hascisc *m.*

hasn't [ˈhæznt] = **has not**.

hassle [ˈhæsl] *n (col)* sacco di problemi.

haste [heɪst] *n* fretta.

hasten [ˈheɪsn] *vt* affrettare ♦ *vi* affrettarsi; **I ~ to add that ...** mi preme di aggiungere che ....

hastily [ˈheɪstɪlɪ] *adv* in fretta, precipitosamente.

hasty [ˈheɪstɪ] *adj* affrettato(a), precipitoso(a).

hat [hæt] *n* cappello.

hatbox [ˈhætbɔks] *n* cappelliera.

hatch [hætʃ] *n (NAUT: also:* **~way**) boccaporto; *(BRIT: also:* **service ~**) portello di servizio ♦ *vi* schiudersi ♦ *vt* covare; *(fig: scheme, plot)* elaborare, mettere a punto.

hatchback [ˈhætʃbæk] *n (AUT)* tre *(or*

cinque) porte *f inv.*

hatchet [ˈhætʃɪt] *n* accetta.

hatchet job *n (col)* attacco spietato; **to do a ~ on sb** fare a pezzi qn.

hatchet man *n (col)* tirapiedi *m inv*, scagnozzo.

hate [heɪt] *vt* odiare, detestare ♦ *n* odio; **to ~ to do** *or* **doing** detestare fare; **I ~ to trouble you, but ...** mi dispiace disturbarla, ma ....

hateful [ˈheɪtful] *adj* odioso(a), detestabile.

hatred [ˈheɪtrɪd] *n* odio.

hat trick *n (BRIT SPORT, also fig):* **to get a ~** segnare tre punti consecutivi *(or* vincere per tre volte consecutive).

haughty [ˈhɔːtɪ] *adj* altero(a), arrogante.

haul [hɔːl] *vt* trascinare, tirare ♦ *n (of fish)* pescata; *(of stolen goods etc)* bottino.

haulage [ˈhɔːlɪdʒ] *n* trasporto; autotrasporto.

haulage contractor *n (BRIT: firm)* impresa di trasporti; *(: person)* autotrasportatore *m.*

haulier [ˈhɔːlɪə*], *(US)* **hauler** [ˈhɔːlə*] *n* autotrasportatore *m.*

haunch [hɔːntʃ] *n* anca; **a ~ of venison** una coscia di cervo.

haunt [hɔːnt] *vt (subj: fear)* pervadere; *(: person)* frequentare ♦ *n* rifugio; **a ghost ~s this house** questa casa è abitata da un fantasma.

haunted [ˈhɔːntɪd] *adj (castle etc)* abitato(a) dai fantasmi *or* dagli spiriti; *(look)* ossessionato(a), tormentato(a).

haunting [ˈhɔːntɪŋ] *adj (sight, music)* ossessionante, che perseguita.

Havana [həˈvænə] *n* l'Avana.

═══════════════════════════ *KEYWORD*

have [hæv] *(pt, pp* **had)** *aux vb* **1** *(gen)* avere; essere; **to ~ arrived/gone** essere arrivato(a)/andato(a); **to ~ eaten/slept** avere mangiato/dormito; **he has been kind/promoted** è stato gentile/promosso; **having finished** *or* **when he had finished, he left** dopo aver finito, se n'è andato

2 *(in tag questions):* **you've done it, ~n't you?** l'hai fatto, (non è) vero?; **he hasn't done it, has he?** non l'ha fatto, vero?

3 *(in short answers and questions):* **you've made a mistake — no I ~n't/so I ~** ha fatto un errore — ma no, niente affatto/ sì, è vero; **we ~n't paid — yes we ~!** non abbiamo pagato — ma sì che abbiamo pagato!; **I've been there before, ~ you?** ci sono già stato, e lei?

♦ *modal aux vb (be obliged):* **to ~ (got) to do sth** dover fare qc; **I ~n't got** *or* **I don't ~**

to wear glasses non ho bisogno di portare gli occhiali; **I had better leave** è meglio che io vada
♦ *vt* **1** (*possess, obtain*) avere; **he has (got) blue eyes/dark hair** ha gli occhi azzurri/i capelli scuri; ~ **you got** *or* **do you** ~ **a car/phone?** ha la macchina/il telefono?; **may I** ~ **your address?** potrebbe darmi il suo indirizzo?; **you can** ~ **it for £5** te lo do per 5 sterline
2 (+*noun: take, hold etc*): **to** ~ **a bath** fare un bagno; **to** ~ **breakfast** fare colazione; **to** ~ **a cigarette** fumare una sigaretta; **to** ~ **dinner** cenare; **to** ~ **a drink** bere qualcosa; **to** ~ **lunch** pranzare; **to** ~ **a party** dare *or* fare una festa; **to** ~ **an operation** avere *or* subire un'operazione; **to** ~ **a swim** fare una nuotata; **I'll** ~ **a coffee** prendo un caffè; **let me** ~ **a try** fammi *or* lasciami provare
3: **to** ~ **sth done** far fare qc; **to** ~ **one's hair cut** tagliarsi *or* farsi tagliare i capelli; **he had a suit made** si fece fare un abito; **to** ~ **sb do sth** far fare qc a qn; **he had me phone his boss** mi ha fatto telefonare al suo capo
4 (*experience, suffer*) avere; **to** ~ **a cold/flu** avere il raffreddore/l'influenza; **she had her bag stolen** le hanno rubato la borsa
5 (*phrases*): **you've been had!** ci sei cascato!; **I won't** ~ **it!** (*accept*) non mi sta affatto bene!; *see also* **haves**
► **have in** *vt*: **to** ~ **it in for sb** (*col*) avercela con qn
► **have on** *vt* (*garment*) avere addosso; (*be busy with*) avere da fare; **I don't** ~ **any money on me** non ho soldi con me; ~ **you anything on tomorrow?** (*BRIT*) ha qualcosa in programma per domani?; **to** ~ **sb on** (*BRIT col*) prendere in giro qn
► **have out** *vt*: **to** ~ **it out with sb** (*settle a problem etc*) mettere le cose in chiaro con qn.

haven ['heɪvn] *n* porto; (*fig*) rifugio.
haversack ['hævəsæk] *n* zaino.
haves [hævz] *npl* (*col*): **the** ~ **and the have-nots** gli abbienti e i non abbienti.
havoc ['hævək] *n* confusione *f*, subbuglio; **to play** ~ **with sth** scombussolare qc; **to wreak** ~ **on sth** mettere in subbuglio qc.
Hawaii [hə'waɪiː] *n* le Hawaii.
Hawaiian [hə'waɪjən] *adj* hawaiano(a) ♦ *n* hawaiano/a; (*LING*) lingua hawaiana.
hawk [hɔːk] *n* falco ♦ *vt* (*goods for sale*) vendere per strada.
hawker ['hɔːkə*] *n* venditore *m* ambulante.

hawkish ['hɔːkɪʃ] *adj* violento(a).
hawthorn ['hɔːθɔːn] *n* biancospino.
hay [heɪ] *n* fieno.
hay fever *n* febbre *f* da fieno.
haystack ['heɪstæk] *n* pagliaio.
haywire ['heɪwaɪə*] *adj* (*col*): **to go** ~ perdere la testa; impazzire.
hazard ['hæzəd] *n* (*chance*) azzardo; (*risk*) pericolo, rischio ♦ *vt* (*one's life*) rischiare, mettere a repentaglio; (*remark*) azzardare; **to be a health/fire** ~ essere pericoloso per la salute/in caso d'incendio; **to** ~ **a guess** tirare a indovinare.
hazardous ['hæzədəs] *adj* pericoloso(a), rischioso(a).
hazard pay *n* (*US*) indennità di rischio.
hazard warning lights *npl* (*AUT*) luci *fpl* di emergenza.
haze [heɪz] *n* foschia.
hazel ['heɪzl] *n* (*tree*) nocciolo ♦ *adj* (*eyes*) (color) nocciola *inv*.
hazelnut ['heɪzlnʌt] *n* nocciola.
hazy ['heɪzɪ] *adj* fosco(a); (*idea*) vago(a); (*photograph*) indistinto(a).
H-bomb ['eɪtʃbɔm] *n* bomba H.
h & c *abbr* (*BRIT*) = hot and cold (*water*).
HE *abbr* = high explosive; (*REL, DIPLOMACY*: = His (*or* Her) Excellency) S.E.
he [hiː] *pron* lui, egli; **it is** ~ **who ...** è lui che ...; **here** ~ **is** eccolo; ~-**bear** *etc* orso *etc* maschio.
head [hɛd] *n* testa, capo; (*leader*) capo; (*on tape recorder, computer etc*) testina ♦ *vt* (*list*) essere in testa a; (*group*) essere a capo di; ~**s** (**or tails**) testa (o croce), pari (o dispari); ~ **first** a capofitto; ~ **over heels in love** pazzamente innamorato(a); **£10 a** *or* **per** ~ 10 sterline a testa; **to sit at the** ~ **of the table** sedersi a capotavola; **to have a** ~ **for business** essere tagliato per gli affari; **to have no** ~ **for heights** soffrire di vertigini; **to lose/keep one's** ~ perdere/non perdere la testa; **to come to a** ~ (*fig: situation etc*) precipitare; **to** ~ **the ball** (*SPORT*) dare di testa alla palla.
► **head for** *vt fus* dirigersi verso.
► **head off** *vt* (*threat, danger*) sventare.
headache ['hɛdeɪk] *n* mal *m* di testa; **to have a** ~ aver mal di testa.
headband ['hɛdbænd] *n* fascia per i capelli.
headboard ['hɛdbɔːd] *n* testiera (del letto).
head cold *n* raffreddore *m* di testa.
headdress ['hɛddrɛs] *n* (*of Indian etc*) copricapo; (*of bride*) acconciatura.
headed notepaper ['hɛdɪd-] *n* carta intestata.
header ['hɛdə*] *n* (*BRIT col: FOOTBALL*) colpo

di testa; (: *fall*) caduta di testa.

head-first ['hɛd'fɜːst] *adv* a testa in giù; (*fig*) senza pensare.

headhunt ['hɛdhʌnt] *vt*: **to be ~ed** avere un'offerta di lavoro da un cacciatore di teste.

headhunter ['hɛdhʌntə*] *n* cacciatore *m* di teste.

heading ['hɛdɪŋ] *n* titolo; intestazione *f*.

headlamp ['hɛdlæmp] *n* (*BRIT*) = **headlight**.

headland ['hɛdlənd] *n* promontorio.

headlight ['hɛdlaɪt] *n* fanale *m*.

headline ['hɛdlaɪn] *n* titolo.

headlong ['hɛdlɔŋ] *adv* (*fall*) a capofitto; (*rush*) precipitosamente.

headmaster [hɛd'mɑːstə*] *n* preside *m*.

headmistress [hɛd'mɪstrɪs] *n* preside *f*.

head office *n* sede *f* (centrale).

head-on [hɛd'ɔn] *adj* (*collision*) frontale.

headphones ['hɛdfəunz] *npl* cuffia.

headquarters (HQ) [hɛd'kwɔːtəz] *npl* ufficio centrale; (*MIL*) quartiere *m* generale.

head-rest ['hɛdrɛst] *n* poggiacapo.

headroom ['hɛdrum] *n* (*in car*) altezza dell'abitacolo; (*under bridge*) altezza limite.

headscarf ['hɛdskɑːf] *n* foulard *m inv*.

headset ['hɛdsɛt] *n* = **headphones**.

headstone ['hɛdstəun] *n* (*on grave*) lapide *f*, pietra tombale.

headstrong ['hɛdstrɔŋ] *adj* testardo(a).

head waiter *n* capocameriere *m*.

headway ['hɛdweɪ] *n*: **to make ~** fare progressi *or* passi avanti.

headwind ['hɛdwɪnd] *n* controvento.

heady ['hɛdɪ] *adj* che dà alla testa; inebriante.

heal [hiːl] *vt*, *vi* guarire.

health [hɛlθ] *n* salute *f*; **Department of H~** ≈ Ministero della Sanità.

health care *n* assistenza sanitaria.

health centre *n* (*BRIT*) poliambulatorio.

health food(s) *n(pl)* alimenti *mpl* integrali.

health hazard *n* pericolo per la salute.

Health Service *n*: **the ~** (*BRIT*) ≈ il Servizio Sanitario Statale.

healthy ['hɛlθɪ] *adj* (*person*) in buona salute; (*climate*) salubre; (*food*) salutare; (*attitude etc*) sano(a); (*economy*) florido(a); (*bank balance*) solido(a).

heap [hiːp] *n* mucchio ♦ *vt* ammucchiare; **~s (of)** (*col: lots*) un sacco (di), un mucchio (di); **to ~ favours/praise/gifts** *etc* **on sb** ricolmare qn di favori/lodi/ regali *etc*.

hear, *pt*, *pp* **heard** [hɪə*, hɜːd] *vt* sentire; (*news*) ascoltare; (*lecture*) assistere a;

(*LAW: case*) esaminare ♦ *vi* sentire; **to ~ about** sentire parlare di; (*have news of*) avere notizie di; **did you ~ about the move?** ha sentito del trasloco?; **to ~ from sb** ricevere notizie da qn.

▶**hear out** *vt* ascoltare senza interrompere.

hearing ['hɪərɪŋ] *n* (*sense*) udito; (*of witnesses*) audizione *f*; (*of a case*) udienza; **to give sb a ~** dare ascolto a qn.

hearing aid *n* apparecchio acustico.

hearsay ['hɪəseɪ] *n* dicerie *fpl*, chiacchiere *fpl*; **by ~** *adv* per sentito dire.

hearse [hɜːs] *n* carro funebre.

heart [hɑːt] *n* cuore *m*; **~s** *npl* (*CARDS*) cuori *mpl*; **at ~** in fondo; **by ~** (*learn, know*) a memoria; **to take ~** farsi coraggio *or* animo; **to lose ~** perdere coraggio, scoraggiarsi; **to have a weak ~** avere il cuore debole; **to set one's ~ on sth/on doing sth** tenere molto a qc/a fare qc; **the ~ of the matter** il nocciolo della questione.

heartache ['hɑːteɪk] *n* pene *fpl*, dolori *mpl*.

heart attack *n* attacco di cuore.

heartbeat ['hɑːtbiːt] *n* battito del cuore.

heartbreak ['hɑːtbreɪk] *n* immenso dolore *m*.

heartbreaking ['hɑːtbreɪkɪŋ] *adj* straziante.

heartbroken ['hɑːtbrəukən] *adj* affranto(a); **to be ~** avere il cuore spezzato.

heartburn ['hɑːtbɜːn] *n* bruciore *m* di stomaco.

-hearted ['hɑːtɪd] *suffix*: **a kind~ person** una persona molto gentile.

heartening ['hɑːtnɪŋ] *adj* incoraggiante.

heart failure *n* (*MED*) arresto cardiaco.

heartfelt ['hɑːtfɛlt] *adj* sincero(a).

hearth [hɑːθ] *n* focolare *m*.

heartily ['hɑːtɪlɪ] *adv* (*laugh*) di cuore; (*eat*) di buon appetito; (*agree*) in pieno, completamente; **to be ~ sick of** (*BRIT*) essere veramente stufo di, essere arcistufo di.

heartland ['hɑːtlænd] *n* zona centrale; **Italy's industrial ~** il cuore dell'industria italiana.

heartless ['hɑːtlɪs] *adj* senza cuore, insensibile; crudele.

heartstrings ['hɑːtstrɪŋz] *npl*: **to tug at sb's ~** toccare il cuore a qn, toccare qn nel profondo.

heart-throb ['hɑːtθrɔb] *n* rubacuori *m inv*.

heart-to-heart ['hɑːttə'hɑːt] *adj*, *adv* a cuore aperto.

heart transplant *n* trapianto del cuore.

heartwarming ['hɑːtwɔːmɪŋ] *adj* confortante, che scalda il cuore.

hearty ['hɑːtɪ] adj caloroso(a); robusto(a), sano(a); vigoroso(a).

heat [hiːt] n calore m; (fig) ardore m; fuoco; (SPORT: also: **qualifying** ~) prova eliminatoria; (ZOOL): **in** or (BRIT) **on** ~ in calore ♦ vt scaldare.

►**heat up** vi (liquids) scaldarsi; (room) riscaldarsi ♦ vt riscaldare.

heated ['hiːtɪd] adj riscaldato(a); (fig) appassionato(a); acceso(a), eccitato(a).

heater ['hiːtə*] n stufa; radiatore m.

heath [hiːθ] n (BRIT) landa.

heathen ['hiːðn] adj, n pagano(a).

heather ['hɛðə*] n erica.

heating ['hiːtɪŋ] n riscaldamento.

heat-resistant ['hiːtrɪzɪstənt] adj termoresistente.

heat-seeking ['hiːtsiːkɪŋ] adj che cerca fonti di calore.

heatstroke ['hiːtstrəuk] n colpo di sole.

heatwave ['hiːtweɪv] n ondata di caldo.

heave [hiːv] vt sollevare (con forza) ♦ vi sollevarsi ♦ n (push) grande spinta; **to** ~ **a sigh** emettere or mandare un sospiro.

►**heave to** (pt, pp **hove**) vi (NAUT) mettersi in cappa.

heaven ['hɛvn] n paradiso, cielo; ~ **forbid!** Dio ce ne guardi!; **for** ~'**s sake!** (pleading) per amor del cielo!, per carità!; (protesting) santo cielo!, in nome del cielo!; **thank** ~! grazie al cielo!

heavenly ['hɛvnlɪ] adj divino(a), celeste.

heavily ['hɛvɪlɪ] adv pesantemente; (drink, smoke) molto.

heavy ['hɛvɪ] adj pesante; (sea) grosso(a); (rain) forte; (drinker, smoker) gran (before noun); **it's** ~ **going** è una gran fatica; ~ **industry** industria pesante.

heavy cream n (US) doppia panna.

heavy-duty ['hɛvɪ'djuːtɪ] adj molto resistente.

heavy goods vehicle (HGV) n (BRIT) veicolo per trasporti pesanti.

heavy-handed ['hɛvɪ'hændɪd] adj (clumsy, tactless) pesante.

heavy metal n (MUS) heavy metal m.

heavy-set ['hɛvɪ'sɛt] adj (esp US) tarchiato(a).

heavyweight ['hɛvɪweɪt] n (SPORT) peso massimo.

Hebrew ['hiːbruː] adj ebreo(a) ♦ n (LING) ebraico.

Hebrides ['hɛbrɪdiːz] npl: **the** ~ le Ebridi.

heck [hɛk] (col) excl: **oh** ~! oh no! ♦ n: **a** ~ **of a lot of** un gran bel po' di.

heckle ['hɛkl] vt interpellare e dare noia a (un oratore).

heckler ['hɛklə*] n agitatore/trice.

hectare ['hɛktɑː*] n (BRIT) ettaro.

hectic ['hɛktɪk] adj movimentato(a); (busy) frenetico(a).

hector ['hɛktə*] vt usare le maniere forti con.

he'd [hiːd] = **he would; he had.**

hedge [hɛdʒ] n siepe f ♦ vi essere elusivo(a); **as a** ~ **against inflation** per cautelarsi contro l'inflazione; **to** ~ **one's bets** (fig) coprirsi dai rischi.

►**hedge in** vt recintare con una siepe.

hedgehog ['hɛdʒhɔg] n riccio.

hedgerow ['hɛdʒrəu] n siepe f.

hedonism ['hiːdənɪzəm] n edonismo.

heed [hiːd] vt (also: **take** ~ **of**) badare a, far conto di ♦ n: **to pay (no)** ~ **to, to take (no)** ~ **of** (non) ascoltare, (non) tener conto di.

heedless ['hiːdlɪs] adj sbadato(a).

heel [hiːl] n (ANAT) calcagno; (of shoe) tacco ♦ vt (shoe) rifare i tacchi a; **to bring to** ~ addomesticare; **to take to one's** ~s (col) darsela a gambe, alzare i tacchi.

hefty ['hɛftɪ] adj (person) solido(a); (parcel) pesante; (piece, price) grosso(a).

heifer ['hɛfə*] n giovenca.

height [haɪt] n altezza; (high ground) altura; (fig: of glory) apice m; (: of stupidity) colmo; **what** ~ **are you?** quanto sei alto?; **of average** ~ di statura media; **to be afraid of** ~s soffrire di vertigini; **it's the** ~ **of fashion** è l'ultimo grido della moda.

heighten ['haɪtn] vt innalzare; (fig) accrescere.

heinous ['heɪnəs] adj nefando(a), atroce.

heir [ɛə*] n erede m.

heir apparent n erede m/f legittimo(a).

heiress ['ɛərɛs] n erede f.

heirloom ['ɛəluːm] n mobile m (or gioiello or quadro) di famiglia.

heist [haɪst] n (US col) rapina.

held [hɛld] pt, pp of **hold.**

helicopter ['hɛlɪkɔptə*] n elicottero.

heliport ['hɛlɪpɔːt] n eliporto.

helium ['hiːlɪəm] n elio.

hell [hɛl] n inferno; **a** ~ **of a ...** (col) un(a) maledetto(a) ...; **oh** ~! (col) porca miseria!, accidenti!

he'll [hiːl] = **he will, he shall.**

hell-bent [hɛl'bɛnt] adj (col): **to be** ~ **on doing sth** voler fare qc a tutti i costi.

hellish ['hɛlɪʃ] adj infernale.

hello [hə'ləu] excl buon giorno!; ciao! (to sb one addresses as "tu"); (surprise) ma guarda!

helm [hɛlm] n (NAUT) timone m.

helmet ['hɛlmɪt] n casco.

helmsman ['hɛlmzmən] n timoniere m.

help [hɛlp] n aiuto; (charwoman) donna di

servizio; (*assistant etc*) impiegato/a ♦ *vt*
aiutare; ~! aiuto!; **with the ~ of** con
l'aiuto di; **to be of ~ to sb** essere di aiuto
or essere utile a qn; **to ~ sb (to) do sth**
aiutare qn a far qc; **can I ~ you?** (*in shop*)
desidera?; ~ **yourself (to bread)** si serva
(del pane); **I can't ~ saying** non posso
evitare di dire; **he can't ~ it** non ci può
far niente.

helper ['hɛlpə*] *n* aiutante *m/f*, assistente
m/f.

helpful ['hɛlpful] *adj* di grande aiuto;
(*useful*) utile.

helping ['hɛlpɪŋ] *n* porzione *f*.

helping hand *n:* **to give sb a ~** dare una
mano a qn.

helpless ['hɛlplɪs] *adj* impotente; debole;
(*baby*) indifeso(a).

helplessly ['hɛlplɪslɪ] *adv* (*watch*) senza
poter fare nulla.

helpline ['hɛlplaɪn] *n* ≈ telefono amico;
(*COMM*) servizio *m* informazioni *inv* (*a
pagamento*).

Helsinki ['hɛlsɪŋkɪ] *n* Helsinki *f*.

helter-skelter ['hɛltə'skɛltə*] *n* (*BRIT: in
funfair*) scivolo (a spirale).

hem [hɛm] *n* orlo ♦ *vt* fare l'orlo a.
▶**hem in** *vt* cingere; **to feel ~med in** (*fig*)
sentirsi soffocare.

he-man ['hiːmæn] *n* (*col*) fusto.

hematology [hiːmə'tɔlədʒɪ] *n* (*US*) =
haematology.

hemisphere ['hɛmɪsfɪə*] *n* emisfero.

hemlock ['hɛmlɔk] *n* cicuta.

hemoglobin [hiːməu'gləubɪn] *n* (*US*) =
haemoglobin.

hemophilia [hiːməu'fɪlɪə] *n* (*US*) =
haemophilia.

hemorrhage *n* (*US*) = **haemorrhage**.

hemorrhoids ['hɛmərɔɪdz] *npl* (*US*) =
haemorrhoids.

hemp [hɛmp] *n* canapa.

hen [hɛn] *n* gallina; (*female bird*) femmina.

hence [hɛns] *adv* (*therefore*) dunque; **2 years
~** di qui a 2 anni.

henceforth [hɛns'fɔːθ] *adv* d'ora in poi.

henchman ['hɛntʃmən] *n* (*pej*) caudatario.

henna ['hɛnə] *n* henna.

hen night *n* (*col*) addio al nubilato.

hen party *n* (*col*) festa di sole donne.

henpecked ['hɛnpɛkt] *adj* dominato dalla
moglie.

hepatitis [hɛpə'taɪtɪs] *n* epatite *f*.

her [həː*] *pron* (*direct*) la, l' + *vowel*;
(*indirect*) le; (*stressed, after prep*) lei; *see
note at* **she** ♦ *adj* il(la) suo(a), i(le)
suoi(sue); **I see ~** la vedo; **give ~ a
book** le dia un libro; **after ~** dopo (di)
lei.

herald ['hɛrəld] *n* araldo ♦ *vt* annunciare.

heraldic [hɛ'rældɪk] *adj* araldico(a).

heraldry ['hɛrəldrɪ] *n* araldica.

herb [həːb] *n* erba; ~**s** *npl* (*CULIN*) erbette
fpl.

herbaceous [həː'beɪʃəs] *adj* erbaceo(a).

herbal ['həːbəl] *adj* di erbe; ~ **tea** tisana.

herbicide ['həːbɪsaɪd] *n* erbicida *m*.

herd [həːd] *n* mandria; (*of wild animals,
swine*) branco ♦ *vt* (*drive, gather: animals*)
guidare; (*: people*) radunare; ~**ed
together** ammassati (come bestie).

here [hɪə*] *adv* qui, qua ♦ *excl* ehi!; ~! (*at roll
call*) presente!; ~ **is**, ~ **are** ecco; ~'**s my
sister** ecco mia sorella; ~ **she is** eccola; ~
she comes eccola che viene; **come ~**!
vieni qui!; ~ **and there** qua e là.

hereabouts ['hɪərəbauts] *adv* da queste
parti.

hereafter [hɪər'ɑːftə*] *adv* in futuro; dopo
questo ♦ *n:* **the ~** l'al di là *m*.

hereby [hɪə'baɪ] *adv* (*in letter*) con la
presente.

hereditary [hɪ'rɛdɪtrɪ] *adj* ereditario(a).

heredity [hɪ'rɛdɪtɪ] *n* eredità.

heresy ['hɛrəsɪ] *n* eresia.

heretic ['hɛrətɪk] *n* eretico/a.

heretical [hɪ'rɛtɪkl] *adj* eretico(a).

herewith [hɪə'wɪð] *adv* qui accluso.

heritage ['hɛrɪtɪdʒ] *n* eredità; (*of country,
nation*) retaggio; **our national ~** il nostro
patrimonio nazionale.

hermetically [həː'mɛtɪklɪ] *adv*
ermeticamente; ~ **sealed** ermeticamente
chiuso.

hermit ['həːmɪt] *n* eremita *m*.

hernia ['həːnɪə] *n* ernia.

hero, ~es ['hɪərəu] *n* eroe *m*.

heroic [hɪ'rəuɪk] *adj* eroico(a).

heroin ['hɛrəuɪn] *n* eroina (*droga*).

heroin addict *n* eroinomane *m/f*.

heroine ['hɛrəuɪn] *n* eroina (*donna*).

heroism ['hɛrəuɪzəm] *n* eroismo.

heron ['hɛrən] *n* airone *m*.

hero worship *n* divismo.

herring ['hɛrɪŋ] *n* aringa.

hers [həːz] *pron* il(la) suo(a), i(le) suoi(sue);
a friend of ~ un suo amico; **this is ~**
questo è (il) suo.

herself [həː'sɛlf] *pron* (*reflexive*) si;
(*emphatic*) lei stessa; (*after prep*) se stessa,
sé.

Herts *abbr* (*BRIT*) = **Hertfordshire**.

he's [hiːz] = **he is**; **he has**.

hesitant ['hɛzɪtənt] *adj* esitante,
indeciso(a); **to be ~ about doing sth**
esitare a fare qc.

hesitate ['hɛzɪteɪt] *vi*: **to ~ (about/to do)** esitare (su/a fare); **don't ~ to ask (me)** non aver timore *or* paura di chiedermelo.

hesitation [hɛzɪ'teɪʃən] *n* esitazione *f*; **I have no ~ in saying (that) ...** non esito a dire che ....

hessian ['hɛsɪən] *n* tela di canapa.

heterogeneous [hɛtərəʊ'dʒiːnɪəs] *adj* eterogeneo(a).

heterosexual [hɛtərəʊ'sɛksjʊəl] *adj, n* eterosessuale (*m/f*).

het up [hɛt'ʌp] *adj* agitato(a).

HEW *n abbr* (*US*: = *Department of Health, Education, and Welfare*) *ministero della sanità, della pubblica istruzione e della previdenza sociale.*

hew [hjuː] *vt* tagliare (con l'accetta).

hex [hɛks] (*US*) *n* stregoneria ♦ *vt* stregare.

hexagon ['hɛksəgən] *n* esagono.

hexagonal [hɛk'sægənl] *adj* esagonale.

hey [heɪ] *excl* ehi!

heyday ['heɪdeɪ] *n*: **the ~ of** i bei giorni di, l'età d'oro di.

HF *n abbr* (= *high frequency*) AF.

HGV *n abbr see* **heavy goods vehicle**.

HI *abbr* (*US*) = *Hawaii*.

hi [haɪ] *excl* ciao!

hiatus [haɪ'eɪtəs] *n* vuoto; (*LING*) iato.

hibernate ['haɪbəneɪt] *vi* ibernare.

hibernation [haɪbə'neɪʃən] *n* letargo, ibernazione *f*.

hiccough, hiccup ['hɪkʌp] *vi* singhiozzare ♦ *n* singhiozzo; **to have (the) ~s** avere il singhiozzo.

hick [hɪk] *n* (*US col*) buzzurro/a.

hid [hɪd] *pt of* **hide**.

hidden ['hɪdn] *pp of* **hide** ♦ *adj* nascosto(a); **there are no ~ extras** è veramente tutto compreso nel prezzo; **~ agenda** programma *m* occulto.

hide [haɪd] *n* (*skin*) pelle *f* ♦ *vb* (*pt* **hid**, *pp* **hidden** [hɪd, 'hɪdn]) *vt*: **to ~ sth (from sb)** nascondere qc (a qn) ♦ *vi*: **to ~ (from sb)** nascondersi (da qn).

hide-and-seek ['haɪdən'siːk] *n* rimpiattino.

hideaway ['haɪdəweɪ] *n* nascondiglio.

hideous ['hɪdɪəs] *adj* laido(a); orribile.

hide-out ['haɪdaʊt] *n* nascondiglio.

hiding ['haɪdɪŋ] *n* (*beating*) bastonata; **to be in ~** (*concealed*) tenersi nascosto(a).

hiding place *n* nascondiglio.

hierarchy ['haɪərɑːkɪ] *n* gerarchia.

hieroglyphic [haɪərə'glɪfɪk] *adj* geroglifico(a); **~s** *npl* geroglifici *mpl*.

hi-fi ['haɪ'faɪ] *adj, n abbr* (= *high fidelity*) hi-fi (*m*) *inv*.

higgledy-piggledy ['hɪgldɪ'pɪgldɪ] *adv* alla rinfusa.

high [haɪ] *adj* alto(a); (*speed, respect, number*) grande; (*wind*) forte; (*BRIT CULIN*: *meat, game*) frollato(a); (: *spoilt*) andato(a) a male; (*col*: *on drugs*) fatto(a); (: *on drink*) su di giri ♦ *adv* alto, in alto ♦ *n*: **exports have reached a new ~** le esportazioni hanno toccato un nuovo record; **20m ~** alto(a) 20m; **to pay a ~ price for sth** pagare (molto) caro qc.

highball ['haɪbɔːl] *n* (*US*: *drink*) whisky (*or* brandy) e soda con ghiaccio.

highboy ['haɪbɔɪ] *n* (*US*) cassettone *m*.

highbrow ['haɪbraʊ] *adj, n* intellettuale (*m/f*).

highchair ['haɪtʃɛə*] *n* seggiolone *m*.

high-class ['haɪ'klɑːs] *adj* (*neighbourhood*) elegante; (*hotel*) di prim'ordine; (*person*) di gran classe; (*food*) raffinato(a).

High Court *n* alta corte *f*; *see boxed note*.

HIGH COURT

Nel sistema legale inglese e gallese, la **High Court** *e la "Court of Appeal" compongono la "Supreme Court of Judicature", e si occupa di casi più importanti e complessi. In Scozia, invece, la* **High Court** *è la corte che si occupa dei reati più gravi e corrisponde alla "crown court" inglese.*

higher ['haɪə*] *adj* (*form of life, study etc*) superiore ♦ *adv* più in alto, più in su.

higher education *n* istruzione *f* superiore, istruzione universitaria.

highfalutin [haɪfə'luːtɪn] *adj* (*col*) pretenzioso(a).

high finance *n* alta finanza.

high-flier, high-flyer [haɪ'flaɪə*] *n* (giovane) promessa (*fig*).

high-flying [haɪ'flaɪɪŋ] *adj* (*fig*) promettente.

high-handed [haɪ'hændɪd] *adj* prepotente.

high-heeled [haɪ'hiːld] *adj* a tacchi alti.

highjack ['haɪdʒæk] *vt, n* = **hijack**.

high jump *n* (*SPORT*) salto in alto.

highlands ['haɪləndz] *npl* zona montuosa; **the H~** le Highlands scozzesi.

high-level ['haɪlɛvl] *adj* (*talks etc, COMPUT*) ad alto livello.

highlight ['haɪlaɪt] *n* (*fig*: *of event*) momento culminante ♦ *vt* mettere in evidenza; **~s** *npl* (*in hair*) colpi *mpl* di sole.

highlighter ['haɪlaɪtə*] *n* (*pen*) evidenziatore *m*.

highly ['haɪlɪ] *adv* molto; **~ paid** pagato molto bene; **to speak ~ of** parlare molto bene di.

highly-strung ['haɪlɪ'strʌŋ] *adj* teso(a) di nervi, eccitabile.

highness ['haɪnɪs] n altezza; **Her H**~ Sua Altezza.
high-pitched [haɪ'pɪtʃt] adj acuto(a).
high point n: **the** ~ il momento più importante.
high-powered ['haɪ'pauəd] adj (engine) molto potente, ad alta potenza; (fig: person) di prestigio.
high-pressure ['haɪprɛʃə*] adj ad alta pressione; (fig) aggressivo(a).
high-rise block ['haɪraɪz-] n palazzone m.
high school n (BRIT) scuola secondaria; (US) istituto d'istruzione secondaria; see boxed note.

HIGH SCHOOL

Negli Stati Uniti la **high school** *è un istituto di istruzione secondaria. Si suddivide in "junior high school" (dal settimo al nono anno di corso) e "senior high school" (dal decimo al dodicesimo), dove vengono impartiti sia insegnamenti scolastici che di formazione professionale. In Gran Bretagna molte scuole secondarie si chiamano* **high school**.

---

high season n (BRIT) alta stagione.
high spirits npl buonumore m, euforia; **to be in** ~ essere euforico(a).
high street n (BRIT) strada principale.
highway ['haɪweɪ] n strada maestra; **the information** ~ l'autostrada telematica.
Highway Code n (BRIT) codice m della strada.
highwayman ['haɪweɪmən] n bandito.
hijack ['haɪdʒæk] vt dirottare ♦ n dirottamento; (also: ~**ing**) pirateria aerea.
hijacker ['haɪdʒækə*] n dirottatore/trice.
hike [haɪk] vi fare un'escursione a piedi ♦ n escursione f a piedi; (col: in prices etc) aumento ♦ vt (col) aumentare.
hiker ['haɪkə*] n escursionista m/f.
hiking ['haɪkɪŋ] n escursioni fpl a piedi.
hilarious [hɪ'lɛərɪəs] adj che fa schiantare dal ridere.
hilarity [hɪ'lærɪtɪ] n ilarità.
hill [hɪl] n collina, colle m; (fairly high) montagna; (on road) salita.
hillbilly ['hɪlbɪlɪ] n (US) montanaro/a dal sud degli Stati Uniti; (pej) zotico/a.
hillside ['hɪlsaɪd] n fianco della collina.
hill start n (AUT) partenza in salita.
hilly ['hɪlɪ] adj collinoso(a); montagnoso(a).
hilt [hɪlt] n (fig): **to the** ~ fino in fondo.
him [hɪm] pron (direct) lo, l' + vowel; (indirect) gli; (stressed, after prep) lui; **I see** ~ lo vedo; **give** ~ **a book** gli dia un libro; **after** ~ dopo (di) lui.

Himalayas [hɪmə'leɪəz] npl: **the** ~ l'Himalaia m.
himself [hɪm'sɛlf] pron (reflexive) si; (emphatic) lui stesso; (after prep) se stesso, sé.
hind [haɪnd] adj posteriore ♦ n cerva.
hinder ['hɪndə*] vt ostacolare; (delay) tardare; (prevent): **to** ~ **sb from doing** impedire a qn di fare.
hindquarters ['haɪndkwɔ:təz] npl (ZOOL) posteriore m.
hindrance ['hɪndrəns] n ostacolo, impedimento.
hindsight ['haɪndsaɪt] n senno di poi; **with the benefit of** ~ con il senno di poi.
Hindu ['hɪndu:] n indù m/f inv.
hinge [hɪndʒ] n cardine m ♦ vi (fig): **to** ~ **on** dipendere da.
hint [hɪnt] n accenno, allusione f; (advice) consiglio ♦ vt: **to** ~ **that** lasciar capire che ♦ vi: **to** ~ **at** accennare a; **to drop a** ~ lasciar capire; **give me a** ~ (clue) dammi almeno un'idea, dammi un'indicazione.
hip [hɪp] n anca, fianco; (BOT) frutto della rosa canina.
hip flask n fiaschetta da liquore tascabile.
hip hop n hip-hop m.
hippie ['hɪpɪ] n hippy m/f inv.
hip pocket n tasca posteriore dei calzoni.
hippopotamus, pl ~**es** or **hippopotami** [hɪpə'pɔtəməs, -'pɔtəmaɪ] n ippopotamo.
hippy ['hɪpɪ] n = **hippie**.
hire ['haɪə*] vt (BRIT: car, equipment) noleggiare; (worker) assumere, dare lavoro a ♦ n nolo, noleggio; **for** ~ da nolo; (taxi) libero(a); **on** ~ a nolo.
▶**hire out** vt noleggiare, dare a nolo or noleggio, affittare.
hire(d) car n (BRIT) macchina a nolo.
hire purchase (HP) n (BRIT) acquisto (or vendita) rateale; **to buy sth on** ~ comprare qc a rate.
his [hɪz] adj, pron il(la) suo(sua), i(le) suoi(sue); **this is** ~ questo è (il) suo.
hiss [hɪs] vi fischiare; (cat, snake) sibilare ♦ n fischio; sibilo.
histogram ['hɪstəgræm] n istogramma m.
historian [hɪ'stɔ:rɪən] n storico/a.
historic(al) [hɪ'stɔrɪk(l)] adj storico(a).
history ['hɪstərɪ] n storia; **there's a long** ~ **of that illness in his family** ci sono molti precedenti (della malattia) nella sua famiglia.
histrionics [hɪstrɪ'ɔnɪks] n istrionismo.
hit [hɪt] vt (pt, pp **hit**) colpire, picchiare; (knock against) battere; (reach: target) raggiungere; (collide with: car) urtare contro; (fig: affect) colpire; (find: problem)

incontrare ♦ *n* colpo; (*success, song*)
successo; **to ~ the headlines** far titolo; **to
~ the road** (*col*) mettersi in cammino; **to
~ it off with sb** andare molto d'accordo
con qn; **to get a ~/10,000 ~s** (*COMPUT*)
trovare una pagina Web/10.000 pagine
Web; **our web page had 10,000 hits last
month** lo scorso mese il nostro sito ha
avuto 10.000 visitori.
►**hit back** *vi*: **to ~ back at sb** restituire il
colpo a qn.
►**hit out at** *vt fus* sferrare dei colpi contro;
(*fig*) attaccare.
►**hit (up)on** *vt fus* (*answer*) imbroccare,
azzeccare; (*solution*) trovare (per caso).
hit-and-run driver ['hɪtænd'rʌn-] *n* pirata *m*
della strada.
hitch [hɪtʃ] *vt* (*fasten*) attaccare; (*also: ~
up*) tirare su ♦ *n* (*difficulty*) intoppo,
difficoltà *f inv*; **technical ~** difficoltà
tecnica; **to ~ a lift** fare l'autostop.
►**hitch up** *vt* (*horse, cart*) attaccare.
hitch-hike ['hɪtʃhaɪk] *vi* fare l'autostop.
hitch-hiker ['hɪtʃhaɪkə*] *n* autostoppista
m/f.
hi-tech ['haɪ'tɛk] *adj* high-tech *inv*, a
tecnologia avanzata.
hitherto ['hɪðə'tuː] *adv* finora.
hit list *n* libro nero.
hitman ['hɪtmæn] *n* (*col*) sicario.
hit-or-miss ['hɪtə'mɪs] *adj* casuale; **it's ~
whether ...** è in dubbio se ...; **the service
in this hotel is very ~** il servizio
dell'albergo lascia a desiderare.
hit parade *n* hit-parade *f*.
HIV *n abbr* (= *human immunodeficiency virus*)
virus *m inv* di immunodeficienza; **~-
negative/-positive** sieronegativo(a)/
sieropositivo(a).
hive [haɪv] *n* alveare *m*; **the shop was a ~ of
activity** (*fig*) c'era una grande attività nel
negozio.
►**hive off** *vt* (*col*) separare.
hl *abbr* (= *hectolitre*) hl.
HM *abbr* (= *His (or Her) Majesty*) S.M. (= *Sua
Maestà*).
HMG *abbr* (*BRIT*) = *His (or Her) Majesty's
Government*.
HMI *n abbr* (*BRIT SCOL*: = *His (or Her) Majesty's
Inspector*) ≈ ispettore *m* scolastico.
HMO *n abbr* (*US*: = *Health Maintenance
Organization*) organo per la salvaguardia
della salute pubblica.
HMS *abbr* (*BRIT*) = *His (or Her) Majesty's
Ship*.
HNC *n abbr* (*BRIT*: = *Higher National
Certificate*) diploma di istituto tecnico o
professionale.

HND *n abbr* (*BRIT*: = *Higher National Diploma*)
diploma in materie tecniche equivalente
ad una laurea.
hoard [hɔːd] *n* (*of food*) provviste *fpl*; (*of
money*) gruzzolo ♦ *vt* ammassare.
hoarding ['hɔːdɪŋ] *n* (*BRIT*) tabellone *m* per
affissioni.
hoarfrost ['hɔːfrɔst] *n* brina.
hoarse [hɔːs] *adj* rauco(a).
hoax [həʊks] *n* scherzo; falso allarme.
hob [hɔb] *n* piastra (con fornelli).
hobble ['hɔbl] *vi* zoppicare.
hobby ['hɔbɪ] *n* hobby *m inv*, passatempo.
hobby-horse ['hɔbɪhɔːs] *n* cavallo a
dondolo; (*fig*) chiodo fisso.
hobnail(ed) boots ['hɔbneɪl(d)-] *n* scarponi
mpl chiodati.
hobnob ['hɔbnɔb] *vi*: **to ~ (with)** mescolarsi
(con).
hobo ['həʊbəʊ] *n* (*US*) vagabondo.
hock [hɔk] *n* (*BRIT: wine*) vino del Reno; (*of
animal, CULIN*) garretto; (*col*): **to be in ~**
avere debiti.
hockey ['hɔkɪ] *n* hockey *m*.
hocus-pocus ['həʊkəs'pəʊkəs] *n* (*trickery*)
trucco; (*words: of magician*) abracadabra
m inv; (: *jargon*) parolone *fpl*.
hod [hɔd] *n* (*TECH*) cassetta per portare i
mattoni.
hodgepodge ['hɔdʒpɔdʒ] *n* = **hotchpotch**.
hoe [həʊ] *n* zappa ♦ *vt* (*ground*) zappare.
hog [hɔg] *n* maiale *m* ♦ *vt* (*fig*) arraffare; **to
go the whole ~** farlo fino in fondo.
Hogmanay [hɔgmə'neɪ] *n* (*SCOTTISH*) ≈ San
Silvestro.
hogwash ['hɔgwɔʃ] *n* (*col*) stupidaggini *fpl*.
hoist [hɔɪst] *n* paranco ♦ *vt* issare.
hoity-toity [hɔɪtɪ'tɔɪtɪ] *adj* (*col*)
altezzoso(a).
hold [həʊld] *vb* (*pt, pp* **held** [hɛld]) *vt* tenere;
(*contain*) contenere; (*keep back*)
trattenere; (*believe*) mantenere;
considerare; (*possess*) avere, possedere;
detenere ♦ *vi* (*withstand pressure*) tenere;
(*be valid*) essere valido(a) ♦ *n* presa; (*fig*)
potere *m*; (*NAUT*) stiva; **~ the line!** (*TEL*)
resti in linea!; **to ~ office** (*POL*) essere in
carica; **to ~ sb responsible for sth**
considerare *or* ritenere qn responsabile
di qc; **to ~ one's own** (*fig*) difendersi
bene; **he ~s the view that ...** è del parere
che ...; **to ~ firm *or* fast** resistere bene,
tenere; **to catch *or* get (a) ~ of** afferrare;
to get ~ of (*fig*) trovare; **to get ~ of o.s.**
trattenersi.
►**hold back** *vt* trattenere; (*secret*) tenere
celato(a); **to ~ sb back from doing sth**
impedire a qn di fare qc.

►**hold down** *vt* (*person*) tenere a terra; (*job*) tenere.

►**hold forth** *vi* fare *or* tenere una concione.

►**hold off** *vt* tener lontano ♦ *vi* (*rain*): **if the rain ~s off** se continua a non piovere.

►**hold on** *vi* tener fermo; (*wait*) aspettare; **~ on!** (*TEL*) resti in linea!

►**hold on to** *vt fus* tenersi stretto(a) a; (*keep*) conservare.

►**hold out** *vt* offrire ♦ *vi* (*resist*): **to ~ out (against)** resistere (a).

►**hold over** *vt* (*meeting etc*) rimandare, rinviare.

►**hold up** *vt* (*raise*) alzare; (*support*) sostenere; (*delay*) ritardare; (*traffic*) rallentare; (*rob: bank*) assaltare.

holdall ['həuldɔ:l] *n* (*BRIT*) borsone *m*.

holder ['həuldə*] *n* (*of ticket, title*) possessore/posseditrice; (*of office etc*) incaricato/a; (*of passport, post*) titolare; (*of record*) detentore/trice.

holding ['həuldɪŋ] *n* (*share*) azioni *fpl*, titoli *mpl*; (*farm*) podere *m*, tenuta.

holding company *n* holding *f inv*.

holdup ['həuldʌp] *n* (*robbery*) rapina a mano armata; (*delay*) ritardo; (*BRIT: in traffic*) blocco.

hole [həul] *n* buco, buca ♦ *vt* bucare; **~ in the heart** (*MED*) morbo blu; **to pick ~s in** (*fig*) trovare da ridire su.

►**hole up** *vi* nascondersi, rifugiarsi.

holiday ['hɔlədɪ] *n* vacanza; (*from work*) ferie *fpl*; (*day off*) giorno di vacanza; (*public*) giorno festivo; **to be on ~** essere in vacanza; **tomorrow is a ~** domani è festa.

holiday camp *n* (*BRIT: for children*) colonia (di villeggiatura); (*also:* **holiday centre**) ≈ villaggio (di vacanze).

holiday-maker ['hɔlədɪmeɪkə*] *n* (*BRIT*) villeggiante *m/f*.

holiday pay *n* stipendio delle ferie.

holiday resort *n* luogo di villeggiatura.

holiday season *n* stagione *f* delle vacanze.

holiness ['həulɪnɪs] *n* santità.

holistic [həu'lɪstɪk] *adj* olistico(a).

Holland ['hɔlənd] *n* Olanda.

holler ['hɔlə*] *vi* gridare, urlare.

hollow ['hɔləu] *adj* cavo(a), vuoto(a); (*fig*) falso(a); vano(a) ♦ *n* cavità *f inv*; (*in land*) valletta, depressione *f*.

►**hollow out** *vt* scavare.

holly ['hɔlɪ] *n* agrifoglio.

hollyhock ['hɔlɪhɔk] *n* malvone *m*.

holocaust ['hɔləkɔ:st] *n* olocausto.

hologram ['hɔləgræm] *n* ologramma *m*.

hols [hɔlz] *npl*: **the ~** le vacanze.

holster ['həulstə*] *n* fondina (di pistola).

holy ['həulɪ] *adj* santo(a); (*bread*) benedetto(a); (*ground*) consacrato(a); **the H~ Father** il Santo Padre.

Holy Communion *n* la Santa Comunione.

Holy Ghost, Holy Spirit *n* Spirito Santo.

Holy Land *n*: **the ~** la Terra Santa.

holy orders *npl* ordini *mpl* (sacri).

homage ['hɔmɪdʒ] *n* omaggio; **to pay ~ to** rendere omaggio a.

home [həum] *n* casa; (*country*) patria; (*institution*) casa, ricovero ♦ *cpd* (*life*) familiare; (*cooking etc*) casalingo(a); (*ECON, POL*) nazionale, interno(a); (*SPORT: team*) di casa; (*: match, win*) in casa ♦ *adv* a casa; in patria; (*right in: nail etc*) fino in fondo; **at ~** a casa; **to go** (*or* **come**) **~** tornare a casa (*or* in patria); **it's near my ~** è vicino a casa mia; **make yourself at ~** si metta a suo agio.

►**home in on** *vt fus* (*missiles*) dirigersi (automaticamente) verso.

home address *n* indirizzo di casa.

home-brew [həum'bru:] *n* birra *or* vino fatto(a) in casa.

homecoming ['həumkʌmɪŋ] *n* ritorno.

home computer *n* home computer *m inv*.

Home Counties *npl* contee *fpl* intorno a Londra.

home economics *n* economia domestica.

home ground *n* (*fig*): **to be on ~** essere sul proprio terreno.

home-grown [həum'grəun] *adj* nostrano(a), di produzione locale.

home help *n* (*BRIT*) collaboratore familiare per persone bisognose stipendiato dal comune.

homeland ['həumlænd] *n* patria.

homeless ['həumlɪs] *adj* senza tetto; spatriato(a); **the ~** *npl* i senzatetto.

home loan *n* prestito con garanzia immobiliare.

homely ['həumlɪ] *adj* semplice, alla buona; accogliente.

home-made [həum'meɪd] *adj* casalingo(a).

Home Office *n* (*BRIT*) ministero degli Interni.

homeopathy *etc* [həumɪ'ɔpəθɪ] (*US*) = **homoeopathy** *etc*.

home page *n* (*COMPUT*) home page *f inv*.

home rule *n* autogoverno.

Home Secretary *n* (*BRIT*) ministro degli Interni.

homesick ['həumsɪk] *adj*: **to be ~** avere la nostalgia.

homestead ['həumstɛd] *n* fattoria e terreni.

home town n città f inv natale.

home truth n: **to tell sb a few ~s** dire a qn qualche amara verità.

homeward ['həumwəd] adj (journey) di ritorno.

homeward(s) ['həumwəd(z)] adv verso casa.

homework ['həumwə:k] n compiti mpl (per casa).

homicidal [hɔmɪ'saɪdl] adj omicida.

homicide ['hɔmɪsaɪd] n (US) omicidio.

homily ['hɔmɪlɪ] n omelia.

homing ['həumɪŋ] adj (device, missile) autocercante; **~ pigeon** piccione m viaggiatore.

homoeopath, (US) **homeopath** ['həumɪəupæθ] n omeopatico.

homoeopathic, (US) **homeopathic** ['həumɪəu'pæθɪk] adj omeopatico(a).

homoeopathy, (US) **homeopathy** [həumɪ'ɔpəθɪ] n omeopatia.

homogeneous [hɔməu'dʒi:nɪəs] adj omogeneo(a).

homogenize [hə'mɔdʒənaɪz] vt omogenizzare.

homosexual [hɔməu'sɛksjuəl] adj, n omosessuale (m/f).

Hon. abbr = **honourable; honorary**.

Honduras [hɔn'djuərəs] n Honduras m.

hone [həun] vt (sharpen) affilare; (fig) affinare.

honest ['ɔnɪst] adj onesto(a); sincero(a); **to be quite ~ with you** ... se devo dirle la verità ....

honestly ['ɔnɪstlɪ] adv onestamente; sinceramente.

honesty ['ɔnɪstɪ] n onestà.

honey ['hʌnɪ] n miele m; (US col) tesoro, amore m.

honeycomb ['hʌnɪkəum] n favo ♦ vt (fig): **~ed with tunnels** etc pieno(a) di gallerie etc.

honeymoon ['hʌnɪmu:n] n luna di miele, viaggio di nozze.

honeysuckle ['hʌnɪsʌkl] n caprifoglio.

Hong Kong ['hɔŋ'kɔŋ] n Hong Kong f.

honk [hɔŋk] n (AUT) colpo di clacson ♦ vi suonare il clacson.

Honolulu [hɔnə'lu:lu:] n Honolulu f.

honorary ['ɔnərərɪ] adj onorario(a); (duty, title) onorifico(a).

honour, (US) **honor** ['ɔnə*] vt onorare ♦ n onore m; **in ~ of** in onore di.

hono(u)rable ['ɔnərəbl] adj onorevole.

hono(u)r-bound ['ɔnə'baund] adj: **to be ~ to do** dover fare per una questione di onore.

hono(u)rs degree n (SCOL) laurea (con corso di studi di 4 o 5 anni); see boxed note.

HONOURS DEGREE

In Gran Bretagna esistono titoli universitari di diverso livello. Gli studenti che conseguono ottimi risultati e che approfondiscono una o più materie possono ottenere l'**honours degree**. Questo titolo, abbreviato in **Hons.**, viene posto dopo il titolo ottenuto (ad esempio BA Hons); vedi anche **ordinary degree**.

---

honours list n (BRIT) elenco ufficiale dei destinati al conferimento di onorificenze; see boxed note.

HONOURS LIST

La **honours list** è un elenco di cittadini britannici e del Commonwealth che si sono distinti in campo imprenditoriale, militare, sportivo ecc, meritando il conferimento di un titolo o di una decorazione da parte del sovrano. Ogni anno vengono redatte due honours lists, una a Capodanno e una in occasione del compleanno del sovrano.

Hons. [ɔnz] abbr (SCOL) = **hono(u)rs degree**.

hood [hud] n cappuccio; (BRIT AUT) capote f; (US AUT) cofano; (col) malvivente m/f.

hooded ['hudɪd] adj (robber) mascherato(a).

hoodlum ['hu:dləm] n malvivente m/f.

hoodwink ['hudwɪŋk] vt infinocchiare.

hoof, pl **~s** or **hooves** [hu:f, hu:vz] n zoccolo.

hook [huk] n gancio; (for fishing) amo ♦ vt uncinare; (dress) agganciare; **to be ~ed on** (col) essere fanatico di; **~s and eyes** gancetti; **by ~ or by crook** in un modo o nell'altro.

▶**hook up** vt (RADIO, TV etc) allacciare, collegare.

hooligan ['hu:lɪgən] n giovinastro, teppista m.

hooliganism ['hu:lɪgənɪzəm] n teppismo.

hoop [hu:p] n cerchio.

hoot [hu:t] vi (AUT) suonare il clacson; (owl) gufare ♦ n colpo di clacson; **to ~ with laughter** farsi una gran risata.

hooter ['hu:tə*] n (AUT) clacson m inv; (NAUT, at factory) sirena.

hoover ® ['hu:və*] n (BRIT) aspirapolvere m inv ♦ vt pulire con l'aspirapolvere.

hooves [hu:vz] npl of **hoof**.

hop [hɔp] vi saltellare, saltare; (on one foot) saltare su una gamba ♦ n salto; **~s** npl luppoli mpl.

hope [həup] vt, vi sperare ♦ n speranza; **I ~**

so/not spero di sì/no.

hopeful ['həupful] *adj* (*person*) pieno(a) di speranza; (*situation*) promettente; **I'm ~ that she'll manage to come** ho buone speranze che venga.

hopefully ['həupfulɪ] *adv* con speranza; **~ he will recover** speriamo che si riprenda.

hopeless ['həuplɪs] *adj* senza speranza, disperato(a); (*useless*) inutile.

hopelessly ['həuplɪslɪ] *adv* (*live etc*) senza speranza; (*involved, complicated*) spaventosamente; (*late*) disperatamente, irrimediabilmente; **I'm ~ confused/lost** sono completamente confuso/perso.

hopper ['hɔpə*] *n* (*chute*) tramoggia.

horde [hɔːd] *n* orda.

horizon [hə'raɪzn] *n* orizzonte *m*.

horizontal [hɔrɪ'zɔntl] *adj* orizzontale.

hormone ['hɔːməun] *n* ormone *m*.

hormone replacement therapy *n* terapia ormonale (*usata in menopausa*).

horn [hɔːn] *n* corno; (*AUT*) clacson *m inv*.

horned [hɔːnd] *adj* (*animal*) cornuto(a).

hornet ['hɔːnɪt] *n* calabrone *m*.

horny ['hɔːnɪ] *adj* corneo(a); (*hands*) calloso(a).

horoscope ['hɔrəskəup] *n* oroscopo.

horrendous [hɔ'rɛndəs] *n* orrendo(a).

horrible ['hɔrɪbl] *adj* orribile, tremendo(a).

horrid ['hɔrɪd] *adj* orrido(a); (*person*) antipatico(a).

horrific [hɔ'rɪfɪk] *adj* (*accident*) spaventoso(a); (*film*) orripilante.

horrify ['hɔrɪfaɪ] *vt* lasciare inorridito(a).

horrifying ['hɔrɪfaɪɪŋ] *adj* terrificante.

horror ['hɔrə*] *n* orrore *m*.

horror film *n* film *m inv* dell'orrore.

horror-struck ['hɔrəstrʌk], **horror-stricken** ['hɔrəstrɪkn] *adj* inorridito(a).

hors d'œuvre [ɔː'dəːvrə] *n* antipasto.

horse [hɔːs] *n* cavallo.

horseback ['hɔːsbæk]: **on ~** *adj, adv* a cavallo.

horsebox ['hɔːsbɔks] *n* carro *or* furgone *m* per il trasporto dei cavalli.

horse chestnut *n* ippocastano.

horse-drawn ['hɔːsdrɔːn] *adj* tirato(a) da cavallo.

horsefly ['hɔːsflaɪ] *n* tafano, mosca cavallina.

horseman ['hɔːsmən] *n* cavaliere *m*.

horseplay ['hɔːspleɪ] *n* giochi *mpl* scatenati.

horsepower (hp) ['hɔːspauə*] *n* cavallo (vapore) (c/v).

horse-racing ['hɔːsreɪsɪŋ] *n* ippica.

horseradish ['hɔːsrædɪʃ] *n* rafano.

horseshoe ['hɔːsʃuː] *n* ferro di cavallo.

horse show *n* concorso ippico, gare *fpl*

ippiche.

horse-trading ['hɔːstreɪdɪŋ] *n* mercanteggiamento.

horse trials *npl* = **horse show**.

horsewhip ['hɔːswɪp] *vt* frustare.

horsewoman ['hɔːswumən] *n* amazzone *f*.

horsey ['hɔːsɪ] *adj* (*col: person*) che adora i cavalli; (*appearance*) cavallino(a), da cavallo.

horticulture ['hɔːtɪkʌltʃə*] *n* orticoltura.

hose [həuz] *n* (*also:* **~pipe**) tubo; (*also:* **garden ~**) tubo per annaffiare.

▶**hose down** *vt* lavare con un getto d'acqua.

hosepipe ['həuzpaɪp] *n see* **hose**.

hosiery ['həuzɪərɪ] *n* (*in shop*) (reparto di) calze *fpl* e calzini *mpl*.

hospice ['hɔspɪs] *n* ricovero, ospizio.

hospitable [hɔ'spɪtəbl] *adj* ospitale.

hospital ['hɔspɪtl] *n* ospedale *m*; **in ~,** (*US*) **in the ~** all'ospedale.

hospitality [hɔspɪ'tælɪtɪ] *n* ospitalità.

hospitalize ['hɔspɪtəlaɪz] *vt* ricoverare (in *or* all'ospedale).

host [həust] *n* ospite *m*; (*TV, RADIO*) presentatore/trice; (*REL*) ostia; (*large number*): **a ~ of** una schiera di ♦ *vt* (*TV programme, games*) presentare.

hostage ['hɔstɪdʒ] *n* ostaggio/a.

host country *n* paese *m* ospite, paese che ospita.

hostel ['hɔstl] *n* ostello; (*for students, nurses etc*) pensionato; (*for homeless people*) ospizio, ricovero; (*also:* **youth ~**) ostello della gioventù.

hostelling ['hɔstəlɪŋ] *n*: **to go (youth) ~** passare le vacanze negli ostelli della gioventù.

hostess ['həustɪs] *n* ospite *f*; (*AVIAT*) hostess *f inv*; (*in nightclub*) entraineuse *f inv*.

hostile ['hɔstaɪl] *adj* ostile.

hostility [hɔ'stɪlɪtɪ] *n* ostilità *f inv*.

hot [hɔt] *adj* caldo(a); (*as opposed to only warm*) molto caldo(a); (*spicy*) piccante; (*fig*) accanito(a); ardente; violento(a), focoso(a); **to be ~** (*person*) aver caldo; (*thing*) essere caldo(a); (*METEOR*) far caldo.

▶**hot up** (*BRIT col*) *vi* (*situation*) farsi più teso(a); (*party*) scaldarsi ♦ *vt* (*pace*) affrettare; (*engine*) truccare.

hot-air balloon [hɔt'ɛə-] *n* mongolfiera.

hotbed ['hɔtbɛd] *n* (*fig*) focolaio.

hotchpotch ['hɔtʃpɔtʃ] *n* (*BRIT*) pot-pourri *m*.

hot dog *n* hot dog *m inv*.

hotel [həu'tɛl] *n* albergo.

hotelier [həu'tɛljeɪ] *n* albergatore/trice.

hotel industry n industria alberghiera.
hotel room n camera d'albergo.
hot flush n (BRIT) scalmana, caldana.
hotfoot ['hɔtfut] adv di gran carriera.
hothead ['hɔthɛd] n (fig) testa calda.
hotheaded [hɔt'hɛdɪd] adj focoso(a),
eccitabile.
hothouse ['hɔthaus] n serra.
hot line n (POL) telefono rosso.
hotly ['hɔtlɪ] adv violentemente.
hotplate ['hɔtpleɪt] n fornello; piastra
riscaldante.
hotpot ['hɔtpɔt] n (BRIT CULIN) stufato.
hot potato n (BRIT col) patata bollente; **to
drop sb/sth like a** ~ mollare subito qn/qc.
hot seat n (fig) posto che scotta.
hot spot n (fig) zona calda.
hot spring n sorgente f termale.
hot-tempered [hɔt'tɛmpəd] adj irascibile.
hot-water bottle [hɔt'wɔːtə-] n borsa
dell'acqua calda.
hot-wire ['hɔtwaɪə*] vt (col: car) avviare
mettendo in contatto i fili
dell'accensione.
hound [haund] vt perseguitare ♦ n segugio;
the ~**s** la muta.
hour ['auə*] n ora; **at 30 miles an** ~ a 30
miglia all'ora; **lunch** ~ intervallo di
pranzo; **to pay sb by the** ~ pagare qn a
ore.
hourly ['auəlɪ] adj (ad) ogni ora; (rate)
orario(a) ♦ adv ogni ora; ~ **paid** adj
pagato(a) a ore.
house n [haus] (pl ~**s** ['hauzɪz]) (also: firm)
casa; (POL) camera; (THEAT) sala;
pubblico; spettacolo ♦ vt [hauz] (person)
ospitare; **at** (or **to**) **my** ~ a casa mia; **the
H**~ **(of Commons/Lords)** (BRIT) la Camera
dei Comuni/Lords; **the H**~ **(of
Representatives)** (US) ≈ la Camera dei
Deputati; **on the** ~ (fig) offerto(a) dalla
casa.
house arrest n arresti mpl domiciliari.
houseboat ['hausbəut] n house boat f inv.
housebound ['hausbaund] adj confinato(a)
in casa.
housebreaking ['hausbreɪkɪŋ] n furto con
scasso.
house-broken ['hausbrəukn] adj (US) =
house-trained.
housecoat ['hauskəut] n vestaglia.
household ['haushəuld] n famiglia, casa.
householder ['haushəuldə*] n padrone/a di
casa; (head of house) capofamiglia m/f.
household name n nome m che tutti
conoscono.
househunting ['haushʌntɪŋ] n: **to go** ~
mettersi a cercar casa.

housekeeper ['hauskiːpə*] n governante f.
housekeeping ['hauskiːpɪŋ] n (work)
governo della casa; (also: ~ **money**) soldi
mpl per le spese di casa; (COMPUT) ausilio.
houseman ['hausmən] n (BRIT MED) ≈
interno.
house-owner ['hausəunə*] n possessore m/f
di casa.
house plant n pianta da appartamento.
house-proud ['hauspraud] adj che è
maniaco(a) della pulizia.
house-to-house ['haustə'haus] adj
(collection) di porta in porta; (search) casa
per casa.
house-train ['haustreɪn] vt (pet animal)
addestrare a non sporcare in casa.
house-trained ['haustreɪnd] adj (BRIT:
animal) che non sporca in casa.
house-warming party ['hauswɔːmɪŋ-] n
festa per inaugurare la casa nuova.
housewife ['hauswaɪf] n massaia,
casalinga.
housework ['hauswɔːk] n faccende fpl
domestiche.
housing ['hauzɪŋ] n alloggio ♦ cpd (problem,
shortage) degli alloggi.
housing association n cooperativa
edilizia.
housing benefit n (BRIT) contributo
abitativo (ad affittuari e a coloro che
comprano una casa).
housing conditions npl condizioni fpl di
abitazione.
housing development, (BRIT) **housing
estate** n zona residenziale con case
popolari e/o private.
hovel ['hɔvl] n casupola.
hover ['hɔvə*] vi (bird) librarsi; (helicopter)
volare a punto fisso; **to** ~ **round sb**
aggirarsi intorno a qn.
hovercraft ['hɔvəkrɑːft] n hovercraft m inv.
hoverport ['hɔvəpɔːt] n porto per
hovercraft.
how [hau] adv come; ~ **are you?** come sta?;
~ **do you do?** piacere!, molto lieto!; ~ **far
is it to …?** quanto è lontano …?; ~ **long
have you been here?** da quanto tempo sta
qui?; ~ **lovely!** che bello!; ~ **many?**
quanti(e)?; ~ **much?** quanto(a)?; ~ **many
people/much milk?** quante persone/
quanto latte?; ~ **old are you?** quanti anni
ha?; ~'**s life?** (col) come va (la vita)?; ~
about a drink? che ne diresti di andare a
bere qualcosa?; ~ **is that …?** com'è che
… + sub?
however [hau'ɛvə*] adv in qualsiasi modo
or maniera che; (+ adjective) per quanto
+ sub; (in questions) come ♦ conj

comunque, però.
howitzer ['hauɪtsə*] *n* (*MIL*) obice *m*.
howl [haul] *n* ululato ♦ *vi* ululare.
howler ['haulə*] *n* marronata.
howling ['haulɪŋ] *adj*: **a ~ wind** *or* **gale** un vento terribile.
HP *n abbr* (*BRIT*) *see* **hire purchase**.
hp *abbr* (*AUT*) *see* **horsepower**.
HQ *n abbr* (= *headquarters*) Q.G.
HR *n abbr* (*US*) = **House of Representatives**; (= *human resources: department*) ufficio personale; (: *staff*) risorse umane.
HRH *abbr* (= *His (or Her) Royal Highness*) S.A.R.
hr(s) *abbr* (= *hour(s)*) h.
HRT *n abbr* = **hormone replacement therapy**.
HS *abbr* (*US*) = **high school**.
HST *abbr* (= *Hawaiian Standard Time*) *fuso orario*.
HT *abbr* (= *high tension*) A.T.
HTML *n abbr* (= *hypertext markup language*) HTML *m*.
hub [hʌb] *n* (*of wheel*) mozzo; (*fig*) fulcro.
hubbub ['hʌbʌb] *n* baccano.
hubcap ['hʌbkæp] *n* (*AUT*) coprimozzo.
HUD *n abbr* (*US*) = *Department of Housing and Urban Development*.
huddle ['hʌdl] *vi*: **to ~ together** rannicchiarsi l'uno contro l'altro.
hue [hjuː] *n* tinta; **~ and cry** *n* clamore *m*.
huff [hʌf] *n*: **in a ~** stizzito(a); **to take the ~** mettere il broncio.
huffy ['hʌfɪ] *adj* (*col*) stizzito(a), indispettito(a).
hug [hʌg] *vt* abbracciare; (*shore, kerb*) stringere ♦ *n* abbraccio, stretta; **to give sb a ~** abbracciare qn.
huge [hjuːdʒ] *adj* enorme, immenso(a).
hulk [hʌlk] *n* carcassa.
hulking ['hʌlkɪŋ] *adj*: **~ (great)** grosso(a) e goffo(a).
hull [hʌl] *n* (*of ship*) scafo.
hullabaloo [hʌləbə'luː] *n* (*col*: *noise*) fracasso.
hullo [hə'ləu] *excl* = **hello**.
hum [hʌm] *vt* (*tune*) canticchiare ♦ *vi* canticchiare; (*insect, plane*) ronzare ♦ *n* (*also ELEC*) ronzio; (*of traffic, machines*) rumore *m*; (*of voices etc*) mormorio, brusio.
human ['hjuːmən] *adj* umano(a) ♦ *n* (*also: ~ being*) essere *m* umano.
humane [hjuː'meɪn] *adj* umanitario(a).
humanism ['hjuːmənɪzəm] *n* umanesimo.
humanitarian [hjuːmænɪ'tɛərɪən] *adj* umanitario(a).
humanity [hjuː'mænɪtɪ] *n* umanità; **the humanities** gli studi umanistici.

humanly ['hjuːmənlɪ] *adv* umanamente.
humanoid ['hjuːmənɔɪd] *adj* che sembra umano(a) ♦ *n* umanoide *m/f*.
human rights *npl* diritti *mpl* dell'uomo.
humble ['hʌmbl] *adj* umile, modesto(a) ♦ *vt* umiliare.
humbly ['hʌmblɪ] *adv* umilmente, modestamente.
humbug ['hʌmbʌg] *n* inganno; sciocchezze *fpl*; (*BRIT*: *sweet*) caramella alla menta.
humdrum ['hʌmdrʌm] *adj* monotono(a), tedioso(a).
humid ['hjuːmɪd] *adj* umido(a).
humidifier [hjuː'mɪdɪfaɪə*] *n* umidificatore *m*.
humidity [hjuː'mɪdɪtɪ] *n* umidità.
humiliate [hjuː'mɪlɪeɪt] *vt* umiliare.
humiliation [hjuːmɪlɪ'eɪʃən] *n* umiliazione *f*.
humility [hjuː'mɪlɪtɪ] *n* umiltà.
humorist ['hjuːmərɪst] *n* umorista *m/f*.
humorous ['hjuːmərəs] *adj* umoristico(a); (*person*) buffo(a).
humour, (*US*) **humor** ['hjuːmə*] *n* umore *m* ♦ *vt* (*person*) compiacere; (*sb's whims*) assecondare; **sense of ~** senso dell'umorismo; **to be in a good/bad ~** essere di buon/cattivo umore.
humo(u)rless ['hjuːmələs] *adj* privo(a) di umorismo.
hump [hʌmp] *n* gobba.
humpback ['hʌmpbæk] *n* schiena d'asino; (*BRIT*: *also*: **~ bridge**) ponte *m* a schiena d'asino.
humus ['hjuːməs] *n* humus *m*.
hunch [hʌntʃ] *n* gobba; (*premonition*) intuizione *f*; **I have a ~ that** ho la vaga impressione che.
hunchback ['hʌntʃbæk] *n* gobbo/a.
hunched [hʌntʃt] *adj* incurvato(a).
hundred ['hʌndrəd] *num* cento; **about a ~ people** un centinaio di persone; **~s of people** centinaia *fpl* di persone; **I'm a ~ per cent sure** sono sicuro al cento per cento.
hundredweight ['hʌndrɪdweɪt] *n* (*BRIT*) = *50.8 kg; 112 lb*; (*US*) = *45.3 kg; 100 lb.*
hung [hʌŋ] *pt, pp of* **hang**.
Hungarian [hʌŋ'gɛərɪən] *adj* ungherese ♦ *n* ungherese *m/f*; (*LING*) ungherese *m*.
Hungary ['hʌŋgərɪ] *n* Ungheria.
hunger ['hʌŋgə*] *n* fame *f* ♦ *vi*: **to ~ for** desiderare ardentemente.
hunger strike *n* sciopero della fame.
hungover [hʌŋ'əuvə*] *adj* (*col*): **to be ~** avere i postumi della sbornia.
hungrily ['hʌŋgrəlɪ] *adv* voracemente; (*fig*) avidamente.
hungry ['hʌŋgrɪ] *adj* affamato(a); **to be ~**

aver fame; ~ **for** (*fig*) assetato di.
hung up *adj* (*col*) complessato(a).
hunk [hʌŋk] *n* bel pezzo.
hunt [hʌnt] *vt* (*seek*) cercare; (*SPORT*) cacciare ♦ *vi* andare a caccia ♦ *n* caccia.
►**hunt down** *vt* scovare.
hunter ['hʌntə*] *n* cacciatore *m*; (*BRIT*: *horse*) cavallo da caccia.
hunting ['hʌntɪŋ] *n* caccia.
hurdle ['hɜːdl] *n* (*SPORT, fig*) ostacolo.
hurl [hɜːl] *vt* lanciare con violenza.
hurling ['hɜːlɪŋ] *n* (*SPORT*) hurling *m*.
hurly-burly ['hɜːlɪ'bɜːlɪ] *n* chiasso, baccano.
hurrah, hurray [hu'rɑː, hu'reɪ] *excl* urra!, evviva!
hurricane ['hʌrɪkən] *n* uragano.
hurried ['hʌrɪd] *adj* affrettato(a); (*work*) fatto(a) in fretta.
hurriedly ['hʌrɪdlɪ] *adv* in fretta.
hurry ['hʌrɪ] *n* fretta ♦ *vi* affrettarsi ♦ *vt* (*person*) affrettare; (*work*) far in fretta; **to be in a** ~ aver fretta; **to do sth in a** ~ fare qc in fretta; **to** ~ **in/out** entrare/ uscire in fretta; **to** ~ **back/home** affrettarsi a tornare indietro/a casa.
►**hurry along** *vi* camminare in fretta.
►**hurry away, hurry off** *vi* andarsene in fretta.
►**hurry up** *vi* sbrigarsi.
hurt [hɜːt] *vb* (*pt, pp* **hurt**) *vt* (*cause pain to*) far male a; (*injure, fig*) ferire; (*business, interests etc*) colpire, danneggiare ♦ *vi* far male ♦ *adj* ferito(a); **I** ~ **my arm** mi sono fatto male al braccio; **where does it** ~? dove ti fa male?
hurtful ['hɜːtful] *adj* (*remark*) che ferisce.
hurtle ['hɜːtl] *vt* scagliare ♦ *vi*: **to** ~ **past/ down** passare/scendere a razzo.
husband ['hʌzbənd] *n* marito.
hush [hʌʃ] *n* silenzio, calma ♦ *vt* zittire; ~! zitto(a)!
►**hush up** *vt* (*fact*) cercare di far passare sotto silenzio.
hush-hush ['hʌʃ'hʌʃ] *adj* (*col*) segretissimo(a).
husk [hʌsk] *n* (*of wheat*) cartoccio; (*of rice, maize*) buccia.
husky ['hʌskɪ] *adj* roco(a) ♦ *n* cane *m* eschimese.
hustings ['hʌstɪŋz] *npl* (*BRIT POL*) comizi *mpl* elettorali.
hustle ['hʌsl] *vt* spingere, incalzare ♦ *n* pigia pigia *m inv*; ~ **and bustle** trambusto.
hut [hʌt] *n* rifugio; (*shed*) ripostiglio.
hutch [hʌtʃ] *n* gabbia.
hyacinth ['haɪəsɪnθ] *n* giacinto.
hybrid ['haɪbrɪd] *adj* ibrido(a) ♦ *n* ibrido.
hydrant ['haɪdrənt] *n* (*also*: **fire** ~) idrante

m.
hydraulic [haɪ'drɔlɪk] *adj* idraulico(a).
hydraulics [haɪ'drɔlɪks] *n* idraulica.
hydrochloric [haɪdrə'klɔrɪk] *adj*: ~ **acid** acido cloridrico.
hydroelectric [haɪdrəʊɪ'lɛktrɪk] *adj* idroelettrico(a).
hydrofoil ['haɪdrəfɔɪl] *n* aliscafo.
hydrogen ['haɪdrədʒən] *n* idrogeno.
hydrogen bomb *n* bomba all'idrogeno.
hydrophobia [haɪdrə'fəʊbɪə] *n* idrofobia.
hydroplane ['haɪdrəʊpleɪn] *n* idrovolante *m*.
hyena [haɪ'iːnə] *n* iena.
hygiene ['haɪdʒiːn] *n* igiene *f*.
hygienic [haɪ'dʒiːnɪk] *adj* igienico(a).
hymn [hɪm] *n* inno; cantica.
hype [haɪp] *n* (*col*) clamorosa pubblicità.
hyperactive [haɪpər'æktɪv] *adj* iperattivo(a).
hypermarket ['haɪpəmɑːkɪt] *n* (*BRIT*) ipermercato.
hypertension [haɪpə'tɛnʃən] *n* (*MED*) ipertensione *f*.
hypertext ['haɪpə,tɛkst] *n* (*COMPUT*) ipertesto.
hyphen ['haɪfn] *n* trattino.
hypnosis [hɪp'nəʊsɪs] *n* ipnosi *f*.
hypnotic [hɪp'nɔtɪk] *adj* ipnotico(a).
hypnotism ['hɪpnətɪzəm] *n* ipnotismo.
hypnotist ['hɪpnətɪst] *n* ipnotizzatore/trice.
hypnotize ['hɪpnətaɪz] *vt* ipnotizzare.
hypoallergenic [haɪpəʊælə'dʒɛnɪk] *adj* ipoallergico(a).
hypochondriac [haɪpə'kɔndrɪæk] *n* ipocondriaco/a.
hypocrisy [hɪ'pɔkrɪsɪ] *n* ipocrisia.
hypocrite ['hɪpəkrɪt] *n* ipocrita *m/f*.
hypocritical [hɪpə'krɪtɪkl] *adj* ipocrita.
hypodermic [haɪpə'dɜːmɪk] *adj* ipodermico(a) ♦ *n* (*syringe*) siringa ipodermica.
hypotenuse [haɪ'pɔtɪnjuːz] *n* ipotenusa.
hypothermia [haɪpəʊ'θɜːmɪə] *n* ipotermia.
hypothesis, *pl* **hypotheses** [haɪ'pɔθɪsɪs, -siːz] *n* ipotesi *f inv*.
hypothetical [haɪpəʊ'θɛtɪkl] *adj* ipotetico(a).
hysterectomy [hɪstə'rɛktəmɪ] *n* isterectomia.
hysteria [hɪ'stɪərɪə] *n* isteria.
hysterical [hɪ'stɛrɪkl] *adj* isterico(a); **to become** ~ avere una crisi isterica.
hysterics [hɪ'stɛrɪks] *npl* accesso di isteria; (*laughter*) attacco di riso; **to have** ~ avere una crisi isterica.

I i

I, i [aɪ] n (letter) I, i f or m inv; **I for Isaac,** (US) **I for Item** ≈ I come Imola.

I [aɪ] pron io ♦ abbr (= island, isle) Is.

IA abbr (US) = Iowa.

IAEA n abbr = **International Atomic Energy Agency**.

IBA n abbr (BRIT: = Independent Broadcasting Authority) organo di controllo sulle reti televisive.

Iberian [aɪ'bɪərɪən] adj iberico(a).

Iberian Peninsula n: the ~ la Penisola iberica.

IBEW n abbr (US: = International Brotherhood of Electrical Workers) associazione internazionale degli elettrotecnici.

ib(id). ['ɪb(ɪd)] abbr (= ibidem: from the same source) ibid.

i/c abbr (BRIT) = **in charge**.

ICBM n abbr (= intercontinental ballistic missile) ICBM m inv.

ICC n abbr (= International Chamber of Commerce) C.C.I. f; (US: = Interstate Commerce Commission) commissione per il commercio tra gli stati degli USA.

ice [aɪs] n ghiaccio; (on road) gelo ♦ vt (cake) glassare; (drink) mettere in fresco ♦ vi (also: ~ over) ghiacciare; (also: ~ up) gelare; **to keep sth on** ~ (fig: plan, project) mettere da parte (per il momento), accantonare.

Ice Age n era glaciale.

ice axe n piccozza da ghiaccio.

iceberg ['aɪsbə:g] n iceberg m inv; **tip of the** ~ (also fig) punta dell'iceberg.

icebox ['aɪsbɔks] n (US) frigorifero; (BRIT) reparto ghiaccio; (insulated box) frigo portatile.

icebreaker ['aɪsbreɪkə*] n rompighiaccio m inv.

ice bucket n secchiello del ghiaccio.

ice-cap ['aɪskæp] n calotta polare.

ice-cold [aɪs'kəuld] adj gelato(a).

ice cream n gelato.

ice-cream soda n (gelato) affogato al seltz.

ice cube n cubetto di ghiaccio.

iced [aɪst] adj (drink) ghiacciato(a); (coffee, tea) freddo(a); (cake) glassato(a).

ice hockey n hockey m su ghiaccio.

Iceland ['aɪslənd] n Islanda.

Icelander ['aɪsləndə*] n islandese m/f.

Icelandic [aɪs'lændɪk] adj islandese ♦ n (LING) islandese m.

ice lolly n (BRIT) ghiacciolo.

ice pick n piccone m per ghiaccio.

ice rink n pista di pattinaggio.

ice-skate ['aɪsskeɪt] n pattino da ghiaccio ♦ vi pattinare sul ghiaccio.

ice-skating ['aɪsskeɪtɪŋ] n pattinaggio sul ghiaccio.

icicle ['aɪsɪkl] n ghiacciolo.

icing ['aɪsɪŋ] n (AVIAT etc) patina di ghiaccio; (CULIN) glassa.

icing sugar n zucchero a velo.

ICJ n abbr see **International Court of Justice**.

icon ['aɪkɔn] n icona; (COMPUT) immagine f.

ICR n abbr (US) = Institute for Cancer Research.

ICRC n abbr (= International Committee of the Red Cross) CICR m.

ICT n abbr (BRIT SCOL: = Information and Communications Technology) informatica.

ICU n abbr see **intensive care unit**.

icy ['aɪsɪ] adj ghiacciato(a); (weather, temperature) gelido(a).

ID (US) = Idaho; (= identification document) documento di identità.

I'd [aɪd] = **I would; I had**.

Ida. abbr (US) = Idaho.

ID card n = **identity card**.

IDD n abbr (BRIT TEL: = International direct dialling) teleselezione f internazionale.

idea [aɪ'dɪə] n idea; **good** ~! buon'idea!; **to have an** ~ **that** ... aver l'impressione che ...; **I haven't the least** ~ non ne ho la minima idea.

ideal [aɪ'dɪəl] adj, n ideale (m).

idealist [aɪ'dɪəlɪst] n idealista m/f.

ideally [aɪ'dɪəlɪ] adv perfettamente, assolutamente; ~ **the book should have** ... l'ideale sarebbe che il libro avesse ....

identical [aɪ'dɛntɪkl] adj identico(a).

identification [aɪdɛntɪfɪ'keɪʃən] n identificazione f; **means of** ~ carta d'identità.

identify [aɪ'dɛntɪfaɪ] vt identificare ♦ vi: **to** ~ **with** identificarsi con.

Identikit ® [aɪ'dɛntɪkɪt] n: ~ **(picture)** identikit m inv.

identity [aɪ'dɛntɪtɪ] n identità f inv.

identity card n carta d'identità.

identity parade n (BRIT) confronto all'americana.

ideological [aɪdɪə'lɔdʒɪkəl] adj ideologico(a).

ideology [aɪdɪ'ɔlədʒɪ] n ideologia.
idiocy ['ɪdɪəsɪ] n idiozia.
idiom ['ɪdɪəm] n idioma m; (phrase) espressione f idiomatica.
idiomatic [ɪdɪə'mætɪk] adj idiomatico(a).
idiosyncrasy [ɪdɪəu'sɪŋkrəsɪ] n idiosincrasia.
idiot ['ɪdɪət] n idiota m/f.
idiotic [ɪdɪ'ɔtɪk] adj idiota.
idle ['aɪdl] adj inattivo(a); (lazy) pigro(a), ozioso(a); (unemployed) disoccupato(a); (question, pleasures) ozioso(a) ♦ vi (engine) girare al minimo; **to lie** ~ stare fermo, non funzionare.
►**idle away** vt (time) sprecare, buttar via.
idleness ['aɪdlnɪs] n ozio; pigrizia.
idler ['aɪdlə*] n ozioso/a, fannullone/a.
idle time n tempi mpl morti.
idol ['aɪdl] n idolo.
idolize ['aɪdəlaɪz] vt idoleggiare.
idyllic [ɪ'dɪlɪk] adj idillico(a).
i.e. abbr (= id est: that is) cioè.
if [ɪf] conj se ♦ n: **there are a lot of** ~**s and buts** ci sono molti se e ma; **I'd be pleased** ~ **you could do it** sarei molto contento se potesse farlo; ~ **necessary** se (è) necessario; ~ **only he were here** se solo fosse qui; ~ **only to show him my gratitude** se non altro per esprimergli la mia gratitudine.
iffy ['ɪfɪ] adj (col) incerto(a).
igloo ['ɪɡlu:] n igloo m inv.
ignite [ɪɡ'naɪt] vt accendere ♦ vi accendersi.
ignition [ɪɡ'nɪʃən] n (AUT) accensione f; **to switch on/off the** ~ accendere/spegnere il motore.
ignition key n (AUT) chiave f dell'accensione.
ignoble [ɪɡ'nəubl] adj ignobile.
ignominious [ɪɡnə'mɪnɪəs] adj vergognoso(a), ignominioso(a).
ignoramus [ɪɡnə'reɪməs] n ignorante m/f.
ignorance ['ɪɡnərəns] n ignoranza; **to keep sb in** ~ **of sth** tenere qn all'oscuro di qc.
ignorant ['ɪɡnərənt] adj ignorante; **to be** ~ **of** (subject) essere ignorante in; (events) essere ignaro(a) di.
ignore [ɪɡ'nɔ:*] vt non tener conto di; (person, fact) ignorare.
ikon ['aɪkɔn] n = **icon**.
IL abbr (US) = Illinois.
ILA n abbr (US: = International Longshoremen's Association) associazione internazionale degli scaricatori di porto.
ill [ɪl] adj (sick) malato(a); (bad) cattivo(a) ♦ n male m; **to take** or **be taken** ~ ammalarsi; **to feel** ~ star male; **to**

speak/think ~ **of sb** parlar/pensar male di qn.
I'll [aɪl] = **I will, I shall.**
Ill. abbr (US) = Illinois.
ill-advised [ɪləd'vaɪzd] adj (decision) poco giudizioso(a); (person) mal consigliato(a).
ill-at-ease [ɪlət'i:z] adj a disagio.
ill-considered [ɪlkən'sɪdəd] adj (plan) avventato(a).
ill-disposed [ɪldɪs'pəuzd] adj: **to be** ~ **towards sb/sth** essere maldisposto(a) verso qn/qc or nei riguardi di qn/qc.
illegal [ɪ'li:ɡl] adj illegale.
illegally [ɪ'li:ɡəlɪ] adv illegalmente.
illegible [ɪ'ledʒɪbl] adj illeggibile.
illegitimate [ɪlɪ'dʒɪtɪmət] adj illegittimo(a).
ill-fated [ɪl'feɪtɪd] adj nefasto(a).
ill-favoured, (US) ill-favored [ɪl'feɪvəd] adj sgraziato(a), brutto(a).
ill feeling n rancore m.
ill-gotten ['ɪlɡɔtn] adj: ~ **gains** maltolto.
ill health n problemi mpl di salute.
illicit [ɪ'lɪsɪt] adj illecito(a).
ill-informed [ɪlɪn'fɔ:md] adj (judgement, speech) pieno(a) di inesattezze; (person) male informato(a).
illiterate [ɪ'lɪtərət] adj analfabeta, illetterato(a); (letter) scorretto(a).
ill-mannered [ɪl'mænəd] adj maleducato(a), sgarbato(a).
illness ['ɪlnɪs] n malattia.
illogical [ɪ'lɔdʒɪkl] adj illogico(a).
ill-suited [ɪl'su:tɪd] adj (couple) mal assortito(a); **he is** ~ **to the job** è inadatto a quel lavoro.
ill-timed [ɪl'taɪmd] adj intempestivo(a), inopportuno(a).
ill-treat [ɪl'tri:t] vt maltrattare.
ill-treatment [ɪl'tri:tmənt] n maltrattamenti mpl.
illuminate [ɪ'lu:mɪneɪt] vt illuminare; ~**d sign** insegna luminosa.
illuminating [ɪ'lu:mɪneɪtɪŋ] adj chiarificatore(trice).
illumination [ɪlu:mɪ'neɪʃən] n illuminazione f.
illusion [ɪ'lu:ʒən] n illusione f; **to be under the** ~ **that** avere l'impressione che.
illusive [ɪ'lu:sɪv], **illusory** [ɪ'lu:sərɪ] adj illusorio(a).
illustrate ['ɪləstreɪt] vt illustrare.
illustration [ɪlə'streɪʃən] n illustrazione f.
illustrator ['ɪləstreɪtə*] n illustratore/trice.
illustrious [ɪ'lʌstrɪəs] adj illustre.
ill will n cattiva volontà.
ILO n abbr (= International Labour Organization) OIL f.
I'm [aɪm] = **I am.**

image ['ɪmɪdʒ] n immagine f; (public face) immagine (pubblica).

imagery ['ɪmɪdʒərɪ] n immagini fpl.

imaginable [ɪ'mædʒɪnəbl] adj immaginabile, che si possa immaginare.

imaginary [ɪ'mædʒɪnərɪ] adj immaginario(a).

imagination [ɪmædʒɪ'neɪʃən] n immaginazione f, fantasia.

imaginative [ɪ'mædʒɪnətɪv] adj immaginoso(a).

imagine [ɪ'mædʒɪn] vt immaginare.

imbalance [ɪm'bæləns] n squilibrio.

imbecile ['ɪmbəsiːl] n imbecille m/f.

imbue [ɪm'bjuː] vt: to ~ sth with impregnare qc di.

IMF n abbr see **International Monetary Fund**.

imitate ['ɪmɪteɪt] vt imitare.

imitation [ɪmɪ'teɪʃən] n imitazione f.

imitator ['ɪmɪteɪtə*] n imitatore/trice.

immaculate [ɪ'mækjulət] adj immacolato(a); (dress, appearance) impeccabile.

immaterial [ɪmə'tɪərɪəl] adj immateriale, indifferente; it is ~ whether poco importa se or che + sub.

immature [ɪmə'tjuə*] adj immaturo(a).

immaturity [ɪmə'tjuərɪtɪ] n immaturità, mancanza di maturità.

immeasurable [ɪ'mɛʒərəbl] adj incommensurabile.

immediacy [ɪ'miːdɪəsɪ] n immediatezza.

immediate [ɪ'miːdɪət] adj immediato(a).

immediately [ɪ'miːdɪətlɪ] adv (at once) subito, immediatamente; ~ next to proprio accanto a.

immense [ɪ'mɛns] adj immenso(a); enorme.

immensity [ɪ'mɛnsɪtɪ] n (of size, difference) enormità; (of problem etc) vastità.

immerse [ɪ'məːs] vt immergere.

immersion heater [ɪ'məːʃən-] n (BRIT) scaldaacqua m inv a immersione.

immigrant ['ɪmɪgrənt] n immigrante m/f; (already established) immigrato/a.

immigration [ɪmɪ'greɪʃən] n immigrazione f.

immigration authorities npl ufficio stranieri.

immigration laws npl leggi fpl relative all'immigrazione.

imminent ['ɪmɪnənt] adj imminente.

immobile [ɪ'məubaɪl] adj immobile.

immobilize [ɪ'məubɪlaɪz] vt immobilizzare.

immoderate [ɪ'mɔdərɪt] adj (person) smodato(a), sregolato(a); (opinion, reaction, demand) eccessivo(a).

immodest [ɪ'mɔdɪst] adj (indecent) indecente, impudico(a); (boasting) presuntuoso(a).

immoral [ɪ'mɔrl] adj immorale.

immorality [ɪmə'rælɪtɪ] n immoralità.

immortal [ɪ'mɔːtl] adj, n immortale (m/f).

immortalize [ɪ'mɔːtəlaɪz] vt rendere immortale.

immovable [ɪ'muːvəbl] adj (object) non movibile; (person) irremovibile.

immune [ɪ'mjuːn] adj: ~ (to) immune (da).

immune system n sistema m immunitario.

immunity [ɪ'mjuːnɪtɪ] n (also fig: of diplomat) immunità; **diplomatic** ~ immunità diplomatica.

immunization [ɪmjunaɪ'zeɪʃən] n immunizzazione f.

immunize ['ɪmjunaɪz] vt immunizzare.

imp [ɪmp] n folletto, diavoletto; (child) diavoletto.

impact ['ɪmpækt] n impatto.

impair [ɪm'pɛə*] vt danneggiare.

impaired [ɪm'pɛəd] adj indebolito(a).

-impaired [ɪm'pɛəd] suffix: **visually**~ videoleso(a).

impale [ɪm'peɪl] vt impalare.

impart [ɪm'pɑːt] vt (make known) comunicare; (bestow) impartire.

impartial [ɪm'pɑːʃl] adj imparziale.

impartiality [ɪmpɑːʃɪ'ælɪtɪ] n imparzialità.

impassable [ɪm'pɑːsəbl] adj insuperabile; (road) impraticabile.

impasse [æm'pɑːs] n impasse f inv.

impassioned [ɪm'pæʃənd] adj appassionato(a).

impassive [ɪm'pæsɪv] adj impassibile.

impatience [ɪm'peɪʃəns] n impazienza.

impatient [ɪm'peɪʃənt] adj impaziente; **to get** or **grow** ~ perdere la pazienza.

impeach [ɪm'piːtʃ] vt accusare, attaccare; (public official) mettere sotto accusa.

impeachment [ɪm'piːtʃmənt] n (LAW) imputazione f.

impeccable [ɪm'pɛkəbl] adj impeccabile.

impecunious [ɪmpɪ'kjuːnɪəs] adj povero(a).

impede [ɪm'piːd] vt impedire.

impediment [ɪm'pɛdɪmənt] n impedimento; (also: **speech** ~) difetto di pronuncia.

impel [ɪm'pɛl] vt (force): **to** ~ **sb (to do sth)** costringere or obbligare qn (a fare qc).

impending [ɪm'pɛndɪŋ] adj imminente.

impenetrable [ɪm'pɛnɪtrəbl] adj impenetrabile.

imperative [ɪm'pɛrətɪv] adj imperativo(a); necessario(a), urgente; (voice) imperioso(a) ♦ n (LING) imperativo.

imperceptible [ɪmpə'sɛptɪbl] adj impercettibile.

imperfect [ɪm'pəːfɪkt] adj imperfetto(a);

(*goods etc*) difettoso(a) ♦ *n* (LING: *also*: ~ tense) imperfetto.

imperfection [ɪmpəˈfɛkʃən] *n* imperfezione *f*; (*flaw*) difetto.

imperial [ɪmˈpɪərɪəl] *adj* imperiale; (*measure*) legale.

imperialism [ɪmˈpɪərɪəlɪzəm] *n* imperialismo.

imperil [ɪmˈpɛrɪl] *vt* mettere in pericolo.

imperious [ɪmˈpɪərɪəs] *adj* imperioso(a).

impersonal [ɪmˈpəːsənl] *adj* impersonale.

impersonate [ɪmˈpəːsəneɪt] *vt* impersonare; (THEAT) imitare.

impersonation [ɪmpəːsəˈneɪʃən] *n* (LAW) usurpazione *f* d'identità; (THEAT) imitazione *f*.

impersonator [ɪmˈpəːsəneɪtə*] *n* (*gen*, THEAT) imitatore/trice.

impertinence [ɪmˈpəːtɪnəns] *n* impertinenza.

impertinent [ɪmˈpəːtɪnənt] *adj* impertinente.

imperturbable [ɪmpəˈtəːbəbl] *adj* imperturbabile.

impervious [ɪmˈpəːvɪəs] *adj* impermeabile; (*fig*): ~ **to** insensibile a; impassibile di fronte a.

impetuous [ɪmˈpɛtjuəs] *adj* impetuoso(a), precipitoso(a).

impetus [ˈɪmpətəs] *n* impeto.

impinge [ɪmˈpɪndʒ]: **to** ~ **on** *vt fus* (*person*) colpire; (*rights*) ledere.

impish [ˈɪmpɪʃ] *adj* malizioso(a), birichino(a).

implacable [ɪmˈplækəbl] *adj* implacabile.

implant [ɪmˈplɑːnt] *vt* (MED) innestare; (*fig*: *idea*, *principle*) inculcare.

implausible [ɪmˈplɔːzɪbl] *adj* non plausibile.

implement *n* [ˈɪmplɪmənt] attrezzo; (*for cooking*) utensile *m* ♦ *vt* [ˈɪmplɪmɛnt] effettuare.

implicate [ˈɪmplɪkeɪt] *vt* implicare.

implication [ɪmplɪˈkeɪʃən] *n* implicazione *f*; **by** ~ implicitamente.

implicit [ɪmˈplɪsɪt] *adj* implicito(a); (*complete*) completo(a).

implicitly [ɪmˈplɪsɪtlɪ] *adv* implicitamente.

implore [ɪmˈplɔː*] *vt* implorare.

imply [ɪmˈplaɪ] *vt* insinuare; suggerire.

impolite [ɪmpəˈlaɪt] *adj* scortese.

imponderable [ɪmˈpɔndərəbl] *adj* imponderabile.

import *vt* [ɪmˈpɔːt] importare ♦ *n* [ˈɪmpɔːt] (COMM) importazione *f*; (*meaning*) significato, senso ♦ *cpd* (*duty, licence etc*) d'importazione.

importance [ɪmˈpɔːtns] *n* importanza; **to be of great/little** ~ importare molto/poco,

essere molto/poco importante.

important [ɪmˈpɔːtnt] *adj* importante; **it's not** ~ non ha importanza; **it is** ~ **that** è importante che + *sub*.

importantly [ɪmˈpɔːtəntlɪ] *adv* (*pej*) con (un'aria d')importanza; **but, more** ~, ... ma, quel che più conta *or* importa, ...

importation [ɪmpɔːˈteɪʃən] *n* importazione *f*.

imported [ɪmˈpɔːtɪd] *adj* importato(a).

importer [ɪmˈpɔːtə*] *n* importatore/trice.

impose [ɪmˈpəuz] *vt* imporre ♦ *vi*: **to** ~ **on sb** sfruttare la bontà di qn.

imposing [ɪmˈpəuzɪŋ] *adj* imponente.

imposition [ɪmpəˈzɪʃən] *n* imposizione *f*; **to be an** ~ **on** (*person*) abusare della gentilezza di.

impossibility [ɪmpɔsəˈbɪlɪtɪ] *n* impossibilità.

impossible [ɪmˈpɔsɪbl] *adj* impossibile; **it is** ~ **for me to leave now** mi è impossibile venir via adesso.

impostor [ɪmˈpɔstə*] *n* impostore/a.

impotence [ˈɪmpətns] *n* impotenza.

impotent [ˈɪmpətnt] *adj* impotente.

impound [ɪmˈpaund] *vt* confiscare.

impoverished [ɪmˈpɔvərɪʃt] *adj* impoverito(a).

impracticable [ɪmˈpræktɪkəbl] *adj* impraticabile.

impractical [ɪmˈpræktɪkl] *adj* non pratico(a).

imprecise [ɪmprɪˈsaɪs] *adj* impreciso(a).

impregnable [ɪmˈprɛgnəbl] *adj* (*fortress*) inespugnabile; (*fig*) inoppugnabile; irrefutabile.

impregnate [ˈɪmprɛgneɪt] *vt* impregnare; (*fertilize*) fecondare.

impresario [ɪmprɪˈsɑːrɪəu] *n* impresario/a.

impress [ɪmˈprɛs] *vt* impressionare; (*mark*) imprimere, stampare; **to** ~ **sth on sb** far capire qc a qn.

impression [ɪmˈprɛʃən] *n* impressione *f*; **to be under the** ~ **that** avere l'impressione che; **to make a good/bad** ~ **on sb** fare una buona/cattiva impressione a *or* su qn.

impressionable [ɪmˈprɛʃnəbl] *adj* impressionabile.

impressionist [ɪmˈprɛʃənɪst] *n* impressionista *m/f*.

impressive [ɪmˈprɛsɪv] *adj* impressionante.

imprint [ˈɪmprɪnt] *n* (PUBLISHING) sigla editoriale.

imprinted [ɪmˈprɪntɪd] *adj*: ~ **on** impresso(a) in.

imprison [ɪmˈprɪzn] *vt* imprigionare.

imprisonment [ɪmˈprɪznmənt] *n*

imprigionamento.

improbable [ɪmˈprɔbəbl] *adj* improbabile; (*excuse*) inverosimile.

impromptu [ɪmˈprɔmptjuː] *adj* improvvisato(a) ♦ *adv* improvvisando, così su due piedi.

improper [ɪmˈprɔpə*] *adj* scorretto(a); (*unsuitable*) inadatto(a), improprio(a); sconveniente, indecente.

impropriety [ɪmprəˈpraɪətɪ] *n* sconvenienza; (*of expression*) improprietà.

improve [ɪmˈpruːv] *vt* migliorare ♦ *vi* migliorare; (*pupil etc*) fare progressi.

▸**improve (up)on** *vt fus* (*offer*) aumentare.

improvement [ɪmˈpruːvmənt] *n* miglioramento; progresso; **to make ~s to** migliorare, apportare dei miglioramenti a.

improvisation [ɪmprəvaɪˈzeɪʃən] *n* improvvisazione *f.*

improvise [ˈɪmprəvaɪz] *vt, vi* improvvisare.

imprudence [ɪmˈpruːdns] *n* imprudenza.

imprudent [ɪmˈpruːdnt] *adj* imprudente.

impudence [ˈɪmpjudns] *n* impudenza.

impudent [ˈɪmpjudnt] *adj* impudente, sfacciato(a).

impugn [ɪmˈpjuːn] *vt* impugnare.

impulse [ˈɪmpʌls] *n* impulso; **to act on ~** agire d'impulso *or* impulsivamente.

impulse buy *n* acquisto fatto d'impulso.

impulsive [ɪmˈpʌlsɪv] *adj* impulsivo(a).

impunity [ɪmˈpjuːnɪtɪ] *n*: **with ~** impunemente.

impure [ɪmˈpjuə*] *adj* impuro(a).

impurity [ɪmˈpjuərɪtɪ] *n* impurità *f inv.*

IN *abbr* (*US*) = *Indiana.*

══════════════ *KEYWORD*

in [ɪn] *prep* **1** (*indicating place, position*) in; ~ **the house/garden** in casa/giardino; ~ **the box** nella scatola; ~ **the fridge** nel frigorifero; **I have it** ~ **my hand** ce l'ho in mano; ~ **town/the country** in città/campagna; ~ **school** a scuola; ~ **here/there** qui/lì dentro

2 (*with place names: of town, region, country*): ~ **London** a Londra; ~ **England** in Inghilterra; ~ **the United States** negli Stati Uniti; ~ **Yorkshire** nello Yorkshire

3 (*indicating time: during, in the space of*) in; ~ **spring/summer** in primavera/estate; ~ **1988** nel 1988; ~ **May** in *or* a maggio; **I'll see you** ~ **July** ci vediamo a luglio; ~ **the afternoon** nel pomeriggio; **at 4 o'clock** ~ **the afternoon** alle 4 del pomeriggio; **I did it** ~ **3 hours/days** l'ho fatto in 3 ore/giorni; **I'll see you** ~ **2**

weeks *or* ~ **2 weeks' time** ci vediamo tra 2 settimane; **once** ~ **a hundred years** una volta ogni cento anni

4 (*indicating manner etc*) a; ~ **a loud/soft voice** a voce alta/bassa; ~ **pencil** a matita; ~ **English/French** in inglese/francese; ~ **writing** per iscritto; **the boy** ~ **the blue shirt** il ragazzo con la camicia blu

5 (*indicating circumstances*): ~ **the sun** al sole; ~ **the shade** all'ombra; ~ **the rain** sotto la pioggia; **a rise** ~ **prices** un aumento dei prezzi

6 (*indicating mood, state*): ~ **tears** in lacrime; ~ **anger** per la rabbia; ~ **despair** disperato(a); ~ **good condition** in buono stato, in buone condizioni; **to live** ~ **luxury** vivere nel lusso

7 (*with ratios, numbers*): **1** ~ **10** 1 su 10; **20 pence** ~ **the pound** 20 pence per sterlina; **they lined up** ~ **twos** si misero in fila per due; ~ **hundreds** a centinaia

8 (*referring to people, works*) in; **the disease is common** ~ **children** la malattia è comune nei bambini; ~ **(the works of) Dickens** in Dickens, nelle opere di Dickens

9 (*indicating profession etc*) in; **to be** ~ **teaching** fare l'insegnante, insegnare; **to be** ~ **publishing** lavorare nell'editoria

10 (*after superlative*) di; **the best** ~ **the class** il migliore della classe

11 (*with present participle*): ~ **saying this** dicendo questo, nel dire questo

12: ~ **that** *conj* poiché

♦ *adv*: **to be** ~ (*person: at home, work*) esserci; (*train, ship, plane*) essere arrivato(a); (*in fashion*) essere di moda; **their party is** ~ il loro partito è al potere; **to ask sb** ~ invitare qn ad entrare; **to run/limp** *etc* ~ entrare di corsa/zoppicando *etc*

♦ *n*: **the ~s and outs of the problem** tutti gli aspetti del problema.

in., ins *abbr* = **inch(es).**

inability [ɪnəˈbɪlɪtɪ] *n* inabilità, incapacità; ~ **to pay** impossibilità di pagare.

inaccessible [ɪnəkˈsɛsɪbl] *adj* inaccessibile.

inaccuracy [ɪnˈækjurəsɪ] *n* inaccuratezza; inesattezza; imprecisione *f.*

inaccurate [ɪnˈækjurət] *adj* inaccurato(a); (*figures*) inesatto(a); (*translation*) impreciso(a).

inaction [ɪnˈækʃən] *n* inazione *f.*

inactivity [ɪnækˈtɪvɪtɪ] *n* inattività.

inadequacy [ɪnˈædɪkwəsɪ] *n* insufficienza.

inadequate [ɪnˈædɪkwət] *adj* insufficiente.

inadmissible [ɪnədˈmɪsəbl] *adj*

inammissibile.

inadvertent [ɪnəd'vɔːtənt] adj involontario(a).

inadvertently [ɪnəd'vɔːtntlɪ] adv senza volerlo.

inadvisable [ɪnəd'vaɪzəbl] adj sconsigliabile.

inane [ɪ'neɪn] adj vacuo(a), stupido(a).

inanimate [ɪn'ænɪmət] adj inanimato(a).

inapplicable [ɪn'æplɪkəbl] adj inapplicabile.

inappropriate [ɪnə'prəuprɪət] adj disadatto(a); (word, expression) improprio(a).

inapt [ɪn'æpt] adj maldestro(a); fuori luogo.

inaptitude [ɪn'æptɪtjuːd] n improprietà.

inarticulate [ɪnɑː'tɪkjulət] adj (person) che si esprime male; (speech) inarticolato(a).

inasmuch as [ɪnəz'mʌtʃæz] adv in quanto che; (seeing that) poiché.

inattention [ɪnə'tɛnʃən] n mancanza di attenzione.

inattentive [ɪnə'tɛntɪv] adj disattento(a), distratto(a); negligente.

inaudible [ɪn'ɔːdɪbl] adj che non si riesce a sentire.

inaugural [ɪ'nɔːgjurəl] adj inaugurale.

inaugurate [ɪ'nɔːgjureɪt] vt inaugurare; (president, official) insediare.

inauguration [ɪnɔː'gjuˈreɪʃən] n inaugurazione f; insediamento in carica.

inauspicious [ɪnɔːs'pɪʃəs] adj poco propizio(a).

in-between [ɪnbɪ'twiːn] adj fra i (or le) due.

inborn [ɪn'bɔːn] adj (feeling) innato(a); (defect) congenito(a).

inbred [ɪn'brɛd] adj innato(a); (family) connaturato(a).

inbreeding [ɪn'briːdɪŋ] n incrocio ripetuto di animali consanguinei; unioni fpl fra consanguinei.

Inc. abbr see **incorporated**.

Inca ['ɪŋkə] adj (also: ~n) inca inv ♦ n inca m/f inv.

incalculable [ɪn'kælkjuləbl] adj incalcolabile.

incapability [ɪnkeɪpə'bɪlɪtɪ] n incapacità.

incapable [ɪn'keɪpəbl] adj: ~ (of doing sth) incapace (di fare qc).

incapacitate [ɪnkə'pæsɪteɪt] vt: to ~ sb from doing rendere qn incapace di fare.

incapacitated [ɪnkə'pæsɪteɪtɪd] adj (LAW) inabilitato(a).

incapacity [ɪnkə'pæsɪtɪ] n incapacità.

incarcerate [ɪn'kɑːsəreɪt] vt imprigionare.

incarnate adj [ɪn'kɑːnɪt] incarnato(a) ♦ vt ['ɪnkɑːneɪt] incarnare.

incarnation [ɪnkɑː'neɪʃən] n incarnazione f.

incendiary [ɪn'sɛndɪərɪ] adj incendiario(a)

♦ n (bomb) bomba incendiaria.

incense n ['ɪnsɛns] incenso ♦ vt [ɪn'sɛns] (anger) infuriare.

incense burner n incensiere m.

incentive [ɪn'sɛntɪv] n incentivo.

incentive scheme n piano di incentivazione.

inception [ɪn'sɛpʃən] n inizio, principio.

incessant [ɪn'sɛsnt] adj incessante.

incessantly [ɪn'sɛsntlɪ] adv di continuo, senza sosta.

incest ['ɪnsɛst] n incesto.

inch [ɪntʃ] n pollice m (= 25 mm; 12 in a foot); **within an ~ of** a un pelo da; **he wouldn't give an ~** (fig) non ha ceduto di un millimetro.

►**inch forward** vi avanzare pian piano.

inch tape n (BRIT) metro a nastro (da sarto).

incidence ['ɪnsɪdns] n incidenza.

incident ['ɪnsɪdnt] n incidente m; (in book) episodio.

incidental [ɪnsɪ'dɛntl] adj accessorio(a), d'accompagnamento; (unplanned) incidentale; ~ **to** marginale a; ~ **expenses** npl spese fpl accessorie.

incidentally [ɪnsɪ'dɛntəlɪ] adv (by the way) a proposito.

incidental music n sottofondo (musicale), musica di sottofondo.

incident room n (POLICE) centrale f delle operazioni (per indagini).

incinerate [ɪn'sɪnəreɪt] vt incenerire.

incinerator [ɪn'sɪnəreɪtə*] n inceneritore m.

incipient [ɪn'sɪpɪənt] adj incipiente.

incision [ɪn'sɪʒən] n incisione f.

incisive [ɪn'saɪsɪv] adj incisivo(a); tagliante; acuto(a).

incisor [ɪn'saɪzə*] n incisivo.

incite [ɪn'saɪt] vt incitare.

incl. abbr = **including, inclusive (of)**.

inclement [ɪn'klɛmənt] adj inclemente.

inclination [ɪnklɪ'neɪʃən] n inclinazione f.

incline n ['ɪnklaɪn] pendenza, pendio ♦ vb [ɪn'klaɪn] vt inclinare ♦ vi: **to ~ to** tendere a; **to be ~d to do** tendere a fare; essere propenso(a) a fare; **to be well ~d towards sb** essere ben disposto(a) verso qn.

include [ɪn'kluːd] vt includere, comprendere; **the tip is/is not ~d** la mancia è compresa/esclusa.

including [ɪn'kluːdɪŋ] prep compreso(a), incluso(a); ~ **tip** mancia compresa, compresa la mancia.

inclusion [ɪn'kluːʒən] n inclusione f.

inclusive [ɪn'kluːsɪv] adj incluso(a), compreso(a); **£50, ~ of all surcharges** 50 sterline, incluse tutte le soprattasse.

inclusive terms *npl* (*BRIT*) prezzo tutto compreso.

incognito [ɪnkɔg'niːtəu] *adv* in incognito.

incoherent [ɪnkəu'hɪərənt] *adj* incoerente.

income ['ɪnkʌm] *n* reddito; **gross/net** ~ reddito lordo/netto; ~ **and expenditure account** conto entrate ed uscite.

income support *n* (*BRIT*) sussidio di indigenza *or* povertà.

income tax *n* imposta sul reddito.

income tax inspector *n* ispettore *m* delle imposte dirette.

income tax return *n* dichiarazione *f* annuale dei redditi.

incoming ['ɪnkʌmɪŋ] *adj* (*passengers*) in arrivo; (*government, tenant*) subentrante; ~ **tide** marea montante.

incommunicado [ɪnkəmjunɪ'kɑːdəu] *adj*: **to hold sb** ~ tenere qn in segregazione.

incomparable [ɪn'kɔmpərəbl] *adj* incomparabile.

incompatible [ɪnkəm'pætɪbl] *adj* incompatibile.

incompetence [ɪn'kɔmpɪtns] *n* incompetenza, incapacità.

incompetent [ɪn'kɔmpɪtnt] *adj* incompetente, incapace.

incomplete [ɪnkəm'pliːt] *adj* incompleto(a).

incomprehensible [ɪnkɔmprɪ'hɛnsɪbl] *adj* incomprensibile.

inconceivable [ɪnkən'siːvəbl] *adj* inimmaginabile.

inconclusive [ɪnkən'kluːsɪv] *adj* improduttivo(a); (*argument*) poco convincente.

incongruous [ɪn'kɔŋgruəs] *adj* poco appropriato(a); (*remark, act*) incongruo(a).

inconsequential [ɪnkɔnsɪ'kwɛnʃl] *adj* senza importanza.

inconsiderable [ɪnkən'sɪdərəbl] *adj*: **not** ~ non trascurabile.

inconsiderate [ɪnkən'sɪdərət] *adj* sconsiderato(a).

inconsistency [ɪnkən'sɪstənsɪ] *n* (*of actions etc*) incongruenza; (*of work*) irregolarità; (*of statement etc*) contraddizione *f*.

inconsistent [ɪnkən'sɪstnt] *adj* incoerente; poco logico(a); contraddittorio(a); ~ **with** in contraddizione con.

inconsolable [ɪnkən'səuləbl] *adj* inconsolabile.

inconspicuous [ɪnkən'spɪkjuəs] *adj* incospicuo(a); (*colour*) poco appariscente; (*dress*) dimesso(a); **to make o.s.** ~ cercare di passare inosservato(a).

inconstant [ɪn'kɔnstnt] *adj* incostante.

incontinence [ɪn'kɔntɪnəns] *n* incontinenza.

incontinent [ɪn'kɔntɪnənt] *adj* incontinente.

incontrovertible [ɪnkɔntrə'vəːtəbl] *adj* incontrovertibile.

inconvenience [ɪnkən'viːnjəns] *n* inconveniente *m*; (*trouble*) disturbo ♦ *vt* disturbare; **to put sb to great** ~ creare degli inconvenienti a qn.

inconvenient [ɪnkən'viːnjənt] *adj* scomodo(a); **that time is very** ~ **for me** quell'ora mi è molto scomoda, non è un'ora adatta per me.

incorporate [ɪn'kɔːpəreɪt] *vt* incorporare; (*contain*) contenere.

incorporated [ɪn'kɔːpəreɪtɪd] *adj*: ~ **company** (*US: abbr* **Inc.**) società *f inv* registrata.

incorrect [ɪnkə'rɛkt] *adj* scorretto(a); (*statement*) impreciso(a).

incorrigible [ɪn'kɔrɪdʒəbl] *adj* incorreggibile.

incorruptible [ɪnkə'rʌptɪbl] *adj* incorruttibile.

increase *n* ['ɪnkriːs] aumento ♦ *vi* [ɪn'kriːs] aumentare; **to be on the** ~ essere in aumento; **an** ~ **of £5/10%** un aumento di 5 sterline/del 10%.

increasing [ɪn'kriːsɪŋ] *adj* (*number*) crescente.

increasingly [ɪn'kriːsɪŋlɪ] *adv* sempre più.

incredible [ɪn'krɛdɪbl] *adj* incredibile.

incredulous [ɪn'krɛdjuləs] *adj* incredulo(a).

increment ['ɪnkrɪmənt] *n* aumento, incremento.

incriminate [ɪn'krɪmɪneɪt] *vt* compromettere.

incriminating [ɪn'krɪmɪneɪtɪŋ] *adj* incriminante.

incubate ['ɪnkjubeɪt] *vt* (*eggs*) covare ♦ *vi* (*egg*) essere in incubazione; (*disease*) avere un'incubazione.

incubation [ɪnkju'beɪʃən] *n* incubazione *f*.

incubation period *n* (periodo di) incubazione *f*.

incubator ['ɪnkjubeɪtə*] *n* incubatrice *f*.

inculcate ['ɪnkʌlkeɪt] *vt*: **to** ~ **sth in sb** inculcare qc a qn, instillare qc a qn.

incumbent [ɪn'kʌmbənt] *adj*: **it is** ~ **on him to do ...** è suo dovere fare ... ♦ *n* titolare *m/f*.

incur [ɪn'kəː*] *vt* (*expenses*) incorrere; (*debt*) contrarre; (*loss*) subire; (*anger, risk*) esporsi a.

incurable [ɪn'kjuərəbl] *adj* incurabile.

incursion [ɪn'kəːʃən] *n* incursione *f*.

Ind. *abbr* (*US*) = *Indiana*.

indebted [ɪn'dɛtɪd] *adj*: **to be** ~ **to sb** (**for**) essere obbligato(a) verso qn (per).

indecency [ɪn'diːsnsɪ] *n* indecenza.
indecent [ɪn'diːsnt] *adj* indecente.
indecent assault *n* (*BRIT*) aggressione *f* a scopo di violenza sessuale.
indecent exposure *n* atti *mpl* osceni in luogo pubblico.
indecipherable [ɪndɪ'saɪfərəbl] *adj* indecifrabile.
indecision [ɪndɪ'sɪʒən] *n* indecisione *f*.
indecisive [ɪndɪ'saɪsɪv] *adj* indeciso(a); (*discussion*) non decisivo(a).
indeed [ɪn'diːd] *adv* infatti; veramente; **yes ~!** certamente!
indefatigable [ɪndɪ'fætɪɡəbl] *adj* infaticabile, instancabile.
indefensible [ɪndɪ'fɛnsəbl] *adj* (*conduct*) ingiustificabile.
indefinable [ɪndɪ'faɪnəbl] *adj* indefinibile.
indefinite [ɪn'dɛfɪnɪt] *adj* indefinito(a); (*answer*) vago(a); (*period, number*) indeterminato(a).
indefinitely [ɪn'dɛfɪnɪtlɪ] *adv* (*wait*) indefinitamente.
indelible [ɪn'dɛlɪbl] *adj* indelebile.
indelicate [ɪn'dɛlɪkɪt] *adj* (*tactless*) indelicato(a), privo(a) di tatto; (*not polite*) sconveniente.
indemnify [ɪn'dɛmnɪfaɪ] *vt* indennizzare.
indemnity [ɪn'dɛmnɪtɪ] *n* (*insurance*) assicurazione *f*; (*compensation*) indennità, indennizzo.
indent [ɪn'dɛnt] *vt* (*TYP: text*) far rientrare dal margine.
indentation [ɪndɛn'teɪʃən] *n* dentellatura; (*TYP*) rientranza; (*dent*) tacca.
indented [ɪn'dɛntɪd] *adj* (*TYP*) rientrante.
indenture [ɪn'dɛntʃə*] *n* contratto *m* formazione *inv*.
independence [ɪndɪ'pɛndns] *n* indipendenza.
Independence Day *n* (*US*) *see boxed note.*

---

independent [ɪndɪ'pɛndnt] *adj* indipendente.
independently [ɪndɪ'pɛndntlɪ] *adv* indipendentemente; separatamente; **~ of** indipendentemente da.
in-depth ['ɪn'dɛpθ] *adj* approfondito(a).

indescribable [ɪndɪ'skraɪbəbl] *adj* indescrivibile.
indestructible [ɪndɪ'strʌktəbl] *adj* indistruttibile.
indeterminate [ɪndɪ'təːmɪnɪt] *adj* indeterminato(a).
index ['ɪndɛks] *n* (*pl ~es: in book*) indice *m*; (*: in library etc*) catalogo; (*pl* **indices** ['ɪndɪsiːz]: *ratio, sign*) indice *m*.
index card *n* scheda.
index finger *n* (dito) indice *m*.
index-linked ['ɪndɛks'lɪŋkt], (*US*) **indexed** ['ɪndɛkst] *adj* legato(a) al costo della vita.
India ['ɪndɪə] *n* India.
Indian ['ɪndɪən] *adj*, *n* indiano(a).
Indian ink *n* inchiostro di china.
Indian Ocean *n*: **the ~** l'Oceano Indiano.
Indian Summer *n* (*fig*) estate *f* di San Martino.
India paper *n* carta d'India, carta bibbia.
India rubber *n* caucciù *m*.
indicate ['ɪndɪkeɪt] *vt* indicare ♦ *vi* (*BRIT AUT*): **to ~ left/right** mettere la freccia a sinistra/a destra.
indication [ɪndɪ'keɪʃən] *n* indicazione *f*, segno.
indicative [ɪn'dɪkətɪv] *adj* indicativo(a) ♦ *n* (*LING*) indicativo; **to be ~ of sth** essere indicativo(a) or un indice di qc.
indicator ['ɪndɪkeɪtə*] *n* (*sign*) segno; (*AUT*) indicatore *m* di direzione, freccia.
indices ['ɪndɪsiːz] *npl of* **index**.
indict [ɪn'daɪt] *vt* accusare.
indictable [ɪn'daɪtəbl] *adj* passibile di pena; **~ offence** atto che costituisce reato.
indictment [ɪn'daɪtmənt] *n* accusa.
indifference [ɪn'dɪfrəns] *n* indifferenza.
indifferent [ɪn'dɪfrənt] *adj* indifferente; (*poor*) mediocre.
indigenous [ɪn'dɪdʒɪnəs] *adj* indigeno(a).
indigestible [ɪndɪ'dʒɛstɪbl] *adj* indigeribile.
indigestion [ɪndɪ'dʒɛstʃən] *n* indigestione *f*.
indignant [ɪn'dɪɡnənt] *adj*: **~ (at sth/with sb)** indignato(a) (per qc/contro qn).
indignation [ɪndɪɡ'neɪʃən] *n* indignazione *f*.
indignity [ɪn'dɪɡnɪtɪ] *n* umiliazione *f*.
indigo ['ɪndɪɡəʊ] *adj*, *n* indaco (*inv*).
indirect [ɪndɪ'rɛkt] *adj* indiretto(a).
indirectly [ɪndɪ'rɛktlɪ] *adv* indirettamente.
indiscreet [ɪndɪ'skriːt] *adj* indiscreto(a); (*rash*) imprudente.
indiscretion [ɪndɪ'skrɛʃən] *n* indiscrezione *f*; imprudenza.
indiscriminate [ɪndɪ'skrɪmɪnət] *adj* (*person*) che non sa discernere; (*admiration*) cieco(a); (*killings*) indiscriminato(a).
indispensable [ɪndɪ'spɛnsəbl] *adj* indispensabile.

indisposed [ɪndɪ'spəuzd] *adj* (*unwell*) indisposto(a).

indisposition [ɪndɪspə'zɪʃən] *n* (*illness*) indisposizione *f*.

indisputable [ɪndɪ'spjuːtəbl] *adj* incontestabile, indiscutibile.

indistinct [ɪndɪ'stɪŋkt] *adj* indistinto(a); (*memory, noise*) vago(a).

indistinguishable [ɪndɪ'stɪŋgwɪʃəbl] *adj* indistinguibile.

individual [ɪndɪ'vɪdjuəl] *n* individuo ♦ *adj* individuale; (*characteristic*) particolare, originale.

individualist [ɪndɪ'vɪdjuəlɪst] *n* individualista *m/f*.

individuality [ɪndɪvɪdju'ælɪtɪ] *n* individualità.

individually [ɪndɪ'vɪdjuəlɪ] *adv* singolarmente, uno(a) per uno(a).

indivisible [ɪndɪ'vɪzɪbl] *adj* indivisibile.

Indochina ['ɪndəu'tʃaɪnə] *n* Indocina.

indoctrinate [ɪn'dɔktrɪneɪt] *vt* indottrinare.

indoctrination [ɪndɔktrɪ'neɪʃən] *n* indottrinamento.

indolent ['ɪndələnt] *adj* indolente.

Indonesia [ɪndəu'niːzɪə] *n* Indonesia.

Indonesian [ɪndəu'niːzɪən] *adj, n* indonesiano(a); (*LING*) indonesiano.

indoor ['ɪndɔː*] *adj* da interno; (*plant*) d'appartamento; (*swimming pool*) coperto(a); (*sport, games*) fatto(a) al coperto.

indoors [ɪn'dɔːz] *adv* all'interno; (*at home*) in casa.

indubitable [ɪn'djuːbɪtəbl] *adj* indubitabile.

induce [ɪn'djuːs] *vt* persuadere; (*bring about*) provocare; **to ~ sb to do sth** persuadere qn a fare qc.

inducement [ɪn'djuːsmənt] *n* incitamento; (*incentive*) stimolo, incentivo.

induct [ɪn'dʌkt] *vt* insediare; (*fig*) iniziare.

induction [ɪn'dʌkʃən] *n* (*MED: of birth*) parto indotto.

induction course *n* (*BRIT*) corso di avviamento.

indulge [ɪn'dʌldʒ] *vt* (*whim*) compiacere, soddisfare; (*child*) viziare ♦ *vi*: **to ~ in sth** concedersi qc; abbandonarsi a qc.

indulgence [ɪn'dʌldʒəns] *n* lusso (che uno si permette); (*leniency*) indulgenza.

indulgent [ɪn'dʌldʒənt] *adj* indulgente.

industrial [ɪn'dʌstrɪəl] *adj* industriale; (*injury*) sul lavoro; (*dispute*) di lavoro.

industrial action *n* azione *f* rivendicativa.

industrial estate *n* zona industriale.

industrialist [ɪn'dʌstrɪəlɪst] *n* industriale *m*.

industrialize [ɪn'dʌstrɪəlaɪz] *vt* industrializzare.

industrial park *n* (*US*) zona industriale.

industrial relations *npl* relazioni *fpl* industriali.

industrial tribunal *n* (*BRIT*) ≈ Tribunale *m* Amministrativo Regionale.

industrial unrest *n* (*BRIT*) agitazione *f* (sindacale).

industrious [ɪn'dʌstrɪəs] *adj* industrioso(a), assiduo(a).

industry ['ɪndəstrɪ] *n* industria; (*diligence*) operosità.

inebriated [ɪ'niːbrɪeɪtɪd] *adj* ubriaco(a).

inedible [ɪn'ɛdɪbl] *adj* immangiabile; non commestibile.

ineffective [ɪnɪ'fɛktɪv] *adj* inefficace.

ineffectual [ɪnɪ'fɛktʃuəl] *adj* inefficace; incompetente.

inefficiency [ɪnɪ'fɪʃənsɪ] *n* inefficienza.

inefficient [ɪnɪ'fɪʃənt] *adj* inefficiente.

inelegant [ɪn'ɛlɪgənt] *adj* poco elegante.

ineligible [ɪn'ɛlɪdʒɪbl] *adj* (*candidate*) ineleggibile; **to be ~ for sth** non avere il diritto a qc.

inept [ɪ'nɛpt] *adj* inetto(a).

ineptitude [ɪ'nɛptɪtjuːd] *n* inettitudine *f*, stupidità.

inequality [ɪnɪ'kwɔlɪtɪ] *n* ineguaglianza.

inequitable [ɪn'ɛkwɪtəbl] *adj* iniquo(a).

ineradicable [ɪnɪ'rædɪkəbl] *adj* inestirpabile.

inert [ɪ'nɜːt] *adj* inerte.

inertia [ɪ'nɜːʃə] *n* inerzia.

inertia-reel seat belt [ɪ'nɜːʃə'riːl-] *n* cintura di sicurezza con arrotolatore.

inescapable [ɪnɪ'skeɪpəbl] *adj* inevitabile.

inessential [ɪnɪ'sɛnʃl] *adj* non essenziale.

inestimable [ɪn'ɛstɪməbl] *adj* inestimabile, incalcolabile.

inevitable [ɪn'ɛvɪtəbl] *adj* inevitabile.

inevitably [ɪn'ɛvɪtəblɪ] *adv* inevitabilmente; **as ~ happens ...** come immancabilmente succede ....

inexact [ɪnɪg'zækt] *adj* inesatto(a).

inexcusable [ɪnɪks'kjuːzəbl] *adj* imperdonabile.

inexhaustible [ɪnɪg'zɔːstɪbl] *adj* inesauribile; (*person*) instancabile.

inexorable [ɪn'ɛksərəbl] *adj* inesorabile.

inexpensive [ɪnɪk'spɛnsɪv] *adj* poco costoso(a).

inexperience [ɪnɪk'spɪərɪəns] *n* inesperienza.

inexperienced [ɪnɪk'spɪərɪənst] *adj* inesperto(a), senza esperienza; **to be ~ in sth** essere poco pratico di qc.

inexplicable [ɪnɪk'splɪkəbl] *adj* inesplicabile.

inexpressible [ɪnɪk'sprɛsəbl] *adj*

inesprimibile.

inextricable [ɪnɪk'strɪkəbl] *adj* inestricabile.

infallibility [ɪnfælə'bɪlɪtɪ] *n* infallibilità.

infallible [ɪn'fælɪbl] *adj* infallibile.

infamous ['ɪnfəməs] *adj* infame.

infamy ['ɪnfəmɪ] *n* infamia.

infancy ['ɪnfənsɪ] *n* infanzia.

infant ['ɪnfənt] *n* bambino/a.

infantile ['ɪnfəntaɪl] *adj* infantile.

infant mortality *n* mortalità infantile.

infantry ['ɪnfəntrɪ] *n* fanteria.

infantryman ['ɪnfəntrɪmən] *n* fante *m*.

infant school *n* (*BRIT*) scuola elementare (*per bambini dall'età di 5 a 7 anni*).

infatuated [ɪn'fætjueɪtɪd] *adj*: ~ **with** infatuato(a) di; **to become** ~ **(with sb)** infatuarsi (di qn).

infatuation [ɪnfætju'eɪʃən] *n* infatuazione *f*.

infect [ɪn'fɛkt] *vt* infettare; ~**ed with** (*illness*) affetto(a) da; **to become** ~**ed** (*wound*) infettarsi.

infection [ɪn'fɛkʃən] *n* infezione *f*.

infectious [ɪn'fɛkʃəs] *adj* (*disease*) infettivo(a), contagioso(a); (*person, laughter*) contagioso(a).

infer [ɪn'fəː*] *vt*: **to** ~ **(from)** dedurre (da), concludere (da).

inference ['ɪnfərəns] *n* deduzione *f*, conclusione *f*.

inferior [ɪn'fɪərɪə*] *adj* inferiore; (*goods*) di qualità scadente ♦ *n* inferiore *m/f*; (*in rank*) subalterno/a; **to feel** ~ sentirsi inferiore.

inferiority [ɪnfɪərɪ'ɔrətɪ] *n* inferiorità.

inferiority complex *n* complesso di inferiorità.

infernal [ɪn'fəːnl] *adj* infernale.

inferno [ɪn'fəːnəu] *n* inferno.

infertile [ɪn'fəːtaɪl] *adj* sterile.

infertility [ɪnfəː'tɪlɪtɪ] *n* sterilità.

infested [ɪn'fɛstɪd] *adj*: ~ **(with)** infestato(a) (di).

infidelity [ɪnfɪ'dɛlɪtɪ] *n* infedeltà.

in-fighting ['ɪnfaɪtɪŋ] *n* lotte *fpl* intestine.

infiltrate ['ɪnfɪltreɪt] *vt* (*troops etc*) far penetrare; (*enemy line etc*) infiltrare ♦ *vi* infiltrarsi.

infinite ['ɪnfɪnɪt] *adj* infinito(a); **an** ~ **amount of time/money** un'illimitata quantità di tempo/denaro.

infinitely ['ɪnfɪnɪtlɪ] *adv* infinitamente.

infinitesimal [ɪnfɪnɪ'tɛsɪməl] *adj* infinitesimale.

infinitive [ɪn'fɪnɪtɪv] *n* infinito.

infinity [ɪn'fɪnɪtɪ] *n* infinità; (*also MATH*) infinito.

infirm [ɪn'fəːm] *adj* infermo(a).

infirmary [ɪn'fəːmərɪ] *n* ospedale *m*; (*in school, factory*) infermeria.

infirmity [ɪn'fəːmɪtɪ] *n* infermità *f inv*.

inflamed [ɪn'fleɪmd] *adj* infiammato(a).

inflammable [ɪn'flæməbl] *adj* infiammabile.

inflammation [ɪnflə'meɪʃən] *n* infiammazione *f*.

inflammatory [ɪn'flæmətərɪ] *adj* (*speech*) incendiario(a).

inflatable [ɪn'fleɪtəbl] *adj* gonfiabile.

inflate [ɪn'fleɪt] *vt* (*tyre, balloon*) gonfiare; (*fig*) esagerare; gonfiare; **to** ~ **the currency** far ricorso all'inflazione.

inflated [ɪn'fleɪtɪd] *adj* (*style*) gonfio(a); (*value*) esagerato(a).

inflation [ɪn'fleɪʃən] *n* (*ECON*) inflazione *f*.

inflationary [ɪn'fleɪʃənərɪ] *adj* inflazionistico(a).

inflexible [ɪn'flɛksɪbl] *adj* inflessibile, rigido(a).

inflict [ɪn'flɪkt] *vt*: **to** ~ **on** infliggere a.

infliction [ɪn'flɪkʃən] *n* inflizione *f*; afflizione *f*.

in-flight ['ɪnflaɪt] *adj* a bordo.

inflow ['ɪnfləu] *n* afflusso.

influence ['ɪnfluəns] *n* influenza ♦ *vt* influenzare; **under the** ~ **of** sotto l'influenza di; **under the** ~ **of drink** sotto l'influenza *or* l'effetto dell'alcool.

influential [ɪnflu'ɛnʃl] *adj* influente.

influenza [ɪnflu'ɛnzə] *n* (*MED*) influenza.

influx ['ɪnflʌks] *n* afflusso.

inform [ɪn'fɔːm] *vt*: **to** ~ **sb (of)** informare qn (di) ♦ *vi*: **to** ~ **on sb** denunciare qn; **to** ~ **sb about** mettere qn al corrente di.

informal [ɪn'fɔːml] *adj* (*person, manner*) alla buona, semplice; (*visit, discussion*) informale; (*invitation*) non ufficiale; "**dress** ~" "non è richiesto l'abito scuro"; ~ **language** linguaggio colloquiale.

informality [ɪnfɔː'mælɪtɪ] *n* semplicità, informalità; carattere *m* non ufficiale.

informally [ɪn'fɔːməlɪ] *adv* senza cerimonie; (*invite*) in modo non ufficiale.

informant [ɪn'fɔːmənt] *n* informatore/trice.

informatics [ɪnfə'mætɪks] *n* informatica.

information [ɪnfə'meɪʃən] *n* informazioni *fpl*; particolari *mpl*; **to get** ~ **on** informarsi su; **a piece of** ~ un'informazione; **for your** ~ a titolo d'informazione, per sua informazione.

information bureau *n* ufficio *m* informazioni *inv*.

information processing *n* elaborazione *f* delle informazioni.

information retrieval *n* ricupero delle informazioni.

information superhighway *n* autostrada informatica.

information technology (IT) *n*
informatica.
informative [ɪnˈfɔːmətɪv] *adj* istruttivo(a).
informed [ɪnˈfɔːmd] *adj* (*observer*) (ben)
informato(a); **an ~ guess** un'ipotesi
fondata.
informer [ɪnˈfɔːməʳ] *n* informatore/trice.
infra dig [ˈɪnfrəˈdɪg] *adj abbr* (*col*: = *infra*
dignitatem: *beneath one's dignity*)
indecoroso(a).
infra-red [ɪnfrəˈrɛd] *adj* infrarosso(a).
infrastructure [ˈɪnfrəstrʌktʃəʳ] *n*
infrastruttura.
infrequent [ɪnˈfriːkwənt] *adj* infrequente,
raro(a).
infringe [ɪnˈfrɪndʒ] *vt* infrangere ♦ *vi*: **to ~**
on calpestare.
infringement [ɪnˈfrɪndʒmənt] *n*: **~ (of)**
infrazione *f* (di).
infuriate [ɪnˈfjuərɪeɪt] *vt* rendere furioso(a).
infuriating [ɪnˈfjuərɪeɪtɪŋ] *adj* molto
irritante.
infuse [ɪnˈfjuːz] *vt* (*with courage*,
enthusiasm): **to ~ sb with sth** infondere
qc a qn, riempire qn di qc.
infusion [ɪnˈfjuːʒən] *n* (*tea etc*) infuso,
infusione *f*.
ingenious [ɪnˈdʒiːnjəs] *adj* ingegnoso(a).
ingenuity [ɪndʒɪˈnjuːɪtɪ] *n* ingegnosità.
ingenuous [ɪnˈdʒɛnjuəs] *adj* ingenuo(a).
ingot [ˈɪŋgət] *n* lingotto.
ingrained [ɪnˈgreɪnd] *adj* radicato(a).
ingratiate [ɪnˈgreɪʃɪeɪt] *vt*: **to ~ o.s. with sb**
ingraziarsi qn.
ingratiating [ɪnˈgreɪʃɪeɪtɪŋ] *adj* (*smile*,
speech) suadente, cattivante; (*person*)
compiacente.
ingratitude [ɪnˈgrætɪtjuːd] *n* ingratitudine *f*.
ingredient [ɪnˈgriːdɪənt] *n* ingrediente *m*;
elemento.
ingrowing [ˈɪngrəʊɪŋ], **ingrown** [ˈɪngrəʊn]
adj: **~ (toe)nail** unghia incarnita.
inhabit [ɪnˈhæbɪt] *vt* abitare.
inhabitable [ɪnˈhæbɪtəbl] *adj* abitabile.
inhabitant [ɪnˈhæbɪtnt] *n* abitante *m/f*.
inhale [ɪnˈheɪl] *vt* inalare ♦ *vi* (*in smoking*)
aspirare.
inhaler [ɪnˈheɪləʳ] *n* inalatore *m*.
inherent [ɪnˈhɪərənt] *adj*: **~ (in or to)**
inerente (a).
inherently [ɪnˈhɪərəntlɪ] *adv* (*easy, difficult*)
di per sé; **~ lazy** pigro di natura.
inherit [ɪnˈhɛrɪt] *vt* ereditare.
inheritance [ɪnˈhɛrɪtəns] *n* eredità.
inhibit [ɪnˈhɪbɪt] *vt* (*PSYCH*) inibire; **to ~ sb**
from doing impedire a qn di fare.
inhibited [ɪnˈhɪbɪtɪd] *adj* (*person*) inibito(a).
inhibiting [ɪnˈhɪbɪtɪŋ] *adj* che inibisce.

inhibition [ɪnhɪˈbɪʃən] *n* inibizione *f*.
inhospitable [ɪnhɔsˈpɪtəbl] *adj* inospitale.
in-house [ˈɪnˈhaus] *adj* effettuato(a) da
personale interno, interno(a) ♦ *adv*
(*training*) all'interno dell'azienda.
inhuman [ɪnˈhjuːmən] *adj* inumano(a),
disumano(a).
inhumane [ɪnhjuːˈmeɪn] *adj* inumano(a),
disumano(a).
inimitable [ɪˈnɪmɪtəbl] *adj* inimitabile.
iniquity [ɪˈnɪkwɪtɪ] *n* iniquità *f inv*.
initial [ɪˈnɪʃl] *adj* iniziale ♦ *n* iniziale *f* ♦ *vt*
siglare; **~s** *npl* iniziali *fpl*; (*as signature*)
sigla.
initialize [ɪˈnɪʃəlaɪz] *vt* (*COMPUT*)
inizializzare.
initially [ɪˈnɪʃəlɪ] *adv* inizialmente, all'inizio.
initiate [ɪˈnɪʃɪeɪt] *vt* (*start*) avviare;
intraprendere; iniziare; (*person*) iniziare;
to ~ sb into sth iniziare qn a qc; **to ~**
proceedings against sb (*LAW*) intentare
causa a *or* contro qn.
initiation [ɪnɪʃɪˈeɪʃən] *n* iniziazione *f*.
initiative [ɪˈnɪʃətɪv] *n* iniziativa; **to take the**
~ prendere l'iniziativa.
inject [ɪnˈdʒɛkt] *vt* (*liquid*) iniettare; (*person*)
fare una puntura a; (*fig: money*): **to ~ into**
immettere in.
injection [ɪnˈdʒɛkʃən] *n* iniezione *f*, puntura;
to have an ~ farsi fare un'iniezione *or*
una puntura.
injudicious [ɪndʒuˈdɪʃəs] *adj* poco saggio(a).
injunction [ɪnˈdʒʌŋkʃən] *n* (*LAW*)
ingiunzione *f*, intimazione *f*.
injure [ˈɪndʒəʳ] *vt* ferire; (*wrong*) fare male
or torto a; (*damage: reputation etc*)
nuocere a; (*feelings*) offendere; **to ~ o.s.**
farsi male.
injured [ˈɪndʒəd] *adj* (*person, leg etc*)
ferito(a); (*tone, feelings*) offeso(a); **~**
party (*LAW*) parte *f* lesa.
injurious [ɪnˈdʒuərɪəs] *adj*: **~ (to)** nocivo(a)
(a), pregiudizievole (per).
injury [ˈɪndʒərɪ] *n* ferita; (*wrong*) torto; **to**
escape without ~ rimanere illeso.
injury time *n* (*SPORT*) tempo di ricupero.
injustice [ɪnˈdʒʌstɪs] *n* ingiustizia; **you do**
me an ~ mi fa un torto, è ingiusto verso
di me.
ink [ɪŋk] *n* inchiostro.
ink-jet printer [ˈɪŋkdʒɛt-] *n* stampante *f* a
getto d'inchiostro.
inkling [ˈɪŋklɪŋ] *n* sentore *m*, vaga idea.
inkpad [ˈɪŋkpæd] *n* tampone *m*, cuscinetto
per timbri.
inky [ˈɪŋkɪ] *adj* macchiato(a) *or* sporco(a)
d'inchiostro.
inlaid [ˈɪnleɪd] *adj* incrostato(a); (*table etc*)

intarsiato(a).

inland *adj* ['ɪnlənd] interno(a) ♦ *adv* [ɪn'lænd] all'interno; ~ **waterways** canali e fiumi *mpl* navigabili.

Inland Revenue *n* (*BRIT*) Fisco.

in-laws ['ɪnlɔːz] *npl* suoceri *mpl*; famiglia del marito (*or* della moglie).

inlet ['ɪnlɛt] *n* (*GEO*) insenatura, baia.

inlet pipe *n* (*TECH*) tubo d'immissione.

inmate ['ɪnmeɪt] *n* (*in prison*) carcerato/a; (*in asylum*) ricoverato/a.

inmost ['ɪnməust] *adj* più profondo(a), più intimo(a).

inn [ɪn] *n* locanda.

innards ['ɪnədz] *npl* (*col*) interiora *fpl*, budella *fpl*.

innate [ɪ'neɪt] *adj* innato(a).

inner ['ɪnə*] *adj* interno(a), interiore.

inner city *n* centro di una zona urbana.

innermost ['ɪnəməust] *adj* = **inmost**.

inner tube *n* camera d'aria.

innings ['ɪnɪŋz] *n* (*CRICKET*) turno di battuta; (*BRIT fig*): **he has had a good** ~ ha avuto molto dalla vita.

innocence ['ɪnəsns] *n* innocenza.

innocent ['ɪnəsnt] *adj* innocente.

innocuous [ɪ'nɔkjuəs] *adj* innocuo(a).

innovation [ɪnəu'veɪʃən] *n* innovazione *f*.

innuendo, ~**es** [ɪnju'ɛndəu] *n* insinuazione *f*.

innumerable [ɪ'njuːmrəbl] *adj* innumerevole.

inoculate [ɪ'nɔkjuleɪt] *vt*: **to** ~ **sb with sth/against sth** inoculare qc a qn/qn contro qc.

inoculation [ɪnɔkju'leɪʃən] *n* inoculazione *f*.

inoffensive [ɪnə'fɛnsɪv] *adj* inoffensivo(a), innocuo(a).

inopportune [ɪn'ɔpətjuːn] *adj* inopportuno(a).

inordinate [ɪ'nɔːdɪnɪt] *adj* eccessivo(a).

inordinately [ɪ'nɔːdɪnətlɪ] *adv* smoderatamente.

inorganic [ɪnɔː'gænɪk] *adj* inorganico(a).

in-patient ['ɪnpeɪʃənt] *n* ricoverato/a.

input ['ɪnput] *n* (*ELEC*) energia, potenza; (*of machine*) alimentazione *f*; (*of computer*) input *m* ♦ *vt* (*COMPUT*) inserire, introdurre.

inquest ['ɪnkwɛst] *n* inchiesta.

inquire [ɪn'kwaɪə*] *vi* informarsi ♦ *vt* domandare, informarsi di *or* su; **to** ~ **about** informarsi di *or* su, chiedere informazioni su; **to** ~ **when/where/whether** informarsi di quando/su dove/se.

▶**inquire after** *vt fus* (*person*) chiedere di; (*sb's health*) informarsi di.

▶**inquire into** *vt fus* indagare su, fare delle indagini *or* ricerche su.

inquiring [ɪn'kwaɪərɪŋ] *adj* (*mind*) inquisitivo(a).

inquiry [ɪn'kwaɪərɪ] *n* domanda; (*LAW*) indagine *f*, investigazione *f*; **to hold an** ~ **into sth** fare un'inchiesta su qc.

inquiry desk *n* (*BRIT*) banco delle informazioni.

inquiry office *n* (*BRIT*) ufficio *m* informazioni *inv*.

inquisition [ɪnkwɪ'zɪʃən] *n* inquisizione *f*, inchiesta; (*REL*): **the I**~ l'Inquisizione.

inquisitive [ɪn'kwɪzɪtɪv] *adj* curioso(a).

inroads ['ɪnrəudz] *npl*: **to make** ~ **into** (*savings, supplies*) intaccare (seriamente).

insane [ɪn'seɪn] *adj* matto(a), pazzo(a); (*MED*) alienato(a).

insanitary [ɪn'sænɪtərɪ] *adj* insalubre.

insanity [ɪn'sænɪtɪ] *n* follia; (*MED*) alienazione *f* mentale.

insatiable [ɪn'seɪʃəbl] *adj* insaziabile.

inscribe [ɪn'skraɪb] *vt* iscrivere; (*book etc*): **to** ~ (**to sb**) dedicare (a qn).

inscription [ɪn'skrɪpʃən] *n* iscrizione *f*; (*in book*) dedica.

inscrutable [ɪn'skruːtəbl] *adj* imperscrutabile.

inseam ['ɪnsiːm] *n* (*US*): ~ **measurement** lunghezza interna.

insect ['ɪnsɛkt] *n* insetto.

insect bite *n* puntura *or* morsicatura di insetto.

insecticide [ɪn'sɛktɪsaɪd] *n* insetticida *m*.

insect repellent *n* insettifugo.

insecure [ɪnsɪ'kjuə*] *adj* malsicuro(a); (*person*) insicuro(a).

insecurity [ɪnsɪ'kjuərɪtɪ] *n* mancanza di sicurezza.

insensible [ɪn'sɛnsɪbl] *adj* insensibile; (*unconscious*) privo(a) di sensi.

insensitive [ɪn'sɛnsɪtɪv] *adj* insensibile.

insensitivity [ɪnsɛnsɪ'tɪvɪtɪ] *n* mancanza di sensibilità.

inseparable [ɪn'sɛprəbl] *adj* inseparabile.

insert *vt* [ɪn'səːt] inserire, introdurre ♦ *n* ['ɪnsəːt] inserto.

insertion [ɪn'səːʃən] *n* inserzione *f*.

in-service ['ɪn'səːvɪs] *adj* (*course, training*) dopo l'assunzione.

inshore [ɪn'ʃɔː*] *adj* costiero(a) ♦ *adv* presso la riva; verso la riva.

inside ['ɪn'saɪd] *n* interno, parte *f* interiore; (*of road*: *BRIT*) sinistra; (: *US, in Europe etc*) destra ♦ *adj* interno(a), interiore ♦ *adv* dentro, all'interno ♦ *prep* dentro, all'interno di; (*of time*): ~ **10 minutes** entro 10 minuti; ~**s** *npl* (*col*) ventre *m*; ~

out *adv* alla rovescia; **to turn sth ~ out** rivoltare qc; **to know sth ~ out** conoscere qc a fondo; **~ information** informazioni *fpl* riservate; **~ story** storia segreta.

inside forward *n* (*SPORT*) mezzala, interno.

inside lane *n* (*AUT*) corsia di marcia.

inside leg measurement *n* (*BRIT*) lunghezza interna.

insider [ɪn'saɪdə*] *n* uno(a) che ha le mani in pasta.

insider dealing, insider trading *n* (*STOCK EXCHANGE*) insider trading *m inv*.

insidious [ɪn'sɪdɪəs] *adj* insidioso(a).

insight ['ɪnsaɪt] *n* acume *m*, perspicacia; (*glimpse, idea*) percezione *f*; **to gain** *or* **get an ~ into sth** potersi render conto di qc.

insignia [ɪn'sɪgnɪə] *npl* insegne *fpl*.

insignificant [ɪnsɪg'nɪfɪknt] *adj* insignificante.

insincere [ɪnsɪn'sɪə*] *adj* insincero(a).

insincerity [ɪnsɪn'sɛrɪtɪ] *n* falsità, insincerità.

insinuate [ɪn'sɪnjueɪt] *vt* insinuare.

insinuation [ɪnsɪnju'eɪʃən] *n* insinuazione *f*.

insipid [ɪn'sɪpɪd] *adj* insipido(a), insulso(a).

insist [ɪn'sɪst] *vi* insistere; **to ~ on doing** insistere per fare; **to ~ that** insistere perché + *sub*; (*claim*) sostenere che.

insistence [ɪn'sɪstəns] *n* insistenza.

insistent [ɪn'sɪstənt] *adj* insistente.

insofar [ɪnsəu'fɑː*] *conj*: **~ as** in quanto.

insole ['ɪnsəul] *n* soletta; (*fixed part of shoe*) tramezza.

insolence ['ɪnsələns] *n* insolenza.

insolent ['ɪnsələnt] *adj* insolente.

insoluble [ɪn'sɔljubl] *adj* insolubile.

insolvency [ɪn'sɔlvənsɪ] *n* insolvenza.

insolvent [ɪn'sɔlvənt] *adj* insolvente.

insomnia [ɪn'sɔmnɪə] *n* insonnia.

insomniac [ɪn'sɔmnɪæk] *n* chi soffre di insonnia.

inspect [ɪn'spɛkt] *vt* ispezionare; (*BRIT*: *ticket*) controllare.

inspection [ɪn'spɛkʃən] *n* ispezione *f*; controllo.

inspector [ɪn'spɛktə*] *n* ispettore/trice; controllore *m*.

inspiration [ɪnspə'reɪʃən] *n* ispirazione *f*.

inspire [ɪn'spaɪə*] *vt* ispirare.

inspired [ɪn'spaɪəd] *adj* (*writer, book etc*) ispirato(a); **in an ~ moment** in un momento d'ispirazione.

inspiring [ɪn'spaɪərɪŋ] *adj* stimolante.

inst. [ɪnst] *abbr* (*BRIT COMM*: = *instant*) c.m. (=*corrente mese*).

instability [ɪnstə'bɪlɪtɪ] *n* instabilità.

install [ɪn'stɔːl] *vt* installare.

installation [ɪnstə'leɪʃən] *n* installazione *f*.

installment plan *n* (*US*) acquisto a rate.

instalment, (*US*) **installment** [ɪn'stɔːlmənt] *n* rata; (*of TV serial etc*) puntata; **to pay in ~s** pagare a rate.

instance ['ɪnstəns] *n* esempio, caso; **for ~** per *or* ad esempio; **in that ~** in quel caso; **in the first ~** in primo luogo.

instant ['ɪnstənt] *n* istante *m*, attimo ♦ *adj* immediato(a); urgente; (*coffee, food*) in polvere; **the 10th ~** il 10 corrente (mese).

instantaneous [ɪnstən'teɪnɪəs] *adj* istantaneo(a).

instantly ['ɪnstəntlɪ] *adv* immediatamente, subito.

instant replay *n* (*US TV*) replay *m inv*.

instead [ɪn'stɛd] *adv* invece; **~ of** invece di; **~ of sb** al posto di qn.

instep ['ɪnstɛp] *n* collo del piede; (*of shoe*) collo della scarpa.

instigate ['ɪnstɪgeɪt] *vt* (*rebellion, strike, crime*) istigare a; (*new ideas etc*) promuovere.

instigation [ɪnstɪ'geɪʃən] *n* istigazione *f*; **at sb's ~** per *or* in seguito al suggerimento di qn.

instil [ɪn'stɪl] *vt*: **to ~ (into)** inculcare (in).

instinct ['ɪnstɪŋkt] *n* istinto.

instinctive [ɪn'stɪŋktɪv] *adj* istintivo(a).

instinctively [ɪn'stɪŋktɪvlɪ] *adv* per istinto.

institute ['ɪnstɪtjuːt] *n* istituto ♦ *vt* istituire, stabilire; (*inquiry*) avviare; (*proceedings*) iniziare.

institution [ɪnstɪ'tjuːʃən] *n* istituzione *f*; istituto (d'istruzione); istituto (psichiatrico).

institutional [ɪnstɪ'tjuːʃənl] *adj* istituzionale; **~ care** assistenza presso un istituto.

instruct [ɪn'strʌkt] *vt* istruire; **to ~ sb in sth** insegnare qc a qn; **to ~ sb to do** dare ordini a qn di fare.

instruction [ɪn'strʌkʃən] *n* istruzione *f*; **~s (for use)** istruzioni per l'uso.

instruction book *n* libretto di istruzioni.

instructive [ɪn'strʌktɪv] *adj* istruttivo(a).

instructor [ɪn'strʌktə*] *n* istruttore/trice; (*for skiing*) maestro/a.

instrument ['ɪnstrumənt] *n* strumento.

instrumental [ɪnstru'mɛntl] *adj* (*MUS*) strumentale; **to be ~ in sth/in doing sth** avere un ruolo importante in qc/nel fare qc.

instrumentalist [ɪnstru'mɛntəlɪst] *n* strumentista *m/f*.

instrument panel *n* quadro *m* portastrumenti *inv*.

insubordinate [ɪnsə'bɔːdənɪt] *adj* insubordinato(a).

insubordination [ɪnsəbɔːdə'neɪʃən] *n* insubordinazione *f*.

insufferable [ɪn'sʌfrəbl] *adj* insopportabile.

insufficient [ɪnsə'fɪʃənt] *adj* insufficiente.

insufficiently [ɪnsə'fɪʃəntlɪ] *adv* in modo insufficiente.

insular ['ɪnsjulə*] *adj* insulare; (*person*) di mente ristretta.

insulate ['ɪnsjuleɪt] *vt* isolare.

insulating tape ['ɪnsjuleɪtɪŋ-] *n* nastro isolante.

insulation [ɪnsju'leɪʃən] *n* isolamento.

insulin ['ɪnsjulɪn] *n* insulina.

insult *n* ['ɪnsʌlt] insulto, affronto ♦ *vt* [ɪn'sʌlt] insultare.

insulting [ɪn'sʌltɪŋ] *adj* offensivo(a), ingiurioso(a).

insuperable [ɪn'sjuːprəbl] *adj* insormontabile, insuperabile.

insurance [ɪn'ʃuərəns] *n* assicurazione *f*; **fire/life** ~ assicurazione contro gli incendi/sulla vita; **to take out** ~ **(against)** fare un'assicurazione (contro), assicurarsi (contro).

insurance agent *n* agente *m* d'assicurazioni.

insurance broker *n* broker *m inv* d'assicurazioni.

insurance policy *n* polizza d'assicurazione.

insurance premium *n* premio assicurativo.

insure [ɪn'ʃuə*] *vt* assicurare; **to** ~ **sb** *or* **sb's life** assicurare qn sulla vita; **to be** ~**d for £5000** essere assicurato per 5000 sterline.

insured [ɪn'ʃuəd] *n*: **the** ~ l'assicurato/a.

insurer [ɪn'ʃuərə*] *n* assicuratore/trice.

insurgent [ɪn'sɜːdʒənt] *adj* ribelle ♦ *n* insorto/a, rivoltoso/a.

insurmountable [ɪnsə'mauntəbl] *adj* insormontabile.

insurrection [ɪnsə'rɛkʃən] *n* insurrezione *f*.

intact [ɪn'tækt] *adj* intatto(a).

intake ['ɪnteɪk] *n* (*TECH*) immissione *f*; (*of food*) consumo; (*of pupils etc*) afflusso.

intangible [ɪn'tændʒɪbl] *adj* intangibile.

integral ['ɪntɪɡrəl] *adj* integrale; (*part*) integrante.

integrate ['ɪntɪɡreɪt] *vt* integrare.

integrated circuit *n* (*COMPUT*) circuito integrato.

integration [ɪntɪ'ɡreɪʃən] *n* integrazione *f*; **racial** ~ integrazione razziale.

integrity [ɪn'tɛɡrɪtɪ] *n* integrità.

intellect ['ɪntəlɛkt] *n* intelletto.

intellectual [ɪntə'lɛktjuəl] *adj, n* intellettuale (*m/f*).

intelligence [ɪn'tɛlɪdʒəns] *n* intelligenza; (*MIL etc*) informazioni *fpl*.

intelligence quotient (IQ) *n* quoziente *m* d'intelligenza (Q.I.).

Intelligence Service *n* servizio segreto.

intelligence test *n* test *m inv* d'intelligenza.

intelligent [ɪn'tɛlɪdʒənt] *adj* intelligente.

intelligible [ɪn'tɛlɪdʒɪbl] *adj* intelligibile.

intemperate [ɪn'tɛmpərət] *adj* immoderato(a); (*drinking too much*) intemperante nel bere.

intend [ɪn'tɛnd] *vt* (*gift etc*): **to** ~ **sth for** destinare qc a; **to** ~ **to do** aver l'intenzione di fare.

intended [ɪn'tɛndɪd] *adj* (*insult*) intenzionale; (*effect*) voluto(a); (*journey, route*) progettato(a).

intense [ɪn'tɛns] *adj* intenso(a); (*person*) di forti sentimenti.

intensely [ɪn'tɛnslɪ] *adv* intensamente; profondamente.

intensify [ɪn'tɛnsɪfaɪ] *vt* intensificare.

intensity [ɪn'tɛnsɪtɪ] *n* intensità.

intensive [ɪn'tɛnsɪv] *adj* intensivo(a).

intensive care *n* terapia intensiva; ~ **unit (ICU)** *n* reparto terapia intensiva.

intent [ɪn'tɛnt] *n* intenzione *f* ♦ *adj*: ~ **(on)** intento(a) (a), immerso(a) (in); **to all** ~**s and purposes** a tutti gli effetti; **to be** ~ **on doing sth** essere deciso a fare qc.

intention [ɪn'tɛnʃən] *n* intenzione *f*.

intentional [ɪn'tɛnʃənl] *adj* intenzionale, deliberato(a).

intentionally [ɪn'tɛnʃənəlɪ] *adv* apposta.

intently [ɪn'tɛntlɪ] *adv* attentamente.

inter [ɪn'tɜː*] *vt* sotterrare.

interact [ɪntər'ækt] *vi* agire reciprocamente, interagire.

interaction [ɪntər'ækʃən] *n* azione *f* reciproca, interazione *f*.

interactive [ɪntər'æktɪv] *adj* interattivo(a).

intercede [ɪntə'siːd] *vi*: **to** ~ **(with sb/on behalf of sb)** intercedere (presso qn/a favore di qn).

intercept [ɪntə'sɛpt] *vt* intercettare; (*person*) fermare.

interception [ɪntə'sɛpʃən] *n* intercettamento.

interchange *n* ['ɪntətʃeɪndʒ] (*exchange*) scambio; (*on motorway*) incrocio pluridirezionale ♦ *vt* [ɪntə'tʃeɪndʒ] scambiare; sostituire l'uno(a) per l'altro(a).

interchangeable [ɪntə'tʃeɪndʒəbl] *adj* intercambiabile.

intercity [ɪntə'sɪtɪ] *adj*: ~ **(train)** ≈ (treno) rapido.

intercom ['ɪntəkɔm] *n* interfono.

interconnect [ɪntəkə'nɛkt] *vi* (*rooms*) essere in comunicazione.

intercontinental ['ɪntəkɔntɪ'nɛntl] *adj* intercontinentale.

intercourse ['ɪntəkɔːs] *n* rapporti *mpl*; (*sexual* ~) rapporti sessuali.

interdependent [ɪntədɪ'pɛndənt] *adj* interdipendente.

interest ['ɪntrɪst] *n* interesse *m*; (*COMM*: *stake, share*) interessi *mpl* ♦ *vt* interessare; **compound/simple** ~ interesse composto/semplice; **business** ~**s** attività *fpl* commerciali; **British** ~**s in the Middle East** gli interessi (commerciali) britannici nel Medio Oriente.

interested ['ɪntrɪstɪd] *adj* interessato(a); **to be** ~ **in** interessarsi di.

interest-free ['ɪntrɪst'friː] *adj* senza interesse.

interesting ['ɪntrɪstɪŋ] *adj* interessante.

interest rate *n* tasso di interesse.

interface ['ɪntəfeɪs] *n* (*COMPUT*) interfaccia.

interfere [ɪntə'fɪə*] *vi*: **to** ~ **(in)** (*quarrel, other people's business*) immischiarsi (in); **to** ~ **with** (*object*) toccare; (*plans*) ostacolare; (*duty*) interferire con.

interference [ɪntə'fɪərəns] *n* interferenza.

interfering [ɪntə'fɪərɪŋ] *adj* invadente.

interim ['ɪntərɪm] *adj* provvisorio(a) ♦ *n*: **in the** ~ nel frattempo; ~ **dividend** (*COMM*) acconto di dividendo.

interior [ɪn'tɪərɪə*] *n* interno; (*of country*) entroterra ♦ *adj* interiore, interno(a).

interior decorator, interior designer *n* decoratore/trice (d'interni).

interjection [ɪntə'dʒɛkʃən] *n* interiezione *f*.

interlock [ɪntə'lɔk] *vi* ingranarsi ♦ *vt* ingranare.

interloper ['ɪntələupə*] *n* intruso/a.

interlude ['ɪntəluːd] *n* intervallo; (*THEAT*) intermezzo.

intermarry [ɪntə'mærɪ] *vi* imparentarsi per mezzo di matrimonio; sposarsi tra parenti.

intermediary [ɪntə'miːdɪərɪ] *n* intermediario/a.

intermediate [ɪntə'miːdɪət] *adj* intermedio(a); (*SCOL*: *course, level*) medio(a).

interment [ɪn'təːmənt] *n* (*formal*) inumazione *f*.

interminable [ɪn'təːmɪnəbl] *adj* interminabile.

intermission [ɪntə'mɪʃən] *n* pausa; (*THEAT*, *CINE*) intermissione *f*, intervallo.

intermittent [ɪntə'mɪtnt] *adj* intermittente.

intermittently [ɪntə'mɪtntlɪ] *adv* a intermittenza.

intern *vt* [ɪn'təːn] internare ♦ *n* ['ɪntəːn] (*US*) medico interno.

internal [ɪn'təːnl] *adj* interno(a); ~ **injuries** lesioni *fpl* interne.

internally [ɪn'təːnəlɪ] *adv* all'interno; "**not to be taken** ~" "per uso esterno".

Internal Revenue (Service) (IRS) *n* (*US*) Fisco.

international [ɪntə'næʃənl] *adj* internazionale ♦ *n* (*BRIT SPORT*) partita internazionale.

International Atomic Energy Agency (IAEA) *n* Agenzia Internazionale per l'Energia Atomica (IAEA).

International Court of Justice (ICJ) *n* Corte *f* Internazionale di Giustizia.

international date line *n* linea del cambiamento di data.

internationally [ɪntə'næʃnəlɪ] *adv* a livello internazionale.

International Monetary Fund (IMF) *n* Fondo monetario internazionale (F.M.I.).

international relations *npl* rapporti *mpl* internazionali.

internecine [ɪntə'niːsaɪn] *adj* sanguinoso(a).

internee [ɪntəː'niː] *n* internato/a.

Internet ['ɪntə,nɛt] *n*: **the** ~ Internet *f*.

internment [ɪn'təːnmənt] *n* internamento.

interplay ['ɪntəpleɪ] *n* azione e reazione *f*.

Interpol ['ɪntəpɔl] *n* Interpol *f*.

interpret [ɪn'təːprɪt] *vt* interpretare ♦ *vi* fare da interprete.

interpretation [ɪntəːprɪ'teɪʃən] *n* interpretazione *f*.

interpreter [ɪn'təːprɪtə*] *n* interprete *m/f*.

interpreting [ɪn'təːprɪtɪŋ] *n* (*profession*) interpretariato.

interrelated [ɪntərɪ'leɪtɪd] *adj* correlato(a).

interrogate [ɪn'tɛrəugeɪt] *vt* interrogare.

interrogation [ɪntɛrəu'geɪʃən] *n* interrogazione *f*; (*of suspect etc*) interrogatorio.

interrogative [ɪntə'rɔgətɪv] *adj* interrogativo(a) ♦ *n* (*LING*) interrogativo.

interrogator [ɪn'tɛrəgeɪtə*] *n* interrogante *m/f*.

interrupt [ɪntə'rʌpt] *vt* interrompere.

interruption [ɪntə'rʌpʃən] *n* interruzione *f*.

intersect [ɪntə'sɛkt] *vt* intersecare ♦ *vi* (*roads*) intersecarsi.

intersection [ɪntə'sɛkʃən] *n* intersezione *f*; (*of roads*) incrocio.

intersperse [ɪntə'spəːs] *vt*: **to** ~ **with** costellare di.

intertwine [ɪntə'twaɪn] *vt* intrecciare ♦ *vi* intrecciarsi.

interval ['ɪntəvl] n intervallo; (BRIT SCOL) ricreazione f, intervallo; **bright ~s** (in weather) schiarite fpl; **at ~s** a intervalli.
intervene [ɪntə'viːn] vi (time) intercorrere; (event, person) intervenire.
intervention [ɪntə'vɛnʃən] n intervento.
interview ['ɪntəvjuː] n (RADIO, TV etc) intervista; (for job) colloquio ♦ vt intervistare; avere un colloquio con.
interviewee [ɪntəvjuː'iː] n (TV) intervistato/a; (for job) chi si presenta ad un colloquio di lavoro.
interviewer ['ɪntəvjuːə*] n intervistatore/trice.
intestate [ɪn'tɛsteɪt] adj intestato(a).
intestinal [ɪn'tɛstɪnl] adj intestinale.
intestine [ɪn'tɛstɪn] n intestino; **large/small ~** intestino crasso/tenue.
intimacy ['ɪntɪməsɪ] n intimità.
intimate adj ['ɪntɪmət] intimo(a); (knowledge) profondo(a) ♦ vt ['ɪntɪmeɪt] lasciar capire.
intimately ['ɪntɪmɪtlɪ] adv intimamente.
intimation [ɪntɪ'meɪʃən] n annuncio.
intimidate [ɪn'tɪmɪdeɪt] vt intimidire, intimorire.
intimidation [ɪntɪmɪ'deɪʃən] n intimidazione f.
into ['ɪntu] prep dentro, in; **come ~ the house** vieni dentro la casa; **~ pieces** a pezzi; **~ Italian** in italiano; **to change pounds ~ dollars** cambiare delle sterline in dollari.
intolerable [ɪn'tɔlərəbl] adj intollerabile.
intolerance [ɪn'tɔlərns] n intolleranza.
intolerant [ɪn'tɔlərnt] adj: **~ (of)** intollerante (di).
intonation [ɪntəu'neɪʃən] n intonazione f.
intoxicate [ɪn'tɔksɪkeɪt] vt inebriare.
intoxicated [ɪn'tɔksɪkeɪtɪd] adj inebriato(a).
intoxication [ɪntɔksɪ'keɪʃən] n ebbrezza.
intractable [ɪn'træktəbl] adj intrattabile; (illness) difficile da curare; (problem) insolubile.
intranet ['ɪntrənɛt] n Intranet f.
intransigence [ɪn'trænsɪdʒəns] n intransigenza.
intransigent [ɪn'trænsɪdʒənt] adj intransigente.
intransitive [ɪn'trænsɪtɪv] adj intransitivo(a).
intra-uterine device (IUD) [ɪntrə'-juːtəraɪn-] n dispositivo intrauterino (IUD).
intravenous [ɪntrə'viːnəs] adj endovenoso(a).
in-tray ['ɪntreɪ] n raccoglitore m per le carte in arrivo.
intrepid [ɪn'trɛpɪd] adj intrepido(a).

intricacy ['ɪntrɪkəsɪ] n complessità f inv.
intricate ['ɪntrɪkət] adj intricato(a), complicato(a).
intrigue [ɪn'triːg] n intrigo ♦ vt affascinare ♦ vi complottare, tramare.
intriguing [ɪn'triːgɪŋ] adj affascinante.
intrinsic [ɪn'trɪnsɪk] adj intrinseco(a).
introduce [ɪntrə'djuːs] vt introdurre; **to ~ sb (to sb)** presentare qn (a qn); **to ~ sb to** (pastime, technique) iniziare qn a; **may I ~ ...?** permette che le presenti ...?
introduction [ɪntrə'dʌkʃən] n introduzione f; (of person) presentazione f; **a letter of ~** una lettera di presentazione.
introductory [ɪntrə'dʌktərɪ] adj introduttivo(a); **an ~ offer** un'offerta di lancio; **~ remarks** osservazioni fpl preliminari.
introspection [ɪntrəu'spɛkʃən] n introspezione f.
introspective [ɪntrəu'spɛktɪv] adj introspettivo(a).
introvert ['ɪntrəuvəːt] adj, n introverso(a).
intrude [ɪn'truːd] vi (person) intromettersi; **to ~ on** (person) importunare; **~ on** or **into** (conversation) intromettersi in; **am I intruding?** disturbo?
intruder [ɪn'truːdə*] n intruso/a.
intrusion [ɪn'truːʒən] n intrusione f.
intrusive [ɪn'truːsɪv] adj importuno(a).
intuition [ɪntjuː'ɪʃən] n intuizione f.
intuitive [ɪn'tjuːɪtɪv] adj intuitivo(a); dotato(a) di intuito.
inundate ['ɪnʌndeɪt] vt: **to ~ with** inondare di.
inure [ɪn'juə*] vt: **to ~ (to)** assuefare (a).
invade [ɪn'veɪd] vt invadere.
invader [ɪn'veɪdə*] n invasore m.
invalid n ['ɪnvəlɪd] malato/a; (with disability) invalido/a ♦ adj [ɪn'vælɪd] (not valid) invalido(a), non valido(a).
invalidate [ɪn'vælɪdeɪt] vt invalidare.
invalid chair n (BRIT) sedia a rotelle.
invaluable [ɪn'væljuəbl] adj prezioso(a); inestimabile.
invariable [ɪn'vɛərɪəbl] adj costante, invariabile.
invariably [ɪn'vɛərɪəblɪ] adv invariabilmente; **she is ~ late** è immancabilmente in ritardo.
invasion [ɪn'veɪʒən] n invasione f.
invective [ɪn'vɛktɪv] n invettiva.
inveigle [ɪn'viːgl] vt: **to ~ sb into (doing) sth** circuire qn per (fargli fare) qc.
invent [ɪn'vɛnt] vt inventare.
invention [ɪn'vɛnʃən] n invenzione f.
inventive [ɪn'vɛntɪv] adj inventivo(a).
inventiveness [ɪn'vɛntɪvnɪs] n inventiva.

inventor [ɪn'vɛntə*] *n* inventore *m*.
inventory ['ɪnvəntrɪ] *n* inventario.
inventory control *n* (*COMM*) controllo delle giacenze.
inverse [ɪn'vəːs] *adj* inverso(a) ♦ *n* inverso, contrario; **in ~ proportion (to)** in modo inversamente proporzionale (a).
inversely [ɪn'vəːslɪ] *adv* inversamente.
invert [ɪn'vəːt] *vt* invertire; (*object*) rovesciare.
invertebrate [ɪn'vəːtɪbrɪt] *n* invertebrato.
inverted commas [ɪn'vəːtɪd-] *npl* (*BRIT*) virgolette *fpl*.
invest [ɪn'vɛst] *vt* investire; (*fig: time, effort*) impiegare; (*endow*): **to ~ sb with sth** investire qn di qc ♦ *vi* fare investimenti; **to ~ in** investire in, fare (degli) investimenti in; (*acquire*) comprarsi.
investigate [ɪn'vɛstɪgeɪt] *vt* investigare, indagare; (*crime*) fare indagini su.
investigation [ɪnvɛstɪ'geɪʃən] *n* investigazione *f*; (*of crime*) indagine *f*.
investigative [ɪn'vɛstɪgətɪv] *adj*: **~ journalism** giornalismo investigativo.
investigator [ɪn'vɛstɪgeɪtə*] *n* investigatore/trice; **a private ~** un investigatore privato, un detective.
investiture [ɪn'vɛstɪtʃə*] *n* investitura.
investment [ɪn'vɛstmənt] *n* investimento.
investment income *n* reddito da investimenti.
investment trust *n* fondo comune di investimento.
investor [ɪn'vɛstə*] *n* investitore/trice; (*shareholder*) azionista *m/f*.
inveterate [ɪn'vɛtərət] *adj* inveterato(a).
invidious [ɪn'vɪdɪəs] *adj* odioso(a); (*task*) spiacevole.
invigilate [ɪn'vɪdʒɪleɪt] *vt, vi* (*BRIT SCOL*) sorvegliare.
invigilator [ɪn'vɪdʒɪleɪtə*] *n* (*BRIT*) chi sorveglia agli esami.
invigorating [ɪn'vɪgəreɪtɪŋ] *adj* stimolante; vivificante.
invincible [ɪn'vɪnsɪbl] *adj* invincibile.
inviolate [ɪn'vaɪələt] *adj* inviolato(a).
invisible [ɪn'vɪzɪbl] *adj* invisibile.
invisible assets *npl* (*BRIT*) beni *mpl* immateriali.
invisible ink *n* inchiostro simpatico.
invisible mending *n* rammendo invisibile.
invitation [ɪnvɪ'teɪʃən] *n* invito; **by ~ only** esclusivamente su *or* per invito; **at sb's ~** dietro invito di qn.
invite [ɪn'vaɪt] *vt* invitare; (*opinions etc*) sollecitare; (*trouble*) provocare; **to ~ sb (to do)** invitare qn (a fare); **to ~ sb to**

dinner invitare qn a cena.
▶**invite out** *vt* invitare fuori.
▶**invite over** *vt* invitare (a casa).
inviting [ɪn'vaɪtɪŋ] *adj* invitante, attraente.
invoice ['ɪnvɔɪs] *n* fattura ♦ *vt* fatturare; **to ~ sb for goods** inviare a qn la fattura per le *or* delle merci.
invoke [ɪn'vəuk] *vt* invocare.
involuntary [ɪn'vɔləntrɪ] *adj* involontario(a).
involve [ɪn'vɔlv] *vt* (*entail*) richiedere, comportare; (*associate*): **to ~ sb (in)** implicare qn (in); coinvolgere qn (in); **to involve o.s. in sth** (*politics etc*) impegnarsi in qc.
involved [ɪn'vɔlvd] *adj* involuto(a), complesso(a); **to feel ~** sentirsi coinvolto(a); **to become ~ with sb** (*socially*) legarsi a qn; (*emotionally*) legarsi sentimentalmente a qn.
involvement [ɪn'vɔlvmənt] *n* implicazione *f*; coinvolgimento; impegno; partecipazione *f*.
invulnerable [ɪn'vʌlnərəbl] *adj* invulnerabile.
inward ['ɪnwəd] *adj* (*movement*) verso l'interno; (*thought, feeling*) interiore, intimo(a); *see also* **inward(s)**.
inwardly ['ɪnwədlɪ] *adv* (*feel, think etc*) nell'intimo, entro di sé.
inward(s) ['ɪnwəd(z)] *adv* verso l'interno.
I/O *abbr* (*COMPUT*: = *input/output*) I/O.
IOC *n abbr* (= *International Olympic Committee*) CIO *m* (= *Comitato Internazionale Olimpico*).
iodine ['aɪəudiːn] *n* iodio.
IOM *abbr* (*BRIT*) = *Isle of Man*.
ion ['aɪən] *n* ione *m*.
Ionian Sea [aɪ'əunɪən-] *n*: **the ~** il mare Ionio.
ioniser ['aɪənaɪzə*] *n* ionizzatore *m*.
iota [aɪ'əutə] *n* (*fig*) briciolo.
IOU *n abbr* (= *I owe you*) pagherò *m inv*.
IOW *abbr* (*BRIT*) = *Isle of Wight*.
IPA *n abbr* (= *International Phonetic Alphabet*) I.P.A. *m*.
IP address *n* (*COMPUT*) indirizzo IP.
IQ *n abbr* = **intelligence quotient**.
IRA *n abbr* (= *Irish Republican Army*) I.R.A. *f*; (*US*) = *individual retirement account*.
Iran [ɪ'rɑːn] *n* Iran *m*.
Iranian [ɪ'reɪnɪən] *adj* iraniano(a) ♦ *n* iraniano/a; (*LING*) iranico.
Iraq [ɪ'rɑːk] *n* Iraq *m*.
Iraqi [ɪ'rɑːkɪ] *adj* iracheno(a) ♦ *n* iracheno/a.
irascible [ɪ'ræsɪbl] *adj* irascibile.
irate [aɪ'reɪt] *adj* irato(a).

Ireland ['aɪələnd] n Irlanda; **Republic of** ~ Repubblica d'Irlanda, Eire f.

iris, ~**es** ['aɪrɪs, -ɪz] n iride f; (BOT) giaggiolo, iride.

Irish ['aɪrɪʃ] adj irlandese ♦ npl: **the** ~ gli Irlandesi.

Irishman ['aɪrɪʃmən] n irlandese m.

Irish Sea n: **the** ~ il mar d'Irlanda.

Irishwoman ['aɪrɪʃwumən] n irlandese f.

irk [əːk] vt seccare.

irksome ['əːksəm] adj seccante.

IRN n abbr (= Independent Radio News) agenzia d'informazioni per la radio.

IRO n abbr (= International Refugee Organization) O.I.R. f (= Organizzazione Internazionale per i Rifugiati).

iron ['aɪən] n ferro; (for clothes) ferro da stiro ♦ adj di or in ferro ♦ vt (clothes) stirare; see also **irons**.

▶**iron out** vt (crease) appianare; (fig) spianare; far sparire.

Iron Curtain n (HIST): **the** ~ la cortina di ferro.

iron foundry n fonderia.

ironic(al) [aɪ'rɔnɪk(l)] adj ironico(a).

ironically [aɪ'rɔnɪklɪ] adv ironicamente.

ironing ['aɪənɪŋ] n (act) stirare m; (clothes) roba da stirare.

ironing board n asse f da stiro.

iron lung n (MED) polmone m d'acciaio.

ironmonger ['aɪənmʌŋgə*] n (BRIT) negoziante m in ferramenta; ~**'s (shop)** n negozio di ferramenta.

iron ore n minerale m di ferro.

irons ['aɪənz] npl (chains) catene fpl.

ironworks ['aɪənwəːks] n ferriera.

irony ['aɪrənɪ] n ironia.

irrational [ɪ'ræʃənl] adj irrazionale; irragionevole; illogico(a).

irreconcilable [ɪrɛkən'saɪləbl] adj irreconciliabile; (opinion): ~ **with** inconciliabile con.

irredeemable [ɪrɪ'diːməbl] adj (COMM) irredimibile.

irrefutable [ɪrɪ'fjuːtəbl] adj irrefutabile.

irregular [ɪ'rɛgjulə*] adj irregolare.

irregularity [ɪrɛgju'lærɪtɪ] n irregolarità f inv.

irrelevance [ɪ'rɛləvəns] n inappropriatezza.

irrelevant [ɪ'rɛləvənt] adj non pertinente.

irreligious [ɪrɪ'lɪdʒəs] adj irreligioso(a).

irreparable [ɪ'rɛprəbl] adj irreparabile.

irreplaceable [ɪrɪ'pleɪsəbl] adj insostituibile.

irrepressible [ɪrɪ'prɛsəbl] adj irrefrenabile.

irreproachable [ɪrɪ'prəutʃəbl] adj irreprensibile.

irresistible [ɪrɪ'zɪstɪbl] adj irresistibile.

irresolute [ɪ'rɛzəluːt] adj irresoluto(a), indeciso(a).

irrespective [ɪrɪ'spɛktɪv]: ~ **of** prep senza riguardo a.

irresponsible [ɪrɪ'spɔnsɪbl] adj irresponsabile.

irretrievable [ɪrɪ'triːvəbl] adj (object) irrecuperabile; (loss) irreparabile.

irreverent [ɪ'rɛvərnt] adj irriverente.

irrevocable [ɪ'rɛvəkəbl] adj irrevocabile.

irrigate ['ɪrɪgeɪt] vt irrigare.

irrigation [ɪrɪ'geɪʃən] n irrigazione f.

irritable ['ɪrɪtəbl] adj irritabile.

irritant ['ɪrɪtənt] n sostanza irritante.

irritate ['ɪrɪteɪt] vt irritare.

irritation [ɪrɪ'teɪʃən] n irritazione f.

IRS n abbr (US) see **Internal Revenue Service**.

is [ɪz] vb see **be**.

ISA ['aɪsə] n abbr (= individual savings account) forma di investimento detassata.

ISBN n abbr (= International Standard Book Number) I.S.B.N. m.

Islam ['ɪzlɑːm] n Islam m.

island ['aɪlənd] n isola; (also: traffic ~) salvagente m.

islander ['aɪləndə*] n isolano/a.

isle [aɪl] n isola.

isn't ['ɪznt] = **is not**.

isolate ['aɪsəleɪt] vt isolare.

isolated ['aɪsəleɪtɪd] adj isolato(a).

isolation [aɪsə'leɪʃən] n isolamento.

isotope ['aɪsəutəup] n isotopo.

ISP n abbr (COMPUT: = Internet service provider) ISP m inv.

Israel ['ɪzreɪl] n Israele m.

Israeli [ɪz'reɪlɪ] adj, n israeliano(a).

issue ['ɪʃjuː] n questione f, problema m; (outcome) esito, risultato; (of banknotes etc) emissione f; (of newspaper etc) numero; (offspring) discendenza ♦ vt (rations, equipment) distribuire; (orders) dare; (book) pubblicare; (banknotes, cheques, stamps) emettere ♦ vi: to ~ (from) uscire (da), venir fuori (da); at ~ in gioco, in discussione; to avoid the ~ evitare la discussione; to take ~ with sb (over sth) prendere posizione contro qn (riguardo a qc); to confuse or obscure the ~ confondere le cose; to make an ~ of sth fare un problema di qc; to ~ sth to sb, ~ sb with sth consegnare qc a qn.

Istanbul [ɪstæn'buːl] n Istanbul f.

isthmus ['ɪsməs] n istmo.

IT n abbr see **information technology**.

==================== KEYWORD

it [ɪt] *pron* **1** (*specific: subject*) esso(a) (*mostly omitted in Italian*); (: *direct object*) lo(la), l'; (: *indirect object*) gli(le); **where's my book?** — ~'s **on the table** dov'è il mio libro? — è sulla tavola; **what is** ~? che cos'è?; (*what's the matter?*) cosa c'è?; **where is** ~? dov'è?; **I can't find** ~ non lo (*or* la) trovo; **give** ~ **to me** dammelo (*or* dammela); **about/from/of** ~ ne; **I spoke to him about** ~ gliene ho parlato; **what did you learn from** ~? quale insegnamento ne hai tratto?; **I'm proud of** ~ ne sono fiero; **in/to/at** ~ ci; **did you go to** ~? ci sei andato?; **I wasn't at** ~ non c'ero; **above/over** ~ sopra; **below/under** ~ sotto; **in front of/behind** ~ lì davanti/dietro

2 (*impers*): ~'s **raining** piove; ~'s **Friday tomorrow** domani è venerdì; ~'s **6 o'clock** sono le 6; ~'s **2 hours on the train** sono *or* ci vogliono 2 ore di treno; **who is** ~? — ~'s **me** chi è? — sono io.

Italian [ɪ'tæljən] *adj* italiano(a) ♦ *n* italiano/a; (*LING*) italiano; **the** ~s gli Italiani.

italic [ɪ'tælɪk] *adj* corsivo(a); ~s *npl* corsivo.

Italy ['ɪtəlɪ] *n* Italia.

ITC *n abbr* (*BRIT*: = *Independent Television Commission*) *organo di controllo sulle reti televisive.*

itch [ɪtʃ] *n* prurito ♦ *vi* (*person*) avere il prurito; (*part of body*) prudere; **to be** ~**ing to do** non veder l'ora di fare.

itchy ['ɪtʃɪ] *adj* che prude; **my back is** ~ ho prurito alla schiena.

it'd ['ɪtd] = **it would; it had.**

item ['aɪtəm] *n* articolo; (*on agenda*) punto; (*in programme*) numero; (*also:* **news** ~) notizia; ~s **of clothing** capi *mpl* di abbigliamento.

itemize ['aɪtəmaɪz] *vt* specificare.

itemized bill ['aɪtəmaɪzd-] *n* conto dettagliato.

itinerant [ɪ'tɪnərənt] *adj* ambulante.

itinerary [aɪ'tɪnərərɪ] *n* itinerario.

it'll ['ɪtl] = **it will, it shall.**

ITN *n abbr* (*BRIT*: = *Independent Television News*) *agenzia d'informazioni per la televisione.*

its [ɪts] *adj, pron* il(la) suo(a), i(le) suoi(sue).

it's [ɪts] = **it is; it has.**

itself [ɪt'sɛlf] *pron* (*emphatic*) esso(a) stesso(a); (*reflexive*) si.

ITV *n abbr* (*BRIT*: = *Independent Television*) *rete televisiva indipendente; see boxed note.*

ITV

La **ITV** *è un'azienda televisiva privata che comprende una serie di emittenti regionali, la prima delle quali è stata aperta nel 1955. Si autofinanzia tramite la pubblicità ed è sottoposta al controllo di un ente ufficiale, la "ITC"; vedi anche* **BBC**.

IUD *n abbr* = **intra-uterine device.**

I've [aɪv] = **I have.**

ivory ['aɪvərɪ] *n* avorio.

Ivory Coast *n* Costa d'Avorio.

ivory tower *n* torre *f* d'avorio.

ivy ['aɪvɪ] *n* edera.

Ivy League *n* (*US*) *see boxed note.*

IVY LEAGUE

Ivy League *è il termine usato per indicare le otto università più prestigiose degli Stati Uniti nordorientali (Brown, Columbia, Cornell, Dartmouth College, Harvard, Princeton, University of Pennsylvania e Yale).*

================== **J j**

J, j [dʒeɪ] *n* (*letter*) J, j *f or m inv*; **J for Jack,** (*US*) **J for Jig** ≈ J come Jersey.

JA *n abbr see* **judge advocate.**

J/A *abbr see* **joint account.**

jab [dʒæb] *vt*: **to** ~ **sth into** affondare *or* piantare qc dentro ♦ *vi*: **to** ~ **at** dare colpi a ♦ *n* colpo; (*MED: col*) puntura.

jabber ['dʒæbə*] *vt, vi* borbottare.

jack [dʒæk] *n* (*AUT*) cricco; (*BOWLS*) boccino, pallino; (*CARDS*) fante *m*.

▶**jack in** *vt* (*col*) mollare.

▶**jack up** *vt* sollevare sul cricco; (*raise: prices etc*) alzare.

jackal ['dʒækl] *n* sciacallo.

jackass ['dʒækæs] *n* (*also fig*) asino, somaro.

jackdaw ['dʒækdɔ:] *n* taccola.

jacket ['dʒækɪt] *n* giacca; (*of book*) copertura; **potatoes in their** ~s (*BRIT*) patate *fpl* con la buccia.

jacket potato *n* patata cotta al forno con la buccia.

jack-in-the-box ['dʒækɪndəbɒks] *n* scatola a sorpresa (con pupazzo a molla).

jack-knife ['dʒæknaɪf] *vi*: **the lorry ~d** l'autotreno si è piegato su se stesso.

jack-of-all-trades [dʒækəv'ɔːltreɪdz] *n* uno che fa un po' di tutto.

jack plug *n* (*BRIT*) jack plug *f inv.*

jackpot ['dʒækpɒt] *n* primo premio (in denaro).

Jacuzzi ® [dʒə'kuːzɪ] *n* vasca per idromassaggio Jacuzzi ®.

jade [dʒeɪd] *n* (*stone*) giada.

jaded ['dʒeɪdɪd] *adj* sfinito(a), spossato(a).

jagged ['dʒægɪd] *adj* sbocconcellato(a); (*cliffs etc*) frastagliato(a).

jaguar ['dʒægjuə*] *n* giaguaro.

jail [dʒeɪl] *n* prigione *f* ♦ *vt* mandare in prigione.

jailbird ['dʒeɪlbəːd] *n* avanzo di galera.

jailbreak ['dʒeɪlbreɪk] *n* evasione *f.*

jailer ['dʒeɪlə*] *n* custode *m* del carcere.

jalopy [dʒə'lɒpɪ] *n* (*col*) macinino.

jam [dʒæm] *n* marmellata; (*of shoppers etc*) ressa; (*also*: **traffic ~**) ingorgo ♦ *vt* (*passage etc*) ingombrare, ostacolare; (*mechanism, drawer etc*) bloccare; (*RADIO*) disturbare con interferenze ♦ *vi* (*mechanism, sliding part*) incepparsi, bloccarsi; (*gun*) incepparsi; **to get sb out of a ~** tirare qn fuori dai pasticci; **to ~ sth into** forzare qc dentro; infilare qc a forza dentro; **the telephone lines are ~med** le linee sono sovraccariche.

Jamaica [dʒə'meɪkə] *n* Giamaica.

Jamaican [dʒə'meɪkən] *adj, n* giamaicano(a).

jamb [dʒæm] *n* stipite *m.*

jam-packed [dʒæm'pækt] *adj*: **~ (with)** pieno(a) zeppo(a) (di), strapieno(a) (di).

jam session *n* improvvisazione *f* jazzistica.

Jan. *abbr* (= *January*) gen., genn.

jangle ['dʒæŋgl] *vi* risuonare; (*bracelet*) tintinnare.

janitor ['dʒænɪtə*] *n* (*caretaker*) portiere *m*; (*SCOL*) bidello.

January ['dʒænjuərɪ] *n* gennaio; *for phrases see also* **July.**

Japan [dʒə'pæn] *n* Giappone *m.*

Japanese [dʒæpə'niːz] *adj* giapponese ♦ *n* (*pl inv*) giapponese *m/f*; (*LING*) giapponese *m.*

jar [dʒɑː*] *n* (*container*) barattolo, vasetto ♦ *vi* (*sound*) stridere; (*colours etc*) stonare ♦ *vt* (*shake*) scuotere.

jargon ['dʒɑːgən] *n* gergo.

jarring ['dʒɑːrɪŋ] *adj* (*sound, colour*) stonato(a).

Jas. *abbr* = *James.*

jasmin(e) ['dʒæzmɪn] *n* gelsomino.

jaundice ['dʒɔːndɪs] *n* itterizia.

jaundiced ['dʒɔːndɪst] *adj* (*fig*) invidioso(a) e critico(a).

jaunt [dʒɔːnt] *n* gita.

jaunty ['dʒɔːntɪ] *adj* vivace; disinvolto(a), spigliato(a).

Java ['dʒɑːvə] *n* Giava.

javelin ['dʒævlɪn] *n* giavellotto.

jaw [dʒɔː] *n* mascella; **~s** (*TECH*: *of vice etc*) morsa.

jawbone ['dʒɔːbəʊn] *n* mandibola.

jay [dʒeɪ] *n* ghiandaia.

jaywalker ['dʒeɪwɔːkə*] *n* pedone(a) indisciplinato(a).

jazz [dʒæz] *n* jazz *m.*

▶**jazz up** *vt* rendere vivace.

jazz band *n* banda *f* jazz *inv.*

jazzy ['dʒæzɪ] *adj* vistoso(a), chiassoso(a).

JCB ® *n* scavatrice *f.*

JCS *n abbr* (*US*) = Joint Chiefs of Staff.

JD *n abbr* (*US*: = *Doctor of Laws*) titolo di studio; (: = *Justice Department*) *ministero della Giustizia.*

jealous ['dʒɛləs] *adj* geloso(a).

jealously ['dʒɛləslɪ] *adv* (*enviously*) con gelosia; (*watchfully*) gelosamente.

jealousy ['dʒɛləsɪ] *n* gelosia.

jeans [dʒiːnz] *npl* (blue-)jeans *mpl.*

Jeep ® [dʒiːp] *n* jeep *m inv.*

jeer [dʒɪə*] *vi*: **to ~ (at)** fischiare; beffeggiare; *see also* **jeers.**

jeering ['dʒɪərɪŋ] *adj* (*crowd*) che urla e fischia ♦ *n* fischi *mpl*; parole *fpl* di scherno.

jeers ['dʒɪəz] *npl* fischi *mpl.*

jelly ['dʒɛlɪ] *n* gelatina.

jellyfish ['dʒɛlɪfɪʃ] *n* medusa.

jeopardize ['dʒɛpədaɪz] *vt* mettere in pericolo.

jeopardy ['dʒɛpədɪ] *n*: **in ~** in pericolo.

jerk [dʒəːk] *n* sobbalzo, scossa; sussulto; (*col*) povero scemo ♦ *vt* dare una scossa a ♦ *vi* (*vehicles*) sobbalzare.

jerkin ['dʒəːkɪn] *n* giubbotto.

jerky ['dʒəːkɪ] *adj* a scatti; a sobbalzi.

jerry-built ['dʒɛrɪbɪlt] *adj* fatto(a) di cartapesta.

jerry can ['dʒɛrɪ-] *n* tanica.

Jersey ['dʒəːzɪ] *n* Jersey *m.*

jersey ['dʒəːzɪ] *n* maglia, jersey *m.*

Jerusalem [dʒə'ruːsələm] *n* Gerusalemme *f.*

jest [dʒɛst] *n* scherzo; **in ~** per scherzo.

jester ['dʒɛstə*] *n* (*HISTORY*) buffone *m.*

Jesus ['dʒiːzəs] *n* Gesù *m*; **~ Christ** Gesù Cristo.

jet [dʒɛt] *n* (*of gas, liquid*) getto; (*AUT*) spruzzatore *m*; (*AVIAT*) aviogetto.

jet-black ['dʒɛt'blæk] *adj* nero(a) come l'ebano, corvino(a).

jet engine *n* motore *m* a reazione.

jet lag *n* (problemi *mpl* dovuti allo) sbalzo dei fusi orari.

jetsam ['dʒɛtsəm] *n* relitti *mpl* di mare.

jet-setter ['dʒɛtsɛtə*] *n* membro del jet set.

jettison ['dʒɛtɪsn] *vt* gettare in mare.

jetty ['dʒɛtɪ] *n* molo.

Jew [dʒuː] *n* ebreo.

jewel ['dʒuːəl] *n* gioiello.

jeweller, (*US*) **jeweler** ['dʒuːələ*] *n* orefice *m*, gioielliere/a; ~'**s** (shop) *n* oreficeria, gioielleria.

jewellery, (*US*) **jewelry** ['dʒuːəlrɪ] *n* gioielli *mpl*.

Jewess ['dʒuːɪs] *n* ebrea.

Jewish ['dʒuːɪʃ] *adj* ebreo(a), ebraico(a).

JFK *n abbr* (*US*) = *John Fitzgerald Kennedy International Airport*.

jib [dʒɪb] *n* (*NAUT*) fiocco; (*of crane*) braccio ♦ *vi* (*horse*) impennarsi; **to ~ at doing sth** essere restio a fare qc.

jibe [dʒaɪb] *n* beffa.

jiffy ['dʒɪfɪ] *n* (*col*): **in a ~** in un batter d'occhio.

jig [dʒɪg] *n* (*dance, tune*) giga.

jigsaw ['dʒɪgsɔː] *n* (*tool*) sega da traforo; (*also:* ~ **puzzle**) puzzle *m inv.*

jilt [dʒɪlt] *vt* piantare in asso.

jingle ['dʒɪŋgl] *n* (*advert*) sigla pubblicitaria ♦ *vi* tintinnare, scampanellare.

jingoism ['dʒɪŋgəuɪzəm] *n* sciovinismo.

jinx [dʒɪŋks] *n* (*col*) iettatura; (*person*) iettatore/trice.

jitters ['dʒɪtəz] *npl* (*col*): **to get the ~** aver fifa.

jittery ['dʒɪtərɪ] *adj* (*col*) teso(a), agitato(a); **to be ~** aver fifa.

jiujitsu [dʒuː'dʒɪtsuː] *n* jujitsu *m.*

job [dʒɔb] *n* lavoro; (*employment*) impiego, posto; **a part-time/full-time ~** un lavoro a mezza giornata/a tempo pieno; **that's not my ~** non è compito mio; **he's only doing his ~** non fa che il suo dovere; **it's a good ~ that ...** meno male che ...; **just the ~!** proprio quello che ci vuole!

jobber ['dʒɔbə*] *n* (*BRIT STOCK EXCHANGE*) *intermediario tra agenti di cambio.*

jobbing ['dʒɔbɪŋ] *adj* (*BRIT: workman*) a ore, a giornata.

Jobcentre ['dʒɔbsɛntə*] *n* ufficio di collocamento.

job creation scheme *n* progetto per la creazione di nuovi posti di lavoro.

job description *n* caratteristiche *fpl* (di un lavoro).

jobless ['dʒɔblɪs] *adj* senza lavoro, disoccupato(a) ♦ *npl*: **the ~** i senza lavoro.

job lot *n* partita di articoli disparati.

job satisfaction *n* soddisfazione *f* nel lavoro.

job security *n* sicurezza del posto di lavoro.

job share *vi* fare un lavoro ripartito ♦ *n* lavoro ripartito.

job specification *n* caratteristiche *fpl* (di un lavoro).

jockey ['dʒɔkɪ] *n* fantino, jockey *m inv* ♦ *vi*: **to ~ for position** manovrare per una posizione di vantaggio.

jockey box *n* (*US AUT*) vano portaoggetti.

jockstrap ['dʒɔkstræp] *n* conchiglia (*per atleti*).

jocular ['dʒɔkjulə*] *adj* gioviale; scherzoso(a).

jog [dʒɔg] *vt* urtare ♦ *vi* (*SPORT*) fare footing, fare jogging; **to ~ along** trottare; (*fig*) andare avanti pian piano; **to ~ sb's memory** stimolare la memoria di qn.

jogger ['dʒɔgə*] *n* persona che fa footing *or* jogging.

jogging ['dʒɔgɪŋ] *n* footing *m*, jogging *m.*

john [dʒɔn] *n* (*US col*): **the ~** il gabinetto.

join [dʒɔɪn] *vt* unire, congiungere; (*become member of*) iscriversi a; (*meet*) raggiungere; riunirsi a ♦ *vi* (*roads, rivers*) confluire ♦ *n* giuntura; **to ~ forces (with)** allearsi (con *or* a); (*fig*) mettersi insieme (a); **will you ~ us for dinner?** viene a cena con noi?; **I'll ~ you later** vi raggiungo più tardi.

►**join in** *vt fus* unirsi a, prendere parte a, partecipare a ♦ *vi* partecipare.

►**join up** *vi* arruolarsi.

joiner ['dʒɔɪnə*] *n* falegname *m.*

joinery ['dʒɔɪnərɪ] *n* falegnameria.

joint [dʒɔɪnt] *n* (*TECH*) giuntura; giunto; (*ANAT*) articolazione *f*, giuntura; (*BRIT CULIN*) arrosto; (*col: place*) locale *m* ♦ *adj* comune; (*responsibility*) collettivo(a); (*committee*) misto(a).

joint account (J/A) *n* (*at bank etc*) conto in comune.

jointly ['dʒɔɪntlɪ] *adv* in comune, insieme.

joint ownership *n* comproprietà.

joint-stock company ['dʒɔɪntstɔk-] *n* società *f inv* per azioni.

joist [dʒɔɪst] *n* trave *f.*

joke [dʒəuk] *n* scherzo; (*funny story*) barzelletta ♦ *vi* scherzare; **to play a ~ on** fare uno scherzo a.

joker ['dʒəukə*] *n* buffone/a, burlone/a; (*CARDS*) jolly *m inv.*

joking ['dʒəukɪŋ] *n* scherzi *mpl.*

jollity ['dʒɔlɪtɪ] *n* allegria.

jolly ['dʒɒlɪ] adj allegro(a), gioioso(a) ♦ adv (BRIT col) veramente, proprio ♦ vt (BRIT): **to ~ sb along** cercare di tenere qn su (di morale); **~ good!** (BRIT) benissimo!

jolt [dʒəult] n scossa, sobbalzo ♦ vt urtare.

Jordan ['dʒɔːdən] n (country) Giordania; (river) Giordano.

Jordanian [dʒɔːˈdeɪnɪən] adj, n giordano(a).

joss stick ['dʒɒs-] n bastoncino d'incenso.

jostle ['dʒɒsl] vt spingere coi gomiti ♦ vi farsi spazio coi gomiti.

jot [dʒɒt] n: **not one ~** nemmeno un po'.

▶**jot down** vt annotare in fretta, buttare giù.

jotter ['dʒɒtə*] n (BRIT) quaderno; blocco.

journal ['dʒəːnl] n (newspaper) giornale m; (periodical) rivista; (diary) diario.

journalese [dʒəːnəˈliːz] n (pej) stile m giornalistico.

journalism ['dʒəːnəlɪzəm] n giornalismo.

journalist ['dʒəːnəlɪst] n giornalista m/f.

journey ['dʒəːnɪ] n viaggio; (distance covered) tragitto; **a 5-hour ~** un viaggio or un tragitto di 5 ore.

jovial ['dʒəuvɪəl] adj gioviale, allegro(a).

jowl [dʒaul] n mandibola; guancia.

joy [dʒɔɪ] n gioia.

joyful ['dʒɔɪful], **joyous** ['dʒɔɪəs] adj gioioso(a), allegro(a).

joyride ['dʒɔɪraɪd] n: **to go for a ~** rubare una macchina per farsi un giro.

joyrider ['dʒɔɪraɪdə*] n chi ruba una macchina per andare a farsi un giro.

joystick ['dʒɔɪstɪk] n (AVIAT) barra di comando; (COMPUT) joystick m inv.

JP n abbr see **Justice of the Peace**.

Jr. abbr = **junior**.

jubilant ['dʒuːbɪlnt] adj giubilante; trionfante.

jubilation [dʒuːbɪˈleɪʃən] n giubilo.

jubilee ['dʒuːbɪliː] n giubileo; **silver ~** venticinquesimo anniversario.

judge [dʒʌdʒ] n giudice m/f ♦ vt giudicare; (consider) ritenere; (estimate: weight, size etc) calcolare, valutare ♦ vi: **judging** or **to ~ by his expression** a giudicare dalla sua espressione; **as far as I can ~** a mio giudizio; **I ~d it necessary to inform him** ho ritenuto necessario informarlo.

judge advocate (JA) n (MIL) magistrato militare.

judg(e)ment ['dʒʌdʒmənt] n giudizio; (punishment) punizione f; **in my ~** a mio giudizio; **to pass ~ (on)** (LAW) pronunciare un giudizio (su); (fig) dare giudizi affrettati (su).

judicial [dʒuːˈdɪʃl] adj giudiziale, giudiziario(a).

judiciary [dʒuːˈdɪʃɪərɪ] n magistratura.

judicious [dʒuːˈdɪʃəs] adj giudizioso(a).

judo ['dʒuːdəu] n judo.

jug [dʒʌg] n brocca, bricco.

jugged hare [dʒʌgd-] n (BRIT) lepre f in salmì.

juggernaut ['dʒʌgənɔːt] n (BRIT: huge truck) bestione m.

juggle ['dʒʌgl] vi fare giochi di destrezza.

juggler ['dʒʌglə*] n giocoliere/a.

Jugoslav ['juːgəuslɑːv] adj, n = **Yugoslav**.

jugular ['dʒʌgjulə*] adj: **~ (vein)** vena giugulare.

juice [dʒuːs] n succo; (of meat) sugo; **we've run out of ~** (col: petrol) siamo rimasti a secco.

juicy ['dʒuːsɪ] adj succoso(a).

jukebox ['dʒuːkbɒks] n juke-box m inv.

Jul. abbr (= July) lug., lu.

July [dʒuːˈlaɪ] n luglio; **the first of ~** il primo luglio; **(on) the eleventh of ~** l'undici luglio; **in the month of ~** nel mese di luglio; **at the beginning/end of ~** all'inizio/alla fine di luglio; **in the middle of ~** a metà luglio; **during ~** durante (il mese di) luglio; **in ~ of next year** a luglio dell'anno prossimo; **each** or **every ~** ogni anno a luglio; **~ was wet this year** ha piovuto molto a luglio quest'anno.

jumble ['dʒʌmbl] n miscuglio ♦ vt (also: **~ up**, **~ together**) mischiare, mettere alla rinfusa.

jumble sale n ≈ vendita di beneficenza; see boxed note.

JUMBLE SALE

La **jumble sale** è un mercatino dove vengono venduti vari oggetti, per lo più di seconda mano; viene organizzata in chiese, scuole o circoli ricreativi. I proventi delle vendite vengono devoluti in beneficenza o usati per una giusta causa.

---

jumbo ['dʒʌmbəu] adj: **~ jet** jumbo-jet m inv; **~ size** formato gigante.

jump [dʒʌmp] vi saltare, balzare; (start) sobbalzare; (increase) rincarare ♦ vt saltare ♦ n salto, balzo; sobbalzo; (SHOWJUMPING) salto; (fence) ostacolo; **to ~ the queue** (BRIT) passare davanti agli altri (in una coda).

▶**jump about** vi fare salti, saltellare.

▶**jump at** vt fus (fig) cogliere or afferrare al volo; **he ~ed at the offer** si affrettò ad accettare l'offerta.

▶**jump down** vi saltare giù.

▶**jump up** vi saltare in piedi.

jumped-up ['dʒʌmptʌp] *adj* (*BRIT pej*) presuntuoso(a).

jumper ['dʒʌmpə*] *n* (*BRIT: pullover*) maglia; (*US: pinafore dress*) scamiciato; (*SPORT*) saltatore/trice.

jump leads, (*US*) **jumper cables** *npl* cavi *mpl* per batteria.

jump-start ['dʒʌmpstɑːt] *vt* (*car*) far partire spingendo; (*fig*) dare una spinta a, rimettere in moto.

jump suit *n* tuta.

jumpy ['dʒʌmpɪ] *adj* nervoso(a), agitato(a).

Jun. *abbr* (= *June*) giu.

Jun., Junr *abbr* = **junior**.

junction ['dʒʌŋkʃən] *n* (*BRIT: of roads*) incrocio; (*of rails*) nodo ferroviario.

juncture ['dʒʌŋktʃə*] *n*: **at this ~** in questa congiuntura.

June [dʒuːn] *n* giugno; *for phrases see also* **July.**

jungle ['dʒʌŋgl] *n* giungla.

junior ['dʒuːnɪə*] *adj, n*: **he's ~ to me (by 2 years), he's my ~ (by 2 years)** è più giovane di me (di 2 anni); **he's ~ to me** (*seniority*) è al di sotto di me, ho più anzianità di lui.

junior high school *n* (*US*) scuola media (*da 12 a 15 anni*).

junior minister *n* (*BRIT POL*) *ministro che non fa parte del Cabinet.*

junior partner *n* socio meno anziano.

junior school *n* (*BRIT*) scuola elementare (*da 8 a 11 anni*).

juniper ['dʒuːnɪpə*] *n*: **~ berry** bacca di ginepro.

junk [dʒʌŋk] *n* (*rubbish*) chincaglia; (*ship*) giunca ♦ *vt* disfarsi di.

junk bond *n* (*COMM*) titolo *m* spazzatura *inv*.

junk dealer *n* rigattiere *m*.

junket ['dʒʌŋkɪt] *n* (*CULIN*) giuncata; (*BRIT col: also:* ~**ing**): **to go on a ~, go ~ing** fare bisboccia.

junk food *n* porcherie *fpl*, cibo a scarso valore nutritivo.

junkie ['dʒʌŋkɪ] *n* (*col*) drogato/a.

junk mail *n* posta *f* spazzatura *inv*.

junk room *n* (*US*) ripostiglio.

junk shop *n* chincaglieria.

junta ['dʒʌntə] *n* giunta.

Jupiter ['dʒuːpɪtə*] *n* (*planet*) Giove *m*.

jurisdiction [dʒuərɪs'dɪkʃən] *n* giurisdizione *f*; **it falls *or* comes within/outside our ~** è/ non è di nostra competenza.

jurisprudence [dʒuərɪs'pruːdəns] *n* giurisprudenza.

juror ['dʒuərə*] *n* giurato/a.

jury ['dʒuərɪ] *n* giuria.

jury box *n* banco della giuria.

juryman ['dʒuərɪmən] *n* = **juror**.

just [dʒʌst] *adj* giusto(a) ♦ *adv*: **he's ~ done it/left** lo ha appena fatto/è appena partito; **~ as I expected** proprio come me lo aspettavo; **~ right** proprio giusto; **~ 2 o'clock** le 2 precise; **we were ~ going** stavamo uscendo; **I was ~ about to phone** stavo proprio per telefonare; **~ as he was leaving** proprio mentre se ne stava andando; **it was ~ before/enough/ here** era poco prima/appena assai/ proprio qui; **it's ~ me** sono solo io; **it's ~ a mistake** non è che uno sbaglio; **~ missed/caught** appena perso/preso; **~ listen to this!** senta un po' questo!; **~ ask someone the way** basta che tu chieda la strada a qualcuno; **it's ~ as good** è altrettanto buono; **it's ~ as well you didn't go** per fortuna non ci sei andato; **not ~ now** non proprio adesso; **~ a minute!, ~ one moment!** un attimo!

justice ['dʒʌstɪs] *n* giustizia; **Lord Chief J~** (*BRIT*) presidente *m* della Corte d'Appello; **this photo doesn't do you ~** questa foto non ti fa giustizia.

Justice of the Peace (JP) *n* giudice *m* conciliatore.

justifiable [dʒʌstɪ'faɪəbl] *adj* giustificabile.

justifiably [dʒʌstɪ'faɪəblɪ] *adv* legittimamente, con ragione.

justification [dʒʌstɪfɪ'keɪʃən] *n* giustificazione *f*; (*TYP*) giustezza.

justify ['dʒʌstɪfaɪ] *vt* giustificare; (*TYP etc*) allineare, giustificare; **to be justified in doing sth** avere ragione di fare qc.

justly ['dʒʌstlɪ] *adv* giustamente.

justness ['dʒʌstnɪs] *n* giustezza.

jut [dʒʌt] *vi* (*also:* ~ **out**) sporgersi.

jute [dʒuːt] *n* iuta.

juvenile ['dʒuːvənaɪl] *adj* giovane, giovanile; (*court*) dei minorenni; (*books*) per ragazzi ♦ *n* giovane *m/f*, minorenne *m/f*.

juvenile delinquency *n* delinquenza minorile.

juvenile delinquent *n* delinquente *m/f* minorenne.

juxtapose ['dʒʌkstəpəuz] *vt* giustapporre.

juxtaposition [dʒʌkstəpə'zɪʃən] *n* giustapposizione *f*.

K k

K, k [keɪ] *n* (*letter*) K, k *f or m inv*; **K for King** ≈ K come Kursaal.

K *n abbr* (= *one thousand*) mille ♦ *abbr* (*BRIT*: = *Knight*) *titolo*; (= *kilobyte*) K.

kaftan ['kæftæn] *n* caffettano.

Kalahari Desert [kælə'hɑːrɪ-] *n* Deserto di Calahari.

kale [keɪl] *n* cavolo verde.

kaleidoscope [kə'laɪdəskəup] *n* caleidoscopio.

kamikaze [kæmɪ'kɑːzɪ] *adj* da kamikaze.

Kampala [kæm'pɑːlə] *n* Kampala *f.*

Kampuchea [kæmpu't∫ɪə] *n* Kampuchea *f.*

kangaroo [kæŋgə'ruː] *n* canguro.

Kans. *abbr* (*US*) = *Kansas.*

kaput [kə'put] *adj* (*col*) kaputt *inv.*

karaoke [kɑːrə'əukɪ] *n* karaoke *m inv.*

karate [kə'rɑːtɪ] *n* karate *m.*

Kashmir [kæ∫'mɪə*] *n* Kashmir *m.*

Kazakhstan [kæzæk'stɑːn] *n* Kazakistan *m.*

KC *n abbr* (*BRIT LAW*: = *King's Counsel*) avvocato della Corona; *see also* **QC.**

kebab [kə'bæb] *n* spiedino.

keel [kiːl] *n* chiglia; **on an even ~** (*fig*) in uno stato normale.

► **keel over** *vi* (*NAUT*) capovolgersi; (*person*) crollare.

keen [kiːn] *adj* (*interest, desire*) vivo(a); (*eye, intelligence*) acuto(a); (*competition*) serrato(a); (*edge*) affilato(a); (*eager*) entusiasta; **to be ~ to do** *or* **on doing sth** avere una gran voglia di fare qc; **to be ~ on sth** essere appassionato(a) di qc; **to be ~ on sb** avere un debole per qn; **I'm not ~ on going** non mi va di andare.

keenly ['kiːnlɪ] *adv* (*enthusiastically*) con entusiasmo; (*acutely*) vivamente; in modo penetrante.

keenness ['kiːnnɪs] *n* (*eagerness*) entusiasmo.

keep [kiːp] *vb* (*pt, pp* **kept** [kɛpt]) *vt* tenere; (*hold back*) trattenere; (*feed: one's family etc*) mantenere, sostentare; (*a promise*) mantenere; (*chickens, bees, pigs etc*) allevare ♦ *vi* (*food*) mantenersi; (*remain: in a certain state or place*) restare ♦ *n* (*of castle*) maschio; (*food etc*): **enough for his** ~ abbastanza per vitto e alloggio; **to ~ doing sth** continuare a fare qc; fare qc di continuo; **to ~ sb from doing/sth from happening** impedire a qn di fare/che qc succeda; **to ~ sb busy/a place tidy** tenere qn occupato(a)/un luogo in ordine; **to ~ sb waiting** far aspettare qn; **to ~ an appointment** andare ad un appuntamento; **to ~ a record** *or* **note of sth** prendere nota di qc; **to ~ sth to o.s.** tenere qc per sé; **to ~ sth (back) from sb** celare qc a qn; **to ~ time** (*clock*) andar bene; **~ the change** tenga il resto; *see also* **keeps.**

► **keep away** *vt*: **to ~ sth/sb away from sb** tenere qc/qn lontano da qn ♦ *vi*: **to ~ away (from)** stare lontano (da).

► **keep back** *vt* (*crowds, tears, money*) trattenere ♦ *vi* tenersi indietro.

► **keep down** *vt* (*control: prices, spending*) contenere, ridurre; (*retain: food*) trattenere, ritenere ♦ *vi* tenersi giù, stare giù.

► **keep in** *vt* (*invalid, child*) tenere a casa; (*SCOL*) trattenere a scuola ♦ *vi* (*col*): **to ~ in with sb** tenersi buono qn.

► **keep off** *vt* (*dog, person*) tenere lontano da ♦ *vi* stare alla larga; **your hands off!** non toccare!, giù le mani!; "**~ off the grass**" "non calpestare l'erba".

► **keep on** *vi* continuare; **to ~ on doing** continuare a fare.

► **keep out** *vt* tener fuori ♦ *vi* restare fuori; "**~ out**" "vietato l'accesso".

► **keep up** *vi* mantenersi ♦ *vt* continuare, mantenere; **to ~ up with** tener dietro a, andare di pari passo con; (*work etc*) farcela a seguire; **to ~ up with sb** (*in race etc*) mantenersi al passo con qn.

keeper ['kiːpə*] *n* custode *m/f*, guardiano/a.

keep-fit [kiːp'fɪt] *n* ginnastica.

keeping ['kiːpɪŋ] *n* (*care*) custodia; **in ~ with** in armonia con; in accordo con.

keeps [kiːps] *n*: **for ~** (*col*) per sempre.

keepsake ['kiːpseɪk] *n* ricordo.

keg [kɛg] *n* barilotto.

Ken. *abbr* (*US*) = *Kentucky.*

kennel ['kɛnl] *n* canile *m.*

Kenya ['kɛnjə] *n* Kenia *m.*

Kenyan ['kɛnjən] *adj, n* Keniano(a), Keniota (*m/f*).

kept [kɛpt] *pt, pp of* **keep.**

kerb [kəːb] *n* (*BRIT*) orlo del marciapiede.

kerb crawler [-'krɔːlə*] *n* chi va in macchina in cerca di una prostituta.

kernel ['kəːnl] *n* nocciolo.

kerosene ['kɛrəsiːn] *n* cherosene *m.*

ketchup ['kɛt∫əp] *n* ketchup *m inv.*

kettle ['kɛtl] n bollitore m.
kettle drum n timpano.
key [kiː] n (gen, MUS) chiave f; (of piano, typewriter) tasto; (on map) leg(g)enda ♦ cpd (vital: position, industry etc) chiave inv.
► **key in** vt (text) introdurre da tastiera.
keyboard ['kiːbɔːd] n tastiera ♦ vt (text) comporre su tastiera.
keyboarder ['kiːbɔːdə*] n dattilografo(a).
keyed up [kiːd'ʌp] adj: to be ~ essere agitato(a).
keyhole ['kiːhəul] n buco della serratura.
keyhole surgery n chirurgia mininvasiva.
keynote ['kiːnəut] n (MUS) tonica; (fig) nota dominante.
keypad ['kiːpæd] n tastierino numerico.
key ring n portachiavi m inv.
keystroke ['kiːstrəuk] n battuta (di un tasto).
kg abbr (= kilogram) Kg.
KGB n abbr KGB m.
khaki ['kɑːkɪ] adj, n cachi (m).
kibbutz [kɪ'buts] n kibbutz m inv.
kick [kɪk] vt calciare, dare calci a ♦ vi (horse) tirar calci ♦ n calcio; (of rifle) contraccolpo; (thrill): **he does it for ~s** lo fa giusto per il piacere di farlo.
► **kick around** vi (col) essere in giro.
► **kick off** vi (SPORT) dare il primo calcio.
kick-off ['kɪkɔf] n (SPORT) calcio d'inizio.
kick-start ['kɪkstɑːt] n (also: ~er) pedale m d'avviamento.
kid [kɪd] n ragazzino/a; (animal, leather) capretto ♦ vi (col) scherzare ♦ vt (col) prendere in giro.
kid gloves npl: to treat sb with ~ trattare qn coi guanti.
kidnap ['kɪdnæp] vt rapire, sequestrare.
kidnapper ['kɪdnæpə*] n rapitore/trice.
kidnapping ['kɪdnæpɪŋ] n sequestro (di persona).
kidney ['kɪdnɪ] n (ANAT) rene m; (CULIN) rognone m.
kidney bean n fagiolo borlotto.
kidney machine n rene m artificiale.
Kilimanjaro [kɪlɪmən'dʒɑːrəu] n: **Mount** ~ il monte Kilimangiaro.
kill [kɪl] vt uccidere, ammazzare; (fig) sopprimere; sopraffare; ammazzare ♦ n uccisione f; to ~ time ammazzare il tempo.
► **kill off** vt sterminare; (fig) eliminare, soffocare.
killer ['kɪlə*] n uccisore m, killer m inv; assassino/a.
killer instinct n: to have a/the ~ essere spietato(a).

killing ['kɪlɪŋ] n assassinio; (massacre) strage f; (col): **to make a** ~ fare un bel colpo.
kill-joy ['kɪldʒɔɪ] n guastafeste m/f inv.
kiln [kɪln] n forno.
kilo ['kiːləu] n abbr (= kilogram) chilo.
kilobyte ['kɪləbaɪt] n kilobyte m inv.
kilogram(me) ['kɪləugræm] n chilogrammo.
kilometre, (US) **kilometer** ['kɪləmiːtə*] n chilometro.
kilowatt ['kɪləuwɔt] n chilowatt m inv.
kilt [kɪlt] n gonnellino scozzese.
kilter ['kɪltə*] n: out of ~ fuori fase.
kimono [kɪ'məunəu] n chimono.
kin [kɪn] n see next of kin, kith.
kind [kaɪnd] adj gentile, buono(a) ♦ n sorta, specie f; (species) genere m; to be two of a ~ essere molto simili; **would you be ~ enough to …?, would you be so ~ as to …?** sarebbe così gentile da …?; **it's very ~ of you (to do)** è molto gentile da parte sua (di fare); in ~ (COMM) in natura; (fig): **to repay sb in** ~ ripagare qn della stessa moneta.
kindergarten ['kɪndəgɑːtn] n giardino d'infanzia.
kind-hearted [kaɪnd'hɑːtɪd] adj di buon cuore.
kindle ['kɪndl] vt accendere, infiammare.
kindling ['kɪndlɪŋ] n frasche fpl, ramoscelli mpl.
kindly ['kaɪndlɪ] adj pieno(a) di bontà, benevolo(a) ♦ adv con bontà, gentilmente; **will you ~ …** vuole … per favore; **he didn't take it** ~ se l'è presa a male.
kindness ['kaɪndnɪs] n bontà, gentilezza.
kindred ['kɪndrɪd] adj imparentato(a); ~ **spirit** spirito affine.
kinetic [kɪ'nɛtɪk] adj cinetico(a).
king [kɪŋ] n re m inv.
kingdom ['kɪŋdəm] n regno, reame m.
kingfisher ['kɪŋfɪʃə*] n martin m inv pescatore.
kingpin ['kɪŋpɪn] n (TECH, fig) perno.
king-size(d) ['kɪŋsaɪz(d)] adj super inv; gigante; (cigarette) extra lungo(a).
kink [kɪŋk] n (of rope) attorcigliamento; (in hair) ondina; (fig) aberrazione f.
kinky ['kɪŋkɪ] adj (fig) eccentrico(a); dai gusti particolari.
kinship ['kɪnʃɪp] n parentela.
kinsman ['kɪnzmən] n parente m.
kinswoman ['kɪnzwumən] n parente f.
kiosk ['kiːɔsk] n edicola, chiosco; (BRIT: also: **telephone** ~) cabina (telefonica); (: also: **newspaper** ~) edicola.
kipper ['kɪpə*] n aringa affumicata.
Kirghizia [kəː'gɪzɪə] n Kirghizistan.

kiss [kɪs] n bacio ♦ vt baciare; **to ~ (each other)** baciarsi; **to ~ sb goodbye** congedarsi da qn con un bacio; **~ of life** (BRIT) respirazione f bocca a bocca.

kissagram ['kɪsəgræm] n servizio di recapito a domicilio di messaggi e baci augurali.

kit [kɪt] n equipaggiamento, corredo; (set of tools etc) attrezzi mpl; (for assembly) scatola di montaggio; **tool ~** cassetta or borsa degli attrezzi.

►**kit out** vt (BRIT) attrezzare, equipaggiare.

kitbag ['kɪtbæg] n zaino; sacco militare.

kitchen ['kɪtʃɪn] n cucina.

kitchen garden n orto.

kitchen sink n acquaio.

kitchen unit n (BRIT) elemento da cucina.

kitchenware ['kɪtʃɪnwɛə*] n stoviglie fpl; utensili mpl da cucina.

kite [kaɪt] n (toy) aquilone m; (ZOOL) nibbio.

kith [kɪθ] n: **~ and kin** amici e parenti mpl.

kitten ['kɪtn] n gattino/a, micino/a.

kitty ['kɪtɪ] n (money) fondo comune.

kiwi fruit ['kiːwiː-] n kiwi m inv.

KKK n abbr (US) = Ku Klux Klan.

Kleenex ® ['kliːnɛks] n fazzolettino di carta.

kleptomaniac [klɛptəu'meɪnɪæk] n cleptomane m/f.

km abbr (= kilometre) km.

km/h abbr (= kilometres per hour) km/h.

knack [næk] n: **to have a ~ (for doing)** avere una pratica (per fare); **to have the ~ of** avere l'abilità di; **there's a ~ to doing this** c'è un trucco per fare questo.

knackered ['nækəd] adj (col) fuso(a).

knapsack ['næpsæk] n zaino, sacco da montagna.

knave [neɪv] n (CARDS) fante m.

knead [niːd] vt impastare.

knee [niː] n ginocchio.

kneecap ['niːkæp] n rotula ♦ vt gambizzare.

knee-deep ['niː'diːp] adj: **the water was ~** l'acqua ci arrivava alle ginocchia.

kneel [niːl] vi (pt, pp knelt [nɛlt]) inginocchiarsi.

kneepad ['niːpæd] n ginocchiera.

knell [nɛl] n rintocco.

knelt [nɛlt] pt, pp of **kneel**.

knew [njuː] pt of **know**.

knickers ['nɪkəz] npl (BRIT) mutandine fpl.

knick-knack ['nɪknæk] n ninnolo.

knife [naɪf] n (pl knives) coltello ♦ vt accoltellare, dare una coltellata a; **~, fork and spoon** coperto.

knife edge n: **to be on a ~** (fig) essere appeso(a) a un filo.

knight [naɪt] n cavaliere m; (CHESS) cavallo.

knighthood ['naɪthud] n cavalleria; (title): **to get a ~** essere fatto cavaliere.

knit [nɪt] vt fare a maglia; (fig): **to ~ together** unire ♦ vi lavorare a maglia; (broken bones) saldarsi.

knitted ['nɪtɪd] adj lavorato(a) a maglia.

knitting ['nɪtɪŋ] n lavoro a maglia.

knitting machine n macchina per maglieria.

knitting needle n ferro (da calza).

knitting pattern n modello (per maglia).

knitwear ['nɪtwɛə*] n maglieria.

knives [naɪvz] npl of **knife**.

knob [nɔb] n bottone m; manopola; (BRIT): **a ~ of butter** una noce di burro.

knobbly ['nɔblɪ], (US) **knobby** ['nɔbɪ] adj (wood, surface) nodoso(a); (knee) ossuto(a).

knock [nɔk] vt (strike) colpire; urtare; (fig: col) criticare ♦ vi (engine) battere; (at door etc): **to ~ at/on** bussare a ♦ n bussata; colpo, botta; **he ~ed at the door** ha bussato alla porta; **to ~ a nail into sth** conficcare un chiodo in qc.

►**knock down** vt abbattere; (pedestrian) investire; (price) abbassare.

►**knock off** vi (col: finish) smettere (di lavorare) ♦ vt (strike off) far cadere; (col: steal) sgraffignare, grattare; **to ~ off £10** fare uno sconto di 10 sterline.

►**knock out** vt stendere; (BOXING) mettere K.O., mettere fuori combattimento.

►**knock over** vt (object) far cadere; (pedestrian) investire.

knockdown ['nɔkdaun] adj (price) fortemente scontato(a).

knocker ['nɔkə*] n (on door) battente m.

knocking ['nɔkɪŋ] n colpi mpl.

knock-kneed [nɔk'niːd] adj che ha le gambe ad x.

knockout ['nɔkaut] n (BOXING) knock out m inv.

knockout competition n (BRIT) gara ad eliminazione.

knock-up ['nɔkʌp] n (TENNIS etc) palleggio; **to have a ~** palleggiare.

knot [nɔt] n nodo ♦ vt annodare; **to tie a ~** fare un nodo.

knotty ['nɔtɪ] adj (fig) spinoso(a).

know [nəu] vt (pt knew, pp known [njuː, nəun]) sapere; (person, author, place) conoscere ♦ vi sapere; **to ~ that ...** sapere che ...; **to ~ how to do** sapere fare; **to get to ~ sth** venire a sapere qc; **I ~ nothing about it** non ne so niente; **I don't ~ him** non lo conosco; **to ~ right from wrong** distinguere il bene dal male; **as far as I ~**

... che io sappia ..., per quanto io ne
sappia ...; **yes, I** ~ sì, lo so; **I don't** ~ non
lo so.
know-all [ˈnəʊɔːl] *n* (*BRIT pej*) sapientone/a.
know-how [ˈnəʊhaʊ] *n* tecnica; pratica.
knowing [ˈnəʊɪŋ] *adj* (*look etc*) d'intesa.
knowingly [ˈnəʊɪŋlɪ] *adv* consapevolmente;
di complicità.
know-it-all [ˈnəʊɪtɔːl] *n* (*US*) = **know-all**.
knowledge [ˈnɒlɪdʒ] *n* consapevolezza;
(*learning*) conoscenza, sapere *m*; **to have
no** ~ **of** ignorare, non sapere; **not to my**
~ che io sappia, no; **to have a working** ~
of Italian avere una conoscenza pratica
dell'italiano; **without my** ~ a mia
insaputa; **it is common** ~ **that** ... è
risaputo che ...; **it has come to my** ~ **that**
... sono venuto a sapere che ....
knowledgeable [ˈnɒlɪdʒəbl] *adj* ben
informato(a).
known [nəʊn] *pp of* **know** ♦ *adj* (*thief, facts*)
noto(a); (*expert*) riconosciuto(a).
knuckle [ˈnʌkl] *n* nocca.
▶**knuckle down** *vi* (*col*): **to** ~ **down to
some hard work** mettersi sotto a
lavorare.
▶**knuckle under** *vi* (*col*) cedere.
knuckleduster [ˈnʌkldʌstə*] *n* tirapugni *m
inv*.
KO *abbr* (= *knock out*) *n* K.O. *m* ♦ *vt* mettere
K.O.
koala [kəʊˈɑːlə] *n* (*also*: ~ **bear**) koala *m inv*.
kook [kuːk] *n* (*US col*) svitato/a.
Koran [kɔˈrɑːn] *n* Corano.
Korea [kəˈriːə] *n* Corea; **North/South** ~
Corea del Nord/Sud.
Korean [kəˈriːən] *adj, n* coreano(a).
kosher [ˈkəʊʃə*] *adj* kasher *inv*.
kowtow [ˈkaʊˈtaʊ] *vi*: **to** ~ **to sb** mostrarsi
ossequioso(a) verso qn.
Kremlin [ˈkrɛmlɪn] *n*: **the** ~ il Cremlino.
KS *abbr* (*US*) = *Kansas*.
Kt *abbr* (*BRIT*: = *Knight*) titolo.
Kuala Lumpur [ˈkwɑːləˈlumpuə*] *n* Kuala
Lumpur *f*.
kudos [ˈkjuːdɒs] *n* gloria, fama.
Kurd [kəːd] *n* curdo/a.
Kuwait [kuˈweɪt] *n* Kuwait *m*.
Kuwaiti [kuˈweɪtɪ] *adj, n* kuwaitiano(a).
kW *abbr* (= *kilowatt*) kw.
KY, Ky. *abbr* (*US*) = *Kentucky*.

= L l

L, I [ɛl] *n* (*letter*) L, l *f or m inv*; **L for Lucy,** (*US*)
L for Love ≈ L come Livorno.
L *abbr* (= *lake*) l; (= *large*) taglia grande;
(= *left*) sin.; (*BRIT AUT*) = **learner**.
l *abbr* (= *litre*) l.
LA *n abbr* (*US*) = *Los Angeles* ♦ *abbr* (*US*)
= *Louisiana*.
La. *abbr* (*US*) = *Louisiana*.
lab [læb] *n abbr* (= *laboratory*) laboratorio.
Lab. *abbr* (*Canada*) = *Labrador*.
label [ˈleɪbl] *n* etichetta, cartellino; (*brand*:
of record) casa ♦ *vt* etichettare;
classificare.
labor *etc* [ˈleɪbə*] (*US*) = **labour** *etc*.
laboratory [ləˈbɔrətərɪ] *n* laboratorio.
Labor Day *n* (*US*) festa del lavoro; *see boxed
note*.

---

laborious [ləˈbɔːrɪəs] *adj* laborioso(a).
labor union *n* (*US*) sindacato.
Labour [ˈleɪbə*] *n* (*BRIT POL*: *also*: **the** ~
Party) il partito laburista, i laburisti.
labour, (*US*) **labor** [ˈleɪbə*] *n* (*task*) lavoro;
(*workmen*) manodopera; (*MED*) travaglio
del parto, doglie *fpl* ♦ *vi*: **to** ~ (**at**) lavorare
duro (a); **to be in** ~ (*MED*) avere le doglie.
labo(u)r camp *n* campo dei lavori forzati.
labo(u)r cost *n* costo del lavoro.
labo(u)r dispute *n* conflitto tra lavoratori
e datori di lavoro.
labo(u)red [ˈleɪbəd] *adj* (*breathing*) affa-
ticato(a); (*style*) elaborato(a), pesante.
labo(u)rer [ˈleɪbərə*] *n* manovale *m*; (*on
farm*) lavoratore *m* agricolo.
labo(u)r force *n* manodopera.
labo(u)r-intensive [leɪbərɪnˈtɛnsɪv] *adj* che
assorbe molta manodopera.
labo(u)r market *n* mercato del lavoro.
labo(u)r pains *npl* doglie *fpl*.
labo(u)r relations *npl* relazioni *fpl*

industriali.

labo(u)r-saving ['leɪbəseɪvɪŋ] adj che fa risparmiare fatica or lavoro.

labo(u)r unrest n agitazioni fpl degli operai.

labyrinth ['læbɪrɪnθ] n labirinto.

lace [leɪs] n merletto, pizzo; (of shoe etc) laccio ♦ vt (shoe) allacciare; (drink: fortify with spirits) correggere.

lacemaking ['leɪsmeɪkɪŋ] n fabbricazione f dei pizzi or dei merletti.

laceration [læsə'reɪʃən] n lacerazione f.

lace-up ['leɪsʌp] adj (shoes etc) con i lacci, con le stringhe.

lack [læk] n mancanza, scarsità ♦ vt mancare di; **through** or **for** ~ **of** per mancanza di; **to be ~ing (in)** mancare di.

lackadaisical [lækə'deɪzɪkl] adj disinteressato(a), noncurante.

lackey ['lækɪ] n (also fig) lacchè m inv.

lacklustre, (US) **lackluster** ['læklʌstə*] adj (surface) opaco(a); (style) scialbo(a); (eyes) spento(a).

laconic [lə'kɔnɪk] adj laconico(a).

lacquer ['lækə*] n lacca; **hair** ~ lacca per (i) capelli.

lacy ['leɪsɪ] adj (like lace) che sembra un pizzo.

lad [læd] n ragazzo, giovanotto; (BRIT: in stable etc) mozzo or garzone m di stalla.

ladder ['lædə*] n scala; (BRIT: in tights) smagliatura ♦ vt smagliare ♦ vi smagliarsi.

laden ['leɪdn] adj: ~ (**with**) carico(a) or caricato(a) (di); **fully** ~ (truck, ship) a pieno carico.

ladle ['leɪdl] n mestolo.

lady ['leɪdɪ] n signora; **L~ Smith** lady Smith; **the ladies' (toilets)** i gabinetti per signore; **a ~ doctor** una dottoressa.

ladybird ['leɪdɪbəːd], (US) **ladybug** ['leɪdɪbʌg] n coccinella.

lady-in-waiting ['leɪdɪɪn'weɪtɪŋ] n dama di compagnia.

ladykiller ['leɪdɪkɪlə*] n dongiovanni m inv.

ladylike ['leɪdɪlaɪk] adj da signora.

ladyship ['leɪdɪʃɪp] n: **your L~** signora contessa etc.

lag [læg] n = **time** ~ ♦ vi (also: ~ **behind**) trascinarsi ♦ vt (pipes) rivestire di materiale isolante.

lager ['laːgə*] n lager m inv.

lager lout n (BRIT col) giovinastro ubriaco.

lagging ['lægɪŋ] n rivestimento di materiale isolante.

lagoon [lə'guːn] n laguna.

Lagos ['leɪgɔs] n Lagos f.

laid [leɪd] pt, pp of **lay**.

laid-back [leɪd'bæk] adj (col) rilassato(a).

lain [leɪn] pp of **lie**.

lair [lɛə*] n covo, tana.

laissez-faire [lɛseɪ'fɛə*] n liberismo.

laity ['leɪətɪ] n laici mpl.

lake [leɪk] n lago.

Lake District n: **the** ~ (BRIT) la regione dei laghi.

lamb [læm] n agnello.

lamb chop n cotoletta d'agnello.

lambskin ['læmskɪn] n (pelle f d')agnello.

lambswool ['læmzwul] n lamb's wool m.

lame [leɪm] adj zoppo(a); ~ **duck** (fig: person) persona inetta; (: firm) azienda traballante.

lamely ['leɪmlɪ] adv (fig) in modo poco convincente.

lament [lə'mɛnt] n lamento ♦ vt lamentare, piangere.

lamentable ['læməntəbl] adj doloroso(a); deplorevole.

laminated ['læmɪneɪtɪd] adj laminato(a).

lamp [læmp] n lampada.

lamplight ['læmplaɪt] n: **by** ~ a lume della lampada.

lampoon [læm'puːn] n satira.

lamppost ['læmppəust] n lampione m.

lampshade ['læmpʃeɪd] n paralume m.

lance [laːns] n lancia ♦ vt (MED) incidere.

lance corporal n (BRIT) caporale m.

lancet ['laːnsɪt] n (MED) bisturi m inv.

Lancs [læŋks] abbr (BRIT) = Lancashire.

land [lænd] n (as opposed to sea) terra (ferma); (country) paese m; (soil) terreno; (estate) terreni mpl, terre fpl ♦ vi (from ship) sbarcare; (AVIAT) atterrare; (fig: fall) cadere ♦ vt (obtain) acchiappare; (passengers) sbarcare; (goods) scaricare; **to go/travel by** ~ andare/viaggiare per via di terra; **to own** ~ possedere dei terreni, avere delle proprietà (terriere); **to** ~ **on one's feet** cadere in piedi; (fig: to be lucky) cascar bene.

▶**land up** vi andare a finire.

landed gentry ['lændɪd-] n proprietari mpl terrieri.

landfill site ['lændfɪl-] n discarica dove i rifiuti vengono sepolti.

landing ['lændɪŋ] n (from ship) sbarco; (AVIAT) atterraggio; (of staircase) pianerottolo.

landing card n carta di sbarco.

landing craft n mezzo da sbarco.

landing gear n (AVIAT) carrello d'atterraggio.

landing stage n pontile m da sbarco.

landing strip n pista d'atterraggio.

landlady ['lændleɪdɪ] n padrona or

proprietaria di casa.

landlocked ['lændlɔkt] *adj* senza sbocco sul mare.

landlord ['lændlɔːd] *n* padrone *m or* proprietario di casa; (*of pub etc*) oste *m*.

landlubber ['lændlʌbə*] *n* marinaio d'acqua dolce.

landmark ['lændmɑːk] *n* punto di riferimento; (*fig*) pietra miliare.

landowner ['lændəunə*] *n* proprietario(a) terriero(a).

landscape ['lænskeɪp] *n* paesaggio.

landscape architect, landscape gardener *n* paesaggista *m/f*.

landscape painting *n* (*ART*) paesaggistica.

landslide ['lændslaɪd] *n* (*GEO*) frana; (*fig: POL*) valanga.

lane [leɪn] *n* (*in country*) viottolo; (*in town*) stradetta; (*AUT, in race*) corsia; **shipping ~** rotta (marittima).

language ['læŋgwɪdʒ] *n* lingua; (*way one speaks*) linguaggio; **bad ~** linguaggio volgare.

language laboratory *n* laboratorio linguistico.

language school *n* scuola di lingue.

languid ['læŋgwɪd] *adj* languente; languido(a).

languish ['læŋgwɪʃ] *vi* languire.

lank [læŋk] *adj* (*hair*) liscio(a) e opaco(a).

lanky ['læŋkɪ] *adj* allampanato(a).

lanolin(e) ['lænəlɪn] *n* lanolina.

lantern ['læntn] *n* lanterna.

Laos [lauz] *n* Laos *m*.

lap [læp] *n* (*of track*) giro; (*of body*): **in** *or* **on one's ~** in grembo ♦ *vt* (*also: ~ up*) papparsi, leccare ♦ *vi* (*waves*) sciabordare.

►**lap up** *vt* (*fig: compliments, attention*) bearsi di.

La Paz [læ'pæz] *n* La Paz *f*.

lapdog ['læpdɔg] *n* cane *m* da grembo.

lapel [lə'pɛl] *n* risvolto.

Lapland ['læplænd] *n* Lapponia.

Lapp [læp] *adj* lappone ♦ *n* lappone *m/f*; (*LING*) lappone *m*.

lapse [læps] *n* lapsus *m inv*; (*longer*) caduta; (*fault*) mancanza; (*in behaviour*) scorrettezza ♦ *vi* (*law, act*) cadere; (*ticket, passport*) scadere; **to ~ into bad habits** pigliare cattive abitudini; **~ of time** spazio di tempo; **a ~ of memory** un vuoto di memoria.

laptop ['læptɔp] *n* (*also: ~ computer*) lap-top *m inv*.

larceny ['lɑːsənɪ] *n* furto.

lard [lɑːd] *n* lardo.

larder ['lɑːdə*] *n* dispensa.

large [lɑːdʒ] *adj* grande; (*person, animal*) grosso(a) ♦ *adv*: **by and ~** generalmente; **at ~** (*free*) in libertà; (*generally*) in generale; nell'insieme; **to make ~r** ingrandire; **a ~ number of people** molta gente; **on a ~ scale** su vasta scala.

largely ['lɑːdʒlɪ] *adv* in gran parte.

large-scale ['lɑːdʒ'skeɪl] *adj* (*map, drawing etc*) in grande scala; (*reforms, business activities*) su vasta scala.

lark [lɑːk] *n* (*bird*) allodola; (*joke*) scherzo, gioco.

►**lark about** *vi* fare lo stupido.

larva, *pl* **larvae** ['lɑːvə, -iː] *n* larva.

laryngitis [lærɪn'dʒaɪtɪs] *n* laringite *f*.

larynx ['lærɪŋks] *n* laringe *f*.

lasagne [lə'zænjə] *n* lasagne *fpl*.

lascivious [lə'sɪvɪəs] *adj* lascivo(a).

laser ['leɪzə*] *n* laser *m*.

laser beam *n* raggio *m* laser *inv*.

laser printer *n* stampante *f* laser *inv*.

lash [læʃ] *n* frustata; (*also: eye~*) ciglio ♦ *vt* frustare; (*tie*) legare.

►**lash down** *vt* assicurare (con corde) ♦ *vi* (*rain*) scrosciare.

►**lash out** *vi*: **to ~ out (at** *or* **against sb/sth)** attaccare violentemente (qn/qc); **to ~ out (on sth)** (*col: spend*) spendere un sacco di soldi (per qc).

lashing ['læʃɪŋ] *n* (*beating*) frustata, sferzata; **~s of** (*BRIT col*) un mucchio di, una montagna di.

lass [læs] *n* ragazza.

lasso [læ'suː] *n* laccio ♦ *vt* acchiappare con il laccio.

last [lɑːst] *adj* ultimo(a); (*week, month, year*) scorso(a), passato(a) ♦ *adv* per ultimo ♦ *vi* durare; **~ week** la settimana scorsa; **~ night** ieri sera, la notte scorsa; **at ~** finalmente, alla fine; **~ but one** penultimo(a); **the ~ time** l'ultima volta; **it ~s (for) 2 hours** dura 2 ore.

last-ditch ['lɑːst'dɪtʃ] *adj* ultimo(a) e disperato(a).

lasting ['lɑːstɪŋ] *adj* durevole.

lastly ['lɑːstlɪ] *adv* infine, per finire, per ultimo.

last-minute ['lɑːstmɪnɪt] *adj* fatto(a) (*or* preso(a)) all'ultimo momento.

latch [lætʃ] *n* serratura a scatto.

►**latch on to** *vt fus* (*cling to: person*) attaccarsi a, appiccicarsi a; (*: idea*) afferrare, capire.

latchkey ['lætʃkiː] *n* chiave *f* di casa.

late [leɪt] *adj* (*not on time*) in ritardo; (*far on in day etc*) tardi *inv*; tardo(a); (*recent*) recente, ultimo(a); (*former*) ex; (*dead*) defunto(a) ♦ *adv* tardi; (*behind time, schedule*) in ritardo; **to be (10 minutes)** ~ essere in ritardo (di 10 minuti); **to work** ~ lavorare fino a tardi; ~ **in life** in età avanzata; **of** ~ di recente; **in the** ~ **afternoon** nel tardo pomeriggio; **in** ~ **May** verso la fine di maggio; **the** ~ **Mr X** il defunto Signor X.

latecomer ['leɪtkʌmə*] *n* ritardatario/a.

lately ['leɪtlɪ] *adv* recentemente.

lateness ['leɪtnɪs] *n* (*of person*) ritardo; (*of event*) tardezza, ora tarda.

latent ['leɪtnt] *adj* latente; ~ **defect** vizio occulto.

later ['leɪtə*] *adj* (*date etc*) posteriore; (*version etc*) successivo(a) ♦ *adv* più tardi; ~ **on today** oggi più tardi.

lateral ['lætərl] *adj* laterale.

latest ['leɪtɪst] *adj* ultimo(a), più recente; **at the** ~ al più tardi; **the** ~ **news** le ultime notizie.

latex ['leɪtɛks] *n* latice *m.*

lath, ~**s** [læθ, læðz] *n* assicella.

lathe [leɪð] *n* tornio.

lather ['lɑːðə*] *n* schiuma di sapone ♦ *vt* insaponare ♦ *vi* far schiuma.

Latin ['lætɪn] *n* latino ♦ *adj* latino(a).

Latin America *n* America Latina.

Latin American *adj* sudamericano(a).

latitude ['lætɪtjuːd] *n* latitudine *f*; (*fig: freedom*) libertà d'azione.

latrine [lə'triːn] *n* latrina.

latter ['lætə*] *adj* secondo(a); più recente ♦ *n*: **the** ~ quest'ultimo, il secondo.

latterly ['lætəlɪ] *adv* recentemente, negli ultimi tempi.

lattice ['lætɪs] *n* traliccio; graticolato.

lattice window *n* finestra con vetrata a losanghe.

Latvia ['lætvɪə] *n* Lettonia.

Latvian ['lætvɪən] *adj* lettone *inv* ♦ *n* lettone *m/f*; (*LING*) lettone *m.*

laudable ['lɔːdəbl] *adj* lodevole.

laudatory ['lɔːdətrɪ] *adj* elogiativo(a).

laugh [lɑːf] *n* risata ♦ *vi* ridere.

►**laugh at** *vt fus* (*misfortune etc*) ridere di; **I** ~**ed at his joke** la sua barzelletta mi fece ridere.

►**laugh off** *vt* prendere alla leggera.

laughable ['lɑːfəbl] *adj* ridicolo(a).

laughing ['lɑːfɪŋ] *adj* (*face*) ridente; **this is no** ~ **matter** non è una cosa da ridere.

laughing gas *n* gas *m* esilarante.

laughing stock *n*: **the** ~ **of** lo zimbello di.

laughter ['lɑːftə*] *n* riso; risate *fpl.*

launch [lɔːntʃ] *n* (*of rocket, product etc*) lancio; (*of new ship*) varo; (*boat*) scialuppa; (*also*: **motor** ~) lancia ♦ *vt*

(*rocket, product*) lanciare; (*ship, plan*) varare.

►**launch out** *vi*: **to** ~ **out (into)** lanciarsi (in).

launching ['lɔːntʃɪŋ] *n* lancio; varo.

launch(ing) pad *n* rampa di lancio.

launder ['lɔːndə*] *vt* lavare e stirare.

Launderette ® [lɔːn'drɛt], (*US*) **Laundromat** ® ['lɔːndrəmæt] *n* lavanderia (automatica).

laundry ['lɔːndrɪ] *n* lavanderia; (*clothes*) biancheria; **to do the** ~ fare il bucato.

laureate ['lɔːrɪət] *adj see* **poet laureate.**

laurel ['lɔrl] *n* lauro, alloro; **to rest on one's** ~**s** riposare *or* dormire sugli allori.

Lausanne [ləu'zæn] *n* Losanna.

lava ['lɑːvə] *n* lava.

lavatory ['lævətrɪ] *n* gabinetto.

lavatory paper *n* (*BRIT*) carta igienica.

lavender ['lævəndə*] *n* lavanda.

lavish ['lævɪʃ] *adj* abbondante; sontuoso(a); (*giving freely*): ~ **with** prodigo(a) di, largo(a) in ♦ *vt*: **to** ~ **sth on sb/sth** profondere qc a qn/qc.

lavishly ['lævɪʃlɪ] *adv* (*give, spend*) generosamente; (*furnished*) sontuosamente, lussuosamente.

law [lɔː] *n* legge *f*; **against the** ~ contro la legge; **to study** ~ studiare diritto; **to go to** ~ (*BRIT*) ricorrere alle vie legali; **civil/criminal** ~ diritto civile/penale.

law-abiding ['lɔːəbaɪdɪŋ] *adj* ubbidiente alla legge.

law and order *n* l'ordine *m* pubblico.

lawbreaker ['lɔːbreɪkə*] *n* violatore/trice della legge.

law court *n* tribunale *m*, corte *f* di giustizia.

lawful ['lɔːful] *adj* legale.

lawfully ['lɔːfəlɪ] *adv* legalmente.

lawless ['lɔːlɪs] *adj* senza legge; illegale.

Law Lords *npl* ≈ Corte *f* Suprema.

lawmaker ['lɔːmeɪkə*] *n* legislatore *m.*

lawn [lɔːn] *n* tappeto erboso.

lawnmower ['lɔːnməuə*] *n* tosaerba *m or f inv.*

lawn tennis *n* tennis *m* su prato.

law school *n* facoltà *f inv* di legge.

law student *n* studente/essa di legge.

lawsuit ['lɔːsuːt] *n* processo, causa; **to bring a** ~ **against** intentare causa a.

lawyer ['lɔːjə*] *n* (*consultant, with company*) giurista *m/f*; (*for sales, wills etc*) ≈ notaio; (*partner, in court*) ≈ avvocato/essa.

lax [læks] *adj* (*conduct*) rilassato(a); (*person: careless*) negligente; (: *on discipline*) permissivo(a).

laxative ['læksətɪv] *n* lassativo.

laxity ['læksɪtɪ] *n* rilassatezza; negligenza.

lay [leɪ] *pt of* **lie** ♦ *adj* laico(a); secolare ♦ *vt* (*pt, pp* **laid** [leɪd]) posare, mettere; (*eggs*) fare; (*trap*) tendere; (*plans*) fare, elaborare; **to ~ the table** apparecchiare la tavola; **to ~ the facts/one's proposals before sb** presentare i fatti/delle proposte a qn; **to get laid** (*col!*) scopare (*!*); essere scopato(a) (*!*).

▶**lay aside, lay by** *vt* mettere da parte.

▶**lay down** *vt* mettere giù; **to ~ down the law** (*fig*) dettar legge.

▶**lay in** *vt* fare una scorta di.

▶**lay into** *vt fus* (*col: attack, scold*) aggredire.

▶**lay off** *vt* (*workers*) licenziare.

▶**lay on** *vt* (*water, gas*) installare, mettere; (*provide: meal etc*) fornire; (*paint*) applicare.

▶**lay out** *vt* (*design*) progettare; (*display*) presentare; (*spend*) sborsare.

▶**lay up** *vt* (*to store*) accumulare; (*ship*) mettere in disarmo; (*subj: illness*) costringere a letto.

layabout ['leɪəbaut] *n* sfaccendato/a, fannullone/a.

lay-by ['leɪbaɪ] *n* (*BRIT*) piazzola (di sosta).

lay days *npl* (*NAUT*) stallie *fpl*.

layer ['leɪə*] *n* strato.

layette [leɪ'ɛt] *n* corredino (per neonato).

layman ['leɪmən] *n* laico; profano.

lay-off ['leɪɔf] *n* sospensione *f*, licenziamento.

layout ['leɪaut] *n* lay-out *m inv*, disposizione *f*; (*PRESS*) impaginazione *f*.

laze [leɪz] *vi* oziare.

laziness ['leɪzɪnɪs] *n* pigrizia.

lazy ['leɪzɪ] *adj* pigro(a).

lb. *abbr* (= *libra: pound*) lb.

lbw *abbr* (*CRICKET*: = *leg before wicket*) *fallo dovuto al fatto che il giocatore ha la gamba davanti alla porta.*

LC *n abbr* (*US*) = *Library of Congress.*

lc *abbr* (*TYP*) = **lower case**.

L/C *abbr* = **letter of credit**.

LCD *n abbr see* **liquid crystal display**.

Ld *abbr* (*BRIT*: = *lord*) titolo.

LDS *n abbr* (*BRIT*: = *Licentiate in Dental Surgery*) *specializzazione dopo la laurea*; (= *Latter-day Saints*) *Chiesa di Gesù Cristo dei Santi dell'Ultimo Giorno.*

LEA *n abbr* (*BRIT*: = *local education authority*) ≈ Provveditorato degli Studi.

lead [liːd] *n* (*front position*) posizione *f* di testa; (*distance, time ahead*) vantaggio; (*clue*) indizio; (*ELEC*) filo (elettrico); (*for dog*) guinzaglio; (*THEAT*) parte *f* principale; [lɛd] (*metal*) piombo; (*in pencil*) mina ♦ *vb* (*pt, pp* **led** [lɛd]) *vt* menare,

guidare, condurre; (*induce*) indurre; (*be leader of*) essere a capo di; (*: orchestra*: *BRIT*) essere il primo violino di; (*: US*) dirigere; (*SPORT*) essere in testa a ♦ *vi* condurre, essere in testa; **to be in the ~** (*SPORT*) essere in testa; **to take the ~** (*SPORT*) passare in testa; (*fig*) prendere l'iniziativa; **to ~ to** menare a; condurre a; portare a; **to ~ astray** sviare; **to ~ sb to believe that ...** far credere a qn che ...; **to ~ sb to do sth** portare qn a fare qc.

▶**lead away** *vt* condurre via.

▶**lead back** *vt* riportare, ricondurre.

▶**lead off** *vt* portare ♦ *vi* partire da.

▶**lead on** *vt* (*tease*) tenere sulla corda.

▶**lead on to** *vt* (*induce*) portare a.

▶**lead up to** *vt fus* portare a; (*fig*) preparare la strada per.

leaded ['lɛdɪd] *adj* (*petrol*) con piombo; **~ windows** vetrate *fpl* (artistiche).

leaden ['lɛdn] *adj* di piombo.

leader ['liːdə*] *n* capo; leader *m inv*; (*in newspaper*) articolo di fondo; **they are ~s in their field** (*fig*) sono all'avanguardia nel loro campo; **the L~ of the House** (*BRIT*) il capo della maggioranza ministeriale.

leadership ['liːdəʃɪp] *n* direzione *f*; **under the ~ of ...** sotto la direzione *or* guida di ...; **qualities of ~** qualità *fpl* di un capo.

lead-free ['lɛdfriː] *adj* senza piombo.

leading ['liːdɪŋ] *adj* primo(a); principale; **a ~ question** una domanda tendenziosa; **~ role** ruolo principale.

leading lady *n* (*THEAT*) prima attrice.

leading light *n* (*person*) personaggio di primo piano.

leading man *n* (*THEAT*) primo attore.

lead pencil [lɛd-] *n* matita con la mina di grafite.

lead poisoning [lɛd-] *n* saturnismo.

lead time [liːd-] *n* (*COMM*) tempo di consegna.

lead weight [lɛd-] *n* piombino, piombo.

leaf [liːf] *n* (*pl* **leaves**) foglia; (*of table*) ribalta; **to turn over a new ~** (*fig*) cambiar vita; **to take a ~ out of sb's book** (*fig*) prendere esempio da qn.

▶**leaf through** *vt* (*book*) sfogliare.

leaflet ['liːflɪt] *n* dépliant *m inv*; (*POL, REL*) volantino.

leafy ['liːfɪ] *adj* ricco(a) di foglie.

league [liːg] *n* lega; (*FOOTBALL*) campionato; **to be in ~ with** essere in lega con.

league table *n* classifica.

leak [liːk] *n* (*out*) fuga; (*in*) infiltrazione *f*; (*fig: of information*) fuga di notizie ♦ *vi* (*roof, bucket*) perdere; (*liquid*) uscire; (*shoes*) lasciar passare l'acqua ♦ *vt*

(*liquid*) spandere; (*information*) divulgare.
▶**leak out** *vi* uscire; (*information*)
trapelare.

leakage ['liːkɪdʒ] *n* (*of water, gas etc*) perdita.

leaky ['liːkɪ] *adj* (*pipe, bucket, roof*) che
perde; (*shoe*) che lascia passare l'acqua;
(*boat*) che fa acqua.

lean [liːn] *adj* magro(a) ♦ *n* (*of meat*) carne *f*
magra ♦ *vb* (*pt, pp* **leaned** *or* **leant** [lɛnt]) *vt*:
to ~ sth on appoggiare qc su ♦ *vi* (*slope*)
pendere; (*rest*): **to ~ against** appoggiarsi
contro; essere appoggiato(a) a; **to ~ on**
appoggiarsi a.
▶**lean back** *vi* sporgersi indietro.
▶**lean forward** *vi* sporgersi in avanti.
▶**lean out** *vi*: **to ~ out (of)** sporgersi (da).
▶**lean over** *vi* inclinarsi.

leaning ['liːnɪŋ] *n*: **~ (towards)** propensione
f (per) ♦ *adj* inclinato(a), pendente; **the L~**
Tower of Pisa la torre (pendente) di Pisa.

leant [lɛnt] *pt, pp of* **lean.**

lean-to ['liːntuː] *n* (*roof*) tettoia; (*building*)
edificio con tetto appoggiato ad altro
edificio.

leap [liːp] *n* salto, balzo ♦ *vi* (*pt, pp* **leaped** *or*
leapt [lɛpt]) saltare, balzare; **to ~ at an**
offer afferrare al volo una proposta.
▶**leap up** *vi* (*person*) alzarsi d'un balzo,
balzare su.

leapfrog ['liːpfrɒg] *n* gioco della cavallina
♦ *vi*: **to ~ over sb/sth** saltare (alla
cavallina) qn/qc.

leapt [lɛpt] *pt, pp of* **leap.**

leap year *n* anno bisestile.

learn, *pt, pp* **learned** *or* **learnt** [ləːn, -t] *vt, vi*
imparare; **to ~ how to do sth** imparare a
fare qc; **to ~ that ...** apprendere che ...;
to ~ about sth (*SCOL*) studiare qc; (*hear*)
apprendere qc; **we were sorry to ~ that it**
was closing down la notizia della
chiusura ci ha fatto dispiacere.

learned ['ləːnɪd] *adj* erudito(a), dotto(a).

learner ['ləːnə*] *n* principiante *m/f*;
apprendista *m/f*; **he's a ~ (driver)** (*BRIT*)
sta imparando a guidare.

learning ['ləːnɪŋ] *n* erudizione *f*, sapienza.

learnt [ləːnt] *pt, pp of* **learn.**

lease [liːs] *n* contratto d'affitto ♦ *vt*
affittare; **on ~** in affitto.
▶**lease back** *vt* effettuare un lease-back
inv.

leaseback ['liːsbæk] *n* lease-back *m inv.*

leasehold ['liːshəuld] *n* (*contract*) contratto
di affitto (*a lungo termine con responsabilità*
simili a quelle di un proprietario) ♦ *adj* in
affitto.

leash [liːʃ] *n* guinzaglio.

least [liːst] *adj*: **the ~** + *noun* il(la) più

piccolo(a), il(la) minimo(a); (*smallest*
amount of) il(la) meno ♦ *adv*: **the ~**
+ *adjective*: **the ~ beautiful girl** la ragazza
meno bella; **the ~ expensive** il(la) meno
caro(a); **I have the ~ money** ho meno
denaro di tutti; **at ~** almeno; **not in the ~**
affatto, per nulla.

leather ['lɛðə*] *n* (*soft*) pelle *f*; (*hard*) cuoio
♦ *cpd* di *or* in pelle; di cuoio; **~ goods**
pelletteria, pelletterie *fpl.*

leave [liːv] *vb* (*pt, pp* **left** [lɛft]) *vt* lasciare;
(*go away from*) partire da ♦ *vi* partire,
andarsene ♦ *n* (*time off*) congedo; (*MIL,*
also: consent) licenza; **to be left** rimanere;
there's some milk left over c'è rimasto
del latte; **to take one's ~ of** congedarsi
di; **he's already left for the airport** è già
uscito per andare all'aeroporto; **to ~**
school finire la scuola; **~ it to me!** ci
penso io!, lascia fare a me!; **on ~** in
congedo; **on ~ of absence** in permesso;
(*public employee*) in congedo; (*MIL*) in
licenza.
▶**leave behind** *vt* (*also fig*) lasciare
indietro; (*forget*) dimenticare.
▶**leave off** *vt* non mettere; (*BRIT col: stop*):
to ~ off doing sth smetterla *or* piantarla
di fare qc.
▶**leave on** *vt* lasciare su; (*light, fire, cooker*)
lasciare acceso(a).
▶**leave out** *vt* omettere, tralasciare.

leaves [liːvz] *npl of* **leaf.**

leavetaking ['liːvteɪkɪŋ] *n* commiato, addio.

Lebanese [lɛbə'niːz] *adj, n* (*pl inv*) libanese
(*m/f*).

Lebanon ['lɛbənən] *n* Libano.

lecherous ['lɛtʃərəs] *adj* lascivo(a),
lubrico(a).

lectern ['lɛktəːn] *n* leggio.

lecture ['lɛktʃə*] *n* conferenza; (*SCOL*)
lezione *f* ♦ *vi* fare conferenze; fare
lezioni; (*reprove*) rimproverare, fare una
ramanzina a; **to ~ on** fare una
conferenza su; **to give a ~ (on)** (*BRIT*) fare
una conferenza (su); fare lezione (su).

lecture hall *n* aula magna.

lecturer ['lɛktʃərə*] *n* (*speaker*)
conferenziere/a; (*BRIT: at university*)
professore/essa, docente *m/f*; **assistant ~**
(*BRIT*) ≈ professore(essa) associato(a);
senior ~ (*BRIT*) ≈ professore(essa)
ordinario(a).

lecture theatre *n* = **lecture hall.**

LED *n abbr* (*ELEC:* = *light-emitting diode*)
diodo a emissione luminosa.

led [lɛd] *pt, pp of* **lead.**

ledge [lɛdʒ] *n* (*of window*) davanzale *m*; (*on*
wall etc) sporgenza; (*of mountain*) cornice

f, cengia.

ledger ['lɛdʒə*] *n* libro maestro, registro.

lee [li:] *n* lato sottovento; **in the ~ of** a ridosso di, al riparo di.

leech [li:tʃ] *n* sanguisuga.

leek [li:k] *n* porro.

leer [lɪə*] *vi:* **to ~ at sb** gettare uno sguardo voglioso (*or* maligno) su qn.

leeward ['li:wəd] *adj* sottovento *inv* ♦ *n* lato sottovento; **to ~** sottovento.

leeway ['li:weɪ] *n* (*fig*): **to have some ~** avere una certa libertà di agire.

left [lɛft] *pt, pp of* **leave** ♦ *adj* sinistro(a) ♦ *adv* a sinistra, a sinistra; **on the ~, to the ~** a sinistra; **the L~** (*POL*) la sinistra.

left-click ['lɛftklɪk] *vi* (*COMPUT*): **to ~ on** fare clic con il pulsante sinistro del mouse su.

left-hand drive ['lɛfthænd-] *n* (*BRIT*) guida a sinistra.

left-handed [lɛft'hændɪd] *adj* mancino(a); **~ scissors** forbici *fpl* per mancini.

left-hand side ['lɛfthænd-] *n* lato *or* fianco sinistro.

leftie ['lɛftɪ] *n*: **a ~** (*col*) uno/a di sinistra.

leftist ['lɛftɪst] *adj* (*POL*) di sinistra.

left-luggage (office) [lɛft'lʌgɪdʒ-] *n* deposito *m* bagagli *inv*.

left-overs ['lɛftəuvəz] *npl* avanzi *mpl,* resti *mpl*.

left wing *n* (*MIL, SPORT*) ala sinistra; (*POL*) sinistra ♦ *adj*: **left-wing** (*POL*) di sinistra.

left-winger [lɛft'wɪŋə*] *n* (*POL*) uno/a di sinistra; (*SPORT*) ala sinistra.

lefty ['lɛftɪ] *n* = **leftie**.

leg [lɛg] *n* gamba; (*of animal*) zampa; (*of furniture*) piede *m*; (*CULIN: of chicken*) coscia; (*of journey*) tappa; **lst/2nd ~** (*SPORT*) partita di andata/ritorno; **~ of lamb** (*CULIN*) cosciotto d'agnello; **to stretch one's ~s** sgranchirsi le gambe.

legacy ['lɛgəsɪ] *n* eredità *f inv*; (*fig*) retaggio *m*.

legal ['li:gl] *adj* legale; **to take ~ action** *or* **proceedings against sb** intentare un'azione legale contro qn, far causa a qn.

legal adviser *n* consulente *m/f* legale.

legality [lɪ'gælɪtɪ] *n* legalità.

legalize ['li:gəlaɪz] *vt* legalizzare.

legally ['li:gəlɪ] *adv* legalmente; **~ binding** legalmente vincolante.

legal tender *n* moneta legale.

legation [lɪ'geɪʃən] *n* legazione *f*.

legend ['lɛdʒənd] *n* leggenda.

legendary ['lɛdʒəndərɪ] *adj* leggendario(a).

-legged ['lɛgɪd] *suffix*: **two~** a due gambe (*or* zampe), bipede.

leggings ['lɛgɪŋz] *npl* ghette *fpl*.

leggy ['lɛgɪ] *adj* dalle gambe lunghe.

legibility [lɛdʒɪ'bɪlɪtɪ] *n* leggibilità.

legible ['lɛdʒəbl] *adj* leggibile.

legibly ['lɛdʒəblɪ] *adv* in modo leggibile.

legion ['li:dʒən] *n* legione *f*.

legionnaire [li:dʒə'nɛə*] *n* legionario; **~'s disease** morbo del legionario.

legislate ['lɛdʒɪsleɪt] *vi* legiferare.

legislation [lɛdʒɪs'leɪʃən] *n* legislazione *f*; **a piece of ~** una legge.

legislative ['lɛdʒɪslətɪv] *adj* legislativo(a).

legislator ['lɛdʒɪsleɪtə*] *n* legislatore/trice.

legislature ['lɛdʒɪslətʃə*] *n* corpo legislativo.

legitimacy [lɪ'dʒɪtɪməsɪ] *n* legittimità.

legitimate [lɪ'dʒɪtɪmət] *adj* legittimo(a).

legitimize [lɪ'dʒɪtɪmaɪz] *vt* (*gen*) legalizzare, rendere legale; (*child*) legittimare.

legless ['lɛglɪs] *adj* (*BRIT col*) sbronzo(a), fatto(a).

leg-room ['lɛgru:m] *n* spazio per le gambe.

Leics *abbr* (*BRIT*) = *Leicestershire*.

leisure ['lɛʒə*] *n* agio, tempo libero; ricreazioni *fpl*; **at ~** all'agio; **a proprio comodo**.

leisure centre *n* centro di ricreazione.

leisurely ['lɛʒəlɪ] *adj* tranquillo(a); fatto(a) con comodo *or* senza fretta.

leisure suit *n* (*BRIT*) tuta (da ginnastica).

lemon ['lɛmən] *n* limone *m*.

lemonade [lɛmə'neɪd] *n* limonata.

lemon cheese, lemon curd *n* crema di limone (*che si spalma sul pane etc*).

lemon juice *n* succo di limone.

lemon squeezer *n* spremiagrumi *m inv*.

lemon tea *n* tè *m inv* al limone.

lend, *pt, pp* **lent** [lɛnd, lɛnt] *vt*: **to ~ sth (to sb)** prestare qc (a qn); **to ~ a hand** dare una mano.

lender ['lɛndə*] *n* prestatore/trice.

lending library ['lɛndɪŋ-] *n* biblioteca circolante.

length [lɛŋθ] *n* lunghezza; (*section: of road, pipe etc*) pezzo, tratto; **~ of time** periodo (di tempo); **what ~ is it?** quant'è lungo?; **it is 2 metres in ~** è lungo 2 metri; **to fall full ~** cadere lungo disteso; **at ~** (*at last*) finalmente, alla fine; (*lengthily*) a lungo; **to go to any ~(s) to do sth** fare qualsiasi cosa pur di *or* per fare qc.

lengthen ['lɛŋθən] *vt* allungare, prolungare ♦ *vi* allungarsi.

lengthways ['lɛŋθweɪz] *adv* per il lungo.

lengthy ['lɛŋθɪ] *adj* molto lungo(a).

leniency ['li:nɪənsɪ] *n* indulgenza, clemenza.

lenient ['li:nɪənt] *adj* indulgente, clemente.

leniently ['liːnɪəntlɪ] *adv* con indulgenza.
lens [lɛnz] *n* lente *f*; (*of camera*) obiettivo.
Lent [lɛnt] *n* Quaresima.
lent [lɛnt] *pt, pp of* **lend**.
lentil ['lɛntl] *n* lenticchia.
Leo ['liːəu] *n* Leone *m*; **to be ~** essere del Leone.
leopard ['lɛpəd] *n* leopardo.
leotard ['liːətɑːd] *n* calzamaglia.
leper ['lɛpə*] *n* lebbroso/a.
leper colony *n* lebbrosario.
leprosy ['lɛprəsɪ] *n* lebbra.
lesbian ['lɛzbɪən] *n* lesbica ♦ *adj* lesbico(a).
lesion ['liːʒən] *n* (*MED*) lesione *f*.
Lesotho [lɪ'suːtu] *n* Lesotho *m*.
less [lɛs] *adj, pron, adv* meno; **~ than you/ever** meno di lei/che mai; **~ than half** meno della metà; **~ and ~** sempre meno; **the ~ he works** ... meno lavora ...; **than £1/a kilo/3 metres** meno di una sterlina/un chilo/3 metri; **~ 5%** meno il 5%.
lessee [lɛ'siː] *n* affittuario/a, locatario/a.
lessen ['lɛsn] *vi* diminuire, attenuarsi ♦ *vt* diminuire, ridurre.
lesser ['lɛsə*] *adj* minore, più piccolo(a); **to a ~ extent** *or* **degree** in grado *or* misura minore.
lesson ['lɛsn] *n* lezione *f*; **a maths ~** una lezione di matematica; **to give ~s in** dare *or* impartire lezioni di; **it taught him a ~** (*fig*) gli è servito di lezione.
lessor ['lɛsɔː*, lɛ'sɔː*] *n* locatore/trice.
lest [lɛst] *conj* per paura di + *infinitive*, per paura che + *sub*.
let, *pt, pp* **let** [lɛt] *vt* lasciare; (*BRIT: lease*) dare in affitto; **to ~ sb do sth** lasciar fare qc a qn, lasciare che qn faccia qc; **to ~ sb know sth** far sapere qc a qn; **to ~ sb have sth** dare qc a qn; **he ~ me go** mi ha lasciato andare; **~ the water boil and** ... fate bollire l'acqua e ...; **~'s go** andiamo; **~ him come** lo lasci venire; **"to ~"** "affittasi".
▶**let down** *vt* (*lower*) abbassare; (*dress*) allungare; (*hair*) sciogliere; (*disappoint*) deludere; (*BRIT: tyre*) sgonfiare.
▶**let go** *vi* mollare ♦ *vt* mollare; (*allow to go*) lasciare andare.
▶**let in** *vt* lasciare entrare; (*visitor etc*) far entrare; **what have you ~ yourself in for?** in che guai *or* pasticci sei andato a cacciarti?
▶**let off** *vt* (*allow to go*) lasciare andare; (*firework etc*) far partire; (*smell etc*) emettere; (*subj: taxi driver, bus driver*) far scendere; **to ~ off steam** (*fig col*) sfogarsi, scaricarsi.
▶**let on** *vi* (*col*): **to ~ on that** ... lasciar capire che ....
▶**let out** *vt* lasciare uscire; (*dress*) allargare; (*scream*) emettere; (*rent out*) affittare, dare in affitto.
▶**let up** *vi* diminuire.
let-down ['lɛtdaun] *n* (*disappointment*) delusione *f*.
lethal ['liːθl] *adj* letale, mortale.
lethargic [lɛ'θɑːdʒɪk] *adj* letargico(a).
lethargy ['lɛθədʒɪ] *n* letargia.
letter ['lɛtə*] *n* lettera; **~s** *npl* (*LITERATURE*) lettere; **small/capital ~** lettera minuscola/maiuscola; **~ of credit** lettera di credito; **documentary ~ of credit** lettera di credito documentata.
letter bomb *n* lettera esplosiva.
letterbox ['lɛtəbɔks] *n* buca delle lettere.
letterhead ['lɛtəhɛd] *n* intestazione *f*.
lettering ['lɛtərɪŋ] *n* iscrizione *f*; caratteri *mpl*.
letter-opener ['lɛtərəupnə*] *n* tagliacarte *m inv*.
letterpress ['lɛtəprɛs] *n* (*method*) rilievografia.
letter quality *n* (*of printer*) qualità di stampa.
letters patent *npl* brevetto di invenzione.
lettuce ['lɛtɪs] *n* lattuga, insalata.
let-up ['lɛtʌp] *n* (*col*) interruzione *f*.
leukaemia, (*US*) **leukemia** [luː'kiːmɪə] *n* leucemia.
level ['lɛvl] *adj* piatto(a), piano(a); orizzontale ♦ *n* livello; (*also*: **spirit ~**) livella (a bolla d'aria) ♦ *vt* livellare, spianare; (*gun*) puntare (verso); (*accusation*): **to ~ (against)** lanciare (a *or* contro) ♦ *vi* (*col*): **to ~ with sb** essere franco(a) con qn; **to be ~ with** essere alla pari di; **a ~ spoonful** (*CULIN*) un cucchiaio raso; **to draw ~ with** (*team*) mettersi alla pari di; (*runner, car*) affiancarsi a; **A ~s** *npl* (*BRIT*) ≈ esami *mpl* di maturità; **O ~s** *npl* (*BRIT: formerly*) diploma di istruzione secondaria conseguito a 16 anni in Inghilterra e Galles, ora sostituito dal GCSE; **on the ~** piatto(a); (*fig*) onesto(a).
▶**level off, level out** *vi* (*prices etc*) stabilizzarsi; (*ground*) diventare pianeggiante; (*aircraft*) volare in quota.
level crossing *n* (*BRIT*) passaggio a livello.
level-headed [lɛvl'hɛdɪd] *adj* equilibrato(a).
levelling, (*US*) **leveling** ['lɛvlɪŋ] *adj* (*process, effect*) di livellamento.
level playing field *n*: **to compete on a ~** (*fig*) competere ad armi pari.
lever ['liːvə*] *n* leva ♦ *vt*: **to ~ up/out** sollevare/estrarre con una leva.

leverage ['liːvərɪdʒ] *n*: ~ **(on** *or* **with)** ascendente *m* (su).

levity ['lɛvɪtɪ] *n* leggerezza, frivolità.

levy ['lɛvɪ] *n* tassa, imposta ♦ *vt* imporre.

lewd [luːd] *adj* osceno(a), lascivo(a).

lexicographer [lɛksɪ'kɔɡrəfə*] *n* lessicografo/a.

lexicography [lɛksɪ'kɔɡrəfɪ] *n* lessicografia.

LGV *n abbr* (*BRIT*: = *Large Goods Vehicle*) automezzo pesante.

LI *abbr* (*US*) = *Long Island*.

liabilities [laɪə'bɪlətɪz] *npl* debiti *mpl*; (*on balance sheet*) passivo.

liability [laɪə'bɪlətɪ] *n* responsabilità *f inv*; (*handicap*) peso.

liable ['laɪəbl] *adj* (*subject*): ~ **to** soggetto(a) a; passibile di; (*responsible*): ~ **(for)** responsabile (di); (*likely*): ~ **to do** propenso/a a fare; **to be** ~ **to a fine** essere passibile di multa.

liaise [liː'eɪz] *vi*: **to** ~ **(with)** mantenere i contatti (con).

liaison [liː'eɪzɔn] *n* relazione *f*; (*MIL*) collegamento.

liar ['laɪə*] *n* bugiardo/a.

libel ['laɪbl] *n* libello, diffamazione *f* ♦ *vt* diffamare.

libellous, (*US*) **libelous** ['laɪbləs] *adj* diffamatorio(a).

liberal ['lɪbərl] *adj* liberale; (*generous*): **to be** ~ **with** distribuire liberalmente ♦ *n* (*POL*): **L**~ liberale *m/f*.

Liberal Democrat *n* liberal-democratico(a).

liberality [lɪbə'rælɪtɪ] *n* (*generosity*) generosità, liberalità.

liberalize ['lɪbərəlaɪz] *vt* liberalizzare.

liberal-minded [lɪbərl'maɪndɪd] *adj* tollerante.

liberate ['lɪbəreɪt] *vt* liberare.

liberation [lɪbə'reɪʃən] *n* liberazione *f*.

liberation theology *n* teologia della liberazione.

Liberia [laɪ'bɪərɪə] *n* Liberia.

Liberian [laɪ'bɪərɪən] *adj*, *n* liberiano(a).

liberty ['lɪbətɪ] *n* libertà *f inv*; **at** ~ **to do** libero(a) di fare; **to take the** ~ **of** prendersi la libertà di, permettersi di.

libido [lɪ'biːdəʊ] *n* libido *f*.

Libra ['liːbrə] *n* Bilancia; **to be** ~ essere della Bilancia.

librarian [laɪ'brɛərɪən] *n* bibliotecario/a.

library ['laɪbrərɪ] *n* biblioteca.

library book *n* libro della biblioteca.

libretto [lɪ'brɛtəʊ] *n* libretto.

Libya ['lɪbɪə] *n* Libia.

Libyan ['lɪbɪən] *adj*, *n* libico(a).

lice [laɪs] *npl of* **louse**.

licence, (*US*) **license** ['laɪsns] *n* autorizzazione *f*, permesso; (*COMM*) licenza; (*RADIO, TV*) canone *m*, abbonamento; (*also*: **driving** ~, (*US*) **driver's** ~) patente *f* di guida; (*excessive freedom*) licenza; **import** ~ licenza di importazione; **produced under** ~ prodotto su licenza.

licence number *n* (*BRIT AUT*) numero di targa.

license ['laɪsns] *n* (*US*) = **licence** ♦ *vt* dare una licenza a; (*car*) pagare la tassa di circolazione *or* il bollo di.

licensed ['laɪsnst] *adj* (*for alcohol*) che ha la licenza di vendere bibite alcoliche.

licensed trade *n* commercio di bevande alcoliche con licenza speciale.

licensee [laɪsən'siː] *n* (*BRIT*: *of pub*) detentore/trice di autorizzazione alla vendita di bevande alcoliche.

license plate *n* (*esp US AUT*) targa (automobilistica).

licentious [laɪ'sɛnʃəs] *adj* licenzioso(a).

lichen ['laɪkən] *n* lichene *m*.

lick [lɪk] *vt* leccare; (*col*: *defeat*) suonarle a, stracciare ♦ *n* leccata; **a** ~ **of paint** una passata di vernice.

licorice ['lɪkərɪs] *n* = **liquorice**.

lid [lɪd] *n* coperchio; **to take the** ~ **off sth** (*fig*) smascherare qc.

lido ['laɪdəʊ] *n* piscina all'aperto; (*part of the beach*) lido, stabilimento balneare.

lie [laɪ] *n* bugia, menzogna ♦ *vi* mentire, dire bugie; (*pt* **lay**, *pp* **lain** [leɪ, leɪn]) (*rest*) giacere, star disteso(a); (*in grave*) giacere, riposare; (*of object*: *be situated*) trovarsi, essere; **to tell** ~**s** raccontare *or* dire bugie; **to** ~ **low** (*fig*) latitare.

▶**lie about, lie around** *vi* (*things*) essere in giro; (*person*) bighellonare.

▶**lie back** *vi* stendersi.

▶**lie down** *vi* stendersi, sdraiarsi.

▶**lie up** *vi* (*hide*) nascondersi.

Liechtenstein ['lɪktənstaɪn] *n* Liechtenstein *m*.

lie detector *n* macchina della verità.

lie-down ['laɪdaʊn] *n* (*BRIT*): **to have a** ~ sdraiarsi, riposarsi.

lie-in ['laɪɪn] *n* (*BRIT*): **to have a** ~ rimanere a letto.

lieu [luː] *n*: **in** ~ **of** invece di, al posto di.

Lieut. *abbr* (= *lieutenant*) Ten.

lieutenant [lɛf'tɛnənt, (*US*) luː'tɛnənt] *n* tenente *m*.

lieutenant-colonel [lɛf'tɛnənt'kəːnl, (*US*) luː'tɛnənt'kəːnl] *n* tenente colonnello.

life [laɪf] *n* (*pl* **lives**) vita ♦ *cpd* di vita; della vita; a vita; **country/city** ~ vita di campagna/di città; **to be sent to prison for** ~ essere condannato all'ergastolo; **true to** ~ fedele alla realtà; **to paint from** ~ dipingere dal vero.

life annuity n rendita vitalizia.

life assurance n (BRIT) = **life insurance**.

lifebelt ['laɪfbɛlt] n (BRIT) salvagente m.

lifeblood ['laɪfblʌd] n (fig) linfa vitale.

lifeboat ['laɪfbəut] n scialuppa di salvataggio.

life expectancy n durata media della vita.

lifeguard ['laɪfgɑːd] n bagnino.

life imprisonment n ergastolo.

life insurance n assicurazione f sulla vita.

life jacket n giubbotto di salvataggio.

lifeless ['laɪflɪs] adj senza vita.

lifelike ['laɪflaɪk] adj che sembra vero(a); rassomigliante.

lifeline ['laɪflaɪn] n cavo di salvataggio.

lifelong ['laɪflɔŋ] adj per tutta la vita.

life preserver n (US) salvagente m; giubbotto di salvataggio; (BRIT) sfollagente m inv.

lifer ['laɪfə*] n (col) ergastolano/a.

life-raft ['laɪfrɑːft] n zattera di salvataggio.

life-saver ['laɪfseɪvə*] n bagnino.

life sentence n (condanna all')ergastolo.

life-sized ['laɪfsaɪzd] adj a grandezza naturale.

life span n (durata della) vita.

life style n stile m di vita.

life support system n (MED) respiratore m automatico.

lifetime ['laɪftaɪm] n: **in his** ~ durante la sua vita; **in a** ~ nell'arco della vita; in tutta la vita; **the chance of a** ~ un'occasione unica.

lift [lɪft] vt sollevare, levare; (steal) prendere, rubare ♦ vi (fog) alzarsi ♦ n (BRIT: elevator) ascensore m; **to give sb a** ~ (BRIT) dare un passaggio a qn.

▶**lift off** vt togliere ♦ vi (rocket) partire; (helicopter) decollare.

▶**lift out** vt tirar fuori; (troops, evacuees etc) far evacuare per mezzo di elicotteri (or aerei).

▶**lift up** vt sollevare, alzare.

lift-off ['lɪftɔf] n decollo.

ligament ['lɪgəmənt] n legamento.

light [laɪt] n luce, lume m; (daylight) luce, giorno; (lamp) lampada; (AUT: rear ~) luce di posizione; (: headlamp) fanale m; (for cigarette etc): **have you got a** ~? ha da accendere? ♦ vt (pt, pp **lighted** or **lit** [lɪt]) (candle, cigarette, fire) accendere; (room) illuminare ♦ adj (room, colour) chiaro(a); (not heavy, also fig) leggero(a) ♦ adv (travel) con poco bagaglio; ~**s** npl (AUT:

traffic ~s) semaforo; **in the** ~ **of** alla luce di; **to turn the** ~ **on/off** accendere/ spegnere la luce; **to come to** ~ venire in luce; **to cast** or **shed** or **throw** ~ **on** gettare luce su; **to make** ~ **of sth** (fig) prendere alla leggera qc, non dar peso a qc.

▶**light up** vi illuminarsi ♦ vt illuminare.

light bulb n lampadina.

lighten ['laɪtn] vi schiarirsi ♦ vt (give light to) illuminare; (make lighter) schiarire; (make less heavy) alleggerire.

lighter ['laɪtə*] n (also: **cigarette** ~) accendino; (boat) chiatta.

light-fingered [laɪt'fɪŋgəd] adj lesto(a) di mano.

light-headed ['laɪt'hɛdɪd] adj stordito(a).

light-hearted ['laɪt'hɑːtɪd] adj gioioso(a), gaio(a).

lighthouse ['laɪthaus] n faro.

lighting ['laɪtɪŋ] n illuminazione f.

lighting-up time ['laɪtɪŋʌp-] n (BRIT) orario per l'accensione delle luci.

lightly ['laɪtlɪ] adv leggermente; **to get off** ~ cavarsela a buon mercato.

light meter n (PHOT) esposimetro.

lightness ['laɪtnɪs] n chiarezza; (in weight) leggerezza.

lightning ['laɪtnɪŋ] n lampo, fulmine m; **a flash of** ~ un lampo, un fulmine.

lightning conductor, (US) **lightning rod** n parafulmine m.

lightning strike n (BRIT) sciopero m lampo inv.

light pen n penna luminosa.

lightship ['laɪtʃɪp] n battello m faro inv.

lightweight ['laɪtweɪt] adj (suit) leggero(a); (boxer) peso leggero inv.

light year ['laɪtjɪə*] n anno m luce inv.

Ligurian [lɪ'gjuərɪən] adj, n ligure (m/f).

like [laɪk] vt (person) volere bene a; (activity, object, food): **I** ~ **swimming/that book/ chocolate** mi piace nuotare/quel libro/il cioccolato ♦ prep come ♦ adj simile, uguale ♦ n: **the** ~ uno(a) uguale; **I would** ~, **I'd** ~ mi piacerebbe, vorrei; **would you** ~ **a coffee?** gradirebbe un caffè?; **if you** ~ se vuoi; **to be/look** ~ **sb/sth** somigliare a qn/ qc; **what's he** ~? che tipo è?, com'è?; **what's the weather** ~? che tempo fa?; **that's just** ~ **him** è proprio da lui; **something** ~ **that** qualcosa del genere; **I feel** ~ **a drink** avrei voglia di bere qualcosa; **there's nothing** ~ ... non c'è niente di meglio di or niente come ...; **his** ~**s and dislikes** i suoi gusti.

likeable ['laɪkəbl] adj simpatico(a).

likelihood ['laɪklɪhud] n probabilità; **in all** ~

con ogni probabilità, molto probabilmente.

likely ['laɪklɪ] *adj* probabile; plausibile; **he's** ~ **to leave** probabilmente partirà, è probabile che parta; **not** ~! (*col*) neanche per sogno!

like-minded ['laɪk'maɪndɪd] *adj* che pensa allo stesso modo.

liken ['laɪkən] *vt*: **to** ~ **sth to** paragonare qc a.

likeness ['laɪknɪs] *n* (*similarity*) somiglianza.

likewise ['laɪkwaɪz] *adv* similmente, nello stesso modo.

liking ['laɪkɪŋ] *n*: ~ (**for**) simpatia (per); debole *n* (per); **to be to sb's** ~ essere di gusto *or* gradimento di qn; **to take a** ~ **to sb** prendere qn in simpatia.

lilac ['laɪlək] *n* lilla *m inv* ♦ *adj* lilla *inv*.

Lilo ® ['laɪləʊ] *n* materassino gonfiabile.

lilt [lɪlt] *n* cadenza.

lilting ['lɪltɪŋ] *adj* melodioso(a).

lily ['lɪlɪ] *n* giglio; ~ **of the valley** mughetto.

Lima ['li:mə] *n* Lima.

limb [lɪm] *n* membro; **to be out on a** ~ (*fig*) sentirsi spaesato *or* tagliato fuori.

limber ['lɪmbə*]: **to** ~ **up** *vi* riscaldarsi i muscoli.

limbo ['lɪmbəʊ] *n*: **to be in** ~ (*fig*) essere lasciato(a) nel dimenticatoio.

lime [laɪm] *n* (*tree*) tiglio; (*fruit*) limetta; (*GEO*) calce *f*.

lime juice *n* succo di limetta.

limelight ['laɪmlaɪt] *n*: **in the** ~ (*fig*) alla ribalta, in vista.

limerick ['lɪmərɪk] *n poesiola umoristica di cinque versi.*

limestone ['laɪmstəʊn] *n* pietra calcarea; (*GEO*) calcare *m*.

limit ['lɪmɪt] *n* limite *m* ♦ *vt* limitare; **weight/speed** ~ limite di peso/di velocità; **within** ~**s** entro certi limiti.

limitation [lɪmɪ'teɪʃən] *n* limitazione *f*, limite *m*.

limited ['lɪmɪtɪd] *adj* limitato(a), ristretto(a); ~ **edition** edizione *f* a bassa tiratura.

limited (liability) company (Ltd) *n* (*BRIT*) ≈ società *f inv* a responsabilità limitata (S.r.l.).

limitless ['lɪmɪtlɪs] *adj* illimitato(a).

limousine ['lɪməzi:n] *n* limousine *f inv*.

limp [lɪmp] *n*: **to have a** ~ zoppicare ♦ *vi* zoppicare ♦ *adj* floscio(a), flaccido(a).

limpet ['lɪmpɪt] *n* patella.

limpid ['lɪmpɪd] *adj* (*poet*) limpido(a).

linchpin ['lɪntʃpɪn] *n* acciarino, bietta; (*fig*) perno.

Lincs *abbr* (*BRIT*) = Lincolnshire.

line [laɪn] *n* (*gen, COMM*) linea; (*rope*) corda; (*wire*) filo; (*of poem*) verso; (*row, series*) fila, riga; coda ♦ *vt* (*clothes*): **to** ~ (**with**) foderare (di); (*box*): **to** ~ (**with**) rivestire *or* foderare (di); (*subj: trees, crowd*) fiancheggiare; **to cut in** ~ (*US*) passare avanti; **in his** ~ **of business** nel suo ramo (di affari); **on the right** ~**s** sulla buona strada; **a new** ~ **in cosmetics** una nuova linea di cosmetici; **hold the** ~ **please** (*BRIT TEL*) resti in linea per cortesia; **to be in** ~ **for sth** (*fig*) essere in lista per qc; **in** ~ **with** d'accordo con, in linea con; **to bring sth into** ~ **with sth** mettere qc al passo con qc; **to draw the** ~ **at (doing) sth** (*fig*) rifiutarsi di fare qc; **to take the** ~ **that ...** essere del parere che ....

▶**line up** *vi* allinearsi, mettersi in fila ♦ *vt* mettere in fila; **to have sth** ~**d up** avere qc in programma; **to have sb** ~**d up** avere qn in mente.

linear ['lɪnɪə*] *adj* lineare.

lined [laɪnd] *adj* (*paper*) a righe, rigato(a); (*face*) rugoso(a); (*clothes*) foderato(a).

line feed *n* (*COMPUT*) avanzamento di una interlinea.

linen ['lɪnɪn] *n* biancheria, panni *mpl*; (*cloth*) tela di lino.

line printer *n* stampante *f* parallela.

liner ['laɪnə*] *n* nave *f* di linea; **dustbin** ~ sacchetto per la pattumiera.

linesman ['laɪnzmən] *n* guardalinee *m inv*, segnalinee *m inv*.

line-up ['laɪnʌp] *n* allineamento, fila; (*also*: **police** ~) confronto all'americana; (*SPORT*) formazione *f* di gioco.

linger ['lɪŋgə*] *vi* attardarsi; indugiare; (*smell, tradition*) persistere.

lingerie ['lænʒəri:] *n* biancheria intima (femminile).

lingering ['lɪŋgərɪŋ] *adj* lungo(a); persistente; (*death*) lento(a).

lingo, ~**es** ['lɪŋgəʊ] *n* (*pej*) gergo.

linguist ['lɪŋgwɪst] *n* linguista *m/f*; poliglotta *m/f*.

linguistic [lɪŋ'gwɪstɪk] *adj* linguistico(a).

linguistics [lɪŋ'gwɪstɪks] *n* linguistica.

lining ['laɪnɪŋ] *n* fodera; (*TECH*) rivestimento (interno); (*of brake*) guarnizione *f*.

link [lɪŋk] *n* (*of a chain*) anello; (*connection*) legame *m*, collegamento; (*COMPUT*) link, collegamento ♦ *vt* collegare, unire, congiungere; (*COMPUT*) creare un collegamento con ♦ *vi* (*COMPUT*): **to** ~ **to a site** creare un collegamento con un sitio; **rail** ~ collegamento ferroviario; *see also* **links.**

▶**link up** vt collegare, unire ♦ vi riunirsi; associarsi.

links [lɪŋks] npl pista or terreno da golf.

link-up ['lɪŋkʌp] n legame m; (of roads) nodo; (of spaceships) aggancio; (RADIO, TV) collegamento.

linoleum [lɪ'nəʊlɪəm] n linoleum m inv.

linseed oil ['lɪnsiːd-] n olio di semi di lino.

lint [lɪnt] n garza.

lintel ['lɪntl] n architrave f.

lion ['laɪən] n leone m.

lion cub n leoncino.

lioness ['laɪənɪs] n leonessa.

lip [lɪp] n labbro; (of cup etc) orlo; (insolence) sfacciataggine f.

liposuction ['lɪpəʊsʌkʃən] n liposuzione f.

lipread ['lɪpriːd] vi leggere sulle labbra.

lip salve n burro di cacao.

lip service n: **to pay ~ to sth** essere favorevole a qc solo a parole.

lipstick ['lɪpstɪk] n rossetto.

liquefy ['lɪkwɪfaɪ] vt liquefare ♦ vi liquefarsi.

liqueur [lɪ'kjʊə*] n liquore m.

liquid ['lɪkwɪd] n liquido ♦ adj liquido(a).

liquid assets npl attività fpl liquide, crediti mpl liquidi.

liquidate ['lɪkwɪdeɪt] vt liquidare.

liquidation [lɪkwɪ'deɪʃən] n liquidazione f; **to go into ~** andare in liquidazione.

liquidator ['lɪkwɪdeɪtə*] n liquidatore m.

liquid crystal display (LCD) n visualizzazione f a cristalli liquidi.

liquidity [lɪ'kwɪdɪtɪ] n (COMM) liquidità.

liquidize ['lɪkwɪdaɪz] vt (BRIT CULIN) passare al frullatore.

liquidizer ['lɪkwɪdaɪzə*] n (BRIT CULIN) frullatore m (a bocca).

liquor ['lɪkə*] n alcool m.

liquorice ['lɪkərɪs] n liquirizia.

Lisbon ['lɪzbən] n Lisbona.

lisp [lɪsp] n difetto nel pronunciare le sibilanti.

lissom ['lɪsəm] adj leggiadro(a).

list [lɪst] n lista, elenco; (of ship) sbandamento ♦ vt (write down) mettere in lista; fare una lista di; (enumerate) elencare; (COMPUT) stampare (un prospetto di) ♦ vi (ship) sbandare; **shopping ~** lista or nota della spesa.

listed building ['lɪstəd-] n (ARCHIT) edificio sotto la protezione delle Belle Arti.

listed company n società quotata in Borsa.

listen ['lɪsn] vi ascoltare; **to ~ to** ascoltare.

listener ['lɪsnə*] n ascoltatore/trice.

listeria [lɪs'tɪərɪə] n listeria.

listing ['lɪstɪŋ] n (COMPUT) lista stampata.

listless ['lɪstlɪs] adj svogliato(a); apatico(a).

listlessly ['lɪstlɪslɪ] adv svogliatamente; apaticamente.

list price n prezzo di listino.

lit [lɪt] pt, pp of **light**.

litany ['lɪtənɪ] n litania.

liter ['liːtə*] n (US) = **litre**.

literacy ['lɪtərəsɪ] n il sapere leggere e scrivere.

literacy campaign n lotta contro l'analfabetismo.

literal ['lɪtərl] adj letterale.

literally ['lɪtərəlɪ] adv alla lettera, letteralmente.

literary ['lɪtərərɪ] adj letterario(a).

literate ['lɪtərɪt] adj che sa leggere e scrivere.

literature ['lɪtərɪtʃə*] n letteratura; (brochures etc) materiale m.

lithe [laɪð] adj agile, snello(a).

lithography [lɪ'θɒɡrəfɪ] n litografia.

Lithuania [lɪθju'eɪnɪə] n Lituania.

Lithuanian [lɪθju'eɪnɪən] adj lituano(a) ♦ n lituano/a; (LING) lituano.

litigate ['lɪtɪɡeɪt] vt muovere causa a ♦ vi litigare.

litigation [lɪtɪ'ɡeɪʃən] n causa.

litmus ['lɪtməs] n: **~ paper** cartina di tornasole.

litre, (US) liter ['liːtə*] n litro.

litter ['lɪtə*] n (rubbish) rifiuti mpl; (young animals) figliata ♦ vt sparpagliare; lasciare rifiuti in; **~ed with** coperto(a) di.

litter bin n (BRIT) cestino per rifiuti.

litter lout, (US) litterbug ['lɪtəbʌɡ] n persona che butta per terra le cartacce o i rifiuti.

little ['lɪtl] adj (small) piccolo(a); (not much) poco(a) ♦ adv poco; **a ~** un po' (di); **a ~ milk** un po' di latte; **with ~ difficulty** senza fatica or difficoltà; **~ by ~** a poco a poco; **as ~ as possible** il meno possibile; **for a ~ while** per un po'; **to make ~ of** dare poca importanza a; **~ finger** mignolo.

little-known ['lɪtl'nəʊn] adj poco noto(a).

liturgy ['lɪtədʒɪ] n liturgia.

live vi [lɪv] vivere; (reside) vivere, abitare ♦ adj [laɪv] (animal) vivo(a); (issue) scottante, d'attualità; (wire) sotto tensione; (broadcast) diretto(a); (ammunition: not blank) carico(a); (unexploded) inesploso(a); **to ~ in London** abitare a Londra; **to ~ together** vivere insieme, convivere.

▶**live down** vt far dimenticare (alla gente).

▶**live in** vi essere interno(a); avere vitto e

alloggio.

▶**live off** *vi* (*land, fish etc*) vivere di; (*pej: parents etc*) vivere alle spalle *or* a spese di.

▶**live on** *vt fus* (*food*) vivere di ♦ *vi* sopravvivere, continuare a vivere; **to ~ on £50 a week** vivere con 50 sterline la settimana.

▶**live out** *vi* (*BRIT: students*) essere esterno(a) ♦ *vt:* **to ~ out one's days** *or* **life** trascorrere gli ultimi anni.

▶**live up** *vt:* **to ~ it up** (*col*) fare la bella vita.

▶**live up to** *vt fus* tener fede a, non venir meno a.

live-in ['lɪvɪn] *adj* (*col: partner*) convivente; (*servant*) che vive in casa; **he has a ~ girlfriend** la sua ragazza vive con lui.

livelihood ['laɪvlɪhud] *n* mezzi *mpl* di sostentamento.

liveliness ['laɪvlɪnəs] *n* vivacità.

lively ['laɪvlɪ] *adj* vivace, vivo(a).

liven up ['laɪvn-] *vt* (*room etc*) ravvivare; (*discussion, evening*) animare.

liver ['lɪvə*] *n* fegato.

liverish ['lɪvərɪʃ] *adj* che soffre di mal di fegato; (*fig*) scontroso(a).

Liverpudlian [lɪvə'pʌdlɪən] *adj* di Liverpool ♦ *n* abitante *m/f* di Liverpool; originario/a di Liverpool.

livery ['lɪvərɪ] *n* livrea.

lives [laɪvz] *npl of* **life**.

livestock ['laɪvstɔk] *n* bestiame *m*.

live wire [laɪv-] *n* (*col: fig*): **to be a ~** essere pieno(a) di vitalità.

livid ['lɪvɪd] *adj* livido(a); (*furious*) livido(a) di rabbia, furibondo(a).

living ['lɪvɪŋ] *adj* vivo(a), vivente ♦ *n:* **to earn** *or* **make a ~** guadagnarsi la vita; **cost of ~** costo della vita, carovita *m*; **within ~ memory** a memoria d'uomo.

living conditions *npl* condizioni *fpl* di vita.

living expenses *npl* spese *fpl* di mantenimento.

living room *n* soggiorno.

living standards *npl* tenore *m* di vita.

living wage *n* salario sufficiente per vivere.

lizard ['lɪzəd] *n* lucertola.

llama ['lɑːmə] *n* lama *m inv*.

LLB *n abbr* (= *Bachelor of Laws*) ≈ laurea in legge.

LLD *n abbr* (= *Doctor of Laws*) titolo di studio.

LMT *abbr* (*US:* = *Local Mean Time*) tempo medio locale.

load [ləud] *n* (*weight*) peso; (*ELEC, TECH, thing carried*) carico ♦ *vt:* **to ~ (with)** (*lorry, ship*) caricare (di); (*gun, camera*) caricare (con); **a ~ of**, **~s of** (*fig*) un sacco di; **to ~ a program** (*COMPUT*) caricare un programma.

loaded ['ləudɪd] *adj* (*dice*) falsato(a); (*question, word*) capzioso(a); (*col: rich*) pieno(a) di soldi.

loading bay ['ləudɪŋ-] *n* piazzola di carico.

loaf [ləuf] *n* (*pl* **loaves**) pane *m*, pagnotta ♦ *vi* (*also: ~* **about,** *~* **around**) bighellonare.

loam [ləum] *n* terra di marna.

loan [ləun] *n* prestito ♦ *vt* dare in prestito; **on ~** in prestito.

loan account *n* conto dei prestiti.

loan capital *n* capitale *m* di prestito.

loan shark *n* (*col: pej*) strozzino(a).

loath [ləuθ] *adj:* **to be ~ to do** essere restio(a) a fare.

loathe [ləuð] *vt* detestare, aborrire.

loathing ['ləuðɪŋ] *n* aborrimento, disgusto.

loathsome ['ləuðsəm] *adj* (*gen*) ripugnante; (*person*) detestabile, odioso(a).

loaves [ləuvz] *npl of* **loaf**.

lob [lɔb] *vt* (*ball*) lanciare.

lobby ['lɔbɪ] *n* atrio, vestibolo; (*POL: pressure group*) gruppo di pressione ♦ *vt* fare pressione su.

lobbyist ['lɔbɪɪst] *n* appartenente *m/f* ad un gruppo di pressione.

lobe [ləub] *n* lobo.

lobster ['lɔbstə*] *n* aragosta.

lobster pot *n* nassa per aragoste.

local ['ləukl] *adj* locale ♦ *n* (*BRIT: pub*) ≈ bar *m inv* all'angolo; **the ~s** *npl* la gente della zona.

local anaesthetic *n* anestesia locale.

local authority *n* autorità locale.

local call *n* (*TEL*) telefonata urbana.

local government *n* amministrazione *f* locale.

locality [ləu'kælɪtɪ] *n* località *f inv*; (*position*) posto, luogo.

localize ['ləukəlaɪz] *vt* localizzare.

locally ['ləukəlɪ] *adv* da queste parti; nel vicinato.

locate [ləu'keɪt] *vt* (*find*) trovare; (*situate*) collocare.

location [ləu'keɪʃən] *n* posizione *f*; **on ~** (*CINE*) all'esterno.

loch [lɔx] *n* lago.

lock [lɔk] *n* (*of door, box*) serratura; (*of canal*) chiusa; (*of hair*) ciocca, riccio ♦ *vt* (*with key*) chiudere a chiave; (*immobilize*) bloccare ♦ *vi* (*door etc*) chiudersi; (*wheels*) bloccarsi, incepparsi; **~ stock and barrel** (*fig*) in blocco; **on full ~** (*BRIT AUT*) a tutto sterzo.

▶**lock away** *vt* (*valuables*) tenere

(rinchiuso(a)) al sicuro; (*criminal*) metter dentro.

▶**lock out** *vt* chiudere fuori; **to ~ workers out** fare una serrata.

▶**lock up** *vi* chiudere tutto (a chiave).

locker ['lɔkə*] *n* armadietto.

locket ['lɔkɪt] *n* medaglione *m*.

lockjaw ['lɔkdʒɔ:] *n* tetano.

lockout ['lɔkaut] *n* (*INDUSTRY*) serrata.

locksmith ['lɔksmɪθ] *n* magnano.

lock-up ['lɔkʌp] *n* (*prison*) prigione *f*; (*cell*) guardina; (*also:* ~ **garage**) box *m inv*.

locomotive [ləukə'məutɪv] *n* locomotiva.

locum ['ləukəm] *n* (*MED*) medico sostituto.

locust ['ləukəst] *n* locusta.

lodge [lɔdʒ] *n* casetta, portineria; (*FREEMASONRY*) loggia ♦ *vi* (*person*): **to ~ (with)** essere a pensione (presso *or* da) ♦ *vt* (*appeal etc*) presentare, fare; **to ~ a complaint** presentare un reclamo; **to ~ (itself) in/between** piantarsi dentro/fra.

lodger ['lɔdʒə*] *n* affittuario/a; (*with room and meals*) pensionante *m/f*.

lodging ['lɔdʒɪŋ] *n* alloggio; *see also* **board**; **lodgings**.

lodging house *n* (*BRIT*) casa con camere in affitto.

lodgings ['lɔdʒɪŋz] *npl* camera d'affitto; camera ammobiliata.

loft [lɔft] *n* soffitta; (*AGR*) granaio; (*US*) appartamento ricavato da solaio (*or* granaio *etc*).

lofty ['lɔftɪ] *adj* alto(a); (*haughty*) altezzoso(a); (*sentiments, aims*) nobile.

log [lɔg] *n* (*of wood*) ceppo; (*book*) = **logbook** ♦ *n abbr* = **logarithm** ♦ *vt* registrare.

▶**log in, log on** *vi* (*COMPUT*) aprire una sessione (*con codice di riconoscimento*).

▶**log off, log out** *vi* (*COMPUT*) terminare una sessione.

logarithm ['lɔgərɪðm] *n* logaritmo.

logbook ['lɔgbuk] *n* (*NAUT, AVIAT*) diario di bordo; (*AUT*) libretto di circolazione; (*of lorry driver*) registro di viaggio; (*of events, movement of goods etc*) registro.

log cabin *n* capanna di tronchi.

log fire *n* fuoco di legna.

logger ['lɔgə*] *n* boscaiolo, taglialegna *m inv*.

loggerheads ['lɔgəhɛdz] *npl*: **at ~ (with)** ai ferri corti (con).

logic ['lɔdʒɪk] *n* logica.

logical ['lɔdʒɪkəl] *adj* logico(a).

logically ['lɔdʒɪkəlɪ] *adv* logicamente.

logistics [lɔ'dʒɪstɪks] *n* logistica.

logjam ['lɔgdʒæm] *n*: **to break the ~** superare l'impasse.

logo ['ləugəu] *n* logo *m inv*.

loin [lɔɪn] *n* (*CULIN*) lombata; **~s** *npl* reni *fpl*.

loin cloth *n* perizoma *m*.

loiter ['lɔɪtə*] *vi* attardarsi; **to ~ (about)** indugiare, bighellonare.

loll [lɔl] *vi* (*also:* ~ **about**) essere stravaccato(a).

lollipop ['lɔlɪpɔp] *n* lecca lecca *m inv*.

lollipop man, lollipop lady *n* (*BRIT*) *see boxed note*.

LOLLIPOP MAN/LADY

*In Gran Bretagna il **lollipop man** e la **lollipop lady** sono persone incaricate di regolare il traffico in prossimità delle scuole e di aiutare i bambini ad attraversare la strada; usano una paletta la cui forma ricorda quella di un lecca lecca, in inglese, appunto, "lollipop".*

---

lollop ['lɔləp] *vi* (*BRIT*) camminare (*or* correre) goffamente.

lolly ['lɔlɪ] *n* (*col*) lecca lecca *m inv*; (*also:* **ice ~**) ghiacciolo; (*money*) grana.

Lombardy ['lɔmbədɪ] *n* Lombardia.

London ['lʌndən] *n* Londra.

Londoner ['lʌndənə*] *n* londinese *m/f*.

lone [ləun] *adj* solitario(a).

loneliness ['ləunlɪnɪs] *n* solitudine.

lonely ['ləunlɪ] *adj* solitario(a); (*place*) isolato(a); **to feel ~** sentirsi solo(a).

lonely hearts *adj*: **~ ads, ~ column** messaggi *mpl* personali.

lone parent *n* (*unmarried: mother*) ragazza madre; (*: father*) ragazzo padre; (*divorced*) genitore *m* divorziato(a); (*widowed*) genitore rimasto vedovo.

loner ['ləunə*] *n* solitario/a.

lonesome ['ləunsəm] *adj* solo(a).

long [lɔŋ] *adj* lungo(a) ♦ *adv* a lungo, per molto tempo ♦ *n*: **the ~ and the short of it is that ...** (*fig*) a farla breve ... ♦ *vi*: **to ~ for sth/to do** desiderare qc/di fare; non veder l'ora di aver qc/di fare; **he had ~ understood that ...** aveva capito da molto tempo che ...; **how ~ is this river/course?** quanto è lungo questo fiume/corso?; **6 metres ~** lungo 6 metri; **6 months ~** che dura 6 mesi, di 6 mesi; **all night ~** tutta la notte; **he no ~er comes** non viene più; **~ before** molto tempo prima; **before ~** (+ *future*) presto, fra poco; (+ *past*) poco tempo dopo; **~ ago** molto tempo fa; **don't be ~!** faccia presto!; **I shan't be ~** non ne avrò per molto; **at ~ last** finalmente; **in the ~ run** alla fin fine; **so** *or* **as ~ as** sempre che + *sub*.

long-distance [lɔŋ'dɪstəns] *adj* (*race*) di

fondo; (*call*) interurbano(a).
long-haired ['lɔŋ'hɛəd] *adj* (*person*) dai
capelli lunghi; (*animal*) dal pelo lungo.
longhand ['lɔŋhænd] *n* scrittura normale.
longing ['lɔŋɪŋ] *n* desiderio, voglia, brama
♦ *adj* di desiderio; pieno(a) di nostalgia.
longingly ['lɔŋɪŋlɪ] *adv* con desiderio.
longitude ['lɔŋgɪtjuːd] *n* longitudine *f*.
long johns [-dʒɔnz] *npl* mutande *fpl* lunghe.
long jump *n* salto in lungo.
long-lost ['lɔŋlɔst] *adj* perduto(a) da tempo.
long-playing ['lɔŋpleɪɪŋ] *adj*: ~ **record (LP)**
(disco) 33 giri *m inv*.
long-range [lɔŋ'reɪndʒ] *adj* a lunga portata;
(*weather forecast*) a lungo termine.
longshoreman ['lɔŋʃɔːmən] *n* (*US*)
scaricatore *m* (di porto), portuale *m*.
long-sighted [lɔŋ'saɪtɪd] *adj* (*BRIT*) presbite;
(*fig*) lungimirante.
long-standing ['lɔŋstændɪŋ] *adj* di vecchia
data.
long-suffering [lɔŋ'sʌfərɪŋ] *adj*
estremamente paziente; infinitamente
tollerante.
long-term ['lɔŋtəːm] *adj* a lungo termine.
long wave *n* (*RADIO*) onde *fpl* lunghe.
long-winded [lɔŋ'wɪndɪd] *adj* prolisso(a),
interminabile.
loo [luː] *n* (*BRIT col*) W.C. *m inv*, cesso.
loofah ['luːfə] *n* luffa.
look [luk] *vi* guardare; (*seem*) sembrare,
parere; (*building etc*): **to ~ south/on to
the sea** dare a sud/sul mare ♦ *n* sguardo;
(*appearance*) aspetto, aria; ~**s** *npl* aspetto;
bellezza; **to ~ like** assomigliare a; **to ~
ahead** guardare avanti; **it ~s about 4
metres long** sarà lungo un 4 metri; **it ~s
all right to me** a me pare che vada bene;
to have a ~ at sth dare un'occhiata a qc;
to have a ~ for sth cercare qc.
►**look after** *vt fus* occuparsi di, prendersi
cura di; (*keep an eye on*) guardare, badare
a.
►**look around** *vi* guardarsi intorno.
►**look at** *vt fus* guardare.
►**look back** *vi*: **to ~ back at sth/sb** voltarsi
a guardare qc/qn; **to ~ back on** (*event,
period*) ripensare a.
►**look down on** *vt fus* (*fig*) guardare
dall'alto, disprezzare.
►**look for** *vt fus* cercare.
►**look forward to** *vt fus* non veder l'ora di;
I'm not ~ing forward to it non ne ho
nessuna voglia; ~**ing forward to hearing
from you** (*in letter*) aspettando tue notizie.
►**look in** *vi*: **to ~ in on sb** (*visit*) fare un
salto da qn.
►**look into** *vt fus* (*matter, possibility*)

esaminare.
►**look on** *vi* fare da spettatore.
►**look out** *vi* (*beware*): **to ~ out (for)** stare
in guardia (per).
►**look out for** *vt fus* cercare; (*watch out for*):
to ~ out for sb/sth guardare se arriva
qn/qc.
►**look over** *vt* (*essay*) dare un'occhiata a,
riguardare; (*town, building*) vedere;
(*person*) esaminare.
►**look round** *vi* (*turn*) girarsi, voltarsi; (*in
shops*) dare un'occhiata; **to ~ round for
sth** guardarsi intorno cercando qc.
►**look through** *vt fus* (*papers, book*)
scorrere; (*telescope*) guardare
attraverso.
►**look to** *vt fus* stare attento(a) a; (*rely on*)
contare su.
►**look up** *vi* alzare gli occhi; (*improve*)
migliorare ♦ *vt* (*word*) cercare; (*friend*)
andare a trovare.
►**look up to** *vt fus* avere rispetto per.
look-out ['lukaut] *n* posto d'osservazione;
guardia; **to be on the ~ (for)** stare in
guardia (per).
look-up table ['lukʌp-] *n* (*COMPUT*) tabella
di consultazione.
loom [luːm] *n* telaio ♦ *vi* sorgere; (*fig*)
minacciare.
loony ['luːnɪ] *adj*, *n* (*col*) pazzo(a).
loop [luːp] *n* cappio; (*COMPUT*) anello.
loophole ['luːphəul] *n* via d'uscita;
scappatoia.
loose [luːs] *adj* (*knot*) sciolto(a); (*screw*)
allentato(a); (*stone*) cadente; (*clothes*)
ampio(a), largo(a); (*animal*) in libertà,
scappato(a); (*life, morals*) dissoluto(a);
(*discipline*) allentato(a); (*thinking*) poco
rigoroso(a), vago(a) ♦ *vt* (*untie*)
sciogliere; (*slacken*) allentare; (*free*)
liberare; (*BRIT: arrow*) scoccare; ~
connection (*ELEC*) filo che fa contatto; **to
be at a ~ end** *or* (*US*) **at ~ ends** (*fig*) non
saper che fare; **to tie up ~ ends** (*fig*)
avere ancora qualcosa da sistemare.
loose change *n* spiccioli *mpl*, moneta.
loose-fitting ['luːsfɪtɪŋ] *adj* ampio(a).
loose-leaf ['luːsliːf] *adj*: ~ **binder** *or* **folder**
raccoglitore *m*.
loose-limbed [luːs'lɪmd] *adj* snodato(a),
agile.
loosely ['luːslɪ] *adv* lentamente;
approssimativamente.
loosely-knit ['luːslɪ'nɪt] *adj* non
rigidamente strutturato(a).
loosen ['luːsn] *vt* sciogliere.
►**loosen up** *vi* (*before game*) sciogliere i
muscoli, scaldarsi; (*col: relax*) rilassarsi.

loot [luːt] n bottino ♦ vt saccheggiare.
looter ['luːtə*] n saccheggiatore/trice.
looting ['luːtɪŋ] n saccheggio.
lop [lɔp] vt (also: ~ **off**) tagliare via, recidere.
lop-sided ['lɔp'saɪdɪd] adj non equilibrato(a), asimmetrico(a).
lord [lɔːd] n signore m; **L~ Smith** lord Smith; **the L~** (REL) il Signore; **the (House of) L~s** (BRIT) la Camera dei Lord.
lordly ['lɔːdlɪ] adj nobile, maestoso(a); (arrogant) altero(a).
lordship ['lɔːdʃɪp] n (BRIT): **your L~** Sua Eccellenza.
lore [lɔː*] n tradizioni fpl.
lorry ['lɔrɪ] n (BRIT) camion m inv.
lorry driver n (BRIT) camionista m.
lose, pt, pp **lost** [luːz, lɔst] vt perdere; (pursuers) distanziare ♦ vi perdere; **to ~ (time)** (clock) ritardare; **to ~ no time (in doing sth)** non perdere tempo (a fare qc); **to get lost** (person) perdersi, smarrirsi; (object) andare perso or perduto.
loser ['luːzə*] n perdente m/f; **to be a good/ bad ~** saper/non saper perdere.
loss [lɔs] n perdita; **to cut one's ~es** rimetterci il meno possibile; **to make a ~** subire una perdita; **to sell sth at a ~** vendere qc in perdita; **to be at a ~** essere perplesso(a); **to be at a ~ to explain sth** non saper come fare a spiegare qc.
loss adjuster n (INSURANCE) responsabile m/f della valutazione dei danni.
loss leader n (COMM) articolo a prezzo ridottissimo per attirare la clientela.
lost [lɔst] pt, pp of **lose** ♦ adj perduto(a); **~ in thought** immerso or perso nei propri pensieri; **~ and found property** n (US) oggetti mpl smarriti; **~ and found** n (US) ufficio oggetti smarriti.
lost property n (BRIT) oggetti mpl smarriti; **~ office** or **department** ufficio oggetti smarriti.
lot [lɔt] n (at auctions) lotto; (destiny) destino, sorte f; **the ~** tutto(a) quanto(a); tutti(e) quanti(e); **a ~** molto; **a ~ of** una gran quantità, un sacco di; **~s of** molto(a); **to draw ~s (for sth)** tirare a sorte (per qc).
lotion ['ləuʃən] n lozione f.
lottery ['lɔtərɪ] n lotteria.
loud [laud] adj forte, alto(a); (gaudy) vistoso(a), sgargiante ♦ adv (speak etc) forte; **out ~** ad alta voce.
loudhailer [laud'heɪlə*] n (BRIT) portavoce m inv.
loudly ['laudlɪ] adv fortemente, ad alta voce.

loudspeaker [laud'spiːkə*] n altoparlante m.
lounge [laundʒ] n salotto, soggiorno; (of hotel) salone m; (of airport) sala d'attesa ♦ vi oziare; starsene colle mani in mano.
lounge bar n bar m inv con servizio a tavolino.
lounge suit n (BRIT) completo da uomo.
louse [laus] n (pl **lice**) pidocchio.
▶**louse up** vt (col) rovinare.
lousy ['lauzɪ] adj (fig) orrendo(a), schifoso(a).
lout [laut] n zoticone m.
louvre, (US) **louver** ['luːvə*] adj (door, window) con apertura a gelosia.
lovable ['lʌvəbl] adj simpatico(a), carino(a); amabile.
love [lʌv] n amore m ♦ vt amare; voler bene a; **to ~ to do: I ~ to do** mi piace fare; **I'd ~ to come** mi piacerebbe molto venire; **to be in ~ with** essere innamorato(a) di; **to fall in ~ with** innamorarsi di; **to make ~** fare l'amore; **~ at first sight** amore a prima vista, colpo di fulmine; **to send one's ~ to sb** mandare i propri saluti a qn; **~ from Anne, ~, Anne** con affetto, Anne; **"15 ~"** (TENNIS) "15 a zero".
love affair n relazione f.
love child n figlio/a dell'amore.
loved ones [lʌvd-] npl: **my ~** i miei cari.
love-hate relationship ['lʌv'heɪt-] n rapporto amore-odio inv.
love letter n lettera d'amore.
love life n vita sentimentale.
lovely ['lʌvlɪ] adj bello(a); (delicious: smell, meal) buono(a); **we had a ~ time** ci siamo divertiti molto.
lover ['lʌvə*] n amante m/f; (amateur): **a ~ of** un(un')amante di; un(un')appassionato(a) di.
lovesick ['lʌvsɪk] adj malato(a) d'amore.
lovesong ['lʌvsɔŋ] n canzone f d'amore.
loving ['lʌvɪŋ] adj affettuoso(a), amoroso(a), tenero(a).
low [ləu] adj basso(a) ♦ adv in basso ♦ n (METEOR) depressione f ♦ vi (cow) muggire; **to feel ~** sentirsi giù; **to reach a new** or **an all-time ~** toccare il livello più basso or il minimo; **to turn (down) ~** vt abbassare.
low-alcohol [ləu'ælkəhɔl] adj a basso contenuto alcolico.
lowbrow ['ləubrau] adj (person) senza pretese intellettuali.
low-calorie ['ləu'kælərɪ] adj a basso contenuto calorico.
low-cut ['ləukʌt] adj (dress) scollato(a).
low-down ['ləudaun] adj (mean) ignobile

♦ *n* (*col*): **he gave me the ~ on it** mi ha messo al corrente dei fatti.

lower ['ləuə*] *adj, adv comparative of* **low** ♦ *vt* (*gen*) calare; (*reduce: price*) abbassare, ridurre; (*resistance*) indebolire.

lower case *n* minuscolo.

low-fat ['ləu'fæt] *adj* magro(a).

low-key ['ləu'ki:] *adj* moderato(a); (*operation*) condotto(a) con discrezione.

lowland ['ləulənd] *n* bassopiano, pianura.

low-level ['ləulɛvl] *adj* a basso livello; (*flying*) a bassa quota.

low-loader ['ləuləudə*] *n* camion *m* a pianale basso.

lowly ['ləulɪ] *adj* umile, modesto(a).

low-lying [ləu'laɪŋ] *adj* a basso livello.

low-paid [ləu'peɪd] *adj* mal pagato(a).

low-rise ['ləuraɪz] *adj* di altezza contenuta.

low-tech ['ləu'tɛk] *adj* a basso contenuto tecnologico.

loyal ['lɔɪəl] *adj* fedele, leale.

loyalist ['lɔɪəlɪst] *n* lealista *m/f*.

loyalty ['lɔɪəltɪ] *n* fedeltà, lealtà.

loyalty card *n carta che offre sconti a clienti abituali.*

lozenge ['lɔzɪndʒ] *n* (*MED*) pastiglia; (*GEOM*) losanga.

LP *n abbr* (= *long-playing record*) LP *m*.

LPG *n abbr* (= *liquefied petroleum gas*) GPL (= *gas di petrolio liquefatto*).

L-plate *n* ≈ contrassegno P principiante; *see boxed note.*

LPN *n abbr* (*US*: = *Licensed Practical Nurse*) ≈ infermiera diplomata.

LRAM *n abbr* (*BRIT*: = *Licentiate of the Royal Academy of Music*) *specializzazione dopo la laurea.*

LSD *n abbr* (= *lysergic acid diethylamide*) L.S.D. *m*; (*BRIT*: = *pounds, shillings and pence*) *sistema monetario in vigore in Gran Bretagna fino al 1971.*

LSE *n abbr* = *London School of Economics.*

LT *abbr* (*ELEC*: = *low tension*) B.T.

Lt. *abbr* (= *lieutenant*) Ten.

Ltd *abbr* (*COMM*) = **limited**.

lubricant ['lu:brɪkənt] *n* lubrificante *m*.

lubricate ['lu:brɪkeɪt] *vt* lubrificare.

lucid ['lu:sɪd] *adj* lucido(a).

lucidity [lu:'sɪdɪtɪ] *n* lucidità.

luck [lʌk] *n* fortuna, sorte *f*; **bad ~** sfortuna, mala sorte; **good ~** (buona) fortuna; **to be in ~** essere fortunato(a); **to be out of ~** essere sfortunato(a).

luckily ['lʌkɪlɪ] *adv* fortunatamente, per fortuna.

luckless ['lʌklɪs] *adj* sventurato(a).

lucky ['lʌkɪ] *adj* fortunato(a); (*number etc*) che porta fortuna.

lucrative ['lu:krətɪv] *adj* lucrativo(a), lucroso(a), profittevole.

ludicrous ['lu:dɪkrəs] *adj* ridicolo(a), assurdo(a).

ludo ['lu:dəu] *n* ≈ gioco dell'oca.

lug [lʌg] *vt* trascinare.

luggage ['lʌgɪdʒ] *n* bagagli *mpl*.

luggage rack *n* portabagagli *m inv*.

luggage van, (*US***) luggage car** *n* (*RAIL*) bagagliaio.

lugubrious [lu'gu:brɪəs] *adj* lugubre.

lukewarm ['lu:kwɔ:m] *adj* tiepido(a).

lull [lʌl] *n* intervallo di calma ♦ *vt* (*child*) cullare; (*person, fear*) acquietare, calmare.

lullaby ['lʌləbaɪ] *n* ninnananna.

lumbago [lʌm'beɪgəu] *n* lombaggine *f*.

lumber ['lʌmbə*] *n* roba vecchia ♦ *vt* (*BRIT col*): **to ~ sb with sth/sb** affibbiare *or* rifilare qc/qn a qn ♦ *vi* (*also*: ~ **about**, ~ **along**) muoversi pesantemente.

lumberjack ['lʌmbədʒæk] *n* boscaiolo.

lumber room *n* (*BRIT*) sgabuzzino.

lumber yard *n* segheria.

luminous ['lu:mɪnəs] *adj* luminoso(a).

lump [lʌmp] *n* pezzo; (*in sauce*) grumo; (*swelling*) gonfiore *m* ♦ *vt* (*also*: ~ **together**) riunire, mettere insieme.

lump sum *n* somma globale.

lumpy ['lʌmpɪ] *adj* (*sauce*) grumoso(a).

lunacy ['lu:nəsɪ] *n* demenza, follia, pazzia.

lunar ['lu:nə*] *adj* lunare.

lunatic ['lu:nətɪk] *adj, n* pazzo(a), matto(a).

lunatic asylum *n* manicomio.

lunch [lʌntʃ] *n* pranzo, colazione *f*; **to invite sb to** *or* **for ~** invitare qn a pranzo *or* a colazione.

lunch break *n* intervallo del pranzo.

luncheon ['lʌntʃən] *n* pranzo.

luncheon meat *n* ≈ mortadella.

luncheon voucher *n* buono *m* pasto *inv*.

lunch hour *n* = **lunch break**.

lunchtime ['lʌntʃtaɪm] *n* ora di pranzo.

lung [lʌŋ] *n* polmone *m*.

lung cancer *n* cancro del polmone.

lunge [lʌndʒ] *vi* (*also*: ~ **forward**) fare un balzo in avanti; **to ~ at sb** balzare su qn.

lupin ['luːpɪn] *n* lupino.

lurch [ləːtʃ] *vi* vacillare, barcollare ♦ *n* scatto improvviso; **to leave sb in the ~** piantare in asso qn.

lure [luə*] *n* richiamo; lusinga ♦ *vt* attirare (con l'inganno).

lurid ['luərɪd] *adj* sgargiante; (*details etc*) impressionante.

lurk [ləːk] *vi* stare in agguato.

luscious ['lʌʃəs] *adj* succulento(a); delizioso(a).

lush [lʌʃ] *adj* lussureggiante.

lust [lʌst] *n* lussuria; cupidigia; desiderio; (*fig*): ~ **for** sete *f* di.

►**lust after** *vt fus* bramare, desiderare.

luster ['lʌstə*] *n* (*US*) = **lustre**.

lustful ['lʌstful] *adj* lascivo(a), voglioso(a).

lustre, (*US*) **luster** ['lʌstə*] *n* lustro, splendore *m*.

lusty ['lʌstɪ] *adj* vigoroso(a), robusto(a).

lute [luːt] *n* liuto.

Luxembourg ['lʌksəmbəːg] *n* (*state*) Lussemburgo *m*; (*city*) Lussemburgo *f*.

luxuriant [lʌg'zjuərɪənt] *adj* lussureggiante.

luxurious [lʌg'zjuərɪəs] *adj* sontuoso(a), di lusso.

luxury ['lʌkʃərɪ] *n* lusso ♦ *cpd* di lusso.

LV *n abbr* (*BRIT*) = **luncheon voucher**.

LW *abbr* (*RADIO*: = *long wave*) O.L.

Lycra ® ['laɪkrə] *n* lycra ® *f inv*.

lying ['laɪɪŋ] *n* bugie *fpl*, menzogne *fpl* ♦ *adj* (*statement, story*) falso(a); (*person*) bugiardo(a).

lynch [lɪntʃ] *vt* linciare.

lynx [lɪŋks] *n* lince *f*.

Lyons ['laɪənz] *n* Lione *f*.

lyre ['laɪə*] *n* lira.

lyric ['lɪrɪk] *adj* lirico(a); ~**s** *npl* (*of song*) parole *fpl*.

lyrical ['lɪrɪkl] *adj* lirico(a).

lyricism ['lɪrɪsɪzəm] *n* lirismo.

M m

M, m [ɛm] *n* (*letter*) M, m *f or m inv*; **M for Mary,** (*US*) **M for Mike** ≈ M come Milano.

M *n abbr* (*BRIT*: = *motorway*): **the M8** ≈ l'A8 ♦ *abbr* (= *medium*) taglia media.

m *abbr* (= *metre*) m; = **mile; million**.

MA *n abbr* (*SCOL*) *see* **Master of Arts**; (*US*) = *military academy* ♦ (*US*) = *Massachusetts*.

mac [mæk] *n* (*BRIT*) impermeabile *m*.

macabre [mə'kɑːbrə] *adj* macabro(a).

macaroni [mækə'rəunɪ] *n* maccheroni *mpl*.

macaroon [mækə'ruːn] *n* amaretto (*biscotto*).

mace [meɪs] *n* mazza; (*spice*) macis *m or f*.

Macedonia [mæsɪ'dəunɪə] *n* Macedonia.

Macedonian [mæsɪ'dəunɪən] *adj* macedone ♦ *n* macedone *m/f*; (*LING*) macedone *m*.

machinations [mækɪ'neɪʃənz] *npl* macchinazioni *fpl*, intrighi *mpl*.

machine [mə'ʃiːn] *n* macchina ♦ *vt* (*dress etc*) cucire a macchina; (*TECH*) lavorare (a macchina).

machine code *n* (*COMPUT*) codice *m* di macchina, codice assoluto.

machine gun *n* mitragliatrice *f*.

machine language *n* (*COMPUT*) linguaggio *m* macchina *inv*.

machine-readable [mə'ʃiːnriːdəbl] *adj* (*COMPUT*) leggibile dalla macchina.

machinery [mə'ʃiːnərɪ] *n* macchinario, macchine *fpl*; (*fig*) macchina.

machine shop *n* officina meccanica.

machine tool *n* macchina utensile.

machine washable *adj* lavabile in lavatrice.

machinist [mə'ʃiːnɪst] *n* macchinista *m/f*.

macho ['mætʃəu] *adj* macho *inv*.

mackerel ['mækrəl] *n* (*pl inv*) sgombro.

mackintosh ['mækɪntɔʃ] *n* impermeabile *m*.

macro... ['mækrəu] *prefix* macro....

macroeconomics ['mækrəuiːkə'nɔmɪks] *n* macroeconomia.

mad [mæd] *adj* matto(a), pazzo(a); (*foolish*) sciocco(a); (*angry*) furioso(a); **to go ~** impazzire, diventar matto; ~ **(at or with sb)** furibondo(a) (con qn); **to be ~ (keen) about** or **on sth** (*col*) andar pazzo or matto per qc.

madam ['mædəm] *n* signora; **M~ Chairman** Signora Presidentessa.

madcap ['mædkæp] *adj* (*col*) senza senso, assurdo(a).

mad cow disease *n* encefalite *f* bovina spongiforme.

madden ['mædn] *vt* fare infuriare.

maddening ['mædnɪŋ] *adj* esasperante.

made [meɪd] *pt, pp* of **make**.

Madeira [mə'dɪərə] *n* (*GEO*) Madera; (*wine*) madera *m*.

made-to-measure ['meɪdtə'mɛʒə*] *adj* (*BRIT*) fatto(a) su misura.

madhouse ['mædhaus] *n* (*also fig*) manicomio.

madly ['mædlɪ] *adv* follemente; (*love*) alla follia.

madman ['mædmən] *n* pazzo, alienato.

madness ['mædnɪs] *n* pazzia.
Madrid [mə'drɪd] *n* Madrid *f*.
Mafia ['mæfɪə] *n* mafia *f*.
mag. [mæg] *n abbr* (*BRIT col*) = **magazine**
(*PRESS*).
magazine [mægə'ziːn] *n* (*PRESS*) rivista;
(*MIL: store*) magazzino, deposito; (*of
firearm*) caricatore *m*.
maggot ['mægət] *n* baco, verme *m*.
magic ['mædʒɪk] *n* magia ♦ *adj* magico(a).
magical ['mædʒɪkəl] *adj* magico(a).
magician [mə'dʒɪʃən] *n* mago/a.
magistrate ['mædʒɪstreɪt] *n* magistrato;
giudice *m/f*.
magistrates' court *n see* **crown court**.
magnanimous [mæg'nænɪməs] *adj*
magnanimo(a).
magnate ['mægneɪt] *n* magnate *m*.
magnesium [mæg'niːzɪəm] *n* magnesio.
magnet ['mægnɪt] *n* magnete *m*, calamita.
magnetic [mæg'netɪk] *adj* magnetico(a).
magnetic disk *n* (*COMPUT*) disco
magnetico.
magnetic tape *n* nastro magnetico.
magnetism ['mægnɪtɪzəm] *n* magnetismo.
magnification [mægnɪfɪ'keɪʃən] *n*
ingrandimento.
magnificence [mæg'nɪfɪsns] *n*
magnificenza.
magnificent [mæg'nɪfɪsnt] *adj* magnifico(a).
magnify ['mægnɪfaɪ] *vt* ingrandire.
magnifying glass ['mægnɪfaɪɪŋ-] *n* lente *f*
d'ingrandimento.
magnitude ['mægnɪtjuːd] *n* grandezza;
importanza.
magnolia [mæg'nəʊlɪə] *n* magnolia.
magpie ['mægpaɪ] *n* gazza.
mahogany [mə'hɔgənɪ] *n* mogano ♦ *cpd* di
or in mogano.
maid [meɪd] *n* domestica; (*in hotel*)
cameriera; **old ~** (*pej*) vecchia zitella.
maiden ['meɪdn] *n* fanciulla ♦ *adj* (*aunt etc*)
nubile; (*speech, voyage*) inaugurale.
maiden name *n* nome *m* nubile *or* da
ragazza.
mail [meɪl] *n* posta ♦ *vt* spedire (per posta);
by ~ per posta.
mailbox ['meɪlbɔks] *n* (*US*) cassetta delle
lettere; (*COMPUT*) mailbox *f inv*.
mailing list ['meɪlɪŋ-] *n* elenco d'indirizzi.
mailman ['meɪlmæn] *n* (*US*) portalettere *m
inv*, postino.
mail-order ['meɪlɔːdə*] *n* vendita (*or*
acquisto) per corrispondenza ♦ *cpd*: **~
firm** *or* **house** ditta di vendita per
corrispondenza.
mailshot ['meɪlʃɔt] *n* mailing *m inv*.
mail train *n* treno postale.

mail truck *n* (*US AUT*) = **mail van**.
mail van *n* (*BRIT: AUT*) furgone *m* postale;
(*:RAIL*) vagone *m* postale.
maim [meɪm] *vt* mutilare.
main [meɪn] *adj* principale ♦ *n* (*pipe*)
conduttura principale; **the ~s** (*ELEC*) la
linea principale; **~s operated** *adj* che
funziona a elettricità; **in the ~** nel
complesso, nell'insieme.
main course *n* (*CULIN*) piatto principale,
piatto forte.
mainframe ['meɪnfreɪm] *n* (*also*: ~
computer) mainframe *m inv*.
mainland ['meɪnlənd] *n* continente *m*.
mainline ['meɪnlaɪn] *adj* (*RAIL*) della linea
principale ♦ *vb* (*drugs slang*) *vt* bucarsi di
♦ *vi* bucarsi.
main line *n* (*RAIL*) linea principale.
mainly ['meɪnlɪ] *adv* principalmente,
soprattutto.
main road *n* strada principale.
mainstay ['meɪnsteɪ] *n* (*fig*) sostegno
principale.
mainstream ['meɪnstriːm] *n* (*fig*) corrente *f*
principale.
maintain [meɪn'teɪn] *vt* mantenere; (*affirm*)
sostenere; **to ~ that ...** sostenere che ....
maintenance ['meɪntənəns] *n*
manutenzione *f*; (*alimony*) alimenti *mpl*.
maintenance contract *n* contratto di
manutenzione.
maintenance order *n* (*LAW*) obbligo degli
alimenti.
maisonette [meɪzə'net] *n* (*BRIT*)
appartamento a due piani.
maize [meɪz] *n* granturco, mais *m*.
Maj. *abbr* (*MIL*) = **major**.
majestic [mə'dʒestɪk] *adj* maestoso(a).
majesty ['mædʒɪstɪ] *n* maestà *f inv*.
major ['meɪdʒə*] *n* (*MIL*) maggiore *m* ♦ *adj*
(*greater, MUS*) maggiore; (*in importance*)
principale, importante ♦ *vi* (*US SCOL*): **to
~** (**in**) specializzarsi (in); **a ~ operation**
(*MED*) una grossa operazione.
Majorca [mə'jɔːkə] *n* Maiorca.
major general *n* (*MIL*) generale *m* di
divisione.
majority [mə'dʒɔrɪtɪ] *n* maggioranza ♦ *cpd*
(*verdict*) maggioritario(a).
majority holding *n* (*COMM*): **to have a ~**
essere maggiore azionista.
make [meɪk] *vt* (*pt, pp* **made** [meɪd]) fare;
(*manufacture*) fare, fabbricare; (*cause to
be*): **to ~ sb sad** *etc* rendere qn triste *etc*;
(*force*): **to ~ sb do sth** costringere qn a
fare qc, far fare qc a qn; (*equal*): **2 and 2
~ 4** 2 più 2 fa 4 ♦ *n* fabbricazione *f*;
(*brand*) marca; **to ~ it** (*in time etc*)

arrivare; (*succeed*) farcela; **what time do you ~ it?** che ora fai?; **to ~ good** *vi* (*succeed*) aver successo ♦ *vt* (*deficit*) colmare; (*losses*) compensare; **to ~ do with** arrangiarsi con.

►**make for** *vt fus* (*place*) avviarsi verso.

►**make off** *vi* svignarsela.

►**make out** *vt* (*write out*) scrivere; (*understand*) capire; (*see*) distinguere; (: *numbers*) decifrare; (*claim, imply*): **to ~ out (that)** voler far credere (che); **to ~ out a case for sth** presentare delle valide ragioni in favore di qc.

►**make over** *vt* (*assign*): **to ~ over (to)** passare (a), trasferire (a).

►**make up** *vt* (*invent*) inventare; (*parcel*) fare ♦ *vi* conciliarsi; (*with cosmetics*) truccarsi; **to be made up of** essere composto di *or* formato da.

►**make up for** *vt fus* compensare; ricuperare.

make-believe ['meɪkbɪliːv] *n*: **a world of ~** un mondo di favole; **it's just ~** è tutta un'invenzione.

maker ['meɪkə*] *n* fabbricante *m*; creatore/trice, autore/trice.

makeshift ['meɪkʃɪft] *adj* improvvisato(a).

make-up ['meɪkʌp] *n* trucco.

make-up bag *n* borsa del trucco.

make-up remover *n* struccatore *m*.

making ['meɪkɪŋ] *n* (*fig*): **in the ~** in formazione; **he has the ~s of an actor** ha la stoffa dell'attore.

maladjusted [mælə'dʒʌstɪd] *adj* disadattato(a).

maladroit [mælə'drɔɪt] *adj* maldestro(a).

malaise [mæ'leɪz] *n* malessere *m*.

malaria [mə'lɛərɪə] *n* malaria.

Malawi [mə'lɑːwɪ] *n* Malawi *m*.

Malay [mə'leɪ] *adj* malese ♦ *n* malese *m/f*; (*LING*) malese *m*.

Malaya [mə'leɪə] *n* Malesia.

Malayan [mə'leɪən] *adj, n* = **Malay**.

Malaysia [mə'leɪzɪə] *n* Malaysia.

Malaysian [mə'leɪzɪən] *adj, n* malaysiano(a).

Maldives ['mɔːldaɪvz] *npl*: **the ~** le (isole) Maldive.

male [meɪl] *n* (*BIO, ELEC*) maschio ♦ *adj* (*gen, sex*) maschile; (*animal, child*) maschio(a); **~ and female students** studenti e studentesse.

male chauvinist *n* maschilista *m*.

male nurse *n* infermiere *m*.

malevolence [mə'lɛvələns] *n* malevolenza.

malevolent [mə'lɛvələnt] *adj* malevolo(a).

malfunction [mæl'fʌŋkʃən] *n* funzione *f* difettosa.

malice ['mælɪs] *n* malevolenza.

malicious [mə'lɪʃəs] *adj* malevolo(a); (*LAW*) doloso(a).

malign [mə'laɪn] *vt* malignare su; calunniare.

malignant [mə'lɪgnənt] *adj* (*MED*) maligno(a).

malingerer [mə'lɪŋgərə*] *n* scansafatiche *m/f inv*.

mall [mɔːl] *n* (*also:* **shopping ~**) centro commerciale.

malleable ['mælɪəbl] *adj* malleabile.

mallet ['mælɪt] *n* maglio.

malnutrition [mælnjuː'trɪʃən] *n* denutrizione *f*.

malpractice [mæl'præktɪs] *n* prevaricazione *f*; negligenza.

malt [mɔːlt] *n* malto ♦ *cpd* (*whisky*) di malto.

Malta ['mɔːltə] *n* Malta.

Maltese [mɔːl'tiːz] *adj, n* (*pl inv*) maltese (*m/f*); (*LING*) maltese *m*.

maltreat [mæl'triːt] *vt* maltrattare.

mammal ['mæml] *n* mammifero.

mammoth ['mæməθ] *n* mammut *m inv* ♦ *adj* enorme, gigantesco(a).

man [mæn] *n* (*pl* **men**) uomo; (*CHESS*) pezzo; (*DRAUGHTS*) pedina ♦ *vt* fornire d'uomini; stare a; essere di servizio a.

Man. *abbr* (*Canada*) = Manitoba.

manacles ['mænəklz] *npl* manette *fpl*.

manage ['mænɪdʒ] *vi* farcela ♦ *vt* (*be in charge of*) occuparsi di; (*shop, restaurant*) gestire; **to ~ without sth/sb** fare a meno di qc/qn; **to ~ to do sth** riuscire a far qc.

manageable ['mænɪdʒəbl] *adj* maneggevole; (*task etc*) fattibile.

management ['mænɪdʒmənt] *n* amministrazione *f*, direzione *f*; gestione *f*; (*persons: of business, firm*) dirigenti *mpl*; (: *of hotel, shop, theatre*) direzione *f*; **"under new ~"** "sotto nuova gestione".

management accounting *n* contabilità di gestione.

management buyout *n* acquisto di una società da parte dei suoi dirigenti.

management consultant *n* consulente *m/f* aziendale.

manager ['mænɪdʒə*] *n* direttore *m*; (*of shop, restaurant*) gerente *m*; (*of artist*) manager *m inv*; **sales ~** direttore *m* delle vendite.

manageress [mænɪdʒə'rɛs] *n* direttrice *f*; gerente *f*.

managerial [mænə'dʒɪərɪəl] *adj* dirigenziale.

managing director (MD) ['mænɪdʒɪŋ-] *n* amministratore *m* delegato.

Mancunian [mæŋ'kjuːnɪən] *adj* di Manchester ♦ *n* abitante *m/f* di

Manchester; originario/a di Manchester.
mandarin ['mændərɪn] n (*person, fruit*)
mandarino.
mandate ['mændeɪt] n mandato.
mandatory ['mændətərɪ] *adj*
obbligatorio(a); ingiuntivo(a).
mandolin(e) ['mændəlɪn] n mandolino.
mane [meɪn] n criniera.
maneuver [mə'nuːvə*] *etc* (*US*)
= **manoeuvre** *etc*.
manful ['mænful] *adj* coraggioso(a),
valoroso(a).
manfully ['mænfəlɪ] *adv* valorosamente.
manganese [mæŋgə'niːz] n manganese *m*.
mangetout ['mɔnʒ'tuː] n pisello dolce,
taccola.
mangle ['mæŋgl] *vt* straziare; mutilare ♦ *n*
strizzatoio.
mango, ~**es** ['mæŋgəu] n mango.
mangrove ['mæŋgrəuv] n mangrovia.
mangy ['meɪndʒɪ] *adj* rognoso(a).
manhandle ['mænhændl] *vt* (*treat roughly*)
malmenare; (*move by hand: goods*)
spostare a mano.
manhole ['mænhəul] n botola stradale.
manhood ['mænhud] n età virile; virilità.
man-hour ['mænauə*] n ora di lavoro.
manhunt ['mænhʌnt] n caccia all'uomo.
mania ['meɪnɪə] n mania.
maniac ['meɪnɪæk] n maniaco/a.
manic ['mænɪk] *adj* maniacale.
manic-depressive ['mænɪkdɪ'prɛsɪv] *adj*
maniaco-depressivo(a) ♦ *n* persona
affetta da mania depressiva.
manicure ['mænɪkjuə*] n manicure *f inv*.
manicure set n trousse *f inv* della
manicure.
manifest ['mænɪfɛst] *vt* manifestare ♦ *adj*
manifesto(a), palese ♦ *n* (*AVIAT, NAUT*)
manifesto.
manifestation [mænɪfɛs'teɪʃən] n
manifestazione *f*.
manifesto [mænɪ'fɛstəu] n manifesto.
manifold ['mænɪfəuld] *adj* molteplice ♦ *n*
(*AUT etc*): **exhaust** ~ collettore *m* di
scarico.
Manila [mə'nɪlə] n Manila.
manil(l)a [mə'nɪlə] *adj* (*paper, envelope*)
manilla *inv*.
manipulate [mə'nɪpjuleɪt] *vt* (*tool*)
maneggiare; (*controls*) azionare; (*limb,
facts*) manipolare.
manipulation [mənɪpju'leɪʃən] n
maneggiare *m*; capacità di azionare;
manipolazione *f*.
mankind [mæn'kaɪnd] n umanità, genere *m*
umano.
manliness ['mænlɪnɪs] n virilità.

manly ['mænlɪ] *adj* virile; coraggioso(a).
man-made ['mæn'meɪd] *adj* sintetico(a);
artificiale.
manna ['mænə] n manna.
mannequin ['mænɪkɪn] n (*dummy*)
manichino; (*fashion model*) indossatrice *f*.
manner ['mænə*] n maniera, modo; ~**s** *npl*
maniere *fpl*; (**good**) ~**s** buona educazione
f, buone maniere; **bad** ~**s** maleducazione
f; **all** ~ **of** ogni sorta di.
mannerism ['mænərɪzəm] n vezzo, tic *m inv*.
mannerly ['mænəlɪ] *adj* educato(a), civile.
manoeuvrable, (*US*) **maneuverable**
[mə'nuːvrəbl] *adj* facile da manovrare;
(*car*) maneggevole.
manoeuvre, (*US*) **maneuver** [mə'nuːvə*]
vt manovrare ♦ *vi* far manovre ♦ *n*
manovra; **to** ~ **sb into doing sth**
costringere abilmente qn a fare qc.
manor ['mænə*] n (*also*: ~ **house**) maniero.
manpower ['mænpauə*] n manodopera.
**Manpower Services Commission
(MSC)** n (*BRIT*) ente nazionale per
l'occupazione.
manservant, *pl* **menservants**
['mænsə:vənt, 'mɛn-] n domestico.
mansion ['mænʃən] n casa signorile.
manslaughter ['mænslɔ:tə*] n omicidio
preterintenzionale.
mantelpiece ['mæntlpi:s] n mensola del
caminetto.
mantle ['mæntl] n mantello.
man-to-man ['mæntə'mæn] *adj, adv* da
uomo a uomo.
Mantua ['mæntjuə] n Mantova.
manual ['mænjuəl] *adj, n* manuale (*m*).
manual worker n manovale *m*.
manufacture [mænju'fæktʃə*] *vt*
fabbricare ♦ *n* fabbricazione *f*,
manifattura.
manufactured goods *npl* manufatti *mpl*.
manufacturer [mænju'fæktʃərə*] n
fabbricante *m*.
manufacturing industries
[mænju'fæktʃərɪŋ-] *npl* industrie *fpl*
manifatturiere.
manure [mə'njuə*] n concime *m*.
manuscript ['mænjuskrɪpt] n manoscritto.
many ['mɛnɪ] *adj* molti(e) ♦ *pron* molti(e),
un gran numero; **a great** ~ moltissimi(e),
un gran numero (di); ~ **a ... molti(e) ...,
più di un(a) ...; **too** ~ **difficulties** troppe
difficoltà; **twice as** ~ due volte tanto;
how ~? quanti(e)?
Maori ['maurɪ] *adj, n* maori (*m/f*) *inv*.
map [mæp] n carta (geografica) ♦ *vt* fare
una carta di.
▶**map out** *vt* tracciare un piano di; (*fig*:

career, holiday, essay) pianificare.
maple ['meɪpl] *n* acero.
mar [mɑː*] *vt* sciupare.
Mar. *abbr* (= *March*) mar.
marathon ['mærəθən] *n* maratona ♦ *adj*: **a ~ session** una seduta fiume.
marathon runner *n* maratoneta *m/f*.
marauder [mə'rɔːdə*] *n* saccheggiatore *m*; predatore *m*.
marble ['mɑːbl] *n* marmo; (*toy*) pallina, bilia; **~s** *n* (*game*) palline, bilie.
March [mɑːtʃ] *n* marzo; *for phrases see also* **July**.
march [mɑːtʃ] *vi* marciare; sfilare ♦ *n* marcia; (*demonstration*) dimostrazione *f*; **to ~ into a room** entrare a passo deciso in una stanza.
marcher ['mɑːtʃə*] *n* dimostrante *m/f*.
marching ['mɑːtʃɪŋ] *n*: **to give sb his ~ orders** (*fig*) dare il benservito a qn.
march-past ['mɑːtʃpɑːst] *n* sfilata.
mare [mɛə*] *n* giumenta.
marg [mɑːdʒ] *n abbr* (*col*) = **margarine**.
margarine [mɑːdʒə'riːn] *n* margarina.
marge [mɑːdʒ] *n abbr* (*col*) = **margarine**.
margin ['mɑːdʒɪn] *n* margine *m*.
marginal ['mɑːdʒɪnl] *adj* marginale; **~ seat** (*POL*) seggio elettorale ottenuto con una stretta maggioranza.
marginally ['mɑːdʒɪnəlɪ] *adv* (*bigger, better*) lievemente, di poco; (*different*) un po'.
marigold ['mærɪɡəʊld] *n* calendola.
marijuana [mærɪ'wɑːnə] *n* marijuana.
marina [mə'riːnə] *n* marina.
marinade *n* [mærɪ'neɪd] marinata ♦ *vt* ['mærɪneɪd] = **marinate**.
marinate ['mærɪneɪt] *vt* marinare.
marine [mə'riːn] *adj* (*animal, plant*) marino(a); (*forces, engineering*) marittimo(a) ♦ *n* fante *m* di marina; (*US*) marine *m inv*.
marine insurance *n* assicurazione *f* marittima.
marital ['mærɪtl] *adj* maritale, coniugale; **~ status** stato coniugale.
maritime ['mærɪtaɪm] *adj* marittimo(a).
maritime law *n* diritto marittimo.
marjoram ['mɑːdʒərəm] *n* maggiorana.
mark [mɑːk] *n* segno; (*stain*) macchia; (*of skid etc*) traccia; (*BRIT SCOL*) voto; (*SPORT*) bersaglio; (*currency*) marco; (*BRIT TECH*): **M~ 2/3** 1a/2a serie *f* ♦ *vt* segnare; (*stain*) macchiare; (*BRIT SCOL*) dare un voto a; correggere; (*SPORT: player*) marcare; **punctuation ~s** segni di punteggiatura; **to be quick off the ~** (*in doing*) (*fig*) non perdere tempo (per fare); **up to the ~** (*in efficiency*) all'altezza; **to ~ time** segnare il passo.
▶**mark down** *vt* (*reduce: prices, goods*) ribassare, ridurre.
▶**mark off** *vt* (*tick off*) spuntare, cancellare.
▶**mark out** *vt* delimitare.
▶**mark up** *vt* (*price*) aumentare.
marked ['mɑːkt] *adj* spiccato(a), chiaro(a).
markedly ['mɑːkɪdlɪ] *adv* visibilmente, notevolmente.
marker ['mɑːkə*] *n* (*sign*) segno; (*bookmark*) segnalibro.
market ['mɑːkɪt] *n* mercato ♦ *vt* (*COMM*) mettere in vendita; (*promote*) lanciare sul mercato; **to play the ~** giocare *or* speculare in borsa; **to be on the ~** essere (messo) in vendita *or* in commercio; **open ~** mercato libero.
marketable ['mɑːkɪtəbl] *adj* commercializzabile.
market analysis *n* analisi *f* di mercato.
market day *n* giorno di mercato.
market demand *n* domanda del mercato.
market economy *n* economia di mercato.
market forces *npl* forze *fpl* di mercato.
market garden *n* (*BRIT*) orto industriale.
marketing ['mɑːkɪtɪŋ] *n* marketing *m*.
marketplace ['mɑːkɪtpleɪs] *n* (*piazza del*) mercato; (*world of trade*) piazza, mercato.
market price *n* prezzo di mercato.
market research *n* indagine *f or* ricerca di mercato.
market value *n* valore *m* di mercato.
marking ['mɑːkɪŋ] *n* (*on animal*) marcatura di colore; (*on road*) segnaletica orizzontale.
marksman ['mɑːksmən] *n* tiratore *m* scelto.
marksmanship ['mɑːksmənʃɪp] *n* abilità nel tiro.
mark-up ['mɑːkʌp] *n* (*COMM: margin*) margine *m* di vendita; (: *increase*) aumento.
marmalade ['mɑːməleɪd] *n* marmellata d'arance.
maroon [mə'ruːn] *vt* (*fig*): **to be ~ed (in *or* at)** essere abbandonato(a) (in) ♦ *adj* bordeaux *inv*.
marquee [mɑː'kiː] *n* padiglione *m*.
marquess, marquis ['mɑːkwɪs] *n* marchese *m*.
Marrakech, Marrakesh [mærə'kɛʃ] *n* Marrakesh *f*.
marriage ['mærɪdʒ] *n* matrimonio.
marriage bureau *n* agenzia matrimoniale.
marriage certificate *n* certificato di matrimonio.
marriage guidance, (*US*) **marriage counseling** *n* consulenza matrimoniale.
marriage of convenience *n* matrimonio

di convenienza.

married ['mærɪd] *adj* sposato(a); (*life, love*) coniugale, matrimoniale.

marrow ['mærəʊ] *n* midollo; (*vegetable*) zucca.

marry ['mærɪ] *vt* sposare, sposarsi con; (*subj: father, priest etc*) dare in matrimonio ♦ *vi* (*also*: **get married**) sposarsi.

Mars [mɑːz] *n* (*planet*) Marte *m*.

Marseilles [mɑː'seɪlz] *n* Marsiglia.

marsh [mɑːʃ] *n* palude *f*.

marshal ['mɑːʃl] *n* maresciallo; (*US*: fire ~) capo; (: *police* ~) capitano; (*for demonstration, meeting*) membro del servizio d'ordine ♦ *vt* adunare.

marshalling yard ['mɑːʃlɪŋ-] *n* scalo smistamento.

marshmallow [mɑːʃ'mæləʊ] *n* (*BOT*) altea; (*sweet*) caramella soffice e gommosa.

marshy ['mɑːʃɪ] *adj* paludoso(a).

marsupial [mɑː'suːpɪəl] *adj, n* marsupiale (*m*).

martial ['mɑːʃl] *adj* marziale.

martial arts *npl* arti *fpl* marziali.

martial law *n* legge *f* marziale.

Martian ['mɑːʃən] *n* marziano/a.

martin ['mɑːtɪn] *n* (*also*: **house** ~) balestruccio.

martyr ['mɑːtə*] *n* martire *m/f* ♦ *vt* martirizzare.

martyrdom ['mɑːtədəm] *n* martirio.

marvel ['mɑːvl] *n* meraviglia ♦ *vi*: **to** ~ **(at)** meravigliarsi (di).

marvellous, (*US*) **marvelous** ['mɑːvələs] *adj* meraviglioso(a).

Marxism ['mɑːksɪzəm] *n* marxismo.

Marxist ['mɑːksɪst] *adj, n* marxista (*m/f*).

marzipan ['mɑːzɪpæn] *n* marzapane *m*.

mascara [mæs'kɑːrə] *n* mascara *m inv*.

mascot ['mæskət] *n* mascotte *f inv*.

masculine ['mæskjulɪn] *adj* maschile ♦ *n* genere *m* maschile.

masculinity [mæskju'lɪnɪtɪ] *n* mascolinità.

MASH [mæʃ] *n abbr* (*US MIL*: = *mobile army surgical hospital*) ospedale *di campo di unità mobile dell'esercito*.

mash [mæʃ] *vt* (*CULIN*) passare, schiacciare.

mashed [mæʃt] *adj*: ~ **potatoes** purè *m* di patate.

mask [mɑːsk] *n* (*gen, ELEC*) maschera ♦ *vt* mascherare.

masochism ['mæsəkɪzəm] *n* masochismo.

masochist ['mæsəkɪst] *n* masochista *m/f*.

mason ['meɪsn] *n* (*also*: **stone**~) scalpellino; (*also*: **free**~) massone *m*.

masonic [mə'sɔnɪk] *adj* massonico(a).

masonry ['meɪsnrɪ] *n* muratura.

masquerade [mæskə'reɪd] *n* ballo in maschera; (*fig*) mascherata ♦ *vi*: **to** ~ **as** farsi passare per.

mass [mæs] *n* moltitudine *f*, massa; (*PHYSICS*) massa; (*REL*) messa ♦ *vi* ammassarsi; **the** ~**es** le masse; **to go to** ~ andare a *or* alla messa.

Mass. *abbr* (*US*) = *Massachusetts*.

massacre ['mæsəkə*] *n* massacro ♦ *vt* massacrare.

massage ['mæsɑːʒ] *n* massaggio ♦ *vt* massaggiare.

masseur [mæ'sɜː*] *n* massaggiatore *m*.

masseuse [mæ'sɜːz] *n* massaggiatrice *f*.

massive ['mæsɪv] *adj* enorme, massiccio(a).

mass market *n* mercato di massa.

mass media *npl* mass media *mpl*.

mass meeting *n* riunione *f* generale; (*huge*) adunata popolare.

mass-produce ['mæsprə'djuːs] *vt* produrre in serie.

mass production *n* produzione *f* in serie.

mast [mɑːst] *n* albero; (*RADIO, TV*) pilone *m* (a traliccio).

mastectomy [mæs'tɛktəmɪ] *n* mastectomia.

master ['mɑːstə*] *n* padrone *m*; (*ART etc*, *teacher: in primary school*) maestro; (: *in secondary school*) professore *m*; (*title for boys*): **M~ X** Signorino X ♦ *vt* domare; (*learn*) imparare a fondo; (*understand*) conoscere a fondo; ~ **of ceremonies (MC)** *n* maestro di cerimonie; **M~'s degree** *n see* *boxed note*.

MASTER'S DEGREE

Il **Master's degree** *è il riconoscimento che viene conferito a chi segue un corso di specializzazione dopo aver conseguito un "Bachelor's degree". Vi sono diversi tipi di Master's Degree; i più comuni sono il "Master of Arts (MA)" e il "Master of Science (MSc)" che si ottengono dopo aver seguito un corso e aver presentato una tesi originale. Per il "Master of Letters (MLitt)" e il "Master of Philosophy (MPhil)" è invece sufficiente presentare la tesi; vedi anche* **doctorate***.*

master disk *n* (*COMPUT*) disco *m* master *inv*, disco principale.

masterful ['mɑːstəful] *adj* autoritario(a), imperioso(a).

master key *n* chiave *f* maestra.

masterly ['mɑːstəlɪ] *adj* magistrale.

mastermind ['mɑːstəmaɪnd] *n* mente *f* superiore ♦ *vt* essere il cervello di.

masterpiece ['mɑːstəpiːs] n capolavoro.
master plan n piano generale.
master stroke n colpo maestro.
mastiff ['mæstɪf] n mastino inglese.
masturbate ['mæstəbeɪt] vi masturbare.
masturbation [mæstə'beɪʃən] n
masturbazione f.
mat [mæt] n stuoia; (also: **door**~) stoino,
zerbino ♦ adj = **matt**.
match [mætʃ] n fiammifero; (game) partita,
incontro; (fig) uguale m/f; matrimonio;
partito ♦ vt intonare; (go well with) andare
benissimo con; (equal) uguagliare ♦ vi
intonarsi; **to be a good** ~ andare bene.
▶**match up** vt intonare.
matchbox ['mætʃbɔks] n scatola per
fiammiferi.
matching ['mætʃɪŋ] adj ben assortito(a).
matchless ['mætʃlɪs] adj senza pari.
mate [meɪt] n compagno/a di lavoro; (col:
friend) amico/a; (animal) compagno/a; (in
merchant navy) secondo ♦ vi accoppiarsi
♦ vt accoppiare.
material [mə'tɪərɪəl] n (substance) materiale
m, materia; (cloth) stoffa ♦ adj materiale;
(important) essenziale; ~s npl (equipment
etc) materiali mpl; occorrente m.
materialistic [mətɪərɪə'lɪstɪk] adj
materialistico(a).
materialize [mə'tɪərɪəlaɪz] vi
materializzarsi, realizzarsi.
materially [mə'tɪərɪəlɪ] adv dal punto di
vista materiale; sostanzialmente.
maternal [mə'təːnl] adj materno(a).
maternity [mə'təːnɪtɪ] n maternità ♦ cpd di
maternità; (clothes) pre-maman inv.
maternity benefit n sussidio di
maternità.
maternity hospital n ≈ clinica ostetrica.
matey ['meɪtɪ] adj (BRIT col) amicone(a).
math [mæθ] n abbr (US) = **mathematics**.
mathematical [mæθə'mætɪkl] adj
matematico(a).
mathematician [mæθəmə'tɪʃən] n
matematico/a.
mathematics [mæθə'mætɪks] n
matematica.
maths [mæθs] n abbr (BRIT) = **mathematics**.
matinée ['mætɪneɪ] n matinée f inv.
mating ['meɪtɪŋ] n accoppiamento.
mating call n chiamata all'accoppiamento.
mating season n stagione f degli amori.
matriarchal [meɪtrɪ'ɑːkl] adj matriarcale.
matrices ['meɪtrɪsiːz] npl of **matrix**.
matriculation [mətrɪkju'leɪʃən] n
immatricolazione f.
matrimonial [mætrɪ'məunɪəl] adj
matrimoniale, coniugale.

matrimony ['mætrɪmənɪ] n matrimonio.
matrix, pl matrices ['meɪtrɪks, 'meɪtrɪsiːz] n
matrice f.
matron ['meɪtrən] n (in hospital)
capoinfermiera; (in school) infermiera.
matronly ['meɪtrənlɪ] adj da matrona.
matt [mæt] adj opaco(a).
matted ['mætɪd] adj ingarbugliato(a).
matter ['mætə*] n questione f; (PHYSICS)
materia, sostanza; (content) contenuto;
(MED: pus) pus m ♦ vi importare; **it doesn't**
~ non importa; (I don't mind) non fa
niente; **what's the** ~? che cosa c'è?; **no** ~
what qualsiasi cosa accada; **that's**
another ~ quello è un altro affare; **as a** ~
of course come cosa naturale; **as a** ~ **of**
fact in verità; **it's a** ~ **of habit** è una
questione di abitudine; **printed** ~ stampe
fpl; **reading** ~ (BRIT) qualcosa da leggere.
matter-of-fact [mætərəv'fækt] adj
prosaico(a).
matting ['mætɪŋ] n stuoia.
mattress ['mætrɪs] n materasso.
mature [mə'tjuə*] adj maturo(a); (cheese)
stagionato(a) ♦ vi maturare; stagionare;
(COMM) scadere.
mature student n studente universitario
che ha più di 25 anni.
maturity [mə'tjuərɪtɪ] n maturità.
maudlin ['mɔːdlɪn] adj lacrimoso(a).
maul [mɔːl] vt lacerare.
Mauritania [mɔrɪ'teɪnɪə] n Mauritania.
Mauritius [mə'rɪʃəs] n Maurizio.
mausoleum [mɔːsə'lɪəm] n mausoleo.
mauve [məuv] adj malva inv.
maverick ['mævərɪk] n (fig) chi sta fuori del
branco.
mawkish ['mɔːkɪʃ] adj sdolcinato(a);
insipido(a).
max. abbr = **maximum**.
maxim ['mæksɪm] n massima.
maxima ['mæksɪmə] npl of **maximum**.
maximize ['mæksɪmaɪz] vt (profits etc)
massimizzare; (chances) aumentare al
massimo.
maximum ['mæksɪməm] adj massimo(a) ♦ n
(pl **maxima**) massimo.
May [meɪ] n maggio; for phrases see also **July**.
may [meɪ] vi (conditional: **might**) (indicating
possibility): **he** ~ **come** può darsi che
venga; (be allowed to): ~ **I smoke?** posso
fumare?; ~ **I sit here?** le dispiace se mi
siedo qua?; (wishes): ~ **God bless you!**
Dio la benedica!; **he might be there** può
darsi che ci sia; **he might come** potrebbe
venire, può anche darsi che venga; **I**
might as well go potrei anche
andarmene; **you might like to try** forse le

piacerebbe provare.

maybe ['meibi:] *adv* forse, può darsi; ~ **he'll** ... può darsi che lui ... +*sub*, forse lui ...; ~ **not** forse no, può darsi di no.

mayday ['meideɪ] *n* S.O.S. *m*, mayday *m inv*.

May Day *n* il primo maggio.

mayhem ['meihɛm] *n* cagnara.

mayonnaise [meɪə'neɪz] *n* maionese *f*.

mayor [mɛə*] *n* sindaco.

mayoress ['mɛərɛs] *n* sindaco (*donna*); moglie *f* del sindaco.

maypole ['meɪpəul] *n palo ornato di fiori attorno a cui si danza durante la festa di maggio*.

maze [meiz] *n* labirinto, dedalo.

MB *abbr* (*COMPUT*) = megabyte; (*Canada*) = Manitoba.

MBA *n abbr* (= *Master of Business Administration*) *titolo di studio*.

MBE *n abbr* (*BRIT*: = *Member of the Order of the British Empire*) *titolo*.

MBO *n abbr see* **management buyout**.

MC *n abbr see* **master of ceremonies**; (*US*: = *Member of Congress*) *membro del Congresso*.

MCAT *n abbr* (*US*: = *Medical College Admissions Test*) *esame di ammissione a studi superiori di medicina*.

MD *n abbr* (= *Doctor of Medicine*) *titolo di studio*; (*COMM*) *see* **managing director** ♦ *abbr* (*US*) = *Maryland*.

Md. *abbr* (*US*) = *Maryland*.

MDT *abbr* (*US*: = *Mountain Daylight Time*) *ora legale delle Montagne Rocciose*.

ME *abbr* (*US*) = *Maine* ♦ *n abbr* (*MED*: = *myalgic encephalomyelitis*) sindrome *f* da affaticamento cronico; (*US*) *see* **medical examiner**.

me [mi:] *pron* mi, m' + *vowel*; (*stressed, after prep*) me; **it's** ~ sono io; **it's for** ~ è per me.

meadow ['mɛdəu] *n* prato.

meagre, (*US*) **meager** ['mi:gə*] *adj* magro(a).

meal [mi:l] *n* pasto; (*flour*) farina; **to go out for a** ~ mangiare fuori.

meals on wheels *n* (*BRIT*) distribuzione *f* di pasti caldi a domicilio (*per persone malate o anziane*).

mealtime ['mi:ltaim] *n* l'ora di mangiare.

mealy-mouthed ['mi:lɪmauðd] *adj* che parla attraverso eufemismi.

mean [mi:n] *adj* (*with money*) avaro(a), gretto(a); (*unkind*) meschino(a), maligno(a); (*US*: *vicious*: *animal*) cattivo(a); (: *person*) perfido(a); (*average*) medio(a) ♦ *vt* (*pt, pp* **meant** [mɛnt]) (*signify*) significare, voler dire; (*intend*): **to** ~ **to do**

aver l'intenzione di fare ♦ *n* mezzo; (*MATH*) media; **to be meant for** essere destinato(a) a; **do you** ~ **it?** dice sul serio?; **what do you** ~? che cosa vuol dire?; *see also* **means**.

meander [mɪ'ændə*] *vi* far meandri; (*fig*) divagare.

meaning ['mi:nɪŋ] *n* significato, senso.

meaningful ['mi:nɪŋful] *adj* significativo(a); (*relationship*) valido(a).

meaningless ['mi:nɪŋlɪs] *adj* senza senso.

meanness ['mi:nnɪs] *n* avarizia; meschinità.

means [mi:nz] *npl* mezzi *mpl*; **by** ~ **of** per mezzo di; (*person*) a mezzo di; **by all** ~ ma certo, prego.

means test *n* (*ADMIN*) accertamento dei redditi (*per una persona che ha chiesto un aiuto finanziario*).

meant [mɛnt] *pt, pp of* **mean**.

meantime ['mi:ntaim], **meanwhile** ['mi:nwail] *adv* (*also*: **in the** ~) nel frattempo.

measles ['mi:zlz] *n* morbillo.

measly ['mi:zlɪ] *adj* (*col*) miserabile.

measurable ['mɛʒərəbl] *adj* misurabile.

measure ['mɛʒə*] *vt, vi* misurare ♦ *n* misura; (*ruler*) metro; **a litre** ~ una misura da un litro; **some** ~ **of success** un certo successo; **to take** ~s **to do sth** prendere provvedimenti per fare qc.

▶**measure up** *vi*: **to** ~ **up (to)** dimostrarsi *or* essere all'altezza (di).

measured ['mɛʒəd] *adj* misurato(a).

measurement ['mɛʒəmənt] *n* (*act*) misurazione *f*; (*measure*) misura; **chest/hip** ~ giro petto/fianchi; **to take sb's** ~**s** prendere le misure di qn.

meat [mi:t] *n* carne *f*; **cold** ~**s** (*BRIT*) affettati *mpl*; **crab** ~ polpa di granchio.

meatball ['mi:tbɔ:l] *n* polpetta di carne.

meat pie *n torta salata in pasta frolla con ripieno di carne*.

meaty ['mi:tɪ] *adj* che sa di carne; (*fig*) sostanzioso(a); (*of person*) corpulento(a); (*of part of body*) carnoso(a); ~ **meal** pasto a base di carne.

Mecca ['mɛkə] *n* La Mecca; (*fig*): **a** ~ (**for**) la Mecca (di).

mechanic [mɪ'kænɪk] *n* meccanico; *see also* **mechanics**.

mechanical [mɪ'kænɪkəl] *adj* meccanico(a).

mechanical engineering *n* (*science*) ingegneria meccanica; (*industry*) costruzioni *fpl* meccaniche.

mechanics [mə'kænɪks] *n* meccanica ♦ *npl* meccanismo.

mechanism ['mɛkənɪzəm] *n* meccanismo.

mechanization [mɛkənaɪ'zeɪʃən] *n*
meccanizzazione *f*.
MEd *n abbr* (= *Master of Education*) *titolo di studio.*
medal ['mɛdl] *n* medaglia.
medallion [mɪ'dælɪən] *n* medaglione *m*.
medallist, (*US*) **medalist** ['mɛdəlɪst] *n*
(*SPORT*) vincitore/trice di medaglia.
meddle ['mɛdl] *vi*: **to ~ in** immischiarsi in,
mettere le mani in; **to ~ with** toccare.
meddlesome ['mɛdlsəm], **meddling**
['mɛdlɪŋ] *adj* (*interfering*) che mette il naso
dappertutto; (*touching things*) che tocca
tutto.
media ['miːdɪə] *npl* (*PRESS, RADIO, TV*) media
mpl; (*means*) *pl of* **medium**.
media circus *n* carrozzone *m*
dell'informazione.
mediaeval [mɛdɪ'iːvl] *adj* = **medieval**.
median ['miːdɪən] *n* (*US: also:* ~ **strip**)
banchina *f* spartitraffico *inv*.
media research *n* sondaggio tra gli utenti
dei mass media.
mediate ['miːdɪeɪt] *vi* interporsi; fare da
mediatore/trice.
mediation [miːdɪ'eɪʃən] *n* mediazione *f*.
mediator ['miːdɪeɪtə*] *n* mediatore/trice.
Medicaid ['mɛdɪkeɪd] *n* (*US*) *assistenza
medica ai poveri.*
medical ['mɛdɪkl] *adj* medico(a); ~
(**examination**) visita medica.
medical certificate *n* certificato medico.
medical examiner (ME) *n* (*US*) *medico
incaricato di indagare la causa di morte
in circostanze sospette.*
medical student *n* studente/essa di
medicina.
Medicare ['mɛdɪkeə*] *n* (*US*) *assistenza
medica agli anziani.*
medicated ['mɛdɪkeɪtɪd] *adj* medicato(a).
medication [mɛdɪ'keɪʃən] *n* (*drugs etc*)
medicinali *mpl*, farmaci *mpl*.
medicinal [mɛ'dɪsɪnl] *adj* medicinale.
medicine ['mɛdsɪn] *n* medicina.
medicine chest *n* armadietto
farmaceutico.
medicine man *n* stregone *m*.
medieval [mɛdɪ'iːvl] *adj* medievale.
mediocre [miːdɪ'əukə*] *adj* mediocre.
mediocrity [miːdɪ'ɔkrɪtɪ] *n* mediocrità.
meditate ['mɛdɪteɪt] *vi*: **to ~ (on)** meditare
(su).
meditation [mɛdɪ'teɪʃən] *n* meditazione *f*.
Mediterranean [mɛdɪtə'reɪnɪən] *adj*
mediterraneo(a); **the ~ (Sea)** il (mare)
Mediterraneo.
medium ['miːdɪəm] *adj* medio(a) ◆ *n* (*pl*
media: *means*) mezzo; (*pl* **mediums**:

person) medium *m inv*; **the happy ~** una
giusta via di mezzo; *see also* **media**.
medium-dry ['miːdɪəm'draɪ] *adj* demisec
inv.
medium-sized ['miːdɪəmsaɪzd] *adj* (*tin etc*)
di grandezza media; (*clothes*) di taglia
media.
medium wave *n* (*RADIO*) onde *fpl* medie.
medley ['mɛdlɪ] *n* selezione *f*.
meek [miːk] *adj* dolce, umile.
meet [miːt], *pt, pp* **met** *vt* incontrare;
(*for the first time*) fare la conoscenza di;
(*fig*) affrontare; far fronte a; soddisfare;
raggiungere ◆ *vi* incontrarsi; (*in session*)
riunirsi; (*join: objects*) unirsi ◆ *n* (*BRIT
HUNTING*) raduno (dei partecipanti alla
caccia alla volpe); (*US SPORT*) raduno
(sportivo); **I'll ~ you at the station** verrò
a prenderla alla stazione; **pleased to ~
you!** lieto di conoscerla!, piacere!
▶**meet up** *vi*: **to ~ up with sb** incontrare
qn.
▶**meet with** *vt fus* incontrare; **he met with
an accident** ha avuto un incidente.
meeting ['miːtɪŋ] *n* incontro; (*session: of
club etc*) riunione *f*; (*interview*) intervista;
(*formal*) colloquio; (*SPORT: rally*) raduno;
she's at a ~ (*COMM*) è in riunione; **to call
a ~** convocare una riunione.
meeting place *n* luogo d'incontro.
megabyte ['mɛgəbaɪt] *n* megabyte *m inv*.
megalomaniac [mɛgələu'meɪnɪæk] *n*
megalomane *m/f*.
megaphone ['mɛgəfəun] *n* megafono.
megawatt ['mɛgəwɔt] *n* megawatt *m inv*.
melancholy ['mɛlənkəlɪ] *n* malinconia ◆ *adj*
malinconico(a).
mellow ['mɛləu] *adj* (*wine, sound*) ricco(a);
(*person, light*) dolce; (*colour*) caldo(a);
(*fruit*) maturo(a) ◆ *vi* (*person*) addolcirsi.
melodious [mɪ'ləudɪəs] *adj* melodioso(a).
melodrama ['mɛləudrɑːmə] *n* melodramma
m.
melodramatic [mɛlədrə'mætɪk] *adj*
melodrammatico(a).
melody ['mɛlədɪ] *n* melodia.
melon ['mɛlən] *n* melone *m*.
melt [mɛlt] *vi* (*gen*) sciogliersi, struggersi;
(*metals*) fondersi; (*fig*) intenerirsi ◆ *vt*
sciogliere, struggere; fondere; (*person*)
commuovere; **~ed butter** burro fuso.
▶**melt away** *vi* sciogliersi completamente.
▶**melt down** *vt* fondere.
meltdown ['mɛltdaun] *n* melt-down *m inv*.
melting point ['mɛltɪŋ-] *n* punto di fusione.
melting pot ['mɛltɪŋ-] *n* (*fig*) crogiolo; **to be
in the ~** essere ancora in discussione.
member ['mɛmbə*] *n* membro; (*of club*)

socio/a, iscritto/a; (*of political party*) iscritto/a; ~ **country/state** n paese m/stato membro; **M~ of Parliament (MP)** n (*BRIT*) deputato; **M~ of the European Parliament (MEP)** n eurodeputato; **M~ of the House of Representatives (MHR)** n (*US*) membro della Camera dei Rappresentanti.

membership ['mɛmbəʃɪp] n iscrizione f; (*numero d'*)iscritti mpl, membri mpl.

membership card n tessera (di iscrizione).

membrane ['mɛmbreɪn] n membrana.

memento [mə'mɛntəu] n ricordo.

memo ['mɛməu] n appunto; (*COMM etc*) comunicazione f di servizio.

memoir ['mɛmwɑː*] n memoria; ~**s** npl memorie fpl, ricordi mpl.

memo pad n blocchetto per appunti.

memorable ['mɛmərəbl] adj memorabile.

memorandum, pl **memoranda** [mɛmə'rændəm, -də] n appunto; (*COMM etc*) comunicazione f di servizio; (*DIPLOMACY*) memorandum m inv.

memorial [mɪ'mɔːrɪəl] n monumento commemorativo ♦ adj commemorativo(a).

Memorial Day n (*US*) see boxed note.

MEMORIAL DAY
*Negli Stati Uniti il **Memorial Day** è una festa nazionale per la commemorazione di tutti i soldati americani caduti in guerra. Le celebrazioni sono tenute ogni anno l'ultimo lunedì di maggio.*

---

memorize ['mɛməraɪz] vt imparare a memoria.

memory ['mɛmərɪ] n (*gen, COMPUT*) memoria; (*recollection*) ricordo; **in** ~ **of** in memoria di; **to have a good/bad** ~ aver buona/cattiva memoria; **loss of** ~ amnesia.

men [mɛn] npl of **man**.

menace ['mɛnɪs] n minaccia; (*col: nuisance*) peste f ♦ vt minacciare; **a public** ~ un pericolo pubblico.

menacing ['mɛnɪsɪŋ] adj minaccioso(a).

menagerie [mɪ'nædʒərɪ] n serraglio.

mend [mɛnd] vt aggiustare, riparare; (*darn*) rammendare ♦ n rammendo; **on the** ~ in via di guarigione.

mending ['mɛndɪŋ] n rammendo; (*items to be mended*) roba da rammendare.

menial ['miːnɪəl] adj da servo; umile.

meningitis [mɛnɪn'dʒaɪtɪs] n meningite f.

menopause ['mɛnəupɔːz] n menopausa.

menservants ['mɛnsəːvənts] npl of **manservant**.

men's room n: **the** ~ (*esp US*) la toilette degli uomini.

menstruate ['mɛnstrueɪt] vi mestruare.

menstruation [mɛnstru'eɪʃən] n mestruazione f.

menswear ['mɛnzwɛə*] n abbigliamento maschile.

mental ['mɛntl] adj mentale; ~ **illness** malattia mentale.

mental hospital n ospedale m psichiatrico.

mentality [mɛn'tælɪtɪ] n mentalità f inv.

mentally ['mɛntlɪ] adv: **to be** ~ **handicapped** essere minorato psichico.

menthol ['mɛnθɔl] n mentolo.

mention ['mɛnʃən] n menzione f ♦ vt menzionare, far menzione di; **don't** ~ **it!** non c'è di che!, prego!; **I need hardly** ~ **that** … inutile dire che …; **not to** ~, **without** ~**ing** per non parlare di, senza contare.

mentor ['mɛntɔː*] n mentore m.

menu ['mɛnjuː] n (*set* ~, *COMPUT*) menù m inv; (*printed*) carta.

menu-driven ['mɛnjuːdrɪvn] adj (*COMPUT*) guidato(a) da menù.

MEP n abbr see **Member of the European Parliament.**

mercantile ['məːkəntaɪl] adj mercantile; (*law*) commerciale.

mercenary ['məːsɪnərɪ] adj venale ♦ n mercenario.

merchandise ['məːtʃəndaɪz] n merci fpl ♦ vt commercializzare.

merchandiser ['məːtʃəndaɪzə*] n merchandiser m inv.

merchant ['məːtʃənt] n (*trader*) commerciante m; (*shopkeeper*) negoziante m; **timber/wine** ~ negoziante di legno/vino.

merchant bank n (*BRIT*) banca d'affari.

merchantman ['məːtʃəntmən] n mercantile m.

merchant navy, (*US*) **merchant marine** n marina mercantile.

merciful ['məːsɪful] adj pietoso(a), clemente.

mercifully ['məːsɪflɪ] adv con clemenza; (*fortunately*) per fortuna.

merciless ['məːsɪlɪs] adj spietato(a).

mercurial [məː'kjuərɪəl] adj (*unpredictable*) volubile.

mercury ['məːkjurɪ] n mercurio.

mercy ['məːsɪ] n pietà f; (*REL*) misericordia; **to have** ~ **on sb** aver pietà di qn; **at the** ~ **of** alla mercé di.

mercy killing n eutanasia.

mere [mɪə*] adj semplice; **by a** ~ **chance**

per mero caso.

merely ['mɪəlɪ] *adv* semplicemente, non ... che.

merge [mɜːdʒ] *vt* unire; (*COMPUT: files, text*) fondere ♦ *vi* fondersi, unirsi; (*COMM*) fondersi.

merger ['mɜːdʒə*] *n* (*COMM*) fusione *f.*

meridian [mə'rɪdɪən] *n* meridiano.

meringue [mə'ræŋ] *n* meringa.

merit ['mɛrɪt] *n* merito, valore *m* ♦ *vt* meritare.

meritocracy [mɛrɪ'tɔkrəsɪ] *n* meritocrazia.

mermaid ['mɜːmeɪd] *n* sirena.

merriment ['mɛrɪmənt] *n* gaiezza, allegria.

merry ['mɛrɪ] *adj* gaio(a), allegro(a); **M~ Christmas!** Buon Natale!

merry-go-round ['mɛrɪgəʊraʊnd] *n* carosello.

mesh [mɛʃ] *n* maglia; rete *f* ♦ *vi* (*gears*) ingranarsi; **wire** ~ rete metallica.

mesmerize ['mɛzməraɪz] *vt* ipnotizzare; affascinare.

mess [mɛs] *n* confusione *f*, disordine *m*; (*fig*) pasticcio; (*MIL*) mensa; **to be (in) a** ~ (*house, room*) essere in disordine (*or* molto sporco); (*fig: marriage, life*) essere un caos; **to be/get o.s. in a** ~ (*fig*) essere/cacciarsi in un pasticcio.

▶**mess about, mess around** *vi* (*col*) trastullarsi.

▶**mess about** *or* **around with** *vt fus* (*col*) gingillarsi con; (*plans*) fare un pasticcio di.

▶**mess up** *vt* sporcare; fare un pasticcio di; rovinare.

message ['mɛsɪdʒ] *n* messaggio; **to get the** ~ (*fig col*) capire l'antifona.

message switching *n* (*COMPUT*) smistamento messaggi.

messenger ['mɛsɪndʒə*] *n* messaggero/a.

Messiah [mɪ'saɪə] *n* Messia *m.*

Messrs, Messrs. ['mɛsəz] *abbr* (*on letters*: = *messieurs*) Spett.

messy ['mɛsɪ] *adj* sporco(a); disordinato(a); (*confused: situation etc*) ingarbugliato(a).

Met [mɛt] *n abbr* (*US*) = *Metropolitan Opera.*

met [mɛt] *pt, pp of* **meet** ♦ *adj abbr* (= *meteorological*): **the M~ Office** l'Ufficio Meteorologico.

metabolism [mɛ'tæbəlɪzəm] *n* metabolismo.

metal ['mɛtl] *n* metallo ♦ *vt* massicciare.

metallic [mɛ'tælɪk] *adj* metallico(a).

metallurgy [mɛ'tælədʒɪ] *n* metallurgia.

metalwork ['mɛtlwɜːk] *n* (*craft*) lavorazione *f* del metallo.

metamorphosis, *pl* **-phoses**

[mɛtə'mɔːfəsɪs, -iːz] *n* metamorfosi *f inv.*

metaphor ['mɛtəfə*] *n* metafora.

metaphysics [mɛtə'fɪzɪks] *n* metafisica.

mete [miːt]: **to** ~ **out** *vt fus* infliggere.

meteor ['miːtɪə*] *n* meteora.

meteoric [miːtɪ'ɔrɪk] *adj* (*fig*) fulmineo(a).

meteorite ['miːtɪəraɪt] *n* meteorite *m.*

meteorological [miːtɪərə'lɔdʒɪkl] *adj* meteorologico(a).

meteorology [miːtɪə'rɔlədʒɪ] *n* meteorologia.

meter ['miːtə*] *n* (*instrument*) contatore *m*; (*parking* ~) parchimetro; (*US*) = **metre**.

methane ['miːθeɪn] *n* metano.

method ['mɛθəd] *n* metodo; ~ **of payment** modo *or* modalità *f inv* di pagamento.

methodical [mɪ'θɔdɪkl] *adj* metodico(a).

Methodist ['mɛθədɪst] *adj, n* metodista (*m/f*).

methylated spirits ['mɛθɪleɪtɪd-] *n* (*BRIT*: *also*: **meths**) alcool *m* denaturato.

meticulous [mɛ'tɪkjuləs] *adj* meticoloso(a).

metre, (*US*) **meter** ['miːtə*] *n* metro.

metric ['mɛtrɪk] *adj* metrico(a); **to go** ~ adottare il sistema metrico decimale.

metrical ['mɛtrɪkl] *adj* metrico(a).

metrication [mɛtrɪ'keɪʃən] *n* conversione *f* al sistema metrico.

metric system *n* sistema *m* metrico decimale.

metric ton *n* tonnellata.

metronome ['mɛtrənəʊm] *n* metronomo.

metropolis [mɪ'trɔpəlɪs] *n* metropoli *f inv.*

metropolitan [mɛtrə'pɔlɪtən] *adj* metropolitano(a).

Metropolitan Police *n* (*BRIT*): **the** ~ la polizia di Londra.

mettle ['mɛtl] *n* coraggio.

mew [mjuː] *vi* (*cat*) miagolare.

mews [mjuːz] *n* (*BRIT*): ~ **flat** *appartamentino ricavato da una vecchia scuderia.*

Mexican ['mɛksɪkən] *adj, n* messicano(a).

Mexico ['mɛksɪkəʊ] *n* Messico.

Mexico City *n* Città del Messico.

mezzanine ['mɛtsəniːn] *n* mezzanino.

MFA *n abbr* (*US*: = *Master of Fine Arts*) *titolo di studio.*

mfr *abbr* = **manufacture; manufacturer**.

mg *abbr* (= *milligram*) mg.

Mgr *abbr* (= *Monseigneur, Monsignor*) mons.; (*COMM*) = **manager**.

MHR *n abbr* (*US*) *see* **Member of the House of Representatives**.

MHz *abbr* (= *megahertz*) MHz.

MI *abbr* (*US*) = *Michigan*.

MI5 *n abbr* (*BRIT*: = *Military Intelligence, section five*) *agenzia di controspionaggio.*

MI6 *n abbr* (*BRIT*: = *Military Intelligence, section 6*) *agenzia di spionaggio.*

MIA *abbr* = **missing in action.**

miaow [miːˈau] *vi* miagolare.

mice [maɪs] *npl of* **mouse.**

Mich. *abbr* (*US*) = *Michigan.*

microbe [ˈmaɪkrəub] *n* microbio.

microbiology [maɪkrəubaɪˈɔlədʒɪ] *n* microbiologia.

microchip [ˈmaɪkrəutʃɪp] *n* microcircuito integrato, chip *m inv.*

microcomputer [maɪkrəukəmˈpjuːtə*] *n* microcomputer *m inv.*

microcosm [ˈmaɪkrəukɔzəm] *n* microcosmo.

microeconomics [maɪkrəuiːkəˈnɔmiks] *n* microeconomia.

microfiche [ˈmaɪkrəufiːʃ] *n* microfiche *f inv.*

microfilm [ˈmaɪkrəufilm] *n* microfilm *m inv* ♦ *vt* microfilmare.

microlight [ˈmaɪkrəulaɪt] *n* aereo *m* biposto *inv.*

micrometer [maɪˈkrɔmɪtə*] *n* micrometro, palmer *m inv.*

microphone [ˈmaɪkrəfəun] *n* microfono.

microprocessor [maɪkrəuˈprəusɛsə*] *n* microprocessore *m.*

micro-scooter [ˈmaɪkrəuskuːtə*] *n* monopattino.

microscope [ˈmaɪkrəskəup] *n* microscopio; **under the** ~ al microscopio.

microscopic [maɪkrəˈskɔpɪk] *adj* microscopico(a).

microwavable, microwaveable [ˈmaɪkrəuweɪvəbl] *adj* adatto(a) al forno a microonde.

microwave [ˈmaɪkrəuweɪv] *n* (*also*: ~ **oven**) forno a microonde.

mid [mɪd] *adj*: ~ **May** metà maggio; ~ **afternoon** metà pomeriggio; **in** ~ **air** a mezz'aria; **he's in his** ~ **thirties** avrà circa trentacinque anni.

midday [mɪdˈdeɪ] *n* mezzogiorno.

middle [ˈmɪdl] *n* mezzo; centro; (*waist*) vita ♦ *adj* di mezzo; **I'm in the** ~ **of reading it** sto proprio leggendolo ora; **in the** ~ **of the night** nel mezzo della notte.

middle age *n* mezza età.

middle-aged [mɪdlˈeɪdʒd] *adj* di mezza età.

Middle Ages *npl*: **the** ~ il Medioevo.

middle class *adj* (*also*: **middle-class**) ≈ borghese ♦ *n*: **the** ~ **(es)** ≈ la borghesia.

Middle East *n*: **the** ~ il Medio Oriente.

middleman [ˈmɪdlmæn] *n* intermediario; agente *m* rivenditore.

middle management *n* quadri *mpl* intermedi.

middle name *n* secondo nome *m.*

middle-of-the-road [ˈmɪdləvðəˈrəud] *adj* moderato(a).

middleweight [ˈmɪdlweɪt] *n* (*BOXING*) peso medio.

middling [ˈmɪdlɪŋ] *adj* medio(a).

midge [mɪdʒ] *n* moscerino.

midget [ˈmɪdʒɪt] *n* nano/a.

midi system [ˈmɪdɪ-] *n* (*hi-fi*) compatto.

Midlands [ˈmɪdləndz] *npl contee del centro dell'Inghilterra.*

midnight [ˈmɪdnaɪt] *n* mezzanotte *f*; **at** ~ a mezzanotte.

midriff [ˈmɪdrɪf] *n* diaframma *m.*

midst [mɪdst] *n*: **in the** ~ **of** in mezzo a.

midsummer [mɪdˈsʌmə*] *n* mezza *or* piena estate *f.*

midway [mɪdˈweɪ] *adj, adv*: ~ **(between)** a mezza strada (fra).

midweek [mɪdˈwiːk] *adv, adj* a metà settimana.

midwife, *pl* **midwives** [ˈmɪdwaɪf, -vz] *n* levatrice *f.*

midwifery [ˈmɪdwɪfərɪ] *n* ostetrica.

midwinter [mɪdˈwɪntə*] *n* pieno inverno.

miffed [mɪft] *adj* (*col*) seccato(a).

might [maɪt] *vb see* **may** ♦ *n* potere *m*, forza.

mighty [ˈmaɪtɪ] *adj* forte, potente ♦ *adv* (*col*) molto.

migraine [ˈmiːgreɪn] *n* emicrania.

migrant [ˈmaɪgrənt] *n* (*bird, animal*) migratore *m*; (*person*) migrante *m/f*; nomade *m/f* ♦ *adj* migratore(trice); nomade; (*worker*) emigrato(a).

migrate [maɪˈgreɪt] *vi* migrare.

migration [maɪˈgreɪʃən] *n* migrazione *f.*

mike [maɪk] *n abbr* (= *microphone*) microfono.

Milan [mɪˈlæn] *n* Milano *f.*

mild [maɪld] *adj* mite; (*person, voice*) dolce; (*flavour*) delicato(a); (*illness*) leggero(a) ♦ *n* birra leggera.

mildew [ˈmɪldjuː] *n* muffa.

mildly [ˈmaɪldlɪ] *adv* mitemente; dolcemente; delicatamente; leggermente; **to put it** ~ a dire poco.

mildness [ˈmaɪldnɪs] *n* mitezza; dolcezza; delicatezza; non gravità.

mile [maɪl] *n* miglio; **to do 20** ~**s per gallon** ≈ usare 14 litri per cento chilometri.

mileage [ˈmaɪlɪdʒ] *n* distanza in miglia, ≈ chilometraggio.

mileage allowance *n* rimborso per miglio.

mileometer [maɪˈlɔmɪtə*] *n* (*BRIT*) = **milometer.**

milestone [ˈmaɪlstəun] *n* pietra miliare.

milieu [ˈmiːljəː] *n* ambiente *m.*

militant [ˈmɪlɪtnt] *adj, n* militante (*m/f*).

militarism ['mɪlɪtərɪzəm] *n* militarismo.
militaristic [mɪlɪtə'rɪstɪk] *adj* militaristico(a).
military ['mɪlɪtərɪ] *adj* militare ♦ *n*: **the ~** i militari, l'esercito.
military service *n* servizio militare.
militate ['mɪlɪteɪt] *vi*: **to ~ against** essere d'ostacolo a.
militia [mɪ'lɪʃə] *n* milizia.
milk [mɪlk] *n* latte *m* ♦ *vt* (*cow*) mungere; (*fig*) sfruttare.
milk chocolate *n* cioccolato al latte.
milk float *n* (*BRIT*) furgone *m* del lattaio.
milking ['mɪlkɪŋ] *n* mungitura.
milkman ['mɪlkmən] *n* lattaio.
milk shake *n* frappé *m inv.*
milk tooth *n* dente *m* di latte.
milk truck *n* (*US*) = **milk float**.
milky ['mɪlkɪ] *adj* lattiginoso(a); (*colour*) latteo(a).
Milky Way *n* Via Lattea.
mill [mɪl] *n* mulino; (*small: for coffee, pepper etc*) macinino; (*factory*) fabbrica; (*spinning ~*) filatura ♦ *vt* macinare ♦ *vi* (*also: ~ about*) formicolare.
millennium, *pl* **~s** *or* **millennia** [mɪ'lɛnɪəm, -'lɛnɪə] *n* millennio.
millennium bug *n* baco di fine millennio.
miller ['mɪlə*] *n* mugnaio.
millet ['mɪlɪt] *n* miglio.
milli... ['mɪlɪ] *prefix* milli....
milligram(me) ['mɪlɪgræm] *n* milligrammo.
millilitre, (*US*) **milliliter** ['mɪlɪliːtə*] *n* millilitro.
millimetre, (*US*) **millimeter** ['mɪlɪmiːtə*] *n* millimetro.
milliner ['mɪlɪnə*] *n* modista.
millinery ['mɪlɪnərɪ] *n* modisteria.
million ['mɪljən] *n* milione *m*.
millionaire [mɪljə'nɛə*] *n* milionario, ≈ miliardario.
millipede ['mɪlɪpiːd] *n* millepiedi *m inv.*
millstone ['mɪlstəun] *n* macina.
millwheel ['mɪlwiːl] *n* ruota di mulino.
milometer [maɪ'lɔmɪtə*] *n* ≈ contachilometri *m inv.*
mime [maɪm] *n* mimo ♦ *vt, vi* mimare.
mimic ['mɪmɪk] *n* imitatore/trice ♦ *vt* (*subj: comedian*) imitare; (: *animal, person*) scimmiottare.
mimicry ['mɪmɪkrɪ] *n* imitazioni *fpl*; (*ZOOL*) mimetismo.
Min. *abbr* (*BRIT POL*: = *ministry*) Min.
min. *abbr* (= *minute, minimum*) min.
minaret [mɪnə'rɛt] *n* minareto.
mince [mɪns] *vt* tritare, macinare ♦ *vi* (*in walking*) camminare a passettini ♦ *n* (*BRIT*

CULIN) carne *f* tritata; **he does not ~ (his) words** parla chiaro e tondo.
mincemeat ['mɪnsmiːt] *n frutta secca tritata per uso in pasticceria.*
mince pie *n specie di torta con frutta secca.*
mincer ['mɪnsə*] *n* tritacarne *m inv.*
mincing ['mɪnsɪŋ] *adj* lezioso(a).
mind [maɪnd] *n* mente *f* ♦ *vt* (*attend to, look after*) badare a, occuparsi di; (*be careful*) fare attenzione a, stare attento(a) a; (*object to*): **I don't ~ the noise** il rumore non mi dà alcun fastidio; **do you ~ if ...?** le dispiace se ...?; **I don't ~** non m'importa; **~ you, ...** sì, però va detto che ...; **never ~** non importa, non fa niente; **it is on my ~** mi preoccupa; **to change one's ~** cambiare idea; **to be in two ~s about sth** essere incerto su qc; **to my ~** secondo me, a mio parere; **to be out of one's ~** essere uscito(a) di mente; **to keep sth in ~** non dimenticare qc; **to bear sth in ~** tener presente qc; **to have sb/sth in ~** avere in mente qn/qc; **to have in ~ to do** aver l'intenzione di fare; **it went right out of my ~** mi è completamente passato di mente, me ne sono completamente dimenticato; **to bring** *or* **call sth to ~** riportare *or* richiamare qc alla mente; **to make up one's ~** decidersi; **"~ the step"** "attenzione allo scalino".
mind-boggling ['maɪndbɔglɪŋ] *adj* (*col*) sconcertante.
-minded ['maɪndɪd] *adj*: **fair~** imparziale; **an industrially~ nation** una nazione orientata verso l'industria.
minder ['maɪndə*] *n* (*child ~*) bambinaia; (*bodyguard*) guardia del corpo.
mindful ['maɪndful] *adj*: **~ of** attento(a) a; memore di.
mindless ['maɪndlɪs] *adj* idiota; (*violence, crime*) insensato(a).
mine [maɪn] *pron* il(la) mio(a), *pl* i(le) miei(mie); **this book is ~** questo libro è mio ♦ *n* miniera; (*explosive*) mina ♦ *vt* (*coal*) estrarre; (*ship, beach*) minare.
mine detector *n* rivelatore *m* di mine.
minefield ['maɪnfiːld] *n* campo minato.
miner ['maɪnə*] *n* minatore *m*.
mineral ['mɪnərəl] *adj* minerale ♦ *n* minerale *m*; **~s** *npl* (*BRIT: soft drinks*) bevande *fpl* gasate.
mineralogy [mɪnə'rælədʒɪ] *n* mineralogia.
mineral water *n* acqua minerale.
minesweeper ['maɪnswiːpə*] *n* dragamine *m inv.*
mingle ['mɪŋgl] *vt* mescolare, mischiare

♦ *vi*: **to ~ with** mescolarsi a, mischiarsi con.

mingy ['mɪndʒɪ] *adj* (*col: amount*) misero(a); (: *person*) spilorcio(a).

miniature ['mɪnətʃə*] *adj* in miniatura ♦ *n* miniatura.

minibus ['mɪnɪbʌs] *n* minibus *m inv*.

minicab ['mɪnɪkæb] *n* (*BRIT*) ≈ taxi *m inv*.

minicomputer ['mɪnɪkəm'pju:tə*] *n* minicomputer *m inv*.

Minidisc ® ['mɪnɪdɪsk] *n* minidisc *m inv*.

minim ['mɪnɪm] *n* (*MUS*) minima.

minima ['mɪnɪmə] *npl of* **minimum**.

minimal ['mɪnɪml] *adj* minimo(a).

minimalist ['mɪnɪməlɪst] *adj, n* minimalista (*m/f*).

minimize ['mɪnɪmaɪz] *vt* minimizzare.

minimum ['mɪnɪməm] *n* (*pl* **minima**) minimo ♦ *adj* minimo(a); **to reduce to a ~** ridurre al minimo; **~ wage** salario minimo garantito.

minimum lending rate (MLR) *n* (*BRIT*) ≈ tasso ufficiale di sconto (T.U.S.).

mining ['maɪnɪŋ] *n* industria mineraria ♦ *adj* minerario(a); di minatori.

minion ['mɪnjən] *n* (*pej*) caudatario; favorito/a.

mini-series ['mɪnɪsɪəri:z] *n* miniserie *f inv*.

miniskirt ['mɪnɪskə:t] *n* minigonna.

minister ['mɪnɪstə*] *n* (*BRIT POL*) ministro; (*REL*) pastore *m* ♦ *vi*: **to ~ to sb** assistere qn; **to ~ to sb's needs** provvedere ai bisogni di qn.

ministerial [mɪnɪs'tɪərɪəl] *adj* (*BRIT POL*) ministeriale.

ministry ['mɪnɪstrɪ] *n* (*BRIT POL*) ministero; (*REL*): **to go into the ~** diventare pastore.

mink [mɪŋk] *n* visone *m*.

mink coat *n* pelliccia di visone.

Minn. *abbr* (*US*) = *Minnesota*.

minnow ['mɪnəu] *n* pesciolino d'acqua dolce.

minor ['maɪnə*] *adj* minore, di poca importanza; (*MUS*) minore ♦ *n* (*LAW*) minorenne *m/f*.

Minorca [mɪ'nɔ:kə] *n* Minorca.

minority [maɪ'nɔrɪtɪ] *n* minoranza; **to be in a ~** essere in minoranza.

minster ['mɪnstə*] *n* cattedrale *f* (*annessa a monastero*).

minstrel ['mɪnstrəl] *n* giullare *m*, menestrello.

mint [mɪnt] *n* (*plant*) menta; (*sweet*) pasticca di menta ♦ *vt* (*coins*) battere; **the (Royal) M~,** (*US*) **the (US) M~** la Zecca; **in ~ condition** come nuovo(a) di zecca.

mint sauce *n* salsa di menta.

minuet [mɪnju'ɛt] *n* minuetto.

minus ['maɪnəs] *n* (*also:* ~ **sign**) segno meno ♦ *prep* meno.

minuscule ['mɪnəskju:l] *adj* minuscolo(a).

minute *adj* [maɪ'nju:t] minuscolo(a); (*detail*) minuzioso(a) ♦ *n* ['mɪnɪt] minuto; (*official record*) processo verbale, resoconto sommario; **~s** *npl* verbale *m*, verbali *mpl*; **it is 5 ~s past 3** sono le 3 e 5 (minuti); **wait a ~!** (aspetta) un momento!; **at the last ~** all'ultimo momento; **up to the ~** ultimissimo; **in ~ detail** minuziosamente.

minute book *n* libro dei verbali.

minute hand *n* lancetta dei minuti.

minutely [maɪ'nju:tlɪ] *adv* (*by a small amount*) di poco; (*in detail*) minuziosamente.

minutiae [mɪ'nju:ʃɪi:] *npl* minuzie *fpl*.

miracle ['mɪrəkl] *n* miracolo.

miraculous [mɪ'rækjuləs] *adj* miracoloso(a).

mirage ['mɪrɑ:ʒ] *n* miraggio.

mire ['maɪə*] *n* pantano, melma.

mirror ['mɪrə*] *n* specchio ♦ *vt* rispecchiare, riflettere.

mirror image *n* immagine *f* speculare.

mirth [mə:θ] *n* gaiezza.

misadventure [mɪsəd'vɛntʃə*] *n* disavventura; **death by ~** (*BRIT*) morte *f* accidentale.

misanthropist [mɪ'zænθrəpɪst] *n* misantropo/a.

misapply [mɪsə'plaɪ] *vt* impiegare male.

misapprehension ['mɪsæprɪ'hɛnʃən] *n* malinteso.

misappropriate [mɪsə'prəuprɪeɪt] *vt* appropriarsi indebitamente di.

misappropriation ['mɪsəprəuprɪ'eɪʃən] *n* appropriazione *f* indebita.

misbehave [mɪsbɪ'heɪv] *vi* comportarsi male.

misbehaviour, (*US*) **misbehavior** [mɪsbɪ'heɪvjə*] *n* comportamento scorretto.

misc. *abbr* = **miscellaneous**.

miscalculate [mɪs'kælkjuleɪt] *vt* calcolare male.

miscalculation ['mɪskælkju'leɪʃən] *n* errore *m* di calcolo.

miscarriage ['mɪskærɪdʒ] *n* (*MED*) aborto spontaneo; **~ of justice** errore *m* giudiziario.

miscarry [mɪs'kærɪ] *vi* (*MED*) abortire; (*fail: plans*) andare a monte, fallire.

miscellaneous [mɪsɪ'leɪnɪəs] *adj* (*items*) vario(a); (*selection*) misto(a); **~ expenses** spese varie.

miscellany [mɪ'sɛlənɪ] *n* raccolta.

mischance [mɪs'tʃɑ:ns] *n*: **by (some) ~** per

sfortuna.

mischief ['mɪstʃɪf] n (naughtiness)
birichineria; (harm) male m, danno;
(maliciousness) malizia.

mischievous ['mɪstʃɪvəs] adj (naughty)
birichino(a); (harmful) dannoso(a).

misconception [mɪskən'sɛpʃən] n idea
sbagliata.

misconduct [mɪs'kɔndʌkt] n cattiva
condotta; **professional** ~ reato
professionale.

misconstrue [mɪskən'struː] vt interpretare
male.

miscount [mɪs'kaunt] vt, vi contare male.

misdeed [mɪs'diːd] n (old) misfatto.

misdemeanour, (US) **misdemeanor**
[mɪsdɪ'miːnə*] n misfatto; infrazione f.

misdirect [mɪsdɪ'rɛkt] vt mal indirizzare.

miser ['maɪzə*] n avaro.

miserable ['mɪzərəbl] adj infelice;
(wretched) miserabile; (weather)
deprimente; **to feel** ~ sentirsi avvilito or
giù di morale.

miserably ['mɪzərəblɪ] adv (fail, live, pay)
miseramente; (smile, answer)
tristemente.

miserly ['maɪzəlɪ] adj avaro(a).

misery ['mɪzərɪ] n (unhappiness) tristezza;
(pain) sofferenza; (wretchedness) miseria.

misfire [mɪs'faɪə*] vi far cilecca; (car
engine) perdere colpi.

misfit ['mɪsfɪt] n (person) spostato/a.

misfortune [mɪs'fɔːtʃən] n sfortuna.

misgiving(s) [mɪs'gɪvɪŋ(z)] n(pl) dubbi mpl,
sospetti mpl; **to have ~s about sth** essere
diffidente or avere dei dubbi per quanto
riguarda qc.

misguided [mɪs'gaɪdɪd] adj sbagliato(a);
poco giudizioso(a).

mishandle [mɪs'hændl] vt (treat roughly)
maltrattare; (mismanage) trattare male.

mishap ['mɪshæp] n disgrazia.

mishear [mɪs'hɪə*] vt, vi irreg capire male.

mishmash ['mɪʃmæʃ] n (col) minestrone m,
guazzabuglio.

misinform [mɪsɪn'fɔːm] vt informare male.

misinterpret [mɪsɪn'təːprɪt] vt interpretare
male.

misinterpretation ['mɪsɪntəːprɪ'teɪʃən] n
errata interpretazione f.

misjudge [mɪs'dʒʌdʒ] vt giudicare male.

mislay [mɪs'leɪ] vt irreg smarrire.

mislead [mɪs'liːd] vt irreg sviare.

misleading [mɪs'liːdɪŋ] adj ingannevole.

misled [mɪs'lɛd] pt, pp of **mislead**.

mismanage [mɪs'mænɪdʒ] vt gestire male;
trattare male.

mismanagement [mɪs'mænɪdʒmənt] n

cattiva amministrazione f.

misnomer [mɪs'nəumə*] n termine m
sbagliato or improprio.

misogynist [mɪ'sɔdʒɪnɪst] n misogino.

misplace [mɪs'pleɪs] vt smarrire; collocare
fuori posto; **to be ~d** (trust etc) essere
malriposto(a).

misprint ['mɪsprɪnt] n errore m di stampa.

mispronounce [mɪsprə'nauns] vt
pronunziare male.

misquote [mɪs'kwəut] vt citare
erroneamente.

misread [mɪs'riːd] vt irreg leggere male.

misrepresent [mɪsrɛprɪ'zɛnt] vt travisare.

Miss [mɪs] n Signorina; **Dear ~ Smith** Cara
Signorina; (more formal) Gentile
Signorina.

miss [mɪs] vt (fail to get) perdere;
(appointment, class) mancare a; (escape,
avoid) evitare; (notice loss of: money etc)
accorgersi di non avere più; (regret the
absence of): **I ~ him/it** sento la sua
mancanza, lui/esso mi manca ♦ vi
mancare ♦ n (shot) colpo mancato; (fig):
that was a near ~ c'è mancato poco; **the
bus just ~ed the wall** l'autobus per un
pelo non è andato a finire contro il muro;
you're ~ing the point non capisce.

►**miss out** vt (BRIT) omettere.

►**miss out on** vt fus (fun, party) perdersi;
(chance, bargain) lasciarsi sfuggire.

Miss. abbr (US) = Mississippi.

missal ['mɪsl] n messale m.

misshapen [mɪs'ʃeɪpən] adj deforme.

missile ['mɪsaɪl] n (AVIAT) missile m; (object
thrown) proiettile m.

missile base n base f missilistica.

missile launcher n lancia-missili m inv.

missing ['mɪsɪŋ] adj perso(a), smarrito(a);
to go ~ sparire; ~ **person** scomparso/a,
disperso/a; ~ **in action** (MIL) disperso/a.

mission ['mɪʃən] n missione f; **on a ~ to sb**
in missione da qn.

missionary ['mɪʃənrɪ] n missionario/a.

misspell [mɪs'spɛl] vt (irreg: like **spell**)
sbagliare l'ortografia di.

misspent [mɪs'spɛnt] adj: **his ~ youth** la sua
gioventù sciupata.

mist [mɪst] n nebbia, foschia ♦ vi (also: ~
over, ~ **up**) annebbiarsi; (BRIT: windows)
appannarsi.

mistake [mɪs'teɪk] n sbaglio, errore m
♦ vt (irreg: like **take**) sbagliarsi di;
fraintendere; **to ~ for** prendere per; **by ~**
per sbaglio; **to make a ~** (in writing,
calculating etc) fare uno sbaglio or un
errore; **to make a ~ about sb/sth**
sbagliarsi sul conto di qn/su qc.

mistaken [mɪsˈteɪkən] *pp of* **mistake** ♦ *adj*
(*idea etc*) sbagliato(a); **to be ~** sbagliarsi.
mistaken identity *n* errore *m* di persona.
mistakenly [mɪsˈteɪkənlɪ] *adv* per errore.
mister [ˈmɪstə*] *n* (*col*) signore *m*; *see* **Mr**.
mistletoe [ˈmɪsltəu] *n* vischio.
mistook [mɪsˈtuk] *pt of* **mistake**.
mistranslation [mɪstrænsˈleɪʃən] *n*
traduzione *f* errata.
mistreat [mɪsˈtriːt] *vt* maltrattare.
mistress [ˈmɪstrɪs] *n* padrona; (*lover*)
amante *f*; (*BRIT SCOL*) insegnante *f*.
mistrust [mɪsˈtrʌst] *vt* diffidare di ♦ *n*: ~
(**of**) diffidenza (nei confronti di).
mistrustful [mɪsˈtrʌstful] *adj*: ~ (**of**)
diffidente (nei confronti di).
misty [ˈmɪstɪ] *adj* nebbioso(a), brumoso(a).
misty-eyed [ˈmɪstɪˈaɪd] *adj* trasognato(a).
misunderstand [mɪsʌndəˈstænd] *vt, vi irreg*
capire male, fraintendere.
misunderstanding [mɪsʌndəˈstændɪŋ] *n*
malinteso, equivoco.
misunderstood [mɪsʌndəˈstud] *pt, pp of*
misunderstand.
misuse *n* [mɪsˈjuːs] cattivo uso; (*of power*)
abuso ♦ *vt* [mɪsˈjuːz] far cattivo uso di;
abusare di.
MIT *n abbr* (*US*) = *Massachusetts Institute of*
Technology.
mite [maɪt] *n* (*small quantity*) briciolo; (*BRIT*:
small child): **poor ~!** povera creaturina!
miter [ˈmaɪtə*] *n* (*US*) = **miter**.
mitigate [ˈmɪtɪgeɪt] *vt* mitigare; (*suffering*)
alleviare; **mitigating circumstances**
circostanze *fpl* attenuanti.
mitigation [mɪtɪˈgeɪʃən] *n* mitigazione *f*;
alleviamento.
mitre, (*US*) **miter** [ˈmaɪtə*] *n* mitra;
(*CARPENTRY*) giunto ad angolo retto.
mitt(en) [ˈmɪt(n)] *n* mezzo guanto;
manopola.
mix [mɪks] *vt* mescolare ♦ *vi* mescolarsi ♦ *n*
mescolanza; preparato; **to ~ sth with sth**
mischiare qc a qc; **to ~ business with**
pleasure unire l'utile al dilettevole; **cake**
~ preparato per torta.
▶**mix in** *vt* (*eggs etc*) incorporare.
▶**mix up** *vt* mescolare; (*confuse*)
confondere; **to be ~ed up in sth** essere
coinvolto in qc.
mixed [mɪkst] *adj* misto(a).
mixed-ability [ˈmɪkstəˈbɪlɪtɪ] *adj* (*class etc*)
con alunni di capacità diverse.
mixed bag *n* miscuglio, accozzaglia; **it's a**
~ c'è un po' di tutto.
mixed blessing *n*: **it's a ~** ha i suoi lati
positivi e negativi.
mixed doubles *npl* (*SPORT*) doppio misto.

mixed economy *n* economia mista.
mixed grill *n* (*BRIT*) misto alla griglia.
mixed marriage *n* matrimonio misto.
mixed-up [mɪkstˈʌp] *adj* (*confused*)
confuso(a).
mixer [ˈmɪksə*] *n* (*for food: electric*)
frullatore *m*; (: *hand*) frullino; (*person*): **he**
is a good ~ è molto socievole.
mixer tap *n* miscelatore *m*.
mixture [ˈmɪkstʃə*] *n* mescolanza; (*blend: of*
tobacco etc) miscela; (*MED*) sciroppo.
mix-up [ˈmɪksʌp] *n* confusione *f*.
MK *abbr* (*BRIT TECH*) = **mark**.
mk *abbr* (*HIST*) = **mark** (*currency*).
mkt *abbr* = **market**.
MLitt *n abbr* (= *Master of Literature, Master of*
Letters) *titolo di studio*.
MLR *n abbr* (*BRIT*) *see* **minimum lending rate**.
mm *abbr* (= *millimetre*) mm.
MN *abbr* (*BRIT*) = **Merchant Navy**; (*US*)
= *Minnesota*.
MO *n abbr* = *medical officer*; (*US col*: = *modus*
operandi) modo d'agire ♦ *abbr* (*US*)
= *Missouri*.
m.o. *abbr* = **money order**.
moan [məun] *n* gemito ♦ *vi* gemere; (*col*:
complain): **to ~ (about)** lamentarsi (di).
moaner [ˈməunə*] *n* (*col*) uno/a che si
lamenta sempre.
moaning [ˈməunɪŋ] *n* gemiti *mpl*.
moat [məut] *n* fossato.
mob [mɔb] *n* folla; (*disorderly*) calca; (*pej*):
the ~ la plebaglia ♦ *vt* accalcarsi intorno
a.
mobile [ˈməubaɪl] *adj* mobile ♦ *n* (*ART*)
mobile *m inv*; **applicants must be ~** (*BRIT*) i
candidati devono essere disposti a
viaggiare.
mobile home *n* grande roulotte *f inv*
(*utilizzata come domicilio*).
mobile phone *n* telefonino.
mobile shop *n* (*BRIT*) negozio ambulante.
mobility [məuˈbɪlɪtɪ] *n* mobilità; (*of*
applicant) disponibilità a viaggiare.
mobilize [ˈməubɪlaɪz] *vt* mobilitare ♦ *vi*
mobilitarsi.
moccasin [ˈmɔkəsɪn] *n* mocassino.
mock [mɔk] *vt* deridere, burlarsi di ♦ *adj*
falso(a).
mockery [ˈmɔkərɪ] *n* derisione *f*; **to make a**
~ of rendere ridicolo.
mocking [ˈmɔkɪŋ] *adj* derisorio(a).
mockingbird [ˈmɔkɪŋbəːd] *n* mimo
(*uccello*).
mock-up [ˈmɔkʌp] *n* modello dimostrativo;
abbozzo.
MOD *n abbr* (*BRIT*) = **Ministry of Defence**; *see*
defence.

mod cons ['mɔd'kɔnz] npl abbr (BRIT) = **modern conveniences**.

mode [məud] n modo; (of transport) mezzo; (COMPUT) modalità f inv.

model ['mɔdl] n modello; (person: for fashion) indossatore/trice; (: for artist) modello/a ♦ vt modellare ♦ vi fare l'indossatore (or l'indossatrice) ♦ adj (small-scale: railway etc) in miniatura; (child, factory) modello inv; **to ~ clothes** presentare degli abiti; **to ~ sb/sth on** modellare qn/qc su.

modem ['məudɛm] n modem m inv.

moderate ['mɔdərɪt] adj moderato(a) ♦ n (POL) moderato/a ♦ vb ['mɔdəreɪt] vi moderarsi, placarsi ♦ vt moderare.

moderately ['mɔdərɪtlɪ] adv (act) con moderazione; (expensive, difficult) non troppo; (pleased, happy) abbastanza, discretamente; **~ priced** a prezzo modico.

moderation [mɔdə'reɪʃən] n moderazione f, misura; **in ~** in quantità moderata, con moderazione.

moderator ['mɔdəreɪtə*] n moderatore/ trice; (REL) moderatore in importanti riunioni ecclesiastiche.

modern ['mɔdən] adj moderno(a); **~ conveniences** comodità fpl moderne; **~ languages** lingue fpl moderne.

modernization [mɔdənaɪ'zeɪʃən] n rimodernamento, modernizzazione f.

modernize ['mɔdənaɪz] vt modernizzare.

modest ['mɔdɪst] adj modesto(a).

modesty ['mɔdɪstɪ] n modestia.

modicum ['mɔdɪkəm] n: **a ~ of** un minimo di.

modification [mɔdɪfɪ'keɪʃən] n modificazione f; **to make ~s** fare or apportare delle modifiche.

modify ['mɔdɪfaɪ] vt modificare.

modish ['məudɪʃ] adj (liter) à la page inv.

Mods [mɔdz] n abbr (BRIT: = (Honour) Moderations) esame all'università di Oxford.

modular ['mɔdjulə*] adj (filing, unit) modulare.

modulate ['mɔdjuleɪt] vt modulare.

modulation [mɔdju'leɪʃən] n modulazione f.

module ['mɔdjuːl] n modulo.

Mogadishu [mɔgə'dɪʃuː] n Mogadiscio f.

mogul ['məugl] n (fig) magnate m, pezzo grosso; (SKI) cunetta.

MOH n abbr (BRIT: = Medical Officer of Health) ≈ ufficiale m sanitario.

mohair ['məuhɛə*] n mohair m.

Mohammed [məu'hæmɪd] n Maometto.

moist [mɔɪst] adj umido(a).

moisten ['mɔɪsn] vt inumidire.

moisture ['mɔɪstʃə*] n umidità; (on glass) goccioline fpl di vapore.

moisturize ['mɔɪstʃəraɪz] vt (skin) idratare.

moisturizer ['mɔɪstʃəraɪzə*] n idratante f.

molar ['məulə*] n molare m.

molasses [məu'læsɪz] n molassa.

mold [məuld] etc (US) = **mould** etc.

Moldavia [mɔl'deɪvɪə], **Moldova** [mɔl'dəuvə] n Moldavia.

Moldavian [mɔl'deɪvɪən], **Moldovan** [mɔl'dəuvən] adj moldavo(a).

mole [məul] n (animal) talpa; (spot) neo.

molecule ['mɔlɪkjuːl] n molecola.

molehill ['məulhɪl] n cumulo di terra sulla tana di una talpa.

molest [məu'lɛst] vt molestare.

mollusc, (US) mollusk ['mɔləsk] n mollusco.

mollycoddle ['mɔlɪkɔdl] vt coccolare, vezzeggiare.

Molotov cocktail ['mɔlətɔf-] n (bottiglia) Molotov f inv.

molt [məult] vi (US) = **moult**.

molten ['məultən] adj fuso(a).

mom [mɔm] n (US) = **mum**.

moment ['məumənt] n momento, istante m; importanza; **at the ~** al momento, in questo momento; **for the ~** per il momento, per ora; **in a ~** tra un momento; **"one ~ please"** (TEL) "attenda, prego".

momentarily ['məuməntərɪlɪ] adv per un momento; (US: very soon) da un momento all'altro.

momentary ['məuməntərɪ] adj momentaneo(a), passeggero(a).

momentous [məu'mɛntəs] adj di grande importanza.

momentum [məu'mɛntəm] n velocità acquisita, slancio; (PHYSICS) momento; **to gather ~** aumentare di velocità; (fig) prendere or guadagnare terreno.

mommy ['mɔmɪ] n (US) mamma.

Mon. abbr (= Monday) lun.

Monaco ['mɔnəkəu] n Monaco f.

monarch ['mɔnək] n monarca m.

monarchist ['mɔnəkɪst] n monarchico/a.

monarchy ['mɔnəkɪ] n monarchia.

monastery ['mɔnəstərɪ] n monastero.

monastic [mə'næstɪk] adj monastico(a).

Monday ['mʌndɪ] n lunedì m inv; for phrases see also **Tuesday**.

Monegasque [mɔnə'gæsk] adj, n monegasco(a).

monetarist ['mʌnɪtərɪst] n monetarista m/f.

monetary ['mʌnɪtərɪ] adj monetario(a).

money ['mʌnɪ] n denaro, soldi mpl; **to make ~** (person) fare (i) soldi; (business)

rendere; **danger** ~ (*BRIT*) indennità di
rischio; **I've got no** ~ **left** non ho più
neanche una lira.

moneyed ['mʌnɪd] *adj* ricco(a).

moneylender ['mʌnɪlɛndə*] *n* prestatore *m*
di denaro.

moneymaker ['mʌnɪmeɪkə*] *n* (*BRIT col:
business*) affare *m* d'oro.

moneymaking ['mʌnɪmeɪkɪŋ] *adj* che rende
(bene *or* molto), lucrativo(a).

money market *n* mercato monetario.

money order *n* vaglia *m inv.*

money-spinner ['mʌnɪspɪnə*] *n* (*col*)
miniera d'oro (*fig*).

money supply *n* liquidità monetaria.

Mongol ['mɔŋgəl] *n* mongolo/a; (*LING*)
mongolo.

mongol ['mɔŋgəl] *adj, n* (*MED*) mongoloide
(*m/f*).

Mongolia [mɔŋ'gəulɪə] *n* Mongolia.

Mongolian [mɔŋ'gəulɪən] *adj* mongolico(a)
♦ *n* mongolo/a; (*LING*) mongolo.

mongoose ['mɔŋguːs] *n* mangusta.

mongrel ['mʌŋgrəl] *n* (*dog*) cane *m*
bastardo.

monitor ['mɔnɪtə*] *n* (*BRIT SCOL*) capoclasse
m/f; (*US SCOL*) chi sorveglia agli esami;
(*TV, COMPUT*) monitor *m inv* ♦ *vt*
controllare; (*foreign station*) ascoltare le
trasmissioni di.

monk [mʌŋk] *n* monaco.

monkey ['mʌŋkɪ] *n* scimmia.

monkey business *n* (*col*) scherzi *mpl.*

monkey nut *n* (*BRIT*) nocciolina
americana.

monkey wrench *n* chiave *f* a rullino.

mono ['mɔnəu] *adj* mono *inv*; (*broadcast*) in
mono.

mono... ['mɔnəu] *prefix* mono....

monochrome ['mɔnəkrəum] *adj*
monocromo(a).

monocle ['mɔnəkl] *n* monocolo.

monogamous [mə'nɔgəməs] *adj*
monogamo(a).

monogamy [mə'nɔgəmɪ] *n* monogamia.

monogram ['mɔnəgræm] *n* monogramma
m.

monolith ['mɔnəlɪθ] *n* monolito.

monologue ['mɔnəlɔg] *n* monologo.

monoplane ['mɔnəupleɪn] *n* monoplano.

monopolize [mə'nɔpəlaɪz] *vt*
monopolizzare.

monopoly [mə'nɔpəlɪ] *n* monopolio;
Monopolies and Mergers Commission
(*BRIT*) commissione *f* antimonopoli.

monorail ['mɔnəureɪl] *n* monorotaia.

monosodium glutamate (MSG)
[mɔnə'səudɪəm'gluːtəmeɪt] *n* glutammato di

sodio.

monosyllabic [mɔnəsɪ'læbɪk] *adj*
monosillabico(a); (*person*) che parla a
monosillabi.

monosyllable ['mɔnəsɪləbl] *n* monosillabo.

monotone ['mɔnətəun] *n* pronunzia (*or*
voce *f*) monotona; **to speak in a** ~ parlare
con voce monotona.

monotonous [mə'nɔtənəs] *adj*
monotono(a).

monotony [mə'nɔtənɪ] *n* monotonia.

monoxide [mɔ'nɔksaɪd] *n*: **carbon** ~ ossido
di carbonio.

monsoon [mɔn'suːn] *n* monsone *m.*

monster ['mɔnstə*] *n* mostro.

monstrosity [mɔn'strɔsɪtɪ] *n* mostruosità *f
inv.*

monstrous ['mɔnstrəs] *adj* mostruoso(a).

Mont. *abbr* (*US*) = *Montana.*

montage [mɔn'tɑːʒ] *n* montaggio.

Mont Blanc [mɔblɑ̃] *n* Monte *m* Bianco.

month [mʌnθ] *n* mese *m*; **300 dollars a** ~
300 dollari al mese; **every** ~ (*happen*)
tutti i mesi; (*pay*) mensilmente, ogni
mese.

monthly ['mʌnθlɪ] *adj* mensile ♦ *adv* al
mese; ogni mese ♦ *n* (*magazine*) rivista
mensile; **twice** ~ due volte al mese.

monument ['mɔnjumənt] *n* monumento.

monumental [mɔnju'mɛntl] *adj*
monumentale; (*fig*) colossale.

monumental mason *n* lapidario.

moo [muː] *vi* muggire, mugghiare.

mood [muːd] *n* umore *m*; **to be in a good/
bad** ~ essere di buon/cattivo umore; **to
be in the** ~ **for** essere disposto(a) a, aver
voglia di.

moody ['muːdɪ] *adj* (*variable*)
capriccioso(a), lunatico(a); (*sullen*)
imbronciato(a).

moon [muːn] *n* luna.

moonbeam ['muːnbiːm] *n* raggio di
luna.

moon landing *n* allunaggio.

moonlight ['muːnlaɪt] *n* chiaro di luna ♦ *vi*
fare del lavoro nero.

moonlighting ['muːnlaɪtɪŋ] *n* lavoro nero.

moonlit ['muːnlɪt] *adj* illuminato(a) dalla
luna; **a** ~ **night** una notte rischiarata
dalla luna.

moonshot ['muːnʃɔt] *n* lancio sulla luna.

moonstruck ['muːnstrʌk] *adj* lunatico(a).

moony ['muːnɪ] *adj* (*eyes*) sognante.

Moor [muə*] *n* moro/a.

moor [muə*] *n* brughiera ♦ *vt* (*ship*)
ormeggiare ♦ *vi* ormeggiarsi.

moorings ['muərɪŋz] *npl* (*chains*) ormeggi
mpl; (*place*) ormeggio.

Moorish ['muərɪʃ] *adj* moresco(a).
moorland ['muələnd] *n* brughiera.
moose [muːs] *n* (*pl inv*) alce *m*.
moot [muːt] *vt* sollevare ♦ *adj*: ~ **point** punto discutibile.
mop [mɔp] *n* lavapavimenti *m inv*; (*also:* ~ **of hair**) zazzera ♦ *vt* lavare con lo straccio; **to** ~ **one's brow** asciugarsi la fronte.
►**mop up** *vt* asciugare con uno straccio.
mope [məup] *vi* fare il broncio.
►**mope about, mope around** *vi* trascinarsi *or* aggirarsi con aria avvilita.
moped ['məuped] *n* (*BRIT*) ciclomotore *m*.
MOR *adj abbr* (*MUS*: = *middle-of-the-road*): ~ **music** musica leggera.
moral ['mɔrəl] *adj* morale ♦ *n* morale *f*; ~**s** *npl* moralità.
morale [mɔ'rɑːl] *n* morale *m*.
morality [mə'rælɪtɪ] *n* moralità.
moralize ['mɔrəlaɪz] *vi*: **to** ~ (**about**) fare il (*or* la) moralista (riguardo), moraleggiare (riguardo).
morally ['mɔrəlɪ] *adv* moralmente.
moral victory *n* vittoria morale.
morass [mə'ræs] *n* palude *f*, pantano.
moratorium [mɔrə'tɔːrɪəm] *n* moratoria.
morbid ['mɔːbɪd] *adj* morboso(a).

===================== *KEYWORD*

more [mɔː*] *adj* **1** (*greater in number etc*) più; ~ **people/letters than we expected** più persone/lettere di quante ne aspettavamo; **I have** ~ **wine/money than you** ho più vino/soldi di te; **I have** ~ **wine than beer** ho più vino che birra
2 (*additional*) altro(a), ancora; **do you want (some)** ~ **tea?** vuole dell'altro tè?, vuole ancora del tè?; **I have no** *or* **I don't have any** ~ **money** non ho più soldi
♦ *pron* **1** (*greater amount*) più; ~ **than 10** più di 10; **it cost** ~ **than we expected** è costato più di quanto ci aspettassimo; **and what's** ~ **...** e per di più ...
2 (*further or additional amount*) ancora; **is there any** ~**?** ce n'è ancora?; **there's no** ~ non ce n'è più; **a little** ~ ancora un po'; **many/much** ~ molti(e)/molto(a) di più
♦ *adv*: ~ **dangerous/easily (than)** più pericoloso/facilmente (di); ~ **and** ~ sempre di più; ~ **and** ~ **difficult** sempre più difficile; ~ **or less** più o meno; ~ **than ever** più che mai; **once** ~ ancora (una volta), un'altra volta; **no** ~, **not any** ~ non ... più; **I have no** ~ **money, I haven't any** ~ **money** non ho più soldi.

moreover [mɔː'rəuvə*] *adv* inoltre, di più.

morgue [mɔːg] *n* obitorio.
MORI ['mɔːrɪ] *n abbr* (*BRIT*: = *Market & Opinion Research Institute*) *istituto di sondaggio*.
moribund ['mɔrɪbʌnd] *adj* moribondo(a).
morning ['mɔːnɪŋ] *n* mattina, mattino; (*duration*) mattinata; **in the** ~ la mattina; **this** ~ stamattina; **7 o'clock in the** ~ le 7 di *or* della mattina.
morning-after pill ['mɔːnɪŋ'ɑːftə-] *n* pillola del giorno dopo.
morning sickness *n* nausee *fpl* mattutine.
Moroccan [mə'rɔkən] *adj*, *n* marocchino(a).
Morocco [mə'rɔkəu] *n* Marocco.
moron ['mɔːrɔn] *n* deficiente *m/f*.
moronic [mə'rɔnɪk] *adj* deficiente.
morose [mə'rəus] *adj* cupo(a), tetro(a).
morphine ['mɔːfiːn] *n* morfina.
morris dancing ['mɔrɪs-] *n* (*BRIT*) *antica danza tradizionale inglese*.
Morse [mɔːs] *n* (*also:* ~ **code**) alfabeto Morse.
morsel ['mɔːsl] *n* boccone *m*.
mortal ['mɔːtl] *adj*, *n* mortale (*m*).
mortality [mɔː'tælɪtɪ] *n* mortalità.
mortality rate *n* tasso di mortalità.
mortar ['mɔːtə*] *n* (*CONSTR*) malta; (*dish*) mortaio.
mortgage ['mɔːgɪdʒ] *n* ipoteca; (*in house buying*) mutuo ipotecario ♦ *vt* ipotecare; **to take out a** ~ contrarre un mutuo (*or* un'ipoteca).
mortgage company *n* (*US*) società *f inv* immobiliare.
mortgagee [mɔːgɪ'dʒiː] *n* creditore *m* ipotecario.
mortgagor ['mɔːgɪdʒə*] *n* debitore *m* ipotecario.
mortician [mɔː'tɪʃən] *n* (*US*) impresario di pompe funebri.
mortified ['mɔːtɪfaɪd] *adj* umiliato(a).
mortise lock ['mɔːtɪs-] *n* serratura incastrata.
mortuary ['mɔːtjuərɪ] *n* camera mortuaria; obitorio.
mosaic [məu'zeɪɪk] *n* mosaico.
Moscow ['mɔskəu] *n* Mosca.
Moslem ['mɔzləm] *adj*, *n* = **Muslim**.
mosque [mɔsk] *n* moschea.
mosquito, ~**es** [mɔs'kiːtəu] *n* zanzara.
mosquito net *n* zanzariera.
moss [mɔs] *n* muschio.
mossy ['mɔsɪ] *adj* muscoso(a).
most [məust] *adj* la maggior parte di; il più di ♦ *pron* la maggior parte ♦ *adv* più; (*work, sleep etc*) di più; (*very*) molto, estremamente; **the** ~ (*also:* + *adjective*) il(la) più; ~ **fish** la maggior parte dei

pesci; ~ **of** la maggior parte di; ~ **of them** quasi tutti; **I saw** ~ ho visto più io; **at the (very)** ~ al massimo; **to make the** ~ **of** trarre il massimo vantaggio da.

mostly ['məustlɪ] *adv* per lo più.

MOT *n abbr* (*BRIT*: = *Ministry of Transport*): **the** ~ **(test)** *revisione obbligatoria degli autoveicoli*.

motel [məu'tɛl] *n* motel *m inv*.

moth [mɔθ] *n* farfalla notturna; tarma.

mothball ['mɔθbɔ:l] *n* pallina di naftalina.

moth-eaten ['mɔθi:tn] *adj* tarmato(a).

mother ['mʌðə*] *n* madre *f* ♦ *vt* (*care for*) fare da madre a.

mother board *n* (*COMPUT*) scheda madre.

motherhood ['mʌðəhud] *n* maternità.

mother-in-law ['mʌðərɪnlɔ:] *n* suocera.

mother-of-pearl [mʌðərəv'pə:l] *n* madreperla.

mother's help *n* bambinaia.

mother-to-be [mʌðətə'bi:] *n* futura mamma.

mother tongue *n* madrelingua.

mothproof ['mɔθpru:f] *adj* antitarmico(a).

motif [məu'ti:f] *n* motivo.

motion ['məuʃən] *n* movimento, moto; (*gesture*) gesto; (*at meeting*) mozione *f*; (*BRIT: also*: **bowel** ~) evacuazione *f* ♦ *vt, vi*: **to** ~ **(to) sb to do** fare cenno a qn di fare; **to be in** ~ (*vehicle*) essere in moto; **to set in** ~ avviare; **to go through the** ~**s of doing sth** (*fig*) fare qc pro forma.

motionless ['məuʃənlɪs] *adj* immobile.

motion picture *n* film *m inv*.

motivate ['məutɪveɪt] *vt* (*act, decision*) dare origine a, motivare; (*person*) spingere.

motivated ['məutɪveɪtɪd] *adj* motivato(a).

motivation [məutɪ'veɪʃən] *n* motivazione *f*.

motive ['məutɪv] *n* motivo ♦ *adj* motore(trice); **from the best** ~**s** con le migliori intenzioni.

motley ['mɔtlɪ] *adj* eterogeneo(a), molto vario(a).

motor ['məutə*] *n* motore *m*; (*BRIT col*: *vehicle*) macchina ♦ *adj* motore(trice).

motorbike ['məutəbaɪk] *n* moto *f inv*.

motorboat ['məutəbəut] *n* motoscafo.

motorcade ['məutəkeɪd] *n* corteo di macchine.

motorcar ['məutəka:] *n* automobile *f*.

motorcoach ['məutəkəutʃ] *n* (*BRIT*) pullman *m inv*.

motorcycle ['məutəsaɪkl] *n* motocicletta.

motorcyclist ['məutəsaɪklɪst] *n* motociclista *m/f*.

motoring ['məutərɪŋ] *n* (*BRIT*) turismo automobilistico ♦ *adj* (*accident*) d'auto, automobilistico(a); (*offence*) di guida; ~

holiday vacanza in macchina.

motorist ['məutərɪst] *n* automobilista *m/f*.

motorize ['məutəraɪz] *vt* motorizzare.

motor oil *n* olio lubrificante.

motor racing *n* (*BRIT*) corse *fpl* automobilistiche.

motor scooter *n* motorscooter *m inv*.

motor vehicle *n* autoveicolo.

motorway ['məutəweɪ] *n* (*BRIT*) autostrada.

mottled ['mɔtld] *adj* chiazzato(a), marezzato(a).

motto, ~es ['mɔtəu] *n* motto.

mould, (US) mold [məuld] *n* forma, stampo; (*mildew*) muffa ♦ *vt* formare; (*fig*) foggiare.

mo(u)lder ['məuldə*] *vi* (*decay*) ammuffire.

mo(u)lding ['məuldɪŋ] *n* (*ARCHIT*) modanatura.

mo(u)ldy ['məuldɪ] *adj* ammuffito(a).

moult, (US) molt [məult] *vi* far la muta.

mound [maund] *n* rialzo, collinetta.

mount [maunt] *n* monte *m*, montagna; (*horse*) cavalcatura; (*for jewel etc*) montatura ♦ *vt* montare; (*horse*) montare a; (*exhibition*) organizzare; (*attack*) sferrare, condurre; (*picture, stamp*) sistemare ♦ *vi* salire; (*get on a horse*) montare a cavallo; (*also*: ~ **up**) aumentare.

mountain ['mauntɪn] *n* montagna ♦ *cpd* di montagna; **to make a** ~ **out of a molehill** fare di una mosca un elefante.

mountain bike *n* mountain bike *f inv*.

mountaineer [mauntɪ'nɪə*] *n* alpinista *m/f*.

mountaineering [mauntɪ'nɪərɪŋ] *n* alpinismo; **to go** ~ fare dell'alpinismo.

mountainous ['mauntɪnəs] *adj* montagnoso(a).

mountain range *n* catena montuosa.

mountain rescue team *n* ≈ squadra di soccorso alpino.

mountainside ['mauntɪnsaɪd] *n* fianco della montagna.

mounted ['mauntɪd] *adj* a cavallo.

mourn [mɔ:n] *vt* piangere, lamentare ♦ *vi*: **to** ~ **(for sb)** piangere (la morte di qn).

mourner ['mɔ:nə*] *n* parente *m/f* (*or* amico/ a) del defunto.

mourning ['mɔ:nɪŋ] *n* lutto ♦ *cpd* (*dress*) da lutto; **in** ~ in lutto.

mouse, pl mice [maus, maɪs] *n* topo; (*COMPUT*) mouse *m inv*.

mousetrap ['maustræp] *n* trappola per i topi.

moussaka [mu'sɑ:kə] *n* moussaka.

mousse [mu:s] *n* mousse *f inv*.

moustache [məs'tɑ:ʃ] *n* baffi *mpl*.

mousy ['mausɪ] *adj* (*person*) timido(a); (*hair*)

né chiaro(a) né scuro(a).

mouth, ~s [mauθ, -ðz] *n* bocca; (*of river*) bocca, foce *f*; (*opening*) orifizio.

mouthful ['mauθful] *n* boccata.

mouth organ *n* armonica.

mouthpiece ['mauθpiːs] *n* (*MUS*) bocchino; (*TEL*) microfono; (*of breathing apparatus*) boccaglio; (*person*) portavoce *m/f*.

mouth-to-mouth ['mauθtə'mauθ] *adj*: ~ **resuscitation** respirazione *f* bocca a bocca.

mouthwash ['mauθwɔʃ] *n* collutorio.

mouth-watering ['mauθwɔːtərɪŋ] *adj* che fa venire l'acquolina in bocca.

movable ['muːvəbl] *adj* mobile.

move [muːv] *n* (*movement*) movimento; (*in game*) mossa; (: *turn to play*) turno; (*change of house*) trasloco ♦ *vt* muovere, spostare; (*emotionally*) commuovere; (*POL: resolution etc*) proporre ♦ *vi* (*gen*) muoversi, spostarsi; (*traffic*) circolare; (*also:* ~ **house**) cambiar casa, traslocare; **to ~ towards** andare verso; **to ~ sb to do sth** indurre *or* spingere qn a fare qc; **to get a ~ on** affrettarsi, sbrigarsi; **to be ~d** (*emotionally*) essere commosso(a).

►**move about, move around** *vi* (*fidget*) agitarsi; (*travel*) viaggiare.

►**move along** *vi* muoversi avanti.

►**move away** *vi* allontanarsi, andarsene.

►**move back** *vi* indietreggiare; (*return*) ritornare.

►**move forward** *vi* avanzare ♦ *vt* avanzare, spostare in avanti; (*people*) far avanzare.

►**move in** *vi* (*to a house*) entrare (*in una nuova casa*).

►**move off** *vi* partire.

►**move on** *vi* riprendere la strada ♦ *vt* (*onlookers*) far circolare.

►**move out** *vi* (*of house*) sgombrare.

►**move over** *vi* spostarsi.

►**move up** *vi* avanzare.

movement ['muːvmənt] *n* (*gen*) movimento; (*gesture*) gesto; (*of stars, water, physical*) moto; ~ **(of the bowels)** (*MED*) evacuazione *f*.

mover ['muːvə*] *n* proponente *m/f*.

movie ['muːvɪ] *n* film *m inv*; **the ~s** il cinema.

movie camera *n* cinepresa.

moviegoer ['muːvɪɡəuə*] *n* (*US*) frequentatore/trice di cinema.

moving ['muːvɪŋ] *adj* mobile; (*causing emotion*) commovente; (*instigating*) animatore(trice).

mow, pt mowed, pp mowed or mown [məu, -n] *vt* falciare; (*grass*) tagliare.

►**mow down** *vt* falciare.

mower ['məuə*] *n* (*also:* **lawn** ~) tagliaerba *m inv*.

mown [məun] *pp of* **mow**.

Mozambique [məuzəm'biːk] *n* Mozambico.

MP *n abbr* = *Military Police*; (*Canada*) = *Mounted Police*; (*BRIT*) *see* **Member of Parliament**.

MP3 *n* MP3 *m inv*.

MP3 player *n* lettore *m* MP3.

mpg *n abbr* = *miles per gallon* (*30 mpg = 9.4 l. per 100 km*).

mph *n abbr* = *miles per hour* (*60 mph = 96 km/h*).

MPhil *n abbr* (= *Master of Philosophy*) *titolo di studio.*

MPS *n abbr* (*BRIT*) = *Member of the Pharmaceutical Society.*

Mr, Mr. ['mɪstə*] *n*: ~ **X** Signor X, Sig. X.

MRC *n abbr* (*BRIT*: = *Medical Research Council*) *ufficio governativo per la ricerca medica in Gran Bretagna e nel Commonwealth.*

MRCP *n abbr* (*BRIT*) = *Member of the Royal College of Physicians.*

MRCS *n abbr* (*BRIT*) = *Member of the Royal College of Surgeons.*

MRCVS *n abbr* (*BRIT*) = *Member of the Royal College of Veterinary Surgeons.*

Mrs, Mrs. ['mɪsɪz] *n*: ~ **X** Signora X, Sig.ra X.

MS *n abbr* (*US*: = *Master of Science*) *titolo di studio;* (= *manuscript*) *ms;* (*MED*) = **multiple sclerosis** ♦ *abbr* (*US*) = *Mississippi.*

Ms, Ms. [mɪz] *n* (= *Miss or Mrs*): ~ **X** ≈ Signora X, Sig.ra X.

MSA *n abbr* (*US*: = *Master of Science in Agriculture*) *titolo di studio.*

MSc *n abbr see* **Master of Science**.

MSG *abbr see* **monosodium glutamate**.

MSP *n abbr* = *Member of the Scottish Parliament.*

MST *abbr* (*US*: = *Mountain Standard Time*) *ora invernale delle Montagne Rocciose.*

MSW *n abbr* (*US*: = *Master of Social Work*) *titolo di studio.*

MT *n abbr* = *machine translation* ♦ (*US*) = *Montana.*

Mt *abbr* (*GEO*: = *mount*) M.

mth *abbr* (= *month*) m.

MTV *n abbr* = **music television**.

=================================== *KEYWORD*

much [mʌtʃ] *adj, pron* molto(a); **he's done so ~ work** ha lavorato così tanto; **I have as ~ money as you** ho tanti soldi quanti ne hai tu; **how ~ is it?** quant'è?; **it's not ~** non è tanto; **it costs too ~** costa troppo; **as ~ as you want** quanto vuoi

♦ *adv* **1** (*greatly*) molto, tanto; **thank you very** ~ molte grazie; **I like it very/so** ~ mi piace moltissimo/così tanto; ~ **to my amazement** con mio enorme stupore; **he's very** ~ **the gentleman** è il vero gentiluomo; **I read as** ~ **as I can** leggo quanto posso; **as** ~ **as you** tanto quanto te **2** (*by far*) molto; **it's** ~ **the biggest company in Europe** è di gran lunga la più grossa società in Europa **3** (*almost*) grossomodo, praticamente; **they're** ~ **the same** sono praticamente uguali.

muck [mʌk] *n* (*mud*) fango; (*dirt*) sporcizia.
▶**muck about, muck around** *vi* (*col*) fare lo stupido; (: *waste time*) gingillarsi; (*tinker*) armeggiare.
▶**muck in** *vi* (*BRIT col*) mettersi insieme.
▶**muck out** *vt* (*stable*) pulire.
▶**muck up** *vt* (*col: dirty*) sporcare; (: *spoil*) rovinare.
muckraking ['mʌkreɪkɪŋ] *n* (*fig col*) caccia agli scandali ♦ *adj* scandalistico(a).
mucky ['mʌkɪ] *adj* (*dirty*) sporco(a), lordo(a).
mucus ['mjuːkəs] *n* muco.
mud [mʌd] *n* fango.
muddle ['mʌdl] *n* confusione *f*, disordine *m*; pasticcio ♦ *vt* (*also*: ~ **up**) mettere sottosopra; confondere; **to be in a** ~ (*person*) non riuscire a raccapezzarsi; **to get in a** ~ (*while explaining*) imbrogliarsi.
▶**muddle along** *vi* andare avanti a casaccio.
▶**muddle through** *vi* cavarsela alla meno peggio.
muddle-headed [mʌdl'hɛdɪd] *adj* (*person*) confusionario(a).
muddy ['mʌdɪ] *adj* fangoso(a).
mud flats *npl* distesa fangosa.
mudguard ['mʌdgɑːd] *n* parafango.
mudpack ['mʌdpæk] *n* maschera di fango.
mud-slinging ['mʌdslɪŋɪŋ] *n* (*fig*) infangamento.
muesli ['mjuːzlɪ] *n* müsli *m inv*.
muff [mʌf] *n* manicotto ♦ *vt* (*shot, catch etc*) mancare, sbagliare; **to** ~ **it** sbagliare tutto.
muffin ['mʌfɪn] *n* specie di pasticcino *soffice da tè*.
muffle ['mʌfl] *vt* (*sound*) smorzare, attutire; (*against cold*) imbacuccare.
muffled ['mʌfld] *adj* smorzato(a), attutito(a).
muffler ['mʌflə*] *n* (*scarf*) sciarpa (pesante); (*US AUT*) marmitta; (*on motorbike*) silenziatore *m*.
mufti ['mʌftɪ] *n*: **in** ~ in borghese.

mug [mʌg] *n* (*cup*) tazzone *m*; (*for beer*) boccale *m*; (*col: face*) muso; (: *fool*) scemo/a ♦ *vt* (*assault*) assalire; **it's a** ~**'s game** (*BRIT*) è proprio (una cosa) da fessi.
▶**mug up** *vt* (*BRIT col: also*: ~ **up on**) studiare bene.
mugger ['mʌgə*] *n* aggressore *m*.
mugging ['mʌgɪŋ] *n* aggressione *f* (a scopo di rapina).
muggins ['mʌgɪnz] *n* (*col*) semplicione/a, sprovveduto/a.
muggy ['mʌgɪ] *adj* afoso(a).
mug shot *n* (*col*) foto *f inv* segnaletica.
mulatto, ~**es** [mjuː'lætəu] *n* mulatto/a.
mulberry ['mʌlbərɪ] *n* (*fruit*) mora (di gelso); (*tree*) gelso, moro.
mule [mjuːl] *n* mulo.
mull [mʌl]: **to** ~ **over** *vt* rimuginare.
mulled [mʌld] *adj*: ~ **wine** vino caldo.
multi... ['mʌltɪ] *prefix* multi....
multi-access [mʌltɪ'æksɛs] *adj* (*COMPUT*) ad accesso multiplo.
multicoloured, (*US*) **multicolored** ['mʌltɪkʌləd] *adj* multicolore, variopinto(a).
multifarious [mʌltɪ'fɛərɪəs] *adj* molteplice, svariato(a).
multilateral [mʌltɪ'lætərəl] *adj* (*POL*) multilaterale.
multi-level ['mʌltɪlɛvl] *adj* (*US*) = **multistorey**.
multimillionaire [mʌltɪmɪljə'nɛə*] *n* multimiliardario/a.
multinational [mʌltɪ'næʃənl] *adj, n* multinazionale (*f*).
multiple ['mʌltɪpl] *adj* multiplo(a); molteplice ♦ *n* multiplo; (*BRIT: also*: ~ **store**) *grande magazzino che fa parte di una catena*.
multiple choice *n* esercizi *mpl* a scelta multipla.
multiple crash *n* serie *f inv* di incidenti a catena.
multiple sclerosis *n* sclerosi *f* a placche.
multiplex ['mʌltɪplɛks] *n* (*also*: ~ **cinema**) cinema *m inv* multisale *inv*.
multiplication [mʌltɪplɪ'keɪʃən] *n* moltiplicazione *f*.
multiplication table *n* tavola pitagorica.
multiplicity [mʌltɪ'plɪsɪtɪ] *n* molteplicità.
multiply ['mʌltɪplaɪ] *vt* moltiplicare ♦ *vi* moltiplicarsi.
multiracial [mʌltɪ'reɪʃəl] *adj* multirazziale.
multistorey ['mʌltɪ'stɔːrɪ] *adj* (*BRIT: building, car park*) a più piani.
multitude ['mʌltɪtjuːd] *n* moltitudine *f*.
mum [mʌm] *n* (*BRIT*) mamma ♦ *adj*: **to keep** ~ non aprire bocca; ~**'s the word!** acqua

in bocca!

mumble ['mʌmbl] vt, vi borbottare.

mumbo jumbo ['mʌmbəʊ-] n (col) parole fpl incomprensibili.

mummify ['mʌmɪfaɪ] vt mummificare.

mummy ['mʌmɪ] n (BRIT: mother) mamma; (embalmed) mummia.

mumps [mʌmps] n orecchioni mpl.

munch [mʌntʃ] vt, vi sgranocchiare.

mundane [mʌn'deɪn] adj terra a terra inv.

Munich ['mjuːnɪk] n Monaco f (di Baviera).

municipal [mjuː'nɪsɪpl] adj municipale.

municipality [mjuːnɪsɪ'pælɪtɪ] n municipio.

munitions [mjuː'nɪʃənz] npl munizioni fpl.

mural ['mjʊərəl] n dipinto murale.

murder ['mɜːdə*] n assassinio, omicidio ♦ vt assassinare; **to commit** ~ commettere un omicidio.

murderer ['mɜːdərə*] n omicida m, assassino.

murderess ['mɜːdərɪs] n omicida f, assassina.

murderous ['mɜːdərəs] adj micidiale.

murk [mɜːk] n oscurità, buio.

murky ['mɜːkɪ] adj tenebroso(a), buio(a).

murmur ['mɜːmə*] n mormorio ♦ vt, vi mormorare; **heart** ~ (MED) soffio al cuore.

MusB(ac) n abbr (= Bachelor of Music) titolo di studio.

muscle ['mʌsl] n muscolo.

▶**muscle in** vi immischiarsi.

muscular ['mʌskjʊlə*] adj muscolare; (person, arm) muscoloso(a).

muscular dystrophy n distrofia muscolare.

MusD(oc) n abbr (= Doctor of Music) titolo di studio.

muse [mjuːz] vi meditare, sognare ♦ n musa.

museum [mjuː'zɪəm] n museo.

mush [mʌʃ] n pappa.

mushroom ['mʌʃrʊm] n fungo ♦ vi (fig) svilupparsi rapidamente.

mushy ['mʌʃɪ] adj (of food) spappolato(a); (sentimental) sdolcinato(a).

music ['mjuːzɪk] n musica.

musical ['mjuːzɪkəl] adj musicale ♦ n (show) commedia musicale.

music(al) box n carillon m inv.

musical chairs n gioco delle sedie (in cui bisogna sedersi non appena cessa la musica); (fig) scambio delle poltrone.

musical instrument n strumento musicale.

music centre n impianto m stereo inv monoblocco inv.

music hall n teatro di varietà.

musician [mjuː'zɪʃən] n musicista m/f.

music stand n leggio.

musk [mʌsk] n muschio.

musket ['mʌskɪt] n moschetto.

muskrat ['mʌskræt] n topo muschiato.

musk rose n (BOT) rosa muschiata.

Muslim ['mʌzlɪm] adj, n musulmano(a).

muslin ['mʌzlɪn] n mussola.

musquash ['mʌskwɒʃ] n (fur) rat musqué m inv.

mussel ['mʌsl] n cozza.

must [mʌst] aux vb (obligation): **I** ~ **do it** devo farlo; (probability): **he** ~ **be there by now** dovrebbe essere arrivato ormai; **I** ~ **have made a mistake** devo essermi sbagliato ♦ n: **this programme/trip is a** ~ è un programma/viaggio da non perdersi.

mustache ['mʌstæʃ] n (US) = **moustache**.

mustard ['mʌstəd] n senape f, mostarda.

mustard gas n iprite f.

muster ['mʌstə*] vt radunare; (also: ~ **up**: strength, courage) fare appello a.

mustiness ['mʌstɪnɪs] n odor di muffa or di stantio.

mustn't ['mʌsnt] = **must not**.

musty ['mʌstɪ] adj che sa di muffa or di rinchiuso.

mutant ['mjuːtənt] adj, n mutante (m).

mutate [mjuː'teɪt] vi subire una mutazione.

mutation [mjuː'teɪʃən] n mutazione f.

mute [mjuːt] adj, n muto(a).

muted ['mjuːtɪd] adj (noise) attutito(a), smorzato(a); (criticism) attenuato(a); (MUS) in sordina; (: trumpet) con sordina.

mutilate ['mjuːtɪleɪt] vt mutilare.

mutilation [mjuːtɪ'leɪʃən] n mutilazione f.

mutinous ['mjuːtɪnəs] adj (troops) ammutinato(a); (attitude) ribelle.

mutiny ['mjuːtɪnɪ] n ammutinamento ♦ vi ammutinarsi.

mutter ['mʌtə*] vt, vi borbottare, brontolare.

mutton ['mʌtn] n carne f di montone.

mutual ['mjuːtʃʊəl] adj mutuo(a), reciproco(a).

mutually ['mjuːtʃʊəlɪ] adv reciprocamente.

Muzak ® ['mjuːzæk] n (often pej) musica di sottofondo.

muzzle ['mʌzl] n muso; (protective device) museruola; (of gun) bocca ♦ vt mettere la museruola a.

MV abbr (= motor vessel) M/N, m/n.

MVP n abbr (US SPORT: = most valuable player) titolo ottenuto da sportivo.

MW abbr (RADIO: = medium wave) O.M.; (= megawatt) megawatt m inv.

my [maɪ] adj il(la) mio(a), pl i(le) miei(mie).

Myanmar ['maɪænmɑ:*] *n* Myanma.
myopic [maɪ'ɔpɪk] *adj* miope.
myriad ['mɪrɪəd] *n* miriade *f*.
myself [maɪ'sɛlf] *pron* (*reflexive*) mi;
(*emphatic*) io stesso(a); (*after prep*) me.
mysterious [mɪs'tɪərɪəs] *adj* misterioso(a).
mystery ['mɪstərɪ] *n* mistero.
mystery story *n* racconto del mistero.
mystic ['mɪstɪk] *adj, n* mistico(a).
mystical ['mɪstɪkəl] *adj* mistico(a).
mystify ['mɪstɪfaɪ] *vt* mistificare; (*puzzle*)
confondere.
mystique [mɪs'tiːk] *n* fascino.
myth [mɪθ] *n* mito.
mythical ['mɪθɪkl] *adj* mitico(a).
mythological [mɪθə'lɔdʒɪkl] *adj*
mitologico(a).
mythology [mɪ'θɔlədʒɪ] *n* mitologia.

N n

N, n [ɛn] *n* (*letter*) N, n *f or m inv*; **N for Nellie,**
(*US*) **N for Nan** ≈ N come Napoli.
N *abbr* (= *north*) N.
NA *n abbr* (*US:* = *Narcotics Anonymous*)
*associazione in aiuto dei
tossicodipendenti*; (*US*) = *National
Academy.*
n/a *abbr* (= *not applicable*) non pertinente.
NAACP *n abbr* (*US*) = *National Association for
the Advancement of Colored People.*
NAAFI ['næfɪ] *n abbr* (*BRIT:* = *Navy, Army, &
Air Force Institutes*) *organizzazione che
gestisce negozi, mense ecc. per il
personale militare.*
nab [næb] *vt* (*col*) beccare, acchiappare.
NACU *n abbr* (*US*) = *National Association of
Colleges and Universities.*
nadir ['neɪdɪə*] *n* (*ASTRONOMY*) nadir *m*;
(*fig*) punto più basso.
nag [næg] *n* (*pej: horse*) ronzino; (*person*)
brontolone/a ♦ *vt* tormentare ♦ *vi*
brontolare in continuazione.
nagging ['nægɪŋ] *adj* (*doubt, pain*)
persistente ♦ *n* brontolii *mpl*, osservazioni
fpl continue.
nail [neɪl] *n* (*human*) unghia; (*metal*) chiodo
♦ *vt* inchiodare; **to ~ sb down to a date/
price** costringere qn a un appuntamento/
ad accettare un prezzo; **to pay cash on
the ~** (*BRIT*) pagare a tamburo battente.

nailbrush ['neɪlbrʌʃ] *n* spazzolino da *or* per
unghie.
nailfile ['neɪlfaɪl] *n* lima da *or* per unghie.
nail polish *n* smalto da *or* per unghie.
nail polish remover *n* acetone *m*, solvente
m.
nail scissors *npl* forbici *fpl* da *or* per
unghie.
nail varnish *n* (*BRIT*) = **nail polish.**
Nairobi [naɪ'rəʊbɪ] *n* Nairobi *f*.
naïve [naɪ'iːv] *adj* ingenuo(a).
naïveté [nɑːiːv'teɪ], **naivety** [naɪ'iːvtɪ] *n*
ingenuità *f inv*.
naked ['neɪkɪd] *adj* nudo(a); **with the ~ eye**
a occhio nudo.
nakedness ['neɪkɪdnɪs] *n* nudità.
NAM *n abbr* (*US*) = *National Association of
Manufacturers.*
name [neɪm] *n* nome *m*; (*reputation*) nome,
reputazione *f* ♦ *vt* (*baby etc*) chiamare;
(*person, object*) identificare; (*price, date*)
fissare; **by ~** di nome; **she knows them all
by ~** li conosce tutti per nome; **in the ~
of** in nome di; **what's your ~?** come si
chiama?; **my ~ is Peter** mi chiamo Peter;
to take sb's ~ and address prendere
nome e indirizzo di qn; **to make a ~ for
o.s.** farsi un nome; **to get (o.s.) a bad ~**
farsi una cattiva fama *or* una brutta
reputazione; **to call sb ~s** insultare qn.
name dropping *n menzionare qualcuno
per fare bella figura.*
nameless ['neɪmlɪs] *adj* senza nome.
namely ['neɪmlɪ] *adv* cioè.
nameplate ['neɪmpleɪt] *n* (*on door etc*)
targa.
namesake ['neɪmseɪk] *n* omonimo.
nan bread [nɑːn-] *n tipo di pane indiano
poco lievitato di forma allungata.*
nanny ['nænɪ] *n* bambinaia.
nanny goat *n* capra.
nap [næp] *n* (*sleep*) pisolino; (*of cloth*)
peluria ♦ *vi*: **to be caught ~ping** essere
preso alla sprovvista; **to have a ~**
schiacciare un pisolino.
NAPA *n abbr* (*US:* = *National Association of
Performing Artists*) *associazione nazionale
degli artisti di palcoscenico.*
napalm ['neɪpɑːm] *n* napalm *m*.
nape [neɪp] *n*: **~ of the neck** nuca.
napkin ['næpkɪn] *n* tovagliolo; (*BRIT: for
baby*) pannolino.
Naples ['neɪplz] *n* Napoli *f*.
Napoleonic [nəpəʊlɪ'ɔnɪk] *adj*
napoleonico(a).
nappy ['næpɪ] *n* (*BRIT*) pannolino.
nappy liner *n* (*BRIT*) fogliettino igienico.
narcissistic [nɑːsɪ'sɪstɪk] *adj*

narcisistico(a).

narcissus, pl **narcissi** [nɑː'sɪsəs, -saɪ] n narciso.

narcotic [nɑː'kɔtɪk] n (MED) narcotico; ~**s** npl (drugs) narcotici, stupefacenti mpl.

nark [nɑːk] vt (BRIT col) scocciare.

narrate [nə'reɪt] vt raccontare, narrare.

narration [nə'reɪʃən] n narrazione f.

narrative ['nærətɪv] n narrativa ♦ adj narrativo(a).

narrator [nə'reɪtə*] n narratore/trice.

narrow ['nærəu] adj stretto(a); (resources, means) limitato(a), modesto(a); (fig): to take a ~ view of avere una visione limitata di ♦ vi restringersi; to have a ~ escape farcela per un pelo; to ~ sth down to ridurre qc a.

narrow gauge adj (RAIL) a scartamento ridotto.

narrowly ['nærəulɪ] adv: Maria ~ escaped drowning per un pelo Maria non è affogata; he ~ missed hitting the cyclist per poco non ha investito il ciclista.

narrow-minded [nærəu'maɪndɪd] adj meschino(a).

NAS n abbr (US) = National Academy of Sciences.

NASA ['næsə] n abbr (US: = National Aeronautics and Space Administration) N.A.S.A. f.

nasal ['neɪzl] adj nasale.

Nassau ['næsɔː] n Nassau f.

nastily ['nɑːstɪlɪ] adv con cattiveria.

nastiness ['nɑːstɪnɪs] n (of person, remark) cattiveria; (: spitefulness) malignità.

nasturtium [nəs'təːʃəm] n cappuccina, nasturzio (indiano).

nasty ['nɑːstɪ] adj (person, remark) cattivo(a); (: spiteful) maligno(a); (smell, wound, situation) brutto(a); to turn ~ (situation) mettersi male; (weather) guastarsi; (person) incattivirsi; it's a ~ business è una brutta faccenda, è un brutto affare.

NAS/UWT n abbr (BRIT: = National Association of Schoolmasters/Union of Women Teachers) sindacato di insegnanti in Inghilterra e Galles.

nation ['neɪʃən] n nazione f.

national ['næʃənl] adj nazionale ♦ n cittadino/a.

national anthem n inno nazionale.

National Curriculum n (BRIT) ≈ programma m scolastico ministeriale (in Inghilterra e Galles).

national debt n debito pubblico.

national dress n costume m nazionale.

National Guard n (US) milizia nazionale

(volontaria, in ogni stato).

National Health Service (NHS) n (BRIT) servizio nazionale di assistenza sanitaria, ≈ S.A.U.B. f.

National Insurance n (BRIT) ≈ Previdenza Sociale.

nationalism ['næʃnəlɪzəm] n nazionalismo.

nationalist ['næʃnəlɪst] adj, n nazionalista (m/f).

nationality [næʃə'nælɪtɪ] n nazionalità f inv.

nationalization [næʃnəlaɪ'zeɪʃən] n nazionalizzazione f.

nationalize ['næʃnəlaɪz] vt nazionalizzare.

nationally ['næʃnəlɪ] adv a livello nazionale.

national park n parco nazionale.

national press n stampa a diffusione nazionale.

National Security Council n (US) consiglio nazionale di sicurezza.

national service n (MIL) servizio militare.

National Trust n sovrintendenza ai beni culturali e ambientali; see boxed note.

NATIONAL TRUST

Fondato nel 1895, il **National Trust** è un'organizzazione che si occupa della tutela e salvaguardia di edifici e monumenti di interesse storico e di territori di interesse ambientale nel Regno Unito.

---

nation-wide ['neɪʃənwaɪd] adj diffuso(a) in tutto il paese ♦ adv in tutto il paese.

native ['neɪtɪv] n abitante m/f del paese; (in colonies) indigeno/a ♦ adj indigeno(a); (country) natio(a); (ability) innato(a); a ~ of Russia un nativo della Russia; a ~ speaker of French una persona di madrelingua francese; ~ language madrelingua.

Native American n discendente di tribù dell'America settentrionale.

Nativity [nə'tɪvɪtɪ] n (REL): the ~ la Natività.

nativity play n recita sulla Natività.

NATO ['neɪtəu] n abbr (= North Atlantic Treaty Organization) N.A.T.O. f.

natter ['nætə*] (BRIT col) vi chiacchierare ♦ n chiacchierata.

natural ['nætʃrəl] adj naturale; (ability) innato(a); (manner) semplice; **death from ~ causes** (LAW) morte f per cause naturali.

natural childbirth n parto indolore.

natural gas n gas m metano.

natural history n storia naturale.

naturalist ['nætʃrəlɪst] n naturalista m/f.

naturalization [nætʃrəlaɪ'zeɪʃən] n

naturalizzazione *f*; acclimatazione *f*.

naturalize ['nætʃrəlaɪz] *vt*: **to be ~d**
(*person*) naturalizzarsi.

naturally ['nætʃrəlɪ] *adv* naturalmente; (*by
nature*: *gifted*) di natura.

naturalness ['nætʃrəlnɪs] *n* naturalezza.

natural resources *npl* risorse *fpl* naturali.

natural selection *n* selezione *f* naturale.

natural wastage *n* (*INDUSTRY*)
diminuzione *f* di manodopera (*per
pensionamento, decesso etc*).

nature ['neɪtʃə*] *n* natura; (*character*)
natura, indole *f*; **by ~** di natura;
documents of a confidential ~ documenti
mpl di natura privata.

-natured ['neɪtʃəd] *suffix*: **ill~**
maldisposto(a).

nature reserve *n* (*BRIT*) parco naturale.

nature trail *n percorso tracciato in parchi
nazionali ecc con scopi educativi.*

naturist ['neɪtʃərɪst] *n* naturista *m/f*.

naught [nɔːt] *n* = **nought**.

naughtiness ['nɔːtɪnɪs] *n* cattiveria.

naughty ['nɔːtɪ] *adj* (*child*) birichino(a),
cattivello(a); (*story, film*) spinto(a).

nausea ['nɔːsɪə] *n* (*MED*) nausea; (*fig:
disgust*) schifo.

nauseate ['nɔːsɪeɪt] *vt* nauseare; far schifo
a.

nauseating ['nɔːsɪeɪtɪŋ] *adj* nauseante; (*fig*)
disgustoso(a).

nauseous ['nɔːsɪəs] *adj* nauseabondo(a);
(*feeling sick*): **to be ~** avere la nausea.

nautical ['nɔːtɪkl] *adj* nautico(a).

nautical mile *n* miglio nautico *or* marino.

naval ['neɪvl] *adj* navale.

naval officer *n* ufficiale *m* di marina.

nave [neɪv] *n* navata centrale.

navel ['neɪvl] *n* ombelico.

navigable ['nævɪgəbl] *adj* navigabile.

navigate ['nævɪgeɪt] *vt* percorrere
navigando ♦ *vi* navigare; (*AUT*) fare da
navigatore.

navigation [nævɪ'geɪʃən] *n* navigazione *f*.

navigator ['nævɪgeɪtə*] *n* (*NAUT, AVIAT*)
ufficiale *m* di rotta; (*explorer*) navigatore
m; (*AUT*) copilota *m/f*.

navvy ['nævɪ] *n* manovale *m*.

navy ['neɪvɪ] *n* marina; **Department of the
N~** (*US*) Ministero della Marina.

navy(-blue) ['neɪvɪ('bluː)] *adj* blu scuro *inv*.

Nazareth ['næzərɪθ] *n* Nazareth *f*.

Nazi ['nɑːtsɪ] *adj, n* nazista (*m/f*).

NB *abbr* (= *nota bene*) N.B.; (*Canada*) = *New
Brunswick*.

NBA *n abbr* (*US*: = *National Basketball
Association*) ≈ F.I.P. *f* (= *Federazione
Italiana Pallacanestro*); = *National Boxing*

Association.

NBC *n abbr* (*US*: = *National Broadcasting
Company*) *compagnia nazionale di
radiodiffusione.*

NBS *n abbr* (*US*: = *National Bureau of
Standards*) *ufficio per la normalizzazione.*

NC *abbr* (*COMM etc*: = *no charge*) gratis; (*US*)
= *North Carolina.*

NCC *n abbr* (*US*) = *National Council of
Churches.*

NCO *n abbr see* **non-commissioned**.

ND, N. Dak. *abbr* (*US*) = *North Dakota*.

NE *abbr* (*US*) = *Nebraska*; *New England*.

NEA *n abbr* (*US*) = *National Education
Association.*

neap [niːp] *n* (*also*: **~tide**) marea di
quadratura.

Neapolitan [nɪə'pɔlɪtən] *adj, n*
napoletano(a).

near [nɪə*] *adj* vicino(a); (*relation*)
prossimo(a) ♦ *adv* vicino ♦ *prep* (*also*: **~ to**)
vicino a, presso; (*time*) verso ♦ *vt*
avvicinarsi a; **to come ~** avvicinarsi; **~
here/there** qui/lì vicino; **£25,000 or ~est
offer** (*BRIT*) 25.000 sterline trattabili; **in
the ~ future** in un prossimo futuro; **the
building is ~ing completion** il palazzo è
quasi terminato *or* ultimato.

nearby [nɪə'baɪ] *adj* vicino(a) ♦ *adv* vicino.

Near East *n*: **the ~** il Medio Oriente.

nearer ['nɪərə*] *adj* più vicino(a) ♦ *adv* più
vicino.

nearly ['nɪəlɪ] *adv* quasi; **not ~** non ...
affatto; **I ~ lost it** per poco non lo
perdevo; **she was ~ crying** era lì lì per
piangere.

near miss *n*: **that was a ~** c'è mancato
poco.

nearness ['nɪənɪs] *n* vicinanza.

nearside ['nɪəsaɪd] *n* (*right-hand drive*) lato
sinistro; (*left-hand drive*) lato destro ♦ *adj*
sinistro(a); destro(a).

near-sighted [nɪə'saɪtɪd] *adj* miope.

neat [niːt] *adj* (*person, room*) ordinato(a);
(*work*) pulito(a); (*solution, plan*) ben
indovinato(a), azzeccato(a); (*spirits*)
liscio(a).

neatly ['niːtlɪ] *adv* con ordine; (*skilfully*)
abilmente.

neatness ['niːtnɪs] *n* (*tidiness*) ordine *m*;
(*skilfulness*) abilità.

Nebr. *abbr* (*US*) = *Nebraska*.

nebulous ['nɛbjuləs] *adj* nebuloso(a); (*fig*)
vago(a).

necessarily ['nɛsɪsrɪlɪ] *adv*
necessariamente; **not ~** non è detto, non
necessariamente.

necessary ['nɛsɪsrɪ] *adj* necessario(a); **if ~**

se necessario.

necessitate [nɪ'sɛsɪteɪt] vt rendere necessario(a).

necessity [nɪ'sɛsɪtɪ] n necessità f inv; **in case of** ~ in caso di necessità.

neck [nɛk] n collo; (of garment) colletto ♦ vi (col) pomiciare, sbaciucchiarsi; ~ **and** ~ testa a testa; **to stick one's** ~ **out** (col) rischiare (forte).

necklace ['nɛklɪs] n collana.

neckline ['nɛklaɪn] n scollatura.

necktie ['nɛktaɪ] n (esp US) cravatta.

nectar ['nɛktə*] n nettare m.

nectarine ['nɛktərɪn] n nocepesca.

née [neɪ] adj: ~ **Scott** nata Scott.

need [niːd] n bisogno ♦ vt aver bisogno di; **I** ~ **to do it** lo devo fare, bisogna che io lo faccia; **you don't** ~ **to go** non deve andare, non c'è bisogno che lei vada; **a signature is** ~**ed** occorre or ci vuole una firma; **to be in** ~ **of, have** ~ **of** aver bisogno di; **£10 will meet my immediate** ~**s** 10 sterline mi basteranno per le necessità più urgenti; **in case of** ~ in caso di bisogno or necessità; **there's no** ~ **for ...** non c'è bisogno or non occorre che ...; **there's no** ~ **to do ...** non occorre fare ...; **the** ~**s of industry** le esigenze dell'industria.

needle ['niːdl] n ago; (on record player) puntina ♦ vt punzecchiare.

needlecord ['niːdlkɔːd] n (BRIT) velluto a coste sottili.

needless ['niːdlɪs] adj inutile; ~ **to say, ...** inutile dire che ....

needlessly ['niːdlɪslɪ] adv inutilmente.

needlework ['niːdlwəːk] n cucito.

needn't ['niːdnt] = need not.

needy ['niːdɪ] adj bisognoso(a).

negation [nɪ'geɪʃən] n negazione f.

negative ['nɛgətɪv] n (PHOT) negativa, negativo; (ELEC) polo negativo; (LING) negazione f ♦ adj negativo(a); **to answer in the** ~ rispondere negativamente or di no.

negative equity n situazione in cui l'ammontare del mutuo su un immobile supera il suo valore sul mercato.

neglect [nɪ'glɛkt] vt trascurare ♦ n (of person, duty) negligenza; **state of** ~ stato di abbandono; **to** ~ **to do sth** trascurare or tralasciare di fare qc.

neglected [nɪ'glɛktɪd] adj trascurato(a).

neglectful [nɪ'glɛktful] adj (gen) negligente; **to be** ~ **of sb/sth** trascurare qn/qc.

negligee ['nɛglɪʒeɪ] n négligé m inv.

negligence ['nɛglɪdʒəns] n negligenza.

negligent ['nɛglɪdʒənt] adj negligente.

negligently ['nɛglɪdʒəntlɪ] adv con

negligenza.

negligible ['nɛglɪdʒɪbl] adj insignificante, trascurabile.

negotiable [nɪ'gəuʃɪəbl] adj negoziabile; (cheque) trasferibile; (road) transitabile.

negotiate [nɪ'gəuʃɪeɪt] vi negoziare ♦ vt (COMM) negoziare; (obstacle) superare; (bend in road) prendere; **to** ~ **with sb for sth** trattare con qn per ottenere qc.

negotiating table [nɪ'gəuʃɪeɪtɪŋ-] n tavolo delle trattative.

negotiation [nɪgəuʃɪ'eɪʃən] n trattativa; (POL) negoziato; **to enter into** ~**s with sb** entrare in trattative (or intavolare i negoziati) con qn.

negotiator [nɪ'gəuʃɪeɪtə*] n negoziatore/trice.

Negress ['niːgrɪs] n negra.

Negro ['niːgrəu] adj, n (pl ~**es**) negro(a).

neigh [neɪ] vi nitrire.

neighbour, (US**) neighbor** ['neɪbə*] n vicino/a.

neighbo(u)rhood ['neɪbəhud] n vicinato.

neighbourhood watch n (BRIT: also: ~ **scheme**) sistema di vigilanza reciproca in un quartiere.

neighbo(u)ring ['neɪbərɪŋ] adj vicino(a).

neighbo(u)rly ['neɪbəlɪ] adj: **he is a** ~ **person** è un buon vicino.

neither ['naɪðə*] adj, pron né l'uno(a) né l'altro(a), nessuno(a) dei(delle) due ♦ conj neanche, nemmeno, neppure ♦ adv: ~ **good nor bad** né buono né cattivo; **I didn't move and** ~ **did Claude** io non mi mossi e nemmeno Claude; **...** ~ **did I refuse ...**, ma non ho nemmeno rifiutato.

neo... ['niːəu] prefix neo....

neolithic [niːəu'lɪθɪk] adj neolitico(a).

neologism [nɪ'ɔlədʒɪzəm] n neologismo.

neon ['niːɔn] n neon m.

neon light n luce f al neon.

neon sign n insegna al neon.

Nepal [nɪ'pɔːl] n Nepal m.

nephew ['nɛvjuː] n nipote m.

nepotism ['nɛpətɪzəm] n nepotismo.

nerd [nəːd] n (col) sfigato/a, povero(a) fesso/a.

nerve [nəːv] n nervo; (fig) coraggio; (impudence) faccia tosta; **he gets on my** ~**s** mi dà ai nervi, mi fa venire i nervi; **a fit of** ~**s** una crisi di nervi; **to lose one's** ~ (self-confidence) perdere fiducia in se stesso; **I lost my** ~ (courage) mi è mancato il coraggio.

nerve centre n (ANAT) centro nervoso; (fig) cervello, centro vitale.

nerve gas n gas m nervino.

nerve-racking ['nəːvrækɪŋ] adj che spezza i

nervi.

nervous ['nəːvəs] *adj* nervoso(a).

nervous breakdown *n* esaurimento nervoso.

nervously ['nəːvəslɪ] *adv* nervosamente.

nervousness ['nəːvəsnɪs] *n* nervosismo.

nervous wreck *n*: **to be a ~** (*col*) essere nevrastenico(a).

nervy ['nəːvɪ] *adj* agitato(a), nervoso(a).

nest [nɛst] *n* nido; **~ of tables** tavolini *mpl* cicogna *inv*.

nest egg *n* (*fig*) gruzzolo.

nestle ['nɛsl] *vi* accoccolarsi.

nestling ['nɛslɪŋ] *n* uccellino di nido.

net [nɛt] *n* rete *f*; (*fabric*) tulle *m*; **the N~** (*Internet*) Internet *f* ♦ *adj* netto(a) ♦ *vt* (*subj: person*) ricavare un utile netto di; (*deal, sale*) dare un utile netto di; **~ of tax** netto, al netto di tasse; **he earns £10,000 ~ per year** guadagna 10.000 sterline nette all'anno.

netball ['nɛtbɔːl] *n specie di pallacanestro*.

net curtains *npl* tende *fpl* di tulle.

Netherlands ['nɛðələndz] *npl*: **the ~** i Paesi Bassi.

net profit *n* utile *m* netto.

netsurfer ['nɛtsəːfə*] *n* navigatore/trice in Internet.

nett [nɛt] *adj* = **net**.

netting ['nɛtɪŋ] *n* (*for fence etc*) reticolato; (*fabric*) tulle *m*.

nettle ['nɛtl] *n* ortica.

network ['nɛtwəːk] *n* rete *f*.

neuralgia [njuə'rældʒə] *n* nevralgia.

neurological [njuərə'lɔdʒɪkl] *adj* neurologico(a).

neurosis, *pl* **neuroses** [njuə'rəusɪs, -siːz] *n* nevrosi *f inv*.

neurotic [njuə'rɔtɪk] *adj, n* nevrotico(a).

neuter ['njuːtə*] *adj* neutro(a) ♦ *n* neutro ♦ *vt* (*cat etc*) castrare.

neutral ['njuːtrəl] *adj* neutro(a); (*person, nation*) neutrale ♦ *n* (*AUT*): **in ~** in folle.

neutrality [njuː'trælɪtɪ] *n* neutralità.

neutralize ['njuːtrəlaɪz] *vt* neutralizzare.

Nev. *abbr* (*US*) = *Nevada*.

never ['nɛvə*] *adv* (non...) mai; **~ again** mai più; **I'll ~ go there again** non ci vado più; **~ in my life** mai in vita mia; *see also* **mind**.

never-ending [nɛvər'ɛndɪŋ] *adj* interminabile.

nevertheless [nɛvəðə'lɛs] *adv* tuttavia, ciò nonostante, ciò nondimeno.

new [njuː] *adj* nuovo(a); (*brand new*) nuovo(a) di zecca; **as good as ~** come nuovo.

New Age *adj, n* New Age (*f*) *inv*.

newborn ['njuːbɔːn] *adj* neonato(a).

newcomer ['njuːkʌmə*] *n* nuovo(a) venuto(a).

new-fangled ['njuːfæŋgld] *adj* (*pej*) stramoderno(a).

new-found ['njuːfaund] *adj* nuovo(a).

Newfoundland ['njuːfənlənd] *n* Terranova.

New Guinea *n* Nuova Guinea.

newly ['njuːlɪ] *adv* di recente.

newly-weds ['njuːlɪwɛdz] *npl* sposini *mpl*, sposi *mpl* novelli.

new moon *n* luna nuova.

newness ['njuːnɪs] *n* novità.

news [njuːz] *n* notizie *fpl*; (*RADIO*) giornale *m* radio; (*TV*) telegiornale *m*; **a piece of ~** una notizia; **good/bad ~** buone/cattive notizie; **financial ~** (*PRESS*) pagina economica e finanziaria; (*RADIO, TV*) notiziario economico.

news agency *n* agenzia di stampa.

newsagent ['njuːzeɪdʒənt] *n* (*BRIT*) giornalaio.

news bulletin *n* (*RADIO, TV*) notiziario.

newscaster ['njuːzkɑːstə*] *n* (*RADIO, TV*) annunciatore/trice.

newsdealer ['njuːzdiːlə*] *n* (*US*) = **newsagent**.

newsflash ['njuːzflæʃ] *n* notizia *f* lampo *inv*.

newsletter ['njuːzlɛtə*] *n* bollettino (*di ditta, associazione*).

newspaper ['njuːzpeɪpə*] *n* giornale *m*; **daily ~** quotidiano; **weekly ~** settimanale *m*.

newsprint ['njuːzprɪnt] *n* carta da giornale.

newsreader ['njuːzriːdə*] *n* = **newscaster**.

newsreel ['njuːzriːl] *n* cinegiornale *m*.

newsroom ['njuːzrum] *n* (*PRESS*) redazione *f*; (*RADIO, TV*) studio.

news stand *n* edicola.

newsworthy ['njuːzwəːðɪ] *adj* degno(a) di menzione (*per radio, TV ecc*); **to be ~** fare notizia.

newt [njuːt] *n* tritone *m*.

new town *n* (*BRIT*) *nuovo centro urbano creato con fondi pubblici*.

New Year *n* Anno Nuovo; **Happy ~!** Buon Anno!; **to wish sb a happy ~** augurare Buon Anno a qn.

New Year's Day *n* il Capodanno.

New Year's Eve *n* la vigilia di Capodanno.

New York [-'jɔːk] *n* New York *f*, Nuova York *f*; (*also:* **~ State**) stato di New York.

New Zealand [-'ziːlənd] *n* Nuova Zelanda ♦ *adj* neozelandese.

New Zealander [-'ziːləndə*] *n* neozelandese *m/f*.

next [nɛkst] *adj* prossimo(a) ♦ *adv* accanto; (*in time*) dopo; **~ to** *prep* accanto a; **~ to**

nothing quasi niente; ~ **time** adv la prossima volta; ~ **week** la settimana prossima; **the** ~ **week** la settimana dopo or seguente; **the week after** ~ fra due settimane; **the** ~ **day** il giorno dopo, l'indomani; ~ **year** l'anno prossimo or venturo; "**turn to the** ~ **page**" "vedi pagina seguente"; **who's** ~? a chi tocca?; **when do we meet** ~? quando ci rincontriamo?

next door adv accanto.

next of kin n parente m/f prossimo(a).

NF n abbr (BRIT POL: = National Front) partito di estrema destra ♦ abbr (Canada) = **Newfoundland**.

NFL n abbr (US) = National Football League.

Nfld. abbr (Canada) = **Newfoundland**.

NG abbr (US) = National Guard.

NGO n abbr = non-governmental organization.

NH abbr (US) = New Hampshire.

NHL n abbr (US: = National Hockey League) ≈ F.I.H.P. f (= Federazione Italiana Hockey e Pattinaggio).

NHS n abbr (BRIT) see **National Health Service**.

NI abbr = **Northern Ireland**; (BRIT) = **National Insurance**.

Niagara Falls [naɪ'ægərə-] npl: **the** ~ le cascate del Niagara.

nib [nɪb] n (of pen) pennino.

nibble ['nɪbl] vt mordicchiare.

Nicaragua [nɪkə'rægjuə] n Nicaragua m.

Nicaraguan [nɪkə'rægjuən] adj, n nicaraguense (m/f).

Nice [niːs] n Nizza.

nice [naɪs] adj (holiday, trip) piacevole; (flat, picture) bello(a); (person) simpatico(a), gentile; (taste, smell, meal) buono(a); (distinction, point) sottile.

nice-looking ['naɪslukɪŋ] adj bello(a).

nicely ['naɪslɪ] adv bene; **that will do** ~ andrà benissimo.

niceties ['naɪsɪtɪz] npl finezze fpl.

nick [nɪk] n tacca ♦ vt intaccare; tagliare; (col: steal) rubare; (: BRIT: arrest) beccare; **in the** ~ **of time** appena in tempo; **in good** ~ (BRIT col) decente, in buono stato; **to** ~ o.s. farsi un taglietto.

nickel ['nɪkl] n nichel m; (US) moneta da cinque centesimi di dollaro.

nickname ['nɪkneɪm] n soprannome m ♦ vt soprannominare.

Nicosia [nɪkə'siːə] n Nicosia.

nicotine ['nɪkətiːn] n nicotina.

nicotine patch n cerotto antifumo (a base di nicotina).

niece [niːs] n nipote f.

nifty ['nɪftɪ] adj (col: car, jacket) chic inv; (: gadget, tool) ingegnoso(a).

Niger ['naɪdʒə*] n Niger m.

Nigeria [naɪ'dʒɪərɪə] n Nigeria.

Nigerian [naɪ'dʒɪərɪən] adj, n nigeriano(a).

niggardly ['nɪgədlɪ] adj (person) tirchio(a), spilorcio(a); (allowance, amount) misero(a).

nigger ['nɪgə*] n (col!: highly offensive) negro/a.

niggle ['nɪgl] vt assillare ♦ vi fare il(la) pignolo(a).

niggling ['nɪglɪŋ] adj pignolo(a); (detail) insignificante; (doubt, pain) persistente.

night [naɪt] n notte f; (evening) sera; **at** ~ la notte; la sera; **by** ~ di notte; **in the** ~, **during the** ~ durante la notte; **the** ~ **before last** l'altro ieri notte; l'altro ieri sera.

night-bird ['naɪtbəːd] n uccello notturno; (fig) nottambulo/a.

nightcap ['naɪtkæp] n bicchierino prima di andare a letto.

night club n locale m notturno.

nightdress ['naɪtdrɛs] n camicia da notte.

nightfall ['naɪtfɔːl] n crepuscolo.

nightie ['naɪtɪ] n camicia da notte.

nightingale ['naɪtɪŋgeɪl] n usignolo.

night life n vita notturna.

nightly ['naɪtlɪ] adj di ogni notte or sera; (by night) notturno(a) ♦ adv ogni notte or sera.

nightmare ['naɪtmɛə*] n incubo.

night porter n portiere m di notte.

night safe n cassa continua.

night school n scuola serale.

nightshade ['naɪtʃeɪd] n: **deadly** ~ (BOT) belladonna.

nightshift ['naɪtʃɪft] n turno di notte.

night-time ['naɪttaɪm] n notte f.

night watchman n guardiano notturno.

nihilism ['naɪɪlɪzəm] n nichilismo.

nil [nɪl] n nulla m; (SPORT) zero.

Nile [naɪl] n: **the** ~ il Nilo.

nimble ['nɪmbl] adj agile.

nine [naɪn] num nove.

9-11 n 11 settembre.

nineteen [naɪn'tiːn] num diciannove.

ninety ['naɪntɪ] num novanta.

ninth [naɪnθ] num nono(a).

nip [nɪp] vt pizzicare ♦ vi (BRIT col): **to** ~ **out/down/up** fare un salto fuori/giù/di sopra ♦ n (pinch) pizzico; (drink) goccio, bicchierino.

nipple ['nɪpl] n (ANAT) capezzolo.

nippy ['nɪpɪ] adj (weather) pungente; (BRIT: car, person) svelto(a).

nit [nɪt] n (of louse) lendine m; (col: idiot) cretino/a, scemo/a.

nit-pick ['nɪtpɪk] vi (col) cercare il pelo

nell'uovo.
nitrogen ['naɪtrədʒən] *n* azoto.
nitroglycerin(e) [naɪtrəʊ'glɪsəriːn] *n* nitroglicerina.
nitty-gritty ['nɪtɪ'grɪtɪ] *n* (*col*): **to get down to the** ~ venire al sodo.
nitwit ['nɪtwɪt] *n* (*col*) scemo/a.
NJ *abbr* (*US*) = New Jersey.
NLF *n abbr* (= National Liberation Front) ≈ F.L.N. *m.*
NLRB *n abbr* (*US*: = National Labor Relations Board) organismo per la tutela dei lavoratori.
NM, N. Mex. *abbr* (*US*) = New Mexico.

═══════════════ *KEYWORD*

no [nəʊ] *adv* (*opposite of "yes"*) no; **are you coming?** — ~ (**I'm not**) viene? — no (non vengo); **would you like some more?** — ~ **thank you** ne vuole ancora un po'? — no, grazie; **I have** ~ **more wine** non ho più vino
♦ *adj* (*not any*) nessuno(a); **I have** ~ **money/time/books** non ho soldi/tempo/libri; ~ **student would have done it** nessuno studente lo avrebbe fatto; **there is** ~ **reason to believe** ... non c'è nessuna ragione per credere ...; "~ **parking**" "divieto di sosta"; "~ **smoking**" "vietato fumare"; "~ **entry**" "ingresso vietato"; "~ **dogs**" "vietato l'accesso ai cani"
♦ *n* (*pl* ~**es**) no *m inv*; **I won't take** ~ **for an answer** non accetterò un rifiuto.

no. *abbr* (= number) n.
nobble ['nɒbl] *vt* (*BRIT col*: bribe: person) comprare, corrompere; (: person to speak to, criminal) bloccare, beccare; (*RACING*: horse, dog) drogare.
Nobel prize [nəʊ'bɛl-] *n* premio Nobel.
nobility [nəʊ'bɪlɪtɪ] *n* nobiltà.
noble ['nəʊbl] *adj, n* nobile (*m*).
nobleman ['nəʊblmən] *n* nobile *m*, nobiluomo.
nobly ['nəʊblɪ] *adv* (selflessly) generosamente.
nobody ['nəʊbədɪ] *pron* nessuno.
no-claims bonus ['nəʊkleɪmz-] *n* bonus malus *m inv*.
nocturnal [nɒk'təːnl] *adj* notturno(a).
nod [nɒd] *vi* accennare col capo, fare un cenno; (sleep) sonnecchiare ♦ *vt*: **to** ~ **one's head** fare di sì col capo ♦ *n* cenno; **they** ~**ded their agreement** accennarono di sì (col capo).
►**nod off** *vi* assopirsi.
no-fly zone [nəʊ'flaɪ-] *n* zona di interdizione aerea.

noise [nɔɪz] *n* rumore *m*; (*din, racket*) chiasso.
noiseless ['nɔɪzlɪs] *adj* silenzioso(a).
noisily ['nɔɪzɪlɪ] *adv* rumorosamente.
noisy ['nɔɪzɪ] *adj* (street, car) rumoroso(a); (person) chiassoso(a).
nomad ['nəʊmæd] *n* nomade *m/f*.
nomadic [nəʊ'mædɪk] *adj* nomade.
no man's land *n* terra di nessuno.
nominal ['nɒmɪnl] *adj* nominale.
nominate ['nɒmɪneɪt] *vt* (propose) proporre come candidato; (elect) nominare.
nomination [nɒmɪ'neɪʃən] *n* nomina; candidatura.
nominee [nɒmɪ'niː] *n* persona nominata; candidato/a.
non... [nɒn] *prefix* non....
non-alcoholic ['nɒnælkə'hɒlɪk] *adj* analcolico(a).
non-breakable [nɒn'breɪkəbl] *adj* infrangibile.
nonce word ['nɒns-] *n* parola coniata per l'occasione.
nonchalant ['nɒnʃələnt] *adj* incurante, indifferente.
non-commissioned [nɒnkə'mɪʃnd] *adj*: ~ **officer (NCO)** sottufficiale *m*.
non-committal [nɒnkə'mɪtl] *adj* evasivo(a).
nonconformist [nɒnkən'fɔːmɪst] *n* anticonformista *m/f*; (*BRIT REL*) dissidente *m/f* ♦ *adj* anticonformista.
non-contributory [nɒnkən'trɪbjutərɪ] *adj*: ~ **pension scheme** or (*US*) **plan** sistema di pensionamento con i contributi interamente a carico del datore di lavoro.
non-cooperation ['nɒnkəʊɒpə'reɪʃən] *n* non cooperazione *f*, non collaborazione *f*.
nondescript ['nɒndɪskrɪpt] *adj* qualunque *inv*.
none [nʌn] *pron* (not one thing) niente; (not one person) nessuno(a); ~ **of you** nessuno(a) di voi; **I have** ~ non ne ho nemmeno uno; **I have** ~ **left** non ne ho più; ~ **at all** proprio niente; (not one) nemmeno uno; **he's** ~ **the worse for it** non ne ha risentito.
nonentity [nɒ'nɛntɪtɪ] *n* persona insignificante.
non-essential [nɒnɪ'sɛnʃl] *adj* non essenziale ♦ *n*: ~**s** superfluo, cose *fpl* superflue.
nonetheless ['nʌnðə'lɛs] *adv* nondimeno.
non-event [nɒnɪ'vɛnt] *n* delusione *f*.
non-executive [nɒnɪg'zɛkjutɪv] *adj*: ~ **director** direttore *m* senza potere esecutivo.
non-existent [nɒnɪg'zɪstənt] *adj*

inesistente.
non-fiction [nɔn'fɪkʃən] *n* saggistica.
non-flammable [nɔn'flæməbl] *adj*
ininfiammabile.
non-intervention ['nɔnɪntə'vɛnʃən] *n* non
intervento.
no-no ['nəunəu] *n*: **it's a ~!** (*undesirable*) è
inaccettabile!; (*forbidden*) non si può
fare!
non obst. *abbr* (= *non obstante*:
notwithstanding) nonostante.
no-nonsense [nəu'nɔnsəns] *adj* che va al
sodo.
non-payment [nɔn'peɪmənt] *n* mancato
pagamento.
nonplussed [nɔn'plʌst] *adj* sconcertato(a).
non-profit-making [nɔn'prɔfɪtmeɪkɪŋ] *adj*
senza scopo di lucro.
nonsense ['nɔnsəns] *n* sciocchezze *fpl*; ~!
che sciocchezze!, che assurdità!; **it is ~**
to say that ... è un'assurdità *or* non ha
senso dire che ....
nonsensical [nɔn'sɛnsɪkl] *adj* assurdo(a),
ridicolo(a).
non-shrink [nɔn'ʃrɪŋk] *adj* (*BRIT*)
irrestringibile.
non-skid [nɔn'skɪd] *adj* antisdrucciolo(a).
non-smoker ['nɔn'sməukə*] *n* non
fumatore/trice.
non-starter [nɔn'stɑːtə*] *n*: **it's a ~** è fallito
in partenza.
non-stick ['nɔn'stɪk] *adj* antiaderente,
antiadesivo(a).
non-stop ['nɔn'stɔp] *adj* continuo(a); (*train,
bus*) direttissimo(a) ♦ *adv* senza sosta.
non-taxable [nɔn'tæksəbl] *adj*: ~ **income**
reddito non imponibile.
non-U [nɔn'juː] *adj abbr* (*BRIT col*) = *non-
upper class.*
non-volatile [nɔn'vɔlətaɪl] *adj*: ~ **memory**
(*COMPUT*) memoria permanente.
non-voting [nɔn'vəutɪŋ] *adj*: ~ **shares**
azioni *fpl* senza diritto di voto.
non-white ['nɔn'waɪt] *adj* di colore ♦ *n*
persona di colore.
noodles ['nuːdlz] *npl* taglierini *mpl*.
nook [nuk] *n*: ~**s and crannies** angoli *mpl*.
noon [nuːn] *n* mezzogiorno.
no one ['nəuwʌn] *pron* = **nobody.**
noose [nuːs] *n* nodo scorsoio, cappio;
(*hangman's*) cappio.
nor [nɔː*] *conj* = **neither** ♦ *adv* see **neither.**
norm [nɔːm] *n* norma.
normal ['nɔːml] *adj* normale ♦ *n*: **to return
to ~** tornare alla normalità.
normality [nɔː'mælɪtɪ] *n* normalità.
normally ['nɔːməlɪ] *adv* normalmente.
Normandy ['nɔːməndɪ] *n* Normandia.

north [nɔːθ] *n* nord *m*, settentrione *m* ♦ *adj*
nord *inv*, del nord, settentrionale ♦ *adv*
verso nord.
North Africa *n* Africa del Nord.
North African *adj, n* nordafricano(a).
North America *n* America del Nord.
North American *adj, n* nordamericano(a).
Northants [nɔː'θænts] *abbr* (*BRIT*)
= *Northamptonshire.*
northbound ['nɔːθbaund] *adj* (*traffic*)
diretto(a) a nord; (*carriageway*) nord *inv*.
north-east [nɔːθ'iːst] *n* nord-est *m*.
northerly ['nɔːðəlɪ] *adj* (*wind*) del nord;
(*direction*) verso nord.
northern ['nɔːðən] *adj* del nord,
settentrionale.
Northern Ireland *n* Irlanda del Nord.
North Pole *n*: **the ~** il Polo Nord.
North Sea *n*: **the ~** il mare del Nord.
North Sea oil *n* petrolio del mare del
Nord.
northward(s) ['nɔːθwəd(z)] *adv* verso nord.
north-west [nɔːθ'wɛst] *n* nord-ovest *m*.
Norway ['nɔːweɪ] *n* Norvegia.
Norwegian [nɔː'wiːdʒən] *adj* norvegese ♦ *n*
norvegese *m/f*; (*LING*) norvegese *m*.
nos. *abbr* (= *numbers*) nn.
nose [nəuz] *n* naso; (*of animal*) muso ♦ *vi*
(*also*: ~ **one's way**): **to pay through the ~ (for sth)** (*col*) pagare
(qc) un occhio della testa.
▶**nose about, nose around** *vi* aggirarsi.
nosebleed ['nəuzbliːd] *n* emorragia nasale.
nose-dive ['nəuzdaɪv] *n* picchiata.
nose drops *npl* gocce *fpl* per il naso.
nosey ['nəuzɪ] *adj* curioso(a).
nostalgia [nɔs'tældʒɪə] *n* nostalgia.
nostalgic [nɔs'tældʒɪk] *adj* nostalgico(a).
nostril ['nɔstrɪl] *n* narice *f*; (*of horse*) frogia.
nosy ['nəuzɪ] *adj* = **nosey.**
not [nɔt] *adv* non; ~ **at all** niente affatto;
(*after thanks*) prego, s'immagini; **you must
~** *or* **mustn't do this** non deve fare
questo; **he isn't ...** egli non è ...; **I hope ~**
spero di no.
notable ['nəutəbl] *adj* notevole.
notably ['nəutəblɪ] *adv* notevolmente; (*in
particular*) in particolare.
notary ['nəutərɪ] *n* (*also*: ~ **public**) notaio.
notation [nəu'teɪʃən] *n* notazione *f*.
notch [nɔtʃ] *n* tacca.
▶**notch up** *vt* (*score, victory*) marcare,
segnare.
note [nəut] *n* nota; (*letter, banknote*)
biglietto ♦ *vt* prendere nota di; **to take ~
of** prendere nota di; **to take ~s** prendere
appunti; **to compare ~s** (*fig*) scambiarsi
le impressioni; **of ~** eminente,

importante; **just a quick ~ to let you know** ... ti scrivo solo due righe per informarti ....

notebook ['nəutbuk] *n* taccuino; (*for shorthand*) bloc-notes *m inv*.

note-case ['nəutkeis] *n* (*BRIT*) portafoglio.

noted ['nəutid] *adj* celebre.

notepad ['nəutpæd] *n* bloc-notes *m inv*, blocchetto.

notepaper ['nəutpeipə*] *n* carta da lettere.

noteworthy ['nəutwə:ði] *adj* degno(a) di nota, importante.

nothing ['nʌθiŋ] *n* nulla *m*, niente *m*; **he does ~** non fa niente; **~ new** niente di nuovo; **for ~** (*free*) per niente; **~ at all** proprio niente.

notice ['nəutis] *n* avviso; (*of leaving*) preavviso; (*BRIT: review: of play etc*) critica, recensione *f* ♦ *vt* notare, accorgersi di; **to take ~ of** fare attenzione a; **to bring sth to sb's ~** far notare qc a qn; **to give sb ~ of sth** avvisare qn di qc; **to give ~, hand in one's ~** (*subj: employee*) licenziarsi; **without ~** senza preavviso; **at short ~** con un breve preavviso; **until further ~** fino a nuovo avviso; **advance ~** preavviso; **to escape** *or* **avoid ~** passare inosservato; **it has come to my ~ that** ... sono venuto a sapere che ....

noticeable ['nəutisəbl] *adj* evidente.

notice board *n* (*BRIT*) tabellone *m* per affissi.

notification [nəutifi'keiʃən] *n* annuncio; notifica; denuncia.

notify ['nəutifai] *vt*: **to ~ sth to sb** notificare qc a qn; **to ~ sb of sth** avvisare qn di qc; (*police*) denunciare qc a qn.

notion ['nəuʃən] *n* idea; (*concept*) nozione *f*.

notions ['nəuʃənz] *npl* (*US: haberdashery*) merceria.

notoriety [nəutə'raiəti] *n* notorietà.

notorious [nəu'tɔ:riəs] *adj* famigerato(a).

notoriously [nəu'tɔ:riəsli] *adv* notoriamente.

Notts [nɔts] *abbr* (*BRIT*) = Nottinghamshire.

notwithstanding [nɔtwiθ'stændiŋ] *adv* nondimeno ♦ *prep* nonostante, malgrado.

nougat ['nu:ga:] *n* torrone *m*.

nought [nɔ:t] *n* zero.

noun [naun] *n* nome *m*, sostantivo.

nourish ['nʌriʃ] *vt* nutrire.

nourishing ['nʌriʃiŋ] *adj* nutriente.

nourishment ['nʌriʃmənt] *n* nutrimento.

Nov. *abbr* (= *November*) nov.

Nova Scotia ['nəuvə'skəuʃə] *n* Nuova Scozia.

novel ['nɔvl] *n* romanzo ♦ *adj* nuovo(a).

novelist ['nɔvəlist] *n* romanziere/a.

novelty ['nɔvəlti] *n* novità *f inv*.

November [nəu'vɛmbə*] *n* novembre *m*; *for phrases see also* **July**.

novice ['nɔvis] *n* principiante *m/f*; (*REL*) novizio/a.

NOW [nau] *n abbr* (*US*: = *National Organization for Women*) ≈ U.D.I. *f* (= *Unione Donne Italiane*).

now [nau] *adv* ora, adesso ♦ *conj*: **~ (that)** adesso che, ora che; **right ~** subito; **by ~** ormai; **just ~: that's the fashion just ~** è la moda del momento; **I saw her just ~** l'ho vista proprio adesso; **I'll read it just ~** lo leggo subito; **~ and then, ~ and again** ogni tanto; **from ~ on** da ora in poi; **in 3 days from ~** fra 3 giorni; **between ~ and Monday** da qui a lunedì, entro lunedì; **that's all for ~** per ora basta.

nowadays ['nauədeiz] *adv* oggidì.

nowhere ['nəuwɛə*] *adv* in nessun luogo, da nessuna parte; **~ else** in nessun altro posto.

no-win situation [nəu'win-] *n*: **to be in a ~** aver perso in partenza.

noxious ['nɔkʃəs] *adj* nocivo(a).

nozzle ['nɔzl] *n* (*of hose etc*) boccaglio.

NP *n abbr* = **notary public**.

NS *abbr* (*Canada*) = **Nova Scotia**.

NSC *n abbr* (*US*) = **National Security Council**.

NSF *n abbr* (*US*) = *National Science Foundation*.

NSPCC *n abbr* (*BRIT*) = *National Society for the Prevention of Cruelty to Children*.

NSW *abbr* (*Australia*) = *New South Wales*.

NT *n abbr* (= *New Testament*) N.T. ♦ *abbr* (*Canada*) = *Northwest Territories*.

nth [ɛnθ] *adj*: **for the ~ time** (*col*) per l'ennesima volta.

nuance ['nju:ɑ:ns] *n* sfumatura.

nubile ['nju:bail] *adj* nubile; (*attractive*) giovane e desiderabile.

nuclear ['nju:kliə*] *adj* nucleare; (*warfare*) atomico(a).

nuclear disarmament *n* disarmo nucleare.

nuclear family *n* famiglia nucleare.

nuclear-free zone ['nju:kliə'fri:-] *n* zona denuclearizzata.

nucleus, *pl* **nuclei** ['nju:kliəs, 'nju:kliai] *n* nucleo.

NUCPS *n abbr* (*BRIT*) = *National Union of Civil and Public Servants*.

nude [nju:d] *adj* nudo(a) ♦ *n* (*ART*) nudo; **in the ~** tutto(a) nudo(a).

nudge [nʌdʒ] *vt* dare una gomitata a.

nudist ['nju:dist] *n* nudista *m/f*.

nudity ['nju:dɪtɪ] n nudità.
nugget ['nʌgɪt] n pepita.
nuisance ['nju:sns] n: **it's a** ~ è una seccatura; **he's a** ~ lui dà fastidio; **what a** ~**!** che seccatura!
NUJ n abbr (BRIT: = National Union of Journalists) sindacato nazionale dei giornalisti.
nuke [nju:k] n (col) bomba atomica.
null [nʌl] adj: ~ **and void** nullo(a).
nullify ['nʌlɪfaɪ] vt annullare.
NUM n abbr (BRIT: = National Union of Mineworkers) sindacato nazionale dei dipendenti delle miniere.
numb [nʌm] adj intorpidito(a) ♦ vt intorpidire; ~ **with** (fear) paralizzato(a) da; (grief) impietrito(a) da; ~ **with cold** intirizzito(a) (dal freddo).
number ['nʌmbə*] n numero ♦ vt numerare; (include) contare; **a** ~ **of** un certo numero di; **telephone** ~ numero di telefono; **wrong** ~ (TEL) numero sbagliato; **the staff** ~**s 20** gli impiegati sono in 20.
numbered account ['nʌmbəd-] n (in bank) conto numerato.
number plate n (BRIT AUT) targa.
Number Ten n (BRIT: = 10 Downing Street) residenza del Primo Ministro del Regno Unito.
numbness ['nʌmnɪs] n intorpidimento; (due to cold) intirizzimento.
numbskull ['nʌmskʌl] n (col) imbecille m/f, idiota m/f.
numeral ['nju:mərəl] n numero, cifra.
numerate ['nju:mərɪt] adj (BRIT): **to be** ~ saper far di conto.
numerical [nju:'mɛrɪkl] adj numerico(a).
numerous ['nju:mərəs] adj numeroso(a).
nun [nʌn] n suora, monaca.
nunnery ['nʌnərɪ] n convento.
nuptial ['nʌpʃəl] adj nuziale.
nurse [nə:s] n infermiere/a; (also: ~**maid**) bambinaia ♦ vt (patient, cold) curare; (baby: BRIT) cullare; (: US) allattare, dare il latte a; (hope) nutrire.
nursery ['nə:sərɪ] n (room) camera dei bambini; (institution) asilo; (for plants) vivaio.
nursery rhyme n filastrocca.
nursery school n scuola materna.
nursery slope n (BRIT SKI) pista per principianti.
nursing ['nə:sɪŋ] n (profession) professione f di infermiere (or di infermiera) ♦ adj (mother) che allatta.
nursing home n casa di cura.
nurture ['nə:tʃə*] vt allevare; nutrire.
NUS n abbr (BRIT: = National Union of

Students) sindacato nazionale degli studenti.
NUT n abbr (BRIT: = National Union of Teachers) sindacato nazionale degli insegnanti.
nut [nʌt] n (of metal) dado; (fruit) noce f (or nocciola or mandorla etc) ♦ adj (chocolate etc) alla nocciola etc; **he's** ~**s** (col) è matto.
nutcase ['nʌtkeɪs] n (col) mattarello/a.
nutcrackers ['nʌtkrækəz] npl schiaccianoci m inv.
nutmeg ['nʌtmɛg] n noce f moscata.
nutrient ['nju:trɪənt] adj nutriente ♦ n sostanza nutritiva.
nutrition [nju:'trɪʃən] n nutrizione f.
nutritionist [nju:'trɪʃənɪst] n nutrizionista m/f.
nutritious [nju:'trɪʃəs] adj nutriente.
nutshell ['nʌtʃɛl] n guscio di noce; **in a** ~ in poche parole.
nutty ['nʌtɪ] adj di noce (or nocciola or mandorla etc); (BRIT col) tocco(a), matto(a).
nuzzle ['nʌzl] vi: **to** ~ **up to** strofinare il muso contro.
NV abbr (US) = Nevada.
NWT abbr (Canada) = Northwest Territories.
NY abbr (US) = New York.
NYC abbr (US) = New York City.
nylon ['naɪlɔn] n nailon m; ~**s** npl calze fpl di nailon.
nymph [nɪmf] n ninfa.
nymphomaniac [nɪmfəu'meɪnɪæk] adj, n ninfomane (f).
NYSE abbr (US) = New York Stock Exchange.

O o

O, o [əu] n (letter) O, o f or m inv; (US SCOL: = outstanding) ≈ ottimo; (number: TEL etc) zero; **O for Oliver,** (US) **O for Oboe** ≈ O come Otranto.
oaf [əuf] n zoticone m.
oak [əuk] n quercia ♦ cpd di quercia.
OAP n abbr (BRIT) see **old-age pensioner**.
oar [ɔ:*] n remo; **to put** or **shove one's** ~ **in** (fig col) intromettersi.
oarsman ['ɔ:zmən], **oarswoman** ['ɔ:zwumən] n rematore/trice.
OAS n abbr (= Organization of American

States) O.S.A. *f* (= *Organizzazione degli Stati Americani*).

oasis, *pl* **oases** [əu'eɪsɪs, əu'eɪsiːz] *n* oasi *f inv.*

oath [əuθ] *n* giuramento; (*swear word*) bestemmia; **to take the** ~ giurare; **on** ~ (*BRIT*) *or* **under** ~ sotto giuramento.

oatmeal ['əutmiːl] *n* farina d'avena.

oats [əuts] *npl* avena.

obdurate ['ɔbdjurɪt] *adj* testardo(a); incallito(a); ostinato(a), irremovibile.

OBE *n abbr* (*BRIT*: = *Order of the British Empire*) titolo.

obedience [ə'biːdɪəns] *n* ubbidienza; **in** ~ **to** conformemente a.

obedient [ə'biːdɪənt] *adj* ubbidiente; **to be** ~ **to sb/sth** ubbidire a qn/qc.

obelisk ['ɔbɪlɪsk] *n* obelisco.

obese [əu'biːs] *adj* obeso(a).

obesity [əu'biːsɪtɪ] *n* obesità.

obey [ə'beɪ] *vt* ubbidire a; (*instructions, regulations*) osservare ♦ *vi* ubbidire.

obituary [ə'bɪtjuərɪ] *n* necrologia.

object *n* ['ɔbdʒɪkt] oggetto; (*purpose*) scopo, intento; (*LING*) complemento oggetto ♦ *vi* [əb'dʒɛkt]: **to** ~ **to** (*attitude*) disapprovare; (*proposal*) protestare contro, sollevare delle obiezioni contro; **I** ~! mi oppongo!; **he** ~**ed that ...** obiettò che ...; **do you** ~ **to my smoking?** la disturba se fumo?; **what's the** ~ **of doing that?** a che serve farlo?; **expense is no** ~ non si bada a spese.

objection [əb'dʒɛkʃən] *n* obiezione *f*; (*drawback*) inconveniente *m*; **if you have no** ~ se non ha obiezioni; **to make** *or* **raise an** ~ sollevare un'obiezione.

objectionable [əb'dʒɛkʃənəbl] *adj* antipatico(a); (*smell*) sgradevole; (*language*) scostumato(a).

objective [əb'dʒɛktɪv] *n* obiettivo ♦ *adj* obiettivo(a).

objectivity [ɔbdʒɪk'tɪvɪtɪ] *n* obiettività.

object lesson *n*: ~ **(in)** dimostrazione *f* (di).

objector [əb'dʒɛktə*] *n* oppositore/trice.

obligation [ɔblɪ'geɪʃən] *n* obbligo, dovere *m*; (*debt*) obbligo (di riconoscenza); "**without** ~" "senza impegno"; **to be under an** ~ **to sb/to do sth** essere in dovere verso qn/di fare qc.

obligatory [ə'blɪgətərɪ] *adj* obbligatorio(a).

oblige [ə'blaɪdʒ] *vt* (*force*): **to** ~ **sb to do** costringere qn a fare; (*do a favour*) fare una cortesia a; **to be** ~**d to sb for sth** essere grato a qn per qc; **anything to** ~! (*col*) questo e altro!

obliging [ə'blaɪdʒɪŋ] *adj* servizievole, compiacente.

oblique [ə'bliːk] *adj* obliquo(a); (*allusion*) indiretto(a) ♦ *n* (*BRIT TYP*): ~ **(stroke)** barra.

obliterate [ə'blɪtəreɪt] *vt* cancellare.

oblivion [ə'blɪvɪən] *n* oblio.

oblivious [ə'blɪvɪəs] *adj*: ~ **of** incurante di; inconscio(a) di.

oblong ['ɔblɔŋ] *adj* oblungo(a) ♦ *n* rettangolo.

obnoxious [əb'nɔkʃəs] *adj* odioso(a); (*smell*) disgustoso(a), ripugnante.

oboe ['əubəu] *n* oboe *m*.

obscene [əb'siːn] *adj* osceno(a).

obscenity [əb'sɛnɪtɪ] *n* oscenità *f inv.*

obscure [əb'skjuə*] *adj* oscuro(a) ♦ *vt* oscurare; (*hide: sun*) nascondere.

obscurity [əb'skjuərɪtɪ] *n* oscurità; (*obscure point*) punto oscuro; (*lack of fame*) anonimato.

obsequious [əb'siːkwɪəs] *adj* ossequioso(a).

observable [əb'zəːvəbl] *adj* osservabile; (*appreciable*) notevole.

observance [əb'zəːvns] *n* osservanza; **religious** ~**s** pratiche *fpl* religiose.

observant [əb'zəːvnt] *adj* attento(a).

observation [ɔbzə'veɪʃən] *n* osservazione *f*; (*by police etc*) sorveglianza.

observation post *n* (*MIL*) osservatorio.

observatory [əb'zəːvətrɪ] *n* osservatorio.

observe [əb'zəːv] *vt* osservare.

observer [əb'zəːvə*] *n* osservatore/trice.

obsess [əb'sɛs] *vt* ossessionare; **to be** ~**ed by** *or* **with sb/sth** essere ossessionato da qn/qc.

obsession [əb'sɛʃən] *n* ossessione *f*.

obsessive [əb'sɛsɪv] *adj* ossessivo(a).

obsolescence [ɔbsə'lɛsns] *n* obsolescenza; **built-in** *or* **planned** ~ (*COMM*) obsolescenza programmata.

obsolescent [ɔbsə'lɛsnt] *adj* obsolescente.

obsolete ['ɔbsəliːt] *adj* obsoleto(a); (*word*) desueto(a).

obstacle ['ɔbstəkl] *n* ostacolo.

obstacle race *n* corsa agli ostacoli.

obstetrician [ɔbstə'trɪʃən] *n* ostetrico/a.

obstetrics [ɔb'stɛtrɪks] *n* ostetrica.

obstinacy ['ɔbstɪnəsɪ] *n* ostinatezza.

obstinate ['ɔbstɪnɪt] *adj* ostinato(a).

obstreperous [əb'strɛpərəs] *adj* turbolento(a).

obstruct [əb'strʌkt] *vt* (*block*) ostruire, ostacolare; (*halt*) fermare; (*hinder*) impedire.

obstruction [əb'strʌkʃən] *n* ostruzione *f*; ostacolo.

obstructive [əb'strʌktɪv] *adj* ostruttivo(a); che crea impedimenti.

obtain – of

obtain [əb'teɪn] *vt* ottenere ♦ *vi* essere in uso; **to ~ sth (for o.s.)** procurarsi qc.
obtainable [əb'teɪnəbl] *adj* ottenibile.
obtrusive [əb'truːsɪv] *adj* (*person*) importuno(a); (*smell*) invadente; (*building etc*) imponente e invadente.
obtuse [əb'tjuːs] *adj* ottuso(a).
obverse ['ɔbvəːs] *n* opposto, inverso.
obviate ['ɔbvɪeɪt] *vt* ovviare a, evitare.
obvious ['ɔbvɪəs] *adj* ovvio(a), evidente.
obviously ['ɔbvɪəslɪ] *adv* ovviamente; ~! certo!; ~ **not!** certo che no!; **he was ~ not drunk** si vedeva che non era ubriaco; **he was not ~ drunk** non si vedeva che era ubriaco.
OCAS *n abbr* = *Organization of Central American States*.
occasion [ə'keɪʒən] *n* occasione *f*; (*event*) avvenimento ♦ *vt* cagionare; **on that ~ in** quell'occasione, quella volta; **to rise to the ~** mostrarsi all'altezza della situazione.
occasional [ə'keɪʒənl] *adj* occasionale; **I smoke an ~ cigarette** ogni tanto fumo una sigaretta.
occasionally [ə'keɪʒənəlɪ] *adv* ogni tanto; **very ~** molto raramente.
occasional table *n* tavolino.
occult [ɔ'kʌlt] *adj* occulto(a) ♦ *n*: **the ~** l'occulto.
occupancy ['ɔkjupənsɪ] *n* occupazione *f*.
occupant ['ɔkjupənt] *n* occupante *m/f*; (*of boat, car etc*) persona a bordo.
occupation [ɔkju'peɪʃən] *n* occupazione *f*; (*job*) mestiere *m*, professione *f*; **unfit for ~** (*house*) inabitabile.
occupational [ɔkju'peɪʃənl] *adj* (*disease*) professionale; (*hazard*) del mestiere; ~ **accident** infortunio sul lavoro.
occupational guidance *n* (*BRIT*) orientamento professionale.
occupational pension scheme *n sistema pensionistico programmato dal datore di lavoro.*
occupational therapy *n* ergoterapia.
occupier ['ɔkjupaɪə*] *n* occupante *m/f*.
occupy ['ɔkjupaɪ] *vt* occupare; **to ~ o.s. by doing** occuparsi a fare; **to be occupied with sth/in doing sth** essere preso da qc/occupato a fare qc.
occur [ə'kəː*] *vi* accadere; (*difficulty, opportunity*) capitare; (*phenomenon, error*) trovarsi; **to ~ to sb** venire in mente a qn.
occurrence [ə'kʌrəns] *n* caso, fatto; presenza.
ocean ['əuʃən] *n* oceano; ~**s of** (*col*) un sacco di.
ocean bed *n* fondale *m* oceanico.

ocean-going ['əuʃəngəuɪŋ] *adj* d'alto mare.
Oceania [əuʃɪ'ɑːnɪə] *n* Oceania.
ocean liner *n* transatlantico.
ochre, (*US*) **ocher** ['əukə*] *adj* ocra *inv*.
o'clock [ə'klɔk] *adv*: **it is one ~** è l'una; **it is 5 ~** sono le 5.
OCR *n abbr see* **optical character reader**; **optical character recognition**.
Oct. *abbr* (= *October*) ott.
octagonal [ɔk'tægənl] *adj* ottagonale.
octane ['ɔkteɪn] *n* ottano; **high-~ petrol** *or* (*US*) **gas** benzina ad alto numero di ottani.
octave ['ɔktɪv] *n* ottavo.
October [ɔk'təubə*] *n* ottobre *m*; *for phrases see also* **July.**
octogenarian [ɔktəudʒɪ'nɛərɪən] *n* ottuagenario/a.
octopus ['ɔktəpəs] *n* polpo, piovra.
odd [ɔd] *adj* (*strange*) strano(a), bizzarro(a); (*number*) dispari *inv*; (*left over*) in più; (*not of a set*) spaiato(a); **60-~** 60 e oltre; **at ~ times** di tanto in tanto; **the ~ one out** l'eccezione *f*.
oddball ['ɔdbɔːl] *n* (*col*) eccentrico/a.
oddity ['ɔdɪtɪ] *n* bizzarria; (*person*) originale *m/f*.
odd-job man [ɔd'dʒɔb-] *n* tuttofare *m inv*.
odd jobs *npl* lavori *mpl* occasionali.
oddly ['ɔdlɪ] *adv* stranamente.
oddments ['ɔdmənts] *npl* (*BRIT COMM*) rimanenze *fpl*.
odds [ɔdz] *npl* (*in betting*) quota; **the ~ are against his coming** c'è poca probabilità che venga; **it makes no ~** non importa; **at ~ in** contesa; **to succeed against all the ~** riuscire contro ogni aspettativa; ~ **and ends** avanzi *mpl*.
odds-on [ɔdz'ɔn] *adj* (*col*) probabile; ~ **favourite** (*RACING*) favorito(a).
ode [əud] *n* ode *f*.
odious ['əudɪəs] *adj* odioso(a), ripugnante.
odometer [ɔ'dɔmɪtə*] *n* odometro.
odour, (*US*) **odor** ['əudə*] *n* odore *m*.
odo(u)rless ['əudəlɪs] *adj* inodoro(a).
OECD *n abbr* (= *Organization for Economic Cooperation and Development*) O.C.S.E. *f* (= *Organizzazione per la Cooperazione e lo Sviluppo Economico*).
oesophagus, (*US*) **esophagus** [iː'sɔfəgəs] *n* esofago.
oestrogen, (*US*) **estrogen** ['iːstrəudʒən] *n* estrogeno.

========================= *KEYWORD*

of [ɔv, əv] *prep* **1** (*gen*) di; **a boy ~ 10** un ragazzo di 10 anni; **a friend ~ ours** un nostro amico; **that was kind ~ you** è stato

molto gentile da parte sua
2 (*expressing quantity, amount, dates etc*)
di; **a kilo ~ flour** un chilo di farina; **how
much ~ this do you need?** quanto gliene
serve?; **there were four ~ them** (*people*)
erano in quattro; (*objects*) ce n'erano
quattro; **three ~ us went** tre di noi sono
andati; **the 5th ~ July** il 5 luglio; **a quarter
~ 4** (*US*) le 4 meno un quarto
3 (*from, out of*) di, in; **made ~ wood**
(fatto) di *or* in legno.

Ofcom ['ɔfkɔm] *n abbr* (*BRIT*: = *Office of
Communications*) *organismo de
regolamentazione delle
telecomunicazioni.*

=================== *KEYWORD*

off [ɔf] *adv* **1** (*distance, time*): **it's a long way
~** è lontano; **the game is 3 days ~** la
partita è tra 3 giorni
2 (*departure, removal*) via; **to go ~ to
Paris** andarsene a Parigi; **I must be ~**
devo andare via; **to take ~ one's coat**
togliersi il cappotto; **the button came ~** il
bottone è venuto via *or* si è staccato; **10%
~** con lo sconto del 10%
3 (*not at work*): **to have a day ~** avere un
giorno libero; **to be ~ sick** essere assente
per malattia
♦ *adj* (*engine*) spento(a); (*tap*) chiuso(a);
(*cancelled*) sospeso(a); (*BRIT*: *food*)
andato(a) a male; **to be well/badly ~**
essere/non essere benestante; **the lid was
~** non c'era il coperchio; **I'm afraid the
chicken is ~** (*BRIT*: *not available*) purtroppo
il pollo è finito; **on the ~ chance** nel caso;
to have an ~ day non essere in forma;
that's a bit ~, isn't it? (*fig col*) non è molto
carino, vero?
♦ *prep* **1** (*motion, removal etc*) da; (*distant
from*) a poca distanza da; **a street ~ the
square** una strada che parte dalla piazza;
5km ~ the road a 5km dalla strada; **~ the
coast** al largo della costa; **a house ~ the
main road** una casa che non è sulla
strada principale
2: **to be ~ meat** non mangiare più la
carne.

offal ['ɔfl] *n* (*CULIN*) frattaglie *fpl.*
offbeat ['ɔfbiːt] *adj* eccentrico(a).
off-centre, (*US*) **off-center** [ɔf'sɛntə*] *adj*
storto(a), fuori centro.
off-colour ['ɔf'kʌlə*] *adj* (*BRIT*: *ill*) malato(a),
indisposto(a); **to feel ~** sentirsi poco
bene.
offence, (*US*) **offense** [ə'fɛns] *n* (*LAW*)

contravvenzione *f*; (: *more serious*) reato;
to give ~ to offendere; **to take ~ at**
offendersi per; **to commit an ~**
commettere un reato.
offend [ə'fɛnd] *vt* (*person*) offendere ♦ *vi*: **to
~ against** (*law, rule*) trasgredire.
offender [ə'fɛndə*] *n* delinquente *m/f*;
(*against regulations*) contravventore/trice.
offending [ə'fɛndɪŋ] *adj* (*often hum*): **the ~
word/object** la parola incriminata/
l'oggetto incriminato.
offense [ə'fɛns] *n* (*US*) = **offence**.
offensive [ə'fɛnsɪv] *adj* offensivo(a); (*smell
etc*) sgradevole, ripugnante ♦ *n* (*MIL*)
offensiva.
offer ['ɔfə*] *n* offerta, proposta ♦ *vt* offrire
"**on ~**" (*COMM*) "in offerta speciale"; **to
make an ~ for sth** fare un'offerta per qc;
to ~ sth to sb, **~ sb sth** offrire qc a qn; **to
~ to do sth** offrirsi di fare qc.
offering ['ɔfərɪŋ] *n* offerta.
offhand [ɔf'hænd] *adj* disinvolto(a),
noncurante ♦ *adv* all'impronto; **I can't tell
you ~** non posso dirglielo su due piedi.
office ['ɔfɪs] *n* (*place*) ufficio; (*position*)
carica; **doctor's ~** (*US*) ambulatorio; **to
take ~** entrare in carica; **through his
good ~s** con il suo prezioso aiuto; **O~ of
Fair Trading** (*BRIT*) *organismo di
protezione contro le pratiche
commerciali abusive.*
office automation *n* automazione *f*
d'ufficio, burotica.
office bearer *n* (*of club etc*) membro
dell'amministrazione.
office block, (*US*) **office building** *n*
complesso di uffici.
office boy *n* garzone *m*.
office hours *npl* orario d'ufficio; (*US MED*)
orario di visite.
office manager *n* capoufficio *m/f*.
officer ['ɔfɪsə*] *n* (*MIL etc*) ufficiale *m*; (*of
organization*) funzionario; (*also*: **police ~**)
agente *m* di polizia.
office work *n* lavoro d'ufficio.
office worker *n* impiegato/a d'ufficio.
official [ə'fɪʃl] *adj* (*authorized*) ufficiale ♦ *n*
ufficiale *m*; (*civil servant*) impiegato/a
statale; funzionario.
officialdom [ə'fɪʃəldəm] *n* burocrazia.
officially [ə'fɪʃəlɪ] *adv* ufficialmente.
official receiver *n* curatore *m*
fallimentare.
officiate [ə'fɪʃɪeɪt] *vi* (*REL*) ufficiare; **to ~ as
Mayor** esplicare le funzioni di sindaco; **to
~ at a marriage** celebrare un
matrimonio.
officious [ə'fɪʃəs] *adj* invadente.

offing ['ɔfɪŋ] n: **in the** ~ (fig) in vista.
off-key [ɔf'kiː] adj stonato(a) ♦ adv fuori
tono.
off-licence ['ɔflaɪsns] n (BRIT) spaccio di
bevande alcoliche; see boxed note.

OFF-LICENCE

In Gran Bretagna e in Irlanda, gli **off-licences**
sono esercizi pubblici specializzati nella vendita
strettamente regolamentata di bevande
alcoliche, per la quale è necessario avere
un'apposita licenza. In genere sono aperti fino
a tarda sera.

---

off-limits [ɔf'lɪmɪts] adj (esp US) in cui vige
il divieto d'accesso.
off line adj, adv (COMPUT) off line inv, fuori
linea; (: switched off) spento(a).
off-load ['ɔfləud] vt scaricare.
off-peak ['ɔf'piːk] adj (ticket etc) a tariffa
ridotta; (time) non di punta.
off-putting ['ɔfputɪŋ] adj (BRIT) un po'
scostante.
off-season ['ɔfsiːzn] adj, adv fuori stagione.
offset ['ɔfsɛt] vt irreg (counteract) contro-
bilanciare ♦ n (also: ~ printing) offset m.
offshoot ['ɔfʃuːt] n (fig) diramazione f.
offshore [ɔf'ʃɔː*] adj (breeze) di terra;
(island) vicino alla costa; (fishing)
costiero(a); ~ **oilfield** giacimento
petrolifero in mare aperto.
offside ['ɔf'saɪd] adj (SPORT) fuori gioco;
(AUT: with right-hand drive) destro(a);
(: with left-hand drive) sinistro(a) ♦ n
destra; sinistra.
offspring ['ɔfsprɪŋ] n prole f, discendenza.
offstage [ɔf'steɪdʒ] adv dietro le quinte.
off-the-cuff [ɔfðə'kʌf] adv improvvisando.
off-the-job ['ɔfðə'dʒɔb] adj: ~ **training**
addestramento fuori sede.
off-the-peg ['ɔfðə'pɛg], (US) **off-the-rack**
['ɔfðə'ræk] adv prêt-à-porter.
off-the-record ['ɔfðə'rɛkɔːd] adj
ufficioso(a) ♦ adv in via ufficiosa.
off-white ['ɔfwaɪt] adj bianco sporco inv.
Ofgem ['ɔfdʒɛm] n abbr (BRIT: = Office of Gas
and Electricity Markets) organo
indipendente di controllo per la tutela
dei consumatori.
often ['ɔfn] adv spesso; **how** ~ **do you go?**
quanto spesso ci va?; **as** ~ **as not** quasi
sempre.
Ofwat ['ɔfwɔt] n abbr (BRIT: = Office of Water
Services) in Inghilterra e Galles, organo
indipendente di controllo per la tutela
dei consumatori.
ogle ['əugl] vt occhieggiare.

ogre ['əugə*] n orco.
OH abbr (US) = Ohio.
oh [əu] excl oh!
OHMS abbr (BRIT) = On His (or Her) Majesty's
Service.
oil [ɔɪl] n olio; (petroleum) petrolio; (for
central heating) nafta ♦ vt (machine)
lubrificare.
oilcan ['ɔɪlkæn] n oliatore m a mano; (for
storing) latta da olio.
oil change n cambio dell'olio.
oilfield ['ɔɪlfiːld] n giacimento
petrolifero.
oil filter n (AUT) filtro dell'olio.
oil-fired ['ɔɪlfaɪəd] adj a nafta.
oil gauge n indicatore m del livello
dell'olio.
oil industry n industria del petrolio.
oil level n livello dell'olio.
oil painting n quadro a olio.
oil refinery n raffineria di petrolio.
oil rig n derrick m inv; (at sea) piattaforma
per trivellazioni subacquee.
oilskins ['ɔɪlskɪnz] npl indumenti mpl di tela
cerata.
oil slick n chiazza d'olio.
oil tanker n petroliera.
oil well n pozzo petrolifero.
oily ['ɔɪlɪ] adj unto(a), oleoso(a); (food)
untuoso(a).
ointment ['ɔɪntmənt] n unguento.
OK abbr (US) = Oklahoma.
O.K., okay [əu'keɪ] excl d'accordo! ♦ vt
approvare ♦ n: **to give sth one's** ~
approvare qc ♦ adj: **is it** ~?, **are you** ~?
tutto bene?; **it's** ~ **with** or **by me** per me
va bene; **are you** ~ **for money?** sei a posto
coi soldi?
Okla. abbr (US) = Oklahoma.
old [əuld] adj vecchio(a); (ancient) antico(a),
vecchio(a); (person) anziano(a),
anziano(a); **how** ~ **are you?** quanti anni
ha?; **he's 10 years** ~ ha 10 anni; ~**er
brother/sister** fratello/sorella maggiore;
any ~ **thing will do** va bene qualsiasi
cosa.
old age n vecchiaia.
old-age pensioner (OAP) ['əuldeɪdʒ-] n
(BRIT) pensionato/a.
old-fashioned ['əuld'fæʃnd] adj
antiquato(a), fuori moda; (person)
all'antica.
old maid n zitella.
old people's home n ricovero per
anziani.
old-style ['əuldstaɪl] adj (di) vecchio
stampo inv.
old-time ['əuldtaɪm] adj di una volta.

old-timer [əuld'taɪmə*] n veterano/a.
old wives' tale n vecchia superstizione f.
O levels npl (BRIT: formerly) diploma di istruzione secondaria conseguito a 16 anni in Inghilterra e Galles, ora sostituito dal GCSE.
olive ['ɔlɪv] n (fruit) oliva; (tree) olivo ♦ adj (also: ~-green) verde oliva inv.
olive oil n olio d'oliva.
Olympic [əu'lɪmpɪk] adj olimpico(a); **the ~ Games, the ~s** i giochi olimpici, le Olimpiadi.
OM n abbr (BRIT: = Order of Merit) titolo.
Oman [əu'mɑːn] n Oman m.
OMB n abbr (US: = Office of Management and Budget) servizio di consulenza al Presidente in materia di bilancio.
omelet(te) ['ɔmlɪt] n omelette f inv; **ham/ cheese** ~ omelette al prosciutto/al formaggio.
omen ['əumən] n presagio, augurio.
ominous ['ɔmɪnəs] adj minaccioso(a); (event) di malaugurio.
omission [əu'mɪʃən] n omissione f.
omit [əu'mɪt] vt omettere; **to ~ to do sth** tralasciare or trascurare di fare qc.
omnivorous [ɔm'nɪvərəs] adj onnivoro(a).
ON abbr (Canada) = Ontario.

═══════════════════════ KEYWORD

on [ɔn] prep **1** (indicating position) su; ~ **the wall** sulla parete; ~ **the left** a or sulla sinistra; **I haven't any money** ~ **me** non ho soldi con me
2 (indicating means, method, condition etc): ~ **foot** a piedi; ~ **the train/plane** in treno/ aereo; ~ **the telephone** al telefono; ~ **the radio/television** alla radio/televisione; **to be** ~ **drugs** drogarsi; ~ **holiday** in vacanza; **he's** ~ **£16,000 a year** guadagna 16.000 sterline all'anno; **this round's** ~ **me** questo giro lo offro io
3 (referring to time): ~ **Friday** venerdì; ~ **Fridays** il or di venerdì; ~ **June 20th** il 20 giugno; ~ **Friday, June 20th** venerdì, 20 giugno; **a week** ~ **Friday** venerdì a otto; ~ **his arrival** al suo arrivo; ~ **seeing this** vedendo ciò
4 (about, concerning) su, di; **information** ~ **train services** informazioni sui collegamenti ferroviari; **a book** ~ **Goldoni/physics** un libro su Goldoni/di or sulla fisica
♦ adv **1** (referring to dress, covering): **to have one's coat** ~ avere indosso il cappotto; **to put one's coat** ~ mettersi il cappotto; **what's she got** ~? cosa indossa?; **she put her boots/gloves/hat** ~ si mise gli stivali/i guanti/il cappello; **screw the lid** ~ **tightly** avvita bene il coperchio
2 (further, continuously): **to walk** ~, **go** etc continuare, proseguire; **to read** ~ continuare a leggere; ~ **and off** ogni tanto; **from that day** ~ da quel giorno in poi; **it was well** ~ **in the evening** era sera inoltrata
♦ adj **1** (in operation: machine, TV, light) acceso(a); (: tap) aperto(a); (: brake) inserito(a); **is the meeting still** ~? (in progress) la riunione è ancora in corso?; (not cancelled) è confermato l'incontro?; **there's a good film** ~ **at the cinema** danno un buon film al cinema; **when is the film** ~? quando c'è questo film?; **my father's always** ~ **at me to get a job** (col) mio padre mi tormenta sempre perché trovi un lavoro
2 (col): **that's not** ~! (not acceptable) non si fa così!; (not possible) non se ne parla neanche!

───────────────────────

once [wʌns] adv una volta ♦ conj non appena, quando; ~ **he had left/it was done** dopo che se n'era andato/fu fatto; **at** ~ subito; (simultaneously) a un tempo; **all at** ~ (tutto) ad un tratto; ~ **a week** una volta alla settimana; ~ **more** ancora una volta; **I knew him** ~ un tempo or in passato lo conoscevo; ~ **and for all** una volta per sempre; ~ **upon a time there was** … c'era una volta ….
oncoming ['ɔnkʌmɪŋ] adj (traffic) che viene in senso opposto.

═══════════════════════ KEYWORD

one [wʌn] num uno(a); ~ **hundred and fifty** centocinquanta; ~ **day** un giorno; **it's** ~ **(o'clock)** è l'una; **to be** ~ **up on sb** essere avvantaggiato(a) rispetto a qn; **to be at** ~ **(with sb)** andare d'accordo (con qn)
♦ adj **1** (sole) unico(a); **the** ~ **book which** l'unico libro che; **the** ~ **man who** l'unico che
2 (same) stesso(a); **they came in the** ~ **car** sono venuti nella stessa macchina
♦ pron **1**: **this** ~ questo(a); **that** ~ quello(a); **which** ~ **do you want?** quale vuole?; **I've already got** ~**/a red** ~ ne ho già uno/uno rosso; ~ **by** ~ uno per uno
2: **another** ~ l'un l'altro; **to look at** ~ **another** guardarsi; **to help** ~ **another** aiutarsi l'un l'altro or a vicenda
3 (impersonal) si; ~ **never knows** non si

sa mai; **to cut ~'s finger** tagliarsi un dito; **to express ~'s opinion** esprimere la propria opinione; **~ needs to eat** bisogna mangiare.

one-armed bandit ['wʌnɑːmd-] *n* slot-machine *f inv.*

one-day excursion ['wʌndeɪ-] *n* (*US*) biglietto giornaliero di andata e ritorno.

One-hundred share index ['wʌnhʌndrəd-] *n indice borsistico del Financial Times.*

one-man ['wʌn'mæn] *adj* (*business*) diretto(a) *etc* da un solo uomo.

one-man band *n suonatore ambulante con vari strumenti.*

one-off [wʌn'ɔf] (*BRIT col*) *n* fatto eccezionale ♦ *adj* eccezionale.

one-parent family ['wʌnpɛərənt-] *n* famiglia monogenitore.

one-piece ['wʌnpiːs] *adj* (*bathing suit*) intero(a).

onerous ['ɔnərəs] *adj* (*task, duty*) gravoso(a); (*responsibility*) pesante.

oneself [wʌn'sɛlf] *pron* si; (*after prep*) sé, se stesso(a); **to do sth (by) ~** fare qc da sé.

one-shot [wʌn'ʃɔt] *n* (*US*) = **one-off.**

one-sided [wʌn'saɪdɪd] *adj* (*decision, view*) unilaterale; (*judgement, account*) parziale; (*game, contest*) impari *inv.*

one-time ['wʌntaɪm] *adj* ex *inv.*

one-to-one ['wʌntəwʌn] *adj* (*relationship*) univoco(a).

one-upmanship [wʌn'ʌpmənʃɪp] *n*: **the art of ~** l'arte *f* di primeggiare.

one-way ['wʌnweɪ] *adj* (*street, traffic*) a senso unico.

ongoing ['ɔngəuɪŋ] *adj* in corso; in attuazione.

onion ['ʌnjən] *n* cipolla.

on line *adj* (*COMPUT*) on line *inv*, in linea; (*: switched on*) acceso(a).

onlooker ['ɔnlukə*] *n* spettatore/trice.

only ['əunlɪ] *adv* solo, soltanto ♦ *adj* solo(a), unico(a) ♦ *conj* solo che, ma; **an ~ child** un figlio unico; **not ~** non solo; **I ~ took one** ne ho preso soltanto uno, non ne ho preso che uno; **I saw her ~ yesterday** l'ho vista appena ieri; **I'd be ~ too pleased to help** sarei proprio felice di essere d'aiuto; **I would come, ~ I'm very busy** verrei volentieri, solo che sono molto occupato.

ono *abbr* = **or nearest offer;** *see* **near.**

onset ['ɔnsɛt] *n* inizio; (*of winter*) arrivo.

onshore ['ɔnʃɔː*] *adj* (*wind*) di mare.

onslaught ['ɔnslɔːt] *n* attacco, assalto.

Ont. *abbr* (*Canada*) = Ontario.

on-the-job ['ɔnðə'dʒɔb] *adj*: **~ training** addestramento in sede.

onto ['ɔntu] *prep* su, sopra.

onus ['əunəs] *n* onere *m*, peso; **the ~ is upon him to prove it** sta a lui dimostrarlo.

onward(s) ['ɔnwəd(z)] *adv* (*move*) in avanti; **from this time ~** d'ora in poi.

onyx ['ɔnɪks] *n* onice *f.*

oops [ups] *excl* ops! (*esprime rincrescimento per un piccolo contrattempo*); **~-a-daisy!** oplà!

ooze [uːz] *vi* stillare.

opacity [əu'pæsɪtɪ] *n* opacità.

opal ['əupl] *n* opale *m or f.*

opaque [əu'peɪk] *adj* opaco(a).

OPEC ['əupɛk] *n abbr* (= *Organization of Petroleum-Exporting Countries*) O.P.E.C. *f.*

open ['əupn] *adj* aperto(a); (*road*) libero(a); (*meeting*) pubblico(a); (*admiration*) evidente, franco(a); (*question*) insoluto(a); (*enemy*) dichiarato(a) ♦ *vt* aprire ♦ *vi* (*eyes, door, debate*) aprirsi; (*flower*) sbocciare; (*shop, bank, museum*) aprire; (*book etc: commence*) cominciare; **in the ~ (air)** all'aperto; **the ~ sea** il mare aperto, l'alto mare; **~ ground** (*among trees*) radura; (*waste ground*) terreno non edificato; **to have an ~ mind (on sth)** non avere ancora deciso (su qc).

▶**open on to** *vt fus* (*subj: room, door*) dare su.

▶**open out** *vt* aprire ♦ *vi* aprirsi.

▶**open up** *vt* aprire; (*blocked road*) sgombrare ♦ *vi* aprirsi.

open-air [əupn'ɛə*] *adj* all'aperto.

open-and-shut ['əupnən'ʃʌt] *adj*: **~ case** caso indubbio.

open day *n* (*BRIT*) giornata di apertura al pubblico.

open-ended [əupn'ɛndɪd] *adj* (*fig*) aperto(a), senza limiti.

opener ['əupnə*] *n* (*also*: **can ~**, **tin ~**) apriscatole *m inv.*

open-heart [əupn'hɑːt] *adj*: **~ surgery** chirurgia a cuore aperto.

opening ['əupnɪŋ] *n* apertura; (*opportunity*) occasione *f*, opportunità *f inv*; sbocco; (*job*) posto vacante.

opening night *n* (*THEAT*) prima.

open learning *n sistema educativo secondo il quale lo studente ha maggior controllo e gestione delle modalità di apprendimento.*

openly ['əupnlɪ] *adv* apertamente.

open-minded [əupn'maɪndɪd] *adj* che ha la mente aperta.

open-necked ['əupnnɛkt] *adj* col collo slacciato.

openness ['əupnnɪs] *n* (*frankness*) franchezza, sincerità.

open-plan ['əupn'plæn] *adj* senza pareti divisorie.

open prison *n istituto di pena dove viene data maggiore libertà ai detenuti.*

open sandwich *n* canapè *m inv.*

open shop *n fabbrica o ditta dove sono accolti anche operai non iscritti ai sindacati.*

Open University *n* (*BRIT*) *see boxed note.*

OPEN UNIVERSITY

La **Open University (OU)***, fondata in Gran Bretagna nel 1969, organizza corsi universitari per corrispondenza o via Internet, basati anche su lezioni che vengono trasmesse dalla BBC per radio e per televisione e su corsi estivi.*

---

opera ['ɔpərə] *n* opera.

opera glasses *npl* binocolo da teatro.

opera house *n* opera.

opera singer *n* cantante *m/f* d'opera *or* lirico(a).

operate ['ɔpəreit] *vt* (*machine*) azionare, far funzionare; (*system*) usare ♦ *vi* funzionare; (*drug, person*) agire; **to ~ on sb (for)** (*MED*) operare qn (di).

operatic [ɔpə'rætik] *adj* dell'opera, lirico(a).

operating ['ɔpəreitiŋ] *adj* (*COMM: costs etc*) di gestione; (*MED*) operatorio(a).

operating room *n* (*US*) = **operating theatre.**

operating system *n* (*COMPUT*) sistema *m* operativo.

operating theatre *n* (*MED*) sala operatoria.

operation [ɔpə'reiʃən] *n* operazione *f*; **to be in ~** (*machine*) essere in azione *or* funzionamento; (*system*) essere in vigore; **to have an ~ (for)** (*MED*) essere operato(a) (di).

operational [ɔpə'reiʃənl] *adj* operativo(a); (*COMM*) di gestione, d'esercizio; (*ready for use or action*) in attività, in funzione.

operative ['ɔpərətiv] *adj* (*measure*) operativo(a) ♦ *n* (*in factory*) operaio/a; **the ~ word** la parola chiave.

operator ['ɔpəreitə*] *n* (*of machine*) operatore/trice; (*TEL*) centralinista *m/f*.

operetta [ɔpə'retə] *n* operetta.

ophthalmologist [ɔfθæl'mɔlədʒist] *n* oftalmologo/a.

opinion [ə'pinjən] *n* opinione *f*, parere *m*; **in my ~** secondo me, a mio avviso; **to seek a second ~** (*MED etc*) consultarsi con un altro medico *etc*.

opinionated [ə'pinjəneitid] *adj* dogmatico(a).

opinion poll *n* sondaggio di opinioni.

opium ['əupiəm] *n* oppio.

opponent [ə'pəunənt] *n* avversario/a.

opportune ['ɔpətjuːn] *adj* opportuno(a).

opportunist [ɔpə'tjuːnist] *n* opportunista *m/f*.

opportunity [ɔpə'tjuːniti] *n* opportunità *f inv*, occasione *f*; **to take the ~ to do** *or* **of doing** cogliere l'occasione per fare.

oppose [ə'pəuz] *vt* opporsi a; **~d to** contrario(a) a; **as ~d to** in contrasto con.

opposing [ə'pəuziŋ] *adj* opposto(a); (*team*) avversario(a).

opposite ['ɔpəzit] *adj* opposto(a); (*house etc*) di fronte ♦ *adv* di fronte, dirimpetto ♦ *prep* di fronte a ♦ *n* opposto, contrario; (*of word*) contrario; **"see ~ page"** "vedere pagina a fronte".

opposite number *n* controparte *f*, corrispondente *m/f*.

opposite sex *n*: **the ~** l'altro sesso.

opposition [ɔpə'ziʃən] *n* opposizione *f*.

oppress [ə'pres] *vt* opprimere.

oppression [ə'preʃən] *n* oppressione *f*.

oppressive [ə'presiv] *adj* oppressivo(a).

opprobrium [ə'prəubriəm] *n* (*formal*) obbrobrio.

opt [ɔpt] *vi*: **to ~ for** optare per; **to ~ to do** scegliere di fare; **to ~ out of** (*BRIT: of NHS*) scegliere di non far più parte di; (*of agreement, arrangement*) scegliere di non partecipare a.

optical ['ɔptikl] *adj* ottico(a).

optical character reader/recognition (OCR) *n* lettore *m* ottico/lettura ottica di caratteri.

optical fibre *n* fibra ottica.

optician [ɔp'tiʃən] *n* ottico.

optics ['ɔptiks] *n* ottica.

optimism ['ɔptimizəm] *n* ottimismo.

optimist ['ɔptimist] *n* ottimista *m/f*.

optimistic [ɔpti'mistik] *adj* ottimistico(a).

optimum ['ɔptiməm] *adj* ottimale.

option ['ɔpʃən] *n* scelta; (*SCOL*) materia facoltativa; (*COMM*) opzione *f*; **to keep one's ~s open** (*fig*) non impegnarsi; **I have no ~** non ho scelta.

optional ['ɔpʃənl] *adj* facoltativo(a); (*COMM*) a scelta; **~ extra** optional *m inv*.

opulence ['ɔpjuləns] *n* opulenza.

opulent ['ɔpjulənt] *adj* opulento(a).

OR *abbr* (*US*) = Oregon.

or [ɔː*] *conj* o, oppure; (*with negative*): **he hasn't seen ~ heard anything** non ha visto né sentito niente; **~ else** se no, altrimenti; oppure.

oracle ['ɔrəkl] *n* oracolo.

oral [ˈɔːrəl] *adj* orale ♦ *n* esame *m* orale.

orange [ˈɔrɪndʒ] *n* (*fruit*) arancia ♦ *adj* arancione.

orangeade [ɔrɪndʒˈeɪd] *n* aranciata.

oration [ɔːˈreɪʃən] *n* orazione *f*.

orator [ˈɔrətə*] *n* oratore/trice.

oratorio [ɔrəˈtɔːrɪəu] *n* oratorio.

orb [ɔːb] *n* orbe *m*.

orbit [ˈɔːbɪt] *n* orbita ♦ *vt* orbitare intorno a; **to be in/go into ~ (round)** essere/entrare in orbita (attorno a).

orbital [ˈɔːbɪtl] *n* (*also*: **~ motorway**) raccordo anulare.

orchard [ˈɔːtʃəd] *n* frutteto; **apple ~** meleto.

orchestra [ˈɔːkɪstrə] *n* orchestra; (*US*: *seating*) platea.

orchestral [ɔːˈkɛstrəl] *adj* orchestrale; (*concert*) sinfonico(a).

orchestrate [ˈɔːkɪstreɪt] *vt* (*MUS*, *fig*) orchestrare.

orchid [ˈɔːkɪd] *n* orchidea.

ordain [ɔːˈdeɪn] *vt* (*REL*) ordinare; (*decide*) decretare.

ordeal [ɔːˈdiːl] *n* prova, travaglio.

order [ˈɔːdə*] *n* ordine *m*; (*COMM*) ordinazione *f* ♦ *vt* ordinare; **to ~ sb to do** ordinare a qn di fare; **in ~** in ordine; (*of document*) in regola; **in ~ of size** in ordine di grandezza; **in ~ to do** per fare; **in ~ that** affinché +*sub*; **a machine in working ~** una macchina che funziona bene; **to be out of ~** (*machine*, *toilets*) essere guasto(a); (*telephone*) essere fuori servizio; **to place an ~ for sth with sb** ordinare qc a qn; **to the ~ of** (*BANKING*) all'ordine di; **to be under ~s to do sth** avere l'ordine di fare qc; **a point of ~** una questione di procedura; **to be on ~** essere stato ordinato; **made to ~** fatto su commissione; **the lower ~s** (*pej*) i ceti inferiori.

order book *n* copiacommissioni *m inv*.

order form *n* modulo d'ordinazione.

orderly [ˈɔːdəlɪ] *n* (*MIL*) attendente *m* ♦ *adj* (*room*) in ordine; (*mind*) metodico(a); (*person*) ordinato(a), metodico(a).

order number *n* numero di ordinazione.

ordinal [ˈɔːdɪnl] *adj* (*number*) ordinale.

ordinary [ˈɔːdnrɪ] *adj* normale, comune; (*pej*) mediocre ♦ *n*: **out of the ~** diverso dal solito, fuori dell'ordinario.

ordinary degree *n* laurea; *see boxed note*.

ORDINARY DEGREE

Il corso universitario di studi che porta al conferimento del "Bachelor's degree" può

---

*avere una durata diversa, a seconda del profitto dello studente. Chi non è interessato a proseguire gli studi oltre tre anni di corso può optare per l'***ordinary degree***; vedi anche* **honours degree**.

---

ordinary seaman (OS) *n* (*BRIT*) marinaio semplice.

ordinary shares *npl* azioni *fpl* ordinarie.

ordination [ɔːdɪˈneɪʃən] *n* ordinazione *f*.

ordnance [ˈɔːdnəns] *n* (*MIL*: *unit*) (reparto di) sussistenza.

Ordnance Survey map *n* (*BRIT*) ≈ carta topografica dell'IGM.

ore [ɔː*] *n* minerale *m* grezzo.

Ore(g). *abbr* (*US*) = Oregon.

organ [ˈɔːgən] *n* organo.

organic [ɔːˈgænɪk] *adj* organico(a).

organism [ˈɔːgənɪzəm] *n* organismo.

organist [ˈɔːgənɪst] *n* organista *m/f*.

organization [ɔːgənaɪˈzeɪʃən] *n* organizzazione *f*.

organize [ˈɔːgənaɪz] *vt* organizzare; **to get ~d** organizzarsi.

organized crime [ˈɔːgənaɪzd-] *n* criminalità organizzata.

organized labour [ˈɔːgənaɪzd-] *n* manodopera organizzata.

organizer [ˈɔːgənaɪzə*] *n* organizzatore/trice.

orgasm [ˈɔːgæzəm] *n* orgasmo.

orgy [ˈɔːdʒɪ] *n* orgia.

Orient [ˈɔːrɪənt] *n*: **the ~** l'Oriente *m*.

oriental [ɔːrɪˈɛntl] *adj*, *n* orientale (*m/f*).

orientate [ˈɔːrɪənteɪt] *vt* orientare.

orifice [ˈɔrɪfɪs] *n* orifizio.

origin [ˈɔrɪdʒɪn] *n* origine *f*; **country of ~** paese *m* d'origine.

original [əˈrɪdʒɪnl] *adj* originale; (*earliest*) originario(a) ♦ *n* originale *m*.

originality [ərɪdʒɪˈnælɪtɪ] *n* originalità.

originally [əˈrɪdʒɪnəlɪ] *adv* (*at first*) all'inizio.

originate [əˈrɪdʒɪneɪt] *vi*: **to ~ from** venire da, essere originario(a) di; (*suggestion*) provenire da; **to ~ in** nascere in; (*custom*) avere origine in.

originator [əˈrɪdʒɪneɪtə*] *n* iniziatore/trice.

Orkneys [ˈɔːknɪz] *npl*: **the ~** (*also*: **the Orkney Islands**) le (isole) Orcadi.

ornament [ˈɔːnəmənt] *n* ornamento; (*trinket*) ninnolo.

ornamental [ɔːnəˈmɛntl] *adj* ornamentale.

ornamentation [ɔːnəmɛnˈteɪʃən] *n* decorazione *f*, ornamento.

ornate [ɔːˈneɪt] *adj* molto ornato(a).

ornithologist [ɔːnɪˈθɔlədʒɪst] *n* ornitologo/a.

ornithology [ɔ:nɪ'θɔlədʒɪ] *n* ornitologia.
orphan ['ɔ:fn] *n* orfano/a ♦ *vt*: **to be ~ed** diventare orfano.
orphanage ['ɔ:fənɪdʒ] *n* orfanotrofio.
orthodox ['ɔ:θədɔks] *adj* ortodosso(a).
orthopaedic, *(US)* **orthopedic** [ɔ:θə'pi:dɪk] *adj* ortopedico(a).
OS *abbr* (*BRIT*: = *Ordnance Survey*) ≈ IGM *m* (= *Istituto Geografico Militare*); (: *NAUT*) *see* **ordinary seaman**; (: *DRESS*) = **outsize**.
O.S. *abbr* = **out of stock**.
oscillate ['ɔsɪleɪt] *vi* oscillare.
OSHA *n abbr* (*US*: = *Occupational Safety and Health Administration*) amministrazione per la sicurezza e la salute sul lavoro.
Oslo ['ɔzləu] *n* Oslo *f*.
ostensible [ɔs'tɛnsɪbl] *adj* preteso(a); apparente.
ostensibly [ɔs'tɛnsɪblɪ] *adv* all'apparenza.
ostentation [ɔstɛn'teɪʃən] *n* ostentazione *f*.
ostentatious [ɔstɛn'teɪʃəs] *adj* pretenzioso(a); ostentato(a).
osteopath ['ɔstɪəpæθ] *n* specialista *m/f* di osteopatia.
ostracize ['ɔstrəsaɪz] *vt* dare l'ostracismo a.
ostrich ['ɔstrɪtʃ] *n* struzzo.
OT *abbr* (= *Old Testament*) V.T.
OTB *n abbr* (*US*: = *off-track betting*) puntate effettuate fuori dagli ippodromi.
OTE *abbr* (= *on-target earnings*) stipendio compreso le commissioni.
other ['ʌðə*] *adj* altro(a) ♦ *pron*: **the ~** l'altro(a); **the ~s** gli altri; **the ~ day** l'altro giorno; **some ~ people have still to arrive** (alcuni) altri devono ancora arrivare; **some actor or ~** un certo attore; **somebody or ~** qualcuno; **~ than** altro che; **a parte che; the car was none ~ than Roberta's** la macchina era proprio di Roberta.
otherwise ['ʌðəwaɪz] *adv*, *conj* altrimenti; **an ~ good piece of work** un lavoro comunque buono.
OTT *abbr* (*col*) = **over the top**; *see* **top**.
otter ['ɔtə*] *n* lontra.
OU *n abbr* (*BRIT*) *see* **Open University**.
ouch [autʃ] *excl* ohi!, ahi!
ought, *pt* **ought** [ɔ:t] *aux vb*: **I ~ to do it** dovrei farlo; **this ~ to have been corrected** questo avrebbe dovuto essere corretto; **he ~ to win** dovrebbe vincere; **you ~ to go and see it** dovreste andare a vederlo, fareste bene ad andarlo a vedere.
ounce [auns] *n* oncia (= *28.35 g; 16 in a pound*).
our [auə*] *adj* il(la) nostro(a), *pl* i(le) nostri(e).

ours [auəz] *pron* il(la) nostro(a), *pl* i(le) nostri(e).
ourselves [auə'sɛlvz] *pron pl* (*reflexive*) ci; (*after preposition*) noi; (*emphatic*) noi stessi(e); **we did it (all) by ~** l'abbiamo fatto (tutto) da soli.
oust [aust] *vt* cacciare, espellere.

══════════════════════ *KEYWORD*

out [aut] *adv* (*gen*) fuori; **~ here/there** qui/là fuori; **to speak ~ loud** parlare forte; **to have a night ~** uscire una sera; **to be ~ and about** *or* (*US*) **around again** essere di nuovo in piedi; **the boat was 10 km ~** la barca era a 10 km dalla costa; **the journey ~** l'andata; **3 days ~ from Plymouth** a 3 giorni da Plymouth
♦ *adj*: **to be ~** (*gen*) essere fuori; (*unconscious*) aver perso i sensi; (*style, singer*) essere fuori moda; **before the week was ~** prima che la settimana fosse finita; **to be ~ to do sth** avere intenzione di fare qc; **he's ~ for all he can get** sta cercando di trarne il massimo profitto; **to be ~ in one's calculations** aver sbagliato i calcoli
♦ **out of** *prep* **1** (*outside, beyond*) fuori di; **to go ~ of the house** uscire di casa; **to look ~ of the window** guardare fuori dalla finestra
2 (*because of*) per; **~ of pity** per pietà; **~ of boredom** per noia
3 (*origin*) da; **made ~ of wood** (fatto) di *or* in legno; **to drink ~ of a cup** bere da una tazza
4 (*from among*): **~ of 10** su 10
5 (*without*) senza; **~ of petrol** senza benzina; **it's ~ of stock** (*COMM*) è esaurito.

outage ['autɪdʒ] *n* (*esp US*: *power failure*) interruzione *f or* mancanza di corrente elettrica.
out-and-out ['autəndaut] *adj* vero(a) e proprio(a).
outback ['autbæk] *n* zona isolata; (*in Australia*) interno, entroterra.
outbid, *pt*, *pp* **outbid** [aut'bɪd] *vt* fare un'offerta più alta di.
outboard ['autbɔ:d] *n*: **~ (motor)** (motore *m*) fuoribordo.
outbound ['autbaund] *adj*: **~ (for *or* from)** in partenza (per *or* da).
outbreak ['autbreɪk] *n* scoppio; epidemia.
outbuilding ['autbɪldɪŋ] *n* dipendenza.
outburst ['autbə:st] *n* scoppio.
outcast ['autkɑ:st] *n* esule *m/f*; (*socially*) paria *m inv*.

outclass [aut'klɑːs] vt surclassare.
outcome ['autkʌm] n esito, risultato.
outcrop ['autkrɔp] n affioramento.
outcry ['autkraɪ] n protesta, clamore m.
outdated [aut'deɪtɪd] adj (custom, clothes) fuori moda; (idea) sorpassato(a).
outdistance [aut'dɪstəns] vt distanziare.
outdo [aut'duː] vt irreg sorpassare.
outdoor [aut'dɔː*] adj all'aperto.
outdoors [aut'dɔːz] adv fuori; all'aria aperta.
outer ['autə*] adj esteriore; ~ **suburbs** estrema periferia.
outer space n spazio cosmico.
outfit ['autfɪt] n equipaggiamento; (clothes) abito; (col: organization) organizzazione f.
outfitter ['autfɪtə*] n (BRIT): "**(gent's) ~s**" "confezioni da uomo".
outgoing ['autgəuɪŋ] adj (president, tenant) uscente; (means of transport) in partenza; (character) socievole.
outgoings ['autgəuɪŋz] npl (BRIT: expenses) spese fpl.
outgrow [aut'grəu] vt irreg (clothes) diventare troppo grande per.
outhouse ['authaus] n costruzione f annessa.
outing ['autɪŋ] n gita; escursione f.
outlandish [aut'lændɪʃ] adj strano(a).
outlast [aut'lɑːst] vt sopravvivere a.
outlaw ['autlɔː] n fuorilegge m/f ♦ vt (person) mettere fuori della legge; (practice) proscrivere.
outlay ['autleɪ] n spesa.
outlet ['autlɛt] n (for liquid etc) sbocco, scarico; (for emotion) sfogo; (for goods) sbocco, mercato; (also: retail ~) punto di vendita; (US ELEC) presa di corrente.
outline ['autlaɪn] n contorno, profilo; (summary) abbozzo, grandi linee fpl.
outlive [aut'lɪv] vt sopravvivere a.
outlook ['autluk] n prospettiva, vista.
outlying ['autlaɪɪŋ] adj periferico(a).
outmanoeuvre, (US) **outmaneuver** [autmə'nuːvə*] vt (rival etc) superare in strategia.
outmoded [aut'məudɪd] adj passato(a) di moda; antiquato(a).
outnumber [aut'nʌmbə*] vt superare in numero.
out-of-court [autəv'kɔːt] adj extragiudiziale ♦ adv (settle) senza ricorrere al tribunale.
out-of-date [autəv'deɪt] adj (passport, ticket) scaduto(a); (theory, idea) sorpassato(a), superato(a); (custom) antiquato(a); (clothes) fuori moda.
out-of-the-way ['autəvðə'weɪ] adj (remote)

fuori mano; (unusual) originale, insolito(a).
outpatient ['autpeɪʃənt] n paziente m/f esterno(a).
outpost ['autpəust] n avamposto.
outpouring ['autpɔːrɪŋ] n (fig) torrente m.
output ['autput] n produzione f; (COMPUT) output m inv ♦ vt emettere.
outrage ['autreɪdʒ] n oltraggio; scandalo ♦ vt oltraggiare.
outrageous [aut'reɪdʒəs] adj oltraggioso(a).
outrider ['autraɪdə*] n (on motorcycle) battistrada m inv.
outright adv [aut'raɪt] completamente; schiettamente; apertamente; sul colpo ♦ adj ['autraɪt] completo(a); schietto(a) e netto(a).
outrun [aut'rʌn] vt irreg superare (nella corsa).
outset ['autsɛt] n inizio.
outshine [aut'ʃaɪn] vt irreg (fig) eclissare.
outside [aut'saɪd] n esterno, esteriore m ♦ adj esterno(a), esteriore; (remote, unlikely): **an ~ chance** una vaga possibilità ♦ adv fuori, all'esterno ♦ prep fuori di, all'esterno di; **at the ~** (fig) al massimo; ~ **left/right** n (FOOTBALL) ala sinistra/destra.
outside broadcast n (RADIO, TV) trasmissione f in esterno.
outside lane n (AUT) corsia di sorpasso.
outside line n (TEL) linea esterna.
outsider [aut'saɪdə*] n (in race etc) outsider m inv; (stranger) straniero/a.
outsize ['autsaɪz] adj enorme; (clothes) per taglie forti.
outskirts ['autskəːts] npl sobborghi mpl.
outsmart [aut'smɑːt] vt superare in astuzia.
outspoken [aut'spəukən] adj molto franco(a).
outspread ['autsprɛd] adj (wings) aperto(a).
outstanding [aut'stændɪŋ] adj eccezionale, di rilievo; (unfinished) non completo(a); non evaso(a); non regolato(a); **your account is still ~** deve ancora saldare il conto.
outstay [aut'steɪ] vt: **to ~ one's welcome** diventare un ospite sgradito.
outstretched [aut'strɛtʃt] adj (hand) teso(a); (body) disteso(a).
outstrip [aut'strɪp] vt (also fig) superare.
out-tray ['auttreɪ] n raccoglitore m per le carte da spedire.
outvote [aut'vəut] vt: **to ~ sb (by)** avere la maggioranza rispetto a qn (per); **to ~ sth (by)** respingere qc (per).
outward ['autwəd] adj (sign, appearances)

esteriore; (*journey*) d'andata.

outwardly ['autwədlɪ] *adv* esteriormente; in apparenza.

outweigh [aut'weɪ] *vt* avere maggior peso di.

outwit [aut'wɪt] *vt* superare in astuzia.

oval ['əuvl] *adj, n* ovale (*m*).

Oval Office *n* (*US*) *see boxed note*.

OVAL OFFICE

L'**Oval Office** *è una grande stanza di forma ovale nella "White House", la Casa Bianca, dove ha sede l'ufficio del Presidente degli Stati Uniti. Spesso il termine è usato per indicare la stessa presidenza degli Stati Uniti.*

---

ovarian [əu'vɛərɪən] *adj* ovarico(a).

ovary ['əuvərɪ] *n* ovaia.

ovation [əu'veɪʃən] *n* ovazione *f*.

oven ['ʌvn] *n* forno.

ovenproof ['ʌvnpruːf] *adj* da forno.

oven-ready ['ʌvnrɛdɪ] *adj* pronto(a) da infornare.

ovenware ['ʌvnwɛə*] *n* vasellame *m* da mettere in forno.

over ['əuvə*] *adv* al di sopra; (*excessively*) molto, troppo ♦ *adj* (*or adv*) (*finished*) finito(a), terminato(a); (*too much*) troppo; (*remaining*) che avanza ♦ *prep* su; sopra; (*above*) al di sopra di; (*on the other side of*) di là di; (*more than*) più di; (*during*) durante; ~ **here** qui; ~ **there** là; **all** ~ (*everywhere*) dappertutto; (*finished*) tutto(a) finito(a); ~ **and** ~ (**again**) più e più volte; ~ **and above** oltre (a); **to ask sb** ~ invitare qn (a passare); **now** ~ **to our Rome correspondent** diamo ora la linea al nostro corrispondente da Roma; **the world** ~ in tutto il mondo; **she's not** ~ **intelligent** (*BRIT*) non è troppo intelligente; **they fell out** ~ **money** litigarono per una questione di denaro.

over... ['əuvə*] *prefix*: ~**abundant** sovrabbondante.

overact [əuvər'ækt] *vi* (*THEAT*) esagerare *or* strafare la propria parte.

overall *adj, n* ['əuvərɔːl] *adj* totale ♦ *n* (*BRIT*) grembiule *m* ♦ *adv* [əuvər'ɔːl] nell'insieme, complessivamente; ~**s** *npl* tuta (da lavoro).

overall majority *n* maggioranza assoluta.

overanxious [əuvər'æŋkʃəs] *adj* troppo ansioso(a).

overawe [əuvər'ɔː] *vt* intimidire.

overbalance [əuvə'bæləns] *vi* perdere l'equilibrio.

overbearing [əuvə'bɛərɪŋ] *adj* imperioso(a),

prepotente.

overboard ['əuvəbɔːd] *adv* (*NAUT*) fuori bordo, in acqua; **to go** ~ **for sth** (*fig*) impazzire per qc.

overbook [əuvə'buk] *vt* sovrapprenotare.

overcapitalize [əuvə'kæpɪtəlaɪz] *vt* sovraccapitalizzare.

overcast ['əuvəkɑːst] *adj* coperto(a).

overcharge [əuvə'tʃɑːdʒ] *vt*: **to** ~ **sb for sth** far pagare troppo caro a qn per qc.

overcoat ['əuvəkəut] *n* soprabito, cappotto.

overcome [əuvə'kʌm] *vt irreg* superare; sopraffare; ~ **with grief** sopraffatto(a) dal dolore.

overconfident [əuvə'kɔnfɪdənt] *adj* troppo sicuro(a) (di sé), presuntuoso(a).

overcrowded [əuvə'kraudɪd] *adj* sovraffollato(a).

overcrowding [əuvə'kraudɪŋ] *n* sovraffollamento; (*in bus*) calca.

overdo [əuvə'duː] *vt irreg* esagerare; (*overcook*) cuocere troppo; **to** ~ **it, to** ~ **things** (*work too hard*) lavorare troppo.

overdose ['əuvədəus] *n* dose *f* eccessiva.

overdraft ['əuvədrɑːft] *n* scoperto (di conto).

overdrawn [əuvə'drɔːn] *adj* (*account*) scoperto(a).

overdrive ['əuvədraɪv] *n* (*AUT*) overdrive *m inv*.

overdue [əuvə'djuː] *adj* in ritardo; (*recognition*) tardivo(a); (*bill*) insoluto(a); **that change was long** ~ quel cambiamento ci voleva da tempo.

overemphasis [əuvər'ɛmfəsɪs] *n*: ~ **on sth** importanza eccessiva data a qc.

overemphasize [əuvər'ɛmfəsaɪz] *vt* dare un'importanza eccessiva a.

overestimate [əuvər'ɛstɪmeɪt] *vt* sopravvalutare.

overexcited [əuvərɪk'saɪtɪd] *adj* sovraeccitato(a).

overexertion [əuvərɪg'zəːʃən] *n* logorio (fisico).

overexpose [əuvərɪk'spəuz] *vt* (*PHOT*) sovraesporre.

overflow *vi* [əuvə'fləu] traboccare ♦ *n* ['əuvəfləu] eccesso; (*also*: ~ **pipe**) troppopieno.

overfly [əuvə'flaɪ] *vt irreg* sorvolare.

overgenerous [əuvə'dʒɛnərəs] *adj* troppo generoso(a).

overgrown [əuvə'grəun] *adj* (*garden*) ricoperto(a) di vegetazione; **he's just an** ~ **schoolboy** è proprio un bambinone.

overhang [əuvə'hæŋ] *irreg vt* sporgere da ♦ *vi* sporgere.

overhaul *vt* [əuvə'hɔːl] revisionare ♦ *n*

['əuvəhɔːl] revisione *f.*

overhead *adv* [əuvə'hɛd] di sopra ♦ *adj* ['əuvəhɛd] aereo(a); (*lighting*) verticale ♦ *n* (*US*) = **overheads.**

overheads ['əuvəhɛdz] *npl* (*BRIT*) spese *fpl* generali.

overhear [əuvə'hɪə*] *vt irreg* sentire (per caso).

overheat [əuvə'hiːt] *vi* surriscaldarsi.

overjoyed [əuvə'dʒɔid] *adj* pazzo(a) di gioia.

overkill ['əuvəkɪl] *n* (*fig*) strafare *m.*

overland ['əuvəlænd] *adj, adv* per via di terra.

overlap *vi* [əuvə'læp] sovrapporsi ♦ *n* ['əuvəlæp] sovrapposizione *f.*

overleaf [əuvə'liːf] *adv* a tergo.

overload [əuvə'ləud] *vt* sovraccaricare.

overlook [əuvə'luk] *vt* (*have view of*) dare su; (*miss*) trascurare; (*forgive*) passare sopra a.

overlord ['əuvəlɔːd] *n* capo supremo.

overmanning [əuvə'mænɪŋ] *n* eccedenza di manodopera.

overnight *adv* [əuvə'naɪt] (*happen*) durante la notte; (*fig*) tutto ad un tratto ♦ *adj* ['əuvənaɪt] di notte; fulmineo(a); **he stayed there** ~ ci ha passato la notte; **if you travel** ~ ... se viaggia di notte ...; **he'll be away** ~ passerà la notte fuori.

overpass ['əuvəpɑːs] *n* cavalcavia *m inv.*

overpay [əuvə'peɪ] *vt*: **to** ~ **sb by £50** pagare 50 sterline in più a qn.

overplay [əuvə'pleɪ] *vt* dare troppa importanza a; **to** ~ **one's hand** sopravvalutare la propria posizione.

overpower [əuvə'pauə*] *vt* soppraffare.

overpowering [əuvə'pauərɪŋ] *adj* irresistibile; (*heat, stench*) soffocante.

overproduction ['əuvəprə'dʌkʃən] *n* sovrapproduzione *f.*

overrate [əuvə'reɪt] *vt* sopravvalutare.

overreach [əuvə'riːtʃ] *vt*: **to** ~ **o.s.** volere strafare.

overreact [əuvərɪ'ækt] *vi* reagire in modo esagerato.

override [əuvə'raɪd] *vt* (*irreg: like* **ride**) (*order, objection*) passar sopra a; (*decision*) annullare.

overriding [əuvə'raɪdɪŋ] *adj* preponderante.

overrule [əuvə'ruːl] *vt* (*decision*) annullare; (*claim*) respingere.

overrun [əuvə'rʌn] *vt irreg* (*MIL: country etc*) invadere; (*time limit etc*) superare, andare al di là di ♦ *vi* protrarsi; **the town is** ~ **with tourists** la città è invasa dai turisti.

overseas [əuvə'siːz] *adv* oltremare; (*abroad*) all'estero ♦ *adj* (*trade*) estero(a); (*visitor*)

straniero(a).

oversee [əuvə'siː] *vt irreg* sorvegliare.

overseer ['əuvəsɪə*] *n* (*in factory*) caposquadra *m.*

overshadow [əuvə'ʃædəu] *vt* (*fig*) eclissare.

overshoot [əuvə'ʃuːt] *vt irreg* superare.

oversight ['əuvəsaɪt] *n* omissione *f*, svista; **due to an** ~ per una svista.

oversimplify [əuvə'sɪmplɪfaɪ] *vt* rendere troppo semplice.

oversleep [əuvə'sliːp] *vi irreg* dormire troppo a lungo.

overspend [əuvə'spɛnd] *vi irreg* spendere troppo; **we have overspent by 5000 dollars** abbiamo speso 5000 dollari di troppo.

overspill ['əuvəspɪl] *n* eccedenza di popolazione.

overstaffed [əuvə'stɑːft] *adj*: **to be** ~ avere troppo personale.

overstate [əuvə'steɪt] *vt* esagerare.

overstatement [əuvə'steɪtmənt] *n* esagerazione *f.*

overstay [əuvə'steɪ] *vt*: **to** ~ **one's welcome** trattenersi troppo a lungo (come ospite).

overstep [əuvə'stɛp] *vt*: **to** ~ **the mark** superare ogni limite.

overstock [əuvə'stɔk] *vt* sovrapprovvigionare, sovraimmagazzinare.

overstretched [əuvə'strɛtʃt] *adj* sovraccarico(a); (*budget*) arrivato(a) al limite.

overstrike *n* ['əuvəstraɪk] (*on printer*) sovrapposizione *f* (di caratteri) ♦ *vt irreg* [əuvə'straɪk] sovrapporre.

overt [əu'vɔːt] *adj* palese.

overtake [əuvə'teɪk] *vt irreg* sorpassare.

overtaking [əuvə'teɪkɪŋ] *n* (*AUT*) sorpasso.

overtax [əuvə'tæks] *vt* (*ECON*) imporre tasse eccessive a, tassare eccessivamente; (*fig: strength, patience*) mettere alla prova, abusare di; **to** ~ **o.s.** chiedere troppo alle proprie forze.

overthrow [əuvə'θrəu] *vt irreg* (*government*) rovesciare.

overtime ['əuvətaɪm] *n* (*lavoro*) straordinario; **to do** *or* **work** ~ fare lo straordinario.

overtime ban *n* rifiuto sindacale a fare gli straordinari.

overtone ['əuvətəun] *n* (*also:* ~**s**) sfumatura.

overture ['əuvətʃuə*] *n* (*MUS*) ouverture *f inv*; (*fig*) approccio.

overturn [əuvə'tɔːn] *vt* rovesciare ♦ *vi* rovesciarsi.

overview ['əuvəvjuː] *n* visione *f* d'insieme.

overweight [əuvəˈweɪt] *adj* (*person*) troppo grasso(a); (*luggage*) troppo pesante.

overwhelm [əuvəˈwelm] *vt* sopraffare; sommergere; schiacciare.

overwhelming [əuvəˈwelmɪŋ] *adj* (*victory*) schiacciante; (*desire*) irresistibile; **one's ~ impression is of heat** l'impressione dominante è quella di caldo.

overwhelmingly [əuvəˈwelmɪŋlɪ] *adv* in massa.

overwork [əuvəˈwəːk] *vt* far lavorare troppo ♦ *vi* lavorare troppo, strapazzarsi.

overwrite [əuvəˈraɪt] *vt* (*COMPUT*) ricoprire.

overwrought [əuvəˈrɔːt] *adj* molto agitato(a).

ovulation [ɔvjuˈleɪʃən] *n* ovulazione *f*.

owe [əu] *vt* dovere; **to ~ sb sth, to ~ sth to sb** dovere qc a qn.

owing to [ˈəuɪŋtuː] *prep* a causa di.

owl [aul] *n* gufo.

own [əun] *adj* proprio(a) ♦ *vt* possedere ♦ *vi* (*BRIT*): **to ~ to sth** ammettere qc; **to ~ to having done sth** ammettere di aver fatto qc; **a room of my ~** la mia propria camera; **to get one's ~ back** vendicarsi; **on one's ~** tutto(a) solo(a); **can I have it for my (very) ~?** posso averlo tutto per me?; **to come into one's ~** mostrare le proprie qualità.

► **own up** *vi* confessare.

own brand *n* (*COMM*) etichetta propria.

owner [ˈəunə*] *n* proprietario/a.

owner-occupier [ˈəunərˈɔkjupaɪə*] *n* proprietario/a della casa in cui abita.

ownership [ˈəunəʃɪp] *n* possesso; **it's under new ~** ha un nuovo proprietario.

own goal *n* (*also fig*) autogol *m inv*.

ox, *pl* **oxen** [ɔks, ˈɔksn] *n* bue *m*.

Oxbridge [ˈɔksbrɪdʒ] *n* le università di Oxford e/o Cambridge; *see boxed note*.

Oxfam [ˈɔksfæm] *n abbr* (*BRIT*: = *Oxford Committee for Famine Relief*) organizzazione per aiuti al terzo mondo.

oxide [ˈɔksaɪd] *n* ossido.

Oxon. [ˈɔksn] *abbr* (*BRIT*: = *Oxoniensis*) = *of Oxford*.

oxtail [ˈɔksteɪl] *n*: **~ soup** minestra di coda di bue.

oxyacetylene [ˈɔksɪəˈsetɪliːn] *adj* ossiacetilenico(a); **~ burner, ~ lamp** cannello ossiacetilenico.

oxygen [ˈɔksɪdʒən] *n* ossigeno.

oxygen mask *n* maschera ad ossigeno.

oxygen tent *n* tenda ad ossigeno.

oyster [ˈɔɪstə*] *n* ostrica.

oz. *abbr* = **ounce**.

ozone [ˈəuzəun] *n* ozono.

ozone-friendly [ˈəuzəunˈfrendlɪ] *adj* che non danneggia lo strato d'ozono.

P p

P, p [piː] *n* (*letter*) P, p *f or m inv*; **P for Peter** ≈ P come Padova.

P *abbr* = **president; prince**.

p *abbr* (= *page*) p; (*BRIT*) = **penny, pence**.

PA *n abbr see* **personal assistant; public address system** ♦ *abbr* (*US*) = *Pennsylvania*.

pa [pɑː] *n* (*col*) papà *m inv*, babbo.

p.a. *abbr* = **per annum**.

PAC *n abbr* (*US*) = *political action committee*.

pace [peɪs] *n* passo; (*speed*) passo; velocità ♦ *vi*: **to ~ up and down** camminare su e giù; **to keep ~ with** camminare di pari passo a; (*events*) tenersi al corrente di; **to put sb through his ~s** (*fig*) mettere qn alla prova; **to set the ~** (*running*) fare l'andatura; (*fig*) dare il la or il tono.

pacemaker [ˈpeɪsmeɪkə*] *n* (*MED*) pacemaker *m inv*, stimolatore *m* cardiaco; (*SPORT*) chi fa l'andatura.

pacific [pəˈsɪfɪk] *adj* pacifico(a) ♦ *n*: **the P~ (Ocean)** il Pacifico, l'Oceano Pacifico.

pacification [pæsɪfɪˈkeɪʃən] *n* pacificazione *f*.

pacifier [ˈpæsɪfaɪə*] *n* (*US*: *dummy*) succhiotto, ciuccio (*col*).

pacifist [ˈpæsɪfɪst] *n* pacifista *m/f*.

pacify [ˈpæsɪfaɪ] *vt* pacificare; (*soothe*) calmare.

pack [pæk] *n* (*packet*) pacco; (*COMM*) confezione *f*; (*US*: *of cigarettes*) pacchetto; (*of goods*) balla; (*of hounds*) muta; (*of wolves*) branco; (*of thieves etc*) banda; (*of cards*) mazzo ♦ *vt* (*goods*) impaccare, imballare; (*in suitcase etc*) mettere; (*box*) riempire; (*cram*) stipare, pigiare; (*press down*) tamponare; turare; (*COMPUT*) comprimere, impaccare ♦ *vi*: **to ~ (one's bags)** fare la valigia; **to send sb ~ing** (*col*) spedire via qn.

▶**pack in** (*BRIT col*) *vi* (*watch, car*) guastarsi
♦ *vt* mollare, piantare; ~ **it in!** piantala!
▶**pack off** *vt* (*person*) spedire.
▶**pack up** *vi* (*BRIT col: machine*) guastarsi;
(: *person*) far fagotto ♦ *vt* (*belongings,
clothes*) mettere in una valigia; (*goods,
presents*) imballare.
package ['pækɪdʒ] *n* pacco; balla; (*also:* ~
deal) pacchetto; forfait *m inv* ♦ *vt* (*goods*)
confezionare.
package holiday *n* (*BRIT*) vacanza
organizzata.
package tour *n* viaggio organizzato.
packaging ['pækɪdʒɪŋ] *n* confezione *f*,
imballo.
packed [pækt] *adj* (*crowded*) affollato(a); ~
lunch (*BRIT*) pranzo al sacco.
packer ['pækə*] *n* (*person*) imballatore/
trice.
packet ['pækɪt] *n* pacchetto.
packet switching [-swɪtʃɪŋ] *n* (*COMPUT*)
commutazione *f* di pacchetto.
pack ice ['pækaɪs] *n* banchisa.
packing ['pækɪŋ] *n* imballaggio.
packing case *n* cassa da imballaggio.
pact [pækt] *n* patto, accordo; trattato.
pad [pæd] *n* blocco; (*for inking*) tampone *m*;
(*col: flat*) appartamentino ♦ *vt* imbottire
♦ *vi:* **to** ~ **about/in** *etc* camminare/entrare
etc a passi felpati.
padded cell ['pædɪd-] *n* cella imbottita.
padding ['pædɪŋ] *n* imbottitura; (*fig*)
riempitivo.
paddle ['pædl] *n* (*oar*) pagaia ♦ *vi* sguazzare
♦ *vt* (*boat*) fare andare a colpi di pagaia.
paddle steamer *n* battello a ruote.
paddling pool ['pædlɪŋ-] *n* piscina per
bambini.
paddock ['pædək] *n* recinto; paddock *m inv.*
paddy ['pædɪ] *n* (*also:* ~ **field**) risaia.
padlock ['pædlɔk] *n* lucchetto ♦ *vt* chiudere
con il lucchetto.
padre ['pɑːdrɪ] *n* cappellano.
Padua ['pædʒuə] *n* Padova.
paediatrician, (*US*) **pediatrician**
[piːdɪə'trɪʃən] *n* pediatra *m/f.*
paediatrics, (*US*) **pediatrics** [piːdɪ'ætrɪks]
n pediatria.
paedophile, (*US*) **pedophile** ['piːdəufaɪl]
adj, n pedofilo(a).
pagan ['peɪgən] *adj, n* pagano(a).
page [peɪdʒ] *n* pagina; (*also:* ~ **boy**)
fattorino; (: *at wedding*) paggio ♦ *vt* (*in
hotel etc*) (far) chiamare.
pageant ['pædʒənt] *n* spettacolo storico;
grande cerimonia.
pageantry ['pædʒəntrɪ] *n* pompa.
page break *n* interruzione *f* di pagina.

pager ['peɪdʒə*] *n* cicalino, cercapersone
m.
paginate ['pædʒɪneɪt] *vt* impaginare.
pagination [pædʒɪ'neɪʃən] *n* impaginazione
f.
pagoda [pə'gəudə] *n* pagoda.
paid [peɪd] *pt, pp of* **pay** ♦ *adj* (*work, official*)
rimunerato(a); **to put** ~ **to** (*BRIT*) mettere
fine a.
paid-up ['peɪdʌp], (*US*) **paid in** ['peɪdɪn] *adj*
(*member*) che ha pagato la sua quota;
(*share*) interamente pagato(a); ~ **capital**
capitale *m* interamente versato.
pail [peɪl] *n* secchio.
pain [peɪn] *n* dolore *m*; **to be in** ~ soffrire,
aver male; **to have a** ~ **in** aver male *or* un
dolore a; **to take** ~**s to do** mettercela
tutta per fare; **on** ~ **of death** sotto pena
di morte.
pained [peɪnd] *adj* addolorato(a), afflitto(a).
painful ['peɪnful] *adj* doloroso(a), che fa
male; (*difficult*) difficile, penoso(a).
painfully ['peɪnfəlɪ] *adv* (*fig: very*) fin troppo.
painkiller ['peɪnkɪlə*] *n* antalgico,
antidolorifico.
painstaking ['peɪnzteɪkɪŋ] *adj* sollecito(a).
paint [peɪnt] *n* (*for house etc*) tinta, vernice
f; (*ART*) colore *m* ♦ *vt* (*ART, walls*)
dipingere; (*door etc*) verniciare; **a tin of** ~
un barattolo di tinta *or* vernice; **to** ~ **the
door blue** verniciare la porta di azzurro;
to ~ **in oils** dipingere a olio.
paintbox ['peɪntbɔks] *n* scatola di colori.
paintbrush ['peɪntbrʌʃ] *n* pennello.
painter ['peɪntə*] *n* (*artist*) pittore *m*;
(*decorator*) imbianchino.
painting ['peɪntɪŋ] *n* (*activity: of artist*)
pittura; (: *of decorator*) imbianchino;
verniciatura; (*picture*) dipinto, quadro.
paint-stripper ['peɪntstrɪpə*] *n* prodotto
sverniciante.
paintwork ['peɪntwəːk] *n* (*BRIT*) tinta; (: *of
car*) vernice *f.*
pair [pɛə*] *n* (*of shoes, gloves etc*) paio; (*of
people*) coppia; duo *m inv*; **a** ~ **of scissors/
trousers** un paio di forbici/pantaloni.
▶**pair off** *vi:* **to** ~ **off (with sb)** fare coppia
(con qn).
pajamas [pə'dʒɑːməz] *npl* (*US*) pigiama *m.*
Pakistan [pɑːkɪ'stɑːn] *n* Pakistan *m.*
Pakistani [pɑːkɪ'stɑːnɪ] *adj, n* pakistano(a).
PAL [pæl] *n abbr* (*TV:* = *phase alternation line*)
PAL *m.*
pal [pæl] *n* (*col*) amico/a, compagno/a.
palace ['pæləs] *n* palazzo.
palatable ['pælɪtəbl] *adj* gustoso(a).
palate ['pælɪt] *n* palato.
palatial [pə'leɪʃəl] *adj* sontuoso(a),

sfarzoso(a).

palaver [pəˈlɑːvə*] *n* chiacchiere *fpl*; storie *fpl*.

pale [peɪl] *adj* pallido(a) ♦ *vi* impallidire ♦ *n*: **to be beyond the** ~ aver oltrepassato ogni limite; **to grow** *or* **turn** ~ (*person*) diventare pallido(a), impallidire; **to** ~ **into insignificance (beside)** perdere d'importanza (nei confronti di); ~ **blue** azzurro *or* blu pallido *inv*.

paleness [ˈpeɪlnɪs] *n* pallore *m*.

Palestine [ˈpælɪstaɪn] *n* Palestina.

Palestinian [pælɪsˈtɪnɪən] *adj, n* palestinese (*m/f*).

palette [ˈpælɪt] *n* tavolozza.

paling [ˈpeɪlɪŋ] *n* (*stake*) palo; (*fence*) palizzata.

palisade [pælɪˈseɪd] *n* palizzata.

pall [pɔːl] *n* (*of smoke*) cappa ♦ *vi*: **to** ~ (**on**) diventare noioso(a) (a).

pallet [ˈpælɪt] *n* (*for goods*) paletta.

pallid [ˈpælɪd] *adj* pallido(a), smorto(a).

pallor [ˈpælə*] *n* pallore *m*.

pally [ˈpælɪ] *adj* (*col*) amichevole.

palm [pɑːm] *n* (ANAT) palma, palmo; (*also*: ~ **tree**) palma ♦ *vt*: **to** ~ **sth off on sb** (*col*) rifilare qc a qn.

palmist [ˈpɑːmɪst] *n* chiromante *m/f*.

Palm Sunday *n* Domenica delle Palme.

palpable [ˈpælpəbl] *adj* palpabile.

palpitation [pælpɪˈteɪʃən] *n* palpitazione *f*; **to have** ~**s** avere le palpitazioni.

paltry [ˈpɔːltrɪ] *adj* derisorio(a); insignificante.

pamper [ˈpæmpə*] *vt* viziare, accarezzare.

pamphlet [ˈpæmflət] *n* dépliant *m inv*; (*political etc*) volantino, manifestino.

pan [pæn] *n* (*also*: **sauce**~) casseruola; (*also*: **frying** ~) padella ♦ *vi* (CINE) fare una panoramica; **to** ~ **for gold** (lavare le sabbie aurifere per) cercare l'oro.

panacea [pænəˈsɪə] *n* panacea.

panache [pəˈnæʃ] *n* stile *m*.

Panama [ˈpænəmɑː] *n* Panama *m*.

Panama Canal *n* canale *m* di Panama.

Panamanian [pænəˈmeɪnɪən] *adj, n* panamense (*m/f*).

pancake [ˈpænkeɪk] *n* frittella.

Pancake Day *n* (BRIT) martedì *m* grasso.

pancake roll *n* crêpe ripiena di verdure alla cinese.

pancreas [ˈpæŋkrɪəs] *n* pancreas *m inv*.

panda [ˈpændə] *n* panda *m inv*.

panda car *n* (BRIT) auto *f* della polizia.

pandemonium [pændɪˈməunɪəm] *n* pandemonio.

pander [ˈpændə*] *vi*: **to** ~ **to** lusingare; concedere tutto a.

p & h *abbr* (US: = postage and handling) affrancatura e trasporto.

P & L *abbr* (= profit and loss) P.P.

p & p *abbr* (BRIT: = postage and packing) affrancatura ed imballaggio.

pane [peɪn] *n* vetro.

panel [ˈpænl] *n* (*of wood, cloth etc*) pannello; (RADIO, TV) giuria.

panel game *n* (BRIT) quiz *m inv* a squadre.

panelling, (US) **paneling** [ˈpænəlɪŋ] *n* rivestimento a pannelli.

panellist, (US) **panelist** [ˈpænəlɪst] *n* partecipante *m/f* (al quiz, alla tavola rotonda *etc*).

pang [pæŋ] *n*: **to feel** ~**s of remorse** essere torturato(a) dal rimorso; ~**s of hunger** spasimi *mpl* della fame; ~**s of conscience** morsi *mpl* di coscienza.

panhandler [ˈpænhændlə*] *n* (US col) accattone/a.

panic [ˈpænɪk] *n* panico ♦ *vi* perdere il sangue freddo.

panic buying [-baɪɪŋ] *n* accaparramento.

panicky [ˈpænɪkɪ] *adj* (*person*) pauroso(a).

panic-stricken [ˈpænɪkstrɪkən] *adj* (*person*) in preda al panico; (*look*) terrorizzato(a).

pannier [ˈpænɪə*] *n* (*on bicycle*) borsa.

panorama [pænəˈrɑːmə] *n* panorama *m*.

panoramic [pænəˈræmɪk] *adj* panoramico(a).

pansy [ˈpænzɪ] *n* (BOT) viola del pensiero.

pant [pænt] *vi* ansare.

panther [ˈpænθə*] *n* pantera.

panties [ˈpæntɪz] *npl* slip *m*, mutandine *fpl*.

pantihose [ˈpæntɪhəuz] *n* (US) collant *m inv*.

panto [ˈpæntəu] *n* (BRIT col) *see* **pantomime**.

pantomime [ˈpæntəmaɪm] *n* (*at Christmas*) spettacolo natalizio; (*tecnica*) pantomima; *see boxed note*.

PANTOMIME

In Gran Bretagna la **pantomime** *(abbreviata in* **panto***) è una sorta di libera interpretazione delle favole più conosciute che vengono messe in scena nei teatri durante il periodo natalizio. Gli attori principali sono la dama, "dame", che è un uomo vestito da donna, il protagonista, "principal boy", che è una donna travestita da uomo, e il cattivo, "villain". È uno spettacolo per tutta la famiglia, che prevede la partecipazione del pubblico.*

---

pantry [ˈpæntrɪ] *n* dispensa.

pants [pænts] *npl* (BRIT) mutande *fpl*, slip *m*; (US: trousers) pantaloni *mpl*.

pantsuit [ˈpæntsuːt] *n* (US) completo *m or* tailleur *m inv* pantalone *inv*.

papacy ['peɪpəsɪ] n papato.
papal ['peɪpəl] adj papale, pontificio(a).
paparazzi [pæpə'rætsiː] npl paparazzi mpl.
paper ['peɪpə*] n carta; (also: **wall**~) carta da parati, tappezzeria; (also: **news**~) giornale m; (study, article) saggio; (exam) prova scritta ♦ adj di carta ♦ vt tappezzare; **a piece of** ~ (odd bit) un pezzo di carta; (sheet) un foglio (di carta); **to put sth down on** ~ mettere qc per iscritto; see also **papers**.
paper advance n (on printer) avanzamento della carta.
paperback ['peɪpəbæk] n tascabile m; edizione f economica ♦ adj: ~ **edition** edizione f tascabile.
paper bag n sacchetto di carta.
paperboy ['peɪpəbɔɪ] n (selling) strillone m; (delivering) ragazzo che recapita i giornali.
paper clip n graffetta, clip f inv.
paper handkerchief n fazzolettino di carta.
paper mill n cartiera.
paper money n cartamoneta, moneta cartacea.
paper profit n utile m teorico.
papers ['peɪpəz] npl (also: **identity** ~) carte fpl, documenti mpl.
paper shop n (BRIT) giornalaio (negozio).
paperweight ['peɪpəweɪt] n fermacarte m inv.
paperwork ['peɪpəwɔːk] n lavoro amministrativo.
papier-mâché ['pæpɪeɪ'mæʃeɪ] n cartapesta.
paprika ['pæprɪkə] n paprica.
Pap test, Pap smear ['pæp-] n (MED) pap-test m inv.
par [pɑː*] n parità, pari f; (GOLF) norma; **on a** ~ **with** alla pari con; **at/above/below** ~ (COMM) alla/sopra la/sotto la pari; **above/below** ~ (gen, GOLF) al di sopra/al di sotto della norma; **to feel below** or **under** or **not up to** ~ non sentirsi in forma.
parable ['pærəbl] n parabola (REL).
parabola [pə'ræbələ] n parabola (MATH).
parachute ['pærəʃuːt] n paracadute m inv ♦ vi scendere col paracadute.
parachute jump n lancio col paracadute.
parachutist ['pærəʃuːtɪst] n paracadutista m/f.
parade [pə'reɪd] n parata; (inspection) rivista, rassegna ♦ vt (fig) fare sfoggio di ♦ vi sfilare in parata; **a fashion** ~ (BRIT) una sfilata di moda.
parade ground n piazza d'armi.
paradise ['pærədaɪs] n paradiso.
paradox ['pærədɔks] n paradosso.
paradoxical [pærə'dɔksɪkl] adj paradossale.
paradoxically [pærə'dɔksɪklɪ] adv paradossalmente.
paraffin ['pærəfɪn] n (BRIT): ~ **(oil)** paraffina; **liquid** ~ olio di paraffina.
paraffin heater n (BRIT) stufa al cherosene.
paraffin lamp n (BRIT) lampada al cherosene.
paragon ['pærəgən] n modello di perfezione or di virtù.
paragraph ['pærəgrɑːf] n paragrafo; **to begin a new** ~ andare a capo.
Paraguay ['pærəgwaɪ] n Paraguay m.
Paraguayan [pærə'gwaɪən] adj, n paraguaiano(a).
parallel ['pærəlɛl] adj (also COMPUT) parallelo(a); (fig) analogo(a) ♦ n (line) parallela; (fig, GEO) parallelo; ~ **(with** or **to)** parallelo(a) (a).
paralysis, pl **paralyses** [pə'rælɪsɪs, -siːz] n paralisi f inv.
paralytic [pærə'lɪtɪk] adj paralitico(a); (BRIT col: drunk) ubriaco(a) fradicio(a).
paralyze ['pærəlaɪz] vt paralizzare.
paramedic [pærə'mɛdɪk] n paramedico.
parameter [pə'ræmɪtə*] n parametro.
paramilitary [pærə'mɪlɪtərɪ] adj paramilitare.
paramount ['pærəmaunt] adj: **of** ~ **importance** di capitale importanza.
paranoia [pærə'nɔɪə] n paranoia.
paranoid ['pærənɔɪd] adj paranoico(a).
paranormal [pærə'nɔːml] adj paranormale.
paraphernalia [pærəfə'neɪlɪə] n attrezzi mpl, roba.
paraphrase ['pærəfreɪz] vt parafrasare.
paraplegic [pærə'pliːdʒɪk] n paraplegico(a).
parapsychology [pærəsaɪ'kɔlədʒɪ] n parapsicologia.
parasite ['pærəsaɪt] n parassita m.
parasol ['pærəsɔl] n parasole m inv.
paratrooper ['pærətruːpə*] n paracadutista m (soldato).
parcel ['pɑːsl] n pacco, pacchetto ♦ vt (also: ~ **up**) impaccare.
▶**parcel out** vt spartire.
parcel bomb n (BRIT) pacchetto esplosivo.
parcel post n servizio pacchi.
parch [pɑːtʃ] vt riardere.
parched ['pɑːtʃt] adj (person) assetato(a).

parchment ['pɑːtʃmənt] n pergamena.
pardon ['pɑːdn] n perdono; grazia ♦ vt perdonare; (LAW) graziare; ~! scusi!; ~ me! mi scusi!; **I beg your** ~! scusi!; **(I beg your)** ~?, (US) ~ **me?** prego?
pare [pɛə*] vt (BRIT: nails) tagliarsi; (: fruit etc) sbucciare, pelare.
parent ['pɛərənt] n padre m (or madre f); ~s npl genitori mpl.
parentage ['pɛərəntɪdʒ] n natali mpl; **of unknown** ~ di genitori sconosciuti.
parental [pə'rɛntl] adj dei genitori.
parent company n società madre f inv.
parenthesis, pl **parentheses** [pə'rɛnθɪsɪs, -siːz] n parentesi f inv; **in parentheses** fra parentesi.
parenthood ['pɛərənthud] n paternità or maternità.
parenting ['pɛərəntɪŋ] n mestiere m di genitore.
Paris ['pærɪs] n Parigi f.
parish ['pærɪʃ] n parrocchia; (civil) ≈ municipio ♦ adj parrocchiale.
parish council n (BRIT) ≈ consiglio comunale.
parishioner [pə'rɪʃənə*] n parrocchiano/a.
Parisian [pə'rɪzɪən] adj, n parigino(a).
parity ['pærɪtɪ] n parità.
park [pɑːk] n parco; (public) giardino pubblico ♦ vt, vi parcheggiare.
parka ['pɑːkə] n eskimo.
parking ['pɑːkɪŋ] n parcheggio; **"no** ~" "sosta vietata".
parking lights npl luci fpl di posizione.
parking lot n (US) posteggio, parcheggio.
parking meter n parchimetro.
parking offence n (BRIT) infrazione f al divieto di sosta.
parking place n posto di parcheggio.
parking ticket n multa per sosta vietata.
parking violation n (US) = **parking offence**.
Parkinson's ['pɑːkɪnsənz] n (also: ~ disease) morbo di Parkinson.
parkway ['pɑːkweɪ] n (US) viale m.
parlance ['pɑːləns] n: **in common/modern** ~ nel gergo or linguaggio comune/ moderno.
parliament ['pɑːləmənt] n parlamento; see boxed note.

PARLIAMENT

Nel Regno Unito il Parlamento, **Parliament**, è formato da due camere: la "House of

Commons", e la "House of Lords". Nella "House of Commons" siedono 650 parlamentari, chiamati "MPs", eletti per votazione diretta del popolo nelle rispettive circoscrizioni elettorali, le "constituencies". Le sessioni del Parlamento sono presiedute e moderate dal presidente della Camera, lo "Speaker". Alla "House of Lords", i cui poteri sono più limitati, in passato si accedeva per nomina o per carica ereditaria mentre ora le cariche ereditarie sono state ridotte e in futuro verranno abolite.

parliamentary [pɑːlə'mɛntərɪ] adj parlamentare.
parlour, (US) **parlor** ['pɑːlə*] n salotto.
parlous ['pɑːləs] adj periglioso(a).
Parmesan [pɑːmɪ'zæn] n parmigiano.
parochial [pə'rəukɪəl] adj parrocchiale; (pej) provinciale.
parody ['pærədɪ] n parodia.
parole [pə'rəul] n: **on** ~ in libertà per buona condotta.
paroxysm ['pærəksɪzəm] n (MED) parossismo; (of anger, laughter, coughing) convulso; (of grief) attacco.
parquet ['pɑːkeɪ] n: ~ **floor(ing)** parquet m.
parrot ['pærət] n pappagallo.
parrot fashion adv in modo pappagallesco.
parsimonious [pɑːsɪ'məunɪəs] adj parsimonioso(a).
parsley ['pɑːslɪ] n prezzemolo.
parsnip ['pɑːsnɪp] n pastinaca.
parson ['pɑːsn] n prete m; (Church of England) parroco.
part [pɑːt] n parte f; (of machine) pezzo; (THEAT etc) parte, ruolo; (MUS) voce f; parte ♦ adj in parte ♦ adv = **partly** ♦ vt separare ♦ vi (people) separarsi; (roads) dividersi; **to take** ~ **in** prendere parte a; **to take sb's** ~ parteggiare per qn; **on his** ~ da parte sua; **for my** ~ per parte mia; **for the most** ~ in generale; nella maggior parte dei casi; **for the better** ~ **of the day** per la maggior parte della giornata; **to be** ~ **and parcel of** essere parte integrante di; **to take sth in good/bad** ~ prendere bene/male qc; ~ **of speech** (LING) parte del discorso.
▶**part with** vt fus separarsi da; rinunciare a.
partake [pɑː'teɪk] vi irreg (formal): **to** ~ **of** sth consumare qc, prendere qc.
part exchange n (BRIT): **in** ~ in pagamento parziale.
partial ['pɑːʃl] adj parziale; **to be** ~ **to** avere un debole per.
partially ['pɑːʃəlɪ] adv in parte.
participant [pɑː'tɪsɪpənt] n: ~ **(in)**

partecipante *m/f* (a).
participate [pɑːˈtɪsɪpeɪt] *vi*: to ~ (in) prendere parte (a), partecipare (a).
participation [pɑːtɪsɪˈpeɪʃən] *n* partecipazione *f*.
participle [ˈpɑːtɪsɪpl] *n* participio.
particle [ˈpɑːtɪkl] *n* particella.
particular [pəˈtɪkjulə*] *adj* particolare; speciale; (*fussy*) difficile; meticoloso(a); ~s *npl* particolari *mpl*, dettagli *mpl*; (*information*) informazioni *fpl*; in ~ in particolare, particolarmente; to be very ~ about essere molto pignolo(a) su; I'm not ~ per me va bene tutto.
particularly [pəˈtɪkjulərl] *adv* particolarmente; in particolare.
parting [ˈpɑːtɪŋ] *n* separazione *f*; (*BRIT: in hair*) scriminatura ♦ *adj* d'addio; ~ shot (*fig*) battuta finale.
partisan [pɑːtɪˈzæn] *n* partigiano/a ♦ *adj* partigiano(a); di parte.
partition [pɑːˈtɪʃən] *n* (*POL*) partizione *f*; (*wall*) tramezzo.
partly [ˈpɑːtlɪ] *adv* parzialmente; in parte.
partner [ˈpɑːtnə*] *n* (*COMM*) socio/a; (*SPORT*) compagno/a; (*at dance*) cavaliere/dama.
partnership [ˈpɑːtnəʃɪp] *n* associazione *f*; (*COMM*) società *f inv*; to go into ~ (with) mettersi in società (con), associarsi (a).
part payment *n* acconto.
partridge [ˈpɑːtrɪdʒ] *n* pernice *f*.
part-time [ˈpɑːtˈtaɪm] *adj, adv* a orario ridotto, part-time (*inv*).
part-timer [ˈpɑːtˈtaɪmə*] *n* (*also*: part-time worker) lavoratore/trice part-time.
party [ˈpɑːtɪ] *n* (*POL*) partito; (*team*) squadra; gruppo; (*LAW*) parte *f*; (*celebration*) ricevimento, serata; festa; dinner ~ cena; to give *or* throw a ~ dare una festa *or* un party; to be a ~ to a crime essere coinvolto in un reato.
party line *n* (*POL*) linea del partito; (*TEL*) duplex *m inv*.
party piece *n*: to do one's ~ (*BRIT col*) esibirsi nel proprio pezzo forte a una festa, cena etc.
party political broadcast *n* comunicato radiotelevisivo di propaganda.
pass [pɑːs] *vt* (*gen*) passare; (*place*) passare davanti a; (*exam*) passare, superare; (*candidate*) promuovere; (*overtake, surpass*) sorpassare, superare; (*approve*) approvare ♦ *vi* passare; (*SCOL*) essere promosso(a) ♦ *n* (*permit*) lasciapassare *m inv*; permesso; (*in mountains*) passo, gola; (*SPORT*) passaggio; (*SCOL: also*: ~ mark): to get a ~ prendere la sufficienza; to ~ for passare per; could you ~ the

vegetables round? potrebbe far passare i contorni?; to make a ~ at sb (*col*) fare delle proposte *or* delle avances a qn; things have come to a pretty ~ (*BRIT*) ecco a cosa siamo arrivati.
►**pass away** *vi* morire.
►**pass by** *vi* passare ♦ *vt* trascurare.
►**pass down** *vt* (*customs, inheritance*) tramandare, trasmettere.
►**pass on** *vi* (*die*) spegnersi, mancare ♦ *vt* (*hand on*): to ~ on (to) (*news, information, object*) passare (a); (*cold, illness*) attaccare (a); (*benefits*) trasmettere (a); (*price rises*) riversare (su).
►**pass out** *vi* svenire; (*BRIT MIL*) uscire dall'accademia.
►**pass over** *vi* (*die*) spirare ♦ *vt* lasciare da parte.
►**pass up** *vt* (*opportunity*) lasciarsi sfuggire, perdere.
passable [ˈpɑːsəbl] *adj* (*road*) praticabile; (*work*) accettabile.
passage [ˈpæsɪdʒ] *n* (*gen*) passaggio; (*also*: ~way) corridoio; (*in book*) brano, passo; (*by boat*) traversata.
passenger [ˈpæsɪndʒə*] *n* passeggero/a.
passer-by [pɑːsəˈbaɪ] *n* passante *m/f*.
passing [ˈpɑːsɪŋ] *adj* (*fig*) fuggevole; to mention sth in ~ accennare a qc di sfuggita.
passing place *n* (*AUT*) piazzola (di sosta).
passion [ˈpæʃən] *n* passione *f*; amore *m*; to have a ~ for sth aver la passione di *or* per qc.
passionate [ˈpæʃənɪt] *adj* appassionato(a).
passion fruit *n* frutto della passione.
passive [ˈpæsɪv] *adj* (*also LING*) passivo(a).
passive smoking *n* fumo passivo.
passkey [ˈpɑːskiː] *n* passe-partout *m inv*.
Passover [ˈpɑːsəuvə*] *n* Pasqua ebraica.
passport [ˈpɑːspɔːt] *n* passaporto.
passport control *n* controllo *m* passaporti *inv*.
passport office *n* ufficio *m* passaporti *inv*.
password [ˈpɑːswəːd] *n* parola d'ordine.
past [pɑːst] *prep* (*further than*) oltre, di là di; dopo; (*later than*) dopo ♦ *adv*: to run ~ passare di corsa; to walk ~ passare ♦ *adj* passato(a); (*president etc*) ex *inv* ♦ *n* passato; quarter/half ~ four le quattro e un quarto/e mezzo; ten/twenty ~ four le quattro e dieci/venti; he's ~ forty ha più di quarant'anni; it's ~ midnight è mezzanotte passata; for the ~ few days da qualche giorno; in questi ultimi giorni; for the ~ 3 days negli ultimi 3 giorni; in the ~ in *or* nel passato; (*LING*) al

passato; **I'm** ~ **caring** non me ne importa più nulla; **to be** ~ **it** (BRIT col: person) essere finito(a).

pasta ['pæstə] n pasta.

paste [peɪst] n (glue) colla; (CULIN) pâté m inv; pasta ♦ vt collare; **tomato** ~ concentrato di pomodoro.

pastel ['pæstl] adj pastello inv.

pasteurized ['pæstəraɪzd] adj pastorizzato(a).

pastille ['pæstl] n pastiglia.

pastime ['pɑːstaɪm] n passatempo.

past master n (BRIT): **to be a** ~ **at** essere molto esperto(a) in.

pastor ['pɑːstə*] n pastore m.

pastoral ['pɑːstərl] adj pastorale.

pastry ['peɪstrɪ] n pasta.

pasture ['pɑːstʃə*] n pascolo.

pasty n ['pæstɪ] pasticcio di carne ♦ adj ['peɪstɪ] pastoso(a); (complexion) pallido(a).

pat [pæt] vt accarezzare, dare un colpetto (affettuoso) a ♦ n: **a** ~ **of butter** un panetto di burro; **to give sb/o.s. a** ~ **on the back** (fig) congratularsi or compiacersi con qn/se stesso; **he knows it (off)** ~, (US) **he has it down** ~ lo conosce or sa a menadito.

patch [pætʃ] n (of material) toppa; (spot) macchia; (of land) pezzo ♦ vt (clothes) rattoppare; **a bad** ~ (BRIT) un brutto periodo.

▶**patch up** vt rappezzare.

patchwork ['pætʃwɜːk] n patchwork m.

patchy ['pætʃɪ] adj irregolare.

pate [peɪt] n: **a bald** ~ una testa pelata.

pâté ['pæteɪ] n pâté m inv.

patent ['peɪtnt] n brevetto ♦ vt brevettare ♦ adj patente, manifesto(a).

patent leather n cuoio verniciato.

patently ['peɪtntlɪ] adv palesemente.

patent medicine n specialità f inv medicinale.

patent office n ufficio brevetti.

paternal [pə'tɜːnl] adj paterno(a).

paternity [pə'tɜːnɪtɪ] n paternità.

paternity suit n (LAW) causa di riconoscimento della paternità.

path [pɑːθ] n sentiero, viottolo; viale m; (fig) via, strada; (of planet, missile) traiettoria.

pathetic [pə'θɛtɪk] adj (pitiful) patetico(a); (very bad) penoso(a).

pathological [pæθə'lɔdʒɪkl] adj patologico(a).

pathologist [pə'θɔlədʒɪst] n patologo/a.

pathology [pə'θɔlədʒɪ] n patologia.

pathos ['peɪθɔs] n pathos m.

pathway ['pɑːθweɪ] n sentiero, viottolo.

patience ['peɪʃns] n pazienza; (BRIT CARDS) solitario; **to lose one's** ~ spazientirsi.

patient ['peɪʃnt] n paziente m/f; malato/a ♦ adj paziente; **to be** ~ **with sb** essere paziente or aver pazienza con qn.

patiently ['peɪʃntlɪ] adv pazientemente.

patio ['pætɪəu] n terrazza.

patriot ['peɪtrɪət] n patriota m/f.

patriotic [pætrɪ'ɔtɪk] adj patriottico(a).

patriotism ['pætrɪətɪzəm] n patriottismo.

patrol [pə'trəul] n pattuglia ♦ vt pattugliare; **to be on** ~ fare la ronda; essere in ricognizione; essere in perlustrazione.

patrol boat n guardacoste m inv.

patrol car n autoradio f inv (della polizia).

patrolman [pə'trəulmən] n (US) poliziotto.

patron ['peɪtrən] n (in shop) cliente m/f; (of charity) benefattore/trice; ~ **of the arts** mecenate m/f.

patronage ['pætrənɪdʒ] n patronato.

patronize ['pætrənaɪz] vt essere cliente abituale di; (fig) trattare con condiscendenza.

patronizing ['pætrənaɪzɪŋ] adj condiscendente.

patron saint n patrono.

patter ['pætə*] n picchiettio; (sales talk) propaganda di vendita ♦ vi picchiettare.

pattern ['pætən] n modello; (SEWING etc) modello (di carta), cartamodello; (design) disegno, motivo; (sample) campione m; **behaviour** ~s tipi mpl di comportamento.

patterned ['pætənd] adj a disegni, a motivi; (material) fantasia inv.

paucity ['pɔːsɪtɪ] n scarsità.

paunch [pɔːntʃ] n pancione m.

pauper ['pɔːpə*] n indigente m/f; ~**'s grave** fossa comune.

pause [pɔːz] n pausa ♦ vi fare una pausa, arrestarsi; **to** ~ **for breath** fermarsi un attimo per riprender fiato.

pave [peɪv] vt pavimentare; **to** ~ **the way for** aprire la via a.

pavement ['peɪvmənt] n (BRIT) marciapiede m; (US) pavimentazione f stradale.

pavilion [pə'vɪlɪən] n padiglione m; tendone m; (SPORT) edificio annesso ad un campo sportivo.

paving ['peɪvɪŋ] n pavimentazione f.

paving stone n lastra di pietra.

paw [pɔː] n zampa ♦ vt dare una zampata a; (subj: person: pej) palpare.

pawn [pɔːn] n pegno; (CHESS) pedone m; (fig) pedina ♦ vt dare in pegno.

pawnbroker ['pɔːnbrəukə*] n prestatore m su pegno.

pawnshop ['pɔːnʃɔp] n monte m di pietà.

pay [peɪ] n (gen) paga ♦ vb (pt, pp **paid** [peɪd]) vt pagare; (be profitable to: also fig) convenire a ♦ vi pagare; (be profitable) rendere; **to ~ attention (to)** fare attenzione (a); **I paid £5 for that record** quel disco l'ho pagato 5 sterline; **how much did you ~ for it?** quanto l'ha pagato?; **to ~ one's way** pagare la propria parte; (company) coprire le spese; **to ~ dividends** (fig) dare buoni frutti.
▶**pay back** vt rimborsare.
▶**pay for** vt fus pagare.
▶**pay in** vt versare.
▶**pay off** vt (debts) saldare; (creditor) pagare; (mortgage) estinguere; (workers) licenziare ♦ vi (scheme) funzionare; (patience) dare dei frutti; **to ~ sth off in instalments** pagare qc a rate.
▶**pay out** vt (money) sborsare, tirar fuori; (rope) far allentare.
▶**pay up** vt saldare.
payable ['peɪəbl] adj pagabile; **to make a cheque ~ to sb** intestare un assegno a (nome di) qn.
pay award n aumento salariale.
pay day n giorno di paga.
PAYE n abbr (BRIT: = pay as you earn) pagamento di imposte tramite ritenute alla fonte.
payee [peɪ'iː] n beneficiario/a.
pay envelope n (US) busta f paga inv.
paying ['peɪɪŋ] adj: **~ guest** ospite m/f pagante, pensionante m/f.
payload ['peɪləud] n carico utile.
payment ['peɪmənt] n pagamento; **advance ~** (part sum) anticipo, acconto; (total sum) pagamento anticipato; **deferred ~, ~ by instalments** pagamento dilazionato or a rate; **in ~ for, in ~ of** in pagamento di; **on ~ of £5** dietro pagamento di 5 sterline.
pay packet n (BRIT) busta f paga inv.
payphone ['peɪfəun] n cabina telefonica.
payroll ['peɪrəul] n ruolo (organico); **to be on a firm's ~** far parte del personale di una ditta.
pay slip n (BRIT) foglio m paga inv.
pay station n (US) cabina telefonica.
PBS n abbr (US: = Public Broadcasting Service) servizio che collabora alla realizzazione di programmi per la rete televisiva nazionale.
PBX abbr (= private branch exchange) sistema telefonico con centralino.
PC n abbr see **personal computer**; (BRIT) see **police constable** ♦ abbr (BRIT) = **Privy Councillor** ♦ adj abbr = **politically correct**.
pc abbr = **per cent**; (= postcard) C.P.

p/c abbr = **petty cash**.
PCB n abbr see **printed circuit board**.
pcm abbr = per calendar month.
PD n abbr (US) = **police department**.
pd abbr = **paid**.
PDA n abbr (= personal digital assistant) PDA m inv.
PDQ abbr (col) = pretty damn quick.
PDSA n abbr (BRIT: = People's Dispensary for Sick Animals) assistenza veterinaria gratuita.
PDT abbr (US: = Pacific Daylight Time) ora legale del Pacifico.
PE n abbr (= physical education) ed. fisica ♦ abbr (Canada) = Prince Edward Island.
pea [piː] n pisello.
peace [piːs] n pace f; (calm) calma, tranquillità; **to be at ~ with sb/sth** essere in pace con qn/qc; **to keep the ~** (subj: policeman) mantenere l'ordine pubblico; (: citizen) rispettare l'ordine pubblico.
peaceable ['piːsəbl] adj pacifico(a).
peaceful ['piːsful] adj pacifico(a), calmo(a).
peacekeeping ['piːskiːpɪŋ] n mantenimento della pace; **~ force** forza di pace.
peace offering n (fig) dono in segno di riconciliazione.
peach [piːtʃ] n pesca.
peacock ['piːkɔk] n pavone m.
peak [piːk] n (of mountain) cima, vetta; (mountain itself) picco; (fig) massimo; (: of career) acme f.
peak-hour ['piːkauə*] adj (traffic etc) delle ore di punta.
peak hours npl ore fpl di punta.
peak period n periodo di punta.
peak rate n tariffa massima.
peaky ['piːkɪ] adj (BRIT col) sbattuto(a).
peal [piːl] n (of bells) scampanio, carillon m inv; **~s of laughter** scoppi mpl di risa.
peanut ['piːnʌt] n arachide f, nocciolina americana.
peanut butter n burro di arachidi.
pear [pɛə*] n pera.
pearl [pəːl] n perla.
peasant ['pɛznt] n contadino/a.
peat [piːt] n torba.
pebble ['pɛbl] n ciottolo.
peck [pɛk] vt (also: ~ **at**) beccare; (: food) mangiucchiare ♦ n colpo di becco; (kiss) bacetto.
pecking order ['pɛkɪŋ-] n (fig) ordine m gerarchico.
peckish ['pɛkɪʃ] adj (BRIT col): **I feel ~** ho un languorino.
peculiar [pɪ'kjuːlɪə*] adj strano(a), bizzarro(a); (particular: importance, qualities) particolare; **~ to** tipico(a) di,

caratteristico(a) di.

peculiarity [pɪkjuːlɪ'ærɪtɪ] n peculiarità f inv; (oddity) bizzarria.

pecuniary [pɪ'kjuːnɪərɪ] adj pecuniario(a).

pedal ['pɛdl] n pedale m ♦ vi pedalare.

pedal bin n (BRIT) pattumiera a pedale.

pedantic [pɪ'dæntɪk] adj pedantesco(a).

peddle ['pɛdl] vt (goods) andare in giro a vendere; (drugs) spacciare; (gossip) mettere in giro.

peddler ['pɛdlə*] n venditore m ambulante.

pedestal ['pɛdəstl] n piedestallo.

pedestrian [pɪ'dɛstrɪən] n pedone/a ♦ adj pedonale; (fig) prosaico(a), pedestre.

pedestrian crossing n (BRIT) passaggio pedonale.

pedestrian mall n (US) zona pedonale.

pedestrian precinct n (BRIT) zona pedonale.

pediatrics [piːdɪ'ætrɪks] n (US) = **paediatrics**.

pedigree ['pɛdɪgriː] n stirpe f; (of animal) pedigree m inv ♦ cpd (animal) di razza.

pedlar ['pɛdlə*] n = **peddler**.

pee [piː] vi (col) pisciare.

peek [piːk] vi guardare furtivamente.

peel [piːl] n buccia; (of orange, lemon) scorza ♦ vt sbucciare ♦ vi (paint etc) staccarsi.

▶**peel back** vt togliere, levare.

peeler [piːlə*] n: **potato** ~ sbucciapatate m inv.

peelings ['piːlɪŋz] npl bucce fpl.

peep [piːp] n (BRIT: look) sguardo furtivo, sbirciata; (sound) pigolio ♦ vi (BRIT) guardare furtivamente.

▶**peep out** vi (BRIT) mostrarsi furtivamente.

peephole ['piːphəul] n spioncino.

peer [pɪə*] vi: **to** ~ **at** scrutare ♦ n (noble) pari m inv; (equal) pari m/f inv, uguale m/f.

peerage ['pɪərɪdʒ] n dignità di pari; pari mpl.

peerless ['pɪəlɪs] adj impareggiabile, senza pari.

peeved [piːvd] adj stizzito(a).

peevish ['piːvɪʃ] adj stizzoso(a).

peg [pɛg] n (tent ~) picchetto; (for coat etc) attaccapanni m inv; (BRIT: also: **clothes** ~) molletta ♦ vt (clothes) appendere con le mollette; (BRIT: groundsheet) fissare con i picchetti; (fig: prices, wages) fissare, stabilizzare; **off the** ~ confezionato(a).

pejorative [pɪ'dʒɔrətɪv] adj peggiorativo(a).

Pekin [piː'kɪn], **Peking** [piː'kɪŋ] n Pechino f.

pekin(g)ese [piːkɪ'niːz] n pechinese m.

pelican ['pɛlɪkən] n pellicano.

pelican crossing n (BRIT AUT)

attraversamento pedonale con semaforo a controllo manuale.

pellet ['pɛlɪt] n pallottola, pallina.

pell-mell ['pɛl'mɛl] adv disordinatamente.

pelmet ['pɛlmɪt] n mantovana; cassonetto.

pelt [pɛlt] vt: **to** ~ **sb (with)** bombardare qn (con) ♦ vi (rain) piovere a dirotto ♦ n pelle f.

pelvis ['pɛlvɪs] n pelvi f inv, bacino.

pen [pɛn] n penna; (for sheep) recinto; (US col: prison) galera; **to put** ~ **to paper** prendere la penna in mano.

penal ['piːnl] adj penale.

penalize ['piːnəlaɪz] vt punire; (SPORT) penalizzare; (fig) svantaggiare.

penal servitude [-'səːvɪtjuːd] n lavori mpl forzati.

penalty ['pɛnltɪ] n penalità f inv; sanzione f penale; (fine) ammenda; (SPORT) penalizzazione f; (FOOTBALL: also: ~ **kick**) calcio di rigore.

penalty area n (BRIT SPORT) area di rigore.

penalty clause n penale f.

penalty kick n (FOOTBALL) calcio di rigore.

penalty shoot-out [-'ʃuːtaut] n (FOOTBALL) rigori mpl.

penance ['pɛnəns] n penitenza.

pence [pɛns] npl (BRIT) of **penny**.

penchant ['pãːʃãːŋ] n debole m.

pencil ['pɛnsl] n matita ♦ vt (also: ~ **in**) scrivere a matita.

pencil case n astuccio per matite.

pencil sharpener n temperamatite m inv.

pendant ['pɛndnt] n pendaglio.

pending ['pɛndɪŋ] prep in attesa di ♦ adj in sospeso.

pendulum ['pɛndjuləm] n pendolo.

penetrate ['pɛnɪtreɪt] vt penetrare.

penetrating ['pɛnɪtreɪtɪŋ] adj penetrante.

penetration [pɛnɪ'treɪʃən] n penetrazione f.

penfriend ['pɛnfrɛnd] n (BRIT) corrispondente m/f.

penguin ['pɛŋgwɪn] n pinguino.

penicillin [pɛnɪ'sɪlɪn] n penicillina.

peninsula [pə'nɪnsjulə] n penisola.

penis ['piːnɪs] n pene m.

penitence ['pɛnɪtns] n penitenza.

penitent ['pɛnɪtnt] adj penitente.

penitentiary [pɛnɪ'tɛnʃərɪ] n (US) carcere m.

penknife ['pɛnnaɪf] n temperino.

Penn(a). abbr (US) = Pennsylvania.

pen name n pseudonimo.

pennant ['pɛnənt] n banderuola.

penniless ['pɛnɪlɪs] adj senza un soldo.

Pennines ['pɛnaɪnz] npl: **the** ~ i Pennini.

penny, pl **pennies** or **pence** ['pɛnɪ, 'pɛnɪz, pɛns] n penny m (pl pence); (US) centesimo.

penpal ['pɛnpæl] *n* corrispondente *m/f*.

penpusher ['pɛnpuʃə*] *n* (*pej*) scribacchino/a.

pension ['pɛnʃən] *n* pensione *f*.

▶**pension off** *vt* mandare in pensione.

pensionable ['pɛnʃənəbl] *adj* (*person*) che ha diritto a una pensione, pensionabile; (*age*) pensionabile.

pensioner ['pɛnʃənə*] *n* (*BRIT*) pensionato/a.

pension fund *n* fondo pensioni.

pensive ['pɛnsɪv] *adj* pensoso(a).

pentagon ['pɛntəgən] *n* pentagono; **the P~** (*US POL*) il Pentagono; *see boxed note*.

PENTAGON

Il **Pentagon** *è un edificio a pianta pentagonale che si trova ad Arlington, in Virginia, nel quale hanno sede gli uffici del Ministero della Difesa degli Stati Uniti. Il termine* **Pentagon** *è usato anche per indicare la dirigenza militare del paese.*

Pentecost ['pɛntɪkɔst] *n* Pentecoste *f*.

penthouse ['pɛnthaus] *n* appartamento (di lusso) nell'attico.

pent-up ['pɛntʌp] *adj* (*feelings*) represso(a).

penultimate [pɪ'nʌltɪmət] *adj* penultimo(a).

penury ['pɛnjurɪ] *n* indigenza.

people ['piːpl] *npl* gente *f*; persone *fpl*; (*citizens*) popolo ♦ *n* (*nation, race*) popolo ♦ *vt* popolare; **old ~** i vecchi; **young ~** i giovani; **~ at large** il grande pubblico; **a man of the ~** un uomo del popolo; **4/ several ~ came** 4/parecchie persone sono venute; **the room was full of ~** la stanza era piena di gente; **~ say that ...** si dice *or* la gente dice che ....

PEP [pɛp] *n* = **personal equity plan**.

pep [pɛp] *n* (*col*) dinamismo.

▶**pep up** *vt* vivacizzare; (*food*) rendere più gustoso(a).

pepper ['pɛpə*] *n* pepe *m*; (*vegetable*) peperone *m* ♦ *vt* pepare.

peppermint ['pɛpəmɪnt] *n* (*plant*) menta peperita; (*sweet*) pasticca di menta.

pepperoni [pɛpə'rəunɪ] *n* salsiccia piccante.

pepperpot ['pɛpəpɔt] *n* pepaiola.

peptalk ['pɛptɔːk] *n* (*col*) discorso di incoraggiamento.

per [pə:*] *prep* per; a; **~ hour** all'ora; **~ kilo** *etc* il chilo *etc*; **~ day** al giorno; **~ week** alla settimana; **~ person** a testa, a *or* per persona; **as ~ your instructions** secondo le vostre istruzioni.

per annum *adv* all'anno.

per capita *adj, adv* pro capite.

perceive [pə'siːv] *vt* percepire; (*notice*) accorgersi di.

per cent *adv* per cento; **a 20 ~ discount** uno sconto del 20 per cento.

percentage [pə'sɛntɪdʒ] *n* percentuale *f*; **on a ~ basis** a percentuale.

percentage point *n* punto percentuale.

perceptible [pə'sɛptɪbl] *adj* percettibile.

perception [pə'sɛpʃən] *n* percezione *f*; sensibilità; perspicacia.

perceptive [pə'sɛptɪv] *adj* percettivo(a); perspicace.

perch [pə:tʃ] *n* (*fish*) pesce *m* persico; (*for bird*) sostegno, ramo ♦ *vi* appollaiarsi.

percolate ['pə:kəleɪt] *vt* filtrare.

percolator ['pə:kəleɪtə*] *n* caffettiera a pressione; caffettiera elettrica.

percussion [pə'kʌʃən] *n* percussione *f*; (*MUS*) strumenti *mpl* a percussione.

peremptory [pə'rɛmptərɪ] *adj* perentorio(a).

perennial [pə'rɛnɪəl] *adj* perenne ♦ *n* pianta perenne.

perfect *adj, n* ['pə:fɪkt] *adj* perfetto(a) ♦ *n* (*also*: **~ tense**) perfetto, passato prossimo ♦ *vt* [pə'fɛkt] perfezionare; mettere a punto; **he's a ~ stranger to me** mi è completamente sconosciuto.

perfection [pə'fɛkʃən] *n* perfezione *f*.

perfectionist [pə'fɛkʃənɪst] *n* perfezionista *m/f*.

perfectly ['pə:fɪktlɪ] *adv* perfettamente; **I'm ~ happy with the situation** sono completamente soddisfatta della situazione; **you know ~ well** sa benissimo.

perforate ['pə:fəreɪt] *vt* perforare.

perforated ulcer ['pə:fəreɪtɪd-] *n* (*MED*) ulcera perforata.

perforation [pə:fə'reɪʃən] *n* perforazione *f*; (*line of holes*) dentellatura.

perform [pə'fɔ:m] *vt* (*carry out*) eseguire, fare; (*symphony etc*) suonare; (*play, ballet*) dare; (*opera*) fare ♦ *vi* suonare; recitare.

performance [pə'fɔ:məns] *n* esecuzione *f*; (*at theatre etc*) rappresentazione *f*, spettacolo; (*of an artist*) interpretazione *f*; (*of player etc*) performance *f*; (*of car, engine*) prestazione *f*; **the team put up a good ~** la squadra ha giocato una bella partita.

performer [pə'fɔ:mə*] *n* artista *m/f*.

performing [pə'fɔ:mɪŋ] *adj* (*animal*) ammaestrato(a).

performing arts *npl*: **the ~** le arti dello spettacolo.

perfume ['pə:fju:m] *n* profumo ♦ *vt* profumare.

perfunctory [pə'fʌŋktərɪ] *adj* superficiale, per la forma.

perhaps [pə'hæps] *adv* forse; ~ **he'll come** forse verrà, può darsi che venga; ~ **so/ not** forse sì/no, può darsi di sì/di no.

peril ['pɛrɪl] *n* pericolo.

perilous ['pɛrɪləs] *adj* pericoloso(a).

perilously ['pɛrɪləslɪ] *adv*: **they came ~ close to being caught** sono stati a un pelo dall'esser presi.

perimeter [pə'rɪmɪtə*] *n* perimetro.

perimeter wall *n* muro di cinta.

period ['pɪərɪəd] *n* periodo; (*HISTORY*) epoca; (*SCOL*) lezione *f*; (*full stop*) punto; (*US FOOTBALL*) tempo; (*MED*) mestruazioni *fpl* ♦ *adj* (*costume, furniture*) d'epoca; **for a ~ of three weeks** per un periodo di *or* per la durata di tre settimane; **the holiday ~** (*BRIT*) il periodo delle vacanze.

periodic [pɪərɪ'ɔdɪk] *adj* periodico(a).

periodical [pɪərɪ'ɔdɪkl] *adj* periodico(a) ♦ *n* periodico.

periodically [pɪərɪ'ɔdɪklɪ] *adv* periodicamente.

period pains *npl* (*BRIT*) dolori *mpl* mestruali.

peripatetic [pɛrɪpə'tɛtɪk] *adj* (*salesman*) ambulante; (*BRIT*: *teacher*) peripatetico(a).

peripheral [pə'rɪfərəl] *adj* periferico(a) ♦ *n* (*COMPUT*) unità *f inv* periferica.

periphery [pə'rɪfərɪ] *n* periferia.

periscope ['pɛrɪskəup] *n* periscopio.

perish ['pɛrɪʃ] *vi* perire, morire; (*decay*) deteriorarsi.

perishable ['pɛrɪʃəbl] *adj* deperibile.

perishables ['pɛrɪʃəblz] *npl* merci *fpl* deperibili.

perishing ['pɛrɪʃɪŋ] *adj* (*BRIT col*): **it's ~ (cold)** fa un freddo da morire.

peritonitis [pɛrɪtə'naɪtɪs] *n* peritonite *f*.

perjure ['pə:dʒə*] *vt*: **to ~ o.s.** spergiurare.

perjury ['pə:dʒərɪ] *n* (*LAW*: *in court*) falso giuramento; (*breach of oath*) spergiuro.

perk [pə:k] *n* vantaggio.

▶**perk up** *vi* (*cheer up*) rianimarsi.

perky ['pə:kɪ] *adj* (*cheerful*) vivace, allegro(a).

perm [pə:m] *n* (*for hair*) permanente *f* ♦ *vt*: **to have one's hair ~ed** farsi fare la permanente.

permanence ['pə:mənəns] *n* permanenza.

permanent ['pə:mənənt] *adj* permanente; (*job, position*) fisso(a); (*dye, ink*) indelebile; ~ **address** residenza fissa; **I'm not ~ here** non sono fisso qui.

permanently ['pə:mənəntlɪ] *adv*

definitivamente.

permeable ['pə:mɪəbl] *adj* permeabile.

permeate ['pə:mɪeɪt] *vi* penetrare ♦ *vt* permeare.

permissible [pə'mɪsɪbl] *adj* permissibile, ammissibile.

permission [pə'mɪʃən] *n* permesso; **to give sb ~ to do sth** dare a qn il permesso di fare qc.

permissive [pə'mɪsɪv] *adj* tollerante; **the ~ society** la società permissiva.

permit *n* ['pə:mɪt] permesso; (*entrance pass*) lasciapassare *m* ♦ *vt*, *vi* [pə'mɪt] permettere; **fishing ~** licenza di pesca; **to ~ sb to do** permettere a qn di fare, dare il permesso a qn di fare; **weather ~ting** tempo permettendo.

permutation [pə:mju'teɪʃən] *n* permutazione *f*.

pernicious [pə:'nɪʃəs] *adj* pernicioso(a), nocivo(a).

pernickety [pə'nɪkɪtɪ] *adj* (*col*: *person*) pignolo(a); (: *task*) da certosino.

perpendicular [pə:pən'dɪkjulə*] *adj*, *n* perpendicolare (*f*).

perpetrate ['pə:pɪtreɪt] *vt* perpetrare, commettere.

perpetual [pə'pɛtjuəl] *adj* perpetuo(a).

perpetuate [pə'pɛtjueɪt] *vt* perpetuare.

perpetuity [pə:pɪ'tju:ɪtɪ] *n*: **in ~** in perpetuo.

perplex [pə'plɛks] *vt* lasciare perplesso(a).

perplexing [pə'plɛksɪŋ] *adj* che lascia perplesso(a).

perquisites ['pə:kwɪzɪts] *npl* (*also*: **perks**) benefici *mpl* collaterali.

persecute ['pə:sɪkju:t] *vt* perseguitare.

persecution [pə:sɪ'kju:ʃən] *n* persecuzione *f*.

perseverance [pə:sɪ'vɪərəns] *n* perseveranza.

persevere [pə:sɪ'vɪə*] *vi* perseverare.

Persia ['pə:ʃə] *n* Persia.

Persian ['pə:ʃən] *adj* persiano(a) ♦ *n* (*LING*) persiano; **the (~) Gulf** il Golfo Persico.

Persian cat *n* gatto persiano.

persist [pə'sɪst] *vi*: **to ~ (in doing)** persistere (nel fare); ostinarsi (a fare).

persistence [pə'sɪstəns] *n* persistenza; ostinazione *f*.

persistent [pə'sɪstənt] *adj* persistente; ostinato(a); (*lateness, rain*) continuo(a); ~ **offender** (*LAW*) delinquente *m/f* abituale.

persnickety [pə'snɪkɪtɪ] *adj* (*US col*) = **pernickety**.

person ['pə:sn] *n* persona; **in ~** di *or* in persona, personalmente; **on** *or* **about**

one's ~ (*weapon*) su di sé; (*money*) con sé; **a ~ to ~ call** (*TEL*) una chiamata con preavviso.

personable ['pɔːsnəbl] *adj* di bell'aspetto.

personal ['pɔːsnl] *adj* personale; individuale; ~ **belongings,** ~ **effects** oggetti *mpl* d'uso personale; **a ~ interview** un incontro privato.

personal allowance *n* (*TAX*) quota del reddito non imponibile.

personal assistant (PA) *n* segretaria personale.

personal call *n* (*TEL*) chiamata con preavviso.

personal column *n* messaggi *mpl* personali.

personal computer (PC) *n* personal computer *m inv*.

personal details *npl* dati *mpl* personali.

personal equity plan *n* (*FINANCE*) *fondo di investimento azionario con agevolazioni fiscali destinato al piccolo risparmiatore.*

personal identification number (PIN) *n* (*COMPUT, BANKING*) numero di codice segreto.

personality [pɔːsə'nælɪtɪ] *n* personalità *f inv*.

personally ['pɔːsnəlɪ] *adv* personalmente.

personal organizer *n* agenda; (*electronic*) agenda elettronica.

personal property *n* beni *mpl* personali.

personal stereo *n* walkman ® *m inv*.

personify [pɔː'sɔnɪfaɪ] *vt* personificare.

personnel [pɔːsə'nɛl] *n* personale *m*.

personnel department *n* ufficio del personale.

personnel manager *n* direttore/trice del personale.

perspective [pə'spɛktɪv] *n* prospettiva; **to get sth into** ~ ridimensionare qc.

Perspex ® ['pɔːspɛks] *n* (*BRIT*) *tipo di resina termoplastica.*

perspicacity [pɔːspɪ'kæsɪtɪ] *n* perspicacia.

perspiration [pɔːspɪ'reɪʃən] *n* traspirazione *f*, sudore *m*.

perspire [pə'spaɪə*] *vi* traspirare.

persuade [pə'sweɪd] *vt*: **to ~ sb to do sth** persuadere qn a fare qc; **to ~ sb of sth/ that** persuadere qn di qc/che.

persuasion [pə'sweɪʒən] *n* persuasione *f*; (*creed*) convinzione *f*, credo.

persuasive [pə'sweɪsɪv] *adj* persuasivo(a).

pert [pɔːt] *adj* (*bold*) sfacciato(a), impertinente; (*hat*) spiritoso(a).

pertaining [pɔː'teɪnɪŋ]: ~ **to** *prep* che riguarda.

pertinent ['pɔːtɪnənt] *adj* pertinente.

perturb [pə'tɔːb] *vt* turbare.

perturbing [pə'tɔːbɪŋ] *adj* inquietante.

Peru [pə'ruː] *n* Perù *m*.

perusal [pə'ruːzl] *n* attenta lettura.

Peruvian [pə'ruːvjən] *adj, n* peruviano(a).

pervade [pə'veɪd] *vt* pervadere.

pervasive [pə'veɪsɪv] *adj* (*smell*) penetrante; (*influence*) dilagante; (*gloom, feelings*) diffuso(a).

perverse [pə'vɔːs] *adj* perverso(a).

perversion [pə'vɔːʃən] *n* pervertimento, perversione *f*.

perversity [pə'vɔːsɪtɪ] *n* perversità.

pervert *n* ['pɔːvɔːt] pervertito/a ♦ *vt* [pə'vɔːt] pervertire.

pessimism ['pɛsɪmɪzəm] *n* pessimismo.

pessimist ['pɛsɪmɪst] *n* pessimista *m/f*.

pessimistic [pɛsɪ'mɪstɪk] *adj* pessimistico(a).

pest [pɛst] *n* animale *m* (*or* insetto) pestifero; (*fig*) peste *f*.

pest control *n* disinfestazione *f*.

pester ['pɛstə*] *vt* tormentare, molestare.

pesticide ['pɛstɪsaɪd] *n* pesticida *m*.

pestilence ['pɛstɪləns] *n* pestilenza.

pestle ['pɛsl] *n* pestello.

pet [pɛt] *n* animale *m* domestico; (*favourite*) favorito/a ♦ *vt* accarezzare ♦ *vi* (*col*) fare il petting; ~ **lion** *etc* leone *m etc* ammaestrato.

petal ['pɛtl] *n* petalo.

peter ['piːtə*]: **to ~ out** *vi* esaurirsi; estinguersi.

petite [pə'tiːt] *adj* piccolo(a) e aggraziato(a).

petition [pə'tɪʃən] *n* petizione *f* ♦ *vi* richiedere; **to ~ for divorce** presentare un'istanza di divorzio.

pet name *n* (*BRIT*) nomignolo.

petrified ['pɛtrɪfaɪd] *adj* (*fig*) morto(a) di paura.

petrify ['pɛtrɪfaɪ] *vt* pietrificare; (*fig*) terrorizzare.

petrochemical [pɛtrə'kɛmɪkl] *adj* petrolchimico(a).

petrodollars ['pɛtrəudɔləz] *npl* petrodollari *mpl*.

petrol ['pɛtrəl] *n* (*BRIT*) benzina.

petrol bomb *n* (*BRIT*) (bottiglia) molotov *f inv*.

petrol can *n* (*BRIT*) tanica per benzina.

petrol engine *n* (*BRIT*) motore *m* a benzina.

petroleum [pə'trəulɪəm] *n* petrolio.

petroleum jelly *n* vaselina.

petrol pump *n* (*BRIT*: *in car, at garage*) pompa di benzina.

petrol station *n* (*BRIT*) stazione *f* di rifornimento.

petrol tank *n* (*BRIT*) serbatoio della

benzina.
petticoat ['pɛtɪkəʊt] *n* sottana.
pettifogging ['pɛtɪfɔgɪŋ] *adj* cavilloso(a).
pettiness ['pɛtɪnɪs] *n* meschinità.
petty ['pɛtɪ] *adj* (*mean*) meschino(a);
(*unimportant*) insignificante.
petty cash *n* piccola cassa.
petty officer *n* sottufficiale *m* di marina.
petulant ['pɛtjulənt] *adj* irritabile.
pew [pjuː] *n* panca (di chiesa).
pewter ['pjuːtə*] *n* peltro.
Pfc *abbr* (*US MIL*) = *private first class.*
PG *n abbr* (*CINE:* = *parental guidance*)
consenso dei genitori richiesto.
PG13 *abbr* (*US CINE:* = *Parental Guidance 13*)
vietato ai minori di 13 anni non
accompagnati dai genitori.
PGA *n abbr* (= *Professional Golfers
Association*) associazione dei giocatori di
golf professionisti.
PH *n abbr* (*US MIL:* = *Purple Heart*)
decorazione per ferite riportate in
guerra.
PHA *n abbr* (*US:* = *Public Housing
Administration*) amministrazione per
l'edilizia pubblica.
phallic ['fælɪk] *adj* fallico(a).
phantom ['fæntəm] *n* fantasma *m*.
Pharaoh ['fɛərəʊ] *n* faraone *m*.
pharmaceutical [fɑːmə'sjuːtɪkl] *adj*
farmaceutico(a) ♦ *n*: ~s prodotti *mpl*
farmaceutici.
pharmacist ['fɑːməsɪst] *n* farmacista *m/f*.
pharmacy ['fɑːməsɪ] *n* farmacia.
phase [feɪz] *n* fase *f*, periodo ♦ *vt*: to ~ sth
in/out introdurre/eliminare qc
progressivamente.
PhD *n abbr* = *Doctor of Philosophy.*
pheasant ['fɛznt] *n* fagiano.
phenomenon, *pl* **phenomena**
[fə'nɔmɪnən, -nə] *n* fenomeno.
phew [fjuː] *excl* uff!
phial ['faɪəl] *n* fiala.
philanderer [fɪ'lændərə*] *n* donnaiolo.
philanthropic [fɪlən'θrɔpɪk] *adj*
filantropico(a).
philanthropist [fɪ'lænθrəpɪst] *n* filantropo.
philatelist [fɪ'lætəlɪst] *n* filatelico/a.
philately [fɪ'lætəlɪ] *n* filatelia.
Philippines ['fɪlɪpiːnz] *npl* (*also:* **Philippine
Islands**): the ~ le Filippine.
philosopher [fɪ'lɔsəfə*] *n* filosofo/a.
philosophical [fɪlə'sɔfɪkl] *adj* filosofico(a).
philosophy [fɪ'lɔsəfɪ] *n* filosofia.
phlegm [flɛm] *n* flemma.
phlegmatic [flɛg'mætɪk] *adj* flemmatico(a).
phobia ['fəʊbjə] *n* fobia.
phone [fəʊn] *n* telefono ♦ *vt* telefonare a

♦ *vi* telefonare; **to be on the** ~ avere il
telefono; (*be calling*) essere al telefono.
►**phone back** *vt, vi* richiamare.
phone book *n* guida del telefono, elenco
telefonico.
phone box, phone booth *n* cabina
telefonica.
phone call *n* telefonata.
phonecard ['fəʊnkɑːd] *n* scheda telefonica.
phone-in ['fəʊnɪn] *n* (*BRIT RADIO, TV*)
trasmissione radiofonica o televisiva con
intervento telefonico degli ascoltatori.
phone tapping [-tæpɪŋ] *n* intercettazioni
fpl telefoniche.
phonetics [fə'nɛtɪks] *n* fonetica.
phoney ['fəʊnɪ] *adj* falso(a), fasullo(a) ♦ *n*
(*person*) ciarlatano.
phonograph ['fəʊnəgrɑːf] *n* (*US*) giradischi
m inv.
phony ['fəʊnɪ] *adj, n* = **phoney**.
phosphate ['fɔsfeɪt] *n* fosfato.
phosphorus ['fɔsfərəs] *n* fosforo.
photo ['fəʊtəʊ] *n* foto *f inv.*
photo... ['fəʊtəʊ] *prefix* foto....
photocall ['fəʊtəʊkɔːl] *n* convocazione di
fotoreporter a scopo pubblicitario.
photocopier ['fəʊtəʊkɔpɪə*] *n*
fotocopiatrice *f*.
photocopy ['fəʊtəʊkɔpɪ] *n* fotocopia ♦ *vt*
fotocopiare.
photoelectric [fəʊtəʊɪ'lɛktrɪk] *adj*: ~ **cell**
cellula fotoelettrica.
Photofit ® ['fəʊtəʊfɪt] *n* photofit *m inv.*
photogenic [fəʊtəʊ'dʒɛnɪk] *adj*
fotogenico(a).
photograph ['fəʊtəgræf] *n* fotografia ♦ *vt*
fotografare; **to take a** ~ **of sb** fare una
fotografia a *or* fotografare qn.
photographer [fə'tɔgrəfə*] *n* fotografo.
photographic [fəʊtə'græfɪk] *adj*
fotografico(a).
photography [fə'tɔgrəfɪ] *n* fotografia.
photo opportunity *n* opportunità di
scattare delle foto ad un personaggio
importante.
Photostat ® ['fəʊtəʊstæt] *n* fotocopia.
photosynthesis [fəʊtəʊ'sɪnθəsɪs] *n*
fotosintesi *f*.
phrase [freɪz] *n* espressione *f*; (*LING*)
locuzione *f*; (*MUS*) frase *f* ♦ *vt* esprimere;
(*letter*) redigere.
phrasebook ['freɪzbʊk] *n* vocabolarietto.
physical ['fɪzɪkl] *adj* fisico(a); ~
examination visita medica; ~ **education**
educazione *f* fisica; ~ **exercises**
ginnastica.
physically ['fɪzɪklɪ] *adv* fisicamente.
physician [fɪ'zɪʃən] *n* medico.

physicist ['fɪzɪsɪst] n fisico.
physics ['fɪzɪks] n fisica.
physiological [fɪzɪə'lɔdʒɪkəl] adj fisiologico(a).
physiology [fɪzɪ'ɔlədʒɪ] n fisiologia.
physiotherapist [fɪzɪəu'θɛrəpɪst] n fisioterapista m/f.
physiotherapy [fɪzɪəu'θɛrəpɪ] n fisioterapia.
physique [fɪ'ziːk] n fisico.
pianist ['piːənɪst] n pianista m/f.
piano [pɪ'ænəu] n pianoforte m.
piano accordion n (BRIT) fisarmonica (a tastiera).
piccolo ['pɪkələu] n ottavino.
pick [pɪk] n (tool: also: ~-axe) piccone m ♦ vt scegliere; (gather) cogliere; (scab, spot) grattarsi ♦ vi: **to ~ and choose** scegliere con cura; **take your ~** scelga; **the ~ of** il fior fiore di; **to ~ one's nose** mettersi le dita nel naso; **to ~ one's teeth** stuzzicarsi i denti; **to ~ sb's brains** farsi dare dei suggerimenti da qn; **to ~ pockets** borseggiare; **to ~ a fight/quarrel with sb** attaccar rissa/briga con qn; **to ~ one's way through** attraversare stando ben attento a dove mettere i piedi.
▶**pick off** vt (kill) abbattere.
▶**pick on** vt fus (person) avercela con.
▶**pick out** vt scegliere; (distinguish) distinguere.
▶**pick up** vi (improve) migliorarsi ♦ vt raccogliere; (collect) passare a prendere; (AUT: give lift to) far salire; (learn) imparare; (RADIO, TV, TEL) captare; **to ~ o.s. up** rialzarsi; **to ~ up where one left off** riprendere dal punto in cui ci si era fermati; **to ~ up speed** acquistare velocità.
pickaxe, (US) **pickax** ['pɪkæks] n piccone m.
picket ['pɪkɪt] n (in strike) scioperante m/f che fa parte di un picchetto; picchetto ♦ vt picchettare.
picket line n cordone m degli scioperanti.
pickings ['pɪkɪŋz] npl (pilferings): **there are good ~ to be had here** qui ci sono buone possibilità di intascare qualcosa sottobanco.
pickle ['pɪkl] n (also: ~s: as condiment) sottaceti mpl; (fig): **in a ~** nei pasticci ♦ vt mettere sottaceto; mettere in salamoia.
pick-me-up ['pɪkmiːʌp] n tiramisù m inv.
pickpocket ['pɪkpɔkɪt] n borsaiolo.
pickup ['pɪkʌp] n (BRIT: on record player) pick-up m inv; (small truck: also: ~ truck, ~ van) camioncino.
picnic ['pɪknɪk] n picnic m inv ♦ vi fare un picnic.
picnicker ['pɪknɪkə*] n chi partecipa a un picnic.
pictorial [pɪk'tɔːrɪəl] adj illustrato(a).
picture ['pɪktʃə*] n quadro; (painting) pittura; (photograph) foto(grafia); (drawing) disegno; (TV) immagine f; (film) film m inv ♦ vt raffigurarsi; **the ~s** (BRIT) il cinema; **to take a ~ of sb/sth** fare una foto a qn/di qc; **we get a good ~ here** (TV) la ricezione qui è buona; **the overall ~** il quadro generale; **to put sb in the ~** mettere qn al corrente.
picture book n libro illustrato.
picture messaging [-'mɛsɪdʒɪŋ] n picture messaging m, invio di messaggini con disegni.
picturesque [pɪktʃə'rɛsk] adj pittoresco(a).
picture window n finestra panoramica.
piddling ['pɪdlɪŋ] adj (col) insignificante.
pidgin English ['pɪdʒɪn-] n inglese semplificato misto ad elementi indigeni.
pie [paɪ] n torta; (of meat) pasticcio.
piebald ['paɪbɔːld] adj pezzato(a).
piece [piːs] n pezzo; (of land) appezzamento; (DRAUGHTS etc) pedina; (item): **a ~ of furniture/advice** un mobile/consiglio ♦ vt: **to ~ together** mettere insieme; **in ~s** (broken) in pezzi; (not yet assembled) smontato(a); **to take to ~s** smontare; **~ by ~** poco alla volta; **a 10p ~** (BRIT) una moneta da 10 pence; **a six-~ band** un complesso di sei strumentisti; **in one ~** (object) intatto; **to get back all in one ~** (person) tornare a casa incolume or sano e salvo; **to say one's ~** dire la propria.
piecemeal ['piːsmiːl] adv pezzo a pezzo, a spizzico.
piece rate n tariffa a cottimo.
piecework ['piːswəːk] n (lavoro a) cottimo.
pie chart n grafico a torta.
Piedmont ['piːdmɔnt] n Piemonte m.
pier [pɪə*] n molo; (of bridge etc) pila.
pierce [pɪəs] vt forare; (with arrow etc) trafiggere; **to have one's ears ~d** farsi fare i buchi per gli orecchini.
piercing ['pɪəsɪŋ] adj (cry) acuto(a).
piety ['paɪətɪ] n pietà, devozione f.
piffling ['pɪflɪŋ] adj insignificante.
pig [pɪg] n maiale m, porco.
pigeon ['pɪdʒən] n piccione m.
pigeonhole ['pɪdʒənhəul] n casella ♦ vt classificare.
pigeon-toed ['pɪdʒən'təud] adj che cammina con i piedi in dentro.
piggy bank ['pɪgɪ-] n salvadanaio.
pigheaded ['pɪg'hɛdɪd] adj caparbio(a),

cocciuto(a).

piglet ['pɪglɪt] *n* porcellino.

pigment ['pɪgmənt] *n* pigmento.

pigmentation [pɪgmən'teɪʃən] *n* pigmentazione *f*.

pigmy ['pɪgmɪ] *n* = **pygmy**.

pigskin ['pɪgskɪn] *n* cinghiale *m*.

pigsty ['pɪgstaɪ] *n* porcile *m*.

pigtail ['pɪgteɪl] *n* treccina.

pike [paɪk] *n* (*spear*) picca; (*fish*) luccio.

pilchard ['pɪltʃad] *n* specie di sardina.

pile [paɪl] *n* (*pillar, of books*) pila; (*heap*) mucchio; (*of carpet*) pelo ♦ *vb* (*also*: ~ **up**) *vt* ammucchiare ♦ *vi* ammucchiarsi; **in a** ~ ammucchiato; *see also* **piles**.

▶**pile on** *vt*: **to** ~ **it on** (*col*) esagerare, drammatizzare.

piles [paɪlz] *npl* (*MED*) emorroidi *fpl*.

pileup ['paɪlʌp] *n* (*AUT*) tamponamento a catena.

pilfer ['pɪlfə*] *vt* rubacchiare ♦ *vi* fare dei furtarelli.

pilfering ['pɪlfərɪŋ] *n* rubacchiare *m*.

pilgrim ['pɪlgrɪm] *n* pellegrino/a.

pilgrimage ['pɪlgrɪmɪdʒ] *n* pellegrinaggio.

pill [pɪl] *n* pillola; **to be on the** ~ prendere la pillola.

pillage ['pɪlɪdʒ] *vt* saccheggiare.

pillar ['pɪlə*] *n* colonna.

pillar box *n* (*BRIT*) cassetta delle lettere (a colonnina).

pillion ['pɪljən] *n* (*of motor cycle*) sellino posteriore; **to ride** ~ viaggiare dietro.

pillory ['pɪlərɪ] *n* berlina ♦ *vt* mettere alla berlina.

pillow ['pɪləu] *n* guanciale *m*.

pillowcase ['pɪləukeɪs], **pillowslip** ['pɪləuslɪp] *n* federa.

pilot ['paɪlət] *n* pilota *m/f* ♦ *cpd* (*scheme etc*) pilota *inv* ♦ *vt* pilotare.

pilot boat *n* pilotina.

pilot light *n* fiammella di sicurezza.

pimento [pɪ'mɛntəu] *n* peperoncino.

pimp [pɪmp] *n* mezzano.

pimple ['pɪmpl] *n* foruncolo.

pimply ['pɪmplɪ] *adj* foruncoloso(a).

PIN *n abbr see* **personal identification number**.

pin [pɪn] *n* spillo; (*TECH*) perno; (*BRIT*: *drawing* ~) puntina da disegno; (*BRIT ELEC*: *of plug*) spinotto ♦ *vt* attaccare con uno spillo; ~**s and needles** formicolio; **to** ~ **sb against/to** inchiodare qn contro/a; **to** ~ **sth on sb** (*fig*) addossare la colpa di qc a qn.

▶**pin down** *vt* (*fig*): **to** ~ **sb down** obbligare qn a pronunziarsi; **there's something strange here but I can't quite**

~ **it down** c'è qualcosa di strano qua ma non riesco a capire cos'è.

pinafore ['pɪnəfɔ:*] *n* grembiule *m* (senza maniche).

pinafore dress *n* scamiciato.

pinball ['pɪnbɔ:l] *n* flipper *m inv*.

pincers ['pɪnsəz] *npl* pinzette *fpl*.

pinch [pɪntʃ] *n* pizzicotto, pizzico ♦ *vt* pizzicare; (*col*: *steal*) grattare ♦ *vi* (*shoe*) stringere; **at a** ~ in caso di bisogno; **to feel the** ~ (*fig*) trovarsi nelle ristrettezze.

pinched [pɪntʃt] *adj* (*drawn*) dai lineamenti tirati; (*short*): ~ **for money/space** a corto di soldi/di spazio; ~ **with cold** raggrinzito dal freddo.

pincushion ['pɪnkuʃən] *n* puntaspilli *m inv*.

pine [paɪn] *n* (*also*: ~ **tree**) pino ♦ *vi*: **to** ~ **for** struggersi dal desiderio di.

▶**pine away** *vi* languire.

pineapple ['paɪnæpl] *n* ananas *m inv*.

pine cone *n* pigna.

pine needles *npl* aghi *mpl* di pino.

ping [pɪŋ] *n* (*noise*) tintinnio.

Ping-Pong ® ['pɪŋpɔŋ] *n* ping-pong ® *m*.

pink [pɪŋk] *adj* rosa *inv* ♦ *n* (*colour*) rosa *m inv*; (*BOT*) garofano.

pinking shears ['pɪŋkɪŋ-] *n* forbici *fpl* a zigzag.

pin money *n* (*BRIT*) denaro per le piccole spese.

pinnacle ['pɪnəkl] *n* pinnacolo.

pinpoint ['pɪnpɔɪnt] *vt* indicare con precisione.

pinstripe ['pɪnstraɪp] *n* stoffa gessata; (*also*: ~ **suit**) gessato.

pint [paɪnt] *n* pinta (*BRIT* = *0.57 l*; *US* = *0.47 l*); (*BRIT col*: *of beer*) ≈ birra piccola.

pinup ['pɪnʌp] *n* pin-up girl *f inv*.

pioneer [paɪə'nɪə*] *n* pioniere/a ♦ *vt* essere un pioniere in.

pious ['paɪəs] *adj* pio(a).

pip [pɪp] *n* (*seed*) seme *m*; (*time signal on radio*) segnale *m* orario.

pipe [paɪp] *n* tubo; (*for smoking*) pipa; (*MUS*) piffero ♦ *vt* portare per mezzo di tubazione; ~**s** *npl* (*also*: **bag**~**s**) cornamusa (scozzese).

▶**pipe down** *vi* (*col*) calmarsi.

pipe cleaner *n* scovolino.

piped music [paɪpt-] *n* musica di sottofondo.

pipe dream *n* vana speranza.

pipeline ['paɪplaɪn] *n* conduttura; (*for oil*) oleodotto; (*for natural gas*) metanodotto; **it is in the** ~ (*fig*) è in arrivo.

piper ['paɪpə*] *n* piffero; suonatore/trice di cornamusa.

pipe tobacco *n* tabacco da pipa.

piping ['paɪpɪŋ] *adv*: ~ **hot** bollente.

piquant ['piːkənt] *adj* (*sauce*) piccante; (*conversation*) stimolante.

pique [piːk] *n* picca.

piracy ['paɪərəsɪ] *n* pirateria.

pirate ['paɪərət] *n* pirata *m* ♦ *vt* (*record, video, book*) riprodurre abusivamente.

pirate radio *n* (*BRIT*) radio pirata *f inv.*

pirouette [pɪruˈɛt] *n* piroetta ♦ *vi* piroettare.

Pisces ['paɪsiːz] *n* Pesci *mpl;* **to be** ~ essere dei Pesci.

piss [pɪs] *vi* (*col!*) pisciare; ~ **off!** vaffanculo! (*!*).

pissed [pɪst] *adj* (*BRIT col*: *drunk*) ubriaco(a) fradicio(a).

pistol ['pɪstl] *n* pistola.

piston ['pɪstən] *n* pistone *m.*

pit [pɪt] *n* buca, fossa; (*also*: **coal** ~) miniera; (*also*: **orchestra** ~) orchestra ♦ *vt*: **to** ~ **sb against sb** opporre qn a qn; ~**s** *npl* (*AUT*) box *m;* **to** ~ **o.s. against** opporsi a.

pitapat ['pɪtəˈpæt] *adv* (*BRIT*): **to go** ~ (*heart*) palpitare, battere forte; (*rain*) picchiettare.

pitch [pɪtʃ] *n* (*throw*) lancia; (*MUS*) tono; (*of voice*) altezza; (*fig*: *degree*) grado, punto; (*also*: **sales** ~) discorso di vendita, imbonimento; (*BRIT SPORT*) campo; (*NAUT*) beccheggio; (*tar*) pece *f* ♦ *vt* (*throw*) lanciare ♦ *vi* (*fall*) cascare; (*NAUT*) beccheggiare; **to** ~ **a tent** piantare una tenda; **at this** ~ a questo ritmo.

pitch-black [pɪtʃˈblæk] *adj* nero(a) come la pece.

pitched battle [pɪtʃt-] *n* battaglia campale.

pitcher ['pɪtʃə*] *n* brocca.

pitchfork ['pɪtʃfɔːk] *n* forcone *m.*

piteous ['pɪtɪəs] *adj* pietoso(a).

pitfall ['pɪtfɔːl] *n* trappola.

pith [pɪθ] *n* (*of plant*) midollo; (*of orange*) parte *f* interna della scorza; (*fig*) essenza, succo; vigore *m.*

pithead ['pɪthɛd] *n* (*BRIT*) imbocco della miniera.

pithy ['pɪθɪ] *adj* conciso(a); vigoroso(a).

pitiable ['pɪtɪəbl] *adj* pietoso(a).

pitiful ['pɪtɪful] *adj* (*touching*) pietoso(a); (*contemptible*) miserabile.

pitifully ['pɪtɪfəlɪ] *adv* pietosamente; **it's** ~ **obvious** è penosamente chiaro.

pitiless ['pɪtɪlɪs] *adj* spietato(a).

pittance ['pɪtns] *n* miseria, magro salario.

pitted ['pɪtɪd] *adj*: ~ **with** (*potholes*) pieno(a) di; (*chickenpox*) butterato(a) da.

pity ['pɪtɪ] *n* pietà ♦ *vt* aver pietà di, compatire, commiserare; **to have** *or* **take** ~ **on sb** aver pietà di qn; **it is a** ~ **that you can't come** è un peccato che non possa venire; **what a** ~! che peccato!

pitying ['pɪtɪɪŋ] *adj* compassionevole.

pivot ['pɪvət] *n* perno ♦ *vi* imperniarsi.

pixel ['pɪksl] *n* (*COMPUT*) pixel *m inv.*

pixie ['pɪksɪ] *n* folletto.

pizza ['piːtsə] *n* pizza.

placard ['plækɑːd] *n* affisso.

placate [pləˈkeɪt] *vt* placare, calmare.

placatory [pləˈkeɪtərɪ] *adj* conciliante.

place [pleɪs] *n* posto, luogo; (*proper position, rank, seat*) posto; (*house*) casa, alloggio; (*home*): **at/to his** ~ a casa sua; (*in street names*): **Laurel P**~ via dei Lauri ♦ *vt* (*object*) posare, mettere; (*identify*) riconoscere; individuare; (*goods*) piazzare; **to take** ~ aver luogo; succedere; **out of** ~ (*not suitable*) inopportuno(a); **I feel rather out of** ~ **here** qui mi sento un po' fuori posto; **in the first** ~ in primo luogo; **to change** ~**s with sb** scambiare il posto con qn; **to put sb in his** ~ (*fig*) mettere a posto qn, mettere qn al suo posto; **from** ~ **to** ~ da un posto all'altro; **all over the** ~ dappertutto; **he's going** ~**s** (*fig col*) si sta facendo strada; **it is not my** ~ **to do it** non sta a me farlo; **how are you** ~**d next week?** com'è messo la settimana prossima?; **to** ~ **an order with sb (for)** (*COMM*) fare un'ordinazione a qn (di).

placebo [pləˈsiːbəu] *n* placebo *m inv.*

place mat *n* sottopiatto; (*in linen etc*) tovaglietta.

placement ['pleɪsmənt] *n* collocamento; (*job*) lavoro.

place name *n* toponimo.

placenta [pləˈsɛntə] *n* placenta.

placid ['plæsɪd] *adj* placido(a), calmo(a).

placidity [pləˈsɪdɪtɪ] *n* placidità.

plagiarism ['pleɪdʒjərɪzəm] *n* plagio.

plagiarist ['pleɪdʒjərɪst] *n* plagiario/a.

plagiarize ['pleɪdʒjəraɪz] *vt* plagiare.

plague [pleɪg] *n* peste *f* ♦ *vt* tormentare; **to** ~ **sb with questions** assillare qn di domande.

plaice [pleɪs] *n* (*pl inv*) pianuzza.

plaid [plæd] *n* plaid *m inv.*

plain [pleɪn] *adj* (*clear*) chiaro(a), palese; (*simple*) semplice; (*frank*) franco(a), aperto(a); (*not handsome*) bruttino(a); (*without seasoning etc*) scondito(a); naturale; (*in one colour*) tinta unita *inv* ♦ *adv* francamente, chiaramente ♦ *n* pianura; **to make sth** ~ **to sb** far capire chiaramente qc a qn; **in** ~ **clothes** (*police*) in borghese.

plain chocolate n cioccolato fondente.

plainly ['pleɪnlɪ] *adv* chiaramente; (*frankly*) francamente.

plainness ['pleɪnnɪs] n semplicità.

plain speaking *n*: **there has been some** ~ **between the two leaders** i due leader si sono parlati chiaro.

plaintiff ['pleɪntɪf] n attore/trice.

plaintive ['pleɪntɪv] *adj* (*voice, song*) lamentoso(a); (*look*) struggente.

plait [plæt] n treccia ♦ *vt* intrecciare; **to** ~ **one's hair** farsi una treccia (*or* le trecce).

plan [plæn] n pianta; (*scheme*) progetto, piano ♦ *vt* (*think in advance*) progettare; (*prepare*) organizzare; (*intend*) avere in progetto ♦ *vi*: **to** ~ **(for)** far piani *or* progetti (per); **to** ~ **to do** progettare di fare, avere l'intenzione di fare; **how long do you** ~ **to stay?** quanto conta di restare?

plane [pleɪn] n (*AVIAT*) aereo; (*tree*) platano; (*tool*) pialla; (*ART, MATH etc*) piano ♦ *adj* piano(a), piatto(a) ♦ *vt* (*with tool*) piallare.

planet ['plænɪt] n pianeta m.

planetarium [plænɪ'tɛərɪəm] n planetario.

plank [plæŋk] n tavola, asse f.

plankton ['plæŋktən] n plancton m.

planned economy [plænd-] n economia pianificata.

planner ['plænə*] n pianificatore/trice; (*chart*) calendario; **town** *or* (*US*) **city** ~ urbanista m/f.

planning ['plænɪŋ] n progettazione f; (*POL, ECON*) pianificazione f; **family** ~ pianificazione delle nascite.

planning permission n (*BRIT*) permesso di costruzione.

plant [plɑːnt] n pianta; (*machinery*) impianto; (*factory*) fabbrica ♦ *vt* piantare; (*bomb*) mettere.

plantation [plæn'teɪʃən] n piantagione f.

plant pot n (*BRIT*) vaso (di fiori).

plaque [plæk] n placca.

plasma ['plæzmə] n plasma m.

plaster ['plɑːstə*] n intonaco; (*also*: ~ **of Paris**) gesso; (*BRIT: also*: **sticking** ~) cerotto ♦ *vt* intonacare; ingessare; (*cover*): **to** ~ **with** coprire di; (*col: mud etc*) impiastricciare; **in** ~ (*BRIT: leg etc*) ingessato(a).

plasterboard ['plɑːstəbɔːd] n lastra di cartone intonaco.

plaster cast n (*MED*) ingessatura, gesso; (*model, statue*) modello in gesso.

plastered ['plɑːstəd] *adj* (*col*) ubriaco(a) fradicio(a).

plasterer ['plɑːstərə*] n intonacatore m.

plastic ['plæstɪk] n plastica ♦ *adj* (*made of plastic*) di *or* in plastica; (*flexible*) plastico(a), malleabile; (*art*) plastico(a).

plastic bag n sacchetto di plastica.

plastic bullet n pallottola di plastica.

plastic explosive n esplosivo al plastico.

plasticine ® ['plæstɪsiːn] n plastilina ®.

plastic surgery n chirurgia plastica.

plate [pleɪt] n (*dish*) piatto; (*sheet of metal*) lamiera; (*PHOT*) lastra; (*TYP*) cliché m inv; (*in book*) tavola; (*on door*) targa, targhetta; (*AUT: number* ~) targa; (*dishes*): **gold** ~ vasellame m d'oro; **silver** ~ argenteria.

plateau, ~s *or* ~**x** ['plætəu, -z] n altipiano.

plateful ['pleɪtful] n piatto.

plate glass n vetro piano.

platen ['plætən] n (*on typewriter, printer*) rullo.

plate rack n scolapiatti m inv.

platform ['plætfɔːm] n (*stage, at meeting*) palco; (*BRIT: on bus*) piattaforma; (*RAIL*) marciapiede m; **the train leaves from** ~ **7** il treno parte dal binario 7.

platform ticket n (*BRIT*) biglietto d'ingresso ai binari.

platinum ['plætɪnəm] n platino.

platitude ['plætɪtjuːd] n luogo comune.

platoon [plə'tuːn] n plotone m.

platter ['plætə*] n piatto.

plaudits ['plɔːdɪts] *npl* plauso.

plausible ['plɔːzɪbl] *adj* plausibile, credibile; (*person*) convincente.

play [pleɪ] n gioco; (*THEAT*) commedia ♦ *vt* (*game*) giocare a; (*team, opponent*) giocare contro; (*instrument, piece of music*) suonare; (*play, part*) interpretare ♦ *vi* giocare; suonare; recitare; **to bring** *or* **call into** ~ (*plan*) mettere in azione; (*emotions*) esprimere; ~ **on words** gioco di parole; **to** ~ **a trick on sb** fare uno scherzo a qn; **they're** ~**ing at soldiers** stanno giocando ai soldati; **to** ~ **for time** (*fig*) cercare di guadagnar tempo; **to** ~ **into sb's hands** (*fig*) fare il gioco di qn.

▶**play about, play around** *vi* (*person*) divertirsi; **to** ~ **about** *or* **around with** (*fiddle with*) giocherellare con; (*idea*) accarezzare.

▶**play along** *vi*: **to** ~ **along with** (*fig: person*) stare al gioco di; (*: plan, idea*) fingere di assecondare ♦ *vt* (*fig*): **to** ~ **sb along** tenere qn in sospeso.

▶**play back** *vt* riascoltare, risentire.

▶**play down** *vt* minimizzare.

▶**play on** *vt fus* (*sb's feelings, credulity*) giocare su; **to** ~ **on sb's nerves** dare sui nervi a qn.

▶**play up** *vi* (*cause trouble*) fare i capricci.

playact ['pleɪækt] vi fare la commedia.
playboy ['pleɪbɔɪ] n playboy m inv.
played-out ['pleɪd'aut] adj spossato(a).
player ['pleɪə*] n giocatore/trice; (THEAT) attore/trice; (MUS) musicista m/f.
playful ['pleɪful] adj giocoso(a).
playgoer ['pleɪɡəuə*] n assiduo(a) frequentatore(trice) di teatri.
playground ['pleɪɡraund] n (in school) cortile m per la ricreazione; (in park) parco m giochi inv.
playgroup ['pleɪɡruːp] n giardino d'infanzia.
playing card ['pleɪɪŋ-] n carta da gioco.
playing field ['pleɪɪŋ-] n campo sportivo.
playmaker ['pleɪmeɪkə*] n (SPORT) playmaker m inv.
playmate ['pleɪmeɪt] n compagno/a di gioco.
play-off ['pleɪɔf] n (SPORT) bella.
playpen ['pleɪpɛn] n box m inv.
playroom ['pleɪruːm] n stanza dei giochi.
plaything ['pleɪθɪŋ] n giocattolo.
playtime ['pleɪtaɪm] n (SCOL) ricreazione f.
playwright ['pleɪraɪt] n drammaturgo/a.
plc abbr (BRIT) see **public limited company.**
plea [pliː] n (request) preghiera, domanda; (excuse) scusa; (LAW) (argomento di) difesa.
plea bargaining n (LAW) patteggiamento.
plead [pliːd] vt patrocinare; (give as excuse) addurre a pretesto ♦ vi (LAW) perorare la causa; (beg): **to ~ with sb** implorare qn; **to ~ for sth** implorare qc; **to ~ guilty/not guilty** (defendant) dichiararsi colpevole/innocente.
pleasant ['plɛznt] adj piacevole, gradevole.
pleasantly ['plɛzntlɪ] adv piacevolmente.
pleasantry ['plɛzntrɪ] n (joke) scherzo; (polite remark): **to exchange pleasantries** scambiarsi i convenevoli.
please [pliːz] vt piacere a ♦ vi (think fit): **do as you ~** faccia come le pare; **~!** per piacere!; **my bill, ~** il conto, per piacere; **~ yourself!** come ti (or le) pare!; **~ don't cry!** ti prego, non piangere!
pleased [pliːzd] adj (happy) felice, lieto(a); **~ (with)** (satisfied) contento(a) (di); **we are ~ to inform you that ...** abbiamo il piacere di informarla che ...; **~ to meet you!** piacere!
pleasing ['pliːzɪŋ] adj piacevole, che fa piacere.
pleasurable ['plɛʒərəbl] adj molto piacevole, molto gradevole.
pleasure ['plɛʒə*] n piacere m; **with ~** con piacere, volentieri; **"it's a ~"** "prego"; **is this trip for business or ~?** è un viaggio

d'affari o di piacere?
pleasure cruise n crociera.
pleat [pliːt] n piega.
plebiscite ['plɛbɪsɪt] n plebiscito.
plebs [plɛbz] npl (pej) plebe f.
plectrum ['plɛktrəm] n plettro.
pledge [plɛdʒ] n pegno; (promise) promessa ♦ vt impegnare; promettere; **to ~ support for sb** impegnarsi a sostenere qn; **to ~ sb to secrecy** far promettere a qn di mantenere il segreto.
plenary ['pliːnərɪ] adj plenario(a); **in ~ session** in seduta plenaria.
plentiful ['plɛntɪful] adj abbondante, copioso(a).
plenty ['plɛntɪ] n abbondanza; **~ of** tanto(a), molto(a); un'abbondanza di; **we've got ~ of time to get there** abbiamo un sacco di tempo per arrivarci.
pleurisy ['pluərɪsɪ] n pleurite f.
Plexiglas ® ['plɛksɪɡlɑːs] n (US) plexiglas ® m.
pliable ['plaɪəbl] adj flessibile; (person) malleabile.
pliers ['plaɪəz] npl pinza.
plight [plaɪt] n situazione f critica.
plimsolls ['plɪmsəlz] npl (BRIT) scarpe fpl da tennis.
plinth [plɪnθ] n plinto; piedistallo.
PLO n abbr (= Palestine Liberation Organization) O.L.P. f.
plod [plɔd] vi camminare a stento; (fig) sgobbare.
plodder ['plɔdə*] n sgobbone m.
plodding ['plɔdɪŋ] adj lento(a) e pesante.
plonk [plɔŋk] (col) n (BRIT: wine) vino da poco ♦ vt: **to ~ sth down** buttare giù qc bruscamente.
plot [plɔt] n congiura, cospirazione f; (of story, play) trama; (of land) lotto ♦ vt (mark out) fare la pianta di; rilevare; (: diagram etc) tracciare; (conspire) congiurare, cospirare ♦ vi congiurare; **a vegetable ~** (BRIT) un orticello.
plotter ['plɔtə*] n cospiratore/trice; (COMPUT) plotter m inv, tracciatore m di curve.
plough, (US) **plow** [plau] n aratro ♦ vt (earth) arare.
▶**plough back** vt (COMM) reinvestire.
▶**plough through** vt fus (snow etc) procedere a fatica in.
ploughing, (US) **plowing** ['plauɪŋ] n aratura.
ploughman, (US) **plowman** ['plaumən] n aratore m; **~'s lunch** (BRIT) semplice pasto a base di pane e formaggio.
ploy [plɔɪ] n stratagemma m.

pls *abbr* = **please**.

pluck [plʌk] *vt* (*fruit*) cogliere; (*musical instrument*) pizzicare; (*bird*) spennare ♦ *n* coraggio, fegato; **to ~ one's eyebrows** depilarsi le sopracciglia; **to ~ up courage** farsi coraggio.

plucky ['plʌkɪ] *adj* coraggioso(a).

plug [plʌg] *n* tappo; (*ELEC*) spina; (*AUT: also:* **spark(ing)** ~) candela ♦ *vt* (*hole*) tappare; (*col: advertise*) spingere; **to give sb/sth a ~** fare pubblicità a qn/qc.

▶**plug in** (*ELEC*) *vi* inserire la spina ♦ *vt* attaccare a una presa.

plughole ['plʌghəʊl] *n* (*BRIT*) scarico.

plum [plʌm] *n* (*fruit*) susina ♦ *cpd:* ~ **job** (*col*) impiego ottimo *or* favoloso.

plumage ['plu:mɪdʒ] *n* piume *fpl*, piumaggio.

plumb [plʌm] *adj* verticale ♦ *n* piombo ♦ *adv* (*exactly*) esattamente ♦ *vt* sondare.

▶**plumb in** *vt* (*washing machine*) collegare all'impianto idraulico.

plumber ['plʌmə*] *n* idraulico.

plumbing ['plʌmɪŋ] *n* (*trade*) lavoro di idraulico; (*piping*) tubature *fpl*.

plumbline ['plʌmlaɪn] *n* filo a piombo.

plume [plu:m] *n* piuma, penna; (*decorative*) pennacchio.

plummet ['plʌmɪt] *vi* cadere a piombo.

plump [plʌmp] *adj* grassoccio(a) ♦ *vt:* **to ~ sth (down) on** lasciar cadere qc di peso su.

▶**plump for** *vt fus* (*col*) decidersi per.

▶**plump up** *vt* sprimacciare.

plunder ['plʌndə*] *n* saccheggio ♦ *vt* saccheggiare.

plunge [plʌndʒ] *n* tuffo ♦ *vt* immergere ♦ *vi* (*dive*) tuffarsi; (*fall*) cadere, precipitare; **to take the ~** (*fig*) saltare il fosso; **to ~ a room into darkness** far piombare una stanza nel buio.

plunger ['plʌndʒə*] *n* (*for blocked sink*) sturalavandini *m inv*.

plunging ['plʌndʒɪŋ] *adj* (*neckline*) profondo(a).

plural ['plʊərl] *adj, n* plurale (*m*).

plus [plʌs] *n* (*also:* ~ **sign**) segno più ♦ *prep* più ♦ *adj* (*MATH, ELEC*) positivo(a); **ten/ twenty ~** più di dieci/venti; **it's a ~** (*fig*) è un vantaggio.

plus fours *npl* calzoni *mpl* alla zuava.

plush [plʌʃ] *adj* lussuoso(a) ♦ *n* felpa.

plutonium [plu:'təʊnɪəm] *n* plutonio.

ply [plaɪ] *n* (*of wool*) capo; (*of wood*) strato ♦ *vt* (*tool*) maneggiare; (*a trade*) esercitare ♦ *vi* (*ship*) fare il servizio; **three ~ (wool)** lana a tre capi; **to ~ sb with drink** dare da bere continuamente a qn.

plywood ['plaɪwud] *n* legno compensato.

PM *n abbr* (*BRIT*) see **prime minister**.

p.m. *adv abbr* (= *post meridiem*) del pomeriggio.

PMS *n abbr* (= *premenstrual syndrome*) sindrome *f* premestruale.

PMT *n abbr* (= *premenstrual tension*) sindrome *f* premestruale.

pneumatic [nju:'mætɪk] *adj* pneumatico(a); ~ **drill** martello pneumatico.

pneumonia [nju:'məʊnɪə] *n* polmonite *f*.

PO *n abbr* (= *Post Office*) ≈ P.T. (= *Poste e Telegrafi*) ♦ *abbr* (*NAUT*) = **petty officer**.

po *abbr* = **postal order**.

POA *n abbr* (*BRIT:* = *Prison Officers' Association*) sindacato delle guardie carcerarie.

poach [pəʊtʃ] *vt* (*cook*) affogare; (*steal*) cacciare (*or* pescare) di frodo ♦ *vi* fare il bracconiere.

poached [pəʊtʃt] *adj* (*egg*) affogato(a).

poacher ['pəʊtʃə*] *n* bracconiere *m*.

poaching ['pəʊtʃɪŋ] *n* caccia (*or* pesca) di frodo.

PO box *n abbr see* **post office box**.

pocket ['pɒkɪt] *n* tasca ♦ *vt* intascare; **to be out of ~** rimetterci; **to be £5 in/out of ~** (*BRIT*) trovarsi con 5 sterline in più/in meno; **air ~** vuoto d'aria.

pocketbook ['pɒkɪtbuk] *n* (*wallet*) portafoglio; (*notebook*) taccuino; (*US: handbag*) busta.

pocket knife *n* temperino.

pocket money *n* paghetta, settimana.

pockmarked ['pɒkmɑːkt] *adj* (*face*) butterato(a).

pod [pɒd] *n* guscio ♦ *vt* sgusciare.

podgy ['pɒdʒɪ] *adj* grassoccio(a).

podiatrist [pɒ'diːətrɪst] *n* (*US*) callista *m/f*.

podiatry [pɒ'diːətrɪ] *n* (*US*) mestiere *m* di callista.

podium ['pəʊdɪəm] *n* podio.

POE *n abbr* = *port of embarkation*; *port of entry*.

poem ['pəʊɪm] *n* poesia.

poet ['pəʊɪt] *n* poeta/essa.

poetic [pəʊ'ɛtɪk] *adj* poetico(a).

poet laureate *n* (*BRIT*) poeta *m* laureato; *see boxed note*.

POET LAUREATE

In Gran Bretagna il **poet laureate** *è un poeta che riceve un vitalizio dalla casa reale britannica e che ha l'incarico di scrivere delle poesie commemorative in occasione delle festività ufficiali.*

poetry ['pəʊɪtrɪ] n poesia.
poignant ['pɔɪnjənt] adj struggente.
point [pɔɪnt] n (gen) punto; (tip: of needle etc) punta; (BRIT ELEC: also: **power** ~) presa (di corrente); (in time) punto, momento; (SCOL) voto; (main idea, important part) nocciolo; (also: **decimal** ~): **2 ~ 3 (2.3)** 2 virgola 3 (2,3) ♦ vt (show) indicare; (gun etc): **to ~ sth at** puntare qc contro ♦ vi mostrare a dito; **~s** npl (AUT) puntine fpl; (RAIL) scambio; **to ~ to** indicare; (fig) dimostrare; **to make a ~** fare un'osservazione; **to get the ~** capire; **to come to the ~** venire al fatto; **when it comes to the ~** quando si arriva al dunque; **to be on the ~ of doing sth** essere sul punto di or stare (proprio) per fare qc; **to be beside the ~** non entrarci; **to make a ~ of doing sth** non mancare di fare qc; **there's no ~ (in doing)** è inutile (fare); **in ~ of fact** a dire il vero; **that's the whole ~!** precisamente!, sta tutto lì!; **you've got a ~ there!** giusto!, ha ragione!; **the train stops at Carlisle and all ~s south** il treno ferma a Carlisle e in tutte le stazioni a sud di Carlisle; **good ~s** vantaggi mpl; (of person) qualità fpl; **~ of departure** (also fig) punto di partenza; **~ of order** mozione f d'ordine; **~ of sale** (COMM) punto di vendita; **~ of view** punto di vista.
▶**point out** vt far notare.
point-blank ['pɔɪnt'blæŋk] adv (also: **at ~ range**) a bruciapelo; (fig) categoricamente.
pointed ['pɔɪntɪd] adj (shape) aguzzo(a), appuntito(a); (remark) specifico(a).
pointedly ['pɔɪntɪdlɪ] adv in maniera inequivocabile.
pointer ['pɔɪntə*] n (stick) bacchetta; (needle) lancetta; (clue) indizio; (advice) consiglio; (dog) pointer m, cane m da punta.
pointless ['pɔɪntlɪs] adj inutile, vano(a).
poise [pɔɪz] n (balance) equilibrio; (of head, body) portamento; (calmness) calma ♦ vt tenere in equilibrio; **to be ~d for** (fig) essere pronto(a) a.
poison ['pɔɪzn] n veleno ♦ vt avvelenare.
poisoning ['pɔɪznɪŋ] n avvelenamento.
poisonous ['pɔɪznəs] adj velenoso(a); (fumes) venefico(a), tossico(a); (ideas, literature) pernicioso(a); (rumours, individual) perfido(a).
poke [pəʊk] vt (fire) attizzare; (jab with finger, stick etc) punzecchiare; (put): **to ~ sth in(to)** spingere qc dentro ♦ n (jab) colpetto; (with elbow) gomitata; **to ~**

one's head out of the window mettere la testa fuori dalla finestra; **to ~ fun at sb** prendere in giro qn.
▶**poke about** vi frugare.
poker ['pəʊkə*] n attizzatoio; (CARDS) poker m.
poker-faced ['pəʊkə'feɪst] adj dal viso impassibile.
poky ['pəʊkɪ] adj piccolo(a) e stretto(a).
Poland ['pəʊlənd] n Polonia.
polar ['pəʊlə*] adj polare.
polar bear n orso bianco.
polarize ['pəʊləraɪz] vt polarizzare.
Pole [pəʊl] n polacco/a.
pole [pəʊl] n (of wood) palo; (ELEC, GEO) polo.
poleaxe, (US) poleax ['pəʊlæks] vt (fig) stendere.
pole bean n (US) fagiolino.
polecat ['pəʊlkæt] n puzzola; (US) moffetta.
Pol. Econ. ['pɔlɪkɔn] n abbr = political economy.
polemic [pə'lɛmɪk] n polemica.
pole star n stella polare.
pole vault n salto con l'asta.
police [pə'liːs] n polizia ♦ vt mantenere l'ordine in; (streets, city, frontier) presidiare; **a large number of ~ were hurt** molti poliziotti sono rimasti feriti.
police car n macchina della polizia.
police constable (PC) n (BRIT) agente m di polizia.
police department n (US) dipartimento di polizia.
police force n corpo di polizia, polizia.
policeman [pə'liːsmən] n poliziotto, agente m di polizia.
police officer n = police constable.
police record n: **to have a ~** avere precedenti penali.
police state n stato di polizia.
police station n posto di polizia.
policewoman [pə'liːswumən] n donna f poliziotto inv.
policy ['pɔlɪsɪ] n politica; (of newspaper, company) linea di condotta, prassi f inv; (also: **insurance** ~) polizza (d'assicurazione); **to take out a ~** (INSURANCE) stipulare una polizza di assicurazione.
policy holder n assicurato/a.
policy-making ['pɔlɪsɪmeɪkɪŋ] n messa a punto di programmi.
polio ['pəʊlɪəʊ] n polio f.
Polish ['pəʊlɪʃ] adj polacco(a) ♦ n (LING) polacco.
polish ['pɔlɪʃ] n (for shoes) lucido; (for floor)

cera; (*for nails*) smalto; (*shine*) lucentezza, lustro; (*fig*: *refinement*) raffinatezza ♦ *vt* lucidare; (*fig*: *improve*) raffinare.

►**polish off** *vt* (*work*) sbrigare; (*food*) mangiarsi.

polished ['pɔlıʃt] *adj* (*fig*) raffinato(a).

polite [pə'laıt] *adj* cortese; **it's not ~ to do that** non è educato *or* buona educazione fare questo.

politely [pə'laıtlı] *adv* cortesemente.

politeness [pə'laıtnıs] *n* cortesia.

politic ['pɔlıtık] *adj* diplomatico(a).

political [pə'lıtıkl] *adj* politico(a).

political asylum *n* asilo politico.

politically [pə'lıtıklı] *adv* politicamente.

politically correct *adj* politicamente corretto(a).

politician [pɔlı'tıʃən] *n* politico.

politics ['pɔlıtıks] *n* politica ♦ *npl* idee *fpl* politiche.

polka ['pɔlkə] *n* polca.

polka dot *n* pois *m inv*.

poll [pəul] *n* scrutinio; (*votes cast*) voti *mpl*; (*also*: **opinion ~**) sondaggio (d'opinioni) ♦ *vt* ottenere; **to go to the ~s** (*voters*) andare alle urne; (*government*) indire le elezioni.

pollen ['pɔlən] *n* polline *m*.

pollen count *n* tasso di polline nell'aria.

pollination [pɔlı'neıʃən] *n* impollinazione *f*.

polling ['pəulıŋ] *n* (*BRIT POL*) votazione *f*, votazioni *fpl*; (*TEL*) interrogazione *f* ciclica.

polling booth *n* (*BRIT*) cabina elettorale.

polling day *n* (*BRIT*) giorno delle elezioni.

polling station *n* (*BRIT*) sezione *f* elettorale.

pollster ['pəulstə*] *n* chi esegue sondaggi d'opinione.

poll tax *n* (*BRIT*) *imposta locale sulla persona fisica* (*non più in vigore*).

pollutant [pə'lu:tənt] *n* sostanza inquinante.

pollute [pə'lu:t] *vt* inquinare.

pollution [pə'lu:ʃən] *n* inquinamento.

polo ['pəuləu] *n* polo.

polo neck *n* collo alto; (*also*: **~ sweater**) dolcevita ♦ *adj* a collo alto.

poly ['pɔlı] *n abbr* (*BRIT*) = **polytechnic**.

poly bag *n* (*BRIT col*) borsa di plastica.

polyester [pɔlı'ɛstə*] *n* poliestere *m*.

polygamy [pə'lıgəmı] *n* poligamia.

polygraph ['pɔlıgrɑːf] *n* macchina della verità.

Polynesia [pɔlı'niːzıə] *n* Polinesia.

Polynesian [pɔlı'niːzıən] *adj*, *n* polinesiano(a).

polyp ['pɔlıp] *n* (*MED*) polipo.

polystyrene [pɔlı'staıriːn] *n* polistirolo.

polytechnic [pɔlı'tɛknık] *n* (*college*) istituto superiore ad indirizzo tecnologico.

polythene ['pɔlıθiːn] *n* politene *m*.

polythene bag *n* borsa di plastica.

polyurethane ['pɔlı'juərıθeın] *n* poliuretano.

pomegranate ['pɔmıgrænıt] *n* melagrana.

pommel ['pɔml] *n* pomo ♦ *vt* = **pummel**.

pomp [pɔmp] *n* pompa, fasto.

pompom ['pɔmpɔm] *n* pompon *m inv*.

pompous ['pɔmpəs] *adj* pomposo(a); (*person*) pieno(a) di boria.

pond [pɔnd] *n* stagno; (*in park*) laghetto.

ponder ['pɔndə*] *vi* riflettere, meditare ♦ *vt* ponderare, riflettere su.

ponderous ['pɔndərəs] *adj* ponderoso(a), pesante.

pong [pɔŋ] *n* (*BRIT col*) *n* puzzo ♦ *vi* puzzare.

pontiff ['pɔntıf] *n* pontefice *m*.

pontificate [pɔn'tıfıkeıt] *vi* (*fig*): **to ~ (about)** pontificare (su).

pontoon [pɔn'tuːn] *n* pontone *m*; (*BRIT CARDS*) ventuno.

pony ['pəunı] *n* pony *m inv*.

ponytail ['pəunıteıl] *n* coda di cavallo.

pony trekking [-trɛkıŋ] *n* (*BRIT*) escursione *f* a cavallo.

poodle ['puːdl] *n* barboncino, barbone *m*.

pooh-pooh [puː'puː] *vt* deridere.

pool [puːl] *n* (*of rain*) pozza; (*pond*) stagno; (*artificial*) vasca; (*also*: **swimming ~**) piscina; (*sth shared*) fondo comune; (*COMM*: *consortium*) pool *m inv*; (*US*: *monopoly trust*) trust *m inv*; (*billiards*) *specie di biliardo a buca* ♦ *vt* mettere in comune; **typing ~**, (*US*) **secretary ~** servizio comune di dattilografia; **to do the (football) ~s** ≈ fare la schedina; giocare al totocalcio.

poor [puə*] *adj* povero(a); (*mediocre*) mediocre, cattivo(a) ♦ *npl*: **the ~** i poveri.

poorly ['puəlı] *adv* poveramente; (*badly*) male ♦ *adj* indisposto(a), malato(a).

pop [pɔp] *n* (*noise*) schiocco; (*MUS*) musica pop; (*US col*: *father*) babbo; (*col*: *drink*) bevanda gasata ♦ *vt* (*put*) mettere (in fretta) ♦ *vi* scoppiare; (*cork*) schioccare; **she ~ped her head out** (*of the window*) sporse fuori la testa.

►**pop in** *vi* passare.

►**pop out** *vi* fare un salto fuori.

►**pop up** *vi* apparire, sorgere.

pop concert *n* concerto *m* pop *inv*.

popcorn ['pɔpkɔːn] *n* pop-corn *m*.

pope [pəup] *n* papa *m*.

poplar ['pɔplə*] *n* pioppo.

poplin ['pɔplın] *n* popeline *f*.

popper ['pɔpə*] n (BRIT) bottone m automatico, bottone a pressione.

poppy ['pɔpɪ] n papavero.

poppycock ['pɔpɪkɔk] n (col) scempiaggini fpl.

Popsicle ® ['pɔpsɪkl] n (US) ghiacciolo.

populace ['pɔpjuləs] n popolo.

popular ['pɔpjulə*] adj popolare; (fashionable) in voga; **to be ~ (with)** (person) essere benvoluto(a) or ben visto(a) (da); (decision) essere gradito(a) (a); **a ~ song** una canzone di successo.

popularity [pɔpju'lærɪtɪ] n popolarità.

popularize ['pɔpjuləraɪz] vt divulgare; (science) volgarizzare.

populate ['pɔpjuleɪt] vt popolare.

population [pɔpju'leɪʃən] n popolazione f.

population explosion n forte espansione f demografica.

populous ['pɔpjuləs] adj popolato(a).

pop-up menu ['pɔpʌp-] n (COMPUT) menu m inv a comparsa.

porcelain ['pɔːslɪn] n porcellana.

porch [pɔːtʃ] n veranda.

porcupine ['pɔːkjupaɪn] n porcospino.

pore [pɔː*] n poro ♦ vi: **to ~ over** essere immerso(a) in.

pork [pɔːk] n carne f di maiale.

pork chop n braciola or costoletta di maiale.

porn [pɔːn] (col) n pornografia ♦ adj porno inv.

pornographic [pɔːnə'græfɪk] adj pornografico(a).

pornography [pɔː'nɔgrəfɪ] n pornografia.

porous ['pɔːrəs] adj poroso(a).

porpoise ['pɔːpəs] n focena.

porridge ['pɔrɪdʒ] n porridge m.

port¹ [pɔːt] n porto; (opening in ship) portello; (NAUT: left side) babordo; (COMPUT) porta; **to ~** (NAUT) a babordo; **~ of call** (porto di) scalo.

port² [pɔːt] n (wine) porto.

portable ['pɔːtəbl] adj portatile.

portal ['pɔːtl] n portale m.

portcullis [pɔːt'kʌlɪs] n saracinesca.

portent ['pɔːtɛnt] n presagio.

porter ['pɔːtə*] n (for luggage) facchino, portabagagli m inv; (doorkeeper) portiere m, portinaio; (US RAIL) addetto ai vagoni letto.

portfolio [pɔːt'fəuliəu] n (POL: office; ECON) portafoglio; (of artist) raccolta dei propri lavori.

porthole ['pɔːthəul] n oblò m inv.

portico ['pɔːtɪkəu] n portico.

portion ['pɔːʃən] n porzione f.

portly ['pɔːtlɪ] adj corpulento(a).

portrait ['pɔːtreɪt] n ritratto.

portray [pɔː'treɪ] vt fare il ritratto di; (character on stage) rappresentare; (in writing) ritrarre.

portrayal ['pɔːtreɪəl] n ritratto; rappresentazione f.

Portugal ['pɔːtjugl] n Portogallo.

Portuguese [pɔːtju'giːz] adj portoghese ♦ n (pl inv) portoghese m/f; (LING) portoghese m.

Portuguese man-of-war [-mænəv'wɔː*] n (jellyfish) medusa.

pose [pəuz] n posa ♦ vi posare; (pretend): **to ~ as** atteggiarsi a, posare a ♦ vt porre; **to strike a ~** mettersi in posa.

poser ['pəuzə*] n domanda difficile; (person) = **poseur**.

poseur [pəu'zɔː*] n (pej) persona affettata.

posh [pɔʃ] adj (col) elegante; (family) per bene ♦ adv (col): **to talk ~** parlare in modo snob.

position [pə'zɪʃən] n posizione f; (job) posto ♦ vt mettere in posizione, collocare; **to be in a ~ to do sth** essere nella posizione di fare qc.

positive ['pɔzɪtɪv] adj positivo(a); (certain) sicuro(a), certo(a); (definite) preciso(a); definitivo(a).

posse ['pɔsɪ] n (US) drappello.

possess [pə'zɛs] vt possedere; **like one ~ed** come un ossesso; **whatever can have ~ed you?** cosa ti ha preso?

possession [pə'zɛʃən] n possesso; (object) bene m; **to take ~ of sth** impossessarsi or impadronirsi di qc.

possessive [pə'zɛsɪv] adj possessivo(a).

possessiveness [pə'zɛsɪvnɪs] n possessività.

possessor [pə'zɛsə*] n possessore/ posseditrice.

possibility [pɔsɪ'bɪlɪtɪ] n possibilità f inv; **he's a ~ for the part** è uno dei candidati per la parte.

possible ['pɔsɪbl] adj possibile; **it is ~ to do it** è possibile farlo; **if ~** se possibile; **as big as ~** il più grande possibile; **as far as ~** nei limiti del possibile.

possibly ['pɔsɪblɪ] adv (perhaps) forse; **if you ~ can** se le è possibile; **I cannot ~ come** proprio non posso venire.

post [pəust] n (BRIT: mail, letters, delivery) posta; (: collection) levata; (job, situation) posto; (pole) palo; (trading ~) stazione f commerciale ♦ vt (BRIT: send by post) impostare; (MIL) appostare; (notice) affiggere; (BRIT: appoint): **to ~ to** assegnare a; **by ~** (BRIT) per posta; **by return of ~** (BRIT) a giro di posta; **to keep sb ~ed** tenere qn al corrente.

post... [pəust] *prefix* post...; ~-**1990** dopo il 1990.
postage ['pəustɪdʒ] *n* affrancatura.
postage stamp *n* francobollo.
postal ['pəustəl] *adj* postale.
postal order *n* vaglia *m inv* postale.
postbag ['pəustbæg] *n* (*BRIT*) sacco postale, sacco della posta.
postbox ['pəustbɔks] *n* cassetta delle lettere.
postcard ['pəustkɑːd] *n* cartolina.
postcode ['pəustkəud] *n* (*BRIT*) codice *m* (di avviamento) postale.
postdate ['pəust'deɪt] *vt* (*cheque*) postdatare.
poster ['pəustə*] *n* manifesto, affisso.
poste restante [pəust'rɛstɑ̃ːnt] *n* (*BRIT*) fermo posta *m*.
posterior [pɔs'tɪərɪə*] *n* (*col*) deretano, didietro.
posterity [pɔs'tɛrɪtɪ] *n* posterità.
poster paint *n* tempera.
post exchange (PX) *n* (*US MIL*) spaccio militare.
post-free [pəust'friː] *adj*, *adv* (*BRIT*) franco di porto.
postgraduate ['pəust'grædjuət] *n* laureato/a che continua gli studi.
posthumous ['pɔstjuməs] *adj* postumo(a).
posthumously ['pɔstjuməslɪ] *adv* dopo la mia (*or* sua *etc*) morte.
posting ['pəustɪŋ] *n* (*BRIT*) incarico.
postman ['pəustmən] *n* postino.
postmark ['pəustmɑːk] *n* bollo *or* timbro postale.
postmaster ['pəustmɑːstə*] *n* direttore *m* di un ufficio postale.
Postmaster General *n* ≈ ministro delle Poste.
postmistress ['pəustmɪstrɪs] *n* direttrice *f* di un ufficio postale.
post-mortem [pəust'mɔːtəm] *n* autopsia; (*fig*) analisi *f inv* a posteriori.
postnatal ['pəust'neɪtl] *adj* post-parto *inv*.
post office *n* (*building*) ufficio postale; (*organization*) poste *fpl*.
post office box (PO box) *n* casella postale (C.P.).
post-paid ['pəust'peɪd] *adj* già affrancato(a).
postpone [pəust'pəun] *vt* rinviare.
postponement [pəust'pəunmənt] *n* rinvio.
postscript ['pəustskrɪpt] *n* poscritto.
postulate ['pɔstjuleɪt] *vt* postulare.
posture ['pɔstʃə*] *n* portamento; (*pose*) posa, atteggiamento ♦ *vi* posare.
postwar ['pəust'wɔː*] *adj* del dopoguerra.
posy ['pəuzɪ] *n* mazzetto di fiori.

pot [pɔt] *n* (*for cooking*) pentola; casseruola; (*for plants, jam*) vaso; (*piece of pottery*) ceramica; (*col: marijuana*) erba ♦ *vt* (*plant*) piantare in vaso; **to go to** ~ (*col*) andare in malora; ~**s of** (*BRIT col*) un sacco di.
potash ['pɔtæʃ] *n* potassa.
potassium [pə'tæsɪəm] *n* potassio.
potato, ~**es** [pə'teɪtəu] *n* patata.
potato crisps, (*US*) **potato chips** *npl* patatine *fpl*.
potato flour *n* fecola di patate.
potato peeler *n* sbucciapatate *m inv*.
potbellied ['pɔtbɛlɪd] *adj* (*from overeating*) panciuto(a); (*from malnutrition*) dal ventre gonfio.
potency ['pəutnsɪ] *n* potenza; (*of drink*) forza.
potent ['pəutnt] *adj* potente, forte.
potentate ['pəutnteɪt] *n* potentato.
potential [pə'tɛnʃl] *adj* potenziale ♦ *n* possibilità *fpl*; **to have** ~ essere promettente.
potentially [pə'tɛnʃəlɪ] *adv* potenzialmente.
pothole ['pɔthəul] *n* (*in road*) buca; (*BRIT: underground*) marmitta.
potholer ['pɔthəulə*] *n* (*BRIT*) speleologo/a.
potholing ['pɔthəulɪŋ] *n* (*BRIT*): **to go** ~ fare la speleologia.
potion ['pəuʃən] *n* pozione *f*.
potluck [pɔt'lʌk] *n*: **to take** ~ tentare la sorte.
potpourri [pəu'purɪ] *n* (*dried petals etc*) miscuglio di petali essiccati profumati; (*fig*) pot-pourri *m inv*.
pot roast *n* brasato.
potshot ['pɔtʃɔt] *n*: **to take** ~**s at** tirare a casaccio contro.
potted ['pɔtɪd] *adj* (*food*) in conserva; (*plant*) in vaso; (*fig: shortened*) condensato(a).
potter ['pɔtə*] *n* vasaio ♦ *vi* (*BRIT*): **to** ~ **around,** ~ **about** lavoracchiare; **to** ~ **round the house** sbrigare con calma le faccende di casa; ~'**s wheel** tornio (da vasaio).
pottery ['pɔtərɪ] *n* ceramiche *fpl*; **a piece of** ~ una ceramica.
potty ['pɔtɪ] *adj* (*BRIT col: mad*) tocco(a) ♦ *n* (*child's*) vasino.
potty-trained ['pɔtɪtreɪnd] *adj* che ha imparato a farla nel vasino.
pouch [pautʃ] *n* borsa; (*ZOOL*) marsupio.
pouf(fe) [puːf] *n* (*stool*) pouf *m inv*.
poultice ['pəultɪs] *n* impiastro, cataplasma *m*.
poultry ['pəultrɪ] *n* pollame *m*.
poultry farm *n* azienda avicola.
poultry farmer *n* pollicoltore/trice.

pounce [pauns] *vi*: **to ~ (on)** balzare addosso (a), piombare (su) ♦ *n* balzo.

pound [paund] *n* (*weight:* = *453g, 16 ounces*) libbra; (*money:* = *100 pence*) (lira) sterlina; (*for dogs*) canile *m* municipale ♦ *vt* (*beat*) battere; (*crush*) pestare, polverizzare ♦ *vi* (*beat*) battere, martellare; **half a ~** mezza libbra; **a five-~ note** una banconota da cinque sterline.

pounding ['paundɪŋ] *n*: **to take a ~** (*fig*) prendere una batosta.

pound sterling *n* sterlina.

pour [pɔ:*] *vt* versare ♦ *vi* riversarsi; (*rain*) piovere a dirotto.

▶**pour away, pour off** *vt* vuotare.

▶**pour in** *vi* (*people*) entrare in fiotto; **to come ~ing in** (*water*) entrare a fiotti; (*letters*) arrivare a valanghe; (*cars, people*) affluire in gran quantità.

▶**pour out** *vi* (*people*) riversarsi fuori ♦ *vt* vuotare; versare.

pouring ['pɔ:rɪŋ] *adj*: **~ rain** pioggia torrenziale.

pout [paut] *vi* sporgere le labbra; fare il broncio.

poverty ['pɔvətɪ] *n* povertà, miseria.

poverty line *n* soglia di povertà.

poverty-stricken ['pɔvətɪstrɪkən] *adj* molto povero(a), misero(a).

poverty trap *n* (*BRIT*) circolo vizioso della povertà.

POW *n abbr* = **prisoner of war**.

powder ['paudə*] *n* polvere *f* ♦ *vt* spolverizzare; (*face*) incipriare; **~ed milk** latte *m* in polvere; **to ~ one's nose** incipriarsi il naso; (*euphemism*) andare alla toilette.

powder compact *n* portacipria *m inv*.

powder keg *n* (*fig: area*) polveriera; (*: situation*) situazione *f* esplosiva.

powder puff *n* piumino della cipria.

powder room *n* toilette *f inv* (per signore).

powdery ['paudərɪ] *adj* polveroso(a).

power ['pauə*] *n* (*strength*) potenza, forza; (*ability, POL: of party, leader*) potere *m*; (*MATH*) potenza; (*ELEC*) corrente *f* ♦ *vt* fornire di energia; azionare; **to be in ~** essere al potere; **to do all in one's ~ to help sb** fare tutto quello che si può per aiutare qn; **the world ~s** le grandi potenze; **mental ~s** capacità *fpl* mentali.

powerboat ['pauəbəut] *n* (*BRIT*) motobarca, imbarcazione *f* a motore.

power cut *n* (*BRIT*) interruzione *f or* mancanza di corrente.

powered ['pauəd] *adj*: **~ by** azionato(a) da; **nuclear-~ submarine** sottomarino a propulsione atomica.

power failure *n* guasto alla linea elettrica.

powerful ['pauəful] *adj* potente, forte.

powerhouse ['pauəhaus] *n* (*fig: person*) persona molto dinamica; **a ~ of ideas** una miniera di idee.

powerless ['pauəlɪs] *adj* impotente, senza potere.

power line *n* linea elettrica.

power of attorney *n* procura.

power point *n* (*BRIT*) presa di corrente.

power station *n* centrale *f* elettrica.

power steering *n* (*AUT: also:* **power-assisted steering**) servosterzo.

powwow ['pauwau] *n* riunione *f*.

pp *abbr* (= *pages*) pp.; (= *per procurationem*: *by proxy*): **~ J. Smith** per il Signor J. Smith.

PPE *n abbr* (*BRIT SCOL*: = *philosophy, politics, and economics*) corso di laurea.

PPS *n abbr* (*BRIT*: = *parliamentary private secretary*) parlamentare che assiste un ministro; = *post postscriptum*.

PQ *abbr* (*Canada*) = *Province of Quebec*.

PR *n abbr see* **proportional representation**; **public relations** ♦ *abbr* (*US*) = *Puerto Rico*.

Pr. *abbr* = **prince**.

practicability [præktɪkə'bɪlɪtɪ] *n* praticabilità.

practicable ['præktɪkəbl] *adj* (*scheme*) praticabile.

practical ['præktɪkl] *adj* pratico(a).

practicality [præktɪ'kælɪtɪ] *n* (*of plan*) fattibilità; (*of person*) senso pratico; **practicalities** dettagli *mpl* pratici.

practical joke *n* beffa.

practically ['præktɪklɪ] *adv* (*almost*) quasi, praticamente.

practice ['præktɪs] *n* pratica; (*of profession*) esercizio; (*at football etc*) allenamento; (*business*) gabinetto; clientela ♦ *vt, vi* (*US*) = **practise**; **in ~** (*in reality*) in pratica; **out of ~** fuori esercizio; **2 hours' piano ~** 2 ore di esercizio al pianoforte; **it's common ~** è d'uso; **to put sth into ~** mettere qc in pratica; **target ~** pratica di tiro.

practice match *n* partita di allenamento.

practise, (*US*) **practice** ['præktɪs] *vt* (*work at: piano, one's backhand etc*) esercitarsi a; (*train for: skiing, running etc*) allenarsi a; (*a sport, religion*) praticare; (*method*) usare; (*profession*) esercitare ♦ *vi* esercitarsi; (*train*) allenarsi; **to ~ for a match** allenarsi per una partita.

practised ['præktɪst] *adj* (*BRIT: person*) esperto(a); (*: performance*) da virtuoso(a); (*: liar*) matricolato(a); **with a ~ eye** con occhio esperto.

practising ['præktɪsɪŋ] *adj* (*Christian etc*) praticante; (*lawyer*) che esercita la professione; (*homosexual*) attivo(a).

practitioner [præk'tɪʃənə*] *n* professionista *m/f*; (*MED*) medico.

pragmatic [præg'mætɪk] *adj* prammatico(a).

Prague [prɑːg] *n* Praga.

prairie ['prɛərɪ] *n* prateria.

praise [preɪz] *n* elogio, lode *f* ♦ *vt* elogiare, lodare.

praiseworthy ['preɪzwɜː:ðɪ] *adj* lodevole.

pram [præm] *n* (*BRIT*) carrozzina.

prance [prɑːns] *vi* (*horse*) impennarsi.

prank [præŋk] *n* burla.

prat [præt] *n* (*BRIT col*) cretino/a.

prattle ['prætl] *vi* cinguettare.

prawn [prɔːn] *n* gamberetto.

pray [preɪ] *vi* pregare.

prayer [prɛə*] *n* preghiera.

prayer book *n* libro di preghiere.

pre... [priː] *prefix* pre...; **~-1970** prima del 1970.

preach [priːtʃ] *vt, vi* predicare; **to ~ at sb** fare la predica a qn.

preacher ['priːtʃə*] *n* predicatore/trice; (*US: minister*) pastore *m*.

preamble [prɪ'æmbl] *n* preambolo.

prearranged [priːə'reɪndʒd] *adj* organizzato/a in anticipo.

precarious [prɪ'kɛərɪəs] *adj* precario(a).

precaution [prɪ'kɔːʃən] *n* precauzione *f*.

precautionary [prɪ'kɔːʃənərɪ] *adj* (*measure*) precauzionale.

precede [prɪ'siːd] *vt, vi* precedere.

precedence ['prɛsɪdəns] *n* precedenza; **to take ~ over** avere la precedenza su.

precedent ['prɛsɪdənt] *n* precedente *m*; **to establish** *or* **set a ~** creare un precedente.

preceding [prɪ'siːdɪŋ] *adj* precedente.

precept ['priːsɛpt] *n* precetto.

precinct ['priːsɪŋkt] *n* (*round cathedral*) recinto; (*US: district*) circoscrizione *f*; **~s** *npl* (*neighbourhood*) dintorni *mpl*, vicinanze *fpl*; **pedestrian ~** zona pedonale; **shopping ~** (*BRIT*) centro commerciale.

precious ['prɛʃəs] *adj* prezioso(a) ♦ *adv* (*col*): **~ little/few** ben poco/pochi; **your ~ dog** (*ironic*) il suo amatissimo cane.

precipice ['prɛsɪpɪs] *n* precipizio.

precipitate *adj* [prɪ'sɪpɪtɪt] (*hasty*) precipitoso(a) ♦ *vt* [prɪ'sɪpɪteɪt] accelerare.

precipitation [prɪsɪpɪ'teɪʃən] *n* precipitazione *f*.

precipitous [prɪ'sɪpɪtəs] *adj* (*steep*) erto(a), ripido(a).

précis, *pl* **précis** ['preɪsiː, -z] *n* riassunto.

precise [prɪ'saɪs] *adj* preciso(a).

precisely [prɪ'saɪslɪ] *adv* precisamente; **~!** appunto!

precision [prɪ'sɪʒən] *n* precisione *f*.

preclude [prɪ'kluːd] *vt* precludere, impedire; **to ~ sb from doing** impedire a qn di fare.

precocious [prɪ'kəuʃəs] *adj* precoce.

preconceived [priːkən'siːvd] *adj* (*idea*) preconcetto(a).

preconception [priːkən'sɛpʃən] *n* preconcetto.

precondition [priːkən'dɪʃən] *n* condizione *f* necessaria.

precursor [priː'kɜːsə*] *n* precursore *m*.

predate [priː'deɪt] *vt* (*precede*) precedere.

predator ['prɛdətə*] *n* predatore *m*.

predatory ['prɛdətərɪ] *adj* predatore(trice).

predecessor ['priːdɪsɛsə*] *n* predecessore/a.

predestination [priːdɛstɪ'neɪʃən] *n* predestinazione *f*.

predetermine [priːdɪ'tɜːmɪn] *vt* predeterminare.

predicament [prɪ'dɪkəmənt] *n* situazione *f* difficile.

predicate ['prɛdɪkɪt] *n* (*LING*) predicativo.

predict [prɪ'dɪkt] *vt* predire.

predictable [prɪ'dɪktəbl] *adj* prevedibile.

predictably [prɪ'dɪktəblɪ] *adv* (*behave, react*) in modo prevedibile; **~ she didn't arrive** come era da prevedere, non è arrivata.

prediction [prɪ'dɪkʃən] *n* predizione *f*.

predispose [priːdɪs'pəuz] *vt* predisporre.

predominance [prɪ'dɔmɪnəns] *n* predominanza.

predominant [prɪ'dɔmɪnənt] *adj* predominante.

predominantly [prɪ'dɔmɪnəntlɪ] *adv* in maggior parte; soprattutto.

predominate [prɪ'dɔmɪneɪt] *vi* predominare.

pre-eminent [priː'ɛmɪnənt] *adj* preminente.

pre-empt [prɪ'ɛmpt] *vt* acquistare per diritto di prelazione; (*fig*) anticipare.

pre-emptive [prɪ'ɛmptɪv] *adj*: **~ strike** azione *f* preventiva.

preen [priːn] *vt*: **to ~ itself** (*bird*) lisciarsi le penne; **to ~ o.s.** agghindarsi.

prefab ['priːfæb] *n* casa prefabbricata.

prefabricated [priː'fæbrikeɪtɪd] *adj* prefabbricato(a).

preface ['prɛfəs] *n* prefazione *f*.

prefect ['priːfɛkt] *n* (*BRIT: in school*) *studente/essa con funzioni disciplinari*; (*in Italy*) prefetto.

prefer [prɪ'fəː*] vt preferire; (LAW: charges, complaint) sporgere; (: action) intentare; **to ~ coffee to tea** preferire il caffè al tè.
preferable ['prɛfrəbl] adj preferibile.
preferably ['prɛfrəblɪ] adv preferibilmente.
preference ['prɛfrəns] n preferenza; **in ~ to sth** piuttosto che qc.
preference shares npl (BRIT) azioni fpl privilegiate.
preferential [prɛfə'rɛnʃəl] adj preferenziale; **~ treatment** trattamento di favore.
preferred stock [prɪ'fəːd-] npl (US) = **preference shares**.
prefix ['priːfɪks] n prefisso.
pregnancy ['prɛgnənsɪ] n gravidanza.
pregnancy test n test m inv di gravidanza.
pregnant ['prɛgnənt] adj incinta adj f; (animal) gravido(a); (fig: remark, pause) significativo(a); **3 months ~** incinta di 3 mesi.
prehistoric ['priːhɪs'tɔrɪk] adj preistorico(a).
prehistory [priː'hɪstərɪ] n preistoria.
prejudge [priː'dʒʌdʒ] vt pregiudicare.
prejudice ['prɛdʒudɪs] n pregiudizio; (harm) torto, danno ♦ vt pregiudicare, ledere; (bias): **to ~ sb in favour of/against** disporre bene/male qn verso.
prejudiced ['prɛdʒudɪst] adj (person) pieno(a) di pregiudizi; (view) prevenuto(a); **to be ~ against sb/sth** essere prevenuto contro qn/qc.
prelate ['prɛlət] n prelato.
preliminaries [prɪ'lɪmɪnərɪz] npl preliminari mpl.
preliminary [prɪ'lɪmɪnərɪ] adj preliminare.
prelude ['prɛljuːd] n preludio.
premarital ['priː'mærɪtl] adj prematrimoniale.
premature ['prɛmətʃuə*] adj prematuro(a); (arrival) (molto) anticipato(a); **you are being a little ~** è un po' troppo precipitoso.
premeditated [priː'mɛdɪteɪtɪd] adj premeditato(a).
premeditation [priːmɛdɪ'teɪʃən] n premeditazione f.
premenstrual tension [priː'mɛnstruəl-] n (MED) tensione f premestruale.
premier ['prɛmɪə*] adj primo(a) ♦ n (POL) primo ministro.
première ['prɛmɪɛə*] n prima.
premise ['prɛmɪs] n premessa.
premises ['prɛmɪsɪz] npl locale m; **on the**

~ **sul posto**; **business ~** locali commerciali.
premium ['priːmɪəm] n premio; **to be at a ~** (fig: housing etc) essere ricercatissimo; **to sell at a ~** (shares) vendere sopra la pari.
premium bond n (BRIT) obbligazione f a premio.
premium deal n (COMM) offerta speciale.
premium gasoline n (US) super f.
premonition [prɛmə'nɪʃən] n premonizione f.
preoccupation [priːɔkju'peɪʃən] n preoccupazione f.
preoccupied [priː'ɔkjupaɪd] adj preoccupato(a).
prep [prɛp] n abbr (SCOL: = preparation) studio ♦ adj abbr: **~ school** = **preparatory school**.
prepackaged [priː'pækɪdʒd] adj già impacchettato(a).
prepaid [priː'peɪd] adj pagato(a) in anticipo; (envelope) affrancato(a).
preparation [prɛpə'reɪʃən] n preparazione f; **~s** npl (for trip, war) preparativi mpl; **in ~ for sth** in vista di qc.
preparatory [prɪ'pærətərɪ] adj preparatorio(a); **~ to sth/to doing sth** prima di qc/di fare qc.
preparatory school n (BRIT) scuola elementare privata; (US) scuola superiore privata; see boxed note.

PREPARATORY SCHOOL

In Gran Bretagna, la **prep(aratory) school** è una scuola privata frequentata da bambini dai 7 ai 13 anni in vista dell'iscrizione alla "public school". Negli Stati Uniti, invece, è una scuola superiore privata che prepara i ragazzi che si iscriveranno al "college".

---

prepare [prɪ'pɛə*] vt preparare ♦ vi: **to ~ for** prepararsi a.
prepared [prɪ'pɛəd] adj: **~ for** preparato(a) a; **~ to** pronto(a) a; **to be ~ to help sb** (willing) essere disposto or pronto ad aiutare qn.
preponderance [prɪ'pɔndərns] n preponderanza.
preposition [prɛpə'zɪʃən] n preposizione f.
prepossessing [priːpə'zɛsɪŋ] adj simpatico(a), attraente.
preposterous [prɪ'pɔstərəs] adj assurdo(a).
prerecord ['priːrɪ'kɔːd] vt registrare in anticipo; **~ed broadcast** trasmissione f registrata; **~ed cassette** (musi)cassetta.
prerequisite [priː'rɛkwɪzɪt] n requisito

indispensabile.

prerogative [prɪˈrɔgətɪv] *n* prerogativa.

presbyterian [prezbɪˈtɪərɪən] *adj, n* presbiteriano(a).

presbytery [ˈprezbɪtərɪ] *n* presbiterio.

preschool [ˈpriːˈskuːl] *adj* (*age*) prescolastico(a); (*child*) in età prescolastica.

prescribe [prɪˈskraɪb] *vt* prescrivere; (*MED*) ordinare; ~**d books** (*BRIT SCOL*) testi *mpl* in programma.

prescription [prɪˈskrɪpʃən] *n* prescrizione *f*; (*MED*) ricetta; **to make up** *or* (*US*) **fill a** ~ preparare *or* fare una ricetta; "**only available on** ~" "ottenibile solo dietro presentazione di ricetta medica".

prescription charges *npl* (*BRIT*) ticket *m inv*.

prescriptive [prɪˈskrɪptɪv] *adj* normativo(a).

presence [ˈprezns] *n* presenza; ~ **of mind** presenza di spirito.

present [ˈpreznt] *adj* presente; (*wife, residence, job*) attuale ♦ *n* regalo; (*also*: ~ **tense**) tempo presente ♦ *vt* [prɪˈzent] presentare; (*give*): **to** ~ **sb with sth** offrire qc a qn; **to be** ~ **at** essere presente a; **those** ~ i presenti; **at** ~ al momento; **to make sb a** ~ **of sth** regalare qc a qn.

presentable [prɪˈzentəbl] *adj* presentabile.

presentation [prezn'teɪʃən] *n* presentazione *f*; (*gift*) regalo, dono; (*ceremony*) consegna ufficiale; **on** ~ **of the voucher** dietro presentazione del buono.

present-day [ˈprezntdeɪ] *adj* attuale.

presenter [prɪˈzentə*] *n* (*BRIT RADIO, TV*) presentatore/trice.

presently [ˈprezntlɪ] *adv* (*soon*) fra poco, presto; (*at present*) al momento; (*US: now*) adesso, ora.

preservation [prezə'veɪʃən] *n* preservazione *f*, conservazione *f*.

preservative [prɪˈzɔːvətɪv] *n* conservante *m*.

preserve [prɪˈzɔːv] *vt* (*keep safe*) preservare, proteggere; (*maintain*) conservare; (*food*) mettere in conserva ♦ *n* (*for game, fish*) riserva; (*often pl*: *jam*) marmellata; (: *fruit*) frutta sciroppata.

preside [prɪˈzaɪd] *vi* presiedere.

presidency [ˈprezɪdənsɪ] *n* presidenza; (*US*: *of company*) direzione *f*.

president [ˈprezɪdənt] *n* presidente *m*; (*US*: *of company*) direttore/trice generale.

presidential [prezɪˈdenʃl] *adj* presidenziale.

press [pres] *n* (*tool, machine*) pressa; (*for wine*) torchio; (*newspapers*) stampa;

(*crowd*) folla ♦ *vt* (*push*) premere, pigiare; (*doorbell*) suonare; (*squeeze*) spremere; (: *hand*) stringere; (*clothes*: *iron*) stirare; (*pursue*) incalzare; (*insist*): **to** ~ **sth on sb** far accettare qc da qn; (*urge, entreat*): **to** ~ **sb to do** *or* **into doing sth** fare pressione su qn affinché faccia qc ♦ *vi* premere; accalcare; **to go to** ~ (*newspaper*) andare in macchina; **to be in the** ~ (*in the newspapers*) essere sui giornali; **we are** ~**ed for time** ci manca il tempo; **to** ~ **for sth** insistere per avere qc; **to** ~ **sb for an answer** insistere perché qn risponda; **to** ~ **charges against sb** (*LAW*) sporgere una denuncia contro qn.

▶**press ahead** *vi*: **to** ~ **ahead (with)** andare avanti (con).

▶**press on** *vi* continuare.

press agency *n* agenzia di stampa.

press clipping *n* ritaglio di giornale.

press conference *n* conferenza stampa.

press cutting *n* = **press clipping**.

press-gang [ˈpresgæŋ] *vt*: **to** ~ **sb into doing sth** costringere qn a viva forza a fare qc.

pressing [ˈpresɪŋ] *adj* urgente ♦ *n* stiratura.

press officer *n* addetto/a stampa *inv*.

press release *n* comunicato stampa.

press stud *n* (*BRIT*) bottone *m* a pressione.

press-up [ˈpresʌp] *n* (*BRIT*) flessione *f* sulle braccia.

pressure [ˈpreʃə*] *n* pressione *f* ♦ *vt* = **to put** ~ **on**; **high/low** ~ alta/bassa pressione; **to put** ~ **on sb** fare pressione su qn.

pressure cooker *n* pentola a pressione.

pressure gauge *n* manometro.

pressure group *n* gruppo di pressione.

pressurize [ˈpreʃəraɪz] *vt* pressurizzare; (*fig*): **to** ~ **sb (into doing sth)** fare delle pressioni su qn (per costringerlo a fare qc).

pressurized [ˈpreʃəraɪzd] *adj* pressurizzato(a).

Prestel ® [ˈprestel] *n* Videotel ® *m inv*.

prestige [presˈtiːʒ] *n* prestigio.

prestigious [presˈtɪdʒəs] *adj* prestigioso(a).

presumably [prɪˈzjuːməblɪ] *adv* presumibilmente; ~ **he did it** penso *or* presumo che l'abbia fatto.

presume [prɪˈzjuːm] *vt* supporre; **to** ~ **to do** (*dare*) permettersi di fare.

presumption [prɪˈzʌmpʃən] *n* presunzione *f*; (*boldness*) audacia.

presumptuous [prɪˈzʌmpʃəs] *adj* presuntuoso(a).

presuppose [priːsəˈpəuz] *vt* presupporre.

pre-tax [pri:'tæks] *adj* al lordo d'imposta.

pretence, (*US*) **pretense** [prɪ'tɛns] *n* (*claim*) pretesa; (*pretext*) pretesto, scusa; **to make a ~ of doing** far finta di fare; **on** *or* **under the ~ of doing sth** con il pretesto *or* la scusa di fare qc; **she is devoid of all ~** non si nasconde dietro false apparenze.

pretend [prɪ'tɛnd] *vt* (*feign*) fingere ♦ *vi* far finta; (*claim*): **to ~ to sth** pretendere a qc; **to ~ to do** far finta di fare.

pretense [prɪ'tɛns] *n* (*US*) = **pretence.**

pretension [prɪ'tɛnʃən] *n* (*claim*) pretesa; **to have no ~s to sth/to being sth** non avere la pretesa di avere qc/di essere qc.

pretentious [prɪ'tɛnʃəs] *adj* pretenzioso(a).

preterite ['prɛtərɪt] *n* preterito.

pretext ['pri:tɛkst] *n* pretesto; **on** *or* **under the ~ of doing sth** col pretesto di fare qc.

pretty ['prɪtɪ] *adj* grazioso(a), carino(a) ♦ *adv* abbastanza, assai.

prevail [prɪ'veɪl] *vi* (*win, be usual*) prevalere; (*persuade*): **to ~ (up)on sb to do** persuadere qn a fare.

prevailing [prɪ'veɪlɪŋ] *adj* dominante.

prevalent ['prɛvələnt] *adj* (*belief*) predominante; (*customs*) diffuso(a); (*fashion*) corrente; (*disease*) comune.

prevarication [prɪværɪ'keɪʃən] *n* tergiversazione *f*.

prevent [prɪ'vɛnt] *vt* prevenire; **to ~ sb from doing** impedire a qn di fare.

preventable [prɪ'vɛntəbl] *adj* evitabile.

preventative [prɪ'vɛntətɪv] *adj* preventivo(a).

prevention [prɪ'vɛnʃən] *n* prevenzione *f*.

preventive [prɪ'vɛntɪv] *adj* preventivo(a).

preview ['pri:vju:] *n* (*of film*) anteprima.

previous ['pri:vɪəs] *adj* precedente; anteriore; **I have a ~ engagement** ho già (preso) un impegno; **~ to doing** prima di fare.

previously ['pri:vɪəslɪ] *adv* prima.

prewar ['pri:'wɔ:*] *adj* anteguerra *inv*.

prey [preɪ] *n* preda ♦ *vi*: **to ~ on** far preda di; **it was ~ing on his mind** gli rodeva la mente.

price [praɪs] *n* prezzo; (*BETTING: odds*) quotazione *f* ♦ *vt* (*goods*) fissare il prezzo di; valutare; **what is the ~ of ...?** quanto costa ...?; **to go up** *or* **rise in ~** salire *or* aumentare di prezzo; **to put a ~ on sth** valutare *or* stimare qc; **he regained his freedom, but at a ~** ha riconquistato la sua libertà, ma a caro prezzo; **what ~ his promises now?** (*BRIT*) a che valgono ora

le sue promesse?; **to be ~d out of the market** (*article*) essere così caro da diventare invendibile; (*producer, nation*) non poter sostenere la concorrenza.

price control *n* controllo dei prezzi.

price-cutting ['praɪskʌtɪŋ] *n* riduzione *f* dei prezzi.

priceless ['praɪslɪs] *adj* di valore inestimabile; (*col: amusing*) impagabile, spassosissimo(a).

price list *n* listino (dei) prezzi.

price range *n* gamma di prezzi; **it's within my ~** rientra nelle mie possibilità.

price tag *n* cartellino del prezzo.

price war *n* guerra dei prezzi.

pricey ['praɪsɪ] *adj* (*col*) caruccio(a).

prick [prɪk] *n* puntura ♦ *vt* pungere; **to ~ up one's ears** drizzare gli orecchi.

prickle ['prɪkl] *n* (*of plant*) spina; (*sensation*) pizzicore *m*.

prickly ['prɪklɪ] *adj* spinoso(a); (*fig: person*) permaloso(a); **~ heat** sudamina.

pride [praɪd] *n* orgoglio; superbia ♦ *vt*: **to ~ o.s. on** essere orgoglioso(a) di; vantarsi di; **to take (a) ~ in** tenere molto a; essere orgoglioso di; **to take a ~ in doing** andare orgoglioso di fare; **to have ~ of place** (*BRIT*) essere al primo posto.

priest [pri:st] *n* prete *m*, sacerdote *m*.

priestess ['pri:stɪs] *n* sacerdotessa.

priesthood ['pri:sthud] *n* sacerdozio.

prig [prɪg] *n*: **he's a ~** è compiaciuto di se stesso.

prim [prɪm] *adj* pudico(a); contegnoso(a).

primacy ['praɪməsɪ] *n* primato.

prima facie ['praɪmə'feɪʃɪ] *adj*: **to have a ~ case** (*LAW*) presentare una causa in apparenza fondata.

primal ['praɪml] *adj* primitivo(a).

primarily ['praɪmərɪlɪ] *adv* principalmente.

primary ['praɪmərɪ] *adj* primario(a); (*first in importance*) primo(a) ♦ *n* (*US: election*) primarie *fpl; see boxed note*.

PRIMARY

Negli Stati Uniti, attraverso le **primaries** *viene fatta una prima scrematura dei candidati dei partiti alle elezioni presidenziali. La scelta definitiva del candidato da presentare alla presidenza si basa sui risultati delle* **primaries** *e ha luogo durante le "Conventions" dei partiti, che si tengono in luglio e in agosto.*

---

primary colour *n* colore *m* fondamentale.

primary school *n* (*BRIT*) scuola elementare; *see boxed note*.

primate *n* (*REL*: ['praɪmɪt], *ZOOL*: ['praɪmeɪt]) primate *m.*

prime [praɪm] *adj* primario(a), fondamentale; (*excellent*) di prima qualità ♦ *n*: **in the ~ of life** nel fiore della vita ♦ *vt* (*gun*) innescare; (*pump*) adescare; (*fig*) mettere al corrente.

prime minister (PM) *n* primo ministro.

primer ['praɪmə*] *n* (*book*) testo elementare; (*paint*) vernice *f* base *inv.*

prime time *n* (*RADIO*, *TV*) fascia di massimo ascolto.

primeval [praɪ'miːvl] *adj* primitivo(a).

primitive ['prɪmɪtɪv] *adj* primitivo(a).

primrose ['prɪmrəuz] *n* primavera.

primus (stove) ® ['praɪməs-] *n* (*BRIT*) fornello a petrolio.

prince [prɪns] *n* principe *m.*

prince charming *n* principe *m* azzurro.

princess [prɪn'sɛs] *n* principessa.

principal ['prɪnsɪpl] *adj* principale ♦ *n* (*of school, college etc*) preside *m/f*; (*money*) capitale *m*; (*in play*) protagonista *m/f.*

principality [prɪnsɪ'pælɪtɪ] *n* principato.

principally ['prɪnsɪplɪ] *adv* principalmente.

principle ['prɪnsɪpl] *n* principio; **in ~** in linea di principio; **on ~** per principio.

print [prɪnt] *n* (*mark*) impronta; (*letters*) caratteri *mpl*; (*fabric*) tessuto stampato; (*ART, PHOT*) stampa ♦ *vt* imprimere; (*publish*) stampare, pubblicare; (*write in capitals*) scrivere in stampatello; **out of ~** esaurito(a).

▶**print out** *vt* (*COMPUT*) stampare.

printed circuit board (PCB) [prɪntɪd-] *n* circuito stampato.

printed matter [prɪntɪd-] *n* stampe *fpl.*

printer ['prɪntə*] *n* tipografo; (*machine*) stampante *m.*

printhead ['prɪnthɛd] *n* testa di stampa.

printing ['prɪntɪŋ] *n* stampa.

printing press *n* macchina tipografica.

print-out ['prɪntaut] *n* tabulato.

print wheel *n* margherita.

prior ['praɪə*] *adj* precedente ♦ *n* (*REL*) priore *m*; **~ to doing** prima di fare; **without ~ notice** senza preavviso; **to have a ~ claim to sth** avere un diritto di precedenza su qc.

priority [praɪ'ɔrɪtɪ] *n* priorità *f inv*, precedenza; **to have** *or* **take ~ over sth** avere la precedenza su qc.

priory ['praɪərɪ] *n* monastero.

prise [praɪz] *vt*: **to ~ open** forzare.

prism ['prɪzəm] *n* prisma *m.*

prison ['prɪzn] *n* prigione *f.*

prison camp *n* campo di prigionia.

prisoner ['prɪznə*] *n* prigioniero/a; **to take sb ~** far prigioniero qn; **the ~ at the bar** l'accusato, l'imputato; **~ of war** prigioniero/a di guerra.

prissy ['prɪsɪ] *adj* per benino.

pristine ['prɪstiːn] *adj* originario(a); intatto(a); puro(a).

privacy ['prɪvəsɪ] *n* solitudine *f*, intimità.

private ['praɪvɪt] *adj* privato(a); personale ♦ *n* soldato semplice; *"~"* (*on envelope*) "riservata"; **in ~** in privato; **in (his) ~ life** nella vita privata; **he is a very ~ person** è una persona molto riservata; **~ hearing** (*LAW*) udienza a porte chiuse; **to be in ~ practice** essere medico non convenzionato (con la mutua).

private enterprise *n* iniziativa privata.

private eye *n* investigatore *m* privato.

private limited company *n* (*BRIT*) società per azioni non quotata in Borsa.

privately ['praɪvɪtlɪ] *adv* in privato; (*within o.s.*) dentro di sé.

private parts *npl* (*ANAT*) parti *fpl* intime.

private property *n* proprietà privata.

private school *n* scuola privata.

privation [praɪ'veɪʃən] *n* (*state*) privazione *f*; (*hardship*) privazioni *fpl*, stenti *mpl.*

privatize ['praɪvɪtaɪz] *vt* privatizzare.

privet ['prɪvɪt] *n* ligustro.

privilege ['prɪvɪlɪdʒ] *n* privilegio.

privileged ['prɪvɪlɪdʒd] *adj* privilegiato(a); **to be ~ to do sth** avere il privilegio *or* l'onore di fare qc.

privy ['prɪvɪ] *adj*: **to be ~ to** essere al corrente di.

Privy Council *n* (*BRIT*) Consiglio della Corona; *see boxed note.*

Privy Councillor *n* (*BRIT*) Consigliere *m* della Corona.

prize [praɪz] *n* premio ♦ *adj* (*example, idiot*)

perfetto(a); (*bull, novel*) premiato(a) ♦ *vt* apprezzare, pregiare.

prize-fighter ['praɪzfaɪtə*] *n* pugile *m* (*che si batte per conquistare un premio*).

prize giving *n* premiazione *f*.

prize money *n* soldi *mpl* del premio.

prizewinner ['praɪzwɪnə*] *n* premiato/a.

prizewinning ['praɪzwɪnɪŋ] *adj* vincente; (*novel, essay etc*) premiato(a).

PRO *n abbr* = **public relations officer**.

pro [prəu] *n* (*SPORT*) professionista *m/f*; **the ~s and cons** il pro e il contro.

pro- [prəu] *prefix* (*in favour of*) filo...; **~Soviet** *adj* filosovietico(a).

pro-active [prəu'æktɪv] *adj*: **to be ~** agire d'iniziativa.

probability [prɔbə'bɪlɪtɪ] *n* probabilità *f inv*; **in all ~** con ogni probabilità.

probable ['prɔbəbl] *adj* probabile; **it is ~/ hardly ~ that ...** è probabile/poco probabile che ... + *sub*.

probably ['prɔbəblɪ] *adv* probabilmente.

probate ['prəubɪt] *n* (*LAW*) omologazione *f* (*di un testamento*).

probation [prə'beɪʃən] *n* (*in employment*) periodo di prova; (*LAW*) libertà vigilata; (*REL*) probandato; **on ~** (*employee*) in prova; (*LAW*) in libertà vigilata.

probationary [prəu'beɪʃənərɪ] *adj*: **~ period** periodo di prova.

probe [prəub] *n* (*MED, SPACE*) sonda; (*enquiry*) indagine *f*, investigazione *f* ♦ *vt* sondare, esplorare; indagare.

probity ['prəubɪtɪ] *n* probità.

problem ['prɔbləm] *n* problema *m*; **to have ~s with the car** avere dei problemi con la macchina; **what's the ~?** che cosa c'è?; **I had no ~ in finding her** non mi è stato difficile trovarla; **no ~!** ma certamente!, non c'è problema!

problematic [prɔblə'mætɪk] *adj* problematico(a).

problem-solving ['prɔbləmsɔlvɪŋ] *n* risoluzione *f* di problemi.

procedure [prə'siːdʒə*] *n* (*ADMIN, LAW*) procedura; (*method*) metodo.

proceed [prə'siːd] *vi* (*go forward*) avanzare, andare avanti; (*go about it*) procedere; (*continue*): **to ~ (with)** continuare; **to ~ to** andare a; passare a; **to ~ to do** mettersi a fare; **to ~ against sb** (*LAW*) procedere contro qn; **I am not sure how to ~** non so bene come fare.

proceedings [prə'siːdɪŋz] *npl* misure *fpl*; (*LAW*) procedimento; (*meeting*) riunione *f*; (*records*) rendiconti *mpl*; atti *mpl*.

proceeds ['prəusiːdz] *npl* profitto, incasso.

process ['prəusɛs] *n* processo; (*method*)

metodo, sistema *m* ♦ *vt* trattare; (*information*) elaborare ♦ *vi* [prə'sɛs] (*BRIT formal: go in procession*) sfilare, procedere in corteo; **we are in the ~ of moving to ...** stiamo per trasferirci a ....

processed cheese, (*US*) **process cheese** *n* formaggio fuso.

processing ['prəusɛsɪŋ] *n* trattamento; elaborazione *f*.

procession [prə'sɛʃən] *n* processione *f*, corteo; **funeral ~** corteo funebre.

pro-choice [prəu'tʃɔɪs] *adj* per la libertà di scelta di gravidanza.

proclaim [prə'kleɪm] *vt* proclamare, dichiarare.

proclamation [prɔklə'meɪʃən] *n* proclamazione *f*.

proclivity [prə'klɪvɪtɪ] *n* tendenza, propensione *f*.

procrastination [prəukræstɪ'neɪʃən] *n* procrastinazione *f*.

procreation [prəukrɪ'eɪʃən] *n* procreazione *f*.

Procurator Fiscal ['prɔkjureɪtə-] *n* (*Scottish*) procuratore *m*.

procure [prə'kjuə*] *vt* (*for o.s.*) procurarsi; (*for sb*) procurare.

procurement [prə'kjuəmənt] *n* approvvigionamento.

prod [prɔd] *vt* dare un colpetto a ♦ *n* (*push, jab*) colpetto.

prodigal ['prɔdɪgl] *adj* prodigo(a).

prodigious [prə'dɪdʒəs] *adj* prodigioso(a).

prodigy ['prɔdɪdʒɪ] *n* prodigio.

produce *n* ['prɔdjuːs] (*AGR*) prodotto, prodotti *mpl* ♦ *vt* [prə'djuːs] produrre; (*to show*) esibire, mostrare; (*proof of identity*) produrre, fornire; (*cause*) cagionare, causare; (*THEAT*) mettere in scena.

producer [prə'djuːsə*] *n* (*THEAT*) direttore/ trice; (*AGR, CINE*) produttore *m*.

product ['prɔdʌkt] *n* prodotto.

production [prə'dʌkʃən] *n* produzione *f*; (*THEAT*) messa in scena; **to put into ~** mettere in produzione.

production agreement *n* (*US*) accordo sui tempi di produzione.

production line *n* catena di lavorazione.

production manager *n* production manager *m inv*, direttore *m* della produzione.

productive [prə'dʌktɪv] *adj* produttivo(a).

productivity [prɔdʌk'tɪvɪtɪ] *n* produttività.

productivity agreement *n* (*BRIT*) accordo sui tempi di produzione.

productivity bonus *n* premio di produzione.

Prof. *abbr* (= *professor*) Prof.

profane [prə'feɪn] *adj* profano(a); (*language*) empio(a).

profess [prə'fɛs] *vt* professare; **I do not ~ to be an expert** non pretendo di essere un esperto.

professed [prə'fɛst] *adj* (*self-declared*) dichiarato(a).

profession [prə'fɛʃən] *n* professione *f*; **the ~s** le professioni liberali.

professional [prə'fɛʃənl] *n* (*SPORT*) professionista *m/f* ♦ *adj* professionale; (*work*) da professionista; **he's a ~ man** è un professionista; **to take ~ advice** consultare un esperto.

professionalism [prə'fɛʃnəlɪzəm] *n* professionismo.

professionally [prə'fɛʃnəlɪ] *adv* professionalmente, in modo professionale; (*SPORT: play*) come professionista; **I only know him ~** con lui ho solo rapporti di lavoro.

professor [prə'fɛsə*] *n* professore *m* (*titolare di una cattedra*); (*US: teacher*) professore/essa.

professorship [prə'fɛsəʃɪp] *n* cattedra.

proffer ['prɔfə*] *vt* (*remark*) profferire; (*apologies*) porgere, presentare; (*one's hand*) porgere.

proficiency [prə'fɪʃənsɪ] *n* competenza, abilità.

proficient [prə'fɪʃənt] *adj* competente, abile.

profile ['prəufaɪl] *n* profilo; **to keep a low ~** (*fig*) cercare di passare inosservato *or* di non farsi notare troppo; **to maintain a high ~** mettersi in mostra.

profit ['prɔfɪt] *n* profitto; beneficio ♦ *vi*: **to ~ (by *or* from)** approfittare (di); **~ and loss account** conto perdite e profitti; **to make a ~** realizzare un profitto; **to sell sth at a ~** vendere qc con un utile.

profitability [prɔfɪtə'bɪlɪtɪ] *n* redditività.

profitable ['prɔfɪtəbl] *adj* redditizio(a); (*fig: beneficial*) vantaggioso(a); (: *meeting, visit*) fruttuoso(a).

profit centre *n* centro di profitto.

profiteering [prɔfɪ'tɪərɪŋ] *n* (*pej*) affarismo.

profit-making ['prɔfɪtmeɪkɪŋ] *adj* a scopo di lucro.

profit margin *n* margine *m* di profitto.

profit-sharing ['prɔfɪtʃeərɪŋ] *n* compartecipazione *f* agli utili.

profits tax *n* (*BRIT*) imposta sugli utili.

profligate ['prɔflɪgɪt] *adj* (*dissolute: behaviour*) dissipato(a); (: *person*) debosciato(a); (*extravagant*): **he's very ~ with his money** è uno che sperpera i suoi soldi.

pro forma ['prəu'fɔːmə] *adv*: **~ invoice** fattura proforma.

profound [prə'faund] *adj* profondo(a).

profuse [prə'fjuːs] *adj* infinito(a), abbondante.

profusely [prə'fjuːslɪ] *adv* con grande effusione.

profusion [prə'fjuːʒən] *n* profusione *f*, abbondanza.

progeny ['prɔdʒɪnɪ] *n* progenie *f*; discendenti *mpl*.

programme, (*US*) **program** ['prəugræm] *n* programma *m* ♦ *vt* programmare.

program(m)er ['prəugræmə*] *n* programmatore/trice.

program(m)ing ['prəugræmɪŋ] *n* programmazione *f*.

program(m)ing language *n* linguaggio di programmazione.

progress *n* ['prəugrɛs] progresso ♦ *vi* [prə'grɛs] (*go forward*) avanzare, procedere; (*in time*) procedere; (*also*: **make ~**) far progressi; **in ~** in corso.

progression [prə'grɛʃən] *n* progressione *f*.

progressive [prə'grɛsɪv] *adj* progressivo(a); (*person*) progressista.

progressively [prə'grɛsɪvlɪ] *adv* progressivamente.

progress report *n* (*MED*) bollettino medico; (*ADMIN*) rendiconto dei lavori.

prohibit [prə'hɪbɪt] *vt* proibire, vietare; **to ~ sb from doing sth** vietare *or* proibire a qn di fare qc; **"smoking ~ed"** "vietato fumare".

prohibition [prəuɪ'bɪʃən] *n* (*US*) proibizionismo.

prohibitive [prə'hɪbɪtɪv] *adj* (*price etc*) proibitivo(a).

project *n* ['prɔdʒɛkt] (*plan*) piano; (*venture*) progetto, (*SCOL*) studio, ricerca ♦ *vb* [prə'dʒɛkt] *vt* proiettare ♦ *vi* (*stick out*) sporgere.

projectile [prə'dʒɛktaɪl] *n* proiettile *m*.

projection [prə'dʒɛkʃən] *n* proiezione *f*; sporgenza.

projectionist [prə'dʒɛkʃənɪst] *n* (*CINE*) proiezionista *m/f*.

projection room *n* (*CINE*) cabina *or* sala di proiezione.

projector [prə'dʒɛktə*] *n* proiettore *m*.

proletarian [prəulɪ'tɛərɪən] *adj, n* proletario(a).

proletariat [prəulɪ'tɛərɪət] *n* proletariato.

pro-life [prəu'laɪf] *adj* per il diritto alla vita.

proliferate [prə'lɪfəreɪt] *vi* proliferare.

proliferation [prəlɪfə'reɪʃən] *n* proliferazione *f*.

prolific [prə'lɪfɪk] *adj* prolifico(a).

prologue, (*US*) **prolog** ['prəulɔg] *n* prologo.

prolong [prə'lɔŋ] *vt* prolungare.

prom [prɔm] *n abbr* = **promenade**, **promenade concert**; (*US*: *ball*) ballo studentesco; *see boxed note*.

PROM

In Gran Bretagna i **Proms** (= *promenade concerts*) *sono concerti di musica classica, i più noti dei quali sono quelli eseguiti nella Royal Albert Hall a Londra. Prendono il nome dal fatto che in origine il pubblico li ascoltava stando in piedi o passeggiando. Negli Stati Uniti, invece, con* **prom** *si intende il ballo studentesco di un'università o di un college.*

---

promenade [prɔmə'nɑːd] *n* (*by sea*) lungomare *m*.

promenade concert *n* concerto (*con posti in piedi*).

promenade deck *n* (*NAUT*) ponte *m* di passeggiata.

prominence ['prɔmɪnəns] *n* prominenza; importanza.

prominent ['prɔmɪnənt] *adj* (*standing out*) prominente; (*important*) importante; **he is ~ in the field of ...** è un'autorità nel campo di ....

prominently ['prɔmɪnəntlɪ] *adv* (*display, set*) ben in vista; **he figured ~ in the case** ha avuto una parte di primo piano nella faccenda.

promiscuity [prɔmɪs'kjuːɪtɪ] *n* (*sexual*) rapporti *mpl* multipli.

promiscuous [prə'mɪskjuəs] *adj* (*sexually*) di facili costumi.

promise ['prɔmɪs] *n* promessa ♦ *vt, vi* promettere; **to make sb a ~** fare una promessa a qn; **a young man of ~** un giovane promettente; **to ~ (sb) to do sth** promettere (a qn) di fare qc.

promising ['prɔmɪsɪŋ] *adj* promettente.

promissory note ['prɔmɪsərɪ-] *n* pagherò *m inv*.

promontory ['prɔməntrɪ] *n* promontorio.

promote [prə'məut] *vt* promuovere; (*venture, event*) organizzare; (*product*) lanciare, reclamizzare; **the team was ~d to the second division** (*BRIT FOOTBALL*) la squadra è stata promossa in serie B.

promoter [prə'məutə*] *n* (*of sporting event*) organizzatore/trice; (*of cause etc*) sostenitore/trice.

promotion [prə'məuʃən] *n* promozione *f*.

prompt [prɔmpt] *adj* rapido(a), svelto(a); puntuale; (*reply*) sollecito(a) ♦ *adv* (*punctually*) in punto ♦ *n* (*COMPUT*) guida ♦ *vt* incitare; provocare; (*THEAT*) suggerire a; **at 8 o'clock ~** alle 8 in punto; **to ~ sb to do** spingere qn a fare.

prompter ['prɔmptə*] *n* (*THEAT*) suggeritore *m*.

promptly ['prɔmptlɪ] *adv* prontamente; puntualmente.

promptness ['prɔmptnɪs] *n* prontezza; puntualità.

prone [prəun] *adj* (*lying*) prono(a); **~ to** propenso(a) a, incline a; **to be ~ to illness** essere soggetto(a) a malattie; **she is ~ to burst into tears if ...** può facilmente scoppiare in lacrime se ....

prong [prɔŋ] *n* rebbio, punta.

pronoun ['prəunaun] *n* pronome *m*.

pronounce [prə'nauns] *vt* pronunziare ♦ *vi*: **to ~ (up)on** pronunziare su; **they ~d him unfit to drive** lo hanno dichiarato inabile alla guida.

pronounced [prə'naunst] *adj* (*marked*) spiccato(a).

pronouncement [prə'naunsmənt] *n* dichiarazione *f*.

pronunciation [prənʌnsɪ'eɪʃən] *n* pronunzia.

proof [pruːf] *n* prova; (*of book*) bozza; (*PHOT*) provino; (*of alcohol*): **70% ~** ≈ 40° in volume ♦ *vt* (*tent, anorak*) impermeabilizzare ♦ *adj*: **~ against** a prova di.

proofreader ['pruːfriːdə*] *n* correttore/trice di bozze.

prop [prɔp] *n* sostegno, appoggio ♦ *vt* (*also*: **~ up**) sostenere, appoggiare; (*lean*): **to ~ sth against** appoggiare qc contro *or* a.

Prop. *abbr* (*COMM*) = **proprietor**.

propaganda [prɔpə'gændə] *n* propaganda.

propagation [prɔpə'geɪʃən] *n* propagazione *f*.

propel [prə'pɛl] *vt* spingere (in avanti), muovere.

propeller [prə'pɛlə*] *n* elica.

propelling pencil [prə'pɛlɪŋ-] *n* (*BRIT*) matita a mina.

propensity [prə'pɛnsɪtɪ] *n* tendenza.

proper ['prɔpə*] *adj* (*suited, right*) adatto(a), appropriato(a); (*seemly*) decente; (*authentic*) vero(a); (*col: real*) *n* + vero(a) e proprio(a); **to go through the ~ channels** (*ADMIN*) seguire la regolare procedura.

properly ['prɔpəlɪ] *adv* decentemente; (*really, thoroughly*) veramente.

proper noun *n* nome *m* proprio.

property ['prɔpətɪ] *n* (*things owned*) beni *mpl*;

(*land, building*, CHEM *etc*) proprietà *f inv*.
property developer *n* (BRIT) costruttore *m* edile.
property owner *n* proprietario/a.
property tax *n* imposta patrimoniale.
prophecy ['prɔfɪsɪ] *n* profezia.
prophesy ['prɔfɪsaɪ] *vt* predire, profetizzare.
prophet ['prɔfɪt] *n* profeta *m*.
prophetic [prə'fɛtɪk] *adj* profetico(a).
proportion [prə'pɔːʃən] *n* proporzione *f*; (*share*) parte *f* ♦ *vt* proporzionare, commisurare; **to be in/out of** ~ **to** *or* **with sth** essere in proporzione/sproporzionato rispetto a qc; **to see sth in** ~(*fig*) dare il giusto peso a qc.
proportional [prə'pɔːʃənl] *adj* proporzionale.
proportional representation (PR) *n* rappresentanza proporzionale.
proportionate [prə'pɔːʃənɪt] *adj* proporzionato(a).
proposal [prə'pəuzl] *n* proposta; (*plan*) progetto; (*of marriage*) proposta di matrimonio.
propose [prə'pəuz] *vt* proporre, suggerire ♦ *vi* fare una proposta di matrimonio; **to** ~ **to do** proporsi di fare, aver l'intenzione di fare.
proposer [prə'pəuzə*] *n* (BRIT: *of motion*) proponente *m/f*.
proposition [prɔpə'zɪʃən] *n* proposizione *f*; (*proposal*) proposta; **to make sb a** ~ proporre qualcosa a qn.
propound [prə'paund] *vt* proporre, presentare.
proprietary [prə'praɪətərɪ] *adj*: ~ **article** prodotto con marchio depositato; ~ **brand** marchio di fabbrica.
proprietor [prə'praɪətə*] *n* proprietario/a.
propriety [prə'praɪətɪ] *n* (*seemliness*) decoro, rispetto delle convenienze sociali.
propulsion [prə'pʌlʃən] *n* propulsione *f*.
pro rata [prəu'rɑːtə] *adv* in proporzione.
prosaic [prəu'zeɪɪk] *adj* prosaico(a).
Pros. Atty. *abbr* (US) = **prosecuting attorney**.
proscribe [prə'skraɪb] *vt* proscrivere.
prose [prəuz] *n* prosa; (SCOL: *translation*) traduzione *f* dalla madrelingua.
prosecute ['prɔsɪkjuːt] *vt* intentare azione contro.
prosecuting attorney ['prɔsɪkjuːtɪŋ-] *n* (US) ≈ procuratore *m*.
prosecution [prɔsɪ'kjuːʃən] *n* (LAW) azione *f* giudiziaria; (*accusing side*) accusa.
prosecutor ['prɔsɪkjuːtə*] *n* (*also*: **public** ~)

≈ procuratore *m* della Repubblica.
prospect *n* ['prɔspɛkt] prospettiva; (*hope*) speranza ♦ *vb* [prə'spɛkt] *vt* esplorare ♦ *vi*: **to** ~ **for gold** cercare l'oro; **there is every** ~ **of an early victory** tutto lascia prevedere una rapida vittoria; *see also* **prospects**.
prospecting [prə'spɛktɪŋ] *n* prospezione *f*.
prospective [prə'spɛktɪv] *adj* (*buyer*) probabile; (*legislation, son-in-law*) futuro(a).
prospector [prə'spɛktə*] *n* prospettore *m*; **gold** ~ cercatore *m* d'oro.
prospects ['prɔspɛkts] *npl* (*for work etc*) prospettive *fpl*.
prospectus [prə'spɛktəs] *n* prospetto, programma *m*.
prosper ['prɔspə*] *vi* prosperare.
prosperity [prɔ'spɛrɪtɪ] *n* prosperità.
prosperous ['prɔspərəs] *adj* prospero(a).
prostate ['prɔsteɪt] *n* (*also*: ~ **gland**) prostata, ghiandola prostatica.
prostitute ['prɔstɪtjuːt] *n* prostituta; **male** ~ uomo che si prostituisce.
prostitution [prɔstɪ'tjuːʃən] *n* prostituzione *f*.
prostrate *adj* ['prɔstreɪt] prostrato(a) ♦ *vt* [prɔ'streɪt]: **to** ~ **o.s.** (*before sb*) prostrarsi.
protagonist [prə'tægənɪst] *n* protagonista *m/f*.
protect [prə'tɛkt] *vt* proteggere, salvaguardare.
protection [prə'tɛkʃən] *n* protezione *f*; **to be under sb's** ~ essere sotto la protezione di qn.
protectionism [prə'tɛkʃənɪzəm] *n* protezionismo.
protection racket *n* racket *m inv*.
protective [prə'tɛktɪv] *adj* protettivo(a); ~ **custody** (LAW) protezione *f*.
protector [prə'tɛktə*] *n* protettore/trice.
protégé ['prəutɪʒeɪ] *n* protetto.
protégée ['prəutɪʒeɪ] *n* protetta.
protein ['prəutiːn] *n* proteina.
pro tem [prəu'tɛm] *adv abbr* (= *pro tempore*: *for the time being*) pro tempore.
protest *n* ['prəutɛst] protesta ♦ *vt, vi* [prə'tɛst] protestare; **to do sth under** ~ fare qc protestando; **to** ~ **against/about** protestare contro/per.
Protestant ['prɔtɪstənt] *adj, n* protestante (*m/f*).
protester, protestor [prə'tɛstə*] *n* (*in demonstration*) dimostrante *m/f*.
protest march *n* marcia di protesta.
protocol ['prəutəkɔl] *n* protocollo.
prototype ['prəutətaɪp] *n* prototipo.
protracted [prə'træktɪd] *adj* tirato(a) per le

lunghe.

protractor [prə'træktə*] n (GEOM) goniometro.

protrude [prə'tru:d] vi sporgere.

protuberance [prə'tju:bərəns] n sporgenza.

proud [praud] adj fiero(a), orgoglioso(a); (pej) superbo(a); **to be ~ to do sth** essere onorato(a) di fare qc; **to do sb ~** non far mancare nulla a qn; **to do o.s. ~** trattarsi bene.

proudly ['praudlı] adv con orgoglio, fieramente.

prove [pru:v] vt provare, dimostrare ♦ vi: **to ~ correct** etc risultare vero(a) etc; **to ~ o.s.** mostrare le proprie capacità; **to ~ o.s./itself (to be) useful** etc mostrarsi or rivelarsi utile etc; **he was ~d right in the end** alla fine i fatti gli hanno dato ragione.

Provence [prɔvãs] n Provenza.

proverb ['prɔvə:b] n proverbio.

proverbial [prə'və:bıəl] adj proverbiale.

provide [prə'vaıd] vt fornire, provvedere; **to ~ sb with sth** fornire or provvedere qn di qc; **to be ~d with** essere dotato or munito di.

►**provide for** vt fus provvedere a.

provided [prə'vaıdıd] conj: ~ **(that)** purché + sub, a condizione che + sub.

Providence ['prɔvıdəns] n Provvidenza.

providing [prə'vaıdıŋ] conj purché + sub, a condizione che + sub.

province ['prɔvıns] n provincia.

provincial [prə'vınʃəl] adj provinciale.

provision [prə'vıʒən] n (supply) riserva; (supplying) provvista; rifornimento; (stipulation) condizione f; ~**s** npl (food) provviste fpl; **to make ~ for** (one's family, future) pensare a; **there's no ~ for this in the contract** il contratto non lo prevede.

provisional [prə'vıʒənl] adj provvisorio(a) ♦ n: **P~** (Irish POL) provisional m inv.

provisional licence n (BRIT AUT) ≈ foglio m rosa inv.

provisionally [prə'vıʒnəlı] adv provvisoriamente; (appoint) a titolo provvisorio.

proviso [prə'vaızəu] n condizione f; **with the ~ that** a condizione che + sub, a patto che + sub.

Provo ['prɔvəu] n abbr (col) = **Provisional**.

provocation [prɔvə'keıʃən] n provocazione f.

provocative [prə'vɔkətıv] adj (aggressive) provocatorio(a); (thought-provoking) stimolante; (seductive) provocante.

provoke [prə'vəuk] vt provocare; incitare; **to ~ sb to sth/to do** or **into doing sth** spingere qn a qc/a fare qc.

provoking [prə'vəukıŋ] adj irritante, esasperante.

provost ['prɔvəst] n (BRIT: of university) rettore m; (Scottish) sindaco.

prow [prau] n prua.

prowess ['prauıs] n prodezza; **his ~ as a footballer** le sue capacità di calciatore.

prowl [praul] vi (also: ~ **about**, ~ **around**) aggirarsi furtivamente ♦ n: **on the ~** in cerca di preda.

prowler ['praulə*] n tipo sospetto (che s'aggira con l'intenzione di rubare, aggredire etc).

proximity [prɔk'sımıtı] n prossimità.

proxy ['prɔksı] n procura; **by ~** per procura.

PRP n abbr (= performance related pay) retribuzione f commensurata al rendimento.

prude [pru:d] n puritano/a.

prudence ['pru:dns] n prudenza.

prudent ['pru:dnt] adj prudente.

prudish ['pru:dıʃ] adj puritano(a).

prune [pru:n] n prugna secca ♦ vt potare.

pry [praı] vi: **to ~ into** ficcare il naso in.

PS n abbr (= postscript) P.S.

psalm [sɑ:m] n salmo.

PSAT ® n abbr (US) = Preliminary Scholastic Aptitude Test.

PSBR n abbr (BRIT: = public sector borrowing requirement) fabbisogno di prestiti per il settore pubblico.

pseud ['sju:d] n (BRIT col: intellectually) intellettualoide m/f; (: socially) snob m/f inv.

pseudo- ['sju:dəu] prefix pseudo....

pseudonym ['sju:dənım] n pseudonimo.

PST abbr (US: = Pacific Standard Time) ora invernale del Pacifico.

psyche ['saıkı] n psiche f.

psychedelic [saıkı'dɛlık] adj psichedelico(a).

psychiatric [saıkı'ætrık] adj psichiatrico(a).

psychiatrist [saı'kaıətrıst] n psichiatra m/f.

psychiatry [saı'kaıətrı] n psichiatria.

psychic ['saıkık] adj (also: ~**al**) psichico(a); (person) dotato(a) di qualità telepatiche.

psycho ['saıkəu] n (col) folle m/f.

psychoanalyse [saıkəu'ænəlaız] vt psicanalizzare.

psychoanalysis, pl -ses [saıkəuə'nælısıs, -siːz] n psicanalisi f inv.

psychoanalyst [saıkəu'ænəlıst] n psicanalista m/f.

psychological [saıkə'lɔdʒıkl] adj psicologico(a).

psychologist [saı'kɔlədʒıst] n psicologo/a.

psychology [saı'kɔlədʒı] n psicologia.

psychopath ['saɪkəupæθ] *n* psicopatico/a.
psychosis, *pl* **psychoses** [saɪ'kəusɪs, -siːz]
n psicosi *f inv.*
psychosomatic [saɪkəusə'mætɪk] *adj*
psicosomatico(a).
psychotherapy [saɪkəu'θɛrəpɪ] *n*
psicoterapia.
psychotic [saɪ'kɔtɪk] *adj, n* psicotico(a).
PT *n abbr* (*BRIT:* = *physical training*) ed. fisica.
pt *abbr* (= *pint; point*) pt.
Pt. *abbr* (*in place names:* = *Point*) Pt.
PTA *n abbr* (= *Parent-Teacher Association*)
associazione genitori e insegnanti.
Pte. *abbr* (*BRIT MIL*) = *private.*
PTO *abbr* (= *please turn over*) v.r. (= *vedi
retro*).
PTV *n abbr* (*US*) = *pay television, public
television.*
pub [pʌb] *n abbr* (= *public house*) pub *m inv;*
see boxed note.

PUB

In Gran Bretagna e in Irlanda i **pubs** *sono
locali dove vengono servite bibite alcoliche ed
analcoliche e dove è anche possibile mangiare.
Sono punti di ritrovo dove spesso si può
giocare a biliardo, a freccette o guardare la
televisione. Le leggi che regolano la vendita
degli alcolici sono molto severe in Gran
Bretagna e quindi gli orari di apertura e di
chiusura vengono osservati scrupolosamente.*

pub crawl *n:* **to go on a** ~ (*BRIT col*) fare il
giro dei pub.
puberty ['pjuːbətɪ] *n* pubertà.
pubic ['pjuːbɪk] *adj* pubico(a), del pube.
public ['pʌblɪk] *adj* pubblico(a) ♦ *n* pubblico;
in ~ in pubblico; **the general** ~ il
pubblico; **to make sth** ~ render noto *or* di
pubblico dominio qc; **to be** ~ **knowledge**
essere di dominio pubblico; **to go** ~
(*COMM*) emettere le azioni sul mercato.
public address system (PA) *n* impianto
di amplificazione.
publican ['pʌblɪkən] *n* (*BRIT*) gestore *m* (*or*
proprietario) di un pub.
publication [pʌblɪ'keɪʃən] *n* pubblicazione
f.
public company *n* ≈ società *f inv* per
azioni (*costituita tramite pubblica
sottoscrizione*).
public convenience *n* (*BRIT*) gabinetti *mpl.*
public holiday *n* (*BRIT*) giorno festivo,
festa nazionale.
public house *n* (*BRIT*) pub *m inv.*
publicity [pʌb'lɪsɪtɪ] *n* pubblicità.
publicize ['pʌblɪsaɪz] *vt* fare (della)

pubblicità a, reclamizzare.
public limited company (plc) *n* ≈ società
per azioni a responsabilità limitata
(*quotata in Borsa*).
publicly ['pʌblɪklɪ] *adv* pubblicamente.
public opinion *n* opinione *f* pubblica.
public ownership *n* proprietà pubblica *or*
sociale; **to be taken into** ~ essere
statalizzato(a).
public prosecutor *n* pubblico ministero;
~**'s office** ufficio del pubblico ministero.
public relations *n* pubbliche relazioni *fpl.*
public relations officer *n* addetto/a alle
pubbliche relazioni.
public school *n* (*BRIT*) scuola privata; (*US*)
scuola statale; *see boxed note.*

PUBLIC SCHOOL

In Inghilterra le **public schools** *sono scuole o
collegi privati di istruzione secondaria, spesso
di un certo prestigio. In Scozia e negli Stati
Uniti, invece, le* **public schools** *sono scuole
pubbliche gratuite amministrate dallo stato.*

public sector *n* settore *m* pubblico.
public service vehicle (PSV) *n* (*BRIT*)
mezzo pubblico.
public-spirited [pʌblɪk'spɪrɪtɪd] *adj* che ha
senso civico.
public transport, (*US*) **public
transportation** *n* mezzi *mpl* pubblici.
public utility *n* servizio pubblico.
public works *npl* lavori *mpl* pubblici.
publish ['pʌblɪʃ] *vt* pubblicare.
publisher ['pʌblɪʃə*] *n* editore *m;* (*firm*)
casa editrice.
publishing ['pʌblɪʃɪŋ] *n* (*industry*) editoria;
(*of a book*) pubblicazione *f.*
publishing company *n* casa *or* società
editrice.
puce [pjuːs] *adj* color pulce *inv.*
puck [pʌk] *n* (*ICE HOCKEY*) disco.
pucker ['pʌkə*] *vt* corrugare.
pudding ['pudɪŋ] *n* budino; (*dessert*) dolce
m; **black** ~, (*US*) **blood** ~ sanguinaccio;
rice ~ budino di riso.
puddle ['pʌdl] *n* pozza, pozzanghera.
puerile ['pjuəraɪl] *adj* puerile.
Puerto Rico ['pwɔːtəu'riːkəu] *n* Portorico.
puff [pʌf] *n* sbuffo; (*also:* **powder** ~)
piumino ♦ *vt* (*also:* ~ **out:** *sails, cheeks*)
gonfiare ♦ *vi* uscire a sbuffi; (*pant*) ansare;
to ~ **out smoke** mandar fuori sbuffi di
fumo.
puffed [pʌft] *adj* (*col: out of breath*) senza
fiato.
puffin ['pʌfɪn] *n* puffino.

puff pastry, (US) **puff paste** n pasta sfoglia.

puffy ['pʌfɪ] adj gonfio(a).

pugnacious [pʌg'neɪʃəs] adj combattivo(a).

pull [pul] n (tug) strattone m, tirata; (of moon, magnet, the sea etc) attrazione f; (fig) influenza ♦ vt tirare; (muscle) strappare, farsi uno strappo a ♦ vi tirare; **to give sth a** ~ tirare su qc; **to** ~ **a face** fare una smorfia; **to** ~ **to pieces** fare a pezzi; **to** ~ **one's punches** (BOXING) risparmiare l'avversario; **not to** ~ **one's punches** (fig) non avere peli sulla lingua; **to** ~ **one's weight** dare il proprio contributo; **to** ~ **o.s. together** ricomporsi, riprendersi; **to** ~ **sb's leg** prendere in giro qn; **to** ~ **strings (for sb)** muovere qualche pedina (per qn).

▶**pull about** vt (BRIT: handle roughly: object) strapazzare; (: person) malmenare.

▶**pull apart** vt (break) fare a pezzi.

▶**pull down** vt (house) demolire; (tree) abbattere.

▶**pull in** vi (AUT: at the kerb) accostarsi; (RAIL) entrare in stazione.

▶**pull off** vt (deal etc) portare a compimento.

▶**pull out** vi partire; (withdraw) ritirarsi; (AUT: come out of line) spostarsi sulla mezzeria ♦ vt staccare; far uscire; (withdraw) ritirare.

▶**pull over** vi (AUT) accostare.

▶**pull round** vi (unconscious person) rinvenire; (sick person) ristabilirsi.

▶**pull through** vi farcela.

▶**pull up** vi (stop) fermarsi ♦ vt (uproot) sradicare; (stop) fermare.

pulley ['pulɪ] n puleggia, carrucola.

pull-out ['pulaut] n inserto ♦ cpd staccabile.

pullover ['puləuvə*] n pullover m inv.

pulp [pʌlp] n (of fruit) polpa; (for paper) pasta per carta; (magazines, books) stampa di qualità e di tono scadenti; **to reduce sth to** ~ spappolare qc.

pulpit ['pulpɪt] n pulpito.

pulsate [pʌl'seɪt] vi battere, palpitare.

pulse [pʌls] n polso; **to feel** or **take sb's** ~ sentire or tastare il polso a qn.

pulses ['pʌlsəz] npl (CULIN) legumi mpl.

pulverize ['pʌlvəraɪz] vt polverizzare.

puma ['pjuːmə] n puma m inv.

pumice (stone) ['pʌmɪs-] n (pietra) pomice f.

pummel ['pʌml] vt dare pugni a.

pump [pʌmp] n pompa; (shoe) scarpetta ♦ vt pompare; (fig: col) far parlare; **to** ~ **sb for information** cercare di strappare delle informazioni a qn.

▶**pump up** vt gonfiare.

pumpkin ['pʌmpkɪn] n zucca.

pun [pʌn] n gioco di parole.

punch [pʌntʃ] n (blow) pugno; (fig: force) forza; (tool) punzone m; (drink) ponce m ♦ vt (hit): **to** ~ **sb/sth** dare un pugno a qn/qc; **to** ~ **a hole (in)** fare un buco (in).

▶**punch in** vi (US) timbrare il cartellino (all'entrata).

▶**punch out** vi (US) timbrare il cartellino (all'uscita).

punch-drunk ['pʌntʃdrʌŋk] adj (BRIT) stordito(a).

punch(ed) card ['pʌntʃ(t)-] n scheda perforata.

punch line n (of joke) battuta finale.

punch-up ['pʌntʃʌp] n (BRIT col) rissa.

punctual ['pʌŋktjuəl] adj puntuale.

punctuality [pʌŋktju'ælɪtɪ] n puntualità.

punctually ['pʌŋktjuəlɪ] adv puntualmente; **it will start** ~ **at 6** comincerà alle 6 precise or in punto.

punctuate ['pʌŋktjueɪt] vt punteggiare.

punctuation [pʌŋktju'eɪʃən] n interpunzione f, punteggiatura.

punctuation mark n segno d'interpunzione.

puncture ['pʌŋktʃə*] n (BRIT) foratura ♦ vt forare; **to have a** ~ (AUT) forare (una gomma).

pundit ['pʌndɪt] n sapientone/a.

pungent ['pʌndʒənt] adj piccante; (fig) mordace, caustico(a).

punish ['pʌnɪʃ] vt punire; **to** ~ **sb for sth/ for doing sth** punire qn per qc/per aver fatto qc.

punishable ['pʌnɪʃəbl] adj punibile.

punishing ['pʌnɪʃɪŋ] adj (fig: exhausting) sfiancante.

punishment ['pʌnɪʃmənt] n punizione f; (fig col): **to take a lot of** ~ (boxer) incassare parecchi colpi; (car) essere messo(a) a dura prova.

punk [pʌŋk] n (person: also: ~ **rocker**) punk m/f inv; (music: also: ~ **rock**) musica punk, punk rock m; (US col: hoodlum) teppista m.

punt [pʌnt] n (boat) barchino; (FOOTBALL) colpo a volo; (Irish) sterlina irlandese ♦ vi (BRIT: bet) scommettere.

punter ['pʌntə*] n (BRIT: gambler) scommettitore/trice.

puny ['pjuːnɪ] adj gracile.

pup [pʌp] n cucciolo/a.

pupil ['pjuːpl] n allievo/a; (ANAT) pupilla.

puppet ['pʌpɪt] n burattino.

puppet government n governo fantoccio.

puppy ['pʌpɪ] n cucciolo/a, cagnolino/a.

purchase ['pəːtʃɪs] n acquisto, compera;

(*grip*) presa ♦ *vt* comprare; **to get a ~ on**
(*grip*) trovare un appoggio su.
purchase order *n* ordine *m* d'acquisto,
ordinazione *f*.
purchase price *n* prezzo d'acquisto.
purchaser ['pɔːtʃɪsə*] *n* compratore/trice.
purchase tax *n* (*BRIT*) tassa d'acquisto.
purchasing power ['pɔːtʃɪsɪŋ-] *n* potere *m*
d'acquisto.
pure [pjuə*] *adj* puro(a); **a ~ wool jumper**
un golf di pura lana; **it's laziness ~ and
simple** è pura pigrizia.
purebred ['pjuəbrɛd] *adj* di razza pura.
purée ['pjuəreɪ] *n* purè *m inv*.
purely ['pjuəlɪ] *adv* puramente.
purge [pɔːdʒ] *n* (*MED*) purga; (*POL*)
epurazione *f* ♦ *vt* purgare; (*fig*) epurare.
purification [pjuərɪfɪ'keɪʃən] *n*
purificazione *f*.
purify ['pjuərɪfaɪ] *vt* purificare.
purist ['pjuərɪst] *n* purista *m/f*.
puritan ['pjuərɪtən] *adj, n* puritano(a).
puritanical [pjuərɪ'tænɪkl] *adj* puritano(a).
purity ['pjuərɪtɪ] *n* purità.
purl [pɔːl] *n* punto rovescio ♦ *vt* lavorare a
rovescio.
purloin [pɔː'lɔɪn] *vt* rubare.
purple ['pɔːpl] *adj* di porpora; viola *inv*.
purport [pɔː'pɔːt] *vi*: **to ~ to be/do**
pretendere di essere/fare.
purpose ['pɔːpəs] *n* intenzione *f*, scopo; **on
~** apposta, di proposito; **for illustrative ~s**
a titolo illustrativo; **for teaching ~s** per
l'insegnamento; **for the ~s of this
meeting** agli effetti di questa riunione; **to
no ~** senza nessun risultato, inutilmente.
purpose-built ['pɔːpəs'bɪlt] *adj* (*BRIT*)
costruito(a) allo scopo.
purposeful ['pɔːpəsful] *adj* deciso(a),
risoluto(a).
purposely ['pɔːpəslɪ] *adv* apposta.
purr [pɔː*] *n* fusa *fpl* ♦ *vi* fare le fusa.
purse [pɔːs] *n* borsellino; (*US: handbag*)
borsetta, borsa ♦ *vt* contrarre.
purser ['pɔːsə*] *n* (*NAUT*) commissario di
bordo.
purse snatcher [-'snætʃə*] *n* (*US*)
scippatore *m*.
pursue [pə'sjuː] *vt* inseguire; essere alla
ricerca di; (*inquiry, matter*) approfondire.
pursuer [pə'sjuːə*] *n* inseguitore/trice.
pursuit [pə'sjuːt] *n* inseguimento;
(*occupation*) occupazione *f*, attività *f inv*; **in
(the) ~ of sth** alla ricerca di qc; **scientific
~s** ricerche *fpl* scientifiche.
purveyor [pə'veɪə*] *n* fornitore/trice.
pus [pʌs] *n* pus *m*.
push [puʃ] *n* spinta; (*effort*) grande sforzo;

(*drive*) energia ♦ *vt* spingere; (*button*)
premere; (*thrust*): **to ~ sth (into)** ficcare
qc (in); (*fig*) fare pubblicità a ♦ *vi*
spingere; premere; **to ~ a door open/
shut** aprire/chiudere una porta con una
spinta o spingendola; **to be ~ed for
time/money** essere a corto di tempo/
soldi; **she is ~ing 50** (*col*) va per i 50; **to ~
for** (*better pay, conditions etc*) fare
pressione per ottenere; "~" (*on door*)
"spingere"; (*on bell*) "suonare"; **at a ~**
(*BRIT col*) in caso di necessità.
►**push aside** *vt* scostare.
►**push in** *vi* introdursi a forza.
►**push off** *vi* (*col*) filare.
►**push on** *vi* (*continue*) continuare.
►**push over** *vt* far cadere.
►**push through** *vt* (*measure*) far
approvare.
►**push up** *vt* (*total, prices*) far salire.
push-bike ['puʃbaɪk] *n* (*BRIT*) bicicletta.
push-button ['puʃbʌtn] *adj* a pulsante.
pushchair ['puʃtʃɛə*] *n* passeggino.
pusher ['puʃə*] *n* (*also*: **drug ~**)
spacciatore/trice (di droga).
pushover ['puʃəuvə*] *n* (*col*): **it's a ~** è un
lavoro da bambini.
push-up ['puʃʌp] *n* (*US*) flessione *f* sulle
braccia.
pushy ['puʃɪ] *adj* (*pej*) troppo
intraprendente.
puss, pussy(-cat) [pus, 'pusɪ(kæt)] *n* micio.
put, *pt, pp* **put** [put] *vt* mettere, porre; (*say*)
dire, esprimere; (*a question*) fare;
(*estimate*) stimare ♦ *adv*: **to stay ~** non
muoversi; **to ~ sb to bed** mettere qn a
letto; **to ~ sb in a good/bad mood**
mettere qn di buon/cattivo umore; **to ~
sb to a lot of trouble** scomodare qn; **to ~
a lot of time into sth** dedicare molto
tempo a qc; **to ~ money on a horse**
scommettere su un cavallo; **how shall I ~
it?** come dire?; **I ~ it to you that ...** (*BRIT*)
io sostengo che ....
►**put about** *vi* (*NAUT*) virare di bordo ♦ *vt*
(*rumour*) diffondere.
►**put across** *vt* (*ideas etc*) comunicare, far
capire.
►**put aside** *vt* (*lay down: book etc*) mettere
da una parte, posare; (*save*) mettere da
parte; (*in shop*) tenere da parte.
►**put away** *vt* (*clothes, toys etc*) mettere
via.
►**put back** *vt* (*replace*) rimettere (a posto);
(*postpone*) rinviare; (*delay*) ritardare; (*set
back: watch, clock*) mettere indietro; **this
will ~ us back 10 years** questo ci farà
tornare indietro di 10 anni.

►**put by** vt (*money*) mettere da parte.

►**put down** vt (*parcel etc*) posare, mettere giù; (*pay*) versare; (*in writing*) mettere per iscritto; (*suppress: revolt etc*) reprimere, sopprimere; (*attribute*) attribuire.

►**put forward** vt (*ideas*) avanzare, proporre; (*date*) anticipare.

►**put in** vt (*application, complaint*) presentare.

►**put in for** vt fus (*job*) far domanda per; (*promotion*) far domanda di.

►**put off** vt (*postpone*) rimandare, rinviare; (*discourage*) dissuadere.

►**put on** vt (*clothes, lipstick etc*) mettere; (*light etc*) accendere; (*play etc*) mettere in scena; (*concert, exhibition etc*) allestire, organizzare; (*extra bus, train etc*) mettere in servizio; (*food, meal*) servire; (*brake*) mettere; (*assume: accent, manner*) affettare; (*col: tease*) prendere in giro; (*inform, indicate*): **to ~ sb on to sb/sth** indicare qn/qc a qn; **to ~ on weight** ingrassare; **to ~ on airs** darsi delle arie.

►**put out** vt mettere fuori; (*one's hand*) porgere; (*light etc*) spegnere; (*person: inconvenience*) scomodare; (*dislocate: shoulder, knee*) lussarsi; (*: back*) farsi uno strappo a ♦ vi (*NAUT*): **to ~ out to sea** prendere il largo; **to ~ out from Plymouth** partire da Plymouth.

►**put through** vt (*caller*) mettere in comunicazione; (*call*) passare; **~ me through to Miss Blair** mi passi la signorina Blair.

►**put together** vt mettere insieme, riunire; (*assemble: furniture*) montare; (*: meal*) improvvisare.

►**put up** vt (*raise*) sollevare, alzare; (*pin up*) affiggere; (*hang*) appendere; (*build*) costruire, erigere; (*increase*) aumentare; (*accommodate*) alloggiare; (*incite*): **to ~ sb up to doing sth** istigare qn a fare qc; **to ~ sth up for sale** mettere in vendita qc.

►**put upon** vt fus: **to be ~ upon** (*imposed on*) farsi mettere sotto i piedi.

►**put up with** vt fus sopportare.

putrid ['pjuːtrɪd] adj putrido(a).

putt [pʌt] vt (*ball*) colpire leggermente ♦ n colpo leggero.

putter ['pʌtə*] n (*GOLF*) putter m inv ♦ vi (*US*) = **potter**.

putting green ['pʌtɪŋ-] n green m inv; campo da putting.

putty ['pʌtɪ] n stucco.

put-up ['putʌp] adj: **~ job** montatura.

puzzle ['pʌzl] n enigma m, mistero; (*jigsaw*) puzzle m ♦ vt confondere, rendere perplesso(a) ♦ vi scervellarsi; **to be ~d about sth** domandarsi il perché di qc; **to ~ over** (*sb's actions*) cercare di capire; (*mystery, problem*) cercare di risolvere.

puzzling ['pʌzlɪŋ] adj (*question*) poco chiaro(a); (*attitude, set of instructions*) incomprensibile.

PVC n abbr (= *polyvinyl chloride*) P.V.C. m.

Pvt. abbr (*US MIL*) = **private**.

PW n abbr (*US*) = **prisoner of war**.

pw abbr = **per week**.

PX n abbr (*US MIL*) see **post exchange**.

pygmy ['pɪgmɪ] n pigmeo/a.

pyjamas, (*US***) pajamas** [pə'dʒɑːməz] npl pigiama m; **a pair of ~** un pigiama.

pylon ['paɪlən] n pilone m.

pyramid ['pɪrəmɪd] n piramide f.

Pyrenees [pɪrə'niːz] npl: **the ~** i Pirenei.

Pyrex ® ['paɪrɛks] n Pirex ® m inv ♦ cpd: **~ dish** pirofila.

python ['paɪθən] n pitone m.

Q q

Q, q [kjuː] n (*letter*) Q, q f or m inv; **Q for Queen** ≈ Q come Quarto.

Qatar [kæ'tɑː*] n Qatar m.

QC n abbr (*BRIT*: = *Queen's Counsel*) avvocato della Corona.

QED abbr (= *quod erat demonstrandum*) qed.

QM n abbr see **quartermaster**.

q.t. n abbr (*col*: = *quiet*): **on the ~** di nascosto.

qty abbr = **quantity**.

quack [kwæk] n (*of duck*) qua qua m inv; (*pej: doctor*) ciarlatano/a.

quad [kwɔd] n abbr = **quadrangle; quadruple; quadruplet**.

quadrangle ['kwɔdræŋgl] n (*MATH*) quadrilatero; (*courtyard*) cortile m.

quadruped ['kwɔdruped] n quadrupede m.

quadruple [kwɔ'drupl] adj quadruplo(a) ♦ n quadruplo ♦ vt quadruplicare ♦ vi quadruplicarsi.

quadruplet [kwɔ'druːplɪt] n uno/a di quattro gemelli.

quagmire ['kwægmaɪə*] n pantano.

quail [kweɪl] n (*ZOOL*) quaglia ♦ vi: **to ~ at** or **before** perdersi d'animo davanti a.

quaint [kweɪnt] adj bizzarro(a); (*old-*

fashioned) antiquato(a) e pittoresco(a).

quake [kweɪk] *vi* tremare ♦ *n abbr* = **earthquake**.

Quaker ['kweɪkə*] *n* quacchero/a.

qualification [kwɔlɪfɪ'keɪʃən] *n* (*degree etc*) qualifica, titolo; (*ability*) competenza, qualificazione *f*; (*limitation*) riserva, restrizione *f*; **what are your ~s?** quali sono le sue qualifiche?

qualified ['kwɔlɪfaɪd] *adj* qualificato(a); (*able*) competente, qualificato(a); (*limited*) condizionato(a); **~ for/to do** qualificato(a) per/per fare; **he's not ~ for the job** non ha i requisiti necessari per questo lavoro; **it was a ~ success** è stato un successo parziale.

qualify ['kwɔlɪfaɪ] *vt* abilitare; (*limit: statement*) modificare, precisare ♦ *vi*: **to ~ (as)** qualificarsi (come); **to ~ (for)** acquistare i requisiti necessari (per); (*SPORT*) qualificarsi (per *or* a); **to ~ as an engineer** diventare un perito tecnico.

qualifying ['kwɔlɪfaɪŋ] *adj* (*exam*) di ammissione; (*round*) eliminatorio(a).

qualitative ['kwɔlɪtətɪv] *adj* qualitativo(a).

quality ['kwɔlɪtɪ] *n* qualità *f inv* ♦ *cpd* di qualità; **of good ~** di buona qualità; **of poor ~** scadente; **~ of life** qualità della vita.

quality control *n* controllo di qualità.

quality papers *npl*, **quality press** *n* (*BRIT*): **the ~** la stampa d'informazione; *see boxed note.*

QUALITY PRESS

Il termine **quality press** *si riferisce ai quotidiani o ai settimanali che offrono un'informazione seria ed approfondita. Questi giornali si differenziano da quelli popolari, i "tabloid", per formato e contenuti. Questa divisione tra tipi di giornali riflette il tradizionale divario tra classi sociali nella società britannica; vedi anche* **tabloid press***.*

---

qualm [kwɑːm] *n* dubbio; scrupolo; **to have ~s about sth** avere degli scrupoli per qc.

quandary ['kwɔndrɪ] *n*: **in a ~** in un dilemma.

quango ['kwæŋgəu] *n abbr* (*BRIT*: = *quasi-autonomous non-governmental organization*) *commissione consultiva di nomina governativa.*

quantifiable ['kwɔntɪfaɪəbl] *adj* quantificabile.

quantitative ['kwɔntɪtətɪv] *adj* quantitativo(a).

quantity ['kwɔntɪtɪ] *n* quantità *f inv*; **in ~** in grande quantità.

quantity surveyor *n* (*BRIT*) geometra *m* (*specializzato nel calcolare la quantità e il costo del materiale da costruzione*).

quantum leap ['kwɔntəm-] *n* (*fig*) enorme cambiamento.

quarantine ['kwɔrntiːn] *n* quarantena.

quark [kwɑːk] *n* quark *m inv*.

quarrel ['kwɔrl] *n* lite *f*, disputa ♦ *vi* litigare; **to have a ~ with sb** litigare con qn; **I've no ~ with him** non ho niente contro di lui; **I can't ~ with that** non ho niente da ridire su questo.

quarrelsome ['kwɔrəlsəm] *adj* litigioso(a).

quarry ['kwɔrɪ] *n* (*for stone*) cava; (*animal*) preda ♦ *vt* (*marble etc*) estrarre.

quart [kwɔːt] *n* due pinte *fpl*, ≈ litro.

quarter ['kwɔːtə*] *n* quarto; (*of year*) trimestre *m*; (*district*) quartiere *m*; (*US, Canada: 25 cents*) quarto di dollaro, 25 centesimi ♦ *vt* dividere in quattro; (*MIL*) alloggiare; **~s** *npl* alloggio; (*MIL*) alloggi *mpl*, quadrato; **a ~ of an hour** un quarto d'ora; **it's a ~ to 3, (US) it's a ~ of 3** sono le 3 meno un quarto, manca un quarto alle 3; **it's a ~ past 3, (US) it's a ~ after 3** sono le 3 e un quarto; **from all ~s** da tutte le parti *or* direzioni; **at close ~s** a distanza ravvicinata.

quarterback ['kwɔːtəbæk] *n* (*US FOOTBALL*) quarterback *m inv*.

quarter-deck ['kwɔːtədɛk] *n* (*NAUT*) cassero.

quarter final *n* quarto di finale.

quarterly ['kwɔːtəlɪ] *adj* trimestrale ♦ *adv* trimestralmente ♦ *n* periodico trimestrale.

quartermaster (QM) ['kwɔːtəmɑːstə*] *n* (*MIL*) furiere *m*.

quartet(te) [kwɔː'tɛt] *n* quartetto.

quarto ['kwɔːtəu] *adj, n* in quarto (*m*) *inv*.

quartz [kwɔːts] *n* quarzo ♦ *cpd* di quarzo; (*watch, clock*) al quarzo.

quash [kwɔʃ] *vt* (*verdict*) annullare.

quasi- ['kweɪzaɪ] *prefix* quasi + *noun*; quasi, pressoché + *adjective*.

quaver ['kweɪvə*] *n* (*BRIT MUS*) croma ♦ *vi* tremolare.

quay [kiː] *n* (*also:* **~side**) banchina.

Que. *abbr* (*Canada*) = **Quebec**.

queasy ['kwiːzɪ] *adj* (*stomach*) delicato(a); **to feel ~** aver la nausea.

Quebec [kwɪ'bɛk] *n* Quebec *m*.

queen [kwiːn] *n* (*gen*) regina; (*CARDS etc*) regina, donna.

queen mother *n* regina madre.

Queen's speech *n* (*BRIT*) *see boxed note.*

QUEEN'S SPEECH

Durante la sessione di apertura del Parlamento britannico il sovrano legge un discorso redatto dal primo ministro, il **Queen's speech** *(se si tratta della regina), che contiene le linee generali del nuovo programma politico.*

---

queer [kwɪə*] *adj* strano(a), curioso(a); (*suspicious*) dubbio(a), sospetto(a); (*BRIT: sick*): **I feel** ~ mi sento poco bene ♦ *n* (*col*) finocchio.

quell [kwɛl] *vt* domare.

quench [kwɛntʃ] *vt* (*flames*) spegnere; **to** ~ **one's thirst** dissetarsi.

querulous ['kwɛrʊləs] *adj* querulo(a).

query ['kwɪərɪ] *n* domanda, questione *f*; (*doubt*) dubbio ♦ *vt* mettere in questione; (*disagree with, dispute*) contestare.

quest [kwɛst] *n* cerca, ricerca.

question ['kwɛstʃən] *n* domanda, questione *f* ♦ *vt* (*person*) interrogare; (*plan, idea*) mettere in questione *or* in dubbio; **to ask sb a** ~, **put a** ~ **to sb** fare una domanda a qn; **to bring** *or* **call sth into** ~ mettere in dubbio qc; **the** ~ **is** ... il problema è ...; **it's a** ~ **of doing** si tratta di fare; **there's some** ~ **of doing** c'è chi suggerisce di fare; **beyond** ~ fuori di dubbio; **out of the** ~ fuori discussione, impossibile.

questionable ['kwɛstʃənəbl] *adj* discutibile.

questioner ['kwɛstʃənə*] *n* interrogante *m/f*.

questioning ['kwɛstʃənɪŋ] *adj* interrogativo(a) ♦ *n* interrogatorio.

question mark *n* punto interrogativo.

questionnaire [kwɛstʃə'nɛə*] *n* questionario.

queue [kjuː] *n* coda, fila ♦ *vi* fare la coda; **to jump the** ~ passare davanti agli altri (in una coda).

quibble ['kwɪbl] *vi* cavillare.

quick [kwɪk] *adj* rapido(a), veloce; (*reply*) pronto(a); (*mind*) pronto(a), acuto(a) ♦ *adv* rapidamente, presto ♦ *n*: **cut to the** ~ (*fig*) toccato(a) sul vivo; **be** ~! fa presto!; **to be** ~ **to act** agire prontamente; **she was** ~ **to see that** ... ha visto subito che ....

quicken ['kwɪkn] *vt* accelerare, affrettare; (*rouse*) animare, stimolare ♦ *vi* accelerare, affrettarsi.

quick fix *n* soluzione *f* tampone *inv*.

quicklime ['kwɪklaɪm] *n* calce *f* viva.

quickly ['kwɪklɪ] *adv* rapidamente, velocemente; **we must act** ~ dobbiamo agire tempestivamente.

quickness ['kwɪknɪs] *n* rapidità; prontezza; acutezza.

quicksand ['kwɪksænd] *n* sabbie *fpl* mobili.

quickstep ['kwɪkstɛp] *n* tipo di ballo simile al fox-trot.

quick-tempered [kwɪk'tɛmpəd] *adj* che si arrabbia facilmente.

quick-witted [kwɪk'wɪtɪd] *adj* pronto(a) d'ingegno.

quid [kwɪd] *n* (*pl inv*: *BRIT col*) sterlina.

quid pro quo ['kwɪdprəʊ'kwəʊ] *n* contraccambio.

quiet ['kwaɪət] *adj* tranquillo(a), quieto(a); (*reserved*) quieto(a), taciturno(a); (*ceremony*) semplice; (*not noisy: engine*) silenzioso(a); (*not busy: day*) calmo(a), tranquillo(a); (*colour*) discreto(a) ♦ *n* tranquillità, calma ♦ *vt, vi* (*US*) = **quieten**; **keep** ~! sta zitto!; **on the** ~ di nascosto; **I'll have a** ~ **word with him** gli dirò due parole in privato; **business is** ~ **at this time of year** questa è la stagione morta.

quieten ['kwaɪətn] (*BRIT: also*: ~ **down**) *vi* calmarsi, chetarsi ♦ *vt* calmare, chetare.

quietly ['kwaɪətlɪ] *adv* tranquillamente, calmamente; silenziosamente.

quietness ['kwaɪətnɪs] *n* tranquillità, calma; silenzio.

quill [kwɪl] *n* penna d'oca.

quilt [kwɪlt] *n* trapunta; **continental** ~ piumino.

quin [kwɪn] *n* *abbr* = **quintuplet**.

quince [kwɪns] *n* (mela) cotogna; (*tree*) cotogno.

quinine [kwɪ'niːn] *n* chinino.

quintet(te) [kwɪn'tɛt] *n* quintetto.

quintuplet [kwɪn'tjuːplɪt] *n* uno/a di cinque gemelli.

quip [kwɪp] *n* battuta di spirito.

quire ['kwaɪə*] *n* ventesima parte di una risma.

quirk [kwəːk] *n* ghiribizzo; **by some** ~ **of fate** per un capriccio della sorte.

quit, *pt, pp* **quit** *or* **quitted** [kwɪt] *vt* lasciare, partire da ♦ *vi* (*give up*) mollare; (*resign*) dimettersi; **to** ~ **doing** smettere di fare; ~ **stalling!** (*US col*) non tirarla per le lunghe!; **notice to** ~ (*BRIT*) preavviso (*dato all'inquilino*).

quite [kwaɪt] *adv* (*rather*) assai; (*entirely*) completamente, del tutto; **I** ~ **understand** capisco perfettamente; ~ **a few of them** non pochi di loro; ~ **(so)!** esatto!; ~ **new** proprio nuovo; **that's not** ~ **right** non è proprio esatto; **she's** ~ **pretty** è piuttosto carina.

quits [kwɪts] *adj*: ~ **(with)** pari (con); **let's call it** ~ adesso siamo pari.

quiver ['kwɪvə*] *vi* tremare, fremere ♦ *n* (*for arrows*) faretra.

quiz [kwɪz] n (game) quiz m inv; indovinello ♦ vt interrogare.
quizzical ['kwɪzɪkəl] adj enigmatico(a).
quoits [kwɔɪts] npl gioco degli anelli.
quorum ['kwɔːrəm] n quorum m.
quota ['kwəʊtə] n quota.
quotation [kwəʊ'teɪʃən] n citazione f; (of shares etc) quotazione f; (estimate) preventivo.
quotation marks npl virgolette fpl.
quote [kwəʊt] n citazione f ♦ vt (sentence) citare; (price) dare, indicare, fissare; (shares) quotare ♦ vi: to ~ from citare; to ~ for a job dare un preventivo per un lavoro; ~s npl (col) = quotation marks; in ~s tra virgolette; ~ ... unquote (in dictation) aprire le virgolette ... chiudere le virgolette.
quotient ['kwəʊʃənt] n quoziente m.
qv abbr (= quod vide: which see) v.
qwerty keyboard ['kwəːtɪ-] n tastiera qwerty inv.

R r

R, r [ɑ:*] n (letter) R, r f or m inv; **R for Robert**, (US) **R for Roger** ≈ R come Roma.
R abbr (= Réaumur (scale)) R; (= river) F; (= right) D; (US CINE: = restricted) ≈ vietato; (US POL) = **Republican**; (BRIT) = Rex, Regina.
RA n abbr (BRIT) = Royal Academy, Royal Academician ♦ abbr = rear admiral.
RAAF n abbr = Royal Australian Air Force.
Rabat [rə'bɑːt] n Rabat f.
rabbi ['ræbaɪ] n rabbino.
rabbit ['ræbɪt] n coniglio ♦ vi: to ~ (on) (BRIT) blaterare.
rabbit hole n tana di coniglio.
rabbit hutch n conigliera.
rabble ['ræbl] n (pej) canaglia, plebaglia.
rabid ['ræbɪd] adj rabbioso(a); (fig) fanatico(a).
rabies ['reɪbiːz] n rabbia.
RAC n abbr (BRIT: = Royal Automobile Club) ≈ A.C.I. m (= Automobile Club d'Italia).
raccoon [rə'kuːn] n procione m.
race [reɪs] n razza; (competition, rush) corsa ♦ vt (person) gareggiare (in corsa) con; (horse) far correre; (engine) imballare

♦ vi correre; **the human** ~ la razza umana; **he** ~**d across the road** ha attraversato la strada di corsa; **to** ~ **in/ out** etc precipitarsi dentro/fuori etc.
race car n (US) = racing car.
race car driver n (US) = racing driver.
racecourse ['reɪskɔːs] n campo di corse, ippodromo.
racehorse ['reɪshɔːs] n cavallo da corsa.
race relations npl rapporti razziali.
racetrack ['reɪstræk] n pista.
racial ['reɪʃl] adj razziale.
racial discrimination n discriminazione f razziale.
racialism ['reɪʃəlɪzəm] n razzismo.
racialist ['reɪʃəlɪst] adj, n razzista (m/f).
racing ['reɪsɪŋ] n corsa.
racing car n (BRIT) macchina da corsa.
racing driver n (BRIT) corridore m automobilista.
racism ['reɪsɪzəm] n razzismo.
racist ['reɪsɪst] adj, n (pej) razzista (m/f).
rack [ræk] n rastrelliera; (also: **luggage** ~) rete f, portabagagli m inv; (also: **roof** ~) portabagagli ♦ vt torturare, tormentare; **magazine** ~ portariviste m inv; **shoe** ~ scarpiera; **toast** ~ portatoast m inv; **to go to** ~ **and ruin** (building) andare in rovina; (business) andare in malora or a catafascio; **to** ~ **one's brains** scervellarsi.
▶**rack up** vt accumulare.
racket ['rækɪt] n (for tennis) racchetta; (noise) fracasso, baccano; (swindle) imbroglio, truffa; (organized crime) racket m inv.
racketeer [rækɪ'tɪə*] n (US) trafficante m/f.
racoon [rə'kuːn] n = raccoon.
racquet ['rækɪt] n racchetta.
racy ['reɪsɪ] adj brioso(a); piccante.
RADA ['rɑːdə] n abbr (BRIT) = Royal Academy of Dramatic Art.
radar ['reɪdɑ:*] n radar m ♦ cpd radar inv.
radar trap n controllo della velocità con radar.
radial ['reɪdɪəl] adj (also: ~-**ply**) radiale.
radiance ['reɪdɪəns] n splendore m, radiosità.
radiant ['reɪdɪənt] adj raggiante; (PHYSICS) radiante.
radiate ['reɪdɪeɪt] vt (heat) irraggiare, irradiare ♦ vi (lines) irradiarsi.
radiation [reɪdɪ'eɪʃən] n irradiamento; (radioactive) radiazione f.
radiation sickness n malattia da radiazioni.
radiator ['reɪdɪeɪtə*] n radiatore m.
radiator cap n tappo del radiatore.

radiator grill n (AUT) mascherina, calandra.

radical ['rædɪkl] adj radicale.

radii ['reɪdɪaɪ] npl of **radius**.

radio ['reɪdɪəu] n radio f inv ♦ vt (information) trasmettere per radio; (one's position) comunicare via radio; (person) chiamare via radio ♦ vi: **to ~ to sb** comunicare via radio con qn; **on the ~** alla radio.

radio... ['reɪdɪəu] prefix radio....

radioactive ['reɪdɪəu'æktɪv] adj radioattivo(a).

radioactivity ['reɪdɪəuæk'tɪvɪtɪ] n radioattività.

radio announcer n annunciatore/trice della radio.

radio-controlled ['reɪdɪəukən'trəuld] adj radiocomandato(a), radioguidato(a).

radiographer [reɪdɪ'ɔgrəfə*] n radiologo/a (tecnico).

radiography [reɪdɪ'ɔgrəfɪ] n radiografia.

radiologist [reɪdɪ'ɔlədʒɪst] n radiologo/a (medico).

radiology [reɪdɪ'ɔlədʒɪ] n radiologia.

radio station n stazione f radio inv.

radio taxi n radiotaxi m inv.

radiotelephone ['reɪdɪəu'tɛlɪfəun] n radiotelefono.

radiotherapist ['reɪdɪəu'θɛrəpɪst] n radioterapista m/f.

radiotherapy ['reɪdɪəu'θɛrəpɪ] n radioterapia.

radish ['rædɪʃ] n ravanello.

radium ['reɪdɪəm] n radio.

radius, pl **radii** ['reɪdɪəs, -ɪaɪ] n raggio; (ANAT) radio; **within a ~ of 50 miles** in un raggio di 50 miglia.

RAF n abbr (BRIT) see **Royal Air Force**.

raffia ['ræfɪə] n rafia.

raffish ['ræfɪʃ] adj dal look trasandato.

raffle ['ræfl] n lotteria ♦ vt (object) mettere in palio.

raft [rɑːft] n zattera.

rafter ['rɑːftə*] n trave f.

rag [ræg] n straccio, cencio; (pej: newspaper) giornalaccio; (for charity) iniziativa studentesca a scopo benefico ♦ vt (BRIT) prendere in giro; **~s** npl stracci mpl, brandelli mpl; **in ~s** stracciato.

rag-and-bone man ['rægən'bəun-] n straccivendolo.

ragbag ['rægbæg] n (fig) guazzabuglio.

rag doll n bambola di pezza.

rage [reɪdʒ] n (fury) collera, furia ♦ vi (person) andare su tutte le furie; (storm) infuriare; **it's all the ~** fa furore; **to fly**

into a ~ andare or montare su tutte le furie.

ragged ['rægɪd] adj (edge) irregolare; (cuff) logoro(a); (appearance) pezzente.

raging ['reɪdʒɪŋ] adj (all senses) furioso(a); **in a ~ temper** su tutte le furie.

rag trade n (col): **the ~** l'abbigliamento.

rag week n (BRIT) see boxed note.

raid [reɪd] n (MIL) incursione f; (criminal) rapina; (by police) irruzione f ♦ vt fare un'incursione in; rapinare; fare irruzione in.

raider ['reɪdə*] n rapinatore/trice; (plane) aeroplano da incursione.

rail [reɪl] n (on stair) ringhiera; (on bridge, balcony) parapetto; (of ship) battagliola; (for train) rotaia; **~s** npl binario, rotaie fpl; **by ~** per ferrovia, in treno.

railcard ['reɪlkɑːd] n (BRIT) tessera di riduzione ferroviaria.

railing(s) ['reɪlɪŋ(z)] n(pl) ringhiere fpl.

railway ['reɪlweɪ], (US) **railroad** ['reɪlrəud] n ferrovia.

railway engine n (BRIT) locomotiva.

railway line n (BRIT) linea ferroviaria.

railwayman ['reɪlweɪmən] n (BRIT) ferroviere m.

railway station n (BRIT) stazione f ferroviaria.

rain [reɪn] n pioggia ♦ vi piovere; **in the ~** sotto la pioggia; **it's ~ing** piove; **it's ~ing cats and dogs** piove a catinelle.

rainbow ['reɪnbəu] n arcobaleno.

raincoat ['reɪnkəut] n impermeabile m.

raindrop ['reɪndrɔp] n goccia di pioggia.

rainfall ['reɪnfɔːl] n pioggia; (measurement) piovosità.

rainforest ['reɪnfɔrɪst] n foresta pluviale or equatoriale.

rainproof ['reɪnpruːf] adj impermeabile.

rainstorm ['reɪnstɔːm] n pioggia torrenziale.

rainwater ['reɪnwɔːtə*] n acqua piovana.

rainy ['reɪnɪ] adj piovoso(a).

raise [reɪz] n aumento ♦ vt (lift) alzare, sollevare; (build) erigere; (increase) aumentare; (a protest, doubt, question) sollevare; (cattle, family) allevare; (crop) coltivare; (army, funds) raccogliere; (loan) ottenere; (end: siege, embargo) togliere; **to ~ one's voice** alzare la voce; **to ~ sb's**

hopes accendere le speranze di qn; **to ~ one's glass to sb/sth** brindare a qn/qc; **to ~ a laugh/a smile** far ridere/sorridere.

raisin ['reizn] *n* uva secca.

Raj [rɑ:dʒ] *n*: **the ~** l'impero britannico (*in India*).

rajah ['rɑ:dʒə] *n* ragià *m inv*.

rake [reik] *n* (*tool*) rastrello; (*person*) libertino ♦ *vt* (*garden*) rastrellare; (*with machine gun*) spazzare ♦ *vi*: **to ~ through** (*fig*: *search*) frugare tra.

rake-off ['reikɔf] *n* (*col*) parte *f* percentuale.

rakish ['reikiʃ] *adj* dissoluto(a); disinvolto(a).

rally ['ræli] *n* (*POL etc*) riunione *f*; (*AUT*) rally *m inv*; (*TENNIS*) scambio ♦ *vt* riunire, radunare ♦ *vi* raccogliersi, radunarsi; (*sick person, STOCK EXCHANGE*) riprendersi.

►**rally round** *vt fus* raggrupparsi intorno a; venire in aiuto di.

rallying point ['ræliiŋ-] *n* (*POL, MIL*) punto di riunione, punto di raduno.

RAM [ræm] *n abbr* (*COMPUT*: = *random access memory*) RAM *f*.

ram [ræm] *n* montone *m*, ariete *m*; (*device*) ariete ♦ *vt* conficcare; (*crash into*) cozzare, sbattere contro; percuotere; speronare.

ramble ['ræmbl] *n* escursione *f* ♦ *vi* (*pej*: *also*: **~ on**) divagare.

rambler ['ræmblə*] *n* escursionista *m/f*.

rambling ['ræmbliŋ] *adj* (*speech*) sconnesso(a); (*BOT*) rampicante; (*house*) tutto(a) nicchie e corridoi.

rambunctious [ræm'bʌŋkʃəs] *adj* (*US*) = **rumbustious**.

RAMC *n abbr* (*BRIT*) = *Royal Army Medical Corps*.

ramification [ræmifi'keiʃən] *n* ramificazione *f*.

ramp [ræmp] *n* rampa; (*AUT*) dosso artificiale.

rampage [ræm'peidʒ] *n*: **to go on the ~** scatenarsi in modo violento ♦ *vi*: **they went rampaging through the town** si sono scatenati in modo violento per la città.

rampant ['ræmpənt] *adj* (*disease etc*) che infierisce.

rampart ['ræmpɑ:t] *n* bastione *m*.

ram raiding [-reidiŋ] *n* *il rapinare un negozio sfondandone la vetrina con un veicolo rubato.*

ramshackle ['ræmʃækl] *adj* (*house*) cadente; (*car etc*) sgangherato(a).

ran [ræn] *pt of* **run**.

ranch [rɑ:ntʃ] *n* ranch *m inv*.

rancid ['rænsid] *adj* rancido(a).

rancour, (*US*) **rancor** ['ræŋkə*] *n* rancore

m.

R&B *n abbr* = *rhythm and blues*.

R&D *n abbr see* **research and development**.

random ['rændəm] *adj* fatto(a) *or* detto(a) per caso; (*COMPUT, MATH*) casuale ♦ *n*: **at ~** a casaccio.

random access *n* (*COMPUT*) accesso casuale.

R & R *n abbr* (= *rest and recreation*) ricreazione *f*.

randy ['rændi] *adj* (*col*) arrapato(a); lascivo(a).

rang [ræŋ] *pt of* **ring**.

range [reindʒ] *n* (*of mountains*) catena; (*of missile, voice*) portata; (*of products*) gamma; (*MIL*: *also*: **shooting ~**) campo di tiro; (*also*: **kitchen ~**) fornello, cucina economica ♦ *vt* (*place*) disporre, allineare; (*roam*) vagare per ♦ *vi*: **to ~ over** coprire; **to ~ from ... to** andare da ... a; **price ~** gamma di prezzi; **do you have anything else in this price ~?** ha nient'altro su *or* di questo prezzo?; **within (firing) ~ a** portata di tiro; **~d left/right** (*text*) allineato(a) a destra/sinistra.

ranger ['reindʒə*] *n* guardia forestale.

Rangoon [ræŋ'gu:n] *n* Rangun *f*.

rank [ræŋk] *n* fila; (*MIL*) grado; (*BRIT*: *also*: **taxi ~**) posteggio di taxi ♦ *vi*: **to ~ among** essere nel numero di ♦ *adj* (*smell*) puzzolente; (*hypocrisy, injustice*) vero(a) e proprio(a); **the ~s** (*MIL*) la truppa; **the ~ and file** (*fig*) la gran massa; **to close ~s** (*MIL, fig*) serrare i ranghi; **I ~ him sixth** gli do il sesto posto, lo metto al sesto posto.

rankle ['ræŋkl] *vi*: **to ~ (with sb)** bruciare (a qn).

rank outsider *n* outsider *m/f inv*.

ransack ['rænsæk] *vt* rovistare; (*plunder*) saccheggiare.

ransom ['rænsəm] *n* riscatto; **to hold sb to ~** (*fig*) esercitare pressione su qn.

rant [rænt] *vi* vociare.

ranting ['ræntiŋ] *n* vociare *m*.

rap [ræp] *n* (*noise*) colpetti *mpl*; (*at a door*) bussata ♦ *vt* dare dei colpetti a; bussare a.

rape [reip] *n* violenza carnale, stupro ♦ *vt* violentare.

rape(seed) oil ['reip(si:d)-] *n* olio di ravizzone.

rapid ['ræpid] *adj* rapido(a).

rapidity [rə'piditi] *n* rapidità.

rapidly ['ræpidli] *adv* rapidamente.

rapids ['ræpidz] *npl* (*GEO*) rapida.

rapist ['reipist] *n* violentatore *m*.

rapport [ræ'pɔ:*] *n* rapporto.

rapt [ræpt] adj (attention) rapito(a), profondo(a); **to be ~ in contemplation** essere in estatica contemplazione.

rapture ['ræptʃə*] n estasi f inv; **to go into ~s over** andare in solluchero per.

rapturous ['ræptʃərəs] adj estatico(a).

rare [rɛə*] adj raro(a); (CULIN: steak) al sangue; **it is ~ to find that ...** capita di rado or raramente che ... + sub.

rarebit ['rɛəbɪt] n see **Welsh rarebit.**

rarefied ['rɛərɪfaɪd] adj (air, atmosphere) rarefatto(a).

rarely ['rɛəlɪ] adv raramente.

raring ['rɛərɪŋ] adj: **to be ~ to go** (col) non veder l'ora di cominciare.

rarity ['rɛərɪtɪ] n rarità f inv.

rascal ['rɑːskl] n mascalzone m.

rash [ræʃ] adj imprudente, sconsiderato(a) ♦ n (MED) eruzione f; **to come out in a ~** avere uno sfogo.

rasher ['ræʃə*] n fetta sottile (di lardo or prosciutto).

rasp [rɑːsp] n (tool) lima ♦ vt (speak: also: ~ out) gracchiare.

raspberry ['rɑːzbərɪ] n lampone m.

raspberry bush n lampone m (pianta).

rasping ['rɑːspɪŋ] adj stridulo(a).

Rastafarian [ræstə'fɛərɪən] adj, n rastafariano(a).

rat [ræt] n ratto.

ratable ['reɪtəbl] adj = **rateable.**

ratchet ['rætʃɪt] n: **~ wheel** ruota dentata.

rate [reɪt] n (proportion) tasso, percentuale f; (speed) velocità f inv; (price) tariffa ♦ vt valutare; stimare; **to ~ sb/sth as** valutare qn/qc come; **to ~ sb/sth among** annoverare qn/qc tra; **to ~ sb/sth highly** stimare molto qn/qc; **at a ~ of 60 kph** alla velocità di 60 km all'ora; **~ of exchange** tasso di cambio; **~ of flow** flusso medio; **~ of growth** tasso di crescita; **~ of return** tasso di rendimento; **pulse ~** frequenza delle pulsazioni; see also **rates.**

rateable value ['reɪtəbl-] n (BRIT) valore m imponibile (agli effetti delle imposte comunali).

ratepayer ['reɪtpeɪə*] n (BRIT) contribuente m/f (che paga le imposte comunali).

rates [reɪts] npl (BRIT) imposte fpl comunali.

rather ['rɑːðə*] adv piuttosto; (somewhat) abbastanza; (to some extent) un po'; **it's ~ expensive** è piuttosto caro; (too much) è un po' caro; **there's ~ a lot** ce n'è parecchio; **I would** or **I'd ~ go** preferirei andare; **I had ~ go** farei meglio ad andare; **I'd ~ not leave** preferirei non partire; **or ~** (more accurately) anzi, per essere (più) precisi; **I ~ think he won't**

come credo proprio che non verrà.

ratification [rætɪfɪ'keɪʃən] n ratificazione f.

ratify ['rætɪfaɪ] vt ratificare.

rating ['reɪtɪŋ] n classificazione f; punteggio di merito; (NAUT: category) classe f; (: sailor: BRIT) marinaio semplice.

ratings ['reɪtɪŋz] npl (RADIO, TV) indice m di ascolto.

ratio ['reɪʃɪəu] n proporzione f; **in the ~ of 2 to 1** in rapporto di 2 a 1.

ration ['ræʃən] n razione f ♦ vt razionare.

rational ['ræʃənl] adj razionale, ragionevole; (solution, reasoning) logico(a).

rationale [ræʃə'nɑːl] n fondamento logico; giustificazione f.

rationalization [ræʃnəlaɪ'zeɪʃən] n razionalizzazione f.

rationalize ['ræʃnəlaɪz] vt razionalizzare.

rationally ['ræʃnəlɪ] adv razionalmente; logicamente.

rationing ['ræʃnɪŋ] n razionamento.

ratpack ['rætpæk] n (BRIT col) stampa scandalistica.

rat poison n veleno per topi.

rat race n carrierismo, corsa al successo.

rattan [ræ'tæn] n malacca.

rattle ['rætl] n tintinnio; (louder) rumore m di ferraglia; (object: of baby) sonaglino; (: of sports fan) raganella ♦ vi risuonare, tintinnare; fare un rumore di ferraglia ♦ vt agitare; far tintinnare; (col: disconcert) sconcertare.

rattlesnake ['rætlsneɪk] n serpente m a sonagli.

ratty ['rætɪ] adj (col) incavolato(a).

raucous ['rɔːkəs] adj sguaiato(a).

raucously ['rɔːkəslɪ] adv sguaiatamente.

raunchy ['rɔːntʃɪ] adj (col: person) allupato(a); (: voice, song) libidinoso(a).

ravage ['rævɪdʒ] vt devastare.

ravages ['rævɪdʒɪz] npl danni mpl.

rave [reɪv] vi (in anger) infuriarsi; (with enthusiasm) andare in estasi; (MED) delirare ♦ n: **a ~ (party)** un rave ♦ adj (scene, culture, music) del fenomeno rave ♦ cpd: **~ review** (col) critica entusiastica.

raven ['reɪvən] n corvo.

ravenous ['rævənəs] adj affamato(a).

ravine [rə'viːn] n burrone m.

raving ['reɪvɪŋ] adj: **~ lunatic** pazzo(a) furioso(a).

ravings ['reɪvɪŋz] npl vaneggiamenti mpl.

ravioli [rævɪ'əulɪ] n ravioli mpl.

ravish ['rævɪʃ] vt (delight) estasiare.

ravishing ['rævɪʃɪŋ] adj incantevole.

raw [rɔː] adj (uncooked) crudo(a); (not

processed) greggio(a); (*sore*) vivo(a); (*inexperienced*) inesperto(a); **to get a ~ deal** (*col: bad bargain*) prendere un bidone; (: *harsh treatment*) venire trattato ingiustamente.

Rawalpindi [rɔːl'pɪndɪ] *n* Rawalpindi *f*.

raw material *n* materia prima.

ray [reɪ] *n* raggio.

rayon ['reɪɔn] *n* raion *m*.

raze [reɪz] *vt* radere, distruggere; (*also*: ~ **to the ground**) radere al suolo.

razor ['reɪzə*] *n* rasoio.

razor blade *n* lama di rasoio.

razzle(-dazzle) ['ræzl('dæzl)] *n* (*BRIT col*): **to be/go on the ~** darsi alla pazza gioia.

razzmatazz ['ræzmə'tæz] *n* (*col*) clamore *m*.

RC *abbr* = **Roman Catholic**.

RCAF *n abbr* = *Royal Canadian Air Force*.

RCMP *n abbr* = *Royal Canadian Mounted Police*.

RCN *n abbr* = *Royal Canadian Navy*.

RD *abbr* (*US POST*) = *rural delivery*.

Rd *abbr* = *road*.

RDC *n abbr* (*BRIT*) *see* **rural district council**.

RE *n abbr* (*BRIT MIL*: = *Royal Engineers*) ≈ G.M. (= *Genio Militare*); (*BRIT*) = **religious education**.

re [riː] *prep* con riferimento a.

reach [riːtʃ] *n* portata; (*of river etc*) tratto ♦ *vt* raggiungere; arrivare a ♦ *vi* stendersi; (*stretch out hand: also*: ~ **down**, ~ **over**, ~ **across** *etc*) allungare una mano; **out of/within ~** (*object*) fuori/a portata di mano; **within easy ~ (of)** (*place*) a breve distanza (di), vicino (a); **to ~ sb by phone** contattare qn per telefono; **can I ~ you at your hotel?** la posso contattare al suo albergo?

▶**reach out** *vi*: **to ~ out for** stendere la mano per prendere.

react [riː'ækt] *vi* reagire.

reaction [riː'ækʃən] *n* reazione *f*.

reactionary [riː'ækʃənrɪ] *adj, n* reazionario(a).

reactor [riː'æktə*] *n* reattore *m*.

read, *pt, pp* **read** [riːd, rɛd] *vi* leggere ♦ *vt* leggere; (*understand*) intendere, interpretare; (*study*) studiare; **do you ~ me?** (*TEL*) mi ricevete?; **to take sth as read** (*fig*) dare qc per scontato.

▶**read out** *vt* leggere ad alta voce.

▶**read over** *vt* rileggere attentamente.

▶**read through** *vt* (*quickly*) dare una scorsa a; (*thoroughly*) leggere da cima a fondo.

▶**read up** *vt*, **read up on** *vt fus* studiare bene.

readable ['riːdəbl] *adj* leggibile; che si

legge volentieri.

reader ['riːdə*] *n* lettore/trice; (*book*) libro di lettura; (*BRIT: at university*) *professore con funzioni preminenti di ricerca*.

readership ['riːdəʃɪp] *n* (*of paper etc*) numero di lettori.

readily ['rɛdɪlɪ] *adv* volentieri; (*easily*) facilmente.

readiness ['rɛdɪnɪs] *n* prontezza; **in ~** (*prepared*) pronto(a).

reading ['riːdɪŋ] *n* lettura; (*understanding*) interpretazione *f*; (*on instrument*) indicazione *f*.

reading lamp *n* lampada da studio.

reading room *n* sala di lettura.

readjust [riːə'dʒʌst] *vt* raggiustare ♦ *vi* (*person*): **to ~ (to)** riadattarsi (a).

ready ['rɛdɪ] *adj* pronto(a); (*willing*) pronto(a), disposto(a); (*quick*) rapido(a); (*available*) disponibile ♦ *n*: **at the ~** (*MIL*) pronto a sparare; (*fig*) tutto(a) pronto(a); **~ for use** pronto per l'uso; **to be ~ to do sth** essere pronto a fare qc; **to get ~** *vi* prepararsi ♦ *vt* preparare.

ready cash *n* denaro in contanti.

ready-cooked [rɛdɪ'kukt] *adj* già cotto(a).

ready-made [rɛdɪ'meɪd] *adj* prefabbricato(a); (*clothes*) confezionato(a).

ready reckoner [-'rɛkənə*] *n* (*BRIT*) prontuario di calcolo.

ready-to-wear [rɛdɪtə'wɛə*] *adj* prêt-à-porter *inv*.

reagent [riː'eɪdʒənt] *n*: **chemical ~** reagente *m* chimico.

real [rɪəl] *adj* reale; vero(a) ♦ *adv* (*US col: very*) veramente, proprio; **in ~ terms** in realtà; **in ~ life** nella realtà.

real ale *n* birra ad effervescenza naturale.

real estate *n* beni *mpl* immobili.

realism ['rɪəlɪzəm] *n* (*also ART*) realismo.

realist ['rɪəlɪst] *n* realista *m/f*.

realistic [rɪə'lɪstɪk] *adj* realistico(a).

reality [riː'ælɪtɪ] *n* realtà *f inv*; **in ~** in realtà, in effetti.

realization [rɪəlaɪ'zeɪʃən] *n* (*awareness*) presa di coscienza; (*of hopes, project etc*) realizzazione *f*.

realize ['rɪəlaɪz] *vt* (*understand*) rendersi conto di; (*a project, COMM: asset*) realizzare; **I ~ that ...** mi rendo conto *or* capisco che ....

really ['rɪəlɪ] *adv* veramente, davvero.

realm [rɛlm] *n* reame *m*, regno.

real time *n* (*COMPUT*) tempo reale.

Realtor ® ['rɪəltɔː*] *n* (*US*) agente *m* immobiliare.

ream [riːm] *n* risma; **~s** (*fig col*) pagine e

pagine *fpl.*

reap [ri:p] *vt* mietere; (*fig*) raccogliere.

reaper ['ri:pə*] *n* (*machine*) mietitrice *f.*

reappear [ri:ə'pɪə*] *vi* ricomparire, riapparire.

reappearance [ri:ə'pɪərəns] *n* riapparizione *f.*

reapply [ri:ə'plaɪ] *vi*: **to ~ for** fare un'altra domanda per.

reappraisal [ri:ə'preɪzl] *n* riesame *m.*

rear [rɪə*] *adj* di dietro; (*AUT*: *wheel etc*) posteriore ♦ *n* didietro, parte *f* posteriore ♦ *vt* (*cattle, family*) allevare ♦ *vi* (*also*: **~ up**: *animal*) impennarsi.

rear admiral *n* contrammiraglio.

rear-engined ['rɪə'ɛndʒɪnd] *adj* (*AUT*) con motore posteriore.

rearguard ['rɪəgɑ:d] *n* retroguardia.

rearm [ri:'ɑ:m] *vt, vi* riarmare.

rearmament [ri:'ɑ:məmənt] *n* riarmo.

rearrange [ri:ə'reɪndʒ] *vt* riordinare.

rear-view mirror ['rɪəvju:-] *n* (*AUT*) specchio retrovisivo.

reason ['ri:zn] *n* ragione *f*; (*cause, motive*) ragione, motivo ♦ *vi*: **to ~ with sb** far ragionare qn; **to have ~ to think** avere motivi per pensare; **it stands to ~ that** è ovvio che; **the ~ for/why** la ragione *or* il motivo di/per cui; **with good ~** a ragione; **all the more ~ why you should not sell it** ragione di più per non venderlo.

reasonable ['ri:znəbl] *adj* ragionevole; (*not bad*) accettabile.

reasonably ['ri:znəblɪ] *adv* ragionevolmente; **one can ~ assume that** ... uno può facilmente supporre che ....

reasoned ['ri:znd] *adj* (*argument*) ponderato(a).

reasoning ['ri:znɪŋ] *n* ragionamento.

reassemble [ri:ə'sɛmbl] *vt* riunire; (*machine*) rimontare.

reassert [ri:ə'sɜ:t] *vt* riaffermare.

reassurance [ri:ə'ʃuərəns] *n* rassicurazione *f.*

reassure [ri:ə'ʃuə*] *vt* rassicurare; **to ~ sb of** rassicurare qn di *or* su.

reassuring [ri:ə'ʃuərɪŋ] *adj* rassicurante.

reawakening [ri:ə'weɪknɪŋ] *n* risveglio.

rebate ['ri:beɪt] *n* rimborso.

rebel *n* ['rɛbl] ribelle *m/f* ♦ *vi* [rɪ'bɛl] ribellarsi.

rebellion [rɪ'bɛljən] *n* ribellione *f.*

rebellious [rɪ'bɛljəs] *adj* ribelle.

rebirth [ri:'bə:θ] *n* rinascita.

rebound *vi* [rɪ'baund] (*ball*) rimbalzare ♦ *n* ['ri:baund] rimbalzo.

rebuff [rɪ'bʌf] *n* secco rifiuto ♦ *vt* respingere.

rebuild [ri:'bɪld] *vt irreg* ricostruire.

rebuke [rɪ'bju:k] *n* rimprovero ♦ *vt* rimproverare.

rebut [rɪ'bʌt] *vt* rifiutare.

rebuttal [rɪ'bʌtl] *n* rifiuto.

recalcitrant [rɪ'kælsɪtrənt] *adj* recalcitrante.

recall [rɪ'kɔ:l] *vt* (*gen, COMPUT*) richiamare; (*remember*) ricordare, richiamare alla mente ♦ *n* richiamo; **beyond ~** irrevocabile.

recant [rɪ'kænt] *vi* ritrattarsi; (*REL*) fare abiura.

recap ['ri:kæp] *n* ricapitolazione *f* ♦ *vt* ricapitolare ♦ *vi* riassumere.

recapture [ri:'kæptʃə*] *vt* riprendere; (*atmosphere*) ricreare.

recd. *abbr* = **received**.

recede [rɪ'si:d] *vi* allontanarsi; ritirarsi; calare.

receding [rɪ'si:dɪŋ] *adj* (*forehead, chin*) sfuggente; **he's got a ~ hairline** è stempiato.

receipt [rɪ'si:t] *n* (*document*) ricevuta; (*act of receiving*) ricevimento; **to acknowledge ~ of** accusare ricevuta di; **we are in ~ of** ... abbiamo ricevuto ....

receipts [rɪ'si:ts] *npl* (*COMM*) introiti *mpl.*

receivable [rɪ'si:vəbl] *adj* (*COMM*) esigibile; (*: owed*) dovuto(a).

receive [rɪ'si:v] *vt* ricevere; (*guest*) ricevere, accogliere; **"~d with thanks"** (*COMM*) "per quietanza".

Received Pronunciation (RP) *n* (*BRIT*) see *boxed note.*

RECEIVED PRONUNCIATION

Si chiama **Received Pronunciation (RP)**
l'accento dell'inglese parlato in alcune parti del sud-est dell'Inghilterra. In esso si identifica l'inglese "standard" delle classi colte, privo di inflessioni regionali e adottato tradizionalmente dagli annunciatori della BBC. È anche l'accento standard dell'inglese insegnato come lingua straniera.

---

receiver [rɪ'si:və*] *n* (*TEL*) ricevitore *m*; (*RADIO*) apparecchio ricevente; (*of stolen goods*) ricettatore/trice; (*LAW*) curatore *m* fallimentare.

receivership [rɪ'si:vəʃɪp] *n* curatela; **to go into ~** andare in amministrazione controllata.

recent ['ri:snt] *adj* recente; **in ~ years** negli ultimi anni.

recently ['ri:sntlɪ] *adv* recentemente; **as ~ as** ... soltanto ...; **until ~** fino a poco

tempo fa.
receptacle [rɪ'sɛptɪkl] *n* recipiente *m*.
reception [rɪ'sɛpʃən] *n* (*gen*) ricevimento;
(*welcome*) accoglienza; (*TV*) ricezione *f*.
reception centre *n* (*BRIT*) centro di
raccolta.
reception desk *n* (*in hotel*) reception *f inv*;
(*in hospital, at doctor's*) accettazione *f*; (*in
large building, offices*) portineria.
receptionist [rɪ'sɛpʃənɪst] *n* receptionist *m/f
inv*.
receptive [rɪ'sɛptɪv] *adj* ricettivo(a).
recess [rɪ'sɛs] *n* (*in room*) alcova; (*POL etc:
holiday*) vacanze *fpl*; (*US LAW: short break*)
sospensione *f*; (*US SCOL*) intervallo.
recession [rɪ'sɛʃən] *n* (*ECON*) recessione *f*.
recharge [riː'tʃɑːdʒ] *vt* (*battery*) ricaricare.
rechargeable ['riː'tʃɑːdʒəbl] *adj*
ricaricabile.
recipe ['rɛsɪpɪ] *n* ricetta.
recipient [rɪ'sɪpɪənt] *n* beneficiario/a; (*of
letter*) destinatario/a.
reciprocal [rɪ'sɪprəkl] *adj* reciproco(a).
reciprocate [rɪ'sɪprəkeɪt] *vt* ricambiare.
recital [rɪ'saɪtl] *n* recital *m inv*; concerto (di
solista).
recite [rɪ'saɪt] *vt* (*poem*) recitare.
reckless ['rɛkləs] *adj* (*driver etc*)
spericolato(a); (*spender*) incosciente.
recklessly ['rɛkləslɪ] *adv* in modo
spericolato; da incosciente.
reckon ['rɛkən] *vt* (*count*) calcolare;
(*consider*) considerare, stimare; (*think*): **I
~ that ...** penso che ... ♦ *vi* contare,
calcolare; **to ~ without sb/sth** non tener
conto di qn/qc; **he is somebody to be ~ed
with** è uno da non sottovalutare.
▶**reckon on** *vt fus* contare su.
reckoning ['rɛknɪŋ] *n* conto; stima; **the day
of ~** il giorno del giudizio.
reclaim [rɪ'kleɪm] *vt* (*land*) bonificare;
(*demand back*) richiedere, reclamare.
recline [rɪ'klaɪn] *vi* stare sdraiato(a).
reclining [rɪ'klaɪnɪŋ] *adj* (*seat*) ribaltabile.
recluse [rɪ'kluːs] *n* eremita *m*, recluso/a.
recognition [rɛkəg'nɪʃən] *n*
riconoscimento; **to gain ~** essere
riconosciuto(a); **in ~ of** in *or* come segno
di riconoscimento per; **transformed
beyond ~** irriconoscibile.
recognizable ['rɛkəgnaɪzəbl] *adj*: **~ (by)**
riconoscibile (a *or* da).
recognize ['rɛkəgnaɪz] *vt*: **to ~ (by/as)**
riconoscere (a *or* da/come).
recoil [rɪ'kɔɪl] *vi* (*gun*) rinculare; (*spring*)
balzare indietro; (*person*): **to ~ (from)**
indietreggiare (davanti a) ♦ *n* (*of gun*)
rinculo.

recollect [rɛkə'lɛkt] *vt* ricordare.
recollection [rɛkə'lɛkʃən] *n* ricordo; **to the
best of my ~** per quello che mi ricordo.
recommend [rɛkə'mɛnd] *vt* raccomandare;
(*advise*) consigliare; **she has a lot to ~ her**
ha molti elementi a suo favore.
recommendation [rɛkəmɛn'deɪʃən] *n*
raccomandazione *f*; consiglio.
recommended retail price (RRP)
[rɛkə'mɛndɪd-] *n* (*BRIT*) prezzo
raccomandato al dettaglio.
recompense ['rɛkəmpɛns] *vt*
ricompensare; (*compensate*) risarcire ♦ *n*
ricompensa; risarcimento.
reconcilable ['rɛkənsaɪləbl] *adj* conciliabile.
reconcile ['rɛkənsaɪl] *vt* (*two people*)
riconciliare; (*two facts*) conciliare,
quadrare; **to ~ o.s. to** rassegnarsi a.
reconciliation [rɛkənsɪlɪ'eɪʃən] *n*
riconciliazione *f*; conciliazione *f*.
recondition [riːkən'dɪʃən] *vt* rimettere a
nuovo; rifare.
reconnaissance [rɪ'kɔnɪsns] *n* (*MIL*)
ricognizione *f*.
reconnoitre, (US) reconnoiter
[rɛkə'nɔɪtə*] (*MIL*) *vt* fare una ricognizione
di ♦ *vi* fare una ricognizione.
reconsider [riːkən'sɪdə*] *vt* riconsiderare.
reconstitute [riː'kɔnstɪtjuːt] *vt* ricostituire.
reconstruct [riːkən'strʌkt] *vt* ricostruire.
reconstruction [riːkən'strʌkʃən] *n*
ricostruzione *f*.
reconvene [riːkən'viːn] *vt* riconvocare ♦ *vi*
radunarsi.
record *n* ['rɛkɔːd] ricordo, documento; (*of
meeting etc*) nota, verbale *m*; (*register*)
registro; (*file*) pratica, dossier *m inv*;
(*COMPUT*) record *m inv*, registrazione *f*;
(*also*: **police ~**) fedina penale sporca;
(*MUS: disc*) disco; (*SPORT*) record *m inv*,
primato ♦ *vt* [rɪ'kɔːd] (*set down*) prendere
nota di; (*relate*) raccontare; (*COMPUT,
MUS: song etc*) registrare; **public ~s**
archivi *mpl*; **Italy's excellent ~** i brillanti
successi italiani; **in ~ time** a tempo di
record; **to keep a ~ of** tener nota di; **to
set the ~ straight** mettere le cose in
chiaro; **off the ~** *adj* ufficioso(a) ♦ *adv*
ufficiosamente; **he is on ~ as saying that
...** ha dichiarato pubblicamente che ....
record card *n* (*in file*) scheda.
recorded delivery letter [rɪ'kɔːdɪd-] *n*
(*BRIT POST*) lettera raccomandata.
recorder [rɪ'kɔːdə*] *n* (*LAW*) avvocato che
funge da giudice; (*MUS*) flauto diritto.
record holder *n* (*SPORT*) primatista *m/f*.
recording [rɪ'kɔːdɪŋ] *n* (*MUS*) registrazione
f.

recording studio *n* studio di registrazione.

record player *n* giradischi *m inv.*

recount [rɪ'kaunt] *vt* raccontare, narrare.

re-count *n* ['riːkaunt] (*POL: of votes*) nuovo conteggio ♦ *vt* [riː'kaunt] ricontare.

recoup [rɪ'kuːp] *vt* ricuperare; **to ~ one's losses** ricuperare le perdite, rifarsi.

recourse [rɪ'kɔːs] *n:* **to have ~ to** ricorrere a.

recover [rɪ'kʌvə*] *vt* ricuperare ♦ *vi* (*from illness*) rimettersi (in salute), ristabilirsi; (*country, person: from shock*) riprendersi.

re-cover [riː'kʌvə*] *vt* (*chair etc*) ricoprire.

recovery [rɪ'kʌvərɪ] *n* ricupero; ristabilimento; ripresa.

recreate [riːkrɪ'eɪt] *vt* ricreare.

recreation [rɛkrɪ'eɪʃən] *n* ricreazione *f;* svago.

recreational [rɛkrɪ'eɪʃənəl] *adj* ricreativo(a).

recreational drug *n droga usata saltuariamente.*

recreational vehicle (RV) *n* (*US*) camper *m inv.*

recrimination [rɪkrɪmɪ'neɪʃən] *n* recriminazione *f.*

recruit [rɪ'kruːt] *n* recluta ♦ *vt* reclutare.

recruitment [rɪ'kruːtmənt] *n* reclutamento.

rectangle ['rɛktæŋgl] *n* rettangolo.

rectangular [rɛk'tæŋgjulə*] *adj* rettangolare.

rectify ['rɛktɪfaɪ] *vt* (*error*) rettificare; (*omission*) riparare.

rector ['rɛktə*] *n* (*REL*) parroco (*anglicano*); (*in Scottish universities*) personalità eletta dagli studenti per rappresentarli.

rectory ['rɛktərɪ] *n* presbiterio.

rectum ['rɛktəm] *n* (*ANAT*) retto.

recuperate [rɪ'kjuːpəreɪt] *vi* ristabilirsi.

recur [rɪ'kəː*] *vi* riaccadere; (*idea, opportunity*) riapparire; (*symptoms*) ripresentarsi.

recurrence [rɪ'kʌrəns] *n* ripresentarsi *m;* riapparizione *f.*

recurrent [rɪ'kʌrənt] *adj* ricorrente.

recurring [rɪ'kʌrɪŋ] *adj* (*MATH*) periodico(a).

recycle [riː'saɪkl] *vt* riciclare.

red [rɛd] *n* rosso; (*POL: pej*) rosso/a ♦ *adj* rosso(a); **in the ~** (*account*) scoperto; (*business*) in deficit.

red alert *n* allarme *m* rosso.

red-blooded ['rɛd'blʌdɪd] *adj* (*col*) gagliardo(a).

red-brick university ['rɛdbrɪk-] *n* (*BRIT*) *università di recente formazione; see boxed note.*

RED-BRICK UNIVERSITY

In Gran Bretagna, con **red-brick university** *(letteralmente, università di mattoni rossi) si indicano le università istituite tra la fine dell'Ottocento e i primi del Novecento, per contraddistinguerle dalle università più antiche, i cui edifici sono di pietra; vedi anche* **Oxbridge.**

---

red carpet treatment *n* cerimonia col gran pavese.

Red Cross *n* Croce *f* Rossa.

redcurrant ['rɛdkʌrənt] *n* ribes *m inv.*

redden ['rɛdn] *vt* arrossare ♦ *vi* arrossire.

reddish ['rɛdɪʃ] *adj* rossiccio(a).

redecorate [riː'dɛkəreɪt] *vt* tinteggiare (e tappezzare) di nuovo.

redeem [rɪ'diːm] *vt* (*debt*) riscattare; (*sth in pawn*) ritirare; (*fig, also REL*) redimere.

redeemable [rɪ'diːməbl] *adj* con diritto di riscatto; redimibile.

redeeming [rɪ'diːmɪŋ] *adj* (*feature*) che salva.

redefine [riːdɪ'faɪn] *vt* ridefinire.

redemption [rɪ'dɛmpʃən] *n* (*REL*) redenzione *f;* **past** *or* **beyond ~** irrecuperabile.

redeploy [riːdɪ'plɔɪ] *vt* (*MIL*) riorganizzare lo schieramento di; (*resources*) riorganizzare.

redeployment [riːdɪ'plɔɪmənt] *n* riorganizzazione *f.*

redevelop [riːdɪ'vɛləp] *vt* ristrutturare.

redevelopment [riːdɪ'vɛləpmənt] *n* ristrutturazione *f.*

red-handed [rɛd'hændɪd] *adj:* **to be caught ~** essere preso(a) in flagrante *or* con le mani nel sacco.

redhead ['rɛdhɛd] *n* rosso/a.

red herring *n* (*fig*) falsa pista.

red-hot [rɛd'hɔt] *adj* arroventato(a).

redirect [riːdaɪ'rɛkt] *vt* (*mail*) far seguire.

redistribute [riːdɪ'strɪbjuːt] *vt* ridistribuire.

red-letter day ['rɛdlɛtə-] *n* giorno memorabile.

red light *n:* **to go through a ~** (*AUT*) passare col rosso.

red-light district [rɛd'laɪt-] *n* quartiere *m* luce rossa *inv.*

red meat *n* carne *f* rossa.

redness ['rɛdnɪs] *n* rossore *m;* (*of hair*) rosso.

redo [riː'duː] *vt irreg* rifare.

redolent ['rɛdələnt] *adj:* **~ of** che sa di; (*fig*) che ricorda.

redouble [riː'dʌbl] *vt*: **to ~ one's efforts** raddoppiare gli sforzi.

redraft [riː'drɑːft] *vt* fare una nuova stesura di.

redress [rɪ'drɛs] *n* riparazione *f* ♦ *vt* riparare; **to ~ the balance** ristabilire l'equilibrio.

Red Sea *n*: **the ~** il mar Rosso.

redskin ['rɛdskɪn] *n* pellerossa *m/f*.

red tape *n* (*fig*) burocrazia.

reduce [rɪ'djuːs] *vt* ridurre; (*lower*) ridurre, abbassare; **"~ speed now"** (*AUT*) "rallentare"; **to ~ sth by/to** ridurre qc di/a; **to ~ sb to silence/despair/tears** ridurre qn al silenzio/alla disperazione/in lacrime.

reduced [rɪ'djuːst] *adj* (*decreased*) ridotto(a); **at a ~ price** a prezzo ribassato *or* ridotto; **"greatly ~ prices"** "grandi ribassi".

reduction [rɪ'dʌkʃən] *n* riduzione *f*; (*of price*) ribasso; (*discount*) sconto.

redundancy [rɪ'dʌndənsɪ] *n* licenziamento (per eccesso di personale); **compulsory ~** licenziamento; **voluntary ~** *forma di cassa integrazione volontaria*.

redundancy payment *n* (*BRIT*) indennità *f inv* di licenziamento.

redundant [rɪ'dʌndnt] *adj* (*BRIT: worker*) licenziato(a); (*detail, object*) superfluo(a); **to make ~** (*BRIT*) licenziare (per eccesso di personale).

reed [riːd] *n* (*BOT*) canna; (*MUS: of clarinet etc*) ancia.

re-educate [riː'ɛdjukeɪt] *vt* rieducare.

reedy ['riːdɪ] *adj* (*voice, instrument*) acuto(a).

reef [riːf] *n* (*at sea*) scogliera; **coral ~** barriera corallina.

reek [riːk] *vi*: **to ~ (of)** puzzare (di).

reel [riːl] *n* bobina, rocchetto; (*TECH*) aspo; (*FISHING*) mulinello; (*CINE*) rotolo ♦ *vt* (*TECH*) annaspare; (*also*: **~ up**) avvolgere ♦ *vi* (*sway*) barcollare, vacillare; **my head is ~ing** mi gira la testa.

▶**reel off** *vt* snocciolare.

re-election [riːɪ'lɛkʃən] *n* rielezione *f*.

re-enter [riː'ɛntə*] *vt* rientrare in.

re-entry [riː'ɛntrɪ] *n* rientro.

re-export *vt* [riːɪk'spɔːt] riesportare ♦ *n* [riː'ɛkspɔːt] merce *f* riesportata, riesportazione *f*.

ref [rɛf] *n abbr* (*col*: = *referee*) arbitro.

ref. *abbr* (*COMM*: = *with reference to*) sogg.

refectory [rɪ'fɛktərɪ] *n* refettorio.

refer [rɪ'fəː*] *vt*: **to ~ sth to** (*dispute, decision*) deferire qc a; **to ~ sb to**

(*inquirer: for information*) indirizzare qn a; (*reader: to text*) rimandare qn a; **he ~red me to the manager** mi ha detto di rivolgermi al direttore.

▶**refer to** *vt fus* (*allude to*) accennare a; (*apply to*) riferire a; (*consult*) rivolgersi a; **~ring to your letter** (*COMM*) in riferimento alla Vostra lettera.

referee [rɛfə'riː] *n* arbitro; (*TENNIS*) giudice *m* di gara; (*BRIT: for job application*) referenza ♦ *vt* arbitrare.

reference ['rɛfrəns] *n* riferimento; (*mention*) menzione *f*, allusione *f*; (*for job application: letter*) referenza; lettera di raccomandazione; (: *person*) referenza; (*in book*) rimando; **with ~ to** riguardo a; (*COMM: in letter*) in *or* con riferimento a; **"please quote this ~"** (*COMM*) "si prega di far riferimento al numero di protocollo".

reference book *n* libro di consultazione.

reference library *n* biblioteca per la consultazione.

reference number *n* (*COMM*) numero di riferimento.

referendum, *pl* **referenda** [rɛfə'rɛndəm, -də] *n* referendum *m inv*.

referral [rɪ'fəːrəl] *n* deferimento; (*MED*) richiesta (di visita specialistica).

refill *vt* [riː'fɪl] riempire di nuovo; (*pen, lighter etc*) ricaricare ♦ *n* ['riːfɪl] (*for pen etc*) ricambio.

refine [rɪ'faɪn] *vt* raffinare.

refined [rɪ'faɪnd] *adj* raffinato(a).

refinement [rɪ'faɪnmənt] *n* (*of person*) raffinatezza.

refinery [rɪ'faɪnərɪ] *n* raffineria.

refit *n* ['riːfɪt] (*NAUT*) raddobbo ♦ *vt* [riː'fɪt] (*ship*) raddobbare.

reflate [riː'fleɪt] *vt* (*economy*) rilanciare.

reflation [riː'fleɪʃən] *n* rilancio.

reflationary [riː'fleɪʃənərɪ] *adj* nuovamente inflazionario(a).

reflect [rɪ'flɛkt] *vt* (*light, image*) riflettere; (*fig*) rispecchiare ♦ *vi* (*think*) riflettere, considerare.

▶**reflect on** *vt fus* (*discredit*) rispecchiarsi su.

reflection [rɪ'flɛkʃən] *n* riflessione *f*; (*image*) riflesso; (*criticism*): **~ on** giudizio su; attacco a; **on ~** pensandoci sopra.

reflector [rɪ'flɛktə*] *n* (*also AUT*) catarifrangente *m*.

reflex ['riːflɛks] *adj* riflesso(a) ♦ *n* riflesso.

reflexive [rɪ'flɛksɪv] *adj* (*LING*) riflessivo(a).

reform [rɪ'fɔːm] *n* riforma ♦ *vt* riformare.

reformat [rɪ'fɔːmæt] *vt* (*COMPUT*) riformattare.

Reformation [rɛfə'meɪʃən] n: **the** ~ la Riforma.

reformatory [rɪ'fɔ:mətərɪ] n (US) riformatorio.

reformed [rɪ'fɔ:md] adj cambiato(a) (per il meglio).

reformer [rɪ'fɔ:mə*] n riformatore/trice.

refrain [rɪ'freɪn] vi: **to** ~ **from doing** trattenersi dal fare ♦ n ritornello.

refresh [rɪ'frɛʃ] vt rinfrescare; (subj: food, sleep) ristorare.

refresher course [rɪ'frɛʃə-] n (BRIT) corso di aggiornamento.

refreshing [rɪ'frɛʃɪŋ] adj (drink) rinfrescante; (sleep) riposante, ristoratore(trice); (change etc) piacevole; (idea, point of view) originale.

refreshment [rɪ'frɛʃmənt] n (eating, resting etc) ristoro; ~(s) rinfreschi mpl.

refrigeration [rɪfrɪdʒə'reɪʃən] n refrigerazione f.

refrigerator [rɪ'frɪdʒəreɪtə*] n frigorifero.

refuel [ri:'fjuəl] vt rifornire (di carburante) ♦ vi far rifornimento (di carburante).

refuge ['rɛfju:dʒ] n rifugio; **to take** ~ **in** rifugiarsi in.

refugee [rɛfju'dʒi:] n rifugiato/a, profugo/a.

refugee camp n campo (di) profughi.

refund n ['ri:fʌnd] rimborso ♦ vt [rɪ'fʌnd] rimborsare.

refurbish [ri:'fə:bɪʃ] vt rimettere a nuovo.

refurnish [ri:'fə:nɪʃ] vt ammobiliare di nuovo.

refusal [rɪ'fju:zəl] n rifiuto; **to have first** ~ **on sth** avere il diritto d'opzione su qc.

refuse n ['rɛfju:s] rifiuti mpl ♦ vt, vi [rɪ'fju:z] rifiutare; **to** ~ **to do sth** rifiutare or rifiutarsi di fare qc.

refuse collection n raccolta di rifiuti.

refuse disposal n sistema m di scarico dei rifiuti.

refusenik [rɪ'fju:znɪk] n ebreo a cui il governo sovietico impediva di lasciare il paese.

refute [rɪ'fju:t] vt confutare.

regain [rɪ'geɪn] vt riguadagnare; riacquistare, ricuperare.

regal ['ri:gl] adj regale.

regale [rɪ'geɪl] vt: **to** ~ **sb with sth** intrattenere qn con qc.

regalia [rɪ'geɪlɪə] n insegne fpl reali.

regard [rɪ'gɑ:d] n riguardo, stima ♦ vt considerare, stimare; **to give one's** ~**s** porgere i suoi saluti a; **(kind)** ~**s** cordiali saluti; **as** ~**s**, **with** ~ **to** riguardo a.

regarding [rɪ'gɑ:dɪŋ] prep riguardo a, per quanto riguarda.

regardless [rɪ'gɑ:dlɪs] adv lo stesso; ~ **of** a

dispetto di, nonostante.

regatta [rɪ'gætə] n regata.

regency ['ri:dʒənsɪ] n reggenza.

regenerate [rɪ'dʒɛnəreɪt] vt rigenerare; (feelings, enthusiasm) far rinascere ♦ vi rigenerarsi; rinascere.

regent ['ri:dʒənt] n reggente m.

reggae ['rɛgeɪ] n reggae m.

régime [reɪ'ʒi:m] n regime m.

regiment n ['rɛdʒɪmənt] reggimento ♦ vt ['rɛdʒɪmɛnt] irreggimentare.

regimental [rɛdʒɪ'mɛntl] adj reggimentale.

regimentation [rɛdʒɪmɛn'teɪʃən] n irreggimentazione f.

region ['ri:dʒən] n regione f; **in the** ~ **of** (fig) all'incirca di.

regional ['ri:dʒənl] adj regionale.

regional development n sviluppo regionale.

register ['rɛdʒɪstə*] n registro; (also: **electoral** ~) lista elettorale ♦ vt registrare; (vehicle) immatricolare; (luggage) spedire assicurato(a); (letter) assicurare; (subj: instrument) segnare ♦ vi iscriversi; (at hotel) firmare il registro; (make impression) entrare in testa; **to** ~ **a protest** fare un esposto; **to** ~ **for a course** iscriversi a un corso.

registered ['rɛdʒɪstəd] adj (design) depositato(a); (BRIT: letter) assicurato(a); (student, voter) iscritto(a).

registered company n società iscritta al registro.

registered nurse n (US) infermiere(a) diplomato(a).

registered office n sede f legale.

registered trademark n marchio depositato.

registrar ['rɛdʒɪstrɑ:*] n ufficiale m di stato civile; segretario.

registration [rɛdʒɪs'treɪʃən] n (act) registrazione f; iscrizione f; (AUT: also: ~ **number**) numero di targa.

registry ['rɛdʒɪstrɪ] n ufficio del registro.

registry office n (BRIT) anagrafe f; **to get married in a** ~ ≈ sposarsi in municipio.

regret [rɪ'grɛt] n rimpianto, rincrescimento ♦ vt rimpiangere; **I** ~ **that I/he cannot help** mi rincresce di non poter aiutare/ che lui non possa aiutare; **we** ~ **to inform you that** ... siamo spiacenti di informarla che ....

regretfully [rɪ'grɛtfəlɪ] adv con rincrescimento.

regrettable [rɪ'grɛtəbl] adj deplorevole.

regrettably [rɪ'grɛtəblɪ] adv purtroppo, sfortunatamente.

regroup [ri:'gru:p] vt raggruppare ♦ vi

raggrupparsi.

regt *abbr* (= *regiment*) Reg.

regular ['rɛgjulə*] *adj* regolare; (*usual*) abituale, normale; (*listener, reader*) fedele; (*soldier*) dell'esercito regolare; (*COMM*: *size*) normale ♦ *n* (*client etc*) cliente *m/f* abituale.

regularity [rɛgju'lærɪtɪ] *n* regolarità *f inv*.

regularly ['rɛgjuləlɪ] *adv* regolarmente.

regulate ['rɛgjuleɪt] *vt* regolare.

regulation [rɛgju'leɪʃən] *n* (*rule*) regola, regolamento; (*adjustment*) regolazione *f* ♦ *cpd* (*MIL*) di ordinanza.

rehabilitate [riːə'bɪlɪteɪt] *vt* (*criminal, drug addict, invalid*) ricuperare, reinserire.

rehabilitation ['riːəbɪlɪ'teɪʃən] *n* (*see vb*) ricupero, reinserimento.

rehash [riː'hæʃ] *vt* (*col*) rimaneggiare.

rehearsal [rɪ'həːsəl] *n* prova; **dress** ~ prova generale.

rehearse [rɪ'həːs] *vt* provare.

rehouse [riː'hauz] *vt* rialloggiare.

reign [reɪn] *n* regno ♦ *vi* regnare.

reigning ['reɪnɪŋ] *adj* (*monarch*) regnante; (*champion*) attuale.

reimburse [riːɪm'bəːs] *vt* rimborsare.

rein [reɪn] *n* (*for horse*) briglia; **to give sb free** ~ (*fig*) lasciare completa libertà a qn.

reincarnation [riːɪnkɑː'neɪʃən] *n* reincarnazione *f*.

reindeer ['reɪndɪə*] *n* (*pl inv*) renna.

reinforce [riːɪn'fɔːs] *vt* rinforzare.

reinforced concrete [riːɪn'fɔːst-] *n* cemento armato.

reinforcement [riːɪn'fɔːsmənt] *n* (*action*) rinforzamento; ~**s** *npl* (*MIL*) rinforzi *mpl*.

reinstate [riːɪn'steɪt] *vt* reintegrare.

reinstatement [riːɪn'steɪtmənt] *n* reintegrazione *f*.

reissue [riː'ɪʃjuː] *vt* (*book*) ristampare, ripubblicare; (*film*) distribuire di nuovo.

reiterate [riː'ɪtəreɪt] *vt* reiterare, ripetere.

reject *n* ['riːdʒɛkt] (*COMM*) scarto ♦ *vt* [rɪ'dʒɛkt] rifiutare, respingere; (*COMM*: *goods*) scartare.

rejection [rɪ'dʒɛkʃən] *n* rifiuto.

rejoice [rɪ'dʒɔɪs] *vi*: **to** ~ **(at** *or* **over)** provare diletto (in).

rejoinder [rɪ'dʒɔɪndə*] *n* (*retort*) replica.

rejuvenate [rɪ'dʒuːvəneɪt] *vt* ringiovanire.

rekindle [riː'kɪndl] *vt* riaccendere.

relapse [rɪ'læps] *n* (*MED*) ricaduta.

relate [rɪ'leɪt] *vt* (*tell*) raccontare; (*connect*) collegare ♦ *vi*: **to** ~ **to** (*refer to*) riferirsi a; (*get on with*) stabilire un rapporto con.

related [rɪ'leɪtɪd] *adj* imparentato(a); collegato(a), connesso(a); ~ **to** imparentato(a) con; collegato(a) *or* connesso(a) con.

relating [rɪ'leɪtɪŋ]: ~ **to** *prep* che riguarda, rispetto a.

relation [rɪ'leɪʃən] *n* (*person*) parente *m/f*; (*link*) rapporto, relazione *f*; **in** ~ **to** con riferimento a; **diplomatic/international** ~**s** rapporti diplomatici/internazionali; **bear a** ~ **to** corrispondere a.

relationship [rɪ'leɪʃənʃɪp] *n* rapporto; (*personal ties*) rapporti *mpl*, relazioni *fpl*; (*also*: **family** ~) legami *mpl* di parentela; (*affair*) relazione *f*; **they have a good** ~ vanno molto d'accordo.

relative ['rɛlətɪv] *n* parente *m/f* ♦ *adj* relativo(a); (*respective*) rispettivo(a).

relatively ['rɛlətɪvlɪ] *adv* relativamente; (*fairly, rather*) abbastanza.

relax [rɪ'læks] *vi* rilasciarsi; (*person: unwind*) rilassarsi ♦ *vt* rilasciare; (*mind, person*) rilassare; ~! (*calm down*) calma!

relaxation [riːlæk'seɪʃən] *n* rilasciamento; rilassamento; (*entertainment*) ricreazione *f*, svago.

relaxed [rɪ'lækst] *adj* rilasciato(a); rilassato(a).

relaxing [rɪ'læksɪŋ] *adj* rilassante.

relay ['riːleɪ] *n* (*SPORT*) corsa a staffetta ♦ *vt* (*message*) trasmettere.

release [rɪ'liːs] *n* (*from prison*) rilascio; (*from obligation*) liberazione *f*; (*of gas etc*) emissione *f*; (*of film etc*) distribuzione *f*; (*record*) disco; (*device*) disinnesto ♦ *vt* (*prisoner*) rilasciare; (*from obligation, wreckage etc*) liberare; (*book, film*) fare uscire; (*news*) rendere pubblico(a); (*gas etc*) emettere; (*TECH: catch, spring etc*) disinnestare; (*let go*) rilasciare; lasciar andare; sciogliere; **to** ~ **one's grip** mollare la presa; **to** ~ **the clutch** (*AUT*) staccare la frizione.

relegate ['rɛləgeɪt] *vt* relegare; (*SPORT*): **to be** ~**d** essere retrocesso(a).

relent [rɪ'lɛnt] *vi* cedere.

relentless [rɪ'lɛntlɪs] *adj* implacabile.

relevance ['rɛləvəns] *n* pertinenza; ~ **of sth to sth** rapporto tra qc e qc.

relevant ['rɛləvənt] *adj* pertinente; (*chapter*) in questione; ~ **to** pertinente a.

reliability [rɪlaɪə'bɪlɪtɪ] *n* (*of person*) serietà; (*of machine*) affidabilità.

reliable [rɪ'laɪəbl] *adj* (*person, firm*) fidato(a), che dà affidamento; (*method*) sicuro(a); (*machine*) affidabile.

reliably [rɪ'laɪəblɪ] *adv*: **to be** ~ **informed** sapere da fonti sicure.

reliance [rɪ'laɪəns] *n*: ~ **(on)** dipendenza (da).

reliant [rɪ'laɪənt] *adj*: **to be ~ on sth/sb** dipendere da qc/qn.

relic ['rɛlɪk] *n* (*REL*) reliquia; (*of the past*) resto.

relief [rɪ'liːf] *n* (*from pain, anxiety*) sollievo; (*help, supplies*) soccorsi *mpl*; (*of guard*) cambio; (*ART, GEO*) rilievo; **by way of light ~** come diversivo.

relief map *n* carta in rilievo.

relief road *n* (*BRIT*) circonvallazione *f*.

relieve [rɪ'liːv] *vt* (*pain, patient*) sollevare; (*bring help*) soccorrere; (*take over from*: *gen*) sostituire; (: *guard*) rilevare; **to ~ sb of sth** (*load*) alleggerire qn di qc; **to ~ sb of his command** (*MIL*) esonerare qn dal comando; **to ~ o.s.** (*euphemism*) fare i propri bisogni.

relieved [rɪ'liːvd] *adj* sollevato(a); **to be ~ that ...** essere sollevato(a) (dal fatto) che ...; **I'm ~ to hear it** mi hai tolto un peso con questa notizia.

religion [rɪ'lɪdʒən] *n* religione *f*.

religious [rɪ'lɪdʒəs] *adj* religioso(a).

religious education *n* religione *f*.

relinquish [rɪ'lɪŋkwɪʃ] *vt* abbandonare; (*plan, habit*) rinunziare a.

relish ['rɛlɪʃ] *n* (*CULIN*) condimento; (*enjoyment*) gran piacere *m* ♦ *vt* (*food etc*) godere; **to ~ doing** adorare fare.

relive [riː'lɪv] *vt* rivivere.

reload [riː'ləud] *vt* ricaricare.

relocate [riːləu'keɪt] *vt* (*business*) trasferire ♦ *vi*: **to ~ in** trasferire la propria sede a.

reluctance [rɪ'lʌktəns] *n* riluttanza.

reluctant [rɪ'lʌktənt] *adj* riluttante, mal disposto(a); **to be ~ to do sth** essere restio a fare qc.

reluctantly [rɪ'lʌktəntlɪ] *adv* di mala voglia, a malincuore.

rely [rɪ'laɪ]: **to ~ on** *vt fus* contare su; (*be dependent*) dipendere da.

remain [rɪ'meɪn] *vi* restare, rimanere; **to ~ silent** restare in silenzio; **I ~, yours faithfully** (*BRIT*: *in letters*) distinti saluti.

remainder [rɪ'meɪndə*] *n* resto; (*COMM*) rimanenza.

remaining [rɪ'meɪnɪŋ] *adj* che rimane.

remains [rɪ'meɪnz] *npl* resti *mpl*.

remand [rɪ'mɑːnd] *n*: **on ~** in detenzione preventiva ♦ *vt*: **to ~ in custody** rinviare in carcere; trattenere a disposizione della legge.

remand home *n* (*BRIT*) riformatorio, casa di correzione.

remark [rɪ'mɑːk] *n* osservazione *f* ♦ *vt* osservare, dire; (*notice*) notare ♦ *vi*: **to ~ on sth** fare dei commenti su qc.

remarkable [rɪ'mɑːkəbl] *adj* notevole; eccezionale.

remarry [riː'mærɪ] *vi* risposarsi.

remedial [rɪ'miːdɪəl] *adj* (*tuition, classes*) di riparazione.

remedy ['rɛmədɪ] *n*: **~ (for)** rimedio (per) ♦ *vt* rimediare a.

remember [rɪ'mɛmbə*] *vt* ricordare, ricordarsi di; **I ~ seeing it, I ~ having seen it** (mi) ricordo di averlo visto; **she ~ed to do it** si è ricordata di farlo; **~ me to your wife and children!** saluti sua moglie e i bambini da parte mia!

remembrance [rɪ'mɛmbrəns] *n* memoria; ricordo.

Remembrance Sunday *n* (*BRIT*) *see boxed note.*

REMEMBRANCE SUNDAY

Nel Regno Unito, la domenica più vicina all'11 di novembre, data in cui fu firmato l'armistizio con la Germania nel 1918, ricorre il **Remembrance Sunday**, *giorno in cui vengono commemorati i caduti in guerra. In questa occasione molti portano un papavero di carta appuntato al petto in segno di rispetto.*

---

remind [rɪ'maɪnd] *vt*: **to ~ sb of sth** ricordare qc a qn; **to ~ sb to do** ricordare a qn di fare; **that ~s me!** a proposito!

reminder [rɪ'maɪndə*] *n* richiamo; (*note etc*) promemoria *m inv*.

reminisce [rɛmɪ'nɪs] *vi*: **to ~ (about)** abbandonarsi ai ricordi (di).

reminiscences [rɛmɪ'nɪsnsɪz] *npl* reminiscenze *fpl*, memorie *fpl*.

reminiscent [rɛmɪ'nɪsnt] *adj*: **~ of** che fa pensare a, che richiama.

remiss [rɪ'mɪs] *adj* negligente; **it was ~ of me** è stata una negligenza da parte mia.

remission [rɪ'mɪʃən] *n* remissione *f*; (*of fee*) esonero.

remit [rɪ'mɪt] *vt* rimettere.

remittance [rɪ'mɪtəns] *n* rimessa.

remnant ['rɛmnənt] *n* resto, avanzo; **~s** *npl* (*COMM*) scampoli *mpl*; fine *f* serie.

remonstrate ['rɛmənstreɪt] *vi* protestare; **to ~ with sb about sth** fare le proprie rimostranze a qn circa qc.

remorse [rɪ'mɔːs] *n* rimorso.

remorseful [rɪ'mɔːsful] *adj* pieno(a) di rimorsi.

remorseless [rɪ'mɔːslɪs] *adj* spietato(a).

remote [rɪ'məut] *adj* remoto(a), lontano(a); (*person*) distaccato(a); **there is a ~ possibility that ...** c'è una vaga possibilità che ... + *sub*.

remote control *n* telecomando.

remote-controlled [rɪ'məutkən'trəuld] *adj* telecomandato(a).

remotely [rɪ'məutlɪ] *adv* remotamente; (*slightly*) vagamente.

remould ['riːməuld] *n* (*BRIT: tyre*) gomma rivestita.

removable [rɪ'muːvəbl] *adj* (*detachable*) staccabile.

removal [rɪ'muːvəl] *n* (*taking away*) rimozione *f*; soppressione *f*; (*from house*) trasloco; (*from office: sacking*) destituzione *f*; (*MED*) ablazione *f*.

removal man *n* (*BRIT*) addetto ai traslochi.

removal van *n* (*BRIT*) furgone *m* per traslochi.

remove [rɪ'muːv] *vt* togliere, rimuovere; (*employee*) destituire; (*stain*) far sparire; (*doubt, abuse*) sopprimere, eliminare; **first cousin once ~d** cugino di secondo grado.

remover [rɪ'muːvə*] *n* (*for paint*) prodotto sverniciante; (*for varnish*) solvente *m*; **make-up ~** struccatore *m*.

remunerate [rɪ'mjuːnəreɪt] *vt* rimunerare.

remuneration [rɪmjuːnə'reɪʃən] *n* rimunerazione *f*.

Renaissance [rə'neɪsəns] *n*: **the ~** il Rinascimento.

rename [riː'neɪm] *vt* ribattezzare.

rend, *pt, pp* **rent** [rɛnd, rɛnt] *vt* lacerare.

render ['rɛndə*] *vt* rendere; (*CULIN: fat*) struggere.

rendering ['rɛndərɪŋ] *n* (*MUS etc*) interpretazione *f*.

rendez-vous ['rɔndɪvuː] *n* appuntamento; (*place*) luogo d'incontro; (*meeting*) incontro ♦ *vi* ritrovarsi; (*spaceship*) effettuare un rendez-vous.

rendition [rɛn'dɪʃən] *n* (*MUS*) interpretazione *f*.

renegade ['rɛnɪgeɪd] *n* rinnegato/a.

renew [rɪ'njuː] *vt* rinnovare; (*negotiations*) riprendere.

renewable [rɪ'njuːəbl] *adj* riutilizzabile; **~ energy**, **~s** fonti *mpl* di energia rinnovabile.

renewal [rɪ'njuːəl] *n* rinnovamento; ripresa.

renounce [rɪ'nauns] *vt* rinunziare a; (*disown*) ripudiare.

renovate ['rɛnəveɪt] *vt* rinnovare; (*art work*) restaurare.

renovation [rɛnə'veɪʃən] *n* rinnovamento; restauro.

renown [rɪ'naun] *n* rinomanza.

renowned [rɪ'naund] *adj* rinomato(a).

rent [rɛnt] *pt, pp of* **rend** ♦ *n* affitto ♦ *vt* (*take for rent*) prendere in affitto; (*car, TV*)

noleggiare, prendere a noleggio; (*also: ~ out*) dare in affitto; (*car, TV*) noleggiare, dare a noleggio.

rental ['rɛntl] *n* (*cost: on TV, telephone*) abbonamento; (: *on car*) nolo, noleggio.

rent boy *n* (*BRIT col*) giovane prostituto.

renunciation [rɪnʌnsɪ'eɪʃən] *n* rinnegamento; (*self-denial*) rinunzia.

reopen [riː'əupən] *vt* riaprire.

reopening [riː'əupnɪŋ] *n* riapertura.

reorder [riː'ɔːdə*] *vt* ordinare di nuovo; (*rearrange*) riorganizzare.

reorganize [riː'ɔːgənaɪz] *vt* riorganizzare.

Rep *abbr* (*US POL*) = **representative**; **Republican**.

rep [rɛp] *n abbr* (*COMM*: = *representative*) rappresentante *m/f*; (*THEAT*: = *repertory*) teatro di repertorio.

repair [rɪ'pɛə*] *n* riparazione *f* ♦ *vt* riparare; **in good/bad ~** in buona/cattiva condizione; **under ~** in riparazione.

repair kit *n* corredo per riparazioni.

repair man *n* riparatore *m*.

repair shop *n* (*AUT etc*) officina.

repartee [rɛpɑː'tiː] *n* risposta pronta.

repast [rɪ'pɑːst] *n* (*formal*) pranzo.

repatriate [riː'pætrɪeɪt] *vt* rimpatriare.

repay [riː'peɪ] *vt irreg* (*money, creditor*) rimborsare, ripagare; (*sb's efforts*) ricompensare.

repayment [riː'peɪmənt] *n* rimborsamento; ricompensa.

repeal [rɪ'piːl] *n* (*of law*) abrogazione *f*; (*of sentence*) annullamento ♦ *vt* abrogare; annullare.

repeat [rɪ'piːt] *n* (*RADIO, TV*) replica ♦ *vt* ripetere; (*pattern*) riprodurre; (*promise, attack, also COMM: order*) rinnovare ♦ *vi* ripetere.

repeatedly [rɪ'piːtɪdlɪ] *adv* ripetutamente, spesso.

repeat order *n* (*COMM*): **to place a ~ (for)** rinnovare l'ordinazione (di).

repel [rɪ'pɛl] *vt* respingere.

repellent [rɪ'pɛlənt] *adj* repellente ♦ *n*: **insect ~** prodotto *m* anti-insetti *inv*; **moth ~** anti-tarmico.

repent [rɪ'pɛnt] *vi*: **to ~ (of)** pentirsi (di).

repentance [rɪ'pɛntəns] *n* pentimento.

repercussion [riːpə'kʌʃən] *n* (*consequence*) ripercussione *f*.

repertoire ['rɛpətwɑː*] *n* repertorio.

repertory ['rɛpətərɪ] *n* (*also: ~ theatre*) teatro di repertorio.

repertory company *n* compagnia di repertorio.

repetition [rɛpɪ'tɪʃən] *n* ripetizione *f*; (*COMM: of order etc*) rinnovo.

repetitious [rɛpɪ'tɪʃəs] *adj* (*speech*) pieno(a) di ripetizioni.

repetitive [rɪ'pɛtɪtɪv] *adj* (*movement*) che si ripete; (*work*) monotono(a); (*speech*) pieno(a) di ripetizioni.

replace [rɪ'pleɪs] *vt* (*put back*) rimettere a posto; (*take the place of*) sostituire; (*TEL*): "~ **the receiver**" "riattaccare".

replacement [rɪ'pleɪsmənt] *n* rimessa; sostituzione *f*; (*person*) sostituto/a.

replacement part *n* pezzo di ricambio.

replay ['riːpleɪ] *n* (*of match*) partita ripetuta; (*of tape, film*) replay *m inv*.

replenish [rɪ'plɛnɪʃ] *vt* (*glass*) riempire; (*stock etc*) rifornire.

replete [rɪ'pliːt] *adj*: ~ **(with)** ripieno(a) (di); (*well-fed*) sazio(a) (di).

replica ['rɛplɪkə] *n* replica, copia.

reply [rɪ'plaɪ] *n* risposta ♦ *vi* rispondere; **in** ~ in risposta; **there's no** ~ (*TEL*) non risponde (nessuno).

reply coupon *n* buono di risposta.

report [rɪ'pɔːt] *n* rapporto; (*PRESS etc*) cronaca *f*; (*BRIT: also*: **school** ~) pagella ♦ *vt* riportare; (*PRESS etc*) fare una cronaca su; (*bring to notice: occurrence*) segnalare; (: *person*) denunciare ♦ *vi* (*make a report*) fare un rapporto (*or* una cronaca); (*present o.s.*): **to** ~ **(to sb)** presentarsi (a qn); **to** ~ **(on)** fare un rapporto (su); **it is** ~**ed that** si dice che; **it is** ~**ed from Berlin that** ... ci è stato riferito da Berlino che ....

report card *n* (*US, Scottish*) pagella.

reportedly [rɪ'pɔːtɪdlɪ] *adv*: **she is** ~ **living in Spain** si dice che vive in Spagna.

reported speech [rɪ'pɔːtɪd-] *n* (*LING*) discorso indiretto.

reporter [rɪ'pɔːtə*] *n* (*PRESS*) cronista *m/f*, reporter *m inv*; (*RADIO*) radiocronista *m/f*; (*TV*) telecronista *m/f*.

repose [rɪ'pəuz] *n*: **in** ~ in riposo.

repossess [riːpə'zɛs] *vt* rientrare in possesso di.

repossession order [riːpə'zɛʃən-] *n* ordine *m* di espropriazione.

reprehensible [rɛprɪ'hɛnsɪbl] *adj* riprensibile.

represent [rɛprɪ'zɛnt] *vt* rappresentare.

representation [rɛprɪzɛn'teɪʃən] *n* rappresentazione *f*; ~**s** *npl* (*protest*) protesta.

representative [rɛprɪ'zɛntətɪv] *n* rappresentativo/a; (*COMM*) rappresentante *m* (di commercio); (*US: POL*) deputato/a ♦ *adj*: ~ **(of)** rappresentativo(a) (di).

repress [rɪ'prɛs] *vt* reprimere.

repression [rɪ'prɛʃən] *n* repressione *f*.

repressive [rɪ'prɛsɪv] *adj* repressivo(a).

reprieve [rɪ'priːv] *n* (*LAW*) sospensione *f* dell'esecuzione della condanna; (*fig*) dilazione *f* ♦ *vt* sospendere l'esecuzione della condanna a; accordare una dilazione a.

reprimand ['rɛprɪmɑːnd] *n* rimprovero ♦ *vt* rimproverare, redarguire.

reprint ['riːprɪnt] *n* ristampa ♦ *vt* ristampare.

reprisal [rɪ'praɪzl] *n* rappresaglia; **to take** ~**s** fare delle rappresaglie.

reproach [rɪ'prəutʃ] *n* rimprovero ♦ *vt*: **to** ~ **sb with sth** rimproverare qn di qc; **beyond** ~ irreprensibile.

reproachful [rɪ'prəutʃful] *adj* di rimprovero.

reproduce [riːprə'djuːs] *vt* riprodurre ♦ *vi* riprodursi.

reproduction [riːprə'dʌkʃən] *n* riproduzione *f*.

reproductive [riːprə'dʌktɪv] *adj* riproduttore(trice); riproduttivo(a).

reproof [rɪ'pruːf] *n* riprovazione *f*.

reprove [rɪ'pruːv] *vt* (*action*) disapprovare; (*person*): **to** ~ **(for)** biasimare (per).

reproving [rɪ'pruːvɪŋ] *adj* di disapprovazione.

reptile ['rɛptaɪl] *n* rettile *m*.

Repub. *abbr* (*US POL*) = **Republican**.

republic [rɪ'pʌblɪk] *n* repubblica.

republican [rɪ'pʌblɪkən] *adj, n* repubblicano(a).

repudiate [rɪ'pjuːdɪeɪt] *vt* ripudiare.

repugnant [rɪ'pʌgnənt] *adj* ripugnante.

repulse [rɪ'pʌls] *vt* respingere.

repulsion [rɪ'pʌlʃən] *n* ripulsione *f*.

repulsive [rɪ'pʌlsɪv] *adj* ripugnante, ripulsivo(a).

reputable ['rɛpjutəbl] *adj* di buona reputazione; (*occupation*) rispettabile.

reputation [rɛpju'teɪʃən] *n* reputazione *f*; **he has a** ~ **for being awkward** ha la fama di essere un tipo difficile.

repute [rɪ'pjuːt] *n* reputazione *f*.

reputed [rɪ'pjuːtɪd] *adj* reputato(a); **to be** ~ **to be rich/intelligent** *etc* essere ritenuto(a) ricco(a)/intelligente *etc*.

reputedly [rɪ'pjuːtɪdlɪ] *adv* secondo quanto si dice.

request [rɪ'kwɛst] *n* domanda; (*formal*) richiesta ♦ *vt*: **to** ~ **(of** *or* **from sb)** chiedere (a qn); **at the** ~ **of** su richiesta di; "**you are** ~**ed not to smoke**" "si prega di non fumare".

request stop *n* (*BRIT: for bus*) fermata facoltativa *or* a richiesta.

requiem ['rɛkwɪəm] *n* requiem *m or f inv*.

require [rɪ'kwaɪə*] *vt* (*need*: *subj*: *person*) aver bisogno di; (: *thing, situation*) richiedere; (*want*) volere; esigere; (*order*) obbligare; **to ~ sb to do sth/sth of sb** esigere che qn faccia qc/qc da qn; **what qualifications are ~d?** che requisiti ci vogliono?; **~d by law** prescritto dalla legge; **if ~d** in caso di bisogno.

required [rɪ'kwaɪəd] *adj* richiesto(a).

requirement [rɪ'kwaɪəmənt] *n* (*need*) esigenza; (*condition*) requisito; **to meet sb's ~s** soddisfare le esigenze di qn.

requisite ['rɛkwɪzɪt] *n* cosa necessaria ♦ *adj* necessario(a); **toilet ~s** articoli *mpl* da toletta.

requisition [rɛkwɪ'zɪʃən] *n*: **~ (for)** richiesta (di) ♦ *vt* (*MIL*) requisire.

reroute [ri:'ru:t] *vt* (*train etc*) deviare.

resale ['ri:'seɪl] *n* rivendita.

resale price maintenance (RPM) *n* prezzo minimo di vendita imposto.

rescind [rɪ'sɪnd] *vt* annullare; (*law*) abrogare; (*judgement*) rescindere.

rescue ['rɛskju:] *n* salvataggio; (*help*) soccorso ♦ *vt* salvare; **to come/go to sb's ~** venire/andare in aiuto a *or* di qn.

rescue party *n* squadra di salvataggio.

rescuer ['rɛskjuə*] *n* salvatore/trice.

research [rɪ'sə:tʃ] *n* ricerca, ricerche *fpl* ♦ *vt* fare ricerche su ♦ *vi*: **to ~ (into sth)** fare ricerca (su qc); **a piece of ~** un lavoro di ricerca; **~ and development (R&D)** ricerca e sviluppo.

researcher [rɪ'sə:tʃə*] *n* ricercatore/trice.

research work *n* ricerche *fpl*.

resell [ri:'sɛl] *vt irreg* rivendere.

resemblance [rɪ'zɛmbləns] *n* somiglianza; **to bear a strong ~ to** somigliare moltissimo a.

resemble [rɪ'zɛmbl] *vt* assomigliare a.

resent [rɪ'zɛnt] *vt* risentirsi di.

resentful [rɪ'zɛntful] *adj* pieno(a) di risentimento.

resentment [rɪ'zɛntmənt] *n* risentimento.

reservation [rɛzə'veɪʃən] *n* (*booking*) prenotazione *f*; (*doubt*) dubbio; (*protected area*) riserva; (*BRIT AUT*: *also*: **central ~**) spartitraffico *m inv*; **to make a ~ (in an hotel/a restaurant/on a plane)** prenotare (una camera/una tavola/un posto); **with ~s** (*doubts*) con le dovute riserve.

reservation desk *n* (*US*: *in hotel*) reception *f inv*.

reserve [rɪ'zə:v] *n* riserva ♦ *vt* (*seats etc*) prenotare; **~s** *npl* (*MIL*) riserve *fpl*; **in ~** in serbo.

reserve currency *n* valuta di riserva.

reserved [rɪ'zə:vd] *adj* (*shy*) riservato(a); (*seat*) prenotato(a).

reserve price *n* (*BRIT*) prezzo di riserva, prezzo *m* base *inv*.

reserve team *n* (*BRIT SPORT*) seconda squadra.

reservist [rɪ'zə:vɪst] *n* (*MIL*) riservista *m*.

reservoir ['rɛzəvwɑ:*] *n* serbatoio; (*artificial lake*) bacino idrico.

reset [ri:'sɛt] *vt* (*COMPUT*) azzerare.

reshape [ri:'ʃeɪp] *vt* (*policy*) ristrutturare.

reshuffle [ri:'ʃʌfl] *n*: **Cabinet ~** (*POL*) rimpasto governativo.

reside [rɪ'zaɪd] *vi* risiedere.

residence ['rɛzɪdəns] *n* residenza; **to take up ~** prendere residenza; **in ~** (*queen etc*) in sede; (*doctor*) fisso.

residence permit *n* (*BRIT*) permesso di soggiorno.

resident ['rɛzɪdənt] *n* (*gen, COMPUT*) residente *m/f*; (*in hotel*) cliente *m/f* fisso(a) ♦ *adj* residente.

residential [rɛzɪ'dɛnʃəl] *adj* di residenza; (*area*) residenziale.

residue ['rɛzɪdju:] *n* resto; (*CHEM, PHYSICS*) residuo.

resign [rɪ'zaɪn] *vt* (*one's post*) dimettersi da ♦ *vi*: **to ~ (from)** dimettersi (da), dare le dimissioni (da); **to ~ o.s. to** rassegnarsi a.

resignation [rɛzɪg'neɪʃən] *n* dimissioni *fpl*; rassegnazione *f*; **to tender one's ~** dare le dimissioni.

resilience [rɪ'zɪlɪəns] *n* (*of material*) elasticità, resilienza; (*of person*) capacità di recupero.

resilient [rɪ'zɪlɪənt] *adj* elastico(a); (*person*) che si sa riprende facilmente.

resin ['rɛzɪn] *n* resina.

resist [rɪ'zɪst] *vt* resistere a.

resistance [rɪ'zɪstəns] *n* resistenza.

resistant [rɪ'zɪstənt] *adj*: **~ (to)** resistente (a).

resolute ['rɛzəlu:t] *adj* risoluto(a).

resolution [rɛzə'lu:ʃən] *n* (*resolve*) fermo proposito, risoluzione *f*; (*determination*) risolutezza; (*on screen*) risoluzione *f*; **to make a ~** fare un proposito.

resolve [rɪ'zɔlv] *n* risoluzione *f* ♦ *vi* (*decide*): **to ~ to do** decidere di fare ♦ *vt* (*problem*) risolvere.

resolved [rɪ'zɔlvd] *adj* risoluto(a).

resonance ['rɛzənəns] *n* risonanza.

resonant ['rɛzənənt] *adj* risonante.

resort [rɪ'zɔ:t] *n* (*town*) stazione *f*; (*place*) località *f inv*; (*recourse*) ricorso ♦ *vi*: **to ~ to** far ricorso a; **seaside/winter sports ~** stazione *f* balneare/di sport invernali; **as**

a last ~ come ultima risorsa.

resound [rɪ'zaund] vi: **to ~ (with)** risonare (di).

resounding [rɪ'zaundɪŋ] adj risonante.

resource [rɪ'sɔːs] n risorsa; **~s** npl risorse fpl; **natural ~s** risorse naturali; **to leave sb to his (or her) own ~s** (fig) lasciare che qn si arrangi (per conto suo).

resourceful [rɪ'sɔːsful] adj pieno(a) di risorse, intraprendente.

resourcefulness [rɪ'sɔːsfəlnɪs] n intraprendenza.

respect [rɪs'pɛkt] n rispetto; (point, detail): **in some ~s** sotto certi aspetti ♦ vt rispettare; **~s** npl ossequi mpl; **to have or show ~ for** aver rispetto per; **out of ~ for** per rispetto or riguardo a; **with ~ to** rispetto a, riguardo a; **in ~ of** quanto a; **in this ~** per questo riguardo; **with (all) due ~ I ...** con rispetto parlando, io ....

respectability [rɪspɛktə'bɪlɪtɪ] n rispettabilità.

respectable [rɪs'pɛktəbl] adj rispettabile; (quite big: amount etc) considerevole; (quite good: player, result etc) niente male inv.

respectful [rɪs'pɛktful] adj rispettoso(a).

respective [rɪs'pɛktɪv] adj rispettivo(a).

respectively [rɪs'pɛktɪvlɪ] adv rispettivamente.

respiration [rɛspɪ'reɪʃən] n respirazione f.

respirator ['rɛspɪreɪtə*] n respiratore m.

respiratory ['rɛspərətərɪ] adj respiratorio(a).

respite ['rɛspaɪt] n respiro, tregua.

resplendent [rɪs'plɛndənt] adj risplendente.

respond [rɪs'pɔnd] vi rispondere.

respondent [rɪs'pɔndənt] n (LAW) convenuto/a.

response [rɪs'pɔns] n risposta; **in ~ to** in risposta a.

responsibility [rɪspɔnsɪ'bɪlɪtɪ] n responsabilità f inv; **to take ~ for sth/sb** assumersi or prendersi la responsabilità di qc/per qn.

responsible [rɪs'pɔnsɪbl] adj (liable): **~ (for)** responsabile (di); (trustworthy) fidato(a); (job) di (grande) responsabilità; **to be ~ to sb (for sth)** dover rispondere a qn (di qc).

responsibly [rɪs'pɔnsəblɪ] adv responsabilmente.

responsive [rɪs'pɔnsɪv] adj che reagisce.

rest [rɛst] n riposo; (stop) sosta, pausa; (MUS) pausa; (support) appoggio, sostegno; (remainder) resto, avanzi mpl ♦ vi riposarsi; (remain) rimanere, restare; (be supported): **to ~ on** appoggiarsi su ♦ vt

(lean): **to ~ sth on/against** appoggiare qc su/contro; **to set sb's mind at ~** tranquillizzare qn; **the ~ of them** gli altri; **to ~ one's eyes** or **gaze on** posare lo sguardo su; **~ assured that ...** stia tranquillo che ...; **it ~s with him to decide** sta a lui decidere.

restart [riː'stɑːt] vt (engine) rimettere in marcia; (work) ricominciare.

restaurant ['rɛstərɔŋ] n ristorante m.

restaurant car n (BRIT) vagone m ristorante.

rest cure n cura del riposo.

restful ['rɛstful] adj riposante.

rest home n casa di riposo.

restitution [rɛstɪ'tjuːʃən] n (act) restituzione f; (reparation) riparazione f.

restive ['rɛstɪv] adj agitato(a), impaziente; (horse) restio(a).

restless ['rɛstlɪs] adj agitato(a), irrequieto(a); **to get ~** spazientirsi.

restlessly ['rɛstlɪslɪ] adv in preda all'agitazione.

restock [riː'stɔk] vt rifornire.

restoration [rɛstə'reɪʃən] n restauro; restituzione f.

restorative [rɪ'stɔrətɪv] adj corroborante, ristorativo(a) ♦ n ricostituente m.

restore [rɪ'stɔː*] vt (building) restaurare; (sth stolen) restituire; (peace, health) ristorare.

restorer [rɪs'tɔːrə*] n (ART etc) restauratore/trice.

restrain [rɪs'treɪn] vt (feeling) contenere, frenare; (person): **to ~ (from doing)** trattenere (dal fare).

restrained [rɪs'treɪnd] adj (style) contenuto(a), sobrio(a); (manner) riservato(a).

restraint [rɪs'treɪnt] n (restriction) limitazione f; (moderation) ritegno; **wage ~** restrizioni fpl salariali.

restrict [rɪs'trɪkt] vt restringere, limitare.

restricted area [rɪs'trɪktɪd-] n (AUT) zona a velocità limitata.

restriction [rɪs'trɪkʃən] n restrizione f, limitazione f.

restrictive [rɪs'trɪktɪv] adj restrittivo(a).

restrictive practices npl (INDUSTRY) pratiche restrittive di produzione.

rest room n (US) toletta.

restructure [riː'strʌktʃə*] vt ristrutturare.

result [rɪ'zʌlt] n risultato ♦ vi: **to ~ in** avere per risultato; **as a ~ (of)** in or di conseguenza (a), in seguito (a); **to ~ (from)** essere una conseguenza (di), essere causato(a) (da).

resultant [rɪ'zʌltənt] adj risultante,

conseguente.

resume [rɪ'zjuːm] *vt, vi* (*work, journey*) riprendere; (*sum up*) riassumere.

résumé ['reɪzjuːmeɪ] *n* riassunto; (*US: curriculum vitae*) curriculum vitae *m inv*.

resumption [rɪ'zʌmpʃən] *n* ripresa.

resurgence [rɪ'səːdʒəns] *n* rinascita.

resurrection [rɛzə'rɛkʃən] *n* risurrezione *f*.

resuscitate [rɪ'sʌsɪteɪt] *vt* (*MED*) risuscitare.

resuscitation [rɪsʌsɪ'teɪʃən] *n* rianimazione *f*.

retail ['riːteɪl] *n* (vendita al) minuto ♦ *cpd* al minuto ♦ *vt* vendere al minuto ♦ *vi*: **to ~ at** essere in vendita al pubblico al prezzo di.

retailer ['riːteɪlə*] *n* commerciante *m/f* al minuto, dettagliante *m/f*.

retail outlet *n* punto di vendita al dettaglio.

retail price *n* prezzo al minuto.

retail price index *n* indice *m* dei prezzi al consumo.

retain [rɪ'teɪn] *vt* (*keep*) tenere, serbare.

retainer [rɪ'teɪnə*] *n* (*servant*) servitore *m*; (*fee*) onorario.

retaliate [rɪ'tælieɪt] *vi*: **to ~ (against)** vendicarsi (di); **to ~ on sb** fare una rappresaglia contro qn.

retaliation [rɪtælɪ'eɪʃən] *n* rappresaglie *fpl*; **in ~ for** per vendicarsi di.

retaliatory [rɪ'tælɪətərɪ] *adj* di rappresaglia, di ritorsione.

retarded [rɪ'tɑːdɪd] *adj* ritardato(a); (*also*: **mentally ~**) tardo(a) (di mente).

retch [rɛtʃ] *vi* aver conati di vomito.

retentive [rɪ'tɛntɪv] *adj* ritentivo(a).

rethink ['riː'θɪŋk] *vt* ripensare.

reticence ['rɛtɪsns] *n* reticenza.

reticent ['rɛtɪsnt] *adj* reticente.

retina ['rɛtɪnə] *n* retina.

retinue ['rɛtɪnjuː] *n* seguito, scorta.

retire [rɪ'taɪə*] *vi* (*give up work*) andare in pensione; (*withdraw*) ritirarsi, andarsene; (*go to bed*) andare a letto, ritirarsi.

retired [rɪ'taɪəd] *adj* (*person*) pensionato(a).

retirement [rɪ'taɪəmənt] *n* pensione *f*.

retirement age *n* età del pensionamento.

retiring [rɪ'taɪərɪŋ] *adj* (*person*) riservato(a); (*departing: chairman*) uscente.

retort [rɪ'tɔːt] *n* (*reply*) rimbecco; (*container*) storta ♦ *vi* rimbeccare.

retrace [riː'treɪs] *vt* ricostruire; **to ~ one's steps** tornare sui propri passi.

retract [rɪ'trækt] *vt* (*statement*) ritrattare; (*claws, undercarriage, aerial*) ritrarre, ritirare ♦ *vi* ritrarsi.

retractable [rɪ'træktəbl] *adj* retrattile.

retrain [riː'treɪn] *vt* (*worker*) riaddestrare.

retraining [rɪ'treɪnɪŋ] *n* riaddestramento.

retread *vt* [riː'trɛd] (*AUT: tyre*) rigenerare ♦ *n* ['riːtrɛd] gomma rigenerata.

retreat [rɪ'triːt] *n* ritirata; (*place*) rifugio ♦ *vi* battere in ritirata; (*flood*) ritirarsi; **to beat a hasty ~** (*fig*) battersela.

retrial [riː'traɪəl] *n* nuovo processo.

retribution [rɛtrɪ'bjuːʃən] *n* castigo.

retrieval [rɪ'triːvəl] *n* ricupero.

retrieve [rɪ'triːv] *vt* (*sth lost*) ricuperare, ritrovare; (*situation, honour*) salvare; (*COMPUT*) ricuperare.

retriever [rɪ'triːvə*] *n* cane *m* da riporto.

retroactive [rɛtrəu'æktɪv] *adj* retroattivo(a).

retrograde ['rɛtrəugreɪd] *adj* retrogrado(a).

retrospect ['rɛtrəspɛkt] *n*: **in ~** guardando indietro.

retrospective [rɛtrə'spɛktɪv] *adj* retrospettivo(a); (*law*) retroattivo(a) ♦ *n* (*ART*) retrospettiva.

return [rɪ'təːn] *n* (*going or coming back*) ritorno; (*of sth stolen etc*) restituzione *f*; (*COMM: from land, shares*) profitto, reddito; (*: of merchandise*) resa; (*report*) rapporto; (*reward*): **in ~ (for)** in cambio (di) ♦ *cpd* (*journey, match*) di ritorno; (*BRIT: ticket*) di andata e ritorno ♦ *vi* tornare, ritornare ♦ *vt* rendere, restituire; (*bring back*) riportare; (*send back*) mandare indietro; (*put back*) rimettere; (*POL: candidate*) eleggere; **~s** *npl* (*COMM*) incassi *mpl*; profitti *mpl*; **by ~ of post** a stretto giro di posta; **many happy ~s (of the day)!** auguri!, buon compleanno!

returnable [rɪ'təːnəbl] *adj*: **~ bottle** vuoto a rendere.

returner [rɪ'təːnə*] *n* donna che ritorna al lavoro dopo la maternità.

returning officer [rɪ'təːnɪŋ-] *n* (*BRIT POL*) funzionario addetto all'organizzazione delle elezioni in un distretto.

return key *n* (*COMPUT*) tasto di ritorno.

reunion [riː'juːnɪən] *n* riunione *f*.

reunite [riːjuː'naɪt] *vt* riunire.

rev [rɛv] *n abbr* (= *revolution: AUT*) giro ♦ *vb* (*also*: **~ up**) *vt* imballare ♦ *vi* imballarsi.

revaluation [riːvælju'eɪʃən] *n* rivalutazione *f*.

revamp ['riː'væmp] *vt* rinnovare; riorganizzare.

rev counter *n* contagiri *m inv*.

Rev(d). *abbr* = **reverend**.

reveal [rɪ'viːl] *vt* (*make known*) rivelare, svelare; (*display*) rivelare, mostrare.

revealing [rɪ'viːlɪŋ] *adj* rivelatore(trice); (*dress*) scollato(a).

reveille [rɪ'væli] n (MIL) sveglia.
revel ['rɛvl] vi: **to ~ in sth/in doing** dilettarsi di qc/a fare.
revelation [rɛvə'leɪʃən] n rivelazione f.
reveller ['rɛvlə*] n festaiolo/a.
revelry ['rɛvlrɪ] n baldoria.
revenge [rɪ'vɛndʒ] n vendetta; (in game etc) rivincita ♦ vt vendicare; **to take ~** vendicarsi; **to get one's ~ (for sth)** vendicarsi (di qc).
revengeful [rɪ'vɛndʒful] adj vendicatore(trice); vendicativo(a).
revenue ['rɛvənjuː] n reddito.
reverberate [rɪ'vəːbəreɪt] vi (sound) rimbombare; (light) riverberarsi.
reverberation [rɪvəːbə'reɪʃən] n (of light, sound) riverberazione f.
revere [rɪ'vɪə*] vt venerare.
reverence ['rɛvərəns] n venerazione f, riverenza.
Reverend ['rɛvərənd] adj (in titles) reverendo(a).
reverent ['rɛvərənt] adj riverente.
reverie ['rɛvərɪ] n fantasticheria.
reversal [rɪ'vəːsl] n capovolgimento.
reverse [rɪ'vəːs] n contrario, opposto; (back) rovescio; (AUT: also: ~ **gear**) marcia indietro ♦ adj (order) inverso(a); (direction) opposto(a) ♦ vt (turn) invertire, rivoltare; (change) capovolgere, rovesciare; (LAW: judgement) cassare ♦ vi (BRIT AUT) fare marcia indietro; **in ~ order** in ordine inverso; **to go into ~** fare marcia indietro.
reverse-charge call n (BRIT TEL) telefonata con addebito al ricevente.
reverse video n reverse video m.
reversible [rɪ'vəːsəbl] adj (garment) double-face inv; (procedure) reversibile.
reversing lights [rɪ'vəːsɪŋ-] npl (BRIT AUT) luci fpl per la retromarcia.
reversion [rɪ'vəːʃən] n ritorno.
revert [rɪ'vəːt] vi: **to ~ to** tornare a.
review [rɪ'vjuː] n rivista; (of book, film) recensione f ♦ vt passare in rivista; fare la recensione di; **to come under ~** essere preso in esame.
reviewer [rɪ'vjuːə*] n recensore/a.
revile [rɪ'vaɪl] vt insultare.
revise [rɪ'vaɪz] vt (manuscript) rivedere, correggere; (opinion) emendare, modificare; (study: subject, notes) ripassare; **~d edition** edizione riveduta.
revision [rɪ'vɪʒən] n revisione f; ripasso; (revised version) versione f riveduta e corretta.
revitalize [riː'vaɪtəlaɪz] vt ravvivare.
revival [rɪ'vaɪvəl] n ripresa; ristabilimento;

(of faith) risveglio.
revive [rɪ'vaɪv] vt (person) rianimare; (custom) far rivivere; (hope, courage) ravvivare; (play, fashion) riesumare ♦ vi (person) rianimarsi; (hope) ravvivarsi; (activity) riprendersi.
revoke [rɪ'vəuk] vt revocare; (promise, decision) rinvenire su.
revolt [rɪ'vəult] n rivolta, ribellione f ♦ vi rivoltarsi, ribellarsi; **to ~ (against sb/sth)** ribellarsi a (qn/qc).
revolting [rɪ'vəultɪŋ] adj ripugnante.
revolution [rɛvə'luːʃən] n rivoluzione f; (of wheel etc) rivoluzione, giro.
revolutionary [rɛvə'luːʃənrɪ] adj, n rivoluzionario(a).
revolutionize [rɛvə'luːʃənaɪz] vt rivoluzionare.
revolve [rɪ'vɔlv] vi girare.
revolver [rɪ'vɔlvə*] n rivoltella.
revolving [rɪ'vɔlvɪŋ] adj girevole.
revolving door n porta girevole.
revue [rɪ'vjuː] n (THEAT) rivista.
revulsion [rɪ'vʌlʃən] n ripugnanza.
reward [rɪ'wɔːd] n ricompensa, premio ♦ vt: **to ~ (for)** ricompensare (per).
rewarding [rɪ'wɔːdɪŋ] adj (fig) soddisfacente; **financially ~** conveniente dal punto di vista economico.
rewind [riː'waɪnd] vt irreg (watch) ricaricare; (ribbon etc) riavvolgere.
rewire [riː'waɪə*] vt (house) rifare l'impianto elettrico di.
reword [riː'wəːd] vt formulare or esprimere con altre parole.
rewritable [riː'raɪtəbl] adj riscrivibile.
rewrite [riː'raɪt] vt irreg riscrivere.
Reykjavik ['reɪkjaviːk] n Reykjavik f.
RFD abbr (US POST) = rural free delivery.
RGN n abbr (BRIT: = Registered General Nurse) infermiera diplomata (dopo corso triennale).
Rh abbr (= rhesus) Rh.
rhapsody ['ræpsədɪ] n (MUS) rapsodia; (fig) elogio stravagante.
rhesus negative ['riːsəs-] adj (MED) Rh-negativo(a).
rhesus positive adj (MED) Rh-positivo(a).
rhetoric ['rɛtərɪk] n retorica.
rhetorical [rɪ'tɔrɪkl] adj retorico(a).
rheumatic [ruː'mætɪk] adj reumatico(a).
rheumatism ['ruːmətɪzəm] n reumatismo.
rheumatoid arthritis ['ruːmətɔɪd-] n artrite f reumatoide.
Rhine [raɪn] n: **the ~** il Reno.
rhinestone ['raɪnstəun] n diamante m falso.
rhinoceros [raɪ'nɔsərəs] n rinoceronte m.
Rhodes [rəudz] n Rodi f.

Rhodesia [rəu'diːʒə] *n* Rhodesia.
Rhodesian [rəu'diːʒən] *adj, n* Rhodesiano(a).
rhododendron [rəudə'dɛndrn] *n* rododendro.
Rhone [rəun] *n*: **the** ~ il Rodano.
rhubarb ['ruːbɑːb] *n* rabarbaro.
rhyme [raɪm] *n* rima; (*verse*) poesia ♦ *vi*: **to** ~ **(with)** fare rima (con); **without** ~ **or reason** senza capo né coda.
rhythm ['rɪðm] *n* ritmo.
rhythmic(al) ['rɪðmɪk(əl)] *adj* ritmico(a).
rhythmically ['rɪðmɪkəlɪ] *adv* con ritmo.
rhythm method *n* metodo Ogino-Knauss.
RI *abbr* (*US POST*) = *Rhode Island* ♦ *n abbr* (*BRIT*) = *religious instruction*.
rib [rɪb] *n* (*ANAT*) costola ♦ *vt* (*tease*) punzecchiare.
ribald ['rɪbəld] *adj* licenzioso(a), volgare.
ribbed [rɪbd] *adj* (*knitting*) a coste.
ribbon ['rɪbən] *n* nastro; **in** ~**s** (*torn*) a brandelli.
rice [raɪs] *n* riso.
ricefield ['raɪsfiːld] *n* risaia.
rice pudding *n* budino di riso.
rich [rɪtʃ] *adj* ricco(a); (*clothes*) sontuoso(a); **the** ~ *npl* i ricchi; ~**es** *npl* ricchezze *fpl*; **to be** ~ **in sth** essere ricco di qc.
richly ['rɪtʃlɪ] *adv* riccamente; (*dressed*) sontuosamente; (*deserved*) pienamente.
rickets ['rɪkɪts] *n* rachitismo.
rickety ['rɪkɪtɪ] *adj* zoppicante.
rickshaw ['rɪkʃɔː] *n* risciò *m inv*.
ricochet ['rɪkəʃeɪ] *n* rimbalzo ♦ *vi* rimbalzare.
rid, *pt, pp* **rid** [rɪd] *vt*: **to** ~ **sb of** sbarazzare *or* liberare qn di; **to get** ~ **of** sbarazzarsi di.
riddance ['rɪdns] *n*: **good** ~! che liberazione!
ridden ['rɪdn] *pp of* **ride**.
riddle ['rɪdl] *n* (*puzzle*) indovinello ♦ *vt*: **to be** ~**d with** essere crivellato(a) di.
ride [raɪd] *n* (*on horse*) cavalcata; (*outing*) passeggiata; (*distance covered*) cavalcata; corsa ♦ *vb* (*pt* **rode**, *pp* **ridden** [rəud, 'rɪdn]) *vi* (*as sport*) cavalcare; (*go somewhere*: *on horse, bicycle*) andare (a cavallo or in bicicletta *etc*); (*journey*: *on bicycle, motorcycle, bus*) andare, viaggiare ♦ *vt* (*a horse*) montare, cavalcare; **to go for a** ~ andare a fare una cavalcata; andare a fare un giro; **can you** ~ **a bike?** sai andare in bicicletta?; **we rode all day/all the way** abbiamo cavalcato tutto il giorno/per tutto il tragitto; **to** ~ **a horse/ bicycle/camel** montare a cavallo/in bicicletta/in groppa a un cammello; **to** ~

at anchor (*NAUT*) essere alla fonda; **horse** ~ cavalcata; **car** ~ passeggiata in macchina; **to take sb for a** ~ (*fig*) prendere in giro qn; fregare qn.
►**ride out** *vt*: **to** ~ **out the storm** (*fig*) mantenersi a galla.
rider ['raɪdə*] *n* cavalcatore/trice; (*jockey*) fantino; (*on bicycle*) ciclista *m/f*; (*on motorcycle*) motociclista *m/f*; (*in document*) clausola addizionale, aggiunta.
ridge [rɪdʒ] *n* (*of hill*) cresta; (*of roof*) colmo; (*of mountain*) giogo; (*on object*) riga (in rilievo).
ridicule ['rɪdɪkjuːl] *n* ridicolo ♦ *vt* mettere in ridicolo; **to hold sb/sth up to** ~ mettere in ridicolo qn/qc.
ridiculous [rɪ'dɪkjuləs] *adj* ridicolo(a).
riding ['raɪdɪŋ] *n* equitazione *f*.
riding school *n* scuola d'equitazione.
rife [raɪf] *adj* diffuso(a); **to be** ~ **with** abbondare di.
riffraff ['rɪfræf] *n* canaglia, gentaglia.
rifle ['raɪfl] *n* carabina ♦ *vt* vuotare.
►**rifle through** *vt fus* frugare.
rifle range *n* campo di tiro; (*at fair*) tiro a segno.
rift [rɪft] *n* fessura, crepatura; (*fig: disagreement*) incrinatura.
rig [rɪg] *n* (*also*: **oil** ~: *on land*) derrick *m inv*; (: *at sea*) piattaforma di trivellazione ♦ *vt* (*election etc*) truccare.
►**rig out** *vt* (*BRIT*) attrezzare; (*pej*) abbigliare, agghindare.
►**rig up** *vt* allestire.
rigging ['rɪgɪŋ] *n* (*NAUT*) attrezzatura.
right [raɪt] *adj* giusto(a); (*suitable*) appropriato(a); (*not left*) destro(a) ♦ *n* (*title, claim*) diritto; (*not left*) destra ♦ *adv* (*answer*) correttamente; (*not on the left*) a destra ♦ *vt* raddrizzare; (*fig*) riparare ♦ *excl* bene!; **the** ~ **time** l'ora esatta; **to be** ~ (*person*) aver ragione; (*answer*) essere giusto(a) *or* corretto(a); **to get sth** ~ far giusto qc; **you did the** ~ **thing** ha fatto bene; **let's get it** ~ **this time!** cerchiamo di farlo bene stavolta!; **to put a mistake** ~ (*BRIT*) correggere un errore; ~ **now** proprio adesso; subito; ~ **away** subito; ~ **before/after** subito prima/dopo; **to go** ~ **to the end of sth** andare fino in fondo a qc; ~ **against the wall** proprio contro il muro; ~ **ahead** sempre diritto; proprio davanti; ~ **in the middle** proprio nel mezzo; **by** ~**s** di diritto; **on the** ~, **to the** ~ a destra; ~ **and wrong** il bene e il male; **to have a** ~ **to sth** aver diritto a qc; **film** ~**s** diritti di riproduzione cinematografica; ~ **of way** diritto di

passaggio; (*AUT*) precedenza.
right angle *n* angolo retto.
right-click ['raɪtklɪk] *vi* (*COMPUT*): **to ~ on** fare clic con il pulsante destro del mouse su.
righteous ['raɪtʃəs] *adj* retto(a), virtuoso(a); (*anger*) giusto(a), giustificato(a).
righteousness ['raɪtʃəsnɪs] *n* rettitudine *f*, virtù *f*.
rightful ['raɪtful] *adj* (*heir*) legittimo(a).
rightfully ['raɪtfəlɪ] *adv* legittimamente.
right-handed [raɪt'hændɪd] *adj* (*person*) che adopera la mano destra.
right-hand man ['raɪthænd-] *n* braccio destro (*fig*).
right-hand side *n* lato destro.
rightly ['raɪtlɪ] *adv* bene, correttamente; (*with reason*) a ragione; **if I remember ~** se mi ricordo bene.
right-minded [raɪt'maɪndɪd] *adj* sensato(a).
rights issue *n* (*STOCK EXCHANGE*) emissione *f* di azioni riservate agli azionisti.
right wing *n* (*MIL*, *SPORT*) ala destra; (*POL*) destra ♦ *adj*: **right-wing** (*POL*) di destra.
right-winger [raɪt'wɪŋə*] *n* (*POL*) uno/a di destra; (*SPORT*) ala destra.
rigid ['rɪdʒɪd] *adj* rigido(a); (*principle*) rigoroso(a).
rigidity [rɪ'dʒɪdɪtɪ] *n* rigidità.
rigidly ['rɪdʒɪdlɪ] *adv* rigidamente.
rigmarole ['rɪgmərəul] *n* tiritera; commedia.
rigor ['rɪgə*] *n* (*US*) = **rigour**.
rigor mortis ['rɪgə'mɔːtɪs] *n* rigidità cadaverica.
rigorous ['rɪgərəs] *adj* rigoroso(a).
rigorously ['rɪgərəslɪ] *adv* rigorosamente.
rigour, (*US*) rigor ['rɪgə*] *n* rigore *m*.
rig-out ['rɪgaut] *n* (*BRIT col*) tenuta.
rile [raɪl] *vt* irritare, seccare.
rim [rɪm] *n* orlo; (*of spectacles*) montatura; (*of wheel*) cerchione *m*.
rimless ['rɪmlɪs] *adj* (*spectacles*) senza montatura.
rimmed [rɪmd] *adj* bordato(a); cerchiato(a).
rind [raɪnd] *n* (*of bacon*) cotenna; (*of lemon etc*) scorza.
ring [rɪŋ] *n* anello; (*also*: **wedding ~**) fede *f*; (*of people, objects*) cerchio; (*of spies*) giro; (*of smoke etc*) spirale *f*; (*arena*) pista, arena; (*for boxing*) ring *m inv*; (*sound of bell*) scampanio; (*telephone call*) colpo di telefono ♦ *vb* (*pt* **rang**, *pp* **rung** [ræŋ, rʌŋ]) *vi* (*person, bell, telephone*) suonare; (*also*: **~ out**: *voice, words*) risuonare; (*TEL*) telefonare ♦ *vt* (*BRIT TEL*: *also*: **~ up**)

telefonare a; **to give sb a ~** (*TEL*) dare un colpo di telefono a qn; **that has the ~ of truth about it** questo ha l'aria d'essere vero; **to ~ the bell** suonare il campanello; **the name doesn't ~ a bell (with me)** questo nome non mi dice niente.
►**ring back** *vt*, *vi* (*BRIT TEL*) richiamare.
►**ring off** *vi* (*BRIT TEL*) mettere giù, riattaccare.
ring binder *n* classificatore *m* a anelli.
ring finger *n* anulare *m*.
ringing ['rɪŋɪŋ] *n* (*of bell*) scampanio; (: *louder*) scampanellata; (*of telephone*) squillo; (*in ears*) fischio, ronzio.
ringing tone *n* (*BRIT TEL*) segnale *m* di libero.
ringleader ['rɪŋliːdə*] *n* (*of gang*) capobanda *m*.
ringlets ['rɪŋlɪts] *npl* boccoli *mpl*.
ring road *n* (*BRIT*) raccordo anulare.
ring tone *n* (*TEL*) suoneria.
rink [rɪŋk] *n* (*also*: **ice ~**) pista di pattinaggio; (*for roller-skating*) pista di pattinaggio (a rotelle).
rinse [rɪns] *n* risciacquatura; (*hair tint*) cachet *m inv* ♦ *vt* sciacquare.
Rio (de Janeiro) ['riːəu(dədʒə'nɪərəu)] *n* Rio de Janeiro *f*.
riot ['raɪət] *n* sommossa, tumulto ♦ *vi* tumultuare; **a ~ of colours** un'orgia di colori; **to run ~** creare disordine.
rioter ['raɪətə*] *n* dimostrante *m/f* (*durante dei disordini*).
riot gear *n*: **in ~** in assetto di guerra.
riotous ['raɪətəs] *adj* tumultuoso(a); che fa crepare dal ridere.
riotously ['raɪətəslɪ] *adv*: **~ funny** che fa crepare dal ridere.
riot police *n* ≈ la Celere.
RIP *abbr* (= *requiescat or requiescant in pace*) R.I.P.
rip [rɪp] *n* strappo ♦ *vt* strappare ♦ *vi* strapparsi.
►**rip up** *vt* stracciare.
ripcord ['rɪpkɔːd] *n* cavo di spiegamento.
ripe [raɪp] *adj* (*fruit*) maturo(a); (*cheese*) stagionato(a).
ripen ['raɪpən] *vt* maturare ♦ *vi* maturarsi; stagionarsi.
ripeness ['raɪpnɪs] *n* maturità.
rip-off ['rɪpɔf] *n* (*col*): **it's a ~!** è un furto!
riposte [rɪ'pɔst] *n* risposta per le rime.
ripple ['rɪpl] *n* increspamento, ondulazione *f*; mormorio ♦ *vi* incresparsi ♦ *vt* increspare.
rise [raɪz] *n* (*slope*) salita, pendio; (*hill*) altura; (*increase*: *in wages*) aumento; (: *in prices, temperature*) rialzo, aumento; (*fig*:

to power etc) ascesa ♦ *vi* (*pt* **rose,** *pp* **risen**
[rəʊz, 'rɪzn]) alzarsi, levarsi; (*prices*)
aumentare; (*waters, river*) crescere; (*sun,
wind*) levarsi; (*also*: ~ **up**: *rebel*) insorgere; ribellarsi; **to give** ~ **to** provocare,
dare origine a; **to** ~ **to the occasion**
dimostrarsi all'altezza della situazione.

rising ['raɪzɪŋ] *adj* (*increasing: number*)
sempre crescente; (*prices*) in aumento;
(*tide*) montante; (*sun, moon*) nascente,
che sorge ♦ *n* (*uprising*) sommossa.

rising damp *n* infiltrazioni *fpl* d'umidità.

rising star *n* (*also fig*) astro nascente.

risk [rɪsk] *n* rischio ♦ *vt* rischiare; **to take** *or*
run the ~ **of doing** correre il rischio di
fare; **at** ~ in pericolo; **at one's own** ~ a
proprio rischio e pericolo; **fire/health** ~
rischio d'incendio/per la salute; **I'll** ~ **it** ci
proverò lo stesso.

risk capital *n* capitale *m* di rischio.

risky ['rɪskɪ] *adj* rischioso(a).

risqué ['riːskeɪ] *adj* (*joke*) spinto(a).

rissole ['rɪsəul] *n* crocchetta.

rite [raɪt] *n* rito; **last** ~**s** l'estrema unzione.

ritual ['rɪtjuəl] *adj, n* rituale (*m*).

rival ['raɪvl] *n* rivale *m/f*; (*in business*)
concorrente *m/f* ♦ *adj* rivale; che fa concorrenza ♦ *vt* essere in concorrenza con;
to ~ **sb/sth in** competere con qn/qc in.

rivalry ['raɪvəlrɪ] *n* rivalità; concorrenza.

river ['rɪvə*] *n* fiume *m* ♦ *cpd* (*port, traffic*)
fluviale; **up/down** ~ a monte/valle.

riverbank ['rɪvəbæŋk] *n* argine *m*.

riverbed ['rɪvəbed] *n* alveo (fluviale).

riverside ['rɪəsaɪd] *n* sponda del fiume.

rivet ['rɪvɪt] *n* ribattino, rivetto ♦ *vt*
ribadire; (*fig*) concentrare, fissare.

riveting ['rɪvɪtɪŋ] *adj* (*fig*) avvincente.

Riviera [rɪvɪ'ɛərə] *n*: **the (French)** ~ la Costa
Azzurra; **the Italian** ~ la Riviera.

Riyadh [rɪ'jɑːd] *n* Riad *f*.

RMT *n abbr* (= *National Union of Rail,
Maritime and Transport Workers*) *sindacato
dei Ferrovieri, Marittimi e Trasportatori.*

RN *n abbr* (*BRIT*) = **Royal Navy;** (*US*)
= **registered nurse.**

RNA *n abbr* (= *ribonucleic acid*) R.N.A. *m.*

RNLI *n abbr* (*BRIT*: = *Royal National Lifeboat
Institution*) *associazione volontaria che
organizza e dispone di scialuppe di
salvataggio.*

RNZAF *n abbr* = *Royal New Zealand Air
Force.*

RNZN *n abbr* = *Royal New Zealand Navy.*

road [rəud] *n* strada; (*small*) cammino; (*in
town*) via; **main** ~ strada principale;
major/minor ~ strada con/senza diritto
di precedenza; **it takes 4 hours by** ~ sono

4 ore di macchina (*or* in camion *etc*); **on
the** ~ **to success** sulla via del successo;
"~ up" (*BRIT*) "attenzione: lavori in corso".

road accident *n* incidente *m* stradale.

roadblock ['rəudblɔk] *n* blocco stradale.

road haulage *n* autotrasporti *mpl.*

roadhog ['rəudhɔg] *n* pirata *m* della strada.

road map *n* carta stradale.

road rage *n* aggressività al volante.

road safety *n* sicurezza sulle strade.

roadside ['rəudsaɪd] *n* margine *m* della
strada; **by the** ~ a lato della strada.

roadsign ['rəudsaɪn] *n* cartello stradale.

roadsweeper ['rəudswiːpə*] *n* (*BRIT*: *person*)
spazzino.

road user *n* utente *m/f* della strada.

roadway ['rəudweɪ] *n* carreggiata.

roadworks ['rəudwəːks] *npl* lavori *mpl*
stradali.

roadworthy ['rəudwəːðɪ] *adj* in buono stato
di marcia.

roam [rəum] *vi* errare, vagabondare ♦ *vt*
vagare per.

roar [rɔː*] *n* ruggito; (*of crowd*) tumulto; (*of
thunder, storm*) muggito ♦ *vi* ruggire;
tumultuare; muggire; **to** ~ **with laughter**
scoppiare dalle risa.

roaring ['rɔːrɪŋ] *adj*: **a** ~ **fire** un bel fuoco;
to do a ~ **trade** fare affari d'oro; **a** ~
success un successo strepitoso.

roast [rəust] *n* arrosto ♦ *vt* (*meat*) arrostire.

roast beef *n* arrosto di manzo.

roasting ['rəustɪŋ] *n* (*col*): **to give sb a** ~
dare una lavata di capo a qn.

rob [rɔb] *vt* (*person*) rubare; (*bank*)
svaligiare; **to** ~ **sb of sth** derubare qn di
qc; (*fig: deprive*) privare qn di qc.

robber ['rɔbə*] *n* ladro; (*armed*) rapinatore *m.*

robbery ['rɔbərɪ] *n* furto, rapina.

robe [rəub] *n* (*for ceremony etc*) abito; (*also*:
bath~) accappatoio ♦ *vt* vestire.

robin ['rɔbɪn] *n* pettirosso.

robot ['rəubɔt] *n* robot *m inv.*

robotics ['rəubɔtɪks] *n* robotica.

robust [rəu'bʌst] *adj* robusto(a); (*material*)
solido(a).

rock [rɔk] *n* (*substance*) roccia; (*boulder*)
masso; roccia; (*in sea*) scoglio; (*BRIT*:
sweet) zucchero candito ♦ *vt* (*swing gently:
cradle*) dondolare; (: *child*) cullare; (*shake*)
scrollare, far tremare ♦ *vi* dondolarsi;
oscillare; **on the** ~**s** (*drink*) col ghiaccio;
(*ship*) sugli scogli; (*marriage etc*) in crisi;
to ~ **the boat** (*fig*) piantare grane.

rock and roll *n* rock and roll *m.*

rock-bottom ['rɔk'bɔtəm] *n* (*fig*) stremo; **to
reach** *or* **touch** ~ (*price*) raggiungere il
livello più basso; (*person*) toccare il

fondo.

rock climber *n* rocciatore/trice, scalatore/trice.

rock climbing *n* roccia.

rockery ['rɔkərɪ] *n* giardino roccioso.

rocket ['rɔkɪt] *n* razzo; (*MIL*) razzo, missile *m* ♦ *vi* (*prices*) salire alle stelle.

rocket launcher [-lɔːntʃə*] *n* lanciarazzi *m inv*.

rock face *n* parete *f* della roccia.

rock fall *n* caduta di massi.

rocking chair ['rɔkɪŋ-] *n* sedia a dondolo.

rocking horse *n* cavallo a dondolo.

rocky ['rɔkɪ] *adj* (*hill*) roccioso(a); (*path*) sassoso(a); (*unsteady: table*) traballante.

Rocky Mountains *npl*: **the ~** le Montagne Rocciose.

rod [rɔd] *n* (*metallic, TECH*) asta; (*wooden*) bacchetta; (*also*: **fishing ~**) canna da pesca.

rode [rəud] *pt of* **ride**.

rodent ['rəudnt] *n* roditore *m*.

rodeo ['rəudɪəu] *n* rodeo.

roe [rəu] *n* (*species: also*: **~ deer**) capriolo; (*of fish: also*: **hard ~**) uova *fpl* di pesce; **soft ~** latte *m* di pesce.

roe deer *n* (*species*) capriolo; (*female deer: pl inv*) capriolo femmina.

rogue [rəug] *n* mascalzone *m*.

roguish ['rəugɪʃ] *adj* birbantesco(a).

role [rəul] *n* ruolo.

role model *n* modello (di comportamento).

role-play ['rəulpleɪ], **role-playing** ['rəulpleɪɪŋ] *n* il recitare un ruolo, role-playing *m inv*.

roll [rəul] *n* rotolo; (*of banknotes*) mazzo; (*also*: **bread ~**) panino; (*register*) lista; (*sound: of drums etc*) rullo; (*movement: of ship*) rullio ♦ *vt* rotolare; (*also*: **~ up**: *string*) aggomitolare; (*also*: **~ out**: *pastry*) stendere ♦ *vi* rotolare; (*wheel*) girare; **cheese ~** panino al formaggio.

▶**roll about, roll around** *vi* rotolare qua e là; (*person*) rotolarsi.

▶**roll by** *vi* (*time*) passare.

▶**roll in** *vi* (*mail, cash*) arrivare a bizzeffe.

▶**roll over** *vi* rivoltarsi.

▶**roll up** *vi* (*col: arrive*) arrivare ♦ *vt* (*carpet, cloth, map*) arrotolare; (*sleeves*) rimboccare; **to ~ o.s. up into a ball** raggomitolarsi.

roll call *n* appello.

rolled gold [rəuld-] *adj* d'oro laminato.

roller ['rəulə*] *n* rullo; (*wheel*) rotella.

rollerblades ['rəuləbleɪdz] *npl* pattini *mpl* in linea.

roller blind *n* (*BRIT*) avvolgibile *m*.

roller coaster *n* montagne *fpl* russe.

roller skates *npl* pattini *mpl* a rotelle.

rollicking ['rɔlɪkɪŋ] *adj* allegro(a) e chiassoso(a).

rolling ['rəulɪŋ] *adj* (*landscape*) ondulato(a).

rolling pin *n* matterello.

rolling stock *n* (*RAIL*) materiale *m* rotabile.

roll-on-roll-off ['rəulɔn'rəulɔf] *adj* (*BRIT: ferry*) roll-on roll-off *inv*.

roly-poly ['rəulɪ'pəulɪ] *n* (*BRIT CULIN*) rotolo di pasta con ripieno di marmellata.

ROM [rɔm] *n abbr* (*COMPUT:* = read-only memory*) ROM *f*.

Roman ['rəumən] *adj*, *n* romano(a).

Roman Catholic *adj*, *n* cattolico(a).

romance [rə'mæns] *n* storia (*or* avventura *or* film *m inv*) romantico(a); (*charm*) poesia; (*love affair*) idillio.

Romanesque [rəumə'nɛsk] *adj* romanico(a).

Romania [rəu'meɪnɪə] *n* Romania.

Romanian [rəu'meɪnɪən] *adj* romeno(a) ♦ *n* romeno/a; (*LING*) romeno.

Roman numeral *n* numero romano.

romantic [rə'mæntɪk] *adj* romantico(a); sentimentale.

romanticism [rə'mæntɪsɪzəm] *n* romanticismo.

Romany ['rɔmənɪ] *adj* zingaresco(a) ♦ *n* (*person*) zingaro/a; (*LING*) lingua degli zingari.

Rome [rəum] *n* Roma.

romp [rɔmp] *n* gioco chiassoso ♦ *vi* (*also*: **~ about**) giocare chiassosamente; **to ~ home** (*horse*) vincere senza difficoltà, stravincere.

rompers ['rɔmpəz] *npl* pagliaccetto.

rondo ['rɔndəu] *n* (*MUS*) rondò *m inv*.

roof [ruːf] *n* tetto; (*of tunnel, cave*) volta ♦ *vt* coprire (con un tetto); **~ of the mouth** palato.

roof garden *n* giardino pensile.

roofing ['ruːfɪŋ] *n* materiale *m* per copertura.

roof rack *n* (*AUT*) portabagagli *m inv*.

rook [ruk] *n* (*bird*) corvo nero; (*CHESS*) torre *f* ♦ *vt* (*cheat*) truffare, spennare.

rookie ['rukɪ] *n* (*col: esp MIL*) pivellino/a.

room [ruːm] *n* (*in house*) stanza, camera; (*in school etc*) sala; (*space*) posto, spazio; **~s** *npl* (*lodging*) alloggio; "**~s to let**", (*US*) "**~s for rent**" "si affittano camere"; **is there ~ for this?** c'è spazio per questo?, ci sta anche questo?; **to make ~ for sb** far posto a qn; **there is ~ for improvement** si potrebbe migliorare.

rooming house ['ruːmɪŋ-] *n* (*US*) *casa in*

cui si affittano camere o appartamentini ammobiliati.

roommate ['ru:mmeɪt] *n* compagno/a di stanza.

room service *n* servizio da camera.

room temperature *n* temperatura ambiente.

roomy ['ru:mɪ] *adj* spazioso(a); (*garment*) ampio(a).

roost [ru:st] *n* appollaiato ♦ *vi* appollaiarsi.

rooster ['ru:stə*] *n* gallo.

root [ru:t] *n* radice *f* ♦ *vt* (*plant, belief*) far radicare; **to take** ~ (*plant*) attecchire, prendere; (*idea*) far presa; **the** ~ **of the problem is that** ... il problema deriva dal fatto che ....

▶**root about** *vi* (*fig*) frugare.

▶**root for** *vt fus* (*col*) fare il tifo per.

▶**root out** *vt* estirpare.

root beer *n* (*US*) bibita dolce a base di estratto di erbe e radici.

rope [rəup] *n* corda, fune *f*; (*NAUT*) cavo ♦ *vt* (*box*) legare; (*climbers*) legare in cordata; **to** ~ **sb in** (*fig*) coinvolgere qn; **to know the** ~**s** (*fig*) conoscere i trucchi del mestiere.

rope ladder *n* scala di corda.

ropey ['rəupɪ] *adj* (*col*) scadente, da quattro soldi; **to feel** ~ (*ill*) sentirsi male.

rosary ['rəuzərɪ] *n* rosario; roseto.

rose [rəuz] *pt of* **rise** ♦ *n* rosa; (*also:* ~ **bush**) rosaio; (*on watering can*) rosetta ♦ *adj* rosa *inv*.

rosé ['rəuzeɪ] *n* vino rosato.

rosebed ['rəuzbɛd] *n* roseto.

rosebud ['rəuzbʌd] *n* bocciolo di rosa.

rosebush ['rəuzbʊʃ] *n* rosaio.

rosemary ['rəuzmərɪ] *n* rosmarino.

rosette [rəu'zɛt] *n* coccarda.

ROSPA ['rɔspə] *n abbr* (*BRIT*: = *Royal Society for the Prevention of Accidents*) ≈ E.N.P.I. *m* (= *Ente Nazionale Prevenzione Infortuni*).

roster ['rɔstə*] *n*: **duty** ~ ruolino di servizio.

rostrum ['rɔstrəm] *n* tribuna.

rosy ['rəuzɪ] *adj* roseo(a).

rot [rɔt] *n* (*decay*) putrefazione *f*; (*col: nonsense*) stupidaggini *fpl* ♦ *vt, vi* imputridire, marcire; **dry/wet** ~ *funghi parassiti del legno*; **to stop the** ~ (*BRIT fig*) salvare la situazione.

rota ['rəutə] *n* tabella dei turni; **on a** ~ **basis** a turno.

rotary ['rəutərɪ] *adj* rotante.

rotate [rəu'teɪt] *vt* (*revolve*) far girare; (*change round: crops*) avvicendare; (*: jobs*) fare a turno ♦ *vi* (*revolve*) girare.

rotating [rəu'teɪtɪŋ] *adj* (*movement*) rotante.

rotation [rəu'teɪʃən] *n* rotazione *f*; **in** ~ a turno, in rotazione.

rote [rəut] *n*: **to learn sth by** ~ imparare qc a memoria.

rotor ['rəutə*] *n* rotore *m*.

rotten ['rɔtn] *adj* (*decayed*) putrido(a), marcio(a); (*: teeth*) cariato(a); (*dishonest*) corrotto(a); (*col: bad*) brutto(a); (*: action*) vigliacco(a); **to feel** ~ (*ill*) sentirsi proprio male.

rotting ['rɔtɪŋ] *adj* in putrefazione.

rotund [rəu'tʌnd] *adj* grassoccio(a); tondo(a).

rouble, (*US*) **ruble** ['ru:bl] *n* rublo.

rouge [ru:ʒ] *n* belletto.

rough [rʌf] *adj* aspro(a); (*person, manner: coarse*) rozzo(a), aspro(a); (*: violent*) brutale; (*district*) malfamato(a); (*weather*) cattivo(a); (*plan*) abbozzato(a); (*guess*) approssimativo(a) ♦ *n* (*GOLF*) macchia; ~ **estimate** approssimazione *f*; **to** ~ **it** far vita dura; **to play** ~ far il gioco pesante; **to sleep** ~ (*BRIT*) dormire all'addiaccio; **to feel** ~ (*BRIT*) sentirsi male; **to have a** ~ **time (of it)** passare un periodaccio; **the sea is** ~ **today** c'è mare grosso oggi.

▶**rough out** *vt* (*draft*) abbozzare.

roughage ['rʌfɪdʒ] *n* alimenti *mpl* ricchi di cellulosa.

rough-and-ready ['rʌfən'rɛdɪ] *adj* rudimentale.

rough-and-tumble ['rʌfən'tʌmbl] *n* zuffa.

roughcast ['rʌfkɑːst] *n* intonaco grezzo.

rough copy, rough draft *n* brutta copia.

roughen ['rʌfn] *vt* (*a surface*) rendere ruvido(a).

rough justice *n* giustizia sommaria.

roughly ['rʌflɪ] *adv* (*handle*) rudemente, brutalmente; (*make*) grossolanamente; (*approximately*) approssimativamente; ~ **speaking** grosso modo, ad occhio e croce.

roughness ['rʌfnɪs] *n* asprezza; rozzezza; brutalità.

roughshod ['rʌfʃɔd] *adv*: **to ride** ~ **over** (*person*) mettere sotto i piedi; (*objection*) passare sopra a.

rough work *n* (*at school etc*) brutta copia.

roulette [ru:'lɛt] *n* roulette *f*.

Roumania *etc* [ru:'meɪnɪə] = **Romania** *etc*.

round [raund] *adj* rotondo(a) ♦ *n* tondo, cerchio; (*BRIT*: *of toast*) fetta; (*duty*: *of policeman, milkman etc*) giro; (*: of doctor*) visite *fpl*; (*game*: *of cards, in competition*) partita; (*BOXING*) round *m inv*; (*of talks*) serie *f inv* ♦ *vt* (*corner*) girare; (*bend*) prendere; (*cape*) doppiare ♦ *prep* intorno a ♦ *adv*: **right** ~, **all** ~ tutt'attorno; **the long way** ~ il giro più lungo; **all the year** ~

tutto l'anno; **in** ~ **figures** in cifra tonda; **it's just** ~ **the corner** (*also fig*) è dietro l'angolo; **to ask sb** ~ invitare qn (a casa propria); **I'll be** ~ **at 6 o'clock** ci sarò alle 6; **to go** ~ fare il giro; **to go** ~ **to sb's (house)** andare da qn; **to go** ~ **an obstacle** aggirare un ostacolo; **go** ~ **the back** passi da dietro; **to go** ~ **a house** visitare una casa; **enough to go** ~ abbastanza per tutti; **she arrived** ~ **(about) noon** è arrivata intorno a mezzogiorno; ~ **the clock** 24 ore su 24; **to go the** ~**s** (*illness*) diffondersi; (*story*) circolare, passare di bocca in bocca; **the daily** ~ (*fig*) la routine quotidiana; ~ **of ammunition** cartuccia; ~ **of applause** applausi *mpl*; ~ **of drinks** giro di bibite; ~ **of sandwiches** (*BRIT*) sandwich *m inv*.

▶**round off** *vt* (*speech etc*) finire.

▶**round up** *vt* radunare; (*criminals*) fare una retata di; (*prices*) arrotondare.

roundabout ['raundəbaut] *n* (*BRIT AUT*) rotatoria; (*at fair*) giostra ♦ *adj* (*route, means*) indiretto(a).

rounded ['raundɪd] *adj* arrotondato(a); (*style*) armonioso(a).

rounders ['raundəz] *npl* (*game*) gioco simile al baseball.

roundly ['raundlɪ] *adv* (*fig*) chiaro e tondo.

round robin *n* (*SPORT*: *also*: ~ **tournament**) ≈ torneo all'italiana.

round-shouldered [raund'ʃəuldəd] *adj* dalle spalle tonde.

round trip *n* (viaggio di) andata e ritorno.

roundup ['raundʌp] *n* raduno; (*of criminals*) retata; **a** ~ **of the latest news** un sommario *or* riepilogo delle ultime notizie.

rouse [rauz] *vt* (*wake up*) svegliare; (*stir up*) destare; provocare; risvegliare.

rousing ['rauzɪŋ] *adj* (*speech, applause*) entusiastico(a).

rout [raut] *n* (*MIL*) rotta ♦ *vt* mettere in rotta.

route [ruːt] *n* itinerario; (*of bus*) percorso; (*of trade, shipping*) rotta; **"all** ~**s"** (*AUT*) "tutte le direzioni"; **the best** ~ **to London** la strada migliore per andare a Londra; **en** ~ **for** in viaggio verso; **en** ~ **from ... to** viaggiando da ... a.

route map *n* (*BRIT*: *for journey*) cartina di itinerario; (*for trains etc*) pianta dei collegamenti.

routine [ruː'tiːn] *adj* (*work*) corrente, abituale; (*procedure*) solito(a) ♦ *n* (*pej*) routine *f*, tran tran *m*; (*THEAT*) numero; (*COMPUT*) sottoprogramma *m*; **daily** ~ orario quotidiano; ~ **procedure**

prassi *f*.

roving ['rəuvɪŋ] *adj* (*life*) itinerante.

roving reporter *n* reporter *m inv* volante.

row[1] [rəu] *n* (*line*) riga, fila; (*KNITTING*) ferro; (*behind one another: of cars, people*) fila ♦ *vi* (*in boat*) remare; (*as sport*) vogare ♦ *vt* (*boat*) manovrare a remi; **in a** ~ (*fig*) di fila.

row[2] [rau] *n* (*noise*) baccano, chiasso; (*dispute*) lite *f* ♦ *vi* litigare; **to make a** ~ far baccano; **to have a** ~ litigare.

rowboat ['rəubəut] *n* (*US*) barca a remi.

rowdiness ['raudɪnɪs] *n* baccano; (*fighting*) zuffa.

rowdy ['raudɪ] *adj* chiassoso(a); turbolento(a) ♦ *n* teppista *m/f*.

rowdyism ['raudɪɪzəm] *n* teppismo.

rowing ['rəuɪŋ] *n* canottaggio.

rowing boat *n* (*BRIT*) barca a remi.

royal ['rɔɪəl] *adj* reale.

Royal Academy *n* (*BRIT*) *see boxed note.*

Royal Air Force (RAF) *n* (*BRIT*) *aeronautica militare britannica.*

royal blue *adj* blu reale *inv*.

royalist ['rɔɪəlɪst] *adj, n* realista (*m/f*).

Royal Navy (RN) *n* (*BRIT*) *marina militare britannica.*

royalty ['rɔɪəltɪ] *n* (*royal persons*) (membri *mpl* della) famiglia reale; (*payment: to author*) diritti *mpl* d'autore; (: *to inventor*) diritti di brevetto.

RP *n abbr* (*BRIT*: = *received pronunciation*) pronuncia standard.

RPI *abbr* (*BRIT*: = *retail price index*) ≈ Indice dei prezzi al consumo.

rpm *abbr* (= *revolutions per minute*) giri/min.

RR *abbr* (*US* = *railroad*) Ferr.

R&R *n abbr* (*US MIL*: = *rest and recreation*) *permesso per militari.*

RRP *n abbr* (*BRIT*) *see* **recommended retail price.**

RSA *n abbr* (*BRIT*) = *Royal Society of Arts*; *Royal Scottish Academy.*

RSI *n abbr* (*MED*: = *repetitive strain injury*) *lesione al braccio tipica di violinisti e terminalisti.*

RSPB *n abbr* (*BRIT*: = *Royal Society for the Protection of Birds*) ≈ L.I.P.U. *f* (= *Lega*

Italiana Protezione Uccelli).
RSPCA *n abbr* (*BRIT*: = *Royal Society for the Prevention of Cruelty to Animals*) ≈ E.N.P.A. *m* (= *Ente Nazionale per la Protezione degli Animali).*
RSVP *abbr* (= *répondez s'il vous plaît*) R.S.V.P.
RTA *n abbr* (= *road traffic accident*) incidente *m* stradale.
Rt Hon. *abbr* (*BRIT*: = *Right Honourable*) ≈ On. (= *Onorevole).*
Rt Rev. *abbr* (= *Right Reverend*) Rev.
rub [rʌb] *n* (*with cloth*) fregata, strofinata; (*on person*) frizione *f*, massaggio ♦ *vt* fregare, strofinare; frizionare; **to ~ sb up** *or* (*US*) ~ **sb the wrong way** lisciare qn contro pelo.
▶**rub down** *vt* (*body*) strofinare, frizionare; (*horse*) strigliare.
▶**rub in** *vt* (*ointment*) far penetrare (massaggiando *or* frizionando).
▶**rub off** *vi* andare via; **to ~ off on** lasciare una traccia su.
▶**rub out** *vt* cancellare ♦ *vi* cancellarsi.
rubber ['rʌbə*] *n* gomma.
rubber band *n* elastico.
rubber bullet *n* pallottola di gomma.
rubber plant *n* ficus *m inv.*
rubber ring *n* (*for swimming*) ciambella.
rubber stamp *n* timbro di gomma.
rubber-stamp [rʌbə'stæmp] *vt* (*fig*) approvare senza discussione.
rubbery ['rʌbərɪ] *adj* gommoso(a).
rubbish ['rʌbɪʃ] *n* (*from household*) immondizie *fpl*, rifiuti *mpl*; (*fig: pej*) cose *fpl* senza valore; robaccia; (*nonsense*) sciocchezze *fpl* ♦ *vt* (*col*) sputtanare.
rubbish bin *n* (*BRIT*) pattumiera.
rubbish dump *n* luogo di scarico.
rubbishy ['rʌbɪʃɪ] *adj* (*BRIT col*) scadente, che non vale niente.
rubble ['rʌbl] *n* macerie *fpl*; (*smaller*) pietrisco.
ruble ['ruːbl] *n* (*US*) = **rouble.**
ruby ['ruːbɪ] *n* rubino.
RUC *n abbr* (*BRIT*: = *Royal Ulster Constabulary*) forza di polizia dell'Irlanda del Nord.
rucksack ['rʌksæk] *n* zaino.
ructions ['rʌkʃənz] *npl* putiferio, finimondo.
rudder ['rʌdə*] *n* timone *m.*
ruddy ['rʌdɪ] *adj* (*face*) fresco(a); (*col: damned*) maledetto(a).
rude [ruːd] *adj* (*impolite: person*) scortese, rozzo(a); (: *word, manners*) grossolano(a), rozzo(a); (*shocking*) indecente; **to be ~ to sb** essere maleducato con qn.
rudely ['ruːdlɪ] *adv* scortesemente;

grossolanamente.
rudeness ['ruːdnɪs] *n* scortesia; grossolanità.
rudiment ['ruːdɪmənt] *n* rudimento.
rudimentary [ruːdɪ'mɛntərɪ] *adj* rudimentale.
rue [ruː] *vt* pentirsi amaramente di.
rueful ['ruːful] *adj* mesto(a), triste.
ruff [rʌf] *n* gorgiera.
ruffian ['rʌfɪən] *n* briccone *m*, furfante *m.*
ruffle ['rʌfl] *vt* (*hair*) scompigliare; (*clothes, water*) increspare; (*fig: person*) turbare.
rug [rʌg] *n* tappeto; (*BRIT: for knees*) coperta.
rugby ['rʌgbɪ] *n* (*also:* ~ **football**) rugby *m.*
rugged ['rʌgɪd] *adj* (*landscape*) aspro(a); (*features, determination*) duro(a); (*character*) brusco(a).
rugger ['rʌgə*] *n* (*col*) rugby *m.*
ruin ['ruːɪn] *n* rovina ♦ *vt* rovinare; (*spoil: clothes*) sciupare; ~**s** *npl* rovine *fpl*, ruderi *mpl*; **in** ~**s** in rovina.
ruination [ruːɪ'neɪʃən] *n* rovina.
ruinous ['ruːɪnəs] *adj* rovinoso(a); (*expenditure*) inverosimile.
rule [ruːl] *n* (*gen*) regola; (*regulation*) regolamento, regola; (*government*) governo; (*dominion etc*): **under British** ~ sotto la sovranità britannica ♦ *vt* (*country*) governare; (*person*) dominare; (*decide*) decidere ♦ *vi* regnare; decidere; (*LAW*) dichiarare; **to ~ against/in favour of/on** (*LAW*) pronunciarsi a sfavore di/in favore di/su; **it's against the** ~**s** è contro le regole *or* il regolamento; **by** ~ **of thumb** a lume di naso; **as a** ~ normalmente, di regola.
▶**rule out** *vt* escludere; **murder cannot be** ~**d out** non si esclude che si tratti di omicidio.
ruled [ruːld] *adj* (*paper*) vergato(a).
ruler ['ruːlə*] *n* (*sovereign*) sovrano/a; (*leader*) capo (dello Stato); (*for measuring*) regolo, riga.
ruling ['ruːlɪŋ] *adj* (*party*) al potere; (*class*) dirigente ♦ *n* (*LAW*) decisione *f.*
rum [rʌm] *n* rum *m* ♦ *adj* (*BRIT col*) strano(a).
Rumania *etc* [ruː'meɪnɪə] = **Romania** *etc.*
rumble ['rʌmbl] *n* rimbombo; brontolio ♦ *vi* rimbombare; (*stomach, pipe*) brontolare.
rumbustious [rʌm'bʌstʃəs] *adj* (*person*): **to be** ~ essere un terremoto.
rummage ['rʌmɪdʒ] *vi* frugare.
rumour, (*US*) **rumor** ['ruːmə*] *n* voce *f* ♦ *vt*: **it is** ~**ed that** corre voce che.
rump [rʌmp] *n* (*of animal*) groppa.
rumple ['rʌmpl] *vt* (*hair*) arruffare, scompigliare; (*clothes*) spiegazzare,

sgualcire.

rump steak *n* bistecca di girello.

rumpus ['rʌmpəs] *n* (*col*) baccano; (: *quarrel*) rissa; **to kick up a** ~ fare un putiferio.

run [rʌn] *n* corsa; (*outing*) gita (in macchina); (*distance travelled*) percorso, tragitto; (*series*) serie *f inv*; (*THEAT*) periodo di rappresentazione; (*SKI*) pista ♦ *vb* (*pt* **ran**, *pp* **run** [ræn, rʌn]) *vt* (*operate*: *business*) gestire, dirigere; (: *competition*, *course*) organizzare; (: *hotel*) gestire; (: *house*) governare; (*COMPUT*: *program*) eseguire; (*water*, *bath*) far scorrere; (*force through*: *rope*, *pipe*): **to** ~ **sth through** far passare qc attraverso; (*to pass*: *hand*, *finger*): **to** ~ **sth over** passare qc su ♦ *vi* correre; (*pass*: *road etc*) passare; (*work*: *machine*, *factory*) funzionare, andare; (*bus*, *train*: *operate*) far servizio; (: *travel*) circolare; (*continue*: *play*, *contract*) durare; (*slide*: *drawer*, *flow*: *river*, *bath*) scorrere; (*colours*, *washing*) stemperarsi; (*in election*) presentarsi come candidato; **to go for a** ~ andare a correre; (*in car*) fare un giro (in macchina); **to break into a** ~ mettersi a correre; **a** ~ **of luck** un periodo di fortuna; **to have the** ~ **of sb's house** essere libero di andare e venire in casa di qn; **there was a** ~ **on ...** c'era una corsa a ...; **in the long** ~ alla lunga; in fin dei conti; **in the short** ~ sulle prime; **on the** ~ in fuga; **to make a** ~ **for it** scappare, tagliare la corda; **I'll** ~ **you to the station** la porto alla stazione; **to** ~ **a risk** correre un rischio; **to** ~ **errands** andare a fare commissioni; **the train** ~**s between Gatwick and Victoria** il treno collega Gatwick alla stazione Victoria; **the bus** ~**s every 20 minutes** c'è un autobus ogni 20 minuti; **it's very cheap to** ~ comporta poche spese; **to** ~ **on petrol** *or* (*US*) **gas/on diesel/off batteries** andare a benzina/a diesel/a batterie; **to** ~ **for the bus** fare una corsa per prendere l'autobus; **to** ~ **for president** presentarsi come candidato per la presidenza; **their losses ran into millions** le loro perdite hanno raggiunto i milioni; **to be** ~ **off one's feet** (*BRIT*) doversi fare in quattro.

▶**run about** *vi* (*children*) correre qua e là.

▶**run across** *vt fus* (*find*) trovare per caso.

▶**run away** *vi* fuggire.

▶**run down** *vi* (*clock*) scaricarsi ♦ *vt* (*AUT*) investire; (*criticize*) criticare; (*BRIT*: *reduce*: *production*) ridurre gradualmente; (: *factory*, *shop*) rallentare l'attività di; **to be** ~ **down** (*battery*) essere scarico(a);

(*person*) essere giù (di corda).

▶**run in** *vt* (*BRIT*: *car*) rodare, fare il rodaggio di.

▶**run into** *vt fus* (*meet*: *person*) incontrare per caso; (: *trouble*) incontrare, trovare; (*collide with*) andare a sbattere contro; **to** ~ **into debt** trovarsi nei debiti.

▶**run off** *vi* fuggire ♦ *vt* (*water*) far defluire; (*copies*) fare.

▶**run out** *vi* (*person*) uscire di corsa; (*liquid*) colare; (*lease*) scadere; (*money*) esaurirsi.

▶**run out of** *vt fus* rimanere a corto di; **I've** ~ **out of petrol** *or* (*US*) **gas** sono rimasto senza benzina.

▶**run over** *vt* (*AUT*) investire, mettere sotto ♦ *vt fus* (*revise*) rivedere.

▶**run through** *vt fus* (*instructions*) dare una scorsa a.

▶**run up** *vt* (*debt*) lasciar accumulare; **to** ~ **up against** (*difficulties*) incontrare.

runaround ['rʌnəraund] *n* (*col*): **to give sb the** ~ far girare a vuoto qn.

runaway ['rʌnəweɪ] *adj* (*person*) fuggiasco(a); (*horse*) in libertà; (*truck*) fuori controllo; (*inflation*) galoppante.

rundown ['rʌndaun] *n* (*BRIT*: *of industry etc*) riduzione *f* graduale dell'attività di.

rung [rʌŋ] *pp of* **ring** ♦ *n* (*of ladder*) piolo.

run-in ['rʌnɪn] *n* (*col*) scontro.

runner ['rʌnə*] *n* (*in race*) corridore *m*; (*on sledge*) pattino; (*for drawer etc*, *carpet*) guida.

runner bean *n* (*BRIT*) fagiolino.

runner-up [rʌnər'ʌp] *n* secondo(a) arrivato(a).

running ['rʌnɪŋ] *n* corsa; direzione *f*; organizzazione *f*; funzionamento ♦ *adj* (*water*) corrente; (*commentary*) simultaneo(a); **6 days** ~ 6 giorni di seguito; **to be in/out of the** ~ **for sth** essere/non essere più in lizza per qc.

running costs *npl* (*of business*) costi *mpl* d'esercizio; (*of car*) spese *fpl* di mantenimento.

running head *n* (*TYP*, *WORD PROCESSING*) testata, titolo corrente.

running mate *n* (*US POL*) candidato alla vicepresidenza.

runny ['rʌnɪ] *adj* che cola.

run-off ['rʌnɔf] *n* (*in contest*, *election*) confronto definitivo; (*extra race*) spareggio.

run-of-the-mill ['rʌnəvðə'mɪl] *adj* solito(a), banale.

runt [rʌnt] *n* (*also pej*) omuncolo; (*ZOOL*) animale *m* più piccolo del normale.

run-through ['rʌnθruː] *n* prova.

run-up ['rʌnʌp] n (BRIT): ~ **to sth** periodo
che precede qc.
runway ['rʌnweɪ] n (AVIAT) pista (di
decollo).
rupture ['rʌptʃə*] n (MED) ernia ♦ vt: **to** ~
o.s. farsi venire un'ernia.
rural ['ruərl] adj rurale.
rural district council (RDC) n (BRIT)
consiglio (amministrativo) di distretto
rurale.
ruse [ruːz] n trucco.
rush [rʌʃ] n corsa precipitosa; (of crowd)
afflusso; (hurry) furia, fretta; (current)
flusso; (BOT) giunco ♦ vt mandare or
spedire velocemente; (attack: town etc)
prendere d'assalto ♦ vi precipitarsi; **is
there any** ~ **for this?** è urgente?; **we've
had a** ~ **of orders** abbiamo avuto una
valanga di ordinazioni; **I'm in a** ~ **(to do)**
ho fretta or premura (di fare); **gold** ~
corsa all'oro; **to** ~ **sth off** spedire con
urgenza qc; **don't** ~ **me!** non farmi
fretta!
▶**rush through** vt (meal) mangiare in
fretta; (book) leggere in una scorsa frettolosa
a; (town) attraversare in fretta; (COMM:
order) eseguire d'urgenza ♦ vt fus (work)
sbrigare frettolosamente.
rush hour n ora di punta.
rush job n (urgent) lavoro urgente.
rush matting n stuoia.
rusk [rʌsk] n fetta biscottata.
Russia ['rʌʃə] n Russia.
Russian ['rʌʃən] adj russo(a) ♦ n russo/a;
(LING) russo.
rust [rʌst] n ruggine f ♦ vi arrugginirsi.
rustic ['rʌstɪk] adj rustico(a) ♦ n (pej)
cafone/a.
rustle ['rʌsl] vi frusciare ♦ vt (paper) far
frusciare; (US: cattle) rubare.
rustproof ['rʌstpruːf] adj inossidabile.
rustproofing ['rʌstpruːfɪŋ] n trattamento
antiruggine.
rusty ['rʌstɪ] adj arrugginito(a).
rut [rʌt] n solco; (ZOOL) fregola; **to be in a** ~
(fig) essersi fossilizzato(a).
rutabaga [ruːtə'beɪgə] n (US) rapa svedese.
ruthless ['ruːθlɪs] adj spietato(a).
ruthlessness ['ruːθlɪsnɪs] n spietatezza.
RV abbr (= revised version) versione
riveduta della Bibbia ♦ n abbr (US) see
recreational vehicle.
rye [raɪ] n segale f.

S, s [ɛs] n (letter) S, s f or m inv; (US SCOL:
= satisfactory) ≈ sufficiente; **S for Sugar**
≈ S come Savona.
S abbr (= saint) S.; (= south) S; (on clothes)
= small.
SA abbr = **South Africa; South America.**
Sabbath ['sæbəθ] n (Jewish) sabato;
(Christian) domenica.
sabbatical [sə'bætɪkl] adj: ~ **year** anno
sabbatico.
sabotage ['sæbətɑːʒ] n sabotaggio ♦ vt
sabotare.
saccharin(e) ['sækərɪn] n saccarina.
sachet ['sæʃeɪ] n bustina.
sack [sæk] n (bag) sacco ♦ vt (dismiss)
licenziare, mandare a spasso; (plunder)
saccheggiare; **to get the** ~ essere
mandato a spasso; **to give sb the** ~
licenziare qn, mandare qn a spasso.
sackful ['sækful] n: **a** ~ **of** un sacco di.
sacking ['sækɪŋ] n tela di sacco; (dismissal)
licenziamento.
sacrament ['sækrəmənt] n sacramento.
sacred ['seɪkrɪd] adj sacro(a).
sacred cow n (fig: person) intoccabile m/f;
(: institution) caposaldo; (: idea, belief)
dogma m.
sacrifice ['sækrɪfaɪs] n sacrificio ♦ vt
sacrificare; **to make** ~**s (for sb)** fare (dei)
sacrifici (per qn).
sacrilege ['sækrɪlɪdʒ] n sacrilegio.
sacrosanct ['sækrəusæŋkt] adj
sacrosanto(a).
sad [sæd] adj triste; (deplorable)
deplorevole.
sadden ['sædn] vt rattristare.
saddle ['sædl] n sella ♦ vt (horse) sellare; **to
be** ~**d with sth** (col) avere qc sulle spalle.
saddlebag ['sædlbæg] n bisaccia; (on
bicycle) borsa.
sadism ['seɪdɪzəm] n sadismo.
sadist ['seɪdɪst] n sadico/a.
sadistic [sə'dɪstɪk] adj sadico(a).
sadly ['sædlɪ] adv tristemente; (regrettably)
sfortunatamente; ~ **lacking in**
penosamente privo di.
sadness ['sædnɪs] n tristezza.
sadomasochism [seɪdəu'mæsəkɪzəm] n

sadomasochismo.

sae *abbr* (*BRIT*) = **stamped addressed envelope**; *see* **stamp**.

safari [sə'fɑːrɪ] *n* safari *m inv*.

safari park *n* zoosafari *m inv*.

safe [seɪf] *adj* sicuro(a); (*out of danger*) salvo(a), al sicuro; (*cautious*) prudente ♦ *n* cassaforte *f*; ~ **from** al sicuro da; ~ **and sound** sano(a) e salvo(a); ~ **journey!** buon viaggio!; **(just) to be on the** ~ **side** per non correre rischi; **to play** ~ giocare sul sicuro; **it is** ~ **to say that** ... si può affermare con sicurezza che ....

safe bet *n*: **it's a** ~ è una cosa sicura.

safe-breaker ['seɪfbreɪkə*] *n* (*BRIT*) scassinatore *m*.

safe-conduct [seɪf'kɔndʌkt] *n* salvacondotto.

safe-cracker ['seɪfkrækə*] *n* = **safe-breaker**.

safe-deposit ['seɪfdɪpɔzɪt] *n* (*vault*) caveau *m inv*; (*box*) cassetta di sicurezza.

safeguard ['seɪfgɑːd] *n* salvaguardia ♦ *vt* salvaguardare.

safe haven *n* zona sicura *or* protetta.

safekeeping ['seɪf'kiːpɪŋ] *n* custodia.

safely ['seɪflɪ] *adv* sicuramente; sano(a) e salvo(a); prudente; **I can** ~ **say** ... posso tranquillamente asserire ....

safe passage *n* passaggio sicuro.

safe sex *n* sesso sicuro.

safety ['seɪftɪ] *n* sicurezza; ~ **first!** la prudenza innanzitutto!

safety belt *n* cintura di sicurezza.

safety catch *n* sicura.

safety net *n* rete *f* di protezione.

safety pin *n* spilla di sicurezza.

safety valve *n* valvola di sicurezza.

saffron ['sæfrən] *n* zafferano.

sag [sæg] *vi* incurvarsi; afflosciarsi.

saga ['sɑːgə] *n* saga; (*fig*) odissea.

sage [seɪdʒ] *n* (*herb*) salvia; (*man*) saggio.

Sagittarius [sædʒɪ'tɛərɪəs] *n* Sagittario; **to be** ~ essere del Sagittario.

sago ['seɪgəu] *n* sagù *m*.

Sahara [sə'hɑːrə] *n*: **the** ~ **Desert** il Deserto del Sahara.

Sahel [sæ'hɛl] *n* Sahel *m*.

said [sɛd] *pt, pp of* **say**.

Saigon [saɪ'gɔn] *n* Saigon *f*.

sail [seɪl] *n* (*on boat*) vela; (*trip*): **to go for a** ~ fare un giro in barca a vela ♦ *vt* (*boat*) condurre, governare ♦ *vi* (*travel: ship*) navigare; (: *passenger*) viaggiare per mare; (*set off*) salpare; (*SPORT*) fare della vela; **they** ~**ed into Genoa** entrarono nel porto di Genova.

▶**sail through** *vt fus* (*fig*) superare senza difficoltà ♦ *vi* farcela senza difficoltà.

sailboat ['seɪlbəut] *n* (*US*) barca a vela.

sailing ['seɪlɪŋ] *n* (*sport*) vela; **to go** ~ fare della vela.

sailing boat *n* barca a vela.

sailing ship *n* veliero.

sailor ['seɪlə*] *n* marinaio.

saint [seɪnt] *n* santo/a.

saintly ['seɪntlɪ] *adj* da santo(a); santo(a).

sake [seɪk] *n*: **for the** ~ **of** per, per amore di; **for pity's** ~ per pietà; **for the** ~ **of argument** tanto per fare un esempio; **art for art's** ~ l'arte per l'arte.

salad ['sæləd] *n* insalata; **tomato** ~ insalata di pomodori.

salad bowl *n* insalatiera.

salad cream *n* (*BRIT*) (tipo di) maionese *f*.

salad dressing *n* condimento per insalata.

salad oil *n* olio da tavola.

salami [sə'lɑːmɪ] *n* salame *m*.

salaried ['sælərɪd] *adj* stipendiato(a).

salary ['sælərɪ] *n* stipendio.

salary scale *n* scala dei salari.

sale [seɪl] *n* vendita; (*at reduced prices*) svendita, liquidazione *f*; "**for** ~" "in vendita"; **on** ~ in vendita; **on** ~ **or return** da vendere o rimandare; **a closing-down** *or* (*US*) **liquidation** ~ una liquidazione; ~ **and lease back** *n* lease back *m inv*.

saleroom ['seɪlrum] *n* sala delle aste.

sales assistant *n* (*BRIT*) commesso/a.

sales clerk *n* (*US*) commesso/a.

sales conference *n* riunione *f* marketing e vendite.

sales drive *n* campagna di vendita, sforzo promozionale.

sales force *n* personale *m* addetto alle vendite.

salesman ['seɪlzmən] *n* commesso; (*representative*) rappresentante *m*.

sales manager *n* direttore *m* commerciale.

salesmanship ['seɪlzmənʃɪp] *n* arte *f* del vendere.

sales tax *n* (*US*) imposta sulle vendite.

saleswoman ['seɪlzwumən] *n* commessa.

salient ['seɪlɪənt] *adj* saliente.

saline ['seɪlaɪn] *adj* salino(a).

saliva [sə'laɪvə] *n* saliva.

sallow ['sæləu] *adj* giallastro(a).

sally forth, sally out ['sælɪ-] *vi* uscire di gran carriera.

salmon ['sæmən] *n* (*pl inv*) salmone *m*.

salmon trout *n* trota (di mare).

saloon [sə'luːn] *n* (*US*) saloon *m inv*, bar *m inv*; (*BRIT AUT*) berlina; (*ship's lounge*) salone *m*.

SALT [sɔːlt] *n abbr* (= *Strategic Arms Limitation Talks/Treaty*) S.A.L.T. *m*.

salt [sɔːlt] n sale m ♦ vt salare ♦ cpd di sale; (CULIN) salato(a); **an old** ~ un lupo di mare.
▶**salt away** vt ammucchiare, mettere via.
salt cellar n saliera.
salt-free ['sɔːlt'friː] adj senza sale.
saltwater ['sɔːltwɔːtə*] adj (fish etc) di mare.
salty ['sɔːltɪ] adj salato(a).
salubrious [sə'luːbrɪəs] adj salubre; (fig: district etc) raccomandabile.
salutary ['sæljutərɪ] adj salutare.
salute [sə'luːt] n saluto ♦ vt salutare.
salvage ['sælvɪdʒ] n (saving) salvataggio; (things saved) beni mpl salvati or recuperati ♦ vt salvare, mettere in salvo.
salvage vessel n scialuppa di salvataggio.
salvation [sæl'veɪʃən] n salvezza.
Salvation Army n Esercito della Salvezza.
salver ['sælvə*] n vassoio.
salvo, ~es ['sælvəu] n salva.
Samaritan [sə'mærɪtən] n: **the ~s** (organization) ≈ telefono amico.
same [seɪm] adj stesso(a), medesimo(a) ♦ pron: **the ~** lo(la) stesso(a), gli(le) stessi(e); **the ~ book as** lo stesso libro di (or che); **on the ~ day** lo stesso giorno; **at the ~ time** allo stesso tempo; **all** or **just the ~** tuttavia; **to do the ~** fare la stessa cosa; **to do the ~ as sb** fare come qn; **the ~ again** (in bar etc) un altro; **they're one and the ~** (person/thing) sono la stessa persona/cosa; **and the ~ to you!** altrettanto a lei!; ~ **here!** anch'io!
sample ['sɑːmpl] n campione m ♦ vt (food) assaggiare; (wine) degustare; **to take a ~** prelevare un campione; **free ~** campione omaggio.
sanatorium, pl sanatoria [sænə'tɔːrɪəm, -rɪə] n sanatorio.
sanctify ['sæŋktɪfaɪ] vt santificare.
sanctimonious [sæŋktɪ'məunɪəs] adj bigotto(a), bacchettone(a).
sanction ['sæŋkʃən] n sanzione f ♦ vt sancire, sanzionare; **to impose economic ~s on** or **against** adottare sanzioni economiche contro.
sanctity ['sæŋktɪtɪ] n santità.
sanctuary ['sæŋktjuərɪ] n (holy place) santuario; (refuge) rifugio; (for wildlife) riserva.
sand [sænd] n sabbia ♦ vt cospargere di sabbia; (also: ~ **down**: wood etc) cartavetrare; see also **sands**.
sandal ['sændl] n sandalo.
sandbag ['sændbæg] n sacco di sabbia.
sandblast ['sændblɑːst] vt sabbiare.

sandbox ['sændbɔks] n (US: for children) buca di sabbia.
sandcastle ['sændkɑːsl] n castello di sabbia.
sand dune n duna di sabbia.
sander ['sændə*] n levigatrice f.
sandpaper ['sændpeɪpə*] n carta vetrata.
sandpit ['sændpɪt] n (BRIT: for children) buca di sabbia.
sands [sændz] npl spiaggia.
sandstone ['sændstəun] n arenaria.
sandstorm ['sændstɔːm] n tempesta di sabbia.
sandwich ['sændwɪtʃ] n tramezzino, panino, sandwich m inv ♦ vt (also: ~ **in**) infilare; **cheese/ham** ~ sandwich al formaggio/prosciutto; **to be ~ed between** essere incastrato(a) fra.
sandwich board n cartello pubblicitario (portato da un uomo sandwich).
sandwich course n (BRIT) corso di formazione professionale.
sandwich man n uomo m sandwich inv.
sandy ['sændɪ] adj sabbioso(a); (colour) color sabbia inv, biondo(a) rossiccio(a).
sane [seɪn] adj (person) sano(a) di mente; (outlook) sensato(a).
sang [sæŋ] pt of **sing**.
sanguine ['sæŋgwɪn] adj ottimista.
sanitarium, pl sanitaria [sænɪ'tɛərɪəm, -rɪə] n (US) = **sanatorium**.
sanitary ['sænɪtərɪ] adj (system, arrangements) sanitario(a); (clean) igienico(a).
sanitary towel, (US) **sanitary napkin** n assorbente m (igienico).
sanitation [sænɪ'teɪʃən] n (in house) impianti mpl sanitari; (in town) fognature fpl.
sanitation department n (US) nettezza urbana.
sanity ['sænɪtɪ] n sanità mentale; (common sense) buon senso.
sank [sæŋk] pt of **sink**.
San Marino [sænmə'riːnəu] n San Marino f.
Santa Claus [sæntə'klɔːz] n Babbo Natale.
Santiago [sæntɪ'ɑːgəu] n (also: ~ **de Chile**) Santiago (del Cile) f.
sap [sæp] n (of plants) linfa ♦ vt (strength) fiaccare.
sapling ['sæplɪŋ] n alberello.
sapphire ['sæfaɪə*] n zaffiro.
sarcasm ['sɑːkæzm] n sarcasmo.
sarcastic [sɑː'kæstɪk] adj sarcastico(a); **to be ~** fare del sarcasmo.
sarcophagus, pl sarcophagi [sɑː'kɔfəgəs, -gaɪ] n sarcofago.
sardine [sɑː'diːn] n sardina.
Sardinia [sɑː'dɪnɪə] n Sardegna.

Sardinian [sɑːˈdɪnɪən] *adj, n* sardo(a).
sardonic [sɑːˈdɔnɪk] *adj* sardonico(a).
sari [ˈsɑːrɪ] *n* sari *m inv.*
SARS [sɑːz] *n abbr* (= *severe acute respiratory syndrome*) SARS *f*, polmonite atipica.
sartorial [sɑːˈtɔːrɪəl] *adj* di sartoria.
SAS *n abbr* (*BRIT MIL*: = *Special Air Service*) reparto dell'esercito britannico specializzato in operazioni clandestine.
SASE *n abbr* (*US*: = *self-addressed stamped envelope*) busta affrancata e con indirizzo.
sash [sæʃ] *n* fascia.
sash window *n* finestra a ghigliottina.
SAT *n abbr* (*US*) = *Scholastic Aptitude Test.*
sat [sæt] *pt, pp of* **sit**.
Sat. *abbr* (= *Saturday*) sab.
Satan [ˈseɪtən] *n* Satana *m.*
satanic [səˈtænɪk] *adj* satanico(a).
satchel [ˈsætʃl] *n* cartella.
sated [ˈseɪtɪd] *adj* soddisfatto(a); sazio(a).
satellite [ˈsætəlaɪt] *adj, n* satellite (*m*).
satellite television *n* televisione *f* via satellite.
satiate [ˈseɪʃɪeɪt] *vt* saziare.
satin [ˈsætɪn] *n* satin *m* ♦ *adj* di *or* in satin; **with a ~ finish** satinato(a).
satire [ˈsætaɪə*] *n* satira.
satirical [səˈtɪrɪkl] *adj* satirico(a).
satirist [ˈsætərɪst] *n* (*writer etc*) scrittore(trice) *etc* satirico(a); (*cartoonist*) caricaturista *m/f.*
satirize [ˈsætɪraɪz] *vt* satireggiare.
satisfaction [sætɪsˈfækʃən] *n* soddisfazione *f*; **has it been done to your ~?** ne è rimasto soddisfatto?
satisfactory [sætɪsˈfæktərɪ] *adj* soddisfacente.
satisfied [ˈsætɪsfaɪd] *adj* (*customer*) soddisfatto(a); **to be ~ (with sth)** essere soddisfatto(a) (di qc).
satisfy [ˈsætɪsfaɪ] *vt* soddisfare; (*convince*) convincere; **to ~ the requirements** rispondere ai requisiti; **to ~ sb (that)** convincere qn (che), persuadere qn (che); **to ~ o.s. of sth** accertarsi di qc.
satisfying [ˈsætɪsfaɪɪŋ] *adj* soddisfacente.
SATs *n abbr* (*BRIT*: = *standard assessment tasks or tests*) *esame di fine anno sostenuto dagli allievi delle scuole pubbliche inglesi a 7, 11 o 14 anni.*
satsuma [sætˈsuːmə] *n agrume di provenienza giapponese.*
saturate [ˈsætʃəreɪt] *vt*: **to ~ (with)** saturare (di).
saturated fat [ˈsætʃəreɪtɪd-] *n* grassi *mpl* saturi.
saturation [sætʃəˈreɪʃən] *n* saturazione *f.*

Saturday [ˈsætədɪ] *n* sabato; *for phrases see also* **Tuesday.**
sauce [sɔːs] *n* salsa; (*with meat, fish*) sugo.
saucepan [ˈsɔːspən] *n* casseruola.
saucer [ˈsɔːsə*] *n* piattino.
saucy [ˈsɔːsɪ] *adj* impertinente.
Saudi Arabia [ˈsaudɪ-] *n* Arabia Saudita.
Saudi (Arabian) *adj, n* saudita (*m/f*).
sauna [ˈsɔːnə] *n* sauna.
saunter [ˈsɔːntə*] *vi* andare a zonzo, bighellonare.
sausage [ˈsɔsɪdʒ] *n* salsiccia; (*salami etc*) salame *m.*
sausage roll *n* rotolo di pasta sfoglia ripieno di salsiccia.
sauté [ˈsəuteɪ] *adj* (*CULIN*: *potatoes*) saltato(a); (: *onions*) soffritto(a) ♦ *vt* far saltare; far soffriggere.
savage [ˈsævɪdʒ] *adj* (*cruel, fierce*) selvaggio(a), feroce; (*primitive*) primitivo(a) ♦ *n* selvaggio/a ♦ *vt* attaccare selvaggiamente.
savagery [ˈsævɪdʒrɪ] *n* crudeltà, ferocia.
save [seɪv] *vt* (*person, belongings, COMPUT*) salvare; (*money*) risparmiare, mettere da parte; (*time*) risparmiare; (*food*) conservare; (*avoid: trouble*) evitare ♦ *vi* (*also*: **~ up**) economizzare ♦ *n* (*SPORT*) parata ♦ *prep* salvo, a eccezione di; **it will ~ me an hour** mi farà risparmiare un'ora; **to ~ face** salvare la faccia; **God ~ the Queen!** Dio salvi la Regina!
saving [ˈseɪvɪŋ] *n* risparmio ♦ *adj*: **the ~ grace of** l'unica cosa buona di; **~s** *npl* risparmi *mpl*; **to make ~s** fare economia.
savings account *n* libretto di risparmio.
savings bank *n* cassa di risparmio.
saviour, (*US*) **savior** [ˈseɪvjə*] *n* salvatore *m.*
savour, (*US*) **savor** [ˈseɪvə*] *n* sapore *m*, gusto ♦ *vt* gustare.
savoury, (*US*) **savory** [ˈseɪvərɪ] *adj* saporito(a); (*dish*: *not sweet*) salato(a).
savvy [ˈsævɪ] *n* (*col*) arguzia.
saw [sɔː] *pt of* **see** ♦ *n* (*tool*) sega ♦ *vt* (*pt* **sawed**, *pp* **sawed** *or* **sawn** [sɔːn]) segare; **to ~ sth up** fare a pezzi qc con la sega.
sawdust [ˈsɔːdʌst] *n* segatura.
sawmill [ˈsɔːmɪl] *n* segheria.
sawn [sɔːn] *pp of* **saw.**
sawn-off [ˈsɔːnɔf], (*US*) **sawed-off** [ˈsɔːdɔf] *adj*: **~ shotgun** fucile *m* a canne mozze.
saxophone [ˈsæksəfəun] *n* sassofono.
say [seɪ] *n*: **to have one's ~** fare sentire il proprio parere; **to have a** *or* **some ~** avere voce in capitolo ♦ *vt* (*pt, pp* **said** [sɛd]) dire; **could you ~ that again?** potrebbe ripeterlo?; **to ~ yes/no** dire di

sì/di no; **she said (that) I was to give you this** ha detto di darle questo; **my watch ~s 3 o'clock** il mio orologio fa le 3; **shall we ~ Tuesday?** facciamo martedì?; **that doesn't ~ much for him** non torna a suo credito; **when all is said and done** a conti fatti; **there is something** *or* **a lot to be said for it** ha i suoi lati positivi; **that is to ~** cioè, vale a dire; **to ~ nothing of** per non parlare di; **~ that ...** mettiamo *or* diciamo che ...; **that goes without ~ing** va da sé.

saying ['seɪɪŋ] *n* proverbio, detto.

SBA *n abbr* (*US*: = *Small Business Administration*) organismo ausiliario per piccole imprese.

SC *n abbr* (*US*) = **supreme court** ♦ *abbr* (*US*) = *South Carolina.*

s/c *abbr* (= *self-contained*) indipendente.

scab [skæb] *n* crosta; (*pej*) crumiro/a.

scabby ['skæbɪ] *adj* crostoso(a).

scaffold ['skæfəʊld] *n* impalcatura; (*gallows*) patibolo.

scaffolding ['skæfəldɪŋ] *n* impalcatura.

scald [skɔːld] *n* scottatura ♦ *vt* scottare.

scalding ['skɔːldɪŋ] *adj* (*also*: ~ **hot**) bollente.

scale [skeɪl] *n* scala; (*of fish*) squama ♦ *vt* (*mountain*) scalare; **pay ~** scala dei salari; **~ of charges** tariffa; **on a large ~** su vasta scala; **to draw sth to ~** disegnare qc in scala; **small-~ model** modello in scala ridotta; *see also* **scales.**

▶**scale down** *vt* ridurre (proporzionalmente).

scaled-down [skeɪld'daʊn] *adj* su scala ridotta.

scale drawing *n* disegno in scala.

scale model *n* modello in scala.

scales [skeɪlz] *npl* bilancia.

scallion ['skæljən] *n* cipolla; (*US*: *shallot*) scalogna; (: *leek*) porro.

scallop ['skɔləp] *n* pettine *m*.

scalp [skælp] *n* cuoio capelluto ♦ *vt* scotennare.

scalpel ['skælpl] *n* bisturi *m inv.*

scalper ['skælpə*] *n* (*US col*: *of tickets*) bagarino.

scam [skæm] *n* (*col*) truffa.

scamp [skæmp] *n* (*col: child*) peste *f.*

scamper ['skæmpə*] *vi*: **to ~ away, ~ off** darsela a gambe.

scampi ['skæmpɪ] *npl* scampi *mpl.*

scan [skæn] *vt* scrutare; (*glance at quickly*) scorrere, dare un'occhiata a; (*poetry*) scandire; (*TV*) analizzare; (*RADAR*) esplorare ♦ *n* (*MED*) ecografia.

scandal ['skændl] *n* scandalo; (*gossip*) pettegolezzi *mpl.*

scandalize ['skændəlaɪz] *vt* scandalizzare.

scandalous ['skændələs] *adj* scandaloso(a).

Scandinavia [skændɪ'neɪvɪə] *n* Scandinavia.

Scandinavian [skændɪ'neɪvɪən] *adj, n* scandinavo(a).

scanner ['skænə*] *n* (*RADAR*, *MED*) scanner *m inv.*

scant [skænt] *adj* scarso(a).

scantily ['skæntɪlɪ] *adv*: **~ clad** *or* **dressed** succintamente vestito(a).

scanty ['skæntɪ] *adj* insufficiente; (*swimsuit*) ridotto(a).

scapegoat ['skeɪpgəʊt] *n* capro espiatorio.

scar [skɑː*] *n* cicatrice *f* ♦ *vt* sfregiare.

scarce [skɛəs] *adj* scarso(a); (*copy, edition*) raro(a).

scarcely ['skɛəslɪ] *adv* appena; **~ anybody** quasi nessuno; **I can ~ believe it** faccio fatica a crederci.

scarcity ['skɛəsɪtɪ] *n* scarsità, mancanza.

scarcity value *n* valore *m* di rarità.

scare [skɛə*] *n* spavento, paura ♦ *vt* spaventare, atterrire; **to ~ sb stiff** spaventare a morte qn; **bomb ~** evacuazione *f* per sospetta presenza di un ordigno esplosivo.

▶**scare away, scare off** *vt* mettere in fuga.

scarecrow ['skɛəkrəʊ] *n* spaventapasseri *m inv.*

scared [skɛəd] *adj*: **to be ~** aver paura.

scaremonger ['skɛəmʌŋgə*] *n* allarmista *m/f.*

scarf, *pl* **scarves** [skɑːf, skɑːvz] *n* (*long*) sciarpa; (*square*) fazzoletto da testa, foulard *m inv.*

scarlet ['skɑːlɪt] *adj* scarlatto(a).

scarlet fever *n* scarlattina.

scarper ['skɑːpə*] *vi* (*BRIT col*) darsela a gambe.

SCART socket ['skɑːt-] *n* presa *f* SCART *inv.*

scarves [skɑːvz] *npl of* **scarf.**

scary ['skɛərɪ] *adj* (*col*) che fa paura.

scathing ['skeɪðɪŋ] *adj* aspro(a); **to be ~ about sth** essere molto critico rispetto a qc.

scatter ['skætə*] *vt* spargere; (*crowd*) disperdere ♦ *vi* disperdersi.

scatterbrained ['skætəbreɪnd] *adj* scervellato(a), sbadato(a).

scattered ['skætəd] *adj* sparso(a).

scatty ['skætɪ] *adj* (*col*) scervellato(a), sbadato(a).

scavenge ['skævɪndʒ] *vi* (*person*): **to ~ (for)** frugare tra i rifiuti (alla ricerca di); (*hyenas etc*) nutrirsi di carogne.

scavenger ['skævəndʒə*] n spazzino.
SCE n abbr = Scottish Certificate of Education.
scenario [sɪ'nɑːrɪəu] n (THEAT, CINE) copione
m; (fig) situazione f.
scene [siːn] n (THEAT, fig etc) scena; (of
crime, accident) scena, luogo; (sight, view)
vista, veduta; **behind the ~s** (also fig)
dietro le quinte; **to appear** or **come on the
~** (also fig) entrare in scena; **the political
~ in Italy** il quadro politico in Italia; **to
make a ~** (col: fuss) fare una scenata.
scenery ['siːnərɪ] n (THEAT) scenario;
(landscape) panorama m.
scenic ['siːnɪk] adj scenico(a);
panoramico(a).
scent [sɛnt] n odore m, profumo; (sense of
smell) olfatto, odorato; (fig: track) pista; **to
put** or **throw sb off the ~** (fig) far perdere
le tracce a qn, sviare qn.
sceptic, (US) **skeptic** ['skɛptɪk] n
scettico/a.
sceptical, (US) **skeptical** ['skɛptɪkl] adj
scettico(a).
scepticism, (US) **skepticism** ['skɛptɪsɪzm]
n scetticismo.
sceptre, (US) **scepter** ['sɛptə*] n scettro.
schedule ['ʃɛdjuːl, (US) 'skɛdjuːl] n
programma m, piano; (of trains) orario; (of
prices etc) lista, tabella ♦ vt fissare; **as ~d**
come stabilito; **on ~** in orario; **to be
ahead of/behind ~** essere in anticipo/
ritardo sul previsto; **we are working to a
very tight ~** il nostro programma di
lavoro è molto intenso; **everything went
according to ~** tutto è andato secondo i
piani or secondo il previsto.
scheduled ['ʃɛdjuːld, (US) 'skɛdjuːld] adj
(date, time) fissato(a); (visit, event) pro-
grammato(a); (train, bus, stop) previsto(a)
(sull'orario); **~ flight** volo di linea.
schematic [skɪ'mætɪk] adj schematico(a).
scheme [skiːm] n piano, progetto; (method)
sistema m; (dishonest plan, plot) intrigo,
trama; (arrangement) disposizione f,
sistemazione f ♦ vt progettare; (plot)
ordire ♦ vi fare progetti; (intrigue)
complottare; **colour ~** combinazione f di
colori.
scheming ['skiːmɪŋ] adj intrigante ♦ n
intrighi mpl, macchinazioni fpl.
schism ['skɪzəm] n scisma m.
schizophrenia [skɪtsə'friːnɪə] n
schizofrenia.
schizophrenic [skɪtsə'frɛnɪk] adj, n
schizofrenico(a).
scholar ['skɔlə*] n erudito/a.
scholarly ['skɔləlɪ] adj dotto(a), erudito(a).
scholarship ['skɔləʃɪp] n erudizione f;

(grant) borsa di studio.
school [skuːl] n scuola; (in university)
scuola, facoltà f inv ♦ cpd scolare,
scolastico(a) ♦ vt (animal) addestrare.
school age n età scolare.
schoolbook ['skuːlbuk] n libro scolastico.
schoolboy ['skuːlbɔɪ] n scolaro.
schoolchild, pl **-children** ['skuːltʃaɪld,
-'tʃɪldrən] n scolaro/a.
schooldays ['skuːldeɪz] npl giorni mpl di
scuola.
schoolgirl ['skuːlɡəːl] n scolara.
schooling ['skuːlɪŋ] n istruzione f.
school-leaver ['skuːlliːvə*] n (BRIT)
≈ neodiplomato/a.
schoolmaster ['skuːlmɑːstə*] n (primary)
maestro; (secondary) insegnante m.
schoolmistress ['skuːlmɪstrɪs] n (primary)
maestra; (secondary) insegnante f.
school report n (BRIT) pagella.
schoolroom ['skuːlruːm] n classe f, aula.
schoolteacher ['skuːltiːtʃə*] n insegnante
m/f, docente m/f; (primary) maestro/a.
schoolyard ['skuːljɑːd] n (US) cortile m
della scuola.
schooner ['skuːnə*] n (ship) goletta,
schooner m inv; (glass) bicchiere m alto da
sherry.
sciatica [saɪ'ætɪkə] n sciatica.
science ['saɪəns] n scienza; **the ~s** le
scienze; (SCOL) le materie scientifiche.
science fiction n fantascienza.
scientific [saɪən'tɪfɪk] adj scientifico(a).
scientist ['saɪəntɪst] n scienziato/a.
sci-fi ['saɪfaɪ] n abbr (col) = **science fiction**.
Scilly Isles ['sɪlɪ'aɪlz] npl, **Scillies** ['sɪlɪz] npl:
the ~ le isole Scilly.
scintillating ['sɪntɪleɪtɪŋ] adj scintillante;
(wit, conversation, company) brillante.
scissors ['sɪzəz] npl forbici fpl; **a pair of ~**
un paio di forbici.
sclerosis [sklɪ'rəusɪs] n sclerosi f.
scoff [skɔf] vt (BRIT col: eat) tranguiare,
ingozzare ♦ vi: **to ~ (at)** (mock) farsi beffe
(di).
scold [skəuld] vt rimproverare.
scolding ['skəuldɪŋ] n lavata di capo,
sgridata.
scone [skɔn] n focaccina da tè.
scoop [skuːp] n mestolo; (for ice cream)
cucchiaio dosatore; (PRESS) colpo
giornalistico, notizia (in) esclusiva.
▶**scoop out** vt scavare.
▶**scoop up** vt tirare su, sollevare.
scooter ['skuːtə*] n (motor cycle) motoretta,
scooter m inv; (toy) monopattino.
scope [skəup] n (capacity: of plan,
undertaking) portata; (: of person) capacità

fpl; (*opportunity*) possibilità *fpl*; **to be within the ~ of** rientrare nei limiti di; **it's well within his ~ to** ... è perfettamente in grado di ...; **there is plenty of ~ for improvement** (*BRIT*) ci sono notevoli possibilità di miglioramento.

scorch [skɔːtʃ] *vt* (*clothes*) strinare, bruciacchiare; (*earth, grass*) seccare, bruciare.

scorched earth policy [skɔːtʃt-] *n* tattica della terra bruciata.

scorcher ['skɔːtʃə*] *n* (*col: hot day*) giornata torrida.

scorching ['skɔːtʃɪŋ] *adj* cocente, scottante.

score [skɔː*] *n* punti *mpl*, punteggio; (*MUS*) partitura, spartito; (*twenty*): **a ~** venti ♦ *vt* (*goal, point*) segnare, fare; (*success*) ottenere; (*cut: leather, wood, card*) incidere ♦ *vi* segnare; (*FOOTBALL*) fare un goal; (*keep score*) segnare i punti; **on that ~** a questo riguardo; **to have an old ~ to settle with sb** (*fig*) avere un vecchio conto da saldare con qn; **~s of people** (*fig*) un sacco di gente; **to ~ 6 out of 10** prendere 6 su 10.

▶**score out** *vt* cancellare con un segno.

scoreboard ['skɔːbɔːd] *n* tabellone *m* segnapunti.

scorecard ['skɔːkɑːd] *n* cartoncino segnapunti.

scoreline ['skɔːlaɪn] *n* (*SPORT*) risultato.

scorer ['skɔːrə*] *n* marcatore/trice; (*keeping score*) segnapunti *m inv*.

scorn [skɔːn] *n* disprezzo ♦ *vt* disprezzare.

scornful ['skɔːnful] *adj* sprezzante.

Scorpio ['skɔːpɪəu] *n* Scorpione *m*; **to be ~** essere dello Scorpione.

scorpion ['skɔːpɪən] *n* scorpione *m*.

Scot [skɒt] *n* scozzese *m/f*.

Scotch [skɒtʃ] *n* whisky *m* scozzese, scotch *m*.

scotch [skɒtʃ] *vt* (*rumour etc*) soffocare.

Scotch tape ® *n* scotch ® *m*.

scot-free ['skɒt'friː] *adj* impunito(a); **to get off ~** (*unpunished*) farla franca; (*unhurt*) uscire illeso(a).

Scotland ['skɒtlənd] *n* Scozia.

Scots [skɒts] *adj* scozzese.

Scotsman ['skɒtsmən] *n* scozzese *m*.

Scotswoman ['skɒtswumən] *n* scozzese *f*.

Scottish ['skɒtɪʃ] *adj* scozzese; **the ~ National Party** partito nazionalista scozzese; **the ~ Parliament** il Parlamento scozzese.

scoundrel ['skaundrl] *n* farabutto/a; (*child*) furfantello/a.

scour ['skauə*] *vt* (*clean*) pulire strofinando; raschiare via; ripulire; (*search*) battere,

perlustrare.

scourer ['skauərə*] *n* (*pad*) paglietta; (*powder*) (detersivo) abrasivo.

scourge [skəːdʒ] *n* flagello.

scout [skaut] *n* (*MIL*) esploratore *m*; (*also*: **boy ~**) giovane esploratore, scout *m inv*.

▶**scout around** *vi* cercare in giro.

scowl [skaul] *vi* accigliarsi, aggrottare le sopracciglia; **to ~ at** guardare torvo.

scrabble ['skræbl] *vi* (*claw*): **to ~ (at)** graffiare, grattare; (*also*: **to ~ about** or **around for sth** cercare affannosamente qc ♦ *n*: **S~** ® Scarabeo ®.

scraggy ['skrægɪ] *adj* scarno(a).

scram [skræm] *vi* (*col*) filare via.

scramble ['skræmbl] *n* arrampicata ♦ *vi* inerpicarsi; **to ~ out** *etc* uscire *etc* in fretta; **to ~ for** azzuffarsi per; **to go scrambling** (*SPORT*) fare il motocross.

scrambled eggs *npl* uova *fpl* strapazzate.

scrap [skræp] *n* pezzo, pezzetto; (*fight*) zuffa; (*also*: **~ iron**) rottami *mpl* di ferro, ferraglia ♦ *vt* demolire; (*fig*) scartare; **~s** *npl* (*waste*) scarti *mpl*; **to sell sth for ~** vendere qc come ferro vecchio.

scrapbook ['skræpbuk] *n* album *m inv* di ritagli.

scrap dealer *n* commerciante *m* di ferraglia.

scrape [skreɪp] *vt*, *vi* raschiare, grattare ♦ *n*: **to get into a ~** cacciarsi in un guaio.

▶**scrape through** *vi* (*succeed*) farcela per un pelo, cavarsela ♦ *vt fus* (*exam*) passare per miracolo, passare per il rotto della cuffia.

scraper ['skreɪpə*] *n* raschietto.

scrap heap *n* mucchio di rottami; **to throw sth on the ~** (*fig*) mettere qc nel dimenticatoio.

scrap merchant *n* (*BRIT*) commerciante *m* di ferraglia.

scrap metal *n* ferraglia.

scrap paper *n* cartaccia.

scrappy ['skræpɪ] *adj* frammentario(a), sconnesso(a).

scrap yard *n* deposito di rottami; (*for cars*) cimitero delle macchine.

scratch [skrætʃ] *n* graffio ♦ *cpd*: **~ team** squadra raccogliticcia ♦ *vt* graffiare, rigare; (*COMPUT*) cancellare ♦ *vi* grattare, graffiare; **to start from ~** cominciare or partire da zero; **to be up to ~** essere all'altezza.

scratch pad *n* (*US*) notes *m inv*, blocchetto.

scrawl [skrɔːl] *n* scarabocchio ♦ *vi* scarabocchiare.

scrawny ['skrɔːnɪ] *adj* scarno(a), pelle e ossa *inv*.

scream [skri:m] *n* grido, urlo ♦ *vi* urlare, gridare; **to ~ at sb (to do sth)** gridare a qn (di fare qc); **it was a ~** (*fig col*) era da crepar dal ridere; **he's a ~** (*fig col*) è una sagoma, è uno spasso.

scree [skri:] *n* ghiaione *m*.

screech [skri:tʃ] *n* strido; (*of tyres, brakes*) stridore *m* ♦ *vi* stridere.

screen [skri:n] *n* schermo; (*fig*) muro, cortina, velo ♦ *vt* schermare, fare schermo a; (*from the wind etc*) riparare; (*film*) proiettare; (*book*) adattare per lo schermo; (*candidates etc*) passare al vaglio; (*for illness*) sottoporre a controlli medici.

screen editing [-ɛdɪtɪŋ] *n* (*COMPUT*) correzione *f* e modifica su schermo.

screening ['skri:nɪŋ] *n* (*MED*) dépistage *m* *inv*; (*of film*) proiezione *f*; (*for security*) controlli *mpl* (di sicurezza).

screen memory *n* (*COMPUT*) memoria di schermo.

screenplay ['skri:npleɪ] *n* sceneggiatura.

screensaver *n* (*COMPUT*) screen saver *m* *inv*.

screen test *n* provino (cinematografico).

screw [skru:] *n* vite *f*; (*propeller*) elica ♦ *vt* avvitare; **to ~ sth to the wall** fissare qc al muro con viti.

▶**screw up** *vt* (*paper, material*) spiegazzare; (*col: ruin*) mandare a monte; **to ~ up one's face** fare una smorfia.

screwdriver ['skru:draɪvə*] *n* cacciavite *m*.

screwed-up ['skru:d'ʌp] *adj* (*col*): **she's totally ~** è nel pallone.

screwy ['skru:ɪ] *adj* (*col*) svitato(a).

scribble ['skrɪbl] *n* scarabocchio ♦ *vt* scribacchiare ♦ *vi* scarabocchiare; **to ~ sth down** scribacchiare qc.

scribe [skraɪb] *n* scriba *m*.

script [skrɪpt] *n* (*CINE etc*) copione *m*; (*in exam*) elaborato *or* compito d'esame; (*writing*) scrittura.

Scripture ['skrɪptʃə*] *n* Sacre Scritture *fpl*.

scriptwriter ['skrɪptraɪtə*] *n* soggettista *m/f*.

scroll [skrəul] *n* rotolo di carta ♦ *vt* (*COMPUT*) scorrere.

scroll bar *n* (*COMPUT*) barra di scorrimento.

scrotum ['skrəutəm] *n* scroto.

scrounge [skraundʒ] *vt* (*col*): **to ~ sth (off or from sb)** scroccare qc (a qn) ♦ *vi*: **to ~ on sb** vivere alle spalle di qn.

scrounger ['skraundʒə*] *n* scroccone/a.

scrub [skrʌb] *n* (*clean*) strofinata; (*land*) boscaglia ♦ *vt* pulire strofinando; (*reject*) annullare.

scrubbing brush ['skrʌbɪŋ-] *n* spazzolone *m*.

scruff [skrʌf] *n*: **by the ~ of the neck** per la collottola.

scruffy ['skrʌfɪ] *adj* sciatto(a).

scrum(mage) ['skrʌm(ɪdʒ)] *n* mischia.

scruple ['skru:pl] *n* scrupolo; **to have no ~s about doing sth** non avere scrupoli a fare qc.

scrupulous ['skru:pjuləs] *adj* scrupoloso(a).

scrupulously ['skru:pjuləslɪ] *adv* scrupolosamente; **he tries to be ~ fair/ honest** cerca di essere più imparziale/ onesto che può.

scrutinize ['skru:tɪnaɪz] *vt* scrutare, esaminare attentamente.

scrutiny ['skru:tɪnɪ] *n* esame *m* accurato; **under the ~ of sb** sotto la sorveglianza di qn.

scuba ['sku:bə] *n* autorespiratore *m*.

scuba diving *n* immersioni *fpl* subacquee.

scuff [skʌf] *vt* (*shoes*) consumare strasciicando.

scuffle ['skʌfl] *n* baruffa, tafferuglio.

scullery ['skʌlərɪ] *n* retrocucina *m or f*.

sculptor ['skʌlptə*] *n* scultore *m*.

sculpture ['skʌlptʃə*] *n* scultura.

scum [skʌm] *n* schiuma; (*pej: people*) feccia.

scupper ['skʌpə*] *vt* (*BRIT*) autoaffondare; (*fig*) far naufragare.

scurrilous ['skʌrɪləs] *adj* scurrile, volgare.

scurry ['skʌrɪ] *vi* sgambare, affrettarsi.

scurvy ['skə:vɪ] *n* scorbuto.

scuttle ['skʌtl] *n* (*NAUT*) portellino; (*also*: **coal ~**) secchio del carbone ♦ *vt* (*ship*) autoaffondare ♦ *vi* (*scamper*): **to ~ away, ~ off** darsela a gambe, scappare.

scythe [saɪð] *n* falce *f*.

SD, S. Dak. *abbr* (*US*) = *South Dakota*.

SDI *n abbr* (= *Strategic Defense Initiative*) S.D.I. *f*.

SDLP *n abbr* (*BRIT POL*) = *Social Democratic and Labour Party*.

sea [si:] *n* mare *m* ♦ *cpd* marino(a), del mare; (*ship, port*) marittimo(a), di mare; **on the ~** (*boat*) in mare; (*town*) di mare; **to go by ~** andare per mare; **by** *or* **beside the ~** (*holiday*) al mare; (*village*) sul mare; **to look out to ~** guardare il mare; **(out) at ~** al largo; **heavy** *or* **rough ~(s)** mare grosso *or* agitato; **a ~ of faces** (*fig*) una marea di gente; **to be all at ~** (*fig*) non sapere che pesci pigliare.

sea bed *n* fondo marino.

sea bird *n* uccello di mare.

seaboard ['si:bɔ:d] *n* costa.

sea breeze *n* brezza di mare.

seafarer ['si:fɛərə*] *n* navigante *m*.

seafaring ['si:fɛərɪŋ] *adj* (*community*) marinaro(a); (*life*) da marinaio.

seafood ['si:fu:d] *n* frutti *mpl* di mare.

sea front *n* lungomare *m*.

seagoing ['si:gəuɪŋ] *adj* (*ship*) d'alto mare.

seagull ['si:gʌl] *n* gabbiano.

seal [si:l] *n* (*animal*) foca; (*stamp*) sigillo; (*impression*) impronta del sigillo ♦ *vt* sigillare; (*decide: sb's fate*) segnare; (*: bargain*) concludere; ~ **of approval** beneplacito.

▶**seal off** *vt* (*close*) sigillare; (*forbid entry to*) bloccare l'accesso a.

sea level *n* livello del mare.

sealing wax ['si:lɪŋ-] *n* ceralacca.

sea lion *n* leone *m* marino.

sealskin ['si:lskɪn] *n* pelle *f* di foca.

seam [si:m] *n* cucitura; (*of coal*) filone *m*; **the hall was bursting at the** ~**s** l'aula era piena zeppa.

seaman ['si:mən] *n* marinaio.

seamanship ['si:mənʃɪp] *n* tecnica di navigazione.

seamless ['si:mlɪs] *adj* senza cucitura.

seamy ['si:mɪ] *adj* malfamato(a); squallido(a).

seance ['seɪɒns] *n* seduta spiritica.

seaplane ['si:pleɪn] *n* idrovolante *m.*

seaport ['si:pɔ:t] *n* porto di mare.

search [sə:tʃ] *n* (*for person, thing*) ricerca; (*of drawer, pockets*) esame *m* accurato; (*LAW: at sb's home*) perquisizione *f* ♦ *vt* perlustrare, frugare; (*scan, examine*) esaminare minuziosamente; (*COMPUT*) ricercare ♦ *vi*: **to** ~ **for** ricercare; **in** ~ **of** alla ricerca di; "~ **and replace**" (*COMPUT*) "ricercare e sostituire".

▶**search through** *vt fus* frugare.

search engine *n* (*COMPUT*) motore *m* di ricerca.

searcher ['sə:tʃə*] *n* chi cerca.

searching ['sə:tʃɪŋ] *adj* minuzioso(a); penetrante; (*question*) pressante.

searchlight ['sə:tʃlaɪt] *n* proiettore *m*.

search party *n* squadra di soccorso.

search warrant *n* mandato di perquisizione.

searing ['sɪərɪŋ] *adj* (*heat*) rovente; (*pain*) acuto(a).

seashore ['si:ʃɔ:*] *n* spiaggia; **on the** ~ sulla riva del mare.

seasick ['si:sɪk] *adj* che soffre il mal di mare; **to be** ~ avere il mal di mare.

seaside ['si:saɪd] *n* spiaggia; **to go to the** ~ andare al mare.

seaside resort *n* stazione *f* balneare.

season ['si:zn] *n* stagione *f* ♦ *vt* condire,

insaporire; **to be in/out of** ~ essere di/fuori stagione; **the busy** ~ (*for shops*) il periodo di punta; (*for hotels etc*) l'alta stagione; **the open** ~ (*HUNTING*) la stagione della caccia.

seasonal ['si:zənl] *adj* stagionale.

seasoned ['si:znd] *adj* (*wood*) stagionato(a); (*fig: worker, actor, troops*) con esperienza; **a** ~ **campaigner** un veterano.

seasoning ['si:znɪŋ] *n* condimento.

season ticket *n* abbonamento.

seat [si:t] *n* sedile *m*; (*in bus, train: place*) posto; (*PARLIAMENT*) seggio; (*centre: of government etc, of infection*) sede *f*; (*buttocks*) didietro; (*of trousers*) fondo ♦ *vt* far sedere; (*have room for*) avere or essere fornito(a) di posti a sedere per; **are there any** ~**s left?** ci sono posti?; **to take one's** ~ prendere posto; **to be** ~**ed** essere seduto(a); **please be** ~**ed** accomodatevi per favore.

seat belt *n* cintura di sicurezza.

seating arrangements ['si:tɪŋ-] *npl* sistemazione *f* or disposizione *f* dei posti.

seating capacity *n* posti *mpl* a sedere.

SEATO ['si:təu] *n abbr* (= *Southeast Asia Treaty Organization*) SEATO *f.*

sea water *n* acqua di mare.

seaweed ['si:wi:d] *n* alghe *fpl.*

seaworthy ['si:wə:ðɪ] *adj* atto(a) alla navigazione.

SEC *n abbr* (*US: = Securities and Exchange Commission*) *commissione di controllo sulle operazioni in Borsa.*

sec. *abbr* = **second.**

secateurs [sɛkə'tə:z] *npl* forbici *fpl* per potare.

secede [sɪ'si:d] *vi*: **to** ~ **(from)** ritirarsi (da).

secluded [sɪ'klu:dɪd] *adj* isolato(a), appartato(a).

seclusion [sɪ'klu:ʒən] *n* isolamento.

second ['sɛkənd] *num* secondo(a) ♦ *adv* (*in race etc*) al secondo posto; (*RAIL*) in seconda ♦ *n* (*unit of time*) secondo; (*in series, position*) secondo/a; (*BRIT SCOL*) *laurea con punteggio discreto*; (*AUT: also:* ~ **gear**) seconda; (*COMM: imperfect*) scarto ♦ *vt* (*motion*) appoggiare; [sɪ'kɔnd] (*employee*) distaccare; **Charles the S**~ Carlo Secondo; **just a** ~! un attimo!; ~ **floor** (*BRIT*) secondo piano; (*US*) primo piano; **to ask for a** ~ **opinion** (*MED*) chiedere un altro *or* ulteriore parere; **to have** ~ **thoughts (about doing sth)** avere dei ripensamenti (quanto a fare qc); **on** ~ **thoughts** *or* (*US*) **thought** a ripensarci, ripensandoci bene.

secondary ['sɛkəndərɪ] *adj* secondario(a).

secondary school n scuola secondaria; *see boxed note.*

SECONDARY SCHOOL

In Gran Bretagna la **secondary school** *è la scuola frequentata dai ragazzi dagli 11 ai 18 anni. Nel paese è obbligatorio andare a scuola fino a 16 anni; vedi anche* **primary school, high school**.

---

second-best [sɛkənd'bɛst] n ripiego; **as a ~** in mancanza di meglio.
second-class [sɛkənd'klɑːs] adj di seconda classe ♦ adv: **to travel ~** viaggiare in seconda (classe); **to send sth ~** spedire qc per posta ordinaria; **~ citizen** cittadino di second'ordine.
second cousin n cugino di secondo grado.
seconder ['sɛkəndə*] n sostenitore/trice.
second-guess ['sɛkənd'gɛs] vt (predict) anticipare; (after the event) giudicare col senno di poi.
second hand n (on clock) lancetta dei secondi.
second-hand [sɛkənd'hænd] adj di seconda mano, usato(a) ♦ adv (buy) di seconda mano; **to hear sth ~** venire a sapere qc da terze persone.
second-in-command ['sɛkəndɪnkə'mɑːnd] n (MIL) comandante m in seconda; (ADMIN) aggiunto.
secondly ['sɛkəndlɪ] adv in secondo luogo.
secondment [sɪ'kɔndmənt] n (BRIT) distaccamento.
second-rate [sɛkənd'reɪt] adj scadente.
Second World War n: **the ~** la seconda guerra mondiale.
secrecy ['siːkrəsɪ] n segretezza.
secret ['siːkrɪt] adj segreto(a) ♦ n segreto; **in ~** in segreto, segretamente; **to keep sth ~ (from sb)** tenere qc segreto (a qn), tenere qc nascosto (a qn); **keep it ~** che rimanga un segreto; **to make no ~ of sth** non far mistero di qc.
secret agent n agente m segreto.
secretarial [sɛkrɪ'tɛərɪəl] adj (work) da segretario/a; (college, course) di segretariato.
secretariat [sɛkrɪ'tɛərɪət] n segretariato.
secretary ['sɛkrətrɪ] n segretario/a; **S~ of State** (US POL) ≈ Ministro degli Esteri; **S~ of State (for)** (BRIT POL) ministro (di).
secretary-general ['sɛkrətrɪ'dʒɛnərl] n segretario generale.
secrete [sɪ'kriːt] vt (MED, ANAT, BIOL) secernere; (hide) nascondere.
secretion [sɪ'kriːʃən] n secrezione f.

secretive ['siːkrətɪv] adj riservato(a).
secretly ['siːkrɪtlɪ] adv in segreto, segretamente.
secret police n polizia segreta.
secret service n servizi mpl segreti.
sect [sɛkt] n setta.
sectarian [sɛk'tɛərɪən] adj settario(a).
section ['sɛkʃən] n sezione f; (of document) articolo ♦ vt sezionare, dividere in sezioni; **the business ~** (PRESS) la pagina economica.
sector ['sɛktə*] n settore m.
secular ['sɛkjulə*] adj secolare.
secure [sɪ'kjuə*] adj (free from anxiety) sicuro(a); (firmly fixed) assicurato(a), ben fermato(a); (in safe place) al sicuro ♦ vt (fix) fissare, assicurare; (get) ottenere, assicurarsi; (COMM: loan) garantire; **to make sth ~** fissare bene qc; **to ~ sth for sb** procurare qc per or a qn.
security [sɪ'kjuərɪtɪ] n sicurezza; (for loan) garanzia; **securities** npl (STOCK EXCHANGE) titoli mpl; **to increase/tighten ~** aumentare/intensificare la sorveglianza; **~ of tenure** garanzia del posto di lavoro, garanzia di titolo or di godimento.
Security Council n: **the ~** il Consiglio di Sicurezza.
security forces npl forze fpl dell'ordine.
security guard n guardia giurata.
security risk n rischio per la sicurezza.
secy. abbr = **secretary**.
sedan [sə'dæn] n (US AUT) berlina.
sedate [sɪ'deɪt] adj posato(a); calmo(a) ♦ vt calmare.
sedation [sɪ'deɪʃən] n (MED): **to be under ~** essere sotto l'azione di sedativi.
sedative ['sɛdɪtɪv] n sedativo, calmante m.
sedentary ['sɛdntrɪ] adj sedentario(a).
sediment ['sɛdɪmənt] n sedimento.
sedition [sɪ'dɪʃən] n sedizione f.
seduce [sɪ'djuːs] vt sedurre.
seduction [sɪ'dʌkʃən] n seduzione f.
seductive [sɪ'dʌktɪv] adj seducente.
see [siː] vb (pt **saw**, pp **seen** [sɔː, siːn]) vt vedere; (accompany): **to ~ sb to the door** accompagnare qn alla porta ♦ vi vedere; (understand) capire ♦ n sede f vescovile; **to ~ that** (ensure) badare che + sub, fare in modo che + sub; **to go and ~ sb** andare a trovare qn; **~ you soon/later/tomorrow!** a presto/più tardi/domani!; **as far as I can ~** da quanto posso vedere; **there was nobody to be ~n** non c'era anima viva; **let me ~** (show me) fammi vedere; (let me think) vediamo (un po'); **~ for yourself** vai a vedere con i tuoi occhi; **I don't know what she ~s in him** non so

che cosa ci trovi in lui.

►**see about** *vt fus* (*deal with*) occuparsi di.

►**see off** *vt* salutare alla partenza.

►**see through** *vt* portare a termine ♦ *vt fus* non lasciarsi ingannare da.

►**see to** *vt fus* occuparsi di.

seed [si:d] *n* seme *m*; (*fig*) germe *m*; (*TENNIS*) testa di serie; **to go to** ~ fare seme; (*fig*) scadere.

seedless ['si:dlɪs] *adj* senza semi.

seedling ['si:dlɪŋ] *n* piantina di semenzaio.

seedy ['si:dɪ] *adj* (*shabby: person*) sciatto(a); (: *place*) cadente.

seeing ['si:ɪŋ] *conj:* ~ (**that**) visto che.

seek [si:k], *pt, pp* **sought** *vt* cercare; **to** ~ **advice/help from sb** chiedere consiglio/ aiuto a qn.

►**seek out** *vt* (*person*) andare a cercare.

seem [si:m] *vi* sembrare, parere; **there** ~**s to be** ... sembra che ci sia ...; **it** ~**s (that)** ... sembra *or* pare che ... + *sub*; **what** ~**s to be the trouble?** cosa c'è che non va?

seemingly ['si:mɪŋlɪ] *adv* apparentemente.

seen [si:n] *pp of* **see**.

seep [si:p] *vi* filtrare, trapelare.

seer [sɪə*] *n* profeta/essa, veggente *m/f*.

seersucker ['sɪəsʌkə*] *n* cotone *m* indiano.

seesaw ['si:sɔ:] *n* altalena a bilico.

seethe [si:ð] *vi* ribollire; **to** ~ **with anger** fremere di rabbia.

see-through ['si:θru:] *adj* trasparente.

segment ['sɛgmənt] *n* segmento.

segregate ['sɛgrɪgeɪt] *vt* segregare, isolare.

segregation [sɛgrɪ'geɪʃən] *n* segregazione *f*.

Seine [seɪn] *n* Senna.

seismic ['saɪzmɪk] *adj* sismico(a).

seize [si:z] *vt* (*grasp*) afferrare; (*take possession of*) impadronirsi di; (*LAW*) sequestrare.

►**seize up** *vi* (*TECH*) grippare.

►**seize (up)on** *vt fus* ricorrere a.

seizure ['si:ʒə*] *n* (*MED*) attacco; (*LAW*) confisca, sequestro.

seldom ['sɛldəm] *adv* raramente.

select [sɪ'lɛkt] *adj* scelto(a); (*hotel, restaurant*) chic *inv*; (*club*) esclusivo(a) ♦ *vt* scegliere, selezionare; **a** ~ **few** pochi eletti *mpl*.

selection [sɪ'lɛkʃən] *n* selezione *f*, scelta.

selection committee *n* comitato di selezione.

selective [sɪ'lɛktɪv] *adj* selettivo(a).

selector [sɪ'lɛktə*] *n* (*person*) selezionatore/trice; (*TECH*) selettore *m*.

self [sɛlf] *n* (*pl* **selves** [sɛlvz]): **the** ~ l'io *m* ♦ *prefix* auto....

self-addressed ['sɛlfə'drɛst] *adj:* ~ **envelope** busta col proprio nome e indirizzo.

self-adhesive [sɛlfəd'hi:zɪv] *adj* autoadesivo(a).

self-assertive [sɛlfə'sə:tɪv] *adj* autoritario(a).

self-assurance [sɛlfə'ʃuərəns] *n* sicurezza di sé.

self-assured [sɛlfə'ʃuəd] *adj* sicuro(a) di sé.

self-catering [sɛlf'keɪtərɪŋ] *adj* (*BRIT*) in cui ci si cucina da sé; ~ **apartment** appartamento (per le vacanze).

self-centred, (*US*) **self-centered** [sɛlf'sɛntəd] *adj* egocentrico(a).

self-cleaning [sɛlf'kli:nɪŋ] *adj* autopulente.

self-confessed [sɛlfkən'fɛst] *adj* (*alcoholic etc*) dichiarato(a).

self-confidence [sɛlf'kɒnfɪdəns] *n* sicurezza di sé.

self-conscious [sɛlf'kɒnʃəs] *adj* timido(a).

self-contained [sɛlfkən'teɪnd] *adj* (*BRIT: flat*) indipendente.

self-control [sɛlfkən'trəul] *n* autocontrollo.

self-defeating [sɛlfdɪ'fi:tɪŋ] *adj* futile.

self-defence, (*US*) **self-defense** [sɛlfdɪ'fɛns] *n* autodifesa; (*LAW*) legittima difesa.

self-discipline [sɛlf'dɪsɪplɪn] *n* autodisciplina.

self-employed [sɛlfɪm'plɔɪd] *adj* che lavora in proprio.

self-esteem [sɛlfɪ'sti:m] *n* amor proprio *m*.

self-evident [sɛlf'ɛvɪdənt] *adj* evidente.

self-explanatory [sɛlfɪk'splænətərɪ] *adj* ovvio(a).

self-governing [sɛlf'gʌvənɪŋ] *adj* autonomo(a).

self-help ['sɛlf'hɛlp] *n* iniziativa individuale.

self-importance [sɛlfɪm'pɔ:tns] *n* sufficienza.

self-indulgent [sɛlfɪn'dʌldʒənt] *adj* indulgente verso se stesso(a).

self-inflicted [sɛlfɪn'flɪktɪd] *adj* autoinflitto(a).

self-interest [sɛlf'ɪntrɪst] *n* interesse *m* personale.

selfish ['sɛlfɪʃ] *adj* egoista.

selfishly ['sɛlfɪʃlɪ] *adv* egoisticamente.

selfishness ['sɛlfɪʃnɪs] *n* egoismo.

selfless ['sɛlflɪs] *adj* altruista.

selflessly ['sɛlflɪslɪ] *adv* altruisticamente.

selflessness ['sɛlflɪsnɪs] *n* altruismo.

self-made man ['sɛlfmeɪd-] *n* self-made man *m inv*, uomo che si è fatto da sé.

self-pity [sɛlf'pɪtɪ] *n* autocommiserazione *f*.

self-portrait [sɛlf'pɔ:trɪt] *n* autoritratto.

self-possessed [sɛlfpə'zɛst] *adj*
controllato(a).
self-preservation ['sɛlfprɛzə'veɪʃən] *n*
istinto di conservazione.
self-raising [sɛlf'reɪzɪŋ], (*US*) **self-rising**
[sɛlf'raɪzɪŋ] *adj*: ~ **flour** miscela di farina e
lievito.
self-reliant [sɛlfrɪ'laɪənt] *adj* indipendente.
self-respect [sɛlfrɪs'pɛkt] *n* rispetto di sé,
amor proprio.
self-respecting [sɛlfrɪs'pɛktɪŋ] *adj* che ha
rispetto di sé.
self-righteous [sɛlf'raɪtʃəs] *adj*
soddisfatto(a) di sé.
self-rising [sɛlf'raɪzɪŋ] *adj* (*US*) = **self-
raising**.
self-sacrifice [sɛlf'sækrɪfaɪs] *n* abnegazione
f.
self-same ['sɛlfseɪm] *adj* stesso(a).
self-satisfied [sɛlf'sætɪsfaɪd] *adj*
compiaciuto(a) di sé.
self-sealing [sɛlf'siːlɪŋ] *adj* autosigillante.
self-service [sɛlf'səːvɪs] *n* autoservizio,
self-service *m*.
self-styled [sɛlf'staɪld] *adj* sedicente.
self-sufficient [sɛlfsə'fɪʃənt] *adj*
autosufficiente.
self-supporting [sɛlfsə'pɔːtɪŋ] *adj*
economicamente indipendente.
self-taught [sɛlf'tɔːt] *adj* autodidatta.
self-test ['sɛlftɛst] *n* (*COMPUT*) autoverifica.
sell, *pt, pp* **sold** [sɛl, səʊld] *vt* vendere ♦ *vi*
vendersi; **to ~ at** *or* **for 100 euros** essere
in vendita a 100 euro; **to ~ sb an idea** (*fig*)
far accettare un'idea a qn.
▶**sell off** *vt* svendere, liquidare.
▶**sell out** *vi*: **to ~ out (to sb/sth)** (*COMM*)
vendere (tutto) (a qn/qc) ♦ *vt* esaurire;
the tickets are all sold out i biglietti sono
esauriti.
▶**sell up** *vi* vendere (tutto).
sell-by date ['sɛlbaɪ-] *n* scadenza.
seller ['sɛlə*] *n* venditore/trice; ~**'s market**
mercato favorevole ai venditori.
selling price ['sɛlɪŋ-] *n* prezzo di vendita.
Sellotape ® ['sɛləʊteɪp] *n* (*BRIT*) nastro
adesivo, scotch ® *m*.
sellout ['sɛlaʊt] *n* (*betrayal*) tradimento; (*of
tickets*): **it was a** ~ registrò un tutto
esaurito.
selves [sɛlvz] *npl of* **self**.
semantic [sɪ'mæntɪk] *adj* semantico(a).
semantics [sɪ'mæntɪks] *n* semantica.
semaphore ['sɛməfɔː*] *n* segnali *mpl* con
bandiere; (*RAIL*) semaforo.
semblance ['sɛmbləns] *n* parvenza,
apparenza.
semen ['siːmən] *n* sperma *m*.

semester [sɪ'mɛstə*] *n* (*US*) semestre *m*.
semi... ['sɛmɪ] *prefix* semi... ♦ *n*: **semi**
= **semidetached (house)**.
semi-breve ['sɛmɪbriːv] *n* (*BRIT*) semibreve
f.
semicircle ['sɛmɪsəːkl] *n* semicerchio.
semicircular ['sɛmɪ'səːkjʊlə*] *adj*
semicircolare.
semicolon [sɛmɪ'kəʊlən] *n* punto e virgola.
semiconductor [sɛmɪkən'dʌktə*] *n*
semiconduttore *m*.
semiconscious [sɛmɪ'kɔnʃəs] *adj*
parzialmente cosciente.
semidetached (house) [sɛmɪdɪ'tætʃt-] *n*
(*BRIT*) casa gemella.
semifinal [sɛmɪ'faɪnl] *n* semifinale *f*.
seminar ['sɛmɪnɑː*] *n* seminario.
seminary ['sɛmɪnərɪ] *n* (*REL*: *for priests*)
seminario.
semiprecious [sɛmɪ'prɛʃəs] *adj*
semiprezioso(a).
semiquaver ['sɛmɪkweɪvə*] *n* (*BRIT*)
semicroma.
semiskilled ['sɛmɪ'skɪld] *adj*: ~ **worker**
operaio(a) non specializzato(a).
semi-skimmed ['sɛmɪ'skɪmd] *adj*
parzialmente scremato(a).
semitone ['sɛmɪtəʊn] *n* (*MUS*) semitono.
semolina [sɛmə'liːnə] *n* semolino.
Sen., sen. *abbr* = **senator; senior**.
senate ['sɛnɪt] *n* senato.
senator ['sɛnɪtə*] *n* senatore/trice.
send [sɛnd], *pt, pp* **sent** *vt* mandare; **to ~ by
post** *or* (*US*) **mail** spedire per posta; **to ~
sb for sth** mandare qn a prendere qc;
to ~ word that ... mandare a dire che ...;
she ~s (you) her love ti saluta
affettuosamente; **to ~ sb to Coventry**
(*BRIT*) dare l'ostracismo a qn; **to ~ sb
to sleep/into fits of laughter** far
addormentare/scoppiare dal ridere qn;
to ~ sth flying far volare via qc.
▶**send away** *vt* (*letter, goods*) spedire;
(*person*) mandare via.
▶**send away for** *vt fus* richiedere per
posta, farsi spedire.
▶**send back** *vt* rimandare.
▶**send for** *vt fus* mandare a chiamare, far
venire; (*by post*) ordinare per posta.
▶**send in** *vt* (*report, application, resignation*)
presentare.
▶**send off** *vt* (*goods*) spedire; (*BRIT SPORT*:
player) espellere.
▶**send on** *vt* (*BRIT*: *letter*) inoltrare; (*luggage
etc*: *in advance*) spedire in anticipo.
▶**send out** *vt* (*invitation*) diramare; (*emit*:
light, heat) mandare, emanare; (: *signals*)
emettere.

▶**send round** *vt* (*letter, document etc*) far circolare.

▶**send up** *vt* (*person, price*) far salire; (*BRIT: parody*) mettere in ridicolo.

sender ['sɛndə*] *n* mittente *m/f*.

send-off ['sɛndɔf] *n*: **to give sb a good ~** festeggiare la partenza di qn.

Senegal [sɛnɪ'gɔːl] *n* Senegal *m*.

Senegalese [sɛnɪgə'liːz] *adj, n* senegalese (*m/f*).

senile ['siːnaɪl] *adj* senile.

senility [sɪ'nɪlɪtɪ] *n* senilità *f*.

senior ['siːnɪə*] *adj* (*older*) più vecchio(a); (*of higher rank*) di grado più elevato ♦ *n* persona più anziana; (*in service*) persona con maggiore anzianità; **P. Jones ~** P. Jones senior, P. Jones padre.

senior citizen *n* anziano/a.

senior high school *n* (*US*) ≈ liceo.

seniority [siːnɪ'ɔrɪtɪ] *n* anzianità; (*in rank*) superiorità.

sensation [sɛn'seɪʃən] *n* sensazione *f*; **to create a ~** fare scalpore.

sensational [sɛn'seɪʃənl] *adj* sensazionale; (*marvellous*) eccezionale.

sense [sɛns] *n* senso; (*feeling*) sensazione *f*, senso; (*meaning*) senso, significato; (*wisdom*) buonsenso ♦ *vt* sentire, percepire; **~s** *npl* (*sanity*) ragione *f*; **it makes ~** ha senso; **there is no ~ in (doing) that** non ha senso (farlo); **~ of humour** (senso dell')umorismo; **to come to one's ~s** (*regain consciousness*) riprendere i sensi; (*become reasonable*) tornare in sé; **to take leave of one's ~s** perdere il lume *or* l'uso della ragione.

senseless ['sɛnslɪs] *adj* sciocco(a); (*unconscious*) privo(a) di sensi.

sensibilities [sɛnsɪ'bɪlɪtɪz] *npl* sensibilità *fsg*.

sensible ['sɛnsɪbl] *adj* sensato(a), ragionevole.

sensitive ['sɛnsɪtɪv] *adj*: **~ (to)** sensibile (a); **he is very ~ about it** è un tasto che è meglio non toccare con lui.

sensitivity [sɛnsɪ'tɪvɪtɪ] *n* sensibilità.

sensual ['sɛnsjuəl] *adj* sensuale.

sensuous ['sɛnsjuəs] *adj* sensuale.

sent [sɛnt] *pt, pp of* **send**.

sentence ['sɛntns] *n* (*LING*) frase *f*; (*LAW: judgement*) sentenza; (: *punishment*) condanna ♦ *vt*: **to ~ sb to death/to 5 years** condannare qn a morte/a 5 anni; **to pass ~ on sb** condannare qn.

sentiment ['sɛntɪmənt] *n* sentimento; (*opinion*) opinione *f*.

sentimental [sɛntɪ'mɛntl] *adj* sentimentale.

sentimentality [sɛntɪmɛn'tælɪtɪ] *n* sentimentalità, sentimentalismo.

sentry ['sɛntrɪ] *n* sentinella.

sentry duty *n*: **to be on ~** essere di sentinella.

Seoul [səul] *n* Seul *f*.

separable ['sɛprəbl] *adj* separabile.

separate *adj* ['sɛprɪt] separato(a) ♦ *vb* ['sɛpəreɪt] *vt* separare ♦ *vi* separarsi; **~ from** separato da; **under ~ cover** (*COMM*) in plico a parte; **to ~ into** dividere in; *see also* **separates**.

separately ['sɛprɪtlɪ] *adv* separatamente.

separates ['sɛprɪts] *npl* (*clothes*) coordinati *mpl*.

separation [sɛpə'reɪʃən] *n* separazione *f*.

Sept. *abbr* (= *September*) sett., set.

September [sɛp'tɛmbə*] *n* settembre *m*; *for phrases see also* **July**.

septic ['sɛptɪk] *adj* settico(a); (*wound*) infettato(a); **to go ~** infettarsi.

septicaemia, (*US*) **septicemia** [sɛptɪ'siːmɪə] *n* setticemia.

septic tank *n* fossa settica.

sequel ['siːkwl] *n* conseguenza; (*of story*) seguito.

sequence ['siːkwəns] *n* (*series*) serie *f inv*; (*order*) ordine *m*; **in ~** in ordine, di seguito; **~ of tenses** concordanza dei tempi.

sequential [sɪ'kwɛnʃəl] *adj*: **~ access** (*COMPUT*) accesso sequenziale.

sequin ['siːkwɪn] *n* lustrino, paillette *f inv*.

Serb [səːb] *adj, n* = **Serbian**.

Serbia ['səːbɪə] *n* Serbia.

Serbian ['səːbɪən] *adj* serbo(a) ♦ *n* serbo/a; (*LING*) serbo.

Serbo-Croat ['səːbəu'krəuæt] *n* (*LING*) serbocroato.

serenade [sɛrə'neɪd] *n* serenata ♦ *vt* fare la serenata a.

serene [sɪ'riːn] *adj* sereno(a), calmo(a).

serenity [sɪ'rɛnɪtɪ] *n* serenità, tranquillità.

sergeant ['sɑːdʒənt] *n* sergente *m*; (*POLICE*) brigadiere *m*.

sergeant major *n* maresciallo.

serial ['sɪərɪəl] *n* (*PRESS*) romanzo a puntate; (*RADIO, TV*) trasmissione *f* a puntate ♦ *cpd* (*number*) di serie; (*COMPUT*) seriale.

serialize ['sɪərɪəlaɪz] *vt* pubblicare a puntate; trasmettere a puntate.

serial killer *n* serial killer *m inv*.

serial number *n* numero di serie.

series ['sɪəriːz] *n* (*pl inv*) serie *f inv*; (*PUBLISHING*) collana.

serious ['sɪərɪəs] *adj* serio(a), grave; **are you ~ (about it)?** parla sul serio?

seriously ['sɪərɪəslɪ] *adv* seriamente; **he's ~**

rich (col: extremely) ha un casino di soldi; **to take sth/sb ~** prendere qc/qn sul serio.

seriousness ['sɪərɪəsnɪs] n serietà, gravità.

sermon ['sɜːmən] n sermone m.

serrated [sɪ'reɪtɪd] adj seghettato(a).

serum ['sɪərəm] n siero.

servant ['sɜːvənt] n domestico/a.

serve [sɜːv] vt (employer etc) servire, essere a servizio di; (purpose) servire a; (customer, food, meal) servire; (apprenticeship) fare; (prison term) scontare ♦ vi (also TENNIS) servire; (soldier etc) prestare servizio; (be useful): **to ~ as/for/to do** servire da/per/per fare ♦ n (TENNIS) servizio; **are you being ~d?** la stanno servendo?; **to ~ on a committee/ jury** far parte di un comitato/una giuria; **it ~s him right** ben gli sta, se l'è meritata; **it ~s my purpose** fa al caso mio.

▶**serve out, serve up** vt (food) servire.

server ['sɜːvə*] n (COMPUT) server sm inv.

service ['sɜːvɪs] n servizio; (AUT: maintenance) revisione f; (REL) funzione f ♦ vt (car, washing machine) revisionare; **the S~s** npl le forze armate; **to be of ~ to sb, to do sb a ~** essere d'aiuto a qn; **to put one's car in for (a) ~** portare la macchina in officina per una revisione; **dinner ~** servizio da tavola.

serviceable ['sɜːvɪsəbl] adj pratico(a), utile; (usable, working) usabile.

service area n (on motorway) area di servizio.

service charge n (BRIT) servizio.

service industries npl settore m terziario.

serviceman ['sɜːvɪsmən] n militare m.

service provider n (COMPUT) provider sm inv.

service station n stazione f di servizio.

serviette [sɜːvɪ'ɛt] n (BRIT) tovagliolo.

servile ['sɜːvaɪl] adj servile.

session ['sɛʃən] n (sitting) seduta, sessione f; (SCOL) anno scolastico (or accademico); **to be in ~** essere in seduta.

session musician n musicista m/f di studio.

set [sɛt] n serie f inv; (RADIO, TV) apparecchio; (TENNIS) set m inv; (group of people) mondo, ambiente m; (CINE) scenario; (THEAT: stage) scene fpl; (: scenery) scenario; (MATH) insieme m; (HAIRDRESSING) messa in piega ♦ adj (fixed) stabilito(a), determinato(a); (ready) pronto(a) ♦ vb (pt, pp set) (place) posare, mettere; (fix) fissare; (assign: task, homework) dare, assegnare; (adjust) regolare; (decide: rules etc) stabilire, fissare; (TYP) comporre ♦ vi (sun)

tramontare; (jam, jelly) rapprendersi; (concrete) fare presa; **to be ~ on doing** essere deciso a fare; **to be all ~ to do sth** essere pronto fare qc; **to be (dead) ~ against** essere completamente contrario a; **~ in one's ways** abitudinario; **a novel ~ in Rome** un romanzo ambientato a Roma; **to ~ to music** mettere in musica; **to ~ on fire** dare fuoco a; **to ~ free** liberare; **to ~ sth going** mettere in moto qc; **to ~ sail** prendere il mare; **a ~ phrase** una frase fatta; **a ~ of false teeth** una dentiera; **a ~ of dining-room furniture** una camera da pranzo.

▶**set about** vt fus (task) intraprendere, mettersi a; **to ~ about doing sth** mettersi a fare qc.

▶**set aside** vt mettere da parte.

▶**set back** vt (progress) ritardare; **to ~ back (by)** (in time) mettere indietro (di); **a house ~ back from the road** una casa a una certa distanza dalla strada.

▶**set in** vi (infection) svilupparsi; (complications) intervenire; **the rain has ~ in for the day** ormai pioverà tutto il giorno.

▶**set off** vi partire ♦ vt (bomb) far scoppiare; (cause to start) mettere in moto; (show up well) dare risalto a.

▶**set out** vi partire; (aim): **to ~ out to do** proporsi di fare ♦ vt (arrange) disporre; (state) esporre, presentare.

▶**set up** vt (organization) fondare, costituire; (record) stabilire; (monument) innalzare.

setback ['sɛtbæk] n (hitch) contrattempo, inconveniente m; (in health) ricaduta.

set menu n menù m inv fisso.

set square n squadra.

settee [sɛ'tiː] n divano, sofà m inv.

setting ['sɛtɪŋ] n ambiente m; (scenery) sfondo; (of jewel) montatura.

setting lotion n fissatore m.

settle ['sɛtl] vt (argument, matter) appianare; (problem) risolvere; (pay: bill, account) regolare, saldare; (MED: calm) calmare; (colonize: land) colonizzare ♦ vi (bird, dust etc) posarsi; (sediment) depositarsi; (also: ~ down) sistemarsi, stabilirsi; (become calmer) calmarsi; **to ~ to sth** applicarsi a qc; **to ~ for sth** accontentarsi di qc; **to ~ on sth** decidersi per qc; **that's ~d then** allora è deciso; **to ~ one's stomach** calmare il mal di stomaco.

▶**settle in** vi sistemarsi.

▶**settle up** vi: **to ~ up with sb** regolare i conti con qn.

settlement ['sɛtlmənt] n (payment)

pagamento, saldo; (*agreement*) accordo; (*colony*) colonia; (*village etc*) villaggio, comunità *f inv*; **in ~ of our account** (*COMM*) a saldo del nostro conto.

settler ['sɛtlə*] *n* colonizzatore/trice.

setup ['sɛtʌp] *n* (*arrangement*) sistemazione *f*; (*situation*) situazione; (*COMPUT*) setup *m inv*.

seven ['sɛvn] *num* sette.

seventeen [sɛvn'tiːn] *num* diciassette.

seventh ['sɛvnθ] *num* settimo(a).

seventy ['sɛvntɪ] *num* settanta.

sever ['sɛvə*] *vt* recidere, tagliare; (*relations*) troncare.

several ['sɛvərl] *adj, pron* alcuni(e), diversi(e); **~ of us** alcuni di noi; **~ times** diverse volte.

severance ['sɛvərəns] *n* (*of relations*) rottura.

severance pay *n* indennità di licenziamento.

severe [sɪ'vɪə*] *adj* severo(a); (*serious*) serio(a), grave; (*hard*) duro(a); (*plain*) semplice, sobrio(a).

severely [sɪ'vɪəlɪ] *adv* (*gen*) severamente; (*wounded, ill*) gravemente.

severity [sɪ'vɛrɪtɪ] *n* severità; gravità; (*of weather*) rigore *m*.

sew, *pt* **sewed**, *pp* **sewn** [səu, səud, səun] *vt, vi* cucire.

▶**sew up** *vt* ricucire; **it is all sewn up** (*fig*) è tutto apposto.

sewage ['suːɪdʒ] *n* acque *fpl* di scolo.

sewage works *n* stabilimento per la depurazione dei liquami.

sewer ['suːə*] *n* fogna.

sewing ['səuɪŋ] *n* cucito.

sewing machine *n* macchina da cucire.

sewn [səun] *pp of* **sew**.

sex [sɛks] *n* sesso; **to have ~ with** avere rapporti sessuali con.

sex act *n* atto sessuale.

sex appeal *n* sex appeal *m inv*.

sex education *n* educazione *f* sessuale.

sexism ['sɛksɪzəm] *n* sessismo.

sexist ['sɛksɪst] *adj* sessista.

sex life *n* vita sessuale.

sex object *n* oggetto sessuale; **to be treated like a ~** (*woman*) essere trattata da donna oggetto.

sextet [sɛks'tɛt] *n* sestetto.

sexual ['sɛksjuəl] *adj* sessuale; **~ assault** violenza carnale; **~ harassment** molestie *fpl* sessuali; **~ intercourse** rapporti *mpl* sessuali.

sexy ['sɛksɪ] *adj* provocante, sexy *inv*.

Seychelles [seɪ'ʃɛlz] *npl*: **the ~** le Seicelle.

SF *n abbr* = **science fiction**.

SG *n abbr* (*US*) = **Surgeon General**.

Sgt. *abbr* (= *sergeant*) serg.

shabbiness ['ʃæbɪnɪs] *n* trasandatezza; squallore *m*; meschinità.

shabby ['ʃæbɪ] *adj* trasandato(a); (*building*) squallido(a), malandato(a); (*behaviour*) meschino(a).

shack [ʃæk] *n* baracca, capanna.

shackles ['ʃæklz] *npl* ferri *mpl*, catene *fpl*.

shade [ʃeɪd] *n* ombra; (*for lamp*) paralume *m*; (*of colour*) tonalità *f inv*; (*US: window ~*) veneziana; (*small quantity*): **a ~ of** un po' *or* un'ombra di ♦ *vt* ombreggiare, fare ombra a; **~s** *npl* (*US: sunglasses*) occhiali *mpl* da sole; **in the ~** all'ombra; **a ~ smaller** un tantino più piccolo.

shadow ['ʃædəu] *n* ombra ♦ *vt* (*follow*) pedinare; **without** *or* **beyond a ~ of doubt** senz'ombra di dubbio.

shadow cabinet *n* (*BRIT POL*) governo *m* ombra *inv*.

shadowy ['ʃædəuɪ] *adj* ombreggiato(a), ombroso(a); (*dim*) vago(a), indistinto(a).

shady ['ʃeɪdɪ] *adj* ombroso(a); (*fig: dishonest*) losco(a), equivoco(a).

shaft [ʃɑːft] *n* (*of arrow, spear*) asta; (*AUT, TECH*) albero; (*of mine*) pozzo; (*of lift*) tromba; (*of light*) raggio; **ventilator ~** condotto di ventilazione.

shaggy ['ʃægɪ] *adj* ispido(a).

shake [ʃeɪk] *vb* (*pt* **shook**, *pp* **shaken** [ʃuk, 'ʃeɪkn]) *vt* scuotere; (*bottle, cocktail*) agitare ♦ *vi* tremare ♦ *n* scossa; **to ~ one's head** scuotere la testa; **to ~ hands with sb** stringere *or* dare la mano a qn.

▶**shake off** *vt* scrollare (via); (*fig*) sbarazzarsi di.

▶**shake up** *vt* scuotere.

shake-up ['ʃeɪkʌp] *n* riorganizzazione *f* drastica.

shakily ['ʃeɪkɪlɪ] *adv* (*reply*) con voce tremante; (*walk*) con passo malfermo; (*write*) con mano tremante.

shaky ['ʃeɪkɪ] *adj* (*hand, voice*) tremante; (*memory*) labile; (*knowledge*) incerto(a); (*building*) traballante.

shale [ʃeɪl] *n* roccia scistosa.

shall [ʃæl] *aux vb*: **I ~ go** andrò.

shallot [ʃə'lɔt] *n* (*BRIT*) scalogna.

shallow ['ʃæləu] *adj* poco profondo(a); (*fig*) superficiale.

sham [ʃæm] *n* finzione *f*, messinscena; (*jewellery, furniture*) imitazione *f* ♦ *adj* finto(a) ♦ *vt* fingere, simulare.

shambles ['ʃæmblz] *n* confusione *f*, baraonda, scompiglio; **the economy is (in) a complete ~** l'economia è nel caos più totale.

shambolic [ʃæm'bɔlɪk] *adj* (*col*) incasinato(a).

shame [ʃeɪm] *n* vergogna ♦ *vt* far vergognare; **it is a ~ (that/to do)** è un peccato (che + *sub/*fare); **what a ~!** che peccato!; **to put sb/sth to ~** (*fig*) far sfigurare qn/qc.

shamefaced ['ʃeɪmfeɪst] *adj* vergognoso(a).

shameful ['ʃeɪmful] *adj* vergognoso(a).

shameless ['ʃeɪmlɪs] *adj* sfrontato(a); (*immodest*) spudorato(a).

shampoo [ʃæm'puː] *n* shampoo *m inv* ♦ *vt* fare lo shampoo a; **~ and set** shampoo e messa in piega.

shamrock ['ʃæmrɔk] *n* trifoglio (*simbolo nazionale dell'Irlanda*).

shandy ['ʃændɪ] *n* birra con gassosa.

shan't [ʃɑːnt] = **shall not**.

shanty town ['ʃæntɪ-] *n* bidonville *f inv*.

SHAPE [ʃeɪp] *n abbr* (= *Supreme Headquarters Allied Powers, Europe*) *supremo quartier generale delle Potenze Alleate in Europa*.

shape [ʃeɪp] *n* forma ♦ *vt* (*clay, stone*) dar forma a; (*fig: ideas, character*) formare; (: *course of events*) determinare; condizionare; (*statement*) formulare; (*sb's ideas*) condizionare ♦ *vi* (*also*: **~ up**: *events*) andare, mettersi; (: *person*) cavarsela; **to take ~** prendere forma; **in the ~ of a heart** a forma di cuore; **to get o.s. into ~** rimettersi in forma; **I can't bear gardening in any ~ or form** detesto il giardinaggio d'ogni genere e specie.

-shaped [ʃeɪpt] *suffix*: **heart-~** a forma di cuore.

shapeless ['ʃeɪplɪs] *adj* senza forma, informe.

shapely ['ʃeɪplɪ] *adj* ben proporzionato(a).

share [ʃɛə*] *n* (*thing received, contribution*) parte *f*; (*COMM*) azione *f* ♦ *vt* dividere; (*have in common*) condividere, avere in comune; **to ~ out (among *or* between)** dividere (tra); **to ~ in** partecipare a.

share capital *n* capitale *m* azionario.

share certificate *n* certificato azionario.

shareholder ['ʃɛəhəuldə*] *n* azionista *m/f*.

share index *n* listino di Borsa.

shark [ʃɑːk] *n* squalo, pescecane *m*.

sharp [ʃɑːp] *adj* (*razor, knife*) affilato(a); (*point*) acuto(a), acuminato(a); (*nose, chin*) aguzzo(a); (*outline*) netto(a); (*curve, bend*) stretto(a), accentuato(a); (*cold, pain*) pungente; (*voice*) stridulo(a); (*person: quick-witted*) sveglio(a); (: *unscrupulous*) disonesto(a); (*MUS*): **C ~** do diesis ♦ *n* (*MUS*) diesis *m inv* ♦ *adv*: **at 2 o'clock ~** alle due in punto; **turn ~ left**

giri tutto a sinistra; **to be ~ with sb** rimproverare qn; **look ~!** sbrigati!

sharpen ['ʃɑːpən] *vt* affilare; (*pencil*) fare la punta a; (*fig*) aguzzare.

sharpener ['ʃɑːpnə*] *n* (*also*: **pencil ~**) temperamatite *m inv*; (*also*: **knife ~**) affilacoltelli *m inv*.

sharp-eyed [ʃɑːp'aɪd] *adj* dalla vista acuta.

sharpish ['ʃɑːpɪʃ] *adv* (*BRIT col: quickly*) subito.

sharply ['ʃɑːplɪ] *adv* (*abruptly*) bruscamente; (*clearly*) nettamente; (*harshly*) duramente, aspramente.

sharp-tempered [ʃɑːp'tɛmpəd] *adj* irascibile.

shatter ['ʃætə*] *vt* mandare in frantumi, frantumare; (*fig: upset*) distruggere; (: *ruin*) rovinare ♦ *vi* frantumarsi, andare in pezzi.

shattered ['ʃætəd] *adj* (*grief-stricken*) sconvolto(a); (*exhausted*) a pezzi, distrutto(a).

shatterproof ['ʃætəpruːf] *adj* infrangibile.

shave [ʃeɪv] *vt* radere, rasare ♦ *vi* radersi, farsi la barba ♦ *n*: **to have a ~** farsi la barba.

shaven ['ʃeɪvn] *adj* (*head*) rasato(a), tonsurato(a).

shaver ['ʃeɪvə*] *n* (*also*: **electric ~**) rasoio elettrico.

shaving ['ʃeɪvɪŋ] *n* (*action*) rasatura; **~s** *npl* (*of wood etc*) trucioli *mpl*.

shaving brush *n* pennello da barba.

shaving cream *n* crema da barba.

shaving soap *n* sapone *m* da barba.

shawl [ʃɔːl] *n* scialle *m*.

she [ʃiː] *pron* ella, lei; **there ~ is** eccola; **~-bear** orsa; **~-elephant** elefantessa; *NB: for ships, countries follow the gender of your translation.*

sheaf, *pl* **sheaves** [ʃiːf, ʃiːvz] *n* covone *m*.

shear [ʃɪə*] *vt* (*pt* **~ed**, *pp* **~ed** *or* **shorn** [ʃɔːn]) (*sheep*) tosare.

▶**shear off** *vi* (*break off*) spezzarsi.

shears ['ʃɪəz] *npl* (*for hedge*) cesoie *fpl*.

sheath [ʃiːθ] *n* fodero, guaina; (*contraceptive*) preservativo.

sheathe [ʃiːð] *vt* rivestire; (*sword*) rinfoderare.

sheath knife *n* coltello (con fodero).

sheaves [ʃiːvz] *npl of* **sheaf**.

shed [ʃɛd] *n* capannone *m* ♦ *vt* (*pt, pp* **shed**) (*leaves, fur etc*) perdere; (*tears*) versare; **to ~ light on** (*problem, mystery*) far luce su.

she'd [ʃiːd] = **she had; she would**.

sheen [ʃiːn] *n* lucentezza.

sheep [ʃiːp] *n* (*pl inv*) pecora.

sheepdog ['ʃiːpdɔg] *n* cane *m* da pastore.
sheep farmer *n* allevatore *m* di pecore.
sheepish ['ʃiːpɪʃ] *adj* vergognoso(a),
timido(a).
sheepskin ['ʃiːpskɪn] *n* pelle *f* di pecora.
sheepskin jacket *n* (giacca di) montone *m*.
sheer [ʃɪə*] *adj* (*utter*) vero(a) (e
proprio(a)); (*steep*) a picco,
perpendicolare; (*transparent*) trasparente
♦ *adv* a picco; **by ~ chance** per puro caso.
sheet [ʃiːt] *n* (*on bed*) lenzuolo; (*of paper*)
foglio; (*of glass*) lastra; (*of metal*) foglio,
lamina.
sheet feed *n* (*on printer*) alimentazione *f* di
fogli.
sheet lightning *n* lampo diffuso.
sheet metal *n* lamiera.
sheet music *n* fogli *mpl* di musica.
sheik(h) [ʃeɪk] *n* sceicco.
shelf, *pl* **shelves** [ʃelf, ʃelvz] *n* scaffale *m*,
mensola.
shelf life *n* (*COMM*) durata di
conservazione.
shell [ʃel] *n* (*on beach*) conchiglia; (*of egg,
nut etc*) guscio; (*explosive*) granata; (*of
building*) scheletro, struttura ♦ *vt* (*peas*)
sgranare; (*MIL*) bombardare,
cannoneggiare.
▶**shell out** *vi* (*col*): **to ~ out (for)** sganciare
soldi (per).
she'll [ʃiːl] = **she will; she shall**.
shellfish ['ʃelfɪʃ] *n* (*pl inv*) (*crab etc*)
crostaceo; (*scallop etc*) mollusco; (*pl: as
food*) crostacei; molluschi.
shellsuit ['ʃelsuːt] *n* tuta di acetato.
shelter ['ʃeltə*] *n* riparo, rifugio ♦ *vt*
riparare, proteggere; (*give lodging to*)
dare rifugio *or* asilo a ♦ *vi* ripararsi,
mettersi al riparo; **to take ~ (from)**
mettersi al riparo (da).
sheltered ['ʃeltəd] *adj* (*life*) ritirato(a);
(*spot*) riparato(a), protetto(a).
shelve [ʃelv] *vt* (*fig*) accantonare,
rimandare.
shelves [ʃelvz] *npl of* **shelf**.
shelving ['ʃelvɪŋ] *n* scaffalature *fpl*.
shepherd ['ʃepəd] *n* pastore *m* ♦ *vt* (*guide*)
guidare.
shepherdess ['ʃepədɪs] *n* pastora.
shepherd's pie *n* timballo di carne
macinata e purè di patate.
sherbet ['ʃɔːbət] *n* (*BRIT: powder*) polvere
effervescente al gusto di frutta; (*US: water
ice*) sorbetto.
sheriff ['ʃerɪf] *n* sceriffo.
sherry ['ʃerɪ] *n* sherry *m inv*.
she's [ʃiːz] = **she is; she has**.
Shetland ['ʃetlənd] *n* (*also:* **the ~s, the ~**

Isles) le (isole) Shetland.
Shetland pony *n* pony *m inv* delle
Shetland.
shield [ʃiːld] *n* scudo ♦ *vt*: **to ~ (from)**
riparare (da), proteggere (da *or* contro).
shift [ʃɪft] *n* (*change*) cambiamento; (*of
workers*) turno ♦ *vt* spostare, muovere;
(*remove*) rimuovere ♦ *vi* spostarsi,
muoversi; **~ in demand** (*COMM*)
variazione *f* della domanda; **the wind has
~ed to the south** il vento si è girato e
soffia da sud.
shift key *n* (*on typewriter*) tasto delle
maiuscole.
shiftless ['ʃɪftlɪs] *adj* fannullone(a).
shift work *n* lavoro a squadre; **to do ~**
fare i turni.
shifty ['ʃɪftɪ] *adj* ambiguo(a); (*eyes*)
sfuggente.
Shiite ['ʃiːaɪt] *adj, n* sciita (*m/f*).
shilling ['ʃɪlɪŋ] *n* (*BRIT*) scellino (= *12 old
pence; 20 in a pound*).
shilly-shally ['ʃɪlɪʃælɪ] *vi* tentennare,
esitare.
shimmer ['ʃɪmə*] *vi* brillare, luccicare.
shimmering ['ʃɪmərɪŋ] *adj* (*gen*) luccicante,
scintillante; (*haze*) tremolante; (*satin etc*)
cangiante.
shin [ʃɪn] *n* tibia ♦ *vi*: **to ~ up/down a tree**
arrampicarsi in cima a/scivolare giù da
un albero.
shindig ['ʃɪndɪg] *n* (*col*) festa chiassosa.
shine [ʃaɪn] *n* splendore *m*, lucentezza ♦ *vb*
(*pt, pp* **shone** [ʃɔn]) *vi* (ri)splendere,
brillare ♦ *vt* far brillare, far risplendere;
(*torch*): **to ~ sth on** puntare qc verso.
shingle ['ʃɪŋgl] *n* (*on beach*) ciottoli *mpl*; (*on
roof*) assicella di copertura.
shingles ['ʃɪŋglz] *n* (*MED*) herpes zoster *m*.
shining ['ʃaɪnɪŋ] *adj* (*surface, hair*) lucente;
(*light*) brillante.
shiny ['ʃaɪnɪ] *adj* lucente, lucido(a).
ship [ʃɪp] *n* nave *f* ♦ *vt* trasportare (via
mare); (*send*) spedire (via mare); (*load*)
imbarcare, caricare; **on board ~** a bordo.
shipbuilder ['ʃɪpbɪldə*] *n* costruttore *m*
navale.
shipbuilding ['ʃɪpbɪldɪŋ] *n* costruzione *f*
navale.
ship chandler [-'tʃɑːndlə*] *n* fornitore *m*
marittimo.
shipment ['ʃɪpmənt] *n* carico.
shipowner ['ʃɪpəunə*] *n* armatore *m*.
shipper ['ʃɪpə*] *n* spedizioniere *m*
(marittimo).
shipping ['ʃɪpɪŋ] *n* (*ships*) naviglio; (*traffic*)
navigazione *f*.
shipping agent *n* agente *m* marittimo.

shipping company n compagnia di navigazione.
shipping lane n rotta (di navigazione).
shipping line n = shipping company.
shipshape ['ʃɪpʃeɪp] adj in perfetto ordine.
shipwreck ['ʃɪprɛk] n relitto; (event) naufragio ♦ vt: **to be ~ed** naufragare, fare naufragio.
shipyard ['ʃɪpjɑːd] n cantiere m navale.
shire ['ʃaɪə*] n (BRIT) contea.
shirk [ʃəːk] vt sottrarsi a, evitare.
shirt [ʃəːt] n (man's) camicia; **in ~ sleeves** in maniche di camicia.
shirty ['ʃəːtɪ] adj (BRIT col) incavolato(a).
shit [ʃɪt] excl (col!) merda(!).
shiver ['ʃɪvə*] n brivido ♦ vi rabbrividire, tremare.
shoal [ʃəul] n (of fish) banco.
shock [ʃɔk] n (impact) urto, colpo; (ELEC) scossa; (emotional) colpo, shock m inv; (MED) shock ♦ vt colpire, scioccare; scandalizzare; **to give sb a ~** far venire un colpo a qn; **to be suffering from ~** essere in stato di shock; **it came as a ~ to hear that ...** è stata una grossa sorpresa sentire che ....
shock absorber n ammortizzatore m.
shocker ['ʃɔkə*] n: **it was a real ~** (col) è stata una vera bomba.
shocking ['ʃɔkɪŋ] adj scioccante, traumatizzante; (scandalous) scandaloso(a); (very bad: weather, handwriting) orribile; (: results) disastroso(a).
shockproof ['ʃɔkpruːf] adj antiurto inv.
shock therapy, shock treatment n (MED) shockterapia.
shock wave n onda d'urto; (fig: usually pl) impatto msg.
shod [ʃɔd] pt, pp of shoe.
shoddy ['ʃɔdɪ] adj scadente.
shoe [ʃuː] n scarpa; (also: horse~) ferro di cavallo; (brake ~) ganascia (del freno) ♦ vt (pt, pp shod [ʃɔd]) (horse) ferrare.
shoebrush ['ʃuːbrʌʃ] n spazzola per le scarpe.
shoehorn ['ʃuːhɔːn] n calzante m.
shoelace ['ʃuːleɪs] n stringa.
shoemaker ['ʃuːmeɪkə*] n calzolaio.
shoe polish n lucido per scarpe.
shoeshop ['ʃuːʃɔp] n calzoleria.
shoestring ['ʃuːstrɪŋ] n stringa (delle scarpe); **on a ~** (fig: do sth) con quattro soldi.
shoetree ['ʃuːtriː] n forma per scarpe.
shone [ʃɔn] pt, pp of shine.
shoo [ʃuː] excl sciò!, via! ♦ vt (also: ~ away, ~ off) cacciare (via).

shook [ʃuk] pt of shake.
shoot [ʃuːt] n (on branch, seedling) germoglio; (shooting party) partita di caccia; (competition) gara di tiro ♦ vb (pt, pp shot [ʃɔt]) vt (game: BRIT) cacciare, andare a caccia di; (person) sparare a; (execute) fucilare; (film) girare ♦ vi (with gun): **to ~ (at)** sparare (a), fare fuoco (su); (with bow): **to ~ (at)** tirare (su); (FOOTBALL) sparare, tirare (forte); **to ~ past sb** passare vicino a qn come un fulmine; **to ~ in/out** entrare/uscire come una freccia.
▶**shoot down** vt (plane) abbattere.
▶**shoot up** vi (fig) salire alle stelle.
shooting ['ʃuːtɪŋ] n (shots) sparatoria; (murder) uccisione f (a colpi d'arma da fuoco); (HUNTING) caccia; (CINE) riprese fpl.
shooting range n poligono (di tiro), tirassegno.
shooting star n stella cadente.
shop [ʃɔp] n negozio; (workshop) officina ♦ vi (also: **go ~ping**) fare spese; **repair ~** officina di riparazione; **to talk ~** (fig) parlare di lavoro.
▶**shop around** vi fare il giro dei negozi.
shopaholic ['ʃɔpə'hɔlɪk] n (col) maniaco/a dello shopping.
shop assistant n (BRIT) commesso/a.
shop floor n (BRIT: fig) operai mpl, maestranze fpl.
shopkeeper ['ʃɔpkiːpə*] n negoziante m/f, bottegaio/a.
shoplift ['ʃɔplɪft] vi taccheggiare.
shoplifter ['ʃɔplɪftə*] n taccheggiatore/trice.
shoplifting ['ʃɔplɪftɪŋ] n taccheggio.
shopper ['ʃɔpə*] n compratore/trice.
shopping ['ʃɔpɪŋ] n (goods) spesa, acquisti mpl.
shopping bag n borsa per la spesa.
shopping centre n centro commerciale.
shop-soiled ['ʃɔpsɔɪld] adj sciupato(a) a forza di stare in vetrina.
shop steward n (BRIT INDUSTRY) rappresentante m sindacale.
shop window n vetrina.
shore [ʃɔː*] n (of sea) riva, spiaggia; (of lake) riva ♦ vt: **to ~ (up)** puntellare; **on ~** a terra.
shore leave n (NAUT) franchigia.
shorn [ʃɔːn] pp of shear.
short [ʃɔːt] adj (not long) corto(a); (soon finished) breve; (person) basso(a); (curt) brusco(a), secco(a); (insufficient) insufficiente ♦ n (also: ~ film) cortometraggio; **it is ~ for** è

l'abbreviazione *or* il diminutivo di; **a ~ time ago** poco tempo fa; **in the ~ term** nell'immediato futuro; **to be ~ of sth** essere a corto di *or* mancare di qc; **to run ~ of sth** rimanere senza qc; **to be in ~ supply** scarseggiare; **I'm 3 ~** me ne mancano 3; **in ~** in breve; **~ of doing** a meno che non si faccia; **everything ~ of** tutto fuorché; **to cut ~** (*speech, visit*) accorciare, abbreviare; (*person*) interrompere; **to fall ~ of** venire meno a; non soddisfare; **to stop ~** fermarsi di colpo; **to stop ~ of** non arrivare fino a; *see also* **shorts.**

shortage ['ʃɔːtɪdʒ] *n* scarsezza, carenza.

shortbread ['ʃɔːtbred] *n* biscotto di pasta frolla.

short-change [ʃɔːt'tʃeɪndʒ] *vt*: **to ~ sb** imbrogliare qn sul resto.

short-circuit [ʃɔːt'səːkɪt] *n* cortocircuito ♦ *vt* cortocircuitare ♦ *vi* fare cortocircuito.

shortcoming ['ʃɔːtkʌmɪŋ] *n* difetto.

short(crust) pastry ['ʃɔːt(krʌst)-] *n* (*BRIT*) pasta frolla.

shortcut ['ʃɔːtkʌt] *n* scorciatoia.

shorten ['ʃɔːtn] *vt* accorciare, ridurre.

shortening ['ʃɔːtnɪŋ] *n* grasso per pasticceria.

shortfall ['ʃɔːtfɔːl] *n* deficienza.

shorthand ['ʃɔːthænd] *n* (*BRIT*) stenografia; **to take sth down in ~** stenografare qc.

shorthand notebook *n* (*BRIT*) bloc-notes *m inv* per stenografia.

shorthand typist *n* (*BRIT*) stenodattilografo/a.

short list *n* (*BRIT*: *for job*) rosa dei candidati.

short-lived ['ʃɔːt'lɪvd] *adj* effimero(a), di breve durata.

shortly ['ʃɔːtlɪ] *adv* fra poco.

shortness ['ʃɔːtnɪs] *n* brevità; insufficienza.

shorts [ʃɔːts] *npl* (*also*: **a pair of ~**) i calzoncini.

short-sighted [ʃɔːt'saɪtɪd] *adj* (*BRIT*) miope; (*fig*) poco avveduto(a).

short-staffed [ʃɔːt'stɑːft] *adj* a corto di personale.

short story *n* racconto, novella.

short-tempered [ʃɔːt'tɛmpəd] *adj* irascibile.

short-term ['ʃɔːttəːm] *adj* (*effect*) di *or* a breve durata.

short time *n* (*INDUSTRY*): **to work ~, be on ~** essere *or* lavorare a orario ridotto.

short wave *n* (*RADIO*) onde *fpl* corte.

shot [ʃɔt] *pt, pp of* **shoot** ♦ *n* sparo, colpo; (*shotgun pellets*) pallottole *fpl*; (*person*)

tiratore *m*; (*try*) prova; (*injection*) iniezione *f*; (*PHOT*) foto *f inv*; **like a ~** come un razzo; (*very readily*) immediatamente; **to fire a ~ at sb/sth** sparare un colpo a qn/qc; **to have a ~ at sth/doing sth** provarci con qc/a fare qc; **a big ~** (*col*) un pezzo grosso, un papavero; **to get ~ of sb/sth** (*col*) sbarazzarsi di qn/qc.

shotgun ['ʃɔtgʌn] *n* fucile *m* da caccia.

should [ʃud] *aux vb*: **I ~ go now** dovrei andare ora; **he ~ be there now** dovrebbe essere arrivato ora; **I ~ go if I were you** se fossi in lei andrei; **I ~ like to** mi piacerebbe; **~ he phone...** se telefonasse....

shoulder ['ʃəʊldə*] *n* spalla; (*BRIT*: *of road*): **hard ~** corsia d'emergenza ♦ *vt* (*fig*) addossarsi, prendere sulle proprie spalle; **to look over one's ~** guardarsi alle spalle; **to rub ~s with sb** (*fig*) essere a contatto con qn; **to give sb the cold ~** (*fig*) trattare qn con freddezza.

shoulder bag *n* borsa a tracolla.

shoulder blade *n* scapola.

shoulder strap *n* bretella, spallina.

shouldn't ['ʃudnt] = **should not.**

shout [ʃaut] *n* urlo, grido ♦ *vt* gridare ♦ *vi* urlare, gridare; **to give sb a ~** chiamare qn gridando.

▶**shout down** *vt* zittire gridando.

shouting ['ʃautɪŋ] *n* urli *mpl*.

shouting match *n* (*col*) vivace scambio di opinioni.

shove [ʃʌv] *vt* spingere; (*col*: *put*): **to ~ sth in** ficcare qc in ♦ *n* spintone *m*; **he ~d me out of the way** mi ha spinto da parte.

▶**shove off** *vi* (*NAUT*) scostarsi.

shovel ['ʃʌvl] *n* pala ♦ *vt* spalare.

show [ʃəʊ] *n* (*of emotion*) dimostrazione *f*, manifestazione *f*; (*semblance*) apparenza; (*exhibition*) mostra, esposizione *f*; (*THEAT, CINE*) spettacolo; (*COMM, TECH*) salone *m*, fiera ♦ *vb* (*pt ~ed, pp* **shown** [ʃəʊn]) *vt* far vedere, mostrare; (*courage etc*) dimostrare, dar prova di; (*exhibit*) esporre ♦ *vi* vedersi, essere visibile; **to ~ sb to his seat/to the door** accompagnare qn al suo posto/alla porta; **to ~ a profit/loss** (*COMM*) registrare un utile/una perdita; **it just goes to ~ that ...** il che sta a dimostrare che ...; **to ask for a ~ of hands** chiedere che si voti per alzata di mano; **to be on ~** essere esposto; **it's just for ~** è solo per far scena; **who's running the ~ here?** (*col*) chi è il padrone qui?

▶**show in** *vt* far entrare.

▶**show off** *vi* (*pej*) esibirsi, mettersi in mostra ♦ *vt* (*display*) mettere in risalto;

(*pej*) mettere in mostra.

▶**show out** *vt* accompagnare alla porta.

▶**show up** *vi* (*stand out*) essere ben visibile; (*col: turn up*) farsi vedere ♦ *vt* mettere in risalto; (*unmask*) smascherare.

showbiz ['ʃəubɪz] *n* (*col*) = **show business**.

show business *n* industria dello spettacolo.

showcase ['ʃəukeɪs] *n* vetrina, bacheca.

showdown ['ʃəudaun] *n* prova di forza.

shower ['ʃauə*] *n* (*also*: ~ **bath**) doccia; (*rain*) acquazzone *m*; (*of stones etc*) pioggia; (*US: party*) *festa* (*di fidanzamento etc*) *in cui si fanno regali alla persona festeggiata* ♦ *vi* fare la doccia ♦ *vt*: **to** ~ **sb with** (*gifts, abuse etc*) coprire qn di; (*missiles*) lanciare contro qn una pioggia di; **to have** *or* **take a** ~ fare la doccia.

shower cap *n* cuffia da doccia.

showerproof ['ʃauəpruːf] *adj* impermeabile.

showery ['ʃauərɪ] *adj* (*weather*) con piogge intermittenti.

showground ['ʃəugraund] *n* terreno d'esposizione.

showing ['ʃəuɪŋ] *n* (*of film*) proiezione *f*.

show jumping *n* concorso ippico (di salto ad ostacoli).

showman ['ʃəumən] *n* (*at fair, circus*) impresario; (*fig*) attore *m*.

showmanship ['ʃəumənʃɪp] *n* abilità d'impresario.

shown [ʃəun] *pp of* **show**.

show-off ['ʃəuɔf] *n* (*col: person*) esibizionista *m/f*.

showpiece ['ʃəupiːs] *n* (*of exhibition*) pezzo forte; **that hospital is a** ~ **is** è un ospedale modello.

showroom ['ʃəurum] *n* sala d'esposizione.

show trial *n* processo a scopo dimostrativo (*spesso ideologico*).

showy ['ʃəuɪ] *adj* vistoso(a), appariscente.

shrank [ʃræŋk] *pt of* **shrink**.

shrapnel ['ʃræpnl] *n* shrapnel *m*.

shred [ʃrɛd] *n* (*gen pl*) brandello; (*fig: of truth, evidence*) briciolo ♦ *vt* fare a brandelli; (*CULIN*) sminuzzare, tagliuzzare; (*documents*) distruggere, sminuzzare.

shredder ['ʃrɛdə*] *n* (*for documents, papers*) distruttore *m* di documenti, sminuzzatrice *f*.

shrew [ʃruː] *n* (*ZOOL*) toporagno; (*fig: pej: woman*) strega.

shrewd [ʃruːd] *adj* astuto(a), scaltro(a).

shrewdness ['ʃruːdnɪs] *n* astuzia.

shriek [ʃriːk] *n* strillo ♦ *vt, vi* strillare.

shrift [ʃrɪft] *n*: **to give sb short** ~ sbrigare qn.

shrill [ʃrɪl] *adj* acuto(a), stridulo(a), stridente.

shrimp [ʃrɪmp] *n* gamberetto.

shrine [ʃraɪn] *n* reliquario; (*place*) santuario.

shrink [ʃrɪŋk] *vb* (*pt* **shrank** [ʃræŋk, ʃrʌŋk]) *vi* restringersi; (*fig*) ridursi ♦ *vt* (*wool*) far restringere ♦ *n* (*col: pej*) psicanalista *m/f*; **to** ~ **from doing sth** rifuggire dal fare qc.

shrinkage ['ʃrɪŋkɪdʒ] *n* restringimento.

shrink-wrap ['ʃrɪŋkræp] *vt* confezionare con plastica sottile.

shrivel ['ʃrɪvl] (*also*: ~ **up**) *vt* raggrinzare, avvizzire ♦ *vi* raggrinzirsi, avvizzire.

shroud [ʃraud] *n* lenzuolo funebre ♦ *vt*: ~**ed in mystery** avvolto(a) nel mistero.

Shrove Tuesday ['ʃrəuv-] *n* martedì *m* grasso.

shrub [ʃrʌb] *n* arbusto.

shrubbery ['ʃrʌbərɪ] *n* arbusti *mpl*.

shrug [ʃrʌg] *n* scrollata di spalle ♦ *vt, vi*: **to** ~ (**one's shoulders**) alzare le spalle, fare spallucce.

▶**shrug off** *vt* passare sopra a; (*cold, illness*) sbarazzarsi di.

shrunk [ʃrʌŋk] *pp of* **shrink**.

shrunken ['ʃrʌŋkən] *adj* rattrappito(a).

shudder ['ʃʌdə*] *n* brivido ♦ *vi* rabbrividire.

shuffle ['ʃʌfl] *vt* (*cards*) mescolare; **to** ~ (**one's feet**) strascicare i piedi.

shun [ʃʌn] *vt* sfuggire, evitare.

shunt [ʃʌnt] *vt* (*RAIL: direct*) smistare; (: *divert*) deviare ♦ *vi*: **to** ~ (**to and fro**) fare la spola.

shunting yard *n* fascio di smistamento.

shush [ʃuʃ] *excl* zitto(a)!

shut, *pt, pp* **shut** [ʃʌt] *vt* chiudere ♦ *vi* chiudersi, chiudere.

▶**shut down** *vt, vi* chiudere definitivamente.

▶**shut off** *vt* (*stop: power*) staccare; (: *water*) chiudere; (: *engine*) spegnere; (*isolate*) isolare.

▶**shut out** *vt* (*person, noise, cold*) non far entrare; (*block: view*) impedire, bloccare; (: *memory*) scacciare.

▶**shut up** *vi* (*col: keep quiet*) stare zitto(a) ♦ *vt* (*close*) chiudere; (*silence*) far tacere.

shutdown ['ʃʌtdaun] *n* chiusura.

shutter ['ʃʌtə*] *n* imposta; (*PHOT*) otturatore *m*.

shuttle ['ʃʌtl] *n* spola, navetta; (*also*: ~ **service**) servizio *m* navetta *inv* ♦ *vi* (*subj: vehicle, person*) fare la spola ♦ *vt* (*to and* *fro: passengers*) portare (avanti e indietro).

shuttlecock ['ʃʌtlkɔk] *n* volano.

shuttle diplomacy *n* frequenti mediazioni *fpl* diplomatiche.

shy [ʃaɪ] *adj* timido(a) ♦ *vi*: **to ~ away from doing sth** (*fig*) rifuggire dal fare qc; **to fight ~ of** tenersi alla larga da; **to be ~ of doing sth** essere restio a fare qc.

shyness ['ʃaɪnɪs] *n* timidezza.

Siam [saɪˈæm] *n* Siam *m*.

Siamese [saɪəˈmiːz] *adj*: ~ **cat** gatto siamese; ~ **twins** fratelli *mpl* (*or* sorelle *fpl*) siamesi.

Siberia [saɪˈbɪərɪə] *n* Siberia.

sibling ['sɪblɪŋ] *n* (*formal*) fratello/sorella.

Sicilian [sɪˈsɪlɪən] *adj, n* siciliano(a).

Sicily ['sɪsɪlɪ] *n* Sicilia.

sick [sɪk] *adj* (*ill*) malato(a); (*vomiting*): **to be ~** vomitare; (*humour*) macabro(a); **to feel ~** avere la nausea; **to be ~ of** (*fig*) averne abbastanza di; **a ~ person** un malato; **to be (off) ~** essere assente perché malato; **to fall** *or* **take ~** ammalarsi.

sickbag ['sɪkbæg] *n* sacchetto (*da usarsi in caso di malessere*).

sick bay *n* infermeria.

sick building syndrome *n* malattia *causata da mancanza di ventilazione e luce naturale.*

sicken ['sɪkn] *vt* nauseare ♦ *vi*: **to be ~ing for sth** (*cold, flu etc*) covare qc.

sickening ['sɪknɪŋ] *adj* (*fig*) disgustoso(a), rivoltante.

sickle ['sɪkl] *n* falcetto.

sick leave *n* congedo per malattia.

sickle-cell anaemia ['sɪklsɛl-] *n* anemia drepanocitica.

sickly ['sɪklɪ] *adj* malaticcio(a); (*causing nausea*) nauseante.

sickness ['sɪknɪs] *n* malattia; (*vomiting*) vomito.

sickness benefit *n* indennità di malattia.

sick pay *n* sussidio per malattia.

sickroom ['sɪkruːm] *n* stanza di malato.

side [saɪd] *n* (*gen*) lato; (*of person, animal*) fianco; (*of lake*) riva; (*face, surface: gen*) faccia; (*: of paper*) facciata; (*fig: aspect*) aspetto, lato; (*team: SPORT*) squadra; (*: POL etc*) parte *f* ♦ *cpd* (*door, entrance*) laterale ♦ *vi*: **to ~ with sb** parteggiare per qn, prendere le parti di qn; **by the ~ of** a fianco di; (*road*) sul ciglio di; ~ **by ~** fianco a fianco; **to take ~s (with)** schierarsi (con); **the right/wrong ~** il dritto/rovescio; **from ~ to ~** da una parte all'altra; ~ **of beef** quarto di bue.

sideboard ['saɪdbɔːd] *n* credenza.

sideboards ['saɪdbɔːdz] (*BRIT*), **sideburns** ['saɪdbəːnz] *npl* (*whiskers*) basette *fpl*.

sidecar ['saɪdkɑː*] *n* sidecar *m inv*.

side dish *n* contorno.

side drum *n* (*MUS*) piccolo tamburo.

side effect *n* (*MED*) effetto collaterale.

sidekick ['saɪdkɪk] *n* (*col*) compagno/a.

sidelight ['saɪdlaɪt] *n* (*AUT*) luce *f* di posizione.

sideline ['saɪdlaɪn] *n* (*SPORT*) linea laterale; (*fig*) attività secondaria.

sidelong ['saɪdlɔŋ] *adj* obliquo(a); **to give a ~ glance at sth** guardare qc con la coda dell'occhio.

side plate *n* piattino.

side road *n* strada secondaria.

sidesaddle ['saɪdsædl] *adv* all'amazzone.

side show *n* attrazione *f*.

sidestep ['saɪdstɛp] *vt* (*question*) eludere; (*problem*) scavalcare ♦ *vi* (*BOXING etc*) spostarsi di lato.

side street *n* traversa.

sidetrack ['saɪdtræk] *vt* (*fig*) distrarre.

sidewalk ['saɪdwɔːk] *n* (*US*) marciapiede *m*.

sideways ['saɪdweɪz] *adv* (*move*) di lato, di fianco; (*look*) con la coda dell'occhio.

siding ['saɪdɪŋ] *n* (*RAIL*) binario di raccordo.

sidle ['saɪdl] *vi*: **to ~ up (to)** avvicinarsi furtivamente a.

SIDS *n* (= *sudden infant death syndrome*) *see* **cot death**.

siege [siːdʒ] *n* assedio; **to lay ~ to** porre l'assedio a.

siege economy *n* economia da stato d'assedio.

Sierra Leone [sɪˈɛrəlɪˈəun] *n* Sierra Leone *f*.

sieve [sɪv] *n* setaccio ♦ *vt* setacciare.

sift [sɪft] *vt* passare al crivello; (*fig*) vagliare ♦ *vi*: **to ~ through** esaminare minuziosamente.

sigh [saɪ] *n* sospiro ♦ *vi* sospirare.

sight [saɪt] *n* (*faculty*) vista; (*spectacle*) spettacolo; (*on gun*) mira ♦ *vt* avvistare; **in ~** in vista; **out of ~** non visibile; **at first ~** a prima vista; **to catch ~ of sth/sb** scorgere qc/qn; **to lose ~ of sb/sth** perdere di vista qn/qc; **to set one's ~s on sth/on doing sth** mirare a qc/a fare qc; **at ~** a vista; **I know her by ~** la conosco di vista.

sighted ['saɪtɪd] *adj* che ha il dono della vista; **partially ~** parzialmente cieco.

sightseeing ['saɪtsiːɪŋ] *n* turismo; **to go ~** visitare una località.

sightseer ['saɪtsiːə*] *n* turista *m/f*.

sign [saɪn] *n* segno; (*with hand etc*) segno, gesto; (*notice*) insegna, cartello; (*road ~*) segnale *m* ♦ *vt* firmare; **as a ~ of** in segno

di; **it's a good/bad** ~ è buon/brutto segno;
to show ~s/no ~ of doing sth
accennare/non accennare a fare qc;
plus/minus ~ segno del più/meno; **to ~
one's name** firmare, apporre la propria
firma.
▶**sign away** vt (rights etc) cedere (con una
firma).
▶**sign in** vi firmare il registro (all'arrivo).
▶**sign off** vi (RADIO, TV) chiudere le
trasmissioni.
▶**sign on** vi (MIL etc: enlist) arruolarsi; (as
unemployed) iscriversi sulla lista
(dell'ufficio di collocamento); (begin
work) prendere servizio; (enrol): **to ~ on
for a course** iscriversi a un corso.
▶**sign out** vi firmare il registro (alla
partenza).
▶**sign over** vt: **to ~ sth over to sb** cedere
qc con scrittura legale a qn.
▶**sign up** (MIL) vt arruolare ♦ vi arruolarsi.
signal ['sɪgnl] n segnale m ♦ vt (person) fare
segno a; (message) comunicare per
mezzo di segnali ♦ vi: **to ~ to sb (to do
sth)** far segno a qn (di fare qc); **to ~ a
left/right turn** (AUT) segnalare un
cambiamento di direzione a sinistra/
destra.
signal box n (RAIL) cabina di manovra.
signalman ['sɪgnlmən] n (RAIL) deviatore m.
signatory ['sɪgnətərɪ] n firmatario/a.
signature ['sɪgnətʃə*] n firma.
signature tune n sigla musicale.
signet ring ['sɪgnət-] n anello con sigillo.
significance [sɪg'nɪfɪkəns] n (of remark)
significato; (of event) importanza; **that is
of no ~** ciò non ha importanza.
significant [sɪg'nɪfɪkənt] adj (improvement,
amount) notevole; (discovery, event)
importante; (evidence, smile)
significativo(a); **it is ~ that ...** è
significativo che ....
significantly [sɪg'nɪfɪkəntlɪ] adv (smile) in
modo eloquente; (improve, increase)
considerevolmente, decisamente.
signify ['sɪgnɪfaɪ] vt significare.
sign language n linguaggio dei muti.
signpost ['saɪnpəust] n cartello indicatore.
silage ['saɪlɪdʒ] n insilato.
silence ['saɪlns] n silenzio ♦ vt far tacere,
ridurre al silenzio.
silencer ['saɪlənsə*] n (on gun, BRIT AUT)
silenziatore m.
silent ['saɪlnt] adj silenzioso(a); (film)
muto(a); **to keep** or **remain ~** tacere,
stare zitto(a).
silently ['saɪlntlɪ] adv silenziosamente, in
silenzio.

silent partner n (COMM) socio
accomandante.
silhouette [sɪlu:'ɛt] n silhouette f inv ♦ vt: **to
be ~d against** stagliarsi contro.
silicon ['sɪlɪkən] n silicio.
silicon chip n chip m inv al silicio.
silicone ['sɪlɪkəun] n silicone m.
silk [sɪlk] n seta ♦ cpd di seta.
silky ['sɪlkɪ] adj di seta, come la seta.
sill [sɪl] n (window~) davanzale m; (AUT)
predellino.
silly ['sɪlɪ] adj stupido(a), sciocco(a); **to do
something ~** fare una sciocchezza.
silo ['saɪləu] n silo.
silt [sɪlt] n limo.
silver ['sɪlvə*] n argento; (money) monete
da 5, 10, 20 o 50 pence; (also: ~**ware**)
argenteria ♦ cpd d'argento.
silver foil, (BRIT) **silver paper** n carta
argentata, (carta) stagnola.
silver-plated [sɪlvə'pleɪtɪd] adj
argentato(a).
silversmith ['sɪlvəsmɪθ] n argentiere m.
silverware ['sɪlvəwɛə*] n argenteria,
argento.
silvery ['sɪlvərɪ] adj (colour) argenteo(a);
(sound) argentino(a).
SIM card ['sɪm-] n (TEL: = Subscriber Identity
Module card) SIM card f inv.
similar ['sɪmɪlə*] adj: ~ **(to)** simile (a).
similarity [sɪmɪ'lærɪtɪ] n somiglianza,
rassomiglianza.
similarly ['sɪmɪləlɪ] adv (in a similar way) allo
stesso modo; (as is similar) così pure.
simile ['sɪmɪlɪ] n similitudine f.
simmer ['sɪmə*] vi cuocere a fuoco lento.
▶**simmer down** vi (fig col) calmarsi.
simper ['sɪmpə*] vi fare lo(la) smorfioso(a).
simpering ['sɪmpərɪŋ] adj lezioso(a),
smorfioso(a).
simple ['sɪmpl] adj semplice; **the ~ truth** la
pura verità.
simple interest n (MATH, COMM) interesse
m semplice.
simple-minded [sɪmpl'maɪndɪd] adj
sempliciotto(a).
simpleton ['sɪmpltən] n semplicione/a,
sempliciotto/a.
simplicity [sɪm'plɪsɪtɪ] n semplicità.
simplification [sɪmplɪfɪ'keɪʃən] n
semplificazione f.
simplify ['sɪmplɪfaɪ] vt semplificare.
simply ['sɪmplɪ] adv semplicemente.
simulate ['sɪmjuleɪt] vt fingere, simulare.
simulation [sɪmju'leɪʃən] n simulazione f.
simultaneous [sɪməl'teɪnɪəs] adj
simultaneo(a).
simultaneously [sɪməl'teɪnɪəslɪ] adv

simultaneamente, contemporaneamente.
sin [sɪn] *n* peccato ♦ *vi* peccare.
Sinai ['saɪnaɪ] *n* Sinai *m*.
since [sɪns] *adv* da allora ♦ *prep* da ♦ *conj* (*time*) da quando; (*because*) poiché, dato che; ~ **then** da allora; ~ **Monday** da lunedì; (**ever**) ~ **I arrived** (fin) da quando sono arrivato.
sincere [sɪn'sɪə*] *adj* sincero(a).
sincerely [sɪn'sɪəlɪ] *adv* sinceramente; **Yours** ~ (*at end of letter*) distinti saluti.
sincerity [sɪn'sɛrɪtɪ] *n* sincerità.
sine [saɪn] *n* (*MATH*) seno.
sinew ['sɪnjuː] *n* tendine *m*; ~**s** *npl* (*muscles*) muscoli *mpl*.
sinful ['sɪnful] *adj* peccaminoso(a).
sing, *pt* **sang**, *pp* **sung** [sɪŋ, sæŋ, sʌŋ] *vt*, *vi* cantare.
Singapore [sɪŋgə'pɔː*] *n* Singapore *f*.
singe [sɪndʒ] *vt* bruciacchiare.
singer ['sɪŋə*] *n* cantante *m/f*.
Singhalese [sɪŋə'liːz] *adj* = **Sinhalese**.
singing ['sɪŋɪŋ] *n* (*of person, bird*) canto; (*of kettle, bullet, in ears*) fischio.
single ['sɪŋgl] *adj* solo(a), unico(a); (*unmarried*: *man*) celibe; (: *woman*) nubile; (*not double*) semplice ♦ *n* (*BRIT*: *also*: ~ **ticket**) biglietto di (sola) andata; (*record*) 45 giri *m inv*; **not a** ~ **one was left** non ne è rimasto nemmeno uno; **every** ~ **day** tutti i santi giorni; *see also* **singles**.
▶**single out** *vt* scegliere; (*distinguish*) distinguere.
single bed *n* letto a una piazza.
single-breasted ['sɪŋglbrɛstɪd] *adj* a un petto.
Single European Market *n*: **the** ~ il Mercato Unico.
single file *n*: **in** ~ in fila indiana.
single-handed [sɪŋgl'hændɪd] *adv* senza aiuto, da solo(a).
single-minded [sɪŋgl'maɪndɪd] *adj* tenace, risoluto(a).
single parent *n* ragazzo padre/ragazza madre; genitore *m* separato; ~ **family** famiglia monoparentale.
single room *n* camera singola.
singles ['sɪŋglz] *npl* (*TENNIS*) singolo; (*US*: *single people*) single *m/f pl*.
singles bar *n* (*esp US*) bar *m inv* per single.
single-sex school ['sɪŋgl'sɛks-] *n* (*for boys*) scuola maschile; (*for girls*) scuola femminile.
singly ['sɪŋglɪ] *adv* separatamente.
singsong ['sɪŋsɔŋ] *adj* (*tone*) cantilenante ♦ *n* (*songs*): **to have a** ~ farsi una cantata.
singular ['sɪŋgjulə*] *adj* (*LING*) singolare; (*unusual*) strano(a), singolare ♦ *n* (*LING*)

singolare *m*; **in the feminine** ~ al femminile singolare.
singularly ['sɪŋgjuləlɪ] *adv* stranamente.
Sinhalese [sɪnhə'liːz] *adj* singalese.
sinister ['sɪnɪstə*] *adj* sinistro(a).
sink [sɪŋk] *n* lavandino, acquaio ♦ *vb* (*pt* **sank**, *pp* **sunk** [sæŋk, sʌŋk]) *vt* (*ship*) (fare) affondare, colare a picco; (*foundations*) scavare; (*piles etc*): **to** ~ **sth into** conficcare qc in ♦ *vi* affondare, andare a fondo; (*ground etc*) cedere, avvallarsi; **he sank into a chair/the mud** sprofondò in una poltrona/nel fango.
▶**sink in** *vi* penetrare; **it took a long time to** ~ **in** ci ho (*or* ha *etc*) messo molto a capirlo.
sinking ['sɪŋkɪŋ] *adj*: **that** ~ **feeling** una stretta allo stomaco.
sinking fund *n* (*COMM*) fondo d'ammortamento.
sink unit *n* blocco lavello.
sinner ['sɪnə*] *n* peccatore/trice.
Sinn Féin [ʃɪn'feɪn] *n* movimento separatista irlandese.
sinuous ['sɪnjuəs] *adj* sinuoso(a).
sinus ['saɪnəs] *n* (*ANAT*) seno.
sip [sɪp] *n* sorso ♦ *vt* sorseggiare.
siphon ['saɪfən] *n* sifone *m* ♦ *vt* (*funds*) trasferire.
▶**siphon off** *vt* travasare (con un sifone).
sir [sə*] *n* signore *m*; **S**~ **John Smith** Sir John Smith; **yes** ~ sì, signore; **Dear S**~ (*in letter*) Egregio signor (*followed by name*); **Dear S**~**s** Spettabile ditta.
siren ['saɪərn] *n* sirena.
sirloin ['səːlɔɪn] *n* controfiletto.
sirloin steak *n* bistecca di controfiletto.
sirocco [sɪ'rɒkəu] *n* scirocco.
sisal ['saɪsəl] *n* sisal *f inv*.
sissy ['sɪsɪ] *n* (*col*) femminuccia.
sister ['sɪstə*] *n* sorella; (*nun*) suora; (*nurse*) infermiera *f* caposala *inv* ♦ *cpd*: ~ **organization** organizzazione *f* affine; ~ **ship** nave *f* gemella.
sister-in-law ['sɪstərɪnlɔː] *n* cognata.
sit, *pt*, *pp* **sat** [sɪt, sæt] *vi* sedere, sedersi; (*dress etc*) cadere; (*assembly*) essere in seduta ♦ *vt* (*exam*) sostenere, dare; **to** ~ **on a committee** far parte di una commissione.
▶**sit about, sit around** *vi* star seduto(a) (senza far nulla).
▶**sit back** *vi* (*in seat*) appoggiarsi allo schienale.
▶**sit down** *vi* sedersi; **to be** ~**ting down** essere seduto(a).
▶**sit in** *vi*: **to** ~ **in on a discussion** assistere ad una discussione.

▶**sit up** vi tirarsi su a sedere; (not go to bed) stare alzato(a) fino a tardi.

sitcom ['sɪtkɔm] n abbr (TV: = situation comedy) sceneggiato a episodi (comico).

sit-down ['sɪtdaun] adj: ~ **strike** sciopero bianco (con occupazione della fabbrica); **a ~ meal** un pranzo.

site [saɪt] n posto; (also: **building** ~) cantiere m; (COMPUT) sito ♦ vt situare.

sit-in ['sɪtɪn] n (demonstration) sit-in m inv.

siting ['saɪtɪŋ] n ubicazione f.

sitter ['sɪtə*] n (for painter) modello/a; (also: **baby** ~) babysitter m/f inv.

sitting ['sɪtɪŋ] n (of assembly etc) seduta; (in canteen) turno.

sitting member n (POL) deputato/a in carica.

sitting room n soggiorno.

sitting tenant n (BRIT) attuale affittuario.

situate ['sɪtjueɪt] vt collocare.

situated ['sɪtjueɪtɪd] adj situato(a).

situation [sɪtju'eɪʃən] n situazione f; "~s vacant/wanted" (BRIT) "offerte/domande di impiego".

situation comedy n (THEAT) commedia di situazione.

six [sɪks] num sei.

six-pack ['sɪkspæk] n (esp US) confezione f da sei.

sixteen [sɪks'tiːn] num sedici.

sixth [sɪksθ] num sesto(a) ♦ n: **the upper/lower ~** (BRIT SCOL) l'ultimo/il penultimo anno di scuola superiore.

sixty ['sɪkstɪ] num sessanta.

size [saɪz] n dimensioni fpl; (of clothing) taglia, misura; (of shoes) numero; (glue) colla; **I take ~ 14 in a dress** ≈ porto la 44 di vestiti; **I'd like the small/large ~** (of soap powder etc) vorrei la confezione piccola/grande.

▶**size up** vt giudicare, farsi un'idea di.

sizeable ['saɪzəbl] adj considerevole.

sizzle ['sɪzl] vi sfrigolare.

SK abbr (Canada) = Saskatchewan.

skate [skeɪt] n pattino; (fish: pl inv) razza ♦ vi pattinare.

▶**skate over, skate around** vi (problem, issue) prendere alla leggera, prendere sottogamba.

skateboard ['skeɪtbɔːd] n skateboard m inv.

skater ['skeɪtə*] n pattinatore/trice.

skating ['skeɪtɪŋ] n pattinaggio.

skating rink n pista di pattinaggio.

skeleton ['skɛlɪtn] n scheletro.

skeleton key n passe-partout m inv.

skeleton staff n personale m ridotto.

skeptic etc ['skɛptɪk] (US) = **sceptic** etc.

sketch [skɛtʃ] n (drawing) schizzo, abbozzo;

(THEAT etc) scenetta comica, sketch m inv ♦ vt abbozzare, schizzare.

sketch book n album m inv per schizzi.

sketch pad n blocco per schizzi.

sketchy ['skɛtʃɪ] adj incompleto(a), lacunoso(a).

skew [skjuː] n (BRIT): **on the ~** di traverso.

skewer ['skjuːə*] n spiedo.

ski [skiː] n sci m inv ♦ vi sciare.

ski boot n scarpone m da sci.

skid [skɪd] n slittamento; (sideways slip) sbandamento ♦ vi slittare; sbandare; **to go into a ~** slittare; sbandare.

skid mark n segno della frenata.

skier ['skiːə*] n sciatore/trice.

skiing ['skiːɪŋ] n sci m.

ski instructor n maestro/a di sci.

ski jump n (ramp) trampolino; (event) salto con gli sci.

skilful, (US) **skillful** ['skɪlful] adj abile.

ski lift n sciovia.

skill [skɪl] n abilità f inv, capacità f inv; (technique) tecnica.

skilled [skɪld] adj esperto(a); (worker) qualificato(a), specializzato(a).

skillet ['skɪlɪt] n padella.

skillful etc ['skɪlful] (US) = **skilful** etc.

skil(l)fully ['skɪlfəlɪ] adv abilmente.

skim [skɪm] vt (milk) scremare; (soup) schiumare; (glide over) sfiorare ♦ vi: **to ~ through** (fig) scorrere, dare una scorsa a.

skimmed milk n latte m scremato.

skimp [skɪmp] vi: **to ~ on**, vt (work) fare alla carlona; (cloth etc) lesinare.

skimpy ['skɪmpɪ] adj misero(a); striminzito(a); frugale.

skin [skɪn] n pelle f; (of fruit, vegetable) buccia; (on pudding, paint) crosta ♦ vt (fruit etc) sbucciare; (animal) scuoiare, spellare; **wet** or **soaked to the ~** bagnato fino al midollo.

skin cancer n cancro alla pelle.

skin-deep [skɪn'diːp] adj superficiale.

skin diver n subacqueo.

skin diving n nuoto subacqueo.

skinflint ['skɪnflɪnt] n taccagno/a, tirchio/a.

skin graft n innesto epidermico.

skinhead ['skɪnhɛd] n skinhead m/f inv.

skinny ['skɪnɪ] adj molto magro(a).

skin test n prova di reazione cutanea.

skintight ['skɪntaɪt] adj aderente.

skip [skɪp] n saltello, balzo; (container) benna ♦ vi saltare; (with rope) saltare la corda ♦ vt (pass over) saltare; **to ~ school** (US) marinare la scuola.

ski pants npl pantaloni mpl da sci.

ski pass n ski pass m inv.

ski pole n racchetta (da sci).

skipper ['skɪpə*] *n* (*NAUT, SPORT*) capitano.
skipping rope ['skɪpɪŋ-] *n* (*BRIT*) corda per saltare.
ski resort *n* località *f inv* sciistica.
skirmish ['skə:mɪʃ] *n* scaramuccia.
skirt [skə:t] *n* gonna, sottana ♦ *vt* fiancheggiare, costeggiare.
skirting board ['skə:tɪŋ-] *n* (*BRIT*) zoccolo.
ski run *n* pista (da sci).
ski suit *n* tuta da sci.
skit [skɪt] *n* parodia; scenetta satirica.
ski tow *n* = **ski lift**.
skittle ['skɪtl] *n* birillo; **~s** *n* (*game*) (gioco dei) birilli *mpl*.
skive [skaɪv] *vi* (*BRIT col*) fare il lavativo.
skulk [skʌlk] *vi* muoversi furtivamente.
skull [skʌl] *n* cranio, teschio.
skullcap ['skʌlkæp] *n* (*worn by Jews*) zucchetto; (*worn by Pope*) papalina.
skunk [skʌŋk] *n* moffetta.
sky [skaɪ] *n* cielo; **to praise sb to the skies** portare alle stelle qn.
sky-blue [skaɪ'blu:] *adj* azzurro(a), celeste.
sky-diving ['skaɪdaɪvɪŋ] *n* caduta libera, paracadutismo acrobatico.
sky-high [skaɪ'haɪ] *adv* (*throw*) molto in alto ♦ *adj* (*col*) esorbitante; **prices have gone ~** (*col*) i prezzi sono saliti alle stelle.
skylark ['skaɪlɑ:k] *n* allodola.
skylight ['skaɪlaɪt] *n* lucernario.
skyline ['skaɪlaɪn] *n* (*horizon*) orizzonte *m*; (*of city*) profilo.
sky marshal *n* agente *m/f* a bordo.
skyscraper ['skaɪskreɪpə*] *n* grattacielo.
slab [slæb] *n* lastra; (*of wood*) tavola; (*of meat, cheese*) pezzo.
slack [slæk] *adj* (*loose*) allentato(a); (*slow*) lento(a); (*careless*) negligente; (*COMM: market*) stagnante; (: *demand*) scarso(a); (*period*) morto(a) ♦ *n* (*in rope etc*) parte *f* non tesa; **business is ~** l'attività commerciale è scarsa; *see also* **slacks**.
slacken ['slækn] (*also: ~ off*) *vi* rallentare, diminuire ♦ *vt* allentare; (*pressure*) diminuire.
slacks [slæks] *npl* pantaloni *mpl*.
slag [slæg] *n* scorie *fpl*.
slag heap *n* ammasso di scorie.
slain [sleɪn] *pp of* **slay**.
slake [sleɪk] *vt* (*one's thirst*) spegnere.
slalom ['slɑ:ləm] *n* slalom *m*.
slam [slæm] *vt* (*door*) sbattere; (*throw*) scaraventare; (*criticize*) stroncare ♦ *vi* sbattere.
slammer ['slæmə*] *n*: **the ~** (*col*) la gattabuia.
slander ['slɑ:ndə*] *n* calunnia; (*LAW*) diffamazione *f* ♦ *vt* calunniare; diffamare.

slanderous ['slɑ:ndrəs] *adj* calunnioso(a); diffamatorio(a).
slang [slæŋ] *n* gergo, slang *m*.
slanging match ['slæŋɪŋ-] *n* (*BRIT col*) rissa verbale.
slant [slɑ:nt] *n* pendenza, inclinazione *f*; (*fig*) angolazione *f*, punto di vista.
slanted ['slɑ:ntɪd] *adj* tendenzioso(a).
slanting ['slɑ:ntɪŋ] *adj* in pendenza, inclinato(a).
slap [slæp] *n* manata, pacca; (*on face*) schiaffo ♦ *vt* dare una manata a; schiaffeggiare ♦ *adv* (*directly*) in pieno; **it fell ~ in the middle** cadde proprio nel mezzo.
slapdash ['slæpdæʃ] *adj* abborracciato(a).
slaphead ['slæphɛd] *n* (*BRIT col*) imbecille *m/f*.
slapstick ['slæpstɪk] *n* (*comedy*) farsa grossolana.
slap-up ['slæpʌp] *adj* (*BRIT*): **a ~ meal** un pranzo (*or* una cena) coi fiocchi.
slash [slæʃ] *vt* squarciare; (*face*) sfregiare; (*fig: prices*) ridurre drasticamente, tagliare.
slat [slæt] *n* (*of wood*) stecca.
slate [sleɪt] *n* ardesia ♦ *vt* (*fig: criticize*) stroncare, distruggere.
slaughter ['slɔ:tə*] *n* (*of animals*) macellazione *f*; (*of people*) strage *f*, massacro ♦ *vt* macellare; trucidare, massacrare.
slaughterhouse ['slɔ:təhaus] *n* macello, mattatoio.
Slav [slɑ:v] *adj, n* slavo(a).
slave [sleɪv] *n* schiavo/a ♦ *vi* (*also: ~ away*) lavorare come uno schiavo; **to ~ (away) at sth/at doing sth** ammazzarsi di fatica *or* sgobbare per qc/per fare qc.
slave driver *n* (*col, pej*) schiavista *m/f*.
slave labour *n* lavoro degli schiavi; (*fig*): **we're just ~ here** siamo solamente sfruttati qui dentro.
slaver ['slævə*] *vi* (*dribble*) sbavare.
slavery ['sleɪvərɪ] *n* schiavitù *f*.
Slavic ['slævɪk] *adj* slavo(a).
slavish ['sleɪvɪʃ] *adj* servile; pedissequo(a).
slavishly ['sleɪvɪʃlɪ] *adv* (*copy*) pedissequamente.
Slavonic [slə'vɔnɪk] *adj* slavo(a).
slay, *pt* **slew**, *pp* **slain** [sleɪ, slu:, sleɪn] *vt* (*formal*) uccidere.
sleazy ['sli:zɪ] *adj* trasandato(a).
sledge [slɛdʒ] *n* slitta.
sledgehammer ['slɛdʒhæmə*] *n* martello da fabbro.
sleek [sli:k] *adj* (*hair, fur*) lucido(a), lucente; (*car, boat*) slanciato(a), affusolato(a).

sleep [sli:p] *n* sonno ♦ *vi* (*pt, pp* **slept** [slɛpt]) dormire ♦ *vt*: **we can ~ 4** abbiamo 4 posti letto, possiamo alloggiare 4 persone; **to have a good night's ~** farsi una bella dormita; **to go to ~** addormentarsi; **to ~ lightly** avere il sonno leggero; **to put to ~** (*patient*) far addormentare; (*animal: euphemistic: kill*) abbattere; **to ~ with sb** (*euphemistic: have sex*) andare a letto con qn.

▶**sleep in** *vi* (*lie late*) alzarsi tardi; (*oversleep*) dormire fino a tardi.

sleeper ['sli:pə*] *n* (*person*) dormiente *m/f*; (*BRIT RAIL: on track*) traversina; (: *train*) treno di vagoni letto.

sleepily ['sli:pɪlɪ] *adv* con aria assonnata.

sleeping ['sli:pɪŋ] *adj* addormentato(a).

sleeping bag *n* sacco a pelo.

sleeping car *n* vagone *m* letto *inv*, carrozza *f* letto *inv*.

sleeping partner *n* (*BRIT COMM*) = **silent partner**.

sleeping pill *n* sonnifero.

sleeping sickness *n* malattia del sonno.

sleepless ['sli:plɪs] *adj* (*person*) insonne; **a ~ night** una notte in bianco.

sleeplessness ['sli:plɪsnɪs] *n* insonnia.

sleepover ['sli:pəuvə*] *n* il *dormire a casa di amici, usato in riferimento a bambini*.

sleepwalk ['sli:pwɔ:k] *vi* camminare nel sonno; (*as a habit*) essere sonnambulo(a).

sleepwalker ['sli:pwɔ:kə*] *n* sonnambulo/a.

sleepy ['sli:pɪ] *adj* assonnato(a), sonnolento(a); (*fig*) addormentato(a); **to be** *or* **feel ~** avere sonno.

sleet [sli:t] *n* nevischio.

sleeve [sli:v] *n* manica; (*of record*) copertina.

sleeveless ['sli:vlɪs] *adj* (*garment*) senza maniche.

sleigh [sleɪ] *n* slitta.

sleight [slaɪt] *n*: **~ of hand** gioco di destrezza.

slender ['slɛndə*] *adj* snello(a), sottile; (*not enough*) scarso(a), esiguo(a).

slept [slɛpt] *pt, pp of* **sleep**.

sleuth [slu:θ] *n* (*col*) segugio.

slew [slu:] *vi* (*also: ~ round*) girare ♦ *pt of* **slay**.

slice [slaɪs] *n* fetta ♦ *vt* affettare, tagliare a fette; **~d bread** pane *m* a cassetta.

slick [slɪk] *adj* (*clever*) brillante; (*insincere*) untuoso(a), falso(a) ♦ *n* (*also: oil ~*) chiazza di petrolio.

slid [slɪd] *pt, pp of* **slide**.

slide [slaɪd] *n* (*in playground*) scivolo; (*PHOT*) diapositiva; (*microscope ~*) vetrino; (*BRIT: also: hair ~*) fermaglio (per capelli); (*in prices*) caduta ♦ *vb* (*pt, pp* **slid** [slɪd]) *vt* far scivolare ♦ *vi* scivolare; **to let things ~** (*fig*) lasciare andare tutto, trascurare tutto.

slide projector *n* proiettore *m* per diapositive.

slide rule *n* regolo calcolatore.

sliding ['slaɪdɪŋ] *adj* (*door*) scorrevole; **~ roof** (*AUT*) capotte *f inv*.

sliding scale *n* scala mobile.

slight [slaɪt] *adj* (*slim*) snello(a), sottile; (*frail*) delicato(a), fragile; (*trivial*) insignificante; (*small*) piccolo(a) ♦ *n* offesa, affronto ♦ *vt* (*offend*) offendere, fare un affronto a; **the ~est** il minimo (*or* la minima); **not in the ~est** affatto, neppure per sogno.

slightly ['slaɪtlɪ] *adv* lievemente, un po'; **~ built** esile.

slim [slɪm] *adj* magro(a), snello(a) ♦ *vi* dimagrire, fare (*or* seguire) una dieta dimagrante.

slime [slaɪm] *n* limo, melma; viscidume *m*.

slimming ['slɪmɪŋ] *adj* (*diet, pills*) dimagrante.

slimy ['slaɪmɪ] *adj* (*also fig: person*) viscido(a); (*covered with mud*) melmoso(a).

sling [slɪŋ] *n* (*MED*) benda al collo ♦ *vt* (*pt, pp* **slung** [slʌŋ]) lanciare, tirare; **to have one's arm in a ~** avere un braccio al collo.

slink, *pt, pp* **slunk** [slɪŋk, slʌŋk] *vi*: **to ~ away**, **~ off** svignarsela.

slinky ['slɪŋkɪ] *adj* (*clothing*) aderente, attillato(a).

slip [slɪp] *n* scivolata, scivolone *m*; (*mistake*) errore *m*, sbaglio; (*underskirt*) sottoveste *f*; (*paper*) bigliettino, tallonecino ♦ *vt* (*slide*) far scivolare ♦ *vi* (*slide*) scivolare; (*move smoothly*): **to ~ into/out of** scivolare in/via da; (*decline*) declinare; **to give sb the ~** sfuggire qn; **a ~ of paper** un foglietto; **a ~ of the tongue** un lapsus linguae; **to ~ sth on/off** infilarsi/togliersi qc; **to let a chance ~ by** lasciarsi scappare un'occasione; **it ~ped from her hand** le sfuggì di mano.

▶**slip away** *vi* svignarsela.

▶**slip in** *vt* introdurre casualmente.

▶**slip out** *vi* uscire furtivamente.

slip-on ['slɪpɔn] *adj* (*gen*) comodo(a) da mettere; (*shoes*) senza allacciatura.

slipped disc ['slɪpt-] *n* spostamento delle vertebre.

slipper ['slɪpə*] *n* pantofola.

slippery ['slɪpərɪ] *adj* scivoloso(a); **it's ~** si scivola.

slip road n (_BRIT_: _to motorway_) rampa di accesso.

slipshod ['slɪpʃɔd] adj sciatto(a), trasandato(a).

slip-up ['slɪpʌp] n granchio (_fig_).

slipway ['slɪpweɪ] n scalo di costruzione.

slit [slɪt] n fessura, fenditura; (_cut_) taglio; (_tear_) strappo ♦ vt (_pt_, _pp_ **slit**) tagliare; **to ~ sb's throat** tagliare la gola a qn.

slither ['slɪðə*] vi scivolare, sdrucciolare.

sliver ['slɪvə*] n (_of glass, wood_) scheggia; (_of cheese, sausage_) fettina.

slob [slɔb] n (_col_) sciattone/a.

slog [slɔg] (_BRIT_) n faticata ♦ vi lavorare con accanimento, sgobbare.

slogan ['sləugən] n motto, slogan m inv.

slop [slɔp] vi (_also_: ~ **over**) traboccare; versarsi ♦ vt spandere; versare ♦ npl: ~**s** acqua sporca; sbobba.

slope [sləup] n pendio; (_side of mountain_) versante m; (_of roof_) pendenza; (_of floor_) inclinazione f ♦ vi: **to ~ down** declinare; **to ~ up** essere in salita.

sloping ['sləupɪŋ] adj inclinato(a).

sloppy ['slɔpɪ] adj (_work_) tirato(a) via; (_appearance_) sciatto(a); (_film etc_) sdolcinato(a).

slosh [slɔʃ] vi (_col_): **to ~ about** or **around** (_person_) sguazzare; (_liquid_) guazzare.

sloshed [slɔʃt] adj (_col_: _drunk_) sbronzo(a).

slot [slɔt] n fessura; (_fig_: _in timetable_, _RADIO_, _TV_) spazio ♦ vt: **to ~ into** introdurre in una fessura.

sloth [sləuθ] n (_vice_) pigrizia, accidia; (_ZOOL_) bradipo.

slot machine n (_BRIT_: _vending machine_) distributore m automatico; (_for amusement_) slot-machine f inv.

slot meter n contatore m a gettoni.

slouch [slautʃ] vi (_when walking_) camminare dinoccolato(a); **she was ~ed in a chair** era sprofondata in una poltrona.

▶**slouch about, slouch around** vi (_laze_) oziare.

Slovak ['sləuvæk] adj slovacco(a) ♦ n slovacco/a; (_LING_) slovacco; **the ~ Republic** la Repubblica Slovacca.

Slovakia [sləu'vækɪə] n Slovacchia.

Slovakian [sləu'vækɪən] adj, n = **Slovak**.

Slovene ['sləuviːn] adj sloveno(a) ♦ n sloveno/a; (_LING_) sloveno.

Slovenia [sləu'viːnɪə] n Slovenia.

Slovenian [sləu'viːnɪən] adj, n = **Slovene**.

slovenly ['slʌvənlɪ] adj sciatto(a), trasandato(a).

slow [sləu] adj lento(a); (_watch_): **to be ~** essere indietro ♦ adv lentamente ♦ vt, vi (_also_: ~ **down**, ~ **up**) rallentare; "~" (_road sign_) "rallentare"; **at a ~ speed** a bassa velocità; **to be ~ to act/decide** essere lento ad agire/a decidere; **my watch is 20 minutes ~** il mio orologio è indietro di 20 minuti; **business is ~** (_COMM_) gli affari procedono a rilento; **to go ~** (_driver_) andare piano; (_in industrial dispute_) fare uno sciopero bianco.

slow-acting ['sləu'æktɪŋ] adj che agisce lentamente, ad azione lenta.

slowly ['sləulɪ] adv lentamente; **to drive ~** andare piano.

slow motion n: **in ~** al rallentatore.

slowness ['sləunɪs] n lentezza.

sludge [slʌdʒ] n fanghiglia.

slug [slʌg] n lumaca; (_bullet_) pallottola.

sluggish ['slʌgɪʃ] adj lento(a); (_business, market, sales_) stagnante, fiacco(a).

sluice [sluːs] n chiusa ♦ vt: **to ~ down** or **out** lavare (con abbondante acqua).

slum [slʌm] n catapecchia.

slumber ['slʌmbə*] n sonno.

slump [slʌmp] n crollo, caduta; (_economic_) depressione f, crisi f inv ♦ vi crollare; **he was ~ed over the wheel** era curvo sul volante.

slung [slʌŋ] pt, pp of **sling**.

slunk [slʌŋk] pt, pp of **slink**.

slur [sləː*] n pronuncia indistinta; (_stigma_) diffamazione f, calunnia; (_MUS_) legatura; (_smear_): ~ **(on)** macchia (su) ♦ vt pronunciare in modo indistinto; **to cast a ~ on sb** calunniare qn.

slurp [sləːp] vt, vi bere rumorosamente ♦ n rumore fatto bevendo.

slurred [sləːd] adj (_pronunciation_) inarticolato(a), disarticolato(a).

slush [slʌʃ] n neve f mista a fango.

slush fund n fondi mpl neri.

slushy ['slʌʃɪ] adj (_snow_) che si scioglie; (_BRIT_: _fig_) sdolcinato(a).

slut [slʌt] n donna trasandata, sciattona.

sly [slaɪ] adj furbo(a), scaltro(a); **on the ~** di soppiatto.

SM n abbr (= _sadomasochism_) sadomasochismo.

smack [smæk] n (_slap_) pacca; (_on face_) schiaffo ♦ vt schiaffeggiare; (_child_) picchiare ♦ vi: **to ~ of** puzzare di; **to ~ one's lips** fare uno schiocco con le labbra.

smacker ['smækə*] n (_col_: _kiss_) bacio; (: _BRIT_: _pound note_) sterlina; (: _US_: _dollar bill_) dollaro.

small [smɔːl] adj piccolo(a); (_in height_) basso(a); (_letter_) minuscolo(a) ♦ n: **the ~ of the back** le reni; **to get** or **grow ~er**

(*stain, town*) rimpicciolire; (*debt, organization, numbers*) ridursi; **to make ~er** (*amount, income*) ridurre; (*garden, object, garment*) rimpicciolire; **in the ~ hours** alle ore piccole; **a ~ shopkeeper** un piccolo negoziante.

small ads *npl* (*BRIT*) piccoli annunci *mpl*.

small arms *npl* armi *fpl* portatili *or* leggere.

small business *n* piccola impresa.

small change *n* moneta, spiccioli *mpl*.

smallholder ['smɔːlhəʊldə*] *n* (*BRIT*) piccolo proprietario.

smallholding ['smɔːlhəʊldɪŋ] *n* (*BRIT*) piccola tenuta.

smallish ['smɔːlɪʃ] *adj* piccolino(a).

small-minded [smɔːl'maɪndɪd] *adj* meschino(a).

smallpox ['smɔːlpɒks] *n* vaiolo.

small print *n* caratteri *mpl* piccoli; (*on document*) parte scritta in piccolo.

small-scale ['smɔːlskeɪl] *adj* (*map, model*) in scala ridotta; (*business, farming*) modesto(a).

small talk *n* chiacchiere *fpl*.

small-time ['smɔːltaɪm] *adj* (*col*) da poco; **a ~ thief** un ladro di polli.

small-town ['smɔːltaun] *adj* (*pej*) provinciale, di paese.

smarmy ['smɑːmɪ] *adj* (*BRIT pej*) untuoso(a), strisciante.

smart [smɑːt] *adj* elegante; (*also fig: clever*) intelligente; (*quick*) sveglio(a) ♦ *vi* bruciare; **the ~ set** il bel mondo; **to look ~** essere elegante; **my eyes are ~ing** mi bruciano gli occhi.

smartcard ['smɑːtkɑːd] *n* smartcard *f inv*, carta intelligente.

smarten up ['smɑːtn-] *vi* farsi bello(a) ♦ *vt* (*people*) fare bello(a); (*things*) abbellire.

smash [smæʃ] *n* (*also: ~-up*) scontro, collisione *f*; (*sound*) fracasso ♦ *vt* frantumare, fracassare; (*opponent*) annientare, schiacciare; (*hopes*) distruggere; (*SPORT: record*) battere ♦ *vi* frantumarsi, andare in pezzi.

▶**smash up** *vt* (*car*) sfasciare; (*room*) distruggere.

smash-hit [smæʃ'hɪt] *n* successone *m*.

smashing ['smæʃɪŋ] *adj* (*col*) favoloso(a), formidabile.

smattering ['smætərɪŋ] *n*: **a ~ of** un'infarinatura di.

smear [smɪə*] *n* macchia; (*MED*) striscio; (*insult*) calunnia ♦ *vt* ungere; (*fig*) denigrare, diffamare; **his hands were ~ed with oil/ink** aveva le mani sporche di olio/inchiostro.

smear campaign *n* campagna diffamatoria.

smear test *n* (*BRIT MED*) Pap-test *m inv*.

smell [smɛl] *n* odore *m*; (*sense*) olfatto, odorato ♦ *vb* (*pt, pp* **smelt** *or* **smelled** [smɛlt, smɛld]) *vt* sentire (l')odore di ♦ *vi* (*food etc*): **to ~ (of)** avere odore (di); (*pej*) puzzare, avere un cattivo odore; **it ~s good** ha un buon odore.

smelly ['smɛlɪ] *adj* puzzolente.

smelt [smɛlt] *pt, pp of* **smell** ♦ *vt* (*ore*) fondere.

smile [smaɪl] *n* sorriso ♦ *vi* sorridere.

smiling ['smaɪlɪŋ] *adj* sorridente.

smirk [smɔːk] *n* sorriso furbo; sorriso compiaciuto.

smith [smɪθ] *n* fabbro.

smithy ['smɪðɪ] *n* fucina.

smitten ['smɪtn] *adj*: **~ with** colpito(a) da.

smock [smɒk] *n* grembiule *m*, camice *m*.

smog [smɒg] *n* smog *m*.

smoke [sməʊk] *n* fumo ♦ *vt, vi* fumare; **to have a ~** fumarsi una sigaretta; **do you ~?** fumi?; **to go up in ~** (*house etc*) bruciare, andare distrutto dalle fiamme; (*fig*) andare in fumo.

smoked [sməʊkt] *adj* (*bacon, glass*) affumicato(a).

smokeless fuel ['sməʊklɪs-] *n* carburante *m* che non dà fumo.

smokeless zone *n* (*BRIT*) zona dove sono vietati gli scarichi di fumo.

smoker ['sməʊkə*] *n* (*person*) fumatore/ trice; (*RAIL*) carrozza per fumatori.

smoke screen *n* cortina fumogena *or* di fumo; (*fig*) copertura.

smoke shop *n* (*US*) tabaccheria.

smoking ['sməʊkɪŋ] *n* fumo; **"no ~"** (*sign*) "vietato fumare"; **he's given up ~** ha smesso di fumare.

smoking compartment, (*US*) **smoking car** *n* carrozza (per) fumatori.

smoky ['sməʊkɪ] *adj* fumoso(a); (*surface*) affumicato(a).

smolder ['sməʊldə*] *vi* (*US*) = **smoulder**.

smoochy ['smuːtʃɪ] *adj* (*col*) romantico(a).

smooth [smuːð] *adj* liscio(a); (*sauce*) omogeneo(a); (*flavour, whisky*) amabile; (*cigarette*) leggero(a); (*movement*) regolare; (*person*) mellifluo(a); (*landing, take-off, flight*) senza scosse ♦ *vt* lisciare, spianare; (*also: ~ out: difficulties*) appianare.

▶**smooth over** *vt*: **to ~ things over** (*fig*) sistemare le cose.

smoothly ['smuːðlɪ] *adv* (*easily*) liscio; **everything went ~** tutto andò liscio.

smother ['smʌðə*] *vt* soffocare.

smoulder, (US) smolder ['sməʊldə*] *vi*
covare sotto la cenere.

SMS *n abbr* (= *short message service*) SMS *m*
(*servizio*).

smudge [smʌdʒ] *n* macchia; sbavatura ♦ *vt*
imbrattare, sporcare.

smug [smʌg] *adj* soddisfatto(a),
compiaciuto(a).

smuggle ['smʌgl] *vt* contrabbandare; **to ~
in/out** (*goods etc*) far entrare/uscire di
contrabbando.

smuggler ['smʌglə*] *n* contrabbandiere/a.

smuggling ['smʌglɪŋ] *n* contrabbando.

smut [smʌt] *n* (*grain of soot*) granello di
fuliggine; (*mark*) segno nero; (*in
conversation etc*) sconcezze *fpl*.

smutty ['smʌtɪ] *adj* (*fig*) osceno(a),
indecente.

snack [snæk] *n* spuntino; **to have a ~** fare
uno spuntino.

snack bar *n* tavola calda, snack bar *m inv.*

snag [snæg] *n* intoppo, ostacolo imprevisto.

snail [sneɪl] *n* chiocciola.

snake [sneɪk] *n* serpente *m.*

snap [snæp] *n* (*sound*) schianto, colpo
secco; (*photograph*) istantanea; (*game*)
rubamazzo ♦ *adj* improvviso(a) ♦ *vt* (*far*)
schioccare; (*break*) spezzare di netto;
(*photograph*) scattare un'istantanea di ♦ *vi*
spezzarsi con un rumore secco; (*fig:
person*) crollare; **to ~ at sb** rivolgersi a
qn con tono brusco; (*subj: dog*) cercare di
mordere qn; **to ~ open/shut** aprirsi/
chiudersi di scatto; **to ~ one's fingers at**
(*fig*) infischiarsi di; **a cold ~** (*of weather*)
un'improvvisa ondata di freddo.

▶**snap off** *vt* (*break*) schiantare.

▶**snap up** *vt* afferrare.

snap fastener *n* bottone *m* automatico.

snappy ['snæpɪ] *adj* rapido(a); **make it ~**!
(*col: hurry up*) sbrigati!, svelto!

snapshot ['snæpʃɔt] *n* istantanea.

snare [snɛə*] *n* trappola.

snarl [snɑːl] *vi* ringhiare ♦ *vt*: **to get ~ed up**
(*wool, plans*) ingarbugliarsi; (*traffic*)
intasarsi.

snatch [snætʃ] *n* (*fig*) furto; (*BRIT: small
amount*): **~es of** frammenti *mpl* di ♦ *vt*
strappare (con violenza); (*steal*) rubare
♦ *vi*: **don't ~**! non strappare le cose di
mano!; **to ~ a sandwich** mangiarsi in
fretta un panino; **to ~ some sleep**
riuscire a dormire un po'.

▶**snatch up** *vt* raccogliere in fretta.

snazzy ['snæzi] *adj* (*col: clothes*) sciccoso(a).

sneak [sniːk] *vi*: **to ~ in/out** entrare/uscire
di nascosto ♦ *vt*: **to ~ a look at sth**
guardare di sottecchi qc.

sneakers ['sniːkəz] *npl* scarpe *fpl* da
ginnastica.

sneaking ['sniːkɪŋ] *adj*: **to have a ~ feeling/
suspicion that ...** avere la vaga
impressione/il vago sospetto che ....

sneaky ['sniːki] *adj* falso(a), disonesto(a).

sneer [snɪə*] *n* ghigno, sogghigno ♦ *vi*
ghignare, sogghignare; **to ~ at sb/sth**
farsi beffe di qn/qc.

sneeze [sniːz] *n* starnuto ♦ *vi* starnutire.

snide [snaɪd] *adj* maligno(a).

sniff [snɪf] *n* fiutata, annusata ♦ *vi* fiutare,
annusare; tirare su col naso; (*in contempt*)
arricciare il naso ♦ *vt* fiutare, annusare;
(*glue, drug*) sniffare.

▶**sniff at** *vt fus*: **it's not to be ~ed at** non è
da disprezzare.

sniffer dog ['snɪfə-] *n* cane *m* poliziotto (*per
stupefacenti o esplosivi*).

snigger ['snɪgə*] *n* riso represso ♦ *vi*
ridacchiare, ridere sotto i baffi.

snip [snɪp] *n* pezzetto; (*bargain*) (*buon*)
affare *m*, occasione *f* ♦ *vt* tagliare.

sniper ['snaɪpə*] *n* franco tiratore *m*,
cecchino.

snippet ['snɪpɪt] *n* frammento.

snivelling ['snɪvlɪŋ] *adj* piagnucoloso(a).

snob [snɔb] *n* snob *m/f inv.*

snobbery ['snɔbəri] *n* snobismo.

snobbish ['snɔbɪʃ] *adj* snob *inv.*

snog [snɔg] *vi* (*col*) pomiciare.

snooker ['snuːkə*] *n* tipo di gioco del
biliardo.

snoop [snuːp] *vi*: **to ~ on sb** spiare qn; **to ~
about** curiosare.

snooper ['snuːpə*] *n* ficcanaso *m/f.*

snooty ['snuːtɪ] *adj* borioso(a), snob *inv.*

snooze [snuːz] *n* sonnellino, pisolino ♦ *vi*
fare un sonnellino.

snore [snɔː*] *vi* russare.

snoring ['snɔːrɪŋ] *n* russare *m.*

snorkel ['snɔːkl] *n* (*of swimmer*) respiratore
m a tubo.

snort [snɔːt] *n* sbuffo ♦ *vi* sbuffare ♦ *vt*
(*drugs slang*) sniffare.

snotty ['snɔtɪ] *adj* moccioso(a).

snout [snaʊt] *n* muso.

snow [snəʊ] *n* neve *f* ♦ *vi* nevicare ♦ *vt*: **to be
~ed under with work** essere sommerso
di lavoro.

snowball ['snəʊbɔːl] *n* palla di neve.

snowbound ['snəʊbaʊnd] *adj* bloccato(a)
dalla neve.

snow-capped ['snəʊkæpt] *adj* (*mountain*)
con la cima coperta di neve; (*peak*)
coperto(a) di neve.

snowdrift ['snəʊdrɪft] *n* cumulo di neve
(*ammucchiato dal vento*).

snowdrop ['snəudrɔp] n bucaneve m inv.
snowfall ['snəufɔːl] n nevicata.
snowflake ['snəufleɪk] n fiocco di neve.
snowman ['snəumæn] n pupazzo di neve.
snowplough, (US) **snowplow** ['snəuplau] n spazzaneve m inv.
snowshoe ['snəuʃuː] n racchetta da neve.
snowstorm ['snəustɔːm] n tormenta.
snowy ['snəuɪ] adj nevoso(a).
SNP n abbr (BRIT POL) = Scottish National Party.
snub [snʌb] vt snobbare ♦ n offesa, affronto.
snub-nosed [snʌb'nəuzd] adj dal naso camuso.
snuff [snʌf] n tabacco da fiuto ♦ vt (also: ~ out: candle) spegnere.
snuff movie n (col) film porno dove una persona viene uccisa realmente.
snug [snʌg] adj comodo(a); (room, house) accogliente, comodo(a); **it's a ~ fit** è attillato.
snuggle ['snʌgl] vi: **to ~ down in bed** accovacciarsi a letto; **to ~ up to sb** stringersi a qn.
snugly ['snʌglɪ] adv comodamente; **it fits ~** (object in pocket etc) entra giusto giusto; (garment) sta ben attillato.
SO abbr (BANKING) = standing order.

===================== *KEYWORD*

so [səu] adv **1** (thus, likewise) così; **if ~ se** è così, quand'è così; **I didn't do it — you did ~!** non l'ho fatto io — sì che l'hai fatto!; **~ do I, ~ am I** anch'io; **it's 5 o'clock — ~ it is!** sono le 5 — davvero!; **I hope ~** lo spero; **I think ~** penso di sì; **quite ~!** esattamente!; **even ~** comunque; **~ far** finora, fin qui; (in past) fino ad allora
2 (in comparisons etc: to such a degree) così; **~ big (that)** così grande (che); **she's not ~ clever as her brother** lei non è (così) intelligente come suo fratello
3: **~ much** adj tanto(a) ♦ adv tanto; **I've got ~ much work/money** ho tanto lavoro/tanti soldi; **I love you ~ much** ti amo tanto; **~ many** tanti(e)
4 (phrases): **10 or ~** circa 10; **~ long!** (col: goodbye) ciao!, ci vediamo!; **~ to speak** per così dire; **~ what?** (col) e allora?, e con questo?
♦ conj **1** (expressing purpose): **~ as to do** in modo or così da fare; **we hurried ~ as not to be late** ci affrettammo per non fare tardi; **~ (that)** affinché + sub, perché + sub
2 (expressing result): **he didn't arrive ~ I left** non è venuto così me ne sono andata; **~ you see, I could have gone** vedi, sarei potuto

andare; **~ that's the reason!** allora è questo il motivo!, ecco perché!

soak [səuk] vt inzuppare; (clothes) mettere a mollo ♦ vi inzupparsi; (clothes) essere a mollo; **to be ~ed through** essere fradicio.
▶**soak in** vi penetrare.
▶**soak up** vt assorbire.
soaking ['səukɪŋ] adj (also: ~ **wet**) fradicio(a).
so-and-so ['səuənsəu] n (somebody) un tale; **Mr/Mrs ~** signor/signora tal dei tali.
soap [səup] n sapone m.
soapbox ['səupbɔks] n palco improvvisato (per orazioni pubbliche).
soapflakes ['səupfleɪks] npl sapone m in scaglie.
soap opera n soap opera f inv.
soap powder n detersivo.
soapsuds ['səupsʌdz] npl saponata.
soapy ['səupɪ] adj insaponato(a).
soar [sɔː*] vi volare in alto; (price, morale, spirits) salire alle stelle.
sob [sɔb] n singhiozzo ♦ vi singhiozzare.
s.o.b. n abbr (US col!: = son of a bitch) figlio di puttana (!).
sober ['səubə*] adj non ubriaco(a); (sedate) serio(a); (moderate) moderato(a); (colour, style) sobrio(a).
▶**sober up** vt far passare la sbornia a ♦ vi farsi passare la sbornia.
sobriety [səu'braɪətɪ] n (not being drunk) sobrietà; (seriousness, sedateness) sobrietà, pacatezza.
sob story n (col, pej) storia lacrimosa.
Soc. abbr (= society) Soc.
so-called ['səu'kɔːld] adj cosiddetto(a).
soccer ['sɔkə*] n calcio.
soccer pitch n campo di calcio.
soccer player n calciatore m.
sociable ['səuʃəbl] adj socievole.
social ['səuʃl] adj sociale ♦ n festa, serata.
social climber n arrampicatore/trice sociale, arrivista m/f.
social club n club m inv sociale.
Social Democrat n socialdemocratico/a.
social insurance n (US) assicurazione f sociale.
socialism ['səuʃəlɪzəm] n socialismo.
socialist ['səuʃəlɪst] adj, n socialista (m/f).
socialite ['səuʃəlaɪt] n persona in vista nel bel mondo.
socialize ['səuʃəlaɪz] vi frequentare la gente; farsi degli amici; **to ~ with** socializzare con.
social life n vita sociale.
socially ['səuʃəlɪ] adv socialmente, in società.

social science *n* scienze *fpl* sociali.
social security *n* previdenza sociale;
Department of S~ S~ (DSS) (*BRIT*) ≈
Istituto di Previdenza Sociale.
social services *npl* servizi *mpl* sociali.
social welfare *n* assistenza sociale.
social work *n* servizio sociale.
social worker *n* assistente *m/f* sociale.
society [sə'saɪətɪ] *n* società *f inv*; (*club*)
società, associazione *f*; (*also*: **high** ~) alta
società ♦ *cpd* (*party, column*) mondano(a).
socioeconomic ['səʊsɪəʊiːkə'nɒmɪk] *adj*
socio-economico(a).
sociological [səʊsɪə'lɒdʒɪkl] *adj*
sociologico(a).
sociologist [səʊsɪ'ɒlədʒɪst] *n* sociologo/a.
sociology [səʊsɪ'ɒlədʒɪ] *n* sociologia.
sock [sɒk] *n* calzino ♦ *vt* (*hit*) dare un pugno
a; **to pull one's ~s up** (*fig*) darsi una
regolata.
socket ['sɒkɪt] *n* cavità *f inv*; (*of eye*) orbita;
(*ELEC*: *also*: **wall** ~) presa di corrente;
(: *for light bulb*) portalampada *m inv.*
sod [sɒd] *n* (*of earth*) zolla erbosa; (*BRIT col!*)
bastardo/a (*!*).
▶**sod off** *vi*: ~ **off!** (*BRIT col!*) levati dalle
palle! (*!*).
soda ['səʊdə] *n* (*CHEM*) soda; (*also*: ~ **water**)
acqua di seltz; (*US*: *also*: ~ **pop**) gassosa.
sodden ['sɒdn] *adj* fradicio(a).
sodium ['səʊdɪəm] *n* sodio.
sodium chloride *n* cloruro di sodio.
sofa ['səʊfə] *n* sofà *m inv.*
Sofia ['səʊfɪə] *n* Sofia.
soft [sɒft] *adj* (*not rough*) morbido(a); (*not
hard*) soffice; (*not loud*) sommesso(a);
(*kind*) gentile; (: *look, smile*) dolce; (*not
strict*) indulgente; (*weak*) debole; (*stupid*)
stupido(a).
soft-boiled ['sɒftbɔɪld] *adj* (*egg*) alla coque.
soft drink *n* analcolico.
soft drugs *npl* droghe *fpl* leggere.
soften ['sɒfn] *vt* ammorbidire; addolcire;
attenuare ♦ *vi* ammorbidirsi; addolcirsi;
attenuarsi.
softener ['sɒfnə*] *n* ammorbidente *m.*
soft fruit *n* (*BRIT*) ≈ frutti di bosco.
soft furnishings *npl* tessuti *mpl* d'arredo.
soft-hearted [sɒft'hɑːtɪd] *adj* sensibile.
softly ['sɒftlɪ] *adv* dolcemente;
morbidamente.
softness ['sɒftnɪs] *n* dolcezza; morbidezza.
soft option *n* soluzione *f* (più) facile.
soft sell *n* persuasione *f* all'acquisto.
soft target *n* obiettivo civile (*e quindi facile
da colpire*).
soft touch *n* (*col*): **to be a** ~ lasciarsi
spillare facilmente denaro.

soft toy *n* giocattolo di peluche.
software ['sɒftwɛə*] *n* software *m.*
software package *n* pacchetto di
software.
soft water *n* acqua non calcarea.
soggy ['sɒgɪ] *adj* inzuppato(a).
soil [sɔɪl] *n* (*earth*) terreno, suolo ♦ *vt*
sporcare; (*fig*) macchiare.
soiled [sɔɪld] *adj* sporco(a), sudicio(a).
sojourn ['sɒdʒəːn] *n* (*formal*) soggiorno.
solace ['sɒlɪs] *n* consolazione *f.*
solar ['səʊlə*] *adj* solare.
solarium, *pl* **solaria** [sə'lɛərɪəm, -rɪə] *n*
solarium *m inv.*
solar plexus [-'plɛksəs] *n* (*ANAT*) plesso
solare.
solar power *n* energia solare.
sold [səʊld] *pt, pp of* **sell.**
solder ['səʊldə*] *vt* saldare ♦ *n* saldatura.
soldier ['səʊldʒə*] *n* soldato, militare *m* ♦ *vi:*
to ~ on perseverare; **toy** ~ soldatino.
sold out *adj* (*COMM*) esaurito(a).
sole [səʊl] *n* (*of foot*) pianta (del piede); (*of
shoe*) suola; (*fish*: *pl inv*) sogliola ♦ *adj*
solo(a), unico(a); (*exclusive*) esclusivo(a).
solely ['səʊllɪ] *adv* solamente, unicamente; **I
will hold you ~ responsible** la
considererò il solo responsabile.
solemn ['sɒləm] *adj* solenne; grave;
serio(a).
sole trader *n* (*COMM*) commerciante *m* in
proprio.
solicit [sə'lɪsɪt] *vt* (*request*) richiedere,
sollecitare ♦ *vi* (*prostitute*) adescare i
passanti.
solicitor [sə'lɪsɪtə*] *n* (*BRIT*: *for wills etc*) ≈
notaio; (*in court*) ≈ avvocato; *see boxed note.*

SOLICITOR

Il **solicitor** *appartiene a una delle due branche
della professione legale britannica (vedi anche*
barrister*). È compito dei* **solicitors** *agire
come consulenti in materia legale, redigere
pratiche, preparare la documentazione legale
per i "barristers". Contrariamente a questi
ultimi, i* **solicitors** *non sono qualificati a
rappresentare una parte nelle corti investite
della potestà di decidere sui reati più gravi.*

---

solid ['sɒlɪd] *adj* (*not hollow*) pieno(a);
(*strong, reliable, not liquid*) solido(a); (*meal*)
sostanzioso(a); (*line*) ininterrotto(a); (*vote*)
unanime ♦ *n* solido; **to be on ~ ground**
essere su terraferma; (*fig*) muoversi su
terreno sicuro; **we waited 2 ~ hours**
abbiamo aspettato due ore buone.
solidarity [sɒlɪ'dærɪtɪ] *n* solidarietà.

solid fuel n combustibile m solido.
solidify [sə'lɪdɪfaɪ] vi solidificarsi ♦ vt solidificare.
solidity [sə'lɪdɪtɪ] n solidità.
solid-state ['sɔlɪdsteɪt] adj (ELEC) a transistor.
soliloquy [sə'lɪləkwɪ] n soliloquio.
solitaire [sɔlɪ'tɛə*] n (game, gem) solitario.
solitary ['sɔlɪtərɪ] adj solitario(a).
solitary confinement n (LAW): **to be in ~** essere in cella d'isolamento.
solitude ['sɔlɪtjuːd] n solitudine f.
solo ['səuləu] n (MUS) assolo.
soloist ['səuləuɪst] n solista m/f.
Solomon Islands ['sɔləmən-] n: **the ~** le isole Salomone.
solstice ['sɔlstɪs] n solstizio.
soluble ['sɔljubl] adj solubile.
solution [sə'luːʃən] n soluzione f.
solve [sɔlv] vt risolvere.
solvency ['sɔlvənsɪ] n (COMM) solvenza, solvibilità.
solvent ['sɔlvənt] adj (COMM) solvibile ♦ n (CHEM) solvente m.
solvent abuse n abuso di colle e solventi.
Somali [sə'mɑːlɪ] adj somalo(a).
Somalia [sə'mɑːlɪə] n Somalia.
Somaliland [səu'mɑːlɪlænd] n paesi mpl del corno d'Africa.
sombre, (US) **somber** ['sɔmbə*] adj scuro(a); (mood, person) triste.

================ *KEYWORD*

some [sʌm] adj **1** (a certain amount or number of): **~ tea/water/cream** del tè/dell'acqua/della panna; **there's ~ milk in the fridge** c'è (del) latte nel frigo; **~ children/apples** dei bambini/delle mele; **after ~ time** dopo un po'; **at ~ length** a lungo
2 (certain: in contrasts) certo(a); **~ people say that ...** alcuni dicono che ..., certa gente dice che ...
3 (unspecified) un(a) certo(a), qualche; **~ woman was asking for you** una tale chiedeva di lei; **~ day** un giorno; **~ day next week** un giorno della prossima settimana; **in ~ form or other** in una forma o nell'altra
♦ pron **1** (a certain number) alcuni(e), certi(e); **I've got ~** (books etc) ne ho alcuni; **~ (of them) have been sold** alcuni sono stati venduti
2 (a certain amount) un po'; **I've got ~** (money, milk) ne ho un po'; **I've read ~ of the book** ho letto parte del libro; **~ (of it)**

was left ne è rimasto un po'; **could I have ~ of that cheese?** potrei avere un po' di quel formaggio?
♦ adv: **~ 10 people** circa 10 persone.

───────────────────

somebody ['sʌmbədɪ] pron qualcuno; **~ or other** qualcuno.
someday ['sʌmdeɪ] adv uno di questi giorni, un giorno o l'altro.
somehow ['sʌmhau] adv in un modo o nell'altro, in qualche modo; (for some reason) per qualche ragione.
someone ['sʌmwʌn] pron = **somebody**.
someplace ['sʌmpleɪs] adv (US) = **somewhere**.
somersault ['sʌməsɔːlt] n capriola; (in air) salto mortale ♦ vi fare una capriola (or un salto mortale); (car) cappottare.
something ['sʌmθɪŋ] pron qualcosa; **~ interesting** qualcosa di interessante; **~ to do** qualcosa da fare; **he's ~ like me** mi assomiglia un po'; **it's ~ of a problem** è un bel problema.
sometime ['sʌmtaɪm] adv (in future) una volta o l'altra; (in past): **~ last month** durante il mese scorso; **I'll finish it ~** lo finirò prima o poi.
sometimes ['sʌmtaɪmz] adv qualche volta.
somewhat ['sʌmwɔt] adv piuttosto.
somewhere ['sʌmwɛə*] adv in or da qualche parte; **~ else** da qualche altra parte.
son [sʌn] n figlio.
sonar ['səunɑː*] n sonar m.
sonata [sə'nɑːtə] n sonata.
song [sɔŋ] n canzone f.
songbook ['sɔŋbuk] n canzoniere m.
songwriter ['sɔŋraɪtə*] n compositore/trice di canzoni.
sonic ['sɔnɪk] adj (boom) sonico(a).
son-in-law ['sʌnɪnlɔː] n genero.
sonnet ['sɔnɪt] n sonetto.
sonny ['sʌnɪ] n (col) ragazzo mio.
soon [suːn] adv presto, fra poco; (early) presto; **~ afterwards** poco dopo; **very/quite ~** molto/abbastanza presto; **as ~ as possible** prima possibile; **I'll do it as ~ as I can** lo farò appena posso; **how ~ can you be ready?** fra quanto tempo sarà pronto?; **see you ~!** a presto!
sooner ['suːnə*] adv (time) prima; (preference): **I would ~ do** preferirei fare; **~ or later** prima o poi; **no ~ said than done** detto fatto; **the ~ the better** prima è meglio è; **no ~ had we left than ...** eravamo appena partiti, quando ....
soot [sut] n fuliggine f.
soothe [suːð] vt calmare.

soothing ['suːðɪŋ] _adj_ (_ointment etc_) calmante; (_tone, words etc_) rassicurante.

SOP _n abbr_ = _standard operating procedure._

sop [sɔp] _n_: **that's only a ~** è soltanto un contentino.

sophisticated [sə'fɪstɪkeɪtɪd] _adj_ sofisticato(a); raffinato(a); (_film, mind_) sottile.

sophistication [səfɪstɪ'keɪʃən] _n_ raffinatezza; (_of machine_) complessità; (_of argument etc_) sottigliezza.

sophomore ['sɔfəmɔː*] _n_ (_US_) studente/ essa del secondo anno.

soporific [sɔpə'rɪfɪk] _adj_ soporifero(a).

sopping ['sɔpɪŋ] _adj_ (_also: ~ **wet**_) bagnato(a) fradicio(a).

soppy ['sɔpɪ] _adj_ (_pej_) sentimentale.

soprano [sə'prɑːnəu] _n_ (_voice_) soprano _m_; (_singer_) soprano _m/f._

sorbet ['sɔːbeɪ] _n_ sorbetto.

sorcerer ['sɔːsərə*] _n_ stregone _m_, mago.

sordid ['sɔːdɪd] _adj_ sordido(a).

sore [sɔː*] _adj_ (_painful_) dolorante; (_col: offended_) offeso(a) ♦ _n_ piaga; **my eyes are ~, I have ~ eyes** mi fanno male gli occhi; **~ throat** mal _m_ di gola; **it's a ~ point** (_fig_) è un punto delicato.

sorely ['sɔːlɪ] _adv_ (_tempted_) fortemente.

sorrel ['sɔrəl] _n_ acetosa.

sorrow ['sɔrəu] _n_ dolore _m_.

sorrowful ['sɔrəuful] _adj_ triste.

sorry ['sɔrɪ] _adj_ spiacente; (_condition, excuse_) misero(a), pietoso(a); (_sight, failure_) triste; **~!** scusa! (_or_ scusi! _or_ scusate!); **to feel ~ for sb** rincrescersi per qn; **I'm ~ to hear that …** mi dispiace (sentire) che …; **to be ~ about sth** essere dispiaciuto _or_ spiacente di qc.

sort [sɔːt] _n_ specie _f_, genere _m_; (_make: of coffee, car etc_) tipo ♦ _vt_ (_also: ~ **out**: papers_) classificare; ordinare; (: _letters etc_) smistare; (: _problems_) risolvere; (_COMPUT_) ordinare; **what ~ of car?** che tipo di macchina?; **I shall do nothing of the ~!** nemmeno per sogno!; **it's ~ of awkward** (_col_) è piuttosto difficile.

sortie ['sɔːtɪ] _n_ sortita.

sorting office ['sɔːtɪŋ-] _n_ ufficio _m_ smistamento _inv._

SOS _n abbr_ S.O.S. _m inv._

so-so ['səusəu] _adv_ così così.

soufflé ['suːfleɪ] _n_ soufflé _m inv._

sought [sɔːt] _pt, pp of_ **seek.**

sought-after ['sɔːtɑːftə*] _adj_ richiesto(a).

soul [səul] _n_ anima; **the poor ~ had nowhere to sleep** il poveraccio non aveva dove dormire; **I didn't see a ~** non ho visto anima viva.

soul-destroying ['səuldɪ'strɔɪɪŋ] _adj_ demoralizzante.

soulful ['səulful] _adj_ pieno(a) di sentimento.

soulless ['səullɪs] _adj_ senz'anima, inumano(a).

soul mate _n_ anima gemella.

soul-searching ['səulsɑːtʃɪŋ] _n_: **after much ~** dopo un profondo esame di coscienza.

sound [saund] _adj_ (_healthy_) sano(a); (_safe, not damaged_) solido(a), in buono stato; (_reliable, not superficial_) solido(a); (_sensible_) giudizioso(a), di buon senso; (_valid: argument, policy, claim_) valido(a) ♦ _adv_: **~ asleep** profondamente addormentato ♦ _n_ (_noise_) suono; rumore _m_; (_GEO_) stretto ♦ _vt_ (_alarm_) suonare; (_also: ~ **out**: opinions_) sondare ♦ _vi_ suonare; (_fig: seem_) sembrare; **to be of ~ mind** essere sano di mente; **I don't like the ~ of it** (_fig: of film etc_) non mi dice niente; (: _of news_) è preoccupante; **it ~s as if …** ho l'impressione che …; **it ~s like French** somiglia al francese; **that ~s like them arriving** mi sembra di sentirli arrivare.

▶**sound off** _vi_ (_col_): **to ~ off (about)** (_give one's opinions_) fare dei grandi discorsi (su).

sound barrier _n_ muro del suono.

soundbite ['saundbaɪt] _n_ frase _f_ incisiva.

sound effects _npl_ effetti _mpl_ sonori.

sound engineer _n_ tecnico del suono.

sounding ['saundɪŋ] _n_ (_NAUT etc_) scandagliamento.

sounding board _n_ (_MUS_) cassa di risonanza; (_fig_): **to use sb as a ~ for one's ideas** provare le proprie idee su qn.

soundly ['saundlɪ] _adv_ (_sleep_) profondamente; (_beat_) duramente.

soundproof ['saundpruːf] _vt_ insonorizzare, isolare acusticamente ♦ _adj_ insonorizzato(a), isolato(a) acusticamente.

sound system _n_ impianto _m_ audio _inv._

soundtrack ['saundtræk] _n_ (_of film_) colonna sonora.

soup [suːp] _n_ minestra; (_clear_) brodo; (_thick_) zuppa; **in the ~** (_fig_) nei guai.

soup course _n_ minestra.

soup kitchen _n_ mensa per i poveri.

soup plate _n_ piatto fondo.

soupspoon ['suːpspuːn] _n_ cucchiaio da minestra.

sour ['sauə*] _adj_ aspro(a); (_fruit_) acerbo(a); (_milk_) acido(a), fermentato(a); (_fig_) acido(a); **to go** _or_ **turn ~** (_milk, wine_) inacidirsi; (_fig: relationship, plans_) guastarsi; **it's ~ grapes** (_fig_) è soltanto invidia.

source [sɔːs] n fonte f, sorgente f; (fig) fonte; **I have it from a reliable ~ that ...** ho saputo da fonte sicura che ....

south [sauθ] n sud m, meridione m, mezzogiorno ♦ adj del sud, sud inv, meridionale ♦ adv verso sud; **(to the) ~ of** a sud di; **the S~ of France** il sud della Francia; **to travel ~** viaggiare verso sud.

South Africa n Sudafrica m.

South African adj, n sudafricano(a).

South America n Sudamerica m, America del sud.

South American adj, n sudamericano(a).

southbound ['sauθbaund] adj (gen) diretto(a) a sud; (carriageway) sud inv.

south-east [sauθ'iːst] n sud-est m.

South-East Asia n Asia sudorientale.

southerly ['sʌðəlɪ] adj del sud.

southern ['sʌðən] adj del sud, meridionale; (wall) esposto(a) a sud; **the ~ hemisphere** l'emisfero australe.

South Pole n Polo Sud.

South Sea Islands npl: **the ~** le isole dei Mari del Sud.

South Seas npl: **the ~** i Mari del Sud.

South Vietnam n Vietnam m del Sud.

southward(s) ['sauθwəd(z)] adv verso sud.

south-west [sauθ'wɛst] n sud-ovest m.

souvenir [suːvə'nɪə*] n ricordo, souvenir m inv.

sovereign ['sɔvrɪn] adj, n sovrano(a).

sovereignty ['sɔvrəntɪ] n sovranità.

soviet ['səuvɪət] adj sovietico(a).

Soviet Union n: **the ~** l'Unione f Sovietica.

sow n [sau] scrofa ♦ vt [səu] (pt ~ed, pp sown [səun]) seminare.

soya ['sɔɪə], (US) **soy** [sɔɪ] n: **~ bean** seme m di soia; **~ sauce** salsa di soia.

sozzled ['sɔzld] adj (BRIT col) sbronzo(a).

spa [spaː] n (resort) stazione f termale; (US: also: **health ~**) centro di cure estetiche.

space [speɪs] n spazio; (room) posto; spazio; (length of time) intervallo ♦ cpd spaziale ♦ vt (also: **~ out**) distanziare; **in a confined ~** in un luogo chiuso; **to clear a ~ for sth** fare posto per qc; **in a short ~ of time** in breve tempo; **(with)in the ~ of an hour/ three generations** nell'arco di un'ora/di tre generazioni.

space bar n (on typewriter) barra spaziatrice.

spacecraft ['speɪskrɑːft] n (pl inv) veicolo spaziale.

spaceman ['speɪsmæn] n astronauta m, cosmonauta m.

spaceship ['speɪsʃɪp] n astronave f, navicella spaziale.

space shuttle n shuttle m inv.

spacesuit ['speɪssuːt] n tuta spaziale.

spacewoman ['speɪswumən] n astronauta f, cosmonauta f.

spacing ['speɪsɪŋ] n spaziatura; **single/ double ~** (TYP etc) spaziatura singola/ doppia.

spacious ['speɪʃəs] adj spazioso(a), ampio(a).

spade [speɪd] n (tool) vanga; pala; (child's) paletta; **~s** npl (CARDS) picche fpl.

spadework ['speɪdwəːk] n (fig) duro lavoro preparatorio.

spaghetti [spə'gɛtɪ] n spaghetti mpl.

Spain [speɪn] n Spagna.

spam [spæm] n (COMPUT) spamming m ♦ vt: **to ~ sb** inviare a qn messaggi pubblicitari non richiesti via email.

span [spæn] n (of bird, plane) apertura alare; (of arch) campata; (in time) periodo, durata ♦ vt attraversare; (fig) abbracciare.

Spaniard ['spænjəd] n spagnolo/a.

spaniel ['spænjəl] n spaniel m inv.

Spanish ['spænɪʃ] adj spagnolo(a) ♦ n (LING) spagnolo; **the ~** npl gli Spagnoli; **~ omelette** frittata di cipolle, pomodoro e peperoni.

spank [spæŋk] vt sculacciare.

spanner ['spænə*] n (BRIT) chiave f inglese.

spar [spaː*] n asta, palo ♦ vi (BOXING) allenarsi.

spare [spɛə*] adj di riserva, di scorta; (surplus) in più, d'avanzo ♦ n (part) pezzo di ricambio ♦ vt (do without) fare a meno di; (afford to give) concedere; (refrain from hurting, using) risparmiare; **to ~** (surplus) d'avanzo; **there are 2 going ~** (BRIT) ce ne sono 2 in più; **to ~ no expense** non badare a spese; **can you ~ the time?** ha tempo?; **I've a few minutes to ~** ho un attimino di tempo; **there is no time to ~** non c'è tempo da perdere; **can you ~ (me) £10?** puoi prestarmi 10 sterline?

spare part n pezzo di ricambio.

spare room n stanza degli ospiti.

spare time n tempo libero.

spare tyre n (AUT) gomma di scorta.

spare wheel n (AUT) ruota di scorta.

sparing ['spɛərɪŋ] adj (amount) scarso(a); (use) parsimonioso(a); **to be ~ with** essere avaro(a) di.

sparingly ['spɛərɪŋlɪ] adv moderatamente.

spark [spaːk] n scintilla.

spark(ing) plug ['spaːk(ɪŋ)-] n candela.

sparkle ['spaːkl] n scintillio, sfavillio ♦ vi scintillare, sfavillare; (bubble) spumeggiare, frizzare.

sparkler ['spaːklə*] n fuoco d'artificio.

sparkling ['spɑːklɪŋ] adj scintillante, sfavillante; (wine) spumante.

sparring partner ['spɑːrɪŋ-] n sparring partner m inv; (fig) interlocutore abituale in discussioni, dibattiti, tavole rotonde ecc.

sparrow ['spærəu] n passero.

sparse [spɑːs] adj sparso(a), rado(a).

spartan ['spɑːtən] adj (fig) spartano(a).

spasm ['spæzəm] n (MED) spasmo; (fig) accesso, attacco.

spasmodic [spæz'mɔdɪk] adj spasmodico(a); (fig) intermittente.

spastic ['spæstɪk] n spastico/a.

spat [spæt] pt, pp of **spit ♦** n (US) battibecco.

spate [speɪt] n (fig): ~ **of** diluvio or fiume m di; **in** ~ (river) in piena.

spatial ['speɪʃəl] adj spaziale.

spatter ['spætə*] vt, vi schizzare.

spatula ['spætjulə] n spatola.

spawn [spɔːn] vt deporre; (pej) produrre **♦** vi deporre le uova **♦** n uova fpl.

SPCA n abbr (US: = Society for the Prevention of Cruelty to Animals) ≈ E.N.P.A. m (= Ente Nazionale per la Protezione degli Animali).

SPCC n abbr (US) = Society for the Prevention of Cruelty to Children.

speak, pt **spoke,** pp **spoken** [spiːk, spəuk, 'spəukn] vt (language) parlare; (truth) dire **♦** vi parlare; **to** ~ **to sb/of** or **about sth** parlare a qn/di qc; ~ **up!** parli più forte!; **to** ~ **at a conference/in a debate** partecipare ad una conferenza/ad un dibattito; ~**ing!** (on telephone) sono io!; **to** ~ **one's mind** dire quello che si pensa; **he has no money to** ~ **of** non si può proprio dire che sia ricco.

▶**speak for** vt fus: **to** ~ **for sb** parlare a nome di qn; **that picture is already spoken for** (in shop) quel quadro è già stato venduto.

speaker ['spiːkə*] n (in public) oratore/trice; (also: **loud**~) altoparlante m; (POL): **the S**~ il presidente della Camera dei Comuni (BRIT) or dei Rappresentanti (US); **are you a Welsh** ~? parla gallese?

speaking ['spiːkɪŋ] adj parlante; **Italian-**~ **people** persone che parlano italiano; **to be on** ~ **terms** parlarsi.

spear [spɪə*] n lancia.

spearhead ['spɪəhɛd] n punta di lancia; (MIL) reparto d'assalto **♦** vt (attack etc) condurre.

spearmint ['spɪəmɪnt] n (BOT etc) menta verde.

spec [spɛk] n (BRIT col): **on** ~ sperando bene; **to buy sth on** ~ comprare qc sperando di fare un affare.

special ['spɛʃl] adj speciale **♦** n (train) treno supplementare; **nothing** ~ niente di speciale; **take** ~ **care** siate particolarmente prudenti.

special agent n agente m segreto.

special correspondent n inviato speciale.

special delivery n (POST): **by** ~ per espresso.

special effects npl (CINE) effetti mpl speciali.

specialist ['spɛʃəlɪst] n specialista m/f; **a heart** ~ (MED) un cardiologo.

speciality [spɛʃɪ'ælɪtɪ], (esp US) **specialty** n specialità f inv.

specialize ['spɛʃəlaɪz] vi: **to** ~ **(in)** specializzarsi (in).

specially ['spɛʃəlɪ] adv specialmente, particolarmente.

special offer n (COMM) offerta speciale.

specialty ['spɛʃəltɪ] n (esp US) = **speciality.**

species ['spiːʃiːz] n (pl inv) specie f inv.

specific [spə'sɪfɪk] adj specifico(a); preciso(a); **to be** ~ **to** avere un legame specifico con.

specifically [spə'sɪfɪklɪ] adv (explicitly: state, warn) chiaramente, esplicitamente; (especially: design, intend) appositamente.

specification [spɛsɪfɪ'keɪʃən] n specificazione f; ~**s** npl (of car, machine) dati mpl caratteristici; (for building) dettagli mpl.

specify ['spɛsɪfaɪ] vt specificare, precisare; **unless otherwise specified** salvo indicazioni contrarie.

specimen ['spɛsɪmən] n esemplare m, modello; (MED) campione m.

specimen copy n campione m.

specimen signature n firma depositata.

speck [spɛk] n puntino, macchiolina; (particle) granello.

speckled ['spɛkld] adj macchiettato(a).

specs [spɛks] npl (col) occhiali mpl.

spectacle ['spɛktəkl] n spettacolo; see also **spectacles.**

spectacle case n (BRIT) fodero per gli occhiali.

spectacles ['spɛktəklz] npl (BRIT) occhiali mpl.

spectacular [spɛk'tækjulə*] adj spettacolare **♦** n (CINE etc) film m inv etc spettacolare.

spectator [spɛk'teɪtə*] n spettatore/trice.

spectator sport n sport m inv come spettacolo.

spectra ['spɛktrə] npl of **spectrum.**

spectre, (US) **specter** ['spɛktə*] n spettro.

spectrum, pl **spectra** ['spɛktrəm, -rə] n spettro; (fig) gamma.

speculate ['spɛkjuleɪt] *vi* speculare; (*try to guess*): **to ~ about** fare ipotesi su.
speculation [spɛkju'leɪʃən] *n* speculazione *f*; congetture *fpl*.
speculative ['spɛkjulətɪv] *adj* speculativo(a).
speculator ['spɛkjuleɪtə*] *n* speculatore/trice.
sped [spɛd] *pt, pp of* **speed**.
speech [spiːtʃ] *n* (*faculty*) parola; (*talk*) discorso; (*manner of speaking*) parlata; (*language*) linguaggio; (*enunciation*) elocuzione *f*.
speech day *n* (*BRIT SCOL*) giorno della premiazione.
speech impediment *n* difetto di pronuncia.
speechless ['spiːtʃlɪs] *adj* ammutolito(a), muto(a).
speech therapy *n* cura dei disturbi del linguaggio.
speed [spiːd] *n* velocità *f inv*; (*promptness*) prontezza; (*AUT: gear*) marcia ♦ *vi* (*pt, pp* **sped** [spɛd]): **to ~ along** procedere velocemente; **the years sped by** gli anni sono volati; (*AUT: exceed ~ limit*) andare a velocità eccessiva; **at ~** (*BRIT*) velocemente; **at full** *or* **top ~** a tutta velocità; **at a ~ of 70 km/h** a una velocità di 70 km l'ora; **shorthand/typing ~s** numero di parole al minuto in stenografia/dattilografia; **a five-~ gearbox** un cambio a cinque marce.
▶**speed up**, *pt, pp* ~**ed up** *vi, vt* accelerare.
speedboat ['spiːdbəut] *n* motoscafo; fuoribordo *m inv*.
speed dating [-deɪtɪŋ] *n sistema di appuntamenti grazie al quale si possono incontrare in pochissimo tempo diverse persone e scegliere eventualmente chi frequentare.*
speedily ['spiːdɪlɪ] *adv* velocemente; prontamente.
speeding ['spiːdɪŋ] *n* (*AUT*) eccesso di velocità.
speed limit *n* limite *m* di velocità.
speedometer [spɪ'dɔmɪtə*] *n* tachimetro.
speed trap *n* (*AUT*) *tratto di strada sul quale la polizia controlla la velocità dei veicoli.*
speedway ['spiːdweɪ] *n* (*SPORT*) pista per motociclismo.
speedy ['spiːdɪ] *adj* veloce, rapido(a); (*reply*) pronto(a).
speleologist [spɛlɪ'ɔlədʒɪst] *n* speleologo/a.
spell [spɛl] *n* (*also*: **magic ~**) incantesimo; (*period of time*) (breve) periodo ♦ *vt* (*pt, pp* **spelt** *or* ~**ed** [spɛlt, spɛld]) (*in writing*)

scrivere (lettera per lettera); (*aloud*) dire lettera per lettera; (*fig*) significare; **to cast a ~ on sb** fare un incantesimo a qn; **he can't ~** fa errori di ortografia; **how do you ~ your name?** come si scrive il suo nome?; **can you ~ it for me?** me lo può dettare lettera per lettera?
spellbound ['spɛlbaund] *adj* incantato(a), affascinato(a).
spelling ['spɛlɪŋ] *n* ortografia.
spelt [spɛlt] *pt, pp of* **spell**.
spend, *pt, pp* **spent** [spɛnd, spɛnt] *vt* (*money*) spendere; (*time, life*) passare; **to ~ time/money/effort on sth** dedicare tempo/soldi/energie a qc.
spending ['spɛndɪŋ] *n*: **government ~** spesa pubblica.
spending money *n* denaro per le piccole spese.
spending power *n* potere *m* d'acquisto.
spendthrift ['spɛndθrɪft] *n* spendaccione/a.
spent [spɛnt] *pt, pp of* **spend** ♦ *adj* (*patience*) esaurito(a); (*cartridge, bullets, match*) usato(a).
sperm [spəːm] *n* sperma *m*.
sperm bank *n* banca dello sperma.
sperm whale *n* capodoglio.
spew [spjuː] *vt* vomitare.
sphere [sfɪə*] *n* sfera.
spherical ['sfɛrɪkl] *adj* sferico(a).
sphinx [sfɪŋks] *n* sfinge *f*.
spice [spaɪs] *n* spezia ♦ *vt* aromatizzare.
spick-and-span ['spɪkən'spæn] *adj* impeccabile.
spicy ['spaɪsɪ] *adj* piccante.
spider ['spaɪdə*] *n* ragno; ~**'s web** ragnatela.
spiel [spiːl] *n* (*col*) tiritera.
spike [spaɪk] *n* punta; ~**s** *npl* (*SPORT*) scarpe *fpl* chiodate.
spike heel *n* (*US*) tacco a spillo.
spiky ['spaɪkɪ] *adj* (*bush, branch*) spinoso(a); (*animal*) ricoperto(a) di aculei.
spill, *pt, pp* **spilt** *or* ~**ed** [spɪl, -t, -d] *vt* versare, rovesciare ♦ *vi* versarsi, rovesciarsi; **to ~ the beans** (*col*) vuotare il sacco.
▶**spill out** *vi* riversarsi fuori.
▶**spill over** *vi*: **to ~ over (into)** (*liquid*) versarsi (in); (*crowd*) riversarsi (in).
spillage ['spɪlɪdʒ] *n* (*event*) fuoriuscita; (*substance*) sostanza fuoriuscita.
spin [spɪn] *n* (*revolution of wheel*) rotazione *f*; (*AVIAT*) avvitamento; (*trip in car*) giretto ♦ *vb* (*pt, pp* **spun** [spʌn]) *vt* (*wool etc*) filare; (*wheel*) far girare; (*BRIT: clothes*) mettere nella centrifuga ♦ *vi* girare; **to ~ a yarn** raccontare una storia; **to ~ a coin** (*BRIT*)

lanciare in aria una moneta.
►**spin out** _vt_ far durare.
spina bifida ['spaɪnə'bɪfɪdə] _n_ spina bifida.
spinach ['spɪnɪtʃ] _n_ spinacio; (_as food_)
spinaci _mpl._
spinal ['spaɪnl] _adj_ spinale.
spinal column _n_ colonna vertebrale,
spina dorsale.
spinal cord _n_ midollo spinale.
spindly ['spɪndlɪ] _adj_ lungo(a) e sottile,
filiforme.
spin doctor _n_ (_col_) esperto di
comunicazioni responsabile
dell'immagine di un partito politico.
spin-dry ['spɪn'draɪ] _vt_ asciugare con la
centrifuga.
spin-dryer [spɪn'draɪə*] _n_ (_BRIT_) centrifuga.
spine [spaɪn] _n_ spina dorsale; (_thorn_) spina.
spine-chilling ['spaɪntʃɪlɪŋ] _adj_
agghiacciante.
spineless ['spaɪnlɪs] _adj_ invertebrato(a),
senza spina dorsale; (_fig_) smidollato(a).
spinner ['spɪnə*] _n_ (_of thread_) tessitore/
trice.
spinning ['spɪnɪŋ] _n_ filatura.
spinning top _n_ trottola.
spinning wheel _n_ filatoio.
spin-off ['spɪnɔf] _n_ applicazione _f_
secondaria.
spinster ['spɪnstə*] _n_ nubile _f_; zitella.
spiral ['spaɪərl] _n_ spirale _f_ ♦ _adj_ a spirale ♦ _vi_
(_prices_) salire vertiginosamente; **the
inflationary** ~ la spirale dell'inflazione.
spiral staircase _n_ scala a chiocciola.
spire ['spaɪə*] _n_ guglia.
spirit ['spɪrɪt] _n_ (_soul_) spirito, anima; (_ghost_)
spirito, fantasma _m_; (_mood_) stato
d'animo, umore _m_; (_courage_) coraggio; ~**s**
npl (_drink_) alcolici _mpl_; **in good** ~**s** di buon
umore; **in low** ~**s** triste, abbattuto(a);
community ~, **public** ~ senso civico.
spirit duplicator _n_ duplicatore _m_ a spirito.
spirited ['spɪrɪtɪd] _adj_ vivace, vigoroso(a);
(_horse_) focoso(a).
spirit level _n_ livella a bolla (d'aria).
spiritual ['spɪrɪtjuəl] _adj_ spirituale ♦ _n_ (_also:_
Negro ~) spiritual _m inv._
spiritualism ['spɪrɪtjuəlɪzəm] _n_ spiritismo.
spit [spɪt] _n_ (_for roasting_) spiedo; (_spittle_)
sputo; (_saliva_) saliva ♦ _vi_ (_pt, pp_ **spat**
[spæt]) sputare; (_fire, fat_) scoppiettare.
spite [spaɪt] _n_ dispetto ♦ _vt_ contrariare, far
dispetto a; **in** ~ **of** nonostante, malgrado.
spiteful ['spaɪtful] _adj_ dispettoso(a);
(_tongue, remark_) maligno(a), velenoso(a).
spitroast ['spɪt'rəust] _vt_ cuocere allo
spiedo.
spitting ['spɪtɪŋ] _n_: "~ **prohibited**" "vietato

sputare" ♦ _adj_: **to be the** ~ **image of sb**
essere il ritratto vivente _or_ sputato di qn.
spittle ['spɪtl] _n_ saliva; sputo.
spiv [spɪv] _n_ (_BRIT col_) imbroglione _m._
splash [splæʃ] _n_ spruzzo; (_sound_) tonfo; (_of
colour_) schizzo ♦ _vt_ spruzzare ♦ _vi_ (_also:_ ~
about) sguazzare; **to** ~ **paint on the floor**
schizzare il pavimento di vernice.
splashdown ['splæʃdaun] _n_ ammaraggio.
splay [spleɪ] _adj_: ~ **footed** che ha i piedi
piatti.
spleen [spliːn] _n_ (_ANAT_) milza.
splendid ['splɛndɪd] _adj_ splendido(a),
magnifico(a).
splendour ['splɛndə*], (_US_) **splendor** ['splɛndə*] _n_
splendore _m._
splice [splaɪs] _vt_ (_rope_) impiombare; (_wood_)
calettare.
splint [splɪnt] _n_ (_MED_) stecca.
splinter ['splɪntə*] _n_ scheggia ♦ _vi_
scheggiarsi.
splinter group _n_ gruppo dissidente.
split [splɪt] _n_ spaccatura; (_fig: division,
quarrel_) scissione _f_ ♦ _vb_ (_pt, pp_ **split**) _vt_
spaccare; (_party_) dividere; (_work, profits_)
spartire, ripartire ♦ _vi_ (_divide_) dividersi;
to do the ~**s** fare la spaccata; **to** ~ **the
difference** dividersi la differenza.
►**split up** _vi_ (_couple_) separarsi, rompere;
(_meeting_) sciogliersi.
split-level ['splɪtlɛvl] _adj_ (_house_) a piani
sfalsati.
split peas _npl_ piselli _mpl_ secchi spaccati.
split personality _n_ doppia personalità.
split second _n_ frazione _f_ di secondo.
splitting ['splɪtɪŋ] _adj_: **a** ~ **headache** un mal
di testa da impazzire.
splutter ['splʌtə*] _vi_ farfugliare;
sputacchiare.
spoil, _pt, pp_ **spoilt** _or_ ~**ed** [spɔɪl, -t, -d] _vt_
(_damage_) rovinare, guastare; (_mar_)
sciupare; (_child_) viziare; (_ballot paper_)
rendere nullo(a), invalidare; **to be** ~**ing
for a fight** morire dalla voglia di litigare.
spoils [spɔɪlz] _npl_ bottino.
spoilsport ['spɔɪlspɔːt] _n_ guastafeste _m/f inv._
spoilt [spɔɪlt] _pt, pp of_ **spoil** ♦ _adj_ (_child_)
viziato(a); (_ballot paper_) nullo(a).
spoke [spəuk] _pt of_ **speak** ♦ _n_ raggio.
spoken ['spəukn] _pp of_ **speak**.
spokesman ['spəuksmən], **spokeswoman**
[-wumən] _n_ portavoce _m/f inv._
spokesperson ['spəukspəːsn] _n_ portavoce
_m/f._
sponge [spʌndʒ] _n_ spugna; (_CULIN: also:_ ~
cake) pan _m_ di Spagna ♦ _vt_ spugnare,
pulire con una spugna ♦ _vi_: **to** ~ **on** _or_
(_US_) **off of** scroccare a.

sponge bag n (BRIT) nécessaire m inv.
sponge cake n pan m di Spagna.
sponger ['spʌndʒə*] n (pej) parassita m/f, scroccone/a.
spongy ['spʌndʒɪ] adj spugnoso(a).
sponsor ['spɒnsə*] n (RADIO, TV, SPORT etc) sponsor m inv; (of enterprise, bill, for fund-raising) promotore/trice ♦ vt sponsorizzare; patrocinare; (POL: bill) presentare; **I ~ed him at 3p a mile** (in fund-raising race) ho offerto in beneficenza 3 penny per ogni miglio che fa.
sponsorship ['spɒnsəʃɪp] n sponsorizzazione f; patrocinio.
spontaneity [spɒntə'neɪɪtɪ] n spontaneità.
spontaneous [spɒn'teɪnɪəs] adj spontaneo(a).
spoof [spuːf] n presa in giro, parodia.
spooky ['spuːkɪ] adj che fa accapponare la pelle.
spool [spuːl] n bobina.
spoon [spuːn] n cucchiaio.
spoon-feed ['spuːnfiːd] vt nutrire con il cucchiaio; (fig) imboccare.
spoonful ['spuːnful] n cucchiaiata.
sporadic [spə'rædɪk] adj sporadico(a).
sport [spɔːt] n sport m inv; (person) persona di spirito; (amusement) divertimento ♦ vt sfoggiare; **indoor/outdoor ~s** sport mpl al chiuso/all'aria aperta; **to say sth in ~** dire qc per scherzo.
sporting ['spɔːtɪŋ] adj sportivo(a); **to give sb a ~ chance** dare a qn una possibilità (di vincere).
sport jacket n (US) = **sports jacket**.
sports car n automobile f sportiva.
sports ground n campo sportivo.
sports jacket n giacca sportiva.
sportsman ['spɔːtsmən] n sportivo.
sportsmanship ['spɔːtsmənʃɪp] n spirito sportivo.
sports page n pagina sportiva.
sports utility vehicle (SUV) n (esp US) fuoristrada m inv.
sportswear ['spɔːtsweə*] n abiti mpl sportivi.
sportswoman ['spɔːtswumən] n sportiva.
sporty ['spɔːtɪ] adj sportivo(a).
spot [spɒt] n punto; (mark) macchia; (dot: on pattern) pallino; (pimple) foruncolo; (place) posto; (also: ~ **advertisement**) spot m inv; (small amount): **a ~ of** un po' di ♦ vt (notice) individuare, distinguere; **on the ~** sul posto; **to do sth on the ~** fare qc immediatamente or lì per lì; **to put sb on the ~** mettere qn in difficoltà; **to come out in ~s** coprirsi di foruncoli.

spot check n controllo senza preavviso.
spotless ['spɒtlɪs] adj immacolato(a).
spotlight ['spɒtlaɪt] n proiettore m; (AUT) faro ausiliario.
spot-on [spɒt'ɒn] adj (BRIT) esatto(a).
spot price n (COMM) prezzo del pronto.
spotted ['spɒtɪd] adj macchiato(a); a puntini, a pallini; **~ with** punteggiato(a) di.
spotty ['spɒtɪ] adj (face) foruncoloso(a).
spouse [spauz] n sposo/a.
spout [spaut] n (of jug) beccuccio; (of liquid) zampillo, getto ♦ vi zampillare.
sprain [spreɪn] n storta, distorsione f ♦ vt: **to ~ one's ankle** storcersi una caviglia.
sprang [spræŋ] pt of **spring**.
sprawl [sprɔːl] vi sdraiarsi (in modo scomposto) ♦ n: **urban ~** sviluppo urbanistico incontrollato; **to send sb ~ing** mandare qn a gambe all'aria.
spray [spreɪ] n spruzzo; (container) nebulizzatore m, spray m inv; (of flowers) mazzetto ♦ cpd (deodorant) spray inv ♦ vt spruzzare; (crops) irrorare.
spread [sprɛd] n diffusione f; (distribution) distribuzione f; (PRESS, TYP: two pages) doppia pagina; (: across columns) articolo a più colonne; (CULIN) pasta (da spalmare) ♦ vb (pt, pp **spread**) vt (cloth) stendere, distendere; (butter etc) spalmare; (disease, knowledge) propagare, diffondere ♦ vi stendersi, distendersi; spalmarsi; propagarsi, diffondersi; **middle-age ~** pancetta; **repayments will be ~ over 18 months** i versamenti saranno scaglionati lungo un periodo di 18 mesi.
spread-eagled ['sprɛdiːgld] adj: **to be** or **lie ~** essere disteso(a) a gambe e braccia aperte.
spreadsheet ['sprɛdʃiːt] n (COMPUT) foglio elettronico.
spree [spriː] n: **to go on a ~** fare baldoria.
sprig [sprɪg] n ramoscello.
sprightly ['spraɪtlɪ] adj vivace.
spring [sprɪŋ] n (leap) salto, balzo; (bounciness) elasticità; (coiled metal) molla; (season) primavera; (of water) sorgente f ♦ vi (pt **sprang**, pp **sprung** [spræŋ, sprʌŋ]) saltare, balzare ♦ vt: **to ~ a leak** (pipe etc) cominciare a perdere; **to walk with a ~ in one's step** camminare con passo elastico; **in ~, in the ~** in primavera; **to ~ from** provenire da; **to ~ into action** entrare (rapidamente) in azione; **he sprang the news on me** mi ha sorpreso con quella notizia.
▶**spring up** vi (problem) presentarsi.

springboard ['sprɪŋbɔːd] n trampolino.
spring-clean [sprɪŋ'kliːn] n (also: ~**ing**)
grandi pulizie fpl di primavera.
spring onion n (BRIT) cipollina.
spring roll n involtino fritto di verdure o
carne tipico della cucina cinese.
springtime ['sprɪŋtaɪm] n primavera.
springy ['sprɪŋɪ] adj elastico(a).
sprinkle ['sprɪŋkl] vt spruzzare; spargere;
to ~ water etc on, ~ **with water etc**
spruzzare dell'acqua etc su; **to ~ sugar**
etc **on**, ~ **with sugar etc** spolverizzare di
zucchero etc; ~**d with** (fig) cosparso(a)
di.
sprinkler ['sprɪŋklə*] n (for lawn etc)
irrigatore m; (for fire-fighting) sprinkler m
inv.
sprinkling ['sprɪŋklɪŋ] n (of water) qualche
goccia; (of salt, sugar) pizzico.
sprint [sprɪnt] n scatto ♦ vi scattare; **the
200-metres** ~ i 200 metri piani.
sprinter ['sprɪntə*] n velocista m/f.
sprite [spraɪt] n elfo, folletto.
spritzer ['sprɪtsə*] n spritz m inv.
sprocket ['sprɔkɪt] n (on printer etc) dente
m, rocchetto.
sprout [spraut] vi germogliare.
sprouts [sprauts] npl (also: **Brussels** ~)
cavolini mpl di Bruxelles.
spruce [spruːs] n abete m rosso ♦ adj
lindo(a); azzimato(a).
▶**spruce up** vt (tidy) mettere in ordine;
(smarten up: room etc) abbellire; **to ~ o.s.
up** farsi bello(a).
sprung [sprʌŋ] pp of **spring**.
spry [spraɪ] adj arzillo(a), sveglio(a).
SPUC n abbr (= Society for the Protection of
Unborn Children) associazione anti-
abortista.
spun [spʌn] pt, pp of **spin**.
spur [spəː*] n sperone m; (fig) sprone m,
incentivo ♦ vt (also: ~ **on**) spronare; **on
the** ~ **of the moment** lì per lì.
spurious ['spjuərɪəs] adj falso(a).
spurn [spəːn] vt rifiutare con disprezzo,
sdegnare.
spurt [spəːt] n getto; (of energy) esplosione f
♦ vi sgorgare; zampillare; **to put in or on
a** ~ (runner) fare uno scatto; (fig: in work
etc) affrettarsi, sbrigarsi.
sputter ['spʌtə*] vi = **splutter**.
spy [spaɪ] n spia ♦ cpd (film, story) di
spionaggio ♦ vi: **to** ~ **on** spiare ♦ vt (see)
scorgere.
spying ['spaɪɪŋ] n spionaggio.
Sq. abbr (in address) = **square**.
sq. abbr (MATH etc) = **square**.
squabble ['skwɔbl] n battibecco ♦ vi

bisticciarsi.
squad [skwɔd] n (MIL) plotone m; (POLICE)
squadra; **flying** ~ (POLICE) volante f.
squad car n (BRIT POLICE) automobile f
della polizia.
squaddie ['skwɔdɪ] n (MIL col) burba.
squadron ['skwɔdrn] n (MIL) squadrone m;
(AVIAT, NAUT) squadriglia.
squalid ['skwɔlɪd] adj sordido(a).
squall [skwɔːl] n burrasca.
squalor ['skwɔlə*] n squallore m.
squander ['skwɔndə*] vt dissipare.
square [skweə*] n quadrato; (in town)
piazza; (US: block of houses) blocco,
isolato; (instrument) squadra ♦ adj
quadrato(a); (honest) onesto(a); (col:
ideas, person) di vecchio stampo ♦ vt
(arrange) regolare; (MATH) elevare al
quadrato ♦ vi (agree) accordarsi; **a ~ meal**
un pasto abbondante; **2 metres** ~ di 2
metri per 2; **1 ~ metre** 1 metro quadrato;
we're back to ~ one (fig) siamo al punto
di partenza; **all** ~ pari; **to get one's
accounts** ~ mettere in ordine i propri
conti; **I'll ~ it with him** (col) sistemo io le
cose con lui; **can you ~ it with your
conscience?** (reconcile) puoi conciliarlo
con la tua coscienza?
▶**square up** vi (BRIT: settle) saldare,
pagare; **to ~ up with sb** regolare i conti
con qn.
square bracket n (TYP) parentesi f inv
quadra.
squarely ['skweəlɪ] adv (directly)
direttamente; (honestly, fairly)
onestamente.
square root n radice f quadrata.
squash [skwɔʃ] n (BRIT: drink): **lemon/
orange** ~ sciroppo di limone/arancia;
(vegetable) zucca; (SPORT) squash m ♦ vt
schiacciare.
squat [skwɔt] adj tarchiato(a), tozzo(a)
♦ vi accovacciarsi; (on property) occupare
abusivamente.
squatter ['skwɔtə*] n occupante m/f
abusivo(a).
squawk [skwɔːk] vi emettere strida
rauche.
squeak [skwiːk] vi squittire ♦ n (of hinge,
wheel etc) cigolio; (of shoes) scricchiolio;
(of mouse etc) squittio.
squeaky ['skwiːkɪ] adj (col) cigolante; **to be
~ clean** (fig) avere un'immagine pulita.
squeal [skwiːl] vi strillare.
squeamish ['skwiːmɪʃ] adj schizzinoso(a);
disgustato(a).
squeeze [skwiːz] n pressione f; (also ECON)
stretta; (credit ~) stretta creditizia ♦ vt

premere; (*hand, arm*) stringere ♦ *vi*: **to ~ in** infilarsi; **to ~ past/under sth** passare vicino/sotto a qc con difficoltà; **a ~ of lemon** una spruzzata di limone.

▶**squeeze out** *vt* spremere.

squelch [skwɛltʃ] *vi* fare ciac; sguazzare.

squib [skwɪb] *n* petardo.

squid [skwɪd] *n* calamaro.

squint [skwɪnt] *vi* essere strabico(a); (*in the sunlight*) strizzare gli occhi ♦ *n*: **he has a ~** è strabico; **to ~ at sth** guardare qc di traverso; (*quickly*) dare un'occhiata a qc.

squire ['skwaɪə*] *n* (*BRIT*) proprietario terriero.

squirm [skwə:m] *vi* contorcersi.

squirrel ['skwɪrəl] *n* scoiattolo.

squirt [skwə:t] *n* schizzo ♦ *vi* schizzare; zampillare.

Sr *abbr* = **senior; sister** (*REL*).

SRC *n abbr* (*BRIT*: = *Students' Representative Council*) *comitato di rappresentanza studenti*.

Sri Lanka [srɪ'læŋkə] *n* Sri Lanka *m*.

SRO *abbr* (*US*: = *standing room only*) solo posti in piedi.

SS *abbr* = **steamship**.

SSA *n abbr* (*US*: = *Social Security Administration*) ≈ Previdenza Sociale.

SST *n abbr* (*US*) = *supersonic transport*.

ST *abbr* (*US*: = *Standard Time*) *ora ufficiale*.

St *abbr* = **saint; street**.

stab [stæb] *n* (*with knife etc*) pugnalata; (*col: try*): **to have a ~ at (doing) sth** provare a fare qc ♦ *vt* pugnalare; **to ~ sb to death** uccidere qn a coltellate.

stabbing ['stæbɪŋ] *n*: **there's been a ~** qualcuno è stato pugnalato ♦ *adj* (*pain, ache*) lancinante.

stability [stə'bɪlɪti] *n* stabilità.

stabilization [steɪbəlaɪ'zeɪʃən] *n* stabilizzazione *f*.

stabilize ['steɪbəlaɪz] *vt* stabilizzare ♦ *vi* stabilizzarsi.

stabilizer ['steɪbəlaɪzə*] *n* (*AVIAT, NAUT*) stabilizzatore *m*.

stable ['steɪbl] *n* (*for horses*) scuderia; (*for cattle*) stalla ♦ *adj* stabile; **riding ~s** maneggio.

staccato [stə'kɑ:təu] *adv* in modo staccato ♦ *adj* (*MUS*) staccato(a); (*sound*) scandito(a).

stack [stæk] *n* catasta, pila; (*col*) mucchio, sacco ♦ *vt* accatastare, ammucchiare; **there's ~s of time to finish it** (*BRIT col*) abbiamo un sacco di tempo per finirlo.

stadium ['steɪdɪəm] *n* stadio.

staff [stɑ:f] *n* (*work force: gen*) personale *m*; (: *BRIT: SCOL*) personale insegnante; (:

servants) personale di servizio; (*MIL*) stato maggiore; (*stick*) bastone *m* ♦ *vt* fornire di personale.

staffroom ['stɑ:fru:m] *n* sala dei professori.

Staffs *abbr* (*BRIT*) = **Staffordshire**.

stag [stæg] *n* cervo; (*BRIT STOCK EXCHANGE*) rialzista *m/f* su nuove emissioni.

stage [steɪdʒ] *n* (*platform*) palco; (*in theatre*) palcoscenico; (*profession*): **the ~** il teatro, la scena; (*point*) fase *f*, stadio ♦ *vt* (*play*) allestire, mettere in scena; (*demonstration*) organizzare; (*fig: perform: recovery etc*) effettuare; **in ~s** per gradi; a tappe; **in the early/final ~s** negli stadi iniziali/finali; **to go through a difficult ~** attraversare un periodo difficile.

stagecoach ['steɪdʒkəutʃ] *n* diligenza.

stage door *n* ingresso degli artisti.

stage fright *n* paura del pubblico.

stagehand ['steɪdʒhænd] *n* macchinista *m*.

stage-manage ['steɪdʒmænɪdʒ] *vt* allestire le scene per; montare.

stage manager *n* direttore *m* di scena.

stagger ['stægə*] *vi* barcollare ♦ *vt* (*person*) sbalordire; (*hours, holidays*) scaglionare.

staggering ['stægərɪŋ] *adj* (*amazing*) incredibile, sbalorditivo(a).

staging post ['steɪdʒɪŋ-] *n* passaggio obbligato.

stagnant ['stægnənt] *adj* stagnante.

stagnate [stæg'neɪt] *vi* (*also fig*) stagnare.

stagnation [stæg'neɪʃən] *n* stagnazione *f*, ristagno.

stag night, stag party *n* festa di addio al celibato.

staid [steɪd] *adj* posato(a), serio(a).

stain [steɪn] *n* macchia; (*colouring*) colorante *m* ♦ *vt* macchiare; (*wood*) tingere.

stained glass window ['steɪnd-] *n* vetrata.

stainless ['steɪnlɪs] *adj* (*steel*) inossidabile.

stain remover *n* smacchiatore *m*.

stair [stɛə*] *n* (*step*) gradino; **~s** *npl* (*flight of ~s*) scale *fpl*, scala.

staircase ['stɛəkeɪs], **stairway** ['stɛəweɪ] *n* scale *fpl*, scala.

stairwell ['stɛəwel] *n* tromba delle scale.

stake [steɪk] *n* palo, piolo; (*BETTING*) puntata, scommessa ♦ *vt* (*bet*) scommettere; (*risk*) rischiare; (*also: ~ out: area*) delimitare con paletti; **to be at ~** essere in gioco; **to have a ~ in sth** avere un interesse in qc; **to ~ a claim (to sth)** rivendicare (qc).

stakeout ['steɪkaut] *n* sorveglianza.

stalactite ['stæləktaɪt] *n* stalattite *f*.

stalagmite ['stæləgmaɪt] *n* stalagmite *f*.

stale [steɪl] *adj* (*bread*) raffermo(a), stantio(a); (*beer*) svaporato(a); (*smell*) di chiuso.

stalemate ['steɪlmeɪt] *n* stallo; (*fig*) punto morto.

stalk [stɔ:k] *n* gambo, stelo ♦ *vt* inseguire ♦ *vi* camminare impettito(a).

stall [stɔ:l] *n* (*BRIT: in street, market etc*) bancarella; (*in stable*) box *m inv* di stalla ♦ *vt* (*AUT*) far spegnere ♦ *vi* (*AUT*) spegnersi, fermarsi; (*fig*) temporeggiare; ~**s** *npl* (*BRIT: in cinema, theatre*) platea; **newspaper/flower** ~ chiosco del giornalaio/del fioraio.

stallholder ['stɔ:lhəʊldə*] *n* (*BRIT*) bancarellista *m/f*.

stallion ['stæljən] *n* stallone *m*.

stalwart ['stɔ:lwət] *n* membro fidato.

stamen ['steɪmɛn] *n* stame *m*.

stamina ['stæmɪnə] *n* vigore *m*, resistenza.

stammer ['stæmə*] *n* balbuzie *f* ♦ *vi* balbettare.

stamp [stæmp] *n* (*postage* ~) francobollo; (*implement*) timbro; (*mark, also fig*) marchio, impronta; (*on document*) bollo; timbro ♦ *vi* (*also*: ~ **one's foot**) battere il piede ♦ *vt* battere; (*letter*) affrancare; (*mark with a* ~) timbrare; ~**ed addressed envelope (sae)** busta affrancata per la risposta.

▶**stamp out** *vt* (*fire*) estinguere; (*crime*) eliminare; (*opposition*) soffocare.

stamp album *n* album *m inv* per francobolli.

stamp collecting *n* filatelia.

stamp duty *n* (*BRIT*) bollo.

stampede [stæm'pi:d] *n* fuggi fuggi *m inv*; (*of cattle*) fuga precipitosa.

stamp machine *n* distributore *m* automatico di francobolli.

stance [stæns] *n* posizione *f*.

stand [stænd] *n* (*position*) posizione *f*; (*MIL*) resistenza; (*structure*) supporto, sostegno; (*at exhibition*) stand *m inv*; (*at market*) bancarella; (*booth*) chiosco; (*SPORT*) tribuna; (*also*: **music** ~) leggio *m* ♦ *vb* (*pt, pp* **stood** [stud]) *vi* stare in piedi; (*rise*) alzarsi in piedi; (*be placed*) trovarsi ♦ *vt* (*place*) mettere, porre; (*tolerate, withstand*) resistere, sopportare; **to make a** ~ prendere posizione; **to take a** ~ **on an issue** prendere posizione su un problema; **to** ~ **for parliament** (*BRIT*) presentarsi come candidato (per il parlamento); **to** ~ **guard** *or* **watch** (*MIL*) essere di guardia; **it** ~**s to reason** è logico; **as things** ~ stando così le cose; **to**

~ **sb a drink/meal** offrire da bere/un pranzo a qn; **I can't** ~ **him** non lo sopporto.

▶**stand aside** *vi* farsi da parte, scostarsi.

▶**stand by** *vi* (*be ready*) tenersi pronto(a) ♦ *vt fus* (*opinion*) sostenere.

▶**stand down** *vi* (*withdraw*) ritirarsi; (*LAW*) lasciare il banco dei testimoni.

▶**stand for** *vt fus* (*signify*) rappresentare, significare; (*tolerate*) sopportare, tollerare.

▶**stand in for** *vt fus* sostituire.

▶**stand out** *vi* (*be prominent*) spiccare.

▶**stand up** *vi* (*rise*) alzarsi in piedi.

▶**stand up for** *vt fus* difendere.

▶**stand up to** *vt fus* tener testa a, resistere a.

stand-alone ['stændələun] *adj* (*COMPUT*) stand-alone *inv*.

standard ['stændəd] *n* modello, standard *m inv*; (*level*) livello; (*flag*) stendardo ♦ *adj* (*size etc*) normale, standard *inv*; (*practice*) normale; (*model*) di serie; ~**s** *npl* (*morals*) principi *mpl*, valori *mpl*; **to be** *or* **come up to** ~ rispondere ai requisiti; **below** *or* **not up to** ~ (*work*) mediocre; **to apply a double** ~ usare metri diversi (nel giudicare *or* fare *etc*); ~ **of living** livello di vita.

standardization [stændədaɪ'zeɪʃən] *n* standardizzazione *f*.

standardize ['stændədaɪz] *vt* normalizzare, standardizzare.

standard lamp *n* (*BRIT*) lampada a stelo.

standard time *n* ora ufficiale.

stand-by ['stændbaɪ] *n* riserva, sostituto; **to be on** ~ (*gen*) tenersi pronto(a); (*doctor*) essere di guardia; **a** ~ **ticket** un biglietto standby; **to fly** ~ essere in lista d'attesa per un volo.

stand-by generator *n* generatore *m* d'emergenza.

stand-by passenger *n* (*AVIAT*) passeggero/a in lista d'attesa.

stand-by ticket *n* (*AVIAT*) biglietto senza garanzia.

stand-in ['stændɪn] *n* sostituto/a; (*CINE*) controfigura.

standing ['stændɪŋ] *adj* diritto(a), in piedi; (*permanent: committee*) permanente; (: *rule*) fisso(a); (: *army*) regolare; (*grievance*) continuo(a); (*duration*): **of 6 months'** ~ che dura da 6 mesi ♦ *n* rango, condizione *f*, posizione *f*; **it's a** ~ **joke** è diventato proverbiale; **he was given a** ~ **ovation** tutti si alzarono per applaudirlo; **a man of some** ~ un uomo di una certa importanza.

standing committee n commissione f permanente.

standing order n (BRIT: at bank) ordine m di pagamento (permanente); ~s npl (MIL) regolamento.

standing room n posto all'impiedi.

stand-off ['stændɔf] n (esp US: stalemate) situazione f di stallo.

standoffish [stænd'ɔfɪʃ] adj scostante, freddo(a).

standpat ['stændpæt] adj (US) irremovibile.

standpipe ['stændpaɪp] n fontanella.

standpoint ['stændpɔɪnt] n punto di vista.

standstill ['stændstɪl] n: at a ~ fermo(a); (fig) a un punto morto; to come to a ~ fermarsi; giungere a un punto morto.

stank [stæŋk] pt of stink.

stanza ['stænzə] n stanza (poesia).

staple ['steɪpl] n (for papers) graffetta; (chief product) prodotto principale ♦ adj (food etc) di base; (crop, industry) principale ♦ vt cucire.

stapler ['steɪplə*] n cucitrice f.

star [stɑ:*] n stella; (celebrity) divo/a; (principal actor) vedette f inv ♦ vi: to ~ (in) essere il (or la) protagonista (di) ♦ vt (CINE) essere interpretato(a) da; four-~ hotel ≈ albergo di prima categoria; 2-~ petrol (BRIT) ≈ benzina normale; 4-~ petrol (BRIT) ≈ super f.

star attraction n numero principale.

starboard ['stɑ:bəd] n dritta; to ~ a dritta.

starch [stɑ:tʃ] n amido.

starched ['stɑ:tʃt] adj (collar) inamidato(a).

starchy ['stɑ:tʃɪ] adj (food) ricco(a) di amido.

stardom ['stɑ:dəm] n celebrità.

stare [stɛə*] n sguardo fisso ♦ vi: to ~ at fissare.

starfish ['stɑ:fɪʃ] n stella di mare.

stark [stɑ:k] adj (bleak) desolato(a); (simplicity, colour) austero(a); (reality, poverty, truth) crudo(a) ♦ adv: ~ naked completamente nudo(a).

starkers ['stɑ:kəz] adj: to be ~ (BRIT col) essere nudo(a) come un verme.

starlet ['stɑ:lɪt] n (CINE) stellina.

starlight ['stɑ:laɪt] n: by ~ alla luce delle stelle.

starling ['stɑ:lɪŋ] n storno.

starlit ['stɑ:lɪt] adj stellato(a).

starry ['stɑ:rɪ] adj stellato(a).

starry-eyed [stɑ:rɪ'aɪd] adj (idealistic, gullible) ingenuo(a); (from wonder) meravigliato(a).

Stars and Stripes npl: the ~ la bandiera a stelle e strisce.

star sign n segno zodiacale.

star-studded ['stɑ:stʌdɪd] adj: a ~ cast un cast di attori famosi.

start [stɑ:t] n inizio; (of race) partenza; (sudden movement) sobbalzo; (advantage) vantaggio ♦ vt cominciare, iniziare; (found: business, newspaper) fondare, creare ♦ vi cominciare; (on journey) partire, mettersi in viaggio; (jump) sobbalzare; to ~ doing sth (in)cominciare a fare qc; at the ~ all'inizio; for a ~ tanto per cominciare; to make an early ~ partire di buon'ora; to ~ (off) with ... (firstly) per prima cosa ...; (at the beginning) all'inizio; to ~ a fire provocare un incendio.

▶**start off** vi cominciare; (leave) partire.

▶**start over** vi (US) ricominciare.

▶**start up** vi cominciare; (car) avviarsi ♦ vt iniziare; (car) avviare.

starter ['stɑ:tə*] n (AUT) motorino d'avviamento; (SPORT: official) starter m inv; (: runner, horse) partente m/f; (BRIT CULIN) primo piatto.

starting handle ['stɑ:tɪŋ-] n (BRIT) manovella d'avviamento.

starting point n punto di partenza.

starting price n prezzo m base inv.

startle ['stɑ:tl] vt far trasalire.

startling ['stɑ:tlɪŋ] adj sorprendente, sbalorditivo(a).

star turn n (BRIT) attrazione f principale.

starvation [stɑ:'veɪʃən] n fame f, inedia; to die of ~ morire d'inedia.

starve [stɑ:v] vi morire di fame; soffrire la fame ♦ vt far morire di fame, affamare; I'm starving muoio di fame.

stash [stæʃ] vt: to ~ sth away (col) nascondere qc.

state [steɪt] n stato; (pomp): in ~ in pompa ♦ vt dichiarare, affermare; annunciare; to be in a ~ essere agitato(a); the ~ of the art il livello di tecnologia (or cultura etc); ~ of emergency stato di emergenza; ~ of mind stato d'animo.

state control n controllo statale.

stated ['steɪtɪd] adj fissato(a), stabilito(a).

State Department n (US) Dipartimento di Stato, ≈ Ministero degli Esteri.

state education n (BRIT) istruzione f pubblica or statale.

stateless ['steɪtlɪs] adj apolide.

stately ['steɪtlɪ] adj maestoso(a), imponente.

stately home n residenza nobiliare (d'interesse storico o artistico spesso aperta al pubblico).

statement ['steɪtmənt] n dichiarazione f; (LAW) deposizione f; (FINANCE) rendiconto;

official ~ comunicato ufficiale; ~ **of account, bank** ~ estratto conto.
state-owned ['steɪt'əund] *adj* statalizzato(a).
States [steɪts] *npl*: **the** ~ (*USA*) gli Stati Uniti.
state school *n* scuola statale.
statesman ['steɪtsmən] *n* statista *m*.
static ['stætɪk] *n* (*RADIO*) scariche *fpl* ♦ *adj* statico(a); ~ **electricity** elettricità statica.
station ['steɪʃən] *n* stazione *f*; (*rank*) rango, condizione *f* ♦ *vt* collocare, disporre; **action** ~s posti *mpl* di combattimento; **to be** ~ed **in** (*MIL*) essere di stanza in.
stationary ['steɪʃənərɪ] *adj* fermo(a), immobile.
stationer ['steɪʃənə*] *n* cartolaio/a; ~'s **shop** cartoleria.
stationery ['steɪʃənərɪ] *n* articoli *mpl* di cancelleria; (*writing paper*) carta da lettere.
station master *n* (*RAIL*) capostazione *m*.
station wagon *n* (*US*) giardinetta.
statistic [stə'tɪstɪk] *n* statistica; *see also* **statistics**.
statistical [stə'tɪstɪkəl] *adj* statistico(a).
statistics [stə'tɪstɪks] *n* (*science*) statistica.
statue ['stætjuː] *n* statua.
statuesque [stætju'ɛsk] *adj* statuario(a).
statuette [stætju'ɛt] *n* statuetta.
stature ['stætʃə*] *n* statura.
status ['steɪtəs] *n* posizione *f*, condizione *f* sociale; (*prestige*) prestigio; (*legal, marital*) stato.
status quo [-'kwəu] *n*: **the** ~ lo statu quo.
status symbol *n* simbolo di prestigio.
statute ['stætjuːt] *n* legge *f*; ~s *npl* (*of club etc*) statuto.
statute book *n* codice *m*.
statutory ['stætjutərɪ] *adj* stabilito(a) dalla legge, statutario(a); ~ **meeting** (*COMM*) assemblea ordinaria.
staunch [stɔːntʃ] *adj* fidato(a), leale ♦ *vt* (*flow*) arrestare; (*blood*) arrestare il flusso di.
stave [steɪv] *n* (*MUS*) rigo ♦ *vt*: **to** ~ **off** (*attack*) respingere; (*threat*) evitare.
stay [steɪ] *n* (*period of time*) soggiorno, permanenza ♦ *vi* rimanere; (*reside*) alloggiare, stare; (*spend some time*) trattenersi, soggiornare; ~ **of execution** (*LAW*) sospensione *f* dell'esecuzione; **to** ~ **put** non muoversi; **to** ~ **with friends** stare presso amici; **to** ~ **the night** passare la notte.
▶**stay behind** *vi* restare indietro.
▶**stay in** *vi* (*at home*) stare in casa.

▶**stay on** *vi* restare, rimanere.
▶**stay out** *vi* (*of house*) rimanere fuori (di casa); (*strikers*) continuare lo sciopero.
▶**stay up** *vi* (*at night*) rimanere alzato(a).
staying power ['steɪɪŋ-] *n* capacità di resistenza.
STD *n abbr* (*BRIT*: = *subscriber trunk dialling*) teleselezione *f*; (= *sexually transmitted disease*) malattia venerea.
stead [stɛd] *n* (*BRIT*): **in sb's** ~ al posto di qn; **to stand sb in good** ~ essere utile a qn.
steadfast ['stɛdfɑːst] *adj* fermo(a), risoluto(a).
steadily ['stɛdɪlɪ] *adv* continuamente; (*walk*) con passo sicuro.
steady ['stɛdɪ] *adj* stabile, solido(a), fermo(a); (*regular*) costante; (*boyfriend etc*) fisso(a); (*person*) calmo(a), tranquillo(a) ♦ *vt* stabilizzare; calmare; **to** ~ **o.s.** ritrovare l'equilibrio.
steak [steɪk] *n* (*meat*) bistecca; (*fish*) trancia.
steakhouse ['steɪkhaus] *n ristorante specializzato in bistecche*.
steal, *pt* **stole**, *pp* **stolen** [stiːl, stəul, 'stəuln] *vt* rubare ♦ *vi* (*thieve*) rubare.
▶**steal away, steal off** *vi* svignarsela, andarsene alla chetichella.
stealth [stɛlθ] *n*: **by** ~ furtivamente.
stealthy ['stɛlθɪ] *adj* furtivo(a).
steam [stiːm] *n* vapore *m* ♦ *vt* trattare con vapore; (*CULIN*) cuocere a vapore ♦ *vi* fumare; (*ship*): **to** ~ **along** filare; **to let off** ~ (*fig*) sfogarsi; **under one's own** ~ (*fig*) da solo, con i propri mezzi; **to run out of** ~ (*fig: person*) non farcela più.
▶**steam up** *vi* (*window*) appannarsi; **to get** ~ed up about sth (*fig*) andare in bestia per qc.
steam engine *n* macchina a vapore; (*RAIL*) locomotiva a vapore.
steamer ['stiːmə*] *n* piroscafo, vapore *m*; (*CULIN*) pentola a vapore.
steam iron *n* ferro a vapore.
steamroller ['stiːmrəulə*] *n* rullo compressore.
steamship ['stiːmʃɪp] *n* piroscafo, vapore *m*.
steamy ['stiːmɪ] *adj* pieno(a) di vapore; (*window*) appannato(a).
steed [stiːd] *n* (*literary*) corsiero, destriero.
steel [stiːl] *n* acciaio ♦ *cpd* di acciaio.
steel band *n* banda di strumenti a percussione (*tipica dei Caribi*).
steel industry *n* industria dell'acciaio.
steel mill *n* acciaieria.
steelworks ['stiːlwəːks] *n* acciaieria.

steely ['sti:lɪ] adj (determination) inflessibile; (gaze) duro(a); (eyes) freddo(a) come l'acciaio.

steep [sti:p] adj ripido(a), scosceso(a); (price) eccessivo(a) ♦ vt inzuppare; (washing) mettere a mollo.

steeple ['sti:pl] n campanile m.

steeplechase ['sti:pltʃeɪs] n corsa a ostacoli, steeplechase m inv.

steeplejack ['sti:pldʒæk] n chi ripara campanili e ciminiere.

steer [stɪə*] n manzo ♦ vt (ship) governare; (car) guidare ♦ vi (NAUT: person) governare; (: ship) rispondere al timone; (car) guidarsi; **to ~ clear of sb/sth** (fig) tenersi alla larga da qn/qc.

steering ['stɪərɪŋ] n (AUT) sterzo.

steering column n piantone m dello sterzo.

steering committee n comitato direttivo.

steering wheel n volante m.

stem [stɛm] n (of flower, plant) stelo; (of tree) fusto; (of glass) gambo; (of fruit, leaf) picciolo ♦ vt contenere, arginare.

▶**stem from** vt fus provenire da, derivare da.

stench [stɛntʃ] n puzzo, fetore m.

stencil ['stɛnsl] n (of metal, cardboard) stampino, mascherina; (in typing) matrice f.

stenographer [stɛ'nɔgrəfə*] n (US) stenografo/a.

stenography [stɛ'nɔgrəfɪ] n (US) stenografia.

step [stɛp] n passo; (stair) gradino, scalino; (action) mossa, azione f ♦ vi: **to ~ forward** fare un passo avanti; **~s** npl (BRIT) = **stepladder**; **~ by ~** un passo dietro l'altro; (fig) poco a poco; **to be in/out of ~ with** (also fig) stare/non stare al passo con.

▶**step down** vi (fig) ritirarsi.

▶**step in** vi fare il proprio ingresso.

▶**step off** vt fus scendere da.

▶**step over** vt fus scavalcare.

▶**step up** vt aumentare; intensificare.

step aerobics n step m inv.

stepbrother ['stɛpbrʌðə*] n fratellastro.

stepchild ['stɛptʃaɪld] n figliastro/a.

stepdaughter ['stɛpdɔ:tə*] n figliastra.

stepfather ['stɛpfɑ:ðə*] n patrigno.

stepladder ['stɛplædə*] n scala a libretto.

stepmother ['stɛpmʌðə*] n matrigna.

stepping stone ['stɛpɪŋ-] n pietra di un guado; (fig) trampolino.

step Reebok ® [-'ri:bɔk] n step m inv.

stepsister ['stɛpsɪstə*] n sorellastra.

stepson ['stɛpsʌn] n figliastro.

stereo ['stɛrɪəu] n (system) sistema m stereofonico; (record player) stereo m inv ♦ adj (also: ~phonic) stereofonico(a); **in ~** in stereofonia.

stereotype ['stɪərɪətaɪp] n stereotipo.

sterile ['stɛraɪl] adj sterile.

sterility [stɛ'rɪlɪtɪ] n sterilità.

sterilization [stɛrɪlaɪ'zeɪʃən] n sterilizzazione f.

sterilize ['stɛrɪlaɪz] vt sterilizzare.

sterling ['stə:lɪŋ] adj (gold, silver) di buona lega; (fig) autentico(a), genuino(a) ♦ n (ECON) (lira) sterlina; **a pound ~** una lira sterlina.

sterling area n area della sterlina.

stern [stə:n] adj severo(a) ♦ n (NAUT) poppa.

sternum ['stə:nəm] n sterno.

steroid ['stɛrɔɪd] n steroide m.

stethoscope ['stɛθəskəup] n stetoscopio.

stevedore ['sti:vɪdɔ:*] n scaricatore m di porto.

stew [stju:] n stufato ♦ vt, vi cuocere in umido; **~ed tea** tè lasciato troppo in infusione; **~ed fruit** frutta cotta.

steward ['stju:əd] n (AVIAT, NAUT, RAIL) steward m inv; (in club etc) dispensiere m; (shop ~) rappresentante m/f sindacale.

stewardess ['stju:ədɛs] n assistente f di volo, hostess f inv.

stewardship ['stju:ədʃɪp] n amministrazione f.

stewing steak ['stju:ɪŋ-], (US) **stew meat** n carne f (di manzo) per stufato.

St. Ex. abbr = **stock exchange**.

stg abbr = **sterling**.

stick [stɪk] n bastone m; (of rhubarb, celery) gambo ♦ vb (pt, pp **stuck** [stʌk]) vt (glue) attaccare; (thrust): **to ~ sth into** conficcare or piantare or infiggere qc in; (col: put) ficcare; (: tolerate) sopportare ♦ vi conficcarsi; tenere; (remain) restare, rimanere; (get jammed: door, lift) bloccarsi; **to ~ to** (one's word, promise) mantenere; (principles) tener fede a; **to get hold of the wrong end of the ~** (fig) capire male; **it stuck in my mind** mi è rimasto in mente.

▶**stick around** vi (col) restare, fermarsi.

▶**stick out, stick up** vi sporgere, spuntare ♦ vt: **to ~ it out** (col) tener duro.

▶**stick up for** vt fus difendere.

sticker ['stɪkə*] n cartellino adesivo.

sticking plaster ['stɪkɪŋ-] n cerotto adesivo.

sticking point n (fig) punto di stallo, impasse f inv.

stickleback ['stɪklbæk] n spinarello.

stickler ['stɪklə*] n: **to be a ~ for** essere

pignolo(a) su, tenere molto a.

stick-on ['stɪkɔn] *adj* (*label*) adesivo(a).

stick shift *n* (*US AUT*) cambio manuale.

stick-up ['stɪkʌp] *n* (*col*) rapina a mano armata.

sticky ['stɪkɪ] *adj* attaccaticcio(a), vischioso(a); (*label*) adesivo(a).

stiff [stɪf] *adj* rigido(a), duro(a); (*muscle*) legato(a), indolenzito(a); (*difficult*) difficile, arduo(a); (*cold*: *manner etc*) freddo(a), formale; (*strong*) forte; (*high*: *price*) molto alto(a); **to be** *or* **feel** ~ (*person*) essere *or* sentirsi indolenzito; **to have a** ~ **neck/back** avere il torcicollo/ mal di schiena; **to keep a** ~ **upper lip** (*BRIT fig*) conservare il sangue freddo.

stiffen ['stɪfn] *vt* irrigidire; rinforzare ♦ *vi* irrigidirsi; indurirsi.

stiffness ['stɪfnɪs] *n* rigidità; indolenzimento; difficoltà; freddezza.

stifle ['staɪfl] *vt* soffocare.

stifling ['staɪflɪŋ] *adj* (*heat*) soffocante.

stigma, *pl* (*BOT, MED*) ~**ta,** (*fig*) ~**s** ['stɪgmə, stɪg'mɑːtə] *n* stigma *m*.

stigmata [stig'mɑːtə] *npl* (*REL*) stigmate *fpl*.

stile [staɪl] *n* cavalcasiepe *m*; cavalcasteccato.

stiletto [stɪ'lɛtəu] *n* (*also*: ~ **heel**) tacco a spillo.

still [stɪl] *adj* fermo(a); (*quiet*) silenzioso(a); (*orange juice etc*) non gassato(a) ♦ *adv* (*up to this time, even*) ancora; (*nonetheless*) tuttavia, ciò nonostante ♦ *n* (*CINE*) fotogramma *m*; **keep** ~! stai fermo!; **he** ~ **hasn't arrived** non è ancora arrivato.

stillborn ['stɪlbɔːn] *adj* nato(a) morto(a).

still life *n* natura morta.

stilt [stɪlt] *n* trampolo; (*pile*) palo.

stilted ['stɪltɪd] *adj* freddo(a), formale; artificiale.

stimulant ['stɪmjulənt] *n* stimolante *m*.

stimulate ['stɪmjuleɪt] *vt* stimolare.

stimulating ['stɪmjuleɪtɪŋ] *adj* stimolante.

stimulation [stɪmju'leɪʃən] *n* stimolazione *f*.

stimulus, *pl* **stimuli** ['stɪmjuləs, 'stɪmjulaɪ] *n* stimolo.

sting [stɪŋ] *n* puntura; (*organ*) pungiglione *m*; (*col*) trucco ♦ *vt* (*pt, pp* **stung** [stʌŋ]) pungere ♦ *vi* bruciare; **my eyes are** ~**ing** mi bruciano gli occhi.

stingy ['stɪndʒɪ] *adj* spilorcio(a), tirchio(a).

stink [stɪŋk] *n* fetore *m*, puzzo ♦ *vi* (*pt* **stank**, *pp* **stunk** [stæŋk, stʌŋk]) puzzare.

stinker ['stɪŋkə*] *n* (*col*) porcheria; (*person*) fetente *m/f*.

stinking ['stɪŋkɪŋ] *adj* (*col*): **a** ~ ... uno schifo di ..., un(a) maledetto(a) ...; ~ **rich** ricco(a) da far paura.

stint [stɪnt] *n* lavoro, compito ♦ *vi*: **to** ~ **on** lesinare su.

stipend ['staɪpɛnd] *n* stipendio, congrua.

stipendiary [staɪ'pɛndɪərɪ] *adj*: ~ **magistrate** magistrato stipendiato.

stipulate ['stɪpjuleɪt] *vt* stipulare.

stipulation [stɪpju'leɪʃən] *n* stipulazione *f*.

stir [stəː*] *n* agitazione *f*, clamore *m* ♦ *vt* rimescolare; (*move*) smuovere, agitare ♦ *vi* muoversi; **to give sth a** ~ mescolare qc; **to cause a** ~ fare scalpore.

▸**stir up** *vt* provocare, suscitare.

stir-fry ['stəː'fraɪ] *vt* saltare in padella ♦ *n* pietanza al salto.

stirring ['stəːrɪŋ] *adj* eccitante; commovente.

stirrup ['stɪrəp] *n* staffa.

stitch [stɪtʃ] *n* (*SEWING*) punto; (*KNITTING*) maglia; (*MED*) punto (di sutura); (*pain*) fitta ♦ *vt* cucire, attaccare; suturare.

stoat [stəut] *n* ermellino.

stock [stɔk] *n* riserva, provvista; (*COMM*) giacenza, stock *m inv*; (*AGR*) bestiame *m*; (*CULIN*) brodo; (*FINANCE*) titoli *mpl*, azioni *fpl*; (*RAIL*: *also*: **rolling** ~) materiale *m* rotabile; (*descent, origin*) stirpe *f* ♦ *adj* (*fig*: *reply etc*) consueto(a); solito(a), classico(a); (*greeting*) usuale; (*COMM*: *goods, size*) standard *inv* ♦ *vt* (*have in stock*) avere, vendere; **well-**~**ed** ben fornito(a); **to have sth in** ~ avere qc in magazzino; **out of** ~ esaurito(a); **to take** ~ (*fig*) fare il punto; ~**s and shares** valori *mpl* di borsa; **government** ~ titoli di Stato.

▸**stock up** *vi*: **to** ~ **up (with)** fare provvista (di).

stockade [stɔ'keɪd] *n* palizzata.

stockbroker ['stɔkbrəukə*] *n* agente *m* di cambio.

stock control *n* gestione *f* magazzino.

stock cube *n* (*BRIT CULIN*) dado.

stock exchange *n* Borsa (valori).

stockholder ['stɔkhəuldə*] *n* (*FINANCE*) azionista *m/f*.

Stockholm ['stɔkhəum] *n* Stoccolma.

stocking ['stɔkɪŋ] *n* calza.

stock-in-trade ['stɔkɪn'treɪd] *n* (*fig*): **it's his** ~ è la sua specialità.

stockist ['stɔkɪst] *n* (*BRIT*) fornitore *m*.

stock market *n* (*BRIT*) Borsa, mercato finanziario.

stock phrase *n* cliché *m inv*.

stockpile ['stɔkpaɪl] *n* riserva ♦ *vt* accumulare riserve di.

stockroom ['stɔkrum] *n* magazzino.

stocktaking ['stɔkteɪkɪŋ] *n* (*BRIT COMM*) inventario.

stocky ['stɔkɪ] *adj* tarchiato(a), tozzo(a).

stodgy ['stɔdʒɪ] adj pesante, indigesto(a).

stoic ['stəuɪk] n stoico/a.

stoical ['stəuɪkəl] adj stoico(a).

stoke [stəuk] vt alimentare.

stoker ['stəukə*] n fochista m.

stole [stəul] pt of **steal** ♦ n stola.

stolen ['stəuln] pp of **steal**.

stolid ['stɔlɪd] adj impassibile.

stomach ['stʌmək] n stomaco; (abdomen) ventre m ♦ vt sopportare, digerire.

stomach ache n mal m di stomaco.

stomach pump n pompa gastrica.

stomach ulcer n ulcera allo stomaco.

stomp [stɔmp] vi: **to ~ in/out** etc entrare/ uscire etc con passo pesante.

stone [stəun] n pietra; (pebble) sasso, ciottolo; (in fruit) nocciolo; (MED) calcolo; (BRIT: weight) = 6.348 kg.; 14 libbre ♦ cpd di pietra ♦ vt lapidare; **within a ~'s throw of the station** a due passi dalla stazione.

Stone Age n: **the ~** l'età della pietra.

stone-cold [stəun'kəuld] adj gelido(a).

stoned [stəund] adj (col: drunk) sbronzo(a); (on drugs) fuori inv.

stone-deaf [stəun'dɛf] adj sordo(a) come una campana.

stonemason ['stəunmeɪsn] n scalpellino.

stonewall [stəun'wɔːl] vi fare ostruzionismo ♦ vt ostacolare.

stonework ['stəunwəːk] n muratura.

stony ['stəunɪ] adj pietroso(a), sassoso(a).

stood [stud] pt, pp of **stand**.

stooge [stuːdʒ] n (col) tirapiedi m/f inv.

stool [stuːl] n sgabello.

stoop [stuːp] vi (also: **have a ~**) avere una curvatura; (bend) chinarsi, curvarsi; **to ~ to sth/doing sth** abbassarsi a qc/a fare qc.

stop [stɔp] n arresto; (stopping place) fermata; (in punctuation) punto ♦ vt arrestare, fermare; (break off) interrompere; (also: **put a ~ to**) porre fine a; (prevent) impedire ♦ vi fermarsi; (rain, noise etc) cessare, finire; **to ~ doing sth** cessare or finire di fare qc; **to ~ sb (from) doing sth** impedire a qn di fare qc; **to ~ dead** fermarsi di colpo; **~ it!** smettila!, basta!.

▶**stop by** vi passare, fare un salto.

▶**stop off** vi sostare brevemente.

▶**stop up** vt (hole) chiudere, turare.

stopcock ['stɔpkɔk] n rubinetto di arresto.

stopgap ['stɔpgæp] n (person) tappabuchi m/f inv; (measure) ripiego ♦ cpd (measures, solution) di fortuna.

stoplights ['stɔplaɪts] npl (AUT) stop mpl.

stopover ['stɔpəuvə*] n breve sosta; (AVIAT) scalo.

stoppage ['stɔpɪdʒ] n arresto, fermata; (of pay) trattenuta; (strike) interruzione f del lavoro.

stopper ['stɔpə*] n tappo.

stop press n ultimissime fpl.

stopwatch ['stɔpwɔtʃ] n cronometro.

storage ['stɔːrɪdʒ] n immagazzinamento; (COMPUT) memoria.

storage heater n (BRIT) radiatore m elettrico che accumula calore.

store [stɔː*] n provvista, riserva; (depot) deposito; (BRIT: department ~) grande magazzino; (US: shop) negozio ♦ vt mettere da parte; conservare; (grain, goods) immagazzinare; (COMPUT) registrare; **to set great/little ~ by sth** dare molta/poca importanza a qc; **who knows what is in ~ for us?** chissà cosa ci riserva il futuro?

▶**store up** vt mettere in serbo, conservare.

storehouse ['stɔːhaus] n magazzino, deposito.

storekeeper ['stɔːkiːpə*] n (US) negoziante m/f.

storeroom ['stɔːrum] n dispensa.

storey, (US) **story** ['stɔːrɪ] n piano.

stork [stɔːk] n cicogna.

storm [stɔːm] n tempesta; (also: **thunder~**) temporale m ♦ vi (fig) infuriarsi ♦ vt prendere d'assalto.

storm cloud n nube f temporalesca.

storm door n controporta.

stormy ['stɔːmɪ] adj tempestoso(a), burrascoso(a).

story ['stɔːrɪ] n storia; racconto; (PRESS) articolo; (US) = **storey**.

storybook ['stɔːrɪbuk] n libro di racconti.

storyteller ['stɔːrɪtɛlə*] n narratore/trice.

stout [staut] adj solido(a), robusto(a); (brave) coraggioso(a); (fat) corpulento(a), grasso(a) ♦ n birra scura.

stove [stəuv] n (for cooking) fornello; (: small) fornelletto; (for heating) stufa; **gas/electric ~** cucina a gas/elettrica.

stow [stəu] vt mettere via.

stowaway ['stəuəweɪ] n passeggero(a) clandestino(a).

straddle ['strædl] vt stare a cavalcioni di.

strafe [strɑːf] vt mitragliare.

straggle ['strægl] vi crescere (or estendersi) disordinatamente; trascinarsi; rimanere indietro; **~d along the coast** disseminati(e) lungo la costa.

straggler ['stræglə*] n sbandato/a.

straggling ['stræglɪŋ], **straggly** ['stræglɪ] adj (hair) in disordine.

straight [streɪt] adj (continuous, direct)

dritto(a); (*frank*) onesto(a), franco(a); (*plain, uncomplicated*) semplice; (*THEAT: part, play*) serio(a); (*col: heterosexual*) eterosessuale ♦ *adv* diritto; (*drink*) liscio ♦ *n*: **the** ~ la linea retta; (*RAIL*) il rettilineo; (*SPORT*) la dirittura d'arrivo; **to put** *or* **get** ~ mettere in ordine, mettere ordine in; **to be (all)** ~ (*tidy*) essere a posto, essere sistemato; (*clarified*) essere chiaro; **ten** ~ **wins** dieci vittorie di fila; ~ **away**, ~ **off** (*at once*) immediatamente; ~ **off**, ~ **out** senza esitare; **I went** ~ **home** sono andato direttamente a casa.

straighten ['streɪtn] *vt* (*also*: ~ **out**) raddrizzare; **to** ~ **things out** mettere le cose a posto.

straight-faced [streɪt'feɪst] *adj* impassibile, imperturbabile ♦ *adv* con il viso serio.

straightforward [streɪt'fɔːwəd] *adj* semplice; (*frank*) onesto(a), franco(a).

strain [streɪn] *n* (*TECH*) sollecitazione *f*; (*physical*) sforzo; (*mental*) tensione *f*; (*MED*) strappo; (*streak, trace*) tendenza; elemento; (*breed*) razza; (*of virus*) tipo ♦ *vt* tendere; (*muscle*) slogare; (*ankle*) storcere; (*friendship, marriage*) mettere a dura prova; (*filter*) colare, filtrare ♦ *vi* sforzarsi; ~**s** *npl* (*MUS*) note *fpl*; **she's under a lot of** ~ è molto tesa, è sotto pressione.

strained [streɪnd] *adj* (*laugh etc*) forzato(a); (*relations*) teso(a).

strainer ['streɪnə*] *n* passino, colino.

strait [streɪt] *n* (*GEO*) stretto; **to be in dire** ~**s** (*fig*) essere nei guai.

straitjacket ['streɪtdʒækɪt] *n* camicia di forza.

strait-laced [streɪt'leɪst] *adj* puritano(a).

strand [strænd] *n* (*of thread*) filo.

strange [streɪndʒ] *adj* (*not known*) sconosciuto(a); (*odd*) strano(a), bizzarro(a).

strangely ['streɪndʒlɪ] *adv* stranamente.

stranger ['streɪndʒə*] *n* (*unknown*) sconosciuto/a; (*from another place*) estraneo/a; **I'm a** ~ **here** non sono del posto.

strangle ['stræŋgl] *vt* strangolare.

stranglehold ['stræŋglhəuld] *n* (*fig*) stretta (mortale).

strangulation [stræŋgju'leɪʃən] *n* strangolamento.

strap [stræp] *n* cinghia; (*of slip, dress*) spallina, bretella ♦ *vt* legare con una cinghia; (*child etc*) punire (con una cinghia).

straphanging ['stræphæŋɪŋ] *n* viaggiare *m* in piedi (*su mezzi pubblici reggendosi a un*

sostegno).

strapless ['stræplɪs] *adj* (*bra, dress*) senza spalline.

strapped [stræpt] *adj*: ~ **for cash** a corto di soldi; **financially** ~ finanziariamente a terra.

strapping ['stræpɪŋ] *adj* ben piantato(a).

Strasbourg ['stræzbɔːg] *n* Strasburgo *f*.

strata ['strɑːtə] *npl of* **stratum**.

stratagem ['strætɪdʒəm] *n* stratagemma *m*.

strategic [strə'tiːdʒɪk] *adj* strategico(a).

strategist ['strætɪdʒɪst] *n* stratega *m*.

strategy ['strætɪdʒɪ] *n* strategia.

stratosphere ['strætəsfɪə*] *n* stratosfera.

stratum, *pl* **strata** ['strɑːtəm, 'strɑːtə] *n* strato.

straw [strɔː] *n* paglia; (*drinking* ~) cannuccia; **that's the last** ~! è la goccia che fa traboccare il vaso!

strawberry ['strɔːbərɪ] *n* fragola.

stray [streɪ] *adj* (*animal*) randagio(a) ♦ *vi* perdersi; allontanarsi, staccarsi (dal gruppo); ~ **bullet** proiettile *m* vagante.

streak [striːk] *n* striscia; (*fig: of madness etc*): **a** ~ **of** una vena di ♦ *vt* striare, screziare ♦ *vi*: **to** ~ **past** passare come un fulmine; **to have** ~**s in one's hair** avere le mèche nei capelli; **a winning/losing** ~ un periodo fortunato/sfortunato.

streaker ['striːkə*] *n* streaker *m/f inv*.

streaky ['striːkɪ] *adj* screziato(a), striato(a).

streaky bacon *n* (*BRIT*) ≈ pancetta.

stream [striːm] *n* ruscello; corrente *f*; (*of people*) fiume *m* ♦ *vt* (*SCOL*) dividere in livelli di rendimento ♦ *vi* scorrere; **to** ~ **in/out** entrare/uscire a fiotti; **against the** ~ controcorrente; **on** ~ (*new power plant etc*) in funzione, in produzione.

streamer ['striːmə*] *n* (*of paper*) stella filante.

stream feed *n* (*on photocopier etc*) alimentazione *f* continua.

streamline ['striːmlaɪn] *vt* dare una linea aerodinamica a; (*fig*) razionalizzare.

streamlined ['striːmlaɪnd] *adj* aerodinamico(a), affusolato(a); (*fig*) razionalizzato(a).

street [striːt] *n* strada, via; **the back** ~**s** le strade secondarie; **to be on the** ~**s** (*homeless*) essere senza tetto; (*as prostitute*) battere il marciapiede.

streetcar ['striːtkɑː*] *n* (*US*) tram *m inv*.

street cred [₊krɛd] *n* (*col*) credibilità presso i giovani.

street lamp *n* lampione *m*.

street lighting *n* illuminazione *f* stradale.

street map, street plan *n* pianta (di una città).

street market n mercato all'aperto.

streetwise ['striːtwaɪz] adj (col) esperto(a) dei bassifondi.

strength [strɛŋθ] n forza; (of girder, knot etc) resistenza, solidità; (of chemical solution) concentrazione f; (of wine) gradazione f alcolica; **on the ~ of** sulla base di, in virtù di; **below/at full ~** con gli effettivi ridotti/al completo.

strengthen ['strɛŋθən] vt rinforzare; (muscles) irrobustire; (economy, currency) consolidare.

strenuous ['strɛnjuəs] adj vigoroso(a), energico(a); (tiring) duro(a), pesante.

stress [strɛs] n (force, pressure) pressione f; (mental strain) tensione f; (accent) accento; (emphasis) enfasi f ♦ vt insistere su, sottolineare; **to be under ~** essere sotto tensione; **to lay great ~ on sth** dare grande importanza a qc.

stressful ['strɛsful] adj (job) difficile, stressante.

stretch [strɛtʃ] n (of sand etc) distesa; (of time) periodo ♦ vi stirarsi; (extend): **to ~ to** or **as far as** estendersi fino a; (be enough: money, food): **to ~ (to)** bastare (per) ♦ vt tendere, allungare; (spread) distendere; (fig) spingere (al massimo); **at a ~** ininterrottamente; **to ~ a muscle** tendere un muscolo; **to ~ one's legs** sgranchirsi le gambe.

▶**stretch out** vi allungarsi, estendersi ♦ vt (arm etc) allungare, tendere; (to spread) distendere; **to ~ out for sth** allungare la mano per prendere qc.

stretcher ['strɛtʃə*] n barella, lettiga.

stretcher-bearer ['strɛtʃəbɛərə*] n barelliere m.

stretch marks npl smagliature fpl.

strewn [struːn] adj: **~ with** cosparso(a) di.

stricken ['strɪkən] adj provato(a); affranto(a); **~ with** colpito(a) da.

strict [strɪkt] adj (severe) rigido(a), severo(a); (: order, rule) rigoroso(a); (: supervision) stretto(a); (precise) preciso(a), stretto(a); **in ~ confidence** in assoluta confidenza.

strictly ['strɪktlɪ] adv severamente; rigorosamente; strettamente; **~ confidential** strettamente confidenziale; **~ speaking** a rigor di termini; **~ between ourselves** ... detto fra noi ....

stride [straɪd] n passo lungo ♦ vi (pt strode, pp stridden [strəud, 'strɪdn]) camminare a grandi passi; **to take in one's ~** (fig: changes etc) prendere con tranquillità.

strident ['straɪdnt] adj stridente.

strife [straɪf] n conflitto; litigi mpl.

strike [straɪk] n sciopero; (of oil etc) scoperta; (attack) attacco ♦ vb (pt, pp struck [strʌk]) vt colpire; (oil etc) scoprire, trovare; (produce, make: coin, medal) coniare; (: agreement, deal) concludere ♦ vi far sciopero, scioperare; (attack) attaccare; (clock) suonare; **to go on** or **come out on ~** mettersi in sciopero; **to ~ a match** accendere un fiammifero; **to ~ a balance** (fig) trovare il giusto mezzo.

▶**strike back** vi (MIL) fare rappresaglie; (fig) reagire.

▶**strike down** vt (fig) atterrare.

▶**strike off** vt (from list) cancellare; (: doctor etc) radiare.

▶**strike out** vt depennare.

▶**strike up** vt (MUS) attaccare; **to ~ up a friendship with** fare amicizia con.

strikebreaker ['straɪkbreɪkə*] n crumiro/a.

striker ['straɪkə*] n scioperante m/f; (SPORT) attaccante m.

striking ['straɪkɪŋ] adj impressionante.

Strimmer ® ['strɪmə*] n tagliabordi m inv.

string [strɪŋ] n spago; (row) fila; sequenza; catena; (COMPUT) stringa, sequenza; (MUS) corda ♦ vt (pt, pp strung [strʌŋ]): **to ~ out** disporre di fianco; **to ~ together** mettere insieme; **the ~s** npl (MUS) gli archi; **~ of pearls** filo di perle; **with no ~s attached** (fig) senza vincoli, senza obblighi; **to get a job by pulling ~s** ottenere un lavoro a forza di raccomandazioni.

string bean n fagiolino.

string(ed) instrument n (MUS) strumento a corda.

stringent ['strɪndʒənt] adj rigoroso(a); (reasons, arguments) stringente, impellente.

string quartet n quartetto d'archi.

strip [strɪp] n striscia; (SPORT): **wearing the Celtic ~** con la divisa del Celtic ♦ vt spogliare; (also: **~ down:** machine) smontare ♦ vi spogliarsi.

strip cartoon n fumetto.

stripe [straɪp] n striscia, riga.

striped ['straɪpt] adj a strisce or righe.

strip light n (BRIT) tubo al neon.

stripper ['strɪpə*] n spogliarellista.

strip-search ['strɪpsəːtʃ] vt: **to ~ sb** perquisire qn facendolo(a) spogliare ♦ n perquisizione f (facendo spogliare il perquisito).

striptease ['strɪptiːz] n spogliarello.

strive, pt **strove,** pp **striven** [straɪv, strəuv, 'strɪvn] vi: **to ~ to do** sforzarsi di fare.

strobe [strəub] n (also: **~ light**) luce f stroboscopica.

strode [strəud] *pt of* **stride**.

stroke [strəuk] *n* colpo; (*of piston*) corsa; (*MED*) colpo apoplettico; (*SWIMMING*: *style*) nuoto; (*caress*) carezza ♦ *vt* accarezzare; **at a ~** in un attimo; **on the ~ of 5** alle 5 in punto, allo scoccare delle 5; **a ~ of luck** un colpo di fortuna; **two-~ engine** motore a due tempi.

stroll [strəul] *n* giretto, passeggiatina ♦ *vi* andare a spasso; **to go for a ~, have** *or* **take a ~** andare a fare un giretto *or* due passi.

stroller ['strəulə*] *n* (*US*) passeggino.

strong [strɒŋ] *adj* (*gen*) forte; (*sturdy: table, fabric etc*) solido(a); (*concentrated, intense: bleach, acid*) concentrato(a); (*protest, letter, measures*) energico(a) ♦ *adv*: **to be going ~** (*company*) andare a gonfie vele; (*person*) essere attivo(a); **they are 50 ~** sono in 50; **~ language** (*swearing*) linguaggio volgare.

strong-arm ['strɒŋɑːm] *adj* (*tactics, methods*) energico(a).

strongbox ['strɒŋbɒks] *n* cassaforte *f*.

stronghold ['strɒŋhəuld] *n* fortezza, roccaforte *f*.

strongly ['strɒŋlɪ] *adv* fortemente, con forza; solidamente; energicamente; **to feel ~ about sth** avere molto a cuore qc.

strongman ['strɒŋmæn] *n* personaggio di spicco.

strongroom ['strɒŋrum] *n* camera di sicurezza.

stroppy ['strɒpɪ] *adj* (*BRIT col*) scontroso(a), indisponente.

strove [strəuv] *pt of* **strive**.

struck [strʌk] *pt, pp of* **strike**.

structural ['strʌktʃərəl] *adj* strutturale; (*CONSTR*) di costruzione; di struttura.

structurally ['strʌktʃrəlɪ] *adv* dal punto di vista della struttura.

structure ['strʌktʃə*] *n* struttura; (*building*) costruzione *f*, fabbricato.

struggle ['strʌgl] *n* lotta ♦ *vi* lottare; **to have a ~ to do sth** avere dei problemi per fare qc.

strum [strʌm] *vt* (*guitar*) strimpellare.

strung [strʌŋ] *pt, pp of* **string**.

strut [strʌt] *n* sostegno, supporto ♦ *vi* pavoneggiarsi.

strychnine ['strɪkniːn] *n* stricnina.

stub [stʌb] *n* mozzicone *m*; (*of ticket etc*) matrice *f*, talloncino ♦ *vt*: **to ~ one's toe (on sth)** urtare *or* sbattere il dito del piede (contro qc).

▶**stub out** *vt*: **to ~ out a cigarette** spegnere una sigaretta.

stubble ['stʌbl] *n* stoppia; (*on chin*) barba ispida.

stubborn ['stʌbən] *adj* testardo(a), ostinato(a).

stubby ['stʌbɪ] *adj* tozzo(a).

stucco ['stʌkəu] *n* stucco.

stuck [stʌk] *pt, pp of* **stick** ♦ *adj* (*jammed*) bloccato(a); **to get ~** bloccarsi.

stuck-up [stʌk'ʌp] *adj* presuntuoso(a).

stud [stʌd] *n* bottoncino; borchia; (*of horses*) scuderia, allevamento di cavalli; (*also*: **~ horse**) stallone *m* ♦ *vt* (*fig*): **~ded with** tempestato(a) di.

student ['stjuːdənt] *n* studente/essa ♦ *cpd* studentesco(a); universitario(a); degli studenti; **a law/medical ~** uno studente di legge/di medicina.

student driver *n* (*US*) conducente *m/f* principiante.

students' union *n* (*BRIT*: *association*) circolo universitario; (: *building*) sede *f* del circolo universitario.

studied ['stʌdɪd] *adj* studiato(a), calcolato(a).

studio ['stjuːdɪəu] *n* studio.

studio flat, (*US*) **studio apartment** *n* appartamento monolocale.

studious ['stjuːdɪəs] *adj* studioso(a); (*studied*) studiato(a), voluto(a).

studiously ['stjuːdɪəslɪ] *adv* (*carefully*) deliberatamente, di proposito.

study ['stʌdɪ] *n* studio ♦ *vt* studiare; esaminare ♦ *vi* studiare; **to make a ~ of sth** fare uno studio su qc; **to ~ for an exam** prepararsi a un esame.

stuff [stʌf] *n* (*substance*) roba; (*belongings*) cose *fpl*, roba ♦ *vt* imbottire; (*animal: for exhibition*) impagliare; (*CULIN*) farcire; **my nose is ~ed up** ho il naso chiuso; **get ~ed!** (*col!*) va' a farti fottere! (*!*); **~ed toy** giocattolo di peluche.

stuffing ['stʌfɪŋ] *n* imbottitura; (*CULIN*) ripieno.

stuffy ['stʌfɪ] *adj* (*room*) mal ventilato(a), senz'aria; (*ideas*) antiquato(a).

stumble ['stʌmbl] *vi* inciampare; **to ~ across** (*fig*) imbattersi in.

stumbling block ['stʌmblɪŋ-] *n* ostacolo, scoglio.

stump [stʌmp] *n* ceppo; (*of limb*) moncone *m* ♦ *vt*: **to be ~ed for an answer** essere incapace di rispondere.

stun [stʌn] *vt* stordire; (*amaze*) sbalordire.

stung [stʌŋ] *pt, pp of* **sting**.

stunk [stʌŋk] *pp of* **stink**.

stunning ['stʌnɪŋ] *adj* (*piece of news etc*) sbalorditivo(a); (*girl, dress*) favoloso(a), stupendo(a).

stunt [stʌnt] *n* bravata; trucco

pubblicitario; (*AVIAT*) acrobazia ♦ *vt* arrestare.

stunted ['stʌntɪd] *adj* stentato(a), rachitico(a).

stuntman ['stʌntmæn] *n* cascatore *m*.

stupefaction [stjuːpɪˈfækʃən] *n* stupefazione *f*, stupore *m*.

stupefy ['stjuːpɪfaɪ] *vt* stordire; intontire; (*fig*) stupire.

stupendous [stjuːˈpɛndəs] *adj* stupendo(a), meraviglioso(a).

stupid ['stjuːpɪd] *adj* stupido(a).

stupidity [stjuːˈpɪdɪtɪ] *n* stupidità.

stupidly ['stjuːpɪdlɪ] *adv* stupidamente.

stupor ['stjuːpə*] *n* torpore *m*.

sturdy ['stɜːdɪ] *adj* robusto(a), vigoroso(a); solido(a).

sturgeon ['stɜːdʒən] *n* storione *m*.

stutter ['stʌtə*] *n* balbuzie *f* ♦ *vi* balbettare.

Stuttgart ['ʃtutgart] *n* Stoccarda.

sty [staɪ] *n* (*of pigs*) porcile *m*.

stye [staɪ] *n* (*MED*) orzaiolo.

style [staɪl] *n* stile *m*; (*distinction*) eleganza, classe *f*; (*hair ~*) pettinatura; (*of dress etc*) modello, linea; **in the latest** ~ all'ultima moda.

styli ['staɪlaɪ] *npl of* **stylus**.

stylish ['staɪlɪʃ] *adj* elegante.

stylist ['staɪlɪst] *n*: **hair** ~ parrucchiere/a.

stylized ['staɪlaɪzd] *adj* stilizzato(a).

stylus, *pl* **styli** *or* **styluses** ['staɪləs, -laɪ] *n* (*of record player*) puntina.

Styrofoam ® ['staɪrəfəum] *n* (*US*) = **polystyrene** ♦ *adj* (*cup*) di polistirene.

suave [swɑːv] *adj* untuoso(a).

sub [sʌb] *n abbr* = **submarine; subscription.**

sub... [sʌb] *prefix* sub..., sotto....

subcommittee ['sʌbkəmɪtɪ] *n* sottocomitato.

subconscious [sʌbˈkɒnʃəs] *adj, n* subcosciente (*m*).

subcontinent [sʌbˈkɒntɪnənt] *n*: **the (Indian)** ~ il subcontinente (indiano).

subcontract *n* [sʌbˈkɒntrækt] subappalto ♦ *vt* [sʌbkənˈtrækt] subappaltare.

subcontractor ['sʌbkənˈtræktə*] *n* subappaltatore/trice.

subdivide [sʌbdɪˈvaɪd] *vt* suddividere.

subdivision ['sʌbdɪvɪʒən] *n* suddivisione *f*.

subdue [səbˈdjuː] *vt* sottomettere, soggiogare.

subdued [səbˈdjuːd] *adj* pacato(a); (*light*) attenuato(a); (*person*) poco esuberante.

sub-editor ['sʌbˈɛdɪtə*] *n* (*BRIT*) redattore(trice) aggiunto(a).

subject ['sʌbdʒɪkt] *n* soggetto, (*citizen etc*) cittadino/a; (*SCOL*) materia ♦ *adj* (*liable*): ~ **to** soggetto(a) a ♦ *vt* [səbˈdʒɛkt]: **to** ~ **to**

sottomettere a; esporre a; ~ **to confirmation in writing** a condizione di ricevere conferma scritta; **to change the** ~ cambiare discorso.

subjection [səbˈdʒɛkʃən] *n* sottomissione *f*, soggezione *f*.

subjective [səbˈdʒɛktɪv] *adj* soggettivo(a).

subject matter *n* argomento; contenuto.

sub judice [sʌbˈdʒuːdɪsɪ] *adj* (*LAW*) sub iudice.

subjugate ['sʌbdʒugeɪt] *vt* sottomettere, soggiogare.

subjunctive [səbˈdʒʌŋktɪv] *adj* congiuntivo(a) ♦ *n* congiuntivo.

sublet [sʌbˈlɛt] *vt*, *vi irreg* subaffittare.

sublime [səˈblaɪm] *adj* sublime.

subliminal [sʌbˈlɪmɪnl] *adj* subliminale.

submachine gun ['sʌbməˈʃiːn-] *n* mitra *m inv*.

submarine [sʌbməˈriːn] *n* sommergibile *m*.

submerge [səbˈmɜːdʒ] *vt* sommergere; immergere ♦ *vi* immergersi.

submersion [səbˈmɜːʃən] *n* sommersione *f*; immersione *f*.

submission [səbˈmɪʃən] *n* sottomissione *f*; (*to committee etc*) richiesta, domanda.

submissive [səbˈmɪsɪv] *adj* remissivo(a).

submit [səbˈmɪt] *vt* sottomettere; (*proposal, claim*) presentare ♦ *vi* sottomettersi.

subnormal [sʌbˈnɔːməl] *adj* subnormale.

subordinate [səˈbɔːdɪnət] *adj, n* subordinato(a).

subpoena [səbˈpiːnə] *n* (*LAW*) citazione *f*, mandato di comparizione ♦ *vt* (*LAW*) citare in giudizio.

subroutine ['sʌbruːtiːn] *n* (*COMPUT*) sottoprogramma *m*.

subscribe [səbˈskraɪb] *vi* contribuire; **to** ~ **to** (*opinion*) approvare, condividere; (*fund*) sottoscrivere; (*newspaper*) abbonarsi a; essere abbonato(a) a.

subscriber [səbˈskraɪbə*] *n* (*to periodical, telephone*) abbonato/a.

subscript ['sʌbskrɪpt] *n* deponente *m*.

subscription [səbˈskrɪpʃən] *n* sottoscrizione *f*; abbonamento; **to take out a** ~ **to** abbonarsi a.

subsequent ['sʌbsɪkwənt] *adj* (*later*) successivo(a); (*further*) ulteriore; ~ **to** in seguito a.

subsequently ['sʌbsɪkwəntlɪ] *adv* in seguito, successivamente.

subservient [səbˈsɜːvɪənt] *adj*: ~ **(to)** remissivo(a) (a), sottomesso(a) (a).

subside [səbˈsaɪd] *vi* cedere, abbassarsi; (*flood*) decrescere; (*wind*) calmarsi.

subsidence [səbˈsaɪdns] *n* cedimento, abbassamento.

subsidiarity [səbsɪdɪˈærɪtɪ] *n* (*POL*) *principio del decentramento del potere.*

subsidiary [səbˈsɪdɪərɪ] *adj* sussidiario(a); accessorio(a); (*BRIT SCOL: subject*) complementare ♦ *n* filiale *f.*

subsidize [ˈsʌbsɪdaɪz] *vt* sovvenzionare.

subsidy [ˈsʌbsɪdɪ] *n* sovvenzione *f.*

subsist [səbˈsɪst] *vi*: **to ~ on sth** vivere di qc.

subsistence [səbˈsɪstəns] *n* esistenza; mezzi *mpl* di sostentamento.

subsistence allowance *n* indennità *f inv* di trasferta.

subsistence level *n* livello minimo di vita.

substance [ˈsʌbstəns] *n* sostanza; (*fig*) essenza; **to lack ~** (*argument*) essere debole.

substance abuse *n* abuso di sostanze tossiche.

substandard [sʌbˈstændəd] *adj* (*goods, housing*) di qualità scadente.

substantial [səbˈstænʃl] *adj* solido(a); (*amount, progress etc*) notevole; (*meal*) sostanzioso(a).

substantially [səbˈstænʃəlɪ] *adv* sostanzialmente; **~ bigger** molto più grande.

substantiate [səbˈstænʃɪeɪt] *vt* comprovare.

substitute [ˈsʌbstɪtjuːt] *n* (*person*) sostituto/a; (*thing*) succedaneo, surrogato ♦ *vt*: **to ~ sth/sb for** sostituire qc/qn a.

substitute teacher *n* (*US*) supplente *m/f.*

substitution [sʌbstɪˈtjuːʃən] *n* sostituzione *f.*

subterfuge [ˈsʌbtəfjuːdʒ] *n* sotterfugio.

subterranean [sʌbtəˈreɪnɪən] *adj* sotterraneo(a).

subtitle [ˈsʌbtaɪtl] *n* (*CINE*) sottotitolo.

subtle [ˈsʌtl] *adj* sottile; (*flavour, perfume*) delicato(a).

subtlety [ˈsʌtltɪ] *n* sottigliezza.

subtly [ˈsʌtlɪ] *adv* sottilmente; delicatamente.

subtotal [sʌbˈtəutl] *n* somma parziale.

subtract [səbˈtrækt] *vt* sottrarre.

subtraction [səbˈtrækʃən] *n* sottrazione *f.*

suburb [ˈsʌbəːb] *n* sobborgo; **the ~s** la periferia.

suburban [səˈbəːbən] *adj* suburbano(a).

suburbia [səˈbəːbɪə] *n* periferia, sobborghi *mpl.*

subversion [səbˈvəːʃən] *n* sovversione *f.*

subversive [səbˈvəːsɪv] *adj* sovversivo(a).

subway [ˈsʌbweɪ] *n* (*US: underground*) metropolitana; (*BRIT: underpass*) sottopassaggio.

subzero [sʌbˈzɪərəu] *adj*: **~ temperatures** *fpl* sotto zero.

succeed [səkˈsiːd] *vi* riuscire, avere successo ♦ *vt* succedere a; **to ~ in doing** riuscire a fare.

succeeding [səkˈsiːdɪŋ] *adj* (*following*) successivo(a); **~ generations** generazioni *fpl* future.

success [səkˈsɛs] *n* successo.

successful [səkˈsɛsful] *adj* (*venture*) coronato(a) da successo, riuscito(a); **to be ~** (**in doing**) riuscire (a fare).

successfully [səkˈsɛsfəlɪ] *adv* con successo.

succession [səkˈsɛʃən] *n* successione *f*; **in ~** di seguito.

successive [səkˈsɛsɪv] *adj* successivo(a); consecutivo(a); **on 3 ~ days** per 3 giorni consecutivi *or* di seguito.

successor [səkˈsɛsə*] *n* successore *m.*

succinct [səkˈsɪŋkt] *adj* succinto(a), breve.

succulent [ˈsʌkjulənt] *adj* succulento(a) ♦ *n* (*BOT*): **~s** piante *fpl* grasse.

succumb [səˈkʌm] *vi* soccombere.

such [sʌtʃ] *adj* tale; (*of that kind*): **~ a book** un tale libro, un libro del genere; **~ books** tali libri, libri del genere; (*so much*): **~ courage** tanto coraggio ♦ *adv*: **~ a long trip** un viaggio così lungo; **~ good books** libri così buoni; **~ a lot of** talmente *or* così tanto(a); **making ~ a noise that** facendo un rumore tale che; **~ a long time ago** tanto tempo fa; **~ as** (*like*) come; **a noise ~ as to** un rumore tale da; **~ books as I have** quei pochi libri che ho; **as ~** come *or* in quanto tale; **I said no ~ thing** non ho detto niente del genere.

such-and-such [ˈsʌtʃənsʌtʃ] *adj* tale (*after noun*).

suchlike [ˈsʌtʃlaɪk] *pron* (*col*): **and ~** e così via.

suck [sʌk] *vt* succhiare; (*subj: baby*) poppare; (: *pump, machine*) aspirare.

sucker [ˈsʌkə*] *n* (*ZOOL, TECH*) ventosa; (*BOT*) pollone *m*; (*col*) gonzo/a, babbeo/a.

suckle [ˈsʌkl] *vt* allattare.

sucrose [ˈsuːkrəuz] *n* saccarosio.

suction [ˈsʌkʃən] *n* succhiamento; (*TECH*) aspirazione *f.*

suction pump *n* pompa aspirante.

Sudan [suːˈdɑːn] *n* Sudan *m.*

Sudanese [suːdəˈniːz] *adj*, *n* sudanese (*m/f*).

sudden [ˈsʌdn] *adj* improvviso(a); **all of a ~** improvvisamente, all'improvviso.

sudden-death [sʌdnˈdɛθ] *n* (*also*: **~ playoff**) (*SPORT*) spareggio, bella.

suddenly [ˈsʌdnlɪ] *adv* bruscamente, improvvisamente, di colpo.

suds [sʌdz] *npl* schiuma (di sapone).

sue [suː] *vt* citare in giudizio ♦ *vi*: **to ~ (for)**

intentare causa (per); **to ~ for divorce** intentare causa di divorzio; **to ~ sb for damages** citare qn per danni.

suede [sweɪd] *n* pelle *f* scamosciata ♦ *cpd* scamosciato(a).

suet ['suɪt] *n* grasso di rognone.

Suez ['suːɪz] *n*: **the ~ Canal** il Canale di Suez.

suffer ['sʌfə*] *vt* soffrire, patire; (*bear*) sopportare, tollerare; (*undergo: loss, setback*) subire ♦ *vi* soffrire; **to ~ from** soffrire di; **to ~ from the effects of alcohol/a fall** risentire degli effetti dell'alcool/di una caduta.

sufferance ['sʌfərəns] *n*: **he was only there on ~** era più che altro sopportato lì.

sufferer ['sʌfərə*] *n* (*MED*): **~ (from)** malato/a (di).

suffering ['sʌfərɪŋ] *n* sofferenza; (*hardship, deprivation*) privazione *f*.

suffice [sə'faɪs] *vi* essere sufficiente, bastare.

sufficient [sə'fɪʃənt] *adj* sufficiente; **~ money** abbastanza soldi.

sufficiently [sə'fɪʃəntlɪ] *adv* sufficientemente, abbastanza.

suffix ['sʌfɪks] *n* suffisso.

suffocate ['sʌfəkeɪt] *vi* (*have difficulty breathing*) soffocare; (*die through lack of air*) asfissiare.

suffocation [sʌfə'keɪʃən] *n* soffocamento; (*MED*) asfissia.

suffrage ['sʌfrɪdʒ] *n* suffragio.

suffuse [sə'fjuːz] *vt*: **to ~ (with)** (*colour*) tingere (di); (*light*) soffondere (di); **her face was ~d with joy** la gioia si dipingeva sul suo volto.

sugar ['ʃugə*] *n* zucchero ♦ *vt* zuccherare.

sugar beet *n* barbabietola da zucchero.

sugar bowl *n* zuccheriera.

sugar cane *n* canna da zucchero.

sugar-coated ['ʃugəkəutɪd] *adj* ricoperto(a) di zucchero.

sugar lump *n* zolletta di zucchero.

sugar refinery *n* raffineria di zucchero.

sugary ['ʃugərɪ] *adj* zuccherino(a), dolce; (*fig*) sdolcinato(a).

suggest [sə'dʒɛst] *vt* proporre, suggerire; (*indicate*) indicare; **what do you ~ I do?** cosa mi suggerisce di fare?

suggestion [sə'dʒɛstʃən] *n* suggerimento, proposta.

suggestive [sə'dʒɛstɪv] *adj* suggestivo(a); (*indecent*) spinto(a), indecente.

suicidal [suɪ'saɪdl] *adj* suicida *inv*; (*fig*) fatale, disastroso(a).

suicide ['suɪsaɪd] *n* (*person*) suicida *m/f*; (*act*) suicidio; **to commit ~** suicidarsi.

suicide attempt, suicide bid *n* tentato suicidio.

suicide bomber *n* attentatore/trice suicida.

suicide bombing *n* attentato suicida.

suit [suːt] *n* (*man's*) completo; (*woman's*) completo, tailleur *m inv*; (*law~*) causa; (*CARDS*) seme *m*, colore *m* ♦ *vt* andar bene a *or* per; essere adatto(a) a *or* per; (*adapt*): **to ~ sth to** adattare qc a; **to be ~ed to sth** (*suitable for*) essere adatto a qc; **well ~ed** (*couple*) fatti l'uno per l'altro; **to bring a ~ against sb** intentare causa a qn; **to follow ~** (*fig*) fare altrettanto.

suitable ['suːtəbl] *adj* adatto(a); appropriato(a); **would tomorrow be ~?** andrebbe bene domani?; **we found somebody ~** abbiamo trovato la persona adatta.

suitably ['suːtəblɪ] *adv* (*dress*) in modo adatto; (*thank*) adeguatamente.

suitcase ['suːtkeɪs] *n* valigia.

suite [swiːt] *n* (*of rooms*) appartamento; (*MUS*) suite *f inv*; (*furniture*): **bedroom/dining room ~** arredo *or* mobilia per la camera da letto/sala da pranzo; **a three-piece ~** un salotto comprendente un divano e due poltrone.

suitor ['suːtə*] *n* corteggiatore *m*, spasimante *m*.

sulfate ['sʌlfeɪt] *n* (*US*) = **sulphate**.

sulfur *etc* ['sʌlfə*] (*US*) = **sulphur** *etc*.

sulk [sʌlk] *vi* fare il broncio.

sulky ['sʌlkɪ] *adj* imbronciato(a).

sullen ['sʌlən] *adj* scontroso(a); cupo(a).

sulphate, (US) sulfate ['sʌlfeɪt] *n* solfato; **copper ~** solfato di rame.

sulphur, (US) sulfur ['sʌlfə*] *n* zolfo.

sulphur dioxide *n* biossido di zolfo.

sulphuric, (US) sulfuric [sʌl'fjuərɪk] *adj*: **~ acid** acido solforico.

sultan ['sʌltən] *n* sultano.

sultana [sʌl'tɑːnə] *n* (*fruit*) uva (secca) sultanina.

sultry ['sʌltrɪ] *adj* afoso(a).

sum [sʌm] *n* somma; (*SCOL etc*) addizione *f*.

▶**sum up** *vt* riassumere; (*evaluate rapidly*) valutare, giudicare ♦ *vi* riassumere.

Sumatra [su'mɑːtrə] *n* Sumatra.

summarize ['sʌməraɪz] *vt* riassumere, riepilogare.

summary ['sʌmərɪ] *n* riassunto ♦ *adj* (*justice*) sommario(a).

summer ['sʌmə*] *n* estate *f* ♦ *cpd* d'estate, estivo(a); **in (the) ~** d'estate.

summer camp *n* (*US*) colonia (estiva).

summerhouse ['sʌməhaus] *n* (*in garden*)

padiglione *m*.

summertime ['sʌmətaɪm] *n* (*season*) estate *f*.

summer time *n* (*by clock*) ora legale (estiva).

summery ['sʌmərɪ] *adj* estivo(a).

summing-up [sʌmɪŋ'ʌp] *n* (*LAW*) ricapitolazione *f* del processo.

summit ['sʌmɪt] *n* cima, sommità; (*POL*) vertice *m*.

summit conference *n* conferenza al vertice.

summon ['sʌmən] *vt* chiamare, convocare; **to ~ a witness** citare un testimone.

▶**summon up** *vt* raccogliere, fare appello a.

summons *n* ordine *m* di comparizione ♦ *vt* citare; **to serve a ~ on sb** notificare una citazione a qn.

sumo ['suːməu] *n* (*also*: ~ **wrestling**) sumo.

sump [sʌmp] *n* (*AUT*) coppa dell'olio.

sumptuous ['sʌmptjuəs] *adj* sontuoso(a).

Sun. *abbr* (= *Sunday*) dom.

sun [sʌn] *n* sole *m*; **in the ~** al sole; **to catch the ~** prendere sole; **they have everything under the ~** hanno tutto ciò che possono desiderare.

sunbathe ['sʌnbeɪð] *vi* prendere un bagno di sole.

sunbeam ['sʌnbiːm] *n* raggio di sole.

sunbed ['sʌnbed] *n* lettino solare.

sunblock ['sʌnblɔk] *n* crema solare a protezione totale.

sunburn ['sʌnbəːn] *n* (*tan*) abbronzatura; (*painful*) scottatura.

sunburnt ['sʌnbəːnt], **sunburned** ['sʌnbəːnd] *adj* abbronzato(a); (*painfully*) scottato(a) dal sole.

sun cream *n* crema solare.

sundae ['sʌndeɪ] *n* coppa di gelato guarnita.

Sunday ['sʌndɪ] *n* domenica; *for phrases see also* **Tuesday**.

Sunday paper *n* giornale *m* della domenica; *see boxed note*.

SUNDAY PAPERS

I **Sunday papers** *sono i giornali che escono di domenica. Sono generalmente corredati da supplementi e riviste di argomento culturale, sportivo e di attualità ed hanno un'alta tiratura.*

Sunday school *n* ≈ scuola di catechismo.

sundial ['sʌndaɪəl] *n* meridiana.

sundown ['sʌndaun] *n* tramonto.

sundries ['sʌndrɪz] *npl* articoli diversi.

sundry ['sʌndrɪ] *adj* vari(e), diversi(e); **all and ~** tutti quanti.

sunflower ['sʌnflauə*] *n* girasole *m*.

sung [sʌŋ] *pp of* **sing**.

sunglasses ['sʌnglɑːsɪz] *npl* occhiali *mpl* da sole.

sunk [sʌŋk] *pp of* **sink**.

sunken ['sʌŋkən] *adj* sommerso(a); (*eyes, cheeks*) infossato(a); (*bath*) incassato(a).

sunlamp ['sʌnlæmp] *n* lampada a raggi ultravioletti.

sunlight ['sʌnlaɪt] *n* (luce *f* del) sole *m*.

sunlit ['sʌnlɪt] *adj* assolato(a), soleggiato(a).

sunny ['sʌnɪ] *adj* assolato(a), soleggiato(a); (*fig*) allegro(a), felice; **it is ~** c'è il sole.

sunrise ['sʌnraɪz] *n* levata del sole, alba.

sunroof ['sʌnruːf] *n* (*on building*) tetto a terrazzo; (*AUT*) tetto apribile.

sunscreen ['sʌnskriːn] *n* crema solare protettiva.

sunset ['sʌnset] *n* tramonto.

sunshade ['sʌnʃeɪd] *n* parasole *m*.

sunshine ['sʌnʃaɪn] *n* (luce *f* del) sole *m*.

sunspot ['sʌnspɔt] *n* macchia solare.

sunstroke ['sʌnstrəuk] *n* insolazione *f*, colpo di sole.

suntan ['sʌntæn] *n* abbronzatura.

suntanned ['sʌntænd] *adj* abbronzato(a).

suntan oil *n* olio solare.

suntrap ['sʌntræp] *n* luogo molto assolato.

super ['suːpə*] *adj* (*col*) fantastico(a).

superannuation [suːpərænjuˈeɪʃən] *n* contributi *mpl* pensionistici; pensione *f*.

superb [suːˈpəːb] *adj* magnifico(a).

Super Bowl *n* (*US SPORT*) Super Bowl *m inv*.

supercilious [suːpəˈsɪlɪəs] *adj* sprezzante.

superconductor [suːpəkənˈdʌktə*] *n* superconduttore *m*.

superficial [suːpəˈfɪʃəl] *adj* superficiale.

superficially [suːpəˈfɪʃəlɪ] *adv* superficialmente.

superfluous [suˈpəːfluəs] *adj* superfluo(a).

superglue ['suːpəgluː] *n* colla a presa rapida.

superhighway ['suːpəhaɪweɪ] *n* (*US*) autostrada; **the information ~** l'autostrada telematica.

superhuman [suːpəˈhjuːmən] *adj* sovrumano(a).

superimpose ['suːpərɪmˈpəuz] *vt* sovrapporre.

superintend [suːpərɪnˈtend] *vt* dirigere, sovraintendere.

superintendent [suːpərɪnˈtendənt] *n* direttore/trice; (*POLICE*) ≈ commissario (capo).

superior [suˈpɪərɪə*] *adj* superiore; (*COMM*:

goods, quality) di prim'ordine, superiore; (*smug: person*) che fa il superiore ♦ *n* superiore *m/f*; **Mother S**~ (*REL*) Madre *f* Superiora, Superiora.

superiority [supɪərɪ'ɔrɪtɪ] *n* superiorità.

superlative [su'pɜ:lətɪv] *adj* superlativo(a), supremo(a) ♦ *n* (*LING*) superlativo.

superman ['su:pəmæn] *n* superuomo.

supermarket ['su:pəmɑ:kɪt] *n* supermercato.

supermodel ['su:pəmɔdl] *n* top model *m/f* *inv*.

supernatural [su:pə'nætʃərəl] *adj* soprannaturale.

supernova [su:pə'nəuvə] *n* supernova.

superpower ['su:pəpauə*] *n* (*POL*) superpotenza.

superscript ['su:pəskrɪpt] *n* esponente *m*.

supersede [su:pə'si:d] *vt* sostituire, soppiantare.

supersonic ['su:pə'sɔnɪk] *adj* supersonico(a).

superstar ['su:pəstɑ:*] *adj, n* superstar (*f*) *inv*.

superstition [su:pə'stɪʃən] *n* superstizione *f*.

superstitious [su:pə'stɪʃəs] *adj* superstizioso(a).

superstore ['su:pəstɔ:*] *n* (*BRIT*) grande supermercato.

supertanker ['su:pətæŋkə*] *n* superpetroliera.

supertax ['su:pətæks] *n* soprattassa.

supervise ['su:pəvaɪz] *vt* (*person etc*) sorvegliare; (*organization*) soprintendere a.

supervision [su:pə'vɪʒən] *n* sorveglianza, supervisione *f*; **under medical** ~ sotto controllo medico.

supervisor ['su:pəvaɪzə*] *n* sorvegliante *m/f*, soprintendente *m/f*; (*in shop*) capocommesso/a; (*at university*) relatore/trice.

supervisory ['su:pəvaɪzərɪ] *adj* di sorveglianza.

supine ['su:paɪn] *adj* supino(a).

supper ['sʌpə*] *n* cena; **to have** ~ cenare.

supplant [sə'plɑ:nt] *vt* soppiantare.

supple ['sʌpl] *adj* flessibile; agile.

supplement *n* ['sʌplɪmənt] supplemento ♦ *vt* [sʌplɪ'mɛnt] completare, integrare.

supplementary [sʌplɪ'mɛntərɪ] *adj* supplementare.

supplementary benefit *n* (*BRIT*) *forma di indennità assistenziale*.

supplier [sə'plaɪə*] *n* fornitore *m*.

supply [sə'plaɪ] *vt* (*goods*): **to** ~ **sth (to sb)** fornire qc (a qn); (*people, organization*): **to**

~ **sb (with sth)** fornire a qn (qc); (*system, machine*): **to** ~ **sth (with sth)** alimentare qc (con qc); (*a need*) soddisfare ♦ *n* riserva, provvista; (*supplying*) approvvigionamento; (*TECH*) alimentazione *f*; **supplies** *npl* (*food*) viveri *mpl*; (*MIL*) sussistenza; **office supplies** forniture *fpl* per ufficio; **to be in short** ~ scarseggiare, essere scarso(a); **the electricity/water/gas** ~ l'erogazione *f* di corrente/d'acqua/di gas; ~ **and demand** la domanda e l'offerta; **the car comes supplied with a radio** l'auto viene fornita completa di radio.

supply teacher *n* (*BRIT*) supplente *m/f*.

support [sə'pɔ:t] *n* (*moral, financial etc*) sostegno, appoggio; (*TECH*) supporto ♦ *vt* sostenere; (*financially*) mantenere; (*uphold*) sostenere, difendere; (*SPORT: team*) fare il tifo per; **they stopped work in** ~ (**of**) hanno smesso di lavorare per solidarietà (con); **to** ~ **o.s.** (*financially*) mantenersi.

supporter [sə'pɔ:tə*] *n* (*POL etc*) sostenitore/trice, fautore/trice; (*SPORT*) tifoso/a.

supporting [sə'pɔ:tɪŋ] *adj* (*wall*) di sostegno.

supporting actor *n* attore *m* non protagonista.

supporting actress *n* attrice *f* non protagonista.

supporting role *n* ruolo non protagonista.

supportive [sə'pɔ:tɪv] *adj* d'appoggio; **I have a** ~ **wife/family** mia moglie/la mia famiglia mi appoggia.

suppose [sə'pəuz] *vt, vi* supporre; immaginare; **to be** ~**d to do** essere tenuto(a) a fare; **always supposing (that) he comes** ammesso e non concesso che venga; **I don't** ~ **she'll come** non credo che venga; **he's** ~**d to be an expert** dicono che sia un esperto, passa per un esperto.

supposedly [sə'pəuzɪdlɪ] *adv* presumibilmente; (*seemingly*) apparentemente.

supposing [sə'pəuzɪŋ] *conj* se, ammesso che + *sub*.

supposition [sʌpə'zɪʃən] *n* supposizione *f*, ipotesi *f inv*.

suppository [sə'pɔzɪtərɪ] *n* supposta, suppositorio.

suppress [sə'prɛs] *vt* reprimere; sopprimere; tenere segreto(a).

suppression [sə'prɛʃən] *n* repressione *f*; soppressione *f*.

suppressor [sə'prɛsə*] *n* (*ELEC etc*)

soppressore *m*.

supremacy [su'prɛməsɪ] *n* supremazia.

supreme [su'pri:m] *adj* supremo(a).

Supreme Court *n* (*US*) Corte *f* suprema; ~ **of Judicature** *corte di giudizio suprema dell'Inghilterra e del Galles.*

supremo [su'pri:məu] *n* autorità *f inv* massima.

Supt. *abbr* (*POLICE*) = **superintendent**.

surcharge ['sə:tʃɑ:dʒ] *n* supplemento; (*extra tax*) soprattassa.

sure [ʃuə*] *adj* sicuro(a); (*definite, convinced*) sicuro(a), certo(a) ♦ *adv* (*col*: *US*): **that ~ is pretty, that's ~ pretty** è veramente *or* davvero carino; ~! (*of course*) senz'altro!, certo!; ~ **enough** infatti; **to make ~ of** assicurarsi di; **to be ~ of sth** essere sicuro di qc; **to be ~ of o.s.** essere sicuro di sé; **I'm not ~ how/why/when** non so bene come/perché/quando + *sub*.

sure-fire ['ʃuəfaɪə*] *adj* (*col*) infallibile.

sure-footed [ʃuə'futɪd] *adj* dal passo sicuro.

surely ['ʃuəlɪ] *adv* sicuramente; certamente; ~ **you don't mean that!** non parlerà sul serio!

surety ['ʃuərətɪ] *n* garanzia; **to go** *or* **stand ~ for sb** farsi garante per qn.

surf [sə:f] *n* (*waves*) cavalloni *mpl*; (*foam*) spuma ♦ *vt*: **to ~ the Net** navigare in Internet.

surface ['sə:fɪs] *n* superficie *f* ♦ *vt* (*road*) asfaltare ♦ *vi* risalire alla superficie; (*fig*: *person*) venire a galla, farsi vivo(a); **on the ~ it seems that ...** (*fig*) superficialmente sembra che ....

surface area *n* superficie *f*.

surface mail *n* posta ordinaria.

surface-to-surface ['sə:fɪstə'sə:fɪs] *adj* (*MIL*) terra-terra *inv*.

surfboard ['sə:fbɔ:d] *n* tavola per surfing.

surfeit ['sə:fɪt] *n*: **a ~ of** un eccesso di; un'indigestione di.

surfer ['sə:fə*] *n* chi pratica il surfing.

surfing ['sə:fɪŋ] *n* surfing *m*.

surge [sə:dʒ] *n* (*strong movement*) ondata; (*of feeling*) impeto; (*ELEC*) sovracorrente *f* transitoria ♦ *vi* (*waves*) gonfiarsi; (*ELEC*: *power*) aumentare improvvisamente; **to ~ forward** buttarsi avanti.

surgeon ['sə:dʒən] *n* chirurgo.

Surgeon General *n* (*US*) ≈ Ministro della Sanità.

surgery ['sə:dʒərɪ] *n* chirurgia; (*BRIT MED*: *room*) studio *or* gabinetto medico, ambulatorio; (: *session*) visita ambulatoriale; (*BRIT*: *of MP etc*) incontri *mpl* con gli elettori; **to undergo ~** subire un intervento chirurgico.

surgery hours *npl* (*BRIT*) orario delle visite *or* di consultazione.

surgical ['sə:dʒɪkl] *adj* chirurgico(a).

surgical spirit *n* (*BRIT*) alcool denaturato.

surly ['sə:lɪ] *adj* scontroso(a), burbero(a).

surmise [sə:'maɪz] *vt* supporre, congetturare.

surmount [sə:'maunt] *vt* sormontare.

surname ['sə:neɪm] *n* cognome *m*.

surpass [sə:'pɑ:s] *vt* superare.

surplus ['sə:pləs] *n* eccedenza; (*ECON*) surplus *m inv* ♦ *adj* eccedente, d'avanzo; **it is ~ to our requirements** eccede i nostri bisogni; ~ **stock** merce *f* in sovrappiù.

surprise [sə'praɪz] *n* sorpresa; (*astonishment*) stupore *m* ♦ *vt* sorprendere; stupire; **to take by ~** (*person*) cogliere di sorpresa; (*MIL*: *town, fort*) attaccare di sorpresa.

surprising [sə'praɪzɪŋ] *adj* sorprendente, stupefacente.

surprisingly [se'praɪzɪŋlɪ] *adv* sorprendentemente; (*somewhat*) ~, **he agreed** cosa (alquanto) sorprendente, ha accettato.

surrealism [sə'rɪəlɪzəm] *n* surrealismo.

surrealist [sə'rɪəlɪst] *adj*, *n* surrealista (*m/f*).

surrender [sə'rɛndə*] *n* resa, capitolazione *f* ♦ *vi* arrendersi ♦ *vt* (*claim, right*) rinunciare a.

surrender value *n* (*COMM*) valore *m* di riscatto.

surreptitious [sʌrəp'tɪʃəs] *adj* furtivo(a).

surrogate ['sʌrəgɪt] *n* (*BRIT*: *substitute*) surrogato ♦ *adj* surrogato(a).

surrogate mother *n* madre *f* sostitutiva.

surround [sə'raund] *vt* circondare; (*MIL etc*) accerchiare.

surrounding [sə'raundɪŋ] *adj* circostante.

surroundings [sə'raundɪŋz] *npl* dintorni *mpl*; (*fig*) ambiente *m*.

surtax ['sə:tæks] *n* soprattassa.

surveillance [sə:'veɪləns] *n* sorveglianza, controllo.

survey *n* ['sə:veɪ] (*comprehensive view*: *of situation, development*) quadro generale; (*study*) indagine *f*, studio; (*in housebuying etc*) perizia; (*of land*) rilevamento, rilievo topografico ♦ *vt* [sə:'veɪ] osservare; esaminare; (*SURVEYING*: *building*) fare una perizia di; (: *land*) fare il rilevamento di.

surveying [sə'veɪɪŋ] *n* (*of land*) agrimensura.

surveyor [sə'veɪə*] *n* perito; (*of land*) agrimensore *m*.

survival [sə'vaɪvl] *n* sopravvivenza; (*relic*)

reliquia, vestigio.

survival course n corso di sopravvivenza.

survival kit n equipaggiamento di prima necessità.

survive [sə'vaɪv] vi sopravvivere ♦ vt sopravvivere a.

survivor [sə'vaɪvə*] n superstite m/f, sopravvissuto/a.

susceptible [sə'sɛptəbl] adj: ~ **(to)** sensibile (a); (disease) predisposto(a) (a).

suspect adj, n ['sʌspɛkt] adj sospetto(a) ♦ n persona sospetta ♦ vt [səs'pɛkt] sospettare; (think likely) supporre; (doubt) dubitare di.

suspected [səs'pɛktɪd] adj presunto(a); **to have a ~ facture** avere una sospetta frattura.

suspend [səs'pɛnd] vt sospendere.

suspended animation n: **in a state of ~** in stato comatoso.

suspended sentence n condanna con la condizionale.

suspender belt [səs'pɛndə*-] n (BRIT) reggicalze m inv.

suspenders [səs'pɛndəz] npl (BRIT) giarrettiere fpl; (US) bretelle fpl.

suspense [səs'pɛns] n apprensione f; (in film etc) suspense m.

suspension [səs'pɛnʃən] n (gen, AUT) sospensione f; (of driving licence) ritiro temporaneo.

suspension bridge n ponte m sospeso.

suspicion [səs'pɪʃən] n sospetto; **to be under ~** essere sospettato; **arrested on ~ of murder** arrestato come presunto omicida.

suspicious [səs'pɪʃəs] adj (suspecting) sospettoso(a); (causing suspicion) sospetto(a); **to be ~ of** o **about sb/sth** nutrire sospetti nei riguardi di qn/qc.

suss out vt (BRIT col): **I've ~ed it/him out** ho capito come stanno le cose/che tipo è.

sustain [səs'teɪn] vt sostenere; sopportare; (suffer) subire.

sustainable [səs'teɪnəbl] adj sostenibile.

sustained [sə'steɪnd] adj (effort) prolungato(a).

sustenance ['sʌstɪnəns] n nutrimento; mezzi mpl di sostentamento.

suture ['suːtʃə*] n sutura.

SUV n abbr see **sports utility vehicle**.

SW abbr (RADIO: = short wave) O.C.

swab [swɔb] n (MED) tampone m ♦ vt (NAUT: also: ~ **down**) radazzare.

swagger ['swægə*] vi pavoneggiarsi.

swallow ['swɔləu] n (bird) rondine f; (of food) boccone m; (of drink) sorso ♦ vt inghiottire; (fig: story) bere.

▶**swallow up** vt inghiottire.

swam [swæm] pt of **swim**.

swamp [swɔmp] n palude f ♦ vt sommergere.

swampy ['swɔmpɪ] adj paludoso(a), pantanoso(a).

swan [swɔn] n cigno.

swank [swæŋk] vi (col: talk boastfully) fare lo spaccone; (: show off) mettersi in mostra.

swan song n (fig) canto del cigno.

swap [swɔp] n scambio ♦ vt: **to ~ (for)** scambiare (con).

SWAPO ['swɑːpəu] n abbr = South-West Africa People's Organization.

swarm [swɔːm] n sciame m ♦ vi formicolare; (bees) sciamare.

swarthy ['swɔːðɪ] adj di carnagione scura.

swashbuckling ['swɔʃbʌklɪŋ] adj (role, hero) spericolato(a).

swastika ['swɔstɪkə] n croce f uncinata, svastica.

SWAT [swɔt] n abbr (US: = Special Weapons and Tactics) reparto speciale di polizia; **a ~ team** uno squadrone del reparto speciale (di polizia).

swat [swɔt] vt schiacciare ♦ n (BRIT: also: **fly ~**) ammazzamosche m inv.

swathe [sweɪð] n fascio ♦ vt: **to ~ in** (bandages, blankets) avvolgere in.

swatter ['swɔtə*] n (also: **fly ~**) ammazzamosche m inv.

sway [sweɪ] vi (building) oscillare; (tree) ondeggiare; (person) barcollare ♦ vt (influence) influenzare ♦ n (rule, power): ~ **(over)** influenza (su); **to hold ~ over sb** dominare qn.

Swaziland ['swɑːzɪlænd] n Swaziland m.

swear, pt **swore**, pp **sworn** [sweə*, swɔː*, swɔːn] vi (witness etc) giurare; (curse) bestemmiare, imprecare ♦ vt: **to ~ an oath** prestare giuramento; **to ~ to sth** giurare qc.

▶**swear in** vt prestare giuramento a.

swearword ['sweəwɔːd] n parolaccia.

sweat [swɛt] n sudore m, traspirazione f ♦ vi sudare; **in a ~** in un bagno di sudore.

sweatband ['swɛtbænd] n (SPORT) fascia elastica (per assorbire il sudore).

sweater ['swɛtə*] n maglione m.

sweatshirt ['swɛtʃɜːt] n maglione m in cotone felpato.

sweatshop ['swɛtʃɔp] n azienda o fabbrica dove i dipendenti sono sfruttati.

sweaty ['swɛtɪ] adj sudato(a); bagnato(a) di sudore.

Swede [swiːd] n svedese m/f.

swede [swiːd] n (BRIT) rapa svedese.

Sweden ['swi:dn] *n* Svezia.
Swedish ['swi:dɪʃ] *adj* svedese ♦ *n* (*LING*) svedese *m*.
sweep [swi:p] *n* spazzata; (*curve*) curva; (*expanse*) distesa; (*range*) portata; (*also*: **chimney** ~) spazzacamino ♦ *vb* (*pt, pp* **swept** [swɛpt]) *vt* spazzare, scopare; (*subj*: *fashion, craze*) invadere ♦ *vi* camminare maestosamente; precipitarsi, lanciarsi; (e)stendersi.
▶**sweep away** *vt* spazzare via; trascinare via.
▶**sweep past** *vi* sfrecciare accanto; passare accanto maestosamente.
▶**sweep up** *vt, vi* spazzare.
sweeper ['swi:pə*] *n* (*person*) spazzino/a; (*machine*) spazzatrice *f*; (*FOOTBALL*) libero.
sweeping ['swi:pɪŋ] *adj* (*gesture*) ampio(a); (*changes, reforms*) ampio(a), radicale; **a ~ statement** un'affermazione generica.
sweepstake ['swi:psteɪk] *n* lotteria (*spesso abbinata alle corse dei cavalli*).
sweet [swi:t] *n* (*BRIT*) dolce *m*; (*candy*) caramella ♦ *adj* dolce; (*fresh*) fresco(a); (*kind*) gentile; (*cute*) carino(a) ♦ *adv*: **to smell/taste** ~ avere un odore/sapore dolce; ~ **and sour** *adj* agrodolce.
sweetbread ['swi:tbrɛd] *n* animella.
sweetcorn ['swi:tkɔ:n] *n* granturco dolce.
sweeten ['swi:tn] *vt* addolcire; zuccherare.
sweetener ['swi:tnə*] *n* (*CULIN*) dolcificante *m*.
sweetheart ['swi:tha:t] *n* innamorato/a.
sweetly ['swi:tlɪ] *adv* dolcemente.
sweetness ['swi:tnɪs] *n* sapore *m* dolce; dolcezza.
sweet pea *n* pisello odoroso.
sweet potato *n* patata americana, patata dolce.
sweetshop ['swi:tʃɔp] *n* (*BRIT*) ≈ pasticceria.
sweet tooth *n*: **to have a ~** avere un debole per i dolci.
swell [swɛl] *n* (*of sea*) mare *m* lungo ♦ *adj* (*col*: *excellent*) favoloso(a) ♦ *vb* (*pt* ~**ed**, *pp* **swollen**, ~**ed** ['swəulən]) *vt* gonfiare, ingrossare; (*numbers, sales etc*) aumentare ♦ *vi* gonfiarsi, ingrossarsi; (*sound*) crescere; (*MED*) gonfiarsi.
swelling ['swɛlɪŋ] *n* (*MED*) tumefazione *f*, gonfiore *m*.
sweltering ['swɛltərɪŋ] *adj* soffocante.
swept [swɛpt] *pt, pp of* **sweep**.
swerve [swə:v] *vi* deviare; (*driver*) sterzare; (*boxer*) scartare.
swift [swɪft] *n* (*bird*) rondone *m* ♦ *adj* rapido(a), veloce.

swiftly ['swɪftlɪ] *adv* rapidamente, velocemente.
swiftness ['swɪftnɪs] *n* rapidità, velocità.
swig [swɪg] *n* (*col*: *drink*) sorsata.
swill [swɪl] *n* broda ♦ *vt* (*also*: ~ **out**, ~ **down**) risciacquare.
swim [swɪm] *n*: **to go for a** ~ andare a fare una nuotata ♦ *vb* (*pt* **swam**, *pp* **swum** [swæm, swʌm]) *vi* nuotare; (*SPORT*) fare del nuoto; (*head, room*) girare ♦ *vt* (*river, channel*) attraversare *or* percorrere a nuoto; **to go** ~**ming** andare a nuotare; **to** ~ **a length** fare una vasca (a nuoto).
swimmer ['swɪmə*] *n* nuotatore/trice.
swimming ['swɪmɪŋ] *n* nuoto.
swimming baths *npl* (*BRIT*) piscina.
swimming cap *n* cuffia.
swimming costume *n* (*BRIT*) costume *m* da bagno.
swimmingly ['swɪmɪŋlɪ] *adv*: **to go** ~ (*wonderfully*) andare a gonfie vele.
swimming pool *n* piscina.
swimming trunks *npl* costume *m* da bagno (*per uomo*).
swimsuit ['swɪmsu:t] *n* costume *m* da bagno.
swindle ['swɪndl] *n* truffa ♦ *vt* truffare.
swindler ['swɪndlə*] *n* truffatore/trice.
swine [swaɪn] *n* (*pl inv*) maiale *m*, porco; (*col!*) porco (*!*).
swing [swɪŋ] *n* altalena; (*movement*) oscillazione *f*; (*MUS*) ritmo; (*also*: ~ **music**) swing *m* ♦ *vb* (*pt, pp* **swung** [swʌŋ]) *vt* dondolare, far oscillare; (*also*: ~ **round**) far girare ♦ *vi* oscillare, dondolare; (*also*: ~ **round**: *object*) roteare; (: *person*) girarsi, voltarsi; **to be in full** ~ (*activity*) essere in piena attività; (*party etc*) essere nel pieno; **a** ~ **to the left** (*POL*) una svolta a sinistra; **to get into the** ~ **of things** entrare nel pieno delle cose; **the road** ~**s south** la strada prende la direzione sud.
swing bridge *n* ponte *m* girevole.
swing door *n* (*BRIT*) porta battente.
swingeing ['swɪndʒɪŋ] *adj* (*BRIT*: *defeat*) violento(a); (: *price increase*) enorme.
swinging ['swɪŋɪŋ] *adj* (*step*) cadenzato(a), ritmico(a); (*rhythm, music*) trascinante; ~ **door** (*US*) porta battente.
swipe [swaɪp] *n* forte colpo; schiaffo ♦ *vt* (*hit*) colpire con forza; dare uno schiaffo a; (*col*: *steal*) sgraffignare; (*credit card etc*) far passare (nell'apposita macchinetta).
swirl [swə:l] *n* turbine *m*, mulinello ♦ *vi* turbinare, far mulinello.
swish [swɪʃ] *adj* (*col*: *smart*) all'ultimo grido, alla moda ♦ *n* (*sound*: *of whip*) sibilo; (: *of skirts, grass*) fruscio ♦ *vi*

sibilare.

Swiss [swɪs] *adj, n* (*pl inv*) svizzero(a).

Swiss French *adj* svizzero(a) francese.

Swiss German *adj* svizzero(a) tedesco(a).

switch [swɪtʃ] *n* (*for light, radio etc*) interruttore *m*; (*change*) cambiamento ♦ *vt* (*also*: ~ **round**, ~ **over**) cambiare; scambiare.

▶**switch off** *vt* spegnere.

▶**switch on** *vt* accendere; (*engine, machine*) mettere in moto, avviare; (*AUT*: *ignition*) inserire; (*BRIT*: *water supply*) aprire.

switchback ['swɪtʃbæk] *n* (*BRIT*) montagne *fpl* russe.

switchblade ['swɪtʃbleɪd] *n* (*also*: ~ **knife**) coltello a scatto.

switchboard ['swɪtʃbɔːd] *n* centralino.

switchboard operator *n* centralinista *m/f*.

Switzerland ['swɪtsələnd] *n* Svizzera.

swivel ['swɪvl] *vi* (*also*: ~ **round**) girare.

swollen ['swəulən] *pp of* **swell** ♦ *adj* (*ankle etc*) gonfio(a).

swoon [swuːn] *vi* svenire.

swoop [swuːp] *n* (*by police etc*) incursione *f*; (*of bird etc*) picchiata ♦ *vi* (*also*: ~ **down**) scendere in picchiata; (*police*): **to** ~ **(on)** fare un'incursione (in).

swop [swɔp] *n, vt* = **swap**.

sword [sɔːd] *n* spada.

swordfish ['sɔːdfɪʃ] *n* pesce *m* spada *inv*.

swore [swɔː*] *pt of* **swear**.

sworn [swɔːn] *pp of* **swear**.

swot [swɔt] *vt* sgobbare su ♦ *vi* sgobbare.

swum [swʌm] *pp of* **swim**.

swung [swʌŋ] *pt, pp of* **swing**.

sycamore ['sɪkəmɔː*] *n* sicomoro.

sycophant ['sɪkəfənt] *n* leccapiedi *m/f*.

sycophantic [sɪkə'fæntɪk] *adj* ossequioso(a), adulatore(trice).

Sydney ['sɪdnɪ] *n* Sydney *f*.

syllable ['sɪləbl] *n* sillaba.

syllabus ['sɪləbəs] *n* programma *m*; **on the** ~ in programma d'esame.

symbol ['sɪmbl] *n* simbolo.

symbolic(al) [sɪm'bɔlɪk(l)] *adj* simbolico(a); **to be** ~ **of sth** simboleggiare qc.

symbolism ['sɪmbəlɪzəm] *n* simbolismo.

symbolize ['sɪmbəlaɪz] *vt* simbolizzare.

symmetrical [sɪ'mɛtrɪkl] *adj* simmetrico(a).

symmetry ['sɪmɪtrɪ] *n* simmetria.

sympathetic [sɪmpə'θɛtɪk] *adj* (*showing pity*) compassionevole; (*kind*) comprensivo(a); ~ **towards** ben disposto(a) verso; **to be** ~ **to a cause** (*well-disposed*) simpatizzare per una causa.

sympathetically [sɪmpə'θɛtɪklɪ] *adv* in

modo compassionevole; con comprensione.

sympathize ['sɪmpəθaɪz] *vi*: **to** ~ **with sb** compatire qn; partecipare al dolore di qn; (*understand*) capire qn.

sympathizer ['sɪmpəθaɪzə*] *n* (*POL*) simpatizzante *m/f*.

sympathy ['sɪmpəθɪ] *n* compassione *f*; **in** ~ **with** d'accordo con; (*strike*) per solidarietà con; **with our deepest** ~ con le nostre più sincere condoglianze.

symphonic [sɪm'fɔnɪk] *adj* sinfonico(a).

symphony ['sɪmfənɪ] *n* sinfonia.

symphony orchestra *n* orchestra sinfonica.

symposium [sɪm'pəuzɪəm] *n* simposio.

symptom ['sɪmptəm] *n* sintomo; indizio.

symptomatic [sɪmptə'mætɪk] *adj*: ~ **(of)** sintomatico(a) (di).

synagogue ['sɪnəgɔg] *n* sinagoga.

sync [sɪŋk] *n* (*col*): **in/out of** ~ in/fuori sincronia; (*fig*: *people*) **they are in** ~ sono in sintonia.

synchromesh [sɪŋkrəu'mɛʃ] *n* cambio sincronizzato.

synchronize ['sɪŋkrənaɪz] *vt* sincronizzare ♦ *vi*: **to** ~ **with** essere contemporaneo(a) a.

synchronized swimming *n* nuoto sincronizzato.

syncopated ['sɪŋkəpeɪtɪd] *adj* sincopato(a).

syndicate ['sɪndɪkɪt] *n* sindacato; (*PRESS*) agenzia di stampa.

syndrome ['sɪndrəum] *n* sindrome *f*.

synonym ['sɪnənɪm] *n* sinonimo.

synonymous [sɪ'nɔnɪməs] *adj*: ~ **(with)** sinonimo(a) (di).

synopsis, *pl* **synopses** [sɪ'nɔpsɪs, -siːz] *n* sommario, sinossi *f inv*.

syntax ['sɪntæks] *n* sintassi *f inv*.

synthesis, *pl* **syntheses** ['sɪnθəsɪs, -siːz] *n* sintesi *f inv*.

synthesizer ['sɪnθəsaɪzə*] *n* (*MUS*) sintetizzatore *m*.

synthetic [sɪn'θɛtɪk] *adj* sintetico(a) ♦ *n* prodotto sintetico; (*TEXTILES*) fibra sintetica.

syphilis ['sɪfɪlɪs] *n* sifilide *f*.

syphon ['saɪfən] *n, vb* = **siphon**.

Syria ['sɪrɪə] *n* Siria.

Syrian ['sɪrɪən] *adj, n* siriano(a).

syringe [sɪ'rɪndʒ] *n* siringa.

syrup ['sɪrəp] *n* sciroppo; (*also*: **golden** ~) melassa raffinata.

syrupy ['sɪrəpɪ] *adj* sciropposo(a).

system ['sɪstəm] *n* sistema *m*; (*network*) rete *f*; (*ANAT*) apparato; **it was a shock to his** ~ è stato uno shock per il suo

organismo.
systematic [sɪstə'mætɪk] *adj* sistematico(a).
system disk *n* (*COMPUT*) disco del sistema.
systems analyst *n* analista *m/f* di sistemi.

T t

T, t [tiː] *n* (*letter*) T, t *m or f inv*; **T for Tommy** ≈ T come Taranto.
TA *n abbr* (*BRIT*) = *Territorial Army*.
ta [taː] *excl* (*BRIT col*) grazie!
tab [tæb] *n abbr* = **tabulator** ♦ *n* (*loop on coat etc*) laccetto; (*label*) etichetta; **to keep ~s on** (*fig*) tenere d'occhio.
tabby ['tæbɪ] *n* (*also*: ~ **cat**) (gatto) soriano, gatto tigrato.
tabernacle ['tæbənækl] *n* tabernacolo.
table ['teɪbl] *n* tavolo, tavola; (*chart*) tabella ♦ *vt* (*motion etc*) presentare; **to lay** *or* **set the ~** apparecchiare *or* preparare la tavola; **to clear the ~** sparecchiare; **league ~** (*FOOTBALL, RUGBY*) classifica; **~ of contents** indice *m*.
tablecloth ['teɪblklɔθ] *n* tovaglia.
table d'hôte [taːbl'dəut] *adj* (*meal*) a prezzo fisso.
table lamp *n* lampada da tavolo.
tablemat ['teɪblmæt] *n* sottopiatto.
table salt *n* sale *m* fino *or* da tavola.
tablespoon ['teɪblspuːn] *n* cucchiaio da tavola; (*also*: ~**ful**) cucchiaiata.
tablet ['tæblɪt] *n* (*MED*) compressa; (: *for sucking*) pastiglia; (*for writing*) blocco; (*of stone*) targa; ~ **of soap** (*BRIT*) saponetta.
table tennis *n* tennis *m* da tavolo, ping-pong ® *m*.
table wine *n* vino da tavola.
tabloid ['tæblɔɪd] *n* (*newspaper*) tabloid *m inv*; **the ~s, the ~ press** i giornali popolari; *see boxed note*.

taboo [tə'buː] *adj, n* tabù (*m inv*).
tabulate ['tæbjuleɪt] *vt* (*data*) tabulare.
tabulator ['tæbjuleɪtə*] *n* tabulatore *m*.
tachograph ['tækəgrɑːf] *n* tachigrafo.
tachometer [tæ'kɔmɪtə*] *n* tachimetro.
tacit ['tæsɪt] *adj* tacito(a).
taciturn ['tæsɪtəːn] *adj* taciturno(a).
tack [tæk] *n* (*nail*) bulletta; (*stitch*) punto d'imbastitura; (*NAUT*) bordo, bordata ♦ *vt* imbullettare; imbastire ♦ *vi* bordeggiare; **to change ~** virare di bordo; **on the wrong ~** (*fig*) sulla strada sbagliata; **to ~ sth on to (the end of) sth** (*of letter, book*) aggiungere qc alla fine di qc.
tackle ['tækl] *n* (*equipment*) attrezzatura, equipaggiamento; (*for lifting*) paranco; (*RUGBY*) placcaggio; (*FOOTBALL*) contrasto ♦ *vt* (*difficulty*) affrontare; (*RUGBY*) placcare; (*FOOTBALL*) contrastare.
tacky ['tækɪ] *adj* colloso(a); ancora bagnato(a); (*col: shabby*) scadente.
tact [tækt] *n* tatto.
tactful ['tæktful] *adj* delicato(a), discreto(a); **to be ~** avere tatto.
tactfully ['tæktfəlɪ] *adv* con tatto.
tactical ['tæktɪkl] *adj* tattico(a).
tactical voting *n* voto tattico.
tactician [tæk'tɪʃən] *n* tattico/a.
tactics ['tæktɪks] *n, npl* tattica.
tactless ['tæktlɪs] *adj* che manca di tatto.
tactlessly ['tæktlɪslɪ] *adv* senza tatto.
tadpole ['tædpəul] *n* girino.
taffy ['tæfɪ] *n* (*US*) caramella *f* mou *inv*.
tag [tæg] *n* etichetta; **price/name ~** etichetta del prezzo/con il nome.
▶**tag along** *vi* seguire.
Tahiti [tə'hiːtɪ] *n* Tahiti *f*.
tail [teɪl] *n* coda; (*of shirt*) falda ♦ *vt* (*follow*) seguire, pedinare; **to turn ~** voltare la schiena; *see also* **head**.
▶**tail away, tail off** *vi* (*in size, quality etc*) diminuire gradatamente.
tailback ['teɪlbæk] *n* (*BRIT*) ingorgo.
tail coat *n* marsina.
tail end *n* (*of train, procession etc*) coda; (*of meeting etc*) fine *f*.
tailgate ['teɪlgeɪt] *n* (*AUT*) portellone *m* posteriore.
tail light *n* (*AUT*) fanalino di coda.
tailor ['teɪlə*] *n* sarto ♦ *vt*: **to ~ sth (to)** adattare qc (alle esigenze di); **~'s (shop)** sartoria (da uomo).
tailoring ['teɪlərɪŋ] *n* (*cut*) taglio.
tailor-made ['teɪlə'meɪd] *adj* (*also fig*) fatto(a) su misura.
tailwind ['teɪlwɪnd] *n* vento di coda.
taint [teɪnt] *vt* (*meat, food*) far avariare;

(*fig*: *reputation*) infangare.
tainted ['teɪntɪd] *adj* (*food*) guasto(a);
(*water, air*) infetto(a); (*fig*) corrotto(a).
Taiwan [taɪ'wɑːn] *n* Taiwan *m*.
Tajikistan [tɑːdʒɪkɪ'stɑːn] *n* Tagikistan *m*.
take [teɪk] *vb* (*pt* **took**, *pp* **taken** [tuk, 'teɪkn])
vt prendere; (*gain*: *prize*) ottenere,
vincere; (*require*: *effort, courage*)
occorrere, volerci; (*tolerate*) accettare,
sopportare; (*hold*: *passengers etc*)
contenere; (*accompany*) accompagnare;
(*bring, carry*) portare; (*conduct*: *meeting*)
condurre; (*exam*) sostenere, presentarsi
a ♦ *vi* (*dye, fire etc*) prendere; (*injection*)
fare effetto; (*plant*) attecchire ♦ *n* (*CINE*)
ripresa; **I ~ it that** suppongo che; **to ~ for
a walk** (*child, dog*) portare a fare una
passeggiata; **to ~ sb's hand** prendere qn
per mano; **to ~ it upon o.s. to do sth**
prendersi la responsabilità di fare qc; **to
be ~n ill** avere un malore; **to be ~n with
sb/sth** (*attracted*) essere tutto preso da
qn/qc; **it won't ~ long** non ci vorrà molto
tempo; **it ~s a lot of time/courage**
occorre *or* ci vuole molto tempo/
coraggio; **it will ~ at least 5 litres**
contiene almeno 5 litri; **~ the first on the
left** prenda la prima a sinistra; **to ~
Russian at university** fare russo
all'università; **I took him for a doctor** l'ho
preso per un dottore. ♦
▶**take after** *vt fus* assomigliare a.
▶**take apart** *vt* smontare.
▶**take away** *vt* portare via; togliere; **to ~
away (from)** sottrarre (da).
▶**take back** *vt* (*return*) restituire; riportare;
(*one's words*) ritirare.
▶**take down** *vt* (*building*) demolire;
(*dismantle*: *scaffolding*) smontare; (*letter
etc*) scrivere.
▶**take in** *vt* (*lodger*) prendere, ospitare;
(*orphan*) accogliere; (*stray dog*)
raccogliere; (*SEWING*) stringere; (*deceive*)
imbrogliare, abbindolare; (*understand*)
capire; (*include*) comprendere, includere.
▶**take off** *vi* (*AVIAT*) decollare ♦ *vt* (*remove*)
togliere; (*imitate*) imitare.
▶**take on** *vt* (*work*) accettare,
intraprendere; (*employee*) assumere;
(*opponent*) sfidare, affrontare.
▶**take out** *vt* portare fuori; (*remove*)
togliere; (*licence*) prendere, ottenere; **to
~ sth out of** tirare qc fuori da; estrarre
qc da; **don't ~ it out on me!** non
prendertela con me!
▶**take over** *vt* (*business*) rilevare ♦ *vi*: **to ~
over from sb** prendere le consegne *or* il
controllo da qn.

▶**take to** *vt fus* (*person*) prendere in
simpatia; (*activity*) prendere gusto a;
(*form habit of*): **to ~ to doing sth** prendere
or cominciare a fare qc.
▶**take up** *vt* (*one's story*) riprendere;
(*dress*) accorciare; (*absorb*: *liquids*)
assorbire; (*accept*: *offer, challenge*)
accettare; (*occupy*: *time, space*) occupare;
(*engage in*: *hobby etc*) mettersi a; **to ~ up
with sb** fare amicizia con qn.
takeaway ['teɪkəweɪ] *adj* (*BRIT*: *food*) da
portar via.
take-home pay ['teɪkhəum-] *n* stipendio
netto.
taken ['teɪkn] *pp of* **take**.
takeoff ['teɪkɔf] *n* (*AVIAT*) decollo.
takeout ['teɪkaut] *adj* (*US*) = **takeaway**.
takeover ['teɪkəuvə*] *n* (*COMM*)
assorbimento.
takeover bid *n* offerta di assorbimento.
takings ['teɪkɪŋz] *npl* (*COMM*) incasso.
talc [tælk] *n* (*also*: **~um powder**) talco.
tale [teɪl] *n* racconto, storia; (*pej*) fandonia;
to tell ~s fare la spia.
talent ['tælənt] *n* talento.
talented ['tæləntɪd] *adj* di talento.
talent scout *n* talent scout *m/f inv*.
talisman ['tælɪzmən] *n* talismano.
talk [tɔːk] *n* discorso; (*gossip*) chiacchiere
fpl; (*conversation*) conversazione *f*;
(*interview*) discussione *f* ♦ *vi* parlare;
(*chatter*) chiacchierare; **to give a ~** tenere
una conferenza; **to ~ about** parlare di;
(*converse*) discorrere *or* conversare su;
to ~ sb out of/into doing dissuadere qn
da/convincere qn a fare; **to ~ shop**
parlare del lavoro *or* degli affari; **~ing of
films, have you seen ...?** a proposito di
film, ha visto ...?
▶**talk over** *vt* discutere.
talkative ['tɔːkətɪv] *adj* loquace,
ciarliero(a).
talking point ['tɔːkɪŋ-] *n* argomento di
conversazione.
talking-to ['tɔːkɪŋtuː] *n*: **to give sb a good
~** fare una bella paternale a qn.
talk show *n* (*TV, RADIO*) intervista
(informale), talk show *m inv*.
tall [tɔːl] *adj* alto(a); **to be 6 feet ~** ≈ essere
alto 1 metro e 80; **how ~ are you?** quanto
è alto?
tallboy ['tɔːlbɔɪ] *n* (*BRIT*) cassettone *m* alto.
tallness ['tɔːlnɪs] *n* altezza.
tall story *n* panzana, frottola.
tally ['tælɪ] *n* conto, conteggio ♦ *vi*: **to ~
(with)** corrispondere (a); **to keep a ~ of
sth** tener il conto di qc.
talon ['tælən] *n* artiglio.

tambourine [tæmbə'ri:n] *n* tamburello.
tame [teɪm] *adj* addomesticato(a); (*fig: story, style*) insipido(a), scialbo(a).
Tamil ['tæmɪl] *adj* tamil *inv* ♦ *n* tamil *m/f inv*; (*LING*) tamil *m*.
tamper ['tæmpə*] *vi*: **to ~ with** manomettere.
tampon ['tæmpɔn] *n* tampone *m*.
tan [tæn] *n* (*also:* **sun~**) abbronzatura ♦ *vt* abbronzare ♦ *vi* abbronzarsi ♦ *adj* (*colour*) marrone rossiccio *inv*; **to get a ~** abbronzarsi.
tandem ['tændəm] *n* tandem *m inv*.
tandoori [tæn'duərɪ] *adj nella cucina indiana, detto di carni o verdure cucinate allo spiedo in particolari forni.*
tang [tæŋ] *n* odore *m* penetrante; sapore *m* piccante.
tangent ['tændʒənt] *n* (*MATH*) tangente *f*; **to go off at a ~** (*fig*) partire per la tangente.
tangerine [tændʒə'ri:n] *n* mandarino.
tangible ['tændʒəbl] *adj* tangibile; **~ assets** patrimonio reale.
Tangier [tæn'dʒɪə*] *n* Tangeri *f*.
tangle ['tæŋgl] *n* groviglio ♦ *vt* aggrovigliare; **to get in(to) a ~** finire in un groviglio.
tango ['tæŋgəu] *n* tango.
tank [tæŋk] *n* serbatoio; (*for processing*) vasca; (*for fish*) acquario; (*MIL*) carro armato.
tankard ['tæŋkəd] *n* boccale *m*.
tanker ['tæŋkə*] *n* (*ship*) nave *f* cisterna *inv*; (*for oil*) petroliera; (*truck*) autobotte *f*, autocisterna.
tanned [tænd] *adj* abbronzato(a).
tannin ['tænɪn] *n* tannino.
tanning ['tænɪŋ] *n* (*of leather*) conciatura.
tannoy ® ['tænɔɪ] *n* (*BRIT*) altoparlante *m*; **over the ~** per altoparlante.
tantalizing ['tæntəlaɪzɪŋ] *adj* allettante.
tantamount ['tæntəmaunt] *adj*: **~ to** equivalente a.
tantrum ['tæntrəm] *n* accesso di collera; **to throw a ~** fare le bizze.
Tanzania [tænzə'nɪə] *n* Tanzania.
Tanzanian [tænzə'nɪən] *adj, n* tanzaniano(a).
tap [tæp] *n* (*on sink etc*) rubinetto; (*gentle blow*) colpetto ♦ *vt* dare un colpetto a; (*resources*) sfruttare, utilizzare; (*telephone conversation*) intercettare; (*telephone*) mettere sotto controllo; **on ~** (*beer*) alla spina; (*fig: resources*) a disposizione.
tap-dancing ['tæpdɑːnsɪŋ] *n* tip tap *m*.
tape [teɪp] *n* nastro; (*also:* **magnetic ~**) nastro (magnetico) ♦ *vt* (*record*)

registrare (su nastro); **on ~** (*song etc*) su nastro.
tape deck *n* piastra di registrazione.
tape measure *n* metro a nastro.
taper ['teɪpə*] *n* candelina ♦ *vi* assottigliarsi.
tape-record ['teɪprɪkɔːd] *vt* registrare (su nastro).
tape recorder *n* registratore *m* (a nastro).
tape recording *n* registrazione *f*.
tapered ['teɪpəd], **tapering** ['teɪpərɪŋ] *adj* affusolato(a).
tapestry ['tæpɪstrɪ] *n* arazzo; tappezzeria.
tape-worm ['teɪpwə:m] *n* tenia, verme *m* solitario.
tapioca [tæpɪ'əukə] *n* tapioca.
tappet ['tæpɪt] *n* punteria.
tar [tɑ:*] *n* catrame *m*; **low-/middle-~ cigarettes** sigarette a basso/medio contenuto di nicotina.
tarantula [tə'ræntjulə] *n* tarantola.
tardy ['tɑ:dɪ] *adj* tardo(a); tardivo(a).
target ['tɑ:gɪt] *n* bersaglio; (*fig: objective*) obiettivo; **to be on ~** (*project*) essere nei tempi (di lavorazione).
target practice *n* tiro al bersaglio.
tariff ['tærɪf] *n* tariffa.
tarmac ['tɑ:mæk] *n* (*BRIT: on road*) macadam *m* al catrame; (*AVIAT*) pista di decollo ♦ *vt* (*BRIT*) macadamizzare.
tarnish ['tɑ:nɪʃ] *vt* offuscare, annerire; (*fig*) macchiare.
tarot ['tærəu] *n* tarocco.
tarpaulin [tɑ:'pɔ:lɪn] *n* tela incatramata.
tarragon ['tærəgən] *n* dragoncello.
tart [tɑ:t] *n* (*CULIN*) crostata; (*BRIT col: pej: woman*) sgualdrina ♦ *adj* (*flavour*) aspro(a), agro(a).
►**tart up** *vt* (*col*): **to ~ o.s. up** farsi bello(a); (*pej*) agghindarsi.
tartan ['tɑ:tn] *n* tartan *m inv*.
tartar ['tɑ:tə*] *n* (*on teeth*) tartaro.
tartar sauce *n* salsa tartara.
task [tɑ:sk] *n* compito; **to take to ~** rimproverare.
task force *n* (*MIL, POLICE*) unità operativa.
taskmaster ['tɑ:skmɑ:stə*] *n*: **he's a hard ~** è un vero tiranno.
Tasmania [tæz'meɪnɪə] *n* Tasmania.
tassel ['tæsl] *n* fiocco.
taste [teɪst] *n* gusto; (*flavour*) sapore *m*, gusto; (*fig: glimpse, idea*) idea ♦ *vt* gustare; (*sample*) assaggiare ♦ *vi*: **to ~ of** (*fish etc*) sapere di, avere sapore di; **what does it ~ like?** che sapore *or* gusto ha?; **it ~s like fish** sa di pesce; **you can ~ the garlic (in it)** (ci) si sente il sapore dell'aglio; **can I have a ~ of this wine?** posso assaggiare

un po' di questo vino?; **to have a ~ of sth**
assaggiare qc; **to have a ~ for sth** avere
un'inclinazione per qc; **to be in bad** or
poor ~ essere di cattivo gusto.
taste bud n papilla gustativa.
tasteful ['teɪstful] adj di buon gusto.
tastefully ['teɪstfəlɪ] adv con gusto.
tasteless ['teɪstlɪs] adj (food) insipido(a);
(remark) di cattivo gusto.
tasty ['teɪstɪ] adj saporito(a), gustoso(a).
tattered ['tætəd] adj see **tatters**.
tatters ['tætəz] npl: **in ~** (also: **tattered**) a
brandelli, sbrindellato(a).
tattoo [tə'tuː] n tatuaggio; (spectacle)
parata militare ♦ vt tatuare.
tatty ['tætɪ] adj (BRIT col) malandato(a).
taught [tɔːt] pt, pp of **teach**.
taunt [tɔːnt] n scherno ♦ vt schernire.
Taurus ['tɔːrəs] n Toro; **to be ~** essere del
Toro.
taut [tɔːt] adj teso(a).
tavern ['tævən] n taverna.
tawdry ['tɔːdrɪ] adj pacchiano(a).
tawny ['tɔːnɪ] adj fulvo(a).
tax [tæks] n imposta, tassa; (on income)
imposte fpl, tasse fpl ♦ vt tassare; (fig:
strain: patience etc) mettere alla prova;
free of ~ esentasse inv, esente da
imposte; **before/after ~** al lordo/netto
delle tasse.
taxable ['tæksəbl] adj imponibile.
tax allowance n detrazione f d'imposta.
taxation [tæk'seɪʃən] n tassazione f; tasse
fpl, imposte fpl; **system of ~** sistema m
fiscale.
tax avoidance n l'evitare legalmente il
pagamento di imposte.
tax collector n esattore m delle imposte.
tax disc n (BRIT AUT) ≈ bollo.
tax evasion n evasione f fiscale.
tax exemption n esenzione f fiscale.
tax exile n chi ripara all'estero per
evadere le imposte.
tax-free [tæks'friː] adj esente da imposte.
tax haven n paradiso fiscale.
taxi ['tæksɪ] n taxi m inv ♦ vi (AVIAT) rullare.
taxidermist ['tæksɪdəːmɪst] n tassidermista
m/f.
taxi driver n tassista m/f.
tax inspector n (BRIT) ispettore m delle
tasse.
taxi rank, (US) **taxi stand** n posteggio dei
taxi.
tax payer n contribuente m/f.
tax rebate n rimborso fiscale.
tax relief n sgravio fiscale.
tax return n dichiarazione f dei redditi.
tax shelter n paradiso fiscale.

tax year n anno fiscale.
TB n abbr (= tuberculosis) TBC f.
tbc abbr (= to be confirmed) da confermarsi.
TD n abbr (US) = **Treasury Department**;
(: FOOTBALL) = **touchdown**.
tea [tiː] n tè m inv; (BRIT: snack: for children)
merenda; **high ~** (BRIT) cena leggera
(presa nel tardo pomeriggio).
tea bag n bustina di tè.
tea break n (BRIT) intervallo per il tè.
teacake ['tiːkeɪk] n (BRIT) panino dolce
all'uva.
teach, pt, pp **taught** [tiːtʃ, tɔːt] vt: **to ~ sb
sth, ~ sth to sb** insegnare qc a qn ♦ vi
insegnare; **it taught him a lesson** (fig) gli
è servito da lezione.
teacher ['tiːtʃə*] n (gen) insegnante m/f; (in
secondary school) professore/essa; (in
primary school) maestro/a; **French ~**
insegnante di francese.
teacher training college n (for primary
schools) ≈ istituto magistrale; (for
secondary schools) scuola universitaria
per l'abilitazione all'insegnamento nelle
medie superiori.
teaching ['tiːtʃɪŋ] n insegnamento.
teaching aids npl materiali mpl per
l'insegnamento.
teaching hospital n (BRIT) clinica
universitaria.
teaching staff n (BRIT) insegnanti mpl,
personale m insegnante.
tea cosy n copriteiera m inv.
teacup ['tiːkʌp] n tazza da tè.
teak [tiːk] n teak m.
tea leaves npl foglie fpl di tè.
team [tiːm] n squadra; (of animals)
tiro.
▶**team up** vi: **to ~ up (with)** mettersi
insieme (a).
team games npl giochi mpl di squadra.
teamwork ['tiːmwəːk] n lavoro di squadra.
tea party n tè m inv (ricevimento).
teapot ['tiːpɔt] n teiera.
tear n [tɛə*] strappo; [tɪə*] lacrima ♦ vb
[tɛə*] (pt **tore,** pp **torn** [tɔː*, tɔːn]) vt
strappare ♦ vi strapparsi; **in ~s** in
lacrime; **to burst into ~s** scoppiare in
lacrime; **to ~ to pieces** or **to bits** or **to
shreds** (also fig) fare a pezzi or a
brandelli.
▶**tear along** vi (rush) correre
all'impazzata.
▶**tear apart** vt (also fig) distruggere.
▶**tear away** vt: **to ~ o.s. away (from sth)**
(fig) staccarsi (da qc).
▶**tear out** vt (sheet of paper, cheque)
staccare.

►**tear up** vt (*sheet of paper etc*) strappare.
tearaway ['tɛərəweɪ] n (*col*) monello/a.
teardrop ['tɪədrɔp] n lacrima.
tearful ['tɪəful] adj piangente, lacrimoso(a).
tear gas n gas m lacrimogeno.
tearoom ['tiːruːm] n sala da tè.
tease [tiːz] vt canzonare; (*unkindly*) tormentare.
tea set n servizio da tè.
teashop ['tiːʃɔp] n (*BRIT*) sala da tè.
Teasmaid ® ['tiːzmeɪd] n macchinetta per fare il tè.
teaspoon ['tiːspuːn] n cucchiaino da tè; (*also:* ~**ful**: *as measurement*) cucchiaino.
tea strainer n colino da tè.
teat [tiːt] n capezzolo; (*of bottle*) tettarella.
teatime ['tiːtaɪm] n ora del tè.
tea towel n (*BRIT*) strofinaccio (per i piatti).
tea urn n bollitore m per il tè.
tech [tɛk] n abbr (*col*) = **technical college**; **technology**.
technical ['tɛknɪkl] adj tecnico(a).
technical college n ≈ istituto tecnico.
technicality [tɛknɪ'kælɪtɪ] n tecnicità; (*detail*) dettaglio tecnico; **on a legal** ~ grazie a un cavillo legale.
technically ['tɛknɪklɪ] adv dal punto di vista tecnico.
technician [tɛk'nɪʃən] n tecnico/a.
technique [tɛk'niːk] n tecnica.
techno ['tɛknəu] n (*MUS*) techno f inv.
technocrat ['tɛknəkræt] n tecnocrate m/f.
technological [tɛknə'lɔdʒɪkl] adj tecnologico(a).
technologist [tɛk'nɔlədʒɪst] n tecnologo/a.
technology [tɛk'nɔlədʒɪ] n tecnologia.
teddy (bear) ['tɛdɪ-] n orsacchiotto.
tedious ['tiːdɪəs] adj noioso(a), tedioso(a).
tedium ['tiːdɪəm] n noia, tedio.
tee [tiː] n (*GOLF*) tee m inv.
teem [tiːm] vi abbondare, brulicare; **to** ~ **with** brulicare di; **it is** ~**ing (with rain)** piove a dirotto.
teenage ['tiːneɪdʒ] adj (*fashions etc*) per giovani, per adolescenti.
teenager ['tiːneɪdʒə*] n adolescente m/f.
teens [tiːnz] npl: **to be in one's** ~ essere adolescente.
tee-shirt ['tiːʃəːt] n = **T-shirt**.
teeter ['tiːtə*] vi barcollare, vacillare.
teeth [tiːθ] npl of **tooth**.
teethe [tiːð] vi mettere i denti.
teething ring ['tiːðɪŋ-] n dentaruolo.
teething troubles npl (*fig*) difficoltà fpl iniziali.
teetotal ['tiː'təutl] adj astemio(a).
teetotaller, (*US*) **teetotaler** ['tiː'təutlə*] n

astemio/a.
TEFL ['tɛfl] n abbr = *Teaching of English as a Foreign Language.*
Teflon ® ['tɛflɔn] n teflon ® m.
Tehran [tɛə'rɑːn] n Tehran f.
tel. abbr (= *telephone*) tel.
Tel Aviv ['tɛlə'viːv] n Tel Aviv f.
telecast ['tɛlɪkɑːst] vt, vi teletrasmettere.
telecommunications ['tɛlɪkəmjuːnɪ'keɪʃənz] n telecomunicazioni fpl.
teleconferencing ['tɛlɪkɔnfərənsɪŋ] n teleconferenza.
telegram ['tɛlɪgræm] n telegramma m.
telegraph ['tɛlɪgrɑːf] n telegrafo.
telegraphic [tɛlɪ'græfɪk] adj telegrafico(a).
telegraph pole n palo del telegrafo.
telegraph wire n filo del telegrafo.
telepathic [tɛlɪ'pæθɪk] adj telepatico(a).
telephone ['tɛlɪfəun] n telefono ♦ vt (*person*) telefonare a; (*message*) telefonare; **to have a** ~, (*BRIT*) **to be on the** ~ (*subscriber*) avere il telefono; **to be on the** ~ (*be speaking*) essere al telefono.
telephone booth, (*BRIT*) **telephone box** n cabina telefonica.
telephone call n telefonata.
telephone directory n elenco telefonico.
telephone number n numero di telefono.
telephone operator n centralinista m/f.
telephone tapping n intercettazione f telefonica.
telephonist [tə'lɛfənɪst] n (*BRIT*) telefonista m/f.
telephoto lens ['tɛlɪfəutəu-] n teleobiettivo.
teleprinter ['tɛlɪprɪntə*] n telescrivente f.
Teleprompter ® ['tɛlɪprɔmptə*] n (*US*) gobbo.
telesales ['tɛlɪseɪlz] n vendita per telefono.
telescope ['tɛlɪskəup] n telescopio ♦ vi chiudersi a telescopio; (*fig: vehicles*) accartocciarsi.
telescopic [tɛlɪs'kɔpɪk] adj telescopico(a); (*umbrella*) pieghevole.
Teletext ® ['tɛlɪtɛkst] n (*system*) teletext m inv; (*in Italy*) televideo.
telethon ['tɛlɪθɔn] n maratona televisiva.
televise ['tɛlɪvaɪz] vt teletrasmettere.
television ['tɛlɪvɪʒən] n televisione f; **on** ~ alla televisione.
television licence n (*BRIT*) abbonamento alla televisione.
television programme n programma m televisivo.
television set n televisore m.
teleworking ['tɛlɪwəːkɪŋ] n telelavoro.
telex ['tɛlɛks] n telex m inv ♦ vt trasmettere

per telex ♦ *vi* mandare un telex; **to ~ sb (about sth)** informare qn via telex (di qc).

tell, *pt, pp* **told** [tɛl, təʊld] *vt* dire; (*relate: story*) raccontare; (*distinguish*): **to ~ sth from** distinguere qc da ♦ *vi* (*have effect*) farsi sentire, avere effetto; **to ~ sb to do** dire a qn di fare; **to ~ sb about sth** dire a qn di qc; raccontare qc a qn; **to ~ the time** leggere l'ora; **can you ~ me the time?** può dirmi l'ora?; **(I) ~ you what ...** so io che cosa fare ...; **I couldn't ~ them apart** non riuscivo a distinguerli.

▶**tell off** *vt* rimproverare, sgridare.

▶**tell on** *vt fus* (*inform against*) denunciare.

teller ['tɛlə*] *n* (*in bank*) cassiere/a.

telling ['tɛlɪŋ] *adj* (*remark, detail*) rivelatore(trice).

telltale ['tɛlteɪl] *adj* (*sign*) rivelatore(trice) ♦ *n* malalingua, pettegolo/a.

telly ['tɛlɪ] *n abbr* (*BRIT col:* = *television*) tivù *f inv.*

temerity [tə'mɛrɪtɪ] *n* temerarietà.

temp [tɛmp] *abbr* (*BRIT col:* = *temporary*) *n* impiegato(a) straordinario(a) ♦ *vi* lavorare come impiegato(a) straordinario(a).

temper ['tɛmpə*] *n* (*nature*) carattere *m*; (*mood*) umore *m*; (*fit of anger*) collera ♦ *vt* (*moderate*) temperare; **to be in a ~** essere in collera; **to keep one's ~** restare calmo; **to lose one's ~** andare in collera.

temperament ['tɛmprəmənt] *n* temperamento.

temperamental [tɛmprə'mɛntl] *adj* capriccioso(a).

temperance ['tɛmpərns] *n* moderazione *f*; (*in drinking*) temperanza nel bere.

temperate ['tɛmprət] *adj* moderato(a); (*climate*) temperato(a).

temperature ['tɛmprətʃə*] *n* temperatura; **to have** *or* **run a ~** avere la febbre.

tempered ['tɛmpəd] *adj* (*steel*) temprato(a).

tempest ['tɛmpɪst] *n* tempesta.

tempestuous [tɛm'pɛstjʊəs] *adj* (*relationship, meeting*) burrascoso(a).

tempi ['tɛmpiː] *npl of* **tempo.**

template, (*US*) **templet** ['tɛmplɪt] *n* sagoma.

temple ['tɛmpl] *n* (*building*) tempio; (*ANAT*) tempia.

templet ['tɛmplɪt] *n* (*US*) = **template.**

tempo, **~s** *or* **tempi** ['tɛmpəʊ, 'tɛmpiː] *n* tempo; (*fig: of life etc*) ritmo.

temporal ['tɛmpərl] *adj* temporale.

temporarily ['tɛmpərərɪlɪ] *adv* temporaneamente.

temporary ['tɛmpərərɪ] *adj* temporaneo(a);

(*job, worker*) avventizio(a), temporaneo(a); **~ secretary** segretaria temporanea; **~ teacher** supplente *m/f.*

temporize ['tɛmpəraɪz] *vi* temporeggiare.

tempt [tɛmpt] *vt* tentare; **to ~ sb into doing** indurre qn a fare; **to be ~ed to do sth** essere tentato di fare qc.

temptation [tɛmp'teɪʃən] *n* tentazione *f.*

tempting ['tɛmptɪŋ] *adj* allettante, seducente.

ten [tɛn] *num* dieci ♦ *n* dieci; **~s of thousands** decine di migliaia.

tenable ['tɛnəbl] *adj* sostenibile.

tenacious [tə'neɪʃəs] *adj* tenace.

tenacity [tə'næsɪtɪ] *n* tenacia.

tenancy ['tɛnənsɪ] *n* affitto; condizione *f* di inquilino.

tenant ['tɛnənt] *n* inquilino/a.

tend [tɛnd] *vt* badare a, occuparsi di; (*sick etc*) prendersi cura di ♦ *vi:* **to ~ to do** tendere a fare; (*colour*): **to ~ to** tendere a.

tendency ['tɛndənsɪ] *n* tendenza.

tender ['tɛndə*] *adj* tenero(a); (*sore*) sensibile; (*fig: subject*) delicato(a) ♦ *n* (*COMM: offer*) offerta; (*money*): **legal ~** valuta (a corso legale) ♦ *vt* offrire; **to put in a ~ (for)** fare un'offerta (per); **to put work out to ~** (*BRIT*) dare lavoro in appalto; **to ~ one's resignation** presentare le proprie dimissioni.

tenderize ['tɛndəraɪz] *vt* (*CULIN*) far intenerire.

tenderly ['tɛndəlɪ] *adv* teneramente.

tenderness ['tɛndənɪs] *n* tenerezza; sensibilità.

tendon ['tɛndən] *n* tendine *m.*

tenement ['tɛnəmənt] *n* casamento.

Tenerife [tɛnə'riːf] *n* Tenerife *f.*

tenet ['tɛnət] *n* principio.

Tenn. *abbr* (*US*) = *Tennessee.*

tenner ['tɛnə*] *n* (*BRIT col*) (banconota da) dieci sterline *fpl.*

tennis ['tɛnɪs] *n* tennis *m.*

tennis ball *n* palla da tennis.

tennis court *n* campo da tennis.

tennis elbow *n* (*MED*) gomito del tennista.

tennis match *n* partita di tennis.

tennis player *n* tennista *m/f.*

tennis racket *n* racchetta da tennis.

tennis shoes *npl* scarpe *fpl* da tennis.

tenor ['tɛnə*] *n* (*MUS, of speech etc*) tenore *m.*

tenpin bowling ['tɛnpɪn-] *n* (*BRIT*) bowling *m.*

tense [tɛns] *adj* teso(a) ♦ *n* (*LING*) tempo ♦ *vt* (*tighten: muscles*) tendere.

tenseness ['tɛnsnɪs] *n* tensione *f.*

tension ['tɛnʃən] *n* tensione *f.*

tent [tɛnt] *n* tenda.

tentacle ['tɛntəkl] *n* tentacolo.

tentative ['tɛntətɪv] *adj* esitante, incerto(a); (*conclusion*) provvisorio(a).

tenterhooks ['tɛntəhuks] *npl*: **on ~** sulle spine.

tenth [tɛnθ] *num* decimo(a).

tent peg *n* picchetto da tenda.

tent pole *n* palo da tenda, montante *m.*

tenuous ['tɛnjuəs] *adj* tenue.

tenure ['tɛnjuə*] *n* (*of property*) possesso; (*of job*) incarico; (*guaranteed employment*): **to have ~** essere di ruolo.

tepid ['tɛpɪd] *adj* tiepido(a).

term [tɜːm] *n* (*limit*) termine *m*; (*word*) vocabolo, termine; (*SCOL*) trimestre *m*; (*LAW*) sessione *f* ♦ *vt* chiamare, definire; **~s** *npl* (*conditions*) condizioni *fpl*; (*COMM*) prezzi *mpl*, tariffe *fpl*; **~ of imprisonment** periodo di prigionia; **during his ~ of office** durante il suo incarico; **in the short/long ~** a breve/lunga scadenza; **"easy ~s"** (*COMM*) "facilitazioni di pagamento"; **to be on good ~s with** essere in buoni rapporti con; **to come to ~s with** (*person*) arrivare a un accordo con; (*problem*) affrontare.

terminal ['tɜːmɪnl] *adj* finale, terminale; (*disease*) nella fase terminale ♦ *n* (*ELEC, COMPUT*) terminale *m*; (*AVIAT, for oil, ore etc*) terminal *m inv*; (*BRIT: also*: **coach ~**) capolinea *m.*

terminate ['tɜːmɪneɪt] *vt* mettere fine a ♦ *vi*: **to ~ in** finire in *or* con.

termination [tɜːmɪ'neɪʃən] *n* fine *f*; (*of contract*) rescissione *f*; **~ of pregnancy** (*MED*) interruzione *f* della gravidanza.

termini ['tɜːmɪnaɪ] *npl of* **terminus**.

terminology [tɜːmɪ'nɔlədʒɪ] *n* terminologia.

terminus, *pl* termini ['tɜːmɪnəs, 'tɜːmɪnaɪ] *n* (*for buses*) capolinea *m*; (*for trains*) stazione *f* terminale.

termite ['tɜːmaɪt] *n* termite *f.*

term paper *n* (*US UNIVERSITY*) saggio scritto da consegnare a fine trimestre.

Ter(r). *abbr* = **terrace**.

terrace ['tɛrəs] *n* terrazza; (*BRIT: row of houses*) fila di case a schiera; **the ~s** *npl* (*BRIT SPORT*) le gradinate.

terraced ['tɛrɪst] *adj* (*garden*) a terrazze; (*in a row: house, cottage etc*) a schiera.

terrain [tɛ'reɪn] *n* terreno.

terrible ['tɛrɪbl] *adj* terribile; (*weather*) bruttissimo(a); (*performance, report*) pessimo(a).

terribly ['tɛrəblɪ] *adv* terribilmente; (*very*

badly) malissimo.

terrier ['tɛrɪə*] *n* terrier *m inv.*

terrific [tə'rɪfɪk] *adj* incredibile, fantastico(a); (*wonderful*) formidabile, eccezionale.

terrify ['tɛrɪfaɪ] *vt* terrorizzare; **to be terrified** essere atterrito(a).

territorial [tɛrɪ'tɔːrɪəl] *adj* territoriale.

territorial waters *npl* acque *fpl* territoriali.

territory ['tɛrɪtərɪ] *n* territorio.

terror ['tɛrə*] *n* terrore *m.*

terror attack *n* attentato terroristico.

terrorism ['tɛrərɪzəm] *n* terrorismo.

terrorist ['tɛrərɪst] *n* terrorista *m/f.*

terrorize ['tɛrəraɪz] *vt* terrorizzare.

terse [tɜːs] *adj* (*style*) conciso(a); (*reply*) laconico(a).

tertiary ['tɜːʃərɪ] *adj* (*gen*) terziario(a); **~ education** (*BRIT*) educazione *f* superiore post-scolastica.

Terylene ® ['tɛrəliːn] *n* (*BRIT*) terital ® *m*, terilene ® *m.*

TESL ['tɛsl] *n abbr* = *Teaching of English as a Second Language.*

TESSA ['tɛsə] *n abbr* (*BRIT*: = *Tax Exempt Special Savings Account*) *deposito a risparmio esente da tasse.*

test [tɛst] *n* (*trial, check*) prova; (: *of goods in factory*) controllo, collaudo; (*MED*) esame *m*; (*CHEM*) analisi *f inv*; (*exam: of intelligence etc*) test *m inv*; (: *in school*) compito in classe; (*also*: **driving ~**) esame *m* di guida ♦ *vt* provare; controllare, collaudare; esaminare; analizzare; sottoporre ad esame; **to put sth to the ~** mettere qc alla prova; **to ~ sth for sth** analizzare qc alla ricerca di qc; **to ~ sb in history** esaminare qn in storia.

testament ['tɛstəmənt] *n* testamento; **the Old/New T~** il Vecchio/Nuovo testamento.

test ban *n* (*also*: **nuclear ~**) divieto di esperimenti nucleari.

test case *n* (*LAW, fig*) caso che farà testo.

testes ['tɛstiːz] *npl* testicoli *mpl.*

test flight *n* volo di prova.

testicle ['tɛstɪkl] *n* testicolo.

testify ['tɛstɪfaɪ] *vi* (*LAW*) testimoniare, deporre; **to ~ to sth** (*LAW*) testimoniare qc; (*gen*) comprovare *or* dimostrare qc; (*be sign of*) essere una prova di qc.

testimonial [tɛstɪ'məunɪəl] *n* (*BRIT: reference*) benservito; (*gift*) testimonianza di stima.

testimony ['tɛstɪmənɪ] *n* (*LAW*) testimonianza, deposizione *f.*

testing ['tɛstɪŋ] *adj* (*difficult: time*) duro(a).

test match *n* (*CRICKET, RUGBY*) partita

internazionale.

testosterone [tɛs'tɔstərəʊn] n testosterone m.

test paper n (SCOL) interrogazione f scritta.

test pilot n pilota m collaudatore.

test tube n provetta.

test-tube baby ['tɛsttjuːb-] n bambino(a) concepito(a) in provetta.

testy ['tɛstɪ] adj irritabile.

tetanus ['tɛtənəs] n tetano.

tetchy ['tɛtʃɪ] adj irritabile, irascibile.

tether ['tɛðə*] vt legare ♦ n: **at the end of one's** ~ al limite (della pazienza).

Tex. abbr (US) = Texas.

text [tɛkst] n testo; (TEL) messaggino, SMS m inv ♦ vt mandare un SMS a.

textbook ['tɛkstbʊk] n libro di testo.

textile ['tɛkstaɪl] n tessile m; ~**s** npl tessuti mpl.

texting ['tɛkstɪŋ] n invio di SMS.

text message n (TEL) messaggino, SMS m inv.

textual ['tɛkstjʊəl] adj testuale, del testo.

texture ['tɛkstʃə*] n tessitura; (of skin, paper etc) struttura.

TGIF abbr (col) = thank God it's Friday.

TGWU n abbr (BRIT: = Transport and General Workers' Union) sindacato degli operai dei trasporti e non specializzati.

Thai [taɪ] adj tailandese ♦ n tailandese m/f; (LING) tailandese m.

Thailand ['taɪlænd] n Tailandia.

thalidomide ® [θə'lɪdəmaɪd] n talidomide ® m.

Thames [tɛmz] n: **the** ~ il Tamigi.

than [ðæn, ðən] conj che; (with numerals, pronouns, proper names): **more** ~ **10/me/ Maria** più di 10/me/Maria; **you know her better** ~ **I do** la conosce meglio di me; **she has more apples** ~ **pears** ha più mele che pere; **it is better to phone** ~ **to write** è meglio telefonare che scrivere; **no sooner did he leave** ~ **the phone rang** non appena uscì il telefono suonò.

thank [θæŋk] vt ringraziare; ~ **you (very much)** grazie (tante); ~ **heavens/God!** grazie al cielo/a Dio!; see also **thanks**.

thankful ['θæŋkful] adj: ~ **(for)** riconoscente (per); ~ **for/that** (relieved) sollevato(a) da/dal fatto che.

thankfully ['θæŋkfəlɪ] adv con riconoscenza; con sollievo; ~ **there were few victims** grazie al cielo ci sono state poche vittime.

thankless ['θæŋklɪs] adj ingrato(a).

thanks [θæŋks] npl ringraziamenti mpl, grazie fpl ♦ excl grazie!; ~ **to** prep grazie a.

Thanksgiving (Day) ['θæŋksgɪvɪŋ-] n (US) giorno del ringraziamento; see boxed note.

THANKSGIVING

Negli Stati Uniti il quarto giovedì di novembre ricorre il **Thanksgiving (Day)**, festa nazionale in ricordo della celebrazione con cui i Padri Pellegrini, i puritani inglesi che fondarono la colonia di Plymouth nel Massachusetts, ringraziarono Dio del buon raccolto del 1621.

============================ *KEYWORD*

that [ðæt] (pl **those**) adj (demonstrative) quel(quell', quello) m; quella(quell') f; ~ **man/woman/book** quell'uomo/quella donna/quel libro; (not "this") quell'uomo/ quella donna/quel libro là; ~ **one** quello(a) là
♦ pron **1** (demonstrative) ciò; (not "this one") quello(a); **who's** ~? chi è quello là?; **what's** ~? cos'è quello?; **is** ~ **you?** sei tu?; **I prefer this to** ~ preferisco questo a quello; ~'**s what he said** questo è ciò che ha detto; **after** ~ dopo; **what happened after** ~? che è successo dopo?; ~ **is (to say)** cioè; **at** or **with** ~ **she ...** con ciò lei ...; **do it like** ~ fallo così

2 (relative: direct) che; (: indirect) cui; **the book** (~) **I read** il libro che ho letto; **the box** (~) **I put it in** la scatola in cui l'ho messo; **the people** (~) **I spoke to** le persone con cui or con le quali ho parlato; **not** ~ **I know of** non che io sappia

3 (relative: of time) in cui; **the day** (~) **he came** il giorno in cui è venuto
♦ conj che; **he thought** ~ **I was ill** pensava che io fossi malato
♦ adv (demonstrative) così; **I can't work** ~ **much** non posso lavorare (così) tanto; ~ **high** così alto; **the wall's about** ~ **high and** ~ **thick** il muro è alto circa così e spesso circa così.

---

thatched [θætʃt] adj (roof) di paglia; ~ **cottage** cottage m inv col tetto di paglia.

Thatcherism ['θætʃərɪzəm] n thatcherismo.

thaw [θɔː] n disgelo ♦ vi (ice) sciogliersi; (food) scongelarsi ♦ vt (food) (fare) scongelare; **it's** ~**ing** (weather) sta sgelando.

============================ *KEYWORD*

the [ðiː, ðə] def art **1** (gen) il(lo, l') m; la(l') f; i(gli) mpl; le fpl; ~ **boy/girl/ink** il ragazzo/ la ragazza/l'inchiostro; ~ **books/pencils** i libri/le matite; ~ **history of** ~ **world** la storia del mondo; **give it to** ~ **postman** dallo al postino; **I haven't** ~ **time/money** non ho tempo/soldi; ~ **rich and** ~ **poor** i ricchi e i poveri; **1.5 euros to** ~ **dollar** 1.5 euro per un dollaro; **paid by** ~ **hour** pagato a ore 2 (*in titles*): **Elizabeth** ~ **First** Elisabetta prima; **Peter** ~ **Great** Pietro il Grande 3 (*in comparisons*): ~ **more he works,** ~ **more he earns** più lavora più guadagna; ~ **sooner** ~ **better** prima è meglio è.

nessuno qui; ~ **has been an accident** c'è stato un incidente 2 (*referring to place*) là, lì; **it's** ~ è là *or* lì; **up/in/down** ~ lassù/là dentro/laggiù; **back** ~ là dietro; **on** ~ lassù; **over** ~ là; **through** ~ di là; **he went** ~ **on Friday** ci è andato venerdì; **it takes two hours to go** ~ **and back** ci vogliono due ore per andare e tornare; **I want that book** ~ voglio quel libro là *or* lì; ~ **he is!** eccolo! 3: ~, ~ (*esp to child*) su, su.

theatre, (*US*) **theater** ['θɪətə*] *n* teatro.
theatre-goer ['θɪətəgəʊə*] *n* frequentatore/trice di teatri.
theatrical [θɪ'ætrɪkl] *adj* teatrale.
theft [θɛft] *n* furto.
their [ðɛə*] *adj* il(la) loro, *pl* i(le) loro.
theirs [ðɛəz] *pron* il(la) loro, *pl* i(le) loro; **it is** ~ è loro; **a friend of** ~ un loro amico.
them [ðɛm, ðəm] *pron* (*direct*) li(le); (*indirect*) gli, loro (*after vb*); (*stressed, after prep: people*) loro; (: *people, things*) essi(e); **I see** ~ li vedo; **give** ~ **the book** dà loro *or* dagli il libro; **give me a few of** ~ dammene un po' *or* qualcuno.
theme [θi:m] *n* tema *m*.
theme park *n* parco dei divertimenti a soggetto.
theme song, theme tune *n* tema musicale.
themselves [ðəm'sɛlvz] *pl pron* (*reflexive*) si; (*emphatic*) loro stessi(e); (*after prep*) se stessi(e); **between** ~ tra (di) loro.
then [ðɛn] *adv* (*at that time*) allora; (*next*) poi, dopo; (*and also*) e poi ♦ *conj* (*therefore*) perciò, dunque, quindi ♦ *adj*: **the** ~ **president** il presidente di allora; **from** ~ **on** da allora in poi; **until** ~ fino ad allora; **and** ~ **what?** e poi?, e allora?; **what do you want me to do** ~**?** allora cosa vuole che faccia?
theologian [θɪə'ləʊdʒən] *n* teologo/a.
theological [θɪə'lɔdʒɪkl] *adj* teologico(a).
theology [θɪ'ɔlədʒɪ] *n* teologia.
theorem ['θɪərəm] *n* teorema *m*.
theoretical [θɪə'rɛtɪkl] *adj* teorico(a).
theorize ['θɪəraɪz] *vi* teorizzare.
theory ['θɪərɪ] *n* teoria; **in** ~ in teoria.
therapeutic(al) [θɛrə'pju:tɪk(l)] *adj* terapeutico(a).
therapist ['θɛrəpɪst] *n* terapista *m/f*.
therapy ['θɛrəpɪ] *n* terapia.

===================== *KEYWORD*

there [ðɛə*] *adv* **1**: ~ **is,** ~ **are** c'è, ci sono; ~ **are 3 of them** (*people*) sono in 3; (*things*) ce ne sono 3; ~ **is no-one here** non c'è

thereabouts ['ðɛərəbauts] *adv* (*place*) nei pressi, da quelle parti; (*amount*) giù di lì, all'incirca.
thereafter [ðɛər'ɑːftə*] *adv* da allora in poi.
thereby [ðɛə'baɪ] *adv* con ciò.
therefore ['ðɛəfɔː*] *adv* perciò, quindi.
there's [ðɛəz] = **there is; there has.**
thereupon [ðɛərə'pɔn] *adv* (*at that point*) a quel punto; (*formal: on that subject*) in merito.
thermal ['θə:ml] *adj* (*currents, spring*) termale; (*underwear, printer*) termico(a); (*paper*) termosensibile.
thermodynamics [θə:məudaɪ'næmɪks] *n* termodinamica.
thermometer [θə'mɔmɪtə*] *n* termometro.
thermonuclear ['θə:məu'nju:klɪə*] *adj* termonucleare.
Thermos ® ['θə:məs] *n* (*also*: ~ **flask**) thermos ® *m inv*.
thermostat ['θə:məstæt] *n* termostato.
thesaurus [θɪ'sɔːrəs] *n* dizionario dei sinonimi.
these [ðiːz] *pl pron, adj* questi(e).
thesis, *pl* **theses** ['θiːsɪs, 'θiːsiːz] *n* tesi *f inv*.
they [ðeɪ] *pl pron* essi(esse); (*people only*) loro; ~ **say that ...** (*it is said that*) si dice che ....
they'd [ðeɪd] = **they would; they had.**
they'll [ðeɪl] = **they will; they shall.**
they're [ðɛə*] = **they are.**
they've [ðeɪv] = **they have.**
thick [θɪk] *adj* spesso(a); (*crowd*) compatto(a); (*stupid*) ottuso(a), lento(a) ♦ *n*: **in the** ~ **of** nel folto di; **it's 20 cm** ~ ha uno spessore di 20 cm.
thicken ['θɪkən] *vi* ispessire ♦ *vt* (*sauce etc*) ispessire, rendere più denso(a).
thicket ['θɪkɪt] *n* boscaglia.
thickly ['θɪklɪ] *adv* (*spread*) a strati spessi; (*cut*) a fette grosse; (*populated*)

thickness ['θɪknɪs] n spessore m.

thickset [θɪk'sɛt] adj tarchiato(a), tozzo(a).

thickskinned [θɪk'skɪnd] adj (fig) insensibile.

thief, pl **thieves** [θiːf, θiːvz] n ladro/a.

thieving ['θiːvɪŋ] n furti mpl.

thigh [θaɪ] n coscia.

thighbone ['θaɪbəun] n femore m.

thimble ['θɪmbl] n ditale m.

thin [θɪn] adj sottile; (person) magro(a); (soup) poco denso(a); (hair, crowd) rado(a); (fog) leggero(a) ♦ vt (hair) sfoltire ♦ vi (fog) diradarsi; (also: ~ out: crowd) disperdersi; **to ~ (down)** (sauce, paint) diluire; **his hair is ~ning** sta perdendo i capelli.

thing [θɪŋ] n cosa; (object) oggetto; (contraption) aggeggio; **~s** npl (belongings) cose fpl; **for one ~** tanto per cominciare; **the best ~ would be to** la cosa migliore sarebbe di; **the ~ is ...** il fatto è che ...; **the main ~ is to ...** la cosa più importante è di ...; **first ~ (in the morning)** come or per prima cosa (di mattina); **last ~ (at night)** come or per ultima cosa (di sera); **poor ~** poveretto/a; **she's got a ~ about mice** è terrorizzata dai topi; **how are ~s?** come va?

think, pt, pp **thought** [θɪŋk, θɔːt] vi pensare, riflettere ♦ vt pensare, credere; (imagine) immaginare; **to ~ of** pensare a; **what did you ~ of them?** cosa ne ha pensato?; **to ~ about sth/sb** pensare a qc/qn; **I'll ~ about it** ci penserò; **to ~ of doing** pensare di fare; **I ~ so** penso or credo di sì; **to ~ well of** avere una buona opinione di; **to ~ aloud** pensare ad alta voce; **~ again!** rifletti!, pensaci su!

▸**think out** vt (plan) elaborare; (solution) trovare.

▸**think over** vt riflettere su; **I'd like to ~ things over** vorrei pensarci su.

▸**think through** vt riflettere a fondo su.

▸**think up** vt ideare.

thinking ['θɪŋkɪŋ] n: **to my (way of) ~** a mio parere.

think tank n gruppo di esperti.

thinly ['θɪnlɪ] adv (cut) a fette sottili; (spread) in uno strato sottile.

thinness ['θɪnnɪs] n sottigliezza; magrezza.

third [θɜːd] n terzo(a) ♦ n terzo/a; (fraction) terzo, terza parte f; (BRIT SCOL: degree) laurea col minimo dei voti.

third-degree burns ['θɜːdɪ'griː-] npl ustioni fpl di terzo grado.

thirdly ['θɜːdlɪ] adv in terzo luogo.

third party insurance n (BRIT)

assicurazione f contro terzi.

third-rate [θɜːd'reɪt] adj di qualità scadente.

Third World n: **the ~** il Terzo Mondo.

thirst [θɜːst] n sete f.

thirsty ['θɜːstɪ] adj (person) assetato(a), che ha sete; **to be ~** aver sete.

thirteen [θɜː'tiːn] num tredici.

thirtieth ['θɜːtɪɪθ] num trentesimo(a).

thirty ['θɜːtɪ] num trenta.

═══════════════════════════ *KEYWORD*

this [ðɪs] (pl **these**) adj (demonstrative) questo(a); **~ man/woman/book** quest'uomo/questa donna/questo libro; (not "that") quest'uomo/questa donna/ questo libro qui; **~ one** questo(a) qui; **~ time** questa volta; **~ time last year** l'anno scorso in questo periodo; **~ way** (in this direction) da questa parte; (in this fashion) così

♦ pron (demonstrative) questo(a); (not "that one") questo(a) qui; **who/what is ~?** chi è/che cos'è questo?; **I prefer ~ to that** preferisco questo a quello; **~ is where I live** io abito qui; **~ is what he said** questo è ciò che ha detto; **they were talking of ~ and that** stavano parlando del più e del meno; **~ is Mr Brown** (in introductions, photo) questo è il signor Brown; (on telephone) sono il signor Brown

♦ adv (demonstrative): **~ high/long** etc alto/lungo etc così; **it's about ~ high** è alto circa così; **I didn't know things were ~ bad** non sapevo andasse così male.

thistle ['θɪsl] n cardo.

thong [θɒŋ] n cinghia.

thorn [θɔːn] n spina.

thorny ['θɔːnɪ] adj spinoso(a).

thorough ['θʌrə] adj (person) preciso(a), accurato(a); (search) minuzioso(a); (knowledge, research) approfondito(a), profondo(a); (cleaning) a fondo.

thoroughbred ['θʌrəbrɛd] n (horse) purosangue m/f inv.

thoroughfare ['θʌrəfɛə*] n strada transitabile; **"no ~"** (BRIT) "divieto di transito".

thoroughgoing ['θʌrəgəuɪŋ] adj (analysis) approfondito(a); (reform) totale.

thoroughly ['θʌrəlɪ] adv accuratamente; minuziosamente; in profondità; a fondo; **he ~ agreed** fu completamente d'accordo.

thoroughness ['θʌrənɪs] n precisione f.

those [ðəuz] pl pron quelli(e) ♦ pl adj quei(quegli) mpl; quelle fpl.

though [ðəʊ] *conj* benché, sebbene ♦ *adv* comunque, tuttavia; **even** ~ anche se; **it's not so easy,** ~ tuttavia non è così facile.

thought [θɔːt] *pt, pp of* **think** ♦ *n* pensiero; (*opinion*) opinione *f*; (*intention*) intenzione *f*; **after much** ~ dopo molti ripensamenti; **I've just had a** ~ mi è appena venuta un'idea; **to give sth some** ~ prendere qc in considerazione, riflettere su qc.

thoughtful ['θɔːtful] *adj* pensieroso(a), pensoso(a); ponderato(a); (*considerate*) premuroso(a).

thoughtfully ['θɔːtfəlɪ] *adv* (*pensively*) con aria pensierosa.

thoughtless ['θɔːtlɪs] *adj* sconsiderato(a); (*behaviour*) scortese.

thoughtlessly ['θɔːtlɪslɪ] *adv* sconsideratamente; scortesemente.

thought-provoking ['θɔːtprəvəukɪŋ] *adj* stimolante.

thousand ['θauzənd] *num* mille; **one** ~ mille; ~**s of** migliaia di.

thousandth ['θauzəntθ] *num* millesimo(a).

thrash [θræʃ] *vt* picchiare; bastonare; (*defeat*) battere.

▶**thrash about** *vi* dibattersi.

▶**thrash out** *vt* dibattere, sviscerare.

thrashing ['θræʃɪŋ] *n*: **to give sb a** ~ = **to thrash sb**.

thread [θrɛd] *n* filo; (*of screw*) filetto ♦ *vt* (*needle*) infilare; **to** ~ **one's way between** infilarsi tra.

threadbare ['θrɛdbɛə*] *adj* consumato(a), logoro(a).

threat [θrɛt] *n* minaccia; **to be under** ~ **of** (*closure, extinction*) rischiare di; (*exposure*) essere minacciato(a) di.

threaten ['θrɛtn] *vi* (*storm*) minacciare ♦ *vt*: **to** ~ **sb with sth/to do** minacciare qn con qc/di fare.

threatening ['θrɛtnɪŋ] *adj* minaccioso(a).

three [θriː] *num* tre.

three-dimensional [θriːdaɪ'mɛnʃənl] *adj* tridimensionale.

three-piece ['θriːpiːs]: ~ **suit** *n* completo (con gilè); ~ **suite** *n* salotto comprendente un divano e due poltrone.

three-ply [θriː'plaɪ] *adj* (*wood*) a tre strati; (*wool*) a tre fili.

three-quarters [θriː'kwɔːtəz] *npl* tre quarti *mpl*; ~ **full** pieno per tre quarti.

three-wheeler [θriː'wiːlə*] *n* (*car*) veicolo a tre ruote.

thresh [θrɛʃ] *vt* (*AGR*) trebbiare.

threshing machine ['θrɛʃɪŋ-] *n* trebbiatrice *f*.

threshold ['θrɛʃhəʊld] *n* soglia; **to be on the** ~ **of** (*fig*) essere sulla soglia di.

threshold agreement *n* (*ECON*) ≈ scala mobile.

threw [θruː] *pt of* **throw**.

thrift [θrɪft] *n* parsimonia.

thrifty ['θrɪftɪ] *adj* economico(a), parsimonioso(a).

thrill [θrɪl] *n* brivido ♦ *vi* eccitarsi, tremare ♦ *vt* (*audience*) elettrizzare; **I was** ~**ed to get your letter** la tua lettera mi ha fatto veramente piacere.

thriller ['θrɪlə*] *n* film *m inv* (*or* dramma *m or* libro) del brivido.

thrilling ['θrɪlɪŋ] *adj* (*book, play etc*) pieno(a) di suspense; (*news, discovery*) entusiasmante.

thrive, *pt* **thrived, throve,** *pp* **thrived, thriven** [θraɪv, θrəʊv, 'θrɪvn] *vi* crescere *or* svilupparsi bene; (*business*) prosperare; **he** ~**s on it** gli fa bene, ne gode.

thriving ['θraɪvɪŋ] *adj* (*industry etc*) fiorente.

throat [θrəʊt] *n* gola; **to have a sore** ~ avere (un *or* il) mal di gola.

throb [θrɒb] *n* (*of heart*) battito; (*of engine*) vibrazione *f*; (*of pain*) fitta ♦ *vi* (*heart*) palpitare; (*engine*) vibrare; (*with pain*) pulsare; **my head is** ~**bing** mi martellano le tempie.

throes [θrəʊz] *npl*: **in the** ~ **of** alle prese con; in preda a; **in the** ~ **of death** in agonia.

thrombosis [θrɒm'bəʊsɪs] *n* trombosi *f*.

throne [θrəʊn] *n* trono.

throng [θrɒŋ] *n* moltitudine *f* ♦ *vt* affollare.

throttle ['θrɒtl] *n* (*AUT*) valvola a farfalla; (*on motorcycle*) (manopola del) gas ♦ *vt* strangolare.

through [θruː] *prep* attraverso; (*time*) per, durante; (*by means of*) per mezzo di; (*owing to*) a causa di ♦ *adj* (*ticket, train, passage*) diretto(a) ♦ *adv* attraverso; **(from) Monday** ~ **Friday** (*US*) da lunedì a venerdì; **I am halfway** ~ **the book** sono a metà libro; **to let sb** ~ lasciar passare qn; **to put sb** ~ **to sb** (*TEL*) passare qn a qn; **to be** ~ (*TEL*) ottenere la comunicazione; (*have finished*) avere finito; **"no** ~ **traffic"** (*US*) "divieto d'accesso"; **"no** ~ **road"** (*BRIT*) "strada senza sbocco".

throughout [θruː'aut] *prep* (*place*) dappertutto in; (*time*) per *or* durante tutto(a) ♦ *adv* dappertutto; sempre.

throughput ['θruːput] *n* (*of goods, materials*) materiale *m* in lavorazione; (*COMPUT*) volume *m* di dati immessi.

throve [θrəʊv] *pt of* **thrive**.

throw [θrəʊ] *n* tiro, getto; (*SPORT*) lancio ♦ *vt* (*pt* **threw,** *pp* **thrown** [θruː, θrəʊn]) tirare, gettare; (*SPORT*) lanciare; (*rider*) disarcionare; (*fig*) confondere; (*pottery*) formare al tornio; **to ~ a party** dare una festa; **to ~ open** (*doors, windows*) spalancare; (*house, gardens etc*) aprire al pubblico; (*competition, race*) aprire a tutti.

▶**throw about, throw around** *vt* (*litter etc*) spargere.

▶**throw away** *vt* gettare *or* buttare via.

▶**throw off** *vt* sbarazzarsi di.

▶**throw out** *vt* buttare fuori; (*reject*) respingere.

▶**throw together** *vt* (*clothes, meal etc*) mettere insieme; (*essay*) buttar giù.

▶**throw up** *vi* vomitare.

throwaway ['θrəuəwei] *adj* da buttare.

throwback ['θrəubæk] *n*: **it's a ~ to** (*fig*) ciò risale a.

throw-in ['θrəuin] *n* (*SPORT*) rimessa in gioco.

thrown [θrəun] *pp of* **throw**.

thru [θru:] *prep, adj, adv* (*US*) = **through**.

thrush [θrʌʃ] *n* (*ZOOL*) tordo; (*MED: esp in children*) mughetto; (: *BRIT: in women*) candida.

thrust [θrʌst] *n* (*TECH*) spinta ♦ *vt* (*pt, pp* **thrust**) spingere con forza; (*push in*) conficcare.

thrusting ['θrʌstɪŋ] *adj* (*troppo*) intraprendente.

thud [θʌd] *n* tonfo.

thug [θʌg] *n* delinquente *m*.

thumb [θʌm] *n* (*ANAT*) pollice *m* ♦ *vt* (*book*) sfogliare; **to ~ a lift** fare l'autostop; **to give sb/sth the ~s up/down** approvare/disapprovare qn/qc.

thumb index *n* indice *m* a rubrica.

thumbnail ['θʌmneil] *n* unghia del pollice.

thumbnail sketch *n* descrizione *f* breve.

thumbtack ['θʌmtæk] *n* (*US*) puntina da disegno.

thump [θʌmp] *n* colpo forte; (*sound*) tonfo ♦ *vi* battere su ♦ *vi* picchiare, battere.

thunder ['θʌndə*] *n* tuono ♦ *vi* tuonare; (*train etc*): **to ~ past** passare con un rombo.

thunderbolt ['θʌndəbəult] *n* fulmine *m*.

thunderclap ['θʌndəklæp] *n* rombo di tuono.

thunderous ['θʌndərəs] *adj* fragoroso(a).

thunderstorm ['θʌndəstɔ:m] *n* temporale *m*.

thunderstruck ['θʌndəstrʌk] *adj* (*fig*) sbigottito(a).

thundery ['θʌndəri] *adj* temporalesco(a).

Thur(s). *abbr* (= *Thursday*) gio.

Thursday ['θə:zdi] *n* giovedì *m inv; for phrases see also* **Tuesday**.

thus [ðʌs] *adv* così.

thwart [θwɔ:t] *vt* contrastare.

thyme [taim] *n* timo.

thyroid ['θairɔid] *n* tiroide *f*.

tiara [ti'ɑ:rə] *n* (*woman's*) diadema *m*.

Tiber ['taibə*] *n*: **the ~** il Tevere.

Tibet [ti'bet] *n* Tibet *m*.

Tibetan [ti'betən] *adj* tibetano(a) ♦ *n* (*person*) tibetano/a; (*LING*) tibetano.

tibia ['tibiə] *n* tibia.

tic [tik] *n* tic *m inv*.

tick [tik] *n* (*sound: of clock*) tic tac *m inv*; (*mark*) segno; spunta; (*ZOOL*) zecca; (*BRIT col*): **in a ~** in un attimo; (*BRIT col: credit*): **to buy sth on ~** comprare qc a credito ♦ *vi* fare tic tac ♦ *vt* spuntare; **to put a ~ against sth** fare un segno di fianco a qc.

▶**tick off** *vt* spuntare; (*person*) sgridare.

▶**tick over** *vi* (*BRIT: engine*) andare al minimo.

ticker tape ['tikə-] *n* nastro di telescrivente; (*US: in celebrations*) stelle *fpl* filanti.

ticket ['tikit] *n* biglietto; (*in shop: on goods*) etichetta; (: *from cash register*) scontrino; (*for library*) scheda; (*US POL*) lista dei candidati; **to get a (parking) ~** (*AUT*) prendere una multa (per sosta vietata).

ticket agency *n* (*THEAT*) agenzia di vendita di biglietti.

ticket collector *n* bigliettaio.

ticket holder *n* persona munita di biglietto.

ticket inspector *n* controllore *m*.

ticket office *n* biglietteria.

tickle ['tikl] *n* solletico ♦ *vt* fare il solletico a, solleticare; (*fig*) stuzzicare; piacere a; far ridere.

ticklish ['tikliʃ] *adj* che soffre il solletico; (*which tickles: blanket, cough*) che provoca prurito.

tidal ['taidl] *adj* di marea.

tidal wave *n* onda anomala.

tidbit ['tidbit] *n* (*US*) = **titbit**.

tiddlywinks ['tidliwiŋks] *n* gioco della pulce.

tide [taid] *n* marea; (*fig: of events*) corso ♦ *vt*: **will £20 ~ you over till Monday?** ti basteranno 20 sterline fino a lunedì?; **high/low ~** alta/bassa marea; **the ~ of public opinion** l'orientamento dell'opinione pubblica.

tidily ['taidili] *adv* in modo ordinato; **to arrange ~** sistemare; **to dress ~** vestirsi per benino.

tidiness ['taidinis] *n* ordine *m*.

tidy ['taidi] *adj* (*room*) ordinato(a), lindo(a); (*dress, work*) curato(a), in ordine; (*person*) ordinato(a); (*mind*) organizzato(a) ♦ *vt* (*also*: ~ **up**) riordinare, mettere in ordine; **to ~ o.s. up** rassettarsi.

tie [taɪ] *n* (*string etc*) legaccio; (*BRIT: also*: **neck~**) cravatta; (*fig: link*) legame *m*; (*SPORT: draw*) pareggio (: *match*) incontro; (*US RAIL*) traversina ♦ *vt* (*parcel*) legare; (*ribbon*) annodare ♦ *vi* (*SPORT*) pareggiare; "**black/white ~**" "**smoking/abito di rigore**"; **family ~s** legami familiari; **to ~ sth in a bow** annodare qc; **to ~ a knot in sth** fare un nodo a qc.

►**tie down** *vt* fissare con una corda; (*fig*): **to ~ sb down to** costringere qn ad accettare.

►**tie in** *vi*: **to ~ in (with)** (*correspond*) corrispondere (a).

►**tie on** *vt* (*BRIT: label etc*) attaccare.

►**tie up** *vt* (*parcel, dog*) legare; (*boat*) ormeggiare; (*arrangements*) concludere; **to be ~d up** (*busy*) essere occupato *or* preso.

tie-break(er) ['taɪbreɪk(ə*)] *n* (*TENNIS*) tie-break *m inv*; (*in quiz*) spareggio.

tie-on ['taɪɔn] *adj* (*BRIT: label*) volante.

tie-pin ['taɪpɪn] *n* (*BRIT*) fermacravatta *m inv*.

tier [tɪə*] *n* fila; (*of cake*) piano, strato.

Tierra del Fuego [tɪ'ɛrədel'fweɪgəu] *n* Terra del Fuoco.

tie tack *n* (*US*) fermacravatta *m inv*.

tiff [tɪf] *n* battibecco.

tiger ['taɪgə*] *n* tigre *f*.

tight [taɪt] *adj* (*rope*) teso(a), tirato(a); (*clothes*) stretto(a); (*budget, programme, bend*) stretto(a); (*control*) severo(a), fermo(a); (*col: drunk*) sbronzo(a) ♦ *adv* (*squeeze*) fortemente; (*shut*) ermeticamente; **to be packed ~** (*suitcase*) essere pieno zeppo; (*people*) essere pigiati; **everybody hold ~!** tenetevi stretti!; *see also* **tights**.

tighten ['taɪtn] *vt* (*rope*) tendere; (*screw*) stringere; (*control*) rinforzare ♦ *vi* tendersi; stringersi.

tight-fisted [taɪt'fɪstɪd] *adj* avaro(a).

tight-lipped ['taɪt'lɪpt] *adj*: **to be ~** essere reticente; (*angry*) tenere le labbra serrate.

tightly ['taɪtlɪ] *adv* (*grasp*) bene, saldamente.

tightrope ['taɪtrəup] *n* corda (da acrobata).

tightrope walker *n* funambolo/a.

tights [taɪts] *npl* (*BRIT*) collant *m inv*.

tigress ['taɪgrɪs] *n* tigre *f* (femmina).

tilde ['tɪldə] *n* tilde *f*.

tile [taɪl] *n* (*on roof*) tegola; (*on floor*) mattonella; (*on wall*) piastrella ♦ *vt* (*floor, bathroom etc*) piastrellare.

tiled [taɪld] *adj* rivestito(a) di tegole; a mattonelle; a piastrelle.

till [tɪl] *n* registratore *m* di cassa ♦ *vt* (*land*) coltivare ♦ *prep, conj* = **until**.

tiller ['tɪlə*] *n* (*NAUT*) barra del timone.

tilt [tɪlt] *vt* inclinare, far pendere ♦ *vi* inclinarsi, pendere ♦ *n* (*slope*) pendio; **to wear one's hat at a ~** portare il cappello sulle ventitré; **(at) full ~** a tutta velocità.

timber ['tɪmbə*] *n* (*material*) legname *m*; (*trees*) alberi *mpl* da legname.

time [taɪm] *n* tempo; (*epoch: often pl*) epoca, tempo; (*by clock*) ora; (*moment*) momento; (*occasion, also MATH*) volta; (*MUS*) tempo ♦ *vt* (*race*) cronometrare; (*programme*) calcolare la durata di; (*remark etc*): **to ~ sth well/badly** scegliere il momento più/meno opportuno per qc; **a long ~** molto tempo; **for the ~ being** per il momento; **from ~ to ~** ogni tanto; **~ after ~, ~ and again** mille volte; **in ~** (*soon enough*) in tempo; (*after some time*) col tempo; (*MUS*) a tempo; **at ~s** a volte; **to take one's ~** prenderla con calma; **in a week's ~** fra una settimana; **in no ~** in un attimo; **on ~** puntualmente; **to be 30 minutes behind/ ahead of ~** avere 30 minuti di ritardo/ anticipo; **5 ~s 5** 5 volte 5, 5 per 5; **what ~ is it?** che ora è?, che ore sono?; **what ~ do you make it?** che ora fa?; **to have a good ~** divertirsi; **they had a hard ~ of it** è stato duro per loro; **~'s up!** è (l')ora!; **to be behind the ~s** vivere nel passato; **I've no ~ for it** (*fig*) non ho tempo da perdere con cose del genere; **he'll do it in his own (good) ~** (*without being hurried*) lo farà quando avrà (un minuto di) tempo; **he'll do it in** *or* (*US*) **on his own ~** (*out of working hours*) lo farà nel suo tempo libero; **the bomb was ~d to explode 5 minutes later** la bomba era stata regolata in modo da esplodere 5 minuti più tardi.

time-and-motion study ['taɪmənd 'məuʃən-] *n* analisi *f inv* dei tempi e dei movimenti.

time bomb *n* bomba a orologeria.

time card *n* cartellino (da timbrare).

time clock *n* orologio *m* marcatempo *inv*.

time-consuming ['taɪmkənsjuːmɪŋ] *adj* che richiede molto tempo.

time difference *n* differenza di fuso orario.

time frame *n* tempi *mpl*.

time-honoured, (*US*) **time-honored** ['taɪmɔnəd] *adj* consacrato(a) dal tempo.

timekeeper ['taɪmkiːpə*] *n* (*SPORT*) cronometrista *m/f*.

time lag *n* intervallo, ritardo; (*in travel*) differenza di fuso orario.
timeless ['taɪmlɪs] *adj* eterno(a).
time limit *n* limite *m* di tempo.
timely ['taɪmlɪ] *adj* opportuno(a).
time off *n* tempo libero.
timer ['taɪmə*] *n* (*in kitchen*) contaminuti *m inv*; (*TECH*) timer *m inv*, temporizzatore *m*.
time-saving ['taɪmseɪvɪŋ] *adj* che fa risparmiare tempo.
time scale *n* tempi *mpl* d'esecuzione.
time-sharing ['taɪmʃɛərɪŋ] *n* (*COMPUT*) divisione *f* di tempo.
time sheet *n* = **time card**.
time signal *n* segnale *m* orario.
time switch *n* interruttore *m* a tempo.
timetable ['taɪmteɪbl] *n* orario; (*programme of events etc*) programma *m*.
time zone *n* fuso orario.
timid ['tɪmɪd] *adj* timido(a); (*easily scared*) pauroso(a).
timidity [tɪ'mɪdɪtɪ] *n* timidezza.
timing ['taɪmɪŋ] *n* sincronizzazione *f*; (*fig*) scelta del momento opportuno, tempismo; (*SPORT*) cronometraggio.
timing device *n* (*on bomb*) timer *m inv*.
timpani ['tɪmpənɪ] *npl* timpani *mpl*.
tin [tɪn] *n* stagno; (*also:* ~ **plate**) latta; (*BRIT: can*) barattolo (di latta), lattina, scatola; (*for baking*) teglia; **a** ~ **of paint** un barattolo di tinta *or* vernice.
tin foil *n* stagnola.
tinge [tɪndʒ] *n* sfumatura ♦ *vt*: ~**d with** tinto(a) di.
tingle ['tɪŋgl] *vi* (*cheeks, skin: from cold*) pungere, pizzicare; (: *from bad circulation*) formicolare.
tinker ['tɪŋkə*] *n* stagnino ambulante; (*gipsy*) zingaro/a.
▶**tinker with** *vt fus* armeggiare intorno a; cercare di riparare.
tinkle ['tɪŋkl] *vi* tintinnare ♦ *n* (*col*): **to give sb a** ~ dare un colpo di telefono a qn.
tin mine *n* miniera di stagno.
tinned [tɪnd] *adj* (*BRIT: food*) in scatola.
tinnitus [tɪ'naɪtəs] *n* (*MED*) ronzio auricolare.
tinny ['tɪnɪ] *adj* metallico(a).
tin-opener ['tɪnəupnə*] *n* (*BRIT*) apriscatole *m inv*.
tinsel ['tɪnsl] *n* decorazioni *fpl* natalizie (*argentate*).
tint [tɪnt] *n* tinta; (*for hair*) shampoo *m inv* colorante ♦ *vt* (*hair*) fare uno shampoo colorante a.
tinted ['tɪntɪd] *adj* (*hair*) tinto(a); (*spectacles, glass*) colorato(a).

tiny ['taɪnɪ] *adj* minuscolo(a).
tip [tɪp] *n* (*end*) punta; (*protective: on umbrella etc*) puntale *m*; (*gratuity*) mancia; (*for coal*) discarica; (*for rubbish*) immondezzaio; (*advice*) suggerimento ♦ *vt* (*waiter*) dare la mancia a; (*tilt*) inclinare; (*overturn: also:* ~ **over**) capovolgere; (*empty: also:* ~ **out**) scaricare; (*predict: winner*) pronosticare; (: *horse*) dare vincente; **he** ~**ped out the contents of the box** ha rovesciato il contenuto della scatola.
▶**tip off** *vt* fare una soffiata a.
tip-off ['tɪpɔf] *n* (*hint*) soffiata.
tipped ['tɪpt] *adj* (*BRIT: cigarette*) col filtro; **steel-**~ con la punta d'acciaio.
Tipp-Ex ® ['tɪpɛks] *n* (*BRIT*) liquido correttore.
tipple ['tɪpl] (*BRIT*) *vi* sbevazzare ♦ *n*: **to have a** ~ prendere un bicchierino.
tipster ['tɪpstə*] *n* (*RACING*) *chi vende informazioni sulle corse e altre manifestazioni oggetto di scommesse.*
tipsy ['tɪpsɪ] *adj* brillo(a).
tiptoe ['tɪptəu] *n*: **on** ~ in punta di piedi.
tiptop ['tɪptɔp] *adj*: **in** ~ **condition** in ottime condizioni.
tirade [taɪ'reɪd] *n* filippica.
tire ['taɪə*] *vt* stancare ♦ *vi* stancarsi ♦ *n* (*US*) = **tyre**.
▶**tire out** *vt* sfinire, spossare.
tired ['taɪəd] *adj* stanco(a); **to be/feel/look** ~ essere/sentirsi/sembrare stanco; **to be** ~ **of** essere stanco *or* stufo di.
tiredness ['taɪədnɪs] *n* stanchezza.
tireless ['taɪəlɪs] *adj* instancabile.
tiresome ['taɪəsəm] *adj* noioso(a).
tiring ['taɪərɪŋ] *adj* faticoso(a).
tissue ['tɪʃuː] *n* tessuto; (*paper handkerchief*) fazzolettino di carta.
tissue paper *n* carta velina.
tit [tɪt] *n* (*bird*) cinciallegra; (*col: breast*) tetta; **to give** ~ **for tat** rendere pan per focaccia.
titanium [tɪ'teɪnɪəm] *n* titanio.
titbit ['tɪtbɪt], (*US*) **tidbit** ['tɪdbɪt] *n* (*food*) leccornia; (*news*) notizia ghiotta.
titillate ['tɪtɪleɪt] *vt* titillare.
titivate ['tɪtɪveɪt] *vt* agghindare.
title ['taɪtl] *n* titolo; (*LAW: right*): ~ **(to)** diritto (a).
title deed *n* (*LAW*) titolo di proprietà.
title page *n* frontespizio.
title role *n* ruolo *or* parte *f* principale.
titter ['tɪtə*] *vi* ridere scioccamente.
tittle-tattle ['tɪtltætl] *n* chiacchiere *fpl*,

pettegolezzi *mpl.*

titular ['tɪtjulə*] *adj* (*in name only*)
nominale.

tizzy ['tɪzɪ] *n* (*col*): **to be in a** ~ essere in
agitazione.

T-junction ['tiː'dʒʌŋkʃən] *n* incrocio a T.

TM *n abbr* (= *transcendental meditation*) M.T.
f; (*COMM*) = **trademark**.

TN *abbr* (*US*) = *Tennessee*.

TNT *n abbr* (= *trinitrotoluene*) T.N.T.
m.

===================== *KEYWORD*

to [tuː, tə] *prep* **1** (*direction*) a; **to go** ~
France/London/school andare in
Francia/a Londra/a scuola; **to go** ~ **town**
andare in città; **to go** ~ **Paul's/the**
doctor's andare da Paul/dal dottore; **the**
road ~ **Edinburgh** la strada per
Edimburgo; ~ **the left/right** a sinistra/
destra
2 (*as far as*) (fino) a; **from here** ~ **London**
da qui a Londra; **to count** ~ **10** contare
fino a 10; **from 40** ~ **50 people** da 40 a 50
persone
3 (*with expressions of time*): **a quarter** ~ **5**
le 5 meno un quarto; **it's twenty** ~ **3** sono
le 3 meno venti
4 (*for, of*): **the key** ~ **the front door** la
chiave della porta d'ingresso; **a letter** ~
his wife una lettera per la moglie
5 (*expressing indirect object*) a; **to give sth**
~ **sb** dare qc a qn; **give it** ~ **me** dammelo;
to talk ~ **sb** parlare a qn; **it belongs** ~
him gli appartiene, è suo; **to be a danger**
~ **sb/sth** rappresentare un pericolo per
qn/qc
6 (*in relation to*) a; **3 goals** ~ **2** 3 goal a 2;
30 miles ~ **the gallon** ≈ 11 chilometri con
un litro; **4 apples** ~ **the kilo** 4 mele in un
chilo
7 (*purpose, result*): **to come** ~ **sb's aid**
venire in aiuto a qn; **to sentence sb** ~
death condannare a morte qn; ~ **my**
surprise con mia sorpresa
♦ *with vb* **1** (*simple infinitive*): ~ **go/eat** *etc*
andare/mangiare *etc*
2 (*following another vb*): **to want/try/start**
~ **do** volere/cercare di/cominciare a fare
3 (*with vb omitted*): **I don't want** ~ non
voglio (farlo); **you ought** ~ devi (farlo)
4 (*purpose, result*) per; **I did it** ~ **help you**
l'ho fatto per aiutarti
5 (*equivalent to relative clause*): **I have**
things ~ **do** ho da fare; **the main thing is**
~ **try** la cosa più importante è provare
6 (*after adjective etc*): **ready** ~ **go**
pronto(a) a partire; **too old/young** ~ …

troppo vecchio(a)/giovane per …
♦ *adv*: **to push the door** ~ accostare la
porta; **to go** ~ **and fro** andare e tornare.

toad [təud] *n* rospo.

toadstool ['təudstuːl] *n* fungo (velenoso).

toady ['təudɪ] *vi* adulare.

toast [təust] *n* (*CULIN*) toast *m*, pane *m*
abbrustolito; (*drink, speech*) brindisi *m inv*
♦ *vt* (*CULIN*) abbrustolire; (*drink to*)
brindare a; **a piece** *or* **slice of** ~ una fetta
di pane abbrustolito.

toaster ['təustə*] *n* tostapane *m inv.*

toastmaster ['təustmɑːstə*] *n* direttore *m*
dei brindisi.

toast rack *n* portatoast *m inv.*

tobacco [tə'bækəu] *n* tabacco; **pipe** ~
tabacco da pipa.

tobacconist [tə'bækənɪst] *n* tabaccaio/a;
~**'s (shop)** tabaccheria.

Tobago [tə'beɪgəu] *n see* **Trinidad and**
Tobago.

toboggan [tə'bɔgən] *n* toboga *m inv*; (*child's*)
slitta.

today [tə'deɪ] *adv, n* (*also fig*) oggi (*m inv*);
what day is it ~? che giorno è oggi?;
what date is it ~? quanti ne abbiamo
oggi?; ~ **is the 4th of March** (oggi) è il 4
di marzo; **the** ~ **paper** il giornale di oggi; **a**
fortnight ~ quindici giorni a oggi.

toddler ['tɔdlə*] *n* bambino/a che impara a
camminare.

toddy ['tɔdɪ] *n* grog *m inv.*

to-do [tə'duː] *n* (*fuss*) storie *fpl.*

toe [təu] *n* dito del piede; (*of shoe*) punta
♦ *vt*: **to** ~ **the line** (*fig*) stare in riga,
conformarsi; **big** ~ alluce *m*; **little** ~
mignolino.

TOEFL ['təufl] *n abbr* = *Test(ing) of English as*
a Foreign Language.

toehold ['təuhəuld] *n* punto d'appoggio.

toenail ['təuneɪl] *n* unghia del piede.

toffee ['tɔfɪ] *n* caramella.

toffee apple *n* (*BRIT*) mela caramellata.

tofu ['təufuː] *n* tofu *m* (*latte di soia non*
fermentato).

toga ['təugə] *n* toga.

together [tə'gɛðə*] *adv* insieme; (*at same*
time) allo stesso tempo; ~ **with** insieme a.

togetherness [tə'gɛðənɪs] *n* solidarietà;
intimità.

toggle switch ['tɔgl-] *n* (*COMPUT*) tasto
bistabile.

Togo ['təugəu] *n* Togo.

togs [tɔgz] *npl* (*col: clothes*) vestiti *mpl.*

toil [tɔɪl] *n* travaglio, fatica ♦ *vi* affannarsi;
sgobbare.

toilet ['tɔɪlət] *n* (*BRIT: lavatory*) gabinetto

♦ *cpd* (*soap etc*) da toletta; **to go to the ~** andare al gabinetto or al bagno.

toilet bag *n* (*BRIT*) nécessaire *m inv* da toilette.

toilet bowl *n* vaso *or* tazza del gabinetto.

toilet paper *n* carta igienica.

toiletries ['tɔɪlɪtrɪz] *npl* articoli *mpl* da toletta.

toilet roll *n* rotolo di carta igienica.

toilet water *n* acqua di colonia.

to-ing and fro-ing ['tuːɪŋən'frəʊɪŋ] *n* (*BRIT*) andirivieni *m inv.*

token ['təʊkən] *n* (*sign*) segno; (*voucher*) buono ♦ *cpd* (*fee, strike*) simbolico(a); **book/record ~** (*BRIT*) buono-libro/-disco; **by the same ~** (*fig*) per lo stesso motivo.

tokenism ['təʊkənɪzəm] *n* (*POL*) concessione *f* pro forma *inv.*

Tokyo ['təʊkjəʊ] *n* Tokyo *f.*

told [təʊld] *pt, pp of* **tell.**

tolerable ['tɔlərəbl] *adj* (*bearable*) tollerabile; (*fairly good*) passabile.

tolerably ['tɔlərəblɪ] *adv* (*good, comfortable*) abbastanza.

tolerance ['tɔlərns] *n* (*also TECH*) tolleranza.

tolerant ['tɔlərnt] *adj:* **~ (of)** tollerante (nei confronti di).

tolerate ['tɔləreɪt] *vt* sopportare; (*MED, TECH*) tollerare.

toleration [tɔlə'reɪʃən] *n* tolleranza.

toll [təʊl] *n* (*tax, charge*) pedaggio ♦ *vi* (*bell*) suonare; **the accident ~ on the roads** il numero delle vittime della strada.

tollbridge ['təʊlbrɪdʒ] *n* ponte *m* a pedaggio.

toll call *n* (*US TEL*) (telefonata) interurbana.

toll-free ['təʊl'friː] (*US*) *adj* senza addebito, gratuito(a) ♦ *adv* gratuitamente; **~ number** ≈ numero verde.

tomato, ~es [tə'mɑːtəʊ] *n* pomodoro.

tomb [tuːm] *n* tomba.

tombola [tɔm'bəʊlə] *n* tombola.

tomboy ['tɔmbɔɪ] *n* maschiaccio.

tombstone ['tuːmstəʊn] *n* pietra tombale.

tomcat ['tɔmkæt] *n* gatto.

tomorrow [tə'mɔrəʊ] *adv, n* (*also fig*) domani (*m inv*); **the day after ~** dopodomani; **a week ~** domani a otto; **~ morning** domani mattina.

ton [tʌn] *n* tonnellata (*BRIT:* = 1016 kg; 20 cwt; *US* = 907 kg; *metric* = 1000 kg); (*NAUT: also:* **register ~**) tonnellata di stazza (= 2.83 cu.m; 100 cu.ft); **~s of** (*col*) un mucchio *or* sacco di.

tonal ['təʊnl] *adj* tonale.

tone [təʊn] *n* tono; (*of musical instrument*) timbro ♦ *vi* intonarsi.

▶**tone down** *vt* (*colour, criticism, sound*) attenuare.

▶**tone up** *vt* (*muscles*) tonificare.

tone-deaf [təʊn'dɛf] *adj* che non ha orecchio (musicale).

toner ['təʊnə*] *n* (*for photocopier*) colorante *m* organico, toner *m.*

Tonga ['tɔŋgə] *n* isole *fpl* Tonga.

tongs [tɔŋz] *npl* tenaglie *fpl;* (*for coal*) molle *fpl;* (*for hair*) arricciacapelli *m inv.*

tongue [tʌŋ] *n* lingua; **~ in cheek** (*fig*) ironicamente.

tongue-tied ['tʌŋtaɪd] *adj* (*fig*) muto(a).

tongue-twister ['tʌŋtwɪstə*] *n* scioglilingua *m inv.*

tonic ['tɔnɪk] *n* (*MED*) ricostituente *m;* (*skin* ~) tonico; (*MUS*) nota tonica; (*also:* ~ **water**) acqua tonica.

tonight [tə'naɪt] *adv* stanotte; (*this evening*) stasera ♦ *n* questa notte; questa sera; **I'll see you ~** ci vediamo stasera.

tonnage ['tʌnɪdʒ] *n* (*NAUT*) tonnellaggio, stazza.

tonne [tʌn] *n* (*BRIT: metric ton*) tonnellata.

tonsil ['tɔnsl] *n* tonsilla; **to have one's ~s out** farsi operare di tonsille.

tonsillitis [tɔnsɪ'laɪtɪs] *n* tonsillite *f;* **to have ~** avere la tonsillite.

too [tuː] *adv* (*excessively*) troppo; (*also*) anche; **it's ~ sweet** è troppo dolce; **I went ~ much** ci sono andato anch'io; **~ much** *adv* troppo ♦ *adj* troppo(a); **~ many** *adj* troppi(e); **~ bad!** tanto peggio!; peggio così!

took [tʊk] *pt of* **take.**

tool [tuːl] *n* utensile *m*, attrezzo; (*fig: person*) strumento ♦ *vt* lavorare con un attrezzo.

tool box *n* cassetta *f* portautensili *inv.*

tool kit *n* cassetta di attrezzi.

toot [tuːt] *vi* suonare; (*with car horn*) suonare il clacson.

tooth [tuːθ], *pl* **teeth** [tuːθ, tiːθ] *n* (*ANAT, TECH*) dente *m;* **to clean one's teeth** lavarsi i denti; **to have a ~ out** *or* (*US*) **pulled** farsi togliere un dente; **by the skin of one's teeth** per il rotto della cuffia.

toothache ['tuːθeɪk] *n* mal *m* di denti; **to have ~** avere il mal di denti.

tooth fairy *n fatina che porta soldini in regalo a un bimbo quando perde un dentino di latte,* ≈ topolino.

toothpaste ['tuːθpeɪst] *n* dentifricio.

toothpick ['tuːθpɪk] *n* stuzzicadenti *m inv.*

tooth powder *n* dentifricio in polvere.

top [tɔp] *n* (*of mountain, page, ladder*) cima; (*of box, cupboard, table*) sopra *m inv*, parte *f* superiore; (*lid: of box, jar*) coperchio; (: *of* *bottle)* tappo; *(toy)* trottola; *(DRESS: blouse etc)* camicia *(or* maglietta *etc)*; *(of pyjamas)* giacca ♦ *adj* più alto(a); *(in rank)* primo(a); *(best)* migliore ♦ *vt (exceed)* superare; *(be first in)* essere in testa a; **on ~ of** sopra, in cima a; *(in addition to)* oltre a; **from ~ to toe** *(BRIT)* dalla testa ai piedi; **at the ~ of the stairs/page/street** in cima alle scale/alla pagina/alla strada; **the ~ of the milk** *(BRIT)* la panna; **at ~ speed** a tutta velocità; **at the ~ of one's voice** *(fig)* a squarciagola; **over the ~** *(col: behaviour etc)* eccessivo(a); **to go over the ~** esagerare.

▶**top up,** *(US)* **top off** *vt* riempire.

topaz ['təupæz] *n* topazio.

top-class ['tɔp'klɑːs] *adj* di prim'ordine.

topcoat ['tɔpkəut] *n* soprabito.

topflight ['tɔpflaɪt] *adj* di primaria importanza.

top floor *n* ultimo piano.

top hat *n* cilindro.

top-heavy [tɔp'hɛvɪ] *adj (object)* con la parte superiore troppo pesante.

topic ['tɔpɪk] *n* argomento.

topical ['tɔpɪkəl] *adj* d'attualità.

topless ['tɔplɪs] *adj (bather etc)* col seno scoperto; **~ swimsuit** topless *m inv.*

top-level ['tɔplɛvl] *adj (talks)* ad alto livello.

topmost ['tɔpməust] *adj* il(la) più alto(a).

top-notch ['tɔp'nɔtʃ] *adj (col: player, performer)* di razza; (: *school, car)* eccellente.

topography [tə'pɔgrəfɪ] *n* topografia.

topping ['tɔpɪŋ] *n (CULIN)* guarnizione *f.*

topple ['tɔpl] *vt* rovesciare, far cadere ♦ *vi* cadere; traballare.

top-ranking ['tɔp'ræŋkɪŋ] *adj* di massimo grado.

top-secret ['tɔp'siːkrɪt] *adj* segretissimo(a).

top-security ['tɔpsɪ'kjuərɪtɪ] *adj (BRIT)* di massima sicurezza.

topsy-turvy ['tɔpsɪ'təːvɪ] *adj, adv* sottosopra *(inv).*

top-up ['tɔpʌp] *n:* **would you like a ~?** vuole che le riempia il bicchiere *(or* la tazza *etc)?*

top-up loan *n (BRIT)* prestito integrativo.

torch [tɔːtʃ] *n* torcia; *(BRIT: electric)* lampadina tascabile.

tore [tɔː*] *pt of* tear.

torment *n* ['tɔːmɛnt] tormento ♦ *vt* [tɔː'mɛnt] tormentare; *(fig: annoy)* infastidire.

torn [tɔːn] *pp of* tear ♦ *adj:* **~ between** *(fig)* combattuto(a) tra.

tornado, ~es [tɔː'neɪdəu] *n* tornado.

torpedo, ~es [tɔː'piːdəu] *n* siluro.

torpedo boat *n* motosilurante *f.*

torpor ['tɔːpə*] *n* torpore *m.*

torrent ['tɔrnt] *n* torrente *m.*

torrential [tɔ'rɛnʃl] *adj* torrenziale.

torrid ['tɔrɪd] *adj* torrido(a); *(fig)* denso(a) di passione.

torso ['tɔːsəu] *n* torso.

tortoise ['tɔːtəs] *n* tartaruga.

tortoiseshell ['tɔːtəʃɛl] *adj* di tartaruga.

tortuous ['tɔːtjuəs] *adj* tortuoso(a).

torture ['tɔːtʃə*] *n* tortura ♦ *vt* torturare.

torturer ['tɔːtʃərə*] *n* torturatore/trice.

Tory ['tɔːrɪ] *adj* tory *inv,* conservatore(trice) ♦ *n* tory *m/f inv,* conservatore/trice.

toss [tɔs] *vt* gettare, lanciare; *(BRIT: pancake)* far saltare; *(head)* scuotere ♦ *n (movement: of head etc)* movimento brusco; *(of coin)* lancio; **to win/lose the ~** vincere/perdere a testa o croce; *(SPORT)* vincere/perdere il sorteggio; **to ~ a coin** fare a testa o croce; **to ~ up for sth** fare a testa o croce per qc; **to ~ and turn** *(in bed)* girarsi e rigirarsi.

tot [tɔt] *n (BRIT: drink)* bicchierino; *(child)* bimbo/a.

▶**tot up** *vt (BRIT: figures)* sommare.

total ['təutl] *adj* totale ♦ *n* totale *m* ♦ *vt (add up)* sommare; *(amount to)* ammontare a; **in ~** in tutto.

totalitarian [təutælɪ'tɛərɪən] *adj* totalitario(a).

totality [təu'tælɪtɪ] *n* totalità.

totally ['təutəlɪ] *adv* completamente.

tote bag ['təut-] *n* sporta.

totem pole ['təutəm-] *n* totem *m inv.*

totter ['tɔtə*] *vi* barcollare; *(object, government)* vacillare.

touch [tʌtʃ] *n* tocco; *(sense)* tatto; *(contact)* contatto; *(FOOTBALL)* fuori gioco *m* ♦ *vt* toccare; **a ~ of** *(fig)* un tocco di; un pizzico di; **to get in ~ with** mettersi in contatto con; **to lose ~** *(friends)* perdersi di vista; **I'll be in ~** mi farò sentire; **to be out of ~ with events** essere tagliato fuori; **the personal ~** una nota personale; **to put the finishing ~es to sth** dare gli ultimi ritocchi a qc.

▶**touch on** *vt fus (topic)* sfiorare, accennare a.

▶**touch up** *vt (improve)* ritoccare.

touch-and-go ['tʌtʃən'gəu] *adj* incerto(a); **it was ~ with the sick man** il malato era tra la vita e la morte.

touchdown ['tʌtʃdaun] *n* atterraggio; *(on sea)* ammaraggio; *(US FOOTBALL)* meta.

touched [tʌtʃt] *adj* commosso(a); *(col)* tocco(a), toccato(a).

touching ['tʌtʃɪŋ] *adj* commovente.
touchline ['tʌtʃlaɪn] *n* (SPORT) linea laterale.
touch-screen ['tʌtʃskriːn] *n* (COMPUT) touch-screen *m inv*, schermo sensibile.
touch-sensitive ['tʌtʃ'sɛnsɪtɪv] *adj* sensibile al tatto.
touch-type ['tʌtʃtaɪp] *vi* dattilografare (senza guardare i tasti).
touchy ['tʌtʃɪ] *adj* (*person*) suscettibile.
tough [tʌf] *adj* duro(a); (*resistant*) resistente; (*meat*) duro(a), tiglioso(a); (*journey*) faticoso(a), duro(a); (*person: rough*) violento(a), brutale ♦ *n* (*gangster etc*) delinquente *m/f*; **~ luck!** che sfortuna!
toughen ['tʌfn] *vt* indurire, rendere più resistente.
toughness ['tʌfnɪs] *n* durezza; resistenza.
toupee ['tuːpeɪ] *n* parrucchino.
tour [tuə*] *n* viaggio; (*also*: **package ~**) viaggio organizzato; (*of town, museum*) visita; (*by artist*) tournée *f inv* ♦ *vt* visitare; **to go on a ~ of** (*region, country*) fare il giro di; (*museum, castle*) visitare; **to go on ~** andare in tournée.
tour guide *n* accompagnatore/trice turistico(a).
touring ['tuərɪŋ] *n* turismo.
tourism ['tuərɪzəm] *n* turismo.
tourist ['tuərɪst] *n* turista *m/f* ♦ *adv* (*travel*) in classe turistica ♦ *cpd* turistico(a); **the ~ trade** il turismo.
tourist class *n* (AVIAT) classe *f* turistica.
tourist office *n* pro loco *f inv*.
tournament ['tuənəmənt] *n* torneo.
tourniquet ['tuənɪkeɪ] *n* (MED) laccio emostatico, pinza emostatica.
tour operator *n* (BRIT) operatore *m* turistico.
tousled ['tauzld] *adj* (*hair*) arruffato(a).
tout [taut] *vi*: **to ~ for** procacciare, raccogliere; cercare clienti per ♦ *n* (BRIT: *also*: **ticket ~**) bagarino; **to ~ sth (around)** (BRIT) cercare di (ri)vendere qc.
tow [təu] *vt* rimorchiare ♦ *n* rimorchio; "**on ~**", (US) "**in ~**" (AUT) "veicolo rimorchiato"; **to give sb a ~** rimorchiare qn.
toward(s) [tə'wɔːd(z)] *prep* verso; (*of attitude*) nei confronti di; (*of purpose*) per; **~ noon/the end of the year** verso mezzogiorno/la fine dell'anno; **to feel friendly ~ sb** provare un sentimento d'amicizia per qn.
towel ['tauəl] *n* asciugamano; (*also*: **tea ~**) strofinaccio; **to throw in the ~** (*fig*) gettare la spugna.
towelling ['tauəlɪŋ] *n* (*fabric*) spugna.
towel rail, (US) **towel rack** *n*

portasciugamano.
tower ['tauə*] *n* torre *f* ♦ *vi* (*building, mountain*) innalzarsi; **to ~ above** *or* **over sb/sth** sovrastare qn/qc.
tower block *n* (BRIT) palazzone *m*.
towering ['tauərɪŋ] *adj* altissimo(a), imponente.
towline ['təulaɪn] *n* (cavo da) rimorchio.
town [taun] *n* città *f inv*; **to go to ~** andare in città; (*fig*) mettercela tutta; **in (the) ~** in città; **to be out of ~** essere fuori città.
town centre *n* centro (città).
town clerk *n* segretario comunale.
town council *n* consiglio comunale.
town crier [-'kraɪə*] *n* (BRIT) banditore/trice.
town hall *n* ≈ municipio.
townie ['taunɪ] *n* (BRIT *col*) uno/a di città.
town plan *n* pianta della città.
town planner *n* urbanista *m/f*.
town planning *n* urbanistica.
township ['taunʃɪp] *n* township *f inv*.
townspeople ['taunzpiːpl] *npl* cittadinanza, cittadini *mpl*.
towpath ['təupɑːθ] *n* alzaia.
towrope ['təurəup] *n* (cavo da) rimorchio.
tow truck *n* (US) carro *m* attrezzi *inv*.
toxic ['tɔksɪk] *adj* tossico(a).
toxin ['tɔksɪn] *n* tossina.
toy [tɔɪ] *n* giocattolo.
▶**toy with** *vt fus* giocare con; (*idea*) accarezzare, trastullarsi con.
toyshop ['tɔɪʃɔp] *n* negozio di giocattoli.
trace [treɪs] *n* traccia ♦ *vt* (*draw*) tracciare; (*follow*) seguire; (*locate*) rintracciare; **without ~** (*disappear*) senza lasciare traccia; **there was no ~ of it** non ne restava traccia.
trace element *n* oligoelemento.
trachea [trə'kɪə] *n* (ANAT) trachea.
tracing paper ['treɪsɪŋ-] *n* carta da ricalco.
track [træk] *n* (*mark: of person, animal*) traccia; (*on tape, SPORT; path: gen*) pista; (: *of bullet etc*) traiettoria; (: *of suspect, animal*) pista, tracce *fpl*; (RAIL) binario, rotaie *fpl*; (COMPUT) traccia, pista ♦ *vt* seguire le tracce di; **to keep ~ of** seguire; **to be on the right ~** (*fig*) essere sulla buona strada.
▶**track down** *vt* (*prey*) scovare; snidare; (*sth lost*) rintracciare.
tracker dog ['trækə-] *n* (BRIT) cane *m* poliziotto *inv*.
track events *npl* (SPORT) prove *fpl* su pista.
tracking station ['trækɪŋ-] *n* (SPACE) osservatorio spaziale.
track meet *n* (US) meeting *m inv* di atletica.
track record *n*: **to have a good ~** (*fig*)

avere un buon curriculum.

tracksuit ['træksuːt] *n* tuta sportiva.

tract [trækt] *n* (*GEO*) tratto, estensione *f*; (*pamphlet*) opuscolo, libretto; **respiratory** ~ (*ANAT*) apparato respiratorio.

traction ['trækʃən] *n* trazione *f*.

tractor ['træktə*] *n* trattore *m*.

trade [treɪd] *n* commercio; (*skill, job*) mestiere *m*; (*industry*) industria, settore *m* ♦ *vi* commerciare; **to** ~ **with/in** commerciare con/in; **foreign** ~ commercio estero; **Department of T~ and Industry** (**DTI**) (*BRIT*) ≈ Ministero del Commercio.

▶**trade in** *vt* (*old car etc*) dare come pagamento parziale.

trade barrier *n* barriera commerciale.

trade deficit *n* bilancio commerciale in deficit.

Trade Descriptions Act *n* (*BRIT*) legge *f* a tutela del consumatore.

trade discount *n* sconto sul listino.

trade fair *n* fiera campionaria.

trade-in ['treɪdɪn] *n*: **to take as a** ~ accettare in permuta.

trade-in price *n* prezzo di permuta.

trademark ['treɪdmɑːk] *n* marchio di fabbrica.

trade mission *n* missione *f* commerciale.

trade name *n* marca, nome *m* depositato.

trade-off ['treɪdɔf] *n* compromesso, accomodamento.

trader ['treɪdə*] *n* commerciante *m/f*.

trade secret *n* segreto di fabbricazione.

tradesman ['treɪdzmən] *n* fornitore *m*; (*shopkeeper*) negoziante *m*.

trade union *n* sindacato.

trade unionist [-'juːnjənɪst] *n* sindacalista *m/f*.

trade wind *n* aliseo.

trading ['treɪdɪŋ] *n* commercio.

trading estate *n* (*BRIT*) zona industriale.

trading stamp *n* bollo premio.

tradition [trə'dɪʃən] *n* tradizione *f*; ~**s** *npl* tradizioni, usanze *fpl*.

traditional [trə'dɪʃənl] *adj* tradizionale.

traffic ['træfɪk] *n* traffico ♦ *vi*: **to** ~ **in** (*pej: liquor, drugs*) trafficare in.

traffic calming [-'kɑːmɪŋ] *n* uso di accorgimenti per rallentare il traffico in zone abitate.

traffic circle *n* (*US*) isola rotatoria.

traffic island *n* salvagente *m*, isola *f* spartitraffico *inv*.

traffic jam *n* ingorgo (del traffico).

trafficker ['træfɪkə*] *n* trafficante *m/f*.

traffic lights *npl* semaforo.

traffic offence *n* (*BRIT*) infrazione *f* al codice stradale.

traffic sign *n* cartello stradale.

traffic violation *n* (*US*) = **traffic offence**.

traffic warden *n* addetto/a al controllo del traffico e del parcheggio.

tragedy ['trædʒədɪ] *n* tragedia.

tragic ['trædʒɪk] *adj* tragico(a).

trail [treɪl] *n* (*tracks*) tracce *fpl*, pista; (*path*) sentiero; (*of smoke etc*) scia ♦ *vt* trascinare, strascicare; (*follow*) seguire ♦ *vi* essere al traino; (*dress etc*) strusciare; (*plant*) arrampicarsi; strisciare; **to be on sb's** ~ essere sulle orme di qn.

▶**trail away, trail off** *vi* (*sound*) affievolirsi; (*interest, voice*) spegnersi a poco a poco.

▶**trail behind** *vi* essere al traino.

trailer ['treɪlə*] *n* (*AUT*) rimorchio; (*US*) roulotte *f inv*; (*CINE*) prossimamente *m inv*.

trailer truck *n* (*US*) autoarticolato.

train [treɪn] *n* treno; (*of dress*) coda, strascico; (*BRIT: series*): ~ **of events** serie *f* di avvenimenti a catena ♦ *vt* (*apprentice, doctor etc*) formare; (*sportsman*) allenare; (*dog*) addestrare; (*memory*) esercitare; (*point: gun etc*): **to** ~ **sth on** puntare qc contro ♦ *vi* formarsi; allenarsi; (*learn a skill*) fare pratica, fare tirocinio; **to go by** ~ andare in *or* col treno; **one's** ~ **of thought** il filo dei propri pensieri; **to** ~ **sb to do sth** preparare qn a fare qc.

train attendant *n* (*US*) addetto/a ai vagoni letto.

trained [treɪnd] *adj* qualificato(a); allenato(a); addestrato(a).

trainee [treɪ'niː] *n* allievo/a; (*in trade*) apprendista *m/f*; **he's a** ~ **teacher** sta facendo tirocinio come insegnante.

trainer ['treɪnə*] *n* (*SPORT*) allenatore/trice; (*of dogs etc*) addestratore/trice; ~**s** *npl* (*shoes*) scarpe *fpl* da ginnastica.

training ['treɪnɪŋ] *n* formazione *f*; allenamento; addestramento; **in** ~ (*SPORT*) in allenamento; (*fit*) in forma.

training college *n* istituto professionale.

training course *n* corso di formazione professionale.

traipse [treɪps] *vi*: **to** ~ **in/out** *etc* entrare/ uscire *etc* trascinandosi.

trait [treɪt] *n* tratto.

traitor ['treɪtə*] *n* traditore/trice.

trajectory [trə'dʒɛktərɪ] *n* traiettoria.

tram [træm] *n* (*BRIT: also*: ~**car**) tram *m inv*.

tramline ['træmlaɪn] *n* linea tranviaria.

tramp [træmp] *n* (*person*) vagabondo/a; (*col: pej: woman*) sgualdrina ♦ *vi* camminare con passo pesante ♦ *vt* (*walk through: town, streets*) percorrere a piedi.

trample ['træmpl] *vt*: **to ~ (underfoot)**
calpestare.

trampoline ['træmpəli:n] *n* trampolino.

trance [trɑːns] *n* trance *f inv*; (*MED*) catalessi
f inv; **to go into a ~** cadere in trance.

tranquil ['træŋkwɪl] *adj* tranquillo(a).

tranquillity, (*US*) **tranquility** [træŋ'kwɪlɪtɪ]
n tranquillità.

tranquillizer, (*US*) **tranquilizer**
['træŋkwɪlaɪzə*] *n* (*MED*) tranquillante *m*.

transact [træn'zækt] *vt* (*business*) trattare.

transaction [træn'zækʃən] *n* transazione *f*;
~s *npl* (*minutes*) atti *mpl*; **cash ~**
operazione *f* in contanti.

transatlantic ['trænzət'læntɪk] *adj*
transatlantico(a).

transcend [træn'sɛnd] *vt* trascendere;
(*excel over*) superare.

transcendental [trænsɛn'dɛntl] *adj*: **~**
meditation meditazione *f* trascendentale.

transcribe [træn'skraɪb] *vt* trascrivere.

transcript ['trænskrɪpt] *n* trascrizione *f*.

transcription [træn'skrɪpʃən] *n* trascrizione
f.

transept ['trænsɛpt] *n* transetto.

transfer *n* ['trænsfə*] (*gen, also SPORT*)
trasferimento; (*POL: of power*) passaggio;
(*picture, design*) decalcomania; (: *stick-on*)
autoadesivo ♦ *vt* [træns'fə:*] trasferire;
passare; decalcare; **by bank ~** tramite
trasferimento bancario; **to ~ the charges**
(*BRIT TEL*) telefonare con addebito al
ricevente.

transferable [træns'fə:rəbl] *adj* trasferibile;
not ~ non cedibile, personale.

transfix [træns'fɪks] *vt* trafiggere; (*fig*): **~ed**
with fear paralizzato dalla paura.

transform [træns'fɔ:m] *vt* trasformare.

transformation [trænsfə'meɪʃən] *n*
trasformazione *f*.

transformer [træns'fɔ:mə*] *n* (*ELEC*)
trasformatore *m*.

transfusion [træns'fju:ʒən] *n* trasfusione *f*.

transgress [træns'grɛs] *vt* (*go beyond*)
infrangere; (*violate*) trasgredire,
infrangere.

tranship [træn'ʃɪp] *vt* trasbordare.

transient ['trænzɪənt] *adj* transitorio(a),
fugace.

transistor [træn'zɪstə*] *n* (*ELEC*) transistor
m inv; (*also*: **~ radio**) radio *f inv* a
transistor.

transit ['trænzɪt] *n*: **in ~** in transito.

transit camp *n* campo (di raccolta)
profughi.

transition [træn'zɪʃən] *n* passaggio,
transizione *f*.

transitional [træn'zɪʃənl] *adj* di transizione.

transitive ['trænzɪtɪv] *adj* (*LING*)
transitivo(a).

transit lounge *n* (*AVIAT*) sala di transito.

transitory ['trænzɪtərɪ] *adj* transitorio(a).

translate [trænz'leɪt] *vt* tradurre; **to ~**
(from/into) tradurre (da/in).

translation [trænz'leɪʃən] *n* traduzione *f*;
(*SCOL: as opposed to prose*) versione *f*.

translator [trænz'leɪtə*] *n* traduttore/trice.

translucent [trænz'lu:snt] *adj* traslucido(a).

transmission [trænz'mɪʃən] *n* trasmissione
f.

transmit [trænz'mɪt] *vt* trasmettere.

transmitter [trænz'mɪtə*] *n* trasmettitore
m.

transparency [træns'pɛərnsɪ] *n* (*PHOT*)
diapositiva.

transparent [træns'pærnt] *adj* trasparente.

transpire [træns'paɪə*] *vi* (*happen*)
succedere; **it finally ~d that** ... alla fine si
è venuto a sapere che ....

transplant *vt* [træns'plɑ:nt] trapiantare ♦ *n*
['trænsplɑ:nt] trapianto; **to have a heart ~**
subire un trapianto cardiaco.

transport *n* ['trænspɔ:t] trasporto ♦ *vt*
[træns'pɔ:t] trasportare; **public ~** mezzi
mpl pubblici; **Department of T~**(*BRIT*)
Ministero dei Trasporti.

transportation ['trænspɔ:'teɪʃən] *n* (*mezzo*
di) trasporto; (*of prisoners*) deportazione
f; **Department of T~** (*US*) Ministero dei
Trasporti.

transport café *n* (*BRIT*) trattoria per
camionisti.

transpose [træns'pəuz] *vt* trasporre.

transsexual [trænz'sɛksjuəl] *adj, n*
transessuale (*m/f*).

transverse ['trænzvɔ:s] *adj* trasversale.

transvestite [trænz'vɛstaɪt] *n* travestito/a.

trap [træp] *n* (*snare, trick*) trappola;
(*carriage*) calesse *m* ♦ *vt* prendere in
trappola, intrappolare; (*immobilize*)
bloccare; (*jam*) chiudere, schiacciare; **to**
set *or* **lay a ~ (for sb)** tendere una
trappola (a qn); **to ~ one's finger in the**
door chiudersi il dito nella porta; **shut**
your ~! (*col*) chiudi quella boccaccia!

trap door *n* botola.

trapeze [trə'pi:z] *n* trapezio.

trapper ['træpə*] *n* cacciatore *m* di animali
da pelliccia.

trappings ['træpɪŋz] *npl* ornamenti *mpl*;
indoratura, sfarzo.

trash [træʃ] *n* (*pej: goods*) ciarpame *m*;
(: *nonsense*) sciocchezze *fpl*; (*US: rubbish*)
rifiuti *mpl*, spazzatura.

trash can *n* (*US*) secchio della spazzatura.

trashy ['træʃɪ] *adj* (*col*) scadente.

trauma ['trɔːmə] *n* trauma *m*.

traumatic [trɔːˈmætɪk] *adj* (*PSYCH, fig*) traumatico(a), traumatizzante.

travel ['trævl] *n* viaggio; viaggi *mpl* ♦ *vi* viaggiare; (*move*) andare, spostarsi ♦ *vt* (*distance*) percorrere; **this wine doesn't ~ well** questo vino non resiste agli spostamenti.

travel agency *n* agenzia (di) viaggi.

travel agent *n* agente *m* di viaggio.

travel brochure *n* dépliant *m* di viaggi.

traveller, (*US*) **traveler** ['trævlə*] *n* viaggiatore/trice; (*COMM*) commesso viaggiatore.

traveller's cheque, (*US*) **traveler's check** *n* assegno turistico.

travelling, (*US*) **traveling** ['trævlɪŋ] *n* viaggi *mpl* ♦ *adj* (*circus, exhibition*) itinerante ♦ *cpd* (*bag, clock*) da viaggio; (*expenses*) di viaggio.

travel(l)ing salesman *n* commesso viaggiatore.

travelogue ['trævəlɔg] *n* (*book, film*) diario *or* documentario di viaggio; (*talk*) conferenza sui viaggi.

travel sickness *n* mal *m* d'auto (*or* di mare *or* d'aria).

traverse ['trævəs] *vt* traversare, attraversare.

travesty ['trævəstɪ] *n* parodia.

trawler ['trɔːlə*] *n* peschereccio (a strascico).

tray [treɪ] *n* (*for carrying*) vassoio; (*on desk*) vaschetta.

treacherous ['trɛtʃərəs] *adj* traditore(trice); **road conditions today are ~** oggi il fondo stradale è pericoloso.

treachery ['trɛtʃərɪ] *n* tradimento.

treacle ['triːkl] *n* melassa.

tread [trɛd] *n* passo; (*sound*) rumore *m* di passi; (*of tyre*) battistrada *m inv* ♦ *vi* (*pt* **trod,** *pp* **trodden** [trɔd, 'trɔdn]) camminare.

►**tread on** *vt fus* calpestare.

treadle ['trɛdl] *n* pedale *m*.

treas. *abbr* = **treasurer**.

treason ['triːzn] *n* tradimento.

treasure ['trɛʒə*] *n* tesoro ♦ *vt* (*value*) tenere in gran conto, apprezzare molto; (*store*) custodire gelosamente.

treasure hunt *n* caccia al tesoro.

treasurer ['trɛʒərə*] *n* tesoriere/a.

treasury ['trɛʒərɪ] *n* tesoreria; (*POL*): **the T~,** (*US*) **the T~ Department** ≈ il Ministero del Tesoro.

treasury bill *n* buono del tesoro.

treat [triːt] *n* regalo ♦ *vt* trattare; (*MED*) curare; (*consider*) considerare; **it was a ~ mi** (*or* ci *etc*) ha fatto veramente piacere;

to ~ sb to sth offrire qc a qn; **to ~ sth as a joke** considerare qc uno scherzo.

treatise ['triːtɪz] *n* trattato.

treatment ['triːtmənt] *n* trattamento; **to have ~ for sth** (*MED*) farsi curare qc.

treaty ['triːtɪ] *n* patto, trattato.

treble [trɛbl] *adj* triplo(a), triplice ♦ *n* (*MUS*) soprano *m/f* ♦ *vt* triplicare ♦ *vi* triplicarsi.

treble clef *n* chiave *f* di violino.

tree [triː] *n* albero.

tree-lined ['triːlaɪnd] *adj* fiancheggiato(a) da alberi.

treetop ['triːtɔp] *n* cima di un albero.

tree trunk *n* tronco d'albero.

trek [trɛk] *n* (*hike*) spedizione *f*; (*tiring walk*) camminata sfiancante ♦ *vi* (*as holiday*) fare dell'escursionismo.

trellis ['trɛlɪs] *n* graticcio, pergola.

tremble ['trɛmbl] *vi* tremare; (*machine*) vibrare.

trembling ['trɛmblɪŋ] *n* tremito ♦ *adj* tremante.

tremendous [trɪˈmɛndəs] *adj* (*enormous*) enorme; (*excellent*) meraviglioso(a), formidabile.

tremendously [trɪˈmɛndəslɪ] *adv* incredibilmente; **he enjoyed it ~** gli è piaciuto da morire.

tremor ['trɛmə*] *n* tremore *m*, tremito; (*also*: **earth ~**) scossa sismica.

trench [trɛntʃ] *n* trincea.

trench coat *n* trench *m inv*.

trench warfare *n* guerra di trincea.

trend [trɛnd] *n* (*tendency*) tendenza; (*of events*) corso; (*fashion*) moda; **~ towards/ away from** tendenza a/ad allontanarsi da; **to set the ~** essere all'avanguardia; **to set a ~** lanciare una moda.

trendy ['trɛndɪ] *adj* (*idea*) di moda; (*clothes*) all'ultima moda.

trepidation [trɛpɪˈdeɪʃən] *n* trepidazione *f*, agitazione *f*.

trespass ['trɛspəs] *vi*: **to ~ on** entrare abusivamente in; (*fig*) abusare di; **"no ~ing"** "proprietà privata", "vietato l'accesso".

trespasser ['trɛspəsə*] *n* trasgressore *m*; **"~s will be prosecuted"** "i trasgressori saranno puniti secondo i termini di legge".

trestle ['trɛsl] *n* cavalletto.

trestle table *n* tavola su cavalletti.

trial ['traɪəl] *n* (*LAW*) processo; (*test: of machine etc*) collaudo; (*hardship*) prova, difficoltà *f inv*; (*worry*) cruccio; **~s** *npl* (*ATHLETICS*) prove *fpl* di qualificazione; **horse ~s** concorso ippico; **to be on ~** essere sotto processo; **~ by jury** processo

penale con giuria; **to be sent for** ~ essere
rinviato a giudizio; **to bring sb to** ~ **(for a
crime)** portare qn in giudizio (per un
reato); **by** ~ **and error** a tentoni.
trial balance n (COMM) bilancio di verifica.
trial basis n: **on a** ~ in prova.
trial run n periodo di prova.
triangle ['traɪæŋgl] n (MATH, MUS)
triangolo.
triangular [traɪ'æŋgjulə*] adj triangolare.
triathlon [traɪ'æθlən] n triathlon m inv.
tribal ['traɪbəl] adj tribale.
tribe [traɪb] n tribù f inv.
tribesman ['traɪbzmən] n membro della
tribù.
tribulation [trɪbju'leɪʃən] n tribolazione f.
tribunal [traɪ'bju:nl] n tribunale m.
tributary ['trɪbju:tərɪ] n (river) tributario,
affluente m.
tribute ['trɪbju:t] n tributo, omaggio; **to pay
~ to** rendere omaggio a.
trice [traɪs] n: **in a** ~ in un attimo.
trick [trɪk] n trucco; (clever act)
stratagemma m; (joke) tiro; (CARDS) presa
♦ vt imbrogliare, ingannare; **to play a** ~
on sb giocare un tiro a qn; **it's a** ~ **of the
light** è un effetto ottico; **that should do
the** ~ (col) vedrai che funziona; **to** ~ **sb
into doing sth** convincere qn a fare qc
con l'inganno; **to** ~ **sb out of sth** fregare
qc a qn.
trickery ['trɪkərɪ] n inganno.
trickle ['trɪkl] n (of water etc) rivolo;
gocciolio ♦ vi gocciolare; **to** ~ **in/out**
(people) entrare/uscire alla spicciolata.
trick question n domanda f trabocchetto
inv.
trickster ['trɪkstə*] n imbroglione/a.
tricky ['trɪkɪ] adj difficile, delicato(a).
tricycle ['traɪsɪkl] n triciclo.
trifle ['traɪfl] n sciocchezza; (BRIT CULIN) ≈
zuppa inglese ♦ adv: **a** ~ **long** un po' lungo
♦ vi: **to** ~ **with** prendere alla leggera.
trifling ['traɪflɪŋ] adj insignificante.
trigger ['trɪgə*] n (of gun) grilletto.
▶**trigger off** vt dare l'avvio a.
trigonometry [trɪgə'nɒmətrɪ] n
trigonometria.
trilby ['trɪlbɪ] n (BRIT: also: ~ **hat**) cappello
floscio di feltro.
trill [trɪl] n (of bird, MUS) trillo.
trilogy ['trɪlədʒɪ] n trilogia.
trim [trɪm] adj ordinato(a); (house, garden)
ben tenuto(a); (figure) snello(a) ♦ n
(haircut etc) spuntata, regolata;
(embellishment) finiture fpl; (on car)
guarnizioni fpl ♦ vt spuntare; (decorate): **to
~ (with)** decorare (con); (NAUT: a sail)

orientare; **to keep in (good)** ~
mantenersi in forma.
trimmings ['trɪmɪŋz] npl decorazioni fpl;
(extras: gen CULIN) guarnizione f.
Trinidad and Tobago ['trɪnɪdæd-] n
Trinidad e Tobago m.
Trinity ['trɪnɪtɪ] n: **the** ~ la Trinità.
trinket ['trɪŋkɪt] n gingillo; (piece of
jewellery) ciondolo.
trio ['tri:əu] n trio.
trip [trɪp] n viaggio; (excursion) gita,
escursione f; (stumble) passo falso ♦ vi
inciampare; (go lightly) camminare con
passo leggero; **on a** ~ in viaggio.
▶**trip up** vi inciampare ♦ vt fare lo
sgambetto a.
tripartite [traɪ'pɑːtaɪt] adj (agreement)
tripartito(a); (talks) a tre.
tripe [traɪp] n (CULIN) trippa; (pej: rubbish)
sciocchezze fpl, fesserie fpl.
triple ['trɪpl] adj triplo(a) ♦ adv: ~ **the
distance/the speed** tre volte più lontano/
più veloce.
triple jump n triplo salto.
triplets ['trɪplɪts] npl bambini(e)
trigemini(e).
triplicate ['trɪplɪkət] n: **in** ~ in triplice
copia.
tripod ['traɪpɒd] n treppiede m.
Tripoli ['trɪpəlɪ] n Tripoli f.
tripper ['trɪpə*] n (BRIT) gitante m/f.
tripwire ['trɪpwaɪə*] n filo in tensione che
fa scattare una trappola, allarme etc.
trite [traɪt] adj banale, trito(a).
triumph ['traɪʌmf] n trionfo ♦ vi: **to** ~ **(over)**
trionfare (su).
triumphal [traɪ'ʌmfl] adj trionfale.
triumphant [traɪ'ʌmfənt] adj trionfante.
trivia ['trɪvɪə] npl banalità fpl.
trivial ['trɪvɪəl] adj (matter) futile; (excuse,
comment) banale; (amount) irrisorio(a);
(mistake) di poco conto.
triviality [trɪvɪ'ælɪtɪ] n frivolezza; (trivial
detail) futilità.
trivialize ['trɪvɪəlaɪz] vt sminuire.
trod [trɒd] pt of **tread**.
trodden ['trɒdn] pp of **tread**.
trolley ['trɒlɪ] n carrello; (in hospital)
lettiga.
trolley bus n filobus m inv.
trollop ['trɒləp] n prostituta.
trombone [trɒm'bəun] n trombone m.
troop [tru:p] n gruppo; (MIL) squadrone m;
~**s** npl (MIL) truppe fpl; ~**ing the colour**
(BRIT: ceremony) sfilata della bandiera.
▶**troop in** vi entrare a frotte.
▶**troop out** vi uscire a frotte.
troop carrier n (plane) aereo per il

trasporto (di) truppe; (*NAUT: also*: **troopship**) nave *f* per il trasporto (di) truppe.

trooper ['truːpə*] *n* (*MIL*) soldato di cavalleria; (*US: policeman*) poliziotto (della polizia di stato).

troopship ['truːpʃɪp] *n* nave *f* per il trasporto (di) truppe.

trophy ['trəufɪ] *n* trofeo.

tropic ['trɒpɪk] *n* tropico; **in the ~s** ai tropici; **T~ of Cancer/Capricorn** tropico del Cancro/Capricorno.

tropical ['trɒpɪkəl] *adj* tropicale.

trot [trɒt] *n* trotto ♦ *vi* trottare; **on the ~** (*BRIT fig*) di fila, uno(a) dopo l'altro(a).

►**trot out** *vt* (*excuse, reason*) tirar fuori; (*names, facts*) recitare di fila.

trouble ['trʌbl] *n* (*problems*) difficoltà *fpl*, problemi *mpl*; (*worry*) preoccupazione *f*; (*bother, effort*) sforzo; (*with sth mechanical*) noie *fpl*; (*POL*) conflitti *mpl*, disordine *m*; (*MED*): **stomach** *etc* **~** disturbi *mpl* gastrici *etc* ♦ *vt* disturbare; (*worry*) preoccupare ♦ *vi*: **to ~ to do** disturbarsi a fare; **~s** *npl* (*POL etc*) disordini *mpl*; **to be in ~** avere dei problemi; (*for doing wrong*) essere nei guai; **to go to the ~ of doing** darsi la pena di fare; **it's no ~!** di niente!; **what's the ~?** cosa c'è che non va?; **the ~ is...** c'è che..., il guaio è che...; **to have ~ doing sth** avere delle difficoltà a fare qc; **please don't ~ yourself** non si disturbi.

troubled ['trʌbld] *adj* (*person*) preoccupato(a), inquieto(a); (*epoch, life*) agitato(a), difficile.

trouble-free ['trʌblfriː] *adj* senza problemi.

troublemaker ['trʌblmeɪkə*] *n* elemento disturbatore, agitatore/trice.

troubleshooter ['trʌblʃuːtə*] *n* (*in conflict*) conciliatore *m*.

troublesome ['trʌblsəm] *adj* fastidioso(a), seccante.

trouble spot *n* zona calda.

troubling ['trʌblɪŋ] *adj* (*thought*) preoccupante; **these are ~ times** questi sono tempi difficili.

trough [trɒf] *n* (*also*: **drinking ~**) abbeveratoio; (*also*: **feeding ~**) trogolo, mangiatoia; (*channel*) canale *m*; **~ of low pressure** (*METEOROLOGY*) depressione *f*.

trounce [trauns] *vt* (*defeat*) sgominare.

troupe [truːp] *n* troupe *f inv*.

trouser press *n* stirapantaloni *m inv*.

trousers ['trauzəz] *npl* pantaloni *mpl*, calzoni *mpl*; **short ~** (*BRIT*) calzoncini *mpl*.

trouser suit *n* (*BRIT*) completo *m or* tailleur *m inv* pantalone *inv*.

trousseau, *pl* **~x** *or* **~s** ['truːsəu, -z] *n*

corredo da sposa.

trout [traut] *n* (*pl inv*) trota.

trowel ['trauəl] *n* cazzuola.

truant ['truənt] *n*: **to play ~** (*BRIT*) marinare la scuola.

truce [truːs] *n* tregua.

truck [trʌk] *n* autocarro, camion *m inv*; (*RAIL*) carro merci aperto; (*for luggage*) carrello *m* portabagagli *inv*.

truck driver, (*US*) **trucker** ['trʌkə*] *n* camionista *m/f*.

truck farm *n* (*US*) orto industriale.

trucking ['trʌkɪŋ] *n* (*esp US*) autotrasporto.

trucking company *n* (*esp US*) impresa di trasporti.

truculent ['trʌkjulənt] *adj* aggressivo(a), brutale.

trudge [trʌdʒ] *vi* trascinarsi pesantemente.

true [truː] *adj* vero(a); (*accurate*) accurato(a), esatto(a); (*genuine*) reale; (*faithful*) fedele; (*wall, beam*) a piombo; (*wheel*) centrato(a); **to come ~** avverarsi; **~ to life** verosimile.

truffle ['trʌfl] *n* tartufo.

truly ['truːlɪ] *adv* veramente; (*truthfully*) sinceramente; (*faithfully*) fedelmente; **yours ~** (*in letter-writing*) distinti saluti.

trump [trʌmp] *n* (*CARDS*) atout *m inv*; **to turn up ~s** (*fig*) fare miracoli.

trump card *n* atout *m inv*; (*fig*) asso nella manica.

trumped-up [trʌmpt'ʌp] *adj* inventato(a).

trumpet ['trʌmpɪt] *n* tromba.

truncated [trʌŋ'keɪtɪd] *adj* tronco(a).

truncheon ['trʌntʃən] *n* sfollagente *m inv*.

trundle ['trʌndl] *vt, vi*: **to ~ along** rotolare rumorosamente.

trunk [trʌŋk] *n* (*of tree, person*) tronco; (*of elephant*) proboscide *f*; (*case*) baule *m*; (*US AUT*) bagagliaio.

trunk call *n* (*BRIT TEL*) (telefonata) interurbana.

trunk road *n* (*BRIT*) strada principale.

trunks [trʌŋks] *npl* (*also*: **swimming ~**) calzoncini *mpl* da bagno.

truss [trʌs] *n* (*MED*) cinto erniario ♦ *vt*: **to ~ (up)** (*CULIN*) legare.

trust [trʌst] *n* fiducia; (*LAW*) amministrazione *f* fiduciaria; (*COMM*) trust *m inv* ♦ *vt* (*have confidence in*) fidarsi di; (*rely on*) contare su; (*entrust*): **to ~ sth to sb** affidare qc a qn; (*hope*): **to ~ (that)** sperare (che); **you'll have to take it on ~** deve credermi sulla parola; **in ~** (*LAW*) in amministrazione fiduciaria.

trust company *n* trust *m inv*.

trusted ['trʌstɪd] *adj* fidato(a).

trustee [trʌs'tiː] *n* (*LAW*)

amministratore(trice) fiduciario(a); (*of school etc*) amministratore/trice.

trustful ['trʌstful] *adj* fiducioso(a).

trust fund *n* fondo fiduciario.

trusting ['trʌstɪŋ] *adj* = **trustful**.

trustworthy ['trʌstwəːðɪ] *adj* fidato(a), degno(a) di fiducia.

trusty ['trʌstɪ] *adj* fidato(a).

truth, ~s [truːθ, truːðz] *n* verità *f inv*.

truthful ['truːθful] *adj* (*person*) sincero(a); (*description*) veritiero(a), esatto(a).

truthfully ['truːθfəlɪ] *adv* sinceramente.

truthfulness ['truːθfəlnɪs] *n* veracità.

try [traɪ] *n* prova, tentativo; (*RUGBY*) meta ♦ *vt* (*LAW*) giudicare; (*test: sth new*) provare; (*strain: patience, person*) mettere alla prova ♦ *vi* provare; **to ~ to do** provare a fare; (*seek*) cercare di fare; **to give sth a ~** provare qc; **to ~ one's (very) best** *or* **one's (very) hardest** mettercela tutta.

▶**try on** *vt* (*clothes*) provare, mettere alla prova; **to ~ it on** (*fig*) cercare di farla.

▶**try out** *vt* provare, mettere alla prova.

trying ['traɪɪŋ] *adj* (*day, experience*) logorante, pesante; (*child*) difficile, insopportabile.

tsar [zɑː*] *n* zar *m inv*.

T-shirt ['tiːʃəːt] *n* maglietta.

TSO *n abbr* (*BRIT: = The Stationery Office*) ≈ Poligrafici *mpl* dello Stato.

T-square ['tiːskwɛə*] *n* riga a T.

TT *adj abbr* (*BRIT col*) = **teetotal** ♦ *abbr* (*US*) = *Trust Territory*.

tub [tʌb] *n* tinozza; mastello; (*bath*) bagno.

tuba ['tjuːbə] *n* tuba.

tubby ['tʌbɪ] *adj* grassoccio(a).

tube [tjuːb] *n* tubo; (*BRIT: underground*) metropolitana; (*for tyre*) camera d'aria; (*col: television*): **the ~** la tele.

tubeless ['tjuːblɪs] *adj* (*tyre*) senza camera d'aria.

tuber ['tjuːbə*] *n* (*BOT*) tubero.

tuberculosis (TB) [tjubəːkjuˈləusɪs] *n* tubercolosi *f*.

tube station *n* (*BRIT*) stazione *f* del metrò.

tubing ['tjuːbɪŋ] *n* tubazione *f*; **a piece of ~** un tubo.

tubular ['tjuːbjulə*] *adj* tubolare.

TUC *n abbr* (*BRIT: = Trades Union Congress*) confederazione *f* dei sindacati britannici.

tuck [tʌk] *n* (*SEWING*) piega ♦ *vt* (*put*) mettere.

▶**tuck away** *vt* riporre.

▶**tuck in** *vt* mettere dentro; (*child*) rimboccare ♦ *vi* (*eat*) mangiare di buon appetito; abbuffarsi.

▶**tuck up** *vt* (*child*) rimboccare.

tuck shop *n* negozio di pasticceria (*in una scuola*).

Tue(s). *abbr* (*= Tuesday*) mar.

Tuesday ['tjuːzdɪ] *n* martedì *m inv*; (**the date) today is ~ 23rd March** oggi è martedì 23 marzo; **on ~** martedì; **on ~s** di martedì; **every ~** tutti i martedì; **every other ~** ogni due martedì; **last/next ~** martedì scorso/prossimo; **~ next** martedì prossimo; **the following ~** (*in past*) il martedì successivo; (*in future*) il martedì dopo; **a week/fortnight on ~, ~ week/ fortnight** martedì fra una settimana/ quindici giorni; **the ~ before last** martedì di due settimane fa; **the ~ after next** non questo martedì ma il prossimo; **~ morning/lunchtime/afternoon/evening** martedì mattina/all'ora di pranzo/ pomeriggio/sera; **~ night** martedì sera; (*overnight*) martedì notte; **~'s newspaper** il giornale di martedì.

tuft [tʌft] *n* ciuffo.

tug [tʌg] *n* (*ship*) rimorchiatore *m* ♦ *vt* tirare con forza.

tug-of-love [tʌgəvˈlʌv] *n* contesa per la custodia dei figli; **~ children** bambini *mpl* coinvolti nella contesa per la custodia.

tug-of-war [tʌgəvˈwɔː*] *n* tiro alla fune.

tuition [tjuːˈɪʃən] *n* (*BRIT: lessons*) lezioni *fpl*; (*US: fees*) tasse *fpl* scolastiche (*or* universitarie).

tulip ['tjuːlɪp] *n* tulipano.

tumble ['tʌmbl] *n* (*fall*) capitombolo ♦ *vi* capitombolare, ruzzolare; (*somersault*) fare capriole ♦ *vt* far cadere; **to ~ to sth** (*col*) realizzare qc.

tumbledown ['tʌmbldaun] *n* cadente, diroccato(a).

tumble dryer *n* (*BRIT*) asciugatrice *f*.

tumbler ['tʌmblə*] *n* bicchiere *m* (senza stelo).

tummy ['tʌmɪ] *n* (*col*) pancia.

tumour, (*US***) tumor** ['tjuːmə*] *n* tumore *m*.

tumult ['tjuːmʌlt] *n* tumulto.

tumultuous [tjuːˈmʌltjuəs] *adj* tumultuoso(a).

tuna ['tjuːnə] *n* (*pl inv*) (*also*: **~ fish**) tonno.

tune [tjuːn] *n* (*melody*) melodia, aria ♦ *vt* (*MUS*) accordare; (*RADIO, TV, AUT*) regolare, mettere a punto; **to be in/out of ~** (*instrument*) essere accordato(a)/ scordato(a); (*singer*) essere intonato(a)/ stonato(a); **to the ~ of** (*fig: amount*) per la modesta somma di; **in ~ with** (*fig*) in accordo con.

▶**tune in** *vi* (*RADIO, TV*): **to ~ in (to)** sintonizzarsi (su).

▶**tune up** *vi* (*musician*) accordare lo strumento.

tuneful ['tju:nful] *adj* melodioso(a).
tuner ['tju:nə*] *n* (*radio set*) sintonizzatore *m*; **piano** ~ accordatore/trice di pianoforte.
tuner amplifier *n* amplificatore *m* di sintonia.
tungsten ['tʌŋstn] *n* tungsteno.
tunic ['tju:nɪk] *n* tunica.
tuning ['tju:nɪŋ] *n* messa a punto.
tuning fork *n* diapason *m inv*.
Tunis ['tju:nɪs] *n* Tunisi *f*.
Tunisia [tju:'nɪzɪə] *n* Tunisia.
Tunisian [tju:'nɪzɪən] *adj*, *n* tunisino(a).
tunnel ['tʌnl] *n* galleria ♦ *vi* scavare una galleria.
tunnel vision *n* (*MED*) riduzione *f* del campo visivo; (*fig*) visuale *f* ristretta.
tunny ['tʌnɪ] *n* tonno.
turban ['tə:bən] *n* turbante *m*.
turbid ['tə:bɪd] *adj* torbido(a).
turbine ['tə:baɪn] *n* turbina.
turbo ['tə:bəu] *n* turbo *m inv*.
turbojet ['tə:bəu'dʒɛt] *n* turboreattore *m*.
turboprop ['tə:bəu'prɒp] *n* turboelica *m inv*.
turbot ['tə:bət] *n* (*pl inv*) rombo gigante.
turbulence ['tə:bjuləns] *n* turbolenza.
turbulent ['tə:bjulənt] *adj* turbolento(a); (*sea*) agitato(a).
tureen [tə'ri:n] *n* zuppiera.
turf [tə:f] *n* terreno erboso; (*clod*) zolla ♦ *vt* coprire di zolle erbose; **the T~** l'ippodromo.
▶**turf out** *vt* (*col*) buttar fuori.
turf accountant *n* (*BRIT*) allibratore *m*.
turgid ['tə:dʒɪd] *adj* (*speech*) ampolloso(a), pomposo(a).
Turin [tjuə'rɪn] *n* Torino *f*.
Turk [tə:k] *n* turco/a.
Turkey ['tə:kɪ] *n* Turchia.
turkey ['tə:kɪ] *n* tacchino.
Turkish ['tə:kɪʃ] *adj* turco(a) ♦ *n* (*LING*) turco.
Turkish bath *n* bagno turco.
Turkish delight *n* gelatine ricoperte di zucchero a velo.
turmeric ['tə:mərɪk] *n* curcuma.
turmoil ['tə:mɔɪl] *n* confusione *f*, tumulto.
turn [tə:n] *n* giro; (*in road*) curva; (*tendency: of mind, events*) tendenza; (*performance*) numero; (*MED*) crisi *f inv*, attacco ♦ *vt* girare, voltare; (*milk*) far andare a male; (*shape: wood, metal*) tornire; (*change*): **to** ~ **sth into** trasformare qc in ♦ *vi* girare; (*person: look back*) girarsi, voltarsi; (*reverse direction*) girarsi indietro; (*change*) cambiare; (*become*) diventare; **to** ~ **into** trasformarsi in; **a good** ~ un buon servizio; **a bad** ~ un brutto tiro; **it**

gave me quite a ~ mi ha fatto prendere un bello spavento; **"no left** ~**"** (*AUT*) "divieto di svolta a sinistra"; **it's your** ~ tocca a lei; **in** ~ a sua volta; a turno; **to take** ~**s (at sth)** fare (qc) a turno; **at the** ~ **of the year/century** alla fine dell'anno/del secolo; **to take a** ~ **for the worse** (*situation, events*) volgere al peggio; (*patient, health*) peggiorare; **to** ~ **left/right** girare a sinistra/destra.
▶**turn about** *vi* girarsi indietro.
▶**turn away** *vi* girarsi (dall'altra parte) ♦ *vt* (*reject: person*) mandar via; (: *business*) rifiutare.
▶**turn back** *vi* ritornare, tornare indietro.
▶**turn down** *vt* (*refuse*) rifiutare; (*reduce*) abbassare; (*fold*) ripiegare.
▶**turn in** *vi* (*col: go to bed*) andare a letto ♦ *vt* (*fold*) voltare in dentro.
▶**turn off** *vi* (*from road*) girare, voltare ♦ *vt* (*light, radio, engine etc*) spegnere.
▶**turn on** *vt* (*light, radio etc*) accendere; (*engine*) avviare.
▶**turn out** *vt* (*light, gas*) chiudere, spegnere; (*produce: goods*) produrre; (: *novel, good pupils*) creare ♦ *vi* (*appear, attend: troops, doctor etc*) presentarsi; **to** ~ **out to be** ... rivelarsi ..., risultare ....
▶**turn over** *vi* (*person*) girarsi; (*car etc*) capovolgersi ♦ *vt* girare.
▶**turn round** *vi* girare; (*person*) girarsi.
▶**turn up** *vi* (*person*) arrivare, presentarsi; (*lost object*) saltar fuori ♦ *vt* (*collar, sound, gas etc*) alzare.
turnabout ['tə:nəbaut], **turnaround** ['tə:nəraund] *n* (*fig*) dietrofront *m inv*.
turncoat ['tə:nkəut] *n* voltagabbana *m/f inv*.
turned-up ['tə:ndʌp] *adj* (*nose*) all'insù.
turning ['tə:nɪŋ] *n* (*in road*) curva; (*side road*) strada laterale; **the first** ~ **on the right** la prima a destra.
turning circle *n* (*BRIT*) diametro di sterzata.
turning point *n* (*fig*) svolta decisiva.
turning radius *n* (*US*) = **turning circle**.
turnip ['tə:nɪp] *n* rapa.
turnout ['tə:naut] *n* presenza, affluenza.
turnover ['tə:nəuvə*] *n* (*COMM: amount of money*) giro di affari; (: *of goods*) smercio; (*CULIN*): **apple** *etc* ~ sfogliatella alle mele *etc*; **there is a rapid** ~ **in staff** c'è un ricambio molto rapido di personale.
turnpike ['tə:npaik] *n* (*US*) autostrada a pedaggio.
turnstile ['tə:nstail] *n* tornella.
turntable ['tə:nteibl] *n* (*on record player*) piatto.

turn-up ['tə:nʌp] n (BRIT: on trousers) risvolto.

turpentine ['tə:pəntaɪn] n (also: **turps**) acqua ragia.

turquoise [tə:kwɔɪz] n (stone) turchese m ♦ adj color turchese; di turchese.

turret ['tʌrɪt] n torretta.

turtle ['tə:tl] n testuggine f.

turtleneck (sweater) ['tə:tlnɛk-] n maglione m con il collo alto.

Tuscan ['tʌskən] adj, n toscano(a).

Tuscany ['tʌskənɪ] n Toscana.

tusk [tʌsk] n zanna.

tussle ['tʌsl] n baruffa, mischia.

tutor ['tju:tə*] n (in college) docente m/f (responsabile di un gruppo di studenti); (private teacher) precettore m.

tutorial [tju:'tɔ:rɪəl] n (SCOL) lezione f con discussione (a un gruppo limitato).

tuxedo [tʌk'si:dəu] n (US) smoking m inv.

TV [ti:'vi:] n abbr (= television) tivù f inv.

TV dinner n pasto surgelato pronto in due minuti.

twaddle ['twɔdl] n scemenze fpl.

twang [twæŋ] n (of instrument) suono vibrante; (of voice) accento nasale ♦ vi vibrare ♦ vt (guitar) pizzicare le corde di.

tweak [twi:k] vt (nose) pizzicare; (ear, hair) tirare.

tweed [twi:d] n tweed m inv.

tweezers ['twi:zəz] npl pinzette fpl.

twelfth [twɛlfθ] num dodicesimo(a).

Twelfth Night n la notte dell'Epifania.

twelve [twɛlv] num dodici; **at** ~ alle dodici, a mezzogiorno; (midnight) a mezzanotte.

twentieth ['twɛntɪɪθ] num ventesimo(a).

twenty ['twɛntɪ] num venti.

twerp [twə:p] n (col) idiota m/f.

twice [twaɪs] adv due volte; ~ **as much** due volte tanto; ~ **a week** due volte alla settimana; **she is** ~ **your age** ha il doppio dei suoi anni.

twiddle ['twɪdl] vt, vi: **to** ~ **(with)** sth giocherellare con qc; **to** ~ **one's thumbs** (fig) girarsi i pollici.

twig [twɪg] n ramoscello ♦ vt, vi (col) capire.

twilight ['twaɪlaɪt] n (evening) crepuscolo; (morning) alba; **in the** ~ nella penombra.

twill [twɪl] n spigato.

twin [twɪn] adj, n gemello(a).

twin(-bedded) room ['twɪn('bɛdɪd)-] n stanza con letti gemelli.

twin beds npl letti mpl gemelli.

twin-carburettor ['twɪnkɑ:bju'rɛtə*] adj a doppio carburatore.

twine [twaɪn] n spago, cordicella ♦ vi (plant) attorcigliarsi; (road) serpeggiare.

twin-engined ['twɪn'ɛndʒɪnd] adj a due motori; ~ **aircraft** bimotore m.

twinge [twɪndʒ] n (of pain) fitta; **a** ~ **of conscience/regret** un rimorso/rimpianto.

twinkle ['twɪŋkl] n scintillio ♦ vi scintillare; (eyes) brillare.

twin town n città f inv gemella.

twirl [twə:l] n piroetta ♦ vt far roteare ♦ vi roteare.

twist [twɪst] n torsione f; (in wire, flex) storta; (in story) colpo di scena; (bend) svolta, piega ♦ vt attorcigliare; (weave) intrecciare; (roll around) arrotolare; (fig) deformare ♦ vi attorcigliarsi; arrotolarsi; (road) serpeggiare; **to** ~ **one's ankle/wrist** (MED) slogarsi la caviglia/il polso.

twisted ['twɪstɪd] adj (wire, rope) attorcigliato(a); (ankle, wrist) slogato(a); (fig: logic, mind) contorto(a).

twit [twɪt] n (col) minchione/a.

twitch [twɪtʃ] n tiratina; (nervous) tic m inv ♦ vi contrarsi; avere un tic.

two [tu:] num due; ~ **by** ~, **in** ~**s** a due a due; **to put** ~ **and** ~ **together** (fig) trarre le conclusioni.

two-bit [tu:'bɪt] adj (esp US: col, pej) da quattro soldi.

two-door [tu:'dɔ:*] adj (AUT) a due porte.

two-faced ['tu:'feɪst] adj (pej: person) falso(a).

twofold ['tu:fəuld] adv: **to increase** ~ aumentare del doppio ♦ adj (increase) doppio(a); (reply) in due punti.

two-piece ['tu:'pi:s] n (also: ~ **suit**) due pezzi m inv; (also: ~ **swimsuit**) (costume m da bagno a) due pezzi m inv.

two-seater ['tu:'si:tə*] n (plane) biposto; (car) macchina a due posti.

twosome ['tu:səm] n (people) coppia.

two-stroke ['tu:strəuk] n (engine) due tempi m inv ♦ adj a due tempi.

two-tone ['tu:təun] adj (colour) bicolore.

two-way ['tu:weɪ] adj (traffic) a due sensi; ~ **radio** radio f inv ricetrasmittente.

TX abbr (US) = Texas.

tycoon [taɪ'ku:n] n: **(business)** ~ magnate m.

type [taɪp] n (category) genere m; (model) modello; (example) tipo; (TYP) tipo, carattere m ♦ vt (letter etc) battere (a macchina), dattilografare; **what** ~ **do you want?** che tipo vuole?; **in bold/italic** ~ in grassetto/corsivo.

type-cast ['taɪpkɑ:st] adj (actor) a ruolo fisso.

typeface ['taɪpfeɪs] n carattere m tipografico.

typescript ['taɪpskrɪpt] *n* dattiloscritto.
typeset ['taɪpsɛt] *vt* comporre.
typesetter ['taɪpsɛtə*] *n* compositore *m*.
typewriter ['taɪpraɪtə*] *n* macchina da scrivere.
typewritten ['taɪprɪtn] *adj* dattiloscritto(a), battuto(a) a macchina.
typhoid ['taɪfɔɪd] *n* tifoidea.
typhoon [taɪ'fuːn] *n* tifone *m*.
typhus ['taɪfəs] *n* tifo.
typical ['tɪpɪkl] *adj* tipico(a).
typify ['tɪpɪfaɪ] *vt* essere tipico(a) di.
typing ['taɪpɪŋ] *n* dattilografia.
typing error *n* errore *m* di battitura.
typing pool *n* ufficio *m* dattilografia *inv*.
typist ['taɪpɪst] *n* dattilografo/a.
typo ['taɪpəu] *n abbr* (*col*: = *typographical error*) refuso.
typography [taɪ'pɒgrəfɪ] *n* tipografia.
tyranny ['tɪrənɪ] *n* tirannia.
tyrant ['taɪərnt] *n* tiranno.
tyre, (*US*) **tire** ['taɪə*] *n* pneumatico, gomma.
tyre pressure *n* pressione *f* (delle gomme).
Tyrol [tɪ'rəul] *n* Tirolo.
Tyrolean [tɪrə'liːən], **Tyrolese** [tɪrə'liːz] *adj*, *n* tirolese (*m/f*).
Tyrrhenian Sea [tɪ'riːnɪən-] *n*: **the ~** il mar Tirreno.

U u

U, u [juː] *n* (*letter*) U, u *m or f inv*; **U for Uncle** ≈ U come Udine.
U *n abbr* (*BRIT CINE*: = *universal*) per tutti.
UAW *n abbr* (*US*: = *United Automobile Workers*) *sindacato degli operai automobilistici*.
UB40 *n abbr* (*BRIT*: = *unemployment benefit form 40*) *modulo per la richiesta del sussidio di disoccupazione*.
U-bend ['juːbɛnd] *n* (*in pipe*) sifone *m*.
ubiquitous [juː'bɪkwɪtəs] *adj* onnipresente.
UCAS ['juːkæs] *n abbr* (*BRIT*) = *Universities and Colleges Admissions Service*.
UDA *n abbr* (*BRIT*: = *Ulster Defence Association*) *organizzazione paramilitare protestante*.
UDC *n abbr* (*BRIT*) = *Urban District Council*.
udder ['ʌdə*] *n* mammella.

UDI *abbr* (*BRIT POL*) = *unilateral declaration of independence*.
UDR *n abbr* (*BRIT*: = *Ulster Defence Regiment*) *reggimento dell'esercito britannico in Irlanda del Nord*.
UEFA [juː'eɪfə] *n abbr* (= *Union of European Football Associations*) U.E.F.A. *f*.
UFO ['juːfəu] *n abbr* (= *unidentified flying object*) UFO *m inv*.
Uganda [juː'gændə] *n* Uganda.
Ugandan [juː'gændən] *adj*, *n* ugandese (*m/f*).
UGC *n abbr* (*BRIT*: = *University Grants Committee*) *organo che autorizza sovvenzioni alle università*.
ugh [əːh] *excl* puah!
ugliness ['ʌglɪnɪs] *n* bruttezza.
ugly ['ʌglɪ] *adj* brutto(a).
UHF *abbr* = *ultra-high frequency*.
UHT *adj abbr* (= *ultra heat treated*): **~ milk** *n* latte *m* UHT.
UK *n abbr see* **United Kingdom**.
Ukraine [juː'kreɪn] *n* Ucraina.
Ukrainian [juː'kreɪnɪən] *adj* ucraino(a) ♦ *n* (*person*) ucraino/a; (*LING*) ucraino.
ulcer ['ʌlsə*] *n* ulcera; **mouth ~** afta.
Ulster ['ʌlstə*] *n* Ulster *m*.
ulterior [ʌl'tɪərɪə*] *adj* ulteriore; **~ motive** secondo fine *m*.
ultimata [ʌltɪ'meɪtə] *npl of* **ultimatum**.
ultimate ['ʌltɪmɪt] *adj* ultimo(a), finale; (*authority*) massimo(a), supremo(a) ♦ *n*: **the ~ in luxury** il non plus ultra del lusso.
ultimately ['ʌltɪmɪtlɪ] *adv* alla fine; in definitiva, in fin dei conti.
ultimatum, *pl* **~s** *or* **ultimata** [ʌltɪ'meɪtəm, -tə] *n* ultimatum *m inv*.
ultrasonic [ʌltrə'sɒnɪk] *adj* ultrasonico(a).
ultrasound [ʌltrə'saund] *n* (*MED*) ecografia.
ultraviolet ['ʌltrə'vaɪəlɪt] *adj* ultravioletto(a).
umbilical [ʌm'bɪlɪkl] *adj*: **~ cord** cordone *m* ombelicale.
umbrage ['ʌmbrɪdʒ] *n*: **to take ~** offendersi, impermalirsi.
umbrella [ʌm'brɛlə] *n* ombrello; **under the ~ of** (*fig*) sotto l'egida di.
umlaut ['umlaut] *n* Umlaut *m inv*.
umpire ['ʌmpaɪə*] *n* arbitro.
umpteen [ʌmp'tiːn] *adj* non so quanti(e); **for the ~th time** per l'ennesima volta.
UMW *n abbr* (= *United Mineworkers of America*) *unione dei minatori d'America*.
UN *n abbr see* **United Nations**.
unabashed [ʌnə'bæʃt] *adj* imperturbato(a).
unabated [ʌnə'beɪtɪd] *adj* non diminuito(a).
unable [ʌn'eɪbl] *adj*: **to be ~ to** non potere, essere nell'impossibilità di; (*not to know how to*) essere incapace di, non sapere.

unabridged [ʌnəˈbrɪdʒd] *adj* integrale.

unacceptable [ʌnəkˈsɛptəbl] *adj* (*proposal, behaviour*) inaccettabile; (*price*) impossibile.

unaccompanied [ʌnəˈkʌmpənɪd] *adj* (*child, lady*) non accompagnato(a); (*singing, song*) senza accompagnamento.

unaccountably [ʌnəˈkauntəblɪ] *adv* inesplicabilmente.

unaccounted [ʌnəˈkauntɪd] *adj*: **two passengers are ~ for** due passeggeri mancano all'appello.

unaccustomed [ʌnəˈkʌstəmd] *adj* insolito(a); **to be ~ to sth** non essere abituato(a) a qc.

unacquainted [ʌnəˈkweɪntɪd] *adj*: **to be ~ with** (*facts*) ignorare, non essere al corrente di.

unadulterated [ʌnəˈdʌltəreɪtɪd] *adj* (*gen*) puro(a); (*wine*) non sofisticato(a).

unaffected [ʌnəˈfɛktɪd] *adj* (*person, behaviour*) naturale, spontaneo(a); (*emotionally*): **to be ~ by** non essere toccato(a) da.

unafraid [ʌnəˈfreɪd] *adj*: **to be ~** non aver paura.

unaided [ʌnˈeɪdɪd] *adv* senza aiuto.

unanimity [juːnəˈnɪmɪtɪ] *n* unanimità.

unanimous [juːˈnænɪməs] *adj* unanime.

unanimously [juːˈnænɪməslɪ] *adv* all'unanimità.

unanswered [ʌnˈɑːnsəd] *adj* (*question, letter*) senza risposta; (*criticism*) non confutato(a).

unappetizing [ʌnˈæpɪtaɪzɪŋ] *adj* poco appetitoso(a).

unappreciative [ʌnəˈpriːʃɪətɪv] *adj* che non apprezza.

unarmed [ʌnˈɑːmd] *adj* (*person*) disarmato(a); (*combat*) senz'armi.

unashamed [ʌnəˈʃeɪmd] *adj* sfacciato(a); senza vergogna.

unassisted [ʌnəˈsɪstɪd] *adj, adv* senza nessun aiuto.

unassuming [ʌnəˈsjuːmɪŋ] *adj* modesto(a), senza pretese.

unattached [ʌnəˈtætʃt] *adj* senza legami, libero(a).

unattended [ʌnəˈtɛndɪd] *adj* (*car, child, luggage*) incustodito(a).

unattractive [ʌnəˈtræktɪv] *adj* privo(a) di attrattiva, poco attraente.

unauthorized [ʌnˈɔːθəraɪzd] *adj* non autorizzato(a).

unavailable [ʌnəˈveɪləbl] *adj* (*article, room, book*) non disponibile; (*person*) impegnato(a).

unavoidable [ʌnəˈvɔɪdəbl] *adj* inevitabile.

unavoidably [ʌnəˈvɔɪdəblɪ] *adv* (*detained*) per cause di forza maggiore.

unaware [ʌnəˈwɛə*] *adj*: **to be ~ of** non sapere, ignorare.

unawares [ʌnəˈwɛəz] *adv* di sorpresa, alla sprovvista.

unbalanced [ʌnˈbælənst] *adj* squilibrato(a).

unbearable [ʌnˈbɛərəbl] *adj* insopportabile.

unbeatable [ʌnˈbiːtəbl] *adj* imbattibile.

unbeaten [ʌnˈbiːtn] *adj* (*team, army*) imbattuto(a); (*record*) insuperato(a).

unbecoming [ʌnbɪˈkʌmɪŋ] *adj* (*unseemly: language, behaviour*) sconveniente; (*unflattering: garment*) che non dona.

unbeknown(st) [ʌnbɪˈnəun(st)] *adv*: **~ to** all'insaputa di.

unbelief [ʌnbɪˈliːf] *n* incredulità.

unbelievable [ʌnbɪˈliːvəbl] *adj* incredibile.

unbelievingly [ʌnbɪˈliːvɪŋlɪ] *adv* con aria incredula.

unbend [ʌnˈbɛnd] *vb* (*irreg*) *vi* distendersi ♦ *vt* (*wire*) raddrizzare.

unbending [ʌnˈbɛndɪŋ] *adj* (*fig*) inflessibile, rigido(a).

unbias(s)ed [ʌnˈbaɪəst] *adj* obiettivo(a), imparziale.

unblemished [ʌnˈblɛmɪʃt] *adj* senza macchia.

unblock [ʌnˈblɔk] *vt* (*pipe, road*) sbloccare.

unborn [ʌnˈbɔːn] *adj* non ancora nato(a).

unbounded [ʌnˈbaundɪd] *adj* sconfinato(a), senza limite.

unbreakable [ʌnˈbreɪkəbl] *adj* infrangibile.

unbridled [ʌnˈbraɪdld] *adj* sbrigliato(a).

unbroken [ʌnˈbrəukən] *adj* (*intact*) intero(a); (*continuous*) continuo(a); (*record*) insuperato(a).

unbuckle [ʌnˈbʌkl] *vt* slacciare.

unburden [ʌnˈbəːdn] *vt*: **to ~ o.s.** sfogarsi.

unbutton [ʌnˈbʌtn] *vt* sbottonare.

uncalled-for [ʌnˈkɔːldfɔː*] *adj* (*remark*) fuori luogo *inv*; (*action*) ingiustificato(a).

uncanny [ʌnˈkænɪ] *adj* misterioso(a), strano(a).

unceasing [ʌnˈsiːsɪŋ] *adj* incessante.

unceremonious [ʌnsɛrɪˈməunɪəs] *adj* (*abrupt, rude*) senza tante cerimonie.

uncertain [ʌnˈsəːtn] *adj* incerto(a); **it's ~ whether ...** non è sicuro se ...; **in no ~ terms** chiaro e tondo, senza mezzi termini.

uncertainty [ʌnˈsəːtntɪ] *n* incertezza.

unchallenged [ʌnˈtʃælɪndʒd] *adj* incontestato(a); **to go ~** non venire contestato, non trovare opposizione.

unchanged [ʌnˈtʃeɪndʒd] *adj* immutato(a).

uncharitable [ʌnˈtʃærɪtəbl] *adj* duro(a), severo(a).

uncharted [ʌn'tʃɑːtɪd] *adj* inesplorato(a).
unchecked [ʌn'tʃɛkt] *adj* incontrollato(a).
uncivilized [ʌn'sɪvɪlaɪzd] *adj* (*gen*)
selvaggio(a); (*fig*) incivile, barbaro(a).
uncle ['ʌŋkl] *n* zio.
unclear [ʌn'klɪə*] *adj* non chiaro(a); **I'm still
~ about what I'm supposed to do** non ho
ancora ben capito cosa dovrei fare.
uncoil [ʌn'kɔɪl] *vt* srotolare ♦ *vi* srotolarsi,
svolgersi.
uncomfortable [ʌn'kʌmfətəbl] *adj*
scomodo(a); (*uneasy*) a disagio,
agitato(a); (*situation*) sgradevole.
uncomfortably [ʌn'kʌmfətəblɪ] *adv*
scomodamente; (*uneasily: say*) con voce
inquieta; (: *think*) con inquietudine.
uncommitted [ʌnkə'mɪtɪd] *adj* (*attitude,
country*) neutrale.
uncommon [ʌn'kɔmən] *adj* raro(a),
insolito(a), non comune.
uncommunicative [ʌnkə'mjuːnɪkətɪv] *adj*
poco comunicativo(a), chiuso(a).
uncomplicated [ʌn'kɔmplɪkeɪtɪd] *adj*
semplice, poco complicato(a).
uncompromising [ʌn'kɔmprəmaɪzɪŋ] *adj*
intransigente, inflessibile.
unconcerned [ʌnkən'səːnd] *adj* (*unworried*)
tranquillo(a); **to be ~ about** non darsi
pensiero di, non preoccuparsi di *or* per.
unconditional [ʌn'kən'dɪʃənl] *adj*
incondizionato(a), senza condizioni.
uncongenial [ʌnkən'dʒiːnɪəl] *adj* (*work,
surroundings*) poco piacevole.
unconnected [ʌnkə'nɛktɪd] *adj* (*unrelated*)
senza connessione, senza rapporto; **to be
~ with** essere estraneo(a) a.
unconscious [ʌn'kɔnʃəs] *adj* privo(a) di
sensi, svenuto(a); (*unaware*)
inconsapevole, inconscio(a) ♦ *n*: **the ~**
l'inconscio; **to knock sb ~** far perdere i
sensi a qn con un pugno.
unconsciously [ʌn'kɔnʃəslɪ] *adv*
inconsciamente.
unconstitutional [ʌnkɔnstɪ'tjuːʃənl] *adj*
incostituzionale.
uncontested [ʌnkən'tɛstɪd] *adj* (*champion*)
incontestato(a); (*POL: seat*) non
disputato(a).
uncontrollable [ʌnkən'trəuləbl] *adj*
incontrollabile, indisciplinato(a).
uncontrolled [ʌnkən'trəuld] *adj* (*child, dog,
emotion*) sfrenato(a); (*inflation, price rises*)
che sfugge al controllo.
unconventional [ʌnkən'vɛnʃənl] *adj* poco
convenzionale.
unconvinced [ʌnkən'vɪnst] *adj*: **to be** *or*
remain ~ non essere convinto(a).
unconvincing [ʌnkən'vɪnsɪŋ] *adj* non

convincente, poco persuasivo(a).
uncork [ʌn'kɔːk] *vt* stappare.
uncorroborated [ʌnkə'rɔbəreɪtɪd] *adj* non
convalidato(a).
uncouth [ʌn'kuːθ] *adj* maleducato(a),
grossolano(a).
uncover [ʌn'kʌvə*] *vt* scoprire.
unctuous ['ʌŋktjuəs] *adj* untuoso(a).
undamaged [ʌn'dæmɪdʒd] *adj* (*goods*) in
buono stato; (*fig: reputation*) intatto(a).
undaunted [ʌn'dɔːntɪd] *adj* intrepido(a).
undecided [ʌndɪ'saɪdɪd] *adj* indeciso(a).
undelivered [ʌndɪ'lɪvəd] *adj* non
recapitato(a); **if ~ return to sender** in
caso di mancato recapito rispedire al
mittente.
undeniable [ʌndɪ'naɪəbl] *adj* innegabile,
indiscutibile.
under ['ʌndə*] *prep* sotto; (*less than*) meno
di; al disotto di; (*according to*) secondo, in
conformità a ♦ *adv* (al) disotto; **from ~
sth** da sotto a *or* dal disotto di qc; **~ there**
là sotto; **in ~ 2 hours** in meno di 2 ore; **~
anaesthetic** sotto anestesia; **~ discussion**
in discussione; **~ repair** in riparazione; **~
the circumstances** date le circostanze.
under... ['ʌndə*] *prefix* sotto..., sub....
under-age [ʌndər'eɪdʒ] *adj* minorenne.
underarm ['ʌndərɑːm] *n* ascella ♦ *adj*
ascellare ♦ *adv* da sotto in su.
undercapitalized [ʌndə'kæpɪtəlaɪzd] *adj*
carente di capitali.
undercarriage ['ʌndəkærɪdʒ] *n* (*BRIT AVIAT*)
carrello (d'atterraggio).
undercharge [ʌndə'tʃɑːdʒ] *vt* far pagare di
meno a.
underclass ['ʌndəklɑːs] *n* sottoproletariato.
underclothes ['ʌndəkləuðz] *npl* biancheria
(intima).
undercover ['ʌndəkʌvə*] *adj* segreto(a),
clandestino(a).
undercurrent ['ʌndəkʌrənt] *n* corrente *f*
sottomarina.
undercut [ʌndə'kʌt] *vt irreg* vendere a
prezzo minore di.
underdeveloped ['ʌndədɪ'vɛləpt] *adj*
sottosviluppato(a).
underdog ['ʌndədɔg] *n* oppresso/a.
underdone [ʌndə'dʌn] *adj* (*CULIN*) poco
cotto(a).
under-employment [ʌndərɪm'plɔɪmənt] *n*
sottoccupazione *f*.
underestimate [ʌndər'ɛstɪmeɪt] *vt*
sottovalutare.
underexposed [ʌndərɪks'pəuzd] *adj* (*PHOT*)
sottoesposto(a).
underfed [ʌndə'fɛd] *adj* denutrito(a).
underfoot [ʌndə'fut] *adv* sotto i piedi.

under-funded ['ʌndə'fʌndɪd] *adj*
insufficientemente sovvenzionato(a).

undergo [ʌndə'gəu] *vt irreg* subire;
(*treatment*) sottoporsi a; **the car is ~ing
repairs** la macchina è in riparazione.

undergraduate [ʌndə'grædjuɪt] *n*
studente(essa) universitario(a) ♦ *cpd:* ~
courses corsi *mpl* di laurea.

underground ['ʌndəgraund] *n*
metropolitana; (*POL*) movimento
clandestino ♦ *adj* sotterraneo(a); (*fig*)
clandestino(a); (*ART, CINE*) underground
inv ♦ *adv* sottoterra; clandestinamente.

undergrowth ['ʌndəgrəuθ] *n* sottobosco.

underhand(ed) [ʌndə'hænd(ɪd)] *adj* (*fig*)
furtivo(a), subdolo(a).

underinsured [ʌndərɪn'ʃuəd] *adj* non
sufficientemente assicurato(a).

underlie [ʌndə'laɪ] *vt irreg* essere alla base
di; **the underlying cause** il motivo di
fondo.

underline [ʌndə'laɪn] *vt* sottolineare.

underling ['ʌndəlɪŋ] *n* (*pej*) subalterno/a,
tirapiedi *m/f inv*.

undermanning [ʌndə'mænɪŋ] *n* carenza di
personale.

undermentioned [ʌndə'mɛnʃənd] *adj*
(riportato(a)) qui sotto *or* qui di seguito.

undermine [ʌndə'maɪn] *vt* minare.

underneath [ʌndə'niːθ] *adv* sotto, disotto
♦ *prep* sotto, al di sotto di.

undernourished [ʌndə'nʌrɪʃt] *adj*
denutrito(a).

underpaid [ʌndə'peɪd] *adj* mal pagato(a).

underpants ['ʌndəpænts] *npl* (*BRIT*)
mutande *fpl*, slip *m inv*.

underpass ['ʌndəpɑːs] *n* (*BRIT*)
sottopassaggio.

underpin [ʌndə'pɪn] *vt* puntellare;
(*argument, case*) corroborare.

underplay [ʌndə'pleɪ] *vt* minimizzare.

underpopulated [ʌndə'pɔpjuleɪtɪd] *adj*
scarsamente popolato(a),
sottopopolato(a).

underprice [ʌndə'praɪs] *vt* vendere a un
prezzo inferiore al dovuto.

underprivileged [ʌndə'prɪvɪlɪdʒd] *adj*
svantaggiato(a).

underrate [ʌndə'reɪt] *vt* sottovalutare.

underscore [ʌndə'skɔː*] *vt* sottolineare.

underseal ['ʌndəsiːl] *vt* rendere stagno il
fondo di.

undersecretary [ʌndə'sɛkrətrɪ] *n*
sottosegretario.

undersell ['ʌndə'sɛl] *vt irreg* (*competitors*)
vendere a prezzi più bassi di.

undershirt ['ʌndəʃəːt] *n* (*US*) maglietta.

undershorts ['ʌndəʃɔːts] *npl* (*US*) mutande

fpl, slip *m inv*.

underside ['ʌndəsaɪd] *n* disotto.

undersigned ['ʌndəsaɪnd] *adj, n*
sottoscritto(a).

underskirt ['ʌndəskəːt] *n* sottoveste *f*.

understaffed [ʌndə'stɑːft] *adj* a corto di
personale.

understand [ʌndə'stænd] *vb* (*irreg: like*
stand) *vt, vi* capire, comprendere; **I ~ that
… sento che …; credo di capire che …; to
make o.s. understood** farsi capire.

understandable [ʌndə'stændəbl] *adj*
comprensibile.

understanding [ʌndə'stændɪŋ] *adj*
comprensivo(a) ♦ *n* comprensione *f*;
(*agreement*) accordo; **on the ~ that … a
patto che *or* a condizione che …; to come
to an ~ with sb** giungere ad un accordo
con qn.

understate [ʌndə'steɪt] *vt* minimizzare,
sminuire.

understatement [ʌndə'steɪtmənt] *n:* **that's
an ~!** a dire poco!

understood [ʌndə'stud] *pt, pp of* **understand**
♦ *adj* inteso(a); (*implied*) sottinteso(a).

understudy ['ʌndəstʌdɪ] *n* sostituto/a,
attore/trice supplente.

undertake [ʌndə'teɪk] *vt irreg*
intraprendere; **to ~ to do sth** impegnarsi
a fare qc.

undertaker ['ʌndəteɪkə*] *n* impresario di
pompe funebri.

undertaking [ʌndə'teɪkɪŋ] *n* impresa;
(*promise*) promessa.

undertone ['ʌndətəun] *n* (*low voice*) tono
sommesso; (*of criticism etc*) vena,
sottofondo; **in an ~** sottovoce.

undervalue [ʌndə'væljuː] *vt* svalutare,
sottovalutare.

underwater [ʌndə'wɔːtə*] *adv* sott'acqua
♦ *adj* subacqueo(a).

underwear ['ʌndəwɛə*] *n* biancheria
(intima).

underweight [ʌndə'weɪt] *adj* al di sotto del
giusto peso; (*person*) sottopeso *inv*.

underworld ['ʌndəwəːld] *n* (*of crime*)
malavita.

underwrite ['ʌndəraɪt] *vt* (*FINANCE*)
sottoscrivere; (*INSURANCE*) assicurare.

underwriter ['ʌndəraɪtə*] *n* sottoscrittore/
trice; assicuratore/trice.

undeserving [ʌndɪ'zəːvɪŋ] *adj:* **to be ~ of**
non meritare, non essere degno di.

undesirable [ʌndɪ'zaɪərəbl] *adj*
indesiderabile, sgradito(a).

undeveloped [ʌndɪ'vɛləpt] *adj* (*land,
resources*) non sfruttato(a).

undies ['ʌndɪz] *npl* (*col*) robina, biancheria

intima da donna.

undiluted [ʌndaɪ'luːtɪd] *adj* non diluito(a).

undiplomatic [ʌndɪplə'mætɪk] *adj* poco diplomatico(a).

undischarged ['ʌndɪs'tʃɑːdʒd] *adj*: ~ **bankrupt** fallito non riabilitato.

undisciplined [ʌn'dɪsɪplɪnd] *adj* indisciplinato(a).

undisguised [ʌndɪs'gaɪzd] *adj* (*dislike, amusement etc*) palese.

undisputed [ʌndɪs'pjuːtɪd] *adj* indiscusso(a).

undistinguished [ʌndɪs'tɪŋgwɪʃt] *adj* mediocre, qualunque.

undisturbed [ʌndɪs'təːbd] *adj* tranquillo(a); **to leave sth** ~ lasciare qc così com'è.

undivided [ʌndɪ'vaɪdɪd] *adj*: **I want your** ~ **attention** esigo tutta la sua attenzione.

undo [ʌn'duː] *vt irreg* disfare.

undoing [ʌn'duːɪŋ] *n* rovina, perdita.

undone [ʌn'dʌn] *pp of* **undo**; **to come** ~ slacciarsi.

undoubted [ʌn'dautɪd] *adj* sicuro(a), certo(a).

undoubtedly [ʌn'dautɪdlɪ] *adv* senza alcun dubbio.

undress [ʌn'drɛs] *vi* spogliarsi.

undrinkable [ʌn'drɪŋkəbl] *adj* (*unpalatable*) imbevibile; (*poisonous*) non potabile.

undue [ʌn'djuː] *adj* eccessivo(a).

undulating ['ʌndjuleɪtɪŋ] *adj* ondeggiante; ondulato(a).

unduly [ʌn'djuːlɪ] *adv* eccessivamente.

undying [ʌn'daɪɪŋ] *adj* imperituro(a).

unearned [ʌn'əːnd] *adj* (*praise, respect*) immeritato(a); ~ **income** rendita.

unearth [ʌn'əːθ] *vt* dissotterrare; (*fig*) scoprire.

unearthly [ʌn'əːθlɪ] *adj* soprannaturale; (*hour*) impossibile.

uneasy [ʌn'iːzɪ] *adj* a disagio; (*worried*) preoccupato(a); **to feel** ~ **about doing sth** non sentirsela di fare qc.

uneconomic(al) ['ʌniːkə'nɔmɪk(l)] *adj* non economico(a), antieconomico(a).

uneducated [ʌn'ɛdjukeɪtɪd] *adj* senza istruzione, incolto(a).

unemployed [ʌnɪm'plɔɪd] *adj* disoccupato(a) ♦ *npl*: **the** ~ i disoccupati.

unemployment [ʌnɪm'plɔɪmənt] *n* disoccupazione *f*.

unemployment benefit, (*US*) **unemployment compensation** *n* sussidio di disoccupazione.

unending [ʌn'ɛndɪŋ] *adj* senza fine.

unenviable [ʌn'ɛnvɪəbl] *adj* poco invidiabile.

unequal [ʌn'iːkwəl] *adj* (*length, objects*)

disuguale; (*amounts*) diverso(a); (*division of labour*) ineguale.

unequalled, (*US*) **unequaled** [ʌn'iːkwəld] *adj* senza pari, insuperato(a).

unequivocal [ʌnɪ'kwɪvəkəl] *adj* (*answer*) inequivocabile; (*person*) esplicito(a), chiaro(a).

unerring [ʌn'əːrɪŋ] *adj* infallibile.

UNESCO [juː'nɛskəu] *n abbr* (= *United Nations Educational, Scientific and Cultural Organization*) U.N.E.S.C.O. *f*.

unethical [ʌn'ɛθɪkəl] *adj* (*methods*) poco ortodosso(a), non moralmente accettabile; (*doctor's behaviour*) contrario(a) all'etica professionale.

uneven [ʌn'iːvn] *adj* ineguale; (*ground*) disuguale, accidentato(a); (*heartbeat*) irregolare.

uneventful [ʌnɪ'vɛntful] *adj* senza sorprese, tranquillo(a).

unexceptional [ʌnɪk'sɛpʃənl] *adj* che non ha niente d'eccezionale.

unexciting [ʌnɪk'saɪtɪŋ] *adj* (*news*) poco emozionante; (*film, evening*) poco interessante.

unexpected [ʌnɪk'spɛktɪd] *adj* inatteso(a), imprevisto(a).

unexpectedly [ʌnɪk'spɛktɪdlɪ] *adv* inaspettatamente.

unexplained [ʌnɪk'spleɪnd] *adj* inspiegato(a).

unexploded [ʌnɪk'spləudɪd] *adj* inesploso(a).

unfailing [ʌn'feɪlɪŋ] *adj* (*supply, energy*) inesauribile; (*remedy*) infallibile.

unfair [ʌn'fɛə*] *adj*: ~ **(to)** ingiusto(a) (nei confronti di); **it's** ~ **that** ... non è giusto che ... + *sub*.

unfair dismissal *n* licenziamento ingiustificato.

unfairly [ʌn'fɛəlɪ] *adv* ingiustamente.

unfaithful [ʌn'feɪθful] *adj* infedele.

unfamiliar [ʌnfə'mɪlɪə*] *adj* sconosciuto(a), strano(a); **to be** ~ **with sth** non essere pratico di qc, non avere familiarità con qc.

unfashionable [ʌn'fæʃnəbl] *adj* (*clothes*) fuori moda *inv*; (*district*) non alla moda.

unfasten [ʌn'fɑːsn] *vt* slacciare; sciogliere.

unfathomable [ʌn'fæðəməbl] *adj* insondabile.

unfavourable, (*US*) **unfavorable** [ʌn'feɪvərəbl] *adj* sfavorevole.

unfavo(u)rably [ʌn'feɪvərəblɪ] *adv*: **to look** ~ **upon** vedere di malocchio.

unfeeling [ʌn'fiːlɪŋ] *adj* insensibile, duro(a).

unfinished [ʌn'fɪnɪʃt] *adj* incompiuto(a).

unfit [ʌnˈfɪt] adj inadatto(a); (ill) non in forma; (incompetent): ~ **(for)** incompetente (in); (: work, MIL) inabile (a); ~ **for habitation** inabitabile.

unflagging [ʌnˈflægɪŋ] adj instancabile.

unflappable [ʌnˈflæpəbl] adj calmo(a), composto(a).

unflattering [ʌnˈflætərɪŋ] adj (dress, hairstyle) che non dona.

unflinching [ʌnˈflɪntʃɪŋ] adj che non indietreggia, risoluto(a).

unfold [ʌnˈfəuld] vt spiegare; (fig) rivelare ♦ vi (view) distendersi; (story) svelarsi.

unforeseeable [ˈʌnfɔːˈsiːəbl] adj imprevedibile.

unforeseen [ʌnfɔːˈsiːn] adj imprevisto(a).

unforgettable [ʌnfəˈgɛtəbl] adj indimenticabile.

unforgivable [ʌnfəˈgɪvəbl] adj imperdonabile.

unformatted [ʌnˈfɔːmætɪd] adj (disk, text) non formattato(a).

unfortunate [ʌnˈfɔːtʃnɪt] adj sfortunato(a); (event, remark) infelice.

unfortunately [ʌnˈfɔːtʃnɪtlɪ] adv sfortunatamente, purtroppo.

unfounded [ʌnˈfaundɪd] adj infondato(a).

unfriendly [ʌnˈfrɛndlɪ] adj poco amichevole, freddo(a).

unfulfilled [ʌnfulˈfɪld] adj (ambition) non realizzato(a); (prophecy) che non si è avverato(a); (desire) insoddisfatto(a); (promise) non mantenuto(a); (terms of contract) non rispettato(a); (person) frustrato(a).

unfurl [ʌnˈfəːl] vt spiegare.

unfurnished [ʌnˈfəːnɪʃt] adj non ammobiliato(a).

ungainly [ʌnˈgeɪnlɪ] adj goffo(a), impacciato(a).

ungodly [ʌnˈgɔdlɪ] adj empio(a); **at an ~ hour** a un'ora impossibile.

ungrateful [ʌnˈgreɪtful] adj ingrato(a).

unguarded [ʌnˈgɑːdɪd] adj: **in an ~ moment** in un momento di distrazione.

unhappily [ʌnˈhæpɪlɪ] adv (unfortunately) purtroppo, sfortunatamente.

unhappiness [ʌnˈhæpɪnɪs] n infelicità.

unhappy [ʌnˈhæpɪ] adj infelice; ~ **with** (arrangements etc) insoddisfatto(a) di.

unharmed [ʌnˈhɑːmd] adj incolume, sano(a) e salvo(a).

UNHCR n abbr (= United Nations High Commission for Refugees) Alto Commissariato delle Nazioni Unite per Rifugiati.

unhealthy [ʌnˈhɛlθɪ] adj (gen) malsano(a); (person) malaticcio(a).

unheard-of [ʌnˈhəːdɔv] adj inaudito(a), senza precedenti.

unhelpful [ʌnˈhɛlpful] adj poco disponibile.

unhesitating [ʌnˈhɛzɪteɪtɪŋ] adj (loyalty) che non vacilla; (reply, offer) pronto(a), immediato(a).

unholy [ʌnˈhəulɪ] adj: **an ~ alliance** un'alleanza nefasta; **he returned at an ~ hour** è tornato ad un'ora indecente.

unhook [ʌnˈhuk] vt sganciare; sfibbiare.

unhurt [ʌnˈhəːt] adj incolume, sano(a) e salvo(a).

unhygienic [ʌnhaɪˈdʒiːnɪk] adj non igienico(a).

UNICEF [ˈjuːnɪsɛf] n abbr (= United Nations International Children's Emergency Fund) U.N.I.C.E.F. m.

unicorn [ˈjuːnɪkɔːn] n unicorno.

unidentified [ʌnaɪˈdɛntɪfaɪd] adj non identificato(a).

uniform [ˈjuːnɪfɔːm] n uniforme f, divisa ♦ adj uniforme.

uniformity [juːnɪˈfɔːmɪtɪ] n uniformità.

unify [ˈjuːnɪfaɪ] vt unificare.

unilateral [juːnɪˈlætərəl] adj unilaterale.

unimaginable [ʌnɪˈmædʒɪnəbl] adj inimmaginabile, inconcepibile.

unimaginative [ʌnɪˈmædʒɪnətɪv] adj privo(a) di fantasia, a corto di idee.

unimpaired [ʌnɪmˈpɛəd] adj intatto(a), non danneggiato(a).

unimportant [ʌnɪmˈpɔːtənt] adj senza importanza, di scarsa importanza.

unimpressed [ʌnɪmˈprɛst] adj niente affatto impressionato(a).

uninhabited [ʌnɪnˈhæbɪtɪd] adj disabitato(a).

uninhibited [ʌnɪnˈhɪbɪtɪd] adj senza inibizioni; senza ritegno.

uninjured [ʌnˈɪndʒəd] adj incolume.

uninspiring [ʌnɪnˈspaɪərɪŋ] adj banale.

uninstall [ʌnɪnˈstɔːl] vt (COMPUT) disinstallare.

unintelligent [ʌnɪnˈtɛlɪdʒənt] adj poco intelligente.

unintentional [ʌnɪnˈtɛnʃənəl] adj involontario(a).

unintentionally [ʌnɪnˈtɛnʃnəlɪ] adv senza volerlo, involontariamente.

uninvited [ʌnɪnˈvaɪtɪd] adj non invitato(a).

uninviting [ʌnɪnˈvaɪtɪŋ] adj (place, food) non invitante, poco invitante; (offer) poco allettante.

union [ˈjuːnjən] n unione f; (also: **trade ~**) sindacato ♦ cpd sindacale; **the U~** (US) gli stati dell'Unione.

unionize [ˈjuːnjənaɪz] vt sindacalizzare, organizzare in sindacato.

Union Jack *n bandiera nazionale britannica.*

Union of Soviet Socialist Republics (USSR) *n (HIST)* Unione *f* delle Repubbliche Socialiste Sovietiche (U.R.S.S.).

union shop *n stabilimento in cui tutti gli operai sono tenuti ad aderire ad un sindacato.*

unique [juːˈniːk] *adj* unico(a).

unisex [ˈjuːnɪsɛks] *adj* unisex *inv.*

Unison [ˈjuːnɪsn] *n (trade union)* sindacato generale dei funzionari.

unison [ˈjuːnɪsn] *n:* **in ~** all'unisono.

unit [ˈjuːnɪt] *n* unità *f inv; (section: of furniture etc)* elemento; *(team, squad)* reparto, squadra; **production** ~ reparto *m* produzione *inv;* **sink** ~ blocco *m* lavello *inv.*

unit cost *n* costo unitario.

unite [juːˈnaɪt] *vt* unire ♦ *vi* unirsi.

united [juːˈnaɪtɪd] *adj* unito(a); *(efforts)* congiunto(a).

United Arab Emirates *npl* Emirati *mpl* Arabi Uniti.

United Kingdom (UK) *n* Regno Unito.

United Nations (Organization) (UN, UNO) *n* (Organizzazione *f* delle) Nazioni Unite (O.N.U.).

United States (of America) (US, USA) *n* Stati *mpl* Uniti (d'America) (USA).

unit price *n* prezzo unitario.

unit trust *n (BRIT COMM)* fondo d'investimento.

unity [ˈjuːnɪtɪ] *n* unità.

Univ. *abbr =* **university**.

universal [juːnɪˈvɔːsl] *adj* universale.

universe [ˈjuːnɪvɔːs] *n* universo.

university [juːnɪˈvɔːsɪtɪ] *n* università *f inv* ♦ *cpd (student, professor, education)* universitario(a); *(year)* accademico(a).

university degree *n* laurea.

unjust [ʌnˈdʒʌst] *adj* ingiusto(a).

unjustifiable [ʌndʒʌstɪˈfaɪəbl] *adj* ingiustificabile.

unjustified [ʌnˈdʒʌstɪfaɪd] *adj* ingiustificato(a); *(TYP)* non allineato(a).

unkempt [ʌnˈkempt] *adj* trasandato(a); spettinato(a).

unkind [ʌnˈkaɪnd] *adj* poco gentile, villano(a).

unkindly [ʌnˈkaɪndlɪ] *adv (speak)* in modo sgarbato; *(treat)* male.

unknown [ʌnˈnəʊn] *adj* sconosciuto(a); ~ **to me …** a mia insaputa …; ~ **quantity** *(MATH, fig)* incognita.

unladen [ʌnˈleɪdn] *adj (ship, weight)* a vuoto.

unlawful [ʌnˈlɔːful] *adj* illecito(a), illegale.

unleaded [ˈʌnˈlɛdɪd] *adj* senza piombo; ~ **petrol** benzina verde *or* senza piombo.

unleash [ʌnˈliːʃ] *vt* sguinzagliare; *(fig)* scatenare.

unleavened [ʌnˈlɛvnd] *adj* non lievitato(a), azzimo(a).

unless [ʌnˈlɛs] *conj* a meno che (non) + *sub;* ~ **otherwise stated** salvo indicazione contraria; ~ **I am mistaken** se non mi sbaglio.

unlicensed [ʌnˈlaɪsənst] *adj (BRIT)* senza licenza per la vendita di alcolici.

unlike [ʌnˈlaɪk] *adj* diverso(a) ♦ *prep* a differenza di, contrariamente a.

unlikelihood [ʌnˈlaɪklɪhud] *adj* improbabilità.

unlikely [ʌnˈlaɪklɪ] *adj* improbabile; *(explanation)* inverosimile.

unlimited [ʌnˈlɪmɪtɪd] *adj* illimitato(a).

unlisted [ʌnˈlɪstɪd] *adj (US TEL):* **to be ~** non essere sull'elenco; *(STOCK EXCHANGE)* non quotato(a).

unlit [ʌnˈlɪt] *adj (room)* senza luce; *(road)* non illuminato(a).

unload [ʌnˈləʊd] *vt* scaricare.

unlock [ʌnˈlɔk] *vt* aprire.

unlucky [ʌnˈlʌkɪ] *adj* sfortunato(a); *(object, number)* che porta sfortuna, di malaugurio; **to be ~** *(person)* essere sfortunato, non avere fortuna.

unmanageable [ʌnˈmænɪdʒəbl] *adj (tool, vehicle)* poco maneggevole; *(situation)* impossibile.

unmanned [ʌnˈmænd] *adj (spacecraft)* senza equipaggio.

unmannerly [ʌnˈmænəlɪ] *adj* maleducato(a).

unmarked [ʌnˈmɑːkt] *adj (unstained)* pulito(a), senza macchie; ~ **police car** civetta della polizia.

unmarried [ʌnˈmærɪd] *adj* non sposato(a); *(man only)* scapolo, celibe; *(woman only)* nubile.

unmarried mother *n* ragazza *f* madre *inv.*

unmask [ʌnˈmɑːsk] *vt* smascherare.

unmatched [ʌnˈmætʃt] *adj* senza uguali.

unmentionable [ʌnˈmenʃnəbl] *adj (vice, topic)* innominabile; *(word)* irripetibile.

unmerciful [ʌnˈmɔːsɪful] *adj* spietato(a).

unmistakable [ʌnmɪsˈteɪkəbl] *adj* indubbio(a); facilmente riconoscibile.

unmitigated [ʌnˈmɪtɪɡeɪtɪd] *adj (disaster etc)* totale, assoluto(a).

unnamed [ʌnˈneɪmd] *adj (nameless)* senza nome; *(anonymous)* anonimo(a).

unnatural [ʌnˈnætʃrəl] *adj* innaturale; contro natura.

unnecessary [ʌnˈnesəsərɪ] *adj* inutile,

superfluo(a).

unnerve [ʌn'nɜːv] *vt* (*subj: accident*) sgomentare; (*: hostile attitude*) bloccare; (*: long wait, interview*) snervare.

unnoticed [ʌn'nəutɪst] *adj*: **to go** *or* **pass** ~ passare inosservato(a).

UNO ['juːnəu] *n abbr see* **United Nations Organization**.

unobservant [ʌnəb'zɜːvənt] *adj*: **to be** ~ non avere spirito di osservazione.

unobtainable [ʌnəb'teɪnəbl] *adj* (*TEL*) non ottenibile.

unobtrusive [ʌnəb'truːsɪv] *adj* discreto(a).

unoccupied [ʌn'ɔkjupaɪd] *adj* (*house*) vuoto(a); (*seat, MIL: zone*) libero(a), non occupato(a).

unofficial [ʌnə'fɪʃl] *adj* non ufficiale; (*strike*) non dichiarato(a) dal sindacato.

unopened [ʌn'əupənd] *adj* (*letter*) non aperto(a); (*present*) ancora incartato(a).

unopposed [ʌnə'pəuzd] *adj* senza incontrare opposizione.

unorthodox [ʌn'ɔːθədɔks] *adj* non ortodosso(a).

unpack [ʌn'pæk] *vi* disfare la valigia (*or* le valigie).

unpaid [ʌn'peɪd] *adj* (*holiday*) non pagato(a); (*work*) non retribuito(a); (*bill, debt*) da pagare.

unpalatable [ʌn'pælətəbl] *adj* (*food*) immangiabile; (*drink*) imbevibile; (*truth*) sgradevole.

unparalleled [ʌn'pærəlɛld] *adj* incomparabile, impareggiabile.

unpatriotic ['ʌnpætrɪ'ɔtɪk] *adj* (*person*) poco patriottico(a); (*speech, attitude*) antipatriottico(a).

unplanned [ʌn'plænd] *adj* (*visit*) imprevisto(a); (*baby*) non previsto(a).

unpleasant [ʌn'plɛznt] *adj* spiacevole; (*person, remark*) antipatico(a); (*day, experience*) brutto(a).

unplug [ʌn'plʌg] *vt* staccare.

unpolluted [ʌnpə'luːtɪd] *adj* non inquinato(a).

unpopular [ʌn'pɔpjulə*] *adj* impopolare; **to make o.s.** ~ **(with)** rendersi antipatico (a); (*subj: politician etc*) alienarsi le simpatie (di).

unprecedented [ʌn'prɛsɪdəntɪd] *adj* senza precedenti.

unpredictable [ʌnprɪ'dɪktəbl] *adj* imprevedibile.

unprejudiced [ʌn'prɛdʒudɪst] *adj* (*not biased*) obiettivo(a), imparziale; (*having no prejudices*) senza pregiudizi.

unprepared [ʌnprɪ'pɛəd] *adj* (*person*) impreparato(a); (*speech*)

improvvisato(a).

unprepossessing [ʌnpriːpə'zɛsɪŋ] *adj* insulso(a).

unpretentious [ʌnprɪ'tɛnʃəs] *adj* senza pretese.

unprincipled [ʌn'prɪnsɪpld] *adj* senza scrupoli.

unproductive [ʌnprə'dʌktɪv] *adj* improduttivo(a); (*discussion*) sterile.

unprofessional ['ʌnprə'fɛʃənl] *adj*: ~ **conduct** scorrettezza professionale.

unprofitable [ʌn'prɔfɪtəbl] *adj* (*financially*) non redditizio(a); (*job, deal*) poco lucrativo(a).

UNPROFOR ['ʌnprəfɔː*] *n abbr* (= *United Nations Protection Force*) reparto di protezione dell'ONU.

unprotected ['ʌnprə'tɛktɪd] *adj* (*sex*) non protetto(a).

unprovoked [ʌnprə'vəukt] *adj* non provocato(a).

unpunished [ʌn'pʌnɪʃt] *adj*: **to go** ~ restare impunito(a).

unqualified [ʌn'kwɔlɪfaɪd] *adj* (*worker*) non qualificato(a); (*in professions*) non abilitato(a); (*success*) assoluto(a), senza riserve.

unquestionably [ʌn'kwɛstʃənəblɪ] *adv* indiscutibilmente.

unquestioning [ʌn'kwɛstʃənɪŋ] *adj* (*obedience, acceptance*) cieco(a).

unravel [ʌn'rævl] *vt* dipanare, districare.

unreal [ʌn'rɪəl] *adj* irreale.

unrealistic [ʌnrɪə'lɪstɪk] *adj* (*idea*) illusorio(a); (*estimate*) non realistico(a).

unreasonable [ʌn'riːznəbl] *adj* irragionevole; **to make** ~ **demands on sb** voler troppo da qn.

unrecognizable [ʌn'rɛkəgnaɪzəbl] *adj* irriconoscibile.

unrecognized [ʌn'rɛkəgnaɪzd] *adj* (*talent, genius*) misconosciuto(a); (*POL: regime*) non ufficialmente riconosciuto(a).

unrecorded [ʌnrɪ'kɔːdɪd] *adj* non documentato(a), non registrato(a).

unrefined [ʌnrɪ'faɪnd] *adj* (*sugar, petroleum*) greggio(a); (*person*) rozzo(a).

unrehearsed [ʌnrɪ'hɜːst] *adj* (*THEAT etc*) improvvisato(a); (*spontaneous*) imprevisto(a).

unrelated [ʌnrɪ'leɪtɪd] *adj*: ~ **(to)** senza rapporto (con); (*by family*) non imparentato(a) (con).

unrelenting [ʌnrɪ'lɛntɪŋ] *adj* implacabile; accanito(a).

unreliable [ʌnrɪ'laɪəbl] *adj* (*person, machine*) che non dà affidamento; (*news, source of information*) inattendibile.

unrelieved [ʌnrɪ'liːvd] *adj* (*monotony*) uniforme.

unremitting [ʌnrɪ'mɪtɪŋ] *adj* incessante, infaticabile.

unrepeatable [ʌnrɪ'piːtəbl] *adj* (*offer*) unico(a).

unrepentant [ʌnrɪ'pɛntənt] *adj* impenitente.

unrepresentative [ʌnrɛprɪ'zɛntətɪv] *adj* atipico(a), poco rappresentativo(a).

unreserved [ʌnrɪ'zɜːvd] *adj* (*seat*) non prenotato(a), non riservato(a); (*approval, admiration*) senza riserve.

unresponsive [ʌnrɪs'pɒnsɪv] *adj* che non reagisce.

unrest [ʌn'rɛst] *n* agitazione *f.*

unrestricted [ʌnrɪ'strɪktɪd] *adj* (*power, time*) illimitato(a); (*access*) libero(a).

unrewarded [ʌnrɪ'wɔːdɪd] *adj* non ricompensato(a).

unripe [ʌn'raɪp] *adj* acerbo(a).

unrivalled, (*US*) **unrivaled** [ʌn'raɪvəld] *adj* senza pari.

unroll [ʌn'rəul] *vt* srotolare.

unruffled [ʌn'rʌfld] *adj* (*person*) calmo(a) e tranquillo(a), imperturbato(a); (*hair*) a posto.

unruly [ʌn'ruːlɪ] *adj* indisciplinato(a).

unsafe [ʌn'seɪf] *adj* pericoloso(a), rischioso(a); ~ **to drink** non potabile; ~ **to eat** non commestibile.

unsaid [ʌn'sɛd] *adj*: **to leave sth** ~ passare qc sotto silenzio.

unsaleable, (*US*) **unsalable** [ʌn'seɪləbl] *adj* invendibile.

unsatisfactory ['ʌnsætɪs'fæktərɪ] *adj* che lascia a desiderare, insufficiente.

unsavoury, (*US*) **unsavory** [ʌn'seɪvərɪ] *adj* (*fig: person*) losco(a); (: *reputation, subject*) disgustoso(a), ripugnante.

unscathed [ʌn'skeɪðd] *adj* incolume.

unscientific ['ʌnsaɪən'tɪfɪk] *adj* poco scientifico(a).

unscrew [ʌn'skruː] *vt* svitare.

unscrupulous [ʌn'skruːpjuləs] *adj* senza scrupoli.

unseat [ʌn'siːt] *vt* (*rider*) disarcionare; (*fig: an official*) spodestare.

unsecured [ʌnsɪ'kjuəd] *adj*: ~ **creditor** creditore *m* chirografario.

unseeded [ʌn'siːdɪd] *adj* (*SPORT*) che non è una testa di serie.

unseemly [ʌn'siːmlɪ] *adj* sconveniente.

unseen [ʌn'siːn] *adj* (*person*) inosservato(a); (*danger*) nascosto(a).

unselfish [ʌn'sɛlfɪʃ] *adj* (*person*) altruista; (*act*) disinteressato(a).

unsettled [ʌn'sɛtld] *adj* (*person, future*) incerto(a); (*question*) non risolto(a); (*weather, market*) instabile; **to feel** ~ sentirsi disorientato(a).

unsettling [ʌn'sɛtlɪŋ] *adj* inquietante.

unshak(e)able [ʌn'ʃeɪkəbl] *adj* irremovibile.

unshaven [ʌn'ʃeɪvn] *adj* non rasato(a).

unsightly [ʌn'saɪtlɪ] *adj* brutto(a), sgradevole a vedersi.

unskilled [ʌn'skɪld] *adj*: ~ **worker** manovale *m.*

unsociable [ʌn'səuʃəbl] *adj* (*person*) poco socievole; (*behaviour*) antipatico(a).

unsocial [ʌn'səuʃəl] *adj*: ~ **hours** orario sconveniente.

unsold [ʌn'səuld] *adj* invenduto(a).

unsolicited [ʌnsə'lɪsɪtɪd] *adj* non richiesto(a).

unsophisticated [ʌnsə'fɪstɪkeɪtɪd] *adj* semplice, naturale.

unsound [ʌn'saund] *adj* (*health*) debole, cagionevole; (*in construction: floor, foundations*) debole, malsicuro(a); (*policy, advice*) poco sensato(a); (*judgment, investment*) poco sicuro(a).

unspeakable [ʌn'spiːkəbl] *adj* (*bad*) abominevole.

unspoken [ʌn'spəukən] *adj* (*words*) non detto(a); (*agreement, approval*) tacito(a).

unsteady [ʌn'stɛdɪ] *adj* instabile, malsicuro(a).

unstinting [ʌn'stɪntɪŋ] *adj* (*support*) incondizionato(a); (*generosity*) illimitato(a); (*praise*) senza riserve.

unstuck [ʌn'stʌk] *adj*: **to come** ~ scollarsi; (*fig*) fare fiasco.

unsubscribe [ʌnsʌb'scraɪb] *vi* (*COMPUT*) disdire l'abbonamento.

unsubstantiated [ʌnsəb'stænʃɪeɪtɪd] *adj* (*rumour, accusation*) infondato(a).

unsuccessful [ʌnsək'sɛsful] *adj* (*writer, proposal*) che non ha successo; (*marriage, attempt*) mal riuscito(a), fallito(a); **to be** ~ (*in attempting sth*) non riuscire; non avere successo; (*application*) non essere considerato(a).

unsuccessfully [ʌnsək'sɛsfəlɪ] *adv* senza successo.

unsuitable [ʌn'suːtəbl] *adj* inadatto(a); (*moment*) inopportuno(a).

unsuited [ʌn'suːtɪd] *adj*: **to be** ~ **for** *or* **to** non essere fatto(a) per.

unsung ['ʌn'sʌŋ] *adj*: **an** ~ **hero** un eroe misconosciuto.

unsupported [ʌnsə'pɔːtɪd] *adj* (*claim*) senza fondamento; (*theory*) non dimostrato(a).

unsure [ʌn'ʃuə*] *adj*: ~ **(of** *or* **about)** incerto(a) (su); **to be** ~ **of o.s.** essere insicuro(a).

unsuspecting [ʌnsə'spɛktɪŋ] *adj* che non sospetta niente.

unsweetened [ʌn'swiːtnd] *adj* senza zucchero.

unswerving [ʌn'swəːvɪŋ] *adj* fermo(a).

unsympathetic ['ʌnsɪmpə'θɛtɪk] *adj* (*attitude*) poco incoraggiante; (*person*) antipatico(a); ~ **(to)** non solidale (verso).

untangle [ʌn'tæŋgl] *vt* sbrogliare.

untapped [ʌn'tæpt] *adj* (*resources*) non sfruttato(a).

untaxed [ʌn'tækst] *adj* (*goods*) esente da imposte; (*income*) non imponibile.

unthinkable [ʌn'θɪŋkəbl] *adj* impensabile, inconcepibile.

unthinkingly ['ʌn'θɪŋkɪŋlɪ] *adv* senza pensare.

untidy [ʌn'taɪdɪ] *adj* (*room*) in disordine; (*appearance, work*) trascurato(a); (*person, writing*) disordinato(a).

untie [ʌn'taɪ] *vt* (*knot, parcel*) disfare; (*prisoner, dog*) slegare.

until [ʌn'tɪl] *prep* fino a; (*after negative*) prima di ♦ *conj* finché, fino a quando; (*in past, after negative*) prima che + *sub*, prima di + *infinitive*; ~ **now** finora; ~ **then** fino ad allora; **from morning** ~ **night** dalla mattina alla sera.

untimely [ʌn'taɪmlɪ] *adj* intempestivo(a), inopportuno(a); (*death*) prematuro(a).

untold [ʌn'təuld] *adj* incalcolabile; indescrivibile.

untouched [ʌn'tʌtʃt] *adj* (*not used etc*) non toccato(a), intatto(a); (*safe: person*) incolume; (*unaffected*): ~ **by** insensibile a.

untoward [ʌntə'wɔːd] *adj* sfortunato(a), sconveniente.

untrained ['ʌn'treɪnd] *adj* (*worker*) privo(a) di formazione professionale; (*troops*) privo(a) di addestramento; **to the** ~ **eye** ad un occhio inesperto.

untrammelled [ʌn'træmld] *adj* illimitato(a).

untranslatable [ʌntrænz'leɪtəbl] *adj* intraducibile.

untrue [ʌn'truː] *adj* (*statement*) falso(a), non vero(a).

untrustworthy [ʌn'trʌstwəːðɪ] *adj* di cui non ci si può fidare.

unusable [ʌn'juːzəbl] *adj* inservibile, inutilizzabile.

unused [ʌn'juːzd] *adj* (*new*) nuovo(a); (*not made use of*) non usato(a), non utilizzato(a); **to be** ~ **to sth/to doing sth** non essere abituato(a) a qc/a fare qc.

unusual [ʌn'juːʒuəl] *adj* insolito(a), eccezionale, raro(a).

unusually [ʌn'juːʒuəlɪ] *adv* insolitamente.

unveil [ʌn'veɪl] *vt* scoprire, svelare.

unwanted [ʌn'wɔntɪd] *adj* non desiderato(a).

unwarranted [ʌn'wɔrəntɪd] *adj* ingiustificato(a).

unwary [ʌn'wɛərɪ] *adj* incauto(a).

unwavering [ʌn'weɪvərɪŋ] *adj* fermo(a), incrollabile.

unwelcome [ʌn'wɛlkəm] *adj* (*gen*) non gradito(a); **to feel** ~ sentire che la propria presenza non è gradita.

unwell [ʌn'wɛl] *adj* indisposto(a); **to feel** ~ non sentirsi bene.

unwieldy [ʌn'wiːldɪ] *adj* poco maneggevole.

unwilling [ʌn'wɪlɪŋ] *adj*: **to be** ~ **to do** non voler fare.

unwillingly [ʌn'wɪlɪŋlɪ] *adv* malvolentieri.

unwind [ʌn'waɪnd] *vb* (*irreg*) *vt* svolgere, srotolare ♦ *vi* (*relax*) rilassarsi.

unwise [ʌn'waɪz] *adj* (*decision, act*) avventato(a).

unwitting [ʌn'wɪtɪŋ] *adj* involontario(a).

unworkable [ʌn'wəːkəbl] *adj* (*plan etc*) inattuabile.

unworthy [ʌn'wəːðɪ] *adj* indegno(a); **to be** ~ **of sth/to do sth** non essere degno di qc/di fare qc.

unwrap [ʌn'ræp] *vt* disfare; (*present*) aprire.

unwritten [ʌn'rɪtn] *adj* (*agreement*) tacito(a).

unzip [ʌn'zɪp] *vt* aprire (la chiusura lampo di); (*COMPUT*) dezippare.

═══════════════════════════ *KEYWORD*

up [ʌp] *prep* su; **he went** ~ **the stairs/the hill** è salito su per le scale/sulla collina; **the cat was** ~ **a tree** il gatto era su un albero; **they live further** ~ **the street** vivono un po' più su nella stessa strada

♦ *adv* **1** (*upwards, higher*) su, in alto; ~ **in the sky/the mountains** su nel cielo/in montagna; ~ **there** lassù; ~ **above** su in alto; ~ **with Leeds United!** viva il Leeds United!

2: **to be** ~ (*out of bed*) essere alzato(a); (*prices, level*) essere salito(a); (*building*) essere terminato(a); (*tent*) essere piantato(a); (*curtains, shutters, wallpaper*) essere su; **"this side** ~**"** "alto"; **to be** ~ **(by)** (*in price, value*) essere salito(a) *or* aumentato(a) (di); **when the year was** ~ (*finished*) finito l'anno; **time's** ~ il tempo è scaduto; **he's well** ~ **in** *or* **on politics** (*BRIT*) è molto informato di *or* sulla politica

3: ~ **to** (*as far as*) fino a; ~ **to now** finora

4: to be ~ to (*depending on*): **it's ~ to you** sta a lei, dipende da lei; (*equal to*): **he's not ~ to it** (*job, task etc*) non ne è all'altezza; (*col: be doing*): **what is he ~ to?** cosa sta combinando?; **what's ~?** (*col: wrong*) che c'è?; **what's ~ with him?** che ha?, che gli prende?
♦ *n:* **~s and downs** alti e bassi *mpl*
♦ *vi* (*col*): **she ~ped and left** improvvisamente se ne andò.

up-and-coming ['ʌpənd'kʌmɪŋ] *adj* pieno(a) di promesse, promettente.
upbeat ['ʌpbiːt] *n* (*MUS*) tempo in levare; (*in economy, prosperity*) incremento ♦ *adj* (*col*) ottimistico(a).
upbraid [ʌp'breɪd] *vt* rimproverare.
upbringing['ʌpbrɪŋɪŋ] *n* educazione *f.*
upcoming ['ʌpkʌmɪŋ] *adj* imminente, prossimo(a).
update [ʌp'deɪt] *vt* aggiornare.
upend [ʌp'ɛnd] *vt* rovesciare.
upfront [ʌp'frʌnt] *adj* (*col*) franco(a), aperto(a) ♦ *adv* (*pay*) subito.
upgrade [ʌp'greɪd] *vt* promuovere; (*job*) rivalutare; (*COMPUT*) far passare a potenza superiore.
upheaval [ʌp'hiːvl] *n* sconvolgimento; tumulto.
uphill [ʌp'hɪl] *adj* in salita; (*fig: task*) difficile ♦ *adv:* **to go ~** andare in salita, salire.
uphold [ʌp'həuld] *vt irreg* approvare; sostenere.
upholstery [ʌp'həulstərɪ] *n* tappezzeria.
upkeep ['ʌpkiːp] *n* manutenzione *f.*
up-market [ʌp'mɑːkɪt] *adj* (*product*) che si rivolge ad una fascia di mercato superiore.
upon [ə'pɔn] *prep* su.
upper ['ʌpə*] *adj* superiore ♦ *n* (*of shoe*) tomaia; **the ~ class** ≈ l'alta borghesia.
upper case *n* maiuscolo.
upper-class [ʌpə'klɑːs] *adj* dell'alta borghesia; (*district*) signorile; (*accent*) aristocratico(a); (*attitude*) snob *inv.*
uppercut ['ʌpəkʌt] *n* uppercut *m inv*, montante *m.*
upper hand *n:* **to have the ~** avere il coltello dalla parte del manico.
Upper House *n:* **the ~** (*in Britain*) la Camera Alta, la Camera dei Lords; (*in US etc*) il Senato.
uppermost ['ʌpəməust] *adj* il(la) più alto(a); predominante; **it was ~ in my mind** è stata la mia prima preoccupazione.
Upper Volta [-'vɔltə] *n* Alto Volta *m.*
upright ['ʌpraɪt] *adj* diritto(a); verticale;

(*fig*) diritto(a), onesto(a) ♦ *n* montante *m.*
uprising ['ʌpraɪzɪŋ] *n* insurrezione *f,* rivolta.
uproar ['ʌprɔː*] *n* tumulto, clamore *m.*
uproarious [ʌp'rɔːrɪəs] *adj* clamoroso(a); (*hilarious*) esilarante; **~ laughter** risata sonora.
uproot [ʌp'ruːt] *vt* sradicare.
upset *n* ['ʌpsɛt] turbamento ♦ *vt* [ʌp'sɛt] (*irreg: like* **set**) (*glass etc*) rovesciare; (*plan, stomach*) scombussolare; (*person: offend*) contrariare; (*: grieve*) addolorare; sconvolgere ♦ *adj* [ʌp'sɛt] contrariato(a); addolorato(a); (*stomach*) scombussolato(a), disturbato(a); **to have a stomach ~** (*BRIT*) avere lo stomaco in disordine *or* scombussolato; **to get ~** contrariarsi; addolorarsi.
upset price *n* (*US, Scottish*) prezzo di riserva.
upsetting [ʌp'sɛtɪŋ] *adj* (*saddening*) sconvolgente; (*offending*) offensivo(a); (*annoying*) fastidioso(a).
upshot ['ʌpʃɔt] *n* risultato; **the ~ of it all was that ...** la conclusione è stata che ....
upside down ['ʌpsaɪd-] *adv* sottosopra; **to turn ~** capovolgere; (*fig*) mettere sottosopra.
upstage ['ʌp'steɪdʒ] *vt:* **to ~ sb** rubare la scena a qn.
upstairs [ʌp'stɛəz] *adv, adj* di sopra, al piano superiore ♦ *n* piano di sopra.
upstart ['ʌpstɑːt] *n* parvenu *m inv.*
upstream [ʌp'striːm] *adv* a monte.
upsurge ['ʌpsəːdʒ] *n* (*of enthusiasm etc*) ondata.
uptake ['ʌpteɪk] *n:* **he is quick/slow on the ~** è pronto/lento di comprendonio.
uptight [ʌp'taɪt] *adj* (*col*) teso(a).
up-to-date ['ʌptə'deɪt] *adj* moderno(a); aggiornato(a).
upturn ['ʌptəːn] *n* (*in luck*) svolta favorevole; (*in value of currency*) rialzo.
upturned ['ʌptəːnd] *adj* (*nose*) all'insù.
upward ['ʌpwəd] *adj* ascendente; verso l'alto.
upwardly-mobile ['ʌpwədlɪ'məubaɪl] *n:* **to be ~** salire nella scala sociale.
upward(s) ['ʌpwəd(z)] *adv* in su, verso l'alto.
URA *n abbr* (*US:* = *Urban Renewal Administration*) amministrazione per il rinnovamento urbano.
Ural Mountains ['juərəl-] *npl:* **the ~** (*also:* **the Urals**) gli Urali, i Monti Urali.
uranium [juə'reɪnɪəm] *n* uranio.
Uranus [juə'reɪnəs] *n* (*planet*) Urano.
urban ['əːbən] *adj* urbano(a).

urbane [əː'beɪn] *adj* civile, urbano(a), educato(a).
urbanization [əːbənaɪ'zeɪʃən] *n* urbanizzazione *f*.
urchin ['əːtʃɪn] *n* monello; **sea** ~ riccio di mare.
Urdu ['uəduː] *n* urdu *m inv*.
urge [əːdʒ] *n* impulso, stimolo ♦ *vt* (*caution etc*) raccomandare vivamente; **to** ~ **sb to do** esortare qn a fare, spingere qn a fare; raccomandare a qn di fare.
▶**urge on** *vt* spronare.
urgency ['əːdʒənsɪ] *n* urgenza; (*of tone*) insistenza.
urgent ['əːdʒənt] *adj* urgente; (*earnest, persistent: plea*) pressante; (: *tone*) insistente, incalzante.
urgently ['əːdʒəntlɪ] *adv* d'urgenza, urgentemente; con insistenza.
urinal ['juərɪnl] *n* (*BRIT: building*) vespasiano; (: *vessel*) orinale *m*, pappagallo.
urinate ['juərɪneɪt] *vi* orinare.
urine ['juərɪn] *n* orina.
urn [əːn] *n* urna; (*also:* **tea** ~) bollitore *m* per il tè.
Uruguay ['juərəgwaɪ] *n* Uruguay *m*.
Uruguayan [juərə'gwaɪən] *adj, n* uruguaiano(a).
US *n abbr see* **United States**.
us [ʌs] *pron* ci; (*stressed, after prep*) noi.
USA *n abbr* (*GEO*) *see* **United States (of America)**; (*MIL*) = *United States Army*.
usable ['juːzəbl] *adj* utilizzabile, usabile.
USAF *n abbr* = *United States Air Force*.
usage ['juːzɪdʒ] *n* uso.
USCG *n abbr* = *United States Coast Guard*.
USDA *n abbr* = *Union of Shop, Distributive, and Allied Workers*.
USDAW ['ʌzdɔː] *n abbr* (*BRIT:* = *Union of Shop, Distributive and Allied Workers*) sindacato dei dipendenti di negozi, reti di distribuzione e simili.
USDI *n abbr* = *United States Department of the Interior*.
use *n* [juːs] uso; impiego, utilizzazione *f* ♦ *vt* [juːz] usare, utilizzare, servirsi di; **she** ~**d to do it** lo faceva (una volta), era solita farlo; **in** ~ in uso; **out of** ~ fuori uso; **to be of** ~ essere utile, servire; **to make** ~ **of sth** far uso di qc, utilizzare qc; **ready for** ~ pronto per l'uso; **it's no** ~ non serve, è inutile; **to have the** ~ **of** poter usare; **what's this** ~**d for?** a che serve?; **to be** ~**d to** avere l'abitudine di; **to get** ~**d to** abituarsi a, fare l'abitudine a.
▶**use up** *vt* finire; (*supplies*) dare fondo a; (*left-overs*) utilizzare.

used [juːzd] *adj* (*car*) d'occasione.
useful ['juːsful] *adj* utile; **to come in** ~ fare comodo, tornare utile.
usefulness ['juːsfəlnɪs] *n* utilità.
useless ['juːslɪs] *adj* inutile; (*unusable: object*) inservibile.
user ['juːzə*] *n* utente *m/f*; (*of petrol, gas etc*) consumatore/trice.
user-friendly ['juːzə'frɛndlɪ] *adj* orientato(a) all'utente.
USES *n abbr* = *United States Employment Service*.
usher ['ʌʃə*] *n* usciere *m*; (*in cinema*) maschera ♦ *vt*: **to** ~ **sb in** far entrare qn.
usherette [ʌʃə'rɛt] *n* (*in cinema*) maschera.
USIA *n abbr* = *United States Information Agency*.
USM *n abbr* = *United States Mint*; *United States Mail*.
USN *n abbr* = *United States Navy*.
USP *n abbr* = *unique selling point or proposition*.
USPHS *n abbr* = *United States Public Health Service*.
USPO *n abbr* = *United States Post Office*.
USS *abbr* = *United States Ship (or Steamer)*.
USSR *n abbr* (*HIST*) *see* **Union of Soviet Socialist Republics**.
usu. *abbr* = **usually**.
usual ['juːʒuəl] *adj* solito(a); **as** ~ come al solito, come d'abitudine.
usually ['juːʒuəlɪ] *adv* di solito.
usurer ['juːʒərə*] *adj* usuraio/a.
usurp [juː'zəːp] *vt* usurpare.
UT *abbr* (*US*) = *Utah*.
utensil [juː'tɛnsl] *n* utensile *m*.
uterus ['juːtərəs] *n* utero.
utilitarian [juːtɪlɪ'tɛərɪən] *adj* utilitario(a).
utility [juː'tɪlɪtɪ] *n* utilità; (*also:* **public** ~) servizio pubblico.
utility room *n* locale adibito alla stiratura dei panni etc.
utilization [juːtɪlaɪ'zeɪʃən] *n* utilizzazione *f*.
utilize ['juːtɪlaɪz] *vt* utilizzare; sfruttare.
utmost ['ʌtməust] *adj* estremo(a) ♦ *n*: **to do one's** ~ fare il possibile *or* di tutto; **of the** ~ **importance** della massima importanza; **it is of the** ~ **importance that ...** è estremamente importante che ... + *sub*.
utter ['ʌtə*] *adj* assoluto(a), totale ♦ *vt* pronunciare, proferire; emettere.
utterance ['ʌtərəns] *n* espressione *f*; parole *fpl*.
utterly ['ʌtəlɪ] *adv* completamente, del tutto.
U-turn ['juːtəːn] *n* inversione *f* a U; (*fig*) voltafaccia *m inv*.
Uzbekistan [ʌzbɛkɪ'stɑːn] *n* Uzbekistan.

V v

V, v [viː] n (*letter*) V, v m or f inv; **V for Victor** ≈ V come Venezia.

v abbr (= *verse*; = *vide: see*) v.; (= *volt*) V.; (= *versus*) contro.

VA, Va. abbr (US) = *Virginia*.

vac [væk] n abbr (*BRIT col*) = **vacation**.

vacancy ['veɪkənsɪ] n (*job*) posto libero; (*room*) stanza libera; **"no vacancies"** "completo"; **have you any vacancies?** (*office*) avete bisogno di personale?; (*hotel*) avete una stanza?

vacant ['veɪkənt] adj (*job, seat etc*) libero(a); (*expression*) assente.

vacant lot n terreno non occupato; (*for sale*) terreno in vendita.

vacate [və'keɪt] vt lasciare libero(a).

vacation [və'keɪʃən] n (*esp US*) vacanze *fpl*; **to take a** ~ prendere una vacanza, prendere le ferie; **on** ~ in vacanza, in ferie.

vacation course n corso estivo.

vaccinate ['væksɪneɪt] vt vaccinare.

vaccination [væksɪ'neɪʃən] n vaccinazione f.

vaccine ['væksiːn] n vaccino.

vacuum ['vækjum] n vuoto.

vacuum bottle n (US) = **vacuum flask**.

vacuum cleaner n aspirapolvere m inv.

vacuum flask n (*BRIT*) thermos ® m inv.

vacuum-packed ['vækjum'pækt] adj confezionato(a) sottovuoto.

vagabond ['vægəbɒnd] n vagabondo/a.

vagary ['veɪgərɪ] n capriccio.

vagina [və'dʒaɪnə] n vagina.

vagrancy ['veɪgrənsɪ] n vagabondaggio.

vagrant ['veɪgrənt] n vagabondo/a.

vague [veɪg] adj vago(a); (*blurred: photo, memory*) sfocato(a); **I haven't the** ~**st idea** non ho la minima or più pallida idea.

vaguely ['veɪglɪ] adv vagamente.

vain [veɪn] adj (*useless*) inutile, vano(a); (*conceited*) vanitoso(a); **in** ~ inutilmente, invano.

valance ['væləns] n volant m inv, balza.

valedictory [vælɪ'dɪktərɪ] adj di commiato.

valentine ['væləntaɪn] n (*also*: ~ **card**) cartolina or biglietto di San Valentino.

valet ['vælɪt] n cameriere m personale.

valet parking n parcheggio effettuato da un dipendente (dell'albergo etc).

valet service n (*for clothes*) servizio di lavanderia; (*for car*) servizio completo di lavaggio.

valiant ['vælɪənt] adj valoroso(a), coraggioso(a).

valid ['vælɪd] adj valido(a), valevole; (*excuse*) valido(a).

validate ['vælɪdeɪt] vt (*contract, document*) convalidare; (*argument, claim*) comprovare.

validity [və'lɪdɪtɪ] n validità.

valise [və'liːz] n borsa da viaggio.

valley ['vælɪ] n valle f.

valour, (US) **valor** ['vælə*] n valore m.

valuable ['væljuəbl] adj (*jewel*) di (grande) valore; (*time*) prezioso(a); ~**s** npl oggetti mpl di valore.

valuation [vælju'eɪʃən] n valutazione f, stima.

value ['væljuː] n valore m ♦ vt (*fix price*) valutare, dare un prezzo a; (*cherish*) apprezzare, tenere a; **to be of great** ~ **to sb** avere molta importanza per qn; **to lose (in)** ~ (*currency*) svalutarsi; (*property*) perdere (di) valore; **to gain (in)** ~ (*currency*) guadagnare; (*property*) aumentare di valore; **you get good** ~ **(for money) in that shop** si compra bene in quel negozio.

value added tax (VAT) n (*BRIT*) imposta sul valore aggiunto (I.V.A.).

valued ['væluːd] adj (*appreciated*) stimato(a), apprezzato(a).

valuer ['væljuə*] n stimatore/trice.

valve [vælv] n valvola.

vampire ['væmpaɪə*] n vampiro.

van [væn] n (*AUT*) furgone m; (*BRIT RAIL*) vagone m.

V and A n abbr (*BRIT*) = *Victoria and Albert Museum*.

vandal ['vændl] n vandalo/a.

vandalism ['vændəlɪzəm] n vandalismo.

vandalize ['vændəlaɪz] vt vandalizzare.

vanguard ['vængɑːd] n avanguardia.

vanilla [və'nɪlə] n vaniglia ♦ cpd (*ice cream*) alla vaniglia.

vanish ['vænɪʃ] vi svanire, scomparire.

vanity ['vænɪtɪ] n vanità.

vanity case n valigetta per cosmetici.

vantage ['vɑːntɪdʒ] n: ~ **point** posizione f or punto di osservazione; (*fig*) posizione vantaggiosa.

vaporize ['veɪpəraɪz] vt vaporizzare ♦ vi vaporizzarsi.

vapour, (US) **vapor** ['veɪpə*] n vapore m.

variable ['vɛərɪəbl] adj variabile; (*mood*)

mutevole ♦ n fattore m variabile, variabile f.

variance ['vɛərɪəns] n: **to be at ~ (with)** essere in disaccordo (con); (facts) essere in contraddizione (con).

variant ['vɛərɪənt] n variante f.

variation [vɛərɪ'eɪʃən] n variazione f; (in opinion) cambiamento.

varicose ['værɪkəʊs] adj: ~ **veins** varici fpl.

varied ['vɛərɪd] adj vario(a), diverso(a).

variety [və'raɪətɪ] n varietà f inv; (quantity): **a wide ~ of** ... una vasta gamma di ...; **for a ~ of reasons** per una serie di motivi.

variety show n spettacolo di varietà.

various ['vɛərɪəs] adj vario(a), diverso(a); (several) parecchi(e), molti(e); **at ~ times** in momenti diversi; (several) diverse volte.

varnish ['vɑːnɪʃ] n vernice f; (for nails) smalto ♦ vt verniciare; **to ~ one's nails** mettersi lo smalto sulle unghie.

vary ['vɛərɪ] vt, vi variare, mutare; **to ~ (with or according to)** variare (con or a seconda di).

varying ['vɛərɪɪŋ] adj variabile.

vase [vɑːz] n vaso.

vasectomy [væ'sɛktəmɪ] n vasectomia.

Vaseline ® ['væsɪliːn] n vaselina.

vast [vɑːst] adj vasto(a); (amount, success) enorme.

vastly ['vɑːstlɪ] adv enormemente.

vastness ['vɑːstnɪs] n vastità.

VAT [væt] n abbr (BRIT) see **value added tax.**

vat [væt] n tino.

Vatican ['vætɪkən] n: **the ~** il Vaticano.

vatman ['vætmæn] n (BRIT col): **the ~** ≈ l'ispettore m dell'IVA; (Inland Revenue) (il) fisco.

vault [vɔːlt] n (of roof) volta; (tomb) tomba; (in bank) camera blindata; (jump) salto ♦ vt (also: ~ **over**) saltare (d'un balzo).

vaunted ['vɔːntɪd] adj: **much-~** tanto celebrato(a).

VC n abbr (BRIT: = Victoria Cross) medaglia al coraggio; = **vice-chairman.**

VCR n abbr see **video cassette recorder.**

VD n abbr see **venereal disease.**

VDU n abbr see **visual display unit.**

veal [viːl] n vitello.

veer [vɪə*] vi girare; virare.

veg. [vɛdʒ] n abbr (BRIT col: = vegetable(s)) ≈ contorno.

vegan ['viːgən] n (BRIT) vegetaliano/a.

vegeburger, veggieburger ['vɛdʒɪbəːgə*] n hamburger m inv vegetariano.

vegetable ['vɛdʒtəbl] n verdura, ortaggio ♦ adj vegetale.

vegetable garden n orto.

vegetarian [vɛdʒɪ'tɛərɪən] adj, n vegetariano(a).

vegetate ['vɛdʒɪteɪt] vi vegetare.

vegetation [vɛdʒɪ'teɪʃən] n vegetazione f.

vegetative ['vɛdʒɪtətɪv] adj (also BOT) vegetativo(a).

vehemence ['viːɪməns] n veemenza, violenza.

vehement ['viːɪmənt] adj veemente, violento(a); profondo(a).

vehicle ['viːɪkl] n veicolo; (fig) mezzo.

vehicular [vɪ'hɪkjulə*] adj: **"no ~ traffic"** "chiuso al traffico di veicoli".

veil [veɪl] n velo ♦ vt velare; **under a ~ of secrecy** (fig) protetto da una cortina di segretezza.

veiled [veɪld] adj (also fig) velato(a).

vein [veɪn] n vena; (on leaf) nervatura; (fig: mood) vena, umore m.

Velcro ® ['vɛlkrəu] n velcro ® m inv.

vellum ['vɛləm] n (writing paper) carta patinata.

velocity [vɪ'lɒsɪtɪ] n velocità f inv.

velour [və'luə*] n velours m inv.

velvet ['vɛlvɪt] n velluto.

vending machine ['vɛndɪŋ-] n distributore m automatico.

vendor ['vɛndə*] n venditore/trice; **street ~** venditore ambulante.

veneer [və'nɪə*] n impiallacciatura; (fig) vernice f.

venerable ['vɛnərəbl] adj venerabile.

venereal disease (VD) [vɪ'nɪərɪəl-] n malattia venerea.

Venetian [vɪ'niːʃən] adj, n veneziano(a).

Venetian blind n (tenda alla) veneziana.

Venezuela [vɛnɪ'zweɪlə] n Venezuela m.

Venezuelan [vɛnɪ'zweɪlən] adj, n venezuelano(a).

vengeance ['vɛndʒəns] n vendetta; **with a ~** (fig) davvero; furiosamente.

vengeful ['vɛndʒful] adj vendicativo(a).

Venice ['vɛnɪs] n Venezia.

venison ['vɛnɪsn] n carne f di cervo.

venom ['vɛnəm] n veleno.

venomous ['vɛnəməs] adj velenoso(a).

vent [vɛnt] n foro, apertura; (in dress, jacket) spacco ♦ vt (fig: one's feelings) sfogare, dare sfogo a.

ventilate ['vɛntɪleɪt] vt (room) dare aria a, arieggiare.

ventilation [vɛntɪ'leɪʃən] n ventilazione f.

ventilation shaft n condotto di aerazione.

ventilator ['vɛntɪleɪtə*] n ventilatore m.

ventriloquist [vɛn'trɪləkwɪst] n ventriloquo/a.

venture ['vɛntʃə*] n impresa (rischiosa) ♦ vt rischiare, azzardare ♦ vi arrischiarsi, azzardarsi; **a business** ~ un'iniziativa commerciale; **to** ~ **to do sth** azzardarsi a fare qc.

venture capital *n* capitale *m* di rischio.

venue ['vɛnjuː] *n* luogo di incontro; (*SPORT*) luogo (designato) per l'incontro.

Venus ['viːnəs] *n* (*planet*) Venere *m*.

veracity [vəˈræsɪtɪ] *n* veridicità.

veranda(h) [vəˈrændə] *n* veranda.

verb [vəːb] *n* verbo.

verbal ['vəːbəl] *adj* verbale; (*translation*) letterale.

verbally ['vəːbəlɪ] *adv* a voce.

verbatim [vəːˈbeɪtɪm] *adv, adj* parola per parola.

verbose [vəːˈbəus] *adj* verboso(a).

verdict ['vəːdɪkt] *n* verdetto; (*opinion*) giudizio, parere *m*; ~ **of guilty/not guilty** verdetto di colpevolezza/non colpevolezza.

verge [vəːdʒ] *n* bordo, orlo; "**soft ~s**" (*BRIT*) "banchina cedevole"; **on the** ~ **of doing** sul punto di fare.

▶**verge on** *vt fus* rasentare.

verger ['vəːdʒə*] *n* (*REL*) sagrestano.

verification [vɛrɪfɪˈkeɪʃən] *n* verifica.

verify ['vɛrɪfaɪ] *vt* verificare; (*prove the truth of*) confermare.

veritable ['vɛrɪtəbl] *adj* vero(a).

vermin ['vəːmɪn] *npl* animali *mpl* nocivi; (*insects*) insetti *mpl* parassiti.

vermouth ['vəːməθ] *n* vermut *m inv.*

vernacular [vəˈnækjulə*] *n* vernacolo.

versatile ['vəːsətaɪl] *adj* (*person*) versatile; (*machine, tool etc*) (che si presta a molti usi.

verse [vəːs] *n* (*of poem*) verso; (*stanza*) stanza, strofa; (*in bible*) versetto; (*no pl*: *poetry*) versi *mpl*; **in** ~ in versi.

versed [vəːst] *adj*: (**well-**)~ **in** versato(a) in.

version ['vəːʃən] *n* versione *f.*

versus ['vəːsəs] *prep* contro.

vertebra, *pl* ~**e** ['vəːtɪbrə, -briː] *n* vertebra.

vertebrate ['vəːtɪbrɪt] *n* vertebrato.

vertebrae ['vəːtɪbriː] *npl of* **vertebra**.

vertical ['vəːtɪkl] *adj, n* verticale (*m*).

vertically ['vəːtɪklɪ] *adv* verticalmente.

vertigo ['vəːtɪgəu] *n* vertigine *f*; **to suffer from** ~ soffrire di vertigini.

verve [vəːv] *n* brio; entusiasmo.

very ['vɛrɪ] *adv* molto ♦ *adj*: **the** ~ **book which** proprio il libro che; ~ **much** moltissimo; ~ **well** molto bene; ~ **little** molto poco; **at the** ~ **end** proprio alla fine; **the** ~ **last** proprio l'ultimo; **at the** ~ **least** almeno; **the** ~ **thought (of it) alarms me** il solo pensiero mi spaventa, sono spaventato solo al pensiero.

vespers ['vɛspəz] *npl* vespro.

vessel ['vɛsl] *n* (*ANAT*) vaso; (*NAUT*) nave *f*; (*container*) recipiente *m.*

vest [vɛst] *n* (*BRIT*) maglia; (: *sleeveless*) canottiera; (*US: waistcoat*) gilè *m inv* ♦ *vt*: **to** ~ **sb with sth, to** ~ **sth in sb** conferire qc a qn.

vested interest *n*: **to have a** ~ **in doing** avere tutto l'interesse a fare; ~**s** *npl* (*COMM*) diritti *mpl* acquisiti.

vestibule ['vɛstɪbjuːl] *n* vestibolo.

vestige ['vɛstɪdʒ] *n* vestigio.

vestment ['vɛstmənt] *n* (*REL*) paramento liturgico.

vestry ['vɛstrɪ] *n* sagrestia.

Vesuvius [vɪˈsuːvɪəs] *n* Vesuvio.

vet [vɛt] *n abbr* (= *veterinary surgeon*) veterinario; (*US: col*) = **veteran** ♦ *vt* esaminare minuziosamente; (*text*) rivedere; **to** ~ **sb for a job** raccogliere delle informazioni dettagliate su qn prima di offrirgli un posto.

veteran ['vɛtərn] *n* veterano; (*also*: **war** ~) reduce *m* ♦ *adj*: **she's a** ~ **campaigner for** ... lotta da sempre per ....

veteran car *n* auto *f inv* d'epoca (*anteriore al 1919*).

veterinarian [vɛtrɪˈnɛərɪən] *n* (*US*) = **veterinary surgeon**.

veterinary ['vɛtrɪnərɪ] *adj* veterinario(a).

veterinary surgeon *n* (*BRIT*) veterinario.

veto ['viːtəu] *n* (*pl* ~**es**) veto ♦ *vt* opporre il veto a; **to put a** ~ **on** opporre il veto a.

vetting ['vɛtɪŋ] *n*: **positive** ~ *indagine per accertare l'idoneità di un aspirante ad una carica ufficiale.*

vex [vɛks] *vt* irritare, contrariare.

vexed [vɛkst] *adj* (*question*) controverso(a), dibattuto(a).

VFD *n abbr* (*US*) = voluntary fire department.

VG *abbr* (*BRIT: SCOL etc*: = *very good*) ottimo.

VHF *abbr* (= *very high frequency*) VHF.

VI *abbr* (*US*) = Virgin Islands.

via [vaɪə] *prep* (*by way of*) via; (*by means of*) tramite.

viability [vaɪəˈbɪlɪtɪ] *n* attuabilità.

viable ['vaɪəbl] *adj* attuabile; vitale.

viaduct ['vaɪədʌkt] *n* viadotto.

vial ['vaɪəl] *n* fiala.

vibes [vaɪbz] *npl* (*col*): **I got good/bad** ~ **ho** trovato simpatica/antipatica l'atmosfera.

vibrant ['vaɪbrənt] *adj* (*sound*) vibrante; (*colour*) vivace, vivo(a).

vibraphone ['vaɪbrəfəun] *n* vibrafono.

vibrate [vaɪˈbreɪt] *vi*: **to** ~ (**with**) vibrare (di); (*resound*) risonare (di).

vibration [vaɪˈbreɪʃən] *n* vibrazione *f.*

vibrator [vaɪˈbreɪtə*] *n* vibratore *m.*

vicar ['vɪkə*] n pastore m.
vicarage ['vɪkərɪdʒ] n presbiterio.
vicarious [vɪ'kɛərɪəs] adj sofferto(a) al posto di un altro; **to get ~ pleasure out of sth** trarre piacere indirettamente da qc.
vice [vaɪs] n (evil) vizio; (TECH) morsa.
vice- [vaɪs] prefix vice ....
vice-chairman [vaɪs'tʃɛəmən] n vicepresidente m.
vice-chancellor [vaɪs'tʃɑ:nsələ*] n (BRIT SCOL) rettore m (per elezione).
vice-president [vaɪs'prɛzɪdənt] n vicepresidente m.
viceroy ['vaɪsrɔɪ] n viceré m inv.
vice squad n (squadra del) buon costume f.
vice versa ['vaɪsɪ'vəːsə] adv viceversa.
vicinity [vɪ'sɪnɪtɪ] n vicinanze fpl.
vicious ['vɪʃəs] adj (remark) maligno(a), cattivo(a); (blow) violento(a); **a ~ circle** un circolo vizioso.
viciousness ['vɪʃəsnɪs] n malignità, cattiveria; ferocia.
vicissitudes [vɪ'sɪsɪtjuːdz] npl vicissitudini fpl.
victim ['vɪktɪm] n vittima; **to be the ~ of** essere vittima di.
victimization [vɪktɪmaɪ'zeɪʃən] n persecuzione f; rappresaglie fpl.
victimize ['vɪktɪmaɪz] vt perseguitare; compiere delle rappresaglie contro.
victor ['vɪktə*] n vincitore m.
Victorian [vɪk'tɔːrɪən] adj vittoriano(a).
victorious [vɪk'tɔːrɪəs] adj vittorioso(a).
victory ['vɪktərɪ] n vittoria; **to win a ~ over sb** riportare una vittoria su qn.
video ['vɪdɪəu] cpd video... ◆ n (~ film) video m inv; (also: ~ **cassette**) videocassetta; (also: ~ **cassette recorder**) videoregistratore m.
video camera n videocamera.
video cassette n videocassetta.
video (cassette) recorder n videoregistratore m.
videodisc ['vɪdɪəudɪsk] n disco ottico.
video game n videogioco.
video nasty n video estremamente violento o porno.
videophone ['vɪdɪəufəun] n videotelefono.
video recording n registrazione f su video.
video tape n videotape m inv.
vie [vaɪ] vi: **to ~ with** competere con, rivaleggiare con.
Vienna [vɪ'ɛnə] n Vienna.
Vietnam, Viet Nam [vjɛt'næm] n Vietnam m.
Vietnamese [vjɛtnə'miːz] adj vietnamita

◆ n vietnamita m/f; (LING) vietnamita m.
view [vjuː] n vista, veduta; (opinion) opinione f ◆ vt (situation) considerare; (house) visitare; **on ~** (in museum etc) esposto(a); **to be in** or **within ~ (of sth)** essere in vista (di qc); **in full ~ of sb** sotto gli occhi di qn; **an overall ~ of the situation** una visione globale della situazione; **in my ~** a mio avviso, secondo me; **in ~ of the fact that** considerato che; **to take** or **hold the ~ that ...** essere dell'opinione che ...; **with a ~ to doing sth** con l'intenzione di fare qc.
viewdata ['vjuːdeɪtə] n (BRIT) sistema di televideo.
viewer ['vjuːə*] n (viewfinder) mirino; (small projector) visore m; (TV) telespettatore/trice.
viewfinder ['vjuːfaɪndə*] n mirino.
viewpoint ['vjuːpɔɪnt] n punto di vista.
vigil ['vɪdʒɪl] n veglia; **to keep ~** vegliare.
vigilance ['vɪdʒɪləns] n vigilanza.
vigilant ['vɪdʒɪlənt] adj vigile.
vigilante [vɪdʒɪ'læntɪ] n cittadino che si fa giustizia da solo.
vigorous ['vɪgərəs] adj vigoroso(a).
vigour, (US) vigor [vɪgə*] n vigore m.
vile [vaɪl] adj (action) vile; (smell) disgustoso(a), nauseante; (temper) pessimo(a).
vilify ['vɪlɪfaɪ] vt diffamare.
villa ['vɪlə] n villa.
village ['vɪlɪdʒ] n villaggio.
villager ['vɪlɪdʒə*] n abitante m/f di villaggio.
villain ['vɪlən] n (scoundrel) canaglia; (criminal) criminale m; (in novel etc) cattivo.
VIN n abbr (US) = vehicle identification number.
vinaigrette [vɪneɪ'grɛt] n vinaigrette f inv.
vindicate ['vɪndɪkeɪt] vt comprovare; giustificare.
vindication [vɪndɪ'keɪʃən] n: **in ~ of** per giustificare; a discolpa di.
vindictive [vɪn'dɪktɪv] adj vendicativo(a).
vine [vaɪn] n vite f; (climbing plant) rampicante m.
vinegar ['vɪnɪgə*] n aceto.
vine grower n viticoltore m.
vine-growing ['vaɪngrəuɪŋ] adj viticolo(a) ◆ n viticoltura.
vineyard ['vɪnjɑːd] n vigna, vigneto.
vintage ['vɪntɪdʒ] n (year) annata, produzione f; **the 1970 ~** il vino del 1970.
vintage car n auto f inv d'epoca.
vintage wine n vino d'annata.
vinyl ['vaɪnl] n vinile m.

viola [vɪ'əulə] n viola.

violate ['vaɪəleɪt] vt violare.

violation [vaɪə'leɪʃən] n violazione f; **in ~ of sth** violando qc.

violence ['vaɪələns] n violenza; (POL etc) incidenti mpl violenti.

violent [vaɪələnt] adj violento(a); **a ~ dislike of sb/sth** una violenta avversione per qn/qc.

violently ['vaɪələntlɪ] adv violentemente; (ill, angry) terribilmente.

violet ['vaɪələt] adj (colour) viola inv, violetto(a) ♦ n (plant) violetta.

violin [vaɪə'lɪn] n violino.

violinist [vaɪə'lɪnɪst] n violinista m/f.

VIP n abbr (= very important person) V.I.P. m/f inv.

viper ['vaɪpə*] n vipera.

viral ['vaɪərəl] adj virale.

virgin ['vɜːdʒɪn] n vergine f ♦ adj vergine inv; **she is a ~** lei è vergine; **the Blessed V~** la Beatissima Vergine.

virginity [vɜː'dʒɪnɪtɪ] n verginità.

Virgo ['vɜːgəu] n (sign) Vergine f; **to be ~** essere della Vergine.

virile ['vɪraɪl] adj virile.

virility [vɪ'rɪlɪtɪ] n virilità.

virtual ['vɜːtjuəl] adj effettivo(a), vero(a); (COMPUT, PHYSICS) virtuale; (in effect): **it's a ~ impossibility** è praticamente impossibile; **the ~ leader** il capo all'atto pratico.

virtually ['vɜːtjuəlɪ] adv (almost) praticamente; **it is ~ impossible** è praticamente impossibile.

virtual reality n realtà f inv virtuale.

virtue ['vɜːtjuː] n virtù f inv; (advantage) pregio, vantaggio; **by ~ of** grazie a.

virtuosity [vɜːtju'ɒsɪtɪ] n virtuosismo.

virtuoso [vɜːtju'əuzəu] n virtuoso.

virtuous ['vɜːtjuəs] adj virtuoso(a).

virulent ['vɪrulənt] adj virulento(a).

virus ['vaɪərəs] n virus m inv.

visa ['viːzə] n visto.

vis-à-vis [viːzə'viː] prep rispetto a, nei riguardi di.

viscount ['vaɪkaunt] n visconte m.

viscous ['vɪskəs] adj viscoso(a).

vise [vaɪs] n (US TECH) = **vice**.

visibility [vɪzɪ'bɪlɪtɪ] n visibilità.

visible ['vizəbl] adj visibile; **~ exports/ imports** esportazioni fpl/importazioni fpl visibili.

visibly ['vɪzəblɪ] adv visibilmente.

vision ['vɪʒən] n (sight) vista; (foresight, in dream) visione f.

visionary ['vɪʒənərɪ] n visionario/a.

visit ['vɪzɪt] n visita; (stay) soggiorno ♦ vt (person) andare a trovare; (place) visitare; **to pay a ~ to** (person) fare una visita a; (place) andare a visitare; **on a private/official ~** in visita privata/ ufficiale.

visiting ['vɪzɪtɪŋ] adj (speaker, professor, team) ospite.

visiting card n biglietto da visita.

visiting hours npl orario delle visite.

visitor ['vɪzɪtə*] n visitatore/trice; (guest) ospite m/f.

visitors' book n libro d'oro; (in hotel) registro.

visor ['vaɪzə*] n visiera.

VISTA ['vɪstə] n abbr (= Volunteers In Service To America) volontariato in zone depresse degli Stati Uniti.

vista ['vɪstə] n vista, prospettiva.

visual ['vɪzjuəl] adj visivo(a); visuale; ottico(a).

visual aid n sussidio visivo.

visual arts npl arti fpl figurative.

visual display unit (VDU) n unità f inv di visualizzazione.

visualize ['vɪzjuəlaɪz] vt immaginare, figurarsi; (foresee) prevedere.

visually ['vɪzjuəlɪ] adv: **~ appealing** piacevole a vedersi; **~ handicapped** con una menomazione della vista.

vital ['vaɪtl] adj vitale; **of ~ importance (to sb/sth)** di vitale importanza (per qn/qc).

vitality [vaɪ'tælɪtɪ] n vitalità.

vitally ['vaɪtəlɪ] adv estremamente.

vital statistics npl (of population) statistica demografica; (col: woman's) misure fpl.

vitamin ['vɪtəmɪn] n vitamina.

vitiate ['vɪʃɪeɪt] vt viziare.

vitreous ['vɪtrɪəs] adj (rock) vetroso(a); (china, enamel) vetrificato(a).

vitriolic [vɪtrɪ'ɒlɪk] adj (fig) caustico(a).

viva ['vaɪvə] n (also: **~ voce**) (esame m) orale.

vivacious [vɪ'veɪʃəs] adj vivace.

vivacity [vɪ'væsɪtɪ] n vivacità.

vivid ['vɪvɪd] adj vivido(a).

vividly ['vɪvɪdlɪ] adv (describe) vividamente; (remember) con precisione.

vivisection [vɪvɪ'sɛkʃən] n vivisezione f.

vixen ['vɪksn] n volpe f femmina; (pej: woman) bisbetica.

viz abbr (= vide licet: namely) cioè.

VLF abbr (= very low frequency) bassissima frequenza.

V-neck ['viːnɛk] n maglione m con lo scollo a V.

VOA n abbr (= Voice of America) voce f dell'America (alla radio).

vocabulary [vəu'kæbjulərɪ] n vocabolario.

vocal ['vəʊkl] *adj* (*MUS*) vocale; (*communication*) verbale; (*noisy*) rumoroso(a).

vocal cords *npl* corde *fpl* vocali.

vocalist ['vəʊkəlɪst] *n* cantante *m/f* (*in un gruppo*).

vocation [vəʊ'keɪʃən] *n* vocazione *f*.

vocational [vəʊ'keɪʃənl] *adj* professionale; ~ **guidance** orientamento professionale; ~ **training** formazione *f* professionale.

vociferous [və'sɪfərəs] *adj* rumoroso(a).

vodka ['vɔdkə] *n* vodka *f inv*.

vogue [vəʊg] *n* moda; (*popularity*) popolarità, voga; **to be in** ~, **be the** ~ essere di moda.

voice [vɔɪs] *n* voce *f* ♦ *vt* (*opinion*) esprimere; **in a loud/soft** ~ a voce alta/bassa; **to give** ~ **to** esprimere.

voice mail *n* servizio di segreteria telefonica.

voice-over ['vɔɪsəʊvə*] *n* voce *f* fuori campo *inv*.

void [vɔɪd] *n* vuoto ♦ *adj*: ~ **of** privo(a) di.

voile [vɔɪl] *n* voile *m*.

vol. *abbr* (= *volume*) vol.

volatile ['vɔlətaɪl] *adj* volatile; (*fig*) volubile.

volcanic [vɔl'kænɪk] *adj* vulcanico(a).

volcano, ~es [vɔl'keɪnəu] *n* vulcano.

volition [və'lɪʃən] *n*: **of one's own** ~ di propria volontà.

volley ['vɔlɪ] *n* (*of gunfire*) salva; (*of stones etc*) raffica, gragnola; (*TENNIS etc*) volata.

volleyball ['vɔlɪbɔːl] *n* pallavolo *f*.

volt [vəʊlt] *n* volt *m inv*.

voltage ['vəʊltɪdʒ] *n* tensione *f*, voltaggio; **high/low** ~ alta/bassa tensione.

voluble ['vɔljubl] *adj* loquace, ciarliero(a).

volume ['vɔljuːm] *n* volume *m*; (*of tank*) capacità *f inv*; ~ **one/two** (*of book*) volume primo/secondo; **his expression spoke** ~**s** la sua espressione lasciava capire tutto.

volume control *n* (*RADIO, TV*) regolatore *m* or manopola del volume.

voluminous [və'luːmɪnəs] *adj* voluminoso(a); (*notes etc*) abbondante.

voluntarily ['vɔləntrɪlɪ] *adv* volontariamente; gratuitamente.

voluntary ['vɔləntərɪ] *adj* volontario(a); (*unpaid*) gratuito(a), non retribuito(a).

voluntary liquidation *n* (*COMM*) liquidazione *f* volontaria.

volunteer [vɔlən'tɪə*] *n* volontario/a ♦ *vi* (*MIL*) arruolarsi volontario; **to** ~ **to do** offrire (volontariamente) di fare.

voluptuous [və'lʌptjuəs] *adj* voluttuoso(a).

vomit ['vɔmɪt] *n* vomito ♦ *vt, vi* vomitare.

voracious [və'reɪʃəs] *adj* (*appetite*) smisurato(a); (*reader*) avido(a).

vote [vəʊt] *n* voto, suffragio; (*cast*) voto; (*franchise*) diritto di voto ♦ *vi* votare ♦ *vt* (*gen*) votare; (*sum of money etc*) votare a favore di; **to** ~ **to do sth** votare a favore di fare qc; **he was** ~**d secretary** è stato eletto segretario; **to put sth to the** ~, **to take a** ~ **on sth** mettere qc ai voti; ~ **for/against** voto a favore/contrario; **to pass a** ~ **of confidence/no confidence** dare il voto di fiducia/sfiducia; ~ **of thanks** discorso di ringraziamento.

voter ['vəʊtə*] *n* elettore/trice.

voting ['vəʊtɪŋ] *n* scrutinio.

voting paper *n* (*BRIT*) scheda elettorale.

voting right *n* diritto di voto.

vouch [vautʃ] *n*: **to** ~ **for** *vt fus* farsi garante di.

voucher ['vautʃə*] *n* (*for meal, petrol*) buono; (*receipt*) ricevuta; **travel** ~ voucher *m inv*, tagliando.

vow [vau] *n* voto, promessa solenne ♦ *vi* giurare; **to take** *or* **make a** ~ **to do sth** fare voto di fare qc.

vowel ['vauəl] *n* vocale *f*.

voyage ['vɔɪɪdʒ] *n* viaggio per mare, traversata.

voyeur [vwɑː'jɜː*] *n* guardone/a.

VP *n abbr* (= *vice-president*) V.P.

vs *abbr* (= *versus*) contro.

VSO *n abbr* (*BRIT*: = *Voluntary Service Overseas*) servizio volontario in paesi sottosviluppati.

VT, Vt. *abbr* (*US*) = *Vermont*.

vulgar ['vʌlgə*] *adj* volgare.

vulgarity [vʌl'gærɪtɪ] *n* volgarità.

vulnerability [vʌlnərə'bɪlɪtɪ] *n* vulnerabilità.

vulnerable ['vʌlnərəbl] *adj* vulnerabile.

vulture ['vʌltʃə*] *n* avvoltoio.

W w

W, w ['dʌbljuː] *n* (*letter*) W, w *m or f inv*; **W for William** ≈ W come Washington.

W *abbr* (= *west*) O; (*ELEC*: = *watt*) w.

WA *abbr* (*US*) = *Washington*.

wad [wɔd] *n* (*of cotton wool, paper*) tampone *m*; (*of banknotes etc*) fascio.

wadding ['wɔdɪŋ] *n* imbottitura.

waddle ['wɔdl] *vi* camminare come una papera.

wade [weɪd] *vi*: **to ~ through** camminare a stento in ♦ *vt* guadare.

wafer ['weɪfə*] *n* (*CULIN*) cialda; (*REL*) ostia; (*COMPUT*) wafer *m inv*.

wafer-thin ['weɪfə'θɪn] *adj* molto sottile.

waffle ['wɒfl] *n* (*CULIN*) cialda; (*col*) ciance *fpl*; riempitivo ♦ *vi* cianciare; parlare a vuoto.

waffle iron *n* stampo per cialde.

waft [wɒft] *vt* portare ♦ *vi* diffondersi.

wag [wæg] *vt* agitare, muovere ♦ *vi* agitarsi; **the dog ~ged its tail** il cane scodinzolò.

wage [weɪdʒ] *n* (*also*: ~**s**) salario, paga ♦ *vt*: **to ~ war** fare la guerra; **a day's ~s** un giorno di paga.

wage claim *n* rivendicazione *f* salariale.

wage differential *n* differenza di salario.

wage earner *n* salariato/a.

wage freeze *n* blocco dei salari.

wage packet *n* (*BRIT*) busta *f* paga *inv*.

wager ['weɪdʒə*] *n* scommessa.

waggle ['wægl] *vt* dimenare, agitare ♦ *vi* dimenarsi, agitarsi.

wag(g)on ['wægən] *n* (*horse-drawn*) carro; (*truck*) furgone *m*; (*BRIT RAIL*) vagone *m* (merci).

wail [weɪl] *n* gemito; (*of siren*) urlo ♦ *vi* gemere; urlare.

waist [weɪst] *n* vita, cintola.

waistcoat ['weɪskəut] *n* panciotto, gilè *m inv*.

waistline ['weɪstlaɪn] *n* (giro di) vita.

wait [weɪt] *n* attesa ♦ *vi* aspettare, attendere; **to ~ for** aspettare; **to keep sb ~ing** far aspettare qn; **~ a moment!** (aspetti un momento!; **"repairs while you ~"** "riparazioni lampo"; **I can't ~ to** ... (*fig*) non vedo l'ora di ...; **to lie in ~ for** stare in agguato a.

▶**wait behind** *vi* rimanere (ad aspettare).

▶**wait on** *vt fus* servire.

▶**wait up** *vi* restare alzato(a) (ad aspettare); **don't ~ up for me** non rimanere alzato per me.

waiter ['weɪtə*] *n* cameriere *m*.

waiting ['weɪtɪŋ] *n*: **"no ~"** (*BRIT AUT*) "divieto di sosta".

waiting list *n* lista d'attesa.

waiting room *n* sala d'aspetto *or* d'attesa.

waitress ['weɪtrɪs] *n* cameriera.

waive [weɪv] *vt* rinunciare a, abbandonare.

waiver ['weɪvə*] *n* rinuncia.

wake [weɪk] *vb* (*pt* **woke**, **~d**, *pp* **woken**, **~d** [wəuk, 'wəukn]) *vt* (*also*: **~ up**) svegliare ♦ *vi* (*also*: **~ up**) svegliarsi ♦ *n* (*for dead person*) veglia funebre; (*NAUT*) scia; **to ~ up to sth** (*fig*) rendersi conto di qc; **in the**

~ of sulla scia di; **to follow in sb's ~** (*fig*) seguire le tracce di qn.

waken ['weɪkn] *vt*, *vi* = **wake**.

Wales [weɪlz] *n* Galles *m*.

walk [wɔːk] *n* passeggiata; (*short*) giretto; (*gait*) passo, andatura; (*path*) sentiero; (*in park etc*) sentiero, vialetto ♦ *vi* camminare; (*for pleasure, exercise*) passeggiare ♦ *vt* (*distance*) fare *or* percorrere a piedi; (*dog*) accompagnare, portare a passeggiare; **10 minutes' ~ from** 10 minuti di cammino *or* a piedi da; **to go for a ~** andare a fare quattro passi; andare a fare una passeggiata; **from all ~s of life** di tutte le condizioni sociali; **to ~ in one's sleep** essere sonnambulo(a); **I'll ~ you home** ti accompagno a casa.

▶**walk out** *vi* (*go out*) uscire; (*as protest*) uscire (in segno di protesta); (*strike*) scendere in sciopero; **to ~ out on sb** piantare in asso qn.

walkabout ['wɔːkəbaut] *n*: **to go (on a) ~** avere incontri informali col pubblico (*durante una visita ufficiale*).

walker ['wɔːkə*] *n* (*person*) camminatore/trice.

walkie-talkie ['wɔːkɪ'tɔːkɪ] *n* walkie-talkie *m inv*.

walking ['wɔːkɪŋ] *n* camminare *m*; **it's within ~ distance** ci si arriva a piedi.

walking holiday *n* vacanza fatta di lunghe camminate.

walking shoes *npl* scarpe *fpl* da passeggio.

walking stick *n* bastone *m* da passeggio.

Walkman ® ['wɔːkmən] *n* walkman ® *m inv*.

walk-on ['wɔːkɒn] *adj* (*THEAT*: *part*) da comparsa.

walkout ['wɔːkaut] *n* (*of workers*) sciopero senza preavviso *or* a sorpresa.

walkover ['wɔːkəuvə*] *n* (*col*) vittoria facile, gioco da ragazzi.

walkway ['wɔːkweɪ] *n* passaggio pedonale.

wall [wɔːl] *n* muro; (*internal, of tunnel, cave*) parete *f*; **to go to the ~** (*fig*: *firm etc*) fallire.

▶**wall in** *vt* (*garden etc*) circondare con un muro.

wall cupboard *n* pensile *m*.

walled [wɔːld] *adj* (*city*) fortificato(a).

wallet ['wɒlɪt] *n* portafoglio.

wallflower ['wɔːlflauə*] *n* violacciocca; **to be a ~** (*fig*) fare da tappezzeria.

wall hanging *n* tappezzeria.

wallop ['wɒləp] *vt* (*col*) pestare.

wallow ['wɒləu] *vi* sguazzare, rotolarsi; **to ~ in one's grief** crogiolarsi nel proprio dolore.

wallpaper ['wɔːlpeɪpə*] *n* carta da parati;

(*COMPUT*) sfondo.

wall-to-wall ['wɔːltə'wɔːl] *adj*: ~ **carpeting** moquette *f*.

walnut ['wɔːlnʌt] *n* noce *f*; (*tree*) noce *m*.

walrus, *pl* ~ *or* ~**es** ['wɔːlrəs] *n* tricheco.

waltz [wɔːlts] *n* valzer *m inv* ♦ *vi* ballare il valzer.

wan [wɔn] *adj* pallido(a), smorto(a); triste.

wand [wɔnd] *n* (*also*: **magic** ~) bacchetta (magica).

wander ['wɔndə*] *vi* (*person*) girare senza meta, girovagare; (*thoughts*) vagare; (*river*) serpeggiare.

wanderer ['wɔndərə*] *n* vagabondo/a.

wandering ['wɔndrɪŋ] *adj* (*tribe*) nomade; (*minstrel, actor*) girovago(a); (*path, river*) tortuoso(a); (*glance, mind*) distratto(a).

wane [weɪn] *vi* (*moon*) calare; (*reputation*) declinare.

wangle ['wæŋgl] (*BRIT col*) *vt* procurare (con l'astuzia) ♦ *n* astuzia.

wanker ['wæŋkə*] *n* (*col!*) segaiolo (*!*); (*as insult*) coglione (*!*) *m*.

want [wɔnt] *vt* volere; (*need*) aver bisogno di; (*lack*) mancare di ♦ *n* (*poverty*) miseria, povertà; ~**s** *npl* (*needs*) bisogni *mpl*; **for** ~ **of** per mancanza di; **to** ~ **to do** volere fare; **to** ~ **sb to do** volere che qn faccia; **you're** ~**ed on the phone** la vogliono al telefono; **"cook** ~**ed"** "cercasi cuoco".

want ads *npl* (*US*) piccoli annunci *mpl*.

wanting ['wɔntɪŋ] *adj*: **to be** ~ **(in)** mancare (di); **to be found** ~ non risultare all'altezza.

wanton ['wɔntn] *adj* sfrenato(a); senza motivo.

war [wɔː*] *n* guerra; **to go to** ~ entrare in guerra.

warble ['wɔːbl] *n* (*of bird*) trillo ♦ *vi* trillare.

war cry *n* grido di guerra.

ward [wɔːd] *n* (*in hospital: room*) corsia; (: *section*) reparto; (*POL*) circoscrizione *f*; (*LAW: child*) pupillo/a.

▶**ward off** *vt* parare, schivare.

warden ['wɔːdn] *n* (*of institution*) direttore/trice; (*of park, game reserve*) guardiano/a; (*BRIT: also*: **traffic** ~) addetto/a al controllo del traffico e del parcheggio.

warder ['wɔːdə*] *n* (*BRIT*) guardia carceraria.

wardrobe ['wɔːdrəub] *n* (*cupboard*) guardaroba *m inv*, armadio; (*clothes*) guardaroba; (*THEAT*) costumi *mpl*.

warehouse ['wɛəhaus] *n* magazzino.

wares [wɛəz] *npl* merci *fpl*.

warfare ['wɔːfɛə*] *n* guerra.

war game *n* war game *m inv*.

warhead ['wɔːhɛd] *n* (*MIL*) testata, ogiva.

warily ['wɛərɪlɪ] *adv* cautamente, con prudenza.

warlike ['wɔːlaɪk] *adj* guerriero(a).

warm [wɔːm] *adj* caldo(a); (*welcome, applause*) caloroso(a); (*person, greeting*) cordiale; (*heart*) d'oro; (*supporter*) convinto(a); **it's** ~ fa caldo; **I'm** ~ ho caldo; **to keep sth** ~ tenere qc al caldo; **with my** ~**est thanks** con i miei più sentiti ringraziamenti.

▶**warm up** *vi* scaldarsi, riscaldarsi; (*athlete, discussion*) riscaldarsi ♦ *vt* scaldare, riscaldare; (*engine*) far scaldare.

warm-blooded ['wɔːm'blʌdɪd] *adj* a sangue caldo.

war memorial *n* monumento ai caduti.

warm-hearted [wɔːm'hɑːtɪd] *adj* affettuoso(a).

warmly ['wɔːmlɪ] *adv* caldamente; calorosamente; vivamente.

warmonger ['wɔːmʌŋgə*] *n* guerrafondaio.

warmongering ['wɔːmʌŋgrɪŋ] *n* bellicismo.

warmth [wɔːmθ] *n* calore *m*.

warm-up ['wɔːmʌp] *n* (*SPORT*) riscaldamento.

warn [wɔːn] *vt* avvertire, avvisare; **to** ~ **sb not to do sth** *or* **against doing sth** avvertire qn di non fare qc.

warning ['wɔːnɪŋ] *n* avvertimento; (*notice*) avviso; **without (any)** ~ senza preavviso; **gale** ~ avviso di burrasca.

warning light *n* spia luminosa.

warning triangle *n* (*AUT*) triangolo.

warp [wɔːp] *n* (*TEXTILES*) ordito ♦ *vi* deformarsi ♦ *vt* deformare; (*fig*) corrompere.

warpath ['wɔːpɑːθ] *n*: **to be on the** ~ (*fig*) essere sul sentiero di guerra.

warped [wɔːpt] *adj* (*wood*) curvo(a); (*fig: character, sense of humour etc*) contorto(a).

warrant ['wɔrnt] *n* (*LAW: to arrest*) mandato di cattura; (: *to search*) mandato di perquisizione ♦ *vt* (*justify, merit*) giustificare.

warrant officer (WO) *n* sottufficiale *m*.

warranty ['wɔrəntɪ] *n* garanzia; **under** ~ (*COMM*) in garanzia.

warren ['wɔrən] *n* (*of rabbits*) tana.

warring ['wɔːrɪŋ] *adj* (*interests etc*) opposto(a), in lotta; (*nations*) in guerra.

warrior ['wɔrɪə*] *n* guerriero/a.

Warsaw ['wɔːsɔː] *n* Varsavia.

warship ['wɔːʃɪp] *n* nave *f* da guerra.

wart [wɔːt] *n* verruca.

wartime ['wɔːtaɪm] *n*: **in** ~ in tempo di guerra.

wary ['wɛərɪ] *adj* prudente; **to be ~ about** *or* **of doing sth** andare cauto nel fare qc.

was [wɔz] *pt of* **be**.

wash [wɔʃ] *vt* lavare; (*sweep, carry: sea etc*) portare, trascinare ♦ *vi* lavarsi ♦ *n:* **to give sth a ~** lavare qc, dare una lavata a qc; **to have a ~** lavarsi; **he was ~ed overboard** fu trascinato in mare (dalle onde).

▶**wash away** *vt* (*stain*) togliere lavando; (*subj: river etc*) trascinare via.

▶**wash down** *vt* lavare.

▶**wash off** *vi* andare via con il lavaggio.

▶**wash up** *vi* lavare i piatti; (*US: have a wash*) lavarsi.

Wash. *abbr* (*US*) = Washington.

washable ['wɔʃəbl] *adj* lavabile.

washbasin ['wɔʃbeɪsn] *n* lavabo.

washcloth ['wɔʃklɔθ] *n* (*US*) pezzuola (per lavarsi).

washer ['wɔʃə*] *n* (*TECH*) rondella.

washing ['wɔʃɪŋ] *n* (*BRIT: linen etc*) bucato; **dirty ~** biancheria da lavare.

washing line *n* (*BRIT*) corda del bucato.

washing machine *n* lavatrice *f*.

washing powder *n* (*BRIT*) detersivo (in polvere).

Washington ['wɔʃɪŋtən] *n* Washington *f*.

washing-up [wɔʃɪŋˈʌp] *n* (*dishes*) piatti *mpl* sporchi; **to do the ~** lavare i piatti, rigovernare.

washing-up liquid *n* (*BRIT*) detersivo liquido (per stoviglie).

wash-out ['wɔʃaut] *n* (*col*) disastro.

washroom ['wɔʃrum] *n* gabinetto.

wasn't ['wɔznt] = was not.

Wasp, WASP [wɔsp] *n abbr* (*US:* = *White Anglo-Saxon Protestant*) W.A.S.P. *m* (*protestante bianco anglosassone*).

wasp [wɔsp] *n* vespa.

waspish ['wɔspɪʃ] *adj* litigioso(a).

wastage ['weɪstɪdʒ] *n* spreco; (*in manufacturing*) scarti *mpl*.

waste [weɪst] *n* spreco; (*of time*) perdita; (*rubbish*) rifiuti *mpl* ♦ *adj* (*material*) di scarto; (*food*) avanzato(a); (*energy, heat*) sprecato(a); (*land, ground: in city*) abbandonato(a); (: *in country*) incolto(a) ♦ *vt* sprecare; (*time, opportunity*) perdere; **~s** *npl* distesa desolata; **it's a ~ of money** sono soldi sprecati; **to go to ~** andare sprecato; **to lay ~** devastare.

▶**waste away** *vi* deperire.

wastebasket ['weɪstbɑːskɪt] *n* = **wastepaper basket**.

waste disposal (unit) *n* (*BRIT*) eliminatore *m* di rifiuti.

wasteful ['weɪstful] *adj* sprecone(a);

(*process*) dispendioso(a).

waste ground *n* (*BRIT*) terreno incolto *or* abbandonato.

wasteland ['weɪstlænd] *n* terra desolata.

wastepaper basket ['weɪstpeɪpə-] *n* cestino per la carta straccia.

waste pipe *n* tubo di scarico.

waste products *npl* (*INDUSTRY*) materiali *mpl* di scarto.

waster ['weɪstə*] *n* (*col*) buono/a a nulla.

watch [wɔtʃ] *n* (*wrist~*) orologio; (*act of watching*) sorveglianza; (*guard:* MIL, NAUT) guardia; (*NAUT: spell of duty*) quarto ♦ *vt* (*look at*) osservare; (: *match, programme*) guardare; (*spy on, guard*) sorvegliare, tenere d'occhio; (*be careful of*) fare attenzione a ♦ *vi* osservare, guardare; (*keep guard*) fare *or* montare la guardia; **to keep a close ~ on sb/sth** tener bene d'occhio qn/qc; **~ how you drive/what you're doing** attento a come guidi/quel che fai.

▶**watch out** *vi* fare attenzione.

watchband ['wɔtʃbænd] *n* (*US*) cinturino da orologio.

watchdog ['wɔtʃdɔg] *n* cane *m* da guardia; (*fig*) sorvegliante *m/f*.

watchful ['wɔtʃful] *adj* attento(a), vigile.

watchmaker ['wɔtʃmeɪkə*] *n* orologiaio/a.

watchman ['wɔtʃmən] *n* guardiano; (*also:* **night ~**) guardiano notturno.

watch stem *n* (*US*) corona di carica.

watch strap *n* cinturino da orologio.

watchword ['wɔtʃwɔːd] *n* parola d'ordine.

water [wɔːtə*] *n* acqua ♦ *vt* (*plant*) annaffiare ♦ *vi* (*eyes*) piangere; **in British ~s** nelle acque territoriali britanniche; **I'd like a drink of ~** vorrei un bicchier d'acqua; **to pass ~** orinare; **to make sb's mouth ~** far venire l'acquolina in bocca a qn.

▶**water down** *vt* (*milk*) diluire; (*fig: story*) edulcorare.

water closet *n* (*BRIT*) W.C. *m inv*, gabinetto.

watercolour, (*US*) **watercolor** ['wɔːtəkʌlə*] *n* (*picture*) acquerello; **~s** *npl* colori *mpl* per acquerelli.

water-cooled ['wɔːtəkuːld] *adj* raffreddato(a) ad acqua.

watercress ['wɔːtəkrɛs] *n* crescione *m*.

waterfall ['wɔːtəfɔːl] *n* cascata.

waterfront ['wɔːtəfrʌnt] *n* (*seafront*) lungomare *m*; (*at docks*) banchina.

water heater *n* scaldabagno.

water hole *n* pozza d'acqua.

water ice *n* (*BRIT*) sorbetto.

watering can ['wɔːtərɪŋ-] *n* annaffiatoio.

water level *n* livello dell'acqua; (*of flood*)

livello delle acque.

water lily n ninfea.

waterline ['wɔːtəlaɪn] n (NAUT) linea di galleggiamento.

waterlogged ['wɔːtəlɔgd] adj saturo(a) d'acqua; imbevuto(a) d'acqua; (football pitch etc) allagato(a).

watermark ['wɔːtəmɑːk] n (on paper) filigrana.

watermelon ['wɔːtəmɛlən] n anguria, cocomero.

water polo n pallanuoto f.

waterproof ['wɔːtəpruːf] adj impermeabile.

water-repellent ['wɔːtərɪ'pɛlənt] adj idrorepellente.

watershed ['wɔːtəʃɛd] n (GEO, fig) spartiacque m.

water-skiing ['wɔːtəskiːɪŋ] n sci m acquatico.

water softener n addolcitore m; (substance) anti-calcare m.

water tank n serbatoio d'acqua.

watertight ['wɔːtətaɪt] adj stagno(a).

water vapour n vapore m acqueo.

waterway ['wɔːtəweɪ] n corso d'acqua navigabile.

waterworks ['wɔːtəwɔːks] npl impianto idrico.

watery ['wɔːtərɪ] adj (colour) slavato(a); (coffee) acquoso(a).

watt [wɔt] n watt m inv.

wattage ['wɔtɪdʒ] n wattaggio.

wattle ['wɔtl] n graticcio.

wave [weɪv] n onda; (of hand) gesto, segno; (in hair) ondulazione f; (fig: of enthusiasm, strikes etc) ondata ♦ vi fare un cenno con la mano; (flag) sventolare ♦ vt (handkerchief) sventolare; (stick) brandire; (hair) ondulare; **short/medium/long** ~ (RADIO) onde corte/medie/lunghe; **the new** ~ (CINE, MUS) la new wave; **to** ~ **sb goodbye, to** ~ **goodbye to sb** fare un cenno d'addio a qn; **he** ~**d us over to his table** ci invitò con un cenno al suo tavolo.

▶**wave aside, wave away** vt (person): **to** ~ **sb aside** fare cenno a qn di spostarsi; (fig: suggestion, objection) respingere, rifiutare; (: doubts) scacciare.

waveband ['weɪvbænd] n gamma di lunghezze d'onda.

wavelength ['weɪvlɛŋθ] n lunghezza d'onda.

waver ['weɪvə*] vi vacillare; (voice) tremolare.

wavy ['weɪvɪ] adj ondulato(a); ondeggiante.

wax [wæks] n cera ♦ vt dare la cera a; (car) lucidare ♦ vi (moon) crescere.

waxworks ['wækswɔːks] npl cere fpl; museo delle cere.

way [weɪ] n via, strada; (path, access) passaggio; (distance) distanza; (direction) parte f, direzione f; (manner) modo, stile m; (habit) abitudine f; (condition) condizione f; **which** ~? — **this** ~ da che parte or in quale direzione? — da questa parte or per di qua; **to crawl one's** ~ **to** ... raggiungere ... strisciando; **he lied his** ~ **out of it** se l'è cavata mentendo; **to lose one's** ~ perdere la strada; **on the** ~ (en route) per strada; (expected) in arrivo; **you pass it on your** ~ **home** ci passi davanti andando a casa; **to be on one's** ~ essere in cammino or sulla strada; **to be in the** ~ bloccare il passaggio; (fig) essere tra i piedi or d'impiccio; **to keep out of sb's** ~ evitare qn; **it's a long** ~ **away** è molto lontano da qui; **the village is rather out of the** ~ il villaggio è abbastanza fuori mano; **to go out of one's** ~ **to do** (fig) mettercela tutta or fare di tutto per fare; **to be under** ~ (work, project) essere in corso; **to make** ~ **(for sb/sth)** far strada (a qn/qc); (fig) lasciare il posto or far largo (a qn/qc); **to get one's own** ~ fare come si vuole; **put it the right** ~ **up** (BRIT) mettilo in piedi dalla parte giusta; **to be the wrong** ~ **round** essere al contrario; **he's in a bad** ~ è ridotto male; **in a** ~ in un certo senso; **in some** ~s sotto certi aspetti; **in the** ~ **of** come; **by** ~ **of** (through) attraverso; (as a sort of) come; "~ **in**" "entrata", "ingresso"; "~ **out**" "uscita"; **the** ~ **back** la via del ritorno; **this** ~ **and that** di qua e di là; "**give** ~" (BRIT AUT) "dare la precedenza"; **no** ~! (col) assolutamente no!

waybill ['weɪbɪl] n (COMM) bolla di accompagnamento.

waylay [weɪ'leɪ] vt irreg tendere un agguato a; attendere al passaggio; (fig): **I got waylaid** ho avuto un contrattempo.

wayside ['weɪsaɪd] n bordo della strada; **to fall by the** ~ (fig) perdersi lungo la strada.

way station n (US RAIL) stazione f secondaria; (fig) tappa.

wayward ['weɪwəd] adj capriccioso(a); testardo(a).

WC n abbr (BRIT: = water closet) W.C. m inv, gabinetto.

WCC n abbr (= World Council of Churches) Consiglio Ecumenico delle Chiese.

we [wiː] pl pron noi; **here** ~ **are** eccoci.

weak [wiːk] adj debole; (health) precario(a); (beam etc) fragile; (tea, coffee) leggero(a);

to grow ~(er) indebolirsi.
weaken ['wiːkən] *vi* indebolirsi ♦ *vt* indebolire.
weak-kneed ['wiːk'niːd] *adj* (*fig*) debole, codardo(a).
weakling ['wiːklɪŋ] *n* smidollato/a; debole *m/f*.
weakly ['wiːklɪ] *adj* deboluccio(a), gracile ♦ *adv* debolmente.
weakness ['wiːknɪs] *n* debolezza; (*fault*) punto debole, difetto.
wealth [wɛlθ] *n* (*money, resources*) ricchezza, ricchezze *fpl*; (*of details*) abbondanza, profusione *f*.
wealthy ['wɛlθɪ] *adj* ricco(a).
wean [wiːn] *vt* svezzare.
weapon ['wɛpən] *n* arma; **~s of mass destruction** armi di distruzione di massa.
wear [wɛə*] *n* (*use*) uso; (*deterioration through use*) logorio, usura; (*clothing*): **sports/baby ~** abbigliamento sportivo/ per neonati ♦ *vb* (*pt* **wore**, *pp* **worn** [wɔː*, wɔːn]) *vt* (*clothes*) portare; mettersi; (*look, smile, beard etc*) avere; (*damage: through use*) consumare ♦ *vi* (*last*) durare; (*rub etc through*) consumarsi; **~ and tear** usura, consumo; **town/evening ~** abiti *mpl* or tenuta da città/sera; **to ~ a hole in sth** bucare qc a furia di usarlo.
▶**wear away** *vt* consumare; erodere ♦ *vi* consumarsi; essere eroso(a).
▶**wear down** *vt* consumare; (*strength*) esaurire.
▶**wear off** *vi* sparire lentamente.
▶**wear on** *vi* passare.
▶**wear out** *vt* consumare; (*person, strength*) esaurire.
wearable ['wɛərəbl] *adj* indossabile.
wearily ['wɪərɪlɪ] *adv* stancamente.
weariness ['wɪərɪnɪs] *n* stanchezza.
wearisome ['wɪərɪsəm] *adj* (*tiring*) estenuante; (*boring*) noioso(a).
weary ['wɪərɪ] *adj* stanco(a); (*tiring*) faticoso(a) ♦ *vt* stancare ♦ *vi*: **to ~ of** stancarsi di.
weasel ['wiːzl] *n* (*ZOOL*) donnola.
weather ['wɛðə*] *n* tempo ♦ *vt* (*wood*) stagionare; (*storm, crisis*) superare; **what's the ~ like?** che tempo fa?; **under the ~** (*fig: ill*) poco bene.
weather-beaten ['wɛðəbiːtn] *adj* (*person*) segnato(a) dalle intemperie; (*building*) logorato(a) dalle intemperie.
weather forecast *n* previsioni *fpl* del tempo, bollettino meteorologico.
weatherman ['wɛðəmæn] *n* meteorologo.
weatherproof ['wɛðəpruːf] *adj* (*garment*) impermeabile.

weather report *n* bollettino meteorologico.
weather vane *n* = **weather cock**.
weave, *pt* **wove**, *pp* **woven** [wiːv, wəuv, 'wəuvn] *vt* (*cloth*) tessere; (*basket*) intrecciare ♦ *vi* (*fig: pt, pp* ~**d**: *move in and out*) zigzagare.
weaver ['wiːvə*] *n* tessitore/trice.
weaving ['wiːvɪŋ] *n* tessitura.
web [wɛb] *n* (*of spider*) ragnatela; (*on foot*) palma; (*fabric, also fig*) tessuto; **the (World Wide) W~** la Rete.
webbed [wɛbd] *adj* (*foot*) palmato(a).
webbing ['wɛbɪŋ] *n* (*on chair*) cinghie *fpl*.
web page *n* (*COMPUT*) pagina *f* web *inv*.
website ['wɛbsaɪt] *n* (*COMPUT*) sito.
wed [wɛd] *vt* (*pt, pp* **wedded**) sposare ♦ *n*: **the newly-~s** gli sposi novelli.
Wed. *abbr* (= *Wednesday*) mer.
we'd [wiːd] = **we had**; **we would**.
wedded ['wɛdɪd] *pt, pp of* **wed**.
wedding ['wɛdɪŋ] *n* matrimonio; **silver/ golden ~** nozze *fpl* d'argento/d'oro.
wedding anniversary *n* anniversario di matrimonio.
wedding day *n* giorno delle nozze *or* del matrimonio.
wedding dress *n* abito nuziale.
wedding present *n* regalo di nozze.
wedding ring *n* fede *f*.
wedge [wɛdʒ] *n* (*of wood etc*) cuneo; (*under door etc*) zeppa; (*of cake*) spicchio, fetta ♦ *vt* mettere una zeppa sotto (*or* in); **to ~ a door open** tenere aperta una porta con un fermo.
wedge-heeled shoes ['wɛdʒhiːld-] *npl* scarpe *fpl* con tacco a zeppa.
wedlock ['wɛdlɔk] *n* vincolo matrimoniale.
Wednesday ['wɛdnzdɪ] *n* mercoledì *m inv*; *for phrases see also* **Tuesday**.
wee [wiː] *adj* (*Scottish*) piccolo(a).
weed [wiːd] *n* erbaccia ♦ *vt* diserbare.
▶**weed out** *vt* fare lo spoglio di.
weed-killer ['wiːdkɪlə*] *n* diserbante *m*.
weedy ['wiːdɪ] *adj* (*man*) allampanato.
week [wiːk] *n* settimana; **once/twice a ~** una volta/due volte alla settimana; **in 2 ~s' time** fra 2 settimane, fra 15 giorni; **Tuesday ~, a ~ on Tuesday** martedì a otto.
weekday ['wiːkdeɪ] *n* giorno feriale; (*COMM*) giornata lavorativa; **on ~s** durante la settimana.
weekend [wiːk'ɛnd] *n* fine settimana *m or f inv*, weekend *m inv*.
weekly ['wiːklɪ] *adv* ogni settimana, settimanalmente ♦ *adj, n* settimanale (*m*).
weep, *pt, pp* **wept** [wiːp, wɛpt] *vi* (*person*)

piangere; (*MED: wound etc*) essudare.
weeping willow ['wi:pɪŋ-] *n* salice *m* piangente.
weepy ['wi:pɪ] *n* (*col*) film *m inv or* storia strappalacrime.
weigh [weɪ] *vt, vi* pesare; **to ~ anchor** salpare *or* levare l'ancora; **to ~ the pros and cons** valutare i pro e i contro.
▶**weigh down** *vt* (*branch*) piegare; (*fig: with worry*) opprimere, caricare.
▶**weigh out** *vt* (*goods*) pesare.
▶**weigh up** *vt* valutare.
weighbridge ['weɪbrɪdʒ] *n* bascula.
weighing machine ['weɪɪŋ-] *n* pesa.
weight [weɪt] *n* peso; **sold by ~** venduto(a) a peso; **~s and measures** pesi e misure; **to put on/lose ~** ingrassare/dimagrire.
weighting ['weɪtɪŋ] *n*: **~ allowance** indennità *f inv* speciale (*per carovita etc*).
weightlessness ['weɪtlɪsnɪs] *n* mancanza di peso.
weightlifter ['weɪtlɪftə*] *n* pesista *m*.
weight training *n*: **to do ~** allenarsi con i pesi.
weighty ['weɪtɪ] *adj* pesante; (*fig*) importante, grave.
weir [wɪə*] *n* diga.
weird [wɪəd] *adj* strano(a), bizzarro(a); (*eerie*) soprannaturale.
weirdo ['wɪədəu] *n* (*col*) tipo/a allucinante.
welcome ['welkəm] *adj* benvenuto(a) ♦ *n* accoglienza, benvenuto ♦ *vt* accogliere cordialmente; (*also:* **bid ~**) dare il benvenuto a; (*be glad of*) rallegrarsi di; **to be ~** essere il(la) benvenuto(a); **to make sb ~** accogliere bene qn; **you're ~** (*after thanks*) prego; **you're ~ to try** provi pure.
welcoming ['welkəmɪŋ] *adj* accogliente.
weld [weld] *n* saldatura ♦ *vt* saldare.
welder ['weldə*] *n* (*person*) saldatore *m*.
welding ['weldɪŋ] *n* saldatura (autogena).
welfare ['welfɛə*] *n* benessere *m*.
welfare state *n* stato sociale.
welfare work *n* assistenza sociale.
well [wel] *n* pozzo ♦ *adv* bene ♦ *adj*: **to be ~** (*person*) stare bene ♦ *excl* allora!; ma!; ebbene!; **~ done!** bravo(a)!; **get ~ soon!** guarisci presto!; **to do ~ in sth** riuscire in qc; **to be doing ~** stare bene; **to think ~ of sb** avere una buona opinione di qn; **I don't feel ~** non mi sento bene; **as ~** (*in addition*) anche; **X as ~ as Y** sia X che Y; **he did as ~ as he could** ha fatto come meglio poteva; **you might as ~ tell me** potresti anche dirmelo; **it would be as ~ to ask** sarebbe bene chiedere; **~, as I was saying** … dunque, come stavo dicendo ….
▶**well up** *vi* (*tears, emotions*) sgorgare.

we'll [wi:l] = **we will; we shall.**
well-behaved ['welbɪ'heɪvd] *adj* ubbidiente.
well-being ['wel'bi:ɪŋ] *n* benessere *m*.
well-bred ['wel'bred] *adj* educato(a), beneducato(a).
well-built ['wel'bɪlt] *adj* (*person*) ben fatto(a).
well-chosen ['wel'tʃəuzn] *adj* (*remarks, words*) ben scelto(a), appropriato(a).
well-developed ['weldɪ'vɛləpt] *adj* sviluppato(a).
well-disposed ['weldɪs'pəuzd] *adj*: **~ to(wards)** bendisposto(a) verso.
well-dressed ['wel'drest] *adj* ben vestito(a), vestito(a) bene.
well-earned ['wel'ə:nd] *adj* (*rest*) meritato(a).
well-groomed ['wel'gru:md] *adj* curato(a), azzimato(a).
well-heeled ['wel'hi:ld] *adj* (*col: wealthy*) agiato(a), facoltoso(a).
well-informed ['welɪn'fɔ:md] *adj* ben informato(a).
Wellington ['welɪŋtən] *n* Wellington *f*.
wellingtons ['welɪŋtənz] *npl* (*also:* **wellington boots**) stivali *mpl* di gomma.
well-kept ['wel'kept] *adj* (*house, grounds, secret*) ben tenuto(a); (*hair, hands*) ben curato(a).
well-known ['wel'nəun] *adj* noto(a), famoso(a).
well-mannered ['wel'mænəd] *adj* ben educato(a).
well-meaning ['wel'mi:nɪŋ] *adj* ben intenzionato(a).
well-nigh ['wel'naɪ] *adv*: **~ impossible** quasi impossibile.
well-off ['wel'ɔf] *adj* benestante, danaroso(a).
well-read ['wel'red] *adj* colto(a).
well-spoken ['wel'spəukn] *adj* che parla bene.
well-stocked ['wel'stɔkt] *adj* (*shop, larder*) ben fornito(a).
well-timed ['wel'taɪmd] *adj* opportuno(a).
well-to-do ['weltə'du:] *adj* abbiente, benestante.
well-wisher ['welwɪʃə*] *n* ammiratore/trice; **letters from ~s** lettere *fpl* di incoraggiamento.
well-woman clinic ['welwumən-] *n* ≈ consultorio (familiare).
Welsh [welʃ] *adj* gallese ♦ *n* (*LING*) gallese *m*; **the ~** *npl* i gallesi; **the ~ National Assembly** il Parlamento gallese.
Welshman, Welshwoman ['welʃmən, -wumən] *n* gallese *m/f*.
Welsh rarebit *n* crostino al formaggio.

welter ['wɛltə*] *n* massa, mucchio.
went [wɛnt] *pt of* **go**.
wept [wɛpt] *pt, pp of* **weep**.
were [wə:*] *pt of* **be**.
we're [wɪə*] = **we are**.
weren't [wə:nt] = **were not**.
werewolf, *pl* **-wolves** ['wɪəwulf, -wulvz] *n* licantropo, lupo mannaro (*col*).
west [wɛst] *n* ovest *m*, occidente *m*, ponente *m* ♦ *adj* (a) ovest *inv*, occidentale ♦ *adv* verso ovest; **the W~** l'Occidente.
westbound ['wɛstbaund] *adj* (*traffic*) diretto(a) a ovest; (*carriageway*) ovest *inv*.
West Country *n*: **the ~** il sud-ovest dell'Inghilterra.
westerly ['wɛstəlɪ] *adj* (*wind*) occidentale, da ovest.
western ['wɛstən] *adj* occidentale, dell'ovest ♦ *n* (*CINE*) western *m inv*.
westerner ['wɛstənə*] *n* occidentale *m/f*.
westernized ['wɛstənaɪzd] *adj* occidentalizzato(a).
West German *adj*, *n* tedesco(a) occidentale.
West Germany *n* Germania Occidentale.
West Indian *adj* delle Indie Occidentali ♦ *n* abitante *m/f* (*or* originario/a) delle Indie Occidentali.
West Indies [-'ɪndɪz] *npl*: **the ~** le Indie Occidentali.
Westminster ['wɛstmɪnstə*] *n* il parlamento (britannico).
westward(s) ['wɛstwəd(z)] *adv* verso ovest.
wet [wɛt] *adj* umido(a), bagnato(a); (*soaked*) fradicio(a); (*rainy*) piovoso(a) ♦ *vt*: **to ~ one's pants** *or* **o.s.** farsi la pipì addosso; **to get ~** bagnarsi; *"~ paint"* "vernice fresca".
wet blanket *n* (*fig*) guastafeste *m/f inv*.
wetness ['wɛtnɪs] *n* umidità.
wet suit *n* tuta da sub.
we've [wi:v] = **we have**.
whack [wæk] *vt* picchiare, battere.
whacked [wækt] *adj* (*col: tired*) sfinito(a), a pezzi.
whale [weɪl] *n* (*ZOOL*) balena.
whaler ['weɪlə*] *n* (*ship*) baleniera.
whaling ['weɪlɪŋ] *n* caccia alla balena.
wharf, *pl* **wharves** [wɔ:f, wɔ:vz] *n* banchina.

═══════════════════════ *KEYWORD*

what [wɔt] *adj* **1** (*in direct/indirect questions*) che; quale; **~ size is it?** che taglia è?; **~ colour is it?** di che colore è?; **~ books do you want?** quali *or* che libri vuole?; **for ~ reason?** per quale motivo?

2 (*in exclamations*) che; **~ a mess!** che disordine!
♦ *pron* **1** (*interrogative*) che cosa, cosa, che; **~'s in there?** cosa c'è lì dentro?; **~ is his address?** qual è il suo indirizzo?; **~ will it cost?** quanto costerà?; **~ are you doing?** che *or* (che) cosa fai?; **~ are you talking about?** di che cosa parli?; **~'s happening?** che *or* (che) cosa succede?; **~ is it called?** come si chiama?; **~ about me?** e io?; **~ about doing …?** e se facessimo …?

2 (*relative*) ciò che, quello che; **I saw ~ you did** ho visto quello che hai fatto; **I saw ~ was on the table** ho visto cosa c'era sul tavolo; **~ I want is a cup of tea** ciò che voglio adesso è una tazza di tè

3 (*indirect use*) (che) cosa; **he asked me ~ she had said** mi ha chiesto che cosa avesse detto; **tell me ~ you're thinking about** dimmi a cosa stai pensando; **I don't know ~ to do** non so cosa fare
♦ *excl* (*disbelieving*) cosa!, come!

whatever [wɔt'ɛvə*] *adj*: **~ book** qualunque *or* qualsiasi libro + *sub*
♦ *pron*: **do ~ is necessary/you want** faccia qualunque *or* qualsiasi cosa sia necessaria/lei voglia; **~ happens** qualunque cosa accada; **no reason ~** *or* **whatsoever** nessuna ragione affatto *or* al mondo; **~ it costs** costi quello che costi.
whatsoever [wɔtsəu'ɛvə*] *adj, pron* = **whatever.**
wheat [wi:t] *n* grano, frumento.
wheatgerm ['wi:tdʒə:m] *n* germe *m* di grano.
wheatmeal ['wi:tmi:l] *n* farina integrale di frumento.
wheedle ['wi:dl] *vt*: **to ~ sb into doing sth** convincere qn a fare qc (con lusinghe); **to ~ sth out of sb** ottenere qc da qn (con lusinghe).
wheel [wi:l] *n* ruota; (*AUT: also:* **steering ~**) volante *m*; (*NAUT*) (ruota del) timone *m* ♦ *vt* spingere ♦ *vi* (*also:* **~ round**) girare.
wheelbarrow ['wi:lbærəu] *n* carriola.
wheelbase ['wi:lbeɪs] *n* interasse *m*.
wheelchair ['wi:ltʃɛə*] *n* sedia a rotelle.
wheel clamp *n* (*AUT*) morsetto *m* bloccaruota *inv*.
wheeler-dealer ['wi:lə'di:lə*] *n* trafficone *m*, maneggione *m*.
wheelie-bin ['wi:lɪbɪn] *n* (*BRIT*) bidone *m* (della spazzatura) a rotelle.
wheeling ['wi:lɪŋ] *n*: **~ and dealing** maneggi *mpl*.
wheeze [wi:z] *n* respiro affannoso ♦ *vi*

ansimare.
wheezy ['wiːzɪ] adj (person) che respira
con affanno; (breath) sibilante.

=============================== KEYWORD

when [wɛn] adv quando; ~ **did it happen?**
quando è successo?
♦ conj 1 (at, during, after the time that)
quando; **she was reading ~ I came in**
quando sono entrato lei leggeva; **that
was ~ I needed you** era allora che avevo
bisogno di te
2 (on, at which): **on the day ~ I met him** il
giorno in cui l'ho incontrato; **one day ~ it
was raining** un giorno che pioveva
3 (whereas) quando, mentre; **you said I
was wrong ~ in fact I was right** mi hai
detto che avevo torto, quando in realtà
avevo ragione.

whenever [wɛn'ɛvə*] adv quando mai ♦ conj
quando; (every time that) ogni volta che; **I
go ~ I can** ci vado ogni volta che posso.
where [wɛə*] adv, conj dove; **this is ~** è qui
che; ~ **are you from?** di dov'è?; ~
possible quando è possibile, se possibile.
whereabouts ['wɛərəbauts] adv dove ♦ n:
sb's ~ luogo dove qn si trova.
whereas [wɛər'æz] conj mentre.
whereby [wɛə'baɪ] adv (formal) per cui.
whereupon [wɛərə'pɔn] adv al che.
wherever [wɛər'ɛvə*] adv dove mai ♦ conj
dovunque + sub; **sit ~ you like** si sieda
dove vuole.
wherewithal ['wɛəwɪðɔːl] n: **the ~ (to do
sth)** i mezzi (per fare qc).
whet [wɛt] vt (appetite etc) stimolare.
whether ['wɛðə*] conj se; **I don't know ~ to
accept or not** non so se accettare o no;
it's doubtful ~ è poco probabile che; ~
you go or not che lei vada o no.
whey [weɪ] n siero.

=============================== KEYWORD

which [wɪtʃ] adj 1 (interrogative: direct,
indirect) quale; ~ **picture do you want?**
quale quadro vuole?; ~ **one?** quale?; ~
one of you did it? chi di voi lo ha fatto?
2: **in ~ case** nel qual caso; **by ~ time** e a
quel punto
♦ pron 1 (interrogative) quale; ~ **(of these)
are yours?** quali di questi sono suoi?; ~ **of
you are coming?** chi di voi viene?
2 (relative) che; (: indirect) cui, il (la)
quale; **the apple ~ you ate/~ is on the
table** la mela che hai mangiato/che è sul
tavolo; **the chair on ~ you are sitting** la
sedia sulla quale or su cui sei seduto; **the**

book of ~ we were speaking il libro del
quale stavamo parlando; **he said he
knew, ~ is true** ha detto che lo sapeva, il
che è vero; **I don't mind ~** non mi
importa quale; **after ~** dopo di che.

whichever [wɪtʃ'ɛvə*] adj: **take ~ book you
prefer** prenda qualsiasi libro che
preferisce; ~ **book you take** qualsiasi
libro prenda; ~ **way you ...** in qualunque
modo lei ... + sub.
whiff [wɪf] n odore m; **to catch a ~ of sth**
sentire l'odore di qc.
while [waɪl] n momento ♦ conj mentre; (as
long as) finché; (although) sebbene + sub;
for a ~ per un po'; **in a ~** tra poco; **all the
~** tutto il tempo; **we'll make it worth your
~** faremo in modo che le valga la pena.
►**while away** vt (time) far passare.
whilst [waɪlst] conj = **while**.
whim [wɪm] n capriccio.
whimper ['wɪmpə*] n piagnucolio ♦ vi
piagnucolare.
whimsical ['wɪmzɪkl] adj (person)
capriccioso(a); (look) strano(a).
whine [waɪn] n gemito ♦ vi gemere;
uggiolare; piagnucolare.
whip [wɪp] n frusta; (for riding) frustino;
(POL: person) capogruppo ♦ vt frustare;
(CULIN: cream etc) sbattere; (snatch)
sollevare (or estrarre) bruscamente; see
boxed note.
►**whip up** vt (cream) montare, sbattere;
(col: meal) improvvisare; (: stir up: support,
feeling) suscitare, stimolare.

┌─────────────────────────────────────┐
│ **WHIP**   │
│   │
│ Nel Parlamento britannico i **whips** sono │
│ parlamentari incaricati di mantenere la │
│ disciplina tra i deputati del loro partito durante │
│ le votazioni e di verificare la loro presenza in │
│ aula.   │
└─────────────────────────────────────┘

whiplash ['wɪplæʃ] n (MED: also: ~ **injury**)
colpo di frusta.
whipped cream ['wɪpt-] n panna montata.
whipping boy ['wɪpɪŋ-] n (fig) capro
espiatorio.
whip-round ['wɪpraund] n (BRIT) colletta.
whirl [wəːl] n turbine m ♦ vt (far) girare
rapidamente; (far) turbinare ♦ vi
turbinare; (dancers) volteggiare; (leaves,
dust) sollevarsi in un vortice.
whirlpool ['wəːlpuːl] n mulinello.
whirlwind ['wəːlwɪnd] n turbine m.
whirr [wəː*] vi ronzare.
whisk [wɪsk] n (CULIN) frusta; frullino ♦ vt

sbattere, frullare; **to ~ sb away** *or* **off** portar via qn a tutta velocità.

whiskers ['wɪskəz] *npl* (*of animal*) baffi *mpl*; (*of man*) favoriti *mpl*.

whisky, (*Irish*, *US*) **whiskey** ['wɪskɪ] *n* whisky *m inv*.

whisper ['wɪspə*] *n* bisbiglio, sussurro; (*rumour*) voce *f* ♦ *vt, vi* bisbigliare, sussurrare; **to ~ sth to sb** bisbigliare qc a qn.

whispering ['wɪspərɪŋ] *n* bisbiglio.

whist [wɪst] *n* (*BRIT*) whist *m*.

whistle ['wɪsl] *n* (*sound*) fischio; (*object*) fischietto ♦ *vi, vt* fischiare; **to ~ a tune** fischiettare un motivetto.

whistle-stop ['wɪslstɔp] *adj*: **~ tour** (*POL, fig*) rapido giro.

Whit [wɪt] *n* Pentecoste *f*.

white [waɪt] *adj* bianco(a); (*with fear*) pallido(a) ♦ *n* bianco; (*person*) bianco/a; **to turn** *or* **go ~** (*person*) sbiancare; (*hair*) diventare bianco; **the ~s** (*washing*) i capi bianchi; **tennis ~s** completo da tennis.

whitebait ['waɪtbeɪt] *n* bianchetti *mpl*.

white-collar worker ['waɪtkɔlə-] *n* impiegato/a.

white elephant *n* (*fig*) oggetto (*or* progetto) costoso ma inutile.

white goods *npl* (*appliances*) elettrodomestici *mpl*; (*linens*) biancheria per la casa.

white-hot [waɪt'hɔt] *adj* (*metal*) incandescente.

White House *n*: **the ~** la Casa Bianca; *see boxed note.*

---

white lie *n* bugia pietosa.

whiteness ['waɪtnɪs] *n* bianchezza.

white noise *n* rumore *m* bianco.

white paper *n* (*POL*) libro bianco.

whitewash ['waɪtwɔʃ] *n* (*paint*) bianco di calce ♦ *vt* imbiancare; (*fig*) coprire.

whiting ['waɪtɪŋ] *n* (*pl inv*) merlango.

Whit Monday *n* lunedì *m inv* di Pentecoste.

Whitsun ['wɪtsn] *n* Pentecoste *f*.

whittle ['wɪtl] *vt*: **to ~ away, ~ down** ridurre, tagliare.

whizz [wɪz] *vi* passare sfrecciando.

whizz kid *n* (*col*) prodigio.

WHO *n abbr* (= *World Health Organization*) O.M.S. *f* (= *Organizzazione mondiale della sanità*).

================== *KEYWORD*

who [hu:] *pron* **1** (*interrogative*) chi; **~ is it?, ~'s there?** chi è?
2 (*relative*) che; **the man ~ spoke to me** l'uomo che ha parlato con me; **those ~ can swim** quelli che sanno nuotare.

whodunit [hu:'dʌnɪt] *n* (*col*) giallo.

whoever [hu:'ɛvə*] *pron*: **~ finds it** chiunque lo trovi; **ask ~ you like** lo chieda a chiunque vuole; **~ told you that?** chi mai gliel'ha detto?

whole [həul] *adj* (*complete*) tutto(a), completo(a); (*not broken*) intero(a), intatto(a) ♦ *n* (*total*) totale *m*; (*sth not broken*) tutto; **the ~ lot** (*of it*) tutto; **the ~ lot** (*of them*) tutti; **the ~ of the time** tutto il tempo; **the ~ of the town** la città intera; **on the ~, as a ~** nel complesso, nell'insieme; **~ villages were destroyed** interi paesi furono distrutti.

wholehearted [həul'hɑ:tɪd] *adj* sincero(a).

wholemeal ['həulmi:l] *adj* (*BRIT: flour, bread*) integrale.

whole note *n* (*US*) semibreve *f*.

wholesale ['həulseɪl] *n* commercio *or* vendita all'ingrosso ♦ *adj* all'ingrosso; (*destruction*) totale.

wholesaler ['həulseɪlə*] *n* grossista *m/f*.

wholesome ['həulsəm] *adj* sano(a); (*climate*) salubre.

wholewheat ['həulwi:t] *adj* = **wholemeal**.

wholly ['həulɪ] *adv* completamente, del tutto.

================== *KEYWORD*

whom [hu:m] *pron* **1** (*interrogative*) chi; **~ did you see?** chi hai visto?; **to ~ did you give it?** a chi lo hai dato?
2 (*relative*) che, *prep* + il (la) quale; **the man ~ I saw** l'uomo che ho visto; **the man to ~ I spoke** l'uomo al *or* con il quale ho parlato; **those to ~ I spoke** le persone alle *or* con le quali ho parlato.

whooping cough ['hu:pɪŋ-] *n* pertosse *f*.

whoops [wu:ps] *excl*: **~-a-daisy!** ops!

whoosh [wuʃ] *n*: **it came out with a ~** (*sauce etc*) è uscito di getto; (*air*) è uscito con un sibilo.

whopper ['wɔpə*] *n* (*col: lie*) balla; (: *large*

thing) cosa enorme.

whopping ['wɔpɪŋ] *adj* (*col: big*) enorme.

whore [hɔ:*] *n* (*pej*) puttana.

========================== KEYWORD

whose [hu:z] *adj* **1** (*possessive: interrogative*) di chi; ~ **book is this?**, ~ **is this book?** di chi è questo libro?; ~ **daughter are you?** di chi sei figlia?; ~ **pencil have you taken?** di chi è la matita che hai preso?
2 (*possessive: relative*): **the man** ~ **son you rescued** l'uomo il cui figlio hai salvato *or* a cui hai salvato il figlio; **the girl** ~ **sister you were speaking to** la ragazza alla cui sorella stavi parlando
♦ *pron* di chi; ~ **is this?** di chi è questo?; **I know** ~ **it is** so di chi è.

Who's Who ['hu:z'hu:] *n* elenco di personalità.

why [waɪ] *adv, conj* perché ♦ *excl* (*surprise*) ma guarda un po'!; (*remonstrating*) ma (via)!; (*explaining*) ebbene!; ~ **not?** perché no?; ~ **not do it now?** perché non farlo adesso?; **the reason** ~ il motivo per cui.

whyever [waɪ'ɛvə*] *adv* perché mai.

WI *n abbr* (*BRIT*: = *Women's Institute*) circolo femminile ♦ *abbr* (*GEO*) = **West Indies**; (*US*) = **Wisconsin**.

wick [wɪk] *n* lucignolo, stoppino.

wicked ['wɪkɪd] *adj* cattivo(a), malvagio(a); (*mischievous*) malizioso(a); (*terrible: prices, weather*) terribile.

wicker ['wɪkə*] *n* vimine *m*; (*also:* ~**work**) articoli *mpl* di vimini.

wicket ['wɪkɪt] *n* (*CRICKET*) porta; area tra le due porte.

wicket keeper *n* (*CRICKET*) ≈ portiere *m*.

wide [waɪd] *adj* largo(a); (*region, knowledge*) vasto(a); (*choice*) ampio(a) ♦ *adv*: **to open** ~ spalancare; **to shoot** ~ tirare a vuoto *or* fuori bersaglio; **it is 3 metres** ~ è largo 3 metri.

wide-angle lens ['waɪdæŋgl-] *n* grandangolare *m*.

wide-awake [waɪdə'weɪk] *adj* completamente sveglio(a).

wide-eyed [waɪd'aɪd] *adj* con gli occhi spalancati.

widely ['waɪdlɪ] *adv* (*different*) molto, completamente; (*believed*) generalmente; ~ **spaced** molto distanziati(e); **to be** ~ **read** (*author*) essere molto letto; (*reader*) essere molto colto.

widen ['waɪdn] *vt* allargare, ampliare.

wideness ['waɪdnɪs] *n* larghezza; vastità; ampiezza.

wide open *adj* spalancato(a).

wide-ranging [waɪd'reɪndʒɪŋ] *adj* (*survey, report*) vasto(a); (*interests*) svariato(a).

widescreen ['waɪdskri:n] *adj* (*television*) a schermo panoramico.

widespread ['waɪdsprɛd] *adj* (*belief etc*) molto *or* assai diffuso(a).

widow ['wɪdəu] *n* vedova.

widowed ['wɪdəud] *adj* (che è rimasto(a)) vedovo(a).

widower ['wɪdəuə*] *n* vedovo.

width [wɪdθ] *n* larghezza; **it's 7 metres in** ~ è largo 7 metri.

widthways ['wɪdθweɪz] *adv* trasversalmente.

wield [wi:ld] *vt* (*sword*) maneggiare; (*power*) esercitare.

wife, *pl* **wives** [waɪf, waɪvz] *n* moglie *f*.

wig [wɪg] *n* parrucca.

wigging ['wɪgɪŋ] *n* (*BRIT col*) lavata di capo.

wiggle ['wɪgl] *vt* dimenare, agitare ♦ *vi* (*loose screw etc*) traballare; (*worm*) torcersi.

wiggly ['wɪglɪ] *adj* (*line*) ondulato(a), sinuoso(a).

wild [waɪld] *adj* (*animal, plant*) selvatico(a); (*countryside, appearance*) selvaggio(a); (*sea*) tempestoso(a); (*idea, life*) folle; (*col: angry*) arrabbiato(a), furibondo(a); (*enthusiastic*): **to be** ~ **about** andar pazzo(a) per ♦ *n*: **the** ~ la natura; ~**s** *npl* regione *f* selvaggia.

wild card *n* (*COMPUT*) carattere *m* jolly *inv*.

wildcat ['waɪldkæt] *n* gatto(a) selvatico(a).

wildcat strike *n* ≈ sciopero selvaggio.

wilderness ['wɪldənɪs] *n* deserto.

wildfire ['waɪldfaɪə*] *n*: **to spread like** ~ propagarsi rapidamente.

wild-goose chase [waɪld'gu:s-] *n* (*fig*) pista falsa.

wildlife ['waɪldlaɪf] *n* natura.

wildly ['waɪldlɪ] *adv* (*applaud*) freneticamente; (*hit, guess*) a casaccio; (*happy*) follemente.

wiles [waɪlz] *npl* astuzie *fpl*.

wilful, (*US*) **willful** ['wɪlful] *adj* (*person*) testardo(a); ostinato(a); (*action*) intenzionale; (*crime*) premeditato(a).

========================== KEYWORD

will [wɪl] *aux vb* **1** (*forming future tense*): **I** ~ **finish it tomorrow** lo finirò domani; **I** ~ **have finished it by tomorrow** lo finirò entro domani; ~ **you do it? – yes I** ~**/no I won't** lo farai? – sì (lo farò)/no (non lo farò); **the car won't start** la macchina non parte
2 (*in conjectures, predictions*): **he** ~ *or* **he'll**

be there by now dovrebbe essere
arrivato a quest'ora; **that ~ be the
postman** sarà il postino
3 *(in commands, requests, offers)*: **~ you be
quiet!** vuoi stare zitto?; **~ you sit down?**
(politely) prego, si accomodi; *(angrily)*
vuoi metterti seduto?; **~ you come?** vieni
anche tu?; **~ you help me?** mi aiuti?, mi
puoi aiutare?; **you won't lose it, ~ you?**
non lo perderai, vero?; **~ you have a cup
of tea?** vorrebbe una tazza di tè?; **I won't
put up with it!** non lo accetterò!
♦ *vt (pt, pp* **~ed): to ~ sb to do** pregare tra
sé perché qn faccia; **he ~ed himself to go
on** continuò grazie a un grande sforzo di
volontà
♦ *n* **1** *(desire)* volontà; **against sb's ~**
contro la volontà *or* il volere di qn; **to do
sth of one's own free ~** fare qc di propria
volontà
2 *(LAW)* testamento; **to make a/one's ~**
fare testamento.

willful ['wɪlful] *adj (US)* = **wilful.**
willing ['wɪlɪŋ] *adj* volonteroso(a) ♦ *n:* **to
show ~** dare prova di buona volontà; **~
to do** disposto(a) a fare.
willingly ['wɪlɪŋlɪ] *adv* volentieri.
willingness ['wɪlɪŋnɪs] *n* buona volontà.
will-o'-the-wisp [wɪləðə'wɪsp] *n (also fig)*
fuoco fatuo.
willow ['wɪləu] *n* salice *m.*
will power *n* forza di volontà.
willy-nilly ['wɪlɪ'nɪlɪ] *adv* volente o nolente.
wilt [wɪlt] *vi* appassire.
Wilts [wɪlts] *abbr (BRIT)* = **Wiltshire.**
wily ['waɪlɪ] *adj* furbo(a).
wimp [wɪmp] *n (col)* mezza calzetta.
win [wɪn] *n (in sports etc)* vittoria ♦ *vb (pt, pp*
won [wʌn]) *vt (battle, prize)* vincere;
(money) guadagnare; *(popularity)*
conquistare; *(contract)* aggiudicarsi ♦ *vi*
vincere.
▶**win over,** *(BRIT)* **win round** *vt*
convincere.
wince [wɪns] *n* trasalimento, sussulto ♦ *vi*
trasalire.
winch [wɪntʃ] *n* verricello, argano.
Winchester disk ['wɪntʃɪstə-] *n (COMPUT)*
disco Winchester.
wind *n* [wɪnd] vento; *(MED)* flatulenza,
ventosità ♦ *vb* [waɪnd] *(pt, pp* **wound**
[waund]) *vt* attorcigliare; *(wrap)*
avvolgere; *(clock, toy)* caricare; *(take
breath away:* [wɪnd]) far restare senza
fiato ♦ *vi (road, river)* serpeggiare; **the ~(s)**
(MUS) i fiati; **into** *or* **against the ~**
controvento; **to get ~ of sth** venire a

sapere qc; **to break ~** scoreggiare *(col)*.
▶**wind down** *vt (car window)* abbassare;
(fig: production, business) diminuire.
▶**wind up** *vt (clock)* caricare; *(debate)*
concludere.
windbreak ['wɪndbreɪk] *n* frangivento.
windcheater ['wɪndtʃiːtə*], *(US)*
windbreaker ['wɪndbreɪkə*] *n* giacca a
vento.
winder ['waɪndə*] *n (BRIT: on watch)* corona
di carica.
windfall ['wɪndfɔːl] *n* colpo di fortuna.
winding ['waɪndɪŋ] *adj (road)* serpeggiante;
(staircase) a chiocciola.
wind instrument *n (MUS)* strumento a
fiato.
windmill ['wɪndmɪl] *n* mulino a vento.
window ['wɪndəu] *n (gen, COMPUT)* finestra;
(in car, train) finestrino; *(in shop etc)*
vetrina; *(also:* **~ pane)** vetro.
window box *n* cassetta da fiori.
window cleaner *n (person)* pulitore *m* di
finestre.
window dressing *n* allestimento della
vetrina.
window envelope *n* busta a finestra.
window frame *n* telaio di finestra.
window ledge *n* davanzale *m.*
window pane *n* vetro.
window-shopping ['wɪndəuʃɔpɪŋ] *n:* **to go
~** andare a vedere le vetrine.
windowsill ['wɪndəusɪl] *n* davanzale *m.*
windpipe ['wɪndpaɪp] *n* trachea.
wind power *n* energia eolica.
windscreen ['wɪndskriːn], *(US)*
windshield ['wɪndʃiːld] *n* parabrezza *m
inv.*
windscreen washer *n* lavacristallo.
windscreen wiper *n* tergicristallo.
windshield ['wɪndʃiːld] *n (US)* =
windscreen.
windsurfing ['wɪndsəːfɪŋ] *n* windsurf *m inv.*
windswept ['wɪndswɛpt] *adj* spazzato(a)
dal vento.
wind tunnel *n* galleria aerodinamica *or*
del vento.
windy ['wɪndɪ] *adj* ventoso(a); **it's ~** c'è
vento.
wine [waɪn] *n* vino ♦ *vt:* **to ~ and dine sb**
offrire un ottimo pranzo a qn.
wine bar *n* enoteca.
wine cellar *n* cantina.
wine glass *n* bicchiere *m* da vino.
wine list *n* lista dei vini.
wine merchant *n* commerciante *m* di
vino.
wine tasting *n* degustazione *f* dei vini.
wine waiter *n* sommelier *m inv.*

wing [wɪŋ] n ala; ~**s** npl (THEAT) quinte fpl.
winger ['wɪŋə*] n (SPORT) ala.
wing mirror n (BRIT) specchietto
retrovisore esterno.
wing nut n galletto.
wingspan ['wɪŋspæn], **wingspread**
['wɪŋsprɛd] n apertura alare, apertura
d'ali.
wink [wɪŋk] n occhiolino, strizzatina
d'occhi ♦ vi ammiccare, fare l'occhiolino.
winkle ['wɪŋkl] n litorina.
winner ['wɪnə*] n vincitore/trice.
winning ['wɪnɪŋ] adj (team) vincente; (goal)
decisivo(a); (charming) affascinante; see
also **winnings**.
winning post n traguardo.
winnings ['wɪnɪŋz] npl vincite fpl.
winsome ['wɪnsəm] adj accattivante.
winter ['wɪntə*] n inverno; **in** ~ d'inverno,
in inverno.
winter sports npl sport mpl invernali.
wintry ['wɪntrɪ] adj invernale.
wipe [waɪp] n pulita, passata ♦ vt pulire
(strofinando); (dishes) asciugare; **to give
sth a** ~ dare una pulita or una passata a
qc; **to** ~ **one's nose** soffiarsi il naso.
▶**wipe off** vt cancellare; (stains) togliere
strofinando.
▶**wipe out** vt (debt) pagare, liquidare;
(memory) cancellare; (destroy)
annientare.
▶**wipe up** vt asciugare.
wire ['waɪə*] n filo; (ELEC) filo elettrico;
(TEL) telegramma m ♦ vt (ELEC: house) fare
l'impianto elettrico di; (: circuit)
installare; (also: ~ **up**) collegare,
allacciare.
wire brush n spazzola metallica.
wire cutters [-kʌtəz] npl tronchese m or f.
wireless ['waɪəlɪs] n (BRIT) telegrafia senza
fili; (set) (apparecchio m) radio f inv ♦ adj
(technology) wireless inv, senza fili.
wire netting n rete f metallica.
wire service n (US) = **news agency**.
wire-tapping ['waɪə'tæpɪŋ] n
intercettazione f telefonica.
wiring ['waɪərɪŋ] n (ELEC) impianto
elettrico.
wiry ['waɪərɪ] adj magro(a) e nerboruto(a).
Wis(c). abbr (US) = Wisconsin.
wisdom ['wɪzdəm] n saggezza; (of action)
prudenza.
wisdom tooth n dente m del giudizio.
wise [waɪz] adj saggio(a); (advice, remark)
prudente; **I'm none the** ~**r** ne so come
prima.
▶**wise up** vi (col): **to** ~ **up to** divenire più
consapevole di.

... wise [waɪz] suffix: **time**~ per quanto
riguarda il tempo, in termini di tempo.
wisecrack ['waɪzkræk] n battuta spiritosa.
wish [wɪʃ] n (desire) desiderio; (specific
desire) richiesta ♦ vt desiderare, volere;
best ~**es** (on birthday etc) i migliori
auguri; **with best** ~**es** (in letter) cordiali
saluti, con i migliori saluti; **give her my
best** ~**es** le faccia i migliori auguri da
parte mia; **to** ~ **sb goodbye** dire
arrivederci a qn; **he** ~**ed me well** mi
augurò di riuscire; **to** ~ **to do/sb to do**
desiderare or volere fare/che qn faccia;
to ~ **for** desiderare; **to** ~ **sth on sb**
rifilare qc a qn.
wishbone ['wɪʃbəun] n forcella.
wishful ['wɪʃful] adj: **it's** ~ **thinking** è
prendere i desideri per realtà.
wishy-washy ['wɪʃɪ'wɔʃɪ] adj insulso(a).
wisp [wɪsp] n ciuffo, ciocca; (of smoke,
straw) filo.
wistful ['wɪstful] adj malinconico(a);
(nostalgic) nostalgico(a).
wit [wɪt] n (gen pl) intelligenza; presenza di
spirito; (wittiness) spirito, arguzia;
(person) bello spirito; **to be at one's** ~**s'
end** (fig) non sapere più cosa fare; **to
have** or **keep one's** ~**s about one** avere
presenza di spirito; **to** ~ adv cioè.
witch [wɪtʃ] n strega.
witchcraft ['wɪtʃkrɑːft] n stregoneria.
witch doctor n stregone m.
witch-hunt ['wɪtʃhʌnt] n (fig) caccia alle
streghe.

===== KEYWORD

with [wɪð, wɪθ] prep **1** (in the company of)
con; **I was** ~ **him** ero con lui; **we stayed** ~
friends siamo stati da amici; **I'll be** ~ **you
in a minute** vengo subito
2 (descriptive) con; **a room** ~ **a view** una
camera con vista (sul mare or sulle
montagne etc); **the man** ~ **the grey hat/
blue eyes** l'uomo con il cappello grigio/
gli occhi blu
3 (indicating manner, means, cause): ~
tears in her eyes con le lacrime agli
occhi; **red** ~ **anger** rosso(a) dalla rabbia;
to shake ~ **fear** tremare di paura;
covered ~ **snow** coperto(a) di neve
4: **I'm** ~ **you** (I understand) la seguo; **I'm
not really** ~ **it today** (col) oggi sono un po'
fuori.

withdraw [wɪθ'drɔː] vb (irreg) vt ritirare;
(money from bank) ritirare, prelevare ♦ vi
ritirarsi; **to** ~ **into o.s.** chiudersi in se
stesso.

withdrawal [wɪθ'drɔːəl] *n* ritiro; prelievo; (*of army*) ritirata; (*MED*) stato di privazione.

withdrawal symptoms *npl* crisi *f* di astinenza.

withdrawn [wɪθ'drɔːn] *pp of* **withdraw** ♦ *adj* distaccato(a).

wither ['wɪðə*] *vi* appassire.

withered ['wɪðəd] *adj* appassito(a); (*limb*) atrofizzato(a).

withhold [wɪθ'həuld] *vt irreg* (*money*) trattenere; (*permission*): **to ~ (from)** rifiutare (a); (*information*): **to ~ (from)** nascondere (a).

within [wɪð'ɪn] *prep* all'interno di; (*in time, distances*) entro ♦ *adv* all'interno, dentro; **~ sight of** in vista di; **~ a mile of** entro un miglio da; **~ the week** prima della fine della settimana; **~ an hour from now** da qui a un'ora; **to be ~ the law** restare nei limiti della legge.

without [wɪð'aut] *prep* senza; **to go** *or* **do ~ sth** fare a meno di qc; **~ anybody knowing** senza che nessuno lo sappia.

withstand [wɪθ'stænd] *vt irreg* resistere a.

witness ['wɪtnɪs] *n* (*person*) testimone *m/f* ♦ *vt* (*event*) essere testimone di; (*document*) attestare l'autenticità di ♦ *vi*: **to ~ to sth/having seen sth** testimoniare qc/di aver visto qc; **to bear ~ to sth** testimoniare qc; **~ for the prosecution/ defence** testimone a carico/discarico.

witness box, (*US*) **witness stand** *n* banco dei testimoni.

witticism ['wɪtɪsɪzəm] *n* spiritosaggine *f*.

witty ['wɪtɪ] *adj* spiritoso(a).

wives [waɪvz] *npl of* **wife**.

wizard ['wɪzəd] *n* mago.

wizened ['wɪznd] *adj* raggrinzito(a).

wk *abbr* = **week**.

Wm. *abbr* = **William**.

WMD *n abbr see* **weapons of mass destruction**.

WO *n abbr see* **warrant officer**.

wobble ['wɔbl] *vi* tremare; (*chair*) traballare.

wobbly ['wɔblɪ] *adj* (*hand, voice*) tremante; (*table, chair*) traballante; (*object about to fall*) che oscilla pericolosamente.

woe [wəu] *n* dolore *m*; disgrazia.

woeful ['wəuful] *adj* (*sad*) triste; (*deplorable*) deplorevole.

wok [wɔk] *n* wok *m inv* (*padella concava usata nella cucina cinese*).

woke [wəuk] *pt of* **wake**.

woken ['wəukn] *pp of* **wake**.

wolf, *pl* **wolves** [wulf, wulvz] *n* lupo.

woman, *pl* **women** ['wumən, 'wɪmɪn] *n*
donna ♦ *cpd*: **~ doctor** *n* dottoressa; **~ friend** *n* amica; **~ teacher** *n* insegnante *f*; **women's page** *n* (*PRESS*) rubrica femminile.

womanize ['wumənaɪz] *vi* essere un donnaiolo.

womanly ['wumənlɪ] *adj* femminile.

womb [wuːm] *n* (*ANAT*) utero.

women ['wɪmɪn] *npl of* **woman**.

Women's (Liberation) Movement *n* (*also*: **Women's Lib**) Movimento per la Liberazione della Donna.

won [wʌn] *pt, pp of* **win**.

wonder ['wʌndə*] *n* meraviglia ♦ *vi*: **to ~ whether** domandarsi se; **to ~ at** essere sorpreso(a) di; meravigliarsi di; **to ~ about** domandarsi di; pensare a; **it's no ~ that** c'è poco *or* non c'è da meravigliarsi che + *sub*.

wonderful ['wʌndəful] *adj* meraviglioso(a).

wonderfully ['wʌndəfəlɪ] *adv* (+ *adjective*) meravigliosamente; (+ *verb*) a meraviglia.

wonky ['wɔŋkɪ] *adj* (*BRIT col*) traballante.

wont [wəunt] *n*: **as is his/her ~** com'è solito/a fare.

won't [wəunt] = **will not**.

woo [wuː] *vt* (*woman*) fare la corte a.

wood [wud] *n* legno; (*timber*) legname *m*; (*forest*) bosco ♦ *cpd* di bosco, silvestre.

wood carving *n* scultura in legno, intaglio.

wooded ['wudɪd] *adj* boschivo(a); boscoso(a).

wooden ['wudn] *adj* di legno; (*fig*) rigido(a); inespressivo(a).

woodland ['wudlənd] *n* zona boscosa.

woodpecker ['wudpɛkə*] *n* picchio.

wood pigeon *n* colombaccio, palomba.

woodwind ['wudwɪnd] *npl* (*MUS*): **the ~** i legni.

woodwork ['wudwəːk] *n* parti *fpl* in legno; (*craft, subject*) falegnameria.

woodworm ['wudwəːm] *n* tarlo del legno.

woof [wuf] *n* (*of dog*) bau bau *m* ♦ *vi* abbaiare; **~, ~!** bau bau!

wool [wul] *n* lana; **to pull the ~ over sb's eyes** (*fig*) fargliela a qn.

woollen, (*US*) **woolen** ['wulən] *adj* di lana ♦ *n*: **~s** indumenti *mpl* di lana.

woolly, (*US*) **wooly** ['wulɪ] *adj* lanoso(a); (*fig: ideas*) confuso(a).

woozy ['wuːzɪ] *adj* (*col*) stordito(a).

word [wəːd] *n* parola; (*news*) notizie *fpl* ♦ *vt* esprimere, formulare; **~ for ~** parola per parola, testualmente; **what's the ~ for "pen" in Italian?** come si dice "pen" in italiano?; **to put sth into ~s** esprimere qc a parole; **in other ~s** in altre parole; **to**

have a ~ **with sb** scambiare due parole con qn; **to have** ~**s with sb** (*quarrel with*) avere un diverbio con qn; **to break/keep one's** ~ non mantenere/mantenere la propria parola; **I'll take your** ~ **for it** la crederò sulla parola; **to send** ~ **of** avvisare di; **to leave** ~ (**with** *or* **for sb**) **that** ... lasciare detto (a qn) che ....

wording ['wɔːdɪŋ] *n* formulazione *f*.

word of mouth *n* passaparola *m*; **I learned it by** *or* **through** ~ lo so per sentito dire.

word-perfect ['wɔːd'pəfɪkt] *adj* (*speech etc*) imparato(a) a memoria.

word processing *n* word processing *m*, elaborazione *f* testi.

word processor *n* word processor *m inv*.

wordwrap ['wɔːdræp] *n* (*COMPUT*) ritorno carrello automatico.

wordy ['wɔːdɪ] *adj* verboso(a), prolisso(a).

wore [wɔː*] *pt of* **wear**.

work [wɔːk] *n* lavoro; (*ART, LITERATURE*) opera ♦ *vi* lavorare; (*mechanism, plan etc*) funzionare; (*medicine*) essere efficace ♦ *vt* (*clay, wood etc*) lavorare; (*mine etc*) sfruttare; (*machine*) far funzionare; **to be at** ~ (**on sth**) lavorare (a qc); **to set to** ~, **to start** ~ mettersi all'opera; **to go to** ~ andare al lavoro; **to be out of** ~ essere disoccupato(a); **to** ~ **one's way through a book** riuscire a leggersi tutto un libro; **to** ~ **one's way through college** lavorare per pagarsi gli studi; **to** ~ **hard** lavorare sodo; **to** ~ **loose** allentarsi; *see also* **works**.

▶**work on** *vt fus* lavorare a; (*principle*) basarsi su; **he's** ~**ing on the car** sta facendo dei lavori alla macchina.

▶**work out** *vi* (*plans etc*) riuscire, andare bene; (*SPORT*) allenarsi ♦ *vt* (*problem*) risolvere; (*plan*) elaborare; **it** ~**s out at £100** fa 100 sterline.

workable ['wɔːkəbl] *adj* (*solution*) realizzabile.

workaholic [wɔːkə'hɔlɪk] *n* stacanovista *m/f*.

workbench ['wɔːkbɛntʃ] *n* banco (da lavoro).

worked up *adj*: **to get** ~ andare su tutte le furie; eccitarsi.

worker ['wɔːkə*] *n* lavoratore/trice; (*esp AGR, INDUSTRY*) operaio/a; **office** ~ impiegato/a.

work force *n* forza lavoro.

work-in ['wɔːkɪn] *n* (*BRIT*) sciopero alla rovescia.

working ['wɔːkɪŋ] *adj* (*day*) feriale; (*tools, conditions*) di lavoro; (*clothes*) da lavoro; (*wife*) che lavora; (*partner*) attivo(a); **in** ~ **order** funzionante; ~ **knowledge** conoscenza pratica.

working capital *n* (*COMM*) capitale *m* d'esercizio.

working class *n* classe *f* operaia *or* lavatrice ♦ *adj*: **working-class** operaio(a).

working man *n* lavoratore *m*.

working party *n* (*BRIT*) commissione *f*.

working week *n* settimana lavorativa.

work-in-progress ['wɔːkɪn'prəugrɛs] *n* (*products*) lavoro in corso; (*value*) valore *m* del manufatto in lavorazione.

workload ['wɔːkləud] *n* carico di lavoro.

workman ['wɔːkmən] *n* operaio.

workmanship ['wɔːkmənʃɪp] *n* (*of worker*) abilità; (*of thing*) fattura.

workmate ['wɔːkmeɪt] *n* collega *m/f*.

workout ['wɔːkaut] *n* (*SPORT*) allenamento.

work permit *n* permesso di lavoro.

works [wɔːks] *n* (*BRIT: factory*) fabbrica ♦ *npl* (*of clock, machine*) meccanismo; **road** ~ **opere stradali**.

works council *n* consiglio aziendale.

work sheet *n* (*COMPUT*) foglio col programma di lavoro.

workshop ['wɔːkʃɔp] *n* officina.

work station *n* stazione *f* di lavoro.

work study *n* studio di organizzazione del lavoro.

worktop ['wɔːktɔp] *n* piano di lavoro.

work-to-rule ['wɔːktə'ruːl] *n* (*BRIT*) sciopero bianco.

world [wɔːld] *n* mondo ♦ *cpd* (*tour*) del mondo; (*record, power, war*) mondiale; **all over the** ~ in tutto il mondo; **to think the** ~ **of sb** pensare un gran bene di qn; **out of this** ~ (*fig*) formidabile; **what in the** ~ **is he doing?** che cavolo sta facendo?; **to do sb a** ~ **of good** fare un gran bene a qn; **W**~ **War One/Two** la prima/seconda guerra mondiale.

world champion *n* campione/essa mondiale.

World Cup *n* (*FOOTBALL*) Coppa del Mondo.

world-famous [wɔːld'feɪməs] *adj* di fama mondiale.

worldly ['wɔːldlɪ] *adj* di questo mondo.

world music *n* musica etnica.

World Series *n*: **the** ~ (*US BASEBALL*) la finalissima di baseball.

world-wide ['wɔːld'waɪd] *adj* universale.

worm [wɔːm] *n* verme *m*.

worn [wɔːn] *pp of* **wear** ♦ *adj* usato(a).

worn-out ['wɔːnaut] *adj* (*object*) consumato(a), logoro(a); (*person*) sfinito(a).

worried ['wʌrɪd] *adj* preoccupato(a); **to be**

~ **about sth** essere preoccupato per qc.

worrier ['wʌrɪə*] *n* ansioso/a.

worrisome ['wʌrɪsəm] *adj* preoccupante.

worry ['wʌrɪ] *n* preoccupazione *f* ♦ *vt*
preoccupare ♦ *vi* preoccuparsi; **to** ~
about *or* **over sth/sb** preoccuparsi di qc/
per qn.

worrying ['wʌrɪɪŋ] *adj* preoccupante.

worse [wəːs] *adj* peggiore ♦ *adv, n* peggio; **a
change for the** ~ un peggioramento; **to
get** ~, **to grow** ~ peggiorare; **he is none
the** ~ **for it** non ha avuto brutte
conseguenze; **so much the** ~ **for you!**
tanto peggio per te!

worsen ['wəːsn] *vt, vi* peggiorare.

worse off *adj* in condizioni (economiche)
peggiori; (*fig*) **you'll be** ~ **this way** così
sarà peggio per lei; **he is now** ~ **than
before** ora è in condizioni peggiori di
prima.

worship ['wəːʃɪp] *n* culto ♦ *vt* (*God*)
adorare, venerare; (*person*) adorare; **Your
W**~ (*to mayor*) signor sindaco; (*to judge*)
signor giudice.

worshipper ['wəːʃɪpə*] *n* adoratore/trice;
(*in church*) fedele *m/f*, devoto/a.

worst [wəːst] *adj* il(la) peggiore ♦ *adv, n*
peggio; **at** ~ al peggio, per male che
vada; **to come off** ~ avere la peggio; **if
the** ~ **comes to the** ~ nel peggior dei
casi.

worst-case ['wəːst'keɪs] *adj*: **the** ~ **scenario**
la peggiore delle ipotesi.

worsted ['wustɪd] *n*: (**wool**) ~ lana
pettinata.

worth [wəːθ] *n* valore *m* ♦ *adj*: **to be** ~
valere; **how much is it** ~? quanto vale?;
it's ~ **it** ne vale la pena; **it's not** ~ **the
trouble** non ne vale la pena; **50 pence** ~
of apples 50 pence di mele.

worthless ['wəːθlɪs] *adj* di nessun valore.

worthwhile ['wəːθ'waɪl] *adj* (*activity*) utile;
(*cause*) lodevole; **a** ~ **book** un libro che
vale la pena leggere.

worthy ['wəːðɪ] *adj* (*person*) degno(a);
(*motive*) lodevole; ~ **of** degno di.

═══════════════════════ *KEYWORD*

would [wud] *aux vb* **1** (*conditional tense*): **if
you asked him he** ~ **do it** se glielo
chiedesse lo farebbe; **if you had asked
him he** ~ **have done it** se glielo avesse
chiesto lo avrebbe fatto

2 (*in offers, invitations, requests*): ~ **you
like a biscuit?** vorrebbe *or* vuole un
biscotto?; ~ **you ask him to come in?** lo
faccia entrare, per cortesia; ~ **you open
the window please?** apra la finestra, per

favore

3 (*in indirect speech*): **I said I** ~ **do it** ho
detto che l'avrei fatto

4 (*emphatic*): **it WOULD have to snow
today!** doveva proprio nevicare oggi!

5 (*insistence*): **she** ~**n't do it** non ha
voluto farlo

6 (*conjecture*): **it** ~ **have been midnight**
sarà stata mezzanotte; **it** ~ **seem so**
sembrerebbe proprio di sì

7 (*indicating habit*): **he** ~ **go there on
Mondays** andava lì ogni lunedì.

would-be ['wudbiː] *adj* (*pej*) sedicente.

wound *vb* [waund] *pt, pp of* **wind** ♦ *n, vt*
[wuːnd] *n* ferita ♦ *vt* ferire; ~**ed in the leg**
ferito(a) alla gamba.

wove [wəuv] *pt of* **weave**.

WP *abbr* (*BRIT col*: = *weather permitting*)
tempo permettendo ♦ *n abbr* = **word
processing; word processor**.

WPC *n abbr* (*BRIT*: = *woman police constable*)
donna poliziotto.

wpm *abbr* (= *words per minute*) p.p.m.

WRAC *n abbr* (*BRIT*: = *Women's Royal Army
Corps*) ausiliarie dell'esercito.

WRAF *n abbr* (*BRIT*: = *Women's Royal Air
Force*) ausiliarie dell'aeronautica
militare.

wrangle ['ræŋgl] *n* litigio ♦ *vi* litigare.

wrap [ræp] *n* (*stole*) scialle *m*; (*cape*)
mantellina ♦ *vt* (*also*: ~ **up**) avvolgere;
(*parcel*) incartare; **under** ~**s** segreto.

wrapper ['ræpə*] *n* (*of book*) copertina; (*on
chocolate*) carta.

wrapping paper ['ræpɪŋ-] *n* carta da
pacchi; (*for gift*) carta da regali.

wrath [rɔθ] *n* collera, ira.

wreak [riːk] *vt* (*destruction*) portare,
causare; **to** ~ **vengeance on** vendicarsi
su; **to** ~ **havoc on** portare scompiglio in.

wreath, **~s** [riːθ, riːðz] *n* corona.

wreck [rɛk] *n* (*sea disaster*) naufragio; (*ship*)
relitto; (*pej: person*) rottame *m* ♦ *vt*
demolire; (*ship*) far naufragare; (*fig*)
rovinare.

wreckage ['rɛkɪdʒ] *n* rottami *mpl*; (*of
building*) macerie *fpl*; (*of ship*) relitti *mpl*.

wrecker ['rɛkə*] *n* (*US: breakdown van*)
carro *m* attrezzi *inv*.

WREN [rɛn] *n abbr* (*BRIT*) membro del
WRNS.

wren [rɛn] *n* (*ZOOL*) scricciolo.

wrench [rɛntʃ] *n* (*TECH*) chiave *f*; (*tug*)
torsione *f* brusca; (*fig*) strazio ♦ *vt*
strappare; storcere; **to** ~ **sth from**
strappare qc a *or* da.

wrest [rɛst] *vt*: **to** ~ **sth from sb** strappare

qc a qn.

wrestle ['rɛsl] *vi*: **to ~ (with sb)** lottare (con qn); **to ~ with** (*fig*) combattere *or* lottare contro.

wrestler ['rɛslə*] *n* lottatore/trice.

wrestling ['rɛslɪŋ] *n* lotta; (*also*: **all-in ~**: *BRIT*) catch *m*, lotta libera.

wrestling match *n* incontro di lotta (*or* lotta libera).

wretch [rɛtʃ] *n* disgraziato/a, sciagurato/a; **little ~!** (*often humorous*) birbante!

wretched ['rɛtʃɪd] *adj* disgraziato(a); (*col: weather, holiday*) orrendo(a), orribile; (: *child, dog*) pestifero(a).

wriggle ['rɪgl] *n* contorsione *f* ♦ *vi* dimenarsi; (*snake, worm*) serpeggiare, muoversi serpeggiando.

wring *pt, pp* **wrung** [rɪŋ, rʌŋ] *vt* torcere; (*wet clothes*) strizzare; (*fig*): **to ~ sth out of** strappare qc a.

wringer ['rɪŋə*] *n* strizzatoio (manuale).

wringing ['rɪŋɪŋ] *adj* (*also*: **~ wet**) bagnato(a) fradicio(a).

wrinkle ['rɪŋkl] *n* (*on skin*) ruga; (*on paper etc*) grinza ♦ *vt* corrugare; raggrinzire ♦ *vi* corrugarsi; raggrinzirsi.

wrinkled ['rɪŋkld], **wrinkly** ['rɪŋklɪ] *adj* (*fabric, paper*) stropicciato(a); (*surface*) corrugato(a), increspato(a); (*skin*) rugoso(a).

wrist [rɪst] *n* polso.

wristband ['rɪstbænd] *n* (*of shirt*) polsino; (*of watch*) cinturino.

wrist watch *n* orologio da polso.

writ [rɪt] *n* ordine *m*; mandato; **to issue a ~ against sb, serve a ~ on sb** notificare un mandato di comparizione a qn.

write, *pt* **wrote,** *pp* **written** [raɪt, rəut, 'rɪtn] *vt, vi* scrivere; **to ~ sb a letter** scrivere una lettera a qn.

▶**write away** *vi*: **to ~ away for** (*information*) richiedere per posta; (*goods*) ordinare per posta.

▶**write down** *vt* annotare; (*put in writing*) mettere per iscritto.

▶**write off** *vt* (*debt*) cancellare; (*depreciate*) deprezzare; (*smash up: car*) distruggere.

▶**write out** *vt* scrivere; (*copy*) ricopiare.

▶**write up** *vt* redigere.

write-off ['raɪtɔf] *n* perdita completa; **the car is a ~** la macchina va bene per il demolitore.

write-protect ['raɪtprə'tɛkt] *vt* (*COMPUT*) proteggere contro scrittura.

writer ['raɪtə*] *n* autore/trice, scrittore/trice.

write-up ['raɪtʌp] *n* (*review*) recensione *f*.

writhe [raɪð] *vi* contorcersi.

writing ['raɪtɪŋ] *n* scrittura; (*of author*) scritto, opera; **in ~** per iscritto; **in my own ~** scritto di mio pugno.

writing desk *n* scrivania, scrittoio.

writing paper *n* carta da scrivere.

written ['rɪtn] *pp of* **write.**

WRNS *n abbr* (*BRIT*: = *Women's Royal Naval Service*) ausiliarie della marina militare.

wrong [rɔŋ] *adj* sbagliato(a); (*not suitable*) inadatto(a); (*wicked*) cattivo(a); (*unfair*) ingiusto(a) ♦ *adv* in modo sbagliato, erroneamente ♦ *n* (*evil*) male *m*; (*injustice*) torto ♦ *vt* fare torto a; **to be ~** (*answer*) essere sbagliato; (*in doing, saying*) avere torto; **you are ~ to do it** ha torto a farlo; **you are ~ about that, you've got it ~** si sbaglia; **to be in the ~** avere torto; **what's ~?** cosa c'è che non va?; **there's nothing ~** va tutto bene; **what's ~ with the car?** cos'ha la macchina che non va?; **to go ~** (*person*) sbagliarsi; (*plan*) fallire, non riuscire; (*machine*) guastarsi; **it's ~ to steal, stealing is ~** è male rubare.

wrongdoer ['rɔŋduːə*] *n* malfattore/trice.

wrong-foot [rɔŋ'fut] *vt* (*SPORT; also fig*) prendere in contropiede.

wrongful ['rɔŋful] *adj* illegittimo(a); ingiusto(a); **~ dismissal** licenziamento ingiustificato.

wrongly ['rɔŋlɪ] *adv* (*accuse, dismiss*) a torto; (*answer, do, count*) erroneamente; (*treat*) ingiustamente.

wrong number *n*: **you have the ~** (*TEL*) ha sbagliato numero.

wrong side *n* (*of cloth*) rovescio.

wrote [rəut] *pt of* **write.**

wrought [rɔːt] *adj*: **~ iron** ferro battuto.

wrung [rʌŋ] *pt, pp of* **wring.**

WRVS *n abbr* (*BRIT*) = *Women's Royal Voluntary Service.*

wry [raɪ] *adj* storto(a).

wt. *abbr* = **weight.**

WV, W. Va. *abbr* (*US*) = *West Virginia.*

WWW *n abbr* (= *World Wide Web*): **the ~** la Rete.

WY, Wyo. *abbr* (*US*) = *Wyoming.*

WYSIWYG ['wɪzɪwɪg] *abbr* (*COMPUT*) = *what you see is what you get.*

X x

X, x [ɛks] *n* (*letter*) X, x *f or m inv*; (*BRIT CINE*: *old*) ≈ film vietato ai minori di 18 anni; **X for Xmas** ≈ X come Xeres.

Xerox ® ['zɪərɔks] *n* (*also*: ~ **machine**) fotocopiatrice *f*; (*photocopy*) fotocopia ♦ *vt* fotocopiare.

XL *abbr* = *extra large*.

Xmas ['ɛksməs] *n abbr* = **Christmas**.

X-rated ['ɛks'reɪtɪd] *adj* (*US*: *film*) ≈ vietato ai minori di 18 anni.

X-ray ['ɛks'reɪ] *n* raggio X; (*photograph*) radiografia ♦ *vt* radiografare; **to have an** ~ farsi fare una radiografia.

xylophone ['zaɪləfəun] *n* xilofono.

Y y

Y, y [waɪ] *n* (*letter*) Y, y *f or m inv*; **Y for Yellow,** (*US*) **Y for Yoke** ≈ Y come Yacht.

yacht [jɔt] *n* panfilo, yacht *m inv*.

yachting ['jɔtɪŋ] *n* yachting *m*, sport *m* della vela.

yachtsman ['jɔtsmən] *n* yachtsman *m inv*.

yam [jæm] *n* igname *m*; (*sweet potato*) patata dolce.

Yank [jæŋk], **Yankee** ['jæŋkɪ] *n* (*pej*) yankee *m/f inv*, nordamericano/a.

yank [jæŋk] *n* strattone *m* ♦ *vt* tirare, dare uno strattone a.

yap [jæp] *vi* (*dog*) guaire.

yard [jɑːd] *n* (*of house etc*) cortile *m*; (*US*: *garden*) giardino; (*measure*) iarda (= *914 mm; 3 feet*); **builder's** ~ deposito di materiale da costruzione.

yardstick ['jɑːdstɪk] *n* (*fig*) misura, criterio.

yarn [jɑːn] *n* filato; (*tale*) lunga storia.

yawn [jɔːn] *n* sbadiglio ♦ *vi* sbadigliare.

yawning ['jɔːnɪŋ] *adj* (*gap*) spalancato(a).

yd. *abbr* = **yard**.

yeah [jɛə] *adv* (*col*) sì.

year [jɪə*] *n* (*gen, SCOL*) anno; (*referring to*

harvest, wine etc) annata; **every** ~ ogni anno, tutti gli anni; **this** ~ quest'anno; ~ **in,** ~ **out** anno dopo anno; **she's three** ~**s old** ha tre anni; **a** *or* **per** ~ all'anno.

yearbook ['jɪəbuk] *n* annuario.

yearly ['jɪəlɪ] *adj* annuale ♦ *adv* annualmente; **twice-**~ semestrale.

yearn [jəːn] *vi*: **to** ~ **for sth/to do** desiderare ardentemente qc/di fare.

yearning ['jəːnɪŋ] *n* desiderio intenso.

yeast [jiːst] *n* lievito.

yell [jɛl] *n* urlo ♦ *vi* urlare.

yellow ['jɛləu] *adj* giallo(a).

yellow fever *n* febbre *f* gialla.

yellowish ['jɛləuɪʃ] *adj* giallastro(a), giallognolo(a).

Yellow Pages ® *npl* pagine *fpl* gialle.

Yellow Sea *n*: **the** ~ il mar Giallo.

yelp [jɛlp] *n* guaito, uggiolio ♦ *vi* guaire, uggiolare.

Yemen ['jɛmən] *n* Yemen *m*.

yen [jɛn] *n* (*currency*) yen *m inv*; (*craving*): ~ **for/to do** gran voglia di/di fare.

yeoman ['jəumən] *n*: **Y**~ **of the Guard** guardiano della Torre di Londra.

yes [jɛs] *adv, n* sì (*m inv*); **to say** ~ (**to**) dire di sì (a), acconsentire (a).

yesterday ['jɛstədɪ] *adv, n* ieri (*m inv*); ~ **morning/evening** ieri mattina/sera; **the day before** ~ l'altro ieri; **all day** ~ ieri tutto il giorno.

yet [jɛt] *adv* ancora; già ♦ *conj* ma, tuttavia; **it is not finished** ~ non è ancora finito; **the best** ~ il migliore finora; **as** ~ finora; ~ **again** di nuovo; **must you go just** ~? deve andarsene di già?; **a few days** ~ ancora qualche giorno.

yew [juː] *n* tasso (*albero*).

Y-fronts ® ['waɪfrʌnts] *npl* (*BRIT*) slip *m inv* da uomo.

YHA *n abbr* (*BRIT*: = *Youth Hostels Association*) Y.H.A. *f*.

Yiddish ['jɪdɪʃ] *n* yiddish *m*.

yield [jiːld] *n* resa; (*of crops etc*) raccolto ♦ *vt* produrre, rendere; (*surrender*) cedere ♦ *vi* cedere; (*US AUT*) dare la precedenza; **a** ~ **of 5%** un profitto *or* un interesse del 5%.

YMCA *n abbr* (= *Young Men's Christian Association*) Y.M.C.A. *m*.

yob(bo) ['jɔb(əu)] *n* (*BRIT col*) bullo.

yodel ['jəudl] *vi* cantare lo jodel *or* alla tirolese.

yoga ['jəugə] *n* yoga *m*.

yog(h)ourt, yog(h)urt ['jəugət] *n* iogurt *m inv*.

yoke [jəuk] *n* giogo ♦ *vt* (*also*: ~ **together**: *oxen*) aggiogare.

yolk [jəuk] *n* tuorlo, rosso d'uovo.
yonder ['jɔndə*] *adv* là.
yonks [jɔŋks] *npl*: **for** ~ (*col*) da una vita.
Yorks [jɔːks] *abbr* (*BRIT*) = Yorkshire.

==================================== KEYWORD

you [juː] *pron* **1** (*subject*) tu; (*: polite form*)
lei; (*: pl*) voi; (*: very formal*) loro; ~ **Italians
enjoy your food** a voi italiani piace
mangiare bene; ~ **and I will go** andiamo
io e te (*or* lei ed io); **if I was** *or* **were** ~ **se**
fossi in te (*or* lei *etc*)
2 (*object: direct*) ti; la; vi; loro (*after vb*);
(*: indirect*) ti; le; vi; loro (*after vb*); **I know**
~ ti (*or* la *or* vi) conosco; **I'll see** ~
tomorrow ci vediamo domani; **I gave it to**
~ **te** l'ho dato; gliel'ho dato; ve l'ho dato;
l'ho dato loro
3 (*stressed, after prep, in comparisons*) te;
lei; voi; loro; **I told YOU to do it** ho detto a
TE (*or* a LEI *etc*) di farlo; **she's younger
than** ~ è più giovane di te (*or* lei *etc*)
4 (*impers: one*) si; **fresh air does** ~ **good**
l'aria fresca fa bene; ~ **never know** non
si sa mai.

you'd [juːd] = **you had; you would.**
you'll [juːl] = **you will; you shall.**
young [jʌŋ] *adj* giovane ♦ *npl* (*of animal*)
piccoli *mpl*; (*people*): **the** ~ i giovani, la
gioventù; **a** ~ **man** un giovanotto; **a** ~
lady una signorina; **a** ~ **woman** una
giovane donna; **the** ~**er generation** la
nuova generazione; **my** ~**er brother** il
mio fratello minore.
youngish ['jʌŋɪʃ] *adj* abbastanza giovane.
youngster ['jʌŋstə*] *n* giovanotto/a; (*child*)
bambino/a.
your [jɔː*] *adj* il(la) tuo(a), *pl* i(le) tuoi(tue);
(*polite form*) il(la) suo(a), *pl* i(le) suoi(sue);
(*pl*) il(la) vostro(a), *pl* i(le) vostri(e);
(*: very formal*) il(la) loro, *pl* i(le) loro.
you're [juə*] = **you are.**
yours [jɔːz] *pron* il(la) tuo(a), *pl* i(le)
tuoi(tue); (*polite form*) il(la) suo(a), *pl* i(le)
suoi(sue); (*pl*) il(la) vostro(a), *pl* i(le)
vostri(e); (*: very formal*) il(la) loro, *pl* i(le)
loro; ~ **sincerely/faithfully** (*in letter*)
cordiali/distinti saluti; **a friend of** ~ un
tuo (*or* suo *etc*) amico; **is it** ~**?** è tuo (*or*
suo *etc*)?
yourself [jɔː'sɛlf] *pron* (*reflexive*) ti; (*: polite
form*) si; (*after prep*) te; se; (*emphatic*) tu
stesso(a); lei stesso(a); **you** ~ **told me** me
l'hai detto proprio tu, tu stesso me l'hai
detto.
yourselves [jɔː'sɛlvz] *pl pron* (*reflexive*) vi; (*:
polite form*) si; (*after prep*) voi; loro;

(*emphatic*) voi stessi(e); loro stessi(e).
youth [juːθ] *n* gioventù *f*; (*young man: pl* ~**s**
[juːðz]) giovane *m*, ragazzo; **in my** ~ da
giovane, quando ero giovane.
youth club *n* centro giovanile.
youthful ['juːθful] *adj* giovane; da giovane;
giovanile.
youthfulness ['juːθfəlnɪs] *n* giovinezza.
youth hostel *n* ostello della gioventù.
youth movement *n* movimento giovanile.
you've [juːv] = **you have.**
yowl [jaul] *n* (*of dog, person*) urlo; (*of cat*)
miagolio ♦ *vi* urlare; miagolare.
yr *abbr* = **year.**
YT *abbr* (*Canada*) = Yukon Territory.
Yugoslav ['juːgəuslɑːv] *adj, n* jugoslavo(a).
Yugoslavia [juːgəu'slɑːvɪə] *n* Jugoslavia.
Yugoslavian [juːgəu'slɑːvɪən] *adj, n*
jugoslavo(a).
Yule log [juːl-] *n* ceppo nel caminetto a
Natale.
yuppie ['jʌpɪ] *adj, n* (*col*) yuppie (*m/f*) *inv*.
YWCA *n abbr* (= *Young Women's Christian
Association*) Y.W.C.A. *m*.

Z z

Z, z [zɛd, (*US*) ziː] *n* (*letter*) Z, z *f or m inv*; **Z
for Zebra** ≈ Z come Zara.
Zaire [zɑː'ɪə*] *n* Zaire *m*.
Zambia ['zæmbɪə] *n* Zambia *m*.
Zambian ['zæmbɪən] *adj, n* zambiano(a).
zany ['zeɪnɪ] *adj* un po' pazzo(a).
zap [zæp] *vt* (*COMPUT*) cancellare.
zeal [ziːl] *n* zelo; entusiasmo.
zealot ['zɛlət] *n* zelota *m/f*.
zealous ['zɛləs] *adj* zelante; premuroso(a).
zebra ['ziːbrə] *n* zebra.
zebra crossing *n* (*BRIT*) (passaggio
pedonale a) strisce *fpl*, zebre *fpl*.
zenith ['zɛnɪθ] *n* zenit *m inv*; (*fig*) culmine *m*.
zero ['zɪərəu] *n* zero; **5° below** ~ 5° sotto
zero.
zero hour *n* l'ora zero.
zero option *n* (*POL*) opzione *f* zero.
zero-rated ['zɪərəu'reɪtɪd] *adj* (*BRIT*) ad
aliquota zero.
zest [zɛst] *n* gusto; (*CULIN*) buccia.
zigzag ['zɪgzæg] *n* zigzag *m inv* ♦ *vi*
zigzagare.
Zimbabwe [zɪm'bɑːbwɪ] *n* Zimbabwe *m*.

Zimbabwean [zɪm'bɑːbwɪən] *adj* dello Zimbabwe.

Zimmer ® ['zɪmə*] *n* (*also*: ~ **frame**) deambulatore *m*.

zinc [zɪŋk] *n* zinco.

Zionism ['zaɪənɪzəm] *n* sionismo.

Zionist ['zaɪənɪst] *adj* sionistico(a) ♦ *n* sionista *m/f*.

zip [zɪp] *n* (*also*: ~ **fastener**, (*US*) ~**per**) chiusura *f* or cerniera *f* lampo *inv*; (*energy*) energia, forza ♦ *vt* (*also*: ~ **up**) chiudere con una cerniera lampo; (*COMPUT*) zippare.

zip code *n* (*US*) codice *m* di avviamento postale.

zither ['zɪðə*] *n* cetra.

zodiac ['zəudɪæk] *n* zodiaco.

zombie ['zɔmbɪ] *n* (*fig*): **like a** ~ come un morto che cammina.

zone [zəun] *n* zona.

zoo [zuː] *n* zoo *m inv*.

zoological [zuə'lɔdʒɪkl] *adj* zoologico(a).

zoologist [zuː'ɔlədʒɪst] *n* zoologo/a.

zoology [zuː'ɔlədʒɪ] *n* zoologia.

zoom [zuːm] *vi*: **to** ~ **past** sfrecciare; **to** ~ **in (on sb/sth)** (*PHOT*, *CINE*) zumare (su qn/qc).

zoom lens *n* zoom *m inv*, obiettivo a focale variabile.

zucchini [zuː'kiːnɪ] *n* (*pl inv*) (*US*) zucchina.

Zulu ['zuːluː] *adj*, *n* zulù (*m/f*) *inv*.

Zürich ['zjuərɪk] *n* Zurigo *f*.

ITALIAN IN ACTION

INGLESE ATTIVO

Contributors/Collaboratori

Loredana Riu   Daphne Day   Gabriella Bacchelli

Coordination/Coordinamento

Isobel Gordon

INTRODUZIONE

Il supplemento INGLESE ATTIVO vi aiuterà ad esprimervi in modo semplice e corretto, usando espressioni tipiche della lingua realmente parlata.

La sezione LOCUZIONI DI BASE contiene centinaia di frasi seguite dalla traduzione degli elementi chiave, utilizzabili nella costruzione di moltissime altre frasi.

Nella sezione sulla corrispondenza troverete diversi modelli di lettere in inglese, sia personali che commerciali, le formule più comuni usate per iniziare e concludere una lettera, indicazioni su dove e come scrivere indirizzo e mittente sulla busta e così via. Troverete anche un esempio di curriculum vitae, una domanda di assunzione e utili consigli su come adattare questi modelli alle vostre particolari esigenze.

C'è inoltre una sezione a parte sull'invio di fax e di messaggi di posta elettronica e sui diversi tipi di conversazioni telefoniche.

Siamo sicuri che, assieme al dizionario, il supplemento INGLESE ATTIVO, sarà uno strumento prezioso per aiutarvi a scrivere e a comunicare in inglese nel modo più corretto, naturale e adatto ad ogni situazione.

INDICE

INTRODUCTION

The aim of ITALIAN IN ACTION is to help you express yourself simply but correctly in fluent, natural Italian.

The SENTENCE BUILDER section provides hundreds of phrases in which the key elements have been translated, providing an invaluable point of reference when you then construct your own sentences.

The section on correspondence provides practical models of personal and business letters, job applications and CVs, together with examples of standard opening and closing formulae and information on how to address an envelope. This section also offers guidance notes to help the user adapt these models to his/her needs.

A separate section covers fax and e-mail correspondence as well as all the expressions you might need to make different types of phone calls.

We hope you will find ITALIAN IN ACTION both relevant and useful and that, used in conjunction with the dictionary, it will improve your understanding and enjoyment of Italian.

CONTENTS

❑ *Gusti e preferenze*

Per dire ciò che ci piace

I **like** cakes.	*Mi piacciono ...*
I **like** things to be in their proper place.	*Mi piace che ...*
I **really liked** the film.	*... mi è piaciuto molto.*
I **love** going to clubs.	*Adoro ...*
What I like best about Matthew are his eyes.	*Quello che mi piace di più ...*
What I enjoy most is an evening with friends.	*La cosa che mi piace di più è ...*
I **very much enjoyed** the trip to the vineyards.	*... mi è piaciuta molto.*
I've never tasted **anything better than** this chicken.	*... niente di meglio di ...*
I've **got a weakness for** chocolate cakes.	*Ho un debole per ...*
You can't beat a good cup of tea.	*Non c'è niente come ...*
There's nothing quite like a nice hot bath!	*Non c'è niente di meglio di ...*
My favourite dish is risotto.	*Il mio ... preferito ...*
Reading is **one of my favourite** pastimes.	*... uno dei miei ... preferiti.*
I **don't mind** being alone.	*Non mi dispiace ...*

Per dire ció che non ci piace

I **don't like** fish.	*Non mi piace ...*
I **don't like** him **at all**.	*... non mi piace per niente.*
I'm **not very keen on** speaking in public.	*Non mi piace molto ...*
I'm **not particularly keen on** the idea.	*Non è che ... mi faccia impazzire.*
I **hate** chemistry.	*Odio ...*
I **loathe** sport.	*Detesto ...*
I **can't stand** being lied to.	*Non sopporto ...*
If there's one thing I hate it's ironing.	*Se c'è una cosa che odio è ...*

Per esprimere una preferenza

I **prefer** pop **to** classical music.	*Preferisco ... alla ...*
I **would rather** live in Rome.	*Preferirei ...*
I'**d rather** starve **than** ask him a favour.	*Preferirei ... piuttosto che ...*

Per esprimere indifferenza

It's all the same to me.	*Per me fa lo stesso.*
I have no particular preference.	*Non ho preferenze.*
As you like.	*Come vuoi.*
It doesn't matter in the least.	*Non ha nessuna importanza.*
I don't mind.	*È indifferente.*

Rivolgendosi ad altri

Do you like chocolate?	*Ti piace ...*
Do you like cooking?	*Ti piace ...*
Which do you like better: football or cricket?	*Cosa preferisci ...*
Which would you rather have: the red one or the black one?	*Quale preferisci ...*
Do you prefer living in the town or in the country?	*Preferisci ...*
What do you like best on television?	*Cosa ti piace di più ...*

❏ *Opinioni*

Per chiedere l'opinione di qualcuno

What do you think about it?	*Cosa ne pensa?*
What do you think about divorce?	*Cosa pensa del ...*
What do you think of his behaviour?	*Come ti sembra ...*
I'd like to know what you think of his work.	*Vorrei sapere cosa pensi del ...*
I would like to know your views on this.	*Mi piacerebbe sapere il suo parere o la sua opinione su ...*
What is your opinion on the team's chances of success?	*Qual è la sua opinione sulle ...*
Could you give me your opinion on this proposal?	*Potrebbe dirmi cosa pensa di ...*
In your opinion, are men and women equal?	*A suo parere o avviso ...*
In your opinion, is this the best solution?	*Secondo lei ...*

Per esprimere un'opinione

You are right.	*Hai ragione.*
He is wrong.	*Ha torto.*
He was wrong to resign.	*Ha sbagliato a ...*
I think it ought to be possible.	*Penso che ...*
I think it's a bit premature.	*Credo che sia ...*
I think it's quite natural.	*Mi sembra che sia ...*
Personally, I think that it's a waste of money.	*Personalmente, ritengo che sia ...*
I have the impression that her parents don't understand her.	*Ho l'impressione che ...*
I'm sure he is completely sincere.	*Sono sicuro che ...*
I'm convinced that there are other possibilities.	*Sono convinto che ...*
In my opinion, he hasn't changed.	*A mio parere o avviso ...*
In my view, he's their best player.	*Secondo me ...*

Per rispondere senza dare un'opinione

It depends.	*Dipende.*
It all depends on what you mean by patriotism.	*Dipende da cosa intendi per ...*
I'd rather not express an opinion.	*Preferisco non pronunciarmi.*
Actually, I've never thought about it.	*A dire il vero, non ci ho mai pensato.*

❏ *Approvazione e accordo*

I think it's an excellent idea.	*Mi sembra una magnifica idea.*
What a good idea!	*Ottima idea!*
I was very impressed by his speech.	*Ho apprezzato moltissimo ...*
It's a very good thing.	*È un'ottima cosa.*
I think you're right to be wary.	*Secondo me hai ragione a ...*
Newspapers **are right to** publish these stories.	*... fanno bene a ...*

You were right to leave your bags in left-luggage.	*Hai fatto bene a ...*
Third World countries **rightly believe that** most pollution comes from developed countries.	*... ritengono giustamente che ...*
You're quite justified in complaining.	*Non hai torto a ...*
I share this view.	*Condivido l'opinione.*
I fully share your concern.	*Condivido pienamente la sua ...*
We support the creation of jobs.	*Siamo favorevoli alla ...*
We are in favour of a united Europe.	*Siamo a favore dell' ...*
It is true that mistakes were made.	*È vero che ...*
I agree with you.	*Sono d'accordo con lei.*
I entirely agree with you.	*Sono assolutamente d'accordo con lei.*

❏ *Disapprovazione e dissenso*

I think he was wrong to borrow so much money.	*Trovo che abbia sbagliato a ...*
It's a pity that you didn't tell me.	*È un peccato che ...*
It is regrettable that they allowed this to happen.	*C'è da rammaricarsi che ...*
I dislike the idea **intensely.**	*... non mi piace per niente.*
I can't stand lies.	*Non sopporto ...*
We are against hunting.	*Siamo contro ...*
We do not condone violence.	*Crediamo che ... sia ingiustificabile o non abbia scusanti.*
I am opposed to compulsory screening.	*Sono contrario al ...*
I don't share this point of view.	*Non condivido questo punto di vista.*
I am disappointed by his attitude.	*Sono deluso del ...*
I am deeply disappointed.	*Sono profondamente deluso.*
You shouldn't have said that.	*Non avresti dovuto ...*
What gives him the right to act like this?	*Che diritto ha di ...*
I disagree.	*Non sono d'accordo.*
We don't agree with them.	*Non siamo d'accordo con ...*
I totally disagree with what he said.	*Non sono affatto d'accordo con ...*

It is **not true to say that** the disaster was inevitable.	*Non è vero che ...*
You are wrong!	*Ti sbagli!*

❑ *Scuse*

Per chiedere scusa

Sorry.	*Scusa.*
Oh, sorry! I've got the wrong number.	*Oh, scusi!*
Sorry to bother you.	*Scusi se la disturbo.*
I'm sorry I woke you.	*Scusa se ...*
I'm terribly sorry about the misunderstanding.	*Sono terribilmente spiacente per ...*
I do apologize.	*La prego di scusarmi.*
We hope our readers **will** excuse this oversight.	*Preghiamo ... di ...*

... ammettendo responsabilità

It's my fault; I should have left earlier.	*È colpa mia, sarei dovuto ...*
I shouldn't have laughed at her.	*Non avrei dovuto ...*
We were wrong not to check this information.	*Abbiamo sbagliato a non ...*
I take full responsibility for what I did.	*Mi assumo la piena responsabilità delle ...*
If only I had done my homework!	*Se solo avessi ...*

... declinando responsabilità

It's not my fault.	*Non è colpa mia.*
It isn't my fault if we're late.	*Non è colpa mia se ...*
I didn't do it on purpose.	*Non l'ho fatto apposta.*
I had no option.	*Non ho potuto fare altrimenti.*
But I thought that it was okay to park here.	*Pensavo che ...*
I thought I was doing the right thing in warning him.	*Credevo di fare bene ad ...*

Per esprimere rammarico

I'm sorry, but it's impossible.	*Mi dispiace, ma ...*
I'm afraid we're fully booked.	*Purtroppo ...*
Unfortunately we are unable to meet your request.	*Purtroppo non siamo in grado di ...*

❑ *Spiegazioni*

Cause

I didn't buy anything **because** I had no money.	*... perché ...*
I arrived late **because of** the traffic.	*... a causa del ...*
Since you insist, I'll come again tomorrow.	*Visto o dato che ...*
As I lived near the library, I used it a lot.	*Siccome ...*
I got through it **thanks to** the support of my friends.	*... grazie all'...*
Given the present situation, finding a job will be difficult.	*Vista o Data ...*
Given that there is an economic crisis, it is difficult to find work.	*Dato che ...*
Considering how many problems we had, we did well.	*Considerando ...*
It was a broken axle **that caused** the derailment.	*È stata ... che ha causato ...*
He resigned **for** health **reasons.**	*... per motivi di ...*
The theatre is closing, **due to** lack of funds.	*... per ...*
The project was abandoned **owing to** legal problems.	*... a causa di ...*
Many cancers **are linked to** smoking.	*... sono legati al ...*
The problem is that people are afraid of computers.	*Il problema è che ...*
The drop in sales **is the result of** high interest rates.	*... è il risultato dei ...*
The quarrel **resulted from** a misunderstanding.	*... ha avuto origine da ...*

Per spiegare le conseguenze di una situazione

I have to leave tonight; **so** I can't come with you.	*... quindi ...*
Distribution has been improved **so that** readers now get their newspaper earlier.	*... cosicché ...*
This cider is fermented for a very short time and is **consequently** low in alcohol.	*... di conseguenza ...*

| Our lack of consultation **has resulted in** a duplication of effort. | ... ha avuto come conseguenza ... |
| **That's why** they are easy to remember. | Ecco perché ... |

❏ *Paragoni*

Gambling **can be compared to** a drug.	Si può paragonare ... a ...
The gas has a smell **that can be compared to** rotten eggs.	... paragonabile a ...
The shape of Italy **is often compared to** a boot.	... è spesso paragonata a ...
The noise **was comparable to** that of a large motorbike.	... era paragonabile a ...
Africa is still underpopulated **compared with** Asia.	Paragonata all'...
In the UK, the rate of inflation increased slightly **compared to** the previous year.	... rispetto all'...
What is so special about a holiday in Florida **as compared to** one in Spain?	... a paragone di ...
This story **is like** a fairy tale.	... sembra ...
He loved this countryside, which **reminded him of** Ireland.	... gli ricordava ...
Frightening levels of unemployment, **reminiscent of those** of the 30s.	... che ricordano ...
The snowboard **is the equivalent** on snow **of** the skateboard.	... è l'equivalente dello ...
This sum **corresponds to** six months' salary.	... corrisponde a ...
A 'bap'? **It's the same thing as** a bread roll.	È esattamente come ...
It comes to the same thing in terms of calories.	... è perfettamente equivalente.
This record **is no better and no worse than** the others.	... non è né meglio né peggio degli ...

Sottolineando le differenze ...

No catastrophe **can compare with** Chernobyl.	... non ha uguali.
Modern factories **cannot be compared with** those our grandparents worked in.	... non si possono paragonare con ...
The actions of this group **are in no way comparable to** those of terrorists.	... non hanno niente in comune con ...
The newspaper reports **differ** on this point.	... si differenziano ...

The history of the United States **in no way resembles** our own.	... non assomiglia affatto alla ...
There are worse things than losing a European cup final.	C'è di peggio che ...
This film **is less** interesting **than** his first one.	... è meno ... del ...
Women's life expectancy is 81 years, **while** men's is 72.	... mentre ...
While the consumption of wine and beer is decreasing, the consumption of bottled water is increasing.	Mentre ...

❏ *Richieste e offerte*

Richieste

I'd like another beer.	Vorrei ...
I'd like to know the times of trains to Edinburgh.	Vorrei ...
Could you give us a hand?	Potresti ...
Can you tell Eleanor the good news?	Puoi ...
Could you please show me the way out?	Potrebbe per cortesia ...
Could I ask you for a few minutes of your time?	Può concedermi ...
Be an angel, pop to the baker's for me.	Sii gentile ...
If you wouldn't mind waiting for a moment.	Se non le dispiace ...
Would you mind opening the window?	Le spiacerebbe ...
Would you be very kind and save my seat for me?	Potrebbe farmi la cortesia di ...
I would be grateful if you could reply as soon as possible.	Le sarei grato se ...

Offerte

I can come and pick you up **if** you like.	Posso ... se ...
I could go with you.	Potrei ...
Do you fancy a bit of Stilton?	Ti va ...
How about a pear tart?	Che ne dici di ...
Would you like to see my photos?	Vi piacerebbe ...

| Would you like to have dinner with me one evening? | Ti andrebbe di ... |
| Do you want me to go and get your car? | Vuoi che ... |

❏ *Consigli e suggerimenti*

Per chiedere un consiglio

What would you do, if you were me?	Cosa faresti, al posto mio?
Would you accept, **if you were me?**	Se fossi in me ...
What's your opinion on this?	Cosa ne pensi?
What, in your opinion, should be done to reduce pollution?	Cosa bisognerebbe fare, secondo voi, per ...
What would you advise?	Cosa consigli?
What would you advise me to do?	Cosa mi consigli di fare?
Which would you recommend, Majorca or Ibiza?	Quale ci consiglia ...
If we were to sponsor a player, **who would you recommend?**	... chi raccomanderesti?
What strategy do you suggest?	Che ... proponi?
How would you deal with unemployment?	Come affrontereste ...

Per dare un suggerimento

If I were you, I'd be a bit wary.	Se fossi in te ...
If I were you I wouldn't say anything.	Al posto tuo ...
Take my advice, buy your tickets in advance.	Se posso darle un consiglio ...
A word of advice: read the instructions.	Un consiglio ...
A useful tip: always have some pasta in your cupboard.	Un consiglio ...
As you like languages, **you ought to** train as a translator.	... dovresti ...
You should see a specialist.	Dovresti ...
You would do well to see a solicitor.	Faresti bene a ...
You would do better to spend the money on a new car.	Faresti meglio a ...

You could perhaps ask someone to go with you.	*Forse potresti ...*
You could try being a little more understanding.	*Potresti ...*
Perhaps you should speak to a plumber about it.	*Forse dovresti ...*
Perhaps we ought to try a different approach.	*Forse dovremmo ...*
Why don't you phone him?	*Perché non ...*
How about renting a video?	*E se ...*
How about 3 March at 10.30am?	*Io proporrei ...*
It might be better to give her money rather than jewellery.	*Forse sarebbe meglio ...*
It would be better to wait a bit.	*Sarebbe meglio ...*

Avvertimenti

I warn you, I intend to get my own back.	*Ti avverto ...*
I'd better warn you that he knows you did it.	*Ti avverto che ...*
Don't forget to keep a copy of your income tax return.	*Ricordati di ...*
Remember: appearances can be deceptive.	*Non fidarti: l'apparenza inganna.*
Beware of buying tickets from touts.	*Diffidate dei ...*
Whatever you do, don't leave your camera in the car.	*Soprattutto, non ... mai ...*
If you don't book early **you risk** being disappointed.	*... rischi di ...*

❏ *Intenzioni e desideri*

Per chiedere a qualcuno cosa intenda fare

What are you going to do?	*Cosa pensi di fare?*
What will you do if you fail your exams?	*Cosa farai se ...*
What are you going to do when you get back? **Do you have anything planned?**	*Cosa conti di fare ... Hai dei progetti?*
Can we expect you next Sunday?	*Vi aspettiamo ...*
Are you planning to spend all of the holiday here?	*Conti di ...*
Are you planning on staying long?	*Conti di ...*

What are you **planning to do with** your collection?	*Cosa conti di fare della ...*
What are you **thinking of doing?**	*Cosa pensi di fare?*
Do you intend to go into teaching?	*Hai intenzione di ...*
Are you thinking of making another film in Europe?	*Conta di ...*

Per esprimere le proprie intenzioni

I was planning to go to New York on 8 July.	*Pensavo di ...*
She plans to go to India for a year.	*Prevede di ...*
There are plans to build a new stadium.	*È prevista ...*
The bank **intends to** close a hundred branches.	*... ha intenzione di ...*
I am thinking of giving up politics.	*Sto pensando di ...*
I have decided to get a divorce.	*Ho deciso di ...*
I have made up my mind to stop smoking.	*Ho deciso di ...*
We never had any intention of talking to the press.	*Non è mai stata nostra intenzione ...*
That's settled, we'll go to Florida in May.	*È deciso ...*
For me, living abroad **is out of the question.**	*... è fuori discussione.*

Desideri

I'd like to be able to play as well as him.	*Vorrei ...*
I'd like to go hang-gliding.	*Mi piacerebbe ...*
I would like my photos to be published.	*Vorrei che ...*
I would like to have had a brother.	*Mi sarebbe piaciuto avere ...*
I want to act in films.	*Voglio ...*
Ian **wanted at all costs** to prevent his boss finding out.	*... voleva a tutti i costi ...*
We wish to preserve our independence.	*È nostro desiderio ...*
I hope to have children.	*Spero di ...*
We hope that children will watch this programme with their parents.	*Ci auguriamo che ...*
Do you dream of winning the lottery?	*Sogni di ...*
I dream of having a big house.	*Il mio sogno sarebbe di ...*

❏ *Obbligo*

I must find somewhere to live.	*Devo ...*
We really must see each other more often!	*Dobbiamo assolutamente ...*
If you're going to Poland, **you must** learn Polish.	*... devi ...*
He made his secretary answer all his calls.	*Esigeva che ...*
My mother **makes me** eat spinach.	*... mi costringe a ...*
The hijackers **demanded that** the plane fly to New York.	*... hanno preteso che ...*
A serious illness **forced me to** cancel my holiday.	*... mi ha costretto a ...*
He was obliged to borrow more and more money.	*Ha dovuto ...*
Mary **had no choice but to** invite him.	*... non poteva fare altro che ...*
The only thing you can do is say no.	*Non puoi fare altro che ...*
Many mothers **have to** work; **they have no other option.**	*... devono ... non hanno scelta.*
She had the baby adopted because **she had no other option.**	*... non poteva fare altrimenti.*
School **is compulsory** until the age of sixteen.	*... è obbligatoria ...*
It is essential to know some history, if we are to understand the situation.	*È indispensabile ...*

❏ *Permesso*

Per chiedere il permesso

Can I use the phone?	*Posso ...*
Can I ask you something?	*Posso ...*
Is it okay if I come now, or is it too early?	*Va bene se ...*
Do you mind if I smoke?	*Le dà fastidio se ...*
Do you mind if I open the window?	*Le spiace se ...*
Would you mind if I had a look in your briefcase, madam?	*Permette che ...*
Could I have permission to leave early?	*Posso ...*

Per concedere il permesso

Do as you please.	*Fate come volete.*
Go ahead!	*Faccia pure!*
No, of course I don't mind.	*No, non ci sono problemi.*
I have nothing against it.	*Non ho niente in contrario.*
Pupils **are allowed to** wear what they like.	*... possono ...*

Per negare il permesso

I forbid you to go out!	*Ti proibisco di ...*
It's forbidden.	*È vietato.*
Smoking in the toilet **is forbidden.**	*È vietato ...*
Child labour is **strictly forbidden by** a UN convention.	*... assolutamente proibito da ...*
No entry.	*Vietato l'ingresso.*
No parking.	*Sosta vietata.*
It's not allowed.	*Non è permesso.*
You are not allowed to swim in the lake.	*È vietato ...*
We weren't allowed to eat or drink while on duty.	*Non potevamo ...*
That's out of the question.	*È fuori discussione.*

❏ *Certezza, probabilità e possibilità*

Certezza

Undoubtedly, there will be problems.	*... senz'altro ...*
There is no doubt that the country's image has suffered.	*Non c'è alcun dubbio che ...*
It's bound to cause trouble.	*Sicuramente ...*
Clearly the company is in difficulties.	*È evidente che ...*
A foreign tourist is **quite obviously** a rare sight here.	*... ovviamente ...*
It is undeniable that she was partly to blame.	*È innegabile che ...*
I am sure you will like my brother.	*Sono sicuro che ...*
I am sure that I will win.	*Sono sicuro di ...*
I'm sure that I won't get bored working with him.	*Sono sicuro che ...*

| I am **certain that** we are on the right track. | *Sono sicuro che ...* |
| I am **convinced that** there are other solutions. | *Sono convinto che ...* |

Probabilità

The price of petrol will **probably** rise.	*È probabile che ...*
Inflation will **very probably** exceed 10%.	*Molto probabilmente ...*
It is highly probable that they will abandon the project.	*È molto probabile che ...*
The trend **is likely** to continue.	*È probabile che ...*
80% of skin problems **undoubtedly** have psychological origins.	*... senza dubbio ...*
They were **no doubt** right.	*... senza dubbio ...*
The construction work **should** start in April.	*... dovrebbero ...*
He must have forgotten to open the windows.	*Deve avere ...*

Possibilità

It's possible.	*È possibile.*
It is possible that they got your name from the electoral register.	*È possibile che ...*
It is not impossible that he has gone to Manchester.	*Non è da escludersi che ...*
That might be more expensive.	*Potrebbe essere ...*
He may have misunderstood.	*Potrebbe avere ...*
This virus **may** be extremely infectious.	*... potrebbe ...*
It may be that it will take time to achieve peace.	*Potrebbe darsi che ...*
In a few months everything **could** change.	*... potrebbe ...*
Perhaps I am mistaken.	*Puo darsi che ...*

❏ *Dubbio, improbabilità e impossibilità*

Dubbio

I'm not sure it's useful.	*Non sono sicuro che sia ...*
I'm not sure I'll manage.	*Non sono sicuro di ...*
I'm not sure that it's a good idea.	*Non sono sicuro che ...*

We **cannot be sure that** the problem will be solved.	*Non sappiamo con certezza se ...*
I very much doubt he'll adapt to not working.	*Dubito fortemente che ...*
Is it wise? **I doubt it.**	*Ne dubito.*
He began **to have doubts about** his doctor's competence.	*... dubitare della ...*
I wonder if we've made much progress in this area.	*Mi domando se ...*
There is no guarantee that a vaccine can be developed.	*Non è sicuro che ...*
Nobody knows exactly what happened.	*Non si sa esattamente ...*

Improbabilità

He **probably won't** change his mind.	*Probabilmente non ...*
It is unlikely that there'll be any tickets left.	*È poco probabile che ...*
I'd be surprised if they had your size.	*Mi sorprenderebbe se ...*
They are not likely to get the Nobel prize for Economics!	*È improbabile che ...*
There is not much chance the growth rate will exceed 1.5%.	*Ci sono poche probabilità che ...*
There's no danger we'll get bored.	*Non c'è pericolo di ...*
It would be amazing if everything went according to plan.	*Sarebbe sorprendente che ...*

Impossibilità

It's impossible.	*È impossibile.*
It is not possible for the government to introduce this bill before the recess.	*Non è possibile per ...*
This information **cannot be** wrong.	*È impossibile che ...*
There is no chance of their helping us.	*Non c'è alcuna possibilità che ...*

❏ *Saluti*

Hello!	*Ciao! o Salve!*
Hi!	*Ciao!*
Good morning!	*Buongiorno!*

Good afternoon!	Buonasera!
Good evening!	Buonasera!
How's it going?	Come va?
How's things?	Come vanno le cose?
How's life?	Come va la vita?
How are you?	Come sta?

Come rispondere

Very well, and you?	Molto bene grazie, e lei?
Fine, thanks.	Bene, grazie.
So-so.	Così così.
Could be worse.	Potrebbe andare peggio.

Per fare le presentazioni

This is Charles.	Questo è ...
Let me introduce you to my girlfriend.	Le presento ...
I'd like you to meet my husband.	Ti voglio far conoscere ...
I don't believe you know one another.	Non credo che vi conosciate.

Cosa dire durante le presentazioni

Pleased to meet you.	Piacere.
How do you do?	Molto piacere.
Hi, I'm Jane.	Ciao, sono ...

Accomiatarsi

Bye!	Ciao!
Goodbye!	Arrivederci!
Good night!	Buonanotte!
See you!	Ci vediamo!
See you later!	A più tardi!

See you soon!	*A presto!*
See you tomorrow!	*A domani!*
See you next week!	*Alla settimana prossima!*
See you Thursday!	*A giovedì!*

Auguri

Happy Birthday!	*Buon compleanno!*
Many happy returns!	*Cento di questi giorni!*
Happy Christmas!	*Buon Natale!*
Happy New Year!	*Buon Anno!*
Happy Anniversary!	*Buon anniversario!*
Congratulations!	*Congratulazioni!* o *Complimenti!*
Welcome!	*Benvenuti!*
Good luck!	*Buona fortuna!*
Safe journey!	*Buon viaggio!*
Get well soon!	*Guarisci presto!*
Take care!	*Stammi bene!*
Have fun!	*Divertiti!*
Cheers!	*Cin cin!* o *Salute!*
Enjoy your meal!	*Buon appetito!*

❏ Corrispondenza

Come intestare una lettera in Gran Bretagna

Francobollo

Il codice di avviamento postale va messo dopo il nome della città o del paese.

Mrs J.M. Mackintosh
129 Strathmore Ave
EDINBURGH
EH11 2AD
UK

Come intestare una lettera negli Stati Uniti

Francobollo

MARK SMITH
968 MICHIGAN ST
SEATTLE WA   98060-1024
USA

Il codice di avviamento postale (**zip code**) va messo dopo il nome della città e l'abbreviazione dello stato.

Abbreviazioni usate comunemente negli indirizzi

Ave = avenue	Dr = drive	Pl = place	Sq = square
Cres = crescent	Gdns = gardens	Rd = road	St = street

Formule di apertura e chiusura standard

Per scrivere a conoscenti o amici

Dear Mr and Mrs Roberts	Yours (*abbastanza formale*)
Dear Kate and Jeremy	With best wishes
Dear Aunt Jane and Uncle Alan	Love from
Dear Granny	Lots of love from (*informale*)

Nella corrispondenza formale

Dear Sirs Dear Sir Dear Madam Dear Sir or Madam Dear Professor Meldrum Dear Ms Gilmour	Yours faithfully Yours sincerely

Per iniziare una lettera indirizzata a conoscenti o amici

It was lovely to hear from you.

Mi ha fatto molto piacere ricevere tue notizie.

Thanks for your letter ...

Grazie per la tua lettera ...

Sorry I haven't written sooner.

Scusami se non ti ho scritto prima.

Per iniziare una lettera formale

Thank you for your letter of ...

La ringrazio per la Sua lettera del ...

In reply to your letter of ...

In risposta alla Sua lettera del ...

With reference to ...

In riferimento a ...

We are writing to you to ...

Le scriviamo per ...

We are pleased to inform you ...

Siamo lieti di comunicarle ...

We regret to inform you ...

Siamo spiacenti di comunicarle ...

Per concludere una lettera indirizzata a conoscenti o amici

Write soon.

Scrivimi presto.

Give my regards to ...

Salutami ...

... sends his/her best wishes.

Saluti da ...

Give my love to ...

Dà un bacio da parte mia a ...

Per chiudere una lettera formale

I look forward to hearing from you.

Resto in attesa di una Sua cortese risposta.

Thanking you in advance for your help.

RingraziandoLa anticipatamente del Suo aiuto.

If you require any further information please do not hesitate to contact me.

Resto a Sua disposizione per eventuali ulteriori informazioni.

❏ *Lettera di ringraziamento*

Indirizzo del mittente.

18 Slateford Ave
Leeds
LS24 3PR

9th May 2004

Data.

Dear Gran and Grandpa,

Thank you both very much for the CDs which you sent me for my birthday. They are two of my favourite groups and I'll really enjoy listening to them.

There's not much news here. I seem to be spending most of my time studying for my exams which start in two weeks. I'm hoping to pass all of them but I'm not looking forward to the Maths exam as that's my worst subject.

Mum says that you're off to Crete on holiday next week, so I hope that you have a great time and come back with a good tan.

Tony sends his love.

With love from

Per le alternative, vedi pag.21.

❏ *Prenotazione alberghiera*

109 Bellview Road
Cumbernauld
CA7 4TX

14th June 2004

Data.

Mrs Elaine Crawford
Manager
Poppywell Cottage
Westleigh
Devon
DV3 8SP

Nome e indirizzo del destinatario della lettera.

Dear Mrs Crawford,

My sister stayed with you last year and has highly recommended your guest house.

I would like to reserve a family room for one week from 18th to 24th August of this year. I would be obliged if you would let me know how much this would be for two adults and two children, and whether you have a room available on those dates.

I hope to hear from you soon.

Yours sincerely,

Andrew Naismith

Questa formula va usata quando si conosce il nome della persona a cui si scrive.

❏ *Lettera di reclamo*

Per le alternative, vedi pag.22.

85 Rush Lane
Triptown
Lancs
LC4 2DT

20th February 2004

Woodpecker Restaurant
145 Main Street
Triptown
Lancs
LC4 3EF

Dear Sir/Madam

I was to have dined in your restaurant last Thursday by way of celebrating my wedding anniversary with my wife and young son but am writing to let you know of our great dissatisfaction.

I had reserved a corner table for two with a view of the lake. However, when we arrived we had to wait for more than 20 minutes for a table and even then, not in the area which I had chosen. There was no highchair for my son as was promised and your staff made no effort whatsoever to accommodate our needs. In fact, they were downright discourteous. Naturally we went elsewhere, and not only have you lost any future custom from me, but I will be sure to advise my friends and colleagues against your establishment.

Yours faithfully

T. Greengage

Questa formula va usata quando non si conosce il nome della persona a cui si scrive.

❏ *Curriculum Vitae*

CURRICULUM VITAE

In caso di titoli di studio italiani, per cercare lavoro in un paese di lingua inglese occorre indicare **"maturità (equivalent of A-levels), laurea (equivalent of BA (Hons))"**.

Name: Rosalind A. Williamson
Address: 11 North Street, Barnton NE6 2BT
Telephone: 01294 476230
E-mail: rosalindw@metalcomp.co.uk
Date of Birth: 18/4/1980
Nationality: British
Marital Status: Single

CAREER

2/97 to date: Sales and Marketing Executive, Metal Company plc, Barnton

11/95-1/97: Marketing Assistant, Metal Company plc

QUALIFICATIONS

1991-1995: University of Newby
BA (Hons) Italian with French – 2:1

1984-1991: Barnton Comprehensive School
A-levels: English Literature (D), French (B), Italian (A)
GCSEs: Art, Chemistry, English Language, English Literature, French, German, Italian, Maths

OTHER SKILLS

Computer literate (Word for Windows, Excel, QuarkXPress), good keyboarding skills, full, clean driving licence.

INTERESTS

Travel (have travelled extensively throughout Europe and North America), riding and sailing.

REFEREES

Ms Alice Bluegown
Sales and Marketing Manager
Metal Company plc
Barnton
NE4 3KL

Dr I.O. Sono
Department of Italian
University of Newby
Newby
S13 2RR

Occorre dare il nome di due persone che possano fornire referenze su di voi al vostro potenziale datore di lavoro. L'ideale sarebbe che almeno una di queste persone sia un precedente datore di lavoro o, se siete studenti, un vostro insegnante.

❏ *Ricerca di lavoro*

11 North Street
Barnton
NE6 2BT

18 August 2004

The Personnel Director
Clifton Manufacturing Ltd
Firebrick House
Clifton
MK45 6RB

Dear Sir or Madam

Questa formula va utilizzata se non si conosce il sesso della persona a cui si sta scrivendo. Se invece si conosce il nome della persona a cui si sta scrivendo, per esempio:
Mrs Lynn Kerr
Personnel Director
Clifton Manufacturing Ltd ecc.
la lettera va iniziata con la seguente formula:
Dear Mrs Kerr

With reference to your advertisement in the Guardian of 15 August, I wish to apply for the position of Marketing Manager in your company.

I am currently employed as a Sales and Marketing Executive for the Metal Company in Barnton where my main role is maintaining and developing links with our customers within the UK and producing material for marketing purposes.

I am interested in this position as it offers an opportunity to apply my sales and marketing skills in a new and challenging direction. I enclose my Curriculum Vitae for your consideration. Please do not hesitate to contact me if you require any further details.

Yours faithfully

Questa formula va usata quando non si conosce il nome della persona a cui si scrive.

Rosalind Williamson

Enc.

= **enclosures.** Da aggiungere se si allegano alla lettera ulteriori informazioni, p. es. un curriculum vitae.

❏ *Convocazione ad un colloquio di lavoro*

> Le aziende spesso inseriscono un numero di riferimento nella corrispondenza per facilitarne l'archiviazione.

CLIFTON MANUFACTURING LTD.

Firebrick House • Clifton MK45 6RB
Tel: (01367) 345 900 • Fax: (01367) 345 901
E-mail: personnel@cliftman.co.uk

Ref: RW/LK

27 August 2004

Ms Rosalind Williamson
11 North Street
Barnton
NE6 2BT

Dear Ms Williamson

Following your recent application for the position of Marketing Manager, I would like to invite you to attend an interview at the above office on Friday 3 September at 11am.

The interview will be conducted by the Sales and Marketing Director and myself and should last approximately one hour.

If this date does not suit please notify Jane Simpson on extension 3287 to arrange an alternative date.

We look forward to meeting you.

Yours sincerely

> Questa formula va usata se la lettera comincia con **Dear Ms Williamson** ecc.

Lynn Kerr

Lynn Kerr (Mrs)
Personnel Director

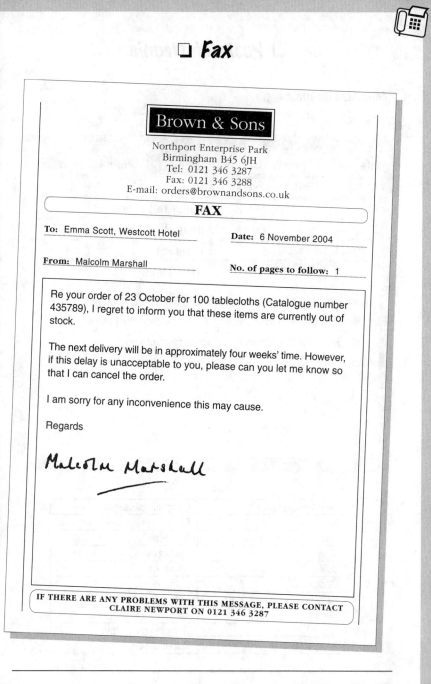

❏ *Fax*

Brown & Sons

Northport Enterprise Park
Birmingham B45 6JH
Tel: 0121 346 3287
Fax: 0121 346 3288
E-mail: orders@brownandsons.co.uk

FAX

To: Emma Scott, Westcott Hotel

Date: 6 November 2004

From: Malcolm Marshall

No. of pages to follow: 1

Re your order of 23 October for 100 tablecloths (Catalogue number 435789), I regret to inform you that these items are currently out of stock.

The next delivery will be in approximately four weeks' time. However, if this delay is unacceptable to you, please can you let me know so that I can cancel the order.

I am sorry for any inconvenience this may cause.

Regards

Malcolm Marshall

IF THERE ARE ANY PROBLEMS WITH THIS MESSAGE, PLEASE CONTACT
CLAIRE NEWPORT ON 0121 346 3287

❑ *Posta elettronica*

Mandare un messaggio

New Message							
File	**Edit**	**View**	**Tools**	**Compose**	**Help**	**Send**	✉

To: andrew@pmdesigns.co.uk	**New**	
Cc:	**Reply to Sender**	
Bcc:	**Reply to All**	
Subject: Meeting	**Forward**	
	Attachment	

Re our conversation this morning, would next Monday morning

10am be convenient for a meeting about the project's progress?

If this doesn't suit, I'm also free Wednesday morning.

Mark

New Message	Componi messaggio
File	File
Edit	Modifica
View	Visualizza
Tools	Strumenti
Compose	Componi
Help	Help
Send	Invia
New	Componi messaggio
Reply to Sender	Rispondi all'autore

❑ Posta elettronica

Ricevere un messaggio

			Meeting			
File	**Edit**	**View**	**Tools**	**Compose**	**Help**	

From: Andrew Collins (andrew@pmdesigns.co.uk)

Sent: 30 November 2004 08.30

To: mark.gordon@typo.co.uk

Subject: Meeting

> In inglese per comunicare a qualcuno il proprio indirizzo di posta elettronica si dice: **"andrew at pmdesigns dot co dot uk"**.

Mark,

Unfortunately I'm away on business all next week. Would it be possible to arrange a working lunch, Thursday or Friday of this week?

Sorry about this!

Andrew

Reply to All	Rispondi a tutti
Forward	Inoltra
Attachment	Inserisci file
To	A
Cc (carbon copy)	Cc
Bcc (blind carbon copy)	Ccn
Subject	Oggetto
From	Da
Sent	Data

❏ *Telefono*

Diversi tipi di telefonate

Local/national call.	Comunicazione urbana/interurbana.
I want to make an international call.	Vorrei chiamare all'estero.
I want to make a reverse-charge call (*Brit*) to a Paris number *o* I want to call a Paris number collect (*US*).	Vorrei fare una chiamata a ... con addebito al destinatario.
How do I get an outside line?	Cosa devo fare per ottenere una linea esterna?

Come chiedere informazioni

What is the number for directory enquiries (*Brit*) *o* directory assistance (*US*)?	Qual è il numero del servizio informazioni?
Can you give me the number of Europost, 20 Cumberland Street, Newquay?	Vorrei il numero di ...
What is the code for Martinique?	Qual è il prefisso del ...
What is the number for the speaking clock?	Qual è il numero dell'ora esatta?

Come ricevere informazioni

The number you require is 0181-613 3297. (*o-one-eight-one six-one-three three-two-nine-seven*)	Il numero da lei richiesto è ...
I'm sorry, there's no listing under that name.	Spiacente, non c'è nessun abbonato con questo nome.
The number you require is ex-directory (*Brit*) *o* unlisted (*US*).	Il numero da lei richiesto è fuori elenco.

Quando l'abbonato risponde

Could I speak to Mr Sanderson, please?	Vorrei *o* Potrei parlare con ...
Could you put me through to Dr Evans, please?	Può passarmi ...
Can I have extension 6578, please?	Può passarmi l'interno ...
I'll call back in half an hour.	Richiamo tra ...
Would you ask him to ring me when he gets back?	Può chiedergli di richiamarmi appena rientra?

Risponde il centralino

Who shall I say is calling?	Chi devo dire?
I'm putting you through.	Glielo passo.

I have a call from Tokyo for Mrs Thomson.	*C'è una chiamata da ...* *per ...*
I've got Miss Martin on the line.	*Ho in linea ...*
Dr Roberts is on another line. Do you want to wait?	*... è occupato sull'altra linea, attende?*
Please hold.	*Attenda, prego.*
There's no reply.	*Non risponde.*
Would you like to leave a message?	*Desidera lasciare un messaggio?*

Messaggi registrati

The number you have dialled has not been recognized. Please hang up.	*Il numero selezionato è inesistente. Si prega di riattaccare.*
The number you have dialled has been changed to 0171-789 0044.	*L'abbonato ha cambiato numero. Il nuovo numero è ...*
All the lines are busy right now. Please try again later.	*A causa dell'ingente traffico, non ci è possibile dar seguito alla sua chiamata. La preghiamo di richiamare più tardi.*
Hello, you have reached Sunspot Insurance. Please wait, your call will be answered shortly.	*Buongiorno, siete in linea con ... Vi preghiamo di attendere: un operatore risponderà appena possibile.*
Hello, you are through to Emma and Matthew Hargreaves. Please leave a message after the tone and we'll get back to you. Thanks.	*Buongiorno, risponde la segreteria telefonica di ... Lasciate un messaggio dopo il bip, sarete richiamati al più presto.*

Per rispondere al telefono

Hello, it's Anne speaking.	*Pronto, sono ...*
Speaking.	*Sono io.*
Who's speaking?	*Chi parla?*

In caso di difficoltà

I can't get through.	*Non riesco a prendere la linea.*
Their phone is out of order.	*Il loro telefono è guasto.*
We have been cut off.	*È caduta la linea.*
I must have dialled the wrong number.	*Credo di aver sbagliato numero.*
We've got a crossed line.	*C'è un'interferenza sulla linea.*
This is a very bad line.	*La linea è molto disturbata.*

❑ Likes, dislikes and preferences

Saying what you like

Mi piacciono i dolci.
I like ...

Mi piace che le cose siano al loro posto.
I like ...

Il film **mi è piaciuto.**
I liked ...

La visita ai vigneti **mi è piaciuta molto.**
I very much enjoyed ...

Adoro andare in discoteca.
I love ...

La cosa che mi piace di più è passare una serata con amici.
What I like most is ...

Il mio piatto **preferito** è il risotto.
My favourite ...

Leggere è **uno dei miei** passatempi **preferiti.**
... one of my favourite ...

Ho un debole per i dolci al cioccolato.
I've got a weakness for ...

Vado matto per la musica jazz.
I'm crazy about ...

Non c'è niente di meglio di un bel bagno caldo!
There's nothing better than ...

Non mi dispiace stare da solo.
I don't mind ...

Saying what you dislike

Non mi piace il pesce.
I don't like ...

Non mi piace molto parlare in pubblico.
I'm not very keen on ...

La birra **non mi piace per niente.**
I don't like ... at all.

Il suo comportamento **non mi piace per niente.**
I don't like ... at all.

Odio la chimica.
I hate ...

Detesto lo sport.
I loathe ...

Non sopporto che mi si dicano bugie.
I can't stand ...

Se c'è una cosa che odio è aspettare sotto la pioggia.
What I hate most is ...

Non è che l'idea **mi faccia impazzire.**
I'm not madly keen on ...

Saying what you prefer

Preferisco il rock **alla** musica classica.
I prefer ... to ...

Preferirei vivere a Parigi.
I would rather ...

Preferirei morire di fame **piuttosto che** chiedergli un favore.
I'd rather ... than ...

Mi piacerebbe di più lavorare a casa.
I'd rather ...

Expressing indifference

Per me fa lo stesso.	*It's all the same to me.*
Non ho preferenze.	*I have no particular preference.*
Come vuole *or* **preferisce.**	*As you like.*
Non ha nessuna importanza.	*It doesn't matter in the least.*
È indifferente.	*I don't mind.*
Fai come credi, **per me è uguale.**	*... it's all the same to me.*

Asking what someone likes

Ti piacciono le patate fritte?	*Do you like ...*
Ti piace cucinare?	*Do you like ...*
Le piace vivere in città?	*Do you like ...*
Cosa preferisci: il mare o la montagna?	*Which do you like better ...*
Quale preferisci: il rosso o il nero?	*Which do you prefer ...*
Preferisci vivere in città o in campagna?	*Do you prefer ...*
Cosa ti piace di più in un uomo?	*What do you like best ...*

❏ Opinions

Asking for opinions

Cosa pensa del divorzio?	*What do you think about ...*
Cosa ne pensa?	*What do you think about it?*
Potrebbe dirmi la sua opinione su questo programma?	*Could you tell me your opinion of ...*
Vorrei sapere cosa pensi del suo lavoro.	*I'd like to know what you think of ...*
Qual è la sua opinione sulle probabilità di successo?	*What is your opinion on ...*
Mi piacerebbe sentire il suo parere su questo problema.	*I'd like to hear your views on ...*
Come ti sembra il suo modo di fare?	*What do you think of ...*
A suo parere, c'è parità tra uomini e donne?	*In your opinion ...*
A suo avviso, lui c'entra?	*In your view ...*
Secondo te, bisognerebbe ripensarci?	*In your opinion ...*

Expressing opinions

Hai ragione.	*You are right.*
Ha torto.	*He is wrong.*
Ha sbagliato a dimettersi.	*He was wrong to ...*
Sono sicuro che sia in buonafede.	*I'm sure he's ...*
Sono convinto che esistano altre soluzioni.	*I'm convinced that ...*
Sono convinto che sia la soluzione migliore.	*I'm sure that it's ...*
Penso che sarà possibile.	*I think ...*
Penso che tu sbagli.	*I think ...*
Credo che sia un po' prematuro.	*I think it's ...*
Credo che sia in ritardo.	*I think he's ...*
Mi sembra che sia normale.	*I think it's ...*
A mio parere, non è cambiato.	*In my opinion ...*
A mio avviso, è il caso di intervenire.	*In my opinion ...*
Per me, ha sbagliato.	*In my view ...*
Secondo me, è stato un grave errore.	*In my view ...*
Personalmente, ritengo che sia denaro sprecato.	*Personally, I think that it's ...*
Ho l'impressione che i suoi non la capiscano.	*I have the impression that ...*

Being noncommittal

Non ho un'opinione precisa al riguardo.	*I have no particular opinion on this.*
A dire il vero, non ci ho mai pensato.	*Actually, I have never thought about it.*
Dipende da cosa intendi per patriottismo.	*It all depends what you mean by ...*
Dipende.	*It depends.*
Preferisco non pronunciarmi.	*I'd rather not express an opinion.*

❏ *Approval and agreement*

Mi sembra una magnifica idea.	*I think it's an excellent idea.*
Ottima idea!	*What a good idea!*

Hai fatto bene a lasciare le valigie al deposito bagagli.	*You were right to ...*
Ho apprezzato moltissimo il suo articolo sul razzismo.	*I was very impressed by ...*
I giornali **fanno bene a** pubblicare queste notizie.	*... are right to ...*
Secondo me lei **ha ragione a** diffidarne.	*I think you're right to ...*
È un'ottima cosa.	*It's a very good thing.*
Non hai torto a lamentarti.	*You're quite justified in ...*
Condivido la sua opinione.	*I share your view.*
Condivido pienamente la sua apprensione.	*I fully share your ...*
Siamo favorevoli alla creazione di posti di lavoro.	*We are in favour of ...*
Siamo a favore dell'Europa unita.	*We are in favour of ...*
Ritengono giustamente che l'inquinamento provenga dalla fabbrica.	*They rightly believe that ...*
Sono d'accordo con lei.	*I agree with you.*
Sono pienamente d'accordo con te.	*I entirely agree with you.*
È vero che ci sono meno matrimoni oggi.	*It is true that ...*

❏ *Disapproval and disagreement*

Non sono d'accordo.	*I disagree.*
Non siamo d'accordo con loro.	*We don't agree with ...*
Non sono affatto d'accordo con quello che ha detto.	*I totally disagree with ...*
Non è vero che il risultato era inevitabile.	*It is not true to say that ...*
Ti sbagli!	*You are wrong!*
Non condivido il punto di vista degli euroscettici.	*I don't share the ... point of view.*
Siamo contro la caccia.	*We are against ...*
L'idea **non mi piace per niente.**	*I dislike ... intensely.*
Non sopporto le bugie.	*I can't stand ...*
La violenza **è ingiustificabile.**	*... cannot be justified.*
Sono contrario al test obbligatorio per l'AIDS.	*I am opposed to ...*
Trovo che abbia sbagliato a chiedere un prestito così grosso.	*I think he was wrong to ...*
Non avresti dovuto parlargli così.	*You shouldn't have ...*
Sono deluso del suo atteggiamento.	*I am disappointed by ...*

Sono profondamente deluso.	*I am deeply disappointed.*
È un peccato che costi così caro.	*It's a pity that ...*
È deplorevole che non siano in grado di trovare una soluzione.	*It is highly regrettable that ...*
Non possiamo permettere che la situazione peggiori.	*We must not allow ...*
Che diritto ha di agire così?	*What gives him the right to ...*

❏ *Apologies*

How to say sorry

Scusi.	*Sorry.*
Oh, scusi! Devo aver sbagliato piano.	*Oh, sorry!*
Scusi se la disturbo.	*Sorry to bother you.*
Scusa se ti ho svegliato.	*I am sorry I ...*
Mi dispiace per tutto quello che è successo.	*I am sorry about ...*
La prego di scusarmi.	*I do apologize.*
Preghiamo i lettori di scusare questa omissione.	*We hope our readers will ...*

Admitting responsibility

È colpa mia, sarei dovuto partire prima.	*It's my fault, I should have ...*
Non avrei dovuto ridere di lei.	*I shouldn't have ...*
Abbiamo sbagliato a non verificare questa informazione.	*We were wrong not to ...*
Mi assumo la piena responsabilità delle mie azioni.	*I take full responsibility for ...*
Purtroppo abbiamo commesso un errore nel conteggio.	*We unfortunately made a mistake ...*

Disclaiming responsibility

Non è colpa mia.	*It's not my fault.*
Non è colpa mia se siamo in ritardo.	*It isn't my fault if ...*
Non l'ho fatto apposta.	*I didn't do it on purpose.*
Non ho potuto fare altrimenti.	*I had no option.*

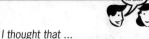

Mi era sembrato di capire che si potesse parcheggiare qui.

I thought that ...

Credevo di far bene a dirglielo.

I thought I was doing the right thing in ...

Apologizing for being unable to do something

Mi dispiace, ma è impossibile.

I'm sorry, but ...

Non posso fare altrimenti.

I have no other option.

Sono spiacente, ma purtroppo siamo al completo.

I'm sorry, but unfortunately ...

Siamo desolati di non poter soddisfare la sua richiesta.

We are very sorry we ...

❏ Explanations

Causes

Sono arrivato in ritardo **a causa del** traffico.

... because of ...

Il programma è stato abbandonato **a causa di** problemi legali.

.... owing to ...

Ha detto che è qui **per via del** fratello.

... because of ...

Sono riuscito a cavarmela **grazie all'**aiuto dei miei amici.

... thanks to ...

Non ho comprato niente **perché** non ho soldi.

... because ...

Visto or **dato che** insisti, tornerò domani.

Since ...

Siccome abitavo vicino alla biblioteca ci andavo spesso.

_As ..._

Vista la situazione attuale, non si può sperare in un miglioramento immediato.

Given ...

Dato che c'è una crisi economica, è difficile trovare lavoro.

Given that ...

Dati i problemi che abbiamo avuto, non ce la siamo cavata male.

Considering ...

È stata la rottura di un asse **che ha causato** il deragliamento.

It was ... that caused ...

Si è dimesso **per motivi di** salute.

... for ... reasons.

Il teatro chiude **per** mancanza di fondi.

... due to ...

Molte forme di tumore **sono legate al** fumo.

... are linked to ...

Il problema è che la gente è intimorita dai computer.

The problem is that ...

Il calo delle vendite **è il risultato dei** tassi d'interesse alti.

... is the result of ...

Consequences

Devo partire stasera, **quindi** non potrò venire con te.	... *so* ...
I contadini ora possono coltivare più terra, **col risultato che** la produzione di riso è aumentata.	... *with the result that* ...
La distribuzione è stata migliorata, **e dunque** i lettori riceveranno prima il loro giornale.	... *and so* ...
Il nuovo sidro viene fermentato molto poco e **di conseguenza** ha un basso contenuto alcolico.	... *consequently* ...
La mancanza di fondi **ha portato ad** un rallentamento del progetto.	... *has resulted in* ...
Sono tutti uguali **e perciò** è facile confondersi.	... *and so* ...

❏ *Comparisons*

Questo trattamento costa poco **se lo si paragona ad** altri.	... *if one compares it to* ...
Si può paragonare il gioco d'azzardo **a** una droga.	... *can be compared to* ...
Il gas di scarico ha un odore **simile a** quello delle uova marce.	... *similar to* ...
Il Vittoriale di d'Annunzio **è spesso paragonato a** una nave.	... *is often compared to* ...
Il rumore **era paragonabile a** quello di una grossa moto.	... *was comparable to* ...
L'Africa è ancora un continente sottopopolato **paragonato all'**Asia.	... *compared with* ...
L'Irlanda, **a paragone dell'**Islanda, ha un clima tropicale.	*Compared to* ...
In Francia, gli investimenti pubblicitari sono aumentati leggermente **rispetto all'**anno precedente.	... *compared to* ...
Questa storia **sembra** una favola.	... *is like* ...
Amava questa campagna che **gli ricordava** l'Irlanda.	... *reminded him of* ...
Livelli di disoccupazione **che ricordano** quelli degli anni '30.	... *reminiscent of* ...
La televisione **è l'equivalente** moderno **dei** circhi romani.	... *is the ... equivalent of* ...
Questa cifra **corrisponde a** sei mesi di stipendio.	... *amounts to* ...
'La schiacciata'? **È la stessa cosa che** la focaccia.	*It's the same thing as* ...
In termini di calorie è **equivalente**.	*It comes to the same thing* ...

Questo disco **non è né migliore né peggiore** dell'ultimo.

... is no better and no worse than ...

Stressing differences

Nessuna catastrofe **può essere paragonata a** quella di Černobyl.

No ... can compare with ...

Le fabbriche moderne **non si possono paragonare a** quelle in cui lavoravano i nostri nonni.

... cannot be compared with ...

Le azioni di questo gruppo **non hanno niente in comune con** le attività terroristiche.

... are in no way comparable to ...

I due personaggi **si differenziano** anche nei loro rapporti con le donne.

... differ ...

La storia degli Stati Uniti **non assomiglia affatto alla** nostra.

... in no way resembles ...

C'è di peggio che perdere la finale di Coppa Europa.

There are worse things than ...

Questo film **è meno** interessante **del** suo film d'esordio.

... is less ... than ...

Questo programma **è più** interessante **rispetto a** quello che ho visto ieri.

... is more ... than ...

La durata media della vita delle donne è di 81 anni, **mentre** quella degli uomini è di 72.

... while ...

❑ *Requests and offers*

Requests

Vorrei un'altra birra.

I'd like ...

Vorrei sapere gli orari dei treni per Padova.

I'd like to ...

Potrebbe darci una mano?

Could you ...

Può dare lei la buona notizia a Cinzia?

Can you ...

Sii gentile, fai un salto in panetteria.

Be an angel ...

Se non le dispiace attendere un attimo ...

If you wouldn't mind ...

Sarebbe così gentile da darci la ricetta?

Would you be so kind as to ...

Potrebbe farmi la cortesia di tenermi il posto?

Would you be very kind and ...

Potrebbe per cortesia indicarmi l'uscita?	*Could you please ...*
Può concedermi qualche minuto?	*Could you spare me ...*
Le spiacerebbe aprire la finestra?	*Would you mind ...*
Gradirei che mi comunicaste la decisione entro venerdì.	*I would be grateful if ...*
Le sarei grato se provvedesse affinché questo non si ripeta più.	*I would be grateful if ...*

Offers

Posso passare a prenderti, **se** vuoi.	*I can ... if ...*
Potrei accompagnarti io.	*I could ...*
Ti va un po' di gelato?	*Do you fancy ...*
Vi piacerebbe vedere le mie foto?	*Would you like to ...*
Che ne diresti di una crostata alle pere?	*Do you fancy ...*
Vuoi che vada a prendere la macchina?	*Do you want me to ...*
Le andrebbe di venire a cena con me una di queste sere?	*Would you like to ...*

❏ *Advice and suggestions*

Asking for advice or suggestions

Cosa faresti, al posto mio?	*What would you do, if you were me?*
È una questione complicata. **Tu cosa ne pensi?**	*What's your opinion?*
Quale ci consiglia, Majorca o Ibiza?	*Which would you recommend ...*
Cosa mi consiglia?	*What would you advise?*
Cosa mi consiglia di fare?	*What would you advise me to do?*
Se volessimo sponsorizzare un corridore, **chi raccomanderebbe?**	*... who would you recommend?*
Che strategia **proponi?**	*What ... do you suggest?*
Cosa bisognerebbe fare, secondo voi, per ridurre l'inquinamento?	*What, in your opinion, should be done to ...*
Come affrontereste la disoccupazione?	*How would you deal with ...*

Offering advice or suggestions

Se posso darle un consiglio, tenga le negative.
If I may give you a bit of advice ...

Un consiglio: leggete le istruzioni.
A word of advice ...

Se fossi in lei non mi fiderei.
If I were you ...

Al posto tuo non ne farei parola.
If I were you ...

Perché non gli telefoni?
Why don't you ...

Lei dovrebbe andare da uno specialista.
You should ...

Forse dovresti parlarne con un idraulico.
Perhaps you should ...

Farebbe bene a consultare un avvocato.
You would do well to ...

Faresti meglio a spendere quei soldi per comprare una macchina nuova.
You would do better to ...

Forse potrebbe chiedere a qualcuno di tradurglielo.
You could perhaps ...

Potresti essere un po' più comprensivo.
You could ...

Dato che hai senso del ritmo **dovresti** imparare a ballare.
... you ought to ...

Forse dovremmo tentare un approccio diverso.
Perhaps we ought to ...

E se noleggiassimo un video?
How about ...

Io proporrei il 3 marzo alle 10 e 30.
How about ...

Sarebbe bello rivedersi a Parigi.
It would be nice to ...

Forse sarebbe meglio regalarle dei soldi anziché dei gioielli.
It might be better to ...

Sarebbe meglio attendere i risultati del referendum.
It would be better to ...

Warnings

Soprattutto, non lasciare **mai** la macchina fotografica in auto.
Whatever you do, don't ...

Diffidate dei bagarini.
Beware of ...

Non fidarti: l'apparenza inganna.
Remember: appearances can be deceptive.

Se non prenoti per tempo **rischi** di non trovare posto.
... you risk ...

Ti avverto, mi vendicherò.
I warn you ...

Si ricordi di tenere una copia della dichiarazione dei redditi.
Don't forget to ...

❏ *Intentions and desires*

Asking what someone intends to do

Che progetti avete?	*What are your plans?*
Cosa conti di fare quando torni? **Hai dei progetti?**	*What are you going to do ... Do you have anything planned?*
Cosa conta di fare della sua collezione?	*What are you planning to do with ...*
Conta di restare molto tempo?	*Are you planning on ...*
Conta di girare un altro film in Europa?	*Are you thinking of ...*
Come pensi di fare?	*What are you thinking of doing?*
Cosa pensi di fare dopo la laurea?	*What are you thinking of doing ...*
Cosa farai se non passi agli esami?	*What will you do if ...*
Vi aspettiamo domenica prossima, d'accordo?	*We'll expect you ...*
Hai intenzione di seguire questa carriera?	*Do you intend to ...*

Talking about intentions

Pensavo di andare ad Ajaccio l'8 luglio.	*I was planning to ...*
Contiamo di vendere oltre centomila dischi.	*We reckon to ...*
Sto pensando di ritirarmi dalla politica.	*I am thinking of ...*
Prevede di trascorrere un anno in India.	*She plans to ...*
È prevista la costruzione di un nuovo stadio.	*There are plans to ...*
Ho deciso di divorziare.	*I have decided to ...*
È deciso, andiamo in Florida.	*That's settled ...*
È mia intenzione dirglielo prima possibile.	*I intend to ...*
La banca **ha intenzione di** chiudere oltre un centinaio di succursali.	*... intends to ...*
Non è mai stata nostra intenzione parlare male della stampa.	*We never had any intention of ...*
Per me vivere all'estero **è fuori discussione**.	*... is out of the question.*

Wishes

Voglio fare del cinema.   *I want to …*

Vorrei suonare come Louis Armstrong.   *I'd like to …*

Vorrei che le mie foto venissero pubblicate.   *I would like …*

Mi piacerebbe fare qualche sport.   *I'd like to …*

Mi sarebbe piaciuto avere un fratello.   *I would have liked to …*

Spero di potermi sposare e avere dei bambini.   *I hope to …*

Ci auguriamo che i bambini guardino questo programma con i genitori.   *We hope that …*

Carlos **voleva a tutti i costi** impedire al capo di scoprirlo.   *… wanted at all costs to …*

Sogni di vincere alla lotteria?   *Do you dream of …*

Il mio sogno è quello di avere una casa grande.   *I dream of …*

È nostro desiderio mantenere buoni rapporti.   *We wish to …*

❏ *Obligation*

Devo trovare un alloggio.   *I must …*

Dobbiamo assolutamente rivederci prima del 23!   *We really must …*

Se vieni in Polonia **devi** imparare il polacco.   *… you must …*

La scuola **è obbligatoria** come il servizio militare.   *… is compulsory …*

Esigeva che la sua guardia del corpo dormisse nel corridoio.   *He made …*

Mia madre **mi costringe a** mangiare spinaci.   *… makes me …*

I dirottatori **hanno chiesto che** l'aereo ripartisse alla volta di New York.   *… demanded that …*

Un attacco d'asma **mi ha costretto a** interrompere il viaggio.   *… forced me to …*

Ha dovuto chiedere in prestito sempre più soldi.   *… was obliged to …*

Non puoi fare altro che rifiutare.   *You have no choice but to …*

Ha dato il bambino in adozione perché **non poteva fare altrimenti.**   *… she had no other option.*

Molte madri **sono obbligate a** lavorare, **non hanno scelta.**   *… have to …; they have no other option.*

È indispensabile conoscere un po' la storia per comprendere la situazione.   *It is essential to …*

❏ *Permission*

Asking for permission

Posso usare il telefono?	*Could I ...*
Posso chiederle qualcosa?	*Can I ...*
Va bene se vengo ora, o è troppo presto?	*Is it alright if ...*
Le spiace se apro la finestra?	*Do you mind if ...*
Le dà fastidio se fumo?	*Do you mind if ...*
Permette che guardi nella sua valigetta, signora?	*Would you mind if ...*
Posso avere il permesso di andare via prima?	*May I have permission to ...*

Giving permission

Fate come volete.	*Do as you please.*
Vai pure!	*Of course you can go!*
Non ho niente in contrario.	*I have nothing against it.*
Alle 8 **mi hanno detto che potevo** andarmene.	*... they told me I could ...*
I ragazzi **possono** uscire due volte alla settimana.	*... are allowed to ...*
Ti permetto di andarci se mi prometti di telefonare quando arrivi.	*I'll let you ...*

Saying something is not allowed

Ti proibisco di uscire!	*I forbid you to ...*
È proibito.	*It's forbidden.*
È vietato fumare nella toilette.	*... is forbidden.*
Vietato l'ingresso.	*No entry.*
Sosta vietata.	*No parking.*
Divieto di sosta.	*No parking.*
Non è permesso.	*It's not allowed.*
Proibisce ai bambini **di** vedere i nonni.	*She forbids ... to ...*
Il lavoro infantile **è formalmente proibito da** una convenzione dell'ONU.	*... is strictly forbidden by ...*
Non potevamo né mangiare né bere, in servizio.	*We weren't allowed to ...*
È fuori discussione.	*That's out of the question.*
Non se ne parla nemmeno.	*It's out of the question.*

❏ *Certainty, probability and possibility*

Certainty

Ci saranno **senz'altro** dei problemi.	*Undoubtedly ...*
È evidente che l'azienda è in difficoltà.	*Clearly ...*
È innegabile che fosse in parte colpa sua.	*It is undeniable that ...*
Non c'è alcun dubbio che l'immagine del paese ne abbia risentito.	*There is no doubt that ...*
Vedere un turista è **ovviamente** una cosa rarissima.	*... quite obviously ...*
Sono sicuro che mio fratello ti piacerà.	*I am sure that ...*
Sono sicuro che siamo sulla pista giusta.	*I am certain that ...*
Sono sicuro di vincere.	*I am sure that I ...*
Ho la certezza di non annoiarmi, lavorando con lui.	*I am sure that ...*
Sono convinto che esistano altre soluzioni.	*I am convinced that ...*

Probability

L'80% dei problemi dermatologici è **senza dubbio** di origine psicologica.	*... undoubtedly ...*
È probabile che il costo della benzina aumenti.	*... probably ...*
Bisogna **probabilmente** rivedere i dati.	*... probably ...*
L'inflazione supererà **molto probabilmente** il 100%.	*... very probably ...*
Deve avere dimenticato di aprire la finestra.	*He must have ...*
I lavori di costruzione **dovrebbero** iniziare ad aprile.	*... should ...*
Potrebbe darsi che stiano osservando le nostre reazioni.	*It is quite possible that ...*

Possibility

È possibile.	*It is possible.*
È possibile che l'America sia stata scoperta dai cinesi.	*It is possible that ...*
Potrebbe essere più costoso.	*That might be ...*
Tra qualche mese **potrebbe** cambiare tutto.	*... could ...*
Questo virus **potrebbe** essere estremamente contagioso.	*... may ...*
Non è da escludersi che sia andato a Parigi.	*It is not impossible that ...*

Può darsi che ci voglia del tempo per concludere la pace. *It may be that …*

Magari sbaglio. *Perhaps …*

❑ *Doubt, improbability and impossibility*

Doubt

Non sono sicuro che sia utile. *I'm not sure it's …*

Non sono sicuro di aver ragione. *I'm not sure …*

Non sono certo che sia una buona idea. *I'm not sure that it's …*

Mi domando se abbiamo fatto molti progressi in questo campo. *I wonder if …*

È saggio? **Ne dubito.** *I doubt it.*

Cominciò a **dubitare della** competenza del proprio medico. *… have doubts about …*

Dubito fortemente che possa adattarsi alla situazione. *I very much doubt …*

Non è sicuro che riesca ad arrivare in tempo. *There is no certainty that …*

Non sappiamo con certezza se è stato lui. *We don't know for sure that …*

Non si sa esattamente cosa sia successo. *Nobody knows exactly …*

Improbability

Probabilmente non cambierà idea. *… probably won't …*

È poco probabile che siano rimasti dei biglietti. *It is unlikely that …*

Mi sorprenderebbe se avessero il tuo numero. *I'd be surprised if …*

Non rischiamo di annoiarci. *There's no danger of …*

Ci sono poche probabilità che il tasso di crescita superi l'1,5%. *It is unlikely that …*

Sarebbe da stupirsi se tutto andasse liscio. *It would be amazing if …*

Impossibility

È impossibile. *It's impossible.*

Non è possibile per l'80% dei giovani continuare gli studi superiori. *It is not possible for …*

È impossibile che quest'informazione sia falsa.

... cannot be ...

Non c'è alcuna possibilità che ci aiutino.

There is no chance of ...

❏ *Greetings*

Ciao!	*Hello!* or *Hi!*
Salve! *(more formal)*	*Hello!*
Come sta?	*How are you?*
Come va?	*How's it going?*
Come vanno le cose?	*How's things?*
Come va la vita?	*How's life?*
Buongiorno!	*Good morning!*
Buonasera!	*Good afternoon!* or *Good evening!*

What to say in reply

Molto bene grazie, e lei?	*Fine thanks, and you?*
Benone!	*Great!*
Così così.	*So-so.*
Non c'è male.	*Not so bad.*

Introductions

Questo è Charles.	*This is ...*
Le presento la mia ragazza.	*May I introduce ...*
Le voglio far conoscere mio marito.	*I'd like you to meet ...*

Replying to an introduction

Piacere.	*Pleased to meet you.*
Molto lieto.	*How do you do*

Leavetaking

Arrivederci!	*Goodbye!*
Buonanotte!	*Good night!*

Ciao!	*Bye!*
Ci vediamo!	*See you!*
A più tardi!	*See you later!*
A presto!	*See you soon!*
A domani!	*See you tomorrow!*
Alla settimana prossima!	*See you next week!*
A giovedì!	*See you Thursday!*

Best wishes

Buon compleanno!	*Happy Birthday!*
Cento di questi giorni!	*Many happy returns!*
Buon anniversario!	*Happy Anniversary!*
Buon Natale!	*Merry Christmas!*
Buon Anno!	*Happy New Year!*
Congratulazioni!	*Congratulations!*
Buon viaggio!	*Safe journey!*
Buon appetito!	*Enjoy your meal!*
Buona fortuna!	*Good luck!*
Divertiti!	*Have fun!*
Cin cin!	*Cheers!*
Buon riposo!	*Sleep well!*
Benvenuti!	*Welcome!*
Guarisci presto!	*Get well soon!*
Stammi bene!	*Take care!*

❏ *Correspondence*

How to address an envelope

Stamp

Gent. Sig.ra Bellini
Via dei Cairoli, 24
50131 FIRENZE

The postcode precedes the name of the town or area.

Common abbreviations used in addresses

Egr. = Egregio	P.zza = Piazza	Spett. = Spettabile
Gent. = Gentile	Sig. = Signor	V. = Via
P.le = Piazzale	Sig.ra = Signora	V.le = Viale

Standard opening and closing formulae

In personal correspondence

Caro Signor Bianchi	Cari saluti *(quite informal)*
Cara Giovanna	A presto
Carissimo Pietro	Ti abbraccio affettuosamente
Cari Anna e Marco	Un abbraccio
Cara zia Bruna	Baci *(very informal)*

In formal correspondence

Egregio Sig. Millo	Distinti saluti
Egr. Dott. Marsi	
Gent. Sig.ra Coretti	Cordiali saluti
Gent. Dott. Milesi	
Spett. Ditta	

Starting a personal letter

Ti ringrazio per la tua lettera.	*Thank you for your letter.*
Mi ha fatto molto piacere ricevere vostre notizie.	*It was lovely to have your news.*
Scusami se rispondo alla tua lettera solo ora, ma purtroppo ...	*Sorry for not replying sooner but unfortunately ...*

Starting a formal letter

In riferimento alla Sua lettera del ...	*Further to your letter of ...*
Le scrivo in seguito alla nostra conversazione telefonica avvenuta il ...	*Further to our telephone conversation of ...*
Desidero innanzitutto ringraziarLa per la Sua lettera.	*Thank you very much for your letter.*
Le scrivo a proposito di ...	*I am writing to you about ...*
Abbiamo il piacere d'informarLa che ...	*We are pleased to inform you that ...*
... ci dispiace doverLa informare che ...	*... we regret to inform you that ...*

Ending a personal letter

Tanti saluti anche a ...	*Best wishes to ...*
Dà un bacione da parte mia anche a ...	*Give my love to ...*
Mi raccomando, scrivimi presto!	*Write soon!*
Non vedo l'ora di avere vostre notizie.	*I look forward to hearing from you.*

Ending a formal letter

RingraziandoLa anticipatamente, Le porgo i miei più cordiali saluti.	*Thanking you in advance. Yours sincerely ...*
In attesa di una Vostra gentile risposta, invio distinti saluti.	*I look forward to hearing from you. Yours sincerely ...*

❏ *Thank you letter*

Livorno, 7 gennaio 2004

Date.

Cari Simona e Gianluca,

grazie ancora per la stupenda festa di Capodanno. È stato un piacere immenso rivedere tanti vecchi amici che avevamo un po' perso di vista.

Non vediamo l'ora di incontrarvi di nuovo per fare una chiacchierata e per mostrarvi le foto che Stefano ha scattato durante la festa. Che ne dite di venire da noi a prendere un aperitivo e vedere le foto? Vi telefoneremo la settimana prossima per accordarci sulla data.

Una caro abbraccio

For alternatives see p51.

Annamaria e Stefano

❏ *Hotel booking*

Massimo Lupini
Via G. Murat, 12
00190 Roma

Roma, 9 maggio 2004

Spett. Direzione
Hotel Roma
Piazza Garibaldi, 4
38100 Trento

Spett. Direzione,

in seguito alla nostra conversazione telefonica del 28 aprile, vi scrivo per prenotare una camera singola per le notti del 16, 17 e 18 c.m. presso il vostro albergo. Arriverò a Trento mercoledì 16 verso le 23 e ripartirò sabato 19 in tarda mattinata.

Vi sarei grato se poteste confermarmi le tariffe e la prenotazione via fax al numero 06-6389836.

In attesa di un vostro gentile riscontro, invio cordiali saluti.

Massimo Lupini

❏ *Letter of complaint*

Sig. e Sig.ra Colli
Via Ibsen, 3
10100 Torino

Torino, 5 gennaio 2004

Hotel da Vinci
Via Cavour, 2
56100 Pisa

Spett. Direzione,

mio marito ed io abbiamo trascorso la notte del 22 dicembre presso il vostro albergo, avendo regolarmente prenotato una camera per quella data. Vi scriviamo per esprimere il nostro disappunto per il servizio riservatoci.

Avevamo chiesto espressamente una camera silenziosa ed invece ci è stata assegnata una camera che dava sulla strada con la conseguenza che il rumore del traffico ci ha tenuti svegli tutta la notte. Come se ciò non bastasse, la mattina dopo è stato impossibile avere la colazione prima della nostra partenza alle 6 e 30.

La sosta presso di voi, che doveva permetterci di riposare nel corso di un lungo viaggio, non ha fatto che stancarci ancora di più.

Non solo non faremo mai più uso del vostro albergo, ma lo sconsiglieremo vivamente ai nostri amici.

Distinti saluti

H. Colli

For alternatives see p52.

❏ *Curriculum Vitae*

CURRICULUM VITAE

If you have British or American qualifications you should give them, followed by a brief description in Italian.

Nome e cognome	Michela Grini
Indirizzo	Piazza Annali 23, Varese
Telefono	0332 45 67 89
Data di nascita	7 novembre 1981
Nazionalità	italiana

Titoli di studio

Diploma di ragioneria conseguito presso l'Istituto Fermi di Varese nel 1989

Diploma di dattilografia conseguito presso l'Istituto Manzoni di Varese.

Lingue

Ottima conoscenza della lingua inglese parlata e scritta

Buona conoscenza della lingua francese parlata e scritta

Esperienze Professionali

1995 a oggi

Asole Costruzioni S.p.A. di Varese, con mansioni di segretaria personale dell'Amministratore unico

1993 - 1995

Presti S.p.A. di Varese, con mansioni di segretaria personale dell'Amministratore

1990 - 1992

Impresa Lanic di Varese, con mansioni di segretaria dattilografa

Varie

Conoscenza dei principali programmi di videoscrittura e di gestione ufficio
Patente di guida

❏ *Job application*

Michela Grini
Piazza Annali, 23
21100 Varese

Varese, 21 ottobre 2004

> INFOCOMP Sistemi Informatici
> Ufficio Assunzioni
> Via del Fiore, 9
> 25100 Brescia

Spett. INFOCOMP,

ho letto con molto interesse il Vostro annuncio
pubblicato su "La Gazzetta di Brescia" di oggi
e vorrei propormi per l'incarico di segretaria
bilingue. Come risulta dalla copia del
curriculum che allego, ho maturato una vasta
esperienza come segretaria, ho un'ottima
conoscenza delle lingue e possiedo buone
conoscenze informatiche.

Resto in attesa di una Vostra cortese risposta
e colgo l'occasione per inviarVi i miei più
cordiali saluti.

Michela Grini

For
alternatives
see p52.

❏ *Invitation to interview*

It is becoming very common to include an e-mail address in correspondence.

INFOCOMP Sistemi Informatici

Via del Fiore, 9 • 25100 BRESCIA
Tel.: 030-4829847 • e-mail: infocomp@com.it

Sig.ra Michela Grini
Piazza Annali, 23
21100 VARESE

Brescia, 29 ottobre 2004

Rif: am6

This is used to aid filing of correspondence.

Gent. Sig.ra Grini,

in risposta alla Sua recente candidatura al posto di segretaria bilingue, sono lieto di invitarLa ad un colloquio con il nostro direttore generale, Dott. Carlo Robini, lunedì 7 novembre alle ore 10 presso i nostri uffici di Brescia.

Qualora fosse impossibilitata a presentarsi al colloquio in tale data, La prego di contattare la nostra segretaria, Sig.ra Maria Ponzi (tel. 030-4829850), per concordare un altro appuntamento.

Cordiali saluti

Giancarlo Marchesini

Dott. Giancarlo Marchesini
Capo Ufficio Personale

The forms of address **Dott.** and **Dott.ssa** precede the names of all graduates.

❏ *Fax*

Studio legale Dott. Bini

Via Ghiberti, 25
33105 FIRENZE
Tel: 055–3453821
Fax: 055–3453822

FAX

Per: Sig. Carlo Salesi

Da: Maria Nelli

Oggetto: richiesta listini

Data: 19 novembre, 2004

Pagine: 1, inclusa questa

Gent. Sig. Salesi,

dovendo acquistare urgentemente 2 stampanti laser per il nostro studio, Le scrivo per avere qualche informazione sulle stampanti fornite dalla Sua ditta. Avremmo bisogno di un modello adatto alla stampa della modulistica per le dichiarazioni dei redditi che possa servire anche per le normali operazioni d'ufficio (invio lettere, ecc.).

Le sarei estremamente grata se potesse inviarmi al più presto via fax un elenco completo delle stampanti attualmente disponibili specificando le caratteristiche tecniche di ciascun esemplare e il prezzo.

Distinti saluti

Maria Nelli

PER PROBLEMI DI RICEZIONE DEL FAX CONTATTARE IL NUMERO
055–3453821

❏ E-mail

Sending messages

Componi messaggio						
File Modifica Visualizza Strumenti	**Componi**	?	Invia ✉			

A: francesca@abc.it	**Componi messaggio**
Cc:	**Rispondi all'autore**
Ccn:	**Rispondi a tutti**
Oggetto: Sono tornata!	**Inoltra**
	Inserisci file

Cara Francesca,

ho ricevuto il tuo messaggio solo oggi dato che sono appena ritornata
da una settimana di vacanza a Rimini. Ti manderò prima possibile
l'indirizzo che mi hai chiesto.

Un bacione,

Cristina

File	File
Modifica	Edit
Visualizza	View
Strumenti	Tools
Componi	Compose
Invia	Send
Componi messaggio	New
Rispondi all'autore	Reply to sender
Rispondi a tutti	Reply to all

❑ E-mail

Receiving messages

		Re: Sono tornata!			
File	Modifica	Visualizza	Strumenti	Componi	?

Da: Francesca Maggi (francesca@abc.it)

Data: 28 giugno, 2004

A: cristina_benelli@abc.it

Oggetto: Re: Sono tornata!

> In Italian, when telling someone your e-mail address you say:
> **"francesca chiocciolina abc punto it"**.

Cara Cristina,

adesso capisco dov'eri finita per tutto questo tempo! Ti sei divertita

a Rimini? Scrivimi presto e raccontami tutto.

Ciao,

Francesca

PS. Non preoccuparti per quell'indirizzo: l'ho già trovato.

Inoltra	Forward
Inserisci file	Attachment
A	To
Cc (copia carbone)	Cc
Ccn (copia carbone nascosta)	Bcc
Oggetto	Subject
Da	From
Data	Sent

❏ *Telephone*

Different types of call

Chiamata urbana/interurbana/internazionale.	*Local/national/international call.*
Vorrei fare una telefonata internazionale.	*I want to make an international call.*
Vorrei fare una telefonata a carico del destinatario	*I want to make a reverse-charge call (Brit) or I want to call collect (US).*

Asking for information

Vorrei il numero della ditta Decapex di Vercelli.	*I'd like the number of ...*
Qual è il prefisso di Livorno?	*What is the code for ...*
Posso telefonare in Colombia direttamente?	*Can I dial direct to ...*
Qual è il prefisso per telefonare in Francia?	*What is the code for calling ...*

Receiving information

Il numero da lei richiesto è: 0432 37 49 95. *(zero quattro tre due tre sette quattro nove nove cinque)*	*The number you require is ...*
Mi dispiace, ma non c'è nessun abbonato con questo nome.	*I'm sorry, but there's no listing under that name.*
Mi dispiace, il numero da lei richiesto è fuori elenco.	*... the number you have asked for is ex-directory (Brit) or unlisted (US).*

When your number answers

Vorrei parlare con il signor Matta, per favore.	*Could I speak to ...*
Mia può passare l'interno 516, per cortesia?	*Could I have extension ...*
Richiamerò più tardi.	*I'll try again later.*
Potrei lasciare un messaggio?	*Can I leave a message?*
Potrebbe chiedergli di chiamarmi quando rientra?	*Would you ask him to call me when he gets back?*

The switchboard operator speaks

Pronto, Hotel Rex, desidera?	*Hello ... can I help you?*
Chi parla, per cortesia?	*Who's calling ...*
Glielo passo subito.	*I'm putting you through now.*
C'è una telefonata in linea da Tokyo per la signora Marelli.	*I have a call from ... for ...*

C'è la signorina Martini **in linea**. / .... is on the line.

Non risponde nessuno. / There's no reply.

Attenda in linea, prego or **Rimanga in linea**, per favore. / Hold the line ...

Vuole lasciare un messaggio? / Would you like to leave a messsage?

Recorded messages

Telecom Italia: **informazione gratuita. Il numero da lei selezionato è inesistente.** / You have not been charged for this call. The number you have dialled has not been recognised

Telecom Italia: **servizio gratuito. L'utente da lei chiamato ha cambiato numero. Attenda in linea senza riagganciare poiché stiamo inoltrando automaticamente la sua chiamata al nuovo numero** 040–45 63 02. **Per le prossime comunicazioni la preghiamo di utilizzare la nuova numerazione.** Grazie. / You have not been charged for this call. This number has been changed. Please hold while we transfer your call. The new number is ...

Benvenuti al servizio assistenza della ditta Se.Ge.Co. / Welcome to ... customer services.

Tutte le linee sono momentaneamente occupate. La preghiamo di attendere. La sua chiamata sarà inoltrata prima possibile. / All the lines are busy right now. Please hold the line and we will deal with your call as soon as possible.

Risponde la segreteria telefonica della famiglia Boni. **Lasciate un messaggio dopo il segnale acustico.** Grazie. / You have reached ... Please leave a message after the tone.

Answering the telephone

Pronto, sono Anna. / Hello, this is ...

Sì, sono io. / Speaking.

Chi parla? / Who's calling?

When in trouble

Non riesco a prendere la linea. / I can't get through.

L'apparecchio è fuori servizio. / The phone is out of order.

È caduta la linea. / We've been cut off.

Ho sbagliato numero. / I must have dialled the wrong number.

C'è un'interferenza sulla linea. / We've got a crossed line.

La linea è molto disturbata. / This is a very bad line.